The New Comprehensive
A-Z Crossword
DICTIONARY

(REVISED EDITION)

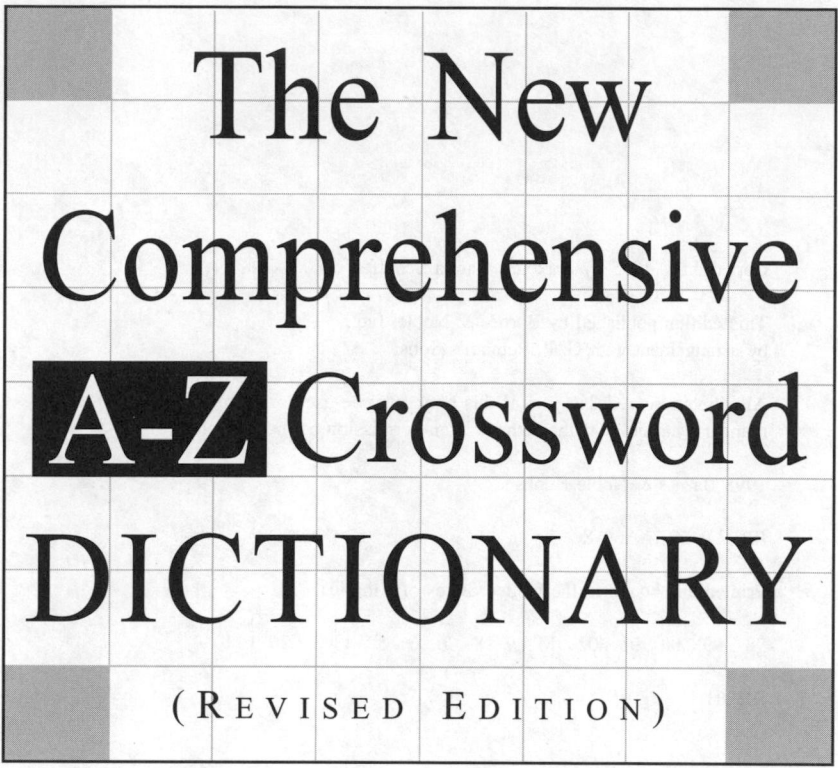

The New Comprehensive A-Z Crossword DICTIONARY

(REVISED EDITION)

compiled by

EDY GARCIA SCHAFFER

BARNES
&NOBLE
BOOKS
NEW YORK

TO MY LIEBLING,

whom I cannot thank enough
for his endless patience
and moral support,

AND TO MY EDITOR,
IRENE PROKOP

I am grateful
for your faith and
belief in my work.

List of
Abbreviations Used

abbr.	*abbreviation*		Mex.	*Mexican*
Austral.	*Australian*		myth.	*mythology*
Brit.	*British*		N.	*North*
colloq.	*colloquial*		naut.	*nautical*
comb. form	*combining form*		obs.	*obsolete*
dial.	*dialectal*		poet.	*poetic*
Eccles.	*Ecclesiastical*		S.	*South*
e.g.	*for example*		Russ.	*Russian*
Eng.	*English*		Scot.	*Scottish*
Fr.	*French*		sl.	*slang*
Ger.	*German*		Sp.	*Spanish*
Gr.	*Greek*		US/U.S.	*United States*
Ital.	*Italian*		var.	*variant*
Lat.	*Latin*			

A

A .... A, AN, AY, PER, EACH
Greek .... ALPHA
Hebrew .... ALEPH
à bas .... DOWN, OPPOSE
à la mode .... STYLISH,
FASHIONABLE
mort .... MORTALLY,
MELANCHOLY
aa .... LAVA
aardvark .... ANTBEAR, ANTEATER
eating place .... ANTHILL,
FORMICARY
Aaron's ally .... HUR
brother .... MOSES
death mount .... HOR
father .... AMRAM
miracle worker .... ROD
mother .... JOCHEBED
rod .... MULLEIN
sister .... MIRIAM
son .... ABIHU, NADAB,
ELEAZAR, ITHAMAR
wife .... ELISHEBA
aba .... ROBE, GARMENT
abaca .... HEMP, FIBER, LUPIS,
LINAGA
product .... ROPE
aback .... BEHIND
taken .... CONFUSED,
STARTLED, SURPRISED
abacus .... SLAB, SOROBAN,
ADDER, CALCULATOR
Abaddon .... HELL, ABYSS,
HADES, SATAN
angel .... APOLLYON
abaft .... AFT, REAR, ASTERN,
BEHIND
abalone .... NACRE, ORMER,
SNAIL, ASSEIR, MOLLUSK,
EARSHELL
abandon ...... DROP, QUIT, DITCH,
LEAVE, WAIVE, DESERT,
VACATE, DISCARD, FORSAKE,
ABDICATE
abandoned .... LEFT, LOST,
FORLORN, DEPRAVED,
DERELICT, DESOLATE,
FORSAKEN, UNBRIDLED
abandonment .... DEFECTION,
DESERTION, DESOLATION
abase .... LOWER, SHAME,
DEMEAN, HUMBLE, DEGRADE,
DISHONOR
abasement .... SHAME,

DEGRADATION, HUMILIATION
abash .... DAUNT, SHAME,
CONFUSE, CONFOUND,
DISCOMFIT, EMBARRASS
abate .... EASE, WANE, QUASH,
DEDUCT, LESSEN, LOOSEN,
SUBSIDE, DECREASE, DIMINISH
abatement .... LETUP, EASEMENT,
REDUCTION
abatis ...... OBSTACLE, BARRICADE
abbatoir .... SHAMBLES,
SLAUGHTERHOUSE
abb .... WOOL, YARN
abba .... BISHOP, FATHER
abbe .... MONK, ABBOT, PRIEST
domain .... ABBACY,
MONASTERY
abbess .... AMMA
domain .... CONVENT,
NUNNERY
who loved Abelard
.... HELOISE
abbey .... PRIORY, CONVENT,
CLOISTER, MONASTERY
head .... ABBOT, PRIOR,
ABBESS
of an .... ABBATIAL
abbot .... ABBE, ABBAS, COARB,
HEGUMEN
assistant .... PRIOR
hero .... ROLLO
abbreviate .... CUT, CLIP, REDUCE,
ABRIDGE, SHORTEN,
CONTRACT
ABC, et al. .... NETWORKS
Power .... CHILE, BRAZIL,
ARGENTINA
abdicate .... QUIT, RESIGN,
RENOUNCE, SURRENDER
abdication .... DEMISSION,
(SE)CESSION
abdomen .... BELLY, PAUNCH,
VENTER, STOMACH
colloquial .... GUT
fluid in .... ASCITES
of the .... ALVINE
abdominal .... VENTRAL
limb, crustacean ...... PLEOPOD
pain .... COLIC, PYROSIS,
COLLYWOBBLES
region .... PUBES
swelling .... BLOAT
abduct .... KIDNAP, CAPTURE
slang .... SNATCH, SHANGHAI

Abdul the Bul Bul .... AMIR
abeam .... BY, ASIDE, BESIDE,
ABREAST
abecedarian .... TYRO, NOVICE,
AMATEUR, LEARNER,
BEGINNER, NEOPHYTE
abed ...... SICK, NAPPING, RESTING,
RETIRED, SLEEPING
Abelard's love .... HELOISE
abele .... PINE, POPLAR
Abel's brother .... CAIN, SETH
parent .... EVE, ADAM
aberrant .... ASTRAY, DEVIANT,
MISTAKEN, WANDERING
slang .... OFF BASE
aberration ...... LAPSE, DELIRIUM,
INSANITY, DEVIATION,
DERANGEMENT
abet .... AID, EGG, HELP, BOOST,
COACH, ASSIST, FOMENT,
INCITE, SECOND, SUCCOR,
UPHOLD
abettor .... BACKER, ADVOCATE,
EXPONENT, PROMOTER
abeyance .... PENDENCY,
SUSPENSION
abhor .... HATE, SHUN, DETEST,
LOATHE, DESPISE
abhorrence ...... ODIUM, HATRED,
DISGUST, AVERSION,
DETESTATION
abide .... LIVE, STAY, (A)WAIT,
DWELL, TARRY, ENDURE,
REMAIN, SUBMIT
abiding .... LASTING, ENDURING
Abi's father .... ZECHARIAH
husband .... AHAZ
mother .... HEZEKIAH
Abie's loved one .... ROSE
abigail .... MAID
Abigail's husband .... DAVID,
NABAL
son .... AMASA
Abihail's daughter .... ESTHER
father .... HURI, ELIAB
husband .... ABISHUR,
REHOBOAM
son .... ZURIEL
Abijah's son .... ASA
ability .... FLAIR, POWER, SKILL,
TALENT, CALIBER, FACULTY,
PROWESS
to borrow .... CREDIT
to feel .... (A)ESTHESIA,

1

.... SENSATION

to read and write

.... LITERACY

Abimelech's brother ...... JOTHAM

father .... GIDEON, ABIATHA

friend .... AHUZZATH

Abital's husband .... DAVID

son .... SHEPHATIAH

abject ...... LOW, BASE, HANGDOG,

PITIFUL, SERVILE, WRETCHED

abjectly afraid .... CRAVEN

abjure .... DENY, SPURN, RECANT,

REJECT, DISAVOW, RENOUNCE,

REPUDIATE

ablation .... SURGERY

ablaze ...... AFIRE, AGLOW, EAGER,

AFLAME, BURNING, EXCITED

able .... CAN, ADEPT, HABILE,

SKILLED, SKILLFUL,

COMPETENT, QUALIFIED

bodied .... STRONG, HEALTHY

to be totaled .... ADDABLE

to pay .... SOLVENT

to read and write

.... LITERATE

to reason .... SANE

willing and _____ ...... READY,

SET

ablegate .... ENVOY

abluent .... SOAP, DETERGENT

ablution .... BATH(ING), WASHING,

CLEANSING

abnegation .... DENIAL

Abner, brother of .... KISH

cousin of .... SAUL

epithet/character LIL

father of .... NER

slayer of .... JOAB

son of .... JAASIEL

wife of .... RIZPAH

abnormal .... ODD, QUEER,

UNUSUAL, IRREGULAR,

UNNATURAL

eye condition .... MYOPIA

mental condition

.... DEMENTIA

Abo .... TURKO

abode ...... HOME, NEST, HABITAT,

DOMICILE, DWELLING,

QUARTERS, RESIDENCE

colloquial .... CONDO, ROOST

of animals ..... DEN, STY, ZOO,

LAIR, HUTCH, WARREN

birds .... COTE, NEST, NIDE,

AERIE, AVIARY

giants .... UTGARD

gods .... MERU, ASGARD,

OLYMPUS

humans .... MIGARD

paradise .... EDEN

sinners' souls .... LIMBO,

PURGATORY

the dead ..... ARALU, HADES,

ORCUS, SHEOL, HEAVEN,

NIRVANA, PARADISE

the Muses .... PARNASSUS

slang .... PAD, DUMP, JOINT

abolish .... END, ANNUL, KILL,

ERASE, CANCEL, REPEAL,

REVOKE, DISCARD, NULLIFY,

RESCIND

aboma ...... BOA, SNAKE, SERPENT

abominable .... VILE, ODIOUS,

HATEFUL, HEINOUS,

OFFENSIVE, UNPLEASANT

Abominable Snowman ...... YETI

abominate .... HATE, ABHOR,

DETEST, LOATHE, EXECRATE

abomination .... HATRED,

PLAGUE, AVERSION, LOATHING

aboriginal .... FIRST, NATAL,

ORIGINAL, PRIMITIVE,

INDIGENOUS

weapon ..... NULLA, BLOWPIPE,

WO(O)MERA, BOOMERANG

aborigine .... NATIVE, INDIGENE

world boxing champ

.... (LIONEL) ROSE

abort .... CHECK, THWART

abortion .... FIASCO, FAILURE,

MISCARRIAGE

illegal .... FETICIDE,

ABORTICIDE

abortive .... FUTILE, FRUITLESS,

UNSUCCESSFUL

abound .... TEEM, SWARM

abounding .... RIFE, COPIOUS,

TEEMING, ABUNDANT,

PLENTIFUL

suffix .... FUL, ULANT

about ...... OF, RE, ANENT, CIRCA,

ALMOST, AROUND, NEARLY,

REGARDING, CONCERNING

face .... REVERSAL,

REVULSION, TURNABOUT,

SOM(M)ERSAULT

above .... ATOP, PAST, OVER,

UPON, ALOFT, BEYOND,

HIGHER, SUPERIOR

board .... FAIR, OPEN, LEGIT,

HONEST, BLAMELESS

poetic .... O'ER

prefix .... HYPER, SUPER,

SUPRA

reproach ...... PURE, INNOCENT,

BLAMELESS

the ear .... EPIOTIC

zero .... PLUS

abra .... PASS, DEFILE

abracadabra ...... SPELL, JARGON,

GIBBERISH

abrade .... RUB, RASP, GRATE,

SAND, WEAR, CHAFE, GRAZE,

ERODE, GRIND, SCRAPE

abrading tool .... FILE, RASP,

GRATER, SANDER, GRINDER

material .... EMERY,

CORUNDUM, ERODENT,

SAND(PAPER)

Abraham's birthplace .... UR

brother .... HARAN, NAHOR

burial place .... MACHPELAH

CAVE

concubine .... HAGAR

father .... TERAH

grandfather .... NAHOR

grandson .... ESAU, JACOB

nephew .... LOT

shrine .... C(K)AABA

son .... ISAAC, MEDAN, SHUAH,

MIDIAN, ZIMRAN, ISHBAK,

JOKSHAN, ISHMAEL

wife .... SARAH, SARAI,

KETURAH

abramis .... CARP, FISH, BREAM

abrasion .... BRUISE, SCRAPE

abrasive .... BORT(Z), EMERY,

QUARTZ, ERODENT, TRIPOLI,

SAND(PAPER)

abraxas ...... GEM, CHARM, STONE

abreast ...... EVEN, EQUAL, LEVEL

of the times .... MODERN,

TRENDY

abri .... DUGOUT, SHELTER

abridge .... EDIT, DIGEST, REDUCE,

SHRINK, CURTAIL, SHORTEN,

CONDENSE

abridg(e)ment .... DIGEST,

SKETCH, EPITOME, SUMMARY,

SYNOPSIS, COMPEND(IUM)

abroad .... AWAY, DISTANT,

OUTSIDE, OVERSEAS

abrogate .... ANNUL, CANCEL,

REPEAL, ABOLISH, RESCIND

abrogation .... ABOLITION,

CESSATION, RESCISSION

abrupt .... CURT, RUDE, GRUFF,

HASTY, STEEP, SUDDEN,

BRUSQUE, UNEXPECTED

abruptly .... SPANG, SUDDENLY

Absalom's captain/cousin

.... AMASA

father .... DAVID

mother .... MAACHAH

sister .... TAMAR

slayer .... JOAB

abscess ...... BOIL, ULCER, FESTER,

PUSTULE

on gums .... GUMBOIL

on skin .... PIMPLE, BLISTER

abscond .... FLEE, ELOPE,

DECAMP, ELOINE, ESCAPE,

LEVANT

absence .... HOOKY, TRUANCY
  from one's country ...... EXILE
  leave of .... EXEAT, PERMIT,
    FURLOUGH
  of feeling .... COLD, NUMB,
    INSENSATE
  government .... ANARCHY
  hair .... ACOMIA, ALOPECIA
  light .... NIGHT, DARKNESS
  money .... BANKRUPT
  motion .... REST, INERTIA
  shame .... BRAZEN
  taste .... AGEUSIA
absent .... OUT, AWAY, GONE
  minded .... LOST, RAPT,
    DREAMY, BEMUSED,
    ABSORBED, DISTRAIT
  without leave .... AWOL
absentee, a kind of ...... TRUANT,
    MALINGERER
  colloquial .... NO-SHOW
absinthe .... GENIPI, LIQUEUR,
    WORMWOOD
absolute .... FULL, PURE, VERY,
  SHEER, STARK, TOTAL, UTTER,
  CERTAIN, PLENARY, SUPREME,
  COMPLETE, DEFINITE
  independence .... ALOD
  rule .... AUTARCHY, DESPOTISM
  ruler .... CZAR, SHAH, TSAR,
    DESPOT, SULTAN
  superlative .... ULTRA, ELATIVE
absolutely ...... SIMPLY, UTTERLY,
  ENTIRELY, DEFINITELY,
    CERTAINLY
  certain .... COCKSURE
  not allowed .... FORBIDDEN
absolution .... PARDON,
  ACQUITTAL, CLEANSING,
  CLEARANCE, REMISSION
absolve .... FREE, CLEAR, PARDON,
  ACQUIT, REMIT, EXONERATE
  in law .... VESTED
  sin .... SHRIVE
absorb .... EAT, BLOT, SUCK,
  DRINK, ENGULF, CONSUME,
  ENGROSS, SWALLOW,
    ASSIMILATE
absorbed .... LOST, (W)RAPT,
  ENRAPT, MERGED
absorbent .... POROUS, SPONGY,
    BIBULOUS
  material .... GAUZE, SPONGE,
    BLOTTER
absquatulate .... FLEE, DECAMP
abstain ...... DENY, AVOID, DESIST,
  FORGO, FORBEAR, REFRAIN
  from .... ESCHEW
  from eating ...... FAST, STARVE
abstainer of a kind .... DRY,
    TEETOTALER

abstemious .... SOBER,
  MODERATE, TEMPERATE
absterge .... WIPE, PURGE,
    CLEAN(SE)
abstinence .... SELF-DENIAL, SELF-
    RESTRAINT
  from alcoholic drinks
  .... SOBRIETY, TEETOTALISM
  sexual .... CELIBACY,
  CHASTITY, CONTINENCE
  total .... TEMPERANCE
abstract .... BRIEF, STEAL, DIGEST,
  PRECIS, REMOVE, RESUME,
  COMPEND, EPITOME,
    SUMMARY
  being .... ENS, ESSE
abstraction .... NOTION,
  PREOCCUPATION
abstruse .... DEEP, HIDDEN,
  SUBTLE, ESOTERIC, RECONDITE
absurd .... WILD, INEPT, SILLY,
  FATUOUS, FOOLISH,
  RIDICULOUS, NONSENSICAL
  colloquial .... RICH
  slang .... COCKEYED
absurdity .... PARADOX,
    NONSENSE
  colloquial .... POPPYCOCK
abundance ...... FOISON, GALORE,
  WEALTH, OPULENCE,
  AFFLUENCE, PLENITUDE
  colloquial .... SCADS
abundant .... RIFE, AMPLE,
  TEEMING, AFFLUENT,
    PLENTIFUL
abuse .... RAIL, SCOLD, INSULT,
  MALIGN, MISUSE, REVILE,
  SLANDER, VIOLATE,
  MALTREAT(MENT), MISTREAT
  a confidence .... BETRAY
abusive .... FOUL, INSOLENT,
  INSULTING, OFFENSIVE
abut .... JOIN, ADJOIN, BORDER
abysmal .... GAPING, YAWNING,
  CAVERNOUS, BOTTOMLESS,
    FATHOMLESS
abyss .... PIT, GULF, HOLE, CHASM,
  CLEFT, CAVITY, DEPTH,
  HOLLOW, TRENCH
  Babylonian mythology
  .... APSU
  below Hades .... TARTARUS
Abyssinia .... AXUM, ETHIOPIA
  ancient capital of .... MEROE
  capital of .... ADDIS ABABA
Abyssinian .... KAF(F)A,
    ETHIOPIAN
  animal ..... KUDU, LION, ORYX,
  ZEBRA, BABOON, GELADA,
  IMPALA, JACKAL, MONKEY,
  GAZELLE, GIRAFFE

  area .... AMHARA, ERITREA
  banana .... ENSETE
  battleground .... ADOWA
  bishop .... ABUNA
  Catholic .... CUSH, GEEZ,
    UNIAT(E)
  city/town .... ADWA, GORE,
  ASSAB, HARAR, JIMMA,
  GONDAR, GAMBELA, NAZRET,
  DESSYE, ASMARA, MAKALE,
  MAGDALA, SODDU, WALDIA
  coin/money .... BESA, HARF,
  AMOLE, GIRSH, SANTIM,
  KHARAF, TALARI, BIRR,
  ASHRAFI, PIASTER
  dialect .... GEEZ, GHESE
  drink .... MESE, BOUSA
  emperor ...... NEGUS, MEMNON,
  MENELIK, SELASSIE
  fly .... ZIMB
  garment .... CHAMMA
  governor .... RAS
  grain/plant .... TEFF
  Hamite ...... AFAR, AGAO, BEJA
  herb .... RAMTIL
  island .... DAHLAK
  lake .... TANA, ABAYA,
  CHAMO, ASSALE, RUDOLF,
  ZWAI, TURKANA, STEFANIE
  language .... GEEZ, ARABIC,
  AMHARIC, SOMALI, TIGRINYA
  lyre .... KISSAR
  measure .... TAT, KUBA,
  SINJER, TANICA, FARSAKH,
    FARSANG
  mountain .... BALE, GUGHE,
    RAS DASHAN
  ox .... GALLA, SANGA
  peninsula .... BURI
  people .... KALA, BEJAS,
  ETHIOP, SOMALIS
  primate .... ABUNA
  prince .... RAS
  princess .... AIDA, ANDROMEDA
  province .... ARUSI, BALE,
  TIGRE, WALLO, SHOA, GOJJAM,
  ERITREA, GONDER, GAMU-
  GOFA, SIDAMO, KAFFA,
  HARAR, WALLAGA
  pygmy .... DOKO
  queen .... CANDACE
  river .... OMO, ABAY, WABI,
  BARO, DAWA, FAFAN, AWASH,
  AKOBO, MAREB, ATBARA,
  BARAKA, TAKKAZE
  rock salt money .... EMOL
  title .... RAS, ABUNA, NEGUS
  tree .... KOSO, CUSSO
  tribe .... AFAR, AGOWS, GALAS,
  TIGRES, DONAKUS, SOMALIS
  tribesman .... SHOA

violin .... MASINKO
weight .... PEK, KASM, NATR,
OKET, ALADA, NETER, RATEL,
WAKEA, WOGIET, FARASULA
wolf .... KABERU
acacia .... BABUL, MYALL, SHRUB,
LOCUST, MIMOSA, WATTLE,
SHITTAH
astringent .... CATECHU
academe .... GROVE
academic ...... CLASSIC, ERUDITE,
LEARNED, PEDANTIC,
SCHOLASTIC
achievement .... DEGREE,
DOCTORATE
costume appendage
.... LIRIPIPE
degree, kind of .... LICENTIATE
paper .... THESIS
academy .... LYCEUM, SCHOOL,
COLLEGE, INSTITUTE
Acadia .... NOVA SCOTIA
acaleph .... JELLYFISH, SEA
NETTLE
acarid ...... MITE, TICK, ARACHNID
acaudal/acaudate .... TAILLESS
accede .... AGREE, YIELD, ASSENT,
COMPLY, CONSENT
accelerant .... CATALYST
accelerate .... REV, RACE, HURRY,
SPEED, HASTEN, QUICKEN,
STEP UP, ADVANCE
accelerator .... GUN, THROTTLE
accent .... BEAT, BURR, MARK,
TONE, DRAWL, ICTUS, PULSE,
TWANG, BROGUE, DIALECT,
STRESS, EMPHASIS
accenting syllable .... ARSIS
accentuate .... STRESS,
EMPHASIZE, HIGHLIGHT,
UNDERLINE, UNDERSCORE
accept .... TAKE, ADMIT, ADOPT,
ALLOW, GRANT, EMBRACE,
RECEIVE, SWALLOW
as true .... ADMIT, CREDIT
eagerly .... LEAP, POUNCE
readily .... DEVOUR, BELIEVE,
SWALLOW
with indulgence ..... CONDONE
without question .... ABIDE,
ENDURE, SUBMIT, TOLERATE
accepted .... APPROVED
not .... OUTCAST, UNWANTED
standard .... PAR, NORM, TYPE,
MODEL
access .... WAY, ROAD, ENTRY,
AVENUE, ENTREE, APPROACH,
ADMISSION
accessible .... OPEN, HANDY,
AVAILABLE, OBTAINABLE
accessory .... AIDE, ALLY, EXTRA,

ADJUNCT, ASSISTANT,
ACCOMPLICE
accident .... CHANCE, HAZARD,
MISHAP, CASUALTY
accidental ...... CASUAL, RANDOM,
FORTUITOUS
accipiter ...... OWL, HAWK, EAGLE
acclaim .... HAIL, LAUD, EXTOL,
PRAISE
acclamation .... CRY, SHOUT,
OVATION, PLAUDIT
word of .... HAIL, AVE, OLE,
RAH, HEIL, BRAVO, BANZAI,
MABUHAY
acclimate .... INURE, ENURE,
SEASON, ACCUSTOM
acclivity .... SLOPE, TALUS,
INCLINE
accolade .... AWARD, HONOR,
PRAISE, LAURELS, TRIBUTE
accommodate .... FIT, LEND,
ADAPT, GRANT, LODGE,
ADJUST, BILLET, OBLIGE
accommodation .... BERTH,
FAVOR, AMENITY, QUARTERS,
LOAN, CONCORD, CONCESSION
accompaniment .... ESCORT,
SPOUSE, SQUIRE, CONSORT
slang .... PARD
accompany .... JOIN, CONVOY,
ESCORT, CHAPERON(E)
accomplish .... DO, ATTAIN,
EFFECT, ACHIEVE, FULFILL,
PERFORM, COMPLETE
accomplished .... ADEPT, EXPERT,
GIFTED, SKILLED, POLISHED,
TALENTED
accomplishment .... DEED, FEAT,
SKILL, TALENT, FRUITION,
REALIZATION
accord ...... GIVE, UNITY, BESTOW,
CONCERT, CONFORM, UNISON,
HARMONY
according to .... PER, ALLA,
PURSUANT
good form .... DE RIGUEUR
law/rule .... FORMAL,
LEGAL(LY), DE REGLE,
LEGITIMATE
morals .... ETHICAL
regulations .... BY THE BOOK
usage .... CUSTOMARY
accordion-like instrument
...... MELODEON, CONCERTINA
accost .... CALL, HAIL, STOP,
GREET, SALUTE, WAYLAY,
ADDRESS
account .... TAB, SAKE, TALE,
SCORE, STORY, REPORT,
COMPUTE, EXPLAIN, NARRATE,
STATEMENT

accountant .... BEAN COUNTER
accounting .... AUDIT, COSTING,
BOOKKEEPING
entry .... ITEM, ASSET, DEBIT,
CREDIT, LIABILITY
form .... LEDGER, JOURNAL
accouter .... ARRAY, DRESS,
EQUIP, OUTFIT
accouterment .... TRAPPING(S),
HABILIMENT
Accra is capital of .... GHANA
accredit .... DEPUTE, APPOINT,
CERTIFY, LICENSE, AUTHORIZE
accrue ...... GROW, AMASS, ENSUE,
ISSUE, RESULT, COLLECT,
INCREASE
accumulate .... BANK, AMASS,
HOARD, STORE, ACCRUE,
GARNER, GATHER, COLLECT
accumulation .... FUND, HEAP,
PILE, HOARD, COLLECTION
accuracy .... TRUTH, PRECISION
of reproduction .... FIDELITY
accurate .... TRUE, EXACT,
CORRECT, PRECISE
accursed .... FEY, CURSED,
DAMNED, DOOMED
accusation .... RAP, BLAME,
CHARGE, INDICTMENT
slang .... FRAME
accuse ...... CITE, BLAME, ALLEGE,
IMPUTE, INDICT, ARRAIGN,
IMPEACH
accustom .... ENURE, INURE,
ADDICT, TOUGHEN,
ACCLIMATE, HABITUATE
accustomed .... USED, WONT,
USUAL, INURED, TRAINED
ace ...... TIB, ONE(R), HERO, TOPS,
STAR, FLYER, EXPERT,
ONESPOT
of clubs .... BASTO
of spades .... SPADILLE
queen combination
.... TENACE
to ten in poker .... STRAIGHT
to ten, same suit
.... (ROYAL)FLUSH
acephalous .... HEADLESS,
LEADERLESS
acerate .... NEEDLELIKE
acerb .... ACID, TART, HARSH,
SHARP, BITTER
acerbate .... VEX, EMBITTER,
IRRITATE
aces, two .... AMBSACE, AMESACE
acetic acid .... ESTER, ACETATE,
VINEGAR
acetone .... ACETOL, KEYSTONE
acetose .... ACID, SOUR
acetum .... VINEGAR

acetylene .... ETHIN(E), TOLANE

ache .... HURT, PAIN, PINE, SMART, THROB, YEARN

Acheron .... HADES, RIVER

tributary .... COCYTUS

achieve .... WIN, GAIN, REACH, ATTAIN, COMPASS, REALIZE, ACCOMPLISH

achievement .... DEED, FEAT, END, RESULT, EXPLOIT, COMPLETION, ATTAINMENT

Achilles .... PELIDES

adviser .... NESTOR

captive .... BRISEIS

charioteer .... AUTOMEDON

friend .... PATROCLUS

horse .... XANTHUS

parent .... PELEUS, THETIS

slayer .... PARIS

teacher .... CHIRON

victim .... HECTOR, TROILUS

vulnerable spot .... HEEL

warrior .... MYRMIDON

achira .... CANNA

achromatic substance ...... LININ

acicular .... SPINY, BRISTLY

acid .... SOUR, TART, ACERB, SHARP, BITING, CAUSTIC, CUTTING

base indicator .... LITMUS

etching .... MORDANT

kind of .... AMINO, BORIC, NITRIC, OLEATE, MURIATIC, PECTIC, SALYCYLIC

neutralizer .... ALKALI

nicotinic .... NIACIN

slang .... LSD

tanning .... CATECHIN

acidity .... ACOR, ACERBITY, SOURNESS

acidulous .... TART

acinus .... RASPBERRY

ack-ack fire .... FLAK

gun .... POMPOM

acknowledge .... OWN, AVOW, SIGN, ADMIT, CONFESS, RECOGNIZE

acknowledgment .... CREDIT, ADMISSION

of liability .... COGNOVIT

acle .... IRONWOOD

acme .... TOP, APEX, PEAK, SUMMIT, PINNACLE

acolyte .... NOVICE, ALTARBOY, THURIFER

acolyte's garb .... COTTA

acomia .... BALDNESS

aconite .... ATIS, WOLFSBANE, MONKSWOOD

acor .... ACIDITY

acorn .... OVEST, FRUIT, MAST,

NUT, CAMATA

barnacle .... SCUTA

cup .... VALONIA

dried .... CAMATA

edible .... BALLOTE

shaped .... BALANOID

acoustic equipment .... SIRENE

vase .... ECHEA

acoustics .... SONICS, PHONICS

acquaint .... TELL, BRIEF, TEACH, VERSE, INFORM, REVEAL, APPRISE

acquainted .... FAMILIAR, (CON)VERSANT, KNOWN

acquiesce .... BOW, AGREE, YIELD, ACCEDE, ASSENT, CONCUR, CONSENT

acquire .... BUY, GET, GAIN, EARN, REAP, OBTAIN, SECURE

in advance .... PREEMPT

knowledge .... LEARN

acquired knowledge
.... EDUCATION

acquisitiveness .... GREED, AVARICE

acquit ...... FREE, PARDON, CLEAR, EXCUSE, ABSOLVE, RELEASE

colloq. .... WHITEWASH

oneself .... BEHAVE

acquittance .... RELEASE, CLEARANCE

acre .... LAND, FIELD

¼ of .... ROOD

acres, 2.47 .... HECTARE

acrid .... SOUR, HARSH, NASTY, SHARP, BITING, BITTER, PUNGENT, VITRIOLIC

acrimonious .... CAUSTIC, BITTER, CUTTING, PEEVISH, SPITEFUL, STINGING

acrimony .... ANGER, SPITE, RANCOR, SPLEEN, ASPERITY

acrobat ...... GYMNAST, TUMBLER, STUNTMAN, AERIALIST, DAREDEVIL

high-wire .... AERIALIST

of India .... NAT

acrobat's equipment .... BARS, POLE, TIGHTROPE, TIGHTWIRE, TRAMPOLINE

forte .... STUNTS, SOM(M)ERSAULTS

net .... TRAMPOLINE

risk .... FALL, SLIP

wear .... TIGHTS, LEOTARD, FLESHINGS

acrogen .... FERN

acrolith .... STATUE

acropolis .... HILL, CADMEA, CITADEL, LARISSA

across .... ON, OVER, BEYOND,

ASTRIDE, ATHWART, TRAVERSE, CROSSWISE, ASTRADDLE

combining form ..... DIA, TRA, TRANS

the board .... BLANKET, OMNIBUS, TOTALLY

acrostic .... AGLA, TELESTIC(H), WORDPLAY

act .... DO, DEED, FEAT, PLAY, SKIT, EMOTE, EDICT, EXERT, MODEL, BEHAVE, PERFORM

according to rules
.... CONFORM

against morality .... SIN

as chairperson .... PRESIDE

before .... FORESTALL, PRECEDE, ANTICIPATE

dishonestly: sl. .... FUDGE

for .... REPRESENT, SUBSTITUTE

helpful .... GOOD TURN

in the interest of
.... ADVANCE, PROMOTE

insincerely .... FAKE, POSE, PRETEND

like .... APE, IMITATE, SIMULATE

of pretending .... FEIGN

of prudence .... CAUTION

of regret .... APOLOGY

official .... LAW, BILL, EDICT, DEGREE

out .... ENACT, MIMIC, PORTRAY

over .... EMOTE, PLAYACT

prima donna's .... TANTRUM

regrettable .... CRIME

silly .... CLOWN

the idler .... LAZE

up .... PRISS

with exaggeration .... HAM, EMOTE

acting by turns ...... ALTERN(ATE)

pertaining to .... THESPIAN, HISTRIONIC

trophy .... OSCAR, EMMY, TONY

action .... DEED, EDICT, WORK, FIGHT, STEP, ACTIVITY, COMBAT, PRACTICE, BEHAVIOR, SUIT, PROCESS, FUNCTION

court .... LAWSUIT

melodramatic .... HEROICS

put into .... ACTUATE, ACTIVATE

put out of .... KO, MAIM, CRIPPLE, DISABLE

symbolic .... CHARADE

to outwit another .... PLOY, BLUFF

to recover property
.... TROVER, REPLEVIN
violent .... RIOT, AFFRAY
where it is ..... ARENA, STAGE,
OVAL, DIAMOND, SCENE,
TABLE, COURT, STADIUM,
(COCK)PIT, RING, FIELD,
COLISEUM
with ridiculous end .... FIASCO
word .... VERB
activate .... SPARK, TRIGGER
activator .... DYNAMO, CATALYST
active .... BUSY, SPRY, ABOUT,
BRISK, AGILE, ASTIR, MOVING,
LIVELY, READY, NIMBLE,
WORKING
one .... DOER
place .... HUB, HIVE
activity .... ADO, STIR, LIFE,
BUSINESS, ACTION, BUSTLE,
EXERCISE, OPERATION
after guessing wrong
.... EATING CROW
forbidden .... NO-NO
actor .... LEAD, HERO, STAR,
MIME, PLAYER, ARTIST,
HISTRIO(N), THESPIAN,
MUMMER, PERFORMER
in farces .... FARCEUR
last line(s) of .... TAG
many-faced .... MUNI,
(LON)CHANEY
minor role .... WALK-ON
mythical .... SPELVIN
of a thousand faces
.... (LON)CHANEY
overacting .... MUGGER
second-rate .... HAM,
BARNSTORMER
veteran .... TROUPER
with speaking part ...... SUPER
actors' aid .... (PRESS)AGENT,
STAND-IN, DRESSER,
PROMPTER
apers .... ZANIES
association .... AEA, AAAA
group .... CAST, TROUPE
hint to .... CUE
improvisation .... AD LIB
in dramatics .... AMATEURS
offstage place .... GREEN
ROOM
part ...... ROLE, LEAD, VILLAIN,
COMIC, HEAVY, STAR(RING)
pest .... HECKLER
actress. See also actor ...... DIVA,
STAR
"blond bombshell"
.... HARLOW
from Brooklyn .... (MAE)WEST
in farces .... FARCEUSE

role sometimes .... INGENUE
with "it" .... (CLARA)BOW
with "oomph"
.... (ANN)SHERIDAN
actual ...... REAL, TRUE, POSIT, DE
FACTO, FACTUAL, GENUINE,
CONCRETE
being .... ESSE
actuality .... FACT, TRUTH,
VERITY, REALITY
actually .... TRULY, IN FACT,
REALLY
actuate .... EGG, MOVE, STIR,
URGE, DRIVE, IMPEL, ROUSE,
START, INCITE, AGITATE,
ACTIVATE, MOTIVATE
acuity .... WIT, EDGE, KEENNESS
acumen ...... WIT, FLAIR, WISDOM,
INSIGHT, KEENNESS, SAGACITY
acute ...... SHARP, FIERCE, SEVERE,
SHREWD, URGENT, CRUCIAL,
INTENSE, CRITICAL
ad .... NOTICE, INSERTION,
PUBLICITY, ADVERTISEMENT
hoc .... MAKESHIFT,
TEMPORARY, TENTATIVE,
PROVISIONAL
in tennis .... ADVANTAGE
infinitum .... FOREVER,
ENDLESSLY, WITHOUT END
interim .... MEANTIME,
MEANWHILE, TEMPORARY
lib .... INVENT, IMPROVISE,
EXTEMPORIZE
sum .... PRESENT
type of .... COVER, INSIDE,
DISPLAY, COLOR(ED),
CLASSIFIED
valorem .... WORTH,
VALUATION
verbum .... LITERAL,
VERBATIM
verse .... JINGLE
A.D., part of .... ANNO, DOMINI
adage .... SAW, MAXIM, MOTTO,
SAYING, PROVERB
subject .... TIDE, TIME
adagio .... SLOW, BALLET(DANCE)
Adam-and-Eve .... ORCHID,
PUTTYROOT
Smith is pseudonym of
.... GOODMAN
adamant .... SET, FIRM, RIGID,
SOLID, UNMOVED
Adamite .... NUDIST
Adam's ale .... WATER
apple .... GUZZLE, LARYNX
flannel .... MULLEIN
grandson .... ENOS, ENOCH
mate of legend .... LILITH
needle .... YUCCA

second mate/rib .... EVE
son .... ABEL, CAIN, SETH
teacher .... RAISEL
adapt .... FIT, MOLD, SUIT, APPLY,
ADJUST, ORIENT, CONFORM
add .... EKE, SUM, TOT, JOIN,
PLUS, TOTAL, UNITE, COMBINE
carbon dioxide .... CHARGE
dash of liquor/spirits
.... LACE, SPIKE
details .... SPELL OUT,
ELABORATE, EMBROIDER
fuel to the flame .... STOKE,
EXCITE, INCITE
insult to injury .... WORSEN,
PROVOKE, AGGRAVATE
member to a board ..... COOPT
on .... AFFIX, RIDER, ATTACH
sugar .... SWEETEN
to .... PLUS, ADORN, ENRICH,
EXPAND, AUGMENT, INCREASE
up ..... SUM, TOT, JIBE, COUNT,
TALLY, TOTAL, CALCULATE
up to .... MEAN, SIGNIFY
adda .... LIZARD
addax .... ANTELOPE
added to .... AND, EKE, PLUS,
ADDITIVE, SUPPLEMENT
addendum .... SEQUEL, ADJUNCT,
APPENDIX, EPILOGUE
adder .... ASP, SNAKE, VIPER,
COUNTER, REPTILE
addict .... FAN, USER, SLAVE,
DEVOTEE
slang .... BUG, NUT, DOPE,
HEAD, FIEND, HOUND, JUNKIE
addicted .... PRONE, HOOKED,
BIBULOUS, DEPENDENT
addiction .... WONT, HABIT,
ALCOHOLISM, DEPENDENCE
adding machine ...... TOTALIZER,
CALCULATOR
Addis Ababa is capital of
.... ABYSSINIA, ETHIOPIA
Addison and ____ .... STEELE
poet .... CLIO, JOSEPH
addition .... AND, ALSO, ELSE,
CODICIL, INCREASE,
ADDEND(A) (UM), APPENDIX
to a bill .... RIDER
to a building .... ELL, ANNEX
to a letter ...... PS, NOTA BENE,
POSTSCRIPT
additional .... MORE, EXTRA,
(AN)OTHER, FURTHER
appearance of a performer
.... ENCORE
name .... ALIAS, PSEUDONYM
pay .... TIP, BONUS
addle .... CONFUSE, FLUSTER,
STUMP, BAFFLE, PERPLEX

slang .... BUFFALO
addlebrained .... STUPID, MUDDLED
addled .... FOGGED, MUDDLED, EMPTY, DAZED, FLOORED
addlepated .... IDIOTIC, PINHEAD, PEABRAIN
address .... HOME, TACT, TALK, ABODE, GREET, ACCOST, DIRECT, SPEECH, ORATION, PETITION, RESIDENCE
army .... APO
navy .... FPO
President's .... WHITE HOUSE
Secretary of Defense's .... PENTAGON
to someone .... DEDICATE
adduce ...... CITE, INFER, PRESENT, ALLEGE, QUOTE, ADVANCE
adeem .... CANCEL, REVOKE
Adelina, singer .... PATTI
Adenauer's sobriquet .... (DER)ALTE
adept .... ACE, DEFT, EXPERT, ADROIT, MASTER, SKILLED, VERSED, DEXTEROUS
adequate .... AMPLE, EQUAL, ENOUGH, SUITABLE, ACCEPTABLE, SUFFICIENT
Adhem _____ .... (BEN)ABOU
adhere .... GLUE, HOLD, ABIDE, CLING, STICK, ATTACH, CLEAVE
adherent .... ITE, IST, ALLY, VOTARY, ZEALOT, DEVOTEE, BELIEVER, DISCIPLE, FOLLOWER, PARTISAN, RETAINER, SERVITOR
adhesive .... GUM, GLUE, TAPE, EPOXY, PASTE, CEMENT, STICKY, PLASTER
adhibit ...... ADMIT, AFFIX, APPLY
adieu .... GOODBY(E), TATA, FAREWELL
adipose .... FAT(TY), OBESE, LARDY, FLESHY, SUETY
slang .... BLIMP, FATSO
adit .... INLET, STULM, INGRESS, ACCESS, PASSAGE, ENTRANCE
adjacent ...... NEAR, NEXT, CLOSE, ADJOINING, CONTIGUOUS
adjective ...... ADNOUN, MODIFIER
ending .... IC, ENT, IAL, IL, ISH, INE, ILE, IST, ITE, IVE, OUS, ICAL, ULAR
verbal .... GERUNDIVE
adjoin ...... ABUT, TOUCH, APPEND
adjourn ...... END, CEASE, CLOSE, RECESS, RETIRE, SUSPEND, PROROGUE
adjudge .... DEEM, AWARD,

DECIDE, DECREE, SETTLE, CONDEMN, SENTENCE
unfit .... CONDEMN, DISQUALIFY, RULE OUT
adjudicate ...... TRY, HEAR, RULE, JUDGE, DECIDE
adjunct .... ANNEX, APPENDAGE
adjust ...... FIT, FIX, SUIT, ADAPT, ALIGN, ATTUNE, ORIENT, SETTLE
adjutant .... AIDE, ALLY, HELPER, ASSISTANT
bird .... STORK, ARGALA, HURGILA, MARABOU
adman .... HUCKSTER, PR MAN, PITCHMAN, PROMOTER, PUBLICIST, COPYWRITER
slang .... FLACK, BARKER, PLUGGER, SPIELER, BALLYHOOER
Admetus' wife .... ALCESTIS
administer ...... RUN, DEAL, GIVE, MANAGE, CONDUCT, HUSBAND, DISPENSE
administration ...... RULE, REIGN, MINISTRY, REGIME(N), MANAGEMENT
administrative .... MANAGING, EXECUTIVE, MINISTERIAL
body .... JUNTA, BOARD, COUNCIL, ASSEMBLY
admiral .... NAVARCH, OFFICER, COMMODORE
of fame .... BYRD, KING, LEAHY, DEWEY, HALSEY, NIMITZ, NELSON, PORTER, FARRAGUT
rank .... VICE, REAR, FLEET, FOUR-STAR
winged .... BUTTERFLY
admire .... LOVE, ESTEEM, REGARD, REVERE, IDOLIZE
admissible .... OK, OKAY, LICIT, ACCEPTABLE
in law .... LIE
admission .... FEE, ACCESS, ENTREE, ADMITTANCE, CONFESSION, CONCESSION
ticket: sl. .... DUCAT
admit ...... OWN, ALLOW, ACCEDE, ACCEPT, CONCEDE, GRANT, PROFESS, RECEIVE
colloquial .... FESS
admitted fact .... DATUM, TRUTH, TRUISM
admixture .... ALLOY, BLEND, SHADE, FLAVOR, COMPOUND
admonish .... WARN, CHIDE, ADVISE, REBUKE, CAUTION, REPROVE, SERMON(IZE)
admonisher .... MENTOR,

ADVISER, MONITOR
admonition .... ADVICE, REPROOF, WARNING, SCOLDING, REPRIMAND
first word of, sometimes .... DON'T
ado .... FUSS, STIR, TO-DO, BUSTLE, EFFORT, POTHER, TROUBLE
adobe .... MUD, CLAY, DOBY, BRICK
adolescence .... TEENS, YOUTH, TEENAGE, NONAGE, PUBERTY
adolescent, designating one .... HIPPIE, TEENAGER, BOBBYSOXER
Adonais, per Shelley ...... KEATS
Adonis' beloved .... APHRODITE
parent ..... CINYRAS, MYRRH(A)
slayer .... (WILD)BOAR
adopt .... ACCEPT, ASSUME, CHOOSE, TAKE ON, ESPOUSE
adore .... DOTE, LOVE, ADMIRE, HONOR, IDOLIZE, REVERE, GLORIFY, WORSHIP
adorn ...... DIGHT, DRESS, GRACE, (BE)DECK, BEAUTIFY, EMBELLISH, DECORATE
with diamonds .... BEGEM
with rich clothing .... CAPARISON
adorner .... DECORATOR, DRESSER, ORNAMENTIST
adrenal hormone .... CORTISONE
Adriana's servant .... LUCE
Adriatic city .... TRIESTE
island .... LAGOSTA
peninsula .... ISTRIA
port .... FIUME, TRIESTE, RIJEKA, RIMINI
resort .... LIDO
seaport .... VALONA, AVLONA
wind .... BORA
adrift .... ASEA, LOST, LOOSE, AWAFT, AFLOAT, UNTIED, FLOATING, DERELICT
adroit .... APT, DEFT, NEAT, ADEPT, HANDY, CLEVER, HABILE, CUNNING, SKILLFUL
adularia .... FELDSPAR, MOONSTONE
adulate .... PRAISE, FLATTER
adulation .... HONOR, GLORY, KUDOS
object of .... HERO, STAR, VICTOR, WINNER, CONQUEROR
slang ...... SWEET TALK, SWEET NOTHINGS
adulator, kind of .... FAN, YESMAN, TOADY, FAWNER, FLATTERER, COURTIER,

7

BOOTLICKER
adult .... MATURE, NUBILE, OF
AGE, GROWN(UP)
insect .... IMAGO
person .... MAN, WOMAN
tadpole .... FROG
wriggler .... MOSQUITO
adulterant, common .... FIZZ,
WATER
adulterate .... MIX, TAINT, CUT,
DEBASE, DEFILE, DILUTE,
DOCTOR, WEAKEN, CORRUPT,
DENATURE
slang .... BAPTIZE
adulterated .... MIXED,
THINNED(OUT), IMPURE,
WATERED(DOWN)
adultery .... TRIANGLE, HANKY-
PANKY, CUCKOLDRY,
INFIDELITY
adumbrate .... HINT, IMPLY,
SKETCH, OBSCURE, FIGURE,
SUGGEST, PREDICT
adust .... BURNT, SCORCHED,
SALLOW, PARCHED
advance .... LOAN, RISE, MARCH,
PUSH, LEND, MOVE, FOSTER,
PROCEED, PROMOTE, FURTHER,
PROGRESS, ATTACK, INCREASE
man .... AGENT, PLAYBROKER
man: sl. .... TEN-PERCENTER
money .... (IM)PREST
notice .... WARNING
payment .... ANTE, ARLES
slowly .... INCH, CREEP
to prospector .... GRUBSTAKE
unit .... VAN(GUARD)
word .... TIP, CLUE
advanced .... OLD, AGED,
MODERN, REFINED,
PERFECTED, FAR(GONE)
in years ..... SENIOR, ELDERLY,
WRINKLED
advancement .... GROWTH,
PROGRESS, HEADWAY,
PROMOTION
advantage .... EDGE, PROFIT, USE,
ODDS, GAIN, BENEFIT,
AMENITY, FOOTHOLD,
LEVERAGE
kind of, in tennis .... AD IN,
AD OUT
take ...... ABUSE, CHEAT, TRICK
advent .... COMING, ARRIVAL,
APPROACH, IMMINENCE
adventitious ...... CASUAL, FLUKY,
ALEATORY, ACCIDENTAL,
EPISODIC
lung sound .... RALE
adventure .... HAP, GEST(E),
MISSION, ESCAPADE, FEAT,

EVENT, QUEST, EXPLOIT,
ARISTEIA
adventurer .... SPECULATOR,
PICAROON, TREKKER,
SPORTSMAN, EXPLORER,
FORTUNE HUNTER
of chance .... GAMBLER
of old .... MERCENARY,
KNIGHT, FREEBOOTER
of speculation .... PLUNGER,
GUNSLINGER, SCALPER,
STOCKBROKER
reckless .... DAREDEVIL,
HELLCAT, FIRE-EATER
upstart .... PARVENU,
TUFTHUNTER, NAME DROPPER
adventurous .... DARING, BOLD,
RASH, RECKLESS, DYNAMIC,
FOOLHARDY
slang .... WILD-ASS
adversary .... FOE, RIVAL, ENEMY,
OPPONENT, FOEMAN,
ANTAGONIST
adverse .... HOSTILE, COUNTER,
OPPOSED, CLASHING,
PERVERSE, CONTRARY,
INIMICAL, UNTOWARD
criticism: sl. .... PAN(NING)
opinion .... CENSURE
reaction, show of .... BOO,
HISS, HOOT, POUT, SCOWL,
RASPBERRY
adversity .... DISASTER, HARDSHIP,
CALAMITY, BLIGHT, MISHAP,
TRAGEDY, GRIEF, MISERY,
POVERTY
slang .... BUMMER, WHAMMY
advertisement .... AD, BLURB,
NOTICE, INSERTION, MESSAGE,
PLACARD, POSTER, AFFICHE,
COMMERCIAL
abbreviation .... AD, ADVT
book jacket .... BLURB
interpolate .... PLUG
make-up .... LAYOUT
outdoor .... POSTER, FLYER,
BILLBOARD, MARQUEE,
HANDBILL, LEAFLET,
SIGNBOARD
radio/television
.... COMMERCIAL
slang .... PLUG, DODGER
advertiser ...... PLUGGER, SPIELER,
HAWKER
kind of .... BARKER
advertising client .... ACCOUNT
colloquial .... BALLYHOO
contract .... ACCOUNT
handbill: sl. .... DODGER
man: colloq. .... PITCHMAN,
HUCKSTER

medium .... NEWSPAPER,
FLYER, TV, MAGAZINE, RADIO,
MARQUEE, BROCHURE,
BILLBOARD
on book jacket .... BLURB
poster .... BILL
praise in .... PUFFERY
statuette .... CLIO
text .... COPY
advice .... COUNSEL, REDE,
PROPOSAL, BRIEFING, REPORT,
AVISO, CAVEAT, MESSAGE,
GUIDANCE
in 1835 .... GO WEST
seek .... CONSULT
to stockholders in 1933
.... SELL, UNLOAD
advise .... COACH, TELL, WARN,
INSTRUCT, INFORM, GUIDE,
DIRECT, APPRISE, CAUTION,
ACQUAINT
and _____ .... CONSENT
colloquial .... KIBITZ
adviser .... MENTOR, MONITOR,
ORIENTER, NESTOR, EGERIA,
CONFIDANT, COUNSELOR
colloquial .... KIBITZER,
BACKSEAT DRIVER
slang .... BUTTINSKY
advisory .... DIRECTIVE,
MONITORY
on weather .... WARNING
advocate .... SIDER, BACKER,
LAWYER, ABETTOR, ESPOUSE,
PLEAD(ER), CHAMPION,
DEFENDER, PREACHER,
APOLOGIST, PROPONENT
colloquial .... FAN, BUFF
of majority rule
.... DEMOCRAT
slang ...... ANGEL, MOUTHPIECE
adytum ...... SANCTUARY, SHRINE,
SANCTUM
adz .... AX(E), HATCHET, CUTTING
TOOL
Aeetes' daughter .... MEDEA
Aegean gulf/sea .... SAROS
inhabitant .... SAMIOTE,
LELEGE
island .... MELOS, LESBOS,
PATMOS, SAMOS, IOS, NIO,
TENOS, MYTILENE
river .... STRUMA
Aegeon's wife .... AEMILIA
Aegir's wife .... RAN
aegis .... SHIELD, ARMOR,
AUSPICES, SAFEGUARD,
PATRONAGE
Aello .... HARPY
Aeneas follower .... ACHATES
great grandson .... BRUT

parent .... VENUS, ANCHISES
son .... ASCANIUS
wife .... CREUSA
Aeneid author .... VERGIL, VIRGIL
first word .... ARMA
hero .... AENEAS
Aengus' mother .... BOANN
Aeolian lyricist .... SAPPHO
Aeolus' brother .... DORUS,
XUTHUS
daughter .... CANACE,
HALCYONE
parent .... ORSEIS, HIPPOTES
son .... ATHAMAS, CRETHEUS,
SALMONEUS
aeon .... AGE, ERA, EON, CYCLE,
PERIOD, ETERNITY, LIFETIME
aeonian .... LASTING, ETERNAL,
AGELESS, INFINITE,
PERPETUAL
aerate .... GASIFY, DISTILL,
WINNOW, FLUIDIZE
aerial .... LOFTY, AIRISH, UNREAL,
ETHEREAL, ANTENNA,
IMAGINARY, TOWERING,
VAPOROUS
battle .... DOGFIGHT
bomb: sl. .... EGG,
BREADBASKET
bombardment .... BLITZ
bombing, describing one
.... SATURATION, CARPET
car suspended from cables
.... TELPHER
navigation aid .... TELERAN
stunt ..... BARREL, ROLL, LOOP,
AEROBATIC, LOOP-THE-LOOP
aerialist ...... ACROBAT, GYMNAST,
BALANCER, WIREWALKER
aerie .... NEST, NIDUS, APIARY,
BEEHIVE
aerobatics .... LOOP, ROLL, TURN,
STUNTS, IMMELMANN
aerobe .... BACTERIUM
aerolite .... METEORITE
aeronaut .... PILOT, AIRMAN,
AVIATOR, SPACEMAN
aeronautics .... AVIATION
aerosol .... SPRAY, ATOMIZER,
CLYSTER, ASPERGIL
aerostat .... BLIMP, BALLOON,
DIRIGIBLE, ZEPPELIN
aerugo .... RUST, PATINA,
VERDIGRIS
aes .... COIN, BRONZE
Aesculapian .... DOCTOR,
MEDICAL, PHYSICIAN
Aesculapius' father .... APOLLO
teacher .... CHIRON
Aesir ...... TYR, LOKI, ODIN, THOR,
VALI, DONAR, FREYA, WODEN,

BALDER
Aesop .... WRITER, FABULIST
home of .... SAMOS
story .... FABLE
aesthete .... GOURMET, VIRTUOSO,
DILETTANTE, CONNOISSEUR
aesthetic ...... ELEGANT, ARTISTIC,
CLASSIC(AL), TASTEFUL,
BEAUTIFUL
slang .... ARTY-CRAFTY
aestival .... SUMMER
aestivate, opposed to
.... HIBERNATE
Aether's father .... EREBUS
Aetolian prince .... TYDEUS
afar .... OFF, AWAY, HAMITE,
REMOTE, DISTANT
affable .... KIND, CIVIL, SUAVE,
BENIGN, GENIAL, DECENT,
POLITE, AMIABLE, URBANE,
CORDIAL, FRIENDLY,
GRACIOUS, OBLIGING,
SOCIABLE
affair .... AMOUR, PARTY,
MATTER, SOIREE, CONCERN,
LIAISON, ROMANCE, BUSINESS,
GATHERING, RECEPTION
afternoon .... MATINEE
class/family .... REUNION
illicit ..... ADULTERY, INTRIGUE
love .... ROMANCE, TRIANGLE
of high school juniors
.... PROM
of honor, usually .... DUEL
of seniors .... HOP
affect .... HIT, SMITE, MOVE,
TOUCH, POSE, STRIKE, SWAY,
FEIGN, PRETEND, IMPRESS,
INFLUENCE
emotionally .... TRAUMATIZE
with pity .... SOFTEN
affectation .... AIRS, POSE, SHAM,
FACADE, CONCEIT, FAKERY,
PRETEXT, PRETENSE, ARTIFICE
of elegance .... FRIPPERY
of prudery .... STUFFINESS
affected .... LURID, POSEY,
MOVED, GARISH, FLASHY,
SHOWY, FEIGNED, FALLAL,
STAGY, AFFLICTED
elegance .... FROUFROU
slang .... PHONY
affecting .... BLEAK, MOVING,
PATHETIC, PITIFUL,
WRETCHED, TOUCHING,
DISMAL, RUEFUL
affection .... LOVE, AMOUR,
RAPTURE, ECSTASY, PASSION,
REGARD, FEELING, ESTEEM,
EMOTION, DISEASE, CHARITY,
FONDNESS

affectionate .... KIND, FOND,
WARM, TENDER, LOVING,
FILIAL, DEVOTED
afferent .... SENSORY
affiance .... ENGAGE, PLIGHT,
PLEDGE, PROMISE, TRUST,
BETROTH(AL)
affianced ...... FIANCE(E), SWORN,
ASSURED, ENGAGED,
PLIGHTED, BETROTHED
slang .... INTENDED
affiant ...... DEPONENT, VOUCHER,
SWEARER, ATTESTER,
TESTATOR
affidavit .... DEPOSITION,
STATEMENT, TESTIMONY
addendum .... JURAT
maker .... AFFIANT, DEPONENT,
TESTATOR
taker .... NOTARY
affiliate .... JOIN, MERGE, ARM,
WING, BAND, UNITE, MEMBER,
CHAPTER, DIVISION, BRANCH,
ASSOCIATE, OFF-SHOOT,
INSIDER
affinity ...... BOND, LINK, KINSHIP,
RELATION(SHIP), RAPPORT,
ATTRACTION, LEANING,
ALLIANCE
slang .... BAG, CUP OF TEA
affirm .... AVER, AVOW, SWEAR,
VOUCH, ASSERT, POSIT,
RATIFY, CONFIRM, NOTARIZE
affirmation .... DICTUM,
SUMPTION, ASSERTION,
SANCTION, CONFIRMATION,
THEOREM, DECLARATION
slang .... SAY-SO
affirmative .... AYE, YES, YEA,
YEP, AMEN, YEAH, NOD,
POSITIVE
consent .... BLESSING
expression .... THUMBS-UP
side of controversy .... PRO
voice/vote .... AYE
affix .... SEAL, GRAFT, ANNEX,
APPEND, ATTACH, STAMP,
FASTEN
afflatus .... IMPULSE, INSPIRATION
afflict .... AIL, VEX, PAIN,
DISTRESS, HARM, HURT,
PINCH, STING, SCATHE,
SICKEN, BURDEN, GRIPE,
TORMENT, TROUBLE,
INDISPOSE
afflicted .... BESET, SOUSED,
RACKED, HURTING, CONFUSED,
WOUNDED, PLASTERED,
TORTURED, STEWED,
DISTRESSED
affliction .... PAIN, GRIEF, WOE,

AILMENT, MALADY, CURSE, SCOURGE, SICKNESS, PLAGUE, ILLNESS, CALAMITY, DISORDER, SUFFERING

affluence .... WEALTH, RICHES, LUCRE, MONEY, OPULENCE, SECURITY, GOLD, PLENTY, ABUNDANCE

slang .... EASY STREET

afflux .... FLOW, DRIFT

afford .... GIVE, BEAR, GRANT, SUPPLY, STAND, SPARE, YIELD, ENABLE

affray .... RIOT, BRAWL, FIGHT, MELEE, SCUFFLE, ASSAULT

affright .... SCARE, ALARM, DAUNT, DISMAY, DREAD, TERRIFY, HORRIFY

affront .... DARE, FACE, MOCK, SNUB, HARASS, INSULT, OFFEND, SLIGHT, OFFENSE, CHALLENGE

affronter .... DARER, INSULTER

affusion .... BAPTISM

affy .... BETROTH, ESPOUSE

Afghan(istan) .... PATHAN, HOUND, SHAWL, DURANI, BLANKET

ameer .... SHERE

capital .... KABUL

carpet/rug .... BUKHARA

city/town .... HERAT, FARSI, BALKH, AYBAK, MOQOR, KALAT, FARAH, KHOLM, TAGAB, TULAK, GARDEZ, GHAZNI, QONDUZ, KUNAR, ZARANJ, BAGHLAN, KANDAHAR, MEYMANEH, CHARIKAR, JALALABAD, TALOQAN, SHEBERGHAN

coin .... PUL, AMANIA

desert .... MARGOW-DASHT-E

garment .... CHADRI

king .... SHAH, ZAHIR

lake .... HELMAND

language .... PASHTO, DARI, PUSHTU, UZBEK, BALUCHI

measure .... JERIB, KAROH

monetary unit .... AFGHANI

mountain .... KOH, SAFEO, SULAIMAN, PAMIRS, HIMALAYAS, HINDU KUSH

native .... SISTANI

nomad .... KUCHI

parliament .... SHURA, JIRGA, WOLESI

pony .... YABU, YABOO

prime minister .... YUSUF

prince .... AMIR, AMEER

range .... PAROPAMISUS

religion .... ISLAM

river .... KABUL, KONAR, TARNAK, HARIRUD, LURAH, HELMAND, FARAHRUD

ruler .... SHER SHAH

salt lake .... NAMAKSAR

sea .... DARYA

title .... KHAN

tribe .... SAFI, ULUS, TURK, KAFIR, TAJIK

tribesman .... PATHAN

valley .... WAKHAN

aficionado .... FAN, DEVOTEE, FOLLOWER, ENTHUSIAST

aflame .... AFIRE, ABLAZE, GLOWING, BURNING

afloat .... ASEA, AWEIGH, RIFE, ADRIFT, UNMOORED, AIRBORNE, CURRENT, UNFIXED, UNSTABLE, RUMORED, IN THE NEWS

afoot .... ASTIR, ABROAD, MOVING, UNDERWAY

aforesaid .... PRIOR, NAMED, FORMER, PREVIOUS, ANTECEDENT

aforethought .... PREPENSE, PREMEDITATED

afoul .... (EN)TANGLED, IN COLLISION

afraid .... COWED, SCARED, TERRIFIED, FRIGHTENED, FEARED, DAUNTED, FEARFUL, PANICKY, TIMOROUS, COWARDLY, DISMAYED

slang .... YELLOW, CHICKEN

afreet .... DEMON, JINNI, JINNEE

afresh .... NEW, NEWLY, OVER, AGAIN, DITTO

French .... BIS, ENCORE

Italian .... DA CAPO

slang .... FROM SCRATCH

African ...... IBO, BANTU, BLACK, HAUS(S)A, KAFFIR, NUBIAN, YORUBA, ETHIOP(IAN), SWAHILI, MANDINGO, HOTTENTOT

American dance .... CAKEWALK

American folksong .... SPIRITUAL

and mulatto offspring .... GRIFF(E)

and white offspring .... MESTEE, MUSTEE, MULATTO

antelope .... ELAND, KOB, ASSE, GEMSBOK, KUDU, IMPALA, ORIBI, GNU, BLESBUCK, BLESBOK, BONGO, ADDAX, PEELE, BUBAL(IS), BUSHBACK, BONTEBOK, BOS(C)HBOK, DUIKER(BOK),

KOODOO

ape .... BABOON

ash .... ATAR

ass .... QUAGGA

aunt .... TANTA

baboon .... DRILL, MANDRILL

bass .... IYO

bat .... HAMMERHEAD

bean .... CALABAR

beer .... POMBE

bird .... LORY, LOURI, TAHA, COLY, UMBER, UMBRETTE, TURAKOO

boat .... DHOW

boss/master .... BAAS

bread .... KISRA

buffalo .... NIARE

burrowing animal .... SURICATE, GERBIL(LE)

bushman .... NEGRILLO

bustard .... KORI, PAAUW

caffeine/nut tree .... KOLA, COLA

camp .... BOMA

canal .... SUEZ

canoe ...... ALMADIA, ALMADIE

cape ...... BON, BLANC, VERDE, PALMAS, AGULHAS, RASASER, BABAOMBY, GOOD HOPE

capital .... ACCRA, LAGOS, PRAIA, RABAT, CAIRO, DAKAR, TUNIS, LOME, BANJUL, NIAMEY, MONROVIA, PORTO NOVO, PRETORIA, CAPE TOWN, MORONI, HARARE, TRIPOLI, FREETOWN, PORT LOUIS, KHARTOUM, BRAZZAVILLE, VICTORIA, ADDIS ABABA, BISSAU, DAR ES SALAAM, LUANDA, KAMPALA, MAPUTO, CONAKRY, LIBREVILLE, KINSHASA, LILONGWE, LUSAKA, KIGALI, BAMAKO, YAOUNDE, DJIBOUTI, MALABO, NAIROBI

carnivore ..... CANNIBAL, LION, RATEL, HYENA, CHEETAH, LEOPARD

catfish .... SHAL

cattle .... NIATA

channel .... MOZAMBIQUE

charm .... GRIGRI, GREEGREE

chief .... KAID, CABOCEER

city/town ...... FES, ORAN, EDE, ADO, ABA, SALE, IWO, ARUSHA, SFAX, TANGIER, ABIDJAN, ILESHA, ILLORIN, ENUGU, JOHANNESBURG, DOUALA, FRANCISTOWN, TABORA, CASABLANCA, BLANTYRE, CONSTANTINE,

MANZINI, GERMISTON, MOMBASA, MARRAKECH, CALABAR, ABEOKUTA, KIKWIT, AZROU, TANGA, CHINGOLA, KIMBERLEY, KUMASI, ROADEPORT, NDOLA, KITWE, KABWE, COTONOU, DURBAN, JINJA

civet .... NANDINE

cloak .... JELAB

coin .... PESA, TOQUE, OKIA, RIAL, GIRSH, RUPIE, TALARI

colonist .... BOER

cony .... DAS, DASSIE

corn .... MEALIE

council .... BAAD, INDABA

country ...... ALGERIA, GHANA, BENIN, GAMBIA, GUINEA, IVORY COAST, LIBERIA, MAURITANIA, NIGERIA, MALI, MOROCCO, EGYPT, NIGER, SENEGAL, CHAD, LIBYA, TUNISIA, TOGO, DJIBOUTI, ETHIOPIA, CONGO, SUDAN, ANGOLA, KENYA, GABON, CAMEROON, ZAIRE, UGANDA, SOMALIA, ZIMBABWE, TANZANIA, ZAMBIA, MADAGASCAR, COMOROS, MOZAMBIQUE, SWAZILAND, MAURITIUS, BOTSWANA, SEYCHELLES

dance .... JUBA, N'GOMA

deity .... NYAMBE, NZAMBI

desert ...... KALAHARI, LIBYAN, SAHARA, GRAND ERG, TANEZROUFT

dialect ..... SAHO, TAAL, FANTI, BANTU, GEEZ, SWAHILI

disease .... NENTA

dish .... COUSCOUS

district .... NUBIA, RAND, RUANDA, NYASSA

dog .... BASENJI

drink .... OMEIRES

eagle .... BERGHAAN

explorer .... AKELEY

falls .... BOYOMA, STANLEY, VICTORIA

ferryboat .... PONT

fish .... CHARACIN

fly .... KIVU, TSETSE

food .... CASSAVA

fox .... ASSE, CAAMA

fruit .... TERFA, TERFEZ

fugitive .... MAROON

gangster .... TSOTSIS

garden .... SHAMBA

garment .... TOBE, KAROSS

gazelle .... ADMI, CORA, NORA, ARIEL

giraffe-like animal .... OKAPI

gold district .... RAND

gorge .... KLOOF

grass .... ALFA, FUNDI, ESPARTO

grass country .... VELD(T)

greenhorn .... IKONA

grivet .... WAAG

groundnut .... GOBBE

guard .... ASKAR

gulf .... ADEN, GABES, SIDRA, GUINEA

gun .... ROER

harp .... NANGA

hartebeest .... TORA

headland .... RAS

helmet .... TOPI, TOPEE

hemp .... IFE

hill .... KOP

hog .... BOSCHVARK

hornbill .... TOCK

horse .... BARB

horse disease .... SURRA

Hottentot .... NAMA

house .... TEMBE

hunting party .... SAFARI

hut .... KRAAL

instrument .... BALAFO, NANGA, REHAB, ZANZE

iris .... IXIA

Islamic sect .... ALMOHADES

island .... AZORES, PEMBA, BIOKO, ANNOBON, MAYOTTE, ST. HELENA, BOURBON, ASCENSION, CAPE VERDE, ZANZIBAR

islands ...... CANARY, MADEIRA

jackal .... DIEB

javelin .... ASSEGAI

lake .... CHAD, ASSALE, NASSER, KARIBA, EDWARD, TANA, TURKANA, VICTORIA, NVASA, VOLTA, NYAS(S)A, LIFU, DEMBEL, RUDOLF, ALBERT, TANGANYIKA

language .... BANTU, TAAL, BERBER, FULANI, MENDE, MOSSI, ARABIC, BALE, SENUFU, SWAHILI, YORUBA

lemur .... MACACO

lily .... ALOE, AGAPANTHUS

livestock .... FE

lynx .... CARACAL

mint plant .... COLEUS

money(shell) .... COWRY, COWRIE

monkey .... GRIVET, MONA, MACAQUE, COLOBUS, GUENON

mortar .... SWISH

Moslem .... BERBER

mountain .... ELGON, KENYA, TOUBKAL, NATAL, KILIMANJARO

mountain pass .... NEK

mountains ...... ATLAS, TIBESTI

musical instrument .... NANGA

narcotic .... DAGGA

native .... IBO, BARI, ASHA, KOPI, FELUP, FULAH, ZULU, SOTIK, MAUMAU, DAMARA, ASHANTI, WATU(T)SI, DAHOMAN, GABUNESE

nurse .... AYAH

palm .... DOOM, DOUM

peasant .... KOPI

pigeon .... NAMAQUA

pine .... RONIER

pirate .... ALGERINE

plant .... ALOE, IXIA, OCRA, CALLA, CALABAR, COLEUS

plateau .... KAROO

poisonous tree .... SASSY

polecat .... MUSANG, ZORIL

port .... ORAN, DAKAR

Portuguese colony .... ANGOLA

pygmy .... ITA, AKKA, NEGRILLO, HOTTENTOT

race .... SOMALI

region .... CONGO, NUBIA, SAHARA, SUDAN, SOUDAN

rhinoceros .... KEITLOA

river ...... NILE, CONGO, KASAI, BLUE NILE, NIGER, WHITE NILE, VAAL, ORANGE, LIMPOPO, RUFIJI, OKOVANGO, VOLTA, UBANGI, ZAIRE, ZAMBEZI

river bed .... DONGA

rosewood .... MULOMPI

rug .... KAROSS

ruminant .... CAMEL

scrub .... BITO

seaport .... ORAN, LAGOS, TUNIS, CASABLANCA

secret society .... MAU-MAU

sect .... COPTIC, ABELITE

servant .... VOLK

sheep .... ZENU

snake .... BOA, ELAP, CERASTES

soldier .... SPAHI, ASKARI

songbird .... LINNET

sorcery .... OBE, OBI, OBEAH

soup powder .... LALO

spear .... ASSAGAI, ASSEGAI

spiritual power .... NGAI

squirrel .... XERUS

stockade .... BOMA, KRAAL, ZAREBA

stork .... ARGALA, MARABOU

tableland .... KAROO

"telegraph" .... TOM-TOM
tick .... TAMPAN
title .... AGA, RAS, AGHA,
BWANA, NEGUS
tree .... COLA, ARTAR, KOLA,
TARFA, BAOBAB, BAKU, SHEA,
BUMBO, SASSY, NJABE,
COPAIBA, AKEE, MOLI,
SAMANDURA
tribal conference ..... PALAVER
tribe .... ABO, KUA, AKAN,
ALAR, BONI, DOMA, GOGO,
HABE, KALI, MAKA, KETU,
NUBA, TIBU, VACA, KAFFIR,
WARI, KREPI, ZULU, BANTU,
KABONGA
trip .... TREK, SAFARI
U.N. president
.... (MONGI)SLIM
valley .... WADI, KLOOF
village .... DORP, STAD, KRAAL
wading bird .... IBIS
war dance .... CALINDA
weasel .... ZORIL(A)
weasel-like animal
.... ICHNEUMON
wheat .... IMPHEE
whip .... KOORBASH
wild cat .... SERVAL
wild hog .... BOAR,
BOSCHVARK, WART(HOG)
wild sheep .... ARUI, UDAD,
AOUDAD
wind .... SAMIEL, SIMOOM,
SIMOON
witchcraft .... OBI, OBEAH
wolf .... AARD
wood .... TEAK, EBONY
worm .... LOA

African-Americans,
discrimination against
.... JIM CROW(ISM)
Africa's ancient name .... LIBYA
Afrikaans .... BOER, TAAL
afro .... HAIRDO, NATURAL,
HAIRSTYLE, COIF(FURE),
HEADDRESS
aft .... TAIL, ABAFT, (A)STERN,
POSTERN
after .... NEXT, PAST, POST,
LATER, SINCE, BEHIND
a fashion ..... MERELY, SIMPLY
a while .... ANON, LATER,
SHORTLY
dinner treat .... CORDIAL
expenses .... NET
the style of .... A LA
afterbirth .... SECUNDINE
afterdeath .... POSTHUMOUS
after-effect .... WAKE, TRACK,
TRAIL, SIDE EFFECT

afterglow .... FLUSH, GLEAM,
GLINT, GLOSS, LUSTER,
SHEEN, SKYLIGHT
afterimage .... SPECTRUM
afterlife .... THE BEYOND, THE
HEREAFTER
aftermath .... EFFECT, RESULT,
ROWEN, SEQUEL, LINEAGE,
SUCCESSOR
afternoon .... POST-MERIDIAN
nap .... SIESTA
party .... TEA
show .... MATINEE
afterpiece .... EPODE, EXODE
of a sort .... ENCORE
aftersong .... EPODE
afterthought .... REGRET, REVIEW,
REMORSE, RETHINKING
French ...... ESPRIT D'ESCALIER
in a letter .... POSTSCRIPT
slang .... FLIPFLOP
afterward .... THEN, LATER,
SUBSEQUENTLY
Aga .... TURK
Agag's slayer .... SAMUEL
again ...... ANEW, MORE, ENCORE,
BESIDES
appear/happen .... RECUR
do/say .... REPEAT
against .... CON, ANTI, CONTRA,
OPPOSED, VERSUS
a person/thing .... HOSTILE,
UNFRIENDLY
a thing, in law .... IN REM
morals .... WICKED, RIBALD,
ILLICIT, OBSCENE, UNETHICAL
prefix .... ANTI, CONTRA
slang .... ASS-BACKWARDS
the current .... UPSTREAM
the grain .... AT ODDS
the law .... ILLEGAL,
UNLAWFUL
the state .... SEDITIOUS,
TREASON(OUS)
agalite .... TALC
agalloch wood .... AGAR, ALOE,
GAROO
agama .... LIZARD, CHAMELEON
Agamemnon rescued her
.... BRISEIS
Agamemnon's brother
.... MENELAUS
children .... ELECTRA,
ORESTES, IPHIGENIA
father .... ATREUS
agamic .... ASEXUAL
Agana is capital of .... GUAM
agape .... HOLE, AJAR, CHASM,
YAWNING, OPENING
agaric .... FUNGUS, MUSHROOM,
TOADSTOOL

agate .... ONYX, RUBY, ACHATE,
MARBLE, TYPE, QUARTZ
agave .... ALOE, PITA, AMOLE,
DATIL, ISTLE, MAGUEY, SISAL,
HENEQUEN
juice drink .... MESCAL,
PULQUE
age .... EON, ERA, TIME, RIPEN,
YEARS, MATURE, EPOCH,
CENTURY, MELLOW, LIFETIME
designating one ...... ICE, OLD,
IRON, STONE, ATOMIC,
BRONZE, GOLDEN, SILVER,
TEEN(S), PUBERTY,
ADOLESCENCE
modern .... JET, SPACE,
ATOMIC, COMPUTER,
ELECTRONIC
of moon on June 1st
.... EPACT
old .... DOTAGE, SENESCE,
SENILITY
pertaining to an .... ERAL,
EVAL, HEYDAY, INNOCENCE
same .... COEVAL
when mammals developed
.... NEOCENE
aged .... RIPE, ANILE, OLD(EN),
SENILE, ELDERLY
agee .... AWRY, ASKEW
Agena .... ATLAS
agency .... MEANS, MEDIUM,
HAND, PROXY, SERVICE,
TRADING, BROKERAGE
news .... UPI, AP, TASS,
REUTERS, DOMEI, MENA,
NCNA, HAVAS
agendum .... RITUAL
Agenor's daughter .... EUROPA
agent .... ENVOY, FACTOR, PROXY,
DEPUTY, BROKER, EMISSARY,
MIDDLEMAN, FACIENT,
LEGMAN, PROCTOR
business .... MANAGER
chemical .... ACID, ALKALI,
REAGENT
cleansing .... SOAP,
TOOTHPASTE, DETERGENT,
ENEMA, PURGATIVE
007 .... BOND
foreign firm .... COMPRADOR
freight/shipping
.... FORWARDER
insurance .... UNDERWRITER
intermediary .... JOBBER,
LIAISON, MIDDLEMAN,
DISTRIBUTOR
legal .... LAWYER, ATTORNEY
narcotics .... FED, NARC
real estate .... BROKER,
REALTOR

Treasury .... T-MAN, REVENUER
undercover .... SPY
undercover work
.... ESPIONAGE
agglomerate .... MASS, LUMP, HEAP, GATHER, CLUSTER
agglomeration .... COHERENCE
aggrandize .... ENLARGE, EXPAND, INCREASE
aggravate ...... TWIT, ANGER, IRK, WORSEN, INTENSIFY
aggregate .... SUM, MASS, TOTAL, GATHER, WHOLE, COMBINED
fruit of strawberry
.... ETAERIO
aggress .... ATTACK, INVADE, PROVOKE
aggression .... WAR, RAID, ASSAULT, ATTACK, INVASION, ONSLAUGHT, HOSTILITY
aggressive .... MILITANT, PEPPY, PUSHY, WARLIKE, DYNAMIC, COMBATIVE, PUSHING, SPIRITED, ZESTFUL, ASSERTIVE
slang .... GO-GO, TRIGGER-HAPPY
aggressor .... RAIDER, INVADER, ATTACKER, OFFENDER, PROVOKER, ASSAILANT
slang .... MUGGER
aggrieve .... WRONG, CRUSH, INJURE, OFFEND, SLIGHT, OPPRESS
aghast .... AMAZED, STUNNED, APPALLED, BEWITCHED, TERRIFIED, ENTRANCED, FROZEN, HORRIFIED
slang .... SCARED SHITLESS
agialid .... BITO
agile .... FAST, KEEN, SPRY, QUICK, PERT, ALERT, FLEET, SHARP, SWIFT, ACTIVE, NIMBLE, LISSOM(E), LIVELY, CHIPPER
aging .... SENESCENT
agio .... PREMIUM, REBATE, SETOFF, EXCHANGE, DISCOUNT, DEDUCTION
slang .... KICKBACK, ROLLBACK
agitate ...... STIR, ALARM, CHURN, ROUSE, EXCITE, WORRY, F(E)AZE, FEEZE, UPSET, SHAKE, INCITE, ROIL, DISTURB, FLUSTER
agitation .... DITHER, RUMPUS, POTHER, TUMULT, TURMOIL, FLURRY, ANXIETY, UPHEAVAL, TEMPEST, CACOPHONY
French .... BROUHAHA

Italian .... FURORE
slang .... HEEBIE-JEEBIES
state of .... AGOG, BOILING, SEETHING, STORMY, TUMULTUOUS
agitator .... INCITER, URGER, RIOTER, EXCITER, MUTINEER, PROVOKER, FIREBRAND, RABBLE-ROUSER, DEMAGOG(UE), ANARCHIST, INCENDIARY
French .... PROVOCATEUR
Aglaia .... GRACE
aglet .... TAG, LACE, SPANGLE
agley .... AWRY
aglow .... ALIT, SHINING, MOONLIT, RADIANT, STARLIT, BLUSHING, BURNING, TINSELED
agnail .... HANGNAIL
agname .... NICKNAME, PET NAME, MONICKER
agnate .... KIN, ALLIED, RELATIVE
Agnew's negativists
.... NATTERING NABOBS
agnomen .... ALIAS, (NICK)NAME, COGNOMEN
agnostic .... CYNIC, NESCIENT, ATHEIST, DOUBTER, SCOFFER, SKEPTIC
Agnus Dei .... HYMN, LAMB, PRAYER
ago ...... BACK, ERST, GONE, PAST, SINCE
agog .... ASTIR, EAGER, MORBID, AQUIVER, CURIOUS, YEASTY, EXPECTANT
agonize .... RACK, FESTER, RANKLE, SUFFER, STRAIN, GRIEVE, TORTURE, TORMENT, WRITHE, STRUGGLE
agonizing struggle .... THROES
agony .... WOE, PAIN, THROE(S), SORROW, DESPAIR, PASSION, DISTRESS, ANGUISH, SUFFERING
"agony ____" of newspaper
.... COLUMN
agora .... ASSEMBLY, MARKETPLACE
coin .... OBOL
agouti .... PACA, RODENT
agrafe .... CLASP, BRACKET
Agram .... ZAGREB
Agra's pride .... TAJ MAHAL
agree .... JIBE, GRANT, MATCH, TALLY, CONCUR, YIELD, ASSENT, APPROVE, COINCIDE, CORRESPOND
agreeable .... PLEASING, SUITABLE, PLEASANT,

WILLING, AMENABLE
odor .... SCENT, AROMA, PERFUME, FRAGRANCE
old style .... AMENE
taste .... SWEET, SAVORY, TOOTHSOME, PALATABLE
agreeableness of letter
.... EUTONY
agreement .... PACT, DEAL, CARTEL, ACCORD, TREATY, MISE, ENTENTE, CONCORD, AMEN, CONTRACT, COVENANT
in opinion .... CONSENSUS
to rent .... LEASE
with conditions .... ESCROW
agrestic .... RURAL, RUSTIC, CRUDE, PASTORAL
agricultural .... FARM, RURAL, BUCOLIC, RUSTIC, AGRARIAN
overseer .... AGRONOME
worker .... OKIE, RYOT, PEASANT
agriculture, goddess of
.... CERES, DEMETER
Agrippa's temple ...... PANTHEON
Agrippina's son .... NERO
agua .... TOAD, WATER
ague .... CHILL, FEVER
Ahab's cabin boy .... PIP
daughter .... ATHALIAH
father .... OMRI
royal palace ..... IVORY HOUSE
ship .... PEQUOD, WHALER
son .... AHAZIAH, JEHORAM
wife .... JEZEBEL
Ahasuerus' minister ...... HAMAN
wife .... ESTHER
Ahaz's father .... JOTHAM
grandson .... MANASSEH
son .... HEZEKIAH
ahead .... FIRST, EARLY, FRONT, BEFORE, FORWARD, WINNING, LEADING
forge .... LEAD, ADVANCE, PROGRESS
French .... A LA MODE
of its time ...... ULTRAMODERN
ahem sound .... COUGH
ahuehuete .... CYPRESS
ai .... SLOTH
aid .... ABET, HELP, SUCCOR, ASSIST, REMEDY, FAVOR, RESCUE, FURTHER
Aida's lover .... R(H)ADAMES
rival .... AMNERIS
aide .... ADJUTANT, DEPUTY, ORDERLY, ASSISTANT, SUBALTERN, LIEUTENANT
memoire .... MEMORANDUM
aiglet .... TAG, POINT
aigrette .... EGRET

ail .... PAIN, BOTHER, SUFFER
aileron part .... TAB
ailing .... ILL, SICK, HURTING,
                UNDER THE WEATHER
ailment .... ILLNESS, DEFECT,
      MALADY, DISEASE, DISORDER,
                    COMPLAINT
  minor .... PIP
aim .... END, GOAL, POINT, ASPIRE,
      TARGET, SIGHT, INTENT,
      PURPOSE, DIRECTION,
      AMBITION, OBJECT(IVE)
aimless .... FUTILE, USELESS,
      POINTLESS, DESULTORY,
                HAPHAZARD
  scribble .... DOODLE
  wanderer of sorts .... JEW,
      NOMAD, ROVER, TRAMP
ain .... OWN
air .... ARIA, MEIN, SONG, TUNE,
      MANNER, MELODY, CARRIAGE,
               ATMOSPHERE
  apparatus .... FAN, SCUBA,
      BLOWER, AERATOR
  bends .... AEROEMBOLISM
  boundary .... FRONT
  castle .... (DAY)DREAM,
      AUTISM, FANTASY, REVERIE,
               STARGAZE
  combining form .... AERO,
                AER(I)
  current .... EDDY, STREAM
  currents, rising ...... ANABATIC
  expose to .... AERATE
  fear of .... AEROPHOBIA
  fill with .... AERATE, GAS UP
  filled film of liquid
      .... BUBBLE
  force girl .... WASP, WREN
  fresh/pure .... OZONE
  friction .... WINDAGE
  gauge .... AEROMETER
  group .... RAF, USAF, WING,
                ESCADRILLE
  hero .... ACE
  in motion .... WIND, BREEZE,
                ZEPHYR
  in violent agitation .... STORM,
      TORNADO, CYCLONE, TEMPEST,
        TYPHOON, WHIRLWIND
  mass .... ISOTHERM
  navigation officer
      .... AVIGATOR
  navigation system
      .... SHORAN, TELERAN
  of .... AERIAL
  open .... ALFRESCO
  passage/pipe .... FLUE,
      NOSTRIL, VENT(IDUCT)
  pertaining to .... AURAL,
                AERIAL

  pipe .... FLUE, VENTIDUCT
  plant .... ORCHID, EPIPHYTE
  pocket .... TURBULENCE
  poisonous/unwholesome
      .... MIASMA, MALARIA
  race marker .... PYLON
  raid ..... BLITZ(KRIEG), STRAFE,
           BOMBARDMENT
  route .... SKYWAY
  shaft ..... BLOWHOLE, NOSTRIL,
                SPIRACLE
  show .... FLYING CIRCUS
  spirit .... SYLPH, ARIEL
  stream producer .... FAN,
      BELLOWS, PROPELLER
  taxi .... SHUTTLE
  tight .... HERMETIC
  unhealthfulness .... POLLUTION
  upper .... OZONE, ETHER
aircraft .... SPAD, AIRPLANE,
      AUTOGIRO, TRIMOTOR,
      GLIDER, HELICOPTER,
      ZEPPELIN, DIRIGIBLE,
              HYDROPLANE
  abrupt climb .... CHANDELLE
  air from propeller ...... DOWN-
      WASH, SLIPSTREAM
  altitude controller .... BALLAST
  altitude indicator
      .... ALTIMETER, STATOSCOPE
  attack with gunfire .... STRAFE
  battle .... DOGFIGHT
  body .... FUSELAGE
  bombs .... EGGS
  carried by another
      .... PICKABACK
  carrier ..... FLAT-TOP, HORNET,
      YORKTOWN, SARATOGA,
      LEXINGTON, AMERICA,
              ENTERPRISE
  climb, sudden .... ZOOM
  commercial .... LINER, AIRLINE
  delivery of sold .... FERRY
  designer ..... FOKKER, CURTISS,
               SIKORSKY
  detector .... RADAR
  dome .... BLISTER
  enclosed part .... NACELLE
  engine cover .... COWLING
  engineless .... GLIDER,
              SAILPLANE
  flapping .... FLUTTER,
      ORTHOPTER, ORNITHOPTER
  flight .... HOP, TRIP,
           BARNSTORM
  flight record .... LOG
  formation .... FLIGHT,
           ECHELON
  front .... NOSE
  fuel, antiknock .... TRIPTANE
  group .... WING, ECHELON,

      SQUADRON, ESCADRILLE
  gun turret shield .... DOME,
             BLISTER
  heavier than air .... AERODYNE
  idle propeller of ...... FEATHER
  landing position ...... PANCAKE
  landing/take-off strip
      .... RUNWAY
  launcher on ship
      .... CATAPULT
  lever .... (JOY)STICK
  maneuver on ground ..... TAXI
  manufacturer .... BOEING,
      CESSNA, DOUGLAS, LOCKHEED
  military scouting
      .... GRASSHOPPER
  movable flap .... GILL,
      RUDDER, AILERON
  navigation aid .... LORAN,
      BEACON, SHORAN, TELERAN
  notice to pilots .... NOTAM
  obsolete .... CANARD
  opening for missile ..... BOMB
               BAY
  pilotless .... DRONE
  pilot's place .... COCKPIT
  propeller .... PROP, ROTOR,
              AIRSCREW
  recovery from a dive
      .... PULLOUT
  runner for landing .... SKID
  shed/shelter .... HANGAR,
      AIRDROME, AERODROME
  small .... FLIVVER
  stabilizer .... FIN, AIRFOIL,
            EMPENNAGE
  struts arrangement
      .... CABANE
  stunts .... AEROBATICS, SPIN,
      (BARREL)ROLL, LOOP (-THE-
      LOOP), IMMELMAN (TURN)
  tail part .... FIN, RUDDER,
      ELEVATOR, STABILIZER
  towed target .... DROGUE
  throttle .... GUN
  turn .... BANK, LOOP, BARREL
              LOOP
  twisting force .... TORQUE
  type .... JET, LINER, FIGHTER,
      AMPHIBIAN, TWOSEATER,
      MONOPLANE, BOMBER,
           COMMERCIAL
  war .... MIG, SPAD, ZERO,
      STUKA, BOMBER, FIGHTER,
      SABREJET, SUPERCOBRA,
      MIRAGE, SPITFIRE, CORSAIR,
          SUPERFORT
  water landing gear
      .... PONTOON
  window .... BOMB BAY

wing section for banking .... AILERON

wing support .... STRUT, CABANE

airdrome. See **airport**

airedale .... TERRIER

airfoil .... TAB, PLANE

airing .... OUTING, REVEALING, EXPRESSION, VENTILATION

airline schedule .... TIMETABLE

airmail, by .... PAR AVION

airman .... PILOT, AVIATOR, BARNSTORMER

mythological .... ICARUS

non-flying .... KIWI

would-be .... DODO

airplane. See **aircraft**

airport .... (AIR)DROME, HANGAR, AERODROME

busiest .... O'HARE

marker .... PYLON

part .... APRON, TOWER, RUNWAY, LANDING FIELD

paving .... TARMAC

queue .... TAXIS

air-raid shelter .... ABRI, BUNKER, DUGOUT

airs, given to .... VAIN, PRISSY, SNOOTY, SNOBBISH

airship .... AERO, BLIMP, BALLOON, ZEPPELIN, DIRIGIBLE

airsick .... QUALMY, QUEASY, NAUSEOUS

slang .... PUKY, PUKISH

airtight .... FOOLPROOF, HERMETIC(AL)

airy .... GAY, LIGHT, BREEZY, JAUNTY, ETHEREAL

aisle .... LANE, NAVE, PATH, ALLEY, CHANNEL, CORRIDOR, PASSAGEWAY

tread the middle .... WED, MARRY

treader of the middle .... BRIDE(GROOM)

ait .... EYOT, HOLM, ISLE(T)

Aix-la-Chapelle .... AACHEN

Ajaccio is capital of .... CORSICA

Ajax, father of .... TELEMON

the _____ .... LESS

akin .... SIB, LIKE, AGNATE, GERMANE, RELATED

Al Smith character .... JEFF, MUTT

ala .... WING

Alabama bay .... MOBILE, PERDIDO, BON SECOUR

capital .... MONTGOMERY

channel .... GRANTS PASS

city/town .... PELL, TROY,

SELMA, LINDEN, MOBILE, GADSDEN, DECATUR, ANNISTON, CORONA, FLORENCE, HUNTSVILLE, BIRMINGHAM, PRICHARD, TUSCALOOSA

county .... LEE, BIBB, CLAY, DALE, BLOUNT, LAMAR, COFFEE, DALLAS, MOBILE, MORGAN, SHELBY, ELMORE, WALKER, WILCOX, BALDWIN, CALHOUN, COLBERT, DE KALB, HOUSTON, JACKSON, MADISON, MARSHALL, JEFFERSON, LAUDERDALE, LIMESTONE, MONTGOMERY

creek .... SANDY, PIGEON, ESCAMBIA, MULBERRY

island .... HERBES

lake .... LAY, WEISS, JORDAN, HARDING, WHEELER, BANKHEAD, PICKWICK, GREAT ROCK

mountain .... SAND, CHEAHA, LOOKOUT

river .... ELK, PEA, COOSA, CAHABA, LITTLE, MOBILE, SIPSEY, TENSAW, ALABAMA, PERDIDO, SEPULGA, CHATTOOGA, TENNESSEE, TOMBIGBEE

state bird ..... YELLOWHAMMER

state flower .... CAMELLIA

state nickname .... COTTON, HEART OF DIXIE

alabaster .... SILK, SATIN, IVORY, GYPSUM, VELVET, MINERAL, GRAPHITE

alackaday .... ALAS, WOE IS ME

alacrity .... ZEAL, AGILITY, CELERITY, VITALITY, RAPIDITY, RASHNESS, QUICKNESS, READINESS

Aladdin's lamp .... WISH-BRINGER

servant .... GENIE, JINNI

alamandite .... GARNET

alameda .... WALK, PROMENADE

alamo .... POPLAR

Alamo hero .... BOWIE, CROCKETT

in Texas .... SHRINE, MISSION

Alamogordo county .... OTERO

Alan, actor .... ALDA, LADD

author .... PATON

aland .... DOG

alange .... DRAB, DULL, DREARY

alantin .... INULIN

alar .... PTERO, WINGED, WINGLIKE, WINGSHAPED

Alaric's men .... GOTHS

alarm .... CALL, ALERT, PANIC, SCARE, SIREN, AROUSE,

SIGNAL, WARN(ING)

bell .... TOCSIN

poetic .... ALARUM

system for short .... DEWS

whistle .... BLAST, SIREN(E), FOGHORN

alarming .... AWING, FAZING, SERIOUS, CHILLING, CRITICAL, MENACING

alarmist .... SCAREMONGER

slang .... WORRY WART

alas .... ALACKADAY, WOE (IS ME)

Alaska capital .... JUNEAU

former capital .... SITKA

Purchase in 1867, to some .... FOLLY

Alaskan auk .... ARRIES

bay .... DRY, ICY, HAZEN, MUZON, NORTON, TOGIAK, BRISTOL, CHIGNIK, PAVLOF, CORDOVA, GLACIER, TWO ARM, YAKUTAT

bear .... KODIAK

blizzard .... PURGA

canal .... SEYMOUR

cape .... ICY, HALKETT, LISBURNE, MENDENHALL, WRANGELL, FAIRWEATHER, CONSTANTINE, KRUSENSTERN

city/town .... NOME, KENAI, SITKA, BETHEL, KODIAK, SEWARD, VALDEZ, COLLEGE, CORDOVA, SKAGWAY, WRANGELL, ANCHORAGE, FAIRBANKS, KETCHIKAN

garment .... PARKA

glacier .... MUIR, GUYOT, BERING, COLUMBIA, MALASPINA

highway .... ALCAN

Indian .... TLINGIT, TLINKIT

inlet .... COOK, DEASE, PORT WELLS, PORT HEIDEN

island .... HALL, KING, KUIU, UNGA, KAYAK, KISKA, OTTER, SANAK, UMNAK, AGATTU, AKUTAN, KNIGHT, KODIAK, MARMOT, WALRUS, ETOLIN, MITKOF, STUART, BARANOF, YAKOBI

islands ..... FOX, RAT, SEMICHI, ALEUTIAN, PRIBILOF, ANDREANOF

lake .... CLARK, MUYAKUK, SELAWIK, BECHAROF

mining town .... NOME

monument .... KATMAI

mountain .... ADA, BEAR, BONA, COOK, HAYES, KENAI, DOUGLAS, FORAKER, SANFORD, MCKINLEY, MICHELSON,

15

VANCOUVER, DEVILS PAW, WEST POINT, FAIRWEATHER, KATES NEEDLE

mountains .... BAIRD, COAST, TAYLOR, WARING, CHUGASH, ENDICOTT

native .... DENE, ALEUT, ESKIMO

peak .... MCKINLEY

peninsula .... UNGA, KENAI, SEWARD

range .... BROOKS, ALEUTIAN

river ..... TAKU, FIRTH, KOBUK, MEADE, STONY, WHITE, YUKON, COPPER, INNOKO, NOATAK, TANANA, NOWITNA, SUSITNA, TAZLINA, COLVILLE, CHANDALAR, MATANUSKA, PORCUPINE

seaport .... KETCHIKAN

state bird .... WILLOW PTARMIGAN

state flower .... FORGET-ME-NOT

state nickname .... THE LAST FRONTIER

tree .... SPRUCE

valley .... MATANUSKA

vehicle .... SLED

volcano .... KISKA, KATMAI, PAVLOF, TANAGA, REDOUBT, MAKUSHIN, SHISHALDIN

alb .... ROBE, VESTMENT

alba .... SONG, AUBADE

albacore .... FISH, TUNNY, BONITO, MACKEREL

Albanese, soprano .... LICIA

Albanian .... GHEG

capital .... TIRANA, TIRANE

city/town .... FIER, BERAT, KORCE, VLORE, DURRES, KAVAJE, ELBASAN, SHKODER

dialect .... GEG, CHAM, TOSK

king .... ZOG

island .... SAZAN

lake .... OHRID, PRESPA, SCUTARI

money .... LEK, QUINTAR

mountain .... KORAB

river .... DRIN, VIJOSE

sea .... ADRIATIC

seaport .... SCUTARI

soldier .... PALIKAR

spy .... CICERO

strait .... OTRANTO

Albany is capital of .... NEW YORK

albatross .... GONY, NELLY, MALLEMUCK

Albee's Alice .... TINY

albeit .... YET, STILL, EVEN IF,

ALTHOUGH

Alberta resource .... OIL

scenery .... BANFF

albinism .... ALPHOSIS, BLONDNESS, WHITENESS

Albion .... ENGLAND

adjective for .... PERFIDIOUS

albite .... FELDSPAR

album .... RECORD, REGISTER, SCRAPBOOK

albumen .... GLAIR

alburnum .... SAPWOOD

alcaide .... JAILER, WARDEN

Alcestis' husband ...... ADMETUS

alchemical .... HERMETIC

alchemist, pioneer .... THOTH

alchemy, work on .... ALMAGEST

alchitran .... TAR, PITCH

Alcides .... HERCULES

Alcinous' garden .... SCHERIA

alcohol ...... BREW, GROG, LOTUS, LIQUOR, SPIRITS, BEVERAGE, SCHNAPPS, INTOXICANT

antiseptic .... IODINE, PEROXIDE, MERTHIOLATE

chemical .... BORAX, ACETONE, AMMONIA, BROMIDE, BENZOATE

crystal .... TALITOL

depressant .... OPIUM, CODEINE, MORPHINE

fuel .... GAS, ETHANOL, PROPELLANT

ingredient .... AMYL, ETHYL, METHYL

slang .... BOOZE

solid .... STEROL

alcoholic .... WINY, ADDICT, VINOUS, DRUNKARD

drink .... GIN, RUM, TOT, MEAD, WINE, VODKA, POSSET, WHISKEY

drink from rice/molasses .... SAKE, ARRACK

drunkard .... WASSAILER, DIPSOMANIAC

haunt of .... SKIDROW

liquor .... MESCAL, TIPPLE

liquor, craving for ...... THIRST

liquor from wine/fruit .... BRANDY, COGNAC

liquor smuggler .... RUMRUNNER

liquor to an Indian .... FIREWATER

slang .... LUSH, WINO, BOOZER, SPONGE

sugar .... TROSSE

Alcoran .... KORAN

Alcott heroine .... JO, AMY, MEG, BETH

alcove .... BAY, NOOK, BOWER, NICHE, ORIEL, RECESS

Alda, Frances .... DIVA, SOPRANO

aldehyde, liquid .... CITRAL

alder .... ROSE, ARN, SAGE, ALNUS

alderman .... REEVE, SOLON, SENATOR, LEGISLATOR

ale .... MOM, NOG(G), BEER, BOCK, FLIP, YILL, ALEGAR, LAGER, STOUT, STINGO, PORTER

flavor .... HOPS

ingredient .... HOPS, MALT, YEAST

measure .... GILL, PINT, NOGGIN

mug .... TOBY, STEIN

sour/vinegar .... ALEGAR

strong .... NAPPY, STINGO

alec .... (FISH)SAUCE

Alecto .... FURY

alee, opposite of .... STOSS, AWEATHER

alehouse .... BAR, INN, PUB, BISTRO, SALOON, TAVERN

slang .... SPEAKEASY

alembic .... STILL, RETORT, DISTILLER

Alencon is capital of .... ORNE

product .... LACE

Aleppo native .... SYRIAN

alert .... GLEG, KEEN, AWAKE, AWARE, READY, WARNING, VIGILANT, ON THE BALL

Aleut .... UNUNGUN

Aleutian fish .... GREENLING

isle .... ADAK, ATKA, ATTU

alewife .... FISH, HERRING, POMPANO, WALLEYE

Alexander .... KING, POPE, SEROV, FLEMING, THE GREAT, ARCHIPELAGO

Hamilton's downfall ..... DUEL

the Great's battle site .... ISSUS, GRANICUS, HYDASPES, GAUGAMELA

eastern conquest .... SIWA, SUSA, BABYLON, SAMARIA, PARSEPOLIS

enemy .... BATIS, PORUS, DARIUS

father .... PHILIP

general .... ANTIPATER

kingdom .... MACEDONIA

southern conquest .... ACCO, GAZA, TYRE, AZOTUS, ASHKELON, STRATO'S TOWER

Alexandria, patriarch ...... PAPA

Alexandrian courtesan .... THAIS

mathematician .... PTOLEMY

theologian .... ARIUS

writer .... ORIGEN

alfalfa .... PEA, MEDIC, FODDER, LUCERN(E), SATIVA
alforja .... SADDLEBAG
alfresco .... OPEN-AIR, OUTDOOR(S), OUTSIDE
alga .... NORI, SCUM, DESMID, DIATOM, SEAWEED, NOSTOC, CONFERVA, ANABAENA, SPYROGYRA
filament .... TRICHOMA
algae genus .... ALARIA
like .... ALGOID
algarroba .... TREE, CAROB, CALDEN, LOCUST, (HONEY)MESQUITE
Algebar .... ORION
Algeria, Roman name .... POMARIA
Algerian cape .... BOUGAROUN
capital .... ALGIERS
cavalryman .... SPAHI
city/town .... BONE, ORAN, MEDEA, SAIDA, SETIF, BISKRA, BOUGIE, TIEMCEN, GHARDALA, TOUGGOURT, CONSTANTINE
city section .... CASBAH
desert .... IGUIDI, SAHARA, GRAND ERG, TANEZROUFT
governor .... DEY
grass .... ESPARTO
guerrilla chieftain .... ZBIRI
infantryman .... TURCO
lagoon .... AURES
minority group .... BERBERS
money .... DINAR
mountain .... TAHAT, CHELIA
native .... BERBER, KABYLE
native quarters .... CASBAH, KASBAH
port ..... BONE, ORAN, ALGIERS
president .... BELLA, BOUMEDIENNE
river .... CHELIF, MEDJERDA
ruler .... BEY
salt lake .... CHERGUI, MEIRHIR
soldier .... SPAHI, TURCO, SPAHEE
weight .... ROTL
algesis .... ACHE, PAIN
algia, as suffix .... PAIN
algid .... COLD, CHILLY
algolagnia .... SADISM, MASOCHISM
Algonquian friend .... NETOP
Indian .... SAC, CREE, MIAMI, LENAPE, OTTAWA, ARAPAHO(E), SHAWNEE
Indian money .... SEAWANT, SE(A)WAN
algor .... CHILL
algum ...... ALMUG, SANDALWOOD

Ali Baba .... WOODCUTTER
brother of .... CASSIM
helper of .... MORGIANA
word(s) of .... (OPEN)SESAME
alias .... ANONYM, HANDLE, PSEUDONYM, ALSO KNOWN AS, OTHERWISE KNOWN
letters before .... AKA
alibi .... PLEA, FEINT, DEVICE, EXCUSE, REFUGE, COVER(-UP), PRETEXT
slang .... COP-OUT
alible ...... NUTRITIVE, NOURISHING
Alice's cat .... DINAH
alidade .... DIOPTER
alien .... METIC, EXOTIC, ADVERSE, FOREIGN(ER), OUTSIDER, STRANGER, OUTLANDER
from outer space .... MARTIAN, SAUCERMAN
alienate .... WEAN, MADDEN, DIVIDE, SUBVERT, DISUNITE, ESTRANGE, TRANSFER, BRAINWASH, DISAFFECT
alienist .... PSYCHIATRIST
slang .... HEADSHRINKER
alight .... LAND, DEBUS, PERCH, ROOST, DEPLANE, DESCEND, DISMOUNT, STEP DOWN
align .... TRUE, ALINE, ARRAY, LEVEL, STRAIGHTEN
alignment .... UNION, FUSION, LINAGE
slang .... HOOKUP, CAHOOTS
alike ...... AKIN, SAME, MATCHED, SIMILAR
aliment .... PAP, FOOD, PABULUM, NUTRITION
alimentary canal .... ENTERON
motion .... PERISTALSIS
alimony .... AID, PENSION, SUBSIDY, SUPPORT
aliped creature .... BAT
aliquot .... PRIME, DIGITAL, NUMERAL
alit .... AGLOW, LANDED, RADIANT, DISMOUNTED
alive .... PERT, SPRY, ALERT, QUICK, LIVELY, LIVING, ANIMATED
and kicking .... HEALTHY
to .... COGNIZANT, IN THE KNOW
alkali .... LYE, SALT, SODA, POTASH, ANTACID, SALTWORT
alkaline .... LIME, OXIDE
solution .... LYE
alkaloid .... ARICIN, CAFFEIN(E), ESERINE, ARABINE, CODEINE, DITAMIN, SINAPIN, CAPSAICIN, QUININ(E), MORPHINE,

BERBERIN(E), MESCALINE
bean .... ESERIN
hemlock .... CONIN(E)
mushroom .... MUSCARINE
poison(ous) .... CONIN, CURARE, BRUCIN(E), TROPIN(E), THEBAINE, MUSCARIN(E)
sedative .... CODEIN(E)
tea .... THEINE
alkanet .... DYE, ANCHUSA, BUGLOSS
alkene .... OLEFIN
all .... ANY, SUM, FULL, WHOLE, ENTIRE, PLENARY, PLENUM, EVERY(ONE), TOTAL(ITY)
aboard .... ALOFT, ANCHORS AWEIGH
around ..... HANDY, VERSATILE
at once .... SUDDENLY
but .... ALMOST, NEARLY
clear .... SAFE, UNINDEBTED
combining form .... PAN, OMNI
comprehensive .... OMNIBUS, UNIVERSAL
consuming .... STIFLING, SILENCING
creating .... OMNIFIC
creation .... UNIVERSE
ears .... RAPTLY, ATTENTIVE
embracing .... WHOLE, THOROUGH
fired .... FANATIC(AL)
fours .... SEVEN UP
in .... TIRED, WEARY, FATIGUED, ON HIS LAST LEGS
in all .... MAINLY, OVERALL, ALTOGETHER
inclusive ...... WHOLE, INFINITE
in music .... TUTTI
in the mind .... IMAGINARY
out .... ABSOLUTE, WHOLE-HOG, DOWNRIGHT
over .... THROUGHOUT
overs .... QUALM, ANXIETY
pervading .... THOROUGH
powerful .... ALMIGHTY, OMNIPOTENT
present .... EVERYWHERE
religions, believer in .... OMNIST
right .... YES, GOOD, OKAY, AGREED, HONEST
seed .... KNOTWEED, GOOSEFOOT
seed herb .... RADIOLA
seeing .... OMNISCIENT
set .... READY, PREPPED
shook up .... STARTLED
spice .... PIMIENTO,

(MYRTLE)BERRY

"the ___ horses"
.... KING'S

the world, to Shakespeare
.... STAGE

the same .... NEVERTHELESS

the time .... ALWAYS

the way .... TO THE LIMIT

there .... SANE, NORMAL,
MENTALLY SOUND

things considered
.... BROADLY, GENERALLY

thumbs .... CLUMSY,
AWKWARD, BUMBLING

time .... UNSURPASSED

together .... JOINTLY

All Saints' Day observance
.... HALLOWEEN, HALLOWMASS

Allah .... MANITOU, THE GREAT
SPIRIT

allan .... GULL

allanite .... CERINE, ORTHITE

allay .... CALM, EASE, QUIET,
SLAKE, ASSURE, PACIFY,
ASSUAGE, GRATIFY, MOLLIFY,
SATIATE, RELIEVE

allegation .... PLEA, CLAIM,
REMARK, AVERMENT,
STATEMENT, PROFESSION

allege .... STATE, ACCUSE, AFFIRM,
ASSERT, TESTIFY

alleged electric force .... ELOD

force .... OD, ODYLE

Allegheny city .... OLEAN

allegiance .... DUTY, FEALTY,
LOYALTY, DEVOTION

allegorical .... PARABOLIC

allegory .... FABLE, PARABLE

alleluia .... CHEER, PAEAN

Allen, ___ .... IRA, FRED,
ETHAN, STEVE

allergic .... AVERSE, SENSITIVE

reaction .... COLD, RASH,
NAUSEA, SNEEZE

skin condition .... HIVES,
ECZEMA, URTICARIA

to firearms .... GUNSHY

allergy .... DISEASE, REACTION,
SENSITIVITY

common cause of .... MITE,
MOLD, POLLEN, DANDER,
CEREAL, FEATHER,
HOUSEDUST, SHELLFISH,
STRAWBERRY

medicine for .... BENADRYL

physician .... ALLERGIST

symptom of .... RASH,
VOMITING, ITCHY SWELLING

alleviate .... EASE, ALLAY,
LESSEN, LIGHTEN, MITIGATE

alleviation .... RELIEF

alley .... MIB, TAW, LANE, PATH,
ROAD, WALK, AISLE, BYPASS,
MARBLE, STREET, PASSAGE

blind .... DEAD END, CUL DE
SAC

cat .... HOMELESS

closed at one end .... DEAD
END

allheal .... PLANT, SELFHEAL,
VALERIAN

alliance .... AXIS, BLOC, UNION,
FUSION, LEAGUE, TREATY,
SODALITY

of nations .... UN, AXIS, OAS,
NATO, SEATO, BIG FIVE

of parties .... COALITION

of woman and man
.... MARRIAGE

allied .... AKIN, BOUND, YOKED,
JOINED, LINKED, UNITED,
COUPLED, KNOTTED,
MARRIED, RELATED, SIMILAR

alligator .... CAIMAN, CAYMAN,
LIZARD, LEATHER, SAURIAN,
CROCODILE

pear ..... AVOCADO, AGUACATE

allium .... LEEK, ONION, GARLIC

allocate .... GIVE, METE, ALLOT,
GRANT, ASSIGN, DETAIL,
DISTRIBUTE

allot ...... DOLE, SHARE, EARMARK

allotment .... SHARE, QUOTA,
RATION, PORTION, STIPEND,
ALIMONY, SUBSIDY

allow .... LET, GIVE, OPINE, YIELD,
BESTOW, ADMIT, EXTEND,
PERMIT, SUFFER, PROVIDE,
TOLERATE

free use .... LEND

to become known .... LEAK

allowable variance
.... TOLERANCE

allowance .... QUOTA, RATION,
WAIVER, SUPPORT, DISCOUNT,
REDUCTION, CONCESSION

depreciation .... AGIO

food .... RATION, CORODY

loss of weight .... DRAFT

slang .... KICKBACK

small .... PITTANCE

waste .... TRET, DRAFT

weight .... TARE

alloy .... METAL, AMALGAM,
MIXTURE

aluminum .... ALNICO,
DURALUMIN

black .... NIELLO

cheap jewelry .... TOMBAK,
TOMBAC(K)

copper-nickel-zinc
.... ALBATA, ELECTRUM

copper-tin .... BRONZE

copper-tin-zinc .... OROIDE

copper-zinc .... BRASS

gold-like ..... AROIDE, ORMOLU

gold-silver .... ASEM,
ELECTRUM

iron-carbon .... STEEL

lead-tin .... TERNE, PEWTER

mercury .... AMALGAM

nickel-steel .... INVAR

nonferrous .... TULA

pewter-like .... BIDRI

sulfur .... NIELLO

three-metal .... TERNARY

tin-copper-antimony
.... BABBIT, BRITANNIA

tin-copper-lead .... PEWTER

tin-zinc .... OROIDE

with aluminum ...... CALORIZE

yellow .... AICH

alloyed .... BASE, SHAM, MIXED,
TAINTED, SPURIOUS,
CHEAPENED, INSINCERE

allude .... CITE, HINT, IMPLY,
REFER, REMARK

allure .... BAIT, SWAY, TOLE,
CHARM, DECOY, SNARE,
TEMPT, ENTICE, ATTRACT

allurement .... CHARM, CONNING,
GLAMOUR, (SEX)APPEAL,
CHARISMA, SEDUCTION,
FASCINATION

slang .... SNOW JOB, SOFT-
SOAP

alluring ...... EXOTIC, APPEALING,
RAVISHING

allusion .... HINT, TOUCH,
INKLING, INNUENDO,
OVERTONE, INFERENCE

allusive .... IRONIC, SUGGESTIVE

alluvial clay .... ADOBE

deposit ..... MUD, SILT, PLACER

fan .... DELTA

matter .... GEEST

alluvion .... SILT, FLOOD

ally .... JOIN, LINK, CRONY,
COHORT, FRIEND, HELPER,
COMPEER, PARTNER

alma mater .... SCHOOL, COLLEGE

almanac .... CALENDAR,
YEARBOOK

astronomical .... EPHEMERIS

almandine .... GARNET, SPINEL

almighty .... SUPREME,
HALLOWED, OMNIPOTENT,
ALL-POWERFUL

Almighty ...... GOD, THE CREATOR

almond .... NUT, TREE, JORDAN,
BADAM, KANARI, LIGHT TAN,
AMYGDALA

emulsion .... ORGEAT

eyed .... SLANT-EYED
flavored liquor .... RATAFIA
oil .... AMARIN
shaped .... AMYGDALOID
almost .... CLOSE, NEARLY
alms .... DOLE, CHARITY
box .... ARCA
giver .... ALMONER,
PHILANTHROPIST
almshouse .... HOSPICE,
BEADHOUSE, POORHOUSE
almsman .... PAUPER, INDIGENT
almuce .... AMICE, TIPPET,
HEADDRESS
alnus .... ALDER
alod .... ESTATE, ALODIUM,
FREEHOLD
aloe .... DRUG, LILY, AGAVE,
MAGUEY
derivative .... ALOIN
aloft ...... UP, ASOAR, IN THE AIR,
UPWARD, SKYWARD,
OVERHEAD
aloha .... LOVE, GOODBYE,
WELCOME, FAREWELL,
GREETING
alone .... LONE, ONLY, SOLE,
SOLO, SINGLE, UNPAIRED, BY
ONESELF, SOLITARY
on stage .... SOLA, SOLUS
along .... ON, BESIDE, ONWARD,
LENGTHWISE
side .... ABREAST
the way .... ENROUTE
with .... AND
aloof .... COLD, APART, FRIGID,
OFFISH, DISTANT, RESERVED,
STANDOFFISH
alopecia .... ACOMIA, BALDNESS
aloud .... LOUDLY, CLEARLY,
AUDIBLY, DISTINCTLY
alow .... BELOW, UNDER
alp .... PEAK, MOUNTAIN
alpaca .... PACO, WOOL, CLOTH,
RUMINANT
like animal .... LLAMA,
VICUNA, GUANACO
alpen .... HILLY, KNOBBY,
ROLLING
alpha .... STAR, DENEB, FIRST,
START, INITIAL
rays .... BETA
Alpha and Omega .... BEGINNING
AND END
alphabet .... ABC'S, BASICS,
PRIMER, RUDIMENTS
character .... OGAM, RUNE,
LETTER
Kashmir .... SARADA
teacher .... ABECEDARIAN

alphabetical list, kind of
.... CATALOG(UE),
CONCORDANCE
Alpine .... NORDIC
animal .... IBEX, CHAMOIS
dance .... GAVOT
danger .... AVALANCHE
dress .... DIRNDL
goat .... IBEX, STEINBOK
herdsman .... SENN
house/hut .... CHALET
pass .... COL, (MONT)CENIS,
SIMPLON
plant .... EDELWEISS
primrose .... AURICULA
river .... RHONE
wind .... BISE, BORA, FOEHN
Alps .... CHAIN, TIROL, TYROL,
MOUNTAIN RANGE
highest peak ..... MONT BLANC
French .... MASSIF
mountain .... BERNINA,
JUNGFRAU, MATTERHORN,
MONT BLANC
pass .... CENIS
Spanish .... SIERRA,
CORDILLERA
already .... ERE, YET, STILL,
BEFORE, ERENOW, PRIORLY,
EARLIER, PREVIOUSLY
Alsatian .... POLICE DOG,
WHITEFRIARS
alsike .... CLOVER, FODDER
also .... AND, TOO, MORE, PLUS,
ALONG, EXTRA, BESIDES,
LIKEWISE
known as .... AKA, ALIAS
ran .... LOSER
Altair .... STAR
altar ...... BOMOS, TABLE, HESTIA,
SHRINE, ESCHARA, SCROBIS
area around .... CHANCEL
boy .... ACOLYTE, THURIFER
carpet .... PEDALE
cloth .... PALL, DOSSAL,
DOSSEL, HAPLOMA, CORPORAL,
VESPERAL
constellation .... ARA
curtain .... RIDDEL
enclosure .... BEMA
end of the church .... APSE
endowed .... CHANTRY
offering .... ALTARAGE,
EUCHARIST
part .... PISCINA, PREDELLA
piece .... DIPTYCH, TRIPTYCH
rail .... SEPTUM
screen/veil .... REREDOS,
ANTEPENDIUM
shelf .... GRADIN, RETABLE
slab/top .... MENSA

table .... CREDENCE
altazimuth of astronomer
.... ABA
alter .... FIX, TURN, VARY,
ADJUST, ADAPT, AMEND,
SHIFT, CHANGE, MODIFY,
MUTATE, REVAMP, REVISE,
CONVERT, DISTORT, PERMUTE
ego .... FRIEND, STOOGE,
ONESELF, INTIMATE, SIDEKICK,
CONFIDANT
alteration .... CHANGE, SWITCH,
REVISION
slang .... FLIP-FLOP
altercation .... SPAT, TIFF,
BICKER, FRACAS, STRIFE,
DISPUTE, QUARREL,
ARGUMENT, SQUABBLE
alternate .... DUMMY, PROXY,
OTHER, SHIFT, SECOND,
ROTATE, STAND-IN,
EXCHANGE, SUBSTITUTE
slang .... RINGER
alternating current .... AC,
ELECTRICITY
alternative .... OR, AND/OR,
CHOICE, EITHER, OPTION,
LOOPHOLE
alternator .... DYNAMO,
GENERATOR
althea .... HOLLYHOCK
Althea .... HEALER
althorn .... SAXHORN
although .... YET, WHEN, STILL,
WHILE, ALBEIT, EVEN IF,
RATHER, IN SPITE OF
altitude .... HEIGHT, STATURE,
ELEVATION
measuring device
.... OROMETER, ALTIMETER
altogether .... IN ALL, FULLY,
WHOLLY, ROUNDLY,
ENTIRELY, OUTRIGHT
the .... NUDITY, BIRTHDAY SUIT
Altona .... HAMBURG
altruism .... CHARITY, LARGESS,
GOODWILL
altruist, one kind of
.... SAMARITAN
opposite of .... EGOIST
alum .... SALT, EMETIC,
ASTRINGENT
aluminum compound
.... BAUXITE, TERMITE
ore .... BAUXITE
oxide .... RUBY, TOPAZ,
ALUMINA, CORUNDUM
alumnus .... GRAD(UATE)
alveary .... (BEE)HIVE
alveolar ...... GINGIVAL, THROATY
alveolate .... HOLEY,

POCKMARKED, HONEYCOMBED

always .... AY, E'ER, EVER, FOREVER, STEADILY, CONSTANTLY, INVARIABLY

poetic .... ETERNE

alyssum .... MADWORT

ama .... CUP, VESSEL

amadou .... PUNK, TINDER, STYPTIC

amah .... AYAH, MAID, NANNY, NURSE, WENCH, SERVANT

British .... TWEENY

French .... BONNE

amain .... GREATLY, HASTILY, FORCIBLY, MIGHTILY

Amakusa port .... AMUTA

Amalekite king .... AGAG

amalgam .... ALLOY, BLEND, COMBO, PASTE, MIXTURE, COMPOUND, COMBINATION

amalgamate .... MIX, FUSE, MERGE, UNIFY, COMBINE, BLEND, COALESCE, SYNDICATE

amalgamating pan .... TINA

amalgamation .... MERGER, METALLURGY

amanuensis .... WRITER, RECORDER, SECRETARY, SCRIBBLER, SCRIVENER

amaranth ...... FLOWER, PIGWEED, TUMBLEWEED

amaranthine .... IMMORTAL, UNFADING, DEATHLESS, EVERLASTING

amaryllis .... BULB, AGAVE, BELLADONNA, PLANT, SHEPHERDESS

amass .... HEAP, PILE, HOARD, STACK, STOCK, STORE, GATHER, MUSTER, COLLECT, COMPILE, ACCUMULATE

Amata's daughter ...... LATINIA, LAVINIA

amateur ...... DUB, TYRO, NOVICE, TRIFLER, NEOPHYTE, GREENHORN, DILETTANTE

athlete's goal .... OLYMPICS

boxing championship .... GOLDEN GLOVES

colloquial .... SIMON PURE

opposite of .... EXPERT, PRO(FESSIONAL)

painter .... DABBLER

radio operator .... HAM

standing .... AMATEURISM

thief, sometime .... SHOPLIFTER

amateurish .... INEPT, CLUMSY, AWKWARD, UNSKILLED, UNTRAINED

slang .... HALF-BAKED

Amati .... FIDDLE, NICOLO, VIOLIN, PICCOLO

amative .... LOVING, EROTIC, AMOROUS

amatol .... EXPLOSIVE

amaurosis .... BLINDNESS

amaze .... STUN, MARVEL, PERPLEX, BEWILDER, ASTONISH, SURPRISE

amazed .... AGOG, AWED, AGHAST, PUT OUT, MESMERIZED

slang .... FLABBERGASTED

amazement .... AWE, WONDER, SPECTACLE

amazing event .... MIRACLE

trick .... MAGIC, SLEIGHT OF HAND

Amazon .... ANT, TITAN, RIVER, WOMAN, PARROT, VIRAGO, GIANTESS, MANHANDLER

cetacean .... INIA

estuary/mouth .... PARA

fish .... LEPIDOSIREN

part of .... SOLIMOES

stone/gem .... AMAZONITE

tributary .... APA, JURUA, JAPURA, JAVARI, JAVARY, TAPAJOZ

valley Indian .... TAPUYAN

Amazonian .... WARLIKE, MASCULINE

ambagious .... DEVIOUS, INDIRECT, CIRCUITOUS

ambary .... FIBER, PLANT, NALITA

ambassador ...... AGENT, ENVOY, EMISSARY, DIPLOMAT, MINISTER

papal .... LEGATE, NUNCIO

amber .... RESIN, YELLOW

fish .... MEDREGAL

like ......: AMBROID, AMBEROID

ambergris .... PERFUMERY, SECRETION

ambi: comb. form .... BOTH

ambidextrous .... CRAFTY, CUNNING, VERSATILE, TWO-FACED, TWO-HANDED

ambience .... CIRCLE, MILIEU, ENVIRONS, VICINITY

ambient .... ENCIRCLING, ROUNDABOUT

ambiguous ...... VAGUE, PATCHY, DELPHIC, JUMBLED, OBSCURE, RAMBLING, UNCERTAIN

ambit .... SCOPE, BOUNDS, EXTENT, LIMITS, REGION, SPHERE, CIRCUIT

ambition .... AIM, END, GOAL, WISH, DESIRE, MOTIVE, PURPOSE, ASPIRATION

ambivalent .... FICKLE, IRONIC, DUBIOUS

amble .... GAIT, PACE, TROT, MOSEY, STROLL, WADDLE

ambling .... CRAWLING, CREEPING, HITCHING

horse .... PADNAG

ambo .... STAND, PULPIT, LECTERN

Ambracian Gulf .... ARTA

ambrosia .... MANNA, SALAD, NECTAR, BEEHEAD, DESSERT, RAGWEED

ambrosial .... SWEET, TASTY, FRAGRANT, DELICIOUS

drink .... AMRITA

ambry .... NICHE, CLOSET, LOCKER, PANTRY, CUPBOARD

ambsace .... BAD LUCK, TWO ACES, DOUBLE ACES

ambulance chaser, so called .... SHYSTER, PETTIFOGGER

ambulant .... ON FOOT, WALKING

seller .... PEDDLER

ambulator .... PEDOMETER

ambush .... TRAP, BLITZ, ATTACK, WAYLAY, ASSAULT, SURPRISE, BUSHWHACK

ameliorate .... BETTER, UPLIFT, IMPROVE, NURTURE, RELIEVE, UPGRADE, MITIGATE

amen .... YES, DONE, AGREED, VERILY, EXACTLY, SO BE IT, APPROVAL

slang .... RIGHTO

amenable .... PLIANT, WILLING, OBEDIENT, AGREEABLE, RECEPTIVE

slang .... GAME

to existing conditions .... ADAPTIVE

to reason .... BROADMINDED, OPEN-MIND(ED)

to requests .... ACCOMMODATING

to suggestions ..... SUBMISSIVE

amend .... ALTER, CHANGE, MODIFY, CORRECT, IMPROVE, REVISE, RECTIFY, REWRITE

amendment .... CLAUSE, PROVISO, REVISION, CORRECTION

tricky .... JOKER, RIDER

amends .... PAYMENT, REDRESS, REQUITAL, SQUARING, ATONEMENT, INDEMNITY

amenities ...... MORES, DECORUM, COMFORTS, NICETIES, SOCIAL GRACES

observance of the .... PUNCTILIO

amenity .... BLISS, NICENESS, CIVILITY, COURTESY,

GENIALITY

ament .... CHAT, GOLEM, IDIOT, MORON, SPIKE, CATKIN, CATTAIL, IMBECILE, SIMPLETON

amerce .... FINE, PUNISH, PENALIZE

America ...... US, USA, STATESIDE, THE STATES, THE AMERICAS, UNITED STATES, LAND OF LIBERTY, UNITED STATES OF AMERICA

identified discoverer of ...... (CHRISTOPHER) COLUMBUS

national personification of .... COLUMBIA, UNCLE SAM, BROTHER JONATHAN

reputed discoverer of .... ERIC, VOTAN, (AMERIGO)VESPUCCI

slang .... UNCLE SUGAR, YANKEE-LAND

American .... YANK(EE), GRINGO, WESTERN, AMERICANO

aborigine .... INDIAN

admiral .... KING, SIMS, DEWEY, CARNEY, HALSEY, NIMITZ, KINKAID, FARRAGUT

aircraft carrier .... HORNET, AMERICA, KENNEDY, SARATOGA, YORKTOWN, LEXINGTON, ENTERPRISE, THEODORE ROOSEVELT

antelope .... BLESBOK, SASSABY

anthologist .... UNTERMEYER

archaeologist .... ANDREWS

"architect" of the Vietnam war .... MCNAMARA

artist .... WEST, HICKS, KENT, FLAGG, CADMUS, PEALE, HOMER, BENTON, COPLEY, INNESS

astronaut .... GLENN, SCOTT, WHITE, YOUNG, BORMAN, ALDRIN, ANDERS, CERNAN, CONRAD, LOVELL, COLLINS, GRISSOM, SCHIRRA, SHEPARD, MCDIVITT, MITCHELL, STAFFORD, ARMSTRONG, CUNNINGHAM

author/writer ..... SHAW, ASCH, AMES, BAUM, BUCK, MEAD, GREY, PUZO, PYLE, POE, ALGER, CRANE, URIS, HARTE, HALEY, HENRY, MOORE, RILEY, STONE, VIDAL, TWAIN, WYLIE, ALCOTT, CAPOTE, FERBER, HAILEY, HERSEY, HOLMES, KRANTZ, LORING, LUDLUM, LONDON, MAILER, RUNYON, SCHARY, EMERSON, GARDNER, LOWELL, O'NEILL, SAROYAN, YERBY, SANDBURG, FAULKNER, MICHENER, HEMINGWAY, SPILLANE, STEINBECK, CALDWELL, TARKINGTON, BENCHLEY, LONGFELLOW, BRADBURY, BURROUGHS, DICKINSON, WILLIAMS

badger .... CARCAJOU

balladeer .... GUTHRIE

balsam .... TOLU

battle scene ..... PERSIAN GULF

battle scene, Philippines .... BATAAN, MANILA BAY, CORREGIDOR

battleship .... ALABAMA, MISSOURI, WISCONSIN, MASSACHUSETTS

bear .... MUSQUAW

beauty .... (RED)ROSE

bingo .... LOTTO

biologist .... MULLER

bird .... ROBIN, COLIN, GUAN, TOWHEE, RHEA, GROUSE, SPARROW, CONDOR, STARLING, JUNCO, BOBOLINK

bishop .... SHEEN

buzzard .... VULTURE

cactus .... CEREUS, SAGUARO

capital lobbyist .... RAINMAKER

capitalist .... ASTOR, BARUCH

cardinal .... CUSHING, BRENNAN, SPELLMAN

caricaturist .... NAST

cartoonist .... CAPP, FISHER, DISNEY, ARNO, NAST, HERBLOCK, CONRAD, SANDERS, OLIPHANT, DARCY, HESSE, MAULDIN

chameleon .... ANOLI

choreographer .... FOKINE

coin .... CENT, PENNY, DIME, NICKEL, EAGLE, QUARTER

columbo .... GENTIAN

commodore .... PERRY

composer .... BERLIN, IVES, PORTER, PAINE, NEVIN, KERN, COPLAND

Confederate soldier .... REB(EL), BUTTERNUT

contralto .... (MARIAN)ANDERSON

critic .... HALE, AYRES

dancer of fame .... (MARTHA)GRAHAM

dinosaur .... BRONTOSAURUS

diplomat .... HARRIMAN, GIBSON, BOHLEN, DULLES, GREW, LODGE, KISSINGER

dog .... ALCO

dramatist .... HART, BARRY, ODETS, CROUSE, WILLIAMS

driest state .... NEVADA

duck .... BUFFLEHEAD

editor .... BOK, LUCE, MENCKEN, WALLACE, DANA, SMITH, GREELY, DAVIS, PARKER, MICHAELS

educator .... CONANT, FISK, NEILSON, ELIOT, KIRK, HUME, HUTCHINS, MANN, WASHINGTON

elk .... WAPITI

evangelist .... GRAHAM

evergreen .... FIR, PINE

explorer .... ELLSWORTH, BYRD, PEARY, FREMONT, LEWIS, CLARK, CARSON

fashion designer .... STARR, CHARLES

feminist .... CATT, PAUL, STONE, STANTON

financier ...... ASTOR, BARUCH, MORGAN, GOULD, LAWSON

finch .... JUNCO, SISKIN

flag .... OLD GLORY

flag maker .... ROSS

flycatcher .... PHOEBE

fowl .... WYANDOTTE

frontier scout .... HICKOK

frontiersman .... BOONE, CARSON, CROCKETT

fur merchant .... ASTOR

game .... GOLF, BASEBALL, FOOTBALL, POKER, (ICE)HOCKEY, TENNIS, BASKETBALL

general ...... LEE, GRANT, ORD, SHERMAN, BRADLEY, BURNSIDE, MACARTHUR, STILLWELL, EISENHOWER, OTIS, RENO, SCOTT, POPE, BUELL, LEMAY, MEADE, SCHWARZKOPF

general of the army .... PERSHING, MACARTHUR, EISENHOWER

geologist .... DANA

girl of 1890's .... GIBSON

grapes .... NIAGARA

"Great Communicator" .... (RONALD)REAGAN

"Great Emancipator" .... (ABRAHAM)LINCOLN

Great White Father .... PRESIDENT

guitarist .... GUTHRIE

hake .... LING

historian ...... BAILEY, HYMAN, ROBINSON, SCHLESINGER

horse .... PINTO, BRONCO, MUSTANG

horticulturist .... BURBANK
hospital ship .... MERCY, COMFORT
humorist .... COBB, NYE, NASH, ROGERS, LARDNER, ADE, TWAIN, BENCHLEY
illustrator ..... FLAGG, NEWELL, ROCKWELL
imaginary town .... PODUNK
Indian .... REE, HUPA, HOH, YUMA, TEWA, KOSO, CREE, NOZI, SERI, HOPI, UTE, PIMA, COOS, SIOUX, OTOE, CROW, POMO, MIAMI, KIOWA, APACHE, SENECA, PECOS, LENAPE, BILOXI, MAKAH, OSAGE, ARIKARA, UINTA, LUMMI, MANDAN, KANSA, SANTEE, PAWNEE, KUSAN, CADDO, SALINA, MODOC, LIPAN, MAIDU, MOQUI, TETON, CHINOOK
and African-American descent ..... SAMBO, GRIFF(E)
ax .... TOMAHAWK
baby .... PAPOOSE
beads .... WAMPUM
dwelling .... TEPEE, LODGE, WIGWAM
greeting .... NETOP
grunt .... UGH
language .... NA-DENE
peace offering .... PIPE
pipe .... CALUMET
pony .... PINTO, CAYUSE
trophy .... SCALP
woman's husband .... SQUAWMAN
insurance capital .... HARTFORD
inventor .... EDISON, HOWE, OTIS, MORSE, FULTON, WHITNEY
isthmus .... PANAMA
ivy .... WOODVINE
Japanese .... NISEI, ISSEI, KIBEI
journalist .... DANA, REID, BIGELOW, BROWN, GUNTHER
jurist .... TANEY, MARSHALL, COOLEY, PAINE, MOORE, TAFT, LANDIS, CARDOZO
jute .... MALLOW
Kennel Club .... AKC
keno .... BINGO, LOTTO
larch .... TAMARACK
lawyer .... PAINE, DARROW
leopard .... JAGUAR
lexicographer .... WEBSTER
light wood .... BALSA
lion .... PUMA, COUGAR
lizard .... ANOLE, ANOLI, BASILISK
lynx .... BOBCAT
mammal ...... OTTER, OPOSSUM
Marine .... GYRENE, LEATHERNECK
Marines' slogan .... ALWAYS FAITHFUL
Lat. .... SEMPER FIDELIS
Mexican name for .... GRINGO
monetary unit .... DOLLAR
money market .... WALL STREET
monkey .... CAPUCHIN, TITI, TEETEE, SAPAJOU
national military cemetery .... ARLINGTON
national military park .... SHILOH
naturalist .... MUIR, BAIRD, AUDUBON, SETON, ANDREWS
nature writer .... BEEBE
naval historian .... MAHAN
Navy enlisted man .... BLUEJACKET
Navy gripe session .... MAST
newspaper, oldest .... COURANT
newspaper publisher .... FIELDS, HEARST, SCRIPPS
night hawk .... PISK
nightshade .... POKEHEED, HENBANE, BELLADONNA
novelist .... FAULKNER, FERBER, STEELE, BALDWIN
nuclear physicist .... TELLER
nutmeg .... CALABASH
"Old Fox" .... (GEORGE)WASHINGTON
"Old Hickory" .... (ANDREW)JACKSON
"Old Rough and Ready" .... (ZACHARY)TAYLOR
operatic singer .... ALDA, FARRAR, STEVENS, PRICE, CALLAS
orator .... OTIS, BRYAN, HENRY
painter ...... SARGENT, BENTON, INNESS, CURRY, LUKS, RYDER, BELLOWS, HOMER, SLOAN, PETERS
painter of animals .... SETON
painter of birds ...... AUDUBON
paper money ...... GREENBACK, LONG GREEN
patriot .... REVERE, ROSS, HALE, HENRY, OTIS, ALLEN, PAINE
patron saint, humorously .... TAMMANY
philanthropist .... RIIS, FORD, CARNEGIE, BARTON, CHANNING, HEARST, ROCKEFELLER
philosopher .... DURANT
physicist .... TESLA, LAWRENCE, VAN ALLEN
pianist .... DUCHIN, CLIBURN, LEVANT
pioneer .... BOONE
pirate .... (CAPTAIN)KIDD
playwright .... SAROYAN, ODETS, MILLER, COWARD, ASCH, KAUFMAN, WILLIAMS
plover .... KILLDEER
poet .... POE, BENET, ELIOT, TATE, SANDBURG, AUDEN, NASH, FROST, LINDSAY, LANIER, GUEST, WHITTIER
poetess .... MILLAY, MOORE, STEIN, LOWELL
political scientist .... NEUSTADT, ROSSITER, MACGREGOR
portraitist .... PEALE, STUART
president .... BUSH, FORD, POLK, TAFT, ADAMS, GRANT, HAYES, NIXON, TYLER, ARTHUR, CARTER, HOOVER, MONROE, PIERCE, REAGAN, TAYLOR, TRUMAN, WILSON, CLINTON, HARDING, JACKSON, JOHNSON, KENNEDY, LINCOLN, MADISON, BUCHANAN, COOLIDGE, FILLMORE, GARFIELD, HARRISON, MCKINLEY, VAN BUREN, CLEVELAND, JEFFERSON, ROOSEVELT, EISENHOWER, WASHINGTON
president's wife .... FIRST LADY
primitive painter .... GRANDMA MOSES
professor of drama ..... BAKER
psychologist .... WATSON
publisher .... HEARST, OCHS, FIELDS, SCRIPPS, NEWHOUSE, MCCORMICK, WEIL, MILLER, HOWARD, BARR, LUCE, KNIGHT, COWLES, GANNETT
quail .... COLIN
railroad magnate .... REA, HARRIMAN
Red Cross organizer .... BARTON
reformer .... RIIS
Revolution soldier .... BUCKSKIN
river .... MISSISSIPPI, TENNESSEE, SACRAMENTO, OHIO, RAPIDAN, HUDSON, ALABAMA, COLORADO,

WABASH, MISSOURI, PEARL, THAMES, COLUMBIA
rodent .... RABBIT, BEAVER, SQUIRREL
sculptor ..... BORGLUM, SMITH, CALDER, PROCTOR
shipyard .... GROTON
shrub .... CHICO, WAHOO
singer .... SINATRA, CLARK, DURBIN, PRESLEY, PAGE, MATHIS, JACKSON, DAVIS, MARTIN, HOUSTON, NELSON, ROGERS, GARLAND, TUCKER, LANZA, CROSBY, EDDY, PRIDE, STREISAND, KITT, BENNETT, MANDRELL, LYNN, RICH, RICHIE, ROSS, HORNE, FRANCIS, BAEZ, NEWTON, WILLIAMS
soldier .... GI, SAMMY, YANKEE, DOGFACE, SAD SACK, DOUGHBOY
songbird .... GREENLET
songwriter .... PORTER, BERLIN, RODGERS
soprano .... CALLAS, PONS, STEBER, ALDA, SILLS, MUNSEL, STEVENS
statesman .... JAY, RUSK, BAKER, LODGE, LOGAN, VANCE, BARUCH, BENTON, BLAINE, DULLES, ROGERS, CLAY, ACHESON, KISSINGER, DAVIS, STIMSON, STEVENSON
suffragist .... CATT
surgeon .... MAYO, PARRAN
thrush .... WAGTAIL
tree .... CALABASH, MAPLE, OAK, REDWOOD, PINE, SYCAMORE, ELM, ASH, FIR, SEQUOIA, WALNUT, BUTTONWOOD
vice-president .... BURR, BUSH, FORD, GORE, KING, ADAMS, AGNEW, DAWES, NIXON, TYLER, ARTHUR, COLFAX, CURTIS, DALLAS, GARNER, HAMLIN, HOBART, MORTON, QUAYLE, TRUMAN, WILSON, BARKLEY, CALHOUN, CLINTON, JOHNSON, MONDALE, SHERMAN, WALLACE, WHEELER, COOLIDGE, FILLMORE, HUMPHREY, MARSHALL, TOMPKINS, VAN BUREN, FAIRBANKS, HENDRICKS, JEFFERSON, ROOSEVELT, STEVENSON, ROCKEFELLER, BRECKENRIDGE
volcano .... SHASTA, SAINT HELENS, LASSEN

weather phenomenon .... SMOG, SMAZE, POGONIP
widgeon .... BALDPATE
wild sheep .... ARGALI, BIGHORN
winter fog .... POGONIP
wolf .... COYOTE
woman governor, first .... ROSS
writer in Yiddish .... ASCH
writer of fables .... ADE
writer of the national anthem .... KEY
yew .... HEMLOCK
Americans, in Key's words .... THE FREE
Amerind .... OTOE, REDSKIN, CREE, INDIAN, ESKIMO
symbol .... XAT
amethyst .... VIOLET, QUARTZ, PURPLE, CORUNDUM
amethystine .... ORCHID, LILAC, MAGENTA, MAUVE, LAVENDER
amiable .... KIND, CORDIAL, GENIAL, AFFABLE, LOVABLE, GRACIOUS
amianthus .... ASBESTOS
amicable .... PEACEFUL, FRIENDLY, HARMONIOUS
amice .... CAPE, COWL, HOOD, ALMUCE, TIPPET
amicus curiae ...... JURAT, JUDGE, BARRISTER, LAWYER, OMBUDSMAN
slang .... MOUTHPIECE
amid(st) .... AMONG(ST), MIDST, TWIXT, BETWEEN
amidine .... STARCH
Amiens river .... SOMME
amigo .... CHUM, BUDDY, FRIEND, COMRADE
British .... MATE
French .... CAMARADE
amino acid .... PROTEIN, PROLIN(E), PEPTIDE, LACTAM, LYSINE, LEUCINE
amiss .... AWRY, FAULTY, ASKEW, WRONG, ERRANT, ASTRAY, MISPLACED
slang .... COCKEYED
amity ...... GOODWILL, HARMONY, AFFINITY, FRIENDSHIP
Amman is capital of .... JORDAN
Ammon .... ZEUS, JUPITER
ammonia .... LOX, ETHER, COOLANT, FERTILIZER
compound .... AMIN(E), AMIDE, DIAMINE
in water solution .... HARTSHORN
ammoniac .... CEMENT, GUM

RESIN, STIMULANT
ammunition .... MEANS, BULLETS, GUNPOWDER, SHELLS, GRENADES, POWDER AND SHOT
box .... CANISTER
carrier .... CAISSON
depot .... ARMORY, ARSENAL, MAGAZINE
slang .... AMMO
amnesia .... FUGUE, MEMORY-GAP
slang .... BLACKOUT
amnesty .... STAY, PARDON, IMMUNITY, REPRIEVE, REMISSION
amnion .... MEMBRANE
of eardrum .... TYMPANUM
amoeba .... MOLD, GERM, FUNGUS, MICROBE, PROTOZOON
amok .... AMUCK, KILLER, VIOLENT, BERSERK, RABID, FRENZIED
slang .... HOG-WILD
amole .... ROOT, SOAP, AGAVE
among .... IN, WITH, MID(ST), AMID(ST), BETWIXT
amontillado .... SHERRY
amor .... LOVE, EROS
amoretto .... CUPID
amorous .... LOVING, EROTIC, SPOONY, PASSIONATE
look .... OGLE, LEER
amorphous .... FORMLESS, VAGUE, SHAPELESS
mass .... GLOB
amort .... LIFELESS, SPIRITLESS
Amos' partner .... ANDY
amount caught ...... HAUL, CATCH
lost by waste ...... DECREMENT
of boastful words .... MOUTHFUL
of gossip .... EARFUL
of medicine .... DOSE, DOSAGE
of stake in gambling ..... MISE
offered at auction .... BID
possessed .... RATAL
produced .... OUTPUT
used .... CONSUMPTION
amour propre .... SELF-LOVE, SELF-ESTEEM, SELF-RESPECT
amperage .... WATTAGE
ampere .... WEBER
ampersand .... AND
amphetamine .... METHEDRINE
amphibian .... FROG, TOAD, NEWT, BATRACHIA, ANURAN, SALAMANDER
order .... BUFO, ANURAN
tailed .... CAUDATE
tank .... ALLIGATOR

tree .... HYLA
young .... TADPOLE
amphibious carnivore ...... MINK,
SEAL, OTTER
vehicle .... DUCK, AMTRAC
amphibole .... ASBESTOS,
MINERAL, EDENITE, URALITE,
TREMOLITE
Amphion's father .... ZEUS
mother .... ANTIOPE
stone-walled city .... THEBES
wife .... NIOBE
amphioxus .... LANCELET
amphipod .... SHRIMP, SAND
FLEA, CRUSTACEAN
amphitheater ...... ARENA, BOWL,
GALLERY, GRANDSTAND
entrance .... VOMITORY
natural .... CIRQUE
amphora .... JAR, URN, VASE
ample .... FULL, MANY, MUCH,
ROOMY, ENOUGH, PLENTY,
ABUNDANT, COPIOUS,
SPACIOUS
poetic .... ENOW
amplification factor .... MU
amplify .... WIDEN, EXPAND,
ENLARGE, MAGNIFY, INCREASE
amplifying device .... LASER,
MASER
amply fleshed .... OBESE
amputate .... LOP, CUT OFF,
CHOP, PRUNE, SEVER
Amu Darya .... OXUS
amuck .... WILD, BERSERK,
FRANTIC, BARESARK
amulet .... CHARM, TALISMAN,
PERIAPT
Philippine ..... ANTING-ANTING
Amundsen, explorer ...... ROALD
Amun-Re's wife .... MUT
Amur tributary .... ARGUN,
USSURI, SUNGARI
amuse .... HUMOR, REGALE,
DIVERT, DELIGHT, BEGUILE,
ENTERTAIN
amusement .... FUN, GAME,
SPORT, DIVERSION
amusing .... FUNNY, DROLL,
RISIBLE, HUMOROUS
moment during a tragedy
.... COMIC-RELIEF
amygdala .... ALMOND, TONSIL
Amy's sister .... JO, MEG, BETH
an .... ONE, PER, EACH, ANYONE
ana .... DATA, MEMOIR, BITS,
ANECDOTES, COLLECTION
anabaena .... ALGA
anaconda .... BOA, SNAKE,
CONSTRICTOR
anadem .... GARLAND, WREATH

anadromous .... SEA-RUNNING
an(a)esthetic .... GAS, OPIATE,
DULLING, NUMBING,
SEDATIVE, ANALGESIC
drug .... ETHER, COCAINE,
PROCAINE
anagram .... REBUS, RIDDLE,
CHARADE, WORDPLAY,
LOGOGRIPH
game .... LOGOMACHY
anal .... TRIM, RECTAL, KOSHER,
PEDANTIC
disorder .... FISSURE,
HEMORRHOIDS
analgesic .... OPIATE, ANODYNE,
PAIN-KILLER
common .... ASPIRIN
narcotic .... CODEINE,
MORPHINE
analogous .... MATCHING,
SIMILAR, PARALLEL
analogy .... SIMILE, LIKENESS,
METAPHOR, COMPARISON
analysis .... TEST, STUDY, REVIEW,
WRITE-UP, DEDUCTION
analyst .... TESTER, EXAMINER
clinical .... PSYCHIATRIST
gold/ore .... ASSAYER
analyze .... ASSAY, STUDY,
DEDUCE, SIFT, DISSECT,
EXAMINE, CLASSIFY, ASSORT,
THEORIZE
grammatically .... PARSE,
CONJUGATE
anamnesis .... REMEMBRANCE
Ananias .... LIAR
wife of .... SAPPHIRA
anarchic .... LAWLESS, UNRULY
anarchist .... REBEL, RADICAL,
AGITATOR, OUTLAW,
TERRORIST, NIHILIST,
EXTREMIST
slang .... RED
anarchy .... CHAOS, TURMOIL,
VIOLENCE, DISORDER
anasarca .... EDEMA, DROPSY
anathema .... HEX, CURSE,
DECRIAL, DAMNATION
anathematize .... BAN, CUSS,
HEX, DAMN, (AC)CURSE,
BLAST, REVILE, BLASPHEME
Anatole, novelist .... FRANCE
Anatolia .... ASIA MINOR
Anatolian capital .... ANKARA
goddess .... MA
native .... HITTITE
rug .... KURDISTAN
anatomical model, of an
.... CLASTIC
model of human body
.... MANIKIN

network .... RETE
walls .... SEPTA
anatomy .... BODY, SCIENCE,
PHYSIQUE, SKELETON,
STRUCTURE
dealing with muscles
.... MYOLOGY
microscopic study of cells
.... CYTOLOGY
microspic study of tissues
.... HISTOLOGY
of animals .... ZOOTOMY
of organisms .... BIOLOGY
of regions .... TOPOLOGY
ancestor ...... ROOT, SIRE, ELDER,
FAMILY, FOREBEAR, STOCK,
FOREFATHER
Irish .... MIL, MILED
ancestral .... AVAL, AVITAL,
MATERNAL, PATERNAL,
PARENTAL
spirits .... LARES, MANES
ancestry .... KIN, FAMILY,
DESCENT, LINEAGE, KINDRED,
PEDIGREE
common .... CONSANGUINITY
Anchises' son .... (A)ENEAS
anchor .... CAT, FIX, TIE, BIND,
MOOR, REST, KEDGE, HOOK,
BERTH, FASTEN
chain .... CABLE
fluke .... BILL
heaviest of a ship ...... BOWER
lift .... CAT, WEIGH
lifting device .... CAPSTAN,
WINDLASS
man/person .... MC, EMCEE,
ENDMAN, COMMENTATOR
part .... ARM, RING, PALM,
STOCK, FLUKE, CROWN, SHANK
place of .... CATHEAD
slightly raised .... ATRIP
small .... KEDGE, KILLICK,
KILLOCK, GRAPNEL
tackle .... CAT
anchorage .... FEE, RADE,
HARBOR, MARINA, DOCKAGE,
(ROAD)STEAD, MOORAGE
anchored .... FIXED, STUCK, TIED,
HELD, RIVETED, CHAINED,
FASTENED
anchorite .... HERMIT, ABSTAINER,
RECLUSE, ASCETIC, ANCHORET
opposed to .... C(O)ENOBITE
anchovy .... SPRAT, HERRING
pear .... MANGO
sauce .... ALEC
anchusa .... ALKANET, BUGLOSS
ancient ...... ELD, AGED, OLD(EN),
ANTIQUE, ARCHAIC,
PRIMEVAL, HOARY, DISTANT

PAST

Alexandrian writer .... ORIGEN

alphabetical character

.... RUNE

Briton .... CELT, PICT

Chinese .... SERES

city .... EUS, TYRE, NICAEA,
CORINTH, THEBES, NINEVEH

country .... ARAM, ELAM,
GAUL, EOLIS, MEDEA

court .... EYRE, LEET

drink .... MORAT

Egyptian king .... PHARAOH,
RAMESES

Egyptian scrolls .... PAPYRI

Greek invader .... DORIAN

language .... LATIN, GREEK,
SANSKRIT

lyre .... ASOR

manuscript .... CODEX

musical instrument ...... ASOR,
LUTE, REBEC, CITHARA

Persian .... MEDE

priests .... MAGI

sword .... ESTOC

tax .... CRO

temple .... NAOS

times .... YORE

warship ..... GALLEON, BIREME,
GALLEY, LONG SHIP

weapon ...... MACE, DAG, PIKE,
SLING, SPEAR, HALBERD,
ARQUEBUS

wicked city .... SODOM,
BABYLON, GOMORRAH

Ancient Mariner's victim

.... ALBATROSS

ancillary .... AID, HELPER,
SERVANT, AUXILIARY,
SUBORDINATE

ancon .... ELBOW, CONSOLE

and ...... TOO, PLUS, AS WELL AS,
MOREOVER, ALSO,
AMPERSAND

not .... NOR

others .... ET AL

so on/so forth .... USW,
ETC(ETERA)

Andalusian .... SPANISH,
LEGHORN, SPANIARD

port .... CADIZ

province .... JAEN

Andean .... PAMPERO

peak, 21,201 ft. .... ILLIMANI

Andersen, Christian .... HANS

Anderson, actress .... LONI

singer .... MARIAN

writer .... MAXWELL,
SHERWOOD

Andes .... MOUNTAIN

camel-like animal ..... LLAMA,

ALPACA, VICUNA, GUANACO

deer .... PUDU

grass .... ICHU

mountain .... HUILA, MISTI,
POTOSI, SORATA, COTOPAXI,
HUASCARAN, ILLAMPU,
CHIMBORAZO

peak .... ACONCAGUA

plain .... LLANO, PARAMO

plateau .... PUNA

rodent .... CHINCHILLA

ruminant ..... LLAMA, ALPACA,
GUANACO

volcano .... MISTI, OMATE,
CHIMBORAZO

wind .... PAMPERO

andiron .... (FIRE)DOG, HESSIAN

Andre, John, for example

.... SPY

Andress, actress .... URSULA

Andrew .... APOSTLE

Andrews, ___ ...... DANA, JULIE

androgen ...... HORMONE, STEROID

Andromache's husband

.... HECTOR

Andromeda's husband

.... PERSEUS

Andy .... HARDY, DEVINE,
GRIFFITH, WILLIAMS

cartoon character .... GUMP

Gump's wife .... MIN

partner of .... AMOS

anecdotage .... ANA, TALES

anecdotes, expert in

.... RACONTEUR

anele .... OIL, ANOINT

anemia .... CHLOROSIS

symptom of .... CHILL,
FATIGUE, FAINTING,
HEADACHE, DIZZINESS

type of .... APLASTIC,
PERNICIOUS, HEMOLYTIC

anemic .... WAN, PALE, PALLOR,
COLORLESS, BILIOUS,
BLOODLESS

anemone .... PLANT, POLYP,
ANIMAL, SNOWDROP, ACTINIA,
WINDFLOWER

anent .... INRE, ABOUT,
REGARDING, CONCERNING

aneroid .... BAROMETER

anes .... ONCE

anesthesia .... NUMBNESS,
UNFEELING

type of .... LOCAL, DENTAL,
SPINAL, GENERAL

anet .... DILL(SEED)

anew .... AGAIN, AFRESH, ONCE
MORE

do .... REPEAT, RESUME

angel .... CHERUB, PATRON, SERAF,

SPIRIT, SERAPH(IM),
MESSENGER

fallen .... LUCIFER

gold-digger's .... SUGAR
DADDY

loyal .... MICHAEL

of bottomless pit

.... APOLLYON

of Broadway, etc. .... SUGAR
DADDY, FINANCIER

of death ...... AZRAEL, DANITE,
SAMUEL

of music .... ISRAFIL

rebel .... AZAZEL, LUCIFER

Angeli, actress .... PIER

angelic .... SAINTLY, CHERUBIC

messenger .... GABRIEL

Angelica .... ARCHANGEL

angels collectively .... HIERARCHY

angelus .... BELL, PRAYER,
VESPER, DEVOTION

anger .... IRE, IRK, FURY, RILE,
ANNOY, WRATH, DANDER,
ENRAGE, INCENSE

fit of .... RAGE, TIFF, PIQUE,
CHOLER, TEMPER, TANTRUM

give vent to .... FUME, RAGE

angina .... CROUP

type of .... PECTORIS,
VINCENT'S, ABDOMINAL

angioma .... TUMOR

Angkor relics .... RUINS, TEMPLES

temple ruins .... BAYON

Wat/Vat .... TEMPLE

angle .... BEND, FISH, PLOT,
SLANT, POINT, TRICK, ANCON,
CORNER, RADIAN, ASPECT,
SCHEME, INTRIGUE

branch .... AXIL

for .... WOO, HUNT, SEEK

formed by aircraft .... YAW

in geology .... HADE

leafstalk .... AXIL

measuring device

.... GONIOMETER

off .... SWERVE

outside .... CANT

pipe .... TEE

trench .... ZIG

with no .... AGONIC

angler ...... NETTER, FISHER(MAN),
TROLLER, SCHEMER,
TRICKSTER

angler's basket .... CREEL

delight .... BITE, STRIKE

need .... ROD, BAIT, HOOK,
LINE, CREEL, LICENSE

Angleterre .... LACE

Anglian kingdom .... DEIRA

Anglican anthem ...... AGNUS DEI

Anglo-French battle site
.... CRECY
Anglo-Indian empire founder
.... CLIVE
kingdom .... KENT
man, rich ...... NAWAB, NABOB
nurse .... AMAH, AYAH
title of address .... BABU
troop .... RESSALA
woman, rich .... BEGUM
Anglo-Saxon .... ENGLISH
armor .... HAUBERK
assembly .... GEMOT(E)
coin .... ORA, SCEAT
consonant .... ETH, EDH
court .... GEMOT(E)
folk hero .... BEOWULF
freeman .... THANE
hunter's attendant .... GILLY,
GILLIE
king .... EDGAR
king's council .... WITAN
kingdom .... ESSEX, MERCIA
lord's attendant .... THANE,
THEGN
noble/prince .... ATHELING
slave .... ESNE
warrior .... THANE, THEGN
Angola capital .... LUANDA
port .... LOBITO, LUANDA
Angora ...... CAT, GOAT, ANKARA,
RABBIT
goat .... CHAMAL
goat fabric .... MOHAIR
angostura .... BARK, TONIC,
FLAVOR, BOLIVAR
angry .... HOT, MAD, SORE,
CROSS, FIERY, IRATE, RILED,
RAGING, WROTH, PIQUED,
STORMY, INCENSED,
INDIGNANT
creature .... AMOK, AMUCK,
BERSERK, WET HEN, SOREHEAD
expression .... SNORT
look .... GLARE, SCOWL,
GLOWER
anguillid .... EEL
anguine .... SNAKELIKE
anguish .... WOE, PAIN, DOLOR,
AGONY, DISTRESS, SORROW,
MISERY, SADNESS, PANG,
GRIEF, DESPAIR, TORMENT,
HEARTACHE
angular .... BONY, GAUNT,
CORNERED
opposite of .... AGONIC
anhydrous .... DRY, PARCHED
ani .... CUCKOO
anil .... SHRUB, INDIGO
anile .... WEAK, CRONE, INFIRM
aniline, dye/red .... MAGENTA,

FUCHSIN
anima .... SOUL, PRINCIPLE
animadversion .... CRITICISM,
NITPICKING
animal .... BEAST, BESTIAL,
BRUTE, GROSS, SENSUAL,
EROTIC, UNCOUTH, CREATURE,
SAVAGE, LUSTFUL
anatomy .... ZOOTOMY
ant-eating .... ECHIDNA,
ANTBEAR, AARDVARK,
PANGOLIN, TAMANDUA
antlered .... ELK, STAG,
CARIBOU, MOOSE, (REIN)DEER
aquatic .... SEAL, MINK,
OTTER, SEACOW, WHALE,
WALRUS
arboreal ..... AI, UNAU, KOALA,
SLOTH, TARSIER, SQUIRREL
armor .... PLATE, SHELL,
ARMATURE, CARAPACE
"armored" .... ARMADILLO
badgerlike .... RATEL
baggage carrier .... SUMPTER
body .... SOMA
bone-like covering
.... CARAPACE
born prematurely .... SLINK
breast .... THORAX, BRISKET
bristly .... HOG, BOAR,
PORCUPINE
burrowing .... MOLE, BROCK,
BADGER, MARMOT, GOPHER,
ARMADILLO, RATEL, WOMBAT,
GROUNDHOG
butting .... GOAT, SHEEP
castrated .... CAPON, OX, STAG,
STEER, GELDING, BARROW
cat family .... FELID, FELINE
clumsy .... JUMBO
coat .... FUR, HAIR, PELT,
WOOL, PELAGE
collection .... ZOO, MENAGERIE
coop .... HUTCH
dam builder .... OTTER
decay poison .... PTOMAIN(E)
dial. .... CRITTER
disease .... GID, ROT,
ANTHRAX, STAGGERS, RABIES,
GLANDERS, HEAVES,
RINDERPEST
doctor .... VET(ERINARIAN)
enclosure .... CAGE, PEN,
CORRAL
fat .... LARD, SUET, GREASE,
TALLOW
fierce .... OUTLAW
flying .... BAT, LEMUR
food .... FODDER, FORAGE
footless .... APOD
footprint .... PUG

game-killer .... VERMIN
giraffe-like .... OKAPI
handler .... TAMER, TRAINER
hibernating .... BEAR,
WOODCHUCK
hide .... FELL, PELT
homing instinct
.... ORIENTATION
hornless .... POLLARD
humped .... ZEBU, BISON,
CAMEL, DROMEDARY
imaginary .... SNARK
inferior: sl. .... PLUG
innards .... HA(R)SLET
large .... RHINO, BEHEMOTH,
ELEPHANT, PACHYDERM
lean, scrawny .... SCRAG
leopard-like .... CHEETAH
life in a region .... FAUNA
life, a study of .... ZOOLOGY
like an .... THEROID
living inside another
.... ENTEZOON
magnetism .... HYPNOTISM,
MESMERISM
male .... BUCK, BULL, JACK
marsupial .... KOALA, TAIT,
WOMBAT, KANGAROO,
(O)POSSUM, PHALANGER
microscopic .... ROTIFER
mixed breed .... MULE,
HYBRID, MONGREL
mouth opening .... RICTUS
multi-celled .... METAZOA
multi-segmented
.... CENTIPEDE
mythical ..... GRIFFIN, GRIFFON
neck hair .... MANE
"necklace" .... TORQUES
nipple .... DUG
noise .... ROAR, BARK, MEW,
GROWL, GRUNT, HOWL, SNORT,
BELLOW, HISS, OINK, WHINE,
YELP, SQUEAK, SQUEAL
of an .... ZOOID
of mixed parentage
.... HYBRID, MONGREL
one-celled .... MONAD, PROTIS,
PROTOZOAN, STENTOR,
RHIZOPOD
one-horned .... BADAK,
UNICORN, RHINO(CEROS)
pack .... SUMPTER
passage/shelter .... BURROW,
TUNNEL
pen .... STY, HUTCH, CORRAL
Peruvian .... LLAMA, ALPACA
pet .... CAT, DOG, CADE,
COSSET, POODLE
pictures painter ..... LANDSEER
plant life .... BIOS, BIOTA

pound .... PINFOLD
scent .... FOIL
sea .... ORC
sexual excitement .... RUT, HEAT, ESTRUS
skin ..... FUR, FELL, HIDE, PELT
skin dealer .... FELLMONGER
skin disease .... MANGE
simplest form of
.... AM(O)EBA
snouted .... COATI, TAPIR
spiny .... PORCUPINE
spirits .... FRISKINESS
spot on face of .... BLAZE
spotted .... PIEBALD, DAPPLE(D)
starch .... GLYCOGEN
stomach .... MAW, CRAW
stories, collection of
.... BESTIARY
striped .... TIGER, ZEBRA, QUAGGA
tanned hide of .... CROP
ten-footed .... DECAPOD
thigh .... HAM
trail .... PUG, FOIL, SLOT, SPUR, SPOOR
trainer .... LEHR (LEW)
trap .... DEADFALL
tusked .... WALRUS, WARTHOG, ELEPHANT
uncontrollable .... OUTLAW
vital organs .... PLUCK
weasel family .... PEKAN
web-footed .... BEAVER, DUCKBILL, PLATYPUS
with no nervous system
.... ACRITA
with pouch for young
.... KOALA, KANGA(ROO)
worship .... DEMONISM
young .... CUB, CALF, FOAL, JOEY, BUNNY, COLT, HEIFER, PIGLET, BULLOCK
animalcule .... ROTIFER
animals born at one time
.... FALL, LITTER
brood of young .... TEAM
carrying their young
.... MARSUPIAL
collectively .... ZOOLOGY
disease from .... ZOONOSIS
driven together .... HERD, COFFLE
male of some ...... BULL, TOM, BOAR, BUCK, STAG
molt of some .... EXUVIAE
painter of .... SETON, BONHEUR
rearing/culture of
.... HUSBANDRY
tied together .... COFFLE

animate .... CHEER, VIVIFY, INSPIRE, (EN)LIVEN, QUICKEN, ENERGIZE, STIMULATE
animated .... CARTOON, CARICATURE
producer .... LANTZ, DISNEY
bird .... WOODPECKER
character ...... MAGOO, POPEYE
dog .... PLUTO
duck .... DONALD
person .... GRIG
animating principle .... SOUL
animation ...... PEP, LIFE, VERVE, BRIO, ELAN, ENERGY, SPIRIT, VITALITY, VIVACITY
anime .... COPAL, RESIN
animist .... IDEALIST
animosity .... HATE, HATRED, FEUD, ENMITY, GRUDGE, SPITE, RANCOR, DISLIKE, ANIMUS, ILL WILL, HOSTILITY
animus .... MIND, GRUDGE, PASSION, PURPOSE, SPIRIT, VENDETTA
anion, opposite of .... CATION
anise .... ANET, FLAVOR, DILL(SEED)
anisette .... CORDIAL, LIQUEUR
Ankara .... ANGORA
is capital of .... TURKEY, ANATOLIA
ankh .... CRUX, CROSS, ANSATA
ankle .... CUIT, JOINT, TARSI, TARSUS
bone ...... TALUS, ASTRAGALUS
deep .... SHALLOW
iron .... BASIL
joint protuberance
.... MALLEOLUS
pertaining to .... TARSAL, TALARIC
anklet ...... SOCK, CHAIN, BANGLE, FETTER
ankyloglossia .... TONGUE-TIE
anlace .... DAGGER
anlage .... PROTON
Ann, actress .... SOTHERN, SHERIDAN
and Andy .... RAGDOLLS
anna .... COIN
¼ of .... PICE
16 of them .... RUPEE
Annabel Lee author .... POE
annalist .... RECORDER
annals .... RECORD, HISTORY, ARCHIVES, CHRONICLES
Annamese .... MONGOL(IAN)
capital .... HUE
coin .... QUAN
measure .... GON, MAU, SAO, TAO

Annapolis, former name
.... ANNE ARUNDEL
institution .... USNA, ACADEMY
student .... CADET, MIDSHIPMAN
annatto .... DYE
anneal .... BAKE, FIRE, FUSE, GLAZE, TEMPER
annealing oven .... KILN, LEER
annelid .... WORM, LEECH, CHAETOPOD
annex .... ELL, WING, CONNECT, ATTACH(MENT)
Annie Oakley .... PASS, (FREE)TICKET
Annie's anxieties .... WHIMWHAM
annihilate .... END, KILL, SLAY, ERASE, PURGE, CANCEL, ABOLISH, ERADICATE, DESTROY, WIPE OUT, DEMOLISH
anniversary, 25th .... SILVER
50th .... GOLDEN
100th .... CENTENNIAL
anno ——— .... MUNDI, REGNI, DOMINI
annotate .... EDIT, GLOSS, REVIEW, CRITIQUE
annotation .... NOTE, RECORD, APOSTIL, COMMENT, FOOTNOTE, GLOSSARY, REFERENCE
announce .... STATE, HERALD, REPORT, AFFIRM, NOTIFY, DECLARE, PROCLAIM
announcement .... AD, BLURB, OBIT(UARY), NOTICE, BULLETIN
printed .... CARD
annoy .... IRK, TRY, VEX, FASH, GRATE, TEASE, MOLEST, PESTER, DISTURB, (BE)DEVIL, PROVOKE
annoyance .... PEST, NUISANCE, TROUBLE, VEXATION, TAILTWISTER
expression of .... BAH, OH MY, SCOWL, GLOWER, GRIMACE
plane-ride .... BUMP, TURBULENCE
annoyed .... RILED, PEEVED, IRRITATED
annoyer .... PEST, HECKLER, HARASSER
camp .... GNAT, MOSQUITO
annoyingly urgent
.... IMPORTUNATE
annual .... RECORD, YEARLY, JOURNAL, ETESIAN, YEARBOOK, PERIODICAL
bean .... URD

headache of a sort .... INCOME TAX
income .... RENTES
movie award .... OSCAR
plant .... OKRA
prize .... NOBEL, PULITZER
produce .... CROP
TV award .... EMMY
annually ...... YEARLY, PER YEAR, SEASONAL
annuity .... RENTE, INCOME, PENSION, SUBSIDY, TONTINE, INSURANCE
annul .... UNDO, VOID, CANCEL, NEGATE, RECALL, REPEAL, NULLIFY, RETRACT, REVOKE, RESCIND, VACATE, WAIVE, INVALIDATE
as a veto .... OVERRIDE
in law .... QUASH
annular .... ROUND, CIRCULAR, RINGLIKE
die .... DOD
annulate .... RINGED
annulet .... CIRCLET, GROMMET
in heraldry .... VAIR, VERT, VIRE, CREST, CORONET
annum .... YEAR
annunciate .... ANNOUNCE
anodyne .... BALM, DRUG, OPIATE, SOOTHER, PACIFIER, SEDATIVE
anoint .... OIL, ANELE, BLESS, ENTHRONE, ENOIL, CONSECRATE
anomalous .... ODD, KINKY, DEVIANT, IMPROPER, ABNORMAL, IRREGULAR
anomaly ...... ODDITY, DEVIATION
anon .... SOON, AGAIN, AFRESH, THENCE, THEREAT, SHORTLY, DIRECTLY, IMMEDIATELY, ANONYMOUS
anonym .... ALIAS, PSEUDONYM
anonymity .... PRIVACY, SECLUSION
anonymous .... UNKNOWN, PRIVATE, NAMELESS, INCOGNITO
anorak .... JACKET
garment like .... PARKA
another .... ELSE, NEW, EXTRA, SPARE, SECOND, OTHER, DIFFERENT, FURTHER, ADDITIONAL
calling .... ALIAS
set of clothes .... CHANGE
time .... ONCE AGAIN
ansate .... HANDLED
anschluss .... UNION
anserine .... STUPID, FOOLISH, GOOSELIKE

answer .... REPLY, RESPONSE, DEFENSE, RESPOND, REBUT(TAL), RIPOSTE, REJOIN(DER)
back .... ECHO, PROVOKE
in kind .... RETORT
insolently .... SWEAR
purpose of .... DO, SERVE, RESOLVE, SATISFY
unfavorable .... REBUFF
answerable .... LIABLE, ACCOUNTABLE, RESPONSIBLE
ant .... ANAY, EMMET, AMAZON, PISMIRE, TERMITE
bear .... AARDVARK
black .... KELEP
combining form .... MYRMECO
cow .... APHID
eater .... MANIS, ECHIDNA, AARDVARK, PANGOLIN, TAMANDUA
genus .... FORMICA
kind of .... SOLDIER
nest .... HILL, FORMICARY
thrush .... PITTA
anta ...... PIER, COLUMN, PILASTER
antacid .... ALKALI, MAGNESIA
Antaeus' father .... POSEIDON
killer .... HERCULES
mother .... GE
antagonism .... ANIMUS, ENMITY, ANTIPATHY, HOSTILITY, OPPOSITION
antagonist .... FOE, RIVAL, OPPONENT, ADVERSARY
antagonistic .... HOSTILE, OPPOSED, UNFRIENDLY
Antarctic ...... SEA, ZONE, OCEAN, CIRCLE, CONTINENT
bird .... PENGUIN
explorer .... BYRD, ROSS, AMUNDSEN
icebreaker .... ATKA
sea .... ROSS, WEDDEL
Antares .... MARS, RED STAR
antbear .... AARDVARK
ante .... PAY, PONY, PRICE, RAISE, STAKE
as prefix .... PRIOR, BEFORE
bellum .... PRE-WAR
chamber .... WAITING ROOM
natal .... PRE-BIRTH
up: sl. .... SWEETEN THE POT
antebrachium .... FOREARM
antecedence .... PRIORITY, PRECEDENCE
antecedent ...... PRIOR, ANCESTOR, PRECEDING
antecedents .... ANCESTRY
antedate .... PRECEDE, PREDATE
antediluvian .... OLD

antelope ...... GOA, BEIRA, NILGAI, SASIN, SAIGA, TAKIN, OTEROP, GAZELLE, BUBALIS, BUBALINE
African .... GNU, KOB, ASSE, KUDU, ORYX, TORA, ELAND, KONZE, ORIBI, ADDAX, BONGO, WANTO, NAGOR, IMPALA, KOODOO, DIKDIK, GEMSBOK, SASSABY, DUIKER(BOK), STEINBOK
American .... BLESBOK, SASSABY
ancient .... PYGARG
female .... DOE
goat .... SEROW, CHAMOIS
Himalayan .... CHIRU, GORAL
like .... BOVID
male .... BUCK
pygmy .... ORIBI
red .... PALLA(H), REEDBOK
sheep-like .... SAIGA
striped .... BONGO, OTEROP
tawny .... ORIBI
young .... KID
antenna .... PALP, AERIAL, FEELER, ANTENNULE
part of .... LEAD IN
anterior .... FRONT, PRIOR, EARLIER, FORWARD, PREVIOUS, PRECEDING
opposite of .... POSTERIOR
anteroom .... LOBBY
anthelion .... HALO, AUREOLE
anthem ..... SONG, MOTET, AGNUS DEI
anther .... STAMEN
anthesis .... BLOOM
anthocyanin .... PIGMENT
anthologist .... COMPILER
anthology .... ANA, POTPOURRI, COLLECTION, COLLECTANEA, COMPILATION
Anthony, _____ .... SUSAN
anthozoan .... CORAL, POLYP, ANEMONE
anthracite .... COAL
pieces/refuse .... CULM
anthrax .... BOIL, PUSTULE, CARBUNCLE
anthropoid .... APE, LAR, GIBBON, MONKEY, SIMIAN, GORILLA, MANLIKE, ORANG(UTAN), CHIMPANZEE, TROGLODYTE
anthropophagi .... CANNIBALS
anthropophagy .... CANNIBALISM
anti .... CON, FOE, CONTRA, AGAINST, HOSTILE, OPPOSED, OPPOSER
knock fuel .... TRIPTANE
knock fuel ingredient .... BROMINE

labor union contract
.... YELLOW DOG

social one .... LONER

antiaircraft artillery .... ACK-
ACK, POMPOM, TRIPLE-A

cannon .... BOFORS

gunfire .... FLAK, ACK-ACK

missile .... NIKE

target aiming device
.... PREDICTOR

antiar .... TREE, UPAS, POISON

antibiotic .... PENICILLIN,
STREPTO(MYCIN),
AUREOMYCIN, TETRACYCLINE

antibody dissolving bacteria,
etc. .... LYSIN(E)

antic .... DIDO, CAPER, CLOWN,
COMIC, PRANK, STUNT

anticipate .... HOPE, AWAIT,
EXPECT, FORESEE, PRECEDE

anticipating .... PROLEPSIS

anticlimax .... DROP, DESCENT,
DECREASE

antidote .... SODA, REMEDY,
SERUM, NEUTRALIZER

for acid .... ALKALI

for madness .... CHRYSOLITE

for poison .... TREACLE

Antigone's parent .... JOCASTA,
OEDIPUS

sister .... ISMENE

uncle .... CREON

antihemophilic factor
.... GLOBULIN

Antilles, _____ .... LESSER,
GREATER

island .... CUBA, ARUBA

native .... CARIB(BEAN)

antimacassar .... TIDY

antimalaria remedy
.... ATABRIN(E), ATEBRIN,
QUININE

antimony ...... REGULUS, STIBIUM

source .... STIBNITE

Antiope's son .... AMPHION

antipasto ...... RELISH, APPETIZER,
HORS D'OEUVRE

antipathy .... HATE, ODIUM, SPITE,
ENMITY, HATRED, MALICE,
DISGUST, DISLIKE, AVERSION

antiphon .... HYMN, PSALM

antipodean .... AUSTRALIAN

antipodes .... OPPOSITES

antiquate .... OUTDATE, OUTMODE

antiquated .... OLD, FOSSIL,
PASSE, ARCHAIC, DEFUNCT,
EXPIRED, EXTINCT, OUT OF
DATE, OBSOLETE

antique .... OLD, AGED, RELIC,
ANCIENT, ARTIFACT

antiques, where usually found
.... MUSEUM, CURIO SHOP

antiquity .... ELD, PAST, YORE,
VESTIGE, PALEOLOGY,
SENIORITY

antiseptic .... EGOL, BORIC,
EUSOL, EUPAD, IODIN(E),
LYSOL, ARNICA, ALCOHOL,
SALOL, PICROL, ARGYROL,
RETINOL, TACHIOL,
CATECHOL, CRESOL,
CHLORINE, FORMALIN,
STERILE, CARVACROL,
GERMICIDE, LISTERINE,
DISINFECTANT

surgery pioneer .... LISTER

antisubmarine vessel
.... CORVET(TE)

antithesis .... REVERSE,
CONTRAST, CONTRARY

antitoxin .... SERUM

for snake venom
.... ANTIVENIN

antler .... HORN

branch .... BAY, BEZ, BROW,
PRONG

furry skin .... VELVET

main shaft .... BEAM

part of .... PALM

point .... TINE, PRONG

unbranched .... SPIKE,
DAG(UE)

antlered animal .... ELK, STAG,
MOOSE, CARIBOU, (REIN)DEER

antlers of stag .... ATTIRE

antlion larva .... DOODLEBUG

Antony, _____ .... MARK

antra .... SINUSES

antre/antrum .... CAVE, CAVERN,
CAVITY

ants, pertaining to .... FORMIC

anurous .... ACAUDAL, ACAUDATE,
TAILLESS

amphibian .... FROG, TOAD

Anubis .... HERMES

Anu's husband .... ANAT

anvil .... JAW, BLOCK, INCUS,
TEEST, STITHY

block .... STOCK

user .... (BLACK)SMITH

Anvil City .... NOME

anxiety ...... CARE, FEAR, DREAD,
WORRY, STRAIN, CONCERN,
TENSION, MISGIVING

disorder .... PANIC, NEUROSIS

anxious .... EAGER, UNEASY,
TENSE, QUALMY, NERVOUS,
IMPATIENT

any .... AN, ALL, PART, SOME,
WHICHEVER

anything .... AT ALL, AUGHT

badly matched .... CENTO

of least value .... PLACK,
TRIFLE

of value .... ASSET

small .... PINHEAD

that stirs .... FILLIP

aoristic .... INDEFINITE

aorta ...... ARTERY, BLOOD VESSEL

aoudad .... ARUI, SHEEP

apace .... FAST, SPEEDY,
SWIFT(LY)

Apache .... THUG, DANCE, INDIAN,
GANGSTER, LANGUAGE

chief .... COCHISE, GERONIMO

ap(p)anage .... DOWRY, ADJUNCT,
SUPPORT, ENDOWMENT,
PERQUISITE

apart .... AWAY, ASIDE, SPLIT,
ASUNDER, DETACHED, ADRIFT,
DISTINCT, SEPARATE

prefix .... DIS

apartheid .... SECLUSION,
SEGREGATION

apartment .... FLAT, ROOM,
CONDO, SUITE, DUPLEX

at top of building
.... PENTHOUSE

British .... CHAMBERS

for women .... HAREM

house, English .... MANSION

style .... HIGH-RISE

without elevator ...... WALK-UP

apatetic .... DECEIVING, IMITATIVE

apathetic .... COLD, ALOOF,
DISMAL, DISTANT, RESTIVE,
UNMOVED, HEEDLESS,
LISTLESS, INDIFFERENT

apathy .... DESPAIR, BOREDOM,
COOLNESS, ALOOFNESS,
UNCONCERN, DISINTEREST

ape .... KRA, COPY, GIBBON,
MONKEY, SIMIAN, GORILLA,
IMITATE, PRIMATE, SIAMANG,
ORANG(UTAN)

kind of .... MIME, CLOWN,
MIMIC, JESTER

sound .... CHATTER

apeman .... ALALUS

of fiction .... TARZAN

Apennines people .... SABINES

aper ...... MIME, MIMIC, IMITATOR

apercu .... DIGEST, GLANCE,
INSIGHT

aperient .... LAXATIVE

apéritif .... DRINK, COCKTAIL,
APPETIZER

wine .... DUBONNET

aperture .... GAP, HOLE, SLOT,
VENT, STOMA, OPENING,
ORIFICE

apery .... MIMICRY, IMITANCY,

apes .... SIMIA IMITATION

apes .... SIMIA

apetalous .... PETALLESS

apex .... TIP, TOP, ACME, CUSP, PEAK, CREST, POINT, CLIMAX, HEIGHT, PINIAL, SUMMIT, VERTEX, ZENITH

covering .... EPI

of elbow .... ANCON

rounded .... RETUSE

aphasia .... ALALIA

treatment of .... SPEECH THERAPY

type of ..... NOMINAL, GLOBAL, RECEPTIVE, EXPRESSIVE

aphid .... LOUSE, INSECT

sucking tube .... NECTARY

aphorism .... SAW, ADAGE, AXIOM, MAXIM, MOTTO, VERSE, GNOME, SAYING, DICTUM, EPIGRAM, PROVERB

aphrodisiac ... ERINGO, ERYNGO, LOVE POTION

substance ..... HONEY, GINGER, GINSENG

Aphrodite .... VENUS, URANIA, GODDESS, BUTTERFLY

love of .... ARES, ADONIS

mother of .... DIONE

priestess of .... HERO

son of .... EROS, (A)ENEAS

temple site of .... PAPHOS

aphta .... THRUSH

apian .... BEELIKE

apiary .... NEST, BEEHIVE

apiculture .... BEEKEEPING

apiece .... PER, EACH

apish .... SILLY, AFFECTED, IMITATIVE

aplomb ...... POISE, CONTROL, AIR, NERVE, SECURITY, ASSURANCE, CONFIDENCE, FLAMBOYANCE

fellow of .... FOP, DUDE, DANDY, ORATOR, COXCOMB, BRAGGART, BLUFFER, (PEA)COCK

apnea .... ASPHYXIA

apocalypse ...... BOOK, FORECAST, EXPOSURE, PROPHECY, MYSTICISM, REVELATION

apocalyptic .... GLOOMY, OMINOUS, MENACING, SINISTER, PROPHETIC

apocopate .... ELIDE, SHORTEN

apocope .... ELISION

apocryphal .... SPURIOUS, COUNTERFEIT

book .... ESDRA, TOBIT

apodal .... FOOTLESS

apogee .... PEAK, CROWN, CLIMAX, PINNACLE

Apollo ...... HELIOS, PHOEBUS, SUN GOD, SPACECRAFT

astronaut ..... ALDRIN, ANDERS, BORMAN, LOVELL, COLLINS

birthplace of .... DELOS

festival of .... DELIA

giant killed by .... OTUS

instrument of ...... BOW, LYRE, LUTE

mother of .... LETO, LATONA

oracle of .... DELOS

oracle site .... DELPHI

priest of ..... ABARIS, CALCHAS

serpent slain by .... PYTHON

sister of .... DIANA, ARTEMIS

son of .... ION, IAMUS

spring sacred to ..... CASTALIA

temple site of .... DELOS

twin of .... ARTEMIS

vale .... TEMPE

Apollyon .... ANGEL, DEVIL, SATAN, DESTROYER, EVIL SPIRIT

apologia .... EXCUSE, APOLOGY, EXPLANATION

apologue .... FABLE, ALLEGORY

apomixis .... APOGAMY

apoplectic with _____ ...... RAGE

apoplexy .... STROKE, SEIZURE, PARALYSIS

aport .... NEAR, LEFT(SIDE)

apostasy .... BETRAYAL, DESERTION

apostate .... DEFECTOR, DESERTER, RENEGADE, RECREANT, TURNCOAT

apostil .... FOOTNOTE, ANNOTATION

apostle .... DISCIPLE, PREACHER, CONVERTER, EVANGELIST, MISSIONARY

biblical .... JOHN, JUDE, JAMES, PAUL, JUDAS, ANDREW, PHILIP, THOMAS, MATTHEW, BARNABAS, MATTHIAS, SIMON PETER, BARTHOLOMEW

of the Franks .... REMI

of the Goths .... ULFILAS

of the Indians .... ELIOT

thirteenth .... MATTHIAS

Apostles John and James .... BOANERGES

teaching of .... DIDACHE

apostolic .... PAPAL, PONTIFICAL

See .... ROME, BISHOPRIC

apothecary .... CHEMIST, DRUGGIST, PHARMACIST

measure .... PINT, DRAM, MINIM, OUNCE, GALLON

store .... PHARMACY

weight .... DRAM, GRAIN, OUNCE, POUND, SCRUPLE

apothegm .... ADAGE, AXIOM, MAXIM, DICTUM, SAYING, APHORISM

apotheosis .... ASCENSION, ELEVATION, EXALTATION

apotheosize .... DEIFY, EXALT, GLORIFY, IDEALIZE

Appalachian range ...... RAMAPO

appal(l) .... AWE, STUN, DAUNT, SHOCK, DISMAY, ASTOUND, HORRIFY, TERRIFY, PETRIFY, FRIGHTEN, SICKEN, ASTONISH

apparatus .... RIG, DEVICE, TOOL, GADGET, TACKLE, GEAR, MACHINE, UTENSIL, APPLIANCE, IMPLEMENT, INSTRUMENT

air blowing .... BELLOWS

air cooling .... FAN

artificial respiration .... PULMOTOR

beauty shop .... DRYER, (HAIR)DRIER

binding .... BALER

blacksmith's .... FORGE

carpenter's .... SAW, DRILL, PLANE, HAMMER, SANDER

dentist's .... DRILL

doctor's .... STETHOSCOPE

farmer's .... PLOW, BALER, HARROW, LISTER, PICKER, WINDROWER

for bacteria cultures .... INCUBATOR

gardener's ...... RAKE, MOWER, SHOVEL

hauling/hoisting .... CRANE, WINCH, FORKLIFT, WINDLASS

machine shop .... LATHE

plumber's .... WRENCH

surgeon's ..... PROBE, SCALPEL

underwater breathing .... SCUBA, SNORKEL, AQUALUNG

water-drawing .... PUMP

weaver's .... LOOM

apparel ...... GARB, GEAR, DRESS, HABIT, CLOTHES, ATTIRE, COSTUME, GARMENT, RAIMENT, CLOTHING

apparent .... CLEAR, PLAIN, OVERT, PATENT, EVIDENT, OBVIOUS, SEEMING, VISIBLE

apparently .... CLEARLY, PLAINLY, VISIBLY, EVIDENTLY, SEEMINGLY

apparition .... GHOST, IMAGE, MIRAGE, VISION, WRAITH, PHANTOM, SPECTER, EIDOLON,

SPECTER

of living person .... FETCH

appassionata .... PASSIONATE, IMPASSIONED

appeal ...... ASK, BEG, SUE, CALL, PRAY, SEEK, SUIT, PLEAD, CHARM, IMPLORE, PROTEST, PETITION, ATTRACTION

sex: sl. .... IT, OOMPH

appealing .... ALLURING, PLEADING, ENTICING, BEGGING, CATCHING, WINSOME, RAVISHING

appear .... ACT, COME, LOOK, LOOM, SEEM, ARISE, ARRIVE, ATTEND, EMERGE, SHOW UP

appearance .... AIR, LOOK, MIEN, ADVENT, ARRIVAL, SHOW, PRESENCE, SEMBLANCE

appease .... CALM, ALLAY, PACIFY, LESSEN, SOFTEN, SLAKE, SOOTHE, ASSUAGE, QUENCH, COMFORT, MOLLIFY, PLACATE, RELIEVE, SATISFY

appeasement, kind of .... SOP

appellation .... NAME, TITLE, NAMING, BAPTISM, DESIGNATION, CHRISTENING

append .... ADD, TAG, CLIP, AFFIX, ANNEX, ATTACH

appendage .... ARM, LEG, TAIL, LIMB, WING, JOINT, BRANCH, SHADOW, ADJUNCT, FIXTURE, ADDITION

crab .... FEELER, ANTENNA

fish .... FIN, BARBEL

leaf .... STIPULE

lobster .... PALP(US)

grain .... AWN, BEARD

threadlike .... CIRRUS

appendix .... ORGAN, RIDER, CODICIL, ADDENDUM, OUTGROWTH, POSTSCRIPT

appertain .... BELONG, RELATE

appetence .... DESIRE, THIRST, CRAVING, APPETITE

appetite .... YEN, ZEST, GUSTO, TASTE, DESIRE, SPIRIT, CRAVING, PASSION, STOMACH, APPETENCE

abnormal .... BULIMIA

for alcoholic drink
.... DIPSOMANIA

for food .... HUNGER

for something .... TASTE, TOOTH

for sweets .... SWEET TOOTH

for water .... THIRST

huge .... GARGANTUAN

insatiable .... GREED, VORACITY

loss of .... ANOREXIA

pertaining to .... ORECTIC

appetizer .... CANAPE, TIDBIT, WHETTER, ANTIPASTO, HORS D'OEUVRE

drink ...... COCKTAIL, APERITIF, DUBONNET

appetizing .... TASTY, SAVORY, PLEASING, TEMPTING, DELICIOUS

applaud ...... HAIL, LAUD, CHEER, EXTOL, ACCLAIM, PRAISE, COMMEND, GIVE A HAND

applauder .... FAN, ROOTER, CHEERER, CLAPPER

applauders' group ...... CLAQUE, CHEERING SQUAD

applause .... HAND, CHEER, ECLAT, PRAISE, PLAUDIT, APPROVAL

round of .... OVATION

word of .... OLE, HEAR, BANZAI, BRAVO, HOORAY, HURRAH, MABUHAY

apple .... MAY, CRAB, LOVE, POME, SORB, FRUIT, GRIMES, GOLDEN, PIPPIN, RUSSET, COSTARD, WINESAP, GREENING, JONATHAN, PEARMAIN, QUEENING, DELICIOUS, GRAVENSTEIN

acid .... MALIC

brownish autumn .... RUSSET

butter .... JAM

center .... CORE

color .... RED, GREEN, YELLOW

cooking .... NEWTON, PIPPIN, GRANNY SMITH

crushed pulp .... POMACE

custard .... ANONA

disease .... STIPPEN

elongated .... CODLING

fall variety .... FAMEUSE, WEALTHY

fermented drink .... CIDER

for backing .... BIFFIN

fried .... ROLPENS

inferior .... CODLIN(G)

jack .... BRANDY

juice .... CIDER

kin .... POME, QUINCE, TOMATO

love .... TOMATO

of one's eye .... PET, JEWEL, DARLING, FAVORITE

Persian .... PEACH

pie, deep-dish .... PAN DOWDY

polisher .... TOADY, FLATTERER

pudding .... BROWN BETTY

red .... MCINTOSH

red winter .... BALDWIN

Russian .... ASTRACHAN

seed/stone .... PIP, PYRENE

seller .... COSTER

shaped fruit .... QUINCE

tosser: myth. .... ERIS

tree .... SORB, WILDING, SAPODILLA

unripe .... CODLING

variety .... NON(E)SUCH

wild .... CRAB

worm .... MOTH

apples, pertaining to ...... MALIC

applesauce .... PUREE, RELISH, DESSERT

colloquial .... HOKUM, BALONEY, NONSENSE

applethorne .... EPIGENE

appliance ...... USE, TOOL, USAGE, DEVICE, MACHINE, UTENSIL, EQUIPMENT, IMPLEMENT

electrical/household ..... IRON, OVEN, MIXER, RANGE, BLENDER, FREEZER, TOASTER, DISHWASHER, CAN OPENER, PERCOLATOR, DISPOSAL, REFRIGERATOR, MICROWAVE OVEN

applicable .... LEGAL, USABLE, FITTING, RELEVANT, SUITABLE, PERTINENT

application .... USE, FORM, OFFER, REMEDY, APPEAL, REQUEST, PROPOSAL, DILIGENCE, RELEVANC(E)Y

medical .... BANDAGE, PLASTER, COMPRESS, DRESSING

applied decoration .... OIL, GESSO, PAINT, APPLIQUE

science .... TECHNOLOGY

apply ...... ASK, PUT, USE, COVER, PLACE, DEVOTE, ASSIGN, BESTOW, EMPLOY, LAY ON, FILE FOR, REQUEST

force .... EXERT, PRESS, DEMAND, ENFORCE

friction ...... RUB, RASP, GRATE

justice .... BRING TO BOOK

oneself .... STRIVE

pressure .... COERCE, INFLUENCE

to .... VEIL, SHIELD

appoggiatura .... THANK YOU, GRACE NOTE

appoint ...... HIRE, NAME, ASSIGN, CHARGE, DETAIL, CHOOSE, ENGAGE, EMPLOY, PLACE, NOMINATE, ORDAIN, DESIGNATE

again .... RENAME

as agent .... DEPUTE, DEPUTIZE, DELEGATE

in lieu of .... PROXY
to benefice .... COLLATE
appointment .... DATE, TRYST,
   DECREE, HIRING, NAMING,
   MEETING, ELECTION,
   INTERVIEW, ENGAGEMENT
appointments ...... GEAR, THINGS,
   FURNITURE, TRAPPINGS,
   BELONGINGS
apportion ...... DEAL, DOLE, GIVE,
   HAND, METE, ALLOT, SHARE,
   ASSIGN, PARCEL, DIVIDE,
   PRORATE
apposite .... APT, FIT, PAT, RIGHT,
   PROPER, GERMANE, RELEVANT
appraisal .... RATING, SURVEY,
   GAUGING, PRICING, ANALYSIS,
   ESTIMATE, EVALUATION
appraise .... RATE, GA(U)GE,
   GRADE, JUDGE, PRICE, WEIGH,
   ASSAY, ASSESS, COMPUTE,
   MEASURE, (E)VALUATE
appraiser .... RATER, ASSAYER,
   ASSESSOR, SURVEYOR,
   ESTIMATOR
appreciable .... REAL, CONCRETE,
   MATERIAL, PALPABLE,
   TANGIBLE, NOTICEABLE
appreciate .... PRIZE, VALUE,
   ESTEEM, NOTICE, CHERISH,
   REALIZE, UNDERSTAND
fondly .... LOVE, SAVOR
highly ...... IDOLIZE, TREASURE
in value .... INCREASE
with respect .... REVERE,
   VENERATE
appreciation .... THANKS,
   RESPECT, COURTESY,
   GRATITUDE, RECOGNITION
of value .... GAIN
apprehend .... NAB, HOLD, HENT,
   CATCH, ARREST, SENSE,
   GRASP, DETAIN, SEIZE,
   CAPTURE, PERCEIVE
apprehension .... FEAR, DOUBT,
   ALARM, ARREST, QUALM,
   ANXIETY, CONCERN, CAPTURE,
   PERCEPTION
apprehensive .... EDGY, ANXIOUS,
   UNEASY, WORRIED, TENSE,
   FEARFUL, NERVOUS, PANICKY,
   PERTURBED
apprentice .... TYRO, DEVIL,
   NOVICE, ROOKIE, LEARNER,
   TRAINEE, BEGINNER,
   NEOPHYTE, HELPER,
   GREENHORN
apprenticeship .... TRAINING,
   PROBATION
contract .... INDENTURE
apprise .... TELL, ADVISE, INFORM,

NOTIFY, ACQUAINT
apprised ...... AWARE, INFORMED,
   COGNIZANT
approach .... COME, NEAR, ONSET,
   ACCESS, ADVENT, STEP UP,
   PASSAGE, OVERTURE
stealthily .... STALK
toward each other
   .... CONVERGE
approbation ...... FAVOR, ASSENT,
   CONSENT, BLESSING, TRIBUTE,
   APPROVAL, SANCTION
appropriate .... APT, DUE, FIT,
   TAKE, ADOPT, SEIZE, STEAL,
   MEET, RIGHT, TIMELY,
   PROPER, POCKET, GERMANE,
   PREEMPT, APPOSITE,
   BECOMING, SUITABLE
honestly .... PURCHASE
improperly ...... COVET, STEAL,
   USURP
approval .... ASSENT, CONSENT,
   SUPPORT, AGREEMENT,
   SANCTION
kind of .... IMPRIMATUR
sign of .... NOD
word of .... GO, OK(AY),
   SHOOT
approve .... PASS, ACCEPT,
   RATIFY, CERTIFY, CONFIRM,
   ENDORSE, SANCTION
approving mention
   .... ACCOLADE, CITATION
approximate .... NEAR, CLOSE,
   ROUGH, INEXACT, APPROACH,
   PARALLEL
approximately .... ABOUT,
   ALMOST, MAINLY, MOSTLY,
   NEARLY, ON THE AVERAGE,
   ROUGHLY, VIRTUALLY
appurtenance ...... PART, ANNEX,
   ADJUNCT, ADDITION
appurtenant .... GERMANE,
   ACCESSORY, PERTINENT
aprenaceous .... SANDY
apres .... AFTER
six .... SEPT
apricot .... UME, ANSU, TREE,
   COLOR, FRUIT, DRUPE,
   YELLOWISH-ORANGE
cordial .... PERSICO
April Dancer's colleague
   .... NOEL
15 initials .... IRS
apron .... BELT, FLAP, SHIELD,
   PINAFORE
child's .... BIB, BISHOP
painter's .... SMOCK
apropos .... APT, PAT, GEARED,
   TIMELY, FITTING, IN PASSING,
   BY THE WAY, RELEVANT,

OPPORTUNE, SUITABLE,
   PERTAINING
apse .... ARCH, DOME, APSIS,
   STEEPLE, PROJECTION
dome cover .... CONCHA
apt .... DEFT, PRONE, QUICK,
   CLEVER, FITTING, LIKELY,
   PROPER, INCLINED, RELEVANT,
   SUITABLE
apteral .... WINGLESS
apteryx .... MOA, BIRD, ROA, KIWI
aptitude .... BENT, GIFT, FLAIR,
   KNACK, GENIUS, ABILITY,
   TALENT, FITNESS, LEANING,
   KEENNESS, DEXTERITY
aptly chosen .... FELICITOUS
Apulia's capital .... BARI
aqua .... WATER, LIQUID,
   SOLUTION
fortis .... NITRIC ACID
pura .... DISTILLED WATER
vitae .... BRANDY, LIQUOR,
   ALCOHOL
aquamarine .... GEM, BERYL,
   COLOR, PIGMENT, BLUISH-
   GREEN
aquarium .... (WATER)TANK,
   FISHPOND
fish .... GUPPY
large marine ..... OCEANARIUM
plant .... FANWORT
small .... FISHBOWL
aquatic .... MARINE, WATERY,
   OCEANIC, WATER-DWELLING
animal .... MINK, NEWT,
   OTTER, BEAVER
bird .... AUK, COOT, DUCK,
   GULL, LOON, SWAN, GOOSE,
   GREBE, SCAUP, PELICAN,
   PENGUIN, FLAMINGO
entertainment .... AQUACADE
mammal .... MINK, SEAL,
   OTTER, WHALE, DUGONG,
   SEACOW, MANATEE
movie character .... FLIPPER
performer .... SEAL, DIVER,
   WHALE, DOLPHIN, FLIPPER
plant .... LILY, SEAWEED
vertebrate .... FISH
aqueduct .... PIPE, CANAL,
   TRENCH, CHANNEL, CONDUIT,
   PASSAGE
of Sylvius .... ITER
aqueous .... WATERY
solution .... JAVEL
Aquila .... EAGLE, CONSTELLATION
star .... ALTAIR
aquiline .... BEAKED, HOOKED
ara .... ALTAR, MACAW,
   CONSTELLATION
Arab .... WAIF, GAMIN, GYPSY,

ANSAR, HORSE, NOMAD, TATAR, URCHIN, SEMITE, BEDOUIN, SARACEN
arabesque .... BAROQUE, ELABORATE
Arabia .... SAUDI, PENINSULA
poetic .... ARABY
Arabian abode .... DAR
antelope .... ADDAX
ape .... BABOON
beverage .... BOSA(H), BOZA, LEBAN
bird of fable .... ROC
camel .... DROMEDARY
capital .... ADEN, SAN'A, BAGHDAD, MUSCAT, MANAMA, TEHRAN, RIYADH, ABU DHABI
chief .... SAYID, SHERIF
chieftain .... AMIR, EMIR, REIS, AMEER, EMEER, SHEIK(H)
chieftain's domain
.... EMIRATE
city/town .... GAZA, JIDDA, MECCA, AHVAZ, MUSCAT, ARBELA, ABADAN, TEBUK, KIRKUK, MEDINA, ARADA, HODEIDA, DHAMAR, MAIDA, TABRIZ, DAMMAN, HAMADAN, AL KUWAIT, DHANK, BAKHTARAN
cloth .... ABA
coffee .... MOCHA
coin .... TALARI
country .... IRAN, IRAQ, OMAN, QATAR, YEMEN, SYRIA, JORDAN, KUWAIT, BAHRAIN, LEBANON, SAUDI ARABIA
demon/evil spirit .... AFRIT(E), AFREET, EBLIS, GENIE, JINN(I)
dervish of story .... AGIB
desert ..... LUT, KAVIR, NEFUD, DAHANA, MARGOW, SYRIAN
dromedary .... BELOOL, HEJEEN
father .... ABU, ABOU
garment .... ABA, HAI(C)K
gazelle .... ARIEL
gulf ..... ADEN, OMAN, MASIRA, PERSIAN
head cord .... AGAL
island .... DAS, YAS, ARWAD, PERIM, MASIRA, ZIRKO, ZUQAR, BUBIYAN, TIRAN, KAMARAN, MASHABI, SOCOTRA
jasmine .... BELA
javelin ..... JER(R)ID, JER(R)EED
judge/magistrate .... CADI
kingdom .... SABA, SHEBA, JORDAN
labor/peasant .... FELLAH
language .... ARABIC

letter .... BA, FA, HA, RA, TA, YA, ZA, AYN, GAF, KAF, THA, JIM, KHA, DAL, DAD, LAM, MIM, NUN, SAD, SIN, ZAY, WAW, ALIF, DHAL, SHIN, GHAYN
measure ...... ARDEB, COVID(O)
measure, grain .... SAA, TOMAN
mock battle .... JER(R)ID, JER(E)ED
monarchy .... YEMEN
monetary unit .... DINAR, RIAL, RIYAL, DIRHAM
Moslem .... WAHABI
mountain .... SABIR, SHAM, MANAR, ANEIZA, HERMON, TROODOS
Nights Bassorah .... BASRA
Nights spirit .... GENIE
nomad .... SLEB
oasis .... DOUMA
palm .... DOUM
peninsula .... ADEN, SINAI
potentate .... SALADIN
prince .... SHERIF
religion .... ISLAM
river ...... DEZ, KONAR, KABUL, LURAH, KHABUR, LITANI, HARIRUD, HELMAND, MURGHAB, ORANTES, TIGRIS, EUPHRATES
ruler .... EMIR, EMEER, SHEIK(H), SULTAN
sacred territory .... HARAM
sailboat .... DHOW
Scripture .... ALCORAN
sea .... RED, DEAD
Sea river .... INDUS
seaport .... ADEN, MOCHA
sheikhdom .... KUWAIT
state .... OMAN, YEMEN
strait .... MANDEB, TIRAN
sultanate .... OMAN
sword .... SCIMITAR
system of numerals
.... ALGORISM
tambourine .... TAAR, DAIRA, DAIRE
teacher .... ULEMA
tent village .... DOUAR
tribal chief .... SHEIK(H)
veil .... YASMAK
wagon .... ARABA
weight .... DIRHEM
wind .... SAMIEL, SIMOOM
Arabic acid .... ARABIN
arabinose .... SUGAR, PENTOSE
arable .... FERTILE, TILLABLE
araceous .... AROID
plant .... ARUM, LILY, TARO,

CABBAGE
Arachne .... SPIDER
arachnid .... MITE, TICK, ACARID, SPIDER, SCORPION
segment .... SOMITE, TELSON
arachnoid, space below
.... CISTERNA
structure .... WEB
arado .... LAND
Arafat org. .... PLO
Aram .... SYRIA
arbalest .... CROSSBOW
Arbela .... ERBIL
arbiter .... JUDGE, EXPERT, OVERMAN, MEDIATOR, AUTHORITY
archaic .... DAYSMAN
baseball .... UMP(IRE)
boxing/basketball
.... REF(EREE)
fashion .... DIOR, BALMAIN, DESIGNER, STYLIST
of taste .... GOURMET, GOURMAND
arbitrary .... UNFAIR, ARROGANT, CARELESS, ABSOLUTE, DESPOTIC, WHIMSICAL, CAPRICIOUS, HIGH-HANDED
arbitrator .... JUDGE, ARBITER, MEDIATOR, JUSTICE, MIDDLEMAN, OVERMAN, MODERATOR
arbor .... BEAM, TREE, AXLE, BOWER, SHAFT, PERGOLA, SPINDLE, TRELLIS
vitae .... THUJA
Arboreal ...... DENDRAL, TREELIKE
amphibian .... TREETOAD
creature ..... AI, UNAU, KOALA, SLOTH, COLUGO, TARSIER, SQUIRREL
arbored .... TREED
arbutus .... BERRY, PLANT, SHRUB, MAYFLOWER
arc .... BOW, ARCH, CURVE
chord .... SINE
of 90 degrees .... QUADRANT
sky .... RAINBOW
arcade .... LOGGIA, PIAZZA, GALLERY, PORTICO, ARCATURE
Arcadian .... RUSTIC, SIMPLE, BUCOLIC, PASTORAL, PEACEFUL, SHEPHERD
princess .... AUGE
Arcady .... ARCADIA
arcane .... HIDDEN, SECRET, ESOTERIC
arcanum .... ELIXIR, REMEDY, SECRET, MYSTERY
arch ...... ARC, SLY, BEND, DOME,

FOOT, HEEL, MAIN, CHIEF, PRIME, CLEVER, CURVE, CRAFTY, FORNIX, CUNNING, PRINCIPAL
as combining form ..... RULER
curved inside .... INTRADOS
enemy/fiend ..... DEVIL, SATAN
lower part .... IMPOST, SPRINGER
of bridge .... SPAN
of heaven .... COPE
of spears over shoulders .... YOKE
of the foot .... INSTEP
over eye .... (EYE)BROW
pointed .... OGEE, OGIVE
side of .... HAUNCH
underside .... SOFFIT
archaic .... OLD, OLDEN, ANCIENT, ANTIQUE, HISTORIC, OUTDATED, OBSOLETE
command .... HEST
archangel .... SATAN, URIEL, GABRIEL, MICHAEL, RAPHAEL, ANGELICA
archbishop .... PONTIFF, PRELATE, PRIMATE, DIOCESAN, HIERARCH
of Canterbury .... ANSELM, BECKET, CRANMER
subordinate of ..... SUFFRAGAN
archbishopric .... SEE, APOSTOLIC
arched .... COPED, CONVEX, HUMPED, CURVED, CONCAVE, VAULTED
passageway .... ARCADE
way .... CLOISTER
arch(a)eological find in 1887 .... SIDON
arch(a)eologist's concern .... RUINS, RELIC, ARTIFACT
archer .... BOWMAN, SHOOTER, CONSTELLATION
angel .... CUPID
buff .... TOXOPHILITE
of story .... ROBIN HOOD, (WILLIAM) TELL
of the sky .... SAGITTARIUS
protective band .... BRACER
target .... CLOUT, ROVER
archery, of .... SAGITTARY
arches, row of .... ARCUATION
archetype .... IDEAL, IMAGE, MODEL, EXAMPLE, PATTERN, ORIGINAL, PROTOTYPE
archfiend .... SATAN
archil .... DYE, LICHEN
archimage .... WIZARD, MAGICIAN
archipelago .... SULU, COLON, MALAY, PAUMOTO, TUAMOTU, BISMARCK

architect .... MAKER, ARTIST, BUILDER, CREATOR, PLANNER, DESIGNER
architectural .... TECTONIC
column .... PILASTER
concave molding .... CAVETTO
design .... SPANDREL
drawing .... EPURE
feature .... NAVE
ornament ..... DENTIL, CORBEIL
pier .... ANTA
type .... DORIC, IONIC, MAYAN, GOTHIC, MODERN, BAROQUE
archly .... PERTLY, SAUCILY
archon .... RULER, MAGISTRATE
Arctic .... COLD, COOL, CHILLY, POLAR, FRIGID, ICY, NORTH(ERN), OVERSHOE
base .... ETAH, THULE
bird .... AUK, ROTCH(E), DOVEKEY, JUNCO, DOVEKIE, GUILLEMOT
dog .... SAMO, SAMOYED(E), MALEMUTE
explorer ...... RAE, ERIC, KANE, PEARY
goose .... BRANT
gulf .... OB
gull ...... XEMA, BURGOMASTER
home .... IGLU, IGLOO
jacket .... PARKA, ANORAK
native .... ALEUT, ESKIMO
phenomenon .... BERG
pinniped .... SEAL
plain .... TUNDRA
seagull .... KITTIWAKE
tribesman .... LAPP
wasteland .... TUNDRA
arcuate .... ARCHED, CURVED
arcubalist .... CROSSBOWMAN
Arden, ____ .... EVE, TONI, ENOCH, ELIZABETH
ardent .... AVID, KEEN, EAGER, WARM, FERVENT, PASSIONATE
devotion .... ZEAL
partisan .... DEVOTEE, FANATIC
spirits .... GIN, LIQUOR, WHISKY
ardor .... ELAN, FIRE, HEAT, ZEAL, FERVOR, VERVE, WARMTH, PASSION
arduous .... HARD, DIFFICULT, ENERGETIC, LABORIOUS
area .... SCOPE, RANGE, FIELD, EXTENT, REGION, ZONE, DISTRICT, VICINITY
around moving body .... PERIPTER
between leaf veins .... AREOLA
measure of .... ARE, ACRE, DECARE, HECTARE, CENTIAR(E)

on bird's bill .... CERE
small .... CLOSE, AREOLA
areaway .... YARD, COURT, PASSAGE
areca .... PALM, BETEL
arena .... RING, FIELD, PIT, BOWL, RINK, LISTS, OVAL, STAGE, SPHERE, STADIUM, THEATER, BULLRING
kind of ..... COURT, (COCK)PIT, DIAMOND, GRIDIRON
arenaceous ...... SANDY, ARENOSE
arenite .... SANDSTONE
areo, as combining form .... MARS
areola .... RING, ROUND, SPACE, CIRCLE, HOLLOW
Ares .... MARS
parent of .... HERA, ZEUS
sister of .... ERIS
arete .... CREST, RIDGE, ARISTA
Arethusa .... NYMPH, ORCHID
argal .... ERGO, HENCE, SHEEP, ARGALI, TARTAR, THEREFORE
argala .... STORK, MARABOU, ADJUTANT
argali .... SHEEP, AOUDAD, BIGHORN
argent .... SILVER(Y)
Argentina's capital ...... BUENOS AIRES
Argentine armadillo ...... PELUDO
bay .... BLANCA, GRANDE
cape .... SAN DIEGO, DOS BAHIAS, SAN ANTONIO, TRES PUNTAS
city/town .... AZUL, CONCORDIA, AVELLANEDA, SALTA, BOLIVAR, ESCOBAR, CAMPANA, CORRIENTES, JUJUY, POSADAS, MENDOZA, CORDOBA, CONCEPCION, CASILDA, MAR DEL PLATA, RIO CUARTO, RIVADAVIA, TIGRE, ZARATE, BARADERO, MORON, ROSARIO, SANTIAGO, SAN JUAN, TRES ARROYOS, GODOY CRUZ
crested bird .... SERIEMA
gulf .... NUEVO, SAN JORGE, SAN MATIAS
highest point .... CERRO ACONGCAGUA
Indian .... PAMPEAN
island .... LENNOX, STATEN, TRINIDAD
lake .... VIEDMA, FAGNANO, BUENOS AIRES, ARGENTINO, MAR CHIQUITA, NAHUEL HUAPI
language .... SPANISH
monetary unit .... AUSTRAL

mountain ...... ANDES, CONICO, PISSIS, RINCON, DEL TORO, ACONGCAGUA, ZAPALERI, MERCEDARIO, TRONADOR, TUPUNGATO, CAMPANARIO
plain .... PAMPAS
port .... ROSARIO, LA PLATA
president .... PERON, MENEM, ILLIA, ONGANIA, ALFONSIN
province .... BUENOS AIRES, MISIONES, CATAMARCA, SANTIAGO DEL ESTERO, CORRIENTES, ENTRE RIOS, SALTA, FORMOSA, MENDOZA, CHACO, CORDOBA, SANTA FE, JUJUY, TUCUMAN, SAN JUAN, CHUBUT, LA PAMPA, DISTRITO FEDERAL
region ..... GRAN CHACO, PUNA DE ATACAMA, PETAGONIA, CHACO CENTRAL, CHACO AUSTRAL
river .... ATUEL, CHICO, BERMEJO, COLORADO, URUGUAY, PILCOMAYO, SALI, DULCE, DIAMANTE, GALLEGOS, FELICIANO, CHUBUT, SALADO, QUINTO, SALTO, NEUQUEN, MENDOZA, COYLE, PARANA, TERCERO, LIMAY, TEUCO, TARIJA
salt deposit .... ARIZARO
seaport .... LA PLATA
"sleeping beauty"
.... (MARIA)TELLO
timber tree .... TALA
tune .... GATO
volcano .... LANIN, MAIPO, DOMUYO, PETEROA
wage earner ..... DESCAMISADO
waterfall ..... GRANDE, IGUAZU
argil .... CLAY
Argo .... SHIP, CONSTELLATION
argol .... TARTAR
Argolis native .... AGIVE
vale of .... NEMEA
Argonaut .... JASON, ACASTUS, MELEAGER
of the gold rush .... FORTY-NINER
ship .... ARGO
argosy .... SHIP, FLEET, VESSEL
argot .... CANT, LINGO, SLANG, JARGON, PATOIS, DIALECT
argue ...... JAW, DEBATE, OBJECT, REASON, CONTEND, DISCUSS, DISPUTE, WRANGLE
for argument's sake
.... ARGUFY
in court .... PRAY, PLEAD, REBUT, CONTEST

price/terms .... HAGGLE, HIGGLE, BARGAIN
argument .... CASE, TOPIC, DEBATE, HASSLE, POLEMIC, DISCUSSION
about words .... LOGOMACHY
kind of .... CON, PRO, RHUBARB
lovers' .... SPAT, QUARREL
to justify .... DEFENSE, REBUTTAL
argumentation .... DIALECTICS
argumentative .... COMBATIVE, ERISTICAL, LITIGIOUS, POLEMICAL, CONTENTIOUS
Argus .... GIANT, WATCHMAN
eyed .... VIGILANT, OBSERVANT
aria .... AIR, SOLO, SONG, TUNE, MELODY, REFRAIN
brilliant flourish ..... CADENZA
like an .... ARIOSO
arias .... SOLI
Ariadne's father .... MINOS
love .... THESEUS
arid .... DRY, BARREN, JEJUNE, TORRID, STERILE, ANHYDROUS, UNFERTILE
region .... DESERT
region, U.S. .... DUST BOWL
ariel .... GAZELLE
Ariel .... SPIRIT, SATELLITE
Ariel's compeer .... SPRITE
master .... PROSPERO
Aries .... RAM, CONSTELLATION
arietta .... AIR, ARIA, SONG, MELODY
arikara .... REE
ariose .... MELODIC, SONGLIKE
arioso .... MELODIOUS
composer .... BACH
arise .... GROW, GET UP, ISSUE, STAND, WAKEN, AWAKE, ASCEND, EMANATE
arista .... AWN, BEARD, BRISTLE
aristocracy ...... ELITE, NOBILITY, OLIGARCHY
aristocrat ...... SNOB, NOBLEMAN, HIGH-BORN
Athenian/Greek ...... EUPATRID
Roman .... PATRICIAN
Russian .... BOYAR
Spanish .... GRANDEE, HIDALGO
aristocratic .... PATRICIAN
aristocrats collectively
.... NOBILITY, NOBLESSE
Aristotle .... STAGIRITE
birthplace .... STAGIRA
follower .... PERIPATETIC
logic .... DEDUCTIVE, SYLLOGISM

teacher of .... PLATO
arithmetic, common .... LOGISTIC
Arizona capital .... PHOENIX
city/town .... MESA, YUMA, TEMPE, PEORIA, PRESCOTT, CHANDLER, TUCSON, NOGALES, WINSLOW, FLAGSTAFF, SCOTTSDALE, KINGMAN, CASA GRANDE
Cochise county seat
.... BISBEE
county .... GILA, PIMA, APACHE, GRAHAM, LA PAZ, PINAL, MOHAVE, NAVAJO, GREENLEE, MARICOPA, YUMA, COCHISE, YAVAPAI
dam .... DAVIS, HOOVER, COOLIDGE, PAINTED ROCK
desert .... YUMA, PAINTED
highest point ...... HUMPHREYS PEAK
Indian ...... HANO, HOPI, TEWA, MOQUI, APACHE, NAVAHO, NAVAJO, YUMA, PAIUTE
lake .... MEAD, ALAMO, APACHE, CANYON, HAVASU, POWELL, SAGUARO
mountain .... ORD, ELDEN, WOODY, GRAHAM, LEMMON, TRUMBULL, FOUR PEAKS
nut .... PINON
river .... GILA, SALT, BLACK, PARIA, VERDE, WHITE, COLORADO
state bird .... WREN
state flower
.... SAGUARO(CACTUS)
state nickname .... GRAND CANYON
tourist sight .... GRAND CANYON, PETRIFIED FOREST
ark .... BOAT, REFUGE
animals/birds .... PAIRS
builder .... NOE, NOAH
landing place
.... (MOUNT)ARARAT
porter .... BEN
Arkansas capital .... LITTLE ROCK
city/town .... CAMDEN, MAGNOLIA, HARRISON, EL DORADO, BLYTHEVILLE, FORT SMITH, PINE BLUFF, TEXARKANA, FAYETTEVILLE, CONWAY, HORSESHOE BEND
county .... CLAY, POPE, MILLER, BOONE, ASHLEY, IZARD, CHICOT, POINSETT, BENTON, GARLAND, GREENE, YELL, LOGAN, OUACHITA, LEE, PULASKI, FAULKNER, BAXTER, MONROE, NEWTON, DREW,

PERRY, CONWAY, UNION, CRITTENDEN, WHITE, WASHINGTON

highest point .... MAGAZINE MOUNTAIN

Indian .... OSAGE, CHEROKEE

lake .... BEAVER, GREESON, NORFOLK, NIMROD, WINONA, CONWAY, BLUE SHOALS

mountain .... MAGAZINE, POTEAU, REEVES KNOB

river .... RED, BLACK, BUFFALO, OUACHITA, CACHE, SALINE, MULBERRY, SPRING, LITTLE RED, CADDO, LITTLE MISSOURI

state bird .... MOCKINGBIRD

state flower .... APPLE BLOSSOM

state nickname .... WONDER, LAND OF OPPORTUNITY

tourist sight .... CRATER OF DIAMONDS

arles ...... ANTE, TOKEN, EARNEST, PREPAYMENT

arm ...... LIMB, BRANCH, WEAPON, FORTIFY, FURNISH, TENTACLE

badge .... BRASSARD

band .... BRACER

bone .... ULNA, HUMERUS

bone, pertaining to ..... ULNAR

cover .... SLEEVE

extendible .... PANTOGRAPH

hole .... SCYE

in-arm .... OXTER

joint .... ELBOW, WRIST

length of .... REACH

like .... BRACHIAL

of the sea .... BAY, FIORD, FIRTH, FJORD, INLET

shield .... BUCKLER

armada .... FLEET

armadillo .... APAR(A), PEBA, POYOU, TATOU

shell .... CARAPACE

6-banded .... PELUDO

3-banded .... APAR, MATACO

12-banded .... TATOUAY

Armageddon .... (LAST)BATTLE

author .... URIS

maybe .... MEGIDDO

armament ...... ARMS, ORDNANCE, WEAPONRY, EQUIPMENT

factory .... KRUPP, SKODA

armature .... ARMOR

armchair .... FAUTEUIL

armed band .... POSSE

conflict .... WAR, BATTLE

escort .... CONVOY, BODYGUARD

fleet .... NAVY

galley .... AESC

guard .... SENTRY, SENTINEL

Armenia's capital .... ERIVAN

mountain .... ARARAT

river .... ARAS

armet .... HELMET

armiger .... SQUIRE, ARMOR BEARER

armistice ...... TRUCE, CEASE-FIRE

armlet .... BANGLE

armoire ...... CABINET, CUPBOARD

armor ...... MAIL, PLATE, BARD(E), SHIELD

arm ..... BRASSARD, BRASSART, PALLETTE

back .... CUIRASS

bearer .... SQUIRE, ARMIGER

body ...... TACE, CULET, TASSE, LORICA, CUIRASS, SURCOAT

breast .... CUIRASS

chain .... MAIL

clamp/hook .... AGRAFFE

elbow to shoulder .... BRASSARD

foot .... SOLLERET

hand .... GAUNTLET

head .... VISOR, BEAVER, ARMET, BASINET, HELMET, HAUBERK, SCONCE

horse .... BARD(E), TESTIERE

jacket .... GIPON, JUPON

joint .... GUSSET

leg .... JAMB(E), GREAVE

neck/throat .... GORGET

plate .... LAME, MASCLE

rings .... BRIGANDINE

shirt cover .... CAMISADO

shoulder .... AILETTE, PAULDRON

snail's .... SHELL

thigh .... CUISH, TUILE, CUISSE, TASSET

tunic .... GIPON, JUPON

turtle's .... CARAPACE

unworn .... BARESARK

armored .... MAILED, COVERED, EQUIPPED

animal .... ARMADILLO

person of old .... KNIGHT

ship ...... MONITOR, IRONCLAD, MERRIMAC

vehicle .... TANK

armorial .... HERALDIC

bearings/ensigns .... HERALDRY

armory ...... ARSENAL, HERALDRY

orator's .... WORDS, CLICHES

armpit .... ALA, OXTER, AXILLA

swelling .... BUBO

arms .... WARFARE, WEAPONS, INSIGNIA

creature with eight .... OCTOPOD, OCTOPUS

of the night, so-called .... DARKNESS

repository .... ARSENAL

army .... HOST, DROVE, HORDE, COLONY, LEGION, TROOP, THRONG, ARMED FORCES

acronym .... SNAFU

car .... JEEP

caterer/follower .... SUTLER

chaplain .... PADRE, PRIEST

engineer .... SAPPER

front of .... VAN(GUARD)

group .... UNIT, CORPS, COMPANY, BRIGADE, PLATOON, SQUAD(RON), REGIMENT

insignia of rank .... BAR, LEAF, STAR, EAGLE, STRIPE

instructor ..... DRILL SERGEANT

mascot .... MULE

meal .... CHOW, MESS

mounted sentinel .... VEDETTE, VIDETTE

of animals .... HERD, PACK

of birds .... FLOCK

of insects .... SWARM

of lions .... PRIDE

of the .... MILITARY

rank .... MAJOR, CAPTAIN, COLONEL, GENERAL, PRIVATE, CORPORAL, SERGEANT, LIEUTENANT

vehicle .... JEEP, TANK, AMTRAC, WEAPONS CARRIER

Arnaz, _____ .... DESI, LUCIE

Arndt (Felix) piece .... NOLA

arnica .... PLANT, ANTISEPTIC

Arnold (Matthew) character .... RUSTUM, SOHRAB

aroid .... ARUM, TARO, TANIA, ARACEOUS

aroma ...... ODOR, SAVOR, SMELL, FLAVOR, FRAGRANCE

aromatic .... SPICY, SAVORY, ODOROUS, PUNGENT, FRAGRANT

bark .... ANGOSTURA, CASCARILLA

berry .... CUBEB

beverage .... COFFEE

condiment .... SPICE

fruit .... NUTMEG

gum .... BALM, MYRRH, ARALIA, BALSAM

herb ...... MINT, ANISE, THYME, CARAWAY, FLEAWORT

leaf .... BAY, BUCHU, LAUREL

liquid .... BAYRUM

oil .... BALM

ointment .... NARD

plant .... MINT, NARD, SAGE,
BASIL, CARUM, ANGELICA,
WORMWOOD, ARTEMISIA
resin .... COPALM, COPAIBA
root .... GINSENG
seed .... DILL, ANISE,
CUM(M)IN, FENNEL, GUAIAC
smoke .... FUME, INCENSE
spice .... MACE, CLOVE,
NUTMEG
tree .... BALSAM, FIRPINE
weed .... TANSY
wood .... CEDAR, BASSWOOD
Arouet's nickname .... ZOZO
around ...... ABOUT, CIRCA, CLOSE
TO, NEARBY, EVERYWAY
arouse ...... FAN, FIRE, SPUR, STIR,
PIQUE, FOMENT, EXCITE,
INCITE, ANIMATE, INFLAME
Arpachshad's brother .... LUD,
ARAM, ELAM, ASHUR
father .... SHEM
grandfather .... NOAH
son .... SHELAH
arpeggio .... ROULADE
arraign .... CITE, ACCUSE,
CHARGE, INDICT, IMPEACH
arrange .... FIX, SET, SORT,
ADAPT, ADJUST, DESIGN,
MARSHAL, PREPARE, CLASSIFY
a coiffure .... TEASE
by twos .... MATE, PAIR
for battle .... DEPLOY
for reference .... FILE
in advance .... PLAN, PREPARE,
SCHEDULE
in files .... STACK
in new groupings .... REALIGN
in threes .... TERNATE
methodically .... FILE,
ALPHABETIZE
the hair .... COMB, DRESS
arrangement .... FILE, PLAN,
ORDER, DESIGN, LAYOUT,
SETUP, AGREEMENT,
SETTLEMENT, TABULATION
literary .... COMPOSITION
musical .... LIED, SONG,
SONATA
arrant .... BAD, BOLD, EVIL, VILE,
HEINOUS, ATROCIOUS,
NOTORIOUS, OUT AND OUT,
WICKED, UNMITIGATED
arras .... TAPESTRY
array ...... DRESS, ORDER, ATTIRE,
FINERY, MARSHAL, DECK-OUT,
TURN-OUT
arrear(s) .... BEHIND, BACKLOG,
DEFICIT, SHORTFALL
arrest .... NAB, CURB, HALE,
HOLD, NICK, STEM, COLLAR,

STOP, CATCH, CHECK, SEIZE
slang .... BUST, PINCH
writ .... CAPLAS
arrival, scheduled: abbr.
.... ETA
arrive .... COME, LAND, REACH,
APPEAR, ATTAIN
arrivederci .... GOODBY, SO
LONG, FAREWELL
arrogance .... AIRS, PRIDE,
BLUSTER, BRAVADO,
HAUTEUR, HUBRIS,
INSOLENCE, SNOBBERY
arrogant .... COCKY, LOFTY,
PROUD, HAUGHTY, CAVALIER,
STUCK-UP, FLIPPANT,
SNOBBISH, OVERBEARING, ON
ONE'S HIGH HORSE
arrogate .... GRAB, CLAIM, USURP,
ASSUME, ACQUIRE, CAPTURE,
CONFISCATE
arrow .... BOLT, DART, SHAFT,
POINTER, SAGITTA
ancient .... QUARREL
barb .... FLUKE
blunt .... BUTT, SHAFT
body of .... STELE
case .... QUIVER
crossbow .... BOLT
feather .... VANE
feather-fitter .... PLUMIER
feathered .... VIRE
like .... SAGITTAL
notch for bowstring ..... NOCK
poetic .... REED
poison .... INEE, UPAS,
CURARE, URARI, ANTIAR(IN)
put feather on .... FLEDGE,
FLETCH
user .... ARCHER, BOWMAN
arrowroot .... PIA, ARUM, CANNA,
ARARAO, TAPIOCA
arrows, quiverful of .... SHEAF
Arrowsmith, Mrs. .... LEORA
arrowwood .... WAHOO,
DOGWOOD, VIBURNUM
arrowworm .... SAGITTA
arroyo .... PIT, WADI, BROOK,
GULLY, HONDO, RIVULET,
STREAM(BED)
arse .... RUMP, BUTTOCKS
arsenal .... ARMORY, SUPPLY,
STOREHOUSE
Arsene, Monsieur .... LUPIN
arsenic .... POISON
acid salt .... ARSENATE
combining form .... ARSENO
compound .... ARSENIDE
powder .... SALVARSAN
sulfide .... REALGAR
symbol .... AS

arsis .... ICTUS, UPBEAT
arsonist .... NERC, BURNER,
FIREBUG, PYROMANIAC
art .... CRAFT, DANCE, DRAMA,
MUSIC, SKILL, TRICK,
CUNNING, ARTIFICE, SCIENCE,
PAINTING
exhibition .... SALON
gallery .... TATE, FREER,
SALON
Latin .... ARS
movement of 1920's .... DADA
objects .... VERTU, VIRTU
of argumentation
.... DIALECTICS
bookbinding ..... BIBLIOPEGY
carving/engraving
.... GLYPTICS
devising dances
.... CHORE(O)GRAPHY
discourse .... RHETORIC
disputation .... ERISTIC,
POLEMICS
dwarfing trees/plants
.... BONSAI
horsemanship .... MANEGE
mapping ...... CHOROGRAPHY
motion pictures
.... CINEMATICS
public speaking
.... ELOCUTION
teaching .... DIDACTIC
style .... DADA, GENRE,
CUBISM, MODERN, BAROQUE,
FAUVISM, ARABESQUE, ART
DECO, GOTHICISM, PURISM,
ART NOUVEAU, IMPRESSIONISM
work .... OIL
work, formless
.... ABSTRACTION(ISM)
work, inferior .... POTBOILER
artal, singular of .... ROTL
artel .... COOPERATIVE
Artemis .... DELIA, DIANA,
PHOEBE, GODDESS
birthplace .... DELOS
father .... ZEUS
mother ..... LETO, LATONA
twin .... APOLLO
victim .... ORION
artemisia .... WORMWOOD
arterial obstruction .... EMBOLUS
artery .... AORTA, STREET,
CHANNEL, BLOOD VESSEL
neck .... CAROTID
pulse .... ICTUS
artful .... SLY, WILY, ADROIT,
CRAFTY, CUNNING, POLITIC,
DECEITFUL
arthritis .... CLOT, DROP, GOUT,
SWELLING, STIFFNESS,

INFLAMMATION

treatment .... ACTH, HEAT, ANTIBIOTICS, VERATRIA, CORTISONE, VERATRIN(E)

type .... SEPTIC, PYOGENIC, RHEUMATOID, DEGENERATIVE

arthropod .... INSECT, ARACHNID, MYRIAPOD, MILLEPEDE, CRUSTACEAN

segmented part .... SOMITE, TELSON

arthropoda .... PHYLA

Arthur. See **King Arthur**

Arthur, actress .... BEA

Arthur Conan .... DOYLE

character .... SHERLOCK HOLMES

title .... SIR

of tennis .... ASHE

Arthurian enchantress .... VIVIAN

tales compiler .... LOOMIS, MALORY

artichoke .... PLANT, TUBER, CYNARA, CHOROGI, SUNFLOWER

kin .... CARDOON

leaf stalks .... CHARD

article .... ITEM, PART, ESSAY, PAPER, PIECE, THING, REPORT, STORY, OBJECT, FEATURE

definite .... THE

in a document .... CLAUSE

indefinite .... A, AN

of faith/belief .... CREDO, CREED

of personal property .... CHATTEL

articles, miscellaneous .... RUMMAGE

of excellence .... IMPERIALS

of virtu .... CURIO, BIBELOT

sold together .... TIE-IN

articulate .... UTTER, JOINTED, DISTINCT, EXPLICIT, LITERATE, ENUNCIATE, EXPRESSIVE

articulated joint .... HINGE

speech sound .... LENIS

artifice .... HOAX, RUSE, CRAFT, FRAUD, GUILE, BLUFF, DODGE, DEVICE, DECEIT, TRICK(ERY), WILE, STRATAGEM

artificial ...... FAKE, MOCK, FALSE, BOGUS, PLASTIC, SHAM, SPURIOUS, AFFECTED, POSTICHE, IMITATION, SIMULATED, SYNTHETIC, UNNATURAL

appearance .... DISGUISE

bait .... LURE, DECOY

butter .... OLEO, MARGARINE

copy of nature ...... SYNTHESIS

fly ...... DUN, NYMPH, DOCTOR, COACHMAN

foodstuff .... ERSATZ

ivory .... IVORIDE

jewelry .... PASTE

language .... IDO, ESPERANTO

respiration apparatus .... PULMOTOR

smile of a sort .... SIMPER

sweetener .... ASPARTAME, CYCLAMATE, SACCHARIN

teeth .... DENTURE

waterway .... CANAL

artillery .... GUNNERY, ORDNANCE

abbreviation .... ORD

anti-aircraft .... POMPOM, ACK-ACK, TRIPLE-A

fire angle measurement .... MIL

man .... GUNNER, LASCAR, CANNONER

type of ..... MOBILE, MOUNTED

wagon .... CAMION, CAISSON

artisan .... ARTIST, CRAFTSMAN, TRADESMAN

artist .... DANCER, ETCHER, PAINTER, PIANIST, COLORIST, PERFORMER, MINIATURIST, SCULPTOR, PORTRAITIST

abbreviation on painting .... PNXT

clay .... POTTER

modern .... DALI

unconventional ..... BOHEMIAN

artistic style .... GUSTO

artist's colony .... TAOS, GREENWICH, LATIN QUARTER

copy .... TRACING

frock .... SMOCK

medium .... OIL, CLAY, BRONZE, CANVAS, PASTEL, MARBLE, TEMPERA

milieu .... STUDIO, ATELIER

mixing board .... PALETTE

name on painting .... DELINEAVIT

stand/frame .... EASEL

artless .... NAIF, FRANK, CRUDE, CLUMSY, NAIVE, PLAIN, SIMPLE, NATURAL, INGENUOUS

woman/girl .... INGENUE

artlessness .... NAIVETE, INNOCENCE, SIMPLICITY

arts and _____ .... CRAFTS, LETTERS, SCIENCES

votary .... PATRON, ESTHETE, CONNOISSEUR

artwork .... PIECE, CREATION, PAINTING, SCULPTURE, COMPOSITION

great(est) .... MASTERPIECE

literary .... CLASSIC(S)

tawdry .... KITSCH

arum .... LILY, TARO, AROID, CALLA, CALADIUM

genus .... ARALES

aruspex .... SEER, SOOTHSAYER

Aryan .... MEDE, SLAV

god .... AGNI

language .... SANSKRIT

as .... FOR, LIKE, THUS, SINCE, QUA, WHILE, THOUGH, BECAUSE

a rule .... GENERALLY

far as .... TO

if .... QUASI

much as .... NO LESS

said above .... DITTO

soon as .... ONCE

to .... CONCERNING

usual: music .... SOLITO

well as .... AND

written: music .... STA

As You Like It character .... JACQUES, ROSALIND

scene .... ARDEN

Asa .... KING(OF JUDAH)

ally of .... BEN-HADAD

father of .... ABIJAH, ABIJAM

grandfather of ...... REHOBOAM

son of .... JEHOSHAPHAT

asafetida .... LASER, RESIN, FERULA

asarum .... PLANT, GINGER

asbestos .... BOARD, SILICATE, AMPHIBOLE

ASCAP member .... AUTHOR, COMPOSER, PUBLISHER

ascarid .... (PIN)WORM, HOOKWORM, ROUNDWORM

ascend ...... SOAR, CLIMB, UPRISE, (A)RISE, CLAMBER, MOUNT, SCALE(THE HEIGHTS)

ascendancy .... RISE, MASTERY, SUPREMACY, DOMINATION, PREDOMINANCE

ascent .... RISE, JUMP, RAMP, UPLIFT, STAIRCASE, SLOPE, UPSURGE, UPSWING, ACCLIVITY

ascertain .... SEE, FIND, LEARN, ENSURE, VERIFY, CERTIFY, DISCOVER, DETERMINE, ESTABLISH

ascertainment .... ASSURANCE, CERTAINTY

ascetic .... MONK, YOGA, FAKIR, ESSENE, HERMIT, STOIC, RECLUSE, AUSTERE, EREMITE, PURITAN, STYLITE, MONASTIC, ANCHORET, ANCHORITE

asceticism .... FASTING, PENANCE,

AUSTERITY, (SELF)DENIAL
Asch name .... SHOLEM, SHOLOM
asci .... (SPORE)SAC
ascidian .... TUNICATE
ascot .... SCARF, (NECK)TIE
ascribe .... IMPLY, ATTACH,
ASSIGN, IMPUTE, (AC)CREDIT,
ATTRIBUTE
aseptic .... STERILE, SANITARY
asexual .... AGAMIC, NEUTER,
SEXLESS
reproduction .... FISSION
Asgard .... ASGARTH
bridge to .... BIFROST
watchman of .... HEIMDALL
ash .... TREE, WOOD, ARTAR,
EMBER, PALLOR, POWDER,
RESIDUE
can .... DUSTBIN
can: sl. .... DEPTH BOMB,
DEPTH CHARGE
fruit ..... KEY, MAPLE, SAMARA
gray .... CINEREOUS
holder of cremated body
.... URN
mountain .... ROWAN
pertaining to .... CINERARY
solution .... LYE
tree juice .... MANNA
Ash Wednesday to Easter
.... LENT
ashamed .... ABASHED, HUMBLED,
CHAGRINED, MORTIFIED,
EMBARRASSED
Ashanti capital .... KUMASI
ashen/ashy .... WAN, GRAY, PALE,
LIVID, WHITE, PALLID
Asher's brother .... GAD
daughter .... SERAH
father .... JACOB
mother .... ZILPAH
son .... ISUI, BERIAH
ashes .... RUINS, POWDER,
REMAINS
ashlar .... BEAM, PLANK, STONE
ashram .... COMMUNE, RETREAT
Ashtoreth ...... ISHTAR, ASTARTE,
GODDESS
Asia Minor .... ANATOLIA
bishop .... (ST) NICHOLAS
city .... GAZA, MYRA, TROY,
TYRE, ISSUS, NICAEA, SARDIS,
ANTIOCH, EPHESUS,
CHALCEDON
country .... CARIA, LYCIA,
LYDIA, MYSIA, CILICIA,
PHRYGIA, PISIDIA
district .... IONIA, TROAD
Greek city .... MILETUS
island .... SAMOS
kingdom .... PONTUS

mountain .... IDA
people .... HITTITES
province .... GALATIA,
LYCAONIA
region .... EOLIS, IONIA, TROAS
river .... IRIS, CAICUS,
GRANICUS
sheep .... KARAKUL,
BROADTAIL
tree .... SYCAMORE
Asiatic ancient people ...... SERES
ass .... ONAGER
bean .... SOY(A)
bird .... MINA, MYNA(H), PITTA
cat ..... OUNCE, TIGER, SIAMESE
cattle .... ZEBU
civet .... ZIBET(H)
coin, Annam .... QUAN
Arabia .... QURSH
China .... LI, FEN, TAEL,
TIAO, YUAN
India ..... ANNA, FELS, HOON,
PICE, TARA, RUPEE
Iran .... PUL, LARI, POUL,
RIAL, DARIC, DINAR, MOHUR
Iraq .... FILS, DINAR
Laos .... AT
Malaya .... TRA(H)
Nepal .... MOHAR
Siam/Thailand .... ANNA,
BAHT, TICAL
Singapore .... CENT
country .... ANNAM, BURMA,
CHINA, KOREA, SIKKIM, INDIA,
NEPAL, IRAN, IRAQ, VIETNAM,
SYRIA, THAILAND(SIAM), LAOS,
TIBET, MALAYSIA, ARABIA,
CAMBODIA, PAKISTAN,
SINGAPORE
country, ancient .... ELAM,
ACCAD, MEDEA, EOLIA
cow .... ZO(H), ZOBO
deer ...... AXIS, SASIN, SAMBAR
desert .... GOBI
disease .... BERIBERI
fiber .... HEMP, RAMIE
finch .... SISKIN
gangster/thug .... DACOIT
gazelle ...... AHU, CORA, ARIEL
ginger/herb .... CARDAMOM,
CARDAMUM
goat antelope .... SEROW
grass .... CITRONELLA
grassland .... MAIDAN
hog .... BABIRUSA
isthmus .... KRA
kingdom .... ELAM, IRAN,
IRAQ, SIAM, AN(N)AM, KOREA,
NEPAL
lake .... ARAL, BAIKAL
lemur .... LORIS, MACACO

medicine man .... SHAMAN
millet .... DARI
monkey .... MACAQUE
mountain .... ALTAI
native .... HUN, TAI, YUIT,
MONGOL, KOREAN, CHINESE,
TA(R)TAR, AN(N)AMESE,
INNUIT, SIAMESE, TIBETAN
nomad .... TATAR
palm .... NIPA, ARECA, BETEL
peninsula .... KOREA, MALAY
perennial plant .... RAMIE
plague .... CHOLERA
plain .... CHOL
plant ...... HEMP, ODAL, RAMIE,
SESAME, GINSENG, TAMPALA
port .... AMOY, MACAO,
SAIGON, HAIPHONG, SHANGHAI
river .... ILI, AMUR, LENA,
ONON, OXUS, YALU, INDUS,
PEARL, MEKONG, YELLOW,
YANGTZE
rodent .... CONY, PIKA,
MARMOT
ruminant .... YAK, ZEBU
sardine .... LOUR
sea .... ARAL, AZOL, CHINA
sheep .... ARGALI
shrub .... TEA, TCHE, THEA
snowstorm .... BURAN
storm .... TYPHOON
tea .... CHA, PEKOE, OOLONG
trade wind .... MONSOON
tree .... ACLE, DITA, TEAK,
NARRA, SIRIS, BANYAN
tribe .... LAI, TAI, AKHA,
AOUL, KHAS, BUGI, KADU,
KUKI, TATAR, UZBEG
weight .... TAEL, CATTY
wild hog ...... BOAR, BABIRUSA
wild sheep .... RASSE
aside .... BY, ALOOF, AWAY,
APART, BESIDE
from .... EXCEPT, EXCLUDING
set .... TABLE, RESERVE
stage .... AD LIB, WHISPER
asinine ...... INANE, NUTTY, SILLY,
MULISH, STUPID, FOOLISH,
IDIOTIC
ask .... BEG, QUIZ, QUERY,
DEMAND, INVITE, INQUIRE,
SOLICIT, QUESTION
a series of questions
.... INTERROGATE
for a handout .... TOUCH
for a loan: sl. .... BRACE
reverently .... PRAY
asker .... REQUESTER
askew .... AGEE, ALOP, AWRY,
ASLANT, OBLIQUE
asleep .... DEAD, DOZING,

DORMANT, NAPPING, INACTIVE, SLEEPING

at the _____ .... SWITCH

Asmara is capital of .... ERITREA

asor .... LYRE

asp .... SNAKE, VIPER

on headdress .... URAEUS

asparagus tip/stalk .... SPEAR

aspect .... LOOK, MIEN, VIEW, PHASE, OUTLOOK, APPEARANCE

general .... FACIES

aspen .... POPLAR, SHAKING, QUIVERING, TREMBLING, FLUTTERING

asper .... COIN

asperity .... RIGOR, PUNGENCY, HARSHNESS, ROUGHNESS, SHARPNESS

asperse ...... SLUR, LIBEL, REVILE, VILIFY, SLANDER

aspersion .... SLUR, BAPTISM, SLANDER, INNUENDO

asphalt .... BITUMEN, UINTAITE, GILSONITE

like mineral .... ALBERTITE

asphyxia .... APNEA, ACROTISM

asphyxiate .... STRANGLE, SUFFOCATE

aspic .... MOLD, JELLY, RELISH, LAVENDER

aspirant .... CANDIDATE, CONTENDER

aspiration .... GOAL, BREATH, DESIRE, AMBITION

aspire .... HOPE, LONG, SEEK, YEARN, DESIRE, BREATHE, STRIVE(FOR)

aspirin .... TABLET

ass .... DOLT, FOOL, BURRO, DONKEY, ONAGER, SIMPLETON

female .... JENNY

hybrid .... ZEBRASS

male .... JACK

young .... FOAL

assa .... CAAMA

assagai .... SPEAR, JAVELIN

assai .... PALM, DRINK

assail .... BESET, ATTACK, SET UPON, ASSAULT, CRITICIZE

assailant .... ATTACKER, AGGRESSOR

Assamese capital .... SHILLONG

dialect .... LHOTA

Mongol .... GARO, NAGA

native .... AHOM

shrub .... TEA

silkworm .... ERI(A)

tribe .... AO, AKA, AHOM, GARO, NAGA

assassin .... THUG, BRAVO,

GUNMAN, KILLER, HITMAN, SLAYER, MURDERER

Abel's/Biblical .... CAIN

character .... DEFAMER, ROORBACH, SMEARER, SLANDERER

Garfield's .... GUITEAU

Kennedy's (John F.) .... OSWALD

Kennedy's (Robert) .... SIRHAN

Lincoln's .... BOOTH

origin of word .... HASHISM

assassinate .... KILL, SLAY, MURDER

assault .... RAID, RAPE, ONSET, ATTACK, CHARGE, OFFENSE

and battery .... BEATING

prolonged .... SIEGE

prolonged verbal .... TIRADE

assaulter .... MUGGER, RAPIST, OFFENDER

assay ...... TEST, WEIGH, ANALYZE, ANALYSIS, APPRAISE

assaying cup .... CUPEL

assemblage ...... CROWD, THRONG, COUNCIL, MEETING, CONCLAVE, GATHERING

assemble .... MEET, UNITE, COLLECT, COMPILE, CONVENE, HUDDLE, MUSTER, SHEAVE, ROUND UP, (FOR)GATHER

assembly .... BEVY, GROUP, ARRAY, RALLY, CAUCUS, GALAXY, MEETING, SESSION, HUSTINGS, AUDIENCE, GATHERING

legislative .... CONGRESS

line .... PLANT, FACTORY

of witches .... COVEN

assent .... ACCEPT, COMPLY, CONSENT, AGREE(MENT), CONCUR(RENCE)

show .... NOD

sign of .... NOD, THUMBS UP

word of .... YES, AMEN, OKAY, YES SIREE, RIGHT ON

assert .... SAY, AVER, STATE, AFFIRM, DECLARE

as a fact .... CLAIM, POSIT, ALLEGE

formally .... ALLEGATE

positively .... SWEAR

assess ...... DUN, FINE, LEVY, TAX, RATE, APPRAISE

assessment ...... FEE, TAX, RATAL, WORTH, ANALYSIS, VALUE, APPRAISAL, ESTIMATE, VALUATION

assessor .... JUDGE, RATER, APPRAISER

asset .... ESTATE, RESOURCE, PROPERTY, ADVANTAGE, POSSESSION

personal .... WIT, TACT, CHARM, BEAUTY, CHARISMA

assets and liabilities ...... ESTATE

asseverate .... AVER, STATE, ASSERT, CERTIFY, TESTIFY

assiduous .... BUSY, FEISTY, DILIGENT, ENERGETIC

assign .... ALLOT, APPOINT, ALLOCATE, RELEGATE, TRANSFER, DESIGNATE

cause/reason .... ASCRIBE, ATTRIBUTE

parts in play .... CAST

assignation .... TRYST, RENDEZVOUS

assimilate .... ABSORB, DIGEST, UNDERSTAND

facts .... LEARN

assimilation of learning .... EDUCATION

assist .... AID, HELP, ATTEND, SECOND, SUPPORT

assistance .... AID, HAND, HELP, SUCCOR, COMFORT

government .... WELFARE, SUBSIDY

in kind .... ALMS, DOLE

to disaster victims ...... RELIEF

assistant .... AIDE, DEPUTY, HELPER, ADJUTANT, AUXILIARY

first, of a sort .... RIGHT-HAND(MAN)

general's .... AIDE-DE-CAMP

in charge of a gambling table .... CROUPIER

of bishop .... VERGER, COADJUTOR

pastor .... CURATE

to an abbot .... PRIOR

assize ...... OYER, INQUEST, COURT SESSIONS

associate ...... ALLY, JOIN, CRONY, CONNECT, PARTNER, CONFRERE, COLLEAGUE

in crime .... ACCOMPLICE

with others .... HOBNOB

association .... CLUB, LINK, LEAGUE, SOCIETY, AFFINITY, FRATERNITY, ORGANIZATION

business firms' .... CARTEL

football .... SOCCER

merchants' .... HANSE

mutual aid .... ARTEL

mutual protection .... GUILD

oldest in membership .... DEAN

scholars', etc. .... ACADEMY

workers' .... UNION
assoil .... ATONE, PARDON,
ABSOLVE
assonance .... PUN
assort .... MATCH, CLASSIFY,
HARMONIZE
assorted .... MIX, VARIOUS,
MISCELLANEOUS
assortment .... OLIO, MIXTURE,
VARIETY, COLLECTION
of types .... FONTS
assuage .... CALM, ALLAY,
LESSEN, PACIFY, RELIEVE,
MITIGATE
assume .... FEIGN, INFER, AFFECT,
PRETEND, ARROGATE,
SUPPOSE, SIMULATE,
UNDERTAKE
a part .... ACT, IMITATE
an attitude .... POSE
another's personality
.... IMPERSONATE
as a fact .... POSIT
control .... TAKE OVER
without right .... USURP
assumed .... STAGY, FICTITIOUS
character .... ROLE
identity for disguise
.... INCOGNITO
name .... ALIAS, PSEUDONYM
personality .... IMPERSONATION
assumer of other personality
.... IMPOSTOR
assumption .... NOTION,
PRETENSE, PRESUMPTION
assurance .... BELIEF, PLEDGE,
PROMISE, CERTAINTY,
GUARANTEE, CONFIDENCE
assuredly .... CERTAINLY,
DECIDEDLY
assurgent ...... RISING, ASCENDING
Assyrian .... AMORITE, S(H)EMITE
capital .... NINEVEH
chief deity .... AS(S)UR,
AS(S)HUR
city .... HARA, OPIS, AKKAD,
ARBELA
god ..... IRA, SIN, ANAT, NABO,
AS(S)UR, HADAD, ASHUR,
NUSKU, NINIB, TAMMUS
goddess .... NANA, ALLATU,
IS(H)TAR, SARPANIT
king .... PUL, SARGON(II)
mountain .... ZAGROS
original capital .... ASHUR
pyramid .... ZIKURAT,
ZIGGURAT
queen .... SEMIRAMIS
river .... ZAB, ADHIAN
warrior .... SARGON
weight .... COLA

Astaire, _____ .... FRED, ADELE
dancing partner .... RITA
astatic ...... UNSTABLE, UNSTEADY
aster .... DAISY, OXEYE, TANSY,
FLOWER, ZINNIA, TANGLEFOOT
asterisk .... MARK, SIGN, STAR
astern .... AFT, BAFT, REAR,
ABAFT, BACKWARD
asteroid .... EROS, CERES, PALLAS,
STARFISH, STARLIKE
asthenic .... FEEBLE
asthma medicine ...... GRINDELIA
asthmatic breath ...... WHEEZE
astigmatism .... AMETROPIA
astir .... AGOG, ABOUT, AWAKE,
MOVING
Astolat maid .... ELAINE
astonish .... AMAZE, ASTOUND,
SURPRISE
Astor, Lady
.... (NANCY)LANGHORNE
astound .... STUN, AMAZE, SHOCK,
BEWILDER, CONFOUND
astraddle .... ACROSS, ASTRIDE
Astraea .... VIRGO, GODDESS
astragal(us) .... TALUS,
ANKLEBONE
astrakham .... PELT, WOOL,
APPLE, CLOTH, KARAKUL
astral .... ASTER, STARRY,
STELLAR
astray .... LOST, AMISS, IN ERROR,
OFF COURSE, WANDERING
astrict ...... BIND, LIMIT, RESTRICT
astringent .... ALUM, COTO,
HARSH, STERN, CASHOO,
SEVERE, TANNIN, CATECHU,
STYPTIC(AL)
fruit .... SLOE
gum .... KINO
material .... CATECHU
resin .... MASTIC
root .... BISTORT
salt .... ALUM
astrolabe .... ALIDAD(E)
astrologer .... STARGAZER,
ASTRONOMER
ancient ..... MAGUS, CHALDEAN
French .... NOSTRADAMUS
legendary .... MERLIN
astrological .... CHALDEAN
belief .... SIDERISM
diagram .... SCHEME
astrology, work on
.... ALMAGEST
astromonk .... BONNY
astronaut .... MOONMAN,
SPACEMAN
American .... GLENN, WHITE,
YOUNG, SCOTT, ANDERS,
BORMAN, ALDRIN, LOVELL,

CONRAD, CERNAN, GORDON,
COLLINS, GRISSOM, BEAN,
SHEPARD, MCDIVITT,
ARMSTRONG, EISELE,
CUNNINGHAM, SCHIRRA,
MITCHELL, STAFFORD
Russian .... GAGARIN,
KOMAROV
astronaut's perfect .... A-OK
astronautic activity .... LUNAR
PROBE
vehicle .... APOLLO, GEMINI,
MARINER, WESTAR, SKYLAB,
SKYNET, SOYUZ, COSMOS,
SPUTNIK, SURVEYOR,
COMSTAR, SHINSEI, COLUMBIA,
AURORA, FRIENDSHIP, OHSUMI,
CHALLENGER
astronomer .... METON, BRAHE,
PTOLEMY, STARGAZER
astronomical .... HUGE, LARGE,
URANIC, CELESTIAL
almanac .... EPHEMERIS
arc .... AZIMUTH
cloud .... NEBULA
cycle .... SAROS
instrument .... ORRERY
intersecting points ...... NODES
measure .... APSIS, PARSEC
phenomenon .... PULSAR,
QUASAR
shadow .... UMBRA, PENUMBRA
astronomy, work on
.... ALMAGEST
astute .... KEEN, WILY, CLEVER,
CRAFTY, CUNNING, CANNY,
SHARP, SHREWD
Astyanax's parent .... HECTOR,
ANDROMACHE
Asunción is capital of
.... PARAGUAY
asunder .... APART, SEPARATED
Aswan .... DAM(SITE)
ancient name of .... SYENE
asylum .... HAVEN, HOME,
REFUGE, RETREAT, SHELTER,
ORPHANAGE, SANCTUARY
describing a kind of
.... POLITICAL
inmate ...... LUNATIC, REFUGEE
asymmetric(al) .... UNEVEN,
IRREGULAR
at .... BY, IN, ON, TO, NEAR
a distance .... AFAR
_____ (addled) ...... SIXES AND
SEVENS
all .... ANY, AUGHT
all times .... EVER, ALWAYS
an angle .... ALIST, ATILT
fault .... GUILTY
full length .... FLAT(LING)

hand .... HERE, NEAR(BY), PRESENT
hand: poet. .... ANEAR
home .... IN, RECEIVING
large .... FREE, LOOSE, ABROAD
last .... ENFIN, FINALLY, ULTIMATELY
no time .... NEVER
odds .... HOSTILE
once ..... STAT, PRONTO, RIGHT NOW, IMMEDIATELY
right angle to a ship's keel .... ABEAM
sea .... LOST
that time .... THEN
the age of .... AET(AT)
the same time .... COEVAL
variance .... DIFFERENT
atabal ...... TABOR, (KETTLE)DRUM
Atahualpa .... INCA, KING
Atalanta's victor .... HIPPOMENES
ataman .... COSSACK
atap .... NIPA, PALM
Ataturk, Kemal .... MUSTAFA
Ate .... AVENGER
atelier .... STUDIO, WORKSHOP
worker .... MODEL, ARTIST, PAINTER
athanasia .... IMMORTALITY
atheist .... INFIDEL, AGNOSTIC, FREE-THINKER, NON-BELIEVER
atheling ..... PRINCE, NOBLE(MAN)
Athena .... NIKE, PALLAS, MINERVA
shield .... (A)EGIS
title of .... ALEA
Athenian .... ATTIC
aristocrat .... EUPATRID
astronomer .... METON
citadel .... ACROPOLIS
clan .... OBE
coin .... CHALCUS
courtesan .... THAIS
demagogue .... CLEON
general .... CIMON, CLEON, NICIAS, ARISTIDES, MILTIADES
judge/juryman .... DICAST
lawgiver .... SOLON
magistrate/ruler .... ARCHON
market .... AGORA
money .... OBOL
political subdivision .... PHYLE
room .... CELLA, ADYTUM
sculptor .... PHIDIAS
seaport .... PIRAEUS
statesman .... CIMON, PERICLES, ARISTIDES, ALCIBIADES
temple .... NIKE, ZEUS, PARTHENON
tribunal .... AREOPAGUS

Athens founder .... CECROPS
athirst .... AVID, EAGER, PARCHED
athlete .... BOXER, CAGER, RACER, GOLFER, JUMPER, PLAYER
sometimes called .... PRO, STAR
athlete's crown .... LAUREL
dream .... OLYMPICS, CHAMPIONSHIP
foot .... RINGWORM
jump .... BROAD
jump with pole .... VAULT
speed event ...... DASH, SPRINT
throw .... PASS, DISCUS, JAVELIN
trainer .... COACH, GYMNAST, HANDLER
athletic .... BRAWNY
contest, 5 events .... PENTATHLON
contest, 10 events .... DECATHLON
exercises .... CALISTHENICS, GYMNASTIC(S)
field .... OVAL, COURT, DIAMOND, STADIUM, COLISEUM
group .... CREW, FIVE, NINE, TEAM, ELEVEN
prize .... AGON, MEDAL, MONEY, TROPHY
athletics .... GAMES, SPORTS, EXERCISES, GYMNASTICS
athodyd .... RAMJET
athwart .... ACROSS, AGAINST, OBLIQUE, CROSSWISE
atilt .... TILTING, INCLINED
atingle .... AGOG, EXCITED, TINGLING
atis .... CONITE
Atlanta is capital of .... GEORGIA
atlantes .... TELAMON
Atlantic coast fish .... TAUTOG, RED DRUM
first solo flier of .... LINDBERGH
island, famed ...... ST. HELENA
sea .... SARGASSO
tributary .... MIN(H)O, SENEGAL
atlas .... MAP, BOOK, CHART, GRAPH, FORMAT, PILLAR, VERTEBRA
Atlas' daughter .... MAIA, HYAD(E), PLEIAD, CALYPSO
name .... AGENA
wife .... PLEIONE
Atli .... HUN, KING
wife .... GUDRUN
atman .... EGO, SOUL
atmosphere ...... AIR, AURA, TONE
in some cities .... SMOG,

SMAZE
measuring instrument .... ATMOMETER
over nation .... AIRSPACE
atmospheric condition .... CLIMATE, WEATHER
gas .... ARGON
phenomenon .... HAIL, STORM, CYCLONE, RAINBOW, TEMPEST, TORNADO, TYPHOON, HURRICANE
pressure .... BARIC
atoll .... BIKINI, (CORAL)ISLAND
pool .... LAGOON
atom ...... JOT, ION, IOTA, MONAD, SPECK, PROTON, MOLECULE, PARTICLE
bomb target, WW II .... NAGASAKI, HIROSHIMA
charged .... ION
negatively charged .... ELECTRON
of specified atomic number .... NUCLIDE
part .... ION, PROTON
smasher .... SYNCHROTON
smashing .... FISSION
type of .... ISOBAR, NORMAL, NEUTRAL, ISOTERE
with valence of two ..... DYAD
atomic .... MINUTE, ISOTERIC, MOLECULAR
particle .... NEUTRON, PROTON, ELECTRON, NEUTRINO
physicist .... BOHR, RABI, UREY, FERMI, COMPTON, MILLIKAN, SCIENTIST
submarine ..... SKATE, TRITON, NAUTILUS, SCORPION
atomize .... SPRAY, VAPORIZE, PULVERIZE
atomizer .... SPRAYER, SPRINKLER
atomy .... DWARF, PIGMY, PYGMY, SKELETON
atone .... REPAY, ASSOIL, REDEEM, EXPIATE, MAKE AMENDS, APOLOGIZE
atonement ...... AMENDS, REFUND, PENANCE, REDRESS, REDEMPTION, REPARATION
atonic sound .... SURD
atoning .... PIACULAR, EXPIATORY, APOLOGETIC
atrabilious .... CROSS, MOROSE
atramentous .... INKY
Atreus' brother .... THYESTES
father .... PELOPS
son .... MENELAUS, AGAMEMNON
atrium ...... HALL, ROOM, COURT, CAVITY, CHAMBER, ENTRANCE

atrocious .... BAD, BASE, VILE, CRUEL, BRUTAL, WICKED, HATEFUL, HEINOUS, VIOLENT

atrocity .... ABUSE, BADNESS, CRUELTY, SAVAGERY, BARBARITY, OUTRAGE, TORTURE, BRUTALITY

a physical ...... DWARF, FREAK, GNOME, MONSTER

visual .... EYESORE

atrophy .... SHRINKAGE, DEGENERATION, DETERIORATION

of horse's muscles .... SWEENY

of person's joints .... ARTHRITIS

Atropos .... FATE, WEIRD(SISTERS)

attach ...... ADD, TIE, JOIN, TACK, AFFIX, SEIZE, APPEND, CONNECT

attaché .... DIPLOMAT

kind of .... PRESS, MILITARY

attached .... FOND, DEVOTED, SEIZED, APPENDED

to branch .... SESSILE

attachment .... LOVE, SEIZURE, ADDITION, DEVOTION, AFFECTION, APPENDAGE

attack .... HIT, SIC, LUNGE, SALVO, ONSET, CHARGE, ASSAIL, POUNCE, ASSAULT, OFFENSIVE, STRIKE, VOLLEY, ONSLAUGHT

artillery .... CANNONADE

at close range .... POTSHOT

diversionary .... FEINT

fierce .... ONSLAUGHT

for quick victory .... BLITZ(KRIEG)

in words/writing .... LASH, BASTE, SQUIB, LAMPOON

kind of .... BLIND, SNEAK, VERBAL, WARLIKE, BLITZ(KRIEG), SURPRISE, TACTICAL, STRATEGIC

prolonged .... SIEGE

reputation ...... LIBEL, DEFAME, MALIGN, SLANDER

signal .... WARISON

sudden .... FORAY

swift, overwhelming .... BLITZ(KRIEG)

swift, surprise .... RAID

verbally .... BLAST, BERATE

violent, intense .... ONSLAUGHT

warning of ..... ALARM, ALERT

attacker .... RAIDER, INVADER, OFFENDER, AGGRESSOR, ASSAILANT

attain .... WIN, EARN, GAIN, REACH, ACHIEVE, SUCCEED

fame .... ARRIVE

attainment .... SKILL, SUCCESS, FRUITION, LEARNING, EDUCATION, ACHIEVEMENT

attaint .... CONDEMN, CONVICT, CORRUPT, DISGRACE, DISHONOR, ATTAINDER

attar .... OIL, PERFUME, (ROSE)EXTRACT

variation .... OTTO

attempt .... TRY, STAB, ESSAY, ATTACK, EMBARK, VENTURE, ENDEAVOR

failed .... MISS

attend .... HEAR, HEED, SERVE, ESCORT, LISTEN, BE PRESENT, ACCOMPANY

attendance .... GATE, HOUSE, TURN-OUT, PRESENCE, GATHERING

describing some .... SRO, FULL, FULL-HOUSE, STANDING ROOM

full .... PLENARY

attendant ...... SERVER, SERVANT, RETAINER, SERVITOR, CONCOMITANT

bridegroom's .... BEST MAN

fact .... CIRCUMSTANCE

hunter's .... GILLY, GILLIE, GUNBEARER

knight's .... SQUIRE

on horseback .... OUTRIDER

patient's .... NURSE

personal .... VALET

queen's .... CONSORT

attendants, group of ...... COURT, TRAIN, RETINUE, ENTOURAGE

attended by all .... PLENARY

attent .... HEEDFUL

attention .... EAR, CARE, HEED, LOOK, NOTICE, REGARD, SCRUTINY, CONSIDERATION

getter .... HEADLINE

getting sound .... PST, SST, AHEM, PSST, COUGH, HIST, YELL, WHISTLE

getting word .... HEY

holding .... GRIPPING

order of .... PRIORITY

attentive .... ALERT, MINDFUL, WATCHFUL, OBSERVANT, THOUGHTFUL

attenuate .... DILUTE, LESSEN, RAREFY, THIN OUT, WEAKEN

attest .... VOUCH, AFFIRM, DEPOSE, CERTIFY, DEMONSTRATE

as witness .... TESTIFY

in earnest .... SWEAR

attestation, formal/solemn .... OATH

sign of official .... SEAL, SIGNATURE

attic .... GARRET, (COCK)LOFT, MANSARD, ATHENIAN

bird .... NIGHTINGALE

part of .... DORMER

salt .... WIT

Attica, capital of .... ATHENS

king .... CECROPS

native .... METIC

township .... DEME

valley .... LCARIA

Attican .... ATHENIAN

Attila .... HUN, ATLI, KING, ETZEL

adjective for .... SCOURGE

attire .... RIG, GARB, ROBE, ARRAY, DRESS, FINERY, CLOTHES, RAIMENT, CLOTHING

man's complete .... SUIT

masquerader's .... COSTUME

military/police .... UNIFORM

religious/riding .... HABIT

soldier's, sometimes .... FATIGUES

stag's .... ANTLERS

winter's .... SNOW

woman's .... GOWN

Attis' love .... CYBELE

Attlee, ____ .... CLEMENT

attitude .... MOOD, MANNER, BEARING, FEELING, OPINION, POSTURE, DISPOSITION

strike an .... AIR, POSE

attract ...... DRAW, LURE, CHARM, CAPTIVATE, FASCINATE

animal/fish .... BAIT

attention/curiosity .... INTEREST

misleadingly .... SEDUCE

attraction .... CHARM, APPEAL, GRAVITY, MAGNET(ISM)

attractive .... CUTE, PRETTY, ALLURING, ENGAGING, FETCHING, PLEASING

girl, describing one ..... SEXY, PINUP, CURVACEOUS, WHISTLEBAIT

girl's body: sl. .... CHASSIS

irresistibly .... BEWITCHING

powerfully .... MAGNETIC

price to buyer .... CHEAP, BARGAIN, CUT-RATE

temptingly .... SEDUCTIVE

very .... STUNNING

attribute .... TRAIT, ASSIGN, IMPUTE, REASON, ASCRIBE, QUALITY, ACCREDIT

of an M.C. .... WIT

of good workers .... LOYALTY,

THOROUGHNESS
attribution .... BLAME, ETIOLOGY, IMPUTATION
attrition .... EROSION, FRICTION, REPENTANCE
battle of .... SIEGE, BESIEGEMENT
attune .... HARMONIZE, RECONCILE
to the times .... UPDATE, MODERNIZE
aubade .... ALBA, MATIN
counterpart .... SERENADE
auberge .... INN, HOSTEL(RY)
auburn .... TITIAN, (REDDISH)BROWN
auction .... ROUP, SALE, SELL, VENDUE
price .... BID, UPSET
auctioneer's hammer .... GAVEL, MALLET
platform .... BLOCK
word .... SOLD, GOING
audacious .... BOLD, SAUCY, DARING, BRAZEN, INSOLENT, RECKLESS
audacity .... GALL, BRASS, CHEEK, CRUST, DARING, COURAGE, BOLDNESS, TEMERITY, IMPUDENCE, INSOLENCE
audible .... ALOUD, CLEAR, HEARD, HEARABLE
audience .... HEARING, ASSEMBLY, ONLOOKERS, INTERVIEW, RECEPTION
kind of .... AUDITION
official .... DURBAR
part of, sometimes .... STANDEES
audio-visual aid ...... FILM, TAPE, SLIDE, MOCK-UP
audiphone .... HEARING AID
audition .... TEST, HEARING, TRY-OUT
auditor .... CPA, HEARER, LISTENER, ACCOUNTANT
auditorium .... HALL, THEATER
auditory .... OTIC, AURAL, AURICULAR
Audubon, John .... PAINTER, NATURALIST, ORNITHOLOGIST
Augean .... FILTHY, STABLE, CORRUPT
auger .... TOOL
groove of .... POD
relative .... AWL, BORER, DRILL, GIMLET, WIMBLE
type of .... SHIP, SCREW, LIP RING
aught .... NAUGHT, ZERO, NOTHING, ANYTHING
augment .... ADD, EKE, RAISE, SWELL, EXPAND, EXTEND, FATTEN, ENLARGE, INCREASE
augur .... BODE, PORTEND, AUSPEX, DIVINER, PRESAGE, PROPHET, FORETELL, PROPHESY, SOOTHSAYER
augury .... OMEN, SIGN, PORTENT, PROPHECY, DIVINATION
august .... GRAND, NOBLE, EXALTED, SUBLIME, IMPOSING, MAGNIFICENT
body, so-called .... SENATE, CONGRESS, SUPREME COURT
August, first .... LAMMAS
Augustan .... ELEGANT, CLASSICAL
Age writer .... OVID
Augustinian .... FRIAR
Augustus title .... PRINCEPS
wife .... LIVIA
auk .... ALCA, MURRE, PUFFIN, ROTCH(E), DOVEKEY, DOVEKIE
family .... ALCIDINE
genus .... ALLE, URIA
small .... ROTCH(E)
aulic .... SUAVE, COURTLY, PRINCELY
Auntie of stage/movies .... MAME
aura ...... AIR, MILIEU, AMBIENCE, ENVIRONS, EMANATION, ATMOSPHERE
of splendor .... NIMBUS
aural .... OTIC, AURICULAR
aureate .... GILDED, GOLDEN, ORNATE, BRILLIANT
aureole .... HALO, GLORY, CORONA
auric .... GOLDEN
acid salt .... AURATE
auricle .... EAR, PINNA
auriculate .... EARED
auriform .... EAR-SHAPED
Auriga .... WAGONER
aurist .... OTOLOGIST
instrument .... OTOSCOPE
aurochs .... OX, URUS, BISON
Aurora .... EOS, DAWN, BOREALIS, AUSTRALIS
auroral .... EOAN, BRIGHT, RADIANT, ROSEATE
aurum .... AU, GOLD
auscultation .... LISTENING
Ausonia .... ITALY
auspex .... SEER, AUGUR, SOOTHSAYER
auspice(s) .... EGIS, OMEN, SUPPORT, APPROVAL, PROPHECY, PATRONAGE, DIVINATION
auspicious .... LUCKY, TIMELY, FAVORABLE, FORTUNATE, PROMISING, PROPITIOUS, SUCCESSFUL
start in a theater .... FULL HOUSE, SRO SIGN
start of a speech .... APPLAUSE, LAUGHTER
austere ...... COLD, HARSH, RIGID, STERN, SEVERE, SIMPLE, ASCETIC, SPARTAN, RIGOROUS
austral .... SOUTHERN, SOUTHERLY
Australasia .... OCEANIA
Australian .... ANZAC, AUSSIE, ANTIPODEAN
aborigine .... MARA, MAORI, MYALL, BUSHMAN
aborigine weapon ...... NULLA, WO(O)MERA, BOOMERANG
acacia .... MYALL, WATTLE
anteater .... ECHIDNA
arboreal/bearlike animal .... KOALA
badger .... WOMBAT, BANDICOOT
bay .... SHARK, SMOKY, COLLIER, REPULSE, STREAKY, PORTLAND, DISCOVERY, LACEPEDE, ENCOUNTER, PORT PHILLIP
bee .... KARBI
beef-wood .... BELAR
bird .... ARA, LORY, ARARA, LOWAN, LEIPOA, EM(E)U, MALLEE, MEGAPOD, LORIKEET, PARDALOTE
boomerang .... KILEY, KYLIE
brushwood .... MALLEE
bushman .... ABO
bushranger .... HIGHWAYMAN
cake .... BROWNIE
cane .... WADDY
cape ..... HOWE, YORK, GREEN, OTWAY, WESSEL, BOWLING, MANIFOLD
capital .... CANBERRA
catlike animal .... LINSANG
cedar .... TOON(A)
chick .... SHEILA
city/town .... AYR, MOE, ALBURY, ASPLEY, ARARAT, ADELAIDE, BALLARAT, HOBART, BRIGHTON, BRISBANE, CANBERRA, CANTERBURY, GLADSTONE, DAVENPORT, CHELSEA, CONCORD, DARWIN, LIVERPOOL, MELBOURNE, PERTH, MANLY, BENDIGO, FORBES, SYDNEY, SEYMOUR, HAWTHORN, NEWCASTLE, ROMA, WARWICK, WINDSOR, ORANGE, PARKES, WAVERLEY
clover .... NARDOO

club of aborigines ..... WADDY
cockatoo .... GALAH
coin .... DUMP, SHILLING
cry/call .... COOEE, COOEY,
                      CODER
dasyure .... YABBI
Davis Cup player .... ROY,
      HOAD, ROCHE, STOLLE,
      EMERSON, NEWCOMBE
desert .... GIBSON, GREAT
      SANDY, SIMPSON, TANAMI,
      GREAT VICTORIA
explorer .... BASS, COOK
eucalyptus .... MALLEE
festival .... CORROBORI,
      CORROBOREE
fish .... MADO, BARRAMUNDA
fish with lungs .... CERATODUS
flycatcher .... FANTAIL
gale .... BUSTER
goldfish .... FANTAIL
grass .... SPINIFEX
gulf .... CARPENTARIA,
  SPENCER, VAN DIEMEN, JOSEPH
      BONAPARTE
gum tree .... TUART, KAR(R)I
harrier/hawk .... KAHU
hinterland .... OUTBACK
horse .... WALER, BRUMBY,
      BRUMBIE, WARRAGAL
hut .... MIMI, MIAM(IA)
island ..... MURION, TASMANIA,
      MONTE BELLO, WESSEL,
      CUMBERLAND, THURSDAY,
      WELLESLEY
kangaroo .... WOLABA,
      WOLARU, WALLABY
kingfisher .... HALCYON
lake .... AULD, DORA, CAREY,
      COWAN, BLANCHE, EYRE,
      FROME, DUNDAS, NASH,
      MACKAY, GREGORY,
      AMADEUS, CARNEGIE, NEALE,
  SERPENTINE, DISAPPOINTMENT
language .... ENGLISH
laughing bird .... GIGAS,
      DACELO, KOOKABURRA
lizard .... GOANNA, MOLOCH
marsupial .... KOALA, TAIT,
      YABBI, WOMBAT, DASYURE,
      KANGAROO, BANDICOOT,
      PHALANGER
measure of capacity ..... ARNA
mining refuse .... MULLOCK
mole .... PLATYPUS
mountain .... ISA, BLUE,
  MAGNET, KOSCIUSKO, BARKER,
  BARTLE FRERE, ZIEL, BRUCE,
      MARGARET, MORGAN,
      WOODROFFE
mountain range .... GREY,

      FLINDERS
native ..... ABO, MARA, MYALL,
      MAORI, BUSHMAN
ostrich .... EM(E)U
oven .... UMU
parrot .... GALAH, CORELLA,
      ROSELLA, COCKATOO,
      COCKATEEL, PARAKEET,
      BUDGERIGAR
peninsula .... EYRE
pepper .... KAVA
pigeon .... WONGA
pine .... DAMMAR
plain .... NULLARBOR
plant .... WARATAN
plateau .... KIMBERLEY
prime minister .... HOLT,
      GORTON
"puritan" .... WOWSER
river ...... DALY, SWAN, ROPER,
  MURRAY, DARLING, FINKE,
  PAROO, FITZROY, MARGARET,
      GEORGINA, COOPERS,
  THOMSON, BARCOO, VICTORIA,
      STURT, DIAMANTINA
salt sea .... GREGORY
sea .... CORAL, TIMOR,
      ARAFURA
sea mile .... NAUT
seaport .... PERTH, DARWIN,
      SYDNEY, BRISBANE
shark .... MAKO
shield .... MULGA
shrub .... CORREA
sight .... KOALA, KANGAROO
soldier .... ANZAC
spear-throwing device
  .... WO(O)MERA
state .... VICTORIA, WESTERN
  AUSTRALIA, NORTHERN
  TERRITORY, SOUTH
  AUSTRALIA, NEW SOUTH
      WALES, TASMANIA,
      QUEENSLAND
strait .... BASS, DUNDAS,
      TORRES, CLARENCE
tennis star .... HOAD, ROY,
      LAVER, STOLLE, ROCHE,
      EMERSON, NEWCOMBE
territory .... PAPUA
traveler .... SWAGMAN
tree ..... BELAR, BILLA, MYALL,
  PENDA, QUADANG, BOREE,
  MARARA, ACACIA, TODART,
      QUANDONG
tree-dwelling animal
  .... KOALA
walking stick .... WADDY
wild dog .... DINGO
wild horse .... BRUMBIES
wilderness .... OUTBACK

Austria: Ger. .... OSTERREICH
Austrian amphibian .... OLM
capital .... VIENNA
chancellor .... DOLLFUSS
city/town .... GRAZ, LEOBEN,
  LINZ, VIENNA, INNSBRUCK,
  DORNBIRN, SALZBURG,
  KLAGENFURT, STEYR,
  KAPPENBERG, WIEN, WEIS,
  TRAUN, ZELTWEG, WOLFSBERG
coin .... DUCAT, FLORIN,
  HELLER, GROSCHEN, KRONE,
  KRUE(T)ZER, GULDEN,
      GUILDER
composer .... MOZART,
      STRAUSS
country dance .... LANDLER
folk dance .... DREHER
grass .... MARRAM
highest point
  .... GROSSGLOCKNER
hunter .... JAGER, YAGER
language .... GERMAN
lake .... BODENSEE,
  CONSTANCE, NEUSIEDLER SEE
measure, dry .... MUTH
measure, liquid .... FASS
monetary unit .... CROWN,
  KRONE, SCHILLING
mountain .... ALLGAU, CARNIC,
  BAVARIAN, OTZTAL,
  GROSSGLOCKNER, WILDSPITZE,
      ZUGSPITZE
name prefix .... VON
native .... TYROLESE
pass ..... BRENNER, SEMMERING
physicist .... MACH
province .... STYRIA, TIROL,
  CARINTHIA, SALZBURG,
  BURGENLAND, VORARLBERG
psychiatrist ..... ADLER, FREUD
range .... HOHE, NIEDERE,
      KARAWANKEN
rifleman .... JAGER, YAGER
river .... DANUBE, INN, ENNS,
  DRAU, MARCH, MUR, RAAB,
  DONAU, RHINE, THAYA,
      TRAUN, SALZACH
ruling family .... HABSBURG
ski champ .... SAILER,
      SCHRANZ
soprano .... JERITZA
violinist ..... MORINI, KREISLER
writer .... KAFKA
autarchy .... DESPOTISM
authentic ...... PURE, REAL, TRUE,
  VALID, GENUINE, ORIGINAL,
      VERITABLE
authenticate .... SEAL, ATTEST,
      VERIFY, CONFIRM
author .... DOER, FATHER,

WRITER, CREATOR, COMPILER, FOUNDER, ORIGINATOR

concern of .... PLOT, STYLE

of America the Beautiful
.... BATES

of many works
.... POLYGRAPH

unknown .... ANON(YMOUS)

authoritative .... RULING, OFFICIAL, MAGISTRAL, POWERFUL, CONTROLLING

rule of law .... ORDINANCE

authority .... FORCE, POWER, LICENSE, INFLUENCE

letter of .... BREVE, BILLET

point as .... CITE, QUOTE

authorization .... BILLET, FIAT, LICENSE, MANDATE, WARRANT, SANCTION, CLEARANCE, PERMISSION

authorize ...... ALLOW, EMPOWER, ENABLE, ENTRUST, DEPUTE, ACCREDIT, DEPUTIZE, GIVE LEAVE, SANCTION, CERTIFY, PERMIT, LEGALIZE, COMMISSION, VALIDATE

authorized .... LEGAL, LEGIT(IMATE)

auto. See also **automobile**
'.................. CAR, MOTORCAR, AUTOMOBILE

clean .... SIMONIZE

colloquial .... BUS

court .... MOTEL

explosion .... BACKFIRE

for hire .... CAB, TAXI(CAB)

obsolete .... MODEL T, REO, FLIVVER, PACKARD

old .... CRATE, JALOPY

old style .... LANDAU, VICTORIA, CABRIOLET

panel .... DASHBOARD

prefix .... MANU

racetrack .... MOTORDROME

racing champion .... CLARK, MEARS, PETTY, UNSER, BODINE, ANDRETTI, WALTRIP, ALLISON, JONES, EARNHARDT, WALLACE, FITTIPALDI

shelter .... BARN, GARAGE, CARPORT

supercharged: colloq.
.... HOTROD

type .... SEDAN, COUPE, TUDOR, HARDTOP, BERLIN(E), ROADSTER, CONVERTIBLE

autobiography ...... MEMOIR, LIFE STORY

autochton ...... NATIVE, INDIGENE, ABORIGINE

autocracy .... DESPOTISM,

DICTATORSHIP

autocrat .... TSAR, MOGUL, CAESAR, DESPOT, DICTATOR

automat .... RESTAURANT

automatic .... PISTOL, MECHANICAL, SELF-OPERATING, REFLEX, SPONTANEOUS

action, kind of .... TIC, REFLEX

coal stoker .... HOPPER

clothes cleaner
.... LAUNDROMAT

writing .... GRAPHOSPASM, WRITER'S ITCH

automation .... ELECTRONICS, SELF-ACTION, CYBERNATION

automaton .... GOLEM, ROBOT, ANDROID

automobile. See also **auto**
.... BUS, (MOTOR)CAR, WHEELS

accessory .... MUFFLER

baggage compartment
.... BOOT, TRUNK

body ...... BERLIN(E), TONNEAU

canvas-topped
.... CONVERTIBLE

decrepit .... CRATE, FLIVVER

fast .... CLIPPER

framework .... CHASSIS

furnishings .... TRIM

hood .... BONNET

lamp .... HEADLIGHT

like a coupe .... CABRIOLET

model .... V-EIGHT

mudguard .... FENDER

operator .... RACER, DRIVER

part .... BRAKE, BUMPER, FENDER, CLUTCH, CHASSIS, IGNITION, ALTERNATOR, RADIATOR, CARBURETOR, HOOD, GEAR, HORN, CHOKE, TAILLIGHT, GENERATOR, STARTER, SPEEDOMETER, FAN, GAUGE, HEADLIGHT, MUFFLER, EXHAUST(PIPE), OIL, COWL, DISTRIBUTOR, WINDSHIELD, TRANSMISSION

speed .... HIGH, LOW

starter .... IGNITION

two-door .... COUPE

with folding top
.... CABRIOLET

automotive boo-boo .... EDSEL

autonomous .... FREE, SEPARATE, INDEPENDENT

autopsy ...... NECROPSY, INQUEST, DISSECTION, POST-MORTEM

Autry, ____ .... GENE

autumn ...... FALL, HARVEST TIME

flower .... ASTER

auxiliary .... SUB, AIDE, ALLY, HELPER, ASSISTANT, COADJUTOR, SUBSIDIARY, SUBSTITUTE

word .... VERB

avail .... USE, SERVE, PROFIT, BENEFIT, UTILIZE

available .... FREE, OPEN, HANDY, READY, USABLE, ON HAND, PRESENT, VACANT, ACCESSIBLE

money .... CASH

avalanche .... PLENTY, PLETHORA, LANDSLIDE, SNOWSLIDE, LAVISHING

lily .... WILDFLOWER

Avalon .... ISLE, AVILION

avant garde .... VANGUARD, FORERUNNER

avarice .... LUST, GREED, CUPIDITY, GLUTTONY

avaricious ...... GREEDY, MISERLY, COVETOUS, GRIPPLE, GRASPING, STINGY, RAVENOUS

avast .... HALT, STOP, CEASE

avaunt .... AROINT, BEGONE

ave .... HAIL, GREETING, FAREWELL, SALUTATION

avena .... OAT, GRASS

avenaceous .... OATEN

avenge .... PUNISH, REQUITE, RETORT, COUNTER, REVENGE, RETALIATE

avenger .... ATE, NEMESIS, VINDICATOR

avenging .... VINDICTIVE

spirit ...... ATE, FURY, ALECTO, MEGAERA, TISIPHONE

avenue .... LANE, PIKE, ACCESS, DRIVE, ROADWAY, ALLEY, PASS(AGE), OUTLET, PROMENADE, MEANS, THOROUGHFARE

of shops .... MALL

of trees .... ARCADE

aver .... AFFIRM, ALLEGE, ASSERT, DECLARE

average .... MEAN, USUAL, MEDIAN, NORM(AL), ORDINARY, STANDARD

averse .... LOATH, AGAINST, OPPOSED, RELUCTANT, UNWILLING

aversion .... HATE, DISLIKE, ANTIPATHY, REVULSION, REPUGNANCE

avert ...... WARD, AVOID, HINDER, DEVIATE, THWART, PREVENT, FRUSTRATE

a blow .... DUCK

a draft .... DODGE

a thrust .... PARRY
Avesta language .... ZEND
aviary ...... VOLERY, BIRD(S)CAGE
aviate .... FLY
aviator .... FLYER, PILOT, AIRMAN
  free-lance .... BARNSTORMER
  hazard .... BLACKOUT
  signal .... CONTACT
  with five kills .... ACE
aviatrix, famous
  .... (AMELIA)EARHART
avid .... KEEN, EAGER, ARDENT,
  GREEDY
avifauna .... ORNIS
avion .... AIRPLANE
avis indica .... APUS
aviso ...... BOAT, ADVICE, NOTICE,
  INFORMATION
avital .... ANCESTRAL
avocado .... PEAR, TREE, FRUIT,
  AGUACATE
  Mexican .... COYO
avocation .... HOBBY, PASTIME,
  SIDELINE
avocet .... COOT, STILT, STORK,
  GODWIT, PLOVER
avoid .... MISS, SHUN, SHIRK,
  ESCAPE, REFRAIN, SIDESTEP
  a blow .... DUCK
  a person .... SNUB
  a plea, in law .... QUASH
  commitment .... HEDGE, HEM
  AND HAW
  conscription .... DODGE
  crowds .... SHUN, EVADE
  responsibility .... SHIRK
  something harmful
  .... ESCHEW
  voting .... ABSTAIN
  work .... SHIRK, MALINGER,
  GOLDBRICK
avoidable .... PREVENTABLE
avoidance .... SHUNNING,
  ESCHEWAL, ANNULMENT,
  ABSTINENCE
  of battle .... FABIAN
  of duty/tax payment
  .... EVASION
  of game .... DEFAULT
  slang .... COP-OUT
avoirdupois .... WEIGHT,
  POUNDAGE, HEAVINESS,
  EMBONPOINT
  1⅓ pounds .... CATTY
avouch .... AVOW, AFFIRM,
  TESTIFY, GUARANTEE
avow .... AVER, ADMIT, ASSERT,
  CONFESS, DECLARE, DISCLOSE,
  ACKNOWLEDGE
avowal .... WORD, SHRIFT,
  STATEMENT, ACCEPTANCE,

CONFESSION
avowed .... ALLEGED, CLAIMED,
  PLEDGED
awa .... KAVA, MILKFISH
  Scottish .... AWAY
await .... BIDE, FACE, ATTEND,
  IMPEND, LOITER, HANG
  AROUND, EXPECT, CONFRONT,
  ANTICIPATE
awake .... KEEN, ALERT, ROUSE,
  ACTIVE, KNOWING, ACTIVATE,
  CONSCIOUS, UNSLEEPING
awakening .... REVIVAL
award ...... GRANT, MEDAL, PRIZE,
  DECREE, REWARD, DECISION,
  JUDGMENT, ADJUDGE,
  SETTLEMENT
  in sports .... LETTER
  journalism/literature/music
  .... PULITZER
  kind of .... BOOBY PRIZE
  movie .... OSCAR
  peace/medicine/economics
  .... NOBEL
  TV .... EMMY
aware .... HEP, HIP, ALERT,
  COGNIZANT, INFORMED,
  CONSCIOUS, SENSIBLE, ON TO,
  PERCEPTIVE
awash .... AFLOAT, FLOODED,
  DRENCHED, FLOATING
away ...... OFF, OUT, GONE, APART,
  FAR-OFF, ABSENT, ABROAD,
  ELSEWHERE
  from mouth .... ABORAL
  from the shore .... SEAWARD
  from wind .... ALEE
  prefix .... AB
away, ____ (shrink) .... SHY
awe .... FEAR, DREAD, TERROR,
  WONDER, RESPECT,
  REVERENCE, VENERATION
aweather .... WINDWARD
  opposite of .... ALEE
awesome .... GREAT, LOFTY,
  EERIE, BIZARRE, FEARFUL,
  DREADFUL, TERRIBLE,
  APPALLING, ASTONISHING
awful .... BAD, UGLY, HORRID,
  HIDEOUS, IMPOSING,
  DREADFUL, TERRIBLE,
  APPALLING
awfully .... VERY, EXTREMELY
awkward .... BULKY, INEPT,
  CLUMSY, IGNORANT,
  NESCIENT, GAUCHE,
  UNWIELDY, MALADROIT
  age .... ADOLESCENCE
  boat .... ARK, DROGHER
  person .... GAWK, LOUT,
  DUFFER, GALOOT, RUSTIC,

SIMPLETON
  stroke .... FOOZLE
awl .... AUGER, ELSIN, BODKIN,
  GIMLET
  for picking typeset .... BODKIN
  shaped .... SUBULATE
  type of .... PEG, SEWING
  with chisel head .... BRADAWL
awn .... BARB, SETA, BEARD,
  FIBER, ARISTA
awned .... ARISTATE
awning .... CANVAS, MARQUEE,
  SHELTER, SUNSHADE
  of bed/door .... CANOPY
  Roman .... VELARIUM
AWOL .... OVER THE HILL
awry .... AGEE, ASKEW, AMISS,
  AGLEY, CROOKED, OBLIQUE,
  TIPSY, WRONG, DISTORTED
  slang .... COCKEYED
ax(e) .... ADZ, HATCHET
  bonehead .... TOMAHAWK
  cut of .... KERF
  head, prehistoric .... CELT
  Indian/stone .... TOMAHAWK
  like tool .... ADZ(E)
  "the" ..... LAYOFF, DISMISSAL,
  DISCHARGE
  type of .... HATCHET,
  HALBERT, HALBERD, POLEAX,
  TOMAHAWK, BATTLE-AX
axial .... KEY, MIDDLE, ROTARY,
  CENTRAL
axil .... ALA, ANGLE
axilla .... ARMPIT
axillary .... ALAR
axiom .... MAXIM, BELIEF,
  PREMISE, PRINCIPLE
axis deer .... CHITAL
  member .... JAPAN,
  (NAZI)GERMANY,
  (FASCIST)ITALY
axle .... BAR, ROD, ARBOR,
  SPINDLE
  bearing .... HOTBOX
ayah .... AMAH, (NURSE)MAID
ayatollah .... LEADER, TEACHER
ay(e) .... YEA, YES, EVER, YEAH,
  ALAS, ALWAYS, AFFIRMATIVE
aye-aye .... LEMUR
Aymara's cousin .... INCA
ayuntamiento .... CITY HALL,
  TOWN HALL
azalea .... SHRUB, FLOWER,
  LAUREL
Azerbaijan's capital .... BAKU
  chief city .... TABRIZ
  native .... TURK
  other spelling
  .... AZERBAIDZHAN

azinuth ...... HORIZON, ALTITUDE, (COMPASS)DIRECTION
azo, as combining form
.... NITROGEN
Azores city/town .... HORTA, PONTA DELGADA, LAJES DO PICO, VILA DO PORTO, ANGRADO HEROISMO
district .... HORTA, PONTA DELGADA, ANGRA DO HEROISMO

island ..... PICO, SANTA MARIA, GRACIOSA, CORVO, SAO MIGUEL, FLORES, TERCEIRA, FAIAL, SAO JORGE
port .... HORTA
volcano .... PICO
azote .... NITROGEN
azoth .... MERCURY, QUICKSILVER
azothic .... NITRIC
Aztec .... NAHUATLAN
country .... AZTLAN

emperor .... MONTEZUMA
god .... XIPE, EECATL
hero .... NATA
language .... NAHUATL
spear .... ATLATL
temple .... TEOPAN
azure .... CYANIC, (SKY)BLUE, CELESTE, CERULEAN
azygous .... ODD, SINGLE, MATELESS
azym .... BREAD

B

B .... SECOND, INFERIOR, SECONDARY
B .... GUN, SHOT
girl .... BARGIRL, BARMAID
Greek .... BETA
Hebrew .... BETH
in chemistry .... BORON
in chess .... BISHOP
letter .... BE, BEE, BETA
picture (movies): sl.
.... QUICKIE
ba .... SOUL
Ba, in chemistry .... BARIUM
baa .... BLEAT
bleater .... LAMB, SHEEP
Baal .... IDOL, (SUN)GOD
Baalist .... IDOLATER
Bab .... BABUDDIN
babbitt ...... UPSTART, PHILISTINE, BUSINESSMAN
Babbitt, _____ .... ISAAC, IRVING, GEORGE
babble .... GAB, BLAB, RAVE, PRATE, GIBBER, GOSSIP, GURGLE, JABBER, MURMUR, BLABBER, CHATTER, PRATTLE
babbling .... DIZZY, GIDDY, RAMBLING, INCOHERENT
babe .... BABY, GIRL, INFANT
in the woods .... NAIVE
Babe Ruth's forte ...... HOMERUN
Babel .... TOWER, JARGON, TUMULT, CONFUSION
babirusa .... HOG
baboo .... SIR, CLERK, TITLE
baboon .... APE, CHACMA, (MAN)DRILL
babu .... SIR, TITLE
babul .... ACACIA
babushka .... SCARF, KERCHIEF
baby .... TOT, BABE, SPOIL, YOUNG, INFANT, CHILD, CODDLE, PAMPER, CHRISOM, INDULGE, SUCKLING,

OFFSPRING
ailment .... CROUP
bathtub .... BASSINET, BATHINETTE
bed .... CRIB, CRADLE
bedroom .... NURSERY
boots/shoes .... BOOTEES
breechcloth .... DIAPER
cap .... BIGGIN, BONNET
carriage .... PRAM, BUGGY, STROLLER, GO-CART, PERAMBULATOR
diaper .... TOWEL, NAPKIN
food .... PAP, FORMULA
garment/outfit .... CREEPER, LAYETTE
goose .... GOSLING
grand .... PIANO
head's soft spot
.... FONTANEL(LE)
hooter .... OWLET
Indian .... PAPOOSE
Italian .... BAMBINO
jacket .... SACK, SACQUE
Kermit .... TADPOLE
pacifier .... NIPPLE, TEETHING RING
pants .... SOAKERS
powder .... TALC
premature .... PREEMIE
robe, baptismal .... CHRISOM
sitter ...... AMAH, AUNT, AYAH, NANNY, NURSE
sitter's problem .... BRAT, CRYBABY
sound .... CROW, MEWL
Spanish ..... NENA, NIÑA, NIÑO
swan .... CYGNET
talk/word .... DADA, LISP, BABBLE
teething toy .... CORAL, PACIFIER
tickle .... KOOCHY-KOO
toy .... BAUBLE

babyish .... CHILDISH
Babylonia .... SHINAR, SHINOR
founder .... SEMIRAMIS
Babylonian ...... NATIVE, WICKED
abode of dead .... ARALU
canal .... JESUF
chief god ...... ANU, BEL, HEA, ENKI
chief goddess .... IS(H)TAR
city .... AKKAD, CUNAXA
deity .... ANU, BEL, HEA, ALALU, MERODACH
division .... ELAM, NITUK, SUMER
god .... EA, ZU, ANU, BEL, UTU, ADAD, ADDU, NABU, NEBO, UTUG, DAGAN, ENLIL, MARDUK, NINIB, NANNAR, ANSHAR, RAMMAN, TAMMUZ, SIRIS, SHAMASH
goddess ...... AYA, BAU, ERUA, GULA, NANA(I), NINA, ARURU, ISHTAR
hero .... ETANA
monarch .... ALOROS
neighbor .... ELAMITE
numeral .... SAR(OS)
people .... SUMERIAN
priestess .... ENTUM
river .... TIGRIS
storm god .... ADAD
temple .... BEL, ISTAR
tower .... ZIGGURAT
weight .... MINA
baby's breath .... PLANT, MADDER, HYACINTH, GYPSOPHILA
face, sometimes .... EGGY
piggy .... TOE
bac .... VAT, CISTERN
baccarat .... (CARD)GAME, CHEMIN DE FER
baccate .... PULPY
bacchanal .... ORGY, CAROUSER

cry .... EVOE
bacchante .... M(A)ENAD,
CAROUSER
Bacchus .... GOD, DIONYSUS
devotee .... SATYR, TOPER,
M(A)ENAD, BACCHANT
bachelor .... SINGLE, DIVORCÉ,
WIDOWER, GRADUATE,
CELIBATE
bait .... SPINSTER
girl .... VIRGIN, OLD MAID
bachelor's button .... TANSY,
KNAPWEED, CORNFLOWER
degree .... BACCALAUREATE
party .... STAG
Bach's composition ...... ARIOSO
back .... AID, TUB, VAT, ABET,
FUND, HIND, REAR, SECOND,
ENDORSE, FINANCE, SPONSOR,
SUPPORT, REVERSE, PROMOTE
and fill .... VEER, ZIGZAG
and forth .... SEESAW,
ALTERNATE
at the/near the .... RETRAL
book .... ISSUE, EDITION
book's .... SPINE
call .... REVOKE, WITHDRAW
climb on .... MOUNT
country .... HINTERLAND
cramp .... CRICK
door/gate/entrance
.... POSTERN, REAR ENTRY
down/out ..... YIELD, RETREAT,
WITHDRAW
flow .... EBB, RECEDE
in zoology .... TERGUM
lying on .... SUPINE
of animal ...... RIDGE, DORSUM
of head .... POLL
of insects .... NOTUM
of neck .... NAPE, NUCHA,
SCRAG, SCRUFF
of skull .... NION, OCCIPITAL
on one's .... HELPLESS,
BEDRIDDEN
pain .... STITCH
part .... DERRIERE
part: comb. form .... NOTO
part of skull .... OCCIPUT
pertaining to the ...... DORSAL,
TERGAL
porch .... STOOP
scratcher .... TOADY
seat, carriage .... DICKEY,
RUMBLE
seat driver: colloq. .... WIFE
slapper .... SOFT-SOAPER
take word .... RECALL,
RECANT, RETRACT, REPUDIATE
talk: colloq. .... LIP, SASS,
RETORT

the field .... BET
to back .... BEHIND, TANDEM
toward .... RETRAL
turn one's .... IGNORE
up .... SECOND, FINANCE,
SUPPORT, SUSTAIN
wound .... STAB
backache .... LUMBAGO
backbite .... DEFAME, ATTACK,
MALIGN, REVILE, SLANDER,
VILIFY, TRADUCE
backbone .... PLUCK, RIDGE,
SPINE, COURAGE, VERTEBRA,
SPINAL COLUMN
having .... VERTEBRATE
of animal .... CHINE
of fish .... GRATE
of the land .... FARMER
backbreaker .... HERCULEAN
TASK
backbreaking .... HEAVY, TIRING,
ARDUOUS, ONEROUS,
DIFFICULT, HERCULEAN,
STRENUOUS
backburner .... SUSPENSION,
UNESSENTIAL
backdoor .... COVERT, SECRET,
FURTIVE, POSTERN,
CLANDESTINE
backdrop .... SETTING, SCENE(RY)
backed .... FAVORED, REINFORCED
backer .... ALLY, DONOR, FUNDER,
PATRON, SPONSOR, FINANCER
stage show ..... ANGEL, SUGAR
DADDY, FAIRY GODMOTHER
backfire .... FAIL, RECOIL,
BOOMERANG, EXPLOSION
backgammon ...... BOARD GAME,
TRIC(K)TRAC(K)
exposed man .... BLOT
game series .... RUBBER
background .... SETTING,
ANCESTRY, TRAINING,
EDUCATION, EXPERIENCE
backhanded .... SHIFTY, ABUSIVE,
INSOLENT, INSINCERE,
SARCASTIC
way of catching a ball
.... AWKWARD
backhouse .... PRIVY
backlash .... BOUNCE, IMPACT,
REBUFF, RECOIL, REACTION
backless .... SPINELESS
dress .... DECOLLETE
person .... COWARD, YELLOW
seat .... STOOL, OTTOMAN
backlog .... PILE-UP, RESERVE,
FIREWOOD, ACCUMULATION
backpack .... KNAPSACK
backset .... RELAPSE
backside .... RUMP, BUTTOCKS

backslide .... FALL, TRIP, SLIP,
LAPSE, REVERT, RELAPSE
backtrack ...... RETREAT, ABOUT-
FACE
backup .... ALTERNATE
backward .... SHY, SLOW,
BASHFUL, DELAYED, REVERSE,
REARWARD, RETARDED
backwater .... BAYOU
channel .... BILLABONG
backwoods .... PRIMITIVE
backwoodsman ...., RUSTIC,
HILLBILLY
bacon, bring home the ...... WIN,
SUCCEED
coating .... RIND
cut .... RASHER
side of .... FLITCH, GAMMON
strip .... LARDO(O)N
bacteremia .... INFECTION
bacteria .... GERMS, MICROBE
culture .... AGAR, STAIN
destroyer/killer .... LYSIN,
ALEXIN, BACTERICIDE
free of .... ASEPTIC
mass of .... CLUMP
organ of locomotion
.... FLAGELLUM
causing food poisoning/
diphtheria
.... SALMONELLA
responsible for tetanus
.... CLOSTRIDIA
rod-shaped .... BACILLI
S and comma-shaped
.... VIBRIO
spherical .... COCCI
spiral-shaped .... SPIRILLA
bacteriologist's wire .... OESE
bacterium .... FUNGUS, BACILLUS
plural of .... BACTERIA
Bactria .... BALKH
bactrian .... CAMEL
bad .... ILL, BASE, EVIL, MEAN,
UNFIT, WICKED, ROTTEN,
HATEFUL, HEINOUS, SINFUL,
SPOILED, INFERIOR
blood .... HATE, ENMITY,
ANIMOSITY, RESENTMENT
boy .... IMP, RASCAL
breath .... HALITOSIS
character .... DISHONOR
check: sl. .... RUBBER
combining form .... MAL, MIS,
DIS
debt .... UNCOLLECTIBLE
deed .... DISSERVICE
faith .... DECEIT
for one's health ..... HARMFUL
girl/woman ..... DOXY, QUEAN,
TRAMP, FLOOZY, WHORE,

HARLOT, FLOOZIE, TART, HUSSY, TROLLOP, STRUMPET, PROSTITUTE
guy .... VILLAIN
habit .... VICE
humor .... TIFF, TEMPER
influence .... ILL-WIND, ROTTEN EGG
language .... CURSING, SWEARING, PROFANITY
liquor: colloq. .... BOUSE
loser's reaction .... SOUR GRAPES
luck ..... CESS, JINX, AMESACE, AMBSACE, HOODOO, MISHAP, WANION, MISFORTUNE
luck man .... JONAH, JONAS
man (of the old West) .... GUNMAN, DESPERADO
mannered person .... BOOR, CLOD, GOON, LOUT, S.O.B., THUG, STINKER
mouth .... DEFAME, MALIGN, REVILE, SLANDER, CRITICIZE
move .... BALK, FALL, SLIP, ERROR, BLUNDER, MISSTEP
name .... ILL-REPUTE
news .... PROBLEM, TROUBLE
prefix .... CACO, MAL(O)
quality .... INFERIOR, DEFECTIVE
smell .... REEK, STENCH, MEPHITIS
smell of oil/fats .... RANCID
smelling .... MEPHITIC, STINKING, MALODOROUS
sport .... CRYBABY
taste .... VULGARITY, IMPROPRIETY
temper .... BILE, ANGER, SPLEEN
temper sign .... TANTRUM
tempered .... GRUFF, DORTY, SURLY, TESTY, CRUSTY, CRANKY, GRUMPY, WASPISH, SNAPPISH, PEEVISH, GRUMPISH, IRRITABLE, SPLENETIC
tempered person .... FURY, SHREW, VIRAGO, HOTHEAD
treatment .... ABUSE, TORTURE, OPPRESSION
badak .... RHINO
badge .... PIN, MARK, SIGN, EMBLEM, SYMBOL, INSIGNIA
Japanese .... MON
of braid .... CORDON
of honor .... MEDAL
of ribbon .... CORDON
on arm .... BRASSARD
on hat .... COCKADE
badger ...... NAG, ANNOY, HARRY,

HARASS, HECKLE, WORRY, TEASE, PESTER, TORMENT
animal .... HAWKER, BROCK, WOMBAT, BANDICOOT
Canadian .... CARCAJOU
European .... BROCK
game .... BLACKMAIL
genus .... MELES
honey .... RATEL
Java .... TELEDU
like animal .... PAHMI, MARMOT
Badger State .... WISCONSIN
badgered .... BESET, NEEDLED, PLAGUED
badinage .... TALK, TEASE, BANTER, CHATTER
badlands .... WASTE
Badlands mountain .... BUTTE
badly .... ILLY, POORLY, HARMFULLY, WICKEDLY
colloquial ..... MUCH, GREATLY
off .... HARD-UP
badminton .... DRINK, (COURT)GAME
cork .... SHUTTLECOCK
racket .... BATTLEDORE
Baedeker .... GUIDEBOOK
Baffin's discovery .... SEA, ISLAND
baffle .... BALK, FOIL, BLOCK, ELUDE, EVADE, STUMP, BOGGLE, PUZZLE, MUFFLE, WONDER, CONFUSE, MYSTIFY, THWART, BEWILDER, NONPLUS, CONFOUND, FRUSTRATE
baffling ...... ELUSIVE, CONFUSING, UNSCRUTABLE
device .... WALL, SCREEN
problem .... POSER, PUZZLE, DILEMMA, MYSTERY, QUANDARY
question ...... ENIGMA, PUZZLE, RIDDLE, CONUNDRUM
bag .... SAC, CYST, POKE, TRAP, CATCH, PURSE, POUCH, SEIZE, UDDER, LUGGAGE, SATCHEL, SUITCASE, CONTAINER
floating .... BALLOON
for books, papers, etc. .... BRIEFCASE
kind of .... DUFFEL, RECEPTACLE
making material .... FLAX, HEMP, JUTE, PAPER, BURLAP, SACKING
slang .... WOMAN, CAPTURE
sleeping .... SACK
toilette .... MUSETTE

with perfumed powder .... SACHET
bagasse .... MEGASS(E), (CANE)REFUSE
bagatelle .... TRIFLE
baggage .... LUGGAGE, TRUNKS, VALISES, SUITCASES
boy .... PORTER
car/wagon .... FOURGON
carrier .... HAM(M)AL, PORTER, REDCAP
slang .... GIRL, SAUCY, WOMAN
baggie .... BELLY, STOMACH
baggy .... LOOSE, PUFFED, BULGING, UNPRESSED
bagman: Eng. .... SALESMAN
bagnio .... CABANA, PRISON, BROTHEL, BATHHOUSE
Bagnold .... ENID
bagpipe .... DRONE, LOURE, MUSETTE, DOODLESACK
drone .... BOURDON
flute/part .... CHANTER
music .... PIBROCH
play/sound .... SKIRL
bagworm .... LARVA, CATERPILLAR
Bah! .... FIE, ROT, TUT, RATS, NUTS, PSHAW
Bahamas capital .... NASSAU
cay .... GUN, RUM, LONG, EXUMA, PLANA, VERDE, SAMANA, FLAMINGO
channel .... SANTAREN, TONGUE OF THE OCEAN
island .... CAT, LONG, ANDROS, ABACO, EXUMA, ACKLINS, HARBOUR, MAYAGUANA, ELEUTHERA, RAGGED, CROOKED, INAGUA, BIMINI, WATLING, NEW PROVIDENCE
major language .... ENGLISH
monetary unit .... BAHAMIAN DOLLAR
mountain .... ALVERNIA
premier .... PINDLING
Bahia .... (SAO)SALVADOR
Bahr ____, Egyptian name for the Nile .... ENNIL
Bahrain capital .... MANAMA, MANAMEH
city .... MUHURRAQ
language .... ARABIC
religion .... ISLAM
bail .... BOND, LADE, SCOOP, BUCKET, PLEDGE, FREE, RELEASE, SECURITY, PALISADES, FORTIFICATION
bond ..... SURETY, GUARANTEE, INSURANCE
one who needs ...... DETAINEE,

PRISONER

out .... JUMP, RELEASE, PARACHUTE

Bailey, lexicographer
.... NATHANIEL

bailiff .... REEVE, MARSHAL, SHERIFF, STEWARD, OVERSEER, TIPSTAFF, CONSTABLE

bailiwick .... FIELD, DOMAIN, REGION, SPHERE, DISTRICT, HOMEGROUND, JURISDICTION

bain-marie .... PAN

bairn ...... SON, CHILD, DAUGHTER

bait ...... DUPE, GOAD, LURE, RIDE, DECOY, SNARE, TRAP, TEASE, TEMPT, HECKLE, ENTICE(MENT), BADGER, HECTOR, SEDUCE, ATTRACT, GUDGEON

drop .... DIP, DAP

fish .... CHUM, LURE

take .... BITE

baize ...... CLOTH, DRAPE, DOMETT

bake .... COOK, FIRE, BROIL, ROAST, ANNEAL, HARDEN, DRY UP

with crumbs .... ESCALOP, SCALLOP

baked Alaska .... PIE, DESSERT

clay .... TILE

dishes, etc. .... CROCKERY

pot .... OLLA

baker bird .... HORNERO

baker's cyst .... BURSA

dozen .... THIRTEEN

equipment .... MIXER, TIMER, BEATER, BLENDER

itch .... RASH, PSORIASIS

job .... KNEAD

kneading trough .... BRAKE

material .... FLOUR, YEAST, LEAVEN

shovel .... PEEL

tool/utensil .... PAN, WHIP, KNIFE, SIEVE, BOWL, SPOON, CUTTER, TURNER, PASTRY BAG, SPATULA, STRAINER

baking chamber ...... KILN, OAST, OVEN

dish .... RAMEKIN, SCALLOP, RAMEQUIN, CASSEROLE

instruction .... RECIPE

pit: Hawaiian .... IMU

soda .... SALERATUS

baksheesh .... TIP, ALMS, GRATUITY

bal _____ .... MASQUE, TABARIN

Balaam's beast .... ASS

balalaika .... GUITAR

balance ...... EVEN, LEVEL, LIBRA, MATCH, POISE, ADJUST, EXCESS, OFFSET, SCALES, SQUARE, SURPLUS, EQUAL(IZE), REMAINDER, SYMMETRY, STABILITY, EQUILIBRIUM

crossbar of .... BEAM

of sales .... ATRY

sheet .... FINANCIAL STATEMENT

state of .... EQUIPOISE

weighing .... STEELYARD

balancer .... HALTER, ACROBAT, GYMNAST, WIRE WALKER, TIGHTROPE WALKER

of books .... ACCOUNTANT

balancing weight .... BALLAST

balas .... SPINEL

balata gum .... CHICLE

Balboa's ocean .... PACIFIC

balcony .... LOGE, TIER, PORCH GAZEBO, LOGGIA, GALLERY, PORTICO, TERRACE, MEZZANINE

bald .... BARE, BLUNT, FRANK, GLABROUS, HAIRLESS, PLAIN, TREELESS, UNADORNED

headed man .... PILGARLIC

baldachin ...... CANOPY, BROCADE

Balder, giant victim of ...... LOKI

parent of .... ODIN, FRIGG

slayer of .... HODER, HODUR

wife of .... NANNA

balderdash .... PALAVER, NONSENSE, RIGMAROLE

baldness ...... ACOMIA, ALOPECIA, CALVITIES

baldpate .... WIDGEON

cover .... WIG, TOUPEE

baldric .... BELT

Baldwin .... APPLE

cousin .... WINESAP

bale .... WOE, BAIL, BUNDLE, SORROW, PACKAGE, DISASTER, DEJECTION

Balearic Island .... MAJORCA, MENORCA, MINORCA, MALLORCA

capital .... PALMA

city/town .... INCA, ARTA, ALAYOR, SOLLER, FELANITX, POLLENSA, MANACOR, CIUDADELA, ANDRAITX, DRAGONERA

is province of .... SPAIN

language .... CATALAN

baleen .... WHALEBONE

balefire .... PYRE, BONFIRE

baleful .... BAD, EVIL, DEADLY, HOSTILE, HURTFUL, SINISTER, INJURIOUS

baler .... TIER, BUNDLER

Bali holy day .... NJEPI

balk .... JIB, SHY, FOIL, STOP, ERROR, REBEL, HINDER, THWART, BLUNDER

Balkan .... SLAV, SERB(IAN), BULGAR(IAN), SLOVENE

state .... GREECE, ALBANIA, BULGARIA, ROMANIA, YUGOSLAVIA

balker, congenital .... ASS, MULE, DONKEY

Balkh .... BACTRIA

balky .... RESTIVE, CONTRARY, STUBBORN, OBSTINATE

ball .... SHOT, DANCE, GLOBE, IVORY, COTILLION, BULLET, PLANET, SPHERE, GLOBULE, PROJECTILE

and chain: sl. .... WIFE

batted high .... FLY

game .... KENO, RUGBY, TENNIS, BASEBALL, FOOTBALL, CRICKET, BOWLING, LACROSSE, SOCCER, BASKETBALL

have a: sl. .... ENJOY

hit for practice .... FUNGO

low .... LINER

metal .... BEARING

metal, athletics .... HAMMER, SHOTPUT

of electric discharge
.... CORPOSANT

of meat/rice .... PINDA

of perfume mixture
.... POMANDER

of yarn/thread .... CLEW

on the .... ALERT, EFFICIENT

play: sl. .... COOPERATE

rolling, get the .... START

rope missile .... BOLA(S)

sign displayer .... PAWNSHOP

supporter .... TEE

swing bat at .... SWAT

throwing device .... TRAP

tiny .... GLOBULE

up .... MUDDLE, CONFUSE

used in jai alai .... PELOTA

ballad .... LAY, POEM, SONG, CALYPSO, DERRY, CHANSON, CHANTEY, SPIRITUAL

hero .... LOCHINVAR

monger .... POETASTER

singer .... MINSTREL, TROUBADOUR

stanza, rhyme of .... ABCB

word .... DERRY

ballast .... STABILIZE(R)

ballerina .... DANSEUSE, TOE DANCER

descriptive word for a
.... PRIMA, ASOLUTA
famous .... FONTEYN, RASCH,
MARKOVA, SHEARER,
ULANOVA, TALLCHIEF
finale .... TWIRL, PIROUETTE
forte .... TOE-DANCE,
PIROUETTE
garb of .... TUTU
ballet .... ADAGIO, DANCE,
BEZANT, MASQUE,
CHOREOGRAPHY
dance solo .... PAS SEUL
dancer .... BALLERINA,
DANSEUSE, CORYPHEE,
FIGURANT
dancer's buoyancy ..... BALON
director .... IMPRESARIO
famous .... SWAN LAKE
jump .... JETE, ENTRECHAT
movement .... PLIE
number .... TOE DANCE
number between acts
.... INTERMEZZO
Petipa's .... RAYMONDA
posture .... ARABESQUE
step .... PAS, GLISSADE
turn .... FOUETTE, PIROUETTE
wear .... TUTU, TIGHTS,
LEOTARD
ballista .... CATAPULT
ballistic missile launching
.... BLAST-OFF
launching place .... PAD
storage place .... SILO
warhead .... PAYLOAD
balloon .... BAG, KITE, BLIMP,
SWELL, INFLATE, DIRIGIBLE,
BALL, AEROSTAT, RUBBERBAG
altitude controller .... BALLAST
bag/covering .... ENVELOPE
ballast/mooring line
.... DRAGROPE
basket .... CAR, NACELLE
cabin .... GONDOLA
gas .... HELIUM, HYDROGEN
pilot .... AERONAUT
shape of ..... ROUND, SAUSAGE
trial .... TEST, FEELER
vine .... HEARTSEED
ballot ...... SLATE, VOICE, CHOICE,
TICKET, VOTE(S), VOTING
straw .... POLL
ballroom dance .... WALTZ,
REDOWA
balls tosser .... JUGGLER
ballyhoo .... PLUG, TALK, TOUT,
UPROAR, ADVERTISE, WRITE-
UP, HYPERBOLE, PUBLICITY,
PROPAGANDA
balm .... OIL, RESIN, SALVE,

SOOTH, ANODYNE,
FRAGRANCE, BALSAM,
UNGUENT, OINTMENT,
SEDATIVE, ANALGESIC
for divorce .... ALIMONY
for injury .... DAMAGES
kind of ..... ARNICA, MENTHOL,
GLYCERIN, LANOLIN, VASELINE
of Gilead .... FIR, OIL,
BALSAM, POPLAR, OINTMENT
Balmoral .... CAP, CASTLE,
PETTICOAT
balmy .... MILD, SOFT, CRAZY,
MOONY, GENTLE, FOOLISH,
HEALING, IDIOTIC, FRAGRANT,
SOOTHING
balneal .... BATH(ING)
baloney .... ROT, BUNK, HUMBUG,
BOLOGNA, SAUSAGE,
BUNCOMBE, NONSENSE
balsa .... RAFT, TREE, WOOD,
CORKWOOD
like wood .... BONGO
balsam .... GUM, BALM, TOLU,
MUSK, RESIN, COPAIBA,
IMPATIENS, LIQUIDAMBAR
gum resin .... BALM, STORAX
Swiss .... RIGA
tree .... TOLU
Balt .... ESTH
Baltic gulf .... RIGA
island .... DAGO, OS(S)EL,
ALSEN
port .... KIEL, RIGA, MEMEL,
REVAL, STETTIN
river .... ODER
Sea city .... LIBAU, LIEBAJA
seaport .... ROSTOCK
state .... LITHUANIA, LATVIA,
ESTONIA, FINLAND
Baltimore oriole ...... HANGBIRD,
HANGNEST, GOLDEN ROBIN
stove .... LATROBE
Balto-Slav .... LETT
Baluchistan capital .... QUETTA
city/town .... BELA, DADU,
MACH, NUSHKI, PISHIN,
MASTUNG, GANDAVA,
BARKHAN, KHUZDAR, LORALAI
grain .... JOWAR
mountain .... HALA
race .... BRAHOES
river .... BOLAN, MOOLA
ruler .... KHAN, SIRDAR
tribe .... REKI
tribesman .... MARI
balustrade .... POST, FENCE,
RAILING, BAN(N)ISTER
Balzac's father .... GORIOT
bambino: Ital. .... CHILD,
BABY(BOY)

Bambi's aunt .... ENA
bamboo ...... CANE, REED, GRASS,
SEDGE, RATTAN, TONKIN
bear .... PANDA
curtain ...... BARRIER, SECRECY
like .... REEDY
shoot pickle .... ACHAR
stalk .... REED
bamboozle .... DUPE, CHEAT,
TRICK, PUZZLE, BUFFALO,
HOCUS-POCUS
ban .... TABU, CURSE, TABOO,
FORBID, CONDEMN,
BLOCKADE, GOVERNOR,
EXCOMMUNICATION, PROHIBIT,
PROCLAMATION
Bana, daughter of .... USHA
banal .... CORNY, TRITE, STALE,
TRIVIAL, HACKNEYED
banality .... CLICHE, PLATITUDE
banana .... FEI, ENSETE, PLANTAIN
bunch/cluster .... HAND
disease .... MOSAIC
like fruit/tropical
.... PLANTAIN
of the .... MUSACEOUS
oil: sl. .... NONSENSE
Philippine .... SABA, SAGING,
LACATAN, LATUNDAN
plant .... MUSA, PESANG
bananas: sl. ...... CRAZY, WACKY,
BONKERS, EXCITED
band .... BELT, TAPE, GROUP,
COLLAR, BINDING, COMPANY,
GIRDLE, GATHER, FASCIA,
COPULA, FILAMENT, STRAP,
STRIP, STRIPE, CROWD,
FILLET, ORCHESTRA
across escutcheon .... FESS
aid .... PLASTER, DRESSING
brain .... LIGULA
deputized/sheriff's .... POSSE
head .... AGAL, CORONET
ecclesiastical .... ORPHREY
leader .... SHAW, CUGAT,
JAMES, CHORAGUS, VALLEE,
WHITEMAN
leaders .... CHORAGI
master .... CONDUCTOR
mourning .... WEED
narrow .... TAPE, STRIA(E)
of soldiers .... COHORT
of stone on wall .... CORDON
ornamental .... CORONET
priest's arm .... PHANO,
FANO(N), FANUM
together .... JOIN
wheel .... RIGGER
bandage .... GAUZE, SPICA, STUPE,
SPONGE, SWATH(E), LIGATE,
LIGATURE, POULTICE

in surgery .... FASCIA
shaped .... LIGULATE
used as compress .... DOSSIL
bandan(n)a ...... (HAND)KERCHIEF
bandeau .... (HAIR)RIBBON,
BRASSIERE
banderilla .... DART
banderole .... FLAG, PENNANT,
BANNEROL, STREAMER
bandicoot .... RAT, BADGER
bandit .... ROBBER, OUTLAW,
BRIGAND, LADRONE,
HIGHWAYMAN
more than one .... BANDITTI
banditry .... PLUNDER,
BRIGANDAGE
bandleader .... CHORAGUS
bandmaster .... SOUSA,
CONDUCTOR
bandog ...... MASTIFF, WATCHDOG,
BLOODHOUND
bandoline .... POMADE
bandore ...... PANDORA, PANDORE
bandwagon riders ...... WINNERS
bandy .... CLUB, BOWED,
CHAFFER, GIVE-AND-TAKE,
EXCHANGE
legs .... BOWED
some are .... LEGS
bane .... HARM, PEST, RUIN,
CURSE, VENOM, POISON
baneful .... BAD, DEADLY,
RUINOUS, VENOMOUS,
PERNICIOUS
Banff National Park lake
.... LOUISE
bang .... HIT, BEAT, SLAM, CLOSE,
STRIKE, EXPLOSION
slang .... PLEASURE,
ENJOYMENT
up .... BRUISE, DAMAGE
Bangalore, where it is
.... MYSORE
banged-up .... A-ONE,
EXCELLENT, WELL DONE
Bangkok is capital of ...... SIAM,
THAILAND
Thai name of .... KRUNG THEP
bangle .... ANKLET, ARMLET,
BRACELET
bangs .... FRINGE, HAIRDO,
HAIRCUT
banian .... SHIRT, MERCHANT
banish .... EXILE, EXPEL, DEPORT,
DISMISS, RELEGATE, PUNISH,
PROSCRIBE, EXPATRIATE
banister .... BALUSTER,
HANDRAIL, BALUSTRADE
banjo .... SAMISEN
string sound ...... TUM, TWANG
bank .... BEACH, RELY, RIDGE,

SHORE, SHOAL, VAULT,
DEPEND, HILLSIDE,
DEPOSITORY
clerk .... TELLER
employee .... RUNNER
kind of .... EYE, POOL, BLOOD,
PIGGY, DOMESTIC
note .... BILL, PAPER MONEY
river .... RIPA
river, pert. to .... RIPARIAN
teller's window .... WICKET
vole .... MOUSE
bankbook .... PASSBOOK
banker .... LAMONT, GIANNINI,
MORGAN, SHROFF,
ROTHSCHILD
banking game .... FARO
bankroll .... WAD
colloquial .... FINANCE,
CAPITALIZE
bankrupt .... BROKE, RUINED,
FAILURE, DESTITUTE,
INSOLVENT, PENNILESS
abbreviation .... BKPT
banner .... FLAG, ENSIGN,
BLAZON, PENNON, LEADING,
PENNANT, GONFALON,
FOREMOST, BANDEROLE
headline .... STREAMER
bannock .... CAKE
banquet .... MEAL, FEAST, DINNER
rich, luxurious ...... LUCULLAN
banquette ...... BENCH, SIDEWALK
banshee .... SPIRIT
bant .... DIET
bantam .... FOWL, SMALL,
MIDGET, PINT-SIZE
publication .... TABLOID,
VESTBOOK, POCKETBOOK
banteng .... OX, TSINE
banter .... JEST, JOSH, CHAFF,
TEASE, BADINAGE, RAILLERY,
PERSIFLAGE, PLEASANTRY
bantling .... BRAT, YOUNGSTER
Bantu .... JAGA, KAF(F)IR
Congo .... RUA, WARUA,
BAKALAI
language .... ILA, SUTO,
RONGA
lion .... SIMBA
nation .... GOGO
native .... ZULU, YAKU,
DUALA, SWAZI, BASUTO
speaking people
.... BECHUANA
tribe .... BAYA, BULE, JAGA,
HAKU, GOMA, RAVI, RORI,
PONDO
banzai ...... CRY, CHEER, CHARGE,
GREETING
baobab .... TREE, FIBER

leaves, dried/powdered
.... LALO
baptism .... RITE, NAMING,
INITIATION, PURIFICATION
for example .... SACRAMENT
of fire .... TEST, ORDEAL
baptismal basin .... FONT, LAVER,
BAPTISTERY
cloth/robe .... CHRISOM
oil .... CHRISM
water .... LAVER
baptize .... DIP, NAME, PURIFY,
CLEANSE, CHRISTEN, INITIATE,
SPRINKLE
bar .... PUB, ROD, BISTRO, HINDER,
HURDLE, OPPOSE, COUNTER,
EXCLUDE, STRIPE, BARRIER,
LAWYERS, TAPROOM,
DRAMSHOP, OBSTRUCT,
TAPHOUSE, WINESHOP
chisel-pointed .... SPUDDER
dividing .... MULLION
door .... STANG
employee ..... B-GIRL, TENDER,
TAPSTER
for holding hair ..... BARRETTE
for mining .... GAD
habitué .... BARFLY
iron ingot .... BLOOM
legally .... ESTOP
of _____ .... SOAP, METAL,
JUSTICE, CHOCOLATE
of justice .... COURT
of loom .... EASER
order .... CHASER, PEANUTS,
(TROPICAL)DRINK
pin .... BROOCH
room .... SALOON, TAPROOM
sinister .... BATON
slang .... GIN MILL
soap frame .... SESS
square metal .... BILLET
supporting .... FID
used with fulcrum ...... LEVER
Bara, actress .... THEDA
barb ...... AWN, JAG, FLUE, FLUKE,
HORSE, SPIKE, SPINE, STING,
PIGEON, BRISTLE, SHARPNESS
of feather .... HARL, HERL
of wit .... STING
small .... BARBEL, BARBULE
Barbados fish .... GUPPY
native .... BIM, BARBADIAN
Barbara .... BUSH, EDEN, HALE,
RUSH, WALTERS
barbarian .... HUN, GOTH(IC),
BEAST, BRUTE, SAVAGE,
VANDAL, PRIMITIVE
barbarism .... SOLECISM,
IGNORANCE
barbarity .... CRUELTY,

SAVAGERY, VIOLENCE, BRUTALITY

barbarized term/word .... CORRUPTION

barbarous .... CRUEL, BRUTAL, GOTHIC, VULGAR, IGNORANT, PRIMITIVE

Barbary ape .... MAGOT

horse .... BARB

state .... ALGIERS, TUNIS, MOROCCO, TRIPOLI

barbate .... AWNED, BEARDED

barbecue .... BROIL, BURGOO, COOKOUT, ROAST, ROTISSERIE

bar .... SPIT, SKEWER

site .... PATIO, BEACH, BACKYARD

barbed .... HOOKED, CUTTING, STINGING, UNCINATE

dart .... BANDERILLA

missile .... DART, ARROW, SPEAR, HARPOON

point .... FLUE

spear .... GAFF

tool .... HOOK

wire blaster .... BANGALORE

wire obstacle .... ABAT(T)IS

barbel ...... BARB, FISH, BARBULE

fish .... WATTLE

fish with ..... MULLET, CATFISH

barber .... SHAVE(R), SNIPPER, TONSOR, HAIRCUTTER

of Seville .... FIGARO

shop chore .... SHAVE, HAIRCUT, HAIR STYLE

work .... TONSORIAL

barber's call .... NEXT

barbet .... BIRD, POODLE

barbital .... DRUG, VERONAL

barbiturate .... SEDATIVE

slang .... UPPERS, DOWNERS, UPPIES, DOWNIES

Barcarolle composer .... CHOPIN

bard .... POET, SCOP, DRUID, RUNER, MINSTREL, VERSIFIER

Bard of Avon .... SHAKESPEARE

Bard's river .... AVON

specialty .... LAY

bare .... MERE, NUDE, EMPTY, NAKED, STARK, BARREN, STRIP, EXPOSE, SIMPLE, DIVULGE, UNCLOTHED

faced .... OPEN, BRAZEN, SHAMELESS, IMPUDENT, UNCONCEALED

foot .... UNSHOD, SHOELESS

foot pilgrim, car-buyer .... SUCKER

footed .... DISCALCED

headed .... HATLESS, UNCOVERED

in mind .... EMPTY-HEADED

naked .... DENUDE

rock, standing .... SCAR

barely .... JUST, ONLY, HARDLY, MERELY, MEAGERLY, SCANTILY, SCARCELY

bargain .... (GOOD)BUY, CHEAP, BARTER, HAGGLE, TRADE, DICKER, HIGGLE, CONTRACT, NEGOTIATE

closed: colloq. .... DEAL

hunter .... SHOPPER

place .... BASEMENT

strike a .... AGREE

bargainer's delight .... BUYS, REBATE, SALE(S), CUTRATES, DISCOUNT

favorite spot .... BASEMENT

barge .... PUNT, SCOW, CASCO, WHERRY, COLLIDE, (HOUSE)BOAT, LIGHTER

heavy .... HOY

in .... CRASH, ENTER

load of coal .... KEEL

river .... GONDOLA

baric .... BAROMETER

barilla .... SALTWORT

barite .... SPAR

barium monoxide/oxide .... BARYTA

sulfate .... BARITE

bark .... BAY, TAN, YAP, RIND, SKIN, SNAP, TREE, WOOF, BARQUE, BRUISE, YELP, CORTEX, (SAIL)BOAT

aromatic .... CASCARILLA

bitter .... NIEPA, NIOTA, ANGOSTURA, CHINCHONA

buckthorn .... CASCARA

cloth/mulberry .... TAPA

drug from .... BEBEERINE

fiber .... BAST

flavoring .... SASSAFRAS

fragrant .... CANELLA

inner .... BAST, LIBER

laxative .... BEARWOOD

louse .... APHID, APHIS

medicinal ...... COTO, PEREIRA, CHINCHONA

of fear/pain .... YELP

pertaining to .... CORTICAL

remover/stripper ...... SPUDDER

shrill .... YIP, YELP

soap .... QUILLAI

spice/tonic .... CANELLA

tree .... RIND, NIEPA

yielding quinine .... CINCHONA

barkeeper/barman ...... TAPSTER, PUBLICAN, BARTENDER

barker .... TOUT, SPIELER

aide of .... SHILL

talk of .... SPIEL, PATTER

barking .... LATRANT

barley .... BERE, BIGG, GRASS, CEREAL, TSAMBA

beard .... AWN

Indian .... PAPOOSE

liquor .... WHISK(E)Y

meal cake .... BANNOCK

steeped .... MALT

water/drink .... PTISAN

barm .... YEAST

barmy: Brit. sl. .... SILLY, IDIOTIC

barn .... MEWS, SHED, STABLE, BUILDING

bar/pole .... BAIL

bird .... OWL

compartment .... BAY

cow .... BYRE

gallery .... LOFT

owl .... TYTO

part for hay/grain .... (HAY)MOW, (HAY)LOFT

barnacle .... GOOSE, CIRRIPED, SHELLFISH

of a sort .... BUR(R)

Barnacle Bill: sl. .... TAR, SAILOR

barnacles: Brit. colloq. .... EYEGLASSES

barnstorm .... CAMPAIGN

Barnum ...... PHINEAS, SHOWMAN

elephant .... JUMBO

midget .... TOM THUMB

specialty .... CIRCUS

barnyard denizen ...... COW, HEN, COCK, GOAT, TURKEY, ROOSTER

pest .... FOX, WEASEL

sound .... BAA, MOO, CROW, BLEAT, CACKLE

barometer .... ANEROID, OROMETER, STATOSCOPE

barometric .... BARIC

line .... ISOBAR

baron .... TITLE, MAGNATE, (BEEF)SIRLOIN, NOBLEMAN, CAPITALIST

heir apparent of .... MASTER

main dwelling of .... HALL

wife of .... LADY, BARONESS

Baron Munchausen .... PEARL

compiler .... RASPE

baronet's addition to name .... BART

baronial .... GRAND, SHOWY

barony, Japanese .... HAN

baroque .... ORNATE, ROCOCO

barque .... BARK, VESSEL, SAILBOAT

barracks .... ETAPE, CASERN, GARRISON

barracuda .... SPET, PICUDA, SENNET

barrage .... DAM, ATTACK, VOLLEY, BARRIER, BOMBARD, WALL, BACKSTOP, DRUMFIRE

barramunda .... CERATODUS

barranca .... GORGE, RAVINE

barrel .... KEG, VAT, BUTT, CASK, TIERCE, SPEED UP, TUBE, CYLINDER, KILDERKIN

cork/stopper .... BUNG

groove .... CROZE

house .... BAR, SALOON, TAVERN

like container .... DRUM

maker/worker .... COOPER, HOOPER

one part .... FIRKIN

part .... HOOP, STAVE

rim .... CHIMB, CHIME, CHINE

stave .... LAG

staves, set .... SHOOK

barrelful .... CASK

barren .... ARID, BARE, LEAN, BLEAK, BORING, STARK, EMPTY, EFFETE, STERILE, JEJUNE, INFERTILE, DEVOID, UNFRUITFUL

land .... USAR, DESERT, DUSTBOWL

barret .... CAP, BIRETTA

barrette .... BAR, CLASP

barricade .... BARRIER, WALL, OBSTACLE, ABAT(T)IS, FENCE, BLOCKADE, PALISADE, SCREEN, CONSTRUCT, STOCKADE, ROADBLOCK

Barrie (James) play .... MARY ROSE

barrier .... WALL, SCREEN, HINDRANCE, OBSTACLE, RAMPART, OBSTRUCTION

of logs/river .... BOOM

of stakes .... PALISADE, STOCKADE

barrio .... SUBURB

chief .... DAT(T)O

barrister .... LAWYER, ATTORNEY, COUNSELOR

headwear .... WIG

barrow .... PIG, CITY, HILL, MOUND, TRUCK, TUMULUS, HANDCART

type of .... HAND, WHEEL

Barrymore, ___ .... DREW, JOHN, ETHEL, LIONEL, MAURICE

Bart .... BARONET

barter ...... SWAP, TRADE, TRUCK, EXCHANGE

bartizan .... TURRET

Bartlett .... PEAR

Baruch, statesman ...... BERNARD

barytron ...... MESON, MESOTRON

bas bleu .... BLUE-STOCKING

basal .... BASIC, FUNDAMENTAL

basalt .... ROCK, POTTERY

source .... LAVA

basaltic rock .... TRAP, WHIN, GREENSTONE

bascule .... SEESAW

base .... BED, VILE, MEAN, LOW, ROOT, BASIS, FELON, ABJECT, MENIAL, BOTTOM, FLOOR, IMPURE, IGNOBLE, FOUNDATION, HEADQUARTERS

architectural .... SOCLE, PLINTH

attached to .... SESSILE

baseball .... BAG, SACK

coal tar .... ANILINE

hit in baseball .... SINGLE, TRIPLE, TWO-BAGGER

of bird's bill .... CERE

of column .... DADO, PLINTH, PEDESTAL

root .... RADIX

baseball abbreviation .... ERA, RBI

backstop .... CAGE

base .... SACK, PLATE

batting practice .... FUNGO

bungler in .... MUFF

catcher .... RECEIVER

catcher-pitcher combination .... BATTERY

club .... BAT

commissioner .... KUHN, FRICK, LANDIS, VINCENT, CHANDLER, GIAMATTI

curve .... HOOK

earned run average .... ERA

event .... SERIES

field/ground .... DIAMOND

field dispute .... RHUBARB

Hall of Fame name .... AARON, RUTH, COBB, GEHRIG, CAMPANELLA, OTT, SISLER, DIMAGGIO, BANKS, BERRA, YOUNG, MACK, MANTLE, ROBINSON, RICE, MAYS, DEAN, MUSIAL, PLANK, STENGEL, KOUFAX, MARICHAL, CHANDLER, CLEMENTE

hit: sl. .... CLOUT

mistake .... ERROR

pitch ..... SLIDER, CURVE, DROP BALL, SPITBALL, KNUCKLE BALL, FAST BALL

pitch aimed at batter's head .... BEANBALL

pitcher's fault .... BALK

pitcher's stand ..... BOX, SLAB, MOUND

pitcher's warm-up area .... BULLPEN

play ..... ASSIST, DOUBLE, PUT-OUT, SQUEEZE

player of fame .... RUTH, COBB, DIMAGGIO, DEAN, MANTLE, RICE, MAYS, KOUFAX, REESE, SPAHN, ROSE, AARON, ROBINSON, OTT, MARICHAL, MARIS, RYAN, MCCOVEY, JACKSON, WINFIELD, BONDS, CLARK, STEWART, VALENZUELA, HENDERSON, MIZE, PERRY, BENCH, WILLIAMS

player's miss at bat .... FAN, STRIKEOUT

player's position .... SHORTSTOP, PITCHER, CATCHER, FIRST BASE, LEFTFIELD, SECOND BASE, THIRD BASE, RIGHTFIELD, CENTERFIELD

player's shelter .... DUGOUT

Rule 8.02's concern .... SPITBALL

run(s) batted in .... RBI

seventh inning habit of fans .... STRETCH

stadium .... PARK

tactic .... BUNT

team/club .... METS, WHITESOX, CARDINALS, TWINS, SENATORS, TIGERS, PADRES, GIANTS, ORIOLES, ATHLETICS, PHILLIES, ASTROS, YANKEES, BRAVES, ANGELS, INDIANS, REDSOX, DODGERS, PIRATES, MARINERS, BLUE JAYS

team players .... NINE

term .... HOMERUN, LINE DRIVE, FLY BALL, WALK, BASE ON BALLS, BUNT, FIELDER'S CHOICE, CLEAN-UP, GROUND BALL, POP UP, LEFT STRANDED, TOP HALF, BOTTOM, INNING, TYING RUN, PINCH HIT, STOLEN BASE, BASES LOADED, DESIGNATED HITTER

VIP .... UMP(IRE), PITCHER, COMMISSIONER

baseball's Dean .... DIZZY, DAFFY

"fall classic" .... WORLD SERIES

Hank/Henry .... AARON

Mel .... OTT

"Mister Cub" .... BANKS

"Preacher" .... ROE

Ruth .... BABE
"Say Hey" kid .... MAYS
Sparky .... LYLE
"Stretch" .... MCCOVEY
"The Lip"
.... (LEO)DUROCHER
Yogi .... BERRA
baseborn .... BASTARD,
          ILLEGITIMATE
based on 10 .... DECIMAL
baseless .... UNFOUNDED,
          GROUNDLESS, UNSUPPORTED
report/rumor .... HOAX,
          CANARD, IDLE TALK
basely .... IGNOBLY
bash .... PARTY, SMASH, SPREE,
          STRIKE, WINGDING
Bashan King .... OG
Bashaw's title .... AGHA, AGA,
          PASHAM KEMAL, PACHA
bashful .... COY, SHY, TIMID,
          RETIRING, DIFFIDENT,
          SHEEPISH
Bashful of fairy tale ...... DWARF
Bashkir's capital .... UFA
basic .... PRIMARY, ESSENTIAL,
          ELEMENTAL, NATURAL,
          FUNDAMENTAL
law .... CHARTER,
          CONSTITUTION
part .... ROOT, CORNERSTONE
rule .... LAW, CANON,
          PRINCIPLE
basics .... ABC(S)
basidiomycete .... RUST, SMUT,
          MUSHROOM, FUNGUS,
          PUFFBALL
basil .... HERB, PLANT
basilica .... PALACE, TEMPLE,
          LATERAN, COURTROOM
basilisk ...... LIZARD, COCKATRICE
basin .... PAN, BOWL, DOCK, BAY,
          POND, SINK, LAVER, VESSEL,
          RESERVOIR
altar .... PISCINA
holy water .... FONT, ASPER,
          SORIUM, STOOP, STOUP
in geology .... TALA
ornamental .... CUVETTE
basinet .... BASNET, HELMET
basis .... BASE, GROUND,
          FOUNDATION, ROOT, FOOTING
of argument .... PREMISE
bask ...... HEAT, REVEL, FLOURISH,
          SUN(BATHE), SWELTER,
          LUXURIATE
basket .... POT, CAUL, DOSSER,
          GABION, HAMPER, PANNIER,
          SCUTTLE
abbreviation .... BKT
baby .... BASSINET

balloon .... CAR, NACELLE
coal/ore .... CORF, SCUTTLE
fiber .... RAFFIA
figs ..... CABAS, FRAIL, TAPNET
fish .... CREEL, WICKER
fruits/grains/vegetables
..... PUNNET, POTTLE, SCUTTLE,
          CALATHUS
hop-picker's .... BIN
material .... RUSH, OSIER,
          RAFFIA, WILLOW, REED,
          WOOD, WICKER, BAMBOO,
          RATTAN, SPLINT
official papers .... HANAFER
pack animal .... DOSSER,
          PANNIER
pelotari's .... CESTA
raisins .... FRAIL
rummy .... CANASTA
sculptured .... CORBEIL
symbol of abundance
.... CALATHUS
wicker .... CORF, HANAFER,
          BASSINET
basketball basket .... CAGE, HOOP
club (NBA):
Atlanta .... HAWKS
Boston .... CELTICS
Charlotte .... HORNETS
Chicago .... BULLS
Cleveland .... CAVALIERS
Dallas .... MAVERICKS
Denver .... NUGGETS
Detroit .... PISTONS
Golden State ...... WARRIORS
Houston .... ROCKETS
Indiana .... PACERS
Los Angeles .... LAKERS,
          CLIPPERS
Miami .... HEAT
Milwaukee .... BUCKS
Minnesota
.... TIMBERWOLVES
New Jersey .... NETS
New York .... KNICKS,
          KNICKERBOCKERS
Orlando .... MAGIC
Philadelphia ...... (SEVENTY-)
          SIXERS
Phoenix .... SUNS
Portland .... TRAILBLAZERS
Sacramento .... KINGS
San Antonio .... SPURS
Seattle .... (SUPER)SONICS
Utah .... JAZZ
Washington .... BULLETS
maneuver .... PRESS, LAY-UP,
DRIBBLE, FREEZE, FAST BREAK
player .... GUARD, CAGER,
          CENTER, FORWARD
player of fame .... WEST,

          GALE, GREER, LUCAS, REED,
          BAYLOR, BRADLEY, BARRY,
          CHAMBERLAIN, JABBAR,
          DEBUSSCHERE, RUSSELL,
          THOMPSON, JORDAN, JOHNSON
team .... FIVE, QUINT(ET)
basking shark .... SAILFISH
basque .... BLOUSE, BODICE,
          TUNIC
Basque .... IBERIAN
cap .... BERET
game .... PELOTA
land .... EUZKADI
pelota player .... PELOTARI
province .... ALVA, BISCAY,
          SOULE, LABOURD, NAVARRA,
          VISCAYA, GUIPUZCOA
Basra native .... IRAQI
bass .... LOW, BAST, DEEP
black .... CHUB
double .... VIOL
double-reed .... OBOE,
          BASSOON
European .... BRASSE
horn .... TUBA
like fish .... SNAPPER
sea .... JEWFISH
stop of organ .... BOURDON
viol .... CONTRABASS
voice .... DRONE
wind instrument ...... HELICON
basset .... DOG, HOUND
horn .... CLARINET
bassinet .... BASKET, CRADLE,
          (BABY)BED
bassoon .... OBOE, WOODWIND
basswood .... LINDEN, LIME(TREE),
          WAHOO
bast .... BARK, BASS, FIBER,
          RAMIE, PHLOEM
fiber .... CATENA
like .... LIBRIFORM
bastard .... SHAM, FRAUD,
          BYBLOW, COUNTERFEIT,
          ILLEGITIMATE, MISBEGOT(TEN)
wing of bird .... ALULA
baste .... SEW, BEAT, TACK,
          ABUSE, STRIKE, THRASH,
          MOISTEN
bastille .... TOWER, PRISON,
          FORTRESS
bastinado .... ROD, STICK,
          CUDGEL
bastion .... BULWARK, DEFENSE
Basutoland capital ...... MASERU
bat .... CLUB, STICK, CUDGEL,
          CHUNK, FLYING FOX,
          NOCTULE, HAMMERHEAD
an eye .... WINK, BLINK
blood-sucking .... VAMPIRE
colloquial .... BLOW, WINK,

BLINK, SPEED, SPREE, FLUTTER
flying .... KALONG
for .... DEFEND, ADVOCATE
hold on .... GRIP
like/wing-footed .... ALIPED
like fish .... GURNARD,
    GURNET, (STING)RAY
manure .... GUANO
mining .... SHALE
Ping-Pong .... PADDLE
tennis .... RACKET, RACQUET
batch ...... LOT, RUN, SET, GROUP,
    SERIES
bate ...... SOAK, REDUCE, DIMINISH
bateau .... BOAT
batfish .... RAY, SKATE,
    (FLYING)GURNARD, DIABOLO,
    STINGRAY, STINGAREE
bath .... DIP, SOAK, WASH, STEEP,
    PLUNGE, ABLUTION
kind of .... MILK, SAUNA,
    SHOWER, SWEDISH, TURKISH,
    JACUZZI, WHIRLPOOL
therapeutic .... WET PACK
tub .... TOSH
Bath's river .... AVON
bathe .... WET, LAVE, WASH,
    MOISTEN, SUFFUSE
bathhouse ...... BAGNIO, CABANA,
    SAUNA
bathing, of .... BALNEAL
suit .... BIKINI
batho: as prefix .... DEPTH
batholite .... GRANITE
bathos .... ANTICLIMAX
bathroom .... HEAD, TOILET,
    WATER CLOSET
fixture .... TUB, URINAL,
    COMMODE
baths .... THERMAE
Bathsheba's father .... ANMIEL
husband .... DAVID, URIA(H)
mother .... SHEBA
son .... SOLOMON, NATHAN,
    SHIMEA, SHOBATH
Bathurst is capital of
    .... GAMBIA
batiste .... LINEN, MUSLIN,
    CAMBRAI
batman .... ORDERLY, SERVANT
slang .... GOFER
baton .... ROD, STAFF, STICK,
    TRUNCHEON
fairy's .... WAND
jester's .... BAUBLE
race .... RELAY
twirler .... MAJORETTE
wielder ...... SOUSA, BEECHAM,
    MAGICIAN, WALTER,
    BERNSTEIN, CONDUCTOR,
    TOSCANINI

batrachian .... FROG, TOAD,
    AMPHIBIAN
bats .... LOCO, CRAZY
batten .... FASTEN, THRIVE,
    OVERFEED, WOODSTRIP
batter .... RAM, BEAT, POUND,
    SMASH
cake .... PANCAKE, WAFFLE,
    CRUMPET, FLAPJACK
in cricket .... BATSMAN
battered baby syndrome
    .... CHILD ABUSE
battering machine .... RAM
ram of ship .... BEAK
battery .... CELL, ARRAY, ATTACK,
    BEATING, ARTILLERY
compartment .... CELL
floating .... PRAM
kind of .... SOLAR, STORAGE
material .... ACID
part .... ANODE, PLATE,
    CATHODE
partner of .... ASSAULT
plate .... GRID
batting, manner of .... FUNGO
order .... LINEUP
battle .... WAR, FIGHT, COMBAT,
    CONTEST, CONFLICT, SIEGE,
    ATTACK, HOSTILITIES
area .... RING, ARENA, FIELD,
    FRONT, SECTOR, THEATER,
    BEACHHEAD, NO-MAN'S-LAND
avoidance .... FABIAN
ax .... GISARME, HATCHET,
    TWIBIL(L), TOMAHAWK
ax: sl. .... NAG, SHREW,
    AMAZON, VIRAGO
combatant .... SOLDIER,
    WARRIOR
cry .... BANZAI, REBEL-YELL,
    TOM-TOM, TO HORSE,
    (WAR)WHOOP
dress .... ARMOR
fatigue .... TRAUMA
formation .... ARRAY,
    ECHELON, PHALANX, HERSE,
    DEPLOYMENT
of politicians .... CAMPAIGN
of the _____ .... SEXES
of wits ..... BANTER, REPARTEE
of words .... DEBATE,
    ARGUMENT
plane .... SPAD, FIGHTER,
    SPITFIRE, ZERO, BOMBER,
    SABREJET
relic .... SCAR, TROPHY
royal .... MELEE, BRAWL,
    RUMBLE, FREE-FOR-ALL
scarred fighter ...... VET(ERAN)
site, 1776 .... LONG ISLAND
site, 1991 .... PERSIAN GULF

trophy of Indian .... SCALP
victim .... CASUALTY
Battle of Hastings site
    .... SENLAR
battledore .... BAT, CLUB,
    PADDLE, RACKET
battlement .... FORT, BASTION,
    RAMPART
part of .... MERLON,
    EMBRASURE, CRENEL(LE)
Battles of 1429 .... ORLEANS
battleship .... GALLEON, CRUISER,
    MAN O(F) WAR, DESTROYER,
    DREADNAUGHT
gun turret .... CUPOLA
slang .... BATTLE WAGON
battue .... HUNT, MASSACRE
batty .... CRAZY, INSANE,
    ECCENTRIC
bauble ...... TOY, BEAD, DOODAD,
    GEWGAW, GIMCRACK, TRIVIA,
    TRINKET
baudekin .... BROCADE,
    BALDACHIN
baudrons: Scot .... CAT
Bauhaus school founder
    .... GROPIUS
Bavaria, capital of .... MUNICH
German name .... BAYERN
Bavarian city .... HOF,
    BAYREUTH, NUREMBERG
river .... ISAR, EGER, MAIN,
    ILLER
weight .... GRAN
bawbee .... COIN, HALF-PENNY
bawd .... MADAM, PROCURESS
bawdy .... LEWD, GROSS, COARSE,
    RIBALD, OBSCENE, INDECENT
house .... BAGNIO, BROTHEL
bawl ...... CRY, SOB, HOWL, YELL,
    WEEP, SHOUT, BELLOW
out/colloquial .... SCOLD,
    REPROVE, REPRIMAND
bay .... ARCH, BARK, COVE, BIGHT,
    INLET, ALCOVE, WING,
    BAYOU, ESTUARY, HOWL,
    FIORD, ULULATE
bring to .... TREE, CORNER
color .... ROAN, CHESTNUT
horse .... ROAN, BAYARD,
    SORREL
keep at .... HOLD(OFF)
name of .... VOE, BAFFIN,
    BISCAY, MANILA, CAMPECHE,
    GALVESTON
sound ...... BARK, HOWL, PEAL,
    BLARE, NEIGH
sweet .... BREWSTER
tree .... LAUREL
window .... ORIEL, PAUNCH,
    MIRADOR, (POT)BELLY

Bay of Biscay city/resort
.... BIARRITZ
of Biscay river .... LOIRE
State .... MASSACHUSETTS
bayard .... HORSE, KNIGHT
Baylor eleven .... BEARS
bayou .... CREEK, INLET,
BACKWATER, EVERGLADES
bazaar ...... MART, SHOP, RIALTO,
MARKET(PLACE)
church/club .... FAIR, SALE
bbl. .... BARREL
bdl. .... BUNDLE
be .... ARE, EXIST, OCCUR,
BELONG, HAPPEN, TAKE
PLACE
a match .... COPE
a success .... CLICK
a tenant farmer .... SHARE-
CROP
at habitually .... HAUNT,
FREQUENT
cool! .... SIMMER DOWN
deficient .... WANT
elated .... TREAD ON AIR
glad .... REJOICE
jubilant .... EXULT
obligated to .... OWE
of use .... AVAIL, UTILE,
SERVICEABLE
off .... ERR
on one's guard .... BEWARE
overly fond .... DOTE, ADORE
silent, in music .... TACE(T)
still .... SSH, HUSH, QUIET,
SHUT-UP
successful .... ARRIVE
suitable .... BELONG
thrifty .... WASTE NOT, WANT
NOT
your age .... BEHAVE
beach .... SANDS, SHORE, GROUND,
STRAND, COAST(LINE)
bath house .... CABANA
bird .... SANDERLING
California .... PEBBLE,
IMPERIAL
fixture .... LIFESAVER,
UMBRELLA, LIFEGUARD,
SUNBATHER
Florida .... MIAMI, ORMOND,
POMPANO
Hawaii .... WAIKIKI
on the: colloq.
.... UNEMPLOYED
panhandler ..... BEACHCOMBER
pest .... SANDFLY
problem .... EROSION
walk .... BOARDWALK,
ESPLANADE
wave over .... COMBER

beacon .... BEAM, BUOY, GUIDE,
PHAROS, SIGNAL, SIGNAL
FIRE, LIGHTHOUSE
light .... CRESSET
on summit .... PIKE
Beaconsfield, Earl of
.... DISRAELI
bead .... DROP, BUBBLE, BALL,
PELLET, GLOBULE
draw one on .... AIM
for trimming dresses
.... BUGLE
gun muzzle's .... SIGHT
money .... PEAG, WAMPUM
beaded moisture .... DEW
beadhouse .... ALMSHOUSE
beading .... GADROON
beadle .... MESSENGER, MACE-
BEARER
of fiction .... BUMBLE
beads .... NECKLACE
Indian .... PEAG(E), WAMPUM
of perspiration .... SWEAT
prayer .... ROSARY, CHAPLET
beadsman .... BEGGAR, PRAYER
beagle .... DOG, HOUND
beak .... NEB, NIB, BILL, NOSE,
ROSTRUM
like process .... ROSTELLUM
of a pitcher .... SPOUT
ship's .... RAM, PROW
slang .... NOSE, SNOUT, JUDGE,
MAGISTRATE
trim with .... PREEN
beaked .... HOOKED, CROOKED,
AQUILINE
beaker .... CUP, GOBLET
beam .... RAY, GLOW, SHINE,
SIGNAL, SMILE, RADIATE,
DIRECT, ASHLAR, JOIST,
GLEAM, RAFTER, CROSSBAR,
SCANTLING
architectural .... TEMPLET,
TEMPLATE
monochromatic .... LASER
off the .... LOST, AMISS,
WRONG
on the .... KEEN, ALERT, RIGHT
supporting .... GIRDER
tie .... BALK
underside .... SOFFIT
beaming .... HAPPY, RADIANT,
SMILING
beamy .... BROAD, BRIGHT,
JOYOUS, MASSIVE
bean .... GOA, POD, SEED, LIMA,
SOY(A), ARBOR, PINTO,
TONKA, LEGUME
counter .... ACCOUNTANT
dish .... SUCCOTASH
flour/meal .... FARINA

fly .... MIDAS
kidney ..... HARICOT, FRIJOL(E)
like plant .... SAINFOIN
lima .... HABA
locust .... CAROB
Mexican .... FRIJOL(E)
mottled .... PINTO
oil .... CASTOR
Oriental .... MONGO, MUNGO
parasite .... BEETLE, WEEVIL
poisonous .... CALABAR
restaurant .... BEANERY
sauce .... SOY
seed .... SOY, PULSE
shaped seed, other plants
.... COFFEE
slang .... HEAD, MIND, BRAIN
soy .... SOJA
stalk/stem .... HA(U)LM
tree .... CAROB, CATALPA
used for counting .... BEANO
versatile .... SOY(A)
white .... PEA
yonka .... GUAIAC
beanie/beany .... (SKULL)CAP
beano .... BINGO
beans, don't know: sl. ...... DUMB
full of: sl. .... ALL WET
spill the: colloq. .... LET THE
CAT OUT OF THE BAG
bear .... HOLD, TOTE, WEAR,
CARRY, ENDURE, SUFFER,
SHOW, CONVEY, SUSTAIN,
ALLOW, BRUIN, STAND,
TOLERATE, TRANSPORT
black-and-white .... PANDA
brown .... URSUS
down .... PUSH, PRESS
down on .... CHARGE
honey .... KINKAJOU
in mind .... REMEMBER
like .... URSINE, URSIFORM
like animal ..... KOALA, PANDA
out .... CONFIRM, SUPPORT,
CORROBORATE
sky .... URSA
squeeze of a .... HUG
Syrian .... DUBB
that was a nymph
.... CALLISTO
variety .... BLACK, BROWN,
HONEY, POLAR, GRIZZLY
with .... ENDURE, PUT UP,
TOLERATE
witness .... ATTEST, TESTIFY
woolly .... WOOBUT,
CATERPILLAR
young .... CUB, WHELP
bearberry .... HOLLY, SHRUB
bearcat .... CIVET, PANDA
beard .... BARB, DEFY, GOATEE,

BARBEL, IMPERIAL, WHISKERS, BURNSIDES
disease of the .... SYCOSIS
grain .... AWN, ARISTA
hairlike .... CRINITE
pointed ..... GOATEE, VANDYKE
red .... BARBAROSSA
short growth .... STUBBLE
the lion .... TAME, SUBDUE
bearded .... AWNED, HAIRY, GOATEED, BARBATE, HIRSUTE, ARISTATE, WHISKERED
butter .... GOA
grass .... RYE
one .... IRIS
seal .... MAKLUK
beardless .... SHAVEN, YOUNG, CALLOW, HAIRLESS, YOUTHFUL
bearer in India .... SIRDAR
of the world: myth ...... ATLAS
bearing ...... AIR, MIEN, MANNER, RELATION, CARRIAGE, MEANING, CONDUCT, DEMEANOR, PRESENCE, CARRYING
twins .... BIPAROUS
writer's name .... ONYMOUS
bearish .... RUDE, ROUGH, CROSS, SURLY
bear's breech .... ACANTHUS
foot .... HELLEBORE
skin .... (FOR)CAP
bearwood .... CASCARA
beast .... BRUTE, ANIMAL, QUADRUPED
huge .... MONSTER, BEHEMOTH, MASTODON
like .... THEROID
of burden .... ASS, MULE, BURRO, CAMEL, YAK, LLAMA, DONKEY, ONAGER, CARABAO
of prey .... LION, TIGER, WOLVERINE
beastly .... BESTIAL, ILL-BRED, RUDE, BRUTAL, VULGAR, BRUSQUE, THEROID, HARSH, DISGUSTING
beasts, king of .... LION
beat .... MIX, CANE, RHYTHM, PULSE, PULSATE, POUND, POMMEL, CADENCE, WHIP, FLOG, FLAIL, FORGE, THROB, BATTER, ACCENT, LACE, DEFEAT, CONQUER, TEMPO, PUMMEL, TROUNCE, DRUB, THRASH, LAMBASTE
back .... REPEL, REPULSE
colloquial .... WHALE, LARRUP, SHELLACK
dead .... CHEAT, WELSHER

group member .... BEATNIK
in a race .... OUTRAN
in foil .... FOLIATE
in journalism .... SCOOP, ASSIGNMENT
into plate/thin .... MALLEATE
it! ...... SCAT, GET LOST, SHOO, SCRAM
off .... REJECT, RESIST
on the .... IN TUNE, ATEMPO, ATTUNED
police .... ROUND
repeatedly ..... FLOG, CLOBBER
slang .... LAM, PASTE, POOP OUT, TIRED, EXHAUSTED
soles of feet with stick .... BASTINADO
soundly .... DRUB, ROUT, WALLOP, OVERWHELM
to softness .... MASH
up .... MAUL, THRASH
with stick .... CLUB, DRUB, CUDGEL, BASTINADO
with whip .... FLOG, LASH
beatable .... WEAK, VINCIBLE, VULNERABLE
beaten path .... TRAIL
beatific .... JOYFUL, BLISSFUL
beatify .... BLESS, HALLOW, SANCTIFY
beating .... DEFEAT, PULSATION, PUNISHMENT
of person .... BATTERY
underbrush to flush game .... BATTUE, BATTING
Beatles, former manager of .... EPSTEIN
one of the .... LENNON, STARR, HARRISON, MCCARTNEY
beatnik .... HEPCAT, HIPSTER, BOHEMIAN
Beatrice's lover .... DANTE
beau .... LOVER, FELLOW, COURTER, SUITOR, SWEETHEART
colloquial .... BF, SPARK
geste .... GALLANTRY
ideal .... NERO
monde .... JET SET
monde's center .... SALON
plural of .... BEAUX
Beau Brummell ...... FOP, DANDY
beaucaire .... MONSIEUR
beaut .... LULU
beautician .... COIFFURIST, HAIRSTYLIST, HAIRDRESSER, MANICURIST
beautiful .... CUTE, FAIR, LOVELY, COMELY, PRETTY, STUNNING, DAINTY, ELEGANT, HANDSOME, ATTRACTIVE

eyes .... TULIPS
girl: sl. .... LULU
poetic .... BEAUTEOUS
slang ..... SHARP, PRETTY AS A PICTURE
woman .... PERI, NYMPH, CHARMER, GODDESS, HEBE, VENUS, HOURI, ENCHANTRESS
beauty, a .... ACE, LULU, DOLL, PERFECT, DAZZLER, STUNNER, KNOCKOUT
famous .... CLEOPATRA, APHRODITE, HELEN OF TROY
reigning .... BELLE
of form, etc. .... GRACE
parlor dye .... HENNA
parlor specialty .... SET, WAVE, FACIAL, MASSAGE, SHAMPOO, PERMANENT, HAIRCUT, MANICURE, MAKE-UP, DYE, PEDICURE
parlor worker .... MASSEUR, HAIRDRESSER, BEAUTICIAN, HAIRSTYLIST, MANICURIST, BARBER, PEDICURIST
shop .... SALON, PARLOR
spot .... MOLE, PATCH
beaver .... FUR, (SILK)HAT, ANIMAL
den of .... LODGE
describing one/beaverlike? .... EAGER
eager .... DOER, HUSTLER
fur hat/of armor .... CASTOR
like animal .... COYPU, NUTRIA
oily substance .... CASTOR(EUM)
skin .... PLEW
Beaver State .... OREGON
bebop .... JAZZ
because .... SINCE, OWING TO, INASMUCH
bêche-de-mer ...... TREPANG, SEA CUCUMBER
beck ...... NOD, BECKON, STREAM, SUMMON
partner of .... CALL
beckon .... CALL, LURE, ENTICE, SIGNAL, SUMMON
becloud .... DARKEN, MUDDLE, CONFUSE
become .... GROW, SUIT, BEFIT, CHANGE, TURN INTO, BEHOOVE, DEVELOP
cheese-like .... CASEFY
different .... CHANGE
dull .... BORE, PALL, HEBETATE
extinct .... DIE
forfeit .... LAPSE
less stern .... THAW, RELENT, SOFTEN

red in face ...... FLUSH, BLUSH, COLOR

shabby .... GO TO SEED

void for cause .... LAPSE

well .... HEAL

becoming .... FIT, PROPER, SEEMLY

bed .... COT, KIP, BASE, BUNK, SACK, COUCH, BOTTOM, RESTING PLACE, PALLET, STRATUM

and board .... HOME, KEEP

awning .... CANOPY

baby's .... CRIB, CRADLE

built-in .... BUNK, BERTH

canopy .... TESTER

clothes .... LINEN, SHAMS, SHEETS, RUFFLES, PILLOWS, BLANKETS

coils .... SPRINGS

covering ...... COVERLET, PUFF, QUILT, COMFORTER, TESTER, (BED)SPREAD

curtain/drapery .... VALANCE

frame .... STEAD

hanging .... HAMMOCK

kind of .... ROSES, OYSTER

maker .... CHAMBERMAID

of plants .... GARDEN

of roses: colloq. .... COMFORT, EASE, LUXURY

ore .... REEF

pest .... BEDBUG

river .... CHANNEL

size .... TWIN, FULL, KING, QUEEN, SINGLE

slang .... BAG, DOSS, SACK

small .... COT, CRIB, PALLET, BASSINET

straw .... PALLET

stream .... WADI, WADY, DONGA, ARROYO

type .... DAY, BUNK, SOFA, BERTH, HAMMOCK, TRUNDLE, ROLL-AWAY, FOLDING, HOSPITAL, WATER, FOUR-POSTER, MATRIMONIAL

bedaub .... PAINT, SMEAR, SMUDGE

bedbug .... CIMEX, CHINCH, VERMIN

bedding, hay/leaves/straw .... LITTER

Bede, ____ .... ADAM, THE VENERABLE

bedeck .... TRIM, ADORN, EMBELLISH

bedevil .... WORRY, HARASS, PESTER, PLAGUE, TORMENT

bedew .... MOISTEN

bedfellow .... ASSOCIATE, CO-

WORKER, COMPANION

bedizen .... ADORN

bedlam .... ASYLUM, UPROAR, TURMOIL, DISORDER, MADHOUSE, CONFUSION

Bedloe island .... LIBERTY

bedmate .... WIFE, SPOUSE, HUSBAND

Bedouin ...... ARAB, RIFF, NOMAD, BERBER, WANDERER

headband cord .... AGAL

home of .... SAHARA

tribe .... ABSI, AMALEKITE

bedraggled .... UNTIDY, UNKEMPT, UNCOMBED

bedrock .... BOTTOM

bedroom .... CABIN, CHAMBER, CUBICLE

caretaker .... CHAMBERMAID

eyes .... GAZE, GLOWER

bedside character .... DOCTOR, NURSE, (BABY)SITTER

manners, describing .... BALMY, GENTLE, CHEERFUL, SOOTHING, REASSURING

bedstead ...... CHARPAI, CHARPOY, FOUR-POSTER

bedtime .... CURFEW

story: colloq. ..... YARN, FAIRY TALE, EXPLANATION

bedwarf .... BELITTLE

bee .... APIS, INSECT, SOCIAL, MEETING, GATHERING, WORKER, STINGER, HYMENOPTERA

balm ..... PLANT, (OSWEGO)TEA

bird .... FLYCATCHER

birling .... ROLEO

colony/workplace .... HIVE

eater/martin .... KINGBIRD

family .... APIDAE, APOIDEA

female .... QUEEN

girl named after .... MELISSA

glue/caulking substance .... PROPOLIS

hive/house .... NIDUS, SKEP, APIARY

in one's bonnet .... KINK

keeper ..... APIARIAN, APIARIST

keeping .... APICULTURE

killer .... ROBBERFLY

kind of .... QUEEN, DRONE, WORKER, SEWING, BUMBLE, SPELLING, QUILTING, SHUCKING

like/of a .... APIAN

male .... DRONE

nest-building .... CARDER

nose of .... LOR(UM)

plant .... BALM, CLOVER,

SPIDERFLOWER

pollen brush of .... SCOPA

secretion .... WAX

social .... WASP, HORNET

sound ...... HUM, BUZZ, DRONE

tree .... LINDEN, BASSWOOD

wax .... CEROTIC

beebread .... AMBROSIA

beech .... NUT, TREE, WOOD, ROBLE

beechnuts .... MAST

beef .... OX, COW, BULL, MEAT, STEER, CATTLE

alternative .... VEAL

braised .... POT ROAST

cattle breed .... ANGUS, GALLOWAY, GUERNSEY, HEREFORD, HOLSTEIN

colloquial .... GRIPE, PEEVE, COMPLAIN(T)

corned/tinned .... BULLY

cut .... RIBS, CHUCK, RUMP, ROUND, BRISKET, LOIN, SHANK, KNUCKLE, SADDLE, SIRLOIN

dish .... MIROTON, PASTRAMI, MEATLOAF, STEW, CHILI-CON-CARNE

double sirloin .... BARON

dried .... JERKY, BUCCAN, CHARQUI

food for explorers .... PEM(M)ICAN

nearest shoulder .... CLOD

roast ..... POT, ROLLED, BLADE, (PRIME)RIB, RUMP, CHUCK, LONDON BROIL

rolled .... PASTRAMI

slang .... BRAWN, MUSCLE

steak .... CLUB, CUBED, T-BONE, RIB-EYE, SIRLOIN, TENDERLOIN, PORTERHOUSE, FLANK, FILLET, MINUTE, NEW YORK, SALISBURY

stew .... GOULASH, POT-AU-FEU

tea .... BROTH

up .... FATTEN, INCREASE, STRENGTHEN

Beef State .... NEBRASKA

beefeater .... ESCORT, YEOMAN, GUARDSMAN

beefwood .... TOA

beefy ...... HEAVY, MEATY, STOUT, BRAWNY, FLESHY, MUSCULAR, CORPULENT

beehive .... SKEP, APIARY, BEEGUM, WORKPLACE

Beehive State .... UTAH

beekeeper ... APIARIAN, SKEPPER, APIARIST, SKEPPIST

beeline .... SHORTCUT

Beelzebub .... DEVIL, SATAN
beep .... CALL, HONK, PEAL, TOOT,
SOUND
beer ...... ALE, BOCK, SUDS, MALT,
KVAS(S), LAGER, STOUT,
PORTER, BITTERS, WEISS,
PILSNER, BEVERAGE
cask ..... KEG, TUN, PUNCHEON
cup/mug .... TOBY, STEIN,
SEIDEL
flavor .... HOPS, MULL
foam .... BEAD, HEAD, FROTH
glass .... SCHOONER
house .... INN, PUB, FARO,
GARDEN, PARLOR, SALOON,
TAVERN
ingredient/material .... HOPS,
MALT, MASH, MEAL, YEAST
inventor/king .... GAMBRINUS
kind of .... DARK, LIGHT,
GINGER
make .... BREW
party .... WASSAIL
plant .... HOPS, BREWERY
slang .... SUDS
sour .... KVAS(S)
spiced/sweetened .... FLIP
strong .... MUM, STINGO
sweeten and flavor .... MULL
weak .... SWIPES
beery .... TIPSY, DRUNKEN,
MAUDLIN
bees, feeding on .... APIVOROUS
genus of .... APIS
pertaining to .... APIAN
structure of wax cells made
by .... HONEYCOMB
study of .... APIOLOGY
substance produced by
.... HONEY
beet .... ROOT, CHARD, PLANT,
MANGEL
crushed .... MEGASS(E)
sugar .... SUCROSE,
SACCHAROSE
Beethoven's Archduke, e.g.
.... TRIO
birthplace .... BONN
composition .... MINUET,
MISSA SOLEMNIS
forte .... SONATA
opera .... FIDELIO
teacher .... NEEFE, HAYDN
third symphony .... EROICA
beetle .... DOR, CLUB, MELOE,
SCARAB, WEEVIL, ELATER(ID),
CURCULIO, EARWIG, MALLET,
SKIPJACK, SAWYER, SNAPPER,
WHIRLIGIG
blister .... MELOID
browed .... SULLEN,

FROWNING, SCOWLING
buzzing/click .... DOR,
ELATER, SNAPPER
dung .... COCKCHAFER
fruit-eater ...... JUNE BUG, FIG-
EATER
gaudy .... LADYBUG, LADYBIRD
grain .... CADELLE
grapevine .... THRIP
ground .... AMARA
head .... NITWIT, BLOCKHEAD
larva .... GRUB, BEEWOLF,
GRUGRU, CADELLE
like charm .... SCARAB
like insect .... EARWIG
order of .... COLEOPTERA
sacred to Egyptians
.... SCARAB
snouted .... CURCULIO
tree .... GIRDLER
wing cover .... SHARD,
ELYTRON
with club-shaped feelers
.... CLAVICORN
wood .... SAWYER
beetling .... PROJECTING,
OVERHANGING
befall .... HAP, COME, PASS,
OCCUR, BETIDE, HAPPEN
befit .... FIT, SUIT, BECOME,
BEHOOVE
befitting .... PROPER, SUITABLE,
APPROPRIATE
holiness .... SAINTLY
befog .... BLUR, CONFUSE,
OBSCURE
befool ...... DUPE, TRICK, DECEIVE
before .... ERE, AHEAD, PRIOR,
FORWARD, PREVIOUS,
FORMERLY, PRECEDING
all others .... FIRST
corn and form .... UNI
craftsy .... ARTSY
long .... ANON, SOON,
SHORTLY, PRESENTLY
mentioned .... SAME, DITTO
prefix .... PRE, ANTE
befoul .... SOIL, DIRTY
befuddle .... CONFUSE, STUPEFY
beg .... ASK, PRAY, MOOCH,
PLEAD, BESEECH, ENTREAT,
IMPLORE, REQUEST,
IMPORTUNE, PANHANDLE
off .... EXCUSE, ASK OUT,
DECLINE
the question .... EVADE
beget .... SIRE, FATHER, PRODUCE,
ENGENDER, GENERATE,
PROCREATE
beggar .... FAKIR, LAZAR, RANDY,
PAUPER, RASCAL, DERVISH,

LAZZARONE, PLEADER,
PANHANDLER, MENDICANT,
SCHNORRER
equipment of .... TINCUP
gift to .... ALMS, HANDOUT
roving .... FAKIR, GANGREL,
GABERLUNZIE
speech of .... CANT
beggarly .... MEAN, PETTY
beggars' lice .... BUR(R),
CLEAVERS
patron saint .... GILES
begging, practice of
...... MENDICITY, MENDICANCY
begin .... OPEN, ARISE, START,
COMMENCE, INITIATE, LEAD
OFF, ORIGINATE
beginner .... TIRO, TYRO, NOVICE,
ROOKIE, ACOLYTE, PUPIL,
NEOPHYTE, FRESHMAN,
GREENHORN, APPRENTICE
beginning .... GERM, ROOT,
INFANCY, ONSET, ORIGIN,
START, OPENING, GENESIS,
OUTSET, KICKOFF, INITIAL,
BIRTH, PREFACE, INCEPTION
Begone! .... SCAT, SHOO, BEAT IT,
SCRAM, AROINT, AVAUNT,
GET LOST
begrime ...... SOIL, DIRTY, SMEAR,
SMUDGE
begrudge .... ENVY, COVET,
REFUSE, GRUMBLE, OBJECT TO
beguile .... LURE, CHARM,
MISLEAD, DELUDE, DIVERT,
VAMP, AMUSE, COZEN,
DECEIVE
beguilements .... ARTS
Beguin .... BEGHARD
begum Indian .... PRINCESS
behalf .... SAKE, SIDE, BENEFIT,
STEAD, INTEREST, ADVANTAGE
behave .... ACT, BEAR, CARRY,
DEPORT, COMPORT, CONDUCT
foolishly .... FRIBBLE
behavior .... ACTION, BEARING,
CONDUCT, MANNERS,
ACTUATION
in polite society
.... ETIQUETTE
science of .... ETHOLOGY
behead .... DECOLLATE,
DECAPITATE
behemoth ...... BEAST, ELEPHANT,
HIPPO(POTAMUS)
behest .... ORDER, BIDDING,
COMMAND
behind .... LATE, ABAFT, ASTERN,
(A)REAR, DELAYED,
BACKWARD
colloquial .... BUTTOCKS

on payment of debt .... IN ARREARS

time(s) .... LATE, PASSE, TARDY, OVERDUE, OUTMODED

Behold! .... LO, SEE, VOILA

beholden ...... OBLIGED, INDEBTED

behoove .... INCUMBENT UPON

beige .... TAN, ECRU, GRAYISH

being .... LIFE, ENTITY, PERSON, CREATURE, EXISTENCE

abstract .... ENS, ENTIA

actual .... ESSE

essential .... ENS

individual .... MONAD

Beirut is capital of .... LEBANON

bejewel .... BEGEM

Bela Lugosi's pet .... BAT

belabor ...... BEAT, WHIP, POUND, ATTACK

belated .... TARDY

belay .... HOLD, STOP, SECURE

belaying cleat .... KEVEL, BOLLARD

belch .... BURP, EMIT, GUSH, VOMIT, ERUCT(ATE)

beldam .... HAG, CRONE, ALECTO, MEGAER, ERINYES

beleaguer .... BESIEGE, SURROUND

beleaguerment .... SIEGE

Belem is capital of .... PARA

belemite .... THUNDERSTONE

belfry .... BELL TOWER

dweller .... BAT

Belgian .... FLEMING, FLEMISH, WALLOON

battlesite in WWI .... YPRES

canal .... ALBERT

capital .... BRUSSELS

city/town .... AALST, ANTWERP, ARLON, ALOST, BALEN, GHENT, BERCHEM, JETTE, BRUGES, DEURNE, MONS, DOORNIK, LIEGE, SPA, LOUVAIN, TOURNAI, HUY, ROULERS, MECHELEN, NAMEN, YPRES, SERAING, BOOM, OSTEND, JEMAPPES, VORST, HOBOKEN, VILVORDE, HASSELT, ZOTTEGEM

commune .... ANS, ATH, NAMUR, VORST, JETTE, LEDE, NIEL, ROUX, SPA, TAMINES

Congo river .... UELE

currency unit .... BELGA, FRANC

dog .... SCHIPPERKE

fascist party .... REX

forest .... ARDENNES

hare/rodent .... LEPORID

highest point .... BOTRANGE

king, former .... ALBERT, LEOPOLD, BAUDOUIN

marble .... RANCE, RANSE

mountain .... VAALSERBERG, BOTRANGE, WEISSERSTEIN

plateau .... HOHE VENN, SCHNEE EIFEL, ZITTERWALD

police .... GENDARME

port .... OSTEND

possession, former ..... CONGO

province ...... ANTWERP, LIEGE, EAST FLANDERS, NAMUR, WEST FLANDERS, HAINAUT, BRABANT, LIMBURG, LUXEMBOURG

queen .... ASTRID

reclaimed land .... POLDER

resort .... SPA, OSTEND

river .... LYS, YSER, DYLE, DEOLE, DENDER, MARK, NETHE, LESSE, SENNE, MEUSE, SAMBRE, RUPEL, OURTHE, SEMOIS, SCHELDE, VESDRE

sea .... NORTH

seaport .... OSTEND, ZEBRUGGE

statesman .... SPAAK

textile center .... GHENT

violinist .... YSAYE

watering place .... SPA

Belgrade .... BEOGRAD

is capital of .... YUGOSLAVIA

Belial .... ANGEL, SATAN

belie .... DENY, DISGUISE, DISPROVE

belief .... ISM, MIND, VIEW, TRUST, OPINION, FAITH, CREED, DOCTRINE, CREDENCE, CONVICTION

based on .... DOXIC

beyond .... INCREDIBLE

in communication through contemplation .... MYSTICISM

in genii .... DEMONISM

in ghosts .... EODOLISM

in one god .... THEISM

Mideast .... ISLAM

beliefs .... ETHOS

set of .... CREDO, CREED

believe .... RELY, COUNT, ASSUME, CREDIT, EXPECT, TRUST, CHERISH, SUPPOSE

believer .... IST, ELITIST, TRUSTER

easy .... GULLIBLE, CREDULOUS

in God .... DEIST, THEIST

in rule by superior people .... ELITIST

in spirits .... ANIMIST

of all religions .... OMNIST

believing .... CREANT

belittle .... KNOCK, DEMEAN, SLIGHT, MINIMIZE, RIDICULE, DEPRECATE, BEDWARF, DISCREDIT, DISPARAGE, DEPRECIATE

Belize's former name .... HONDURAS

bell .... GONG, ROAR, BELLOW, CAMPANA, CARILLON

alarm .... TOCSIN

call to prayer .... ANGELUS

clapper .... TONGUE

flat .... GONG

flower .... RAMPION, CAMPANULA

jar .... CLOCHE

man ..... RINGER, (TOWN)CRIER

ring by hammer .... CHIME

ringer .... SEXTON

ringing device .... CHIME

sound ..... DONG, PEAL, KNELL, TING, TOLL, RING, CLANG, TING-A-LING

striker .... HAMMER, CLAPPER

tongue .... CLAPPER

tower ...... BELFRY, COMPANILE

town in story .... ADANO

belladonna .... MANICON, NIGHTSHADE

alkaloid/drug .... ATROPIN(E)

lily .... AMARYLLIS

bellboy .... PAGE, BELLHOP

call to .... FRONT

colloquial .... BUTTONS

belle .... BEAUTY

Belle of the West .... STARR

belles-lettres .... LITERATURE

bellhop. See **bellboy**

bellicose .... HOSTILE, WARLIKE, BELLIGERENT

belligerence .... WAR, BELLICOSITY

belligerent .... WARLIKE, BELLICOSE, PUGNACIOUS, COMBATANT, CONTENTIOUS, AGGRESSIVE, QUARRELSOME, PROTAGONIST

right of a .... ANGARY

Bellini .... PAINTER

pupil of .... TITIAN

son of ...... GENTILE, GIOVANNI

Bellini's (Vincenzo) opera .... NORMA

Bellona's brother .... MARS

bellow .... BELL, ROAR, WAIL

bellows .... BLOWER

bells, set of .... CHIME(S), CARILLON

bellwether .... SHEEP, LEADER

belly .... WAME, WOMB, BULGE, TUMMY, BAGGIE, VENTER, ABDOMEN, STOMACH

laugh .... ROAR, GUFFAW,

CHORTLE
near/on the .... VENTRAL
protruding .... PAUNCH, BAY
WINDOW, BREADBASKET
bellyache: colloq. .... GRIPE,
COMPLAIN
bellyband .... CINCH, GIRTH
bellybutton .... NAVEL
bellyful .... SURFEIT
belong .... OWN, VEST IN,
PERTAIN, APPERTAIN
belonging to certain people
.... NATIVE, ENDEMIC,
INDIGENOUS
belongings .... ASSETS, ESTATE,
EFFECTS, CHATTELS,
PROPERTY, POSSESSION(S)
beloved ...... LIEF, ANGEL, LOVER,
DARLING, SWEETHEART
colloquial .... HONEYBUNCH
physician .... LUKE
below .... ALOW, LOWER,
(BE)NEATH, INFERIOR,
(UNDER)NEATH, SUBORDINATE
combining form .... HYP(O)
the belt: sl. ...... FOUL, UNFAIR
belt ...... OBI, AREA, BAND, BLOW,
CUFF, SASH, STRAP, CESTUS,
CORDON, ZOSTER, BALDRIC,
GIRDLE, CIRCUIT, ZONE,
CINCTURE, CINGULUM
case .... HOLSTER
fancy .... SASH
imaginary, heavenly
.... ZODIAC
slang .... DECK, CLOBBER
sword .... BALDRIC
tighten .... RETRENCH,
ECONOMIZE
Beltane .... MAYDAY
beluga .... WHALE, WHITEFISH,
DOLPHIN, STURGEON
roe/eggs .... CAVIAR
belvedere .... GALLERY, PAVILION,
SUMMERHOUSE
bema .... CHANCEL, PLATFORM
bemoan .... WAIL, LAMENT,
DEPLORE
bemuse .... MUDDLE, CONFUSE,
STUPEFY, DISTRACT
ben .... SON, PEAK, PARLOR
relative .... IBN
Ben .... HOGAN, GAZZARA
Jonson's comedy ...... EPICENE
Jonson's plague .... GOUT
bench ...... SEAT, COURT, EXEDRA,
GALLERY, SETTEE,
WORKTABLE
church .... PEW
in sports .... SIDELINE
judges' .... BANC

of authority .... DRIVER'S SEAT
"the" .... JUDICIARY
tool .... VISE
warmer .... JUDGE
bend .... BOW, ARCH, KINK, TURN,
WALE, CROFT, GIVE,
FLEX(URE), CROOK, SHAPE,
CURVE, RELENT, YIELD,
STOOP, SOFTEN
and bob .... NID
as of light, heat .... REFRACT
back .... REFLEX
in adoration .... KNEEL
in stream .... HOOK
in timber .... SNY
inward .... INTROVERT
knee in worship
.... GENUFLECT
light wave .... REFRACT
sinister .... BATON
the arm .... FLEX
bender .... ORGY, SPREE, WASSAIL
bending .... BIGHT, ZIGZAG,
FLEXION, FLECTION
bends, having two .... BIFLEX
the .... CRAMPS
bendy .... OKRA
bene .... BOON, (WILD)HOG,
PRAYER
vale .... FAREWELL
beneath .... BELOW, UNDER,
UNWORTHY OF
combining form .... HYP(O)
the skin .... SUBCUTANEOUS
benedict .... BACHELOR, CELIBATE
benedictine .... NUN, MONK,
LIQUEUR
benediction ...... GRACE, BENISON,
BLESSING, INVOCATION
benefaction .... BOON
benefactor .... PATRON,
SYMPATHIZER
benefic ...... KINDLY, CHARITABLE
benefice, appoint to a
.... COLLATE
first income of .... ANNAT
holder .... APPROPRIATOR
of a sort .... SINECURE
revenue .... ANNAT(E)S
temporary .... COMMENDAM
beneficial .... BENIGN, USEFUL,
HELPFUL
beneficiary .... USEE, DONEE
benefit .... GAIN, GOOD, HELP,
SAKE, FAVOR, AVAIL, ASSIST,
PROFIT, ADVANTAGE
benevolent .... KIND, HUMANE,
AMIABLE, LIBERAL, OBLIGING,
CORDIAL, GENEROUS,
CHARITABLE
order .... ELKS

Bengal bison .... GAUR
capital .... CALCUTTA
city .... PATNA
cotton .... ADATI
grass .... MILLET
groom .... SAICE
light .... FIREWORK
native .... KOL, BANIAN,
BENGALI
Ben-Gurion's wife .... PAULA
benighted .... LOST
benign ...... KIND(LY), HARMLESS,
BENEFICIAL, GRACIOUS,
FAVORABLE
tumor/cyst .... ADENOMA
benjamin .... GUM, BENZOIN
Benjamin .... FAVORITE SON
father of .... JACOB
Franklin's musical
instrument
.... HARMONICA
son of .... ARD, EHI, ROSH
benne .... SESAME
bennet .... HEMLOCK, VALERIAN
Benny, comedian .... JACK
devised characteristic of
.... STINGINESS
bent .... SET, BOUND, GRASS,
TASTE, CROOKED, FLAIR,
BIASED, CURVED, PROPENSITY,
APTITUDE, INCLINED,
DISTORTED, DESIRE, WARPED,
TWISTED, TENDENCY,
INCLINATION
backward .... RETRORSE
easily .... SUPPLE, PLIABLE
like a knee .... GENICULATE
Bentley's sleuth .... TRENT
benumb .... HEBETATE
benzedrine .... INHALANT,
STIMULANT
benzene .... BENZOL, SOLVENT
Beowulf, monster slain by
.... GRENDEL
bequeath .... WILL, ENDOW,
LEAVE, HAND DOWN
bequest .... LEGACY, HERITAGE,
ENDOWMENT, INHERITANCE
berate .... SCOLD, REBUKE,
UPBRAID
Berber .... RIFF, KABYLE, HAMITE,
MOSLEM, TUAREG
chief .... CAID
dialect .... TUAREG
hermit .... MARABOUT
tribe .... DAZA, RIFF, TEDA
tribesman .... KABYLE
berceuse .... LULLABY
bereave ...... ROB, STRIP, DEPRIVE
bereavement .... LOSS,
DEPRIVATION

63

expression of .... CONDOLENCE
bereft .... LORN, LONELY,
DEPRIVED(OF)
beret .... CAP, BIRETTA
berg .... ICE
bergamot .... PEAR, MONARDA,
HORSEMINT
Bergen's Mortimer .... SNERD
Berger, singer .... ERNA
Bergerac's sore point ...... NOSE
Bergman, actress .... INGRID
beriberi .... DROPSY
medicine .... THIAMIN(E)
Bering Sea river .... YUKON
Berkshire .... HOG
county seat .... READING
race course .... ASCOT
Berlin .... CITY, CARRIAGE
bonnet .... EASTER
district .... SPANDAU
hit .... REMEMBER
is capital of
.... (EAST)GERMANY
prison .... SPANDAU
river .... SPREE
sight (no longer) .... WALL
songwriter .... IRVING
berm .... LEDGE, TERRACE
Bermuda capital .... HAMILTON
arrowroot .... ARARAO
grass .... DOOB, DOUB
product .... ONION
to pleasure seekers
.... PLAYGROUND
Bern is capital of
.... SWITZERLAND
Bernese Alps mountain
.... WETTERHORN
bernicle .... GOOSE
berry .... BOCCA, GRAPE, BANANA,
CURRANT, MADRONA, ACINUS,
TOMATO, ALLSPICE
branch .... CANE
cigarette .... CUBEB
combining form .... BACCI
fragrant .... MYRTLE
grape .... ACINUS
like .... BACCATE
slang .... DOLLAR
bersagliere .... RIFLEMAN,
SHARPSHOOTER
berseem .... CLOVER
berserk .... AMOK, AMUCK,
BARESARK
Bert .... LAHR, PARKS
berth .... BED, BUNK, POSITION,
SLIP, PLACE, ABODE, DOCK,
ANCHORAGE, LODGING,
COMPARTMENT
Pullman car .... LOWER, UPPER
bertha .... COLLAR

Bertha, Big .... CANNON
beruffled .... FURBELOWED
beryl .... EMERALD, MINERAL,
MORGANITE, AQUAMARINE
beseech .... BEG, PRAY, HOUND,
IMPLORE, ENTREAT, PRESS,
PLEAD, PETITION, URGE,
COAX, SOLICIT
beset ...... HARRY, HARASS, STUD,
ATTACK, BESIEGE, ASSAIL,
OBSESS, PESTER
beshow .... SABLEFISH
beshrew: arch. .... CURSE
beside .... BY, NEAR, CLOSE,
ABREAST, ALONGSIDE
oneself .... MAD, SORE, ANGRY
prefix .... PAR, PARA
besides .... TOO, ALSO, ELSE,
EXCEPT, FURTHER, MOREOVER
besiege .... PLAGUE, PESTER,
BESET, CROWD, HARASS,
INVEST, BELEAGUER,
OVERWHELM, SURROUND
besieger's explosive ...... PETARD
protective cover
.... MANT(E)LET
besmirch ...... SOIL, DIRTY, STAIN,
SULLY, DEFAME, TARNISH
besom .... BROOM
bespangle .... STUD, STAR,
DECORATE
bespatter .... SOIL, SMEAR,
SPLASH
bespeak .... SHOW, RESERVE
Bessemer process product
.... STEEL
best .... TOPS, CHOICE, DEFEAT,
OUTWIT, SURPASS, UTMOST,
EXCELLENT
colloquial .... TOPFLIGHT
combining form .... ARISTO
man at wedding
...... GROOMSMAN, PARANYMPH
part ...... ELITE, CREAM, MEAT,
CHOICE, FLOWER
seller .... HIT, BIBLE
wishes ...... CONGRATULATIONS
bestial .... VILE, BRUTAL, ANIMAL,
BRUTISH, SAVAGE, BEASTLIKE
bestiary book author .... BORGES
bestow .... GIVE, AWARD, CONFER,
DEVOTE, DONATE, PRESENT,
BEQUEATH
generously .... LAVISH
bestrew .... SCATTER
bestride .... STRADDLE
bet .... PLAY, STAKE, WAGER,
GAMBLE, PARLAY,
PROPOSITION
against card dealer .... PUNT
at dice .... FADE

colloquial .... ENTRY,
CANDIDATE
fail to pay .... WELSH
in an election ...... CANDIDATE
in roulette .... BAS
sure win .... IN THE BAG
to win in horse race .... ON
THE NOSE
without odds .... ITOI
you! .... CERTAINLY, YES
INDEED
betake ...... GO, REPAIR, JOURNEY
Betancourt .... MONK, CURATE
bête noire .... LEPER, PARIAH,
BUGBEAR, OUTCAST
of nursery .... CROUP
betel .... SIRI, PLANT, PEPPER
leaf .... PAN, BUYO
nut .... SERI, CATECHU
palm .... ARECA, PINANG
pepper .... IKMO, ITMO
Betelgeuse .... STAR
bethel .... CHAPEL, CHURCH
betide .... OCCUR, BEFALL,
HAPPEN
betimes .... SOON, EARLY,
QUICKLY, PROMPTLY
betoken .... AUGUR, DENOTE,
FORESHOW, INDICATE
beton .... CONCRETE
betray .... SELL, DECEIVE, REVEAL,
DIVULGE, VICTIMIZE
betrayal .... PERFIDY
betrayer .... TRAITOR, SEDUCER,
DECEIVER
Biblical .... JUDAS(ISCARIOT)
betroth .... AFFY, ENGAGE,
PLIGHT, AFFIANCE
betrothal .... PROMISE,
ENGAGEMENT
betrothed person .... FIANCE,
FIANCEE
Betsy Ross creation .... FLAG
slang .... GAT, GUN,
EQUALIZER
Bette .... DAVIS, MIDLER
better .... BEAT, MEND, AMEND,
IMPROVE, OUTDO, EXCEL,
RELIEVE, SURPASS
half: colloq. .... WIFE
looking .... CUTER,
HANDSOMER
betting system .... PARLAY, PARI-
MUTUEL
another way: colloq. ..... ROLL
loser's .... MARTINGAL(E)
between .... AMID, MIDDLE,
BETWIXT, INTERMEDIATE
bee and dee .... CEE
come ...... BUTT IN, INTERFERE
go- .... AGENT, MEDIUM,

MEDIATOR
in law .... MESNE
meals treat .... SODA, SNACK
Michigan and Ontario
.... ERIE
prefix .... DIA, META, INTER
the lines ...... UNSAID, HIDDEN,
IMPLIED
Thomas and Edison ..... ALVA
you and me .... SECRET
betwixt and between .... MIDDLE
Bevan's nickname .... NYE
bevel .... CANT, EDGE, BEZEL,
SLANT
out .... REAM
ship timber .... SNAPE
to join .... MITER, MITRE
beveled angle/surface ...... SPLAY
beverage .... ADE, ALE, TEA,
BOZA, KAVA, MATE, SAKE,
SOUR, WINE, COFFEE, DRINK,
NOG(G), TOKAY, LEBAN,
POTABLE
add liquor to .... LACE
almond-flavored .... RATAFIA
beer-lemonade .... SHANDY
brandy, sugar, spice
.... TODDY
carbonated .... POP, SODA
caffeinated .... TEA, COFFEE
Christmas .... EGGNOG
fermented .... MEAD, SAKE
from evergreen leaves
.... MATE
from leaves .... TEA
from meat extract ...... BROTH,
BEEF-TEA
from molasses .... RUM
fruit(crushed) .... SMASH
hot milk .... POSSET
maker .... TEABAG
palm sap .... TODDY
sour ..... LIME-ADE, LEMONADE
vermouth, etc. .... BRONX
wine .... NEGUS, BISHOP,
VERMOUTH
with anise .... KUMMEL
beverages, place for .... BAR,
CELLAR(ET)
bevy .... COVEY, FLOCK
bewail .... WEEP, MOURN, GRIEVE,
LAMENT, DEPLORE, COMPLAIN
beware .... SHUN, AVOID, BE ON
GUARD, WATCH, LOOKOUT
bewilder .... DAZE, STUMP,
PUZZLE, CONFUSE, MYSTIFY,
PERPLEX
bewildering .... MAZY
bewitch .... HEX, CHARM,
ENCHANT, ENTRANCE,
FASCINATE

bewitchment .... SPELL
bey .... DEY, GOVERNOR
Beyoglu .... PERA
beyond .... PAST, YONDER, LATER,
REMOTE, FARTHER, FURTHER,
OVER, EXCEEDING
colloquial ...... GOD-FORSAKEN
combining form .... SUR,
META, PARA, ULTRA
compare .... PEERLESS,
MATCHLESS
reach .... UNATTAINABLE, FAR-
OFF, OUT-OF-THE-WAY
Bezaleel's father: myth. ...... URI
bezant .... COIN, BALLET
bezel .... RIM, FACET, FLANGE,
TEMPLATE
bhang .... HEMP
Bhutan capital(summer)
.... TASHI-CHHO
capital(winter) .... PUNAKHA
people .... BHOTIYA
pine .... KAIL
ruler .... MAHARAJA(H)
bi: prefix .... TWO, TWICE
Biafran leader .... OJUKWU
Bialystok .... BELOSTOK
biannual .... BIENNIAL, SEMI-
ANNUAL
bias .... BENT, SWAY, TWIST,
SLOPE, TENDENCY, PREJUDICE,
DIAGONAL, INFLUENCE,
PARTIALITY
biased .... UNFAIR, UNJUST,
BIGOTED, PARTIAL, PARTISAN,
ONE-SIDED, PREJUDICED,
NARROW-MINDED
person .... BIGOT
bib .... APRON, DRINK, DICKEY,
IMBIBE, NAPKIN, TIPPLE
and tucker .... CLOTHES
companion of .... TUCKER
bibb .... BIBCOCK
bibber .... DRINKER, TOPER,
TIPPLER
bibcock .... BIBB, FAUCET
bibelot ...... CURIO, VERTU, VIRTU,
ARTIFACT, BRIC-A-BRAC
Bible books of New Testament
.... JOHN, LUKE, MARK,
MATTHEW, ACTS,
CORINTHIANS, GALATIANS,
EPHESIANS, PHILIPPIANS,
JAMES, COLOSSIANS,
TIMOTHY, TITUS,
THESSALONIANS, HEBREWS,
ROMANS, PHILEMON, JUDE,
PETER, REVELATION
books of Old Testament
...... RUTH, EXODUS, NUMBERS,
GENESIS, LEVITICUS, JUDGES,

DEUTERONOMY, KINGS,
JOSHUA, SAMUEL, EZRA,
ESTHER, CHRONICLES, JOB,
PSALMS, PROVERBS, ISAIAH,
AMOS, JEREMIAH, EZEKIEL,
LAMENTATIONS, JOEL, HOSEA,
DANIEL, MICAH, JONAH,
OBADIAH, NAHUM, HAGGAI,
MALACHI, ZECHARIAH,
NEHEMIAH, ZEPHANIAH
reading .... PSALM
the .... HOLY WRIT, HOLY
SCRIPTURES
translator .... ULFILA(S)
version .... DOUAI, DOUAY,
HAGGADAH, KING JAMES,
TORAH, TALMUD, MASORAH,
HALAKAH, PESHITO, VULGATE,
APOCRYPHA
biblical ...... SACRED, SCRIPTURAL,
PROPHETIC, EXEGETIC,
EVANGELICAL, TALMUDIC,
CANONICAL, APOSTOLIC,
APOCRYPHAL
ancient first-aid ..... WINE AND
OIL
angel .... GABRIEL
animal .... OX, FOX, GOAT,
DEER, LION, ORYX, MULE,
CAMEL, HORSE, SHEEP, IBEX,
DONKEY, JACKAL, BEAR,
GAZELLE, LEOPARD, WILD ASS,
CROCODILE
armies .... SABAOTH
ascetic order .... ESSENE
assassin .... CAIN
bird .... RAVEN, ROCK-DOVE,
TURTLE-DOVE
cave .... MACHPELAH,
ADULLAM
character .... ABEL, AMOS,
AMNON, ABNER, AARON, EVE,
CAIN, ADAM, ANNAS, NABAL,
ANTIPAS, ABIGAIL, EZRA,
ESAU, ENOS, JOHN, LEAH,
AQUILA, ABINADAB, ELIAS,
HAGAR, HEROD, DEMETRIUS,
DELILAH, NOAH, MOSES,
PRISCILLA, JONAH, JOSIAH,
ICHABOD, LABAN, NAOMI,
ELIJAH, SIMON, SALOME,
PILATE, TAMAR, TOBIAH,
TIMOTHY, PAUL, VARUS,
BARNABAS
charioteer .... JEHU
city .... NOB, GATH, GAZA,
EKRON, BABEL, HEBRON, DAN,
GOLM, KABUL, RESEN, SODOM,
KANAH, HAZOR, RAMAH,
ACCO, TYRE, ZOAR, HELEPH,
ENDOR, SARID, CHINNERETH,

BETH-SHAN, BETH-ANATH, IBLEAM, OPHRAH, GALILEE, DOTHAM, JUTBAH, MEGIDDO, GILGAL, TIRZAH, JABNEEL, MEDEBA, NAARAN, JOKMEAM, DIBON, PEREA, JERUSALEM, BETHEL, SHILOH, TAPPUAH, RAMAH, ASHDOD, ASHKELON, RABBAH, MIZPAH, JERICHO, MICHMETHATH, BEER-SHEBA, AROER, TIMNAH, CAESAREA, GOMORRAH, BETH-SHEMESH

city built by Antipas .... TIBERIAS

city of refuge .... BEZER, SHECHEM, HEBRON, KEDESH, GOLAN, RAMOTH-GILEAD

cliffs .... MOAB

coin .... PRUTAH, SHEKEL, DRACHMA, TETRADRACHMA, SESTERCE, OCTADRACHMA

cony .... HYRAX

country .... PUL, SHEBA, EDOM, GILEAD, ASSYRIA, SEIR, SEBA, CANAAN, ENON, CHALDEA

curser .... BALAAM

desert .... PARAN

expression .... SELAH

fishing village ...... BETHSAIDA

flight .... EXODUS

flower .... IRIS, TULIP, NARCISSUS, DANDELION, HYACINTH, SAFFRON CROCUS, ANEMONE, STAR OF BETHLEHEM

food .... BARLEY, MANNA, LENTIL, WALNUT, CUCUMBER

forest .... HERETH

fruit .... FIG, DATE, GRAPE, APRICOT, OLIVE, POMEGRANATE

giant .... ANAK, ENIM, GOLIATH

gift-bearer(s) .... MAGI, GASPAR, MELCHIOR, BALTHASAR

Hades .... SHEOL

herb ..... CORIANDER, CHICORY, CASTOR-BEAN, WORMWOOD, WATERCRESS

hill .... ZION, MOREH

hill country ..... JUDEA, JUDAH

hosts .... SABAOTH

hunter .... ESAU, NIMROD

island .... CAUDA

judge .... ELI, ELON, EHUD, GIDEON, JEPHTHAH, ABDON, IBZAN, SAMSON, JAIR, TOLA, OTHNIEL

king .... OG, ASA, AGAG, ABIJAM, DAVID, SOLOMON, REHOBOAM, ABIMELECH,

JEHORAM, JEHOSHAPHAT, HEROD, UZZIAH, JOTHAM, MANASSEH, HEZEKIAH, JEHOAHAZ, JEHOIAKIM, AHAZ, BAASHA, JOSIAH, ZEDEKIAH, JEHOIACHIN, AHAB, JEHU, JEROBOAM, OMRI, JEHOASH, AHAZIAH, SAUL, HOSHEA, MENAHEM, RAMSES, MELCHIZEDEK

king, assassinated .... ELAH, SHALLUM, ZECHARIAH, NADAB, JOASH, AMAZIAH, PEKAH, PEKAHIAH, AMON, JEHORAM

king who committed suicide .... ZIMRI

kingdom .... ELAM, MOAB, ISRAEL, SHEBA, JUDAH, SAMARIA

lake .... HULEH

land .... NOD, TOB, EDOM, GOSHEN

land of cedars .... LEBANON

language .... ARAMIC

lawgiver .... MOSES

Levitical city .... GEBA, BILEAM, REHOB, MISHAL, JAHAZ, ABDON, HAMMATH, GEZER, JOKNEAM, DABERATH, ALMON, GIBEON, KARTHAN, JATTIR, JUTTA, ANATHOTH, AIJALON, TAANACH, DEBIR, GIBBETHON

liar .... ANANIAS, SAPPHIRA

lion .... ARI

lyrelike instrument .... SACKBUT

mass migration .... EXODUS

measure of capacity .... HIN, OMER, EPHAH, HOMER, KAB, BATH, BUSHEL, LOG, LETHECH

measure of length ..... FINGER, SPAN, CUBIT, REED, HANDBREATH, FATHOM, FURLONG

merchant .... TUBAL

mount .... ABLA, HOR, EBAL, NAIN, PEOR, HOREB, NEBO, SIER, SINAI, TABOR, ARARAT, GILEAD, OLIVET, HERMON, GILBOA, MORIAH

name ...... ARAM, AROM, EBAL, EBED, GADDI, ONO, ANIM, REBA, ASOM, IVAH, IRA, ABIAM, AMASA, AHIRA, SERED, MAGOG, ISHMAEL, UR, HELI, MERAB, VASHTI, IRAD, ELAH, GOMER, ULAM

oldster .... ENOS

ornament .... URIM

passage used .... TEXT

password .... SHIBBOLETH

patriarch .... ADAM, ENOS, SETH, SHEM, ABRAHAM, ISAAC, JACOB, PELEG, JOB, TERAH, NOAH, JARED, REU, JOSEPH, LAMECH

people .... SEMITICS, EGYPTIANS, SUMARIANS, AKKADIANS, CANAANITES, GUTIANS, ISRAELITES, HEBREWS, AMALEKITES, BEDOUINS, AMMONITES, MOABITES, PHILISTINES, ROMANS, PHOENICIANS, ASSYRIANS, JUDAHITES, PERSIANS, BABYLONIANS, JEWS, MACEDONIANS, SELEUCIDS, PTOLEMIES, GALILEANS, HASMONEANS, PHARISEES, SAMARITANS

place .... ENON, ENDOR, SHILOH, JORDAN

place of dishonor .... GOD'S LEFT HAND

place of torment .... GEHENNA

plant .... FLAX, MYRRH, **CITRON, WILLOW**, COTTON, **ONION, CASSIA,** MYRTLE, FRANKINCENSE

plateau .... EASTERN, TRANSJORDAN

pool .... GIBEON, SILOAM

precious stone .... LIGURE, TURQUOISE, JACINTH

preposition .... UNTO

priest .... ELI, LEVI, ANNAS, AARON, JANNEUS, HYRCANUS, ARISTOBULUS

promised land .... CANAAN

pronoun .... THEE

prophet .... AMOS, EZRA, SAMUEL, HOSEA, JONAH, MICAH, MOSES, ELISHA, ELIJAH, ISAIAH, DANIEL, JOEL, EZEKIEL, JEREMIAH, HOLY MAN, ZOROASTER

prophetess .... DEBORAH

queen .... SHEBA, ESTHER, CANDACE, VASHTI, ATHALIAH

queen mother .... JEZEBEL

rich man .... DIVES

river .... NILE, JORDAN, ABANA, ARNON, TIGRIS, JABBOK, YARMUK, EUPHRATES

sacred objects .... URIM

scribe .... EZRA, BARUCH

sea .... DEAD, OF REEDS, AEGEAN, OF GALILEE

serpent .... NEHUSHTAN

sheep-owner .... NABAL

shepherd .... ABEL, AMOS

site of Calvary ..... GOLGOTHA
skeptic .... THOMAS
skipper .... NOAH
spice .... STACTE
spring ...... AIN, ESEK, MARY'S
WELL, SILOAM
spy .... CALEB
step-pyramid structure
.... ZIGGURAT
stopping place .... MARAH
symbol of danger .... VIPER,
SERPENT
fertility .... DOLPHIN
prayer .... FRANKINCENSE
suffering .... MYRRH
virtue .... GOLD
system of writing
.... CUNEIFORM
tax collector .... MATTHEW
temptress .... EVE, DELILAH
thief .... BARABBAS
timber .... ALMUG
tower .... EDAR, BABEL
town .... ENDOR, CANA,
ARBELA, NAIN, BETHEL, BETH-
AVEN, BETH-ARBEL,
BETHLEHEM, BETH-BARAH,
NAZARETH, CAPERNAUM,
GINAE, BALAH, EMMAUS,
SEBASTE, GENNESARET,
BETHANY, MAGDALA,
LEBONAH
treasure city .... PITHOM,
RAAMSES
tree ...... ACACIA, CEDAR, OAK,
ALMOND, LAUREL, CYPRESS,
TAMARISK
tribe ...... DAN, LEVI, MOABITE,
NAPHTALI, HEBREW, ISSACHAR,
ASHER, MIDIANITE, AMMONITE,
MANASSEH
valley .... BACA, NEMEA,
JORDAN, ELAH, SIDDIM,
SOREK, HINNOM, KIDRON,
JEZREEL, TYROPOEON
verb ending .... ETH
verb form .... HAST
victim .... ABEL
vineyard owner .... NABOTH
volcano ..... HORNS OF HATTIN
walled city .... MEGIDDO,
SHECHEM
wanderer .... CAIN
weed .... TARE
weight .... BEKA, MINA,
GERAH, POUND, SHEKEL,
TALENT
wicked priest .... SIMON
wild ox .... REEM
wilderness .... MAON, ZIPH,
JUDEA, PARAN

wise men .... MAGI
word .... MENE, RACA, SELAH
bibliographer's abbr. ...... OBED
bibliotheca .... LIBRARY,
CATALOG(UE)
bibulous ...... DRUNK, ABSORBENT,
ALCOHOLIC
festival .... ALE, BACCHANALIA
party .... WASSAIL
person .... SOT, TOPER,
BACCHANT, TIPPLER,
DRUNKARD
bicarbonate .... SODA, BICARB
bice .... BLUE, PIGMENT, VERDITER
bicephalous .... TWO-HEADED
bicker .... ARGUE, CAVIL,
FLUTTER, WRANGLE,
QUARREL, SQUABBLE,
GURGLE, DISPUTE
bicuspid .... TOOTH
bicycle .... BIKE, VELOCIPEDE
rider's seat .... SADDLE
two-seater .... TANDEM
bid .... ASK, OFFER, EFFORT,
TENDER, COMMAND,
INVITATION, OVERTURE
in bridge .... DECLARATION
return .... RECALL
bidarka .... CANOE
bidding ...... COMMAND, REQUEST,
SUMMONS, INVITATION,
(BE)HEST
biddy .... HEN, CHICKEN
bide .... STAY, WAIT, DWELL,
RESIDE, CONTINUE
bield .... SHELTER
bienvenue .... WELCOME
bier .... PYRE, COFFIN, HEARSE,
LITTER, FERETORY,
CATAFALQUE
bifacial .... JANUS, TWO-FACED
biff .... BOX, HIT, CUFF, STRIKE
biffin .... APPLES
bifid .... FORKED, CLEFTED
bifurcate ...... FORKED, BRANCHED
big .... HUGE, LOUD, LARGE,
SIZABLE, MASSIVE, BULKY,
NOBLE, IMPRESSIVE, POMPOUS,
ENORMOUS, WEIGHTY, MAN-
SIZE
and clumsy .... HULKING,
LUBBER(LY)
and strong ..... BURLY, HUSKY,
BRAWNY
casino .... TEN
hand .... TREMENDOUS
OVATION
house: sl. .... PRISON
pill .... BOLUS
shot: sl. .... VIP, BRASS,
BIGWIG, FATCAT

show: sl. .... THREE RING
CIRCUS
teethed .... MACRODONT
toe .... HALLUX
toe ailment .... GOUT, BURSITIS
top .... CIRCUS, TENT(ROOF)
tree .... REDWOOD, SEQUOIA
truck .... MACK
with child .... PREGNANT
Big Ben .... CLOCK
Ben's place .... TOWER,
LONDON
Bertha .... CANNON
Bertha, where cast .... ESSEN
Dipper .... URSA MAJOR
Five member, WWI
.... JAPAN, ITALY, FRANCE
Five member, WWII
.... CHINA, FRANCE, RUSSIA
Horn .... RIVER, MOUNTAIN
Muddy .... MISSOURI
Plain .... GRAND PRAIRIE
River .... MISSISSIPPI
biggest and best portion
.... LION'S SHARE
bighead .... CONCEIT, EGOTISM
bighorn .... SHEEP, ARGALI
bight .... BAY, GULF, CORNER,
FORK, LOOP, HOLLOW, CURVE
bignonia tree .... CALABASH
bigot .... RACIST, ZEALOT
Bigtop name .... RINGLING,
BARNUM, BAILEY
bigwig: colloq. .... VIP, STAR,
FATCAT, TOPBRASS
Oriental .... AGA
Bihar's capital .... PATNA
bijou .... JEWEL, TRINKET
bikini .... ATOLL
on the beach .... SWIMSUIT
upper .... BRA
bilateral .... TWO-SIDED,
RECIPROCAL
bilbo .... RAPIER, SHACKLES
bile .... GALL, ANGER, CHOLER,
TEMPER, BITTERNESS
black .... MELANCHOLY
combining form .... CHOLE,
CHOL(O)
yellow .... CHOLER
bilestone .... GALLSTONE
bilge .... BULGE, SWELL
slang .... NONSENSE
bilingual .... DIGLOT
bilious .... BITTER, CROSS,
LIVERISH, GREEN, BAD-
TEMPERED
biliousness .... NAUSEA
bilk ...... GYP, DECEIVE, DEFRAUD,
CHEAT(ER), SWINDLE(R)
bill .... DUN, NEB, TAB, BEAK,

POSTER, STATEMENT, BELLOW, ACCOUNT, HALBERD, LIST, WILLIAM, RECKONING, ROAR, CHARGE, GREENBACK

and coo .... PET, KISS

fill the .... SUIT, QUALIFY

five-dollar .... VEE

foot the .... PAY

joker in a .... RIDER

of exchange .... DRAFT

of exchange dealer .... CAMBIST

of fare .... MENU, CARTE

of lading .... CARGO LIST

part of .... NEB, CERE

pass through mutual aid .... LOGROLL

stroke with .... PECK, PREEN

one-dollar .... BUCK

two-dollar .... DEUCE

ten-dollar .... TENNER, SAWBUCK

100-dollar .... C-NOTE, CENTURY

1000-dollar .... GRAND

Bill of Rights ...... MAGNA CARTA

billboard ...... POSTER, HOARDING, SIGNBOARD

billet ...... PUT UP, LODGING, POST, QUARTER(S), POSITION

doux .... LOVE LETTER

billfish .... GAR, SKIPPER, SAILFISH, SPEARFISH

billfold .... CASE, WALLET, POCKETBOOK

billhead .... LETTERHEAD

billiards .... POOL

ball .... IVORY

red ball .... CARAMBOLA

shot .... CAROM, MASSE

stick .... CUE

billing .... LISTING, DUNNING, FIGURES, INVOICE, STATEMENT

billingsgate lingo .... FOUL, VULGAR, ABUSIVE

billion .... MILLIARD

billow .... BORE, RISE, ROLL, WAVE, SWELL, EAGRE, SURGE

billy .... CAN, CLUB, STICK, KETTLE, TRUNCHEON

billycock .... HAT, DERBY

bilsted .... TREE, SWEET GUM

Bimini legend ...... FOUNTAIN OF YOUTH

bimonthly .... BIMENSAL, SEMI-MONTHLY

bin .... BOX, CONTAINER, RECEPTACLE, COMPARTMENT

fish .... KENCH

fodder .... CRATCH

for baby .... CRIB, PLAY-PEN

for ship's coal, fuel oil .... BUNKER

storage .... HUTCH

binal .... TWOFOLD

binate .... DOUBLE

binaural .... STEREO

bind .... TIE, GIRD, HOLD, ROPE, TAPE, SECURE, ATTACH, RESTRAIN

as to a mast .... LASH UP

matrimonially .... WED, MARRY

mouth .... GAG

together .... FASTEN

together by rope .... FRAP

wound .... BANDAGE

binder .... BAND, CORD, ROPE, BALER, BANDAGE

binding .... TYING, CONFINING, BANDAGE, MANDATORY, OBLIGATORY, RESTRICTIVE

device, police ...... HANDCUFFS

document .... CONTRACT

machine .... BALER

substance .... TAR, GLUE, PASTE, ADHESIVE

bindle-stiff .... HOBO, TRAMP

bine .... HOP, STEM

Bing crooner .... CROSBY

fruit .... CHERRY

binge .... BOUT, LARK, ORGY, FLING, SPREE, TEAR, BENDER, WASSAIL, CAROUSAL, ESCAPADE

aftermath of .... HANGOVER

kind of ..... EATING, DRINKING, SHOPPING

slang .... PAINT THE TOWN RED

bingo .... KENO, BEANO, LOTTO

binocle .... TELESCOPE, OPERA GLASS, FIELD GLASS

biocatalyst .... HORMONE, VITAMIN

biographer, Ludwig .... EMIL

biographical sketch ...... PROFILE

biography .... MEMOIR, LIFE STORY, HISTORY

biological .... BIOTIC(AL)

change .... MUTATION

division .... GENERA

factor .... GENE

group .... SPECIES

reproductive cell ...... GAMETE

biology, branch of ...... GENETICS

of behavior .... ETHOLOGY

Bion .... POET

opposed to .... MORPHON

bionomics .... ECOLOGY

biped .... MAN, TWO-FOOTED

birch .... BIRK, CANE, ALDER, BETULA, HAZELNUT, WHIP, HORNBEAM, IRONWOOD

birchbark .... BOAT, CANOE

bird .... CROW, DOVE, KIWI, MYNA, FOWL, FLYER, RAIL, SWAN, PARROT, SHRIKE

adjutant .... STORK, ARGALA, MARABOU

African .... COLY, LORY, LOURI, UMBER, TURAKOO, UMBRETTE

air route .... FLYWAY

albatross .... NELLY

American .... RHEA, JUNCO, TOWHEE

Andean .... CONDOR

apteryx .... IAO, KIWI

aquatic .... AUK, DUCK, GOOSE, GULL, LOON, SWAN, SCAUP, PELICAN, PENGUIN

Arctic .... XEMA, FULMAR, LONGSPUR

Asiatic ..... MINA, MYNA, PITA, PITTA

attack .... SWOOP, POUNCE

auk family .... DOVEKIE, ALCA, PUFFIN, ROTCH(E)

Australian .... EMU, KOEL, ARA, ARARA, COOEE, EMEW, KAHU, LEIPOA, COCKATOO, PARDALOTE

baker .... HORNERO

bastard wing .... ALULA

beach .... SANDERLING

beak ..... NEB, NIB, BILL, LORA

beak part .... MANDIBLE

beaky .... TOUCAN

bell .... MAKO

big-footed .... MEGAPOD

bill (see beak)

bittern .... HERON

black .... ANI, CROW, ROOK, RAVEN, MERL(E), GRACKLE, AMSEL, OUSEL, THRUSH

blue .... JAY, IRENA

blue-footed .... TITI

bobolink .... ORTALAN

bobwhite .... QUAIL, COLIN, PARTRIDGE

Brazilian .... TOUCAN, CARIAMA, SERIEMA

bright-colored .... HOOPOE, TOUCAN, TOURACO

bristle-billed .... BARBET

broad-billed ..... DUCK, SCAUP, SPOONBILL

brood .... NIDE, COVEY

butcher .... SHRIKE

call .... PIPE

caress .... BILL

carrion .... CROW, URUBU, VULTURE

catcher .... FOWLER
catching at night .... BATFOWL
chameleonic .... PTARMIGAN
chatterer .... JAY, COTINGA,
    (MAG)PIE, STONECHAT,
    WAXWING, WHEAT-EATER
class of .... AVES
claw-winged .... HOA(C)TZIN
cockateel .... PARROT
cockatoo .... ARARA
"collar" .... RUFF, TORQUES
colloquial .... PERSON
colored beak .... PUFFIN
cormorant .... GUANAY
corvine .... DAW, CROW,
    RAVEN
courlan .... JACAMAR,
    TINAMOU
crane .... SERIEMA,
    DEMOISELLE
craw .... MAW
crest .... COP, TUFT, HOOD,
    CALOT(TE)
crested .... BLUEJAY,
    HOA(C)TZIN, COCKATOO,
    QUE(T)ZAL
crocodile .... TROCHILUS
crop .... MAW, CRAW
crow .... CORBY, CHOUGH,
    CORBIE
crow-like .... ROOK, MAGPIE,
    CORVINE
cry .... CAW, WEEP, ROAR,
    BELLOW, SHRIEK
cuckoo .... ANI, ANO, KOEL
disease .... GAPES
diving ..... AUK, GREBE, LOOM,
    LOON, DUCKER, SMEW, PUFFIN,
    OSPREY, ALCIDINE, DIDAPPER
dodo .... GEESE
dog .... SETTER, POINTER
duck family .... SMEW,
    MERGANSER
duck-like .... COOT, GOOSE
dunlin .... STIB, SANDPIPER
eagle, sea .... ERN(E)
eagle's nest .... AERIE, EYRIE
East Indies .... SHAMA, BESRA,
    SHAHIN, REDPOOL, PEREGRINE
Egyptian sacred .... IBIS
emu-like .... CASSOWARY
European .... REED, AMSEL,
    GLEDE, TEREK, REDSTART,
    OUSEL, SEDGE, WOODCOCK
extinct .... MOA, DODO, MAMO,
    GREAT AUK, NOTORNIS,
    SOLITAIRE
eye tissue .... PECTEN
fabulous .... ROC, PHOENIX
falcon .... MERLIN, BESRA,
    SAKER, TERCEL, REDPOOL,

PEREGRINE
fantailed .... PEACOCK
feather .... PENNA
feather-legged .... GROUSE
feather under the wing
    .... AXILLAR
feathers .... PLUMAGE
feathers near mouth
    .... VIBRISSA
feet for perching ...... ENSESSO
fighting .... AMADAVAT
finch ..... SERIN, MORO, SISKIN,
    BUNTING, CANARY, LINNET,
    TOWHEE, SPARROW, CARDINAL
finch-like .... CHEWINK,
    GROSBEAK
fish-eating .... ERN, OSPREY,
    KINGFISHER, OWL, LOON,
    GOOSANDER, AUK, GREBE,
    SKIMMER, PELICAN,
    MERGANSER, TERN, PUFFIN,
    CORMORANT, TERN, PUFFIN,
    PETREL, HERON, DARTER,
    GANNET
fish egg–eating .... DIPPER
fish-hawk .... OSPREY
flightless .... AUK, MOA, KAGU,
    DODO, PENGUIN, WEKA, KIWI,
    OSTRICH, NOTORNIS,
    CASSOWARY, RHEA, EM(E)U,
    RATITE, APTERYX, TINAMOU
flock .... POD, COVEY
fluid spraying .... HOUBARA
flycatcher .... KINGBIRD,
    OSCINE, PEWEE, PHOEBE
footless: heraldry
    .... MARTLET
for food .... CAPON
forelimb .... WING
fork-tailed .... PETREL
frigate .... IWA
fruit-eating .... BARBET,
    PARROT, TROGON, TOUCAN,
    OILBIRD
fulmar .... NELLY
game bird .... QUAIL, SNIPE,
    GROUSE, TURNIX, PHEASANT
game-killer .... VERMIN
gluttonous/greedy
    .... CORMORANT
goatsucker .... GUACHARO
goldfinch .... REDCAP
goose .... GANDER
grouse .... GORCOCK,
    BLACKCOCK
guan .... ORTALIS
gull, pert. to .... LARINE
gull, sea .... MEW, TERN,
    KITTIWAKE
gull-like .... SKUA, TERN,
    JAEGER

harsh-voiced .... MACAW
Hawaiian .... IWA, IIWI, MAMO,
    OOAA, ALALA
hawk .... EYAS, KAHU, KITE,
    GOSHAWK, CARACARA
heron .... IBIS, SOCO, EGRET,
    BITTERN
hind toe .... HALLUX
homing instinct
    .... ORIENTATION
honey-eating .... IAO, TUI,
    MOHO, MANUAO
hood-like crest ..... CALOT(TE)
house .... COOP, COTE, NEST,
    NIDE, AVIARY, VOLERY
humming .... AVE, SYLPH,
    COLIBRI, TROCHILUS
hunter .... FOWLER
hunting .... HAWK, FALCON
immortalized by Poe
    .... RAVEN
Indian .... SARUS, ARGALA,
    SHAMA, JACANA, AMADAVIT
insectivorous ..... TODY, TERN,
    VIREO, HARRIER, SWALLOW,
    NIGHTJAR, JACAMAR,
    NUTHATCH, HOOPOE, BEE-
    EATER, HERON, SWIFT,
    HORNBILL, STORK, EGRET,
    ROLLER, WOODPECKER
jackdaw .... COE, DAW, KAE
jay-like .... PIET, MOTMOT
killing of .... AVACIDE
kite .... GLEDE
known for straight flight
    .... CROW
lake .... LOON
lamellirostral .... DUCK, SWAN,
    GOOSE
lapwing .... WEEP, PEWIT,
    PLOVER
laughing .... DACELO, LOON,
    GIGAS, KOOKABURRA
large .... EMU, MOA, KITE,
    GUAN, JABIRU, OSTRICH
largest species .... OSTRICH
Latin for .... AVIS
leaf-walker .... JACANA
leg outgrowth .... SPUR,
    CALCAR
leg strap .... JESS
legendary .... ROC
life .... ORNIS
like in appearance
    .... ORNITHOID
limicoline .... STILT, AVOCET
long-billed ...... IBIS, CREEPER,
    NUTHATCH
long-legged .... IBIS, AGAMI,
    HERON, BUSTARD, CRANE,
    EGRET, SERIEMA, STILT,

WADER, FLAMINGO
long-necked .... SWAN, CRANE,
   EGRET, HERON, FLAMINGO
loon-like .... GREBE
love-making .... BILL AND COO
lyre .... MENURA
magpie .... PIET
male ..... TOM, COCK, GANDER,
   ROOSTER, BANTAM, GOBBLER
marsh .... COOT, RAIL, SORA,
   BITTERN, STILT, GALLINULE
martin .... MARTLET
meadow .... LARK, BOBOLINK
migratory .... PLOVER,
   BOBOLINK, WOODCOCK, KNOT,
   SANDPIPER, WHIN,
   WHEATEATER
mina .... STARLING
monkey-faced .... OWL
morepork .... RURU
mound-building .... LEIPOA,
   MEGAPOD
mouth opening .... RICTUS
mythical .... ROC, PHOENIX
nail of .... CLAW
national .... EAGLE
nest-collector .... OOLOGIST
nocturnal .... OWL, GUACHARO,
   GOATSUCKER
noisy .... BLUEJAY
non-flying (see flightless)
non-passerine .... TODY,
   HOOPOE, HORNBILL,
   KINGFISHER
note .... PIPE, CHIRP, TWEET
ocean .... FULMAR, PETREL,
   MALEMUCK, ALBATROSS
of Jove .... EAGLE
of Paradise .... APUS
of peace .... DOVE
of prey .... HAWK, FALCON,
   ERN(E), EAGLE, BATHAWK,
   GLEDE, GOSHAWK, BUZZARD,
   KITE, KESTREL, ACCIPETER,
   OWL, CONDOR, ELANET,
   VULTURE, PEREGRINE
of Sinbad .... ROC
on a quarter .... EAGLE
one-year old .... ANNOTINE
orange-colored .... ORIOLE
order of .... RASORES
oscine .... CHAT, CROW,
   SHRIKE, VIREO, ORIOLE, LARK,
   BUNTING, TANAGER
ostrich-like ..... EM(E)U, RHEA,
   RATITE, TINAMOU
owl: Samoan .... LULU
owl variety .... SNOW,
   BARRED, GREAT-HORNED
parakeet .... BUDGIE
parrot ..... KEA, KAKAM, LORY,

KAKAPOS, COCKATOO
parson .... POE, TUI
partridge .... QUAIL, SEESEE,
   BOBTAIL
partridge-like .... TINAMOU,
   TINAMIDA
passerine .... PITA, ORIOLE,
SPARROW, STARLING, TANAGER
patch on throat .... GORGET
pelican-like .... SOLAN
perching .... LARK, FINCH,
   OSCINE, SHRIKE, BUNTING
Persian .... BULBUL
pertaining to .... AVIAN,
   AVINE, ORNITHIC
Peruvian .... GUANAY
petrel .... TITI, FULMAR
pewee .... PEWIT, PHOEBE
plover-like .... LAPWING,
   KILLDEER
protuberance .... SPUR,
   CALCAR
quail .... BOBWHITE,
   PARTRIDGE
queer: colloq. .... LOCO,
   IDIOT(IC), ECCENTRIC
rail .... COOT, MOHO, SORA,
   CRAKE, SCOTER, SULTANA,
   GALLINULE
rail-like .... COURLAN
rain .... PLOVER
razor-billed .... AUK, MURRE
rear young .... FLEDGE
red-backed sandpiper
   .... PURRE
red-eyed .... VIREO
reed .... BOBOLINK
ring-dove .... CUSHAT
robber .... DAW, SKUA,
   JA(E)GER
ruffed .... REEVE, GROUSE,
   PIGEON, PARTRIDGE,
   SANDPIPER
running swift .... COURSER
sacred .... IBIS
Samoan .... IAO, LULU
sandpiper .... KNOT, REEVE,
   DUNLIN, GREENSHANK
scaup duck .... BLACKHEAD
screamer .... CHAJA
sea .... ERN(E), GULL, SKUA,
   TERN, SCAUP, GANNET,
   MURRE(LET), PETREL, PUFFIN,
   JAEGER, ALBATROSS, SCOTER,
   CORMORANT
secretary-bird
   .... SAGITTARIIDAE
seed-eating .... EMU, CROW,
   JUNCO, NUTHATCH, FINCH,
   MACAW, CHICKADEE, PIGEON,
   SPARROW, GROSBEAK,

CANARY, PARROT, OSTRICH,
   BUNTING, CARDINAL
sheep-killer .... KEA
shore .... RAIL, SORA, SNIPE,
   STILT, AVOCET, PLOVER,
   SANDPIPER, WILLET,
   PRATINCOLE
short-tailed .... BREVE, PLOVER
singing .... OSCINE
skin around eye .... ORBIT
small .... TIT, PIPIT, WREN,
   TODY, TITMOUSE, BIRDIE,
   CHICKADEE, FINCH, BLUET,
   COSTA, VIREO, TOMTIT, SYLPH,
   VERDIN, PEWEE, COLIBRI,
   SERIN, MANAKIN, SAPPHO
smallest species .... (BEE)
   HUMMINGBIRD
snake .... ANHINGA
snipe .... CURLEW, GODWIT,
   DOWITCHER
snipe-like .... WILLET
song .... LARK, PIPE, OUZEL,
   ROBIN, LINNET, BLUEBIRD,
   CANARY, SHAMA, BOBOLINK
sorrel .... OCA
sound .... COO, CAW, TWEET,
   PEEP, CHIRP, HONK, QUACK,
   SHRIEK, CHATTER, ROAR,
   WEEP, CROW, WHOOP,
   BELLOW, CHIRRUP, SCREECH,
   TIRALEE, TWITTER
South American .... GUAN,
   JACU, TURCO, TOUCAN, SYLPH,
   JACANA, TINAMOU, SERIEMA,
   WARRIOR, GUACHARO
space on head .... LORE
sparrow .... TOWHEE, BUNTING,
   PEABODY
starling .... MINA, MYNA,
   MINAH
stib .... DUNLIN
stitch .... IHI
stupid .... DODO, GOOSE,
   NODDY
swallow .... MARTLET
swallow-like .... SWIFT,
   MARTIN, HIRUNDINE
swan .... WHOOPER
swimming .... SWAN, DUCK,
   GREBE, LOON, PENGUIN,
   PHALAROPE, AUK, GULL,
   PELICAN, TERN, PETREL,
   MOORHEN
symbolic .... DOVE, OWL,
   EAGLE, STORK
tail feathers .... TRAIN,
   RECTRIX
tail hump .... UROPYGIUM
talking .... PARROT, MINA,
   MYNA(H)

thief .... DAW, ROOK, SKUA, JA(E)GER

three-toed .... STILT, TURNIX

thrush .... THROSTLE

titmouse .... VERDIN, BLUECAP, CHICKADEE

toe .... HALLUX

top of its head .... PILEUM

towhee .... CHEWINK, SPARROW

trill .... TIRALEE

tropical .... ANI, BARBET, MACAW, JACANA, TROGON, JACAMAR, TOUCAN, JABIRU

trumpeter ..... AGAMI, (BLACK) SWAN

turkey .... TOM, GOBBLER

turkey-like .... CURASSOW

"tuxedo" .... PENGUIN

type of stork .... MARABOU, MAGUARI

unfledged .... SQUAB

vulture .... URUBU, CONDOR

wading .... COOT, RAIL, CURLEW, HERON, AVOCET, EGRET, JACANA, WILLET, CRANE, IBIS, FLAMINGO, SORA, STORK, KILLDEER, SNIPE, STILT, JABIRU, BOATBILL, UMBRETTE, UMBER, GALLINULE

wagtail .... PIPIT

warbler .... REDSTART, TROCHILUS, BLACKPOLL, CHICKADEE, NIGHTINGALE

water .... PELICAN, HYACINTH

water-carrier .... ALBATROSS

weaver .... TAHA, MUNIA

web-footed .... DUCK, AUK, COOT, LOON, GOOSE

whiskered .... BULBUL

white-plumed .... EGRET, SHRIKE

white-tailed .... ERN(E)

wing .... PINION

wing outgrowth .... CALCAR

wing part .... SPUR, ALULA, CALCAR

wing quills .... FLAG

with changing color .... PTARMIGAN

with irregular flight .... PEWIT, LAPWING

with scalelike feathers .... PENGUIN

woman .... AVIATRIX

woodpigeon .... RINGDOVE

yellow-hammer .... FINCH, CUCKOO, FLICKER

young .... CHICK, OWLET, EAGLET, EYAS, CYGNET, GOSLING, NESTLING,

FLEDGLING

birds .... AVES

breeding place .... HERONRY, ROOKERY, HATCHERY

care of .... AVICULTURE

eggs, study of .... OOLOGY

flight south .... MIGRATION

follower of ...... BIRDWATCHER

food plant .... FERN, VIOLET, TREFOIL

habitat of .... FOREST, WOODLAND

of a feather .... LOOK-ALIKES

of a region .... ORNIS

of singing .... OSCINE

pertaining to .... AVIAN, AVINE, ORNITHIC

raising of .... AVICULTURE

reservation .... (GAME) SANCTUARY

study of .... ORNITHOLOGY

bird's-eye view .... SYNOPSIS

biretta .... CAP, BARRET, BERETA, BERRETA, BERRETTA

birk .... BIRCH

birl ...... SPIN, WHIRR, REVOLVE

birling .... LOGROLLING

bee .... ROLOE

object of .... BALANCE

what lumberjacks use for .... LOGS

birr .... FORCE, ENERGY, ONRUSH, SPEECH

birth .... ORIGIN, DESCENT, GENESIS, BEGINNING, BLESSED EVENT

at no cost? .... BORN FREE

before .... PRENATAL

before full-term .... PREMATURITY

control ...... FAMILY PLANNING

control advocate .... SANGER

control device .... PILL, CONDOM, DIAPHRAGM, CONTRACEPTIVE

defect .... ABNORMALITY

Jesus' .... NATIVITY

of a baby, bottom-first .... BREECH DELIVERY

of high .... NOBLE, ROYALTY

of one's .... NATAL

of two .... BIPAROUS

pains .... LABOR

rate .... NATALITY

root .... TRILLIUM

birthmark .... MOLE, BLEMISH, N(A)EVUS, FRECKLE, STRAWBERRY (MARK)

birthright .... HERITAGE, PATRIMONY, INHERITANCE

seller .... ESAU

birthstone, January ...... GARNET

February .... AMETHYST

March .... JASPER, AQUAMARINE, BLOODSTONE

April .... DIAMOND

May .... AGATE, EMERALD

June .... PEARL, MOONSTONE

July .... ONYX, RUBY

August .... SARDONYX, CARNELIAN

September .... SAPPHIRE

October .... OPAL

November .... TOPAZ

December .... ZIRCON, TURQUOISE

birthwort .... ASARUM, CLEMATITE, ARISTOLOCHIA

bis .... BI, TWICE, ENCORE, REPEAT

Biscay .... BASQUE

island .... YEU

biscuit .... BUN, RUSK, SNAP, COOKY, SCONE, CRACKER, COOKIE, PANAL, POPOVER, WAFER, SIMNEL, RATAFEE, MACAROON, ZWIEBACK

in ceramics .... BISQUE

knotted .... PRETZEL

sweetened .... RUSK

bisect .... FORK, DIVIDE

bisexual .... BIPARTITE, BISEXED

bishop .... EPARCH, PONTIFF, PRELATE, CHESSMAN, OVERSEER

in chess .... ALFIN

of Rome .... POPE

vestment .... DALMATIC

weed .... AMMI, GOUT

bishop's assistant .... VERGER, COAD, COADJUTOR

cap/headdress .... MITER, HURA, MITRE, MITERWORT

deputy .... VICAR

first year's revenue .... ANNAT

lap cloth .... GREMIAL

letter .... PASTORAL

robe .... CHIMAR, CHIMER(E)

seat ..... SEE, BEMA, CATHEDRA

see .... EPISCOPATE

skullcap .... ZUCCHETTO

staff .... CROOK, CROSIER, CROZIER

staff bearer .... VERGER

throne .... CATHEDRA

title .... ABBA, PRIMATE

vestment .... ROCHET, COPE, GREMIAL, SURPLICE

bishopric .... SEE, DIOCESE

bishops collectively .... EPISCOPACY

bison .... AUROCHS, BOVINE, BUFFALO

crossed with cattle .... CATALO

pride of .... MANE

bisque .... SOUP, BISCUIT, ICE CREAM, CERAMICS

bissextile .... LEAP YEAR

bistort .... ASTRINGENT

bistro .... BAR, CAFE, CABARET, WINESHOP, NIGHTCLUB, RESTAURANT

habitué .... BARFLY

bit .... ORT, IOTA, MOTE, WHIT, CHECK, CURB, SPECK, COIN, PIECE, MORSEL, MOMENT, SMALL, NIPPED, BLADE, GOBBET

by bit .... GRADUALLY

colloquial .... STITCH

holder .... BRACE

least .... WHIT

of comic business .... GAG

of gossip .... TIDBIT

player .... EXTRA

small .... NIP

tool .... DRILL

bitch ...... BRACH, SHREW, VIXEN, WHELP, TIGRESS, LIONESS

slang .... SCOLD, GRIPE, BOTCH, COMPLAIN, SPOIL, GRUMBLE

Bitch of Buchenwald ...... (ILSE) KOCH

bitchy .... CROSS, CRANKY

bite .... CUT, NIP, GRIP, HOLD, STING, NIBBLE, CORRODE, MOUTHFUL, SNACK, MORSEL, CHEW, PINCH, PARTAKE

bit by bit .... CHEW, GNAW, MASTICATE

colloquial .... SNACK, LUNCH

down hard .... CHAMP

impatiently .... FRET

in dentistry .... OCCLUSION

off .... CROP

one's nail .... FRET, WORRY

sharply/suddenly .... KNAP, SNAP

tentative .... NIBBLE

the bullet .... CONFRONT

the dust .... FALL, LOSE

the hand that feeds one .... BE UNGRATEFUL

with acid .... ETCH

biting ...... KEEN, SHARP, CAUSTIC, CUTTING, STINGING, NIPPY, PUNGENT, MORDACIOUS, ACRID, PIERCING, SARCASTIC

Bitolj .... MONASTIR

bits .... ANA

bitstock .... BRACE

bitt .... DECK, POST

bitter ...... ACERB, ACRID, HARSH, SEVERE, PAINFUL, TART, CUTTING, GRIEVOUS, SORE, PUNGENT, VIRULENT

apple .... COLOCYNTH

bark .... ANGOSTURA

cassava product .... TAPIOCA

combining form .... PICRO

compound .... AMARINE

cynic .... TIMON

drug/herb .... ALOE

end .... LIMIT, FINALE, UNTIL DEATH

feeling .... HATE, RANCOR, SPITE, GRUDGE, ACRIMONY

flavoring agent .... ASARUM

liquid from brine ..... BITTERN

nut .... KOLA

plant substance .... ALUM, ALOIN, LUPULIN

vetch .... ERS

bittern .... BIRD, SOCO

bitterness .... ILL WILL, HATE, REGRET, RANCOR, PUNGENCY, ACERBITY, VILE, RESENTMENT

bitters .... TONIC

bitterweed .... RAGWEED

bitumen .... PITCH, MALTHA, ASPHALT

bivalent .... DIATOMIC

bivalve .... CLAM, MUSSEL, SCALLOP, MOLLUSK, OYSTER, QUAHOG, PIDDOCK

bivouac .... CAMP, ETAPE, BARRACKS, ENCAMP(MENT)

bizarre .... ODD, LURID, QUEER, FANTASTIC, OUTRE, GROTESQUE

Bizet opera .... CARMEN

Bjorn of tennis .... BORG

blab .... GOSSIP, CHATTER, PRATTLE

blabber .... GOSSIP, BABBLE, TATTLE, TATTLER

blabbermouth .... TATTLETALE, GOSSIPMONGER

black .... JET, EBON, SABLE, WICKED, RAVEN, COLLY, JETTY, ATROUS, INKY, AFRICAN (AMERICAN), DARK(NESS)

alder .... SHRUB, WINTERBERRY

alloy .... NIELLO

and-blue .... LIVID, BRUISED

and-tan .... DOG, TERRIER, RAT TERRIER

and-white .... OPPOSITES, PRINT, WRITING, PHOTOGRAPH

art .... MAGIC, SORCERY

bass .... (GAME) FISH

beer .... DANTZIC

bile, having .... MOROSE, MELANCHOLY

bird .... DAW, CROW, MERLE, RAVEN

bread ingredient .... RYE

buck .... SASIN

chimney product .... SOOT

coal .... ATROUS

coffee .... CAFE NOIR

combining form .... ATRO, MELAN(O)

country .... MIDLANDS

cuckoo .... ANI

diamonds .... COAL

eye: colloq. .... SHAME, MOUSE, SHINER, DISHONOR

eyed nymph .... HOURI

eyed pea .... COWPEA

eyed Susan .... KETMIE, RUDBECKIA, (YELLOW) DAISY

feline .... PANTHER

fever .... KALA-AZAR

fin snapper .... SESI

flag .... JOLLY ROGER

garnet .... MELANITE

gold .... OIL

gum .... NYSSA, TUPELO, PEPPERIDGE

hair and eyes ...... BRUNET(TE)

haw .... VIBURNUM, SHEEPBERRY

hole .... DUNGEON

ink item .... ASSET

knot .... FUNGUS

lead .... GRAPHITE

letter .... UNLUCKY, UNFORTUNATE

letter type .... CAXTON

lustrous .... RAVEN

magic ...... VOODOO, SORCERY, WITCHCRAFT

make .... NIGRIFY

mark .... DISREPUTE

mineral .... JET, COAL, IRIDE

nightshade .... MOREL

pepper .... SEASONING

race .... NEGRO

rhinoceros .... BORELE

rot/rust .... FUNGUS

saltwort .... GLAUX

sheep: colloq. .... BAD ONE, PRODIGAL

silver .... STEPHANITE

snake .... RACER

suit cards .... CLUBS, SPADES

swan .... TRUMPETER

tea .... BOHEA

tern .... DARR

tie ...... BOW, (DINNER) JACKET

very .... JETTY

vomit .... YELLOW FEVER

water .... PYROSIS
widow .... SPIDER
wood .... EBONY
Black Death .... (BUBONIC)
PLAGUE
Earth area .... OREL
Forest .... SCHWARZWALD
Friar .... DOMINICAN
Hand .... CAMMORA, MAF(F)IA,
BLACKMAILERS
Maria .... (POLICE) WAGON,
PADDY WAGON, PATROL
WAGON
Monk .... BENEDICTINE
Plague .... BUBONIC
Power leader .... BROWN,
NEWTON, CARMICHAEL
Prince .... EDWARD
Rod .... USHER
Sea .... EUXINE
city .... YALTA, ODESSA
empire .... TREBIZOND
fish .... HAUSEN
inlet .... AZOV
of the .... PONTIC
peninsula .... CRIMEA
port .... ANAPA, VARNA,
ODESSA
resort .... YALTA
Shirt .... NAZI, FASCIST
blackamoor .... NEGRO
blackball .... OPPOSE, REJECT,
BOYCOTT
Blackbeard .... PIRATE, (EDWARD)
TEACH, PRIVATEER
blackbeetle .... COCKROACH
blackberry .... BUSH, VINE,
BRAMBLE
blackbird .... ANI, CROW, RAVEN,
MERL(E), COWBIRD, GRACKLE,
JACKDAW, THRUSH, STARLING
European .... OUSEL, OUZEL
blackboard .... SLATE
blackboy ...... PLANT, GRASS TREE
blackcap .... BIRD, CHICKADEE,
RASPBERRY
blackcock .... (MALE) GROUSE
blackdamp .... GAS
blacken .... TAR, INK, SOIL,
NIGRIFY, SMEAR, DARKEN,
VILIFY, EXECRATE, SLANDER,
JAPAN, TARNISH, DENIGRATE
blackened with soot .... COLLIED
blackface .... BOLD, MINSTREL
Blackfeet .... INDIAN
blackfellow: Austral. ...... MAORI
blackfin snapper .... SESI
blackfish .... TAUTOG, WHALE,
SWART
blackguard .... CAD, VULGAR,
ABUSIVE, VILLAIN,

SCOUNDREL
Blackhawk .... SAC
blackhead .... DUCK, PLUG,
COMEDO, PIMPLE
blackheart .... CHERRY
blackhearted .... EVIL-MINDED,
CRUEL, WICKED, MALEVOLENT
blacking .... SHOE POLISH
blackjack .... OAK, MUG, COERCE,
BLUDGEON, SHANGHAI, CARD
GAME, TWENTY-ONE
blackleg .... FUNGUS, RABIES,
ANTHRAX
blacklist .... CENSURE, CONDEMN,
DENOUNCE, OSTRACIZE
blackly ...... ANGRILY, GLOOMILY,
MENACINGLY
blackmail .... BADGER, COERCE,
TRIBUTE, CHANTAGE,
EXTORTION
blackmailer .... CAMMORA,
MAF(F)IA, VAMPIRE
blackmarket .... BOOTLEG,
UNDER-THE-TABLE
blackness .... NEGRITUDE
blackout .... ECLIPSE, BROWNOUT,
PASS OUT
kind of .... FAINT(ING),
SWOON, AMNESIA, SYNCOPE
news .... HUSH-UP, CENSORSHIP
blackpoll .... WARBLER,
REDSTART, CHICKADEE
blacksmith .... LOHAR, FARRIER
block .... ANVIL
chisel .... HARDY
furnace .... FORGE
shop .... SMITHY, STITHY
tool .... FULLER
blacksnake ...... RACER, COLUBER
blacktail .... MULEDEER
fish .... DASSY
blackthorn ...... HAW, CANE, SLOE
blacktop .... TAR, COVER,
ASPHALT, PAVEMENT
blackwater fever .... MALARIA
blackwood .... BITI, EBONY
blackwort .... COMFREY
bladder ...... BAG, AIR-SAC, URINE
RESERVOIR, VESICA
combining form .... VISICO
container .... STOMACH
deposit .... CALCULUS
infection .... CYSTITIS
problem .... INCONTINENCE
surgery to remove the
.... CYSTECTOMY
bladdernose ...... (HOODED) SEAL
bladderworm .... HYDATID,
CYSTICERCUS
blade .... OAR, LEAF, VANE, KNIFE,
RUNNER, SWORD(SMAN)

grass .... SPEAR
in botany/leaf .... LAMINA
sword ..... TOLEDO, DAMASCUS
bladebone .... SCAPULA
blah: sl. .... ROT, DULL, NONSENSE
blain .... SORE, BULLA, BLISTER,
PUSTULE
Blakely, _____ ...... RONEE, SUSAN
Blake's symbol .... ZOA
blame .... RAP, FAULT, ACCUSE,
CENSURE, CONDEMN,
REPROACH, CRITICIZE,
ACCUSATION
blamed: colloq. .... DAMNED
blameless .... PURE, CLEAN,
HONEST, INNOCENT, SPOTLESS
Blanc, _____ .... MEL
blanch .... PALE, SCALD, BLEACH,
WHITEN, ETIOLATE
blancmange .... FLUMMERY
bland .... MILD, SOFT, GENTLE,
SMOOTH, AFFABLE, SUAVE,
SOOTHING, TEMPERATE
blandation .... BLARNEY,
FLATTERY
blandish .... COAX, CAJOLE,
FLATTER
blank .... CLEAR, EMPTY,
UNWRITTEN, WHITE, BARREN,
UNFILLED, (DE)VOID,
MARKLESS
check of a sort .... CARTE
BLANCHE
draw a .... FAIL, LOSE, ZERO,
ZILCH
in baseball .... SHUTOUT
in printing .... QUAD
interval between words
.... SPACE
look .... POKER FACE
look, describing one
.... VACANT
sheet in book .... FLYLEAF
space .... GAP, VOID, HIATUS
blanket .... COVER, AFGHAN,
SHEET, COVERLET,
OVERSPREAD
approval .... CARTE BLANCHE
authority .... FULL POWER(S)
horse .... MANTA
Mexican .... SERAPE
worn as cloak .... PONCHO
blankety-blank .... DAMNED,
BLASTED, CONFOUNDED,
EXPLETIVE
blankminded .... IGNORANT,
OBLIVIOUS, UNKNOWING
blare .... BLAZON
trumpet's .... FANFARE,
TANTARA
blarney ...... COAX, FLAM, STONE,

SOFT TALK, WHEEDLE, FLATTERY

blasé ...... BORED, SATED, WEARY, SATIATED

blaspheme .... ABUSE, CURSE, REVILE, PROFANE

blasphemous .... FOUL, VILE, ABUSIVE, CURSING, IMPIOUS, IRREVERENT

blasphemy .... IMPIETY, PROFANITY, SACRILEGE

Blass or Beene .... DESIGNER

blast .... GUST, SEAR, ATTACK, BLIGHT, BLOW-UP, ERUPTION, EXPLODE, EXPLOSION

furnace .... FORGE, SMELTER

furnace part .... MANTLE, BOSH, TROMPE, TUYERE

of horn .... TOOT

off step .... COUNT DOWN

sluice .... SOW

blat .... BLAB, BLEAT, BLURT

blatant .... GAUDY, NOISY, SHOWY, COARSE, FLASHY, VULGAR, BOISTEROUS, VOCIFEROUS, LOUDMOUTHED

blather .... NONSENSE, FOOLISH TALK

blaubok .... ETAAC, ANTELOPE

blaze .... FIRE, FLAME, FLARE, FLASH, SHINE, OUTBURST

away ...... SHOOT, (RAPID) FIRE

on animal's face .... SPOT

star .... NOVA

blazer .... JACKET

blazes, go to .... HELL, BE DAMNED

blazing .... AFIRE

star .... COMET, TORCH LILY

blazon .... DISPLAY, EMBLEM, BLARE, PROCLAIM, COAT OF ARMS

bleach .... BLANCH, CHLORE, PURIFY, WHITEN, LIGHTEN, ETIOLATE, DECOLORIZE

by sunning .... INSOLATE

bleaching powder ...... CHLORIDE

vat .... KEIR, KIER

bleak ...... DIM, RAW, BARE, COLD, PALE, DREAR, STARK, DISMAL, DREARY, GLOOMY, DESOLATE, TREELESS

blear .... DIM, BLUR, MISTY, BLURRED, INDISTINCT

bleary-eyed ...... TEARY, RHEUMY, DULL-WITTED

bleat .... BAA, CRY, MAA, BLAT, WHINE

bleater .... CALF, GOAT, LAMB, SHEEP, WHINER, CRYBABY

bleb .... BULLA, BUBBLE, BLISTER,

VESICLE

bleed .... LEAK, OOZE, SUCK, FLOW, EXTORT, SUFFER, EMIT BLOOD

certain way .... LEECH

white .... IMPOVERISH

bleeder ...... LEECH, HEMOPHILIAC

bleeding .... HEMORRHAGE

gums .... GINGIVITIS

heart .... DICENTRA

stoppage of .... HEMOSTASIS

stopper .... HEMOSTAT

uncontrollable .... HEMOPHILIA

within the brain .... CEREBRAL HEMORRHAGE

bleffert .... SQUALL

blemish .... MAR, BLOT, DENT, DEFACE, MARK, FLAW, FAULT, SPECK, SMIRCH, STAIN, DEFECT, DEFORMITY, MACULATE, TARNISH

cloth .... AMPER

on an olive .... SCAB

on reputation .... DISGRACE, DISHONOR

skin .... MOLE, SCAR, NEVUS, PIMPLE, FRECKLE, NAEVUS, BIRTHMARK

blemished ...... FAULTY, MARRED, KELOIDAL

blench .... FADE, PALE, AVOID, EVADE, SHRINK, CRINGE, SHUN, FLINCH, WHITEN, SIDESTEP

blend .... MERGE, FUSE, MELD, MINGLE, MIX(TURE), HARMONIZE

colors .... FONDU

into .... MERGE, COMBINE, CONVERT

blende .... ORE, SPHALERITE

blenny .... GUNNEL, SHANNY

blended .... MERGED, MIXED, ATTUNED, COMBINED

blesbok .... NUNNI, ANTELOPE

bless .... ENDOW, FAVOR, HALLOW, BEATIFY, GLORIFY, PRAISE, SANCTIFY, CONSECRATE

against evil .... SAIN

blessed .... DIVINE, SACRED, JOYFUL, BLISSFUL, HALLOWED, HOLY, BEATIFIED, CONSECRATED

event .... BIRTH

Blessed Sacrament

.... EUCHARIST

blessing .... BOON, GIFT, SAIN, GRACE, BENISON, APPROVAL, INVOCATION, BEATITUDE, BENEDICTION

at meal .... GRACE

blet .... FRUIT DECAY

blight .... NIP, FIRE, RUIN, RUST, SMUT, BLAST, DECAY, DISEASE, MILDEW, DESTROY, SEAR, TAINT, ADVERSITY, IMPAIR, FRUSTRATE

blighted .... RUINED, RUSTY, SEEDY, DAMAGED, DECREPIT, ROTTEN, SPOILED, WRECKED

blighter .... VAGABOND

blimp: colloq. .... AIRSHIP

blind .... SEEL, COVER, DARK(EN), SHADE, EYELESS, SCREEN, RECKLESS, SHUTTER, DAZZLE, OBSCURE, SIGHTLESS

a hawk .... SEEL

aid for the ...... CANE, SEEING-EYE DOG

alley .... DEADEND, IMPASSE, CUL-DE-SAC

as a ____ .... BAT

bargain .... PIG-IN-A-POKE

daters .... STRANGERS

dolphin .... SUSU

faith ...... DOTAGE, CREDULITY, GULLIBILITY

fear .... PANIC

flower girl .... NIDIA

god .... HOTH, HODER

gut .... CECUM

impulse .... ATE, NOTION

love, usually ..... INFATUATION

pig/tiger: sl. .... SPEAKEASY

shot .... HIT-OR-MISS

slang .... DRUNK

spot .... SCOTOMA

spot: colloq. .... WEAKNESS, IGNORANCE

staggers .... GID, MEGRIM, VERTIGO

system of printing for the .... BRAILLE

temporarily .... DAZZLE, ECLIPSE

to .... ASLEEP, UNAWARE, OBLIVIOUS

window .... VENETIAN

blindage .... CAMOUFLAGE, DISGUISE, SMOKE-SCREEN

blinder .... SEEL, WINKER, BLINKER

blinders .... GOGGLES, EYE-PATCH

blindfold .... SEEL, COVER, OBSCURE, MISLEAD, HOODWINK

blindly .... GROPINGLY

blindness .... CECITY, ABLEPSIA, TYPHLITIS, TYPHLOSIS

color .... MONOCHROMATISM

common cause of .... CATARACT, GLAUCOMA

day .... HEMERALOPIA
night .... NYCTALOPIA
river .... ONCHOCERCIASIS
snow .... NIPHABLEPSIA
blinds .... PERSIENNES
blindstory .... GALLERY
blindworm .... ORVET
blink .... BAT, WINK, IGNORE,
FLUTTER, NICTATE, TWINKLE
blinker .... EYE, BLINDER
blintz .... PASTRY, PANCAKE,
FLAPJACK
blip .... SIGNAL
bliss .... JOY, GAIETY, GLORY,
ECSTASY, HARMONY,
DELIGHT, RAPTURE, FELICITY
place of .... EDEN, HEAVEN,
UTOPIA, ELYSIUM, PARADISE
blissful .... HAPPY, JOYOUS,
ELYSIAN, SUBLIME
blister .... BLEB, BLAIN, BULLA,
VESICLE, VESICATE
beetle .... SPANISH FLY
causing .... VESICANT
cloth .... YAW
containing pus .... PUSTULE
on neck .... MALANDERS
blistered .... PUFFED, BULLATE
blistering agent .... VESICANT,
SPISPASTIC
reprimand .... TONGUE-
LASHING
blithe .... GAY, AIRY, GLAD,
JOVIAL, MERRY, CAREFREE,
CHEERFUL, LIGHTHEARTED
spirit, Shakespearean
.... ARIEL
blithering .... JABBERING
blitz .... ATTACK, CHARGE,
DESTROY, OVERWHELM
blitzkrieg .... RAID, WARFARE
of a sort .... COUP, COUP
D'ETAT, COUP DE MAIN
blizzard .... SNOWSTORM,
WINDSTORM
in Alaska .... PURGA
blk. .... BULK, BLACK, BLOCK
bloat .... PUFF, SWELL, TUMEFY,
AMPLIFY, INFLATE, DRUNKARD
bloated .... CURED, OBESE,
TURGID, BULGING, FLUSHED,
POMPOUS, SWOLLEN,
CORPULENT
bloater .... FISH, HERRING,
MACKEREL
blob .... BEAD, SPLASH,
DROP(LET), SPLOTCH
bloc .... BAND, BODY, RING,
GROUP, CLIQUE, TEAM,
UNION, ALLIANCE
block .... DAM, MOLD, SPRAG,

HAMPER, HINDER, IMPEDE,
OCCLUDE, OBSTACLE,
STONEWALL
butcher's .... CHOPPING BOARD
casks' .... QUOIN
for nails on wall .... NOG
go to the .... AUCTION, UP FOR
SALE
hawser .... BITT
house .... FORT
ice .... SERAC
letter .... HANDPRINTING
mechanical .... PULLEY
metal .... NUT
of metal type .... QUAD
of stamps .... PANE
of wood .... NOG, CHUMP,
DEADEYE
set against wheel .... TRIG
small .... TESSERA
up .... DAM, CLOG, CHOKE,
STEM, BLOCKADE, OBSTRUCT
wedge-shaped .... QUOIN
blockade .... ISOLATE, BOTTLE-UP,
SHUTDOWN, STOPPAGE,
ROADBLOCK
runner of a sort
.... SMUGGLER,
CONTRABANDIST
blockhead ...... ASS, CLOD, FOOL,
IDIOT, OAF, DOLT, MUTT,
DUNCE, PINHEAD, BUNGLER,
STOCK, NITWIT, NUM(B)SKULL
blocky .... PUDGY, CHUNKY,
STOCKY
bloke: sl. ...... OAF, CHAP, JOKER,
BUGGER, FELLOW, JASPER
vulgar .... MUCKER
blond(e) .... LACE, WOMAN,
TOWHEAD, FAIR-HAIRED,
FLAXEN-HAIRED
kind of .... ASH, PEROXIDE,
PLATINUM, HONEY,
STRAWBERRY
Blonde Bombshell of movies
.... HARLOW
blood .... GORE, LIFE, SERUM,
KINDRED, KINSHIP, LINEAGE,
PEDIGREE, LIFE-FLUID
accumulation in body
.... CONGESTION
and thunder .... THEATRICS,
CLOAK-AND-DAGGER
bad .... ANGER, HATRED,
ANIMOSITY, ANTAGONISM
brother .... BUDDY, FRIEND,
RELATIVE
cancer/disease .... LEUKEMIA
cell .... MONOCYTE
clot ...... GORE, CRUOR, GRUME

clot formation
.... THROMBOSIS
clotting remedy .... HISTONE
color .... RED, SANGUINE
colored .... HEMATIC
coloring matter .... CRUOR,
HEMOGLOBIN
combining form .... HEMA,
HEM(O), HAEMO, HEMAT,
SANGUI, HEMATO, HAEMATO
condition .... LITHEMIA
congestion .... HYPEREMIA
corpuscle structure
.... STROMA
coughing up/spitting
.... HEMOPTYSIS
covered/filled with ...... GORY,
HEMATOSE
emulsion .... CHYLE
escaping from its vessel
.... HEMORRHAGE
excess of .... PLETHORA
feud .... VENDETTA
flow, stoppage of .... STASIS
flowing from wound
.... GORE, CRUOR
fluid part of .... PLASMA
formation .... HEMATOSIS
having to do with
.... H(A)EMIC, H(A)EMAL
in the urine .... HEMATURIA
iron deficiency .... ANEMIA
is thicker than _____
.... WATER
kin .... GENS, RELATIVE
like .... HEMOID, HEMATOID
money .... CRO, WERGELD,
HUSH-MONEY
movement .... CIRCULATION
of gods .... ICHOR
of the .... HEMIC,
SANGUINEOUS
oxygen carrier
.... HEMOGLOBIN
particles in .... CORPUSCLES
pertaining to .... HEMATIC
poisoning .... SEPSIS,
TOXEMIA, COPR(A)EMIA,
PY(A)EMIA, SAPR(A)EMIA,
SEPTICEMIA
pressure drug ..... ADRENALIN,
HISTAMINE, EPINEPHRINE
pressure hormone .... ACTH,
RENIN
pressure instrument
.... (SPHYGMO) MANOMETER
pudding .... SAUSAGE
red .... CRIMSON, SANGUINE
red cell .... ERYTHROCYTE
red corpuscle, abnormally
large .... MACROCYTE

red corpuscle, abnormally small .... MICROCYTE
relation ...... KIN, SIB, FAMILY, RELATIVE
solvent .... LYSIN(E)
sport .... FOX-HUNTING, COCKFIGHTING
stream foreign matter .... CLOT, (AIR) BUBBLE, EMBOLUS
study of .... HEMATOLOGY
substance in .... OPSONIN
sucking insect .... FLEA, TABANID, LOUSE, BEDBUG, GADFLY, HORSEFLY, CONENOSE, MOSQUITO
sucking monster .... LAMIA
thirsty one ...... LEECH, LOMIA, VAMPIRE
transferred to another person .... TRANSFUSION
vessel .... VEIN, AORTA, ARTERY, CAPILLARY
vessel, dilated .... VARIX
vessel disorder .... SCURVY
vessel obstruction .... EMBOLISM
vessels network .... RETE
vomiting .... HEMATEMESIS
watery part of .... SERA, SERUM
white cell .... LEUKOCYTE
with reduced corpuscles .... AN(A)EMIA
bloodbath ...... PURGE, CARNAGE, KILLING, MASSACRE
bloodcurdling .... DREADFUL, TERRIBLE, FRIGHTFUL, TERRIFYING, HORRIFYING
blooded .... PUREBRED, PEDIGREED, THOROUGHBRED
bloodhound .... SLEUTH, MANHUNTER, HUNTING DOG
bloodied .... GORY
bloodily ...... CRUELLY, SAVAGELY
bloodless ...... COLD, PALE, WEAK, AN(A)EMIC
bloodletting .... BLEEDING, LEECHING, BLOODSHED
art of .... PHLEBOTOMY, VENESECTION
bloodline .... PEDIGREE, DESCENT, LINEAGE, ANCESTRY
bloodroot .... POPPY, PUCCOON, SANGUINARIA
bloodshed .... SLAUGHTER, CARNAGE, KILLING, VIOLENCE
much .... GORY
bloodshot .... RED
bloodstone .... QUARTZ, HEMATITE, BIRTHSTONE,

HELIOTROPE
bloodsucker .... FLEA, MITE, TICK, DEERFLY, VAMPIRE, EXTORTER, LEECH, PARASITE, EXTORTIONIST
bloodthirsty .... CRUEL, WARLIKE, PITILESS, HOMICIDAL, MURDEROUS, SANGUINARY
bloody .... RED, GORY, BLEEDING, CRIMSON
bloom .... BLOW, PRIME, RIPEN, FLOWER, BLOSSOM, FLOURISH
life's .... HEYDAY
bloomer .... ERROR, BLUNDER, MISTAKE, TROUSERS
bloomery .... FORGE, HEARTH, FURNACE
blooming ...... FLORID, THRIVING, BLOSSOMING, FLOWERING, FLOURISHING
colloquial .... UTTER, CONFOUNDED
too early .... RATH(E)
blooper .... BONER, HOWLER, BOO-BOO, SCREW-UP
blossom .... BUD, BLOOM, FLOWER, MELLOW, SPROUT, FLOREATE, FLOURISH
blot .... DAB, MAR, SPOT, STAIN, SULLY, SMUDGE, SMEAR, EXPUNGE, DISGRACE
in printing .... MACKLE
out .... ERASE, CANCEL, DELETE, OBSCURE, DESTROY, WIPE OFF
blotch ...... MARK, SMEAR, STAIN, MACULA, MOTTLE
blotchy .... SPOTTED
blotter .... RECORD, SPONGE, ABSORBENT
usual keeper of .... POLICE
blotto: sl. .... SOT, DRUNK, STONED, UNCONSCIOUS
blouse .... MIDDY, SHIRT, BODICE, SMOCK, WAIST, SHIRTWAIST
front .... JABOT
Korean silk .... CHIMA
under pinafore .... GUIMPE
with tight waist .... BASQUE
blow .... BRAG, BUFF, HUFF, LASH, SWAT, THUD, BLAST, PUFF, BURST, SHOCK, STORM, GALE, WALLOP, MISFORTUNE
about ...... SPREAD, CIRCULATE
colloquial .... FETE, TREAT, SPEND
down .... TOPPLE
dull-sounding .... DUNT
for blow .... TIT FOR TAT, RETALIATION
gently .... WAFT

horn .... TOOT
horn: colloq. ..... BRAG, BOAST
hot and cold .... WAVER, HESITATE, FLUCTUATE, VACILLATE
in: colloq. .... ARRIVE
off .... RANT, TALK, ERUPT, EXPLODE
off chaff .... WINNOW
off steam .... WANTON, CAROUSE, DEBAUCH
on the head .... NOB, CONK
on the knuckles .... RAP
one's mind: sl. .... FREAK OUT
one's nose: archaic .... SNET
one's top off: colloq. .... RAGE, RAVE, EXPLODE
out .... SPEW, ERUPT, EXPEL
over .... COOL, PASS, DISSIPATE
resounding .... WHACK
sharp and quick .... CLIP
slang .... FLEE, LEAVE, SCRAM, SQUANDER
stormily .... BLUSTER
the whistle .... BETRAY, SNITCH, SQUEAL, DISCLOSE
unexpected .... BOLT, SNEAKPUNCH
up .... ERUPT, ENLARGE, EXPLODE, INFLATE
whistle .... TOOT, BLAST, SIREN
with club .... DRUB, CUDGEL
with fist .... POKE, PASTE
blower .... FAN, BELLOWS, WHALE, BRAGGART, VENTILATOR
blowgun ...... SPRAYER, SUMPITAN
missile .... DART, PELLET
blowhole .... FLUE, NOSTRIL, BREATHER
of whale .... SPIRACLE
blowing mammal .... WHALE
blown .... RANCID, BLASTED, EXPOSED, RAVAGED, WINDSWEPT
blowoff: sl. .... BOASTER
blowout .... FEAST, BANQUET, TREAT, PARTY, CELEBRATION
one result of a ...... FLAT TIRE
blowpipe .... BLOWGUN
blowup: colloq. .... BLOAT, OUTBURST, EXPLOSION
blowy .... GUSTY, WINDY, BLUSTERY
blowzy .... FROWZY, SLOVENLY
woman .... SLUT, SLATTERN
blubber ...... CRY, WEEP, (WHALE) FAT
piece of .... LIPPER
strip .... FLENSE
blucher .... SHOE, (HALF)BOOT
bludgeon ...... BAT, CLUB, BULLY,

COERCE, CUDGEL
blue .... SAD, ANIL, AZURE, DELFT, LIVID, PERSE, SMALT, COBALT, GLOOMY, CELESTE, DEJECTED, DEPRESSED
back .... TROUT
bird .... JAY
blood .... NOBLE, ROYALTY, NOBILITY, ARISTOCRAT
book .... DIRECTORY, SOCIAL REGISTER
chip .... STOCK
chips: colloq. .... TOPS, VALUABLE, EXCELLENT
collar worker .... LABORER, UNSKILLED
combining form .... CYAN
days .... MONDAYS
deathly ...... WAN, PALE, EERIE
deep .... ULTRAMARINE
devil: sl. .... DOWNER
devils .... DUMPS, DELIRIUM
dyestuff .... ANIL, WOAD, INDIGO
fin .... TUNA, HERRING
flag .... IRIS, FLOWER
flower .... LARKSPUR
fox .... FUR
gas .... OZONE
grass .... POA
grayish ..... BICE, TEAL, PERSE, SLATE, AZURINE
gum .... TREE, EUCALYPTUS
in the face .... HAGGARD, HYSTERICAL
jeans .... LEVIS, DENIMS, DUNGAREES
language .... PROFANITY
mineral .... IOLITE
movie .... PORNOGRAPHY
or green .... EMAIL
out of the .... SURPRISE, UNEXPECTED, UNFORESEEN
peacock .... PAON
pencil ...... CUT, EDIT, DELETE, REVISE, CORRECT
penciled .... DELED, DELETED
peter .... SIGNAL FLAG
pigment .... BICE, SMALT
pill .... LAXATIVE
pointer shark .... MAKO
racer .... SNAKE
ribbon .... BADGE, AWARD, FIRST (PRIZE), DECORATION
river, so called .... DANUBE
shade .... ALICE, AZURE
star .... VEGA
stem ..... GRASS, ANDROPOGON
the .... SEA, SKY, HEAVEN
wing teal .... GARGANEY
Blue Eagle of New Deal .... NRA

Grotto home .... CAPRI
Nile country .... ETHIOPIA
Bluebeard, latest .... LANDRU
wife of .... FATIMA
bluebell ...... COWSLIP, HAREBELL, HYACINTH
bluebonnet .... CAP, LUPINE, SCOTS(MAN)
bluebottle .... FLY, BLOWFLY, HYACINTH, CORNFLOWER
bluecap .... TITMOUSE
bluecoat .... SOLDIER, POLICEMAN
bluegill .... SUNFISH
Bluegrass State .... KENTUCKY
bluejack .... VITRIOL
bluejacket .... MARINE, SAILOR, SOLDIER, ENLISTED MAN
slang .... GOB, SWABBER
bluenose: colloq. .... PURITAN, NOVA SCOTIAN
bluepoint .... OYSTER
blueprint .... MAP, SKETCH, DIAGRAM, OUTLINE, CYANOTYPE
blues .... MEGRIM, DOLDRUMS, DUMPS, (FOLK)SONG, MULLIGRUBS
bluestocking .... PEDANTIC, SCHOLASTIC
bluestone .... VITRIOL
bluet .... PLANT, INNOCENCE
blueweed .... BUGLOSS
bluff ...... FOOL, SCARE, BLUSTER, MISLEAD, BRUSQUE, BRAVADO, BLUNT, BAMBOOZLE, FOURFLUSH(ER)
in poker ...... RAISE, COUNTER-RAISE
rounded .... MORRO
bluffer .... LIAR, IMPOSTOR, FOURFLUSHER
bluing material .... INDIGO
bluish gray ...... PEARL, MERL(E), BICE, SLATE, CESIUM, CAESIUS
green ..... AQUA, AQUAMARINE
red .... MALLOW
white metallic element .... ZINC
blunder .... SLIP, ERR(OR), GAFFE, BUNGLE, MISTAKE, STUMBLE, FLOUNDER
in social etiquette .... FAUX PAS, SOLECISM
stupid: sl. .... BONER
blunderbore .... OGRE
blunderbuss .... GUN
blunt .... CURT, DULL, BLUFF, GRUFF, INERT, OBTUND, TERSE, OBTUSE, BRUSQUE, DOWNRIGHT, OUTSPOKEN
arrow .... BUTTSHAFT

end .... CHUMP
end of hammer .... POLL
headed bullet .... DUMDUM
refusal .... REBUFF
blur .... DIM, HAZE, BLOT, CLOUD, STAIN, MACKLE, OBSCURE, MACULATE
on film/photo .... FOG
blurb .... WRITE-UP, PUBLICITY, ANNOUNCEMENT, AD(VERTISEMENT)
blurt .... BLABBER, DIVULGE
blush .... COLOR, FLUSH, MANTLE, REDDEN
at first .... OFFHAND, INITIALLY
cause of .... ANGER, SHAME, EXCITEMENT, GUILT, DISCOMFITURE, EMBARRASSMENT
blushing .... GLOWING, COLORING, REDDENING
bluster ...... RANT, BULLY, BLOW, STORM, BRAVADO, RAGE, THREATEN
blustering .... WINDY, NOISY, SWASH, VIOLENT
blustery .... GUSTY, WINDY
blvd. .... BOULEVARD
bo: sl. .... HOBO, TRAMP, VAGRANT
tree .... PIPAL
boa .... SCARF, SNAKE, PYTHON, ANACONDA, CONSTRICTOR
ringed .... ABOMA
boar .... HOG, PIG, SUS, SWINE, BARROW
flesh, picked .... BRAWN
for example .... TUSKER
tooth .... TUSK
board .... FOOD, PLANT, GET ON, TABLE, EMBARK, CLOSE UP, COUNCIL, TRIBUNAL, PLANCH(E), FACILITIES
and lodging .... KEEP
artist's .... PALETTE
for holding mortar ...... HAWK
from sugarcane residue .... CELOTEX
game .... CHESS, DARTS, CHECKERS, MONOPOLY, BACKGAMMON, PA(R)CHISI
member ..... REGENT, TRUSTEE, DIRECTOR
on bus .... EMBUS
on plane .... EMPLANE, ENPLANE
on train .... ENTRAIN
Board, the Big: abbr. ...... NYSE
boarding house .... INN, DORM, LODGING, PENSION, DORMITORY

house lodger .... GUEST, EATER, ROOMER
boards, the ...... STAGE, THEATER
boardwalk .... TRAIL, PATHWAY
boarish .... SWINISH
boast .... BRAG, CROW, CLAIM, ENJOY, VAUNT, FLAUNT, ROISTER, GASCONADE
empty .... BLUFF
of .... GLOAT, MAGNIFY
boaster .... GASCON, BLOWOFF, BRAGGART, BRAGGADOCIO
of one's patriotism ...... JINGO
slang .... WINDBAG, LOUDMOUTH
boastful .... VAIN, PROUD, ARROGANT, THRASONICAL
air .... BRAVADO, SWAGGER
talk .... GAS, BRAG, HOT AIR, GASCONADE, FANFARONADE
walk .... STRUT, SWAGGER
boasting .... CROWING, BRAGGADOCIO, RODOMONTADE
boat .... GIG, TUB, RAFT, SHIP, FERRY, VESSEL, STEAMER, FREIGHTER, (WATER)CRAFT
African .... DHOW
American river .... CANOE
ancient .... BIREME, GALLEY, CORACLE, GALLEON, TRIREME
awkward .... ARK, DROGHER
basin .... MARINA
Bolivian .... BALSA
Canadian .... BATEAU
canoe-like .... PIROGUE
captain .... SKIPPER
captain of story .... AHAB, NEMO, BLIGH
Ceylon/E. Indies .... DONI, DHONI, DINGEY
Chinese .... JUNK, SAMPAN
clumsy .... ARK, TUB, HULK, HOOKER, DROGHER
dispatch .... AVISO, OOLAK
Dutch Indies .... PRAAM, HOOKER
Egyptian .... BARIS, SANDAL
English .... COBLE
Eskimo .... KYAK, KAYAK, UMIAK, OOMIAK, BIDARKEE, BIDARKA
ferry .... BAC
fishing .... DORY, COBLE, SMACK, DOGGER, CORACLE, TRAWLER
flat-bottomed .... BATEAU, DORY, KEEL, PUNT, BARGE, SCOW, SLOOP, PONTOON
for gathering shellfish
.... DREDGER

freight .... SCOW, BARGE, TRAMP, WHERRY, LIGHTER
French .... CARAVELLE
front .... BOW, FORE, PROW
helm .... TILLER
Indian .... DHOW, MASOOLA
Indian river .... ALMADIA
Italian .... GONDOLA
landing .... LST
Levantine .... BUM, SAIC, XEBEC, KETCH
mail .... PACKET
Malayan .... PAHI, PRAH, PRAO, PRAU, PROA, TOUP
marker .... BUOY
Mediterranean .... SET(T)EE
merchant .... ARGOSY
narrow/light .... CANOE
Netherlands .... BILANDER
Nile river .... SANDAL
North Sea .... DOGGER
old .... HULK, HOOKER
on vessel ...... JOLLY, PINNACE
on warship .... DINGHY, LAUNCH
Philippine ...... BATEL, BANCA, CASCO
pole-propelled .... PUNT, CASCO, GONDOLA
propeller ..... OAR, POLE, SAIL, SCULL, PADDLE
race .... REGATTA
racing .... SCULL, SHELL, YACHT
raft/two-hulled
.... CATAMARAN
rear end of .... AFT, STERN
river .... BARGE, CANOE, FERRY, PACKET, SAMPAN, WHERRY
row .... COBLE, SHELL, DINGHY, SKIFF, WHERRY
rudder .... WHEEL, TILLER
sail .... SKIFF, SMACK
scout .... VEDETTE, VIDETTE
shallow, small .... COCKLE
shaped .... SCAPHOID, NAVICULAR
shaped ornament .... NEF
ship's .... YAWL, PINNACE
sink deliberately ...... SCUTTLE
slow .... ARK, TRAMP, BUCKET, DROGHER
small .... COG, DORY, SKIFF, COCKLE, DINGHY, JIGGER, SHALLOP
steering part .... WHEEL, RUDDER, TILLER
tender .... HOY
three-oared .... RANDAN
tiller .... WHEEL, RUDDER

timber .... KEEL
towing .... TUG
two-masted .... DOGGER, PIRAGUA, PIROGUE
boating .... ROWING, SAILING, CRUISING
boatman .... OARSMAN, PADDLER, POLER, VOYAGEUR, GONDOLIER
on Styx .... CHARON
boats, small fleet of .... FLOTILLA
boatswain .... BOSUN
whistle .... PIPE
Boaz' son .... OBED
wife .... RUTH
bob ...... RAP, DOCK, SLED, FLOAT, CURTSY, HAIRCUT, PENDANT, REFRAIN, SHORTEN
bait .... DIB
British: sl. .... SHILLING
bobbery .... ROW, HUBBUB
bobbin .... PIN, PIRN, REEL, SPOOL
lace .... CLUNY
of weaver's shuttle .... PIRN
bobbin's holder .... CREEL, SPINDLE
bobby .... POLICEMAN
soxer: colloq. .... TEENAGER
station of a .... POINT
bobcat .... LYNX, WILDCAT
bobolink .... SORA, ORTALAN, RICEBIRD, SONGBIRD
bobsled .... TOBOGGAN
bobwhite .... COLIN, QUAIL, PARTRIDGE
bocaccio .... COD, ROCKFISH
bocca .... BERRY
Boccaccio's work
.... DECAMERON
Boche ...... HUN, JERRY, GERMAN, SQUAREHEAD
bock .... BEER
bode .... OMEN, AUGUR, PORTEND, PRESAGE
bodega: Sp. .... CELLAR, WAREHOUSE
bodice .... VEST, CHOLL, WAIST, BASQUE, CORSAGE
front piece .... JABOT
posy .... CORSAGE
bodily .... SOMATIC, ENTIRE, WHOLLY, PHYSICAL
bodkin .... DAGGER, NEEDLE, HAIRPIN, STILETTO, EYELETEER
body ...... FIGURE, PERSON, SOMA, GROUP, ANATOMY, ASSEMBLAGE
animal/as a whole .... SOMA
appetite .... LUST

beautiful, adjective for .... SEXY, SEDUCTIVE
build .... PHYSIQUE
coldness .... CHILL
combining form .... SOMA, SOMAT(O)
dead .... CORSE, CORPSE, CADAVER, CARCASS
duct .... MEATUS
fats .... LIPIDS, STEROLS, TRIGLYCERIDES
heavenly .... SUN, MOON, STAR, COMET, PLANET
injury .... TRAUMA
internal organs .... VITALS, INNARDS
joint ...... KNEE, WAIST, ELBOW
judicial ...... COURT, TRIBUNAL
language ...... SHRUG, MOTION, GESTURE
main .... TORSO, TRUNK
odor .... SWEAT, STENCH
odor: colloq. .... BO
odor treatment .... DEODORANT, ANTIPERSPIRANT
of advisers .... CABINET
assistants .... STAFF
horse .... BARREL
laws .... CODE
learning .... LORE
men .... ARMY, POSSE, SQUAD, TROOP, PLATOON
nobility .... PEERAGE
plant .... SOMA
representatives .... DELEGATION
retainers ..... SUITE, RETINUE, ENTOURAGE
the/pertaining to the .... SOMATIC, CORPOR(E)AL
troops .... COMPANY, DIVISION, REGIMENT
vertebra .... CENTRUM
water .... BAY, SEA, COVE, LAKE, POND, POOL, OCEAN, BAYOU, RIVER, CHANNEL, BROOK, CANAL, GULF, LAGOON, STRAIT, FIORD, STREAM, RESERVOIR
writing .... TEXT, THEME
opening .... FORAMEN
orbiting around planet .... SATELLITE
orbiting around sun .... PLANET
politic .... WEAL, STATE, SOCIETY
servant .... VALET
shop .... GARAGE
slang .... CHASSIS

trunk of .... TORSO
weakness .... DEBILITY
body's framework ...... SKELETON
largest organ .... SKIN
bodyguard ...... ESCORT, RETINUE, PROTECTOR
slang .... TORPEDO
Boeotia's capital .... THEBES
Boer dialect .... TAAL
general .... BOTHA, HERTZOG
statesman .... HERTZOG
troops .... COMMANDO
War town besieged .... MAFEKING
Boers' victim .... MATABELE
bog .... FEN, MIRE, MOOR, MARSH, OOZE, QUAG, SWAMP, MORASS, MUSKEG, QUAGMIRE
berry .... CRANBERRY
orchid .... CALYPSO
peat .... MOSS
product .... PEAT
trotter .... IRISH(MAN)
bogey .... BOGY, BOGIE, MONSTER, BUGABOO, BUGBEAR, (HOB)GOBLIN, SPECTER
in golf .... ONE OVER PAR
bogeyman .... GHOUL, GHOST, SCARER, PHANTOM, HOBGOBLIN
bogged down .... STALLED
boggle .... AMAZE, BOTCH, BUNGLE, ASTOUND, CONFUSE, HESITATE, QUIBBLE, SCRUPLE, EQUIVOCATE
boggy .... MIRY, MARSHY, QUAGGY, SWAMPY
tract .... MORASS
bogie: Brit. .... CART, TRUCK
bogus .... FAKE, SHAM, SPURIOUS, COUNTERFEIT
colloq. ...... PHONY, DOCTORED
bogy. See **bogey**
bohea .... (BLACK)TEA
Bohemia .... CECHY
Bohemian .... ARTY, GYPSY, ARTIST, DILETTANTE
city .... PRAHA, PILSEN
composer .... MAHLER
dance .... POLKA, REDOWA, TALIAN
garnet .... PYROPE
general .... ZISKA, ZIZKA
Girl .... ARLINE
hotsprings site ..... CARLSBAD, KARLSBAD
martyr .... HUS(S)
mountain .... ERZ
patron saint .... WENCESLAUS
reformer .... HUS(S)
river .... EGER, ISER, OHRE

town .... CARLSBAD
Bohr, physicist .... NIELS
boil .... COOK, FUME, RAGE, SORE, ANGER, CHURN, BUBBLE, ANTHRAX, SEETHE, PUSTULE, LUMP, FURUNCLE, CARBUNCLE
eyelid .... STY
slow .... STEW, SIMMER
boiled rice: Philippines .... KANIN
rice with meat, spiced .... PILAF, PILAFF, PILAU
shirt: sl. .... BRAGGART, POPINJAY
boiler .... TANK, COPPER, FURNACE, CA(U)LDRON
coating inside of .... SCALE
covering .... LAG(GING)
safety device .... HYDROSTAT
to tend a .... STOKE
vent .... TUBE
boiling .... COOKING, BUBBLING, SCALDING, SEETHING
over .... AFIRE, ABLAZE, FLUSHED, STEAMING
point .... HIGH TEST
slang .... HOT UNDER THE COLLAR
boisterous .... ROWDY, ROUGH, TURBULENT, NOISY, STORMY, RIOTOUS, VIOLENT, VOCIFEROUS
fun .... JINK(S)
bola .... WEAPON
Spanish .... BALL
bolar .... CLAYEY, CLAYISH
bold ...... BRAVE, DARING, FIERCE, FRESH, FEARLESS, INTREPID, AUDACIOUS
and brazen .... SHAMELESS
and courageous .... HEROIC
and daring .... DEFIANT, CHALLENGING
and free .... MOD
and resolute .... HARDY
and strong ..... LUSTY, MIGHTY
faced .... PERT, BRASSY, SAUCY, FORWARD, IMPUDENT
front .... BLUFF
girl .... HOYDEN, TOMBOY
boldness .... CHEEK, PLUCK, DEFIANCE, COURAGE, TEMERITY
bole .... CLAY, STEM, TREE, STALK, TRUNK
bolero .... VEST, DANCE
composer of .... RAVEL
boletus .... TOADSTOOL
bolide .... METEOR, FIREBALL
Bolivar .... COIN, (THE) LIBERATOR
Bolivian boat .... BALSA

capital .... SUCRE, LA PAZ

city/town ...... SUCRE, PUNATA,
ORURO, CAMIRI, TARIJA,
POTOSI, COBIJA, TRINIDAD,
VIACHA

export .... TIN

Indian .... ITE, ITEN, CHOLO,
URO, LECA, MOJO, AYMARA

lagoon .... GAIBA, CACERES,
COLORADA, HUATUNAS,
MANDIORE

lake .... POOPO, COIPASA,
ROGAGUA, TITICACA

language .... AYMARA,
QUECHUA, SPANISH

llama .... ALPACA

money .... PESO, TOMINE,
BOLIVIANO

mountain .... JARA, ILLAMPU,
CHOVORECA, ANCOHUMA,
PUPUYA, SAJAMA,
HUANCHUPA, ZAPALERI,
TOCORPURI

mountains .... CHARAGUA,
BLOOMFIELD

plains .... GRAND CHACO

river ..... BENI, ABUNA, LAUCA,
BOOPI, CLARO, BARRAS,
BLANCO, NEGRO, PIRAY,
GRANDE, MAMORE, RAPULO,
MIZQUE, MADIDI, YATA,
PARAGUAY, BERMEJO,
MACHUPO, CANDELARIA

salt deposit .... COIPASA,
UYUNI, EMPEXA, CHALLVIRI

seat of government .... LA PAZ

swamp ..... IZOZOG, LIVERPOOL

volcano .... OLLAGUE

weight .... LIBRA

boll .... POD, BULB, CAPSULE

weevil .... BEETLE, PICUDO

bollard .... BITT, POST, DEADHEAD

bollix: sl. ...... BUNGLE, BOTCH UP

bolo .... KNIFE, MACHETE

bologna .... SAUSAGE

slang .... BALONEY

Bolshevik .... RUSSIAN,
COMMUNIST

leader .... LENIN, TROTSKY

secret police ...... NKVD, OGPU

bolster .... PAD, PROP, CUSHION,
PILLOW, SUPPORT, REINFORCE

the spirit .... ELATE

bolt .... BAR, PIN, ROD, RUN,
LOCK, PAWL, ROLL, FLASH,
ARROW, LATCH, RIVET,
SHAFT, COTTER, DEFECT,
DECAMP, PINTLE, LIGHTNING

fastener .... NUT

hastily .... DASH (OFF)

pivot .... PINTLE

together .... ELOPE

turner .... SPANNER

bolter .... SIEVE, SIFTER,
DEFECTOR, DESERTER,
ESCAPEE, RUNAWAY

bolthead .... FLASH, ALEMBIC

bolus .... LUMP, MASS, PILL

boma .... BOA, PYTHON

bomb .... ATOM, TEAR, SHELL,
FIREBALL, ATTACK, GRENADE,
BLAST, MISSILE, EXPLOSIVE

aerial: sl. .... EGG,
BREADBASKET

colloquial .... MOLOTOV
COCKTAIL

defective .... DUD

kind of .... ATOM, ATOMIC,
TEAR, FISSION, NEUTRON,
HYDROGEN, INCENDIARY

pit .... CRATER

powerful .... BLOCKBUSTER

shelter .... ABRI, BUNKER,
DUGOUT, FOXHOLE

slang .... FAIL, FLOP

small .... GRENADE

sound on way .... BUZZ,
WHINE

underwater .... ASHCAN,
DEPTH-CHARGE

bombard .... BLITZ, SHELL,
ATTACK, BATTER, STRAFE

bombardment .... SIEGE, AIR
RAID, BARRAGE, DRUMFIRE,
CANNONADE, SHELLFIRE,
BLITZKRIEG

bombardon .... OBOE, TUBA,
ORGAN, BASSOON

bombast .... RANT, BOAST,
HUMBUG, BLUSTER, FUSTIAN

bombastic .... TURGID,
FLAMBOYANT, FLOWERY,
OROTUND, POMPOUS, VOCAL,
GRANDIOSE, PLETHORIC

style .... TUMID

Bombay bigwig .... RANA

city .... POONA, SURAT

native .... MARATHA,
MAHRATTA

bomber .... AIR-RAIDER,
DESTROYER, LIBERATOR

aircraft, British .... JAGUAR,
HARRIER, TORNADO,
BUCCANEER

aircraft, French .... JAGUAR

aircraft, German .... TORNADO

aircraft, Italian .... TORNADO

aircraft, U.S. .... TIGER,
HARRIER, SKYHAWK, FALCON,
THUNDERBOLT, STEALTH,
STRATOFORTRESS

aircraft, U.S.S.R. .... FITTER,

BADGER, BLINDER, FLOGGER

approach of .... RUN

crewman .... GUNNER, FLIER,
PILOT, AVIATOR, NAVIGATOR,
BOMBARDIER

famed .... ENOLA GAY

gunner's place in ...... TURRET

bombinate .... HUM, DRONE

bombing .... AIR ASSAULT,
SHELLING, STRAFING

describing a kind of
.... CARPET, PRECISION,
TACTICAL, STRATEGIC,
SATURATION

halt .... TRIBUTE TO PEACE

mission .... SORTIE

raid starting place
.... SHANGRI-LA

victim ..... EVACUEE, REFUGEE,
CIVILIAN

bombproof shelter ...... BUNKER,
DUGOUT, CASEMATE

bombshell, sort of .... SCANDAL,
SHOCKER, SURPRISE,
SENSATION

bombycid .... IO, MOTH, EGGER

bombyx .... ERI(A), SILKWORM

bon ami .... FRIEND

mot .... QUIP, (APT) SAYING,
WITTICISM

vivant ...... EPICURE, GOURMET,
GOURMAND

bona fide .... REAL, ON-THE-
LEVEL, RIGHTFUL, GENUINE,
AUTHENTIC

fides .... HONESTY, GOOD
FAITH

bonanza .... (GOLD)MINE,
WINDFALL, PROSPERITY

Bonaparte .... LOUIS, LUCIEN,
JEROME, NAPOLEON,
EMPEROR, CORSICAN

bonbon .... CANDY, SUGARPLUM

bonbonniere .... CANDYBOX

bond .... TIE, VOW, JOIN, DUTY,
LINK, UNION, SURETY,
SHACKLE, PLEDGE, CONTRACT,
SLAVE, COVENANT,
AGREEMENT, GUARANTEE,
CONNECTION

marriage .... KNOT

part of .... COUPON

bondage .... YOKE, PEONAGE,
SUBJECTION, SERFDOM,
SLAVERY, CAPTIVITY,
ENSLAVEMENT, SERVITUDE

bondman ...... CARL, ESNE, SERF,
BONDSMAN, CHURL, HELOT,
SLAVE, VASSAL, VILLEIN,
GUARANTOR

bone .... OS, RIB, CUBE, DICE,

FEMUR, SCAPULA, CLAVICLE, SKULL, STERNUM, VERTEBRA
ankle .... TARSUS
arched .... RIB
arm .... ULNA, HUMERUS
break .... FRACTURE
breast .... STERNUM
canals, of .... HAVERSIAN
cavity .... CYST, SINUS, ANTRUM
change to .... OSSIFY
cheek .... MALAR
colloquial .... DICE
combining form .... OSTE(O)
decay .... OSITE, CARIES
disease ...... RICKETS, RACHITIS
ear ...... ANVIL, INCUS, STAPES, HAMMER, TYMPANIC
elevation, knoblike .... TUBERCLE
face .... MAXILLA
fatty tissue .... MARROW
finger .... PHALANGE
flat .... BLADE
forelimb .... HUMERUS
formation .... OSTOSIS
growth on .... EXOTOSIS
inflammation .... OSTEITIS
joint inflammation .... ARTHRITIS
leg ...... FEMUR, TIBIA, FIBULA, PATELLA
like .... OSTEOID, OSSEOUS
malignant growth in .... CANCER
marrow, of the .... MYELOID
nasal .... VOMER
of contention, literally .... WOMAN
of sorts .... FUNNY
of sternum .... STERNAL
of thigh .... FEMUR
of wrist .... CARPUS, CARPAL(E)
opening .... FORAMEN
organic basis .... OSSEIN
pelvic .... ILIUM
pertaining to .... OSTEAL
sac between joints ...... BURSA
scraper .... XYSTER
skull ...... FRONTAL, PARIETAL, TEMPORAL, MANDIBULA
small .... OSSICLE
spine .... SACRUM, VERTEBRA
to pick .... GRUDGE
turn into .... OSSIFY
U-shaped .... HYOID
bonehead .... DOLT, FOOL, NITWIT
boneless fish/meat .... FIL(L)ET
boner .... GOOF, ERROR, BLOOPER, BLUNDER

bones .... DICE, OSSA
as in a song .... DRY
combining form .... OSTE(O)
container for .... OSSUARY
outward curving of, in legs .... BOWLEGS
boneset .... AGUEWEED
bonfire .... BLAZE, BALEFIRE
kind of .... CAMPFIRE
bongo .... DRUM, ANTELOPE
bonhomie .... AFFABLE, PLEASANT, GOOD NATURE
boniface .... HOST, LANDLORD, INNKEEPER
Bonin Island .... OGASAWARA
bonito .... FISH, TUNA, MACKEREL
bonne .... NURSEMAID, MAIDSERVANT
foi: Fr. .... HONESTY
bonnet .... CAP, HAT, HOOD, POKE, HEADDRESS
folding ...... CALASH, CALECHE
projecting rim .... BRIM
woman's .... CAPOTE
Bonnet's cousin .... TAM
bonnie/bonny ...... FINE, PRETTY, HANDSOME, BEAUTIFUL
bonnyclabber .... (CURDLED) MILK
bonus .... TIP, GIFT, BOUNTY, PREMIUM, DIVIDEND
bony .... THIN, OSSEAN, ANGULAR, OSSEOUS, SCRAGGY, OSTEAL, SCLEROUS, EMACIATED
outgrowth .... SURFER'S NODULE
part of nose .... BRIDGE
plate/scale .... SCUTE
tissue inflammation .... OSTEITIS
bonze .... MONK
boo .... HISS, HOOT, JEER
boob: sl. ...... FOOL, DUNCE, IDIOT
booboo .... SNAFU
booby .... BOOB, DOLT, DUPE, LOSER, FOOL, DUNCE, NITWIT
colloquial .... LOONY
prize scores .... LOWS
slang .... DUFFER, DUMBBELL
trap .... PITFALL
trap, lethal .... MINE
boodle .... MOB, LOOT, LOT, CABOODLE, BRIBE, CROWD
boogie-woogie .... JAZZ, ROCK-AND-ROLL
boohoo ...... CRY, SOB, WEEP(ING)
boojum .... SNARK
book .... TEXT, TOME, ENTER, LIBER, PRIMER, REGISTER, ENGAGE, RECORD, READER, ACCUSE, INDICT, VOLUME,

PUBLICATION, SCHEDULE
about saints .... PASSIONAL
announcement .... BLURB
back of .... SPINE
Bible .... SCRIPTURES
blank sheet of .... FLYLEAF
case for .... FOREL, FORRIL
circulating agency .... LIBRARY
collection .... LIBRARY, BIBLIOTHECA
collector .... BIBLIOPHILE
combining form .... BIBLIO
cover fastener .... HASP
division .... CHAPTER
end .... FINIS
ever-changing .... ATLAS
first page .... FRONTISPIECE
foreign exchange ..... CAMBIST
installment .... FASCICLE
introduction .... ISAGOGE, PREFACE, FOREWORD
jacket ad .... BLURB
large .... TOME, FOLIO, VOLUME
leaf .... PAGE
leaf turned down .... DOG-EAR
left-hand page .... VERSO
lining .... DOUBLURE
make-up ..... FORMAT, LAYOUT
marginal comment .... MARGENT
of accounts .... LEDGER, BANKBOOK, CASHBOOK, JOURNAL
charts/maps .... ATLAS
church service forms .... ORDINAL, ORDINARY
classified words .... GLOSSARY, THESAURUS, DICTIONARY
devotions .... MISSAL
feasts .... ORDO
fiction .... NOVEL
gospel .... LUKE, MARK, JOHN, MATTHEW
hours .... HORA(E)
Jewish law .... TALMUD
knowledge .... (EN)CYCLOPEDIA
listings .... DIRECTORY
loose leaves .... CAHIER
musical composition .... OPUS
nobility/nobles ...... PEERAGE
psalms .... PSALTER(Y)
public records .... LIBER
rolled script .... SCROLL
stories of same author .... OMNIBUS

synonyms/antonyms .... THESAURUS
on plants .... HERBAL
on saints' lives .... HAGIOLOGY
on strange subjects .... CURIOSA
operatic .... LIBRETTO
page size .... DUODECIMO
palm .... TARA, TALIERA
paper cover .... JACKET
part .... PAGE, COVER, INDEX, CHAPTER, FLYLEAF, JACKET, COLUMN, SECTION, TITLE, GLOSSARY, FOREWORD, PREFACE, FRONTISPIECE, TABLE OF CONTENTS
reference, familiar .... WEBSTER'S, ROGET'S, THESAURUS, DICTIONARY
sampler .... BROWSER
school .... TEXT
section .... LEAF, PAGE, INDEX, CHAPTER
shape and size .... FORMAT
shelves, set of .... STACK
size ..... DEMY, FOLIO, QUARTO
technical description of .... COLLATION
the .... BIBLE
title page .... FRONTISPIECE
unbound .... BROCHURE, PAMPHLET
bookbinding .... BIBLIOPEGY
material .... SUPER, SKIVER, VELLUM, BUCKRAM, MOROCCO
style .... GROLIER
bookie: sl. .... BET TAKER
booking .... ENGAGEMENT, RESERVATION
agent: sl. .... TEN-PERCENTER
bookish .... SCHOLARLY, ERUDITE, LEARNED, LITERARY, STODGY, PEDANTIC, STUDIOUS
bookkeeper .... ACCOUNTANT, ACTUARY, RECORDER
illegal act of .... EMBEZZLEMENT
mentor of .... AUDITOR
bookkeeping .... ACCOUNTING
book .... LEDGER, JOURNAL
column .... DEBIT, CREDIT, ASSETS, LIABILITIES, NET WORTH
item .... LOSS, INCOME, EXPENSE, PROFIT, RENTAL, CASH, BALANCE, INTEREST
booklet .... PAPERBACK, BANTAM, POCKETBOOK
unstitched .... FOLDER, BROCHURE

bookmaker .... EDITOR, COMPILER, GAMBLER, PRINTER, PUBLISHER
slang .... BOOKIE
bookmakers collectively .... RING
bookplate .... EX LIBRIS
books .... LEDGER, ACCOUNT
collection of .... LIBRARY
of public records .... LIBRI
of the Bible .... APOCRYPHA, NEW TESTAMENT, OLD TESTAMENT
bookseller .... BOOKMAN, STATIONER, BIBLIOPOLE, BOOKDEALER
catalogue of ...... BIBLIOTHECA
bookselling .... BIBLIOPOLY
bookstall .... NEWS STAND
bookstore reading .... BROWSING
bookworm .... PEDANT, SCHOLAR, BOOKLOVER
boom .... JIB, GROW, ROAR, SPAR, BOOST, RESOUND, BARRIER, SPRIT, FLOURISH, PROSPERITY
boom can .... ACE
Boomer State .... OKLAHOMA
boomerang .... KILEY, KYLIE, WEAPON
in a way .... RECOIL, REBOUND, BACKFIRE, KICKBACK, RICOCHET
boon .... GAY, BENE, FAVOR, MERRY, BENEFIT, REQUEST, BLESSING, PLEASANT
companion .... HAIL FELLOW
boondocks .... WOODLAND, HINTERLAND, WILDERNESS
Boone, _____ .... PAT, DEBBY, DANIEL, RICHARD
boor ...... OAF, CLOD, LOUT, TYKE, ROWDY, CHUFF, CHURL, CLOWN, RUSTIC, PEASANT
boorish .... RUDE, ROUGH, VULGAR, AWKWARD, UNCOUTH, ILL-MANNERED
boost .... LIFT, RAISE, PUSH UP, SUPPORT, INCREASE
slang .... PLUG
booster .... ROOTER, PROMOTER
shot .... VACCINE, INJECTION
slang .... SHOPLIFTER
boot ...... KICK, STOG(E)Y, STOGIE, BROGAN, BUSKIN, DISMISS, PAC(K), GALOSH(E), RECRUIT
Eskimo .... KAMIK
kind of .... ZIPPER
named after German field marshal .... BLUCHER
part of .... VAMP
slang ...... DISMISS, DISCHARGE
to .... BESIDES, IN ADDITION

Boot of Europe, so-called .... ITALY
bootee .... CLOTH SHOE
Bootes .... HERDSMAN, PLOWMAN, CONSTELLATION
brightest star in .... ARCTURUS
bootblack .... ATTENDANT, SHOESHINER
booth .... SHED, KIOSK(O), STALL, STAND, STORE
Oriental market .... SOOK
bootlace .... LACET
tip .... AGLET
bootleg .... SMUGGLE, BLACK-MARKET
whisky maker .... MOONSHINER
bootlegger .... SMUGGLER, RACKETEER, RUMRUNNER
bootlegger's ware .... ALKY, POTEEN, WHISKY, MOONSHINE
bootless ...... LAME, VAIN, FUTILE, BARREN, USELESS, HOPELESS
bootlick .... FAWN, PANDER, FLATTER
bootlicker .... TOADY, YESMAN, SYCOPHANT
boots .... SHOES
and saddles .... BUGLE CALL
high, waterproof ...... WADERS
booty .... LOOT, PELF, SWAG, PRIZE, GAINS, SPOILS, PLUNDER
booze .... DRINK, LIQUOR, WHISKY
boozy .... DRUNK
bop .... JAZZ
slang .... HIT, BLOW, PUNCH, STRIKE
borax .... FLUX, TINCAL
Borch, Dutch painter .... TER
Bordeaux .... WINE, MEDOC, CLARET
bordel(lo) .... BROTHEL
bordelaise .... SAUCE
border .... RIM, BRIM, EDGE, MARGE, MARGIN, FRINGE, RAND, BRINK, BOUNDARY, SIDE, LIMBUS, FRONTIER
customs gate .... BARRIER
design .... GUILLOCHE
land in dispute .... MARCH
on .... ABUT
on stamps .... TRESSURE
raise and ridge .... MILL
river .... YALU, MEKONG
wall .... DADO
bordered ...... HEMMED, FLANKED, TRIMMED
by seven hills .... ROMA, ROME
borderline .... DOUBTFUL,

borders, at times .... AREAS IN DISPUTE
bore .... DRAG, HOLE, WAVE, DRILL, WEARY, BURROW, ANNOY, CUT, TIRE, PIERCE, ENDURED
gun .... CHASE, GAUGE, CALIBER, CALIBRE
mine shaft .... TREPAN
out .... REAM
river .... EAGRE
slang .... DRAG
boreal .... NORTHERN, NORTHERLY, NORTHWIND
bored .... BLASE, FED UP
boredom .... ENNUI, TEDIUM
sign of .... YAWN
borele .... RHINO(CEROS)
borer .... AWL, AUGER, DRILL, BEETLE, GIMLET, ANNOYER, INSECT, TERMITE, SHIPWORM
Borges' (Jorge) forte .... BESTIARY
(Victor) forte .... PIANO
Borgia, _____ .... CESARE, LUCREZIA
boric acid .... ANTISEPTIC
salts .... BORATE
boring .... DULL, TEDIOUS, STODGY, TRITE, TIRESOME
person .... PEST, NUISANCE
tool .... AWL, AUGER, DRILL, GIMLET, JUMPER, WIMBLE
borings .... CHIPS, FLAKES
born .... NEE, INNATE, DELIVERED
dead .... STILLBORN
out of wedlock ...... BASTARD, BASEBORN
together with ..... CONGENITAL
yesterday .... NAIVE, INNOCENT, CHILDLIKE
being .... NASCENT
borne .... SUSTAINED, CARRIED
Borneo (South) .... KALIMANTAN
apartment .... LONGHOUSE
ape .... ORANG
burrowing animal ..... TELEDU
cape .... PUTING
hornbill .... KENYALANG
is part of .... INDONESIA
mountain .... RAYA
mountains ...... IRAN, MULLER, SCHWANER
native .... DYAK
pepper plant .... ARA
river .... BARITO, MAHAKAM, PEMBUANG
squirrel .... PENTAIL
town .... BUNTOK, SAMPIT, AMUNTAI, BARABAI, MALINAU,

KETAPANG, KANDANGAN
tribe ...... IBAN, DYAK, DAYAK, KAYAN, KENYAH, DELABIT, MELANAUS
Borodin's prince .... IGOR
boron and one other element .... BORIDE
borough .... BURG, TOWN
citizen .... BURGESS
borrow .... USE, COPY, TAKE, ADOPT, FILCH, OBTAIN, PIRATE, ACQUIRE
bort .... DIAMOND, ABRASIVE
borzoi .... DOG, WOLFHOUND
bos(s) .... COW, BEEF
bosc .... PEAR
cousin of .... ANJOU
boscage .... GROVE, THICKET, SHRUBBERY
bosh: colloq. ...... ROT, NONSENSE
bosk. See **boscage**
bosky .... WOODED
bo's'n/bosun .... BOATSWAIN
bosom ...... BUST, MIDST, BREAST, CHERISH, EMBRACE
buddy .... INTIMATE
Bosporous rowboat .... CAIQUE
boss .... KNOB, STUD, CHIEF, LEADER, MASTER, SACHEM, DOMINEER, FOREMAN, EMPLOYER, SUPERVISOR, MANAGER, HEAD(MAN)
low-profile, with no real power .... FIGUREHEAD
on shield .... UMBO
political .... CACIQUE
bossanova .... DANCE
bossy .... ARBITRARY, STUDDED, BITCHY, PUSHY, HIGH-HANDED, DICTATORIAL, DOMINEERING
Boston .... WALTZ, BEANTOWN, CARD GAME
baseball team ....:.. RED SOX
basketball team .... CELTICS
city near .... MALDEN, CHELSEA, MEDFORD, CAMBRIDGE
cultured person/snob .... BRAHMIN
famed name .... CABOT, FILENE, LOWELL, EMERSON
historical event, 1770 .... MASSACRE
historical event, 1773 ..... TEA PARTY
houseplant .... FERN
is capital of .... MASSACHUSETTS
Orchestra word .... POPS
symbol of .... CODFISH

Bostonian .... HUBBITE
bot(t) .... LARVA, MAGGOT
botanical angle .... AXIL
feat .... GRAFT
sac .... THECA
botanist .... BROWN, MENDEL
botany .... PHYTOLOGY
botch .... FAIL, FLUB, GOOF, MESS, MUFF, BUNGLE, SPOIL, LOUSE (UP), FUMBLE
both .... TWO, ALIKE, EQUALLY, TOGETHER
prefix .... AMBI
bother .... ADO, AIL, FUSS, ANNOY, WORRY, HARASS, MOLEST, PESTER, TROUBLE
Bothnia .... ALAND
botryose .... RACEMOSE
bottle .... VIAL, CRUET, FLASK, JUG, DECANTER, CARAFE, CARBOY, COSTREL, FLAGON, PHIAL, MAGNUM
containing garden .... TERRARIUM
fancy with wicker casing/earthenware .... DEMIJOHN
for acids/liquids .... CARBOY
for condiments .... CRUET, CASTER
hit the .... BOOZE
indentation at bottom .... KICK
medicine .... TENREC
perfume .... FLACON
shaped vessel .... FLASK
size .... FIFTH, GALLON, MAGNUM
stopper .... CORK
top .... CAP, CROWN
up, as emotions ...... SUPPRESS
utility/preserving liquid temperature ..... THERMOS
vinegar .... CRUET
water/wine .... CARAFE, DECANTER
bottleneck ...... SNAG, HINDRANCE
bottlenose .... DOLPHIN, PORPOISE
bottom .... BED, BASE, LAST, ROOT, SHIP, LOWEST, SOURCE
colloquial .... BUTTOCKS
of ship .... KEEL
bottomless .... ABYSMAL
pit/gulf .... HELL, ABYSS, ABADDON, UNDERWORLD
bottoms .... HOLM
boudoir .... BOWER, DRESSING ROOM
bouffant .... FULL, PUFFED
bouffe .... COMIC OPERA
bough .... LIMB, TWIG, BRANCH
of tree .... RAMAGE
boughpot .... BOWPOT, BOUQUET,

JARDINIERE
bougie .... WAX, CANDLE
bouillabaisse .... SOUP, CHOWDER
bouillon .... CUBE, BROTH
Boulder Dam designer
.... SAVAGE
boulevard .... AVENUE, STREET,
CONCOURSE, PROMENADE
Boumedienne, Algerian
president .... HOUARI
bounce .... JUMP, LEAP, BUMP,
DASH, BOUND, EXPEL, THUMP,
SPIRIT, DISMISS, SPRING,
REBOUND
along .... SKITTER
British .... BLUSTER,
IMPUDENCE
on water surface .... DAP
slang ...... DASH, EJECT, EXPEL,
SPIRIT, DISMISS
bouncing .... BIG, BUXOM, LUSTY,
HEALTHY
bound .... JUMP, LEAP, TIED,
LIMIT, SWORN, HEADED,
OBLIGED, SADDLED WITH,
PLEDGED, DESTINED
bundle .... BALE
collection of maps ...... ATLAS
horse's .... VAULT, CURVET
boundaries, mark off
.... DEMARCATE
boundary ...... LINE, MERE, METE,
AMBIT, LIMIT, VERGE,
CONFINES, BORDER, BUTTING
combining form .... ORI
common .... CONTERMINAL,
CONTERMINOUS
outer .... PERIMETER
bounden .... FORCED, OBLIGED,
COMPELLED, INDEBTED
bounder .... CAD, BOOR,
SCOUNDREL
Bounding Main .... OCEAN,
(OPEN) SEA
boundless .... VAST, ENDLESS,
ETERNAL, COUNTLESS,
INFINITE, UNLIMITED
bounds .... AMBIT, SCOPE,
CONFINES, LIMITS
out of .... OFF LIMITS,
PROHIBITED
partner of .... LEAPS
bounteous .... AMPLE, ABUNDANT,
GENEROUS, PLENTIFUL
bounty .... TIP, BONUS, GRANT,
REWARD, PREMIUM,
ALLOWANCE, SUBSIDY,
LARGESSE, GENEROSITY
bouquet .... ODOR, POSY,
CORSAGE, AROMA, SPRAY,
SCENT, GARLAND, NOSEGAY,

PERFUME, FRAGRANCE
Bourbon .... REUNION, WHISKY,
REACTIONARY
bourg .... TOWN, VILLAGE
bourgeois .... FAIR, SMUG,
AVERAGE, ORDINARY,
PASSABLE, SHOPKEEPER,
COMMONPLACE,
MIDDLECLASS, RESPECTABLE
bourgeoisie .... CAPITALISTS,
MIDDLECLASSES
bourn(e) .... GOAL, BROOK,
DOMAIN, STREAM, OBJECTIVE
bourse .... (STOCK) EXCHANGE
bouse .... BOOZE, DRINK, HOIST,
LIQUOR, CAROUSE
bout ...... GO, GAME, TURN, FLING,
MATCH, ROUND, CONTEST
colloquial .... SETTO
of pugilists .... BOXING
boutique .... SPECIALTY SHOP(PE),
STORE, BAZAAR
boutonniere ...... POSY, BOUQUET,
BUTTONHOLE
location/zone .... LAPEL
Bovary, Mme. .... EMMA
bovid .... OX, GOAT, SHEEP,
CATTLE, ANTELOPE
bovine .... OX, COW, BULL, SLOW,
CATTLE, STOLID, PATIENT,
TAURINE
Asiatic .... YAK
Celebes .... ANOA
male .... BULL, STEER
tuberculosis .... GAPES
bow .... NOD, BEND, CURVE,
STOOP, YIELD, SUBMIT
and arrow art .... ARCHERY
decorative .... RIBBON
down to .... KOWTOW
maker .... BOWYER
of eyeglasses .... BRIDGE
of ship ..... BEAK, FORE, PROW
of woman's dress ...... BUSTLE
of wood .... YEW
Oriental .... SALAAM
ornamental/ribbon .... KNOT
out .... RETIRE
shaped .... ARCUATE
bowdlerize .... CENSOR, PURIFY,
EXPURGATE
bowed .... BENT, ARCHED,
CURVED, SURRENDERED
bowel .... COLON, INTESTINE,
DEPTH, ENTRAIL, INTERIOR
movement, abnormal
.... RUNS, DIARRHEA
movement stimulant
.... LAXATIVE, CATHARTIC
pains .... GRIPES

sounds, audible
.... BORBORYGMI
bowels .... VITALS, INNARDS,
INSIDES, VISCERA, INTESTINES
clearer .... LAXATIVE,
CATHARTIC, PURGATIVE
purge of .... CATHARSIS
slang .... GUTS
bower .... ARBOR, ALCOVE,
ANCHOR, BOUDOIR, COTTAGE,
ENCLOSURE, GROTTO,
PERGOLA, RETREAT
bowery .... FARM, LEAFY,
DISTRICT, PLANTATION
"Bowery Boys" member
.... GORCEY
bowfin .... AMIA, GANOID,
DOGFISH, MUDFISH
bowhead .... WHALE
bowie .... HUNTING KNIFE
bowl .... CUP, DISH, ROLL,
TUREEN, BASIN, VESSEL,
CRATER, ARENA, STADIUM
drinking .... MAZER, MAZARD
flower .... JARDINIERE
for pounding substance
.... MORTAR
over .... STAGGER, ASTONISH,
OVERWHELM
punch .... MONTEITH
sound .... BOO, RAH, YELL,
BOOLA, CHEERS
toilet .... CLOACA
Bowl, name of U.S. athletic
collegiate .... SUN, ROSE,
COTTON, ORANGE, FIESTA,
SUGAR, TANGERINE
bowleg .... BANDY, VARUS,
TALIPES
bowler .... DERBY, KEGLER
bowling .... TENPINS, DUCKPINS
alley .... LANE
alley track .... RUNWAY
center mark .... JACK
first-ball target .... KINGPIN
game division .... FRAME
green .... LAWN, RINK
seven/ten pins .... CORNERS
term .... BREAK, SPARE,
GUTTER-BALL, STRIKE
three splits in a row
.... GOOSE
three strikes in a row
.... TURKEY
twelve strikes in a row
.... PERFECT GAME
widest split .... GOALPOSTS
bowls .... TENPINS, NINEPINS,
SKITTLES
bowman .... ARCHER, OARSMAN
bowse .... DRINK

bowstring .... CORD, GARROTE
sound .... TWANG
bowwow .... BARK
box .... BIN, BIFF, CASE, CUFF,
    CHEST, CARTON, SPAR,
    RECEPTACLE
cash .... TILL, REGISTER
fish .... KENCH
for a dead body .... COFFIN,
    CASKET
carrying cosmetics
    .... VANITY CASE
confining birds/animals
    .... CAGE
fodder .... CRIB, MANGER
money/valuables .... KIST,
    COFFER
powdered tobacco
    .... SNUFFBOX
relics .... RELIQUARY
specimen coins ..... PIX, PYX
storing ingredients/food
    .... BIN
tea, etc. .... CADDY,
    CANISTER
funnel-shaped .... HOPPER
in .... CORNER, ENCLOSE
like sleigh .... PUNG
of explosives .... CAISSON
office receipts .... TAKE
office window .... WICKET
office window sign,
    sometimes .... SRO
score item .... HITS, RUNS,
    ERRORS
seat .... LOGE
small .... CASKET
strong .... SAFE
tool .... KIT, CHEST
voice .... LARYNX
boxcar, in dice .... CRAP, TWELVE
boxer .... DOG, PUG(ILIST),
    SLUGGER, RINGSTER,
    PRIZEFIGHTER
colloquial .... PUG, MAULER,
    BEAKBUSTER, BRUISER,
    MITTSLINGER
boxer's arm length .... REACH
combination .... ONE-TWO
    PUNCH
hands: colloq. .... MITTS
practice aide .... SPARRING
    PARTNER
savior, sometimes .... GONG
second/trainer .... HANDLER
trademark .... CAULIFLOWER
    EARS
boxing bouts collectively
    .... CARD
champion .... CLAY, BAER,
    LOUIS, CARNERA, DEMPSEY,

ALI, ORTIZ, TUNNEY, WILLARD,
LEONARD, DOUGLAS, CORBETT,
WALCOTT, GRIFFITH, COKES,
    HARADA, TYSON, VILLA,
    SCHMELING
decision .... TKO, KO, DRAW,
    NO-CONTEST
glove .... CESTUS
match .... GO, BOUT, SETTO,
    FISTICUFFS
of/pertaining to .... FISTIC
official .... REF(EREE)
period .... ROUND
pre-bout need .... WEIGH-IN
promoter .... (TEX) RICHARD,
    (BOB) ARUM, (DAN) DUVA,
    (DON) KING
sanctioning body .... WBC,
    IBF, WBA
science of .... FISTICUFFS
wrestling contest
    .... PANCRATIUM
boxwood .... TREE, SERON, SHRUB
boy .... LAD, YOUTH, YOUNGSTER,
    SPRIG, NIPPER, MAN-CHILD,
    TAD, GOSOON, STRIPLING
age of .... PUBERTY
assistant .... JACK
attendant .... PAGE
colloquial .... BUB, KID,
    BUSTER, SON(NY), SHAVER
friend: colloq. .... LOVER,
    BEAU, ESCORT, SWEETHEART
Scottish .... GALLAN(T)
Boy Scout assembly/gathering
    .... CAMPOREE, JAMBOREE
daily object .... GOOD TURN
founder .... BADEN-POWELL
group .... DEN, PACK, TROOP,
    PATROL
hiking gear .... HAVERSACK
motto .... BE PREPARED
new .... TENDERFOOT
popular image of .... DO-
    GOODER
boycott .... AVOID, SHUN,
    BLACKBALL
in a way .... STRIKE,
    OSTRACIZE
Boz, pseudonym .... DICKENS
BPOE .... ELKS
bra .... BRASSIERE
Brabant's princess .... ELSA
brabble .... ARGUE, CHATTER,
    QUARREL, SQUABBLE
brace .... BIT, BIND, PAIR, GIRDER,
    BRACKET, COUPLE, PROP,
    BITSTOCK, FASTENER, SPLINT,
    TIGHTEN, STIMULATE
bracelet .... BAND, CHAIN, ARMIL,
    BANGLE, ARMLET, HANDCUFF,

    WRISTLET
bracer .... DRINK, TONIC,
    REFRESHER, STIMULANT
braces .... GALLUSES
British: sl. .... SUSPENDERS
brachial .... ARMLIKE
brachyuran .... CRAB,
    CRUSTACEAN
bracing .... REFRESHING, TONIC,
    INVIGORATING
bracken .... FERN, BRAKE
bracket .... ANCON, CONSOLE,
    CORDEL, GROUP,
    CLASSIFICATION
brackish .... BRINY, SALTY,
    NAUSEOUS
bract ...... GLUME, PALEA, SPATHE
cluster .... COMA
grass .... GLUME
brad .... TACK, SPRIG, (WIRE)
    NAIL
brae: Scot. .... BANK, HILLSIDE
brag .... BOAST(ER), CROW,
    VAUNT, BRAGGART,
    GASCONADE
braggadocio .... BOASTING,
    HEROICS, BOMBAST,
    CHAUVINISM
braggart .... GASBAG, BOASTER,
    BRAGGER, GASCON,
    PRETENDER
slang .... WINDBAG,
    BLOWHARD
Bragi's parent ...... ODIN, FRIGGA
Brahma .... FOWL, CATTLE,
    CREATOR
Brahman bull .... ZEBU
rule .... SUTRA, SUTTA
title .... AYA
wiseman .... PUNDIT
Brahmin: Hindu .... PRIEST
braid .... BAND, PLAT, LACET,
    PLAIT, QUEUE, TRESS, WEAVE
decoration .... CORDON
of gold thread .... GALLOON
trimming .... RICKRACK,
    GALLOON, SOUTACHE
zigzag .... RICKRACK
braided material .... SENNIT
brain .... MIND, INTELLECT,
    MENTALITY, INTELLIGENCE,
    CONTROL CENTER
action .... COGITATION,
    CEREBRATION
and the spinal cord
    .... CENTRAL NERVOUS SYSTEM
bleeding within the
    .... HEMORRHAGE
blood clot in the
    .... HEMATOMA
canal/passage .... ITER

collection of pus in the
.... ABSCESS
colloquial .... GRAY MATTER
congenital absence of the
.... ANENCEPHALY
covering .... SKULL, MATER,
MENINGES
damage .... DEMENTIA
disease .... KURU, TUMOR,
APHASIA, ALZHEIMER'S
disorder .... MIGRAINE,
NARCOLEPSY
fever .... ENCEPHALITIS
fissure/groove .... SULCUS
fold .... GYRUS
"food" .... FISH
function .... SPEECH, EMOTION,
THOUGHT
hat .... THINKING CAP
infection within the
...... MENINGITIS, ENCEPHALITIS
lack of oxygen in the
.... HYPOXIA
layer of gray matter
.... CORTEX
linking nerve fibers
.... CORPUS CALLOSUM
lowest section of the .... STEM
membrane .... PIA MATER,
DURA MATER, ARACHNOID
nerve cells ...... GRAY MATTER
nerve fibers .... WHITE
MATTER
of the/pertaining to
.... CEREBRAL, CEREBRIC
opening .... PYLA
pan .... SKULL, CRANIUM
part .... PONS, STEM,
CEREBRUM, CEREBELLUM,
MEDULLA, MIDBRAIN,
FOREBRAIN
ridge .... HIPPOCAMPUS
structure of nerve fibers
.... FORNIS
surgery .... LOBOTOMY
tissue .... TELA
truster: sl. .... EXPERT,
ADVISER, EGGHEAD
tumor .... GLIOMA,
MENINGIOMA
water on the
.... HYDROCEPHALUS
X-ray ..... IMAGING, SCANNING,
ANGIOGRAPHY
brainchild .... IDEA, PLAN,
FANCY, CREATION
brainless .... FOOLISH, STUPID,
IDIOTIC
brains .... INTELLECT,
INTELLIGENCE
slang .... IDEAMAN, KNOWHOW,

MASTERMIND
brainstorm .... INSPIRATION,
PLAN, BRIGHT IDEA, CONCEPT,
CEREBRATION
brainwash .... ALIENATE,
MISINFORM, INDOCTRINATE
brainy .... WISE, SHARP, SMART,
INTELLIGENT, WITTY,
INTELLECTUAL
brake .... CURB, FERN, STOP,
CHECK, CLUMP, HARROW,
BRACKEN, KNEADER, RETARD,
SLOW DOWN, THICKET
for woman's tongue
.... BRANKS
part .... SHOE
Bram Stoker's thriller
.... DRACULA
bramble .... BRIER, SHRUB,
DEWBERRY, BLACKBERRY,
RASPBERRY
brambling .... FINCH
brambly .... THORNY, PRICKLY
bran .... HUSK, SKIN, GRAIN
COVERING
meal, etc. mixture .... MASH
branch .... ARM, PART, BOUGH,
LIMB, TWIG, RAMUS, SPRIG,
BROOK, DIVIDE, DIVISION,
SHOOT, OFFSHOOT, RIVULET,
RAMIFY, FURCATE, FURCATION
angle .... AXIL
in biology .... RAMUS
like .... RAMOUS
of family .... STIRPS
of learning .... ART(S), OLOGY,
SCIENCE, DISCIPLINE
off .... FORK, DIVERGE
out .... GROW, SPREAD,
DEPLOY, DISPERSE
railroad .... SPUR, SIDING
trim .... LOP
branched ...... RAMOSE, RAMOUS,
RAMIFORM
branches, bearing many
.... RAMOSE
branchine .... GILLS
branching .... ARBORESCENT
branchlet .... SPRAY
brand .... SEAR, MARK, DISGRACE,
LABEL, STAIN, STAMP,
TRADEMARK, STIGMA(TIZE)
goose .... BRANT
new .... FRESH, UNUSED
brandish .... WAVE, SHAKE,
SWING, FLAUNT, FLOURISH
brandling .... WORM, FISHBAIT
brandy .... MARC, COGNAC,
AQUA-VITAE
and soda .... PEG
cocktail .... SIDECAR,

ALEXANDER
cordial .... ROSOLIO
branks .... BIT, BRIDLE
brant .... GOOSE
brantail .... BIRD, REDSTART
brash .... RASH, HASTY, BOLD,
IMPUDENT, INSOLENT,
PYROSIS, SHOWER, FRAGMENT,
FRAGILE, BRITTLE, IMPETUOUS
Brasilia, designer of
.... NIEMEYER
is capital of .... BRAZIL
brass .... ALLOY, METAL
as imitation gold ..... ORMOLU
colloquial .... GALL,
BOLDNESS, IMPUDENCE
color .... AENEOUS
combining form .... CHALCO
hat: sl. .... BIGWIG, VIP,
GENERAL, OFFICER,
DIGNITARY, EXECUTIVE
knuckles .... BLACKJACK
like alloy .... LATTEN
mythical man of .... TALOS
plate, kind of .... CYMBAL
slang .... BUCKS, MONEY
tacks .... FACTS, DETAILS,
PARTICULARS
brassard .... BADGE, ARMBAND
brassica .... COLE, TURNIP,
CABBAGE, BROCCOLI
brassie, for example .... GOLF
CLUB
brassiere .... BRA, UPLIFT,
BANDEAU
slang .... FALSIES
brassworker .... BRAZIER
brassy .... BOLD, LOUD, SHOWY,
FORWARD, IMPUDENT,
INSOLENT
brat .... IMP, RAG, PEST, CHILD,
CLOTH, MANTLE, URCHIN,
BANTLING
brattice .... PARAPET,
BREASTWORK
brattle .... RATTLE, CLATTER,
SCAMPER
bravado .... BLUFF, BLUSTER,
BOLDNESS, COCKINESS
brave .... BOLD, DEFY, MANLY,
HEROIC, PLUCKY,
COURAGEOUS, VALIANT,
STOUT-HEARTED
front, usually .... BLUFF
Indian .... WARRIOR
bravery ...... GRIT, VALOR, NERVE,
COURAGE, HEROISM
bravo .... KILLER, ASSASSIN,
DESPERADO
Bravo! .... OLE, CHEER, WELL
DONE, APPLAUSE, VERY

GOOD, EXCELLENT
bravura .... DASH, DARING, BRILLIANCE, TECHNIQUE
braw ...... FINE, CHIC, EXCELLENT
brawl .... ROW, FRAY, RIOT, MELEE, FIGHT, BROIL, FREE-FOR-ALL, FRACAS, UPROAR, SCUFFLE
brawler .... HECTOR, HOODLUM, HOOLIGAN
brawling .... NOISY, ROWDY
brawn .... FLESH, MUSCLE, STRENGTH, HEADCHEESE
colloquial .... BEEF
brawny .... ROBUST, SINEWY, STRONG, STURDY, MUSCULAR, STRAPPING
bray .... CRUSH, LAUGH, POUND, GRIND, GUFFAW, HEEHAW, THRASH, SPREAD, TRITURATE
brayer, in printing .... ROLLER
braze .... SOLDER
brazen .... BOLD, HARSH, IMPUDENT, SHAMELESS
brazier and grill .... HIBACHI
Brazilian aborigine .... ANDOA, CARIB, AMIRANHA
armadillo ...... TATU, TATOUAY
bay .... BUZIOS, MARAJO, SEPETIBA, GUANABARA
bird .... ARA, AGAMI, JABIRU, SERIEMA
"Black Pearl" .... PELE
cape .... FRIO, ORANGE, CASSIPORE
capital .... BRASILIA
capital, former .... RIO
channel .... SUL
city/town .... PARA, BELEM, CEARA, CUIABA, CAMPINAS, FRANCA, JUNDIAL, MANAUS, RIO, LONDRINA, FORTALEZA, NATAL, SAO PAULO, MARINGA, OLINDA, RIO DE JANEIRO, OSASCO, MARILIA, TERESINA
coin .... CENTAVO, (MIL)REI, MOIDORE
crested bird .... SERIEMA
dam .... FURNAS, ITAIPU
dance .... SAMBA
drink .... ASSAI
estate .... PAZENDA
estuary .... PARA
fiber .... IMBE
footballer .... PELE, TOSTAO
forest .... MATTA, MATTO
heron .... SOCO
holly .... MATE
Indian ...... MURA, PURU, TUPI, ARARA, CARIB, GUANA, ACROA, ZAPARO, TAPUYAN

ipecac .... EVEA
island .... GRANDE, MARACA, CARDOSO, MARAJO, BAILIQUE, COMPRIDA, BANANAL, CAVIANA, MEXIANA
killers .... JAGUNCOS
lagoon .... MIRIM, PATOS, MANGUEIRA
lake .... FEIA, AIAMA, ARARUAMA
language .... PORTUGUESE
long-legged bird ...... SERIEMA
macaw .... ARARA
measure, dry .... MOIO
measure, liquid .... PIPA
medicinal plant ...... AYAPANA
money .... CONTO, CRUZADO, (MIL)REI, CRUZEIRO
mountain .... JAUARI, URUCUN, LOMBARDA, PICO DA NEBLINA
nut .... PARA, CASTANA, COQUILLA
orchid .... DICHEA
palm .... ASSAI, PIAS(S)AVA, BABASSU, JUPATI, CARNAUBA
parrot .... ARA(RA), MACAW, TIRBA
plant .... MANIOC, MANIHOT
port ..... BELEM, CEARA, PARA, BAHIA, NATAL, RECIFE, PELOTAS
president .... COLLOR DE MELLO
quartz .... CACO
religion .... CATHOLIC
resort .... BELEM
river .... ACRE, AMAZON, GRAJAU, ARAGUAIA, AMAPARI, BALSAS, BRANCO, GRANDE, ICA, FEIO, GURUPI, MADEIRA, PARA, PARU, CLARO, IRIRI, TEFE, JAVARI, ITAPI, IGUACO, IVAL, JARI, JURUA, JAPURA, MANSO, MIRANDA, MAPUERA, RONURO, PARDO, RIBEIRA, TURVO, PARANA, PARNAIBA, TIBAGI, TAPAJOS, TACUTU, VERDE, URUBU, URUGUAI
rubber port .... MANAUS
rubber tree .... ULE, HULE, SERINGA
seaport .... RIO, BELEM, NATAL, SANTOS
state .... ACRE, ALAGOAS, BAHIA, CEARA, AMAZONAS, SERGIPE, PARAIBA, MARANHAO, GOIAS, PARANA, SAO PAULO, PARA, PIAUI, RIO DE JANEIRO
stork .... JABIRU
tapir .... ANTA

tea plant .... MATE
territory .... AMAPA, RORAIMA, RONDONIA
title of respect .... DOM
tree .... APA, ANDA, MURURE, ARAROBA, PARANAPINE
tree bark .... PEREIRA
tree powder .... ARAROBA
waterfall .... IGUAZU
weight .... ONCA, ARROBA, LIBRA, QUINTAL
wood .... BRASIL, SATINE
Brazil's original name .... VERACRUZ
breach .... GAP, HOLE, RIFT, OPENING, HERNIA, RUPTURE, BREAK, SPLIT, BREAKTHROUGH
of etiquette .... FAUX PAS, SOLECISM, IMPROPRIETY
of relations .... RENT, RIFT, SCHISM
of the peace ...... RIOT, BRAWL
of trust .... BETRAYAL
bread .... AZYM, FOOD, LOAF, RUSK, CRUST, GLUTEN, PONE, MUFFIN, BROTCHEN
and-butter .... LIVELIHOOD, EVERYDAY, YOUTHFUL, COMMONPLACE
and-butter letter .... GRACENOTE
blessed .... HOST, EULOGIA
boiled and flavored ...... CUSH, PANADA
break .... EAT, DINE
crisp coating ...... RIND, CRUST
dough .... SPONGE
Eucharist .... HOST
from heaven .... MANNA
garnish .... SIPPET
hard .... HARDTACK
Hebrew .... AZYM
in one baking .... BATCH
ingredient .... FLOUR, YEAST, LEAVEN
maker .... BAKER
part .... RIND, CRUMB, CRUST
roll .... BAGEL
soaked in beef broth .... BREWIS
soaked in milk .... SOP
soaked in soup/gravy .... SIPPET
spread .... OLEO, BUTTER, JAM, JELLY, MARGARINE
St. John's .... CAROB
sweet, raised .... RUSK
toasted/fried .... SIPPET
unleavened .... HARDTACK
white .... MANCHET

breadbasket .... GRANARY
  slang .... BELLY, STOMACH,
    (AERIAL) BOMB
breadfruit .... RIMA(S)
breadth .... SCOPE, WIDTH,
    EXPANSE
breadwinner: colloq. .... PAPA,
    DADDY, EARNER
break .... GAP, BUST, RUIN, SNAP,
  PAUSE, HIATUS, CAESURA,
  CRASH, CRACK, DEMOTE,
  SHATTER, FRACTURE, SMASH,
  RUPTURE, DISCLOSE, SURPASS,
    QUARREL
  a code .... DECIPHER
  a record .... SURPASS
  a story .... DISCLOSE
  away .... BOLT, ESCAPE,
    SEPARATE
  colloquial .... ESCAPE
  down .... CRY, CRUSH, GIVE
    WAY, ANALYZE, ITEMIZE,
    DEMOLISH
  from habit .... WEAN
  in .... ENTER, INTRUDE,
    INTERRUPT
  in a beginner .... TRAIN
  in a line of verse .... CAESURA
  in rock strata .... FAULT
  in the dike .... CREVASSE
  in two .... SNAP
  into parts .... DIFFRACT
  into pieces ..... BURST, SMASH,
    SHATTER
  of day .... DAWN, MORN,
    DAYBREAK
  off ..... STOP, SEVER, SEPARATE
  off connection .... SECEDE
  one's heart .... CRUSH
  out .... ERUPT, ESCAPE
  popular to workers .... REST,
    COFFEE
  prison .... ESCAPE
  religious law/moral principle
  .... SIN
  slang .... BOON, CHANCE,
    ADVANTAGE
  through .... PIERCE, PENETRATE
  through eggshell .... PIP
  up .... DISPERSE, SEPARATE
  up marriage .... DIVORCE
breakable ...... BRITTLE, FRAGILE,
    DELICATE
breakbone fever .... DENGUE
breakdown .... COLLAPSE,
  BURNOUT, CRACKUP, FAILURE
breaker .... KEG, WAVE, EAGRE,
    COMBER
breakers .... SURF
breakfast and lunch ...... BRUNCH
  food .... CEREAL, FARINA,

    OATMEAL
  last .... DEJEUNER
  nook .... ALCOVE
breaking of bones ...... FRACTURE
  waves .... BREACH
breakneck .... FAST, WILD,
  DARING, DANGEROUS
breakthrough .... BREACH,
  DISCOVERY, INFILTRATION
breakup .... END, RUIN,
  DISBAND(MENT), DISPERSION,
  SPLIT, COLLAPSE, STOPPAGE,
  DISSOLUTION, SEPARATION
breakwater .... DIKE, MOLE, PIER,
  JETTY, BULWARK, SEA WALL
bream .... CHAD, PORGY,
  ABRAMIS, SPAROID, SUNFISH
  Japanese .... TAI
breast .... BUST, BOSOM, CHEST,
    OPPOSE, PETTO
  animal's .... BRISKET
  disorder .... TUMOR, CANCER
  inflammation .... MASTITIS
  lump .... CYST
  meat cut .... BRISKET
  of the .... PECTORAL
  plate .... CUIRASS
  reconstruction
  .... MAMMOPLASTY
  shaped .... MASTOID
  surgical removal of
  .... MASTECTOMY
breastbone .... STERNUM
  flat .... RATITE
  of the .... STERNAL
breastfeed .... NURSE, SUCKLE
breastpin .... BROOCH
breastplate .... (A)EGIS, URIM,
    PLASTRON
breastwork .... BARRIER,
  REDOUBT, BRATTICE,
    BARRICADE
breath .... AIR, LIFE, PUFF, ODOR,
  WIND, WHIFF, BREEZE,
  HALITUS, WHISPER, MOMENT,
    RESPIRATION
  asthmatic/whistling
  .... WHEEZE
  bad/odorous .... HALITOSIS
  catch one's .... GASP, GULP,
    PANT, PAUSE
  forced noisily .... SNORT
  of life .... PNEUMA
  of wind .... FLATUS
  out of .... WINDED
  save one's .... REST, STOP,
    SHUT UP
  sweetener .... CACHOU, MINT,
    LOZENGE
  taking .... EXCITING,
  THRILLING, STARTLING,

    STIRRING, SURPRISING
breathe .... INHALE, EXHALE,
  BLOW, MURMUR, RESPIRE
  hard .... GASP, PANT, HEAVE
  in .... SUCK, INHALE
  noisily .... SNORE, HASSEL,
    HAZZLE
  one's last .... DIE, EXPIRE
  out .... EXHALE, SUSPIRE
  out noisily .... SNORE, SNORT
  tentatively, as it were
  .... SNIFF
  with whistling sound
  .... WHEEZE
breather .... GILL, NOSE, NARES
  of fish .... GILL
  of whale .... BLOWHOLE,
    SPIRACLE
  slang ...... REST, BREAK, PAUSE
breathing .... ALIVE, LIVING,
  EXHALING, INHALING,
    RESPIRATION
  abnormal/rapid .... PANTING,
    HYPERPNEA
  device .... RESPIRATOR,
    VENTILATOR
  device, underwater
  .... SNORKEL
  difficult/painful ...... DYSPNEA,
  DISPNOEA, DYSPNOEA,
    DYSPNOIA
  harsh .... RALE, SNORE
  hole .... NOSE, NOSTRIL,
    SPIRACLE
  smooth .... LENE
  sound .... RALE, SNORE,
  STRIDOR, RHONEUS
  space: colloq. .... REST, ROOM,
    RESPITE
breathless .... AGOG, DEAD,
  EAGER, EXCITED, AIRLESS,
  GASPING, PANTING, STIFLING,
  OVERCOME, (SHORT)-WINDED
bree: Scot. .... BROTH
breech .... RUMP, BEHIND,
  BOTTOM, BUTTOCKS, REAR
    END, DERRIERE
  loading rifle .... CHASSEPOT
breechblock signature,
  ballistics ...... IDENTIFICATION
breechcloth .... LOIN(CLOTH)
  Polynesian .... MALO
breechclout .... G-STRING
breeches ...... TRUNKS, TROUSERS,
  SLOPS, KNICKERS,
    PANTALOONS
  riding .... JODHPURS
  Scottish .... TREWS
  too big for one's .... PROUD,
  ARROGANT, OVERBEARING,
  SWELL-HEAD(ED)

breeching .... BRIDLE, SADDLE, HARNESS
breed .... LINE, KIND, RACE, REAR, HATCH, RAISE, CREATE, STOCK, VARIETY, MULTIPLY, STRAIN, GENERATE, ORIGINATE, CLASS, SPECIES, (RE)PRODUCE
cat .... ANGORA, PERSIAN, SIAMESE
cattle .... DEVON, GUERNSEY, HEREFORD
chicken .... BANTAM, LEGHORN, RHODE ISLAND
dog .... BOXER, BEAGLE, POODLE, (BASSET) HOUND, COLLIE, TERRIER, SPANIEL, BULLDOG, DOBERMAN PINSCHER, DALMATIAN, GERMAN SHEPHERD, CHIHUAHUA, RETRIEVER
horse .... ARABIAN, TROTTER, PONY, PALOMINO, CLYDESDALE
breeding ...... CULTURE, LINEAGE, REARING, TRAINING, ORIGIN, BACKGROUND, UPBRINGING
place .... NEST, NIDUS, ROOKERY, STUD FARM
breeze .... AIR, GENTLE WIND
colloquial .... COMMOTION, DISTURBANCE
refreshing .... CALLER
slight .... BREATH, ZEPHYR
water rippling ...... CAT'S PAW
breezing horse in a race .... EASY WINNER
breezy .... AIRY, BRISK, LIVELY, CAREFREE
Bremen's river .... WESER
Brenner .... PASS
Breslau river .... ODER, OSAR
Breton .... CELT
breve .... WRIT, ORDER, BILLET, LETTER
brevet .... COMMISSION
breviary .... PORTAS, COMPEND
brevity .... BRIEFNESS, SHORTNESS, TERSENESS, CONCISENESS
is the soul of _____ .... WIT
of expression .... LACONISM
brew .... ALE, BEER, TEA, PLOT, CONCOCT, LAGER, PUNCH, STEEP, SCHEME, DISTILL
brewer's ferment .... LOB(B)
grain .... BARLEY
need .... MALT
tub .... KEEVE
vat .... TUN
yeast .... BARM
brewery .... DISTILLERY
refuse ..... LEES, DRAFF, DREGS

brewing, one .... GYLE
brewis ...... BREAD, (BEEF) BROTH
Brezhnev, _____ .... LEONID
Briareus, what it had many of .... HANDS
bribe .... SOP, BAIT, LURE, BONUS, GRAFT, BOODLE, SUBORN, OVERTIP, CORRUPT
collector .... BAGMAN
money .... BOODLE, SLUSH (FUND)
slang .... FIX, PAYOLA, SQUARE, GREASE THE PALM, KICKBACK, HUSH MONEY
bribery .... GRAFT, PAY-OFF, BRIBING, CORRUPTION
bric-a-brac .... CURIO, VIRTU, BIBELOT, KNICK-KNACKS
brick ...... BAR, NOG, CLAY, TILE, ADOBE, BLOCK
burned partly .... BAT, BUR(R), CLINKER
carrier/trough for .... HOD
colloquial .... FINE FELLOW
compressed coal dust .... BRIQUET
cracked .... CHUFF
hard .... CLINKER
making material .... PUG, MARL
masonry .... NOGGING
refuse .... SAMEL
sun dried .... ADOBE
up .... PAVE
worker .... MASON
bricklayer .... MASON
helper of .... HODMAN
tool of .... TROWEL
bricks, pile of .... HACK
brickwork .... MASONRY
bricole .... CATAPULT
bridal .... NUBILE, MARITAL, NUPTIAL, WEDDING
path .... AISLE
wreath .... SHRUB, SPIREA
Bridalveil .... WATERFALL
bride ...... WIFE, SPOUSE, FIANCEE, BETROTHED
in needle-work .... TIE, LOOP
bride's trailer .... MAID
bridesmaid .... PARANYMPH
bridewell ...... GAOL, JAIL, PRISON
bridge .... LINK, SPAN, BAILEY, CARD GAME, CAUSEWAY, PONTOON, CONNECT, RIALTO, TRESTLE, VIADUCT, CANTILEVER
bid/coup .... SLAM
boo-boo: var. .... RENEG
builder .... EADS
calls .... BIDS

card game .... AUCTION, CONTRACT
card game position .... TRUMP, EAST, WEST, NORTH, SOUTH
contestants .... PAIRS
declaration .... BID
defeat .... SET
dental .... FALSE TEETH
expert .... GOREN
floating .... PONTOON
gaffe .... RENEGE
game series .... RUBBER
hand without trumps .... CHICANE
holding .... TENACE
kind of .... DRAW, FOOT, BAILEY, HANGING
Midgard to Asgard .... BIFROST
move/maneuver .... FINESSE
''no game'' .... NIL
of bow instrument .... PONTICELLO
of musical instrument .... MAGAS
over gorge, etc. .... VIADUCT
part ...... SPAN, WALK, GIRDER, TRESTLE
pathway .... CATWALK
railroad .... TRESTLE
support .... PIER, GIRDER, TRUSS, PONTOON, ABUTMENT
term .... BID, NIL, BOOK, GOBY, PASS, RUFF, SLAM, TENACE
to Paradise .... ALSIRAT
tricks .... BOOK
type .... DRAW, TOLL, BASCULE, FLOATING, CANTILEVER, SUSPENSION
Bridges, _____ .... BEAU, JEFF, LLOYD
bridgework .... TOOTH-FOR-A-TOOTH
bridle ...... CURB, REIN, HARNESS, RESTRAIN
part .... BIT, REINS, HEADSTALL, NOSE-BAND
wise animal .... HORSE
brief .... SHORT, CURT, PITHY, TERSE, FLEETING, CONCISE, INSTRUCT, SUCCINCT, SUMMARY
biography .... VITA
case .... BAG, SATCHEL, PORTFOLIO
halt en route .... STOPOVER
in expression .... CURT, BLUNT, TERSE, LACONIC
in law .... BREVE

note .... JOT, MEMO
sleep .... NAP, DOZE, SNOOZE
summary .... GIST, FILL-IN,
RESUME, EPITOME
telegraphic message .... FLASH
time .... FLASH, MOMENT,
SECOND
briefed .... INFORMED,
FAMILIARIZED
briefing .... NEWS, REPORT,
ACCOUNT, TIDINGS, BULLETIN,
ORDERS, INSTRUCTIONS
briefly .... IN SUM, IN SHORT,
SHORTLY, MOMENTARILY
briefs .... UNDERSHORTS
brier .... BUSH, PIPE, HEATH,
THORN, BRAMBLE
briery .... SPINY, THORNY,
PRICKLY
brig ...... SHIP, PRISON, STOCKADE,
GUARDHOUSE
brigade .... GROUP
fire, need of a .... BUCKET
brigadier general .... OFFICER,
COMMANDER
rank below .... COLONEL
brigand .... THUG, BANDIT,
PIRATE, LADRONE, ROBBER,
HIGHWAYMAN
Brigham City resident
.... UTAHAN
bright .... GAY, ROSY, LIVELY,
BRAINY, QUICK, SHARP,
SMART, CHEERFUL, LUMINOUS,
LUSTROUS, ASTUTE, CANNY,
CUNNING, CLEVER, BRILLIANT,
RADIANT, SHINING, KEEN,
ROSEATE, RELUCENT
and cheerful .... SUNNY
colored bird .... ORIOLE,
TANAGER
colored fish .... OPAH,
WRASSE, CATALINA
combining form .... HELI(O)
idea: colloq. ...... BRAINCHILD,
BRAINSTORM, INSPIRATION
saying .... BON MOT,
WITTICISM
star .... NOVA
youngster .... PRODIGY
youngster: sl. .... WHIZ KID
brighten .... GLADDEN, POLISH,
FURBISH, CHEER (UP),
(EN)LIVEN, INSPIRE, LIGHTEN
brightness .... GLOSS, LUSTER,
SHEEN, ACUMEN, APTITUDE,
KEENNESS, RADIANCE,
LUMINOSITY
Bright's disease .... NEPHRITIS
brill .... TURBOT, FLATFISH
brilliance .... ECLAT, GLITTER,

RADIANCE, SPLENDOR
brilliant .... GAY, GEM, VIVID,
BRAINY, QUICK-WITTED,
PRISMATIC, EMINENT,
TALENTED, MAGNIFICENT
array .... GALAXY
facet of .... CULET
gathering .... SALON,
CONCLAVE, CONGRESS
red-yellow color
.... GRAYSTONE
shade of blue .... PEACOCK
stroke/stratagem .... COUP
tennis stroke .... ACE
brim .... LIP, RIM, EDGE, BRINK
of bonnet .... POKE
of cap .... BILL
brimless cap .... FEZ, TAM,
BERET, BARRET, BIRETTA
brimmer .... BUMPER
brimming .... FULL, SUFFUSED
brimstone ...... SULFUR, SULPHUR
brindled .... TABBY, BANDED
brine .... SEA, OCEAN, SOUSE,
TEARS, SALT WATER
shrimp .... ARTEMIA
to salt residue .... BITTERN
bring .... FETCH, CARRY, CONVEY,
TRANSFER, TRANSPORT
a good price .... COMMAND
about ...... CAUSE, ACCOMPLISH
around .... CONVINCE,
PERSUADE
back .... RETURN, RESTORE
down .... LOWER
foot down .... VETO, STAMP
forth .... EAN, CREATE, SPAWN,
PRODUCE, ENGENDER
forth young ..... HATCH, YEAN,
WHELP
forward .... SHOW, PRESENT,
CARRY OVER, INTRODUCE
home the bacon: colloq.
.... WIN, EARN
in .... USHER, ARREST, IMPORT,
CAPTURE
in as price .... FETCH
in forcefully .... THRUST,
INTRUDE, INTERTRUDE
into court .... SUE, HALE,
ARRAIGN
on/upon oneself .... INCUR
one's lunch .... BROWNBAG
out .... EDUCE, EXPOSE, ELICIT,
REVEAL, DISPLAY, PRESENT,
PUBLISH, INTRODUCE
ruin upon .... DAMN
to .... REVIVE
bay .... TREE, CORNER
bear .... EXERT, PRESS,
PRESSURE

completion .... FINISH,
FINALIZE
light ...... REVEAL, UNCOVER,
UNEARTH, DISCLOSE
mind .... RECALL, REMIND,
REMEMBER, RECOLLECT
naught .... RUIN, UNDO,
DESTROY, NULLIFY
standstill .... STALL,
STALEMATE, STATUS QUO
together .... AMASS, GATHER,
ASSEMBLE, CONFLATE
under control .... TAME
up .... REAR, BROACH,
PROPOSE, INTRODUCE
up the ____ .... REAR
bringer of bad luck .... JINX
bringing to central point
.... AFFERENT
brink .... BRIM, EDGE, VERGE
brinkmanship, exponent of
.... DULLES
briny .... SALTY
deep .... SEA, OCEAN
brio .... ZEST, ANIMATION,
VIVACITY
brioche .... ROLL
briquet .... BRICK
brisk .... SPRY, ALERT, ACTIVE,
BUSY, SHARP, ZIPPY, FRISKY,
QUICK, LIVELY, SPANKING,
BUSTLING, ENERGETIC
colloquial .... SNAPPY
in music .... ALLEGRO
brisket .... BREAST, MEAT CUT
brisling .... FISH, SPRAT, SARDINE
bristle .... HAIR, SETA, STAND,
CHAETA, STIFFEN, STUBBLE,
TRICHOME
combining form .... SETI
hooked .... BARB
like growth .... AWN, SETA,
ARISTA, BARBEL, STUBBLE
pertaining to .... SETAL
ruffed animal .... BOAR
shaped .... SETIFORM
surgical .... SETON
bristles, covered with ...... HISPID
having .... SETOSE, STRIGOSE,
SETACEOUS
tuft of .... PAPPUS
bristletail .... THYSANURAN
bristling .... IRATE, ECHINATE
bristly .... HAIRY, HISPID, SETOSE,
HIRSUTE, HORRENT, SHAGGY,
TUFTED, PRICKLY, ROUGH,
SCOPATE, ACICULAR
animal .... HOG, BOAR,
PORCUPINE
Bristol paper .... PASTEBOARD
Britain .... ALBION, ENGLAND,

BRITANNIA, GREAT BRITAIN,
UNITED KINGDOM
ancients .... PICTS, SILURES
mythical king ..... BRAN, BRUT
of .... BRITANNIC
part of .... WALES, ENGLAND,
SCOTLAND
B'rith, _____ .... BNAI
British .... BRITON, ENGLISH,
LIMEY, SAXON, BLIGHTY
ache .... STOUND
active .... NIPPY
actor .... OLIVIER, AHERNE,
ARLISS, COWARD, DONAT,
EVANS, GRANGER, MARSHALL,
RATHBONE
actress .... GWYN, KERR,
LEIGH, GARSON, NEAGLE,
ANDREWS, COLLINS, OBERON,
REDGRAVE
admiral .... BEATTY, NELSON
airforce .... RAF
ale .... NOG(G)
altogether .... JOLLY
amah .... TWEENY
ambiguous .... DICEY, CHANCY
ament .... CLOT
amicus curiae ..... BARMASTER
ancient inhabitants ..... CELTS,
BRYTTAS
anger .... WAX
apartment .... FLAT, CHAMBERS
apartment house ..... MANSION
archaeologist .... KENYON
architect .... ADAM, WREN,
SCOTT
armor bearer .... SQUIRE,
ARMIGER
army bugle call .... POST
army fur hat .... BUSBY
army staff officer: sl.
.... BRASSHAT
assurer .... UNDERWRITER
author .... MEE, MORE, DORAN,
ARLEN, SHUTE, CAINE, BACON,
LANDOR, ROGET, BARRIE,
BELLOC, AUSTEN, WAUGH,
DEFOE, MILNE, OPIE, READE,
STERNE
authoress .... ELIOT, AUSTEN,
BRONTE, COLLINS, CHRISTIE
baby carriage .... PRAM
baby hood/cap .... BIGGIN
bagman .... SALESMAN
bailiff .... REEVE, STEWARD
ballerina .... FONTEYN
bar .... PUB
bard, ancient .... SCOP
barge .... WHERRY
baseball-like game
.... ROUNDERS

basket .... CORF
bathe .... TUB
bay .... RYE, BUDE, LYME,
MOUNTS, CARDIGAN,
FALMOUTH, LIVERPOOL,
MORECAMBE, BIGBURY,
SWANSEA, THE WASH,
TREMADOC, BARNSTAPLE
beak ...... JUDGE, MAGISTRATE,
SCHOOLMASTER
beastly: colloq. .... VERY
bed .... DOSS
beer .... SWIPES
bit .... SPOT
blackbird .... THRUSH
blackleg .... SCAB, CHEAT,
CROOK, GYPPER, GAMBLER,
SWINDLER
blighter: sl. .... CHAP, FELLOW,
RASCAL
blighty: sl. .... HOME,
ENGLAND
bloke .... COVE, JOHNNY
bloody: sl. ..... VERY, CURSED,
DAMNED
boat, ancient .... CORACLE
boatman .... BARGEE
bolt .... SNIB
book on the aristocracy
.... BRETT'S
borough .... BURGH, LEEDS
bottoms .... HOLM
boy .... NIPPER
boy's school ..... ETON, RUGBY
brandy soda .... PEG
bread .... MANCHET
bulrush .... CATTAIL
bunk .... DOSS
buttercup .... CROWTREE
buttocks: sl. .... BUM
canal laborer .... NAVVY
cape .... CORNWALL
capital .... LONDON
captain's boat .... GALLEY
car name .... ROVER, AUSTIN
carbine .... STEN
card game .... PATIENCE
card sharp .... BLACKLEG
carol singer .... WAIT
cascade .... LADORE
cash: sl. .... RHINO
cask .... KILDERKIN
cat-boat .... UNA
cathedral city ...... ELY, YORK,
TRURO
cavalry .... YEOMANRY
certainly .... RATHER
channel ...... SOLENT, ENGLISH,
BRISTOL, SPITHEAD
Channel island .... SARK,
HERM, JERSEY, ALDERNEY,

GUERNSEY
Channel isle .... WIGHT
Channel, river to .... ORNE,
RANCE, SEINE, SOMME
chap .... COVE
chase .... CHEVY
cheese .... STILTON
chemist .... BOYLE, FARADAY
chief, ancient ...... PENDRAGON
chinaware .... SPODE,
CHELSEA, WEDGWOOD
cigarette: sl. .... GASPER
circuit court .... EYRE
city/town .... ELY, LEEDS,
BARNET, BARKING, BASILDON,
BRADFORD, BRISTOL,
BROMLEY, HAMMERSMITH,
BIRMINGHAM, DOVER,
LONDON, CANTERBURY,
EALING, CAMBRIDGE,
COVENTRY, CAMDEN, CHESTER,
HASTINGS, DURHAM, LAMBETH,
GREENWICH, POOLE,
LANCASTER, LIVERPOOL, HULL,
PLYMOUTH, MANCHESTER,
NEWHAM, OLDHAM,
NOTTINGHAM, YORK,
SHEFFIELD, STOCKPORT,
OXFORD, TORBAY, THURROCK,
WARLEY, HALIFAX, LEICESTER,
WAKEFIELD, WESTMINSTER
clown .... GRIMALDI
cluster .... PLUMP
coachman .... JARVEY
coal carrier .... CORF
coal mine room .... BORD
coin .... PENCE, PENNY,
GEORGE, GUINEA, FARTHING,
SOVRAN, SHILLING,
SOV(EREIGN)
coin, old .... ANGEL, GROAT,
CAROLUS
college .... BALLIOL
college servant .... GYP
college steward ...... MANCIPLE
colonial official
.... PROCONSUL
Columbia capital .... VICTORIA
Columbia Indian .... HAIDA
comedian .... TOOLE
composer .... ARNE, ELGAR,
COATES, DELIUS, BRITTEN
conductor .... BEECHAM,
SARGENT, BARBIROLI
conservative party .... TORY
corner .... HERN
coronation rite .... UNCTION
country festival .... ALE
country gentleman ..... SQUIRE
county .... AVON, LONDON,
BEDFORD, DORSET, ESSEX,

SHIRE, DURHAM, BUCKINGHAM, YORK, BERKSHIRE, CHESHIRE, OXFORD, SURREY, SUSSEX, DERBY, DEVON, GLOUCESTER, KENT, CORNWALL, LINCOLN, NORFOLK, SUFFOLK, SOMERSET, MIDLANDS, NOTTINGHAM, WIGHT, WILTS, CUMBRIA, TYNE-AND-WEAR, WARWICK
courage .... PECKER
court .... EYRE, LEET, SOC, HUSTINGS
cow .... RUNT
crazy .... POTTY
crook .... BLACKLEG
crow .... BRAN
crown jewel .... KOHINUR, KOHINOOR
cue ball .... MASSE
dance, ancient .... MORRIS
dandy .... TOFF, (BEAU) BRUMMEL
dealer .... MONGER
demolish .... RASE
derby hat .... BOWLER
dessert .... FLAN
diarist .... PEPYS, BURNEY, EVELYN
diplomat .... EDEN, LLOYD
divine .... INGE, DONNE
dramatist .... SHAW, MARLOWE, READE, PINERO, SITWELL, PEELE, TOBIN, SHAKESPEARE
drunk: sl. .... SCREWED
dump truck .... TIPPER
dupe .... MUGGINS
dynasty .... TUDOR, STUART
early conqueror .... HORSA, HENGIST, NORMANS
elevator .... LIFT
emblem .... ROSE
emperor of India
.... PADISHAH
entry .... CLOSE
essayist .... ELLA, LAMB
estuary .... HUMBER
exam for honors .... TRIPOS
explorer .... ROSS, CABOT, SCOTT, HUDSON, LANG, BAFFIN, BURTON, RALEIGH, FROBISHER, STEELE, STANLEY
expression .... BULLY, I SAY, CHEERIO
fashion model .... TWIGGY
fell .... DOWN, HILL, MOOR
fellow .... CHAP, COVE
field marshal .... HAIG
field marshal at Arlington
.... DILL

financier .... RHODES, GRESHAM
first overlord .... EGBERT
firth .... SOLWAY
fishing boat .... COBLE, HOOKER
flashlight .... TORCH
food .... TUCK
fool .... MUGGINS
foolish .... SPOON(E)Y
forest .... NEW, ARDEN, SHERWOOD
fox hunter .... PINK
franchise .... SOC
free tenant .... DRENG
freeman .... CEORL, CHURL, THANE
gambler who cheats
.... BLACKLEG
gasoline .... PETROL
general .... BRADDOCK
geologist .... LYELL
giant of legend .... MAGOG
good-by .... PIPPIP
government .... WHITEHALL
grain cradle .... CADER
grove .... SPINNEY
Guiana's capital
.... GEORGETOWN
gum .... DEXTRIN
gumshoe: sl. .... TEC
gun .... STEN, ENFIELD
hackney driver .... JARVEY
hamlet .... DORP
handball .... FIVES
handbook on peers
.... BRETT'S
hare .... PUSS
hawker .... CHAPMAN
hayfork .... PIKEL
head .... CONK
headland .... NAZE
hedgerow .... REW
highball .... STINGER
highwayman .... TURPIN
hills .... MENDIP, CHEVIOT, CHILTERN, CLEVELAND, COTSWOLD, SOUTH DOWNS
historian .... BEDE, ACTON, GROTE, GIBBON
Honduras's new name
.... BELIZE
hooligan .... SPIV
horse .... PRAD, SCREW, GARRON
horse dealer .... COPER
house-dress .... OVERALL
humorist .... STERNE
hunt .... CHEVY
hunting cry .... CHEVY, YOICKS

hunting dog .... LURCHER
hut .... NISSEN
hymnodist .... LYTE, NEALE
ID mark ...... BROAD ARROW
India, founder of .... IVAN
Indian coin .... ANNA
Indian monetary unit
.... ANNA, RUPEE
Indian nursemaid .... AMAH, AYAH
Indian province .... SIND, ASSAM
informer ..... SPY, NOSE, NARK
innkeeper .... PUBLICAN
island ...... ELY, HOLY, LUNDY, MERSEA, TRESCO, SHEPPEY
island in Atlantic
.... ASCENSION
island in Indian Ocean
.... MAURITIUS
island near Borneo
.... LABUAN
islands .... SCILLY, CHANNEL
isle .... ELY, MAN, IRELAND
king .... HAL, JAMES, EDWARD, GEORGE, HAROLD
king, ancient
.... A(E)THELSTAN
king, legendary .... BELI, BRAN, BRUT, ARTHUR, LUD, KNUT, CANUTE
labor strike(r) .... TURN-OUT
laborer .... NAVVY, PROLE
lake .... CONISTON
landowner ...... THANE, SQUIRE
language, ancient ...... CYMRIC
language, major ...... ENGLISH, WELSH, GAELIC
lay doggo .... HID
lecturer .... READER
legislator .... COMMONER
legislature .... PARLIAMENT
letter Z .... ZED
lexicographer .... FOWLER, GOWERS
liberal party .... WHIG
loan money .... PREST
lodgings .... DIGS
lunch .... TIFFIN
machine gun .... BREN
mail .... POST
male sheep .... TUP
malt liquor .... PORTER
manufacturing city ..... LEEDS, BIRMINGHAM
marine: sl. .... JOLLY
mark on government
property .... BROAD ARROW
martyr .... ALBAN
meal .... (HIGH) TEA

measure, former .... ELL
measure, imperial liquid and
     dry ...... GILL, PECK, PINT,
     BUSHEL, GALLON, FLUID
     DRAM, FLUID OUNCE, QUART,
     MINIM, KILDERKIN
mendicant order .... FRIARS
merry-making .... RANT
mild oath .... GOR
military police .... REDCAP
military school
     .... SANDHURST
mine wagon .... CORF, ROLLEY
minister of state .... PEEL,
     PITT, WALPOLE
mint box .... PYX
miser .... SCREW
molasses .... TREACLE
money .... POUND, STERLING,
     PENCE, FARTHING, SHILLING
money advanced to enlisted
men .... PREST
money: sl. .... RHINO
monk .... B(A)EDA
monk historian .... BEDE
mop .... MALKIN
mountain ...... AXE EDGE, PEEL
     FELL, CROSS FELL, SKIDDAW,
     BROWN WILLY, HIGH
     WILLHAYS
mountains .... PENINE,
     PRESELI, CUMBRIAN
murderer .... ARAM
national park ...... DARTMOOR,
     EXMOOR, YORKSHIRE DALES
naturalist .... SLOANE
navigator .... DRAKE
navy enlisted man
     .... BLUEJACKET
nimble .... NIPPY
noble .... DUKE, LORD, EARL,
     BARON, PRINCE, VISCOUNT
noblewoman ..... DAME, LADY,
     DUCHESS, PRINCESS
nonsense! .... HAVERS
North America .... CANADA
novelist ..... DICKENS, BRONTE,
     CAINE, CRONIN, ARTHUR,
     HUXLEY, MACHEN, RAMEE,
     READE, STERNE
nurse .... SISTER
oak .... ROBUR
oatmeal pudding .... MUSH
odd .... RUM
officer's servant .... BATMAN
orator .... BURKE, PITT,
     WILLIAM
Order .... GARTER
ore carrier .... CORF
outcry of blame .... DIRDUM
outlet .... POINT

ox .... RUNT
Pacific protectorate .... TONGA
pail .... ESHIN
pain .... STOUND
painter .... OPIE, ORPEN,
     PAYNTER, ROMNEY, TURNER,
     CONSTABLE
parish official .... OVERSEER
parliament member
     .... BURGESS
parliamentary record
     .... HANSARD
passageway ..... CLOSE, SMOOT
path .... PAD
patron saint .... ST. GEORGE
peddler .... CHAPMAN
peninsula .... LIZARD,
     PURBECK, HOLDERNESS
people, ancient .... ICENI
petty .... POTTY
philosopher .... HUME, JOAD,
     BACON, RUSSELL, SPENCER
physician .... ROSS
physicist ..... BOYLE, FARADAY
pianist .... BAUER
pickpocket .... PRIG
playwright .... SHAW, PEELE
pluck .... PECKER
pocket .... SACK
poet ...... HUGH, LANG, AUDEN,
     BLAKE, BYRON, AUSTIN,
     KEATS, DONNE, ELIOT,
     MACNEICE, MASEFIELD, GRAY,
     SITWELL, SPENCER
poet, earliest .... SCOP,
     CAEDMON
poet laureate .... DAY-LEWIS,
     AUSTIN, CIBBER, MASEFIELD
poetess .... SITWELL,
     BROWNING
Point .... DODMAN, PRAWLE,
     MANACLE, HARTLAND,
     PORTLAND, GIBRALTAR
policeman ...... BOBBY, PEELER
policeman's station ...... POINT
political party .... TORY,
     WHIG, LABOR, CONSERVATIVE
political philosopher
     .... BURKE
Pope .... ADRIAN (IV)
port ..... HULL, COWES, DOVER,
     POOLE, BRISTOL, PRESTON,
     LIVERPOOL
pot herb .... CLARY
pottery/porcelain .... SPODE
prefab shelter .... NISSEN
prep school, first-year boy
     .... SQUIT
     second-year boy ...... SQUIRT
     third-year boy .... JOLLY,
     GOOD FELLOW

prime minister ..... PEEL, PITT,
     ASQUITH, CHURCHILL, LAW,
     BALDWIN, CHAMBERLAIN,
     CANNING, ATTLEE, BALFOUR,
     EDEN, MAJOR, THATCHER,
     HOME, WILSON, MACMILLAN
prime minister called
     Ironside .... PITT
prime minister called the
     Iron Lady ...... THATCHER
prime minister with the cigar
     .... CHURCHILL
prime minister with the
     umbrella
     .... CHAMBERLAIN
prince ...... CHARLES, ANDREW,
     PHILIP, HARRY, EDWARD,
     WILLIAM
princess .... DIANA, ANNE,
     URSULA, MARGARET, SARAH,
     EUGENIE, BEATRICE
printer .... CAXTON
printing type .... RUBY
prison .... GAOL, DARTMOOR
prison: sl. .... QUAD, QUOD
property tax .... RATE
psychologist .... ELLIS
publisher .... BEAVERBROOK
pudding ..... MUSH, ROLY-POLY
pupil: sl. .... SCUM
Quaker .... PENN
queen .... ANNE, MARY,
     VICTORIA, ELIZABETH
queen, ancient .... BOADICEA
queer .... RUM
quick .... NIPPY
race course site .... ASCOT,
     NEWMARKET, EPSOM (DOWNS)
RAF fighter-bomber
     .... JAGUAR, SPITFIRE,
     BUCCANEER, HARRIER,
     TORNADO
rage .... WAX
raincoat .... WATERPROOF
range/stove .... KITCHENER
Reformation leader
     .... SEYMOUR
reformer .... SPENCE
resort .... BATH, MARGATE,
     BLACKPOOL
retail store .... WAREHOUSE
river .... ALN, AIRE, AVON,
     CAM, DART, COLNE, KENNET,
     DON, DEE, THAMES, MERSEY,
     ESK, DOVE, EDEN, HODDER,
     VER, LEA, OUSE, HUMBER,
     EXE, LUNE, TRENT, MEDWAY,
     TYNE, RIBBLE, PARRETT, URE,
     NENE, SWALE, SEVERN, USK,
     TEST, YARE, STOUR, WEY,
     TEES, TAW, TAMAR

river lowland .... HOLM, BOTTOMS
road .... PAD
rock singer .... (MICK) JAGGER
routine .... ROTA
royal family .... TUDOR, YORK, STUART, WINDSOR
royal guard officer .... EXON
royal house ..... TUDOR, YORK, WINDSOR, STUART, HANOVER, CLARENCE, HIGHGROVE, SUNNINGHILL
royal household official .... GROOM
royal stables .... MEWS
royal yacht .... BRITANNIA
rubbish! .... HAVERS
ruins .... STONEHENGE
ruler, early ...... OFFA, EGBERT
ruling family .... TUDOR, YORK, WINDSOR
sailor .... LIMEY
saint .... AARON, ALBAN
salary .... SCREW
salesman .... BAGMAN
saloon-keeper .... PUBLICAN
sandhill .... DENE
scarecrow .... MALKIN
school, prep .... ETON, RUGBY, HARROW, LUDGROVE
schoolboy servant .... FAG
schoolmaster ..... ARAM, BEAK
schoolteacher .... MASTER, MISTRESS
scientist .... DARWIN
Scilly island .... TRESCO, ST. MARY'S, ST. MARTIN'S, HUGH TOWN
sea .... IRISH, NORTH
seaman .... RATING
seaport ..... GRIMSBY, RABAUL, BOOTLE, MARGATE, DOVER, WHITBY, BIRKENHEAD
seat in a theater .... STALL
sedan .... SALOON
sentimental .... SOPPY
serf .... ESNE, THRALL
sergeant-at-law cap .... BIGGIN
sheriff's aid .... BULLDOG
sidewalk artist .... SCREEVER
silly .... SPOON(E)Y
slaughterhouse .... KNACKER
sleep: sl. .... DOSS
smack .... HOOKER
smart .... STOUND
smock .... OVERALL
snarl .... GIRN
social event .... ASCOT
socialist .... FABIAN
soldier .... ATKINS, LIMEY, TOMMY, REDCOAT

soldier's furlough/leave .... BLIGHTY
solitaire .... PATIENCE
songbird .... BULBUL, BULLFINCH
Sound .... PLYMOUTH
spa .... BATH, MARGATE
spark .... SPUNK
spot .... BIT
spy .... NARK, NOSE, ANDRE
stage .... PLATEAU
statesman .... PITT, EDEN, BURKE, CLIVE, GREY, HOARE, VILLIERS
steal .... PRIG
stool pigeon: sl. .... NARK
strait .... DOVER
strange .... RUM
streetcar .... TRAM
student, senior .... PREPOS(I)TOR
subdivision .... SHIRE
surgeon .... LISTER
swell dresser .... TOFF
symbol ..... LION, (JOHN) BULL
tax .... GELD, SESS, EXCISE
taxable .... RATABLE
tea .... ELM
teacher .... MISTER CHIPS
tent .... MARQUEE
term for amusement ..... BEER AND SKITTLES
term for good time .... BASH
thanks .... TAS
theologian .... ALCUIN
theorist .... LASKI
thicket .... SPINNEY
thief .... PRIG
tin mine .... STANNARY
title .... SIR, DUKE, EARL, BARON, PRINCE
toast .... CHEERS
tobacco bit .... SCREW
tourist/traveler .... TRIPPER
trader .... MONGER
trout .... SEWEN, SEWIN
truck .... LORRY
tutor .... MASTER
25 pounds: sl. .... PONY
unit of measure .... STACK
university .... OXFORD, CAMBRIDGE
university disciplinarian .... BULLDOG
university official ...... BEADLE
university student .... SOPHISTER
very .... JOLLY
village .... DORP, ARAWE, BOURG
wage earner .... PROLE

waiter .... POTMAN
warrior .... CNUT
wasteland .... HEATH
waterways .... LODES
Wave .... WREN
weight .... TON, KEEL, MAST, STONE
weight for wool .... TOD
whisky-soda .... STINGER
willow herb .... ROSEBAY
woman politician .... (LADY) ASTOR, (MARGARET) THATCHER
woman servant .... SLAVEY
woman, slovenly .... MALKIN
wood pigeon .... CULVER
woodland area .... WEALD
work horse .... GARRAN
World War I commander .... HAIG
wrap .... RUG
Briton, early .... CELT, JUTE, PICT, ANGLE, ICENI
Brittany .... ARMORICA, BRETAGNE
brittle .... BRASH, CRISP, FRAIL, CRACKLY, FRAGILE, VITREOUS
bones disorder .... OSTEOPOROSIS
peanut .... CANDY
Brno name .... (JOSIP) TITO
bro. .... BROTHER
broach .... AWL, TAP, HOLE, OPEN, SPIT, RIMER, CHISEL, LAUNCH, REAMER, SKEWER, BRING UP, INTRODUCE
broad .... WIDE, CLEAR, GENERAL, LIBERAL, SPACIOUS, EXTENSIVE, SWEEPING, TOLERANT, WIDESPREAD
band: heraldry .... FESS
slang .... WOMAN
broadbill .... DUCK, GAPER, RAYA, SCAUP, SPOONBILL
broadbrim: colloq. .... HAT, FRIEND, QUAKER
broadcast .... SOW, SHOW, PROGRAM, PUBLISH, ANNOUNCE, STREW, SPREAD, SCATTER, TELECAST, TRANSMIT
broadcasting ...... ON AIR, AIRING
system/network .... ABC, ESPN, CBS, CNN, NBC
broadcloth .... PIMA
broaden .... EXPAND, EXTEND, WIDEN, SPREAD
broadleaf .... TOBACCO
broadminded .... LIBERAL, RECEPTIVE, TOLERANT, UNBIASED, UNDERSTANDING

broadside .... ABUSE, SALVO, ATTACK
broadsword .... BILL, CLAYMORE, CUTLASS, GLA(I)VE
broadtail .... SHEEP, KARAKUL, ASTRAKHAN
Broadway character .... ANGEL, HOOFER, PRESS AGENT, SUGAR DADDY
  event .... PLAY, SHOW
  girls, former .... FLORADORA
  impresario .... MERRICK
  Joe .... NAMATH
  (nick)name ...... COHAN, BILLY ROSE, FLO ZIEGFELD
  restaurateur .... SARDI
  square .... HERALD
  super hit .... MAN OF LA MANCHA
  venture .... PLAY, REVUE, MUSICAL(E)
Brobdingnagian .... GIANT, GIGANTIC
brocade ...... BROCHE, BAUDEKIN, BALDACHIN
  gold .... KINCOB
  Japanese .... NISHIKI
broccoli .... CAULIFLOWER
brochette .... SKEWER
brochure ...... BOOKLET, LEAFLET, PAMPHLET
brock .... BADGER
brocket .... DEER, PITA, SPITTER
brogan ...... BOOT, SHOE, BROGUE
brogue .... SHOE, ACCENT, PRONUNCIATION
  Scotch .... TRICK, DECEPTION
broil .... BAKE, COOK, RIOT, BRAWL, GRILL, BRAISE, ROAST, BARBECUE
broiled meat .... BARBECUE
broiler .... PAN, OVEN, CAPON, CHICKEN, GRIDIRON
broke: sl. ...... NEEDY, BANKRUPT, MONEYLESS, PENNILESS
broken .... TORN, TAMED, CRUSHED, SMASHED, VIOLATED, BUSTED, SPLINTERED, INTERRUPTED
  apart .... RUPTURE
  bone .... FRACTURE
  colloquial .... OUSTED, DEPOSED, DISMISSED
  down .... SICK, RUINED, CRUSHED, CHATTERED, DECREPIT, DESTROYED, SHAKY, USELESS, WRECKED
  grain husk .... BRAN
  heart .... ANGUISH, DESPAIR
  ice .... BRASH
  in .... TRAINED

mass of clouds .... RACK
  off .... LOOSE, DETACHED
  piece .... FRAGMENT
  pieces of masonry .... RUBBLE
  pieces of pottery .... SHARDS
  rainbow .... WINDGALL
  spike of grain .... CHOB
  stone debris .... RUBBLE
  tooth .... DENTAL FRACTURE
  wind .... HEAVES
broker .... AGENT, DEALER, FACTOR, JOBBER, MIDDLEMAN
  business of .... AGIOTAGE
  order to .... BUY, SELL, UNLOAD
  real estate .... REALTOR
brokerage .... AGIOTAGE
  fee .... AGIO
brolly .... UMBRELLA, PARACHUTE
Brom Bones's lack .... HEAD
bromide .... SOP, CALMANT, SEDATIVE, TRANQUILIZER
  overuse of .... BROMISM
  side effect of .... TREMOR, CONFUSION
bromine .... HALOGEN
bromo .... DOSE
bronchial tube .... TRACHEA, WINDPIPE
bronchitis, complication of .... PLEURISY, PNEUMONIA
  form of .... ACUTE, CHRONIC
  remedy .... GRINDELIA
bronc(h)o .... PONY, HORSE, MUSTANG
  buster .... RIDER, TAMER, COWBOY
Bronte, _____ .... ANNE, EMILY, CHARLOTTE
  biographer .... GERIN
  brother .... BRANWELL
  family's native village .... HAWORTH
  husband of Charlotte .... NICHOLLS
  pseudonym of Anne .... ACTON BELL
  pseudonym of Charlotte .... CURRER BELL
  pseudonym of Emily .... ELLIS BELL
  work .... JANE EYRE, WUTHERING HEIGHTS
bronto as combining form .... THUNDER, HUGENESS
brontosaurus .... DINOSAUR
Bronx .... BOROUGH, COCKTAIL
  cheer ..... BOO, BOOING, HOOT, RASPBERRY
  cheerer's feeling .... SCORN, DISGUST, DERISION, RIDICULE

bronze ...... TAN, ALLOY, COPPER, LATTEN, AENEOUS
  coating/crust of .... PATINA
  coin/Roman .... AES
  ''gold'' ..... ORMOLU, VERMEIL
  green coating .... VERD, PATINA, ANTIQUE, VERDIGRIS
  tool .... CELT
brooch .... PIN, CLIP, OUCH, CAMEO, CLASP
brood .... MOPE, SULK, FLOCK, HATCH, HOVER, THINK, PONDER, LITTER, SIT(ON EGGS), COGITATE, FAMILY, REFLECT, MEDITATE
  of birds .... COVEY, CLUTCH
  chicks .... HATCH, CLUTCH
  ducks .... TEAM
  family .... CHILDREN
  fish .... SPAWN
  goats/sheep .... FLOCK
  hawks/eagles .... AERIE
  pheasants .... NIDE
  pigs .... FARROW
  over .... FRET, PINE, WORRY, GRIEVE
brooder .... HEN, COOP, HENNERY, WORRIER
  slang .... SOURPUSS
brooding hen's sound .... CLUCK, CACKLE
brook .... GILL, GHYLL, RUN, BEAR, RILL(ET), RUNNEL, RIVULET, RUNLET, CREEK, ENDURE, STREAM
  trout .... SALTER
Brooke .... SHIELDS
brooklime .... VERONICA
Brooklyn Dodgers' nickname .... SUPERBAS
  Institute .... PRATT
  island .... CONEY
  resident of .... BROOKLYNITE
brookweed .... PIMPERNEL
broom .... BRUSH, CLEANER, SHRUB, SWEEP, WHISK
  grass/material .... ZACATON
  made of twigs .... BESOM
broomcorn grain .... HIRSE
broth .... BREE, BROO, SOUP, GRUEL, POTAGE, CONSOMME
  cabbage/greens .... KALE
brothel .... KIP, BORDEL(LO), WASTE, BAGNIO, BAWDYHOUSE
  keeper .... BAWD, MADAM, PROCURESS
brother .... FRA, FRIAR, PEER, SIBLING, FELLOW, FRATER
  colloquial .... BUB, BROD
  Fritz's .... HANS

brotherhood .... ELKS, UNION, KINSHIP, ORDER, SODALITY, FRATERNITY, ASSOCIATION
brotherly .... FRATERNAL
brougham .... CARRIAGE, LIMOUSINE, AUTOMOBILE
brought aboard ship .... PIPED
about .... CAUSED
up .... BRED, REARED, BROACHED, INTRODUCED
up by hand .... CADE
up without reason .... LUGGED INTO
brouhaha .... ADO, STIR, HUBBUB, UPROAR, COMMOTION
brow .... CREST, BRAE, EDGE, EYEBROW, SUMMIT, FOREHEAD
browbeat .... COW, BULLY, DAUNT, HECTOR, PETRIFY, BAMBOOZLE, SCARE, TERRIFY, INTIMIDATE
brown .... DUN, TAN, BEIGE, ROAST, BISTER, RUSSET, SEPIA, SIENNA, SORREL, TAWNY, TOAST, UMBER
apple .... RUSSET
betty .... (APPLE) PUDDING
coal .... LIGNITE
dark ...... BRUNET, CHOCOLATE
kiwi .... ROA
light .... TAN, ECRU, BEIGE, KHAKI, PONGEE
paper .... KRAFT
pigment .... BISTER, BISTRE, SIENNA, UMBER
quickly .... SEAR
reddish .... RUST, AUBURN, CHESTNUT
reddish horse .... SORREL
seaweed .... KELP
shoes .... TANS, CORDOVAN
skinned people .... THAIS, MALAY(ANS), FILIPINOS, INDONS, CHAMORROS
study ..... REVERIE, DAYDREAM
thrasher .... SONGBIRD
tone .... SEPIA
yellow .... HAZEL, PABLO
Brown, actress .... VANESSA
Bess .... MUSKET
Shirt .... NAZI, HITLERITE
Browne, _____ .... SAM
browned in deep fat .... RISSOLE
brownie .... CAKE, ELF, NIS, FAIRY, GNOME, GOBLIN, DWARF, CAMERA, KOBOLD, PIXIE, GIRL SCOUT
Browning's home in Italy .... ASOLO
poem .... PARACELSUS

brownish .... DUN
gray .... TAUPE
purple .... PUCE
red .... MAROON, RUFOUS, CORDOVAN, TERRA-COTTA
yellow .... AMBER, BUFF, TAWNY
brownout ...... DIMOUT, DIMMING
brownstone front .... STOOP, FACADE
sign .... TO LET, ROOMS
browntail .... MOTH
browse .... PRY, FEED, SCAN, GLANCE, GRAZE, NIBBLE, CANVASS, LOOK AROUND, EXPLORE
Broz, Josip .... TITO
brucine .... ALKALOID
bruin .... BEAR
bruise ...... JAM, BATTER, SHINER, CRUSH, CONTUSE, CONTUSION, DISCOLORATION
application for/remedy .... ARNICA, COLD COMPRESS
around the eye .... BLACK EYE
medical term for a .... ECCHYMOSIS
bruiser .... BOXER, BULLY, ABUSER, BEATER, FIGHTER
bruising implement ...... PESTLE, CLUB, STICK, CUDGEL
bruit ...... TELL, CLAMOR, RUMOR, GOSSIP, REPORT, SPREAD, PUBLISH, BROADCAST
brumal .... COLD, HIEMAL, SLEETY, WINTRY, AUTUMNAL
brume .... FOG, MIST, VAPOR
brummagem: colloq. ...... FAKE, CHEAP, GAUDY
brumous .... FOGGY, MISTY
Brunei's capital .... BANDAR SERI BEGAWAN
city .... SERIA
language ..... MALAY, CHINESE, ENGLISH
monetary unit .... (BRUNEI) DOLLAR
religion ...... ISLAM, BUDDHISM
ruler .... SULTAN
Brunhild (Brunnhilde, Brynhild) .... QUEEN, VALKYRIE
brother-in-law .... SIGURD
fate of .... SLEEP
husband of .... GUNNAR, GUNTHER
mother of .... ERDA
savior of .... SIEGFRIED
sister-in-law of .... GUDRUN, GUTHRUN
Brunn .... BRNO

brunt .... FORCE, SHOCK, IMPACT, STRESS
brush .... COMB, FITCH, GRAZE, PAINT, BROSSE, POLISH, CLEAN, SWEEP, DUSTER, TOUCH, THICKET, SKIRMISH
aside .... SNUB, IGNORE, SLIGHT, SWEEP (OUT)
for sweeping .... BROOM
lightly .... SCUFF, TOUCH UP
like .... SCOPULATE
material .... ZACATON
off .... SNUB, REBUFF, DISMISS(AL), LEAVE OUT IN THE COLD
up .... NEATEN, CLEAN UP, PRACTICE, REHEARSE
brushwood .... BRAKE, COPSE, SCRUB, COPPICE, UNDERBRUSH
fence .... WEIR
brushwork .... PAINTING
brushy .... BUSHY, BRISTLY
brusque .... CURT, BLUFF, BLUNT, GRUFF, NASTY, SHORT, ABRUPT
slang .... HIGH HAT
Brussels carpet .... TOURNAI
is capital of .... BELGIUM
sprouts .... CABBAGE
brut .... DRY
brutal .... FELL, RUDE, CRUEL, FERAL, FERINE, SAVAGE, COARSE, INFERNAL, DEVILISH, RUTHLESS, COLDBLOODED
behavior .... BARBARISM
soldier .... PANDOUR
taskmaster .... LEGREE
brutalize .... MAUL, BATTER, ILL-USE, TERRORIZE
brute ...... BEAST, GROSS, ANIMAL, STUPID, INSENSATE, SCOUNDREL
"_____ Brute?" .... ET TU
Brynner, actor .... YUL
bryophyte ...... MOSS, LIVERWORT
bryozoan .... CORAL, HYDRA, POLYP, SEAPEN, SEA ANEMONE, POLYZOAN
Brythonic sea god .... LER
bskt. .... BASKET
bub: colloq. ...... BOY, BROTHER
bubaline .... ANTELOPES, HARTEBEESTS
bubble .... BEAD, BLOB, BOIL, FOAM, GLOBULE
air .... BLEB
archaic .... CHEAT, HUSTLE, SWINDLE
flagrantly .... PERK
maker .... GUM
over .... EXULT, OVERFLOW

up .... BOIL, SPURT
with excitement/joy ..... GUSH,
    RAVE, EFFUSE
bubbler of a sort .... BROOK,
    (WATER) FOUNTAIN
bubbles, full of .... BUBBLY,
    HUBBLY, CHAMPAGNE
sound of .... GURGLING
bubbling .... FIZZY, SPARKLING,
    EFFERVESCENT
bubbly: sl. .... CHAMPAGNE
bubonic plague carrier .... RAT,
    FLEA
buccal .... MALAR
buccaneer .... GRILL, PIRATE,
    CORSAIR, SEA ROBBER
ancient .... VIKING
base, one-time .... HAITI
Bucephalus .... STEED,
    (WAR)HORSE
Buceresti .... BUCHAREST
Bucharest is capital of
    .... ROMANIA
buck .... HARE, HART, STAG, MALE
    DEER, BILLY GOAT, BUNNY,
    DANDY, SAWHORSE
and wing .... TAP-DANCE
antler of .... ADVANCER
black/Indian .... SASIN
colloquial .... DEFY, FIGHT,
    RESIST
four-year-old .... SORE
less than a year old ..... FAWN
_____ (military rating)
    .... PRIVATE, SERGEANT
off .... UNSEAT, UPROOT,
    DISMOUNT
pass the .... SHUN, EVADE,
    SHIRK
red .... PALLAH
slang .... GREEN, DOLLAR
    (BILL)
up: colloq. .... BRACE UP,
    CHEER UP, ENCOURAGE
water .... KOB
young .... PUP, CUB, KID,
    COLT, (SCHOOL)BOY, LAD,
    WHELP, LADDIE
Buck, novelist .... PEARL
buckaroo .... RIDER, COWBOY,
    TRAINER
buckboard .... CARRIAGE
bucket .... BAIL, KEEL, PAIL,
    SCOOP, VESSEL, CANNIKIN
butter/fish .... KIT
coal/mining ..... TUB, SCUTTLE
handle .... BAIL
kick the .... DIE
make of a .... OAKEN
Scottish .... STOUP
Buckeye State .... OHIO

Buckingham .... PALACE
buckish .... FOPPISH
buckle .... BOW, JOIN, KINK,
    OUCH, WARP, CATCH, CLASP,
    FASTEN, GRAPPLE
ancient .... FIBULA
part of .... TONGUE
under .... BEND, GIVE IN,
    YIELD, SUBMIT, COLLAPSE
buckler .... ARMOR, TARGE,
    (ARM)SHIELD
bucko .... BULLY
buckra, in Africa .... WHITEMAN
buckram .... RIGID, STIFF,
    STARCHED
buckthorn ...... WAHOO, CASCARA
buckwheat tree ...... TITI, TEETEE
weed ...... DOCK, JUNK, JUNCO,
    LOCO, TARE
bucolic .... RURAL, RUSTIC,
    POETIC, AGRESTIC, ARCADIAN,
    GEORGIC, GEOPONIC,
    PASTORAL
sound .... BAA, LOW, MOO,
    BLEAT, CROW, CACKLE
bud .... BULB, GERM, SHOOT,
    SPROUT, BURGEON,
    PULLULATE
dried .... CLOVE
for grafting .... (S)CION
large and compact .... HEAD
like outgrowth .... GEMMA
nip in the .... STOP, CHECK,
    CURTAIL
of society .... DEB
on a flower stalk .... BULBIL
potato .... EYE
scale .... CATAPHYLL
variation .... SPORT
Bud Fisher's creation .... MUTT,
    JEFF, CICERO
Budapest is capital of
    .... HUNGARY
Buddha .... FO, GAUTAMA,
    TEACHER
cousin of .... ANANDA
Japanese .... AMIDA, AMITA
mother of .... MAYA
tree of .... PIPAL
Buddhism, fate in .... KARMA
form of .... LAMAISM
founder of .... GAUTAMA
hatred .... DOSA
perfect blessedness
    .... NIRVANA
religious language .... PALI
Buddhist angel .... DEVA
cause of infinite existence
    .... NIDANA
church .... TERA, PAGODA
column/pillar .... LAT

dialect/language/tongue
    .... PALI
fate .... KARMA
festival .... BON
final release (from all desires
    and passion) .... NIRVANA
gateway .... TORAN
hell .... NARAKA
holy city .... LASSA, LHASA
holy man/title of respect
    .... MAHATMA
literature .... SUTRA
monastery .... TERA
monk .... BO, LAMA, BONZE,
    TALAPOIN
mound/monument .... STUPA
mountain .... OMEI
novice .... GOYIM
paradise .... JODO
priest .... BO, LAMA, BONZE,
    MAHATMA
religious observances
    .... DHARMA
saint .... AR(A)HAT
scripture .... SUTRA, SUTTA
sect, Japanese .... ZEN
shrine .... TOPE, STUPA,
    DAGOBA
Siamese .... LAO
temple .... PAGODA, VIHARA
buddle .... DRAIN, TROUGH
buddy .... BOY, PAL, CRONY,
    COMRADE, COMPANION
British: sl. .... CULLY
buddy .... PALLY
Buddy .... RICH, HOLLY
budge .... FUR, MOVE, ALTER,
    SHIFT, POMPOUS, LAMBSKIN
budgerigar .... BUDGIE, PARAKEET
budget .... BAG, POUCH, STOCK,
    ESTIMATE, SCHEDULE,
    PROPOSAL, APPROPRIATION
anything .... ALLOW,
    APPORTION
plan .... FORECAST,
    INSTALLMENT
buds, pickled .... CAPERS
put forth .... SHOOT, SPROUT,
    BURGEON
bueno: Sp. .... GOOD, VERY WELL,
    SOUND, HEALTHY
Buenos Aires is capital of
    .... ARGENTINA
buenos dias: Sp. ...... GOOD DAY,
    GREETING, GOOD MORNING
buff .... BLOW, SHINE, POLISH,
    LEATHER, SPINDLE
colloquial .... FAN, DEVOTEE,
    ENTHUSIAST, AFICIONADO
in the .... NUDE, NAKED
the fingernails ...... SMOOTHEN

buffalo .... OX, ARNI, BISON, PERPLEX, CONFOUND
bird .... COWBIRD
bug .... BEETLE
Celebes .... ANOA
crossed with cattle .... CAT(T)ALO
female .... COW
hybrid .... CAT(T)ALO
Philippine .... CARABAO, TIMARAU, TIMARAW
skin ...... BUFF, HIDE, LEATHER
slang .... BULLY, BAMBOOZLE
S. African .... NIARE
wild .... ARNA
Buffalo Bill ...... (WILLIAM) CODY
buffer .... SOCK, BARRIER, BUMPER, CUSHION, ABSORBER
for the floor .... POLISHER
buffet .... BLOW, TOSS, SLAP, PUNCH, TABLE, COUNTER, CREDENZA, SIDEBOARD
meals .... SPREADS, SMORGASBORD
buffeted: poetic .... TOST
bufflehead .... DUCK, BUTTERBALL
buffo .... CLOWN, COMIC, OPERA SINGER
voice of a .... BASS
buffoon ...... FOOL, ZANY, CLOWN, DROLL, JESTER, MIME(R), PRANKSTER, (MERRY)ANDREW, PUNCH, COMEDIAN, HARLEQUIN, PUNCHINELLO
buffoonery ...... COMEDY, FROLIC, CLOWNING, DROLLERY, SLAPSTICK
bufo: Latin .... TOAD
bug .... FLY, NIT, GERM, GNAT, MITE, CIMEX, BEETLE, INSECT, CONENOSE, HOBGOBLIN
living on other insects .... ASSASSIN
river .... NAREW
slang .... TAP, WIRE, FLAW, ANGER, ANNOY, ADDICT, BOTHER, DEFECT, DEVOTEE, ENTHUSIAST, MICROPHONE
spray .... REPELLANT
with built-in light ..... FIREFLY
with sucking beak .... ASSASSIN
bugaboo .... BUGBEAR, NIGHTMARE, MUMBO-JUMBO, HEEBIE-JEEBIES, SCARECROW
African .... GOGO, BOGIE
bugbear ...... BOGY, (HOB)GOBLIN
of a kind .... OGRE, DEMON
bugger ...... CHAP, LOUSE, CREEP, STINKER, SODOMITE
buggy .... CAR, AUTO, CART,

PRAM, SHAY, CHAISE, CARRIAGE, PERAMBULATOR
bughouse: sl. .... ASYLUM, MADHOUSE, NUTHOUSE
bugle ...... BEAD, HORN, CLARION, MINT PLANT, BOOTS AND SADDLES
call ...... TAPS, RALLY, SIGNAL, RETREAT, ASSEMBLY, TANTARA, TAT(T)OO, REVEILLE
carabao horn .... TAMBULI
note .... TIRALEE
signal .... TATTOO
sound .... BLARE
yellow .... IVA
bugloss .... ANCHUSA
bugs: sl. .... DIPPY, LOONY, CRAZY, NUTTY, INSANE
buhr .... WHETSTONE
build .... BODY, FORM, MAKE, REAR, ERECT, CONSTRUCT, RAISE, STATURE, PHYSIQUE
a lawn .... SOD
up: colloq. .... PLUG, PRAISE, PUBLICITY
builder .... MAKER, PRODUCER, CRAFTSMAN
kind of .... ENGINEER, ARCHITECT, STONEMASON, LANDSCAPER, STONECUTTER
knot of .... CLOVEHITCH
building .... PILE, EDIFICE, ERECTION, STRUCTURE
caretaker .... JANITOR, CONCIERGE, CUSTODIAN
crowded .... WARREN
cylindrical .... SILO
behind a big one .... BACKHOUSE
external corner of .... QUOIN
for abode ...... HOUSE, CONDO, TOWN-HOUSE, APARTMENT, CONDOMINIUM
bowling ...... LANES, ALLEYS
coed's residence (in school campus) .... DORM, DORMITORY
exhibits .... MUSEUM, ARCHIVES, PAVILION
famous dead persons .... PANTHEON
fodder .... SILO
fruit-growing .... GRAPERY
gambling .... CASINO
grains .... GRANARY, ELEVATOR
lodging/residential .... HOTEL, HOSTELRY
musical performances .... MUSIC HALL, THEATER, OPERA HOUSE, AUDITORIUM

races/games .... HIPPODROME
sociality .... CLUBHOUSE
storage of merchandise .... WAREHOUSE
worship .... CHAPEL, CHURCH, TEMPLE, CATHEDRAL, SYNAGOGUE
high-rise/tall .... TOWER, PYRAMID, SKYSCRAPER
inscription on .... EPIGRAPH
logger's .... SAWMILL
material .... ADOBE, BRICK, WOOD, STAFF, STONE, CEMENT, LUMBER, MARBLE, MORTAR, CONCRETE
projecting ornament .... GARGOYLE
projection .... BAY, APSE
roadside, for travelers .... MOTEL, MOTOR-COURT
round .... ROTUNDA
site .... LOT, STEADING
U.S. Department of Defense .... PENTAGON
wing .... BAY, ELL, ANNEX
built-in bed .... BUNK, BERTH
Bukhara product .... RUG
bulb .... BUD, LEEK, SEGO, ONION, GARLIC, HYACINTH
edible .... CAMAS(S)
glass .... AMPOULE
like root .... TUBEROSE
like stem, plant with .... CORM, TUBER, CROCUS
lily .... SEGO, CAMAS
lily, dried .... SQUILL
plant .... SEGO, TULIP
segment .... CLOVE
Bulba, ____ .... TARAS
bulbous plant .... GARLIC, TUBEROSE
bulbul .... SONGBIRD, NIGHTINGALE
Bulgarian .... SLAV, CHUVASH
cape .... EMINE, KALIAKRA
capital .... SOFIA
city ..... RUSE, VARNA, PERNIK, SHUMEN, SLIVEN, VIDIN, DOBRICH, GABROVO, YAMBOL, PLOVDIV, HASKOVO
coin/money .... LEV, LEW, DINAR, STOTINKA
czar/tsar .... BORIS
king .... SIMEON
mountain .... RUJEN, MIDZHUR, MUSALA
mountains .... BALKAN
Moslem .... POMAK
president .... ZHIVKOV
queen .... MARGARITA
river ..... VIT, MESTA, DANUBE,

STRUMA, TIMOK, MARITSA
sea .... BLACK
seaport .... VARNA
weight .... OKA, OKE
bulge .... BAG, HUMP, LUMP,
BLOAT, FLARE, PROTRUDE,
PROJECTION, SWELL(ING)
of belly: sl. ...... BAY WINDOW
of skull .... INION
bulging .... TUMID, TOROSE,
TOROUS, BELLIED, BLOATED,
GIBBOUS, TUBEROUS
bulimia, in medicine
.... HUNGER, DIETING
bulk .... SIZE, MASS, AMOUNT,
TOTAL, VOLUME, EXPANSE,
MAJORITY, QUANTITY,
AGGREGATE
additive .... FILLER
bulkhead .... WALL, PARTITION,
EMBANKMENT
bulky .... BIG, HEFTY, LARGE,
MASSY, MASSIVE
boat .... ARK
bull .... LIE, MALE, SEAL, TORO,
STEER, TAURO, TAURUS
castrated .... BULLOCK
cry .... BELLOW
of/like a .... TAURIN(E)
of Hercules .... CRETAN
of myth .... MINATOUR
sacred: Egypt. .... APIS
shoot the: sl. .... CHAT
slang .... COP, CRAP,
MALARKEY, NONSENSE, JOHN
LAW, POLICEMAN
young .... STOT, BULLOCK
Bull, John .... ENGLAND
bulla .... BLEB, BLAIN, BLISTER,
PUSTULE, VESICLE
bullace .... PLUM, TREE
bullbat .... NIGHTHAWK
bulldog .... PUG, MASTIFF,
REVOLVER
color .... BRINDLE
soft-nosed .... DUMDUM
trait ...... COURAGE, BOLDNESS,
DARING, DEFIANCE, TENACITY
bulldogging place .... RODEO
"Bulldogs" .... ELIS
bulldoze .... RAZE, BULLY, LEVEL,
FORCE, COERCE, FLATTEN,
BROWBEAT, FRIGHTEN
bullet .... BALL, SHOT, LEAD,
SLUG, PELLET, MISSILE
charge container
.... CARTRIDGE
kind of ...... DUMDUM, TRACER
metal covering .... JACKET
size .... CALIBER
bulletin ...... REPORT, STATEMENT,

NEWS(LETTER), PUBLICATION
kind of .... MEDICAL,
WEATHER
bulletproof shield
.... MANT(E)LET
bullets, for short .... AMMO
bullfight cheer .... OLE
bullfighter .... MATADOR,
PICADOR, TOREADOR
assistant .... PICADOR
mantle .... CAPA
on foot .... TORERO
queue of .... COLETA
bullfighting dart .... BANDERILLA
participant ...... BANDERILLERO
bullfinch .... OLP, HEDGE,
REDBIRD, SONGBIRD
bullfrog's cry .... BOOM
bullhead .... FISH, CATFISH,
SCULPIN
bullheaded .... STUBBORN,
HEADSTRONG
animal, of a sort .... MULE
bullion before coinage
.... INGOT, BAR, GOLD,
BILLOT, SILVER
bullish .... OPTIMISTIC
time .... RISE
Bullitt director .... YATES
bullock .... OX, STEER, STIRK
bull's-eye .... CENTER, TARGET
circle next to .... INNER
bully .... BUCKO, PIMP, THUG,
HUFF, BRUISER, BROWBEAT,
TYRANT, HECTOR, CORNED
BEEF, BRAWLER, BULLDOZE,
BAMBOOZLE
colloquial .... FINE, GOOD,
WELL DONE
tree .... BALATA
bulrush .... TULE, PAPYRUS
British .... CATTAIL
bulwark .... WALL, SCONCE,
DEFENSE, RAMPART,
EARTHWORK, BREAKWATER,
PROTECTION
bum .... HOBO, LOAF, IDLER,
LOAFER, SPONGER, VAGRANT
a ride .... HITCH(HIKE)
ambulant .... VAGRANT
British: sl. .... BUTTOCKS
check, describing one
.... BOUNCING
_____ (frame-up) .... RAP
bumble .... BLUNDER
bumblebee .... DOR
bump .... JOLT, LUMP, NODE,
STUB, JOSTLE, COLLIDE,
KNOCK, STRIKE, SWELLING
off: sl. .... KILL, MURDER
slang .... REPLACE

bumper .... TOAST, BARRIER,
BRIMMER
auto .... GUARD
crop .... LARGE, ABUNDANT
sticker .... SLOGAN
bum(p)kin .... CLOD, LOUT, RUBE,
YAHOO, YOKEL
ship's .... BOOM, SPAR
bumpkins .... CAVES
bumptious ...... PROUD, PUSHING,
ARROGANT, CONCEITED
bumpy .... JERKY, ROUGH,
JOLTING, TURBULENT
bun .... CHIGNON, KNOT, LOAF,
ROLL
bunch .... LOT, CYME, TUFT,
CROWD, GROUP, BUNDLE,
CLUSTER, COLLECTION
grass .... STIPA
of branches .... COMA
of grapes .... BOTRYOID
of sheaves ...... SHOCK, SHOOK
small .... WISP
bunchberry .... DOGWOOD
bunco: colloq. .... CHEAT, CROOK,
CON MAN, HUSTLER,
SWINDLER
buncombe .... BUNK, HUMBUG,
BOMBAST, TWADDLE,
MALARKEY
bund .... LEAGUE, CONFEDERATION
Oriental .... QUAY,
EMBANKMENT
bundle .... BALE, PACK, BUNCH,
SHEAF, GROUP, GATHER,
PACKET, PARCEL, PACKAGE
of fibers, leaves ...... FASCICLE
of hay/straw ...... WASE, TRUSS
of joy: colloq. .... BABY
of rods .... FASCES
of sheaves of grain
.... SHOCK, STOOK
of sticks/twigs .... FAGOT,
FASCINE
slang .... RICHES, WEALTH
small .... FASCICLE
bundling device .... BALER
bung .... CORK, PLUG, CLOSE,
STOPPER
slang .... BRUISE, DAMAGE
bungalow .... COTTAGE
bungle .... BOTCH, MESS (UP),
SPOIL, LOUSE (UP), FOOZLE,
FUMBLE, BLUNDER, FLOUNDER
a golf stroke .... DUB
a play .... MUFF
slang .... BOLLIX
bungling .... MALADROIT
bunion .... BURSA
bunk .... BED, COT, BERTH, SLEEP
British: sl. .... DOSS

slang .... HOKUM, HOOEY,
HUMBUG, EYEWASH,
BUNCOMBE, BOSH, TWADDLE,
NONSENSE
bunker ...... BIN, TANK, SANDTRAP
bunko. See **bunco**
bunny .... RABBIT
Playboy's .... HOSTESS
tail .... SCUT
time .... EASTER
bunt ...... TAP, BAT, SMUT, SHOVE
with horn: Brit. .... BUTT,
STRIKE
bunting .... FLAG, PENNANT, BIRD,
FINCH, ORTOLAN, ETAMINE,
STREAMER
migratory .... DICKCISSEL
Bunyan's ox .... BABE
buoy .... BOB, DAN, BEACON,
MARKER, FLOAT, MAKE FAST,
SIGNAL, SPEED-UP
for mooring boat ..... DOLPHIN
type .... CAN, BELL, SPAR,
WHISTLE
up .... BOOST, INSPIRE,
SUSTAIN, ENCOURAGE
buoyancy .... BOUNCE, GAIETY,
LEVITY, LIGHTNESS, FLOTAGE,
RESILIENCE
buoyant .... LIGHT, BOUNCY,
ELASTIC, HOPEFUL, SPRINGY
bur .... WEED, SEEDCASE
buran .... WINDSTORM
burble .... BUBBLE, GURGLE
burbot .... CUSK, LING, MARIA
burd: obs. .... LADY
burden .... LOAD, CHARGE,
CUMBER, INCUBUS, PRESSURE,
OPPRESS, WEIGHT, WEIGH
DOWN
bearer .... AMASA, ATLAS,
PORTER
beast of .... ASS, MULE,
BURRO, CAMEL, DONKEY
of a song .... REFRAIN
of proof .... ONUS, EVIDENCE
squaw's .... PAPOOSE
burdened .... TAXED
burdensome .... HEAVY,
WEIGHTY, CUMBERSOME,
ONEROUS, OPPRESSIVE
burdock .... BURR, CLITE,
COCKLEBUR
bureau ...... DESK, CHEST, OFFICE,
DRESSER, BRANCH, SECTION,
HIGHBOY, CHIFFONIER
top cover .... SCARF
bureaucracy .... BODY POLITIC,
OFFICIALDOM, OFFICIOUSNESS
petty .... BEADLEDOM
bureaucratic failing: colloq.

.... RED TAPE
burg .... CITY, TOWN, VILLAGE
lord of .... BURGRAVE
burgeon ...... BUD, GROW, SPROUT
in a way .... TRIPLE,
MUSHROOM
burgess .... CITIZEN, FREEMAN
Burgess's invention .... GOOP
burgh .... TOWN, BOROUGH
burglar .... THIEF, ROBBER,
HOUSE-BREAKER
hazard of .... ALARM BELL
loot of .... SWAG
slang .... YEGG
burgomaster .... GULL, MAYOR
burgonet .... HELMET, MORION
burgoo .... SCUP, GRUEL,
BARBECUE, PORRIDGE
Burgundy, kingdom of .... ARLES
wine .... CHABLIS
burial .... INTERMENT, SEPULTURE,
INHUMATION
box ...... BIER, CASKET, COFFIN
clothes .... SHROUD,
CEREMENT, CERECLOTH
grave marker ...... HEADSTONE,
TABLET, TOMBSTONE
ground for the poor
.... POTTER'S FIELD
heap/mound .... BARROW,
TUMULUS
pertaining to .... FUNERAL,
FUNERARY
pile .... PYRE
place .... PIT, TOMB, CRYPT,
CATACOMB, CEMETERY,
MAUSOLEUM, SEPULCHER,
GRAVE(YARD)
procession .... CORTEGE
vault .... SEPULTURE
burin .... GRAVER
like tool .... CHISEL
burke .... MURDER, SUPPRESS,
SUFFOCATE
Burke's subject .... PEERAGE
Burkitt's tumor ...... LYMPHOMA
burl .... KNOT, VENEER
Burl, actor .... IVES
burlesque .... FARCE, COMEDY,
PARODY, CARICATURE,
VAUDEVILLE
number ...... SKIT, STRIP-TEASE
burley .... TOBACCO
burly ...... GROSS, HEAVY, HUSKY,
MUSCULAR
Burma Road's other name
.... (THE) HUMP
terminus .... LASHIO
Burmese bay .... COMBERMERE
Buddhist .... MON, PROME
cape .... NEGRAIS

capital .... RANGOON
capital, former .... AVA
channel .... COCO, HEYWOOD
chief .... BO(H)
city/town .... MANDALAY,
AKYAB, CHAUK, BASSEIN,
INSEIN, MERGUI, MOULMEIN,
PYE, HENZADA, PAKOKKU,
LASHIO, TAVOY, SITTWE,
THATON, TOUNGOO, WAKEMA
dagger .... DAH, DOW
demon .... NAT
distinguished .... U THANT
district .... PROME
division .... PEGU, RANGOON,
SAGAING, IRRAWADY,
MANDALAY
ethnic group .... MONS, CHINS,
NAGAS, KARENS, KACHINS
garment/sarong .... LONGYI
gate .... TORAN
gibbon .... LAR
girl .... MIMA
governor .... WUN, WOON
gulf .... MARTABAN
hill .... CHIN, NAGA, KACHIN
hillman/Mongol .... LAI
island ...... RAMREE, CHEDUBA,
KALEGAUK, TENASSERIM
knife .... DOW, KAH, KHAO
lake .... INLE, INDAWGYI
language .... CHIN, BURMESE,
SHAN, KAREN, KAYAH, KACHIN
measure .... DHA, BYEE, SEIT
measure, distance .... TAUN
monetary unit .... KYAT
monk .... BO
mountain .... LOILENG,
VICTORIA, HKAKABO RAZI,
KHAO LUANG
mountain range .... ARAKAN
musical instrument ...... TURR,
TORAN
native .... WA, LAI, WAS,
KADU, KUKI, PEGUAN
pagoda .... PHAYA
pass .... AMYA, CHAUKAN,
PANGSAU, THREE PAGODAS
peasant .... TAO
premier/statesman ...... U NU
river .... MU, MON, MEKONG,
SALWEEN, KALADAN,
MANIPUR, ATARAN, SITTANG,
IRRAWADDY
robber .... DACOIT
shelter .... ZAYAT
shrimp .... NAPEE
spirit .... NAT
tree .... ACLE
tribe .... TAI, SHAN
weight .... VIS(S), KYAT,

RUAY, TICAL

burn .... FIRE, CHAR, BLAZE, GLOW, SEAR, CONSUME, SCORCH, DESTROY, OXIDIZE

a dead body to ashes .... CREMATE

cause to .... IGNITE

degree of .... FIRST, SECOND, THIRD

down .... RAZE

hair ends .... SINGE

incense .... CENSE

mark .... ESCHAR

mark of sun ..... TAN, SUNTAN

mark with hot iron .... BRAND

nap of cloth/slightly .... SINGE

Scottish .... STREAM

the midnight oil .... BONE, CRAM, LUCUBRATE

the road .... RACE, BARREL, SPEED (UP)

to stop infection .... CAUTERIZE

treatment of ...... ANTIBIOTICS, SKIN-GRAFTING

unsteadily .... FLICKER

up: colloq. .... FUME, IRK, ANGER, ENRAGE, SEETHE, IRRITATE

with hot fluid/steam .... SCALD

with hot iron/needle .... BRAND, CAUTERIZE

without flame .... SMO(U)LDER

burned up: sl. .... HURT, SORE, ANGRY

burner .... ARGAND, BUNSEN, FURNACE, FIREPLACE, CREMATORY, INCINERATOR

burning .... AFIRE, EAGER, BOILING, ABLAZE, AFLAME, FERVENT, FEVERISH

bush ...... WAHOO, FRAXINELLA

coal container .... BRASIER, BRAZIER

container for a material .... SMUDGE POT

container for incense .... CENSER

for gain/malicious ...... ARSON

glass .... LENS

mountain .... VOLCANO

process .... COMBUSTION

sensation .... HEAT, CAUSALGIA

stick .... BRAND

with anger .... WILD, IRATE, RABID, FURIOUS

with desire .... PASSIONATE

woodpile outdoors .... BONFIRE, CAMPFIRE

vapor from .... FUME, SMOKE

burnish .... SHINE, POLISH, FURBISH

an error/fault .... GLOSS

Burns's negatives .... NAES

sweetheart .... (HIGHLAND) MARY

burnsides .... MUTTON CHOPS, BEARD, WHISKERS

burnt .... ADUST

sugar .... CARAMEL

burp: sl. .... BELCH

burr .... POD, DRILL, ROUGH EDGE, SEEDCASE

in wood .... KNAR

plant/weed .... TEASEL, BURDOCK, THISTLE, COCKLEBUR

Burr, _____ .... AARON, RAYMOND

burro .... ASS, DONKEY

female .... MARE

burrow .... DIG, HOLE, TUNNEL

burrowing animal .... HARE, MOLE, BROCK, RATEL, BADGER, GERBIL(LE), TELEDU, WOMBAT, ARMADILLO

crustacean .... SQUILL(A)

mammal of S. Africa .... SURICATE

mollusk .... PIDDOCK

rodent .... VOLE

tortoise .... GOPHER

Burrows of Broadway .... ABE

Burr's daughter .... THEO

burry .... PRICKLY

bursa .... SAC, POUCH

inflammation of a .... BURSITIS

near the toe .... BUNION

operation to remove .... BURSECTOMY

bursal .... FISCAL

bursar .... TREASURER

burse .... PURSE

Scottish .... SCHOLARSHIP

bursitis, form of .... STUDENT'S ELBOW, CLERGYMAN'S KNEE, HOUSEMAID'S KNEE

treatment of .... DRAINAGE, ICEPACK, ANTIBIOTICS

burst .... BUST, REND, BULGE, BREACH, BREAK OPEN, SPLIT, EXPLODE, RUPTURE

forth .... ERUPT

into pieces suddenly .... SHATTER

of anger .... HUFF

of artillery, as a salute .... SALVO

of cheers .... OVATION, SALVO, APPLAUSE

of energy .... RALLY, SPASM, SPURT

of lightning .... FLASH

of thunder .... CLAP

open .... POP

open, as a seedpod .... DEHISCE

sudden .... GUST

bursting tire .... BLOW-OUT

Burundi capital ...... BUJUMBURA

city/town ...... BURURI, GITEGA

king .... (MWAMI) MWAMBUTSA

lake .... TANGANYIKA

language .... KIRUNDI, FRENCH, SWAHILI

money .... FRANC, CENTIME

native .... BANTU, PYGMY, BAHUTU, WATUSI

river .... RUZIZI

tribe .... BAHUTU, WATUTSI

bury .... SINK, INTER, INURN, INHUME, IMMERSE, CONCEAL, COVER, SEPULCHER

the hatchet .... RECONCILE

to hoard/hide .... CACHE

bus .... JITNEY, (MOTOR)COACH, VEHICLE, CONVEYANCE

colloquial .... FAMILY CAR, AUTO(MOBILE)

for excursion ..... CHARABANC, TOURING CAR

busby .... HAT

wearer .... HUSSAR

bush .... TOD, TAIL, BRIER, HEDGE, SHRUB, THICKET

beat around the .... HINT, FENCE, QUIBBLE, MISLEAD

burning .... WAHOO

league .... MINORS

leaguer .... SECOND-RATER, SECOND-STRINGER

slang .... BEARD

bushbuck .... ANTELOPE

bushed .... TIRED, SPENT, FATIGUED, DRAINED, EXHAUSTED

bushel, in tailoring .... ALTER, MEND

⅛ of .... GALLON

¼ of .... PECK

bushelman .... TAILOR

bushels, 11⅔ .... HOMER

32 or 36 .... CHALDRON

bushes, stunted .... SCRUB

bushing .... LINING

bushman .... PYGMY, NEGRILLO

bushmaster .... SNAKE, VIPER

bushranger .... HIGHWAYMAN

bushwhack .... AMBUSH

bushwhacker .... RAIDER,

GUERRILLA, (BACK)WOODSMAN, UNDERGROUND RESISTANCE

bushy .... DENSE, HAIRY, SHAGGY, WOODED

clump .... TOD

tail .... BRUSH

business .... TASK, WORK, TRADE, AFFAIR, VENTURE, COMMERCE, INDUSTRY, OCCUPATION, ENTERPRISE, PROFESSION

abbreviation ..... INC, LTD, CO, CORP

agent .... BROKER, SYNDIC, SALESMAN, COMPRADOR

association .... SYNDICATE, PARTNERSHIP

burden .... PAYLOAD

cartel .... TRUST, ALLIANCE, SYNDICATE

connection .... CONTACT

cycle, part of .... BOOM, SLUMP, SETBACK, FAILURE, PEAK, DEPRESSION, PROSPERITY

establishment .... BANK, MART, FIRM, STORE, COMPANY, SHOP, MARKET, CORPORATION

event ..... BOOM, DEAL, SLUMP, MERGER, TAKE-OVER, GROWTH, STRIKE, RECESSION

firm .... HOUSE

location .... SITE, STAND

monopoly .... CARTEL, CONTROL, CORNER

offshoot .... FRANCHISE

schedule .... AGENDA, PLAN, PROGRAM

secrets, spy on .... KEEK

slump .... RECESSION, SLOW-DOWN, DEPRESSION

solicitor ...... BIDDER, BARKER, RUNNER

transaction .... DEAL, BARGAIN, CONTRACT

upsurge .... BOOM, FLOURISH

businessman .... BANKER, BROKER, MANAGER, TRADER, MERCHANT, DEALER, FINANCIER, EXECUTIVE

conventional .... BABBITT

Latin of .... INRE

one kind of .... ENTREPRENEUR

busk .... READY, OUTFIT, PREPARE

busker .... MINSTREL

buskin .... BOOT, DRAMA, TRAGEDY

busline, end of .... TERMINUS

buss .... KISS

colloquial .... PECK, SMACK

slang .... SMOOCH

bust .... BOSOM, CHEST, BREAK, BURST, BREAST

colloquial .... FLING, SPREE, FAILURE

figure ...... STATUE, STATUETTE

form/shape .... TAILLE

in .... INTRUDE

in business .... COLLAPSE, FOLD UP, GO BANKRUPT

slang ..... BOOBS, ARREST, HIT, BLOW, PUNCH, DEMOTE

stock market .... CRASH

bustard .... BIRD, OTIS, TARDA

busted .... BEAT, BANKRUPT, (FLAT) BROKE

from jail .... SPRUNG

buster of a kind .... TRUST BREAKER

slang .... BOY

Buster's friend .... TIGE

bustle .... ADO, TO-DO, FUSS, STIR, HASTE, HURRY, RUSTLE, FLURRY, POTHER

colloquial .... HOOPLA

companion of .... HUSTLE

of woman's dress .... BOW, PADDING

busy .... AT IT, ACTIVE, ENGAGED, EMPLOYED, OCCUPIED, ASTIR, WORKING, DILIGENT, ENGROSSED, ASSIDUOUS

creature .... ANT, BEE, OTTER

place .... HIVE

sound .... HUM

busybody .... GOSSIP, KIBITZER, MEDDLER, QUIDNUNC, SNOOP(ER), EAVESDROPPER

but .... YET, EVEN, SAVE, STILL, EXCEPT(ING), ALTHOUGH, MERELY, UNLESS, HOWEVER

Scottish .... OUTER, OUTSIDE, OUTER ROOM

butch .... TOMBOY

butcher ...... KILL, CUT UP, MEAT-CUTTER, MEAT-SELLER, BOTCH, SPOIL, SLAUGHTER

bird .... SHRIKE

hook of .... GAFF, GAMBREL

shop of .... SHAMBLES

tool of .... CLEAVER, BONER, KNIFE, STEEL

butler .... STEWARD, MAJORDOMO, MAITRE D'HOTEL

concern of .... WINE CELLAR, PANTRY, SILVER(WARE)

butt .... RAM, TUP, ABUT, CASK, PUSH, STRIKE, TARGET, BARREL, LAUGHINGSTOCK

fish .... TURBOT, HALIBUT

in .... MEDDLE, INTRUDE, INTERFERE, INTERVENE

of cigar(ette) .... STUB

of criticism usually .... SCAPEGOAT

of goat .... RAM

of joke, figuratively ...... GOAT

of many jokes .... MOTHER-IN-LAW

of tree .... STUMP

of whip .... CROP

slang .... BUTTOCKS, CIGARET(TE)

butte .... HILL, MESA, MOUND

butter .... OIL, GHEE, CREAM, SPREAD

and-eggs .... PLANT, TOADFLAX

and-flour mix .... ROUX

bucket .... KIT

buffalo milk .... GHEE

color for .... ANATTO, AN(N)ATTO

India .... GHI, GHEE

like .... OLEO, BUTTERINE, MARGARINE, BUTYRACEOUS

lump/portion of .... PAT

making contrivance .... CHURN

roll .... BRIOCHE

substitute .... OLEO, SUINE, BUTTERINE, MARGARINE

tree .... SHEA

tub .... KIT, CHURN, FIRKIN

up .... FLATTER

butterball .... BUFFLEHEAD

slang .... FATSO, FATTY

butterbean .... LIMA

buttercup .... CROWTOE, GOLDILOCKS, GOLDTHREAD, GOLDEN SEAL

buttered crumbs/crust .... GRATIN

butterfingers .... CLUMSY, DUFFER, FUMBLER, GOOFER, MUFFER

butterfish .... GUNNEL

butterflies, order of .... LEPIDOPTERA

butterfly .... IO, KIHO, SATYR, ADMIRAL, FRENATE, GRAYLING, MONARCH, FRITILLARY, NYMPHALID, SKIPPER, VANESSA, TROILUS, VICEROY, SWALLOWTAIL

admiral .... ATALANTA

combining form .... CALIGO

fish .... PARU, BLENNY

large .... IDALIA

larva .... CATERPILLAR

lily .... SEGO

named after goddess .... DIANA, APHRODITE

peacock .... IO
proboscis/tongue-like organ
.... LINGUA
small .... BLUE
butternut .... SOUARI
buttery .... LARDER, PANTRY,
SPENCE, STOREROOM
butting animal .... RAM, GOAT,
CARABAO
buttinsky .... INTRUDER, MEDDLER
buttocks .... ASS, BUM, ARSE,
BUTT, NATES, PRAT, BREECH,
SEAT, RUMP, BEHIND,
DERRIERE, HIPS, FUNDAMENT,
POSTERIOR
button .... KNOB, KNOP, STUD,
DISK, LOOP, EMBLEM, FASTEN
cover .... FLY, FLAP
fencing sword .... FOIL
the lips .... SHUT UP
buttonhole .... HOLD, SLIT,
DETAIN, EYELET
flower .... GARDENIA,
CARNATION
buttonholer .... BORE
buttons .... BELLBOY, (HOTEL)
PAGE
and _____ .... BOWS
Buttons, actor .... RED
buttonwood .... SYCAMORE
buttress .... PIER, PROP, STAY,
BRACE, BOLSTER, SUPPORT
butts and bounds
.... BOUNDARIES
buxom .... CURVY, JOLLY, JOVIAL,
MERRY, PLUMP, COMELY,
ENDOWED, SHAPELY,
HEALTHY
buy .... ACQUIRE, PROCURE,
SPEND, PURCHASE
at one's risk .... CAVEAT
EMPTOR
back .... REDEEM
good: colloq. .... BARGAIN,
(DIRT)CHEAP
in/into .... INVEST

off .... BRIBE
up .... CORNER, MONOPOLIZE
what one is saying, as gospel
truth .... TRUST, BELIEVE,
SWALLOW
buyer .... EMPTOR, VENDEE,
BROWSER, CONSUMER,
CUSTOMER, AGENT, SHOPPER,
PURCHASER
and seller .... DEALER, JOBBER,
TRADER, IMPORTER, RETAILER,
WHOLESALER
and seller of stolen goods
.... FENCE, BOOTLEGGER
of illegal drugs .... (DRUG)
DEALER, (DRUG) PUSHER
of office .... BARRATER
of old horses .... KNACKER
of smuggled contraband
.... BLACK-MARKETEER
buyers' strike .... BOYCOTT
buying to gain monopoly
.... COEMPTION
buzz .... HUM, DRONE, GOSSIP,
CALL, SIGNAL, WHIRR,
WHISPER
bomb: Ger. .... ROBOT
colloquial .... TELEPHONE
off! .... SCRAM
buzzard ...... TESA, HAWK, BUTEO,
OSPREY, FALCON,
COCKCHAFER, PREYER,
HARRIER, DUCKHAWK
honey .... BEEHAWK
moor .... HARPY
turkey .... VULTURE
buzzer signal .... CALL, ALARM
buzzing sound ...... HUM, DRONE
by .... AT, PER, NEAR, ASIDE,
BESIDE, BEYOND, ALONGSIDE,
PAST, THROUGH
a whisker .... BARELY
and by .... ANON, SOON,
SHORTLY
birth .... NEE, NATAL
hand .... PERSONAL

hand: prefix .... MANU
means of .... PER, THROUGH
pass .... SHUNT, DETOUR,
SWERVE, EVADE, DEVIATE,
SHIFT, AVOID, CIRCUIT
right .... DEJURE
the day .... PER DIEM
way of .... VIA, THROUGH
word of mouth .... ORAL,
PAROL, VERBAL
work .... HOBBY, SIDELINE,
AVOCATION
byblow .... BASTARD
bye .... RUN, ODD MAN,
INCIDENTAL
bye .... TATA, GOODBYE
Byelorussian city .... MOGILEV
bygone .... PAST
byname .... SURNAME, NICKNAME
byplay .... ADLIB
byre .... COWBARN
product .... MILK
Byron, name of .... NOEL,
GEORGE, GORDON
poem by .... BEPPO
Byronic .... PROUD, IRONIC,
CYNICAL, ROMANTIC
byssus .... FLAX, LINEN
bystander .... ONLOOKER,
WITNESS, SPECTATOR
bystreet .... ALLEY
byway/bypath ...... LANE, ALLEY,
SIDEROAD, SIDESTREET
byword .... ADAGE, MAXIM,
SAYING, PROVERB
Byzantine coin .... BEZANT
emperor .... ALEXIUS,
HERACLIUS
emperor's scepter ..... FERULA
empress .... ZOE
logothete, so-called
.... (WOODROW) WILSON
works of art .... ICONS
Byzantium capital .... ISTANBUL,
CONSTANTINOPLE

C

C grade in school ...... AVERAGE,
MEDIOCRE
Greek .... GAMMA
in a sequence group .... THIRD
in music .... KEYNOTE
in quality .... PASSABLE, THIRD
CLASS
letter .... CEE
mark under .... CEDILLA

Roman numeral .... HUNDRED,
100, CENTURY
symbol for .... CONSTANT
Ca, in chemistry .... CALCIUM
Caaba .... SHRINE
site .... MECCA
camma .... ASSE, FOX
cab .... TAXI, FIACRE, HACKNEY,
CALASH, HANSOM, CARRIAGE

driver .... HACK, CABBIE,
CABETTE
CAB subjects .... AIRLINES
cabal .... PLOT, JUNTA, JUNTO,
CLIQUE, INTRIGUE, FACTION,
SCHEME, CONSPIRACY
man .... PLOTTER
cabala ...... MYSTERY, OCCULTISM
cabalist .... MYSTIC

cabalistic ...... SECRET, ESOTERIC, MYSTERIOUS

caballero ...... KNIGHT, CAVALIER, GENTLEMAN, HORSEMAN

cabana ...... HUT, CABIN, BAGNIO, COTTAGE, BATHHOUSE

cabaret .... CAFE, SALOON, TAVERN, BARROOM, TAPROOM, NIGHTCLUB, COCKTAIL LOUNGE

slang .... BLIND PIG, HONKY-TONK, SPEAKEASY

cabbage ...... KAIL, KALE, SAVOY, OXHEART, COLE(WORT), KOHLRABI, VEGETABLE

broth .... KALE

fermented .... SAUERKRAUT

garden .... KALEYARD

plant like .... COLE

salad/shredded .... SLAW, COLE SLAW

tree .... PALM, YABA, PALMETTO

variety .... CAULIFLOWER

cabby .... HACK, CABBIE, CAB-DRIVER, TAXI-DRIVER

caber .... BEAM, POLE

cabin .... HUT, SHED, SHACK, CABANA, COTTAGE, LOGHOUSE

baloon/dirigible ...... GONDOLA

boy .... DECKHAND, ATTENDANT

cruiser .... SPEEDBOAT

ship's main .... SALON, SALOON, STATEROOM

ship's upper .... DECKHOUSE

Swiss .... CHALET

cabinet .... BOX, BUHL, CASE, CHEST, BUREAU, CLOSET, ALMIRAH, ARMOIRE

composition .... ADVISERS

describing one .... KITCHEN, PRESIDENTIAL

for dishes/food ..... CUPBOARD

for radio/TV .... CONSOLE

for wines .... CELLARET

government .... ADVISORY BOARD COUNCIL, MINISTRY

wood .... KOA, TEAK, CEDAR, NARRA, WALNUT, ROSEWOOD

cable .... ROPE, WIRE, CHAIN, CORD, MESSAGE, TELEGRAM

car .... ELPHER, TELFER

kind of .... JUMP(ER), IGNITION, ELECTRIC, TELEVISION, UNDERGROUND

old .... JUNK

used as brace .... STAY

cabob .... (ROAST) MEAT

holder .... SPIT, SKEWER

cabochon .... (GEM)STONE

caboodle .... ALL, LOT, GROUP

companion of .... KIT

caboose ...... CAB, COMPARTMENT

ship's .... GALLEY, KITCHEN

cabrilla .... FISH, GROUPER, REDHIND

cacao alkaloid ...... THEOBROMINE

product .... COCOA, CHOCOLATE

seed powder .... BROMA

cachalot .... SPERM-WHALE, PHYSETER

cache .... HIDE, HOARD, STORE, STASH, SCREEN, SECRETE, CONCEAL, HIDING PLACE

cachet ...... SEAL, STAMP, WAFER, CAPSULE

cachinate .... LAUGH

cacholong .... OPAL

cachou .... CATECHU, LOZENGE

cacique ...... LORD, CHIEF, PRINCE, LEADER, SACHEM, ORIOLE, TROUPIAL

cackle .... CLACK, LAUGH, CHATTER, PRATTLE

cackler .... HEN, GOOSE

cacoethes .... ITCH, MANIA

cacophonous .... AJAR, HARSH, OFF-KEY, DISCORDANT

cacophony ... DIN, BABEL, NOISE

cactus .... AGAVE, NOPAL, CHOLLA, CEREUS, MESCAL, PEYOTE, PRICKLY-PEAR, OPUNTIA, SAGUARO

fruit .... FIG, COCHAL

like plant .... SPURGE, STAPELIA, EUPHORBIA

plant .... TUNA

plant process .... SPINE

spineless .... CHAUTE

cad .... HEEL, HOOD, WORM, KNAVE, MUCKER, RASCAL, BOUNDER, SCOUNDREL

cadaver .... BODY, COR(P)SE, CARCASS, REMAINS

preserved .... MUMMY

slang .... STIFF

cadaverous .... PALE, ASHEN, WAN, GAUNT, HAGGARD, GHASTLY, GHOSTLY, SALLOW, LIVID, PALLID

caddis worm .... CADEW

caddish .... BOORISH, ILL-BRED, LOUTISH, UNCOUTH

Caddoan Indian .... REE, PAWNEE

caddy/caddie .... CARRIER, (TEA)BOX, ATTENDANT, CONTAINER

cade .... JUNIPER

cadelle .... LARVA

cadence .... BEAT, LILT, ICTUS, ACCENT, STRESS, DROOP, RHYTHM

recite in .... CHIME

cadent .... FALLING, RHYTHMICAL

cadenza .... RIFF, CADENCE

cadet .... SON, YOUTH, STUDENT

designating one .... DODO, AIR, NAVAL, PLEBE, MILITARY

mark against .... DEMERIT

military .... DRAFTEE, PRIVATE, RECRUIT

naval ...... MIDDY, MIDSHIPMAN

cadge .... BEG, BUM, HAWK, MOOCH, PEDDLE, SPONGE

cadger .... BEGGAR, HAWKER, PANHANDLER, VENDOR, PEDDLER

cadgy .... LEWD, MERRY, WILD, WANTON, EXUBERANT, LUSTFUL

cadi .... JUDGE, MAGISTRATE

Cadmean-like victory .... PYRRHIC

Cadmus' daughter .... INO, SEMELE

parent .... AGENOR

sister .... EUROPA

wife .... HARMONIA

cadre .... CELL, GROUP, NUCLEUS, INNER CIRCLE, FRAMEWORK

caduceus .... ROD, WAND, BATON, STAFF, SCEPTER

bearer .... HERMES, MERCURY

Caen river .... ORNE

Caesar .... RULER, TYRANT, SALAD, JULIUS, EMPEROR, AUTOCRAT, DICTATOR

augur who warned .... SPURINNA

assassin of .... BRUTUS, CASCA, CASSIUS

love of .... SERVILIA

mistress of .... EUNOE, CLEO(PATRA)

partner of Sid .... COCA

Pompey battle site .... THAPSUS

wife of .... UXOR, POMPEIA

Caesarian "offspring" .... CALENDAR

Caesarian/Cesarean section .... SURGERY, OPERATION, HYSTEROTOMY

first performed in .... ROME

Caesarism .... AUTOCRACY

Caesars, one of the .... JULIUS, GAIUS, NERO, GALBA, OTHO, TITUS, CLAUDIUS, AUGUSTUS, DOMITIAN, TIBERIUS,

VESPASIAN, VITELLIUS
caesura ...... REST, BREAK, PAUSE
cafe .... BISTRO, COFFEE,
CANTEEN, SNACK BAR,
SALOON, DINER, CABARET,
COFFEE SHOP, ESTAMINET,
RESTAURANT
au ____ .... LAIT
card .... MENU
owner .... RESTAURA(N)TEUR
room .... DIVAN
society member ...... PLAYBOY
cafeteria .... AUTOMAT
caffein(e) .... STIMULANT
effect of too much
.... NAUSEA, ANXIETY,
INSOMNIA, FATIGUE,
IRRITABILITY
source ..... TEA, COLA, COCOA,
COFFEE, KOLA NUT
tea .... THEIN(E)
caftan .... ROBE
cage .... GIG, PEN, BARS, JAIL,
CONFINE, ENCLOSURE
birds', large .... AVIARY
elevator .... CAR
for trapping fish .... CREEL
hauling/hawks' .... MEW
poultry .... COOP
occupant .... PET, BIRD,
ANIMAL, TELLER, CASHIER,
CONVICT, PRISONER
cagey .... SLY, WILY, CLEVER,
CUNNING, TRICKY, SHIFTY
cahier .... REPORT, NOTEBOOK
cahoots, in .... LEAGUE, TIE-UP,
ALLIANCE, COLLUSION,
COMPLICITY, CONNIVANCE
caiman .... ALLIGATOR
Cain .... MURDERER
brother of .... ABEL, SETH
descendant of .... JUBAL
land of .... NOD
parent of .... EVE, ADAM
son of .... ENOCH
caique .... ROWBOAT, SAILBOAT
caird .... GYPSY, IDLER, TINKER,
VAGRANT
cairn ...... LANDMARK, MEMORIAL
cairngorm .... QUARTZ
Cairene .... EGYPTIAN
Cairo is capital of .... EGYPT
shopping district .... MOUSSKY
caisson ...... BOX, CHEST, WAGON,
TUMBREL, TUMBRIL
content of .... AMMO,
EXPLOSIVES, AMMUNITION
disease .... BENDS
man in a .... SANDHOG
occasional use of ...... HEARSE
caitiff .... BASE, EVIL, MEAN,

CRAVEN, POLTROON
cajeput .... LAUREL
cajole .... COAX, BEGUILE,
FLATTER, BLANDISH,
WHEEDLE
slang .... SNOW
cajolery .... PALAVER, LIP-SERVICE
slang .... SNOW JOB
cake .... CLOT, LUMP, MASS, RUSK,
CIMBAL, HARDEN, PASTRY,
GEL, CURD, SOLIDIFY,
THICKEN
barley meal .... BANNOCK
batter ...... CRUMPET, CRULLER,
FRITTER
chocolate .... BROWNIE
corn .... PONE
covering ...... ICING, FROSTING,
MERINGUE
fish/meat .... PATTY
in pipe bowl .... DOTTLE
kind of .... FRUIT, POUND,
LAYER, SPONGE, WHITE
mixture .... BATTER
porous .... SPONGE
pressed tobacco .... PLUG
rich/without flour .... TORTE
ring-shaped .... DONUT,
DOUGHNUT
rum .... BABA
seed .... WIG
small .... BUN, TART, COOKY,
ROLL, COOKIE, ECLAIR
sweet .... SIMNEL
takes the .... WINS, EXCELS,
ECLIPSES, OUTSHINES
tea .... SCONE
thin .... WAFER, JUMBLE
Spanish .... TORTILLA
India style .... POORI
tiny, griddle .... SILVER-
DOLLAR PANCAKE
topped with shredded cheese
and spices ...... STREUSEL
traditional, fruit and nut-
filled .... STOLLEN
cakes and ale, life of
.... HEDONISM
cakewalk .... DANCE, STRUT,
SWAGGER
calabash .... GOURD, SHELL
calaber .... FUR, SQUIRREL
calaboose .... GAOL, JAIL, PRISON,
STATE PEN
Calais' English neighbor
.... DOVER
calamary .... SQUID
calamine ...... LOTION, OINTMENT
calamitous .... FATAL, DEADLY,
TRAGIC, RUINOUS,
DISASTROUS

calamity .... WOE, BLOW, MISERY,
REVERSE, DISASTER, MISHAP,
HARDSHIP, CATASTROPHE
calamus .... QUILL,COMA]
PALM (TREE), RATTAN,
SWEETFLAG
calcar .... SPUR
calced .... SHOD
calcine .... BURN, OXIDIZE
calcined metal/residue .... CALX
calcium carbonate .... TUFA,
CALCITE, CALICHE
carbonate, of ..... CALCAREOUS
crust .... SINTER
gypsum .... PLASTER
oxide .... (QUICK)LIME
phosphate .... APATITE
sulphate .... HEPAR, GYPSUM,
PLASTER
calculate .... COUNT, GUESS,
APPRAISE, DEEM, FIGURE,
COMPUTE, THINK, RECKON,
SUPPOSE, ESTIMATE
calculating .... SHREWD,
CUNNING, CAUTIOUS,
DESIGNING, SCHEMING
device .... TABLE, ABACUS,
COMPUTER, CASH REGISTER,
TABULATOR, SLIDE RULE
calculation, of .... LOGISTIC
calculi, of .... LITHIC
calculus ...... ADDING, ESTIMATION
combining form .... LITHO
dental .... TARTAR
in urinary tract
.... GALLSTONE, BLADDER
STONE
Calcutta is capital of
.... BENGAL
calderite .... GARNET
caldron .... BOILER, KETTLE
Caleb's companion ...... JOSHUA
Caledonia .... SCOTLAND
calefy .... HEAT, WARM
calendar .... LOG, LIST, DIARY,
YEAR, DOCKET, ALMANAC,
JOURNAL, REGISTER,
MENOLOGY, SCHEDULE
church .... ORDO
of business .... AGENDA
type of .... JULIAN, NEW
STYLE, GREGORIAN
calender .... MANGLE, DERVISH
calenture .... FEVER
calesa .... CAB, CALASH, CALECHE,
CARRIAGE
calf .... COW, BOSS(Y), LEG,
SHANK, BOVINE, WEANER
cry .... BLAT, BLEAT
for slaughter .... FATLING
front .... SHIN

hide/skin .... KIP
leather .... ELK
like a .... VITULINE
meat .... VEAL
motherless/stray .... DOGY,
DOGIE, MAVERICK
of the leg .... SURA
of the leg, pertaining to
.... SURAL
skin parchment .... VELLUM
suckling .... BOB
unbranded .... MAVERICK
Caliban's master .... PROSPERO
mother .... SYCORAX
caliber .... BORE, SIZE, GAUGE,
ABILITY, METTLE, QUALITY
calibrate .... CHECK, PROBE,
MEASURE, GRADUATE
in advance .... PRESET
calico .... (COTTON) CLOTH,
SPOTTED, DAPPLED,
VARICOLORED
bass .... CRAPPIE
East Indies .... SALLOO
horse .... PONY, PINTO,
PIEBALD
loin cloth .... LAVA-LAVA
printing .... TEER, LAPIS
printing material
...... LACTARENE, TRAGACANTH
California .... EL DORADO
army base .... ORD
bay .... CARMEL, MONTEREY,
MORRO, MISSION, EMERALD,
BODEGA, GRIZZLY, HUMBOLDT,
HALF-MOON, SAN FRANCISCO,
SAN DIEGO, SAN PEDRO,
SUISUN, SANTA MONICA
bulrush .... TULE
canal ..... COACHELLA, FRIANT-
KERN
cape .... VIZCAINO,
MENDOCINO, SAN MARTIN
capital .... SACRAMENTO
capital, former ..... MONTEREY
channel .... GOLDEN GATE,
SANTA CRUZ, SANTA BARBARA
city/town .... FRESNO, SAN
JOSE, LOS ANGELES, LODI, SAN
FRANCISCO, SAN DIEGO, SANTA
CRUZ, CHINO, SALINAS, LONG
BEACH, NAPA, MURRIETA,
RIVERSIDE, VALLEJO,
BAKERSFIELD, CARMEL,
BARSTOW, ANAHEIM, PALM
SPRINGS, BERKELEY, DUBLIN,
CASTRO VALLEY, DALY,
STOCKTON, TEMECULA,
POMONA, ONTARIO, PASADENA,
HOLLYWOOD, BEVERLY HILLS,
ALTURAS, OAKLAND,

MODESTO, SAN MATEO, SAN
LEANDRO, BELMONT, BENICIA,
CONCORD, PALO ALTO, SAN
CLEMENTE, NEWARK, SANTA
BARBARA, ESCONDIDO, SANTA
MARIA, REDDING, REDWOOD,
BURBANK, EUREKA,
HUNTINGTON BEACH, DOWNEY,
ORANGE, HAYWARD, VISALIA,
MOUNTAIN VIEW, FALLBROOK,
NEWPORT BEACH, COMPTON,
SAN BERNARDINO, OTAY,
YUBA, WALNUT CREEK
college .... MILLS, DELTA,
CYPRESS, BAKERSFIELD,
POMONA, PACIFIC-UNION,
WHITTIER, IRVINE VALLEY,
SADDLEBACK
county ...... ALPINE, ALAMEDA,
BUTTE, AMADOR, BIG BEAR, EL
DORADO, CALAVERAS,
COLUSA, CONTRA COSTA,
KERN, FRESNO, DEL NORTE,
INYO, GLENN, HUMBOLDT,
LAKE, KINGS, LOS ANGELES,
MARIN, LASSEN, MADERA,
MARIPOSA, MENDOCINO,
MONO, MODOC, MERCED,
NEVADA, NAPA, MONTEREY,
RIVERSIDE, ORANGE, SAN
BENITO, SACRAMENTO,
PLACER, SAN BERNARDINO,
PLUMES, SAN FRANCISCO, SAN
DIEGO, SAN JOAQUIN, SAN
MATEO, SANTA BARBARA,
SANTA CRUZ, SANTA CLARA,
SIERRA, SHASTA, SISKIYOU,
SOLANO, SONOMA, SUTTER,
YUBA, TEHAMA, STANISLAUS,
YOLO, TULARE, TRINITY,
VENTURA, TUOLUMNE
creek .... MILL, PINE,
ALAMEDA, COTTONWOOD,
WALNUT, WILLOW, SOUTH
COW
date capital .... INDIO
desert .... MOJAVE
fish .... CABEZON, GRUNION
gold rusher .... ARGONAUT
governor ..... BROWN, REAGAN,
WILSON
grape picker .... BRACERO
grape pickers' strike
.... HUELGA
gulf ..... SANTA CATALINA, THE
FARALLONS
herb .... AMOLE
holly .... TOYON
Indian ...... YUKI, POMO, HUPA,
YUROK, WAPPO, PAIUTE,
PATWIN

island .... ANGEL, BROOKS,
MARE, ALCATRAZ, CORONADO,
SANTA ROSA, SANTA CRUZ,
TREASURE, SAN MIGUEL,
ANACAPA, YERBA BUENA,
BETHEL, SAN CLEMENTE
kingfish .... OPAH, PINTADO,
WHITING
lake ..... CLEAR, TAHOE, MEISS,
MERCED, TULARE, PERRIS,
FOLSOM, SHASTA, CHABOT,
TURLOCK, CROWLEY, TULE,
ELSINORE, SKINNER, CADIZ,
OWENS, ARROWHEAD,
FLORENCE, SAN ANDREAS,
VAIL, EL MIRAGE,
SILVERWOOD, EAGLE, HAVASU,
PYRAMID, BRISTOL, ALMANOR,
OROVILLE
laurel .... MYRTLE, CAJEPUT,
CAJUPUT
mountain .... AGUANGA,
WILSON, SHASTA, KLAMATH,
MUIR, WHITNEY, EAGLE
CRAGS, MARBLE, MONTARA,
PALOMAR, INGALLS, HOFFMAN,
HAMILTON, TAMALPAIS, SCOTT
BAR
mountain, highest ...... MOUNT
WHITNEY
mountains .... GRAPEVINE,
CHOCOLATE, PROVIDENCE,
INYO, SAN BERNARDINO,
SISKIYOU, TEHACHAPI,
WHIPPLE, SIERRA NEVADA
oak .... ROBLE, ENCINA
observatory .... PALOMAR
olive .... MANZANILLO
park .... YOSEMITE, GAVIOTA,
REDWOOD, SEQUOIA, LASSEN,
CHANNEL ISLANDS
pass .... BADGER, DONNER,
SONORA, ALTAMONT
peak ...... HAT, LASSEN, FREEL,
QUARTZ, FREMONT, OWENS,
WHEELER, TELESCOPE
pioneer .... SUTTER
point .... ANO-NUEVO, DUME,
LOPEZ, ARGUELLO, ARENA,
BONITA, COOPER, REYES,
BUCHON, DUXBURY, TOMALES,
PESCADERO
point, highest .... MOUNT
WHITNEY
range .... ARGUS, CASCADE,
AMARGOSA, PANAMINT
ranges .... COAST
river .... EEL, MAD, NOYO,
ALAMO, ESTRELLA, SALMON,
CARMEL, CUYAMA, KERN,
RUSSIAN, AMARGOSA, KINGS,

KLAMATH, FEATHER, MERCED, NAVARRO, REDWOOD, MOKULUMNE, SACRAMENTO, PIT, SALINAS, COLORADO, LOST, TRINITY, TRUCKEE, YUBA, SMITH, SAN JOAQUIN
rockfish .... RE(I)NA
sea lake .... SALTON
shrub .... SALAL, KUMQUAT, OLEANDER
state bird .... QUAIL
state flower .... (GOLDEN) POPPY
state motto .... EUREKA!, (I HAVE FOUND IT)
state nickname .... GOLDEN, GRAPE
state tree .... REDWOOD, SEQUOIA
time: abbr. .... PST
tourist site .... DISNEYLAND, SAN FRANCISCO CABLE CARS, DEATH VALLEY MONUMENT, INYO FOREST, MUIR WOODS, PINNACLES MONUMENT
university, state .... CHICO, FRESNO, FULLERTON, LONG BEACH, LOS ANGELES, SACRAMENTO, BERKELEY, SAN JOSE, SAN FRANCISCO, NORTHRIDGE, SAN DIEGO, DAVIS, POLYTECHNIC, HAYWARD, STANFORD
valley .... NAPA, DEATH, CARMEL, MORENO, FOUNTAIN, SIMI, TEMESCAL, YOSEMITE, IMPERIAL, SAN JOAQUIN, SQUAW, SAN FERNANDO, HIDDEN, PANAMINT
volcano .... LASSEN
California–U.S. Military Air
Force Base .... BEALE, CASTLE, GEORGE, EDWARDS, MARCH, MATHER, NORTON, OXNARD, MCCLELLAN, TRAVIS, VANDENBERG
Army Base .... OAKLAND, FORT ORD, PRESIDIO
Army Depot .... SHARPE, SIERRA, SACRAMENTO
Marine Corps Air Station .... EL TORO
Marine Corps Base ...... CAMP PENDLETON, TWENTY-NINE PALMS
Marine Corps Recruit Depot .... SAN DIEGO
Naval Air Station .... LEMOORE, MOFFETT
Naval Weapons Center .... CHINA LAKE

Navy Yard .... MARE ISLAND
Pacific Missile Test Center .... POINT MUGU
Caligula .... BOOTIKIN
caliph .... ALI, EMIR, IMAM, OMAR, HAKIM, OMMIAD
calisthenics .... ATHLETICS, WORKOUT, EXERCISE(S), GYMNASTICS
system .... DEL SARTE
calix .... CUP, CHALICE
calk/caulk .... SEAL, BLOCK, CLOSE, PLUG UP, CHINSE, STOP
calker .... STAVER
calking/caulking material .... TAR, OAKUM, PITCH
call .... CRY, DUB, DIAL, NAME, PAGE, LABEL, SUMMON, CONVOKE, ANNOUNCE
a bluff .... DARE, FACE
a spade a spade .... TELL IT LIKE IT IS
army .... DRAFT
attention to .... SPECIFY, REFER TO
auction .... BID
baseball ...... OUT, SAFE, FOUL, STRIKE
boy .... PAGE, BELLHOP, BELLMAN
creditor's .... DUN
down .... CHIDE, SCOLD, REBUKE, UPBRAID, CRITICIZE
for .... ASK, DEMAND, SUMMON, CONVOKE
for aid .... APPEAL
for help .... SOS
for hogs .... SOOK
for repetition .... ENCORE
for silence .... HIST, HUSH, SHUSH
forth .... EVOKE, AROUSE, ELICIT, EXCITE, KINDLE
girl .... HOOKER, HOSTESS, PROSTITUTE
greeting .... AVE, HAIL
hotel lobby .... PAGE
in .... INVITE, SUMMON
in gambling .... BET, WAGER
in poker .... SEE
in question .... IMPUGN
off .... CANCEL
on .... SEE, TAP, VISIT
out .... YELL, ROUSE, SHOUT, ANNOUNCE
prayer .... ADAN, AZAN
to account .... CITE, CHARGE, ARRAIGN
to arms, medieval .... BAN
to attract attention .... HEY,

HIST, PSST
to mind .... RECALL, REMEMBER, REMINISCE
to the hounds: var. ...... YOICK
to witness .... OBTEST
together .... GATHER, COLLECT, CONVENE, CONVOKE, SUMMON, ASSEMBLE
up .... BUZZ, DIAL, RING UP, (TELE)PHONE
upon .... CHOOSE, ENJOIN, COMMAND, DESIGNATE
within .... CLOSE, NEARBY
word at flip of coin .... HEADS, TAILS
calla .... ARUM, LILY
Callas, operatic soprano .... MARIA
callboy .... PAGE, BELLHOP, BUTTONS
called .... NAMED, YCLEPT
caller .... GUEST, VISITOR
from minaret .... MUEZZIN
midnight .... CRIER
persistent .... DUTY
calligrapher .... PENMAN, COPYIST, LETTER-MAKER
calligraphy .... FINE HANDWRITING, SCRIPT, ARTISTIC PENMANSHIP
calling .... JOB, TASK, WORK, DUTY, CAREER, METIER, PURSUIT, TRADE, MISSION, VOCATION, BUSINESS, FUNCTION, POSITION, PROFESSION, OCCUPATION
Calliope .... MUSE
Callisto .... NYMPH, CONSTELLATION
callous .... HARD, TOUGH, PITILESS, HARD-BOILED, UNFEELING, THICKSKINNED
growth .... CORN
render .... NUMB, SEAR, HARDEN, LANGUID, INDIFFERENT
calloused .... BONY, HORNY, CORNEOUS
callow .... GREEN, YOUNG, IMMATURE, UNFLEDGED
bird .... FEATHERLESS
person ...... YOUTH, FLEDGLING
Calloway .... CAB
callus, horse's .... CHESTNUT
on toe .... CORN
calm .... COOL, LULL, ABATE, ALLAY, STILL, SOBER, PACIFY, PLACID, PACIFIC, PLACATE, SERENE, COMPOSED, IMPASSIVE, SEDATE, SMOOTH, SOOTHE, TRANQUIL

before the ____ .... STORM
cool and ____ .... COLLECTED
down! .... COOL IT
calmness, mental/emotional
.... ATARAXIA
calmative .... BALM, DRUG,
OPIATE, SEDATIVE
calomel ...... POWDER, CATHARTIC
caloric .... HEAT, THERMAL
calorie .... THERM(E)
counter .... DIETER, MILADY,
DIABETIC
counter's standby
.... CYCLAMATE, NUTRA-
SWEET, SACCHARIN
-free .... WATER
source of .... FAT, PROTEIN,
ALCOHOL, CARBOHYDRATE
calories, count(ing) .... DIET(ING)
measured as .... ENERGY
pertaining to .... THERMAL
calotte .... CREST, (SKULL)CAP
Calpurnia's husband
.... (JULIUS) CAESAR
caltrop .... THISTLE
calumet .... (PEACE) PIPE
user of .... INDIAN, REDSKIN
calumniate .... SLUR, LIBEL,
DEFAME, MALIGN, ASPERSE,
REVILE, SLANDER
slang .... BADMOUTH
calumnious .... ABUSIVE,
CAUSTIC, CRITICAL, LIBELOUS
calumny .... SLUR, LIBEL,
SCANDAL, SLANDER,
ASPERSION, DEFAMATION
Calvary .... ARAM, GOLGOTHA,
BURIAL PLACE, (PLACE OF A)
SKULL
Calve, soprano .... EMMA,
ROQUER
Calvinist of Toulouse ...... CALAS
Calvinist(ic) .... GENEVAN,
DOGMATIC, GENEVESE
calvities .... BALDNESS
Calydonian boar killer
.... MELEAGER
Calypso .... SONG, DANCE, LILT,
NYMPH, MUSIC, BALLAD,
CHANT(EY), FLOWER, ORCHID
island of .... OGYGIA
calypster .... ALULA
calyx leaf .... PETAL, SEPAL
part .... GALEA
cam .... CATCH, WIPER,
COG(WHEEL), TAPPET,
TRIPPER, TRIPPET
wheel projection .... LOBE
camaraderie .... COMRADESHIP,
FELLOWSHIP
camalig .... HUT, GRANARY,

WAREHOUSE
camarilla .... CABAL, CLIQUE
camasa .... LOBELIA, QUAMASH
Cambodia .... CAMBOJA,
CAMBODGE, KAMPUCHEA
capital .... PNOM PENH, PHNOM
PENH
capital, ancient .... ANGKOR
city/town ..... KAMPOT, KULEN,
KRACHEH, PAOY PET, SUONG,
LUMPHAT, SIEMPANG, PAILIN,
SAMBOR, TAKEV, VIROCHEY,
POUTHISAT
gulf .... THAILAND
island .... KAOH KONG, KAOH
RUNG, KAOH TANG
lake .... TONLE SAP
money of .... RIEL
mountains .... DANGREK
native of .... KHMER
neighbor .... LAOS, VIETNAM,
THAILAND
plain .... JONCS
premier .... NOL
river ..... MEKONG, SREPOK, LA
DRANG
ruins .... ANGKOR WAT
seaport .... KAMPOT
skirt .... SAMPORT
cambogia .... (GUM) RESIN
cambrai .... LINEN, BATISTE
cambric .... LAWN, LINEN,
COTTON, PERCALE
Cambridge U. college servant
.... GYP
exam for honors .... TRIPOS
head/fellow .... DON
student .... SIZAR, SIZER,
CANTAB, OPTIME
came about .... AROSE, BEGAN,
CAUSED, HAPPENED
down .... (A)LIT, FELL,
DROPPED, SETTLED,
DESCENDED
camel .... OONT, BELOOL, DELOUL,
HEJEEN, ARABIAN, GUANACO,
BACTRIAN, RUMINANT,
DROMEDARY
back breaker .... STRAW
driver .... SARWAN
feature .... HUMP
hair cloth/fabric .... ABA,
CAMLET, CAMLOT, CASHMERE
hair robe .... ABA
keeper .... OBIL
like animal .... LLAMA,
GUANACO
load .... FARDEL
milk, fermented .... KUMISS,
KOUMIS(S)
rawhide .... SHAGREEN

seat on ..... HOUDAH, HOWDAH
sometimes called ship of the
____ .... DESERT
camellia .... JAPONICA
camelopard .... GIRAFFE
Camelot's lady .... ENID
sport .... TILT, JOUST,
TOURNEY
source of fame .... ARTHUR,
KNIGHTS, ROUND TABLE
Camenas .... NYMPHS
cameo .... GEM, MEDAL(LION),
EMBOSSMENT, ANAGLYPH,
PORTRAYAL
cutting tool .... SPADE
opposed to .... INTAGLIO
stone .... ONYX, SARDONYX
camera .... BOX, KODAK, LUCIDA,
CHAMBER, BROWNIE,
POLAROID
film protector .... CARTRIDGE
holder .... CASE
kind of .... CANDID, PORTRAIT,
TELEVISION
light bulb .... FLASH
opening .... APERTURE
part .... LENS, FINDER,
SHUTTER
platform .... DOLLY
portable .... KODAK
shot .... STILL
____, sketching aid
.... OBSCURA
stand/support .... TRIPOD
tube .... ORTHICON, CATHODE
RAY
cameraman .... SHUTTERBUG,
SNAPSHOOTER,
PHOTOGRAPHER
camerlingo .... CARDINAL,
CHAMBERLAIN
Cameroon .... CAMEROUN
bight .... BIAFRA
capital .... YAOUNDE
city/town .... DOUALA, KUMBA,
GAROUA, BAMENDA, WUM,
TIKO, MAROUA
language .... FANG, DUALA,
FULANI, FRENCH, ENGLISH
money .... FRANC, CENTIME
mountain .... CAMEROON
native .... ABO
religion .... ISLAM
river .... BENUE, CROSS, DJA,
DONGA, KADEI, IVINDO, LOM,
LOGONE, MBERE, SANGA
Camille author .... DUMAS
beloved of .... ARMAND
role actress .... GARBO
camion .... DRAY, TRUCK, WAGON
camise .... SHIRT, SMOCK

camisole .... JACKET
camlet .... CLOTH, PONCHO
camomile .... MAYWEED
Camorra .... (SECRET) SOCIETY
   like group .... MAF(F)IA
   member's specialty
   .... MURDER, BLACKMAIL,
      EXTORTION, TERRORISM
camouflage .... HIDE, MASK,
   BEFOG, CONCEAL, DISGUISE,
      DECEPTION
   expert .... CAMOUFLEUR
camouflaging material .... VEIL,
   PAINT, SMOKE, LEAVES
camp ...... ETAPE, TABOR, CLIQUE,
   BIVOUAC, ENCAMP(MENT)
   barricaded by wagons
   .... LA(A)GER
   besiegers' .... LEAGUER
   follower .... DOXY, FIRE,
   DAVID, GROUND, SUTLER,
      VIVANDIERE
   kind of .... BOOT, TRAILER,
   BOY SCOUTS, DETENTION,
   INTERNMENT, CONCENTRATION
   military .... BASE, BARRACKS
   out .... MAROON, ROUGH IT
   outdoor facility .... TENT,
      LATRINE
   pertaining to .... CASTRAL
   political .... PARTY, FACTION
   privy/toilet .... LATRINE
campagna .... PLAIN
campaign .... PLAN, DRIVE,
   CANVASS, CRUSADE,
   BARNSTORM, ELECTIONEER
   against an idea .... JIHAD
   for .... ESPOUSE
   goal, charity .... FUND-RAISING
   goal, military .... VICTORY
   goal, political .... ELECTION
   kind of .... SMEAR, WHISTLE-
      STOP
   matters .... ISSUES
   military .... WAR, CONFLICT,
      HOSTILITIES
   motive .... CAUSE
   war .... TACTICS, STRATEGY
   word .... PROMISE, REELECT
campaigner .... STUMPER
   military .... SOLDIER, VETERAN
campanile ...... BELFRY, STEEPLE,
      (BELL)TOWER
campanula .... RAMPION,
      HAREBELL
Campbell, singer .... GLEN
camper's equipment .... TENT,
   POLES, STAKES, LANTERN,
      SLEEPING BAG
   kit .... DUFFEL, DUFFLE
campesino .... PEASANT

camphol .... BORNEOL
camphor ball .... MOTHBALL
   -like .... BORNEOL
   oil .... SAFROL(E)
   tree .... EVERGREEN
campo .... PLAIN, PLAZA,
   DISTRICT, FLATLAND
campstool-shaped chair
   .... CURULE
campus ...... QUAD, YARD, FIELD,
   QUADRANGLE,
   SCHOOLGROUNDS
   building .... DORM, SCHOOL,
   GYM(NASIUM)
   feature on some .... IVY
   group .... FRAT, SORORITY,
      FRATERNITY
   VIP .... DEAN, PREXY,
      ATHLETE
can .... JUG, TIN, PAIL, MAY, BE
   ABLE, CONTAINER
   fruit .... PRESERVE
   slang .... JAIL, PRISON, FIRE,
   EXPEL, LAY OFF, DISMISS,
   JOHN, TOILET, BUTTOCKS,
      DISCHARGE
Canaan's brother .... CUSH,
   EGYPT, LIBYA
   father .... HAM
   grandfather .... NOAH
   son .... HETH, SIDON
Canaanites' ancient god
   .... MOLECH
   god of fertility .... BAAL
   goddess of fertility
   .... ASHERAH
Canada, Lower .... QUEBEC
Canada's _____ 67 .... EXPO
Canadian .... CANUCK
   airport .... GANDER
   basin .... FOXE, KANE
   bay .... FUNDY, JAMES, BAFFIN,
   HUDSON, UNGAVA, GEORGIAN
   boatman/woodsman
   .... VOYAGEUR
   canal .... WELLAND
   cape .... RAY, RACE, SABLE,
      CHIDLEY
   capital .... OTTAWA
   channel .... FOXE, PARRY,
      MCLINTOCK
   city/town .... HULL, BANFF,
   LEVIS, CALGARY, MONTREAL,
   GUELPH, BRANDON, HAMILTON,
   MOOSE JAW, DARTMOUTH,
   EDMONTON, MEDICINE HAT,
   HALIFAX, MONCTON,
   NANAIMO, REGINA, SUDBURY,
   KINGSTON, SASKATOON,
   VANCOUVER, TORONTO,
   VICTORIA, WINDSOR, WINNIPEG

crookneck .... CUSHAW
emblem .... MAPLE
farmer .... HABITAN(T)
folk singer .... LIGHTFOOT
football scrimmage .... ROUGE
   game .... LA CROSSE
   game preserve .... JASPER
   gannet .... MARGOT
   gold field .... KLONDIKE
   goose ..... BRANT(A), OUTARDE
   grape .... ISABELLA
   humorist .... LEACOCK
   Indian ..... CREE, DENE, HAIDA,
   SIOUX, MICMAC, TAKU, TINNE,
      SARCEE
   island .... BANKS, BAFFIN,
   DEVON, BATHURST, MANSEL,
   ELLESMERE, ANTICOSTI,
   MELVILLE, NEWFOUNDLAND,
   FOGO, SABLE, VANCOUVER,
   SOMERSET, VICTORIA
   islands ..... OTTAWA, BELCHER,
      MAGDALEN
   lake ..... CREE, ABITIBI, MINTO,
   RAINY, ATHABASCA, GREAT
   BEAR, GREAT SLAVE, LOUISE,
   KLUANE, KOOTENAY, SWAN,
   OKANAGAN, MANITOBA,
   SELWYN, WOODS, WILLISTON,
   TESLIN, REINDEER, WINNIPEG
   land measure .... ARPENT
   language ..... FRENCH, ENGLISH
   lynx .... PISHU, CARCAJOU
   money .... DOLLAR
   mountain ..... LOGAN, ROBSON,
   ALBERTA, CARLETON,
   COLUMBIA, D'UBERVILLE,
      FAIRWEATHER
   mountains ...... COAST, ROCKY,
      TORNGAT
   national park .... YOHO,
   FUNDY, BANFF, JASPER,
   GLACIER, PACIFIC RIM,
   NAHANNI, TERRA NOVA
   official, town president
   .... REEVE
   peak .... (MOUNT) LOGAN
   peninsula ..... GASPE, BOOTHIA
   policeman .... MOUNTIE
   porcupine .... URSON
   prairie province ...... ALBERTA,
   MANITOBA, SASKATCHEWAN
   prime minister .... LAURIER,
   MARONEY, PEARSON, TRUDEAU
   province .... ALBERTA, BRITISH
   COLUMBIA, MANITOBA, NEW
   BRUNSWICK, NEWFOUNDLAND,
   NOVA SCOTIA, ONTARIO,
   PRINCE EDWARD ISLAND,
   QUEBEC, SASKATCHEWAN,
   NORTHWEST TERRITORIES,

YUKON TERRITORY
provincial capital
.... EDMONTON, VICTORIA,
WINNIPEG, FREDERICTON, ST.
JOHN'S, HALIFAX, TORONTO,
CHARLOTTE TOWN, QUEBEC,
REGINA, WHITEHORSE,
YELLOWKNIFE
resort/scenic region ..... GASPE
river .... TRENT, FINLAY,
LIARD, FRASER, MACKENZIE,
PELLY, PEACE, MISTASSIBI,
NELSON, OTTAWA, PERIBONCA,
STEWART, SAINT LAWRENCE,
STIKINE, SASKATCHEWAN,
PEEL, SKEENA, SLAVE, YUKON
river into Pacific .... NASS
rodent .... LEMMING
settler .... SOURDOUGH
squaw .... MAHALA
strait .... CABOT, DAVIS,
NARES, HECATE
summer resort .... BANFF
territory .... YUKON
canaille .... MOB, RABBLE,
RIFFRAFF
canal .... DITCH, CHANNEL,
CULVERT, PASSAGE,
WATERWAY, ERIE, KIEL, SUEZ,
ACEQUIA, CONDUIT, PANAMA,
WELLAND
bank .... BERM(E)
boat .... GONDOLA
boat tower .... MULE
ear .... SCALA, MEATUS
enclosed part .... LOCK
from mouth to anus
.... ENTERON, ALIMENTARY
TRACT
in anatomy/zoology .... VAS,
DUCT, TUBE
lock gate .... WICKET
Suez: colloq. .... SOO
worker .... NAVVY
zone seaport .... BALBOA
zone town ...... ANCON, GATUN
canape .... COUCH, DIVAN,
APPETIZER
spread .... CAVIAR, CHEESE,
SARDINE
canard ...... DUCK, HOAX, RUMOR,
HUMBUG, FICTION, HEARSAY,
AIRPLANE, SCUTTLEBUTT
canary .... DANCE, FINCH,
ROLLER, SONGBIRD, SONGSTER
color .... YELLOW
hybrid .... MULE
kin .... SERIN
seed .... ALPIST
yellow .... MELINE
Canary .... WINE

island .... LA PALMA,
LANZAROTE, TENERIF(FE),
GOMERA, FUERTEVENTURA,
HIERRO, GRAN CANARIA
island mount .... TEIDE, TEYDE
island seaport .... LAS PALMAS
island wine, dry, white
.... SACK
island wine, sweet
.... MADEIRA
canasta play/score .... MELD
Canaveral, Cape .... KENNEDY
Canberra is capital of
.... AUSTRALIA
cancel .... END, STOP, VOID,
ANNUL, ERASE, REMIT,
OFFSET, RECALL, EXPUNGE,
NULLIFY, REPEAL, REVOKE,
RESCIND
deletion made .... STET
in printing .... KILL, OMIT,
DELE(TE)
cancellation in publishing/
printing .... EDITING,
DELETION, BLUE PENCILING
mark on mail .... STAMP,
CACHET, POSTMARK
of debt .... WRITE-OFF
of marriage .... SPLIT-UP,
DIVORCE, ANNULMENT
cancer .... TUMOR, GROWTH,
NEOPLASM, CARCINOMA,
SCIRRHOUS
bone .... FIBROSARCOMA,
EWING'S SARCOMA,
CHONDROSARCOMA,
OSTEOSARCOMA
-causing agent .... ALCOHOL,
TOBACCO, SUNLIGHT
chemical element used in
treatment of .... RADON,
RADIUM
describing .... BENIGN,
MALIGNANT
in the lymph nodes and
spleen .... LYMPHOMA,
HODGKIN'S DISEASE
like .... CANCROID
non-malignant .... BENIGN
of the blood .... LEUKEMIA
of the skin .... MELANOMA,
CARCINOMA
producing substance
.... CARCINOGEN
surgery, bone .... AMPUTATION
surgery, breast
.... LUMPECTOMY,
MASTECTOMY
surgery, colon .... COLECTOMY
treatment ..... CHEMOTHERAPY,
RADIATION THERAPY

Cancer, Zodiac sign .... CRAB
candelabrum .... CANDELABRA,
CANDLESTICK
candent ...... GLOWING, SPARKING,
(WHITE)HOT
candescent .... LUSTROUS,
SHINING, GLOWING, RADIANT
Candia .... CRETE, HERAKLEION
candid ...... OPEN, BLUNT, FRANK,
DIRECT, HONEST, SIMPLE,
STRAIGHT-FORWARD,
TRUTHFUL, BRUSQUE,
GUILELESS, UPFRONT,
OUTSPOKEN, UNGUARDED
Candida author .... SHAW
candidate .... NOMINEE,
ASPIRANT, APPLICANT,
OFFICE-SEEKER
for graduation .... SENIOR
for knighthood .... ESQUIRE
for mending .... TEAR
kind of .... REBEL, LAME
DUCK, FAVORITE, OFFICIAL,
INDEPENDENT
candidates' list .... BALLOT,
SLATE, TICKET
platform .... HUSTINGS
staple ...... PLEDGES, PROMISES
winning score .... MAJORITY,
PLURALITY
candidiasis .... THRUSH,
MONILIASIS
candied .... GLACE, GLAZED,
HONEYED, SUGARED
fruit/nut .... COMFIT,
SWEETMEAT
rind .... CITRON
candies, imitation of
.... CONFETTI
Candiot .... CRETAN
candle .... DIP, LIGHT, TAPER,
CANDELA, RUSHLIGHT
holder .... HEARST, SCONCE,
CANDELABRA, GIRANDOLE,
CHANDELIER
kind of .... RUSH, CORPSE,
VOTARY, BAYBERRY
lighter .... TAPER
maker/seller .... CHANDLER
material .... WAX, WICK,
CARNAUBA, TALLOW,
OZOCERITE
part .... WICK, SNAST
religious ..... VOTIVE, PASCHAL
slang .... GLIM
spike .... PRICKET
wax .... TAPER, BOUGIE,
CARNAUBA
wick's end .... SNUFF
candlelight .... DUSK, EVENING,
TWILIGHT

candlenut .... AMA
candles, storeroom of
.... CHANDLERY
candlestick ...... CRUSIE, LAMPAD,
SCONCE, PRICKET
branched .... JESSE,
GIRANDOLE, CANDELABRA,
CANDELABRUM
ornamental .... LUSTRE,
FLAMBEAU
shelf .... GRADIN(E)
candor .... HONESTY, FAIRNESS,
FRANKNESS, SINCERITY
candy ...... KISS, BONBON, COMFIT,
DULCIFY, CONFETTO,
CONFECTION, SWEETEN,
SWEETS, SWEETMEAT
chewy .... TAFFY, TOFFY,
TOFFEE, CARAMEL, TOOTSIE
ROLL
coating .... DRAGEE
cough drop .... LOZENGE
crisp .... BRITTLE
favorite .... TURTLE
filler .... FONDANT
flavor .... LIME, CHOCOLATE,
LICORICE, BUTTERSCOTCH
fudge-like .... PANOCHA,
PENUCHE
gelatinous .... JELLYBEAN
hard: sl. .... JAWBREAKER
jelly-like .... PASTE
nutty .... NOUGAT, PRALINE
on a stick .... LOLLIPOP,
LOLLYPOP
piece .... POP, DROP, GOODY,
WAFER
pull .... PARTY
seller .... BUCHER,
CONFECTIONER
soft .... FUDGE,
MARSHMALLOW
candytuft .... MUSTARD
cane ...... ROD, BEAT, FLAY, FLOG,
STEM, WADDY, CRUTCH,
HICKORY, RAT(T)AN,
(WALKING) STICK
flogging .... SWISH
like a .... FERULACEOUS
metal cap .... SHOE, FERRULE
plant .... BAMBOO, RATTAN
strip .... SPLINT
sugar .... SACROSE,
SACCHAROSE
walking .... MALACCA
canella .... SPICE, CINNAMON
Canfield (D.) play .... SOLO
cangue-like device .... PILLORY
Canicula .... DOG-STAR, SIRIUS
canicular ...... TORRID, (SIZZLING)
HOT

canine. See also dog .... DOG,
FOX, WOLF, JACKAL,
EYETOOTH
disease .... MANGE, RABIES,
DRONCIT, CORONAVIRUS,
PARAINFLU, DISTEMPER
mongrel .... CUR, TYKE
tooth .... FANG, TUSH,
LANIARY
canister .... BOX, CAN, CADDY,
CARTON, CONTAINER
canker .... ROT, RUST, SORE,
DECAY, FUNGUS, MILDEW,
TAINT, INFECT, CORRUPT
canna .... ACHIRA
cannabin .... RESIN
cannabis .... HEMP, HASHISH
canned .... TINNED, PRESERVED
beef .... BULLY
food poisoning ...... BOTULISM
food toxin .... BOTULIN
slang ...... SACKED, DISMISSED,
GOT THE AX, CASHIERED
Cannes .... RESORT
cannibal .... SAVAGE, MAN-EATER,
CARNIVORE
human food of .... LONG PIG
cannikin .... CAN, CUP, PAIL,
BUCKET
cannon .... MORTAR, HOWITZER,
FIELDPIECE, ORDNANCE, BIG
BERTHA, (CRACK)GUN
ball .... MISSILE, PROJECTILE
collectively .... ARTILLERY
dummy .... QUAKER
firing material .... LANIARD,
LANYARD, LINSTOCK
fodder, so-called .... SOLDIERS
harness for men .... BRICOLE
in billiards .... CAROM
kick of .... RECOIL
mounted .... GINGAL, JINGAL
old .... ASPIC, DRAKE, FALCON,
CULVERIN
pivot .... TRUNNION
oriental .... LANTAKA
platform .... TERREPLEIN
shot .... PROJECTILE
cannonade .... BLITZ, SALVO,
STRAFE, BARRAGE, GUNFIRE,
BLITZKRIEG, BOMBARDMENT
cannonball: sl. .... SWOOP, RAPID,
POUNCE, THUNDERBOLT
cannoneer .... GUNNER,
ARTILLERYMAN
cannonry .... BATTERY,
ORDNANCE, ARTILLERY
cannular .... TUBULAR
canny .... WARY, ASTUTE,
SHREWD, CLEVER, CAREFUL,
CUNNING, WILY, SHARP,

CAUTIOUS
canoe ...... BOAT, DUGOUT, PITPAN
African .... BONGO, ALMADIA
air chamber .... SPONSON
Arctic .... KAYAK
dugout ...... PIRAGUA, PIROGUE
Eskimo .... KAIAK, KAYAK,
UMIAK, BIDARKA
Hawaii .... WAAPA
Malabar .... TONEE
Malay .... PAHI, PRAU, PROA,
PRAH(O)
Maori .... WAKA
mover .... PADDLER
Philippine ..... BANCA, BANKA,
CASCO
propeller .... POLE, PADDLE
with outrigger/sail .... PROA
canon .... LAW, CODE, RULE,
DECREE, CRITERION
in music .... ROUND
law expert .... DECRETIST
of the Mass prayer
.... MEMENTO
canoness .... NUN, NOVICE
canonical .... PAPAL, ABBATIAL,
DIVINE, ACCEPTED, APPROVED,
RUBRICAL, PRESCRIBED
hour .... MATINS, PRIME,
TERCE, TIERCE, SEXT, NONES,
LAUDS, VESPERS, COMPLIN
law, Moslem .... SHERI
canonicals ...... ALB, COPE, HOOD,
GOWN, ROBE, AMICE, FROCK,
HABIT, BIRETTA, CASSOCK,
BANDS, STOLE, FANON,
MANIPLE, SCARF, SURPLICE,
VESTMENTS
canonize .... DEIFY, EXALT, BLESS,
SANCTIFY, GLORIFY, HALLOW,
PURIFY, ENSHRINE
canonized person .... SAINT
canons, group of .... CHAPTER
canopy .... CIEL, COPE, DAIS,
HOWDAH, TENT, COVER,
AWNING
altar .... CIBORIUM, BALDACHIN
bed/tomb .... TESTER
boat/cart .... TILT
of heaven .... VAULT
over the earth .... SKY
support .... BAIL
canorous .... CLEAR, MUSICAL,
PLEASING, MELODIOUS
cant ...... LEAN, TILT, TOSS, TURN,
LINGO, ANGLE, ARGOT,
JARGON, PATTER, PATOIS,
SLANT, SLOPE, INCLINE,
SWAY, SHIFT, SWERVE,
SLANG, CAREEN, DIALECT,
TRITE, SNIVEL, SNUFFLE

hook .... PEAV(E)Y
cantabile .... SONGLIKE
cantaloup(e) .... (MUSK)MELON
cantankerous .... CROSS,
CRANKY, BAD-TEMPERED, ILL-
NATURED, CONTENTIOUS,
BELLICOSE, GRUMPY, ORNERY,
PERVERSE
fellow .... CURMUDGEON
person: colloq. .... CRANK,
GROUCH
person: sl. .... SOREHEAD,
SOURPUSS
cantata .... ARIA, CHORALE,
CHORUSES, PASTORALE,
ORATORIO, VOCAL SOLOS
dramatic/pastoral .... MOTET,
HYMN, SERENATA
canteen .... FLASK, BOTTLE, PX,
SHOP, FLACON, WATERBAG,
POST EXCHANGE,
COMMISSARY
canter .... GAIT, LOPE, GALLOP
Canterbury, archbishop of
.... ANSELM, CRANMER,
DUNSTAN
bell .... CAMPANULA
bell variety .... CUP AND
SAUCER
murdered archbishop
.... BECKET
Tales' author .... CHAUCER
Tales' heroine .... GRISELDA
Tales' inn .... TABARD
cantharides .... IRRITANT,
SPANISH FLY, STIMULANT
singular of .... CANTHARIS
canticle .... ODE, HYMN, SONG,
CHANT, PAEAN, PSALM,
BRAVURA, INTROIT
Canticle of Canticles .... SONG
OF SOLOMON, SONG OF SONGS
cantina .... DINER, CANTEEN,
SNACK BAR, SALOON
cantle ...... PIECE, SLICE, PORTION
canto .... PASSUS, STANZA
Archaic .... FIT
obsolete .... SONG, BALLAD
Canton .... BILLET, CORNER,
COUNTY, REGION, BORDURE,
SECTION, DISTRICT,
QUARTER(S), QUADRANS
crepe .... SILK
flannel .... NAP
is capital of .... KWANGTUNG
is former name of
..... GUANGZHOU, KWANGCHOW
river .... PEARL
river island .... MACAO,
MACAU
cantor .... SINGER, MELODIST,

CHAZ(Z)AN, PRECENTOR
cantrip .... PRANK, TRICK,
(MAGIC) SPELL
cantullate .... SING
cantus .... SONG, MELODY
Canuck .... CANADIAN
canvas .... DUCK, CLOTH, SAIL(S),
TENT(S), (OIL) PAINTING
arena .... BOXING RING
boat .... CANOE
cover ...... TARP, TILT, AWNING
like fabric .... WIGAN
shelter ....: TENT
ship's .... JIB, MIZZEN,
SPANKER, STUDDING,
FOREROYAL
waterproofed ..... TARP(AULIN)
canvasback .... DUCK
relative .... SCAUP, REDHEAD
canvass .... SEEK, DISCUSS,
CAMPAIGN, EXAMINE, SOLICIT
voters .... POLL, SURVEY,
ELECTIONEER
canvasser .... POLLER
canyon .... GAP, DALE, DELL,
VALE, CLEFT, GULCH,
ARROYO, CREVICE, RAVINE,
VALLEY
entrance .... JAWS
mouth .... ABRA
wall .... CLIFF
canzone .... POEM, MADRIGAL
canzonet ...... LILT, CENTO, SONG,
MATIN(S)
caoutchouc .... RUBBER,
ELATERITE
source ..... ULE, CEARA, LATEX
cap .... FEZ, TAM, COIF, COIL,
BERET, TOP, COVER,
HEADGEAR, HAT, LID, BEANIE,
HEADPIECE, HOOD, DOME,
SURPASS
a-pie .... ENTIRELY,
DOWNRIGHT, HEAD TO FOOT
academic .... MORTARBOARD
and bells wearer ...... (COURT)
JESTER
bottle .... CROWN, CAPSULE
brim .... VISOR
brimless .... FEZ, TAM,
BIRETTA, CALOT(TE), PILEUS,
BALMORAL, BERET, TARBOOSH
child's .... BIGGIN
children's/women's
.... BONNET
close/fitting .... COIF, TOQUE
decoration .... POMPON,
COCKADE, FEATHER
ecclesiastical .... BERET,
BARRET, BIRET(TA)

horseman's/with flap
.... MONTERO
jester's .... COCKSCOMB
Jewish priest's .... MITER,
MITRE
kind of .... PERCUSSION,
MORTARBOARD
knitted .... THRUM
lawyer's .... COIF
military .... BUSBY, KEPI,
HAVELOCK, SHAKO, PERSHING
mushroom's .... PILEUS
Oriental .... FEZ, CALPAC,
KALPAK, TURBAN
part .... BILL, BRIM, VISOR
Scottish .... TAM, BALMORAL
shaped .... PILEATE
sheepskin .... CALPAC, KALPAK
skull .... COIF, CALOT(TE),
PILEUS
slang .... LID
square .... BIRETTA
tube .... CAPSULE
turned up front .... COCKUP
visor .... BILL
winter .... TUQUE
capable .... APT, ABLE, ADROIT,
SKILLED, COMPETENT, FIT,
EFFICIENT, QUALIFIED
of being climbed
.... SCALABLE
of being felt .... TACTILE
of being introduced from
abroad .... IMPORTABLE
of being repaired .... FIXABLE,
MENDABLE
of being turned outward
.... REVERSIBLE
of defense .... TENABLE
of following advice
.... AMENABLE
of motion .... MOTILE
of moving .... MOBILE
capacious .... AMPLE, ROOMY,
SPACIOUS
capacitor .... CONDENSER
capacity .... ABILITY, CONTENT,
VIRTUE, SIZE, VOLUME,
FUNCTION, FACULTY, GIFT,
APTITUDE, ABLENESS, STATUS,
POSITION
for feeling .... SENTIENCE
slang .... WHAT IT TAKES
caparison .... OUTFIT,
ADORNMENT, TRAP(PINGS),
TROUSSEAU
horse's .... BRIDLE, SADDLE,
HARNESS, BLINDERS
cape .... NESS, MANTA, MANTLE,
ORALE, POINT, TALMA,
FORELAND, TONGUE,

HEADLAND, MANTILLA, MANTELET, PENINSULA, PROMONTORY
cotton .... MANTA
Dutch .... TAAL, AFRIKAANS
ecclesiastical ..... COPE, AMICE
fur .... ERMINE, PALATINE, PELERINE, COLLARET(TE)
hanging part .... TIPPET
hooded .... AMICE, ALMUCE, MOZ(Z)ETTA
land's .... RAS
like garment .... DOLMAN
Mexican .... SERAPE
muslin/3-cornered .... FICHU
papal .... FANON, FANUM, ORALE, PHANO
sleeveless .... INVERNESS
vestment resembling ..... COPE
women's .... SHAWL
worn for disguise .... CLOAK
Cape Cod food fish .... CERO
Verde Islands capital .... PRAIA
Verde Islands native .... SERER
Capek (Karel) character .... ROBOT
play .... RUR
capelin .... SMELT
Capella ...... KID, STAR, SHE-GOAT
caper .... DIDO, JUMP, LEAP, SKIP, ANTIC, FRISK, CAVORT, GAMBOL, PRANCE, TRICK, CAPRIOLE, CURLICUE, TITTUP, OATCAKE, ROLLICK
criminal .... HEIST, RIP-OFF, ROBBERY
plant .... CAPPARIS
capillary .... VEINLET, MINUTE, SLENDER, HAIRLIKE, BLOOD VESSEL, ARTERIOLE
action .... REPULSION, ATTRACTION
tumor .... ANGIOMA
capital .... CASH, FUNDS, CHIEF, MONEY, ASSETS, RESOURCES, BACKING, PURSE STRINGS, PRINCIPAL, METROPOLIS
body .... SENATE, CONGRESS
business .... STOCK
city ..... SEAT OF GOVERNMENT
colloquial .... EXCELLENT, FIRST RATE, FIRST CLASS
is part of ____ column .... ARCHITECTURAL
letter ..... INITIAL, UPPER-CASE, MAJUSCULE
make .... ABUSE, EXPLOIT
punishment .... HANGING, EXECUTION, DEATH PENALTY, ELECTROCUTION

ship ..... BATTLESHIP, CRUISER, DREADNAUGHT
too little .... SHOESTRING
Capital actress .... (OLYMPIA) DUKAKIS
gospel singer .... (MAHALIA) JACKSON
rock star .... (RICK) SPRINGFIELD
capitalist .... BARON, BACKER, SPONSOR, FINANCER
slang .... ANGEL
capitalize .... BACK, FUND, FINANCE
on .... CASH IN, PROFIT BY
capitate .... HEAD-SHAPED
Capitol .... STATEHOUSE
capitulary .... ORDINANCES
capitulate .... CEDE, YIELD, SUBMIT, SUCCUMB, SURRENDER
capon .... CHICKEN, ROOSTER
caporal .... TOBACCO
capote .... TOP, HOOD, COVER, BONNET, OVERCOAT, RAINCOAT
capouch .... HOOD, CAPUCHE
capra .... SHE-GOAT
Capri .... ISLE
capriccio .... WHIM, PRANK
caprice .... FANCY, FREAK, DESIRE, NOTION, VAGARY, CROTCHET, WHIM(SY), HUMORESQUE
capricious .... FANCY, FICKLE, ERRATIC, FLIGHTY, MOONISH, WAYWARD, ECCENTRIC, FANTASTIC, ROVING, HOITY-TOITY, WHIMSICAL
Capricorn .... GOAT, CONSTELLATION
capriole .... JUMP, LEAP, CAPER
capsize .... KEEL, TIP-OVER, INVERT, UPSET, OVERTURN, TOPPLE-OVER, TURN-TURTLE
capsicum .... PEPPER, CAYENNE, PAPRICA, PAPRIKA
capstan .... WHIM, WINCH, WINDLASS
bar .... LEVER
drum .... RUNDLE
top .... DRUMHEAD
capsule .... CAP, POD, PILL, AMPULE, AMPOULE, CACHET, SEAL, WAFER, CONTAINER
egg .... OVISAC
form into a .... CAPSULATE
plant .... BOLL
spore .... THECA
version .... PRECIS, SYNOPSIS
capsulize ...... ABRIDGE, SHORTEN,

CONDENSE
captain .... CHIEF, LEAD(ER), OFFICER, HEAD(MAN)
Absalom's .... AMASA
allowance of .... PRIMAGE
boat of the .... GIG
dialectic .... CAP'N
in a restaurant ...... MAITRE D, HEADWAITER
of factory/construction workers .... FOREMAN
of province/state .... GOVERNOR
of ship, fiction .... AHAB, NEMO, BLIGH, QUEEG
rank below, in merchant ship .... MATE
rank below, U.S. Navy .... COMMANDER
ship's .... MASTER, SKIPPER
Captain Cook's discovery .... SANDWICH (ISLANDS)
Hook's companion .... SMEE
Nemo's creator .... VERNE
Police .... CHIEF, COMMISSIONER
caption .... LEGEND, HEADING, HEADLINE, SUBHEAD, (SUB)TITLE
subject of .... PICTURE, EXHIBIT
captious .... TRICKY, CAVILING, CATTY, FAULT-FINDING, (HYPER)CRITICAL
captivate .... CHARM, ALLURE, ENAMOR, BEWITCH, ATTRACT, ENCHANT, ENTHRALL, FASCINATE
captive .... DETAINEE, PRISONER
bail of .... RANSOM
burden of .... YOKE
captivity .... DURESS, BONDAGE, CONFINEMENT, IMPRISONMENT
capture ...... BAG, COP, NAB, NET, TAKE, CATCH, ARREST, SNARE, ENTRAP, SEIZE, SEIZURE
slang .... COLLAR
captured object .... PRIZE
capuche. See **capouch**
Capuchin .... MONK, FRIAR, CLOAK, MONEY, SAPAJOU
monkey .... SAI
caput .... HEAD, DOOMED
capybara .... HOG, CAVY, RODENT
car .... AUTO, MACHINE, ROADSTER, VEHICLE, AUTOMOBILE
baggage .... FOURGON
balloon .... NACELLE
bar .... AXLE

battered .... HEAP
bubble of .... BLISTER
buslike, luxurious
.... LIMOUSINE
checkup, repair .... OVERHAUL
closed .... SEDAN
compartment .... TRUNK
decrepit .... HEAP, CRATE,
                                        JALOPY
dome .... BLISTER
for hire .... CAB, TAXI,
                      TAXICAB, LIMOUSINE
hyped-up .... HOTROD, MACH
                      (I), RACER, MUSTANG
in a building .... LIFT, CAGE,
                                     ELEVATOR
kind of .... COUPE, SEDAN,
      USED, TOWN, MOTOR, RACER,
      CLOSED, UTILITY, RAILROAD,
      LUXURY, ARMORED, TOURING,
                          STATION WAGON,
                              SECONDHAND
mine .... HUTCH
old, broken-down: sl. .... DOG,
                                        JALOPY
old-make .... REO, T-MODEL
on rails .... STREETCAR
part .... TIRE, WHEEL, BUMPER,
      FENDER, MUFFLER, ENGINE,
      RADIATOR, HEADLIGHT, WIPER,
      IGNITION, WINDSHIELD, GAS
      TANK, TURN SIGNAL
shoes .... FOUR TIRES
suspended .... TELFER, LIFT,
      TROLLEY, TELPHER, ELEVATOR,
                                     MONORAIL
tassle .... TOGGLE
touring .... PHAETON
train's last .... CABOOSE
versatile .... JEEP
with folded top
.... CONVERTIBLE
carabao ...... BUFFALO, TAMARAU,
                                     TAMARAW
horn bugle .... TAMBULI
carabineer .... HORSEMAN,
                              CAVALRYMAN
carabinieri .... POLICE
caracal .... FUR, LYNX
caracara .... HAWK, FALCON
Caracas is capital of
.... VENEZUELA
carack .... GALLEON
caracole .... TURN, WHEEL
caracul .... FUR, SHEEP
carafe .... BOTTLE, DECANTER
caramel .... CANDY, BURNT
                                        SUGAR
carangoid .... CERO, FISH,
      CAVALLA, YELLOWJACK,
      POMPANO, YELLOWTAIL

carapace .... LORICA, CRUST,
      COVERING, SHELL, SHIELD
animal with .... CRAB, TURTLE,
      TORTOISE, TERRAPIN,
                              ARMADILLO
material .... CHITIN
under part of .... PLASTRON
caravan ...... VAN, TOUR, WAGON,
      TRAIN, PROCESSION
Arabian .... CAFILA
of a kind .... SAFARI
of horsemen/carriages
.... CAVALCADE
of vehicles .... MOTORCADE
stopping place .... OASIS,
      SERAI, INN, CARAVANSARY
caravansary .... INN, KHAN,
      HOSTELRY, SERAI, IMARET
caravel ...... SHIP, BEETLE, VESSEL
of history .... NINA, PINTA
caraway .... SEED, PLANT, SPICE
cooky .... SEED CAKE
carbide, tungsten ...... CARBOLOY
carbine .... STEN, RIFLE, MUSKET,
                                     ESCOPET
firearm resembling
.... PETRONEL
carbohydrate .... SUGAR, PECTIN,
      INULIN, STARCH, LEVULIN,
      LICHENIN, CELLULOSE
most familiar .... SUGAR,
                                        STARCH
most important .... STARCH
source of .... GLUCOSE,
      FRUCTOSE, GALACTOSE,
      LACTOSE, MALTOSE, SUCROSE,
      STARCH, CELLULOSE
suffix .... OSE
type of .... DISACCHARIDES,
      MONOSACCHARIDES,
      POLYSACCHARIDES
carbolic acid .... PHENOL
carbon .... COAL, COKE, LEAD,
                                        CRAYON
atom and two oxygen atoms
.... (CARBON) DIOXIDE
combine chemically with
.... CARBURET
copy: colloq. .... REPLICA,
      DOUBLE, DUPLICATE,
      LIKENESS, LOOK ALIKE,
      FACSIMILE, (SPITTING) IMAGE
dioxide, cooled and
      compressed .... DRY ICE
iron alloy .... PEARLITE
monoxide ...... POISONOUS GAS
pencil .... CHARCOAL,
                                     GRAPHITE
precious/pure .... DIAMOND
product .... SOOT
carbonado .... HACK, MEAT,

SLASH, DIAMOND
carbonate of lime
.... STALACTITE, CALCITE,
                              STALAGMITE
carbonize .... CHAR
carborundum .... EMERY,
                                     ABRASIVE
tool .... GRINDSTONE
carboy .... BOTTLE
carbuncle ...... PIMPLE, ANTHRAX,
                      CLUSTER OF BOILS
common site of .... NAPE,
                                     BUTTOCKS
carburetant .... BENZENE,
                                     GASOLINE
carcajou .... LYNX, BADGER,
      COUGAR, WOLVERINE
carcass .... BODY, BONES,
      SKELETON, FRAMEWORK
of a ship .... HULL
carcinoma .... CANCER,
      MALIGNANT TUMOR
surgery .... MASTECTOMY
card .... ACE, PAM, JACK, LIST,
      KING, TREY, CARTE, BRUSH,
      QUEEN, COMB, DEUCE,
      KNAVE, JOKER, CHART,
      PASTEBOARD
calling .... IDENTIFICATION
cheat ...... BLACKLEG, SHARPER
colloquial .... CHARACTER
combination .... MELD,
                                        TENACE
dealer .... TALLIER
dealer's leftovers .... STOCK,
                                        TALON
file .... CATALOG(UE)
fortune-telling .... TAROT
French .... CARTE
game .... LOO, FARO, MONTE,
      SOLITAIRE, WHIST, BACCARAT,
      BEZIQUE, MUGGINS, CRIBBAGE,
      SLAPJACK, PEDRO, CASINO,
      HEARTS, BRIDGE, CANASTA,
      POKER, FANTAN, PINOCHLE,
      TWENTY-ONE, BLACKJACK,
      SEVEN-UP, ECARTE, NULLO,
      PATIENCE, GIN RUMMY, BRAG,
      QUADRILLE
game "adviser" ..... KIBITZER
game, 18th century .... OMBER
game extra hand .... KITTY,
                                        WIDOW
game for one .... SOLITAIRE
game for two .... ECARTE,
      PIQUET, COONCAN, CONQUIAN
game holding .... HAND
game like bridge .... VINT
game like rummy
.... COONCAN, CONQUIAN
game shuffler .... DEALER

game, solitaire .... CANFIELD
game term .... BID, BYE, PASS,
CHECK, TRUMP, FLUSH, DEAL,
RAISE
game, 3-hand .... SKAT
game win .... GIN, SLAM, VOLE
games, authority on
.... HOYLE
holding .... HAND, TENACE
honor .... ACE
in faro .... SODA
kind of .... PASTE, PLAYING,
CALLING, COMPASS, POST(AL),
GREETING, WEDDING, BUSINESS
missing .... LOOSE DEUCE
playing .... PASTEBOARD
sharp .... BLACKLEG
slang .... FLAKE, ODDBALL,
CRACKPOT
suit, same .... FLUSH
three-spot .... TREY
two-spot .... DEUCE
wild .... JOKER
with four spots .... QUATRE
wool .... COMB, ROVE, TEASE
cardamom ...... POD, HERB, SEED,
GINGER
cardboard box .... CARTON
cardialgin .... HEARTBURN
cardigan .... JACKET, SWEATER,
WAMPUS, WAM(M)US
cardinal .... MAIN, CHIEF,
SONGBIRD, CLERIC, PRELATE,
RED, CLOAK, FINCH, PIVOTAL,
PRINCIPAL, TOPMOST
American .... REDBIRD
chair of .... THRONE
is one .... PRINCE
office of .... DATARY, DATARIA
rank/position of
.... CARDINALATE
sign of rank .... RED HAT
skullcap of .... ZUCCHETTO
title of honor .... EMINENCE
vestment .... DALMATIC
cardinals' meeting room
.... CONCLAVE
carding machine cylinder
.... SWIFT
cardioid .... HEART-SHAPED
cards, fortune-telling ...... TAROTS
held .... HAND
highest .... HONORS
left after dealing .... CAT,
STOCK, TALON
player who cuts .... PONE
spots on playing .... PIPS
that are discarded by all the
players .... CRIB
care .... HEED, CHARGE, CONCERN,
WORRY, ANXIETY, CAUTION,

CUSTODY, PRUDENCE,
TUTELAGE
for .... LOVE, MIND, NURSE,
WATCH, (AT)TEND, PROVIDE
of the aged .... MEDICARE
careen .... TIP, HEEL, LIST, SWAY,
LEAN, TILT, LURCH, BIAS,
SPEED, SLANT, INCLINE
career .... CALLING, PURSUIT,
RACE, LIFEWORK, VOCATION,
DASH, RUSH, SPEED, GALLOP,
OCCUPATION, PROFESSION
careful .... WARY, CHARY, EXACT,
HEEDFUL, ACCURATE,
DISCREET, PRUDENT,
CAUTIOUS, DAINTY, FINICAL,
GUARDED, STUDIED,
PAINSTAKING, METICULOUS
carefully .... GINGERLY, WITH
CARE
careless ...... LAX, RASH, CASUAL,
SLACK, SLOPPY, ARTLESS,
LISTLESS, CAREFREE,
RECKLESS, CURSORY,
SLIPSHOD, NEGLIGENT,
REMISS, HEEDLESS,
NONCHALANT
caress .... PET, BILL, KISS,
CUDDLE, DANDLE, EMBRACE,
CODDLE, FONDLE, NUZZLE,
NESTLE, STROKE, SNUGGLE
bear's .... HUG
bird's .... BILL, PECK
dove's .... BILL (AND COO)
Scottish .... DAUT, DAWT
slang .... NECK
caretaker .... KEEPER, CUSTODIAN
apartment .... CONCIERGE
house of .... LODGE
museum/library ...... CURATOR
of government, temporary
.... REGENT
property .... TRUSTEE
careworn .... WEARY, ANXIOUS,
HAGGARD, WORRIED
cargo .... LOAD, LADING, FREIGHT,
PORTAGE, SHIPMENT
boat .... SCOW, OILER, TANKER,
TRADER, FREIGHTER
cast overboard ship
.... JETSAM
from wrecked ship
.... FLOTSAM
hot .... CONTRABAND
put on .... LADE, LOAD
ship's .... BULK
space in ship .... HOLD
carhop .... WAITER, WAITRESS
Carib .... GALIBI, INDIAN
Caribbean dance .... LIMBO
island .... AVES, ARUBA,

BONAIRE
port .... COLON, ARUBA
witchcraft .... OBEAH
caribe .... PIRAYA
caribou .... REINDEER
male .... STAG
caricature .... COPY, PARODY,
SATIRE, BURLESQUE,
TRAVESTY, MIMICRY,
PRETENSE, DISTORTION
colloquial .... TAKE-OFF
means of expression
.... CARTOON, LAMPOON,
BURLESQUE
caricaturist .... SATIRIST,
CARTOONIST
Berger .... OSCAR
carinate .... KEEL-SHAPED
carillon .... PEAL
cariole .... CART, CARRIAGE
cark .... ANNOY, WORRY
carl .... CHURL, BONDMAN,
VILLEIN
carline ...... HAG, WITCH, WOMAN
Carlton's (hotel) partner
.... RITZ
Carmelite .... (WHITE) FRIAR
Carmen composer .... BIZET
Carmichael (Hoagy) hit song
.... STARDUST
carminative seeds ...... CARAWAY
carmine .... RED, CRIMSON
carnage .... BLOODSHED, KILLING,
BUTCHERY, MASSACRE,
MURDER, SHAMBLES,
SLAUGHTER
carnal .... WILD, RAKISH, BODILY,
SEXUAL, FLESHY, MUNDANE,
GENTILE, SENSUAL, WORLDLY
carnation .... FLOWER, PICOTEE,
RED, ROSY-PINK, DIANTHUS
carnauba .... PALM
product .... WAX
carnelian .... QUARTZ,
CHALCEDONY
carnival .... FAIR, GALA,
FESTIVAL, FETE, FESTIVITY,
EXHIBITION, CIRCUS,
REVELRY, MERRYMAKING
character .... SHILL, BARKER,
GRIFTER
famous .... MARDI GRAS
feature ...... PARADE, PAGEANT,
RIDES, CONFETTI, SIDESHOWS
gambling operator .... GRIFTER
hawker's spot .... PITCH
carnivore ...... DOG, MINK, URSUS,
LION, WOLF, PUMA, OTTER,
BEAR, (POLE)CAT, FOUMART,
GENET, TIGER, LEOPARD,
HYENA, RATEL, SERVAL,

COUGAR, OCELOT, OPPOSUM, SEAL, LYNX, WEASEL
diet .... MEAT, FLESH
opposed to .... HERBIVORE
carnivorous insect .... MANTIS
reptile .... MONITOR, TUATARA, ALLIGATOR, CROCODILE
carnotite ...... MINERAL, URANIUM
carob .... POD, TREE, LOCUST, ALGAROBA
carol ...... LILT, SING, SONG, TRILL
Christmas .... NOEL
singers .... WAIT
Carol .... BURNETT, CHANNING
Caroline, diminutive of
.... CARRIE
island .... YAP, TRUK, BELAU (PALAU), POHNPEI (PONAPE)
Carolinian .... TARHEEL
carom .... RECOIL, REBOUND, RICOCHET
carotene .... VITAMIN A
common source of
.... CARROT, TOMATO
carotid .... ARTERY
and the basilar artery (medical) .... CIRCLE OF WILLIS
carousal ...... ORGY, TEAR, BINGE, SPREE, REVELRY, WASSAIL
carouse .... DRINK, FEAST, QUAFF, BOUSE, SPREE, REVEL, SWILL, TIPPLE, DEBAUCH
carousel .... MERRY-GO-ROUND, LILIOM, WHIRLIGIG
carouser .... SPONGE, REVELER
colloq. .... BARFLY, BOOZER
carp .... NAG, BLEAK, CAVIL, LOACH, TENCH, CRITICIZE
Japanese .... KOI
kin .... MINNOW
like fish .... IDE, DACE, GOLDFISH
minnow .... SHINER
red-eye .... RUDD
carpal tunnel syndrome
.... NUMBNESS, TINGLING, WEAKNESS
affected part of .... HAND, INDEX FINGER, THUMB, MIDDLE FINGERS
Carpatho-Ukraine .... RUTHENIA
carpel .... ACHENE
carpels, united .... PISTIL
carpenter .... JOINER, WRIGHT, CABINETMAKER, WOODWORKER, CONSTRUCTION WORKER
groove of .... DADO
joint of .... MITER, MORTISE
tool of ..... SAW, ADZE, BEVEL,

PLANE, CHISEL, DRILL, HAMMER, SQUARE
with six legs .... ANT
Carpenter .... KAREN, SCOTT
carpet .... MAT, RUG, COVER, TAPIS, COVERING, FOOTCLOTH, FLOOR, TAPETE, FLOORING
Afghan .... HERAT
call on the ..... REBUKE, CHEW OUT, REPRIMAND
city .... AGRA, TOURNAI
English .... WILTON
holder .... HOOK, TACK
India .... AGRA, DRUGGET
kind of .... WALL-TO-WALL, DRUGGET, MOQUETTE, ORIENTAL, HOOKED, WELCOME
material .... MOHAIR, MOQUETTE, CHENILLE, BEARSKIN, DRUGGET, SYNTHETIC FIBER
Persian .... KALI
roll out the red .... BID WELCOME, DO THE HONORS, WELCOME WITH OPEN ARMS
carpetbagger .... CON-MAN, CON-ARTIST, POLITICIAN, SLICKER, PROMOTER, SHARPIE, ADVENTURER
carping .... CAPTIOUS, CRITICAL
carport .... GARAGE
carpus .... WRIST
bone .... CARPAL(E)
carrack .... VESSEL, GALLEON
carrageen .... IRISH-MOSS, SEAWEED
carreta .... CART
carriage ...... AIR, GIG, RIG, SHAY, CARIOLE, POISE, BEARING, CHAISE, SULKY, VOITURE, MIEN, PORTANCE, CONVEYANCE, CART, CONDUCT, BEHAVIOR, EQUIPAGE, ROCKAWAY, WAGON, STANHOPE
attendant .... FLUNKEY, OUTRIDER, OUTRUNNER
baby .... GO-CART, PRAM, BUGGY, CLARENCE, PERAMBULATOR
berlin(e) .... BAROUCHE
closed .... COUPE
dog .... DALMATIAN
driver .... HACK(MAN), COACHMAN
driver's seat .... DICK(E)Y
folding top .... CALASH, CALECHE, PHAETON
for hire .... HACK, FIACRE, HANSOM, RICKSHAW

for state occasions
.... CAROCHE
four-wheeled .... CHAISE, BERLIN(E), PHAETON, CLARENCE, DEARBORN, BUCKBOARD, BAROUCHE, LANDAU, TARANTAS, VICTORIA
French .... FIACRE
hackney .... FLY
hood/top .... CAPOTE
horse-drawn .... SURREY
horseless .... CAR, AUTO(MOBILE)
Java .... SADO
low-wheeled .... CALASH, TARANTAS
luggage space .... RUMBLE
man-drawn .... JINRIKSHA, RICKSHA(W)
one-horse .... SHAY, TRAP, CHAISE, CALESIN, CARIOLE, CARRYALL
Philippine .... CALESA, CARETELA, CARROMATA, CALESIN, TARTANILLA
pole .... SHAFT, THILL
Russian .... TROIKA, TARANTAS(S)
seat .... RUMBLE
servant's seat in .... DICKEY, RUMBLE
single-seat .... STANHOPE
two-wheeled ..... SULKY, TRAP, CALECHE, CURRICLE, CARETELA, CALESA, CALASH, CHAISE, HERDIC, TILBURY
with collapsible top
...... CHAISE, CALASH, BRITSKA, CALECHE
with liveried attendants
.... EQUIPAGE
carried .... TOTED, BORNE, SWAYED, TRANSPORTED
a message .... CONVEYED
a motion .... ADOPTED
away .... RAPT, ENGROSSED, OVERWHELMED
something heavy ...... LUGGED
carrier .... TOTER, BEARER, TRANSPORTER, MESSENGER
air .... AIRPLANE
armor .... SQUIRE, ARMIGER
bad luck .... JINX
bird .... HOMING PIGEON
coal/brick/mortar .... HOD, CORF
common .... SHIP, AIRLINER, SUBWAY, TRAIN, STREETCAR, TAXI, MASS-TRANSIT, OCEANLINER
in a depot/airport ...... PORTER

in a railway station
.... REDCAP
in a port/pier .... STEVEDORE
of disease virus .... VECTOR
of God's message ..... ANGEL,
CLERIC, PREACHER
of mail .... POSTMAN
Oriental .... HAMAL
Spanish .... CARGADOR
water .... BHEESTY, BHEESTIE
carrion ...... FILTHY, DECOMPOSE,
ROTTEN, DECAYING
crow .... VULTURE
Carroll (Lewis) forte .... PARODY
heroine .... ALICE
carron oil .... LINIMENT
carrot .... (EDIBLE) ROOT,
VEGETABLE
color .... YELLOW, ORANGE-
RED
family .... PARSLEY
first cultivated in
.... AFGHANISTAN
like-plant .... PARSNIP
nutritive substance of
.... CAROTENE
oil tube .... VITTA
wild .... QUEEN ANNE'S LACE
carroty .... CRECY, ORANGE, RED-
HAIRED
carrousel. See carousel
carry ...... LUG, WIN, BEAR, LEAD,
TOTE, SWAY, FETCH, CONVEY,
CART, SUSTAIN, TRANSMIT,
TRANSPORT, UPHOLD
across water .... FERRY
away .... RAVE, EXCITE
off .... ABDUCT, KIDNAP,
STEAL, SWIPE
on .... NAG, RANT, WAGE,
URGE, FOLLOW, PURSUE,
CONDUCT, CONTINUE
on person .... WEAR
out ...... OBEY, STAGE, EFFECT,
EXECUTE, ACCOMPLISH
out a promise .... FULFILL
over .... POSTPONE
partner of .... CASH
too far .... AMPLIFY, MAGNIFY,
OVERDO, OVERKILL
weight .... COUNT
carryall .... (TOTE) BAG, BASKET,
CARRIAGE
kind of .... BUS
carrying away .... EFFERENT
unborn child .... ENCEINTE,
PREGNANT
Carson .... KIT, JOHNNY
City is capital of ...... NEVADA
cart .... VAN, BOGY, DRAY,
LORRY, HAUL, CARRY,

CARIOLE, WAIN, WAGON,
TRUNDLE
ammunition .... CAISSON,
TUMBREL, TUMBRIL
hand .... PRAM, DOLLY
low, heavy .... DRAY
pullers .... OXEN
racing .... CHARIOT
two-wheeled .... SULKY
carte .... CARD, MENU, BILL OF
FARE, QUART(E)
blanche of a sort .... BLANK
CHECK
cartel .... POOL, COMBINE, UNION,
AGREEMENT, MONOPOLY
of a sort .... TRUST,
SYNDICATE
Carter Dickson pseudonym
.... CARR
Carthage, capital of .... CARALIS
destroyer of .... ROMANS,
SCIPIO
foe of .... CATO
founder of .... DIDO
god of .... MOLOCH
goddess .... TANIT
of .... PUNIC
queen of .... DIDO
Roman idea of ..... FAITHLESS,
TREACHEROUS
wars of .... PUNIC
Carthaginian conqueror
.... HANNIBAL
general .... HAMILCAR,
HANNIBAL, HASDRUBAL
Carthusian .... NUN, MONK,
EREMITE
order founder .... (SAINT)
BRUNO
cartilage .... TISSUE, GRISTLE
cell .... CHONDROCYTES
combining form ..... CHONDRO
dog tongue's .... LYTTA
gel-like substance
.... COLLAGEN
type of .... FIBRO, ELASTIC,
HYALINE
cartograph .... MAP, PLAT, CHART
cartographer .... MAPPER,
CHARTIST, MERCATOR
opus of .... ATLAS
cartographical half .... HEMI
cartography .... SURVEYING,
TOPOGRAPHY
cartoon .... COMICS, SKETCH,
DRAWING, COMIC STRIP
kind of .... EDITORIAL,
CARICATURE
slang .... FUNNIES
vocals .... BALLOONS
cartoonist .... DRAWER,

CRAYONIST, CARICATURIST,
NAST, CAPP, DISNEY,
SKETCHER, (PETER) ARNO,
(DAVID) LOW, KIRBY,
ADDAMS, SOGLOW, OLIPHANT,
SCHULTZ, TRUDEAU
cartoons .... COMICS, STRIPS
cartridge ...... CASE, SHOT, SHELL
box .... CARTOUCH(E)
container .... CLIP
kind of .... INK, FILM, TAPE
cartwheel .... HAT, HANDSPRING
slang .... COIN
caruncle .... COMB, GILL, WATTLE
Caruso, opera singer .... ENRICO
carvacrol .... ANTISEPTIC,
DISINFECTANT
carve .... CUT(UP), SLIT, INCISE,
CHISEL, SLICE, (EN)GRAVE,
FORM, SHAPE, SCULPT
carved .... GRAVEN, GLYPHIC,
FORMED, SHAPED, MODELED,
CHISELED, ENGRAVED,
ENCHASED, TAILORED
figure .... GLYPH, INTAGLIO
gem .... CAMEO
image .... BUST, STATUE
carver .... ARTIST, GRAVER,
SCULPTOR, SCULPTRESS,
STONECUTTER
carving .... MOLD, BRONZE,
SCULPTURE, SILHOUETTE
art .... GLYPTICS
in low relief .... ANAGLYPHY
stone .... CAMEO
tool .... CHISEL
Cary Grant ...... (ARCHIE) LEACH
casaba .... (MUSK)MELON
fruit-like .... CANTALOUPE
Casal's (Pablo) instrument
.... CELLO
cascade ...... FALL, LINN, SHOWER,
WATERFALL
cascara ...... WAHOO, BEARWOOD,
BUCKTHORN
case .... BOX, CASK, DEED, CRATE,
CAPSULE, CONTAINER, AFFAIR,
MATTER, EXAMPLE, INSTANCE,
LOOK OVER, CAUSE, EVENT,
QUESTION, SUIT, HANDBAG,
VALISE, ACTION, SHEATH,
SITUATION
armadillo's/turtle's
.... CARAPACE
auto tire .... SHOE
book .... FOREL
bullet .... CARTRIDGE
chalice linen .... BURSE
egg .... SHELL
for arnica .... BRUISE

for liquor bottles
.... CELLARET
fruit .... RIND
grammatical .... DATIVE,
    ABLATIVE, ACCUSATIVE,
    GENITIVE, NOMINATIVE
gun .... HOLSTER
hospital .... PATIENT
in any .... ANYHOW
in: sl. .... DIE
insect larva's .... INDUSIUM
legal .... SUIT, LITIGATION
of explosives .... PETARD
pea .... POD
portrait .... LOCKET
pupa .... COCOON
remains' .... COFFIN, CASKET
sausage .... INTESTINE
seed .... POD
ship .... HULL
slang .... LOOK OVER,
    EXAMINE
small .... ETUI, GRIP, ETWEE,
    PYXIS, CAPSULE
toiletry .... ETUI, ETWEE,
    COMPACT
trial site .... VENUE
casein preparation .... LACTARENE
synthetic fabric .... LANITAL
casemate .... ENCLOSURE
describing a .... ARMORED,
    SHELLPROOF
casement .... FRAME, WINDOW
casern .... BARRACKS
cash ...... BILLS, (READY) MONEY,
    COINS, SPECIE, CURRENCY
advance .... ARLES, IMPREST
and carry .... AS IS
box .... TILL, REGISTER
note .... VOUCHER
note of sorts .... IOU
on delivery .... COD
ready .... TILL
receipts/payments handler
.... TELLER, CASHIER
register sign .... NO SALE
cashaw .... CUSHAW, SQUASH
cashbook .... LEDGER
cashew .... MANGO, ANACARD,
    PISTACHIO
French .... (A)CAJOU
oil .... CARDOL
cashier .... PURSER, TELLER, FIRE,
    CLERK, BURSAR, DISCARD,
    DISMISS, DISCHARGE
cashmere .... WOOL, KASHMIR
cashoo .... CATECHU
Cashin, dress designer
.... BONNIE
casing .... HULL, COVER, SHELL,
    FRAME, SHEATH(ING)

casino .... CARD GAME,
    SUMMERHOUSE
cask .... KEG, TUN, VAT, BUTT,
    BARECA, BARREL, FIRKIN,
    DRUM, HOGSHEAD, PUNCHEON
bulge .... BILGE
content measurer
.... GA(U)GER
cork/stopper .... BUNG
forty-two-gallon .... TIERCE
four-gallon .... TUB
groove .... CROZE
maker .... COOPER, HOOPER
rim .... CHIMB, CHIME, CHINE
small .... RUN(D)LET
stave .... LAG
staves, set .... SHOOK
casket .... BOX, PIX, CHEST,
    COFFIN
carrier .... PALLBEARER
for sacred relics .... CIST,
    KIST, RELIQUARY
for valuables .... COFFER
Casmurro or Pedro .... DOM
Caspary (Vera) play ...... LAURA
Caspian Sea fish .... BELUGA,
    STURGEON
tributary .... KURA, URAL,
    VOLGA
casque .... HELMET
cassaba. See **casaba**
Cassandra .... SEERESS,
    PREDICTOR, PROPHETESS
descriptive of .... LIAR
parent of .... PRIAM, HECUBA
cassava ...... JUCA, ROOT, MANIOC,
    MANIHOT
product .... BREAD, STARCH,
    TAPIOCA
casserite .... TINSTONE
casserole .... STEW, RAGOUT,
    BAKING DISH, SERVING DISH
chicken/tuna .... TETRAZZINI
eggplant .... PARMIGIANA
cassete .... HOLDER, CARTRIDGE
cassia .... BARK, CINNAMON
cathartic drug .... SENNA
family .... LAUREL
cassimere .... CASHMERE, WOOLEN
    CLOTH
Cassini, designer .... OLEG
Cassiopeia's chair .... STARS,
    CONSTELLATION
daughter .... ANDROMEDA
husband .... CEPHEUS
cassis .... LIQUEUR
cassock .... SOUTANE, CLERIC,
    CLERGYMAN, VESTMENT
belt .... SURCINGLE
cassowary .... BIRD, RATITE
bird like .... EMU, RHEA,

    OSTRICH
descriptive of ...... FLIGHTLESS
cast .... FORM, HURL, MOLD, TOSS,
    PITCH, HEAVE, FOUND, THROW
a stone .... FLING, SLING
about .... LOOK, DEVISE,
    SEARCH
amorous glances .... OGLE
aside/away ..... VOID, DISCARD,
    ABANDON, DISREGARD
ballot .... VOTE
ballot, affirmative .... VOTE
    YES
ballot, negative .... VOTE NO
blame on .... REFLECT,
    DISCREDIT
down .... HURL, REJECT,
    DISOWN, DEPRESS
founded .... FUSIL(E)
horn .... MEW
in printing .... STEREOTYPE,
    ELECTROTYPE
iron .... HARD METAL, RIGID
medical .... PLASTER,
    POULTICE
metal .... PIG IRON
metal mass .... PIG, INGOT,
    BULLION
of characters .... TROUPE,
    DRAMATIS PERSONAE
off .... DUMP, SHED, SLOUGH,
    DISCARD, EXUVIATE
off a lover .... JILT
off by animal .... MOLT
out .... OUST, EJECT, EXPEL,
    EVICT
thing .... FLY, NET, BAIT, DICE,
    VOTE, ANCHOR, BALLOT
up/forth ..... VOMIT, THROW UP
with matrix .... MOLD
Castalia .... SPRING
castanea .... CHESTNUT
castaway .... WAIF, PARIAH,
    OUTCAST
a kind of ..... LEPER, OUTLAW,
    FUGITIVE
shipwreck's .... MAROON,
    DERELICT
caste .... GENS, RANK, CLASS,
    SOCIAL SYSTEM
castellan .... KEEPER, MASTER,
    CHATELAIN, CUSTODIAN,
    WARDEN, GOVERNOR
castellate .... ARM, ENTRENCH,
    FORTIFY
caster .... CRUET, STAND, BOTTLE,
    ROLLER, PITCHER, FISHERMAN,
    TRUCKLE, TRUNDLE
castigate .... DOCK, LASH,
    CORRECT, CHASTEN,
    CHASTISE, REBUKE, PUNISH,

CRITICAL: CRITICIZE
Castile .... SOAP
designating part of .... NUEVA,
VIEJA
province .... AVILA
river .... EBRO
casting mold .... DIE, MATRICE
place .... FOUNDRY
castle .... FORT, HOME, PALACE,
BASTION, FORTRESS,
MANSION, ROOK, CHESS PIECE,
STRONGHOLD
attackers' explosive
.... PETARD
court .... BAILEY
creek/ditch/defense ...... MOAT
entrance .... POSTERN
French .... CHATEAU
governor/warden
.... CASTELLAN
in the air .... BUBBLE,
DAYDREAM, ILLUSION,
REVERIE, PIE IN THE SKY
keep .... DONJON
keeper .... CASTELLAN,
CHATELAIN
lady of the .... CHATELAINE
open space .... WARD
tower .... KEEP, DONJON,
BARRICAN
underground cell .... DUNGEON
VIP .... KING, KNIGHT
wall .... BAIL(EY)
warden .... CONSTABLE
Castles' dance .... BUNNY HOP,
CASTLE WALK
castoff .... JUNK, TRASH,
GARBAGE, REFUSE, REJECT,
SHED, ORPHAN, DEADWOOD,
DISOWNED, ABANDONED
castor .... HAT, BEAN, CRUET,
BEAVER
bean protein .... RICIN
oil .... CATHARTIC, LUBRICANT,
PURGATIVE
oil plant poison .... RICIN
silk .... ERI(A)
Castor .... STAR
and Pollux ..... TWINS, GEMINI,
DIOSCURI
father of .... ZEUS
killer of .... IDAS
mother of .... LEDA
twin brother of .... POLLUX
castrate ...... GELD, SPAY, ALTER,
UNMAN, CAPONIZE, DESEX,
DISABLE, ENERVATE,
EMASCULATE, STERILIZE
slang .... FIX, DEBALL
castrated .... GIBBED, IMPOTENT
animal .... STAG, NEUTER

boar .... HOG
bull .... OX
cattle .... STEER
horse .... GELDING
male cat .... GIB
man .... EUNUCH, CASTRATO
pig .... BARROW
rooster/cock .... CAPON
sheep .... WETHER
casual .... IDLE, CHANCE,
RANDOM, PASSING, AIMLESS,
CARELESS, OFFHAND,
CURSORY, INFORMAL,
INCIDENTAL, PERFUNCTORY
slang .... HAPPY-GO-LUCKY
casualty .... VICTIM, ACCIDENT,
MISHAP, CALAMITY, DISASTER,
DEATH, INJURY, FATALITY
casuist .... QUIBBLER
alleged .... JESUIT
of a sort .... SOPHIST
casuistic .... SPECIOUS, PLAUSIBLE,
DECEPTIVE
casus .... CASE, EVENT,
HAPPENING, OCCURRENCE
belli result .... WAR
cat .... FELINE, TIGER, ANGORA,
LION, COUGAR, LEOPARD,
PUMA, CIVET, GENET(TE),
FELID, BAUDRONS, LYNX,
MALKIN, MAWKIN, OCELOT,
MARGAY, PANTHER, PUSS(Y)
brier .... SMILAX
burglar .... ROBBER
castrated male .... GIB
colloquial .... KITTY, PUSSY
domestic .... MANX
drinking way of .... LAP
epithet .... BAUDRONS
eyed animal .... LYNX
family .... FELI(DAE), FELINE
fastest .... CHEETAH
female .... QUEEN, TABBY,
GRIMALKIN
grinning, proverbial
.... CHESHIRE
like animal .... LINSANG,
GENET(TE), ZIBET(H)
mice-hunting .... MOUSER
move like a .... PUSSYFOOT
musk-yielding .... CIVET
nap .... DOZE
o-nine-tails .... WHIP
of the .... FELINE
pet .... ANGORA, MALTESE,
PERSIAN, SIAMESE
ring-tailed .... SERVAL
sound ...... MEW, MEOW, PURR,
ROAR, MIAOW, MIAUL,
CATERWAUL
spotted .... JAGUAR, OCELOT,

MARGAY, SERVAL
striped .... TIGER
young .... KITTEN
cata, as prefix ...... AWAY, DOWN,
AGAINST, THROUGH,
BACKWARD
catachresis, victim of .... (MRS.)
MALAPROP
cataclysm ...... DELUGE, DEBACLE,
DISASTER, UPHEAVAL, HAVOC,
CATASTROPHE
kind of .... WAR, FLOOD,
EARTHQUAKE
catacomb .... CRYPT, TOMB,
VAULT, LOCULUS, CEMETERY
catafalque .... BIER
catalase .... ENZYME
catalo .... BISON, BOVINE,
BUFFALO
catalogue ...... LIST, INDEX, BOOK,
ROLL, RECORD, CLASSIFY,
ARRANGE, REGISTER,
SCHEDULE
bookseller's ...... BIBLIOTHECA
box .... CARD FILE
of goods, etc. .... STOCK,
INVENTORY
of saints .... HAGIOLOGY
official .... CANON
Catalonian poet-musician
.... TROUBADOR
catalyst .... URGER, INCITER,
REAGENT, ACTIVATOR,
PROVOKER, CAUSER,
INSTIGATOR
catamaran .... BOAT, RAFT,
BALSA, FLOAT
catamenia .... MENSTRUATION
catamite .... PUNK
catamount .... LYNX, PUMA,
COUGAR
cataplasm .... POULTICE
catapult ...... FIRE, HURL, HURTLE,
LAUNCH, BRICOLE, TAKEOFF,
BALLISTA, ONAGER,
TREBUCHET
kin of .... MANGONEL
projectile .... PELLET
cataract .... LINN, FALLS, DELUGE,
CASCADE, DOWNPOUR,
WATERFALL, EYE DISEASE
catarrh .... COLD, RHEUM
cigarette for .... CUBEB
nasal .... CORYZA
catastasis .... EXORDIUM
catastrophe ...... RUIN, ACCIDENT,
CALAMITY, DISASTER,
DOWNFALL, ADVERSITY,
PERDITION, UPHEAVAL,
MISFORTUNE
in geology .... CATACLYSM

in health .... PAROXYSM
Catawba .... WINE, GRAPE, INDIAN
catch .... NAB, GRAB, HOOK, NAIL,
   TAKE, (EN)TRAP, SEIZE,
   CAPTURE, RATCHET
at straws .... HOPE FOR THE
   BEST
breath .... GASP, PANT
fish .... HAUL, SEINE
in a bill .... JOKER, RIDER
in a ship .... TRIP
of clock .... DETENT
on ..... CLICK, FOLLOW, GET IT,
   GET THE PICTURE, REALIZE,
   UNDERSTAND
phrase .... MOTTO, SLOGAN,
   WARCRY
releaser .... PAWL, DETENT,
   TRIPPER
sight of .... ESPY, SPOT,
   DESCRY, DETECT, DISCERN
slang .... COLLAR
taken in a robbery ..... BOOTY
the eye .... GLARE, APPEAR,
   MEET THE GAZE
up .... GAIN ON, OVERHAUL,
   OVERTAKE
with the _____ .... GOODS
Catch 22 author .... HELLER
catchall .... BASKET, (RAG)BAG,
   HANDBAG, ET AL,
   ETC (ETERA)
one kind of .... ATTIC,
   CLOSET, GARAGE
catcher .... TAKER, CAPTOR,
   NABBER, ATHLETE, BASEMAN
catching .... TAKING, FETCHING,
   ALLURING, ATTRACTIVE,
   INFECTIVE, INFECTIOUS,
   VIRULENT, CONTAGIOUS
catchment, kind of ...... CISTERN,
   RESERVOIR
catchpenny .... CHEAP,
   WORTHLESS
catchpole .... TAX-GATHERER,
   CHICKEN-CHASER
catchup .... CATSUP, KETCHUP
catchword .... CUE, KEY, CLUE,
   HINT, MOTTO, PHRASE,
   SLOGAN
catchy .... FITFUL, TRICKY,
   DECEPTIVE, DECEIVING,
   ERRATIC, MISLEADING
slang .... FISHY
cate .... DAINTY, DELICACY
catechism .... GUIDE, MANUAL,
   HANDBOOK
catechize .... TEACH
catechu .... CUTCH, CASHOO,
   GAMBLER
like gum .... KINO

catechumen ...... PUPIL, STUDENT,
   CONVERT, NEOPHYTE
categorical .... DIRECT, ABSOLUTE,
   EXPLICIT, POSITIVE
categorize .... SORT, LABEL,
   TITLE, COLLATE, CLASSIFY
category .... CLASS, GRADE,
   GENRE, GROUP, ORDER,
   FAMILY, GENUS, SPECIES,
   DIVISION
catena .... SERIES, CHAIN
catenate .... LINK
cater .... SELL, SERVE, SUPPLY,
   FEED, PANDER, PURVEY,
   PROVIDE
to one's whim or mood
   .... HUMOR, INDULGE
cateran .... ROBBER
catercornered .... CROSSWISE,
   DIAGONAL(LY)
caterer .... PURVEYOR, SUPPLIER
army .... SUTLER
kind of .... PIMP, PANDERER,
   PROCURER
caterpillar .... WERI, SLUG,
   LARVA, LOOPER, CUTWORM,
   WOOBUT, WEBWORM,
   WOOLLYBEAR
disease .... WILT
hair .... SETA
Caterpillar treaded vehicle
   .... TANK, CAT, AMTRAC,
   HALF-TRACK, TRACTOR
caterwaul .... HOWL, WAIL,
   MIAUL, SCREAM, SCREECH
catface .... SCAR
catfish .... SHAL, DORAD,
   DOCMAC, BULLHEAD,
   BULLPOUT, TANDAN, SCULPIN,
   SILURID
electric .... RAAD
Catfish Row resident .... BESS,
   PORGY
catgut ...... STRING, VIOLIN, CORD,
   CATLING, WHIPCORD
catharsis ...... PURGING, RELEASE,
   CLEANSING
cathartic .... ALOE, ALOIN,
   CASSIA, PHYSIC, CALOMEL,
   GAMBOGS, EMETIC, LAXATIVE,
   EVACUANT, CASTOR OIL,
   APERIENT, PURGATIVE,
   HEALING, PURGING, REMEDIAL
drug .... SENNA
from flax .... LININ
resin .... SCAMMONY
Cathay .... CHINA
cathedra .... SEE, THRONE
cathedral .... CHURCH, DUOMO,
   TEMPLE, MINSTER, BASILICA,
   OFFICIAL, AUTHORITATIVE

city .... ELY, AMIENS,
   CHARTRES, R(H)EIMS
clergyman .... CANON
famous .... NOTRE DAME
passage .... SLYPE
presiding official .... DEAN
private land of .... CLOSE
Cather, novelist .... WILLA,
   SIBERT
Catherine, mother of 3 kings
   .... MEDICI
the Great .... TSARINA
the Great's favorite
   .... POTEMKIN
Catholic .... GENERAL, LIBERAL,
   TOLERANT, UNIVERSAL
lay society .... SODALITY
tribunal .... ROTA
tribunal member ...... AUDITOR
catholicon ...... ELIXIR, CURE-ALL,
   PANACEA
cation .... ION
catkin .... CHAT, PUSSY,
   AMENT(A), CATTAIL
tree .... BIRCH, POPLAR,
   WILLOW
catlike .... SLY, FURTIVE,
   NOISELESS, STEALTHY
animal .... LINSANG
catling .... KNIFE, CATGUT
catnap .... DOZE
catnip .... NEP
catouse .... UPROAR
cats and dogs, sometimes
   .... ENEMIES
Cats classic .... MEMORIES
cat's eye .... GEM, QUARTZ,
   CHATOYANT, CHRYSOBERYL
paw .... PAD, DUPE, KNOT,
   PAWN, TOOL, STOOGE
whisker(s) .... VIBRISSA(E)
Catt, American suffragist
   .... CARRIE
cattail .... DODD, TULE,
   (BUL)RUSH, CATKIN, RAUPO,
   REED(MACE)
cattiness .... SPITE, ENMITY,
   MEANNESS, VENDETTA
cattle .... KINE, NOWT, OXEN,
   BOVID, BOVINE, LIVESTOCK
beef .... STEER, HOLSTEIN
black .... ANGUS, KERRY,
   WELSH
boat .... TARTAN
breed .... ANGUS, DEVON,
   DEXTER, DURHAM, GALLOWAY,
   SUSSEX, BRAHMAN, HEREFORD,
   JERSEY, HOLSTEIN, LONGHORN
castrated male .... STEER
catcher .... HAYWARD
catching rope .... BOLA

crossed with bison/buffalo .... CAT(T)ALO
dairy .... JERSEY, KERRY, GUERNSEY, HEREFORD
dealer .... DROVER
dewlap .... JOWL
disease .... GID, BOTS, GARGET, NAGANA, ANTHRAX, LOCO, MEASLES, MURRAIN, LUMPY-JAW, TEXAS-FEVER, SCOURS, SHAKES, STAGGERS
dwarf .... DEVON, NIATA
dysentery .... SCOURS
enclosure .... KRAAL, RODEO, CORRAL
epidemic .... RINDERPEST
farm .... RANCH, ESTANCIA
farm manager .... RANCHER
fat .... SUET, TALLOW
feed for hire .... GIST
feed from linseed .... OIL CAKE
female that has given birth .... COW
female under 24 months of age .... HEIFER
fodder .... FARRAGO
foot of .... HOOF
frenzied run .... STAMPEDE
grazing land .... RANGE, PASTURE
group .... HERD, DROVE
hedge .... OXER
herdsman .... VAQUERO
hybrid .... CAT(T)ALO
male .... BULL
nervous ailment .... STAGGERS
parasite .... TICK
parasitic larva .... WARBLE
pen .... YARD, KRAAL, CORRAL
plague (same as epidemic)
polled .... MUL(L)EY
ranch man .... COWBOY, VAQUERO
raiser .... RANCHER, STOCKMAN
round-up .... RODEO, WRANGLE
short-horned .... DURHAM
stall .... CRIB
stealer/thief .... RUSTLER
stealing .... RUSTLING
tender .... COWHEAD, VAQUERO
tormentor .... GNAT
urine .... STALE
vertigo .... MEGRIM
cattleman ...... DROVER, HERDER, RANCHER, STOCKMAN
catty ...... MEAN, BITCHY, FELINE, PETTISH, MALICIOUS, SHREWISH, SPITEFUL
person .... VERMIN
catwalk .... BRIDGE, PATHWAY,

PLATFORM
Caucasian .... ARYAN, TATAR, IRANIAN, WHITE MAN
carpet/rug .... BAKU, KUBA
Central .... OSSET
goat .... TUR
language .... GEORGIAN, SEMITIC, CIRCASSIAN
race .... SEMITE
Caucasus inhabitant .... OSSET(IAN)
region .... OSSETIA
river .... KUBAN
wild goat .... TUR
caucho tree .... ULE
caucus .... CONFAB, MEETING
room, descriptive of a .... SMOKY, SMOKE-FILLED
caudad, opposed to .... CEPHALAD
caudal appendage .... TAIL
caudillo .... LEADER, DICTATOR, COMMANDER
Caudillo, El .... FRANCO
caudle .... DRINK, GRUEL
caught .... RAPT, STUCK, SEIZED
by the police .... ARRESTED
short ...... HURRIED, SURPRISED
up in .... AMID, TANGLED
with the _____ .... GOODS
caul .... VEIL
cauld .... COLD
cauldron .... POT, VAT, BOILER, COPPER, KETTLE
caulicle .... STEM
cauliflower .... VEGETABLE
crossed with broccoli .... BROCCOFLOWER
ear ..... DEFORMITY, DEFORMED
eared one/row character .... PUG, BOXER, PUGILIST
variety .... CABBAGE, BROCCOLI
caulis .... STEM, STALK
caulk .... SEAL, BLOCK, CHINK, CHINSE, STOP UP
caulking material .... TAR, OAKUM
causal connective .... FOR, AFTER, SINCE, BECAUSE, THEREFORE
cause .... MAKE, BASE, BASIS, EFFECT, GROUND, MOTIVE, INDUCE, ORIGIN, REASON, OCCASION, MOVEMENT
bad luck .... HEX, JINK
celebre, usual .... CASE, TRIAL, SCANDAL
destruction of cells .... LYSE
for divorce .... GROUND(S)
for war .... CASUS BELLI

in law .... (LAW)SUIT
impelling .... MAINSPRING
of Archimedes' cry, "Eureka!" .... IDEA
spasm .... CONVULSE
to arch .... ROACH
to continue .... PERPETUATE
to do unwillingly .... PRESS, COERCE
to endure .... TOUGHEN
to fight .... EMBROIL
to grow .... REAR
to happen .... BRING, EFFECTUATE
to happen suddenly .... PRECIPITATE
to remember .... REMIND
wonderment .... AWE
causerie ...... CHAT, TALK, PLEAD, APERCU, DEBATE, PARLEY, DISCOURSE, DISCUSSION
causes or origins, science of .... (A)ETIOLOGY
causeuse .... SOFA, TETE-A-TETE
causeway .... ROAD, CAUSEY, HIGHWAY, PASSAGE
causing abortion .... ECBOLIC
disaster .... MALEFIC
little or no pain ..... INDOLENT
sneezing .... ERRHINE
caustic .... LIME, TART, BITING, HOSTILE, CUTTING, CORROSIVE, MORDANT, SNAPPISH, MORDACIOUS, SEVERE, SARCASTIC, SARDONIC, SHARP, STINGING, VITRIOLIC
agent ..... LYE, ACID, ERODENT
of wit .... IRONIC
soda .... SODIUM HYDROXIDE
solution .... LYE
substance, burn with .... CAUTERIZE
temper .... CROSS, TESTY, ORNERY, SNAPPISH
cauterant .... ACID, MOXA, BURNER, CAUTERY
cauterize ...... BURN, CHAR, SEAR, SCORCH, OXIDIZE
cauterizing agent .... MOXA
chemical to destroy warts .... SILVER NITRATE
caution .... BAIL, CARE, ALERT, TIP-OFF, WARN(ING), PRUDENCE, ADVICE, ADMONISH, ADMONITION
cautious .... WARE, WARY, ALERT, CHARY, CAREFUL, GUARDED, MINDFUL, PRUDENT, CIRCUMSPECT
general .... FABIUS

cavalcade ...... PARADE, PAGEANT, CARAVAN, PROCESSION
cavalier .... GAY, PROUD, ESCORT, KNIGHT, GENTLEMAN, HORSEMAN, GALLANT, ARROGANT, HAUGHTY
cavalla .... CERO, FISH, HORES, CARANGOID
cavalry .... HORSE, TROOPS, HORSEMEN, HORSE SOLDIERS, HUSSARS, DRAGOONS
attack obstacle/hazard .... CALTRAP, CALTROP
bugle call .... BOOTS AND SADDLES
command .... TO HORSE, CHARGE, DISMOUNT
commander .... HIPPARCH
flag .... CORNET
horse .... WALER, TROOPER
soldier .... LANCE(R), SPAHI
standard .... LABARUM
sword .... SABER
unit .... SQUADRON
cavalryman .... RIDER, DRAGOON, LANCER, TROOP(ER)
Algerian ..... SPAHI, CAMELEER
French .... CARABINEER, CHASSEUR, CARABINIER
German .... U(H)LAN
Hungarian/Croatian .... HUSSAR
mount of Algerian ..... CAMEL
Russian .... COSSACK
Turkish .... SPAHI, SPAHEE
weapon of .... LANCE, SABER
cavatina .... SONG, MELODY
cave .... DEN, LAIR, ANTRE, PIT, GROTTO, ANTRUM, HOLE, HOLLOW, RECESS
at a volcano's mouth .... CRATER
dweller .... BAT, BEAR, LION, TROLL, HERMIT, TROGLODYTE
dwelling .... SPEL(A)EAN
explorer .... SPELUNKER
for shelter/refuge ..... BURROW
formation .... STALACTITE, STALAGMITE
in .... SINK, STOVE, YIELD, SUBMIT, COLLAPSE
man ..... HERMIT, TROGLODYTE
man-made .... CRYPT
man's time .... STONE AGE
of a .... SPELEAN
poetic .... GROT, ANTRE
caveat ...... WRIT, NOTICE, ADVICE, CAUTION, WARNING, GUIDANCE, ADMONITION
Cavell, nurse .... EDITH
cavern .... LAIR, ANTRE, GROT(TO)

Hebrides Island ...... FINGAL'S CAVE
caves, inhabiting .... SPELEAN
researcher of .... SPELEOLOGIST
science of .... SPELEOLOGY
caviar .... ROE, RELISH
connoisseur .... GOURMET, RUSSIAN, GOURMAND
fish .... STERLET, STURGEON
material ...... ROE, (FISH) EGGS
source of .... SALMON, SHAD, STERLET, STURGEON
cavil .... CARP, BICKER, DIFFER, OBJECT, PROTEST, QUIBBLE, DISAGREE
cavities, full of .... CAVERNOUS
cavity .... PIT, CELL, HOLE, FOSSA, ANTRUM, HOLLOW, DENT, POCKET, OPENING
animal tissue .... LOCULUS
cause of dental .... PLAQUE
combining form .... C(O)ELE
crystal-lined .... GEODIC
crystal-lined rock .... VOOG, VUGG, VUGH, GEODE
dental .... CARIES, TOOTH DECAY
embryonic .... COELOM(E)
eye .... ORBIT
for excretion or secretion .... FOLLICLE
heart .... ATRIUM
honeycomb .... CELL, ALVEOLUS
in anatomy ..... BURSA, FOSSA, SINUS, ANTRUM, LACUNA, ALVEOLUS
in biology .... LACUNA
in zoology .... CLOACA, ALVEOLUS
membrane .... VESICLE
nose/nasal ...... SINUS, ATRIUM
of abdominal .... COELIAC
on the cheek or chin .... DIMPLE
outlet .... ORIFICE
plant tissue .... LOCULUS
cavort .... LEAP, ROMP, SKIP, CAPER, FROLIC, PRANCE
cavy .... PACA, RODENT, CAPYBARA, GUINEA PIG
caw sounder .... CROW, RAVEN
Cawdor castle site .... NAIRN
cay .... KEY, (CORAL) REEF, (SAND) BANK
cayene .... CANARY, PEPPER, CHILIES, CAPSICUM
cayman .... YAKI, ALLIGATOR
cayuse .... PONY
cowpoke's .... HOSS

Ceara .... FORTALEZA
cease .... END, HALT, STOP, DESIST, REFRAIN, DISCONTINUE
-fire .... TRUCE
nautical .... AVAST
prematurely .... ABORT
ceased to be .... DIED, EXPIRED
ceaseless .... ENDLESS, INCESSANT, ETERNAL, CONTINUAL, CONTINUOUS, CONSTANT, PERENNIAL, PERSISTENT
Cechy .... BOHEMIA
Cecrops ...... KING, MAN-DRAGON
daughter of .... HERSE
cecum .... POUCH, CHAMBER
cedar .... WOOD, THUJA, DEODAR, SAVIN(E), TOONA, CONIFER, JUNIPER
Himalayan .... DEODAR
cedarbird .... WAXWING
cede .... GRANT, YIELD, ASSIGN, SURRENDER, SUBMIT, TRANSFER, HAND OVER, RELINQUISH
Cedric .... (WAR)CHIEF
ward of .... ROWENA
cedula .... PERMIT, CERTIFICATE
ceiba fibers .... KAPOK, SILK-COTTON
ceil .... LINE, COVER
ceiling ...... ROOF, COVER, CANOPY
arched .... VAULT
decorated .... PLAFOND
division .... TRAVE
hit the: colloq. .... RAGE, RAVE, ERUPT, BLUSTER
mine .... ASTEL
of sunken panels .... LACUNAR
of the universe .... SKY
picture .... MURAL
plasterwork .... PARGET(ING)
rounded .... DOME, CUPOLA
section .... PANEL
sketcher .... MICHELANGELO
Celaeno .... HARPY
celandine .... PILEWORT
celanese .... RAYON
Celebes .... SULAWESI
city .... MACASSAR
ox .... ANOA
celebrant at mass .... PRIEST
celebrate ...... FETE, HALLOW, DO HONOR TO, OBSERVE, SOLEMNIZE, KEEP, SIGNALIZE, COMMEMORATE
in song .... CAROL
celebrated .... NOTED, FAMOUS, FESTIVE, EMINENT, RENOWNED, OBSERVED, SOLEMNIZED

archaic .... NOTORIOUS
celebration .... RITE, FANFARE,
FETE, FESTIVITY, REJOICING
campus .... HOMECOMING
gala .... FIESTA
kind of .... CORONATION,
HOLIDAY, INAUGURATION
with much drinking
.... WASSAIL, CAROUSAL
celebrities' meeting place
.... SALON
celebrity .... FAME, HERO, IDOL,
VIP, LION, STAR, RENOWN,
BIG NAME, NOTABLE,
EMINENCE
treat like a .... LIONIZE
celerity .... HASTE, SPEED, HURRY,
DISPATCH, QUICKNESS,
SWIFTNESS
celery .... PLANT, SMALLAGE,
VEGETABLE
like plant .... UDO
celesta for example
.... IDIOPHONE
celeste .... BLUE, AZURE
Celeste, actress .... HOLM
celestial .... HOLY, DIVINE,
ETHEREAL, HEAVENLY,
URANIC, OLYMPIAN,
SUPERNAL
being .... ANGEL, CHERUB,
SERAPH
body .... SUN, STAR, MOON,
COMET, PLANET
circle .... HALO, COLURE
empire .... CHINA
group .... SOLAR SYSTEM
happiness ...... BLISS, ECSTASY
phenomenon .... COMET,
ECLIPSE, RAINBOW
slang .... CHINAMAN
vault .... EMPYREAN
celibacy .... CHASTITY,
SINGLENESS, BACHELORHOOD,
MISOGAMY, SPINSTERHOOD
celibate .... CHASTE, VIRGIN,
SINGLE, BACHELOR, SPINSTER,
UNMARRIED
former .... BENEDICT
one kind of .... MONK, OLD
MAID, PRIEST
cell .... EGG, GERM, OVUM, CADRE,
PROTOPLASM
cavity .... VACUOLE
center .... NUCLEUS
combining form .... CYTE,
CYTO
destruction .... CYTOLYSIS
division ...... MEIOSIS, MITOSIS,
SPIREME
fluid material ...... CYTOPLASM

formation .... CYTOGENESIS
formed by two gametes
.... ZYGOTE
framework .... STROMA
honeycomb .... ALVEOLUS
monks' .... MONASTERY
nerve .... NEURON(E)
network .... CYTOSKELETON
nucleus .... MESOPLAST
nuns' .... CONVENT
occupant .... INMATE
occurrence ...... FERTILIZATION
of animals/birds .... CAGE
of convicts .... JAIL, PRISON
regulators .... ENZYMES
small .... CELLULE, PAPILLA
stinging .... NEMATOCYST
study of the .... CYTOLOGY
vesicle .... LYSOSOME,
PEROXISOME
wall .... PARIES
wall rib .... RAPHE
with electric charge
.... BATTERY
cella .... NAOS, TEMPLE
cellar .... PANTRY, STOREROOM,
WINE-STOCK
location of .... BASEMENT
man in charge of ...... BUTLER
room .... VAULT
wine .... VAULT, BUTTERY
celled structure .... PRISON,
CONVENT, HONEYCOMB,
MONASTERY
cells, change in .... CATAPLASIA
consisting of .... LOCULAR,
CELLULAR
form into .... CELLULATE
mass of/ovum-formed mass
of .... MORULA
the gray .... BRAIN
union of .... ZYGOSIS
water-conducting
.... TRACHEID
cellular .... LOCULAR, ALVEOLATE
celluloid: colloq. .... MOVIES,
(MOVIE) FILM
cellulose fiber/fabric ...... RAYON,
CELANESE
wrapping material
.... CELLOPHANE
Celt .... GAEL, SCOT, IRISH,
WELSH, BRETON, CHISEL
Celtic .... ERSE, IRISH
chief's heir .... TANIST
dart .... COLP
god .... LER, AENGUS
island of paradise .... AVALON
judge/priest .... DRUID
king .... BELI
language .... MANX, WELSH,

BRETON, CYMRIC
lord .... TANIST
people of Wales .... CYMRIC
religious order .... DRUID
sea god .... LER
sea robber .... FOMOR
cement ...... JOIN, GROUT, MASTIC,
ADHESIVE, MALTHA, SOLDER
ingredient .... CLAY, LIME,
WATER
like substance .... GLUE,
PASTE, MUCILAGE
material .... MARL
mixture .... PUTTY, MORTAR,
SLURRY
patch with .... SLUSH
pipe joints/sealing .... LUTE
smoothing tool .... TROWEL
wall .... STUCCO
cemetery ...... GRAVEYARD, GOD'S
ACRE, BONEYARD, ACROPOLIS,
NECROPOLIS
underground .... CATACOMB(S)
cenobite .... MONK, ESSENE,
RECLUSE
dwelling .... CONVENT,
MONASTERY
opposed to .... ANCHORITE
cenotaph .... TOMB, MONUMENT
cense .... THURIFY
censer .... THURIBLE
censor .... CUT, CRITIC, KILL,
REVIEWER, STIFLE, (S)QUASH,
WATCHDOG, RED PENCIL,
FAULTFINDER
kind of .... EDITOR
tool of movie .... SCISSORS
censorious .... CRITICAL
censorship of movie scenes
.... CUTS
speech .... GAG
censure .... RAP, LASH, TASK,
BLAME, ASPERSE, IMPEACH,
DECRY, CRITICISM, CRITICIZE,
CHIDE, REPROVE, UPBRAID,
CONDEMN(ATION), OBLOQUY
census .... COUNT
literally .... HEAD COUNTING,
NOSE COUNTING
taker .... ENUMERATOR
cent .... COIN, PENNY, COPPER
five .... NICKEL
one hundred of them
.... DOLLAR
one tenth of .... MILL
per .... HUNDRED
ten of them .... DIME
twenty-five of them
.... QUARTER
centaur .... CHIRON, NESSUS,
SAGITTARY

father of .... IXION
killed by Hercules ..... NESSUS
centavo .... COIN
centenary .... CENTURY
center .... HUB, MID, CORE,
HEART, FOCUS, LOCUS,
NUCLEUS, PIVOT, MIDDLE
at, in or near .... CENTRIC
farthest from .... DISTAL
having common
.... CONCENTRIC
line .... AXIS
line of verse .... CESURA
moving from .... CENTRIFUGAL
moving toward
.... CENTRIPETAL
nearest the .... PROXIMAL
non-revolving ..... DEAD POINT
of activity .... HUB, HIVE,
FOCUS, GANGLION
of an old-fashioned party
.... QUILT
of attention .... FOCUS,
CONFLUX, FOCAL POINT
of attraction .... CYNOSURE
of command
.... HEADQUARTERS
of energy/force ..... GANGLION
of mass .... CENTROID
of operations .... THEATER
of target ...... EYE, BULL'S-EYE
toward .... ENTAD, MESIAL
wheel's .... HUB
centerpiece .... DOILY, EPERGNE
centesimal .... HUNDREDTH
unit .... GRADE
centesimo, 100 of them .... LIRA,
PESO, BALBOA
centiare, 100 of them .... ARE
centimes, five .... SOU
100 .... FRANC
centipede .... BUG, EARWIG,
INSECT, CHILOPOD, MYRIAPOD,
ARTHROPOD
legs, front pair .... FANGS
relative .... MILLEPEDE
cento .... PATCHWORK
central .... HUB, AXIAL, MAIN,
BASIC, CHIEF, FOCAL, PRIME,
MID(DLE), PRINCIPAL
and guiding .... POLAR
figure .... HERO, STAR, VIP,
ATHLETE, HEROINE
line .... AXIS
mark of target ..... BULL'S-EYE
number .... MEDIAN
part .... CORE, NUCLEUS
point(s) .... FOCUS, FOCI,
NODE, PIVOT, ESSENCE
point of an earthquake
.... EPICENTER

Central African capital
.... BANGUI
African president ...... DACKO,
BOKASSA
American bird .... JUNCO,
CACIQUE, MANAKIN,
CURASSOW
country .... BELIZE, PANAMA,
COSTA RICA, GUATEMALA,
(EL) SALVADOR, HONDURAS,
NICARAGUA
ethnic group .... BANDA,
AZANDE, MBAKA
fiber plant .... MAGUEY,
HENEQUEN
hat/plant .... JIPIJAPA
monkey .... MARMOSET
parrot ...... MACAW, AMAZON
rodent .... PACA, AGOUTI
sash .... TOBE
stinging ant .... KELEP
tortoise .... HICATEE
tree .... EBO(E), AMATE
vulture .... URUBU, ATRATA
wildcat .... EYRA, MARGAY
centralize .... MEET, FOCUS,
UNITE, CONVERGE
centrifugal force, cause of
.... INERTIA
in physiology .... EFFERENT
centripetal, in physiology
.... AFFERENT
century .... AGE, SIECLE,
HUNDRED
plant (fiber) .... ALOE, PITA,
AGAVE, MAGUEY, TEQUILA
ceorl .... CHURL, FREEMAN
cephalad, opposed to
.... CAUDAD
cephalopod .... SQUID, MOLLUSK,
OCTOPUS, CUTTLE(FISH)
Cepheus' daughter
.... ANDROMEDA
wife .... CASSIOPEIA
ceraceous .... WAXY, WAXLIKE
Ceram .... SERANG
ceramic .... CLAY, ENAMEL
mixes .... FRITS
pigment .... SMALTINE
plaque .... TILE
roofing material .... PANTILE
ceramics, of .... FICTILE
product .... TILE, BASALT,
CLOISONNE, EARTHENWARE,
CLAYWARE, CHINAWARE,
POTTERY, PORCELAIN
ceramist .... POTTER
cerate .... WAX, SALVE, OINTMENT
ceratodus .... BARRAMUNDA
ceratin product ...... CORN, HAIR,
HORN, NAIL

ceratoid/ceratose .... HORNY
Cerberus .... DOG
concern of .... HADES
descriptive of .... THREE-
HEADED
cere .... WAX, MEMBRANE
cereal .... GRAIN, GRASS
flour .... FARINA
food ...... RICE, SAMP, HOMINY,
OATMEAL
grain .... OAT, RYE, CORN,
MAIZE, WHEAT, MILLET
grass .... OAT, RYE, WHEAT,
RAGGEE, MILLET, RAG(G)I,
RAGGY
ground .... GRITS, HOMINY
husk .... BRAN
meal .... FARINA
spike .... COB, EAR
stem .... HA(U)LM, STALK
cerebral ...... MENTAL, INTERNAL,
INTELLECTUAL
palsy .... EPILEPSY, NEURALGIA
palsy, type of .... DIPLEGIA,
HEMIPLEGIA, QUADRIPLEGIA
thrombosis .... CLOT-
FORMATION
thrombosis result ...... STROKE
vitamin, so-called .... LSD
cerebrate .... THINK, PONDER,
COGITATE
cerebrum, cortex of .... MANTLE
cerecloth ...... SHROUD, CEREMENT
ceremonial ...... FORMAL, RITUAL,
SOLEMN
bow .... CURTSY, SALAAM
dance .... PAVAN(E)
drink .... TOAST
entrance/exit signal
.... SENNET
procession .... PARADE,
CORTEGE, CAVALCADE
trumpet call .... SENNET
ceremonious ...... PRIM, FORMAL,
POMPOUS, STATELY
act .... SALUTE, SALAAM
display .... BLARE, FANFARE
leave-taking .... CONGE(E)
motion .... FLOURISH
show of homage .... KOWTOW,
SALAAM
trumpet call .... TAPS
ceremony .... POMP, RITE,
FUNCTION, RITUAL,
FORMALITY, OBSERVANCE,
PUNCTILIO
hypocritical .... MUMMERY
kind of ..... PARADE, WEDDING
military .... REVIEW
official .... OATH-TAKING,
INAUGURATION

religious .... MASS, BURIAL
Ceres .... PLANET, DEMETER,
GODDESS, ASTEROID
parent of .... OPS, SATURN
cereus .... CACTUS
Cerigo Island .... KYTHERA
cerise .... RED
cerium dioxide .... CERIA
silicate .... CERITE
cero .... CAVALLA
combining form .... WAX
fish resembling ..... MACKEREL
certain .... FIXED, SOME, SURE,
TRUE, APODITIC, POSITIVE,
RELIABLE, SPECIFIED
absolutely .... COCKSURE
armrest .... SLING
birthdays .... MILESTONE
choir voice .... ALTO,
SOPRANO
count .... POLLEN
fishermen .... EELERS
friends .... FAIR-WEATHER
word puzzles .... ACROSTICS
certainly .... SURELY, INDEED, OF
COURSE
archaic .... IWIS
certainty .... FACT, SURETY,
SHOO-IN, ASSURANCE,
GUARANTEE, CERTITUDE
certificate .... DOCUMENT,
RECORD, TESTIMONIAL
graduation .... DIPLOMA
insurance .... POLICY
money .... SCRIP
of transfer .... BILL OF SALE
price .... PAR VALUE
Spanish .... CEDULA
certification ...... OK, TESTIMONY,
ATTESTATION
certify .... DEPOSE, ASSURE,
STATE, ATTEST, TESTIFY,
NOTARIZE, AFFIRM, VOUCH,
VERIFY, DECLARE
certitude. See **certainty**
cerulean ...... AZURE, (SKY) BLUE
cerumen .... EARWAX
ceruse .... COSMETIC, WHITE LEAD
Cervantes, author .... MIGUEL
cervine .... DOE, DEER, ELK, STAG,
CERVID
Cesare, basso .... SIEPI
cespitose ...... MATTED, TURF-LIKE
cess .... TAX, ASSESSMENT
cessation ...... END, HALT, FINISH,
LET-UP, CEASING, STOP(PAGE),
SURCEASE
of activity, temporary
.... LULL, PAUSE, BREAK,
RESPITE
of hostilities .... PEACE

of war, temporary ...... TRUCE,
CEASEFIRE
cession .... CEDING, YIELDING
cessionary .... ASSIGNEE
cesspool ...... DUMP, SEWER, SUMP
cestode .... TAPEWORM
cestoid .... RIBBONLIKE
cestus .... BELT, GIRDLE
cesura .... PAUSE
cetacean .... INIA, SUSU, DOLPHIN,
GRAMPUS, WHALE, PORPOISE
Arctic .... NARWAL,
NARWHAL(E)
tusked .... NARWHAL
Cetus .... WHALE, CONSTELLATION
Ceylon .... SINHALA, SRI LANKA
Ceylon(ese) .... TAMIL,
CINGALESE, SIN(G)HALESE
aborigine ..... TODA, VEDDA(H)
ape .... MAHA
Buddhist temple site
.... KANDY
capital .... COLOMBO
city/town .... GALLE, KANDY,
JAFFNA, TRINCOMALEE
export .... TEA
fortress town .... GALLE
garment .... SARONG
grass .... CHENA, PATANA
hill dweller .... TODA
language .... PALI, INDIO,
TAMIL, TELUGU, KANARESE,
MALAYALAM
lotus .... NELUMBO
monkey .... MAHA, LANGUR,
TOQUE, WANDEROO
moss .... AGAR, GULAMAN
moss derivative .... ALEC
native .... TODA, TAMIL,
CINGALESE, DRAVIDIAN,
VEDDA(H), SIN(G)HALESE
palm .... TALIPOT
policeman .... PEON
rat .... BANDICOOT
seaport .... GALLE, JAFFNA
snake .... ANACONDA
strait .... PALK
tea .... PEKOE
trading vessel .... D(H)ONI
tree .... PALMYRA
water lily .... NELUMBO
CGS, part of .... CENTIMETER,
GRAM, SECOND
unit .... ERG, DYNE
cha .... TEA
chablis .... WINE
chabouk .... HORSEWHIP
chacma .... BABOON
Chad, capital of ...... N'DJAMENA
city/town .... KELO, PALA,
SARH, DOBA, BONGOR,

ABECHE, FIANGA, KOUMRA,
MOUNDOU
ethnic group .... SARA, MASSA,
KANEMBOU
lake .... CHAD, FITTRI
language ..... ARABIC, FRENCH,
BAGIRMI, MOUDANG
money .... FRANC
mountain .... EMI KOUSSI
mountains .... TIBESTI
plateau .... ENNEDI
president .... TOMBALBAYE
region .... KANEM, SUDAN,
WADAI, BAGUIRMI
river .... SARA, OUHAM, PENDE,
SHARI, LOGONE
chaeta .... SETA, SPINE, BRISTLE
chaetopod .... ANNELID
chafe .... IRK, RUB, GALL, RASP,
ANNOY, STING, ABRADE,
INFLAME, IRRITATE,
EXCORIATE
at the bit .... FRET
chafer .... BEETLE, SCARAB, ROSE-
BUG, FOOD-WARMER
chaff .... BRAN, HUSK, BANTER,
TEASING
like/mixed with .... ACEROSE
like bract .... PALEA
chaffer .... BANDY, HAGGLE,
HIGGLE, BARGAIN(ING)
chaffinch .... (SONG)BIRD
chaffy ...... ACEROSE, WORTHLESS
chafing .... GALLING
dish .... CRESSET
result of .... SORE, FROTH
chagrin .... VEXATION,
DISCOMFITURE,
MORTIFICATION
chain ...... IRON, CATENA, FETTER,
SERIES, SHACKLE, LINKWORK
ball and .... WIFE
decorative .... CHATELAINE
form into a .... CATENATE
mail .... BYRNIE, HAUBERK
mail, like .... ARMURE
mountain .... RANGE,
CORDILLERA
of logical reasoning
.... SORITES
of reasoning ..... CONSECUTION
part .... LINK
pulling .... TUG
smoker, for example
.... ADDICT
TV-radio .... NETWORK
chair .... SEAT, BENCH, PLACE,
CENTER, OFFICE, SETTEE,
ROCKER, POSITION
arrangement .... SEATING
back part .... SPLAT

backless ..... STOOL, OTTOMAN
bar connecting legs .... ROUND
board .... SLAT
bowlegged .... CURULE
cover .... TIDY
covered .... SEDAN
litter-like .... KAGO
making material .... SPLAT
of authority/state ...... THRONE
on elephant's back
.... HOUDAH, HOWDAH
on poles .... SEDAN
part .... ARM, LEG, RUNG,
    SEAT, ROUND, SPLAT, BOTTOM
portable .... SEDAN, LITTER,
    PALANQUIN
take the .... PRESIDE
weaver .... CANER
chairman of sorts .... MC,
    EMCEE, TOASTMASTER
chaise .... SHAY, BUGGY,
    CARRIAGE, SHANDRYDAN
longue .... CHAIR
chalaza .... TREAD
chalcedony .... ONYX, AGATE,
    CHERT, JASPER, CAT'S-EYE,
    QUARTZ, SARD(INE),
    CARNELIAN, (CHRYSO)PRASE
Chaldean .... SORCERER,
    ASTROLOGER
astronomical cycle ...... SAROS
city .... UR
chalet .... HUT, CABIN, COTTAGE
chalice .... AMA, CUP, CALIX,
    GRAIL, GOBLET
cloth .... PALL
covering .... ASTERISKOS
flower .... DAFFODIL
veil .... AER
chalk .... TALLY, CRAYON,
    CALCITE, WHITING,
    LIMESTONE
composition .... SEASHELLS
linseed oil mixture ...... PUTTY
up .... SCORE
chalkstone .... TOPHUS
chalky silicate .... TALC
challenge .... DARE, DEFY, STUMP,
    DEMAND, QUESTION, QUERY,
    DISPUTE, EXCEPTION
as false .... IMPUGN
hurled .... DEFI, GAGE
means .... SLAP
to a duel/written .... CARTEL
challenging .... DEFIANT, BOLD,
    DARING, EXCITING, BAFFLING,
    BELLICOSE
Cham .... KHAN
chamber .... CAMERA,
    (BED)ROOM, COUNCIL,
    CAMARILLA

for dead .... VAULT
judge's .... CAMERA
of a .... CAMERAL
pot .... JORDAN
underground .... VAULT
chambered creature of poetry
.... NAUTILUS
chamberlain .... STEWARD,
    TREASURER
Oriental potentate's
.... EUNUCH
chambers, legislature of two
.... BICAMERAL
chambray .... GINGHAM
chameleon .... LIZARD,
    LACERT(IL)IAN
like .... FICKLE, CHANGEABLE
like creature .... AGAMA
chamfer .... BEVEL, GROOVE,
    FLUTING
chamois .... AOUDAD, SHAMMY,
    ANTELOPE
animal like .... GORAL,
    KLIPSPRINGER
habitat .... ALPS
champ .... CHEW, MUNCH
colloquial .... CHAMPION
champagne .... WINE
bottle .... JEROBOAM
brand .... POMMERY
bucket .... ICER
capital/center .... TROYES
driest .... BRUT
for example .... FIZ(Z)
of teas, so-called
.... DARJEELING
champignon .... MUSHROOM
champion .... VICTOR, WINNER,
    DEFEND(ER), ESPOUSE,
    PALADIN, CHAMP, BACKER,
    ADVOCATE, SUPPORTER,
    SQUIRE, PROTECTOR
auto racing ...... MOSS, CLARK,
    PETTY, ALLISON, UNSER,
    ANDRETTI, EARNHARDT
boxer .... ALI, CLAY, LOUIS,
    VILLA, HARADA, ELORDE,
    DEMPSEY, GRIFFITH, TYSON,
    SPINKS, FRAZIER, PATTERSON,
    LEONARD, FOREMAN
golf .... HOGAN, SNEAD, JONES,
    PALMER, PLAYER, KITE,
    STRANGE, NICKLAUS, SANDERS,
    MILLER, TREVINO, WATSON,
    NORMAN, RODRIGUEZ,
    BALLESTEROS, CRENSHAW
heroic .... KNIGHT, PALADIN
marathon .... BIKILA
pole vault .... SEAGREN,
    BIZZARRO
soccer football .... PELE

tennis .... ASHE, HOAD, KING,
    GRAF, EVERT, TILDEN, LAVER,
    SELES, SANCHEZ, SABATINI,
    BECKER, CONNORS,
    NEWCOMBE, SAMPRAS, CASH,
    EDBERG, MCENROE, AGASSI,
    SANTANA, GONZALES,
    COURIER, GIBSON, CHANG,
    NAVRATILOVA
wrestling .... TAKTI
yacht racing .... INTREPID
1934 world heavyweight
.... BAER
1960 decathlon .... RAFER
    JOHNSON
Chan expression .... AH SO
chance .... HAP, LUCK, RISK,
    GAMBLE, HAZARD, RANDOM,
    LOT, FATE, CASUAL,
    FORTUITY, KARMA, KISMET,
    POTLUCK
betting .... ODDS
big .... OPPORTUNITY
by .... ACCIDENTAL(LY)
goddess of .... TYCHE,
    FORTUNA
on .... MEET, ENCOUNTER
to hit .... AT BAT
chancel .... SACRARIUM
part .... BEMA, RAILING
part surrounded by ..... ALTAR
screen .... JUBE
seats .... SEDILIA
chancellor .... JUDGE, MINISTER
chances ...... EDGE, ODDS, LAW OF
    AVERAGES, ADVANTAGE
chancre ...... SORE, ULCER, LESION
chandelier .... CORONA,
    ELECTROLIER, GASELIER,
    CANDELABRA
describing a .... HANGING,
    PENDULOUS, SUSPENDED
pendant .... LUSTER,
    LAVALIERE
change ...... VARY, ADAPT, ALTER,
    AMEND, MODIFY, MUTATE,
    TURN, FLUX, MUTATION,
    SHIFT, REVISION, DEVIATION
bad habits/conduct
.... REFORM
color .... FADE
course ..... HAUL, TACK, VEER,
    SWERVE
current flow .... RECTIFY
direction .... CANT, TACK,
    TURN, VEER, DEVIATE
in linguistics .... UMLAUT
in religion .... CONVERSION
into liquid .... LIQUEFY
into steel .... ACIERATE
of mind, feeling .... CAPRICE

of life .... MENOPAUSE
party .... BOLT, DEFECT
places/residence .... MOVE
policy .... TACK, DEMARCHE
secret signals .... RECODE
sentence .... COMMUTE
small .... COINS
stocks/bonds to cash
.... REDEEM
tack .... JIBE
the knot .... RETIE
to direct current .... RECTIFY
trains .... TRANSFER
wall decor .... REPANEL,
                              REPAPER
changeable .... FLUID, FICKLE,
       ADRIFT, MOBILE, ERRATIC,
           PROTEAN, MUTABLE,
            VOLATILE, ROVING,
         CAPRICIOUS, WHIMSICAL
person .... CHAMELEON
changeling .... OAF, DOLT, CHILD,
       IDIOT, TURNCOAT, DOUBLE,
           BACK-UP, STAND-IN
Changsa is capital of .... HUNAN
channel .... KILL, NECK, CHUTE,
        SHOOT, COURSE, STRAIT,
         DUCT, PASSAGE, RUNNEL,
        MEDIUM, CONDUIT, RUNWAY
artificial .... CANAL, FLUME,
               SLUICE(WAY)
between cliffs .... GAT
cutting sandbank .... SWASH
direct .... PIPELINE
entrance .... CHOPS
excess water .... SPILLWAY
fence .... WEIR
in physics .... WAVELENGTH
inland .... GAT
marker .... BUOY
narrow .... STRIA
obstruction .... WEIR
of unpredictable currents
.... EURIPUS
principal/main .... ARTERY
vertical .... GLYPH
water .... RACE(WAY)
Channel, English .... (THE)
                              SOLENT
island .... SARK, JERSEY,
       ALDERNEY, GUERNSEY
Island official .... JURAT
swimmer, English ..... EDERLE
channeled .... ROUTED, GROOVED,
    FLUTED, COURSED, FURROWED
channels .... MEDIA
5 .... SENSES
chanson .... SONG, LYRIC, BALLAD
chant .... INTONE, MELODY,
        CANTICLE, SINGSONG,
               INTONATION

poetic .... WARBLE
repetitive .... LITANY
chantage .... BLACKMAIL
chanterelle .... MUSHROOM
chanteuse .... SINGER
chantey .... (SAILOR)SONG
chanticleer .... COCK, ROOSTER
chantilly .... LACE
chantry .... ALTAR, CHAPEL
chaos .... MESS, JUMBLE,
        DISORDER, CONFUSION
Archaic .... ABYSS, CHASM
in language .... BABEL
in printing .... PI
chaotic .... VAGUE, MUDDLED,
       FORMLESS, DISORDERLY
chap ...... GUY, JAW, KIBE, BLOW,
        CHEEK, SKATE, KNOCK,
          BUGGER, ROUGHEN
colloquial .... BOY, MAN,
                            FELLOW
chapeau .... HAT, HEADGEAR
chapel .... CHURCH, TEMPLE,
        VESTRY, SANCTUARY
clergyman .... CHAPLAIN
Egyptian mortuary's
.... MASTABA(H)
medieval church .... GALILEE
private .... ORATORY
sailors' .... BETHEL
small ...... CHANTRY, ORATORY
Vatican .... SISTINE
chaperon ...... DUEN(N)A, ESCORT,
        MATRON, MONITOR,
             ACCOMPANY
strict .... DRAGON
chapfallen .... DEPRESSED,
                         HUMILIATED
chaplain .... PADRE, PRIEST,
      MINISTER, CLERGYMAN
prison .... ORDINARY
chaplet .... WREATH, GARLAND
poetic .... ANADEM
Chaplin .... CHARLIE
chapman .... DEALER, HAWKER,
     MERCHANT, TRADER, PEDDLER
chaps .... JAW, CHEEK, CHOPS,
                        CHAPAREJOS
of hound .... FLEWS
chapter .... PART, LOCAL,
       BRANCH, SECTION, EPISODE,
         POST, VERSE, DIVISION
fraternity .... LODGE
of a .... CAPITULAR
char .... SEAR, BURN(UP),
       CINDERS, TROUT, SCORCH
charabanc .... BUS
character ...... CODE, KIND, ROLE,
        CLASS, TENOR, NATURE,
        CIPHER, TRAIT, REPUTE
alphabet .... LETTERS

ancient alphabetical ..... RUNE,
                              OGHAM
assassination .... LIBEL,
                            SLANDER
element in .... ETHOS
giver .... TONER
ill-tempered .... VINEGAR
in .... APPROPRIATE
in a play .... ACTOR
musical ...... CLEF, NOTE, REST
odd .... CRANK, ECCENTRIC
of community .... ETHOS
police ..... CONVICT, CRIMINAL,
     LAW-BREAKER, MALEFACTOR
quality of .... METTLE
representing a word
.... LOGOGRAM
set .... ALPHABET
sour .... VINEGAR
strength of .... GRISTLE
characteristic .... TRAIT,
        QUALITY, DISTINCTIVE,
        TYPICAL, PECULIARITY
expression .... IDIOM
marks .... INDICIA
taste .... FLAVOR
characters, drama/play
.... PERSONAE
of slums .... DEAD-END
characterize .... MARK, DEPICT,
           DEFINE, DESCRIBE
charade .... PUZZLE, TRAVESTY,
          RIDDLE, WORD GAME,
               PANTOMIME
charcoal .... CARBON, LIGNITE,
        BLACKEN, BONEBLACK
burner .... BRAZIER
burning brazier .... HIBACHI
combining form .... CARB(O)
pencil .... FUSAIN
powdered .... POUNCE
residue .... BREEZE
use of .... FILTER
chard .... BEET, LEAFSTALK
chare .... CHORE
charge .... FEE, COST, DEBIT,
     ASSESS, IMPUTE, COMMAND,
               DASH, INSTRUCT,
     INDICT(MENT), RUSH, BLAME,
       ACCUSE, BURDEN, ATTACK,
       STRIKE, ATTRIBUTE, BLAST,
         FILL, CARE, CUSTODY
in court .... ARRAIGN
kind of .... CAVALRY
mail .... POSTAGE
on property .... TAX, LIEN
restaurant/tavern .... TIP,
          COVER, CORKAGE
road .... TOLL
school .... TUITION
solemnly .... ADJURE

to expense/loss .... DEBIT
to experience .... WRITE OFF
with crime .... INDICT
Charge of the Light _____
.... BRIGADE
charged .... TENSE, FRAUGHT
particle .... ION
water .... SODA
charger .... STEED, WARHORSE
Archaic .... PLATTER,
DESTRIER
chariot .... ESSED(E), QUADRIGA
race .... AGON
race course .... HIPPODROME
race site, ancient .... CIRCUS,
COLOSSEUM
charioteer .... WAGONER
constellation .... AURIGA
furious .... JEHU
of fiction .... BEN HUR
charisma .... AURA, GIFT, GRACE,
CHARM, APPEAL
Charisse, dancer .... CYD
charitable institution .... MISSION
charity .... ALMS, DOLE, LARGESS,
PITY, GRACE, MERCY,
BOUNTY, ALTRUISM,
KINDNESS, PHILANTHROPHY,
GENEROSITY
fair .... KERMIS, KERMESS
sale .... BAZA(A)R, RUMMAGE
charivari .... SERENADE
charlatan .... FAKER, FRAUD,
QUACK, IMPOSTOR, EMPIRIC,
PHON(E)Y, SCIOLIST,
PRETENDER
Charlemagne .... EMPEROR,
CARLO MAGNO
father of .... PEPIN (THE
SHORT)
gift to Rinaldo .... BAYARD
grandfather of .... MARTEL
knight(s) of .... PALADIN,
TWELVE, DOUZEPERS
nephew of .... ROLAND,
ORLANDO
peer .... OLIVER, ROLAND,
ORLANDO
soubriquet .... (THE) GREAT
Charles Dickens's pseudonym
.... BOZ
Charles' Wain .... AURIGA, BIG
DIPPER, URSA MAJOR
charleyhorse .... CRAMP
Charlie ...... RICH, PRIDE, BROWN
Brown expression .... RATS
charlock .... WEED, MUSTARD
charlotte .... LOTTA, LOTTY,
LOTTIE, DESSERT, PUDDING
Charlotte .... AMALIE
charm .... GRACE, SPELL,

ENAMOR, ENDEAR, ENCHANT,
HYPNOTIZE, FETISH,
FASCINATE, BEWITCH,
ATTRACT, INCANTATION
African .... OBI, JUJU, OBEAH
against evil/injury .... AMULET
bracelet disc .... BANGLE
good luck .... TALISMAN
jewel .... SCARAB
magic .... JUJU
charmer .... EXORCIST, MAGICIAN,
ENCHANTER, SORCERER
female .... SIREN
of German legend .... LORELEI
charming .... DAZZLING,
ENCHANTING, DELIGHTFUL,
WINNING, WINSOME
strangely .... ELFIN
charnel house .... TOMB,
OSSUARY
of a sort .... MORTUARY,
PANTHEON
Charon .... FERRYMAN
fee .... OBOL
river .... STYX
charpoy (charpai) .... COT,
BEDSTEAD
charqui .... BEEF
char(r) .... TROUT
chart .... MAP, PLOT, GRAPH,
LAYOUT, OUTLINE
charter ...... HIRE, GRANT, LEASE,
LET, RENT, LICENSE,
FRANCHISE
fundamental .... CONSTITUTION
package .... TOUR
Charteris (Leslie) detective
.... (THE) SAINT
forte of .... WHODUNITS
Chartres river .... EURE
chartreuse .... LIQUEUR,
YELLOWISH-GREEN
chary .... SHY, CAREFUL,
CAUTIOUS
Charybdis .... WHIRLPOOL
rock opposite/companion
.... SCYLLA
chase .... FRET, HUNT, SHAG,
DISPEL, REPEL, FOLLOW,
ENGRAVE, PURSUE, PURSUIT
after .... GET, SECURE,
RETRIEVE
continually .... HOUND
flies .... SHAG
object of .... FOX, GAME,
HARE, ESCAPEE, RAINBOW
off .... ROUT
the .... VENERY
Chase .... CHEVY
chaser .... SODA, WASH, DRINK,
CHISEL, GRAVER, HUNTER

ambulance .... SHYSTER
chasing tool ...... CHISEL, TRACER
chasm .... GAP, RIFT, ABYSS,
CLEFT, CANYON, HIATUS
in a glacier .... CREVASSE
chasseur .... HUNTER, SERVANT,
HUNTSMAN
chassis .... FRAME
slang .... BODY
chaste ...... PURE, CLEAN, SIMPLE,
DECENT, MODEST, VESTAL,
PROPER, VIRTUOUS, REFINED,
SEVERE, CELIBATE, INNOCENT
woman .... VIRGIN
chasten .... HUMBLE, PUNISH,
SUBDUE, CHASTISE
chastise .... SPANK, PUNISH,
CASTIGATE, DISCIPLINE
physically .... FLOG, WHIP
verbally .... SCOLD, BERATE
chastity .... PURITY, CELIBACY,
VIRTUE, DECENCY, VIRGINITY
vower of .... NUN, MONK,
PRIEST, VESTAL
chat .... TALK, CONVERSE,
CONVERSATION
colloquial .... CONFAB
French .... CAUSERIE
friendly .... COSE, COZE
hippie's: sl. .... RAP
of maple .... SAMARA
of plantain .... SPIKE
of willow ...... AMENT, CATKIN
slang .... BULL SESSION
chateau .... CASTLE
entrance .... PORTE
mistress of .... CHATELAINE
chatelain .... CASTELLAN
chatelaine .... PIN, ETUI, CHAIN,
CLASP, BROOCH
chatoyant .... GEM, CAT'S-EYE
chattel .... CHOSE, GOODS
Archaic .... SLAVE
chatter .... GAB, JAW, YAK, BLAB,
CLACK, PRATE, CACKLE,
BABBLE, TALK, TATTLE,
GIBBER, GOSSIP, PATTER,
BLABBER, PALAVER, PRATTLE
Aussie: colloq. .... YABBER
ceaselessly .... LALLYGAG
gossipy .... TATTLE
incoherent .... JABBER
slang .... CHIN
unintelligible .... GIBBER
chatterbox .... JAY, MAGPIE
chatterer, bird .... JAY, PIET,
MAGPIE, COTINGA, WAXWING
Chaucer pilgrim .... REEVE
poet .... GEOFFREY
songs .... CHAUNTS
title .... DAN

work .... CANTERBURY TALES
chauffer .... STOVE, HEATER
chauffeur .... DRIVER
chaussure .... BOOT, SHOE,
SLIPPER, FOOTWEAR
chauvinist .... JINGO
Chavante .... OTI
chazan .... CANTOR
cheap .... TINNY, COMMON, BASE,
MEAN, RAFFISH, PICAYUNE,
LOW, INEXPENSIVE, TWO-
PENNY
and showy .... TINHORN
but sturdy jackknife
.... BARLOW
colloquial .... BRUMMAGEN,
DIME-A-DOZEN
hotel .... RATTRAP
in Spanish .... BARATO
jewelry .... TRINKET
jewelry peddler .... DUFFER
price ...... BARGAIN, CUT-RATE,
REDUCED
race horse .... PLATER
slang .... TWO-BIT, DIRT-CHEAP
cheapest theater seats
.... GALLERY
cheapskate .... MISER, PIKER,
NIGGARD, TIGHTWAD
cheat .... FOB, FUB, GYP, BILK,
COZE, DUPE, GAFF, NICK,
MUMP, FINAGLE, FOIL, SHAM,
HUMBUG, HUSTLE, DECEIVE,
(DE)FRAUD, SWINDLE(R),
SHORT-CHANGE, WELSH(ER),
VICTIMIZE
by fraud .... FLEECE
colloquial ..... BUNCO, DIDDLE,
GOUGE, PHONY
easy to .... GULLIBLE
in schoolwork .... CRIB
slang .... CON, CLIP, MUMP,
STICK, CHISEL, FOURFLUSH
through trickery .... COZEN,
GOUGE, JUGGLE
cheated, person easily .... DUPE,
GULL, VICTIM
colloquial .... SUCKER
cheater in school .... CRIBBER
mean .... JUDAS, JACKAL
cheaters: sl. .... FALSIES,
CONTACTS, (EYE)GLASSES
chebec .... FLYCATCHER
Checchi, Signora .... DUSE
check .... CURB, REIN, DETAIN,
CONTROL, REBUFF, CHEQUE,
VERIFY, ASCERTAIN,
RESTRAIN(T), COUNTERACT
abruptly .... NIP IN THE BUD
accounts .... AUDIT
bad .... KITE, RUBBER

bleeding .... STEM, STANCH
colloquial ..... RIGHT, CORRECT
completely .... HALT, STOP
describing bad one ..... STALE,
RUBBER, BOUNCING
float a .... PREDATE
flow .... DAM, STEM, STANCH
growth/development .... NIP,
STUNT, HINDER
heads, in airplane ...... COUNT,
TALLY
in .... REPORT, REGISTER
infection by burning
.... CAUTERIZE
manuscript .... EDIT
mark .... TICK
money .... DRAFT, ORDER
-out place .... COUNTER
rain .... STUB, DEFERRAL
restaurant .... TAB, CHIT
slang .... ARREST
speed .... BRAKE
unemployment .... DOLE
up .... PROBE, VERIFY,
EXPLORE
checker .... DICE, CASHIER
Archaic .... CHESSBOARD
checkerberry .... WINTERGREEN
checkered ...... VARIED, RUBBERY,
MANY-SIDED, TATTERSALL
cloth .... PLAID, TARTAN
checkers .... GAME, DRAUGHTS
checking account .... FUNDS
block .... SPRAG
checklist .... INDEX
checkmate .... STOP, CORNER,
END, ROUT, BAFFLE, DEFEAT,
STYMIE, THWART, FRUSTRATE
checkup .... PHYSICAL, SPOT-
CHECK
Cheddar .... CHEESE
cheddite .... EXPLOSIVE
cheek .... JAW, CHAP, CHOP, GENA,
JOWL, HALF-FACE, BOLDNESS,
AUDACITY, TEMERITY
bone .... MALAR
buttocks: sl. .... TUSH
by jowl ...... CLOSE, FAMILIAR,
INTIMATE
colloquial .... GALL, BRASH,
BRASS, NERVE, IMPUDENCE,
INSOLENCE, SAUCE, SAUCINESS
gangrene .... NOMA
glow of .... BLOOM
hair growth .... SIDEBURN
hollow .... DIMPLE
muscle .... BUCCINATOR
of the .... GENAL, JUGAL,
MALAR, BUCCAL
pouch .... ALFORJA
to cheek ...... CLOSE, CHUMMY

tongue in .... INSINCERE, TWO-
FACED
cheeks and mouth .... CHOPS
cheeky: colloq. .... COCKY,
SAUCY, BRASSY
cheep .... PEEP, CHIRP
cheer .... ROOT, ELATE, SHOUT,
GAIETY, COMFORT, APPLAUD,
YELL, GLADDEN, (EN)LIVEN,
MIRTH, SOLACE, ENCOURAGE
approving .... ATTABOY
bullring .... OLE
college .... RAH, HURRAH
English .... HEAR
French .... VIVE
Italian .... VIVA, BRAVO
Japanese .... BANZAI
kind of .... BRONX
Mexican .... VIVA
Nazi .... HEIL
Philippine .... MABUHAY
Spanish .... OLE
up .... CONSOLE, COMFORT,
BRIGHTEN, (EN)LIVEN
cheerer .... FAN, ROOTER
cheerful .... GAY, HAPPY, BRIGHT,
JOLLY, LIVELY, MERRY,
CHIRPY, RIANT, SUNNY,
BLITHE
cheerfully bright .... SUNNY
cheering thing .... RAY OF
SUNSHINE
cheerio: Brit. .... HELLO,
GOODBYE
cheerless .... SAD, COLD, DRAB,
GRAY, BLEAK, DISMAL,
DREARY, JOYLESS
cheers .... TOAST
cheery ...... GAY, BRIGHT, LIVELY
cheese .... CREAM, CURDS,
MYSOST
a house of .... COTTAGE
American .... BLUE, COON,
BRICK, COLBY, CREAM,
COTTAGE, CHEDDAR,
LONGHORN, MONTEREY JACK,
NEUFCHATEL, TILLAMOOK
and pastry specialists
.... DANES
and toast dish .... RAREBIT,
WELSH-RABBIT
basis of .... CASEIN
crust .... GRATIN
Danish .... BLUE, SAMSOE
dish .... FONDUE, QUICHE,
RAREBIT, SOUFFLE, RACLETTE
dry, hard .... ROMANO
drying frame .... HACK
Dutch .... EDAM, GOUDA,
COTTAGE
English .... CHEDDAR,

STILTON, CAERPHILLY
enthusiast .... MOUSE
family .... BLUE, WHEY,
DUTCH, FRESH, SWISS,
CHEDDAR, RIPENED,
PARMESAN, PROVOLONE
French .... BRIE, MUENSTER,
CAMEMBERT, ROQUEFORT,
PETIT-SUISSE, PORT DU SALUT
from curds .... GOUDA
from milk, directly
.... NATURAL
German .... LIMBURGER
goat's/ewe's milk
.... ROQUEFORT
Greek .... FETA
Italian ...... ROMANO, FONTINA,
RICOTTA, PARMESAN, BEL-
PAESE, GORGONZOLA,
PROVOLONE, MOZZARELLA
like .... CASEOUS
main type of .... NATURAL,
PASTEURIZED
making substance ..... RENNET
Norwegian .... GJETOST,
JARLSBERG
piece of .... WEDGE
Scottish .... KEBBOCK
Sovetsk, formerly .... TILSIT
Swiss ..... COTTAGE, GRUYERE,
RACLETTE, SAPSAGO,
EMMENTHALER
tang .... NIP
texture .... MILD, SHARP
white, cured in brine .... FETA
whole milk .... DUNLOP
cheesecake: sl. .... PIN-UP
cheesy .... CASEOUS
slang .... POOR, TACKY,
CRUMMY, SHABBY, INFERIOR
cheetah .... GUEPARD, LEOPARD
chef .... (CHIEF) COOK,
CULINARIAN
Chek(h)ov, writer .... ANTON
chela .... CLAW, PINC(H)ERS
India .... NOVICE, DISCIPLE
cheloid .... TUMOR
chelonian ...... TURTLE, TORTOISE
chemical catalyst .... REAGENT
change .... REACTION
combining capacity
.... VALENCE
compound ...... AMIDE, AMINE,
DIENE, CERIA, ESTER, BORIDE,
IODINE, ISOMER, KETONE,
ENOL, TOULENE, ELATERIN
compounds, describing
.... LABILE
element ...... ARGON, HALOGEN
element 43 .... MASURIUM
ink remover .... ERADICATOR

prefix .... OXA, ACETO, AMIDO,
AMINO
radical .... BUTYL, TOLYL
reaction .... CATALYSIS
reagent .... CATALYST,
CATALYSER
salt .... SAL, ESTER, BORATE,
NITRE, IODATE
substance .... AMIDE, LININ
suffix .... YL, ANE, ENE, OSE,
OLIC, YLENE
unit .... TITER, TITRE
word ending .... OL, INE, ENOL
chemin de fer .... RAILROAD,
BACCARAT
chemise ...... SLIP, SARK, CYMAR,
LINGERIE
colloquial .... SHIMMY, UNDIES
chemisette .... TUCKER
chemist ...... ANALYST, DRUGGIST,
PHARMACIST
flask of .... BOLTHEAD
pot of .... ALUDEL
chemistry, suffix in .... ENE, INE,
OLE, OSE
Chemulpo .... INCHON, JINSEN
chenille .... DOG, CORD
Chenpao to Russians
.... DAMANSKY
Cheops .... KHUFU
edifice built by .... PYRAMID
cherish .... ADORE, PRIZE, VALUE,
FOSTER, EMBOSOM, REVERE,
NURTURE, TREASURE, NURSE,
HARBOR, HOLD DEAR
companion in marriage vow
.... LOVE, OBEY
Cherokee sage .... SEQUOYAH
cheroot .... CIGAR
cherry .... DRUPE, RUDDY,
CAPULIN, MARASCA,
AMARELLE, MORELLO,
OXHEART, BLACKHEART
disease .... BLACKKNOT
like color/red .... CERISE
product .... JAM, PIE
sour .... EGRIOT
stone .... NUTLET
sweet/wild .... GEAN,
MAZZARD, BIGAROON
cherrystone .... CLAM, NUTLET,
QUAHOG
chersonese .... PENINSULA
cherub .... AMOR, ANGEL, EROTE,
LAMBKIN, SERAPH, INNOCENT
cherubic .... ANGELIC
chess castle .... ROOK
certain defeat in
.... CHECKMATE
champion .... FISHER, KARPOV,
LASKER, KASPAROV,

PETROSIAN, BOTVINNIK,
SPASSKY, CAPABLANCA
corner piece .... ROOK
defeated at .... MATED
expert .... HOYLE
opening .... CHASSE, GAMBIT
piece .... KING, PAWN, ROOK,
QUEEN, CASTLE, BISHOP,
KNIGHT
sacrifice .... GAMBIT
term .... CHECKMATE,
SELFMATE, EN PASSANT
wins .... MATES
chest .... BOX, ARCA, KIST,
BOSOM, COFFER, LOCKER,
CASE, BREAST, BUREAU,
CASKET, CABINET, THORAX
a kind of ..... TOOL, CAMPHOR,
MEDICINE, TREASURE,
COMMUNITY
animal .... BRISKET
bone .... RIB
cavity membrane ...... PLEURA
clothes .... TRUNK
combining form ..... STETH(O)
for money/valuables
.... COFFER, CASKET
for storage .... HUTCH
for supplies .... WANIGAN
human .... THORAX
located on the .... PECTORAL
of drawers .... LOWBOY,
COMMODE, CHIFFONIER,
HIGHBOY, TALLBOY
of sacred utensils .... CIST
sacred .... ARK, ARCA
Scottish .... KIST
small .... CASKET
sound .... RALE
tool .... KIT
vibration .... FREMITUS
Chesterfield .... LORD, SOFA,
TOPCOAT
Chesterfieldian .... SUAVE,
URBANE, ELEGANT
chessman .... PAWN
chestnut ...... MAST, TREE, HORSE,
OLDIE, MARRON, BUCKEYE
Chinese .... LING
colloquial .... JOKE, CLICHE
pod .... BUR
Polynesian .... RATA
preserved in syrup
.... MARRONS
tree .... CHINCAPIN,
CHINQUAPIN
water .... LING
chevalier .... NOBLE, GALLANT
Archaic .... KNIGHT
Cheviot .... OVINE, SHEEP
chevron .... BAR, STRIPE

shape .... VEE
symbol of ...... RANK, SERVICE
chevrotain .... NAPU, DEERLET
chevy .... FRET, HUNT, CHASE
chew .... GNAW, GRIND, CUD,
CHAMP, MUNCH, MUMBLE,
BITE, (S)CRUNCH, MASTICATE
inability to .... AMOSESIS
leaf to .... BETEL
the cud .... PONDER, RUMINATE
the fat .... CHAT, GOSSIP
the scenery .... EMOTE
chewing gum ingredient
.... CHICLE, MASTIC
gum tree .... SAPODILLA
tobacco piece .... PLUG
chewink .... FINCH, TOWHEE
chewy confection .... GUM,
TAFFY, CARAMEL
Chiang Kai-shek .... GISSIMO
party of .... KUOMINTANG
wife of .... MEI-LING
Chianti .... (RED) WINE
Chiapas, capital of ...... TUXTLA
chiaus: Turk. .... EMISSARY,
SERGEANT
chibouk .... (TOBACCO) PIPE
chic ..... SMART, MODISH, JAUNTY,
ELEGANT, STYLISH, SUAVE,
NATTY, DAPPER, POLISHED
Chicago .... WINDY CITY
airport/hub .... O'HARE
baseball team .... WHITESOX
basketball team .... BULLS
business/theater area ..... LOOP
feature .... STOCKYARDS
football team .... BEARS
personage .... SANDBURG
"Wall Street" .... LA SALLE
chicalote .... POPPY
chicane .... TRICK, QUIBBLE
chicanery ...... HOAX, DECEPTION,
TRICKERY
Chichen Itza native ...... MAYAN
chichi .... ARTY, ELEGANT
chick ...... CHILD, PEEPER, SHEILA
pea ..... GRAM, PLANT, FODDER
chickadee .... BIRD, TOMTIT,
TITMOUSE
chickaree .... SQUIRREL
chicken .... FOWL, BIDDY, BIRD,
SHANGHAI
breast (deformity), cause of
.... RICKETS
breed .... JAVA, ANCONA,
BANTAM, CORNISH, HAMBURG,
MINORCA, (WHITE) LEGHORN,
DORKING, CAMPINE, SUMATRA,
SULTAN, RHODE ISLAND RED,
RHODE ISLAND WHITE,
WYANDOTTE, PLYMOUTH ROCK

castrated .... CAPON
chaser .... SHOO, CATCHPOLE
dish/meat course
.... GALANTINE
feed .... CORN, MEAL, GRAIN,
BARLEY
feed: sl. .... COINS, DIMES,
PEANUTS, PIDDLING, CHEAP,
NEGLIGIBLE, SMALL CHANGE
female .... HEN, LAYER
five-toed .... HOUDAN
hearted/livered .... TIMID,
GUTLESS, COWARDLY,
YELLOW, WEAKLING
little .... ALARMIST
male .... COCK, ROOSTER
noodle scoop .... LADLE
out .... FALTER, COLD FEET
pen/cage .... COOP, RUNWAY
pen/cage material .... WIRE
pox .... VARICELLA
resting place .... PERCH,
ROOST
slang .... PANSY, SISSY,
COWARD, MAMA'S BOY,
CRYBABY
small .... BANTAM
snake .... BOBA
sound .... CLUCK, CACKLE
switch .... PANIC BUTTON
young .... CHICK, FRYER,
POULT, PEEPER, BROILER,
PULLET
chickens, collectively
.... POULTRY
enclosure for .... RUNWAY
heated shelter for
.... BROODER
chicken's route ...... SIDE TO SIDE
chickeny TV role .... MISTER
PEEPERS
chickweed .... ALSINE, ALSONE,
SPURR(E)Y, STITCHWORT
chicle .... SAPOTA
product ..... BALATA, CHEWING
GUM
source .... SAPODILLA
chico .... SHRUB, GREASEWOOD
chicory .... ENDIVE, SUCCORY
use for .... COFFEE
chide .... BLAME, SCOLD, BERATE,
LASH, REBUKE, REPROVE,
LECTURE, UPBRAID, CRITICIZE
chider .... RATER, CRITIC
chief .... ARCH, HEAD, MAIN,
ELDER, LEADER, CAPTAIN,
PRIME, STELLAR, FOREMOST,
CENTRAL, STAPLE, SUPERIOR,
COMMANDER, PRINCIPAL
actor .... HERO, LEAD, STAR
barrio .... DATO, DATU,

CABEZA
Canaan .... SISERA
character .... HERO, HEROINE
colloquial .... BOSS
commander-in .... CINC
commodity/product
.... STAPLE
Cossack .... ATAMAN, HETMAN
excellence ..... FORTE, TALENT,
STRONG-POINT
executive .... PRESIDENT
Indian .... BRANT, COCHISE,
SACHEM, GERONIMO,
POWHATAN, TECUMSEH,
SAGAMORE, SITTING BULL
ingredient .... BASE
Italian .... DUCE
Moslem .... REIS
of foreign mission
.... NUNCIO, AMBASSADOR
of state .... KING, RULER,
PRESIDENT
of workmen .... FOREMAN,
OVERSEER
official .... PREMIER, PRIME
MINISTER
singer .... CANTOR
Spanish .... JEFE
support .... MAINSTAY
Chief Justice, U.S. ...... WARREN,
TANEY, MARSHALL
chiefly ...... MAINLY, IN THE MAIN,
LARGELY, MOSTLY,
ESPECIALLY
chieftain .... LEADER
Indian .... SACHEM
political .... BOSS
Scandinavian .... JARL
chield .... YOUTH
chiffon .... SILK
chigger .... FLEA, LARVA, CHIGOE
chigoe .... FLEA, LARVA, CHIGGER
Chihli .... HOPEI
Chihuahua .... (TOY) DOG
chilblain ...... PERNIO, KIBE, SORE
child .... KID, TOD, TOT, CHIT,
BOY, BABE, BABY, INFANT,
GIRL, SON, ISSUE, DAUGHTER,
KIDDIE, KIDDY, PRODUCT
abnormal .... OAF
bad-tempered/ugly .... ELF,
CHANGELING
bastard .... BY-BLOW
bear of .... TEDDY
beggar's employer
.... PADRONE
bib .... DICKEY
cap/hood of .... BIGGIN
colloquial .... CHIT, TIKE,
TYKE, CHICK, LAMBKIN,
TODDLER

combining form .... PED,
P(A)EDO
dirty, ragged ..... RAGAMUFFIN
feet of .... PETTITOES
game of .... PEEKABOO, RED
ROVER
hand of .... PUD
homeless .... WAIF
impudent/unruly .... BRAT
in the old school, unlucky
.... DUNCE
like .... NAIVE
little .... MOPPET
milk source .... WET NURSE
mischievous .... ELF, IMP,
BRAT, URCHIN, LIMB,
JACKANAPES
murder of .... PROLICIDE,
INFANTICIDE
murder of one's .... FILICIDE
noble born .... CHILDE
of .... FILIAL
of illegitimate birth
.... BASTARD, BASEBORN
of light and day, so-called
.... EROS
of mixed blood .... MESTEE,
MUSTEE, MESTIZO, GRIFFE,
MULATTO, HALF-BREED, HALF-
CASTE
of the street .... ARAB, WAIF,
GAMIN
of the Sun .... INCA
pinafore .... SLIP, TIER, DICKEY
playroom .... NURSERY
pretty .... DOLL
relation to parent
.... FILIATION
sans parents .... ORPHAN
savings bank of ..... SAVE-ALL
spoiled .... BRAT, COCKNEY
substitute .... CHANGELING
teacher/trainer ..... GOVERNESS
tiny .... PEEWEE
toy of .... PEG TOP
undershirt .... WAIST
unweaned .... SUCKLING
walk of ...... PADDLE, TODDLE,
WADDLE
childbearing .... NASCENCY,
PARTURITION
primitive custom .... COUVADE
childbirth .... DELIVERY,
PARTURITION
confinement .... LYING-IN
discharge after .... LOCHIA
pains .... LABOR, TRAVAIL,
BIRTH THROES
childhood writings, etc.
.... JUVENALIA
childing .... PREGNANT

childish .... ANILE, SILLY,
ASININE, FOOLISH, PUERILE,
SENILE, IMMATURE,
INFANTILE, BABYISH,
BRATTISH, JUVENILE, WEAK,
CREDULOUS, YOUTHFUL
state due to age .... DOTAGE
talk .... BABBLE, PRATTLE
walk .... TODDLE, WADDLE
childhood disease .... MUMPS,
MEASLES
childlike .... NAIF, NAIVE, SOFT,
TRUSTFUL, GIRLISH, SILLY,
TRUSTING, INNOCENT
adult .... IDIOT, MORON
speech .... LISP
children .... OFFSPRING, PROGENY
book for .... JUVENILE
colloquial .... (SMALL) FRY
of family .... BROOD, FLOCK
of heaven and earth, alleged
.... TITANS
of Israel .... JEWS, HEBREWS
of the mist .... NIBELUNG
study of .... PEDOLOGY
without .... NONPAROUS
children's book author .... MILNE,
OUIDA, RAMEE
book, doll in .... GOLLIWOG
disease .... MUMPS, MEASLES,
RICKETS, RACHITIS
doctor .... PEDIATRIST,
PEDIATRICIAN
game .... TAG, JACKSTONE
garments .... SMALLS
jacket .... PALETOT
mouth disease .... APHTHA,
THRUSH
patron saint .... SANTA
(CLAUS)
pinafore .... TIER
playroom .... NURSERY
playsuit .... ROMPERS
wasting condition
.... MARASMUS
Chile, meaning of .... SNOW
Chilean aborigine .... INCA
archipelago .... CHONOS,
GUAYANECO
bay ...... COOK, EYRE, DARWIN,
INUTIL, MORENO, NASSAU,
COPIAPO, ADVENTURE,
INGLESA, SKYRING
cape .... HORN, CHOROS,
DESEADO, BASCUNAN
capital .... SANTIAGO
channel .... BEAGLE,
COCKBURN, BALLENERO,
CONCEPCION
city/town .... ANGOL, ARICA,
PENCO, CALAMA, BARRANCAS,

LA SERENA, CONCEPCION,
MAIPU, CHILLAN, IQUIQUE,
RANCAGUA, PUENTE ALTO,
OSORNO, ANTOFAGASTA, LOTA,
RENCA, QUILPUE, TEMUCO,
TALCAHUANO, VALDIVIA,
VALPARAISO, TALCA, VINA
DEL MAR
coastal wind .... SURES
coin .... COLON, ESCUDO,
CENTAVO
court dance .... CUECA
deer .... PUDU
desert .... ATACAMA
evergreen/shrub .... MAQUI
gulf .... ANCUD, ARAUCO,
GUAFO, CORONADOS,
TRINIDAD, ELEFANTES, PENAS,
TRES MONTES
island .... ANGAMOS, BYRON,
DAWSON, CHATHAM, GUAFO,
CAMPANA, ESMERALDA, LUZ,
LENNOX, HOSTE, GORDON,
MOCHA, CHILOE,
LONDONDERRY, NALCAYEC,
MADRE DE DIOS, PIAZZI, PRAT,
PICTON, NUEVA, TRANQUI,
TENQUEHUEN, WOLLASTON,
WELLINGTON
islands .... CHAUQUES,
GRAFTON, HERMITE, WEEK,
WOOD, PAJAROS
lagoon .... ACULEO, BLANCA
lake .... TORO, PALENA,
BLANCO, BUENOS AIRES,
RUPANCO, COCHRANE, RANCO,
YELCHO, VILLARRICA
language .... SPANISH
monetary unit .... PESO,
ESCUDO
mountain .... MACA, CONICO,
RINCON, AGUAS CALIENTES, AP
IWAN, CAMPANARIO,
MELIMOYU, LADRILLERO,
TRONADOR, MURALLON, OJOS
DEL SALADO, ZAPALERI, TRES
CRUCES
palm tree .... COQUITO
peninsula ...... HARDY, LACUY,
TRES MONTES, TAITAO,
STAINES, TUMBES, WHARTON
pianist .... ARAU
president .... ALLENDE
region .... ANTOFAGASTA,
ATACAMA, COQUIMBO, MAULE,
BIOBIO, LOS LAGOS,
SANTIAGO, MAGALLANES,
TARAPACA, VALPARAISO
river ...... ACONCAGUA, BAKER,
BRAVO, BIOBIO, CARMEN,
CHOAPA, CAMARONES,

GRANDE, HUASCO, IMPERIAL, LAUCA, ELQUI, LA LIGUA, LAJA, LOA, LLUTA, MAIPO, RAPEL, MAULE, PASCUA, BUENO, TOLTEN, SIMPSON
salt deposit .... ATACAMA, GRANDE, BELLA VISTA, MIRAJE, LLAMARA, SURIRE, PINTADOS
saltpeter .... NITER
seaport .... LOTA, ARICA
strait .... MAGELLAN, MAGALLANES
tree .... PELU, ULMO, ROBLE, RAULI, QUILLAI
volcano .... MAIPU, LASTARRIA, CORCOVADO, LANIN, MINCHINMAVIDA, LLAIMA, TACORA, SOCOMPA
chili con _____ .... CARNE
flavored dish .... ENCHILADA
chiliad .... THOUSAND
chill .... AGUE, COOL, ALGOR, FROST, COLD(NESS), DEPRESS, SHAKES, DISCOURAGE, SHIVERING, DISPIRIT
chilling device .... ICER, REFRIGERATOR
material .... ICE
chills and fever .... AGUE, MALARIA
chilly .... RAW, COLD, ALGID, CRISP, BLEAK, BRISK, BITING, FROSTY, WINTRY
chilopod .... CENTIPEDE
chimar .... ROBE
chimb .... RIM
chime .... RIM, BELL, PEAL, DOORBELL, HARMONY
in .... JOIN, AGREE, ACCEDE, CONCUR, JUMP AT, INTERRUPT
chimera .... FANCY, FANTASY, ILLUSION, MIRAGE, MONSTER
desert traveler's .... OASIS, WATER
sailor's .... LAND
chimerical .... FANCIFUL, NOTIONAL, FANTASTIC, UNREAL, FERTILE, IMAGINARY, VISIONARY, WHIMSICAL
chimney .... SPOUT, TEWEL, FUNNEL, (SMOKE)STACK
bird .... SWIFT, SWALLOW
carbon .... SOOT
corner .... FIRESIDE, (INGLE)NOOK
cover ..... COWL, MITER, MITRE
lining .... PARGET
of volcano .... VENT
piece .... PAREL, MANTEL
pipe .... FLUE

pot .... TALLBOY
screen .... BONNET
swallow .... SWIFT
chimpanzee .... APE, JOCKO, TROGLODYTE
relative ...... GIBBON, GORILLA, ORANGUTAN
chin flesh .... GILL
hairy growth .... BEARD, GOATEE
hollow/cleft .... DIMPLE
pertaining to .... GENIAL, MENTAL
slang ..... GAB, TALK, CHATTER
China .... SPODE, CATHAY
capital .... PEKING
made with clay .... BONE
Sea region .... ANNAM
chinaware .... CHINA, DISHES, DRESDEN, CROCKERY, PORCELAIN, STONEWARE
chincapin .... CHESTNUT
chinch .... BEDBUG
chinche .... SKUNK
chinchilla .... FUR, RODENT
relative .... VISCACHA
chine .... SILK, RIDGE, SPINE, RAVINE, BACKBONE
Chinese .... MIAO, SINO, SERIC, SINIC, ORIENTAL
A-bomb site .... LOP NOR
alimentary paste ..... WANTON, WONTON
American dish .... SUBGUM, CHOP SUEY, CHOWMEIN
ancient dominant religion .... CONFUCIANISM
arithmetical device .... ABACUS
aromatic root .... GINSENG
art/customs expert .... SINOLOGUE
artichoke .... CHOROGI
association .... TONG
autumn .... CH'IU
bamboo stick .... WHANGEE
bay .... HANGZHOU WAN
bean .... ADSUKI
boat .... JUNK, SAMPAN, TONGKANG
brand on goods .... CHOP
Buddhism .... FOISM
Buddhist monk/priest .... LAMA
bugaboo .... YELLOW PERIL
cape .... OLWAMPI
capital .... PEKING, BEIJING
capital, former .... CHUNGKING
Caucasian tribesman .... LOLO
cauterizing agent .... MOXA
channel .... BASHI

characters in Japanese .... MANA
chestnut .... LING
chicken .... GAI
city/town ...... AMOY, CANTON, KIRIN, ANSHAN, CHUNGKING, FUSHUN, CHENGDU, CHANGCHUN, HENGYANG, GUANGZHOU, TSINAN, FOOCHOW, GUIYANG, KALGAN, KUNMING, HANGCHOW, LUDA, LANZHOU, KWANGCHOW, NANJING, QIGIHAR, QINGDAO, SIAN, QUANZHOU, SHANGHAI, MUKDEN, SHENYANG, TANGSHAN, TZEPO, TIENTSIN, TSINGTAO, SUCHOW, TSINAN, YANGCHOW, ZIBO, WUHAN, ZHENGHOU
club .... TONG
coat .... MANDARIN
coin ..... LI, TAEL, TIAO, YUAN, LIANG
coin, early .... PU
coin with hole .... CASH
combining form .... SINO, CHINO
Communist leader .... MAO, PIAO, PING, CHOU, ZHAO
custom peculiar to .... SINICISM
department .... FU
dependency .... TIBET
desert .... GOBI
dialect .... CANTONESE, PEKIN(G)ESE
dialect, official ..... MANDARIN
dictator .... MAO (TSE-TUNG)
dog .... CHOW, PEKIN(G)ESE
duck eggs, preserved .... PIDAN
dynasty .... HAN, WEI, YIN, CHOU, HSIA, LIAO, MING, SUNG, T'ANG, YUAN, SHANG, MANCHU, MONGOL, TA CHING
dynasty, first .... HSIA
dynasty, last .... MANCHU
eating implement .... CHOPSTICKS
emperor .... HUANG, KUBLAI
emperor, last .... PU-YI
empress .... HOU
empress, last .... TZU-HSI
exercise .... T'AI CHI
eyes, describing .... SLIT, ALMOND
factory .... HONG
feudal state .... WEI
fiber plant .... RAMIE
fish .... TREPANG
flute .... TCHE

fruit .... LOQUAT
gambling game, cards
.... FAN-TAN
game with tiles
.... MAHJONG(G)
gateway .... PAILOU
gelatin/glue .... AGAR
god .... JOSS, SHEN
gong ...... TAM-TAM, TOM-TOM
grape .... WAMPEE
guild .... TONG
gulf .... BO HAI, TONKIN
hairdo .... PIGTAIL
Han city .... HANKOW,
          HANYANG, WUCHANG
harbor craft .... SAMPAN
herb .... GINGER, GINSENG
highest point .... MOUNT
                              EVEREST
ideograph .... KANJI
idol .... JOSS
import duties .... HAIKWAN
incense .... JOSS STICK
indigo .... ISATIS
invention .... GUNPOWDER
island .... AMOY, MATSU,
  DONGSHA, HAINAN, HUNGTOW,
     QUEMOY, YUHUAN, PINGTAN,
     MACAU, TAIWAN (FORMOSA)
islands .... TACHEN, YUSHAN,
                    PESCADORES
kingdom, old .... WEI
laborer .... COOLIE
lake .... BAGRAX, ER HAI, NAM
  CO, KHANKA, DIAN CHI, KOKO
  NOR, LOP NUR, EBINUR HU,
                    POYANG HU
language .... YI, SHAN,
  CHUANG, MONGOL, CHINESE,
    MIAO, UIGUR, KAZAKH,
        MANDARIN, TIBETAN
language/customs, study of
.... SINOLOGY
license .... CHOP
lord of lower world .... YENLO
magnolia .... YULAN
Manchu dynasty .... TA CHING
mandarin's residence
.... YAMEN
measure .... LI, CHIH, TSUN,
                          CHANG
medicinal herb .... GINSENG
metropolis .... WUHAN
mile LI
military academy
.... WHAMPOA
monetary unit ...... FEN, YUAN
money .... TAEL, SYCEE
Mongol .... MANCHU
Mongol dynasty .... YUAN

Mongol dynasty founder
.... KUBLAI
monk .... LAMA, BONZE
mountain .... LUSHAN,
  KONGUR, GONGGA, EVEREST,
    MUZTAG, MUZTAGATA,
    YUSHAN, YAGRADAGZE
Nationalist party
.... KUOMINTANG
noodles .... MEIN
notable name .... SOONG
nuclear center .... LOP NOR,
                        LANCHOW
numeral, 1 to 10 .... YIH, URH,
  SAN, SZE, WOO, LUH, TSIEH,
        PA, KEW, SHIH
nurse/servant .... AMAH
nut .... LYCHEE, LICHI
official .... KUAN, KWAN,
                      MANDARIN
official seal .... CHOP
oil tree .... TUNG
omelet .... FOOYONG
orange .... MANDARIN
ounce .... TAEL
pagoda .... TAA
pagoda: var. .... TAAG
pear .... PYRUS
peninsula .... LIAOTUNG
peony .... MOUTAN
permit .... CHOP
philosopher .... MOTI,
  YUTANG, MENCIUS, MENG-TSE,
                      CONFUCIUS
phoenix .... FENG, HUANG
pickles .... CHOWCHOW
pine .... MATSU
plant .... MOXA, RAMIE,
                        GINSENG
poet .... LI PO
political party .... TONG,
                    KUOMINTANG
porcelain .... CELADON
port .... AMOY, CANTON,
  TSINGTAO, DAIREN, ICHANG,
      TIENTSIN, SHANGHAI
pottery .... MING
pound .... CATTY
prefix .... SINO
president .... SUN (YAT-SEN)
priest .... LAMA
principle .... TAO, YIN, YANG
province .... ANHUI, GANSU,
  HOPEI, FUJIAN, GUANGDONG,
  HUPEI, HONAN, KIANGSI,
  KIANGSU, HUNAN, LIAONING,
  KIRIN, SHANSI, SHENSI,
  SHANTUNG, CHEKIANG,
  SZECHWAN, TSINGHAI,
  YUNNAN, KWEICHOW, XIZANG,
        KWANGTUNG

provincial tax .... LIKIN
punishment .... CANGUE
puzzle .... TANGRAM
race designation .... YELLOW
rebellion of 1900 .... BOXER
religion .... ISLAM, TAOISM,
    BUDDHISM, CONFUCIANISM
river .... AMUR, PEARL, HAN
  SHUI, HAILAR HE, YELLOW,
  FEN HE, HOTAN HE, MEKONG,
  YANGTZE, SALWEEN, TUMEN,
  WEI-HE, WU JIANG, YUEN,
      YUAN, YALU, YALONG
river boat .... SAMPAN
sacred peak .... OMEI
sacred tree .... WU TUNG
salutation .... KOWTOW
satin .... PEKIN
sauce .... SOY
scripture, a .... CHING
sea cucumber .... TREPANG
season .... CH'UN, HSIA, CH'IU,
                        TUNG
secret society .... TONG
sedge .... MATI
shark fins .... YU CHI
silk .... SHA, PEKIN, PONGEE,
  SHANTUNG, TUSSA(H), TUSSER
silkworm .... SINA, TASAR
silver ingot/money ...... SYCEE
sky .... TIEN
slang .... CHINK
soapberry .... LICHEE, LITCHI
society ...... HUI, TONG, BOXER
son .... TAI
soup material .... TREPANG,
                    BIRD'S NEST
spring .... CH'UN
squash .... CASHAW, CUSHAW
stamp .... CHOP
statesman .... KOO
string money .... TIAO
summer .... HSIA
tea .... CHA, TSIA, BOHEA,
  CONGO(U), HYSON, OOLONG,
                    SOUCHONG
team work .... GUNG HO
temple .... TAA, JOSSHOUSE
trading boat .... TONGKANG
treatment by needles
.... ACUPUNCTURE
treaty port .... AMOY,
                      SHANGHAI
tree .... TUNG, GINK(GO),
              LOQUAT, WUTUNG
truth/way .... TAO
unicorn .... LIN, CHLLIN
walking stick .... WHANGEE
warehouse .... HONG
waterwheel .... NORIA
wax .... PELA

weight .... LI, FAN, HAO, TAEL, CATTY, LIANG, PICUL
wine vessel .... TSUN
winter/wood oil .... TUNG
work together .... GUNG HO
wormwood .... MOXA
yellow .... SIL
chink .... RIMA, SLIT, CRACK, CRANNY, CREVICE, FISSURE
filler .... GROUT
Chink: sl. .... CHINESE
chinks, full of .... RIMOSE, RIMOUS
chinky .... RIMOUS
Chinook .... WIND, INDIAN, SALMON
Indian .... FLATHEAD
lily/bulb .... QUAMASH
powwow .... WAWA
chinquapin .... TREE, (CHEST)NUT
chinse .... CALK, CLOSE
chintz .... CLOTH
chip .... BIT, CUT, CHOP, SCRAP, NICK, FLAKE, PIECE, SLICE, FRAGMENT, SPLINTER
in .... ANTE, CONTRIBUTE
of stone .... SPALL, GALLET
off the old block .... JUNIOR, SON(NY)
on one's shoulder .... GRUDGE, RANCOR
chipmunk ...... CHIPPY, TRACKEE, SQUIRREL
cheek pouch .... ALFORJA
cousin of .... GOPHER
chippendale furniture leg .... CABRIOLE
chipper .... ADZ, PERT, CHIRP, CHISEL, LIVELY, TWITTER
colloquial .... BABBLE, CHATTER
Chippewa ...... INDIAN, OJIBWA(Y)
chippy ...... CHIPMUNK, SPARROW, PROSTITUTE
chips' companion .... FISH
chirk .... LIVELY, CHEERFUL
chiro, as combining form .... HAND
chirographer .... PENMAN
chiromancer .... PALMIST
Chiron .... CENTAUR
forte of .... MEDICINE
pupil of .... ACHILLES, HERCULES
chiropodist .... PEDICURIST
advice of .... FOOTBATH
chiropter .... BAT, ALIPED
chirp .... PEEP, CHEEP, TWEET, TWITTER
chirper .... BIRD, CICADA, NESTLING, FLEDGLING

chirrup .... CHIRP, TWEET
chirurgeon .... SURGEON
chisel .... CUT, PARE, TRIM, BURIN, CARVE, GOUGE, HARDY, BROACH, CHASER, FIRMER, GRAVER, TOOLER, ENGRAVE, SCULP(T)
bar .... SPUDDER
broad-faced .... DROVE
colloquial .... CHEAT, SWINDLE
in ..... ENCROACH, MUSCLE (IN)
mason's .... POMMEL
part .... TANG
polishing .... SLICK
primitive/stone .... CELT
slang .... GYP, SCREW
stonemason's .... QUARREL
chiseled profile .... ROMAN, CLASSICAL
chiseler .... CHEAT(ER), CROOK, GYPPER, SWINDLER
chit .... NOTE, SHOOT, SPROUT
colloquial ...... IOU, TAB, GIRL, CHILD
of a kind .... BILL, MEMO, VOUCHER
chitchat .... TALK, GOSSIP
chiton .... LIMPET, GARMENT, MOLLUSK
chitter .... SHIVER, TWITTER
chive ...... ONION, SITHE, FLAVOR, GARLIC
chiv(v)y ...... FRET, HUNT, CHASE, HARRY
chlamys .... CLOAK, MANTLE
Chloe and others .... AUNTS
love of .... DAPHNIS
chloride .... MURIATE
chlorine .... IODINE, BROMINE, HALOGEN
chloroform, for one .... SOLVENT, ANESTHETIC
chlorophyll .... ETIOLIN
chock .... BLOCK, CLEAT, TRIG, SPRAG, WEDGE
chockablock .... CROWDED
chocolate .... CANDY, DRINK
cake .... BROWNIE
candy filling .... FONDANT
flavored .... MOCHA
mixer .... MOLINET
powder .... COCOA
source/tree .... CACAO
substitute .... CAROB
choice ...... PICK, DESIRE, OPTION, SELECTION, PREFERENCE
between two evils .... DILEMMA
food .... DELICACY
make a .... OPT
morsel .... TIDBIT

object/role .... PLUM
of words .... DICTION
other .... ALTERNATIVE
part ...... MEAT, CREAM, ELITE, MARROW
word .... EITHER
choices for getting there somehow .... HOOK AND CROOK
choir boy's collar .... ETON
leader .... CHORAGUS
leader's aide .... SUCCENTOR
of a .... CHORAL
place in church .... LOFT, GALLERY
section .... ALTO, TENOR
vestment ..... COTTA, SURPLICE
choke .... JAM, PLUG, STIFLE, SMOTHER, OBSTRUCT, THROTTLE, SUFFOCATE
by squeezing throat .... STRANGLE
by stuffing mouth .... GAG
to death .... BURKE
up .... CLOG
with iron collar ...... GARROTE
choked up: colloq. .... SPEECHLESS
choker .... COLLAR, FUR(PIECE), NECKTIE, NECKLACE
cholecyst .... (GALL)BLADDER
choler .... FIT, IRE, BILE, RAGE, ANGER, WRATH
cholera bacillus .... COMMA
type of ..... MORBUS, NOSTRAS, INFANTUM
choleric .... ANGRY, IRATE, TESTY, IRASCIBLE, IRRITABLE
cholesterol .... LIPID
good form of .... HDL
harmful form of .... LDL
product .... GALLSTONE
cholla .... CACTUS
chololith .... GALLSTONE
Chomo-lungma .... EVEREST
chondroma .... TUMOR
choose .... OPT, CULL, PICK, WALE, ADOPT, DECIDE, PREFER, SELECT, EMBRACE, DESIGNATE
for office .... ELECT
your _____ .... EXIT, WILD, PARTNER
choosing, right of .... OPTION
choosy .... FUSSY, FINICKY, FINICAL, FASTIDIOUS, PARTICULAR
chop .... AXE, CUT, DICE, FELL, HEW, JAW, LOP, HACK, CHEEK, CLEAVE, MINCE, STRIKE

down .... FELL, RAZE, LEVEL
in China, India .... SEAL,
           PERMIT, LICENSE
off .... PRUNE
stroke, in tennis .... SLICE
up .... HACKLE
chop-chop .... AT ONCE,
    PROMPTLY, QUICKLY
chophouse .... RESTAURANT
Chinese .... CUSTOMSHOUSE
specialty .... STEAK
chopine .... SHOE, PATTEN
Chopin's (Frederic) country
    .... POLAND
love .... (GEORGE) SAND
work .... ETUDE
chopper .... AX(E), MOLAR
meat .... CLEAVER
slang .... HELICOPTER
chopping blows with hand
    .... KARATE
surface .... BLOCK
tool .... AX(E), CLEAVER,
    HATCHET
choppy .... ROUGH, JOLTING
chops .... JAWS, JOWL, PORK,
    MOUTH
choral .... HYMNAL, SINGING
composition .... MOTET
music .... CANTATA, ORATORIO
chord .... CORD, STRING,
    HARMONY
dissonance .... WOLF
playing of notes in
    succession ...... ARPEGGIO
3-tone .... TRIAD
chordate .... VERTEBRATE
example of a .... MAN
chore .... (ODD) JOB, TASK,
    CHARE, STINT, HOUSEWORK,
    ASSIGNMENT
doctor's .... ROUNDS
list .... AGENDA
choreographer of note
    .... ANTON, BALANCHINE
choreography .... DANCE,
    DANCING, BALLET, DEPICTION,
    PORTRAYAL
chorine .... STEPPER, CHORUS GIRL
chorister's garment .... CASSOCK
chorography .... MAP
choroid membrane .... TAPETUM
chortle .... SNORT, CHUCKLE
chorus .... CHOIR, UNISON
girl: colloq. .... CHORINE
leader .... CHORAGUS,
    CONDUCTOR
line .... DANCERS
of a .... CHORAL, CHORIC
of song ...... BURDEN, REFRAIN
chose .... CHATTEL

Chosen .... KOREA
chosen one .... ELECTEE
Chou, Chinese bigwig .... EN LAI
chough .... CROW
chouse .... DUPE, CHEAT,
    SWINDLE(R)
chow .... DOG, FOOD, MEAL
chowchow .... OLIO, MIXED,
    PICKLES, ASSORTED
chowder ingredient .... CLAM
christen .... NAME, BAPTIZE
Christian .... HUMAN, DECENT,
    GENTILE, BELIEVER,
    CHURCHMAN
abbreviation .... XTIAN
bishop of the Goths
    .... ULFILA(S)
church .... ORANT, BASILICA
church as a whole
    .... CATHOLIC
church of Egypt .... COPT
church, the .... HERITAGE
love feast .... AGAPE
non .... PAGAN, PAYNIM,
    HEATHEN
Oriental .... UNIAT
pulpit .... AMBO
religion founder .... JESUS
Science founder .... BAKER
Science healer
    .... PRACTITIONER
theologian .... ORIGEN
traitor .... TRADITOR
Christiania, formerly .... OSLO
was capital of .... NORWAY
Christians, all .... CHURCH
Christie .... AGATHA
Christmas ...... NOEL, YULE(TIDE)
abbreviation .... XMAS
bonanza .... GIFTS
cake/fruitcake .... SIMNEL
carol .... NOEL, NOWEL
crib .... CRECHE
day .... NATIVITY
decorative item .... SEAL,
    MISTLETOE
drink .... EGGNOG
favorite figure .... SANTA
    (CLAUS)
gift container .... STOCKING
masked funster .... MUMMER
mock-up of Nativity
    .... CRECHE
musician .... WAIT
pantomime .... GUISER,
    MUMMER
season .... YULE(TIDE)
song .... NOEL, CAROL
song, Hilaire Belloc's
    .... SAILOR'S CAROL
street singer .... WAIT,

    CAROLER
time entertainment
    .... PANTOMIME
tree .... PINE, HOLLY
vehicle .... SLED, SLEIGH
worker .... ELF
chromosome load .... GENES
chronic .... ROOTED, CONSTANT,
    HABITUAL, CONFIRMED,
    RECURRING, PERSISTENT
chronicle .... ANNAL(S), DIARY,
    RECORD, ACCOUNT, HISTORY
chronicler .... ANNALIST,
    RECORDER, HISTORIAN
chronological .... DATED, IN
    SEQUENCE
chronometer .... WATCH
chrysalis .... PUPA, COCOON
chrysanthemum ...... MUM, KIKU,
    DAISY, FLOWER, POMPON,
    COSTMARY, MARGUERITE
badge: Jap. .... MON
Chrysler cars of 1928–1961
    .... DESOTOS
chrysolite .... OLIVINE, PERIDOT
chub .... (BLACK)BASS
chubby .... OBESE, PLUMP, STOUT,
    ROTUND
one .... BUTTERBALL
chuck .... TOSS, CAST(OFF),
    THROW, DISCARD
slang .... FOOD, GRUB, MEAT
chuckle .... CLUCK, LAUGH,
    GIGGLE, CHORTLE, SNICKER
chucklehead .... DOLT, IDIOT
chuckleheaded .... STUPID
chuddar .... SHAWL
Chudskoe lake .... PEIPUS
chuff .... BOOR, BRICK, CHURL
chum .... PAL, BUDDY, CRONY,
    FRIEND, ROOMMATE
in fishing .... BAIT
chummy .... BOSOM, FAMILIAR,
    FRIENDLY, INTIMATE
chump .... BOOB, FOOL
chunk .... BAT, HUNK, LUMP,
    HUNCH, PIECE, SLAB, GOBBET,
    PORTION
chunky .... BURLY, HEFTY,
    PORTLY, SQUAT, STOUT,
    STOCKY, THICKSET,
    CORPULENT
church .... SECT, CHAPEL,
    MINSTER, TEMPLE, HOUSE OF
    GOD, HOUSE OF WORSHIP,
    DENOMINATION
altar attendant .... ACOLYTE
altar offerings .... ALTARAGE
archaic .... FANE
area .... TRANSEPT
basin .... FONT, STOUP,

LAVABO, PISCINA
bell/ringer .... SEXTON
bell tower .... BELFRY
bench/seat .... PEW, STALL
benefice .... LIVING
benefice, holding of
.... INCUMBENCY
benefit/fund-raising sale
.... BAZAAR
bishop's .... CATHEDRAL
body of .... NAVE
Buddhist .... PAGODA
building .... ECCLESIA
calendar .... ORDO
caretaker ..... SEXTON, VERGER
chancel .... BEMA
cathedral .... LATERAN,
MINSTER
chandelier .... CORONA
chapel .... CHANTRY, ORATORY
choir leader .... CHORAGUS,
CHORISTER, PRECENTOR
composition .... MOTET
contribution to .... TITHE
council/group .... SYNOD,
CONSISTORY
court .... ROTA, CLASSIS,
CONSISTORY
cup .... CHALICE
dignitary .... DEAN, POPE,
BISHOP, LEGATE, NUNCIO,
PRELATE, PRIMATE, CARDINAL
director .... CHORAGUS,
PRECENTOR
dish .... PATEN
dissenter .... SECTARY,
APOSTATE
district .... PARISH, DIOCESE
division in a .... SCHISM
doorkeeper/guard ..... OSTIARY
elder .... PRESBYTER
endowment to a
.... PATRIMONY
festival .... EASTER
finale .... AMEN
French .... EGLISE
gallery .... JUBE, LOFT
governing group .... CLASSIS
government .... HIERARCHY
grave-digger .... SEXTON
grounds .... PRECINCT
having no .... CHURCHLESS
head .... PONTIFF
Italian .... DUOMO
jurisdiction .... SEE,
BISHOPRIC, OBEDIENCE
land/property .... GLEBE
language .... LATIN
law .... CANON
lay leader .... ELDER
leader .... HIERARCH

lectern .... AMBO, ROSTRUM
living .... BENEFICE
loft .... JUBE
main part .... NAVE
members .... FOLD, FLOCK,
ECCLESIA, PARISHIONERS
monastery's .... MINSTER
morning service .... LAUD,
MATIN
Moslem .... MOSQUE
music .... HYMN, PSALM,
CANTATA
of Latter Day Saints
.... MORMON
office ...... BENEFICE, MINISTRY
office, sale of .... SIMONY
officer .... ELDER, BEADLE,
SEXTON, VERGER, ORDINARY,
PRESBYTER, SACRIST(AN)
part .... PEW, APSE, BEMA,
ALTAR, VESTRY, CHANCEL,
ORATORY, STEEPLE, SACRISTY,
TRANSEPT
place for shrines
.... FERETORY
poetic .... FANE
porch .... PARVIS, GALILEE
practice of peace ...... IRENICS
private/secret meeting
.... CONCLAVE
reader .... LECTOR
reading stand .... AMBO,
LECTERN, ROSTRUM
recess .... APSE
regular attender .... CHURCH-
GOER
revenue .... TITHE, BENEFICE
rite ..... (HIGH) MASS, BAPTISM,
BENEDICTION, COMMUNION,
MATRIMONY
Roman .... BASILICA
room for sacred vessels
.... VESTRY, SACRISTY
sale of offices, etc.
.... SIMONY, BARRATRY
sanctuary .... SACRARIUM
Scottish .... KIRK
screen .... ICONASTASIS
seamen's .... BETHEL
seat for clergy .... SEDILIA
separation from .... SCHISM
service/ceremony .... LAUD,
MASS, NONES, TE DEUM
service clothes
.... CANONICALS
service invocation
.... BENEDICTION
service reader .... LECTOR
service reading .... LECTION
singers' group .... CHOIR
tax .... TITHE

tower .... BELFRY, STEEPLE
tower top .... SPIRE
tribunal .... ROTA
vault .... CRYPT
vestibule .... NARTHEX
vestment room .... VESTRY,
SACRISTY
washbowl .... LAVABO
woman assistant
.... DEACONESS
Yiddish .... SHUL
Churchill Downs event .... RACE,
DERBY
Churchill's (W.) daughter
.... SARAH
forte .... PROSE
hobby .... BRICKLAYING
lady .... CLEMENTINE
nickname .... WINNIE
son .... RANDOLPH
son-in-law .... SOAMES
trademark .... CIGAR, VEE SIGN
churchly .... CLERICAL, PASTORAL
churchman .... CANON, ELDER,
BELIEVER, VICAR, BISHOP,
CLERGY, PASTOR, PRIEST,
CARDINAL, MINISTER,
ECCLESIASTIC
churchyard .... PARVIS, GOD'S
ACRE
churl .... OAF, BOOR, HIND, LOUT,
CARL(E), KNAVE, CEORL,
FREEMAN, PEASANT, VARLET,
YOKEL, VILLEIN
churlish .... DOUR, SURLY,
RUSTIC, SULLEN, BOORISH
churn .... BEAT, STIR, WHIP,
SHAKE, SEETHE, AGITATE
rotator .... DASHER
chute .... SHOOT, SLIDE, RAPIDS,
HOPPER, RUNWAY, ROLLWAY,
TROUGH, WATERFALL
for logs .... FLUME
chutney .... RELISH
chutzpah .... NERVE
Chuvash .... BULGARIAN
cibol .... ONION
ciborium .... CUP, PYX, CANOPY
cicada .... LOCUST
vibrating membrane of
.... TIMBAL
cicatricle .... TREAD
cicatrix .... SCAR
Cicero .... TULLY, MARCUS
target of .... CATILINE
cicerone .... GUIDE, DRAGOMAN
Cid .... LEADER
play, author of ..... CORNEILLE
name of .... RUY, (RODRIGO)
DIAZ
sword of .... COLADA

cider .... (APPLE) JUICE, PERKIN, SYTHER, VINEGAR
pear juice .... PERRY
spiced/sweetened .... FLIP
sweeten .... MULL
ci-devant .... LATE, FORMER, RECENT
cigar .... WEED, CLARO, SMOKE, CORONA, CHEROOT, CULEBRA, HAVANA, LONDRES, TOBACCO, COLORADO, BELVEDERE, PANATEL(L)A, PERFECTO
box .... HUMIDOR
butt .... STUB, SNIPE
cheap .... TOBY, STOGIE, STOG(E)Y
descriptive of a .... MADURO
end .... ETTE
Philippine .... MANILA
puff .... DRAG
self-lighting .... LOCOFOCO
Spanish .... PURO, CIGARRO
tree, e.g. .... CATALPA
cigarette, berry .... CUBEB
brand ..... KENT, CAMEL, TRUE, SALEM, DUNHILL, PALL MALL, PIEDMONT, WINSTON, MARLBORO, CHESTER(FIELD)
butt .... STUB, SNIPE
ingredient .... TOBACCO
kind of .... REGULAR, KING-SIZE, FILTER-TIP
lighter .... VESUVIAN
marijuana .... REEFER
material .... MAKINGS
non-tobacco .... CUBEB, REEFER, MARIJUANA
piece .... STICK
product .... TAR, NICOTINE
puff .... DRAG
slang .... COFFIN NAIL, FAG, BUTT, GASPER
smoke cleaner .... FILTER
smoke cooler .... MENTHOL
smoking aid .... PIPE
cigarfish .... SCAD
cilice .... HAIRCLOTH
cilium/cilia .... EYELASH(ES)
cimex .... BEDBUG
Cimmerian .... DARK, BLACK, GLOOMY
cinch .... GIRTH, FASTEN
lead-pipe .... SNAP
slang .... SURE THING
cinchona ...... BARK, TREE, QUILL
alkaloid .... QUINIDINE, QUININE
Cincinnati ball club .... REDS, REDLEGS
family .... TAFT(S)
managers .... REDHEADS

cincture .... BELT, GIRDLE, ENCLOSURE, WAISTBAND
cinder .... ASH(ES), SLAG
like lava .... SCORIA
sifter .... RIDDLE
Cinderella of Pop .... HOPKIN
cinema .... MOVIE, THEATER, MOTION PICTURE
cinerarium .... URN
cinerator .... FURNACE, CREMATORY
cingulum .... BELT, GIRDLE
cinnabar .... ORE, PIGMENT, SINOPLE, VERMILION
cinnamon .... BARK, SPICE, CANELLA
adulterant .... CASSIA
roll .... QUILL
stone .... GARNET, ESSONITE
cinquefoil .... CLOVER, FIVE-FINGER, POTENTILLA
cion .... BUD, GRAFT, SHOOT
Cipango .... JAPAN
cipher .... CODE, ZERO, DEVICE, OUGHT, NAUGHT, MONOGRAM, NONENTITY
system .... CODES
cipolin .... MARBLE
circa .... ABOUT
Circe .... TEMPTRESS, ENCHANTRESS
home of .... AEAEA
circle .... DISK, LOOP, RING, CLIQUE, CIRQUE, COTERIE, SET, GROUP, ENCIRCLE, WHIRL, ZODIAC
angle/arc .... RADIAN
describing one .... VICIOUS
flattened .... OVAL
half a .... HEMICYCLE
imaginary celestial .... COLURE
of guards .... CORDON
of light .... HALO, NIMB, CORONA
part ..... ARC, RADIUS, SECANT, SECTOR, DIAMETER, CIRCUMFERENCE
poetic .... RONDURE
quarter section .... OVOLO, QUADRANT
Circle, imaginary and parallel to equator .... ARCTIC, ANTARCTIC
circuit .... LAP, TOUR, LOOP, AMBIT, CYCLE, ORBIT, ROUND, ROUTE, CURVET, DISTRICT
court/judges' .... EYRE
in radio .... HOOKUP
of a utility system .... MAIN
track .... LAP

circuitous .... DEVIOUS, ROUNDABOUT
circuity .... ZIGZAG, INDIRECT
circular .... BILL, ROUND, BULLETIN, PAMPHLET, GLOBULAR, SPHERICAL
band .... HOOP, RING, BRACELET
course .... OVAL, RACETRACK
cross section .... TERETE
eyelet .... GROMMET
figure/line .... RING
form .... GYRE
letter, papal ...... ENCYCLICAL
motion ...... EDDY, GYRE, SPIN, WHIRL, ROTATE, GYRATION
plate .... DISC, DISH, DISK
saw .... EDGER
space .... CIRQUE
step .... AMBIT
turn .... LOOP
wall of dome .... DRUM
wheel .... RUNDLE
circulate .... PASS, ISSUE, DIFFUSE, SPREAD, GET AROUND, PUBLISH, MOVE AROUND
circumference ...... AMBIT, GIRTH, PERIPHERY
circumlocution .... AMBAGE, VERBIAGE, PERIPHRASE, PERIPHRASIS
circumnavigator, first .... MAGELLAN
circumscribe .... LIMIT, CONFINE, ENCIRCLE, ENCOMPASS
circumspect .... SAFE, WARY, CAREFUL, PRUDENT, CAUTIOUS
circumspection .... PRUDENCE
circumstance .... FACT, STATE, CASE, STATUS, DETAIL, CONDITION
companion of .... POMP
circumvent .... SKIRT, ESCHEW, OUTWIT, SIDESTEP
circus .... ARENA, CIRQUE, CARNIVAL, (TENT) SHOW
animal .... BEAR, LION, SEAL, ELEPHANT
arena .... RING, HIPPODROME
colloquial .... BIG TOP
director .... RINGMASTER
horse .... GRAY
laborer .... ROUSTER, ROUSTABOUT
man .... LION TRAINER
minor attraction .... SIDE SHOW
name, bigtime .... BAILEY, BARNUM, RINGLING
net .... TRAMPOLIN(E)
perennial .... CLOWN

performer .... FLEA, SEAL,
CLOWN, ACROBAT, AERIALIST,
TUMBLER, UNICYCLIST,
JUGGLER, EQUESTRIEN(NE)
ring cover .... TANBARK
swing .... TRAPEZE
vehicle .... CARAVAN
cirque ...... RING, CIRCLE, CIRCUS,
AMPHITHEATER
cirriped .... BARNACLE,
CRUSTACEAN
cirrus .... CLOUDS, FEELERS,
TENDRIL
cloud .... MARE'S-TAIL
cirsoid .... VARIX, VARICOSE
cisco .... HERRING, (WHITE)FISH
cist .... TOMB, CHEST
cistern .... VAC, VAT, (RAIN) TANK
in anatomy .... SAC, CAVITY
natural .... RESERVOIR
cit .... CITIZEN, TOWNMAN
citadel .... FORT, TOWER, CASTLE,
REFUGE, FORTRESS,
ACROPOLIS, STRONGHOLD
of justice, so-called .... COURT
Russian .... KREMLIN
cital .... SUMMONS
citation .... NOTICE, SUMMONS,
QUOTATION, REFERENCE
favorable .... ACCOLADE,
COMMENDATION
cite .... CALL, QUOTE, MENTION,
SUMMON
loosely .... PARAPHRASE
cithern .... CITOLE
cities, between .... INTERURBAN
citified: colloq. .... URBAN
citizen .... NATIVE, BURGESS,
DENIZEN, FREEMAN, SUBJECT,
CIVILIAN, NATIONAL,
RESIDENT, INHABITANT
army .... MILITIA
French .... CITOYEN
of the world ..... COSMOPOLITE
citizenry, local
.... HOMETOWNERS
citizens, assembly of
.... ECCLESIA
of .... CIVIC, CIVIL
citrine .... FALSE TOPAZ
citron .... LIME, ETROG, LEMON
fruit of, symbol of Sukkoth
.... ESROG
citrus drink .... ADE, LIMEADE,
LEMONADE, ORANGEADE
citrus fruit .... LIME, LEMON,
CITRON, ORANGE, MANDARIN,
BERGAMOT, GRAPEFRUIT
disease .... PSOROSIS
membrane .... RAG
oil .... BERGAMOT

skin .... ZEST
city .... TOWN, COSMOPOLIS,
METROPOLIS, MUNICIPALITY
bishop's .... SEE
business section
.... DOWNTOWN
cathedral .... ELY, YORK,
R(H)EIMS, CHARTRES
colloquial .... BURG, BURH,
BIG TOWN
district .... WARD
father .... ALDERMAN,
COUNCILOR
fellow: sl. .... DUDE
gangster .... PLUG-UGLY
great .... MEGALOPOLIS
hall .... AYUNTAMIENTO
heavenly .... SION, ZION
main .... METROPOLIS
of a .... CIVIC, URBAN,
MUNICIPAL
of sin/wicked .... SODOM,
BABYLON, GOMORRAH
of the leaning tower .... PISA
of the Rhine .... MAINZ
of vice .... BABYLON
official .... MAYOR,
ALDERMAN, COUNCILOR
on the Red River .... FARGO
on the sea .... PORT
Pearl of the Orient
.... MANILA
pertaining to .... CIVIC, URBAN
prename .... LAS, LOS
problem .... SMOG, CRIME,
SLUMS, TRAFFIC, POVERTY
square .... PARK
state ...... VATICAN, SINGAPORE
steel .... ESSEN
subdivision .... WARD,
SECTION, PRECINCT
vice center .... TENDERLOIN
windy .... CHICAGO
wonder .... AGRA
City of Angels .... BANGKOK
Bridges .... BRUGES
Brotherly Love
.... PHILADELPHIA
David .... JERUSALEM
Kings .... LIMA
Lights .... PARIS
Masts .... LONDON
Pillars .... IREM
Refuge .... BEZER, GOLAN,
HEBRON, KEDESH, MEDINA,
RAMOTH, SECHEM
Saints .... MONTREAL
Seven Hills .... ROME
the Dead .... NECROPOLIS
the Gods .... ASGARD
civet .... CAT, FUR, DEDES, FOSSA,

RASSE, ZIBET, MUSANG,
NANDINE
like animal .... GENET(TE),
SURICATE
odor .... MUSK(LIKE)
of the .... VIVERINE
civil .... LAY, CIVIC, POLITE,
COURTLY, URBANE, SECULAR,
CIVILIZED, TEMPORAL,
COURTEOUS
magistrate .... SYNDIC
marriage performer ..... JUDGE
wrong .... TORT
Civil War admiral .... FARRAGUT
battlefield .... SHILOH,
ATLANTA, ANTIETAM, BULL
RUN, GETTYSBURG
before the .... ANTEBELLUM
cartoonist .... NAST
division .... BLUE AND GRAY,
NORTH AND SOUTH,
CONFEDERATE AND REBEL
general .... LEE, POPE, HOOD,
EWELL, GRANT, MEADE,
BRAGG, BUELL, SCOTT,
HOOKER, FREMONT,
MCCLELLAN, SHERMAN,
SHERIDAN
soldier .... REB, YANKEE
vet .... GAR
volunteer .... ZOUAVE
civilian .... CITIZEN, CIV(V)IES,
RESIDENT, NONMILITARY,
NONCOMBATANT
clothes .... MUFTI
civilization .... CULTURE
cradle of .... ASIA
civilize .... REFINE, RECLAIM,
EDUCATE, CULTIVATE
clabber .... MILK, CURDLE
clack ...... BLAB, PRATE, CHATTER
clad .... ROBED, ATTIRED,
CLOTHED, DRESSED
claim .... AVER, RIGHT, TITLE,
ALLEGE, ASSERT, CONTEND
legal ...... LIEN, PLEA, DEMAND
mining .... STAKE
on property .... LIEN
without right .... ARROGATE
claimant, kind of .... PRETENDER
clairvoyance .... INSIGHT,
INTUITION, DIVINATION
clairvoyant .... SEER
clam .... MYA, MOLLUSK
hard-shell .... QUAHOG,
QUAHAUG
joint of .... HINGE
killer .... WINKLE
razor .... SOLEN
shell .... TEST, SHUCK
shell opening .... GAPE

soft-shell .... STEAMER
young .... LITTLENECK
clamant .... NOISY, URGENT
clambake .... OUTING, PICNIC,
RALLY, COOKOUT
clamber .... SHIN, CLIMB, CRAWL,
SCALE, SCRAMBLE
clammy .... DAMP, MOIST,
SWEATY
clamor .... DIN, RIOT, NOISE, HUE,
GAFF, OUTCRY, UPROAR,
YAMMER
for .... LEVY, DEMAND,
REQUIRE
clamorous .... LOUD, NOISY,
SHRILL, DINNING, VOCIFEROUS
clamp .... GRIP, VISE, FASTENER
like device .... CHUCK
clan .... GENS, SEPT, TRIBE,
GROUP, CLIQUE, FAMILY
leader .... THANE, TANIST,
CHIEFTAIN
of a .... GENTILE
pattern .... TARTAN
quarrel .... FEUD
symbol .... TOTEM
clandestine .... SLY, SECRET,
HIDDEN, VEILED, FURTIVE,
ILLICIT, UNDERCOVER,
UNDERHAND, SURREPTITIOUS
meeting, usually .... TRYST,
RENDEZVOUS
clang ...... TOLL, DING, PEAL, RING
clangor .... DIN, PEAL, JANGLE
clannish .... TRIBAL
clap .... BLOW, SLAM, SLAP,
STRIKE, APPLAUD
clapboard .... SIDING
clapper, bell .... TONGUE
claptrap .... BOSH, HOKUM,
DRIVEL, HEROICS
claque(ur) .... FAN, ROOTER,
APPLAUDER
Clara .... BOW, BARTON
or Barbara .... SANTA
clare .... MINT
clarence .... CARRIAGE
Clarence, lawyer .... DARROW
claret .... WINE, BORDEAU
clarify .... CLEAR(UP), DEFINE,
FILTER, PURIFY, REFINE,
EXPLAIN, EXPOUND, SETTLE,
ELUCIDATE
lard .... RENDER
clarinet .... REED
forerunner .... CHALUMEAU
socket .... BIRN
clarinetist, bandleader
.... (ARTIE) SHAW
clarion .... TRUMPET
clarity ...... CLEARNESS, LUCIDITY

Clark .... ROY, DICK
claro .... CIGAR
clarry .... MINT
clash .... DIFFER, COLLIDE,
CONFLICT, DISAGREE
clasp .... HUG, HASP, HOOK, OUCH,
CINCH, BUCKLE, ENFOLD,
FIBULA, TASSEL, EMBRACE,
FASTENING
hair .... BARRETTE
ornamental .... BROOCH
class .... ILK, KIND, RATE, SORT,
TYPE, ORDER, KIDNEY, RANK,
SPECIES, CATEGORY
first .... A-ONE, BEST
of animal/plant .... GENUS
of ruling deities
.... MONARCHY, THEARCHY
scientific .... GENUS, GENERA
slang ...... QUALITY, TOP-RATE,
EXCELLENCE
social .... CASTE
classic ...... OLD, SIMPLE, ANTIQUE
car .... REO
classical language .... GREEK,
LATIN, ROMAN
music ..... SONATA, CONCERTO,
SYMPHONY
non .... MODERN, POPULAR,
ROMANTIC
classics annotator .... SCHOLIAST
classification .... LABEL,
GROUPING, CATEGORY
of diseases .... NOSOLOGY
science of .... TAXONOMY
classified (information)
.... SECRET
classify .... LIST, RATE, SORT,
TYPE, LABEL, ASSORT,
ARRANGE, CATALOGUE
classis .... ROTA
classy .... CHIC, ELEGANT, STYLISH
clatter .... DIN, HUBBUB, HURTLE,
RATTLE, BRATTLE
Claude .... RAINS, MONET
claudicant .... LAME, LIMPING
clavichord .... SPINET
clavicle .... COLLARBONE
clavier .... KEYBOARD
common .... PIANO
claviform .... CLAVATE, CLUB-
SHAPED
claw .... HOOK, NAIL, TALON,
NIPPER, POUNCE, UNGUIS,
UNGULA, SCRATCH
having/like a .... UNGUAL
like process .... CALCAR
of crustacean .... CHELA,
PINCER
pincer-like .... CHELIFORM
retract .... SHEATHE

claws .... UNCI
clay .... LOAM, LUTE, MARL,
ARGIL, LOESS, KAOLIN(E),
SAGGAR, SAGGER, FIGULINE,
LATERITE, LITHOMARGE
baked ...... BOLE, TILE, ADOBE,
BRICK
case .... SAGGAR, SAGGER,
SEGGAR
chunk/lump of/disk .... BAT
clump of .... CLOD
desert .... ADOBE
earthy/ore-bearing ..... OCHER,
OCHRE
formation .... SHALE
granite .... PETUNTSE
layer .... SLOAM
like/pertaining to .... BOLAR
mixture .... LOAM, CEMENT,
PUDDLE
molded .... PUG
oven .... TANDOOR
paste .... PATE
pigeon .... TARGET
pigeon shoot .... SKEET
plastic .... PUG
porcelain .... PASTE, KAOLIN
potter's .... ARGIL, PASTE,
FIGULINE
rock .... MUDSTONE
sieve .... LAUN
thinned .... SLIP
tobacco pipe .... DUDEEN
wad .... BAT
water mixture .... SLURRY
white .... PETUNTSE
clayey .... BOLAR, LUTOSE
cement .... LUTE
soil .... BOLE, LOAM, MALM,
MARL, LOESS
claymore .... (BROAD)SWORD
clean ...... PURE, CHASTE, SINLESS,
ABSTERGE, SPOTLESS,
UNSOILED
and draw fowl .... DRESS
as a _____ .... WHISTLE
breast, make a .... CONFESS
by rubbing ...... SCOUR, SCRUB
clothes .... LAUNDER
copy .... LEGIBLE, READABLE
hands .... INNOCENT
of impurities .... PURGE,
PURIFY
ship's bottom .... BREAM,
GRAVE
slang .... SPIC AND SPAN
slate .... RASA, TABULA
up .... WASH, FINISH, SPRUCE
with abrasive .... SCOUR,
SCRAPE
with broom .... SWEEP

with mop .... SWAB
cleaner .... SOAP, SWEEPER, MAID,
    JANITOR, CHARWOMAN
cleaning cloth .... RAG
powder .... ARIEL, PUMICE
cleanse .... PURGE, PURIFY,
    FRESHEN, DETERGE,
    FUMIGATE, DEODORIZE,
    STERILIZE
cleansing substance ...... BORAX,
    SOAP, ARIEL, DETERGENT,
    PURGATIVE, ABSTERGENT
clear .... RID, FREE, PURE,
    HURDLE, LIQUID, LUCENT,
    SHEER, CLARIFY, EVIDENT,
    PLAIN, APPARENT, LUCULENT,
    OBVIOUS, (PEL)LUCID
a magnetic tape .... ERASE
a path .... MAKE WAY
as _____ .... CRYSTAL
conscience .... INNOCENT
cut .... SHARP, DISTINCT,
    TRENCHANT
day/weather ...... FAIR, SUNNY,
    CLOUDLESS, STORMLESS,
    UNCLOUDED
of charges .... ACQUIT,
    ABSOLVE, EXONERATE
out .... GO, LEAVE, DECAMP,
    DEPART, VACATE
perfectly .... LUCID, LIMPID
profit .... NET
sky .... ETHER
textile .... DIAPHANOUS
the way! .... GANGWAY
throat audibly ..... HEM, HAWK
title .... UNENCUMBERED
to the mind .... PLAIN,
    DISTINCT, PALPABLE
up .... SOLVE, CLARIFY,
    EXPLAIN, STRAIGHTEN
clearance .... LEEWAY, MARGIN,
    ADJUSTMENT
of charges .... ACQUITTAL
of disease symptoms
    .... REMISSION
sale .... BARGAIN, RUMMAGE
cleareyed .... AWARE, PERCEPTIVE
clearing, wood .... GLADE
cleat .... KEVEL, PITON, BATTON
make secure around
    .... BELAY
cleavage .... GULF, RIFT, CLEFT,
    FISSION, DIVISION
cleave .... REND, RIVE, CLING,
    SEVER, SPLIT, STICK, ADHERE,
    BREAK, DIVIDE, SUNDER
cleaver .... FROE, FROW, RIVER,
    CHOPPER
sky .... LIGHTNING
cleek .... HOOK

cleft ...... GAP, RIFT, SPLIT, CRACK,
    CREVICE, FISSURE, FORKED,
    DIVIDED, SCISSURE
easily .... FISSILE
Clemenceau's soubriquet
    .... TIGER, TIGRE
clemency .... GRACE, MERCY,
    LENIENCY, MILDNESS
Clemens's pen name ...... MARK
    TWAIN
clement .... MILD, LENIENT,
    MERCIFUL
clench .... GRIP, CLINCH
clenched hand .... FIST
Cleopatra .... FATHER'S GLORY
Cleopatra's domain .... NILE,
    EGYPT
killer .... ASP
lover .... (MARK) ANTONY,
    (JULIUS) CAESAR
maid .... IRAS
mascara .... KOHL
Needle .... OBELISK
river .... NILE
son .... CAESARION
title .... QUEEN
clepe .... CALL, NAME
clepsydra .... (WATER) CLOCK,
    WATERGLASS
clergy .... ABBACY, MINISTRY,
    PRIESTHOOD, THE CLOTH,
    PAPACY, FIRST ESTATE
clergyman .... ABBE, CANON,
    CLERIC, CURATE, DIVINE,
    PADRE, PARSON, PASTOR,
    PRIEST, BISHOP, PRELATE,
    MINISTER, RABBI, DIOCESAN,
    CARDINAL, RECTOR, IMAM,
    VICAR, CHAPLAIN
and author .... SHEEN
church service vestment
    .... CANONICALS
colloquial .... DOMINIE
degree of .... STB
position/garment .... FROCK,
    CASSOCK, SURPLICE
residence of .... MANSE,
    RECTORY, PARSONAGE
salary of .... PREBEND
with the military .... PADRE,
    CHAPLAIN
clerical .... PASTORAL
abbr. .... ECCL
cap .... BIRETTA
collar .... RABATO, REBATO
vestment .... ALB, AMICE,
    FANON, ORALE, SURPLICE
clerisy .... INTELLECTUALS
clerk .... SCRIBE, SALESMAN,
    SECRETARY, SCRIVENER,
    TYPIST, OFFICE WORKER

Clerk's Tale heroine
    .... GRISELDA
Cleveland waterfront .... ERIE
clever .... CUTE, ADEPT, SLICK,
    SMART, ADROIT, BRIGHT,
    HABILE, CUNNING, SKILLFUL,
    TALENTED
as a fox .... VULPINE
remark: sl. .... MOT, CRACK,
    NIFTY
retort .... SALLY, BON MOT,
    REPARTEE, RIPOST(E),
    WITTICISM
stratagem .... COUP
cleverly amusing .... WITTY
done/said .... NEAT
clew .... KEY, TIP, BALL, CLUE,
    THREAD
cliche .... TRUISM, BANALITY,
    PLATITUDE
click .... PAWL, AGREE, CATCH,
    JIBE, SNICK, PALLET, SUCCEED
beetle .... DOR(R), ELATER
clicking sound .... TICK
client .... BUYER, PATRON,
    CUSTOMER
without .... BRIEFLESS
clientele .... TRADE, PATRONS,
    CLIENTAGE, CUSTOMERS,
    PATRONAGE
cliff .... CRAG, SCAR, BLUFF,
    PALISADE, PRECIPICE
debris .... TALUS
edge .... BROW
fissure .... CHINE
fissure for climbing
    .... CHIMNEY
rock pile .... TALUS
shelf .... LEDGE
cliffs, channel between .... GAT
line of .... PALISADES
climacteric .... CRUCIAL
woman's .... MENOPAUSE
climate .... SKY, WEATHER
study of .... METEOROLOGY
climax .... ACME, APOGEE,
    SUMMIT, ZENITH, PINNACLE,
    PEAK, APEX, CULMINATION
climb ...... RISE, MOUNT, ASCEND,
    SCALE, ASCENT, CLAMBER
a rope/pole .... SHIN
down .... DESCEND
climbers .... VINES
social .... SNOBS, PARVENU
climbing .... RISING, SCALING
adapted for .... SCANSORIAL
by attachment .... SCANDENT
iron .... SPUR, PITON, CRAMPON
means of .... LADDER
palm .... RATTAN
plant process .... TENDRIL

vine .... HOP, IVY, PEA, BINE, LIANA, LIANE, BRYONY

wall by ladder .... ESCALADE

clime .... REALM, REGION, CLIMATE, COUNTRY

clinch .... HUG, GRIP, NAIL, CLOSE, GRASP, RIVET, FASTEN, GRAPPLE

argument .... SETTLE

breaker .... REFEREE

nautical .... KNOT, NOOSE, CLENCH

slang .... EMBRACE

cling .... HOLD, GRASP, STICK, ADHERE, COHERE

clingfish .... REMORA, TESTAR

clinic .... WARD, SEMINAR, DISPENSARY

clink .... JAIL, RING, PRISON

clinker .... SLAG, BRICK

built .... LAPSTRAKE

clinking sound .... TINKLE

clinquant .... TINSEL(ED)

"Clinton's ditch" .... ERIE (CANAL)

Clio .... MUSE

Clio's field .... HISTORY

sister .... ERATO

clip .... CUT, MOW, GRIP, TRIM, SCAR, FASTEN, SHORTEN

colloquial .... HIT, PACE, CHEAT, PUNCH, SPEED, SWINDLE

ornamental .... BROOCH

Scottish .... COLL

slang .... GYP

clipped .... CURT, TERSE

clipper .... SHIP, AIRPLANE, SHEARER

barber's .... SCISSORS

clippings .... SCRAPS

clique .... SET, RING, CIRCLE, COTERIE, FACTION

advisers' .... CABAL, CAMARILLA

cloaca .... PRIVY, SEWER

cloak .... PALL, WRAP, GREGO, MANTUA, CONCEAL, CHLAMYS, GARMENT, DISGUISE

and-dagger group .... CIA, OSS, OGPU

blanket-like .... PONCHO, SERAPE

fur-lined .... PELISSE

hood of .... COWL

hooded .... CAMAIL, CAPOTE, BURNOUS, BURNOOSE, CARDINAL

over armor .... TABARD, SURCOAT

room .... CLOSET, VESTIARY

short ..... GREGO, MANT(E)LET, MANTILLA

Spanish .... CAPA, MANTA

used as raincoat .... PONCHO

woman's .... MANTEAU, CARDINAL

clobber .... HIT, BEAT, MAUL, DEFEAT

slang .... PUMMEL

cloche .... HAT, (GLASS) JAR

clock .... HOROLOGE, HOURGLASS, TIME(PIECE)

face of .... DIAL

in .... ARRIVE, REGISTER

inhabitant .... CUCKOO

kind of .... ALARM, RADIO, SUNDIAL, CHRONOGRAPH, CHRONOMETER, GRANDFATHER

London's famed .... BIG BEN

maker/dealer ...... HOROLOGER, HOROLOGIST

part .... DIAL, HAND, PAWL, BUNDY, CHIME, CLICK, PALLET, PENDULUM

ship-shaped .... NEF

slang .... TICKER

sound .... CHIME, TICK(TOCK)

watcher .... IDLER

water .... CLEPSYDRA

work device .... METRONOME

clocker .... TIMER

clocklike .... PRECISE, REGULAR

clockwise .... SUNWISE

clockwork .... EVENLY, PRECISELY

clod ...... DOLT, LUMP, SOIL, LOUT, BUMPKIN, EARTH, HILLBILLY

clodhopper .... BOOR, SHOE, PLOWMAN

clodpate/clodpoll .... DOLT, FOOL, BLOCKHEAD

clog .... JAM, SHOE, CHOKE, BLOCK, DANCE, SABOT, HAMPER, HINDER, IMPEDE, PATTEN, CHOPINE, GALOSH(E)

cloggy .... STICKY

cloisonne finish .... ENAMEL

cloister .... STOA, ABBEY, FRIARY, PRIORY, CONVENT, RETREAT, NUNNERY, MONASTERY

dweller .... NUN, MONK, ABBOT, ABBESS

cloistered ...... PRIVATE, RETIRED, ISOLATED, SECLUDED

clone .... COPY, REPLICA

original .... ORTET

close .... CAP, END, LOCK, SEAL, FINALE, FINISH, COMPACT, OCCLUDE, CONCLUDE, INTIMATE, SHUT(IN), STINGY, SULTRY

after opening .... RESEAL

British .... ENTRY, PASSAGE

building .... PADLOCK

by .... (A)NEAR, NIGH

conclusively .... CLINCH

down/up ..... FOLD, QUIT, STOP

fist .... CLENCH

fitting .... SNUG, (SKIN)TIGHT

hermetically .... SEAL

in .... ENCLOSE, ENCIRCLE, SURROUND

in music .... CODA

mouthed .... TACITURN

mouthed one .... CLAM

of day .... EVENTIDE

poetic .... NIGH, ANEAR

tightly .... CORK, SEAL

to the wind .... LUFF

violently .... SLAM

closed at one end .... BLIND

closefisted .... CHEAP, FRUGAL, STINGY, MISERLY, NIGGARDLY

closet ...... ROOM, AMBRY, CUDDY, PRIVY, LOCKER, TOILET, CUPBOARD

closing passage in music .... CODA

word .... AMEN

closure .... END, SEAL, BLOCKADE, CLOTURE, STOPPAGE, BOTTLENECK, OBSTRUCTION, BARRIER, CONCLUSION

clot .... GOUT, JELL, CRUOR, GRUME, COAGULATE

preventing substance .... HEPARIN

cloth .... BRAT, WOOF, GOODS, SERGE, DENIM, FABRIC, TEXTILE, TWILL, COTTON, MUSLIN, TRICOT, RAYON, FIBER, MATERIAL

a sample piece of .... SWATCH

altar .... PALL, VESPERAL

baptismal .... CHRISOM

bark .... TAPA

buff-colored .... NANKIN, NANKEEN

calico .... DOWLAS

camel's hair ..... ABA, CAMLET

chalice .... PALL

cheap .... MUNGO

checkered ...... PLAID, TARTAN

coarsely woven .... BURLAP

corded .... DIMITY, BENGALI

cotton ..... JEAN, DRILL, CHINO, CRASH, CALICO, CANVAS, DENIM, MANTA, CHINTZ, HOLLAND, MUSLIN, MADRAS, GINGHAM, NANKEEN, PERCALE

cover .... TILT, DRAPE

cretonne .... TOILE

crinkled .... CRAPE, CREPE
curtain .... TAPIS
damask-like .... LAMPAS
dealer .... DRAPER, MERCER,
                CLOTHIER
diagonal weave .... TWILL
dressing .... GAUZE, STUPE
drying .... TOWEL
drying frame .... TENTER
edge .... SELVAGE
end part of .... FAG
equal to 2¼ inches .... NAIL
fiber .... NAP, FLAX, SILK,
       LINEN, RAMIE, COTTON
figured .... BROCADE,
     JACQUARD, BROCATEL(LE)
fine cotton .... PERCALINE
fine, thin .... BATISTE
finishing machine ..... BEETLE,
              CALENDER
flaxen .... LINEN
flaw .... RIP, SNAG, TEAR
floor covering .... RUG
for face sweat ...... VERONICA,
            SUDARIUM
for sheets, pillowcases
.... MUSLIN, PERCALE
frieze-like .... RATTEEN
gauzy .... BAREGE, ILLUSION
glazed .... CHINTZ, JACONET
glossy .... SILK, SATIN,
     SATEEN, CALAMANCO,
     LUSTRING, LUTESTRING
goat's hair .... ABA
gold .... CYPRUS, CYPRESS
hairy surface .... NAP
handwoven .... TAPESTRY
hanging in folds ..... DRAPERY
heavy .... MACE
hemp, unbleached .... CANVAS
jute .... GUNNY
knot .... BURL
leftover pieces (from bolt)
.... REMNANTS
lightweight .... DELAINE
linen .... DRILL, TOILE,
      DOWLAS, HOLLAND
linen with striped pattern
.... SEERSUCKER
loin .... LAVA-LAVA
make of ..... WOVEN, KNITTED,
      PRESSED, EMBOSSED
maker .... DRAPER, WEAVER
making spy .... KEEK
material ..... FLAX, HAIR, SILK,
    SKIN, WOOL, FIBER, RAYON,
          COTTON
measure ...... ELL, NAIL, YARD,
          METER
measure equal to 30 yards
.... BOLT

medicated .... STUPE
metallic .... LAME
method of dyeing designs on
.... BATIK
mix-colored .... MOTLEY
mulberry bark .... TAPA
mummy .... BYSSUS
nautical .... SAIL, CANVAS
needlework on
.... EMBROIDERY
ornamental .... DOSSAL
ornamentally designed
.... LACE, DAMASK, LAMPAS
penitent's .... SACKCLOTH
plaid .... TARTAN
plush-like .... BOLIVIA
powder .... SACHET
rib .... CORD
ribbed .... CORDUROY
ridge .... RIB, WALE
selvage .... LIST
sheer .... TOILE, CHIFFON
silk .... SATIN, CHIFFON,
  CREPE, TAFFETA, LUSTRING,
   PONGEE, CHARMEUSE,
  SARCENET, LEVANTINE
soft .... SILK, SATIN,
         GOSSAMER
stiffening .... WIGAN
strip .... LIST
strips for decoration
.... BUNTING
surface .... NAP
synthetic .... NYLON, RAYON,
         DACRON
table .... NAPKIN
tapestry .... TAPIS
texture .... WALE
the .... CLERGY
thin, stiff .... ORGANZA
to wrap dead person in
.... BYSSUS, SHROUD,
        CEREMENT
triangular .... GORE
twilled .... JEAN, DENIM,
   CHINO, PLAID, SERGE,
      LEVANTINE
umbrella .... GLORIA
upholstering .... TABARET,
     BROCATEL(LE)
veil .... BAREGE
velvet-like .... PANNE
wall hanging .... TAPESTRY
waste .... RAG
waterproof .... GOSSAMER
waxed .... CEREMENT
wiping .... TOWEL, NAPKIN
with decorative pictures
.... TAPESTRY
with diagonal weave .... DRILL

with raised design
.... BROCHE, BROCADE
with satin strips ...... TABARET
with uncut loops .... TERRY
wool(en)—See woolen
worn like a scarf .... STOLE
woven with a pebbly pattern
.... SHARKSKIN
clothe ...... DON, RIG, GARB, ROBE,
   DRAPE, DRESS, ENDUE, EQUIP,
      INVEST
clothed .... CLAD, ATTIRED,
   DRESSED, COSTUMED,
     INVESTED
clothes ...... WEAR, DRESS, ATTIRE,
   RAIMENT, APPAREL,
   GARMENTS, GARB,
  HABILIMENT, TOGGERY
basket .... HAMPER
bride's .... TROUSSEAU, BRIDAL
      OUTFIT
cheap .... SLOPS
chest .... BUREAU, DRESSER
civilian .... PLAIN, CIVVIES
closet .... VESTRY, WARDROBE,
     CLOAKROOM
collection of .... OUTFIT,
   ENSEMBLE, WARDROBE
colloquial .... DUDS, RAGS,
    TOGS, THREADS
fancier ..... FOP, DUDE, DANDY
formal .... TUX, TAILS,
  TUXEDO, EVENING GOWN
gaudy .... FRIPPERY
line .... SEAM
moth .... TINEA
ordinary .... MUFTI
party .... FINERY, GLAD RAGS
pertaining to .... VESTIARY
place for .... BUREAU, CLOSET,
   DRESSER, WARDROBE
powder .... SACHET
press .... IRON, ARMOIRE
rack .... VALET
ragged .... TATTERS
set of .... SUIT, ENSEMBLE
splendid .... REGALIA
stand .... RACK, TREE
to be washed/soiled
.... LAUNDRY
work .... APRON, DENIM,
  JEANS, SMOCK, COVERALL,
  UNIFORM, DUNGAREES
worn .... SECOND-HAND,
   HAND-ME-DOWNS
clotheshorse: colloq. .... FOP,
  DUDE, DANDY, COXCOMB
famed .... (BEAU) BRUMMEL
clothespress .... ARMOIRE
clothier Strauss .... LEVI
clothing .... GARB, ATTIRE,

APPAREL, COSTUME, RAIMENT, HABILIMENT
ID .... NAMETAPE
of men's .... SARTORIAL
pin .... AGLET
store ..... CLOTHIERS, SWEATER SHOP, DRESS SHOP, TOGGERY, HABERDASHERY
store stiff .... MANNEQUIN
Clotho ...... FATE, WEIRD, SPINNER
clotting protein .... GLOBULIN
cloture .... CLOSING, CLOSURE
cloud .... DIM, FOG, GLOOM, HAZE, SULLY, DARKEN, OBSCURE
combining form .... NEPHO
composition .... GAS, DUST, SMOKE, STEAM, WATER, VAPOR
formation .... CIRRUS, NIMBUS, CUMULUS, STRATUS
like mass .... COMA, NEBULA
nine .... JOY, BLISS, ECSTASY
of dust/smoke/gas .... MIST
photo of .... NEPHOGRAM
region .... SKY
small .... CLOUDLET
surrounding gods ...... NIMBUS
cloudburst ...... RAIN, DOWNPOUR
cloudless .... CLEAR, SUNNY, BRIGHT
clouds, fleecy .... CIRRUS
broken mass of .... (W)RACK
combining form .... NEPHO
cumulus .... WOOLPACK
in the ...... FANCIFUL, REVERIE, DAYDREAMING
study of .... NEPHOLOGY
wind-driven .... SCUD
cloudy .... DIM, HAZY, GLOOMY, MISTY, DARK, TURBID, LOWERING, FOGGY, NEBULOUS, NUBILOUS, SHADY, OVERCAST, TROUBLED
clough .... GORGE, RAVINE
clout .... HIT, RAP, BLOW, CUFF, SLAP, SWAT, KNOCK
colloquial .... PULL, POWER, IMPACT, INFLUENCE
clove ...... BUD, SPICE, CARNATION
cloven ...... CLEFT, SPLIT, DIVIDED
footed ...... DEVILISH, SATANIC, FISSIPED
hoofed .... BISULCATE
clover ...... HERB, ALSIKE, LADINO, NARDOO, BERSEEM, ALFALFA, MELILOT, TREFOIL, SHAMROCK, THREE-LEAF
family .... LEGUME
genus .... TRIFOLIUM
in ..... COMFORT, CORNUCOPIA, PROSPERITY

plant resembling .... MEDIC
yield .... HONEY
cloverland .... LEA
cloverleaf .... CROSSWAY, CROSSROAD
clown .... APER, BOOR, LOUT, MIME, ZANY, BUFFO, COMIC, JESTER, BUFFOON, COMEDIAN, HARLEQUIN, PUNCHINELLO
forte of a .... JOKES, ANTICS, PRANKS, TRICKS, ACT SILLY, (TOM)FOOLERY
garment of .... MOTLEY
of a sort: sl. .... CUTUP
Shakespearean play .... FESTE, LAVACHE
woman .... BUFFA
clownish .... RUDE, CLUMSY, BOORISH, ARTLESS, AWKWARD
cloy ...... BORE, GLUT, PALL, SATE, SATIATE, SURFEIT
cloying .... SUGARY, LUSCIOUS
club .... MAUL, STICK, CUDGEL, HIT, BEAT, STRIKE, CLIQUE, SOCIETY, BLUDGEON
aborigine's .... WADDY
armor-breaking/heavy .... MACE
baseball .... BAT
benefit sale .... BAZAAR, RUMMAGE
billiards .... CUE, MACE
college .... SORORITY, FRAT(ERNITY)
for beating cloth .... BEETLE
for sandtraps .... (SAND)WEDGE
golf .... IRON, WOOD, CLEEK, DRIVER, PUTTER
hockey .... BANDY
hold on .... GRIP
house figure .... PRO
local division .... CHAPTER
manager .... STEWARD
member, certain .... LIAR
metal-headed .... MACE
military service .... USO
moss .... LYCOPOD
payment .... DUES
policeman's .... BILLY, TRUNCHEON
polo .... MALLET
service .... LIONS, JAYCEES, ROTARY, KIWANIS
shaped .... CLAVATE, CLAVIFORM
social .... BRIDGE, COTERIE, SORORITY
women's ...... ZONTA, SOROSIS, SORORITY
wooden .... MAUL

clubby .... CLANNISH, SOCIABLE
clubfoot .... TALIPES
clubfooted .... TALIPED
clubman .... LION, FELLOW, JAYCEE, MEMBER, ROTARIAN, INSIDER, KIWANIAN, ASSOCIATE
clubs .... SUIT
clucking sound .... CLACK
clue ...... TIP, CLEW, HINT, GUIDE, POINTER
major .... KEY
clumber .... DOG, SPANIEL
clump .... LUMP, MASS, BUNCH, PATCH, CLUSTER, THICKET
bushy .... TOD
of bushes .... SHAW
of earth .... CLOD
of ivy, etc. .... TOD
of trees .... BOSK, TUFT, GROVE, MOTT(E)
clumps, growing in .... CEPITOSE
clumsy .... LUMPY, GAWKY, GAUCHE, OAFISH, AWKWARD, INEPT, BUMBLING, UNGAINLY, INELEGANT, MALADROIT
and stupid .... LOUTISH
boat .... ARK, BARGE, DROGHER
person .... OX, OAF, JUMBO, LUBBER, LUMMOX
player .... DUB
sometimes called .... LEFT-HANDED
thing .... JUMBO
walker .... WADDLER
worker .... BUNGLER, COBBLER, DABBLER, DABSTER
Cluny product .... LACE
clupeid .... SHAD, HERRING, SARDINE
cluster .... KNOT, TUFT, BUNCH, CLUMP, GLOME, GROUP, SORUS, GLOMERATION
arranged in .... AGMINATE
banana .... HAND
bracts .... COMA
compact .... GLOMERULE
fibers .... FASCICLE
flowers .... CYME, RACEME, PANICLE
fruits .... BUNCH
leaves .... FASCICLE
of notes: music .... TREBLE
of seven stars .... PLEIADES
of shrubs/trees .... CLUMP
of spore cases .... SORUS
clustered .... TUFTED, GLOMERATE
clusters, growing in .... ACERVATE
clutch .... GRAB, GRIP, HOLD,

GRASP, SEIZE, SNATCH, COLLAR, SQUEEZE, EMBRACE
clutches .... GRIP, POWER, CONTROL, CUSTODY
clutter .... MESS, DEBRIS, BUSTLE, JUMBLE, LITTER, DISORDER
clyster .... ENEMA
Clytemnestra's daughter
.... ELECTRA
husband .... AGAMEMNON
lover .... AEGISTHUS
mother .... LEDA
son/killer .... ORESTES
coach .... BUS, CAR, HELP, TEACH, TUTOR, TRAIN, CARRIAGE, VEHICLE, TEACHER, DIRECTOR
athletic .... TRAINER
dog .... DALMATIAN
for hire .... HACK, FIACRE, HANSOM
for state occasions
.... CAROCHE
four-horse drawn .... TALLYHO
roof/top of .... IMPERIAL
coachman ...... FLY, HACK, JEHU, LURE, DRIVER
coaction .... FORCE, COERCION, COMPULSION
coagulate .... SET, CAKE, CLOT, CURD, JELL, CURDLE, CLABBER, CONGEAL, THICKEN
coagulated mass .... CLOT
substance/deposit .... CRUD
coagulating substance
.... RENNET, RENNIN, STYPTIC, COAGULIN, PRECIPITIN
coagulation, blood .... CLOT, THROMBOSIS
coal ...... COKE, CARBON, LIGNITE, ANTHRACITE, BITUMINOUS
barge load of .... KEEL
bin .... BUNKER
box .... BIN, DAN, HOD
bucket/hod .... SCUTTLE
burner .... BRASIER
container of live ...... BRAZIER
deposit .... SEAM
digger/miner .... PITMAN, COLLIER
distillate .... TAR
dust .... ASH, CULM, DUFF, SMUT, SLACK
feeder .... STOKER
glowing piece of/live
.... EMBER, GLEED
grade of .... WALLSEND
impurities/waste .... CULM, CLINKER
leavings .... SLACK
like substance .... JET
lump/mass .... COB

measure .... PEA, CHALDRON
mine .... PIT, COLLIERY
bed .... WINNING
carrier .... TUB, TRAM
gas ..... METHANE, FIREDAMP
roof prop .... SPRAG
shaft .... PIT, WINNING
wagon .... CORF
miner's consumption
.... ANTHRACOSIS
oil ...... KEROSENE, PETROLEUM
partially burned .... CINDER
pieced .... LUMP
region .... RUHR, SAAR
screening device .... TROMMEL
ship .... COLLIER
shovel .... SCOOP
sieve .... TROMMEL
size of .... EGG, NUT, PEA, WALLSEND
stoker .... HOPPER
tar compound ...... SACCHARIN
tar derivative .... PITCH, CRESOL, BITUMEN, CREOSOTE, TOLUENE, TOLUOL(E)
tar dye .... EOSIN, ALIZARIN
truck/wagon .... CORF, TRAM
coalesce ...... MIX, BLEND, MERGE, JOIN, UNITE, COMBINE
coalescence .... UNION, MERGER
coalfish .... CUDDY, POLLACK
coalition .... UNION, FUSION, AXIS, BLOC, LEAGUE, MERGER, ENTENTE, ALLIANCE
coals, rake over the ...... ROAST, RACK, CENSURE, CRITICIZE
coarse .... BAWDY, CRASS, CRUDE, GROSS, HARSH, ROUGH, RIBALD, VULGAR, LOWBRED, OBSCENE, RUDE, UNCOUTH, UNREFINED, BROAD, INDELICATE
cloth .... JUTE, LENO, DENIM, SCRIM, BURLAP
corn meal/hominy .... GRITS, SAMP
fiber .... TOW
flour .... MEAL
lace .... MACRAME
material .... REP(P)
meal .... GROUT
coast .... BEACH, GLIDE, SLIDE, RIVAGE, SEASIDE, (SEA)SHORE, SHORELINE, WATERFRONT
line curve .... BIGHT
of the .... LITTORAL
on aircraft .... VOLPLANE
Coast Guard boat .... CUTTER
girl .... SPAR
coastal .... LITTORAL

coaster .... SLED, TOBOGGAN
glass/bottle .... MAT, DISK, TRAY
coasting vehicle .... SKI, SLED, TOBOGGAN, SURFBOARD
coat .... TOG, COVER, LAYER, JACKET, KIRTLE, GARMENT, RAGLAN, PROTECT, COVERING, ULSTER, SWALLOW-TAIL
animal .... FUR, SKIN, WOOL
arm-pinning/madman's
.... STRAITJACKET
close-fitting ...... COATEE, NEW MARKET
daytime .... CUTAWAY
double-breasted .... REEFER, MACKINAW
formal .... TAILS, CUTAWAY
fur-lined .... PELISSE
hanger .... PEG
icy .... RIME, (HOAR)FROST
kind of ...... TOP, OVER, TURN, DUSTER, TRENCH
leather .... JACK
long .... REDINGOTE
long-sleeved .... CAFTAN, KAFTAN
loose .... SACK, PALETOT
of a mammal .... FUR, HAIR, PELAGE
of alloy .... PATINA
of armor .... BRIGANDINE
of arms .... CREST, BLAZON, SHIELD, HERALDRY
of arms band .... BATON, TRESSURE
of arms edge .... BORDURE
of gold/with gold .... GILD, GILT
of icing .... GLACE
of mail .... ARMOR, BYRNIE, HAUBERK
of metal .... PLATE
of the earth .... CRUST
outer .... RIND
person in white .... DOCTOR
slang .... TOG
sleeveless .... JACK
slit .... VENT
soldier's .... TUNIC
thin .... VENEER
waterproof .... SLICKER, MACKINTOSH
with aluminum ...... CALORIZE
with brass .... BRAZE
with metal .... PLATE
with tar .... PAY
woman's .... DOLMAN, REEFER, REDINGOTE
worn as armor ..... GAMBESON
coati-like animal .... RACCOON

coating .... FILM, LAYER, COVERING, CRUSTATION
boiler's inside .... FUR
for photographic plates/ wounds .... COLLODION
fruit .... BLOOM
glossy .... GLAZE, ENAMEL
icy .... SLEET, (HOAR)FROST
metal/on copper, bronze .... PATINA, PATINE
on ceiling .... PARGET
on eyes .... GLAZE
outer .... HIDE, HUSK, RIND, SHELL
plant .... TEGUMENT
pottery .... GLAZE, ENAMEL
thin .... VENEER
wall .... PARGET
coax .... TEASE, CAJOLE, BLARNEY, WHEEDLE, BLANDISH, PERSUADE
cob .... EAR, SWAN, HORSE, (SEA)GULL
coal .... COBBLES
cobalt .... RADIUM, ISOTOPE
color .... DARK BLUE
symbol .... CO
Cobb, baseball player .... TY
cobble .... MEND, PAVE, PATCH
cobbler .... SOLER, CRISPIN, (SHOE)MENDER
block of .... LAST
form/tool of .... AWL
coble .... ROWBOAT, (FISHING)BOAT
cobra ...... NAGA, MAMBA, SNAKE, VIPER, ELAPINE
fighter .... MONGOOSE
headdress .... URAEUS
cobweb .... TRAP, GOSSAMER
describing a .... FILMY, GAUZY, FLIMSY
material .... FIBROID
Coca, comedienne ...... IMOGENE
Coca-Cola product .... TAB, FRESCA
cocaine .... DOPE, (HARD)DRUG, ALKALOID, NARCOTIC, ANESTHETIC, STIMULANT
addict .... SNOWBIRD
describing use of .... ADDICTIVE, DANGEROUS
slang .... COKE, JUNK, SNOW
source .... COCA, CUCA
Cochin-China capital .... SAIGON
cochineal .... DYE
pigment .... LAKE
silver-gray .... BLANCO
cochlear canal .... SCALA
cochleate .... SPIRAL
cock .... TAP, CROW, FAUCET,

LEADER, ROOSTER
-a-hoop .... ELATED, CONCEITED
-and-bull story .... HOAX, YARN, CANARD
comb of .... CARUNCLE
fighting .... HEELER
young .... COCKEREL
cockade .... KNOT, ROSETTE
cockateel .... PARROT
cockatoo .... ARARA, PARROT
cockatrice ...... SERPENT, BASILISK
cockboat .... COG, TENDER
cockchafer .... DOR, BEETLE, BUZZARD
cockcrow .... DAWN, MORN
cocker ...... PET, CODDLE, FONDLE, PAMPER, SPANIEL
cockerel .... ROOSTER
cockeyed: sl. ...... AWRY, DRUNK, SCREWY, ABSURD, CROOKED, TWISTED, CROSS-EYED
cockfight .... SPAR
cockiness .... CONCEIT, ARROGANCE
cockle ...... BOAT, WEED, PUCKER, DARNEL, WRINKLE, SHELLFISH
cocklebur .... BURDOCK, RAGWEED
cockloft .... ATTIC, GARRET
cockney .... EGG, CHILD, DIALECT
famous .... HORNSBY
Cockney's pal .... MATEY
steed .... ORSE
cockpit .... ARENA, CABIN
occupant .... PILOT
Cockpit of Europe, so-called .... BELGIUM
cockroach .... WATERBUG
cockscomb ...... CAP, FOP, DANDY
cockspur .... (HAW)THORN
cocktail .... (MIXED)DRINK, BRONX, MARTINI, APPETIZER, SIDECAR, STINGER, MANHATTAN
fruit .... MACEDOINE
ingredient .... BITTERS
lethal .... MOLOTOV
measure .... SPLIT
mixer .... BLENDER, SHAKER, BARTENDER
room .... LOUNGE
rum .... ZOMBI(E), DAIQUIRI
tidbit .... OLIVE
with pickled onion .... GIBSON
with legs .... HORSE
cocky .... VAIN, SAUCY, FORWARD, PERT, HAUGHTY, ARROGANT, CONCEITED IMMODEST
colloquial ...... SWELL-HEADED
ones .... ROOSTERS

coco .... PALM(TREE)
cocoa .... BROMA, CHOCOLATE
bean, crushed .... NIBS
coconut .... PALM
husk fiber .... COIR
liquid .... MILK
meat, dried .... COPRA(H), COPPERAH
oil source .... COPRA
cocoon .... POD, CASE, THECA
covering .... FLOSS
fiber .... SILK
in zoology .... FOLLICLE
occupant .... PUPA
silkworm .... CLEW
Cocos Islands .... KEELING
cod ...... CUSK, LING, GADID, FISH, BURBOT, GLASHAN, BOCACCIO, WHITING
Archaic .... BAG
fishing bait .... CAP(E)LIN
kin .... HAKE
young .... SCROD
COD, part of .... ON, CASH, COLLECT, DELIVERY
coda .... FINALE
coddle .... PET, BABY, PAMPER, PARBOIL, SPOONFEED
again .... REPET
code .... LAW, CODEX, CIPHER, NORM, RULE, SALIC
breaker .... KEY
certain .... AREA
church .... CANON
emperor's .... NAPOLEON
kind of .... PENAL
message in .... CRYPTOGRAM
moral .... ETHICS
of a kind .... PASSWORD
of laws .... HAMMURABI
operator .... TELEGRAPHER
word, GI's radio .... ABLE, ECHO, OVER, BAKER, ROGER
codfish .... CUSK, LING, GADID, TORSK, BURBOT, GADOID, GLASHAN
young .... SCROD
codger .... CHURL, MISER, FELLOW, ECCENTRIC
codicil .... RIDER, APPENDIX
codling .... APPLE, SCROD
Cody, American plainsman .... (BUFFALO)BILL
coelenterate .... HYDRA, ANEMONE, ACALEPH(E), JELLYFISH
larva of .... PLANULA
coenurus .... LARVA
host of .... SHEEP
coerce .... COW, MAKE, FORCE, COMPEL, DRAGOON,

CONSTRAIN
colloquial .... BULLY,
BULLDOZE
coercion .... DURESS,
COMPULSION, AGAINST ONE'S
WILL
slang .... HEAT, PRESSURE
coercive indoctrination
.... BRAINWASHING
coetaneous .... COEVAL
Coeur d'Alene Indian
.... SALISHAN
de Lion .... RICHARD (I)
coeval .... COETANEOUS,
COINCIDENT, SYNCHRONOUS,
CONTEMPORARY
coexist ...... MESH, MATCH, AGREE,
COINCIDE, HARMONIZE
coffee .... CAFE, JAVA, MOCHA,
SHRUB, BRAZIL, MADDER,
SUMATRA, EXPRESSO,
CAPPUCCINO
alcoholic condition .... LACE
alkaloid .... CAFFEIN(E)
bean .... NIBS
blend .... MOCHA
box/can .... CANISTER
break .... RESPITE, TIME-OFF,
TAKE FIVE
brewer .... URN, SILEX
cake .... KUCHEN
cup .... DEMITASSE
cup stand .... ZARF
extract .... CAFFEIN(E)
grinder .... MILL
house .... CAFE
kind of/type .... DRIP, INSTANT
making container .... URN,
SILEX, PERCOLATOR
mixture/substitute
.... CHICORY, SUCCORY
plantation .... FINCA
pot .... URN, BIGGIN,
DRIPOLATOR, PERCOLATOR
room .... DIVAN
slang .... MUD, JAVA
tree .... CHICOT
coffer .... ARK, LOCK, CHEST,
VAULT, STRONGBOX
coffers .... CHEST, FUNDS,
TREASURY
coffin .... BIER, CASKET, LITTER,
PINE BOX, BURIAL BOX
carrier .... HEARSE, CAISSON,
PALLBEARER
cover .... PALL
nail: sl. .... CIGARETTE
stand .... BIER, CATAFALQUE
stone .... SARCOPHAGUS
cog ...... GEAR, PAWL, CHEAT, LIE,
TOOTH, WHEEL, DECEIVE,

(COCK)BOAT, SWINDLE
cogent .... VALID, STRONG,
POTENT, COMPELLING,
CONVINCING
cogitate ...... CHEW, MULL, MUSE,
THINK, PONDER, CONSIDER,
REFLECT, MEDITATE
cognac .... BRANDY
cognate .... AKIN, RELATED
cognition .... NOESIS, PERCEPTION
cognizance .... KEN, NOTICE,
INSIGHT, KNOWLEDGE,
AWARENESS
cognizant .... HEP, ON TO,
AWARE, CONSCIOUS
slang .... IN THE KNOW
cognize .... KNOW, NOTICE,
DISCERN, REALIZE, PERCEIVE
cognomen .... NICKNAME,
(SUR)NAME
cognoscente .... CONNOISSEUR
cogon .... GRASS
cogwheel .... GEAR, PINION
cohabit .... SLEEP TOGETHER
Cohan's song .... OVER THERE
coheir .... PARCENER
cohere .... CLASP, CLING, HOLD,
STICK, ADHERE
coherence .... UNITY
coherent .... STICKY, UNITED,
CONSISTENT
cohort .... ALLY, BAND,
ACCOMPLICE
one third of .... MANIPLE
cohune .... PALM
coif .... HAIRDO, SKULLCAP
coiffeur .... HAIRDRESSER
coiffure ...... HAIRDO, HAIRSTYLE,
HEADDRESS
kind of .... AFRO
pad .... RAT
quickie .... WIG, PERUKE,
TOUPEE, PERIWIG
style .... BUN, CHAR, BRAID,
CHIGNON, PIGTAIL
coign .... CORNER
coil .... CURL, LOOP, WIND, TWIST,
CIRCLE, SPIRAL, ROLL,
WHORL, CONVOLVE
cable/rope .... FAKE
in a ball .... CLEW
yarn .... SKEIN
coiled .... SPIRY, TORTILE,
HELICOID, CONVOLUTE
coiling .... WINDING
creature .... BOA, SNAKE,
PYTHON, CONSTRICTOR
coin .... MINT, MONEY, CHANGE,
DEVISE, INVENT, SPECIE
Abyssinian .... BESA, GIRSH,
TALARI

Afghanistan ...... PUL, AMANIA
Albanian .... LEK
Algerian .... CENTIME
American (U.S.) .... CENT,
DIME, EAGLE, PENNY, DOLLAR,
NICKEL, QUARTER
Anglo-Saxon ...... ORA, SCEAT
Angola .... LWEI
Annam .... QUAN
Arabian .... TALARI
Argentine .... CENTAVO
Australian .... CENT
Austrian .... DUCAT, KRONE,
GULDEN
back of .... VERSO
biblical .... BEKA, MITE,
SHEKEL, TALENT
box .... PIX, PYX
Bahamian .... CENT
Brazilian .... CENTAVO,
(MIL)REI, MOIDORE
Bulgarian .... LEV, LEW,
DINAR, STOTINKA
Burmese .... PYA
Chilean .... COLON, ESCUDO,
CENTAVO
Chinese ..... PU, FEN, TAEL, LI,
TIAO, LIANG
coating .... BLOOM
collector .... NUMISMATIST
Colombian .... CENTAVO
Costa Rican .... CENTIMO
counterfeit .... RAP, SLUG,
TOKEN
cross-figured .... KREU(T)ZER
Cuban .... CENTAVO
cut edges of .... NIG
Czech .... DUCAT, KRONE(N)
Danish .... ORA, ORE, ORAS,
CROWN, KRONE(N)
design .... INCUSE
drop .... SLOT
Dutch .... DALER, FLORIN,
GULDEN, STIVER, GUILDER
Dutch East Indies .... BONK,
DUIT
Ecuadorian .... SUCRE,
CENTAVO
edge .... NIG
Egyptian ..... PIASTER, PIASTRE
El Salvador .... CENTAVO
English .... ORA, GROAT,
PENCE, FLORIN, GUINEA,
UNITE, TESTON, CAROLUS
Ethiopian .... GIRSH, TALARI
expert .... NUMISMATIST
French .... ECU, SOU, LOUIS,
BESANT, BEZANT, AGNEL,
OBOLE, PISTOLE
front of .... OBVERSE
Gambian .... BUTUT

German .... MARK, KRONE, TALER, THALER
Greek .... OBOL, OBOLI, STATER, DRACHMA
Hebrew .... GERAH, SHEKEL
hole .... SLOT
Hungarian .... GARA, PENGO, FILLER
Icelandic .... AURAR, EYRIR, KRONE
imitation .... SLUG
India .... PIE, ANNA, MOHUR, RUPEE, PICE, PAISA
into money .... MINT, MONETIZE
Iranian .... RIAL, DARIC, PUL, POUL, DINAR, MOHUR, STATER, TOMAN, PAHLAVI
Iraqi .... DINAR
Irish .... RAP, PENNY
Italian ..... LIRA, LIRE, TESTER, SCUDO, SOLDO, TESTON, CENTESIMO
Japanese .... RIN, SEN
Jewish .... GERAH, SHEKEL
large .... CARTWHEEL
Latvian .... LAT, LATU
Lithuanian .... LIT, LITAI, LITAS, RUBLE
making metal .... FLAN
metal .... FLAN, PLANCHET
metallic .... SPECIE
Mexican .... PESO, CUARTO, CENTAVO
money .... MINT
Moroccan .... RIAL
Nepalese .... MOHAR
Norwegian .... ORE, CROWN, KRONE
Oman .... GAZ, GOZ, BAIZA, GHAZI
Oriental .... DINAR
Persian .... DARIC, DINAR
Peruvian .... SOL, DINERO, PESETA, CENTAVO
pewter .... TRA
plant .... MINT
Polish .... DUCAT, ZLOTY
Portuguese .... (MIL)REI
reverse side .... VERSO
ridges .... KNURL
Roman ...... AS, AES, SOLIDUS, DENARIUS, SESTERCE
Rumanian ...... LEU, LEY, BANI
Russian .... COPEC, KOPEK, RUBLE, KOPECK, CHERVONETS
Scandinavian .... KRONAR
Serbian .... DINAR
shaped .... NUMMULAR
Sicilian .... SCUDO
side .... VERSO, OBVERSE

slang .... INVENT
small value .... MITE, PICAYUNE
South American .... CONDOR
space for date, etc.
.... EXERGUE
Spanish .... DURO, PESO, REAL, DOBLA, PESETA, PISTOLE
Spanish colonial
.... PISTAREEN
Swedish .... ORE, KRONA, KRONER
Swiss .... BATZ, FRANC
tester .... SHROFF
Thailand .... AT, ATT, BAHT, CATTY, TICAL, TIKAL
tin .... TRA
Turkish .... LIRA, ASPER, PARA, ALTUN, MAHBUB, PIASTER, PIASTRE
Venetian .... BETSO, DUCAT
Venezuelan .... PESO
Yugoslav .... DINAR
coincide .... AGREE, CONCUR
coiner of words .... NEOLOGIST
coins .... MONEY, PENCE, SILVER
collection of/study of
.... NUMISMATICS
collector of ...... NUMISMATIST
pertaining to ...... NUMISMATIC
roll of .... ROULEAU
small .... CHANGE
sound of .... JINGLE
coke .... COAL, FUEL
measure .... CHALDRON
residue .... BREEZE
slang .... COCAIN(E)
col .... GAP, PASS
colander ...... PAN, SIEVE, SIFTER, STRAINER
Colchis princess .... MEDEA
cold .... ICY, BLEAK, ALGID, GELID, RHEUM, CHILLY, MARBLY, FROSTY, CATARRH, GLACIAL
and damp .... DANK
be .... SHIVER, SHUDDER, TREMBLE
blooded ...... CRUEL, CALLOUS, PITILESS, HEARTLESS
blooded creature .... FISH
congeal by .... FREEZE
dish .... SLAW, SALAD
extremely .... GELID, FRIGID, FROZEN, FREEZING
head .... CORYZA
hearted .... SELFISH, UNKIND, RUTHLESS
leave out in the .... SNUB, ELIDE, IGNORE, ABANDON, NEGLECT, DISREGARD

prefix .... CYRO
Scottish .... CAULD
season .... WINTER
shoulder .... CUT, SNUB, REBUFF, SLIGHT, BRUSH-OFF
sore .... HERPES, LABIALIS
steel .... BLADE, SWORD
stinging .... NIP, NIPPING, CUTTING, PIERCING
tableland .... PUNA
very .... GELID, FRIGID, WINTRY, FREEZING, STONE-COLD, HYPERBOREAN
weather wear .... PARKA, ANORAK, GLOVES, EARMUFFS, EARFLAPS, THERMALS
Cold War weapon
.... PROPAGANDA
coldness of body .... CHILL
cole .... KALE, RAPE, CABBAGE
Cole .... NATALIE, NAT KING
coleopter .... BEETLE, WEEVIL
coleslaw .... SALAD
Colette heroine .... GIGI
colewort .... KALE, CABBAGE, COLLARD
colic .... ILEUS
in the bile, cause of .... STONE
kind of .... INFANTILE, INTESTINAL
stone .... JADE
colima .... IRONWOOD
colin .... QUAIL, BOBWHITE
coliseum .... ARENA, STADIUM
collaborator .... LAVAL, QUISLING
what he gives enemy ...... AID, COMFORT
collage of a sort .... MOSAIC
collagen .... PROTEIN
disease .... ARTHRITIS
collapse .... FAIL, CAVE IN, SLUMP, FALL IN, FOLD UP, RUIN, DEFLATE, DOWNFALL, EXHAUSTION, BREAKDOWN
collapsible hat .... GIBUS
collar .... ETON, RUFF, GORGET, PARRAL, PARREL, CARCANET, DICKY, NECKBAND, NECKWEAR
ancient metal .... TORQUE
bird with feathered
.... GROUSE, PARTRIDGE
bird's .... FLANGE
bone .... CLAVICLE
clerical .... RABATO
colloquial .... CHOKER
detachable .... TUCKER
edging .... FRAISE
English schoolboy's ..... ETON
fastener .... STUD
frilled/pleated .... RUFF

high .... FRAISE
horse's .... HARNESS
neck, describing
.... ORTHOPEDIC
ornamental .... CARCANET
projecting .... FLANGE
slang .... NAB, CATCH, ARREST,
CAPTURE
strangling .... GAROTTE,
GARROTE
turned down .... FALL,
RABATO
woman's ...... BERTHA, DICKEY
collard .... KALE
collared .... TORQUATE
collate .... ALIGN, GATHER,
COMPARE, COMPILE
collateral ...... SURETY, RELATED,
PARALLEL
collation .... TEA, MEAL,
FORMATION, PLACEMENT
colleague .... PARTNER,
ASSOCIATE, CONFRERE
collect .... REAP, AMASS, GARNER,
GATHER, COMPILE, ROUND UP,
ASSEMBLE, SCRAPE UP,
FLOCK, HUDDLE,
ACCUMULATE
grains leftovers/in bits
.... GLEAN
in church mass .... PRAYER
collectanea ...... CORPUS, MEDLEY,
MENAGERIE, ANTHOLOGY
collected .... CALM, COOL, POISED,
SERENE, COMPOSED,
AMASSED, STORED
collection ...... BEVY, HEAP, LUMP,
PACK, BUNCH, GROUP, STORE,
GALAXY, REPERTORY,
ASSEMBLAGE, COMPILATION
a complete .... SET
anecdotes .... ANA
animal fables .... BESTIARY
animals .... ZOO, HERD,
art works .... GALLERY
assorted .... MISCELLANY,
MISCELLANEA
books .... LIBRARY,
BIBLIOTHECA
Brahman maxims .... SUTRA
bridal clothes ...... TROUSSEAU
coins .... NUMISMATICS
commentaries .... GLOSSARY
documents/of writings
.... PAPERS
dried plants .... HERBARIUM
essays/opinions
.... SYMPOSIUM
explanatory notes
.... GLOSSARY
facts .... ANA, DATA

information about person
.... DOSSIER
large .... RAFF, RAFT,
MULTITUDE
laws ...... CODE, JURIS, CORPUS
literary .... ANALECTA,
ANALECTS
logs on river .... DRIVE
Norse poetry .... EDDA
of a great number of people
together .... THRONG,
MULTITUDE
of news clippings/souvenirs/
pictures .... SCRAPBOOK
operas, songs, etc.
.... REPERTOIRE
paintings/statues ..... GALLERY
piano pieces .... GRADUS
poems, etc. .... ANTHOLOGY
postage stamps ..... PHILATELY
prayers for mass .... MISSAL
precious .... TREASURE
reminiscences .... ANA,
MEMOIRS
saints' lives .... HAGIOLOGY,
LEGENDARY
sayings .... ANA
things .... CONGERIES
tools .... KIT
types .... PI(E)
collective .... GENERAL,
COMBINED, COOPERATING
bargaining result
.... CONTRACT
farm .... KOL(K)HOZ
security group .... NATO,
SEATO, UNITED NATIONS
collectively .... WHOLLY,
TOGETHER
collectivism .... SOCIALISM
collector .... BUFF, DUNNER,
EXPERT, FANCIER,
CONNOISSEUR
art/curios .... VIRTUOSO
bank .... RUNNER
birds' eggs .... OOLOGIST
book .... BIBLIOPHILE
coin .... NUMISMATIST
excise tax .... GA(U)GER
fare .... CONDUCTOR
gem .... LAPIDARY
item for a .... CURIO, RELIC,
MASTER, BIBELOT, FIRST
EDITION, FIRST ISSUE
jokes .... CERF
Munchausen's tales ..... RASPE
phonograph record
.... DISCOPHILE
plants .... HERBALIST
shell .... CONCHOLOGIST
stamps .... PHILATELIST

collector's milieux .... FLEA
MARKETS
colleen .... GIRL, LASS
college .... SCHOOL, ACADEMY,
INSTITUTE, UNIVERSITY
athletic team .... VARSITY
building .... GYM, LAB,
DORM(ITORY)
campus .... QUAD
cheer .... YELL, RAH(RAH)
cheerleader: Jap. ...... OENDAN
course: abbr. .... BOT, ENG,
ANAT, ARCH, BIOL, MED,
ECON, MATH, TRIG, ZOOL
dance .... HOP, PROM
dining hall .... REFECTORY
exams .... MIDTERMS
fellow .... DON
founded by Henry VI
.... ETON
freshman .... FROSH
get-together .... REUNION
girl .... COED
graduate(s) .... ALUMNUS,
ALUMNI
grounds .... CAMPUS,
QUAD(RANGLE)
group .... SORORITY,
FRAT(ERNITY)
half year .... SEMESTER
hall .... AULA
honor society .... ARISTA
league symbol .... IVY(LEAF)
lecturer .... PRELECTOR
living quarters .... HALL,
DORM(ITORY)
of attendance .... ALMA
MATER
office .... DEANERY
official .... DEAN, REGENT,
PROVOST, REGISTRAR
on the Thames .... ETON
optional subject ...... ELECTIVE
organization .... CLUB,
FRATERNITY, SORORITY
permit for absence ...... EXEAT
president .... PREXY
publication .... ANNUAL,
YEARBOOK
rank .... DEGREE
scholars' .... ULEMA
servant .... GYP
student .... JUNIOR, SENIOR,
FRESHMAN, SOPHOMORE
students' revelry
.... GAUDEAMUS
teacher .... PROF(ESSOR)
treasurer .... BURSAR
colleges' sports group .... NCAA,
IVY LEAGUE
collegiate .... VARSITY

collide .... BUMP, CLASH, CONFLICT, CRASH, HURTLE
collie .... (SHEEP)DOG
of book .... LAD, LASSIE
of movies .... LASSIE
collier ...... SHIP, PITMAN, TENDER, (COAL)MINER
colliery .... (COAL)MINE
tunnel .... ADIT
Collins and Mix .... TOMS
collinsia .... FIGWORT
collision .... CRASH, PILEUP, CONFLICT, SMASHUP
colloquial ..... FENDER-BENDER
force of .... IMPACT
result .... CONCUSSION
colloidal dispersion in fluid
.... SOL
solution .... GEL
collop .... PIECE, SLICE
colloquial .... INFORMAL, IDIOMATIC, VERNACULAR, CHATTY, CONVERSATIONAL
affirmative .... YEP, YEAH
negative .... NARY, NOPE, NO WAY, NOT ON YOUR LIFE
term of address .... MAC
colloquialism ...... IDIOM, SLANG, PATOIS
Colloquies author ...... ERASMUS
colloquy .... CHAT, TALK, PARLEY, RAPPING, CONFERENCE
collude .... CONSPIRE
colly .... SOOT, GRIME, BLACKEN
collyrium .... EYEWASH, EYEWATER
collywobbles .... COLIC
colocynth .... VINE, APPLE, BITTER
cologne ...... TOILET WATER, ROSE WATER, LOTION, BAY RUM
Colombia bay .... CHOCO, GUAPI, HUMBOLDT, BUENAVENTURA
cape .... AUGUSTA, LA VELA, LA AGUJA, CORRIENTES
capital .... BOGOTA
city/town .... CALI, PASTO, NEIVA, CIENAGA, CARTAGENA, ENVIGADO, BUENAVENTURA, MANIZALES, BARRANQUILLA, MEDELLIN, BUCARAMANGA, TULUA, CUCUTA, MONTERIA, IBAGUE, PALMIRA, PEREIRA, ZARZAL, SEVILLA, SOLEDAD
coin .... REAL, CENTAVO
division .... AMAZONAS, ATLANTICO, ANTIOQUIA, CAUCA, BOYACA, BOLIVAR, NARINO, CALDAS, CORDOBA, CESAR, SUCRE, MAGDALENA
extinct language .... ARDA
falls .... ANGOSTURA, SALTO GRANDE

gulf .... URABA, CUPICA, . TORTUGAS, TIBUGA, MORROSQUILLO
Indian .... MIRANA
island .... FUERTE, GRANDE, GORGONA, CUSACHON, NAIPO, PROVIDENCIA, BARU, SANTA CATALINA
lake .... UVA, LAGUNA, CHAIRA, DE TOTA, MAPIRIPAN
language .... SPANISH
monetary unit .... PESO
mountain .... HUILA, TOLIMA, CAZUELEJA
peninsula .... GUAJIRA
plains .... LLANOS
port .... LORICA, CARTAGENA
religion .... CATHOLIC
river .... AGUARICO, ARIARI, ARAUCA, AMAZON, BITA, CAUCA, CUSIANA, CESAR, GUAINLA, GUAVIARE, META, ISANA, LOSADA, MUCO, MIRA, PUTUMAYO, PAUTO, NECHI, SALDANA, SINU, SUAREZ, ORINOCO, TOMO, TARAIRA, SOGAMOSO, UPIA, YARI, VICHADA
volcano .... PASTO, PURACE
colon .... LARGE INTESTINE
cancer .... LYMPHOMA, CARCINOID TUMOR
examination .... COLONOSCOPY
examination instrument
.... COLONOSCOPE
layer of the ..... SEROUS COAT, MUCOUS COAT, SUBMUCOUS COAT
section of the .... SIGMOID, ASCENDING, DESCENDING, TRANSVERSE
surgical removal of
.... COLECTOMY
colonel's command .... REGIMENT
insigne .... EAGLE
navy counterpart ...... CAPTAIN
colonial newscaster .... CRIER
senate member ...... DECURION
colonist .... PIONEER, PLANTER, SETTLER
Indian greeting to .... NETOP
colonize .... SETTLE, ESTABLISH, POPULATE
colonizing insect .... ANT, BEE
colonnade .... GALLERY, PORTICO
colony .... PLANTATION, SETTLEMENT
bees .... SWARM
of insects .... NEST
colophony .... ROSIN

color .... DYE, BLUSH, FLUSH, HUE, PIGMENT, PAINT, STAIN, TINT, RED, BICE, BLUE, SEPIA, TINCT, GREEN, WHITE, YELLOW, CHROMO, EBONY, CORAL, COBALT
adding pigment .... STAINER
also called meadow lark
.... ACORN
animal .... ROAN, PINTO, FAWN, TAUPE, DAPPLE, TAWNY, BRINDLE
band .... FASCIA
blindness .... DALTONISM
blue ..... BICE, AZURE, COBALT, CELESTE, CYANEAN, LAPIS-LAZULI, CERULEAN, CYANINE, TURQUOISE, INDIGO, AQUAMARINE
brown .... HAZEL, ALESAN, TAUPE, TAWNY, UMBER, SUNTAN
brownish-red .... MAROON, CHESTNUT, BURGANDY
brownish-yellow .... ECRU, BUFF, AMBER
change .... BLUSH, FLUSH, MANTLE, REDDEN
changing substance
.... ALTERANT
combining form
.... CHROMAT(O)
expert .... DYER
fixer .... MORDANT, FIXATIVE
fixer, in dyeing .... BASE
flesh ...... PINKISH, INCARNATE, INCARNADINE
for French victory
.... MAGENTA
gradation .... TINT, TONE, SHADE
green .... JADE, OLIVE, MYRTLE, EMERALD, ABSINTHE, SHAMROCK, CHARTREUSE, VERDANT, TERRE-VERTE, VERDET, VIRIDIAN
in music .... TIMBRE
intensity .... CHROMA
lack of .... PALLOR
lacking .... ALBINO
lightly .... TINT, TINGE
lose .... FADE, PALE
mallow .... MAUVE
neutral .... SAND, BLACK, GRAY, GREGE, WHITE
of caution .... AMBER
of dust .... KHAKI
of pure marble .... WHITE
of ship's flag under
quarantine .... YELLOW

of telephones on highway
.... BLUE
opposite to white .... BLACK
orange .... APRICOT,
CAROTENE, MARIGOLD,
PUMPKIN, CARNELIAN,
TANGERINE, TERRA-COTTA
painter .... TITIAN
pale .... PASTEL
patch of .... FLECK
pertaining to .... CHROMATIC
pink .... MALLOW, ORCHID,
BEGONIA, CARNATION,
SALMON, PEACH-RED,
PRIMROSE, TEA ROSE
primary/prismatic .... RED,
BLUE, GREEN, INDIGO,
ORANGE, VIOLET, YELLOW
purple .... GRAPE, FUCHSIA,
LILAC, LAVENDER, AMETHYST,
PRUNE, ORCHID, VIOLET,
RAISIN, MAGENTA, PLUM,
MAUVE(INE)
quality of .... HUE, TINT,
TONE, PURITY, LIGHTNESS,
CHROMA, BRIGHTNESS
red ...... RUBY, POPPY, CLARET,
SIENA, DAMASK, CARMINE,
CRIMSON, REALGAR,
CARDINAL, SCARLET,
STRAWBERRY
reddish-brown .... OXBLOOD,
ROAN, RUSSET, CORDOVAN
reddish-yellow .... AUBURN,
TITIAN
small amount of .... TINT,
TINGE
splash .... BLOB
streak .... LACE, FLECK
white .... BONE, BLOND,
IVORY, EGGSHELL, PLATINUM,
ALABASTER
with red ocher .... RADDLE,
REDDLE
yellow .... CREAM, AMBER,
LEMON, MAIZE, CANARY,
STRAW, GOLDEN, CHAMOIS,
CHAMPAGNE, SUNFLOWER
Colorado capital .... DENVER
city/town ...... ASPEN, PUEBLO,
BOULDER, AURORA, ALAMOSA,
CRAIG, DURANGO, GREELEY,
LOVELAND, LEADVILLE,
LITTLETON, MONTROSE,
STERLING, LAKEWOOD,
CORTEZ, GRAND JUNCTION,
THORNTON, TRINIDAD,
WALSENBURG, WESTMINSTER,
LAMAR, WHEAT RIDGE,
COLORADO SPRINGS
county .... ADAMS, BOULDER,

DELTA, CHEYENNE, ARAPAHOE,
DENVER, CONEJOS, CHAFFEE,
EAGLE, ELBERT, DOUGLAS,
GRAND, FREMONT, EL PASO,
LAKE, GARFIELD, GUNNISON,
JEFFERSON, KIT CARSON,
LOGAN, LARIMER, LA PLATA,
MESA, MOFFAT, MONTEZUMA,
OTERO, MORGAN, MONTROSE,
PITKIN, PUEBLO, PROWERS, RIO
GRANDE, RIO BLANCO, ROUTT,
SUMMIT, SAGUACHE, PARK,
OURAY, SEDGWICK, WELD,
YUMA, TELLER
creek .... BEAR, BEAVER, BIG
SANDY, BIG GRIZZLY, CLAY,
CEBOLLA, CRESTONE, CROW,
DISAPPOINTMENT, HORSE,
DOUGLAS, FOUNTAIN, KIOWA,
MUDDY, LANDSMAN, OWL,
POT, PAWNEE, TROUT, TIMPAS,
TOMICHI
feature .... MESA
highest point .... MOUNT
ELBERT
Indian .... UTE, ARAPAHOE
lake .... BARR, CLAY, TWIN,
MEREDITH, GROUNDHOG,
AVERY, GRANBY, CHEESMAN,
HENRY, SAN CRISTOBAL,
ELECTRA, TRAPPERS,
SWEITZER, SWEETWATER
mountain .... BALD, ELBERT,
MESA, BAKER, ETHEL, SHEEP,
EVANS, PARKVIEW, HESPERUS,
HOLY CROSS, POLE CREEK,
YALE, HARVARD, PRINCETON,
ADAMS, ANTERO, POWELL,
SILVER, BENNETT, JUNIPER,
LINCOLN, LONE CONE, ZIRKEL,
MASSIVE, SHERMAN, SNEFFELS
mountains .... WET, ROCKY,
LARAMIE, LA GARITA, SAN
JUAN, SAN MIGUEL, SANGRE
DE CRISTO
mountain range .... GORE,
PARK, FRONT, RABBIT EARS,
SAWATCH, MEDICINE BOW
park .... ESTES, MESA VERDE,
ROCKY MOUNTAIN
pass .... VAIL, MUDDY,
MILNER, BUFFALO, CAMERON,
SCOFIELD, RABBIT EARS, LOS
PINOS, WILKERSON, KEBLER,
ROLLINGS, WILLOW CREEK
peak .... LONGS, ELBERT,
CASTLE, CONEJOS, ARAPAHOE,
PAGODA, HERMOSA, EL
DIENTE, PIKES, WETTERHORN,
WINDOM, ZENOBIA
phenomenon .... RAINBOW

Pittsburgh of .... PUEBLO
resort .... VAIL, ASPEN,
MANITOU
river ...... ELK, EAGLE, PIEDRA,
PINOS, LARAMIE, MANCOS,
SLATE, ILLINOIS, COLORADO,
RIO GRANDE, WHITE, DOLORES,
ARKANSAS, SMOKY HILL,
PURGATOIRE, TAYLOR,
CONEJOS, YAMPA, TRINCHERA
River lake .... MEAD
state bird .... LARK
state flower .... COLUMBINE
state motto .... NIL SINE
NUMINE, (NOTHING WITHOUT
GOD)
state nickname .... ROVER,
CENTENNIAL
tourist site ...... ROYAL GORGE,
BLACK CANYON, U.S. DENVER
MINT, DINOSAUR MONUMENT,
tunnel ..... GUNNISON, ALVA B.
ADAMS
coloration .... DYEING, TINTING,
STAINING
coloratura .... OPERATIC
soprano .... DIVA, PRIMA
DONNA
colored .... HUED, TINCT, SHADED
chalk .... CRAYON, PASTEL
glass .... SMALTO
highly .... PRISMAL
many .... MULTI, PRISMATIC
paper .... STREAMERS
skin .... MELANO, MELANOID
view .... BIAS, PREJUDICE
colorfast .... INDELIBLE
colorful .... VIVID, BRIGHT,
TECHNICOLOR
bird .... TODY, PARROT,
MOTMOT, ORIOLE, PEACOCK,
QUETZAL, JACAMAR,
CARDINAL, BUNTING,
KINGFISHER, TROGON,
TANAGER, TOUCAN-BARBET,
STARLING
less .... PALER
life, describing a
.... CHECKERED
spectacle .... PAGEANT(RY),
EXTRAVAGANZA
coloring agent for plants
.... CHLOROPHYLL
for crayon .... PASTEL
matter ..... DYE, MORIN, PAINT,
STAIN, ENAMEL, RUDDLE,
PIGMENT
method, fabric .... TIEDYE
colorist .... DYER
colorless .... WAN, DULL, PALE,
ASHEN, PASTY, PALLID

colloquial .... BLAH
combining form .... LEUKO
person .... ALBINO, NONENTITY
colors, artist's .... PALETTE
having three .... TRICHOIC
science of .... CHROMATICS,
CHROMATOLOGY,
SPECTROMETRY
the .... FLAG
colossal .... HUGE, LARGE,
ENORMOUS, GIGANTIC
beast .... WHALE, BEHEMOTH,
LEVIATHAN
Colossi of Memnon, actually
.... AMUNHOTEP
colossus .... GIANT, TITAN,
STATUE, MONSTER
sculptor of the .... CHARES
colt .... FOAL, HORSE, YOUTH,
BOLLARD, REVOLVER
revolver: sl. .... HOG-LEG,
PEACEMAKER
coltish .... FRISKY
Colts or Rams .... ELEVEN
columbary .... DOVECOTE
Columbia eleven .... LIONS
River catch .... SALMON
River port .... ASTORIA
columbine .... FLOWER,
AQUILEGIA
columbite .... DIANITE
columbium .... NIOBIUM
columbo .... GENTIAN
Columbus' birthplace .... GENOA
Day month .... OCTOBER
discovery ..... AMERICA, CUBA,
COSTA RICA
navigator of .... PINZON
ship/caravel .... NINA, PINTA,
SANTA MARIA
starting point .... PALOS
column .... SHAFT, PILLAR,
PILASTER
base .... PLINTH
Buddhist .... LAT
capital of a .... CHAPITER
convex swelling .... ENTASIS
designating a .... DORIC, IONIC
figure, female .... CARYATID
figure, male .... TELAMON,
ATLANTES
foundation .... SOCLE
in architecture .... CAPITAL
of troops, ships, etc.
.... FORMATION
ornament .... GRIFFE
part of .... BASE, SHAFT,
CAPITAL
shaft .... SCAPE
square .... ANTA, PIER
substitute for .... ATLAS,

ATLANTES
support of .... BASE, PLINTH,
PEDESTAL
top of .... CAPITAL
writer's .... NEWS, ARTICLE
columnist .... WRITER, NEWSMAN,
REPORTER, NEWS ANALYST,
CAEN, ALSOP, PEARSON,
WESTON, LIPPMANN,
WINCHELL
advantage sought by a
.... SCOOP
identification of .... BY-LINE
news source of .... GRAPEVINE
specialty of .... RUMORS
columns, row of .... COLONNADE,
PERISTYLE
colza .... COLE(SEED), RAPESEED
coma .... TORPOR, TRANCE,
STUPOR, CATALEPSY
having a .... COMATOSE
comate, in botany .... HAIRY,
TUFTED
comatose .... TORPID
comb .... SCRAPE, SEARCH
horse .... CURRY
like implement .... RIPPER
like structure .... CTEN
of fowl ...... CREST, CARUNCLE
the hair .... DRESS, TEASE
wool .... CARD, TEASE
combat ...... DUEL, FIGHT, STOUR,
BATTLE, OPPOSE, FRACAS,
STRIFE, WARFARE, CONFLICT,
SKIRMISH
challenge to .... CARTEL
end of mortal .... DEATH
formal, between two persons
.... DUEL
mortal .... AMORT
operation .... MISSION
place .... LISTS
to decide issue .... DERAIGN
troops .... NAVY, MARINE,
ARMY, AIR FORCE, CAVALRY,
PARATROOPERS, INFANTRY
with lances .... TILT, JOUST
combatant .... G.I., FIGHTER,
SOLDIER, WARRIOR
combative .... WARLIKE,
MILITANT, OFFENSIVE,
AGGRESSIVE, FORCEFUL,
PUGNACIOUS
comber .... WAVE
combination ...... ALLOY, BLEND,
POOL, UNION, MERGER,
MIXTURE, ALLIANCE,
AMALGAM, COALITION,
FUSION, ARRANGEMENT
slang .... COMBO
combine .... FUSE, JOIN, UNITE,

ABSORB, MERGE, COMPOUND,
CENTRALIZE, AMALGAMATE
kind of .... COALITION,
SYNDICATE
resources .... POOL
combined .... ALLIED, UNITED
combining form for
alike .... ISO
among .... INTER
another .... HETERO
angle .... GONIO
asunder .... DICH(O)
aviation .... AER
bad .... CAC(O), MAL
below .... INFERO
between .... INTER
bile .... CHOL(O), CHOLE
blood .... HEMA, HEM(O),
HEMATO, SANGUI
body fluid .... SERO
both .... AMBI
brass .... CHALCO
bright .... HELI(O)
bristles .... CHAET(O)
broad .... EURY, PLAT(Y)
cartilage .... CHONDRO
cavity .... C(O)ELE
cell .... CYTE
circular .... CYCL(O)
cold .... CRY(O)
color .... CHROMAT(O)
copper .... CUPRI
corpse .... NECR(O)
curl .... CIRRI
cutter .... TOME
death .... NECR(O)
depth .... BATHO
different .... HETER(O)
digit .... DACTYL(O)
double .... DIPL(O)
drawing .... GRAPHO
dreadful .... DINO
dry .... XER(O)
dung .... COPR(O)
earth .... GEO
end .... TEL(O)
English .... ANGLO
entire .... HOLO
equal .... ISO, EQUI, PARI
external .... ECT(O)
eye defect .... OPIA
far .... TELE
fatty .... LIP(O)
feather .... PTERO
feces .... COPR(O)
feet .... PED(E), PEDI
female .... GYN(O), GYNOUS
fermentation .... ZYMO
fever .... FEBRI
fine .... LEPT(O)
finger .... DACTYL(O)

firm .... STERE(O)
fish .... PISCI
flat .... PLAT(Y)
flesh .... SARC(O)
flow .... RHEO
freezing .... CRY(O)
French .... GALLO
fruit .... CARP(O)
fungus .... MYC(O)
gall .... CHOL(O), CHOLE
gaseous .... AERI
glass .... HYALO
God .... THEO
grain .... GRANI
gyrating .... GYRO
hair .... CHAET(O)
hand .... CHIRO, CHEIRO
hatred .... MIS(O)
height .... HYPSO
hidden .... CRYPT(O)
hide .... DERMAT(O)
horn .... CERAT(O), KERATO
horse .... HIPPO
hundred .... CENTI, HECT(O)
identical .... ISO
inner .... END(O)
insect(s) .... ENTOMO
inside .... INTRA, INTRO
intestine .... ENTER(O)
iron .... FERRO
latest .... NEO, CENE
liking .... PHIL(E)
lime .... CALCI
lip .... CHIL(O)
little .... MICR(O)
liver .... HEPAT(O)
male/man/masculine
.... ANDR(O)
many .... POLY
Mars .... AREO
middle .... MESO
milky .... GALACT(O)
minute .... MICR(O)
moon .... LUNI
moving .... KINETO
much .... POLY
nitrogen .... AZO
one and a half .... SESQUI
one tenth of .... DECI
other .... HETER(O)
outside .... ECT(O)
people .... ETHN(O)
personal .... IDIO
pointed .... STYL(O)
poor .... CAC(O)
prickly .... ECHIN(O)
race .... ETHN(O)
radiant .... HELI(O)
rainbow .... IRIDO
recent .... NEO
red .... ERYTHR(O)

rib(s) .... COST(O)
ribbon .... TENE
secondary .... DEUT(O),
DEUTER(O)
secret .... CRYPT(O)
self .... AUTO
seven .... HEPT(A), SEPTEM
shaft .... SCAPI
sham .... PSEUD(O)
sharp .... STYL(O)
short .... BRACHY
similar .... ISO
simple/single .... HAPL(O)
skin ...... DERM(O), DERMAT(O)
sleep .... HYPN(O)
slender .... LEPT(O)
small .... MICR(O)
solid .... STERE(O)
sound .... PHONE
spiny .... ECHIN(O)
spiral .... GYRO, HELIC(O)
stalk .... SCAPI
stationary .... STAT
stomach .... GASTR(O)
stone .... LITE, LITH, LYTE
sun .... HELI(O)
swelling .... CELE
tallow .... SEBI
teeth .... DENT(I), ODONT(O)
ten .... DEC(A)
terrible .... DINO
thin .... LEPT(O)
thousand .... KILO
tissue .... HIST(O)
transparent .... HYAL(O)
tree .... DENDR(I), DENDRO,
DENDRON
tumor .... CELE
twin/two .... DIPL(O)
universe .... COSM(O)
water .... HYDR(O)
wave .... CYMO
wax .... CERO, SEBI
weight .... BARO
whole .... HOLO
wing .... PTERO
within .... ESO, END(O), INTRA,
INTRO
woman ...... GYN(E)O, GYNOUS
wood .... HYL(O)
wool .... LANI
world .... COSM(O)
worship .... LATRY
writing .... GRAPHO
yellow(ish) .... LUTEO
combo .... TRIO
combustible .... FIERY,
BURNABLE, EXCITABLE,
(IN)FLAMMABLE
combustion .... FIRE, FLAME,
SPARK, BURNING

come .... REACH, APPEAR, BEFALL,
ARRIVE, RESULT
about .... OCCUR, HAPPEN
across ..... GIVE, MEET, PAY UP
afterwards .... ENSUE
around .... VISIT, YIELD,
REVIVE
back .... RECUR, RETURN,
REJOIN, RESPONSE
before .... PRECEDE, PREDATE
between .... DIVIDE,
INTERVENE
by .... GAIN, ACQUIRE
down .... LAND, ALIGHT,
DISEMBARK
forth .... EMERGE, EMERSE,
APPROACH
forward .... RISE, ADVANCE,
OFFER, VOLUNTEER
in first .... WIN
in second/third .... LOSE
into .... GET, ACQUIRE,
INHERIT, RECEIVE
into view .... LOOM, PEEP,
PEER, BEHOLD
on! .... HURRY(UP), ON THE
DOUBLE
ons ..... BAITS, LURES, DECOYS
ons victim .... SUCKER
out .... ARISE, APPEAR, EMERGE
out number .... SEVEN, ELEVEN
out even .... TIE, DRAW, DEAD-
HEAT
through a crisis ..... TURN THE
TIDE
to grips with .... TANGLE,
EMBROIL
to mind .... OCCUR, RECALL
to pass .... OCCUR, HAPPEN,
UNDERGO, TRANSPIRE
to rest .... DECIDE, SETTLE
to terms .... AGREE, CONCUR
together .... (FOR)GATHER,
ASSEMBLE
up .... SOAR, ARISE, CLIMB
up to .... EQUAL, MATCH
upon ...... HAP, MEET, CHANCE,
STUMBLE ON
comeback .... RETORT, RETURN,
RIPOSTE, REVIVAL, REPARTEE,
REJOINDER
comedian .... CARD, ZANY,
BUFFO, COMIC, JESTER,
FUNSTER, PIERROT
circus .... CLOWN
deadpan .... KEATON
foil of .... STOOGE,
STRAIGHTMAN
forte .... GAGS, JOKES, WIT,
CRACKS, HORSEPLAY,
TOMFOOLERY

missile of .... PIE
of note .... (BOB)HOPE,
FERNANDEL, (BUSTER)KEATON,
(JACK)BENNY, (JERRY)LEWIS,
(BERT)LAHR, (RED)SKELTON,
(OLIVER)HARDY,
(STAN)LAUREL, (LOU)HOLTZ,
(MYRON)COHEN,
(LOU)COSTELLO
comedienne .... (FANNY)BRICE,
(LUCILLE)BALL, (ZAZU)PITTS,
(IMOGENE)COCA,
(ROSEANNE)BARR
comedo .... BLACKHEAD
comedy .... FARCE, HUMOR,
PARODY, SATIRE, BURLESQUE,
AMUSEMENT, HORSEPLAY,
SLAPSTICK
character .... ZANY, PIERROT
muse of .... THALIA
of errors .... FIASCO
Powell, Lombard ..... MY MAN
GODFREY
symbol .... SOCK
comely .... FAIR, GAINLY, PRETTY,
HANDSOME, PLEASING,
LOVELY, ATTRACTIVE,
DECOROUS, GOOD-LOOKING
woman .... BUXOM
comestible(s) .... FOOD, EDIBLE,
EATABLE, VICTUAL
comet .... BIELA'S, HALLEY'S,
SWIFT'S, ALCOCK'S, HOLMES'
envelope .... COMA
head's part .... NUCLEUS
nucleus and coma .... HEAD
part .... TAIL, TRAIN
comeuppance: sl. ...... REVENGE,
TIT-FOR-TAT, PUNISHMENT
comfit .... CANDY, PRALINE,
CONFECTION, SWEETMEAT
comfort .... EASE, CHEER,
LUXURY, SOLACE, SOOTHE,
CONSOLE, PLEASURE
station .... SHELTER
comfortable .... COSE, COZY,
SNUG, HOMEY, SERENE,
PLEASING
chair .... ROCKER
slang .... HUNKY-DORY
comforter ...... QUILT, COVERLET,
BEDSPREAD, PACIFIER
comic .... DROLL, FUNNY,
AMUSING, COMICAL,
COMEDIAN, HILARIOUS,
HUMOROUS, LAUGHABLE
afterpiece .... EXODE
element in play .... HOKUM
famous character .... POGO
kind of .... STAND-UP
opera .... BUFFA, BUFFO,

BOUFFE
relief .... SKIT, AFTERPIECE
strip .... CARTOONS
strip brat .... HANS, FRITZ,
DENNIS THE MENACE
strip character ..... LULU, JEFF,
MUTT, JIGGS, NANCY, SLUGGO,
MILQUETOAST, (LIL)ABNER,
(ETTA)KETT
strip vocals .... BALLOON(S)
theatrical sketch .... SKIT
with wooden sword
.... HARLEQUIN
comical .... ZANY, DROLL, FUNNY,
CLOWNISH, FARCICAL,
HUMOROUS
very .... KILLING,
SIDESPLITTING
coming .... ADVENT, APPROACH
early in the day .... RATH(E)
from outside .... ALIEN,
FOREIGN, ENTHETIC,
EXTRANEOUS
of tide .... FLUX
out party .... DEBUT
to an end .... MORIBUND
comity .... COURTESY, POLITENESS
comma .... MARK, PAUSE
shaped organism .... VIBRIO
command .... ORDER, COMPEL,
BEHEST, BID(DING), DEMAND,
ORDAIN, ENJOIN, DIRECT,
ENJOIN, REQUIRE, INSTRUCT,
DICTATE
authoritative .... MANDATE
level of .... ECHELON
market .... CORNER,
MONOPOLIZE
official .... DECREE
station .... POST
to a cat .... SCAT
to a dog ...... SIT, STAY, FETCH
to helmsman .... STEADY
to horse ...... GEE, HAW, WHOA
to huskies .... MUSH
commandeer .... SEIZE, USURP
commander .... LEADER,
CAPTAIN, SKIPPER
Egyptian .... SIRDAR
in-chief, U.S. .... PRESIDENT
of 1000 men: Rom.
.... CHILIARCH
of the sea .... ADMIRAL
rod/staff of .... WARDER
commanding .... EXACTING,
DEMANDING, DOMINATING,
INSISTENT, IMPRESSIVE
commandment .... LAW, RULE,
ORDER, PRECEPT
in Judaism .... MITZVAH

Commandments, the Ten
.... DECALOG(UE)
commando .... RAIDER, SABOTEUR
assignment .... MISSION
specialty ..... RAID, SABOTAGE,
DEMOLITION
comme ci, comme ca ...... SO-SO
comme il faut .... PROPER,
FITTING
commemorate .... OBSERVE,
CELEBRATE, RECOGNIZE,
REMEMBER, REMINISCE
commemorative .... MEMORIAL
piece .... MEDAL
pillar .... STELE
commence .... OPEN, BEGIN,
START, LEAD OFF, LAUNCH
commencement .... OPENING,
START, INCEPTION, BEGINNING
address .... VALEDICTORY
dole .... DIPLOMA
exercise .... GRADUATION
commend .... CITE, LAUD, EXALT,
EXTOL, PRAISE, ACCLAIM,
APPROVE, ENTRUST
commensal .... ORGANISM,
BACTERIUM, INQUILINE
commensurate .... EVEN, EQUAL,
ACCORDANT, PARALLEL,
EQUITABLE
comment .... TALK, REMARK,
DESCANT, OPINION,
ANNOTATION
adverse .... CRITICISM
at bottom of page
.... FOOTNOTE
derisive .... JEER
favorable .... RAVE, KUDOS,
PRAISE
marginal .... MARGENT
on disapprovingly
.... ANIMADVERT
wordless .... SIGH
commentary .... MEMOIR,
REMARK, CRITIQUE,
CRITICISM, DISCOURSE,
DISCUSSION, VERSION,
OBSERVATION
commentator .... CRITIC,
REVIEWER, ANNOTATOR
newspaper .... EDITOR,
COLUMNIST
commerce .... TRADE, BARTER,
TRAFFIC, BUSINESS
commercial .... TRADING,
MERCANTILE
agent .... CONSUL
paper, worthless .... KITE
rubber stamp .... RUSH
spy .... KEEK
writer .... ADMAN

comminate .... BAN, CURSE

commingle .... BLEND, MERGE, (INTER)MIX

comminute .... MILL, CRUSH, GRIND, PULVERIZE

comminution, product of .... DUST, TALC, POWDER

commiserate ...... PITY, CONDOLE, TOUCH, SOFTEN, EMPATHIZE

commiseration ...... PITY, MERCY, EMPATHY, COMPASSION

commissary ...... STORE, DEPUTY, CANTEEN

colloquial .... PX

commission ...... ORDER, DEPUTE, COUNCIL, ASSIGN, EMPOWER, APPOINT, DELEGATE, AUTHORITY, ENGAGE, NOMINATE, AUTHORIZE

grafter's .... KICKBACK

slang .... RAKE-OFF

commissure .... SEAM, JOINT

commit .... DO, BIND, ENGAGE, CONSIGN, ENTRUST, PERFORM

in mind .... MEMORIZE

perjury .... LIE, FORSWEAR, BEAR FALSE WITNESS

to paper .... RECORD

commitment .... PLEDGE, CONCERN, PROMISE, INVOLVEMENT

commix .... BLEND

commode .... CHEST, BUREAU, TOILET, WASHSTAND, CHIFFONIER

commodious .... ROOMY, SPACIOUS

commodity ...... GOODS, WARE(S), STAPLE, ARTICLE, PRODUCT

control of .... OLIGOPOLY

common ...... LOW, JOINT, USUAL, COARSE, MUTUAL, PUBLIC, SHARED, AVERAGE, GENERAL, ILLBRED, ORDINARY, STANDARD

abbreviation .... ETC

arithmetic .... LOGISTIC

carrier .... BUS, COACH, TRAIN, AIRLINE

cold .... RHEUM

connector .... AND

contraction .... I'VE, ISN'T, WE'VE, AREN'T

footing .... PAR

fund .... POOL

interest faction .... SECT

laborer: sl. .... BOHUNK

market milieu .... EUROPE

people .... FOLKS, DEMOS, PLEBE, PLEBS, MASSES, POPULACE, HOI-POLLOI

people, of the .... GRASS ROOTS

run .... RUCK

saying .... SAW, ADAGE, PROVERB

sense .... SAVVY, GUMPTION

statistic .... AVERAGE MAN

sweetener .... PLEASE

talk .... RUMOR, GOSSIP, HEARSAY

to both sexes .... EPICENE

Common Sense author .... PAINE

commoner .... PLEB, CITIZEN, YEOMAN, FREEMAN, LOWBORN, SUBJECT, PLEBEIAN, ROTURIER

commonly accepted .... VULGATE

supposed .... PUTATIVE

commonplace .... BANAL, PROSE, PROSY, TRITE, USUAL, HUMDRUM, PROSAIC, TEDIOUS, STALE, EVERYDAY, BOURGEOIS

expression .... CLICHE, TRUISM, BROMIDE, PLATITUDE

commotion ...... ADO, ROW, FUSS, MUSS, STIR, TO-DO, FLURRY, HUBBUB, POTHER, SHINDY, TUMULT, UPROAR, TURMOIL, UNREST, FERMENT, DISORDER, BROUHAHA, HURLYBURLY

commove .... EXCITE

communal ...... COMMON, PUBLIC

marriage .... HETAERISM

commune .... TALK, CONFER, MIR, CONSULT, CONVERSE, ANS, ATH, EDE, EPE, KIBBUTZ

communicable .... CONTAGIOUS

communicate .... TALK, SPEAK, CONVEY, IMPART, TRANSMIT

with .... WRITE, CONVERSE, CORRESPOND

communication ...... NOTE, NEWS, LIAISON, MESSAGE, TIDINGS, INFORMATION

form of .... CODE, ORAL, TALK, LETTER, SIGNAL

means of .... SIGN, WIRE, WORD, CABLE, MEDIA, RADIO, TELEGRAPH, TELEPHONE, CARRIER-PIGEON

communications initials .... RCA, ITT

link between US & USSR .... HOTLINE

satellite .... TELSTAR

signal set .... CODE

communicative .... OUTGOING, TALKATIVE

communion .... TALK, UNITY,

CONCORD, SHARING

cloth .... CORPORAL

cup .... AMA

plate .... PATEN

table .... CREDENCE

Communion, Holy .... EUCHARIST, SACRAMENT

communism, exponent of .... MARX, LENIN, STALIN, ENGELS

Communist .... RED, LEFTIST

curtain .... IRON, BAMBOO

Party member .... COMRADE

policy body .... POLITBURO

prominent .... CHOU

spy .... BURGESS, MACLEAN, PHILBY

youth league .... COMSOMOL

community .... BODY, TOWN, PUBLIC, SOCIETY, DISTRICT, PARTNERSHIP

of creatures .... COLONY

of Greek monks/hermits .... SKETE

of peasants: Russ. .... MIR

commutator .... RHEOTROPE

commute .... TRAVEL, EXCHANGE, INTERCHANGE

commuter .... PASSENGER

Comoro island .... MAYOTTE

Islands capital .... MORONI

neighbor of .... ALDABRA

comose .... HAIRY

compact .... CASE, MINI, NEAT, BRIEF, DENSE, TERSE, THICK, SOLID, CONCISE, SERRIED, CONDENSE, AGREEMENT

among individuals/parties, etc. .... CONTRACT, COVENANT

between nations .... TREATY

cosmetics .... VANITY

mass .... WAD

companion .... PAL, CHUM, FERE, ALLY, MATE, ESCORT, FRIEND, CRONY, COMPANY, PARTNER, ASSOCIATE

animal .... PET

at meals .... COMMENSAL

close .... BUDDY, COMRADE, INTIMATE, BOSOM FRIEND

colloquial .... SIDEKICK

constant .... SHADOW, ALTER EGO

of alpha .... OMEGA

back .... FORTH

beck .... CALL

bed .... BOARD

beginning .... END

betwixt .... BETWEEN

bill .... COO

black .... BLUE, WHITE
bolts .... NUTS
bread .... BUTTER
breaking .... ENTERING
cake .... ALE
cash .... CARRY
cease .... DESIST
cloak .... DAGGER
come .... GO
deaf .... DUMB
draw .... QUARTER
easy-come .... EASY-GO
ebb .... FLOW
far .... AWAY, WIDE
fair .... SQUARE
fast .... LOOSE
fire .... BRIMSTONE
fits .... STARTS
flotsam .... JETSAM
foot-loose .... FANCY-FREE
free .... EASY, CLEAR
get-up .... GO
give .... TAKE
heart .... SOUL
hook .... CROOK, LADDER,
              LINE-AND-SINKER
hue .... CRY
huff .... PUFF
kiss .... MAKE UP
kit .... CABOODLE
kith .... KIN
life .... DEATH
live .... LET LIVE
loud .... CLEAR
man .... WIFE
might .... MAIN
mortise .... TENON
night .... DAY
nip .... TUCK
null .... VOID
on .... OFF
open .... SHUT(CASE),
              ABOVEBOARD
oro .... PLATA
over .... ABOVE
pick .... CHOOSE
pins .... NEEDLES
red .... WHITE AND BLUE
rock .... ROLL
snick .... SNEE
song .... DANCE
spick .... SPAN
Stars .... STRIPES
stocks .... BONDS
straight .... NARROW
stuff .... NONSENSE
thunder .... LIGHTNING
to .... FRO
Tom .... DICK AND HARRY
toss .... TURN
trial .... ERROR

tried .... TRUE
up .... DOWN, COMING
wear .... TEAR
wheel .... AXLE
wine .... DINE
wrack .... RUIN
companionable .... GENIAL,
              AMIABLE, FRIENDLY,
              COMPATIBLE
companionship .... SHARING,
              SOCIETY, SODALITY,
              FELLOWSHIP
companionway .... WALK,
              STAIR(S)
company .... BAND, FIRM, GROUP,
              TROOP, SOCIETY
amusing .... CAST
colloquial .... GUEST(S),
              VISITOR(S)
commander .... CAPTAIN
of hunters .... SAFARI
of players .... TEAM, TROUPE
of soldiers .... TROOPS
of soldiers mounted on
              horses .... CAVALRY
of ten soldiers .... DECURION
of travelers .... CARAVAN,
              CARAVANSARY
part .... SEPARATE
comparable .... ALIKE, CLOSE,
              PARALLEL, SIMILAR
comparative .... RELATIVE
compare .... TEST, LIKEN, RELATE,
              CONFRONT, CONTRAST
beyond .... PEERLESS,
              MATCHLESS, NONPAREIL
critically .... COLLATE
compared .... MATCHED
to .... THAN, AGAINST
comparison .... ANALOGY, SIMILE,
              LIKENESS
example .... AVERAGE,
              STANDARD
compartment ...... BOOTH, STALL,
              LOCKER
desk, for filing papers
              .... PIGEONHOLE
grain/hay .... BAY
in aircraft .... CAPSULE
of car, describing .... GLOVE
small/sleeping .... CUBICLE
compass .... GAIN, BOUND,
              GAMUT, RANGE, REACH,
              SCOPE, DEFINE, EXTENT,
              ENCIRCLE, SURROUND
beam .... TRAMMEL
cardinal point .... EAST, WEST,
              NORTH, SOUTH
case/housing .... BINNACLE
dial .... CARD
face .... DIAL

kind of .... DRAWING,
              GYROSIN, MAGNETIC,
              MARINER'S, SURVEYOR'S
part .... AIRT, GIMBAL,
              NEEDLE, HOUSING, TRAMMEL
plant .... ROSINWEED
point .... N, E, W, S, NE, NW,
              SE, SW, ENE, ESE, NNE, NNW,
              SSE, SSW, WNW, WSE, AIRT,
              R(H)UMB, QUARTER
sight .... VANE
zero of .... NORTH
compassion .... PITY, RUTH,
              GRACE, HEART, MERCY,
              EMPATHY, TENDERNESS
compatible .... ATTUNED,
              SUITABLE, CONGENIAL,
              CONGRUOUS
compatriot .... COUNTRYMAN
compeer .... PEER, EQUAL,
              MATCH, COMRADE
compel ...... MAKE, DRIVE, FORCE,
              PRESS, COERCE, OBLIGE,
              IMPOSE ON, REQUIRE,
              CONSTRAIN
compelled: Arch. .... FAIN
compelling .... COGENT,
              INTIMIDATING
influence .... DURESS,
              PRESSURE
compend .... BREVIARY
compendium ...... DIGEST, PRECIS,
              SUMMARY, ABSTRACT,
              SYLLABUS, SYNOPSIS
compensation .... FEE, PAY,
              REWARD, REDRESS,
              EQUIVALENT
for loss .... DAMAGES,
              INDEMNITY
for services .... WAGE,
              SALARY, STIPEND
compete .... VIE, RIVAL, CONTEND
competence .... SKILL, ABILITY,
              CAPACITY, PROFICIENCY
competent .... APT, FIT, ABLE,
              CAPABLE, SKILLED, EFFICIENT
mentally .... SANE
competition .... MATCH, STRIFE,
              CONTEST, RIVALRY, TOURNEY,
              OPPOSITION
competitive .... RIVAL, VYING,
              OPPOSING, CUTTHROAT
competitor .... ENTRY, RIVAL,
              ENTRANT, COMPETER,
              CORRIVAL, CONTENDER,
              CONTESTANT
Compiegne river .... OISE
compilation .... SELECTION,
              COLLECTION
of anecdotes .... MEMOIRS

of alphabetized words and
definitions
.... DICTIONARY
of stories, poems
.... ANTHOLOGY
compile .... EDIT, AMASS, GATHER,
SELECT, ARRANGE, COLLECT
compiler .... CERF, RILEY,
AUTHOR, GLOSSARIST,
ANTHOLOGIST,
ENCYCLOPEDIST
Arthurian tales .... MALORY
English words .... ROGET
population data .... CENSUS
TAKER
quotations .... BARTLETT
complacent .... SMUG, BLASE,
COCKY, CONTENT, PLEASED
complain ...... BEEF, CARP, CRAB,
FRET, FUSS, KICK, MOAN,
GRIPE, GROAN, WHINE,
ACCUSE, BEWAIL, GROUSE,
MURMUR, YAMMER,
GRUMBLE, PROTEST,
BELLYACHE
complainant .... ACCUSER,
CLAIMANT, LITIGANT,
PLAINTIFF
complainer, habitual ...... BITCH,
GROUCH, GROUSER
complaining .... PEEVISH,
QUERULOUS
cry .... WHINE
complaint .... KICK, PEEVE,
WHINE, CLAMOR, GROUSE,
CHARGE, AILMENT, ILLNESS,
PROTEST, SQUAWK,
GRIEVANCE
muttered .... MURMUR
part of .... GRAVAMEN
slang .... BITCHING,
BELLYACHING
complaisant ...... KINDLY, POLITE,
FLEXIBLE, OBLIGING,
AGREEABLE
complement ...... EXTRA, OFFSET,
FULFILL, NEUTRALIZE
complementary
.... SUPPLEMENTAL
complete .... END, FULL, RANK,
SOLID, UTTER, WHOLE,
CLINCH, CAP, ENTIRE, FINISH,
INTACT, TOTAL, ACHIEVE,
CONCLUDE, OUTRIGHT,
THOROUGH
attendance .... PLENARY
collection .... SET
consumption ...... EXHAUSTION
defeat .... ROUT
disorder .... CHAOS
entity .... INTEGER

growth .... MATURITY
in all respects .... PERFECT
not .... PARTIAL
set of games .... SERIES
completed .... DONE, OVER,
ENDED, FINISHED
completely .... FULLY, WHOLLY,
DOWNRIGHT, BAG AND
BAGGAGE
developed .... FULL-FLEDGED
from ____ .... A TO Z
occupied .... BUSY, RAPT,
ENGROSSED
united .... SOLIDARITY
completion ..... END, FILL, CLOSE,
FINAL, FINISH, OUTCOME,
FRUITION, CONCLUSION
complex ...... KNOTTY, MIXED UP,
TANGLE, NETWORK,
INVOLVED, INTRICATE,
COMPLICATED
get .... THICKEN
kind of .... OEDIPUS,
INFERIORITY
complexion .... HUE, TINT, COLOR,
ASPECT, SKIN TEXTURE
complexity .... INTRICACY
compliant .... WEAK, DOCILE,
PASSIVE, PATIENT, OBEDIENT,
DUTIFUL, YIELDING,
TRACTABLE
complicate .... CONFUSE,
PERPLEX, INVOLVE,
COMPOUND
complicated .... KNOTTY,
COMPLEX, INVOLVED
complication .... MESS, SNAG,
NODUS, SNARL, TANGLE
compliment .... LAUD, TOAST,
PRAISE, COMMEND,
CONGRATULATE
exaggerated .... FLATTERY
kind of .... LEFT-HANDED
complimentary .... FREE, GRATIS
complot .... CONSPIRE,
CONSPIRACY
comply .... OBEY, ACCEDE,
SUBMIT, CONFORM
compo .... MORTAR, PLASTER
component .... PART, UNIT,
FACTOR, MEMBER, ELEMENT,
FEATURE
of atom .... PROTON
comport .... ACT, FIT, SUIT,
BEHAVE
comportment .... CONDUCT,
BEHAVIOR
compos mentis .... SANE
non .... MAD, CRAZY, INSANE
compose .... FRAME, WRITE,
ADJUST, CREATE, INDITE,

CONSTITUTE
differences .... RECONCILE
in printing .... TYPE
composed .... CALM, COOL, STAID,
WROTE, UNRUFFLED,
COLLECTED
composer .... INDITER, ARTIST,
HARMONIST, TUNESMITH,
BACH, BIZET, SONGWRITER,
FOOTE, HAYDN, RAVEL,
ROREM, STYNE, WEBER,
CHOPIN, MOZART, WAGNER,
DEBUSSY, PUCCINI,
BEETHOVEN, STRAVINSKY
arranger Peter .... MATZ
great .... MAESTRO
in printing shop
.... LINOTYPIST, TYPESETTER
of Aida .... VERDI
of Carmen .... BIZET
of La Boheme .... PUCCINI
of La Valse .... RAVEL
of marches .... SOUSA
of Messiah .... HANDEL
of Narcissus .... NEVIN
of poems ...... BARD, RHYMER,
VERSIFIER
of Thais .... MASSENET
of The Rosary .... NEVIN
opera .... BIZET, LEHAR, VERDI,
WAGNER, MENOTTI, DONIZETTI
composers' group .... ASCAP
composite .... MIXTURE,
COMPOUND, INTEGRAL
composition .... OPUS, ESSAY,
SETUP, THEME, CONTENTS
artistic .... PIECE
for nine instruments
.... NONET
for organ .... TOCCATA
for piano .... ETUDE, BALLADE,
TOCCATA
for practice .... ETUDE
for seven .... SEPTET(TE)
for three .... TRIO
for two .... DUET
hodgepodge musical
.... CENTO, MEDLEY
musical .... OPUS, ETUDE,
MOTET, RONDO, SUITE,
SONATA, CONCERTO,
FANTASIA, RONDEAU,
NOCTURNE, ORATORIO,
SERENADE
operatic .... SCENA
polyphonic .... FUGUE
sacred .... HYMN, MOTET,
PSALM, CANTICLE
compositor .... LINOTYPIST,
TYPESETTER
guide of .... JIGGER

compost heap part .... HUMUS

composure .... AIR, POISE, APLOMB, CALMNESS, SERENITY, CONTROL, SANG-FROID

compound .... MIX, YARD, ALLOY, MAKE UP, COMBINE, CONCOCT

carbon .... CARBIDE

of silica .... GLASS

raceme .... PANICLE

word .... CONJUGATE

words' separation of parts .... TMESIS

comprador .... BUYER

comprehend .... SEE, KNOW, GRASP, CONCEIVE, INCLUDE, REALIZE, EMBRACE, UNDERSTAND

comprehensible .... EXOTERIC, INTELLIGIBLE

comprehension ...... GRIP, GRASP, COMMAND, MASTERY

thru intellect .... NOESIS

comprehensive .... ALL-EMBRACING

comprehensiveness .... WIDTH

compress .... PAD, WRING, DOSSIL, CROWD, REDUCE, ABRIDGE, SQUEEZE, CONTRACT

comprise ...... EMBODY, CONTAIN, INCLUDE

compromise .... TRIM, ADJUST, BARGAIN, ENDANGER, NEGOTIATE, MEDIATE, GIVE AND TAKE

compulsion .... DRAFT, FORCE, DURESS, COACTION, COERCION, PRESSURE, CONSTRAINT

compulsive .... FORCIBLE, IRRESISTIBLE

craze, obsession, etc. .... MANIA

person, kind of ...... GAMBLER

petty thievery .... KLEPTOMANIA

compulsory .... COERCIVE, STRINGENT, MANDATORY, COMPELLING, OBLIGATORY

military service .... LEVY, DRAFT, CONSCRIPTION

compunction .... QUALM, REMORSE, SCRUPLE, PENITENCE

compurgation .... CLEARANCE

computation .... CALCULATION

compute .... FIGURE, RECKON, CALCULATE

computer .... ADDER, MACHINE, PROCESSOR, CALCULATOR

communication device .... MODEM

fictional .... HAL

floppy disk .... DISKETTE

fodder .... DATA, INPUT

language .... ALGOL, BASIC, COBOL, PILOT, PASCAL, SNOBOL, FORTRAN

movable pointer .... CURSOR

need .... DISK

physical part .... HARDWARE

program that instructs .... SOFTWARE

storage device .... DRUM

system peripheral .... TERMINAL

terminology:

billionth of a second .... NANOSECOND

eliminate error .... DEBUG

erratic signal .... BLIP

erratic speed variation .... FLUTTER

error .... BUG

first in, first out .... FIFO

garbage in, garbage out .... GIGO

group of bits .... BYTE

information .... DATA, INPUT, OUTPUT, RECORD

information store .... MEMORY

interrupt .... BREAK

list of program options .... MENU

look for data .... SEARCH

malfunction .... CRASH

not in operation .... DOWN

one million bytes .... MEGABYTE

output on paper .... HARD COPY

output on screen .... DISPLAY

pattern of dots printer .... MATRIX

run a program ...... EXECUTE

set of instructions .... PROGRAM

systems linkage .... INTERFACE

unwanted data ..... GARBAGE

type of .... IBM, ANALOG, DIGITAL

worker .... OPERATOR, PROGRAMMER

computerize .... AUTOMATE

computing device .... ABACUS, COMPTOMETER, SLIDE RULE

comrade ...... PAL, MATE, BUDDY, FRIEND, FRATER, PARTNER, KAMERAD, COMPANION, TOVARISCH

comte .... COUNT

con ...... ANTI, BILK, READ, STEER, STUDY, PERUSE, AGAINST

amore .... TENDERLY, WITH LOVE

man .... SHILL, GRIFTER, STEEPER, SWINDLER

over .... SCAN

slang .... SWINDLE, HOODWINK, CONFIDENCE

vessel .... STEER

con's confines .... SLAMMER

concatenate .... LINK(ED)

concave .... ARCHED, HOLLOW

molding ..... SCOTIA, CAVETTO

conceal .... HIDE, MASK, STOW, VEIL, CLOAK, COVER, SECRETE

goods .... CACHE, HOARD, ELOI(G)N

in a way .... PALM

in law .... ELOIN

concealed .... COVERT, HIDDEN, PERDUE, CLANDESTINE

sharpshooter .... SNIPER

concealment .... DISGUISE, INCOGNITO, CAMOUFLAGE

attack from .... SNIPE, AMBUSH, AMBUSCADE

concede .... ADMIT, ALLOW, GRANT, YIELD

conceit ...... SIDE, PRIDE, NOTION, VANITY, EGO(ISM), TYMPANY, SELF-ESTEEM

colloquial .... BIGHEAD, SWELLHEAD

conceited .... COCKY, PROUD, BOASTFUL, EGO(T)ISTIC, VAIN(GLORIOUS)

colloquial .... STUCK-UP

person .... PEACOCK, EGO(T)IST

conceive .... THINK, DEVISE, CREATE, IDEATE, IMAGINE, VISUALIZE, IMPREGNATE

concenter ...... FOCUS, CONVERGE

concentrate .... AIM, FOCUS, CENTER, COLLECT, LOCALIZE

concentrated .... DENSE, CENTRAL

concentration .... ALERTNESS, DILIGENCE, ATTENTION

camp, German .... DACHAU, STALAG

concept .... IDEA, NOTION, THOUGHT

combining form .... IDEO

conceptual .... IDEAL

conception .... HENT, IDEA, IDEATION, PREGNANCY

product of .... EMBRYO,

BRAINCHILD

concern .... CARE, AFFAIR,
AFFECT, REGARD, RELATE,
WORRY, ANXIETY, DISTURB,
INTEREST, TROUBLE, LOOKOUT
of ecologist ..... ENVIRONMENT
concerned .... UNEASY, ANXIOUS,
WORRIED, UNCERTAIN
concerning .... INRE, ABOUT,
ANENT, REGARDING
concert .... ACCORD, CONCORD,
HARMONY
ceremony .... PROGRAM
hall .... ODEUM, AUDITORIUM
in .... TOGETHER
master's instrument .... VIOLIN
musical/dance performance
.... RECITAL
organizer .... IMPRESARIO
outdoor platform
.... BANDSHELL
concerted .... JOINT, COMMON,
MUTUAL UNITED, COMBINED
concertina kin .... ACCORDION
concession .... GRANT, RIGHT,
STAND, FRANCHISE, PRIVILEGE
kind of .... SOP
conch .... SHELL
concha .... APSE
Conchobar's intended
.... DEIRDRE
concierge .... JANITOR, PORTER,
CARETAKER, DOORKEEPER
conciliar .... ADVISORY
conciliate .... CALM, ALLAY,
PACIFY, SOOTHE, APPEASE,
MOLLIFY, PLACATE,
SMOOTH(DOWN)
conciliatory .... KIND, PEACEABLE,
BENEVOLENT
offering .... SOP
theology .... IRENICS
concise ...... BRIEF, PITHY, SHORT,
TERSE, LACONIC, SUCCINCT
summary of facts .... PRECIS
conclamation .... SHOUT
conclave .... SYNOD, MEETING
conclude ...... END, CLOSE, INFER,
DEDUCE, FINISH, SETTLE,
RESOLVE, TERMINATE
a speech .... PERORATE
concluding passage in music
.... CODA, FINALE, STRETTA,
STRETTO
conclusion .... END(ING), FINIS(H),
RESULT, OUTCOME,
JUDGMENT, DECISION,
TERMINATION
in .... LASTLY
judge's .... FINDING
conclusive .... FINAL, DECISIVE

blow: sl. .... HAYMAKER,
SOCKDOLAGER, SOCKDOLOGER
point .... CLINCHER
concoct .... MIX, BREW, PLAN,
HATCH, DEVISE, COOK-UP,
COMPOUND, DREAM-UP,
TRUMP-UP
concoction, liquid .... TEA,
COFFEE, COCKTAIL
concomitant .... ANNEX,
ADDITIVE, ATTENDANT
concord .... ACCORD, UNITY,
UNISON, TREATY, ONENESS,
RAPPORT, HARMONY,
ALLIANCE
in music .... EUPHONY,
HOMOPHONY
Concord .... GRAPE
concordance .... AGREEMENT
concordant .... AGREEABLE,
ATTUNED, HARMONIOUS
concordat .... COMPACT, ENTENTE,
COVENANT, AGREEMENT
Concorde, for short .... SST
concourse .... CROWD, ARCADE,
PASSAGE, SQUARE, THRONG
concrete .... REAL, ACTUAL,
SOLID, BETON, EXACT,
SPECIFIC, DEFINITE, TANGIBLE
being .... ENS
concubinage .... HETAERISM,
HETAIRISM
concubine .... HETAERA,
MISTRESS, PARAMOUR
in harem .... ODALISK,
ODALISQUE
concupiscence .... LUST
concur .... AGREE, ACCEDE,
ASSENT, CONSENT, COINCIDE
colloquial .... JIBE
concurrence .... ACCORD, UNISON,
HARMONY, AGREEMENT
concussion .... BLOW, SHOCK,
IMPACT, SHAKING
condemn .... DAMN, DOOM,
DECRY, BLAME, CENSURE,
CONVICT, DENOUNCE
condemnation .... DECRIAL,
DOOM, DAMNATION,
CONVICTION
condemned .... DAMNED
heretic's garment
.... SANBENITO
condense .... CUT, SHORTEN,
THICKEN, ABRIDGE,
COMPRESS, COMPACT,
CONTRACT, INSPISSATE
condensed form .... CAPSULE
moisture .... DEW
condenser .... CAPACITOR
condescend .... DEIGN, STOOP

condescending ...... PATRONIZING,
HAUGHTY, HOITY-TOITY
condign .... FITTING, DESERVED,
SUITABLE
condiment .... MACE, SAUCE,
SPICE, PEPPER, RELISH,
MUSTARD, PAPRICA, PAPRIKA,
VINEGAR, SEASONING,
HORSERADISH
bottle/container .... CRUET,
CASTER
condition .... IF, FIG, CASE, RANK,
CLASS, STATE, FETTLE,
STATUS, POSTURE, STATION,
ACCUSTOM, POSITION,
STANDING, PROVISION
accompanying
.... CIRCUMSTANCE
contract .... TERM, PROVISO,
STIPULATION
of body .... HEALTH, FITNESS
of cycle/development
.... PHASE, STAGE
of decline .... DECADENCE
of great danger/trouble
.... CRISIS
of great vitality .... STHENIA
of hardship/difficulty
.... PINCH
of oblivion .... LIMBO
of payment .... TERMS
of servitude .... BONDAGE,
SLAVERY
of stupor ..... COMA, NARCOSIS
sudden, unexpected
.... EMERGENCY
conditional .... PENDING
bond .... ESCROW
freedom .... BAIL
release .... PAROLE
surrender .... CAPITULATION
conditioned .... LIMITED,
CONTINGENT
for subsequent purchase
.... PRESOLD
conditioning .... TRAINING, TUNE-
UP, ADJUSTMENT
conditions of possession
.... TENURE
condole .... LAMENT, COMFORT,
CONSOLE, COMMISERATE
condolence .... PITY, SYMPATHY
condominium .... (CO-OP)
APARTMENT
condone .... PARDON, FORGIVE,
EXCUSE, ABSOLVE, OVERLOOK
condor .... VULTURE
conduce .... LEAD, TEND,
CONTRIBUTE
conduct .... MIEN, WAGE,
BEARING, BEHAVE, DEMEAN,

HANDLE, MANAGE, BEHAVIOR, DEMEANOR, EXECUTE, TRANSACT
improperly .... MISMANAGE
in polite society .... ETIQUETTE
under guard .... CONVOY, ESCORT

conductor .... LEADER, MAESTRO, MANAGER, DIRECTOR, OPERATOR, CONVEYOR, TRANSMITTER
colloquial .... TIME BEATER
orchestra ..... BOULEZ, MEHTA, BEECHAM, ORMANDY, BERNSTEIN, TOSCANINI, BARBIROLLI
platform of .... PODIUM
stick .... BATON
tourists' ..... GUIDE, CICERONE, DRAGOMAN
woman .... QUACH

conduit .... MAIN, PIPE, CHANNEL, DRAIN, SEWER

cone .... SPIRE, BOBBIN, FUNNEL
bearing tree .... FIR, YEW, PINE, CEDAR, LARCH, ZAMIA, SPRUCE, CONIFER, CYPRESS, JUNIPER, PINASTER
seed-bearing .... STROBIL(E)
shaped ..... CONIC(AL), PINEAL, CONOID(AL), PYRAMIDAL, TURBINATE, CONIFEROUS
shaped paper container .... CORNUCOPIA
shaped pile .... COCK
shaped yarn roll .... COP
spiral .... HELIX

conepate .... SKUNK

coney .... DAMAN, HYRAX, RABBIT, RODENT

confab .... CHAT, TALK, POWWOW

confection .... SWEET, BONBON, COMFIT, CONFITURE, SWEETMEAT
almond .... NOUGAT, MARZIPAN, MARCHPANE
cold .... ICE CREAM
flavor .... VANILLA
nutty .... PRALINE
sugar .... CANDY
Turkish .... HALVAH

confederacy .... SOUTH, ALLIANCE
foe .... UNION

confederate .... ALLY, REB(EL), ACCOMPLICE

Confederate general .... LEE, BRAGG, EWELL, HAMPTON, LONGSTREET
president .... DAVIS
soldier, Civil War .... REB

confederation .... BUND

confer ...... GIVE, GRANT, AWARD, ENDOW, BESTOW, DISCUSS, CONVERSE
privately .... COLLOGUE

conference .... CONFAB, JUNTA, PARLEY, MEETING, PALAVER
church .... COUNCIL
Indian .... POWWOW
Midwest .... BIG TEN
private .... CAUCUS, HUDDLE, TETE-A-TETE
site of 1943 .... CAIRO, TEHERAN
site of 1945 .... YALTA
sitting of a .... SESSION

conferred, thing .... FAVOR, HONOR, RIGHT, TITLE, DEGREE

conferring respect .... HONORIFIC

confess .... OWN, AVOW, BARE, ADMIT, REVEAL
slang .... SING, PEACH, SQUEAL

confession .... AVOWAL, ADMISSION, REVELATION
of faith .... CREDO, CREED

Confessions author .... ROUSSEAU

confetti ...... CANDIES, PAPER BITS

confidant(e) .... FRIEND, INTIMATE

confide .... TELL, TRUST, DIVULGE, ENTRUST, BARE ONE'S MIND

confidence .... FAITH, TRUST, BELIEF, SECRET, PRIVACY, BOLDNESS, ASSURANCE
game .... BUNCO, BUNKO, SHELL GAME, SWINDLE, THIMBLERIG
game item .... CUP, SEED, NUTSHELL
man ...... CON, SHILL, GRIFTER, STEEPER, SWINDLER
show of .... BRAVADO

confident .... BOLD, SURE, SECURE, ASSURED, CERTAIN, POSITIVE

confidential .... SECRET, PRIVATE, ESOTERIC, INTIMATE
advisers' group .... CABAL, CAMARILLA
between you and me .... OFF THE RECORD
disclosure/warning .... TIP-OFF

confiding .... OPEN, NAIVE, TRUSTFUL, TRUSTING

configuration .... FORM, SHAPE, CONTOUR, OUTLINE, GROUPING

confine .... BOX, HEM, PEN, TIE, CAGE, JAIL, LIMIT, DETAIN, FETTER, IMMURE, ASTRICT, IMPRISON, RESTRICT

to a place .... LOCALIZE

confined .... BOUND, ENCLOSED, PENT-UP, SHUT-IN
in circulation .... CLOSE

confinement .... CUSTODY, CAPTIVITY, DETENTION, ENCLOSURE, RESTRAINT
cause of .... ILLNESS, CHILDBIRTH, CONVICTION
place of .... JAIL, ASYLUM, PRISON, HOSPITAL

confirm .... PROVE, ATTEST, RATIFY, VERIFY, VALIDATE, CORROBORATE, SUBSTANTIATE

confirmation .... RITE, EVIDENCE, SACRAMENT, VERIFICATION

confirmed .... TRIED, ARRANT, TESTED, VESTED, CHRONIC, HABITUAL, INVETERATE

confiscate .... TAKE, SEIZE, GRAB, ANNEX, SNATCH, USURP, ESCHEAT, COMMANDEER, APPROPRIATE

confiture .... CANDY, PRESERVE, SWEETMEAT

conflagration .... FIRE, BLAZE, COMBUSTION

conflict .... JAR, CLASH, FIGHT, STOUR, BATTLE, COMBAT, STRIFE, CONTEST, DISCORD, HOSTILITY, STRUGGLE
armed .... WAR
of characters in drama .... AGON
of interest .... BREACH, TUSSLE, CONTROVERSY

conflicting .... HOSTILE, CONTRARY, OPPOSING

confluence .... CROWD, GATHERING, CLUSTERING

conform .... ADAPT, AGREE, SHAPE UP, EXEMPLIFY

conforming to morals ..,............................ ETHICAL

conformist .... STICKLER, ASSENTER
kind of .... YESMAN
non .... HERETIC

conformity .... HABIT, CUSTOM, AGREEMENT, FORMALITY, BY THE BOOK, COMPLIANCE

confound .... ROUT, DISMAY, STUMP, PUZZLE, CONFUSE, PERPLEX, BEWILDER

confraternity ...... BROTHERHOOD

confrere .... ASSOCIATE, COLLEAGUE

confront ...... FACE, MEET, BRAVE, STAND, OPPOSE, RESIST

confuse .... ABASH, RAVEL, FLUMMOX, PUZZLE, MYSTIFY,

PERPLEX, BEWILDER, CONFOUND, DISCONCERT, FLABBERGAST

confused .... ASEA, LOST, MUZZY, ADDLED, HAYWIRE

hopelessly .... OBFUSCATED

turkey .... FLUSTERED BUSTARD

confusion .... ADO, MESS, MOIL, RIOT, MELEE, BEDLAM, JUMBLE, CHAOS, FRACAS, MIX-UP, MUDDLE, HAVOC, RUCKUS, TANGLE, WELTER, DISARRAY, DISORDER

of tongues .... BABEL

sudden .... FLURRY

confutation .... REBUTTAL

confute .... REBUT, DEFEAT, REFUTE, DISPROVE

conge .... FAREWELL, DISMISSAL

congeal .... GEL, SET, JELL, CURDLE, FREEZE, HARDEN, STIFFEN, THICKEN, SOLIDIFY

congealed water (vapor) .... ICE, SNOW

congealer, wound ...... COMFREY

congenial .... BOON, KINDRED, FRIENDLY, PLEASING, AGREEABLE, COMPATIBLE

congenital .... INBORN, INNATE, CONNATE

mark .... MOLE

conger .... EEL

trap .... EELPOT

congeries .... HEAP, PILE, COLLECTION

congest .... JAM, CLOG, PLUG, CHOKE, BLOCK, OVERFILL, OVERCROWD

congestion .... STOPPAGE

conglomerate .... AMASS

conglomeration .... LUMP, MIXTURE, COHESION, HODGEPODGE, MELTING POT

Congo ...... DYE, EEL, TEA, RIVER

capital .... BRAZZAVILLE, KINSHASA

city/town .... EWO, OYO, BOKO, ABALA, KELLE, NKAYI, SEMBE, DONGOU, ZANAGA, GAMBOMA, LOUBOMO, KINKALA, POINTE-NOIRE

dwarf .... AKKA, ACHUAS

ethnic group .... BANTU, BALALI, BATEKE, BAVILI, HAMITE

language ..... BANTU, LINGALA, SWAHILI

mountains .... CRYSTAL

peanut .... NGUBA

premier .... ADOULA, LUMUMBA, TSHOMBE

president .... MOBUTU, YOULOU, KASAVUBU

province .... KIVA, KWILU, KATANGA

red .... SALT

river .... DJA, ALIMA, IVINDO, CONGO, KADEI, OGOOUE, NIARI, SANGHA

river tributary .... UBANGI

tribesman .... SIMBA

congou .... TEA

congratulate .... HAIL, SALUTE, COMMEND, COMPLIMENT, FELICITATE

congratulatory ...... GRATULANT, COMPLIMENTARY

congregate .... GATHER, COLLECT, ASSEMBLE

congregation .... FOLD, FLOCK, CHURCH, PARISH, BRETHREN, ASSEMBLY, ASSEMBLAGE

congress .... MEETING, ASSEMBLY, CONVENTION, LEGISLATURE

Congress attendant .... PAGE

concern of ..... BILLS, BUDGET, RESOLUTIONS

time off .... RECESS

congressman not reelected
.... LAMEDUCK

congruence .... AGREEMENT

congruity ...... FITNESS, HARMONY

congruous .... FIT(TING), SUITABLE

conic section .... CURVE, ELLIPSE, PARABOLA

conical .... FUNNEL-LIKE, FUNNEL-SHAPED

roll of yarn .... COP

shelter .... TIPI, TEPEE

conifer .... FIR, YEW, PINE, CEDAR, LARCH, SPRUCE

coniferous forest .... TAIGA

tree .... FIR, PINE, LARCH

conium .... HEMLOCK

conjecture ...... THEORY, IMAGINE, ASSUMPTION, GUESS(WORK), SURMISE

conjoin .... UNITE, CONNECT

conjoint .... UNITED

conjointly .... TOGETHER

conjugal .... MARITAL, CONNUBIAL, MATRIMONIAL

conjugate .... MATED, UNITE, COUPLE, RELATED

conjugation .... UNION, SYNGAMY

conjunction .... OR, AND, BUT, SINCE, UNION, BLENDING, INCLUSION, COINCIDENCE

in biology .... ZYGOSIS

conjunctivitis .... PINKEYE, TRACHOMA

conjuration ...... MAGIC, SORCERY

conjure .... BEG, CALL UPON, INVOKE, BESEECH, IMPLORE, SUMMON(UP)

conjuror .... MAGE, WIZARD, WARLOCK, MAGICIAN, SORCERER

stick of .... ROD, WAND

words of .... HOCUS-POCUS

conk .... HIT, KNOCK

British slang ..... BLOW, HEAD, NOSE

out .... FAIL

connate .... AKIN, INBORN, INBRED, INNATE, GENETIC, CONGENITAL

connect ...... FUSE, JOIN, LINK, TIE IN, HOOK UP, COUPLE, RELATE, ASSOCIATE

secretly .... TAP

Connecticut, capital of
.... HARTFORD

city/town .... BRIDGEPORT, DANBURY, NEW HAVEN, CANAAN, HAMDEN, NORWALK, MERIDEN, GREENWICH, PUTNAM, BRISTOL, CLINTON, VERNON, STAMFORD, NORWICH, MIDDLETOWN, WATERBURY, NAUGATUCK, TORRINGTON, TRUMBULL, WOODBRIDGE, STRATFORD, WILLIMANTIC

college .... TRINITY, HARTFORD, ST. JOSEPH

county .... TOLLAND, FAIRFIELD, HARTFORD, WINDHAM, LITCHFIELD, NEW HAVEN, MIDDLESEX, NEW LONDON

island .... MASON

lake .... GLEN, BANTAM, ROGERS, PUTNAM, ANDOVER, TYLER, WANGUM, BETHANY, KONOMOC, OXOBOXO, GAILLARD, HAMMONASSET, HIGHLAND, QUASSAPAUG, CHAMBERLAIN, CANDLEWOOD, SPECTACLE, TERRAMUGGUS, WINDWING, WINCHESTER

mountain .... RED, BEAR, CANAAN, MOHAWK, FRISSELL, HAYSTACK, MANITOOK, LAMENTATION

official, borough ...... WARDEN

pond .... MUDGE, PACHAUG

range .... TALCOTT

recreation site .... DINOSAUR PARK, MARK TWAIN HOUSE, MYSTIC AQUARIUM

river .... MAD, BYRAM, MYSTIC,

SALMON, SCANTIC, THAMES, TITICUS, NAUGATUCK, EIGHT MILE, CONNECTICUT, YANTIC, HOUSATONIC

state bird .... ROBIN

state flower .... MOUNTAIN LAUREL

state nickname .... NUTMEG, CONSTITUTION

university .... YALE

connecting body of water .... STRAIT

part .... LINK

pipe .... TEE

strip of land .... ISTHMUS

connection ...... TIE, BOND, NECK, NEXUS, UNION, CONTACT, BRIDGE, KINSHIP, RELATION

close .... LIAISON

connective .... SYNDETIC

tissue .... FASCIA, TENDON, CARTILAGE

tissue disease .... ARTHRITIS

word .... OR, AND, NOR, EITHER, NEITHER

Connelly, playwright .... MARC(US)

Connie .... MACK, FRANCIS

Mack's ballpark .... SHIBE

conning tower adjunct .... PERISCOPE

conniption .... TANTRUM

connivance .... INTRIGUE, TRICKERY, COLLUSION

connive .... PLOT, COLLUDE, CONSPIRE, COOPERATE

conniver ...... PLOTTER, FINAGLER

conniving .... SCHEMING

connoisseur ...... CRITIC, EXPERT, JUDGE, (A)ESTHETE, AUTHORITY, CO(G)NOSCENTE

art .... VIRTUOSO

fine foods/drinks ..... EPICURE, GOURMET, GO(U)RMAND

of gems .... LAPIDARY

connotation .... IMPLICATION

connote .... HINT, IMPLY, SUGGEST

connubial .... MARITAL, NUPTIAL, SPOUSAL, CONJUGAL

conquer .... DEFEAT, MASTER, QUELL, SUBDUE, SUBJUGATE, OVERCOME, OVERRIDE, OVERTHROW, SUPPRESS, VANQUISH

conquerable .... VINCIBLE

conquering .... TAMING

conqueror .... VICTOR

conquest .... VICTORY

of 1954 .... POLIO

conquistador .... CORTEZ, PIZARRO, CONQUEROR

Conrad (Joseph) character .... AXEL, LENA, SEAMAN, MARINER

(Joseph) novel .... VICTORY

Robert Falk .... ROBERT CONRAD

consanguinity .... KINSHIP, AFFINITY, RELATION

conscience, twinge of .... QUALM, REMORSE, SCRUPLE

conscientious objector .... CONCHY

conscious .... (A)WARE, AWAKE, EARNEST, MINDFUL, SENTIENT, COGNIZANT

consciousness ...... WITS, SENSES, INSIGHT, ALERTNESS, DILIGENCE

lose .... FAINT, PASS OUT, SWOON

conscript .... LEVY, DRAFT, FORCE, ENLIST, ENROLL, MUSTER, RECRUIT

conscripted person ...... DRAFTEE

consecrate .... BLESS, ANOINT, VOW, DEVOTE, HALLOW, ORDAIN, DEDICATE, SANCTIFY

consecrated .... BLEST, SACRED

bread .... SACRAMENT

Host's receptacle .... MONSTRANCE

oil .... CHRISM

consecration .... BLESSING

of the bread .... SACRING

consecutive .... ENSUING, FOLLOWING, SUCCESSIVE

consensus .... POLL, ASSENT, OPINION, AGREEMENT, COMMON BELIEF, SYMPOSIUM

consent .... AGREE, ALLOW, GRANT, YIELD, CONCUR, ACCEPT, ACCEDE, APPROVE, PERMISSION, AGREEMENT

consenting .... WILLING

consequence .... END, VALUE, FRUIT, RESULT, SEQUEL, EFFECT, PRODUCT, OUTCOME, CONCERN, IMPORTANCE

person of .... VIP, NABOB, BIGWIG, TYCOON, BIGSHOT

consequential .... MAJOR, IMPORTANT, RESULTANT

consequently .... ERGO, THUS, FINALLY, ACCORDINGLY, AS A RESULT, THEREFORE

conservation .... KEEPING, PROTECTION

conservative ...... TORY, PRUDENT, RIGHT(IST), MODERATE, STABLE, DIEHARD, STANDPAT, UNCHANGING, REACTIONARY

person .... FOG(E)Y

conservatory .... ACADEMY, MUSIC SCHOOL, GREENHOUSE

conserve ...... SAVE(UP), PRESERVE

fruit .... JAM

consider ...... DEEM, HEED, MULL, JUDGE, OPINE, STUDY, WEIGH, REFLECT, PONDER, ENTERTAIN

kindly .... FAVOR

considerable .... BIG, MUCH, LARGE, SIZABLE, WEIGHTY, GREAT DEAL, SUBSTANTIAL

colloquial .... TIDY, GOODLY, PRETTY

considerate .... KIND, THOUGHTFUL

consideration .... FEE, CARE, ESTEEM, REASON, GROUND, REGARD, MOTIVE, THOUGHT, REFLECTION

considering everything ...... ALL IN ALL

consign .... ASSIGN, COMMIT, ENTRUST, DELIVER, RELEGATE

to hell .... DAMN, CONDEMN

consist .... COMPRISE, INCLUDE

consistency .... DENSITY, HARMONY, FIRMNESS, AGREEMENT, SOLIDITY

consistent .... REGULAR, UNIFORM, ACCORDANT, COHERENT

consisting of 100 degrees .... CENTIGRADE

small spaces .... AREOLAR

consolation .... SOP, SOLACE, COMFORT, SYMPATHY

console .... ANCON, CHEER, BRACKET, CABINET, COMFORT, SUPPORT

like bracket .... CORBEL

radio/television .... FLOOR MODEL

the bereaved .... CONDOLE

consolidate .... FUSE, POOL, MERGE, UNITE, COMBINE, FEDERATE, SYNDICATE

consomme .... SOUP, BROTH

consonance .... UNITY, RHYME, CONCORD, HARMONY

consonant, aspirated .... SURD

hard .... FORTIS

unaspirated/smooth .... LENE

voiceless .... ATONIC

consonantal sound ...... SPIRANT

consort .... MATE WIFE, SPOUSE, HUSBAND, COMPEER, PARTNER, COMPANION

Queen Elizabeth's .... PHILIP

Queen Juliana's .... BERNHARD

Queen Victoria's .... ALBERT

Siva's .... DEVI
with ..... ATTEND, ACCOMPANY
consortium .... CARTEL,
COMPACT, COVENANT,
SYNDICATE
conspectus ...... DIGEST, SYNOPSIS
conspicuous .... GLARING, OVERT,
OBVIOUS, SALIENT, EMINENT,
NOTABLE, STRIKING,
PROMINENT, NOTICEABLE
consumption .... WASTE
success .... HIT, ECLAT
conspicuously .... VISIBLY,
CLEARLY, NOTABLY,
FLAGRANTLY
conspiracy .... PLOT, CABAL,
INTRIGUE, TRICKERY,
CONNIVANCE
sneaky .... SKULDUGGERY
to deceive .... CHICANERY
to defraud .... COVIN
conspirator .... TRAITOR,
SCHEMER, CATILINARIAN
conspire .... (COM)PLOT, CONCUR,
COLLUDE, CONNIVE, JOIN IN,
SCHEME, BE IN CAHOOTS
constable .... BULL, WARDEN,
BAILIFF, TROOPER, TIPSTAFF,
POLICE(MAN), PEACE OFFICER
constabulary .... SHERIFFRY,
(STATE)POLICE
constancy .... LOYALTY,
DEVOTION, EVENNESS,
FIRMNESS, STABILITY,
STEADINESS
constant ...... FAST, TRUE, LOYAL,
FIRM, STABLE, STEADY,
CHRONIC, DEVOTED,
FAITHFUL, CONTINUAL
visitor .... FREQUENTER
constantly .... DAY AFTER DAY
Constantine's birthplace
.... NISH
Constantinople .... ISTANBUL,
ISTAMBOUL
foreign quarter .... PERA,
BEYOGLU
inn .... SERAI, IMARET,
CARAVANSARY
constellate .... UNITE, CLUSTER
constellation .... GALAXY,
CLUSTER, ASTERISM,
GATHERING
altar .... ARA
archer .... SAGITTARIUS
arrow .... SAGITTA
balance .... LIBRA
bear .... URSA
bear, the Great .... URSA
MAJOR
bear, the Lesser .... URSA

MINOR
bird of paradise .... APUS
box .... PYXIS
brightest star .... COR
bull .... TAURUS
centaur .... CENTAURUS
charioteer .... AURIGA
crab .... CANCER
crane .... GRUS
cross .... CRUX
crow .... CORVUS
dog .... CANIS
dolphin .... DELPHINUS
dragon .... DRACO
eagle .... AQUILA
equatorial .... CETUS, ORION
fish .... PISCES
fish, the Flying .... VOLANS
fly .... MUSCA
foot .... RIGEL
fox .... VULPECULA
giraffe .... CAMELOPARDUS
goat .... CAPRICORN
hare .... LEPUS
harp .... LYRA
herdsman .... BOOTES
hunter .... ORION
in the Zodiac .... ARIES,
TAURUS, GEMINI, CANCER,
LEO, VIRGO, LIBRA, SCORPIO,
SAGITTARIUS, CAPRICORN(US),
AQUARIUS, PISCES
Indian .... INDUS
lady in the chair
.... CASSIOPEIA
lady, the chained
.... ANDROMEDA
lion .... LEO
lizard .... LACERTA
mast .... MALUS
monarch .... CEPHEUS
net .... RETICULUM
Northern .... LYRA, URSA,
DRACO, BOOTES, CYGNUS,
ARIES, AQUILA, AURIGA,
HYDRA, CEPHEUS, POLARIS,
SCUTUM, PERSEUS, SAGITTA,
LACERTA, PEGASUS, HERCULES,
LEO MINOR, DELPHINUS,
ANDROMEDA, CASSIOPEIA,
VULPECULA
painter .... PICTOR
peacock .... PAVO
ram .... ARIES
raven .... CORVUS
rule .... NORMA
scales .... LIBRA
scorpion .... SCORPIO,
SCORPIUS
sea serpent .... HYDRA
serpent/snake .... SERPENS

ship .... ARGO
Southern .... ARA, APUS,
CRUX, GRUS, PAVO, VELA,
CANIS, CETUS, INDUS, LEPUS,
LUPUS, ORION, MENSA, MUSCA,
NORMA, PYXIS, CARINA,
CORVUS, CAELUM, CRATER,
HYDRUS, ANTLIA, DORADO,
FORNAX, OCTANS, PICTOR,
PUPPIS, TUCANA, VOLANS,
COLUMBA, CIRCINUS, PHOENIX,
SEXTANS, SCULPTOR,
ERIDANUS, CENTAURUS,
MONOCEROS
stern .... PUPPIS
swan .... CYGNUS
table .... MENSA
toucan .... TUCANA
twins .... GEMINI
veil .... VELA
virgin .... VIRGO
water carrier .... AQUARIUS
water serpent .... HYDRUS
whale .... CETUS
winged horse .... PEGASUS
wolf .... LUPUS
woman .... VIRGO
consternation .... FEAR, PANIC,
ALARM, DISMAY, FRIGHT,
HORROR, TERROR,
AMAZEMENT
constipated .... CLOGGED,
COSTIVE
constituency .... VOTERS,
CLIENTELE, ELECTORATE
constituent .... ELECTOR,
ELEMENT, COMPONENT, PART,
VOTER, INTEGRANT
constitution .... CODE, NATURE,
MAKE-UP, CHARTER, BASIC
LAW, STATE, STRUCTURE,
COMPOSITION
addition to .... AMENDMENT
composition of .... BY-LAWS,
ARTICLES, PREAMBLE
state .... CONNECTICUT
constitutional .... BASIC, LAWFUL,
LEGAL, ORGANIC, CHARTERED,
VALID, OFFICIAL, ESSENTIAL
colloquial .... WALK, EXERCISE
constrain .... FORCE, IMPEL,
COMPEL, OBLIGE, STRESS
constraint .... DURESS, COERCION,
STRESS, PRESSURE,
COMPULSION, REPRESSION,
CONFINEMENT
constrict .... LIMIT, HAMPER,
CHOKE, CRAMP, CONTRACT,
STRANGLE, SQUEEZE,
COMPRESS

163

constriction of duct, etc.
.... STENOSIS
constrictor .... BOA, PYTHON, CRUSHER, ANACONDA, SPHINCTER
construct .... FORM, MAKE, REAR, BUILD, ERECT, FRAME, DEVISE, MODEL, COMPOSE, ARRANGE
construction .... BUILDING, CREATION, ERECTION, STRUCTURE, COMPOSITION, INTERPRETATION
battalion member ...... SEABEE
elaborate .... EDIFICE
constructive .... USEFUL, HELPFUL, POSITIVE, BENEFICIAL
arts .... TECTONICS
construe .... READ, INFER, PARSE, EXPLAIN, ANALYZE, RENDER, INTERPRET, TRANSLATE
consuetude .... USE, HABIT, USAGE, CUSTOM, PRACTICE
consul's authority
.... EXEQUATUR
consult .... ADVISE, CONFER, DISCUSS, REFER TO, COMMUNE WITH
consultant, common .... DOCTOR, EXPERT, LAWYER, ENGINEER, TECHNICIAN
consume .... EAT, BURN, DRAIN, DRINK, SPEND, WASTE, USE UP, DEVOUR, EXPEND, CORRODE, DESTROY, EXHAUST
consumed .... BATED, SPENT, REDUCED, WASTED, DEPLETED
by fire .... CREMATED
consumer .... USER, BUYER, EATER, VENDEE
concern .... SHORTAGES
goods .... FOOD, CLOTHING
opposed to .... PRODUCER
consumer's advocate/crusader
.... NADER
loyalty .... BRAND NAME
consummate .... END, PERFECT, FULFILL, COMPLETE, FINISHED, OUTRIGHT, ABSOLUTE, THOROUGH
is what some are .... LIARS, ARTISTS
skill .... FINESSE
consummation ...... END, RESULT, CLIMAX, SUMMIT, OUTCOME, REALIZATION, FULFILLMENT
consumption .... USE, WASTE, ATROPHY, EROSION, WASTAGE, DEPLETION, DESTRUCTION

lung .... TABES, PHTHISIS, TUBERCULOSIS
consumptive .... HECTIC, LUNGER, TABETIC, PHTHISIC, DISEASED, TUBERCULOUS
contact .... MEET, TOUCH, TACTION, TANGENT, ENCOUNTER, CONNECTION
closely .... OSCULATE
in physical .... CONTIGUOUS
mines .... TORPEDOES
contagion .... VIRUS, POISON, MEASLES, VECTION, INFECTION, TRANSFER, SMALLPOX, EPIDEMIC
contagious .... NOXIOUS, CATCHING, INFECTIOUS, COMMUNICABLE
contain .... HOLD, CHECK, HOUSE, EMBODY, ENCLOSE, RESTRAIN, EMBRACE, INCLUDE, COMPRISE
container .... BAG, BOX, CAN, JAR, KEG, TIN, TUN, VAT, PAIL, CRATE, POUCH, BASKET
beer .... KEG, BARREL, GROWLER
cardboard/pasteboard
.... CARTON
cereal .... BOWL
cigarette .... CASE
documents .... HANAPER, BRIEFCASE
dose of medicine ..... CAPSULE
earthenware dish ...... TERRINE
earthenware pot .... PIPKIN
for burning oil .... CRESSET
for carrying drinking water
.... CANTEEN
for carrying paper money/ cards .... WALLET, BILLFOLD
for holding traveling clothes
.... GRIPSACK
for holy oil .... AMPULLA
for liquids ...... EWER, FLAGON
for liquor, flattened .... FLASK, FLASKET
for relics .... CUSTODIAL, RELIQUARY
for serving animal food
.... TROUGH
for serving gravy/sauce
.... GRAVY BOAT
for serving soup .... TUREEN
for table vinegar/oil/honey
.... CRUET, CRUSE
for the sacred host
.... TABERNACLE
for therapy bath ..... SITZBATH
for wine of Holy Communion ..... CHALICE

glass .... BOTTLE, CARBOY
half-gallon .... POTTLE
info .... TARE, NET WEIGHT, GROSS WEIGHT
material for making .... TIN, FLAX, JUTE, GLASS, OSIER, WOOD, STAVE, BURLAP, PAPER, PLASTIC, ALUMINUM
metal .... COPPER
of assorted things .... ATTIC, HANDBAG, CATCHALL
perforated .... DREDGER
perfume .... FLACON
sealed .... CAN, TIN, ENVELOPE
to keep liquids hot/cold
.... THERMOS
to spit into .... CUSPIDOR, SPITTOON
waste .... TRASH CAN
water .... TANK, TROUGH, CISTERN, RESERVOIR
wine .... CARAFE, DECANTER
with wicker casing
.... DEMIJOHN
wooden pail/bucket
.... CANNIKIN
containing air/wind/gases
.... PNEUMATIC
arsenic .... ARSENIOUS
carbon .... ORGANIC
copper .... CUPRIC
defects .... FAULTY
fire .... FIERY, IGNEOUS
gold .... AURIC
iron .... FERRIC
metal/ore ...... METALLIFEROUS
oil .... GREASY, SMOOTH, SLIPPERY, UNCTUOUS
perforations .... FENESTRATE
silver .... LUNAR
sulfur .... SULFIDE
tin .... STANNIC
containment .... ENCLOSURE, INCLUSION
contaminate .... SOIL, DIRTY, TAINT, SPOIL, STAIN, SULLY, BEFOUL, DEFILE, INFECT, CORRUPT, DEPRAVE, POLLUTE
contaminator, air .... SMOG, SMAZE
conte .... TALE, SHORT STORY
contemn .... SCORN, DESPISE
contemplate .... AIM, MUSE, VIEW, GAZE AT, MEAN, PLAN, BEHOLD, INTEND, PONDER, PROPOSE, CONSIDER, REFLECT, MEDITATE
contemplation .... INTENT(ION), EXPECTATION
of embezzlement
...... PECULATION SPECULATION

contemporaneous .... COEVAL, CURRENT, SIMULTANEOUS

contemporary .... MODERN, MODISH, COEVAL, COETANEOUS, PRESENT-DAY, COEXISTENT

contempt .... SCORN, DISDAIN, CONTEMN, DEFIANCE

cry of .... BAH, TUT, PSHAW, FIDDLE-DE-DEE

show of .... FLEER, SNEER, JEER, SNIFF, SNORT

slang .... SLAM

contemptible .... LOW, BASE, MEAN, VILE, ABJECT, PALTRY, SCURVY, DESPISED, SCORNFUL, UNENVIED, OFFENSIVE, DESPICABLE

fellow ...... CAD, HEEL, BLOKE, SKATE, RASCAL, CULLION, SCOUNDREL

contend .... VIE, COPE, FIGHT, ARGUE, BATTLE, OPPOSE, COMPETE

with .... MEET

contender .... ENTRY, RIVAL, COMPETITOR, CONTESTANT

contendere, _____ (not contested) .... NOLO

contending parties .... SIDES, OPPONENTS, PROTAGONISTS

content .... VOLUME, MAKINGS, CAPACITY, SATISFIED

contention .... ROW, STRIFE, CONTEST, DISPUTE, ARGUMENT

in words only .... LOGOMACHY

contentious .... FISTIC, COMBATIVE, LOADED FORBEAR

contents list .... TABLE

unknown purchase ...... GRAB-BAG

contest .... AGON, FIGHT, DISPUTE, RIVALRY, TOURNEY, SKIRMISH, TOURNAMENT

armed .... WAR

boxing .... BOUT

endurance/long distance .... MARATHON

for two, armed .... DUEL

in court/in law .... LAWSUIT, LITIGATE, LITIGATION

judges .... JURY, PANEL

lures .... PRIZES

of knights .... DUEL, TILT, JOUST, TOURNEY

participant .... ENTRY, ENTRANT

second placer ...... RUNNER-UP

winner .... CHAMPION

with lances .... TILT, JOUST

contestant .... SIDE, ENTRY, RIVAL, ENTRANT, CONTENDER, PLAYER COMPETER, COMPETITOR

mercenary .... POTHUNTER

contestants as a whole .... FIELD

context .... SETTING, POSITION, BACKGROUND

contiguity ...... UNION, ABUTMENT

contiguous ...... NEXT, ADJACENT, TOUCHING

continence .... MODERATION, SOBRIETY, SELF-RESTRAINT

continent .... CHASTE, VESTAL, CELIBATE, ABSTINENT, TEMPERATE, ASIA, LANDMASS, MAINLAND, AFRICA, EUROPE, EURASIA, NORTH AMERICA, SOUTH AMERICA, AUSTRALIA, ANTARCTICA

"down under" .... AUSTRALIA

hypothetical .... LEMURIA, CASCADIA

icy .... ANTARCTICA

legendary/lost .... ATLANTIS

Continental Congress president .... HANCOCK

contingency .... HAP, EVENT, CASUALTY, FORTUITY, PROSPECT, EMERGENCY, LIKELIHOOD, INCIDENCE, POSSIBILITY

contingent .... TEAM, GROUP, LIKELY, PENDING, BASED ON, DEPENDENT, INCIDENTAL, HINGING ON, CONDITIONAL, SUBJECT TO

continual .... CONSTANT, ENDLESS, FREQUENT, INCESSANT

change/movement .... FLUX(ION)

continually .... CONSTANTLY, FREQUENTLY, OFTEN(TIMES), REPEATEDLY, NEVER-ENDING

continuance .... ENDURANCE, EXTENSION

in time .... DURATION

continuation .... SEQUEL, ADDITION, DEFERRAL, OFFSHOOT, SEQUENCE, EXTENSION, FOLLOWING, DEFERMENT, RESUMPTION

continue ...... LAST, STAY, GO ON, KEEP-UP, CARRY-ON, STAY, ABIDE, DWELL, ENDURE, PROLONG, PERSIST, PREVAIL, PROCEED, SUSTAIN, MAINTAIN

obsolete .... DURE

tediously .... DRAG

continued story/movie .... SERIAL

continuing ...... STEADY, LASTING, CONSTANT, PERPETUAL, DURABLE, STEADFAST

continuous .... ENDLESS, NONSTOP, CEASELESS, PERENNIAL, UNBROKEN, UNINTERRUPTED

bloom .... EVERGREEN

series .... STREAM

vexation .... HARASSMENT

contort .... WARP, TWIST, DEFORM, DISTORT, DISLOCATE

contortionist .... HOUDINI

contour .... FORM, SHAPE, FIGURE, (OUT)LINE

of head .... PROFILE

of region .... TOPOGRAPHY

contra .... OPPOSITE

contraband .... BANNED, ILLEGAL, SMUGGLED, FORBIDDEN

of a sort .... BOOTLEG

slang .... HOT GOODS

contrabandist .... SMUGGLER, (RUM)RUNNER

contrabass .... VIOL(ONE)

contraception .... STOPPER, HINDRANCE, BIRTH CONTROL

contraceptive device .... IUD, JELLY, CONDOM, THE PILL, DIAPHRAGM

slang .... RUBBER

contract .... VOW, INCUR, NARROW, PLEDGE, SHRINK, (COM)PACT, PROMISE, SHORTEN, AGREEMENT, COVENANT, DOCUMENT

a muscle .... FLEX

betrothal .... HANDFAST, ENGAGEMENT

bridge bid .... SLAM

first paragraph of .... ITEM I

illegal labor ...... YELLOW DOG

marriage .... WEDLOCK, MATRIMONY

of agency .... MANDATE

rental .... LEASE

the brow(s) .... KNIT, FROWN

the lips .... PUCKER(UP)

the skin .... WRINKLE

to marry .... TROTH

to transfer property ...... DEED

work .... INDENTURE

contracted .... CONCISE, REDUCED

contraction .... SYNCOPE, SHORTENING, COMPRESSION, ABBREVIATION

in poetry .... ELISION

of muscles .... SPASM, CRAMPS

of writing .... SHORTHAND,

STENOGRAPHY
contractor .... BUILDER
contradict .... DENY, BELIE, VETO,
REBUT, NEGATE, REFUSE,
REFUTE, GAINSAY
contradiction .... DENIAL,
NEGATION, REBUTTAL,
REFUSAL, INCONSISTENCY
in terms .... ANTILOGY
contradictory .... DENIED,
CONTRARY, NEGATIVE
contralto Nikolaidi .... ELENA
contraption .... GADGET,
CONTRIVANCE
contrary .... WRY, BALKY,
COUNTER, ADVERSE, OPPOSED,
HOSTILE, REVERSE, PERVERSE,
OPPOSITE, OBSTINATE
person .... MARY
to rules .... FOUL
contrast .... LIKEN, COMPARE
with .... DIFFER
contravene .... DEFY, OPPOSE,
VIOLATE, DISAGREE
contretemps .... MISHAP
contribute .... AID, GIVE, HELP,
TEND, SERVE, DONATE
contribution .... DOLE, GIFT,
INPUT, DONATION
form of .... CASH, KIND
small .... MITE
to the Pope .... (PETER'S)
PENCE
contributor .... DONOR, GIVER,
HELPER
newspaper .... COLUMNIST
contrite .... SORRY, PENITENT,
REGRETFUL, REPENTANT
contrition .... REMORSE,
PENITENCE
contrivance .... PLAN, DEVICE,
GADGET, GIMMICK, MACHINE,
INVENTION, CONTRAPTION
contrive .... PLAN, DEVISE,
SCHEME, FINAGLE, PLAY
TRICKS
control .... GRIP, POST, HELM,
REIN, RULE, TEST, CHECK,
DIRECT, MANAGE, COMMAND,
SUBDUE, MASTERY,
RESTRAIN(T)
center .... NUCLEUS
firm, severe .... IRON HAND
frustration .... SEETHE
kind of .... BIRTH, REMOTE
oneself .... KEEP COOL
controversial .... MOOT,
UNCERTAIN, DEBATABLE,
ERISTIC(AL), POLEMIC(AL)
area .... RUHR, SAAR, CHACO,
SABAH, KASHMIR, DAMANSKY

city .... DANZIG
theorist .... DARWIN
theory .... EVOLUTION
controversialist .... ERISTIC
controversy .... DEBATE, DISCORD,
DISPUTE, QUARREL,
ARGUMENT
controvert .... DENY, ARGUE,
DEBATE, DISCUSS, DISPUTE,
REFUTE, OPPUGN, GAINSAY
contumacious .... UNRULY,
DEFIANT, STUBBORN,
REBELLIOUS, DISOBEDIENT,
INSUBORDINATE
contumacy .... DARING, DEFIANCE
contumely .... ABUSE, INSULT,
RUDENESS, INSOLENCE
contusion .... BRUISE, INJURY,
SWELLING
conundrum ...... ENIGMA, PUZZLE,
RIDDLE, MYSTERY, QUESTION
convalesce .... RECOVER,
IMPROVE, RECUPERATE
convalescent, diet of .... SOUP,
GRUEL, LIQUIDS
convallaria .... LILY OF THE
VALLEY
convene .... SIT, CALL, MEET,
GATHER, COLLECT, CONVOKE,
SUMMON, ASSEMBLE
convenience ...... EASE, COMFORT,
UTILITY, FACILITY,
ADVANTAGE,
ACCOMMODATION
convenient .... HANDY, PROPER,
EXPEDIENT, SUITABLE
convent ...... NUNNERY, CLOISTER,
MONASTERY
cubicle .... CELL
dining hall .... REFECTORY
head .... SUPERIOR
inmate .... NUN, MONK,
CENOBITE
member, new .... NEOPHYTE
convention .... RULE, USAGE,
CAUCUS, CUSTOM, MEETING,
CONGRESS, ASSEMBLY,
PRACTICE
choice of .... NOMINEE
man .... DELEGATE
conventional .... SET, USUAL,
ACCEPTED, HABITUAL,
ORTHODOX, BOURGEOIS,
CUSTOMARY
act .... FORMALITY
measure of length .... PACE
converge .... MEET, UNITE
convergence .... FOCUS, FOCAL
POINT
conversant .... HEP, VERSED,
WELL-INFORMED, FAMILIAR

conversation .... CHAT, TALK,
COLLOQUY, DIALOGUE
between two .... DUOLOGUE
idle .... GOSSIP
on Mount Everest ..... SUMMIT
TALK
private .... TETE-A-TETE
starter .... HELLO
to settle dispute .... PARLEY
witty .... REPARTEE
conversational .... CHATTY,
SOCIABLE
comeback .... RETORT, RIPOSTE
digression .... ASIDE
event .... GABFEST
expert of a sort .... WIT
form of writing .... COLLOQUY
phrase .... I SEE, YOU KNOW
slang .... GABBY, WINDY
style, writing in ..... CAUSERIE
converse .... RAP, CHAT, TALK,
OTHER, COMMUNE, DISCUSS,
CONTRARY, OPPOSITE
conversion .... CHANGE
convert .... ADAPT, RENDER,
REMODEL, (EX)CHANGE,
PROSELYTE, TRANSFORM
fat into soap .... SAPONIFY,
SAPONIZE
into money .... REALIZE,
LIQUIDATE
new .... NOVICE, NEOPHYTE
converted .... REBORN
convertible .... MODIFIABLE,
NEGOTIABLE
into cash .... LIQUID
vehicle .... LANDAU, OPEN CAR
convertite .... MAGDALEN
convex .... BANDY, BOWED,
ROUND, CONCAVE
curve .... CAMBER
molding .... TORE, OVOLO,
TORUS, ASTRAGAL
swelling in column
.... ENTASIS
convey .... BEAR, CEDE, DEED,
BRING, CARRY, GRANT,
IMPART, INFORM, TRANSFER,
TRANSMIT, TRANSPORT
beyond jurisdiction ...... ELOIN
by deed .... REMISE
conveyance ...... BUS, CAR, CART,
CARRIER, VEHICLE, CARRIAGE,
SALE, CESSION, DISPOSAL
for dead .... HEARSE
instrument .... DEED
conveying away from center
.... EFFERENT
toward center .... AFFERENT
conveyor basket/car .... TRAM
of property .... ALIENOR

convict .... FELON, CULPRIT, CONDEMN, CRIMINAL, CAPTIVE, PRISONER
privileged .... TRUSTY
slang .... LAG, LIFER, LOSER, TERMER, JAILBIRD
conviction .... DOOM, VIEW, BELIEF, PENALTY, OPINION, SENTENCE, DAMNATION
convicts, squad of .... GANG
convince .... SELL, ASSURE, SATISFY, PERSUADE
convincing .... VALID, COGENT, CREDIBLE, PERSUASIVE
convivial ...... GAY, BOON, JOLLY, MERRY, JOVIAL, FESTIVE, SOCIABLE
drinking .... BOWL, WASSAIL
convocation .... ASSEMBLY
convoke .... CALL, GATHER, SUMMON, CONVENE, ASSEMBLE
convolute ...... COIL, ROLL, TWIRL, TWIST, CONTORT
convoy .... GUARD, ESCORT, CONDUCT, ACCOMPANY
convulse .... STIR, SHAKE, WRING, EXCITE, AGITATE
convulsion .... FIT, PAIN, QUIVER, REVOLT, TWINGE, SPASM, AGITATION, UPHEAVAL
attacks of .... ECLAMPSIA
of rage, etc. .... PAROXYSM
cony .... FUR, DUPE, PIKA, DAMAN, GANAM, HYRAX, DAS(SIE), RABBIT
coo .... CURR, MURMUR
companion of .... BILL
cooer .... DOVE, LOVER, PIGEON
cooing sound .... CURR
cook .... FIX, HEAT, MAKE, CONCOCT, PREPARE
again .... REBOIL, REHEAT
by dry heat .... BAKE
chief .... CHEF
colloquial .... DOCTOR, FALSIFY
galley of .... CUDDY
gently .... CODDLE
in cream .... SHIR(R)
in oil/fat .... FRY
in oven .... BAKE, ROAST
slang .... SPOIL
specialty of .... POTPIE, POT ROAST
up ..... PLOT, DEVISE, CONCOCT
cookbook item .... RECIPE
quantity .... CUPFUL, PINCH, TABLESPOONFUL
cooked meat shop .... DELICATESSEN

partially .... RARE
cooker ...... OVEN, BAKER, GRILL, STOVE, BROILER, TOASTER, BARBECUE, WATERLESS
cookery .... COOKING, (CULINARY) SCIENCE
cookhouse, ship's .... GALLEY
cookie maker .... AMOS, MRS. FIELD
cookies ...... BUNS, CAKES, SNAPS, MACAROON
cooking aid .... SPICE, CONDIMENT
art of .... CUISINE, CULINARY
directions/formula ...... RECIPE
glassware .... PYREX
means of ..... BAKING, FRYING, BOILING, BARBECUE, ROASTING
odor .... NIDOR
outfit .... KITCHEN
pot .... OLLA
stove .... RANGE
stove, portable .... HOTPLATE
style .... CAJUN, CUISINE
vessel .... PAN
cook's choice .... RECIPE
domain aboard ship .... CUDDY, GALLEY
cooky .... BUN, HERMIT, WAFER, JUMBLE, MACAROON, (GINGER)SNAP, LADYFINGER
cool .... FAN, CALM, ALLAY, FREEZE, QUENCH, COMPOSED
calm and ____ .... COLLECTED
color .... BLUE, GRAY, GREEN
hot liquid .... KEEL
make .... ICE, CHILL
one's heels .... WAIT
slang .... NEATO
cooled .... FRAPPE
cooler: sl. .... JAIL, CLINK
Coolidge alma mater .... AMHERST
Dam river .... GILA
singer .... RITA
coolie .... LABORER
woman .... CHANGAR
cooling off .... ON ICE
one's heels .... ARRESTED
coomb .... RAVINE
coon .... RACCOON
coop .... PEN, COTE, HUTCH
fly the .... DECAMP, ESCAPE, ABSCOND
up .... ENCAGE
cooper ...... HOOPER, CASKMAKER
Cooper, actor .... GARY, JACKIE
Mohican hero of .... UNCAS
cooperate .... HELP, COEXIST, PLAY BALL, SIDE WITH
secretly .... COLLUDE,

CONNIVE, CONSPIRE
cooperative ...... CO-OP, ALLIANCE
cooperator .... ALLY
coordinate .... ADAPT, ADJUST, ORGANIZE, HARMONIZE
system .... GRID
Coorg's capital .... MERCARA
coot .... DUCK, FOOL, AVOCET, MUDHEN, SCOTER, NOTORNIS, SHUFFLER, WATERHEN, SIMPLETON
cootie .... LOUSE
cop ...... TOP, CONE, HEAD, CREST
a plea .... CONFESS
club of .... BILLY, STICK, TRUNCHEON
out .... ALIBI, EXCUSE
slang ...... FILCH, SEIZE, STEAL, SWIPE, SNATCH, BULL, DICK, PILFER, FLATFOOT, JOHN LAW, THE FUZZ, POLICEMAN
copacetic .... FINE, GOOD, DANDY, EXCELLENT
copaiba .... TUPI, RESIN
copal .... ANIME, RESIN
copalm .... TREE, RESIN
cope .... SKY, VAULT, CANOPY, HANDLE, MANAGE, CONTEND, FACE, SURVIVE, VESTMENT
Copenhagen is capital of .... DENMARK
copier .... APER, IMITATOR
copious .... LUSH, AMPLE, WORDY, LAVISH, PROFUSE, ABUNDANT, PLENTIFUL
Copland, composer .... AARON
copper .... AES, COIN, METAL, CUPRUM, CA(U)LDRON
alchemist's .... VENUS
alloy .... AROIDE, TOMBAK, TOMBAC(K)
alloy coin .... CASH
and tin alloy .... ORMOLU
coating .... VERD, PATINA, ANTIQUE, VERDIGRIS
coin .... PENNY
color .... REDDISH BROWN
combining form .... CHALCO
gilded .... VERMEIL
nickel .... NICCOLITE
nickel, zinc alloy ...... ALBATA
ore .... CUPRITE, CHALCOCITE
skin .... INDIAN
slang .... POLICEMAN
sulphate .... VITRIOL
tin, zinc alloy .... OROIDE
zinc alloy .... PINCHBECK
copperah .... COPRA
copperhead .... SNAKE, VIPER, NORTHERNER
coppice .... COPSE, THICKET

copse .... BOSK, HOLT, SHAW,
    BUNCH, GROVE, BOSCAGE,
    COPPICE, THICKET
Coptic bishop's title .... ABBA
copula .... BAND, LINK
copulate .... JOIN, MATE, UNITE,
    COUPLE, BREED, COHABIT
copy .... APE, CLONE, MODEL,
    TRACE, ECTYPE, IMITATE,
    FAKE, RESCRIPT, DUPLICATE,
    DITTO, MIRROR, FACSIMILE
closely .... MIMIC
court record .... ESTREAT
document's .... TENOR
of original .... REPLICA
photographic .... PRINT,
    PHOTOSTAT
read .... EDIT, PROOFREAD
slang .... DEAD RINGER
copycat .... APER, MIMIC,
    IMITATOR
copying machine .... XEROX,
    DUPLICATOR, MIMEOGRAPH
copyist .... ARTIST, COPIER,
    SCRIVENER, TRANSCRIBER
copyright .... PATENT
copywriter .... AUTHOR,
    COMPOSER, PUBLICIST
coquet ...... DALLY, FLIRT, TRIFLE
coquette .... VAMP, FLIRT
coquettish .... COY, FICKLE
coquina .... LIMESTONE
coquito .... PALM
cora .... GAZELLE
coracle .... BOAT, CURRACH,
    CURRAGH
coral .... POLYP, SPAWN, STONE,
    ZOOID, POLYPITE, ZOOPHYTE
cavity .... CALICLE
color .... RED, PINK
formation .... REEF, ATOLL,
    SHELF, SHOAL
group/order .... MADREPORE,
    MADREPORARIA
lobster's .... ROE
part .... STOLON
reef island .... CAY, KEY,
    CAPE, HOLM, ISLE, ATOLL,
    ISLET
shape .... MUSHROOM
source .... POLYPS
variety .... APOROSA
corbel .... ANCON, BRACKET,
    CONSOLE
corbeling .... SQUINCH
corbie .... CROW, RAVEN
Corcyra .... CORFU
cord .... BAND, ROPE, CABLE,
    BOND, TWINE, STRING,
    FUNICLE
braided .... SENNIT

cable/rope end's ...... MARLINE
cattle catching .... BOLA
drapery .... TORSADE
head .... AGAL
kind of .... SPINAL
knob lump .... KNOT
strangling .... GAROTTE,
    GARROTE
tip .... TAG, A(I)GLET
trimming .... CHENILLE
umbilical .... FUNICULUS
cordage fiber .... COIR, FERU,
    HEMP, IMBE, JUTE, ABACA,
    AGAVE, ISTLE, SISAL, MAGUEY
grass .... ESPARTO
corded cloth .... REP, POPLIN,
    CORDUROY
Cordelia's father .... LEAR
sister .... REGAN
cordelle .... TASSEL
cordial .... GENIAL, HEARTY,
    KINDLY, AMIABLE, FRIENDLY,
    LIQUEUR, RATAFIA, ROSOLIO,
    ANISETTE, HIPPOCRAS,
    MARASCHINO
apricot .... PERSICO
less .... ICIER
cordierite .... IOLITE
cordite .... EXPLOSIVE
cordon .... BELT, CORD, RING,
    BRAID, CIRCLE, RIBBON
corduroy ...... FUSTIAN, TROUSERS
ridge .... WALE
core .... HEART, CENTER
bone/feather .... PITH
corn ear .... COB
reactor .... PILE
coreopsis .... TICKSEED
corf .... TRUCK, BASKET,
    MINEWAGON
corfu .... CORCYRA, KERKYRA
corium .... SKIN, CUTIS, DERMA,
    DERMIS
Corinthian capital's scroll
    .... VOLUTE
volute .... HELIX
cork ...... TAP, BARK, PLUG, SEAL,
    SPILE, STOPPER, STOPPLE
barrel's .... BUNG
bottle/shallow .... SHIVE
change into .... SUBERIZE
helmet .... TOPI, TOPEE
like .... SUBEROSE
noise .... POP
of a .... SUBERIC
waxy substance
    .... SUBERIN(E)
Cork County port .... COBH
famous feature of
    .... BLARNEY STONE
corker .... LIE, LULU, STOPPER,

    CLINCHER
corking .... EXCELLENT
corkscrew .... BOTTLE OPENER
shape like a .... SPIRAL
corkwood .... BALSA
corm .... BULB, TUBER
plant with .... CROCUS,
    GLADIOLUS
cormorant .... BIRD, SHAG,
    GORMAW, GREEDY, GUANAY;
    GLUTTON(OUS)
corn .... SALT, FLINT, GRAIN,
    CEREAL, KERNEL, PICKLE,
    MAIZE, GRANULE, PAPILLOMA
and beans dish .... SUCCOTASH
belt (per J. Luzzatto)
    .... BOURBON
bin .... CRIB
bread .... PONE, TORTILLA
cake .... JOHNNY-CAKE
color of ripe .... MAIZE
covering .... HUSK
crake .... RAIL, DAKER HEN
flour .... PINOLE
flower .... BLUENOSE
green ear .... TUCKET
ground .... MEAL, FLOUR,
    GRITS, HOMINY
grower .... IOWAN
hair .... TASSEL
hulled .... HOMINY
husk .... SHUCK
imperfect .... NUBBIN
Indian .... MAIZE
lily .... IXIA
liquor .... WHISK(E)Y
meal .... MASA, SAMP, HOMINY
meal, baked/fried
    .... HOECAKE
meal bread/cake .... PONE,
    DODGER
meal dish .... SCRAPPLE
meal dough .... HUSH PUPPY
meal mush .... ATOLE
meal porridge .... MUSH,
    POLENTA, STIRABOUT
meal pudding .... MUSH
mill .... QUERN
porridge .... SAMP
slang .... MUSH
small .... NUBBIN
spike .... EAR
stalk .... STOVER
state .... IOWA
stump .... STUBBLE
toe .... BUNION, CALLUS
variety .... FLINT
cornea bigger than normal
    .... MEGALOCORNEA
disorder of the .... ULCER,
    KERATOCONUS,

KERATOMALACIA

inflammation .... KERATITIS

leucoma of the .... WALLEYE

opacity on .... NEBULA,
LEUCOMA

scratch .... ABRASION

shape .... DOME

smaller than normal
.... MICROCORNEA

corned .... BRINED, SALTED

beef .... BULLY

beef connoisseur .... JIGGS

beef sandwich .... REUBEN

beef's partner .... CABBAGE

cornel .... DOGWOOD

Cornelia Otis .... SKINNER

corneous .... HORNY, HORNLIKE

corner .... BEND, TRAP, TREE,
TURN, BIGHT, COIGN, CURVE,
NICHE, RECESS, REGION

angle .... CANT

chimney/fireplace
.... INGLENOOK

of building .... CANT, QUOIN

of sail .... CLEW

projecting .... COIGN(E)

support .... ARCH, LINTEL,
SQUINCH, CORBELING

the market/prices
.... MONOPOLIZE

cornered .... BENT, AT BAY,
ANGULAR, IMPERILED,
THREATENED

cornerstone .... COIGN(E), QUOIN,
FOUNDATION

of the "underground
economy" .... BLACK
MARKET

cornerwise .... DIAGONALLY

cornet .... CAVALRY FLAG

Cornhusker State .... NEBRASKA

cornice .... STRIP, MOLDING

interior window .... PELMET

projection .... DRIP, CORONA

support .... ANCON

corniculate .... HORNED

Cornish patron saint .... COLIN

town .... ST. IVES

cornu(copia) .... HORN OF PLENTY

Cornwall county seat .... BODMIN

islands .... SCILLY

corny .... BANAL, MUSHY, MUSTY,
STALE, TRITE, SENTIMENTAL

person .... CORNBALL

corolla .... LIGULE, PETALS,
PERIANTH

cuplike part .... CORONA

heraldic .... GALEA

corollary .... ADJUNCT, OFFSHOOT

a .... DEDUCTION, INFERENCE

geometrical .... PORISM

corona .... AURA, HALO, CIGAR,
CROWN, AUREOLE

Corona Australis .... WREATH

coronach .... DIRGE, THRENODY

coronal .... CROWN, DIADEM,
GARLAND

coronary .... ROUND, CIRCULAR

thrombosis .... STROKE, HEART
ATTACK

coronation .... CROWNING

coronet .... CROWN, TIARA,
ANADEM, DIADEM

corporal .... BODILY, PERSONAL

for short .... NCO

infamous .... HITLER

punishment .... FLOGGING,
WHIPPING

rank after .... SERGEANT

tobacco of .... CAPORAL

Corporal, famous/Little
.... NAPOLEON

corporate .... JOINT, COMMON,
UNITED, COMBINED,
ASSOCIATED

corporation .... MERGER,
SYNDICATE, ASSOCIATION

manager .... SYNDIC

corporeal .... SOMAL, BODILY,
SOMATIC, MATERIAL,
PHYSICAL

corps .... BRANCH, COMPANY,
SERVICE

corpse .... LICH, CARCASE
CADAVER, CARCASS

animated .... ZOMBI(E)

dissection .... NECROTOMY

embalmed .... MUMMY

platform for .... BIER

prefix .... NECR(O)

slang .... STIFF

corpsman .... MEDIC

corpulence .... OBESITY, FATNESS,
PORTLINESS

corpulent .... FAT, BULKY, GROSS,
OBESE, PURSY, STOUT,
FLESHY, PORTLY

corpus delicti .... DEAD BODY

corpuscles, lack of red
.... AN(A)EMIA

corral .... PEN, YARD, POUND,
ACQUIRE, ROUND UP,
STOCK(ADE)

correct .... CURE, EDIT, PRIM,
TRUE, AMEND, EMEND,
PROPER, REMEDY, RECTIFY,
ACCURATE

one's fault .... REFORM

correction .... REMEDY, REPAIR,
EDITION, REVISION, DISCIPLINE

correctional house
.... BRIDEWELL, REFORMATORY

correlation .... ANALOGY,
LIKENESS

correlative .... AKIN, COUPLED,
CONNECTED, RELATED,
PARALLEL

pair of .... EITHER-OR,
NEITHER-NOR

correspond .... SUIT, AGREE,
EQUAL, MATCH, TALLY,
WRITE, COINCIDE

correspondence ...... AGREEMENT,
COMMUNICATION

kind of .... BUSINESS,
OFFICIAL, PERSONAL

correspondent, kind of
.... PENPAL, FOREIGN,
STRINGER

corresponding .... IDENTICAL,
EQUIVALENT

corrida celebration .... FIESTA

cry .... OLE

personnel .... TOREROS

corridor .... AISLE, ROUTE,
GALLERY, HALL(WAY),
PASSAGEWAY

corrigenda .... ERRATA

corrigible .... DOCILE, AMENABLE,
REMEDIAL

corrival .... COMPETITOR

corroborant .... TONIC

corroborate ...... ATTEST, RATIFY,
VERIFY, CONFIRM, SUPPORT

corrode ...... ETCH, RUST, DECAY,
GNAW, ERODE, EAT INTO,
WEAR OUT, WEAR AWAY

corroded .... RUSTY, ROTTEN,
CARIOUS, CANKERED, WORN
OUT

corrosive .... ACID, CAUSTIC,
CUTTING, MORDANT,
ESCHAROTIC

corrugate .... PLEAT, FURROW,
GROOVE, WRINKLE

corrugated .... ROUGH, FLUTED,
RUGATE, CRIMPED, GROOVED,
RUGOSE, RUGOUS

corrupt ...... EVIL, SPOIL, DEBASE,
VENAL, DEFILE, INFECT,
ROTTEN, PERVERT, VITIATE

morally .... PUTRID

official .... GRAFTER

one's way ...... BRIBE, SUBORN

corruptible .... ON THE TAKE

corrupting offspring .... HEIR
POLLUTION

corruption .... GRAFT, VENALITY,
DISHONESTY

in hiring relatives
.... NEPOTISM

on the part of a ship's crew
.... BARRATRY

trace of .... TAINT
corsage .... BODICE, FLOWER,
           BOUQUET, NOSEGAY
corsair .... PIRATE, PRIVATEER,
           FREEBOOTER
ship .... XEBEC
corselet .... LORICA, CUIRASS
corset .... BODICE, GIRDLE,
      LORICA, LORLEA, SUPPORT
bone .... BUSK
stiffener .... BUSK, STAY,
           WHALEBONE
Corsican capital .... AJACCIO
famous .... NAPOLEON
seaport .... BASTIA
sheep .... MOUFLON
cortege .... TRAIN, RETINUE,
           PROCESSION
Cortes' loot .... ORO
cortex .... BARK, RIND
corundum .... RUBY, EMERY,
     TOPAZ, AMETHYST, SAPPHIRE
coruscate .... GLEAM, GLITTER,
         SPARKLE, TWINKLE
corvine bird .... CROW, ROOK,
           RAVEN
Corvus .... RAVEN
coryza .... COLD, CATARRH
sign of .... SNEEZE, SNIFFLE
cos ...... COAN, LETTUCE, ROMAINE
cosher .... PAMPER
cosi fan _____ .... TUTTI
cosmetic .... ADORNING,
           BEAUTIFYING
base for .... LANOLIN(E)
cheek/lip .... ROUGE
containing white lead,
       former .... CERUSE
eyelid/eyelash .... KOHL,
           MASCARA
hair .... HENNA
paste .... PACK
skin .... LOTION
use/decorate with .... PAINT
cosmetician Lauder .... ESTEE
cosmetics: sl. .... WARPAINT
cosmic .... VAST, GRANDIOSE
cycle .... EON
ray particle .... MESON
cosmography, branch of
       GEOLOGY, ASTRONOMY,
           GEOGRAPHY
cosmonaut .... SPACEMAN,
    ASTRONAUT, ROCKETMAN
cosmopolitan .... SUAVE, URBANE,
       REFINED, POLISHED
cosmos .... EARTH, GLOBE, ORDER,
    REALM, WORLD, HARMONY,
       THISTLE, UNIVERSE
god of the .... VARUNA
opposed to .... CHAOS

Cossack .... TATAR, RUSSIAN,
           CAVALRYMAN
chief .... ATAMAN, HETMAN
fame of the .... HORSEMANSHIP
whip .... KNOUT
cosset .... PET, LAMB, FONDLE,
           PAMPER
cost ...... PRICE, CHARGE, EXPENSE,
     PAYMENT, SACRIFICE
colloquial .... DAMAGE
exceeding contract price
                 .... OVERRUN
costa .... RIB
Costa Rica bay .... SALINAS,
           CORONADA
cape .... VELAS, BLANCO,
    MATAPALO, SANTA ELENA
capital .... SAN JOSE
city/town .... LIMON, GRECIA,
    NICOYA, CARTAGO, HEREDIA,
    ESPARTA, GOLFITO, PARAISO,
    QUESADA, LIBERIA, ALAHUELA,
    PUNTARENAS, SAN RAMON,
    SANTA CRUZ, SIQUIRRES,
    TURRIALBA, SAN JOSE, SANTO
           DOMINGO
coin .... COLON
discoverer of .... COLUMBUS
gulf .... DULCE, NICOYA
highest point .... CHIRRIPO
           GRANDE
island .... CANO
language .... SPANISH
mountain .... IRAZU,
    GONGORA, CHIRRIPO GRANDE
peak .... BLANCO
peninsula .... NICOYA
port .... LIMON
president .... ARIAS, TREJOS,
           CALDERON
range .... TALAMANCA
river .... SAN JUAN
volcano .... CUILAPA
           MIRAVALLES
costard .... HEAD, APPLE
Costello .... LOU
costly ...... DEAR, PRECIOUS, HIGH-
       PRICED, EXPENSIVE
costmary .... CHRYSANTHEMUM
costrel .... FLASK, BOTTLE
costume ...... (FANCY)DRESS, GET-
     UP, OUTFIT, CLOTHING
colloquial .... RIG, TOG
jewelry ...... BAUBLE, BROOCH,
     GEWGAW, TRINKET
jewelry material .... PASTE,
    OROIDE, ORMOLU, STRASS
masquerade .... DOMINO
matching parts ...... ENSEMBLE
riding .... HABIT
silk material .... SENDAL

wear one in fun .... MUM(M)
cot .... BED, CRIB, CHARPAI,
       CHARPOY, SHELTER
poetic .... COTTAGE
cote .... SHED, SHELTER
coterie .... SET, JUNTO, CIRCLE,
      CLIQUE, CAMARILLA
cotillion .... BALL, DANCE
cotinga .... CHATTERER
Cotswold .... SHEEP
cotta .... SURPLICE
cottage .... HUT, BOWER, VILLA,
    CABIN, CABANA, CASINO,
    CHALET, HOUSE, SHACK,
    SHELTER, BUNGALOW
cheese .... SMEARCASE
cotter .... BOLT, WEDGE
pin .... FORELOCK
cotton .... CLOTH, FABRIC,
    MALLOW, THREAD
and wool cloth .... LINSEY,
           SATINET(TE)
batting fibers .... LINTERS
Bengal .... ADATI
cloth .... JEAN, MULL, PIMA,
    REP(S), REPP, CHINO, DUCKS,
    CRASH, CALICO, CHINTZ,
    KHAKI, MANTA, MADRAS,
    MUSLIN, NANKIN, OXFORD,
    CAMBRIC, ETAMINE, GALATEA,
    NANKEEN, ORGANDY,
    GRENADINE, SEERSUCKER
cloth, canvaslike .... WIGAN
cloth for curtains, etc.
       ..... LAWN, SCRIM, DIMITY
cloth for handkerchiefs, etc.
       .... LAWN, BATISTE
cloth for linings .... SILESIA,
           PERCALINE
cloth for sheets .... MUSLIN,
           PERCALE
cloth, glazed .... CHINTZ,
           JACONET
cloth, glossy .... SATEEN
coarse, for shawls, capes,
       etc. .... MANTA
comb .... CARD
fiber .... LINT(ER), BATTING
fiber knot .... NEP
gauze .... LENO
gum tree .... TUPELO
hosiery/socks .... LISLES
jersey .... T-SHIRT
machine .... GIN, MULE,
    BALER, LINTER, WILLOW(ER)
measure .... LEA, HANK
medical dressing .... LINT,
       GAUZE, SPONGE
pad/piece of .... SPONGE
plug of .... TAMPON
pod .... BOLI, BOLL

printed, brightly colored
.... SARONG
roll of fiber for spinning
.... SLUB
seed cleaner .... GIN, LINTER
seed fiber .... LINTER
sheer .... VOILE
spinning wheel .... CHARK(H)A
stainer .... BUG
thin, lightweight .... NAINSOOK
thread .... LISLE
to .... GET ALONG, HIT IT OFF
tuft .... LOCK
twilled .... JEAN, CHINO,
DENIM
twisted .... ROVE
waste .... LINT, FLOCK
with fleecy nap .... FLANNEL
with glazed/water finish
.... PERCALINE
Cotton State .... ALABAMA
cottonbelt, U.S. .... SOUTH
cottonmouth .... SNAKE
cottontail .... HARE, RABBIT,
LEVERET
cottonwood ...... ALAMO, POPLAR
cottony .... DOWNY, FLUFFY
couch .... LAIR, SOFA, DIVAN,
SQUAB, CANAPE, RECLINE,
LOUNGE, PALLET, SETTEE,
OTTOMAN, DAVENPORT
hanging/swinging
.... HAMMOCK
heavily stuffed with upright
ends .... CHESTERFIELD
like chair ...... CHAISE LONGUE
poetic .... BED
to carry wounded .... LITTER
cougar ...... CAT, PUMA, PAINTER,
PANTHER, CARCAJOU,
CATAMOUNT
cough .... HACK, TUSSIS
barking .... CROUP
candy .... HOARHOUND,
HOREHOUND
drop .... TROCHE, LOZENGE,
PASTILLE
medicine .... GRINDELIA,
EXPECTORANT
medicine base .... SYRUP
of a .... TUSSAL, TUSSIVE
sound like a .... HICCUP
to attract attention .... AHEM
up .... PAY, EJECT, HAND OVER
whooping .... PERTUSSIS
coughing up blood
.... HEMOPTYSIS
pus .... VOMICA
could be Fred's or Steve's
place .... ALLEN'S TOWN
coulee ...... LAVA, GULCH, RAVINE

couloir .... GORGE, GULLY
coulter .... PLOWSHARE
council .... BOARD, JUNTA,
FORUM, CABINET, COMMITTEE
African tribe's .... INDABA
chamber ...... DIVAN, CABINET,
CAMARILLA
church .... SYNOD, CONSISTORY
jury .... PANEL
kind of .... CITY, ADVISORY,
ECUMENICAL
of deacons .... CONSISTORY
of justice .... TRIBUNAL
table .... BOARD
counsel .... REDE, ADVICE,
ADVISE, GUIDE, PROMPT,
SUGGEST
legal .... LAWYER
counselor .... GUIDE, LAWYER,
MENTOR, ADVISER
woman .... EGERIA
count .... ADD, DEEM, RATE,
SCORE, TALLY, RECKON,
FIGURE, ACCOUNT, CONSIDER,
ESTIMATE, (E)NUMERATE
calories .... DIET
down purpose ...... BLAST-OFF,
LAUNCHING
finish .... ESS
in .... INCLUDE
in law .... CHARGE
of population .... CENSUS
on .... RELY, DEPEND
out .... OMIT, FORGET,
EXCLUDE, DISREGARD
palatine .... PALSGRAVE
Count of Monte Cristo
.... DANTES
of Vienne .... DAUPHIN
countenance .... ABET, FACE,
FAVOR, ASPECT, VISAGE,
SUPPORT, SANCTION
counter .... BAR, ADDER, BUFFET,
AGAINST, COMPUTER,
CONTRARY, OPPOSITE
in cards .... MILLE
irritant .... MOXA, SALVE,
SETON, LOTION, MUSTARD,
CALAMINE, OINTMENT,
DEMULCENT
kind of .... GEIGER
sale .... RETAIL
counteract ...... OFFSET, THWART,
CHECK, FRUSTRATE,
NEUTRALIZE
counterattack .... REVENGE,
RETORT, RETALIATION
counterbalance .... EQUIPOISE
counterfeit .... FAKE, BOGUS,
SHAM, FALSE, FORGE(D),
PHON(E)Y, POSTICHE,

IMITATION, SPURIOUS
coin .... SLUG
jewelry .... BRUMMAGEM
counterfeiter .... FORGER, MINTER
counterfeiting .... FORGERY,
PAPER-CAPER
countermand .... CANCEL,
REVOKE, CALL BACK,
NULLIFY, OVERRULE
counterpane .... COVERLET
counterpart .... COPY, MATE,
TWIN, DOUBLE, REPLICA,
LIKENESS, MATCH, PARALLEL,
DUPLICATE
counterpoint .... DESCANT
of .... CONTRAPUNTAL
counterpoise .... BALANCE
countersign .... PASSWORD
countersink .... REAM
countertenor .... ALTO
counterweight .... TARE
countess's title of respect
.... LADY
counting frame .... ABAC(US)
sheep purpose .... SLEEP
ten purpose .... STALL, COOL
OFF
countless .... MYRIAD, UNTOLD,
TEEMING, NUMEROUS
countrified ...... RURAL, HODDEN,
RUSTIC, CORNFED
country .... HOME, LAND, REALM,
STATE, NATION, REGION,
TERRITORY, FATHERLAND
ancient ...... PERSIA, ILLYRIA
bumpkin .... HICK, RUBE,
CHURL, YAHOO, YOKEL,
RUSTIC
dance .... HAY, REEL
dance: Brit. .... COVERLEY
fellow .... CORYDON
gallant/lad .... SWAIN
gentleman .... ESQUIRE,
COVERLEY
girl .... WENCH, PHILLIS,
PHYLLIS
house .... VILLA, CASINO,
HACIENDA
house, of a .... VILLATIC
in law .... PAIS
in the city .... RUS IN URBE
live in the .... RUSTICATE
middle region .... INLAND,
MIDLAND, INTERIOR
of fable .... EL DORADO
of the .... RURAL
officially called principality
.... MONACO, ANDORRA,
LIECHTENSTEIN
on 38th parallel .... KOREA
open, flat .... CHAMPAIGN

open, wild .... WEALD
poetical .... CLIME
pudding .... SASS
social .... BEE, BARNDANCE
ways .... PATHS
countryman .... RUSTIC, CITIZEN,
COMPATRIOT
countryside, of the ...... BUCOLIC
twosome .... HILL AND DALE
county ...... SEAT, SHIRE, DISTRICT
law officer .... SHERIFF
coup .... PLOY, GAMBIT, TACTIC,
STRATEGY, (MASTER)STROKE
d'_____ .... ETAT
de grace .... DEATH BLOW,
LETHAL BLOW
de grace dagger
.... MISERICORD(E)
reporter's .... BEAT, SCOOP
couple ...... DUO, TIE, FEW, DUAD,
DYAD, JOIN, LINK, BRACE,
PAIR, YOKE, CONNECT, UNITE,
SEVERAL, TWO(SOME)
coupled .... JOINED, LINKED,
PAIRED, TEAMED, DOUBLED,
UNITED, GEMINATED
Couples author .... UPDIKE
couplet .... DISTICH
coupling for electric fixtures
.... HICKEY
coupon ...... TICKET, CERTIFICATE
courage .... FACE, GALL, GRIT,
SAND, CHEEK, HEART, NERVE,
PLUCK, SPUNK, VALOR,
METTLE, BRAVERY, BOLDNESS
loss of .... COLDFEET
man of .... HERO, DEMIGOD
pretended .... BRAVADO
slang ..... GUTS, CRUST, MOXIE
symbol of .... TIGER, BULLDOG
woman of .... HEROINE
courageous .... BOLD, BRAVE,
PLUCKY, HARDY, SANDY,
DARING, GRITTY, HEROIC,
SPUNKY, VALIANT, DASHING,
FEARLESS, STOUT(HEARTED)
slang .... GUTSY
courier .... RUNNER, POSTMAN,
ESTAFETTE, MESSENGER
courlan .... LIMPKIN
course .... WAY, FLOW, PATH,
MODE, CYCLE, PASSAGE,
PROCESS, DIRECTION
athletics .... GYMNASTICS
cross-country run
.... LANGLAUF
kind of .... GOLF, RACE
marker .... PYLON
meal ...... DISH, SALAD, VIAND,
ENTREE
of action .... TACK,

PROCEDURE, PROCEEDING
of motion or action
.... ROUTE, TRACK
of official papers
.... CHANNELS
of study .... LESSONS,
CURRICULUM
of travel .... ROUTE, ITINERARY
court .... WOO, HALL, FLIRT,
CAJOLE, ROMANCE, PERISTYLE
action/case .... SUIT, CAUSE,
LAWSUIT, LITIGATION
aggressively .... RUSH
assembly .... LEVEE
castle's .... BAILEY
central/entrance .... ATRIUM
challenge .... RECUSE
church ...... ROTA, CONSISTORY
crier/messenger .... BEADLE
crier's call .... OYES, OYEZ
criminal .... ASSIZE
decree .... ARRET, EDICT
decree, to issue a ...... ORDAIN
enclosed .... PARVIS
equity .... CHANCERY
favorite .... GRACIOSO
game .... SQUASH, TENNIS,
HANDBALL, BADMINTON,
BASKETBALL, RACQUETBALL
hale to .... SUE
hearing .... OYER
jurisdiction .... SOKE
manorial .... LEET
martial defendant .... AWOL,
TRAITOR, DESERTER, MUTINEER
martial in the field
.... DRUMHEAD
minutes .... ACTA
of a/pertaining to .... AULIC
of attendants .... RETINUE,
FOLLOWING
of justice .... BAR, BENCH,
TRIBUNAL
of law .... FORUM
official ..... DA, JUDGE, FISCAL,
JURIST, BAILIFF, JUSTICE,
REFEREE, ATTORNEY
order ..... WRIT, ARRET, EDICT,
DECREE, SUMMONS,
MANDAMUS, SUBPOENA
order extract .... ESTREAT
panel .... JURY
proceeding .... TRIAL, HEARING
room routine .... OATH
ruling, plea for .... MOTION
session .... ASSIZE, HEARING
summons .... CITATION,
SUBPOENA
writ .... OYER, SUMMONS,
SUBPOENA
courted, old style .... SPARK

courteous .... CIVIL, POLITE,
REFINED, URBANE, AMIABLE,
AFFABLE, CORDIAL, GRACIOUS
regard .... RESPECT,
DEFERENCE
courtesan .... THAIS, HARLOT,
WHORE, PROSTITUTE
courtesy .... FAVOR, GRACE,
POLISH, CHIVALRY, CIVILITY,
COMITY, COMPLIMENT,
POLITENESS
courtier .... PUFFER, TOUTER,
TOADY, FLATTERER
courtly .... AULIC, SUAVE,
REFINED, ELEGANT, POLISHED
courtship .... SUIT, PLIGHT,
WOOING, PURSUIT
dance .... CUECA
result of, usually
.... WEDDING, MARRIAGE
through singing ..... SERENADE
Courtship of Miles _____
.... STANDISH
courtyard .... PATIO, ATRIUM,
SQUARE, QUADRANGLE
sunken .... AREAWAY
cousin .... COS, COZ, KIN
busby's .... SHAKO
ferret's .... POLECAT
gnome's .... ELF
kind of .... ONCE REMOVED,
TWICE REMOVED
pewit's .... LARK
Cousteau's challenge .... OCEAN
couteau .... DAGGER
couturier ...... STYLIST, DESIGNER,
DRESSMAKER
fabric of .... LACE, LAME,
SILK, SOIE, VELVET
famed .... DIOR, ADOLFO,
CHANEL, NORELL, BALMAIN,
CASSINI, BERGDORF,
GIVENCHY, GERNREICH, ST.
LAURENT, BALENCIAGA,
MAINBOCHER
cove .... BAY, HOLE, NOOK, INLET,
LAGOON
covenant .... BOND, PACT,
CONTRACT, AGREEMENT,
TESTAMENT
Coventry, goddess of .... GODIVA
cover .... LID, TOP, HIDE, COAT,
CAP, ROOF, WHELM, CANOPY,
ENCASE, SHEATHE,
ENVELOP(E)
a certain hole .... DARN,
PATCH
bottle .... CAP, CROWN
break .... EMERGE
detachable .... BINDER
face .... MASK, VEIL

for a bushing .... SLEEVE
girl .... PIN UP, MODEL
hard .... PLATE, SHELL,
CARAPACE
inner surface .... PAD, LINE
lap .... RUG
leg .... PUTTEE, LEGGING,
CHAUSSES
nipa .... THATCH
ornamental .... SHAM
pie's .... RIND, CRUST
protective .... ARMOR, HELMET,
SHELL, CARAPACE
superficial .... VENEER
thickly .... SMOTHER
thin .... VENEER
thinly .... SKIM
top wall .... CEIL, COPING,
CAPSTONE
under .... HIDDEN, SECRET
up .... HIDE, INTER, CONCEAL
with asphalt .... PAVE
with cloth .... DRAPE
with feathers .... FLEDGE
with jewels .... BEGEM
with moisture .... BEDEW
with plaster .... CEIL
with trappings ...... CAPARISON
coverage, insurance .... RISK
covered .... CARPETED
colonnade .... STOA
entrance .... PORCH
garden .... HOTHOUSE
portico .... GALLERY
vehicle .... VAN
wagon .... SCHOONER,
CONESTOGA
walk .... MALL, STOA, ARCADE,
GALLERY, PORTICO, CLOISTER
with blood .... GORY,
HEMATOSE
with bristles .... HISPID
with climbers .... IVIED
with fine feathers ...... DOWNY
with flakes .... SCURFY,
LEPIDOTE
with frost .... RIMY
with hair .... HISPID, PILOSE,
TOMENTOSE
with leaves .... FOLIOSE
covering .... GARB, SHIELD,
TEGMEN, SHEATHE,
OBSCURING, TEGUMENT,
INTEGUMENT
against the sun .... SHADE,
PARASOL, SHELTER, UMBRELLA
floor .... TILE, BOARDS,
CARPET, TILING, LINOLEUM
for concealment .... MASK,
VEIL, BLINDAGE, CAMOUFLAGE
gloomy .... PALL

glossy/shiny .... SHEEN
head .... CAP, HAT, HOOD,
BERET, BONNET, HELMET
house .... ROOFING, ROOFTOP
material .... TILE, ADOBE,
PATCH, ASPHALT, PLASTER,
CEMENT, CONCRETE,
WALLPAPER
membrane of ovary
.... TUNICA
of clouds .... OVERCAST
of faults or defects
.... WHITEWASH
of reeds .... THATCH
of the skin .... CUTICLE,
EPIDERMIS
protective .... MAIL, ARMOR,
SHELL, LORICA
teeth .... DENTINE
the works .... ENTIRE
thick .... CARPET
waterproof .... TARPAULIN
coverlet .... PALL, QUILT,
BEDSPREAD, COUNTERPANE
covert .... PRIVY, ARCANE,
HIDDEN, VEILED, SECRET,
CLOUDED, CONCEALED
covertly .... UNDER-THE-TABLE
coverup .... WHITEWASH
covet .... ENVY, WANT, CRAVE,
DESIRE
covetous .... GREEDY, ENVIOUS,
AVARICIOUS
covey .... BEVY, BROOD, FLOCK
cow .... BEEF, BOSS, VACA, BULLY,
DAUNT, BOVINE, CRUMMY,
CRUMMIE, FRIGHTEN,
THREATEN, (OVER)AWE,
INTIMIDATE
ad/famous .... ELSIE
barn .... BYRE, STABLE
breed .... ANGUS, DEVON,
JERSEY, KERRY, DEXTER,
GUERNSEY, HEREFORD
call/sound .... LOW, MOO
catcher .... LASSO
cud .... RUMEN
dewlap of .... LAPPET
dialectic ..... CRITTER, CRITTUR
fat .... SUET, TALLOW
fish .... TORO
genus .... BOS
gland .... UDDER
headed deity .... ISIS
hornless .... MUL(L)EY
killer .... WASP
milking .... MILCH
pilot .... PINTANO
polled .... MUL(L)EY
sea .... DUGONG, MANATEE
tuberculosis of .... GRAPE

udder inflammation
.... GARGET
unbranded .... MAVERICK
young .... CALF, STIRK, HEIFER
coward .... SISSY, CRAVEN,
SNEAK, DASTARD, POLTROON
colloquial .... YELLOW,
CHICKEN
descriptive of a/streak of a
.... YELLOW
Coward (Noel) show .... BITTER-
SWEET
song .... NINA
cowardice .... FEAR
symbol of ..... WHITE FEATHER
cowardly ...... CRAVEN, SNEAKING,
DASTARDLY, SPINELESS
animal .... HY(A)ENA
knight of story .... FALSTAFF
person .... CUR, SISSY, CAITIFF,
POLTROON, MAMA'S BOY
slang .... CHICKEN, SCAREDY-
CAT
cowbird .... TROUPIAL
cowboy .... HERDER, COWPOKE,
LLANERO, BUCKAROO,
BUCKAYRO, VAQUERO,
HORSEMAN, WRANGLER,
RANCHER(O), BRONCOBUSTER
Australian .... RINGER,
STOCKMAN
bed .... BUNK
big day of .... RODEO,
ROUNDUP
breeches .... CHAPS
concern of .... CATTLE
friend of/slang ...... PARD(NER)
habitat .... RANCH, RANGE,
PAMPAS
heel device .... SPUR
jacket .... CHAQUETA
kind of .... PUNCHER
original/legendary .... PECOS
BILL
overalls .... LEVIS
rope .... LASSO, REATA, RIATA,
LARIAT
saddlebag .... ALFORJA
show .... RODEO
South American/pampas
.... GAUCHO
trousers .... CHAPS,
CHAPARAJOS
cowcatcher .... FENDER
cowed .... TERRIFIED
cower .... QUAIL, CRINGE,
CROUCH, SHRINK
cowering through fear .... FUNK
Cowes, sight in .... YACHTS
cowfish .... TORO, DUGONG,
GRAMPUS, MANATEE

cowl .... CAPE, HOOD, AMICE, CLOAK
   like headdress .... COUS, ALMUCE
cowlick .... TUFT, FORELOCK
cowpox .... VACCINIA
cows .... KINE
   roundup of .... WRANGLE
cowslip .... BLUEBELL, MAYFLOWER
coxa .... HIP
coxcomb .... POP, DUDE, TOFF, DANDY
coy .... SHY, TIMID, DEMURE, CHARY, MODEST, BASHFUL, RESERVED, RETIRING, DIFFIDENT
coyo .... AVOCADO
coyote .... WOLF
coypu .... NUTRIA, RODENT
coze .... CHAT, TALK
cozen .... CON, BILK, CHEAT, TRICK, DECEIVE
cozy .... SNUG, WARM, CHATTY, HOM(E)Y, COMFORTABLE
   retreat .... DEN, NEST, NOOK
crab .... NAG, CARP, CRANK, GRIPE, SHELLFISH, HORSESHOE, MALACOSTRACAN
   apple .... SCRAB
   claw .... CHELA, NIPPER, PINC(H)ER
   constellation/sign of the Zodiac .... CANCER
   feeler/sense organ .... ANTENNA
   front of .... METOPE
   kind of .... BLUE, HERMIT, FIDDLER, DUNGENESS
   king .... LIMULUS, LIMULOID
   larva .... ZOEA
   like a .... CANCROID
   mantis .... SQUILLA
   one's act .... RUIN, FRUSTRATE
   Scottish .... PARTAN
   shell .... TEST
   upper shell of .... CARAPACE
   walk of ...... SIDLE, SIDEWAYS, SIDEWISE
crabbed .... CRAMPED, SQUEEZED, IRREGULAR
   handwriting .... ILLEGIBLE
crabby .... EDGY, CROSS, PEEVISH, GROUCHY, ILL-TEMPERED
crabfish .... GRAMPLE
Crabtree, actress .... LOTTA
crack ...... POP, REND, RIFT, SNAP, FLAW, BREAK, BURST, CHINK, QUIP, CLEFT, SPLIT, CREVICE
   colloquial ...... SKILLED, FIRST-RATE

deep/glacier .... CREVASSE
down on .... GAG, CENSOR, ASSAULT, SILENCE
filler .... GROUT
in a bone .... FRACTURE
open, as the skin .... CHAP
seal .... CA(U)LK
shot .... MARKSMAN
slang .... TRY, JOKE, GIBE, ATTEMPT
up .... CRASH, COLLAPSE, BREAK DOWN
crackbrained .... CRAZY, NUTTY, INSANE, IDIOTIC
cracked wheat/oats ...... GROATS
cracker .... WAFER, POPPER, BISCUIT, BREAKER, SALTINE, SNAPPER
crackerjack .... ACE, WHIZ, NAILER, EXPERT, WIZARD
crackers, dish of .... PANADA
crackle .... SNAP, SPIT, CREPITATE
cracklings ...... SCRAPS, GREAVES
crackly .... CRISP
cracknel .... BISCUIT, GREAVES, CRACKLINGS
crackpot .... NUT, CRANK, LUNATIC, SCREWBALL
cracks, full of .... CHOPPY, CHAPPED
cracksman .... YEGG, BURGLAR
   slang .... SAFECRACKER
cradle .... BED, CRIB, NEST, CRATE
in mining .... ROCKER
period .... INFANCY
song .... LULLABY
craft .... ART, BOAT, SHIP, CANOE, GUILE, SKILL, TRADE, TALENT, VESSEL, CUNNING, ARTIFICE, OCCUPATION
air .... AIRPLANE, DIRIGIBLE, HELICOPTER
harbor .... SCOW
union of old .... GUILD
water .... BOAT, SHIP, VESSEL
craftsman .... ARTIST, ARTISAN, ARTIFICER
chief .... MAESTRO
metal .... SMITH
crafty .... SLY, FOXY, WILY, ARTFUL, CLEVER, FELINE, SHIFTY, CUNNING, INSIDIOUS
crag .... TOR, ROCK, CLIFF, BOULDER, PRECIPICE
crake .... RAIL
cram .... JAM, BONE, PACK, TUCK, CHOKE, FORCE, STUDY, STUFF
cramp .... CROWD, SPASM, HAMPER, HINDER, CONFINE, CRIPPLE
neck .... KINK, CRICK

slang .... CHARLEY HORSE
crampfish .... TORPEDO
crampon ...... GRAPLIN, GRAPNEL
cranberry disease .... SCALD
crane ...... HERON, STORK, WADER, DERRICK, DEMOISELLE, RUBBERNECK
arm .... JIB
family .... GRUIDAE
framework .... GANTRY
genus .... GRUS
like bird .... CHUNGA, SERIEMA
lift by means of a .... HOIST
pertaining to .... GRUINE
relative .... BUSTARD
ship's .... DAVIT
sound .... CLANG
the neck ...... STRAIN, STRETCH
Crane, Ichabod, rival of .... (BROM) BONES
cranesbill .... GERANIUM
cranial nerve .... VAGUS
cranium .... SKULL
crank .... KEY, WHIM, QUIRK, TWIST, HANDLE, WINDER, CAPRICE
case reservoir .... OILPAN
colloquial ...... CRAB, GROUCH, QUEER, ODDBALL, CRACKPOT, ECCENTRIC
slang .... NUT, SCREWBALL
up .... TURN, WIND, START
cranky .... CROSS, QUEER, GROUCHY, IRRITABLE
cranny .... CHINK, CREVICE
partner of .... NOOK
crap .... DUNG, JUNK, STOOL, TRASH
in dice .... BOXCAR
out .... LOSE
slang .... HOGWASH, NONSENSE, POPPYCOCK, BULL(SHIT)
craps ...... DICE, (GAMBLING)GAME
''come out'' number .... SEVEN, ELEVEN
losing number at first throw .... TWO, THREE, TWELVE
shooter .... GAMBLER
shooter's ''four'' .... JOE, CATER
shooter's throw .... ROLL
throw .... DIE
crape .... WEED, WEEPER
crapehanger .... PESSIMIST
crappie .... SUNFISH
crash .... FALL, BLAST, BREAK, BURST, SMASH, COLLIDE, SHATTER, COLLAPSE, COLLISION
crass ...... CRUDE, GAUDY, GROSS,

ROUGH, COARSE, STUPID, VULGAR

Cratchit's job .... CLERK

crate .... BOX, PACK, BASKET, CASE, ENCASE, HAMPER

maker .... CASER

slang .... JALOPY

crater .... PIT, HOLE, CAVITY, MOUTH, CALDERA, OPENING

lunar .... LINNE

one with .... VOLCANO

cravat .... ASCOT, SCARF, (NECK)TIE, OVERLAY

fabric .... REP

hangman's .... NOOSE

ornament .... STICKPIN

crave .... BEG, NEED, PRAY, SEEK, LONG FOR, COVET, YEARN, HANKER

craven ...... AFRAID, COWARD(LY)

person .... SISSY, CAITIFF, DASTARD, POLTROON

craving ...... YEN, MANIA, DESIRE, HUNGER, THIRST, APPETITE, APPETENCE, OBSESSION

craw .... MAW, CROP, BELLY, GULLET, GIZZARD

crawl .... LAG, INCH, DRAG, CREEP, GROVEL, SLITHER

crawler ...... BABY, WORM, SNAIL, SNAKE, REPTILE

crawling .... PACKED, DRAPED, REPENT, REPTANT, TEEMING, COWERING, CRINGING

crayfish egg .... BERRY

segment .... METAMERE

crayon .... CHALK, PENCIL, CHARCOAL

pastel .... PASTILLE

picture .... PASTEL

craze .... FAD, RAGE, FUROR, MANIA, FASHION, OBSESSION

play/exercise .... HULA-HOOP

women's style .... PANTSUIT, MINISKIRT

crazed .... DAFT, RABID, CUCKOO, INSANE, DEMENTED, MAD(DENED), DERANGED

crazy .... MAD, BUGS, DAFT, LUNY, NUTS, DOTTY, KOOKY, LOONY, POTTY, CUCKOO, INSANE, RABID, KOOKIE, CRACKED

bird .... LOON

person .... MANIAC, LUNATIC, PSYCHOPATH

slang .... LOCO, WACKY, PSYCHO, BANANAS, BONKERS

to kill .... AMOK, AMUCK, BERSERK

creak .... CHIRK, CRICK, GRATE,

SCROOP, SQUEAK

cream .... BEST, GIST, ELITE, PASTE

cleansing .... COLD CREAM, TOOTHPASTE

colored .... ECRU, BEIGE, IVORY, STRAW, OCHERY

cosmetic .... LOTION, SHAMPOO, FACE CREAM

of the crop .... PRIME, CHOICE, CHOSEN, THE BEST

ointment .... SALVE, POMADE

puff .... PASTRY

separator .... CENTRIFUGE

slang .... THRASH

creamy white ...... MILKY, IVORY

crease .... DENT, FOLD, LINE, MARK, MUSS, RUCK, RUGA, RIDGE, RIMPLE, RUMPLE, WRINKLE

creased .... RUGATE, PLEATED

create .... FORM, MAKE, DESIGN, BREED, DEVISE, INVENT, COMPOSE, PRODUCE, ORIGINATE

interest .... DRUM UP

creation .... WORK, COSMOS, GENESIS, PRODUCT, INVENTION

God's .... UNIVERSE

greatest .... MASTERPIECE

creative .... INVENTIVE

writing .... POEM, NOVEL, POETRY, FICTION

creator .... MAKER, AUTHOR, DESIGNER

of an Alice .... ALBEE

of Muppet .... HENSON

of Uncle Remus .... HARRIS

of 007 .... (IAN)FLEMING

Creator, the .... GOD

creature .... MAN, TOOL, BEAST, SLAVE, THING, ANIMAL, MORTAL, PERSON, (HUMAN)BEING

small, imaginary ..... GREMLIN

creche figure .... LAMB, MAGI, MARY, INFANT, JOSEPH, SHEPHERD

part .... CRIB, MANGER

crecopia .... MYTH

credence .... FAITH, TRUST, BELIEF, CREDIT, SURETY, MISSAL STAND

credential .... VOUCHER, AUTHORITY, REFERENCE, CERTIFICATE

credentials .... BADGE, ID CARD

military .... DOG TAG

credenza ...... BUFFET, SIDEBOARD

credibility ...... TRUTH, VERACITY

credible .... LIKELY, TRUSTY, LOGICAL, RELIABLE, PLAUSIBLE, BELIEVABLE

credit .... LOAN, HONOR, TRUST, CHARGE, REBATE, ASCRIBE, BELIEVE, ATTRIBUTE

card organization .... BANKS, DINER'S CLUB

colloquial .... TICK

financial .... BORROWING POWER

for achievement .... KUDOS

creditable ...... HONEST, ETHICAL, CREDIBLE

creditor .... DEBTEE, LENDER, MORTGAGEE, NOTE HOLDER

annoying, insistent .... DUNNER

avaricious .... USURER, LOAN SHARK

exacting .... SHYLOCK

credo .... CREED, TENET, BELIEF

credulous .... GULLIBLE

creed, one such .... NICENE

political .... ISM, DOXY

creek ...... BAY, RIA, KILL, BAYOU, BROOK, INLET, INDIAN, STREAM

creel .... BASKET

user .... ANGLER, FISHERMAN

creep .... FAWN, INCH, CRAWL, SLINK, CRINGE, SLITHER

slang .... DRIP

up on .... SNEAK

creeper .... IVY, VINE, SNAIL, SNAKE

creeping .... REPENT, REPTANT, CRAWLING

charlie, for one .... WEED

plant .... IVY, BINE, VINE, LIANA

creeps, the .... FEAR, HATE, DISGUST, AVERSION, REVULSION

creepy .... EERIE, CRAWLY

creese .... CRIS, KRIS, DAGGER

cremate .... BURN, INCINERATE

cremation .... BURNING, INCINERATION

Hindu .... SUTTEE

crematory .... FURNACE, CINERATOR

Cremona .... AMATI, VIOLIN, STRAD(IVARIUS)

river .... ADDA

violin maker .... AMATI, GUARNERI

crenate .... NOTCHED, SCALLOPED

crenel .... EMBRASURE

crenelate .... NOTCH

Creole ancestry .... FRENCH,

SPANISH
and Indian .... MESTIZO
milieu .... NEW ORLEANS
patois .... GOMBO, GUMBO
rice cake .... CALA
State .... LOUISIANA
creosol .... ANTISEPTIC
crepe suzette .... PANCAKE,
FLAPJACK
crepitate .... RATTLE, CRACKLE
crepuscle .... DUSK, TWILIGHT
crescendo ...... EXPAND, AMPLIFY,
INCREASE
in music .... FORTE, STACCATO
crescent .... CURVE, HALF-CIRCLE,
SCYTHE, SEMI-CIRCLE
moons .... MENISCI
of a .... HORN, BICORN
point of .... CUSP
shape figure .... LUNE,
LUNULA, LUNULE, MENISCUS,
HORSESHOE
shaped .... LUNE, BICORN,
LUNATE, LUNULAR, DEMILUNE,
(SEMI)LUNAR
crescive .... GROWING, INCREASING
cress .... HERB, SALAD, GARNISH
cresset .... TORCH, LANTERN
Cressida's lover .... TROILUS
crest .... CAP, TOP, ACME, APEX,
PEAK, CROWN, RIDGE,
HELMET
a kind of helmet .... TUFT
clergyman's .... CALOTTE
cock's/rooster's .... COMB,
COCKSCOMB
mountain .... ARETE
of bird/fowl .... COMB, CRISTA,
CARUNCLE
wave's .... WHITECAP
crested .... CROWNED, PILEATE,
CORONET(T)ED, CRISTATE(D)
parrot .... COCKATOO,
COCKATEEL, COCKATIEL
royalty .... KING, QUEEN,
MONARCH, SOVEREIGN
crestfallen ...... GLUM, DEJECTED,
HUMBLED, DOWNCAST,
CHAPFALLEN, DISCOURAGED
creta .... CHALK
cretaceous .... CHALKY
Cretan .... MINOAN, CANDIAN
Crete .... KRITI
born painter/sculptor .... EL
GRECO, DOMENIKOS
cape .... KRIOS, SPATHA,
SIDHEROS
capital/seaport .... CANEA,
KHANIA
city/town .... SITIA, SPILI,
VAMOS, ANOYIA, MOIRAI,

KANDANOS, KISSAMOS,
LERAPETRA, KASTELLION,
RETHIMNON, TIMBAKION
escapee .... ICARUS
former name of .... CANDIA
Greek name of .... KRETE,
IRAKLION
guard/watchman of ..... TALOS
gulf .... KHANIA, MESARA,
MERABELLOU
king .... MINOS, IDOMENEUS
King Minos' wife
.... PASIPHAE
mountain .... IDA, IDHI,
SFAKION
mythical beast/monster
.... MINOTAUR
mythical monster's killer
.... THESEUS
mythical monster's mother
.... PASIPHAE
mythical structure
.... LABYRINTH
mythical structure's builder
.... DAEDALUS
princess .... ARIADNE
cretin .... IDIOT, MORON,
SIMPLETON
cretinism .... IDIOCY, MONGOLISM,
RETARDATION
cretonne .... TOILE
crevasse .... PIT, HOLE, ABYSS,
CHASM, SPLIT, FISSURE
crevice .... CHINK, CLEFT,
CRANNY, FISSURE
crevices, full of .... CHINKY,
RIMOSE, FISSURED
crew .... MOB, BAND, GANG, HELP,
TEAM, BUNCH, CROWD,
FORCE, GROUP, STAFF,
COMPANY
member .... OAR, HAND, HIRED
HELP
member, flight .... PILOT,
NAVIGATOR, STEWARD(ESS)
of ship, full ...... COMPLEMENT
relief .... RELAY, RESERVES,
SECOND TEAM
crewel .... YARN
crib .... BED, BIN, BOX, PAD,
PONY, RACK, BOOTH,
MANGER, STALL, TROUGH,
PLAGIARIZE
baby's .... CRADLE
colloquial .... GYP, CHEAT,
FORGE, GOUGE, STEAL
content of .... FODDER
for storing grain .... SILO,
GRANARY
in writing .... PLAGIARISM
worker .... TOOLMAN

cribbage .... CARD GAME
game lost .... LURCH
score .... NOBS, PEGS
crick .... KINK, CRAMP
cricket ...... GRIG, HOOP, CICADA,
INSECT, FOOTSTOOL
bowled ball .... YORKER
club .... BAT
colloquial .... FAIR PLAY
equipment .... BAT, BALL,
WICKET
family .... GRYLLIDAE
inning unplayed .... WICKET
like insect/relative of
.... LOCUST, GRASSHOPPER
positions .... SILLY LEGS
score .... BYE
sound .... CHIRP
team .... ELEVEN
term .... (TICE)BYE
crier .... WAILER, MUEZZIN,
HUCKSTER
crime .... SIN, EVIL, GUILT,
WRONG, BREACH, MISDEED,
OFFENSE, OUTRAGE,
VIOLATION, WRONGDOING,
MALEFACTION
against king .... LESE MAJESTE
against the IRS .... INCOME
TAX EVASION
high ...... TREASON, ESPIONAGE
major .... RAPE, ARSON,
FELONY, MURDER, KIDNAPPING
minor .... MISDEMEANOR
of encroaching on rights,
patents, etc.
.... INFRACTION, INFRINGEMENT
of stealing money by fraud
.... EMBEZZLEMENT
organized .... UNDERWORLD
sophisticated .... CAPER
story question ...... WHODUNIT
syndicate .... MAFIA, COSA
NOSTRA
syndicate member
.... MAFIOSO
where committed .... VENUE
Crimea 1945 Conference site
.... YALTA
Crimean city .... YALTA,
SEVASTOPOL
lamb's fur .... CRIMMER,
KRIMMER
river .... ALMA
sea .... AZOF
seaport .... KERCH, YALTA
strait .... KERCH
criminal .... YEGG, FELON,
OUTLAW, CULPRIT, CONVICT,
SINNER, IMMORAL, GANGSTER,
EVILDOER, OFFENDER,

MISCREANT, WRONGDOER, MALEFACTOR, MALFEASANT
act .... JOB, CRIME
burning .... ARSON
charge .... RAP
colloquial .... CROOK, LOSER
conditional freedom of
.... PAROLE
conditional release of
.... PROBATION
dangerous .... DESPERADO
habitual .... ROUNDER,
SCOFFLAW, RECIDIVIST
lawyer: sl. .... MOUTHPIECE
mark of a .... STIGMA
slang .... HOOD, MOBSTER
unreconstructed .... RECIDIVIST
who purposely burns
property .... ARSONIST
criminals collectively
.... FELONRY
crimp .... CURL, FOLD, WAVE,
BUNCH, FLUTE, PINCH, PLEAT,
PLAIT, GATHER, GOFFER,
CRINKLE
crimple .... NOTCH, WRINKLE
crimson .... RED, BLOODY,
MADDER, CARMINE
Crimson's rival .... YALE
cringe ...... FAWN, COWER, STOOP,
CRAWL, QUAIL, WINCE,
CROUCH, FLINCH, GROVEL,
SHRINK
crinkle ...... FOLD, CRIMP, CREASE,
CRUMPLE, WRINKLE
crinkled paper/cloth .... CREPE
crinkly .... WAVY, CORRUGATED
crinoid .... SEA LILY
crinoline .... PETTICOAT,
(HOOP)SKIRT
cripple .... HURT, LAME, MAIM,
DISABLE, HAMSTRING,
PARALYZE
a horse .... HOCK
of Lepanto .... CERVANTES
walking aid .... CANE, CRUTCH
cripples .... (THE) HALT
patron saint of .... (ST)GILES
crisis ...... PINCH, TRIAL, CRUNCH,
EMERGENCY, TURNING POINT
of disease .... SOLUTION
crisp .... CURT, WAVY, CRUMP,
FIRM, BLUNT, PITHY, STIFF,
BRITTLE, CRUNCHY,
ANIMATED
biscuit .... SNAP, CRACKER
crisper .... CURLER
cristate(d) .... CRESTED
crisscross .... MESH, BRAID,
MATTED, CROSSING,
TRANSVERSE

criterion ...... NORM, RULE, TEST,
CANON, GAUGE, MODEL,
MEASURE, STANDARD
critic .... CARPER, EXPERT,
CENSOR, SLATER, CENSURER,
JUDGE, REVIEWER,
FAULTFINDER
Clive .... BARNES
disapproval of a .... PAN(NING)
inferior .... CRITICASTER
literary .... REVIEWER
loud .... HOOTER
"missile" of, literally
.... EGG, TOMATO
Reed .... REX
uninhibited ..... BOOER, HISSER
work of .... CRITIQUE,
REVIEW(ER)
critical .... ACUTE, RISKY,
URGENT, CAPTIOUS, CRUCIAL,
EXIGENT, EXACTING,
DECISIVE, CENSORIOUS
analysis .... EXEGESIS
mark .... OBELUS
moment .... CRUX, CRISIS,
ZERO HOUR
situation .... CLUTCH
writing .... SATIRE, LAMPOON
criticism .... NOTICE, REMARK,
REPORT, REVIEW, COMMENT,
DESCANT, ANALYSIS,
CRITIQUE, EXEGETICS
abusive .... DIATRIBE
adverse: colloq. .... PAN
colloquial .... WRITE-UP
hostile .... FLAK, SLAM
criticize .... RAP, DAMN, FLAY,
SLAM, BLAME, SLASH, SLATE,
JUDGE, OPPUGN, REVIEW,
CENSURE, BLAST, CONDEMN,
NITPICK, REPROVE,
DENOUNCE, ANIMADVERT
satirically .... ROAST
severely .... SCORE, BERATE
slang .... PAN, RAKE,
BADMOUTH
critique .... REVIEW, SUMMARY,
EPICRISIS, COMMENTARY
croak .... CROUP, GRUMBLE
slang .... DIE
croaker ...... CROW, FROG, RAVEN,
SQUETEAGUE
croaking .... RAUCOUS
Croat .... SLAV
Croatian capital .... ZAGREB
native .... CROAT
necktie/scarf .... CRAVAT
soldier .... PANDOUR
croc .... CROCODILE
crochet .... KINK, KNIT(TING)
crock ...... JAR, POT, SMUT, SOOT,

SHARD, POTSHERD
crockery ...... JARS, POTS, DISHES,
POTTERY, CERAMICS
Crockett, frontiersman
.... DAVEY, DAVID
place of heroism .... ALAMO
crocodile .... YACARE, REPTILE,
SAURIAN
bird .... PLOVER, TROCHILUS
for short .... CROC
India/Malaysia .... GAVIAL,
MUGGAR, MUGGER, MUGGUR
Philippine .... BUAYA
relative ..... CAIMAN, CAYMAN,
ALLIGATOR
teeth picker .... TROCHILUS
Crocodile River .... LIMPOPO
crocus .... IRIS
bulb .... CORM
color .... SAFFRON
croft .... FARM
croissant .... ROLL
cromlech .... TOMB, DOLMEN,
MEGALITH, MONUMENT
Cromwell (Oliver), army of
.... IRONSIDES
soubriquet .... IRONSIDES
title .... LORD PROTECTOR
victory site .... NASEBY
crone .... HAG, ANILE, WITCH,
BELDAM(E), CARLINE
Cronus .... TITAN, SATURN
parent .... GAEA, URANUS
sister of .... TETHYS
son of .... ZEUS
crony .... PAL, CHUM, BUDDY,
COHORT, COMPEER, CONFRERE
cronyism .... FAVORITISM
Cronyn, actor .... HUME
crook .... BEND, HOOK, CURVE
bishop's .... CROSIER
colloquial .... THIEF,
CHEAT(ER), ROBBER,
SWINDLER
in tree branch .... KNEE
crooked .... AGEE, AWRY, BENT,
ASKEW, TIPSY, CURVED,
FALSE, ZIGZAG, WINDING,
DEVIOUS, TORTUOUS,
DISHONEST
slang .... COCKEYED
croon .... HUM, SING
crop .... MAW, CLIP, CRAW, FRUIT,
YIELD, GIZZARD, HARVEST,
PRODUCT
animal feed .... FODDER
picker .... GATHERER
riding .... WHIP
up again .... RECUR
cropper .... FARMER, PEASANT,
SHEARER

colloquial .... RUIN, FAILURE
croquet .... (OUTDOOR) GAME
   equipment .... HOOPS, MALLET,
     WOODEN BALL
   handicap .... BISQUE
   kind of .... ROQUE
   wicket .... ARCH
croquette .... CUTLET
Crosby .... BOB, BING, GARY
   crooner's soubriquet .... THE
     GROANER
crosier ...... CANE, CROOK, CROSS,
   SCEPTER, (PASTORAL) STAFF
cross .... EDGY, FOIL, SPAN,
   SURLY, TESTY, CRANKY,
   OPPOSE, THWART, PEEVISH,
   LIVERISH, FRACTIOUS
   as a Christian symbol
   .... CRUCIFIX
   bearer/carrier .... CRUCIFER
   between a skirt and shorts
   .... SKORT
   between broccoli and
     cauliflower
   .... BROCCOFLOWER
   between tangerine and
     orange .... TANGOR
   breed .... HYBRIDIZE
   by wading/a river .... FORD
   church .... ROOD
   country highway, major
   .... INTERSTATE
   country runner .... HARRIER
   country skiing ...... LANGLAUF
   current .... RIP(TIDE)
   cut .... SAWN
   decoration ..... IRON, VICTORIA
   each other .... INTERSECT
   Egyptian .... ANKH
   examination, of ...... ELENCTIC
   examine .... GRILL,
     INTERROGATE
   eye(d) .... SQUINT,
   STRABISMAL, STRABISMUS
   fertilization .... XENOGAMY
   grained .... CONTRARY
   horizontal beam ..... TRANSOM
   in heraldry/Southern .... CRUX
   inscription .... INRI
   mark X
   off/out .... CANCEL, DELE(TE)
   question .... EXAMINE
   reference .... NOTATE
   shaped .... CRUCIAL,
     CRUCIFORM
   stroke .... SERIF
   up .... CONFUSE, DECEIVE
crossbar .... RUNG
crossbeam .... TRAVE, TREVE,
     TRANSOM
crossbill .... FINCH

genus .... LOXIA
crossbow .... ARBALEST
   missile .... BOLT, QUARREL
crossbreed ..... HYBRID, MONGREL
crossed .... DEFIED, FOILED,
   MARKED, OPPOSED,
   THWARTED, FRUSTRATED
   star .... TRAGIC, ILL-FATED
crossette .... ANCON
crosspiece ...... RUNG, SILL, SPAR,
   CLEAT, LINTEL, TRANSOM
crossruff in whist .... SEESAW
crossthreads .... WOOF
crosswise .... TRANSVERSE
crossword puzzle brew ...... ALE
   inventor of .... ARTHUR
     WYNNE
crotchet .... HOOK, CAPRICE
   half of a .... QUAVER
crotchety person .... CRANK,
   GROUCH, CURMUDGEON
croton bug .... COCKROACH
crouch .... BOW, BEND, COWER,
   STOOP, CRINGE
crouching position .... SQUAT
croup .... ANGINA, CATARRH,
     CRUPPER
   horse's .... RUMP
crouse .... BOLD, PERT, BRISK,
     LIVELY
crouton .... SIPPET
crow .... CAW, BRAG, ROOK,
   CRAKE, GLOAT, (JACK)DAW,
     BLACKBIRD
   constellation/genus
   .... CORVUS
   cry .... CAW
   eat .... RECANT, HUMBLE
     ONESELF
   European, white-spotted
   .... NUTCRACKER
   flight route of .... DIRECT,
     STRAIGHT
   hooded .... GRAYBACK
   Indian .... SIOUX
   kin .... JAY
   like a/of .... CORVINE
   like bird ...... RAVEN, CHOUGH,
     ORIOLE
   over a victory .... BOAST,
     EXULT
   people .... ABSAROKE
crowbar ...... PRY, JEMMY, JIMMY,
   LEVER, EXTRACTOR
crowd .... JAM, MOB, CRAM,
   GANG, HOST, MASS, ROUT,
   DROVE, FLOCK, HORDE,
   PRESS, SERRY, SHOVE,
   THRONG, CONCOURSE,
   GATHERING, MULTITUDE
   busy .... HIVE

close together .... HERD,
     HUDDLE
   colloquial .... SET, CLIQUE
   every which way .... MILL
   fancier .... DIP, ACTOR,
     PICKPOCKET
   in .... ENTER, INTRUDE
   moving .... SWARM
   number .... THREE
   _____ (popular athletes)
   .... PLEASERS
crowded .... DENSE, COMPACT,
   SERRIED, TEEMING, JAM-
     PACKED
crower .... BABY, COCK, BOASTER,
   ROOSTER, BRAGGART
crowfoot flower .... PEONY
crown .... TOP, COIN, HEAD, PATE,
   ADORN, CREST, DIADEM,
   INVEST, INSTALL, WREATHE,
   TREE-TOP, CORONATE,
     ENTHRONE
   bottle .... CAP
   cock's .... COMB
   Egyptian .... ATEF
   for a tooth, artificial .... CAP
   head's .... POLL
   in botany .... CORONA
   in zoology .... CREST
   jewel .... TIARA
   prince .... DAUPHIN,
     HEIR(APPARENT)
   prince, English .... CHARLES
   prince, Japanese .... NARUHITO
   slang .... CONK
   small .... CIRCLET, CORONET
   sun's .... AUREOLA, AUREOLE
   victory .... PRIZE, LAUREL,
   AWARD, TROPHY, GARLAND
crowning .... ULTIMATE
   ceremony .... INVESTITURE
   touch .... CLINCHER,
     DEATHBLOW
crow's feet .... EYE WRINKLES
   nest .... LOOKOUT
crowtoe .... BUTTERCUP
crucial .... SEVERE, TRYING,
   URGENT, CRITICAL, DECISIVE
   point .... CRUX, CRISIS
   spot in game .... SET-POINT
crucible .... TEST, CRUSE, TRIAL,
   ORDEAL, CALDRON, FIREPOT,
     MELTING POT
crucifix .... ROOD, CROSS, SYMBOL
crucifixion, place of Jesus'
   .... CALVARY
crucify .... FLOG, HANG, KILL,
   WHIP, THRASH, BUTCHER,
   EXECUTE, MORTIFY, TORMENT,
     TORTURE
crude .... RAW, BARE, RUDE,

CRASS, GROSS, PLAIN, ROUGH, COARSE, VULGAR, LOWBRED, SKETCHY, UNCOUTH, AGRESTIC, UNREFINED
bed .... DOSS
metal .... ORE
people .... YAHOOS
person .... BOOR
Scottish .... RANDY
shed .... LEAN-TO
sugar .... MELADA, PANOCHA
writing .... GRAFFITI
cruel .... MEAN, HARSH, STONY, BRUTAL, SAVAGE, UNKIND, BESTIAL, BRUTISH, CAUSTIC, PITILESS, RUTHLESS, SPITEFUL, HEARTLESS, COLDBLOODED
behavior .... BEASTLINESS
pleasure-seeker .... SADIST
ruler .... DESPOT, TYRANT
cruet ...... VIAL, CASTER, CASTOR, AMPULLA
cruise .... ROAM, COAST, VOYAGE, WANDER, JOURNEY
cruller .... DONUT, DOUGHNUT, (FRIED)CAKE
crumb ...... BIT, JOT, ORT, SCRAP, MORSEL, FRAGMENT, PARTICLE
ore .... SPALL
crumble .... DECAY, BREAK UP, MO(U)LDER, DISINTEGRATE
easy to .... FRIABLE
crummy .... LOW, SHABBY, INFERIOR
crumple .... RUCK, CRUSH, BUCKLE, WRINKLE, COLLAPSE
crunch .... CHEW, CHAMP, CRUSH, GRIND, MUNCH
cruor .... GORE, BLOOD
crus .... SHIN, SHANK
crusade .... CAUSE, DRIVE, MISSION, CAMPAIGN, MOVEMENT
Moslem .... JEHAD, JIHAD
crusader ...... CATALYST, PILGRIM, TANCRED, TEMPLAR, REFORMER
King Richard .... LION-HEART(ED)
crusaders' foe .... SALADIN, SARACEN
leader .... TANCRED
objective .... REFORM(S)
port .... ACRE
crush .... JAM, BRAY, GRIND, PRESS, QUASH, QUELL, SHAME, SQUASH, SUBDUE, CONQUER, SQUEEZE, SUPPRESS, OVERCOME, VANQUISH, OVERWHELM

colloquial .... LOVE, INFATUATION
into fine particles .... TRITURATE
to softness .... MASH
underfoot .... TRAMPLE
with mortar, pestle .... BRUISE
with teeth .... CHEW
crushed, as a fabric ...... ECRASE
sugarcane refuse .... BAGASSE, MEGASS(E)
crushing defeat .... WATERLOO
Crusoe's creator .... DEFOE
crust .... LOAF, RIND, SCAB, BREAD, SHELL, COATING
fruit-filled .... DUMPLING
metal .... PATINA
slang .... GALL, CHEEK, NERVE, AUDACITY, INSOLENCE
crustacean .... CRAB, PRAWN, ISOPOD, SHRIMP, LOBSTER, COPEPOD, LIMULUS, PAGURID, PAGURIAN, SCHIZOPOD
burrowing .... SQUILLA, MANTIS CRAB
claw .... CHELA
covering .... SHELL
eggs .... ROE, CORAL
feeler .... ANTENNA
horny substance .... CHITIN
limb of .... PLEOPOD
parasitic .... BARNACLE, CIRRIPED
regal .... KING CRAB
segment .... SOMITE, TELSON
skin secretion .... CHITIN
spawn .... ROE, CORAL
10-legged ..... PRAWN, SHRIMP, DECAPOD, LOBSTER, MACRURAN
walking and swimming .... SHRIMP, AMPHIPOD, SANDFLEA
crusty ...... HARSH, HUFFY, SURLY, TESTY, BRUSQUE, HARDENED, ILL-TEMPERED
concoction .... PIE
pieces of bread .... HEELS
spot .... SCAB
crutch .... AID, PROP, STAFF, SUPPORT, WALKING STICK
crux .... CROSS, PUZZLE
ansata .... ANKH
cry .... BEG, SOB, PULE, WAIL, WEEP, YELP, SHOUT, CLAMOR, WHINE, SCREAM
animal's .... BRAY
Australian .... COOEE, COOEY
baby .... MEWL
bacchanal/of Bacchantes .... EVOE

companion of .... HUE
for .... PLEAD, DEMAND, ENTREAT
harsh, loud .... SQUAWK
high-pitched/shrill .... SQUALL, SQUEAL
hunter's .... TALLYHO
like crazy/loudly .... BAWL
loud and confused .... HULLABALOO
mournful/dismal .... YOWL
of calf/goat .... BLEAT
of cheer ..... HOORAY, HURRAH
of child .... MEWL, PULE, WHIMPER
of disapproval .... BOO, HISS, HOOT, CATCALL
of pain .... OUCH
of surrender, 1918 .... KAMERAD
out .... YELL, EXCLAIM, ULULATE, VOCIFERATE
party .... SLOGAN, WATCHWORD, SHIBBOLETH
to the hounds .... YOICKS
wolf .... FALSE ALARM
crybaby .... SOFTY, WEAKLING, POOR LOSER, POOR SPORT
cryogen .... REFRIGERANT
cryogenics .... PHYSICS
crypt .... TOMB, VAULT
cryptic .... OCCULT, SECRET, OBSCURE, ENIGMATIC
cryptographer's stumper .... CODE
cryptogram .... CODE, CIPHER, CRYPTOGRAPH
crystal .... GEM, CLEAR, GLASS, STONE, LIMPID, HEMITROPE
a tiny embryonic .... CRYSTALLITE
clear .... LUCID, PLAIN, OBVIOUS
gazer ...... SEER(ESS), PALMIST, PREDICTOR
gazing .... PALMISTRY
like a .... CRYSTALLOID
pick-up .... DETECTOR
violet .... DYE, STAINER
Crystal, singer .... GAYLE
crystalline .... SHEER, GLASSY, PELLUCID, DIAPHANOUS, TRANSPARENT
alcohol .... CALCIFEROL
alkaloid .... AMARINE, ATROPINE
and granular ...... SACCHAROID
biblical .... BDELLIUM
cloth .... GOSSAMER
compound .... SERINE, BORAZON, CATECHOL,

179

lined stone .... GEODE

material .... GAUZE

mineral .... FELDSPAR

moisture .... DEW

resin .... CANNABIN

salt .... BORAX

substance .... UREA, CARBAZOLE

crystallize .... SET, JELL, HARDEN, CONDENSE, SOLIDIFY, CONGEAL, GRANULATE, (TAKE)FORM, TAKE SHAPE

crystallized sugar/syrup .... CANDY

ctenophores .... NUDA

cub .... WHELP, LIONET, NOVICE, BEGINNER, YOUNGSTER

kind of .... REPORTER

Cub Scout group .... DEN

group leader .... AKELA, DEN CHIEF

Cuba, U.S. base in .... GUANTANAMO

cubage .... VOLUME

Cuban .... HABANERO

archipelago .... SABANA, LOS CANARREOS, LOS COLORADOS

bay ...... PIGS(COCHINOS), NIPE, HONDA, MAISI, JIGUEY, PERROS, MATANZAS, NUEVITAS, SIGUAMEA, BUENAVISTA, GUANTANAMO

bearded one .... (FIDEL)CASTRO

cape .... CRUZ, PEPE, FRANCES, LUCRECIA, CORRIENTES

capital .... HAVANA

castle .... MORRO

cay .... COCO, LARGO, FRAGOSO, GUAJABA, SABINAL, CANTILES

cays .... CAYAMAS, GUZMANES, SAN FELIPE, CINCO BALAS

channel ..... INDIOS, NICHOLAS, CABALLONES, OLD BAHAMA

chess champ ..... CAPABLANCA

cigar .... HAVANA

city/town ...... MORON, REGLA, BAYAMO, PERICO, HOLGUIN, NIQUERO, PALMIRA, CAMAGUEY, CARDENAS, MARIANAO, MATANZAS, REMEDIOS, TRINIDAD, RANCHUELO, GUANTANAMO, GUANABACOA, MANZANILLO, MANICARAGUA, SANTA CLARA, PALMA SORIANO, PINAR DEL RIO, SANCTI SPIRITUS, SANTIAGO DE CUBA

dance .... R(H)UMBA, HABANERA

dictator .... CASTRO, BATISTA

discoverer .... COLUMBUS

drum .... BONGO

food fish .... PINTADO

gulf ...... CAZONES, BATABANO, ANA MARIA, GUACANAYABO

island .... JUVENTUD

lagoon .... LECHE

language .... SPANISH

measure .... VARA, TAREA, MEDIDA

measure for distance .... MILLA, KILOMETRO

measure for grains .... FANEGA

monetary unit .... PESO

mountain .... GRAN PIEDRA, OJO DEL TORO, PICO TURQUINO

mountains .... SIERRA MAESTRA, CUCHILLAS DE TOA, SIERRA DEL CRISTAL

music .... MAMBO

palm leaf .... CHIP

passage .... WINDWARD

peninsula .... ZAPATA, GUANAHACABIBES

premier .... CASTRO

president .... MACHADO, DORTICOS

province .... GRANMA, HABANA, HOLGUIN, CAMAGUEY, MATANZAS, LAS TUNAS, CIENFUEGOS, VILLA CLARA, PINAR DEL RIO, SANTIAGO DE CUBA

river .... CAUTO, SAN PEDRO, JATIBONICO, SAGUA LA GRANDE

rum .... BACARDI

seaport .... MATANZAS, CIENFUEGOS, MANZANILLO

secret police .... PORRA

snake .... JUBA

tempest .... BAYAMO

tobacco .... VUELTA

weight .... KILO, LIBRA, TONELADA

cubbyhole of a sort .... DEN

cube .... CUT, DIE, DICE, CHOP, SOLID

shaped .... CUBICAL

cubeb .... BERRY, CIGARETTE

cubic capacity, ship's .... TONNAGE

content .... VOLUME, CUBATURE

decimeter .... LITER, LITRE

foot per second .... CUSEC

meter .... STERE

cubicle .... DEN, CELL, NOOK, BEDROOM, COMPARTMENT

Cuchulain's wife .... EMER

cuckoldry .... ADULTERY, CONCUBINAGE

cuckoo .... ANI, BIRD, GOWK, KOEL, TOURACO

of the .... CUCULIFORM

slang .... CRAZY, SILLY, FOOLISH

cuckoopint .... ARUM

cucullate .... COWLED, HOODED

cucumber .... PEPO, GOURD, PICKLE, GHERKIN

cool as a .... CALM, POISED, COMPOSED

relish .... PICKLES

cucurbit .... FLASK, GOURD-SHAPED

cucurbitaceous herb .... GOURD, MELON, SQUASH, CUCUMBER

cud .... BITE, CHEW, BOLUS, MORSEL

chew the .... PONDER, RECALL, RUMINATE

chewer's stomach ..... RUMEN, PAUNCH

chewing animal .... COW, DEER, GOAT, BISON, CAMEL, LLAMA, CATTLE, BUFFALO, CARABAO, GIRAFFE, RUMINANT

of chewing tobacco ..... PLUG, QUID, TWIST

variant of .... QUID

cudbear .... DYE, LICHEN

cuddle .... HUG, CLASP, CARESS, CURL UP, FONDLE, NESTLE, EMBRACE, SNUGGLE

cuddly .... ANGELIC, LOVABLE

cuddy .... CABIN, CLOSET, PANTRY, CUPBOARD

cudgel .... BAT, CLUB, DRUB, STAFF, STICK, BASTINADO, SHILLALAH, SHILLELAGH, TRUNCHEON

one's brains .... RACK

cudgels, take up the .... DEFEND

cue .... ROD, TIP, CLUE, HINT, TAIL, SIGNAL

actor's .... CATCHWORD

bridge of .... JIGGER

in music .... PRESA

of hair .... BRAID, QUEUE, PIGTAIL

substitute, billiards .... MACE

cuff .... BOX, HIT, BELT, BIFF, SLAP, CLOUT, FIGHT, STRIKE, HANDCUFF, WRISTBAND

off the .... OFFHAND, IMPROMPTU

Cugat, bandleader .... XAVIER

cuirass .... MAIL, ARMOR, LORLEA, LORIC(A), CORSELET, BREASTPLATE
cuisine .... COOKING, COOKERY, KITCHEN
of the .... CULINARY
cuisine, ____ .... HAUTE
cuisinier .... CHEF, COOK, KITCHENER
cul-de-sac .... BLIND ALLEY
Culbertson, card expert .... ELY
culex pipiens .... MOSQUITO
cull .... SIFT, GLEAN, REJECT, SELECT, PICK OUT
cullis .... GUTTER
cully .... DUPE, MATE, CHEAT, TRICK
British: sl. .... PAL, BUDDY
culm .... COAL, DUST, HA(U)LM
culminate .... END, COME TO A HEAD
culminating point .... CRISIS, HIGH TIDE
culmination .... ACME, CLIMAX, FINISH, FRUITION
sun's .... NOON, ZENITH
Culp, ____ (hobby) .... OVETA
culpa .... FAULT, GUILT
culpa, ____ .... MEA
culpability .... ONUS, BLAME, GUILT
culpable ...... GUILTY, TO BLAME, SINFUL, BLAMABLE, AT FAULT
culprit .... FELON, OFFENDER, CRIMINAL
cult .... FAD, ISM, SECT, VOGUE, BELIEF, WORSHIP
artistic .... DADA
naked .... NUDISM
cultivate .... FARM, GROW, TILL, WORK, NURSE, FOSTER, PURSUE, CHERISH, DEVELOP
cultivated .... TILLED, REFINED, CULTURED, HIGHBROW
land .... FARM, ARADA
plot .... GARDEN
cultivation of soil .... TILTH, CULTURE
cultivator .... TILLER
cultural studies .... ARTS
culture .... ARTS, POLISH, BREEDING, REFINEMENT, CIVILIZATION
medium .... AGAR
of people .... ETHOS
cultured person .... LADY, SCHOLAR, GENTLEMAN
culver .... DOVE, PIGEON
culvert .... DRAIN, CONDUIT, WATERWAY
opening .... INLET

cum .... WITH
cumber .... LOAD, DETER, BURDEN, HAMPER, HINDER, IMPEDE, MEDDLE, OVERLOAD
cumbersome .... CLUMSY, ONEROUS, UNWIELDY, BURDENSOME, HEAVY-LADEN
cumin .... ANISE
cummer .... GODMOTHER
cummerbund .... SASH
cumshaw .... TIP, GRATUITY
cunner .... GILTHEAD
cunning .... SLY, FOXY, WILY, GUILE, CLEVER, ARTFUL, ASTUTE, CRAFT(Y), SHIFTY
as a fox .... VULPINE
person .... KNAVE, SCHEMER, POLITICIAN
cuon .... DHOLE
cup .... BOWL, CALIX, CRATER, CHALICE, CANNIKIN
assaying .... TEST, CUPEL
ceremonial .... AMA
drinking .... MUG, CALIX, TASS, CRUSE, STEIN, STOUP, TAZZA, GOBLET, NOGGIN, RUMMER, TANKARD
druggist's/wine .... BEAKER
flower .... CALYX
gem-cutting .... DOP
holder .... ZARF, SAUCER
knight's quest .... GRAIL
like .... CALICULAR
like spoon .... LADLE
metal .... PANNIKIN
of tea: Brit. colloq.
.... HOBBY, AVOCATION
shaped like a .... HOLLOW, CONCAVE
small, for coffee
.... DEMITASSE
sports championship
..... DAVIS, RYDER, AMERICA'S, WIGHTMAN
to measure liquid .... JIGGER
used at the Last Supper
.... (HOLY)GRAIL
cupbearer of the gods .... HEBE, GANYMEDE
cupboard .... AMBRY, CUDDY, CLOSET, LARDER, PANTRY, ARMOIRE, CABINET
Cupid .... AMOR, EROS
infant .... AMORINO, AMORETTO
mother of .... VENUS
sweetheart of .... PSYCHE
title of .... DAN
cupidity .... LUST, GREED, AVARICE

Cupid's bow, so to speak
.... PUPPY LOVE
cupola .... ARCH, DOME
battleship's .... TURRET
cuprous oxide .... CHALCOCITE
cuprum .... COPPER
cur .... DOG, MUTT, TIKE, TYKE, HOUND, MONGREL
curable .... MENDABLE, MEDICABLE
curacao, orange-flavored
.... COINTREAU
curare .... URALI, URARI, POISON, OURALI, WOORALI, WOURALI
curate .... PRIEST, MINISTER, CLERGYMAN
curative ...... HEALING, REMEDIAL, SANATIVE, SANATORY, MEDICINAL, THERAPEUTIC
curator .... KEEPER, BOOKMAN, GUARDIAN
concern of .... MUSEUM, RELICS, LIBRARY, ARCHIVES
curb .... REIN, CHECK, MARKET, RETARD, SLACKEN, RESTRAIN
colloquial .... LID
for woman's tongue
.... BRANKS
market item ...... BOND, STOCK
curbed .... CONTROLLED
curbing inward .... ADUNC
curbstone .... BORDER
curch .... KERCHIEF
curculio .... BEETLE
curcuma .... GINGER, TURMERIC
curd .... CASEIN
soybean .... TAHO, TOFU, TOKUA
curdle .... CLABBER, CONGEAL, LUMP, SPOIL, THICKEN, COAGULATE
curdled milk .... CLABBER
curdling material .... RENNET, RENNIN
curds with cream .... JUNKET
cure .... HEAL, TREAT, DOCTOR, REMEDY, RELIEVE, RESTORE, REGIMEN, THERAPY, PRESERVE, PHYSIC, MEDICINE, TREATMENT, PRESCRIPTION
all .... ELIXIR, NOSTRUM, PANACEA, CATHOLICON
by salting .... CORN
fish, meat, etc. .... SALT, SMOKE
foods for future use ...... DRY, DEHYDRATE, FREEZE-DRY
French .... PRIEST
fruit by cooking with sugar
.... PRESERVE
hide into leather .... TAN

kind of .... REST, WATER,
PURGATIVE, ACUPUNCTURE
vegetables with brine,
vinegar .... PICKLE
curfew feature .... SIREN,
WHISTLE, LIGHTS OUT
man .... TOWN CRIER
curia official, Catholic
.... DATARY
curio(s) .... VIRTU, GEWGAW,
ANTIQUE, BIBELOT,
GIMCRACK, BRIC-A-BRAC,
KNICKKNACK
collector .... VIRTUOSO
curiosa .... NOVELTIES
curious .... ODD, PRYING,
GOSSIPY, NOS(E)Y, MEDDLING,
MEDDLESOME, INQUISITIVE
colloquial .... SNOOP
one ...... CAT, PRY, SNOOP(ER),
BUSYBODY, QUIDNUNC,
PEEPING TOM
curl .... COIL, ROLL, CRIMP, WAVE,
TRESS, TWIST, RIPPLE,
FRIZ(ZLE)
hair .... SET, MARCEL
of long hair .... RINGLET
snugly ..... CUDDLE, ENSCONCE
the lip .... JEER, SNEER
curled .... SPIRY, CRIMPED,
CRISPATE
curlew .... SNIPE, WHAUP, GODWIT
bird resembling .... WHIMBREL
Curlew River character
.... FERRYMAN
curlicue .... CURL, CURVE, TWIST,
FLOURISH
curling iron .... CRISPER
mark/target .... TEE
match .... BONSPIEL
place .... RINK
curlpaper .... PAPILLOTE
curly .... WAVY, KINKY, SPIRAL
curmudgeon ...... CRAB, GROUCH,
GROWLER
curn .... FEW, GRAIN
curr .... COO, MURMUR
currach .... CORACLE
currant .... BERRY, GRAPE,
SHRUB, RISSEL
genus .... RIBES
syrup .... CASSIS
currency .... CASH, COIN, MONEY,
SPECIE, NEWNESS, FRESHNESS,
PREVALENCE, CIRCULATION
value of .... VALUTA
current .... TIDE, FRESH, MODERN,
COMMON, GOING(ON), IN
VOGUE, EXISTING, STREAM,
PREVAILING
air .... DRAFT

beneath surf .... UNDERTOW
combining form .... RHEO
expenses .... OVERHEAD
measure .... AMPS, AMPERES
opposite .... SETBACK
currently .... NOW, PRESENTLY,
AT PRESENT
currier .... COMBER
Currier and Ives .... PRINTS
curry .... BEAT, COMB, DRUB,
FLOG, STEW, TIDY, CLEAN,
DRESS, GROOM
favor .... FAWN, FLATTER
ingredient .... CUMIN
curse .... BAN, BANE, DAMN,
OATH, SWEAR, REVILE,
ANATHEMA, DENOUNCE,
EXECRATE, BLASPHEME,
MARANATHA, SWEARWORD,
IMPRECATION, MALEDICTION
Archaic ..... WANION, MALISON
colloquial .... CUSS
cursed .... EVIL, ODIOUS, WICKED,
VICTIMIZED
colloquial .... JINXED
curser, biblical .... BALAAM
cursillo founder .... HERVAS
cursive .... FLOWING, RUNNING
cursor .... RUNNER, INDICATOR
cursory .... CASUAL, RANDOM,
SHALLOW, TRIVIAL,
SUPERFICIAL
look .... GLANCE, GLIMPSE
curt .... RUDE, TART, BLUFF,
BLUNT, BRIEF, SHORT, TERSE,
ABRUPT, BRUSQUE, CONCISE,
SNAPPISH
dismissal .... CONGE
curtail .... CUT, CLIP, LESSEN,
REDUCE, DEPRIVE, SHORTEN
curtain .... COVER, DRAPE,
SCREEN, DRAPERY, VEILING
behind stage .... BACKDROP
Cold War .... IRON, BAMBOO
color/shade .... ECRU
holder .... ROD
hung in a doorway
.... PORTIERE
material .... LENO, GAUZE,
NINON, SCRIM, TAPIS,
GRENADINE
of gun fire .... BARRAGE
raiser .... SKIT, PRELIMINARY
rod cover/band .... CORNICE
sash .... TIEBACK
short .... VALANCE
woman's apartment
.... PURDAH
curtains: sl. .... END, DEATH
curtsy .... BOB, BOW, SALUTE
Archaic .... LOUT

curvature .... ARC(H)
curve .... ARC, ARCH, CURL, ESSE,
TURN, CROOK, SINUS,
FLEXURE, HYPERBOLA
baseball pitch/pitcher's
.... HOOK, FASTBALL,
SCREWBALL
double/sharp .... ESS
handwriting .... CURLICUE,
FLOURISH
inward .... INFLECT
mark over vowel .... BREVE
of a column .... ENTASIS
of river .... BEND
path of missile
.... TRAJECTORY
plane .... PARABOLA
S-shaped .... OGEE
to one side .... VEER, SWERVE,
DEFLECT
curved .... BENT, ADUNC, ARCHED,
ARCUATE, FALACTE,
FALCIFORM
bones .... RIBS
in .... CONCAVE
molding .... OGEE
out .... CONVEX
plank, ship's .... SNY
roof .... DOME
surface of arch ..... EXTRADOS
sword .... SCIMITAR
curves, having two .... BIFLEX
curvet ...... LEAP, VAULT, FROLIC,
GAMBOL
curving inward .... ADUNC
cushat .... (RING)DOVE,
(WOOD)PIGEON
cushaw .... SQUASH
cushion .... MAT, PAD, SQUAB,
ABSORB, BUFFER, PILLOW,
SOFTEN, BOLSTER, HASSOCK
of rope, wood, at ship's side
.... FENDER
shock .... BUMPER
Cush's father .... HAM
son .... NIMROD
cushy: sl. .... EASY
cusk .... BURBOT
relative .... COD
cusp of moon .... HORN
cuspid .... FANG, TOOTH
cuspidor .... SPITTOON
cussed ...... MEAN, NASTY, SWORE,
BITCHY, CURSED, ORNERY
custard .... PIE
apple .... PA(W)PAW
apple's cousin .... SWEETSOP
cake .... ECLAIR
dish .... FLAN
like dish .... TIMBALE

Custer's battle site .... LITTLE BIG HORN
nemesis .... SITTING BULL
custodian .... CUSTOS, KEEPER, WARDEN, WARDER, JANITOR, JAILER, CARETAKER, CONCIERGE
museum .... CURATOR
of funds .... TREASURER
of minors .... GUARDIAN
custody .... CARE, WING, TRUST, CHARGE, KEEPING, WARDSHIP, GUARDIANSHIP
take into .... HOLD, ARREST, DETAIN
custom .... USE, WONT, HABIT, USAGE, PRAXIS, PRACTICE
built/made .... TAILORED, MADE-TO-ORDER
with force of law .... MOS, MORES
customable .... TAXABLE
customary .... RULE, USUAL, COMMON, NORMAL, WONTED, REGULAR, HABITUAL, ORDINARY
extras .... ETCETERAS
requirement .... FORMALITY
sidler .... CRAB
usage .... MODE
customer .... USER, BUYER, PATRON, CONSUMER
credit record .... PASSBOOK
present to a .... LAGN(I)APPE
customers ...... TRADE, CLIENTELE
customize .... SPECIALIZE
customs .... MORES
charge .... TAX, DUTY, IMPOST, TARIFF
collector: biblical .... MATTHEW
municipal .... OCTROI
official .... TAXMAN, ASSESSOR, SURVEYOR
station .... PORT OF ENTRY
cut ...... HEW, LOP, NIP, SAW, CLIP, SNIP, SEVER, INCISION, PRUNE(D), TRENCH, CURTAIL
across .... TRANSECT, INTERSECT
and dried .... DULL, FIXED, BORING, RIGGED, ROUTINE
apart piece by piece .... DISSECT
beef .... CHUCK
blubber .... FLENSE
close .... CLIP, CROP, SHAVE
colloquial .... SNUB, IGNORE
companion of ...... DRY, DRIED
corners .... GO DIRECT, SKIP OVER

crop .... REAP, GATHER, HARVEST
crudely .... HACKLE, HAGGLE
dead: colloq. .... SNUB, REBUFF, UPSTAGE, COLD SHOULDER
deep .... GASH
deeper, in engraving .... REENTER
down .... MOW, FELL, RAZE, SLAIN, SMASH, REDUCE
down trees .... LUMBER
edge of coin .... NIG
ends .... LOP, TRIM, SHEAR
expenses ..... SAVE, RETRENCH, ECONOMIZE
glass .... CRYSTAL
grass .... MOW
hair .... BARBER
horse's tail .... DOCK
in .... INTRUDE, INTERRUPT
in cubes .... DICE
in half .... HALVE, BISECT
in length .... ABRIDGE, SHORTEN
in thin slices .... SHAVE
into .... LANCE, INCISE
into small pieces .... DICE, HASH, MINCE
leather .... SKIVE
lengthwise .... SLIT
made by a saw/ax .... KERF
meat/roast/turkey .... CARVE
neck/off head .... BEHEAD, DECAPITATE
notch/slight .... NICK, SNICK
of meat .... CHOP, LOIN, CHINE, CHUCK, STEAK, T-BONE, SIRLOIN, SPARERIB
off ...... BOB, LOP, CLIP, DOCK, SEVER, KERF, POLL, ROACH, INTERCEPT, INTERRUPT
off piece/slice .... CANTLE
off wool .... POLL, SHEAR
out .... OMIT, ELIDE, EXCIDE, EXCEPT, EXCISE, EXSECT, EXSCIND, EXCLUDE, EXTIRPATE
out disk .... TREPAN
out unnecessary parts .... PRUNE
rind/skin .... PARE, PEEL
roughly .... HACK, HACKLE
saw-tooth edge .... PINK
short .... BOB, CLIP, CROP, POLL, STOP, BOBTAIL
slang .... SHARE
spiral grooves .... RIFLE
the mustard ..... ABLE, CAN DO
thin .... SKIVE, SLICE, SLIVER
thru water ...... PLOW, PLOUGH
to pieces .... MINCE, SHRED

to requirement .... TAILOR
to the body/skin .... WOUND
up into parts .... DIVIDE, SEPARATE
V-shaped .... NOTCH
way thru .... PLOW
with axe .... HEW, CHOP, HACK
with scissors .... SNIP
with sweeping stroke .... SLASH
cutback .... REDUCTION
on expenses ...... SAVE, SKIMP, ECONOMIZE, TIGHTEN ONE'S BELT
cutaneous .... DERMAL
cutch .... CATECHU
cute .... COY, DAINTY, SHARP, CANNY, CLEVER, PRETTY, SHREWD, CUNNING
colloquial .... SLICK
one: colloq. .... IMP
cuticle .... SKIN, EPIDERMIS
cutie .... DEARIE
cutis .... DERMA, CORIUM, DERMIS
cutlass .... CURTLE AX, (BROAD)SWORD
cutlery .... FLATWARE, TABLEWARE
item ...... FORK, KNIFE, SPOON, TEASPOON
cutlet, meat .... VEAL
veal .... SCHNITZEL
cutout pattern .... STENCIL
cutpurse .... DIP, THIEF, PICKPOCKET
cutrate .... CHEAP, BARGAIN, REDUCED, MARKED DOWN
cutter ...... BLADE, KNIFE, HEWER, SLICER, BREAKER
garment .... STITCHER, FINISHER
leaf .... ANT, WORM
of life's thread .... ATROPOS
of precious stones .... LAPIDARY
ride covering .... LAPROBE
vessel .... SLED, SLOOP, YACHT, SLEIGH
cutthroat .... THUG, ASSASSIN, STIFF, GRUELING, MURDERER
cutting .... RAW, KEEN, TART, KERF, NIPPY, SHARP, BITING, CAUSTIC, INCISIVE, STINGING, KEEN-EDGED, TRENCHANT
British .... CLIPPING
edge .... LIP
off last letter of word .... APOCOPE
off vowel .... ELISION
part of tool .... BIT, BLADE
plant .... (S)CION

remarks .... DIG, RAP, SWIPE,
INSULT, SARCASM
tool .... AX(E), ADZ(E), BUR,
SAW, BOLO, KNIFE, MOWER,
RAZOR, SCYTHE, SHEARS,
SICKLE, MACHETE, SCISSORS
tool, engraver's .... BURIN,
CHASER, CHISEL, GRAVER
tool holder .... ARBOR
tool seller .... CUTLER
tools .... CUTLERY
tooth .... INCISOR
cuttlefish .... SQUID, BELEMNITE
bone .... POUNCE
ejecting organ .... SIPHON
fluid/secretion .... INK, SEPIA
fossil .... BELEMNITE,
THUNDERSTONE
kin .... SPIRULA
cutup .... CLOWN, HUMORIST,
PRANKSTER
cutwork .... EMBROIDERY,
NEEDLEWORK
cuvette .... BASIN, TEST TUBE
Cuzco Indian .... INCA
location of .... PERU
Cy Young awardee ...... GIBSON,
MCLAIN, SEAVER
cyanic .... BLUE, AZURINE,
CERULEAN
cyanosis .... BLUENESS,
AZURENESS
cyanotype .... BLUEPRINT
Cybele .... OPS, RHEA, KYBELE,
AGDISTIS
beloved of .... ATTIS
daughter of .... JUNO, HERA
father of .... URANUS
husband of .... CRONUS,
SATURN
mother of .... GAEA
son of .... ZEUS, JUPITER
cybernation .... AUTOMATION,
ROBOT CONTROL
cybernaut .... ROBOT
Cyclades .... IOS, ZEA, KEOS,
MILO, DELOS, MELOS, NAXOS,
PAROS, TINOS
cycle .... AGE, RIDE, WHEEL,
ROUND, CIRCLE, PERIOD
of 15 years .... INDICTION
of heavenly body .... ORBIT
of the sun and moon, eclipse
.... SAROS
of years .... EON, EPOCH
vehicle .... BIKE, BICYCLE,
TRICYCLE, MOTORCYCLE
cycloid .... CIRCULAR
cyclone .... GALE, VORTEX,
TORNADO, TWISTER,
TYPHOON, HURRICANE,

WINDSTORM
cyclonic .... ANGRY, RAGING,
STORMY
cyclonite .... EXPLOSIVE
Cyclopean .... HUGE, STRONG,
MASSIVE, ENORMOUS,
GIGANTIC
Cyclops .... GIANT
characteristic of .... ONE-EYED
Odysseus' captor
.... POLYPHEMUS
cyclorama ...... EXHIBIT, PICTURE,
SCENERY, PANORAMA
cyclostome .... HAGFISH, LAMPREY
cyesis .... GESTATION, PREGNANCY
cygnet .... SWAN
Cygnus .... SWAN,
CONSTELLATION
star in .... DENEB
cylinder .... CASK, ROLL, BARREL,
COLUMN, PILLAR
covering .... LAG(GING)
for conveying air, water
.... PIPE, TRUNK
hollow .... DRUM, PIPE, TUBE
in a cylinder .... PISTON
of coins .... ROULEAU
of metal, for dams, dikes
.... GABION
of vascular tissues in plants
.... STELE
part .... END, HEAD, PISTON
printing press .... INKER,
PLATEN, ROLLER
revolving ...... WHEEL, ROLLER
spiral .... HELIX
to roll out dough ..... ROLLING
PIN
tree .... BOLE, TRUNK
water marker .... DANDY,
ROLLER
cylindrical .... TUBULAR,
COLUMNAR, TOROSE, DRUM-
SHAPED, TUBE-SHAPED
and tapered .... TERETE
cyma .... GOLA, MOLDING
cymar .... CHEMISE
cymbals .... TAL, ZEL
cyme .... PHLOX
Cymric .... WELSH, BRETON,
CELTIC
cynic .... DOUBTER, DEFEATIST,
TIMON, RAILER, PESSIMIST,
CRITIC, BELITTLER,
MISANTHROPE
look of .... COLD, LEER,
SMIRK, SNEER
of sorts ..... KNOCKER, SKEPTIC
cynical .... CAPTIOUS, CRITICAL,
DOUBTING, SARCASTIC

cynicism .... IRONY, SATIRE,
SARCASM, PESSIMISM
cynosure .... LODESTAR,
POLESTAR, NORTH STAR
Cynthia .... LUNA, MOON, DIANA,
ARTEMIS
diminutive of .... CINDY
cypress .... SILK, TREE, CLOTH,
SATIN
cyprinoid .... IDE, CHUB, CARP,
DACE, BARBEL, GOLDFISH
Cyprus cape .... GATA, GRECO,
ANDREAS, ARNAUTI
capital .... NICOSIA
city/town .... DHALI, LEFKA,
PAPHOS, KYRENIA, LARNACA,
MORPHOU, LIMASSOL,
FAMAGUSTA
language .... GREEK,
CYPRIOT(E), TURKISH
leader .... MAKARIOS
liquid measure .... CASS
monetary unit
.... (CYPRIOT)POUND
mountain .... TROODOS
native .... CYPRIAN, CYPRIOT
union with Greece ..... ENOSIS
Cyrano, creator of
.... (EDMOND)ROSTAND
shame of .... (LARGE)NOSE
Cyrenaica .... BARCA
capital .... CYRENE
Cytherea ...... VENUS, APHRODITE
cyst .... BAG, SAC, WEN, LUMP,
POUCH, VESICLE
behind the knee .... BAKER'S
infested with amoebas
.... AMEBIASIS
sebaceous .... WEN
type of skin .... DERMOID
with worm larvae
.... HYDATID
czar .... BOSS, TSAR, DESPOT,
EMPEROR, AUTOCRAT,
NICHOLAS
daughter of .... CZAREVNA,
TSAREVNA
heir of .... CZAREVITCH
wife of .... CZARINA, EMPRESS,
TSARINA, CZARITZA
Czechoslovakian .... SLAV,
SLOVAK, BOHEMIAN,
MORAVIAN, SILESIAN
brandy .... SLIVOVITZ
capital .... PRAGUE (PRAHA)
castle .... HRADCANY
city/town .... BRNO, OPAVA,
DECIN, PLZEN, TABOR,
KLADNO, KOSICE, TRNAVA,
ZVOLEN, OLOMOUC, OSTRAVA,

SUMPERK, TEPLICE CHOMUTOV, HANDLOVA, PARDUBICE, BRATISLAVA, BUDEJOVICE, GOTTWALDOV, HRADEC KRALOVE
coin .... DUCAT, KRONEN, HELLER, KORUNA
composer .... DVORAK, JANACEK, SMETANA, (RUDOLF)FRIML
dramatist .... CAPEK
folk hero .... SCHWEIK
forest .... BOHEMIAN
hero .... (JAN)HUS
historian .... PALACKY
language .... CZECH, SLOVAK
leader .... HUSAK, DUBCHEK
measure .... LAN, MIRA

measure, distance .... SAH, LATRO
monetary unit .... KORUNA
mountain .... GERLACHOVKA
mountains .... BESKIDS, JESENIKY, SUDETEN, ERZGEBIRGE, HIGH TATRA, WHITE CARPATHIANS
munition works .... SKODA
news agency .... CETEKA
passage .... JABLUNKA
patriot .... BENES, MASARYK, STEFANIK
premier .... LENART, CERNI(C)K
president .... BENES, HAVEL, MASARYK, NOVOTNY, SVOBODA, GOTTWALD
public square ...... WENCESLAS

rail center .... ZILINA
region ...... PRAHA, JIHOCESKY, BRATISLAVA, SEVEROCESKY, STREDOCESKY, ZAPADOCESKY, VYCHODOCESKY, SEVEROMORAVSKY
republic ..... CZECH SOCIALIST, SLOVAK SOCIALIST
river .... DYJE, HRON, IPEL, LABE, ODER, ODRA, OHRE, VAH, NITRA, ORAVA, HORNAD, DANUBE, MOLDAU, MORAVA, ONDAVA, SAZAVA, TORYSA, UHLAVA, VLTAVA, DUNAJEC, JIHLAVA, LUZNICE, SVITAVA, BEROUNKA
statesman .... BENES
steel works .... SKODA

D

D, Greek .... DELTA
Hebrew .... DALEDH, DALETH
in a sequence .... FOURTH
in chemistry .... DEUTERIUM
letter .... DEE, DELTA
Roman numeral ..... 500, FIVE HUNDRED
symbol for .... DENSITY
DA/D.A. ...... DISTRICT ATTORNEY
dab .... BIT, PAT, TAP, BLOT, PECK, SPOT, PAINT, STAIN, SMEAR, TOUCH, STRIKE, FLATFISH, FLOUNDER
a pitched ball .... BUNT
colloquial .... EXPERT
lightly .... BRUSH, SMOOTH
of salt .... PINCH
dabble .... DIP, WET, POTTER, TRIFLE, SPLASH, TINKER, MOISTEN, SPATTER
in .... SMATTER, TOY WITH
dabbler .... TYRO, DUFFER, AMATEUR, DABSTER, GREENHORN, DILETTANTE
dabchick .... GREBE, DIPPER, DUCKER, DIDAPPER, HELL-DIVER
dabster: colloq. .... EXPERT, DABBLER
dace .... CARP
dacha .... COTTAGE, COUNTRY-HOUSE
dachshund .... (GERMAN)DOG
characteristic ..... LONG BODY, SHORT LEGS, DROOPING EARS
dacoit .... BANDIT, ROBBER
dacron .... FIBER

dactyl, in zoology .... TOE, FINGER
dactylogram .... FINGERPRINT
dad .... FATHER
poetic .... SIRE
daddy ...... DAD, POP, PAPA, POPS, PAPPY, FATHER
kind of: sl. .... SUGAR
longlegs .... CRANE-FLY, SPIDER, SPINNER, CENTIPEDE, HARVESTMAN
dado .... DIE, BEZEL, GROOVE, RABBET, WAINSCOT
daedal .... MAZY, VARIED, RAVELED, ELABORATE, INGENIOUS, INTRICATE, MULTI-COLORED
Daedalus' son .... ICARUS
victim/nephew .... TALOS
daemon .... DEMON, DEVIL, SPIRIT, SPECTER
daffodil .... NARCISSUS
plant resembling ...... JONQUIL
Daffy, baseball player ...... DEAN
colloquial .... CRAZY, SILLY, FOOLISH, SCREWY, GOOFY, WACKY, IDIOTIC
daft .... MAD, CRAZY, SILLY, INSANE, IDIOTIC, WITLESS
slang .... LOCO, LOONY, PSYCHO, COCKEYED
dagger .... DIRK, SNEE, KNIFE, BODKIN, CREESE, WEAPON, STYLET, PIERCER
archaic .... DUDGEON
attached to gun ...... BAYONET
Burmese .... DAH

double, reference mark .... DIESIS
handle .... HAFT, HILT
look .... ANGER, HATRED
mark, in printing .... DIESIS, OBELUS, OBELISK
Malay .... CRIS(S), KRIS, CREESE
medieval .... ANLACE
of mercy .... MISERICORD(E)
old-time .... SNEE
signs in printing .... OBELI
stroke .... STAB, LUNGE, THRUST, STOCCADO
two-edged .... COUTEAU
type of .... DIRK, KRIS, SKEAN, KUTTAR, PONIARD, STILETTO, MISERICORD
wound .... STAB
daguerreotype .... COLLOTYPE, PHOTOSTAT, PHOTOGRAPH
Dahomey .... BENIN
capital .... PORTO NOVO
chief of state .... SOGLO
city/town ...... NIKKI, ABOMEY, COTONOU, LOKOSSA, PARAKOU, NATITIGOU
ethnic group .... FON, ADJA, MAHI, BARIBA, YORUBA
gulf .... GUINEA
language .... MINA, DENDI, SOMBA, BARIBA, YORUBA
monetary unit .... FRANC
mountains .... ATAKORA
native .... FON
region .... SUDAN
river ..... MONO, NIGER, OUEME

seaport .... OUIDAH
Dai Nippon .... JAPAN
Dailey, ____ .... DAN
daily .... DIURNAL, EVERYDAY,
ONCE A DAY, PER DIEM,
QUOTIDIAN
delivery .... MAIL, MILK,
NEWSPAPER
dozen .... EXERCISES,
CONSTITUTIONAL
fare .... DIET
feature article .... COLUMN
newspaper .... JOURNAL
published .... NEWSPAPER
record .... DIARY, JOURNAL
daimio .... NOBLEMAN
retainer of .... SAMURAI
dainties ...... TIDBITS, DELICACIES
dainty .... CUTE, FINE, NEAT,
NICE, RARE, SUBTLE,
DELICATE, EXQUISITE,
FASTIDIOUS
archaic .... CATE
fabric .... SILK, TAFFETA
French .... MIGNON
daiquiri .... COCKTAIL
ingredient .... RUM, LIME
Dairen .... DALNY, TALIEN
dairy .... LACTARY, LACTARIUM
cattle .... JERSEY
farm area .... MILKSHED
maid .... DEY, GOWAN
product .... MILK, CREAM,
BUTTER, CHEESE
shop .... CREAMERY
dais .... STAGE, PODIUM, ESTRADE,
ROSTRUM, TRIBUNE,
PLATFORM
daisy .... OXEYE, SHASTA, GOWAN,
MARGUERITE,
CHRYSANTHEMUM
____ .... MAE
cutter, baseball ..... GROUNDER
English .... GOWAN
dak .... MAIL
Dakar is capital of ...... SENEGAL
natives .... SENEGALESE
Daker hen .... CORN-CRAKE
Dakota Indian .... MANDAN,
SIOUX
Dakotan .... TETON
Dalai Lama .... RULER, BUDDHIST
PRIEST
dale .... DELL, GLEN, VALE, DENE,
DINGLE, VALLEY
Dale .... EVANS, CARNEGIE
Dali, painter .... SALVADOR,
SURREALIST
art of .... SURREALISM
dalles .... RAPIDS
dalliance .... FLIRTATION

dally .... TOY, DELAY, FLIRT, IDLE,
LOITER, TRIFLE, PROLONG
Dalmatian .... DOG, SLAV
decor .... SPOTS
dog's name .... SPOT
dam .... CLOG, DIKE, PLUG,
EMBANK, BARRAGE, BARRIER,
KEEP BACK, MILLPOND
archaic .... MOTHER
builder, animal .... OTTER
designer .... SAVAGE
Egyptian/Nile .... SADD,
ASWAN
for military fortification
.... SANDBAGS
horse .... MARE
in a stream/canal
.... FLOODGATE
in the U.S. .... COULEE,
HOOVER, SHASTA, BOULDER
river .... WEIR, LEVEE
to break force of waves
.... SEAWALL
up a river .... STEM
damage .... MAR, HARM, LOSS,
HURT, ABUSE, DEFECT,
IMPAIR, BRUISE, SCATHE,
INJURE, INJURY
colloquial .... COST, EXPENSE
slang .... BUNG
suit .... TORT, TROVER
damages, claim for ...... TROVER
daman .... CONY, CONEY, HYRAX,
MAMMAL
Damansky to the Chinese
.... CHEN PAO
Damascene .... PLUM
Damascus caliph .... OMMIAD
is capital of .... SYRIA
damask .... LINEN,
(DAMASCUS)STEEL
flower .... ROSE
for hangings .... DORNICK
for vestments, etc.
.... DORNICK, DORNOCK
like cloth .... LAMPAS
dame .... LADY, MADAM, MATRON,
MISTRESS
equivalent title of .... SIR
luring .... DRAWING BROAD
slang .... GAL, GIRL, WOMAN
title of noble .... DUCHESS,
COUNTESS
dammar .... RESIN
damn .... DOOM, CURSE, VILIFY,
CONDEMN, DESTROY
damnation .... RUIN, HAVOC,
PERDITION
damned .... LOST, CURSED,
DEFAMED, ACCURSED,
CONDEMNED, CONVICTED

dialectic .... TARNAL,
TARNATION
the ...... LOST SOULS, SOULS IN
HELL
damning .... SURE, CERTAIN,
CONVINCING
beholder .... EYE-WITNESS
Damocles, word associated
with .... SWORD
damoiselle .... MISS, DAMSEL
Damon and ____ .... PYTHIAS
damp .... WET, DANK, DEWY,
MIST, HUMID, MOIST, STIFLE
and hot .... MUGGY
become .... JIG
dampen .... WET, DARKEN,
SADDEN, DEPRESS, MOISTEN,
DISCOURAGE, DISHEARTEN
the spirits .... DASH, KNOCK
DOWN
damper .... KILLJOY, WET
BLANKET
damsel .... GIRL, LASS, MAID,
MISSY, MAIDEN
fly .... DRAGONFLY
damson .... PLUM
Dan .... SIR, BUOY, MASTER
Cupid .... EROS
Dane .... JUTLANDER
dance .... HOP, BALL, ROMP,
CAPER, GALOP, BALLET,
BUNNYHOP, TRIPPING
African-American folk
.... JUBA, CAKEWALK
arranger/designer
.... CHOREOGRAPHER
attendance .... WAIT ON
Bohemian .... POLKA, REDOWA
Brazilian .... SAMBA, BOSSA-
NOVA
child on knee .... DANDLE
college/school ...... HOP, PROM
colloquial .... DRAG, SHINDIG
costume party
.... MASQUERADE
country ...... HAY, BARN, REEL,
SQUARE, LANDLER
crazed person .... TARANTIST
Cuban .... CONGA, MAMBO,
R(H)UMBA, HABANERA
English .... MORRIS
folk .... HORA, DREHER
for two .... TANGO, WALTZ,
FOXTROT
French .... BAL, GAVOT,
MINUET, GALLIARD,
RIGADOON, FARANDOLA,
QUADRILLE
frontier .... REEL
German .... ALLEMANDE
hall .... GAFF, CASINO,

CABARET, BALLROOM, NIGHTCLUB, DISCOTHEQUE
hall girl .... HOSTESS
Hawaiian .... HULA-(HULA)
Hungarian .... CZARDAS
in a boisterous way .... HORSE AROUND
in a playful manner .... FRISK, FROLIC, GAMBOL
in ragtime .... ONE-STEP
Israeli .... HORA
Italian .... COURANTE
kind of .... TAP, TOE, BELLY, FRUG, POLKA, BALLET, WALTZ, FOXTROT, SOFTSHOE
Latin-American .... CONGA, CHA-CHA
line .... CONGA
lively .... JUBA, REEL, FLING, CONGA, GALOP, CORANTO, GAVOTTE, COURANTE, FANDANGO, HORNPIPE, COTILLION, GALLOPADE, TAMBOURIN, SALTARELLO
mimetic .... HULA
modern .... FRUG, SHAG, DISCO, BOOGIE, LAMBADA, ROCK N'ROLL
music .... JAZZ, SWING, MAMBO, TANGO, VALSE, WALTZ, FOXTROT, RAGTIME, BOOGIE-WOOGIE
of death ...... DANSE MACABRE
of early 1940's ..... JITTERBUG
of 1930 .... SHAG
of 1929 .... CHARLESTON
old .... PAVIN, PAVAN(E), CAROLE
Polish .... POLKA, POLONAISE
polka like .... MAZ(O)URKA
Russian .... KAZATSKA, KAZATSKY
sailor's .... HORNPIPE
Scottish .... REEL
slang .... HOOF
slow, graceful .... ADAGIO, MINUET
South American .... TANGO, CARIOCA
Southwest .... BAILE
Spanish .... TANGO, BOLERO, MORISCO, FANDANGO, FLAMENCO
square .... DOSADOS, HOEDOWN, LANC(I)ERS
stately ..... MINUET, SARABAND
step .... PAS, SHAG, CHASSE, SHUFFLE, CURTSY, GLISSADE
triple time .... JIG
two-fourth time .... GALOP
violent .... APACHE

Virginia .... REEL
war .... PYRRHIC
watcher .... WALLFLOWER
white-tie .... FORMAL
with castanets .... BOLERO, FLAMENCO
with handclapping .... JUBA
with high kicking .... CANCAN
with wooden shoes .... CLOG
dancer .... ARTIST, HOPPER, CHORINE, PRANCER, STEPPER, RAND, ALMA, ALME(H), CASTLE, ROGERS, ZORINA, ASTAIRE
ballet .... RASCH, FONTEYN, NUREYEV, PAVLOVA, SHEARER, ULANOVA, CORYPHEE, FIGURANT, BALLERINA
burlesque .... STRIPPER, ECDYSIAST, STRIPTEASER
co-worker of .... COMET
concern of .... STEPS, RHYTHM, SLIPPERS, CHOREOGRAPHY
costume of .... TUTU, MOTLEY, TIGHTS, LEOTARD
French .... DANSEUR, DANSEUSE
jazz music .... JITTERBUG
kind of .... TAP, TOE, BELLY, LIMBO, APACHE, BALLET, FLAMENCO, STRIPTEASE
noted American .... (MARTHA) GRAHAM
noted fan .... RAND
professional/tap .... HOOFER
shoe of .... CLOG
dancing .... SALTANT, SALTATION, CHOREOGRAPHY
craze for .... TARANTISM, TARENTISM
girl, Biblical .... SALOME
girl, chorus line .... CHORINE
girl, Egyptian .... ALMA, ALME(H)
girl, employed .... TAXI DANCER
girl, feature of discotheque .... GOGO DANCER
girl, Indian .... ALME(H), BAYADEER, BAYADERE, NAUTCH GIRL
girl, Japanese .... GEISHA
horses .... LIPPIZAN(ER)
kind of .... TAP, TOE, CLOG, FRUG, FOLK, BELLY, SQUARE, POLKA, COUNTRY, BALLROOM, MONKEY, SOFTSHOE
master .... MURRAY, ASTAIRE
muse of .... TERPSICHORE

partner, professional .... GIGOLO
place also .... CASINO
position ...... CHEEK TO CHEEK
shoes .... PUMPS
dandelion ...... WEED, KOK-SAGYZ
stalk .... SCAPE
tuft .... PUFFBALL
dander .... SCALES
allergy to .... RHINITIS
colloquial .... IRE, ANGER, WRATH, TEMPER
type of human ...... DANDRUFF
dandify .... DRESS UP, SPRUCE
dandle .... PET, DANCE, CARESS, FONDLE
dandruff .... SCURF, FLAKES, FURFUR, SCALES
dandy .... FOP, BEAU, BUCK, DUDE, PRIG, TOFF, NATTY, COXCOMB
English .... MACARONI
fever .... DENGUE
roll impression .... WATER MARK
slang .... FINE, LULU, DILLY, JOHNNY, JOHNNIE, FIRST RATE, FIRST CLASS
dandyish .... BUCKISH, FOPPISH
danger ...... RISK, PERIL, HAZARD, JEOPARDY
hidden .... AMBUSH, PITFALL
in a body of water .... WHIRLPOOL
sign .... SYMPTOM
signal ...... RED, ALARM, SIREN
that attracts/tempts .... GIN, TRAP, SNARE
dangerous .... RISKY, UNSAFE, PARLOUS, CRITICAL, PERILOUS
and clever .... SHREWD
slang .... HAIRY
dangle .... HANG, LOLL
dangling .... ALOP, LOOSE
Daniel .... BOONE, DEFOE, WEBSTER
Danish .... DANE, PASTRY
astronomer .... BRAHE
cape ...... THE SKAW, SKAGENS ODDE
capital .... COPENHAGEN
channel .... LILLE BAELT, STORE BAELT
cheese .... BRIE, ELBO, TYBO, DANBO, FYNBO, MOLBO, MARIBO, MYCELLA, CAMEMBERT
chieftain .... JARL
city/town ...... VEJLE, ALBORG, LYNGBY, ODENSE, TARNBY, KOLDING, RANDERS,

GENTOFTE, HORSENSE, NAESTVED, ROSKILDE

coin .... ORA, ORE, ORAS, KRONE, RIGSDALER

composer .... NIELSEN

district .... AMT

duchy .... HOLSTEIN

"farmer prince" .... INGOLF

fjord .... ISE

historian .... SAXO

horse .... ZAIN

island .... ALS, FYN, MON, OMO, FEJO, MORS, ROMO, LAESO, SAMSO, AMAGER, SEJERO, ARNHOLT, FALSTER, LOLLAND

king .... CNUT, KNUT, CANUTE, FREDERIK, WALDEMAR

king, Shakespearean .... HAMLET

land measure .... MORGEN

legislature/parliament .... RIGSDAG, FOLKETING

measure, distance .... FOD, MIL, MUL, ALEN

monetary unit .... KRONE

mountain .... TRANEBJERG, YDING SKOVHOJ

native .... DANE

navigator .... BERING

noble .... JARL

novelist .... NEXO

peninsula .... JUTLAND

physicist .... BOHR, OERSTED

pianist .... BORGE

queen .... INGRID

river .... SUSAA, GELSAA, STORAA, GUDENAA

sea .... BALTIC

seaport .... AARHUS, HELSINGOR

sound .... ORESUND

strait .... FEHMARN, KATTEGAT, SKAGERRAK

toast .... SKOAL

weight .... LOD, ORT, VOG, ESER, PUND

dank .... WET, DAMP, DEWY, HUMID, MOIST, MUGGY, CLAMMY

Danny, actor .... KAYE

Danse _____ .... MACABRE

danseuse .... DANCER, CORYPHEE, FIGURANT, BALLERINA

Dante's beloved .... BEATRICE

deathplace .... RAVENNA

work ..... INFERNO, THE DIVINE COMEDY

Danube city .... ULM, LINZ

in German .... DONAU

in Hungarian .... DUNA

in Romanian .... DUNAREA

of .... DANUBIAN

river .... SAU, ULM, ISAR, SAVA, MORAVA

Danzig .... GDANSK

dap .... DAB, DIB, DIP, SKIP, BOUNCE, DIBBLE

daphne .... SHRUB, LAUREL

flower family .... MEZEREUM

Daphne .... NYMPH

Daphnis' lover .... CHLOE

dapper .... CHIC, NEAT, TRIM, NATTY, SMART, SPRUCE, DASHING

slang .... SWANK, SNAZZY

dapple .... PIED, FLECK(ED), MOTTLED, PIEBALD, SPOTTED

poetic .... FREAK

Dar es Salaam is capital of .... TANZANIA

darb .... DART, DILLY

Darcy's forte .... PRIDE

Dardan .... TROJAN

Dardanelles .... STRAIT, HELLESPONT

dare .... TRY, DAST, DEFI, DEFY, FACE, RISK, OPPOSE, ATTEMPT, VENTURE, CHALLENGE

daredevil ...... BOLD, RASH, WILD, RECKLESS, FOOLHARDY

person .... HELLCAT, STUNTMAN, ADVENTURER

daresay ...... DEEM, INFER, THINK, RECKON, BELIEVE, CONCEIVE

Darien .... GULF, ISTHMUS

daring ...... BOLD, WILD, BRAVE, HARDY, RISQUE, BRAVURA, ICARIAN, INTREPID

action .... DERRING-DO

slang .... GOING FOR BROKE

Darius scene of defeat .... ISSUS

dark ...... DIM, EBON, EVIL, INKY, BLACK, DUSKY, MIRK, MURK(Y), UNLIT, SABLE, HIDDEN, RAYLESS, CLOUDY, GLOOMY, SINISTER, TENEBROUS, TENEBREFIC

and dull ...... SOMBER, SOMBRE

area of vision .... SCOTOMA

brown .... SEPIA, BISTER, BISTRE, BRUNET(TE)

colored .... DUSKY, SOMBER, SWARTHY

complexion .... BLACK, MELANO, COLORED, SWARTHY

haired .... MELANOUS, BRUNET(TE)

horse: colloq. .... SLEEPER, LONG-SHOT, OFF-CHANCE

hue .... SWART, SOMBRE

in the .... BLIND, UNAWARE, IGNORANT

marking in marble ..... CLOUD

pigmented .... MELANOID

portending rain ..... LOWERING

red .... LAKY, WINISH

skinned .... SWARTHY, MELANOUS

skinned person .... WOP, DAGO, NEGRO, AFRICAN, NEGRILLO, COLORED, AFRO-AMERICAN, AFRICAN-AMERICAN

wood .... EBONY, MAHOGANY

Dark Age .... BARBARISM

Continent .... AFRICA

darken .... DIM, INK, BLACKEN, (BE)CLOUD, EBONIZE, SHADOW, NEGRIFY, OBSCURE

darkey/darky ...... NEGRO, BLACK MAN

darkish .... BLACKISH

darkness .... DUSK, NIGHT, BLACKNESS, MIDNIGHT, OBSCURITY

combining form .... SCOTO

of hair/skin .... MELANISM

darling .... PET, IDOL, ANGEL, BELOVED, CHERI(E), DEAREST, MINIKIN, FAVORITE, SWEETHEART

colloquial .... DEARY, TOOTS, DEARIE

darn .... FIX, MEND, PATCH

colloquial .... DAMN, CURSE

darnel .... TARE, WEED, COCKLE

darning needle .... DRAGONFLY

dart ...... BARB, BOLT, DASH, FLIT, ARROW, SCOOT, SPEAR, SPURT, THROW, SPRING, MISSILE

darter .... SNAKEBIRD

darts, bullfighter's .... BANDERILLA

Dartmoor .... GAOL, PRISON

Darwinian theory .... EVOLUTION, PANGENESIS

Darwinism .... EVOLUTIONISM

dash .... DART, ELAN, ARDOR, VERVE, WRITE, SMASH, THROW, SPIRIT, SPLASH

against .... LASH

at full speed .... SPRINT

colloquial .... DAM

mark .... HYPHEN

of salt .... BIT

off .... RUSH

one's hopes .... DESTROY, SHATTER, FRUSTRATE

opposed to .... DOT

with force .... CAST, HURL

dashboard .... PANEL
for short .... DASH
dasheen .... TARO, SPROUTS
dasher .... DOLLY
of a churn .... PLUNGER
dashing .... GAY, SHOWY, FLASHY,
JAUNTY, GALLANT, SPIRITED,
GALLOPING
manner .... BRAVURA,
PANACHE, DEVIL-MAY-CARE
dastard .... CAD, CREEP, COWARD,
CRAVEN, POLTROON
dastardly ...... MEAN, COWARDLY
dasyure .... MARSUPIAL
data .... FACTS, FIGURES,
INFORMATION
computer's .... INPUT
device carried by balloon
.... RADIO-SONDE
for pupil's parents
.... PROGRESS REPORT
date .... DAY, FRUIT, TRYST,
ESCORT, TIME, PERIOD,
CALENDS, STEADY,
APPOINTMENT, RENDEZVOUS
abbreviation .... APPT
approximate .... CIRCA
for launching an attack
.... D-DAY
fruit like .... JUJUBE
go on a .... STEP OUT
plum .... KAKI, PERSIMMON
out of .... PASSE, EXPIRED,
OBSOLETE, OLD-FASHIONED
sugar .... GHOOR
tree .... PALM
up to .... FRESH, CURRENT,
MODERN, ABREAST OF,
FASHIONABLE
dated .... PAST, PASSE, DECLASSE,
OBSOLETE, OLD-FASHIONED
dateless .... STAG
dating phrase .... AS OF, AS YET,
UNTIL NOW
datum plane example .... SEA
LEVEL
datura .... JIMSON
daub ...... PAINT, SMEAR, GREASE,
SPREAD, PLASTER, SLUBBER
daughter .... HIJA, FILLE,
OFFSPRING
daughter(s) of Atlas and
Pleione .... PLEIAD(ES)
daunt .... AWE, COW, FAZE,
BULLY, SCARE, DISMAY,
INTIMIDATE
dauntless .... BRAVE, FEARLESS,
UNDAUNTED, INTREPID
davenport .... DESK, SOFA, COUCH
David, for one .... CAMP

David's (King). See **King**
David
Davidoff's subject .... CIGARS
Davis, actress .... BETTE
Davis, Jr. .... SAMMY
davit .... CRANE
Davy Jones's locker
.... SEABOTTOM
daw .... CROW
dawdle .... LAG, IDLE, LOAF,
LINGER, LOITER, PIDDLE,
POTTER, PUTTER
dawdler .... IDLER, MOPER,
GOOFOFF
dawn ...... MORN, SUNUP, AURORA,
SUNRISE, DAYBREAK
crew .... FIRST SHIFT
goddess of .... EOS
herald of .... COCK, LARK,
ROOSTER
pertaining to .... EOAN
to noon .... MORNING
to sunset .... DAYTIME
day ...... AGE, ERA, EPACT, EPOCH,
LIGHT, PERIOD
and night of equal length
.... EQUINOX
bed .... SOFA, COUCH
before .... EVE
every .... DAILY
in court .... CHANCE, HEARING,
OPPORTUNITY
just past .... YESTERDAY
Latin .... DIES
letter .... TELEGRAM
march .... ETAPE
of greatest vigor ...... HEYDAY
Roman .... IDES, NONES
scholar .... EXTERN
star .... SUN
Day, actress ...... DORIS, LARAINE
Dayan .... MOSHE
daybook .... DIARY, JOURNAL
daybreak .... DAWN, MORN,
AURORA, DAWNING, SUNRISE
daydream .... FANCY, FANTASY,
REVERY, IMAGINE, REVERIE
daydreamer .... LOTUS-EATER,
RAINBOW-CHASER
daydreaming .... AUTISM,
REVERIE, UP IN THE CLOUDS
dayfly .... MAY FLY
daylight .... DAWN, SUNLIGHT,
LIMELIGHT, PUBLICITY
slang .... EYES
dayspring .... DAWN, SUNUP,
MORNING, SUNRISE
daytime, pertaining to
.... DIURNAL
days, describing youthful
.... SALAD

gone by .... HISTORY
Dayton suburb .... KETTERING
daze .... STUN, SHOCK, DAZZLE,
STUPOR, TRANCE, STUPEFY,
CONFUSION, BEWILDER(MENT)
dazzle .... BLIND, GLARE, SHINE,
GLITTER, IMPRESS
dazzling .... BRIGHT, GLARING,
BLINDING, PRISMATIC
momentarily .... METEORIC
DC time .... EST
DDE .... IKE
D.D.S. .... DENTIST
DDT .... PESTICIDE, INSECTICIDE
de facto .... ACTUAL, IN FACT
jure .... BY RIGHT
luxe ..... ELEGANT, SUMPTUOUS
De Leon .... PONCE
Maupassant .... GUY
Mille .... CECIL
deacon ...... CLERIC, CLERGYMAN,
ADULTERATE
clergyman above .... PRIEST
deactivate .... DEMOBILIZE
dead .... GONE, (A)MORT,
DEFUNCT, EXTINCT,
DECEASED, DEPARTED,
LIFELESS, INANIMATE
animal pretending to be
.... POSSUM
beat: colloq. .... TIRED, SPENT,
DRAINED, EXHAUSTED
bodies on battlefield
.... CARNAGE
body .... LICH, CORPSE,
CORPUS, CADAVER, CARCASE,
CARCASS
body: sl. .... STIFF
calm .... DOLDRUMS
combining form .... SAPRO
duck .... GONER
end ...... IMPASSE, CUL-DE-SAC,
BLIND ALLEY
end place .... SLUM, GHETTO
flesh .... CARRION
hand .... MORTMAIN
heat .... TIE, PHOTO FINISH
house .... CHARNEL,
MORTUARY, OSSARIUM
pan .... POKERFACE
pan comedian .... KEATON
person .... DECEASED,
DECEDENT
point .... CENTER
recently .... LATE
set .... FIRM, HELL-BENT,
DETERMINED
species .... EXTINCT
stop .... STANDSTILL
tired: sl. ...... BUSHED, POOPED
to .... UNAWARE

to the world .... ASLEEP

when delivered ..... STILLBORN

word preceding name of .... LATE

Dead End Kids member .... GORCEY

Sea find .... SCROLLS

kingdom .... MOAB

river .... JORDAN

scrolls location ..... QUMRAN

deadbeat: sl. .... LEECH, LOAFER, SPONGE(R), WELSHER, FREELOADER

deaden .... DULL, NUMB, BENUMB, DAMPEN, OBTUND, WEAKEN

sound .... MUTE, MUFFLE

deadener, pain .... OPIATE, CODEINE, DEMEROL, ANALGESIC, AN(A)ESTHETIC

deadeye .... SHARPSHOOTER

deadfall .... GIN, TRAP

deadline .... ZERO-HOUR, TIME-LIMIT, TARGET-DATE

deadlock .... TIE, DRAW, IMPASSE, STANDOFF, STALEMATE, STANDSTILL

jury .... HANG, HUNG

deadly .... FATAL FERAL, LETHAL, MORTAL, BANEFUL, HARMFUL, VIRULENT, DANGEROUS, MALIGNANT, INFECTIOUS

Archaic .... FELL

enemy .... NEMESIS

growth .... CANCER

plant .... IVY, UPAS, ERGOT, HEMLOCK, BANEWORT, LOCOWEED, WOLFSBANE, BELLADONNA, NIGHTSHADE

poison ...... ARSENIC, CYANIDE, NICOTINE, STRYCHNINE

sin .... ENVY, LUST, ANGER, PRIDE, SLOTH, GLUTTONY, COVETOUSNESS

snake .... ASP, COBRA

to both sides ..... INTERNECINE

deadpan .... MASK, BLANK, VAGUE

deadweight .... BURDEN

deaf .... SURD, EARLESS, HEEDLESS, UNHEARING

and _____ .... DUMB

and dumb language ...... MOTION, SIGNAL, GESTURE

and dumb person .... LIP READER

deafen .... STUN, SOUNDPROOF

Scottish .... DEAVE

deafening .... NOISY, EAR-SPLITTING

deafness .... IMPAIRED HEARING

at birth .... SENSORINEURAL

type of .... TOTAL, PARTIAL, CONDUCTIVE

deal .... DOLE, GIVE, SALE, ALLOT, TRADE, TREAT, BARTER, BESTOW, FIR WOOD, PINE WOOD, INFLICT, NEGOTIATE, ADMINISTER, DISTRIBUTE

a heavy blow .... SMITE

colloquial .... BARGAIN, AGREEMENT

crookedly .... PALTER

frankly: colloq. .... LEVEL

give-and-take .... (HORSE)TRADE

out .... DOLE, ISSUE

with .... COPE, HANDLE, MANAGE

with a difficult problem .... GRAPPLE

dealer .... BUYER, MONGER, SELLER, TRADER, CHAPMAN, DISTRIBUTOR

cattle .... DROVER

cloth/dry goods .... DRAPER, MERCER, CLOTHIER

cutting tools .... CUTLER

foodstuff .... GROCER

gem .... LAPIDARY

in bonds .... (STOCK)BROKER

in house/lots .... REALTOR

in skins .... FURRIER

right of .... PONE

scrap .... RAGMAN, JUNKMAN

smuggled goods .... BLACK MARKETEER

dealing(s) .... TRADE, COMMERCE, RELATIONS, TRANSACTION(S)

dean .... DOYEN

ecclesiastical .... PREFECT

feminine .... DOYENNE

of a .... DECANAL

residence of .... DEANERY

Dean, baseball player .... DAFFY, DIZZY

deanery .... DECANAL

dean's list .... ACHIEVERS

dear .... LOVE, COSTLY, BELOVED, DARLING, PRECIOUS, CHERISHED, EXPENSIVE

slang .... HONEY, TOOTS

dearie .... DARLING, SWEETHEART

dearness: sl. .... HIGHWAY ROBBERY

dearth .... LACK, FAMINE, PAUCITY, SCARCITY

death .... END, DOOM, LOSS, MORT, DEMISE, DECEASE, PASSING, EXPIRATION, ETERNAL REST

by beheading ...... GUILLOTINE

by burning .... SUTTEE

by hanging, with the .... ROPE, NOOSE

causing .... FATAL, LETHAL, MORTAL

cup .... MUSHROOM

defying .... BOLD

herald of .... BANSHEE, BANSHIE

march/song .... DIRGE

march scene .... BATAAN

mercy .... EUTHANASIA

near .... DYING

noise .... GASP, RATTLE

notice .... OBIT(UARY), NECROLOGY

of .... LETHAL, MORTUARY

painless, easy .... EUTHANASIA

put to .... HANG, KILL, SLAY, EXECUTE, ASSASSINATE

rate .... MORTALITY

rattle .... RALE

ring announcing .... TOLL, KNELL

self-inflicted .... SUICIDE

sentence .... DAMNATION, CONVICTION

sentence, to carry out .... GAS CHAMBER, ELECTRIC CHAIR

slang .... CURTAINS

symbol .... SKULL

toll .... LOSS, KNELL

view of .... THANATOPSIS

deathblow .... COUP DE GRACE

deathless .... LASTING, IMMORTAL

deathlessness .... ATHANASIA, PERPETUITY

death's-head .... SKULL

deathsman .... HANGMAN, EXECUTIONER

deathwatch .... WAKE, VIGIL, BEETLE

deave .... DEAFEN

deb .... BUD, DEBUTANTE

debacle .... ROUT, PANIC, DISASTER, STAMPEDE

debar ...... DENY, FORBID, HINDER, REFUSE, EXCLUDE

debark .... LAND, ALIGHT, UNLOAD

debase .... LOWER, DEFILE, DEMEAN, CORRUPT, DEGRADE, PERVERT, PROFANE, VITIATE, ADULTERATE

liquid .... DILUTE

metal .... ALLOY

morally .... DEBAUCH, DEPRAVE

debasement .... IMPURITY, CORRUPTION

debatable .... MOOT, CONTESTABLE,

QUESTIONABLE, CONTROVERSIAL

debate .... ARGUE, FORUM, PLEAD, REASON, CANVASS, CONTEND, DISCUSS, DISPUTE, PALAVER, CAUSERIE, PHILOSOPHIZE

art of formal .... POLEMICS

ending device .... CLOTURE

pertaining to .... FORENSIC

debater .... POLEMIST, DISPUTANT, POLEMICIST

debauch .... ORGY, RUIN, DEBASE, CORRUPT, DEPRAVE

prolonged .... HELLBENDER

debauchee .... RAKE, ROUE, SATYR, LECHER, LIBERTINE

downfall of .... RIOTOUS LIVING

debauchery .... ORGY, RIOT, CAROUSAL

debenture .... BOND, VOUCHER

debilitate .... WEAKEN, SICKEN, CRIPPLE, DISABLE, ENERVATE, ENFEEBLE

debilitated .... SAPPED, RUN-DOWN

debility .... ATONY, ASTHENIA

debit .... CHARGE

debonair ...... GAY, AIRY, PERKY, SUAVE, GENIAL, JAUNTY, AFFABLE, CAREFREE

urbane fellow .... CITY SLICKER

debouch .... EXPEL, EMERGE, SURFACE

debouche .... OUTLET

debris ...... RUINS, SCREE, TRASH, LITTER, REFUSE, RUBBISH, RUBBLE, DETRITUS

tree prunings .... BRASH

debt ...... LOAN, OWING, ACCOUNT, BORROWING, LIABILITY, OBLIGATION

bad .... NONPAYMENT

evader .... DEADBEAT, DEFAULTER

gambling .... HONORARY

in theology .... SIN

overdue .... ARREAR(S)

relating to .... DEBIT

settlement .... PAYOFF

debtor .... OWER, BORROWER

debtor's note .... IOU

prison .... FLEET

debunk .... EXPOSE, REFUTE, UNMASK

Debussy, composer ...... ACHILLE CLAUDE

composition .... REVERIE

topic of .... SEA

debut .... ENTRANCE,

APPEARANCE, INTRODUCTION, PRESENTATION

debutant(e) .... BUD, DEB

ball .... COTILLION

delight of .... STAGLINE

party for .... COMING OUT

decade .... TEN, DECENNIUM

"Beat" .... THE SIXTIES

decadence .... DECAY, BLIGHT, DECLINE, DETERIORATION

decadent ...... WASTED, DECREPIT, BLASE, CRUMBLING, BROKEN DOWN

decalogue .... CODE, ETHICS

number .... TEN

part of .... COMMANDMENT

Decameron Tales author
.... BOCCACCIO

decamp .... BOLT, FLEE, ABSCOND, CLEAR OUT, RUN AWAY, VAMO(O)SE

decanal .... DEANERY

decant .... POUR, DRAIN, ELUTRIATE

decanter .... BOTTLE, CARAFE

stand .... TANTALUS

decapitate .... BEHEAD, DECOLLATE

decapitation .... EXECUTION

decapod .... CRAB, PRAWN, SQUID, SHRIMP, LOBSTER

decay .... ERODE, SPOIL, EROSION, PUTREFY, GANGRENE, DECOMPOSE

cause of tooth .... PLAQUE

dental/tooth .... CARIES

fruit .... ROT, BLET

into dust .... CRUMBLE

iron/steel .... RUST

moral .... SLOUGH, CORRUPTION

slow, crumbling
.... MO(U)LDER

decayed .... PUTRID, ROTTEN, CARIOUS, CORRUPT

in botany .... DOTY

in fruit .... BLET

decaying .... WANEY, ROTTING, DECLINING

combining form .... SAPRO

dead body .... CARRION

from age .... DOTING

vegetable matter .... DUFF

decease .... DIE, DEATH, DEMISE

deceased .... DEAD, LATE, PARTED, DECEDENT, DEPARTED

deceit .... LIE, WILE, FRAUD, GUILE, COZENAGE, TRICKERY, DECEPTION, IMPOSTURE

archaic .... COVIN

deceitful .... WILY, FALSE, ARTFUL, CRAFTY, SNEAKY, TRICKY, DEVIOUS, CUNNING, DECEPTIVE, DISHONEST

colloquial .... PHONY

face .... MASK

sight .... MIRAGE, ILLUSION, HALLUCINATION

words .... LIES

deceive ...... FOB, FUB, LIE, DUPE, FOOL, COZEN, SPOOF, BETRAY, DELUDE, ENTRAP, HUSTLE, BEGUILE, MISLEAD, SWINDLE, HOODWINK

by flattery .... FLAM

slang .... CON, CLIP

deceiver .... LIAR, CHEAT, FAKER, BETRAYER, IMPOSTOR, SWINDLER

slang .... CONMAN, FOURFLUSHER

victim of: colloq. ...... SUCKER

decelerate .... SLOW DOWN

December decoration .... TINSEL, MISTLETOE

perennial .... SNOW

symbol/VIP .... SANTA (CLAUS)

28th .... CHILDERMAS

decenary .... TITHING

decency ...... DECORUM, HONESTY, GOOD TASTE, PROPRIETY

decennium .... DECADE

decent .... FAIR, KIND, RIGHT, CHASTE, MODEST, PROPER, FITTING, DECOROUS, RESPECTABLE

decentralize .... DISPERSE

deception .... LIE, HOAX, JAPE, RUSE, FRAUD, SPOOF, UNTRUTH, FLIMFLAM, TRICKERY, CHICANERY, DELUSION, FALSEHOOD, IMPOSTURE

deceptive .... SLY, FAKE, FALSE, TRICKY, DELUSIVE, ILLUSORY, AMBIGUOUS, DISGUISED, MISLEADING

front .... BLUFF

game ...... SHELL, THIMBLE-RIG

trick .... FLAM

decide .... FIX, RULE, ELECT, JUDGE, CHOOSE, SETTLE, RESOLVE, CONCLUDE, DETERMINE

issue by combat ...... DERAIGN

judicially .... ADJUDGE

decided .... SET, RULED, CLEAR CUT, SETTLED, DEFINITE

decidedly .... CERTAINLY, DEFINITELY

191

decider of right or wrong .... CASUIST

deciding game to break a tie .... PLAY-OFF

election in case of a tie .... RUN-OFF

vote/voice .... CASTING VOTE

deciduous ...... FADING, FLITTING, TEMPORARY, TRANSIENT

opposed to .... EVERGREEN

decimal .... TENTH, DENARY

base .... TEN

point .... DOT

point system inventor .... STEVIN

system of counting .... ALGORISM

decimate .... DESTROY, MASSACRE, SLAUGHTER

decipher .... READ, DECODE, INTERPRET, TRANSLATE

decipherable .... LEGIBLE, READABLE

decision .... DECREE, FINDING, RESOLVE, VERDICT, GUMPTION, WILL, JUDGMENT, SENTENCE

await .... PEND

basis for/good for the future .... PRECEDENT

decisive .... FIRM, GRIM, FINAL, FATEFUL, CONCLUSIVE

argument .... CLINCHER

point/moment .... CRUX, CLIMAX, CRISIS, CRUCIAL, ZERO HOUR

deck .... TRIM, COVER, FLOOR, CLOTHE, PLATFORM

hand .... SAILOR, TRIMMER, ROUSTABOUT

hit the .... ARISE, GET UP

lowest .... ORLOP

of cards .... PACK

on: colloq. .... READY, ON HAND

out ..... ADORN, ARRAY, DRESS, (BE)DIZEN, CAPARISON

Scottish .... DINK

ship's .... POOP, ORLOP

ship's, upper ...... FORECASTLE

slang .... KNOCK DOWN

the cards .... STACK

declaim .... RANT, ORATE, SPOUT, RECITE, PERORATE

in duplicate .... RANT AND RAVE

declaimer .... ORATOR, RANTER

declamation .... ORATION, ORATORY, HARANGUE, RECITATION

declaration .... AVOWAL, ASSERTION, STATEMENT, AFFIRMATION, PROCLAMATION

in bridge .... BID

of aims .... CHARTER, MANIFESTO

Declaration of Independence

signer ...... WYTHE, HANCOCK

declare .... AVER, STATE, AFFIRM, ALLEGE, ASSERT, PROFESS, PUBLISH, PROCLAIM

guilty ...... CONDEMN, CONVICT

in cards .... MELD

innocent .... CLEAR, ACQUIT, RELEASE, EXONERATE, VINDICATE

legally insane .... DISABLE, INCAPACITATE

true .... CLAIM, SWEAR

untrue .... DENY

vociferously .... THUNDER

war .... CHALLENGE

declared .... ANNOUNCED, BROADCAST, PUBLISHED

declasse .... DATED, PASSE

decline .... DIP, EBB, WANE, AGING, ABATE, DROOP, SLUMP, SPURN, REFUSE, REJECT

an offer .... REFUSE, TURN DOWN

as in price .... SAG

period of .... DECADENCE

declivity .... SCARP, SLOPE

decoct .... DISTILL, EXTRACT

decoction .... TEA, PTISAN, TISANE

decode ...... DECIPHER, TRANSLATE

decollate .... BEHEAD, DECAPITATE

decollete .... LOW-CUT, LOW-NECKED

decolorize .... BLEACH

decompose .... ROT, DECAY, SPOIL, PUTREFY

decomposed .... PUTRID

decompression sickness .... BENDS

decontaminate .... CLEAR, PURIFY

decontrol .... FREE, LIBERATE

decor .... DECORATION

decorate .... DECK, TRIM, ADORN, DRESS, EMBELLISH

food to add color .... GARNISH

in a certain way .... ENSTAR

in a way .... ILLUMINATE

in showy way .... BEDIZEN

with jewels .... BEGEM, ENCRUST

decorated wall .... DADO

decoration .... DECOR, AWARD, RIBBON, GARNISH, ORNAMENT, TRIMMING, ADORNMENT, GARNITURE

as sign of honor .... BADGE, MEDAL

for achievement .... TROPHY

furniture .... BUHL

hat .... COCKADE

military .... PURPLE HEART, SERVICE MEDAL

of a page .... ILLUMINATION

on cloth/material .... APPLIQUE, EMBROIDERY

style of .... ROCOCO

decorative .... SPANGLED, GLITTERING, ORNAMENTAL

anklet/armlet .... BANGLE

band .... SASH

border design .... GUILLOCHE

braid .... CORDON

curve .... ESCALOP, SCALLOP

garland .... FESTOON

knot .... BOW

line in writing .... FLOURISH

plant .... HERB

ribbon .... CORDON, RIBAND

stamp .... SEAL

stroke .... TAG, FLOURISH

decorator .... TRIMMER

of a sort .... GILDER

decorous .... PRIM, PROPER, DIGNIFIED

person .... PRIG

decorticate .... BARK, PARE, PEEL, STRIP

decorum ...... DECENCY, DIGNITY, PROTOCOL, ETIQUETTE, PROPRIETY

decoupage .... ART

decoy .... BAIT, LURE, BLIND, PLANT, ENTICE, ENTRAP

barker's .... SHILL

dog .... TOLLER

gambler's .... SHILL, CAPPER

object of .... GAME

police .... STOOLPIGEON

slang .... STOOLIE

songbird, use .... CAJOLE

decrease .... EBB, DROP, WANE, ABATE, LOWER, TAPER, LESSER, REDUCE, SLACKEN, SUBSIDE, DISCOUNT, DIMINISH, DEPRECIATE

decree .... LAW, FIAT, ARRET, CANON, EDICT, ORDER, (EN)ACT, DECIDE, FIRMAN, ORDAIN, MANDATE, DECISION, RESCRIPT

by judicial sentence .... DECERN

by the Pope .... DECRETAL

judicial .... WRIT

Moslem ruler's .... IRADE

of outlawry .... BAN

papal .... BULL
Russian/official .... UKASE
decrees, collection of papal
.... DECRETAL
decrement .... LOSS, WASTE
opposed to .... INCREMENT
decrepit ...... OLD, WEAK, SENILE,
WORN OUT, BROKEN DOWN,
DELAPIDATED
airplane .... CRATE
automobile ..... CRATE, JALOPY
car: sl. .... DOG
decresent .... WANING
decrier ...... KNOCKER, DEPLORER
decry .... BLAME, CENSURE,
CONDEMN, DENOUNCE,
DISCREDIT, DISPARAGE
decumbent ...... PRONE, TRAILING,
PROSTRATE
opposed to .... SUPINE
decuple .... TENFOLD
decussate .... INTERSECT
dedicate .... APPLY, EXALT,
CONFER, DEVOTE, HALLOW,
ENSHRINE, INSCRIBE
dedication .... ENVOI, ENVOY,
DEVOTION, INSCRIPTION
deduce .... INFER, THINK, ASSUME,
DERIVE, RECKON, BELIEVE,
CONCLUDE
deduct .... DOCK, REMOVE,
SUBTRACT
deductible tax item
.... EXPENSES, (MORTGAGE)
INTEREST, DONATIONS
deduction .... REBATE, DISCOUNT,
REDUCTION, INFERENCE
allowed for loss of weight/
for waste .... DRAFT
kind of .... TARE
opposed to .... INDUCTION
union dues .... CHECKOFF
deed .... ACT, FEAT, GEST(E),
ACTION, EXPLOIT
in .... IN FACT, REALLY
kind of .... SALE, TRANSFER
ownership .... TITLE
deeds .... ACTA
of chivalry .... ERRANTRY
deejay's concern .... DISKS
deem .... JUDGE, OPINE, ASSESS,
REGARD, BELIEVE, CONSIDER
deep .... WISE, ABYSMAL,
ABYSSAL, LEARNED,
ABSTRUSE, PROFOUND
bow .... NOD, CURTSY,
SALAAM, OBEISANCE
crack .... CREVASSE
dish, covered .... TUREEN
dish, fruit pie .... COBBLER
dish, pudding ...... PANDOWDY

gorge .... GULLY, RAVINE
hole .... PIT
red .... CRIMSON, CARNATION
seated .... FIXED, ROOTED,
ENTRENCHED
sleep .... SOPOR, STUPOR,
LETHARGY
sound .... BOOM, RUMBLE
the .... SEA, OCEAN
valley .... CANON, CANYON
voice .... BARITONE
deep south state, U.S.
.... GEORGIA, ALABAMA,
LOUISIANA, MISSISSIPPI
deepfreeze .... REFRIGERATOR
deeply .... INLY
deepset .... CAVERNOUS
deepsix .... DISCARD
deer .... ROE, STAG, BROCKET,
MUNTJAC, MUNTJAK,
RUMINANT, WHITETAIL
American ...... MOOSE, WAPITI,
CARIBOU
Andean .... PUDU
antler .... TAG
antler branch .... POINT
antler shaft .... BEAM
antler, type .... RUSINE
Asiatic .... AHU, ROE, SAMBAR,
SAMBUR
axis .... CHITAL
barking .... KAKAR
distaff .... DOE(S)
entrails .... UMBLES
feeding place .... YARD
female .... DOE, ROE, HIND
flesh .... VENISON
foot .... HOOF
forest cover .... VERT
genus .... RUSA
hart .... STAG
hog .... AXIS, RUSA
horn .... ANTLER
hornless .... POLLARD
horn's second branch ..... BEZ
ANTLER
large .... ELK, MOOSE,
CARIBOU, REINDEER
like giraffe .... OKAPI
male .... HART, STAG,
(ROE)BUCK
maned .... RUSA, SAMBAR
moose-like .... ELK
mouse .... NAPUS
mouse-like .... CHEVROTAIN
mule .... BLACKTAIL
of a .... CERVINE
of India .... AXIS, RUSA
Persian .... MARAL
red .... HART, HIND, STAG,
ELAPHINE

secretion .... MUSK
sexual excitement .... RUT,
ESTRUS
short tail of .... SCUT
small .... ROE, NAPUS,
BROCKET, MUNTJAC,
CHEVROTAIN
spotted .... CHITAL
tail .... FLAG, SCUT
Tibet .... SHOU
track .... SLOT
three-year-old .... SOREL
two-year-old .... TEG,
BROCK(ET), PRICKET
vital organs .... NOMBLES,
NUMBLES, HUMBLE PIE
young .... FAWN, SPITTER
deerlet .... NAPU, CHEVROTAIN
deerlike .... CERVINE
deface .... MAR, MAIM, SCAR,
BLEMISH, MUTILATE,
DISFIGURE
defalcate .... EMBEZZLE
defamation .... ABUSE, LIBEL,
CALUMNY, SLANDER
defamatory .... LIBELOUS
remarks .... MUD
defame .... ABUSE, LIBEL,
MALIGN, REVILE, VILIFY,
SLANDER, TRADUCE,
CALUMNIATE
default .... BREACH, ARREARS,
FAILURE, FORFEIT
colloquial ..... WELSH, RENEGE
defaulter .... EMBEZZLER,
DEFALCATOR
defeat .... WIN, BEAT, BEST, LICK,
LOSS, UNDO, WHIP, WORST,
FOIL, SUBDUE, DESTROY,
REVERSE, TROUNCE,
OVERCOME, VANQUISH
by force .... CONQUER
by small margin .... NOSE
chess .... MATE
decisively .... DRUB, ROUT,
WALLOP, CLOBBER, TROUNCE
disorderly .... ROUT
easy to .... PUSHOVER
incumbent .... UNSEAT
overwhelming .... ROUT,
LACING, MASSACRE,
SHELLACKING
scoreless .... WHITEWASH
soundly .... DRUB, LACE,
SKUNK, WHALE
two ways .... WHIPSAW
unexpectedly .... UPSET
defeated: colloq. .... LICKED
slang .... KAPUT
defeatist, kind of .... PESSIMIST
defecate .... PURIFY, REFINE,

defect .... FLAW, LACK, SPOT, BREAK, FAULT, LACUNA, DEMERIT, FOIBLE, FAILING, WEAKNESS, SHORTCOMING, IMPERFECTION
from a group/cause/country .... BOLT, FLEE, DESERT, RENEGE
in a cloth .... SNAG
in a plan .... KINK
in dry goods .... DAMAGE
in fabric/weave .... SCOB
in hosiery .... RUN
in machine/sl. .... BUG
in wood .... WARP
labial .... HARELIP
slight .... CRACK
superficial skin .... BLEMISH
defection .... DESERTION, SECESSION
defective .... FAULTY, FLAWED, MANQUE, IMPERFECT
bomb .... DUD
car .... LEMON
person .... MORON, CRIPPLE
defector .... RAT, BOLTER, RENEGADE, TURNCOAT
defend .... FIGHT, GUARD, SHIELD, JUSTIFY, PROTECT, GO TO BAT FOR
slang .... STONEWALL
defendable .... TENABLE
defendant .... ACCUSED, CULPRIT, SUSPECT, PRISONER
opposed to .... PLAINTIFF, COMPLAINANT
place of .... DOCK
plea of .... NOLO
statement of .... PLEA
who refuses to plead .... MUTE
defender ...... GUARD, CHAMPION, ADVOCATE, GUARDIAN, PROTECTOR
defense .... REFUGE, BULWARK, PROTECTION, RESISTANCE, FORTIFICATION, JUSTIFICATION
castle's .... MOAT
defendant's .... ALIBI
kind of .... ORAL, SELF, LEGAL, ATTACK
line: Ger. .... LIMES
means of .... ARMOR, SHELL, SPINE, ABATIS, HAUBERK, WEAPON, BARRIER, MUNIMENT, PALISADE, AIR-RAID SHELTER, BARRICADE, SMOKESCREEN
Defense Department monogram .... TAC
defenseless .... BARE, OPEN, WEAK, NAKED, HELPLESS
defensible .... TENABLE, JUSTIFIABLE
defensive .... WATCHFUL, VIGILANT, FORTIFIED, SHIELDING
covering ...... ARMOR, HELMET, SHAKO, (A)EGIS, SHIELD, MAIL, CUIRASS, BREASTPLATE
ditch .... MOAT, FOXHOLE
embankment ..... EARTHWORK, GABIONADE
outwork .... FORTALICE
structure .... FORT, ABATIS, CITADEL, FORTRESS, STOCKADE
wall .... FENCE, BULWARK
defer .... PEND, STAY, DELAY, YIELD, SHELVE, SUBMIT, GIVE IN, SUSPEND, POSTPONE
deference .... RESPECT, YIELDING, OBEISANCE
deferment .... DELAY, RESPITE, MORATORIUM
defi .... DARE, CARTEL, CHALLENGE
defiance .... DARING, THREAT, CONTEMPT, CHALLENGE, REBELLION, RESISTANCE
defiant .... BOLD, INSOLENT, REBELLIOUS, BELLIGERENT
confidence .... BRAVADO
one .... REB, REBEL, CHALLENGER
sound .... YAH
deficiency .... LACK, WANT, DEFECT, ULLAGE, DEFICIT, POORNESS, SHORTAGE
disease .... DROPSY, SCURVY, RICKETS, BERIBERI, PELLAGRA
in supply .... SHORTAGE
of oxygen in body .... ANOXIA
deficient .... SHORT, LACKING, WANTING, DEFECTIVE, INCOMPLETE, INADEQUATE
in volume .... WEAK
deficit .... LACK, SHORTAGE, SHORTFALL
defile .... PASS, DIRTY, GORGE, SULLY, TAINT, RAVINE, VALLEY, BLACKEN, CORRUPT, DEBAUCH, POLLUTE, PROFANE, TARNISH
define .... LIMIT, EXPLAIN, OUTLINE, DESCRIBE, INTERPRET
definite .... EXACT, PLAIN, CERTAIN, PRECISE, EXPLICIT, POSITIVE
definitive .... FINAL, FIXED, DECISIVE, CONCLUSIVE
deflate .... EMPTY, LOWER, REDUCE, EXHAUST, HUMBLE, COLLAPSE
deflated tire .... FLAT
deflect .... BEND, FEND, TURN, AVERT, CURVE, SWING, TWIST, DIVERT, SWERVE, DEVIATE
deflower .... RAVISH
Defoe, character .... CRUSOE, FRIDAY
novelist .... DANIEL
deform .... WARP, CONTORT, MISSHAPE, DISFIGURE
deformed ...... UGLY, DISTORTED, MALFORMED
organism .... TERAS
person .... FREAK, CRIPPLE, HUNCHBACK
deformity .... FLAW, DEFECT, UGLINESS, DISTORTION, IMPERFECTION, DISFIGUREMENT
back .... HUMP, HUNCH
buccal .... HARELIP
foot .... VARUS, TALIPES, CLUBFOOT
of lower limbs .... VARUS, BOWLEGS
of mouth .... CLEFT LIP, CLEFT PALATE
defraud .... GYP, BILK, DUPE, NICK, CHEAT, COZEN, STICK, FLEECE, SWINDLE
defray .... PAY, COVER COST, FOOT THE BILL
defrost .... MELT, THAW, DEICE
deft .... APT, ADROIT, CLEVER, SKILLFUL, DEXTEROUS
defunct ...... DEAD, PAST, EXTINCT
defuse .... CALM, PACIFY, SOOTHE, APPEASE, PLACATE
defy .... DARE, FLOUT, OPPOSE, RESIST, DISOBEY, CONFRONT, CHALLENGE, FLY IN THE FACE OF
degenerate .... DEBASED, DEPRAVED
person .... PIMP, WHORE, LECHER, PERVERT, TROLLOP, SLATTERN
degeneration .... AGING, DETERIORATION
degenerative disorder .... DEMENTIA, BLINDNESS, ARTHRITIS, ALZHEIMER'S DISEASE
deglutition .... SWALLOWING
degradation .... DECLINE, DEMOTION, DOWNGRADE, DEBASEMENT
degrade .... ABASE, DEBASE, DEMEAN, DEMOTE, HUMBLE,

REDUCE, DIMINISH, HUMILIATE

degraded .... SHAMED, DEMOTED, DISGRACED, HUMILIATED

degrading .... MENIAL, INSULTING

degree .... PEG, RANK, RUNG, STEP, LEVEL, STAGE, EXTENT

academic .... BA, BS, MD, LLD, DOCTOR OF LAWS, BACHELOR OF ARTS, DOCTOR OF MEDICINE, BACHELOR OF SCIENCE

highest/utmost .... NTH

of occurrence .... INCIDENCE

of uncertainty .... ENTH

recipient .... HONORAND

suffix .... NESS

to a .... SOMEWHAT

unspecified .... NTH

degust .... SAVOR, TASTE

dehisce .... GAPE, OPEN, BURST, SPREAD, UNFURL

dehiscence .... CHASM, BURSTING, SPLITTING

dehumanized .... BRUTALIZED

dehydrate .... DRY, PARCH, DESSICATE, EVAPORATE

dehydrated .... DRIED, WITHERED, SHRIVELED

dehydration .... DRYING, JERKING, DESSICATION

deice ...... MELT, THAW, DEFROST, UNFREEZE

deictic .... DEMONSTRATIVE

opposed to .... ELENCTIC

deific .... GODLY, DIVINE, GODLIKE

deiform ...... GODLIKE, CELESTIAL

deify .... ADORE, EXALT, EXTOL, PRAISE, GLORIFY, WORSHIP, IDEALIZE, SANCTIFY, APOTHEOSIZE

deign .... STOOP, SUBMIT, LOSE FACE, CONSENT, CONDESCEND

deil: Scot. .... DEVIL

Deirdre's guardian .... CONCHOBAR

deity .... GOD, GODDESS, GODHEAD, GODHOOD, GODSHIP, DIVINITY, PROVIDENCE

agricultural ..... CERES, FLORA, POMONA, DEMETER

Buddhist .... DEVA, BUDDHA

Chinese .... HEU CHI, LEI KUNG, CHANG FEI, LUNG WANG

Egyptian ..... BAST, ISIS, NEPH, PTAH, HORUS, ANUBIS

Germanic .... IDUN, ODIN, FREY, THOR, DONAR, FRIGG, NANNA, WODEN, WOTAN

Hindu .... AGNI, DEVI, ADITI, BRAHMA, DAKSHA, DEVAKI, DHARMA

Japanese .... HOTEI, INARI, HIRUKO, IZANAGI, OMIKAMI, AMATERASU

minor .... GODKIN, DEMIGOD

of commerce .... HERMES

of flocks .... FAUN

of forest/woodland .... PAN, FAUN, SATYR, FAUNUS, ZEPHYRUS

of marriage .... HERA, JUNO, HYMEN

of music/poetry .... ERATO, APOLLO, EUTERPRE, ORPHEUS

of water .... TRITON, NEPTUNE, OCEANUS

secondary .... DEMIURGE

underworld/the nether world .... LOKI, MINOS, ORCUS, CHARON, OSIRIS

deject .... DAMP(EN), DASH, DAUNT, SADDEN, DEPRESS

dejected .... SAD, WEARY, SULLEN, DOWNCAST, DEPRESSED, CRESTFALLEN, BROKENHEARTED

dejection .... GLOOM, GRIEF, DESPAIR, SADNESS, MELANCHOLY

lowest point .... NADIR

dejeuner ...... LUNCH, LUNCHEON, BREAKFAST

delate .... ACCUSE, RELATE, ANNOUNCE, DENOUNCE

delator .... INFORMER

Delaware .... LENI, GRAPE, LENAPE

bay .... DELAWARE, INDIAN RIVER

Bay discoverer .... HUDSON

cape .... HENLOPEN

capital .... DOVER

city/town ...... LEWES, LAUREL, NEWARK, SMYRNA, ELSMERE, MILFORD, SEAFORD, CLAUMONT, BROOKSIDE, WILMINGTON

county .... KENT, SUSSEX, NEW CASTLE

date of state flag: ____ 7, 1787 .... DECEMBER

Indian .... LENAPE

river .... INDIAN, LEIPSIC, CHOPTANK, DELAWARE, BROADKILL, MURDERKILL

River city .... TRENTON

settlers .... SWEDES

state bird .... BLUE HEN

state flower .... PEACH BLOSSOM

state nickname .... FIRST, DIAMOND

delay .... LAG, PEND, SLOW, FLAG, DRAG, DALLY, DEFER(MENT), FALTER, STALL, DETAIN, LINGER

doing something, habitually .... PROCRASTINATE

in getting business done .... RED TAPE

in law .... MORA, LACHES

in law, inexcusable .... LACHES

the advance of progress .... HINDER, IMPEDE, RETARD

until later .... POSTPONE

delayed reaction .... DOUBLE TAKE

delaying action .... STALL

in Congress .... FILIBUSTER

in law .... MORATORY

dele ...... ERASE, CANCEL, DELETE, SLASH, REMOVE

delectable .... YUMMY, DELICIOUS, PLEASING, EXQUISITE

delectation .... DELIGHT, PLEASURE, AMUSEMENT

delegate .... AGENT, ENVOY, DEPUTE, DEPUTY, EMPOWER, ENTRUST, DEPUTIZE, EMISSARY

kind of .... BACKUP, ALTERNATE, ACCREDITED

unofficial .... OBSERVER

delegation .... BODY, MISSION, COMMISSION, CONTINGENT

delete .... DELE, EDIT, ERASE, OMIT, BLOT OUT, EXPUNGE, CROSS OUT, REMOVE

deleterious .... BAD, HARMFUL, HURTFUL, RUINOUS, INJURIOUS, PERNICIOUS, DETRIMENTAL

deletion .... EDITING, ERASURE, OMISSION, BLUE-PENCILING

of word's last letter .... APOCOPE

cancel .... STET

Delia .... ARTEMIS

deliberate .... SLOW, PONDER, CAREFUL, KNOWING, STUDIED, CONSIDER, UNHURRIED, THOUGHTFUL, INTENTIONAL

discourtesy .... CUT, SNUB, REBUFF

Delibes, composer .... LEO

ballet .... NAILA

opera .... LAKME

delicacy .... CATE, CAVIAR, NICETY, TIDBIT, FRAILTY, KICKSAW, FINENESS, NICENESS

gamey .... VENISON
of performance .... FINESSE
delicate .... NICE, FRAIL,
FINE(SPUN), DAINTY, TENDER,
FRAGILE, REFINED, TAFFETA,
TICKLISH, EXQUISITE
delicately pretty .... DAINTY,
MIGNON
delicatessen .... DELI, FOOD SHOP,
FOOD STORE
delicious .... SWEET, TASTY,
YUMMY, SAVORY, LUSCIOUS,
AMBROSIAL, APPETIZING,
PALATABLE, DELIGHTFUL
fruit .... APPLE
delict .... INJURY, OFFENSE,
MISDEMEANOR
delight .... JOY, ELATE, PLEASE,
REGALE, ENCHANT, CHARM,
RAPTURE, REJOICE, ENTRANCE,
PLEASURE
in .... SAVOR
delightful .... ALLURING,
CHARMING, PLEASING
Delilah .... HARLOT, TEMPTRESS
victim of .... SAMSON
delimit .... DEMARCATE
delineate .... DRAW, LIMN, DEPICT,
SKETCH, OUTLINE, PORTRAY,
DESCRIBE
delineation .... PLAN, SKETCH,
DRAWING, PORTRAIT
delineator .... LIMNER
delinquency ...... GUILT, MISDEED,
DEFAULT, NEGLECT,
VIOLATION
record/report: sl. .... GIG
delinquent .... GUILTY, OVERDUE,
CULPABLE, NEGLIGENT,
SINFUL, DEFAULTING,
NEGLECTFUL
a .... JUVENILE
alleged other .... PARENT
debt .... ARREARS
debtor .... DEFAULTER
likely home of .... BOYS'
TOWN, REFORMATORY
person .... SINNER, CULPRIT,
OFFENDER
deliquesce .... MELT, THAW,
LIQUEFY
delirious .... MAD, RAVING,
EXCITED, UNSTABLE
delirium .... MANIA, PANIC,
FRENZY, CONFUSION
severe .... HALLUCINATION
tremens .... JIMJAMS, JITTERS
delitescent ...... HIDDEN, LATENT,
INACTIVE
deliver .... RID, EMIT, FREE, SAVE,
CARRY, SPEAK, UTTER,

CONVEY, RESCUE, HAND
OVER, LIBERATE, TRANSFER,
DISTRIBUTE
goods for sale .... CONSIGN
prematurely .... SLINK
sermon .... PREACH
deliverance .... RESCUE, OPINION,
RELEASE, SALVATION,
REDEMPTION
deliverer .... COURIER, REDEEMER,
LIBERATOR
delivery ...... ADDRESS, TRANSFER,
UTTERANCE, CHILDBIRTH,
PARTURITION, DISTRIBUTION
boy .... JUMPER
of property, legal .... LIVERY
dell .... DALE, GLEN, VALE, SLACK,
DINGLE, RAVINE, VALLEY
denizen .... FARMER
Della, secretary .... STREET
singer .... REESE
dells .... RAPIDS
Delmar, novelist .... VINA
Delos inhabitant .... DELIAN
delouse .... SANITIZE
Delphic .... ORACULAR
priestess .... PYTHIA,
PYTHONESS
seer .... ORACLE
delphinium .... LARKSPUR
delude .... KID, DUPE, FOOL,
CHEAT, TRICK, DECEIVE,
BEGUILE, MISLEAD
deluge .... POUR, FLOOD,
CATARACT, DOWNPOUR,
INUNDATE, CATACLYSM,
INUNDATION
of blood in circulatory
system .... PLETHORA
of words .... SPATE
delul .... CAMEL, DROMEDARY
delusion .... FANCY, MIRAGE,
VISION, FALLACY, FANTASY,
ILLUSION, PARANOIA
of grandeur .... MEGALOMANIA
deluxe .... LUXURIOUS
delve .... DIG, PROBE, FATHOM,
(RE)SEARCH, INVESTIGATE
demagogue .... QUACK,
AGITATOR, MOUNTEBANK,
RABBLE-ROUSER
demand .... CRY, LEVY, NEED,
CLAIM, EXACT, ORDER,
CHARGE, REQUIRE
final .... ULTIMATUM
for identification
.... CHALLENGE
in .... SOUGHT
noisy .... CLAMOR
payment of debt .... DUN
repetition .... ENCORE

with authority .... COMMAND
demandant .... PLAINTIFF
demanding .... STRICT, ARDUOUS,
EXIGENT, EXACTING,
CLAMOROUS, DIFFICULT,
INSISTENT
demarcate .... BOUND, DEFINE,
CONFINE, DELIMIT, RESTRICT
demarcation .... LINE, LIMIT,
BORDER, BOUNDS, BOUNDARY
deme .... TOWNSHIP
demean .... ABASE, HUMBLE,
LOWER, DEGRADE
demeanor .... AIR, MIEN,
MANNER, BEARING, CONDUCT,
BEHAVIOR, CARRIAGE,
PORTANCE
having dignified .... PORTLY
dement .... DERANGE
demented ...... MAD, LOCO, LUNY,
CRAZY, LOONY, CRAZED,
INSANE, FLIGHTY, DERANGED
dementia .... INSANITY
demerit .... FAULT, MINUS,
DEFECT, (BLACK)MARK
slang .... GIG
demerol .... DRUG, SEDATIVE,
ANALGESIC
demesne .... REALM, DOMAIN,
REGION
Demeter .... CERES
demicup .... TASSE
demigod .... HERO, IDOL, DEITY
demilune .... CRESCENT
demise .... WILL, DEATH, CONVEY,
BEQUEST, DECEASE
demission .... ABDICATION,
RESIGNATION
demit .... RESIGN, ABDICATE
demitasse .... (COFFEE)CUP
demobilize .... DISARM, DISBAND,
DISMISS, DISCHARGE, MUSTER
OUT
democracy .... REPUBLIC
world's largest .... INDIA
world's smallest .... SAN
MARINO
Democrat, any .... LOCOFOCO
Democratic Party faction
.... LOCOFOCO
demode ...... PASSE, OUT-OF-DATE,
OLD-FASHIONED
demographic item .... BIRTHS,
DEATHS, MARRIAGES
demoiselle .... CRANE, DAMSEL,
DRAGONFLY
demolish ...... RASE, RAZE, LEVEL,
RUIN, SMASH, WRECK,
DESTROY
demon .... NAT, OGRE, ANITO,
DEVIL, FIEND, GHOST, GHOUL,

GNOME, D(A)EDAL, EVIL SPIRIT

Arabian .... AFRIT, EBLIS, GENIE, JINN(I), AFREET, DAITYA

blood-sucking .... VAMPIRE

female .... LAMIA

Frankenstein's .... MONSTER

little .... ELF

young .... IMP

demoness .... LILITH, INCUBUS, SUCCUBA, SUCCUBUS

demoniac(al) .... CRUEL, FRANTIC, HELLISH, DEVILISH, FIENDISH, DIABOLIC(AL)

demonism .... IDOLATRY, SATANISM

demons, abode of all .... PANDEMONIUM

demonstrable .... APODICTIC, DEDUCIBLE

demonstrate .... SHOW, PROVE, EVINCE, CONFIRM, EXHIBIT

demonstration ...... TEST, PROOF, PROBATION, EXPERIMENT

demonstrative .... EVIDENT, CONVINCING, ILLUSTRATIVE

in grammar .... D(E)ICTIC

pronoun .... THAT, THIS, THESE

demoralize .... WEAKEN, CONFUSE, CORRUPT, DEPRESS, DISCOURAGE, DISHEARTEN

demos .... DEME, MASSES, PEOPLE, POPULACE

demote .... LOWER, DEGRADE, DOWNGRADE

opposed to .... PROMOTE

slang .... BUST, BREAK

demotics .... SOCIOLOGY

Dempsey (Jack) sobriquet .... (MANASSA) MAULER

demulcent ...... SALVE, OINTMENT, SOOTHING

demur .... FALTER, OBJECT, PROTEST, HESITATE, THINK TWICE

demure .... COY, MIM, SHY, PRIM, SOBER, MODEST, SEDATE

demurrer .... PLEA, OBJECTOR, OBJECTION

den .... CAVE, DIVE, ROOM, HAUNT, STUDY, HANGOUT, RETREAT

sacred .... SANCTUM

secret .... MEW, HIDEOUT

wild animal's .... LAIR, LODGE

denarii, 12 .... SOLIDUS

denary .... DECIMAL, TENFOLD

dendritic/dendroid ...... TREELIKE

dene .... DUNE

dengue .... DANDY FEVER,

BREAKBONE FEVER

mosquito carrier of ..... AEDES AEGYPTI

deniable .... DOUBTFUL, SUSPICIOUS

denial ...... REFUSAL, DISAVOWAL, REJECTION, ABSTINENCE, REPUDIATION

in diplomacy/official .... DEMENTI

opposed to .... COMPLIANCE, AFFIRMATIVE

statement of ...... DENEGATION

denier .... COIN, DISOWNER, DISCLAIMER

denigrate ...... DEFAME, ASPERSE, VILIFY, BLACKEN

denim .... FABRIC, (COTTON)CLOTH

use for .... (C)OVERALLS, UNIFORMS

denizen ...... DWELLER, CIT(IZEN), RESIDENT, OCCUPANT, INHABITANT

Denmark. See Danish

Dennis .... DAY, HOPPER

Dennis the _____ .... MENACE

denominate .... CALL, NAME, TITLE

denomination .... SECT, CLASS, ORDER, STYLE, CHURCH, NAMING, CALLING, DESIGNATION

denominational .... SECTARY, SECTARIAN

denote .... MARK, MEAN, EXPRESS, SIGNIFY, SPECIFY, INDICATE

denouement .... END, EFFECT, OUTCOME, SOLUTION

denounce .... CURSE, DECRY, ASSAIL, ACCUSE, CHARGE, CONDEMN, CRITICIZE, EXCORIATE

dense .... CLOSE, GROSS, SOLID, THICK, PACKED, STUPID, COMPACT, POPULOUS

growth of trees .... WOODS, FOREST, JUNGLE

dent .... MAR, DINT, HOLLOW, DIMPLE, INDENTATION

dental device .... FLOSS

drill .... BURR

paste ..... ZIRCATE, DENTIFRICE

dentate .... NOTCHED, SERRATE, TOOTHED

dented .... TOOTHED

denticle .... TOOTH

dentifrice .... ZIRCATE

type of .... GEL, PASTE, POWDER

dentin(e) .... IVORY

dentist: colloq. ..... TOOTH PULLER

drill of .... BURR

pincers of .... FORCEPS

tool of .... PROBE, MIRROR

dentist's aid .... LAUGHING GAS

degree .... DMD

professional helper .... HYGIENIST

dentistry .... ODONTOLOGY

denture .... PLATE, TEETH, BRIDGE

type of .... FULL, PARTIAL, IMMEDIATE

denude .... STRIP

denunciation .... THREAT, CENSURE, ANATHEMA, DIATRIBE, ACCUSATION

Denver is capital of .... COLORADO

deny .... ABJURE, DISOWN, REFUSE, NEGATE, REJECT, DISAVOW, OPPOSE, GAINSAY, FORSWEAR, PROTEST, WITHHOLD, REPUDIATE, CONTRADICT

denying .... NEGATIVE, DENEGATION

deodar .... CEDAR

deodorant .... MUM, PASTILLE, FRESHENER, ANTIPERSPIRANT

drug .... BISMUTH

deontology .... ETHICS

depart ...... DIE, EXIT, LEAVE, GO (AWAY), SET OUT, SKIP OUT

from script .... AD LIB

quickly .... VAMOOSE

secretly .... DECAMP, ABSCOND

slang ..... MOSEY, TODDLE, HIT THE ROAD

departed .... LEFT, PAST, (BY)GONE

the .... DEAD

department .... BUREAU, SECTION, BUSINESS, DIVISION

store, designating a ...... FIVE-AND-TEN

store stairway ...... ESCALATOR

departure .... EXIT, DEATH, EGRESS, LEAVING, PARTING, DEVIATION

from a job due to advanced age .... RETIREMENT

from an area of danger .... EVACUATION

mass/of Israelites from Egypt .... EXODUS

depend .... BANK, HANG, RELY, COUNT, HINGE

dependable .... RELIABLE, STEADFAST, RESPONSIBLE

dependence .... RELIANCE, ADDICTION

dependency .... COLONY,

WARDSHIP, AP(P)ANAGE,
TERRITORY
dependent .... WARD, PROTEGE,
SUBJECT, HANGER-ON,
FOLLOWER, PARASITE,
PENSIONARY, SUBORDINATE
kind of .... SATELLITE
on .... CONTINGENT
depict .... DRAW, LIMN, PAINT,
RENDER, PICTURE, PORTRAY
in words .... DESCRIBE,
DELINEATE
depilate .... PLUCK, SHAVE,
DEHAIR
depilation .... ELECTROLYSIS
deplete .... DRAIN, ERODE, EMPTY,
EXHAUST
deplorable .... SAD, RUEFUL,
WOEFUL, GRIEVOUS,
LAMENTABLE
deplore ...... RUE, DECRY, MOURN,
BEMOAN, BEWAIL, GRIEVE,
LAMENT, REGRET, REPINE
deploy .... SPREAD(OUT)
de plume, _____ .... NOM
deplume .... PLUCK
depone .... DEPOSE, TESTIFY
deponent's statement
.... AFFIDAVIT, TESTIMONY
deport ...... EXILE, EXPEL, BANISH,
BEHAVE, EXPATRIATE
deportment .... MIEN, BEARING,
CONDUCT, BEHAVIOR
depose .... OUST, SWEAR, AFFIRM,
DISBAR, DEPONE, REMOVE,
UNSEAT, TESTIFY, DETHRONE
deposit .... LEES, DREGS, PLEDGE,
PAYMENT, RESIDUE, SECURITY
alluvial .... DELTA, GEEST
body .... CALCULUS
clayey .... MARL
geyser .... SINTER
glacial/water-borne
.... PLACER, MORAINE
mineral .... LODE
money .... PAY IN
on teeth .... TARTAR
sediment .... SILT
waste .... SLUDGE
wine cask ...... ARGAL, ARGOL,
TARTAR
depositary ...... URN, BANK, SAFE,
VAULT, TRUSTEE, DEPOSITORY
deposition .... TESTIMONY
form of .... AFFIDAVIT
depot .... STATION, ENTREPOT,
WAREHOUSE, STOREHOUSE
arms .... ARMORY, ARSENAL
French .... GARE
military .... ARSENAL,
MAGAZINE

deprave .... DEBASE, DEBAUCH,
PERVERT
depraved ...... EVIL, VILE, PUTRID,
CORRUPT, DISSOLUTE
depravity .... CORRUPTION,
TURPITUDE, PERVERSION
deprecate .... BEWAIL, REGRET,
DEPLORE, PROTEST,
DISAPPROVE
depreciate .... FALL, LESSEN,
CHEAPEN, BELITTLE,
DISPARAGE
colloquial .... RUN DOWN
money officially .... DECRY
slang .... KNOCK
depredate .... ROB, PILLAGE,
PLUNDER
depress ...... DENT, LOWER, UPSET,
DAMPEN, DEJECT, SADDEN,
DISHEARTEN
depressant .... SEDATIVE
depressed ...... SAD, BLUE, GLUM,
MOODY, DEJECTED,
DOWNCAST, FLATTENED,
DOWN IN THE MOUTH
depressing .... BLEAK, DISMAL,
DREARY, GLOOMY
periods for some workers
.... BLUE MONDAYS
depression .... DIP, DENT,
HOLLOW, LOWERING,
REDUCTION, ABASEMENT
between hills .... GLEN
between mountains .... COL
emotional feelings of
...... GRIEF, ANXIETY, SADNESS,
DISTRESS, PESSIMISM
in economics .... RECESSION
on the cheek/chin ...... DIMPLE
small .... FOVEA
deprivation .... LOSS, DENIAL
deprive .... STRIP, DENUDE,
USURP, DIVEST, TAKE(AWAY),
DISPOSSESS
of ownership .... EXPROPRIATE
of power to reproduce
.... GELD, CASTRATE,
STERILIZE, EMASCULATE
of sunlight .... ETIOLATE
deprived .... SHORN, (BE)REFT,
CUT OFF, DENUDED
depth ...... SEA, OCEAN, LOWNESS,
DEEPNESS
bomb/charge .... ASHCAN
combining form .... BATHO
of water displaced by ship
.... DRAFT
depurate .... PURIFY
deputation .... DELEGATION
depute .... SEND, APPOINT,
DELEGATE, AUTHORIZE

deputies' group .... POSSE
deputy .... AGENT, ENVOY, PROXY,
VICAR, (DE)LEGATE,
SURROGATE, LIEUTENANT,
VICE-REGENT
Der Alte .... SCHRANZ, ADENAUER
Fuehrer .... HITLER
deracinate .... UPROOT
derange .... UPSET, MESS UP,
CRAZE, DEMENT, CONFUSE,
DISTURB, DISTRACT
deranged .... CRAZY, INSANE
derangement .... TURMOIL,
IMBALANCE
Derby .... HAT, BOWLER, HORSE
RACE
English: colloq.
.... BILLYCOCK
site .... KENTUCKY, EPSOM
DOWNS
winner .... ZEV, SWAPS,
PONDER, ASSAULT, NEEDLES,
TIM TAM, AFFIRMED,
CITATION, WHIRLAWAY, KAUAI
KING, BOLD FORBES,
SECRETARIAT, WAR ADMIRAL,
GATO DEL SOL, GENUINE RISK,
TWENTY GRAND, LUCKY
DEBONAIR, FOOLISH PLEASURE
winner, Triple Crown
.... ASSAULT, AFFIRMED,
CITATION, WHIRLAWAY,
SECRETARIAT, WAR ADMIRAL,
SEATTLE SLEW
derelict .... TRAMP, WRECK,
REMISS, DRIFTER, FLOTSAM,
SLACKER, CASTAWAY,
FORSAKEN
deride .... GIBE, JEER, MOCK,
SCOFF, SCORN, RIDICULE
variant .... FLEAR
derision .... SCORN, DISDAIN,
MOCKERY, CONTEMPT
derisive .... MOCKING, SCORNFUL,
SARCASTIC, DISDAINFUL,
CONTEMPTUOUS
cry .... BOO, HISS, HOOT, RAZZ,
CATCALL
derivation .... ROOT, ORIGIN,
DESCENT
word .... ETYMOLOGY
derive .... GET, DRAW, INFER,
OBTAIN, (D)EDUCE, ORIGINATE
derived from oil .... OLEIC
derm, as suffix .... SKIN,
COVERING
dermatoid .... SKINLIKE
dermis .... SKIN, CUTIS
dernier .... LAST, FINAL
cri .... LAST WORD,
LATEST(STYLE)

derogate .... DECRY, DEFAME, DETRACT, DISPARAGE

derogatory .... ADVERSE, CRITICAL, DEFAMATORY, DETRACTING, HUMILIATING

remark .... SLUR

derrick .... RIG, CRANE, DAVIT, HOIST, STEEVE

part of .... JIB, BEAM, BOOM, SPAR, PULLEY

derriere .... REAR, BEHIND, BUTTOCKS

derring-do .... GEST

derringer .... GUN, PISTOL

derris extraction ...... ROTENONE

derry .... BALLAD

dervish .... FAKIR, BEGGAR, MENDICANT

headgear .... TAJ

Moslem .... SADITE

practice .... HOWLING, WHIRLING

wandering .... CALENDER

Des Moines is capital of

.... IOWA

desalinization .... DESALT

descant .... SONG, MELODY, COMMENT, CRITICISM

descend .... DROP, FALL, PLUNGE, COME DOWN, STEP DOWN, PLUMMET

upon ...... HIT, POUND, ALIGHT, ATTACK, STRIKE

descendant .... BREED, CHILD, SCION, PROGENY, INHERITOR, OFFSPRING

female .... HEIRESS, DAUGHTER

male .... SON, HEIR, SUCCESSOR

of literary work .... SEQUEL

descent .... FALL, LINE, BIRTH, ORIGIN, DECLINE, LINEAGE, ANCESTRY, EXTRACTION, DERIVATION, SUCCESSION

sudden, swift .... SWOOP, POUNCE

describe ..... DRAW, LIMN, LABEL, PAINT, DEFINE, DEPICT, RELATE, NARRATE, PICTURE

briefly again

.... RECAPITULATE

exactly .... DEFINE

grammatically .... PARSE

graphically .... PORTRAY

in detail .... RECOUNT, SPECIFY

description .... SKETCH, ACCOUNT, RELATION, NARRATION

brief .... DIGEST, SUMMARY

detailed .... PARTICULARS

descriptive .... GRAPHIC, STORIED, NARRATIVE

name/title .... EPITHET

poem .... EPIC

word .... LABEL

descry ...... KEN, SEE, ESPY, SPOT, SIGHT, DETECT

Desdemona's husband

.... OTHELLO

slanderer .... IAGO

desecrate .... TAINT, DEBASE, DEFILE, POLLUTE, PROFANE, VIOLATE, DISHONOR

desecration .... BLASPHEMY, SACRILEGE

deseret .... HONEYBEE

desert .... QUIT, LEAVE, MERIT, WASTE, SECEDE, ABANDON, FORSAKE, COLORADO, WILDERNESS

Afghanistan .... DASHTE-MARGOW

African .... NAMIB, LIBYAN, SAHARA, TENERE, ARABIAN, MAKTEIR, KALAHARI, GRAND ERG, ERG-IGUIDI, GUIR-HAMADA, GREAT SAND SEA

animal .... CAMEL

Arabian .... NEFUD, DAHANA, JAFURA, AR-RIMAL, BAHR-ES-SAFI, RUB-AL-KHALI

Arctic .... TUNDRA

Asiatic .... GOBI, THAR, SHAMO, KARA-KUM

Australian .... GIBSON, SIMPSON, GREAT SANDY, GREAT VICTORIA

basin floor .... PLAYA

Chilean .... ATACAMA

China ..... GOBI, ALXA SHAMO, TAKLA MAKAN

dweller .... ARAB(IAN), BEDOUIN

dwelling .... TENT

fertile spot .... OASIS

horse .... ARAB

India .... GREAT INDIAN

Iran .... LUT

Iraq .... SYRIAN

like .... ARID

like condition .... XERIC

Mongolian .... GOBI

Pakistan .... THAR

pertaining to .... EREMIC

plant .... AGAVE, CACTUS, OCOTILLO

plant, tree-like .... SOTOL

pride of the .... CACTI

Russian .... KARA-KUM, KYZYL-KUM

shrub .... RETEM

slang .... DITCH

train .... CARAVAN, CARAVANSARY

Turkestan .... KARA-KUM, KIZIL-KUM

U.S. .... TULE, MOJAVE, PAINTED, ESCALANTE, COLORADO, BLACK ROCK, SMOKE CREEK, WHITE SANDS

valley .... BOLSON

wind .... SIMOOM, SIMOON, SIROCCO

Desert Fox .... ROMMEL

deserted .... LONELY, FORLORN, DESOLATE, SOLITARY, ABANDONED

deserter .... BOLTER, RATTER, RUNAWAY, APOSTATE, FUGITIVE, RENEGADE, RUNAGATE, TURNCOAT

army .... AWOL

describing a .... RAT

desertion .... ESCAPE, FLIGHT, DEFECTION, ABANDONMENT

slang .... COP-OUT

deserts .... DUE

deserve .... EARN, MERIT, ENTITLED TO

deserved reward/punishment

.... DESERT(S)

deservedly .... JUSTLY, WORTHILY

deserving .... WORTHY, MERITORIOUS

punishment .... GUILTY, CULPABLE

desiccant .... DRIER

desiccate .... DRY

desiccated coconut meat

.... COPRA

desideratum .... NEED

design .... AIM, IDEA, PLAN, STYLE, CREATE, SCHEME, PATTERN, PURPOSE, CONTRIVE

having .... FIGURED

highlight .... MOTIF

illustrative .... DIAGRAM

on a page .... VIGNETTE

ornamental .... THEME, DEVICE

rough .... SKETCH

sinister, usually .... PLOT, INTRIGUE

designate .... MARK, NAME, ASSIGN, SELECT, APPOINT, ENTITLE, SPECIFY, INDICATE

again .... RENAME

designated .... SLATED

designation .... TITLE, NAMING, NOMINATION, APPOINTMENT

designator .... SELECTOR

designer .... ARTIST, STYLIST, CREATOR, PLANNER, ARCHITECT of the Wooden Horse .... SINON

designer's forte ...... ORIGINALITY

designing .... WILY, ARTFUL, CRAFTY, CUNNING, SCHEMING

desil .... DEIL

desinence .... SUFFIX

desirable .... IN DEMAND, APPETIZING

part .... MEAT, CREAM

desire .... YEN, NEED, WANT, WILL, WISH, COVET, CRAVE, LIKING, LONGING, PENCHANT

characterized by .... ORECTIC

for sleep .... NARCOLEPSY

overwhelming .... ESTRUS

seat of .... LIVER

strong .... HUNGER

weakest .... VELLEITY

desirer .... LOVER, ASPIRANT

desirous .... AVID, FAIN, KEEN, EAGER, HUNGRY, WISHFUL

desist .... QUIT, STOP, CEASE, ABSTAIN, FORBEAR

desk .... POST, TABLE, PULPIT, BUREAU, COUNTER, ROLLTOP

for prayer .... PRIE DIEU

reading .... AMBO, LECTERN

use of ..... DRAWING, READING, WRITING

writing .... DAVENPORT, SECRETARY, ESCRITOIRE

desman .... MUSK

desmid .... ALGA

desolate .... BLEAK, STARK, BARREN, LONELY, (FOR)LORN, DESERTED, FORSAKEN, SOLITARY, MISERABLE

desolation .... RUIN, WASTE, AGONY, GLOOM, MISERY, SOLITUDE

despair .... WOE, BALE, MISERY, ANGUISH, DESPOND, DESPERATION

desperado .... THUG, BRAVO, OUTLAW, CRIMINAL

hunters .... POSSE

desperate .... RASH, HEROIC, FURIOUS, HOPELESS, RECKLESS

appeal .... SOS

criminal ...... BRAVO, RUFFIAN, DESPERADO

desperation .... FUTILITY, HOPELESSNESS, DESPONDENCY

despicable .... VILE, HATEFUL, ODIOUS, LOW-DOWN, OBNOXIOUS, DETESTABLE, CONTEMPTIBLE

person .... CAD, CHEAT, CROOK, SKUNK, COWARD, GYPPER, COZENER, SCOUNDREL

slang .... SCALY

despise .... HATE, ABHOR, SCORN, DETEST, CONTEMN, DISDAIN

despised .... LOWLY, UNSUNG

despite .... INSULT, MALICE, (AL)THOUGH, IN THE FACE OF, IN THE TEETH OF, NOTWITHSTANDING

despiteful .... HOSTILE

despoil .... ROB, LOOT, RUIN, RAVAGE, PILLAGE, PLUNDER

despoiled: archaic .... REFT

despond .... DESPAIR

despondency ...... BLUES, DUMPS, DISMAY, DESPAIR, DEJECTION

despondent .... DEPRESSED

despot ...... CZAR, TSAR, TYRANT, AUTOCRAT, DICTATOR

Persian .... SATRAP

despotic ruler .... CZAR, SHAH, TSAR

despotism .... TYRANNY, AUTARCHY, AUTOCRACY

despumate .... SKIM

desquamate .... PEEL(OFF)

dessert ...... ICE, FLAN, SWEET(S), MOUSSE, SUNDAE, PARFAIT, CONFECTION

addendum .... CREAM

fruit .... BETTY

fruit juices .... FRAPPE

fruit, gelatin .... CHARLOTTE

item .... PIE, CAKE, FRUITS, PUDDING, ICE CREAM

kind of .... SASS

melon .... BOMBE

milk and gelatin .... BLANC-MANGE

rum .... BABA

spongecake .... TRIFLE

sweetened cream with wine .... SILLABUB, SYLLABUB

desserts .... DUE

destigmatize .... WHITEWASH

destination .... GOAL, ADDRESS, JOURNEY'S END

destine .... LOOM, IMPEND, ORDAIN

destined .... FATED, EXPECTED

destiny .... LOT, DOOM, FATE, LUCK, STAR, FORTUNE

Oriental .... KISMET

destitute .... POOR, NEEDY, DEVOID, HARD-UP, LACKING, FLAT BROKE, DOWN AND OUT

colloquial .... IN THE HOLE

destitution .... NEED, PENURY, POVERTY, INDIGENCE

destrier .... STEED, CHARGER, WARHORSE

destroy .... BURN, RAZE, RUIN,

SACK, SLAY, CRUSH, SMASH, WRECK, RAVAGE, SHATTER, WIPE OUT, DEMOLISH, LAY WASTE, STAMP OUT

by blotting out/effacing .... OBLITERATE

by fire .... GUT

entirely .... ERADICATE, EXTERMINATE

machinery to force agreement .... RATTEN

slang .... TOTAL, TRASH

slowly .... ERODE, WASTE

destroyer .... RUINER, WRECKER

crop .... BLIGHT, LOCUST, DROUGHT

historical .... ATTILA

kind of .... VANDAL, ARSONIST, NIHILIST

military .... BATTLESHIP

of monster .... HERMES, ST. GEORGE

of vermin ...... EXTERMINATOR

of wood .... TERMITE

destruction .... FALL, RUIN, HAVOC, WASTE, WRACK, WRECKAGE, PERDITION

by fire, on purpose ..... ARSON

malicious .... VANDALISM

mass .... GENOCIDE, MASSACRE, SLAUGHTER, DECIMATION

of life by fire/widespread .... HOLOCAUST

of nation .... GENOCIDE

destructive .... DEADLY

insect .... MOTH, LOCUST, TERMITE

liquid .... ACID

natural phenomenon .... STORM, CYCLONE, TORNADO, TYPHOON, HURRICANE, LIGHTNING, FLOOD, EARTHQUAKE

substance .... POISON

to metal .... RUST

destructor .... FURNACE, INCINERATOR

desuetude .... DISUSE

desultory .... FITFUL, RANDOM, AIMLESS, ERRATIC, EXCURSIVE, HAPHAZARD

detach ...... LOOSE, SEVER, UNFIX, SEPARATE, UNFASTEN

detached .... ALONE, ALOOF, SEPARATE, INDIFFERENT

in music .... SPICCATO

detachment .... UNIT, DETAIL, ALOOFNESS, ISOLATION

detail .... ITEM, PART, UNIT, SPECIFY, ENUMERATE,

ASSIGN(MENT), PARTICULAR
attentive to .... METICULOUS
detailed .... ITEMIZED, SPECIFIC,
ASSIGNED, ELABORATE
account .... EXPLICATION
explanation .... EXPOSITION
list .... ROSTER, DIRECTORY,
INVENTORY, ENUMERATION
statement .... RECITAL
details, small and unimportant
.... MINUTIAE
detain ...... HOLD, DELAY, ARREST,
HINDER, CONFINE, RESTRAIN
ship in port .... INTERN
detect ...... SPY, ESPY, FIND, SPOT,
SENSE, TRACE, DESCRY,
NOTICE, DISCERN, DISCOVER,
PERCEIVE
detecting device .... BUG, RADAR,
SONAR, DOWSER FEELER,
ANTENNA, TENTACLE
detection .... ESPIAL, GLIMPSE,
DISCOVERY
radar .... INTERCEPTION
detective ...... TEC, DICK, SLEUTH,
GUMSHOE, SPOTTER,
HAWKSHAW, OPERATIVE,
POLICEMAN
Conan Doyle's .... HOLMES
describing one .... TAIL,
SHADOW, PRIVATE EYE
kind of .... UNDERCOVER,
PLAINCLOTHES
of fiction/movie .... CHAN,
MOTO, NERO, DRAKE, SAINT,
TRACY, TRENT, HOLMES,
POIROT
orchid-loving .... NERO
store .... FLOOR WALKER
story .... MAIGRET
story character .... GOON,
WARDEN, CORONER,
HOODLUM, SHERIFF,
INFORMER, HATCHETMAN,
INVESTIGATOR
detector of sorts ...... BUG, NOSE,
RADAR, SONAR, FEELER,
ANTENNA
detent .... PAWL, CATCH, CLICK
detente ...... TRUCE, COOLING OFF
of a sort ...... RAPPROCHEMENT
detention ...... DELAY, CAPTIVITY,
CONFINEMENT
deter .... BLOCK, IMPEDE,
PREVENT, OBSTRUCT,
DISCOURAGE
deterge .... CLEAN(SE)
detergent .... SOAP, ABLUENT,
SAPONIN, SOLVENT, CLEANSER
compound .... BORON
deteriorate .... ROT, DECAY,

DEBASE, PERISH, WORSEN, GO
BAD, CORRUPT, DEPRECIATE
from disuse .... RUST
determinant .... CAUSE
determinate ...... FIXED, DEFINITE,
SPECIFIC
determination .... WILL,
FIRMNESS, RESOLUTION
determine .... END, JUDGE,
DECIDE, DEFINE, SETTLE,
RESOLVE, SPECIFY, ASCERTAIN
issue by combat ...... DERAIGN
quotient .... DIVIDE
worth of .... EVALUATE,
APPRAISE
determined ...... SET, FIRM, DEAD
SET, RESOLUTE
deterrent ...... STUMBLING BLOCK
of a kind .... FEAR, DOUBT,
SHAME
war .... A-BOMB
detest ...... HATE, ABHOR, LOATHE,
DESPISE, DISLIKE, EXECRATE
detestable ...... ODIOUS, HATEFUL,
HORRID, DAMNABLE,
EXECRABLE, ABOMINABLE
person .... BOOR, LOUT,
COWARD, POLTROON
detestation ...... HATRED, DISLIKE,
LOATHING
dethrone .... OUST, DEPOSE,
UNSEAT, UNCROWN
dethronement, object of
.... KING, RULER, EMPEROR,
CHAMPION
detonate .... GO OFF, SET OFF,
FIRE, EXPLODE, FULMINATE
detonating device .... CAP, PIN,
FUSE, TRIGGER, PERCUSSION
object .... BOMB, SHELL,
SQUIB, BULLET, GRENADE,
DYNAMITE, FIRECRACKER
detour .... TURN, BYPASS, DIVERT,
DEVIATION
detract .... DECRY, BELITTLE,
BACKBITE, CRITICIZE,
DEROGATE, TAKE AWAY,
DISPARAGE, DEPRECIATE
detraction .... LAMPOON,
SCANDAL, CALUMNY,
CRITICISM
detractor .... MUDSLINGER
d'etre, ___ .... RAISON
detriment .... HARM, LOSS,
DAMAGE, INJURY, LIABILITY
detritus .... DEBRIS
Detroit of Italy .... TURIN
product .... CAR, TRUCK,
AUTOMOBILE
suburb .... ECORSE

deuce .... TWO(SPOT)
superior of/topper .... TREY
Deus .... GOD
deus ex ___ .... MACHINA
Deutschland .... GERMANY
devaluate .... LOWER, CHEAPEN,
DEPRECIATE
devastate ...... RAZE, RUIN, SACK,
CRUSH, LEVEL, RAVAGE,
DESTROY, LAY WASTE,
DEMOLISH
devastation .... RUIN, HAVOC,
WRECK, CATASTROPHE,
DESTRUCTION
devel .... BLOW
develop .... GROW, RIPEN,
EVOLVE, MATURE, UNFOLD,
ENLARGE
more fully, as with details
.... AMPLIFY, ELABORATE
plants .... CULTIVATE
start to .... GERMINATE
to make more valuable
.... IMPROVE
to make qualified .... TRAIN
development .... EVENT, CHANGE,
GROWTH, PROGRESS
building ..... HOUSING PROJECT
of fetus .... FETATION,
PREGNANCY
process of .... EVOLUTION
result of .... OUTGROWTH,
CONSEQUENCE
Devi .... MAYA, SAKTI
consort of .... SIVA
father of .... HIMAVAT
deviant .... VARIANT
deviate ...... ROAM, SHEER, STRAY,
RAMBLE, DIVERGE, MEANDER,
GO ADRIFT
from course .... YAW, VEER,
DETOUR, SWERVE, WANDER,
STRAGGLE
from main topic ...... DIGRESS,
DIVAGATE
deviating .... ABERRANT
deviation .... DETOUR, DIVERSION,
DEFLECTION
of a ship/airplane from path
.... DRIFT
sexual .... TRANSVESTISM
deviative .... INDIRECT
device .... PLAN, TOOL, DESIGN,
EMBLEM, GADGET,
MECHANISM
air moistening .... HUMIDOR
aircraft safety ...... PARACHUTE
any: colloq. .... HICK(E)Y,
DOOHICKEY
any: sl. .... DINGUS

consisting of two small telescopes .... BINOCULARS
deceptive/secret .... GIMMICK
fastening .... HASP
for catching criminals/fish .... DRAGNET
for hearing sound .... STETHOSCOPE
for holding stone in jewel cutting .... DIAL
for raising bucket .... WINDLASS
for secret listening .... BUG
gripping .... VISE, CLAMP
hourglass figure .... CORSET, GIRDLE
ingenious .... GADGET
light wave amplifying .... LASER
loosening .... EASER
measuring .... TAPE, RULE(R)
restraining .... BRAKE
sound amplifying .... MASER
thought up .... INVENTION, CONTRIVANCE
time beating ...... METRONOME
to check vibration .... DAMPER
tone muffling .... MUTE, PEDAL
tricky .... RUSE, STRATAGEM
underwater .... SONAR
used at a bee .... QUILT FRAME
devil .... DEMON, FIEND, SATAN, AZAZEL, BELIAL, WRETCH, LUCIFER, MONSTER, OLD NICK, OLD HARRY, OLD SCRATCH
colloquial .... TORMENT
dog: sl. .... MARINE, NAVYMAN, LEATHERNECK
little .... IMP, BRAT
may-care .... CARELESS, RECKLESS, INSOUCIANT, NONCHALANT, HAPPY-GO-LUCKY
Moslem .... SHAITAN
of the .... DIABOLIC
Scottish .... MAHOUND
worship .... IDOLATRY, SATANISM
worshiper .... DIABOLIST
devilfish .... RAY, MANTA, SKATE, SEABAT, OCTOPUS
devilish .... CRUEL, WICKED, HELLISH, INFERNAL, DEMONIAC, DIABOLIC(AL)
devilkin .... IMP
devilment ...... MALICE, MISCHIEF
devil's bones .... DICE
name .... NICK, SATAN, LUCIFER

—— (side for argument's sake) .... ADVOCATE
deviltry ...... DEVILRY, SATANISM, WICKEDNESS, WITCHCRAFT
devious .... SLY, UNTRUE, SHIFTY, TRICKY, CROOKED, ROVING, WINDING, TORTUOUS, CIRCUITOUS, ROUNDABOUT
devise .... GIFT, PLAN, PLOT, COOK, WILL, INVENT, SCHEME, CONCOCT, BEQUEATH, CONTRIVE
devised, not .... INTESTATE
devisor .... TESTATOR
devitalize .... SAP, WEAKEN
devoid .... EMPTY, LACKING, WITHOUT, DESTITUTE
devoir .... DUTY
devolve ...... PASS(ON), TRANSFER, CHANGE HANDS
devote .... GIVE, LEND, APPLY, EMPLOY, DEDICATE, CONSECRATE
devoted .... TRUE, LOYAL, DEVOUT, ADDICTED, FAITHFUL
devotee .... FAN, IST, BUFF, ADDICT, VOTARY, ZEALOT, ENTHUSIAST, FOLLOWER, PARTISAN
avid .... FANATIC
of beauty .... (A)ESTHETE, CONNOISSEUR
of sports, etc. ..... AFICIONADO
of the fine arts .... DILETTANTE
devotion .... ZEAL, ARDOR, PIETY, FEALTY, LOYALTY, FIDELITY
nine-day .... NOVENA
devotions ...... PRAYERS, WORSHIP
devour .... EAT, CONSUME, DESTROY
greedily .... GORGE, GOBBLE, WOLF DOWN
more .... OUTEAT
devout .... GODLY, PIOUS, EARNEST, FERVENT, RELIGIOUS
devoutness .... PIETY
dew .... MIST, MOISTURE
frozen ..... RIME, (HOAR)FROST
dewclaw .... DIGIT
dewlap .... JOWL, PALEA, LAPPET, WATTLE
DEWS, part of .... DISTANT, EARLY, WARNING, SYSTEM
dewy .... DAMP, MOIST
eyed .... AIRY, INNOCENT
dexter .... RIGHT-HAND SIDE
opposed to .... SINISTER
dexterity .... KNACK, SKILL, ADROITNESS, CLEVERNESS

special .... CRAFT
dexterous .... DEFT, ADEPT, HANDY, ADROIT, SKILLFUL
dextral .... RIGHT(HANDED)
dextrose .... SUGAR, GLUCOSE
dhole .... CUON
d'honneur, —— (duel) .... AFFAIRE
di, as prefix ...... TWICE, DOUBLE, TWOFOLD
dia, as prefix .... ACROSS, THROUGH
diabetes, form of .... BRONZE, MELLITUS, INSIPIDUS, GESTATIONAL
injection treatment for .... INSULIN
oral drug to control .... ORINASE, GLIPIZIDE
person who has ...... DIABETIC
diabetics' bread .... GLUTEN
diablerie .... SORCERY, DEVIL(T)RY, MISCHIEF
diabolic .... WICKED, SATANIC, DEVILISH, FIENDISH, INFERNAL
diabolism .... DEMONRY, SORCERY, SATANISM
political .... NAZISM
diacetylmorphine .... HEROIN
diacritical mark .... TILDE, UMLAUT, DIERESIS
diadem .... CROWN, TIARA, HEADBAND
diagnose ...... ANALYZE, EXAMINE
diagnosis .... FINDING, PROGNOSIS
diagnostic in medicine .... SYMPTOM, DIACRITIC
rap .... PERCUSS
diagonal .... TILTED, OBLIQUE, ASLANT, SLANTING
line .... BIAS
line between words .... VIRGULE
diagonally ...... CATER-CORNERED, OBLIQUELY, CATTY-CORNER(ED)
diagram ...... PLAN, PLOT, CHART, GRAPH, SCHEMA, SCHEME, SKETCH, DRAWING, OUTLINE, BLUEPRINT
dial .... CALL, DISK, FACE, TUNE IN, INDICATOR
compass .... CARD
miner's .... COMPASS
pointer .... HAND
dialect ...... CANT, ARGOT, IDIOM, PATOIS, LINGO, SLANG, JARGON, LANGUE, TONGUE, SPEECH, DICTION, LANGUAGE, VERNACULAR
dialects, mixture of ...... LINGUA

FRANCA

dialectician .... LOGICIAN

dialectics .... LOGIC, ARGUMENTATION

dialogue .... LINES, SCRIPT, CONVERSATION, INTERLOCUTION

dialogues of Buddha ...... SUTRA

diamagnetic substance .... ZINC, BISMUTH

diameter .... WIDTH, BREADTH, THICKNESS

measuring device ..... CALIPER

of tube/gun .... BORE, CALIBER

diametrical .... DIRECT, ABSOLUTE, COMPLETE, CONTRARY, OPPOSITE

diamond .... GEM, JEWEL, STONE, FIELD, PLAYGROUND

anniversary .... SIXTIETH

base/facet .... CULET

base, baseball .... SACK

center, ancient ..... GOLCONDA

circular, flat .... RONDEL

crystal/twin crystal .... MACLE

cup .... DOP, DOBB

cut .... FACET, BRIOLETTE

cutter .... LAPIDARY

drill .... CARBONADO

feature .... BASE, HOMEPLATE

habiliment .... MITT

holder .... DOP

in baseball .... INFIELD

in the rough .... CRUDE, UNSHAPED

industrial use .... CUTTING, ABRASIVE, DRILLING

inferior .... BORT

native .... CARBON

official, baseball ..... UMP(IRE)

perfect .... PARAGON

plane figure .... LOZENGE

rough .... BRAIT

shape .... RHOMB(US), PARALLELOGRAM

shaped armor plate .... MASCLE

shaped pattern .... DIAPER

slang .... ICE, SPARKLER, ENGAGEMENT RING

stone, describing a .... DAZZLING, BRILLIANT, SPARKLING, GLITTERING

synthetic .... FABULITE

Diamond of music .... NEIL

State .... DELAWARE

diamondback ...... MOTH, SNAKE, TURTLE, RATTLER, TERRAPIN

diamonds, black .... COAL

or hearts .... RED SUIT

Diana .... DELIA, ARTEMIS

parent of ..... LATONA, JUPITER

poetic .... MOON

dianthus .... CARNATION

diapason .... (ORGAN)STOP, TUNING FORK

diaper ...... DIDY, TOWEL, NAPKIN

diaphanous .... THIN, GAUZY, SHEER, VAGUE, INDISTINCT, TRANSLUCENT, TRANSPARENT

diaphoresis .... SWEAT, PERSPIRATION

diaphragm .... MIDRIFF

device, contraceptive .... PESSARY

pertaining to .... PHRENIC

sound .... HICCUP, HICCOUGH

diarist .... PEPYS, BURNEY, NICOLSON, JOURNALIST

diarrhea, common cause of ...... STRESS, FOOD POISONING

form of .... ACUTE, CHRONIC

diary .... RECORD, DAYBOOK, DIURNAL, JOURNAL, MEMOIRS, CHRONICLE, EPHEMERIS

ship's .... LOG(BOOK)

diaskeuast .... EDITOR

diastase .... ENZYME, AMYLASE

diatomic .... BIVALENT

shell .... FRUSTULE

diatonic, opposed to .... CHROMATIC

scale .... GAMUT

diatribe .... SCREED, TIRADE, PHILIPPIC, DENUNCIATION

Diaz, Mexican president .... PORFIRIO

Rodrigo .... (EL)CID

dib .... BOB, DAP, DIP

dibble .... DIB, DAP, DIP, SOW, FISH, SCATTER

dice .... CUBE, CHOP, CUT(UP), GAME, BONES, CUBES, IVORY, CRAPS, IVORIES, CHECKER

cater of .... FOUR

five on .... CINQUE

game .... NOVUM, HAZARD

game losing throw .... CRAP

six in .... SICE

spot .... PIP

term .... COME, CRAPS, ELEVEN, AMBSACE, NATURAL

three spots .... TREY

throw .... DIE, JOE, ROLL, CATER, CHAPS, BOXCAR, RAILROAD

throw, disallowed ..... NO DICE

throw natural .... SEVEN

trick .... COG

diced .... CUBED

dichroite .... IOLITE

dick: sl. .... DETECTIVE

dickens: colloq. .... DEUCE, DEVIL

Dickens (Charles) beadle .... (MR.) BUMBLE

character ..... PIP, TIM, DORA, GAMP, HEEP, ROSA, FAGIN, BUMBLE, DORRIT, PICKWICK, (JENNY)WREN, (OLIVER)TWIST

dismal swamp of .... EDEN

hero .... CARTON

heroine .... NELL

pen name .... BOZ

pickpocket .... FAGIN

dicker .... TRADE, BARTER, HAGGLE, BARGAIN

dickey ...... BIB, COLLAR, DONKEY, RUMBLE, VESTEE, PINAFORE, (BACK)SEAT, PLASTRON

dicotyledon .... EXOGEN

dictate .... BID, ORDER, ENJOIN, COMMAND, DOMINEER

dictator .... DESPOT, TYRANT, AUTOCRAT

propaganda of .... BIG LIE

dictatorial ...... BOSSY, DESPOTIC, DOGMATIC, ARBITRARY, IMPERIOUS

diction .... EXPRESSION, ENUNCIATION

poor .... CACOLOGY

dictionary .... LEXICON, REFERENCE, WORDBOOK, THESAURUS, VOCABULARY

prosody .... GRADUS

small .... DICT

dictum .... MAXIM, SAY-SO, SAYING, DECISION, PRONOUNCEMENT

didactic .... PEDANTIC

didactics .... PEDAGOGY

didapper .... GREBE, DABCHICK

diddle .... CHEAT, JIGGLE, SWINDLE

Diderot, Fr. philosopher .... DENIS

dido .... ANTIC, CAPER, PRANK

Dido, love of .... AENEAS

realm of .... CARTHAGE

didy .... DIAPER

didymous .... TWIN, DOUBLE

die ...... CUBE, DADO, DICE, MOLD, STAMP, EXPIRE, MATRIX, PERISH, DECEASE, SUCCUMB, PASS AWAY, SUFFOCATE

due to cold .... WINTERKILL

slang .... CROAK, KICK THE BUCKET

Die Fledermaus maid .... ADELE

diehard ...... FANATIC, STUBBORN

dieresis .... UMLAUT

Dies Irae .... HYMN, JUDGMENT DAY

diet .... FAST, FOOD, (DAILY)FARE, CONGRESS, COUNCIL, ASSEMBLY, VICTUALS
course of .... REGIMEN
faulty .... DISTROPHY
old style .... BANT
slang .... GRUB
successfully .... SLIM
dieter's goal .... SLIM
dietetics .... SITOLOGY
differ .... VARY, DEVIATE, EXCEPT, DISSENT, DISAGREE, TAKE ISSUE
difference .... ODDS, VARIETY, DISPUTE, QUARREL, VARIANCE, VARIATION, DISAGREEMENT
between prices bid and asked
.... SPREAD
in years, ideas, beliefs
.... GENERATION GAP
lunar and solar year .... EPACT
different .... ELSE, OTHER, APART, UNLIKE, VARIED, ANOTHER, DIVERSE(E), DISTINCT
combining form .... HETERO
ones .... OTHERS
differentiate .... ALTER, ISOLATE, DISTINGUISH
difficult .... HARD, TOUGH, NOT EASY, KNOTTY, TANGLED, ARDUOUS, COMPLICATED
deed .... FEAT
problem ...... POSER, DILEMMA, GORDIAN(KNOT)
to handle/treat .... STUBBORN
to hold .... SLIPPERY AS AN EEL
to please .... QUEASY, DIFFICILE, DEMANDING
to understand .... ABSTRUSE
difficulty .... SNAG, RIGOR, PLIGHT, SCRAPE, DILEMMA, PROBLEM, STRAITS, TROUBLE, HARDSHIP, QUANDARY
colloq. .... FIX, STEW, PICKLE
crucial .... CRISIS
slang .... JAM
speaking .... APHASIA
that test one's endurance
.... TRIAL, TRIBULATION
trying, severe .... ORDEAL
without solution
.... STALEMATE
writing .... AGRAPHIA
diffidence .... MODESTY, RESERVE, SHYNESS
diffident .... COY, SHY, TIMID, DEMURE, MODEST, BASHFUL
diffract .... SPREAD, SCATTER, DISPERSE

diffuse .... WORDY, SPREAD, RADIATE, SCATTER, PERMEATE, BROADCAST
diffusion .... SPREADING, BROADCASTING, DISSEMINATION
through a membrane
.... OSMOSIS
dig .... JAB, POKE, PROD, SPUD, NUDGE, SPADE, UNEARTH, EXCAVATE
colloquial .... JEER, TAUNT
for metal .... MINE
out .... GOUGE, SCOOP, UPROOT, EXHUME, SHOVEL
slang .... SEE, ENJOY, UNDERSTAND
up .... DELVE, EXHUME, UNCOVER, DISCOVER
with snout .... ROOT, ROUT
digest .... ABSORB, APERCU, PONDER, ABSTRACT, SHORTEN, SUMMARY, SYNOPSIS, CONDENSE, ABRIDGE, SUMMARIZE, ASSIMILATE
the .... PANDECT
digestion .... ABSORPTION
good .... EUPEPSIA
impaired .... DYSPEPSIA
of .... PEPTIC
digestive enzyme .... PAPAIN, PEPSIN
digger .... HOER, MOLE, MINER, WASP, SAPPER, SPADER, SANDHOG, TRENCHER
slang .... AUSTRALIAN, NEW ZEALANDER
digging tool .... HOE, PLOW, SPUD, SPADE, SHOVEL, TROWEL, MATTOCK, PICKAX(E)
dight .... ADORN, EQUIP
digit .... TOE, CIPHER, FIGURE, HALLUX, FINGER, NUMBER, INTEGER
useless .... DEWCLAW
digital .... NUMERAL, NUMERIC, RETENTIVE
computer .... ENIAC
infection .... FELON
digitalis ...... FIGWORT, FOXGLOVE
digits .... HALLUCES
diglot .... BILINGUAL
dignified .... NOBLE, SEDATE, EXALTED, STATELY, DECOROUS
grace/richness .... ELEGANCE
dignify .... ADORN, EXALT, HONOR, ENNOBLE
dignitary .... VIP, BIGWIG, PERSONAGE

dignity .... HONOR, PRIDE, REPUTE, DECORUM, MAJESTY, EMINENCE, NOBILITY, STATELINESS
steeped in .... PRIM, STAID, DEMURE, FORMAL, AFFECTED, DECOROUS, PRIGGISH, CONCEITED
digress .... ROAM, STRAY, RAMBLE, DEVIATE, DIVAGATE
digressions of a sort ...... ASIDES, AD LIBS
dik-dik .... ANTELOPE
dike .... DAM, DITCH, LEVEE, CAUSEWAY, EMBANKMENT
break in a .... CREVASSE
protective mat .... MATTRESS
dilantin, users of ...... EPILEPTICS
dilapidated .... RATTY, RUINED, DECAYED, RUN-DOWN, CRUMBLING, BROKEN-DOWN, RAMSHACKLE
dilapidation .... RUIN, DECAY
dilate .... SWELL, WIDEN, EXPAND, DISTEND, ENLARGE, STRETCH
dilation .... EXPANSION, ENLARGEMENT
cause of eyes' .... WONDER, SURPRISE, INCREDULITY
heart's .... DIASTOLE
pupil's .... MYDRIASIS
dilatory ...... LAGGARD, DELAYING
tactic in Congress
.... FILIBUSTER
dilemma ...... FIX, JAM, TROUBLE, QUANDARY, PREDICAMENT
horn of .... CHOICE, ALTERNATIVE
play's .... NODE
dilettante ...... POSEUR, AMATEUR, DABBLER, TRIFLER, (A)ESTHETE
of a sort .... BOHEMIAN, AFICIONADO
diligence .... INDUSTRY, CONSTANCY, STAGECOACH, APPLICATION, PERSEVERANCE
diligent .... BUSY, ACTIVE, CAREFUL, MINDFUL, SEDULOUS, ATTENTIVE, HARDWORKING
dill(seed) .... ANET, ANISE
dilly .... DARB
colloquial .... LULU, BEAUT, DAISY, PEACH
of the valley .... ECHO
dillydally .... WAIT, DELAY, TARRY, WAVER, LOITER, TRIFLE, HESITATE, VACILLATE
diluent .... SOLVENT
dilute .... THIN, THIN OUT, WATER,

ADULTERATE

slang .... LACE, SPIKE

diluted ...... THIN, WEAK, WASHY, WATERY

diluting substance ...... DILUENT, SOLUTION

dim .... DARK, DULL, FADE, HAZY, FAINT, VAGUE, MIRK(Y), MISTY, DARKEN, GLOOMY, MURK(Y), ECLIPSE, OBSCURE, UNCLEAR

with .... BLEAR, RHEUM

dime .... COIN, TEN CENTS

a-dozen .... CHEAP

novel detective .... (NICK)CARTER

dimension .... AREA, SIZE, SCOPE, EXTENT, HEIGHT, LENGTH, BREADTH, THICKNESS, MEASUREMENT

dimensions, of three .... CUBIC

diminish ...... EBB, WANE, TAPER, (A)BATE, LESSEN, REDUCE, SHRINK, PETER OUT, DWINDLE, DECREASE

by use .... WEAR

diminutive .... WEE, TINY, SMALL, LITTLE, PETITE, MINIKIN

animal .... RUNT

fowl .... BANTAM

helper .... ELF

suffix .... IE, KIN, LET, ULE, ETTE, LING

dimness .... HAZE, OPACITY, DARKNESS, OBSCURITY

dimple .... DENT, HOLLOW, FOSSETTE

dimsighted .... NEARSIGHTED

dimwit .... SAP, CLOD, DOLT, DUNCE, IDIOT, SIMPLETON

din ...... NOISE, OUTCRY, CLAMOR, RACKET, UPROAR

Dinah, singer .... SHORE

dinar .... COIN

dindle .... THRILL, TINGLE, VIBRATE

dine .... EAT, SUP, FEED, MESS, REGALE, SUSTAIN

diner .... EATERY, DINING CAR, RESTAURANT

ding .... RING

dingbat .... STICK, STONE

slang .... SAP(HEAD), BOOB, KLUTZ, DING-A-LING

dinghy .... SABOT, (ROW)BOAT, SHALLOP

dingle .... DALE, DELL, GLEN, VALLEY

dingus .... DEVICE, GADGET

dingy ...... DIRTY, GRIMY, DISMAL, SHABBY, DISCOLORED

dining alcove ...... NOOK, DINETTE

car .... DINER

hall .... MESS, REFECTORY

room .... GRILL, CANTEEN, DINETTE, EATERY, CAFETERIA

table .... BOARD, COUNTER

table companion .... MESSMATE

table ornament .... EPERGNE, CENTERPIECE

dink .... DECK, TRIM

dinkey .... TROLLEY, LOCOMOTIVE

dinky .... SMALL, LITTLE, PIDDLING

dinner .... SUPPER

buffet style ..... SMORGASBORD

course .... ENTREE

jacket .... TUX(EDO)

of .... PRANDIAL

treat .... POT-ROAST, PRIME-RIB

wagon .... TEACART

with toasting, etc. .... BANQUET

dinnerware .... FLATWARE, CHINAWARE, GLASSWARE, TABLEWARE, SILVERWARE

dinosaur .... SAURIAN, SAUROPOD, DIPLODOCUS, ORNITHOPOD

amphibious .... TITANOSAUR

carnivorous/flesh-eating .... MEGALOSAUR, ALLOSAUR(US)

plant-eating .... BRONTOSAUR(US)

type of .... DUCK-BILLED

dint ...... HIT, DENT, SLOG, FORCE, MARK, POWER, EXERTION

diocese .... SEE, REGION, EPARCHY, DISTRICT, BISHOPRIC

Diomedes' father .... TYDEUS

Dionne, quint, ... OLIVA, CECILE, EMELIE, YVONNE, ANNETTE

Dionysian gala .... REVEL

Dionysus' attendant ...... NYMPH, M(A)ENAD

mother .... SEMELE

son .... PRIAPUS

staff .... THYRSUS

diopter .... ALIDADE

diorama .... SIGHT, DISPLAY, EXHIBIT, LANDSCAPE

Dioscuri ...... TWINS, CASTOR AND POLLUX

dip .... BAIL, DROP, LADE, SINK, SOAK, LOWER, CANDLE, PLUNGE

a doughnut .... DUNK

bait .... DAP, DIB(BLE)

in gravy/milk .... SOP

in liquid .... DOUSE, SOUSE,

(IM)MERSE

lightly .... DAP, DIB

slang .... PICKPOCKET

the colors .... SALUTE

diplo: comb. form .... TWO, TWIN, DOUBLE

diploma .... DEGREE, CHARTER, CERTIFICATE

colloquial .... SHEEPSKIN

diplomacy .... TACT, FINESSE, SKILL, PROWESS, STRATEGY

way of .... PROTOCOL

diplomat .... ENVOY, CONSUL, EXPERT, LEGATE, MINISTER, STATESMAN, AMBASSADOR

papal .... NUNCIO

diplomatic .... SUAVE, ARTFUL, POLITIC, TACTFUL, CONSULAR

agreements/ceremonial forms/code .... PROTOCOL

change of policy .... DEMARCHE

corps .... EMBASSY, LEGATION, FOREIGN SERVICE

corps, dean of .... DOYEN

denial .... DEMENTI

dispatch container ...... POUCH

immunity .... DIPPLE

paper .... MEMORIAL

privilege .... IMMUNITY, EXEMPTION

staff member .... ATTACHE

diplopia .... DOUBLE VISION

dipody .... VERSE, SYZYGY, DIMETER

dipper ...... URSA, GREBE, LADLE, OUSEL, OUZEL, SCOOP, PIGGIN

dipsomaniac .... SOT, TOPER, BOOZER, GUZZLER, DRUNKARD, ALCOHOLIC

dipsomaniacs, society of ...... ALCOHOLICS ANONYMOUS

dipterous insect .... GNAT, HOUSEFLY, MOSQUITO

dire .... URGENT, FATEFUL, FEARFUL, DREADFUL, HORRIBLE, TERRIBLE, APPALLING, CALAMITOUS

circumstances .... STRAITS

direct .... AIM, ORDER, POINT, FRANK, MANAGE, STRAIGHT, IMMEDIATE, FIRST-HAND

a helmsman .... CONN

an orchestra .... LEAD, CONDUCT

attention to .... REFER

hit .... ON TARGET, BULL'S EYE

opposite .... ANTITHESIS

proceedings .... PRESIDE

the affairs of state .... RULE, GOVERN

the course/movement of .... GUIDE, STEER

direction .... EAST, LINE, PATH, WEST, NORTH, ORDER, SOUTH, TREND, COURSE, ADDRESS, GUIDANCE, TENDENCY, MANAGEMENT

without fixed .... AIMLESS, ERRATIC, MEANDERING

directions, in all .... ABOUT

directive .... ORDER, COMMAND, INSTRUCTION(S)

directly .... SOON, FLATLY, AS SOON AS, PROMPTLY, INSTANTLY

colloquial .... SPANG

opposite .... DIAMETRICAL

director .... BOSS, GUIDE, LEADER, MASTER, MANAGER, EMPLOYER, MODERATOR, SUPERVISOR

concern of .... SCRIPT

in music .... CONDUCTOR

of a two-wheeled cart, horse-drawn .... CHARIOTEER

of a vessel .... HELMSMAN

of an aircraft .... FLIER, PILOT, AVIATOR

directory .... INDEX, REGISTER

enter in .... LIST

dirge .... HYMN, MASS, SONG, LAMENT, CORONACH, THRENODY, EPICEDIUM

for dead .... REQUIEM

dirigible .... BLIMP, AIRSHIP, BALLOON, ZEPPELIN

bag/covering .... ENVELOPE

cabin .... GONDOLA

gas .... HELIUM

pilot .... AERONAUT

pod .... CAB

diriment .... VOIDING, NULLIFYING

dirk ...... SNEE, DAGGER, PONIARD

dirl .... TINGLE, VIBRATE

dirndl .... SKIRT

dirt ...... MUD, DUST, MUCK, SOIL, EARTH, FILTH, GRIME, GOSSIP

dirty .... FOUL, VILE, MURKY, DEFILE, FILTHY, SOILED, SORDID, OBSCENE, POLLUTE, UNCLEAN

look .... SNEER

place .... HOVEL

writings/pictures .... SMUT, PORNO, PORNOGRAPHY

Dis .... HADES, ORCUS, PLUTO, UNDERWORLD

disability .... HANDICAP, IMPAIRMENT, INCAPACITY

disable .... LAME, MAIM, UNFIT, DAMAGE, IMPAIR, CRIPPLE, HAMSTRING, DISQUALIFY

disadvantage .... HARM, LOSS, DAMAGE, TROUBLE, DRAWBACK, HANDICAP, DETRIMENT

disadvantaged .... NEEDY, INDIGENT

disadvantageous .... HARMFUL

disaffect .... ALIENATE, ESTRANGE

disagree .... CLASH, DIFFER, CONTEND, CONTEST, DISPUTE

disagreeable .... CROSS, CRANKY, UGLY, TESTY, UNSAVORY, OFFENSIVE, UNPLEASANT

situation ...... FIX, JAM, SCOUR, SCRAPE, PREDICAMENT

smell .... FETOR

disagreeably moist and cold .... MUGGY, CLAMMY

moist and hot .... SULTRY, SWELTERING

disagreement ...... ROW, DISPUTE, QUARREL, REFUSAL, ARGUMENT, FRICTION, VARIANCE, DIFFERENCE

result of couple's .... SPAT, SPLIT, DIVORCE, SEPARATION

disallow .... DENY, REFUSE, REJECT

disappear .... GO, FADE, PASS, FLEE, DEPART, ESCAPE, VANISH, DISSOLVE, EVANESCE

gradually .... PETER OUT

when you stand, they .... LAPS

disappearance .... EXIT, ABSENCE, DEPARTURE

disappoint ...... BALK, BILK, FAIL, FOIL, JILT, LET DOWN, DISPLEASE, DISSATISFY

disappointment .... BLOW, CHAGRIN, LETDOWN

disapproval .... CENSURE, DISLIKE, OBJECTION, REJECTION

show of ...... BOO, HISS, HOOT, SNEER, SNORT

disapprove .... DAMN, DENY, VETO, REJECT, CONDEMN, TURN DOWN, CRITICIZE

disarm .... CHARM, PLACATE, DEMILITARIZE

disarming .... SOFT-SPOKEN

disarrange .... MESS(UP), MUSS, MIX UP, RUMPLE, UNSETTLE

disarray .... UPSET, DISORDER, CONFUSION

disarticulate .... AMPUTATE, DISJOINT

disaster .... EVIL, CALAMITY, TRAGEDY, MISFORTUNE, CATASTROPHE

sudden and great .... DEBACLE

disavow .... DENY, ABJURE, DISOWN, DISCLAIM, REPUDIATE

disband .... DISMISS, BREAK UP, DISPERSE, DISSOLVE, SCATTER, DEMOBILIZE

disbar .... EXPEL, EXCLUDE

disbelief in God .... ATHEISM

disbeliever .... DOUBTER, SKEPTIC

disburse .... ALLOT, SPEND, PAY OUT, EXPEND

disc .... DISH, PATEN, PLATE

discalced .... BAREFOOTED

discard .... RID, DROP, JUNK, SHED, CHUCK, SCRAP, REJECT, CAST OFF

card from hand .... THROW

discarded cargo .... JETSAM

discern .... SEE, ESPY, DETECT, NOTICE, DISCOVER, PERCEIVE

beforehand .... FORESEE

discerning ...... ASTUTE, SHREWD, SAPIENT, SAGACIOUS, APPRECIATIVE

discernment .... FLAIR, KNACK, SENSE, TASTE, ACUMEN, APPRECIATION, UNDERSTANDING

discharge ...... DO, EMIT, HANDLE, FLUXION, RELEASE, RELIEVE, REMOVE, EMISSION

a cargo .... OFF-LOAD, UNLADE, UNLOAD

a cargo, as in a heap, mass .... DUMP

a debt .... QUIT, RETIRE, SETTLE, LIQUIDATE

air, gas completely .... EXHAUST

by force .... EJECT, EXPEL

electric .... SHOCK, SPARK

from a job/position .... CASHIER, DISMISS, LAY OFF, DISEMPLOY, GIVE THE AX

from a job/position: sl. .... CAN, FIRE, SACK

from a wound, ulcer .... SANIES

from duty/obligation .... FREE, SPARE, EXCUSE, EXEMPT

from military service .... MUSTER OUT

morbid .... GLEET

of blood, pus .... ISSUE

one's duties .... RENDER, MANAGE, EXECUTE, FULFILL, PERFORM

projectile .... FIRE, SHOOT

pus .... MATURATE, SUPPURATE

waste matter from body
.... EGEST, EXCRETE
disciple .... PUPIL, APOSTLE,
DEVOTEE, FOLLOWER,
ADHERENT
India .... CHELA
disciplinarian .... MARTINET,
STICKLER, CHASTENER
British university .... BULLDOG
stick of a .... FERULE
disciplinary mark .... DEMERIT
discipline .... DRILL, REGIMEN,
CONFORM, PRACTICE,
TRAIN(ING), CORRECT(ION),
PUNISH(MENT), GOVERN,
(SELF)CONTROL, OBEDIENCE
fellow student .... HAZE
disclaim .... DENY, REFUSE,
DISOWN, DISAVOW,
RENOUNCE, REPUDIATE
disclaimer .... DENIAL
in property rights
.... QUITCLAIM
disclose .... BARE, FIND, OPEN,
TELL, REVEAL, UNFOLD,
UNVEIL, IMPART, CONFESS,
DIVULGE, INDICATE
colloquial .... SING
slang .... SQUEAL
disclosure .... EXPOSE,
CONFESSION, REVELATION
confidential .... TIP-OFF
indirect ...... HINT, INTIMATION
to a priest .... SHRIFT
discolor .... FADE, STAIN, STREAK,
BLEMISH
discolored by bruise .... LIVID
discombobulate .... ADDLE,
UPSET, EXCITE, POTHER,
RATTLE, RUFFLE, CONFUSE,
FLUSTER, PERTURB, DISCOMFIT
discomfit ...... JAR, UPSET, ABASH,
RUFFLE, CONFUSE,
EMBARRASS, DISCONCERT
discomfort .... ACHE, PAIN,
DISTRESS, SORENESS,
ANNOYANCE, UNEASINESS
physical .... MALAISE
discommode .... BOTHER,
DISTURB, INCONVENIENCE
discompose .... UPSET, RUFFLE,
AGITATE, DISTURB, FLUSTER,
DISARRANGE, DISCONCERT
disconcert .... JAR, ABASH, FEEZE,
UPSET, RATTLE, THWART,
CONFUSE, DISTURB, PERPLEX,
F(E)AZE, EMBARRASS,
FRUSTRATE, DISCOMPOSE,
FLABBERGAST
disconnect .... SEVER, DETACH,
UNPLUG, SEPARATE,

UNCOUPLE
disconsolate .... SAD, GLOOMY,
FORLORN, MELANCHOLY
discontent .... DISSENT, SORENESS,
VEXATION, RESENTMENT
feeling of .... DYSPHORIA
discontented one .... CRAB,
GRIPER, GROUCH, WHINER,
GRUMBLER, MALCONTENT
discontinue .... HALT, QUIT, STOP,
CEASE, DESIST, DISRUPT,
PAUSE, CALL OFF, SUSPEND
discord .... DIN, ODDS, SPAT, TIFF,
CLASH, BICKER, STRIFE,
CONFLICT, FRICTION,
DISSENSION
discordant ...... AJAR, HARSH, AT
ODDS, OFF-KEY, JARRING,
TUNELESS, EMBROILED,
DISSONANT, CACOPHONOUS
ringing .... JANGLE
discotheque .... CAFE, DISCO,
NIGHTCLUB
discount .... AGIO, ALLOW,
DEDUCT, LESSEN, IGNORE,
REBATE, REDUCE, BELITTLE,
SET ASIDE, SUBTRACT,
DEDUCTION, DISREGARD
discountenance .... ABASH,
CHAGRIN, DISFAVOR, FROWN
AT, DISAPPROVE
discourage .... DAUNT, DETER,
DAMPEN, DISMAY, DEPRESS,
DISHEARTEN, DEMORALIZE
discourse .... TALK, HOMILY,
SERMON, DECLAIM, DISCUSS,
DESCANT, LECTURE, TREATISE,
CONVERSE, CONVERSATION,
DISSERTATE, DISSERTATION
art of .... RHETORIC
Ciceronian .... ORATION
combining form .... LOG(O)
long, tiresome .... SCREED
long, vehement .... TIRADE,
HARANGUE
discourteous .... RUDE, TART,
NASTY, ROUGH, BITING,
COARSE, VULGAR, BRUSQUE,
CAUSTIC, CHURLISH, ILL-
BRED, IMPOLITE
person .... CAD, BOOR, HEEL,
BRUTE, CHURL
discourtesy ...... INSULT, REBUFF,
SLIGHT, DISRESPECT, ILL-
BREEDING
discover .... ESPY, LEARN,
FIND(OUT), DESCRY, DETECT,
REVEAL, UNCOVER, UNEARTH
discoverer's cry .... OHO
discovery .... ESPIAL, FIND(ING),
DETECTION, INVENTION

of 1492 .... AMERICA
of 1521 .... PHILIPPINES
of March 13, 1781
.... URANUS
unexpected .... WINDFALL
discredit .... SLUR, DOUBT,
SHAME, IMPEACH, DISGRACE,
DISHONOR, DISPARAGE
discreditable .... DISGRACEFUL,
HUMILIATING
discredited .... BELIED, REJECTED,
SUSPECT(ED)
discreet .... SHIFTY, CAREFUL,
GUARDED, PRUDENT,
CAUTIOUS
discreetly .... WISELY,
JUDICIOUSLY
discrepancy ...... GAP, VARIANCE,
DIFFERENCE
discrepant .... INCONSISTENT
discrete ...... DISTINCT, SEPARATE,
UNRELATED
discretion .... TACT, OPTION,
CAUTION, SECRECY,
PRUDENCE, JUDGMENT
discretionary .... OPTIONAL,
ARBITRARY, INDEPENDENT
discriminate .... DEMARK, DIVIDE,
SECERN, PREJUDGE,
DEMARCATE, SEGREGATE,
DISTINGUISH, TREAT
UNEQUALLY
discriminating .... NICE, CHOOSY,
REFINED, CRITICAL,
CULTURED, SELECTIVE
discrimination .... BIAS, TASTE,
RACISM, INSIGHT, EXCLUSION,
PREJUDICE, PERCEPTION
discursive .... PROLIX,
WANDERING
discus .... DISK, QUOIT
thrower's statue
.... DISCOBOLUS
discuss .... TALK, ARGUE, DEBATE,
TREAT, ANALYZE, DISPUTE,
EXPLAIN
carefully .... DELIBERATE
formally .... DISSERTATE
in detail .... CANVASS
discussed publicly .... NOTORIOUS
discussion .... DEBATE, ANALYSIS,
DIALOGUE
group .... FORUM, PANEL,
SEMINAR
heated ...... HASSLE, RHUBARB,
SQUABBLE
kind of .... ROUND-TABLE
meeting for .... CONFERENCE
of facts .... TREATISE
secret: sl. .... HUDDLE
slang .... RAP SESSION

disdain .... SCORN, SNEER, SPURN, DESPISE, HAUTEUR, CONTEMPT

disdainful one .... PRIG, SNOB, SCORNER, SNEERER

disease .... MALADY, AILMENT, ILLNESS, DISORDER, SICKNESS, AFFECTION, COMPLAINT

affecting many organs .... WHIPPLE'S

animal .... GID, MANGE, NAGANA, SPAVIN, ANTHRAX

blood .... ANEMIA, TOXEMIA, CLOTTING, LEUKEMIA, POLYCYTHEMIA

bone .... RICKETS, RACHITIS

bone marrow .... CANCER, MYELOMA

brain virus infection .... ENCEPHALITIS

carried by aedes mosquito .... DENGUE, YELLOW FEVER

carried by anopheles mosquito .... MALARIA

carried by tsetse ...... NAGANA

carrier .... BAT, FLY, RAT, TSETSE, VECTOR, MOSQUITO

cause of .... GERM, VIRUS, MICROBE, BACILLUS, PATHOGEN

caused by fungi ...... MYCOSIS, MYCETOMA

causing/leading to .... PECCANT, MORBIFIC

childhood .... MUMPS, MEASLES, RUBELLA

chronic skin .... ROSACEA

chronic tropical .... SPRUE

combining form .... NOS(O)

consumption .... TUBERCULOSIS

contagious/infectious .... FAVUS, NAGANA, PLAGUE, MALARIA, MEASLES, PINK-EYE, SYPHILIS, GONORRHEA, PESTILENCE, TUBERCULOSIS

cranberry .... SCALD

Crohn's .... ENTERITIS

deficiency .... SCURVY, RICKETS, BERIBERI, MARASMUS, PELLAGRA, KWASHIORKOR

dust-caused .... SILICOSIS

epidemic .... PLAGUE, BUBONIC PLAGUE, PESTILENCE

ear .... MYRINGITIS

eye .... MYOPIA, CATARACT, GLAUCOMA, NIGHT BLINDNESS

fluid retention .... EDEMA

germ killer .... ANTIBODY, ANTIBIOTIC

gradual end of .... LYSIS

imaginary .... CRUD

inability to speak ...... MUTISM

indigenous .... ENDEMIC

infection of nails .... PARONYCHIA

inflammation of kidney(s) .... NEPHRITIS

inflammation of lungs .... PNEUMONIA

intestinal .... CHOLERA, MYIASIS

liver ..... CIRRHOSIS, HEPATITIS, PORPHYRIA

lungs .... EMPHYSEMA

malignant ...... FEVER, TUMOR, CANCER, PLAGUE, PESTILENCE

mental .... INSANITY, DERANGEMENT

muscles .... MYOPATHY

nervous .... TIC, CHOREA, TWITCH, EPILEPSY, PELLAGRA

of .... MORBID

acid in stomach .... PEPTIC ULCER

beard .... SYCOSIS

chills and fever .... AGUE, MALARIA

chronic skin disorder .... ACNE

cows .... COWPOX, TAPEWORM

dogs .... RABIES

fowl/poultry .... PIP, ROUP

grasses/rye .... ERGOT

hip .... COXALGIA

horses ...... LAMPAS, SPAVIN, LAMPERS, GLANDERS

joints .... GOUT, ARTHRITIS

kidney .... NEPHROPATHY

kings so-called .... HEMOPHILIA

monkeys ..... YELLOW FEVER

pigs .... BULL NOSE, TAPEWORM, BRUCELLOSIS

rabbits .... TULAREMIA

rats .... PLAGUE

sheep .... GID, ROT, ANTHRAX

wheat .... RUST

origin of/study of .... ETIOLOGY

pancreas .... DIABETES

passage into body ..... ATRIUM

plant .... SMUT

recurrence of .... RELAPSE

recurring .... CHRONIC

scratchy .... ITCH, HIVES, URTICARIA

sexually-transmitted .... SYPHILIS, GONORRHEA, ''THE CLAP''

skin .... ACNE, LUPUS, TINEA, ECZEMA, TETTER, RINGWORM

''slimming'' .... ANOREXIA-NERVOSA

source .... NIDUS

spreader .... CARRIER

swine .... GARGET

tropical .... YAWS, SPRUE

virus .... FLU, POX, COLD, RABIES, MEASLES, RUBELLA, VARIOLA, VIROSIS, INFLUENZA, VARICELLA

warning symptom .... PRODROME

wasting .... TABES, CONSUMPTION

diseased .... ILL, SICK(LY), MORBID, PATHIC, DISABLED, UNSOUND, CONFINED, INCURABLE

beggar .... LAZAR, LEPER

for a long period .... BEDRIDDEN

tissue due to injury .... GANGRENOUS

with impaired digestion .... DYSPEPTIC

diseases, classification of .... NOSOLOGY

deals with the nature of .... PATHOLOGY

deals with treatment and care of .... THERAPY, THERAPEUTICS

examination and analysis of .... DIAGNOSIS

disembark .... LAND, DEBUS, GET OFF, DEPLANE, DETRAIN

disembodied spirit .... SOUL

disembowel .... GUT, DRAW, EVISCERATE

disembowelment, suicide by .... HARAKIRI

disenchant .... DEFLATE, DISILLUSION, DISAPPOINT

disencumber .... RID, FREE, LIGHTEN RELIEVE, UNBURDEN

disendow .... DISINHERIT

disengage .... FREE, DETACH, RELEASE, SEPARATE, UNFASTEN

disentagle .... COMB, RAVEL, UNCURL UNKNOT, UNSNARL, ORGANIZE, EXTRICATE

in football .... UNPILE

disenthrone .... OUST, UNSEAT

disfavor .... HATE, ABHOR, DISLIKE

disfigure .... MAR, MAIM, DEFACE, DEFORM, MANGLE, UGLIFY, DISTORT, MUTILATE

disfigured ...... UGLY, DEFORMED, SCARRED, GROTESQUE
and swollen .... BLOATED
and undersized .... DWARFED
with defective legs
.... BOWLEGGED, BANDY-LEGGED
with excessive scar tissue
.... KELOIDAL
with inflamed skin swelling
.... PIMPLY, PIMPLED
disfigurement ...... SCAR, DEFECT, BLEMISH UGLINESS
disgorge .... EJECT, EMPTY, VOMIT
disgrace ...... BLOT, ODIUM, SLUR, SHAME, TAINT, INFAMY, OBLOQUY, SCANDAL, DISHONOR, IGNOMINY
disgraced ...... CRUSHED, SHAMED, HUMILIATED
disgraceful .... INDIGN, SHOCKING, SCANDALOUS
disgruntle .... DISCONTENT, DISPLEASE, DISSATISFY
disgruntled .... CROSS
one ...... CRYBABY, SOREHEAD, SOURPUSS, AX-GRINDER, CROSSPATCH
disguise ...... MASK, VEIL, CLOAK, SCREEN, CONCEAL, MAKE-UP, CAMOUFLAGE
assumed/in .... INCOGNITO
wearer .... MUMMER
disgust .... REPEL, OFFEND, SICKEN, REPULSE, DISTASTE, NAUSEATE, REPUGNANCE
disgusted .... BORED, FED-UP, SICK AND TIRED
grunt .... UGH
disgusting .... LOUSY, ODIOUS, FULSOME, OFFENSIVE
matter .... FILTH
dish .... BOWL, PATEN, PLATE, COURSE, SAUCER, SERVER, TUREEN, PLATTER, RAMEKIN, RAMEQUIN
appetizer .... PATE, RUMAKI, CANAPES, FRESH OYSTERS, SMOKED SALMON, STUFFED MUSHROOMS
beef .... STEW, ROAST, RAGOUT, TERIYAKI, MEAT LOAF, POT ROAST, CARBONNADE, STROGANOFF, WELLINGTON, BOURGUIGNON, CHATEAUBRIAND
between courses .... ENTREE, ENTREMETS
candy .... COMPOTE, COMPOTIER
cheese .... FONDUE, QUICHE,

RAREBIT, WELSH RABBIT
chicken .... KIEV, BAKED, CURRY, ROAST, POT PIE, A LA KING, FRICASSE, CACCIATORE, TETRAZZINI, CORDON BLEU, ARROZ CON POLLO
choice .... VIAND
colloquial .... FOOD, TREAT, RECIPE, SERVING
cooked on a spit .... HASLET
dessert .... PUDDING, AMBROSIA, SYLLABUB, CHEESECAKE, ZABAGLIONE, BAKED ALASKA, CREPES SUZETTE
duck/duckling .... ROAST, PEKING, SHANGHAI, A-L'ORANGE
eggs .... CREOLE, MORNAY, OMELET, QUICHE, BENEDICT
fancy .... KICKSHAW
for cookies, etc. ...... EPERGNE
for cooking .... CASSEROLE
for cooking over coal
.... BRAZIER
for evaporating liquid
.... CAPSULE
for serving gravy, sauce
.... GRAVY BOAT
fruit .... COMPOTE, EPERGNE, COMPOTIER
highly spiced stew .... OLIO
Hungarian .... GOULASH
lamb .... STEW, CHOPS, CURRY, KABOB, ROAST
main .... ENTREE
maize and pepper ..... TAMALE
make of a ...... GLASS, METAL, CRYSTAL, PLASTIC, PORCELAIN, STONEWARE, EARTHENWARE
Mexican .... TACO, TAMALE, ENCHILADA, CHILI CON CARNE
pasta .... LASAGNA, RAVIOLI, CANNELONI, FETTUCINI, MANICOTTI, SPAGHETTI
pork ..... STEW, CHOPS, ROAST, BURRITO, HOCKS AND BEANS, BARBECUED SPARERIBS
rice .... BAKED, FRIED, PILAF(F)
seafood .... SCAMPI, SCALLOPS, SHRIMP CURRY, THERMIDOR, PAN-FRIED FISH, CLAM FRITTERS, POACHED SALMON/SOLE
served before the roast
.... ENTREE
serving .... TRAY, CROCK, NAPPY, PLATTER, CASSEROLE
side .... ENTREMETS
soup .... GUMBO, POTAGE, BISQUE, GAZPACHO, SPLIT-PEA,

MINESTRONE, VICHYSSOISE, CLAM CHOWDER
soup server .... TUREEN
tasty .... MORSEL
type .... CUP, JAR, BOWL, DEEP, PLATE, SAUCER, CHAFING, TWO-SECTION, WARMING, FLAT-BOTTOMED
veal .... ROAST, MARSALA, PAPRIKA, PICCATA, PARMIGIANA, STEW MILANESE
vegetable .... SALAD, AMANDINE, POLONAISE, STIR-FRIED, RATATOUILLE
dishearten ...... DAUNT, DAMPEN, DEJECT, DISCOURAGE
dishes .... WARE, CHINA
dishevel .... MUSS, RUMPLE, TOUSLE
disheveled .... BLOWZY, UNKEMPT, DISORDERLY
dishonest .... FALSE, LYING, CHEATING, DECEITFUL
card player ...... CHEAT, SHILL, SHARPER, BLACKLEG
lawyer .... SHYSTER, PETTIFOGGER
person .... LIAR, CROOK, CHEATER, STEALER, DECEIVER, SWINDLER
dishonor .... ABUSE, SHAME, INFAMY, DISGRACE, DISCREDIT, DISREPUTE, DISRESPECT
dishonorable .... BASE, SHADY, FOUL, ROTTEN, CROOKED
disillusion .... DISENCHANT
disinclined .... AVERSE, AGAINST, RELUCTANT, UNWILLING
disinfect .... FUMIGATE, STERILIZE
disinfectant ...... LYSOL, CRESOL, IODINE, CHLORINE
disingenuous .... SLY, DISHONEST, INSINCERE
disinherit .... DISOWN
disintegrate .... MELT, DECAY, WEAKEN, BREAKUP, CRUMBLE
by acid .... CORRODE
by water/wind .... ERODE
disinter .... FIND, DIG UP, EXHUME, UNEARTH
disinterested .... NUMB, UNBIASED, IMPARTIAL
disjoin .... CHANGE, SEPARATE
disjoint .... DISLOCATE, DISMEMBER
disk .... PLATE, WHEEL, CIRCLE, PATINA, ROTATOR
bright surrounding saints
.... NIMBUS
for breaking soil ..... HARROW

gem-cutting .... LAP
hockey/ice hockey .... PUCK
jockey .... DEEJAY,
                   ANNOUNCER
like/shaped .... DISCAL,
                   DISCOID
metal .... PATEN
obsolete .... DISCUS
on radio/telephone .... DIAL,
                   FACE
phonograph .... RECORD
poker .... CHIP
sealing .... WAFER
small, computer .... FLOPPY
throwing device .... TRAP
to seal joints .... GASKET
dislike .... HATE, ABHOR, ENMITY,
              DISGUST, DISTASTE,
            AVERSION, ANTIPATHY
intense .... HATRED,
              DETESTATION
dislocate .... SPLAY, UPSET,
             LUXATE, DISJOINT,
             DISARRANGE
dislodge .... EJECT, EVICT, EXPEL,
           REMOVE, DISPLACE
disloyal .... FALSE, UNTRUE,
           RECREANT, FAITHLESS,
      UNFAITHFUL, INCONSTANT
person, kind of .... INGRATE,
          TRAITOR, BETRAYER,
         INFORMER, RENEGADE,
     TURNCOAT, DOUBLE-CROSSER
dismal .... BLEAK, DINGY,
           DREARY, GLOOMY,
             DEPRESSING
dismantle .... RAZE, STRIP,
              DEMOLISH
dismay ...... FEAR, ABASH, DAUNT,
      ALARM, APPAL(L), TERRIFY,
             DISCONCERT
dismember .... DISSECT, DISJOINT
dismiss .... FIRE, OUST, EXPEL,
     LAY OFF, REMOVE, RELEASE,
             DISCHARGE
an organization .... DISBAND
archaic .... DEMIT
colloquial .... BOOT, SACK,
            BRUSH OFF
from command/in disgrace
   .... CASHIER
troops .... DEMOBILIZE
dismissal ...... OUSTER, REMOVAL,
       DISCHARGE, MITTIMUS
curt/abrupt .... CONGE
notice .... PINKSLIP
dismount .... ALIGHT, GET DOWN,
             STEP DOWN
Disney, artist .... ANIMATOR,
             CARTOONIST
dog .... PLUTO

duck .... DAISY, DONALD
duckling .... HUEY, DEWEY,
              LOUIE
goldfish .... CLEO
middle name of .... ELIAS
Mortimer of .... SNERD
movie producer .... WALT
mouse .... MICKEY, MINNIE
pachyderm .... DUMBO
puppet .... PINNOCHIO
disobedient .... UNRULY, DEFIANT,
           INSUBORDINATE
disorder .... MESS, MUSS, RIOT,
   ROIL, CHAOS, HAVOC, UPSET,
    JUMBLE, LITTER, UPROAR,
     CLUTTER, CONFUSION
in .... UPSIDE DOWN
of voices/sounds .... BABEL
place of .... BEDLAM
vague: sl. .... CRUD
disorderly .... MESSY, UNRULY,
    ROWDY, UNTIDY, CHAOTIC,
    RIOTOUS, PELLMELL, SLIPSHOD
crowd .... RABBLE
flight .... ROUT, STAMPEDE
noisy fight .... MELEE
disorganize ...... UPSET, DISBAND,
         DISRUPT, DISSOLVE
disorganized .... HAYWIRE,
     DERANGED, DISORDERLY
disown .... DENY, DISAVOW,
     RENOUNCE, DISCLAIM,
    REPUDIATE, DISINHERIT,
           DISPOSSESS
disparage .... SLUR, DECRY,
    DEMEAN, LESSEN, BELITTLE,
     TRADUCE, PEJORATE,
     VILIPEND, DISCREDIT,
          DEPRECIATE
disparaging remark .... SLUR,
      SMEAR, ASPERSION
disparate ...... UNLIKE, DIFFERENT
disparity .... CONTRAST,
     CLASHING, CONFLICT,
     VARIANCE, INJUSTICE,
          DIFFERENCE
dispassionate .... CALM, COOL,
    EVEN, FAIR, LEVEL-HEADED
dispassionately .... COLDLY
dispatch .... KILL, POST,
    SEND(OFF), HASTE, ROUTE,
    SPEED, LETTER, MESSAGE,
    NEWS STORY, BULLETIN,
    QUICKNESS, PROMPTNESS
across the sea ...... SEND OVER
bearer .... COURIER,
          MESSENGER
boat/vessel .... AVISO
dispatcher .... ROUTER, SENDER
slang .... BUTCHER
dispel .... VANISH, SCATTER, BLOW

    OFF, DISPERSE, DISSOLVE
dispensable .... EXCESS, INFERIOR,
           NEEDLESS
dispensary .... CLINIC,
    PHARMACY, INFIRMARY
dispensation .... FAVOR,
    EXEMPTION, MANAGEMENT,
   ALLOTMENT, DISTRIBUTION
dispense .... EXCUSE, EXEMPT,
    DEAL OUT, DISTRIBUTE
with .... FOREGO, ABSTAIN
dispenser of alms ...... ALMONER
disperse .... SPREAD, SCATTER
system .... COLLOID
dispirited .... BORED, DEJECTED
displace .... MOVE, EXILE,
    DISLODGE, SUPPLANT,
   DISCHARGE, SUPERSEDE
displaced .... HOMELESS
person .... DP, EVACUEE,
    OUTCAST, REFUGEE
displacement .... REMOVAL,
    EJECTION, MIGRATION
display .... SPORT, SHOW(OFF),
    EXPOSE, REVEAL, UNFOLD,
    UNCOVER, MANIFEST,
          EXHIBIT(ION)
brilliant .... POMP, RIOT,
    PARADE, BLAZONRY,
          SPECTACLE
case .... CABINET, COUNTER
empty .... PAGEANT(RY)
frame .... EASEL, SHELF,
          SHELVE
means of .... SHOWCASE,
    (FASHION)SHOW, SHOW-
          WINDOW
of temper .... FIT, FRENZY,
    TANTRUM, OUTBURST
ostentatiously .... WAVE,
    FLAUNT, PARADE
pretentious: colloq.
    .... SPREAD
prominent .... SPLASH
showy ...... BLAZON, FANFARE,
          SPLURGE
superficial .... VENEER
displaying amazement .... WIDE-
          EYED
displease .... VEX, MIFF, ROIL,
    ANGER, ANNOY, PIQUE,
   OFFEND, DISTURB, IRRITATE
displeasure .... IRE, ANGST
disport .... PLAY, FROLIC
disposable .... THROWAWAY
disposal .... RIDDANCE,
          DISPOSITION
of property .... CONVEYANCE
dispose .... ORDER, POSIT,
    ARRANGE, SITUATE
of .... SELL, SETTLE, GIVE

AWAY, CONSUME, LIQUIDATE
disposed .... APT, BENT, PRONE,
MINDED, TENDING, WILLING,
INCLINED
to agree .... AMENABLE
to fight .... COMBATANT,
PUGNACIOUS, BELLIGERENT
disposition .... BENT, MOOD,
MORALE, NATURE, TENDENCY,
ADJUSTMENT, ARRANGEMENT,
TEMPER(AMENT)
of mean .... ORNERY
sour .... TESTY, CRANKY,
GROUCHY, VINEGARY
dispossess .... OUST, EJECT, EVICT,
DISOWN, DIVEST, DEPRIVE,
EXPROPRIATE
disproof .... REFUTATION
disprove .... REBUT, REFUTE,
DEFEAT, CONFUTE, GAINSAY
disputable .... MOOT
at law .... LITIGIOUS
disputant .... ERISTIC
disputation .... DEBATE, POLEMIC
art of .... ERISTIC, POLEMICS
disputatious .... CONTENTIOUS,
CONTROVERSIAL
dispute ...... SPAR, ARGUE, DOUBT,
FLITE, BICKER, DEBATE,
CONTEST, DISCUSS, QUARREL,
CAUSERIE, POLEMICS,
QUESTION, ARGUMENT,
SQUABBLE
angrily ..... CLASH, ALTERCATE
beyond .... SETTLED
noisy .... FRACAS, WRANGLE
petty .... SPAT
disputer .... ARGUER, DEBATER,
OPPOSER, DISSENTER
disqualified .... UNFIT, INELIGIBLE
disqualify .... DISABLE, RULE OUT
disquiet .... FRET, UNEASE,
UNREST, ANXIETY
disquieting .... SCARY, ALARMING,
EXCITING
disquisition .... DISCOURSE
disregard .... DEFY, IGNORE,
DISOBEY, OVERRIDE,
OVERRULE
disregarding rule .... PECCANT
disrepair .... DECAY, DAMAGE,
DECLINE, INUTILITY,
IMPAIRMENT
of body tissue .... ATROPHY
disreputable .... VILE, SHADY,
HEINOUS, RAFFISH, INFAMOUS,
ODOROUS, SHAMEFUL,
UNSAVORY
shrewish woman ..... DEMIREP,
HARRIDAN
disrepute .... SHAME, TAINT,

INFAMY, DISGRACE
disrespect .... SNUB, SLIGHT,
AFFRONT, SARCASM,
CONTEMPT
disrespectful .... RUDE, IMPOLITE,
INSULTING, SARCASTIC
disrobe ...... BARE, STRIP, DIVEST,
UNDRESS
disrupt .... REND, SPLIT, UPSET,
DISTURB, BREAK APART
dissatisfied (one)
.... MALCONTENT
dissatisfy .... VEX, ANGER,
ANNOY, DISPLEASE
dissect .... CUT UP, CUT APART,
ANALYZE, DISMEMBER
dissemble .... LIE, FEIGN,
CONCEAL, PRETEND, DISGUISE,
SIMULATE
dissembler, alleged .... JESUIT
dissembling .... AESOPIC
disseminate .... SOW, STREW,
SPREAD, SCATTER, CIRCULATE,
PROPAGATE
by word of mouth
.... PREACH, BROADCAST
through the press .... PUBLISH,
PUBLICIZE
through the radio
.... BROADCAST
through TV .... TELECAST
dissension .... STRIFE, DISCORD,
QUARREL
in a way .... FLAK
dissent .... DIFFER, OBJECT,
PROTEST, DISAGREE
dissenter .... ANTI, OPPOSER,
SECTARY, OBJECTOR,
SECTARIAN, PROTESTANT,
NONCONFORMIST
dissepiment .... SEPTUM
dissert(ate) .... ARGUE, DISCUSS
dissertation .... ESSAY, PAPER,
THESIS, ARTICLE, LECTURE,
TREATISE, DISCOURSE
disserve .... HARM
disservice .... WRONG, INJURY,
INJUSTICE
dissidence .... DISCORD,
DISCONTENT
dissident .... ANTI, REBEL,
OPPOSER, CONTRARY,
RESISTER, MALCONTENT,
INTRANSIGENT
dissimilar ...... UNLIKE, UNALIKE,
DIFFERENT, DISPARATE
dissimilarity .... ODDS,
DIFFERENCE
dissimulate ...... FEIGN, PRETEND,
DISGUISE
dissipate .... FADE, SPEND, WASTE,

DISPEL, DIFFUSE, SCATTER,
SQUANDER
dissipated man ...... RAKE, ROUE,
DEBAUCHEE
dissociate .... SEPARATE,
DISENGAGE
dissociation, mental
.... PARANOIA
dissolute .... LAX, WILD, LOOSE,
RAKISH, SINFUL, VICIOUS,
LICENTIOUS, PROFLIGATE
person .... RAKE, ROUE,
ADDICT, LECHER
dissolution .... BREAKUP,
DIALYSIS, DISPERSION,
EXPIRATION, SEPARATION
combining form .... LYSIS
dissolve .... END, FADE, MELT,
THAW, VANISH, LIQUEFY
out/and wash away ..... LEACH
dissonance .... DISCORD
from violin group .... WOLF
dissonant .... ATONAL
dissuade .... DETER, REPEL,
DEHORT, RESTRAIN
opposed to .... EXHORT,
PERSUADE
distaff side ...... FEMALE, WOMAN,
WOMEN, WEAKER SEX
distal .... TERMINAL
opposed to .... PROXIMAL
distance .... REACH, FARNESS,
REMOTENESS, MEASUREMENT
around .... CIRCUMFERENCE
between ends .... SPAN
between lines/words ...... GAP,
SPACE
from equator .... LATITUDE
in behavior/manner
.... RESERVE
in radio .... DX
in the .... AFAR
runner .... MILER
shortest .... BEELINE,
STRAIGHTLINE
three-mile, nautical/statute
.... LEAGUE
traveled recorder
.... ODOGRAPH
distant .... FAR, AFAR, AWAY,
ALOOF, FAR OFF, REMOTE,
ABROAD, OVERSEAS,
RESERVED
past .... EARLY
prefix .... TEL(E)
distaste .... DISLIKE, AVERSION
distasteful .... OFFENSIVE,
UNPLEASANT
distemper .... COLOR, PAINT,
MALADY, DISEASE, DISORDER
distend .... BULGE, SWELL,

DILATE, EXPAND, INFLATE, STRETCH
distended .... TURGID
condition .... TYMPANY
distension .... BLOAT, STRAIN
distich .... COUPLET
distill .... BREW, DRIP, DECOCT, PURIFY, TRICKLE
several times .... COHOBATE
distillate .... SPIRIT
distillery .... STILL, BREWERY
mash .... SLOPS
mixing tank .... MASHTUN
waste .... POTASH
distilling apparatus .... STILL, ALEMBIC
refuse .... TAILING
vessel .... RETORT, MATRASS
distinct .... CLEAR, PLAIN, SHARP, EXPLICIT, DEFINITE, SEPARATE, DIFFERENT
part .... UNIT, FEATURE
distinction ...... HONOR, DIGNITY, ELEGANCE, EMINENCE, VARIATION, PROMINENCE
distinctive ...... PRECISE, DEFINITE, PROMINENT, DISTINGUISHING
air .... AURA, ATMOSPHERE
nature .... TRAIT, FLAVOR
taste .... SAVOR, PALATE
distinctly .... CLEARLY, VISIBLY
distinguish .... KNOW, LABEL, HONOR, SECERN, DISCERN, PICK OUT, SEPARATE, DISCRIMINATE, DIFFERENTIATE
distinguished .... FAMOUS, EMINENT, NOTABLE, RENOWNED
man .... DON
distinguishing feature ...... TRAIT, CHARACTERISTIC
moral nature .... ETHOS
distort .... WARP, TWIST, DEFORM, CONTORT, MISREPRESENT
parts of a story, etc. .... GARBLE, MISQUOTE
distorted .... WRY, AWRY, ASKEW, CROOKED
back .... HUMPBACK, HUNCHBACK
foot .... TALIPED, CLUBFOOT(ED)
knee .... KNOCKKNEED
nose .... SNUB-NOSED
distortion .... ABERRATION
ludicrous .... TRAVESTY
of the face .... GRIMACE
distract .... AMUSE, HARASS, CONFUSE
distraction .... AMUSEMENT, DIVERSION

frenzied .... TIZZY
distraint .... POIND
distraught .... MAD, CRAZED, FRANTIC, CONFUSED, HARASSED, BEWILDERED
distress ...... PAIN, AGONY, GRIEF, GRIPE, UPSET, AFFLICT, ANGUISH, ANXIETY, STRAITS, POVERTY, TROUBLE, CALAMITY
signal/call .... SOS, MAYDAY
distribute .... DOLE, METE, ALLOT, DIVIDE, SCATTER, DISH OUT
cards .... DEAL
distributor .... DEALER, MERCHANT
district .... AREA, WARD, ZONE, REGION, SECTOR, CIRCUIT, PRECINCT, TERRITORY
distrust .... ENVY, DOUBT, SUSPECT, UMBRAGE, SUSPICION
disturb ...... ROIL, ANNOY, FEEZE, F(E)AZE, UPSET, WORRY, MOLEST, PESTER, AGITATE, PERTURB, NETTLE, INTERRUPT, DISARRANGE
disturbance .... ROW, BRAWL, HUBBUB, RUMPUS, UPROAR, DISORDER, COMMOTION
unruly .... RIOT
disunion ...... SCHISM, BREAK-UP, DISCORD, SEPARATION
disunite .... PART, DETACH, DIVIDE, SEPARATE
disuse .... WAIVE, ABSTAIN, NEGLECT, DESUETUDE
disused .... OBSOLETE
ditch .... DIKE, DYKE, CANAL, FOSS(E), GULLY, CHANNEL
a suitor .... JILT
barrier .... HAHA
castle .... MOAT
digger .... TRENCHER
filling sticks .... FASCINE
for defense .... TRENCH
road .... GUTTER
slang .... DESERT, CAST OFF, DISCARD
dither .... FLURRY, TWITTER, CONFUSION
in a .... AGOG, EXCITED
dithyramb .... ODE, HYMN, POEM, SONG, SPEECH
dittany .... MINT, FRAXINELLA
ditto ...... COPY, SAME, AGAIN, AS BEFORE, LIKEWISE
ditty .... SONG, REFRAIN
diuretic .... URETIC, URINARY
stimulant .... CANTHARIDES
diurnal .... DAILY, DIARY,

JOURNAL
opposed to .... NOCTURNAL
diva .... SINGER, PRIMA DONNA
forte of .... ARIA, OPERA
Patrice .... MUNSEL
divagate .... STRAY, DIGRESS
divan .... CAFE, SOFA, COUCH, CANAPE, LOUNGE, SETTEE, OTTOMAN
divaricate .... FORK, BRANCH
dive .... DIP, SWOOP, PLUNGE
bomber .... STUKA, AIRPLANE
colloquial .... DEN, SALOON
fancy .... SWAN, GAINER, BACKFLIP
into water .... SUBMERGE
kind of .... NOSE, POWER
slang .... HONKY-TONK
diver, a certain .... PEARLER
bird .... LOON
breathing aid of .... MASK, SCUBA
from airplane .... PARACHUTIST, PARATROOPER
gear of .... TANK, HELMET, AQUALUNG, FLIPPERS, SPEARGUN, (PARA)CHUTE
sickness suffered by .... BENDS
warship .... SUBMARINE
diverge .... FORK, VARY, VEER, DIFFER, SWERVE, DEVIATE, BRANCH OFF
divergent strabismus .... WALLEYE
divergence .... VARIANCE, DEVIATION, VARIATION
divers .... SUNDRY, VARIOUS
diverse .... UNLIKE, VARIED, SEVERAL, DIFFERENT
prefix .... POLY
diversify ...... VARY, BRANCH OUT
diversion .... SPORT, CHANGE, PASTIME, AMUSEMENT, DISTRACTION
diversionary tactic .... FEINT
diversity .... VARIETY
divert .... AMUSE, DEFLECT, DISTRACT, ESTRANGE, ENTERTAIN
divertissement .... BALLET, ENTR'ACTE, DIVERSION, INTERMEZZO
divest .... BARE, STRIP, DENUDE, EXPOSE, DEPRIVE, UNCOVER
divested .... NUDE, NAKED, THREADBARE
divestment .... NUDITY
of outer skin .... ECDYSIS
divide .... PART, ALLOT, HALVE,

SHARE, SPLIT, SUNDER, ALIENATE, SEPARATE, TRANSECT, APPORTION
grammatically ..... PUNCTUATE
into feet .... SCAN
into four parts .... QUARTER
into layers .... FOLIATE
into three .... TRISECT
into two .... HALF, BISECT
voting area ..... GERRYMANDER
divided .... CLEFT, FORKED
equally .... HALVED
in parts .... PARTITE
into 100 degrees
.... CENTIGRADE
into vertical stripes (in
heraldry) .... PALY
dividend .... BONUS, INTEREST
dividing line .... SOLIDUS
wall .... SEPTUM, PARTITION
divination .... GUESS, AUGURY, SORCERY, PROPHECY, HYDROMANCY, NUMEROLOGY, PREDICTION
by communication with the
dead .... NECROMANCY
by figures .... GEOMANCY
by lots .... SORTILEGE
by the stars .... ASTROLOGY
combining form .... MANCY
having powers of ...... MANTIC
method of .... TAROT, AXINOMANCY
pertaining to .... FATIDIC
practice of .... MANTOLOGY
divine ...... HOLY, DREAM, FANCY, GUESS, SACRED, GODLIKE, IMAGINE, HEAVENLY, SUPERNAL, CELESTIAL, DEIFIC, SPIRITUAL, CONJECTURE
bread/food .... MANNA
communication .... ORACLE
favor .... GRACE, BLESSING
intervention .... THEURGY
love .... AGAPE
presence .... SHEKINAH
punishment .... PLAGUE
spirit .... GHOST
tree .... DEVA
word .... LOGOS
work .... MIRACLE
Divine Comedy author .... DANTE
setting .... HELL, PARADISE, PURGATORY
diviner .... SEER, CONJUROR
diving aid .... AQUALUNG
apparatus .... BATHYSCAPH
bell inventor .... EADS
bird .... LOON, GREBE, DUCKER
boat .... SUBMARINE
hazard .... BENDS

divining rod .... WAND
search water with ...... DOWSE
user .... AARON
divinity .... CANDY, DEITY, NUMEN, GOD(HEAD), GODHOOD, THEOLOGY
division .... PART, UNIT, CLASS, GROUP, FISSION, SECTION, SCISSION, PARTITION, SEPARATION
book .... CHAPTER
cell .... MITOSIS
city .... WARD, ZONE, TRACT, PRECINCT
game .... SET, HALF, INNING, CHUKKER, QUARTER
in a group/religious
.... SCHISM
mankind .... RACE
mark of .... OBELUS
opera .... SCENA
play .... ACT, SCENE
poem .... CANTO, VERSE, STANZA
race .... LAP, HEAT
road .... LANE
society .... CASTE
result of .... QUOTIENT
divorce .... PART, SPLIT-UP, SEPARATE
allowance .... ALIMONY
ground for .... ADULTERY, MENTAL CRUELTY, INCOMPATIBILITY
grounds for .... RENO
suit defendant
.... CORRESPONDENT
suit subject .... ALIMONY, CHILD CUSTODY, SETTLEMENT
divorcee .... FEME SOLE
divorcee's alimony .... ESTOVERS
divot .... SOD, TURF
divulge ...... TELL, SPILL, REVEAL, DISCLOSE
divvy: sl. .... SHARE, PORTION
Dixie dish? .... HOMINY GRITS
hat? .... KENTUCKY DERBY
land .... (THE)SOUTH
president .... JIMMY CARTER
river .... ALABAMA
suffix used with .... CRAT
vine .... CAROLINA JASMINE
Dixieite .... ALABAMAN, SOUTHERNER
dixit, ___ .... IPSE
Dixon's partner .... MASON
dizen .... DECK
dizziness ...... VERTIGO, GIDDINESS
attack of .... FAINT
dizzy .... GIDDY, GROGGY, FLIGHTY, VERTIGINOUS

colloquial ..... SILLY, FOOLISH, MIXED-UP
of baseball fame .... DEAN
person: colloq. .... DAME
Djajapura's (Indonesia) neighbor .... SARMI
djebel .... HILL
do .... ACT, MAKE, ENACT, SERVE, CARRY OUT, PERFORM
a constable's job .... RUN-IN
a double take .... REACT, RELOOK
a fall job .... RAKE
a host's job .... GREET
a museum job .... RESTORE
a number on .... BAD-MOUTH
a pocket job .... PICK
a razing job .... BLAST
alone .... SOLO
away with .... RID, KILL, SLAY, ABOLISH
business, in a way .... BARTER
farm work .... SOW, PLOW, REAP, PLANT, HARVEST
in .... KILL, SLAY, DESTROY
it-yourself set .... KIT
handwork .... TAT
make .... EKE
newsroom work .... EDIT
one good .... BE BENEFICIAL
over .... REDECORATE
superficially .... DABBLE
the crawl .... SWIM
the Lindy .... JITTERBUG
well's leader .... NE'ER
without .... SPARE, FOREGO, ABSTAIN
dobbin .... HORSE
dobbin's lunch pail .... NOSE BAG
dobson fly .... SIALID(AN)
doby: colloq. .... ADOBE
doc. .... DOCTOR, DOCUMENT
docile .... TAME, PLIANT, WILLING, OBEDIENT, TRACTABLE, GENTLE (AS A LAMB)
dock ...... BOB, BANG, CLIP, LAND, PIER, QUAY, SLIP, BERTH, HAVEN, JETTY, WHARF, DEDUCT, HARBOR, PENALIZE
area .... MARINA
post .... BOLLARD
prisoner's ...... WITNESS STAND
worker .... LUMPER, STEVEDORE, LONGSHOREMAN
docked tail .... BOB
docket .... LABEL, AGENDA, TICKET, CALENDAR, REGISTER
docking space .... SLIP
doctor .... MEDIC, TREAT, MENDER, TAMPER, FALSIFY,

SURGEON, TEACHER, OSTEOPATH, PHYSICIAN, CHIROPRACTOR, MEDICINE MAN

assistant of .... NURSE, INTERN(E)

certain .... SHRINK

children's .... PEDIATRIST, PEDIATRICIAN

colloquial .... DOC, VET, MEDICO

ear .... OTOLOGIST

eye .... OCULIST

fake/herb .... QUACK

family .... GP, GENERAL PRACTITIONER

frequent prescription of .... REST

heart .... CARDIOLOGIST

hospital ..... INTERN, RESIDENT

inquest .... CORONER

kind of .... QUACK, WITCH, SPECIALIST

Moslem .... HAKIM, HAKEEM

of animals .... VET(ERINARIAN)

of disorders of the mind .... PSYCHIATRIST

of foot/hand diseases .... PODIATRIST, CHIROPODIST

of injury to bones/joints .... ORTHOPEDIST

of the nervous system .... NEUROLOGIST

of women's diseases/ pregnancy .... GYNECOLOGIST, OBSTETRICIAN

skin .... DERMATOLOGIST

teeth .... DENTIST, ORTHODONTIST

doctor's association .... AMA

degree .... MD

oath .... HIPPOCRATIC

rap .... PERCUSS

doctrinaire .... DOGMATIC, VISIONARY, OPINIONATED, DICTATORIAL

person .... BIGOT, RACIST, DOGMATIST, CHAUVINIST

doctrinal .... CREEDAL

doctrine .... ISM, CULT, CREED, DOGMA, TENET, BELIEF, THEORY, PRECEPT, PRINCIPLE

mystical .... CABALA

of salvation .... LEGALISM

religious .... DOXY, CREED, DOGMA

widespread .... GOSPEL

doctrines to be believed .... CREDENDA

document .... DEED, PAPER,

RECORD, CONTRACT

container .... HANAPER

draft .... PROTOCOL

formal .... INSTRUMENT

handwritten by signer .... HOLOGRAPH

legal .... WRIT

of proof .... EVIDENCE

part of .... SEAL

ribbon of .... LAPEL

written .... SCRIPT

documents, collection of .... PAPERS

dodder .... SHAKE, TOTTER, TREMBLE

doddering person .... DOTARD

Dodecanese island .... COS, KOS, SIMI, KASOS, LEROS, PATMOS, RHODES, RODHOS

dodge .... DUCK, RUSE, ELUDE, AVOID, EVADE, PARRY, ESCAPE, SIDESTEP

dodger .... IDLER, ELUDER, EVADER, RASCAL, SHIRKER

equipment .... BUMPER, FENDER

slang .... GOOF-OFF, GOLDBRICK

Dodgers' (baseball) "preacher" .... ROE

dodo in flying school ...... CADET

doe .... DEER

in its 2nd year .... TEG

mate of .... STAG

doer .... ACHIEVER

does gardening .... WEEDS

not understand .... SEES NOT

doff .... VAIL, STRIP, DIVEST, REMOVE, GET RID, TAKE OFF

dog .... LAP, PET, PUG, PUP, ALAN, HUNT, MUTT, SLUT, TYKE, HOUND, POOCH, CANINE, FOLLOW, PURSUE, RATTER, YAPPER, CHENILLE

act of giving birth .... WHELPING

African .... BASENJI

Alaskan .... MALAMUTE, MALEMIUT, MALEMUTE

ape .... BABOON

Arctic ...... HUSKY, MALEMUTE

Australian ..... DINGO, TERRIER

Belgian/Dutch .... GRIFFIN, GRIFFON

bird .... SETTER

breed .... CHOW, BOXER, HUSKY, SPITZ, BEAGLE, COLLIE, POODLE, SETTER, BULLDOG, MALTESE, MASTIFF, POINTER, SAMOYED, SPANIEL, TERRIER, AIREDALE, ALSATIAN,

SHIH TZU, CHIHUAHUA, DACHSHUND, DALMATIAN, GREYHOUND, PEKINGESE, RETRIEVER, SCHNAUZER, GREAT DANE, LHASA APSO, POMERANIAN, ROTTWEILER, WEIMARANER, ST. BERNARD, BASSET(HOUND), GERMAN SHEPHERD, DOBERMAN PINSCHER

of setter ...... IRISH, GORDON, ENGLISH

of spaniel .... TOY, FIELD, COCKER, SUSSEX, CLUMBER, NORFOLK, BLENHEIM, BRITTANY, SPRINGER

of terrier .... FOX, BULL, SKYE, CAIRN, SILKY, WELSH, BORDER, NORWICH, WHEATEN, WIRE-FOX, AIREDALE, LAKELAND, SCOTTISH, SEALYHAM, KERRY-BLUE, YORKSHIRE, BEDLINGTON

Calvin Coolidge's .... ROB ROY

Chinese breed .... CHOW, PEKIN(G)ESE

chops .... FLEWS

coach .... DALMATIAN

collar ring .... TERRET

colloquial .... DOGGY

combining form .... CYNO

command to .... MUSH

constellation .... CANIS

cry .... HOWL

cur .... TYKE

curly-haired .... BARBET, POODLE

days of ____ .... SUMMER

days, month of .... JULY, AUGUST

disease .... MANGE, RABIES, DRONCIT, DISTEMPER, HEARTWORM, BORDETELLA

caused by tick .... LYME

Disney .... PLUTO, TRAMP

Dorothy's .... TOTO

drinking way of .... LAP

droopy-eared .... BASSET, BEAGLE, SPANIEL, DACHSHUND

-eared .... FOLDED, TIME-WORN, WELL-WORN, WORN-DOWN

-eat-dog affair .... RAT RACE

Eskimo .... HUSKY

face of .... MASK

family .... CANIDAE

FDR's .... FALA

female .... SLUT, BITCH, BRACH(ET)

fennel .... HOGWEED, MAYWEED
ferocious .... BANDOG, BULLDOG, BLOODHOUND
fictional .... RAB
footsteps, rhythm of ...... GAIT
formerly called Boarhound .... GREAT DANE
foxhound-like .... HARRIER
French breed .... PAPILLON
French/English .... BULLDOG
genus .... CANIS
George Bush's .... MILLIE
German .... POINTER, SHEPHERD
greyhound .... SALUKI
guard of the underworld/of hell .... CERBERUS
hairless breed .... INCA
hair on neck .... HACKLES
hound .... AFGHAN, BASSET, BEAGLE, GAZELLE, BRACH(ET)
house .... KENNEL
howl of .... BAY, ULULATION
Hungarian guardian .... KUVASZ
Hungarian sheep .... PULI
hunting .... BASSET, BEAGLE, SETTER, HARRIER, MASTIFF, POINTER, BRACH(ET), RETRIEVER
hybrid/of mixed breed .... CUR, MONGREL
in meteorology .... PARHELION
-in-the-manger .... GROUCH, KILLJOY
Japanese .... INU, SPANIEL
large .... MASTIFF, DALMATIAN, GREAT DANE, WEIMARANER, ST. BERNARD, DOBERMAN PINSCHER
largest breed of Japanese .... AKITA
of poodle .... STANDARD
of Schnauzer .... GIANT
of terrier .... AIREDALE
LBJ's/mongrel in White House .... YUKI
lead of .... LEASH
like animal .... JACKAL
like miniature greyhound .... WHIPPET
long-bodied .... DACHSHUND
loss of scent .... FAULT
miniature .... POODLE, PINSCHER, SCHNAUZER
mongrel .... CUR, TYKE
movie/TV .... ASTA, CLEO, NEIL, HOOCH, KELLY, PLUTO, SANDY, BENJIE, LASSIE, DREYFUS, LAD-A-DOG, RIN TIN

TIN
mythological .... CERBERUS
name of .... ACE, REX, ASTA, FALA, FIDO, SPOT, PLUTO, ROVER, SPIKE, BENJIE, LASSIE, SPOTTY, BLACKIE, BROWNIE
non-barking, yodeling .... BASENJI
Nora's .... ASTA
of India .... DHOLE
order .... CARNIVORE
Orphan Annie's .... SANDY
pack .... KENNEL
parasite .... HEARTWORM
part of foot .... PAD, PAW
pendulous upper lips of .... FLEWS
permanent ID method on .... TATTOO
pet .... LAP, POODLE, PEKINESE, CHIHUAHUA, DACHSHUND, LHASA APSO, POMERANIAN
police .... DANE, ALSATIAN, SHEPHERD
pound .... CUR, STRAY, MONGREL
pug-nosed .... PEKIN(G)ESE
rabbit/hare hunter .... HARRIER
racing .... GREYHOUND
retriever .... GOLDEN, LABRADOR
Ronald Reagan's .... REX
rounded ribcage of .... BARREL
Russian .... BORZOI, OWTCHAR, SAMOYED
saliva, result of excessive .... DROOL
Shetland .... SHEEPDOG
short-legged .... BEAGLE, DACHSHUND
show class .... OPEN, PUPPY, NOVICE, AMERICAN-BRED
Siberian ..... HUSKY, SAMOYED
slang .... MUTT, POOCH
sled .... HUSKY
small .... POM, PUG, ALCO, BEAGLE, WHIPPET, KEESHOND, POMERANIAN
smallest .... CHIHUAHUA
spaniel .... COCKER
soft hair on tail of ...... PLUME
"space" .... LAIKA
spaniel ..... COCKER, CLUMBER, SPRINGER
spotted .... DALMATIAN
swift/racing .... WHIPPET, GREYHOUND
tail of .... FLAG
tailless .... SCHIPPERKE
team leader .... OUTRUNNER

terrier .... IRISH, SILKY, SCOTTISH, SEALYHAM, SCHNAUZER, YORKSHIRE
three-headed .... CERBERUS
thumb equivalent of ..... DEW-CLAW
tongue cartilage .... LYTTA
tooth .... FANG, CUSPID, LANIARY
toy .... POM, PUG, PEKE, POODLE, SPANIEL, TERRIER, CHIHUAHUA
traditionally ladies' lap .... TOY
two-toned .... BELTON
U.S. club for registration of purebreds: abbr. ..... AKC
wagon .... DINER
Wales .... SEALYHAM
Welsh .... CORGI, COLLIE, TERRIER
who fathers litter of puppies .... SIRE
wild .... DHOLE, DINGO, JACKAL, TANATE
wire-haired .... GRIFFIN, GRIFFON, POINTER, TERRIER, PINSCHER, SCHNAUZER
with foxlike head .... CORGI
with tan markings .... DOBERMAN PINSCHER
young .... PUP(PY), WHELP
Dog Star .... SIRIUS, PROCYON, CANICULA
of the .... SOTHIC
dogcart .... TRAP
dog-eared .... FOLDED, TIMEWORN
dogface: sl. .... G.I., FOOT SOLDIER, INFANTRYMAN
dogfish .... SHARK, BOWFIN
skin .... SHAGREEN
dogged .... HARRIED, HOUNDED, STUBBORN
dogger .... BOAT
doggerel .... VERSE, JINGLE
doggone! .... DAMN, DARN
doggy .... CANINE, DOGLIKE
dogie .... CALF, WAIF, STRAY, ORPHAN, MAVERICK
dogma .... ISM, CREED, TENET, BELIEF, DOCTRINE
dogmatic .... WILLFUL, OBSTINATE, DICTATORIAL
principle .... DICTA
saying .... DICTUM
dogmatics .... RELIGION, THEOLOGY
dogmatist, a .... CALVINIST
dogmatize .... PROCLAIM
dogs, collectively .... DOGGERY
slang .... FEET

dogtired .... ALL IN
dogwood .... OSIER, CORNEL,
    CORNUS, TUPELO, ASSAGAI,
    ASSEGAI
doilies .... NAPERY
doily .... MAT, NAPKIN
doings .... ACTIVITIES
doited: Scot ...... SENILE, FOOLISH
doldrums .... LULL, CALM, BLUES,
    DUMPS, TEDIUM, DEPRESSION,
    LISTLESSNESS
dole .... ALMS, METE, HANDOUT,
    PITTANCE, DISTRIBUTE
  archaic .... DOLOR, SORROW
  out .... METE, RATION
doleful .... SAD, DISMAL, JOYLESS,
    PENSIVE, UNHAPPY,
    MOURNFUL, LUGUBRIOUS
dolerite .... BASALT
doll .... TOY, CHILD, MAMMET,
    MAUMET, PUPPET, PLAYTHING,
    MARIONETTE
  kind of .... PAPER, BARBIE,
    KEWPIE, VOODOO
  rag .... MOPPET
  real .... LULU
  slang .... BABE, BABY, GIRL,
    DAME, BROAD, CHICK, CUTIE,
    DOLLY, WOMAN, SWEETHEART
  up .... BEAUTIFY, PRETTIFY,
    DRESS(UP), SPRUCE(UP)
dollar .... MONEY, CURRENCY
  bill .... SINGLE
  bill, five: sl. .... FIN, FIVER,
    FIVE-SPOT
  bill, 500: sl. ...... HALF-GRAND
  bill, one: sl. .... BUCK
  bill, 100: sl. .... C-NOTE,
    CENTURY
  bill, 1000: sl. .... GRAND
  bill, ten: sl. .... TENNER,
    SAWBUCK
  bill, twenty: sl. .... DOUBLE
    SAWBUCK
  bill, two: sl. ...... DEUCE, TWO-
    SPOT
  coin part .... CENT, DIME,
    EAGLE, NICKEL, PENNY,
    QUARTER
  coin: sl. .... CARTWHEEL
  Mexican .... PESO
  quarter: sl. .... TWO BITS
  slang .... BUCK, BERRY,
    PLUNK, SMACKER, SIMOLEON
  Spanish .... DURO
dollop .... BLOB, LUMP
dolly .... CART, TRUCK, DASHER,
    LOCOMOTIVE
  child's .... DOLL
  Indian .... TRAY
  slang .... LOTUS

  what it holds .... RIVET
Dolly Varden .... HAT, TROUT
dolman .... COAT, ROBE, WRAP,
    JACKET, MANTLE
dolmen stone .... MEGALITH
dolomite features .... ARETES
Dolomites peak .... MARMOLADA
dolor .... WOE, PANG, AGONY,
    GRIEF, SORROW, ANGUISH
dolorous .... SAD, DOLEFUL,
    FORLORN, TEARFUL,
    MOURNFUL
dolphin .... BUOY, INIA, SUSU,
    BELUGA, SEA HOG, SOOSOO,
    CETACEAN, PORPOISE
  family .... DELPHINIDAE
  frolic of .... GAMBOL
  musician saved by .... ORION
  Spanish .... DORADO
  striker .... SPAR,
    MARTINGAL(E)
  whale .... ORC
dolt .... OAF, SAP, CLOD, FOOL,
    ZANY, DUNCE, NINNY, SCHMO,
    NITWIT, HALFWIT, JACKASS,
    NUMSKULL, DUMBBELL,
    BLOCKHEAD
doltish .... STUPID, WITLESS,
    HALFWITTED
domain .... FIELD, REALM,
    DEMENE, ESTATE, REGION,
    SPHERE, DEMESNE, BAILIWICK,
    TERRITORY
  poetic .... BOURN(E)
dome .... ROOF, VAULT, CUPOLA
  apse's .... CONCHA
  building/hall with
    .... ROTUNDA
  poetic .... MANSION
  slang .... HEAD
  with cupola .... TOPE
Domenico, painter .... EL GRECO
domestic .... TAME, LOCAL,
    HOMELY, MENIAL, NATIVE,
    SLAVEY, ENCHORIC,
    INTERNAL, ENCHORIAL, HOME-
    GROWN
  animal: dia. .... CRITTER,
    CRITTUR
  animal sickness .... SURRA
  establishment .... FAMILY,
    MENAGE, DOMICILE,
    HOUSEHOLD
  fowl .... DORKING, POULTRY
  servant .... (HOUSE)MAID
  type of .... LIVE-IN, SLEEP-IN
  worker .... COOK, MAID,
    BUTLER, SERVANT, GARDENER
domesticate .... REAR, TAME,
    (HOUSE)BREAK, BREED,
    TRAIN, CORRAL, CIVILIZE

domicile .... HOME, ABODE,
    MENAGE, DWELLING,
    HOUSE(HOLD), RESIDENCE
dominance .... CONTROL,
    MASTERY, SUPREMACY
dominant .... RULING, IN
    CONTROL, PRE-EMINENT,
    PREVAILING
dominate .... RULE, REIGN,
    GOVERN, HECTOR, MASTER,
    CONTROL
dominated .... RIDDEN, UNDER
    ONE'S THUMB
domineer .... COW, BREAK,
    BULLY, OPPRESS, LORD OVER,
    OVERBEAR, TYRANNIZE
  husband .... HENPECK
Dominica capital .... ROSEAU
  city .... PORTSMOUTH
  language ..... FRENCH, ENGLISH
  monetary unit .... DOLLAR
Dominican ...... FRIAR, PREACHER
Republic bay .... SAMANA
  cape .... BEATA
  capital ...... SANTO DOMINGO
  city/town .... AZUA, BANI,
    MOCA, NEIBA, LA VEGA,
    SANCHEZ, EL SEIBO, LA
    ROMANA, SANTIAGO
  island .... BEATA, SAONA,
    HISPANIOLA
  language .... SPANISH
  monetary unit .... PESO
  peak .... PICO DUARTE
  president .... BOSCH,
    BALAGUER
dominie .... PASTOR, CLERGYMAN,
    SCHOOLMASTER
dominion .... RULE, SWAY,
    POWER, REALM, REIGN,
    DOMAIN, EMPERY, EMPIRE,
    LORDSHIP
domino .... BONE, LUMP, TILE,
    CLOAK, (HALF)MASK
  spot .... PIP
  variant .... MUGGINS
  with four spots .... QUATRE
dominoes not dealt .... STOCK
don ...... WEAR, PUT ON, ASSUME,
    CLOTHE, INVEST
  Cambridge college ...... HEAD,
    TUTOR, FELLOW
  opposed to .... DOFF
  relative of .... TIA
  river .... DUNA
  Spanish .... NOBLEMAN,
    GENTLEMAN
Don Juan .... RAKE, PHILANDERER
  Juan, greatest
    .... (ANTOINE)DUBOIS
  Juan's mother .... INEZ

Quixote .... MAN OF LA MANCHA
Quixote author .... CERVANTES
Quixote's horse .... ROSINANTE
Quixote's ladylove .... DULCINEA
dona .... LADY, MADAM
Donahue .... PHIL, TROY
Donald Duck, MD .... QUACK DOCTOR
Donar, god of thunder .... THOR
donate .... GIVE, BESTOW, CONFER, TENDER, PRESENT, PROVIDE, CONTRIBUTE
colloquial .... CHIP IN
slang .... KICK IN
donation .... AID, GIFT, HELP, GRANT, ASSISTANCE
generous .... BOUNTY
of a philanthropist .... LARGESSE
periodic .... STIPEND
Donau river ...... DUNA, DANUBE, DUNAREA
done for .... KAPUT, KILLED, RUINED
with .... OVER, ENDED, COMPLETE
with hands .... MANUAL
Donetsk .... STALINO
donjon .... KEEP, TOWER, DUNGEON
donkey .... BURRO, CUDDY, JENNET, ONAGER, DICK(E)Y, (JACK)ASS
and horse offspring ..... MULE, HINNY
animal like a .... QUAGGA
cry .... BRAY
female .... MARE
male .... JACK
man rebuked by .... BALAAM
pet name of .... MOKE
young .... COLT, FOAL
Donna .... REED, SUMMER
Donne and Bradstreet .... POETS
donnybrook .... ADO, RIOT, BRAWL, MELEE, FRACAS, RUCKUS, RUMPUS, FREE-FOR-ALL
donor .... GIVER, GRANTOR, BENEFACTOR, CONTRIBUTOR
Don't ____ that feeds you .... BITE THE HAND
doodad .... BAUBLE, GADGET, GEWGAW, TRINKET, GIMCRACK
doodle .... DAWDLE, SCRAWL, SCRIBBLE
doodlebug .... LARVA

doodlesack .... BAGPIPE
doohickey .... DEVICE, DINGUS, DOODAD, GADGET, DINGBAT, CONTRAPTION
doom ...... FATE, DEATH, DESTINY, CONDEMN, DAMNATION
doomed .... GRIM, FATED, KAPUT, DESTINED, HOPELESS
to death .... FEY
to eternal punishment .... DAMNED
Doone, heroine .... LORNA
husband of .... RIDD
door .... ENTRY, ACCESS, PORTAL, WICKET, BARRIER, PASSAGE
back .... POSTERN
catch .... LATCH
cover .... AWNING, CANOPY
crosspiece .... LINTEL, TRANSOM
fastener/lock ..... HASP, LATCH
for entering .... GATE, INLET, ENTRANCE
frame piece .... TILE
frame(work) ..... SASH, GRATE, GRATING
grating .... GRILLE
handle .... KNOB
joint .... HINGE
knocker .... BELL, RAPPER
leading out .... EXIT, OUTLET
lower half of .... HATCH
part of ..... HASP, KNOB, JAMB, RAIL, SILL, FRAME, LATCH, PANEL, LINTEL, STILE, DOORPOST
rooflike projection .... CANOPY
doorkeeper .... USHER, PORTER, OSTIARY, CONCIERGE, GATEKEEPER
Masonic .... TILER
doorman .... PORTER, SENTRY, JANITOR, CONCIERGE
or maitre d' .... GREETER
doorsill .... THRESHOLD
doorway .... GATE, PORTAL, ENTRANCE
curtain .... PORTIERE
drapery .... LAMBREQUIN
out .... EXIT
sidepost .... JAMB(E)
doozy .... EXCELLENCE
dope .... DRUG, HINT, JUNK, OPIATE, NARCOTIC(S)
addict .... USER, FIEND, JUNKY, ABUSER, JUNKIE, POTHEAD, SNIFFER
out .... SOLVE, FIGURE(OUT)
seller .... PUSHER
slang .... CLOD, DUNCE, NITWIT, STUPID

the .... INFO, LOW-DOWN, DATA, FACTS, SCORE
doped .... SLEEPY, STONED, DRUGGED, OUT COLD
dopester .... ANALYST, SCRUTINEER
dopey .... DAZED, STUPID, CONFUSED, HALF-WITTED
doppelganger .... DOUBLE, WRAITH, REPLICA, SPECTER, DUPLICATE
dor .... BEETLE, BUMBLEBEE
dorado .... DOLPHIN
dorbeetle .... COCKCHAFER
Dorcas .... SEWER TABITHA
dore, ____ (olive wood) .... BRUN
Doric cornice block ...... MUTULE
droplike ornaments .... GUTTA
Dorlcote Mill site .... FLOSS
dormancy .... TORPOR, IDLENESS, INACTION
dormant .... QUIET, STILL, ASLEEP, LATENT, TORPID, RESTING, INACTIVE, QUIESCENT
dormer .... WINDOW, LUTHERN, SKYLIGHT
area .... ATTIC
dormitory .... DORM, HALL, QUARTERS, BOARDINGHOUSE
dormouse .... LEROT, RODENT
acquaintance leaps .... ALICE SPRINGS
dornick .... STONE, DAMASK
dorp .... HAMLET, VILLAGE
dorsal .... BACK, TERGAL
opposed to .... VENTRAL
dorsum .... BACK, TERGUM
dorty .... SULLEN
dory .... (FISHING)BOAT
Dos Passos's trilogy .... USA
dos-a-dos .... SEAT, SOFA
dosage .... DOSE, AMOUNT
dilemma .... MEDICAMENT PREDICAMENT
dose .... DOSAGE, MEASURE, QUANTITY
liquid .... POTION
doss .... BED, BUNK, SLEEP, SNOOZE
dosser .... PANNIER
dossier .... RECORD, (PERSONAL)FILE
dossil ...... TENT, STUPE, PLEDGET, COMPRESS
dot .... JOT, IOTA, MARK, SPOT, WHIT, DOWRY, POINT, TITTLE, SPECK, PERIOD, STIPPLE
dotage .... FONDNESS, SENILITY
dotard .... OCTOGENARIAN

217

describing a .... SENILE
dote .... DROOL, DRIVEL, SLOBBER
    on .... LIKE, ADORE, FANCY
doting .... FOND, AGING,
                DECAYING
dotted .... PIED, DAPPLE,
    MOTTLED, SPOTTED, STIPPLED,
                SPECKLED
    in heraldry .... SEME
dotterel ..... DUPE, GULL, PLOVER
dotty ...... CRAZY, POCKY, FEEBLE,
          SPOTTY, STUDDED
    slang .... DAFFY, DIPPY,
           GOOFY, WACKY
double .... COPY, DUAL, FOLD,
    TWIN, DUPLE, TWICE, BINATE,
    PAIRED, REPEAT, TWOFOLD,
           ALTER EGO
    aces .... AMBSACE, AMESACE
    agent .... SPY, TRAITOR,
             TURNCOAT
    apartment/house .... DUPLEX
    as a substitute in movies/
        plays .... STAND-IN,
           UNDERSTUDY
    bass .... VIOLONE
    check .... VERIFY
    chromosome .... DYAD
    cross: sl. .... DO IN, CHEAT,
    BETRAY, DECEIVE, TREACHERY
    curve .... ESS
    dagger mark .... DIESIS
    dealer .... CHEATER, DECEIVER,
             TWO-TIMER
    dealing .... DUPLICITY, FOUL
                 PLAY
    decker: colloq. ...... SANDWICH
    door part .... SWING
    duo .... TETRAD
    edged .... SHARP, BITING
    exact .... DUPLICATE
    faced .... UNTRUE, INSINCERE
    faced god .... JANUS
    faced person .... HYPOCRITE
    helix .... DNA
    meaning .... EQUIVOKE,
    AMBIGUITY, EQUIVOQUE,
           EQUIVOCACY
    minded .... DOUBTFUL,
    HESITANT, UNCERTAIN,
           UNDECIDED
    moldboard plow .... LISTER
    on the .... QUICKLY
    page spreads .... ADS
    prefix .... DI(S)
    reed instrument .... OBOE,
        SHAWN, BASSOON
    ring .... GEMEL
    ripper/runner .... SLED
    sirloin beef .... BARON
    take .... AFTERTHOUGHT

    talk .... JARGON, GIBBERISH
    tongued ..... TRICKY, DEVIOUS,
        CUNNING, DECEITFUL
    tongued creature .... SNAKE
    tooth .... MOLAR
    tripod .... CAT
    trouble .... RACK AND RUIN
    up .... FOLD, CLENCH
    vision .... DIPLOPIA
doubled .... ECHOED, FOLDED,
              REPEATED
doublet .... COUPLET, POURPOINT,
    TWEEDLEDUM AND
          TWEEDLEDEE
doubletree .... CROSSBAR
doubly .... TWICE, TWOFOLD
doubt .... FEAR, CONCERN,
    MISTRUST, SUSPICION,
    SKEPTICISM, UNCERTAINTY
    about .... WONDER
    beyond .... SURE, CERTAIN
    cause/feel .... MISGIVE
    feeling of .... SCRUPLE
    show .... WAVER, FALTER,
        TEETER, HESITATE
doubter .... THOMAS, SKEPTIC,
           MISSOURIAN
doubtful .... FISHY, MAYBE,
        UNSURE, DUBIOUS
doubting Thomas .... SKEPTIC
douce: Scot. .... PLEASANT
douceur .... TIP, BRIBE
dough .... PASTE, BATTER
    dry strip of .... NOODLE
    fermenting .... LEAVEN
    slang .... CASH, MONEY
    toughener .... GLUTEN
doughboy ...... YANK, DUMPLING,
          INFANTRYMAN
doughnut .... DONUT, CRULLER,
          FRIEDCAKE
    colloquial .... SINKER
    shape .... TORUS
    slang .... TIRE, DUNKER
doughty .... BOLD, BRAVE,
    DARING, GALLANT, VALIANT
doughy .... SOFT, PASTY
doum .... PALM
dour .... GRIM, HARD, HARSH,
    STRICT, STERN, SEVERE,
           SULLEN
Douro .... DUERO
douse .... HIT, DUCK, SOAK,
    DRENCH, EXTINGUISH
dousing .... IMMERSION
dove .... NUN, COOER, CULVER,
        CUSHAT, PIGEON
    Asian/European ..... RINGDOVE
    describing a .... WEAK,
       GENTLE, INNOCENT
    family .... COLUMBIDAE

    genus .... COLUMBA
    kind of .... HOMING, POUTER,
             TUMBLER
    make sound of .... COO,
             MOURN
    opposite of .... HAWK
    shelter ...... COTE, COLUMBARY
    symbol .... PEACE, HOLY
             SPIRIT
dovecote .... COLUMBARY
dovekie .... AUK, ALLE, ROTCH(E),
          GUILLEMOT
dovelike .... GENTLE, ANGELIC
Dover is capital of
    .... DELAWARE
dovetail .... FIT, JOINT, FASTEN
dowager .... WIDOW, MATRON,
          BELDAM(E)
dowdy .... SEEDY, TACKY,
    RAGGED, FRAYED, SHABBY,
    SHODDY, FRAZZLED,
          SLOVENLY
    woman .... FRUMP
dowel .... PIN
    like .... TENON, PINTLE
dower ...... GIFT, DOWRY, ENDOW,
    INVEST, TALENT, BEQUEST,
    ENDOWMENT, INHERITANCE
dowlas .... LINEN, CALICO
down .... FUR, ILL, FELL, HAIR,
    PILE, BELOW, FLOOR, FLUFF,
    UNDER, BENEATH, FEATHERS
    a mound like .... DUNE
    and out .... BANKRUPT,
    HELPLESS, HOPELESS
    at heels .... NEEDY, INDIGENT
    combining form .... CAT(A),
          CATH, KATA
    covered with .... PUBESCENT,
    LANUGINOSE, LANUGINOUS
    duck's .... EIDER
    east .... MAINE, NEW YORK,
          NEW ENGLAND
    facing .... PRONE, PRONATE
    feather .... PLUMULE
    in baseball .... (PUT)OUT
    in bridge .... SET
    in the mouth .... SAD,
    UNHAPPY, DEJECTED,
    (FEELING)LOW, DEPRESSED
    loose particles of .... FUZZ
    plant .... VILLUS
    source of .... EIDER
    the drain .... WASTED
    to-earth one .... REALIST
Down Under .... ANZAC,
    AUSTRALIA, NEW ZEALAND
downcast .... SAD, GLOOMY,
    BASHFUL, DEJECTED
downfall ...... DROP, RUIN, CRASH,
    DEFEAT, FAILURE, COLLAPSE,

LABEFACTION
downgrade ...... DEMOTE, REDUCE
downhearted .... SAD, DASHED, DEJECTED, DEPRESSED, DESPONDENT, DISCOURAGED
downhill, go .... DECLINE, DESCEND
downier .... SOFTER
downpour .... SPATE, DELUGE, SHOWER, TORRENT, RAIN(STORM), CLOUDBURST
downright .... BLUNT, FRANK, PLAIN, SHEER, STARK, DIRECT, UTTERLY, ABSOLUTE
Downs, the .... ROADSTEAD
downtrodden .... ABUSED, OPPRESSED
downward ...... FALLING, SINKING, DESCENDING, PLUMMETING
downwind .... ALEE, LEEWARD
downy .... SOFT, FUZZY, NAPPY, FLEECY, FLOSSY, FLUFFY, VILLOUS, FEATHERY
feather .... PLUMULE
growth .... MOLD, LANUGO
mass .... FLUE
surface/fiber .... NAP
dowry .... GIFT, LEGACY, TALENT, ENDOWMENT
of a .... DOTAL
doxology .... KADDISH
first word .... GLORIA
doxy .... ISM, CREED, DOCTRINE
slang .... HUSSY, WENCH, MISTRESS
doyen .... DEAN, TOP DOG, KINGPIN
doze .... SLEEP, (CAT)NAP, DROWSE, SNOOZE
dozen .... TWELVE
baker's/long .... THIRTEEN
dozing one .... NAPPER
dozy .... DROWSY, SLEEPY
Dr. J in basketball .... (JULIUS)ERVING
No's nemesis .... BOND
Spock, to pals .... BEN
drab ...... DUN, WAN, DULL, SLUT, BORING, LACKLUSTER
drabbet .... LINEN
drach .... DRAM
drachma .... COIN
1/100 of a .... LEPTON
1/6 of a .... OBOL
drachmas (1700) in 1949 .... DOLLAR
Draco .... DRAGON
Draconian .... CRUEL, SEVERE
draff .... LEES, DREGS, REFUSE, SEDIMENT
draft .... DOSE, PULL, DRAIN,

POTION, SKETCH, DRAWING, OUTLINE, POTATION, DRINK(ING), CONSCRIPT
a small .... TASS
animal .... OX, MULE, CARABAO, ELEPHANT
animal and its vehicle .... TEAM
bank .... CHECK
card burner .... DODGER, OBJECTOR
deep .... SWIG
feudal fee to escape .... SCUTAGE
military service .... IMPRESS
of air .... BREEZE
org. .... SSS
draftee .... ROOKIE, RECRUIT, CONSCRIPT
drafts .... CHECKERS
draftsman .... DRAWER, SCRIVENER
drag .... LAG, LUG, TUG, TOW, HALE, HAUL, PULL, SWEEP, TRAIL, DREDGE, GRAPNEL, DRAW OUT, CONTINUE, PROTRACT
feet .... SCUFF(LE)
slang ...... PUFF, RACE, DANCE, INFLUENCE
dragee .... PILL, CANDY
draggletail .... SLUT, SLATTERN
dragnet .... WEB, TRAWL
dragoman ...... GUIDE, CICERONE, INTERPRETER
dragon .... BEAST, MONSTER, FIREDRAKE
archaic .... DRAKE, SNAKE, SERPENT
breath of .... FIRE
deb's .... DUENNA
giant .... FAFNIR
Greek .... LADON
in astronomy .... DRACO
mythical .... BASILISK
slang .... HOTHEAD, FIRE-EATER
slayer .... CADMUS, (ST.)GEORGE
small .... DRAGONET
two-legged .... WIVERN
dragoon .... COERCE, HARASS, TROOPER, CAVALRYMAN
drain .... DRIP, PIPE, DRAFT, EMPTY, SEWER, FILTER, DRAW OFF, DEPLETE, EXHAUST
dry .... DEHYDRATE
for washing ore .... BUDDLE
liquid from .... SAP, TAP, SPOUT
open .... GUTTER, KENNEL

road .... CULVERT
draining hole/pit .... SUMP, CESSPOOL
drained ...... SAPPED, WEAKENED, EXHAUSTED
drake .... DUCK, CANNON, MAY FLY, MALLARD
archaic .... DRAGON
Drake's adversary .... SPANISH ARMADA
dram .... NIP, SIP, SLUG, DRAFT, DRINK
in assaying .... CENTNER
drama .... SHOW, (STAGE)PLAY
climax .... CATASTROPHE
closing section of .... EPILOGUE
comic scenes .... RELIEF
conflict of character ..... AGON
humorous .... COMEDY
in the sport of kings .... TRIPLE CROWN
introduction .... PROLOGUE
Japanese .... KABUKI
main character .... PROTAGONIST
musical .... OPERA, BALLET
opening .... PROTASIS
outdoor .... PAGEANT
pause between acts of .... INTERMISSION
pertaining to .... THESPIAN
section .... ACT
short .... PLAYLET
staging place .... THEATER
tragic .... BUSKIN
with unhappy ending .... TRAGEDY
wordless .... PANTOMIME
writer .... DRAMATIST, PLAYWRIGHT
dramatic .... VIVID, EXCITING, STRIKING
art .... THEATER
impersonator .... DISEUSE
scene/picture .... TABLEAU
dramatics .... THEATRICS, HISTRIONICS
dramatis personae .... CAST, CHARACTERS
dramatist .... PLAYWRIGHT
dramatize .... ENACT, SPLASH
slang .... HAM IT UP
dramshop .... BAR, SALOON
drape ...... FOLD, BAIZE, CURTAIN
draper .... CLOTHIER
drapery .... ARRAS, CLOTH, FABRIC, CURTAIN, TEXTILE, VALANCE
bed .... CANOPY
cloth .... MADRAS, MOREEN

219

cord .... TIEBACK, TORSADE
material ..... VELURE, VELOURS
shelf/door/window
.... LAMBREQUIN
drapes .... CURTAIN
drastic .... RASH, HARSH, SEVERE,
EXTREME
drat .... EXPLETIVE
draught .... SWIG, DRAFT
draughts: Brit. .... CHECKERS
Dravidian .... TELEGU, TELUGU
language .... TAMIL
draw .... TIE, TUG, HAUL, LIMN,
PULL, DRAFT, ALLURE,
DEPICT, SKETCH, ATTRACT,
RECEIVE, STALEMATE,
DISEMBOWEL
after .... TOW
as conclusion .... INFER,
ASSUME, DEDUCE, RECKON
at a cigar(ette) .... PUFF,
DRAG, INHALE
away .... DRAFT, DIVERT
back .... FLINCH, RECEDE,
RETRACT, RETREAT
back in fear .... QUAIL,
COWER, CRINGE, RECOIL
close .... NEAR, APPROACH
forth .... EDUCE, EVOKE, ELICIT
in .... WOO, LURE, ENSNARE
in dots .... STIPPLE
lots .... CAST
off .... DRAFT, SIPHON
off fluid .... TAP
off from dregs .... RACK
out ..... EDUCE, DERIVE, ELICIT,
EXTRACT, PROLONG, STRETCH,
LENGTHEN, CONTINUE,
PROTRACT
out with a ladle .... LADE
sap .... BLEED
the line .... (SET THE) LIMIT
tight ..... FRAP, TENSE, TAUTEN
to scale .... PROTRACT
drawback .... DEFECT, REBATE,
REFUND, HANDICAP,
OBSTACLE, DETERRENT,
SHORTCOMING
drawbridge .... BASCULE,
PONTLEVIS
drawer .... ARTIST, DRAFTSMAN,
DELINEATOR
for money .... TILL
handle of .... KNOB
drawers .... SHORTS
women's .... PANTIES,
PANTALET(TE)S
drawing .... PLAN, CHART,
DESIGN, SKETCH, DIAGRAM,
LOTTERY, ALLURING,
DEPICTION

architect's .... RENDU
architectural .... EPURES
carbon pencil/crayon
.... CHARCOAL
card .... BAIT, DECOY,
CELEBRITY, ENTERTAINER
charcoal .... FUSAIN
force to produce vacuum
.... SUCTION
graphic .... PORTRAYAL,
DELINEATION
humorous .... CARTOON
in dots .... STIPPLE
into the lungs, as of air
.... DRAFT
of load/vehicle .... TRACTION
on walls, etc. .... GRAFFITO
one way to make copy of
.... TRACING
paper .... ATLAS
photographic reproduction of
.... BLUEPRINT
power .... PULL, MAGNET
room .... SALA, SALON,
PARLOR
style of .... CHIAROSCURO
with crayons
.... CALCOGRAPHY
with lead-pointed instrument
.... PLUMBAGO
drawn .... WAN, EVEN, TAUT,
TIED, EQUAL, TENSE, TIRED,
WEARY, HAGGARD
out .... LONG, LENGTHY, LONG-
WINDED
dray .... VAN, CART, WAGON
drayage .... CARTAGE, FREIGHT,
HAULAGE
dread .... AWE, FEAR, ANGST,
FRIGHT, HORROR
dreaded disease .... AIDS,
CANCER, CHOLERA,
LEUKEMIA, SMALLPOX, HEART
ATTACK, TUBERCULOSIS
seizure? .... HOSTILE
TAKEOVER
dreadful .... BAD, DIRE, AWFUL,
HORRID, AWESOME, HIDEOUS,
FEARFUL, SHOCKING,
TERRIBLE
dreadfully: colloq. .... VERY,
BADLY, EXTREMELY
dreadnaught .... WARSHIP,
BATTLESHIP
dream ...... HOPE, FANCY, DESIRE,
VISION, FANTASY, IMAGINE,
DELUSION, ILLUSION
day .... REVERIE
French .... REVE
frightening .... NIGHTMARE
goal .... IDEAL

up .... IMAGINE, CONCEIVE,
CREATE, VISUALIZE
world .... UTOPIA, PARADISE
dreamer .... ROMANTICIST
impractical .... FANTAST,
VISIONARY
of dreams .... WISHFUL
THINKER
dreamily romantic
.... MOONSTRUCK, STARRY-
EYED
dreamland .... SLEEP
dreams, forecast based on
.... ONEIROMANCY
interpret .... REDE
interpretation of
.... ONEIROLOGY
interpreter .... ONEIROCRITIC
dreamy ...... RAPT, MISTY, VAGUE,
UNREAL, FANCIFUL,
ENCHANTED, IMAGINARY,
VISIONARY
from dope smoking .... KEF
person .... POET, PROPHET,
IDEALIST
dreary .... SAD, DULL, GRAY,
DISMAL, GLOOMY, LONELY,
SOMBER, TEDIOUS, CHEERLESS
Scottish .... DREE
dredge .... DRAG, SIFT, DEEPEN,
SPRINKLE
bucket .... CLAMSHELL
shovel .... SCOOP
dree .... DREARY, ENDURE,
SUFFER, TEDIOUS
dregs .... LEES, SCUM, SILT,
DRAFF, FECES, GROUT,
MAGMA, REFUSE, RESIDUE,
SEDIMENT
coffee .... GROUNDS
left in liquor glass
.... HEELTAP
of society .... RIFFRAFF
Dreiser (Theodore) character
.... STOIC, CARRIE
drench .... SOP, WET, SOAK,
DOUSE, SOUSE, SATURATE
drenched .... WET, ASOP, BATHED,
SODDEN, SOAKED, SOPPING,
STEEPED
Dresden .... CHINAWARE,
PORCELAIN
dress .... DON, RIG, TOG, DECK,
GARB, GEAR, TRIM, WEAR,
ADORN, ARRAY, FROCK,
ATTIRE, CLOTHE, APPAREL,
GARMENT, GARNISH, OUTFIT,
RAIMENT, CLOTHING,
DECORATE, EMBELLISH,
ACCOUTERMENT,
ACCOUTREMENT

a horse .... CURRY
accessory .... BAND, BELT,
    SASH, CESTUS, GUIMPE
by rubbing .... DUB
characteristic .... LIVERY
colloquial .... FIG, TOG(S)
cut ...... SACK, A-LINE, SHEATH
designer .... STYLIST
down .... SCOLD, BERATE,
    REPRIMAND
external .... CAPE, COAT,
    CLOAK, SHAWL, STOLE,
    BURNOOSE, WRAP-AROUND
fashion designer .... DIOR,
    BEENE, BLASS, SARMI,
    ADOLFO, CASHIN, CHANEL,
    NORELL, BALMAIN, CASSINI,
    GALANOS, TIFFEAU, BERGDORF,
    GIVENCHY, GERNREICH,
    VALENTINO, BALENCIAGA
feathers .... PREEN
formal .... TUX, GOWN,
    TUXEDO, CUTAWAY, FULL-
    DRESS UNIFORM
flax .... TED
gaudily .... BEDIZEN
hat .... SHAKO, TOPPER, TOP
    HAT
in fine array .... DINK
judge's .... GOWN, ROBE
leather .... DUB, TAN, CURRY
man's full .... TAILS
manner of .... GUISE
material .... LAME, SILK,
    WOOL, LINEN, PIQUE, VOILE,
    MUSLIN, PONGEE, CHIFFON,
    PAISLEY, SHANTUNG,
    GEORGETTE, VELVET(EEN)
odd .... TOG
ornamental slit .... SLASH
pertaining to .... SARTORIAL
rehearsal .... WALK-THROUGH
riding .... HABIT
showily .... FIG
spangle .... SEQUIN
stone .... NIG
style, men's .... NEHRU,
    SWALLOW-TAILED
style, women's .... SACK,
    A-LINE, CHITON, KIRTLE, MUU-
    MUU, PALAZZO, TOPLESS,
    PANTSUIT, CHEONGSAM,
    CRINOLINE, MAXISKIRT,
    MIDISKIRT, MINISKIRT
suit .... TUX(EDO)
trimming .... GIMP, RUCHE,
    PIPING, RICKRACK, SOUTACHE
up .... PRANK, PRIMP, PRINK,
    PRUNE, SPRUCE, DANDIFY
with beak/care .... PREEN
with tails .... CUTAWAY

dressed .... CLAD, GARBED,
    ARRAYED, CLOTHED
pelt .... FUR
shabbily ...... DOWDY, POK(E)Y
smartly .... CHIC, DAPPER
stylishly .... MODISH
to _____ .... KILL
to the _____ ..... NINES, TEETH
dresser .... CHEST, BUREAU,
    CUPBOARD
flashy .... SPIFF
of another person .... VALET
stylish .... FOP, DUDE, TOFF,
    DANDY
dressing .... SAUCE, GARNISH,
    PLEDGET, STUFFING,
    DECORATION
down ...... SCOLDING, CHEWING
    OUT
gown .... ROBE, CAMISE,
    DUSTER, KIMONO, CAMISOLE
medicated .... STUPE, PLASTER,
    POULTICE
room .... CLOSET
soil .... MUCK, MANURE,
    COMPOST
table .... TOILET, VANITY
wheel .... TRUER
wound .... LINT, GAUZE,
    STUPE, DOSSIL, BANDAGE,
    BAND-AID, COMPRESS
dressmaker ...... SEWER, SARTOR,
    STYLIST, TAILOR, MODISTE,
    COUTURIER(E), SEAMSTRESS
dressmaking term .... HEM,
    FACE, GORE, PURL, BASTE,
    GATHER, STITCH, APPLIQUE
dressy ...... CHIC, FANCY, SHOWY,
    SMART, FORMAL, MODISH,
    ELEGANT, STYLISH
Dreyfus' champion
    .... (EMILE)ZOLA
dribble .... DROP, LEAK, DROOL,
    SLAVER, SLABBER, TRICKLE
away .... WASTE, EMACIATE
in basketball .... BOUNCE
in football/soccer .... KICKS
in hockey .... TAP
driblet .... SMIDGEN, PITTANCE
dried coconut meat .... COPRA
flower bud .... CLOVE
grape .... RAISIN
grass .... HAY
orchid tuber .... SALEP
plum .... PRUNE
up .... SERE, BARREN
drier .... KILN, OAST, OVEN,
    SERER, DRYER, BLOWER,
    DESICCANT, DESICCATOR
natural .... SUN, FIRE
driest place in U.S. .... DEATH

    VALLEY
drift .... GIST, PILE, FLOCK, FLOW,
    STRAY, TENOR, TREND,
    INTENT, ESSENCE, MEANING,
    TENDENCY, INCLINATION
away .... FADE, SINK, DWINDLE
ice .... FLOE, SLUDGE
in mining .... HEADING
in nautical usage/off course
    .... SAG
drifter .... HOBO, CLOUD, NOMAD,
    TRAMP, DERELICT,
    VAGABOND, WANDERER
drill .... AWL, BORE, QUIZ, AUGER,
    CLOTH, TRAIN, BABOON,
    GIMLET, PIERCE, EXERCISE,
    PRACTICE, DISCIPLINE
dentist's .... BURR
hall .... ARMORY
team .... SQUAD
drilling equipment .... RIG
machinery support
    .... DERRICK
drink ...... ALE, BIB, TIFF, DRAFT,
    ABSORB, IMBIBE, SWALLOW,
    BEVERAGE, POTATION
a certain way .... LAP
addicted to alcoholic
    .... BIBULOUS
admiral's .... GROG
agave juice .... PULQUE
alcoholic .... GIN, PEG, RUM,
    TOT, BEER, GROG, MEAD,
    SAKE, BOOZE, BRANDY,
    VODKA, COGNAC, LIQUOR,
    SCOTCH, WHISKY, BOURBON,
    SPIRITS, SWIZZLE, LIBATION
ancient .... MEAD, MORAT
appetizer .... BRACER,
    COCKTAIL
aromatic .... JULEP, COFFEE
barley .... PTISAN
beer and lemonade
    .... SHANDY
beerlike, sour .... KVAS(S)
before bedtime ...... NIGHTCAP
before meal .... APERITIF
brandy ...... COGNAC, SIDECAR,
    SANGAREE
brandy and soda .... PEG
Brazilian .... ASSAI
Christmas .... NOG
claret, soda and sugar
    .... BADMINTON
cocktail .... MARTINI,
    HIGHBALL, OLD-FASHIONED
cold .... JULEP, COBBLER
colloquial .... BOOZE,
    MOONSHINE
creme de menthe and cream
    .... GRASSHOPPER

crushed fruit .... SMASH
daintily .... SIP
deep .... SWILL
drug a .... HOCUS
East Indies .... NIPA, SOMA,
                   TODDY
effervescent .... FIZ(Z)
excessively .... TOPE, BOUSE
farewell .... STIRRUP CUP
fermented .... ALE, BEER, RUM,
          MEAD, SAKE, PERRY
for invalids .... CAUDLE
from apples/other fruits
                         CIDER
from fermented grain, with
       hops .... BEER
from fermented molasses
                        RUM
from fermented rice ..... SAKE
from grapes .... WINE,
    BRANDY, COGNAC, MALMSEY,
              CHAMPAGNE
from root extracts ..... GINGER
                       ALE
fruit juice .... ADE
gin .... RICKEY
gin and lime juice ..... GIMLET
granting immortality
                       AMRITA
greedily .... GULP, SWILL,
                     GUZZLE
Greek wine .... RETSINA
habitually .... TOPE, TIPPLE
heartily/heavily .... CAROUSE
honey .... MEAD, MORAT
hot .... GROG, TODDY
hot milk .... SALOOP
iced .... SLING, COBBLER
in great gulps .... SWIG
in honor of/to one's health
                         TOAST
in large quantities ...... QUAFF,
                     SWILL
insipid/weak .... WISH-WASH
Japanese alcoholic/wine
                         SAKE
Mexican .... TEQUILA,
              MARGARITA
mint, etc. .... JULEP, SMASH
mixed .... NOG, MAI-TAI,
    COCKTAIL, HIGHBALL, PINK
      LADY, TOM COLLINS
non-alcoholic .... MINERAL
of beverage with shaved ice
                       FRAPPE
of forgetfulness ..... NEPENTHE
of poison/medicine .... POTION
of rum .... GROG, BUMBO, TOM
               AND JERRY
of sarsaparilla syrup .... MEAD

of spiced, sugared gruel
                       CAUDLE
of the gods .... NECTAR
old-time, fermented ..... MEAD
palm .... NIPA, TUBA
regal .... LAGER
rum and lime juice
                      DAIQUIRI
Russian .... VODKA
sassafras .... SALOOP
short .... DRAM
single .... SHOT, SLUG
slang .... SEA, LUSH, HOOCH,
           OCEAN, SAUCE
slowly .... SIP, NURSE
sly .... NIP
small .... SIP, DRAM, TIFF,
        (S)NIP, SNORT, SNIFTER
soft .... ADE, POP, COLA
spiced .... FLIP, PUNCH, BISHOP
spiced ale .... WASSAIL
stimulant .... BRACER
stirring stick .... MUDDLER
sweet sap .... TODDY
sweetened .... FLIP, NEGUS,
     PUNCH, BISHOP, ORGEAT,
                   POSSET
syrupy, alcoholic .... CORDIAL,
                 LIQUEUR
teenage .... SODA, MALTED
to .... TOAST, SALUTE
to excess .... TOPE, SWILL,
       CAROUSE, INEBRIATE
together .... HOBNOB
vodka and orange juice
                SCREWDRIVER
vodka and tomato juice
              BLOODY MARY
water with syrup .... JULEP
whisky-soda .... HIGHBALL
whisky-vermouth
                 MANHATTAN
wine and honey ..... OENOMEL
wine, water and lemon juice
                   NEGUS
wine, water and spices
                 SANGAREE
drinkable .... POTABLE
drinker ...... SOT, TOPER, BIBBER,
    SOAKER, GUZZLER, CAROUSER,
    IMBIBER, REVELER, TIPPLER,
               TOSSPOT
colloquial .... BARFLY, BOOZER
insatiable alcoholic
                 DIPSOMANIAC
slang .... LUSH, WINO, SOUSE
drinking .... TIFFIN, IMBIBING,
       LIBATION, POTATION
bout ...... BAT, SPREE, BENDER,
      WASSAIL, COMPOTATION
bowl .... JORUM, MAZER,

                 MAZARD
convivial .... BOWL, WASSAIL
cup .... MUG, TASS, TOBY,
       STEIN, BEAKER, NOGGIN,
    RUMMER, SCYPHUS, TANKARD,
              PANNIKIN
excessive .... WASSAIL,
     POTATION, CRAPULENT,
            CRAPULOUS
fountain .... BUBBLER,
           SCUTTLEBUTT
glass .... GOBLET, RUMMER,
     TUMBLER, SCHOONER
mug, leather ..... (BLACK)JACK
party .... ORGY, WASSAIL,
              CAROUSAL
premises .... BAR, INN,
    LOUNGE, SALOON, TAVERN,
    TAPROOM, PUB, ALEHOUSE
salutation ..... TOAST, WASSAIL
spirits/liquor habitually
                 ALCOHOLISM
spree .... BINGE, BOOZE,
    BOUSE, BENDER, WASSAIL,
             CAROUSAL
toast .... SALUD, SKOAL,
    CHEERS, PROSIT, MABUHAY
drip .... DROP, LEAK, SEEP,
              TRICKLE
coffee .... PERCOLATE
edge .... EAVE
slang .... BORE, PEST, CREEP
dripping .... ASOP, SODDEN,
       SOPPY, TRICKLING
wet .... DRENCHED
drive .... GOAD, PROD, PUSH, RIDE,
    RUSH, URGE, FEEZE, FORCE,
    IMPEL, AVENUE, CHARGE,
    ENERGY, HAMMER, CONDUCT,
    CAMPAIGN, PRESSURE
a vehicle/ship .... STEER
away .... SHOO, BANISH
back .... REPEL, REBUFF,
             REPULSE
colloquial .... HUSTLE
from cover .... FLUSH
head first .... RAM, BUTT
in offering .... FOOD,
           DRINK(S), MOVIE
in waiter .... CARHOP
into .... RAM, CRAM, POUND
into, through .... PENETRATE
nail obliquely .... TOE
off quickly: sl. ...... PEEL OUT
onward/forward .... PROPEL
out .... ROUT, ROUST
out by incantation
                 EXORCISE
politician's ...... FUND-RAISING
reformer's .... CRUSADE
together by force .... COERCE,

COMPEL

tree-lined .... AVENUE

with blows .... SLOG

with sudden force ..... THRUST

drivel .... DROOL, SLUSH, BABBLE, SALIVA, SLAVER, MAUNDER, SLOBBER, TWADDLE, NONSENSE

driven obliquely .... TOED

driver .... MOTORIST, MOTORMAN, CHAUFFEUR, STEERSMAN

aircraft .... PILOT, AVIATOR

animal ...... MAHOUT, SKINNER, MULETEER

backseat, usual .... WIFE(Y)

camel .... SARWAN

carriage .... HACK, WHIP, COACHMAN

coach .... JEHU, JARVEY

elephant .... MAHOUT

forklift/heavy machinery .... OPERATOR

gear of .... CRASH HELMET

inept .... FENDER-BENDER

kind of .... PILE, TAMP, HAMMER, MALLET, GOLF CLUB

mule .... MULETEER

of trucks for hauling loads .... TEAMSTER

of wagons .... WAGONER, CHARIOTEER

reckless .... JEHU, MANIAC, SPEEDER, SCORCHER

seat of .... BOX, HELM

slave ..... MARTINET, STICKLER, TASKMASTER

taxi .... CABBY, CABMAN

driving .... PUSHY, RIDING, DYNAMIC, MOTORING, COMPELLING

a .... DRIFT

ambition .... WILL, GET-UP, RESOLVE

desire .... LUST, PASSION, OBSESSION

jealousy .... ENVY

enthusiasm ...... ZEAL, ARDOR, FERVOR, DEVOTION

force, human .... LIBIDO

line .... REIN

drizzle .... MIST, RAIN, SPRAY, MIZZLE, SPRINKLE

drogher .... SAILBOAT

droghiere .... GROCER

droit .... (LEGAL)RIGHT

droll .... ODD, WAG, COMIC, JESTER, AMUSING, BUFFOON, COMICAL, HUMOROUS

finish .... ERY

drome, as suffix .... RUNNING, RACECOURSE

dromedary .... CAMEL, DELUL, MEHARI

dromon(d) .... SHIP

drone .... HUM, BUZZ, IDLER, LOAF(ER), BAGPIPE, AIRPLANE, (HONEY)BEE, MONOTONE

drool. See **drivel**

droop ...... LOP, SAG, BEND, FLAG, LOLL, PEAK, SINK, WILT, NUTATE, SLOUCH, WEAKEN, DECLINE, LANGUISH

drooping .... LOPPY, NUTANT, HANGING, SLOUCH, LANGUID

on one side .... ALOP

droopy ...... WEAK, TIRED, WEARY

drop .... FALL, GOUT, OMIT, FLUNK, GUTTA, LOWER, GLOBULE, DECREASE

bait .... DIB

below surface .... SINK

by/in .... VISIT

drastically, as in value .... COLLAPSE

fish line .... DAP

gently .... DAP, DIP

heavily .... PLOP, FLUMP, PLUMP

in the bucket .... BIT, DOLE, MITE, PITTANCE

in trickles .... DRIP

it .... END, STOP, CEASE

of sweat .... BEAD

one .... MINIM

out .... SECEDE, ABANDON

ready to .... FAINT

sharp .... NOSE DIVE

straight down .... PLUNGE, PLUMMET

sudden .... DIVE, CRASH, SLUMP

the subject .... DISMISS, FORGET(IT)

viscous substance .... BLOB

droplike ornaments .... GUTTA

dropout, for one .... QUITTER

dropper .... PIPET(TE)

droppings .... DUNG, GUANO, MANURE

dropsical .... EDEMIC

dropsy .... (O)EDEMA, ANASARCA, BERIBERI

drosophila .... (FRUIT)FLY

dross .... SCUM, SLAG, WASTE, REFUSE, SCORIA, RUBBISH

drought .... ARIDITY, DRYNESS

plant .... GUAR, CACTUS, XEROPHYTE

droughty .... DRY, ARID

drove .... HERD, CROWD, FLOCK, HORDE

composition of .... HOGS,

SHEEP, CATTLE

drover .... CATTLE DEALER

drown .... FLOOD, DEADEN, MUFFLE, INUNDATE, SUBMERGE, OVERPOWER

drowning, execution by .... NOYADE

drowse .... NAP, NOD, DOZE, SLEEP

drowsiness .... LETHARGY, OSCITANCY

drowsy .... SLEEPY, LETHARGIC, HEAVY-LIDDED

from using drug .... KEF

drub .... HIT, BEAT, LICK, WHIP, KNOCK, THUMP, CUDGEL, THRASH

drubbing .... DEFEAT, BEATING

drudge .... GRUB, MOIL, PLOD, CHORE, GRIND, SCRUB, SLAVE, TOIL(ER), HOUSEKEEPER

literary .... HACK

drudgery .... FAG, RUT, MOIL, CHORE, GRIND, SWEAT, TASKWORK

drug .... HOCUS, SALVE, OPIATE, STUPEFY, MEDICATE, MEDICINE, KNOCK OUT, MORPHINE, NARCOTIC

addict .... USER, ABUSER, JUNKIE, HOPHEAD, POTHEAD, SNOWBIRD

addiction .... HABIT, DEPENDENCE

anabolic/with protein-building effect .... STEROID

antacid .... SELTZER

bitter .... QUASSIA

causing vomit .... EMETIC

cocain(e): sl. ...... COKE, SNOW

compressed form ..... TABLOID

excessive taking of .... OVERDOSE

eye .... MYOTIC, NEOMYCIN, MYDRIATIC

for addicts .... METHADON(E)

for all ailments .... ELIXIR, PANACEA

for allergy ..... ANTIHISTAMINE

for blood pressure .... ADRENALIN

for clearing nasal passages .... DECONGESTANT

for cough .... EXPECTORANT

for drying .... DESICCANT

for epileptic attacks .... DILANTIN

for forgetfulness .... NEPENTHE

for pain relief .... MORPHINE

for perspiration .... BONESET

grinder .... MULLER

heroin: sl. .... JUNK, SMACK
intoxicating .... PEYOTE
laxative .... ALOE, CALOMEL,
 MAGNESIA, CASTOR OIL
LSD: sl. .... ACID
marijuana: sl. .... POT
narcotics .... OPIUM, HEROIN,
 COCAINE
orchid-based .... SALEP
plant .... ALOE, POPPY
slang .... DOPE
soothing/calming
 .... SEDATIVE, TRANQUILIZER
"speed" .... LSD,
 METHEDRINE, AMPHETAMINE
stimulant .... CAFFEINE
drugged .... HIGH, DOPED, DOPEY,
 SPACED OUT, STONED,
 SEDATED
drugget .... MAT, RUG
druggist .... CHEMIST,
 PHARMACIST
container of .... GALLIPOT
drugs, action of .... SYNERGY
drugstore .... PHARMACY,
 APOTHECARY
soap .... SAPO
drum ..... TUM, BARREL, TYMPAN,
 TAMBOUR, CYLINDER
ancient type of .... TIMBREL
beat .... DUB, RATAPLAN,
 RUB-A-DUB-DUB
beat a .... PERCUSS
call .... DIAN, TATTOO
capstan's .... RUNDLE
continuously .... TATTOO
elongated bass .... CONGA
hand .... TABOR, TIMBREL,
 TAMBOURINE
head .... TYMPANUM
jungle/Oriental .... TOMTOM
kettle .... ATABAL
like a/of a .... TYMPANIC
long .... TAMBOURIN
low continuous beating of
 .... RUFFLE
major .... BANDMASTER
major's rod .... BATON
Moorish .... ATABAL
played with hands ..... CONGA,
 BONGO
played with stick
 .... TABORIN(E)
player .... TYMPANIST
primitive ...... TAM-TAM, TOM-
 TOM
signal .... TAPS, TATTOO,
 CHAMADE
small .... TABOR, TABOUR,
 TABRET, TABORET, TABORIN(E)
sound ...... BEAT, ROLL, POUND

string across .... SNARE
with fingers .... THRUM
drumbeat .... DUB, FLAM,
 TATTOO, RATAPLAN,
 RATTATTOO, RAT-TAT-TAT,
 RUB-A-DUB-DUB
continuous .... ROLL, RUFFLE
drumfire .... BARRAGE
drumfish .... WHITING
relative of .... CROAKER
drumlin .... HILL, RIDGE
drummer .... TABORER,
 PERCUSSIONIST
famed .... (GENE)KRUPA
kind of .... SALESMAN
drumming .... BEATING,
 POUNDING, THROBBING,
 THUMPING, THRUMMING
continuous .... TATTOO
drumstick .... TYMP STICK
drunk(ard) ...... SOT, HIGH, SOAK,
 BLIND, BLOAT, BOUSY,
 BOOZY, FRIED, MALTY,
 NAPPY, RUMMY, SOUSE,
 TIGHT, TIPSY, TOPER, BARFLY,
 BLOTTO, GROGGY, LOADED,
 POTTED, STEWED, ROUNDER,
 TIPPLER, TOSSPOT, BIBULOUS,
 COCKEYED, WALLEYED,
 INEBRIATE(D), PLASTERED,
 DIPSOMANIAC, INTOXICATED
drunken .... DIZZY, GIDDY,
 SOUSED, STEWED, BACCHIC,
 SMASHED, INEBRIOUS,
 INTOXICATED
carousal .... BOUT, SPREE,
 REVELRY
carouser .... BACCHANT(E)
celebration .... JAG
party .... WASSAIL,
 BACCHANAL(IA)
spree .... SOAK, BINGE,
 BENDER
drunkenness ...... INTEMPERANCE,
 INTOXICATION
aftereffect of .... HANGOVER
drupe .... PLUM, CHERRY, APRICOT
drupelet .... TRYMA, ACINUS,
 NUTLET
drupelets, fruit of many
 .... GRAPE, RASPBERRY,
 (BLACK)BERRY, LOGANBERRY
druthers .... PERSONAL CHOICE
dry ...... ARID, SEAR, SERE, DRAIN,
 PARCHED, THIRSTY,
 WITHERED, ANHYDROUS,
 DEHYDRATE, (DE)SICCATE
as wine .... SEC, BRUT
cleaning solvent ...... BENZINE,
 NAPHTHA, GASOLINE
colloquial ...... PROHIBITIONIST

combining form .... XERO
fly .... LURE
goods dealer .... DRAPER
grass .... HAY
lake basin .... PLAYA
moderately .... SUBARID
oneself .... TOWEL
opposed to .... WET
run .... TEST, REHEARSAL
spell .... DROUGHT
story, describing .... JEJUNE
style of speaking .... DULL,
 BORING, MATTER-OF-FACT
sucked .... DRAINED, SAPLESS
throat .... HUSKY, HOARSE
to .... SUN, BLOT
tongue, sign of .... THIRST
up ..... PARCH, WIZEN, SHRINK,
 WITHER
with cloth/mop .... SWAB,
 WIPE
with heat .... SUN, BAKE,
 SCORCH, SHRIVEL, TORREFY,
 TORRIFY
dryad .... NYMPH
dryer. See drier
drying away of body tissue
 .... ATROPHY
cloth .... TOWEL
machine .... TEDDER
spread for .... TED
substance that promotes
 .... SICCATIVE
to get a concentrated product
 .... EVAPORATION
dryness .... ARIDITY, ARIDNESS
from lack of rain
 .... DROU(G)HT
from need of water .... THIRST
of mouth .... XEROSTOMIA
of skin/eyeball .... XEROSIS
DST, part of .... TIME, SAVING,
 DAYLIGHT
Du Barry's title .... MADAME,
 COMTESSE
duad .... TWO, DUAL, PAIR,
 COUPLE
dual ...... TWIN, BINARY, DUPLEX,
 DOUBLE, TWOFOLD
campaign promise .... LAW
 AND ORDER
channel audio .... STEREO
dualism, element of .... EVIL,
 GOOD, MIND, MATTER,
 PHYSICAL, SPIRITUAL
dub .... HIT, CALL, POKE, TERM,
 DUFFER, KNIGHT, THRUST,
 DRUMBEAT, (NICK)NAME
dubiety .... UNCERTAINTY
dubious .... LEERY, SHADY,
 SHAKY, VAGUE, UNSURE,

DOUBTFUL, SKEPTICAL,
QUESTIONABLE
dubitation .... DOUBT
Dublin is capital of .... IRELAND
ducal .... DUKEDOM
ducat: sl. ...... (ADMISSION)TICKET
duce .... CHIEF, LEADER
Italian .... MUSSOLINI
Duchess of Windsor
.... (WALLIS)WARFIELD
title of respect .... GRACE
duchy .... REGION, DUKEDOM
duck .... BIRD, DIVE, TERN, AVOID,
CLOTH, DODGE, DOUSE,
BUFFLEHEAD
aquatic stifftail .... OXYURA
Asiatic .... MANDARIN
colloquial .... DARLING
color on wing .... SPECULUM
cry of .... QUACK
dabbling .... ANAS
decoyer .... TOLLER
diving .... SMEW, SCAUP,
POCHARD, REDHEAD,
MERGANSER
downy .... EIDER
fabric .... LINEN, COTTON
family .... ANATIDAE
fish-eating .... GOOSANDER,
MERGANSER
foot membrane .... WEB
genus .... ANAS, ANSER
handsome .... WOOD
Hawaiian .... NENE
hawk .... FALCON, HARRIER
hooded .... MERGUS,
MERGANSER
hunter's screen .... BLIND
large .... MUSCOVY
like .... COOT
long-tailed .... OLDSQUAW
lure .... DECOY
male .... DRAKE
merganser .... SMEW
non-quacking .... MUSCOVY
out .... FLEE, SPLIT
perching .... CAIRINA
pintail .... SMEE
river .... TEAL, WIDGEON
sea/marine .... COOT, EIDER,
SCAUP, SCO(O)TER,
MERGANSER
shooting boat .... SKAG
slang .... JOKER, QUEER,
PERSON
small .... SMEW
torrent .... MERGANETTA-
ARMATA
tufted .... AYTHYA-FULIGULA
use of man-made .... DECOY
walk .... WADDLE

whistling .... DENDROCYGNA
white-faced tree
.... DENDROCYGNA-VIDUATA
wild ..... TEAL, DRAKE, SCAUP,
GADWALL, MALLARD,
WIDGEON, GOLDEN-EYE,
SHELDRAKE, CANVASBACK
young .... DUCKLING
duckbill .... PLATYPUS,
MONOTREME
ducker .... GREBE, DABCHICK
duckpins .... BOWLING
ducks, brood of .... TEAM
collectively .... WATERFOWL
duct .... VAS, FLUE, PIPE, TUBE,
CANAL, CHANNEL, CONDUIT
body .... MEATUS
narrowing of .... STENOSIS
ductile .... PLIANT, ELASTIC,
PLASTIC, PLIABLE, TENSILE,
TRACTILE
ductless gland, of a .... ADRENAL,
THYROID, ENDOCRINE,
PITUITARY
glandlike body .... THYMUS
ducts, of or having
.... VASCULAR
dud .... FLOP, LEMON, FAILURE
duddy: Scot. .... RAGGED
dude ...... FOP, DANDY, COXCOMB
one kind of .... TOURIST
place of .... RANCH
ranch's use .... RESORT
dudeen .... (TOBACCO)PIPE
Dudevant, Baronne
.... (GEORGE)SAND
dudgeon ...... FRET, HILT, ANGER,
PIQUE, RESENTMENT
high .... PET
duds .... TOGS, APPAREL,
CLOTHES, CLOTHING,
RAIMENT, TRAPPINGS
due .... DEBT, OWED, OWING,
RIGHT, PROPER, FITTING,
APROPOS, PAYABLE
one's .... DES(S)ERTS
process .... JUSTICE
to .... BECAUSE
duel .... FIGHT, COMBAT, CONTEST,
RIVALRY
challenge .... CARTEL
mock .... TILT, JOUST
principal of famous ..... BURR,
HAMILTON
victim of .... HAMILTON
dueling code/art .... DUELLO
position .... EN GARDE
duelist .... RIVAL, KNIGHT,
TUSSLER
duenna .... CHAPERON,
GOVERNESS

Duero .... DOURO
dues .... FEE, TAX, CHARGE,
ASSESSMENT
kind of .... TOLL, UNION,
MEMBERSHIP
duet .... DUO, PAIR, TWO(SOME)
duff .... SLACK, PUDDING
slang .... BUTTOCKS
duffel ...... BAG, KIT, COAT, GEAR,
OUTFIT, CLOTHING,
EQUIPMENT
duffer .... DUB, FUMBLER,
LUMMOX, PEDDLER
dug .... TEAT, NIPPLE
dugong .... SEACOW, COWFISH,
MANATEE, HALICORE
food of .... SEAWEED
dugout .... BOAT, BANCA, CANOE,
FOXHOLE, PIRAGUA, PIROGUE,
(BOMB)SHELTER
French/hillside .... ABRI
India .... DONGA
duke, of a .... DUCAL
rank below .... MARQUIS,
MARQUESS
title of respect .... GRACE
wife of .... DUCHESS
dukedom .... DUCHY
dukes: sl. .... FISTS, HANDS
dulcet .... SWEET, ARIOSE, ARIOSO,
HONEYED, SUGARED,
MELODIOUS, ORGAN STOP
dulcify .... APPEASE, MOLLIFY,
SWEETEN
dulcimer .... HARP, SITAR, CITOLE,
PSALTERY
Dulcinea .... SWEETHEART
dull .... FLAT, LOGY, FISHY,
GROSS, HOHUM, PROSY,
VAPID, BORING, STODGY,
HUMDRUM, INSIPID, TEDIOUS,
WITLESS, LISTLESS, BLAH,
STAGNANT, LACKLUSTER
and empty-headed ...... JEJUNE
and slow-moving
.... SLUGGISH, LETHARGIC
become .... HEBETATE
color .... DUN, DRAB, MATTE,
TERNE
edge/point .... BLUNT
finish .... MAT(TE)
grayish brown .... DUN
grossly .... CRASS, STUPID
make .... NUMB, BLUNT,
DEADEN, OBTUND
mentally .... OBTUSE, STUPID,
VACUOUS
period .... LULL, SLACK,
SLUMP
person, describing one
.... BORE, DUNCE, DULLARD

sound .... THUD
without luster .... DIM,
               CLOUDY, OBSCURE
dullard .... OAF, DOLT, LOUT,
      BOOR, DUNCE, MORON,
      NUMSKULL, SIMPLETON
dulled .... JADED
dulse .... SEAWEED
duly .... AS DUE, JUSTLY,
      PROPERLY, FITTINGLY
Dumas character .... ATHOS,
     ARAMIS, PORTHOS, BONIFACE,
           D'ARTAGNAN
novel .... CAMILLE
dumb .... MUTE, SILENT, RETICENT
clucks .... OXEN
clucks, per J. Luzzatto
                        OXES
colloquial .... NAIVE, STUPID,
                 IGNORANT
one .... ASS
show .... APING, MIMING
show figure .... PUPPET,
    PANTOMIME, MARIONETTE
waiter .... ELEVATOR
dumb _____ , **old comic strip**
                       DORA
dumbbell .... IDIOT, MORON,
                   NITWIT
exerciser .... WEIGHT, BARBELL
dum(b)found ...... DAZE, AMAZE,
    ASTOUND, STARTLE, ASTONISH
dumbness ...... MUTISM, APHONIA
dumdum .... BULLET
dummy .... DUPE, MUTE, TOOL,
    STRAWMAN, MANNEQUIN
cannon .... QUAKER
colloquial .... FRONT
field .... SCARECROW
in railroading .... LOCOMOTIVE
kind of ...... PROXY, STAND-IN,
              FIGUREHEAD
ventriloquist's .... SNERD
dump .... DROP, HEAP, JUNK,
    LUMP, PILE, EMPTY OUT,
    CHUCK, UNLOAD, DISCARD,
             DISCHARGE
archaic .... SONG, TUNE
slang .... DITCH
dumpling .... PIE, DOUGH
boiled .... DOUGHBOY
dumps, the .... BLUES, GLOOM,
              DOLDRUMS
dumpy .... PUDGY, SQUAT,
           MELANCHOLY
dun ...... ASK, BILL, BROWN, MAY
    FLY, ARTIFICIAL FLY, DEMAND
             PAYMENT
Duna in German .... DVINA
in Hungarian .... DANUBE
in Russian .... DON

Duncan, dancer .... ISADORA
dunce .... OAF, COOT, DOLT,
    MORON, NANNY, NUMSKULL,
             SIMPLETON
dunderhead .... DOLT, DUNCE,
    FOOL, IDIOT, DULLARD,
             NUMSKULL
dune .... DENE, HILL, RIDGE
dung .... FILTH, MANURE, ORDURE,
    DROPPING(S), EXCREMENT
beetle .... DOR, CHAFER,
              SCARAB
piece .... CHIP
dungarees .... JEANS, LEVIS,
             OVERALLS
dungeon .... PIT, CELL, JAIL,
    TOWER, DONJON, PRISON,
            OUBLIETTE
dungy .... FILTHY
dunk .... DIP, SOUSE
dunker .... SOPPER
dunlin .... SANDPIPER
dunnage .... BAGGAGE
Dunne, actress .... IRENE
dunnite .... EXPLOSIVE
duo .... DUET, PAIR
as combining form .... TWO,
             DOUBLE
plus one .... TRIO
duomo .... CATHEDRAL
dupe .... FOOL, GULL, CON(E)Y,
    CHEAT, HOCUS, TRICK,
    VICTIM, HUMBUG, MUGGINS,
           GREENHORN
kind of .... TOOL, DUMMY,
             CATSPAW
rare .... CULLY
duple .... DOUBLE, TWOFOLD
duplex .... HOUSE, DOUBLE,
           APARTMENT
duplicate .... COPY, DOUBLE,
    REPLICA, FACSIMILE
copy .... ESTREAT
duplicating machine ..... RONEO,
        (XEROX)COPIER,
    MIMEOGRAPH, MULTIGRAPH
duplication .... COPY, REPLICA,
    COUNTERPART, REPRODUCTION
duplicity ...... FRAUD, DECEPTION,
    FALSENESS, DOUBLE-DEALING
durable .... HARDY, STABLE,
    ETERNAL, LASTING,
           PERENNIAL
stage performer .... MAE
    WEST, MARLENE DIETRICH
durability .... AGE, LONGEVITY
duramen .... HEARTWOOD
durance .... IMPRISONMENT
Durante's Goodnight _____
                  MRS. CALABASH
duration ...... TERM, TIME, PERIOD

durbar: India .... HALL,
    AUDIENCE, RECEPTION
dure .... LAST, ENDURE
duress .... COERCION,
    COMPULSION, CONSTRAINT,
           IMPRISONMENT
during .... UNTIL, PENDING,
             THROUGH
durmast .... OAK
duro: Sp. .... PESO, DOLLAR
Duroc-Jersey .... HOG
Durocher, baseball manager
                 LEO, THE LIP
durra .... MILLET, SORGHUM
durum .... FLOUR, WHEAT
Duse, actress .... CHECCHI,
           ELEONORA
burial place .... ASOLO
dusk .... GLOOM, SUNSET,
    EVENFALL, GLOAMING,
    TWILIGHT, CREPUSCLE,
           NIGHTFALL
dusky .... DARK, TAWNY,
    DARKISH, SWART(HY)
dust .... ASH, DIRT, SOIL, SOOT,
    STOUR, EARTH, POLLEN,
    POWDER, SPRINKLE
bite the .... FALL, LOSE
British .... ASHES, RUBBISH
crumble to .... DISINTEGRATE
filter .... INHALER
lick the .... GROVEL, SUCCUMB
of flower .... POLLEN
slang .... MONEY
windblown .... STOUR
dustbin .... ASHCAN
dustbowl .... WASTELAND
duster .... RAG, COAT, WIND,
    WIPER, BROOM, BRUSH
dustheap .... DUMP, JUNKYARD
dusting powder .... TALC
dusty .... DIRTY, SANDY, SOOTY
Dutch. See also **Netherlands**
admiral .... RUYTER
Antilles .... ARUBA
apple, fried .... ROLPENS
astronomer .... HUYGENS
beef .... HUTSPOT
bloomer .... TULIP
botanist .... VRIES
cheese .... EDAM, GOUDA
city .... EDE
coin .... DOIT, DALER, GULDEN,
           STIVER
colonist .... BOER
colonizer .... PATROON
commune .... EDE, DOORN
cupboard .... KAS
dialect in Africa .... TAAL,
          AFRIKAANS
donkey .... EZEL

East Indies island .... JAVA, TIMOR
engraver .... LEYDEN
farm .... BOWERY
fishing boat .... HOOKER
Guiana .... SURINAM
gypsy .... BAZIGAR
Hottentot breed .... GRIQUA
housewife .... VROU(W)
humanist .... ERASMUS
measure .... AAM, KOP, ZAK, ANKER
measure, distance .... DUIM, VOET
metal .... TOMBAC
mistress in South Africa .... NOI
Mrs. .... VROUW
name for the Meuse .... MAAS
native .... BREDAN
navigator .... TASMAN
New Guinea negrito .... TAPIRO
news agency .... ANETA
painter ..... CUYP, GOGH, HALS, LELY, MEER, BORCH, STEEN, LEYDEN, REMBRANDT
philosopher .... SPINOZA
physicist .... HUYGENS, LORENTZ
river .... MAAS
scholar of the Renaissance, noted .... ERASMUS
settler's farm .... BOWERY
ship .... GALLOT, GAL(L)IOT
slang .... GERMAN
South African .... BOER
South African statesman .... KRUGER
statesman .... GROTIUS
theologian .... JANSEN, ERASMUS
title of address .... HEER, MYNHEER
town .... EDE, STAD
uncle .... OOM
vessel, flatbottomed .... FLYBOAT
village .... DOORN
weight .... ONS, LOOD
West Indies .... ANTILLES
woman .... FROU(W), VROUW
Dutchman .... MYNHEER, HOLLANDER
slang .... GERMAN
dutiful .... LOYAL, DOCILE, DUTEOUS, OBEDIENT, COMPLIANT
one .... OBEYER
duty .... JOB, TAX, DEBT, TASK, TOLL, CHORE, EXCISE

accountable .... RESPONSIBILITY
burdensome .... ONUS
imposed legally .... OBLIGATION
in the course of work .... FUNCTION
of tenant to his feudal lord .... FEALTY
on imports ..... IMPOST, TARIFF
to one's country .... ALLEGIANCE
turn of .... TRICK
duumvir .... MAGISTRATE
Dvina river ...... DUNA, DAUGAVA
Dvorak, composer .... ANTON
symphony .... NEW WORLD
dwarf ...... NANO, ATOMY, STUNT, BANTAM, MIDGET, MANAKIN, MANIKIN, OUTSHINE, HOMUNCULUS
African/Asiatic .... PIGMY, PYGMY
animal .... RUNT
antelope .... ORIBI
cattle .... DEVON, NIATA
chestnut .... CHINQUAPIN
describing a .... SHORT STATURE
kind of ...... ELF, GRIG, FREAK, GNOME, PEE WEE
like .... GNOMISH
Norse mythology .... ANDVARI
Philippine ...... AETA, NEGRITO
plant .... ALYSSUM
Scandinavian folklore .... TROLL
Scottish .... BLASTIE
shrub/tree .... BONSAI
slang .... SHRIMP
storybook .... DOC, DOPEY, HAPPY, SLEEPY, BASHFUL, TOM THUMB, THUMBELINA, LILLIPUTIAN
underground/misshapen .... GNOME
dwarfed .... STUMPY, STUNTED, DEFORMED
dwarfish deer .... CHEVROTAIN
dog .... CHIHUAHUA
horse .... PONY
dwarfism .... NANSOMA
dwarfs, any race of .... NIBELUNG
fairy tale .... DOC, DOPEY, HAPPY, GRUMPY, SLEEPY, SNEEZY, BASHFUL
king of .... ALBERICH
dwell .... LIVE, (A)BIDE, LODGE, RESIDE
on .... HARP, REPEAT
slang .... HANG OUT

dweller .... LODGER, RENTER, ROOMER, TENANT, RESIDENT, INHABITANT
on public land .... SQUATTER
prison .... INMATE
dwelling .... HOME, ABODE, HOUSE, RESIDENCE, HABITATION
bear's .... DEN, CAVE
bird's .... CAGE, NEST
fit for .... TENANTABLE
fixed place of .... DOMICILE
high .... AERIE, EYRIE
house .... TENEMENT
imposing .... MANSION
instant .... PREFAB
lion's .... DEN, LAIR
miserable .... HOVEL
mobile/on wheels ..... TRAILER
mollusk's .... SHELL
on artificial island .... CRANNOG
place, kind of .... FLAT, CONDO, APARTMENT
place to which mail is sent .... ADDRESS
royal .... PALACE
slum .... TENEMENT
unsafe .... DEATHTRAP
dwindle .... EBB, ABATE, PETER, LESSEN, SHRINK, DECREASE, DIMINISH
DX, in radio .... DISTANT, DISTANCE
dyad .... PAIR
Dyak blowgun .... SUMPITAN
knife .... PARANG
dye .... DIP, HUE, TINT, WELD, COLOR, FUCUS, STAIN, TAINT, TINGE, BRASIL, CASHOO
aniline .... FUCHSIN, MAGENTA, SAFRANINE
apparatus .... AGER
azo .... CROCEIN(E)
base .... ANILINE, FLAVONE
blue .... WOAD, PASTEL
butter coloring .... ANNATTO
class of .... AZO, VAT, XANTHENE
coal tar .... EOSIN, MAUVE
from whelks .... MUREX
gum .... KINO
hair .... HENNA
Hindu .... ALTA
indigo .... ANIL, ISATIN
ingredient .... TANNIN, ALAZARIN(E)
insect body's .... KERMES
lichen .... ARCHIL
mustard plant .... WOAD

orange .... MANDARIN
plant .... CHAY, AMIL, ANIL,
ANCHUSA, ALKANET, BUGLOSS,
PUCCOON, SUMAC(H),
BLOODROOT
purple .... MUREX, ARCHIL,
ORCHAL, ORCHIL, TURNSOLE
red .... AURIN, CERISE,
EOSIN(E), KERMES, MADDER,
ALKANET, ANCHUSA, FUCHSIN,
COCHINEAL, RHODAMINE,
SOLFERINO
reddish-brown ..... HEMAT(E)IN
source .... LICHEN, CUDBEAR,
NAPTHALENE
substance .... TANNIN
synthetic .... PHTHALEIN,
RHODAMINE
yellow .... FUSTIC
dyed in the wool .... TOTAL,
INGRAINED, STEADFAST,
CONSUMMATE
dyeing astringent .... GAMBIER

color fixer .... MORDANT
liquid/solution container
.... VAT
method .... BAT(T)IK
substance .... TANNIN,
MORDANT, NAPTHOL
dyer .... COLORER, STAINER,
COLORIST
dyestuff .... ANIL, WOAD, CASHOO,
INDIGO, CATECHU, MAGENTA
dyeweed .... WOODWAXEN
dying .... MORIBUND
on the vine .... WITHERING
star .... NOVA
dyke .... DAM, DIKE
dyna as combining form
.... POWER
dynamic ...... POTENT, FORCEFUL,
VIGOROUS, ENERGETIC
opposed to .... STATIC,
ORGANIC
dynamics .... FORCES, STATICS,
KINETICS

dynamite .... EXPLOSIVE
ingredient
.... NITROGLYCERIN(E)
inventor of .... NOBEL
kind of .... TNT
dynamo .... MAGNETO,
GENERATOR
combining form .... POWER
part .... BRUSH, STATOR,
WINDING, ARMATURE,
COMMUTATOR
dynast .... RULER
dynasty, Chinese ... MING, SUNG
dys as prefix .... BAD, ILL
dysfunctional .... IMPAIRED
dysgenic, opposed to
.... EUGENIC
dyspepsia .... INDIGESTION
medicine .... HYDRASTINE
dyspeptic ...... GLOOMY, GROUCHY
dysphoria .... ANXIETY,
DISCOMFORT, DISCONTENT
Dzhugashvili .... STALIN

E

E, Greek .... EPSILON
in a sequence .... FIFTH
in physics .... ENERGY
symbol for ..... EAST, EASTERN
each ...... AN, ALL, PER, ANY ONE,
APIECE, EVERY(ONE)
used in doctor's prescription
.... ANA
Eads (James) invention
.... DIVING BELL
eager .... AGOG, AVID, FAIN,
KEEN, AFIRE, ARDENT,
ANXIOUS, EARNEST, DESIROUS,
IMPATIENT
beaver ..... DYNAMO, HUSTLER,
GO-GETTER
to start .... CHAFING AT THE
BIT
eagerly awaiting/expecting
.... ATIP
eagerness .... ARDOR, DESIRE,
FERVOR, ALACRITY
eagle ...... BIRD, COIN, PREDATOR,
ACCIPITER
beaked .... AQUILINE
biblical .... GIER
brood .... AERIE
constellation .... AQUILA
double-crested .... HARPY
eyed .... SHARP, VIGILANT,
WATCHFUL
family .... FALCON

for one .... SCOUT
Latin .... AQUILA
like/of an .... AQUILINE
like bird .... CONDOR,
VULTURE
nest of .... AERY, AERIE, EYRIE
passenger of .... ETANA
sea .... ERN(E)
young .... EYRY, EYRIE,
EAGLET, AIGLETTE
eaglestone .... ETITE
eagre .... BORE, TIDAL WAVE
Eamon de Valera .... DEV
eanling .... KID, LAMB
ear .... LUG, HANDLE, HEARING,
ATTENTION
anvil .... INCUS
auricle .... PINNA, PAVILION
bone .... AMBOS, ANVIL,
INCUS, HAMMER, STAPES,
TEGMEN, OCCICLE, STIRRUP
canal .... SCALA
cartilage .... HELIX
cauliflower .... HEMATOMA
AURIS
cavity ..... COCHLEA, SACCULE,
UTRICLE
cosmetic surgery on outer
.... OTOPLASTY
degeneration .... DEAFNESS
discharge from infected
.... OTORRHEA

disturber .... DIN
doctor/specialist .... AURIST,
OTOLOGIST
examination .... TOMOGRAPHY,
CT SCANNING
external .... PINNA, CONCHA,
AURICLE
give/lend an .... HEED, LISTEN,
HEARKEN
gland below .... PAROTID
hammer .... MALLEUS
hollow .... CONCHA
in Latin .... AURIS
inflammation/infection
.... OTITIS
inner .... LABYRINTH
instrument .... OTOSCOPE
labyrinth .... SACCULE
like part .... LUG
lobe .... ALA, LUG, EARLAP,
LAPPET
middle .... TYMPANUM
near the ..... PAROTIC, PAROTID
noises within the .... TINNITUS
of corn .... MEALIE
of grain .... SPICA, SPIKE
opening .... FENESTRA
outer rim .... HELIX
pain .... OTALGIA
part ...... LOBE, ANVIL, CANAL,
PINNA, HAMMER,
AURICLE, COCHLEA,

STIRRUP, TYMPANUM, VESTIBULE

pertaining to .... OTIC, AURAL, AURIC

play it by .... AD-LIB, IMPROVISE

prefix .... OTO

projection .... LUG, TRAGUS

science of the .... OTOLOGY

secretion .... WAX, CERUMEN

shaped .... AURIFORM

shaped mollusk .... ORMER, ABALONE

shell .... ORMER, ABALONE, MOLLUSK

stirrup-shaped bone .... STAPES

turn a deaf ...... SNUB, IGNORE

wax .... CERUMEN

wheat .... SPICA

earache .... OTALGIA

eardrop .... EARRING

eardrum .... TYMPANUM

of the .... TYMPANIC

prominence .... UMBO

eared .... AURICULATE

seal .... OTARY

earful .... TIP, GOSSIP, TIRADE, SCOLDING

slang .... INFO, NEWS, THE LOWDOWN

Earhart, aviatrix .... AMELIA

husband of .... (GEORGE)PUTNAM

earl .... NOBLEMAN

deputy of an .... VISCOUNT

wife of an .... COUNTESS

Earl Biggers's sleuth .... (CHARLIE)CHAN

earlier .... PRIOR, FORMER, PREVIOUS

earliest .... PREMIER

early ...... ANON, AHEAD, PROMPT, BETIMES, FORWARD

bird .... FIRST COMER

bird's victim .... WORM

Christian date .... ADI

hour .... FIRST CRACK, HEAD START

in the day/season ..... RATH(E)

Steele and Addison periodical .... TATLER

too .... PREMATURE

earmark .... TAB, SIGN, SPOT, DENOTE, BRAND, LABEL, STAMP, RESERVE, SIGNIFY, IDENTIFY

earn .... WIN, GAIN, RATE, MERIT, DESERVE, WORK FOR

difficultly .... EKE

earnest ...... AVID, EAGER, TOKEN,

ARDENT, INTENT, PLEDGE, FERVENT, INTENSE, SERIOUS, SINCERE, ZEALOUS, ASSURANCE

money .... ARLES, TOKEN, ADVANCE, DEPOSIT, HANDSEL

request .... ENTREATY

earnings .... PAY, WAGES, PROFITS, PAYMENT, INCOME, SALARIES

earphone .... RECEIVER

earpiece .... FLAP

earring .... HOOP, PENDANT, GIRANDOLE

holder .... LOBE

ears .... ANTENNA

all .... ATTENTIVE

having two .... BINAURAL

earsplitting .... LOUD, DEAFENING

earth .... DIRT, DUST, LAND, LOAM, MOLD, SOIL, GLOBE, TERRA, WORLD, GROUND, PLANET, UNIVERSE

combining form .... GEO

crust .... LITHOSPHERE

deposit .... MARL, SILT

division .... ZONE

down to .... NORMAL, REGULAR, PRACTICAL, REALISTIC

eating of .... GEOPHAGY

goddess ..... GE, GAEA, TELLUS

greenish .... TERRE-VERTE

hypothetical figure ...... GEOID

inhabitant/of the .... TELLURIAN

line .... EQUATOR

lump of .... CLOD

pertaining to the .... TERRENE, GEOGRAPHICAL

pig .... AARDVARK

pigment .... UMBEL

poetic .... MARL, VALE

satellite .... ECHO, LUNA, NOVA, ARIEL, CAMEO, MIDAS, SOYUZ, TIROS, VENUS, APOLLO, COSMOS, GEMINI, SKYLAB, VOSTOK, COMSTAR, MARINER, PIONEER, SPUTNIK, COLUMBIA, EXPLORER, SURVEYOR, VANGUARD, CHALLENGER, FRIENDSHIP

shaking .... QUAKE, TREMOR

tamping implement .... BEETLE

thickest layer of .... MANTLE

volcanic .... TRASS

white .... GYPSUM, KAOLIN, MAGNESIA, TERRE ALBA

Eartha, singer .... KITT

earthborn .... LOW, HUMAN,

COMMON, MORTAL, VULGAR

earthbound .... MUNDANE, TERRESTRIAL

earthdrake .... DRAGON

earthen cup .... MUG

jar .... OLLA

earthenware .... JUG, POT, CHINA, POTTERY CERAMICS, CROCK(ERY), PORCELAIN

cooking .... CASSEROLE

fragment .... SHARD

glazed, blue and white .... DELFTWARE

jar .... CROCK

maker .... POTTER

making material .... PUG

pertaining to .... CERAMIC

pot .... PIPKIN

unglazed .... TERRA COTTA

water container .... GOGLET, GURGLET

earthling .... HUMAN, MORTAL, HUMAN BEING, MATERIALIST

earthly ...... MUNDANE, SECULAR, WORLDLY, TERRENE, TELLURIC, TEMPORAL, TELLURIAN, TERRESTRIAL

not .... ETHEREAL, CELESTIAL

opposed to .... SPIRITUAL

earthnut .... POD, TUBER, FUNGUS, PEANUT, TRUFFLE

earthquake .... QUAKE, SEISM, SHOCK, TREMOR, TEMBLOR

combining form ...... S(E)ISMO

echo .... AFTERSHOCK

focus of .... EPICENTER

origin .... EPICENTER

over center of disturbance .... EPIFOCAL

pertaining to .... SEISMAL, SEISMIC

recorder .... RICHTER

slight .... MICROSEISM

starting point .... FOCUS

earthquakes, echo of .... AFTERSHOCK

phenomena of .... SEISMISM

study of .... SEISMOLOGY

earth's treasure guardian .... GNOME

earthshaking: colloq. .... MEMORABLE, MOMENTOUS, THUNDEROUS, SIGNIFICANT

earthwork .... DIKE, AGGER, MOUND, RAMPART, VALLATION, FORTIFICATION

earthworm .... ESS

like an .... LUMBRICOID

earthy .... GROSS, CARNAL, CRUDE, COARSE, SIMPLE, NATURAL, POPULAR, TERRENE,

TEMPORAL
deposit .... MARL
pigment .... OCHRE, SIENNA
earwax .... CERUMEN
earwig .... BEETLE, CENTIPEDE
ease .... REST, POISE, LUXURY,
LOOSEN, RELIEF, COMFORT,
CONTENT, LEISURE, RELIEVE,
FACILITY, PALLIATE
take one's .... RELAX
easel .... TRIPOD, CANVAS HOLDER
easement .... RELIEF, SOLACE,
COMFORT, RIGHT OF ENTRY
in law .... SERVITUDE
easily ...... IDLY, BY FAR, COZILY,
GENTLY, SIMPLY, LIGHTLY,
READILY, FACILELY,
LEISURELY, RELAXEDLY,
COMFORTABLY
affected .... SENSITIVE
angered/annoyed .... TESTY,
CRANKY, GRUMPY, FRETFUL,
IRASCIBLE, IRRITABLE
bent .... LIMBER, PLIANT,
ELASTIC, FLEXIBLE
broken .... BRITTLE, FRAGILE,
DELICATE
cheated/tricked .... GREEN,
GULLIBLE, CREDULOUS,
UNSUSPECTING
frightened .... SCARY,
NERVOUS, PANICKY
handled .... TAME, GENTLE
mixed .... MISCIBLE
offended .... TOUCHY,
SENSITIVE, THIN-SKINNED
pleased .... EASYGOING
remembered .... CATCHY, EYE-
CATCHING
set on fire .... FIERY,
FLAMMABLE, COMBUSTIBLE
tempted .... FRAIL, WEAK-
WILLED
easiness .... EASE, COMFORT,
FACILITY
colloquial .... CINCH, BREEZE
in using hands or body
.... SKILL, DEXTERITY
slang .... SNAP
easing .... RELIEF, REMEDY,
MELLOWING
east .... ASIA, LEVANT, ORIENT
East Indies .... INDONESIA
animal, small .... TARSIER
ape .... GIBBON
arboreal mammal ..... COLUGO
bark .... NIEPA
bird .... ARGUS, LORIKEET
boatman .... SERANG
calico .... SALLOO
cat-like animal .... LINSANG

cedar .... TOON, DEODAR
cereal grass .... RAG(G),
RAGEE
chief .... RAJA(H)
civet .... MUSANG
coin .... CASH
cuckoo .... KOEL
deer .... MUNTJAC
dye .... CHAY
elephant driver .... MAHOUT
fiber (plant) .... JUTE, SUNN
fish .... DORAB
fruit .... DURIAN, DURION,
MANGOSTEEN
garment .... SARONG
grass .... GLAGA, VETIVER
harvest .... RABO
hemp .... SUNN
herb .... PIA, CHAY, CHOY,
SOLA, GINGER, SESAME,
ROSELLE
honeybee .... DINGAR
island .... BALI, CERAM,
SUMATRA
lemur .... COLUGO
litter .... DOOLEE, DOOLI(E),
DOOL(E)Y
mail/mail service .... DAK
medicinal root .... ZEDOARY
mint plant .... COLEUS
monkey .... ENTELLUS
musical instrument .... BINA,
RUANA
myrtle .... CAJEPUT, CAJUPUT
oil plant .... BENNE, SESAME
palm tree .... TALIPOT
parrot .... COCKATOO
peacock-like bird .... ARGUS
perfume .... PATCHOULI
persimmon .... GA(U)B
plant .... AMIL, CHAY, JUTE,
SUNN, AMBARY, BEN(NE),
COLEUS, DERRIS, SESAME,
TURMERIC, PATCHOULI
prince .... RAJA(H)
rat .... KOK
relish .... PICALILI
root .... CHAY, CHOY
sailor .... LASCAR
sauce .... CURRY
seaweed product .... AGAR-
AGAR
shrub .... CUBEB
snake .... KUPPER
spice .... CINNAMON
squirrel .... TAGUAN
tree ..... SAJ, MEE, JACK, POON,
TEAK, TOON, ACANA, PINEY,
SIRIS, BANYAN, DEODAR,
KAMALA, CAJUPUT, CINCHONA,
SAPANWOOD, CALAMANDER,

CHAULMOOGRA
vessel .... PATAMAR
warrior .... SINGH
weight .... CATTY
wood .... ENG, TEAK, TOON,
KOKRA, LIGNALOES
Easter .... PASCH(A)
feast of .... PASCH
fruitcake .... SIMNEL
Island .... RAPANUI
lily .... CALLA
of .... PASCHAL
souvenirs .... EGGS, BUNNIES
the Sunday before .... PALM
third Sunday after
.... JUBILATE
eastern .... ASIATIC, ORIENTAL
league .... IVY
palace .... SERAI, SERAGLIO
rule .... SHAHDOM
ruler .... EMIR, SHAH, EMEER
Eastern Christian .... UNIAT(E)
European .... SLAV
Orthodox church monk
.... CALOYER
Orthodox church prayers
.... EKTENE
Eastwood, actor .... CLINT
easy .... COZY, SOFT, FACILE,
GENTLE, SIMPLE, SMOOTH,
MODERATE, EFFORTLESS,
COMFORTABLE
chair .... ROCKER
course: sl. .... PIPE
gait .... LOPE, CANTER
going .... SMOOTH SAILING
job .... SNAP, CINCH, SINECURE
mark .... DUPE, GULL, PATSY,
SUCKER, PUSHOVER
opposed to .... HARD, TENSE,
TIGHT, TOUGH
slang .... CUSHY
street .... BED OF ROSES, LAP
OF LUXURY, LIFE OF RILEY,
PROSPEROUS CIRCUMSTANCES
take it .... REST, RELAX
to convince .... NAIVE,
GULLIBLE, CREDULOUS
to ''take'' .... TEN
to understand .... SIMPLE,
PELLUCID
easygoing .... LAX, CASUAL,
LENIENT, RELAXED
eat .... SUP, DINE, FEED, GRUB,
FEAST, CONSUME
away ...... FRET, GNAW, ERODE,
CANKER, CORRODE
crow .... SWALLOW ONE'S
PRIDE
greedily .... GAMP, GULP,
WOLF, GORGE, DEVOUR,

GOBBLE, GUTTLE, GORMANDIZE
immoderately .... GLUT, GORGE
into .... RUST, CORRODE
one's heart out .... AGONIZE
one's word .... RECANT, RETRACT, HUMBLE ONESELF
up .... REGALE
eatable .... FOOD, EDIBLE, ESCULENT, COMESTIBLE
eater, heavy .... GLUTTON, TRENCHERMAN
eating capacity, huge .... EDACITY
disorder .... ANOREXIA NERVOSA
hall .... MESS, REFECTORY
implement .... CUTLERY, CHOPSTICK
of .... DIETARY
place .... CAFE, DINER, AUTOMAT, CHOPHOUSE, CHUCKWAGON, RESTAURANT, DINING ROOM, HOTDOG STAND
regulated .... DIET, REGIMEN
eats: colloq. .... FARE, FOOD, MEALS
slang .... CHOW, GRUB
eau .... DEVIE, WATER
de vie .... BRANDY
designating one kind .... COLOGNE, JAVELLE
eaves, trough under ...... GUTTER
eavesdrop ...... BUG, TAP, LISTEN, OVERHEAR
eavesdropper .... SPY, SNOOPER
Eban, Israeli diplomat .... ABBA
ebb .... WANE, RECEDE, REFLUX, FLOW BACK, DECLINE, SUBSIDE
and flow .... TIDE
tide .... NEAP
tide, opposed to .... FLOOD
ebbing .... REFLUX, RECEDING, REFLUENT, RECESSIVE, REFLUENCE, BACKSLIDING
Eber's father .... SHELAH
son .... PELEG, JOKTAN
Eblis .... SATAN
ebon .... DARK, BLACK
ebonite .... VULCANITE
ebonize .... BLACKEN
ebony .... INKY, WOOD, BLACK, JETTY, PITCHY
ebullience .... ELAN, EXUBERANCE
ebullient .... BOILING, EXCITED, BUBBLING, EXUBERANT
ecarte .... CARD GAME
ecce .... LO, SEE, BEHOLD
eccentric .... ODD, OFF, NUTTY, OUTRE, QUEER, CRANK(Y),

W(H)ACKY, BIZARRE, STRANGE, OFF CENTER, ABNORMAL, PECULIAR, CAPRICIOUS
person .... NUT, GEEZER, HERMIT
slang .... BATTY, KOOKY, KOOKIE, ODDBALL
somewhat .... ODDISH
wheel part .... CAM
eccentricity .... KINK, ODDITY, ABERRATION, IDIOSYNCRASY
ecchymosis .... BRUISE
Ecclesiastes, book of .... KOHELETH
ecclesiastic .... FRA, PRIEST, PRELATE, CLERGYMAN
ecclesiastical attendant .... ACOLYTE
banner .... LABARUM
benefice .... GLEBE
cape .... ORALE, MOZ(Z)ETTA
council .... SYNOD
court .... ROTA, CLASSIS
dean .... PREFECT
headdress ...... MITER, BIRETTA
hood .... AMICE
office, trading of .... BARRATRY
proceedings .... ACTA
residence .... ABBEY, MANSE, PRIORY
seat .... SEDILE
skullcap .... BIRETTA
vestment .... ALB, COPE, AMICE, ORALE, STOLE
eccrinology, subject of .... EXCRETION, SECRETION
ecdysis .... MO(U)LT
echidna .... ANTEATER, MONOTREME
echinate .... SPINY, BRISTLY, PRICKLY
animal .... HEDGEHOG, PORCUPINE
echinoderm .... TREPANG, STARFISH, SEA URCHIN
echinus .... SEA URCHIN
echo .... RING, NYMPH, OREAD, PARROT, REPEAT, RESOUND, REVERBERATE
echoing .... RESONANT, RESOUNDING
eclair .... PASTRY
eclampsia .... SEIZURE, CONVULSION
eclat .... FAME, GLORY, PRAISE, RENOWN, ACCLAIM, PLAUDIT, APPLAUSE, SPLENDOR, NOTORIETY
eclectic ...... CHOOSING, SELECTIVE

eclipse .... HIDE, CLOUD, STAIN, DARKEN, CONCEAL, OBSCURE, SURPASS, OUTSHINE, OVERSHADOW
kind of .... LUNAR, SOLAR, TOTAL, PARTIAL, STELLAR
part .... PENUMBRA
eclogue .... POEM, IDYL(L), PASTORAL
ecole .... SCHOOL
attender .... ELEVE
ecological .... ENVIRONAL, ENVIRONMENTAL
ecologist's concern .... ENVIRONMENT
word of advice .... REUSE, RECYCLE
ecology .... BIONOMICS, ECOSYSTEM, CONSERVATION
economic measure, abbr. .... GNP
nest egg .... PENSION TREASURY
policy, kind of .... AUTARKY
system .... COMMUNISM, CAPITALISM
economical ...... CHARY, FRUGAL, STINGY, SPARING, THRIFTY
economize .... SAVE, HOARD, SKIMP, SCRIMP, RETRENCH, TIGHTEN ONE'S BELT
economy .... MENAGE, THRIFT, PARSIMONY, MANAGEMENT
ecru .... TAN, BEIGE, YELLOW
ecstasy .... JOY, BLISS, DELIGHT, RAPTURE, FELICITY
ectad, opposed to .... ENTAD
ectoparasite ...... LEECH, REMORA
ectype .... COPY
ecu .... COIN, SHIELD
Ecuador bay ...... BANKS, MANTA, ISABEL
cape .... ROSA, PASADO, LA PUNTILLA, SAN FRANCISCO
capital of .... QUITO
city/town .... LOJA, MANTA, AMBATO, CUENCA, IBARRA, TULCAN, MACHALA, MILAGRO, QUEVEDO, RIOBAMBA, GUAYAQUIL, ESMERALDAS, PORTOVIEJO
gulf .... GUAYAQUIL
Indian .... CARA, ANDOA, ARDAN, KECHUA, QUECHUA
island .... PUNA, PINTA, BALTRA, PINZON, WENMAN, ESPANOLA, GENOVESA, CULPEPPER, FERNANDINA
islands .... GALAPAGOS
language .... QUECHUA, SPANISH
monetary unit .... SUCRE

mountain .... SANGAY,
CAYAMBE, ANTISANA,
COTOPAXI, CHIMBORAZO
province .... LOJA, NAPO,
AZUAY, EL ORO, GUAYAS,
CARCHI, MANABI, PASTAZA,
COTOPAXI, IMBABURA, LOS
RIOS, PICHINCHA,
CHIMBORAZO, ESMERALDAS,
TUNGURAHUA
river .... MIRA, NAPO, CHIRA,
PINDO, GUAYAS, TUMBES,
ZAMORA, CURARAY, PASTAZA,
AGUARICO, BOBONAZA,
NARANJAL, PUTUMAYO,
ESMERALDAS
seaport .... MANTA,
GUAYAQUIL
volcano .... ANTISANA,
COTOPAXI, CHIMBORAZO
ecumenical .... GLOBAL,
GENERAL, CATHOLIC,
UNIVERSAL, WORLDWIDE
council site .... TRENT
eczema .... HERPES, TETTER,
DERMATITIS
horse's .... MAL(L)ANDERS
edacious .... RAVENOUS,
CONSUMING, DEVOURING,
VORACIOUS
edacity .... GREED, VORACITY
eddo .... ROOT, TARO
eddy .... BORE, SPIN, GURGE,
SURGE, SWIRL, TWIRL, WHIRL,
VORTEX, BACKFLOW,
WHIRLPOOL, WHIRLWIND
edema .... DROPSY, ANASARCA
edemic .... BLOATED, SWOLLEN,
EDEMATOUS
Eden .... GARDEN, HEAVEN,
PARADISE
resident .... EVE, ADAM
river .... PISON
edentate .... SLOTH, ECHIDNA,
AARDVARK, ANTEATER,
BITELESS, TEETHLESS,
TOOTHLESS
edge ...... RIM, CURB, SIDE, BLADE,
BRINK, LEDGE, MARGE,
VERGE, BORDER, FRINGE,
MARGIN
beveled .... CANT
cliff's .... BROW
colloquial .... LEVERAGE,
ADVANTAGE
crater's .... LIP, MOUTH
garment's .... HEM
hat's .... BRIM
in .... ENTER, INTRUDE,
ENCROACH, INFRINGE
keen .... ZEST, SHARP

move along the .... SKIRT
of a molding .... ARRIS
of a river/stream .... BANK
of fabric/paper .... SELVAGE,
SELVEDGE
on .... EAGER, UNEASY,
ANXIOUS, RESTLESS,
IMPATIENT, IRRITABLE
roof's .... EAVE
tool .... AX, ADZ, KNIFE,
RAZOR, CHISEL, NIPPER,
SCYTHE, CLEAVER, SCALPEL,
SHEARS, MATTOCK, SCISSORS
with loops .... PURL, PICOT
edged .... KEEN, ACUTE, SHARP,
CUTTING, KNIFELIKE
object ...... AX(E), BOLO, CELT,
BLADE, KNIFE, RAZOR, SABER,
SWORD, COLTER, DAGGER,
CUTLASS, GROOVER, HATCHET,
MACHETE, TRIMMER
rough .... EROSE
edgewise .... SIDEWAYS, SIDEWISE
glance, with an .... ASKANCE
move .... SKEW, SIDLE
walker .... CRAB
edging .... FRILL, PICOT, RUCHE,
FRINGE, HONING, LIMBUS,
FLOUNCE, TATTING,
FURBELOW, TRIMMING
edgy .... SHARP, TENSE, NERVOUS,
JITTERY, IRRITABLE
slang .... UPTIGHT
edible .... FOOD, EATABLE,
ESCULENT, COMESTIBLE
bulb ...... CAMAS(S), QUAMASH
fungus .... CEPE, MOREL,
MUSHROOM
grain .... CEREAL
plant .... VEGETABLE
root .... YAM, BEET, TARO,
CARROT, GARLIC, MANIOC,
CASSAVA
seed .... PEA, BEAN, PINON,
LENTIL, PEANUT
shoot .... UDO, BAMBOO
starch .... SAGO
tuber .... OCA, YAM, TARO,
SALEP, POTATO
edict .... FIAT, DECREE, MANDATE,
PROCLAMATION
Pope's .... BULL
sultan's .... IRADE
tsar's .... UKASE
edification .... LEARNING,
TEACHING, EDUCATION
edifice .... FABRIC, BUILDING,
STRUCTURE
built by ancient Egyptians
.... PYRAMID

for public worship
.... CHURCH, TEMPLE,
TABERNACLE
large, magnificent ..... PALACE
very tall/high .... TOWER,
SKYSCRAPER
edify .... TEACH, ENNOBLE,
INSTRUCT
Edinburgh is capital of
.... SCOTLAND
poetic .... EDINA
Edirne .... ADRIANOPLE
Edison, inventor
.... THOMAS(ALVA)
edit .... ERASE, DELETE, REVISE,
REDACT, ARRANGE, CORRECT,
PREPARE, BLUE-PENCIL
edition .... COPY, ISSUE, NUMBER,
VOLUME, PRINTING,
IMPRESSION
collector's .... FIRST
early morning newspaper
.... BULLDOG
in which a written work
exists .... TEXT
reissue or new ..... REDACTION
six versions .... HEXAPLA
special .... EXTRA
editor .... CRITIC, REDACTOR,
JOURNALIST
editorial .... ARTICLE, OPINION,
COMMENT(ARY)
main .... LEADER
editorialize .... INDITE, COMPOSE,
EXPOUND, EXPATIATE
Edmonton is capital of
.... ALBERTA
Edna .... BEST, FERBER, MILLAY
Edna Ferber novel .... SO BIG,
SARATOGA
Edo .... TOKYO
Edom .... ESAU, IDUM(A)EA
mountain .... HOR
Edson de Arantes Nacimento
.... PELE, NEGRAO
educate ...... FORM, EDIFY, TEACH,
TRAIN, DEVELOP, INSTRUCT,
CULTIVATE, ENLIGHTEN
educated .... LEARNED, LETTERED,
WELL-VERSED, CULTURED,
LITERATE
education .... LEARNING,
TEACHING, TRAINING,
KNOWLEDGE, ATTAINMENT(S),
EDIFICATION
educational .... INFORMATIVE,
INSTRUCTIVE
facility .... PARK
group .... NEA
institution .... SCHOOL,
ACADEMY, COLLEGE,

SEMINARY, UNIVERSITY, CONSERVATORY

materials .... BOOKS, FILMSTRIPS, RECORDINGS, MOTION PICTURES

educator .... TUTOR, MENTOR, TEACHER, PEDAGOGUE, PROFESSOR, INSTRUCTOR

Hindu .... GURU

music .... MAESTRO

educe .... EVOKE, INFER, DEDUCE, ELICIT, EVOLVE, EXTRACT, DEVELOP, DRAW FORTH

Edward Kennedy Ellington
.... DUKE

specialty .... JAZZ

Edward VII's father .... ALBERT

eek producer .... MOUSE

eel .... GRIG, CARAPO, LAMPREY, ANGUILLID

fish for/method of catching
.... SNIGGLE

fried .... SPITCHCOCK

kind of ...... MORAY, ELECTRIC

large, water .... CONGER

order .... APODES

voracious .... MORAY

young .... ELVER, SNYGGE

eeler .... FISHERMAN

eelgrass .... ZOSTERA, SEA-WRACK

eelpout .... LING, BURBOT

eelworm .... NEMA

eely .... ELUSIVE, SLIPPERY, SNAKELIKE

eerie/eery .... WEIRD, CREEPY, SPOOKY, GHASTLY, GHOSTLY, MACABRE, UNCANNY, ELDRITCH

efface .... BLUR, ODIC, ERASE, CANCEL, DELETE, EXCISE, RUB OUT, BLOT OUT, WIPE OUT, EXPUNGE, OBLITERATE

effect .... CAUSE, FRUIT, ISSUE, TENOR, RESULT, ACHIEVE, MEANING, EFFICACY, AFTERMATH, ACCOMPLISH

in .... ACTUALLY, VIRTUALLY

of an action or process
.... OUTCOME, OFFSHOOT, OUTGROWTH, CONSEQUENCE

produced, as on the mind
.... IMPRESSION

slang .... PAYOFF

effective .... ACTIVE, POTENT, CAPABLE, DYNAMIC, ADEQUATE, EFFICIENT, OPERATIVE, PRODUCTIVE, SUCCESSFUL

effectiveness .... EFFICACY

effects .... PROPERTY, BELONGINGS

effectual .... VALID, EFFECTIVE

effectuate .... ACCOMPLISH

effeminate .... SOFT, WEAK, LYDIAN, UNMANLY, FEMININE, WOMANISH

boy .... SISSY, MILKSOP

person, in a way .... FOP, DANDY

effendi .... SIR, TITLE, MASTER

effervesce .... BOIL, FIZZ, FOAM, HISS, FROTH, FERMENT, SPARKLE

effervescence .... FOAM(ING), VIVACITY, EBULLIENCE, EXUBERANCE, LIVELINESS

effervescent ...... FIZZY, BUBBLING

effete .... ARID, SPENT, WEAK, BARREN, STERILE, DEPLETED, WORN OUT, EXHAUSTED

efficacious .... EFFECTIVE

efficient .... ABLE, CAPABLE, SKILLFUL, COMPETENT, EFFECTIVE

effigy .... COPY, ICON, IMAGE, STATUE, REPLICA, LIKENESS, PORTRAIT, CARICATURE

effloresce .... BLOOM, FLOWER, BLOSSOM(OUT)

effluence .... EMANATION

effluvia .... RAIN

effluvium .... AURA, ODOR, REEK, VAPOR, FLATUS, MIASM(A)

efflux .... OUTFLOW

effluxion .... STREAM, EMANATION

effort .... TRY, NISUS, PAINS, STRAIN, ATTEMPT, CONATUS, ENDEAVOR, EXERTION

colloquial .... PUSH

effortless .... EASY, SIMPLE, NATURAL

effrontery .... GALL, GUTS, BRASS, CHEEK, AUDACITY, BRAZENRY, TEMERITY, IMPUDENCE, INSOLENCE, PRESUMPTION

effulge .... SHINE

effulgence .... GLORY, LUSTER, RADIANCE, SPLENDOR

effuse .... SPREAD

effusive .... GUSHY, GUSHING, EXUBERANT, OVERFLOWING, DEMONSTRATIVE

eft .... NEWT, LIZARD

eftsoon: archaic .... AGAIN, OFTEN, FORTHWITH

e.g., part of .... GRATIA, EXEMPLI

egad .... OATH, EXPLETIVE

Egeria .... NYMPH, ADVISER

egest .... EXCRETE, DISCHARGE

egesta .... FECES, SWEAT, PERSPIRATION

egg .... CELL, OVUM, EMBRYO

capsule ...... OVISAC, OOTHECA

case .... OVISAC

collector .... OOLOGIST

combining form .... OO, OVI

constituent .... YOLK, GLAIR, ALBUMEN

dish .... OMELET(TE)

drink .... NOG(G)

fertilized .... OOSPERM, OOSPORE

immature .... OOCYTE

insect/louse/parasite .... NIT

laying animals .... OVIPARA

laying mammal ...... ECHIDNA, ANTEATER, DUCKBILL, PLATYPUS, MONOTREME

lobster .... BERRY

mollusk's .... OOTHECA

on .... GOAD, PROD, SPUR, URGE, HOUND, INCITE

part .... YOLK, SHELL, WHITE, YELLOW, ALBUMEN

protoplasm .... ARCHIBLAST

relish .... CAVIAR(E)

shaped .... OVAL, OVATE, OVOID, OVIFORM, OBOVOID

shaped, longitudinal section
.... ELLIPTICAL, OBOVATE

slang .... PERSON

small .... OVULE

tester .... CANDLER

unfertilized .... OOSPHERE

white .... GLAIR, ALBUMEN, ALBUMIN

yolk .... VITELLUS, VITELLINE

yolk pigment .... LUTEIN

yolk substance .... LECITHIN

eggbeater .... AGITATOR

egger .... MOTH, BOMBYCID

egghead .... INTELLECTUAL

slang .... HIGHBROW

eggheads collectively .... CLERISY

egglike .... OVULAR, YOLKED

eggs ...... OVA, EXHORTS, INCITES, PROVOKES

fish .... ROE, BERRIES

for breakfast .... SARDOU, BENEDICT

nest of .... CLUTCH

to produce or deposit
.... SPAWN

eggshell color .... ECRU, IVORY, CREAMY

egis .... SHIELD, AUSPICES, PROTECTION, BREASTPLATE, SPONSORSHIP

eglantine .... SWEETBRIER

ego ...... I, SELF, ATMAN, MYSELF, CONCEIT, PERSONALITY

kind of .... ALTER

opposite of .... ID

egocentric .... SELF-CENTERED
egoism .... VANITY, CONCEIT,
INDIVIDUALISM
opposed to .... ALTRUISM
egoist .... PRIG, NARCIST
opposite of .... ALTRUIST
slang .... SWELLHEAD
egotism .... PRIDE, EGOISM,
BIGHEAD, VANITY, EGOMANIA,
SELFISHNESS, SELF-INTEREST
egotistic(al) .... VAIN, COCKY,
SELFISH, PRIGGISH,
CONCEITED, NARCISSISTIC
egregious .... BAD, GROSS, UNDUE,
EXTREME, FLAGRANT,
OUTRIGHT, PRECIOUS
egress .... EXIT, ISSUE, OUTLET,
WAY OUT, OUTFLOW,
EMERGENCE
egret .... HERON, PLUME
Egypt .... MIZRAIM
Egyptian ...... ARAB, COPT, NILOT
alloy .... ASEM
amulet .... MENAT
antelope .... BUBALIS
ape: myth. .... AANI
archaeologist .... SAAD,
RAZEK, SALEH
Asiatic conquerors .... HYKSOS
asp on headdress ...... URAEUS
astronomer .... IMHOTEP
bay .... FOUL, ABU QIR
boat .... FELUCCA
bird .... IBIS, TROCHILUS
bull: myth. .... APIS
canal .... SUEZ
cape .... RAS BANAS, RAS
MUHAMMAD
capital .... CAIRO
capital, ancient .... SAIS,
TANIS, AMARNA, MEMPHIS
captain .... RAIS, REIS
captor of Jerusalem
.... SALADIN
city/town .... GIZA, QENA,
SUEZ, ASWAN, ASYOT, BENHA,
GIRGA, LUXOR, SOHAG,
TAHTA, TANTA, RASHID,
MALLAWI, ZAGAZIG,
DAMANHUR, DAMIETTA, EL
MINYA, ISMAILIA, EL FAIYOM,
PORT SAID, ALEXANDRIA, EL
MANSORA
Christian .... COPT
cobra .... HAJE, URAEUS
coin .... GIRSH, PIASTRE,
BEDIDLIK
commander .... SIRDAR
conquerors .... AMRU,
LYBIANS, NUBIANS, PTOLEMY,
NAPOLEON

cosmetic .... KOHL
cowheaded goddess
.... HATHOR
creator god .... ATUM
crocodile god .... SOBEK
cross .... ANKH, CRUX, ANSATA
dam .... ASWAN
dancing girl .... ALMA(H),
ALME(H), GHAWAZI
dead body, preserved
.... MUMMY
desert .... LIBYAN, SAHARA,
SKETIS, ARABIAN, GREAT SAND
SEA
division .... MAZOR, FAIYUM,
PATHROS
dynasty .... PEPI, SETI, UNAS,
MENES, NECHO, AHMOSE,
CHEOPS, DARIUS, NARMER,
RAMSES, PTOLEMY
dynasty founder .... MENES
elf .... OUPHE
embalmed dead body
.... MUMMY
fabled monster .... SPHINX
falcon-headed god ..... HORUS,
MENTU
fertile land .... GOSHEN
gate .... PYLON
god .... GEB, MIN, ATEN,
ATMU, HAPI, SETH, HORUS,
THOTH, AMEN-RA, ANUBIS,
KHENSU, MNEVIS, WAPUET
god bearer of the ankh
.... PTAH
god judge of the dead
.... OSIRIS
god-king .... PEPI, KHAFRE,
RAMSES, MENKAURE,
SENUSERT, THUTMOSE
god of creation .... PTAH
god of evil .... SET(H)
god of lower world
.... SERAPIS
god of medicine ...... IMHOTEP
god of pleasure .... BES
goddess .... DOR, MUT, NUT,
APET, BAST, ISIS, MAAT, SATI,
(H)ATHOR, SEKHET, SESHAT
governor .... BEY, MUDIR
gulf .... SUEZ, A'QABA, EL
SOLLUM
hairstyle .... SIDELOCK
hare-like animal .... HYRAX
hawk-headed god .... RA
heart .... HATI
heaven ..... AALU, AARU, LALU
high priest .... RANOFER
ibis-headed god .... THOTH
jackal-headed god .... WAPUET
khedive's domain .... DAIRA

king .... TUT, FUAD, MENES,
CHEOPS, FAROUK, PTOLEMY
king of underworld ..... OSIRIS
king, youthful .... TUT
laborer .... FELLAH
lake .... NASSER, BIRKET
QARON
lakes .... BITTER
language .... ARABIC, COPTIC
lighthouse .... PHAROS
lizard .... ADDA
lord of sky .... HORUS
lute .... NABLA
magician .... IMHOTEP
measure .... ARDES
measure, distance .... PIK,
KHET, THEB
measure, dry .... KADA,
ARDEB, KILAH
measure, liquid .... HIN
monetary unit .... POUND
money .... MINA, TALENT,
DRACHMA, PIASTRE
money of account .... ASPER
month .... APAP, TOTH,
MECHIR, MESORE
monument figure
.... CARTOUCH(E)
moon god .... THOTH
mortuary chapel
.... MASTABA(H)
mountain .... SINAI, U'WEINAT,
KATHERINA
mouse .... JERBOA
mullet .... BOURI
mummy cloth .... BYSSUS
name .... GAMAL
native ...... ARAB, COPT, NILOT,
BERBER, NUBIAN
oasis .... SIWA, DAKHLA,
KHARGA, FARAFRA, BAHARIYA
obsolete .... GYPSY
opium .... THEBAINE
party .... WAFD
patron of artists .... PTAH
peasant .... FELLAH
peninsula .... SINAI, PHAROS
Pharaoh .... RAM(E)SES,
AKHENATON
phoenix .... BENU
police .... GHAFIR
port .... SAID
pound .... ROTL
premier .... SAAD
president .... NASSER
queen .... CLEOPATRA,
NEFERTARI, NEFERTITI,
HATSHEPSUT
queen of gods .... SATI
Rameses .... PHARAOH
rattle .... SISTRUM

reed .... PAPYRUS
relic, kind of .... MUMMY
river .... NILE
rock .... PORPHYRY
royal tomb .... PYRAMID
ruler .... KHEDIVE, PHARAOH,
MAMELUKE
sacred beetle .... SCARAB
sacred bird .... BENU, IBIS
sacred bull .... APIS
scribe .... ANI
sea .... RED, MEDITERRANEAN
seaport .... PORT SAID
serpent: myth. .... APEPI
"shepherd kings" .... HYKSOS
singing girl .... ALMA, ALME,
GHAWAZI
site of ruins .... LUXOR,
ABYDOS, AMARNA, KARNAK,
THEBES, MEMPHIS, SAKKARA,
BERENICE, PYRAMIDS
skink .... ADDA
slave-soldier .... MAMELUKE
snake .... ASP
solar deity .... SHU
solar disk/symbol .... ATEN
soul .... KA
spirit .... HAPI
statue, kind of .... SPHINX
stone .... ROSETTA
strait .... TIRAN
structure ...... PYLON, PYRAMID
sultan .... SALADIN
sun .... ATEN
sun god ..... RA, AMON, AMEN-
RA, HORUS
sycamore fig tree .... DAROO
symbol of fertility .... SERAPIS
symbol of life/emblem
.... ANKH
tambourin .... RIKK
Tanis .... ZOAN
temple gate .... PYLON
temple site .... KARNAK
Thebes .... LUXOR
thorn .... BABUL, KIKAR
title .... PASHA, CALIPH
tomb .... MASTABA(H)
tree .... SYCAMORE
verbal shrug .... MA'ALESH
viceroy .... KHEDIVE
waterway .... SUEZ
weight .... KAT, KET, OKA,
OKE, HEML, KHAR, MINA,
OCHA, OHIA, OKIEN, KANTAR
whip .... KURBASH
wind .... KHAMSEEN,
K(H)AMSIN
woman pharaoh
.... HATSHEPSUT

woman singer
.... (OM)KALTHUM
writing form .... DEMOTIC,
HIERATIC, HIEROGLYPHIC
writing material ...... PAPYRUS
Zeus .... AMMON
Egyptologist .... EADY, NIMS,
EMERY, LAUER
eider .... DOWN, (SEA)DUCK
eidolon .... ICON, IMAGE,
PHANTOM
eight ball, behind the
.... DILEMMA, IN A FIX, IN
TROUBLE, ON THE SPOT,
PREDICAMENT
combining form .... OCT(A),
OCT(O)
group of ...... OCTAD, OCTAVE,
OCTET(TE), OCTONARY
hundred forty yards of
cotton .... HANK
multiply by .... OCTUPLE
of .... OCTONARY
of the number .... OCTAL
performers .... OCTET(TE)
series of .... OCTAD
sided figure .... OCTAGON
stringed instrument
.... OCTACHORD
eighteen XVIII
eightfold .... OCTUPLE
eighth day, every .... OCTAN
note .... QUAVER
part of a circle .... OCTANT
eighty .... FOURSCORE
years old .... OCTOGENARIAN
Einstein's birthplace .... ULM
theory .... RELATIVITY
Eire legislature .... DAIL
president .... HYDE
river .... SHANNON
Eisenhower, Gen. .... IKE,
DWIGHT
middle name .... DAVID
wife of .... MAMIE(DOUD)
either ...... ANY, AUGHT, ANY ONE
ejaculate .... SPEW, EJECT,
EXCLAIM, DISCHARGE
eject .... EMIT, OUST, SPEW, VOID,
ERUPT, EVICT, EXPEL, SQUIRT,
DISCARD, DISMISS, DISLODGE,
CAST OUT, DISPLACE
ejecta .... REFUSE
ejection .... EXILE, OUSTER,
RIDDANCE, EVICTION,
EXPULSION
eke .... ADD, INCREASE, LENGTHEN
out .... COPE, MAKE DO,
MANAGE, SURVIVE
el .... THE, WING, RAILWAY,
EXTENSION

El Cid .... RUY, (RODRIGO)DIAZ
Salvador, capital of .... SAN
SALVADOR
city/town .... IZALCO,
CORINTO, METAPAN,
ACAJUTLA, LA PALMA, LA
UNION, USULUTAN,
SONSONATE, SAN MIGUEL,
SAN VICENTE
gulf .... FONSECA
lake .... GUIJA
language .... SPANISH
main export .... COFFEE
monetary unit .... COLON
mountain .... SANTA ANA
port ...... CATUCO, ACAJUTLA
president .... DUARTE,
CRISTIANI
river .... LA PAZ, LEMPA
volcano .... IZALCO
weight .... CAJA, LIBRA
elaborate .... FANCY, ORNATE,
ROCOCO, REFINE, DEVELOP,
DETAILED, EXPATIATE,
INTRICATE, EMBELLISH,
PAINSTAKING
decoration .... FINERY
production .... EXTRAVAGANZA
trimming .... FURBELOW
elaborately made ...... EXQUISITE
Elam's capital .... SUSA,
SHUSHAN
elan ...... ZIP, DASH, ZEST, ARDOR,
ZING, GUSTO, VIGOR, SPIRIT,
VITALITY, VIVACITY
eland .... ANTELOPE
elanet .... HAWK, KITE
elapine .... COBRA, MAMBA
elapse .... DIE, PASS, SLIP(BY),
GLIDE(BY), EXPIRE
elastic .... SUPPLE, BUOYANT,
DUCTILE, SPRINGY, TENSILE,
FLEXIBLE, ADAPTABLE,
RESILIENT, STRETCHABLE
band/strap .... GARTER
material on whale's palate
.... BALEEN, WHALEBONE
substance .... RUBBER
wood .... YEW
elasticity .... BUOYANCY,
DUCTILITY, RESILIENCE
muscular .... TONUS
elate ...... EXALT, EXCITE, PLEASE,
DELIGHT, ENLIVEN, GLADDEN,
GRATIFY, EXHILARATE
elated .... JOYFUL, GLEEFUL,
OVERJOYED, ON CLOUD NINE
elater .... DOR, (CLICK)BEETLE
Elatha's son .... BRES
Elba's important inhabitant
.... NAPOLEON

Elbe .... LABE
   city on the .... MEISSEN
   tributary .... EGER, ISER, OHRE,
               MOLDAU
elbow ...... BEND, ANCON, ANGLE,
   CROWD, JOINT, SHOVE, JOSTLE
   bony tip of the .... FUNNY
               BONE
   inflammation
   .... EPICONDYLITIS
   inflammation, type of
   .... TENNIS ELBOW, GOLFER'S
               ELBOW
   jab with the .... NUDGE
   of the .... ULNAR
   part of the ...... ULNA, RADIUS,
         HUMERUS, OLECRANON
elder .... IVA, SIRE, FORMER,
   SENIOR, ANCIENT, EARLIER,
     ANCESTOR, SUPERIOR
   church .... PRESBYTER
   statesman .... ITO, GENRO,
              SAVANT
elderly .... OLD, AGED, AGING,
   ANILE, SENILE, GRAYING,
     VETERAN, WRINKLED
eldest ...... AINE, OLDEST, SENIOR,
   FIRST-BORN, FIRSTLING
   son .... PRIMOGENITURE
Eldorado's riches .... GOLD,
            DIAMONDS
eldritch ...... EERY, EERIE, WEIRD,
            GHASTLY
Eleanor, diminutive of ...... ELLA,
         NORA, NELL
   variant .... ELINOR
Eleanora, actress .... DUSE
elecampane roots .... INULA
elect ...... OPT, SEAT, VOTE, ELITE,
   CHOOSE, CHOSEN, DECIDE,
     PREFER, SELECT
election .... POLL, CHOICE,
          SELECTION
   casualty .... LAME DUCK
   district .... WARD, PRECINCT
   kind of ..... RUNOFF, GENERAL,
            PRIMARY
   landslide .... WALK-IN
   platform .... ISSUE, PLANK,
   POLICY, PROGRAM, HUSTINGS
   proceedings .... HUSTINGS
   report .... RETURNS
   tour ..... STUMP, WHISTLE STOP
electioneer ...... STUMP, CANVASS,
          CAMPAIGN
elective .... OPTIONAL, ELECTORAL,
        DISCRETIONARY
elector .... VOTER, ELISOR,
     OPTANT, SELECTOR
electorate .... ELECTORS,
       CONSTITUENTS

Electra ...... PLEIAD, SHINING ONE
   brother of .... ORESTES
   parent of .... AGAMEMNON,
         CLYTEMNESTRA
electric .... VOLTAIC, CORDLESS,
   EXCITING, MAGNETIC,
         THRILLING
   bell part .... ARMATURE
   bulb .... GLOBE
   catfish .... RAAD
   chair .... DEATH, HOT SEAT
   circuit .... LOOP
   circuit switch .... TOGGLE
   company employee
   .... READER
   current modulator .... CODER
   current regulator
   .... RHEOSTAT
   device .... RHEO, RESISTOR,
         RHEOSTAT
   engine for towing .... MULE
   eye .... PHOTOCELL
   force unit .... VOLT
   generator .... DYNAMO
   light .... BULB, GLIM, LAMP,
   NEON LAMP, FLUORESCENCE,
     INCANDESCENT LAMP
   particle .... (AN)ION, CATION
   potential .... TENSION
   power .... WATTAGE
   railway, underground
   .... METRO, SUBWAY
   ray .... TORPEDO, NUMBFISH
   unit .... OHM, REL, DYNE,
   ELOD, PERM, VOLT, WATT,
   AMP(ERE), FARAD, HENRY,
     MEGOHM, KILOWATT
   wire .... LINE, CABLE
   wires tube .... RACEWAY
electrical apparatus ...... SPARKER
   appliance .... RANGE, MIXER,
   STOVE, COOKER, FRYPAN,
   BLENDER, TOASTER,
   (FLAT)IRON, COMPACTOR,
     DISHWASHER,
     (MICROWAVE)OVEN
   atom .... ELECTRON
   circuit regulator ...... BOOSTER
   device ..... FUSE, PLUG, RELAY,
   TIMER, DYNAMO, OUTLET,
   CHARGER, RHEOSTAT,
   CAPACITOR, CONDENSER,
     TRANSFORMER
   failure .... SHORT
   force .... ELOD
   machine .... MOTOR, ENGINE,
         GENERATOR
   particle .... (AN)ION, CATION
   phenomenon .... ARC
   system .... WIRING
   terminal .... ANODE,

         ELECTRODE
   unit .... VOLT, WATT, JOULE
   unit of measurement ...... REL,
   BARAD, FARAD, FARADAY,
     HORSEPOWER
electrician ...... WIRER, WIRE MAN
electricity .... LIGHT, POWER
   generator .... EEL
   slang .... JUICE
   unit of .... MHO, OHM, AMPERE
electrified particle .... ION
electrify .... STUN, SHOCK,
   CHARGE, EXCITE, THRILL,
     STARTLE, ENERGIZE
electrode .... GRID, ANODE,
   CATHODE, THERMION,
     CONDUCTOR
electrograph .... WIRE PHOTO
electromagnet .... SOLENOID
electromotive force ...... TENSION,
   VOLT(AGE), PRESSURE
electron .... MESON
   tube .... TRIODE, IGNITRON,
   KENATRON, KLYSTRON,
   MAGNETRON, STROBOTRON
electronic "brain"
   ...... COMPUTER, CALCULATOR
   detector .... RADAR, SONAR
   device .... LASER, MASER,
         ISOTRON
   device connected to wall of
   the heart ..... PACEMAKER
   device to increase electric
   signal strength
   .... AMPLIFIER
   hearing device .... HEARING
         AID
   meter .... DUODIAL,
       VOLTMETER
   recording instrument of
   blood pressure, pulse rate,
   etc. .... POLYGRAPH, LIE
       DETECTOR
   tester .... AMMETER,
       OHMMETER
   transmitting device through
   wave frequencies
   .... RADIO
   tube .... X-RAY, DIODE, STROBE
electroplated .... ANODIZED,
       GALVANIZED
electrum .... ALLOY
eleemosynary ...... FREE, GRATIS,
   GENEROUS, CHARITABLE,
     GRATUITOUS
elegance .... EASE, LUXE, CHARM,
   GRACE, FINISH, POLISH,
   CULTURE, GOOD TASTE,
     REFINEMENT
   affected/excessive ..... PURISM,
       FROUFROU

of manners .... PANACHE
elegant .... CHIC, FINE, POSH,
NOBBY, PLUSH, DELUXE,
REFINED, ARTISTIC,
BECOMING, GRACEFUL,
SUPERB, POLISHED
affectedly .... GENTEEL,
OVERNICE, PURISTIC
in a showy way .... FLOSSY
in manners .... PROPER,
COURTLY, DIGNIFIED
elegiac .... SAD, MOURNFUL,
PLAINTIVE, THRENODIC
elegist ...... GRAY, POET, SHELLEY
elegize .... KNELL, MOURN,
LAMENT, POETICIZE
elegy .... DIRGE, NENIA, REQUIEM,
THRENODY
Shelley's .... ADONAIS
eleme .... FIG
element .... PART, STUFF, FACTOR,
COMPONENT, INGREDIENT
an .... AIR, FIRE, EARTH,
WATER
chemical .... ALKALI, ANTACID,
REAGENT, NEUTRALIZER
extracted .... DERIVATIVE
inert gas .... NEON, HELIUM
nonmetallic chemical
.... SILICON
number 5 .... BORON
number 10 .... NEON
of air .... NEON, ARGON,
HELIUM, OXYGEN, NITROGEN
of anything .... SUBSTANCE
rare-earth .... ERBIUM
similar to another ..... ISOTOPE
smallest particle of an
.... ATOM, MOLECULE
suffix .... IUM
with a valence of one
.... MONAD
with valence six .... HEXAD
with valence two .... DYAD
worthless .... SCUM
elemental .... SIMPLE, PRIMARY,
INCIPIENT, HYPOSTATIC
spirit .... DEMON, GNOME,
SYLPH
elementary .... BASIC, PRIMAL,
SIMPLE, PRIMARY, BEGINNING,
ABC'S, FUNDAMENTAL,
RUDIMENTARY
education .... RUDIMENTS,
INTRODUCTION
school ...... GRAMMAR SCHOOL
elemi .... ANIME, RESIN
elenctic .... REFUTING
opposed to .... D(E)ICTIC
elephant .... HATHI, JUMBO,
TUSKER, PACHYDERM

boy .... SABU
driver .... MAHOUT
extinct .... MAMMOTH,
MASTODON
female .... COW
frenzy of .... MUST
goad .... ANKUS
keeper .... MAHOUT
male .... BULL
maverick/outlaw .... ROGUE
nose .... SNOUT
seat on ..... HOUDAH, HOWDAH
sound .... BELLOW, TRUMPET
tooth .... TUSK
tower on .... CASTLE
trap .... KEDDAH, KHEDAH
tusk .... IVORY
white .... ALBINO
young .... CALF
elephant's ear .... TARO,
BEGONIA
elephantine .... HUGE, VAST,
BULKY, MASSIVE
eleuthera yield .... CASCARILLA
elevate .... BUOY, LIFE, EXALT,
RAISE, JACK UP, HEIGHTEN
elevated .... HIGH, LOFTY,
EMINENT, EDIFYING
railway .... EL, MONORAIL
roadway .... OVERPASS
elevating muscle .... LEVATOR
elevation .... MOUNT, HEIGHT,
UPLIFT, LIFTING, PLATEAU,
ALTITUDE, EMINENCE,
ERECTION
elevator .... HOIST, GRANARY,
WAREHOUSE
aircraft .... AIRFOIL
British .... LIFT
car .... CAGE
kind of .... DUMBWAITER
man .... OTIS
passage for .... SHAFT
pawnbroker's .... SPOUT
eleven's numerals .... ONES
eleventh hour .... CURFEW,
DEADLINE
elf .... FAY, HOB, IMP, NIX, PERI,
PIXY, PUCK, FAIRY, GNOME,
OUPHE, PIXIE, GOBLIN, SPRITE,
BROWNIE
elfdom .... WITCHERY
elfin .... FEY
shelter .... TOADSTOOL
Eli .... HIGH PRIEST
grandson of .... ICHABOD
pupil of .... SAMUEL
son of .... HOPHNI, PHINEHAS
Elia .... LAMB
elicit .... DRAW, EDUCE, EVOKE,
FETCH, EXTORT, EXTRACT

elide .... OMIT, SLUR, LEAVE OUT,
NEGLECT, SUPPRESS
eligibility .... ACCEPTANCE,
QUALIFICATION
eligible .... FIT(TED), SUITABLE,
COMPETENT, DESIRABLE,
QUALIFIED
for draft .... ONE-A
Elijah .... ELIA, ELIAS, PROPHET
diminutive .... LIGE
religious opponent of
.... JEZEBEL
successor of .... ELISHA
Elimelech's daughter-in-law
.... RUTH
son .... MAHLON
wife .... NAOMI
eliminate .... RID, DROP, OMIT,
EJECT, ERASE, EXPEL, SET
ASIDE, REMOVE, EXCLUDE,
EXCRETE, SECRETE,
ERADICATE
tension .... CLEAR THE AIR
Eliot, George .... EVANS
creation .... VERSE
hero .... BEDE, MARNER
heroine .... ROMOLA
Eliot's cruellest month .... APRIL
Elisheba's husband .... AARON
elision .... SYNCOPE, OMISSION,
CONTRACTION
victim of .... VOWEL,
SYLLABLE
elite .... PICK, CREAM, PRIME,
CHOICE, SELECT,
ARISTOCRACY
assemblage .... SALON,
GALAXY
elixir .... POTION, REMEDY,
ARCANUM, CURE-ALL,
NOSTRUM, PANACEA,
CATHOLICON
Elizabeth .... TAYLOR, ASHLEY,
MONTGOMERY
diminutive of .... LIZ, BETH,
BETTY, LISSET(T)E, LIZZIE
Elizabeth I, Queen, adviser
.... CECIL
parent .... BOLEYN,
HENRY(VIII)
tutor .... ASCHAM
Elizabeth II, Queen, daughter
of .... ANNE
daughter-in-law of ..... DIANA,
SARAH
father of .... GEORGE VI
father-in-law of .... ANDREW
granddaughter of .... ZARA,
EUGENIE, BEATRICE
grandson of .... HARRY,
PETER, WILLIAM

husband of .... PHILIP

sister of .... MARGARET

son of ...... ANDREW, EDWARD, CHARLES

son-in-law of .... MARK(PHILLIPS)

elk .... ALCE, LOSH, MOOSE, SAMBAR, WAPITI

male .... BULL

of rank .... EXALTED RULER

Elkanah's son .... SAMUEL

wife .... HANNAH

ell .... WING, EXTENSION

Ella .... RAINES, FITZGERALD

Ellen's lake .... KATRINE

Ellice Islands' old name .... LAGOON

Elliott, actor .... GOULD

ellipse .... OVAL, CURVE, OVATE

ellipsoidal .... OVAL

elliptical .... OVAL, OVATE, OVOID, OBLONG, EGG-SHAPED

elm .... WAHOO

fruit .... SAMARA

Elman, violinist .... MISCHA

Elmo's (St.) fire ...... CORPOSANT

Elohim .... GOD

elongate .... EXTEND, PROLONG, STRETCH, LENGTHEN

elongated .... LONG, OBLONG, PROLATE, PROTRACTED

combining form ...... MACR(O)

elope .... DECAMP, ESCAPE, RUN AWAY, ABSCOND

elopers, usual .... LOVERS

eloquence ...... POWER, FLUENCY, GIFT OF GAB, ORATORY, RHETORIC

eloquent .... FLUENT, LINGUAL, GLIB, ARTICULATE, EXPRESSIVE, VOLUBLE, FLAMBOYANT, ORATORICAL

else .... IF NOT, BESIDES, DIFFERENT, OTHER(WISE)

elsewhere .... AWAY, ALIBI

Elsie's husband .... ELMER

elsin .... AWL

elt .... PORKER

elucidate .... CLEAR, CLARIFY, EXPLAIN, INTERPRET

elude .... FOIL, SHUN, AVOID, DODGE, EVADE, BAFFLE, ESCAPE

elusion ...... EVASION, AVOIDANCE

elusive .... EELY, SHIFTY, TRICKY, EVASIVE, BAFFLING, SLIPPERY

person .... FUGITIVE

thing .... EEL

elutriate .... DECANT, PURIFY

elver .... EEL, CONGER

Elwin, anthropologist .... VERRIER

Ely's famed building .... CATHEDRAL

Elysian .... HAPPY, BLISSFUL

Elysium .... EDEN, HEAVEN, PARADISE

em: colloq. .... THEM

half an .... EN

emaciated .... BONY, THIN, DRAWN, GAUNT, SKINNY, WASTED, HAGGARD, SCRAWNY

colloquial .... SKIN AND BONES

emaciation .... TABES, WASTE, ATROPHY, TENUITY, MARASMUS, THINNESS, SLIGHTNESS

emanate .... EMIT, FLOW, (A)RISE, EXUDE, ISSUE, EFFUSE, EXHALE, SPRING, RADIATE, COME FORTH

emanation(s) ...... AURAE, NITON, EFFLUX, EMISSION, RADIANCE, EMERGENCE, EXHALATION

flower .... AROMA, SCENT, FRAGRANCE

invisible .... AURA, VAPOR

light .... RAY

offensive .... STINK, STENCH

subtle .... AURA, WHIFF

suffocating .... FUME

emancipate ...... FREE, MANUMIT, SET FREE, RELEASE, LIBERATE

emancipation .... LIBERATION, MANUMISSION

emasculate .... GELD, ALTER, UNMAN, WEAKEN, CASTRATE, STERILIZE, DEBILITATE

embalm ...... MUMMIFY, PRESERVE

embalmed body .... MUMMY

embalming fluid .... FORMALIN

embankment .... DAM, BANK, BUND, DIKE, WALL, LEVEE, STAITH

castle .... RAMPART

defensive .... BULWARK

protective mat .... MATTRESS

embar .... STOP, ARREST, CONFINE

embargo .... EXCLUSION, RESTRAINT, PROHIBITION, RESTRICTION

embark ...... SAIL, BEGIN, BOARD, ENGAGE, TACKLE, UNDERTAKE

embarrass .... FAZE, ABASH, SHAME, UPSET, HUMBLE, FLUSTER, NONPLUS, DISCOMFIT, HUMILIATE, DEMORALIZE, DISCONCERT

a speaker .... GRAVEL, HECKLE

embarrassed .... QUEASY, ABASHED, ASHAMED, CRUSHED, SHEEPISH

embarrassing situation .... SCRAPE

embarrassment .... PUDENCY, INHIBITION, CONTRETEMPS

embassy ...... MISSION, LEGATION, CONSULATE

official ..... CONSUL, ATTACHE, AMBASSADOR

embattled .... ARMED, FORTIFIED, AT DAGGERS DRAWN

embellish .... DECK, GILD, PINK, ADORN, EMBOSS, POLISH, TOUCH UP, DECORATE, ORNAMENT, EMBROIDER

embellishment .... FILLIP, TRAPPING, ADORNMENT

ember .... ASH, COAL, IZLE, GLEED, SPARK, CINDER

embezzle .... STEAL, MISUSE, PECULATE, DEFALCATE

embezzlement .... THEFT

embezzler .... CROOK, THIEF, PECULATOR

embitter .... SOUR, ANGER, FESTER, RANKLE, ENVENOM, ACERBATE

emblaze .... KINDLE

emblazon .... ADORN, EXTOL, DECORATE

emblem. See also **symbol** .... SIGN, TOKEN, DEVICE, SYMBOL, INSIGNE, INSIGNIA

authority .... MACE, BADGE, CROWN, GAVEL, ENSIGN, FASCES

Christianity's .... CROSS

clan .... TOTEM

French royal family .... FLEUR-DE-LIS

hat .... COCKADE

heraldic .... CREST, SHIELD, ESCUTCHEON

international .... RED CROSS

Ireland .... SHAMROCK

national .... FLAG

Nazi fascists' .... SWASTIKA

of dawn .... DEW

of immortality .... PHOENIX

of royalty .... CROWN, DIADEM, PURPLE

pirates'/poison ..... SKULL AND CROSSBONES

shield .... IMPRESA

Turkish .... CRESCENT

U.S.A. .... EAGLE

emblematic .... SYMBOLIC, HIEROGLYPH(IC)

embodiment .... IMAGE, AVATAR, EPITOME, RENDITION, EXPRESSION, INCARNATION,

PERSONIFICATION
embody .... JOIN, UNITE, CONTAIN, INCLUDE, COMPRISE, ORGANIZE, INCARNATE, PERSONIFY, INCORPORATE
embolden ...... HEARTEN, INSPIRE, REASSURE, ENCOURAGE
embolism .... BLOCKAGE, OBSTRUCTION, INTERCALATION
type of .... CEREBRAL, PULMONARY
embolus .... FIBRIN
most common type of ..... AIR BUBBLE, BLOOD CLOT
embonpoint .... STOUTNESS, CORPULENCE
embosom ...... CHERISH, SHELTER
emboss ...... STUD, CHASE, RAISE, ENGRAVE, DECORATE
embossed .... CARVED, CHASED, MOLDED, SCULPTED
embossment .... IMPRINT, CONVEXITY, IMPRESSION
embowel .... EVISCERATE
embrace ...... HUG, HOLD, ADOPT, CLASP, INARM, CARESS, CUDDLE, CLUTCH, ENFOLD, ENCLASP, ENCLOSE, ESPOUSE, INCLUDE, WELCOME, ENCIRCLE, COMPRISE
affectionate .... BEARHUG
slang .... CLINCH
embracer .... ARM
embracing .... AMBIENT, ENCOMPASSING
embrasure .... CRENEL(LE)
embrocation .... OIL, LOTION, LINIMENT
embroider .... TAT, PURL, COUCH, EMBOSS, ENHANCE, DECORATE, EMBLAZON, ORNAMENT, EMBELLISH, EXAGGERATE
embroiderer .... NEEDLER
embroidery .... LACEWORK, NEEDLEWORK
design/piece of .... BREDE
frame .... TABARET, TAMBOUR, TABO(U)RET
kind of ..... GROS POINT, PETIT POINT
loop .... PICOT
stitch .... FIGURE EIGHT
style .... CREWEL
worsted yarn used in .... CREWEL
embroil .... MIX UP, MUDDLE, INVOLVE, ENTANGLE
embrown .... TAN
embrue .... WET

embryo .... BUD, CELL, GERM
developed .... FETUS
fertilized .... ZYGOTE
first stage of ..... CONCEPTION, INCIPIENCE
food for .... ENDOSPERM
membrane .... AMNION
middle layer .... MESODERM, MESOBLAST
outer cells .... EPIBLAST
emcee .... MC, NEWSCASTER, COMMENTATOR, TOASTMASTER
emend .... EDIT, AMEND, REDACT, REVISE, CORRECT, REWRITE
emerald ...... GEM, BERYL, GREEN, STONE, SMARAGD
cut .... RECTANGULAR
hiddenite .... LITHIA
Emerald Isle .... EIRE, ERIN, IRELAND
emerge .... SHOW, (A)RISE, ISSUE, COME FORTH, APPEAR
emergence .... EGRESS, SHOWING, OUTGROWTH, APPEARANCE
emergency ...... CRISIS, EXIGENCY
call .... SOS
man .... PINCH-HITTER, TROUBLE-SHOOTER
needing urgent treatment ..... BULLET WOUNDS, CARDIAC ARREST
signal .... FLARE
situation .... PINCH, CLUTCH, CRUNCH
treatment .... FIRST AID
emeritus .... RETIRED
Emerson, actress .... FAYE
essayist, poet .... RALPH WALDO
emery ...... ABRASIVE, CORUNDUM
use for .... FILING, GRINDING, POLISHING
emesis .... VOMITING
emetic ...... ALUM, ALOIN, VOMIT, IPECAC, EVACUANT, CATHARTIC, EXPECTORANT
plant .... TURPETH
emetine .... EXPECTORANT
source .... IPECAC
emigrant .... ALIEN, EMIGRE, LEAVER, SETTLER
emigrate .... MOVE AWAY, LEAVE THE HOMELAND
emigration .... EXODUS, DEPARTURE
emigre, kind of .... EVACUEE, REFUGEE
Emil, author .... LUDWIG
Emile Herzog's pen name .... MAUROIS

psychotherapist .... COUE
Zola book .... NANA
Emily .... POST, BRONTE
eminence .... NOTE, FAME, HEIGHT, REPUTE, DIGNITY
eminent .... GREAT, NOTED, FAMOUS, EXALTED, RENOWNED
emir's domain .... EMIRATE
emissary .... AGENT, ENVOY, (DE)LEGATE, MESSENGER
emission .... ISSUANCE, DISCHARGE
of urine, involuntary .... ENURESIS
emit .... ERUCT, ISSUE, UTTER, EXHALE, EMANATE, RADIATE, DISCHARGE, SEND FORTH
air .... BLOW
amplified light .... LASE
vapor .... REEK
Emma, poet .... LAZARUS
emmet .... ANT, PISMIRE
Emmy .... AWARD, STATUETTE
brother of .... OSCAR
emollient .... OIL, BALM, SALVE
emolument .... PAY, FEE(S), GAIN, WAGE(S), SALARY, STIPEND
emote .... ACT, PERFORM
emotion .... FEAR, HATE, LOVE, ANGER, PATHOS, FEELING, SENTIMENT
center .... HEART
nostalgic .... SENTIMENT(ALITY)
seat of .... LIVER, SPLEEN
self-defeating .... ENVY
strong .... FLAME, PASSION
turn of .... CAPRICE
emotional excitement .... HYSTERIA
illness .... NEUROSIS, DEPRESSION, PSYCHOSIS
injury .... SCAR
play .... MELODRAMA
state .... GRIEF, ECSTASY, MAUDLIN, PASSION
emotionless .... DEAF, NUMB, STOICAL, INSENSATE, UNFEELING
emotive .... MOVING, TOUCHING
empathy .... AFFINITY, SYMPATHY, UNDERSTANDING
emperor .... CZAR, TSAR, CAESAR, DESPOT, AUTOCRAT, PADISHAH, BUTTERFLY, IMPERATOR
decree of .... RESCRIPT
sovereignty of .... EMPERY, EMPIRE

Emperor Constantine's standard .... LABARUM
emphasis .... VALUE, ACCENT, STRESS, WEIGHT, IMPORTANCE
emphasize .... AFFIRM, STRESS, ACCENTUATE, UNDERSCORE
emphatic .... FORCIBLE, POSITIVE, STRIKING
denial .... NEVER
negative .... NOHOW
speech .... BIRR
emphatically .... WITH A CAPITAL
emphysema .... HEAVES
empire .... SWAY, REALM, DOMINION
Empire State .... NEW YORK
empiric ...... QUACK, CHARLATAN MOUNTEBANK
empirical .... BY TRIAL AND ERROR
emplace .... SET
employ .... USE, HIRE, AVAIL, PLACE, DEVOTE, ENGAGE, OCCUPY
employee .... CLERK, HELP(ER), ASSISTANT, HIRED HAND
desk plaque .... NAMEPLATE
employees .... HANDS, PERSONNEL
employer ...... BOSS, USER, HIRER, ENGAGER, MANAGER
employment .... JOB, WORK, CALLING, SERVICE, EXERCISE, OCCUPATION, PROFESSION
contract, illegal .... YELLOW-DOG
emporium .... MART, SHOP, STORE, BAZAAR, MARKET(PLACE)
employee .... FLOORWALKER
empower .... VEST, ENDOW, DEPUTE, ENABLE, PERMIT, ENTITLE, DEPUTIZE, AUTHORIZE
empress .... ZITA, QUEEN, CZARINA
emptiness .... VACUITY, BARENESS
empty .... BARE, IDLE, TEEM, VAIN, BLANK, DRAIN, FLUSH, INANE, (DE)VOID, DEPLETE, EXHAUST, LACKING, VACUOUS, WITHOUT, WORTHLESS
a place or area of people .... EVACUATE
colloquial .... HUNGRY
headed .... SILLY, STUPID, BARE IN MIND
of thought .... VACANT
talk .... FUDGE
talker .... WINDBAG
wind from sail .... SPILL

words .... BOSH
empyema .... PUS
empyreal .... SUBLIME, HEAVENLY, CELESTIAL
empyrean .... SKY, ETHER, FIRMAMENT
EMs .... RANKS, ENLISTED MEN
emu .... RATITE
emu-like bird .... OSTRICH, CASSOWARY
emulate .... APE, VIE, EQUAL, RIVAL, FOLLOW, STRIVE, COMPETE
a butterfly .... FLIT
an ibis .... WADE
Brian Boitano .... SKATE
Currier and Ives .... ETCH
Demosthenes .... ORATE
Dennis Conner .... SAIL
Einstein .... TEACH
Hamill .... SKATE
Jack Horner .... EAT, SIT
John Curry .... SKATE
Lorelei .... TEMPT
Mehta .... LEAD
Riley ...... LIVE THE GOOD LIFE
the lark .... SOAR
emulation .... COPYING, IMITATION
emulsifier .... GUM, MIXER, ARABIC, GELATIN
emunctory .... SKIN, LUNGS, KIDNEYS
en pointe .... ATIP
en route .... ON THE WAY
enable .... ENDOW, EMPOWER
enact ...... DO, MAKE, PASS, PLAY, ACT OUT, ORDER, DECREE, ORDAIN, PERFORM, PORTRAY, LEGISLATE
enactment .... LAW, EDICT, DECREE, PASSAGE, ORDINANCE, LEGISLATION
enamel .... GLAZE, PAINT, SMALTO, COATING, LACQUER, VARNISH, NAIL POLISH
enameled metalware .... TOLE
enamelware .... DISHES, LIMOGES, CERAMICS, UTENSILS, CLOISONNE, PORCELAIN
enamor .... CHARM, CAPTIVATE
encamp .... TENT, PITCH, BIVOUAC
encampment .... CAMPSITE
enceinte .... PREGNANT
enchain .... BIND, FETTER
enchant .... CHARM, PLEASE, BEWITCH, CONJURE, DELIGHT, ENTHRAL(L), FASCINATE
enchanted ...... RAPT, BEWITCHED
enchanting .... MAGIC(AL)
enchantment .... CHARM, SPELL

enchantress .... HAG, MEDEA, SIREN, WITCH, SORCERESS
in Odyssey .... CIRCE
enchiridion .... HANDBOOK
enchorial .... NATIVE, POPULAR
encina .... (LIVE)OAK
encircle .... HEM, GIRD, GIRT, RING, BESET, CORDON, ENLACE, ENGLOBE, ENVIRON, WREATHE, SURROUND, ENCOMPASS
encircling, an .... CINCTURE
enclasp .... HUG, EMBRACE
enclose .... RIM, HEM(IN), FENCE(IN), ENCASE, ENCYST, IMPOUND, CONFINE, ENVELOP
in a globe .... ENSPHERE
securely .... EMBAR
enclosed area .... RING, SEPT, YARD, CORRAL, COMPOUND, STOCKADE
part of aircraft .... NACELLE
space .... COMPOUND, CONFINES
enclosing line .... VERGE
membrane .... TUNICA
enclosure .... PEN, CASE, PALE, WALL, YARD, FENCE, COCOON, GIRDLE, WRAPPER, ENVELOPE, CARTRIDGE
birds/animals ...... CAGE, COTE
cattle .... ATAJO, KRAAL, CORRAL
dogs .... KENNEL
for a dose of medicine .... CAPSULE
for grazing .... WALK
for keeping and studying of animals .... VIVARIUM
for military prisoners .... STOCKADE
for one animal in a stable .... STALL
for small animals/small plants .... TERRARIUM
for stray animals .... POUND
in water .... CRAWL
of wagons for defense .... CORRAL
poultry .... COOP
public telephone .... BOOTH
race track .... PADDOCK
encomiast .... EULOGIST
encomium .... ELOGE, EULOGY, PRAISE, TRIBUTE, PANEGYRIC
encompass .... GIRD, RING, EXTEND, ENVELOP, ENVIRON, INCLUDE, COMPRISE, ENCIRCLE, SURROUND
encore .... BIS, OVER, AGAIN, REPEAT, OVATION, REPETITION

encounter .... FIND, MEET, FIGHT, BATTLE, ENGAGE, COLLIDE, BRUSH, COME UPON, COME ACROSS, CONFRONT, SKIRMISH

encourage .... ABET, SPUR, URGE, BOOST, CHEER, EGG ON, FOSTER, INCITE, HEARTEN, INSPIRE

encroach .... USURP, INVADE, IMPINGE, INTRUDE, VIOLATE, INFRINGE, OVERSTEP, TRESPASS

encroachment .... INTRUSION

encumber .... CLOG, LOAD, BURDEN, HAMPER, HINDER, IMPEDE, SADDLE, OBSTRUCT

encumbered .... INDEBTED

encumbrance .... BURDEN, IMPEDIMENT
in law .... LIEN, CLAIM
kind of .... MORTGAGE

encyclopedic .... EXTENSIVE, COMPREHENSIVE

encyclopedist .... COMPILER, DIDEROT, D'ALEMBERT

end .... AIM, TIP, GOAL, HALT, LAST, SAKE, STOP, TAIL, CLOSE, OMEGA, FINALE, FINIS(H), OBJECT, RESULT, UPSHOT, EXPIRE, PURPOSE, TERMINATE
a pregnancy prematurely .... ABORT(ION)
combining form .... TEL(O)
in music .... FINE
man's sobriquet .... BONES
of a spar .... YARDARM
that is attained .... DESTINATION
thick .... BUTT
toward an .... TELIC
up .... LAND
with old or young .... STER

endanger .... IMPERIL, LAY OPEN, JEOPARDIZE

endangered .... CORNERED, IN PERIL, THREATENED

endearing .... LOVABLE, WINSOME

endearment .... KISS, CARESS, EMBRACE, AFFECTION

endeavor .... AIM, TRY, VIE, SEEK, ESSAY, NISUS, EFFORT, STRIVE, ATTEMPT, STRUGGLE

endemic ...... NATIVE, INDIGENOUS

ending .... FINALE, FINIS(H), CLOSURE, CLOTURE, CROWNING, ULTIMATE, EXPIRATION
comparative .... IER
for land or sea .... SCAPE
for peek or bug .... ABOO

have same .... CONTERMINAL
in chemistry .... ENE
in grammar .... DESINENCE
of a sentence .... PERIOD
with Brooklyn or Gotham .... ITES

endive .... CHICORY, ESCAROLE

endless ...... ETERN(AL), LASTING, UNDYING, INFINITE, BOUNDLESS, INCESSANT, PERPETUAL, CONTINUOUS, EVERLASTING

endmost .... LAST, FARTHEST

endocarp .... STONE

endocrine .... GLAND
designating one ...... OVARIES, THYROID, PANCREAS, PITUITARY, ADRENAL CORTEX

endocrine glands, study of .... ENDOCRINOLOGY

endogamy .... INBREEDING
opposed to .... EXOGAMY

endoparasite .... ENDAMEBA, HOOKWORM

endorse ...... BACK, SIGN, SECOND, APPROVE, SUPPORT, SANCTION, RECOMMEND

endorsement .... NOD, VISA, BACKING, APPROVAL, BLESSING

endow .... VEST, ENDUE, BESTOW, CLOTHE, ENRICH, BEQUEATH

endowment .... BOON, FUND, GIFT, GRANT, TALENT, ABILITY, BEQUEST, DONATION
for graduate student .... FELLOWSHIP
natural .... DOWER, DOWRY

endue .... COVER, DOWER, ENDOW, CLOTHE, FURNISH

endurable .... BEARABLE, TOLERABLE

endurance .... STAMINA, PATIENCE, STRENGTH, FORTITUDE

endure .... BEAR, LAST, LIVE, STAND, STAY, BROOK, HOLD(ON), PERMIT, UNDERGO, TOLERATE

enduring ...... LASTING, LIFELONG

endways .... UPRIGHT, LENGTHWISE

Endymion .... SHEPHERD
lover of .... SELENE

enema .... CLYSTER

enemy .... RIVAL, FOE(MAN), OPPONENT, ADVERSARY, ANTAGONIST, OPPOSING PARTY
alien detained .... INTERNEE
encroacher .... INVADER

kind of .... SWORN, BITTER, PUBLIC

energetic ...... KEEN, LIVE, VIVID, ACTIVE, FORCEFUL
activity .... EXERCISE, EXERTION
one/person .... DOER, DYNAMO, HUSTLER, GO-GETTER
slang .... RARING TO GO

energetically active ...... UP AND DOING

energize .... PEP UP, FORTIFY, ACTIVATE, STIMULATE

energy .... PEP, VIM, ZIP, BIRR, DASH, DRIVE, FORCE, POWER, STEAM, VIGOR
and initiative .... ENTERPRISE
crunch device .... CARPOOL
form of .... HEAT, LIGHT, SOUND, KINETIC, CHEMICAL, ELECTRICAL
luminous .... LIGHT
measure of .... ENTROPY, CALORIE(S)
potential .... ERGAL
slang .... MOXIE, SOCKO, STINGO
source of .... SUN, SOLAR
unit of .... ERG, JOULE

enervate .... SAP, DRAIN, SOFTEN, WEAKEN, UNNERVE, ENFEEBLE, PARALYZE, DEBILITATE

enfeeble .... UNMAN, WEAKEN, DISABLE, EMASCULATE

enfilade .... RAKE, BARRAGE, GUNFIRE

enfin .... AT LAST, FINALLY

enfold .... WRAP, ENLACE, EMBRACE, ENCLOSE, ENVELOP

enforce .... GOAD, LASH, URGE, COMPEL, IMPOSE, OBLIGE

enfranchise .... SET FREE, EMPOWER, LICENSE, QUALIFY, RELEASE, LIBERATE

engage .... BIND, BOOK, HIRE, MESH, EMPLOY, ENLIST, OCCUPY, PLEDGE, RETAIN, BETROTH, RESERVE, AFFIANCE

engaged .... BUSY, EMPLOYED, INVOLVED, OCCUPIED, BETROTHED

engagement .... DATE, TROTH, PROMISE, ENCOUNTER, BETROTHAL, COMMITMENT, APPOINTMENT
assurance .... AVAL

engaging .... SAPID, WINNING, WINSOME, ALLURING, CHARMING, ARRESTING

engender .... BEGET, BREED, CAUSE, PRODUCE, PROMOTE, GENERATE, PROCREATE

engine .... GIN, MOGUL, MOTOR, DEVICE, MACHINE, TURBINE, APPARATUS

compressed air .... RAMJET

cylinder .... PISTON

exhaust noise .... CHUG

knock .... PING

of war .... RAM, ONAGER, CATAPULT, MANGONEL, TREBUCHET

on wheels .... LOCOMOTIVE

part .... CAM, GEAR, BOILER, PISTON, BEARING, CYLINDER, DIFFERENTIAL, TRANSMISSION

platform .... WALK

puff .... PANT

type of .... GAS, JET, FIRE, DIESEL, ROTARY

engineer ...... PLOT, PILOT, SWING, MANAGE, CONTRIVE, PRODUCE, MANEUVER, OPERATOR, EFFECTUATE, MANIPULATE

type of .... ARMY, CIVIL, NAVAL, MARINE, MINING, HIGHWAY, NUCLEAR, CHEMICAL, ELECTRICAL, MECHANICAL

engineer's aid .... OILER, STOKER

place .... CAB

engineless airplane .... GLIDER

England .... ANGLIA, ALBION, EGBERT

personified .... JOHN BULL

revenue offices .... EXCHEQUERS

English. See also **British** .... ANGLE, SILURES, SPIN, ANGELICAN

ale month .... OCTOBER

anthem .... MOTET

architect Christopher .... WREN

author .... LYLY, MILNE

ball game .... ROUNDERS

beefeater .... YEOMAN

chemist .... DAVY

city .... LEEDS, LONDON

coin, old .... ORA, UNITE

composer .... BAX, ARNE

country festival .... ALE

court, old .... LEET

cream .... DEVON

dramatist .... PEELE, PINERO

East India company ship .... INDIAMAN

essayist .... ELIA, BACON, PATER

explorer .... CABOT

fir pole .... UFER

freeman .... THANE

general .... CLIVE

hymnologist .... NEALE

isle .... JERSEY

judicial circuit .... ITER

letter, old .... ETH

metropolis .... LEEDS

novelist .... DEFOE, READE, YATES, BRONTE, STERNE

old money .... ORA

painter .... OPIE, MILLAIS

physicist .... CHADWICK

poet ...... POPE, BLAKE, NOYES, SASSOON

poet of 1700s .... SAVAGE

poet of 19th century ..... ASHE

portrait painter .... SIR JOSHUA REYNOLDS

queen .... ANNE, ELIZABETH

resort .... BATH

river .... EXE, AIRE, TRENT, HUMBER

statesman .... SAVILE

tar .... LIMEY

tourist site .... CASTLE

town .... EPSOM

victory, 100 Years' War .... AGINCOURT

writer of hymns .... WATTS

Englishman .... LIMEY, SAXON, SASSENACH

engram .... TRACE

engrave .... CUT, ETCH, CARVE, CHASE, HATCH, CHISEL, INCISE, STIPPLE

engraver .... CHASER, ETCHER, LAPIDARY

mark of .... REMARQUE

tool/material of .... DIE, BURIN, PLATE, PUNCH, STAMP, STYLE, CHISEL, WOODBLOCK, ETCHING POINT

engraving .... CUT, PRINT, ETCHING

by dots .... STIPPLE

by electrotyping .... CEROGRAPHY

designs on gems ...... GLYPTICS, GLYPTOGRAPHY

means of .... GRAVURE

method .... STIPPLE, MEZZOTINT

on copper or brass .... CHALCOGRAPHY

pertaining to .... GLYPTIC

process .... CEROTYPE, ELECTROTYPE

stone .... INTAGLIO

wood .... XYLOGRAPHY

engross .... ABSORB, ENGAGE, OCCUPY, CONTROL

engrossed .... RAPT, ABSORBED, THOUGHTFUL

engulf .... SWAMP, ENGORGE, ENVELOP, IMMERSE, SWALLOW, (OVER)WHELM

enhance .... ADVANCE, AUGMENT, ELEVATE, HEIGHTEN, INCREASE, INTENSIFY

Enid .... BAGNOLD

husband of: legendary .... GERAINT

enigma .... REBUS, PUZZLE, RIDDLE, SECRET, TEASER, MYSTERY, CONUNDRUM

enigmatic .... CRYPTIC, OBSCURE, BAFFLING, PUZZLING, UNCERTAIN, PERPLEXING, UNEXPLAINED

colloquial .... CLEAR AS MUD

person .... SPHINX

saying .... PARABLE

enisle .... ISOLATE, (SET)APART

enjoin ...... URGE, EXACT, ORDER, CHARGE, DIRECT, EXHORT, (FOR)BID, COUNSEL, REQUIRE

enjoy .... HOLD, LIKE, LOVE, RELISH, POSSESS

books .... READ

with great joy ...... DELIGHT IN

with others .... SHARE

enjoyed oneself greatly ...... HAD A BALL

enjoyment .... FUN, ZEST, GUSTO, DELIGHT, PLEASURE, POSSESSION

enkindle .... FIRE, HEAT, AROUSE, FOMENT, INCITE

enlarge .... GROW, SWELL, WIDEN, DILATE, EXPAND, EXTEND, AMPLIFY, BROADEN, DISTEND, MAGNIFY, INCREASE

hole/bore .... REAM

on/upon .... ELABORATE, EXPATIATE

enlarged picture: colloq. .... BLOWUP

thyroid gland .... GOITER

enlarger .... REAMER

enlighten .... EDIFY, TEACH, INFORM, CLARIFY, EDUCATE, BRIGHTEN, ILLUMINE

enlist .... ENTER, JOIN(UP), SIGN(UP), ENROLL, RECRUIT, VOLUNTEER

enlistment, compulsory .... LEVY, DRAFT, CONSCRIPTION

period .... HITCH

enliven .... CHEER, ELATE, ROUSE, ANIMATE, QUICKEN, REFRESH,

BRIGHTEN, INSPIRIT

enmesh .... KNOT, SNARL, EMBROIL, (EN)TANGLE

enmity .... FEUD, HATE, ANGER, SPITE, ANIMUS, GRUDGE, HATRED, MALICE, RANCOR, DISLIKE, ILL-WILL, ANIMOSITY, ANTIPATHY, HOSTILITY

ennead .... NINE

ennoble .... EXALT, RAISE, UPLIFT, DIGNIFY, GLORIFY

ennui .... BOREDOM, LANGUOR, WEARINESS

Enoch's cousin .... ENOS(H)

father .... CAIN

grandparent .... EVE, ADAM

son .... IRAD, METHUSELAH

wife .... EDNA

enormity .... MIGHT, OUTRAGE, IMMENSITY, MAGNITUDE

enormous .... HUGE, VAST, LARGE, IMMENSE, MAMMOTH, TITANIC, COLOSSAL, GIGANTIC, GARGANTUAN

animal .... BEHEMOTH, MASTODON

number .... GOOGOL

Enos(h)'s cousin .... ENOCH

father .... SETH

grandparent .... EVE, ADAM

grandson .... MAHALEL

son .... KENAN

uncle .... ABEL, CAIN

enough .... AMPLE, EQUAL, QUITE, ADEQUATE, SUFFICIENT

archaic .... ENOW

enrage .... ANGER, FLAME, MADDEN, INCENSE, PROVOKE, INFURIATE

enrapture .... CHARM, PLEASE, BEWITCH, DELIGHT, ENCHANT, ENRAVISH, ENTRANCE, CAPTIVATE

enrich .... LARD, ADORN, ENDOW, BEAUTIFY, CULTIVATE, FERTILIZE

enrobe .... CLOTHE

enroll ...... ENTER, SERVE, ENLIST, JOIN UP, RECORD, REGISTER

enroot .... EMBED, IMPLANT

ens .... BEING, ENTITY, EXISTENCE

Ens. .... ENSIGN

ensconce .... HIDE, SETTLE, CONCEAL, SHELTER

ensemble .... SUIT

enshrine .... DEIFY, CHERISH, IMMORTALIZE

ensiform .... XIPHOID

ensign .... FLAG, BANNER, EMBLEM, GONFALON,

INSIGNIA, ORIFLAMME, STANDARD-BEARER

ensilage .... ENSILE, FODDER

enslave ...... ADDICT, ENTHRAL(L), OPPRESS, DOMINATE

enslavement .... BONDAGE

ensnare .... BAG, NET, BAIT, CATCH, TRICK, ENTICE, (EN)TRAP, SEDUCE, TREPAN, SNIGGLE

ensue .... FOLLOW, HAPPEN, RESULT, SUCCEED, SUPERVENE

ensure .... SECURE, GUARANTEE

entablature, part of .... FRIEZE, CORNICE, ATLANTES, ARCHITRAVE

support .... ATLAS, COLUMN, ATLANTES

entail .... IMPLY, CALL FOR, INVOLVE, REQUIRE

entangle .... MAT, WEB, FOUL, KNOT, RAVEL, (EN)MESH, CONFUSE, EMBROIL, ENSNARE, TWIST, PERPLEX, INVEIGLE

entanglement .... KNOT, INVOLVEMENT

love affair .... TRIANGLE

entellus .... MONKEY

entente ...... TREATY, AGREEMENT

enter .... GO IN, JOIN, POST, BEGIN, COME IN, START, ENROLL, BOARD, INSERT, PIERCE, RECORD, INSCRIBE, REGISTER

clumsily .... BARGE

into conflict .... WAR, ENGAGE, AGGRESS

stealthily .... CREEP IN

enteric fever .... TYPHOID

enterprise ...... ENERGY, SCHEME, PROJECT, VENTURE, GUMPTION, BUSINESS, UNDERTAKING

colloq. .... PUSH

enterprising .... EAGER, AMBITIOUS, ENERGETIC

entertain .... FETE, HOST, AMUSE, TREAT, DIVERT, HARBOR, REGALE, CHERISH, CONSIDER, DWELL UPON

entertainer ...... COMIC, AMUSER, ARTISTE, HOST(ESS), DISEUSE, MAGICIAN, JUGGLER

Allbright .... LOLA

entertaining .... AMUSING, FESTIVE, SPORTIVE, HOSPITABLE

exhibit .... DOGSHOW

entertainment .... FETE, PASTIME, AMUSEMENT, DIVERSION, HOSPITALITY, RECREATION,

SHOW BUSINESS

between acts .... RELIEF, INTERLUDE, INTERMEZZO

by swimmers/divers .... AQUACADE

dramatic .... MASQUE

for all .... GAMES

hoedown .... SQUARE DANCE

of another day .... TENT SHOW

enthrall .... CHARM, BEGUILE, DELIGHT, ENCHANT, ENSLAVE, CAPTIVATE, FASCINATE

enthralled .... RAPT, CHARMED, BEWITCHED, ENTRANCED

enthrone .... SEAT, EXALT

enthuse .... RAVE, REVEL

enthused: sl. .... GUNG-HO

enthusiasm .... ELAN, ZEAL, ARDOR, CRAZE, ECLAT, GUSTO, MANIA, VERVE, FERVOR, FRENZY, SPIRIT, ECSTASY, PASSION

enthusiast .... BUG, FAN, IST, BUFF, ADDICT, ZEALOT, DEVOTEE, FANATIC, AFICIONADO

enthusiastic .... HOT, AVID, KEEN, WARM, EAGER, RABID, ARDENT

appreciation .... GUSTO

entia .... BEINGS

entice .... WOO, BAIT, COAX, LURE, TOLE, TEMPT, CAJOLE, INDUCE, ATTRACT, INVEIGLE

enticed .... ALLURED

enticer .... DECOY, CARROT, SEDUCER, TEMPTRESS

entire .... ALL, TOTAL, WHOLE, INTACT, ABSOLUTE, COMPLETE, LIVELONG, UNDIVIDED

combining form .... HOLO

range/series .... GAMUT

" _____ , entire of itself" (Donne) .... NO MAN IS AN ISLAND

entirely .... WHOLLY, UTTERLY

for Claudius .... IN TOTO

entitle ...... DUB, FIT, CALL, NAME, QUALIFY, AUTHORIZE

entity ...... ENS, ONE, UNIT, BEING, THING, EXISTENCE

entoblast .... ENDODERM

entoil .... ENSNARE

entomb .... BURY, INTER, INURN

entourage .... ROUT, TRAIN, RETINUE, ATTENDANTS

entozoon .... HOOKWORM, PARASITE, TAPEWORM

entr'acte .... INTERVAL, INTERLUDE, INTERMISSION

entrails .... GUTS, OFFAL, BOWELS, UMBLES, INNARDS, INSIDES, VISCERA, INTESTINES

entrance .... ADIT, DOOR, GATE, CHARM, DEBUT, ACCESS, PORTAL, DELIGHT, ENCHANT, INGRESS, OPENING, ADMISSION

back .... POSTERN

court .... ATRIUM

hall .... FOYER, LOBBY, ATRIUM

intrusive .... INVASION

with evil intent .... ENTRY

entrant ...... ENTRY, COMPETITOR, CONTENDER, CONTESTANT

entrants, collectively .... FIELD

entrap .... TANGLE

entreat .... BEG, PRAY, PLEAD, OBTEST, BESEECH, IMPLORE

entreaty .... PLEA, PRAYER, SUPPLICATION

entrechat .... JUMP, LEAP

entree .... DISH, ACCESS, ADMISSION

entrench ...... SECURE, ENCROACH, INFRINGE, TRESPASS

entrepot ...... DEPOT, WAREHOUSE, STOREHOUSE

entrepeneur .... TYCOON, MAGNATE, PROMOTER, ORGANIZER

entresol .... MEZZANINE

entrust .... CHARGE, CONFIDE, CONSIGN, TURN OVER

entry .... DOOR, ACCESS, ENTRANT, RECORD, LISTING, POSTING, INGRESS, ENTRANCE

Annals .... EVENTS

illegal .... INTRUSION, TRESPASS(ING), INVASION OF PRIVACY

in ledger .... ITEM, DEBIT, CREDIT, INCOME, RENT(AL), EXPENSE, INTEREST

marginal .... NOTE

permit .... PASS, VISA, PRATIQUE

entwine .... TWIST, WEAVE, (EN)LACE

enumerate .... DETAIL, (RE)COUNT, NUMBER, TICK OFF

enumeration .... LIST, CENSUS

enumerator, kind of .... NOSE COUNTER

enunciate .... STATE, UTTER, DECLARE, ANNOUNCE, PROCLAIM, PRONOUNCE, ARTICULATE

enunciation .... DICTION

enure .... HARDEN, ACCUSTOM, HABITUATE

enuresis .... URINATION, BED-WETTING

envelop ...... HIDE, WRAP, COVER, ENFOLD, ENCLOSE, INVEST, ENSHROUD, SURROUND

envelope .... CASE, CASING, SHROUD, WRAPPER, COVER(ING)

fetus .... CAUL

for a knife's blade
.... SHEATH(E)

silky .... COCOON

turtle's .... SHELL, CARAPACE

envenom .... MADDEN, POISON, ALIENATE, EMBITTER

enviable .... DESIRED, WINNING

envious .... JEALOUS, GREEN-EYED

person .... ENVIER

environ .... EMBRACE, ENCLOSE, ENCIRCLE, SURROUND

environment .... MILIEU, HABITAT, SETTING, AMBIENCE

slang .... HANGOUT

environmental ...... ECOLOGICAL, SURROUNDING

disease .... ANOXIA, JET-LAG, CHILBLAIN, SEASICKNESS

poison .... POLLUTANT

environs .... LOCALE, PURLIEU, SUBURBS, OUTSKIRTS, VICINITY, PERIPHERY, PRECINCTS

envisage .... EXPECT, FORESEE, PREDICT

envision .... PICTURE, VISUALIZE

envoy .... AGENT, LEGATE, DELEGATE, DIPLOMAT, EMISSARY, MESSENGER, AMBASSADOR

originally .... DEDICATION, POSTSCRIPT

papal .... NUNCIO

envy .... COVET, SPITE, DESIRE, HANKER, MALICE, ILL-WILL, (BE)GRUDGE, JEALOUSY

enzyme ...... ASE, ZYME, MUTASE, OLEASE, PEPSIN(E), RENNET, RENNIN, ZYMASE, CASEASE, EREPSIN, INULASE, MALTASE, OXIDASE, PECTASE, CATALASE, DIASTASE, INVERTASE

action of/producing
.... ZYMOLYSIS

additional component of
.... COENZYME

blood .... THROMBIN

digestive .... LIPASE, AMYLASE, PROTEASE

from bacteria
.... STREPTOKINASE

in saliva .... PTYALIN

in yeast .... LACTASE

protein-splitting .... PAPAIN

eolith .... AX

eon .... AGE, OLAM, EPOCH

eonic .... ERAL

Eos .... DAWN, AURORA, GODDESS

eosin .... DYE, NOPALIN

eparch .... BISHOP, GOVERNOR

eparchy .... DIOCESE

epaulet .... BADGE, PATCH, INSIGNIA, ORNAMENT

epee .... SWORD

ependymona .... GLIOMA

epergne .... CENTERPIECE

ephah, one tenth of .... OMER

ephemera/ephemeron
.... MAYFLY

ephemeral .... MORTAL, MOMENTARY, TRANSIENT, EVANESCENT, TRANSITORY, SHORT-LIVED

ephemeris ...... DIARY, ALMANAC, CALENDAR

Ephraim's brother .... MANASSEH

daughter .... SHEERAH

father .... JOSEPH

grandfather .... JACOB

mother .... ASENATH

son ...... EZER, ELEAD, BERIAH, REPHAH, SHUTHELAH

epic ...... SAGA, GRAND, HOMERIC, HEROIC, IMPOSING, MAJESTIC, NARRATIVE

events, series of .... EPOS

poem ..... EPOS, ILIAD, EPOPEE, (A)ENEID, BEOWULF, ODYSSEY

poetry .... EPOS, EPOPEE, EPOPOEIA

epicarp .... HUSK, RIND

epicedium .... DIRGE

epicene .... NEUTER, SEXLESS

epicenter .... FOCAL POINT

epicure .... GOURMET, GOURMAND, HEDONIST, SENSUIST, SYBARITE

of a kind .... GLUTTON

epicurean ...... APICIAN, SENSUAL, SENSUOUS, SYBARITIC, LUXURY-LOVING

epicurism .... HEDONICS, HEDONISM, GASTRONOMY

Epicurus, philosophy of
.... EPICUREANISM

epidemic .... PLAGUE, DISEASE, PESTILENCE, WIDESPREAD

among plants ..... EPIPHYTOTIC

conquered .... POLIO

most common ...... INFLUENZA

epidermal tissue .... KERATIN
epidermis .... BARK, SKIN,
  CUTICLE, SCARFSKIN,
  INTEGUMENT
epigram .... POEM, ADAGE,
  MAXIM, BON MOT, SAYING,
  MONOSTICH
epigraph .... MOTTO, QUOTATION,
  INSCRIPTION
epilepsy .... FIT, SEIZURE,
  CATALEPSY
  attack of .... GRAND MAL,
  PETIT MAL
epileptic attack, feeling before
  .... AURA
  treatment .... DILANTIN
epilogue .... POSTLUDE,
  POSTSCRIPT
Epimetheus .... TITAN
  brother .... PROMETHEUS
  wife .... PANDORA
epinephrin(e) .... HORMONE,
  ADRENALIN
epinette .... LARCH
epiphany .... (DIVINE)REVELATION
epiphyte .... MOSS, FUNGUS,
  LICHEN, ORCHID
episcopacy .... BISHOPS
episcopal minister .... PRESBYTER
  See .... CATHEDRA
episcopate .... SEE
episode .... EVENT, ACTION,
  INCIDENT, HAP(PENING),
  INSTALLMENT
episodic .... SPASMODIC,
  DIGRESSIVE, DISCURSIVE
epispastic .... VISICANT
episperm .... TESTA
epistaxis .... NOSEBLEED
epistle .... NOTE, LETTER,
  MESSAGE, BILLET(DOUX),
  MISSIVE
  wrote an .... JUDE
epitaph .... RIP, HERE LIES, HIC
  JACET, INSCRIPTION
epithem .... POULTICE
epithet .... OATH, CURSE,
  BYNAME, AGNOMEN,
  MISNOMER, SOBRIQUET
  for Alexander ...... THE GREAT
  Clemenceau .... TIGER
  Eric .... (THE)RED
  Ivan .... (THE)TERRIBLE
  Jackson .... STONEWALL
  Pitt .... IRONSIDE
  Schwarzkopf .... STORMIN'
  NORMAN
epitome ...... GIST, BRIEF, DIGEST,
  SUMMARY, ABSTRACT
epoch ...... AGE, EON, ERA, PERIOD
  Cenozoic .... EOCENE

epochal .... ERAL
epode .... AFTERSONG,
  (LYRIC)POEM
epopee .... EPOS, EPIC(POEM)
epoptic .... MYSTIC
epos .... EPIC
Epsom .... DOWNS, SALT(S)
  Downs event .... DERBY
equable .... CALM, EVEN, SERENE,
  STEADY, UNIFORM, TRANQUIL
equal .... TIE, DRAW, EVEN, SAME,
  ALIKE, MATCH, RIVAL,
  (COM)PEER, PARALLEL
  angled figure .... ISOGON
  combining form .... ISO, EQUI,
  PARI
  distribution of weight
  .... EQUIPOISE
  footing .... PAR
  make .... EQUATE
  quantity .... IDENTIC
  without .... PEERLESS,
  NONPAREIL
Equal Rights party
  .... LOCOFOCO
equalitarian of a kind
  .... DEMOCRAT
equality .... PARITY, BALANCE,
  EQUATION
  of laws/rights .... ISONOMY
  state .... WYOMING
equalizer ...... EVENER, CLINCHER,
  SOCKDOLAGER
equanimity .... POISE, REPOSE,
  CALMNESS, SERENITY,
  COMPOSURE, SANG-FROID,
  SELF-CONTROL
  colloquial .... COOL
equator crosser by ship
  .... SHELLBACK
  passes thru this country
  .... BRAZIL, ECUADOR,
  COLOMBIA
equatorial .... TORRID, SUBSOLAR,
  TROPICAL
Equatorial Guinea capital
  .... MALABO
  city/town .... BATA, LUBA,
  MBINI
  island .... BIOKO, CORISCO
  islands .... ELOBEY
  native .... BUBI, FANG
  president .... MACIAS
  territory ...... BIOKO, RIO MUNI
equestrian ...... RIDER, HORSEMAN
  order of knights .... EQUITES
equilateral figure .... RHOMB,
  TRIANGLE
equilibrist .... BALANCER, ROPE
  WALKER
equilibrium .... PARITY,

  BALANCE, COMPOSURE,
  (EQUI)POISE
  lacking .... ASTASIA
equine .... HORSE, HORSY
  cry .... NEIGH, WHINNY
  disease .... FARCY, LAMPAS,
  SPAVIN, LAMPERS, GLANDERS
  of yore .... MRED
  offspring .... FOAL
  pride of .... MANE
  sound .... SNORT
equip ...... ARM, RIG, GIRD, DIGHT,
  TRAIN, (OUT)FIT, FURNISH,
  APPOINT, PROVIDE
  for military service
  .... ACCOUTER, ACCOUTRE
equipage .... TRAIN, RETINUE,
  OUTFIT, TURN-OUT, CARRIAGE,
  FOLLOWING
equipment .... RIG, GEAR, OUTFIT,
  TACKLE, APPAREL, HARNESS,
  SUPPLIES, FURNISHINGS
equipoise .... EQUILIBRIUM,
  COUNTER-BALANCE
equisetum .... HORSETAIL
equitable .... FAIR, JUST, HONEST,
  ETHICAL, UNBIASED
equitant .... OVERLAPPING
equitation .... MANEGE,
  HORSEMANSHIP
equity .... RIGHT, JUSTICE,
  INTEREST, FAIRNESS, JUSTNESS
Equity initials .... AEA
  member .... ACTOR, PLAYER,
  ACTRESS
equivalent .... SAME, EQUAL,
  WORTH, ANALOG(OUS),
  TANTAMOUNT
equivocal .... EVASIVE, DOUBTFUL,
  AMBIGUOUS, ENIGMATIC,
  UNCERTAIN, UNDECIDED,
  MISLEADING
equivocate ...... HAW, LIE, DODGE,
  EVADE, FENCE, HEDGE,
  PALTER, WEASEL(OUT)
equivocation .... EVASION,
  QUIBBLE, RED-HERRING
equivoke .... PUN, AMBIGUITY
era .... AGE, EON, TIME, EPOCH,
  PERIOD
  flapper .... TWENTIES
eradicate .... ANNUL, ERASE,
  ABOLISH, DESTROY, EPILATE,
  (UP)ROOT, ROOT OUT, WIPE
  OUT, EXTERMINATE
erase .... CANCEL, DELE(TE),
  EFFACE, EXPUNGE,
  OBLITERATE
  slang .... KILL, RUB OUT
erased, can't be .... INDELIBLE
eraser .... RUBBER

Erbil .... ARBELA
ere ...... BEFORE, RATHER, IN TIME,
SOONER THAN
Erebus, place after .... HADES
erect .... REAR, BUILD, EXALT, SET
UP, PITCH, RAISE, STIFF,
CREATE, UPRIGHT, ASSEMBLE,
VERTICAL, CONSTRUCT
erelong .... ANON, SOON
eremite .... HERMIT, RECLUSE
erenow .... HERETOFORE
ergo .... HENCE, THEREFORE
ergon .... ERG, WORK
ergot .... FUNGUS
of rye .... SPUR
eri .... SILKWORM
eria .... BOMBYX
Eric Blair's alma mater
.... ETON
erica .... HEATH(ER)
Erie port .... SANDUSKY
Erin .... EIRE, IERNE, IRELAND,
OLD SOD, HIBERNIA
erinaceous animal .... HEDGEHOG
Erinyes .... ALECTO, FURIES,
MEGAERA, EUMENIDES,
TISIPHONE
eristic .... DISPUTANT,
ARGUMENTATIVE,
CONTROVERSIAL
Eritrea's capital .... ASMARA
neighbor .... ETHIOPIA
seaport .... MASSAUA,
MASSAWA
ermine .... STOAT, WEASEL
fur .... MINEVER, MINIVER
ern .... (SEA)EAGLE
erode .... ABRADE, EAT INTO,
DISINTEGRATE
erodent .... CAUSTIC
Eroica composer .... LISZT
key .... E FLAT
Eros .... GOD, AMOR, CUPID
erose .... GNAWED, UNEVEN,
IRREGULAR
erosion ...... ABRASION, FRICTION,
CORROSION
erotic .... SEXY, CARNAL, SEXUAL,
AMATIVE, AMATORY,
AMOROUS, LESBIAN, PAPHIAN
slang .... X-RATED
err .... NOD, SIN, FALL, SLIP, TRIP,
STRAY, WANDER, BLUNDER,
BARK UP THE WRONG TREE
in construction .... MISMAKE
errand .... TASK, MISSION
boy .... PAGE, CADDIE,
RUNNER, BELLHOP, BUTTONS
errant .... WRONG, ROVING,
TRUANT, ITINERANT,
WANDERING

erratic .... ODD, QUEER, VAGRANT,
OFF AND ON, WAYWARD,
ABNORMAL, PECULIAR,
ECCENTRIC, IRREGULAR,
CAPRICIOUS
erring .... SINNING
Errol, actor .... FLYNN
erroneous .... FALSE, WRONG,
REFUTED, UNTRUE, MISTAKEN
error .... SIN, FALL, MISS, SLIP,
FAULT, GAFFE, LAPSUS,
MISCUE, BLUNDER, FALLACY,
FALSITY, MISTAKE, UNTRUTH,
OVERSIGHT, WRONGDOING
colloquial ..... BONER, HOWLER
companion of .... TRIAL
in etiquette .... FAUX PAS
in naming .... MISNOMER
in one's reasoning .... FLAW
mental .... LAPSE
secretary's .... TYPO
slang .... GOOF, BLOOPER
error(s) in printing ...... ERRATA,
ERRATUM, MISPRINT
ersatz .... ARTIFICIAL, SUBSTITUTE
Erse .... CELT, GAEL, GAELIC
erst .... FIRST, LONG AGO,
FORMERLY
erstwhile .... ONCE, FORMER
erubescent .... REDDISH,
BLUSHING
eruct .... BELCH
erudite .... WISE, LEARNED,
LITERATE, SCHOLARLY
person .... PUNDIT
erudition .... LORE, WISDOM,
LEARNING, SCHOLARSHIP
erupt .... EMIT, BURST, EJECT,
EXPLODE
eruption .... BLAST, BLOW-UP,
OUTBREAK, OUTBURST,
EXPLOSION
of red spots on skin ..... RASH
eryngo .... SEA HOLLY
erysipelas .... CELLULITIS
Esau .... EDOM
brother (twin) of .... JACOB
descendant of .... EDOMITE
father-in-law of .... ELON
father of .... ISAAC
grandson of .... OMAR,
GATAM, KENAZ, TEMAN,
ZEPHO, ZERAH, AMALEK,
MIZZAH, NAHATH
mother of .... REBECCA,
REBEKAH
son of .... JALAM, JEUSH,
KORAH, REUEL, ELIPHAZ
wife of .... ADAH, JUDITH,
BASEMATH, OHOLIBAMAH
escadrille .... SQUADRON

escalade .... SCALE
escalate .... EXPAND, WORSEN,
INTENSIFY
escalator ...... STAIRWAY, MOVING
STAIRCASE
escalop .... MOLLUSK
escapade .... DIDO, CAPER, JAUNT,
PRANK, SPREE, FROLIC,
ADVENTURE
escape .... LAM, FLEE, LEAK, MISS,
AVOID, ELOPE, ELUDE, BOLT,
VENT, EVADE, DEFECT,
FLIGHT, EVASION, DISAPPEAR
colloquial .... SKIP OUT
device from an airplane
.... PARACHUTE
fire .... LADDER
from prison .... JAILBREAK
means of .... LOOPHOLE
narrow .... CLOSE CALL, CLOSE
SHAVE
slang .... GETAWAY, TAKE A
POWDER
escapee ...... REFUGEE, DEFECTOR,
RUNAWAY, DESERTER,
FUGITIVE
escargot .... SNAIL
escarole .... ENDIVE
escarpment .... CLIFF, SLOPE
eschalot .... ONION, SHALLOT,
SCALLION
eschar(a) .... SCAB, BRYOZOAN
escharotic .... CAUSTIC,
CORROSIVE
eschatology subject .... DEATH,
JUDGMENT, IMMORTALITY,
RESURRECTION
escheat .... CONFISCATE
eschew .... SHUN, AVOID
food .... FAST
eschewed by monkey trio
.... EVIL
escort .... DATE, WALK, GUARD,
USHER, ATTEND, CONDUCT,
(E)SQUIRE, RETINUE,
ACCOMPANY
armed .... CONVOY
kind of .... BEAU, POLICE,
OUTRIDER, BODYGUARD
lady's .... CAVALIER,
CABALLERO
paid .... GIGOLO
woman .... DUENNA,
CHAPERONE
escritoire .... DESK, TABLE,
SECRETARY
escrow .... BOND, DEED,
CONTRACT, AGREEMENT
escudo .... COIN
1/100 of .... CENTAVO
esculent .... EDIBLE, EATABLE,

COMESTIBLE
escutcheon .... CREST, (COAT OF)ARMS, TORSE, SHIELD
band .... FESS(E)
border .... ORLE
center .... FESSPOINT
point on .... NOMBRIL
vertical stripe .... PALLET
voided .... ORLE
Esdras .... EZRA, NEHEMIAH, APOCRYPHA
esker (eskar) .... OS, OSAR, RIDGE
Eskimo .... ITA, YUIT, ALEUT, HUSKY, INNUIT, ALASKAN, ESQUIMAU
boat .... UMIAK, OOMIAC
boatman .... KAYAKER
boot .... MUKLUK
canoe .... KAYAK, BAIDAR, OOMIAK, BIDARKA
dog .... HUSKY, MALEMUTE
garment .... PARKA, TEMIAK
Greenland .... ITA
house ...... IGLU, IGLOO, TOPEK
jacket .... ANORAK
knife .... ULU
medicine man .... ANGEKOK
memorial post .... XAT
settlement .... ETAH
transport .... SLED
esne .... SERF, SLAVE
esophagus .... GULA, GULLET, WEASAND
infection .... THRUSH, CANDIDIASIS
inflammation ..... ESOPHAGITIS
muscles contraction in the .... SPASM
narrowing of the .... STRICTURE
pain .... CARDIALGIA
rod for clearing ...... PROBANG
esoteric .... ARCANE, MYSTIC, OCCULT, PRIVATE, CONFIDENTIAL
doctrine .... CABALA
facts .... ESOTERICA
opposed to .... EXOTERIC
esotropia ...... SQUINT, CROSS-EYE
espalier .... LATTICE, TRELLIS, PALISADE
España .... SPAIN
o Alemania .... PAIS
esparto .... GRASS
especial .... SPECIAL, DETAILED, PARTICULAR, NOTEWORTHY, EXCEPTIONAL, OUTSTANDING
especially .... MAINLY, MOSTLY, CHIEFLY, ABOVE ALL
Esperanto .... IDO
deviser .... ZAMENHOF

espionage .... SPYING
American executed for ...... ETHEL ROSENBERG, JULIUS ROSENBERG
esplanade .... WALK, GLACIS, PROMENADE, ROADWAY
espousal .... WEDDING, ADVOCACY, MARRIAGE, BETROTHAL
espouse .... WED, AFFY, MATE, ADOPT, MARRY, ACCEPT, APPROVE, EMBRACE, SUPPORT, ADVOCATE, CRUSADE FOR
esprit de corps .... ELAN, MORALE, SPIRIT, CAMARADERIE
espy .... SEE, SPOT, SIGHT, BEHOLD, DESCRY, DISCERN
Esquimau .... ESKIMO
esquire .... ESCORT, NOBLEMAN, ATTENDANT, GENTLEMAN
ess .... CURVE
essay .... TOY, TEST, PAPER, TRACT, THEME, THESIS, ARTICLE, ATTEMPT, TREATISE
Essay on Man poet .... POPE
essayist .... LAMB, HOLMES, EMERSON
ess .... BEING, ESSENCE, EXISTENCE
essence .... ENS, NUB, ESSE, CORE, GIST, LIFE, PITH, ATTAR, BEING, HEART, ENTITY, KERNEL, FLAVOR, NATURE, ELEMENT, EXTRACT, PERFUME, REALITY, SUBSTANCE
of anything .... JUICE
Essene .... MYSTIC, ASCETIC
essential .... MUST, BASAL, BASIC, FOCAL, VITAL, NEEDFUL, PRIMARY, INHERENT, REQUIRED, INTRINSIC, REQUISITE, HYPOSTATIC
element .... PART
oil .... ATTAR, ESSENCE
oil liquid .... CINEOLE
part .... CORE, PITH, MEMBER
thing .... KEY, THE BOTTOM LINE
Essex city .... ILFORD
essonite .... GARNET
establish .... FIX, SET, ROOT, BUILD, FOUND, CREATE, DECIDE, FIRM UP, SETTLE, VERIFY, CONFIRM, ENSCONCE, ORGANIZE
by evidence .... PROVE
into law .... ENACT
securely .... EMBED, PLANT, RIVET, ENTRENCH
established value .... PAR
establishment .... FIRM, AGENCY,

CORPORATION
domestic .... MENAGE
estafet .... COURIER
estaminet .... CAFE
estancia .... RANCH(O)
estate .... LAND, RANK, ABODE, STATE, ASSETS, STATUS, CAPITAL, EFFECTS, FORTUNE, HOLDINGS, INTEREST, PROPERTY
a freehold .... ALOD, ALLODIUM
as in a tropical region .... PLANTATION
country .... HACIENDA
first .... CLERGY
fourth ...... PRESS, JOURNALISM
holder .... TERMOR
in expectancy ...... REMAINDER
landed .... MANOR, DOMAIN
lands of an .... DEMESNE
overseer .... BAILIFF
pertaining to a noble's .... DUCAL
second .... NOBILITY
Spanish-American .... ESTANCIA
third .... BOURGEOISIE
transfer .... DEMISE
under feudal lord .... FEUD, FIEF
esteem .... FAVOR, HONOR, PRIDE, PRIZE, VALUE, ADMIRE, REGARD, REVERE, RESPECT, WORSHIP
ester .... ACETIN, IODIDE, MALATE, OLEATE, PICRATE, STEARIN, SILICATE, GLYCERIDE
esthesia .... SENSATE
esthete .... CONNOISSEUR
esthetic .... ARTISTIC, TASTEFUL
esthetics .... ARTS
estimable .... WORTHY, DESERVING
estimate .... RATE, GAUGE, JUDGE, VALUE, ASSESS, RECKON, MEASURE, APPRAISE, CRITIQUE, EVALUATE, CALCULATE
in advance .... FORECAST
estimation ...... ESTEEM, REGARD, REPORT, REPUTE, OPINION, APPRAISAL, CRITICISM, CALCULATION
estivate .... SUMMER
opposed to .... HIBERNATE
Estonia, capital of .... TALLINN
city/town of .... NARVA, PARNU, PSKOV, TARTU
Estonian island .... OESEL
lake .... PEIPUS

estop .... BAR, PREVENT, OBSTRUCT
estovers .... NECESSARIES
allowed divorcee ..... ALIMONY
Estrada, actor .... ERIK
estrange .... PART, WEAN, DIVERT, ALIENATE, DISUNITE, SEPARATE, DISAFFECT
estrangement .... RIFT
estray .... WAIF
estriol .... HORMONE, THEELOL
estrone .... HORMONE, THEELIN
estrus .... HEAT, FRENZY
estuary .... ARM, BAY, RIA, LOCH, DELTA, FIORD, FJORD, FIRTH, FRITH, INLET, MOUTH
tidal wave .... BORE, EAGRE
esurient .... GREEDY, HUNGRY, VORACIOUS
et .... AND
al .... OTHERS
etagere .... WHATNOT
etamine .... CLOTH, VOILE
Etanin .... DRACONIS
etape .... ENCAMPMENT, STOREHOUSE
Etats .... UNIS
etc. ...... ET CETERA, AND OTHERS, AND SO FORTH
relative of .... ET AL
etch .... CUT, LINE, CARVE, CHISEL, ENGRAVE
etching .... STIPPLE, LITHOTINT
acid .... MORDANT
for one .... ART
Eteocles, brother of .... POLYNICES
kingdom .... THEBES
parent of .... JOCASTA, OEDIPUS
eternal .... AGELESS, ENDLESS, CONSTANT, FOREVER, INFINITE, (A)EONIAN, TIMELESS, PERPETUAL, EVERLASTING, NEVER ENDING
Eternal City .... ROME
The .... GOD
eternally .... EVER, ALWAYS, FOREVER, EVERMORE, CONSTANTLY, TILL DEATH
eternity ...... (A)EON, OLAM, TIME, INFINITY, IMMORTALITY
etesian .... ANNUAL, PERIODIC, SEASONAL
Ethan Frome's wife .... ZEENA
of '76 .... ALLEN
Ethanim .... TISHRI
ethanol .... (ETHYL)ALCOHOL
Ethel, performer .... MERMAN, BARRYMORE
ether .... AIR, SKY, OZONE, SPACE, HEAVENS

compound .... ESTER
use of .... SOLVENT, ANESTHETIC
ethereal .... AERY, AIRY, LIGHT, FRAGILE, DELICATE, HEAVENLY, SUPERNAL, CELESTIAL
fluid .... ICHOR
salt .... ESTER
ethical .... MORAL, RIGHT, DECENT, HONEST, VIRTUOUS
ethics ...... MORALS, MORAL CODE, STANDARDS, PRINCIPLES
Ethiopia .... ABYSSINIA
Biblical .... CUSH, KUSH
capital of .... ADDIS ABABA
Ethiopian antelope .... DIKDIK
ape .... GELADA
Black Jews .... FALASHA
capital, ancient .... MEROE
city/town .... ADWA, ZULA, ASOSA, ASSAB, AWASA, HARAR, JIMMA, SODDU, ASMARA, DESSYE, GONDAR, MAKALE, NAZRET, ASSELLE, MASSAWA, NAKAMTI, DIREDAWA
coin .... BESA, GIRSH, TALARI
cotton togs .... SHAMMA
district .... HARAR, AMHARA
fly .... ZIMB
Hamite .... AFAR, GALLA
Hamitic tribe member/ tribesman .... FALASHA
ibex .... SAOL, WALIE
king .... NEGUS, MEMNON
kingdom, former ..... AMHARA
lake .... ABABA, CHAMO, TANA, ZWAI, ASSALE, RUDOLF, TURKANA
language .... GEEZ, ARABIC, SIDAMO, SOMALI, AMHARIC
mountain .... BALE, GUGHE, RAS DASHAN
native .... NEGRO
nomadic .... GALLA
president .... HAILE MARIAM
prince .... RAS
province .... BALE, SHOA, ARUSI, HARAR, KAFFA, TIGRE, WALLO, GONDAR, SIDAMO, ERITREA, WALLAGA
queen .... CANDACE
river .... OMO, ABAY, BARO, DAWA, WABI, AKOBO, AWASH, FAFAN, ATBARA, TAKKAZE
seaport .... MASSAUA
table-mountain .... AMBA
title .... RAS, NEGUS
walled city .... GONDAR

wolf .... KABERU
ethnarch .... GOVERNOR
ethnic .... LINEAL, RACIAL, GENETIC, HEATHEN
affiliation .... ETHNICITY
division, ancient .... TRIBE
group .... FOLK, RACE, NATIONALITY
ethologist .... LORENZ
ethos .... BELIEF, MANNER, CULTURE, IDEOLOGY
opposed to .... PATHOS
ethyl .... GASOLINE
alcohol .... ETHANOL
derivative .... ETHER
etiolate .... BLANCH, BLEACH
etiquette ...... CUSTOM, DECORUM, MANNERS, PROPRIETY
breach of .... FAUX PAS, SOLECISM
expert .... POST, BALDRIDGE
required by .... DE RIGUER
Etna .... LAMP, VOLCANO
Eton .... TOWN, SCHOOL
article of wear .... COAT, COLLAR, JACKET
rival of .... HARROW
student .... OPPIDAN
Etruscan god .... LAR(ES), TINIA, TURMS, PENATES
goddess .... UNI, TURAN, MENFRA
king .... PORSENA
Minerva .... MENFRA
Etta of comic strips .... KETT
etude .... OPUS, PIECE, STUDY
etui/etwee .... CASE
item .... NEEDLE
etymological .... LITERAL
etymon .... ROOT, RADIX
Etzel .... ATTILA
eucalyptol .... CINEOLE
eucalyptus .... YATE, MALLEE, IRONBARK
Eucharist .... RITE, HOUSEL, EULOGIA, COMMUNION, SACRAMENT
box .... PIX, PYX
bread .... HOST, WAFER
cloth .... FANON
cup for the consecrated wafers .... CIBORIUM
cup for the wine .... CALIX, CHALICE
oblation .... HOST, WINE, BREAD, OFFERING
to dying person ..... VIATICUM
vessel .... AMA, PATEN
wafer .... HOST
wine of the .... OBLATION
eucharistic plate .... PATEN

service .... LITURGY
vestment ...... FANON, MANIPLE
Euclid .... MATHEMATICIAN
forte of .... GEOMETRY
work on geometry
.... ELEMENTS
eudaemonia .... HAPPINESS
euge .... BRAVO
eugenics, pioneer in ...... GALTON
subject of ...... RACES, BREEDS
eulogia .... EUCHARIST
eulogistic .... ELOGE, MAGNIFIC,
LAUDATORY
eulogize .... LAUD, EXTOL, PRAISE
eulogy .... ELOGE, PRAISE,
TRIBUTE, ENCOMIUM,
PANEGYRIC
Eumenides .... FURIES, ERINYES
eunuch .... GELDING,
CHAMBERLAIN
euphemism for hell .... HECK
euphonium, like .... TUBA
euphony .... METER, MELODY
euphorbia .... SPURGE,
POINSETTIA
euphoria ...... CONTENT, ELATION,
PLEASURE, HAPPINESS,
SMUGNESS, WELL BEING
slang .... HIGH
Euphrosyne .... JOY
euphuism .... BOMBAST
Eurasian in India .... FERINGI,
FERINGHEE
range .... URAL
region, one-time .... TATARY
eureka .... AHA, SEE,
EXCLAMATION
euripus .... STRAIT, CHANNEL
Europa's father .... OGENOR
lover .... ZEUS
European ...... BALT, DANE, FINN,
LAPP, LETT, SERB, SLAV,
FRANK, GREEK, SWEDE,
BOHUNK, FRENCH, ITALIAN,
SPANIARD
alliance: abbr. .... NATO
ancient language .... NORSE
antelope .... CHAMOIS
apple tree .... SORB
aromatic herb .... FLEAWORT
ash tree juice .... MANNA
bay .... BISCAY
beetle .... DORBUG,
COCKCHAFER
bellflower .... RAMPION
bird .... HOOPOE, ROLLER,
TURNIX, REEDLING, WHIMBREL
bison .... AUROCHS
blackbird .... MERLE, OUSEL,
OUZEL
blenny .... SHANNY

"Boot" .... ITALY
brantail .... REDSTART
bunting .... ORTOLAN
buttercup .... GOLDILOCKS
butterfly .... RED ADMIRAL
canal .... KIEL
capital ..... OSLO, BERN, BOON,
ROME, PARIS, SOFIA, ATHENS,
BERLIN, LISBON, LONDON,
MADRID, MOSCOW, TIRANE,
VIENNA, WARSAW, BELFAST,
BELGRADE, BRUSSELS,
BUDAPEST, HELSINKI,
VALLETTA, THE HAGUE,
AMSTERDAM, BUCHAREST,
EDINBURGH, STOCKHOLM,
COPENHAGEN
carp .... BLEAK
catfish .... SILURID
cavalryman .... U(H)LAN,
HUSSAR
cereal grass .... MILLET
chestnut .... MARRON
chicken .... HAMBURG
coal region .... SAAR
commercial weight
.... CENTNER
country .... ITALY, MALTA,
SPAIN, FRANCE, GREECE,
NORWAY, POLAND, SWEDEN,
ALBANIA, AUSTRIA, BELGIUM,
DENMARK, ENGLAND,
FINLAND, GERMANY,
HUNGARY, ICELAND, IRELAND,
ROMANIA, PORTUGAL,
NETHERLANDS, YUGOSLAVIA
country, ancient ..... HELVETIA
crow .... CHOUGH,
NUTCRACKER
deer .... STAG, FALLOW
diving duck .... POCHARD
dog .... SETTER, BULLDOG,
GRIFFON, SPANIEL, TERRIER,
FOXHOUND, SHEPHERD,
GREYHOUND, WOLFHOUND
dormouse .... LEROT
dotterel .... PLOVER
duck .... SMEW, POCHARD,
WIDGEON
falcon .... HOBBY, MERLIN,
LANNER(ET)
finch .... SERIN, SISKIN
fish .... IDE, BOCE, RUDD,
BARBEL, PLAICE, GUDGEON
flatfish .... BRILL
fly .... FRIT
food fish .... SCAD, SAUREL
food seed .... LUPINE
gamebird .... TURNIX
garlic .... MOLY
grosbeak .... HAWFINCH

gulf .... LIONS, BOTHNIA,
FINLAND, TARANTO
hawk .... PUTTOCK
haybird .... BLACKCAP
health resort .... EMS, BADEN
herb .... BASIL, LOVAGE,
TERRAGON, ELECAMPANE
herring .... SPRAT
holly .... ACEBO
in India .... FERINGI
iris .... ORRIS
island .... ELBA, CRETE,
LESVOS, SICILY, CORSICA,
MAJORCA, BORNHOLM,
SARDINIA
islands ..... ORKNEY, CHANNEL,
FRISIAN, LOFOTEN, BALEARIC,
SHETLAND
juniper .... CADE
kite .... GLED(E)
lake .... ONEGA, GENEVA,
LADOGA, BALATON
land .... EIRE
mignonette .... WELD, WOLD
mint .... CLARE, CLAR(R)Y,
HYSSOP
mountain .... EL BRUS
mountains .... ALPS, URAL,
BALKAN, KJOLEN, CAUCASUS,
PYRENESS, CARPATHIAN
mountain goat .... IBEX
mustard herbs .... RAPES
news agency .... HAVAS
nobleman .... EARL, BARON,
COUNT
nomad .... LAPP
oak/tree .... HOLM, DURMAST
oriole .... LORIOT
pea .... LICORICE
plant .... COMFREY, LAVENDER,
LICORICE, ELECAMPANE,
ALFILARIA
plover .... DOTT(E)REL
polecat .... FITCH, FOUMART
poppy .... WINDROSE
principality .... MONACO,
ORANGE, WALACHIA
rabbit .... CONEY
range (see mountains)
ratlike animal .... HAMSTER
ray .... THORNBACK
river ...... PO, BUG, DON, EBRO,
ELBE, ODER, SAVA, ARAKS,
DOURO, DRAVA, LOIRE, RHINE,
RHONE, SEINE, TIBER, VOLGA,
WESER, DANUBE, DONETS,
GARONNE, VISTULA, GUADIANA
river to Caspian Sea
.... VOLGA
river to the Rhine .... MOSEL
robin .... RUDDOCK

rodent .... DORMOUSE
rose .... EGLANTINE
rose tree .... MEDLAR
sea ..... BLACK, NORTH, WHITE,
AEGEAN, BALTIC, BARENTS,
CASPIAN, MARMARA,
ADRIATIC, TYRRHENIAN
shad .... ALOSE
shark .... TOPE
shore bird .... WHIMBREL
shrub .... MEZEREON,
OLEASTER
slang .... BOHUNK
smelt .... SPARLING
songbird .... TIT, MAVIS,
OUSEL, LINNET, THRUSH,
REDWING, THROSTLE,
WHITETHROAT
squirrel .... SUSLIK
strait .... DENMARK, BOSPORUS,
KATTEGAT, GIBRALTAR
sumac .... TEREBINTH
swallow ..... MARTIN, MARTLET
thrush .... MAVIS, OUSEL,
MISSEL, FIELDFARE
tourist quarters .... PENSIONS
volcano .... ETNA
vulture .... LAMMERGEI(E)R
water bird .... GARGANEY
wheat .... SPELT
wild duck .... WI(D)GEON,
SHELDRAKE
wild goose .... GRAYLAG,
GREYLAG
woodpigeon .... CUSHAT,
RINGDOVE
wormwood .... SANTONICA
Eustachian tube .... SALPINX
euthanasia .... MERCY-KILLING
euthenics subject .... RACES,
BREEDS
Eva .... GABOR
Marie .... SAINT
evacuant ...... EMETIC, CATHARTIC
evacuate .... EMIT, QUIT, VOID,
CLEAR, EJECT, EMPTY, EXPEL,
LEAVE, (RE)MOVE, VACATE,
ABANDON, EXCRETE,
WITHDRAW
evacuation .... DEPARTURE
evacuee ...... REFUGEE, DISPLACED
PERSON
evade .... GEE, FOIL, SHUN, AVOID,
DODGE, ELUDE, ESCAPE
direct action ..... SHADOW-BOX
payment .... BILK
the issue .... BEG THE
QUESTION
work .... SHIRK, MALINGER,
GOLDBRICK
evaginate .... EVERT

evaluate .... RATE, ASSAY, GAUGE,
PRICE, VALUE, ASSESS,
ANALYZE, APPRAISE,
ESTIMATE
evaluation .... VIEW, RATING,
OPINION, ANALYSIS,
APPRAISAL
evanesce .... FADE, VANISH,
DISAPPEAR
evanescent .... LOST, MISSING,
FLEETING, EPHEMERAL,
TRANSIENT, VANISHING
evangel .... GOSPEL
evangelical .... APOSTOLIC
Evangeline, author of
.... LONGFELLOW
home of .... ACADIA
locale .... GRAND PRE
evangelist .... JOHN, LUKE, MARK,
MATTHEW, PREACHER,
MISSIONARY, REVIVALIST
Graham .... BILLY
McPherson .... AIMEE
Mormon .... PATRIARCH
Evans, Mary Ann .... ELIOT
evaporate .... DRY, ESCAPE,
VANISH, DISTILL, EMANATE
evaporating quickly
.... VOLATILE
evasion .... SALVO, TRICK,
ELUSION, AVOIDANCE,
SUBTERFUGE, EQUIVOCATION
tax .... NONPAYMENT
evasive .... SHIFTY, TRICKY,
ELUSIVE, EQUIVOCAL
eve .... EVENING
of festival .... VIGIL
even .... FAIR, FLAT, JUST, TIED,
TRUE, EQUAL, LEVEL, PLAIN,
STILL, SMOOTH, STEADY,
UNIFORM, STRAIGHT
break .... FAIR SHAKE
chance .... TOSSUP
colloquial .... QUITS
if .... ALBEIT, THO(UGH),
ALTHOUGH
item .... KEEL
minded/tempered .... CALM,
PLACID, SERENE, EQUABLE
slang .... HUNKY
so .... AT THAT
standing .... PAR
surface .... PLANE
evener .... HALTER, BALANCER,
EQUALIZER
evenfall .... DUSK, TWILIGHT
evenhanded .... FAIR, JUST,
NEUTRAL, IMPARTIAL
evening .... DUSK, SUNDOWN,
GLOAMING, NIGHTFALL
affair .... SOIREE

deadline .... CURFEW
dress .... GOWN, TUXEDO
glory .... SUNSET
love song .... SERENADE
of .... VESPERTINE
poetic .... EEN, EVE, EVEN
prayer/service .... ANGELUS,
VESPER(S), EVENSONG
star .... MOON, VENUS, VESPER,
HESPER(US)
evensong .... VESPERS
event .... CASUS, ISSUE, AFFAIR,
RESULT, HOLIDAY, INCIDENT,
OCCASION, HAPPENING,
OCCURRENCE
causing or provoking war
.... CASUS BELLI
early Boston .... MASSACRE,
TEA PARTY
January .... WHITE SALE
of 1849 .... GOLDRUSH
of June 1953 ..... CORONATION
spurred by Sam Adams,
1773 .... BOSTON TEA
PARTY
sudden .... HAP
eventful .... NEWSY, BUSTLING,
MOMENTOUS
eventide .... DUSK, VESPER,
EVENING, TWILIGHT
eventual .... FINAL, COMING,
ULTIMATE
eventuality .... ADVENT, ARRIVAL,
PROSPECT, CONTINGENCY
eventually .... FINALLY,
ULTIMATELY, IN THE LONG
RUN, SOONER OR LATER
eventuate .... TURN, HAPPEN,
RESULT
ever .... AYE, ONCE, ALWAYS,
FOREVER, ETERNALLY,
REPEATEDLY
Everest conqueror .... (SIR
EDMUND)HILLARY,
(TENZING)NORGAY
inhabitant, alleged .... YETI,
ABOMINABLE SNOWMAN
peak .... LHOTSE
rival .... ANNAPURNA
Everett .... CHAD
everglade .... SWAMPLAND
denizen .... (ALLI)GATOR
Everglade State .... FLORIDA
evergreen .... FRESH, CONIFER,
SAVIN(E), UNFADING,
PERENNIAL, EVER-BLOOMING
bean .... CAROB
genus .... ABIES, PINUS,
CEDRUS
giant .... REDWOOD, SEQUOIA
herb .... GALAX

needles, dried ..... PINE STRAW
oak .... HOLM, ILEX
opposed to .... DECIDUOUS
poisonous .... OLEANDER
shrub .... TITI, ROSEMARY,
OLEANDER, LEATHERWOOD
tree .... FIR, YEW, PINE,
CEDAR, LARCH, OLIVE,
DEODAR, SPRUCE, HEMLOCK,
MADRONA, BALSAM-FIR
tree, nut bearing ...... CASHEW
tree bark .... CASSIA
tree fruit .... CONE
everlasting .... AGELESS,
AGELONG, ETERN(E),
DURABLE, CONSTANT,
ETERNAL, ETERNITY,
UNENDING, CEASELESS,
PERPETUAL
Evert .... CHRIS
everted .... INSIDE OUT
every .... ALL, EACH, ENTIRE
combining form .... PANT(O)
dog has this day? .... NIGHT
TO HOWL
**everybody's unfavorite
(Federal agency)** .... IRS
everyday .... DAILY, USUAL,
COMMON, ROUTINE, HABITUAL
everything .... ALL
slang .... THE WORKS
that .... WHATSO
everywhere .... UBIQUE, ALL
OVER, HIGH AND LOW, ALL
ALONG THE LINE, ALL OVER
THE WORLD
at the same time
..... UBIQUITOUS, OMNIPRESENT
combining form .... OMNI
Eve's first son .... CAIN
husband .... ADAM
second son .... ABEL
third son .... SETH
evict .... OUST, EJECT, EXPEL, PUT
OUT, REMOVE
evidence .... SIGN, PROOF,
INDICATION
based on something witness
heard .... HEARSAY
indirect .... CIRCUMSTANTIAL
indisputable ..... SMOKING GUN
evident ...... OPEN, CLEAR, PLAIN,
PATENT, OBVIOUS, APPARENT,
DISTINCT, MANIFEST,
PALPABLE
evil ...... BAD, BASE, VILE, CURSE,
WRONG, HARMFUL,
DEPRAVITY, PECCANT,
OFFENSIVE, DISGUSTING,
WICKEDNESS, MALEFIC(ENT)
act .... CRIME, IMPIETY

behavior .... CORRUPTION,
IMMORALITY
child .... IMP
colloquial .... JINX
combining form .... MAL
deed .... SIN, PECCANCY
eye .... OGLE, GLOWER,
WHAMMY
for evil .... REVENGE,
RETALIATION
habit .... VICE
intent .... DOLUS, MALICE
intent: law .... MALICE
AFORETHOUGHT
looking .... GRIM, UGLY
minded ..... WICKED, NOXIOUS,
VICIOUS, PRURIENT, SPITEFUL,
LECHEROUS, MALICIOUS,
SALACIOUS, BLACKHEARTED
motivation .... HATE, SPITE,
GRUDGE, HATRED, MALICE,
ILL-WILL, ANIMOSITY,
ANTIPATHY
person .... BULLY, CAITIFF,
HOODLUM, RUFFIAN, VILLAIN,
CRIMINAL, EVILDOER,
GANGSTER, DESPERADO,
MISCREANT
slang .... BAD NEWS
smelling .... STINKING,
MALODOROUS
spirit .... DEMON, FIEND,
DAEMON, INCUBUS, SUCCUBUS,
CACODEMON
spirit, bloodsucker
.... VAMPIRE
spirit, taken by ..... POSSESSED
spirit, woman .... HAG
spirit that feeds on flesh of
the dead .... GHOUL
wishing .... MALIGNANT
evildoer .... SINNER, CON-MAN,
GUN-MAN, BETRAYER,
MURDERER, SCALAWAG,
SWINDLER
convicted .... FELON, CRIMINAL
guilty of treason ..... TRAITOR,
CONSPIRATOR
slang .... RAT, HOOD,
MOBSTER, PLUG-UGLY
with snakes for hair
.... GORGON, MEDUSA
who betrayed Jesus Christ
.... JUDAS ISCARIOT
who betrayed Samson
.... DELILAH
who maliciously destroys
property .... VANDAL
who rules oppressively
.... DESPOT, TYRANT

who turned men into swine
.... CIRCE
who willfully destroys
property by fire
.... ARSONIST, INCENDIARY
evince .... SHOW, DISPLAY,
EXHIBIT, SIGNIFY, INDICATE,
MANIFEST
evincible/evincive ...... APODICTIC
eviscerate ...... GUT, DISEMBOWEL
Evita .... PERON
evitable .... AVOIDABLE
evocation ...... BIDDING, CALLING,
SUMMONS
evoke .... CALL, DRAW, EDUCE,
ELICIT, INVOKE, RECALL,
REMIND, SUMMON, BRING TO
MIND
evolution .... GROWTH, MUTATION,
EXPANSION, DEVELOPMENT
theorist .... DARWIN, LAMARCK
theory of .... DARWINISM
theory of organic
.... LAMARCKISM
**evolutionary development of
plant or animal**
.... PHYLOGENY
evolve .... EXPAND, MATURE,
SEASON, DIG OUT, UNFOLD,
DEVELOP, UNRAVEL, WORK
OUT
Evreux is capital of .... EURE
ewe .... SHEEP
mate of .... RAM
-necked animal .... DOG,
HORSE
"old" .... CRONE
udder inflammation
.... GARGET
ewer .... JUG, PITCHER
ex .... FORMER, PREVIOUS(LY)
fighter .... VET(ERAN)
_____ : from seat of authority
.... CATHEDRAL
libris .... BOOKPLATE
newscaster Newman
.... EDWIN
parte .... ONE-SIDED
post facto .... AFTER THE DEED
preposition .... WITHOUT
spouse .... DIVORCÉ(E)
TV city editor .... ASNER
exacerbate .... IRE, IRK, VEX,
ANNOY, ENRAGE, EMBITTER,
IRRITATE, AGGRAVATE
exact .... LEVY, TAKE, BLEED,
CLAIM, FORCE, WRING,
DEMAND, RIGOROUS, EXTORT,
IMPOSE, SEVERE, STRICT,
CORRECT, LITERAL, PRECISE,
REQUIRE, ACCURATE

copy .... CLONE, DUPLICATE
moment .... POINT
money .... LUG
satisfaction .... AVENGE
translation .... WORD-FOR-
WORD
exacting ones .... PURISTS
exaction .... TAX, TOLL,
EXTORTION
ancient .... TRIBUTE
exactitude .... ACCURACY,
PRECISION
exactly .... TOOT, JUSTLY,
RIGHTLY
the same words ..... VERBATIM
exaggerate .... PUFF, BOAST,
EXPAND, ENHANCE, MAGNIFY,
LAY IT ON, STRETCH,
EMBROIDER, OVERSTATE,
OVEREMPHASIZE
tendency to .... MYTHOMIA
exaggerated .... TALL, OUTRE,
STEEP, OVERDONE, EXCESSIVE,
HIGH-FLOWN, PREPOSTEROUS
comedy .... FARCE
pious feeling .... PIETISM
praise ...... PUFFERY, FLATTERY
spending .... EXTRAVAGANCE
exaggeration ...... YARN, FALSITY,
TALL TALE, DISTORTION,
OVERSTATEMENT
for effect .... HYPERBOLE
of distinguishing features
.... CARICATURE
slang .... COCK-AND-BULL
STORY
exalt .... ELATE, EXTOL, HONOR,
RAISE, PRAISE, UPLIFT,
ELEVATE, GLORIFY
exaltation ...... ASCENT, ELATION,
RAPTURE, ELEVATION,
CONSECRATION
exalted ...... HIGH, LOFTY, NOBLE,
NOTED, TIPSY, STRONG,
EMINENT, HONORED, SUBLIME,
GLORIOUS
examination .... QUIZ, TRIAL,
INQUIRY, SCRUTINY,
TEST(ING), INSPECTION
aid .... X-RAY
colloq. .... EXAM
for uterine cancer .... PAP
TEST
general medical ...... PHYSICAL
of dead body .... AUTOPSY,
NECROPSY
school .... FINAL, MIDTERM
examine .... TEST, LOOK AT,
EXPLORE, INQUIRE, INSPECT
a court decision again
.... REVIEW

a job applicant ..... INTERVIEW
a person for something
concealed .... SEARCH
a witness .... QUESTION,
INTERROGATE
accounts/books .... AUDIT
by touching .... PALPATE
carefully .... SCAN
closely/in detail .... PERUSE,
SCRUTINIZE
for some specific purpose
.... REVIEW, SURVEY
judicially .... TRY
with robbery in mind
.... CASE
examiner .... EYER, CENSOR,
TESTER, INSPECTOR
books of accounts
.... AUDITOR
diagnostic .... PHYSICIAN,
RADIOLOGIST
post mortem .... CORONER
scholastic .... TEACHER,
PROFESSOR
tax .... REVENUER
example ...... CASE, COPY, MODEL,
SAMPLE, PATTERN, INSTANCE,
PARADIGM, SPECIMEN,
STANDARD, PRECEDENT,
(ARCHE)TYPE
examples, perfect .... IDEALS
set of .... PRAXIS
exasperate .... IRK, TRY, VEX,
ROIL, ANGER, ANNOY, PEEVE,
ENRAGE, NETTLE, OFFEND,
RANKLE, RUFFLE, INCENSE,
IRRITATE, INFURIATE
exasperation .... IRE, PIQUE,
ANGER, WRATH, DISGUST
excaudate .... TAILLESS
excavate .... DIG, HOE, SCOOP,
DREDGE, EXHUME, UNEARTH,
HOLLOW OUT
further .... DEEPEN
excavation .... PIT, HOLE, MINE,
SHAFT, CAVITY, HOLLOW,
QUARRY, OPENING
mining .... STOPE
excavator .... DIGGER, DREDGE(R),
SCOOP(ER)
exceed .... BEAT, PASS, EXCEL,
OUTDO, SURPASS, OUTREACH
exceedingly .... UNCO, VERY,
EXTREMELY
archaic .... AMAIN
excel .... BEST, STAR, OUTDO,
EXCEED, ECLIPSE, SURPASS,
TRANSCEND
excellence .... MERIT, VIRTU(E),
GOODNESS, PRESTIGE,
GREATNESS, SUPERIORITY

excellent ...... A-ONE, RARE, TOPS,
SUPER, PEACHY, SUPERB,
CAPITAL, RIPPING, SPLENDID,
TOPNOTCH, BRILLIANT,
OUTSTANDING
except .... BAR, BUT, OMIT, SAVE,
OBJECT, EXCLUDE
for .... ASIDE
that .... UNLESS
exception .... OMISSION,
CHALLENGE, EXCLUSION,
OBJECTION, RESERVATION
in law .... SAVING
take .... DEMUR, OBJECT,
REJECT, RESENT
exceptional .... RARE, SPECIAL,
UNUSUAL, ESPECIAL,
UNCOMMON, OUTSTANDING
excerpt .... QUOTE, SELECT,
EXTRACT, PASSAGE
excess .... EXTRA, NIMIETY,
SURFEIT, OVER(AGE),
PLETHORA, (SUR)PLUS,
REMAINDER, INTEMPERANCE
of solar over lunar year
.... EPACT
excessive .... ULTRA, UNDUE,
EXTREME, EXORBITANT,
IMMODERATE, INORDINATE,
EXTRAVAGANT
affection .... DOTAGE
combining form .... HYPER
demand .... EXACTION,
EXTORTION
formality .... RED TAPE
in belief .... RABID
joy ...... RAPTURE, EXALTATION
saliva secretion ...... PTYALISM
supply .... SPATE
vomiting .... HYPEREMESIS
zeal .... FANATICISM
excessively ...... OVERLY, UNDULY,
EXTREMELY
caustic .... ACRID
detailed report .... RED TAPE
expensive .... PROHIBITIVE
fond .... DOTING
exchange .... SWAP, BANDY,
BARTER, TRUCK, MARKET,
RIALTO, SWITCH, COMMUTE,
COMMERCE
business .... BONDS, SHARES,
STOCKS, CURRENCY
discount/fee/premium
.... AGIO
for money .... SELL
goods .... TRADE
letters .... NYSE
medium .... SYCEE
of shots .... GUNPLAY
stock .... BOURSE

visit .... GAM

exchequer .... FISC, FUNDS, FINANCES, TREASURY

excide .... CUT OUT, EXCISE, REMOVE

excise ...... TAX, DUTY, TOLL, CUT OUT, IMPOST, REMOVE, EXSCIND

tax collector .... GA(U)GER

excitable .... HOT, EDGY, FIERY, NERVOUS, HOT-HEADED

excite .... BURN, RAGE, RANT, RILE, ROIL, PIQUE, (A)ROUSE, SEETHE, STIR(UP), AGITATE, FLUSTER, PROVOKE, STARTLE, TITILLATE

excited ...... AGOG, ASTIR, HET UP, AGITATED, (A)DITHER, BOILING, BURNING, SEETHING

greatly ..... FRANTIC, FRENZIED

nervously .... FEVERISH

slang .... UPTIGHT

state .... FEY

excitement .... BUZZ, FUSS, HEAT, STIR, TO-DO, FEVER, FUROR, TIZZY, THRILL, FLUTTER, COMMOTION

pleasurable .... KICK

reducer .... SEDATIVE

exciting .... HEADY, ELECTRIC, STRIKING, THRILLING

exclaim .... SHOUT, CRY OUT, EJACULATE

exclamation .... AH, BAH, FIE, GEE, HAH, GOSH, NUTS, OH MY, POOH, PUGH, RATS, PSHAW, OUTCRY, SHUCKS, INTERJECTION

of a skeptic .... UNBELIEVABLE

of aversion/disgust .... UGH, PAH

of contempt .... BAH

of disbelief .... UMPH

of joy .... WHOOPEE

of pain .... YOW, OUCH

of praise .... HOSANNA, ADORATION

of regret .... ALAS

of sorrow .... ALACK

of success .... VOILÀ

of triumph .... EUREKA

point .... SCREAMER

to attract attention .... HEY

exclave, example of ...... PRUSSIA

exclude .... BAR, OMIT, EJECT, EXPEL, EXCEPT, REJECT, ISOLATE, BLACKLIST

by general consent .... BANISH, OSTRACIZE

from joining an organization .... BLACKBALL

from some right or privilege .... (DE)BAR

exclusion .... EXILE, BANISHMENT, QUARANTINE, SEGREGATION

exclusive .... ONLY, POSH, SOLE, CLOSED, SELECT, SINGLE

control .... MONOPOLY

of .... EX

set .... ELITE

excommunicate ...... BAN, DAMN, EXPEL, CONDEMN

excommunication .... BAN, ANATHEMA, EXCISION, CONDEMNATION

excoriate .... FLAY, CHAFE, ABRADE, DENOUNCE

excoriation .... ABUSE, ABRASION

excrement .... DUNG, FECES, MANURE, REFUSE

excrescence .... STUD, WART, APPENDAGE, OUTGROWTH

example of ..... HAIR, BUNION, FINGERNAIL

excreta .... SWEAT, URINE

excrete .... EGEST, EXUDE

excretion .... SWEAT, URINE, PERSPIRATION

excruciate .... PAIN, AGONIZE, TORMENT, TORTURE

exculpate .... CLEAR, ACQUIT, ABSOLVE, EXONERATE

excursion .... TOUR, JAUNT, JUNKET, OUTING, (SIDE)TRIP

coach .... CHARABANC

excursive .... RAMBLING, WANDERING

excusable .... VENIAL

excuse .... PLEA, ALIBI, DODGE, SALVO, ABSOLVE, APOLOGY, JUSTIFY, PRETEXT, RELEASE, OVERLOOK

for absence .... ESSOIN

partial .... EXTENUATION

excused .... IMMUNE

execrable .... HATEFUL, ABOMINABLE, DETESTABLE

execrate .... HATE, ABHOR, CURSE, DETEST, LOATHE

execute .... DO, HANG, KILL, SIGN, ENACT, FULFILL, PERFORM

unlawfully .... LYNCH

execution by burning ...... STAKE

by drowning .... NOYADE

by hanging .... SWING, HALTER, STRETCH

executioner .... HANGER, HANGMAN, HEADSMAN, DEATHSMAN

gangland's .... HITMAN, HATCHETMAN

executive .... OFFICER, OFFICIAL

privilege .... PERKS

Executive Mansion .... WHITE HOUSE

exegesis .... EXPLANATION

exemplar .... MODEL, MIRROR, EXAMPLE, PATTERN, (ARCHE)TYPE, SPECIMEN

exempt .... FREE, SPARE, EXCUSE(D), IMMUNE, RELEASE

exemption from punishment .... IMMUNITY, IMPUNITY

temporary .... GRACE

exequies .... FUNERAL, OBSEQUIES

exercise .... USE, DRILL, EXERT, TRAIN, WORRY, HARASS, LESSON, PRAXIS, PERPLEX, PROBLEM, AEROBICS, PRACTICE, EMPLOY(MENT)

exercises, athletic .... RUNNING, SWIMMING, CALISTHENICS

set of .... PRAXIS

squatting .... YOGA

trained .... MANEGE

exert .... STRAIN, STRIVE, EXERCISE, STRUGGLE

oneself to meet a challenge .... RISE TO

slang ..... BURN THE MIDNIGHT OIL

exertion .... DINT, EFFORT, ENERGY

exeunt .... EXIT

exfoliate .... PEEL, SHED, CAST OFF

exhalation .... AURA, FUME, BREATH, HALITUS, EMANATION, EXPIRATION, EVAPORATION

huge .... GIANT SIGH

exhale ...... EXPIRE, BREATHE OUT, EVAPORATE

exhaust .... FAG, TIRE, DRAIN, SPEND, USE UP, DEPLETE

exhausted .... DONE, ALL IN, EMPTY, SPENT, TIRED, EFFETE, USED UP

exhibit .... SHOW, STAGE, EXPOSE, DISPLAY, PRESENTATION

in law ...... PROOF, DOCUMENT, EVIDENCE

of difficult rides .... RODEO

exhibited .... ON VIEW

exhibiting .... SHOWING, FLAUNTING, DISPLAYING

a play of colors .... OPALESCING

exhibition .... FAIR, DISPLAY, PAGEANTRY, SPECTACLE

international .... EXPOSITION

place for historical objects .... MUSEUM

253

place for works of art
.... SALON, GALLERY
exhibitionist .... SHOW-OFF
exhilarate .... ELATE, PEP UP,
ANIMATE, ENLIVEN, GLADDEN,
STIMULATE
exhilaration .... ANIMATION,
LIVELINESS
exhort ...... EGG ON, PROD, URGE,
INCITE, ADMONISH
exhume .... DIG OUT, RECALL,
UNEARTH, DISINTER
exigency .... NEED, CRISIS,
DEMAND, URGENCY,
EMERGENCY
exigent .... URGENT, CRITICAL,
EXACTING, PRESSING
exiguous .... SMALL, LITTLE,
MEAGER, SCANTY
exile .... OUST, EXPEL, DEPORT,
REMOVE, RELEGATE,
BANISH(MENT), EXPATRIATE
island .... ELBA
exist .... BE, IS, ARE, (A)LIVE
existence .... ENS ESSE, LIFE,
BEING, LIVING, PRESENCE,
ACTUALITY
coming into .... NASCENT
type of .... A DOG'S LIFE
existent .... ALIVE, FACTUAL,
PRESENT
existing .... FACT, REAL, ALIVE,
EXTANT
between galaxies
.... INTERGALACTIC
exit .... ISSUE, LEAVE, EGRESS,
OUTLET, WAY OUT,
DEPART(URE)
dramatically ...... GO OUT IN A
BLAZE OF GLORY
surreptitiously .... SNEAK
exocarp .... RIND
exodus .... FLIGHT, HEGIRA,
DEPARTURE, EMIGRATION
hero .... ARI
leader .... MOSES
scene .... RED SEA
Exodus author .... URIS
exogen .... DICOTYLEDON
exogenous .... ENTHETIC
exonerate .... CLEAR, ACQUIT,
ABSOLVE, EXCULPATE
exorbitant .... DEAR, UNDUE,
EXCESSIVE, EXPENSIVE,
IMMODERATE
interest .... USURY
exorcise .... EXPEL, CAST OUT
exorcism .... EXPULSION
exordial .... INTRODUCTORY
exordium .... PROEM, PREFACE,
OPENING, OVERTURE,

BEGINNING
exoteric .... PUBLIC, POPULAR,
EXTERNAL
opposed to .... ESOTERIC
exotic .... RARE, ALIEN, VIVID,
FOREIGN, STRANGE, IMPORTED
expand .... FLAN, SWELL, DILATE,
AMPLIFY, DISTEND, ENLARGE,
INFLATE, INTUMESCE
in a way .... PAD
expanse .... SEA, AREA, OCEAN,
REACH, EXTENT, SPREAD,
BREADTH
expansion ...... GROWTH, OBESITY,
INCREASE, EXTENSION
expatiate .... RANT, DESCANT,
ENLARGE, ELABORATE
expatriate .... EXILE, BANISH,
MIGRANT
expect .... AWAIT, HOPE(FOR),
FORESEE, PREDICT, PRESUME,
ANTICIPATE
huge profits .... SEE DOLLAR
SIGNS
expectant .... ATIP, EAGER
expectantly .... WITH BATED
BREATH
expectation .... HOPE, FAITH,
BELIEF, OUTLOOK, PROSPECT
expecting ...... READY, PREGNANT
expectorant .... EMETIC,
EMETIN(E)
expectorate .... SPIT
expedience .... FITNESS
expedient .... SEEMLY, POLITIC,
FITTING, AUSPICIOUS,
CONVENIENT
expedite .... EASY, HURRY,
HASTEN, SPEED(UP),
FACILITATE
expediter: colloq. .... TICKLER
expedition .... TRIP, HASTE,
MARCH, SPEED, JOURNEY,
DISPATCH
heroic .... QUEST
hunting .... SAFARI
military .... ANABASIS
purpose .... BATTLE,
HUNT(ING), DISCOVERY,
EXPLORATION
religious .... CRUSADE
expeditious ...... EARLY, PROMPT,
SPEEDY
expel .... EMIT, OUST, EJECT,
EVICT, DRIVE OUT,
DISCHARGE
from country .... EXILE,
BANISH, DEPORT, EXPATRIATE
expellant .... EJECTOR
expend .... USE(UP), SPEND,
CONSUME, DISBURSE

expendable .... NEEDLESS,
DISPENSABLE, REPLACEABLE
expenditure .... COSTS, OUTGO,
OUTLAY, OVERHEAD
expense .... FEE, COST, CHARGE,
SACRIFICE
account: sl. .... SWINDLE
SHEET
colloquial .... DAMAGE
expensive .... DEAR, STEEP,
COSTLY, EXORBITANT
experience .... FEEL, HAVE,
UNDERGO
again in imagination
.... RELIVE
harm .... SUFFER
trying .... ORDEAL
experienced .... OLD
experiment .... TRY, TEST, TRIAL,
ATTEMPT, VENTURE
experimental .... TESTING, ON
TRIAL, TENTATIVE
plant .... PILOT
workshop .... LAB(ORATORY)
experimenter .... EMPIRICIST
expert .... ACE, PRO, DEFT, ADEPT,
SHARP, MASTER, DAB(STER),
SKILLFUL
EPA .... ECOL(OGIST)
in canon law .... DISCRETIST
in crafts/arts .... ARTISAN
in fine arts/in taste
.... CONNOISSEUR
in music .... VIRTUOSO
military .... VETERAN
on anecdotes/stories
.... RACONTEUR
on coins .... SHROFF
on figures .... CPA
on food and drinks
.... EPICURE
self-proclaimed .... MAVEN,
MAVIN
shooter .... MARKSMAN
slang .... WHIZ, WIZARD
var. .... MAVIN
expertise .... ART, KNOW-HOW,
SKIL(L)FULNESS
expertly .... ABLY, APTLY
expiate .... ATONE, REDEEM,
REPAIR, SATISFY
expiation .... AMENDS,
ATONEMENT, REPARATION
place of .... PURGATORY
expiatory .... ATONING, PIACULAR,
PURGATIVE
expiration .... END, DEATH
expire .... DIE, END, STOP, CEASE,
PERISH, RUN OUT, TERMINATE
explain .... CLEAR, SOLVE, DEFINE,
DETAIL, CLARIFY, EXPOUND,

DESCRIBE, ELUCIDATE, EXPLICATE, INTERPRET
explanation .... ANSWER, REASON, VERSION, SOLUTION, CLARIFICATION
of Biblical passage .... EXEGESIS
explanatory .... EXEGETIC(AL), CLARIFYING, GLOSSARIAL
expletive .... OATH, CURSE, EXCLAMATION
mild .... DRAT
explicable .... ACCOUNTABLE
explicate .... EXPLAIN, SPELL OUT
explicit .... CLEAR, EXACT, PLAIN, EXPRESS, PRECISE, WRITTEN, DEFINITE, SPECIFIC
explode .... POP, FIRE, BLAST, BURST, CRUMP, BLOW UP, GO OFF, DESTROY, DETONATE, DISCHARGE, DISCREDIT
exploding meteor .... BOLIS, BOLIDE
exploit .... ACT, USE, DEED, FEAT, MILK, GEST(E), ABUSE, ACTION, HEROISM, PROMOTE, UTILIZE
exploration .... QUEST
exploratory .... PRECEDING
surgery .... OPERATION
surgery on abdomen .... LAPARATOMY
surgery on chest .... THORACOTOMY
explore .... NOSE, PROBE, SEARCH, TRAVEL, EXAMINE, INVESTIGATE
explorer .... COOK, ERIC(THE RED), CABOT, LEWIS, OATES, PERRY, HUDSON, PIONEER, RALEIGH, PATHFINDER, TRAILBLAZER
first to reach the South Pole .... (ROALD)AMUNDSEN
polar .... ROSS
Venetian .... (MARCO) POLO
who conquered Mexico .... CORTES, CORTEZ
who discovered America ...... (CHRISTOPHER) COLUMBUS
who discovered Mississippi River .... DE SOTO
who discovered Philippines .... (FERDINAND) MAGELLAN
exploring admiral .... BYRD
explosion .... BLAST, BLOWUP, OUTBURST, DETONATION
explosive .... TNT, BOMB, MINE, SOUP, NITRO, AMATOL, AMYTOL, PETARD, TONITE, CORDITE, DUNNITE, LIGNOSE,

LYDDITE, CHEDDITE, DYNAMITE, ROBURITE, GUNPOWDER
charge, part of .... WARHEAD
material: prefix .... NITR
sound .... POP, BOOM, CHUG, CLAP, WHAM, DETONATION
explosives box .... CAISSON
material .... CELLULOSE
storage place .... MAGAZINE
exponent .... BACKER, SYMBOL, EXAMPLE, ADVOCATE, DEFENDER
in mathematics .... INDEX
export .... SHIP, SEND(OFF), DISPATCH, TRANSMIT
-import .... TRADE
expose .... BARE, OPEN, SHOW, REVEAL, UNMASK, UNVEIL, DISPLAY, EXHIBIT, DISCLOSE
as false ..... DEBUNK, EXPLODE
to danger .... IMPERIL
exposition .... FAIR, SHOW, EXPOSURE, EXHIBITION
expository .... EXEGETIC, EXPLANATORY
expostulate ...... OBJECT, REBUKE, PROTEST, REMONSTRATE
exposure .... AIRING, AVOWAL
expound .... STATE, CLARIFY, EXPLAIN, INTERPRET, ELUCIDATE
express ...... TELL, STATE, UTTER, VOICE, EXTORT, REVEAL, SIGNIFY, EXPLICIT
a notion .... OPINE
differently .... REWORD
dissatisfaction ...... BOO, BEEF, HOOT, GRIPE, COMPLAIN
in numbers .... EVALUATE
road .... PIKE
sympathy .... CONDOLE
expression .... GRIN, LOOK, TERM, TOKEN, SAYING, WORDING, LOCUTION, INDICATION
local .... IDIOM
of agreement .... YEA
chagrin .... OOPS
contempt ...... POOH, GRUNT, SNEER, SNIFF, SNORT
disgust .... PSHAW
pain or grief .... GROAN
reproach/disapproval ..... FIE
sympathy .... CONDOLENCE
thoughts .... SPEECH
outward .... APPEARANCE
pained .... GRIMACE
underbreath .... MUTTER
villain's .... LEER
expressionless .... GLASSY
mien .... DEADPAN, POKERFACE

expressive .... ELOQUENT
action .... GESTURE
expressly .... PLAINLY, PRECISELY, DEFINITELY, ESPECIALLY, EXPLICITLY
expropriate .... DISPOSSESS
expulsion .... OUSTER, EJECTION
kind of .... DEPORTATION
expunge .... ERASE, CANCEL, DELE(TE), EFFACE, WIPE(OUT)
expurgate .... PURGE, CENSOR, PURIFY, CLEANSE, CASTRATE
exquisite .... RARE, REFINED, CHARMING, DELICATE, BEAUTIFUL, MATCHLESS, FASTIDIOUS
exsanguine .... ANEMIC
exscind .... CUT(OUT), EXCISE
exsert .... THRUST, PROTRUDE
exsiccate .... DRY, PARCH
extant .... ALIVE, EXISTING
extemporaneous .... AD LIB, OFFHAND, IMPROMPTU, IMPROVISED
extemporize .... FAKE IT, IMPROVISE
extend .... JUT, OFFER, RENEW, DEPLOY, SPREAD, PROLONG, STRETCH, CONTINUE, LENGTHEN, OUTREACH, PROTRACT
across .... SPAN
extended area .... TRACT
work leave .... SABBATICAL
extension .... SWEEP, EXPANSE, RENEWAL, ADDITION, PROJECTION
building .... ELL, WING
extent ...... AREA, SCOPE, LENGTH, MEASURE, COVERAGE, LATITUDE, MAGNITUDE
of precedence .... LEAD
utmost .... LIMIT
wide .... EXPANSE
extenuate .... LESSEN, PARDON, WEAKEN, DIMINISH, MITIGATE, PALLIATE
extenuating .... JUSTIFYING
exterior .... ECTAL, OUTER, FOREIGN, OUTSIDE, EXTERNAL, EXTRINSIC
covering .... SKIN
of an object .... SURFACE
toward the .... ECTAD
exterminate .... ABOLISH, DESTROY, ERADICATE, EXTIRPATE, ANNIHILATE
extermination .... MAYHEM, DESTRUCTION
mass .... GENOCIDE
exterminator .... NIHILIST,

DESTROYER
of vegetation .... LOCUST
external .... OUTER, EXTERIOR,
EXOTERIC, SUPERFICIAL
combining form .... ECT(O)
covering .... COAT, HIDE, PELT,
SKIN, CRUST, SHEATHE
cover of flower .... PERIANTH
world .... NONEGO
extinct .... DEAD, GONE, DEFUNCT,
OBSOLETE, EXTINGUISHED,
NON-EXISTENT
animal .... MASTODON
auto/vehicle .... EDSEL,
DESOTO
bird .... MOA, DODO, KIWI,
MAMO
elephant .... MAMMOTH
elephant-like animal
.... DINOTHERE
mammal .... GLYPTODONT
ox .... URUS
reptile .... DINOSAUR,
DINOCERAS
extinguish .... DOUSE, DOWSE,
SNUFF, PUT OUT, QUENCH,
SUBDUE, DESTROY, ECLIPSE,
SMOTHER, STAMP ON,
ERADICATE
in law .... NULLIFY
extirpate .... RAZE, UPROOT,
ABOLISH, DESTROY, EXSCIND,
ERADICATE, ANNIHILATE
extol .... LAUD, EXALT, PRAISE,
GLORIFY, COMMEND
extort .... MILK, BLEED, EXACT,
FORCE, MULCT, SCREW,
WREST, WRING, EXTRACT,
SQUEEZE
extortioner .... BLACKMAILER
extra .... ODD, OVER, SPARE,
EXCESS, SURPLUS,
ADDITIONAL
actor ...... SUPER, FIGURANT(E),
SUPERNUMERARY
asset .... PLUS
pay .... BONUS
point kicker .... TOER
extract .... DRAW, ATTAR, EDUCE,
EVOKE, WRING, DISTIL,
ELICIT, EXTORT, EXCERPT,
PULL OUT, SQUEEZE,
QUOTATION
by boiling .... DECOCT
by dissolving .... LEACH
forcibly .... EVULSE
from anything .... ESSENCE
from balsam .... TOLUENE
from plant/vegetable .... JUICE
of court record .... ESTREAT
extraction .... BIRTH, ORIGIN,

DESCENT, LINEAGE, REMOVAL
extractor, kind of .... PUMP,
CORKSCREW
extracurricular activity
.... DEBATING, ATHLETICS,
DRAMATICS
extradite .... REPATRIATE
extraneous .... ALIEN, OUTER,
EXOTIC, FOREIGN, EXTRINSIC
extraordinary .... RARE, UNCO,
GREAT, UNIQUE, NOTABLE,
UNUSUAL, UNCOMMON,
MARVELOUS, REMARKABLE,
EXCEPTIONAL
haste .... RUSH
person .... ONER
extrasensory perception ...... ESP
extravagance .... FOLLY, FRILL
extravagant .... ULTRA, BAROQUE,
PROFUSE, FANCIFUL,
PRODIGAL, WASTEFUL,
EXORBITANT
excessively .... UNREASONABLE
spending .... LAVISH
extravaganza .... REVUE,
SPECTACLE
extreme ...... LAST, FINAL, ULTRA,
ALL OUT, SEVERE, DRASTIC,
RADICAL, FARTHEST,
EXCESSIVE, IMMODERATE,
SUPERLATIVE
emotional pressure .... DURESS
hunger .... FASTING,
STARVATION
limit .... OUTRANCE
opposed to .... MEAN
unction .... SACRAMENT
unction, give .... ANELE
extremely .... UNCO, VERY,
ULTRA, HIGHLY
energetic .... BUSY AS A BEE
fertile .... RANK
fine .... SUPERB
wicked .... HEINOUS
wild .... SAVAGE, RIOTOUS
extremist .... REBEL, RADICAL,
NIHILIST
extremity ...... END, NIB, TIP, TOE,
EDGE, NEED, POLE, DYING,
POINT
extremities .... LIMBS
affliction .... GOUT
extricate .... FREE, RELEASE,
DISENGAGE
extrinsic .... ALIEN, FOREIGN,
OUTWARD, EXTERNAL,
OUTLYING, EXTRANEOUS
extrude .... EJECT, EXPEL,
PROJECT, STICK OUT
extrusive .... EJECTIVE, VOLCANIC
exuberance .... ZEST, BOUNTY,

PLENTY, GAIETY, BONANZA,
EFFUSION, ABUNDANCE
exuberant .... GAY, RANK,
GALORE, LAVISH, FERTILE,
EFFUSIVE
exudate, plant .... GUM, LAC,
RESIN
exudation .... SUDOR, SWEAT,
EMANATION, PERSPIRATION
exude .... EMIT, FLOW, LEAK,
OOZE, REEK, DRAIN, STREAM,
TRICKLE, DISCHARGE
water .... WEEP
exult .... CROW, GLOAT, GLORY,
GLORIFY, REJOICE, JUBILATE
exultant .... JUBILANT
exultation ...... ELATION, JUBILEE,
TRIUMPH
exuviae .... MOLTS, SHELLS
exuviate .... MOLT, SHED, SLOUGH,
CAST OFF
eyas .... HAWK, NESTLING
Eydie, singer .... GORME
eye .... SEE, GAZE, GLIM, LOOK,
VIEW, SIGHT, WATCH,
GLANCE, VISION, EYEBALL,
OBSERVE
abnormally small
.... MICROPHTHALMOS
aching/discomfort
.... EYESTRAIN
artificial, sometimes called
.... GLASS EYE
bean's .... HILUM
black .... MOUSE, SHINER
boldly .... OGLE, STARE
bruise under .... MOUSE,
BLACKEYE
cavity/socket .... ORBIT
central hole/opening of
.... PUPIL
coating/film .... GLAZE
colloquial .... ORB, OPTIC
colored part/membrane
.... IRIS
combining form .... OCUL(O)
congenital defect
.... ALBINISM, NYSTAGMUS
contraction of pupil
.... MYOSIS
correctional device
.... CONTACT LENS
cover .... PATCH
defect .... MYOPIA, OXYOPIA,
DIPLOPIA
dirt .... MOTE
discharge .... RHEUM
disease .... TUMOR, CATARACT,
GLAUCOMA
disorder .... SQUINT,
STRABISMUS, ASTIGMATISM,

NIGHT BLINDNESS
doctor .... OCULIST,
OPHTHALMOLOGIST
drop .... TEAR
dropper .... PIPETTE
examination aid .... SNELLEN'S
CHART
filler .... BEAUTY
filling .... BEAUTIFUL
-for-an-eye .... TALION, TIT
FOR TAT
for detail, an .... CAREFUL,
WATCHFUL
for only one ...... MONOCULAR
framer .... LASH
infection .... TRACHOMA,
CONJUNCTIVITIS
inflammation .... STY, IRITIS
instrument .... ORTHOSCOPE
largest, of any living animal
.... OSTRICH
lashes .... CILIA
layer .... UVEA
lazy .... AMBLYOPIA
magic .... RADAR, SONAR
main lens of .... CORNEA
of the .... OPTIC, OCULAR,
VISUAL
part .... IRIS, LENS, UVEA,
HUMOR, PUPIL, CORNEA,
FOVEA, RETINA, SCLERA,
CHOROID, OPTIC NERVE
pus .... HYPOPYON
shield .... PATCH, VISOR,
BLINDER, BLINKER
simple .... OCELLUS
slang .... PEPPER, WINKER
the displays ..... WINDOW-SHOP
thing with .... STORM, NEEDLE,
POTATO, TARGET, HURRICANE
wash .... EYEMO, MURINE
white of .... SCLERA
worm .... LOA
eyeball dryness .... XEROSIS
front part of outer coat
.... CORNEA

main cavity of .... VITREOUS
HUMOR
tough outer coat of
.... SCLERA
eyebrow .... BREE
cosmetic .... MASCARA
marker .... PENCIL
eyebrows, space between
.... GLABELLA
eyedrops drug .... MURINE,
ESERINE
eyeful ...... STRIKING, ATTRACTIVE,
SIGHT FOR SORE EYES
eyeglasses .... GLIMS, SPECS,
LENSES, GOGGLES, MONOCLE,
BIFOCALS, HARLEQUIN,
LORGNETTE, PINCE NEZ,
SPECTACLES
maker/seller of .... OPTICIAN
sidepieces .... TEMPLES
slang .... SHADES, READERS,
CHEATERS
eyelash .... CILIUM, WINKER
cosmetic .... MASCARA
eyelashes .... CILIA
of .... CILIARY
eyeless .... BLIND
Eyeless in Gaza author
.... HUXLEY
eyelet .... GROMMET, GRUMMET,
OCELLUS, LOOPHOLE,
PEEPHOLE
eyeleteer .... BODKIN, STILETTO
eyelid, corner of .... CANTHUS
cosmetic .... KOHL
drooping .... PTOSIS
inflammation .... STY,
BLEPHARITIS
eyelids, of the .... PALPEBRAL
eye-opener .... SHOCKER
eyes and ears ...... SENSE ORGANS
at, make .... OGLE, FLIRT
be all .... WATCH, LOOK
EAGERLY
colloquial .... SPARKLERS
cover the .... SEEL, HOODWINK,

BLINDFOLD
deep-set .... CAVERNOUS
describing some .... DOE,
EVIL, GREEN, ALMOND,
SHIFTY, DEEPSET, SOULFUL,
SQUINT(Y)
easy on the .... PLEASANT,
BEAUTIFUL, ATTRACTIVE
malalignment of the
.... SQUINT, STRABISMUS
of bean .... HILA
of the .... OCULAR, VISUAL,
OPTICAL
only for, have .... LOVE, WANT
poetic .... ORBS
slang .... LAMPS, DAYLIGHT
swelling .... MOUS(I)E
third .... HAW
tissue .... TARSUS
trouble .... TRACHOMA
"_____ eyes have seen . . ."
.... MINE
eyesight .... VISION
by .... OCULAR
eyesore .... UGLY
eyestalk .... STIPES
eyetooth .... FANG, CANINE,
CUSPID
eyewash .... EYEMO, EXCUSE,
MURINE, FLATTERY,
NONSENSE, COLLYRIUM
eyewink .... HINT, SIGNAL,
INSTANT
eyewitness .... OBSERVER,
ONLOOKER, BYSTANDER,
SPECTATOR
eyot .... AIT, ILE, ISLE(T)
eyra .... WILD CAT
eyre .... TOUR, (CIRCUIT)COURT
eyrie .... NEST, AERIE, EAGLET
Ezekiel .... PROPHET
creature in vision of .... OX,
MAN, LION, EAGLE
Ezida frequenter .... NEBO
Ezra, book about .... ESDRAS

F

F grade in school .... FAILING
in a sequence/group .... SIXTH
in music .... LOUD, FORTE
in temperature .... FAHRENHEIT
is chemical symbol of
.... FLUORINE
letter .... EF, EFF
letters sounding .... GH, PH
plane .... FIGHTER

f.a.s. .... FREE ALONGSIDE SHIP
fabaceous plant .... PEA
Fabian strategy .... DELAY,
AVOIDANCE
Fabius, sobriquet .... CUNCTATOR,
(THE)DELAYER
victim of .... HANNIBAL
fable ...... MYTH, STORY, LEGEND,
FICTION, PARABLE, ALLEGORY,

APOLOG(UE), FALSEHOOD
writer .... ADE, (A)ESOP,
MORALIST, PHAEDRUS
fabled .... UNREAL, MYTHICAL,
LEGENDARY
being .... OGRE, DWARF,
GNOME, SIREN, TITAN, TROLL,
CENTAUR, MINOTAUR
bird .... ROC

fish .... MAH

fables have one .... MORAL
LESSON

fabric .... RAG, CLOTH, ATLAS,
TISSUE, TEXTILE, MATERIAL,
STRUCTURE, CAMEL'S HAIR
Angora .... CAMLET, MOHAIR
any woven .... WEB
carpet .... MOQUETTE
character/quality of
.... TEXTURE
coarse .... MAT, CRASH,
CANVAS, DOWLAS, RATINE
corded .... REP(P), PIQUE,
PADUASOY
cotton .... LENO, MULL,
DENIM, MANTA, PIQUE, SCRIM,
CALICO, DIMITY, CRETON(NE),
MADRAS, MOREEN, MUSLIN,
NANKIN, PENANG, NANKEEN,
NAINSOOK
braided .... GIMP
lightweight .... ETAMINE
resembling velvet
.... VELVETEEN
thin .... GAUZE,
CHEESECLOTH
cravat/tie .... REP, PAISLEY
creased .... KORATRON
crinkled .... CRAPE, CREPE
curtain .... NET, SCRIM
drapery .... MOREEN
edge .... SELVAGE
fall .... WOOL
felt-like .... BAIZE
filling .... WEFT
fine woolen .... CASHMERE
floor cover .... CARPET
glazed .... CAMBRIC
glossy/lustrous .... SATIN,
ETOILE
heavy/with raised design
.... BROCADE
hempen .... BURLAP
jute .... BALINE
kind of .... KNIT, PRINT,
WOOLEN, WORSTED,
SYNTHETIC, WASH-AND-WEAR,
PERMANENT-PRESS
knitted .... TRICOT
light wool .... ALPACA
linen .... SCRIM, DOWLAS
lining .... FLEECE, SATEEN
loose-woven .... ETAMINE
making process .... FELTING,
WEAVING, KNITTING
merchant ..... DRAPER, MERCER
metallic .... LAME
mourning .... ALMA, CRAPE
napped .... FLEECE
net .... TULLE, MALINE

plaid .... TARTAN
printed ..... BAT(T)IK, CHALLIS,
PERCALE
protector .... CAMPHOR
puckered .... PLISSE
resembling velvet ...... PANNE,
TERRY
reversible .... DAMASK
rib .... WALE
ribbed .... CORD, REP(P),
PIQUE, TWILL, TRICOT
rugs .... CHENILLE
satin .... PEKIN, ETOILE
sheer .... GAUZE, NINON,
VOILE, BATISTE, ORGANDY,
ORGANZA
shiny ...... SILK, SATIN, POPLIN,
SATEEN, TAFFETA
silk .... SURAT, FAILLE,
CHIFFON, LUSTRING,
SARCENET, TOBINE,
SHANTUNG, LEVANTINE,
TAFFETA, LUTESTRING
silk, Chinese/Indian
.... CREPE, PONGEE
silk, interwoven with gold or
silver .... SAMITE
stiff .... WIGAN, ORGANDY
stretcher .... TENTER
striped .... DORIA, MADRAS,
DO(O)REA, ZENANA, GALATEA,
BAYADEER, BAYADERE
synthetic .... NYLON, RAYON,
ACETATE, POLYESTER
threads crossing the warp in
a .... WEFT, WOOF
threads running lengthwise
in a .... WARP
towel .... CRASH, TERRY
twilled .... CHINO, SERGE
unwoven, made of bark
.... TAPA
upholstery .... REP, MOREEN,
MOHAIR, BROCATEL
veil .... LACE, TULLE
velvet ...... VELURE, VELOUR(S)
wastes .... MUNGO
watered silk/wavy patterned
.... MOIRE
waterproof .... OILCLOTH,
TARP(AULIN)
wax-coated .... BAT(T)IK
window shades .... HOLLAND
with fuzzy surface .... FELT
with ornamental designs
.... LACE
woolen .... BEIGE, SERGE,
TAMIS, ALPACA, MERINO,
TARTAN, VICUNA, ETAMINE,
ESTAMIN(E)

wool and cotton, napped,
tufted .... CHINCHILLA
worsted .... SERGE, ETAMINE
woven silk .... TRICOT
woven with a pebbly pattern
.... SHARKSKIN

fabricate .... LIE, COIN, VAMP,
CREATE, DEVISE, INVENT,
MAKE(UP), CONCOCT,
CONSTRUCT

fabrication .... LIE, WEB, DECEIT,
FIGMENT, FALSEHOOD,
IMAGINATION

fabricator .... LIAR, MAKER,
FIBBER, FORGER, CREATOR,
INVENTOR, PERJURER,
PRODUCER
forte of .... TALL TALES

fabulist .... ADE, LIAR, (A)ESOP,
GRIMM, LA FONTAINE

fabulous .... MYTHICAL,
LEGENDARY, IMAGINARY,
INCREDIBLE
animal ..... CENTAUR, UNICORN
banker .... ROTHSCHILD
monster .... CHIMERA
place .... EL DORADO
serpent .... BASILISK,
COCKATRICE
tale .... LEGEND

facade .... FACE, MASK, FRONT
main .... FRONTISPIECE

face .... MEET, BRAVE, FACET,
PRIDE, ANSWER, FACADE,
VISAGE, DIAL, (CON)FRONT,
REPUTATION, COUNTENANCE
about ...... TURN TO THE RIGHT
card .... JACK, KING, QUEEN
coin's .... HEAD
colloquial .... PHIZ, BRASS,
CHEEK, SNOOT, AUDACITY
cosmetic .... ROUGE
crease .... LINE, WRINKLE
describing some .... OVAL,
ROUND, HEART-SHAPED
down .... LIE, PRONE, OPPOSE
expressionless .... POKER,
DEADPAN
gem's .... FACET
guard .... MASK, VISOR,
BEAVER
hair .... BEARD
in clubs .... BLACKJACK
obsolete .... MAZARD
of a sort .... DIAL
of rock .... BROW, CLIFF
powder .... TALCUM
slang .... MAP, MUG, PAN,
GALL, MUSH, PUSS, CRUST,
NERVE, KISSER
spot .... FRECKLE

the camera .... POSE
to face .... VIS-A-VIS,
TETE-A-TETE, EYEBALL-TO-
EYEBALL
value .... PAR, WORTH
with stone .... REVET
facelift(ing) .... RENOVATION
benefit? .... NO SAG
facet .... PANE, BEZEL, BEZIL,
CULET, PHASE, ASPECT,
COLLET, FLANGE
facetious .... DROLL, WITTY,
JOCOSE, COMICAL, JOCULAR
person .... WAG, JESTER,
HUMORIST
facetiousness .... WIT
facial adornment .... BEARD,
GOATEE, VANDYKE, IMPERIAL,
MUSTACHE, MUSTACHIO
expression .... GRIN, LEER,
PHIZ, POUT, SCOWL, SMILE,
SMIRK, GRIMACE
paralysis .... BELL'S PALSY
facile .... DEFT, EASY, ADROIT,
FLUENT, AFFABLE
facilitate ...... EASE, HELP, CLEAR,
SMOOTH, FURTHER, QUICKEN
facility ...... EASE, KNACK, MEANS,
SKILL, FLUENCY, DEXTERITY,
CONVENIENCE
facing .... LINER, LINING,
TOWARD, FORNENT, TRIMMING
glacier .... STOSS
inward .... INTRORSE
facsimile .... COPY, REPLICA,
LIKENESS, REPRODUCTION
fact .... FIAT, DATUM, TRUTH,
REALITY, ACTUALITY, NOT A
DREAM, CERTAINTY
of knowing .... KNOWLEDGE
state as a .... AVER, POSIT
faction .... BLOC, SECT, SIDE,
CABAL, CLASH, JUNTO,
CLIQUE, DISCORD, DISSENSION
factional .... PARTISAN
division .... SPLIT, SCHISM,
SPLINTER
factious .... DIVISIVE, PARTISAN,
SEDITIOUS, CONTENTIOUS
factitious .... FORCED, ARTIFICIAL
factor .... PART, AGENT, BASIS,
BROKER, ELEMENT,
CONDITION
biological .... GENE
factory .... MILL, PLANT,
INDUSTRIAL ESTABLISHMENT
country .... HACIENDA
factotum .... AGENT, DO-ALL,
SERVANT, HANDYMAN
facts .... DATA, DETAILS, LOW-
DOWN

slang .... THE DOPE, THE
SCORE
factual .... REAL, TRUE, ACTUAL
facultative .... OPTIONAL,
CONTINGENT
faculty .... KNACK, POWER, SENSE,
TALENT, ABILITY, APTITUDE
of apt expression ..... FELICITY
fad .... MODE, CRAZE, HOBBY,
STYLE, VOGUE, MEGRIM,
FASHION
fade ...... DIM, PALE, PEAK, WANE,
DIE(OUT), WILT, DROOP,
BLEACH, WHITEN, WITHER,
LANGUISH
from sight .... VANISH,
EVANESCE, DISAPPEAR
out .... END, DISSOLVE
faded .... DRAB, DULL, WORN,
DIMMED, WEATHERED,
DISCOLORED
fading .... DYING, EBBING,
WANING, FUGITIVE,
DWINDLING
of fame .... ECLIPSE
quickly .... EVANESCENT,
EVAPORATING
fado .... FOLKSONG
Faerie Queen .... MAB, UNA
character .... ALMA, TALUS,
AMORET, ACRASIA
Fafnir's brother .... REGIN
slayer .... SIGURD
fag .... TIRE, SLAVE, WEARY,
EXHAUST, FATIGUE, PLODDER,
WORKHORSE, DRUDGE(RY),
HOMOSEXUAL
end .... BUTT, RUCK, RUMP,
STUB, STUMP, REMNANT
slang .... CIGARETTE
fagaceous plant .... OAK, BEECH,
CHESTNUT
fagot .... SEW, FASCINE
faience ...... POTTERY, PORCELAIN
fail .... EBB, FLOP, MISS, FLUNK,
PETER OUT, FIZZLE, DEFAULT,
COLLAPSE, MISCARRY
as a motor .... CONK OUT
in duty .... SHIRK, REMISS
in health .... LANGUISH
to catch .... MUFF, FUMBLE
to follow suit .... RENIG,
RENEGE, FAINAIGUE
utterly .... GO TO THE WALL
failing .... FAULT, DEFECT, FOIBLE,
FRAILTY, WEAKNESS
failure .... DUD, LOSS, LAPSE,
(DOWN)FALL, OMISSION,
BREAKDOWN
absolute .... BOMB
colloquial .... BUST, LEMON

complete .... RUIN, CRASH,
FIASCO, WASHOUT,
BANKRUPTCY
in electric power ...... OUTAGE
slang .... BOMB, FLOP, TURKEY
to pay/to prosecute
.... DEFAULT
fain .... GLAD(LY), EAGER, READY,
WILLING, DESIROUS
faineant .... IDLE, LAZY, OTIOSE
faint ...... DIM, WAN, PALE, WEAK,
SWOON, TIMID, FEEBLE, PASS
OUT, SWOUND, UNCLEAR
fainthearted .... TIMID,
COWARDLY
fainting .... SYNCOPATION
fit .... SWOON, SYNCOPE
fair .... EVEN, JUST, COMELY,
BAZA(A)R, DECENT, KERMIS,
LOVELY, PRETTY, SERENE,
AVERAGE, CARNIVAL,
FESTIVAL, HANDSOME,
UNBIASED, BEAUTIFUL,
IMPARTIAL, EXHIBITION,
EXPOSITION
complexion .... LIGHT
game .... DUPE, CHANCE,
TARGET, VICTIM
haired .... PET, BLOND(E),
FAVORITE
place .... BOOTH, STALL,
PAVILION
play .... SQUARE DEAL
portion .... CHUNK
sex .... WOMAN, FEMALE
shake .... TOSSUP
spoken .... GLIB, BLAND,
POLITE, SMOOTH
to middling .... SO-SO,
MODERATE, PASSABLE
weather .... CLEAR, SUNNY,
SUNSHINE, CLOUDLESS
Fairbanks native .... ALASKAN
fairest ...... FLAWLESS, LOVELIEST,
FLOWERLIKE
fairly ...... DULY, FITTING, JUSTLY,
ABOVEBOARD
fairness .... EQUITY, JUSTICE,
JUSTNESS
fairy .... ELF, FAY, ELVE, PERI,
PUCK, PIXY, PIXIE, SPRITE,
HOBGOBLIN, LEPRECHAUN,
TINKERBELL
air .... SYLPH
fort/abode .... LIS(S), SHEE
king .... OBERON
lake dweller .... MORGAN(LE
FAY)
like .... ELFIN
Midsummer Night's Dream
.... COBWEB

queen ...... MAB, UNA, TITANIA
Slavonic .... VILA
story .... LIE, MYTH, TALE,
    FABLE, MARCHEN, ALLEGORY
tale character .... SANDMAN
tale monster .... OGRE
wood .... NYMPH
faith .... CULT, DOXY, CREED,
    DOGMA, TROTH, TRUST,
    BELIEF, LOYALTY, RELIANCE,
        RELIGION
archaic .... FAY
article of .... TENET
bad .... DECEIT, DUPLICITY,
        DISHONESTY
good .... CANDOR, SINCERITY
healer, kind of .... QUACK
matters of .... CREDENDA
of .... PIETISTIC
faithful .... FAST, TRUE, EXACT,
    TRIED, LIEGE, LOYAL,
    DEVOUT, HONEST, DEVOTED,
    CONSTANT, STA(U)NCH,
    LIFELIKE, RELIABLE
friend .... DAMON, ACHATES,
        PYTHIAS
poetic .... LEAL
servant .... SERF, HELOT,
    SLAVE, YES-MAN
faithfully .... EXACTLY, STRICTLY,
        OBEDIENTLY
faithless .... FALSE, UNTRUE,
    DISLOYAL, INCONSTANT,
    PERFIDIOUS, TRAITOROUS
faitour .... ROGUE
fake .... SHAM, BOGUS, CHEAT,
    FALSE, FRAUD, TRICK,
    PHONEY, UNREAL, SPURIOUS,
        COUNTERFEIT
attack .... FEINT
colloquial ..... FEIGN, IMITATE,
        PRETEND
jewelry: colloq.
    .... BRUMMAGEN
faker .... FRAUD, HOAXER,
    HUMBUG, IMPOSTOR,
        SWINDLER
kind of .... QUACK,
        MALINGERER
fakir .... MONK, YOGI, SWAMI,
    BEGGAR, DERVISH,
        MENDICANT
falbala .... FRILL, RUFFLE,
    FLOUNCE, FURBELOW
falcate .... CURVED, HOOKED
falchion .... SWORD
falcon .... HAWK, SAKER, CANNON,
    LUGGER, MERLIN, PEREGRINE,
    LANNER(ET), WINDHOVER,
        SPARROW-HAWK
Asian .... LAGGAR

close eyes of .... SEEL
E. Indian .... BESRA
European .... HOBBY, SAKER,
        KESTREL
eye-blinder .... HOOD, SEEL
female .... LANNER
headed deity ..... RA, MENT(U)
India .... LAGGER, SHAHIN
leg-strap .... JESS
male .... TERCEL, LANNERET
peregrine .... DUCK-HAWK
repair wing of .... IMP
small .... MERLIN, KESTREL
swoop of .... SOUSE
use of .... HUNTING
falconer .... HAWKER
falconer's decoy .... LURE
falconry .... HAWKING
falderal .... GEWGAW, TRIFLE,
        NONSENSE
fall .... DROP, PLOP, RUIN, SLIP,
    PLUNK, SLUMP, SPILL,
    AUTUMN, LITTER, PLUNGE,
    TUMBLE, DESCEND, PLUMMET,
        DECREASE
apart .... BREAK, COLLAPSE
back .... RECEDE, RELAPSE,
        RETREAT
behind .... LAG
"classic" .... WORLD SERIES
flat: sl. .... BOMB
forward .... TOPPLE
from grace/virtue .... LAPSE
guy: sl. .... DUPE, LOSER,
    PATSY, SCAPEGOAT
headlong .... PITCH
heavily .... THUD
in .... AGREE, LINE UP
in drops .... DRIP, RAIN,
    DRIB(BLE), TRICKLE
in line .... FILE
into place .... FORM, COME
        TOGETHER
mortally wounded .... BITE
        THE DUST
on evil days .... GO TO THE
        DOGS
on one's knees .... APOLOGIZE,
    KNEEL, GENUFLECT
out .... SHED, QUARREL
short/through ..... FAIL, CRASH
to .... START, LAUNCH
to pieces .... CRUMBLE,
        DISINTEGRATE
upon .... BESET
fallacious .... DECEPTIVE,
        ERRONEOUS
notion .... IDOLISM
fallacy .... ERROR, IDOLA, IDOLUM,
    MISTAKE, DECEPTION
fallal .... FINERY, FRIPPERY

fallen .... DEAD, DROPPED,
    SILENCED, DEGRADED,
        PROSTRATE
angel .... LOST SOUL,
        RECIDIVIST
fallible .... FISHY, DOUBTFUL
falling .... CADENT
_____ .... DOMINOES THEORY
out .... RIFT, QUARREL
over .... TOPPLE
sickness .... EPILEPSY
star .... METEOR
Fallopian tube .... OVIDUCT,
        SALPINX
fallout .... ATOM BLAST,
    CONTAMINATION,
        RADIOACTIVITY
effect .... AIR POLLUTION
particles .... SNOW, SLEET,
    (COSMIC)DUST
fallow .... BARREN, USELESS,
        UNTILLED
deer .... TEG, DAMA
false .... FAKE, SHAM, BOGUS,
    WRONG, FORGED, HOLLOW,
    UNTRUE, EVASIVE, MISTAKEN,
    SPURIOUS, FAITHLESS,
    UNFOUNDED, ARTIFICIAL,
        MENDACIOUS
belief .... DELUSION
entry .... RINGER
excuse .... RUSE, EVASION,
    PRETEXT, SUBTERFUGE
face .... MASK, DISGUISE
friend .... IAGO, JUDAS,
    TRAITOR, TWO-TIMER
front .... BLUFF, DUMMY
god .... BAAL, IDOL
gossip .... TALE
hair .... PERUKE, TOUPEE,
    (PERI)WIG
jewelry .... PASTE,
        BRUMMAGEN
move .... SLIP, MISSTEP
name .... ALIAS, ANONYM,
    AKA, PSEUDONYM
prefix .... PSEUDO
pretense .... AFFECTATION
reasoning .... IDOLISM
report/rumor .... HOAX,
    CANARD, HODGEPODGE,
        EXAGGERATION
seed cover .... ARILLODE
show .... MAGIC, MASQUERADE
show, make .... FEIGN
show to be .... DEBUNK,
        DISPROVE
step .... TRIP, STUMBLE
story .... YARN, FICTION,
    FUDGE, FARRAGO, TALL TALE
swearing .... PERJURY

teeth .... DENTURE
wing .... ALULA
witness .... LIAR, PERJURER
falsehood .... FIB, LIE, FLAM,
TALE, FABLE, LYING, CANARD,
FICTION, FORGERY, PERJURY,
DECEPTION, UNTRUTH,
PRETENSE, INVENTION,
FABRICATION
colloquial .... BUNK, FRONT
slang .... BLUFF,
FOURFLUSHING
falsies: colloq. .... PADS
falsify .... FIB, FAKE, (BE)LIE,
ALTER, COLOR, FORGE,
GARBLE, PAD(THE BILL),
DISTORT, MISQUOTE
Falstaff's man .... PETO
falter .... HAW, WAVER, FLINCH,
TOTTER, STAMMER, STUMBLE,
HESITATE, VACILLATE
fama .... RUMOR
fame ...... HONOR, GLORY, KUDOS,
NAME, STAR, ECLAT,
RENOWN, REPUTE, PRESTIGE,
REPUTATION
kind of .... NOTORIETY
partner of .... FORTUNE
famed .... NOTED, FAMOUS,
EMINENT, NOTABLE, REPUTED,
NOTORIOUS, CELEBRATED,
WELL-KNOWN
fly catcher .... STAN MUSIAL
Fameuse .... APPLE
familiar .... BOLD, CLOSE,
BRAZEN, COMMON, FORWARD,
VERSANT, ASSUMING,
FRIENDLY, INTIMATE,
ORDINARY
De's .... FOE, NIRO, VITO
for Ann .... NAN
lion .... LEO, MGM
Mac's .... LEOD, LAINE,
MAHON, DONALD, MILLAN,
MURRAY
Mc's .... COY, CREA, CLURE,
ENROE, CARTHY, DOWALL,
KINLEY, AULIFFE, CORMACK,
CORMICK
negative .... AREN'T
O's .... BRIEN, NEILL, TOOLE,
CONNOR
saying .... MOT, SAW, TAG,
ADAGE, MOTTO
sign .... SRO, OPEN, CLOSED,
NO VACANCY, HELP WANTED,
NO LOITERING, BEWARE OF
DOG, NO ADMITTANCE, NO
SOLICITING
Van's .... DYKE, CLEEF,
DEVERE, PATTEN

familiarity .... INTIMACY,
KNOWLEDGE, CORDIALITY
familiarize .... ACQUAINT,
ACCUSTOM
families, quarrel between
.... FEUD
family .... ILK, KIN, CLAN, LINE,
RACE, BREED, GROUP, STOCK,
TRIBE, KINDRED, KINSFOLK,
HOUSEHOLD
acting .... FONDAS
ancient .... DORIA
auto/car .... SEDAN
branch .... STEM, STIRPS
car: colloq. .... BUS
diagram .... TREE
famous .... ESTE, SOONG,
MEDICI, KENNEDY,
ROTHSCHILD, ROCKEFELLER
golfing .... SNEADS
life .... FIRESIDE
meal .... POTLUCK
name .... SURNAME,
COGNOMEN, PATRONYMIC
next door .... NEIGHBOR
of flies .... EMPIDAE
of marine worms
.... NEREIDAE
of spies .... WALKER
pertaining to .... LINEAGE,
DOMESTIC, FAMILIAL
Renaissance ...... ESTE, MEDICI
theatrical .... FOYS
tree .... PEDIGREE
famine ...... HUNGER, STARVATION
famish .... PINCH, STARVE,
EXHAUST
famous .... GRAND, NOTED,
EMINENT, NOTABLE, POPULAR,
RENOWNED, CELEBRATED,
WELL-KNOWN
anthropologist .... MEAD
Arab surgeon ..... ABUL KASIM
aunt .... MAME
ballet .... SWAN LAKE
beachhead .... ANZIO
clergyman .... PEALE
date .... D-DAY
department store maker
.... WANA
diamond .... KOH-I-NOOR
epithet in baseball .... YANKEE
CLIPPER
friend .... DAMON, ACHATES,
PYTHIAS
lake resort .... TAHOE
London Guildhall effigy
.... GOG
murderer .... ARAM, CAIN,
BOOTH, BUNDY, OSWALD
orphan .... ANNIE

postmaster .... JIM FARLEY
ship captain .... NOAH
ski resort .... VAIL, ASPEN
tower .... PISA, BABEL
trio member .... ATHOS,
ARAMIS, PORTHOS
ultimatum reply .... NUTS
unfavorably .... NOTORIOUS
Variety headline ..... HIX-NIX=
STIX-PIX
violin maker .... AMATI
Wagnerian singer ..... LAURITZ
MELCHIOR
Yankees' late Number 7
.... MANTLE
famously .... ROYALLY
famulus ...... SERVANT, ASSISTANT
fan .... BLOW, BUFF, COOL,
EXCITE, FOMENT, ROOTER,
VOTARY, ZEALOT, ADMIRER,
DEVOTEE, AFICIONADO,
ENTHUSIAST
form .... PLICATE
of leaves .... TALIPOT
oriental .... PUNKA(H)
palm .... PALMETTO
Pope's .... FLABELLUM
shaped .... FLABELLATE
slang .... ADDICT
fanatic .... NUT, BIGOT, JINGO,
RABID, ZEALOT, PARTISAN,
BELIEVER, DOGMATIST,
PHRENETIC
murderous .... AMOK, THUG,
BERSERK
fanatical .... FIERY, RABID,
RADICAL, ZEALOUS
fanaticism ...... MANIA, BIGOTRY,
ZEAL(OTRY)
fancied .... UNREAL, IMAGINED,
CONCOCTED, IMAGINARY
fear .... BOG(E)Y, BUGABOO
fancier, kind of .... GOURMET,
GOURMAND, CONNOISSEUR
fanciful .... ODD, AIRY, ANTIC,
AERIAL, QUAINT, UNREAL,
BIZARRE, ILLUSORY,
IMAGINARY, WHIMSICAL,
FANTASTIC, IMAGINATIVE
fancy .... FAD, IDEA, WEEN, WHIM,
DREAM, SHOWY, NOTION,
MEGRIM, ORNATE, VISION,
CAPRICE, DELUSION, ILLUSION
add-on .... FRILL
dive .... SWAN, GAINER,
HEADER
foolish .... CHIMERA
passing .... MOOD
slang .... FLOSSY
fancy-free .... CAREFREE,
UNCHAINED

261

fandango .... DANCE
fane .... CHURCH, SHRINE, TEMPLE,
SANCTUARY
fanfare .... TANTARA, FLOURISH
fanfaron .... BRAGGART
fang .... CLAW, TUSK, TALON,
CUSPID, EYETOOTH, CANINE
TOOTH
fanlight .... TRANSOM
Fannie, writer .... HURST
fanny: sl. .... BUTTOCKS
fanon ...... VANE, ORALE, MANIPLE
fantail .... PIGEON, GOLDFISH
fantasia .... MEDLEY, CAPRICE
fantast ...... DREAMER, VISIONARY
fantastic .... ODD, UNREAL,
BIZARRE, STRANGE,
FABULOUS, WONDROUS,
ECCENTRIC, GROTESQUE,
REMARKABLE, OUTLANDISH
imitation .... PARODY,
TRAVESTY
style .... OUTRE, RACOCO,
BAROQUE
fantasy .... FANCY, WHIMSY,
CAPRICE, ROMANCE, ILLUSION,
PHANTASM, (DAY)DREAM,
MAKE-BELIEVE
far .... TEL, AWAY, REMOTE,
YONDER, DISTANT,
ADVANCED, OUT OF THE WAY
above average .... SUPER
and near .... EVERYWHERE
and wide .... ABROAD
apart .... UNLIKE, DIFFERENT,
DISPARATE
arear .... TAILENDER
combining form .... TELE
cry .... LONG WAY
down/below the surface
.... DEEP
eastern .... ORIENTAL
go .... LAST LONG
left and far right
.... EXTREMES
off .... REMOTE, DISTANT
reaching .... WIDE, BROAD
farce .... MIME, SKIT, EXODE,
COMEDY, PARODY, MOCKERY,
DROLLERY, TRAVESTY,
BURLESQUE
farceur/farceuse .... WAG,
CLOWN, COMEDIAN, JOKER,
JESTER, HUMORIST
farcical .... COMIC, FUNNY,
ABSURD, LUDICROUS,
SLAPSTICK, RIDICULOUS
farcy .... GLANDERS
fardel .... PACK, BUNDLE, BURDEN
fare .... EAT, PAY, DIET, DINE,
FOOD, LUCK, MENU, GET ON,

RESULT, THRIVE, PASSAGE,
OUTCOME, PROSPER,
PASSENGER
farewell .... LAST, VALE, PARTING,
VALEDICTION, LEAVE-TAKING
appearance .... SWANSONG
drink .... STIRRUP-CUP
formal .... CONGE
party .... SEND-OFF
retirement gift .... GOLD
WATCH
word(s) ..... AVE, ADIEU, CIAO,
ADIOS, ALOHA, SO LONG,
BYEBYE, CHEERIO, GOODBYE,
SHALOM, GODSPEED,
ARRIVEDERCI, SAYONARA, AUF
WIEDERSEHEN
farfetched ...... FORCED, REMOTE,
DOUBTFUL, STRAINED,
UNLIKELY
farflung .... WIDE, BROAD,
SWEEPING
farina ...... MEAL, FLOUR, STARCH
farinaceous .... MEALY,
POWDERY, STARCHY
drink .... PTISAN
farinose .... MEALY
farm .... TILL, TORP, RANCH,
GRANGE, HACIENDA,
CULTIVATE
building/structure .... BARN,
SHED, SILO
feature .... COW, HEN, PIG,
DUCK, GOOSE, CHICKEN
grazing .... RANCH(O)
implement .... PLOW, FLAIL,
HARROW, TEDDER
kind of .... DAIRY, OYSTER
machine .... CHURN, REAPER,
SEEDER, TEDDER, PLANTER,
TRACTOR, SCARIFIER
measure .... ACRE
of a .... VILLATIC
small/worked by renter
.... CROFT
tenant .... COTTER, CROFTER
vehicle, large heavy-wheeled
.... WAIN
worker .... HIND, ORRAMAN,
PLOWMAN, CAMPESINO
yard .... BARTON
farmer .... RYOT, SOWER, TILLER,
CROPPER, GRANGER, PEASANT,
PLANTER, HABITAN(T),
HUSBANDMAN
future .... AGGIE
migrant .... OKIE
peasant .... CROFTER
farmers' weather prophet
.... ALMANAC

farmhouse, land nearest
.... INFIELD
farming .... HUSBANDRY,
AGRICULTURE
farmland .... ARABLE LAND,
ACREAGE
faro card .... SODA
form of .... MONTE
Faroes whirlwinds .... OES
farrago .... OLIO, JUMBLE,
MEDLEY, MIXTURE
Farrar, soprano ...... GERALDINE
farrier .... BLACKSMITH,
VETERINARY, VETERINARIAN
farrow .... PIG, LITTER
farseeing .... PROVIDENT
farsighted .... HYPERMETROPIC
one .... SEER, PROPHET
farsightedness .... HYPEROPIA
farther .... BEYOND, REMOTER
India .... INDO-CHINA
farthest ...... ENDMOST, ULTIMATE
back .... REAR, HINDMOST
colloquial ...... GOD-FORSAKEN
fasces carrier .... LICTOR
fascia .... STRIP, FILLET,
BAND(AGE)
fascicle .... CLUSTER
fascinate .... CHARM, ALLURE,
ATTRACT, BEWITCH,
ENCHANT, INTRIGUE,
CAPTIVATE
fascination .... CHARM, SPELL,
WONDER, OBSESSION,
ATTRACTION
fascism .... NAZISM, DESPOTISM,
FALANGISM, DICTATORSHIP
Fascist .... NAZI, FALANGIST
leader .... RAS, FRANCO,
HITLER, MUSSO(LINI)
mayor .... PODESTA
organization in Spain
.... FALANGE
theoretician .... PARETO
fash: Scot. .... VEX, ANNOY,
TROUBLE
fashion .... CUT, FAD, FORM,
KIND, MAKE, MODE, MOLD,
RAGE, SORT, CRAZE, SHAPE,
STYLE, VOGUE, DESIGN,
MANNER, METHOD
designer/VIP .... DIOR,
ADOLFO, CHANEL, NORELL,
BALMAIN, CASSINI, BERGDORF,
GIVENCHY, GERNREICH, ST.
LAURENT, VALENTINO,
BALENCIAGA, MAINBOCHER
figure .... MODEL, CUTTER,
TAILOR, MODISTE, DESIGNER
maker .... TRENDSETTER
model .... TWIGGY, CINDY

CRAWFORD, CHERYL TIEGS, NAOMI CAMPBELL, CLAUDIA SCHIFFER, CHRISTIE BRINKLEY, LINDA EVANGELISTA, PAULINA PORIZKOVA

news .... MAXI, MINI, HEMLINE, NECKLINE

past .... MINISKIRT

plate .... DUDE, DANDY, BEAU(BRUMMELL)

fashionable .... NEW, CHIC, POSH, NOBBY, RITZY, SLEEK, SMART, SWISH, TONEY, DRESSY, MODISH, ALAMODE, STYLISH

gathering .... SALON

society .... BONTON

Fashoda, Sudan town .... KODOK

fast .... DIET, FIRM, APACE, AGILE, FLEET, HASTY, QUICK, RAPID, SWIFT, PRESTO, RAKISH, SECURE, SPEEDY, STARVE, ABSTAIN, DEVOTED, EXPRESS

and loose .... ADRIFT, SHIFTY

break goal .... LAY-UP

combining form .... TACHY

driver .... JEHU

fellow .... SPRINTER

movement .... TANTIVY

plane .... SST

talk .... BLARNEY, GLIB TONGUE

time .... DAYLIGHT-SAVING

fasten .... FIX, TIE, ZIP, BIND, LASH, ROPE, CLOSE, ATTACH, TETHER, CONNECT

boat .... BERTH

firmly ...... NAIL, CHAIN, INFIX, RIVET, SECURE

in a way .... GLUE, PASTE

nautical .... BELAY, BATTEN

fastener .... BITT, CLIP, HASP, SNAP, CLAMP, CLASP, CLEAT, STRAP

slide .... ZIPPER

wire .... STAPLE

wood .... NOG, PEG, PIN

fastening ...... BOLT, LOCK, GLUE, CATCH, CLASP, LATCH, TACH(E), BUCKLE, BUTTON, HOOK(AND EYE)

fastidious .... NICE, PRIM, CHARY, FUSSY, DAINTY, QUEASY, PICKY, FINICAL, FINICKY, PRECISE, CHOOSY, REFINED, CRITICAL, TASTEFUL, PER(S)NICKETY

fastigiate .... CONELIKE

fasting .... ABSTINENCE

period .... LENT, RAMADAN, RAMAZAN

fastness .... STRONGHOLD

fat .... OILY, DUMPY, ESTER, FLAB, GROSS, LARDY, OBESE, PLUMP, PORKY, PUDGY, PUFFY, PURSY, STOUT, THICK, CHUBBY, FLESHY, PORTLY, PINGUID, CORPULENT

and squat .... FUBSY, ROLY-POLY

animal .... LARD, ADEPS, GREASE, TALLOW, ADIPOSE

beef/mutton .... SUET, TALLOW

cat: sl. .... RICH MAN, MILLIONAIRE

chance: sl. .... HOPELESS, NOTHING DOING

chew the .... GAB, CHAT

combining form ..... STEAT(O)

decomposition of .... LIPOLYSIS

hog .... LARD

in butter .... OLEO

in cow's milk .... GHEE

like .... LIPIDE, LIPOID, STEARIC, LIPAROID, UNCTUOUS, UNGUENT(OUS)

liquid part .... OLEIN

lot .... NIX, NOTHING

of .... RICH, FATTY, OLEIC, ADIP(O), ADIPIC, GREASY, TALLOWY, BLUBBERY

of the land .... WEAL, LUXURY, PLENTY

person: sl. ...... BLIMP, TUB(OF LARD), FATSO, HIPPO, HEAVYWEIGHT

refuse (from cooking) .... SLUSH

roasting meat ...... DRIPPING(S)

solid part of .... STEARIN(E)

whale .... BLUBBER

wool .... SUINT, LANOLIN

yielding tree .... SHEA

Fat Tuesday .... MARDI GRAS

Fata Morgana .... FAIRY, MIRAGE

fatal .... FEY, FERAL, VITAL, DEADLY, FUNEST, LETHAL, MORTAL, FATEFUL, RUINOUS, SERIOUS, CRITICAL

fatality .... DEATH, ACCIDENT, CASUALTY, DEADLINESS

fate .... LOT, DOOM, KISMET, DESTINY, FORTUNE, PORTION

Eighteenth Amendment's .... REPEAL

of the USS Missouri .... RECOMMISSIONED

twist of .... IRONY

unhappy .... DOOM, DAMNATION

Fate, mythological .... NONA, MORTA, NORNS, URDUR, CLOTHO, PARCAE, DECUMA, ATROPOS, LACHESIS

fated .... FEY, DOOMED, DESTINED, ORDAINED

fateful .... DIRE, BANEFUL, OMINOUS, DECISIVE, PROPHETIC

Fates, one of the .... NONA, MORTA, NORNS, SKULD, URDUR, CLOTHO, DECUMA, PARCA(E), ATROPOS, LACHESIS

whichever one .... WEIRD

fathead ...... CLOD, DUNCE, IDIOT, STUPID

fatheaded .... DULL, DOPEY, OBTUSE, STUPID

father .... ABBA, PAPA, SIRE, BEGET, PATER, PARENT, PRIEST, CREATOR, FOUNDER, ANCESTOR, FOREBEAR, PROTECTOR

Arabic .... ABU, ABOU

brother of .... UNCLE

colloquial .... PA, DAD, POP, DADDY, PAPPY, OLDMAN

combining form .... PATRI, PATRO

dialectic .... PAW

disciples' .... ZEBEDEE

of all .... JUBAL

of American football .... CAMP

of gods .... ZEUS

of History .... HERODOTUS

of hypnotism .... MESMER

of Medicine ...... HIPPOCRATES

of the Titans .... URANUS

of the U.S. Constitution .... MADISON

of the waltz .... STRAUSS

of Waters .... MISSISSIPPI

pertaining to a .... AGNATE, PATERNAL

relative on side of .... AGNATE

superior .... ABBOT

fathered .... SIRED

fatherhood .... PATERNITY

fatherless .... ORBATE

fatherly .... PARENTAL

fathom ..... DELVE, PLUMB, PROBE, SOUND

one fourth of .... QUARTER

fatigue .... FAG, BORE, JADE, TIRE, WEARY, EXHAUST, WEARINESS

clothes .... DENIM

Fatima descendant ...... SAY(Y)ID

descended from .... FATIMID, FATIMITE

father of .... MOHAMMED

husband of .... BLUEBEARD

sister of .... ANNE, JINNAH

263

step-brother of .... ALI
fatling ...... KID, PIG, CALF, LAMB
fats, having strong attraction for
.... LIPOPHILIC
solvent for .... ETHER
Fats's assertion of song
.... AIN'T MISBEHAVING
fatten .... FEED, NURSE, STUFF,
BATTEN, ENRICH
land .... FERTILIZE
fatty ...... OILY, GREASY, ADIPOSE,
LIPAROID, ALIPHATIC
acid .... ADIPIC, VALERIC
combining form .... LIP(O)
comedian .... ARBUCKLE
liquid .... OLEIN
organic compound .... LIPID
secretion of gland ...... SEBUM
substance from sheep's wool
.... SUINT
substance in decomposed
bodies .... ADIPOCERE
tumor .... LIPOMA
fatuity .... FOLLY, IDIOCY,
STUPIDITY, IMBECILITY
fatuous .... VAIN, INANE, INEPT,
SILLY, ASININE, FOOLISH
slang .... DUMB, SAPPY
faubourg .... SUBURB
fauces .... GULLET, THROAT
faucet .... TAP, BIBB, SPILE,
SPOUT, SPIGOT, (BIB)COCK,
PETCOCK, STOPCOCK
dance .... TAP
flow regulator .... VALVE
leak .... DRIP
fault .... FLAW, LACK, SLIP,
ERROR, LAPSE, DEFECT,
FAILING, BLEMISH, MISDEED,
MISTAKE, WEAKNESS,
IMPERFECTION
amusing .... FOIBLE
antonym of .... VIRTUE
find .... NAG, CARP, CAVIL,
KNOCK, CENSURE, LECTURE,
UPBRAID, COMPLAIN, CRITICIZE
moral .... VICE
slight/trifling ...... PECCADILLO
faultfinder ...... MOMUS, CENSOR,
CRITIC, NAG(GER), KNOCKER,
SCOLDER
faultfinding .... CARPING,
CHIDING, CAPTIOUS,
CAVILING, CRITICAL,
QUERULOUS
faultless .... IDEAL, MODEL,
CORRECT, PARAGON, PERFECT,
FLAWLESS, IMPECCABLE
faulty .... AMISS, PECCANT,
DEFECTIVE, ERRONEOUS
faun .... DEITY, SATYR

fauna's life partner .... FLORA
Fauntleroy .... ERROL, CEDRIC
mother of .... DEAREST
Faunus .... PAN
son .... ACIS
Faure, essayist .... ELIE
Faust, composer of ...... GOUNOD
poem, writer of .... GOETHE
fauteuil .... ARMCHAIR
faux pax .... SLIP, BONER, ERROR,
GAFFE, MISSTEP, FALSE STEP,
SOCIAL BLUNDER
faveolate .... CELLED, ALVEOLATE,
HONEYCOMBED
favonian .... MILD, GENTLE
favor ...... AID, BOON, HELP, LEAN,
LIKE, NOTE, BLESS, GRACE,
LEAVE, LETTER, LIKING,
PREFER, SUPPORT, COURTESY,
GOOD WILL, RESEMBLE, TAKE
AFTER
favorable .... PRO, HELPFUL,
OBLIGING, AUSPICIOUS,
PROPITIOUS, AFFIRMATIVE
in astrology .... TRINE
most .... OPTIMUM
opinion .... ESTEEM
favored .... LUCKY, BETTER,
EXEMPT, GIFTED, BLESSED,
POPULAR, FAVORITE,
PREFERABLE
in the draw .... SEEDED
favoring .... FOR, PRO, APPROVING
favorite .... PET, HERO, IDOL,
MINION, BELOVED, DARLING,
DEAREST, PREFERRED
activity .... HOBBY
activity: Brit. ...... CUP OF TEA
colloq. .... FAIR-HAIRED BOY
son .... BENJAMIN
favoritism .... BIAS, NEPOTISM
favors from public office .... PAP
fawn .... DOE, DEER, CRINGE,
BUCK, GROVEL, FLATTER
fawning .... SERVILE, TOADYING
fay .... ELF, JOIN, FAIRY, SPRITE
archaic .... FAITH
faze ...... ANNOY, DAUNT, RATTLE,
WORRY, AGITATE, DISTURB,
RUFFLE, EMBARRASS,
DISCONCERT
FBI agent .... FED, G-MAN
director, former .... HOOVER
FDR's burial place .... HYDE
PARK
letters .... NRA
Fe, in chemistry .... IRON
fealty .... DUTY, HOMAGE,
LOYALTY, DEVOTION,
FIDELITY, ALLEGIANCE
fear .... AWE, QUALM, SCARE,

WORRY, DISMAY, PHOBIA,
ANXIETY, JITTERS, MISGIVING,
APPREHENSION
excessive .... PHOBIA
frantic, unreasoning ..... PANIC
from sudden danger
.... ALARM
intensely .... DREAD
of animals .... ZOOPHOBIA
becoming insane
.... LYSSOPHOBIA
being alone .... MONOPHOBIA
being idle
.... THAASOPHOBIA
birds .... ORNITHOPHOBIA
blood .... HEMOPHOBIA
cats .... AILUROPHOBIA
children .... PEDOPHOBIA
crossing a street
.... AGYROPHOBIA
crowds .... OCHLOPHOBIA
darkness .... NYCTOPHOBIA
death .... THANATOPHOBIA
dogs .... CYNOPHOBIA
enclosed spaces
.... CLAUSTROPHOBIA
fear .... PHOBOPHOBIA
fire .... PYROPHOBIA
flowers .... ANTHOPHOBIA
flying .... AVIOPHOBIA
food .... SITOPHOBIA
ghosts .... PHASMOPHOBIA
God .... THEOPHOBIA
gold .... AUROPHOBIA
heat .... THERMOPHOBIA
heights .... ACROPHOBIA
ice cold places
.... CRYOPHOBIA
law .... METUS
lightning .... ASTRAPHOBIA
men .... ANDROPHOBIA
mice .... MUSOPHOBIA
monsters ...... TERATOPHOBIA
new things .... NEOPHOBIA
one's own fears
.... PHOBOPHOBIA
open spaces
.... AGORAPHOBIA
pain .... ALGOPHOBIA
poison .... TOXIPHOBIA
putting on weight
.... ANOREXIA
sex .... GENOPHOBIA
snow .... CHIONOPHOBIA
speed .... TACHOPHOBIA
spiders ...... ARACHNEPHOBIA
strangers/foreigners
.... XENOPHOBIA
of the Chinese
.... SINOPHOBIA
English .... ANGLOPHOBIA

French .... GALLOPHOBIA
Germans
.... TEUTONOPHOBIA
number 13
.... TRISKAIDEKAPHOBIA
Russians .... RUSSOPHOBIA
sun .... HELIOPHOBIA
stars .... SIDEROPHOBIA
of thunder ...... BRONTOPHOBIA
travel .... HODOPHOBIA
trees .... DENDROPHOBIA
water .... HYDROPHOBIA
women .... GYNEPHOBIA
work .... ERGOPHOBIA
overwhelming/intense
.... PANIC, TERROR
slang .... HEEBIE-JEEBIES
sudden, shocking .... CHILL,
FRIGHT, SHIVERS
fearful ...... DIRE, PAVID, AFRAID,
TREPID, NERVOUS, TERRIFYING
fearless .... BOLD, BRAVE,
DARING, HEROIC, IMPAVID,
INTREPID
flyer .... ACE
slang .... GUTSY
fearlessness .... STEEL NERVES
fearsome .... SCARY, TIMID,
CHILLING, ALARMING,
TIMOROUS, DREADFUL,
FRIGHTFUL
one .... OGRE
feasible .... LIKELY, POSSIBLE,
WORKABLE, PRACTICABLE
feast .... FETE, REGALE, REPAST,
SPREAD, BANQUET, FESTIVAL
after harvest/for departing
person .... FOY
day: comb. form .... MAS
describing one ...... LUCULLAN
list .... ORDO
outdoor .... PICNIC
Feast of Lots .... PURIM
of the Nativity .... YULE
feastless day .... FERIA
feat ...... ACT, DEED, GEST, STUNT,
EXPLOIT, ACCOMPLISHMENT
feather ...... DOWN, PENNA, PINNA,
PLUME, QUILL, PLUMAGE
arrow .... FLEDGE, FLETCH
barb .... HARL, HERL
cloak .... MAMO
combining form .... PENNI
fine .... EGRET, AIGRETTE
grass .... STIPA
helmet .... PANACHE
like .... PINNATE, PLUMOSE,
PENNIFORM
neckwear .... BOA
part of .... WEB, VANE
prefix .... PTERO

quill .... BARREL, CALAMUS
resembling a .... PINNATE,
PLUMATE
shaft .... SCAPE
shed: arch. .... MEW, MOLT
small ..... PLUMULE, PLUMELET
submarine's .... WAKE
under wing .... AXILIAR
vane of .... VEXILLUM
wing .... PINION
featherbed .... MATTRESS
featherbrained .... DIZZY, GIDDY,
IDIOT, SILLY, SIMPLE,
FOOLISH, FRIVOLOUS
feathered ...... PLUMY, PLUMED,
WINGED, FLEDGED, PENNATED,
PLUMOSE, PLUMAGED
featherer of arrows .... PLUMIER
featherless .... CALLOW
feathers .... DOWN, PLUMAGE
adorn with .... (IM)PLUME
bunch of .... TUFT
bird's wing .... ALULA,
COVERTS
covered with soft ...... DOWNY
for flying .... REMIGES
grow .... FLEDGE
plume of .... PANACHE
pull out the .... PLUCK,
DEPLUME
quill .... CALAMI, BARRELS,
COVERTS
smooth the .... PLUME
soft .... DOWN, EIDER
tail .... RECTRIX
trim the .... PREEN
featherweight ...... BOXER, LIGHT,
TRIVIAL, WRESTLER,
NONENTITY
feathery .... DOWNY, FLUFFY
piece .... BOA
feature .... FILM, FORM, PART,
MOTIF, TRAIT,
CHARACTERISTIC
double .... CHIN
of climber's shoes ...... CLEAT
salient .... MOTIF, HIGHLIGHT
feaze .... FAZE, FEEZE, UNRAVEL
febrile .... FEVERISH
February 2 ...... CANDLEMAS DAY
feces .... DREGS, EGESTA,
SEDIMENT, EXCREMENT
feckless .... WEAK, AIMLESS,
USELESS, CARELESS,
POINTLESS
feculence .... DREGS, FILTH
feculent .... FOUL, FILTHY
fecund .... FERTILE, FRUITFUL,
PROLIFIC, PRODUCTIVE
fecundate .... POLLENATE,
POLLINATE

fecundity .... FERTILITY
Fed .... G-MAN, T-MAN, FBI AGENT
fed up: sl. .... BORED, DISGUSTED,
SATIATED, SURFEITED, SICK
AND TIRED OF
fedayeen leader .... ARAFAT,
HABASH
federate .... UNITE
federation .... UNION, LEAGUE,
ALLIANCE
fedora .... HAT
author of play .... SARDOU
embellishment of .... BAND
fee .... TIP, AGIO, DUES, FEOD,
FIEF, TOLL, CHARGE,
GRATUITY, ASSESSMENT,
HONORARIUM
for settling accounts
.... EXCHANGE
hold in .... OWN, POSSESS
lawyer's .... RETAINER
received for work
.... EMOLUMENT
feeble .... PUNY, WEAK, FRAIL,
WASHY, FLABBY, INFIRM,
FLACCID, RICKETY, DECREPIT
minded .... DOTTY
minded person .... DOLT,
FOOL, AMENT, IDIOT, MORON,
DOTARD, HALF-WIT, IMBECILE
mindedness .... AMENTIA
feed .... EAT, FILL, GRUB, OATS,
BROWSE, COSHER, NOURISH,
PROVIDE, SUBSIST
animal .... FODDER, FORAGE
breast .... NURSE
cattle .... AGIST
colloquial .... CHOW, MEAL
fuel to .... STOKE
the kitty .... ANTE
vat .... SILO
well at other's expense
.... BATTEN
feedback .... RUMBLE, STATIC,
RESPONSE
of speaker's words
.... SIDETONE
feeder .... TRIBUTARY, SUBSIDIARY
Baltic .... ODER
Elbe .... OHRE
Moselle .... SAAR
of furnace .... STOKER
of lines .... STOOGE,
STRAIGHTMAN
Pripyat .... STYR
Rhone .... ISERE
Seine .... OISE
feeding box .... MANGER, TROUGH
feel .... BEAR, PALP, SENSE,
TOUCH, ENDURE, SUFFER,
EXPERIENCE

ability to .... (A)ESTHESIA
able to ..... PASSIBLE, SENSIBLE
about .... GROPE
absence .... MISS
achy .... AIL
compassion .... ACHE
dejected .... REPINE
for .... CARE
like .... INCLINED
out .... SOUND
pity .... YEARN
regret .... RUE, REPENT
sorry .... REGRET
feeler .... BARBEL, PALP(US),
ANTENNA, SMELLER,
TENTACLE
for public opinion .... TRIAL
BALLOON
for wind direction and
velocity .... PILOT
BALLOON
kind of .... POLL, CIRRUS
small .... ANTENNULE
feelers, having .... LONGICORN
feeling .... FIRE, HEART, EMOTION,
OPINION, AWARENESS,
SENSATION, SENTIENCE,
SENTIMENT, TOUCH(ING),
SENSITIVITY
affectionate .... LOVE,
WARMTH, TENDERNESS
capable of .... SENTIENT
impatient .... RESTIVE
of approval/agreement
.... SYMPATHY
arousal .... AGITATION,
EXCITEMENT
being emotionally affected
..... RAPT, MOVED, TOUCHED,
IMPRESSED
bitterness/resentment
.... RANCOR, ANIMOSITY
emotional warmth
.... ARDOR, FERVOR, PASSION
enjoyment/delight
.... PLEASURE
great vigor and liveliness
.... ZEST, GUSTO
ill-being .... DYSPHORIA
overpowering joy
.... ECSTASY
pity/sorrow/sympathy
.... PATHOS, COMPASSION
regret .... REMORSE,
REPENTANCE
vehemence ...... FURY, RAGE,
ANGER
weariness .... ENNUI,
LASSITUDE
wellbeing .... EUPHORIA
show .... EMOTE, REACT

strong/intense .... HEAT
sudden, violent .... SPASM
that something bad will
happen .... HUNCH,
INTUITION, FOREBODING,
PREMONITION
turn of .... WHIM, CAPRICE
feelingly .... HEARTILY,
EMOTIONALLY
feet, care of .... PODIATRY
combining form .... PED(E),
PEDI
5,280 .... A MILE
having .... PEDATE
having many ..... MULTIPED(E)
having three .... TRIPEDAL,
TRIPODAL, TRIPODIC
pertaining to the .... PEDAL,
PODAL, PEDARY
pig's .... PETTITOES
slang .... DOGS
three .... YARD
verse of two .... DIPODY
without .... APOD
feeze .... DRIVE, AGITATE,
DISTURB, DISCONCERT
feign .... ACT, FAKE, ASSUME,
INVENT, PRETEND, SIMULATE,
DISSEMBLE, FABRICATE
sickness .... MALINGER
feigned .... FICTIVE, SIMULAR
feint .... SHAM, BLIND, TRICK,
ARTIFICE, PRETENSE,
DIVERSION
in fencing .... APPEL
feis .... FEAST, FESTIVAL
feisty .... HUFFY, TESTY, CRANKY,
FRISKY, SNAPPISH, BELLICOSE
feldspar .... ALBITE, KAOLIN,
ODINITE, SILICATE, ADULARIA,
ANORTHITE, MOONSTONE,
LABRADORITE
felicitate ...... BLESS, GRATULATE,
COMPLIMENT, CONGRATULATE
felicitation .... BLESSING, BEST
WISHES, COMPLIMENTS
felicitous .... APT, HAPPY, TIMELY,
PERTINENT, APPROPRIATE
felicity .... JOY, BLISS, SONSY,
SONSIE, HAPPINESS
felid .... CAT, FELINE
feline .... SLY, LION, LYNX, PUMA,
PUSS, CATTY, OUNCE, TIGER,
CRAFTY, JAGUAR, CAT(LIKE),
CUNNING, LEOPARD, PANTHER
famous .... ELSA
fierce .... OCELOT
fell .... DROP, CRUEL, CRUSH,
TOPPLE, FLATTEN, CUT DOWN,
GUN DOWN, BRING DOWN,
KNOCK DOWN, PROSTRATE,

RUTHLESS, TERRIBLE
archaic .... DEADLY
of animal .... HIDE, PELT, SKIN
slang .... DECK
felled .... SLAIN, BROKEN,
CONQUERED
fellah: Egyptian .... LABORER,
PEASANT
feller: sl. .... FELLOW
felling .... HAG
fellow. See also **person/man**
.... EGG, CHAP, GENT, JACK,
MATE, PEER, BLOKE, EQUAL,
BUGGER, BUSTER, FRIEND,
COMPEER, CORYDON, PARTNER
archaic .... SIRRAH
big, clumsy .... LOOBY,
LUBBER
British: colloq. .... CULLY
brutish .... YAHOO, HELLION
clumsy .... OAF, LOUT, LOOBY,
MUFFER, FOOZLER,
STUMBLEBUM
colloquial .... BOY, GUY, MAN,
BEAU, PERSON, SUITOR
conceited .... FOP, DUDE,
DANDY, COXCOMB
contemptible .... CAD, SCAB,
VILLAIN, SCOUNDREL
countryman .... COMPATRIOT
faint-hearted .... SISSY,
COWARD
feeling .... KINDNESS,
SYMPATHY, COOPERATION
fine .... TRUMP, GOOD EGG
flashy .... SPORT
foolish .... SOP, FOOL, ZANY,
DUNCE, SIMPLETON
funny ..... WAG, CARD, CLOWN,
JOKER, BUFFOON
lazy .... BUM, SLOUCH
little .... BUB, LAD, SHAVER
mean .... THUG, BUCKO, BULLY
member .... BROTHER,
COMRADE, CONFRERE,
ASSOCIATE, COLLEAGUE
nicknamed Hi .... HIRAM
queer .... CODGER, GEEZER
slang .... GUY, BIRD, BOZO,
GINK, FELLER, HOMBRE
stupid .... ASS, LUG, OAF,
CLOD, GOOF, GANDER, NITWIT,
BLOCKHEAD, LOGGERHEAD
traveler .... ESCORT,
CHAPERON, COMPANION,
SYMPATHIZER
tricky .... KNAVE, ROGUE,
SCAMP, RASCAL, SHYSTER
unprincipled ...... SCAPEGRACE
wicked ..... FIEND, SCOUNDREL
worthless .... BUM, CAD,

ROGUE, SCAMP, RASCAL

young .... CHAP, BLADE,
SPARK, SPRIG, CALLAN(T)

fellowship ...... AMITY, SODALITY,
COMPANY, SORORITY,
ENDOWMENT, BROTHERHOOD,
CAMARADERIE

felly .... DEADLY, CRUELLY,
WHEEL RIM

felo-de-se .... SUICIDE

felon .... CON, BASE, WICKED,
CONVICT, CULPRIT, VILLAIN,
WHITLOW, CRIMINAL

felonious .... BASE, VILE, WRONG,
SINFUL, ILLEGAL, CRIMINAL

felony .... RAPE, ARSON, CRIME,
MURDER, OFFENSE

felt .... FABRIC, SENSED

obliged .... HAD TO,
COMPELLED

felucca .... SHIP

felwort .... GENTIAN, MULLEIN

female .... GIRL, LADY(LIKE),
UNMANLY, FEMININE,
WOMAN(LY), EFFEMINATE

animal .... COW, DAM, EWE,
ROE, SHE, SOW, JILL, MARE,
BITCH, JENNY, VIXEN, LIONESS,
TIGRESS

animal's teat .... DUG

buffalo .... ARNEE

camel .... NAGA

cat .... TABBY

change of life .... MENOPAUSE,
CLIMATERIC

combining form .... GYNE

cow .... HEIFER

deer .... DOE, ROE, HIND,
REINDEER

demon/frumpy .... HAG, LAMIA

dog .... SLUT, BITCH

donkey .... JENNET

elephant .... COW

fascinating .... SIREN

ferret .... JILL

figure, sculptured ...... ORANT,
CARYATID

fox .... VIXEN

gonad .... OVARY

gossip .... TABBY

horse .... MARE

insect .... GYNE

kangaroo .... GIN

lobster .... HEN

mythical .... FURY

pig .... SOW, GILT

praying figure .... ORANT

prophet .... SEERESS,
CASSANDRA

rabbit .... DOE

reproductive organ ..... OVARY

ruff .... REE, REEVE

sandpiper .... REE

servant .... MAID, WENCH

sex .... DISTAFF

sex hormone .... ESTRIOL,
ESTRONE

sheep .... EWE

slang .... BUNNY, FEMME

slave .... DASI, ODALISK

sovereign ..... QUEEN, EMPRESS

swimmer .... MERMAID

warrior .... AMAZON

wolf .... BITCH

feme .... WIFE

sole .... WIDOW, SPINSTER

feminine ...... FEMALE, WOMANLY,
PETTICOAT, EFFEMINATE

suffix .... ESS, INE, ETTE, TRIX,
STRESS

femininity .... MULIEBRITY,
WEAKER SEX

femme .... WIFE, WOMAN

fatale .... VAMP, SIREN,
DELILAH, LORELEI, MATA HARI

femme's spouse .... MARI

femur .... THIGH(BONE)

fen .... BOG, MOOR, MARSH,
SWAMP, MORASS

fence .... PALE, EVADE, PARRY,
RADDLE, BARRIER, DEFENSE,
ENCLOSE, RAIL(ING),
PALISADE, SWORDPLAY

construction site
.... HOARDING

crossing .... STILE

in old style .... EMPALE

material .... PALE, TITE, PICKET

of shrubs .... HEDGE

of stakes .... PALISADE

of woven work .... RADDLE,
WATTLE

part ..... PALING, BARBED WIRE

stake .... PALE, PICKET

step .... STILE

sunken .... (H)AHA

temporary .... HURDLE,
HOARDING

to .... SCRIME

fenced enclosure for grounds
(surrounding a house or
dwelling) .... CURTILAGE

holding cattle and horses
.... CORRAL

holding sheep/cattle
.... KRAAL

military prisoners
.... STOCKADE

fencer .... DUELER, SWORDSMAN

cry of .... HAI, SASA, ON
GUARD

opening position .... EN GARDE

fencing attack .... REPRISE

breastplate .... PLASTROM

dummy for .... PEL

foil .... EPEE

foil guard .... BUTTON

leap .... VOLT

mask .... HELMET

movement .... APPEL

point .... FOIL

position .... CARTE, SIXTE,
QUARTE, QUINTE, TIERCE,
SECONDE, SEPTIME

score .... PUNTO

stroke .... BUTT, APPEL,
LUNGE, RIPOSTE

sword .... EPEE, FOIL, SABRE,
RAPIER

term .... TIERCE, TOUCHE, EN
GARDE, SECONDE

thrust .... BUTT, LUNGE,
PUNTO, REMISE, RIPOSTE,
REPRISE

fend .... HOLD, WARD, AVERT,
PARRY, SHIFT, RESIST

off .... REPEL, REPULSE

off a tackler .... STIFFARM

fender .... BUMPER, MUDGUARD,
BUFFER, SHIELD,
COWCATCHER

damage/foible .... DENT

fenestra .... WINDOW, OPENING

fennec .... FOX

fennel .... HERB, ANISE

fenny .... BOGGY, MARSHY

feod .... FEE, FIEF

feracious .... FRUITFUL

feral .... WILD, FATAL, BRUTAL,
DEADLY, FERINE, GLOOMY,
SAVAGE, UNTAMED,
FUNEREAL, TOMBLIKE

Ferber, Edna .... NOVELIST

heroine .... SELINA

novel .... SO BIG

Ferde, composer .... GROPE

fer de lance .... SNAKE, VIPER

Ferdinand .... BULL, KING, TORO,
EMPEROR

Marcos's wife .... IMELDA

Philippines president
.... MARCOS

Philippines discoverer
.... MAGELLAN

V, wife of .... ISABELLA I

fere .... MATE, PEER, WIFE,
HUSBAND, COMPANION

feretory .... BIER, SHRINE

feria .... FESTIVAL, HOLIDAYS

ferine .... WILD, FERAL, FIERCE

fermata .... HOLD, PAUSE

ferment .... BREW, FRET, RAISE,
SOUR, YEAST, AROUSE,

(EN)ZYME, ACIDIFY, LEAVEN, SEETHE, UNREST, UPROAR, AGITATION, COMMOTION, CURDLE, EFFERVESCE, SACCHARIZE

fermented drink ...... ALE, BEER, MEAD, SAKE, WINE, KUMISS

fermentation .... FUME, SOURING, TUMULT, TURMOIL, YEASTINESS

chemistry of .... ZYMURGY

process .... ZYMOSIS

fermenting agent .... YEAST, ENZYME, LEAVEN, BACTERIA

fern .... BRACKEN, WOODSIA, MOONWORT, MULEWORT, MAIDENHAIR

coarse .... BRAKE

edible .... TARA

filaments .... RHIZOID

flowering .... OSMUND

leaf .... FROND

like plant/perennial stemmed .... ACROGEN

patches .... SORI

petiole .... STIPE

rootstock .... ROI

seed .... SPORE

spore .... SORUS

ferocious .... WILD, CRUEL, FERAL, FIERCE, SAVAGE, BEASTLY

ferocity .... CRUELTY, SAVAGERY, BRUTALITY

Ferrer, actor .... MEL, JOSE

ferret .... HARASS, SEARCH, WEASEL, UNCOVER, UNEARTH

-eyed ...... OBSERVANT, EAGLE-EYED, SHARP-SIGHTED

-eyed giant .... ARGUS

female .... JILL

-like animal .... TAYRA, MONGOOS(E)

out .... SPY, FISH, HUNT, DETECT, DIG UP

relative of .... SKUNK, POLECAT

ferric oxide, anhydrous .... HEMATITE

powder .... ROUGE

ferrotype .... TINTYPE

ferrous sulfate .... COPPERAS

ferrule .... CAP, TIP, RING, BUSHING

ferrum .... IRON

ferry .... PONT, CROSS, CONVEY, AIRDROP, AIRLIFT, SHUTTLE, TRANSPORT

ferryboat .... BAC, PONT, RAFT, SCOW, BARGE, LAUNCH, TENDER

ferryman ...... CHARON, BOATMAN

fertile .... FAT, RANK, RICH, FECUND, PINGUID, FRUITFUL, PROLIFIC, PRODUCTIVE

area .... OASIS

become .... BATTEN

land's surface .... TOPSOIL

mind .... CREATIVE, INVENTIVE, IMAGINATIVE

fertilization .... ENRICHMENT, POLLINATION, PROCREATION, IMPREGNATION

fertilize .... TILL, ENRICH, CULTURE, FRUCTIFY, FECUNDATE, CULTIVATE, POLLINATE

fertilizer .... MARL, GUANO, ALINIT, MANURE, NITRATE, COMPOST, AMMONITE

fertilizing agent .... MILT

ferule .... ROD, HERB, RULER, STICK, FERULA, SCEPTER

fervency ...... HEAT, ZEAL, ARDOR, WARMTH, FERVOR, PASSION

fervent .... HOT, ARDENT, HEATED, EARNEST, GLOWING, PASSIONATE

fervid .... HOT, FIERY, BURNING, FERVENT, INTENSE, FLAMING, FEVERISH, IMPASSIONED

fervor .... ZEAL, ZEST, ARDOR, PASSION, ENTHUSIASM

Fescennine .... VULGAR, OBSCENE

fescue .... GRASS, STICK, STRAW

festal .... GAY, GALA, JOLLY, MERRY, JOVIAL, JOYOUS

fester .... GNAW, HURT, DECAY, RIPEN, RANKLE, ABSCESS, INFECT, PUSTULE, EMBITTER, ULCERATE, SUPPURATE

festering condition .... POX, POCK, ULCER, CANKER, PIMPLE, BLISTER

festival .... ALE, FAIR, FETE, GALA, FEAST, FERIA, FIESTA, CARNIVAL, CELEBRATION, MERRYMAKING

Apollo .... DELIA

Dutch .... KERMIS

paper shower .... CONFETTI

religious .... FIESTA

festive .... GAY, GALA, MERRY, JOLLY, JOVIAL, JOYOUS

festivity .... JOY, MIRTH, PARTY, GAIETY, JOLLITY, REVELRY, MERRIMENT, REJOICING

slang .... BLOWOUT, JAMBOREE

festoon .... LEI, CHAPLET, WREATH, GARLAND, EMBELLISH

festooned .... ADORNED, SPANGLY, STUDDED, BEDECKED,

FLOWERED

feta .... CHEESE

fetal .... BUDDING, EMBRYONIC

fetation .... PREGNANCY

fetch .... GET, DEAL, BRING, CARRY, CHARM, HEAVE, INFER, TRICK, YIELD, ELICIT, WRAITH, GO FOR, ATTRACT, PRODUCE, SELL FOR, RETRIEVE

fetching .... ALLURING, CATCHING, PLEASING, CHARMING, ENGAGING, APPEALING, ATTRACTIVE

fete .... FEAST, REGALE, FESTIVAL, CELEBRATE, ENTERTAIN(MENT)

feterita .... SORGHUM

fetial .... PRIESTS

fetid .... FOUL, OLID, RANK, PUTRID, RANCID, SMELLY, NOISOME, STINKING, (MAL)ODOROUS

fetiparous animal ...... WOMBAT, OPOSSUM, KANGAROO, BANDICOOT, MARSUPIAL

fetish ...... OBI, IDOL, JUJU, ANITO, CHARM, MANIA, OBEAH, TOTEM, AMULET, GRIGRI, VOODOO, TALISMAN, WEAKNESS

fetlock .... TUFT

fetor .... STINK, STENCH

fetter .... BOND, GYVE, IRON, CHECK, HAMPER, HOBBLE, HOGTIE, (EN)CHAIN, SHACKLE, MANACLE, HANDCUFF, RESTRAIN

fettle .... FORM, TRIM, ORDER, SHAPE, STATE, CONDITION

fetus .... EMBRYO

hair of .... LANUGO

malformed .... TERATISM

membrane ..... CAUL, CHORION

membrane that surrounds the .... AMNIOTIC SAC

premature birth of .... MISCARRIAGE

procedure to detect abnormalities of .... AMNIOCENTESIS

waters that surround the .... AMNIOTIC FLUID

feu .... FEE

feud .... FEE, FEOD, FIEF, GRUDGE, RANCOR, STRIFE, QUARREL, REVENGE, RIVALRY, CONFLICT, VENDETTA

feudal .... LORDLY, MAGISTRAL, MASTERFUL, SEIGNIORAL

baron .... THANE

benefice .... FEU, FIEF
estate ..... FEE, FEU, FEOD, FIEF
estate head .... LORD
jurisdiction .... SOC, SOKE
land .... FEOD, BENEFICE
lord .... THANE, SEIGNEUR
retainers .... MEINY, MEINIE
service .... AVERA
slave .... SERF
system .... MONARCHY,
ARISTOCRACY
tax .... TALLAGE, TAIL(L)AGE
tenant/underling .... COTTER,
VASSAL, SOCAGER
tenant's payment .... HERIOT
title .... EARL, BARON
feudalism .... HELOTRY, SERFDOM,
VASSALAGE
feudatory .... FIEF, LIEGE,
VASSAL, SERVILE, SUBJECT
fever ...... HEAT, CAUMA, PYREXIA,
BRUCELLOSIS, TEMPERATURE
blister .... COLD SORE
causing/pertaining to
.... PYRETIC
characterized by .... FEBRILE
chill .... AGUE, ALGOR
intermittent .... OCTAN,
QUARTAN, TERTIAN
kind of .... DANDY, DENGUE,
JUNGLE, YELLOW, MALARIA,
QUARTAN, QUINTAN, SCARLET,
TERTIAN, TROPICAL,
BREAKBONE, BLACKWATER,
YELLOWJACK
mental confusion caused by
high .... DELIRIUM
partner of .... CHILLS
recurring .... QUOTIDIAN
reducer .... PIPERINE,
FEBRIFUGE, ANTIPYRETIC
sore .... HERPES
tropical .... DENGUE,
CALENTURE
undulant .... MALTA
fevered .... HOT, HECTIC,
FLUSHED, DELIRIOUS
feverish .... FIERY, HECTIC,
BURNING, FEBRILE, PYRETIC,
FRANTIC, RESTLESS
few .... CURN, RARE, SCANT,
LITTLE, MEAGER, SCARCE
and far between .... SPARSE,
INFREQUENT
the .... MINORITY
fewer .... LESS
fewest .... LEAST
fey .... FATED, DOOMED
fez-like cap .... TURBAN,
TARBOOSH
wearer ..... SHRINER, EGYPTIAN

fi in hi-fi .... FIDELITY
fiacre .... CAB, CARRIAGE
fiance(e) .... BETROTHED
colloquial .... INTENDED
fiasco .... MESS, BOTCH, FIZZLE,
TURKEY, DEBACLE, FAILURE,
MISFIRE, WASHOUT
fiat .... EDICT, ORDER, DECREE,
COMMAND, SANCTION
fib .... (WHITE)LIE
fibber .... LIAR
fiber .... DATIL, NATURE, THREAD,
FUNICLE, QUALITY, FILAMENT
bark .... TAPA
carpet .... ISTLE
century plant ..... PITA, AGAVE
cleaning tool .... HATCHEL
coconut .... COIR
combing .... CARDING
cordage ..... HEMP, IMBE, PINA,
SUNN, ABACA, SISAL, AMBARI,
AMBARY, MAGUEY, RAFFIA,
FILASSE
East Indies plant .... RAMIE
knot .... NEP
mat/phloegm .... BAST
networks .... RETIA
palm .... TAL, ERUC
plant .... ALOE, FLAX, HEMP,
IXLE, ABACA, ISTLE, RAMIE,
SISAL, AMBARY, COTTON,
MAGUEY
roll of .... SLUB
small .... FIBRIL
strand .... YARN
synthetic .... ORLON, RAYON,
DACRON
tree .... BASS, BAST, BAOBAB
waste .... NOIL, FLOSS
wool .... PILE, STAPLE
woven fabric .... MAT(TING)
fibers, fine .... FUZZ
to clean .... SCUTCH
twist .... ROVE
fibril .... FILAMENT, ROOT HAIR
fibrin .... GLUTEN
fibrous .... ROPY
texture .... DESMOID
fibula .... PIN, BONE, CLASP,
BUCKLE
of the .... PERONEAL
fichu .... CAPE, LACE
fickle .... GIDDY, ERRATIC,
FLIGHTY, MOONISH, MOVABLE,
MUTABLE, UNFIXED,
UNSTABLE, UNSTEADY,
VOLATILE, CHANGEFUL,
WHIMSICAL, CAPRICIOUS,
CHANGEABLE, INCONSTANT
girl .... FLIRT, COQUETTE
fico .... FIG, SNAP, TRIFLE

fictile .... CERAMIC, PLASTIC
fiction .... MYTH, TALE, YARN,
FABLE, NOVEL, FANTASY,
ROMANCE, FALSEHOOD
kingdom of .... OZ
fictional .... MYTHICAL,
LEGENDARY, FABRICATED,
FICTITIOUS, MAKE-BELIEVE
animal .... BAMBI
fictitious .... BOGUS, FALSE,
PHONY, UNREAL, FEIGNED,
ASSUMED, FABULOUS,
MYTHICAL, SPURIOUS,
IMAGINARY
name .... ALIAS, JANE DOE,
JOHN DOE
story .... PIGMENT
fictive .... SHAM, FEIGNED,
FANCIFUL, IMAGINED,
IMAGINARY
fid .... BAR, PIN
fiddle .... KIT, GIGA, VIOL, FIDGET,
TRIFLE, VIOLIN
ancient .... REBEC
bow of .... ARCO
faddle .... FUSS, NONSENSE
fit as a .... HALE
fiddledeedee .... NONSENSE,
RIDICULOUS, WISHY-WASHY
fiddler .... VIOLINIST
crab .... UCA
fiddlestick .... BOW, TRIFLE
fiddlesticks! .... NONSENSE,
MALARKEY, POPPYCOCK
fiddling .... PETTY, USELESS,
TRIFLING
fide, _____ (in good faith)
.... BONA
Fidelio character .... LENORE,
FLORESTAN
fidelity .... FEALTY, LOYALTY,
ACCURACY, DEVOTION,
EXACTNESS, ALLEGIANCE,
FAITHFULNESS
fidget .... TOSS, FRET, FIDDLE,
JITTER, SQUIRM, TWITCH
fidgety .... FUSSY, UNEASY, JERKY,
ACTIVE, NERVOUS, JITTERY,
RESTIVE, RESTLESS
fie .... SHAME
fief .... FEE, FEOD, FEUD, BENEFICE
give or sell .... FEOFF
holder .... FEOFFEE
person granting .... FEOFFER,
FEOFFOR
field .... ACRE, AREA, LAND,
PLAIN, RANGE, REALM,
SPHERE, SAVANNA, CLEARING
border .... RAND
combat/house .... ARENA
cultivated .... GLEBE

enclosed .... AGER, CROFT

glacial .... FIRN, NEVE

glass .... BINOCLE,
BINOCULAR(S)

grassy .... LEA, PASTURE

hospital .... AMBULANCE

mouse .... VOLE

of honor/conflict
.... BATTLEFIELD,
BATTLEGROUND

of work .... LINE, CAREER,
METIER

officer .... MAJOR, COLONEL

open .... CAMPUS

plowed .... ERD

sight ..... SNAKE IN THE GRASS

tent .... MARQUEE

unplowed strip .... RAND

used for grazing ...... PRAIRIE,
GRASSLAND

Field of Dreams .... BASEBALL
DIAMOND

fieldfare .... THRUSH

fiend .... IMP, DEMON, DEVIL,
SATAN, SHAITAN, SHEITAN,
EVILDOER

colloquial .... NUT, BUFF,
ADDICT, (FAN)ATIC

fiendish .... CRUEL, WICKED,
DEMONIC, HELLISH, PECCANT,
SATANIC, VICIOUS, DEVILISH

fierce ...... WILD, LUPINE, SAVAGE,
INTENSE, VIOLENT, FEROCIOUS

as of speech .... SCATHING,
BELLICOSE, TRUCULENT

manner, staring in a
.... GLARING

fiery .... HOT, RED, ARDENT,
FERVID, SULTRY, BLAZING,
GLARING, GLOWING, IGNEOUS,
INFLAMED, SPIRITED,
EXCITABLE, IMPETUOUS,
PASSIONATE, HOT-TEMPERED

fiesta .... FETE, GALA, FERIA,
HOLIDAY, FESTIVAL,
CELEBRATION

fife .... PIPE, FLUTE

fifth columnist .... QUISLING,
TURNCOAT, COLLABORATOR

finger .... PINKY, PINKIE

Fifth Avenue jewelry shop
.... CARTIER

fiftieth anniversary .... JUBILEE

anniversary of a wedding
.... GOLDEN

fifty-fifty ...... EVEN, EQUAL, TOSS-
UP, EVEN-STEVEN

percent .... HALF, MOIETY

third card .... JOKER

two cards .... PACK

fig .... A BIT, A HOOT, DRESS,

SHAPE, RETUND, TRIFLE,
SYCONIUM, TRIFLING

basket .... CABAS

don't care a .... INDIFFERENT

dried .... CARICA

Italian .... FICO

like .... CARICOUS

marigold .... SAMH

parrot .... LORILET

producer .... BANYAN TREE

Smyrna .... ELEME, ELEMI

tree ..... UPAL, PIPAS, BANYAN,
BOTREE

figeater .... BEETLE, JUNE BUG

fight .... ROW, FEUD, FRAY,
BRUSH, RUN-IN, COMBAT,
JOSTLE, AFFRAY, STRIFE,
TUSSLE, CONTEND, QUARREL,
WARFARE, STRUGGLE

a bright sun .... SQUINT

against .... RIVAL, OPPOSE,
RESIST, COMPETE

between countries/factions
.... WAR, BATTLE, CONFLICT,
HOSTILITIES

between two persons, with
deadly weapons .... DUEL

close quarters .... HAND TO
HAND

colloquial .... MIX-UP

desire to .... ANIMUS

fond of .... SCRAPPY

for .... VIE, STRIVE

for a cause .... SERVE,
SUPPORT, CHAMPION

free-for-all .... RIOT, MELEE,
RUMBLE

noisily .... BRAWL, BROIL

of a sort .... DUEL, BOXING

over .... BICKER, DISPUTE,
WRANGLE

program .... CARD

slang .... SCRAP

with feet and fists ..... SAVATE

fighter .... PUG, BOXER, BRAVE,
RIVAL, BATTLER, CONTENDER,
PUGILIST, COMBATANT

for a cause .... MILITANT

frenzied .... AMOK, AMUCK,
BARESARK

kind of .... AIRPLANE

fighting chance of a sort
.... ODDS

gal of 1942 .... WAC, WAAC,
WAAF

man .... SOLDIER, WARRIOR,
LEGIONARY

policy .... MILITANCY

sport .... BOXING, WRESTLING

women of the U.S. Navy
.... WAVES

Fighting Bob, sobriquet
.... EVANS

figment of the mind
.... FANTASM, FANTASY,
PHANTASM(A)

foolish/impossible
.... CHIMERA

figuline .... CLAY, STATUE,
POTTERY, PORCELAIN

figurant .... EXTRA,
(BALLET)DANCER,
SUPERNUMERARY

figuration .... ADORNING,
FORM(ING), SHAPING,
OUTLINE, LIMNING,
DEPICTION, APPEARANCE

figurative .... TYPICAL, IRONICAL,
ALLUSIVE, SYMBOLIC,
COLLOQUIAL, ALLEGORIC(AL),
METAPHOR(ICAL)

language ..... TROPE, IMAGERY,
ALLEGORY

not .... LITERAL

figuratively .... IN A SENSE, SO TO
SPEAK

figure .... BODY, FORM, DIGIT,
IMAGE, SOLID, NUMBER,
RECKON, SYMBOL, COMPUTE,
DIAGRAM, IMAGINE, PICTURE

architectural .... TELAMON,
CARYATID

carved .... GLYPHIC

crescent shaped .... LUNE,
LUNULA

8-sided .... OCTAGON,
OCTANGLE

equal-angled .... ISOGON

4-sided .... SQUARE,
TETRAGON, RECTANGLE,
QUADRANGLE

in a title search .... AREA

of speech .... TROPE, SIMILE,
ZEUGMA, IMAGERY, LITOTES,
METAPHOR, METONYMY,
OXYMORON, HENDIADYS,
HYPERBOLE

on .... RELY, COUNT, DEPEND

ornamental .... DEVICE

out ..... DOPE, SOLVE, DEDUCE,
REASON, COMPUTE,
CALCULATE, UNDERSTAND

oval .... ELLIPSE

part of human .... BUST,
TORSO, TRUNK

skating jump .... LUTZ

10-sided .... DECAGON(AL)

3-sided/3-cornered
.... TRIANGLE

up .... ADD, SUM, TALLY,
TOTAL, COMPUTE

used as support .... ATLAS,

TELEMON, ATLANTES, CARYATID

figured .... PLANNED

figurehead .... DUMMY, PUPPET

figures .... DATA, ADDS UP, STATISTICS

figurine ...... BUST, DOLL, STATUE, CARVING, TANAGRA, MANNEQUIN, STATUETTE

kind of .... SNOWMAN, SCARECROW

well-known ..... EMMY, OSCAR

figwort .... MULLE(I)N, FOXGLOVE, SNAPDRAGON

Fiji bay ...... NATEWA, SAVUSAVU

capital .... SUVA

city/town .... BA, NADI, LAMBASA, LAUTOKA, VATUKOULA

chestnut .... RATA

dependency .... ROTUMA

island ...... KIOA, KORO, NGAU, MOALA, RAMBI, MATUKU, OVALAU, TOTOYA, MBENGGA, THITHIA, VATULELE, VITI LEVU, VANUA LEVU

language .... HINDI, FIJIAN, ENGLISH

mountain .... BATINI, TOMANIIVI

point .... UNDU

tree .... BURI

filament .... BAND, CORD, HAIR, HERL, HARL(E), LIST, TAPE, VEIN, WIRE, CABLE, CHORD, FIBER, FILUM, STRIP, CILIUM, STRAND, THREAD

of a plant .... TENDRIL

spun .... YARN

filamentous .... ROPY, WIRY, HAIRY, STRINGY

filature .... REEL

filbert .... HAZEL(NUT)

filch .... NIM, ROB, STEAL, PILFER, PURLOIN, SHOPLIFT

slang .... SWIPE

file .... ROW, ENTER, CARLET, FOLDER, RECORD, SUBMIT, ARRANGE, CABINET, DOSSIER

away .... STORE

flat .... QUANNET

rough .... RASP

filet .... NET, LACE

filial .... LOVING

duty .... OBEY, HONOR

filibeg .... KILT

filibuster .... OUTTALK, TALKOUT, HINDERER, MERCENARY, ADVENTURER, FREEBOOTER

relative of a .... TALKATHON

filigree .... LACE, TRACERY,

ARABESQUE

filings .... REMAINS, SCRAPINGS

Filipino. See also **Philippines**

.... MORO, TAGALOG, PILIPINO

fill .... PAD, LOAD, PLUG, SATE, STUFF, OCCUPY, SUPPLY, PERVADE, PERMEATE

a need .... SATISFY

in .... BRIEF, INFORM, STANDBY, SUBSTITUTE

in the blanks .... COMPLETE

the tank .... GAS

to excess .... HEAP, CONGEST

with ardor .... FIRE

with hate .... ENVENOM, EMBITTER

with wrath .... INCENSE

fille .... GIRL, MAID, DAUGHTER, SPINSTER

de joie .... PROSTITUTE

filled .... FULL, REPLETE

gold .... BRASS

to capacity .... SATED, CHOCKFUL

with enthusiasm .... EAGER

filler .... SHIM, PADDING, STUFFING

seasoned .... DRESSING

shoe .... INSOLE

fillet .... BAND, BONE, FACIA, LABEL, STRIP, LISTEL, RIBBON, T(A)ENIA

architectural .... ORLE, ORLO

hair .... BAND, SNOOD

narrow .... ORIE, STRIA, ANADEM

filling .... PACKING, PADDING

dentist's ...... GOLD, AMALGAM

for a tooth .... INLAY

material .... PUTTY

place .... GAS STATION, SERVICE STATION

weaving .... WARP, WEFT, WOOF

fillip .... TAP, SNAP, TONIC, EXCITE, STIMULUS

fillister .... GROOVE

filly .... FOAL, MARE

colloquial .... GIRL, WOMAN

film .... BLUR, HAZE, SCUM, MOVIE, SHOOT, COATING, NEGATIVE, PHOTOGRAPH

award-winning ..... GONE WITH THE WIND, THE GRAPES OF WRATH, THE LIFE OF EMILE ZOLA

descriptive of horror .... KNEEKNOCKER

green .... PATINA

part .... REEL

producer Jerry .... WALD

star Edmund, early ...... LOWE

filmy ...... HAZY, GAUZY, BLURRED

cloth .... GOSSAMER

filose .... THREADLIKE, FILAMENTOUS

fils .... SON, YOUTH

English equivalent ..... JUNIOR

filter .... OOZE, SIFT, LEACH, SIEVE, STRAIN, COLATURE, FILTRATE, PERCOLATE

impurities ...... PURIFY, REFINE

screen .... RESEAU

substance .... FELT, SAND, CHARCOAL

through .... SEEP

filth .... DIRT, MUCK, SMUT, SLIME, ORDURE, GARBAGE, SQUALOR, IMPURITY, INDECENCY, FECULENCE, OBSCENITY

filthy .... FOUL, LEWD, RICH, VILE, DIRTY, MUCKY, NASTY, SLIMY, ROTTEN, SMUTTY, OBSCENE, SQUALID, UNCLEAN, FECULENT

animal .... PIG

lucre ..... DIRTY MONEY, DIRTY RICHES

smelly place .... STY, CESSPOOL

filtrate .... FILTER, STRAIN

fin .... VEE, FIVER, PINNA, PROPELLOR, FLIPPER, PINNULE

de _____ .... SIECLE

describing one .... CAUDAL, DORSAL, VENTRAL

footed animal .... PINNIPED

in aeronautics .... RUDDER, AIRFOIL

slang .... HAND

finagle .... CHEAT, RENEGE, WANGLE, MANEUVER

final .... END, LAST, TELIC, DERNIER, DECIDING, DECISIVE, ULTIMATE, CONCLUSIVE

authority .... SAY-SO

CB words ...... OVER AND OUT

discharge .... QUIETUS

judgment .... DOOM

melody .... TAPS

word .... NEVER

word, frequent .... AMEN

finale .... END, CODA, SWAN SONG, CONCLUSION

finally .... EN FIN, AT LAST, IN TIME, IN THE END, DEFINITELY, EVENTUALLY, ONCE AND FOR ALL

finals to students .... BRAIN-DRAIN

finance .... BACK, FUND, SUBSIDIZE, CAPITALIZE, UNDERWRITE

finances .... FUNDS, MONEY, PURSE, BUDGET, ACCOUNTS
financial ...... FISCAL, MONETARY, PECUNIARY
gain, unexpected .... WINDFALL
headache .... ARREARS
independence .... EASY STREET
venture .... FLIER
financially sound/healthy .... SOLVENT, ABOVE WATER
financier .... BANKER, TYCOON, CAPITALIST
finback .... GRASO, WHALE, RORQUAL, RAZORBACK
finch ...... SPINK, CANARY, OSCINE, SISKIN, BUNTING, REDPOLL, SPARROW, GROSBEAK, SNOWBIRD, SONGBIRD
African .... FINK, MORO
American ...... JUNCO, BURION, LINNET, TOWHEE, CHEWINK
canary-like .... SERIN
kin .... CARDINAL
like bird .... TANAGER
small/yellow .... SERIN
find .... GET, ESPY, LEARN, DECIDE, DETECT, OBTAIN, DISCOVER, PERCEIVE
fault .... BEEF, CARP, CAVIL, COMPLAIN
fault continually .... NAG
out .... LEARN, SOLVE, ASCERTAIN
finding ...... VERDICT, JUDGMENT, DISCOVERY, CONCLUSION
fine .... FAIR, KEEN, NICE, PURE, THIN, BULLY, MULCT, SHARP, AMERCE, FLIMSY, DELICATE, EXCELLENT
and ____ .... DANDY
arts .... MUSIC, DANCING, CERAMICS, PAINTING, SCULPTURE, LITERATURE
arts buff .... DILETTANTE
bearing .... BEL AIR
drawn .... SUBTLE
feather .... EGRET
fiddle .... AMATI
fixed by law .... PENALTY
for misconduct .... SCONCE
gravel .... SAND
in law .... CRO
line of letter .... SERIF
point .... NICETY
porcelain .... LIMOGES
powder .... DUST, SOOT
rain .... DRIZZLE
record of .... ESTREAT
thread .... LISLE
fineness .... PURITY, RARITY, TENUITY, DELICACY

finery .... FRILLS, TINSEL, REGALIA, GAUD(ERY), FALDERAL, FRIPPERY, DECORATION
useless .... FALLAL
finespun .... SUBTLE, FRAGILE, DELICATE
finesse .... ART, TACT, CRAFT, SKILL, CUNNING
finest ...... BEST, PRIME, TOPMOST, MATCHLESS
part .... FLOWER
people .... CREAM, ELITE, UPPERCRUST
Fingal's Cave island ...... STAFFA
finger .... DIGIT, STEAL, TOUCH, FEEL, HANDLE, DACTYL(US)
covering/sheath .... COT, STALL
cymbals .... CASTANETS
fifth/smallest .... PINKY, PINKIE
fore .... INDEX, POINTER
game .... MORA
hole of instrument .... VENTAGE
infection/inflammation ...... FELON, AGNAIL, WHITLOW
joint .... KNUCKLE
like .... DIGITATE
little .... PINKIE
middle .... MEDIUS
nail half-moon .... LUNULE
pertaining to .... DIGITAL
ring .... HOOF
slang .... TELL ON, POINT TO, IDENTIFY, INDICATE
snap of .... FILLIP
stall .... COT
stroke .... FLIP
fingerless glove .... MITT
fingerling .... FRY, FISH, PARR, SAMLET
fingernail, care of ...... MANICURE
mark .... LUNULE
fingerprint .... DACTYLOGRAM
mark ..... ARCH, LOOP, WHORL, LUNULE
pattern .... WHIRL
fingers, membrane uniting .... WEB(BING)
finial .... EPI, TIP, APEX, PEAK, SUMMIT
finical .... FUSSY, PRUDISH, EXACTING, FASTIDIOUS, METICULOUS, PARTICULAR
finicky .... PRISSY, PRECISE, OVERNICE
finis .... END, CONCLUSION
finish .... END, STOP, CLOSE, POISE, POLISH, ACCOMPLISH, TERMINATE, PERFECTION
colloquial .... KILL
dull/flat .... MATTE
first by small margin ...... WIN BY A NECK
line .... TAPE, WIRE
lustrous .... ENAMEL
off .... KILL, DESTROY, LIQUIDATE, ANNIHILATE
finished, for short .... THRU
finisher .... EDGER, REAMER, SOCKDOLAGER
finishing school product .... LADY
tool .... LATHE, REAMER
finite .... LIMITED
fink .... SPY, INFORMER, STRIKEBREAKER
Finland .... SUOMI
finnan haddie .... HADDOCK
Finnish .... SUOMI
bath(house) .... SAUNA
canto/poem .... RUNE
capital .... HELSINKI
city/town .... KEMI, OULU, PORI, SALO, ESPOO, KOTKA, LAHTI, NOKIA, RAUMA, TURKU, VAASA, IMATRA, KERAVA, KUOPIO, LIEKSA, JOENSUU, KARHULA, KOKKOLA, MIKKELI, TAMPERE, VARKAUS
coin .... PENNI, MARKKA
composer .... SIBELIUS
dialect .... KARELIAN
epic poem .... KALEVALA
field marshal .... MANNERHEIM
god .... JUMALA
gulf .... BOTHNIA, FINLAND
inlet .... FIORD
island .... KARLO, HAILUOTO, VALLGRUND
islands .... ALAND
lake .... ENARE, INARI, SAIMAA, KEITELE, KOITERE, JUOJARVI, ORIHVESI, PIELINEN, HAUKIVESI, KEMIJARVI, LAPPAJARVI, OULUJARVI, YLIKITKA
language .... SUOMI, FINNISH, SWEDISH
monetary unit .... MARKKA
mountain .... HALTIATUNTURI
native .... LAPP, KARELIAN, LAPLANDER
province .... HAME, KYMI, OULU, LAPPI, VAASA, KUOPIO, MIKKELI, UUSIMAA
river ..... TANA, TORNIO, IIJOKI, MUONIO, KITINEN, KALAJOKI, KEMIJOKI, OULUJOKI, SIMOJOKI, IVALOJOKI
seaport .... (ABO)TURKU

finnikin .... PIGEON
Finno-Ugric language ...... LAPP, MAGYAR, FINNISH, ESTONIAN, HUNGARIAN
Finns .... SUOMI
fiord .... INLET
fipple .... PLUG
fir .... BALSAM, EVERGREEN
  board wood .... DEAL
  pole .... UFER
fire .... BURN, OUST, ARDOR, BLAZE, FEVER, VERVE, ANNEAL, HURL, EXCITE, IGNITE, KINDLE, DISMISS, INSPIRE, (IN)FLAME
  a gun .... SHOOT
  alarm .... BELL, SIREN, WHISTLE, PYROSTAT
  artillery ...... SALVO, BARRAGE
  away .... START
  back .... REREDOS
  basket .... GRATE, CRESSET
  big, destructive .... CONFLAGRATION
  catching .... IGNITION
  clay .... BRICK, SAGGER
  colloquial .... CAN
  combining form .... IGNI, PYRO
  cracker .... PETARD
  damp .... METHANE
  department head .... MARSHAL
  feeder .... STOKER
  god .... AGNI, KAMA, SIVA, VULCAN
  irons .... POKER, TONGS, SHOVEL
  malicious .... ARSON
  of .... IGNEOUS
  on a hearth .... INGLE
  opal .... GIRASOL(E)
  pot .... CRUCIBLE
  principle of .... PHLOGISTON
  produced by .... IGNEOUS
  put out .... DOUSE
  signal .... BEACON
  starting stone .... FLINT
  stir up .... STOKE
  worshiper ...... PARSI, GHEBER, GHEBRE, PARSEE, PYROLATER
Fire Dance composer .... DE FALLA
firearm. See also gun .... GAT, GUN, HAGBUT, IRON, RIFLE, PISTOL, PETRONEL, REVOLVER, DERRINGER
  barrel's end .... MUZZLE
  charge .... LOAD
  hammer .... COCK
firearms protective coating .... COSMOLINE

fireball .... BOLIDE, METEOR
firebrand .... HOTHEAD, AGITATOR
firebug .... ARSONIST, INCENDIARY, PYROMANIAC
firecracker .... PETARD, SNAPPER, SPARKLER, NOISEMAKER
  box for .... MARROON
  broken .... SQUIB
fired clay .... TILE, BRICK
firedamp .... GAS, METHANE
firedog .... ANDIRON
firedrake .... DRAGON
fire-eater ...... DRAGON, HOTSPUR, SPITFIRE
firefly .... BUG, BEETLE, GLIMMER, GLOWWORM
  lighting substance .... LUCIFERIN
fireman .... VAMP, STOKER, FIREFIGHTER, SMOKECHASER
  hat of .... HELMET
  tool of .... LADDER
Firenze .... FLORENCE
fireplace .... GRATE, HEARTH, INGLE(NOOK), SMOKEHOLE
  guard/screen .... FENDER
  ledge .... HOB
  log holder .... ANDIRON, FIREDOG
  part .... HOB, FLUE, SPIT, SHELF, JAMB(E), MANTEL, SCREEN, CHIMNEY
  tool .... POKER, TONGS
fireplug .... HYDRANT, SPRINKLER, EXTINGUISHER
firepower .... GUNFIRE
fireproof .... RESISTANT, UNBURNABLE, INCOMBUSTIBLE, NON-FLAMMABLE
fireside .... HOME, HEARTH
firewater .... RUM, WHISKY
firewood .... LOGS, BAVIN, BILLET, FAG(G)OT, BILLON, KINDLINGS
fireworks .... PETARD, RIPRAP, GERB(E), ROCKETS, SPARKLERS, ROMAN CANDLES
  art of making and using .... PYROTECHNICS
  cluster .... GIRANDOLE
  hissing .... SQUIB, FIZGIGS
  material .... REALGAR
firing .... HURLING, IGNITION, KINDLING, DISMISSAL
  from a position of trust .... CASHIERING
  line .... BATTLEGROUND, KILLING FIELD
  notice .... PINK SLIP
firkin .... TUB
firm .... HARD, FINAL, FIXED, SOLID, STIFF, STEADY, COMPANY, SETTLED, CONSTANT, DECISIVE, RESOLUTE, STEADFAST, STA(U)NCH, DETERMINED, UNFLINCHING
firmament .... SKY, ARCH, VAULT, HEAVEN
  revolving .... PINWHEEL, TOURBILLION
firman .... DECREE, SANCTION
firmer .... CHISEL
firmly .... SECURELY, STRONGLY
  packed .... DENSE, COMPACT
  placed together .... SERRIED
  set .... FIXED, PINNED, ROOTED, RIVETED, EMBEDDED
  united .... SOLID
firmness .... APLOMB, SOLIDITY, STRENGTH, VITALITY
  lacking .... LAX, LIMP, SOFT, LOOSE, FLABBY
  of courage .... GRIT, FORTITUDE
firn .... ICE, NEVE, SNOW
first .... ALPHA, CHIEF, PRIME, INITIAL, EARLIEST, FOREMOST, ORIGINAL, PRINCIPAL
  abbreviation .... ORIG.
  act .... OPENER
  American champion in figure skating .... TENLEY ALBRIGHT
  American civil servant to lie in state in Capitol rotunda .... J. EDGAR HOOVER
  animal named in the Bible .... SERPENT
  appearance .... DEBUT, MAIDEN
  Archbishop of Canterbury .... AUGUSTINE
  black Justice of U.S. Supreme Court .... THURGOOD MARSHALL
  black soloist of Metropolitan Opera House .... MARIAN ANDERSON
  book of the Bible .... ACTS
  born ...... HEIR, EIGNE, ELDEST, OLDEST
  cause .... SOURCE
  circumnavigator .... MAGELLAN
  class ..... A-ONE, TOPS, DANDY, QUALITY, TOPNOTCH, TOP-DRAWER, TOP-FLIGHT
  commisioner of baseball .... LANDIS
  country's flag planted at the South Pole .... NORWAY

day of ancient Roman month .... CALENDS
day of Quakers .... SUNDAY
estate .... CLERGY
female British Prime
    Minister .... MARGARET THATCHER
female U.S. Supreme Court
    Justice .... SANDRA DAY O'CONNOR
female U.S. Surgeon General .... NOVELLO
finger .... INDEX
game/line .... OPENER
Greek philosopher .... THALES
hydrogen bomb explosion
    location .... ENIWETOK
impression .... GAMBIT, BREAKING-IN
in rank .... PREMIER
in seniority .... OLDEST
in time .... PRIMAL
Kentuckian? .... BOONE
king of Israel .... SAUL
king of Rome .... ROMULUS
lady .... EVE
lady of radio in the 40's .... KATE SMITH
lady's mate .... ADAM
letter .... INITIAL
man to orbit the earth .... GAGARIN
man to walk the moon .... ARMSTRONG
man-made satellite .... SPUTNIK
manned suborbital rocket .... MERCURY
martyr of Christianity .... STEPHEN
move .... OVERTURE, INITIATIVE
name in movie lore .... GRETA
name in spies .... MATA
name in Western fiction .... ZANE
name of Guy de Maupassant .... HENRI
native-born U.S. saint .... SETON
night/performance/showing .... OPENING, PREMIERE
nighter .... CRITIC, REVIEWER
of a clone .... ORTET
officer: nautical .... MATE
or second .... RATE
person .... ADAM
person with a palindromic
    name .... EVE
place .... EDEN
Pope .... PETER

prefix .... PROTO
principles .... ABCS
prize .... AWARD, JACKPOT, BLUE RIBBON
rate .... ACE, A-ONE, ONER, TOPS, NOBBY, SUPER, CAPITAL, TOPNOTCH, EXCELLENT, TOPFLIGHT
rate: Anglo-Indian ..... PUCKA, PUKKA
rights .... PRIORITIES
sergeant .... TOPKICK
satellite into orbit .... SPUTNIK
sight .... PRIMA FACIE
sign of the zodiac .... ARIES
space traveler .... GAGARIN
speech, describing .... MAIDEN
stage .... INCIPIENCE
State .... DELAWARE
talking picture, American .... THE JAZZ SINGER
Thanksgiving year .... SIXTEEN TWENTY ONE
U.S. casualty of the Cold
    War .... (JOHN)BIRCH
U.S. president .... (GEORGE)WASHINGTON
U.S. state to grant women
    voting rights .... WYOMING
U.S. vice president to
    become president .... (JOHN)ADAMS
U.S. woman in space .... RIDE
valuable issue .... EDITION
winner of the Indy 500 .... (RAY)HARROUN
winner of the World Series .... BOSTON RED SOX
woman in space .... (VALENTINA)TERESHKOVA
woman to fly solo across the
    Atlantic .... AMELIA EARHART
word of Ethiopia .... ADDIS
word of "Paul Revere's
    Ride" .... LISTEN
year student .... FROSH, PLEB(E), FRESHMAN
year West Pointer .... PLEBE
year's revenue of benefice .... ANNAT

First Lady's husband
    .... PRESIDENT
firsthand .... DIRECT, BRAND-NEW, ORIGINAL
firth .... ARM, KYLE, FIORD, INLET, ESTUARY
fisc .... TREASURY, EXCHEQUER
fiscal ...... NUMMARY, MONETARY, FINANCIAL, PECUNIARY

officer .... BURSAR, PURSER, PROSECUTOR
fish .... GAR, RAY, BASS, CARP, CHUB, DACE, HAKE, LING, OPAH, SHAD, ANGLE, PERCH, SCROD, TRAWL, TROLL, DARTER, SABALO, TARPON, WRASSE, EELPOUT, LABROID, SCULPIN, SNAPPER, BULLHEAD, MACKEREL, PULL OUT, STURGEON, BRAINFOOD
African .... CHARACIN
air bladder .... MAW
air swallowing .... PUFFER, GLOBEFISH, SWELLFISH
appendage .... FIN, BARBEL, FLIPPER
aquarium .... MOLLY, SWORDTAIL
ascending river ...... ANADROM
Atlantic .... TAUTOG
baby .... FRY
bait .... CHUM, HOLA, LURE, LIMPET, MINNOW, SHINER, CAP(E)LIN, LUGWORM, MENBRADEN
ball .... RISSOLE
barbel .... WATTLE
barracuda .... SPET
basket .... CAWL, WEEL, CREEL
batlike ..... GURNET, GURNARD, (STING)RAY
beaked .... SAURY
beard .... BARB(EL)
beluga .... WHITEFISH
bin for salting .... KENCH
boat .... DORY, COBLE, WHALER, TRAWLER
boneless .... FIL(L)ET
bony .... TELEOST
bright-colored .... OPAH, MOLLY, MORAY, WRASSE, PINTANO, COWPILOT, DRAGONET
bucket .... KIT
burbot .... CUSK, LING, EELPOUT
butter .... GUNNEL
butterfly .... PARU, BLENNY
capelin .... SMELT
carangoid .... CAVALLA, POMPANO, YELLOWJACK, YELLOWTAIL
caribe .... PIRAYA, PIRANHA
carp family .... IDE, CHUB, DACE, ROUD, RUD(D), BLEAK, LOACH, ROACH, TENCH, MINNOW, REDFIN
cat .... RAAD
catch .... HAUL
char(r) .... TROUT

chopped .... CHUM
cigar .... SCAD
cleaner .... SCALER
climbing .... ANABAS
clinging ...... REMORA, TESTAR
coal .... POLLACK, POLLOCK
cod family .... CUSK, HAKE,
LING, GADID, BURBOT,
BACALAO, HADDOCK, POLLACK
combining form .... PISCI
cow .... DUGONG, GRAMPUS,
MANATEE
crab and fiddler .... UCA
creature: legendary
.... MERMAN, MERMAID
Cuban .... DIABLO
cure .... BLOAT
cusk .... BURBOT
cuttle .... SEPIA, SQUID
cyprin(o)id .... IDS, DACE,
CARP, ROUD, ORF(E), BLEAK,
BREAM, LOACH, BARBEL,
GOLDFISH
deep sea .... WEEVER
delicacy .... ROE
devil .... SKATE, MANTARAY
dish .... SHADROE,
BOUILLABAISSE
dog .... SHARK, BOWFIN
dolphin .... INIA, CETACEAN,
PORPOISE
drying frame .... HACK
East Indies .... DORAB,
GOURAMI
eating .... PISCIVOROUS
eating animal .... SEAL, OTTER
eating bird .... ERN(E),
OSPREY, PELICAN
eating fish .... ANGLER
edible .... COD, EEL, IDE, BASS,
DORY, PIKE, LOACH, TUNA,
SPRAT, TROUT, TAUTOG,
WRASSE, HADDOCK,
ARAPAIMA, BRISLING,
MACKEREL, BARRACUDA
eel .... LING, ELVER, MORAY,
CONGER, LAMPREY
eel-like .... APOD
eelpout .... BURBOT
eel-shaped .... LEPIDOSIREN
eggs .... ROE, SPAWN
eggs relish .... CAVIAR(E)
elasmobranch .... RAY,
MANTA, SHARK, SKATE,
SAWFISH, MANTA RAY
elongated .... EEL, GAR, PIKE
European .... BLEAK, BREAM,
DACE, UMBER, BARBEL,
BRASSE, PLAICE, SENNET,
WRASSE, SPRAT, TENCH,
BRISLING

eyed on head's top
.... STARGAZER
fabled .... MAH
feeler .... BARBEL
fence .... WEIR, CRAWL
fierce .... PIKE, SHARK,
BLENNY, PIRANHA, SEABASS,
PICKEREL, BARRACUDA
flat ..... DAB, RAY, BUTT, SOLE,
BRILL, FLUKE, SKATE, PLAICE,
TURBOT, HALIBUT, POMPANO,
FLOUNDER
Florida .... BONACI, TARPON
flying .... SAURY, GURNARD
food .... COD, CARP, CERO,
HAKE, LING, SCUP, SHAD,
TUNA, JUREL, MORAY, TROUT,
SMELT, BONITO, MULLET,
PLAICE, GROUPER, POLLACK,
POMPANO, SARDINE, SNAPPER
for .... SEEK, DREDGE, SEARCH,
SOLICIT
fork-tailed .... JUREL,
CAVALLA, POMPANO,
CARANGOID
fresh-water .... IDE, BASS,
DACE, LOACH, TENCH,
ANABAS, DARTER, REDEYE,
CRAPPIE, ARAPAIMA, STONE-
ROLLER
frog .... ANGLER
from boat .... TROLL
full of: poetic .... FINNY
game .... CERO, TROUT,
MARLIN, SALMON, TARPON,
(BLACK)BASS, SWORDFISH
ganoid .... GAR, BOWFIN,
STURGEON
garth .... WEIR
gently .... DAP
genus .... AMIA
gig .... HOOK, SPEAR
gobioid .... GOBY
goby-like .... DRAGONET
grampus .... ORC, DOLPHIN
grasping-tailed
.... HIPPOCAMPUS
green .... PLAICE, SHANNY
grouper .... MERO, (SEA)BASS
grunting .... CROAKER,
GURNARD, PIGFISH
gurnard family ..... SEA ROBIN
haul .... MESS
Hawaiian .... AKU
hawk .... OSPREY
head of .... JOWL
herring .... CISCO, SPRAT,
TARPON, ANCHOVY, OLDWIFE,
PILCHER, SARDINE, MENHADEN,
CLUPE(O)ID, PILCHARD
herring-like .... SHAD,

ALEWIFE
herring, young .... BRIT
hide .... EELSKIN
holy .... HALIBUT
hook .... GIG, GAFF
illegally .... POACH
Japanese .... TAI, FUGU
jelly .... MEDUSA, ACALEPH
jew .... MERO, TARPON,
(SEA)BASS
jurel .... RUNNER
king .... OPAH, PINTADO,
WHITING
lacking pelvic fins .... APOD
lake .... POLLAN
land-walking .... ANABAS
largest freshwater
.... ARAPAIMA
like animal .... LANCELET
line ...... TROT, SNELL, TRAWL,
TROLL
line cork .... BOB
ling .... BURBOT
little .... SMELT, MINNOW,
SARDINE
lizard .... ULAE
loach .... SMERLIN
long-beaked .... GAR, SAURY
lure .... CHUM, SPINNER
mackerel .... TUNA, TUNNY,
BONITO, ALBACORE
mackerel-like .... CERO,
TINKER
male .... MILTER
man-eating .... SHARK
marine ...... CUSK, LING, SCUP,
BLENNY, BONITO, ROBALO,
TARPON, WRASSE, MENHADEN
maskonge .... PIKE
measure .... MEASE
meat, broiled ...... CARBONADO
migration .... RUN
milk .... SABALO
mollusk .... SQUID, OCTOPUS
mucous coating .... SLIME
mythological .... MAH
nest-building .... ACARA
net .... FLEW, FLUE, FYKE,
GILL, SEINE, TRAWL
New Zealand .... IHI
ocean bed .... WEEVER
of .... PISCINE, PISCATORY,
PISCATORIAL
organ of touch .... BARBEL
parasite .... REMORA
parrot .... LORO, LANIA
pen/enclosure .... WEIR,
CRAWL
perch family .... RUFF(E)
perch-like .... ANABAS,
DARTER, CABRILLA

pertaining to .... FINNY, PISCINE, TELEOST, PISCATORY
pickle .... ALEC
piece .... FIL(L)ET
pike .... LUCE, PICKEREL
pike-like/needle .... GAR, ROBALO, BARRACUDA
place for drying .... HACK
poor .... SIMP
porgy .... TAI, SCUP
Polynesian .... ISDA
porpoise .... INIA, DOLPHIN, CETACEAN
primitive .... COELACANTH
rainbow, of Australia
.... MAORI
ray .... MANTA, SKATE
red-eyed .... RUDD
relish .... BOTARGO
reproductive glands .... MILT
resembling .... PISCINE
river ascending .... SHAD, SALMON, ANADROM
rock .... COD, BASS, RE(I)NA, GROUPER
runner .... JUREL
Russian .... STERLET, STURGEON
salmon, young .... PARR, SAMLET
salmon-like .... SMELT
salmonoid .... TROUT, NAMAYCUSH, STEELHEAD
salt-water .... DORY, HAKE, SHAD, TUNA, CYCLOTOME
salting box .... KENCH
sardine .... SPRAT, CLUPEID, HERRING, PILCHARD
sardine-like .... CISCO, ANCHOVY, BRISLING
sauce .... ALEC, ANCHOVY
saurel .... SCAD
scabbard .... HIKU
scale .... GANOID
scaleless .... CATFISH, SCULPIN, BULLHEAD, DRAGONET
schooling .... GRUNION
sculpin family .... CABEZON, BULLHEAD
sea ..... TUNA, SAURY, SCULPIN
sergeant .... ROBALO
serpentine .... EEL
shad-like .... ALEWIFE
shark .... MAKO, TOPE, ANGELFISH
shark family .... CHIMAERA
shark's pilot .... REMORA
shell .... CLAM, CRAB, SLUG, WHELK, LIMPET, SHRIMP, ABALONE, LOBSTER, OCTOPUS, SCALLOP

shrimp-like .... KRILL
sign of zodiac .... PISCES
silver-bellied .... MACKEREL
silvery .... OPAH, SMELT, MULLET, PINTADO
skeleton .... ARETE, ARISTA
slim .... GAR
slimy .... BLENNY
small .... ID(E), FRY, DACE, SMELT, SPELT, SPRAT, DARTER, MINNOW, SAMLET, FINGERLING
smelt .... CAP(E)LIN
snouted .... GAR, SAURY, DOLPHIN, BOARFISH, PICKEREL, PORPOISE, STURGEON
South American .... CARIBE, PIRAYA, PIRANHA, ARAPAIMA
spawning movement
.... ANADROMOUS, CATADROMOUS
spear .... GIG, LEISTER
sperm .... ROE, MILT
spiny .... GOBY, SCULPIN
spiny-headed .... SEA ROBIN
spotted .... OPAH
stewed .... MATELOT(TE)
story .... YARN, EXAGGERATION
St. Peter's .... TILAPIA
sturgeon ..... BELUGA, STERLET
sucking .... REMORA, HAMMERHEAD
swimming bladder ...... SOUND
tank .... STEW, AQUARIUM, VIVARIUM
teleost .... EEL
that recently spawned
.... SHOTTEN
to .... ANGLE, TROLL
toad .... SAPO
trap .... FYKE, GILL, WEIR, CRAWL, CREEL, HATCH, SEINE, TRAWL, EELPOT, KELONG
tropical .... SARGO, ROBALO, SALEMA, SNAPPER, BARRACUDA
trout .... CHAR(R)
tub .... KIT
ugly-looking .... CATFISH
unicorn .... UNIE
upholding universe .... MAH
voracious ...... SHARK, CARIBE, CATFISH, PIRANHA
wahoo .... ONO
wall-eyed .... BLOWFISH
warm-water .... ROBALO
West Indies .... TESTAR
whale .... ORC(A), GRAMPUS, NARWHAL, CACHALOT, CETACEAN
whisker .... BARBEL

whiskered .... CATFISH
whiting ...... HAKE, MENHADEN
with a spoon .... SPIN
with lungs/gills ...... DIPNOAN, CERATODUS, BARRAMUNDA
with staring eyes .... PIKE, PERCH, ALEWIFE, POLLACK
with sucking mouth
.... REMORA, HAGFISH, LAMPREY, CYCLOSTOME
with suction disk .... GOBY
with whiplike tail ...... SKATE, (STING)RAY, STINGAREE
young .... FRY, BRIT, PARR, ELVER, ALEVIN, SAMLET, FINGERLING
fishbait .... CHUM, LUGWORM
fishbowl .... AQUARIUM
fisher ...... SEAL, PEKAN, MARTEN, WEJACK
fisherman .... EELER, ANGLER, FISHER, JACKER, WALTON, WHALER, TRAWLER, TROLLER, PISCATOR
basket .... CREEL
line of .... SNELL
fisherman's bend .... KNOT
hut .... SKEO
fishes, characteristic of
.... ICHTHYIC
fishgig .... SPEAR
fishhook .... GIG, GAFF, DRAIL
end of a .... BARB
line .... SNELL
fishing .... ANGLING, SEEKING, WHALING, PURSUING, TRAWLING, TROLLING, PISCATION
bait .... DRAKE, MAYFLY
basket .... CREEL
boat .... DORY, SMACK, DOGGER, WHALER, CORACLE, SHARPIE, TRAWLER
device .... EELPOT
event .... BITE
float .... BOB
fly .... HACKLE
fly, artificial .... NYMPH
fly trimmer .... HERL
ground/place .... POUND, FISHERY, PISCARY, PISCINA,
kick .... BITE
line with hooks .... BOULTER
net .... FLUE, FYKE, GILL, FLEW, SEINE, TRAWL, TRAMMEL
pertaining to ...... PISCATORIAL
pole .... ROD, TONKIN
reel .... PIRN
right .... PISCARY
season, feast after .... FOY

smack .... DOGGER
spear .... GAFF, HARPOON
spots .... PIERS
vessel .... WHALER, TRAWLER
went .... EELED
fishline leader .... SNELL
fishmonger .... FISHWIFE, FISH
DEALER
fishnet sagging part .... BUNT
fishpond .... TANK, WEIR, PISCINA,
FARM POND
fishskin disease .... ICHTHYOSIS
fishwife .... NAG(GER), MERCHANT
fishy .... DULL, FUNNY, SHADY,
TRICKY, DUBIOUS, DOUBTFUL,
INCREDIBLE, SUSPICIOUS
fish .... RED HERRING
fissile rock .... SHALE
fission .... DECAY, SCISSION,
SPLITTING
kind of .... NUCLEAR
fissure .... RENT, RIFT, RIME,
SEAM, CHINK, CLEFT, CRACK,
SPLIT, CRANNY, CREVICE
in glacier .... CREVASSE
fissures .... RIMAE
full of .... RIMOSE, RIMOUS
fist .... HAND, NIEVE
blow .... PASTE, PUNCH
fight: sl. .... MILL
fistic .... BOXING, PUGILISTIC
fisticuffs ...... BOUT, SPAR, SETTO,
FIGHTING, PUGILISM, BOXING
(MATCH)
fists: sl. .... DUKES
fistula .... PIPE, TUBE, CAVITY
fistulous .... TUBULAR
fit .... APT, PAT, MEET, TRIG,
ATTACK, ADAPT, READY,
RIGHT, KASHER, KOSHER,
PROPER, ELIGIBLE, SUIT(ABLE)
arrow on string .... NOCK
as of disease .... SPASM,
SEIZURE, APOPLEXY,
PAROXYSM, CONVULSION
as of mind inclination
.... WHIM, FANCY, NOTION,
CAPRICE
better .... ABLER
closely, exactly .... FAY
for cultivation .... ARABLE
gamecock with spurs .... HEEL
of pique .... SNIT
of shivers .... AGUE
of temper ..... IRE, HUFF, MIFF,
RAGE, TIFF, ANGER, PIQUE,
TANTRUM, OUTBURST,
CONNIPTION
one inside another .... NEST
out .... RIG, EQUIP, CLOTHE,
FURNISH

to be _____ .... TIED
be drunk .... SORBILE
be tied .... IRATE
drink .... POTABLE
eat .... EDIBLE, KOSHER,
EATABLE, ESCULENT
live in .... HABITABLE
requirement .... TAILOR,
CONFORM
work .... ABLE
together .... MESH, DOVETAIL
fitchew .... POLECAT
fitful .... BROKEN, RESTLESS,
SPORADIC, IRREGULAR,
SPASMODIC, INTERRUPTED,
INTERMITTENT
fitly .... DULY, APTLY, TIMELY,
SUITABLY, APPROPRIATELY
fitness .... APTNESS, UTILITY,
DECORUM, PROPRIETY,
SOUNDNESS
fits and _____ .... STARTS
fitting .... APT, DUE, PAT, MEET,
RIGHT, PROPER, USEFUL,
APROPOS, DECOROUS,
SUITABLE, AUSPICIOUS
fittingly .... DULY, RIGHTLY,
CONDIGNLY, DESERVEDLY
fittings .... FIXTURES,
DECORATIONS, FURNISHINGS
Fitzgerald .... BARRY, F. SCOTT
forte .... SCAT
singer .... ELLA
Fiume .... RIJEKA
five-and-ten cent store
.... DISCOUNT STORE, BARGAIN
BASEMENT
at dice or playing card
.... CINQUE
cards in same suit, sequence
of .... QUINT
-cent coin ...... JITNEY, NICKEL
collection of .... QUINTUPLET
combining form .... PENT(A)
consisting of/fold
.... QUINTUPLE
converging arcs, design of
.... CINQUEFOIL
-day duel protagonist
.... OLIVER, ROLAND
-dollar bill .... FIN, VEE, FIVER
-dollar gold piece .... HALF
EAGLE
-event athletic contest
.... PENTATHLON
finger .... OXLIP, STARFISH,
CINQUEFOIL, POTENTILLA
Goren points .... KING AND
QUEEN
group of .... PENTAD

hundred, card game
.... RUMMY, EUCHRE
hundred fifty foot-pound per
second .... HORSEPOWER
in cards/of trumps in 7-up
.... PEDRO
-lined nonsensical poem
.... LIMERICK
lines, figure of
.... PENTAGRAM
metrical feet ...... PENTAMETER
multiple of .... QUINQUE
-percenter .... FIXER
-petaled .... STARFLOWER
-pointed star .... PENTACLE
rulers, government by
.... PENTARCHY
set of .... QUINARY,
QUINTET(TE)
sided figure .... PENTAGON
-year period .... PENTAD
LUSTRUM
Five Civilized Tribes member
.... CREEK, CHOCTAW,
CHEROKEE, SEMINOLE,
CHICKASAW
Nations member (Indian)
.... CAYUGAS, MOHAWKS,
ONEIDAS, SENECAS,
ONONDAGAS, TUSCARORAS
fiver .... FIN
fives .... HANDBALL
fix .... SET, (A)MEND, LIMIT,
PLACE, RIVET, ADJUST,
DEFINE, FASTEN, FREEZE,
REPAIR, SETTLE, ESTABLISH
a meal/dinner .... PREPARE
a tire .... RECAP
colloquial .... SPAY, SPOT,
SCRAPE, DILEMMA, CASTRATE,
PREDICAMENT
in memory .... CON,
REMEMBER
jewel in setting .... MOUNT
on .... FOCUS
shoes .... SOLE
slang .... BRIBE, HEROIN,
ILLEGAL DRUG
tea .... STEEP
the hose .... DARN
the road .... REPAVE
upon .... DECIDE
fixation .... FOCUS, MANIA,
ATTENTION, OBSESSION,
PREOCCUPATION
slang .... HANGUP
fixative .... MORDANT
fixed .... SET, FIRM, RIGID, STUCK,
FROZEN, MENDED, STEADY,
LIMITED, STABILE, RESOLUTE,
ARRANGED, IMMOVABLE,

STATIONARY

charge item .... TAX, RENT, INTEREST

course .... ROTE

fee .... FLAT RATE

reminder .... SCAR

fixings ...... MAKINGS, TRIMMINGS, ACCESSORIES

fixture ...... FITTING, ATTACHMENT

hanging from ceiling .... CHANDELIER

fixtures .... FITTINGS, EQUIPMENT, PLUMBING, FURNITURE, APPLIANCES

fizgig .... FLIRT, FIREWORK

fizz .... HISS, DRINK, BUBBLE, SPARKLE, CHAMPAGNE

fizzle .... FAIL, FLOP, FIASCO, MISFIRE, COLLAPSE

fizzwater .... SODA

fizzy .... BUBBLING, SPARKLING, EFFERVESCENT

fjeld .... PLATEAU

fjord .... INLET

passage .... GAT

flabbergast .... STUN, ABASH, AMAZE, BOGGLE, ASTONISH, CONFOUND, SURPRISE, DISCONCERT

flabbergasted .... AGHAST, DUMBFOUNDED

flabellum .... FAN

flabby .... SOFT, WEAK, FEEBLE, PULPY, FLESHY, FLACCID

flaccid ...... LIMP, WEAK, FLABBY, FLOPPY, RUBBERY

flacon .... FLASK

flag ...... PINE, SIGN, TIRE, DROOP, BANNER, COLORS, PENNON, SIGNAL, WEAKEN, PENNANT, GONFALON, LANGUISH, STANDARD, STREAMER, ORIFLAMME

American .... OLD GLORY, STARS AND STRIPES

ancient Roman troops' .... VEXILLUM

background .... FIELD

bearer .... CORNET, GUIDON, ANCIENT

championship .... PENNANT

cloth .... BUNTING

corner .... CANTON

deer's .... TAIL

flower/plant .... IRIS

identifying .... BURGEE

little ..... PENNANT, BANNERET, BANNEROL, BANDEROLE

maker Ross .... BETSY

matador's .... MULETA

military .... ENSIGN, GUIDON

STATIONARY

officer ...... ADMIRAL, CAPTAIN

over tomb .... BANDEROL(E)

pirate's .... BLACKJACK, BLACK FLAG, JOLLY ROGER

pole .... SHAFT, STAFF

position .... FANION

rope .... HALYARD

ship's .... BURGEE

signal .... ENSIGN

signal made by a .... WAFT

swallow-tailed/triangular .... BURGEE, PENNON

sweet .... CALAMUS

flagellant .... ALBI

flagellate .... BEAT, FLOG, LASH, WHIP, FLAIL, SPANK, PUMMEL, THRASH, WALLOP

flagellum .... BELT, WHIP, SHOOT, STRAP, THONG, RUNNER

flageolet .... PIPE, FLUTE, RECORDER

flagging .... SLOW, FATIGUED

flagitious .... VILE, WICKED, HEINOUS

flagon .... MUG, JUG, EWER, FLASK, STOUP, BOTTLE, CARAFE

flagrant .... RANK, GROSS, GLARING, NOTORIOUS, SHOCKING, EGREGIOUS, OUTRAGEOUS, SCANDALOUS

flagrante delicto .... RED-HANDED

flagrantly ...... BOLDLY, UNDULY, MEANLY, ARRANTLY, WICKEDLY, VICIOUSLY, CONSPICUOUSLY

flags collectively .... BUNTING

flagship, famed .... SANTA MARIA

official launch .... BARGE

flagstaff .... POLE, SHAFT, STICK

flagstone .... SLAB, BRICK

Flaherty movie film ...... MOANA

flail .... BEAT, WHIP, POUND, PUNISH, THRESH

part .... SWINGLE, SWIP(P)LE

flair .... BENT, GIFT, SKILL, KNACK, STYLE, VERVE, TALENT, ABILITY, BRAVURA, APTITUDE, TENDENCY, DISCERNMENT

flak ...... KNOCK, SWIPE, ACK-ACK, GUNFIRE, CRITICISM

flake .... CHIP, RACK, FLECK, SCALE, SPALL, LAMINA, SHAVING, FLOCCULE, SNOWDUST, SNOWFLAKE

flakes, covered with ...... LEPIDOTE

flaky .... SCALY, POWDERY, SQUAMOSE

slang .... ODD, BATTY, DIPPY, GOOFY, KOOKY, WACKY,

QUEER, ECCENTRIC

flam .... LIE, HOAX, CHEAT, TRICK, HUMBUG, BLARNEY, HOGWASH, CLAPTRAP, DECEPTION

flambeau .... TORCH, CRESSET, LIGHTER, CANDLESTICK

flamboyance .... DASH, PANACHE, FLASHINESS, SHOWINESS

flamboyant .... SHOWY, FRILLY, ORNATE, FLOWERY, POMPOUS, BOMBASTIC, FLAUNTING, HIGHFLOWN, (BE)DAZZLING, GRANDIOSE, STRUTTING, OVERELEGANT, GRANDILOQUENT

pianist .... LIBERACE

flame .... BEAM, FIRE, ZEAL, BLAZE, SPUNK, PASSION

long, narrow .... TONGUE

slang .... BEAU, SWEETHEART

flamen .... PRIEST

flamenco dancer .... GRECO

flamethrower .... WEAPON, BLOWGUN, FLAME SHOOTER

flaming .... FIERY, BRIGHT, BLAZING, EXCITED

flammable ...... FIERY, BURNABLE, COMBUSTIBLE

flan .... TART, BLANK, METAL

Flanders battlesite .... YPRES

native .... FLEMING

river .... YSER

flanerie .... LOAFING

flaneur .... IDLER, LOAFER, ROAMER, TRIFLER, GADABOUT, STROLLER

flange ...... LIP, RIM, EDGE, KNOB, COLLAR

flank .... LOIN, SIDE, SKIRT, BORDER

combining form ..... LAPAR(O)

flannel .... LANA

flannelmouth .... CATFISH

flannels: colloq. ...... UNDERWEAR

flap .... FLY, LAP, TAB, TAG, BEAT, FOLD, SLAP, WHIP, SWING, LAPPET, FLUTTER, UNREST, DISCORD, ARGUMENT

airplane ...... AILERON, AIRFOIL

of flesh .... GILL, DEWLAP, WATTLE

vigorously .... SLAT

wings .... FLICKER

flapjack .... HOT CAKE, PANCAKE, GRIDDLECAKE

flapper .... FIN, FLIPPER, FISHTAIL

flare .... GLOW, BLAZE, BULGE, FLASH, FLECK, GLARE, SHINE, TORCH, FLICKER, OUTBURST

signal .... FUSEE, FUZEE

up ...... BURST, IGNITE, KINDLE

flare-up .... BLOWUP, ERUPTION, OUTBURST, EXPLOSION

flaring .... GAUDY, LURID, GARISH, ABLAZE, AFLAME, BURNING

edge .... FLANGE

star .... NOVA

flash .... BLAZE, BURST, FLARE, GLEAM, GLINT, SPARK, MOMENT, STREAK, GLIMMER, GLITTER, SPARKLE, FLAUNT, EXHIBIT, SCINTILLATE

flood .... GULLY WASHER

in the pan .... DUD, FAILURE, MISFIRE

message .... BULLETIN, NEWS REPORT

of lightning .... BOLT, THUNDERBOLT

out .... EFFULGE

flashback .... RECALL, REVIEW, REMEMBERING, REMINISCENCE

flasher .... BEACON, STREAKER

flashing .... BLINKING, FLICKERING, GLITTERING, SHORT-TERM

flashy .... GAUDY, SHOWY, SNAZZY, SPORTY, DASHING, RAFFISH

flask .... CRUSE, CARAFE, FLACON, BOTTLE, FLAGON, MATARA, CANTEEN, AMPOULE, COSTREL, MATRASS, THERMOS, CUCURBITE

flat ...... WAN, DRAB, DULL, EVEN, LEVEL, PLANE, STALE, SUITE, VAPID, SMOOTH, SOMBER, LOW-LYING, APARTMENT, TASTELESS

and circular .... DISCUS

and even .... HORIZONTAL

bottle .... FLASK

bottom boat .... DORY, PUNT, RAFT, SCOW, BARGE, BATEAU

broke .... POOR, BUSTED, PINCHED, STRAPPED

canopy .... TESTER

colloquial .... DEFLATED

dish .... PLATTER

headed Indian .... CHINOOK

headed nail .... TACK

hill .... MESA

land .... PLAIN

nosed .... PUG, SNUB, SIMOUS

on one's back .... SUPINE

out ...... UTTERLY, EXTREMELY, ABSOLUTE(LY), AT FULL SPEED

paint finish .... PALE, LIGHT, CREAMY, MELLOW, PASTEL, PEARLY, SUBDUED

slang .... BANKRUPT, IN-THE-

HOLE, PENNILESS

stick .... FERULE

stone .... SLAB

surface .... AREA, PLAIN, PLANE, TABULAR

taste .... INSIPID

flatfoot .... PES PLANUS

slang .... COP, POLICEMAN

Flathead .... SALISH, CHINOOK

flatiron .... SADIRON

flatten .... RAZE, CRUSH, PRESS, REDUCE, SUBDUE, CONQUER, EQUALIZE, PROSTRATE, LEVEL OFF, KNOCK DOWN, SMOOTH(EN)

on impact .... SPLAT

flatter .... PET, FAWN(UPON), HUMOR, PLEASE, (OVER)PRAISE, TOADY, ADULATE, BLANDISH, COMPLIMENT, SWEET-TALK

colloquial .... BUTTER UP, SOFT SOAP

slang .... OIL, SNOW, GREASE

flatterer .... PUFFER, TOADY, ADULATOR, COURTIER, FLUNK(E)Y, TOUTER, EULOGIST, SYCOPHANT, COQUETTE, LICKSPIT(TLE)

flattery .... SUGAR, TAFFY, BLARNEY, FAWNING, PALAVER, CAJOLERY, FLUMMERY, TOADYING, ADULATION, SERVILITY, BLANDISHMENT, HONEYED WORDS

slang .... SNOW JOB

flattop: sl. .... (AIRCRAFT)CARRIER

flatulence .... GAS, VANITY

flatulent .... VAIN, WINDY, EJECTIVE, POMPOUS

flatus .... GAS, PUFF

flatware .... TABLEWARE

flatwork .... SHEETS, NAPKINS

flatworm .... PARASITE, PLATYHELMINTH

opposed to .... NEMATODE, ROUNDWORM

type of .... FLUKE, CESTODE, TAPEWORM, TREMATODE

Flaubert heroine .... EMMA

novelist .... GUSTAVE

flaunt .... WAVE, PARADE, DISPLAY, SHOW(OFF), FLUTTER, BRANDISH

flaunting .... CRUDE, GAUDY, SHOWY, FLASHY, GARISH

flautist .... FIFER, BUGLER, FLUTIST, MUSICIAN

flavescent .... YELLOWISH

flavin .... PIGMENT

flavor .... GUST, LACE, ODOR, SALT, AROMA, SAPOR, SAVOR, SMELL, SAUCE, SMACK, TASTE, TINGE, RELISH, SEASON(ING)

drinks/with spice .... MULL

keeping substance

.... ESSENCE

of .... SAPOROUS

penetrating .... TANG

spicy .... GINGER

flavored .... SAPID, SAVORY, SAPOROUS

flavorful .... SAPID, SAVORY, FULL-BODIED, FLAVOROUS

flavoring .... RELISH, ESSENCE, EXTRACT, VANILLA, SEASONER, VANILLIN, CONDIMENT, SEASONING

bulb .... ONION, GARLIC, SHALLOT

for pickles .... DILL

plant .... LEEK, MINT, ANISE, SAGE, BASIL, LAUREL, CELERY, PARSLEY, CAPSICUM

root .... GINGER, LICORICE

seed .... ANISE, POPPY, SESAME, CARAWAY, MUSTARD

spice .... CLOVE, GARLIC, NUTMEG, PEPPER, CAYENNE, OREGANO, CINNAMON, MARJORAM

flavorless .... FLAT, VAPID, INSIPID, SPICELESS, UNSAVORY, TASTELESS

flavorsome .... JUICY, SAPID, TASTY, YUMMY, SAVORY, DELICIOUS, SUCCULENT

flaw .... MAR, GUST, CRACK, KINK, ERROR, FAULT, DEFECT, SQUALL, BLEMISH, MISTAKE

flawed .... FAULTY, ERRONEOUS

entrance .... MISCUE

flawless ...... PERFECT, ACCURATE, POLISHED, SPOTLESS, FAULTLESS, UNSCATHED, UNBLEMISHED

flax .... FIBER, LINEN, BYSSUS

capsule/pod .... BOLL

clean and dress .... HACKLE, HECKLE

cloth .... STUPE, CANVAS, SACKING

comber .... CARD, HACKLE, HATCHEL

dresser .... HACKLE, HECKLE, HATCHEL

fabric .... LINEN

fiber .... TOW, SILVER

filament .... HARL

husk .... SHIVE

like .... TOWY
prepare/soak .... RET
refuse of .... TOW, HARDS,
                              HURDS
remove seeds from ..... RIPPLE
seed .... LINSEED
weed .... TOADFLY
flaxen color .... GOLDEN,
                              BLOND(E)
flay .... ROB, BEAT, CANE, PEEL,
     WHIP, SCOLD, SKIN(ALIVE),
       STRIP, ASSAIL, DENUDE,
        FLEECE, PILLAGE, CASTIGATE,
           CRITICIZE, EXCORIATE
flea .... CHIGOE, JIGGER, JUMPER
               REDBUG, CHIGGER
bitten ..... BLOTCHY, DECREPIT,
        SPLOTCHY, WRETCHED
in one's ear .... ADVICE,
               NOTICE, WARNING
market .... STREET MART, OPEN
        MARKET, RUMMAGE SALE
fleabag .... FLOPHOUSE
fleam .... LANCET, PHLEBOTOME
fleawort .... HERB, PLANTAIN
fleche .... SPIRE
fleck ...... JOT, IOTA, SPOT, FLAKE,
         FREAK, SPECK, TITTLE,
       SPECKLE, FLYSPECK, PARTICLE
flection ...... BEND(ING), FLEXING,
            FLEXURE, TORSION
Fledermaus character .... ADELE
fledge .... BLOOM, RIPEN, MATURE,
               FEATHER(OUT)
fledgling .... INFANT, SAPLING,
         NEOPHYTE, NESTLING,
                  GREENHORN
flee .... FLY, LAM, RUN(AWAY),
      BOLT, SKIP, ELOPE, DECAMP,
       ESCAPE, DESERT, VANISH,
                   ABSCOND
fleece ...... ABB, ROB, COAT, FELL,
       FLAY, HIDE, PILE, WOOL,
        CHEAT, MULCT, SHEAR,
        STEAL, TAUNT, DESPOIL,
                   SWINDLE
cloth .... HODDEN
fleeced .... SHORN
fleecy .... SOFT, WOOLY
fleer ...... GIBE, JEER, LEER, MOCK,
      TWIT, FLOUT, SCOFF, SMIRK,
       SNEER, TAUNT, INSULT,
           REVILE, RUNAWAY,
                   RUNAGATE
fleet .... FLY, FAST, FLIT, NAVY,
     AGILE, GROUP, RAPID, SWIFT,
        MARINE, FLOTILLA
commander's vessel
   .... FLAGSHIP
front of .... VAN
merchant .... ARGOSY

small .... FLOTILLA
Spanish .... ARMADA
unit .... SQUADRON
fleeting .... BRIEF, NIMBLE,
      EPHEMERAL, TRANSIENT,
        PASSING, FUGITIVE,
                   TRANSITORY
Flemish geographer
   .... MERCATOR
mathematician .... STEVIN
painter ..... RUBENS, MEMLING,
      VAN DYCK, FRANCKEN
flense .... SKIN
flesh .... MEAT, PULP,
     (ANIMAL)TISSUE, MANKIND
and blood .... KIN, KINDRED,
       KINFOLK, RELATIVE
become .... CARNIFY
calf .... VEAL
cattle .... BEEF
deer/game animal .... VENISON
eater .... OMNIVORE,
      CARNIVORE, PREDACEAN,
                   OMOPHAGIST
eating .... OMOPHAGOUS,
      PREDACEOUS, PREDACIOUS,
                   CARNIVOROUS
eating, man
   .... CANNIBAL(ISTIC)
eating raw .... OMOPHAGIA
fly .... BLOWFLY
fold of .... COLLOP
of dead body .... CARRION
outgrowth ..... COMB, WATTLE,
                   CARUNCLE
pertaining to .... CARNAL,
       SARCOID, SARCOUS
sheep/lamb .... MUTTON
swine/pig .... PORK
symbol of human body
   .... CLAY
fleshings .... TIGHTS
fleshly .... SEXY, BODILY, CARNAL,
      MORTAL, SEXUAL, SENSUAL,
        WORLDLY, CORPOREAL
fleshpots ...... LUXURY, BROTHEL,
                   BORDELLO
fleshy .... FAT, BEEFY, MEATY,
      OBESE, PLUMP, PULPY, STOUT,
        BRAWNY, ADIPOSE,
                   CORPULENT
fruit .... PEAR, PLUM, POME,
      APPLE, BERRY, DRUPE, MELON,
      BANANA, CHERRY, QUINCE,
        TOMATO, SARCOCARP
fleur-de-lis .... IRIS, LILY,
      INSIGNIA, COAT-OF-ARMS
flex .... BEND, CURL, CURVE,
                   CONTRACT
one's muscles .... GET SET,
      WARM UP, GET READY

flexed .... SKEWED, DEFLECTED
flexibility .... AGILITY, PLIANCY,
      VERSATILITY, ADJUSTABILITY
flexible ..... AGILE, LITHE, DOCILE,
      LIMBER, PLIANT, SUPPLE,
      DUCTILE, ELASTIC, LISSOM(E),
      PLASTIC, TENSILE, TRACTABLE
flexile .... MOBILE, PLIANT
flexing .... FLECTION
flexor .... MUSCLE
flexuous .... PLIANT, PLIABLE,
      TWISTY, TRACTILE, BENDABLE
flexure .... FOLD, CURVE,
      BEND(ING), DEFLECTION
flibbertigibbet .... GIDDYHEAD,
      CHATTERBOX, SCATTERBRAIN
flick .... TAP, DASH, FLIP, SNAP,
      CLICK, FLECK, JIGGLE,
      FLOUNCE, FLYSPECK, STREAK,
                   FLUTTER
slang .... FILM, MOVIE, MOTION
                   PICTURE
Flicka creator .... OHARA
flicker .... FLAP, BLAZE, BLINK,
      WAVER, QUIVER, FLUTTER,
      WOODPECKER,
      YELLOWHAMMER
dialect .... HIGH-HOLE,
                   WOODPECKER
flickering .... FITFUL, ERRATIC,
      LAMBENT, SPORADIC
flier .... PILOT, AIRMAN, AVIATOR,
      LEAFLET, WINGMAN,
      AERONAUT, CIRCULAR,
                   HANDBILL
in a straight stairway ..... STEP
night .... BAT
on an eagle .... ETANA
protected .... EGRET
slang .... GAMBLE, BIRDMAN,
                   SPECULATION
flight .... ESCAPE, EXODUS,
      HEGIRA, HEJIRA, FLEEING,
      SQUADRON, MIGRATION,
                   VOLITATION
between floors .... STAIRS
capable of .... VOLITANT
direction of a ship or plane
   .... COURSE
disorderly .... ROUT
hasty .... SCUTTLE
headlong ...... LAM, STAMPEDE
organ .... WING
short .... HOP
sudden: slang .... LAM
sudden and secret
   .... DECAMPMENT
to get married, secret
   .... ELOPEMENT
type of .... SOLO, TEST,
      MAIDEN, NONSTOP

unit .... STAIR

flightless bird .... EMU, MOA, DODO, KIWI, RHEA, WEKA, RATITE, APTERYX, OSTRICH, PENGUIN, CASSOWARY

flighty .... BARMY, GIDDY, FICKLE, FANCIFUL, FRIVOLOUS, CAPRICIOUS, HOITY-TOITY, LIGHTHEADED, SCATTER-BRAINED

one .... BIRDBRAIN, SOCIAL BUTTERFLY

flimflam ...... LIE, HOCUS, CHEAT, TRICK, HUMBUG, RUBBISH, NONSENSE

flimsy .... POOR, THIN, WEAK, FRAIL, SHEER, FEEBLE, SLEAZY, SLIGHT, FRAGILE, TENUOUS, TRIVIAL, GOSSAMER

flinch ...... COWER, DEMUR, QUAIL, SHRINK, WINCE, BLENCH, CRINGE, RECOIL, RETRACT, RETREAT

flinder .... FRAGMENT, SPLINTER

fling .... CAST, DASH, EMIT, HURL, RUSH, TOSS, SLING, THROW, HURTLE

flint .... CORN, CHERT, SILEX, QUARTZ, SILICA

Flint's outfit .... ZOWIE

flintlock .... MUSKET

flip .... TAP, JERK, PERT, SNAP, TOSS, DRINK, SAUCY, FILLIP, FLIPPANT

in the crypt ..... TURN OVER IN THE GRAVE

slang .... GO BANANAS

talk .... SASS

flippancy .... AIRS, CHEEK, PRIDE, LEVITY, VANITY, BLUSTER

colloquial .... BRASS, SAUCE

slang .... GALL, SASS, CRUST, NERVE

flippant .... AIRY, GLIB, PERT, COCKY, SASSY, SAUCY, BRAZEN

flipped: sl. .... NUTS, NUTTY, BANANAS, BONKERS, FREAKED OUT

flipper .... FIN, PADDLE

relative .... PAW

slang .... HAND

flippered mammal .... SEAL, WALRUS

flirt .... EYE, TOY, OGLE, PLAY, DALLY, TRIFLE, COQUET(TE)

female ...... SIREN, TEMPTRESS, SEDUCTRESS

in the theater .... SOUBRETTE

male .... WOLF

slang .... VAMP

flirtation .... COYNESS, COQUETRY, INTRIGUE, DALLIANCE, HANKY-PANKY

flirtatious ...... FICKLE, ALLURING, SKITTISH, TEMPTING, COQUETTISH

flirting .... TOYING, FOOLING, DALLYING, FIDDLING, TRIFLING

flit ...... FLY, DART, GLIDE, HOVER, WANDER, FLUTTER

flittermouse .... BAT

flivver .... FAIL, CRATE, AIRPLANE, AUTO(MOBILE)

float .... BUOY, CORK, RAFT, RIDE, SELL, SWIM, WAFT, DRIFT, GLIDE, LAUNCH, PONTOON

a loan .... BORROW

fishing line ...... BOB, DOBBER

floater .... ROAMER, DRIFTER, WANDERER, ROLLING STONE

floating .... AWASH, ADRIFT, NATANT, BUOYANT

debris .... FLOTAGE

ice .... BERG, FLOE, GLACIER, CLUMPERS, GROWLERS

island ingredient .... EGGS

leaf .... LILYPAD

plant .... WATERLILY

platform .... RAFT

power of .... FLOTAGE

wreckage .... FLOTSAM

flocculent .... FLAKY, FLUFFY, FLEECY, WOOLLY

flock .... BAND, PACK, BUNCH, BROOD, CROWD, GROUP, TROOP, THRONG, CONGREGATION

of bears .... SLOTH

bees .... HIVE, SWARM, COLONY

birds ...... POD, BEVY, COVEY

cats .... CLOWDER

cattle .... HERD, DROVE

dogs .... KENNEL

elks .... GANG

finches .... CHARM

foxes .... SKULK

geese/wild fowl .... SKEIN, GAGGLE

lions .... PRIDE

locusts/insects .... CLOUD, SWARM

mallards .... SUTE

partridges/quails ...... COVEY

seals .... POD

sheep .... FOLD, HERD, DROVE

whales .... GAM, POD

young animals .... LITTER

pertaining to a .... GREGARIOUS

together .... FUSE, BUNCH UP, ASSEMBLE, CONGREGATE

floe .... GLACIER, (ICE)BERG

flog .... LAM, TAN, BEAT, CANE, GOAD, HIDE, LASH, WHIP, SWISH, PUNISH, LARRUP, THRASH, TROUNCE, SHELLACK, FLAGELLATE

flogging rod .... SWISH, SWITCH

whip .... CHAB(O)UK, KURBASH

flood .... RAIN, SPATE, SWAMP, TORRENT, INUNDATE, OVERFLOW, CLOUDBURST, INUNDATION, OUTPOURING, RAINSTORM, HIGH WATER, UNDERWATER

a great .... DELUGE, CATARACT, CATACLYSM

light .... KLIEG

the engine .... STALL

the market .... GLUT

tidal .... EAGRE

flooded condition .... SPATE, OVERSUPPLY

floodgate ...... DAM, WEIR, HATCH, SLUICE, CONTROL, SPILLWAY

floor .... DECK, DALLE, LEVEL, STORY, PUZZLE, PLANCH(E), SURFACE, PAVEMENT, PLATFORM, KNOCK DOWN

above street level .... ENTRESOL, MEZZANINE

chateau .... ETAGE

cover .... RUG, TILE, WOOD, CARPET, MAT(TING), LINOLEUM

covering, fabric for .... DRUGGET

raised border .... COAMING

show .... ENTERTAINMENT

walker ..... SUPERVISOR, SALES MANAGER

floorcloth .... LINOLEUM

flooring chip/slab .... DALLE, PARQUET, TERRAZZO

floorleader .... WHIP

flop .... DROP, FAIL, FALL, FLAP, LOLL, THUD

colloquial .... BUST, FAILURE

slang .... SLEEP, LAY AN EGG

flophouse .... FLEABAG

denizen .... WINO

flora .... PLANTS

and fauna .... BIOTA

floral .... GARDEN, FLOWERY, FLOWERED

arrangement .... SPRAY, WREATH, BOUQUET, GARLAND, NOSEGAY

arrangement, art of
.... IKEBANA
envelope .... PERIANTH
leaf .... BRACT, SEPAL
organs .... STAMENS
Florence .... FIRENZE, FIORENZA
Florentine friar .... SERVITE
iris .... ORRIS
name .... MEDICI
painter .... LIPPI, SARTO,
    CIMABUE
florescence .... BLOOM(ING),
    BLOSSOM(ING),
    FLOWERING(TIME)
florid ...... ROSY, GAUDY, RUDDY,
    SHOWY, FLORAL, ORNATE,
    FLOWERY, TAFFETA, FANCIFUL
style ...... ROCOCO, ARABESQUE
Florida bay .... PALM, MCKAY,
    TAMPA, CRYSTAL, DEADMAN,
    FLORIDA, BISCAYNE,
    GULLIVAN, APALACHEE,
    CHEVELIER, PENSACOLA,
    WACCASASSA, WHITEWATER,
    HILLSBOROUGH
beach .... VERO, COCOA,
    DEKLE, MIAMI, DELRAY,
    VILANO, BOYNTON, DAYTONA,
    FLAGLER, POMPANO,
    CRESCENT, WEST PALM, FORT
    MYERS, PONTE VEDRA
bird .... ANI, COURLAN,
    LIMPKIN
canal .... TAMIAMI, SNAKE
    CREEK
cape .... SABLE, ROMANO,
    CANAVERAL, SAINT GEORGE
capital of .... TALLAHASSEE
city/town .... DADE, DANIA,
    LARGO, MIAMI, OCALA, PERRY,
    TAMPA, NAPLES, QUINCY,
    PANAMA, ORLANDO, HIALEAH,
    MARGATE, LAKELAND,
    PALATKA, LEESBURG,
    SARASOTA, BRADENTON,
    HOLLYWOOD, MELBOURNE,
    PENSACOLA, CLEARWATER,
    BOCA RATON, FORT MYERS,
    PLANTATION, GAINESVILLE,
    JACKSONVILLE, CORAL
    GABLES, DAYTONA BEACH,
    FORT LAUDERDALE, SAINT
    AUGUSTINE, SAINT
    PETERSBURG
college .... BARRY, TAMPA,
    ROLLINS
county .... BAY, LEE, CLAY,
    DADE, LAKE, LEON, POLK,
    DUVAL, PASCO, CITRUS,
    HARDEE, MARION, MARTIN,
    MONROE, NASSAU, ORANGE,

PUTNAM, SUMTER, WALTON,
    ALACHUA, BREVARD,
    BROWARD, COLLIER, GADSDEN,
    JACKSON, MANATEE, OSCEOLA,
    VOLUSIA, BRADFORD,
    COLUMBIA, ESCAMBIA,
    HERNANDO, OKALOOSA,
    PINELLAS, SARASOTA,
    SEMINOLE, SUWANNEE,
    CHARLOTTE, HIGHLANDS, PALM
    BEACH, SANTA ROSA, SAINT
    JOHNS, SAINT LUCIE,
    HILLSBOROUGH, INDIAN RIVER
creek .... PINE LOG
fish .... MERO, BONACI,
    SALEMA, TETARD, PINTADO,
    CABRILLA
grouper .... BONACI
harbor .... CHARLOTTE,
    EVERGLADES
Indian ...... CALUSA, SEMINOLE
island ...... DOG, PINE, MARCO,
    PINEY, AMELIA, ESTERO,
    TALBOT, CAPTIVA, MERRITT,
    SANIBEL, TREASURE,
    HONEYMOON, SAINT GEORGE
islands .... HOMOSASSA, TEN
    THOUSAND
key .... LONG, VACA, LARGO,
    SANDS, TORCH, GRASSY,
    ELLIOTT, BISCAYNE,
    MATECUMBE, SUGARLOAF,
    BOCA CHICA, OLD RHODES,
    BOCA GRANDE
lake .... DEAD, DORR, HART,
    KERR, LEVY, WEIR, YALE,
    REEDY, APOPKA, BRYANT,
    DEXTER, GEORGE, HARNEY,
    LOWERY, MARIAN, MONROE,
    ORANGE, PLACID, WIMICO,
    WINDER, JACKSON, TALQUIN,
    ARBUCKLE, CRESCENT,
    POINSETT, ALLIGATOR
mountain .... IRON
much of .... LOWLANDS
Naval Air Station
    .... MAYPORT, KEY WEST,
    PENSACOLA
perchlike fish .... CABRILLA
plant .... COONTIE
recreation/historic site .... SEA
    WORLD, MARINELAND, DISNEY
    WORLD, CYPRESS GARDENS,
    RINGLING MUSEUMS, KENNEDY
    SPACE CENTER
resort city .... MIAMI,
    ORLANDO, PALM BEACH
river .... MIAMI, SHOAL,
    BANANA, MYAKKA, AUCILLA,
    MANATEE, S(U)WANEE,
    OKLAWAHA, APALACHICOLA,

CHATTAHOOCHEE,
    CHOCTAWHATCHEE
sapodilla/tree .... BUSTIC
seaport .... TAMPA, PENSACOLA
scenic road .... TAMIAMI
state bird .... MOCKINGBIRD
state flower .... ORANGE
    BLOSSOM
state nickname ...... SUNSHINE,
    EVERGLADE
tortoise .... GOPHER
univeristy .... HEED, NOVA,
    MIAMI, TAMPA, WALDEN,
    STETSON, PALM BEACH
wood oil .... TUNG
florist's specialty .... POSY,
    SPRAY, WREATH, BOUQUET,
    CORSAGE, NOSEGAY
floss .... SILK, FLUFF, SLEAVE
flossy .... SOFT, DOWNY, FANCY,
    CLASSY, FLUFFY, LA-DI-DA,
    ELEGANT
flotage .... FLOTSAM
flotation .... LAUNCHING,
    UNVEILING
flotilla ...... FLEET, SHIPS, ARGOSY
Flotow opera .... MART(H)A
flotsam .... FLOTAGE, DRIFTAGE,
    FLOATAGE
and jetsam .... DRIFTERS,
    VAGRANTS, CASTAWAYS,
    WAIFS AND STRAYS
flounce .... JERK, JUMP, TWIST,
    FALTER, RUFFLE, TOTTER,
    TUMBLE, FALBALA, FURBELOW
flounder .... DAB, SOLE, TOSS,
    FLUKE, GROPE, FUMBLE,
    PLAICE, TURBOT, WALLOP,
    WALLOW, WELTER, HALIBUT,
    STAGGER, FLATFISH,
    STRUGGLE
flour .... MEAL, MILL, DURUM,
    POWDER, BUCKWHEAT
bean/corn .... PINOLE
boiled, thick .... FLUMMERY
cereal .... FARINA
color of .... IVORY, CREAMY-
    WHITE
maker/machine .... MILLER
making product ..... SEMOLINA
mixture .... ROUX, DOUGH,
    PASTE
paste .... PANADA
power .... YEAST
pudding .... DUFF
sieve/sifter .... BOLTER
sprinkle with .... DUST,
    DREDGE, PEPPER
flourish ...... BOOM, GROW, WAVE,
    SWING, TWIRL, WIELD,
    FLAUNT, THRIVE, FANFARE,

PROSPER, SUCCEED, TANTARA, BRANDISH

in an area .... CADENZA

in music .... ROULADE

in signature .... PARAPH

in writing .... TAG

floury .... POWDERY

flout .... JEER, MOCK, FLEER, SCOFF

flow .... RUN, OOZE, WELL, GLIDE, SPOUT, CURRENT, EMANATE

about freely .... CIRCULATE

against/along .... LAVE

and spread .... FLUSH

back .... EBB, RECEDE, REGORGE

combining form .... RHEO

forth .... ISSUE

in drops .... DRIBBLE

of tide .... EBB, FLUX, NEAP, RISE

out .... POUR, EXUDE, ISSUE, SPILL, STREAM

stop .... STEM, STANCH

than can .... FLUID

through .... SEEP

flower .... BEST, PICK, POSY, BLOOM, BLOSSOM, ORNAMENT

amaranth .... PIGWEED

annual .... ASTER

arrangement .... SPRAY, IKEBANA, VERTICIL

aster .... TANGLEFOOT

balsam .... IMPATIENS

bell-shaped .... HYACINTH

bending downward .... CERNUOUS

biennial .... FOXGLOVE

bloom .... ANTHESIS

blue .... VIOLET, LARKSPUR, HYDRANGEA

bract .... PALEA

bud .... KNOT, BULBIL

buds for seasoning .... CAPERS

butterfly-like .... MARIPOSA(LILY)

children, so-called ..... HIPPIES

Christmas .... POINSETTIA

cluster .... CYME, LILAC, TRUSS, UMBEL, CORYMB, RACEME, PANICLE, THYRSUS, CAPITULUM

cormus .... CROCUS, GLADIOLUS

cover of/covering ...... SPATHE, CALYPTRA

cowslip .... MARIGOLD, PRIMROSE

cup-shaped .... CHALICE

daisy .... OX-EYE

daisy-like .... BLACK-EYED SUSAN

Dutch .... TULIP

Easter .... LILY

envelope .... PERIANTH

erica .... HEATH

ericaceous .... AZALEA, LAUREL

extract .... AT(T)AR

fadeless .... AMARANTH, EVERLASTING

fall .... ASTER

field .... DAISY, GOWAN

form of .... PELORIA

fragrant .... ROSE, LILAC, AZALEA, JASMIN(E), HYACINTH, MAGNOLIA, JESSAMINE, HONEYSUCKLE

fringed .... GENTIAN

full-bloomed .... ANTHESIS

garden ...... ROSARY, NURSERY, GREENERY

genus .... ROSA, HEATH, LILIUM, SYRINGA, TAGETES, HIBISCUS

goddess .... FLORA

grower .... GARDENER, NURSERYMAN, HORTICULTURIST

growing, art of .... HORTICULTURE

having only one .... MONANTHOUS

head ...... PANICLE, CAPITULUM

heath .... AZALEA

herbaceous border .... VERBENA

holder .... BED, POT, VASE

honeysuckle .... ELDER, CLOVER

imaginary .... AMARANTH

incipient .... BUD

iris .... ORRIS, ORRICE

leaf ..... BRACT, PALEA, SEPAL, COROLLA

like .... ANTHOID

like animal .... ANEMONE

like ornament .... ROSETTE

lily .... SEGO, CALLA, LOTUS, MARIPOSA

moon .... ACHETE

musk-odored .... MOSCHATEL

night-blooming .... CEREUS

nightshade .... HENBANE, BELLADONNA

of .... FLORAL

of forgetfulness .... LOTUS

of varied colors .... PHLOX

orchid .... ARETHUSA, CYMBIDIUM, WALING-WALING

pansy .... HEARTSEASE

part ..... STEM, AMENT, BRACT, CALYX, OVARY, OVULE, PETAL, SEPAL, STYLE, ANTHER, CARPEL, PISTIL, POLLEN, SPADIX, STAMEN, STIGMA, COROLLA, PEDICEL

perennial .... DAHLIA, AMARANTH

petals .... COROLLA

pink .... TITI, ELDER, CARNATION, RHODORA, HYDRANGEA

pistil .... CARPEL

plot .... BED

pollen-bearing part .... STAMEN

receptacled .... TORUS, THALAMUS

red .... ROSE, OXALIS, CAMELLIA, MARIGOLD

rootstock .... TARO, ORRIS, ORRICE

rose of Sharon .... ALTHEA

roselike .... CAMELLIA

seed .... OVULE

seed-bearing part .... PISTIL

sex cells .... POLLEN

shaped .... FLEURON

showy ..... MARIGOLD, GOLDEN ASTER

small .... FLORET, FLOWERET

spike .... AMENT, SPICA, CATKIN, SPICULE, MIGNONETTE

spring .... TULIP, HYACINTH

stalk .... PETIOLE, PEDUNCLE

stalk bud/bulb .... BULBIL

stand .... EPERGNE, JARDINIERE

summer .... PETUNIA, MARIGOLD, CHRYSANTHEMUM

star .... ASTER

sun prone .... HELIOTROPE

support .... PEDUNCLE

symbol of luxury ...... ORCHID

syringa .... LILAC

the .... PICK, ELECT, ELITE

three-petaled .... ORCHID

turban-like .... TULIP

used for a corsage .... ORCHID

velvety .... PANSY

waterlily .... LOTUS

white .... TITI, ELDER, LILAC, CROCUS, OXALIS, GENTIAN, CAMELLIA, TRILLIUM, HYDRANGEA

wild .... THISTLE

wind .... ANEMONE

windowbox .... PETUNIA

wood sorrel .... OXALIS

yellow .... GOWAN, BENNET, COWSLIP, MARIGOLD

flowered vine .... CLEMATIS

flowering grass .... STIPA

herb .... HEPATICA
more than once a season
.... REMONTANT
plant .... ARUM, FERN, ROSE,
    AVENS, CANNA, YUCCA,
    ORCHID, SPIREA, LUPIN(E),
    LOBELIA, GERANIUM,
    VALERIAN, POINSETTIA
shrub .... BIXA, LILAC, SUMAC,
    AZALEA, SPIREA, MAGNOLIA,
    POINCIANA
vine .... CLEMATIS, WISTERIA
flowerless plant .... FERN,
    LICHEN, AGAMOUS, GENTIAN
flowers, bunch of .... POSY,
    BOUQUET, CORSAGE, NOSEGAY
collectively .... FLOWERAGE
in a spathe .... SPADIX
of/like .... FLORAL, FLOWERY
of Fats fame, two
    .... HONEYSUCKLE ROSE
on woman's shoulder
    .... CORSAGE
sculptured .... CORBEIL
flowery .... FLORID, ORNATE,
    BLOSSOMY, BOMBASTIC,
    FLAMBOYANT, HIGH-FLOWN
girl .... ROSA
flowing .... LOOSE, FLUENT,
    SMOOTH, (AF)FLUX, BILLOWY,
    CURSIVE, GRACEFUL,
    FLUXION, EMANATING
and ebbing .... TIDAL
back .... REFLUX, REFLUENT
freely .... MOBILE
locks .... TRESSES
out .... EFFLUX
together .... CONFLUX,
    CONFLUENT, CONFLUENCE
flown ...... LOOSE, FLUSHED, FLED,
    AT LARGE, FUGITIVE
flu .... INFLUENZA
drug for .... SYMMETREL,
    AMANTADINE
-like illness .... GRIPPE
symptom .... AGUE, FEVER,
    CHILLS, FATIGUE
treatment .... REST,
    ANALGESICS
variety, 1918 .... SPANISH
1957 .... ASIAN
1968 .... HONG KONG
flub ...... BOTCH, ERROR, BUNGLE,
    BLUNDER, FAILURE
slang .... BONER
fluctuant .... WAVY, VARYING,
    UNDULATING
fluctuate ...... VARY, VEER, WAVE,
    SHIFT, SWING, SEE-SAW,
    ALTERNATE, VACILLATE
fluctuating ...... FICKLE, ERRATIC,

    INCONSTANT
fluctuation .... SHIFTING,
    WAVERING, VARIATION
flue .... PIPE, FLUFF, FLUKE,
    SHAFT, FUNNEL, CHIMNEY
dust .... POTASH
fluency .... EASE, FLOW, GRACE,
    GLIBNESS, ELOQUENCE,
    SMOOTHNESS
fluent ...... GLIB, FACILE, SMOOTH,
    FLOWING, ELOQUENT,
    EXPRESSIVE
fluently .... GLIBLY, VIVIDLY
fluff .... ERR, NAP, FLUE, LINT,
    DOWN, BONER, ERROR, FLOSS
fluffy .... DOWNY, LINTY, FLOSSY,
    COTTONY, FEATHERY,
    FLOCCULENT
fluid .... GAS, SAP, SERUM, LIQUID,
    MOBILE, PLASTIC
aeriform .... GAS
body .... BILE, LYMPH
colloidal system .... SOL
life-saving .... BLOOD
matter .... FLUX
part of fruit or vegetable
    .... JUICE
rock .... LAVA
stoppage .... STASIS
fluidity ...... SEROSITY, LIQUIDITY,
    SOLUBLENESS
fluke .... BARB, FLUE, HOOK,
    CLEEK, FLATFISH, FLATWORM,
    FLOUNDER, TREMATODE,
    LUCKY BREAK, STROKE OF
    LUCK
fluky .... CHANCY, UNFORESEEN
flume ...... CHUTE, GORGE, SHUTE,
    OUTLET, RAVINE, SLUICE,
    TROUGH, CHANNEL
flummery .... CUSTARD,
    OATMEAL, RUBBISH,
    FLATTERY, NONSENSE
flummox: sl. .... THWART,
    CONFUSE, PERPLEX
flump .... DROP, THUD, THUMP
flunk .... LOSE, FAIL(URE), FIASCO,
    GIVE UP, NOT PASS, RETREAT
slang .... BUST, WASHOUT
flunk(e)y .... TOADY, LACKEY,
    STOOGE, YES-MAN, FOOTMAN
flunks at Annapolis .... BILGES
fluoresce .... OPALESCE,
    LUMINESCE
fluorescent .... IRIDESCENT,
    OPALESCENT
fluorite .... JADE
fluoroscopy .... X-RAY,
    RADIOSCOPY
flurry .... ADO, GUST, STIR,
    HURRY, AGITATION,

    COMMOTION, CONFUSION
flush .... GLOW, GUSH, RUSH,
    FULL, BLUSH, ELATE, EMPTY,
    RINSE, ROUSE, START, LAVISH,
    EXCITE, REDDEN, THRILL,
    PROFUSE, EXHILARATE
with water .... WASH
flushed .... HOT, RED, AGLOW,
    RUDDY, FLORID, HECTIC,
    BLUSHING, FEVERISH
fluster .... BUSTLE, EXCITE,
    FUDDLE, DITHER, POTHER,
    CONFUSE, BLUSTER,
    UNSETTLE, EMBARRASS
flustered .... AGITATED
flute .... FIFE, PIPE, PIPING,
    GROOVE, CHANNEL
ancient .... TIBIA, HEMIOPE
bagpipe .... CHANTER
blow a .... TOOTLE
Chinese .... (T)CHE
cousin of .... PICCOLO
early form .... RECORDER
India .... MATALAN
-like instrument
    .... FLAGEOLET
part of a .... KEYS, TUBE,
    FIPPLE
player .... FL(A)UTIST TOOTLER
stop .... VENTAGE
fluted .... FOLDED, GROOVED,
    SULCATE(D)
fluting .... GOFFER, GAUFFER,
    GROOVE(S)
architectural .... GADROON,
    GODROON
wavelike .... STRIGIL
flutter .... FLY, FLAP, FLIP, FLIT,
    WHIP, HOVER, SHAKE,
    BUSTLE, WAVE(R), FIDGET,
    QUIVER, FLICKER, TREMBLE,
    TWITTER, AGITATE, VIBRATE,
    PALPITATE
and shift .... RIFFLE
of eyes .... BLINK
flux .... FUSE, BORAX, PURGE,
    ROSIN, FLOW(ING), COURSE,
    MOTION, SOLDER, CURRENT,
    FLUXION, SOLVENT
and reflux .... ALTERNATION,
    UPS AND DOWNS
slang .... TROTS
fluxion ...... FLOWING, DISCHARGE,
    EXCRETION
fly .... BUG, BOLT, DART, FLAP,
    FLEE, FLIT, GNAT, SOAR,
    SCUD, WAVE, WHIR, WING,
    FLOAT, HOVER, MIDGE,
    MUSCA, AVIATE, FLUTTER,
    TACHINA, MOSQUITO
able to ..... VOLANT, VOLITANT

after game .... RAKE
agaric/amanita ..... MUSHROOM
angler's artificial
.... DOWNLOOKER
artificial .... DUN, HARL, HERL,
    ZULU, CAHILL, HACKLE
at .... ATTACK
before the wind .... SCUD
block .... PULLEY
bloodsucking .... GADFLY,
    TABANID
-by-night .... UNSURE,
    UNRELIABLE
case .... ELYTRON
catcher .... TODY, PEWIT,
    PEEWEE, PHOEBE
close to the ground
.... HEDGEHOP
experimental ...... DROSOPHILA
hit .... SWAT
in the ointment ..... OBSTACLE
insect resembling ...... CICADA
let .... THROW
nemesis .... SWATTER
of the .... MUSCID
off .... ESCAPE, RUN AWAY
sheet .... PAMPHLET
slang .... AGILE, SHARP,
    NIMBLE
small .... MITE, PUNKIE
the coop .... BREAK JAIL
to and fro .... VOLITANT
wing cover .... ELYTRON,
    ELYTRUM
flyaway .... ESCAPEE, FLIGHTY,
    STREAMING
flyblow ...... LARVA, SPOIL, TAINT
flyblown .... FILTHY, SPOILED
flycatcher .... TODY, ALDER,
    PEWIT, PE(E)WEE, PHOEBE,
    CHEBEC, FANTAIL, KINGBIRD
flyer, famous .... LINDY,
    LINDBERGH
fearless .... ACE
inky .... CROW, RAVEN
of myth .... ICARUS
stunt of .... LOOP, ROLL
flying .... ALOFT, FLIGHT,
    WINGING, AIRBORNE,
    FLITTING, HOVERING,
    SKYRIDING
act of .... VOLITATION
air matress .... PARAFOIL
airplanes, art or science of
.... AVIATION
capable of .... VOLANT,
    VOLITANT
colors .... SUCCESS, VICTORY
fish .... SAURY, GURNET,
    GURNARD
fox .... BAT, KALONG

gurnard .... GURNET
in an engineless aircraft
.... GLIDING
island, fictional .... LAPUTA
jib .... SAIL
lemur .... COLUGO
lizard's skin fold
.... PATAGIUM, PARACHUTE
machine ...... AERO, AIRCRAFT,
    AIR BALLOON, (AIR)PLANE
marsupial .... PHALANGER
saucer, for short .... UFO
signal .... ROGER
spindrift .... SCUD
squirrel's skin fold
.... PATAGIUM
start .... EDGE, ADVANTAGE
water .... SPRAY
Flying Dutchman .... SHIP,
    SAILOR
Dutchman maiden .... SENTA
Finn .... NURMI
Fortress .... BOMBER
Fortress weapon ...... TAILGUN
Flynn, actor .... ERROL
flyspeck .... DOT, SPOT
flywheel .... WHORL, WHARVE
foal .... COLT, FILLY
foam .... FIZZ, SCUM, SUD(S),
    FROTH, YEAST, BUBBLE,
    SPUME, LATHER
of .... SPUMY, SPUMOUS
poetic .... SEA
foaming .... HEADY, NAPPY
at the mouth .... MAD
foamy ...... SOAPY, SPUMY, SUDSY,
    FROTHY, LATHERY, SPUMOUS
yeast .... BARM
fob .... CHARM, CHEAT, TRICK,
    DECEIVE, PENDANT,
    (WATCH)POCKET
off .... PALM, FOIST
focal .... CHIEF, CENTRAL
point .... HUB, CYNOSURE,
    EPICENTER
focus .... HUB, CORE, HEART,
    POINT, CENTER, NUCLEUS,
    CONVERGE, SPOTLIGHT,
    CENTRALIZE, CONCENTRATE
in .... CLEAR, DISTINCT
focusing device .... LENS
fodder .... HAY, FEED, FOOD,
    OATS, GRASS, STRAW,
    FORAGE, SILAGE, ALFILARIA,
    CORNSTALK, PROVENDER,
    PROVISION
bin .... CRATCH
grain .... KAFFIR
pertaining to .... FORAGE
pit/storage place/tower
.... SILO

plant ...... GRAM, RAPE, VETCH,
    ALSIKE, CLOVER, STOVER,
    ALFALFA, BERSEEM, CHICKPEA,
    SAINFOIN
preservation .... ENSILAGE
rack .... CRATCH
straw .... STOVER
tree pod .... CAROB
trough .... MANGER
foe ...... ENEMY, RIVAL, OPPONENT,
    ADVERSARY, ANTAGONIST
Athenian's .... SPARTAN
of Richelieu .... ATHOS
of shams .... ICONOCLAST
fog .... HAZE, MIST, MURK, BRUME,
    CLOUD, VAPOR, CONFUSE
and smoke .... SMOG
fog(e)y .... DOTARD, MOSSBACK
fogeyish .... FUSTY, SENILE,
    STODGY
foggy .... DIM, MISTY, MURKY,
    CLOUDY, BRUMOUS,
    CONFUSED, NUBILOUS
foghorn .... ALARM, SIGNAL,
    SIREN(E)
foible .... FLAW, VICE, FAULT,
    WHIMSY, FAILING, FRAILTY,
    WEAKNESS
opposed to .... FORTE
foil .... BALK, EPEE, DETER, SPOIL,
    STUMP, SWORD, BAFFLE,
    THWART, FRUSTRATE,
    CIRCUMVENT
comedian's .... STOOGE,
    STRAIGHTMAN
slang ...... CRAMP ONE'S STYLE
foilsman .... FENCER
foist ...... FOB, PALM(OFF), IMPOSE
    ON
Fokine, choreographer
.... MICHEL
fold .... LAP, PLY, BEND, KNIT,
    RUCK, RUGA, WRAP, CLASP,
    CRIMP, DRAPE, FLOCK, LAYER,
    PLAIT, PLEAT, GATHER,
    EMBRACE, ENVELOP, FLEXURE,
    PLICA(TION)
animal's throat .... DEWLAP
coat .... LAPEL
mark .... CREASE
sail .... REEF
sheep .... PEN
skin .... PLICA
slang .... BUST, FAIL
stitched .... TUCK
up .... FAIL, CLOSE, GO UNDER,
    COLLAPSE
folded .... RUGATE, PLEATED,
    DOUBLED, PLICATE
edge .... HEM
part .... PLEAT, PLICA

folder .... COVER, BOOKLET, LEAFLET, PAMPHLET
folding bed .... COT
  hood/bonnet .... CALASH
  leaves, plant with ..... MIMOSA
  money .... ONES, DOLLAR
foliage .... LEAVES, LEAFAGE, UMBRAGE, VERDURE
  mass of .... SPRAY, BOUQUET
folio .... BOOK, PAGE, NUMBER
foliose .... LEAFY, VERDANT
folium .... LOOP
folk ...... KIN, KOLO, RACE, TRIBE, NATION, PEOPLE, PERSONS
  dance .... HORA, DREHER, MORRIS
  tale .... FICTION, MARCHEN
  tale tiny hero ..... TOM THUMB
folklore .... BELIEFS, LEGENDS, SAYINGS, MYTHOLOGY
  character .... OGRE, DWARF, FAIRY, GIANT, TROLL, SANDMAN
folksinger .... BAEZ, IVES
folksong .... LULLABY
folkways .... MORES
follicle .... POD, SAC, GLAND, CAVITY, COCOON, CAPSULE
follies .... REVUE
follow .... TAG, COPY, HEED, OBEY, SEEK, CHASE, ENSUE, TRACE, TRACK, TRAIL, ATTEND, COMPLY, PURSUE, RESULT, CONFORM, IMITATE, SUCCEED, ACCOMPANY
  continually/relentlessly .... DOG, HOUND
  in the footsteps of .... EMULATE
  stealthily/secretly .... STAG, TAIL, SHADOW
  suit .... MODEL AFTER
  up .... PURSUE, GO AFTER
follower .... FAN, IST, ITE, BUFF, MINION, VOTARY, DEVOTEE, PURSUER, ADHERENT, BELIEVER, DISCIPLE, HENCHMAN, PARTISAN, SERVITOR, SUPPORTER
  faithful .... FRIDAY, MYRMIDON
  finger .... BOWL, NAIL, WAVE
  fox or turkey .... TROT
  kind of .... SERVANT, HANGER-ON, ATTENDANT, SATELLITE
  loyal .... LIEGEMAN
  of Arius .... ARIAN
  of forgive .... FORGET
  of Lao-tze .... TAOIST
  of snick .... SNEE
  of theta .... IOTA
  para .... GRAPH, LEGAL, NORMAL

followers, group of .... CULT
following .... SECT, AFTER, TRADE, TRAIN, ENSUING, PURSUIT, RETINUE, EQUIPAGE, ADHERENTS, FOLLOWERS
  this .... HEREAFTER, HENCEFORTH
folly .... IDIOCY, LUNACY, FATUITY, INANITY, FRIVOLITY, SILLINESS, FOOLISHNESS
foment .... ABET, BREW, SPUR, STIR, AROUSE, EXCITE, INCITE, INSTIGATE
fond .... ARDENT, LOVING, TENDER, DEVOTED, FOOLISH, ATTACHED, ENAMORED, AFFECTIONATE
  of: sl. .... STUCK ON
  arguing .... DISPUTATIVE
  fighting .... COMBATIVE, PUGNACIOUS
  foolishly .... DOTING, SMITTEN, UXORIOUS
  luxury, etc. .... EPICUREAN
Fonda .... JANE, HENRY, PETER
fondant .... CANDY
fondle .... HUG, PET, TOUCH, CARESS, COSSET, DANDLE, PAMPER, STROKE, CHERISH, EMBRACE
fondling .... MINION, DARLING, NECKING, PETTING, FAVORITE
fondness .... LOVE, ARDOR, FLAIR, TASTE, DESIRE, LIKING, REGARD, PENCHANT, AFFECTION
font .... BOWL, CASE, FACE, TYPE, BASIN, LAVER, STOOP, STOUP, ORIGIN, SPRING, SOURCE, FOUNTAIN, RESERVOIR
  rite .... BAPTISM
fontal .... ORIGINAL, BAPTISMAL
fontanel(le) .... OUTLET, OPENING
food .... BITE, DIET, FARE, BOARD, TABLE, VIANDS, ALIMENT, EDIBLES, REPAST, NUTRIMENT, NUTRITION, MEAL, COMESTIBLES, NOURISHMENT
  additive: abbr. .... MSG
  allowance .... CORODY, RATION
  and shelter .... KEEP, BOARD
  animal .... FODDER, FORAGE
  archaic .... DAILY BREAD
  being digested .... CHYME
  between meals .... SNACK
  bits .... ORTS, SCRAPS
  cereal .... OAT, CORN, RICE, WHEAT
  chewed, solid .... BROMA
  choice: arch. .... CATE

  colloquial .... CHOW, EATS, GRUB, SPREAD
  concentrated high-energy .... PEMMICAN
  dealer .... GROCER
  desire/need for .... HUNGER
  diet .... FARE, REGIMEN
  disk-shaped .... PATTY
  drying platform .... FLAKE
  fancy .... KICKSAW
  fish .... COD, BASS, CERO, DACE, SHAD, TUNA, PERCH, SCROD, TROUT, SALMON, SARDINE, MACKEREL, SHEEPSHEAD
  fish, Atlantic .... ALEWIFE
  for beginners/infants ...... PAP, PABLUM, PABULUM
  for cattle/goats .... BROWSE
  from heaven .... MANNA
  Hawaiian .... POI
  in a hive .... BEEBREAD
  in Australia: sl. .... TUCKER
  liquid .... SLOP, SOUP, BROTH
  list .... CARTE
  look for .... SCAVENGE
  Maori .... KAI
  needed to sustain life ..... SUSTENANCE, SUBSISTENCE
  non-flesh .... MAIGRE
  of fools .... FLATTERY
  of the gods .... AMRITA, AMBROSIA
  place for ..... LARDER, SPENCE, SPENSE, PANTRY, CUPBOARD
  place for eating .... DINER, EATERY, AUTOMAT, CANTEEN, MESS HALL, CAFE(TERIA), REFECTORY, RESTAURANT, DINING ROOM
  place for eating: colloq. .... GREASY SPOON
  poisoning .... BOTULISM, PTOMAIN(E)
  provider/supplier ..... CATERER
  rack .... FLAKE
  regimen .... DIET
  scrap .... ORT
  served .... HELPING
  serving style .... BUFFET
  shavings/slices .... CHIPS
  shop .... DELICATESSEN
  slang .... FEED, FUEL, SLOP, JUNK FOOD
  soft .... PAP, FLUMMERY
  solid in medicine .... BROMA
  specialist .... DIETARIAN, DIETITIAN
  spoiler .... MOLD, YEAST, ENZYME, BACTERIA
  stock of .... VITTLES,

VICTUALS, PROVISIONS
study of kinds and quantities
.... DIETETICS
style/manner of preparing
.... CUISINE
supplement .... MINERAL,
VITAMIN
taken after a period of
hunger .... REFECTION
thick and semi-solid, made
from milk .... YOGURT
unappetizing .... MESS
wrap .... SARAN
foods, study of .... SITOLOGY,
DIETETICS
foofaraw .... ROW, RIOT, RACKET,
UPROAR
fool .... ASS, OAF, BOOB, DOLT,
DUPE, GABY, JAPE, SIMP,
ZANY, CHUMP, DUNCE, IDIOT,
NINNY, NODDY, TRICK,
DOTARD, NOODLE, DECEIVE,
MISLEAD, MUGGINS,
SAP(HEAD), MOONCALF,
SIMPLETON
around .... TRIFLE
around with .... MEDDLE,
TAMPER
hen .... GROUSE
in a way .... SPOOF
play the .... CLOWN
professional .... JESTER
foolable .... NAIVE, GULLIBLE
foolhardy .... BOLD, RASH, BRASH,
DARING, ICARIAN, RECKLESS
person .... DAREDEVIL
foolish .... MAD, DAFT, RASH,
ZANY, CRAZY, INANE, SILLY,
ABSURD, CUCKOO, SENILE,
STUPID, UNWISE, ASININE,
LUNATIC, PUERILE, TRIVIAL,
ANSERINE, IMPRUDENT,
LUDICROUS, RIDICULOUS
action .... FOLLY,
(TOM)FOOLERY
affection .... DOTAGE
blunder .... HOWLER
fancy .... CHIMERA
from overdrinking
.... SCOTTISH
from old age .... DOITED,
SENILE
slang .... BALMY, BARMY,
DIZZY, GIDDY, GOOFY, KOOKY,
SAPPY, WACKY
talk .... BABBLE, JABBER,
CHATTER, PRATTLE,
BLAB(BER), FLAPDOODLE,
YAKKETY-YAK
undertaking .... FOLLY,
FRIVOLITY, EXTRAVAGANCE

foolishly loving .... FOND
foolishness .... FOLLY, LUNACY,
FATUITY, MISCHIEF, NONSENSE
foolproof .... TIGHT, WIELDY,
(FAIL)SAFE, RESISTANT
fool's bauble .... MAROTTE
gold .... PYRITE
paradise ...... BUBBLE, UTOPIA,
CHIMERA, DAYDREAM, FALSE
HOPE
foot .... BASE, HOOF, WALK,
TREAD, BOTTOM, UNGULA,
TROTTER, EXTREMITY
animal's .... PAD, PAW
and mouth disease
.... MURRAIN
bone of the .... TALUS,
CUBOID, CALCANEUS,
CUNEIFORM, NAVICULAR,
PHALANGES, METATARSALS
child's/woman's .... TOOTSY
colloquial .... PAY, PEG
combining form .... PED(E),
PED(I), POD(E)
deformity .... BUNION,
TALIPES, CLAWFOOT,
CLUBFOOT, FLATFOOT
disease/disorder .... CORN,
GOUT, WART, PODAGRA,
FRACTURE, ARTHRITIS,
INGROWN TOENAIL
disorders, specialist in
.... PODIATRIST
-dragging ..... DELAY, HOLDUP,
RELUCTANCE
fungal infection .... ATHLETE'S
FOOT
inability to raise the
.... FOOTDROP
lever .... PEDAL, TREADLE
metrical .... PAEON, TROCHEE
of 4 syllables .... TETRABRACH
of 3 syllables .... ANAPEST
of 2 syllables .... IAMB
on .... RUNNING, WALKING
on one's .... STANDING
pain .... TARSALGIA
part .... TOE, ARCH, HEEL,
INCH, SHIN, SOLE, ANKLE,
INSTEP
pedal .... TREADLE
pertaining to a .... PEDAL
poetic .... DACTYL, ANAPEST,
IAMB(IC), SPONDEE
prefix .... PED
race .... STEEPLECHASE
science of the .... PODOLOGY
-shaped .... PEDIFORM
soldier .... KERN(E),
INFANTRYMAN
soldier's coat .... JACK

-sole beating .... BASTINADO
sole of .... VOLAR, THENAR,
PLANTAR
sore .... CHILBLAIN
study of .... PODIATRY
swelling .... BUNION
travel gauge .... PEDOMETER
traveler .... HIKER, TRAMP,
JOGGER, RUNNER, WAYFARER,
PEDESTRIAN
with .... PEDATE
footage .... LENGTH, MEASURE,
YARDAGE, DISTANCE
football .... RUGBY, ELEVEN,
RUGGER
association .... SOCCER
bowl .... SUN, HULA, ROSE,
SUPER, COTTON, FIESTA,
ORANGE
coach .... NOLL, ALLEN,
BURNS, DITKA, REESE, SHELL,
LEVY, STAGG, WALSH, WYCHE,
FLORES. MADDEN, ROCKNE,
MORA, PARCELLS, SEIFERT,
KNOX, JOHNSON, ROBINSON
coaching greats, one of
.... HALAS, SHULA, LANDRY
colloquial .... PIGSKIN
commissioner .... BELL,
ROZELLE, TAGLIABUE
conference .... BIG TEN
"Crazy Legs" of
.... (ELROY)HIRSCH
face-off site .... LINE OF
SCRIMMAGE
field .... GRID(IRON)
five-time Super Bowl
champions of ..... FORTY-
NINERS
forefront/unit .... LINE
foul .... CLIP, HOLDING,
FACEMASK, DELAY OF GAME,
LATE HIT, PASS INTERFERENCE
"Galloping Ghost" of
.... (HAROLD RED)GRANGE
Hall of Fame name .... MIX,
BELL, CARR, FORD, HUFF,
HUNT, LANE, OTTO, OWEN
BAUGH, BERRY, BROWN,
CLARK, DAVIS, HALAS, JONES,
LILLY, LYMAN, MOORE,
MUSSO, NEALE, OLSEN, PERRY,
PIHOS, RINGO, SHELL, STARR,
BLANDA, BUTKUS, EWBANK,
GEORGE, GRAHAM, GRANGE,
HEWITT, HINKLE, HIRSCH,
MATSON, PARKER, SAYERS,
STRONG, TAYLOR, THORPE,
TITTLE, TRIPPI, TURNER,
UNITAS, WILLIS, WILSON,
ALWORTH, GIFFORD,

LUCKMAN, MCNALLY, MILLNER, SIMPSON, TUNNELL, LOMBARDI, VAN BUREN, WARFIELD, JURGENSEN, VAN BROCKLIN

kick .... PUNT, SPIRAL

most TD receptions holder, NFL history .... (STEVE)LARGENT

national league .... NFL

official .... JUDGE, LINEMAN, REFEREE

pass .... SPIRAL

player ...... BONO, BURT, CAPP, HILL, KICK, LOTT, MOON, RICE, SIMS, ALLEN, BROWN, BYNER, CLARK, CRAIG, ELWAY, FOUTS, HALEY, KELLY, KRIEG, OKOYE, PERRY, YOUNG, DEBERG, GREEN, AIKMAN, ALZADO, BLANDA, CARTER, CSONKA, HEBERT, GANNON, HARRIS, MARINO, NAMATH, ROCKNE, RYPIEN, TAYLOR, THOMAS, TITTLE, UNITAS, WALKER, WILSON, DORSETT, EVERETT, GABRIEL, LARGENT, MCMAHON, MONTANA, RATHMAN, RIGGINS, SANDERS, SIMPSON, BRADSHAW, MICHAELS, ESIASON, PLUNKETT, STAUBACK, THEISMAN, SCHROEDER, CUNNINGHAM, TESTAVERDE

player: sl. .... GRIDDER

position .... END GUARD, CENTER, KICKER, PUNTER, SAFETY, RECEIVER, QUARTERBACK, (NOSE)TACKLE, RUNNING BACK

ref, sometimes called .... ZEBRA

score .... SAFETY, TOUCHDOWN, FIELD GOAL

slang .... GRID

"Sunday generals" .... QUARTERBACKS

team name, NFL:
Atlanta .... FALCONS
Buffalo .... BILLS
Carolina .... PANTHERS
Chicago .... BEARS
Cincinnati .... BENGALS
Cleveland .... BROWNS
Dallas .... COWBOYS
Denver .... BRONCOS
Detroit .... LIONS
Green Bay .... PACKERS
Houston .... OILERS
Indianapolis .... COLTS
Jacksonville .... JAGUARS

Kansas City .... CHIEFS
Los Angeles .... RAIDERS
Miami .... DOLPHINS
Minnesota .... VIKINGS
New England .... PATRIOTS
New Orleans .... SAINTS
New York .... JETS, GIANTS
Philadelphia .... EAGLES
Phoenix .... CARDINALS
Pittsburgh .... STEELERS
St. Louis .... RAMS
San Diego .... CHARGERS
San Francisco .... FORTY NINERS
Seattle .... SEAHAWKS
Tampa Bay ..... BUCCANEERS
Washington .... REDSKINS

term .... DOWN, KICK, PASS, TACKLE, PUNT, SACK, FUMBLE, HUDDLE, CUTBACK, DEFENSE, OFFENSE, OFFSIDE, PENALTY, INTERFERENCE, INTERCEPTION

footboy .... PAGE

footcloth .... RUG, CARPET

footed, large .... MEGAPOD
single .... MONOPODE

footfall .... STEP, TREAD, STRIDE

foothold .... GRIP, ACCESS, FOOTING
for example .... BEACHHEAD, LODG(E)MENT

footing .... BASIS, SUPPORT, TOEHOLD, WALKING, FOOTHOLD, POSITION

footless .... APOD(AL)
colloq. .... INEPT, CLUMSY

footlights .... KLIEG, STAGE, FLOATS, THEATER, LIMELIGHT, SPOTLIGHT

footlike .... PEDATE
organ .... PES

footloose .... FREE, ROVING, EASYGOING, WANDERING

footman .... PEON, LACKEY, FLUNK(E)Y, SERVANT

footnote .... RECORD, APOSTIL, REFERENCE, ANNOTATION, COMMENTARY
marker ...... OBELUS, ASTERISK
term .... IDEM

footpad .... THUG, BANDIT, ROBBER, BRIGAND, HOLDUPPER, HIGHWAYMAN

footprint .... PAD, CLUE, STEP, TRACK, TREAD, FOOTMARK
animal .... PUG
combining form .... ICHNO
mold .... CAST, MOULAGE
study of .... ICHNOLOGY

footrest .... STOOL, OTTOMAN

foots .... DREGS, SEDIMENT

footsie, play .... FLIRT

footslog .... DRAG, MARCH, STAMP, STOMP, TRAMP, LUMBER

footstalk .... SHANK, PEDICEL

footstep ...... CLOP, STAIR, STRIDE, FOOTFALL
dull sound of a .... PAD
sound of a heavy .... CLUMP

footstone .... TOMBSTONE, GRAVESTONE

footstool ...... CRICKET, HASSOCK, OTTOMAN
wicker .... MORA

footway .... LANE, PATH, TRAIL, SIDEWALK
ship .... CATWALK

footwear .... BOOTS, CLOGS, SHOES, SPATS, SABOTS, SKATES, PATTENS, RUBBERS, FOOTGEAR, SLIPPERS
actor's, of long ago .... BUSKINS
preserve .... SHOETREE
slang .... CLODHOPPERS

footy .... MEAN, PETTY, PALTRY

foozle ...... FLUB, BOTCH, BUNGLE

fop .... DUDE, DANDY, JOHNNY, COXCOMB, JOHNNIE, MACARONI, POPINJAY, EXQUISITE
slang .... TRENDSETTER, CLOTHESHORSE

foppery .... CHIC, CONCEIT, DANDYISM, ELEGANCE, FRIPPERY
slang .... GLAD RAGS

foppish .... SHOWY, CHICHI, LADEDA, LADIDA, BUCKISH, CONCEITED
slang .... RITZY

for .... PRO, IN FAVOR, BECAUSE
aye .... EVER, ALWAYS
each .... PER, EVERY
example .... E.G., VIDE
fear that .... LEST
men only .... STAG
nothing .... FREE, NAUGHT
shame .... FIE
tat, _____ .... TIT
the most part .... MAINLY, LARGELY
the time being .... NONCE, PRO TEM, MEANWHILE
this reason .... HENCE, THEREFORE
what reason .... WHY

forage .... FEED, FOOD, PROG, LOOT, RAID, GRAZE, FODDER, MARAUD, RAVAGE, PASTURE, PLUNDER
crop .... MILO, SORGHUM

plant .... GUAR, ALSIKE, ALFALFA, LUCERN(E)

foramen .... PORE, MEATUS, OPENING

foray .... RAID, MELEE, ATTACK, INROAD, MARAUD, PILLAGE, PLUNDER, INVASION

forbear/forebear .... AVOID, FORGO, SPARE, ENDURE, PARENT, ABSTAIN, REFRAIN, ANCESTOR, TOLERATE

forbearance .... PITY, MERCY, LENIENCE, PATIENCE, RESTRAINT, TOLERANCE

forbearing .... KIND, LENIENT, PATIENT, ENDURING, INDULGENT, TOLERANT

forbears, of ...... AVITAL, LINEAL, PARENTAL, ANCESTRAL

Forbes, novelist .... ESTHER

forbid .... BAN, STOP, VETO, ENJOIN, IMPEDE, INHIBIT, PREVENT, PROHIBIT, INTERDICT, PROSCRIBE

forbiddance .... BAN, NO-NO, VETO, EMBARGO, STOPPAGE, HINDRANCE, INJUNCTION, INTERDICTION

forbidden .... TABU, TABOO, BANNED, ILLEGAL, OFF LIMITS, VERBOTEN, CONTRABAND

city .... LASSA, LHASA

fruit .... APPLE

forbidding .... GRIM, UGLY, STERN, ODIOUS, STRICT, DISTANT, REVOLTING, OFFENSIVE, REPELLANT, REPELLENT, DISAGREEABLE

force .... GAR, GUT, VIM, BIRR, DINT, MAKE, ODYL, BRAWN, DRIVE, IMPEL, MIGHT, POWER, SINEW, VIGOR, COERCE, COMPEL, DURESS, EFFECT, ENERGY, IMPACT, STRAIN, STRESS, IMPETUS, PRESSURE, STRENGTH, VALIDITY, VIOLENCE, CONSTRAIN

armed .... POSSE

back .... REPEL, REPULSE

by .... AMAIN

colloquial .... STEAM

down .... RAM, DETRUDE

driving .... MAINSPRING

-feed .... STUFF, FATTEN

hypothetical .... OD, OG, ELOD, ODYLE

into service ...... LEVY, DRAFT, CONSCRIPT, COMMANDEER

military .... ARMY, NAVY, MARINES, TROOPS,

OCCUPATION

of blow .... BRUNT, IMPACT

of expression/feeling .... EMPHASIS

of habit .... WONT, CUSTOM, PRACTICE

one's way in .... MUSCLE

out .... OUST, ROUT, SPEW, EJECT, EVICT, EXPEL, BANISH, EXCLUDE

rotating .... TORQUE

side of .... FLANK

to the wall .... CORNER

unit of .... DYNE

unit of 1,000 newtons .... STHENE

upon .... IMPOSE, THRUST

forced .... SULKY, HALTING, LABORED, STILTED, UNWILLING, COMPULSORY, INVOLUNTARY

feeding .... GAVAGE

journey .... FLIGHT, HEGIRA

labor .... CORVEE

forceful .... GUTSY, STOUT, VITAL, COGENT, SINEWY, STRONG, TELLING, EMPHATIC, POWERFUL, VIGOROUS, EFFECTIVE, ENERGETIC

forcefully .... FIRMLY, LOUDLY, STRONGLY, VEHEMENTLY

forceless .... WEAK, IMPOTENT

forceps .... TONGS, NIPPER, PINCERS

forces .... UNITS, TROOPS, LEGIONS, SOLDIERY, PERSONNEL, ARMED SERVICE, MILITARY SERVICE

forcible .... MIGHTY, DYNAMIC, VIOLENT, COERCIVE, FORCEFUL

ford .... WADE, CROSS, SHOAL

Ford .... EDSEL, HENRY, GERALD, HARRISON

fore ...... FRONT, PRIOR, FORWARD, ANTERIOR, PREVIOUS, FOREMOST

opposite of .... AFT, BACK, BEHIND

forearm bone .... ULNA

forearmed ...... READY, PREPARED

forebode ...... PORTEND, PREDICT, FORETELL

foreboding .... DARK, OMEN, AUGURY, OMINOUS, PORTENT, PREMONITION, PRESENTIMENT

forecast .... DIVINE, FORESEE, PORTEND, PREDICT, PRESAGE, PREVISE, PROPHESY, PROGNOSIS

forecaster .... SEER, AUGUR,

PROPHET, DOPESTER, SOOTHSAYER, WEATHERMAN

racetrack .... TOUT, TIPSTER

forefather .... ANCESTOR, PROGENITOR

forefinger .... INDEX, POINTER

forefoot .... PAW

part of .... MANUS

forefront .... FRONT, FOREMOST, FRONTAGE, VAN(GUARD)

forego .... DROP, SPARE, WAIVE, DO WITHOUT, ABSTAIN, NEGLECT, OVERLOOK

foregoing .... ABOVE, PREVIOUS, AFORESAID, PRECEDING

foregone .... PAST, FORMER, PREVIOUS

conclusion .... SURETY, SURENESS, CERTAINTY, NECESSITY

forehead .... BROW, TEMPLES, SINCIPUT

animal/bird .... FRONTLET

bone .... FRONTAL

hairy point ..... WIDOW'S PEAK

of the .... METOPIC

foreign .... ALIEN, EXOTIC, ECDEMIC, OUTSIDE, STRANGE, OVERSEAS, PEREGRINE, UNRELATED

affairs .... DIPLOMACY

article .... GERMANDER

bill period of payment .... USANCE

body .... BLEMISH, IMPURITY

exchange .... VALUTA

exchange dealer ...... CAMBIST

lands .... OUTREMER

mission .... EMBASSY, LEGATION, CONSULATE

opposed to .... DOMESTIC

origin .... EXOTIC

quarter .... PERA, ENCLAVE

service officer .... CONSUL, ATTACHE, AMBASSADOR

trade discount .... AGIO

foreigner .... ALIEN, INTRUDER, OUTSIDER, STRANGER, OUTLANDER, TRAMONTANE

in Japan .... GAIJIN

in South Africa .... UITLANDER

foreknowledge .... PRESCIENCE

foreland .... CAPE

forelimb part .... MANUS

forelock .... LINCHPIN, COTTER PIN

foreman ...... GAFFER, OVERSEER, DIRECTOR, SUPERVISOR

foremost .... FIRST, CHIEF, LEADING, PREMIER

part .... BOW, VAN, FRONT

forenoon .... MORNING
forensic .... LEGAL, JUDICIAL,
JURIDICAL, RHETORICAL
medic .... CORONER
foreordain .... (PRE)DESTINE
forerun .... HERALD, PRECEDE,
ANTECEDE, FORESHADOW
forerunner .... SCOUT, HERALD,
ANCESTOR, HARBINGER,
PRECURSOR, PROGNOSTIC,
PREDECESSOR
foreshadow .... PRESAGE,
ADUMBRATE, PREFIGURE
foresight ...... INSIGHT, FORECAST,
PROSPECT, (PRE)VISION,
SAGACITY
foresighted .... EARLY, ASTUTE,
CAUTIOUS, CLAIRVOYANT
foreskin .... PREPUCE
forest .... GROVE, WEALD, WOODS,
JUNGLE, COPPICE, THICKET,
WOODLAND, HINTERLAND,
TIMBERLAND
clearing .... GLADE
cutting right in the/green
growth .... VERT
debris .... SLASH
decaying matter .... DUFF
deity .... PAN, FAUN, NYMPH
fire locator .... ALIDADE
floor layer .... LITTER
humus .... MOR
keeper .... RANGER
kind of .... PINERY, VIRGIN,
PRIMEVAL
of the/pertaining to
.... SYLVAN
open space ..... GLADE, SLASH,
CLEARING
outlying part .... PURLIEU
ox .... ANOA
ranger's post ...... FIRE TOWER
soil .... PODZOL
trees of certain area .... SILVA
trees, the .... SYLVA
warden .... RANGER
forestall .... AVERT, THWART,
PREVENT, STAVE OFF,
ANTICIPATE
Forester's opera .... LORLE
forestry .... WOODCRAFT,
CONSERVATION, SILVICULTURE
forests, coniferous .... TAIGA
foretaste .... WHET, APPETIZER
foretell .... AUGUR, PORTEND,
PREDICT, PRESAGE,
(FORE)BODE, FORECAST,
PROPHESY, VATICINATE,
PROGNOSTICATE
forethought .... PREMEDITATION
foretoken .... OMEN, SIGN,

AUGURY, PROGNOSTIC
foretold .... FORECAST, FORESEEN,
GLIMPSED
foretooth .... INCISOR
forever .... AY(E), ALWAYS, EVER,
ETERN(E), ETERNALLY,
ENDLESSLY, INFINITELY, TIME
WITHOUT END
almost .... EON
and a day: sl. .... TILL HELL
FREEZES OVER
forewarning ...... OMEN, AUGURY,
PORTENT, ADVANCE NOTICE
foreword .... PREFACE, PREAMBLE,
PROLOGUE, FRONTISPIECE,
INTRODUCTION
Forfar .... ANGUS
forfeit .... FINE, GIVE, LOSE,
FORGO, DEFAULT, FOREGO,
PENALTY
for pious purpose
.... DEODAND
forfeited .... GONE, LOST, WASTED
forfeiture .... FINE, LOSS,
PENALTY
of right for cause .... LAPSE
for(e)gather .... MEET, MERGE,
COLLECT, ASSEMBLE,
CONVERGE, ENCOUNTER,
CONGREGATE
forge .... COIN, FORM, MINT,
SHAPE, INVENT, SMITHY,
STITHY, FALSIFY, FOUNDRY,
FURNACE, HAMMER, IMITATE,
BLOOMERY, FABRICATE,
COUNTERFEIT
ahead .... (TAKE THE)LEAD
apparatus .... TROMPE
colloquial .... FUDGE
fireplace of .... HEARTH
tender .... BLACKSMITH
forged .... FAKE, PHONY,
HATCHED, CONCOCTED,
FICTITIOUS
forger .... FAKER, SMITH,
COPYCAT, IMPOSTOR,
PLAGIARIST, METALWORKER,
COUNTERFEITER
forgery ...... MOCK, SHAM, FRAUD,
COINAGE, MINTAGE, SWINDLE,
IMITATION, COUNTERFEIT
slang ..... RIP-OFF, BUM CHECK
forget .... OMIT, DISMISS,
NEGLECT, OVERLOOK
it .... DISREGARD
-me-not .... PLANT, MOUSE-
EAR, MYOSOTIS
forgetful .... CARELESS, HEEDLESS,
NEGLIGENT, OBLIVIOUS,
ABSENTMINDED
one .... AMNESIAC,

PROF(ESSOR), LOTUS-EATER
forgetfulness .... LAPSE, AMNESIA,
OBLIVION, MENTAL BLOCK
colloquial .... BLACKOUT
drug .... NEPENTHE
fruit of .... LOTUS
river of .... LETHE
forgive .... REMIT, EXCUSE,
PARDON, ABSOLVE, CONDONE,
PLACATE, OVERLOOK,
CONCILIATE
a debt .... WRITE OFF
and forget .... LIVE AND LET
LIVE
forgiven .... SPARED, EXCUSED,
REDEEMED, ACQUITTED,
EXONERATED
forgiveness ...... EXCUSE, PARDON,
AMNESTY, REPRIEVE
forgiving .... KIND, HUMANE,
MERCIFUL, PLACABLE,
INDULGENT, CONCILIATORY
forgo. See **forego**
fork .... TINE, BIGHT, BOUGH,
PRONG, TUNER, BISECT,
DIVERGE, BRANCH(OFF),
(BI)FURCATE, SEPARATE,
TABLEWARE
out ...... PAY, GIVE, DOLE OUT,
EXPEND
over: sl. .... KICK IN, PONY UP,
COUGH UP
tuning .... TONOMETER
forked ...... BIFID, CLEFT, ZIGZAG,
ANGULAR, FURCATE, PRONGED
organ/part .... FURCULUM
forlorn .... ALONE, BEREFT,
DESERTED, DESOLATE,
FORSAKEN, HOPELESS,
WRETCHED, MISERABLE
form .... CUT, HEW, SET(UP),
CAST, MAKE(UP), MOLD, POSE,
TRIM, TYPE, BLANK, BUILD,
CARVE, MODEL, SHAPE,
CREATE, FIGURE, RITUAL,
CONTOUR, DEVELOP, OUTLINE,
PATTERN, CEREMONY,
ORGANIZE, FORMALITY
a single unit .... UNITE
by fitting parts together
.... CONSTRUCT
human .... BODY, FRAME,
FIGURE, ANATOMY, PHYSIQUE
into a ball .... CONGLOBE,
CONGLOBATE
into a chain .... CATENATE
into fabric .... KNIT, WEAVE
of a figure/garment
.... SILHOUETTE
alcohol dependence
.... DIPSOMANIA

Athena .... ALEA
bust .... TAILLE
government .... POLITY
obeisance .... BOW,
 KOWTOW, SALAAM,
 GENUFLECTION
oxygen .... OZONE
oval .... OZOID
shortened .... DIGEST,
 ABBREVIATION
square notches in molding
.... CRENELATE
take .... JELL, CRYSTALLIZE,
 MATERIALIZE
to fit requirements .... TAILOR,
 FASHION
formal .... PRIM, EXACT, STIFF,
 FRIGID, PROPER, SOCIAL,
 SOLEMN, STRICT, STUFFY,
 ORDERLY, OUTWARD,
 POMPOUS, CORRECT, PRECISE,
 STARCHY, AFFECTED,
 STYLIZED, DIGNIFIED,
 CEREMONIAL, METHODICAL,
 CEREMONIOUS, TRADITIONAL
agreement .... PACT
argument .... DEBATE
artificially .... STILTED
ceremony/practice .... RITE,
 FUNCTION
choice .... VOTE
dance .... BALL
entrance .... DEBUT
mall .... ALLEE
march .... PROCESSION
talk .... ADDRESS, LECTURE
wear .... TAILS, BLACK TIE,
 EVENING GOWN
formality .... CUSTOM, DECORUM,
 CEREMONY, PROPRIETY,
 CONVENTION
formalize .... DIGNIFY,
 CELEBRATE, SOLEMNIZE
formally .... RITUALLY,
 SOLEMNLY, IN DUE FORM
format .... FORM, PLAN, STYLE,
 DESIGN, LAYOUT, MAKEUP
formation .... ORDER, GROWTH,
 CREATION, STRUCTURE,
 FIGURATION, ARRANGEMENT,
 COMPOSITION
battle .... HERSE, PHALANX
flight/of six or more aircraft
.... SQUADRON
military .... ECHELON
panlike .... PATELLA
side of .... FLANK
formative .... PLIANT, PLASTIC,
 BENDABLE, CREATIVE,
 MORPHOTIC
formed .... BUILT, SETTLED,

COMPOSED, INCORPORATED
at base of mountain(s)
.... PIEDMONT
into a heap .... HILLED
into a rounded mass
.... CONGLOMERATE
on earth's surface .... EPIGENE
former .... EX, ONCE, PRIOR,
 WHILOM, EARLIER, QUONDAM,
 ONE-TIME, PREVIOUS,
 ERST(WHILE)
college gal .... ALUMNA
days/times .... AGO, ELD, PAST,
 YORE
emperor .... CZAR, TSAR,
 KAISER
film star Novarro .... RAMON
name of Annapolis ...... ANNE
 ARUNDEL TOWN
opposed to .... LATTER
ROK name .... RHEE
formerly .... NEE, ONCE, ERENOW,
 WHILOM, USED TO, ONE-TIME,
 SOMETIME, ERST(WHILE)
Palmer peninsula
.... ANTARCTIC
prefix .... EX
formic acid source .... ANT
formicary .... ANTHILL
formicid/formicine .... ANT
formidable ...... MEAN, ARDUOUS,
 AWESOME, FEARFUL,
 DREADFUL, MENACING,
 APPALLING, DIFFICULT,
 TREMENDOUS
formless .... ARUPA, ROUGH,
 UNCUT, VAGUE, RUGGED,
 DEFORMED, CHAOTIC,
 AMORPHOUS, SHAPELESS
void .... CHAOS, DISORDER
Formosa. See Taiwan
formula ...... PLAN, RULE, CREED,
 RECIPE, EQUATION, SOLUTION,
 PRESCRIPTION
formulate .... FRAME, DEVISE,
 ARRANGE, CONCOCT,
 ORGANIZE
fornent .... FACING, OPPOSITE
forsake .... QUIT, LEAVE, DESERT,
 VACATE, ABANDON,
 RENOUNCE
slang .... DITCH
forsaken .... LEFT, (FOR)LORN,
 DROPPED, CAST OFF,
 DESOLATE
forsooth .... INDEED, NO DOUBT
forswear .... DENY, DISOWN,
 NEGATE. REVOKE, DISAVOW,
 PERJURE
fort .... HOLD, KEEP, DONJON,
 BASTION, BULWARK, CITADEL,

FORTRESS, GARRISON,
 PRESIDIO, (ARMY)POST,
 STRONGHOLD
coastal/circular ..... MARTELLO
of fortune .... KNOX
of Moros .... COTTA
opening .... CRENEL
small .... SCONCE, FORTALICE
U.S. .... DIX, ORD, KNOX,
 SUMTER, MCHENRY,
 DONELSON, DUQUESNE
wall .... PARAPET
wooden .... BLOCKHOUSE
Fortaleza .... CEARA
forte .... LOUD, FLAIR, METIER,
 TALENT, SPECIALTY, STRONG
 POINT
opposed to .... FOIBLE
forth .... OUT(OF), ONWARD,
 FORWARD
forthcoming .... NEARING,
 IMMINENT, IMPENDING
forthright .... FRANK, CANDID,
 DIRECT, HONEST, EXPLICIT
forthwith ...... NOW, ANON, SOON,
 AT ONCE, EFTSOON,
 IMMEDIATELY
fortification .... BAIL, FORT,
 ABAT(T)IS, BASTION,
 BULWARK, OUTWORK,
 RAVELIN, REDOUBT,
 FORTRESS, PALISADE,
 EARTHWORK, STRONGHOLD
ditch/moat .... FOSS(E)
material .... GABION
outwork .... FLECHE,
 DEMILUNE, TENAIL(LE)
part of ...... BAIL, PARAPET,
 RAMPART, EMBRASURE,
 BATTLEMENT, BREASTWORK
sloping embankment
.... SCARP, GLACIS
wall .... TALUS
with two parapets .... REDAN
fortified .... ARMED, MANNED,
 BARRICADED, STRENGTHENED
hill .... MERLIN
house .... PEEL
line ...... MAGINOT, WESTWALL,
 SIEGFRIED
place .... REDAN, CASTLE,
 CITADEL, PILLBOX, FORTRESS,
 GARRISON, PRESIDIO
rampart .... BULWARK
tower .... PEEL, DONJON,
 DUNGEON
town .... BURG
fortify .... ARM, MAN, UPHOLD,
 SUSTAIN, BUTTRESS,
 BARRICADE
fortis .... SPEECH SOUND

opposed to .... LENIS
Fortissimo! to musicians
.... PLAY LOUD
fortitude ...... GRIT, GUTS, PLUCK,
SPUNK, COURAGE, STAMINA,
PATIENCE, STRENGTH,
TENACITY, ENDURANCE,
TOUGHNESS
fortnight .... FOURTEEN, TWO
WEEKS
fortnightly .... BI-MONTHLY,
PERIODICAL
fortress .... FORT, TOWER, CASTLE,
BASTION, CITADEL, BASTILLE,
FASTHOLD, FASTNESS,
SAFEHOLD, STRONGHOLD
flying .... SUPERFORT
impregnable, so-called
.... GIBRALTAR, SINGAPORE,
CORREGIDOR
mobile .... TANK
fortuitous ...... CASUAL, CHANCY,
(BY)CHANCE, ACCIDENTAL
Fortuna, Roman .... TYCHE
fortunate .... BLEST, HAPPY,
LUCKY, TIMELY, BLESSED,
FAVORED, OPPORTUNE,
FAVORABLE, AUSPICIOUS,
SUCCESSFUL
fortunately ...... HAPLY, HAPPILY,
LUCKILY, PROPITIOUSLY
fortune .... LOT, FATE, LUCK,
MONEY, STARS, CHANCE,
RICHES, WEALTH, DESTINY,
BLESSING, TREASURES,
PROSPERITY
hunter .... ADVENTURER,
TEMPORIZER
hunter's prize .... HEIR,
HEIRESS
ill .... DOOM, DAMNATION
slang .... PILE(S)
teller .... SEER, AUGUR, GYPSY,
SIBIL, SIBYL, ORACLE,
DIVINER, PALMIST, HARUSPEX,
ASTROLOGER, CRYSTAL-GAZER
teller's cards .... TAROT
telling .... GUESS, DIVINE,
FORESEE, PROPHESY,
PREDICTION, PALM-READING
forty days' fast .... LENT, CARENE
five-degree angle ...... OCTANT
inches .... ELL
niner .... MINER, ARGONAUT
rods .... FURLONG
winks .... DOZE, (CAT)NAP
winks of Spaniard ...... SIESTA
forum .... PANEL, SQUARE,
COUNCIL, ASSEMBLY,
TRIBUNAL, (LAW)COURT,
MARKET(PLACE)

wear .... TOGA
forward .... BOLD, PERT, SEND,
FLIP, AHEAD, EAGER, EARLY,
FRONT, READY, COMING,
FUTURE, PROMPT,
ADVANCE(D), DISPATCH,
TRANSMIT, INTRUSIVE
in development/maturity
.... PRECOCIOUS
in personality .... OFFICIOUS,
AGGRESSIVE
leap .... LUNGE
part .... BOW, FORE, FRONT,
ANTERIOR
tumble .... HEADER
fossa .... PIT, CAVITY, HOLLOW
fosse .... MOAT, DITCH
fossette .... DIMPLE, HOLLOW
fossil .... FOGY, ROCK, RELIC,
PINITE, MINERAL, ANTIQUATED
crinoid .... CRINITE
mollusk .... DOLITE
plants .... CALAMITE
resin .... AMBER, RETINITE
study of .... PALEOBOTANY
fossilize .... PETRIFY
foster .... REAR, SUCKLE, CHERISH,
NOURISH, NURTURE,
PROMOTE, SUPPORT,
ENCOURAGE
child .... STEPSON, FOUNDLING,
FOSTERLING, STEPDAUGHTER
Foster, songwriter ...... STEPHEN
foudroyant .... DAZZLING,
STUNNING
foul .... BAD, EVIL, DIRTY, FILTHY,
SOILED, UNFAIR, ILLEGAL,
SQUALID, UNCLEAN,
FECULENT, INDECENT,
STINKING, LOATHSOME,
UNDERHAND
as of food ...... PUTRID, STALE,
RANCID, ROTTEN
as of language .... OBSCENE,
PROFANE
at pinball .... TILT
dirt .... FILTH
place .... STY
smelling .... OLID, FETID,
ROTTEN, NOISOME
smelling fruit .... DURIAN
smelling plant .... HENBANE
up .... BUNGLE, ENTANGLE
weather .... STORMY
foulard .... SCARF, (NECK)TIE
foumart .... POLECAT
found .... BASE, CAST, AUTHOR,
FATHER, INVENT, CONCEIVE,
DISCOVER, ESTABLISH,
ORIGINATE
on earth's surface .... EPIGENE

thing .... TROVE, DISCOVERY
wanting .... SHORT, FAULTY,
LACKING, INADEQUATE
foundation .... BASE, FUND,
BASIS, BOTTOM, RIPRAP,
PREMISE, LEGACY,
BED(ROCK), ENDOWMENT
garment .... CORSET, GIRDLE,
SUPPORTER
founded .... FUSIL
abbreviation .... EST, ESTAB
on .... FACTUAL, EVIDENTIAL
founder .... FAIL, FALL, SINK,
SLIP, CASTER, SCUTTLE,
STUMBLE, COLLAPSE,
PRODUCER, LAMINITIS,
ORGANIZER, INSTIGATOR,
ORIGINATOR, ESTABLISHER
of Bank of America
.... (AMADEO PETER)GIANNINI
Kentucky Fried Chicken
.... SANDERS
McDonald's restaurant
chain .... (RAY)KROC
Mogul empire .... BABAR
New York Evening Post
...... (ALEXANDER) HAMILTON
Oratory Fathers .... SAINT
PHILIP NERI
Rome .... ROMULUS
Stoicism .... ZENO
the Ethical Culture
Movement .... ADLER
William .... PENN
foundered ...... STUCK, GROUNDED
foundering .... FALLING, SINKING,
PLUNGING, PLUMMETING
foundling .... WAIF, EPPIE,
ORPHAN, WASTREL
place for .... CRECHE
foundry ...... SMITHY, CASTING(S),
IRONWORKS
fount ...... WELL, SOURCE, SPRING
fountain .... JET, WELL, SPRAY,
FOUNT, GEYSER, SOURCE,
SPRING, RESERVOIR
drink/specialty ...... POP, SODA
drinking .... BUBBLER
famed .... TREVI
Mt. Helicon .... HIPPOCRENE
nymph .... NAIAD, EGERIA
of wealth ..... LODE, BONANZA,
GOLD MINE
of youth chaser/seeker
.... PONCE DE LEON
of youth site .... BIMINI
poetic .... FONT
fountainhead .... ORIGIN, SOURCE
fountainpen .... STYLOGRAPH
tube .... BARREL
four .... IV, NUMBER

-bagger .... HOMER(UN)
combining form .... TETRA
dollar gold piece .... STELLA
equal-sided plane figure
.... SQUARE
-footed .... TETRAPOD,
        QUADRUPED
group or set of .... TETRAD,
        H-CLUB, QUATERNION
hundred, the .... ELITE
in hand item .... TEAM,
        ASCOT, COACH, NECKTIE
in sets of .... QUATERNARY
-inch measure .... HAND
-legged speedster .... KELSO
letters, word of
.... TETRAGRAM
lines, poem of .... QUATRAIN
o'clock, the .... PLANT,
        MARVEL-OF-PERU
pecks .... BUSHEL
persons or things, group of
.... QUARTET(TE)
petals, flower with
.... QUATREFOIL
poster .... BED(STEAD)
-sided, four-angled plane
        figure .... TETRAGON,
        RECTANGLE, QUADRANGLE
years, a period of
.... QUADRENNIUM
years, lasting
.... QUADRENNIAL
4-H club's concern .... HEAD,
        HANDS, HEART, HEALTH
fourchette .... WISHBONE
fourflush .... BRAG, BLUFF,
        DECEIVE
fourflusher ...... PHONY, HUMBUG,
        BLUFFER, BRAGGART
game of a .... POKER
fourfold .... QUADRUPLE
fourgon .... CAR, VAN, WAGON,
        TUMBRIL
fourpence .... COIN, GROAT
fours, on all ...... ON HANDS AND
        KNEES
fourscore .... EIGHTY
foursome .... QUARTET
gathering place of .... TEE
foursquare .... FIRM, FRANK,
        HONEST
14 days .... FORTNIGHT
pounds .... STONE
1492 ship .... NINA, PINTA, SANTA
        MARIA
fourth .... QUARTER
canonical hour .... SEXT
class .... SHABBY, INFERIOR,
        LOW GRADE
dimension .... SPACE-TIME

estate ...... MEDIA, (THE)PRESS,
        JOURNALISM
of identical copies
.... QUADRUPLICATE
rate mark .... DEE
var. .... FERTH
foussa .... CIVET
fouter .... PIG
foveola .... VARIOLE
fowl ...... HEN, BIRD, COCK, DUCK,
        BIDDY, GOOSE, TURKEY,
        CHICKEN, ROOSTER, PHEASANT
castrated .... CAPON
comb of .... CARUNCLE
dealer .... POULTER(ER)
disease .... PIP
dish stewed in wine
.... SALMI(S)
domestic .... COCHIN,
        DORKING, LEGHORN, MINORCA,
        POULTRY
flesh below beak ...... WATTLE
forelimb .... WING
leg joint .... HOCK
meat, broiled ...... CARBONADO
outgrowth .... JOWL, SPUR,
        WATTLE
small .... BANTAM
stuffing for .... FARCE
table .... CAPON
wattle .... JOWL
young .... POULT, BROILER,
        POULARD
Fowler .... GENE
fowling piece .... GUN
fowls, domestic .... POULTRY
fox .... TOD, RE(Y)NARD
African .... ASSE, CAAMA,
        FENNEC
face/head of .... MASK
female .... BITCH, VIXEN
flying .... KALONG
hunter/hunter's coat .... PINK
hunter's cry .... TALLYHO
killer .... VULPECIDE
like a .... SLY, CLEVER,
        CUNNING, VULPINE,
        VULPECULAR
male .... DOG
tail .... BRUSH
terrier .... WIREHAIR
terrier, RCA's .... NIPPER
young .... CUB
foxglove .... FIGWORT, DIGITALIS
foxhole ...... PIT, TUNNEL, TRENCH
foxtail .... BRUSH, GRASS
Foxx .... REDD
foxy ...... SLY, CUTE, SOUR, WILY,
        CANNY, SLICK, CLEVER,
        CRAFTY, SHREWD, CUNNING,
        DEVIOUS, VULPINE

foy .... GIFT, FEAST, PRESENT
foyer .... HALL, LOBBY, VESTIBULE
fra .... ABBE, MONK, BROTHER
title of .... MONK, FRIAR
fracas .... BRAWL, MELEE,
        RUMBLE, UPROAR, QUARREL,
        DISTURBANCE
fraction .... BIT, PART, PIECE,
        HALF, SCRAP, DECIMAL,
        PORTION, FRAGMENT
fractious .... MEAN, CROSS,
        UNRULY, TESTY, CRANKY,
        ORNERY, IRRITABLE, FRETFUL,
        PEEVISH
fracture .... BREAK, CRACK, SPLIT,
        DAMAGE, INJURE
fragile ...... WEAK, BRASH, FRAIL,
        FLIMSY, TENDER, BRITTLE,
        DELICATE, FINESPUN,
        BREAKABLE, FRANGIBLE
fragility ...... FRAILTY, DELICACY,
        CRISPNESS
fragment .... BIT, CHIP, PART,
        SNIP, PIECE, SCRAP, SHRED,
        SHIVER, SIPPET, FLINDER,
        SLIVER, MORCEAU, SEGMENT,
        SHATTER, FRACTION
cloth .... RAG, TATTER,
        REMNANT
pottery .... SHARD, SHERD
fragmentary .... BROKEN, SNIPPY,
        PARTIAL, FRACTIONAL
fragrance .... ODOR, AROMA,
        SCENT, INCENSE, PERFUME
of wine/brandy .... BOUQUET
fragrances: rare .... AROMATA
fragrant .... BALMY, OLENT,
        MUSKY, SPICY, SWEET,
        ODOROUS, PERFUMY,
        AROMATIC, REDOLENT
bark .... CANELLA
flower .... ROSE, LILAC,
        JASMINE
gum resin .... MYRRH
oil .... ATTAR, BALSAM
ointment .... (SPIKE)NARD
plant .... PINESAP, LAVENDER
rootstock .... ORRIS
seed ...... DILL, ANISE, ANISEED
shrub .... TIARA
wood .... CEDAR
fraidy-cat ...... COWARD, SCAREDY
        CAT
frail .... WEAK, REEDY, BASKET,
        FINE, THIN, WISPY, FEEBLE,
        FLIMSY, SLIGHT, TENDER,
        FRAGILE, SLENDER, DELICATE
slang .... GIRL, WOMAN
frailty ...... FLAW, FAULT, DEFECT,
        FAILING, TENUITY, DELICACY,
        WEAKNESS, LIGHTNESS,

DAINTINESS

fraise .... RUFF, COLLAR

framb(o)esia .... YAWS

frame ...... FORM, SHAPE, CASING, CREATE, DESIGN, DEVISE, BACKING, COMPOSE, FASHION, MOUNTING, CONSTRUCT

automobile/carriage

.... CHASSIS

bobbins' .... CREEL

body .... BUILD

building's boarding .... SIDING

cloth-stretching .... TENTER

counting .... ABACUS

display .... EASEL

drying .... RACK, HERSE, TENTER

for embroidery

.... TABO(U)RET

for feeding animals

.... HAYRACK

for holding things .... RACK

in baseball .... INNING

of mind .... MOOD, MORALE, SPIRIT(S), TEMPER

of ship .... HULL

openwork .... CAGE

set with spikes/spiked

.... HERSE, PORTCULLIS

soap bar .... SESS

stand .... RACK, EASEL

supporting .... TRESTLE

torch .... CRESSET

up .... RIGGING, INTRIGUE, FALSE ACCUSATION INCRIMINATE

framework .... SHELL, FABRIC, FRAMING, BOUNDARY, CONFINES

basic .... CADRE

bridge support .... TRUSS

ceiling .... BEAM, JOIST

for a fracture .... CAST

for carrying person .... LITTER

for door/window .... SILL, LINTEL, CASEMENT

for traveling crane

.... GANTRY

of a building .... GIRDER

of animal body ..... SKELETON

of rods, sticks, etc.

.... WATTLE

on which to dry skins

.... HERSE

over oil well .... DERRICK

roof support .... TRUSS, RAFTER

franc, 1/100 of .... CENTIME

France. See also French

.... GAUL, GALLIA

novelist .... ANATOLE

Southern .... MIDI

symbol of .... COCK

USA, in .... EUA

franchise .... SOC, SOKE, RIGHT, PATENT, CHARTER, LICENSE, SUFFRAGE, PRIVILEGE

Franciscan .... FRIAR, MINOR, CAPUCHIN

friar .... MINORITE

mission .... ALAMO

Franck, composer .... CESAR

Franco (dictator) title .... (EL) CAUDILLO

francolin .... TITAR, PARTRIDGE

francs, 20 .... LOUIS

frangible ...... FRAGILE, DELICATE, BREAKABLE

frangipani .... JASMIN(E)

neckwear .... LEI

frank .... OPEN, BLUNT, PLAIN, DIRECT, BRAZEN, CANDID, EXEMPT, HONEST, ARTLESS, BRUSQUE, SINCERE, OUTSPOKEN, RIPUARIAN, UNRESERVE

topping .... PICCALILLI

Frank crooner .... SINATRA

or Johnnie .... LOVER

Frankenstein novel authoress

.... SHELLEY

frankfurter ...... WEENY, WIENER, HOTDOG, WEENIE, SAUSAGE

Frankfurter, jurist .... FELIX

frankincense .... OLIBANUM, GUM RESIN

Frankish king .... CLOVIS

law .... SALIC

peasant .... LITUS

franklin .... FREEHOLDER

frankly .... OPENLY, PLAINLY, CANDIDLY, DIRECTLY, HONESTLY

frankness .... CANDOR, RAWNESS, BLUNTNESS, GROSSNESS, VULGARITY, FREEDOM, CANDIDNESS, COARSENESS

Franks, ruler of .... PEPIN, MARTEL

frantic ...... MAD, WILD, EXCITED, FURIOUS, FRENETIC, FRENZIED

make .... PANIC, FRENZY, MADDEN

person ..... MANIAC, DEMONIAC

frap .... TIGHTEN

frappe .... ICED, DRINK, DESSERT, MILKSHAKE

frater .... FRIAR, BROTHER, COMRADE

fraternal .... KIND, FRIENDLY, BROTHERLY, SISTERLY

fraternity .... CLUB, SORORITY,

BROTHERHOOD, (SECRET)SOCIETY

house .... INN, HOSTELRY, DORMITORY

letter .... PSI

local .... CHAPTER

meeting place .... LODGE

to-do .... RUSH, INITIATION

fraternize .... JOIN, ASSOCIATE, MINGLE WITH, COLLABORATE

frau .... WIFE, WOMAN

fraud .... HOAX, JAPE, SHAM, BUNCO, CHEAT, CON MAN, HUMBUG, DECEIT, SWINDLE, ARTIFICE, DECEPTION, FALSEHOOD, IMPOSTURE, TRICK(ERY)

conspiracy to commit

.... COVIN

fraudulent .... FAKE, BOGUS, PHONY, TRICKY, DEVIOUS, GUILEFUL, DECEITFUL

fraught .... BESET, LADEN, FILLED, LOADED, CHARGED

fraxinella .... DITTANY

fray .... RAG, RUB, WEAR, BRAWL, FIGHT, MELEE, RAVEL, BATTLE, FRACAS, FRAZZLE, CONFLICT, SKIRMISH, FREE-FOR-ALL

fraying, cord to stop

.... MARLINE, MARLING

frazzle .... VEX, FRAY, TEAR, SHRED, ABRADE

freak .... FLECK, FLUKE, QUEER, SPORT, WHIM, DAPPLE, STREAK, CAPRICE, ABNORMAL, MONSTROSITY

of nature .... HUNCHBACK, BEARDED LADY, SIAMESE TWIN

out .... BLOW ONE'S MIND

slang .... FLAKE, ODDBALL

freckle .... BLEMISH, LENTIGO

freckled .... BLOTCHY, SPOTTED

Frederick I of Germany

.... BARBAROSSA

the Great's palace .... SANS SOUCI

Fred's cousin .... ALF

free .... LAX, RID, EASE, LISS, OPEN, QUIT, VOID, BROAD, CLEAR, LIBRE, READY, GRATIS, LOOSEN, MANUMIT, RELEASE, UNLEASH, AT LARGE, DETACHED, LIBERATE, LET LOOSE, (FOOT)LOOSE, UNHINDERED

and clear ...... OWN, UNOWING, OUT OF DEBT

and easy .... CASUAL, NATURAL, RELAXED,

CARELESS, FAMILIAR, INFORMAL

-for-all .... FRAY, RIOT, BRAWL, BROIL, FIGHT, MELEE, RUMPUS, RUMBLE, CONTEST, RHUBARB, COMMOTION, BATTLE ROYAL

from bacteria/infection .... ASEPTIC, STERILE

blame ..... ACQUIT, ABSOLVE, EXONERATE

bondage .... EMANCIPATE

dirt .... CLEAN, BRIGHT

discount .... NET

error .... CORRECT, ACCURATE

moisture .... DRY, DEHYDRATE

occupancy/use .... EMPTY, VACANT

restraint .... UNTIE, UNCHAIN, EMANCIPATE

sin .... PURE

suspicion .... CLEAR, ACQUIT, EXCULPATE

hand/scope .... CARTE BLANCHE

lance .... MERCENARY

of charge ..... GRATIS, FREEBIE

of dissimulation .... SINCERE

speech restraint .... GAG, CENSOR

spirit .... LIBERAL, NEUTRAL

swimming organism .... PROTOZOA

throw area in basketball .... KEYHOLE

ticket .... PASS

ticket holder .... DEADHEAD

time .... REST, RECESS, REPOSE, LEISURE

will .... VOLITION

freebie .... GIFT, COUPON

freebooter ...... PIRATE, CATERAN, BUCCANEER, PLUNDERER, FILIBUSTER

freedman ...... LAET, TIRO, THANE

freedom .... RIGHT, LIBERTY, EXEMPTION, FRANCHISE, PRIVILEGE, INDEPENDENCE

from doubt .... CERTAINTY, CERTITUDE

from punishment .... IMMUNITY, IMPUNITY

from sin .... PURITY

kind of .... LICENSE

of action .... LATITUDE

of action or emotion, unrestrained .... ABANDON

to enter .... ENTRY, ACCESS

freehanded .... OPEN, GIVING, GENEROUS, UNSELFISH

freehold .... TITLE, RIGHTS, POSSESSION

estate .... ALOD, ALLOD(IUM)

of a .... ALLODIAL

freeholder .... YEOMAN, FRANKLIN, LANDOWNER

freeloader .... BEGGAR, SPONGE(R), DEADBEAT, DEADHEAD, PARASITE

freeman .... CEORL, CHURL, THANE, BURGESS, CITIZEN, VILLEIN, FRANKLIN

Freeman, actress .... MONA

freemen's assembly .... MOOT

freespoken .... OPEN, FRANK, CANDID, OUTSPOKEN

freestone .... PLUM, PEACH

freethinker .... ATHEIST, AGNOSTIC, LIBERTINE

freeway ...... HIGHWAY, ARTERIAL, SPEEDWAY

block party .... TRAFFIC JAM

feature .... RAMP, ENTRANCE

freewheeling .... NEUTRAL, INDEPENDENT

freewill .... CHOICE, VOLITION, VOLUNTARY, VOLUNTEER

freeze .... DIE, FIX, ICE, NIP, CHILL, FROST, GELATE, HARDEN, CONGEAL, STABILIZE

freezer .... ICER, REFRIGERATOR

item .... (ICE)CUBE

freezing .... FROSTY, CHILLING, ICY-COLD, ICELIKE

freight .... LOAD, CARGO, BURDEN, LADING, SHIPMENT

boat .... SCOW, BARGE

car dumping apparatus .... TIPPLE

steamer .... WHALEBACK

surcharge .... PRIMAGE

train car .... CABOOSE

freighter .... TRAMP, TANKER, TRADER, LIGHTER, SHIPPER, (CARGO)SHIP, STEAMER

area .... HOLD

fremd .... ALIEN, FOREIGN, STRANGE

fremitus .... VIBRATION

French .... GALLIC, FRANCAIS

abbot .... ABBE

abbreviate .... ABREGER

ability .... CAPACITE

able .... HABILE

abortion .... AVORTEMENT

accede/agree .... CONSENTIR

accident .... AVARIE

according .... CONFORME

according to ...... A LA, SELON

accountant .... COMPTABLE

accurate .... PRECIS

across the board .... EN MASSE

actor .... BOYER, CHEVALIER, DELON, FERNANDEL

actress .... CARON

address .... HABILETE

adjust .... REGLER

administrative department .... INTENDANCE

admiral .... DARLAN

ado .... BRUIT, FRACAS

advance .... AVANCER

advance guard .... AVANT-GARDE

adverb .... TROP

advice .... AVIS, CONSEIL

affair of the heart .... AFFAIRE DE COEUR

affix .... APPOSER

affluent .... RICHE

afoot .... A PIED

African colony, former .... MALI

African lake .... (T)CHAD

after .... APRES

afternoon .... APRES-MIDI

again .... ENCORE

against .... CONTRE

agony .... DOULEUR

agreement .... ENTENTE-CORDIALE

airplane .... SPAD, AVION

airship .... AERONAT, AERONEF, DIRIGEABLE

alarm clock .... REVEILLE-MATIN

alcohol .... ALCOOL

ale .... BIERE

Algerian soldier .... TURCO

alien .... EMIGRE(E), ETRANGER

alive .... EN VIE, VIVANT

all .... TOUS, TOUTE

all of you .... VOUS TOUS

alley .... RUELLE

alone .... SEUL

Alp top .... PIC

alphabet .... ABECEDAIRE

Alpine sight .... ADROITE

already .... DEJA

already seen .... DEJA VU

also .... AUSSI

altar .... AUTEL

always .... TOUJOURS

amah .... BONNE

amen .... C'EST CA

amend .... CORRIGER

America .... AMERIQUE

-American .... CREOLE

amiable .... SYMPATHIQUE

amicable .... EN RAPPORT

among .... ENTRE
amount .... MONTANT
amuse .... DIVERTIR
and .... ET
angel .... ANGE
annoy .... GENER
annoyance .... ENNUI
annual income/annuity
.... RENTE
another .... AUTRE
answer .... REPONDRE
ant .... FOURMI
antique .... ANCIEN
anxiety .... SOUCI
anxious .... SOUCIEUX
any/anything .... QUELQUE
apartment .... CHAMBRE
ape .... SINGE, GUENON
appelation .... NOM
apple .... POMME
apple of the eye .... PRUNELLE
apple tree .... POMMIER
April .... AVRIL
apron .... TABLIER
aptly .... A PROPOS
architect .... ARTISAN, LE
                              CORBUSIER
area .... ETENDUE
arm .... BRAS
armful .... BRASSEE
armless .... SANS BRAS
arm band .... BRASSARD
arm chair .... FAUTEUIL
armpit .... AISSELE
army sharpshooter
.... TIRAILLEUR
arrow .... FLECHE
art center .... BARBIZON
art show .... SALON
artfulness .... FINESSE
article .... DA, LA, LE, DES,
        UN, LES, UNS, UNE, UNES,
                                 OBJET
artist/painter .... DORE, COROT,
        DEGAS, LEGER, MANET,
        MONET, DERAIN, INGRES,
        RENOIR, SEURAT, CEZANNE,
        CHARDIN, DAUMIER, LORRAIN,
        MATISSE, POUSSIN, ROUAULT,
        CHAGALL, PISSARRO
ash .... CENDRE
ashtray .... CENDRIER
aside .... DE COTE
assist .... AIDER
astrologer .... NOSTRADAMUS
astronomer .... LAGRANGE
attic .... MANSARDE
auction .... ENCHERE
audience .... AUDITOIRE
August .... AOUT
aunt .... TATA, TANTE

author .... GIDE, HUGO, LOTI,
ZOLA, CAMUS, DUMAS, RENAN,
        STAEL, VERNE, AUTEUR,
        FRANCE, SARTRE, COCTEAU
avail .... SERVIR
average .... MOYEN, COMMUN
avoid .... AVITER
away .... LOIN
awhile .... UN PEU
awl .... ALENE
awning .... TENTE
axe .... HACHE
baby .... BEBE, ENFANT
bachelor .... GARCON
back .... DOS, ARRIERE
backside .... DERRIERE
bacon .... LARD
bacteriologist .... PASTEUR
bad .... MALADE, MAUVAIS
badge .... PLAQUE
bag .... SAC
baker .... BOULANGER
bakery .... BOULANGERIE
bald .... CHAUVE
ball .... BAL, BALLE
ballad .... BALLADE
ballet member .... DANSEUR,
                              DANSEUSE
bamboozle .... TROMPER
bandy-legged .... BANCAL
bank .... BORD, BANQUE,
                                 RIVAGE
bankrupt .... FAILLI
banner ...... FANION, BANNIERE
barber .... COIFFEUR
barefoot .... NU PIEDS
bargain .... MARCHE
bark .... TAN, ECORCE
barn .... GRANGE
barrister .... AVOCAT
base/basis .... FOND
basin .... BOL, CUVETTE
basket ...... PANIER, CORBEILLE
bath .... BAIN
bathroom .... SALLE DE BAIN
bay .... BAIE, GOLFE, SEINE,
                                 BISCAY
be .... ETRE, AVOIR, FAIRE
beach .... UTAH, OMAHA,
                       PLAGE, RIVAGE
bean .... FEVE, HARICOT
beast .... BETE, COCHON
beat .... BATTRE, FRAPPER
beaten .... BATTU
beautiful .... TRES BEAU,
                           MAGNIFIQUE
beauty .... NINON
beauty spot .... MOUCHE
bed .... LIT, COUCHE
bedding .... LITERIE
bedspread .... COUVRELIT

bee .... ABEILLE
beef .... BOEUF
beggar .... GUEUX
behavior .... TENUE
behold .... VOILA
being .... ETRE
belfry .... CLOCHER
Belgian river .... YSER
believe .... CROIRE
belt .... CEINTURON
bench .... BANC, GRADIN
best .... LE MIEUX, LE
                              MEILLEUR
bet .... PARI
betray .... TRAHIR, TROMPER
between .... ENTRE
beverage .... BOISSON
beyond .... OUTRE, AU DELA,
                              PAR DELA
bicycle .... VELO
big .... GROS, VASTE
bigwig .... GROS BONNET
billy goat .... BOUCH
bin .... HUCHE
biologist .... CARREL
bird .... OISEAU
birth .... NAISSANCE
bitter .... ACRE, AMER
bitters .... AIGRE
black .... NOIR(E)
blackmail .... CHANTAGE
bless .... BENIR
blessed .... BENI, SACRE
blind .... AVEUGLE
blood .... SANG
blouse .... CHEMISETTE
blue .... AZUR, BLEU
"Bluebeard" .... LANDRU
boarder .... INTERNE
boarding house/school
.... PENSION(NAT)
boat .... BATEAU
bodice .... GILET, CORSAGE
bond .... RENTE
bone .... OS
book .... LIVRE, CAHIER
boredom .... ENNUI
born .... NEE
bottle case .... CANTINE
box .... BOITE
boy .... GARCON
brainstorm .... IDEE
brandy .... COGNAC
bread .... PAIN
breath .... HALEINE
brewery .... BRASSERIE
bridge .... PONT
briefcase .... SERVIETTE
broken .... CASSE
broker .... COURTIER
broth .... POTAGE

brother .... FRERE
brown .... BRUN
brush .... BROSSE
bullet .... BALLE
bunch .... BOTTE, BOUQUET
bundle .... PAQUET
busybody .... OFFICIEUX
but .... QUE, MAIS
butcher .... BOUCHER
butcher shop .... BOUCHERIE,
       CHARCUTERIE
butterfly .... PAPILLON
cab .... FIACRE
cabbage .... CHOU, CABOCHE
cafe .... ESTAMINET
cake .... GATEAU
call .... APPEL
can .... POT, BIDON
Canadian: sl. .... CANUCK
candle .... CHANDELLE
candy .... BONBON
cape .... CORSE, HAGUE
capital .... PARIS
cap's decoration .... POMPON
car .... RENAULT
card .... CARTE
Cardinal .... MAZARIN,
       RICHELIEU
care .... SOIN, SOUCI
carol .... CHANSON
carpet .... TAPIS
carriage .... FIACRE, VOITURE
cash .... ARGENT
castle .... CHATEAU
cater .... POURVOIR
caterpillar .... CHENILLE
cathedral city .... R(H)EIMS
cauliflower .... CHOUFLEUR
cavalryman .... CARABINIER
chain, Saint Andrew's cross
 .... SAUTOIR
chair .... CHAISE
chalk .... CRAIE
challenge .... DEFI
chat .... CAUSETTE
cheap .... BON MARCHE
cheer .... CHERE, GAIETE
cheese .... BRIE, FROMAGE
chemist .... CURIE, LUSSAC,
       PASTEUR
cherry .... CERISE
chestnut .... MARRON
chicken .... POULET, POUSSIN
chicken pox .... VARICELLE
child .... ENFANT
Christmas .... NOEL
church .... EGLISE
circle .... COTERIE
circumstance .... CAS
citizen .... CITOYEN, HABITANT
city/town ..... GEX, PAU, CAEN,

FOIX, LYON, METZ, NICE,
ORLY, SETE, ST. LO, ARLES,
ARRAS, BLOIS, BREST, CREIL,
DIJON, LILLE, MEAUX, NANCY,
NIMES, REIMS, ROUEN, TOURS,
VICHY, VILLE, AMIENS,
CALAIS, CANNES, CHOLET,
COGNAC, COLMAR, DRANCY,
EVREUX, ISTRES, RENNES,
TOULON, TROYES, VERNON,
ANTIBES, AVIGNON, BAYONNE,
BELFORS, BOURGES, DUNKIRK,
LE MANS, LIMOGES, LORIENT,
LOURDES, ORLEANS, QUIMPER,
ROUBAIX, VALENCE,
BORDEAUX, COLOMBES,
GRENOBLE, LE HAVRE,
SOISSONS, TOULOUSE,
CHANTILLY, MARSEILLE,
TOURCOING, VERSAILLES,
MONTPELLIER, SAINT TROPEZ
clean .... PROPRE
cleric .... ABBE, PRETRE
climb .... ESCALADER
cloak .... MANTEAU
cloth .... DRAP, TOILE
clothes .... VETEMENTS
cloud .... NUAGE
clown .... RUSTRE, BOUFFON,
       PIERROT
coach for hire .... FIACRE
coastal city .... BREST
coffee .... CAFE
cognac .... MARTELL, REMY
       MARTIN
coin .... ECU, SOU, OBOLE,
    FRANC, LIVRE, DENIER,
     TESTON, CENTIME,
      LOUIS(D'OR)
coin, old .... RIAL
cold .... FROID
colony .... TCHAD
color .... COULEUR
color-blind .... DALTONIEN
colored .... COLORE, COLORIE
colorful .... PITTORESQUE
comb .... PEIGNE
combining form .... GALLO
come .... VENIR
come back .... REVENIR
come in .... ENTREZ
comfort .... AISE
commodity tax .... OCTROI
company .... CIE, SOCIETE
composer .... LALO, BIZET,
FAURE, RAVEL, SATIE, D'INDY,
GOUNOD, HALEVY, RAMEAU,
BERLIOZ, DEBUSSY, DE LISLE
concrete .... BETON
conqueror .... CLOVIS
contest .... LUTTE

cook .... CUISINIER(E)
cop .... FLIC
cork .... BOUCHON
corn .... BLE
cost .... PRIX
count .... COMTE
country .... PAYS
county .... DEPARTEMENT
couturier .... DIOR, BALMAIN
cow .... VACHE
coward .... LACHE, POLTRON
cream .... CREME
credit .... FOI
critic .... TAINE
crown .... ECU, SOMMET
crown prince .... DAUPHIN
crown princess ...... DAUPHINE
crude .... CRU
cruet .... BURETTE
crusader .... MONTFORT
crust .... CROUTON
cry for help .... AMOI, AU
       SECOURS
cup .... TASSE
cupboard .... ARMOIRE
cure .... REMEDE
curse .... FLEAU, ANATHEME
curtain .... TOILE, RIDEAU
dagger .... POIGNARD
daisy .... MARGUERITE
dance .... BAL, BRAWL, GAVOT,
   RONDE, APACHE, CANCAN,
    COURANTE, GALLIARD,
    QUADRILLE, BAL MASQUE,
      COTILL(I)ON
daredevil .... CASSECOU
dark .... NOIR
darling/dear .... CHERI
dash .... CHOC, ELAN
daughter .... FILLE
daughter-in-law .... BELLE-
       FILLE
day .... JOUR
dead .... MORT
dead-end .... CUL-DE-SAC
deaf .... SOURD
dean .... DOYEN
debt .... DETTE
December .... DECEMBRE
decisive moment .... CRISE
decoy .... LEURRER
decree .... ARRET
deed .... ACTE, FAIT
delightful .... CHARMANT
depart .... PARTIR
department .... AIN, VAR,
   AUBE, AUDE, CHER, EURE,
    GARD, GERS, JURA, OISE,
    ORNE, NORD, (HAUT)RHIN,
   TARN, AISNE, ALPES, CORSE,
   DOUBS, DROME, ISERE, LOIRE,

MARNE, PARIS, RHONE, SEINE, SOMME, YONNE, ALLIER, ARIEGE, LANDES, LOIRET, MANCHE, SARTHE, SAVOIE, VENDEE, VIENNE, VOSGES, ARDECHE, BELFORT. CORREZE, ESSONNE, GARONNE, GIRONDE, MAYENNE, MOSELLE, ARDENNES, BAS-RHIN, CALVADOS, DORDOGNE, MORBIHAN. VAUCLUSE, YVELINES, FINISTERE

department head ...... PREFECT

depot .... GARE

desert .... MERITE, ABANDONNER

design .... DESSEIN

designer .... AUTEUR

desk .... BUREAU, PUPITRE

detained .... DETENU

detective ..... SURETE, POLICIER

devil .... DEMON, DIABLE

dew .... ROSEE

dialect .... PATOIS, LANGUE D'OC

diamond .... DIAMANT

die .... MOURIR

diet .... REGIME

diplomacy .... SAVOIR-FAIRE

dirt .... CRASSE, SALETE

disease .... MAL, MALADIE

district .... PERCHE, CONTREE

diver .... PLONGEUR

diversion .... JEU

division .... PARTAGE

dog .... CHIEN, GAILLARD

donkey .... ANE, BAUDET

door .... PORTE

down .... BAS

down with .... A BAS

dramatist ..... DUMAS, LESAGE, RACINE, COCTEAU, ETIENNE, MOLIERE, PREVOST, VOLTAIRE

draw-bridge .... PONT-LEVIS

dream .... REVE, SONGE

driver .... COCHER

dry .... SEC

duchy .... ANJOU, VALOIS, AQUITAINE

dugout .... ABRI

duke .... DUC

dungeon .... CACHOT

eagle .... AIGLE

ear .... OREILLE

early .... MATINAL

earn .... GAGNER

earth .... TERRE

east .... EST

eat .... MANGER

edict .... ARRET

eel .... ANGUILLE

egg .... OVE, OEUF, OVALE

eight .... HUIT

elder .... AINE, SUREAU

eleven .... ONZE

emblem .... LILY

emperor ..... LOUIS, NAPOLEON

emphatic word .... TRES

emporium .... ENTREPOT

empress .... EUGENIE, JOSEPHINE

enamel .... EMAIL

enamelware .... LIMOGES

encore! .... BIS

end .... FIN

end, the .... FINIS

enslave .... CAPTIVER

entertainer .... DISEUR, DISEUSE

entrance .... ENTREE

equal .... EGAL, PAREIL

equality .... EGALITE

era .... ERE

eve .... VEILLE

evening .... SOIR

ewe .... BREBIS

exclamation .... HEIN

exist .... ETRE

exit .... SORTIE

expensive .... COUTEUX

expert .... AU FAIT

explorer .... CADILLAC, LA SALLE

eye .... OEIL

eyeglass .... MONOCLE

fabric ...... DRAP, LAME, TOILE, ETOFFE

fabulist .... (LA)FONTAINE

face .... VISAGE

fact .... FAIT

fairy .... FEE

false .... FAUX

false step/error .... FAUX PAS

fan .... EVENTAIL

fascist organization .... CAGOULARD

fashion .... MODE, FACON, BON TON

fashion designer .... DIOR, CHANEL, SAINT LAURENT

fat .... GRAS, GROS

father .... PERE

father-in-law .... BEAU-PERE

fatten .... ENGRAISSER

FBI .... DST

FBI's counterpart ...... SURETE

fear .... PEUR

February .... FEVRIER

fee .... DROIT

feeble .... DABILE

feed .... PATURE, NOURRIR

feed-back .... RETRO-ACTION

feel .... SENTIR

fellow .... CONFRERE

fellow countryman .... COMPATRIOTE

fellowship/sorority/morale .... ESPRIT DE CORPS

female .... DE FEMME

fence ..... CLOTURE, PALISSADE

ferry boat .... BAC

festival .... (DE)FETE

feud .... VENDETTA

feudal tax .... TAILLE

fictitious .... FAUX

field ...... PRE, CHAMP, PRAIRIE

fiend .... DEMON

fight .... COMBATTRE

fighter .... COMBATTANT

fighter plane .... SPAD

file .... LIME, DOSSIER

finally .... ENFIN

find .... TROUVER

fine .... BON, BEAU, AMENDE

fine bearing .... BEL AIR

fine deed .... BEAU GESTE

fine literature .... BELLES LETTRES

finger .... DOIGT

fire .... FEU

fireman .... POMPIER

first .... PREMIER

first prize .... GRAND PRIX

fish .... POISSON

five .... CINQ

flag .... DRAPEAU, FAIBLIR, TRICOLOR

flavor .... SAVEUR

flax .... LIN

flight .... VOL

floor .... PARQUET

flower .... FLEUR

food .... ALIMENT

fool .... SOT, NIAIS

foot .... PIED

foot on the ground ..... PIED A TERRE

footman .... VALET DE PIED

footnote .... APOSTILLE

footstep .... PAS

for .... DE, PAR, POUR

forbidden .... INTERDIT

foreigner .... ETRANGER

forest .... BOIS

formal .... BAL

fortification .... PARADOS

fortification, part of a .... CAPONIERE

forward .... AVANCE, EN AVANT

foundation .... FOND

four .... QUATRE

"Fox, the" .... REYNARD

fragrance .... SUAVE
free .... LIBRE
friar .... FRERE, MOINE
Friday .... VENDREDI
fried potatoes .... CHIPS
friend .... AMI(E)
from .... DE(S), DEPUIS
front .... DEVANT, FACADE
froth .... BAVE
fruit .... POMME, FRUITIER
fun .... DROLERIE
fund .... FONDS, CAISSE
funeral .... FUNEBRE
gala .... FETE
gambler .... JOUEUR
gambling .... JEU(X)
game .... JEU, PARTIE
garbage .... ORDURE(S)
garden .... JARDIN
garlic .... AIL
gate .... PORTE
gauze .... LISSE
general .... KLEBER
genre painter .... WATTEAU
gentle .... DOUX
gentleman .... MONSIEUR
geologist, 17th century
.... CORDIER
geologist, 19th century
.... ELIE DE BEAUMONT
German industrial area
.... SARRE
ghost .... FANTOME, SPECTRE
gift .... CADEAU
gingerbread .... PAIN D'EPICE
girl .... FILLE
give .... DONNER
glance .... APERCU
glass .... VERRE
glassware .... VERRERIE
glove .... GANT
go .... ALLER
goal .... TERME
god .... DIEU
goddess .... DEESSE
good .... BON
goodbye .... ADIEU, AU REVOIR
goodness/goodwill ...... BONTE
goose .... OIE
gossip .... ONDIT, COMMERE
grafted shoot, in gardening
.... ENTE
grape-growing area
.... MEDOC, COGNAC,
BORDEAUX
grass .... GAZON, HERBE
gravy .... JUS
gray/grey .... GRIS
green .... VERT
grindstone .... MEULE
grocer .... EPICIER

grocery .... EPICERIE
ground .... TERRE
guard .... GARDE
guerrillas .... MAQUIS
guest .... INVITE
Guiana capital .... CAYENNE
gulf .... LIONS, AJACCIO, SAINT
MALO, SAINT FLORENT
hack .... COUPER
hair .... CHEVEU(X)
hair net .... RESILLE
hair style .... GOULUE,
CHIGNON
hairdresser .... MARCEL,
FRISEUR, COIFFEUR
half .... DEMI
half-mask .... LOUP
half-year .... SEMESTRE
hall .... SALLE
hand .... MAIN, PALME
handkerchief .... MOUCHOIR
handle .... ANSE, MANCHEE
handwriting .... ECRITURE
happiness .... BONHEUR
happy .... HEUREUX
happy trip .... BON VOYAGE
hat .... CHAPEAU
hat designer .... DACHE
head .... TETE
headache .... MAL DE TETE
health .... SANTE
health resort .... EVIAN
heart .... COEUR
heaven .... CIEL
heavenly .... CELESTE
heavenly being .... ANGE
heir to throne .... DAUPHIN
helmet .... CASQUE, HEAUME
help .... AMOI, SECOURS
here .... ICI, VOICI
hero in romance ...... AMADIS,
BAYARD
heroic verse ..... ALEXANDRINE
heyday .... BEAUX JOURS
hidden .... CACHE, PERDU,
SECRET
high .... HAUT
high society ..... HAUT MONDE
highest point .... MONT BLANC
hill .... COTEAU, COLLINE
hillock .... BUTTE
him .... LE, LUI
his .... SES, SON, LE SIEN
historian .... RENAN, TAINE,
MERIMEE
hole .... TROU
holy .... BENIT, SACRE
Holy Land .... LA TERRE
SAINTE
holy water .... EAU BENITE
honey .... MIEL

hope .... ESPOIR
horn .... CORNE
horse .... CHEVAL
horse stable .... ECURIE
hot .... CHAUD
hour .... HEUR
house .... MAISON
hungry .... AFFAME
hunter .... CHASSEUR
hunting match .... TIR
husband .... MARI
ice .... GLACE
if .... QUAND
import .... PORTEE
impressionist .... DEGAS
impressionest painter
.... MONET
in .... PAR, SUR, DANS
in the manner of .... A LA
income .... RENTE, REVENU
indication .... SIGNE
infantry man .... ZOUAVE,
CHASSEUR
infinitive .... AVOIR
ink .... ENCRE
inn .... AUBERGE
invoice .... FACTURE
iota .... RIEN
IOU .... DETTE
is .... EST
island .... RE, ILE, SEIN,
HYERES, OLERON, USHANT,
CORSICA, BELLE-ILE
island in Indian Ocean
.... REUNION
island off Newfoundland
.... MIQUELON
January .... JANVIER
join .... UNIR
joke .... BLAGUE, BON MOT
joker .... FARCEUR
journalist .... DAUDET
judge .... JUGE
judgment .... ARRET
juice .... JUS, SUC
July .... JUILLET
June .... JUIN
kill .... TUER
kind .... SORTE
king .... ROI, LOUIS, LOUIS
PHILIPPE
king's heir .... DAUPHIN
kingdom ..... ARLES, ROYAUME
kingdom, former .... NAVARRE
kiss .... BAISER
kitchen .... CUISINE
knife .... COUTEAU
know-how .... SAVOIR-FAIRE
lace .... CLUNY, DENTELLE
lady's bag .... ETUI
lagoon .... VACCARES

lake .... GENEVA
lamb .... AGNEAU
land .... TERRE
land measure .... ARPENT
landscape .... PAYSAGE
landscape artist .... COROT
language .... LANGUE
laugh .... RIRE
laughable .... RISIBLE
laundry .... BUANDERIE
law .... LOI, DROIT
lawyer .... AVOCAT
leather .... CUIR
leave .... CONGE
left .... GAUCHE
Legion of Honor member
.... CHEVALIER
legislature .... SENAT
leisure .... LOISIR
lemon .... CITRON
Lent .... LE CAREME
lexicographer .... LAROUSSE
liar .... MENTEUR
life/lifetime .... VIE, VIVANT
likewise .... DEMEME
liking .... GRE
lily .... LIS
line .... LIGNE
lipstick .... BATON DE ROUGE
little .... PEU, PETIT
lively wit .... ESP
lodging place .... GITE
long .... ETENDU
longest river .... LOIRE
love .... AIMER, AMOUR
love affair .... AMOURETTE,
AFFAIRE D'AMOUR
love letter .... BILLET DOUX
lover .... AMANT
loving .... AIMANT, TENDRE
luck .... BONHEUR
luxury .... LUXE
maid (servant) .... BONNE,
FILLE
mail .... POSTE
mail bag .... SAC POSTAL
make .... FAIRE
make believe .... FEINTE
man of letters: 19th century
.... GAUTIER
Manche capital .... ST. LO
mansion ...... HOTEL, CHATEAU
March .... MARS
marshal ...... NEY, FOCH, RUEL,
SAXE, MURAT, JOFFRE,
BAZAINE, MASSENA, TURENNE,
VENDOME
mask .... LOUP
master .... CHEF, MAITRE
masterpiece .... CHEF
D'OEUVRE

match .... EGAL, PAREIL
matchless .... SANS EGAL,
SANS PAREIL
matin lay .... AUBADE
May .... MAI
mayor .... MAIRE
me .... MOI
meager .... MAIGRE, PAUVRE
meal .... REPAS
measure .... PIED, METRE,
MINOT, TOISE, ARPENT, ASSISE,
PORTEE, TONNEAU
measures, old .... AUNE
meat .... VIANDE
meat dish .... SALMI
meaty .... CHARNU
mechanic .... GARAGISTE
medicine .... REMEDE,
MEDICAMENT
menu .... CARTE
menu item .... ENTRECOTE
merchant .... NEGOCIANT
merry .... GAI
midget .... NABOT
migrant/refugee .... EMIGRE
mile .... MILLE
militant .... ACTIVISTE
military ensign
.... ORIFLAMME
military group, large
.... ARMEE
milk .... LAIT
milkman .... LAITIER
mind .... ESPRIT
mink .... VISON
minstrel .... JONGLEUR
mirth .... GAIETE
misdeal .... MALDONNER
misdemeanor .... DELIT
miser .... AVARE
miss .... MANQUE,
MADEMOISELLE
model .... MANNEQUIN
monastery site .... CLUNY
Monday .... LUNDI
money ...... ARGENT, MONNAIE
money account book
.... LIVRE
moneyed .... RICHE
money market .... BOURSE
monetary unit .... FRANC
monk .... MOINE, RELIGIEUX
month .... MOIS
moon .... LUNE
morning .... MATIN
Morocco capital .... MEKNES
most/very .... TRES, LE PLUS
mother .... MERE
mother-in-law .... BELLE-MERE
mountain .... JURA, MONT,
BLANC, FOREZ, MEZENC,

VOSGES, AUVERGNE,
CEVENNES, MONTAGNE, COTE
D'OR, DORE ALPS, FAUCILLES
mountain peak .... PIC
mountain range ..... PYRENESS,
GRAIAN ALPS, COTTIAN ALPS,
MARITIME ALPS
Mrs.: abbr. .... MME
municipal official .... JURAT
museum .... MUSEE, RODIN,
CLUNY, GUIMET, LOUVRE
muslin .... MOUSSELINE
mustard .... MOUTARDE
my .... MA, MON
my dear .... MA CHERE
nail .... CLOU
naked .... DECOUVERT, AU
NATUREL
name .... NOM, RENE, HENRI,
JULIEN, PIERRE, JACQUES,
JEAN(NE), JULIETTE,
MICHEL(LE)
name of Lake Geneva
.... LEMAN
nap .... SIESTE, SOMMEIL
napkin .... SERVIETTE
national .... CITOYEN
national anthem
.... MARSEILLAISE
naturalist .... LAMARCK
naval base .... BREST
navigator .... CARTIER
near .... PRES, PROCHE
neat .... SOIGNE
neck .... COU
need .... BESOIN
needle .... AIGUILLE
negative .... PAS
nerve .... NERF, AUDACE
nest .... NID
neurologist .... CHARCOT
new .... NOUVEAU
news .... NOUVELLES
newspaper .... JOURNAL
newsreel pioneer .... PATHE
night .... NUIT
nightclub .... BOITE DE NUIT
nimble .... LESTE
nine .... NEUF
no .... NON, PAS
nobleman .... DUC, COMTE
none .... NUL, NULLE
noon .... MIDI
north .... NORD
nose .... NEZ
nothing .... RIEN, NEANT
notion .... IDEE
novelist ..... GARD, GIDE, LOTI,
LOUYS, SAGAN, VERNE,
BALZAC, FRANCE, LESAGE,
PROUST, MALRAUX, MAUROIS,

ROMAINS, STENDHAL, ROMANCIER
November .... NOVEMBRE
nursemaid .... BONNE
oath .... VOIRE DIRE
obsession .... IDEE FIXE
October .... OCTOBRE
of .... DE
office .... AGENCE, BUREAU
ogler .... LORGNEUR
oil .... HUILE
old .... ANCIEN
old-fashioned .... DEMODE
omen .... AUGURE
on .... DE, EN, SUR, DANS, DESSUS, ADROITE
on foot .... A PIED
one .... UN(E)
onion .... OIGNON
only .... SEUL
open .... OUVRIR
orchard .... VERGER
orphan .... ORPHELIN
our .... NOS, NOTRE
out .... HORS
over .... SUR
own .... AVOUER
Pacific islands .... MARQUESAS
painter .... COROT, DEGAS, LEGER, MANET, MONET, INGRES, RENOIR, SEURAT, CEZANNE, COURBET, PISSARRO
painter's surface .... MUR
pancake .... CREPE
panegyric .... ELOGE
pantomimist .... PIERROT
paper .... PAPIER
paper maker .... PAPETIER
parent .... MERE, PERE
paring knife .... TRANCHET
parliament .... SENAT
paste .... PATE
pastry .... BABA, ECLAIR, NAPOLEON, PATISSERIE
pate .... TETE, CABOCHE
patron saint .... DENIS
period of time .... TERME
pet .... FAVORI
petticoat .... COTTE, JUPON
philosopher .... TAINE, PASCAL, SARTRE, BERGSON, DIDEROT, DESCARTES
phonetician .... PASSY
physicist .... AMPERE, PERRIN
pilgrim .... PELERIN
pilgrimage town ...... LOURDES
pillow .... OREILLER
plateau ..... MORVAN, LANGRES
playing card .... DIX
playing marble .... BILLE

playwright/diplomat
.... CLAUDEL
plumcake .... BABA
plump .... DODU, GRAS
pocket .... POCHE
poem .... DIT, VERS, VILLANELLE
poet .... MAROT, RACINE, RONSARD, TROUVERE, TROUVEUR, LAMARTINE
police .... GENDARME
police official
.... COMMISSAIRE
police station
.... COMMISSARIAT
pond/pool .... MARE
Pope .... PAPE
porcelain .... SEVRES, LIMOGES
pork .... PORC
pork, pickled .... SALE
porridge .... BOUILLIE
port .... CAEN, SETE, BREST, HAVRE, ROUEN, DIEPPE
porter .... SUISSE, CONCIERGE
possessions .... ILES
possessive pronoun .... MES, MON, SES, NOUS
pout .... MOUE
premier .... HERRIOT, TARDIEU, CLEMENCEAU
preposition .... AVEC
president .... BLUM, COTY, CARNOT, POMPIDOU, (DE)GAULLE, MITTERRAND
president's residence
.... ELYSEE
pressure cooker
.... AUTOCLAVE
pretty .... JOLI(E), GENTIL
priest .... ABBE, CURE, PERE, PRETRE
prime .... ELITE, FLEUR
prime minister .... (MICHEL) ROCARD
prime minister, first woman
.... EDITH CRESSON
prime of life .... ETE, FLEUR DE L'AGE
prize .... PRIX
prize for literature
.... GONCOURT
prize winner .... GAGNANT, LAUREAT
profession .... METIER
profit .... BONI
pronoun ..... JE, TU, IL(S), CES, MES, MOI, TOI, UNE, ELLE, VOUS, VOTRE
prop .... ETAI
Protectorate now part of
Vietnam .... ANNAM

Protestant .... HUGUENOT
Protestant leader ...... MORNAY
Protestant reformer
.... CALVIN
Provencal poet .... MISTRAL
province .... FOIX, ANJOU, AUNIS, BEARN, BERRY, MAINE, ALSACE, ARTOIS, MARCHE, POITOU, GASCONY, GUYENNE, PICARDY, AUVERGNE, BRITTANY, BURGUNDY, DAUPHINE, FLANDERS, LIMOUSIN, LORRAINE, LYONNAIS, NORMANDY, PROVENCE, TOURAINE, CHAMPAGNE, LANGUEDOC, NIVERNAIS, ORLEANAIS, VENAISSIN, BOURBONNAIS, FRANCHE COMTE
punishment .... PEINE
pupil/student .... ELEVE
purchase .... ACHAT
puzzle .... ENIGME
puzzle, crossword .... MOTS CROISES
quality standard .... ALOI
queen .... REINE
quick .... RAPIDE
rabbit .... LAPIN
race-course .... AUTEUIL
racetrack .... PISTE
raffle .... LOTERIE
railroad station .... GARE
rain .... PLUIE
rallying word .... LIBERTE
read .... LIRE
ready .... PRET
real .... VRAI
rebel .... JACOBIN
receipt .... RECU
recess .... NICHE, RECOIN
recipe .... RECETTE
record .... GREFFE, REGISTRE
red .... ROUGE
referee .... ARBITRE
reindeer .... RENNE
relative .... MERE, PERE, FRERE, SOEUR, TANTE
remainder .... RESTE
Republic personified
.... MARIANNE
reserve .... ENCAS
resort .... BAIN, CANNES, MENTON, ANTIBES, RIVIERA, BIARRITZ
rest .... REPOS
revenue .... RENTE
Revolution landmark
.... BASTILLE
Revolution refrain .... CAIRA

Revolutionary calendar,
    month of .... NIVOSE
revolutionist .... MARAT,
    DANTON, CARMAGNOLE
ribbon .... RUBAN, CORDON,
    SAUTOIR
rifle .... CHASSEPOT
rights .... DROITES
river ..... AIN, LOT, ORB, AUBE,
    CHER, EURE, GARD, GERS,
    ISLE, LOIR, OISE, ORNE, SAAR,
    TARN, ADOUR, AISNE, DOUBS,
    DROME, INDRE, ISERE, LOIRE,
    MARNE, MEUSE, RHINE,
    RHONE, RISLE, SAONE, SEINE,
    SOMME, YONNE, ALLIER,
    CREUSE, DRONNE, VIENNE,
    DURANCE, GARONNE,
    HERAULT, GIRONDE, MAYENNE,
    MOSELLE, VILAINE, CHARENTE,
    DORDOGNE
road .... RUE
roast .... ROTI(R)
Roman Catholic .... GALLICAN
room .... SALLE
royal arms symbol ..... FLEUR-
    DE-LIS
royal edict .... ARRET
royal family .... CAPET,
    VALOIS
royal standard ..... ORIFLAMME
royalty .... REINE, ROYAUTE
ruling family .... VALOIS
rumor .... BRUIT, ON DIT
sad(ness) .... TRISTE(SSE)
sale .... VENTE
salt .... SEL
salt pork .... SALE
salt tax .... GABELLE
salt water .... EAU DE MER
salted .... SALEE
same .... MEME
Santa Claus .... PERE NOEL
satin fabric .... ETOILE
satirist .... RABELAIS,
    VOLTAIRE
Saturday .... SAMEDI
saying .... DIT, MOT, DICTON
school .... BANDE, ECOLE
school, secondary/college
    .... LYCEE
sculptor .... RODIN, HOUDON
sea .... MER, NORTH,
    MEDITERRANEAN
sea nymph .... NEREIDE
seaport .... BREST, CALAIS,
    TOULON, LE HAVRE,
    CHERBOURG, MARSEILLE
seasoning .... SECHAGE
seaweed .... ALGUE

second set in a quadrille
    .... LETE
secret intelligence .... SDECE
security .... SURETE, GARANTIE
see .... VOIR
self-esteem .... AMOUR-PROPRE
sell .... VENDRE
senior .... AINE, DOYEN
September .... SEPTEMBRE
seraph .... ANGE
servant ..... BONNE, SERVITEUR
seven .... SEPT
she .... ELLE
sheep .... MOUTON
shell .... COQUE
shelter .... ABRI, GITE,
    COUVERT
shepherd .... PATRE, BERGER
shield .... ECU, ECRAN,
    BOUCLIER
ship .... NAVIRE, VAISSEAU
shoe ...... SOULIER, CHAUSSURE
shoot .... TIRER
shooting gallery .... TIR
shop .... BOUTIQUE
shoplifter .... VOLEUR
short .... BREF, COURT
shout .... CRI
shrimp .... CREVETTE
shrine .... LOURDES
sick .... MALADE
sickness .... MALADIE,
    NAUSEES
sight .... VUE
silk .... SOIE, SOIERIES
silk center .... LYON
sin .... PECHE
sing .... CHANTER
singer .... CHANTEUR
sir .... MONSIEUR
sister .... SOEUR
site of Roman ruins
    .... ORANGE
skater .... PATINEUR
ski champ .... KILLY
skin .... PEAU
sky .... CIEL
slang .... ARGOT
sleep .... SOMMEIL
small .... FIN, PETIT
smell .... ODEUR
smile .... SOURIRE
smoke .... FUMEE
smoker .... FUMEUR
smoking room ..... ESTAMINET
snail .... ESCARGOT
snow .... NIEGE
soap .... SAVON
society .... LE MONDE
soft .... MOU
soldier .... POILU, SOLDAT,

    CHASSEUR, FANTASSIN,
    MILITAIRE, LEGIONNAIRE
soldier hero .... BAYARD
soldier noted for his large
    nose .... CYRANO DE
    BERGERAC
Somaliland capital ...... JIBUTI,
    DJIBOUTI
something for something
    .... QUID PRO QUO
son .... FILS
son-in-law .... GENDRE
song .... CHANSON
soprano .... PONS
soul .... AME
soup .... POTAGE
south .... SUD, (DU)MIDI
speak .... PARLER
speech ...... PAROLE, DISCOURS
spend .... PERDRE
spider .... ARAIGNEE
spinster ..... FILLE NON MARIEE
spirit .... AME, FEU, ELAN,
    ARDEUR, ESPRIT
spot .... TACHE
spring .... SAUT
springtime .... MAI, AVRIL
spy .... ESPION
spy ring/spying
    .... ESPIONNAGE
square .... CARRE
stage .... ETAGE, ESTRADE
stalk .... TIGE
stall, as an engine .... CALER
star .... ASTRE, ETOILE
state .... ETAT
statesman .... BRIAND,
    CARNOT, MAZARIN, REYNAUD,
    CLEMENCEAU
stew .... POT AU FEU
stock exchange .... BOURSE
stoneware .... GRES
stop .... HALTE
storehouse .... DEPOT, ETAPE,
    MAGASIN, ENTREPOT
stork .... CIGOGNE
storm .... ORAGE
stove .... POELE
strait .... DOVER, BONIFACIO
strawberry .... FRAISE
street .... RUE
strong .... FORT, SOLIDE
studio .... ATELIER
stupid .... SOT, BETE
style .... TON, TITRE
stylist .... DIOR
subway .... METRO
Sudan .... MALI
sugar .... SUCRE
summer .... ETE, ESTIVAL
sun .... SOLEIL

Sunday .... DIMANCHE
superfluous .... DETROP
supper .... SOUPER
surnamed .... DIT
sweetbread .... RIS
sweetmeat .... DRAGEE, BON-
BON, SUCRERIE
swimmer .... NAGEUR
sword .... EPEE
taste .... GRE
tattle .... BABIL
tawny .... FAUVE, TANNE
tea .... THE
team .... ATTELAGE
teapot .... THEIERE
tear .... LARME
ten .... DIX
thanks .... MERCI
that ...... CE, CET, CELA, CETTE
the .... LA, LE, LES
thee .... TOI
theft .... VOL
their .... LEUR(S)
them .... EUX, ELLES
then .... DONC, PUIS, ALORS
there! .... VOILA
these .... CES
they .... ILS, ELLES
thin .... MAIGRE
thine .... ATOI
thing .... ETRE, OBJET
think .... PENSER
thirst .... SOIF
thirty .... TRENTE
this .... CE, CET, CETTE
three/third .... TROIS
Thursday .... JEUDI
ticket .... BILLET
tide .... MAREE
tidy .... SOIGNE
tie .... LIER
time .... TEMPS, SAISON
tire .... PNEU
to be .... ETRE
to come in .... ENTRER
to have .... AVOIR
to me .... AMOI
to say .... DIRE
toast .... ROTIE
tobacco .... TABAC
tomato .... TOMATE
tongue .... LANGUE
too .... TROP
tooth .... DENT
town .... VILLE
tree .... ARBRE
trifle .... RIEN
trouble .... AGITER
trough .... AUGE
true .... VRAI
trust .... CONFIANCE

truth .... VERITE
Tuesday .... MARDI
tunnel .... MONT CENIS
twelve .... DOUZE
twelve o'clock midnight
.... MINUIT
twelve peers .... DOUZEPERS
two .... DEUX
ugly .... LAID
uncle .... ONCLE
under .... SOUS
underdog .... OPPRIME
underground fighters
.... MAQUIS
understand .... ENTENDRE
United Kingdom
.... ROYAUME-UNI
United States .... ETATS-UNIS
untrue .... FAUX
up .... HAUT
up-to-date .... AU COURANT
upon .... SUR
upstairs .... D'EN HAUT
use .... EMPLOI
vegetable .... LEGUME
verb .... ETRE, AVOIR
verse .... ALBA, POESIE,
RONDEL, VIRELAY
very .... BIEN, TRES
vest .... GILET
vineyard .... CRU, VIGNE
violin .... VIOLON
violinist
.... (ZINO)FRANCESCATTI
vogue .... BON TON
voucher .... RECU
wagon .... VOITURE
waiter .... GARCON
wall .... MUR
war .... GUERRE
warehouse .... ENTREPOT
wartime capital .... VICHY
water .... EAU
water color .... AQUARELLE
watered silk .... MOIRE
wave .... ONDE
wax .... CIRE
we .... NOUS
weapon .... ARME
Wednesday .... MERCREDI
weight ..... KILO, ONCE, LIVRE,
POIDS, TONNE, GRAMME
well .... BIEN
well-being .... BIEN-ETRE
well-groomed .... SOIGNE(E)
well-timed .... A PROPOS
west .... OUEST
whale .... BALEINE
what/which .... QUEL
wheat .... BLE
when .... QUAND

where .... OU, LA OU
white .... BLANC
who .... QUI
why .... POURQUOI
widow .... VEUVE
will .... VOULOIR
wind .... VENT
wind, cold North ..... MISTRAL
wine ..... VIN, MEDOC, PINARD,
CHABLIS, BORDEAUX,
BURGUNDY, HERMITAGE
wine region .... LOIRE,
ALSACE, ARMAGNAC,
BORDEAUX, COGNAC,
BURGUNDY, CALVADOS,
PROVENCE, CHAMPAGNE,
LANGUEDOC
wing .... ALLE
winter .... HIVER
with .... AVEC
without .... SANS
witless .... SOT, SANS ESPRIT
witness .... TEMOIN
wolf .... LOUP
woman .... FEMME
wood .... BOIS
woodland .... FORET
wool .... LAINE
woolens .... LAINAGE
word .... MOT
work .... TRAVAILLER
world .... MONDE
World War I plane
.... NIEUPORT
worldly .... MONDAIN
worldly-wise woman
.... BLASEE
worry .... ENNUI
worship .... CULTE
wrist .... POIGNET
write .... ECRIRE
writer .... HUGO, DUMAS,
HEINE, RENAN, STAEL, VERNE,
FRANCE, VILLON, MAUROIS,
PROUDHON, VOLTAIRE
writer of fables .... LA
FONTAINE
wrong .... FAUX, ERRONE
yard .... COUR
year .... ANNEE
yearly .... ANNUEL
yellow .... JAUNE
yes .... OUI
yesterday .... HIER
you .... TU, TOI, VOUS
young .... NEUF, JEUNE
your .... TES, TON, VOTRE
youth .... JEUNESSE
Yule .... NOEL
zero .... RIEN
Frenchman .... GAUL, HUGUENOT

famous .... CHARLEMAGNE
frenzied .... MAD, RAVING,
   BERSERK, ENRAGED, FRANTIC,
     MADDING, FRENETIC
 fighter .... AMOK, AMUCK,
    BERSERK, BARESARK
frenzy .... FURY, RAGE, FUROR,
   MANIA, ORGASM, MADNESS,
   HYSTERICS, PANDEMONIUM
freon .... GAS, REFRIGERANT
frequent ...... OFT, OFTEN, HAUNT,
   RESORT, CONSTANT,
   HABITUAL, REPEATED
frequenter of a kind
   .... HABITUE
frequently .... MUCH, OFTEN, A
   LOT, INCESSANTLY
 poetic .... OFT
frere .... FRIAR, BROTHER
fresh .... NEW, RAW, BRISK,
   CLEAN, DRUNK, NOVEL, TIPSY,
   RECENT
 clothes .... CHANGE
 colloquial .... BOLD, PERT,
   SAUCY, SASSY, IMPUDENT
 talk .... LIP
 water alga .... DESMID
 water worm .... NAID
freshen .... REFRESH, SWEETEN
freshener, skin .... LOTION
freshet .... FLOOD, SPATE,
   TORRENT
freshman ...... NOVICE, BEGINNER,
   NEWCOMER, GREENHORN
 Annapolis/West Point
   .... PLEBE
 first banker of .... DAD
 slang .... FROSH
fret .... NAG, VEX, FUME, FUSS,
   GNAW, STEW, CHAFE, CHAMP,
   WORRY, REPINE, COMPLAIN
 British .... CHEVY
fretful .... GRUMPY, GROUCHY,
   PEEVISH, DEJECTED,
   PETULANT, REPINING,
   IRRITABLE
Freud, psychiatrist .... SIGMUND
Freya's dwelling .... FOLKVANG
friable ...... CRISP, FRAIL, MEALY,
   SHORT, BRITTLE, FRAGILE
friar .... FRA, MONK, ABBOT,
   FRATER, LISTER, MONASTIC,
   CARMELITE, BROTHER,
   DOMINICAN, AUGUSTINIAN
 beggar .... SERVITE
 bird .... PIMLICO
 head covering .... COWL,
   CAPUCHE
 of fiction .... TUCK
 robe of .... FROCK
friar's lantern ...... IGNIS FATUUS

friary .... MONASTERY
fricative .... HISS, SPIRANT
friction .... ERASURE, SANDING,
   RUB(BING), ABRASION,
   DISAGREEMENT
 air .... WINDAGE
 match .... FUSEE
Friday, for one .... GIRL
fridge foray .... RAID
fried lightly .... SAUTE(E)D
 slang .... DRUNK
friedcake .... CRULLER,
   DOUGHNUT
friend .... PAL, ALLY, CHUM,
   AMIGO, BUDDY, CRONY,
   NETOP, COMPEER, PATRON,
   INTIMATE, PLAYMATE,
   SUPPORTER, SYMPATHIZER,
   WELL-WISHER
 boy's best ..... MAMA, MOTHER
 close .... SIDEKICK
 Damon's .... PYTHIAS
 faithful ...... DAMON, ACHATES,
   PYTHIAS
 false .... IAGO
 lion's .... ANDROCLES,
   ANDROCLUS
 man's best .... DOG
 Matt Dillon's .... DOC
 of the hungry .... EATERY
 of Trajan and Tacitus
   .... PLINY
 sort of .... FAIR-WEATHER
 special .... FAVORITE
friendly .... AFFABLE, AMIABLE,
   KIND(LY), CORDIAL,
   AMICABLE, INTIMATE,
   FAMILIAR, HOSPITABLE
 dwarf .... LEPRECHAUN
 hint .... TIP
 relations .... AMITY
 sometimes .... REMINDERS
 understanding .... ENTENTE
Friendly Islands .... TONGA
friendship .... AMITY, PEACE,
   HARMONY, BROTHERHOOD
Friesian .... FRIESE
frieze square .... METOPE
frigate .... WARSHIP
 bird .... IWA, ATAFA
 hand .... SALT
Frigga's husband .... ODIN
fright .... AWE, FEAR, ALARM,
   DREAD, PANIC, TERROR
frighten .... AWE, ALARM, DAUNT,
   FEEZE, SCARE, STARTLE,
   TERRIFY, TERRORIZE
frightened .... AFEAR, AFRAID,
   SCARED, ALARMED
 forest .... PETRIFIED
frightful .... HORRIBLE, SHOCKING,

   UNPLEASANT
frigid .... ICY, COLD, STIFF,
   FORMAL, FREEZING,
   HYPERBOREAN
 zone subsoil ...... PERMAFROST
frijol .... BEAN
frill .... EXTRA, JABOT, RUCHE,
   RUFF(LE), FALBALA,
   FURBELOW, TRIMMING,
   ADORNMENT
Frimi (Rudolf) forte
   .... OPERETTA
fringe ...... EDGE, LOMA, BORDER,
   THRUM, MARGIN, (OUT)SKIRT
 benefit ...... BONUS, VACATION,
   INSURANCE
 hairs, etc. .... FIMBRIA
 of Jew's scarf .... ZIZITH
frippery .... FINERY
 useles .... FALLAL
friseur .... HAIRDRESSER
frisk ...... CAPER, CAVORT, FROLIC,
   GAMBOL, TITTUP
 slang .... SEARCH, SHAKE-
   DOWN
frisky .... SPRY, PEPPY, LIVELY,
   PLAYFUL, KITTENISH
 animal .... CAT, DOG, COLT,
   GOAT, PUPPY, KITTEN
Frisson of horror .... GRUE
frith .... INLET, ESTUARY
fritter .... CAKE, DALLY, PIECE,
   SHRED, WASTE, DAWDLE
 away: sl. .... PISS AWAY
frivoled .... TOYED
frivolity .... JOY, GLEE, MIRTH,
   LEVITY, FOOLERY, MADNESS
frivolous .... GIDDY, LIGHT,
   MERRY, PETTY, SILLY,
   PALTRY, FLIGHTY, TRIVIAL,
   FLIPPANT, TRIFLING
frizz .... FRY, CRIMP, SIZZLE,
   FRIZZLE
frizzed ...... CRISP, CURLY, KINKY,
   KINKED, CRAPED, FRIZZY,
   CRIMPED
fro .... AWAY, BACK(WARD)
frock .... COAT, GOWN, ROBE,
   DRESS, SMOCK, TUNIC,
   JERSEY, MANTLE, OVERALL,
   SOUTANE
froe .... CLEAVER
frog .... RANA, TOAD, FROSH,
   ANURAN, PEEPER, PADDOCK,
   POLLYWOG, SALIENTIAN
 farm .... RANARIA
 fish .... ANGLER
 genus .... RANA
 larva .... TADPOLE
 like .... RANINE
 order .... ANURA

slang ..... JUMPER, FRENCHMAN
sound .... CROAK
young .... TADPOLE
froggery .... RANARIA
froggy .... TOADISH
frogman .... DIVER
frolic ...... FUN, GAY, PLAY, ROMP,
CAPER, FRISK, MERRY, PRANK,
SPREE, CAVORT, GAIETY,
GAMBOL, (SKY)LARK,
MERRIMENT
frolicking .... KIDDING AROUND
frolicsome .... FRISKY, PLAYFUL
from .... EX, AWAY, OUT OF
A to Z .... ALPHABET
Ash Wednesday to Easter
.... LENT
bad to ____ .... WORSE
head to foot .... CAP-A-PIE
here .... HENCE
now on .... HENCEFORTH
take .... LESSEN, SUBTRACT
that time/there .... THENCE
the original source ...... FIRST-
HAND
then till now .... SINCE
____ (thoroughly) .... STEM
TO STERN
time immemorial .... AGES
AGO, EVERSINCE
time to time .... SOMETIMES,
OCCASIONALLY
where? .... WHENCE
fromenty .... PUDDING
Frome's (Ethan) wife .... ITU,
ZEENA
frond .... LEAF
frondeur .... CRITIC
front .... VAN, BROW, FACE, FORE,
OBVERSE, FOREHEAD
boat .... BOW, PROW
hoof .... TOE
of building .... FACADE
of coin/medal .... OBVERSE
page box .... EAR
page news .... CRIME,
SCANDAL, CALAMITY,
DISASTER
page sight .... MASTHEAD
position .... FIRING LINE
slang .... DUMMY, STOOGE
frontage .... FACADE
frontal .... FORWARD, METOPIC
frontier .... BOUNDARY,
BORDERLAND, WILDERNESS
settlement .... OUTPOST
vehicle .... STAGE
frontiersman .... CODY, EARP,
BOONE, BOWIE, LOGAN,
CARSON, HICKOK
colloquial .... HILLBILLY

frontlet .... FILLET, FOREHEAD,
HEADBAND
frontispiece .... PREFACE,
PRELUDE, FOREWORD,
INTRODUCTION
fronton .... JAI ALAI
front-runner .... HARBINGER,
PRECURSOR
frosh .... FROG, FRESHMAN
hazer .... SOPH(OMORE)
frost .... ICE, NIP HOAR, RIME,
CHILL, COLDNESS
again .... RE-ICE
froster .... ICER
frosting .... ICING
equipment .... FREEZER, ICER
frosty .... ICY, RIMY, FRORE,
TENSE, HOARY, FROZEN,
AUSTERE, FREEZING,
STRAINED
froth .... FOAM, SCUM, SUDS,
CREAM, SPUME, YEAST,
LATHER
drink's .... HEAD
frothy .... FOAMY, SPUMY,
BUBBLY, TRIFLING
froufrou .... SWISH, RUSTLE
frounce .... CURL, CREASE,
WRINKLE
frow .... WIFE, WOMAN
frown .... LOUR, POUT, SCOWL,
(G)LOWER, GRIMACE,
DISAPPROVE
frowning .... GLUM, SULLEN,
MOROSE, SCOWLING
frowzy .... DIRTY, MUSTY, UNTIDY
woman .... DOWD, SLATTERN
frozen .... ICY, COLD, GELID,
GLACE, CHILLY, GLACIAL,
CONGEALED, MOTIONLESS,
PARALYZED, FROSTBITTEN
carbon dioxide .... DRY ICE
dessert .... ICE, FRAPPE, ICE
CREAM, MOUSSE, SHERBET
dew .... RIME
partly .... FRAPPE
rain ...... SLEET, SNOW(FLAKES)
vapor .... FROST
fructify .... FERTILIZE
fructose .... SUGAR, LEVULOSE
fructuous .... FRUITFUL,
PRODUCTIVE
frugal .... CHARY, CHEAP,
MEAGER, SAVING, PRUDENT,
SPARING, THRIFTY,
ECONOMIC(AL)
frugality .... ECONOMY,
PARSIMONY, THRIFT(INESS)
fruit .... CROP, SLOE, DRUPE,
BERRY, YIELD, PRODUCT,
RESULT, CONSEQUENCE

aggregate .... ETAERIO
apple-shaped .... QUINCE
basket .... POTTLE
bat .... PECA
bear .... FRUCTIFY
bearing no .... ACARPOUS
beech tree .... MAST
berry .... CURRANT,
GOOSEBERRY
berry-like .... STRAWBERRY
boat .... ORANGER
cactus .... FIG
cake .... SIMNEL
candy .... DATE
carbohydrate .... PECTIN
Chinese .... LITCHI, LOQUAT
citrus .... LIME, LEMON,
ORANGE, KUMQUAT
coating .... BLOOM
cocktail/salad ...... MACEDOINE
collective .... SYNCARP
combining form .... CARP(O)
cordial .... RATAFIA
course .... DESSERT
covering .... RIND, EPICARP,
CALYPTRA
cultivation, study of
.... POMOLOGY
date-like .... JUJUBE
dealer .... COSTER
decay .... ROT, BLET
dish ..... COMPOTE, COMPOTIER
dot(s) .... SORI, SORUS
downy bristles .... PAPPUS
dried .... PRUNE, RAISIN
drink/quaff .... ADE
dry .... ACHENE
eating .... FRUGIVOROUS
eating bat .... KALONG, FLYING
FOX, HAMMERHEAD
egg-shaped .... RAMBUTAN
elm/key/maple .... SAMARA
enzyme .... PECTASE
family ...... RUE, ROSE, GOURD,
HEATH, SAXIFRAGE,
SOAPBERRY, CUSTARD-APPLE
filled crust .... DUMPLING
fir .... CONE
flesh .... PULP
fly .... DROSOPHILA
foul-smelling .... DURIAN
fuzzy-skinned .... PEACH
genus .... MALUS, RIBES,
FRAGARIA, FORTUNELLA
gourd .... PEPO, SETON
growing, science of
..... POMOLOGY, HORTICULTURE
hard-shelled .... NUT, GOURD
hawthorne .... HAW
hybrid .... POMA
injury .... BRUISE

inner layer .... ENDOCARP
jelly ingredient .... PECTIN
juice .... MUST, STUM
juice, distilled .... BRANDY
juice, fermented .... WINE,
        VINEGAR
juice drink .... ADE, SHRUB,
  BRANDY, SQUASH, SHERBET,
   LEMONADE, ORANGEADE
juice squeezer .... REAMER
juicy part .... PULP
knife .... CORER, PARER
lemon-like .... CITRON
liquid .... JUICE
melon .... CASABA,
   HONEYDEW, MUSKMELON,
      CANTALOUPE
multiple .... SOROSIS
oak .... ACORN
of discord .... APPLE
of forgetfulness .... LOTUS
of passionflowers
       GRANADILLA
of "virginity" .... CHERRY
oil tube .... VITTA
oily .... OLIVE
one-seeded .... NUT, AKENE
palm .... DATE, COCONUT,
        BETEL NUT
part ..... PIT, CORE, PULP, RIND
peach-like .... NECTARINE
peel .... RIND, ZEST
picker .... OKIE, BRACERO
pie .... TART, COBBLER
pine .... CONE
plant stem .... CANE
"plum of Damascus"
          DAMSON
plum-like .... SLOE,
        PERSIMMON
preserve .... JAM, COMPOTE
prune-like .... MYROBALAN
pulp/residue ...... PAP, POMACE
pulpy .... UVA, DRUPE
refuse .... MARC
rind .... PEEL, EPICARP,
     EXOCARP, CALYPTRA
rosebush .... HIP
rot .... BLET
sculptured .... CORBEIL
seed .... PIP, KERNEL
seller .... COSTER(MONGER)
ship .... ORANGER, FRUITER
skin .... PEEL, RIND, EPICARP
small .... HAW, AKENE,
         ACHENE
sour .... LIME, LEMON
stew .... SASS, SAUCE
stone .... PIP, PIT, NUTLET,
     PYRENE, PUTAMEN
strained .... PUREE

sugar .... FRUCTOSE, LEVULOSE
tomato-like .... POMATO
tree planter, eccentric
     JOHNNY APPLESEED
trees collectively .... ORCHARD
tropical .... DATE, GUAVA,
  MANGO, BANANA, PAPAYA,
   PA(W)PAW, AVOCADO,
   COCONUT, PINEAPPLE
undeveloped .... NUBBIN
vineyard .... GRAPE
winged .... SAMARA
with acid pulp ..... TAMARIND,
      SOURGOURD
with many seeds
      POMEGRANATE
with segmented pulp
      MANGOSTEEN
with sweet pulp, black seeds
       SWEETSOP
fruiter .... SHIP, ORANGER
fruiterer .... COSTER
fruitful .... FECUND, FERTILE,
   PROLIFIC, FERACIOUS,
  FRUCTUOUS, PRODUCTIVE,
       PROFITABLE
make .... FRUCTIFY
fruition .... OUTCOME,
  ATTAINMENT, CULMINATION,
      REALIZATION
fruitless .... VAIN, BARREN,
   FUTILE, OTIOSE, STERILE
undertaking .... FOLLY
fruits, study of .... CARPOLOGY
fruity .... CARPIC
slang .... NUTS, NUTTY
frump .... SLOB, SLOVEN
frumpish .... SHABBY, UNTIDY
frustrate .... BALK, DASH, FOIL,
   AVERT, BAFFLE, DEFEAT,
  HINDER, IMPEDE, THWART,
       NULLIFY
frustration ...... DEFEAT, CHAGRIN
frutescent/fruticose .... SHRUBBY
fry .... FISH, FRIZZ, YOUNG,
   MINNOW, CHILDREN,
      FINGERLING
lightly/quickly .... SAUTE
frying-pan .... SPIDER, SKILLET
fub .... TRICK
fubsy .... PLUMP, SQUAT, ROTUND
fuchsia red .... MAGENTA
fuchsin .... DYE, SOLFERINO
fucoid .... SEAWEED, ROCKWEED
fucus .... DYE, PAINT, SEAWEED
fuddy-duddy ...... DODO, DOTARD,
      OLD FOGY
fudge .... FAKE, CANDY, CHEAT,
  GLOSS, FALSIFY, NONSENSE
Fuego island native .... ONA
fu(e)hrer .... HITLER, LEADER

fuel .... GAS, LOG, OIL, COKE,
   FEED, FIRE, WOOD, STOKE,
   IGNITE, (CHAR)COAL,
     COMBUSTIBLE
brick .... BRIQUET
carrying vessel/ship .... OILER,
    TANKER, TENDER
chemical .... BUTANE
dung .... CHIP
for chafing dishes .... STERNO,
     CANNED HEAT
liquid .... OIL, ALCOHOL,
   GAS(OLINE), PETROL(EUM)
oil .... KEROSENE
turf .... PEAT
type of .... ATOMIC, CANNEL,
   KEROSENE, PARAFFIN
fugacious .... FLEETING,
   EPHEMERAL, TRANSIENT
fugal section .... EPISODE
fugitive .... EXILE, ELOPER,
  ESCAPEE, FLEEING, REFUGEE,
   DESERTER, RUNAWAY,
   FLEETING, RUNAGATE,
   ABSCONDER, TRANSIENT
Negro slave .... MAROON
fugue .... TONAL
concluding passage
     STRETTA, STRETTO
fulcrum .... AXIS, PROP, PIVOT,
       BRACKET
device for holding oar
    OARLOCK, ROWLOCK
filler .... OAR
for an oar .... THOLE
Fulda river .... EDER
fulfill ...... OBEY, EFFECT, REDEEM,
  GRATIFY, PERFORM, REALIZE,
  EXECUTE, SATISFY, COMPLETE,
  IMPLEMENT, ACCOMPLISH
fulfillment .... OUTCOME,
   FRUITION, COMPLETION
fulgent .... RADIANT
fuliginous .... DARK, DUSKY,
   MURKY, SMOKY, SOOTY
full .... SATED, WHOLE, ENTIRE,
   CROWDED, OROTUND,
   REPLETE, COMPLETE,
     PREGNANT
and rounded .... PLUMP
apology .... AMENDE
as a skirt .... BOUFFANT(E)
attendance/meeting
      PLENARY
blast .... BRUTE FORCE
blooded .... HEARTY,
   VIGOROUS, PEDIGREED,
    THOROUGHBRED
blooded horse .... ARAB
bloom .... FLOWERING
blown .... OPEN, MATURE(D)

bodied .... VISCOUS, FLAVORSOME
dress .... TAILS, FORMAL
fig .... SUNDAY CLOTHES
flavored .... MELLOW
fledged .... MATURE
grown .... RIPE, ADULT
house: colloq. .... SRO
measure .... ABUNDANCE, AMPLITUDE
of bog products .... PEATY
of cracks .... RIMOSE
of energy .... PEPPY, SAPPY, SPIRITED
of holes .... PITTED, POCKMARKED
of life .... SPRY, LUSTY, LIVELY, BOUNCING
of: suffix .... OSE, ITOUS, ULENT
of trees .... PINY
of ups and downs .... CHECKERED
of zeal .... AFIRE
scale .... TOTAL, GLOBAL
stop .... PERIOD, STANDSTILL
supply .... GLUT
to the edge/rim ..... BRIMMING
fullness .... PLENUM, SATIETY, SURFEIT, PLENITUDE, REPLETION
fully developed .... WELL-ROUNDED
fulmar .... NELLY, PETREL, MALDUCK, MALLEMUCK
fulminate .... BOOM, ROAR, EXPLODE, THUNDER, DETONATE
fulsome .... FOUL, COARSE, OBNOXIOUS
Fulton's (Robert) invention .... STEAMBOAT
boat .... CLERMONT
fumarole .... HORNITO
fumble .... FLUB, MUFF, FLUFF, GROPE, BOBBLE, BUNGLE
fumbling .... CLUMSY
fume .... GAS, FRET, RAGE, RAVE, REEK, SMOKE, STEAM, VAPOR, SEETHE
fumigant .... PASTILLE, DEODORANT, DEODORIZER
fumigate .... GAS, SANITIZE, DISINFECT
fuming .... RAGING, RAVING, ENRAGED, FURIOUS
fumy .... VAPOROUS
fun ...... JEST, PLAY, JINKS, SPORT, JOLLITY, AMUSEMENT, DIVERSION, MERRIMENT

and games interval .... PLAYTIME
-loving .... GAY
of, make ...... MOCK, RIDICULE
Funafuti .... ATOLL
funambulist .... TIGHTROPE WALKER
kind of .... ACROBAT, AERIALIST
function .... USE, DUTY, RITE, ROLE, WORK, PARTY, SERVE, OFFICE, OPERATE
trigonometry .... SINE, COSINE, TANGENT
functional .... USEFUL
functionary .... OFFICIAL
functionless ...... OTIOSE, USELESS
fund .... CACHE, KITTY, MONEY, STOCK, STORE, OUTLAY, SUPPLY, CAPITAL, COPPERS, RESOURCES
kind of .... SLUSH, TRUST
raiser .... TAGGER
fundament ...... ANUS, BUTTOCKS
fundamental .... BASAL, BASIC, VITAL, ORGANIC, CARDINAL, ORIGINAL, ELEMENTAL, ESSENTIAL, RUDIMENTARY
funeral .... BURIAL, EXEQUIES, INTERMENT, OBSEQUIES
announcement/notice .... OBIT(UARY)
attendants .... CORTEGE, PALLBEARERS
bell .... KNELL
box .... CASKET, COFFIN
"casket team" .... PALLBEARERS
coach/vehicle .... HEARSE
director .... MORTICIAN, UNDERTAKER
fire/pile .... PYRE
hymn .... DIRGE, EPICEDIUM
music .... DIRGE, REQUIEM
ode .... EPICEDIUM
oration .... ELOGE, EULOGY
procession .... EXEQUY, CORTEGE
pyre .... PILE, SUTTER
rite(s) .... EXEQUY, OBSEQUY, OBSEQUIES
song .... DIRGE, ELEGY, NENIA, LAMENT, REQUIEM, THRENODY
funereal ...... SAD, DARK, BLACK, FERAL, DISMAL, GLOOMY, SOLEMN, SOMBER, MOURNFUL, LUGUBRIOUS
fungi ...... SPORE, YEAST, BOLETUS
parasitic .... ERGOT
pertaining to .... AGARIC
spongy material ...... AMADOU

study of .... MYCOLOGY
tissue .... TRAMA
fungous .... SPONGY
fungus .... GERM, RUST, WART, YEAST, BLIGHT, LICHEN, RHIZOPUS, PUFFBALL, TUCKAHOE, BLACKRUST, (BLACK)KNOT
cells/sacs .... ASCI
combining form .... MYC(O)
disease .... ROT, SCAB, BRAND, ERGOT, MYCOSIS
dots .... TELIA
edible .... MOREL, TRUFFLE, EARTHNUT
foul-smelling .... STINKHORN
growth .... MOLD, ERGOT, MILDEW
growth in body .... MYCOSIS
parasitic on animal .... EPIPHYTE
parasitic on trees .... AGARIC
plant .... MOREL, UREDO, AMANITA, MUSHROOM
poisonous .... AMANITINE, TOADSTOOL
seed .... SPORE
smut .... BUNT
spores cluster .... SORUS
thallus of .... MYCELIUM
funicle .... CORD, FIBER
funk .... FEAR, PANIC, SHIRK, COWARD, FRIGHT(EN)
funnel .... CONE, FLUE, CHANNEL, CHIMNEY, SMOKESTACK
funny .... DROLL, ABSURD, AMUSING, COMIC(AL), FARCICAL, HUMOROUS, LAUGHABLE
bone .... HUMERUS
bone site .... ELBOW
colloquial .... ODD, KILLING
line .... GAG
funnyman Foxx .... REDD
fur ...... COAT, DOWN, GRIS, HAIR, HIDE, PELT, SKIN, BUDGE, PELAGE, CARACUL, CRIMMER, KARAKUL, MINIVER, MUSKRAT
bearing animal .... FOX, LYNX, MINK, SEAL, VAIR(E), COYPU, GENET, OTTER, SABLE, BADGER, BEAVER, ERMINE, FITCH(ET), MARTEN, RABBIT, WEASEL, CALABAR, FITCHEW, POLECAT, CHINCHILLA
bearing skins collectively .... PELTRY
cape .... PELERINE
coypu's .... NUTRIA
garment .... WRAP, PARKA, ANORAK

good .... STONEMARTEN
gray .... KRIMMER
hat .... BUSBY, CASTOR
kid pelt .... GALYAK
lamb pelt .... GALYAC
lined cloak .... PELISSE
lynx .... CARACAL
matted .... DAGLOCK
neckpiece .... BOA, STOLE, CHOKER
pertaining to .... PELISSE
piece .... BOA, MUFF, STOLE
rabbit .... CONY, LAPIN
royal .... ERMINE
scarf .... TIPPET
seal .... SEECATCH
squirrel .... VAIR, CALABER
trader, famous .... ASTOR
type of .... FOX, MINK, SEAL, CONEY, GENET, LAPIN, SABLE, BEAVER, ERMINE, MARMOT, MARTEN, NUTRIA, CARACUL, KRIMMER, LEOPARD, MUSKRAT, MOLESKIN, CHINCHILLA
used for trimming, white .... MINIVER
furbelow .... FRILL, JABOT, RUFFLE, FALBALA, FLOUNCE
furbish .... POLISH, BURNISH, BRIGHTEN, RENOVATE
as clothes .... DRY CLEAN
furcate .... BRANCH, FORK(ED)
furculum .... WISHBONE
furfur .... SCURF, DANDRUFF
Furies, one of the .... DIRAE, ALECTO, ERINY(E)S, MEGAERA, EUMENIDES, TISIPHONE
furious .... MAD, ANGRY, WROTH, FIERCE, RAGING, FRANTIC, VIOLENT, FRENZIED, STORMING
furl .... ROLL UP
furlough .... PASS, (SHORE)LEAVE, LIBERTY
furnace .... KILN, OVEN, BLAST, FORGE, BELLOW, CUPOLA, SMITHY, STITHY, CRESSET, SMELTER, BLOOMERY, CREMATORY, CREMATORIUM
air pipe of .... TUYERE
feed/fuel the .... STOKE
for cremation .... (IN)CINERATOR
opening .... STOKEHOLE
part .... BOSH, GRATE, CRUCIBLE

tender .... STOKER
vent .... TUE
furnish ...... LEND, CATER, EQUIP, YIELD, OUTFIT, RENDER, SUPPLY, PLENISH, PROVIDE
with funds .... ENDOW
with weapons .... ARM
furnished with shoes .... SHOD
furnishings .... RIG, GEAR, DECOR, OUTFIT, TRAPPINGS, APPLIANCES, ACCOUTERMENTS
furniture .... GOODS, EQUIPAGE, FIXTURES, FURNISHINGS
convertible .... SOFA BED
decoration/inlaid wood .... BUHL
Duncan .... PHYFE
kind of .... CRADLE
lace decoration ...... MACRAME
leg, kind of .... CABRIOLE
old fashioned office .... ROLLTOP DESK
placement .... CHEST ON CHEST
set .... SUITE
wheel .... CASTER
wood ..... KOA, TEAK, WALNUT
furor .... FURY, RAGE, CRAZE, MANIA, FLURRY, FRENZY, HUBBUB, TUMULT, MADNESS, VIOLENCE
furred .... FURRY, HAIRY, WOOLY, SHAGGY
furrow .... RUT, PLOW, RILL(E), SEAM, STRIA, GROOVE, SULCUS, TRENCH, WRINKLE
for seeds .... DRILL
for planting .... WINDROW
furrowed .... SEAMED, SULCATE
furry ...... BUSHY, DOWNY, HAIRY, NAPPY, FLEECY, FLUFFY, LANATE, PILEOUS, UNSHORN
fellow ..... FOX, OTTER, STOAT, BEAVER, MARTEN, WEASEL
furs collectively .... PELTRY
further .... AID, ABET, AGAIN, ADVANCE, PROMOTE, MOREOVER
furtherance .... PROGRESS, PROMOTION, ADVANCEMENT
furthermore .... TOO, ALSO, BESIDES
furtive .... SLY, WARY, COVERT, SECRET, SHIFTY, SNEAKY, PRIVY, TRICKY, STEALTHY, BACKDOOR, BACKSTAIR, CLANDESTINE
fellow .... SNEAKER

furuncle .... BOIL, ABSCESS
fury .... IRE, RAGE, ANGER, WRATH, ERINYS, FRENZY
furze .... WHIN, GORSE, GORST
fusain .... PENCIL
fuse .... MIX, WELD, BLEND, MERGE, UNITE, (S)MELT, ANNEAL, MINGLE, SOLDER, COALESCE
partly/partially .... FRIT
fused .... FUSIL
fusee .... FLARE, MATCH
fuselage .... NACELLE
fusiform .... ROUNDED
fusil .... FUSED, MUSKET
fusillade .... BURST, SALVO, BARRAGE, DRUMFIRE
fusion .... UNION, MERGER, ALLIANCE, COALITION
fuss .... ADO, ROW, FRET, ROUT, STIR, TO-DO, BUSTLE, FIDGET, BOTHER, KICKUP, POTHER, TINKER
fusspot .... PRIG
fussy .... TENSE, PRISSY, FIDGETY, FINICAL, FINICKY, CRITICAL, HOITY-TOITY, PER(S)NICKETY
one .... NITPICKER
fust .... FADE, RUST, PERISH
fustian .... RANT, BOMBAST, POMPOUS, CORDUROY, VELVETEEN
fustic .... DYE
fustigate ...... FLAY, LASH, ROAST, CASTIGATE
fusty ...... MOLDY, STALE, STUFFY
futile .... IDLE, VAIN, EMPTY, INANE, OTIOSE, USELESS, HOPELESS, FRUITLESS
futility .... DEFEAT, VANITY, DESPAIR, FAILURE, INANITY
future .... LATER, HEREAFTER, POSTERITY
kind of .... ROSEATE
time .... ONE DAY
futuristic .... FATED, COMING, DESTINED, PROBABLE
futurity .... RACE, ADVENT, EVENTUALITY
fuzz .... DOWN, LINT
slang ..... COP, THE LAW, JOHN LAW
fuzzy .... VAGUE, BEMUSED, BLURRED, UNCLEAR, VELVETY
dog .... RAGS
fylfot .... CROSS, SWASTIKA
Fyn Island seaport ...... ODENSE

G

G, Greek .... GAMMA
Hebrew .... GIMEL
in a sequence/group
.... SEVENTH
letter .... GEE
rating of movie .... GENERAL
AUDIENCE
slang .... GRAND, THOUSAND
string .... LOINCLOTH
Ga .... GEORGIA
gab .... TALK, CHATTER
gift of .... GLIBNESS,
ELOQUENCE
gabble .... BLAB, CACKLE, GIBBER,
JABBER, CHATTER, PRATTLE
slang .... CHIN
gabby .... TALKATIVE
gaberlunzie .... BEGGAR
gabion .... CYLINDER
gable .... DORMER, PINION,
AILERON, PEDIMENT
feature .... FINIAL
Gabon, cape .... LOPEZ
capital .... LIBREVILLE
city/town .... OYEM, BITAM,
MOANDA, MOUILA, MAKOKOU,
MOUNANA, LAMBARENE, PORT-
GENTIL
ethnic group ..... PUNU, CHIRA,
LUMBU, ADOUNA, PAHOUIN
lake .... ONANGUE
mountain .... IBOUNZI
president .... (OMAR)BONGO
river .... IVINDO, OGOOUE
Gabor, a .... EVA, MAGDA, ZSA
ZSA
Gabriel .... ARCHANGEL
what he blew .... TRUMPET
gaby .... FOOL, SIMPLETON
gad .... OATH, ROAM, ROVE,
PROWL, SPIKE, RAMBLE,
TRAIPSE, GALLIVANT
Gad, parent of .... JACOB, ZILPAH
son of .... ERI, ARELI
gadabout ...... ROAMER, FLANEUR,
PLAYBOY
gadfly .... PEST, ANNOYER,
TABANID, TORMENTOR
gadget .... DEVICE, DINGUS,
DOODAD, HICKEY, JIGGER,
JIMJAM, GIMMICK,
TECHNOLOGICAL INNOVATION
colloquial .... THINGAMAJIG,
WHATCHUMACALLIT

gadoid, a .... HAKE, CODFISH,
HADDOCK, POLLACK
gadroom .... BEADING, FLUTING
gadwall .... DUCK
Gadzooks .... OATH, EXPLETIVE
Gaea .... GE, TELLUS, GODDESS
son .... TITAN, URANUS
Gael .... CELT, SCOT
Gaelic .... ERSE, MANX, IRISH,
CELT(IC), SCOT(CH)
bard .... OSSIAN
game pole .... CABER
god .... LER, DAGDA, MIDER
poem .... DUAN
spirit .... BANSHEE
sprite .... KELPIE
warrior .... DAGDA
gaff .... HOOK, SPAR, SPUR, SPEAR,
FLEECE
rope .... VANG
slang .... HOAX, TRICK
gaffe ...... BONER, BLUNDER, FAUX
PAS
gaffer .... DODO, OLD MAN,
FOREMAN
gag ...... HOAX, JOKE, QUIP, SCOB,
CHOKE, RETCH, MUFFLE,
MUZZLE, SILENCE, WISECRACK
overworked .... WHEEZE
gage .... PLUM, PLEDGE, SECURITY,
CHALLENGE
gaggle members .... GEESE
Gahlee native .... GALILEAN
gaiety .... FUN, JOLLITY,
FESTIVITY, FRIVOLITY,
MERRIMENT
Gaillard Cut, once ...... CULEBRA
gain .... NET, WIN, EARN, REAP,
LUCRE, REACH, ATTAIN,
PROFIT, BENEFIT, REALIZE
control .... CONQUER
knowledge .... LEARN
slang .... VELVET
gainful .... LUCRATIVE
gainly .... COMELY
gainsay .... DENY, OPPOSE,
REFUTE, CONTRADICT
Gainsborough .... PORTRAIT
gait ...... LOPE, PACE, STEP, WALK,
CANTER, GALLOP, STRIDE
gaiter .... SHOE, SPAT, PUTTEE,
GAMBADE, LEGGING
gal .... GIRL
gala .... FETE, FESTAL, FIESTA,

JOVIAL, JOYOUS, FESTIVE,
FESTIVAL, MERRYMAKING
affair ...... BANQUET, BLOWOUT
galactic .... GLOBAL, LACTIC,
CELESTIAL, PLANETARY
galacto: comb. form ...... MILKY
Galahad, describing .... PURE,
NOBLE
he wrote .... ERSKINE
parent .... ELAINE, LANCELOT
quest of .... (HOLY)GRAIL
Galatea's beloved .... ACIS
lover .... PYGMALION
galaxy ...... BEVY, THRONG, MILKY
WAY, MULTITUDE,
COLLECTION
Galcha .... PAMIR(I)
gale .... GUST, SHRUB, BREEZE,
OUTBURST, WINDSTORM
Gale (Zona), novelist .... BREESE
galena .... ORE, LEAD
galenite .... ORE
Galilean .... CHRISTIAN
sea .... TIBERIAS
the .... JESUS
town .... CANA, MAGDALA,
NAZARETH
galilee .... PORCH, PORTICO
Galileo .... PHYSICIST,
ASTRONOMER
country of .... ITALY
last name of .... GALILEI
theory proven by
.... COPERNICAN
galingale .... ROOT, SEDGE
galiot .... SHIP, GALLEY
galipot .... OLEORESIN,
TURPENTINE
gall ...... VEX, BILE, FELL, ANNOY,
CHAFE, CHEEK, NERVE,
RANCOR, AUDACITY,
TEMERITY
bladder .... CHOLECYST
bladder, of the .... CYSTIC
bladder fluid .... BILE
bladder part .... CERVIX
combining form .... CHOLE,
CHOL(O)
slang .... IMPUDENCE,
INSOLENCE
gallant .... HERO, BULLY, CIVIL,
BRAVE, LOVER, NOBLE,
KNIGHT, GIGOLO, POLITE,
SQUIRE, COURTLY, CAVALIER

gallantry .... CHIVALRY

galleon .... SHIP, ARGOSY, TRADER, CAR(R)ACK

gallery .... POY, LOFT, PORCH, ARCADE, LOGGIA, MUSEUM, PIAZZA, BALCONY, VERANDA, ART-ROOM, CORRIDOR, BELVEDERE

art .... SALON

church .... JUBE

French .... LOUVRE

Italian .... UFFIZI

London ...... TATE, GUILDHALL

gallet .... CHIP, SPALL

galley .... KITCHEN, ROWBOAT, SAILBOAT, PROOF(SHEET)

armed .... AESC, DROMOND

bench .... BANK

Jason's .... ARGO

Mediterranean .... GAL(L)IOT

Roman .... BIREME, TRIREME, UNIREME

ship's .... CABOOSE

slave .... DRUDGE, THRALL

word on a ...... STET, DELE(TE)

work on a .... EDIT, PROOFREAD

Galli-Curci .... AMELITA

Gallia .... GAUL

modern .... FRANCE

Gallic .... FRENCH

chariot .... ESSED

humorist .... (JACQUES)TATI

tribe .... REMI

gallimaufry .... HASH, OLIO, ASSORTMENT, HODGEPODGE

gallinaceous .... RASORIAL

bird .... QUAIL, TURKEY

galling .... PESKY, BITTER, VEXING, CHAFING, ABRASIVE

gallinipper .... MOSQUITO

gallinule .... RAIL, (MUD)HEN

gallipot .... JAR

gallivant ...... GAD, ROAM, PROWL, WANDER

galliwasp .... LIZARD

gallon, half .... POTTLE

gallons, 8 .... BUSHEL

31½ .... BARREL

galloon .... BRAID, RIBBON

gallop .... RUN, GAIT, LOPE, AUBIN, CANTER, TANTIVY

galloping .... SWIFT, FLYING, SPEEDY, DASHING

Galloway .... HORSE, CATTLE

gallows .... TREE, GIBBET, YARDARM, SCAFFOLD

feature of .... NOOSE

gallstone .... CHOLOLITH

galluses ...... BRACES, SUSPENDERS

galoot .... SAP, GOOF, JERK, LOUT,

KLUTZ

galop .... DANCE

galore .... (A)PLENTY, ABUNDANTLY, AMPLY FULL, IN ABUNDANCE

galosh .... BOOT, (OVER)SHOE

galvanic .... EXCITING

galvanize .... SHOCK, EXCITE, STARTLE, ENERGIZE

galvanized .... ANODIZED, (ELECTRO)PLATED

galvanizing material .... ZINC

Galway Bay island .... ARAN

gam ...... POD, CALL, HERD, VISIT, SCHOOL

slang .... LEG

gamb(e) .... LEG, SHANK

gambado .... LEAP, PRANK, GAITER, LEGGING

Gambia capital .... BANJUL

city/town .... BRIKAMA, GEORGETOWN

language .... WOLOF, FULANI, MALINKE, MANDINGO

monetary unit .... DALASI

gambit .... PLOY, RUSE, TRICK, OPENER, MANEUVER

gamble .... BET, RISK, STAKE, WAGER, TOSS UP, GO OUT ON A LIMB

Chinese style .... PLAY FANTAN

reckless .... FLIER, FLYER

gambler .... DARER, DICER, GAMER, BETTOR, PLAYER, THROWER, GAMESTER

in Show Boat .... RAVENAL

kind of ..... PUNTER, PLUNGER, TINHORN, SPECULATOR

small-time .... PIKER

gambler's accomplice ...... SHILL

capital .... STAKE

concern .... ODDS

note .... IOU

odds ...... DOUBLE OR NOTHING

run, at times .... NO LUCK

gambling center .... RENO, CASINO, MONACO, LAS VEGAS, LAKE TAHOE, MONTE CARLO, LAUGHLIN, ATLANTIC CITY

disaster ...... PAIR OF DICE LOST

state capital .... TRENTON, CARSON CITY

table character .... RAKER, BETTOR, DEALER, PLAYER, CROUPIER, KIBITZER

gamboge .... PIGMENT, GUM RESIN

gambol .... DIDO, ROMP, CAPER, LEAP, PLAY, FRISK, FROLIC, CAVORT, CURVET, PRANCE

gambrel .... HOCK, ROOF

Gambrinus' invention ...... BEER

game .... FUN, PLAN, PLAY, PLOY, MATCH, SPORT, FROLIC, CONTEST, AMUSEMENT, DIVERSION, RECREATION

anagrams .... LOGOMACHY

big .... BEAR, LION, HIPPO, RHINO, TIGER, GORILLA, ELEPHANT

board .... CHESS, DARTS, HALMA, CHECKERS

card .... LOO, PAM, FARO, MONTE, OMBER, POKER, TAROT, WHIST, BRIDGE, CASINO, RUMMY, ECARTE, CANASTA, BLACK JACK, TWENTY-ONE

children's ...... TAG, MARBLES, PEEKABOO, JACKSTONE

court ..... TENNIS, BASKETBALL

crossword .... SCRABBLE

dice .... LUDO, CRAPS

divided into chukkers .... POLO

divided into innings .... BASEBALL

divided into quarters .... FOOTBALL, BASKETBALL

first .... OPENER

fish ..... BASS, TROUT, MARLIN, SALMON, TARPON, BARRACUDA

guessing ...... MORA, CHARADE

handball: Eng. .... FIVES

hockey .... SHINN(E)Y

hold scoreless in .... BLANK, SKUNK

killer .... VERMIN

kind of ..... CARD, DICE, KENO, GOLF, BEANO, BINGO, CRICKET, BADMINTON

like billiards .... BAGATELLE

like handball .... JAI ALAI

lottery number .... POLICY

ninepins-like .... SKITTLES

of chance .... LOO, FARO, KENO, BINGO, LOTTO, HAZARD, RAFFLE, LOTTERY

of forfeits .... FILLIPEEN

of marbles .... TAW, MIGS, MIGGLES

of skill .... POOL, CHESS, DARTS, POKER, TENNIS, BOWLING

oriental .... FANTAN

parlor .... LOTTO

pencil .... TICKTACKTOE

period .... SET, INNING, CHUKKAR, CHUKKER, QUARTER

pin .... BOWLING

played on a course .... GOLF

played on horseback ..... POLO

played with tiles .... MAHJONG
point .... RUN, GOAL
preserve .... SANCTUARY
rhyming .... CRAMBO
slang .... PLUCKY, SPORTY
start of .... KICKOFF, TOSS UP
statistic .... SCORE
table net .... PINGPONG
tennis-like .... FIVES
three-handed card .... SKAT
traditional May Day
.... MORRIS DANCE
trail .... SPOOR, TRACK
trap .... GIN
gamecock .... ROOSTER
spur of .... GAFF
gamekeeper .... RANGER, WARDEN
gamete .... EGG
immature .... OOCYTE
gametes' union .... SYNGAMY,
ZYGOSIS
gamic .... SEXUAL
gamin .... TAD, BRAT, PUNK,
WAIF, URCHIN, (STREET)ARAB
gaming cube .... DICE, BONES
tile .... DOMINO
gamma .... MICROGRAM
gammon ...... HAM, FAKE, BACON,
HUMBUG, NONSENSE
gamp .... UMBRELLA
gamut ...... RANGE, SCALE, SCOPE,
EXTENT
gamy .... BOLD, GUTSY, NERVY,
GRITTY, PLUCKY
Gand .... GHENT
gander .... GOOSE, GANNET
take a .... LOOK
Gandhi .... MAHATMA, MOHANDAS
ganef .... GANOV, THIEF
gang ...... MOB, SET, BAND, CREW,
RING, GROUP, HORDE, SQUAD,
CLIQUE
fight .... RUMBLE
head of .... FOREMAN,
RINGLEADER
member .... MOBSTER
Ganges boat .... PUTELEE
city on the .... VARANASI
fish .... SOOSOO
gangland .... UNDERWORLD
gal .... MOLL
gangling .... GAWKY, LANKY,
SPINDLY
gangplank .... RAMP, CATWALK
gangrene .... ROT, DECAY,
NECROSE
gangrenous state .... NECROSIS
gangster .... MUG, THUG, YEGG,
BANDIT, GORILLA, HOODLUM,
HOOLIGAN, RACKETEER,
TOUGH(IE)

bodyguard .... TORPEDO
chief .... RINGLEADER
girl of .... MOLL
gun: sl. .... GAT, ROD, ROSCOE,
EQUALIZER
slang .... GOON, HOOD,
MOBSTER
gangue .... MATRIX
Gangway! .... OPEN UP, MAKE
WAY
gangway's handrail .... MANROPE
gannet .... GOOSE, SOLAN,
GANDER, MARGOT
ganoid .... GAR, AMIA, BOWFIN,
STURGEON
gantlet .... GLOVE
Gantry .... ELMER
Ganymede .... CUPBEARER
gaol .... JAIL, DARTMOOR,
BRIDEWELL
gap .... GULF, HOLE, BREAK,
CHASM, VOID, CLEFT, CRACK,
HIATUS, BREACH, LACUNA,
OPENING, INTERVAL
between peaks .... COL
credibility .... DISTRUST
gape .... GAWK, GAZE, OGLE,
OPEN, PEER, YAUP, YAWN,
YAWP, STARE, SPREAD,
DEHISCE
gapes, the .... RICTUS
gaping ...... AJAR, GAPPY, RICTUS,
ABYSMAL, RINGENT
gar .... SNOOK, GANOID,
STURGEON, NEEDLEFISH
garage .... MEW, CARPORT
garam masala .... CURRY
Garand .... RIFLE
Garapan Island's capital
.... SAIPAN
garb .... DRESS, GUISE, STYLE,
ATTIRE, CLOTHING
for frigid weather .... ANORAK
garbage ...... JUNK, OFFAL, SWILL,
TRASH, WASTE, REFUSE,
SCRAPS, RUBBISH
collect .... SCAVENGE
garble .... JUMBLE, MIX UP,
MUDDLE, CONFUSE, DISTORT
Garbo, actress .... GRETA
role .... CAMILLE
garcon ...... BOY, YOUTH, WAITER,
SERVANT
garden .... ARBOR, GARTH, PITCH,
ARENA, HERBARY, NURSERY,
ORCHARD, PLEASANCE
bed .... PLOT
biblical .... GETHSEMANE
decorative structure
.... TRELLIS
denizen .... FROG, TOAD

first .... EDEN
kind of .... HOTHOUSE,
TERRARIUM, GREENHOUSE
miniature .... TERRARIUM
of England .... KENT
of stone .... CEMETERY
on the Mount of Olives
.... GETHSEMANE
pest .... WEED, APHID, APHIS
plant .... ORACH(E)
rock .... ROCKERY
section .... BED, PLOT
shelter .... GAZEBO
soprano .... MARY
tool .... HOE, RAKE, DIBBLE,
TROWEL
wall/fence .... HAHA
worker .... RAKER, SPADER,
PLANTER
gardener's asset/blessing
.... GREENTHUMB
plague .... WEED, APHID,
BORER, CUTWORM
gardenia .... FLOWER, MADDER
Gardner, actress .... AVA
Erle .... STANLEY
title opener .... THE CASE
Garfield lovers' emotion
.... AILUROPHILIA
garfish .... SNOOK
Gargantua .... KING, GIANT
creator of .... RABELAIS
son .... PANTAGRUEL
gargantuan .... HUGE, VAST,
GIGANTIC, GIANTLIKE
gargle .... WASH, RINSE, LISTERINE
garibaldi .... BLOUSE
garish .... GAUDY, SHOWY
garishness .... GLARE
garland .... LEI, ANADEM, FILLET,
WREATH, CHAPLET, FESTOON
garlic .... MOLY, ALLIUM, RAMSON
part .... CLOVE
garment ...... COAT, ROBE, WRAP,
DRESS, BLOUSE, RAIMENT,
CLOTHING, VESTMENT,
HABILIMENT
corsetlike .... GIRDLE
decoration .... SPANGLE
fastener .... PATTE, AUTOMATIC
flap/fold of .... LAPPET
hooded .... PARKA, ALMUCE
knitted .... JERSEY
loose .... ROBE, TOGA, CYMAR,
BLOUSE, CAFTAN, CAMISE,
DOLMAN, KIMONO, MUUMUU
outer ..... COAT, TOGA, SMOCK,
BLAZER, CAPOTE, JACKET,
KIMONO, PALETOT, SURTOUT,
OVERCOAT, SCAPULAR
patchwork .... CENTO

rain .... PONCHO
scarflike .... TIPPET
sleeveless .... CAPE, VEST,
                      SCAPULAR
tentlike .... CHADRI
tight-fitting .... COTTE
trade spy .... KEEK
trimming .... BEADING
tunic-like ..... CHITON, TABARD
under ...... SLIP, SHIRT, TEDDY,
                     CHEMISE
worker .... SEWER
garments .... COSTUME
garner .... HOARD, STORE,
       GATHER, COLLECT, HARVEST
Garner, actor .... JAMES
garnet .... GEM, RED, PYROPE,
      TACKLE, OLIVINE, ESSONITE,
      MELANITE, ALMANDITE
garnish .... DECK, LARD, TRIM,
      ADORN, OLIVE, FLAVOR,
      RELISH, SEASON, PARSLEY,
      DECORATE, ORNAMENT,
      EMBELLISH
garnishee .... TRUSTEE
garnishment .... LIEN,
      DECORATION
Garrone river tributary .... LOT
garret .... ATTIC, ATELIER,
      MANSARD, (COCK)LOFT
Garrick, actor .... DAVID
garrison .... BILLET, OUTPOST,
      BARRACKS, PRESIDIO,
      (MILITARY)POST
garrote .... SCRAG, STRANGLE
garrulity .... LOQUACITY,
      WORDINESS
garrulous .... GASSY, VOLUBLE,
      TALKATIVE, LOQUACIOUS
Garson, actress .... GREER
garter snake .... ELAP(S)
garth .... WEIR, YARD, GARDEN
gas .... BRAG, FUEL, FUME, ETHER,
      ETHYL, FREON, OZONE,
      RADON, VAPOR, BOMBAST,
      PROPANE, STIBINE, GASOLINE
balloon .... HELIUM
burner ..... BUNSEN, WELSBACH
cigarette lighter .... BUTANE
colorless .... OXAN(E),
      ETHANE, ETHENE
combining form .... AER(O)
condense .... ABSORB
container .... TANK
engine .... PETROL
fill with ...... AERATE, INFLATE
in stomach/intestine
     .... FLATUS, FLATULENCE
inert .... NEON, ARGON
marsh .... METHANE
mask part .... CANISTER

mine .... DAMP
pipe .... FLUE
plant .... BURNING BUSH
slang .... HOT AIR
station device .... PUMP
station employee .... GREASER,
      MECHANIC
step on the .... GUN, HURRY,
      ACCELERATE
used in a blowtorch
     .... ACETYLENE
gascon .... BOASTER, LOUDMOUTH,
      PRETENDER
gasconade .... BRAG, BOAST,
      BLUSTER
gaseous .... AERIFORM
cloud .... NEBULA
combining form .... AERI
compound .... ETHANE
inert element .... NEON
gash ...... CUT, HACK, SLIT, SCORE,
      SLASH, INCISE
gasket .... LINING, PADDING
gasoline .... PETROL
jellied .... NAPALM
kind of .... LEADED,
      UNLEADED
gasp .... PANT, PUFF, CHOKE,
      HEAVE
gastropod .... SNAIL, LIMPET,
      W(H)ELK, MOLLUSK
marine .... MUREX
gastronome .... EPICURE,
      GOURMET, GOURMAND
gastronomy .... EPICURISM
gat .... CHANNEL
gata .... SHARK
gate ...... DOOR, PORTAL, WICKET,
      OPENING
bar .... PORTICULLIS
give the .... SACK, DISMISS,
      DISCHARGE
horse race starting
     .... BARRIER
joint/holder .... HINGE
keeper's dwelling .... LODGE
rear/back .... POSTERN
receipts: colloq. .... TAKE
revolving .... TURNSTILE
slang .... ADMISSION
tower .... BARBICAN
water .... SLUICE, PENSTOCK
gatehouse .... LODGE
gatekeeper .... PORTER
gateway .... PYLON, TORII,
      TORAN(A)
gather .... CULL, FOLD, HERD,
      REAP, (A)MASS, INFER, PLEAT,
      HUDDLE, GARNER, MUSTER,
      PUCKER, SHEAR, SHEAVE,
      COLLECT, HARVEST,

      ASSEMBLE, CONCLUDE
as oysters or logs .... TONG
fabric .... SHIRR
grain .... GLEAN
gathering .... CROWD, RALLY,
      MEET(ING), TURNOUT,
      ASSEMBLY, CONCLAVE,
      ASSEMBLAGE
social ..... BEE, DANCE, PARTY,
      BARBECUE, CLAMBAKE
gator's kin .... CROC
gauche .... CLUMSY, AWKWARD,
      TACTLESS
gaucho .... COWBOY, LLANERO
knife .... MACHETE
milieu .... LLANO, PAMPAS
place .... RANCHO
rope of .... REATA
weapon .... BOLA(S)
gaud .... ADORN, BAUBLE,
      TRINKET, ORNAMENT
gaudiness .... GLARE, GLITTER,
      LOUDNESS, SHOWINESS,
      FLASHINESS, GARISHNESS
gaudy ...... GAY, BRIGHT, SHOWY,
      CHEAP, FLASHY, FLORID,
      GARISH, VULGAR, TAWDRY,
      BLATANT
ornament .... TINSEL
gauge .... RATE, SIZE, JUDGE,
      CALIBER, MEASURE, TEMPLET,
      APPRAISE, ESTIMATE,
      EVALUATE
Gauguin's island home
     .... TAHITI
wife .... METTE
Gaul .... GALLIA, FRENCHMAN
people .... REMI
gaunt .... BONY, GRIM, LANK,
      LEAN, THIN, SPARE, SICKLY,
      HAGGARD, EMACIATED
gauntlet ...... CUFF, GAGE, GLOVE
throw down the .... DEFY,
      CHALLENGE
Gautama .... BUDDHA
gauze .... NET, HAZE, LENO, MIST,
      CREPE, SCRIM, BAREGE,
      TISSUE, BANDAGE
silk .... TIFFANY
gauzy .... FILMY, SHEER,
      DIAPHANOUS, TRANSPARENT
fabric .... LACE, TULLE
gavel .... HAMMER, MALLET
gavial .... CROCODILE
gawk .... OAF, GAPE, GAZE, STARE,
      CUCKOO, SIMPLETON
gawky .... CLUMSY, AWKWARD
one .... LOUT
gay .... JOLLY, MERRY, RIANT,
      BLITHE, BRIGHT, FESTAL,
      JOVIAL, LIVELY, FESTIVE,

——— .... HILARIOUS

rake .... LOTHARIO

tune .... LILT

Gay-Pay-Oo .... GPU, OGPU

successor .... NKVD

gaze .... GAPE, GAWK, LEER, PEER, GLARE, STARE

at .... EYE

intently .... PORE

gazebo .... TURRET, BALCONY

gazelle .... GOA, CORA, KUDU, MOHR, ADDRA, ARIEL, KEVEL, KORIN, CHIKARA, CORINNE

Sudan .... DAMA

gazette .... NEWSPAPER

GBS .... SHAW

was one .... FABIAN

Gdansk .... DANZIG

Ge .... GAEA, GAIA

gear .... CAM, COG, KIT, GARB, DRESS, TOOLS, OUTFIT, TACKLE, EQUIPMENT, BAGGAGE, HARNESS, RIG(GING), OVERDRIVE

for Eric Heiden .... RACING SKATE

rodeo .... RIATAS

shift, for short .... STICK

transmission .... SPEED

geared .... SUITED, TAILORED

gecko .... LIZARD, TARENTE, LACERT(IL)IAN

gee ...... GOLLY, JESUS, GO AHEAD, TURN RIGHT, EXCLAMATION

gee .... RACEHORSE

opposed to .... HAW

geek .... NERD

geese, domestic .... EMDENS

fat .... AXUNGE

formation .... VEE

genus .... ANSER

in the air, flock of .... SKEIN

on land, flock of .... RAFT, GAGGLE

geest .... ALLUVIUM

geetas .... STINGY

Gehenna .... HELL

Gehrig of baseball .... LOU

geisha .... DANCER, HOSTESS, ENTERTAINER, DANCING GIRL

gel .... JELLIFY, COAGULATE

gelatin(e) .... AGAR, ASPIC, GELEE, JELLY, GLUTIN, COLLOID

gelatinous .... VISCID, VISCOUS

geld .... CASTRATE, STERILIZE

gelding .... EUNUCH

Gelett Burgess didn't want to be one .... PURPLE COW

gelid .... ICY, COLD, FROSTY, FROZEN

gelling agent .... AGAR

gem .... JADE, ONYX, OPAL, RUBY, SARD, AGATE, BERYL, JEWEL, STONE, PRIZE, TOPAZ, GARNET, LIGURE, MUFFIN, SPINEL, EMERALD, DIAMOND, PERIDOT, AMETHYST

artificial .... PASTE, RUTILE

believed to be unlucky .... OPAL

biblical .... LIGURE

carved .... CAMEO

carving/engraving .... GLYPTICS

cultured .... PEARL

cut .... BRIOLETTE

cutter/expert .... LAPIDARY

cutting device .... LAP

dealer .... BEERS, CARTIER, LAPIDARY

facet .... BEZEL, CULET

flaw .... FEATHER

precious .... OPAL, RUBY, PEARL, DIAMOND, EMERALD

pseudo .... SPINEL

semi-precious .... TOURMALINE

setting .... BEZEL, CHATON

slang .... ICE, SPARKLER

smart cut .... BRILLIANT

weight .... CARAT, KARAT

Gem State .... IDAHO

gemel .... HINGE

part of .... HOOK, LOOP

Gemini .... TWINS

star .... CASTOR, POLLUX

gemlike .... OPALINE

gemma .... BUD

gems dealer .... LAPIDARY

gemsbok .... ORYX, CHAMOIS, ANTELOPE

gemstone .... IOLITE

gendarme(rie) .... POLICE(MAN)

gender .... SEX, NEUTER, FEMININE, MASCULINE

common .... EPICENE

gene .... FACTOR

material .... DNA, RNA

Gene Autry's team ...... ANGELS

genealogical record .... TREE

genealogy .... TREE, DESCENT, LINEAGE, HERALDRY, PEDIGREE

general ...... RIFE, BROAD, USUAL, COMMON, CURRENT, GENERIC, INCLUSIVE, PANDEMIC, UNIVERSAL, ECUMENICAL, PREVAILING, PREVALENT, WIDESPREAD

arrangement .... FORMAT

direction/course .... TREND

of the Armies .... PERSHING

of the Army ...... MACARTHUR, EISENHOWER

opinion .... CONSENSUS

pardon .... AMNESTY

rule .... CANON

welfare .... COMMONWEAL

Generalissimo .... CHIANG (KAI CHEK)

generally ...... ALWAYS, OVERALL, BY AND LARGE, AS A RULE

generate .... MAKE, BEGET, BREED, PRODUCE, ENGENDER, ORIGINATE, PROCREATE, IMPREGNATE

generation .... AGE, DESCENT, BREEDING, LIFETIME

some of the new .... TEENAGERS

generator .... DYNAMO

generic .... VAGUE, GENERAL, NEBULOUS, INDEFINITE

generosity .... CHARITY, ALTRUISM, PHILANTHROPY

generous .... AMPLE, LAVISH, LIBERAL, GRACIOUS, OBLIGING, UNSELFISH, CHARITABLE, OPEN-HANDED, OPEN-HEARTED

genesis .... BIRTH, ORIGIN, CREATION, BEGINNING

Genesis man .... PELEG

word .... BEGAT

genetic .... GENIC, INNATE, HEREDITARY

stuff .... DNA, RNA

genetics subject .... HEREDITY

geneva .... GIN

Geneva lake .... LEMAN

river .... RHONE

genial .... WARM, JOVIAL, AFFABLE, AMIABLE, CORDIAL, FRIENDLY, PLEASANT, DEBONAIR(E)

genie .... DEMON, GNOME, JINNI, JINNEE, SPIRIT

genius .... GIFT, PIXY, SPIRIT, TALENT, ABILITY, BRILLIANCE

Genoa gulf seaport .... RAPALLO

Genoese city .... LIGURIA

magistrate .... DOGE

genre .... KIND, TYPE, CLASS, STYLE, SPECIES

gens .... CLAN, TRIBE

gent .... GUY

genteel .... NICE, POLITE, ELEGANT, REFINED, WELL-BRED

gentian .... ROOT, FLOWER, COLUMBO, AGUEWEED

gentile .... GOY, PAGAN, HEATHEN, NON-JEW(ISH)

gentle .... MEEK, MILD, SOFT, TAME, AMENE, DOCILE, KINDLY, PLACID, POLITE, LENIENT, TENDER, REFINED, LAMBLIKE

breeze .... ZEPHYR

push .... NUDGE

soul/person .... LAMB

gentleman .... RYE, SIR, GENT, MILORD, SIGNOR, ESQUIRE, GALLANT, CAVALIER, COURTIER

amateur .... CORINTHIAN

attendant .... DONZEL

gentleman's man .... VALET

Gentlemen Prefer Blondes
   author .... (ANITA)LOOS

gentlewoman .... MILADY

gently .... SLOWLY, TENDERLY

Gentoo .... HINDU

gentry .... NOBILITY, ARISTOCRACY

genu .... KNEE

valgum .... KNOCK-KNEE

varum .... BOWLEG

genuflect .... KNEEL, CURTSY

genuine .... REAL, TRUE, LEGIT, RIGHT, VALID, HONEST, SINCERE, AUTHENTIC, SIMON PURE

genus .... KIND, SORT, BREED, CLASS, ORDER, ANALOG, GENDER, SPECIES, VARIETY

ant .... ECITON

birds .... ANSER, CORVUS

bowfin .... AMIA

campion .... SILENE

cats, big .... PANTHERA

cats, small .... FELIS

cattle/cows/ruminant .... BOS

cetaceans .... INIA

chestnuts .... CASTANEA

clams .... MYA

corncrake .... CREX

cranes .... GRUS

dogs .... CANIS

dogwood .... CORNUS

ducks .... ANAS, ANSER

eels .... CONGER

elks/moose .... ALCES

fishes .... ANABAS

fowl .... OLOR

foxes .... VULPES

frogs .... RANA, ANURA

gannet .... SULA

gastropods ...... HARPA, OLIVA, NERITA, TRITON

geese .... ANSER

ginseng .... ARALIA

goats .... CAPRIA

goose barnacles .... LEPAS

gooseberry .... RIBES

goshawks .... ASTUR, BUTEO

grapes .... VITIS

grasses ..... POA, AIRA, AVENA, STIPA, SETARIA

griffon .... GYPS

gulls .... LARI, XEMA, LARUS

herbs ..... ARUM, RUTA, INULA, ASARUM, ANEMONE, TOVARIA

herring .... ALOSA

hogs/pigs/swine .... SUS

honeybee .... APIS

housefly .... MUSCA, FANNIA

insects .... ACARUS, CICADA

lemurs .... GALAGO

lily .... ALOE

lizard .... UTA

man/primate .... HOMO

maple .... ACER

mints .... NEPETA

mollusks .... OLIVA, ANOMIA, NERITA, TEREDO

monkeys .... ATELES

mosquito .... AEDES

mussels .... UNIO

nettles .... URTICA

nuthatch .... SITTA

oats .... AVENA

olives .... OLEA

oysters .... OSTREA

palms .... ARECA

peacock .... PAVO

plants .... ARUM, LANTANA

rhubarb .... RHEUM

sea lettuce .... ULVA

shads .... ALOSA

sheep .... OVIS

shrubs .... ITEA, OLEA, RHUS, ERICA, FUCHSIA

snakes .... BOA, ELAPS, PYTHON

swans .... OLOR, CYGNUS

terns .... STERNA

thistles .... CARLINA

thrushes .... TURDUS

trees .... CELTIS, CORNUS, SAPOTA, CATALPA

turtles .... EMY

wasp .... VESPA

whales .... INIA

wrens .... NANNUS

geode .... VOOG, VUG(H), VUGG, DRUSE, CAVITY

geographer .... VAREN, PTOLEMY, MERCATOR

geography, work on
   .... ALMAGEST

geologic chamber .... CAVE

geological age .... CENOZOIC, PLIOCENE

angle .... HADE

division .... EON, ERA, LIAS, LYAS

epoch .... ECCA, UINTA, EOCENE, MIOCENE, PLIOCENE, OLIGOCENE, PALEOCENE

era .... CENOZOIC, MESOZOIC, PALEOZOIC

formation ...... IONE, TERRANE, TERRAIN, TERRENE, TRIASSIC

ridge .... OSAR

suffix .... ZOIC

geology, part of ...... GEODETICS, PETROLOGY, MINEROLOGY

geomancy .... DIVINATION

geometrical body .... LUNE, PRISM

curve .... PARABOLA

figure ..... CONE, CUBE, ANGLE, PRISM, RHOMB, CIRCLE, SQUARE, ELLIPSE, POLYGON, HELICOID

line .... LOCUS, SECANT

premise .... POSTULATE

principle .... THEOREM

ratio .... PI, SINE

solid .... CONE, CUBE, LUNE, PRISM, PYRAMID

study .... CONICS

term ..... SINE, LOCUS, SECANT, VERSOR, TANGENT, THEOREM

geometry, branch of ...... CONICS

hypothesis .... THEOREM

subject of .... LINE, PLANE, POINT, SOLID

type .... PLANE, SOLID

geophagist .... CLAYEATER

geoponic .... RURAL, RUSTIC, BUCOLIC, PASTORAL

George .... RAFT, DEWEY, GOBEL, LUCAS, SCOTT, SEGAL, PATTON

Bernard .... SHAW

Cukor hit film ...... DINNER AT EIGHT

Eliot .... EVANS

Eliot, weaver of .... MARNER

Herman .... RUTH

georgette .... CREPE

Georgia, capital of ...... ATLANTA

city/town .... ROME, MACON, ALBANY, ATHENS, DALTON, PLAINS, TIFTON, AUGUSTA, GRIFFIN, AMERICUS, COLUMBUS, LA GRANGE, SAVANNAH, VALDOSTA, WAYCROSS, BRUNSWICK, BAINBRIDGE, GAINESVILLE

college .... TIFT, PAINE, BRENAU, SPELMAN

county ...... BIBB, COBB, HALL, POLK, TIFT, WARE, FLOYD,

GLYNN, HENRY, TROUP, BARTOW, CLARKE, COWETA, DE KALB, FULTON, GORDON, NEWTON, THOMAS, WALKER, BALDWIN, BULLOCH, CARROLL, CATOOSA, CHATHAM, CLAYTON, DOUGLAS, HOUSTON, LAURENS, LOWNDES, CHEROKEE, COLQUITT, COLUMBIA, GWINNETT, MUSKOGEE, RICHMOND, ROCKDALE, SPALDING, DOUGHERTY, WHITFIELD

dam .... BARTLETTS FERRY

island .... JEKYLL, SAPELO, WASSAW, OSSABAW, SKIDAWAY, CUMBERLAND

lake .... BANKS, WEISS, BURTON, CARTERS, CHATUGE, SINCLAIR, GOAT ROCK, BLACKSHEAR, WEST POINT, SIDNEY LANIER

mountain .... STONE, SPRINGER, BRASSTOWN BALD

Negro .... GULLAH

peak .... KENNESAW

recreation/historic site
.... HAY HOUSE, ROCK CITY, TALLULAH GORGE, APPALACHIAN TRAIL

river .... COOSA, FLINT, OCONEE, ALAPAHA, SATILLA, TUGALOO, ALTAMAHA, OCMULGEE, S(U)WANEE, SUWANNOOCHEE

seaport .... SAVANNAH

state bird .... THRASHER

state flower .... CHEROKEE ROSE

state nickname .... PEACH, EMPIRE STATE OF THE SOUTH

university .... EMORY, MERCER, OGLETHORPE

Georgian seaport .... BATUM

Geraint .... KNIGHT

wife of .... ENID

geranium .... CRANESBILL

gerbil(l)e .... JERBOA

gerent .... RULER, MANAGER

geriatrics .... NOSTOLOGY

germ .... SEED, VIRUS, EMBRYO, ORIGIN, MICROBE, BACTERIUM

cell .... GAMETE

for short .... STREP

free .... ASEPTIC

German ...... HUN, BOCHE, JERRY, ALEMAN, ALMAIN, JUNKER, DEUTSCHE, TEUTON(IC)

abandon .... AUFGEBEN

above .... UBER

admiral .... SPEE, RAEDER, TIRPITZ

after .... NACH

again .... WIEDER

air .... LUFT

aircraft maker .... DORNIER

airplane .... STUKA, TAUBE

alas .... ACH

all .... ALLE(S)

also .... FERNER

and .... UND

angry .... BOSE

animal/beast .... TIER

answer .... ANTWORTEN

appreciate .... SCHATZEN

approving word .... HOCK

army .... REICHSWEHR

art songs .... LIEDER

artful .... LISTIG

article .... DAS, DER, EIN(E)

ass .... ESEL

assembly hall .... AULA

at no time .... NIE

avenue .... ALLEE

aviator .... FLIEGER

award .... ZUERKENNEN

bacteriologist .... KOCH, LOFFLER

baggage .... GEPACK

bank .... UFER

bath .... BAD

battle .... SCHLACHT

battleship .... TIRPITZ, BISMARCK, (GRAF)SPEE

bay .... BUCHT

beach .... STRAND

bean .... BOHNE

beard .... BART

beautiful .... SCHON

because .... WEIL

bed .... BETT

bee .... BIENE

beer .... BIER, LAGER

believe .... GLAUBEN

betray .... VERRATEN

betroth .... VERLOBEN

black .... SCHWARZ

Black Forest
.... SCHWARZWALD

Black Sea .... SCHWARZES MEER

blanket .... WOLLDECKE

blood .... BLUT

blue .... BLAU

boar .... EBER

bomber .... STUKA

bonnet .... EASTER

book .... BUCH

boots .... HAUSKNECHT

-born architect in U.S.
.... GROPIUS

bottle .... FLASCHE

boy .... JUNGE

bread .... BROT, BROTCHEN

bride .... BRAUT

bridge .... BRUCKE

brother .... BRUDER

brussel sprouts
.... ROSENKOHL

build .... BAUEN

bullet .... KUGEL

burglar .... EINBRECHER

but .... ABER

butcher .... METZGER

buy .... KAUFEN

by .... BEI

cabbage .... KRAUT

cake .... TORTE, KUCHEN, STOLLEN

camp .... LAGER, STALAG

canal .... KIEL

candy .... ZUCKERWERK

car .... WAGEN

carpenter .... ZIMMERMANN

cash .... GELD

cat .... KATZE

cathedral site/city .... ULM, ESSEN, COLOGNE

cavalryman: var. .... ULAN

chancellor .... BRANDT, ERHARD, ADENAUER, BISMARCK

chap .... KERL, SPALT

cheese .... KASE

chicken .... KUCHLEIN

Christmas .... WEIHNACHTEN

Christmas card
.... WEIHNACHTS-KARTE

church .... KIRCHE

circle .... KREIS

clever .... KLUG

cloak .... MANTEL

clock/watch .... UHR

coal region .... RUHR, SAAR, AACHEN

coffee .... KAFFEE

coin .... MARK, KRONE, HELLER, GUILDER, PFENNIG, GROSCHEN, T(H)ALER, KREU(T)ZER

cold .... KALT

come .... KOMMEN

comic hero .... TYLL EULENSPIEGEL

complain .... KLAGEN

composer .... ABT, BACH, WEBER, BRAHMS, FLORIO, WAGNER, STRAUSS

conjunction .... UND

cool .... FRECH, RUHIG

cost .... KOSTEN

cottage .... HUTTE

councilor/counsel .... RAT
count .... GRAF, ZAHLEN
countess .... GRAFIN
counterfeit .... FALSCH
county .... LANDKREIS,
                 GRAFSCHAFT
courage .... MUT
court .... HOF
cousin .... VETTER
cover .... DECKE
cow .... KUH
coward .... FEIGLING
cowboy .... KUHHIRTE
crab .... KRABBE
cradle .... WIEGE
crazy .... VERRUCKT
creator .... SCHOPFER
creature .... GESCHOPF
creature, in folklore .... NIX
credit .... GLAUBE
crime .... VERBRECHEN
criminal .... VERBRECHER
crisis .... KRISE
critic .... KRITIKER
critic/dramatist
.... (GOTTHOLD)LESSING
cross .... KREUZ
crossword puzzle
.... KREUZWORT RATSEL
crowd .... MENGE
crown .... KRONE
cruel .... GRAUSAM
cry of surrender/comrade
.... KAMERAD
daddy .... VATI
dagger .... DOLCH
dam .... EDER, DEICH
dance .... TANZ, COTILLION
dancer .... TANZER
darling .... LIEBLING
data .... ANGABEN
date .... DATUM
day .... TAG
dead .... TOT
deaf .... TAUB
dean .... DEKAN
dear .... LIEB
death .... TOD
debt .... SCHULD
decade .... JAHRZEHNT
December .... DEZEMBER
decorate .... ZIEREN
deed .... TAT
defeat .... SCHLAGEN
defense force ...... LANDSTURM
defenseless .... SCHUTZLOS
deity .... GOTTHEIT
delivery .... ABGABE
demon .... TEUFEL
dentist .... ZAHNARZT
desert .... WUST

dessert .... STREUSEL,
                 NACHTISCH
dictionary .... WORTERBUCH
dine .... SPEISEN
dinner .... MITTAGESSEN
direction .... RICHTUNG
disciple .... JUNGER
disease .... KRANKHEIT
dish .... SCHUSSEL
disk .... SCHEIBE
district .... BEZIRK
do .... TUN
dog .... HUND
doll .... PUPPE
donation/gift .... GABE
donkey .... ESEL
donor .... GEBER
door .... TUR
down .... FLAUM, UNTEN
dozen .... DUTZEND
draw .... ZIEHEN
drawer .... ZIEHER
dream .... TRAUM
dress .... KLEID
drink .... TRUNK, TRINKEN
drop .... TROPFEN
drum .... TROMMEL
dry .... TROCKEN
duchess .... HERZOGIN
duchy .... BADEN, HESSE, LIPPE
duck .... TAUCHEN
duke .... HERZOG
dunce .... DUMMKOPF
duplicate .... DOPPELT
dwarf .... ZWERG
dye .... FARBEN
each/every .... JEDE, JEDER,
                 JEDES
eagle .... ADLER
ear .... OHR
early .... FRUH
earth .... ERDE
earthquake .... ERDBEBEN
east .... OSTEN
Easter .... OSTERN
eat .... ESSEN
ecstasy .... RAUSCH
educate .... ERZIEHEN
eel .... AAL
egg .... EI
egg, hardboiled ..... HARTES-EI
eggplant .... AUBERGINE
egg-shaped .... EIFORMIG
eight .... ACHT
either .... EINE(R)
elder .... ALTER
election .... WAHL
embassy .... BOTSCHAFT
emblem/symbol ...... SINNBILD
emperor .... OTTO, KAISER,
                 WILHELM

empire .... REICH
envy .... NEID
epic .... EPOS
era .... ARA
error .... IRRTUM
estate .... GUT
evening .... ABEND
event .... EREIGNIS
everybody .... JEDERMANN
everything .... ALLES
evil .... UBEL
exclamation ...... ACH, HOCH,
               AUSRUF, HIMMEL
expert .... ERFAHREN
explorer .... BARTH
eye .... AUGE
eyewitness .... AUGENZEUGE
face .... GESICHT
fact .... TATSACHE
fairy .... FEE
fairytale writer .... GRIMM
faith .... GLAUBE
fame .... RUHM
famine .... HUNGERSNOT
far .... WEIT
farmer .... BAUER
fascist .... NAZI
fashion .... MODE
father .... VATER
fear .... FURCHT
feather .... FEDER
February .... FEBRUAR
fee .... HONORAR
feel .... FUHLEN
fellow .... KERL
female .... WEIB
field .... FELD
fight .... KAMPF, GEFECHT
finish .... APPRETUR
fire .... FEUER
first .... ERST
first aid .... ERSTE HILFE
five .... FUNF
flat .... EBEN, FLACH
flight .... FLUG
flirt .... KOKETTE
flower .... BLUME
fog .... NEBEL
folk dance .... ALLEMANDE,
               VOLKSTANZ
folklore .... VOLKSKUNDE
folksong .... VOLKSLIED
follow .... FOLGEN
follower .... NACHFOLGER
follower of a German
philosopher .... HEGELIAN
food .... SPEISE
fool .... NARR
forbid .... VERBIETEN
forbidden .... VERBOTEN
forest .... WALD

forget .... VERGESSEN
fork .... GABEL
four .... VIER
fox .... FUCHS
fraud .... BETRUG
freedom/liberty .... FREIHEIT
Friday .... FREITAG
friend .... FREUND
frog .... FROSCH
from .... AUS, VON
fruit .... OBST
full .... VOLL
gambler/player .... SPIELER
game .... SPIEL
garden .... GARTEN
gardener .... GARTNER
garlic .... KNOBLAUCH
gate .... TOR
gem .... EDELSTEIN
gentleman .... HERR(EN)
germ .... KEIM, BAZILLUS
ghost .... GEIST
ginger .... INGWER
girl .... MADCHEN
give .... GEBEN
glad .... FROH
glance/look .... BLICK
go .... GEHEN
goal/aim .... ZIEL
goat .... ZIEGE
god ..... GOTT, WODEN, WOTAN
goddess .... GOTTIN
golf .... GOLFSPIEL
good .... GUT, GUTEN
good-bye .... AUF WIEDERSEHN
government .... REICH,
      REGIERUNG, HERRSCHAFT
governor .... MARGRAVE,
                  HERRSCHER
grape .... WEINTRAUBE
gray .... GRAU
green .... GRUN
grow .... WERDEN, WACHSEN
grower/planter .... PFLANZER
guard .... WACHE
guest .... GAST
gun .... GEWEHR
gypsy .... ZIGUENER
hair .... HAAR
hairy .... HAARIG
hall .... AULA, SAAL, HALLE
handle .... GRIFF
harlot .... DIRNE
harm .... SCHADEN
hat .... HUT
he .... ER, DER
head .... KOPF
headache .... KOPFWEH
health .... GESUNDHEIT
heart .... HERZ
heat .... HITZE

heaven/sky .... HIMMEL
heir .... ERBE
hero .... HELD, SIEGFRIED
heroine .... HELDIN
high .... HOCH
highway .... AUTOBAHN
historian .... RANKE, HEEREN
hit .... SCHLAG, TREFFER
hog/pig .... SCHWEIN
holiday .... FESTTAG
home .... HAUS, HEIM
honey .... HONIG
honor .... EHRE
hope .... HOFFEN
horse .... PFERD
hospital .... KRANKENHAUS
hot .... HEISS
hour .... STUNDE
housewife .... HAUSFRAU
humbug .... SCHWINDEL
humidity .... NASSE
hunt .... JAGEN
hunter .... JAGER
hypnotist .... MESMER
ice .... EIS
ill .... KRANK
income .... EINKOMMEN
indoor .... HAUSLICH
industrial town .... ESSEN
ink .... TINTE
invasion .... EINFALL
invent .... ERFINDEN
invention .... ERFINDUNG
inventor .... ERFINDER
invitation .... EINLADUNG
irate .... ZORNIG
ire .... ZORN
iron .... EISEN, PLATTEN
ironworks .... EISENHUTTE
it .... ES
itch .... JUCKEN
ivy .... EFEU
Jack .... HANS
janitor .... PFORTNER
January .... JANUAR
joke .... WITZ
joy .... FREUDE
judge .... RICHTER
juice .... SAFT
July .... JULI
jump .... SPRINGEN
June .... JUNI
kennel .... HUNDEHUTTE
key .... SCHLUSSEL
kill .... TOTEN
king .... KONIG, KAISER
king, 936-973 .... OTTO
kingdom .... HESSE, SAXONY,
      HANOVER, PRUSSIA,
                  KONIGREICH
knife .... MESSER

knight .... RITTER, SPRINGER,
                  TANNHAUSER
label .... ZETTEL
lace .... SPITZE
ladies .... DAMEN
lady .... DAME
lady, young .... FRAULEIN
lake .... SEE
land .... BODEN
landlady .... WIRTIN
landlord .... WIRT
language .... SPRACHE
laugh .... LACHEN
law .... RECHT
leaf .... BLATT
league .... BUND
leg .... BEIN
legend's site .... HAMELIN
legislative assembly
.... LANDTAG
lemon .... ZITRONE
lent .... FASTEN
letter .... BRIEF
lettuce .... KOPFSALAT
library .... BIBLIOTHEK
life/live .... LEBEN
lightning .... BLITZ
lion .... LOWE
lip .... LIPPE
lipstick .... LIPPENSTIFT
little .... KLEIN, WENIG
loser .... VERLIERER
love .... LIEBE
love, in tennis .... NULL
lyric .... LIED, GEDICHT
lyric poem .... LIEDER
madam/married woman
.... FRAU
magazine .... WARENLAGER
magic .... ZAUBER
magician .... ZAUBERER
mail .... POST
male .... MANN
man .... MANN, MENSCH
map .... LANDKARTE
marble .... MARMOR
March .... MARZ
master .... HERR, LEHRER,
                  MEISTER
master builder
.... BAUMEISTER
master race .... HERRENVOLK
mathematician .... HESSE
May .... MAI
me .... MIR, MICH
measles .... MASERN, ROSEOLA,
      RUBELLA, RUBEOLA
measure .... KARAT, HALBER,
      KLAFTER, GALLONEN,
      SCHEFFEL, SCHOPPEN,
      KILOGRAMM

meat .... FLEISCH
medicine .... ARZNEI
menu .... SPEISEKARTE
mercenary soldier .... HESSIAN
messenger .... BOTE
middle .... MITTE
Military Intelligence
.... ABWEHR
mimic .... NACHAHMEN
mimist .... SCHARRE
miner .... BERGMANN
minnesinger ...... TANNHAUSER
minstrel .... SPIELMANN
miracle .... WUNDER
mirror .... SPIEGEL
Miss .... FRAULEIN
Mister .... HERR
Monday .... MONTAG
monetary unit .... MARK
money .... GELD
month .... MONAT
moon .... MOND
more .... MEHR
more favorable .... BESSER
morning .... MORGEN
mother .... MUTTER
mountain .... BERG
mouth .... MUND
mug .... BECHER
murder .... MORD
musician .... MUSIKER
musician, legendary .... PIED
PIPER
my .... MEIN
nail .... NAGEL
name prefix .... VON
napkin .... SERVIETTE
nation .... VOLK
naval base .... KIEL, EMDEN
near .... NAHE
neck .... HALS
necklace .... HALSBAND
necktie .... KRAWATTE
needle .... NADEL
negative/no .... NEIN, NICHT
neighbor .... NACHBAR
nephew .... NEFFE
never .... NIE, NIMMER
new .... NEU, FRISCH
newcomer .... ANKOMMLING
news .... NACHRICHT
niece .... NICHTE
night .... NACHT
nine .... NEUN
noble .... EDEL
nobleman .... EDELMANN
noise .... LARM
none .... KEINE(r)
nonsense .... UNSINN
north .... NORDEN
nose .... NASE

number .... ZAHL, NUMMER
oak .... EICHE
of .... AUF, AUS, VON
once .... EINST
one .... EIN
onion .... ZWIEBEL
only .... NUR
open .... OFFEN
operatic soprano .... LEHMANN
orange .... APFELSINE
our(s) .... UNSER
oven .... BACKOFEN
over .... UBER
overcoat .... MANTEL
overture .... VORSPIEL
owl .... EULE
ox .... OCHSE
ox, extinct .... URUS
pain .... WEH
painter .... ERNST, MALER,
GROSZ, HOLBEIN
parents .... ELTERN
parliament .... REICHSTAG
parrot .... PAPAGEI
part .... TEIL
path(way) .... PFAD
patience .... GEDULD
pay .... LOHN
pea .... ERBSE
pea soup .... ERBSENSUPPE
peace .... RUHE, FRIEDE
peacock .... PFAU
peak .... SPITZE
pear .... BIRNE
penalty .... STRAFE
pencil .... BLEISTIFT
people .... VOLK, LEUTE
perfume .... DUFT, PARFUM
pharmacist .... DROGIST
philosopher ...... KANT, HEGEL,
FICHTE, HERDER, CASSIRER
physician .... ARZT
physicist .... HERTZ
pickpocket .... TASCHENDIEB
picture/portrait .... BILD
pirate .... SEERAUBER
plant .... PFLANZE
plate .... TAFEL, PLATTE
playwright ..... SACHS, BRECHT
please .... BITTE
poem .... GEDICHT
poet ..... ARNDT, HEINE, RILKE,
SCHILLER
poison .... GIFT
police .... POLIZEI
policeman .... POLIZIST
potato .... KARTOFFEL
poverty .... ARMUT
POW camp .... STALAG
power .... KRAFT
powerful .... KRAFTIG

pray .... BETEN
prayer .... GEBET
president .... EBERT, HEUSS,
LUBKE, TALER
president, first .... EBERT
pretty .... NETT
principality .... LIPPE
printer .... GUTENBERG
problem .... AUFGABE
profit .... GEWINN
project .... ENTWURF
pronoun .... DU, ICH, SIE, UNS,
WIR
psychiatrist .... KRAEPELIN
pumpkin .... KURBIS
puzzle/riddle .... RATSEL
quarrel .... STREIT
queen .... KONIGIN
question .... FRAGE
rabbit .... KANINCHEN
radio .... RUNDFUNK
railroad .... EISENBAHN
rain .... REGEN
read .... LESEN
ready .... BEREIT
realm .... REICH
receipt .... EMPFANG
red .... ROT
Red Cross .... ROTES KREUZ
redwood .... ROTHOLZ
region .... GEBIET, GEGEND
reply .... ANTWORT
report .... BERICHT
reputation .... RUF
residence .... WOHNUNG
resort/spa .... EMS, BADEN
ribbon .... BAND
rice .... REIS
ride .... RITT
rifleman ..... YAGER, JA(E)GER,
SCHUTZE
ring .... KREIS, LAUTEN
riot .... AUFRUHR
Rip Van Winkle .... KLAUS
river .... STROM
robber .... RAUBER
robbery .... RAUB
robe .... KLEID, TALAR
rodent .... NAGETIER
roof .... DACH
rooster .... HAHN
root .... GRUND
rope .... SEIL
rubber .... GUMMI
rye bread .... ROGGENBROT
sacred place .... ABATON,
HIERON
sale .... VERKAUF
salesman .... VERKAUFER
salmon .... LACHS
salt .... SALZ

salutation .... HEIL
Saturday .... SAMSTAG
sausage .... WURST
saying .... REDE
school .... SCHULE
scientist .... MACH
sculptor .... BILDHAUER
sermon .... PREDIGT
serpent/snake .... SCHLANGE
service .... DIENST
seven .... SIEBEN
she .... SIE
ship/vessel .... SCHIFF
shoplifter .... LADENDIEB
shore .... UFER, STRAND
shout .... SCHREI
show .... ZEIGEN
silk .... SEIDE
sin .... SUNDE
since .... SEIT
siren .... LURLEI, LORELEI
sister .... SCHWESTER
six .... SECHS
slang .... DUTCH, JERRY
Slavic people .... WEND
sleep .... SCHLAF(EN)
small .... KLEIN
snare .... SCHLINGE
snow .... SCHNEE
soap .... SEIFE
society .... VEREIN
soldier .... BOCHE, HEINIE,
                                SOLDAT
son .... SOHN
song .... LIED, GESANG
soul .... SEELE
south .... SUDEN
sparrow .... SPERLING
speak/talk .... REDEN,
                             SPRECHEN
spider .... SPINNE
spirit .... GEIST
spoon .... LOFFEL
spouse .... GATTE, GATTIN
sprite .... FEE, ELFE, KOBOLD
spy .... SPION
stamp .... STANZE, STEMPEL
star .... STERN
state police .... GESTAPO
steel .... STAHL
steeple .... KIRCHTURM
stone .... STEIN
store .... VORRAT
street .... STRASSE
string .... SCHNUR
students' hall .... BURSE
submarine .... U-BOOT
sugar .... ZUCKER
sun .... SONNE
Sunday .... SONNTAG
superior/upper .... OBER

supper .... ABENDESSEN
surgeon .... CHIRURG
suspicion .... VERDACHT
swastika .... HAKENKREUZ
sweet .... LIEBSTE(R)
sword .... SABEL
table .... TAFEL, TISCH
taboo .... VERBOTEN
take .... NEHMEN
tank, armored .... PANZER
tavern .... WIRTSHAUS
teacher .... LEHRER(IN)
ten .... ZEHN
tennis .... NETZBALL
thank .... DANKEN
the .... DAS, DER, DIE
theologian .... EBER
there .... DA, DORT, DAHIN
thing .... DING, SACHE
think .... DENKEN
thirst .... DURST
three .... DREI
Thursday .... DONNERSTAG
time .... ZEIT
tip .... TRINKGELD
title, former .... KAISERIN
title of nobility .... GRAF,
                                 PRINZ
title of respect .... HERR
to .... AN, ZU, AUF, NACH
today .... HEUTE
tooth .... ZAHN
toothache .... ZAHNWEH
tournament .... TURNIER
town .... STADT
train .... ZUG
tree .... BAUM
true .... WAHR
truth .... WAHRHEIT
Tuesday .... DIENSTAG
twenty .... ZWANZIG
twin .... ZWILLING
two .... ZWEI
understand .... VERSTEHEN
up .... OBEN
urchin .... SCHLINGEL
us .... UNS
use .... NUTZEN
valley .... TAL
very .... ECHT, SEHR
victim .... OPFER
village .... DORF
visitor .... BESUCHER
voice .... STIMME
volcano .... VULKAN
wage .... LOHN
waiter .... KELLNER
war .... KRIEG
warning .... WARNUNG
water .... WASSER
wave .... WOGE, WELLE

we .... WIR
wealth .... REICHTUM
weather .... WETTER
wedding .... HOCHZEIT
Wednesday .... MITTWOCH
week .... WOCHE
weight .... GRAMM, TONNE,
                  GEWICHT, KILOGRAMM
west .... WESTEN
what .... WAS, WELCHER
wheat .... WEIZEN
when .... WANN, WENN
where .... WO
whirlpool .... STRUDEL
white .... WEISS
who .... DAS, DER, WER
whole .... GANZ
why .... WARUM
widow .... WITWE
wife/woman ...... FRAU, FROW,
                               FRAULEIN
win .... SIEG
window .... FENSTER
wine .... HOCK, WEIN,
                                MOSELLE
wire .... DRAHT
wish .... WUNSCH
witch .... HEXE
with .... MIT
without .... OHNE
wood .... HOLZ
word .... WORT
work .... ARBEIT
world .... WELT
wrinkle .... WINK
write .... SCHREIBEN
WW II plane .... TAUBE
X ray .... RONTGEN
yawn .... GAHNEN
year .... JAHR
yellow .... GELB
yes .... JA
yet .... NOCH
you .... DU, SIE
young .... JUNG
your .... DEIN, EUER
youth .... JUGEND
zero .... NULL
zodiac .... TIERKREIS
germane .... AKIN, APROPOS,
             RELEVANT, PERTINENT
Germanic people .... CIMBRI
tribesman .... JUTE
Germany .... REICH,
                          DEUTSCHLAND
bay, East .... POMERANIAN,
                         MECKLENBURG
bay, West .... HELGOLAND,
                         MECKLENBURG
cape, East .... ARKONA
capital, East .... BERLIN

capital, West .... BONN
city/town, East .... GERA,
JENA, GOTHA, HALLE, RIESA,
DESSAU, ERFURT, PANKOW,
WEIMAR, WISMAR, WOLFEN,
ZITTAU, BAUTZEN, COTTBUS,
DRESDEN, GORLITZ, LEIPZIG,
POTSDAM, ROSTOCK, STENDAL,
TREPTOW, ZWICKAU,
ARNSTADT, BERNBURG,
EISENACH, KOPENICK,
SCHWERIN, ALTENBERG,
FRANKFURT, BRANDENBURG,
LICHTENBERG
city/town, West ..... HOF, ULM,
KOLN, CELLE, EMDEN, ESSEN,
FULDA, FURTH, HAGEN,
HERNE, MAINZ, NEUSS, TRIER,
AACHEN, AMBERG, BERLIN,
BOCHUM, BREMEN, KASSEL,
LUBECK, MINDEN, MUNICH,
WITTEN, BAMBERG, BOCHOLT,
BOTTROP, COLOGNE,
HAMBURG, HAMELIN,
HANOVER, KOBLENZ,
MUNSTER, SPANDAU,
ARNSBERG, BAYREUTH,
DORTMUND, MANNHEIM,
FRANKFURT, NUREMBERG,
STUTTGART, WOLFSBURG,
DUSSELDORF, SCHONEBERG
district, East ...... GERA, SUHL,
BERLIN, ERFURT, COTTBUS,
DRESDEN, LEIPZIG, POTSDAM,
ROSTOCK, SCHWERIN,
FRANKFURT
forest, East .... SPREEWALD,
THURINGERWALD
forest, West .... BLACK,
BAVARIAN, ODENWALD,
SCHWARZWALD
island, East .... RUGEN,
USEDOM
island, West .... FOHR, SYLT,
AMRUM, JUIST, BALTRUM,
LANGEOOG, HELGOLAND
islands, West .... FRISIAN,
HALLIGEN
lake, West .... AMMERSEE,
BODENSEE, CHIEMSEE,
CONSTANCE, KONIGSSEE
mountain, East
.... FICHTELBERG
mountain, West .... FOLDBERG,
WATZMANN, ZUGSPITZE,
KAISERSTUHL, GROSSER ARBER
mountains, East .... HARZ,
RHON, ERZGEBIRGE
mountains, West .... HARZ,
RHON, HARDT
port ...... ULM, HAFEN, BREMEN

pre-1949 section of
.... RUSSIAN ZONE
range, West .... SWABIAN
JURA, BAVARIAN ALPS
region, East .... SAXONY,
ALTMARK, THURINGIA,
BRANDENBURG
region, West .... SAAR, HEGAU,
ALIGAU, BREISGAU,
SAUERLAND
river, East .... ELBE, ELDE,
ODER, HAVEL, MULDE, PEENE,
SAALE, SPREE, UCKER, WERRA,
ELSTER, NEISSE, WARNOW,
UNSTRUT
river, West .... EMS, INN, ELBE,
HASE, ISAR, LAHN, LECH,
NAAB, OKER, RUHR, SAAR,
ALLER, HUNTE, ILLER, LEINE,
LIPPE, MOSEL, RHINE, SAUER,
WESER, DANUBE, NECKAR,
TAUBER
sea .... NORTH, BALTIC
seaport .... KIEL, EMDEN,
WISMAR
state ...... LAGE, HESSE, STAAT,
BREMEN, BAVARIA, HAMBURG,
SAARLAND, RHINELAND
germicide .... ANTISEPTIC
germinate .... BEGIN, SPROUT,
PULLULATE
Gernreich, designer .... RUDI
Geronimo .... APACHE
foe of .... PALEFACE
greeting .... HOW
Gershwin, songman .... IRA,
GEORGE
Gertrude's friend Alice
.... TOKLAS
gesso .... GYPSUM, PLASTER
Gestapo chief .... HIMMLER
gestation ...... CYESIS, PREGNANCY
gest(e) .... DEED, BEARING,
EXPLOIT, ADVENTURE
gesticulate .... MIME, WAVE,
MOTION, GESTURE
gesture .... GESTE, TOKEN,
ACTION, MOTION, SIGNAL,
MOVEMENT
of contempt .... FIG, FICO
of indifference .... SHRUG
of respect .... BOW, CURTSY
get .... GAIN, OBTAIN, SECURE,
ACQUIRE
a circuit ahead in a race
.... LAP
a fitting .... TRY ON
a peek .... ESPY
a whiff of .... SNIFF
aboard .... EMBARK
about .... MOVE

across .... CONVEY, IMPART
ahead .... ADVANCE, PROSPER
along .... AGE, FARE, AGREE,
CLICK, THRIVE
along on one's own ..... FEND,
MANAGE
along peacefully .... COEXIST
around .... EVADE, SKIRT,
OUTWIT, DECEIVE
at .... GRAB, BRIBE, ARRIVE,
ACQUIRE
away .... ELUDE, DEPART,
ESCAPE
back at .... RETALIATE
back on the bus ..... REBOARD
by .... MANAGE, STRETCH,
SURVIVE
by trickery .... FINAGLE
cold feet .... CHICKEN OUT
cracking .... HURRY, STEP ON
IT
even with .... REVENGE,
RETALIATE
experience .... TASTE
going .... BEGIN, BEGONE,
HASTEN
going to .... IN FOR
hold of .... SEIZE, ACQUIRE
in .... ENTER, REACH, ARRIVE
in arrears .... DEFAULT
in touch .... ANSWER,
CONTACT
in trouble .... BE IN A CORNER,
LOSE ONE'S WAY
in uninvited .... CRASH
in with .... BEFRIEND
it .... SUFFER
it off one's chest ..... CONFESS
it over with .... END
lost .... LEAVE, DEPART, GO
FLY A KITE
married .... TIE THE KNOT
off one's feet .... SIT
on .... DON, BOARD, MOUNT
on one's nerves ..... PROVOKE,
IRRITATE
on the train! ...... ALL ABOARD
one's bearing .... ORIENT
one's dander up .... RILE
one's goat .... IRK, ANNOY,
PIQUE
oneself used to .... INURE
out .... EXIT, PRINT, EXTRACT
out of .... SHIRK
out of line .... NONCONFORM
over .... MOVE, RECOVER
rid of .... DISCARD, DISPOSE
rid of: sl. .... DITCH
set .... READY, PREPARE
stage fright .... CHOKE UP
the better of .... DEFEAT,

OUTWIT

the hang of .... FOLLOW, REALIZE, MASTER

the message .... SEE THE LIGHT

the point .... CATCH ON

to .... ARRIVE

to work .... DIG IN

together ..... BEE, TEA, AMASS, ASSEMBLE, REUNION

together, of a kind .... SEANCE

up .... ARISE, AWAKE

well .... HEAL, MEND, RECOVER

getaway .... ESCAPE

getting going .... UNDER WAY

the gold watch .... RETIRING

Gettysburg general .... LEE, MEADE

orator .... EVERETT, LINCOLN

getup .... WEAR, OUTFIT, COSTUME

geegaw .... GAUD, BAUBLE, DOODAD, TRINKET, FALDEROL, GIMCRACK

geyser .... (HOT)SPRING

mouth of .... CRATER

Ghana cape .... THREE POINTS

capital .... ACCRA

city/town .... HO, WA, ADA, ODA, AXIM, BOLE, KETA, TEMA, TUMU, BAWKU, YENDI, BEKWAI, DUNKWA, ELMINA, KUMASI, NSAWAM, OBUASI, TARKWA, TAMALE, WENCHI, BEREKUM, MAMPONG, PRESTEA, SEKONDI, SUNYANI, WINNEBA, CAPE COAST, KOFORIDUA

coin .... PESEWA

gulf .... GUINEA

lake .... VOLTA

language ..... EWE, TWI, AKAN, FANTE, HAUSA

monetary unit .... CEDI

native .... ASHANTI

"redeemer" .... NKRUMAH

region .... GOLD COAST

river ..... BLACK VOLTA, WHITE VOLTA

ghastly .... GRIM, LURID, GRIS(T)LY, MACABRE, GRUESOME

gha(u)t .... PASS, RANGE

ghee .... BUTTER

Ghent river .... LYS

gherkin .... CUCUMBER

ghetto .... SLUM, JEWRY

visitor .... SLUMMER

ghost .... KER, HANT, MANES, SPOOK, SHADOW, SPIRIT, WRAITH, EIDOLON, PHANTOM, SPECTRE, APPARITION

ghostly .... SPECTRAL, EERIE, SPOOKY

milieu .... HAUNT

ghoul .... DEMON

ghoulish ..... FIENDISH, HORRIBLE, VAMPIRIC, LOATHSOME

GI .... YANK, SAD SACK, GOVERNMENT ISSUE

absentee .... AWOL

address .... APO

bed .... SACK

break .... LEAVE

color .... KHAKI

ex/former .... VET

hangout .... USO

ID .... DOGTAG

Joe .... DOGFACE

ration .... SPAM

rifle .... BAR, GARAND, ARMALITE

runabout of .... JEEP

specialist .... MEDIC

Gian Carlo, composer .... MENOTTI

giant .... BANA, ETEN, LOKI, OGRE, YMER, ATLAS, JOTUN, JUMBO, MIMIR, TITAN, TROLL, BALDER, FAFNIR, GOLIATH

biblical .... ANAK

female .... GIANTESS

hundred-eyed .... ARGUS

hundred-handed ..... BRIAREUS

killer .... JACK, DAVID

living underground ..... TROLL

medieval legendary .... GARGANTUA

mythological .... YMIR

one-eyed .... ALEC, ARGES, CYCLOPS

-sized .... TITANIC

giantess .... GROA, NATT, NORN, URTH, SKULD

giaour .... UNBELIEVER

gib ...... GUT, SALMON, (TOM)CAT, GILBERT

gibbed .... CASTRATED

gibber .... JABBER, CHATTER

gibberish .... JABBER, JARGON, CHATTER, MUMBO-JUMBO

gibbet .... GALLOWS, SCAFFOLD

adjunct .... NOOSE

gibbon .... APE, LAR, WAUWAU, WOUWOU, PRIMATE

Gibbons, composer .... ORLANDO

concern of .... ROME

gibbous .... ROUNDED, HUMPBACKED

gibe .... RIB, JAPE, JEER, FLEER, SCOFF, SNEER, TAUNT, TEASE, DERIDE, HECKLE

giblet .... GIZZARD

Gibraltar cape .... TRAFALGAR

founder of .... GEBIR

old name of .... CALPE

sight .... APE

strait port .... TANGIER

Gibson, Charles .... DANA

girl .... MODEL

tennis champ .... ALTHEA

gibus .... OPERA HAT

gid .... STAGGERS

giddiness .... VERTIGO

giddy .... DIZZY, FICKLE, WHIRLING, HOITY-TOITY

Gide, critic .... ANDRE

gift .... ALMS, BOON, DOLE, BOUNTY, LEGACY, TALENT, ABILITY, BENEFIT, HANDOUT, PRESENT, LARGESS(E), DONATION

bearer .... SANTA

by man to bride .... DOWRY

for good luck .... HANDSEL

from the Magi .... MYRRH

giver .... DONOR

of gab/speech ...... ELOQUENCE

of money for services ..... TIP, GRATUITY

of money, illicit .... BRIBE

recipient .... DONEE

to employee .... BONUS

gifted .... BRAINY, TALENTED

child .... PRODIGY

gig .... NAP, CHAISE, DEMERIT, (ROW)BOAT, CARRIAGE

gigantic .... HUGE, VAST, IMMENSE, MAMMOTH, TITANIC, COLOSSAL, ENORMOUS

statue .... COLOSSUS

giggle .... LAUGH, TITTER, CHUCKLE, SNICKER

giggly sound .... TEHEE

Gigi role player .... HEPBURN

gigolo .... ESCORT

gigot ...... VEAL, MUTTON, SLEEVE

gigue .... JIG

Gil, writer .... BLAS

gila monster .... LIZARD

Gilbert and Sullivan actor .... SAVOYARD

Island .... BERU, MAKIN, TARAWA

gild .... GILT, ADORN, AUREATE

gill .... GIRL, GLEN, BROOK, NOGGIN, WATTLE, SWEETHEART

gillie .... SERVANT, ATTENDANT

gills, 4 .... PINT

gilsonite .... ASPHALT, UINTAITE

gilt .... PIG, SOW, GILD

gilthead .... SCUP, PORGY, BREAM,

CUNNER, SPAROID
gimcrack .... BAUBLE, DOODAD, GAUD(Y), GEWGAW, NOVELTY, TRINKET
gimlet .... WIMBLE
  ingredient .... LIME
gimmick .... ANGLE, GIZMO, GADGET
gimp .... FABRIC, GUIPURE
  colloquial .... VIGOR
gin .... NET, SLOE, TRAP, SNARE, RUM(MY), GENEVA
  flavoring .... SLOE
  liquor .... SCHNAPPS
  mill .... SALOON
  rummy debacle .... BLITZ
ginger .... SPICE, CURCUMA, ENLIVEN, CARDAMOM
  ale-beer .... SHANDYGAFF
  cookies .... SNAPS
Ginger's partner .... FRED
gingerbread .... CAKE, GAUDY, ORNATE, TAWDRY, FRIPPERY
gingerly .... CHARILY, TIMIDLY
gingersnap .... COOKY
gingham ...... CLOTH, CHAMBRAY
gingili .... SESAME
gingko/ginkgo .... ICHO, TREE, MAIDENHAIR
ginseng .... HERB, ROOT
Gioconda, La ...... OPERA, MONA LISA, PORTRAIT
  painter .... DA VINCI
gip .... CHEAT, SWINDLE(R)
gipon .... TUNIC, JACKET
gipsy. (See also **gypsy**) ...... ROM
giraffe .... CAMELOPARD
  feature .... LONG NECK
  like animal .... OKAPI
girandole .... EARRING, PENDANT, FIREWORKS
girasol(e) .... OPAL, SUNFLOWER
gird ...... BIND, GIBE, JEER, EQUIP, ENDUE, SCOFF, STRAP, ENCLOSE, FORTIFY, ENCIRCLE
girder .... IBAR, TBAR, IBEAM, TRUSS
girdle .... BAND, BELT, SASH, GIRT(H), CORSET, ZODIAC, CEST(US), ZOSTER, CINCTURE, CUMMERBUND
  stiffener .... BUSK
girdler .... BEETLER
  world .... TOURIST
girl ...... SIS, TIT, CHIT, JILL, MINX, MISS, BELLE, LASS(IE), FILLE, DAMSEL, MADCAP, MAID(EN)
  attacked by a "swan" .... LEDA
  beautiful .... DOLL, STUNNER
  best friend of .... DIAMONDS

bold .... SLUT, QUEAN, HOYDEN, TOMBOY
  colloquial .... FILLY
  contrary .... MARY
  cover .... MODEL
  cute .... TRICK, PIPPIN
  flirtatious .... FIZGIG
  haircut .... BOB, BANGS, PAGEBOY
  in her early teens .... BOBBY SOXER
  in uniform .... WAC, SPAR, WREN, NURSE, MAJORETTE, CHEERLEADER
  introduced to society .... DEB(UTANTE)
  name meaning .... COLLEEN
  beauty .... ADA
  amiable .... ELMA
  delight .... EDNA
  happiness .... FELICITAS
  holy .... OLGA
  hospitable .... ZENIA
  joyful .... ADA
  noble .... ADELA, ETHEL
  princess .... SARA
  of song .... IDA, SAL, KATE, LILI, LOLA, DAISY, EADIE, FANNY, IRENE, KATIE, SALLY, RAMONA, ADELINE, MARLENE, RIO RITA
  of the 1960s, young .... TEENY-BOPPER
  pert, saucy .... CHIT, MINX, SNIP, FRAIL, HUSSY
  "Rain" .... SADIE
  slang .... TIT, BABE, CHICK, SKIRT, TOMATO, FLOSSIE, SPRING CHICKEN
  student .... COED
  very attractive ...... KNOCKOUT
  young .... MOPPET
Girl Scout .... DAISY, BROWNIE
  founder .... LOW
girlfriend .... STEADY, SWEETHEART
girls' group .... GSA, SORORITY
girth .... BAND, CINCH, STRAP, GIRDLE, ENCIRCLE, CIRCUMFERENCE
gisarme .... HALBERD, BATTLE-AX
gist .... NUB, CORE, CRUX, PITH, POINT, KERNEL, ESSENCE, MEANING, SUMMARY
gitano .... GYPSY
gittern .... CITHER, CITHARA
give .... PAY(OUT), GRANT, AWARD, ENDOW, YIELD, ASSIGN, CONFER, IMPART, PRESENT, HAND OVER
  a bellow .... ROAR

  a buzz .... RING
  a cheer .... ROOT
  a leg up .... AID
  a legal right to .... ENTITLE
  a subsequent showing .... RERUN
  a wavy appearance to .... CRIMP
  an account of .... RELATE
  an instance .... CITE
  and take ...... BANDY, BANTER, EXCHANGE, REPARTEE, HORSE-TRADE
  away .... DONATE, BESTOW, BETRAY, EXPOSE, REVEAL
  back .... RETURN, RESTORE
  birth .... WHELP, FARROW, DELIVER
  birth prematurely .... SLINK
  ear .... HEED, LISTEN, HEARKEN
  expression .... AIR, VOICE, ARTICULATE
  extreme unction to: arch. .... ANELE
  forth .... EMIT, EXUDE, ISSUE, SPOUT
  full consideration to ..... HEAR OUT
  generously .... LAVISH
  goods in return for other goods .... BARTER
  in .... YIELD, CONCEDE
  in law .... REMISE
  it a second try together .... REWED
  medicine to .... DOSE
  new courage .... REMAN
  off .... EMIT
  off fumes .... REEK
  one the business .... PATRONIZE
  opportunity to .... ENABLE
  out .... DOLE, METE
  out a mephitic aura ..... STINK
  party .... THROW
  permission to use .... LEND
  pleasure to .... GRATIFY, SATISFY
  sparingly .... DOLE, STINT
  the ball to (the fullback) .... HAND-OFF
  the raspberry to .... BOO
  the slip .... ELUDE
  title to: arch. .... INTITULE
  up .... QUIT, YIELD, LET GO, WAIVE, FORSAKE, SURRENDER, CAPITULATE
  up formally a high office/ throne .... ABDICATE
  vent to sorrow .... CRY
  way .... BEND, YIELD, LET PASS

wholehearted support .... GO TO BAT FOR

with reluctance ..... BEGRUDGE

giveaway .... DOOR PRIZE, LOSS LEADER

given .... PRONE, ASSUMED

to fighting .... COMBATIVE, PUGNACIOUS

giver's recipient .... TAKER

giving lots and lots ...... RAINING

off light .... LUMINESCENT

gizzard .... GIBLET, STOMACH

glabrous .... BALD, HAIRLESS

glace ...... ICED, FROZEN, CANDIED

glacial .... ICY, COLD, FRIGID

deposit .... ASAR, OSAR, ESKAR, ESKER, PLACER, MORAINE

epoch .... ICE AGE, PLEISTOCENE

formation .... SERAC, DRUMLIN

hill .... KAME, PAHA

ice/snow .... FIRN, NEVE, SERAC

ridge .... ASAR, KAME, OSAR, ESKAR, ESKER, DRUMLIN

snowfield .... FIRN, NEVE

glaciarium feat .... AXEL

glaciate .... FREEZE

glacier .... ICECAP

facing .... STOSS

fissure .... CREVASSE

shaft .... MOULIN

glacis .... SLOPE

glad .... FAIN, HAPPY, BLITHE, PLEASED, WILLING, CHEERFUL

eye .... OGLE

rags .... FINERY, CLOTHES

tidings .... GOSPEL, EVANGEL

gladden .... ELATE

glade .... DELL, LAWN, LAUND, VALLEY, CLEARING

combining form .... NEMO

gladiator ...... LANISTA, WARRIOR

school for .... LUDI

gladiolus .... IRID, IRIS, LILY

bulb .... CORM

gladly .... FAIN, LIEF, READILY, WILLINGLY, WITH PLEASURE

glair .... ALBUMEN

glaive .... SWORD, HALBERD

glamorize .... EXALT, GLORIFY, BEAUTIFY

glamorous .... ALLURING, CHARMING, DAZZLING, GORGEOUS

glamo(u)r .... CHARM, ALLURE

colloquial .... IT, OOMPH

glance .... LEER, LOOK, OGLE, PEEK, FLASH, GLEAM, APERCU, GLIMPSE, ONCE-OVER

off .... GRAZE

sideways .... SQUINT

glancing blow .... SNICK

gland .... PINEAL, SPLEEN, CAROTID, PAROTID, THYROID, FOLLICLE, PANCREAS

milk .... MAMMA

reproductive cell .... GONAD

secretion .... BILE, GALL, URINE, SALIVA, CERUMEN, HORMONE

glanders .... FARCY

glandlike .... ADENOID

glands inflammation

.... ADENITIS

glandular .... ADENOID(AL)

disease ..... GOITER, CRETINISM

tumor .... ADENOMA

glare .... LOOK, BLAZE, FROWN, STARE, GLOWER

glaring .... GARISH, FLAGRANT

Glasgow river .... CLYDE

saint .... MUNGO

glass .... LENS, CALX, PRISM, VERRE, CULLET, MIRROR, RUMMER, SMALTO, CRYSTAL, LALIQUE, TUMBLER

baking dish .... CASSEROLE

bead .... BUGLE

blowpipe .... MATRASS

bottle ..... VIAL, CRUET, PHIAL, CARBOY, CASTER, CASTOR

bowl .... AQUARIUM

brandy .... PONY, SNIFTER

bubble .... BLEB

coloring pigment .... SMALTINE, MAT(T)RASS

combining form ..... HYAL(O), VITRO

cut .... CRYSTAL

cutter .... GLAZIER

cutting tool ..... LAP, DIAMOND

drinking .... GOBLET, TUMBLER

fused .... FRIT(T)

ground .... FRIT

heat-resistant .... SILEX

jar .... BOCAL, CLOCHE

jawed one .... BOXER, PUGILIST

kind of .... LEAD, AGATE, BLOWN, PYREX, STAINED, CRYSTAL

like .... VITRIC, VITREOUS

magnifying .... LOUPE

maker .... GLAZIER

making material .... SAND, FRIT(T), POTASH, SILICA, ZAFFER, SILICON

making rod .... PONTIL

molten .... PARISON

mosaic(work) .... SMALTO, TESSERA

piece .... PANE, SLIVER

roof .... BULL'S-EYE

scraps .... CULLET

toast-drinking .... RUMMER

tube, graduated .... BURET

vessel .... JUG, VASE, VIAL

vial .... AMP(O)ULE

waste .... CULLET

window/unit .... PANE

glasses .... SPECS, GOGGLES

glassware articles .... VITRICS

cooking .... PYREX

glassy .... CLEAR, SHINY, SMOOTH, VITRIC, BRITTLE, FRAGILE, HYALINE, HYALOID, VITREOUS, POLISHED, CRYSTALLINE, TRANSPARENT

body .... TEKTITE

Glaswegian .... SCOT

glaze .... FILM, GLOSS, ENAMEL, COAT(ING), POLISH, VENEER

crack .... CRAZE

glazier .... PUTTIER

burden of .... PANE

glazing machine .... CALENDER

material .... CLAY, KAOLIN

gleam .... RAY, BEAM, GLOW, FLASH, GLINT, LUSTER, GLIMMER, GLISTEN

glean .... REAP, GATHER, COLLECT

glebe .... CLOD, LUMP, TURF, EARTH, FIELD

glede .... KITE

glee .... JOY, MIRTH, GAIETY, ELATION, MERRIMENT

gleed .... COAL, EMBER

Gleek .... TIB

gleeman .... MINSTREL

gleet .... OOZE

glen .... DALE, DELL, VALE, DINGLE, VALLEY

Glengaries .... CAPS, TAMS

Glengary man .... SCOT

Glenn .... FORD, MILLER

glib .... OILY, FACILE, FLUENT, SUAVE, SMOOTH, VOLUBLE

glide .... FLOW, SCUD, SKIP, SKIM, SLIP, COAST, FLOAT, SLIDE, SASHAY

gliding across .... LABILE

step .... GLISSADE

glim .... LAMP, LIGHT, CANDLE

glimmer .... VIEW, BLINK, GLEAM, SHINE, SIGHT, FLICKER

glimpse .... FLASH, GLINT, (SIDE)GLANCE

glint ...... FLASH, GLEAM, GLIMPSE

glioma .... TUMOR

glissade .... GLIDE, SLIDE

glisten ...... FLASH, GLEAM, SHINE, GLITTER, SPARKLE,

glitter .... FLASH, GLINT, GLISTEN, SPANGLE, SPARKLE, BRILLIANCE, CORUSCATE

glittering .... RUTILANT

glittery .... STARRY

gloaming .... DUSK, TWILIGHT

gloat .... BOAST, REVEL, CROW OVER

global .... ROUND, SPHERAL, SPHERICAL, WORLD-WIDE

globe .... ORB, BALL, CLEW, EARTH, SPHERE

thistle .... ARTICHOKE

globe-trotter .... TOURIST, (WORLD)TRAVELER

globefish .... PUFFER

globule .... BEAD, BLOB, DROP(LET)

glockenspiel, instrument like a .... MARIMBA

gloom ...... MURK, BLUES, DUMPS, DIMNESS, SADNESS, DARKNESS

gloomy .... SAD, BLUE, DARK, DOUR, GLUM, MOODY, MURKY, DISMAL, DREAR(Y), MORBID, MOROSE

glop .... GOO, SLIME

gloria .... HALO, HYMN, PAEAN

glorified ...... SAINTLY, REDEEMED

glorify ...... BLESS, EXALT, EXTOL, HONOR, PRAISE, REVERE

gloriole .... HALO

glorious .... GRAND, DIVINE, SUPERB, SPLENDID

glory .... FAME, ECLAT, EXULT, KUDOS, RENOWN, DIGNITY, REJOICE, RADIANCE, SPLENDOR

cloud of .... NIMBUS

head's .... HAIR, HALO, CROWN, TIARA, CORONA, AUREOLE

gloss .... SHEEN, SHINE, LUSTER, POLISH, VENEER, ANNOTATE

over .... FUDGE, WHITEWASH

glossary .... CLAVIS, LEXICON

glossing machine ...... CALENDER

glossolalia .... HYPNOSIS, HYSTERIA

glossy ...... SLEEK, SLICK, SHINING, LUSTROUS, SPECIOUS

fabric ..... SILK, SATIN, SATEEN

poster .... LACQUERED PLACARD

glove .... CUFF, MITT(EN), CESTUS, GA(U)NTLET

kind of .... KID, BOXING, BASEBALL

leather .... KID, MOCHA, SUEDE

glove, _____ (closely associated) .... WERE HAND AND

glow .... FLASH, FLUSH, GLEAM, WARMTH, RADIATE, RADIANCE

glower .... FROWN, GLARE, SCOWL, STARE, GRIMACE

glowerer .... BEETLEBROW

glowing .... ASHINE, CANDENT, FLUSHED, LAMBENT, LUMINOUS

coal .... EMBER

review .... RAVE

glowworm .... FIREFLY

Gluck, composer ...... CHRISTOPH

opera .... ARMIDA

soprano .... ALMA

glucose .... RUTIN, SUGAR

glucoside .... RUTIN, INDICAN, SAPONIN, SINALBIN

glue .... GOO, GUM, PASTE, CEMENT, GELATIN, MUCILAGE

gluey .... PASTY, STICKY

glum ...... SOUR, SULKY, MOROSE, GLOOMY, SULLEN, LONG-FACED

glume .... HUSK, BRACT

glut ...... FILL, CLOY, CRAM, SATE, PACK, GORGE, STUFF, SATIATE, SURFEIT

gluten .... LOAF, BREAD, FIBRIN

glutenous material .... FLOUR

glutinous .... ROPY, GLUEY, STICKY, VISCID

glutton .... HOG, PIG, EPICURE, GO(U)RMAND, CORMORANT

gluttonous ...... GREEDY, HUNGRY, PIGGISH, SWINISH, VORACIOUS

gluttony .... GREED, EDACITY, VORACITY, OVEREATING

glyceride .... ESTER

Glyn, author .... ELINOR

glyph .... CARVING

gnarl .... KNOT, KNUR, SNAG, TWIST, CONTORT

gnarled .... WIRY, ROUGH, KNOTTY, RUGGED

gnash .... BITE, GRATE, GRIND

gnat .... PEST, MIDGE, STINGER, MOSQUITO

gnaw ...... EAT, BITE, CHEW, FRET, CRUNCH, HARASS, NIBBLE, RANKLE, TORMENT

gnawed, appear .... EROSE

gneiss .... FELDSPAR

gnome .... ELF, NIS, BOGIE, DWARF, MAXIM, GOBLIN, KOBOLD, BROWNIE, GREMLIN

gnomon of sundial .... PIN, STYLE

Gnostic sect member .... MANDEAN

GNP, part of .... GROSS, PRODUCT, NATIONAL

gnu .... ANTELOPE, WILDEBEST

go ...... DIE, MOVE, WEND, LEAVE, DEPART, RETIRE, OPERATE, PROCEED

aboard ..... EMBARK, ENPLANE, ENTRAIN

ahead ..... PROCEED, CONTINUE

along ..... AGREE, ACCOMPANY, FOLLOW, COOPERATE, SWIM WITH THE STREAM

around .... SKIRT, DETOUR, CIRCULATE, CIRCUMVENT

astray/wrong .... ERR, SIN, DEVIATE, ABERRATE, MISCARRY

at high speed .... BARREL

away! ..... SCAT, SHOO, SCRAM, GET LOST

back .... RECEDE, RETURN, REVERT, RETREAT

back and forth .... SHUTTLE

back over .... RETRACE

before .... PRECEDE

between .... AGENT, MEDIATOR, MIDDLEMAN

by .... ELAPSE

down ...... FALL, SINK, LOWER, DESCEND

far and wide .... RANGE

first .... LEAD

for .... SUPPORT

for broke .... STRETCH ONE'S LUCK

forth .... SALLY

forward .... ADVANCE

in haste .... SCURRY

left .... PORT

off .... EXPLODE, DETONATE

off course .... VEER, STRAY

on hands and knees .... CREEP

over .... EXCEED, SURPASS

over the wall .... ESCAPE, BREAK JAIL

surfing .... HANG TEN

swiftly: sl. .... SCOOT

tenting .... CAMP OUT

the distance .... FINISH

to _____ (do penance) .... CANOSSA

to bed .... HIT THE HAY, HIT THE SACK

to seed .... DETERIORATE

up .... RISE, CLIMB, ASCEND

goa .... GAZELLE

Goa .... COLONY

capital of .... PANJIM

language .... KONKANI

powder .... ARAROBA

goad .... EGG, GAD, PROD, SPUR,

URGE, ANKUS, PRICK, STICK,
STING, INCITE, NEEDLE
go-ahead .... APPROVAL
goal .... AIM, END, POST, THULE,
INTENT, MOTIVE, OBJECT,
TARGET
falls short of .... MANQUE
goat .... GORAL, ANGORA, BEZOAR,
PASANG
antelope .... GORAL, SEROW
castrated male .... WETHER
constellation .... CAPRICORN
deity .... PAN, FAUN
female .... DOE, CAPRA,
NANNY
genus .... CAPRIA
get one's .... IRK, RILE,
ANNOY, IRRITATE
hair of .... MOHAIR
hair cloth .... ABA, CAMLET
horn .... CORNUCOPIA
leap .... CAPRIOLE
leather .... KID, MOCHA
like .... CAPRINE, HIRCINE
male .... BUCK
pertaining to .... CAPRIC
sucker .... POTOO
under one year old .... KID
wild .... TUR, IBEX, KRAS,
TAIR, TEHR, THAR
wool .... CASHMERE
goatee .... BEARD, VANDYKE,
IMPERIAL
goatfish .... MULLET
goatish .... CAPRINE, HIRCINE
goatman .... FAUN
goatsucker .... POTOO,
NIGHTHAWK
gob .... TAR, LUMP, MASS, SAILOR,
SEAMAN
gobbet .... BIT, LUMP, MASS,
CHUNK, FRAGMENT
gobble .... EAT, SEIZE
gobbledygook .... TALK
gobbler .... TOM, TURKEY
Gobbo .... LAUNCELOT
Gobi .... LAKE, SHAMO, DESERT
gobioid fish .... LOTER
goblet .... TASS, BOCAL, GLASS,
HANAP, CHALICE
drinking .... MAZER, MAZARD
Eucharist .... CHALICE
goblin ...... ELF, HOB, PUCA, PUCK,
POOK, BOGIE, GNOME,
NIS(SE), OUPHE, KOBOLD,
BROWNIE
doglike .... BARHEST
goby .... FISH, MAPO
go-cart .... PRAM, STROLLER
god .... SIVA, DEITY, BRAHMA
agriculture .... NEBO, THOR,

FAUNUS, SATURN
air .... SHU
alcoholic drinks .... SIRIS
appearance of ..... THEOPHANY
Arcadian .... PAN
avarice .... MAMMON
baboon-faced .... THOTH
beauty .... APOLLO
belief in (many)
.... (PAN)THEISM
combining form .... THEO
commerce .... HERMES,
MERCURY
cosmos .... VARUNA
darkness .... SIN, SETH
day .... HOR, HORUS, JANUS
dead .... YAMA, ORCUS,
ANUBIS, OSIRIS
defender .... ANSEL
discord .... LOKE, LOKI
dog-headed .... THOTH
dreams .... MORPHEUS
earth .... BEL, GEB, DAGAN
elephant-headed ..... GANESHA
falcon-headed .... HORUS
false .... BAAL, IDOL,
MAMMON, MOLOCH
fearing .... PIOUS, DEVOUT
fertility .... FREY, OSIRIS
fields .... PAN, FAUN
fire .... AGNI, VULCAN
flocks .... PAN
force .... SHU, PTAH
half-man, half-fish ..... DAGON
harvest .... CRONUS
heaven .... ANU, BEL
herds .... PAN
horses .... POSEIDON
household .... LARES
jackal-headed .... ANUBIS,
WAPUET
justice .... RAMMAN
killer .... DEICIDE
lightning .... AGNI, JUPITER
like .... DEIFIC
love .... AMOR, EROS, KAMA,
CUPID, POTHOS
lower world .... DIS, HADES,
PLUTO, SERAPIS
marriage .... HYMEN
mirth .... COMUS
mischief .... LOKI
moon .... NANNAR
mountains .... ATLAS,
OLYMPUS
music .... BES, APOLLO
offering to .... CORBAN
one-eyed .... ODIN
peace .... FREY, BALDER
pleasure .... BES(A)
praise to .... HOSANNA

prosperity .... FREY
rain .... INDRA, JUPITER
revelry .... COMUS, KOMOS,
BACCHUS
river .... ALPHEUS
sea .... AEGER, DYLAN,
NEREUS, PONTUS, TRITON,
NEPTUNE, POSEIDON
seven-armed .... AGNI
shepherds .... PALES
sky .... ANU, NUT, TYR,
JUPITER
sleep .... HYPNOS, SOMNUS,
MORPHEUS
study of .... THEOLOGY
sun .... RA, SOL, BELI, FREY,
HORUS, NINIB, AMEN-RA,
APOLLO, HELIOS, MITHRAS,
PHOEBUS, SHAMASH
thunder .... THOR, ZEUS,
DONAR, JUPITER
trumpeter of the sea
.... TRITON
two-faced .... AGNI, JANUS
underworld .... DIS, ORCUS,
PLUTO
Vedic .... INDRA
vegetation .... ESUS, ATTIS
victory .... ODIN, ZEUS
war .... ARES, COEL, IR(R)A,
MARS, ODIN, THOR, TYR(R),
AS(S)UR, WODEN
waters .... NEA, FONTUS
winds .... ADDA, EURUS,
AEOLUS, BOREAS
wing-shod .... HERMES,
MERCURY
wisdom .... EA, NEBO, ODIN,
SABU, GANESA
woods .... PAN, SILEN,
SILVANUS
youth .... APOLLO
God .... CREATOR, JEHOVA,
ALMIGHTY
belief in one ..... MONOTHEISM
Bless America composer
.... BERLIN
Godden .... RUMER
goddess .... DEA, DEVI, SHRI,
BEAUTY, LACHESIS
agriculture .... OPS, ISIS,
CERES, DEMETER
air .... HERA
arts and sciences .... CLIO,
MUSE, ERATO, ATHENA,
THALIA, URANIA, EUTERPE,
CALLIOPE, MELPOMENE
astronomy .... URANIA
avenging .... FURY, NEMESIS
beauty .... FREYA, VENUS
birth .... PARCA

cat-headed .... PACHT
chase .... DIAN(A), ARTEMIS
childbirth .... UPIS, LUCINA
comedy .... THALIA
crops .... ANNONA
dawn .... EOS, US(H)AS,
AURORA
death .... DANU, HEL(A)
destiny ...... URD, NORN, URTH,
MOIRA
destruction .... ARA, KALI
discord .... ATE, ERIS
doom .... URTH, WYRD
earth .... GE, LUA, OPS, SEB,
ERDA, GAEA, GAIA, TARI,
ARURU, CERES, TERRA,
ISHTAR, SEMELE, TELLUS,
DEMETER
faith .... FIDES
fate .... NONA, NORN, PARCA
fertility .... ISIS, FAUNA,
ANNONA, ISHTAR, ASTARTE,
ASHTORETH
fields .... FAUNA, TELLUS
fire .... PELE, VESTA, HESTIA
flowers .... FLORA, NANNA,
CHLORIS
fortune .... TYCHE
fountains .... FERONIA
fruits .... POMONA
ghosts .... HECATE
giant .... NORN, URTH
grains .... CERES
harvest .... OPS, CARPO
healing .... EIR, GULA
health .... SALUS, HESTIA,
HYGEIA
heaven .... NUT
history .... CLIO, SAGA
hope .... SPES
horses .... EPONA
hunting ..... DIAN(A), VACUNA,
ARTEMIS
justice .... MAAT, THEMIS,
ASTRAEA
life .... ISIS, LACHESIS
light .... LUCINA
love .... FREYA, VENUS,
HATHOR, SELENE, ARTEMIS,
IS(H)TAR, ASTARTE,
APHRODITE, ASHTORETH
marriage ..... GE, GAEA, HERA,
JUNO
mischief .... ATE, ERIS
moon .... LUNA, DIANA,
HECATE, LUCINA, PHOEBE,
SELENE, ARTEMIS, CYNTHIA
music .... EUTERPE
nature .... CYBELE, ARTEMIS
night .... NOX, NYX, LETO
order .... HARMONIA

Pagan .... ASTARTE
peace .... EIR, PAX, IRENE,
MINERVA
plenty .... OPS
poetry .... ERATO, CALLIOPE
prosperity .... SALUS
rainbow .... IRIS
retribution .... ARA, ATE
revenge .... NEMESIS
seas .... INO, DORIS, SALACIA
seasons .... HORA, HOUR
six-armed, three-headed
.... HECATE
sky .... NUT, FRIGG
splendor .... UMA
spring .... IDUN, VENUS
strife .... ERIS
trees .... POMONA
underworld .... HEL, GAEA,
HECATE, LARUNA
vegetation .... CORA, KORE,
CERES, FLORA
vengeance .... NEMESIS
victory .... NIKE
virtue .... FIDES
volcano .... PELE
war .... ALEA, ENYO, ANATU,
ATHENA, ISHTAR, VACUNA,
BELLONA, MINERVA
waters .... ERUA
weeping .... NIOBE
welfare .... SALUS
wisdom ...... ATHENA, PALLAS,
MINERVA
womanhood .... JUNO, SATI
woods .... DIAN(A), ARTEMIS
youth .... HEBE, IDUN
goddesses of beauty/charm
.... GRACES
of destiny .... FATES
of fate .... NORNS, MOERAE
of nature .... HORAE
godfather .... SPONSOR
godforsaken .... WICKED,
FORLORN, DESOLATE
godhead .... DIVINITY
godless .... PAGAN, WICKED,
IMPIOUS, ATHEISTIC
godlike .... HOLY, DIVINE
godliness .... PIETY
godly .... PIOUS, DEVOUT
person .... SAINT
godmother .... CUMMER
godparent .... SPONSOR
godown .... WAREHOUSE
gods' abode .... MERU, ASGARD
blood .... ICHOR
cupbearer .... HEBE,
GANYMEDE
drink .... NECTAR
king of .... WODEN

messenger .... IRIS, HERMES,
MERCURY
queen of .... HERA, JUNO, SATI
race of .... VANIR
strife among ...... THEOMACHY
God's acre .... CEMETERY
chosen .... ISRAELITE(S)
godsend .... MANNA
Godwin Austen, Mount
.... DAPSANG
godwit .... SNIPE
Goebbels's (Joseph) forte
.... BIG LIE
Goethe or Bach .... JOHANN
Goethe's hero .... FAUST,
WERTHER
heroine .... MIGNON
Gog and ____ .... MAGOG
go-getter .... DOER, TIGER,
HUSTLER, ACHIEVER
goggler .... SCAD, CICHARRA
goggles .... SPECTACLES
Gogol hero .... (TARAS)BULBA
Goidelic language .... ERSE,
MANX
going .... MOVING, LEAVING,
EXPIRING, FLOWING,
OPERATING
balmy .... LOSING ONE'S
MARBLES
get .... BEGIN, START, GET
BUSY
on ..... HAPPENING, OCCURRING
on now ..... LIVE, IN PROGRESS
out .... EXIT, EXODUS,
EGRESS(ION)
strong .... BOOMING
goings-on .... ACTIONS, CONDUCT,
ACTIVITY
goiter .... STRUMA
Golconda .... MINE
gold .... ORO, CYME, GILT,
AU(RUM), RICHES, WEALTH
alchemist's .... SOL
alloy .... ASEM
bar .... INGOT
black .... OIL
braid .... ORRIS
cloth .... LAME
coat with .... GILD
coating .... GILT
coin .... LIRA, ANGEL, DARIC,
DUCAT, EAGLE, KRONE, LOUIS,
MOHUR, OBANG, TOMAN,
SCUDO, GUINEA, PISTOLE,
DOUBLOON, IMPERIAL
content .... CARAT, KARAT
deposit .... PLACER
district, African .... RAND
fineness .... CARAT, KARAT
imitation .... OROIDE, ORMOLU,

PINCHBECK
lace .... ORRIS, FILIGREE
land .... OPHIR
leaf .... FOIL
leaf, imitation .... ORMOLU
like .... AUREATE
like alloy .... ASEM, OROIDE,
ORMOLU
lump .... NUGGET
medalist Biondi .... MATT
medalist, swimming ..... SPITZ
miner .... PANHANDLER
miner, 1849 ...... FORTY-NINER
miners' camp: sl.
.... DIGGINGS
mines region .... KLONDIKE
mosaic .... ORMOLU
native .... NUGGET
pertaining to .... AURIC
rush man .... ARGONAUT
rush site .... YUKON
seeker/searcher .... MINER,
ARGONAUT, PROSPECTOR
separate gravel from ...... PAN
sheet .... FOIL, LATTEN
sometimes .... LEAF
symbol .... AU
Gold Bug author .... POE
Coast .... GHANA
Coast river .... VOLTA
Coast tribe .... AKAN
goldbrick .... LOAF, SHIRK,
MALINGER
gold-digger .... VAMP, FLIRT,
MINER, STRUMPET
"mine of" ...... SUGAR DADDY
target of .... HEIR
golden .... AURIC, GILDED,
YELLOW, AUREATE, PRECIOUS
apples, guardian of ...... IDUN,
ITHUN, HESPERID
ball, king's .... MOUND
color .... DORE
combining form ..... CHRYS(O)
king .... MIDAS
shiner .... DACE, ROACH
token .... WEDDING RING
Golden Age .... MILLENIUM
Boy author .... ODETS
Fleece keeper .... AEETES
Fleece maiden .... HELLE
Fleece searcher .... JASON,
ARGONAUT
Fleece ship .... ARGO
Treasury item ..... ODE, POEM,
SONNET
goldeneye .... BIRD, WHISTLER
goldenrod .... SOLIDAGO
goldfinger, mythological
.... MIDAS
Goldfinger hero .... BOND

goldfinch .... BIRD, REDCAP
goldfinny .... CUNNER
goldfish .... COMET, FANTAIL
Goldie .... HAWN
goldilocks .... BUTTERCUP
Goldsmith, poet .... OLIVER
golem .... ROBOT, AUTOMATON
golf aid .... CADDY, CADDIE
area around the hole
.... GREEN
area for an astronaut
.... MOON
bag item .... TEE, CLUB,
WOOD, IRONS, WEDGE,
PUTTER, CRYING TOWEL
ball material .... BALATA
ball's position .... LIE
"Bantam Ben" of .... BEN
HOGAN
championship cup ...... RYDER
club ..... WOOD, CLEEK, IRONS,
SPOON, BULGER, DRIVER,
JIGGER, MASHIE, PUTTER,
BRASSIE, NIBLICK, (MID)IRON
club part .... TOE, HOSEL
course .... GREEN, LINKS
course hazard .... POND,
WATER, BUNKER, STYMIE,
(SAND)TRAP
eagled a par-three hole in
.... ACED
feat ...... EAGLE, BIRDIE, HOLE-
IN-ONE
first to earn $100,000 in
.... ARNOLD PALMER
goof .... SLICE
hole .... CUP
holes unplayed .... BYE
instructor .... PRO
"Merry Mex" of .... LEE
TREVINO
partner, legendary ...... BOGEY
player Aaron .... TOMMY
Albus .... JIM
Alfredsson .... HELEN
Andrade .... BILLY
Andrews .... DONNA
Aoki .... ISAO
Archer .... GEORGE
Azinger .... PAUL
Baker-Finch .... IAN
Ballesteros .... SEVE
Beck .... CHIP
Bowen .... NANCY
Bradley .... PAT
Brooks .... MARK
Burton .... BRANDIE
Calcavecchia .... MARK
Casper .... BILLY
Charles .... BOB
Clements .... LENNIE

Coe-Jones .... DAWN
Colbert .... JIM
Cook .... JOHN
Couples .... FRED
Crenshaw .... BEN
Crosby .... ELAINE
Daly .... JOHN
Daniel .... BETH
Davies .... LAURA
Dent .... JIM
Descampe .... FLORENCE
Devlin .... BRUCE
Dickinson .... JUDY
Dormann .... DANA
Douglass .... DALE
Duval .... DAVID
Eichelberger .... DAVE
Elkington .... STEVE
Els .... ERNIE
Estes .... BOB
Faldo .... NICK
Faxon .... BRAD
Floyd .... RAY(MOND)
Frost .... DAVID
Funk .... FRED
Gallagher, Jr. .... JIM
Gamez .... ROBERT
Geddes .... JANE
Geiberger .... AL
Gilbert .... LARRY
Green .... TAMMIE
Hill .... MIKE
Hogan .... BEN
Irwin .... HALE
Jacklin .... TONY
Jacobsen .... PETER
Janzen .... LEE
Johnson .... CHRIS, TRISH
Jones .... BOB, ROBERT
Kean .... LAUREL
King .... BETSY
Kite .... TOM
Kobayashi .... HIROMI
Langer .... BERNHARD
Lehman .... TOM
Levi .... WAYNE
Lietzke .... BRUCE
Littler .... GENE
Lopez .... NANCY
Love III .... DAVIS
Maggert .... JEFF
Mallon .... MEG
McGann .... MICHELLE
Merten .... LAURI
Mickelson .... PHIL
Miller .... JOHNNY
Mize .... LARRY
Mochrie .... DOTTIE
Montgomerie .... COLIN
Murphy .... BOB
Nelson .... LARRY

Neumann .... LISELOTTE
Nicklaus .... JACK
Norman .... GREG
Olazabal .... JOSE MARIA
O'Meara .... MARK
Ozaki .... MASASHI
Palmer .... ARNIE, ARNOLD
Pate .... JERRY
Pavin .... COREY
Peete .... CALVIN
Perry .... KENNY
Player .... GARY
Price .... NICK
Ritzman .... ALICE
Robbins .... KELLY
Roberts .... LOREN
Rodriguez .... CHI-CHI
Sanders .... DOUG
Sauers .... GENE
Sheehan .... PATTY
Sigel .... JAY
Singh .... VIJAY
Skinner .... VAL
Snead .... SAM, JC
Stadler .... CRAIG
Steinhauer .... SHERRI
Stephenson .... JAN
Stewart .... PAYNE
Stockton .... DAVE
Strange .... CURTIS
Stricker .... STEVE
Sutton .... HAL
Thompson .... ROCKY
Trevino .... LEE
Venturi .... KEN
Wadkins .... LANNY
Waldorf .... DUFFY
Wargo .... TOM
Watson .... TOM
Woosnam .... IAN
Zarley .... KERMIT
Zembriski .... WALTER
Zoeller .... FUZZY
problem .... STYMIE
score ...... PAR, BOGEY, EAGLE,
    BIRDIE
stroke .... BAFF, CHIP, FADE,
    HOOK, LOFT, PUTT, DRIVE,
    SLICE, SCLAFF
stroke by a duffer .... BAFF
stroke over par .... BOGEY
term .... OB, LIE, TEE, PAR,
    BAFF, BONE, FADE, FORE,
    HOLE, HOOK, LOFT, PUTT,
    GALLERY, TRAP, BOGEY,
    DIVOT, FLAG, DRIVE, EAGLE,
    GREEN, STYMIE, ROUGH, SLICE,
    BIRDIE, BISQUE, DORMIE,
    HAZARD, DOGLEG, FAIRWAY,
    CHILI DIP
tourney ..... OPEN, SKINS, PRO-

AM, MASTERS, SENIORS
tourney played for honor
.... RYDER CUP
turf .... DIVOT
VIP .... PRO
Golf, "Golden Bear" of
.... NICKLAUS
"Great White Shark" of
.... NORMAN
"King" of .... PALMER
Masters champion .... BEN
    HOGAN, SAM SNEAD, TOM
    WATSON, GARY PLAYER, LEE
    TREVINO, TOMMY AARON,
    GENE SARAZEN, ARNOLD
    PALMER, CHARLES COODY,
    JACK NICKLAUS
golfer .... HAAS, KITE, TEER,
    AARON, COODY, FALDO,
    FLOYD, GREEN, HAGEN,
    HOGAN, IRWIN, DALY, JONES,
    MOODY, PAVIN, SNEAD,
    CASPER, LANGER, MILLER,
    NELSON, NORMAN, OMEARA,
    OUIMET, PALMER, PLAYER,
    PRUITT, SUTTON, WATSON,
    AZINGER, COUPLES, JACKLIN,
    LITTLER, MANGRUM,
    SANDERS, SARAZEN, STEWART,
    STRANGE, TREVINO, WADKINS,
    WOOSNAM, ZOELLER,
    CRENSHAW, NICKLAUS,
    CRAMPTON, OLAZABAL,
    RODRIGUEZ, BALLESTEROS,
    CALCAVECCHIA, GEIBERGER,
    DIVOT DIGGER
adviser of, sometimes
.... CADDIE
attire of .... KNICKERS
cry of .... FORE
goal of .... CUP
poor .... DUBBER, HACKER
golfer's org. .... PGA, USGA
golfing glory .... EAGLES
Golgotha .... CALVARY
goliard .... JESTER, MINSTREL
Goliath .... GIANT, PHILISTINE
home of .... GATH
move of .... GIANT STEP
slayer of .... DAVID
golliwogg .... DOLL, OGRE
Golly! .... GEE, GOSH
Gomer's husband .... HOSEA
gomuti .... EJOO, PALM, SAGO
palm .... ARENG(A)
gonad .... OVARY, SPERMARY
gonagra .... GOUT
gondola .... BARGE, CABIN,
    (CANAL)BOAT
man .... POLER, BOATMAN
race .... REGATTA

gondolier .... BOATMAN
song of .... BARCAROLE
work of .... POLING, ROWING
gone .... UP, AGO, OFF, OUT,
    AWAY, DEAD, LOST, USED,
    RUINED, CONSUMED
by .... PAST, PASSED
Gone with the Wind character
.... ASHLEY, MELANIE,
    (RHETT)BUTLER,
    (SCARLETT)O'HARA
goner .... DEAD DUCK
Goneril's father .... LEAR
sister .... REGAN, CORDELIA
gonfalon .... FLAG, BANNER,
    ENSIGN
gong .... BELL, CYMBAL, TAMTAM,
    TOCSIN
gonof/gonoph .... THIEF
gonorrhea .... CLAP
goo .... GLUE, SLUDGE
goober .... PEANUT
grease .... PEANUT BUTTER
good .... BON, MORAL, PUCKA,
    SOUND, VALID, USEFUL,
    GENUINE, LAUDABLE,
    SUITABLE, EFFICIENT,
    UNSPOILED
doing .... BENEFICENT
-for-nothing fellow .... BUM,
    IDLER, ROGUE, LOAFER,
    WASTREL, VAGABOND, NE'ER-
    DO-WELL
health .... PEART
humored .... JOLLY
looking .... FAIR, COMELY,
    PRETTY, HANDSOME
luck bringer .... MASCOT
luck present .... HANDSEL
man .... MODEL, PARAGON
natured .... AMIABLE,
    PLEASANT, EASYGOING
news .... GOSPEL, EVANGEL
order .... EUTAXY
point! .... TOUCHE
references .... CLEAN SLATES
sense .... WIT, JUDGMENT
slang .... SWELL
taste, of .... ESTHETIC
time .... BALL, BASH, SPREE
turn .... FAVOR
will .... GREE
Good Book .... BIBLE
Friday song of Andalusia
.... SAETA
Shepherd .... JESUS
goodbye .... TATA, ADIEU, AU
    REVOIR, SO LONG, FAREWELL
Goodbye, Columbus author
.... ROTH
goodly .... AMPLE, SIZABLE,

PLEASING, SPLENDID
goodman ...... MASTER, HUSBAND
goodness .... MERIT, WORTH,
VIRTUE, BLESSING, KINDNESS
gracious! .... HEAVENS
goods .... STOCK, WARES, EFFECTS,
MERCHANDISE
cast overboard .... LAGAN,
LIGAN, JETSAM, LAGEND,
JETTISON
deliver the ...... FULFILL, COME
ACROSS
movable .... CHATTEL
on hand .... STOCK,
INVENTORY
sold together .... TIE-IN
goody .... CANDY
gooey .... STICKY
goof .... DOLT, FAIL, BONER,
ERR(OR), BOBBLE, BLUNDER
on diamond .... MUFF, FUMBLE
goofy .... GIDDY, SILLY, STUPID,
FOOLISH
Google .... BARNEY
gook .... ORIENTAL, VIETCONG
goon .... THUG, RUFFIAN,
HOOD(LUM), ROUGHNECK
goop's inventor .... BURGESS
goosander .... DUCK, MERGANSER
goose .... BRANT, IDIOT, SOLAN,
GRAYLAG, BARNACLE,
BERNICLE
colloquial .... DUPE, GULL
cry .... HONK, CACKLE
domestic, large .... EMDEN
eggs .... 000, ZERO(S)
foot membrane ..... WEB(BING)
footless .... GANNET
genus .... ANSER
grease .... AXUNGE
male .... GANDER
of a .... ANSERINE
pygmy .... GOSLET
sound .... HISS, CACKLE
stepper .... GERMAN
steppers march, how
.... STIFFLY
young .... GOSLING
gooseberry .... POHA, FABES
goosefoot .... BEET, SPINACH
gooseneck .... LAMP
goose-pimply .... EERIE
gopher .... RODENT, SUSLIK,
TORTOISE
tortoise .... MUNGOFA
Gopher .... MINNESOTAN
State .... MINNESOTA
gorcock .... GROUSE
Gordian knot cutter
.... ALEXANDER
Gordon .... RUTH, FLASH

Gordon's killer .... MAHDI
gore .... STAB, BLOOD, CRUOR,
INSET, GUSSET, PIERCE
gorge .... CLOY, CLUT, GULP,
PASS, SATE, CHASM, FLUME,
GULLY, KLOOF, STUFF,
CANYON, CLOUGH, GULLET,
RAVINE, COULOIR, BARRANCA,
GORMANDIZE
gorgeous .... SUPERB, SPLENDID,
BEAUTIFUL, RESPLENDENT
Gorgeous Gussie .... MORAN
gorget .... COLLAR
Gorgon .... MEDUSA, STHENO,
EURYALE, JEZEBEL
Gorgons' mother .... CETO
watchers .... GRAEAE
gorilla .... APE, TROGLODYTE
slang .... GOON, GANGSTER
walk .... SHAMBLE
Gorki, novelist .... MAXIM
gormandize ...... GORGE, GUTTLE
gormandizer .... FEASTER
gorse .... WHIN, FURZE, SHRUB
gory .... BLOODY
Gosh! .... GEE, GOLLY, PSHAW
goshawk .... BUTEO
Goshen race .... TROT
gospel .... DOGMA, TRUTH,
EVANGEL, DOCTRINE,
EVANGILE
preaching .... EVANGELISM
writer ...... JOHN, LUKE, MARK,
MATTHEW
gossamer ...... FILM(Y), (COB)WEB
gossamery .... THIN, FILMY,
GAUZY, DIAPHANOUS
gossip .... CAT, EME, BUZZ, TALK,
RUMORS, TIDBIT, TITBIT,
BLAB(BER), HEARSAY,
CHITCHAT, BUSYBODY,
CHATTER(ER), TATTLE(R),
SCUTTLEBUTT
bit of .... ONDIT
column unit .... ITEM
malicious .... SLANDER,
BACKBITING
slang .... JAW
gossoon .... BOY
Gotcha! .... AHA, OHO
Goth .... ALARIC, BARBARIAN
Gothic .... BARBAROUS
arch .... OGIVE
architecture feature ..... GABLE
bard .... RUNER
Goths' bishop .... ULFILA(S)
Gotland seaport .... VISBY
Gouda .... CHEESE
gouge .... BENT, ROUT, CHEAT,
CHISEL, GROOVE, (DE)FRAUD,
IMPOSTOR, SWINDLE(R)

goulash .... HASH, STEW, RAGOUT
Gounod opera .... FAUST
opera hero .... ROMEO
gourd ...... PEPO, MELON, SQUASH,
PUMPKIN, CALABASH,
CURCURBIT
pod's substance .... LOOFAH
rattle .... MARACA
shell .... CALABASH
gourmand .... EPICURE, GLUTTON,
GOURMET
anathema to a .... DIET
gourmet .... TASTER, EPICURE,
GO(U)RMAND, GASTRONOME
paradise in London ...... SOHO
gout .... GONAGRA, PODAGRA,
BURSITIS, ARTHRITIS
remedy .... GUACO
govern .... RUN, RULE, REIGN,
GUIDE, DIRECT, MANAGE,
CONTROL, PRESIDE,
MODERATE
archaic .... REGLE
badly .... MISRULE
governess .... NANNY, DUENNA
government .... RULE, STATE,
POLITY, ECONOMY, REGENCY,
REGIME(N), ADMINISTRATION
agent .... SPY
declaration .... MANIFESTO
fiscal problem .... BUDGET
grant ...... SUBSIDY, FRANCHISE
of a .... NATIONAL
of 2 rulers .... DIARCHY
report .... BLUE BOOK, WHITE
PAPER
safety net .... WELFARE
seat .... CAPITAL
without .... ACRACY
governor .... RULER, EPARCH,
VICEROY, REGULATOR
gowan .... DAISY
gown .... ROBE, DRESS, FROCK,
SMOCK, MANTUA, NEGLIGEE
loose, worn in Middle Ages
.... KIRTLE
outer .... SURCOAT
goy .... GENTILE
Gozo's neighbor .... MALTA
GP .... DR., DOCTOR
org. of .... AMA
Graafian follicle .... OVISAC
grab .... HOG, TAKE, ANNEX,
SEIZE, SNATCH, CAPTURE
Gracchus' brother .... GAIUS
grace ...... TACT, ADORN, CHARM,
FAVOR, MERCY, BEAUTY,
ATTEND, PRAYER, DECENCY,
DIGNIFY, CHARISMA,
COURTESY
kind of ..... RESPITE, REPRIEVE,

MORATORIUM
note .... INCIDENTAL
Grace .... KELLY
graceful .... SVELTE, LISSOME,
WILLOWY
bird .... SWAN
creature .... DEER, GAZELLE
piercing wit .... ATTIC SALT
graceless .... CLUMSY, AWKWARD,
INELEGANT
Graces, mother of .... AEGLE
one of the .... JOY, AGLAIA,
THALIA, EUPHROSYNE
gracile .... SLIM, SLENDER
gracious .... BENIGN, GENIAL,
POLITE, URBANE, MERCIFUL
grackle .... DAW, MINA, MYNA(H),
TINKLING, TROUPIAL,
BLACKBIRD
grad .... ALUM
gradate .... BLEND
gradation .... ABLAUT, DEGREE,
NUANCE
grade .... MARK, RANK, RATE,
STEP, LEVEL, DEGREE,
RATING, INCLINE
grader .... PUPIL
gradient .... SLOPE
gradin .... SEAT, STEP, SHELF
gradual .... MODERATE,
LEISURELY, PROGRESSIVE
fall .... DECLINE
reducer .... TAPERER
graduate .... GRAD, PASS,
ALUMNUS
graduated .... SCALAR
glass tube .... BURETTE
graduation ceremony
.... COMMENCEMENT
certificate .... DIPLOMA
dangler .... TASSEL
duo .... CAP AND GOWN
wear .... CLASS RING
Graeae, concern of the
.... GORGONS
describing the .... ONE-EYED
one of the .... DEINO
parent of .... PHORCUS
Graf .... COUNT
graffiti .... SCRAWLS
graft .... BUD, IMP, CLAVE,
(S)CION, INARCH,
CORRUPTION, CROSSBREED,
TRANSPLANT
Graham .... BILLY, MARTHA
grail .... AMA, CUP, CHALICE,
PLATTER
Grail, Holy .... SANGRAAL,
SANGREAL
grain .... BIT, OAT, RYE, CORN,
CURN, MEAL, RICE, SEED,

WALE, SPELT, WHEAT,
CEREAL, KERNEL, KERMES,
MILLET
basket .... SCUTTLE
beard .... AWN, ARISTA
beetle .... CADELLE
black .... URD
building .... GRANARY
chaff .... BRAN
combining form .... GRANI
cracked .... GROATS
cutter .... SCYTHE
disease .... SMUT, ERGOT
elevator .... SILO
exchange .... PIT
fungus .... ERGOT
ground .... SAMP, GRIST, GRITS
hulled .... GRITS, GROATS
husk .... BRAN, GLUME
in kernels .... CORN, MAIZE,
MEALIES
Indian .... CORN, MAIZE
loss through spillage
.... ULLAGE
measure .... MOY, SACK,
CAVAN, CHUPA, GANTA,
BUSHEL, QUARTER
mill .... MANO, QUERN
outer covering .... HUSK
pest .... CADELLE
refuse .... SCOURINGS
row, drying .... WINDROW
shelter .... HUTCH
small .... GRANULE
sorghum .... MILO, KAF(F)IR
stack .... MOW
storehouse .... SILO, GARNER,
GRANARY, ELEVATOR
stumps .... STUBBLE
grains .... SPEAR
3.17 .... CARAT
grainy .... MEALY, GRITTY,
GRANULAR
gram .... PLANT, CHICK-PEA
molecule .... MOL(E)
grama .... GRASS
gramercy .... THANKS
grammar ...... SYNTAX, WORDING,
ACCIDENCE, PHRASEOLOGY
causal connective .... FOR,
SINCE, THEREFORE
expert .... GRAMMARIAN
set of examples/exercises
.... PRAXIS
tense .... PAST, FUTURE,
PERFECT, PRESENT, PAST
PERFECT
grammarian .... PROSODIST
grammatical case .... DATIVE
construction .... SYNTAX,
SYNESIS

description/exercise ..... PARSE
divider .... PARAGRAPH
error .... SOLECISM
goof .... AINT
mark .... ASPER
term .... CASE, MODE, MOOD,
PARSE, STYLE, TENSE, GENDER,
DICTION, CONJUGATE,
PUNCTUATE
gramophone .... VICTROLA,
PHONOGRAPH
grampus .... ORC(A), WHALE,
COWFISH, SPRINGER
relative .... DOLPHIN
Granada, king of .... BOADBIL
granary .... BIN, CRIB, GOLA,
SILO, GARNER, GRANGE,
ELEVATOR, STOREHOUSE
grand ...... LARGE, LOFTY, PIANO,
AUGUST, STATELY, IMPOSING,
MAJESTIC, IMPRESSIVE
jury's word .... IGNORAMUS
mal .... FIT, EPILEPSY
slam .... VOLE, JACKPOT
theft .... LARCENY
Grand _____ .... OLE OPRY
Canal bridge .... RIALTO
Coulee designer .... SAVAGE
Lama .... DALAI LAMA
National site .... AINTREE
Old Party member
.... REPUBLICAN
Pre heroine .... EVANGELINE
grandam .... CRONE
grandchild .... OYE
Grande and others .... RIOS
or Bravo .... RIO
grandee .... PEER, NOBLEMAN
grandeur .... GLORY, DIGNITY,
MAJESTY, EMINENCE,
SPLENDOR
grandfather .... ATAVUS,
PATRIARCH
pertaining to .... AVAL,
AVITAL
grandiloquence .... BOMBAST
grandiloquent .... MAGNIFIC
grandiose .... EPIC, HOMERIC,
POMPOUS, IMPOSING,
BOMBASTIC
Grandma Moses .... ANNA
grandmother .... NANA, GRANNY,
BELDAM(E), GRANDMA
grandparents, having same
.... GERMAN
of/pertaining to .... AVAL
grandson .... NEPOTE
grandstand .... BLEACHERS
play .... STUNT
grange ...... RED, FARM, GRANARY
granger .... FARMER

granite .... ROCK, APLITE, BIOTITE, MUSCOVITE
rock resembling .... GNEISS
granny .... KNOT, GRANDMA
grant .... GIFT, GIVE, AWARD, YIELD, ASSENT, CONFER, PATENT, PERMIT, (CON)CEDE, CONSENT, (RE)MISE, APPANAGE
advance .... SECURE LOAN
by will .... DEMISE
of money .... SUBSIDY, ENDOWMENT
temporary use .... LEND
Grant, U.S. president
.... ULYSSES
granted .... EVEN SO
grantee .... RECIPIENT
Grantland .... RICE
grantor .... DONOR
granular .... SANDY, GRAINY
granulate .... CORN, COARSEN, ROUGHEN
grape .... UVA, BERRY, PINOT, TOKAY, ACINUS, MALAGA, MUSCAT, WAMPEE, CATAWBA, CONCORD, MALMSEY, NIAGARA, DELAWARE, ISABELLA, MALVASIA, MUSCADINE
acid from .... UVIC
coating .... BLOOM
disease .... ESCA, ERINOSE
dried .... PASA, RAISIN
fruit, dried .... CURRANT
jam .... UVATE
jelly .... SAPA
juice .... DIBS, MUST, SAPA, STUM
juice, unfermented .... STUM
juice deposit .... TARTAR
juice liquor .... RAKI, RAKEE
like .... UVA(L), UVIC
preserve .... UVATE
pulp .... RAPE, POMACE
refuse .... MARC, BAGASSE
seed .... ACINUS
sugar ...... GLUCOSE, MALTOSE, DEXTROSE
grapefruit ...... POMELO, PUMELO, SHADDOCK
grapes, art of growing
.... VITICULTURE
bunch .... BOB, BOTRYOID
harvester .... VINTAGER
where grown .... VINEYARD
Grapes of Wrath author
.... STEINBECK
character .... AL, JIM, JOAD, NOAH, OKIE, ROSE, CASEY, CONNIE

grapevine: colloq. ...... HEARSAY, PIPELINE, RUMOR(MILL)
graph .... CHART, DIAGRAM
graphic .... CLEAR, VIVID, LIFELIKE, PICTORIAL
art .... OFFSET, DRAWING, ETCHING, DRYPOINT, PAINTING, PHOTOGRAPHY
style .... ITALICS
graphite .... KISH, LEAD, CARBON, PLUMBAGO
graplin .... CRAMPON
grapnel .... DRAG, ANCHOR, CREEPER, GRAPLIN(E)
grapple .... GRIP, HOLD, LOCK, GRASP, CLUTCH, WRESTLE
grappler .... WRESTLER
grappling iron .... CRAMPON, GRAPLIN, GRAPNEL
grasp ...... SEE, GRAB, GRIP, HENT, HOLD, CLASP, SEIZE, CLUTCH, UNDERSTAND
grass .... OAT, POA, RIE, RYE, CORN, LAWN, NARD, REED, AVENA, BROME, GRAMA, GRAZE, SEDGE, SORGO, WHEAT, BAMBOO, BARLEY, DARNEL, FESCUE, QUITCH, REDTOP, FOXTAIL, PASTURE, VETIVER, ZACATON
Algerian .... ESPARTO
Asiatic .... MILLET
Australian .... ULLA
blade .... SPEAR
blue .... POA
brooms .... ZACATON
bunch .... TUFT
cereal .... OAT, RYE, RICE, RAG(G)I, MILLET, RAGGEE, SORGHUM
clump ...... HASSOCK, TUSSOCK
corn .... KAF(F)IR
country .... VELD(T)
covered soil ...... TURF, SWARD
cutter .... REAPER, SCYTHE, (LAWN)MOWER
dried .... HAY
for thatch .... NETI, ALANG
forage .... GAMA, SORGO, MILLET, REDTOP, SORGHUM, TEOSINTE
genus ...... POA, AVENA, STIPA, SECALE
growth, new .... FOG
hay .... TIMOTHY
husk .... GLUME
Kentucky .... POA, BLUE
killer .... DOWPON, ESTERON
kind of .... ANKEE, BERMUDA
lawn .... REDTOP
leaf .... BLADE, SPEAR

marsh .... REED, SEDGE, SPART, FESCUE
meadow .... POA, FESCUE
mesquite .... GRAMA
moor .... HEATH
ornamental .... EULALIA
paper-making .... ESPARTO
pasture .... GRAMA, FESCUE, REDTOP
pertaining to .... POACEOUS
poisonous .... DARNEL
quaking .... BRIZA
rope-making .... MUNG
rye .... DARNEL, MARCITE
scale .... PALEA
second crop .... ROWEN
sour .... SORREL
swamp .... REED, SEDGE
uncut/ungrazed .... FOG
widow .... DIVORCEE
wiry .... BENT
grasshopper .... GRIG, LOCUST, CRICKET, KATYDID
grassland .... LEA, MEAD, CAMPO, PAMPA, RANGE, SWARD, VELD(T), PASTURE, PRAIRIE, SAVANNA(H)
grassy .... TURFY
ground .... TURF
plain .... CAMPO
grate .... JAR, RUB, FRET, RASP, ANNOY, GRIDE, GRIND, ABRADE, SCRAPE, SCROOP, IRRITATE, FIREPLACE
grateful ...... OBLIGED, BEHOLDEN, THANKFUL
Grateful Dead late lead
guitarist ...... (JERRY) GARCIA
grater .... PEST, VEXER, ANNOYER, CRUSHER, GRINDER
gratification ...... EASE, COMFORT, SATISFACTION
gratify .... SATE, HUMOR, PLEASE, REWARD, INDULGE, SATISFY
gratifying .... PLEASING
gratin .... CRUST
grating .... RASPY, GRILL(E), HOARSE, LATTICE, RASPING, ANNOYING, GRID(IRON)
gratis .... FREE, GRATUITOUS
gratitude ...... THANKS, REQUITAL, APPRECIATION
gratuitous .... FREE, GRATIS
gratuity .... FEE, TIP, BOON, GIFT, PILON, CUMSHAW, PRESENT, VAIL, STIPEND, LAGN(I)APPE, PERQUISITE
graupel .... HAIL, SNOW, SLEET
gravamen .... CHARGE, COMPLAINT, GRIEVANCE
grave ...... TOMB, MOUND, SOBER,

STAID, SEDATE, SOLEMN, SOMBER, OMINOUS, SERIOUS, WEIGHTY, MAUSOLEUM, SEPULCHER
cloth .... SHROUD, CEREMENT
danger .... PERIL
digger .... SEXTON
heap of earth/stone .... MOUND, TUMULUS
marker .... STELE, BARROW, HEADSTONE
robber .... GHOUL
gravel .... SAND, HECKLE, RUBBLE, STONES, PEBBLES, CALCULUS
a boat .... BEACH, GROUND
deposit .... ESKER, GEEST
mound .... OS
ridges .... OSAR
shifter .... RIDDLE
graven ...... CARVED, SCULPTURED
image .... ICON, IDOL, IKON
Gravenstein .... APPLE
graver .... BURIN, CARVER, CHASER, CHISEL, ETCHER, SCULPTOR
Graves' disease .... GOITER
gravestone .... SLAB, STELA, STELE, BARROW, MARKER, MEMORIAL
graveyard .... CEMETERY
gravid .... PREGNANT
gravitate .... DROP, FALL, SINK, SETTLE
gravity .... BURDEN, WEIGHT, PRESSURE, SOLEMNITY, SERIOUSNESS
gravy .... JUS, SAUCE, PROFIT
thickener .... ROUX
gray .... OLD, DULL, ASHEN, DISMAL, BLEAK, HOAR(Y), DREARY, GRIZZLE
brownish .... TAUPE
hair .... GRIZZLE
matter ...... BRAINS, THALAMUS
mole .... TAUPE
grayish .... SLATY
blue .... BICE, TEAL, LIVID, PERSE, AZURINE
brown .... DUN, TAUPE
tan .... BEIGE
graylag .... GOOSE
grayling .... FISH, TROUT, UMBER, BUTTERFLY
graze .... RUB, AGIST, BRUSH, TOUCH, BROWSE, SCRAPE, PASTURE, GLANCE(OFF), SCRATCH
with bullet .... CREASE
grazing land .... (G)RANGE, RANCH(O), PASTURE
rope .... LARIAT, TETHER

grease .... FAT, OIL, DAUB, COOM, LARD, SUET, AXUNGE, LUBRICATE
elbow .... EFFORT
monkey .... MECHANIC
refuse .... SLUSH
slang .... TIP, BRIBE, FLATTERY
greasewood .... CHICO, ORACHE
greasy ...... OILY, FATTY, PINGUID
great .... HUGE, UNCO, MAGNA, NOBLE, INTENSE, TITANIC, IMPOSING, PROFOUND, SUPER(IOR)
artist .... MASTER
artistic work .... MASTER(PIECE)
care .... PAINS
combining form .... MAGNI, MEGA(LO)
grandchild .... IER
grief .... HEARTBREAK
number .... ARMY, HOST, LOTS, HORDE, GALAXY, LEGION
omentum .... CAUL
success .... HIT
toe .... HALLUX
Great Barrier reef/island .... OTEA
Bear .... URSA
Commoner .... CLAY, PITT, BRYAN, STEVENS
Dane .... DOG
Divide .... DEATH, CRISIS
Lakes .... ERIE, HURON, ONTARIO, ST. CLAIR, MICHIGAN, SUPERIOR
Lakes boat .... MACKINAW, WHALEBACK
Lakes fish .... PIKE, CISCO, TULLIBEE, MASKALONGE
Profile .... BARRYMORE
Spirit, Indian .... MANITO
White Father .... PRESIDENT
White Way .... RIALTO, BROADWAY
greatcoat .... PALETOT
Greater Antilles island .... CUBA, JAMAICA, HISPANIOLA, PUERTO RICO
greatest .... BEST, UTMOST, VERIEST, MATCHLESS
amount .... LION'S SHARE
athlete in the world, considered .... DECATHLON WINNER
greatly .... HIGHLY, LARGELY
greaves .... ARMOR, CRACKNEL, CRACKLINGS
grebe .... LOON, GOGOL, DIPPER, DABCHICK, DIDAPPER
Grecian .... GRECO, GREEK,

HELLENIC
theater .... ODEUM
Greco-Egyptian deity .... SERAPIS
Turkish dispute, object of .... CYPRUS
Greece .... ELIS, ACHAEA, ATTICA, HELLAS
of modern .... ROMAIC
prime minister of ...... MITSOTAKIS, PAPANDREOU
to a Greek .... ELLAS
greed(iness) .... AVARICE, AVIDITY, EDACITY, CUPIDITY, GLUTTONY
greedy ...... COVETOUS, ESURIENT, GRASPING, RAVENOUS, VORACIOUS, AVARICIOUS
one .... MISER
Greek .... ATTIC, ARGIVE, CRETAN, IONIAN, ACHAEAN, AEOLIAN, HELLENE, ATHENIAN, HELLENIC
abbess .... AMMA
actor's boot .... BUSKIN
after piece .... EXODE
ancient city .... ELEA
ancient urn .... OLPE
apartment .... ANDRON
architect .... ICTINUS
assembly .... AGORA, BOULE, EKKLESIA
athlete .... MILO
athletic contest .... AGON
Aurora .... EOS
author .... ZENO, AESOP, HOMER, PLATO, TIMON, PINDAR, SAPPHO, PLUTARCH
avenging spirit ..... ATE, FURY, ERINYS
battle site .... MARATHON
bee .... MELISSA
belt .... ZOSTER
beverage .... OENOMEL
bishop .... EPARCH
boatman .... PHAON
bottle .... AMPULLA
bridesmaid .... PARANYMPH
buckle .... FIBULA
canal .... CORINTH
cape .... KRIOS, MALEA, VOUXA, SPATHA, AKRITAS, MATAPAN, KAFIREVS, SIDHEROS, TAINARON
capital .... ATHENS
Catholic .... UNIAT(E)
channel .... EURIPUS
Church, father of ...... ORIGEN
citadel .... ACROPOLIS
city/town .... ARTA, ARGOS, CANEA, DRAMA, KHIOS, LAMIA, NEMEA, POROS,

SAMOS, VOLOS, ALYION,
CANDIA, KHANIA, KOZANI,
LARISA, MEGARA, NAOUSA,
PATRAI, PIRGOS, RODHOS,
SERRAI, SPARTA, THIVAI,
XANTHI, CORINTH, ELASSON,
KALAMAI, KAVALLA, KERKIRA,
KHALKIS, PIRAEUS, PREVEZA,
SALAMIS, VERROIA, AGRINION,
IRAKLION, KASTORIA,
KATERINI, KOMOTINI, MITILLNI,
SALONIKA, TIRNAVOS,
TRIKKALA, TRIPOLIS,
YIANNITSA, THESSALONIKI
city in Asia Minor
.... MELETUS
city in Italy .... SYBARIS
clan .... OBE
clasp .... FIBULA
classical name .... DANAI
coin .... OBOL(I), DRACHMA,
LEPTON, STATER, OBOLUS
colony .... ELEA, IONIA
column .... DORIC, IONIC
comic poet .... MENANDER
commonalty/commune
.... DEME, DEMOS
concert hall .... ODEUM
contest/games .... AGON
counselor .... NESTOR
country .... ELIS, EPIRUS
courtesan ..... THAIS, HETAERA
cross design .... SWASTIKA
cry of sorrow .... AI AI
cup .... DEPAS, SCYPHUS
dance .... PYRRHIC
dialect .... DORIC, IONIC,
(A)EOLIC
dirge .... LINOS
Discordia .... ATE
district .... AONIA, ATTICA,
LOCRIS, ARGOLIS, MEGARIS
earth .... GEOS
elevation .... OSSA
enchantress ..... CIRCE, MEDEA
epic poem .... ILIAD, ODYSSEY,
RHAPSODY
fabulist .... AESOP
farce .... MIME
Fates, one of .... CLOTHO,
ATROPO, LACHESS
feather .... PTERON
festival .... AGON, DELIA,
DIONYSIA
festival, ancient .... HALOA
flask .... OLPE
garment .... CHITON, PEPLOS,
CHLAMYS
geographer .... STRABO
ghost .... KER
giant .... ARGUS, CACUS,

ORION, TITAN, CYCLOPS,
BRIAREUS
giant wrestler .... ANTAEUS
girdle .... ZOSTER
god .... EOS, ARES, EROS,
LETO, ZEUS, CHAOS, HYMEN,
APOLLO, HELIOS, ONIROS,
ARTEMIS, BACCHUS
earth .... BEL
festivity .... COMUS
fire .... VULCAN
flocks .... PAN
heaven(s) .... BEL, ZEUS,
URANUS
hunter .... ORION
love .... EROS
marriage .... HYMEN
medicine .... ASCLEPIUS
mockery .... MOMUS
north wind .... BOREAS
rain .... ZEUS
revelry ..... COMUS, BACCHUS
river .... ERIDANUS
sea .... NEREUS, POSEIDON
sky .... ZEUS, ARGUS
sleep .... HYPNOS, HYPNUS
sun .... APOLLO, HELIOS,
PHOEBUS
supreme .... ZEUS
wealth .... PLUTUS
winds .... EURUS, AEOLUS
wine .... DIONYSUS
war .... ARES
goddess .... DEA
agriculture .... ARTEMIS,
DEMETER
air .... HERA
arts .... ATHENA
beauty .... APHRODITE
chance .... TYCHE
chase .... ARTEMIS
dawn .... EOS
destruction .... ARA
discord .... ERIS
earth .... GAEA, GAIA,
HECATE
fate .... MOERA
flowers .... CHLORIS
ghosts .... HECATE
goblins .... ARTEMIS
health .... HYGEIA
hearth .... HESTIA
heavens .... HERA
hunting .... ARTEMIS
justice .... THEMIS
love .... APHRODITE
marriage .... GAIA, HERA,
DEMETER
memory .... MNEMOSYNE
mischief .... ATE, ERIS
moon .... HECATE, SELENE,

ARTEMIS, ASTARTE
nature .... ARTEMIS
night .... NYX, LEDA, LETO
peace .... IRENE
retribution .... ARA, ATE
seas .... INO, DORIS
sky .... INO
sorcery .... HECATE
strife .... ERIS
vegetation ...... CORA, COTYS
vengeance ..... ARA, NEMESIS
victory .... NIKE
war .... ATHENA, BELLONA
weaving .... ERGANE
wisdom .... ATHENA, PALLAS
witchcraft .... HECATE
women .... HERA
youth .... HEBE
gods, queen of .... HERA
governor .... EPARCH
guerrilla ..... EAM, EDES, ELAS,
KLEPHT
guest .... XENOS
gulf .... ARTA, KHANIA,
MESARA, ARGOLIS, CORINTH,
LAKONIA, MESSINI, SARONIC,
SALONIKA, THERMAIC,
TORONAIC, KIPARISSIA
gymnasium .... XYST,
PAL(A)ESTRA
hat .... PETASOS, PETASUS
headband .... MITER, TAENIA
headland .... ACTIUM
heart .... KARDIA
hedgehog .... ECHINOS
hermit .... GILES
hero .... AJAX, IDAS, JASON,
THESEUS, ALCINOUS
heroine .... LYSISTRATA
historian .... PLUTARCH,
HERODOTUS
holy hill .... ATHOS
hunter: myth. .... ORION
huntress .... ATALANTA
immigrant .... METIC
initiate .... EPOPT(A)
island ...... DIA, IOS, KEA, KOS,
SIMI, ANAFI, CORFU, CRETE,
KASOS, KHIOS, KRITI, LEROS,
MILOS, NAXOS, PAROS, PAXOI,
PSARA, SAMOS, SARIA, SIROS,
THIRA, TILOS, TINOS, ANDROS,
EVVOIA, IKARIA, ITHAKI,
LESVOS, LEVKAS, LIMNOS,
PATMOS, RHODES, SKIROS,
THASOS, AMORGOS, KERKIRA,
KIMOLOS, MIKONOS, NISIROS,
SERIFOS, SKORPIOS
Islands .... OLYMPIA,
CYCLADES, DODECANESE
isthmus .... CORINTH

jar .... AMPHORA
jump .... HALMO
king of Arcadia .... LYCAON
king of Corinth ...... SISYPHUS
king of Crete ...... IDOMENEUS
lake .... VOLVI, PRESPA
language .... KOINE
leper .... LEPRA
leprosy .... ALPHOS
letter .... MU, NU, PI, XI, CHI,
ETA, PHI, PSI, RHO, TAU, BETA,
IOTA, ZETA, ALPHA, DELTA,
GAMMA, KAPPA, OMEGA,
SIGMA, THETA, LAMBDA,
EPSILON, OMICRON, UPSILON
lighthouse .... PHARE
liqueur .... OUZO
love feast .... AGAPE
magistrate .... EPHOR,
ARCHON, DIMIURGE
mantle .... PALLA, CHLAMYS,
PALLIUM, HIMATION
marketplace .... AGORA
marriage .... GAMOS, HYMEN
Mars .... ARES
masses .... DEMOS
mathematician .... EUCLID
measure .... PIC, PIK, BEMA,
PIKI, POUS, ACAENA
mecca .... RUINS
messenger of the gods
.... HERMES
metropolitan .... EPARCH
milestone .... HERMA
militia .... PALIKAR
Modern .... ROMAIC
monks' community ..... SKETE
money .... MINA, TALENT,
DRACHMA
monster: myth. .... HARPY,
HYDRA, LAMIA, SPHINX,
TYPHON, CHIMERA
moralist .... PLUTARCH
mountain ...... IDA, IDHI, OSSA,
ATHOS, PELION, HELICON,
OLYMPUS, PARNASSUS
mountain chain .... PINDUS,
RHODOPE
Muse .... CLIO, ERATO,
THALIA, URANIA, EUTERPE,
CALLIOPE, POLYMNIA
Muses' home .... AONIA
musician .... ARION
mythical flier .... ICARUS
mythical princess ...... EUROPA
native .... SCIOT, CYPRIOT
new .... NEOS
note in music .... NETE
nymph .... HESTIA, OENONE,
ARETHUSA, NEMERTES,
M(A)ENAD, SALMACIS,

(HAMA)DRYAD
official .... EPHOR
orator .... DEMOSTHENES
overseer .... EPHOR
painter .... GRECO, ZEUXIS
parliament .... ROULE
pastoral district .... ARCADIA
pastoral poet .... BION,
THEOCRITUS
patriarch .... ARIUS
peak .... OETA
peninsula .... ACTE, AKTI,
MOREA, SITHONIA, KASSANDRA
people/masses .... DEMOS
personification of conscience
.... AIDOS
philosopher ...... ZENO, PLATO,
TIMON, THALES, DIOGENES,
ARISTOTLE
physician .... GALEN
pillar .... HERMA
pitcher .... OLPE
place for discussions
.... EXEDRA
plain .... OLYMPIA
poem .... EPIC, EPODE, ILIAD,
ODYSSEY
poet .... ARION, HOMER,
HESIOD, PINDAR, ALCAEUS,
THESPIS, ANACREON,
MENANDER
poetess .... SAPPHO
poetry .... EPOS, MELIC
political unit .... EPARCHY
populace .... DEMOS
popular dish .... MOUSSAKA
port .... AULIS
portico .... STOA, XYST
premier .... PAPAGOS
princess .... IRENE
princess: myth. .... IOLE
province .... NOME
race .... GENOS
range .... OETA
region .... CRETE, DORIS,
EPIRUS, IONIAN, THRACE,
THESSALY, MACEDONIA
resistance group .... EAM,
EDES, ELAS
river ...... ARDA, ARTA, EVROS,
NESTOS, PINIOS, VARDAR
rose .... CAMPION
sacred grove .... ALTIS
satirist .... LUCIAN
scarf .... PEPLOS, PEPLUM
scientist .... ARCHIMEDES
sculptor .... MYRON, PHIDIAS
sea .... CRETE, AEGEAN,
IONIAN, MIRTOON
seaport .... ENOS, PATRAS,
SALONIKA

senate .... BOULE
serf .... PENEST
serpent: myth. .... PYTHON
seven .... ZETA
shawl .... PEPLOS, PEPLUM
shepherd, legendary
.... ENDYMION
shield .... PELTA
shipping tycoon ...... ONASSIS,
NIARCHOS
signpost .... HERMA
skeptic .... PYRRHO
skirt, men's .... FUSTANELLA
slave .... PENEST, HETAERA
soldier ...... HOPLITE, PELTAST,
PALIKAR
song .... MELOS
soothsayer .... CALCHAS,
TIRESIAS
sophist .... GORGIAS
sorceress .... CIRCE, MEDEA
soul .... PNEUMA
speaker's dais .... BEMA
spider .... ARACHNE
spirit .... PNEUMA
star .... ASTER
statesman .... PERICLES
Stoic philosopher
.... EPICTETUS
symbol .... ORANT
talking horse .... ARION
temple part .... NAOS, CELLA
theater .... ODEON
theologian .... ARIUS
thread, legendary .... CLEW
time .... CHRONOS
titan .... CRONUS, OCEANUS
town .... SERES
township .... DEME
tragedian .... THESPIS
tribe .... PHYLE
tribe subdivision ..... PHRATRY
troop unit .... TAXIS
trumpet .... SALPINX
underground army/group
.... EAM, EDES, ELAS
''unlucky'' letter .... THETA
valley .... NEMEA, TEMPE
vase .... PYXIS, PELIKE
verb tense .... AOR(IST)
village .... MARATHON
war cry .... ALALA
warrior .... AJAX, ACAMAS,
ACHILLES, DIOMEDES,
ODYSSEUS
wedding song/poem
.... HYMEN(EAL)
weight .... MINA, OBOL(US)
who sold the Trojans on a
horse .... SINON
wine .... OENOMEL

wing .... PTERON
wise man ..... NESTOR, THALES
woman .... GYNE
word .... LOGOS
wrestling school
.... PAL(A)ESTRA
green ...... NEW, RAW, BICE, JADE,
    NILE, VERT, FRESH, LEAFY,
    NAIVE, OLIVE, CALLOW,
    RESEDA, SIMPLE, UNRIPE,
    EMERALD, VERDANT,
    IMMATURE
action .... PUTT
area/spot .... OASIS
bright .... EMERALD
cheese .... SAPSAGO
eyed .... ENVIOUS, JEALOUS
film on copper .... PATINA
golden .... AENEOUS
land .... ERIN
light: colloq. .... OKAY,
    PERMIT, GO-AHEAD,
    AUTHORIZATION
manure .... CLOVER
room .... FOYER
room occupant .... ACTOR
sand .... MARL
shade of .... PEA, BICE, JADE,
    LIME, BERYL, LODEN, OLIVE
sickness .... CHLOROSIS
stamp name .... EIRE
tail .... GRANNOM
vitriol .... COPPERAS
with vegetation .... VERDANT
Green Eggs and Ham author
.... (THEODOR SEUSS)GEISEL
Gables girl .... ANNE
Hat author .... ARLEN
Mansions character ...... ABEL,
    RIMA
Mountain State ...... VERMONT
greenery .... VERDURE
greenheart .... TREE, BEBEERU
greenhorn .... DUPE, TYRO,
    NOVICE, ROOKIE, BEGINNER
greenhouse .... VINERY,
    HOTHOUSE, SOLARIUM,
    VIVARIUM
greening .... APPLE
greenish .... LODEN, VIRESCENT
blue .... BICE, TEAL, NILE,
    TURQUOISE
white .... RESEDA
Greenland base/town ...... THULE
capital .... GODTHAAB
discoverer .... ERIC
feature .... ICECAP
native .... ITA
town/settlement .... ETAH
greenlet .... VIREO, SONGBIRD
greenness .... NEWNESS, VERDURE,

VERDANCY, VIRIDITY
greens .... VEGETABLES
greenshank .... SANDPIPER
greensickness .... ANEMIA,
    CHLOROSIS
greenstone .... JADE, WHIN,
    DIORITE
greensward .... SOD, LAWN, TURF
greet .... HAIL, MEET, ACCOST,
    ADDRESS, WELCOME,
    ENTERTAIN
greeting .... AVE, (ALL)HAIL,
    ALOHA, SALUTE, WELCOME,
    SALUTATION
card .... VALENTINE
gregarious .... SOCIAL, OUTGOING,
    SOCIABLE
grego .... CLOAK
Gregory, actor .... PECK
gremlin .... GNOME, MEDDLER
grenade .... BOMB, SHELL
grenadier .... FISH, INFANTRYMAN
grenadine .... SYRUP, FABRIC,
syrup, source of
.... POMEGRANATE
Grendel .... MONSTER
slayer of .... BEOWULF
Grenoble river .... ISERE
Gretchen .... MARGARET
Gretna Green arrivals
.... ELOPERS, SWEETHEARTS
Gretzky foe .... GOALIE
grew .... SPROUTED
Grey, author .... ZANE
greyhound .... BUS, DOG, SALUKI,
    WHIPPET
arena .... DOG TRACK
grid .... GRATING, ELECTRODE
slang .... FOOTBALL
griddle .... PAN, GRID, PLATE,
    GRILL(ER)
cake .... SCONE, PANCAKE,
    FLAPJACK
gride .... JAR, RASP, GRATE,
    SCRAPE
gridiron .... GRILL(E), GRATING,
    FOOTBALL FIELD
scores, briefly .... TDS
grief .... WOE, PAIN, DOLOR,
    MISERY, SORROW, DESPAIR,
    SADNESS, DISTRESS
Grieg .... NORSE
character .... ASE
dancer .... ANITRA
grievance .... BEEF, GRIPE, SCORE,
    WRONG, GRAVAMEN,
    COMPLAINT, INJUSTICE,
    RESENTMENT
grieve .... CRY, RUE, MOURN,
    LAMENT, REPENT, SADDEN,
    DEPLORE, DISTRESS

unconsolably .... EAT ONE'S
    HEART OUT
grievous .... SAD, SEVERE,
    INTENSE, FLAGRANT,
    LAMENTABLE
griff(e) .... SPUR, MULATTO
griffon .... DOG, GYPS
grifter .... CONMAN
assistant .... SHILL
grig .... EEL, CRICKET
grill ...... BAR, QUIZ, RACK, BROIL,
    ROAST, TAVERN, HIBACHI,
    GRID(IRON), QUESTION,
    INTERROGATE
device .... SPIT
meat-roasting ...... BUCCANEER
grilse .... FISH, SALMON
grim .... DOUR, CRUEL, STERN,
    FIERCE, GRISLY, SAVAGE,
    GHASTLY, MACABRE,
    RESOLUTE, RUTHLESS,
    SINISTER, FORBIDDING
Grim Reaper .... DEATH
grimace .... MUG, MOUE, MOW(E),
    FACE, POUT, FLEER, FROWN,
    SCOWL, MOP, SNEER, SNOOT,
    GLOWER
grimalkin .... CAT, WOMAN
with a grievance .... SORE CAT
grime .... DIRT, SOOT, COLLY,
    SMUTCH
Grimes (Golden) .... APPLE
grimy .... FOUL, DINGY, SOOTY,
    FILTHY
grin .... SMILE, SMIRK
grind .... RUB, BRAY, CHEW, FILE,
    GRIT, HONE, MILL, MULL,
    SAND, TASK, WHET, CRUSH,
    GRATE, GRIDE, CRUNCH,
    POLISH, SHARPEN, DRUDGERY,
    MASTICATE, PULVERIZE,
    TRITURATE
the teeth .... GNASH
grinder .... MILL, HONER, MOLAR,
    TOOTH, CRUSHER
grinding device .... MILL,
    METATE, MORTAR, MULLER,
    MILLSTONE, WHETSTONE
substance .... SAND, EMERY,
    ABRASIVE
grindstone .... HONE, MANO,
    METATE
gringo .... AMERICANO
grinning .... RIDENT
grip ...... BAG, LUG, HOLD, CLAMP,
    CLASP, GRASP, CLUTCH,
    HANDLE, VALISE, CONTROL,
    STAGEHAND
gripe .... BEEF, BITCH, PINCH,
    CLUTCH, HANDLE, MUTTER,
    AFFLICT, GRUMBLE,

COMPLAIN, DISTRESS
slang .... A BONE TO PICK
grip(pe) .... FLU, COLD, COLIC,
INFLUENZA
gripsack .... VALISE
Griqua .... MULATTO
Griselda, like .... MEEK, PATIENT
griseous .... GRAY
grisette .... SHOPGIRL
griskin .... LOIN
grisly .... GRIM, MORBID,
GHASTLY, GRUESOME,
HORRIBLE, FRIGHTFUL
Grissom's first capsule
.... LIBERTY BELL
grist .... MEAL, QUANTITY
for the _____ .... MILL
gristle .... CARTILAGE
grit .... SAND, NERVE, PLUCK,
GRAVEL, COURAGE, STAMINA,
ENDURANCE, FORTITUDE
grith .... SECURITY, SANCTUARY
grits .... MEAL, KASHA, HOMINY
gritty .... BRAVE, SANDY, PLUCKY,
SABULOUS
grivet ...... TOTA, WAAG, GUENON,
MONKEY, VERVET
grizzle .... FRET, GRAY, WORRY,
COMPLAIN
grizzly .... BEAR, GRAYISH
groan .... MOAN
groat .... COIN
grocer .... STOREKEEPER
groceries .... PROVISIONS
Grofe's Donkey _____
.... SERENADE
grog .... RUM, RUMBO
groggery/grogshop .... SALOON
groggy ...... DIZZY, DRUNK, TIPSY,
SLEEPY
groin, of or near .... INGUINAL
swelling .... BUBO
grommet .... RING, BECKET,
EYELET
Gromyko, diplomat ...... ANDREI
groom .... SICE, BRUSH, CURRY,
PREEN, TRAIN, NEATEN, TIDY
(UP), EQUERRY, (H)OSTLER,
BENEDICT, MANSERVANT
horse .... SYCE, COISTREL
grooming process .... TOILETTE
groomsman .... BEST MAN
groove .... RUT, FLUTE, CREASE,
CULLIS, FURROW, SPLINE,
STRIA(E), FLUTING, SULCUS,
ROUTINE
barrel .... CROZE, RIFLING
in architecture .... GLYPH
in iron .... FULLER
masonry ...... RAGGLE, RAGLET
grooved .... LIRATE, STRIATE

grope .... TAY, FEEL, HUNT,
FERDE, PROBE, FUMBLE
for words .... HAW, FALTER,
FLOUNDER
in the dark .... FEEL ONE'S
WAY
Gropius .... GROPE
school .... BAUHAUS
grosbeak .... MORO, FINCH
gross .... RANK, RUDE, BURLY,
BULKY, CRASS, CRUDE,
DENSE, LARGE, THICK, TOTAL,
WHOLE, COARSE, ENTIRE,
VULGAR, GLARING,
FLAGRANT, CORPULENT
opposed to .... NET
grot(to) .... CAVE, SHRINE
grotesque .... ODD, ABSURD,
STRANGE, BAROQUE, BIZARRE,
ABNORMAL, FANTASTIC
Groton product ...... SUBMARINE
grouch .... SULK, GRUMBLE(R)
Groucho .... MARX
grouchy .... CROSS, TESTY,
GRUMPY, ILL-TEMPERED
ground .... SOIL, BASIS, EARTH,
CAUSE, TOPIC, MOTIVE,
REASON, TERRAIN,
FOUNDATION
break .... DIG, START
dig in the .... GRUB
elevation .... RISE
give .... YIELD, RETREAT
hog day .... CANDLEMAS
nut .... GOBBE, PEANUT
parcel of .... SOLUM
pulverizer .... SPIDER
rising .... HURST
unplowed, solid ...... HARDPAN
up .... PULVERIZE
grounded .... ASHORE, GRATED,
ABRADED, WHITTLED
grounder .... DAISY CUTTER
groundhog .... MARMOT,
WOODCHUCK
groundless .... IDLE, BASELESS,
UNFOUNDED, UNJUSTIFIED
groundling .... CREEPER
grounds ...... LEES, BASIS, DREGS,
ESTATE, REASON, GARDENS,
RESIDUE, SEDIMENT
around building .... CLOSE,
COMPOUND
college .... CAMPUS
groundsel .... RAGWORT
groundwork .... BASE, BASIS,
INCEPTION, FOUNDATION
group .... SET, BAND, CREW,
MASS, SORT, UNIT, CLASS,
COVEY, GATHER, CLUSTER,
SEGMENT, ASSEMBLAGE,

COLLECTION
advisers' .... CAMARILLA,
BRAINTRUST
Arafat's .... PLO
athletic .... TEAM
congressional .... BLOC
Civil War: abbr. .... GAR
discussion/gabfest .... BULL
SESSION
distinctive/unique .... ORDER
established in Trygve Lie's
regime .... UNESCO
grid .... ELEVEN
key .... CADRE
matched .... SET
member needing aid .... WEAK
SISTER
of admirers/paid applauders
.... CLAQUE
bananas/grapes .... BUNCH
bears .... SLOTH
bees .... HIVE
birds/goats .... FLOCK
buildings .... PILE
cats .... CLOWDER
cattle/sheep .... HERD
closely related species of
plants, animals
.... GENUS
dogs .... PACK, KENNEL
eight .... OCTAD, OCTAVE,
OCTET(TE)
exclusive people, snobbish
.... CLIQUE
families .... CLAN
fifty: abbr. .... USA
fishes .... SHOAL, SCHOOL
five .... PENTAD, QUINTET,
QUINTUPLETS
fliers .... FLIGHT
foxes .... SKULK
geese .... SKEIN, GAGGLE
girls .... BEVY
hogs/sheep .... DROVE
insects .... SWARM
lions .... PRIDE
modeled figures
.... DIORAMA
nine .... ENNEAD
nonsyllabic phonemes
.... CLUSTER
people associated for social
reasons .... COTERIE
people functioning as a
unit .... BODY
people inside a political
party .... FACTION
people of same nationality,
in one place
.... COLONY

people with same interests
.... RING, CIRCLE
performers .... CAST, TROUPE
players .... TEAM
political intriguers
.... JUNTA, JUNTO
quail .... COVEY
rooms .... SUITE
seals .... POD
seven .... HEPTAD, SEPTET
ships .... FLEET, FLOTILLA
small trees/shrubs .... COPSE
ten .... DECADE
tents .... CAMP
things of the same sort
.... BUNCH, CLUSTER
trees .... GROVE, WOODS,
FOREST, ORCHARD
twenty .... SCORE
twenty priests .... FETIAL
vehicles .... FLEET
whales .... GAM
witches .... COVEN
patriotic .... DAR, SAR
rent-paying .... TENANTRY
singing .... TRIO, CHOIR,
CHORUS, HOOTENANNY
slang .... CABOODLE
social .... TRIBE
top-flight .... ELITE
grouped .... BANDED, RANKED,
SORTED, ARRAYED,
ARRANGED, AGMINATE,
CLASSIFIED
grouper .... MERO, BONACI,
WARSAW, SEABASS
groupie .... FAN, FOLLOWER
grouse .... PINTAIL, SAGE HEN,
PHEASANT, PTARMIGAN
female .... GORHEN
male .... GORCOCK,
BLACKCOCK
slang .... CRAB, GRUMBLE,
COMPLAIN
grout .... LEES, MEAL, DREGS,
MASTIC, MORTAR, GROUNDS,
PORRIDGE, SEDIMENT
grove .... HOLT, TOPE, COPSE,
MOTTE, WOOD(S), BOSK(ET),
BOSCAGE, COPPICE, ORCHARD,
SPINNEY
near Athens .... ACADEME
pines .... PINETUM
where Aristotle taught
.... LYCEUM
grovel ...... FAWN, CRAWL, CREEP,
CRINGE, LICK THE DUST
Grover .... WHALEN
Groves, A-bomb builder
.... LESLIE
grow .... WAX, RAISE, ACCRUE,

SPROUT, THRIVE, ACCRETE,
FLOURISH, CULTIVATE
fast/rapidly .... BOOM,
MUSHROOM
tall and thin .... SPINDLE
together .... KNIT
wearisome .... BORE
grower .... FARMER
growing in couples/pairs
.... BINATE, GEMINATE
one side only .... SECUND
out/outward .... ENATE
up achievement .... AGE OF
DISCRETION
where it is not wanted
.... WEED
growl .... YAR(R), GIRN, GNAR,
HOWL, SNARL, MUTTER,
RUMBLE, GRUMBLE,
COMPLAIN(T)
archaic .... SNAR
growler .... DOG, BEAR
angry .... SNARLER
growler's content .... BEER
grown .... ADULT, MATURE
together .... ADNATE
growth .... WEN, CORN, CYST,
MOLE, SPUR, WART, POLYP,
SHOOT, WATTLE, ACCRETION,
DEVELOPMENT
abnormal body .... TUMOR
in response to force of
gravity .... GEOTROPISM
place of rapid .... HOTBED
process .... NACENCY
skin .... WEN, MOLE, WART
stunted in .... RUNTY,
SCRUBBY
grub .... DIG, LARVA, ASSART,
DRUDGE, MAGGOT, UPROOT,
RUMMAGE
axe .... MATTOCK
slang ..... EAT(S), CHOW, FEED,
FOOD
street .... MILTON
to .... SPUD, SLAVE
grubby .... DINGY, DIRTY, SHABBY
Gruber, composer .... FRANZ
grudge .... ENVY, PEEVE, PIQUE,
SPITE, STINT, ANIMUS,
MALICE, ILLWILL, WITHHOLD
grudging .... ENVIOUS,
RELUCTANT
grue .... ICE, SNOW
gruel .... ATOLE, BROTH, BURGOO,
CAUDLE, LOBLOLLY,
PORRIDGE
grueling .... ARDUOUS,
EXHAUSTING
gruesome .... GRIM, GRISLY,
MORBID, FEARFUL, GHASTLY,

HIDEOUS, MACABRE,
FEARSOME
gruff .... RUDE, BLUNT, HARSH,
ROUGH, SURLY, COARSE,
HOARSE
grugru .... PALM, LARVA
grume .... CLOT
grumble .... FRET, KICK, GRIPE,
GROWL, GROUCH, GROUSE,
MUTTER, REPINE, RUMBLE,
COMPLAIN
grumbler .... GROUCH, REPINER
grumpy .... GLUM, SURLY,
PEEVISH
Grundy, Mrs. .... PRUDE
grunion .... SILVERSIDE
grunt .... RASP, SNORT, COMPLAIN
and groaner .... WRESTLER
grunter .... HOG, PIG
former .... INDIAN
sound of .... OINK
Grus .... CRANE
Gruyere .... CHEESE
guacharo .... (OIL)BIRD
Guadalcanal town .... AOLA
guaiac .... BEAN, SEED, TONKA
Guam .... GUAHAN
American governor
.... SKINNER
bay .... AGAT, PAGO, YLIG,
BAHIA, TUMON, UMATAC,
TALOFOFO
capital .... AGANA
dialect/native .... CHAMORRO
district ..... AGAT, APRA, ASAN,
PITI, TOTO, YIGO, YONA,
TUMON, AGANA, MAITE,
DEDEDO, MERIZO, INARAJAN,
MALOJLOJ, MANGILAO,
SINAJANA, TALOFOFO,
TAMUNING, BARRIGADA,
SANTA RITA, LATTE HEIGHTS,
TUMON HEIGHTS
governor .... ADA, CALVO,
FLORES, BORDALLO,
GUERRERO, GUTIERREZ
governor who committed
suicide
.... (RICARDO)BORDALLO
harbor .... APRA
island .... COCOS, CABRAS
major language .... ENGLISH
monetary unit .... U.S. DOLLAR
mountain ..... LAMLAM, SANTA
ROSA
peninsula .... OROTE
seaport .... APRA (HARBOR)
tourist attraction .... COCOS
ISLAND, TALOFOFO FALLS
tree ..... IPIL, TANGAN-TANGAN
guama .... INGA, GUAVA

Guamanian word(s) for

Guamanian word(s) for:

above	HULO
act	AKTO
actor	AKTA
add	SUMA
advice	PINAGAT
age	IDAT
aid	AYUDA
alien	ESTRANGHERU
all	PURU
alone	MAISA
already	ESTA
also	LOKKUE
altar	ATTAT
American	KANU, AMERIKANU
April	ABRIT, LUMUHU
August	AGOSTO, TENHOS
aunt	TIHA
avocado	ALAGETA
baby	NENI
baby-sitter	CHICHIGUA
bad	MALA
bake	HOTNO
baker	PANADERU
bakery	PANADERIA
ball	BOLA
balloon	LOBU
bamboo	KARISU
betel nut	MAMAON
betel nut palm	PUGUA
big	DANKOLO
bird	PALUMA
blanket	ONNO
blood	HAGA
blue	ASUT
boat	BOTI
book	LEPBLO
boy	LAHI
bridge	TOLLAI
brother	CHELU
burglar	SAKKE
butcher	MATADERU
carnival	FERIA
cheap	BARATU
cheese	KESU
children	FAMAGUON
chopstick	PALITU
circle	SITKULU
city	SIUDAT
clock	RELOS
clown	BUREGO
cockfight	GAYERA, PALITADA
cockfighter	GAYERU
cockpit	RUEDA
cockroach	KUKURACHA
coconut	NIYOK
color	KULOT
contest	HUEGU
cookie	GUYURIA

danger	PILIGRO
darling	KIRIDU
date	FECHA
daughter	HAGA
day	DIA
dead	MATAI
deaf	TANGNGA
dear	NENA
debt	DIBI
December	UMAYANGAN
deed	AKSION
deer	BINADU
devil	DIABLO
dream	GUANIFI
eagle	AGILA
east	HATKATTAN
egg	CHADA
eight	OCHO
eye	MATA
father	TATA
February	MAIMO
female	PALAOAN
fiance	NOBIU
fish	GUIHAN
fisherman	PESKADOT
five	SINKO
flower	FLORES
forward	SIGI
four	KUATRO
fragrant	PAOPAO
free	SAKA
free-loader	ANKAS
Friday	BETNES
friend	GACHONG
giant	HIGANTE
girl	AKKAGA
goat	CHIBA
God	DIOS, YUUS
gold	ORU
good	MAOLEK
grape	UBAS
grass	CHARA
greeting	HAFA ADAI
habit	BISIO
haircut	LAKLAK
happy	FELIS, MAGOF
healthy	BRABU
hear	HANGOK
heir	IRIDERU
here	GAIGE
holiday	GUPOT
house	GUMA
husband/wife	ASAGWA
ill	MALANGU
invoice	RISIBU
jail	KALABOSU
January	ENERU
judge	HUES
July	SEMO
June	MANANAF
late	ATRASAO

laugh	CHALEK
law	LAI
lawsuit	KAOSA
leader	FAGU
life	BIDA
lightning	LAMLAM
love	GUAIYA
lovers	AMANTES
magic	ATTE
man	LAHI
March	MATSO
May	MAYU
meat	KATNE
medicine	AMOT
mermaid	SIRENA
miracle	MILAGRO
Monday	LUNES
monkey	MACHENG
mother	NANA
mountain	SABANA
name	NAAN
necktie	KOTBATA
nephew	SUBRINU
niece	SUBRINA
no	AHE
nonsense	TONTO
noodle	UTDON
north	NOTTE
November	SUMONGSONG
now	PAGO
October	FAGUALO
of	POT
one	ONU
only	UNIKU
parrot	LORU
people	TAOTAO
plant	TANOM
pray/read	FANAITAI
pretty	BUNITA
pumpkin	KALAMASA
race	KARERA
rain	UCHAN
rainbow	ISA
raisins	PASAS
red	AGAGA
rice, cooked	HINEKSA
rice, uncooked	PUGAS
ring	ARAS
road	CHALAN
room	KUATTO
salt	ASIGA
Saturday	SABALU
school	ESKUELA
sea	TASI
sell	BENDE
seller	BIBENDE
September	LUMAMLAM
shark	HALUU
sheep	KINILU
ship	BAPOT
shoes	SAPATOS

signature .... FITMA
sister .... CHELU
sleep .... MAIGO
small .... HAGUI
smile .... CHICHE
smoke .... ASU
snake .... TAKPAPA
snore .... LANNAN
soap .... HABON
son .... IHU
song .... KANTA
south .... HATTAYA
souvenir .... RIKUETDO
spend .... GASTA
star .... ESTREYAS
stop .... BASTA
storm .... PAKYO
strong .... FIGO
sugar .... ASUKAT
Sunday .... DAMENGGO
surprise .... HIGEF
sweet .... MAMES
sword .... ESPADA
tall .... LOKKA
taxes .... ADUANA
teacher .... MAESTRO
thank you ...... SI YUUS MAASE
thief .... LADRON
Thursday .... HUEBES
tobacco .... CHUPA
today .... PAGO
toy .... HUGETI
true .... KLARU
Tuesday .... MATTES
umbrella .... PAYU
understand .... KOMPRENDE
vase .... FLORERU
volcano .... BOTKANU
wait .... NANGGA
waiter .... KAMARERU
walk .... LAHU
war .... GERA
warrior .... GERERU
water .... AGUA
wave .... NAPU
weather .... TIEMPO
Wednesday .... METKOLES
week .... SIMANA
well .... MAOLEK
west .... HATTICHAN
what .... HAFA
white .... APAKA
widow .... BIUDA
wind .... MANGLO
witch .... BRUHA
word .... PALABRA
work .... CHOGUE
wrong .... LACHI
year .... SAKKAN
yellow .... AMARIYU
yes .... HUNGGAN

yesterday .... NIGAP
you .... HAO, HAMYO
young .... HOBEN
your/yours .... MIYU
guanaco-like animal ...... CAMEL, LLAMA
guanay .... CORMORANT
droppings .... GUANO
guano .... MANURE, TUATARA, FERTILIZER
source of .... BATS, GUANAY
Guarani .... TUPI
guarantee .... BOND, VOUCH, ASSURE, INSURE, PLEDGE, SURETY, ENDORSE, PROMISE, WARRANT(Y)
guaranteed ...... CERTIFIED, GOOD AS GOLD
guarantor .... SURETY
guaranty .... SECURITY
guard .... HEDGE, WATCH, CONVOY, DEFEND, PATROL, PICKET, SHIELD, WARDER, OSTIARY, GARRISON, PROTECT(OR), PROTECTION
armed .... SENTRY, SENTINEL
Asgard's .... HEIMDALL
car's .... FENDER
post .... WATCH
ship ...... CONVOY, CORVET(TE)
Guard, ____ (Schutzstaffel) .... ELITE
guarded ...... SAFE, WARY, LEERY, CAUTIOUS
guardhouse .... BRIG, HOOSEGOW
guardian .... CUSTOS, DRAGON, KEEPER, WARDEN, CURATOR, CARETAKER, TRUSTEE, TUTELAR, CUSTODIAN, PROTECTOR
concern of .... WARD
function of .... TUTELAGE
legendary .... ARGUS, CERBERUS
minor's .... TUTOR, CURATOR
of a sort .... WATCHDOG
spirit .... LARES, DAEMON
watchful .... ARGUS
Guatemala babushka .... TZUT
cape .... TRES PUNTAS
capital .... GUATEMALA
city/town .... OCOS, COBAN, IPALA, TIKAL, CHAJUL, GUALAN, JULAPA, PANZOS, SALAMA, SOLOLA, TACANA, ZACAPA, ANTIGUA, AMATITIAN, ESCUINTLA
grass .... TEOSINTE
gulf .... HONDURAS
Indian .... ITZA, MAYA
insect .... KELEP

lake .... GUIJA, IZABAL, ATITLAN, PETEN-ITZA
money .... QUE(T)ZAL
mountains .... MINAS
plain .... PETEN
port .... PUERTO BARRIOS
president ...... PONCE, CEREZO, MENDEZ, AREVALO, ESTRADA, SERRANO
river .... AZUL, CHIXOY, PASION, MOTAGUA, SARSTUN
volcano .... AGUA, FUEGO, TACANA, ATITLAN
guava .... ARACA
guayule .... SHRUB
gudgeon .... BAIT, DUPE, GOBY, GULL, TRICK, MINNOW, TRUNNION
Gudrun, brother of ...... GUNNAR
husband of .... ATLI, SIGURD
rival of .... BRYNHILD
guenon .... MONA, GRIVET, MONKEY, TALAPOIN
guerdon .... CROWN, REWARD
Guernsey .... SHIRT, CATTLE
lily .... NERINE
guerrilla .... REBEL, RAIDER, PARTISAN
guess .... DIVINE, THEORY, SURMISE, ESTIMATE, CONJECTURE, SUPPOSITION
guessing game .... POKER, CHARADE
guesswork .... SURMISE
guest .... CALLER, LODGER, COMPANY, VISITOR
of honor .... LION
paying .... BOARDER
guffaw .... BRAY, ROAR, HEEHAW, LAUGH(TER), HORSELAUGH
deep, hearty .... BELLY LAUGH
Guiana hut .... BENAB
native .... BONI
tree .... MORA
guide .... KEY, CLEW, CLUE, LEAD, PILOT, SCOUT, STEER, CONDUCT, COURIER
mountain .... SHERPA
tourist's .... CICERONE, DRAGOMAN
guidebook .... MANUAL, BAEDEKER, ITINERARY
guided missile .... ICBM. IRBM
guiding .... POLAR, DIRIGENT
example .... PRECEDENT
instrument .... COMPASS
light .... BEACON, LODESTAR, NORTH STAR
rule .... MOTTO, PRINCIPLE
suggestion .... CUE
guidon .... FLAG, PENNANT

Guido note .... UT, ELAMI
  highest .... ELA
  lowest .... GAMUT
guild .... CRAFT, HANSE, UNION
Guild Hall statue .... GOG,
                 MAGOG
guilder .... COIN, GULDEN
guile .... WILE, CRAFT, DECEIT,
       CUNNING, TRICKERY
guileful .... SHREWD, TRICKY
guileless .... OPEN, NAIVE, FRANK,
    CANDID, HONEST, ARTLESS,
              SINCERE
guillemot .... AUK, BIRD, COOT,
       MURR(E), DOVEKIE
  black .... TYSTIE
guillotine .... BEHEAD, MAIDEN
  wagon .... TUMBREL
guilt .... SIN, CRIME, OFFENSE,
    OUTRAGE, CULPA(BILITY)
guiltless .... CLEAR, INNOCENT,
            BLAMELESS
guilty .... NOCENT, AT FAULT,
      CRIMINAL, CULPABLE
guimpe .... BLOUSE
Guinea .... COIN
  cape .... VERGA
  capital .... CONAKRY
  city/town .... LABE, MALI,
    KANKAN, KINDIA, KOUNDARA,
            TELIMELE
  fowl .... PINTADO
  islands .... LOS
  lagoon .... NIMBA
  language .... SUSU, FRENCH,
       FULANI, MANDINGO
  money .... KORI, SYLI
  mountains .... NIMBA
  native .... SUSU, FULANI,
             MALINKE
  pig .... CAVY
  president .... TOURE
  river .... MOA, MILO, BAKOY,
       NIGER, BAFING
  weight ...... AKEY, PISO, UZAN,
             SERON
  young .... KEET
Guinevere's husband
      .... (KING)ARTHUR
  lover .... LANCELOT
guipure .... GIMP, LACE
guise .... GARB, MIEN, CLOAK,
    MANNER, BEHAVIOR,
           PRETENSE
guitar, ancient .... LUTE
  feature .... FRET
  fittings .... CAPO
  fret .... STOP
  like instrument .... ROTE,
    SITAR, CITOLE, CITTERN,

BANDORE, CITHER(N),
GITTERN, PANDORE, SAMISEN,
UKE(LELE), BALALAIKA
old English .... CITHER
plucking implement
  .... PLECTRON, PLECTRUM
ridge .... FRET
guitarist, famed .... SEGOVIA
guitarist's arpeggio .... RASGADO
guitguit .... BIRD
Guitry, playwright .... SACHA
gula .... GULLET
gulch .... ARROYO, CANYON,
    COULEE, RAVINE, VALLEY
gulden .... COIN, GUILDER
gules .... RED
gulf .... GAP, EDDY, ABYSS, BIGHT,
    CLEAVAGE, WHIRLPOOL
Gulf State ...... TEXAS, ALABAMA,
    FLORIDA, LOUISIANA
gull .... COB(B), DUPE, XEMA,
    ALLAN, CHEAT, CULLY,
    PEWEE, PEWIT, GOSLING,
    GUDGEON, KITTIWAKE
  like/of a .... LARINE
  robber .... JA(E)GER
  sea .... COB, MEW, SKUA
gullet .... MAW, CRAW, WEASAND,
           ESOPHAGUS
gullible .... NAIVE, CREDULOUS,
          UNSUSPECTING
Gulliver's Travels author
    .... (JONATHAN)SWIFT
  dwarf .... LILLIPUTIAN
  land .... LAPUTA, LILLIPUT,
          BROBDINGNAG
  people .... YAHOOS
gully .... GUT, SIKE, WADI, DONGA,
    ARROYO, RAVINE, CHANNEL,
           COULOIR
gulp .... BOLT, SWIG, SWALLOW
gum .... ASA, GLUE, KINO, CAROB,
    LATEX, MATTI, RESIN,
    BALATA, CHICLE, RUBBER,
    ADHESIVE, MUCILAGE
  arabic .... ACACIN(E)
  ball machine .... DISPENSER
  black .... TUPELO
  elastic .... RUBBER
  plant .... ULE
  resin ..... BALM, COPAL, ELEMI,
    LOBAN, MYRRH, BALSAM,
    GALBAN, CAMBOGE,
    CAMBOGIA, BDELLIUM,
    OLIBANUM, ASAFETIDA
  resin poison .... ANTIAR
  tree .... KARRI, ACACIA,
    BALATA, COPALM, TUPELO,
         EUCALYPTUS
  up .... CLOG

gumbo .... OKRA, SOUP, GOMART,
            PATOIS
gumboil .... ABSCESS, PARULIS
gummed paper .... STICKER
gummy .... STICKY, VISCID
  substance .... GUTTA
gumption .... NERVE, COURAGE
gums abscess .... GUMBOIL
  inflammation .... GINGIVITIS
  pertaining to .... ULETIC
  source .... FERULA
  the .... ULA
gumshoe .... TEC, RUBBER,
           DETECTIVE
gun .... COLT, LUGER, RIFLE,
    MAXIM, JINGAL, MAUSER,
    MORTAR, PISTOL, CARBINE,
    FIREARM, GATLING,
    REVOLVER, AUTOMATIC
  ancient .... MUSKET,
         HARQUEBUS(E)
  attachment .... SILENCER
  barrel's end .... MUZZLE
  big game .... ROER
  brush .... SWAB
  butt .... STOCK
  caliber .... BORE
  carriage ...... GALLOP, CAISSON
  carriage rope .... PROLONGE
  case .... HOLSTER
  chamber .... GOMER
  crew's shield .... TURRET,
           MANT(E)LET
  dog .... SETTER, POINTER,
          RETRIEVER
  emplacement .... PILLBOX
  girl .... MOLL
  hammer catch of .... SEAR
  muzzle plug .... TAMPION
  part .... PIN, BOLT, BORE,
    BUTT, COCK, LOCK, GOMER,
    SIGHT, STOCK, BARREL,
    BREECH, HAMMER, CHAMBER,
    TRIGGER, CYLINDER,
         MAGAZINE
  pointer .... SIGHT, DOTTER
  sight .... BEAD
  slang .... GAT, ROD, IRON,
    BETSY, PIECE, BARKER,
    ROSCOE, THROTTLE
  small .... DERRINGER
  the motor .... REV
  turret .... CUPOLA, BLISTER
gunboat .... TINCLAD
guncotton plus picric acid
    .... MELINITE
gunfire .... BURST, SALVO,
    VOLLEY, DRUMBEAT,
    SHOOTING, FUSILLADE
gung ho .... AVID, SLOGAN, WORK
           TOGETHER

gunlock catch .... SEAR
gunman .... THUG, TORPEDO,
         GANGSTER
Gunnar's in-law .... SIGURD
 sister .... GUDRUN, GUTHRUN
 wife .... BRYNHILD
gunnel .... FISH, BLENNY,
         GUNWALE
gunner .... STRAFER
gunner's platform .... BANQUETTE
 seat .... TURRET
gunnery .... CANNONS, ARTILLERY
gunny .... BAG, SACK
gunpowder .... TEA, NITER
gunrunner .... SMUGGLER
guns .... WEAPONS, (FIRE)ARMS,
     ORDNANCE, ARTILLERY
 set of heavy .... BATTERY
gunstock .... BUTT
Gunther's wife .... BRUNHILD
gunwale .... GUNNEL
 pin .... THOLE
guppy .... MINNOW
gurgle .... BICKER, BUBBLE,
         BURBLE
gurglet .... GOBLET
gurgling sound producer
 .... BABY, BROOK
gurnard .... GURNET, ROCHET,
    BATFISH, SEA ROBIN
gurnet .... GURNARD
guru .... ADVISER, TEACHER
 pupil of .... CHELA
gush .... JET, EMIT, POUR(OUT),
    ISSUE, SPOUT, SPURT,
        OUTFLOW
 forth .... SPEW
gusher, kind of ...... GEYSER, OIL
     WELL, VOLCANO
gushy .... EFFUSIVE

gusset .... GORE
gust .... BLOW, PUFF, RUSH, TANG,
   BLAST, SAPOR, BREEZE,
   FLURRY, RELISH, OUTBURST
gusto .... ZEST, TASTE, LIKING,
   PALATE, RELISH, DELIGHT,
   PLEASURE, ENJOYMENT
gusty .... WINDY, BLUSTERY
gut .... GULLY, CATGUT, DESTROY,
   DEMOLISH, INTESTINE
guts .... BOWELS, INNARDS,
        ENTRAILS
 slang .... PLUCK, COURAGE,
  FORTITUDE, DETERMINATION
gutta .... DROP, MINIM
gutter .... CURB, SLUM, DITCH,
   CULLIS, KENNEL, TROUGH
guttersnipe .... ARAB, GAMIN,
         URCHIN
guttural ...... DRY, GRUFF, GULAR,
   HUSKY, VELAR, HOARSE,
   RASPING, THROATY
guy .... CHAP, JOSH, ROPE, CHAIN,
    TEASE, FELLOW
 rope .... STAT, STAY, VANG
 with a racket .... MOBSTER
guy's pal/date .... GAL
guzzle .... GULP, SWIG, DRINK,
         SWILL
guzzler .... SOT, TOPER
gymkhana performer .... RIDER,
  ATHLETE, EQUESTRIAN
gymnasium .... GYM, ARENA
gymnast .... TURNER, ACROBAT,
   ATHLETE, TUMBLER
 suit for .... MAILLOT
gymnastics .... TUMBLING,
  ATHLETICS, EXERCISES,
  ACROBATICS, CALISTHENICS
 apparatus .... BUCK

 equipment .... TRAMPOLINE
gymnosophist .... NUDIST
gyp .... CHEAT, CON GAME,
   SERVANT, SWINDLE(R)
gypsophila .... BABY'S BREATH
gypsum .... YESO, GESSO,
   SELENITE, ALABASTER
gypsy .... CALE, CALO, NOMAD,
  ROAMER, ROMANY, TSIGANE,
        ZINGARO
 book LIL
 boy/husband .... ROM
 devil .... BENG
 French .... BOHEMIAN
 gentleman .... ROM, RYE
 girl .... CHAI
 horse .... GRI, GRY, GRASNI
 language .... ROMANY
 non .... GAJO
 opera .... MANERICO
 sea .... BADJAO
 Spanish ...... GITANO, ZINCALO
 thief .... CHOR
 tongue .... CHIB
 village .... GAV
 wagon .... CARAVAN
 winch .... CRAB
 woman .... RANI, ROMI,
        ZINGARA
Gypsy Rose .... LEE
gyrate .... SPIN, TURN, TWIRL,
 WHIRL, ROTATE, SWIVEL,
        REVOLVE
gyrating toy .... TOP
gyrator .... PILOT
gyratory .... WHIRLING
gyre .... WHIRL, VORTEX
gyrene .... MARINE, LEATHERNECK
gyro .... GYROSCOPE
 part .... ROTOR, WHEEL

H

H, letter .... AITCH
 -shaped .... AITCH, ZYGAL
 sound .... ASPIRATE
habanera .... DANCE
habeas corpus ...... WRIT, ORDER
haberdashery .... SHIRTS,
        TOGGERY
habile .... APT, ABLE, ROBE,
    HANDY, CLEVER
habiliment .... DRESS, ATTIRE,
   GARMENT, CLOTHING
habit .... RUT, GARB, WONT,
  DRESS, USAGE, ATTIRE,
  CUSTOM, COSTUME, ROUTINE,
        PRACTICE

 bad .... VICE
 prefix .... ECO
 riding .... JOSEPH, JODHPURS
habitable .... LIV(E)ABLE
habitant ...... DWELLER, RESIDENT
habitation .... HOME, LAIR,
  ABODE, DWELLING
 of a kind .... DEN
habitual .... USUAL, WONTED,
  CHRONIC, ROUTINE,
      CUSTOMARY
habitually silent .... RESERVE,
  RETICENT, TACITURN
habituate .... DRILL, ENURE,
  INURE, ACCUSTOM

 to weather .... ACCLIMATE
habitue .... FREQUENTER
 tavern .... BARFLY
hacienda .... FARM, MINE, RANCH,
  ESTATE, PLANTATION
hack .... AX, CHOP, GASH, COUGH,
  STALE, TRITE, DRUDGE,
  MATTOCK, TAXI(CAB)
 driver .... CABBIE
 literary ..... DEVIL, POETASTER,
      SCRIBBLER
hackbut .... HARQUEBUS
hackie .... CABBIE, TAXI DRIVER
hackle .... CUT, COMB, HAGGLE,
  MANGLE, HATCHEL, FEATHERS

hackmatack ...... LARCH, JUNIPER
hackney .... FLY, FIACRE
  driver .... JARVEY
hackneyed .... DRAB, BANAL,
    STALE, STOCK, TRITE
  expression .... CLICHE,
    PLATITUDE
haddock .... COD, FISH, GADID
Hades ...... DIS, PIT, HELL, ARALU,
    ORCUS, PLUTO, SHEOL,
    ABADDON, AVERNUS
  abyss below .... TARTARUS
  guard .... CERBERUS
  river .... STYX, LETHE,
    ACHERON
  way place to .... EREBUS
hadj .... PILGRIMAGE
haft .... BAIL, HILT, HANDLE
hag .... FURY, CRONE, DEMON,
    HARPY, VIXEN, WITCH,
    VIRAGO, BELDAM(E),
    CARLINE, FELLING, JEZEBEL,
    HARRIDAN
haggard .... WAN, HAWK, DRAWN,
    GAUNT, UNRULY
Haggard novel .... SHE
  singer .... MERLE
haggle .... CHOP, HACK, PRIG,
    CAVIL, MANGLE, BARGAIN,
    CHAFFER, QUIBBLE, WRANGLE
haha .... WALL, FENCE, LAUGH,
    TEHEE
haiku .... POEM
hail .... AVE, AHOY, POUR, CHEER,
    SLEET, ACCOST, SALUTE,
    SHOWER, SIGNAL, ACCLAIM,
    GREET(ING), RAINDROPS
Hailey novel ...... HOTEL, AIRPORT
hair .... FUR, NAP, PILE, SETA,
    DOWN, SHAG, CRINE, ROACH,
    TRESS, THATCH, FILAMENT
  band .... FIL(L)ET
  braid .... CUE, PLAIT, QUEUE,
    PIGTAIL
  bunch of .... WHISK
  cloth .... ABA, CILICE
  coat .... MELOTE
  comb the .... COIF
  combining form .... PILI,
    PIL(O), CHAET(O), TRICHO
  covered with .... HISPID,
    LANATE, PILOSE, SHAGGY,
    TOMENTOSE
  curl of .... LOCK, RINGLET
  curlylike .... CIRROSE
  cut short .... CROP
  disease .... MANGE, SYCOSIS,
    XERASIA, TRICHOSIS
  diseased state .... PLICA
  do the ...... SET, COIF, MARCEL
  dressing .... POMADE,
    BANDOLINE
  dye .... HENNA
  dyer .... ANCIETTE
  face .... BEARD, WHISKER,
    MUSTACHE
  falling out of .... PSILOSIS
  false .... RAT, WIG, JANE,
    PERUKE, TOUPEE
  feeler .... PALP(US)
  fetus .... LANUGO
  fillet .... SNOOD
  fine .... DOWN, FUZZ, PILE
  fringe of .... TUFT
  head .... TOP, CRINE
  knot .... BOB, BUN, CHIGNON
  lock .... TAG, CURL, TRESS
  mass of .... SHOCK
  matted .... SHAG, DAGLOCK
  neck .... MANE, HACKLE
  net .... LINT, SNOOD
  nostril .... VIBRISSA
  of head .... LOCK, POLL,
    THATCH
  ointment .... POMADE
  on abdomen .... PUBES
  pad .... RAT
  piece .... RUG
  pigment .... MELANIN
  pin .... BODKIN
  plant .... PILUS, VILLUS
  prefix .... CRINI
  -raising .... EERIE, SPOOKY
  remove .... BOB, EPILATE,
    TONSURE, DEPILATE
  ribbon .... BANDEAU
  ringlet .... CURL
  roll .... BUN, RAT, PUFF,
    CHIGNON
  rough .... SHAG
  shedding of .... ECDYSIS
  short .... STUBBLE
  shreds .... NOIL
  stray .... WISP
  substance .... KERATIN
  tuft .... FLOCCUS
  unruly .... COWLICK
  unruly head of .... MOP
  wave ..... MARCEL, PERMANENT
hairbreadth ...... CLOSE, NARROW
haircloth .... ABA, CILICE
haircut .... SHINGLE
hairdo .... BUN, BANGS, TETE,
    POODLE, PAGEBOY, COIFFURE,
    POMPADOUR
  unbound .... TRESSES
hairdresser .... CURLER, FRISEUR,
    COIFFEUR, BEAUTICIAN
  at times .... TEASER
  term of .... SET, COIF, RINSE,
    MARCEL, SHAMPOO,
    (COLD)WAVE, PERM(ANENT)
hairiness .... PILOSITY
hairless .... BALD, PELON,
    GLABROUS
  state ..,................... ALOPECIA
hairlike .... TRICHOID
  process .... CILIA, CILIUM
hairline point .... PEAK
hairpiece .... RUG, WIG, FALL,
    PERUKE, TOUPEE
hairpin .... BODKIN
hairs, bunch of .... TUFT, PINICIL
hairsplitter .... QUIBBLER
hairy .... NAPPY, COMATE,
    COMOSE, PILOSE, CRINITE,
    HIRSUTE, PILEOUS, VILLOSE
  Himalayan .... YETI
Hairy Ape .... YANK
Haiti .... HISPANIOLA
Haitian bandit .... CACO
  bay .... BARADERES,
    MANZANILLO
  cape .... MOLE, IROIS
  capital .... PORT-AU-PRINCE
  channel .... SUD, TORTUE
  city/town .... AQUIN, LIMBE,
    HINCHE, JACMEL, JEREMIE,
    GONAIVES, LES CAYES,
    PETIONVILLE, SAINT MARC,
    CAP-HAITIEN, PORT-DE-PAIX
  coin .... GOURDE
  department .... SUD, NORD,
    QUEST, ARTIBONITE, NORD-
    QUEST
  evil spirit .... BAKA, BOKO
  hunter (ox) .... BUCCANEER
  Indian .... TAINO
  island .... VACHE, GONAVE,
    TORTUGA
  king .... CHRISTOPHE
  lake .... SAUMATRE
  language ...... CREOLE, FRENCH
  liberator .... DESSALINES
  lord .... CACIQUE
  money .... GOURDE, CENTIME
  mountain .... MACAYA, LA
    SELLE
  passage .... WINDWARD
  president .... AVRIL, ESTIME,
    ARISTIDE, DUVALIER,
    MAGLIORE, TROUILLOT
  river .... ARTIBONITE, TROIS-
    RIVIERES
  seaport .... CAYES
  voodoo deity .... ZOMBI(E)
  voodoo priest(ess)
    .... MAMALOI, PAPALOI
hake .... GADID, WHITING
  kin of .... COD
hakeem/hakim .... DOCTOR
halberd .... SPEAR, GLA(I)VE,
    GISARME, (BATTLE)AX,

POLEAX(E), PARTISAN
Halberstam book ...... THE BEST AND THE BRIGHTEST
halcyon .... HAPPY, SERENE, PEACEFUL
hale .... DRAG, HAUL, WELL, HEARTY, ROBUST, HEALTHY
half .... DEMI, HEMI, SEMI, MOIETY, FIFTY PERCENT
a fly .... TSE
a goof .... BOO
a sawbuck: sl. .... FIN
a Toscanini? .... SEMI-CONDUCTOR
and half .... MILK, CREAM, FIFTY-FIFTY
and half part .... ALE
assed .... SLIPSHOD
baked .... SOPHOMORIC, AMATEUR(ISH)
boot .... PAC, BUSKIN
breed .... HYBRID, LADINO, MESTEE, MUSTEE, GRIFF(E), MESTIF(F), METIS(SE), MESTIZO, MULATTO
farthing .... MITE
gainer .... ISANDER, (BACK)DIVE
hearted .... LUKEWARM, RELUCTANT, INDECISIVE
hitch .... KNOT
man, half bull ..... BUCENTAUR
man, half dragon ..... CECROPS
man, half fish .... DAGON, MERMAN
man, half goat .... PAN, FAUNUS
man, half horse ...... CENTAUR
mask .... LOUP, DOMINO
moon .... ARC, LUNE, CRESCENT
note, in music .... MINIM
one's better .... WIFE, HUSBAND
penny .... MAG
pint .... SNIP
prefix .... DEMI, HEMI, SEMI
spent before we know what it is .... LIFE
way .... MID
wit .... DOLT, FOOL, IDIOT
witted .... SILLY, STUPID
year's income .... ANNAT
halfway .... MIDDLE, PARTIAL
home .... SECOND BASE
meet .... COMPROMISE
halibut ...... BUTT, SOLE, FLATFISH
Halicarnassus' wonder .... MAUSOLEUM
halicore .... DUGONG, SEACOW, MANATEE

halidom(e) .... HOLINESS
halite .... (ROCK)SALT
halitus .... AURA, VAPOR, BREATH, EXHALATION
hall ...... DORM, SALLE, CORRIDOR, VESTIBULE
concert .... ODEUM
hotel .... FOYER, LOBBY
Odin's/of the slain .... VALHALLA
reception .... COURT, SALON
round .... ROTUNDA
Halley, astronomer ...... EDMUND
constellation .... APUS
discovery .... COMET
halloo .... YELL, SHOUT
hallow .... HOLY, BLESS, SANCTIFY, CONSECRATE
hallowed .... HOLY, SACRED
place .... SHRINE
Halloween option .... TRICK, TREAT
halluces .... DIGITS
hallucination .... ALUSIA, AUTISM, CHIMERA, FANTASY, DELUSION
product of .... MIRAGE
hallucinogen ...... LSD, SEDATIVE, MESCALINE, AMPHETAMINE
drug: sl. .... ACID
source .... FUNGI, PEYOTE
hallux .... (GREAT) TOE
hallway .... CORRIDOR
Halmahera .... GILOLO
halo ...... AURA, GLORY, CORONA, GLORIA, NIMB(US), AUREOLA, AUREOLE, GLORIOLE
halogen .... IODINE, BROMINE, ASTATINE, CHLORINE
compound .... HALIDE
Hals, painter .... FRANS
halt .... LAME, STOP, PAUSE, CEASE, WAVER, HOBBLE
hunter's .... TOHO
the .... CRIPPLES
to a tar .... AVAST
halter .... NOOSE, STRAP
halting place .... INN, ETAPE, OASIS, CARAVANSARY
halve .... BISECT, DIVIDE
ham .... HOCK, MEAT, ACTOR
hog's .... GAMMON
it up .... EMOTE, OVER-ACT
last word of .... WILCO
picnic .... CALI
slang ..... AMATEUR, OVERACT, SHOW-OFF
slice .... RASHER
Ham, parent of, Biblical .... NOAH
son of .... CUSH
hamal .... PORTER

Hambletonian .... HORSE, TROTTER
gait .... TROT
race site .... GOSHEN
hamburg(er) ...... PATTY, STEAK, SANDWICH
Hamilcar's son .... HANNIBAL
Hamite ...... AFAR, GALLA, MASAI, BERBER, LIBYAN, SOMAL(I)
Hamitic language ...... NUMIDIAN
hamlet .... MIR, BURG, DORP, TREF, VILLAGE, THORP(E), CLACHAN
Hamlet and others .... DANES
locale of .... ELSINGOR, ELSINORE
Hamlet's word of contempt .... SIRRAH
Hammarskjold .... DAG
hammer ...... BANG, BEAT, MAUL, KEVEL, BEETLE, FULLER, MALLET, MARTEL, OLIVER, SLEDGE, POUND(ER), MALLEATE
auctioner's .... GAVEL
blow .... POUND
chairman's .... GAVEL
companion of .... TONGS
end/head of .... PEEN, POLL
firearm's .... COCK
kind of .... BALL, DROP, CLAW, PEEN, TRIP
lead .... MADGE
lock .... HOLD
part .... CLAW, HEAD, PEEN
percussion .... PLEXOR, PLESSOR
striking part .... TUP
hammerhead .... BAT, BIRD, FISH, SHARK, UMBRETTE
hammock .... BED, COUCH
hamper .... CRAMP, CRATE, MAUND, HINDER, HOBBLE, IMPEDE, HANAPER, ENCUMBER, TRAMMEL
Hampshire .... HANTS
Hampton Roads protagonist .... MONITOR, MERRIMAC
hamster .... RODENT
hamstring .... LAME, MAIM, TENDON, CRIPPLE, DISABLE
Hamsun, novelist .... KNUT
Han .... DYNASTY
cities .... WUHAN, HANKOW
hanaper .... BASKET, HAMPER
Hancock .... JOHN, SIGNER
hand .... AID, PAW, DEAL, FIST, HELP, MANUS, CLUTCH, CONVEY, WORKER, HOLDING, APPLAUSE, SIGNATURE
at .... READY, NEAR(BY)

baby's .... PUD
below full house .... FLUSH
by .... MANUAL
care .... MANICURE
clapping to music .... TAL
clenched .... FIST
clock .... POINTER
combining form .... CHIRO
companion of .... GLOVE
deformity .... CLAWHAND
drum .... TOMTOM,
              TAMBOURINE
first .... NEW, ORIGINAL
give a .... CLAP, APPLAUD
glass .... MIRROR
grenade .... EGG, PINEAPPLE
holder .... WRIST
jurist .... LEARNED
-me-down .... USED, READY-
       MADE, SECONDHAND
measure .... SPAN
organ .... HURDY-GURDY
out .... DEAL, DOLE
over .... SHELL, DELIVER
palm of .... LOOF, VOLAR,
                  THENAR
pick .... CHOOSE, SELECT
screw .... JACK
slang .... FIN, HAM, PAW, MITT,
                  FLIPPER
sore on .... CHILBLAIN
truck .... DOLLY
upper .... EDGE, ADVANTAGE
without trumps .... CHICANE
written .... MANUSCRIPT
hand, _____ .... PAT
handbag .... ETUI, GRIP, PURSE,
       VALISE, SATCHEL, RETIC(U)LE
handball .... FIVES, PELOTA
handbill ...... LEAF, FLIER, FLYER,
       POSER, DODGER, NOTICE,
                  THROWAWAY
handbook .... TOME, MANUAL,
       BAEDEKER, CATECHISM
handcar .... VELOCIPEDE
handcart .... BARROW
handclasp .... GRIP, SHAKE
handcuffs .... DARBY, FETTER,
       MANACLE, NIPPERS, WRISTLET,
                  BRACELETS
Handel, birthplace of ...... HALLE
forte .... ORATORIO
opus .... NERO, LARGO,
       MESSIAH, BERENICE
handful .... SOME, PLENTY,
                  FISTFUL
of cotton .... WAD
of hay/straw .... WISP
handgun .... PISTOL
handicap .... ODDS, HINDER,
       IMPEDE, HINDRANCE

handily .... DEFTLY, EASILY
handkerchief .... SCARF, SUDARY,
       FOULARD, MALABAR,
                  VERONICA
colloquial .... WIPE(R), HANKIE
large .... MADRAS,
                  BANDAN(N)A
handle .... LUG, ANSA, ANSE,
       BAIL, DEAL, GRIP, HAFT,
       HEFT, HILT, WIELD, SWIPE,
       TREAT, MANAGE, TAKE CARE
awkwardly/clumsily ...... PAW,
                  FUMBLE
ax .... HELVE
bar: colloq. .... MUSTACHE
boat's .... HELM, TILLER
celestial .... ANSA
cup's/pitcher's .... EAR
door .... KNOB
having .... ANSATE
roughly .... PAW, MAUL
rudder .... TILLER
slang .... NAME, MONICKER
whip's .... CROP
handmade .... MANUAL
handmaiden .... SERVANT,
                  ATTENDANT
handout .... DOLE, GIFT,
                  DONATION
handrail, kind of .... MANROPE
hands, clean .... INNOCENT
having two .... BIMANOUS
on hips .... AKIMBO
pertaining to .... MANUAL
warmer .... MUFF
without .... AMANOUS
handsel .... TOKEN, EARNEST,
                  PRESENT
handshake .... GRIP
handsome .... AMPLE, BONNY,
       SHARP, COMELY, GOOD-
       LOOKING, IMPRESSIVE
man .... ADONIS, APOLLO
handspring .... TUMBLE
handstone .... MANO
handwriter, wall .... AGITPROP
handwriting .... SCRIPT,
                  PENMANSHIP
on the wall ...... MENE, TEKEL,
       GRAFFITI, UPHARSIN
pertaining to .... GRAPHIC
study of .... GRAPHOLOGY
handwritten document/will
              .... HOLOGRAPH
handy ...... DEFT, ADROIT, READY,
       HABILE, DEXTEROUS,
                  CONVENIENT
man .... MOZO, JACK-OF-ALL-
                  TRADES
song .... ST. LOUIS BLUES
hang .... LOLL, DRAPE, DROOP,

HOVER, DANGLE, (IM)PEND,
       EXECUTE, SUSPEND
around: colloq. .... HOVER,
       LINGER, LOITER, FREQUENT
down .... LOP, SAG, DROOP,
                  PERPEND
loosely/limply ...... LOP, LOLL,
                  DANGLE
on .... HOLD, WAIT, PERSEVERE
on, in poker .... STAY
out .... HAUNT, HOVER
slang .... STRING
hangar .... SHED, SHELTER,
       (AIR)DROME
area .... APRON
hangbird .... ORIOLE
hangdog .... MEAN
hanger .... EXECUTIONER
on ..... LEECH, TOADY, HEELER,
       DANGLER, HABITUE, PARASITE,
       TRENCHER, FAVOR-SEEKER
hanging .... PENDENT, PENSILE,
       SESSILE, SUSPENDED
apparatus .... GIBBET,
                  GALLOWS
crookedly .... ALOP
limply .... LANK
hangings .... WASH, ARRAS,
       DRAPES, DRAPERY
hangman's noose .... HALTER
rope .... HEMP
hangnail .... WHITLOW
hangout .... DEN, HAUNT,
       RETREAT, STAMPING GROUND
hangover feeling .... NAUSEA,
                  HEADACHE
hank .... COIL, LOOP, SKEIN
hanker .... ITCH, LONG, PINE,
       CRAVE, YEARN
hankering .... YEN, ITCH
hanky-panky .... JUGGLERY,
       DECEPTIVE, TRICK(ER)Y
Hannibal's conqueror ...... SCIPIO
father .... HAMILCAR
defeat/waterloo .... ZAMA
surname .... BARCA
victory site .... CANNAE
Hanoi's holiday .... TET
Hanover beer .... BOCK
hanse .... GUILD, LEAGUE
Hanseatic League .... HANSE
Hansen's disease .... LEPROSY
hansom .... CAB, HACK, CARRIAGE
handspring .... CARTWHEEL
hap .... LUCK, FORTUNE
haphazard .... CASUAL, RANDOM,
       AIMLESS, HIT-OR-MISS
compound word .... HELTER-
                  SKELTER
haphazardly .... ANYHOW
hapless ...... UNLUCKY, LUCKLESS

happen .... OCCUR, BEFALL, BETIDE, COME TO PASS, TRANSPIRE
again .... RECUR
in the end .... EVENTUATE
together .... COINCIDE
happening .... CASUS, EVENT, INCIDENT, OCCASION
before due .... RATH(E), PREMATURE
by chance .... FORTUITOUS
"**happifies**" .... ELATES
happiness .... BLISS, FELICITY
happy .... COSH, GLAD, LUCKY, BLITHE, JOYOUS, CONTENTED
go-lucky .... EASYGOING
medium .... AVERAGE, (GOLDEN)MEAN
times .... HALCYON DAYS
hara-kiri .... SUICIDE, SEPPUKU
harangue .... RANT, ORATE, SPIEL, EXHORT, SCREED, TIRADE, DIATRIBE
Haran's brother .... ABRAM, NAHOR, ABRAHAM
daughter .... MILCAH
father .... TERAH
son .... LOT
harass .... IRK, NAG, VEX, RIDE, ANNOY, BESET, HARRY, TEASE, BOTHER, HECKLE, MOLEST, PESTER, PLAGUE, TORMENT
harbinger .... OMEN, USHER, HERALD, FORETELL, PRECURSOR, FORERUNNER
harbor .... PIER, PORT, HAVEN, MARINA, CONCEAL, SHELTER, ANCHORAGE
and barley .... PEARLS
boat .... TUG
city .... SEAPORT
feature .... PIER, WHARF
guide .... PILOT
laborer .... STEVEDORE
pilot's concern .... TIDE
of mercy .... HOSPITAL
sound .... BELL, CHUG, TOOT, CHURN, (FOG)HORN
wall .... JETTY
hard .... DOUR, FIRM, HARSH, RIGID, SOLID, STERN, STEELY, ADAMANT, ARDUOUS, CALLOUS, DIFFICULT
bed .... PALLET
biscuit .... TACK, CRACKNEL
bitten .... TOUGH, DOGGED
boiled .... TOUGH, CALLOUS
covering .... ARMOR, SHELL
nut to crack .... POSER
prefix .... DIS

problem/puzzle .... POSER, DILEMMA
roll .... BAGEL
rubber .... EBONITE
shell .... LORICA, CARAPACE
shelled animal .... APAR
to find .... RARE
to find in the rain ...... CAB(S)
hardboard .... MASONITE
harden .... GEL, SET, ENURE, STEEL, INURE, OSSIFY, TEMPER, STIFFEN
by heat .... BAKE
hardfisted .... STINGY, MISERLY
hardhanded .... SEVERE
hardhead .... SCULPIN, MENHADEN
hardheaded .... SHREWD, STUBBORN, PRACTICAL
animal .... ASS, MULE, DONKEY
hardihood .... DARING
hardly .... BARELY, FIRMLY, RARELY, NARROWLY, SCARCELY
hardship .... RIGOR, TRIAL, STRAITS, POVERTY
hardtack .... BREAD, WAFER, TOMMY, PANTILE, SEA BISCUITS
hardware .... TOOLS, HOUSEWARES
dealer .... IRONMONGER
slang .... GUNS, WEAPONS
hardwood .... ASH, ELM, OAK, TEAK, EBONY, YAKAL, HICKORY, MAHOGANY
hardy .... BOLD, RASH, TOUGH, DARING, STURDY, DURABLE
Hardy character .... JUDE, TESS
locale .... WESSEX
hare .... CONY, PIKA, PUSS, LEPUS, MALKIN, RABBIT, RODENT, LEPORIDE, LAGOMORPH
and-hounds trail .... TORN PAPER
family .... LEPORID
genus .... LEPUS
hunting dog .... HARRIER
like .... LEPORINE
tail .... SCUT
track .... SLOT, SPOOR
young .... LEVERET
harebrained .... GIDDY, KINKY, DARING, STUPID, FOOLHARDY
harem .... SERAI, ZENANA, SERAGLIO
dweller/slave .... ODALISK, ODALISQUE
room .... ODA(H)
slang .... LOVE NEST
hari-kiri. See **hara-kiri**
haricot ...... STEW, (KIDNEY)BEAN

hark .... HEAR, HIST, LISTEN
harl .... BARB, FILAMENT(S)
harlequin .... MIME, CLOWN, COMIC, BUFFOON
Harlequin, girl of .... COLUMBINE
Harlem painter .... HALS
harlot .... RAHAB, STRUMPET
harm .... MAR, BANE, HURT, ABUSE, INJURE, DAMAGE, INJURY, MALEFIC
harmful .... ILL, NOXAL, NOCENT, BANEFUL, HURTFUL, NOISOME, NOXIOUS, INJURIOUS
gas in mine .... DAMP
very .... DEADLY
harmless ...... NAIVE, INNOCUOUS, INNOXIOUS
harmonica .... MOUTH ORGAN
harmonious .... ORDERLY, SPHERAL, IN ACCORD, CONSONANT
harmonist ...... POET, COMPOSER, MUSICIAN
harmonium .... ORGAN, MELODEON
harmonize .... AGREE, BLEND, (AT)TUNE
harmony .... TONE, TUNE, MUSIC, PEACE, UNISON, BALANCE, CONCORD, RAPPORT, SYMMETRY, AGREEMENT
harness .... RIG, GEAR, DRAFT, EQUIP, GRAITH, INSPAN
bull .... COP
course site .... GOSHEN
maker .... SADDLER
men's .... BRICOLE
part .... BIT, HAME, REIN, TRACE, BRIDLE, COLLAR, HALTER, SADDLE, BLIND(ER)
ring .... TERRET
strap/item .... TRACE, CRUPPER, MARTINGAL(E)
harnessed horses .... SPAN, TEAM
Harold, diminutive of .... HAL
harp .... KOTO, LYRE, NANGA, TRIGON
constellation .... LYRA
like instrument ...... SAMBUKE, DULCIMER, PSALTERY
slang .... IRISHMAN
Harpers Ferry event .... RAID
harpoon .... SPEAR, JAVELIN
barb .... FLUKE
missile like a .... HURLBAT
harpsichord .... SPINET, VIRGINAL
Harpy .... NAG, AELLO, EAGLE, WITCH, BUZZARD, CELAENO, MONSTER, OCYPETE
harquebus .... HAGBUT, FIREARM, HACKBUT

fork .... CROC

harridan .... HAG, NAG, FURY,
SHREW, VIRAGO, JEZEBEL

harried .... BESET

harrier ...... DOG, HAWK, FALCON

Harriet, diminutive of
.... HATTIE

harrow .... VEX, DRAG, BRAKE,
LACERATE

Harrow, rival of .... ETON

harry .... RAID, BESET, TEASE,
HARASS, PESTER, PILLAGE

Harry, Old .... DEVIL, SATAN

harsh .... GRIM, CRUDE, CRUEL,
ROUGH, STARK, STERN,
BITTER, COARSE, SEVERE,
DRASTIC

and dry .... HACKING

critic .... SLATER

sharply .... ACERB

sound .... STRIDOR

taste .... ACERB, BITTER

voiced person .... STENTOR

harsher .... CRUELER

harshness .... RIGOR, ASPERITY

hart .... DEER, STAG

Harte, author .... BRET(T)

character .... AH SIN

hartebeest .... ASSE, TORA,
CAAMA, LECAMA, ANTELOPE

kin of .... SASSABY

hartstongue .... FERN

harum-scarum ...... RASH, WILD,
RECKLESS

haruspex .... PRIEST, SOOTHSAYER

Harvard educator .... PUSEY,
CONANT, LOWELL

man .... CANTAB

newspaper .... CRIMSON

harvest .... CROP, REAP, YIELD

abundant .... BUMPER CROP

feast .... KIRN

festival .... LAMMAS

leftover .... STUMP, STUBBLE

harvesting machine ...... REAPER

harvestman .... DADDY-LONGLEGS

hash .... MINCE, JUMBLE, MEDLEY,
MIX(TURE), RAMEKIN,
MULLIGAN, HODGEPODGE

house: sl. .... JOINT, EATERY

mark: military .... STRIPE

hashish ...... B(H)ANG, CANNABIS,
NARCOTIC, MARIJUANA

source .... HEMP

hasp .... CATCH, SKEIN

hassle ...... FRAY, BRAWL, MELEE,
RUCKUS, SQUABBLE

Hasso, actress .... SIGNE

hassock .... MAT, CUSHION,
TUSSOCK, FOOTSTOOL

haste .... HURRY, SPEED, URGENCY

hasten .... HIE, DASH, RUSH,
HURRY, SPEED(UP), QUICKEN,
ACCELERATE

hasty .... FAST, RASH, BRASH,
QUICK, ABRUPT, URGENT,
TEARING, CURSORY, HURRIED,
IMPATIENT, IMPETUOUS,
IMPULSIVE

effort .... LICK

pudding .... MUSH, SEPON

hat .... CAP, LID, TAM, FELT,
BERET, TOQUE, BONNET,
SCONCE, TOPPER, CAUBEEN,
CHAPEAU, PETASOS, PETASUS,
HEADGEAR

angel's .... HALO

beaver fur .... CASTOR

brimless .... FEZ, TOQUE

chef's .... TOQUE

collapsible .... GIBUS

crown .... POLL

cylindrical .... SHAKO

decoration .... POMPON,
COCKADE

ecclesiastic .... BIRETTA

feature .... BRIM

felt .... FEDORA, HOMBURG

fur .... CONEY, CASTOR

holder .... BANDBOX

hunter's .... TERAI

lining leather .... SKIVER

maker .... MILLINER

making fiber .... BUNTAL,
RAFFIA

material .... FELT, VELOUR(S)

opera .... GIBUS

part .... BAND, BRIM, LINING

pith .... TOPI, TOPEE, HELMET

rack feature .... PRONG

silk .... BEAVER

slang .... LID

small .... COIF

soldier's .... KEPI, BERET,
BUSBY, SHAKO, HAVELOCK

straw .... PANAMA, LEGHORN

style .... HOMBURG, PORKPIE

take off .... DOFF, VAIL

tasseled .... FEZ

that crowned the West
.... STETSON

three-cornered .... TRICORN

trimming .... ROULEAU

woman's ...... TOQUE, CLOCHE,
TURBAN, PILLBOX

hatch .... PLAN, PLOT, DEVISE,
CONCOCT, FISHTRAP,
TRAPDOOR

hatchel .... TEASE

hatchery .... INCUBATOR

hatchet .... AX, TOMAHAWK

man .... GOON

stone .... MOGO

hatchway .... DOOR, SCUTTLE

hate .... ABHOR, ODIUM, SPITE,
ENMITY, LOATHE, MALICE,
PHOBIA, DETEST, DESPISE,
DISLIKE, AVERSION,
ABOMINATE

combining form .... MIS(O)

of foreigners ...... XENOPHOBIA

hateful .... ODIOUS, HEINOUS,
HOSTILE, EXECRABLE,
LOATHSOME, OBNOXIOUS,
REPUGNANT, REPULSIVE,
ABOMINABLE

person .... CAD, TOAD

Hatfield enemy .... MCCOY

hath .... CUBIT

hatred .... HATE, ODIUM, ENMITY,
DISLIKE, ILL WILL, AVERSION,
ANIMOSITY

combining form .... MIS(O)

of change .... MISONEISM

of debate .... MISOLOGY

of mankind ...... MISANTHROPY

of marriage .... MISOGAMY

of women .... MISOGYNY

hats, women's .... MILLINERY

hatrack .... TREE

hatter, woman ...... MILLINER

Hatteras .... CAPE

hauberk .... ARMOR

haughtiness .... HAUTEUR,
ARROGANCE

haughty .... PROUD, SNOOTY,
STUCK-UP, ARROGANT,
CAVALIER

haul ...... LUG, TOW, DRAG, HALE,
DRAW, PULL, SWAG, BOOTY,
BOUSE, CATCH, HEAVE

haulage .... CARTAGE, PORTAGE

hauling car .... VAN

haulm .... HAY, CULM, STEM,
STALK, STRAW

haunch .... HIP, HUCKLE

bone .... ILIUM

part .... HIP, LEG, LOIN, THIGH,
BUTTOCK

haunt ...... DEN, DIVE, LAIR, NEST,
SPOOK, HANG-OUT, PURLIEU,
RETREAT, FREQUENT

in mind .... OBSESS

of literary hacks .... GRUB
STREET

hausfrau .... HOUSEWIFE

hautboy .... OBOE

haute monde .... HIGH SOCIETY

hauteur .... PRIDE, SNOBBERY,
ARROGANCE

Havana ...... CIGAR, (LA)PARASITA

castle .... MORRO

have .... HOLD, ENJOY, POSSESS

a flat .... BLOW A TIRE
a runny nose .... SNIVEL
a session .... SIT, MEET
at .... ATTACK
at bay .... TREE
effect .... TELL
feeling .... SENTIENT
feet .... PEDATE
flavor .... SAPID, TASTY
high objectives .... ASPIRE
it made .... SUCCEED
limits .... FINITE
no worries .... CAREFREE
nothing to do with ...... AVOID
offensive smell .... OLID
on .... WEAR
one too many ...... OVERTIPPLE
relevance .... PERTAIN
ribs .... COSTATE
rough edges .... EROSE,
RAGGED
same origin .... COGNATE,
CONNATE
scruples .... DEMUR
spikes .... TINED, PRONGED
stamina .... LAST
strong desire for .... COVET,
HUNGER
the look .... SEEM
title to .... OWN
haven .... PORT, ASYLUM,
HARBOR, REFUGE, SHELTER,
SANCTUARY
animal's .... PRESERVE
ship's .... ANCHORAGE
haversack .... (CANVAS)BAG
having a dull surface ...... MATTE
a nucleus .... CORED
an incised margin .... EROSE
an old face .... LINED
difficulty ...... IN A HOLE, IN A
MESS
handles .... ANSATE
keen vision .... EAGLE-EYED
lugs/projections .... EARED
no feet .... APOD
omens of success
.... AUSPICIAL
one's marbles .... SANE
rhythm .... CADENT
the shakes .... QUIVERING
two ancestral lines of
descent .... DIPHYLETIC
two sepals or leaves
.... DIPHYLLOUS
havoc .... RUIN
haw .... SLOE, BERRY, FRUIT,
EYELID, FALTER
companion of .... HEM
inflammation .... STY
opposed to .... GEE

Hawaii .... OWYHEE, CROSSROADS
OF THE PACIFIC
author of .... MICHENER
discoverer of .... GAETANO
former status of
.... TERRITORY
garden island .... KAUAI
name in .... DOLE, INOUYE
state bird .... NENE
state flower .... HIBISCUS
state nickname .... ALOHA
valley island .... MAUI
Hawaiian .... KANAKA,
LANGUAGE, POLYNESIAN
acacia .... KOA
apple .... MAILE
association/club .... HUI
baking pit .... IMU
bathing resort .... WAIKIKI
bay .... HILO, HALAWA,
KAHANA, KIHOLO, MAMALA,
WAIMEA, WAIPIO, KANAPOU,
MAALAEA, KAWAIHAE,
NAWILIWILI
beach .... EWA, SUNSET,
WAIKIKI, KAWAILOA,
WAIMANALO, BLACK SAND
bird .... IO, OO, IIWI, KOAE,
MAMO, NENE, NOIO, OMAO,
OOAA, NUKUPUU
blueberry .... OHELO
bonito .... AKU
breech cloth .... MALO
canoe .... WAPA
cape .... KA LAE, KAWAIHOA,
KUMUKAHI
capital .... HONOLULU
channel .... KAIWI, KAUAI,
KALOHI, PAILOLO, KAULAKAHI
chant/song .... MELE
city/town .... AIEA, HILO, LAIE,
KAPAA, KIHEI, KAILUA,
MAKAHA, MOKAPU, WAIMEA,
KAHULUI, KANEOHE, LAHAINA,
WAHIAWA, WAIALUA,
WAILUKU, WAIPAHU,
MAKAKILO, HANAPEPE,
MILILANI, NANAKULI, ALA
MOANA, EWA BEACH,
MAUNAWILI, PEARL CITY
cliff/precipice .... PALI
cloak .... MAMO
cloth .... KAPA, TAPA
coffee .... KONA
county .... MAUI, KAUAI,
HAWAII, KALAWAO, HONOLULU
dance .... HULA
dancer/woman .... WAHINE
desert .... KAU
dress .... MUUMUU
drink .... KAVA

emblem .... LEHUA
falls .... WAILUA, RAINBOW
farewell/greeting .... ALOHA
feast/party .... LUAU
fern .... HEII, IWAIWA
fiber .... WAUKE
fish .... AHI, AKU, ULUA,
LANIA, PALANI
flower .... LEHUA, HIBISCUS
food .... POI, TARO
frigate bird .... IWA
fruit .... POHA
game .... HEI
garland/wreath .... LEI
god .... KANE, KUPO
goddess of fire .... PELE
goose .... NENE, NENI
grass .... HILO
harbor .... PEARL, HONOLULU
hawk .... IO
head .... KOKO, KAUIKI,
DIAMOND
herb .... NOLA
highest point ...... MAUNA KEA
hill .... PUNCHBOWL,
SUGARLOAF
honeyeater .... OO
island ...... FORD, KURE, MAUI,
OAHU, SAND, KAUAI, KAULA,
LANAI, NIHOA, HAWAII,
HIIHAU, LAYSAN, MANANA,
NECKER, MOLOKAI, MOLOKINI,
LISIANSKI
Islands, former name of
.... SANDWICH (ISLANDS)
lagoon .... KEEHI
lake .... SALT, HALALII
language .... POLYNESIAN
lava .... AA
liquor .... AWA, KAWA
lizard fish .... ULAE
loincloth .... PAU, MALO,
MARO
mountain .... KAALA,
HUALALAI, RED HILL,
TANTALUS, LANAIHALE,
MAUNA KEA, PUU KUKUI,
ROUND TOP, WAIALEALE, LUA
MAKIKA
mountain chain .... KOHALA,
KOOLAU, WAIANAE
musical instrument .... PUA,
UKE(LELE)
national park ...... HALEAKALA
neckpiece .... LAI, LEI
newcomer .... MALHINI
noble .... ALII
noddy .... NOIO
nut .... LITCHI
octopus .... HEE
papercloth .... OLONA

pepper .... AVA
plant .... KALO, OLONA
plantation boss .... LUNA
porch .... LANA(I)
port .... HILO
range .... KOOLAU
raven .... ALALA
reef .... MARO
river .... WAIMEA, WAILUKU,
WAINIHA
royal chief .... ALII,
KAMEHAMEHA
seaweed .... LIMU
senator .... INOUYE
shampoo .... LOMILOMI
shrub .... AKIA
singing star .... DON HO
starch .... APII
taro, fermented .... MOD
taro paste .... POI
tern .... NOIO
thrush .... (OL)OMAO
tree .... TI, KOA, AULU, OHIA,
AALII, ALANI, LEHUA, ILIAHI
tree fern .... AMAU, PULU
valley .... MANOA
volcano ...... KILAUEA, MAUNA
KEA, MAUNA LOA
windstorm .... KONA
wood .... KOU, MILO
yam .... HOI
hawfinch .... GROSBEAK
Hawhaw of WW II .... LORD
hawk ...... KITE, ELANITE FALCON,
MERLIN, PEDDLE, CHEATER,
HARRIER, CARACARA
bill of .... PAWL
blind .... SEEL
cage .... MEW
carrier .... CAD
falconry .... BATER
genus .... BUTEO, ACCIPITER
head cover .... SEEL
headed god .... RA, HORUS
leash of .... JESS, LUNE
leg's feather .... FLAG
like bird .... KITE, OSPREY
male .... TERCEL
moth .... SPHINX
nemesis of the .... HOUBARA
opponent of .... DOVE
parrot .... HIA
small ...... EYAS, KITE, ELANET
sparrow .... NISUS
stomach of .... PANNEL
swoop of .... SOUSE
young ...... EYAS, AERIE, EYRIE
hawker .... CADGER, COSTER,
PEDLAR, CHAPMAN, PEDDLER,
FALCONER, HUCKSTER
route of .... WALK

spot/talk of .... PITCH
Hawkeye .... IOWAN
State .... IOWA
Hawkshaw .... DICK, SLEUTH,
DETECTIVE
hawkweed .... DINDLE
hawser frame/holder .... BITT,
BOLLARD
iron .... CALKING
knot .... BEND
post .... BOLLARD
hawthorn .... AZAROLE,
COCKSPUR, MAY(FLOWER)
fruit .... HAW, BERRY
Hawthorne birthplace .... SALEM
character ..... (HESTER)PRYNNE
hay ...... GRASS, CLOVER, FODDER,
ALFALFA, TIMOTHY
bird .... BLACKCAP
box .... MANGER
bundle of .... TRUSS
fever .... ROSE COLD,
POLLINOSIS
fever, cause of .... POLLEN
fodder .... CHAFF
for thatching .... HA(U)LM
grass .... REDTOP
hit the .... SLEEP, RETIRE
lifting tool .... PITCHFORK
pile .... COCK
second crop .... ROWEN
spread the .... TED
storage place .... LOFT
haycock .... COB, RACK, RICK
Hayden, ballerina .... MELISSA
hayloft .... MOW
hayseed .... HICK, RUBE, RUSTIC
haystack .... COB, COIL, GOAF,
MOW, PIKE, RICK
haywire .... AMOK, CRAZY,
DISORDERLY
Hayworth, actress .... RITA
role .... SADIE (THOMPSON)
hazard .... RISK, PERIL, STAKE,
CHANCE, DANGER, WAGER,
VENTURE, JEOPARDY
hazardous .... RISKY, UNSAFE,
PERILOUS, DANGEROUS
haze .... FOG, FILM, GLIN, MIST,
PALL, SMOG, BRUME, VAPOR
hazel .... NUT, TREE, WOOD,
BIRCH, SHRUB
hazelnut .... FILBERT
hazy .... FOGGY, VAGUE, OBSCURE
he .... ANYONE, PERSON
carved it .... SCULPSIT
caused trouble between
Dickens and Thackeray
.... YATES
combining form .... MALE
had no choice .... HOBSON

has the world on his
shoulders .... ATLAS
in chemistry .... HELIUM
is no gentleman .... CAD
Latin .... IPSE
-man, describing a
.... MACHO, VIRILE
painted it .... PNXT, PINXIT
people .... MEN
was slain by Diana ..... ORION
who claimed to rule the
waves .... CANUTE
wrote about man's origin
.... DARWIN
wrote it .... SCRIPSIT
he'll never bite .... A BARKING
DOG
he's at the pearly gates .... PETER
on first .... WHO
head .... NOB, TOP, VAN, MIND,
PATE, POLL, TETE, FRONT,
SKULL, CAPITA, MAZARD,
LEAD(ER), APTITUDE
and shoulders .... BUST
and shoulders cover .... NUBIA
back part .... POLL
band .... FILLET
beer .... FROTH
cold .... CORYZA, SNIFFLES
colloquial .... PATE, WITS,
NODDLE, SCONCE
combining form
.... CEPHAL(O)
counting .... CENSUS,
CAPITATION
cover .... CAP, HAT, COWL,
HAIR, HOOD, HELMET,
TURBAN, WIMPLE
crown of .... PATE, VERTEX
garland .... CHAPLET
hair of .... POLL
like structure .... CAPUT
monastery .... ABBOT
nautical: sl. .... TOILET
newspaper .... CAPTION
of hair .... CRINE
of nunnery .... AMMA
of the ..... CEPHALIC, PARIETAL
off .... AVERT, INTERCEPT
pain .... HEMIALGIA,
HEMICRANIA
protective covering ..... MASK,
HELMET, MORION
shaped like .... CAPITATE
shaved .... TONSURE
shrinker .... ANALYST
skin of .... SCALP
slang .... NOB, NUT, BEAN,
DOME, NOGGIN
start .... LEAD
sweller .... EGO

to foot .... CAP-A-PIE
top of .... PATE, CROWN,
VERTEX
wear .... CAP, HAT, BERET,
BEANIE
wearing crown, describing
.... UNEASY
wrap .... NUBIA, TURBAN,
BURNOOSE, TARBOOSH
wreath .... LAUREL, CHAPLET
Head, ____ (Blue Ridge
range) .... CAESAR'S
headache .... MEGRIM, MIGRAINE,
HEMIALGIA
colloquial .... WORRY,
PROBLEM
type of .... TENSION, MIGRAINE
headband .... AGAL, FILLET,
TAENIA
headdress .... WIG, POUF, TIAR(A),
DIADEM, TOUPEE, TURBAN,
COMMODE, COIFFURE
bishop's .... MITER, MITRE
capelike .... PINNER
cowl-like .... ALMUCE
nun's .... CORNET, WIMPLE
of feathers .... TOPKNOT
used by Arab .... AGAL
widow's .... BANDORE
women's .... POUF, MILLINERY,
POMPADOUR
headgear ...... CAP, HAT, TIAR(A),
TOQUE, HELMET, HARNESS
decorative .... CORONET
headhunter .... DAYAK
heading .... DRIFT, TITLE,
CAPTION, GALLERY
headland .... RAS, CAPE, HOOK,
SPIT, NESS, BLUFF,
PROMONTORY
headless ...... ETETE, ACEPHALOUS
man of fiction
.... (BROM)BONES
headline .... BANNER, SPLASH,
SCREAMER, STREAMER
headliner .... LEAD, ATTRACTION,
(SUPER)STAR
of 1898 .... MAINE
1909 .... PEARY
1914 .... WORLD WAR
1917 .... AEF, DOUGHBOY,
ARMISTICE
1927 .... LINDBERGH
1934 .... DIONNE
1941 .... PEARL HARBOR
1945 .... A-BOMB,
HIROSHIMA
1957 .... SPUTNIK
1959 .... CASTRO
1963 .... KENNEDY
1969 .... MAN ON MOON,

(NEIL)ARMSTRONG
1991 .... WAR IN THE GULF
headlong .... HASTY, RASH(LY),
PELLMELL, RECKLESS
fall .... CROPPER
flight .... LAM, STAMPEDE
headmaster .... RECTOR,
PRINCIPAL
headpiece .... CAP, HELMET
medieval .... ARMET
headquarters .... BASE, SEATS,
MAIN OFFICE
headrest .... PILLOW
headsman .... EXECUTIONER
headspring ...... ORIGIN, SOURCE,
FOUNTAIN
headstone .... STELE, BARROW,
GRAVESTONE
ancient .... DOLMEN,
CROMLECH
headstrong .... RASH, WILLFUL,
STUBBORN, OBSTINATE, SELF-
WILLED
headwaiter .... CAPTAIN
headway :........... GAIN, PROGRESS
of a sort .... DENT
heady .... RASH, NAPPY,
HEADSTRONG
heal .... CURE, EASE, MEND, GET
WELL, REMEDY, REPAIR,
RECONCILE, RECUPERATE
healer .... DOCTOR, SHAMAN
kind of .... FAITH, QUACK,
MEDICINE MAN
healing .... IATRIC, CURATIVE,
REMEDIAL, MEDICINAL,
THERAPEUTIC
substance .... BALM, DRUG,
NOSTRUM, PANACEA, MEDICINE
health .... SALUBRITY,
SOUNDNESS, WELL-BEING
condition .... WELFARE
drinking toast .... SALUD,
CHEERS, PROSIT, MABUHAY
science of .... HYGIENE,
HYGIENICS
healthful .... HYGIENIC,
SALUTARY, WHOLESOME,
SALABRIOUS
healthy .... HALE, WELL, PEPPY,
SOUND, HEARTY, ROBUST,
SALABRIOUS
looking .... TANNED
heap ...... MOW, PILE, RAFF, RAFT,
RUCK, MOUND, (A)MASS,
STACK, SORITE, CONGERIES
colloquial .... LOTS, GREAT
DEAL
combustible .... PYRE
of a .... ACERVAL
of rock fragments ...... DEBRIS

piled by wind .... DRIFT
slang .... CAR
stone .... CAIRN, MOUND,
SCREE
hear .... LEARN, LISTEN,
HARK(EN), HEARKEN
a case again .... RETRY
ye .... OYES, OYEZ
hearer .... AUDITOR, LISTENER
hearing .... OYER, INQUEST,
AUDIENCE, AUDITION,
INTERVIEW
aid .... EAR(PHONE),
AUDIPHONE
court .... TRIAL
of ..... OTIC, AURAL, ACOUSTIC,
AUDITORY
organ .... OTOCYST
range .... EARSHOT
science of .... AUDIOLOGY
hearken .... HEAR, HEED, HIST,
ATTEND, LIST(EN)
Hearn, writer .... LAFCADIO
hearsay .... TALK, RUMOR, GOSSIP,
REPORT
means of spreading
.... GRAPEVINE
hearse .... BIER
cover .... PALL
heart .... COR(E), GIST, GRIT, PITH,
CARDIA, SPIRIT, ESSENCE
action record .... CARDIOGRAM
ailment ...... ANGINA, CARDITIS
attack .... STROKE
auricle(s) .... ATRIA, ATRIUM
beat condition .... FLUTTER,
PALPITATION
beat regulator ..... PACEMAKER
bleeding .... DICENTRA
blood vessel .... AORTA
booster .... LVB, PACER
cavity .... ATRIUM, CAMERA,
AURICLE
colloquial .... TICKER
contraction .... SYSTOLE
deposit .... PLAQUE,
CHOLESTEROL
inflammation .... CARDITIS
leaf .... MEDIC
of a baboon recipient
.... BABY FAE
of the .... CARDIAC
part .... AURICLE, VENTRICLE
point .... FESS
shaped .... CORDATE
sound .... MURMUR
stimulant .... CORDIAL,
DIGITALIS, SPARTEIN(E)
-to-heart .... FRANK, CANDID,
INTIMATE
trouble .... ANGINA

heartache .... WOE, GRIEF, SORROW

heartbeat .... PULSE, THROB, PULSATION

heartbroken .... FORLORN

heartburn .... ENVY, PYROSIS, JEALOUSY, CARDIALGIA

hearten .... CHEER (UP), ENCOURAGE

heartfelt .... GENUINE, SINCERE

hearth ...... HOME, LING, FIRESIDE

goddess of the .... VESTA, HESTIA

heartleaf .... MEDIC

heartless .... COLD, CRUEL, HARSH, UNKIND, CALLOUS, PITILESS, SARDONIC, MERCILESS

hearten .... CHEER(UP), GLADDEN, INSPIRE

hearts/diamonds .... (RED)SUIT

heartrending .... MOVING, PITIFUL, TOUCHING

heartsease .... PANSY, PERSICARY, WALLFLOWER

heartsick .... SAD, ANGUISHED

heartwarming .... GLAD, CHEERY, BLISSFUL, REWARDING

heartwood .... DURA(MEN)

heartworm .... NEMATODE

hearty .... HALE, WELL, LUSTY, GENIAL, ROBUST, SAILOR, STRONG, CORDIAL, VIGOROUS

heat ...... IRE, FIRE, ZEAL, ANGER, ARDOR, CALOR, CAUMA, TEPOR, FEVER, FERVOR, WARM(TH), EXCITEMENT

animal .... RUT

caused by .... THERMIC

combining form ...... THERMO, THERMY

decomposition by .... PYROLYSIS

lightning .... WILDFIRE

meas. .... BTU

oppressive .... SWELTER

pertaining to .... CALEFY, CALORIC, THERMAL, THERMIC

prostration .... SUNSTROKE

rash .... MILIARIA

resistant .... STABILE

unit .... BTU, CALORY, THERM(E), CALORIE

heated .... HOT, AFIRE, ANGRY, FIERY

to whiteness .... CANDENT

heater .... ETNA, OVEN, STOVE, BUNSEN, BURNER

portable .... CHAUFFER

heath .... BENT, MOOR, ERICA, AZALEA

heathen .... PAGAN, PAYNIM, GENTILE, INFIDEL, IRRELIGIOUS

heather .... LING, ERICA, GORSE

heating device .... ETNA, OVEN, STOVE, BOILER, BURNER, RETORT

heaume .... HELMET

heave .... CAST, GASP, HAUL, HEFT, HURL, LIFT, PANT, FLING, RAISE, SWELL

heaven .... SKY, CIEL, EDEN, GLORY, ELYSIUM, PARADISE, FIRMAMENT

arch of .... SKY

combining form .... URANO

edge of .... HORIZON

personified .... URANUS

heavenly .... HOLY, DIVINE, EDENIC, URANIC, ANGELIC, ELYSIAN, ETHEREAL, CELESTIAL

being .... ANGEL, CHERUB, SERAPH(IM)

body .... SUN, MOON, STAR, COMET, METEOR, PLANET

drink .... NECTAR

hunter .... ORION

pasta .... ANGEL HAIR

path .... ORBIT

heavens, belt of .... ZODIAC

heaves .... BROKEN WIND

get the .... RETCH

heavily .... SADLY, BLEAKLY, DENSELY, ONEROUSLY

involved .... UP TO HIS EARS

heavy .... SLOW, GRAVE, INERT, GLOOMY, LEADEN, MASSIVE, SERIOUS, TEDIOUS, WEIGHTY, PONDEROUS

blow .... ONER, HAYMAKER

duty .... TOUGH, RUGGED, STURDY

fingers .... THUMBS

handed .... CRUEL, ARBITRARY, OPPRESSIVE

load .... BURDEN

metal .... LEAD

plus .... OBESE

role .... VILLAIN

step/walk .... SLOG, TROD

weight .... TON

wire .... CABLE

with child .... PREGNANT

heavyweight ...... BOXER, BIGWIG, FIGHTER, PUGILIST

name .... ALI, TYSON

Norton .... KEN

hebdomad .... WEEK, SEVEN

hebetate .... DULL, STUPID

Hebraic law .... TORAH

Hebraism .... JUDAISM

Hebrew .... ZION, DANITE, S(H)EMITE, ISRAELITE

acrostic .... AGLA

alien resident .... GER

ancestor .... EBER

ascetic .... ESSENE, NAZARITE

bible books .... NEBIIM

bread .... AZYM

bride .... KALLAH

brotherhood .... ESSENE

bushel .... EPHA

calendar month:

first .... ABIB, NISAN

second .... ZIV, IYYAR

third .... SIVAN

fourth .... TAMMUZ

fifth .... AV

sixth .... ELUL

seventh ..... TISHRI, ETHANIM

eight ...... BUL, MARCHESVAN

ninth .... KISLEV

tenth .... TEVET, TEBETH

eleventh .... SHEBAT, SHEVAT

twelfth .... ADAR

canonical book .... TALMUD

city .... KIRJATH

coin .... GERAH, SHEKEL

day .... YOM

drum .... TOPH

ear of corn .... ABIB

father .... ABA, ABRAHAM

festival .... PURIM, SEDER

first month .... TISHRI

flute .... NEHILOTH

god .... EL, ADONAI, ELOHIM, YAHWEH, JEHOVAH

greeting .... SHALOM

healer .... ASA

herdsman .... AMOS

high priest .... ELI, EZRA

horn .... SHOFAR, SHOPHAR

hymn .... KADDISH

idols .... TERAPHIM

incantation/melody ...... ELIELI

instrument .... ASOR

judge .... ELI, ELON

juniper .... EZEL

king .... SAUL, DAVID

kingdom .... ISRAEL

language .... RABBINIC

law of Moses .... TORA(H)

lawgiver .... MOSES

letter .... PE(H), A(Y)IN, FEH, JOD, MEM, NUN, TAV, TAW, VAU, WAW, YOD(H), ALEF, BET(H), CAPH, KAPH, KOPH, RESH, S(H)IN, TET(H), ALEPH, CHET(H), GIMEL, SADHE, ZAYIN, LAMED(H), DALETH, SAMEKH

lyre .... ASOR
marriage custom
.... LEVERATE
measure .... HIN, KAB, KOR,
REBA, EPHA(H), (H)OMER
month, old ...... BUL, ETHANIM
my Lord .... ADONAI
name for God .... EL, ADONAI,
ELOHIM
name for Syria .... ARAM
order .... ESSENE
Passover month .... ABIB
perpetual lamp ...... NERTAMID
precept .... TORA(H)
priest .... LEVITE
princess .... SARAH
prophet ..... JOEL, NASI, AMOS,
ELIAS, HOSEA, NAHUM,
DANIEL, HAGGAI, ISAIAH,
EZRA, JONAH, MICAH, ELISHA,
MALACHI, JEREMIAH
prophetess .... DEBORAH
psalms of praise .... HALLEL
quarter .... GHETTO
religion .... JUDAISM,
HEBRAISM
sanctuary .... BAMAH
scarf .... ABNET, TALLITH
scholar ...... AMORA, HALAKIST
scripture marginal notes
.... MASORA
seer .... BALAAM
son .... BEN
teacher .... REBBE, RABBI
ten .... YOD(H)
trader .... BANIAN
tribe .... DAN, LEVITES
universe .... OLAM
weight .... OMER, GERAH,
SHEKEL
white .... LABAN
word .... SELAH
Hebrides island .... IONA, MULL,
SKYE, UIST
hecatomb .... SACRIFICE
heck! .... HELL, INTERJECTION
heckle ...... BAIT, ANNOY, TAUNT,
NEEDLE, HATCHEL
heckler .... BOOER, HOOTER,
HISSER, TEASER, TAUNTER
hectic .... FEBRILE, FEVERED,
FEVERISH, CONSUMPTIVE
hector .... BAIT, HUFF, BULLY,
TEASE, PESTER, HARASS,
BRAWLER, BROWBEAT
Hector, parent of .... PRIAM,
HECUBA
wife of .... ANDROMACHE
Hecuba's children .... PARIS,
HECTOR, TROILUS,
CASSANDRA

husband .... PRIAM
heddle .... CAAM
hedge ...... HAW, HEM, REW, ROW,
BOMA, BUSH, FENCE, WAVER,
BARRIER, HEM AND HAW,
TEMPORIZE, EQUIVOCATE
form a .... PLASH
pant .... PRIVET
trimmer .... PLASHER
hedgehog ...... URCHIN, ECHINOS,
PORCUPINE
like animal .... TENREC
spine .... QUILL
hedgerow .... REW
Hedin, explorer
.... SVEN(ANDERS)
hedonist .... VOLUPTUARY
heebie-jeebies .... JITTERS,
NERVOUSNESS
heed .... MIND, OBEY, RECK,
HEAR(KEN), LISTEN, NOTICE
heedful .... ATTENT(IVE)
heedless .... DEAF, CARELESS,
UNMINDFUL
heehaw .... BRAY, GUFFAW,
LAUGH(TER)
heel ...... CAD, CALX, CANT, LEAN,
LIST, TILT, LOUSE, CAREEN,
BOUNDER
bone .... FIBULA
bone tendon .... ACHILLES
boot's .... DUCE
combining form .... TALO
down at the .... SEEDY,
SHABBY
over .... TILT, CAPSIZE
slang .... RAT
heeled: sl. .... RICH, ARMED,
MONEYED
heeler .... COCK, HANGER-ON
Heflin, actor .... VAN
heft .... PULL, HEAVE, WEIGHT,
INFLUENCE
hefty ...... BULKY, BURLY, HEAVY,
BRAWNY, WEIGHTY
Hegel, philosopher .... GEORG
hegira .... FLIGHT, JOURNEY
destination .... MEDINA
hegumen .... ABBOT
Hehe crop .... MAIZE, MILLET
Heidelberg memento .... SCAR
Heidi's peaks .... ALPS
heifer .... COW, STIRK
maid changed to .... IO
height .... TOP, ACME, SUMMIT,
EXTREME, STATURE,
ALTITUDE, PINNACLE,
TALLNESS, ELEVATION,
LOFTINESS
of play's action .... CLIMAX,
CATASTASIS, DENOUEMENT

prefix .... ALTI
heighten .... ENHANCE, INCREASE,
INTENSIFY
heinous .... ODIOUS, WICKED,
HATEFUL, MONSTROUS,
ABOMINABLE
heir .... SON, SCION, LEGATEE,
(IN)HERITOR
earth .... (THE)MEEK
kind of .... APPARENT
legal .... HERES
to a throne ..... CROWN PRINCE
heirloom .... KEEPSAKE,
SOUVENIR, HERITABLE
heist .... THEFT, HOLDUP,
ROBBERY, BURGLARY
slang .... CAPER
Hejaz capital .... MECCA
city .... MEDINA
Hel .... GODDESS
held .... GRIPPED, DETAINED
capable of being ..... TENABLE
in music .... TENUTO
in trust .... FIDUCIARY
Helen .... ELENA, ELAINE, AILEEN,
EILEEN
diminutive of .... LENA,
NELL(Y)
Mitchell Armstrong
.... MELBA
of Troy's abductor .... PARIS
daughter .... HERMIONE
grandson .... ION
husband .... MENELAUS
mother .... LEDA
son .... DORUS
suitor .... AJAX, PARIS
heliacal .... SOLAR
helianthus .... SUNFLOWER
helical .... TORSE, SPIRAL
helicoid .... SPIRAL
Helicon .... TUBA, MOUNTAIN
dweller .... MUSE
helicopter .... GIRO, CHOPPER,
WHIRLYBIRD
kin .... AUTOGIRO
part .... ROTOR
Heliopolis .... BAALBEK
Helios .... APOLLO, SUN GOD,
HYPERION
daughter of .... CIRCE
father of .... HYPERION
sister of .... ARTEMIS
heliotrope .... TURNSOLE,
(SUN)FLOWER, BLOODSTONE
helix .... SNAIL, SPIRAL, MOLLUSK
hell .... PIT, ABYSS, HADES, SHEOL,
ABADDON, AVERNUS,
GEHENNA, INFERNO,
TARTARUS
biblical .... TOPHET(H)

border of .... LIMBO
capital of .... PANDEMONIUM
diver .... DABCHICK
euphemism for .... HECK
in New Testament
.... GEHENNA
Sherman's .... WAR
Hellas .... GREECE
hellbender ...... SPREE, DEBAUCH,
SALAMANDER
hellbent ...... SET(ON), RESOLVED,
DETERMINED
hellcat .... SHREW, VIXEN, WITCH,
VIRAGO
Hellene .... GREEK
Hellenic Republic .... GREECE
Hellenism .... GRECISM
Hellespont .... DARDANELLES
swimmer .... LEANDER
hellhound .... FIEND, CERBERUS
hellish .... STYGIAN, FIENDISH,
INFERNAL
helm ...... STEER, WHEEL, RUDDER,
TILLER
letters .... ENE
position .... ALEE
Helmer, Mrs. .... NORA
helmet ...... HAT, ARMET, CASQUE,
HEAUME, SALLET, MORION,
SCONCE, BAS(I)NET,
BURGONET
front .... VENTAIL
light .... ARMET
opening .... VUE
part .... VISOR, BEAVER
pith .... TOPI, TOPEE
plume .... PANACHE
shaped .... GALEATE
helminth .... (TAPE)WORM
helmsman .... COX(ON), PILOT,
CONNER, TILLER, STEERSMAN
Heloise, husband of .... ABELARD
helot .... ESNE, SERF, SLAVE
Helot's home .... SPARTA
help .... AID, ABET, SERVE, ASSIST,
RELIEF, WAIT ON, REMEDY,
SERVANT, SUCCO(U)R
bring about .... LEAD TO
me signal .... SOS, MAYDAY
of any kind .... LIFT
over .... TIDE
with the dishes .... DRY
helper .... ALLY, SECOND
helpful .... USEFUL, FAVORABLE
helpless .... LOST, WEAK, FEEBLE,
CRIPPLED, IMPOTENT,
DEPENDENT, SPINELESS
rendered .... HOGTIED
helpmate .... WIFE, SPOUSE
Helsingfors .... HELSINKI
helter-skelter .... AWRY,

CHAOTIC, HAYWIRE, HURRIED,
DISORDERLY, TOPSY-TURVY
helve .... ANSE, HAFT, HANDLE
Helvetia .... SWITZERLAND
hem .... EDGE, LIST, BORDER,
MARGIN, SELVAGE, ENCIRCLE
and haw .... HEDGE, FALTER
in .... BESET, CROWD, FENCE,
CORDON(OFF), ENCLOSE
hematin .... HEME
hematite ...... IRON ORE, LIMONITE
hematoma .... TUMOR
Hemingway, author .... ERNEST
character .... BRETT, PILAR
sobriquet .... PAPA
hemiplegia .... PARALYSIS
hemipterous insect .... LICK,
APHID, BEDBUG
hemitrope .... TWIN
hemlock .... YEW, WEED, CONIUM,
POISON, VALERIAN
alkaloid .... CONIN(E)
poison .... BENNET
hemmed in .... GIRT, CAGED
hemophiliac .... BLEEDER
hemorrhage .... BLEEDING
hemorrhoid .... PILES, TUMOR
hemp .... IFE, TOW, PITA, RINE,
SUNN, ABACA, FIBER, PLANT,
RAMIE, HASHISH
cloth .... CANVAS, SACKING
fabric .... GUNNY, BURLAP
fiber .... TOW, AGAVE, SISAL
filament .... HARL
leaves .... KEF, KIEF, BHANG
narcotic ..... CHARAS, HASHISH,
MARIJUANA
refuse .... TOW, HARDS, HURDS
sisal ..... HENEQUEN, HENEQUIN
shrub .... PUA
hempen cloth .... HESSIAN
hen .... BIRD, FOWL, LAYER,
PULLET, CACKLER, CHICKEN
brooding .... SITTER
fruit .... EGG
hawk .... REDTAIL
roost .... PERCH
slang .... WOMAN
small .... BANTY
sound .... CLUCK, CACKLE,
CHUCK(LE), SQUAWK
spayed .... POULARD
henbane .... NIGHTSHADE
henbit .... MINT, PLANT
hence ...... SO, OFF, AWAY, ERGO,
THEN, THUS, THEREFORE
henchman .... LACKEY, SQUIRE,
ADHERENT, FOLLOWER,
HANGER-ON, ATTENDANT
slang .... YESMAN
henequen .... AGAVE, FIBER,

(SISAL)HEMP
Hengist's brother .... HORSA
kingdom .... KENT
henhouse .... COOP
intercom? .... SQUAWK BOX
henna .... DYE, SHRUB, ALCANA
henpeck .... NAG, HOUND,
DOMINEER
henpecked, a la ...... OBEDIENTLY
Henry Cabot .... LODGE
diminutive of ...... HAL, HANK,
HENNY
IV character .... PETO
VIII .... TUDOR
VIII's forte .... REMARRIAGE
VIII's wife .... PARR, ARAGON,
BOLEYN, CLEVES, HOWARD,
SEYMOUR
hep: sl. ...... ON TO, AWARE, WISE
TO, FAMILIAR, INFORMED
hepatic(a) .... LIVERWORT
Hepburn .... AUDREY,
KATHARINE
role .... GIGI, ONDINE
hepcat .... BEATNIK, HIPSTER,
(SWING)DANCER
cry of .... SOLID
Hephaestus .... VULCAN
heptachord .... LYRE
Hera, husband of .... ZEUS,
JUPITER
mother of .... RHEA
of Romans .... JUNO
rival of .... IO, LEDA, LETO,
EUROPA, THEMIS
son of .... ARES
Herakleion .... CANDIA
Herakles .... HERCULES
herald .... CRIER, USHER, BLAZON,
FORETELL, PROCLAIM,
ANNOUNCE(R), MESSENGER
of good news .... GABRIEL
staff of .... CADUCEUS
heraldic .... ARMORIAL
band .... FESS(E), FILLET,
TRESSURE
bearing .... ENTE, ORLE,
FESS(E), GIRON, LAVER,
PHEON, SALTIRE
cross .... PATEE, PATTE
design .... SEME
device .... CREST
dog: var. .... ALANT
fillet .... ORLE
horizontal band .... FESS
mastiff .... ALAN
shield border .... BORDURE
shield boss .... UMBO
shield stripe .... PALE
star .... ESTOILE
term .... ORLE, SEME, PATTE

triangle .... GIRON
wreath .... ORLE, TORSE
heraldry .... ENTE, ARMORY
bar .... LABEL
bastardy mark .... BATON
bear .... GRISE
bend .... COTISE
bird .... MARTLET
circle .... BEZANT, ANNULET
colter .... LAVER
creature .... LION, PARD, BISSE,
   CANNET, GRIFFON, MARTLET
crest .... MARTLET
cross .... CRUX, SALTIRE
division .... PALE, PALY
dog .... ALAN(T)
face-to-face .... AFFRONTE
grafted .... ENTE
green tincture .... VERT
headless .... ETETE
iris .... LIS
laver .... COLTER
left side .... SINISTER
line .... UNDE, UNDY, URDY,
    DEXTER
manacle .... TIRRET
orange tincture .... TENNE
position of animal .... SEJANT,
   GARDANT, PASSANT
purple .... PURPURE
red tincture .... GULES
row of squares .... COMPANY
shield .... PAVIS
shield bar .... GEMEL
shield-shaped .... PELTATE
shield's center .... FESS
shield's corner .... CANTON
sitting .... ASSIS, SEJANT
snake .... BISSE
standing .... STATANT
voided escutcheon .... ORLE
wavy .... ONDE, UNDE(E),
    NEBULE
herb ...... RUE, DILL, MOLY, RUTA,
   SAGE, WORT, YARB, BASIL,
   GRASS, SEDGE, SEDUM,
   THYME, CATNIP, YARROW,
   CARAWAY, CHERVIL,
   OREGANO, PARSLEY, PARSNIP,
   TARRAGON
Andean .... LLARETA
aromatic .... ANET, DILL, MINT,
   ANISE, BASIL, GINGER,
   FENNEL, DITTANY, GINSENG,
   BERGAMOT, ROSEMARY
aromatic root .... NONDO
aster family .... ARNICA
"bean" .... SAVORY
bean family .... PEA, LOTUS
bennet .... AVENS
bitter .... RUE, ALOE, TANSY,

    GENTIAN
bulbous .... GARLIC
cloverlike .... MEDIC, LUCERNE
coarse .... IVA, ERYNGO,
    ELECAMPANE
common mixture of
  .... BOUQUET GARNI
concoction .... TISANE
decoction .... PTISAN, TISANE
eve/yellow .... IVA
evergreen .... GALAX
flowering .... HEPATICA
forage .... SULLA
fragrant .... BALM
ginger .... ALPINIA
goose foot family .... BLITE
laxative .... SENNA
liked by felines .... CATARIA
magic .... MOLY
medicinal .... RUE, ALOE,
   SENNA, TANSY, ARNICA,
   FENNEL, BONESET
mint family ...... BALM, BASIL,
   CATNIP, HYSSOP, MARJORAM,
   PEPPERMINT, SPEARMINT
mythical .... MOLY
nightshade .... TOMATO,
    HENBANE
of grace .... RUE
parsley family .... CICELY,
    CHERVIL
perennial .... SEGO, SEDUM,
    ORPINE
phlox family .... JACOB'S
    LADDER
pink family .... CAMPION
pod .... OCRA, OKRA
remembrance .... ROSEMARY
root ...... CHAY, CHOY, NONDO,
    GINSENG
snake charm .... MUNGO
spinach-like .... ORACHE
strong-smelling .... RUE,
   RUTA, YARROW
tonic ..... BONESET, CORIANDER
tropical .... GINGER, LOOFA,
    GINSENG
use of .... FOOD, MEDICINE,
   FRAGRANCE, SEASONING
with stinging hairs .... NETTLE
woolly .... POLY
Herb Alpert's swingers
  .... TIJUANA BRASS
herbaceous borders ...... FLOWER
    BEDS
herbage .... GRASS
herbivore .... VEGETARIAN
Hercules .... ALCIDES, HERAKLES,
   STRONG MAN
captive of .... IOLE
death place of .... OETA

monster caught by
  .... ERYMANTHIAN BOAR
monster slain by .... HYDRA
parent of .... ZEUS, ALCMENE
queen slain by ...... HIPPOLYTA
tutor .... CHIRON
victim of .... NESSUS
wife of .... HEBE, DEIANIRA
woman saved by ...... HESIONE
herd .... TEND, CROWD, DROVE,
   FLOCK, CORRAL, RABBLE
animals together .... POD
of horses ..... CAVIYA, HARRAS
of whales .... GAM, POD
herdsman ...... COWBOY, DROVER,
   GAUCHO, VAQUERO,
   RANCHERO, SHEPHERD
constellation .... BOOTES
here .... NOW, HITHER, PRESENT
and _____ .... NOW, THERE
and there .... ABOUT
lies .... HIC JACET
hereafter .... FUTURE
hereditary .... INNATE, LINEAL,
   GENETIC, ANCESTRAL
factor .... GENE
right .... UDAL
ruler .... DYNAST
heredity .... GEN(E), GENETICS
theoretician on .... MENDEL
Hereford .... CATTLE
heres .... HEIR
heresy .... HERETODOXY
heretic .... ARIUS, DISSENTER
burning of .... AUTODAFE
garment of .... SANBENITO
heretofore .... ERENOW
heritable land .... ODAL
heritage .... LEGACY, BEQUEST,
   PATRIMONY, BIRTHRIGHT
heritor .... HEIR
herl .... FLY, BARB
herma ...... SIGNPOST, MILESTONE
hermaphroditic ...... EFFEMINATE
Hermes .... GOD, HERALD,
   MERCURY, MESSENGER
footwear .... TALARIA
gift to Odysseus .... MOLY
hat .... PETASOS, PETASUS
parent of .... MAIA, ZEUS
son of .... PAN
staff of .... CADUCEUS
hermetic .... MYSTIC, SEALED,
    AIRTIGHT
Hermione's brother .... DORUS
husband .... ORESTES
parent .... HELEN, MENELAUS
hermit .... LONER, SANTON,
   THRUSH, ASCETIC, EREMITE,
   RECLUSE, ANCHORET,
    ANCHORITE

crab .... PAGURID, PAGURIAN

hermitage .... WINE, RETREAT, CLOISTER, MONASTERY

hermitic .... SOLITARY

hernia .... BREACH, RUPTURE

support .... TRUSS

hero .... IDOL, LION, STAR, DEMIGOD, PALADIN, CHAMPION, DEFENDER

animal .... AKELA

Babylonian .... ETANA

Crusades .... TANCRED

Faulkner .... ANSER

follower .... INE

legendary .... (EL)CID, AMADIS, PALADIN, TRISTAN, LEONIDES, TRISTRAM

of an Arabian romance .... ANTAR

of many ballads .... ROBIN HOOD

of the Nile .... ADMIRAL NELSON

to some .... SUB

worshiper .... IDOLATER

Hero, lover of .... LEANDER

Herodias' daughter .... SALOME

husband .... ANTIPAS

heroic .... BOLD, DARING, EPIC(AL), GALLANT, SPARTAN, VALIANT

events .... EPOS

narrative .... SAGA, ODYSSEY

poem .... EPIC, EPOS, ILIAD, EPOPEE

verse ...... EPOS, ALEXANDRINE

heroics .... CLAPTRAP

heroin .... HORSE, NARCOTIC

addict .... SNOWBIRD

slang .... SNOW, SMACK

heroine .... DARLING, FAVORITE

C. Brontë's .... EYRE

of Great Expectations .... ESTELLA

of Il Trovatore .... LEONORA

The Maid of Orleans .... JOAN OF ARC

heron .... RAIL, SOCO, CRANE, EGRET, GAULIN, BITTERN, AIGRET(TE), BOATBILL

brood .... EDGE

family .... ARDEIDAE

night .... QUA, SQUAWK

relative of .... GANNET

herpes .... SORE, ECZEMA, TETTER, SHINGLES

designating one .... ZOSTER, SIMPLEX, LABIALIS

herpetology subject ...... REPTILE

herring .... CISCO, SPRAT, TARPON, ANCHOVY, BLUEFIN,

OLDWIFE, PILCHER, SARDINE, MENHADEN, PILCHARD

canned .... SARDINE

cured .... BLOATER

kin .... SHAD

lake .... MELBA

like fish .... CISCO, SPRAT, ALEWIFE, ANCHOVY

measure .... CRAN

pertaining to .... CLUPEOID

red .... BAIT

sauce .... ALEC

slang .... ALEWIFE

that recently spawned .... SHOTTEN

tub .... CADE

young .... BRIT, SMELT, SPARLING

Herriot, premier .... EDOUARD

Herschel's discovery .... URANUS

herse .... PORTCULLIS

Hersey novel town .... ADANO

Herzog's peak .... ANNAPURNA

pen name .... MAUROIS

hesitant .... CHARY, TIMID, UNSURE, WAVERING, RELUCTANT, UNCERTAIN

syllable .... ER

hesitate .... HAW, HEM, DEMUR, PAUSE, WAVER, FALTER, VACILLATE

in speaking .... STAMMER, STUTTER

hesitation .... SCRUPLE, INDECISION, RELUCTANCE

sound of .... ER, UM

Hesperia .... ITALY, SPAIN, BUTTERFLY

Hesperian .... WESTERN

Hesperides ...... AEGLE, GARDEN, HESTIA, NYMPHS

treasure .... APPLES

Hesperus .... STAR, VENUS

fate of .... WRECK

parent .... EOS, ASTRAEUS

Hess, a Nazi .... RUDOLF

pianist .... MYRA

Hessian .... GERMAN, MERCENARY

hest .... ORDER, BID(DING)

Hestia .... NYMPH, VESTA

parent of .... RHEA, CRONUS

het up .... AGOG, EXCITED

hetaera .... SLAVE, THAIS, CONCUBINE, COURTESAN

hetero: combining form .... (AN)OTHER, DIFFERENT

opposed to .... HOMO

heterodox .... HERETICAL

heterogeneous .... MOTLEY, VARIED, DISSIMILAR, MISC(ELLANEOUS)

hetman .... CHIEF, ATAMAN, COSSACK, COMMANDER

hew .... AX, CUT, CHOP, GASH, HACK

hewer .... AXE

hex .... JINX, SPELL, HOODOO, (BE)WITCH, SORCERER

hexad .... SESTET, SEXTET(TE)

Hexham's river .... TYNE

hexapod .... SIX-FOOTED

heyday .... MAY, PEAK, PRIME, YOUTH

Heyerdahl .... THOR

craft .... RA II

Heyward novel .... PORGY

hiatus ...... COL, GAP, VOID, BREAK, PAUSE, LACUNA, OPENING

Hiawatha's bark .... CANOE

hideaway .... WIGWAM

hibachi .... GRILL, BRAZIER

hibernate .... SHACK, SLEEP, WINTER

opposed to .... GESTIVATE

hibernating animal .... BEAR, LEMMING, WOODCHUCK

Hibernia .... ERIN, IRELAND

hibiscus .... TREE, PLANT, SHRUB, MALLOW, GUMAMELA

hic jacet ...... EPITAPH, HERE LIES, INSCRIPTION

hick ...... RUBE, RUSTIC, HAYSEED

hickey .... DEVICE, GADGET

hickory .... CANE, TREE, WOOD, PECAN, SWITCH, (WAL)NUT

fruit .... PIGNUT

nut .... PECAN, TRYMA

tree .... SHAGBARK, SHELLBARK

wattle .... ACACIA

Hidalgo .... NOBLEMAN

state capital .... PACHUCA

hidden .... INNER, PERDU, ARCANE, COVERT, INNATE, LATENT, SECRET, CRYPTIC, OBSCURE

attacker .... SNIPER

fence .... HAHA

provision .... JOKER, RIDER

hide .... BURY, FELL, FLOG, MASK, PELT, SKIN, STOW, VEIL, CLOAK, COVER, STASH, SCREEN, THRASH, CONCEAL, SECRETE, LIE-DOGGO

and hair .... PELAGE

behind words .... HEDGE

calf/lamb .... KIP

for safekeeping .... CACHE

raw .... KIP, SHAGREEN

softening solution .... BATE

hideaway/hideout ...... DEN, LAIR, RETREAT

hidebound .... INFLEXIBLE
hideous ...... GRIM, UGLY, AWFUL,
    GRUESOME, REVOLTING,
    SCABROUS, REPULSIVE,
    UNSIGHTLY
    monster ..... GORGON, MEDUSA
hiding, in .... PERDU
    place .... CACHE
hidrosis .... SWEATING,
    PERSPIRATION
hidrotic .... SUDORIFIC
hie .... RUSH, HURRY, SPEED,
    HASTEN
hiemal .... COLD, BRUMAL,
    WINTRY, HIBERNAL
hierarch .... HIGH PRIEST
hierarchy .... RANK, ORDER,
    ANGELS
hieratic .... PRIESTLY,
    SACERDOTAL
hiero: comb. form .... HOLY,
    SACRED
hieroglyph .... PICTOGRAPH
hieroglyphic .... EMBLEMATIC,
    SYMBOLICAL
hieroglyphics, pillar with
    .... OBELISK
hierophant .... HIGH PRIEST
hifi part .... TWEETER
higgle .... BARGAIN, CHAFFER
higgledy-piggledy .... JUMBLE,
    DISORDER, HELTER-SKELTER
high .... TALL, ALOFT, LOFTY,
    AERIAL, COSTLY, SHRILL,
    TOWERING
    abode .... AERIE, AYRIE
    and dry .... STRANDED
    and low .... EVERYWHERE
    and mighty .... ARROGANT,
    OVERBEARING
    and piping .... TREBLE
    brow .... CULTURED,
    CULTIVATED
    class ...... TONY, ELITE, PLUSH,
    RITZY, QUALITY, SUPERIOR
    colloquial .... STIFF, ELATED
    combining form .... ALTI
    explosive .... TNT
    flown .... FLASHY, GARISH,
    BOMBASTIC
    flyer .... KITE
    grass .... RYE
    hat .... SNUB, SNOOTY, TOPPER,
    SNOB(BISH), STOVEPIPE
    home .... AERIE
    IQ organization/club
    .... MENSA
    jinks .... GLEE, CAPERS,
    PRANKS, REVELRY, FESTIVITY,
    MERRIMENT
    kicks, it has .... CANCAN

    note .... ELA
    note: var. .... EELA
    old time .... SPREE
    peak .... ALP
    pitch .... ALT
    pitched .... SHRILL, TREBLE
    place .... EMINENCE
    prefix .... ALTI
    prestige .... STATUS
    price .... KING'S RANSOM
    priest ...... ELI, AARON, ANNAS,
    PONTIFF
    rank .... ESTATE
    sign .... CUE, SIGNAL
    slang .... DRUNK, SOUSED,
    STINKO, STONED
    society .... BONTON, HAUTE
    MONDE
    sounding .... TENOR, SOPRANO,
    ELEVATED, SONOROUS
    spirited .... FIERY, PROUD,
    SPORTIVE
    stepper .... STRUTTER
    strung .... EDGY, TAUT, JUMPY,
    TENSE, NERVOUS, EXCITABLE,
    SENSITIVE
    tail .... RUN, RUSH, SCURRY,
    SPRINT, HOTFOOT
    time .... NONE TOO SOON
    toned .... LOFTY, MODISH,
    QUALITY, STYLISH
    up .... AERIED
    waters .... FLOOD
    wind .... GALE
High Mass celebrant
    .... DEACON
highball .... DRINK, STINGER
highborn .... BLUE-BLOODED,
    THOROUGHBRED
highboy .... CHEST, BUREAU
highbrow .... SNOB, EGGHEAD,
    ELITIST, LONGHAIR,
    INTELLECTUAL
highest .... SUMMA, SUPREME
    combining form .... ACRO
    mountain .... EVEREST
    note, in music .... ELA
    number of die .... SISE
    point .... APEX, NOON, PEAK,
    APOGEE, CLIMAX, FINIAL,
    VERTEX, ZENITH, PINNACLE
    trump card in napoleon
    .... PAM
highfalutin .... FLIGHTY,
    POMPOUS, PRETENTIOUS
highhanded .... PUSHY,
    ARBITRARY
highland lord .... THANE
    rock .... MONADNOCK
highlander .... GAEL, SCOT,
    TARTAN, PLAIDMAN

    breeches .... TREWS
    pouch .... SPORRAN
    sword of .... CLAYMORE
    weapon of .... DIRK
    wear of .... KILT
Highlands robber ...... CATERAN
highly .... VERY, GREATLY,
    LARGELY, EXTREMELY
    colored .... LURID, VIVID,
    FLORID
    compressed pad .... TIGHTWAD
    decorated .... GAUDY
    excited .... AGOG
    wrought .... D(A)EDAL
highway .... ROAD, AVENUE,
    FREEWAY, (TURN)PIKE
    Alaska-Canada .... ALCAN
    division .... LANE
    fees .... TOLLAGE
    habit .... TAILGATE
    hazard .... SKID
    men .... STATE TROOPERS
    pest .... ROADHOG
    unit .... LANE
highwayman ...... PAD, BRIGAND,
    LADRONE, HIJACKER, ROAD
    AGENT
hijack(er) .... HOLDUP(PER)
hike .... WALK, BOOST, MARCH,
    RAISE, TRAMP
hiker's bag .... KNAPSACK,
    HAVERSACK
hilarious .... GAY, MERRY
    one .... CARD
hilarity .... GLEE, MIRTH, GAIETY,
    MERRIMENT
hilding .... WRETCH
hill .... BRAE, FELL, HEAP, PILE,
    BUTTE, KOP(JE), MOUND,
    MOUNT, BARROW, CUESTA,
    DJEBEL, MONTICULE
    builder/dweller .... ANT
    flat-topped .... MESA
    fortified .... MERLIN
    glacial .... KAME, DRUMLIN
    go over the .... DIE
    isolated .... INCH, BUTTE
    long .... RIDGE
    rounded .... KNOB, MORRO,
    HUMMOCK
    sand .... DENE, DUNE
    small .... HILLOCK
    top .... CAP, TOR, BROW, KNAP,
    CREST
Hillary's conquest .... EVEREST
    Nepalese companion-climber
    .... NORGAY
    other work .... APICULTURE
hillbilly .... RUSTIC
    family member .... MAW, PAW
    food .... TATERS

hillock .... TOFT, TUMP, KNOLL,
KOPJE, MOUND
hills, range of ...... RIDGE, SIERRA
hillside .... BRAE, SLOPE
hollow .... SLACK, CORRIE
hilltop .... TOR, KNAP
Hilo handout .... LEI
hilt .... HAFT, HELVE, HANDLE
wooden .... DUDGEON
Himalayan animal .... OUNCE,
PANDA
antelope .... GORAL, SEROW
bearcat .... PANDA
broadmouth .... RAYA
capital .... GANGTOK,
KATMANDU
country .... NEPAL, SIKKIM
forest .... BHABAR
goat .... KYL, KRAS, TAHR,
TAIR, GORAL
grassland .... TARAI
marmot .... PIA
massif .... ANNAPURNA
Mountains state .... BHUTAN
mystery/humanoid .... YETI
peak .... API, HUMP, NEPAL,
EVEREST
river .... INDUS
sheep .... NAHOOR
tea .... AUCUBA
Himalayas .... (THE) HUMP
hind ...... ROE, BACK, DEER, REAR,
TAIL, RUSTIC, PEASANT,
CABRILLA, POSTERIOR
leg of animal .... HAM
hinder .... BLOCK, DELAY, DETER,
EMBAR, CUMBER, HAMPER,
IMPEDE, RETARD, PREVENT,
OBSTRUCT
hindmost .... LAST
hindquarter .... HAUNCH
hindrance .... BAR, HITCH,
OBSTACLE, IMPEDIMENT
Hindu .... SER, BABU, BANA,
JAIN(A), KOLI, SIKH, TAMIL,
GENTOO
acrobat .... NAT
age of the world .... YUGA
ancestor .... MANU
Anglicized .... BABU
ascetic .... JOGI, MUNI, YATI,
YOGI, FAKIR, SADHU
bandit .... DACOIT
banker .... SOWCAR
barber .... NAI, NAPIT
bear .... BHALU
beggar .... NAGA
betelnut .... SUPARI
boat .... YARAHA
brook .... NALA
bulbul .... KALA

butter .... GHI
call to prayer .... AZAN
caste .... JAT, MAL, KORI, PASI,
TELI, SUDRA, RAJPUT
caste, priestly .... BRAHMAN
cavalry .... RISALA
charitable gift .... ENAM
city .... ABAD
city, holy .... BENARES
cloth .... LUNGI, LUNGEE
congregation .... SAMAJ
cottage .... BARI
court officer .... AMALA
cremation of a widow
.... SATI
cultured .... BRAHMIN
cultured person ...... BRAHMAN
cymbal .... DAL, TAL
dance drama .... RASA
dancing girl .... BAYADERE
deity .... UMA, AGNI, AKAL,
DEVA, DEWA, KAMA, MANU,
RAMA, SIVA, YAMA, BHAGA,
VARUNA, VISHNU, KRISHNA
demon .... RAHU, ASURA
divorce law .... TALAK
drinking pot .... LOTA
dye .... ALTA
ejaculation .... OM
epic .... RAMAYAMA
epic hero .... ARJUNA
essence .... AMRITA
exchange rate .... BATTA
evil spirit .... MARA, ASURA
fair .... MELA
fate .... KARMA
festival .... HOLI, PUJA, DEWALI
flying beings .... GARUDAS
gardener .... MALI
garment .... SARI, DHOTI,
SAREE
gentleman .... SRI, BABU,
BABOO
giant: myth. .... BANA
gnome .... YAKSHA
god .... KA, AGNI, AKAL,
DEVA, KAMA, SIVA, YAMA,
BHAGA, DYAUS, INDRA,
BRAHMA, VARUNA, VISHNU,
GANES(H)A, TRIMURTI,
JAGANNATH
goddess .... UMA, VAC(H),
DEVI, KALI, MAYA, S(H)RI,
SAKTI, SHREE, US(H)AS,
MATRIS, LAKSHMI
gods' abode .... MERU
groom .... SYCE
guitar .... BINA, VINA, SITAR
gypsy .... KARACHEE
handkerchief .... MALABAR
hell .... NARAKA

hero ..... NALA, RAMA, ARJUNA
holy book .... VEDA, SASTRA
holy destination .... HARDWAR,
VARANASI
holy man ...... FAKIR, SADH(U)
immortality .... AMRITA
incarnation .... AVATAR
kingdom .... NEPAL
kismet .... KARMA
kneeling rug .... ASAN
land grant .... ENAM, INAM,
SASAN
language .... SANSKRIT
lawgiver .... MANU
leader .... GANDHI, SIRDAR
loincloth .... DHO(O)TI
lord .... SWAMI
low-caste .... MAL, KORI
magic .... MAYA
master .... MIAN, SAHIB,
SWAMI, SWAMY
Maya .... DEVI, SAKTI
meal .... ATA
measure .... KOS, RYOTS
merchant .... BANIAN
monastic philosophy
.... VEDANTA
money .... ANNA
month .... ASIN, JETH, KUAR,
MAGH, AGHAN, CHAIT,
KA(R)TIK, BAISAKH,
PHA(L)GUN, SA(RA)WAN
mountain .... MERU
mountain pass .... GHAUT
mountaineer .... BHIL
musical instrument ...... VINA,
SAROD, SITAR
mystic word .... OM
Nobel Prize winner
.... TAGORE
noble .... RAJAH
nursemaid .... AYAH
patriarch .... PITRI
peasant .... RYOT
philosophy .... YOGA,
SANKHYA, VEDANTA
pillar .... LAT
poet .... TAGORE, KALIDASA
police station .... THANA
policeman .... SEPOY
pot .... LOTA
prayer carpet/rug .... ASAN
priest .... BRAHMIN
prince .... RANA, RAJA(H),
MAHARAJA
princess .... RANI, RANEE,
MAHARANI
puce .... UDA
pundit .... SWAMI
queen .... RANI, RANEE
ravine .... NALA

religious creed .... JAINISM
religious observances
.... DHARMA
religious devotee .... MUND
religious sect .... SIKHISM
religious teacher .... PIR,
GURU, SWAMI
rites .... ACHAR
sacred literature .... VEDA
sacred river .... GANGA,
GANGES
sage ..... GAUTAMA, MAHATMA
Sanskrit school .... TOL
scarf .... SAREE
scripture ...... AGAMA, SASTRA,
TANTRA
seclusion of women
.... PURDAH
sect .... JAINA
sect member .... SADH, SEIK,
SIKH
serpent .... NAGA
servant .... CELA
slave .... DASIS
soldier .... SEPOY
sorceress .... USHA
soul .... ATMA(N)
sovereignty .... RAJ
spirit .... MARA
summer house .... MAHAL
supreme deity .... VARUNA
swan .... HANSA
teacher .... PIR, GURU,
MULLA(H)
temple .... DEUL
temple tower .... SIKHRA
title .... MIR, RAO, SRI, NAIK,
SIDI, RAJA(H), SAHIB
title of respect .... MIAN,
SAHIB, SWAMI, BAHADUR
trader .... BANIAN, BANYAN
tree .... BO, DAR, PIPAL
trinity .... SIVA, VISHNU,
BRAHMA, TRIMURTI
turban .... PAGRI
underworld king .... YAMA
veranda .... PYAL
water nymph .... APAS
weaver .... TANTI
weight .... SER, TAEL, TOLA,
MAUND
widow .... SATI, SUTTEE
writings .... VEDA
Hinduism .... ANIMISM
cosmic principle .... KARMA
pilgrim's city .... VARANASI
Hindustan hillman .... TODA
magic .... JADU
Mogul emperor .... AKBAR
state .... PUNJAB
Hindustani .... URDU, HINDI

hinge .... AXIS, KNEE, ELBOW,
JOINT, PIVOT, DEPEND
hinny ...... MULE, NEIGH, WHINNY
parent of .... DONKEY
hint .... CUE, CLUE, IMPLY,
ALLUDE, INKLING, POINTER,
TIP(OFF), SUGGEST, INTIMATE
hinterland .... INLAND,
BACKWOODS, BOONDOCKS
hip .... COXA, ILIA, FRUIT,
HAUNCH, HUCKLE
boots .... WADERS
bone .... ILIA, ILIUM, PELVIS
pains .... SCIATICA
pertaining to the .... ILIAC,
SCIATIC
width of: sl. .... BEAM
hipbone .... ILIUM
part of .... PUBIS, ISCHIUM
hippocampus .... SEA HORSE
Hippocrates' birthplace .... COS
Hippocratic _____, doctors'
.... OATH
hippodrome .... ARENA, (RACING)
COURSE
hippopotamus .... SEACOW,
BEHEMOTH, PACHYDERM
hips supporter .... GIRDLE
width .... BEAM
hipster .... HEPCAT, BEATNIK
hircine .... GOATLIKE
hire .... LET, RENT, LEASE,
EMPLOY, ENGAGE, CHARTER
hired applauders .... CLAQUE
assassin .... BRAVO,
CUTTHROAT, HIGHBINDER
hireling .... MERCENARY
Hirondelle .... OISEAU
hirsute .... HAIRY, PILOSE,
SHAGGY, BRISTLY
growth .... HAIR
Hispania .... SPAIN
ancient .... IBERIA
former part of .... PORTUGAL
Hispanic .... SPANISH
Hispaniola .... HAITI
hispid .... HAIRY, SPINY, STRIGOSE
hiss .... SISS, WOOSH, SIBILATE
hisser .... GOOSE, SNAKE,
HECKLER
hissing .... FIZ(Z), FIZZY, SIBILANT
drink .... CHAMPAGNE, SODA
WATER
sound ...... SSH, PSST, WHIZ(Z),
FIZZLE, SIZZLE
hist .... SHUSH
histamine .... GASTRIN
historian .... ANNALIST,
RECORDER, CHRONICLER
historical .... REAL, FAMOUS,
FACTUAL, LEGENDARY

cars .... STANLEY STEAMERS
decade .... MAUVE
lawgiver .... MOSES
period .... ERA
records .... ANNALS, ARCHIVES,
CHRONICLES, MEMORABILIA
history ...... LORE, PAST, ANNALS,
RECORD, ACCOUNT, MEMOIRS,
CHRONICLE, NARRATIVE
famous in .... STORIED
muse of .... CLIO
person's life .... BIOGRAPHY
histrionic .... AFFECTED,
ARTIFICIAL, THEATRICAL
histrionics .... DRAMATICS
hit .... ACE, BAT, BOP, BIFF, BUMP,
CUFF, SLUG, SOCK, SWAT,
CLOUT, KNOCK, SMITE,
SMOTE, POMMEL, STRIKE,
SUCCESS
aloft/as in tennis .... LOB
baseball .... BUNT, SINGLE,
HOMERUN
direct .... BULL'S-EYE
great .... SMASH
hard .... LAM, SLOG, SLUG,
SMITE
it off .... FIT IN
lightly .... TAP
of the early '30s .... GOOD
NEWS
old style .... SMIT
on the head .... BOP, LAM,
BEAN, CONK, BRAIN
or miss .... RANDOM, AIMLESS,
HAPHAZARD
sign .... SRO
the slopes .... SKI
with a quick blow .... SWAT
hitch .... TIE, TUG, KNOT, LIMP,
SNAG, FASTEN, HOBBLE,
OBSTACLE, HINDRANCE
hitchhike .... BUM A RIDE, THUMB
A RIDE
hitchhiker ...... RIDER, PASSENGER
quest of .... LIFT
hitchpost .... PICKET
hither .... HERE, NEARER
partner of .... YON
hitherto .... TO NOW, UNTIL NOW,
HERETOFORE
Hitler's occupation .... HOUSE
PAINTER
rank .... CORPORAL
third .... REICH
title .... FU(E)HRER
wife .... (EVA)BRAUN
Hitlerite .... NAZI
Hittite .... SYRIAN
hive .... SKEP, SWARM, APIARY
dweller .... BEE

hives .... URTICARIA
nettle .... UREDO
remedy for .... BENADRYL
Hizzoner .... MAYOR
HMS Pinafore character
.... BUTTERCUP
Ho! .... HALT, STOP, WHOA
hoar .... GRAY, WHITE
hoard .... HIDE, AMASS, CACHE,
STOCK, STORE, SUPPLY,
RESERVE, TREASURE
hoarder .... MISER, NIGGARD
hoarding .... FENCE, POSTER,
BILLBOARD
animal .... WOODRAT,
SQUIRREL
hoarfrost .... RAG, RIME
hoarse .... GRUFF, HUSKY, ROUPY,
RAUCOUS, THROATY,
CROAKING
hoarseness .... ROUP
hoary .... OLD, GRAY, WHITE,
FROSTY, ANCIENT
hoax .... BAM, GAFF, JOKE, SHAM,
FRAUD, HOCUS, SPOOF, TRICK,
CANARD
hob .... ELF, PEG, LOUT, PUCK,
GOBLIN, RUSTIC
hobble .... LAME, LIMP, HITCH,
FETTER, HAMPER, HINDER
hobbledehoy .... BOY, YOUTH
hobby .... FAD, WHIM, HORSE,
FALCON, PASTIME, AVOCATION
of kings .... PHILATELY
hobgoblin .... ELF, ELVE, PUCK,
BOG(E)Y, GNOME, SPRITE,
BUGBEAR
hobnail .... RUSTIC
hobnob .... MIX, MINGLE,
ASSOCIATE, PAL AROUND,
SOCIALIZE, RUB ELBOWS
hobo .... BO, BUM, TRAMP,
DRIFTER, VAGRANT,
(BINDLE)STIFF
bundle/bedding .... BINDLE
camp .... JUNGLE
city hangout .... SKIDROW
stew .... MULLIGAN
Hobson's choice .... TAKE-IT-OR-
LEAVE-IT
hock .... HAM, PAWN, ANKLE,
JOINT
again .... REPAWN
joint ailment .... SPAVIN
hockey .... SHINNY
arena .... RINK
Bobby of .... ORR
cup .... STANLEY
disk .... PUCK
division of game .... PERIOD
feint .... DEKE

field .... BANDY
goal .... CAGE
player .... GOALIE
puck maneuver .... ICING
scored a goal in .... LIGHTED
THE LAMP
star .... ORR, HULL, GRETZKY
stick .... CAMAN
hockshop .... PAWNSHOP
sign .... BALL
hocus .... HOAX, FRAUD
pocus .... MAGIC, DECEIT,
TRICK(ERY)
hod .... TROUGH, SCUTTLE
hodgepodge .... HASH, MESS,
OLIO, STEW, CENTO, MEDLEY,
FARRAGO, MELANGE,
MIXTURE, POTTAGE,
MISHMASH
hoe .... HACK, TILL
hoecake .... CORN BREAD
hoedown .... SHINDIG
hog .... PIG, GRAB, DUROC, SWINE,
PORK(ER), BABIRUSA
cholera .... ROUGET
deer .... AXIS
fat .... LARD, ADEPS
female .... SOW, GILT
food .... MAST, SLOPS
genus .... SUS
ground .... MARMOT
kind of .... ROAD
male .... BOAR
peanut .... EARTHPEA
plum .... AMRA
thigh .... HAM
vital organ .... HASLET
wild .... BENE, BOAR,
PECCARY, RAZORBACK
young ..... GILT, SHOAT, SHOTE
Hogan's Heroes setting
.... STALAG
hogback .... RIDGE
hogfish .... WRASSE, PORPOISE
hoggish .... FILTHY, GREEDY
hogshead .... CASK, BARREL
content of .... BEER
hogtie .... MANACLE, TRUSS(UP)
hogwash .... SWILL, TRASH,
BALONEY, NONSENSE
hoi polloi .... MASSES,
(THE)MAJORITY
hoist ...... CAT, JACK, LIFT, BOUSE,
HEAVE, RAISE, WINCH, PULL
UP, ELEVATOR
anchor .... WEIGH
hoisted just off bottom .... ATRIP
hoisting device .... GIN, BOOM,
CRANE, DAVIT, SLING, WINCH,
CAPSTAN, DERRICK, FORKLIFT,
WINDLASS

tackle .... CAT
hoity-toity .... FUSSY, GIDDY,
HUFFY, SNOOTY, PETULANT,
ARROGANT, CAPRICIOUS
person .... SNOB
hokeypokey .... ICECREAM,
TRICK(ERY), HOCUS-POCUS
Hokkaido, capital of .... YEZO,
SAPPORO
city .... OTARU
native .... AINU
Hoko Gunto .... PESCADORES
hokum .... BUNK, HUMBUG,
BALONEY, CLAPTRAP,
NONSENSE, APPLESAUCE
hold .... GRIP, STAY, GRASP,
CLUTCH, DETAIN, OCCUPY,
REGARD, SUSTAIN, KEEP
BACK, MAINTAIN, RESTRAIN
a session .... SIT, MEET
back .... DAM, STAY, STEM,
DETER, DETAIN, RETARD,
STIFLE, RESTRAIN
dear .... CHERISH
down .... LIMIT
due to war .... INTERN
fast .... BELAY
firmly .... RIVET
forth .... OFFER, PREACH
in custody .... DETAIN,
IMPOUND
in law .... BIND
off .... REBUFF, POSTPONE
on .... ENDURE, REMAIN,
PERSIST, CONTINUE
one's own .... COPE
out .... LAST, ENDURE, REFUSE,
RESIST
over .... DELAY, POSTPONE
scoreless .... BLANK, BLITZ
ship's .... HATCH
sway .... RULE
the deed of .... OWN
the reins .... GOVERN
up .... DELAY, ELEVATE,
STOPPAGE
your horses! .... WAIT
holder .... OWNER, PAYEE,
POSSESSOR
baby or corn .... CRIB
lease .... LESSEE, RENTER,
TENANT
shish-kebab .... SKEWER
holding .... TENURE, PROPERTY
device .... VISE, CLAMP, CLASP,
TONGS
in custody .... DETENTION
in poker .... PAIR
holdings .... BONDS, STOCKS,
ASSETS, EFFECTS, PROPERTY,
POSSESSIONS

holdout .... STRIKER, RESISTER

holdup .... HEIST, HIJACK, STICKUP, ROBBERY

holdup man .... BANDIT, ROBBER, BRIGAND, FOOTPAD, HIJACKER

hole .... GAP, PIT, BORE, LILL, WELL, CAVITY, HOLLOW, OPENING, ORIFICE, VENT(AGE), APERTURE, EXCAVATION

ace in the .... CLINCHER

air .... SPIRACLE

cloth .... EYELET

coin .... SLOT

embankment .... GIME

enlarger tool .... REAM

gangster's .... HIDEOUT

golf course .... CUP

-in-one, golf .... ACE

of tube, etc. .... BORE

skin .... PORE

sleeve's .... SCYE

up .... DIG IN, HIDE

water .... (SWIMMING)POOL

holes, full of .... PERFORATED

holiday .... FERIA, FIESTA, RECESS, FESTIVAL, VACATION

kind of .... ROMAN, EASTER, WEEKEND, OFFICIAL

of a .... FERIAL

holiness .... SANCTITY

Holland. See also Netherlands
.... CLOTH, DUTCH

capital .... (THE)HAGUE

capital (North) .... HAARLEM

dialect ...... FRISIAN, FRANKISH

gin .... GENEVA, SCHNAP(P)S

seaport .... EDAM

sight in .... WINDMILL

village .... EDE

Hollandaise .... SAUCE

Hollandia .... KOTABARU

hollands .... GIN

holler .... YELL, SHOUT

hollow .... DENT, HOLE, COELO, EMPTY, FALSE, FOSSA, CAVITY, SUNKEN, CONCAVE

cheek's/chin's .... DIMPLE

circular .... CORRIE

opposed to .... SOLID

tile .... KEY

holly .... ASSI, HOLM, ILEX, ACEBO, ERYNGO, YAUPON

hollyhock .... MALLOW, ALTH(A)EA

Hollywood Academy people
.... AWARDERS

award .... OSCAR

columnist .... RONA, GRAHAME, LOUELLA, (HEDDA)HOPPER

industry .... CINEMA, MOVIE(S)

landmark .... CIRO'S

name .... BARA, DUKE, FORD, PECK, WOOD, FONDA, GABLE, GARBO, GRANT, KELLY, LEIGH, NEGRI, TRACY, WAYNE, COOPER, HARLOW, KEATON, MARTIN, MENJOU, TAYLOR, WELLES, DEMILLE, GARDNER, GARLAND, HEPBURN, STEWART, HESTON, SWANSON, CRAWFORD, DIETRICH, PICKFORD

street/locale ...... VINE, SUNSET

writer .... SCENARIST

holm .... AIT, OAK, HOLLY, ISLET, BOTTOMS

oak .... ILEX

Holmes, Sherlock .... DETECTIVE

alter ego .... WATSON

creator of .... (CONAN)DOYLE

favorite word .... ELEMENTARY

holograph .... (MANU)SCRIPT, HANDWRITTEN

Holstein .... CATTLE

holt .... HILL, COPSE, GROVE, WOODS, COPPICE, WILLOWS

holy ...... SANTA, CHASTE, DIVINE, SACRED, BLESSED, SAINTLY, SINLESS, HALLOW(ED)

city ..... ROME, LHASA, MECCA, HARDWAR, VARANASI, JERUSALEM

communion .... EUCHARIST

cross .... ROOD

man .... FAKIR, SAINT, MAHATMA, MARABOUT

oil .... CHRISM

person .... SAINT

picture .... ICON

place .... CHURCH, SHRINE, TEMPLE, SANCTUM, SANCTUARY

prefix .... HAGIO, HIERO

water sprinkling ..... ASPERGES

writings .... SCRIPTURES

Holy Father .... POPE

Grail ..... CHALICE, SANGRAAL, SANGR(E)AL

Grail finder .... GALAHAD

Grail knight .... BORS, AMFORTAS, PARSIPAL, PERCIVAL

Grail knights' enemy
.... KLINGSOR

Land .... PALESTINE

Land visitor .... PALMER, PILGRIM

Sepulcher visitor .... HADJI, PILGRIM

Spirit ..... PNEUMA, PARACLETE

Thursday island
.... ASCENCION

War: Moslem .... JIHAD

Writ .... BIBLE

homage .... HONOR, TRIBUTE, REVERENCE

to saints .... DULIA

hombre ...... CARD, GAME, OMBER

slang .... GUY, MAN, FELLOW

Homburg .... (FELT)HAT

home ...... ROOF, ABODE, ASYLUM, HEARTH, REFUGE, SHELTER, DOMICILE, DWELLING, HOUSEHOLD, RESIDENCE

animal's .... DEN, LAIR, HABITAT

bird's .... NEST, AERIE

for a cruise .... OCEANLINER

for poor/sick .... HOSPICE

-grown .... LOCAL, NATIVE

of Andrew Jackson .... THE HERMITAGE

George Washington
.... MOUNT VERNON

James Madison
.... MONTPELIER

Kodak .... ROCHESTER

the .... DOMESTIC

the Braves .... ATLANTA

the Dolphins .... MIAMI

the Giants .... SAN FRANCISCO

the surrey with the fringe top .... OKLAHOMA

the Uzbek .... ASIA

the Wright Brothers
.... DAYTON

Thomas Jefferson
.... MONTICELLO

pastor's .... MANSE

-run king .... AARON

screen .... TV, TELLY, VIDEO, TELEVISION

spider's .... WEB

stately .... MANOR

Home Sweet Home composer
.... PAYNE

homebody .... RECLUSE, STAY-AT-HOME

of a kind .... TENANT

homecoming, alumni
.... REUNION

homeground .... BASE, BAILIWICK

homeless child .... ARAB, WAIF

tramp .... HOBO

homely ...... UGLY, PLAIN, SIMPLE, HOMESPUN

homemaker .... HOUSEWIFE

homer .... KOR, HOMERUN

Homer enchantress .... CIRCE

epic of .... ILIAD, ODYSSEY

sea nymph .... CALYPSO
translator of .... CHAPMAN
Homeric .... EPIC(AL)
homerun with bases full
.... GRAND SLAM
homesick .... BLUE
homesickness .... NOSTALGIA
excessive .... NOSTOMANIA
homespun .... PLAIN, HOMELY,
SIMPLE, UNPRETENTIOUS,
DOWN-TO-EARTH
cloth .... RUSSET
homestead .... TOFT, MESSUAGE
site .... IN LOT
homesteader .... SOONER,
SETTLER
homestretch .... LAST LAP
homework .... LESSONS
homey .... COZY, FRIENDLY
homicidal .... MURDEROUS
homily .... TALK, SERMON,
LECTURE
homing faculty ...... ORIENTATION
hominy .... SAMP, GRITS
homo .... MAN, PRIMATE
combining form .... LIKE,
SAME, EQUAL
Homo sapiens .... MAN(KIND)
homogeneous .... ALIKE, SIMILAR,
IDENTICAL
homogenize .... EMULSIFY
homonym .... NAMESAKE
homopterous insect .... APHID,
CICADA
homosexual .... GAY, INVERT,
LESBIAN
homunculus .... DWARF
Hondo .... HONSHU
Honduras cape .... FALSO,
CAMARON
capital .... TEGUCIGALPA
city/town .... TELA, YORO,
DANLI, LA PAZ, MORAZAN, LA
CEIBA, CATACAMAS,
CHOLUTECA, COMAYAGUA,
JUTICALPA, OLANCHITO, EL
PARAISO, EL PROGRESO, SANTA
RITA, PUERTO CORTES
gulf .... FONSECA
hero .... LEMPIRA
Indian .... PAYA
island .... UTILA, ROATAN,
GUANAJA
lagoon .... BRUS, CARATASCA
lake .... YOJOA
language .... SPANISH
monetary unit .... LEMPIRA
mountains .... PIJA, COLON,
ESPERANZA
president .... CALLEJAS
river .... COCO, SICO, ULUA,

AGUAN, WANKS, PATUCA,
SULACO, PAULAYA, SEGOVIA,
CHOLUTECA
seaport .... TELA, LA CEIBA
hone .... STROP, YEARN,
GRIND(ER), SHARPEN,
OILSTONE, WHET(STONE)
honest .... FAIR, PURE, WHITE,
FRANK, UPRIGHT, TRUTHFUL
honesty .... HONOR, CANDOR,
PROBITY, MOONWORT,
INTEGRITY
honewort .... PARSLEY
honey .... DEAR, SWEET, DARLING
and mulberry juice .... MORAT
badger .... RATEL
bear .... KINKAJOU
bee .... APIS, DINGAR, DESERET
buzzard .... KITE, PERN
container/holder .... COMB,
CRUSE
creeper .... GUITGUIT
drink .... MEAD, MORAT
eater .... IAO, BEAR, MOHO
fermented .... MEAD
pharmacy .... MEL
plant .... FIGWORT
pollen mix .... BEEBREAD
prefix .... MELI
source .... FLOWER, NECTAR
honeybee genus .... APIS
honeycomb eater .... BEEMOTH
material .... BEESWAX
part .... CELL
honeycombed .... FAVOSE
honeydew .... MELON, NECTAR
honeyed .... SWEET, SUGARY,
CANDIED
words .... FLATTERY
honeymoon haven ...... NIAGARA
FALLS
honeysuckle .... VINE, AZALEA,
CLOVER, WOODBINE,
EGLANTINE
hong .... FACTORY, WAREHOUSE
Hong Kong bay .... REPULSE
capital .... VICTORIA
peninsula .... KOWLOON
honk .... YANG
honker .... GOOSE
honky-tonk: sl. .... DIVE,
SALOON, CABARET
Honolulu airbase .... HICKHAM
exclusive section ...... KAHALA
greeting .... ALOHA
native dance .... HULA
native dancer .... WAHINE
swimming resort ...... WAIKIKI
honor .... FAME, FETE, AWARD,
ECLAT, EXALT, GLORY,
CREDIT, ESTEEM, HOMAGE,

DIGNITY, ENNOBLE, RESPECT,
VENERATE, REVERE(NCE),
DECORATION
with insults .... ROAST
Honor Thy Father author
.... TALESE
honorable .... NOBLE, WORTHY,
UPRIGHT, REPUTABLE
mention .... CITATION
honorarium .... TIP, REWARD
honorary ...... TITULAR, EMERITUS
commission, military
.... BREVET
honors .... AWARDS, TITLES,
ACCOLADE, TRIBUTES
Honshu .... HONDO
bay .... ISE, TOYAMA
city .... KOBE, KURE, KYOTO,
HIMEJI, SENDAI, OKAYAMA,
HIROSHIMA
port .... KOBE
hooch .... BOOTLEG, WHISKEY
hood .... BIGGIN, CAMAIL
airplane's .... NACELLE
bird's .... CREST, CALOT(TE)
carriage's/cloak's ...... CAPOTE
folding ...... CALASH, CALECHE
monk's .... COWL, AMICE,
CAPOUCH, CAPUCHE
part .... CAMAIL, TIPPET
slang .... THUG, GANGSTER
tail of .... LIRIPIPE
hooded ...... COWLED, CUCULLATE
cloak .... CAPUCHIN
garment .... CAPE, PARKA,
CAPOTE
merganser .... SMEW
seal .... BLADDERNOSE
snake .... ADDER, COBRA,
PUFFING
hoodlum ...... GOON, PUNK, THUG,
ROWDY, GANGSTER,
HOOLIGAN, LARRIKIN
hoodoo .... HEX, JINX, VOODOO,
BEWITCH, BAD LUCK
hoodwink .... DUPE, SEEL, CHEAT,
DECEIVE, BLINDFOLD
hooey .... BUNK, NONSENSE
hoof .... PAW, FOOT, UNGULA
like a .... UNGUAL
on the .... ALIVE
paring tool .... BUTTERIS
shaped .... UNGULATE
slang .... DANCE
hoofbeat .... KLOP, CLIP-CLOP
hoofed .... UNGUAL, UNGULATE
hoofer .... (TAP)DANCER
Kelly .... GENE
hook .... BEND, GAFF, GORE,
CLEEK, CROOK, TACH(E),
CLEVIS, JIGGER, GRAMPON,

GRAPNEL, SWINDLE, HEADLAND

and eye .... FASTENER

and loop .... GEMEL, HINGE

colloquial .... LAND, CATCH

like .... FALCATE, UNCINAL

like mark .... CEDILLA

longshoreman's .... BALING

money .... LARI(N)

part .... BARB

shaped .... UNCINAL

hooka(h) .... PIPE, NARG(H)ILE

hooked .... GAFFED, FALCATE, ADUNC(OUS), AQUILINE, UNCINATE

person .... ADDICT

hookey player .... TRUANT

hooklike ...... FALCATE, UNCINATE

process .... UNCUS

hookup .... TIE-UP

hooligan .... SPIV, ROWDY, HOODLUM, RUFFIAN

hoop .... (EAR)RING

shaped handle .... BAIL

hooper .... SWAN, COOPER

hoopla .... BUSTLE, BALLYHOO, EXCITEMENT

hoopster .... CAGER

hoosegow ...... JAIL, POKY, CLINK, PRISON

Hoosier humorist .... ADE

novelist .... TARKINGTON

poet .... RILEY

State .... INDIANA

town .... PERU

hoot ...... BOO, CRY, SASS, SHOUT, WHOOP, ULULATE

sign of a .... SCORN

hooter .... FAN, OWL, HECKLER

Hoover .... DAM, HERBERT

blankets .... NEWSPAPERS

Dam lake .... MEAD

flag .... (EMPTY)POCKET

hop .... LEAP, VINE, CAPER, DANCE, FRISK, SPRING

airplane .... FLIGHT

kiln .... O(A)ST

o'-my-thumb .... DWARF

plant .... LUPULUS

stem .... BINE

hopbrau equipment .... STEINS

hope .... LONG, ASPIRE, DESIRE

container .... CHEST

enormously little .... FAT CHANCE

hopeful .... ASPIRANT, CONTENDER, EXPECTANT, OPTIMISTIC

Hopei .... CHIHLI

capital of .... TIENTSIN

hopeless .... VAIN, FUTILE,

DEJECTED, DESPERATE, BEYOND HOPE

position .... RATTRAP, CHECKMATE

hophead .... ADDICT

Hopi .... MOKI, MOQUI

room of .... KIVA

hopped up .... CHARGED

hopper .... FLEA, FROG, SILO, TOAD, CICADA, LOCUST, CRICKET, KANGAROO

short for a .... ROO

Hopper, columnist .... HEDDA

hops kiln .... O(A)ST

mellowed .... OLDS

powder .... LUPULIN

stem .... BINE

hora .... FOLKDANCE

Horae .... DIKE, HOURS, IRENE, EIRENE, EUNOMIA

horde .... MOB, ARMY, HOST, PACK, CROWD, DROVE, SWARM, LEGION, THRONG

hordeolum .... STY(E)

Horeb ...... MOUNTAIN, (MT.)SINAI

horehound .... MINT, JUICE

horizon .... LIMIT, SKYLINE

arc of the .... AZIMUTH

horizontal .... FLAT, FLUSH, LEVEL, PLANE

band: heraldic .... FRIEZE

position .... PRONE

hormone .... PROLON, ESTRIOL, ESTRONE, GASTRIN, INSULIN, THEELIN, ANDROGEN, ESTROGEN, SECRETIN, ADRENALIN, CORTISONE

horn .... DAG, TUBA, BUGLE, CORNU, PRONG, SIREN, CORNET, CROCKET

bell-like part .... FLARE

bird beak's .... EPITHEMA

blare .... TOOT, FANFARE, TANTARA

combining form .... CERATO

deer .... ANTLER, BALCON, CROCHE

in .... MEDDLE, INTERVENE

insect's .... ANTENNA

like .... CORNU, CORNEOUS

moon's .... CUSP

of a _____ .... DILEMMA

of plenty .... CORNUCOPIA

part of .... MUTE

pierce with .... GORE, HOOK

pout .... CATFISH, BULLHEAD

snail's .... TENTACLE

tissue .... SCUR, KERATIN

unbranched .... DAG

hornbeam .... IRONWOOD

hornbill .... TOCK, HOMARI,

TOUCAN

Hornblower of fiction .... HORATIO

Hornby (Lesley) .... TWIGGY

Horne, singer .... LENA

horneblende .... EDENITE

horned animal .... GNU, RAM, BULL, DEER, IBEX, STAG, RHINO, BUFFALO

horse .... UNICORN

problem .... DILEMMA

viper .... ASP, CERASTES

hornet .... WASP, VESPID, STINGER, YELLOW JACKET

Hornie .... SATAN

hornless .... POLLED, ACEROUS

animal .... MUL(L)EY, POLLARD

hornlike .... CORNU, CERATOID, KERATOID

hornswoggle: sl. .... HUMBUG, BAMBOOZLE

horntail .... INSECT, SAWFLY

horny .... CALLOUS, CORNEOUS

growth ..... CORN, NAIL, WART, KERATOSIS

scale .... NAIL, SCUTE, SCUTUM

skin .... CORN, CALLUS

tissue .... CERATIN

horologe .... CLOCK, WATCH, SUNDIAL, HOURGLASS

horologist .... WATCHMAKER

horoscope ...... ASPECT, FORECAST

division .... CUSP

horrendous .... HORRIBLE

horrible .... DIRE, GRIM, ALARMING, DREADFUL, GRIS(T)LY, HIDEOUS, TERRIBLE, REVOLTING

colloquial .... UGLY, SHOCKING

horrid .... FOUL, UGLY, NASTY, HATEFUL, REPULSIVE, REVOLTING

horrified ...... AGHAST, APPALLED

horrify .... SCARE, APPAL(L), SHOCK, DISMAY, FRIGHTEN

horrifying .... GRUESOME

horror .... DREAD, TERROR, AVERSION, LOATHING

hors de combat .... DISABLED

d'oeuvre .... OLIVE, CANAPE, APPETIZER

horse .... COB, ARAB, BIDET, MOUNT, STEED, BAYARD, DOBBIN, EQUINE, JENNET, PADNAG, SORREL, BOLLARD, CAVALIA

Alexander the Great's .... BUCEPHALUS

ankle .... HOCK

armor .... BARD(E)

back of .... WITHERS

back tumor .... WARBLE
backward movement
.... PASSADE
baggage .... SUMPTER
belly band .... GIRTH
blacksmith .... FARRIER
blanket ...... MANTA, HOUSING,
TRAPPING
blinder .... WINKER
body .... BARREL
box of .... STALL
breaker .... ROUGHRIDER
broken-winded .... WHISTLER
brown ..... BAY, ROAN, SORREL
buyer .... KNACKER
care for pay of .... LIVERY
caretaker .... GROOM, HOSTLER
carriage .... SHAY
castrated .... GELDING
cavalry .... WALER
chestnut .... BUCKEYE
Cisco Kid's .... DIABLO
clean coat of .... CURRY
colloquial .... BANGTAIL
color .... BAY, PIED, ROAN,
PINTO, DAPPLE, SORREL
comber .... GROOM, CURRIER
combining form .... HIPP(O),
KERAT(O)
command to .... GEE, HAW,
WHOA, GIDDAP
dancing .... LIPPIZAN
dappled .... ROAN
dark .... SLEEPER
dealer .... COPER, KNACKER
disease .... GID, BOTS, LOCO,
FARCY, VIVES, HEAVES,
LAMPAS, NAGANA, SPAVIN,
SURRA(H), DOURINE, LAMPERS,
QUITTOR, STAGGERS,
DISTEMPER, STRANGLES,
WHISTLING, MAL(L)ANDERS
dishonestly entered in race
.... RINGER
dock-tailed .... CURTAL
doctor .... VET, FARRIER
donkey offspring .... HINNY
draft .... SHIRE, SUFFOLK,
PERCHERON
eczema .... MALANDERS
exercise place .... PADDOCK
eye cover .... WINKER,
BLINDER
eyelid inflammation ...... HAW
famous ...... OMAHA, ASSAULT,
TRIGGER, CHAMPION,
CITATION, MAN O' WAR,
TRAVELLER, WHIRLAWAY, SEA
BISCUIT, BUCEPHALUS,
SECRETARIAT
female .... DAM, MARE

fictional .... BAYARD,
ROSINANTE
fetlock growth .... GRAGE
fresh .... REMOUNT
from Medusa's body
.... PEGASUS
gait of ...... LOPE, RACK, TROT,
CANTER, GALLOP, WINDING
genus .... EQUUS
golden .... PALOMINO
guide rope .... LONGE
hair .... SETON
half turn .... CARACOLE,
DEMIVOLT
halter .... HACKAMORE
handsome .... ARAB
harness-racing .... PACER
high-spirited .... STEED
hobby .... DADA
hybrid .... ZEBRULA
incisor .... NIPPER
inferior .... NAG, PLUG,
PLATER, SLEEPER
iron .... TRAIN
joint .... HOUGH, FETLOCK
keeper .... GROOM
lame a .... GRAVEL
laugh .... GUFFAW
lead .... PACER
leap .... BUCK, VAULT,
CURVET, GAMBADE, GAMBADO,
CAPRIOLE, CARACOLE
leg part .... HOCK, HOOF,
HOUGH, SHANK, GASKIN,
FETLOCK, PASTERN
longshot .... SLEEPER,
OUTSIDER
losing cause .... NAIL
magic .... BAYARD
male .... COLT, STEED,
GELDING, STALLION
man: myth. .... CENTAUR
master of the .... MARSHAL
mettle .... PRIDE
muscles atrophy .... SWEENY
nearest wheels .... POLER
nervous condition
.... STAGGERS
newborn .... FOAL
non-scratched, in a race
.... STARTER
of mixed breed .... GRADE
of the year, 1994 .... HOLY
BULL
old .... RIP, JADE, HACK, PLUG,
SKATE, PADNAG
opera .... OATER, WESTERN
ornamental covering
.... CAPARISON
pack .... DRUDGE, SUMPTER
paint .... PINTO

parasitic larva .... BOTFLY,
WARBLE
pen .... CORRAL
piebald .... PINTO, CALICO
race .... PACER, PLATER,
SWEEPS, TROTTER, YEARLING,
HANDICAP, STEEPLECHASE
race board .... TOTE
race "triple crown" winner
.... OMAHA, ASSAULT,
AFFIRMED, CITATION,
WHIRLAWAY, SIR BARTON,
COUNT FLEET, GALLANT FOX,
SECRETARIAT, WAR ADMIRAL,
SEATTLE SLEW
racing .... TURF
bet ..... FORECAST, QUINELLA
course .... HIPPODROME
fan .... TURFMAN
meet .... ASCOT, DERBY
official .... STEWARD
radish tree .... BEHEN
rawhide .... SHAGREEN
rearing of .... PESADE
relief .... RELAY
rider .... CAVALRYMAN,
EQUESTRIAN
rider's fall .... SPILL
rider's seat .... SADDLE
riding .... MOUNT, STEED,
PALFREY
river .... HIPPO
Ronald Reagan's .... LITTLE
MAN
round-up .... RODEO
rump .... CROUP, CRUPPER
runaway .... BOLTER
saddle .... MOUNT, PALFREY
shelter .... STALL, STABLE
shoer .... FARRIER
short/thick set .... COB
skin disease .... CALORIS
small .... COB, TIT, PONY,
BIDET, BRONCO, JENNET,
GALLOWAY, GENET(TE),
SHETLAND
sound ...... NIE, NEIGH, SNORT,
WHINNY
spotted .... APPALOOSA
stocky .... COB
sweat .... FOAM, LATHER
swift .... ARAB, PACER, RACER,
CLIPPER, SPANKER
tail .... CLOUD, PRELE
talking .... ARION
tamer .... ROUGHRIDER
tender .... GROOM
tooth .... TUSH, NIPPER
toy .... PONY, SHETLAND
trained .... PACER
training rope/place ..... LONGE

trappings .... HARNESS
turn of .... MANEGE,
  CARACOLE, (DEMI)VOLT
untamed .... BRONCO
war .... CHARGER, COURSER
whip .... CROP, QUIRT
wild .... TARPAN, BRUMBIE,
  BRONC(H)O, MUSTANG
winged .... PEGASUS
winless .... MAIDEN
winning gait .... ROMP
woman's .... PALFREY
worn out .... HACK, JADE,
  PLUG, YAUD, SKATE
worthless ...... NAG, RIP, JADE,
  WEED
young ...... COLT, FOAL, FILLY,
  YEARLING
horseback .... HOGBACK
 on .... A CHEVAL
horsefly .... TABANID
horsehair .... SETON, SNELL
horseman .... RIDER, CABALLERO,
  EQUESTRIAN
 in bullfighting .... PICADOR
horsemanship .... MANEGE,
  EQUITATION
 movement in .... PIAFFER
horsemen .... CAVALRY
 historical .... ROUGHRIDERS
horsemen's parade
  .... CAVALCADE
horsemint .... MONARDA
horseplay .... FUN, JINKS, PRANK,
  COMEDY
horses, ancestors of .... EOHIPPUS
 art of riding .... MANEGE,
  EQUITATION
 certain .... CROPEARS
 collection of .... STUD, STABLE
 herd of .... HARRAS, REMUDA
 hold one's .... PAUSE, SLOW
  DOWN
 left behind in race .... RUCK
 pertaining to .... EQUINE
 school for .... MANEGE
 soldiers on .... CAVALRY
 string of .... STABLE
horseshoe .... RINGER
 gripper .... CALK
 player .... TOSSER
 points .... LEANERS
horseweed .... OXBALM
horsewhip .... CROP, FLOG, LASH,
  QUIRT, CHAB(O)UK
horsy crowd? .... NEIGHBORS
hortatory ...... URGING, ADVISING,
  ADVISORY
Horus .... RA, GOD, SUN
 head of .... HAWK
 parent of .... ISIS, OSIRIS

hosanna .... SHOUT, PRAISE,
  EXCLAMATION
hose .... TUBE, SOCKS, STOCKINGS
 spout .... NOZZLE
Hosea .... OSSE
 daughter of .... UNLOVED
 son of .... JEZREEL
 wife of .... GOMER
hosiery .... HOSE, NYLONS, SOCKS,
  ANKLETS, STOCKINGS
hospice .... INN, ASYLUM, IMARET,
  REFUGE, POORHOUSE
hospitable .... CORDIAL,
  GRACIOUS, RECEPTIVE
hospital .... SICK BAY, INFIRMARY,
  LAZARETTO
 attendant .... ORDERLY
 dispensary .... CLINIC
 division .... WARD, CLINIC,
  PAVILION
 drip IV
 for foundlings .... CRECHE
 for mentally sick
  ...... BUGHOUSE, BOOBY HATCH
 for the poor .... SPITAL,
  LAZARET(TE)
 kind of ...... ASYLUM, MENTAL,
  GENERAL, LYING-IN,
  MATERNITY, SANATORIUM
 ship .... HOPE
 staffer .... RESIDENT
 vehicle .... AMBULANCE
host .... ARMY, BREAD, HORDE,
  LEGION, THRONG, LANDLORD,
  INNKEEPER, MULTITUDE
 a toast .... REGALE
 kind of .... EMCEE
 receptacle .... PYX, PATEN,
  TABERNACLE
hostage .... PAWN, PLEDGE,
  SURETY
hostel(ry) .... INN, TAVERN
hostess .... ATTENDANT,
  ENTERTAINER
 airline .... STEWARDESS
 at times .... USHER, SEATER
 famed .... HOWAR,
  (PERLE)MESTA
hostile .... ENEMY, WARLIKE,
  BELLICOSE, UNFRIENDLY
 feeling .... ANIMUS, GRUDGE,
  RANCOR
hostilities .... BATTLE, COMBAT,
  WAR(FARE), CONFLICT
hostility .... SPITE, ANIMUS,
  ENMITY, HATRED, ILL-WILL,
  FRICTION, ANTAGONISM
hostler .... GROOM
hot .... ANGRY, FIERY, ARDENT,
  BITING, HEATED, HECTIC,
  SULTRY, TORRID, PEPPERY,

  THERMAL, VIOLENT,
  EXCITABLE
 air .... VAPOR, HUMBUG,
  BOASTING, BOMBAST
 and bothered .... UNEASY
 and damp .... MUGGY
 baths .... THERME
 blooded .... LUSTY, ARDENT,
  INTENSE, ZEALOUS, RECKLESS,
  SPIRITED, LUSTFUL,
  PASSIONATE
 cargo .... CONTRABAND
 corner, so-called .... BASE,
  THIRD
 fiddler .... NERO
 goods .... SWAG, STOLEN,
  CONTRABAND
 iron treatment .... CAUTERY
 old style .... CALID
 plate .... STOVE
 seat .... ELECTRIC CHAIR
 slang .... GOOD, FRESH,
  (BRAND)NEW, JUST OUT
 spot .... DESERT
 spot, of a kind .... SAUNA
 spring .... GEYSER, THERME
 springs, of .... THERMAL
 taste .... PEPPERY
 tempered ..... TESTY, IRACUND,
  PEPPERY, EXPLOSIVE
 time .... SUMMER
 water: colloq. .... FIX, JAM,
  PINCH, SCRAPE, TROUBLE
 water hazard .... SCALD
 wind .... SIROCCO
hotbed .... INCITER, TROUBLE
  SPOT
hotchpotch .... MESS, STEW,
  JUMBLE
hotdog .... WIENER
hotel .... INN, PUB, SUITE, TAVERN,
  HOSTEL(RY)
 boy .... PAGE, BUTTONS
 chain .... HYATT, HILTON,
  RAMADA, STATLER, SHERATON,
  HOLIDAY INN
 cheap .... FLEABAG,
  FLOPHOUSE
 dining room .... GRILL
 foyer .... LOBBY
 guest .... PATRON, TRAVELER,
  TRANSIENT
 keeper .... HOST, BONIFACE
 page .... BUTTONS
 reception center
  .... (FRONT)DESK
 resident .... GUEST, PATRON
hotfoot: colloq. .... HIE, RUN,
  RACE, HURRY, HASTEN
hothead .... FIREBRAND
hotheaded .... RASH, FIERY,

HASTY, TESTY, SPUNKY,
WILLFUL, IMPETUOUS
hothouse ...... HOTBED, NURSERY,
GREENERY, VIVARIUM
hotrod .... RACER, JALOPY
hotrods, race of .... DRAG
Hottentot .... NAMA, NEGRO
land .... NAMAQUA
language/tribe .... NAMA,
BUSHMAN
race .... NEGROID
village .... KRAAL
Houdini, magician .... HARRY,
WEISS
hound .... NAG, HUNT, CHASE,
AFGHAN, HARASS, INCITE,
PLAGUE, BRACHET, CERBERUS,
(HUNTING)DOG
female .... BRACH
hunting .... BASSET, BEAGLE,
SETTER, HARRIER,
BLOODHOUND
sad-faced .... BASSET
wolf .... ALAN
hour .... MATIN
hourglass .... HOROLOGE
houri .... NYMPH
hourly .... HORAL, OFTEN,
CONTINUAL, FREQUENT(LY)
house .... HOME, ROOF, LODGE,
CONTAIN, COTTAGE, SHELTER,
THEATER, DOMICILE,
DWELLING
and lot .... PREMISE
bird's .... NEST, AERIE
correctional .... BRIDEWELL,
REFORMATORY
country .... VILLA, CASINO,
extension .... PORCH, VERANDA
feature, suburban ..... PICTURE
WINDOW
fortified .... PEEL
haunter .... SPOOK
ice .... IGLU, IGLOO
instant .... PREFAB
kind of ..... HASH, PENT, POOR,
TOWN, DUPLEX
legislative .... DIET, CONGRESS,
PARLIAMENT
log .... IZBA, CABIN
mud .... DOBE, TEMBE
organ .... PERIODICAL
pertaining to a .... DOMAL
plant .... FERN
poor man's .... HUT, HOVEL,
SHACK
portable .... TENT, TEPEE,
WIGWAM
ranch .... CASITA, GRANGE,
HACIENDA
side covering .... SIDING,

SHINGLE
small, dingy .... HOLE
state visitor's (U.S.) .... BLAIR
stately .... PALACE, MANSION
summer .... RANCH, VILLA,
CASINO, GAZEBO
houseboat .... BARGE
housebreaker .... BURGLAR
housebroken .... TAMED,
TRAINED, DISCIPLINED
housefly genus .... MUSCA,
FANNIA
of the .... MUSCID
household .... HOME, FAMILY,
MENAGE, MAINPOST,
DOMESTIC, DOMICILE
animal .... PET
food supply .... LARDER,
PROVISIONS
gods .... LARES, PENATES
linen .... NAPERY
task .... CHAR(E), CHORE
housekeeping .... MENAGE
housel .... EUCHARIST
houses, buyer of old
.... KNACKER
housesite .... TOFT
housewarming .... INFARE,
(HOUSE)PARTY
housewife .... DAME, HUSSY,
MATRON, HAUSFRAU, SEWING
KIT
concern of .... DIRT, MENU,
SOOT, WASH
housing .... PAD, FRAME,
LODGING, SHELTER, COVERING
engine .... NACELLE
for bells .... STEEPLE
hovel .... HUT, SHED, HUTCH,
SHACK, SHELTER, DWELLING
hover .... FLY, WAVER, LINGER,
FLUTTER, LIBRATE, VACILLATE
how .... MANNER, METHOD
about that! .... JUST IMAGINE
come? .... WHY, WHAT FOR
de-do .... MESS
Merman sang .... BELTED
some like it .... HOT
-to book .... MANUAL
to find out .... ASK
to get to Desire
.... STREETCAR
howdah .... SEAT
howdy ...... HELLO, HOW'S THINGS
however ...... BUT, YET, ANYHOW,
THO(UGH), NEVERTHELESS
howitzer .... CANNON
howl .... WAIL, YOWL, BELLOW,
ULULATE
lustily .... BAWL
howler .... OWL, MONKEY

colloquial .... BLUNDER
hoy .... BARGE
hoyden .... TOMBOY
hr., part of .... MIN, SEC
huaraches .... SANDALS
hub .... AXIS, NAVE, FOCUS,
CENTER, MIDDLE
the .... BOSTON
Hubbard .... SQUASH
Hubbard's (Ron) dianetics
.... SCIENTOLOGY
hubble .... HUMP
bubble .... PIPE, HOOKAH,
HUBBUB, UPROAR
hubbly .... ROUGH, UNEVEN
hubbub .... ADO, DIN, STIR, TO-
DO, NOISE, TUMULT, UPROAR,
RACKET, TURMOIL, BROUHAHA
hubby .... HUSBAND
hubris .... ARROGANCE,
INSOLENCE
huckle .... HIP, HAUNCH
Huckleberry Finn author
.... TWAIN
vehicle of .... RAFT
huckster .... PEDLAR, HAWKER,
VENDOR, PEDDLER,
TRADESMAN
colloquial .... ADMAN
huddle .... CAUCUS, JUMBLE,
ASSEMBLE, CONFERENCE
Hudson cliffs .... PALISADES
River city ..... TROY, YONKERS
River sight .... SINGSING
hue .... CRY, DYE, TINT, TONE,
COLOR, SHADE, TINGE
and cry .... SHOUTING
area .... ANNAM
Huey P., the Kingfish ...... LONG
huff ...... MIFF, PUFF, TIFF, ANGER,
BULLY, HECTOR, OFFEND,
TANTRUM
and puff .... GASP
huffy .... TOUCHY, PETULANT
hug .... FIT, CLASP, CARESS,
CUDDLE, ENFOLD, EMBRACE
kind of .... BEAR, BUNNY
me-tight .... VEST
huge .... LARGE, VAST,
ENORM(OUS), IMMENSE,
MAMMOTH, OUTSIZE, TITANIC,
GIGANTIC
amount .... SCAD
exhalation .... GIANT SIGH
hugger-mugger .... SHUSH,
COVERT, JUMBLE, MUFFLE,
MUDDLE, SECRET, SECRECY
Hugo, novelist .... VICTOR
daughter of .... ADELE
wife of .... ADELE
Huguenot .... PROTESTANT

leader .... CONDE, ADRETS
hula hula .... DANCE
dancer .... WAHINE
hull .... POD, HUSK, CALYX,
SHELL, SHUCK
part of .... KEEL, BILGE
hullabaloo .... ADO, FLAP, TO-DO,
CLAMOR, HUBBUB, TUMULT,
UPROAR, BALLYHOO
hum .... BUZZ, SING, CROON,
DRONE, WHIR(R)
human .... BIPED, WIGHT,
MORTAL, PERSON, ADAMITE,
ANDROID, EARTHLY,
EARTHLING
body .... CORPUS, CARCASS
body model .... MANAKIN,
MANIKIN
chain .... CORDON
conflict in life .... DRAMA
flesh eater .... CANNIBAL
limb .... ARM, LEG
race .... MANKIND
race's father .... NOE, ADAM
soul .... PSYCHE
weakness .... FRAILTY
humane .... KIND, TENDER,
MERCIFUL, CIVILIZED
humanities .... (FINE)ARTS,
LANGUAGES, LITERATURE
humanity .... MERCY, PEOPLE,
MANKIND, KINDNESS,
MORTALITY
humankind .... PEOPLE
humble ...... MEEK, POOR, ABASE,
LOW(LY), DEMEAN, MODEST,
SHAME, PALTRY, DEGRADE,
CHASTISE, HUMILIATE
pie .... CROW, NOMBLES,
NUMBLES
Humboldt, city on the .... ELKO
humbug .... BOSH, DUPE, FLAM,
SHAM, CHEAT, FRAUD,
HOKUM, GAMMON, SLAVER,
IMPOSTOR
compound word ...... JIGGERY-
POKERY
humdinger ...... PIP, AONE, LULU,
ONER, DILLY, WINNER,
SNORTER, EXCELLENT
humdrum .... DRAB, DULL, SOSO,
ROUTINE, MONOTONOUS
humerus .... BONE
kind of nerve in .... RADIAL
site of .... (UPPER)ARM
humid .... WET, DAMP, DANK,
MOIST, SULTRY
humidify .... MOISTEN
humiliate .... ABASE, ABASH,
SHAME, DEMEAN, HUMBLE,
DEGRADE, MORTIFY,

DISGRACE, EMBARRASS
humiliating experience
.... BITTER PILL
humility .... MODESTY, MEEKNESS,
LOWLINESS, SUBMISSION
humming .... BRISK, ACTIVE,
BUZZING, DRONING, SINGING
sound .... DRONE, WHIR(R)
hummingbird .... AVA, BLUET,
COSTA, SYLPH, TOPAZ,
COLIBRI, RACKETTAIL
hummock .... HILL, HUMP,
KNOLL, MOUND, HILLOCK
humor .... WIT, BABY, BILE,
MOOD, WHIM, FANCY, LYMPH,
CHOLER, CODDLE, PHLEGM,
CAPRICE, GRATIFY, INDULGE
bad .... TIFF
ironic(al) .... SARCASM
out of .... CROSS, MOODY,
IRRITABLE
quaint .... DROLLERY
slang .... CORN
humoresque .... CAPRICE
humorist .... ADE, WIT, WAG,
COBB, NASH, JOKER, ROGERS,
(BOB)HOPE, FARCEUR,
BENCHLEY, RABELAIS
alleged .... WEST, BUCHWALD
humorous .... DROLL, FUNNY,
WITTY, JOCOSE, AMUSING,
COMICAL, JOCULAR
awareness .... RISIBILITY
personification .... BARLEY-
CORN
pianist .... BORGE
play .... FARCE, COMEDY
slang suffix .... EROO
verse .... LIMERICK
hump ...... ARCH, BULGE, HUNCH,
HUBBLE, HUMMOCK
of a humpback .... KYPHOS
the .... HIMALAYAS
humpback ...... WHALE, KYPHOSIS
humpbacked .... GIBBOUS
humped animal .... ZEBU,
CAMEL, DROMEDARY
Humpty Dumpty, describing
.... SQUAT
personification .... EGG
humus .... MOLD, SOIL, MULCH
Hun .... ATLI, BOCHE, ETZEL,
ATTILA, GERMAN, SAVAGE,
VANDAL
hunch .... HUMP, HUNK, LUMP,
CHUNK, PREMONITION
Hunchback of Notre Dame
author .... HUGO
character .... ESMERALDA,
QUASIMODO
hundred .... CENTUM

combining form .... CENTI,
HECTO
dollar bill: sl. .... C-NOTE
years .... CENTURY
hundredfold .... CENTUPLE
hundredth .... 100TH, CENTISMAL
abbreviation of .... PCT
hundredweight .... CENTAL,
KANTAR, CENTNER, QUINTAL
hung up .... RANG OFF
Hungarian ...... HUNKY, MAGYAR
capital .... BUDAPEST
cavalryman .... HUSSAR
city/town .... ABA, ACS, ERD,
OZD, VAC, AJKA, ARLO, BAJA,
EGER, GYOR, MAKO, PAKS,
PAPA, PECS, BEKES, GYULA,
CEGLED, SOPRON, SZEGED,
UJPEST, BUDAFOK, KISPEST,
MISKOLC, SZENTES, SZOLNOK,
DEBRECEN, KAPOSVAR,
OROSHAZA, KECSKEMET,
TATABANYA, VARPALOTA
chocolate party .... DOBOS
coin .... PENGO, FILLER
composer .... LEHAR, LISZT,
BARTOK
county .... VAS, PEST, BEKES,
FEJER, HEVES, TOLNA,
NOGRAD, SOMOGY, BARANYA,
KOMAROM, SZOLNOK,
BUDAPEST, CSONGRAD
dance .... CZARDAS
dessert .... STRUDEL
dog .... PULI
dramatist .... MOLNAR
dynasty .... ARPAD
gypsy .... TZIGANE
hero .... NAGY
king .... BELA
kingdom .... SERBIA
lake .... BALATON
language .... MAGYAR
leader .... (BELA)KUN
measure .... AKO
monetary unit .... PENGO,
FORINT, GULDEN
mountain .... KEKES
mountain range .... BUKK,
MATRA, BAKONY, MECSEK
part of .... BANAT
patriot .... KOSSUTH
people .... MAGYAR
pianist .... LISZT
plain .... GREAT ALFOLD
premier .... FOCK, KALLAI
president .... DOBI
regent .... HORTHY
river .... DUNA, EGER, MURA,
RABA, SAJO, ZALA, DRAVA,
KAPOS, KOROS, MAROS, TISZA,

DANUBE, HERNAD, BERETTYO
shepherd's food ...... GOULASH
slang .... HUNKY, HUNKIE
violinist .... AUER
wine .... TOKAY
hunger .... YEN, LUST, PINE,
ACORIA, DESIRE, STARVE,
CRAVING, APPETITE,
ESURIENCE
continuous .... BULIMIA
for home .... NOSTALGIA
striker, famous .... GANDHI
hungry .... AVID, UNFED,
STARVED, ESURIENT,
FAMISHED
go deliberately .... FAST
hunk .... CHIP, LUMP, MASS, SLAB,
CHUNK, HUNCH, PIECE, SLICE
hunks .... MISER, TIGHTWAD
hunky .... WELL, SQUARE,
HUNGARIAN
hunky-dory .... OKAY, GREAT,
SWELL
Huns, king of the .... ATLI,
ETZEL, ATTILA
hunt .... SEEK, CHASE, CHEVY,
HOUND, QUEST, SCOUR,
TRACE, TRAIL, SHOOT,
PURSUE, SEARCH
for lost scent .... CAST
goddess of the .... DIANA,
ARTEMIS
illegally .... POACH
Hunt, actress .... MARSHA
critic, poet .... LEIGH
hunted animals .... GAME
hunter .... JAGER, ORION,
FOWLER, NIMROD, STALKER,
TRAPPER, CHASSEUR,
PREDATOR
aid of .... RETRIEVER
bait of .... DECOY
cap of .... MONTERO
cry of .... TALLYHOO
kind of .... FORTUNE,
TREASURE
prey of .... GAME
screen of .... BLIND
sea .... WHALER
Hunter, actor .... TAB
actress .... KIM
hunters, collectively .... CHASE
org. of .... NRA
hunting art .... CHASE, VENERY
bird .... FALCON
call .... CHEVY, YOICK,
HALLOO, TANTIVY, TALLYHOO
dog .... ALAN(D), HOUND,
BASSET, BEAGLE, SETTER,
POINTER

dog, at times .... TREER
dog's clue .... SCENT
dogs, set of .... PACK
dog's stance .... POINT,
DEADSET
expedition .... SAFARI
ground .... PRESERVE
hat .... TERAI, MONTERO
horn note .... MORT
hound .... BASSET
knife .... BOWIE
living by .... VENATIC
party member .... BEATER,
GUN-BEARER
pertaining to .... VENATIC
huntress: myth. .... DIANA,
ARTEMIS, ATALANTA
hup, sergeant's .... ONE
hupmobile .... AUTO
Hur .... BEN
ally of .... AARON
enemy .... MESSALA
hurdle ...... SLED, SNAG, BARRIER,
OBSTACLE, SURMOUNT,
HINDRANCE
fence on horseback ...... LARK
hurds .... TOW
hurdy-gurdy .... LIRA, ROTA,
(BARREL)ORGAN
hurl .... TOSS, FLING, PITCH,
SLING, THROW, HURTLE,
LAUNCH, CATAPULT, CAST
DOWN
hurlbat .... HARPOON, JAVELIN
hurly-burly .... FUME, BUSTLE,
HUBBUB, TUMULT, UPROAR,
TURMOIL, AGITATION,
BROUHAHA
Hurok, impresario .... SOL
Huron .... LAKE, WYANDO(TE)
hurrah .... OLE, VIVA, WHEE,
CHEER, SHOUT, APPLAUSE
hurricane ...... STORM, CYCLONE,
TORNADO, TYPHOON
center .... EYE
hurried .... SPED, HASTY
and confused .... HELTER-
SKELTER
in music .... AGITATO
hurry .... HIE, DASH, RUSH,
SPEED, FLURRY, HASTE(N),
HUSTLE, URGENCY,
ACCELERATE
along: collog. .... SCOOT
up: inits. .... ASAP
hurrying: sl. .... BALLING THE
JACK
Hurst, novelist .... FANNIE
hurt .... ACHE, HARM, WOUND,
DAMAGE, INJURE, OFFEND

hurtful .... PAINFUL
hurting .... ACHY, CRUEL, BITING,
GNAWING, STINGING
hurtle .... CAST, DASH, HURL,
CLASH, FLING, COLLIDE
husband .... LORD, GROOM,
SPOUSE, CONSORT, GOODMAN,
RESERVE, CONSERVE,
HELPMATE, HELPMEET
and wife .... COUPLE
authority of .... MANUS
bereaved .... WIDOWER
brother of .... LEVIR, IN-LAW
having one .... MONANDRY
prospective .... INTENDED
husbandman .... FARMER,
GRANGER
husbandry .... THRIFT, ECONOMY,
FARMING, TILLAGE,
FRUGALITY, GEOPONICS
hush .... CALM, LULL, SOFT,
QUIET, SHUSH, SILENCE
-hush org. .... CIA
up .... SILENCE, SUPPRESS
husk .... BRAN, HULL, CHAFF,
GLUME, SHELL, SHUCK
rice in the .... PADDY
husky ...... DOG, ESKIMO, HOARSE,
STURDY, ROBUST, MALEMUTE
command to a .... MUSH
hussar .... CAVALRYMAN
gear of .... LANCE(S)
jacket .... DOLMAN
hussy .... CASE, DOXY, ETUI, GIRL,
MINX, SLUT, TART, WENCH,
TROLLOP, SEWING KIT
hustings .... COURT, ASSEMBLY,
PLATFORM, BOONDOCKS
hustle .... JOLT, POKE, PROD,
PUSH, DRIVE, HURRY, SHOVE,
HASTEN, JOSTLE
slang .... CON, SWINDLE
hustler ...... DYNAMO, GO-GETTER
slang .... SWINDLER
hut .... CABIN, HOVEL, SHACK,
CHALET, LEANTO, MIAM(IA),
SHANTY
kind of .... NISSEN QUONSET
hutch .... BIN, HUT, PEN, COOP,
CHEST, TROUGH, WARREN
dweller .... DOE
Huxley, writer .... ALDOUS,
JULIAN
huzza .... CHEER, SHOUT, HURRAH
Hwang Hai .... YELLOW SEA
hyacinth .... GEM, BIRD, BULB,
MUSK, CAMAS, STONE,
FLOWER, BLUEBELL
gem .... TOPAZ, ZIRCON
hyaline .... GLASSY
hyalite .... OPAL

hybrid .... MULE, MIXED, HALFBREED, CROSS(BREED)
  animal .... HINNY, CATALO
  citrus tree .... TANGELO
  dog .... MONGREL
  language .... JARGON
hybridize .... CROSS
hydatid .... CYST
Hyde .... PARK
  creator of Mr. .... RSL
  other self of Mr. .... JEKYLL
Hyderabad city .... GOLCONDA
  ruler .... NIZAM
hydra .... POLYP, HYDROZOAN
Hydra .... SERPENT
  heads and hell's rivers of
  .... ENNEADS
hydrangea .... SHRUB
hydrant .... FIREPLUG
  attachment .... HOSE
hydranth .... ZOOID
hydrocarbon .... BUTANE, CYMENE, MELENE, OCTANE, PINENE, TOLANE, BENZENE, ETHERIN, (M)ETHANE, PROPANE, TERPENE
  aromatic ...... ARENE, CARANE, CHRYSENE
  coal tar .... PYRENE
  compound .... IMINE
  gaseous .... FLUORINE
  liquid .... TOLUENE
  mixture .... MALTHA
  pine tar .... RETENE
  radical .... AMYL, ETHYL
  wax .... MONTAN

hydrocephalus victim
  .... WATERHEAD
hydrocortison .... CORTISOL
hydrogen .... GAS
hydroid .... POLYP
  colony branch .... ZOOID
hydromedusa .... JELLYFISH
hydrometer scale .... BAUME
hydrophobia .... LYSSA, LYTTA, RABIES
hydrous .... WATERY
  (magnesium) silicate .... TALC
hydrozoan .... HYDRA, POLYP, JELLYFISH, MILLEPORE
hygienic .... CLEAN, SANITARY
hyla .... TREETOAD
hymen .... SONG, MAIDENHEAD
hymenopter ...... ANT, BEE, WASP
hymn .... ODE, PAEAN, PSALM, ANTHEM, CHORALE, TE DEUM, CANTICLE, RECESSIONAL
  book .... HYMNAL, GRADUAL, PSALTER
  for the dead .... REQUIEM
  of praise .... LAUD, ANTHEM, MAGNIFICAT
  praising God .... GLORIA, ALLELUIA, ALLELUJAH
hymnoptera .... BEES
hyp .... MELANCHOLIA
hyperbole .... AUXESIS, DISTORTION, EXAGGERATION, OVERSTATEMENT
hyperbolic function .... COSH
Hyperion .... TITAN
  daughter of .... EOS

  parent .... GAEA, URANUS
  son of .... HELIOS
hyphen .... DASH
hypnosis .... TRANCE
hypnotic .... ACETAL, LUMINAL, MESMERIC, SOPORIFIC
  compound .... AMYTAL
  drug .... NEMBUTAL
  force .... OD, ODYL(E)
  state .... TRANCE
hypnotism .... MESMERISM
  founder of .... MESMER
hypnotize ...... CHARM, ENTRANCE
hypochondria ...... HYP, ANXIETY, NEUROSIS, MELANCHOLY
hypochondriac .... NEUROTIC, NOSOMANIA, VALETUDINARIAN
hypocrisy .... CANT, PRETENSE, PHARISAISM, INSINCERITY
hypocrite .... SHAM, PHARISEE, TARTUF(F)E, PRETENDER
hypothesis .... ISM, THEORY
hypothesize .... ASSUME, SUPPOSE
hypothetical .... ASSUMED
  force .... OD, ELOD, ODYL, IDANT
hyrax ...... CONY, DAMAN, RABBIT
hyson .... TEA
hyssop .... MINT, THISTLE
hysteria ...... FIT, PANIC, FRENZY, ANXIETY, JITTERS, MADNESS, DELIRIUM, TARASSIS
hysterical .... WILD, FRENZIED, DELIRIOUS, EMOTIONAL

I

I .... AYE, EGO, SELF
  am to blame .... MEA CULPA
  beam projection .... FLANGE
  believe: Lat. .... CREDO
  excessive use of ..... IOTACISM
  have found it! .... EUREKA
  letter .... IOTA
  pray thee .... PRITHEE
  Remember Mama actress
  .... (IRENE)DUNNE
  Remember Mama author
  .... (KATHRYN)FORBES
Iago's master .... OTHELLO
  wife .... EMILIA
iamb .... FOOT
iambi .... FEET
Iasi .... JASSY
  coin .... LEU
iatric .... MEDICAL, MEDICINAL

Iberia .... SPAIN, PENINSULA
  author of .... MICHENER
Iberian region .... LUSITANIA
ibex ...... TUR, GOAT, KAIL, WALIE, SAKEEN
  habitat .... ALPS, PYRENEES
ibid(em) .... SAME, DITTO
ibis .... HERON, JABIRU
Ibo .... NIGERIAN
Ibsen .... HENDRICK
  character .... ASE, GYNT, NORA, HEDDA, ELLIDA
Icarian-like .... RASH, DARING, FOOLHARDY
Icarus's daughter .... ERIGONE
  parent .... DAEDALUS
ICBM .... ATLAS, MISSILE, MINUTE MAN
ice .... FIRN, FLOE, GRUE, CHILL,

  ROCKS, FREEZE, DESSERT, FROST(ING), SHERBET
  breaker .... ATKA, PICK
  breaking in water .... DEBACLE
  coat .... RIME
  cream .... BISQUE, SUNDAE
  crosser .... ELIZA
  field .... FLOE
  flakes .... SNOW
  floe .... PAN, PACK
  fragments .... BRASH
  hockey disc .... PUCK
  mass .... BERG, FLOE, PACK, SERAC, GLACIER
  of .... GLACIAL
  partly melted .... SLUSH
  pellets .... HAIL
  pinnacle .... SERAC
  rain .... HAIL, SLEET

runner .... SKI, SKATE
sheet .... GLACIER
skate's cousin .... SKI
slang .... DIAMOND(S)
iceberg .... FLOE, LETTUCE
piece from .... CALF
small .... GROWLER
iceboat .... SKIFF
icebox .... FREEZER,
REFRIGERATOR
iced .... GLACE, FRAPPE
Iceland bay .... FAXA, HUNA
cape .... HORN, GERPIR
capital .... REYKJAVIK
city/town .... NES, AKRANES,
HUSAVIK, AKUREYRI,
KEFLAVIK, KOPAVOGUR
district .... SYSSEL
epic .... EDDA
god .... LOKI, ODIN, THOR,
AESIR, WODEN, BALDER
hot spring .... GEYSIR
island .... GRIMSEY, SURTSEY
king .... ATLI
language .... NORSE,
ICELANDIC
literature .... EDDA
measure .... FET, ALEN
monetary unit .... KRONA
NATO base .... KEFLAVIK
parliament .... ALTHING
poet .... SKALD
queen .... BRUNHILD
river .... THJORSA
volcano .... ASKJA, HEKLA
Iceni, queen of .... BOADICEA
Ichabod Crane's rival ...... BROM
work .... PEDAGOGUE
ichneumon .... FLY, MONGOOSE
icing .... FROSTING
icky .... DIRTY, CRAPPY, SHITTY,
STINKY, YECCHY
icon ...... EIKON, IMAGE, PICTURE,
LIKENESS
Ictalurus punctatus ...... CATFISH
icterus .... JAUNDICE
ictus .... FIT, ARSIS, SPASM,
ACCENT, STROKE, UPBEAT,
SEIZURE
icy .... COLD, ALOOF, GELID,
FRIGID, FROSTY, GLACIAL
coat .... RIME
id. .... EGO, IDEM, SAME, IDAHO,
LIBIDO, INSTINCT
ID .... DRIVER'S LICENSE,
(IDENTIFICATION)BADGE
military .... DOG TAG
Idaho .... POTATO STATE
capital .... BOISE
city/town ..... NAMPA, JEROME,
MOSCOW, WEISER, CALDWELL,

LEWISTON, MERIDIAN,
BLACKFOOT, POCATELLO, TWIN
FALLS, IDAHO FALLS
college .... CALDWELL
county .... ADA, BOISE, LATAH,
BONNER, CANYON, CASSIA,
ELMORE, BANNOCK, BINGHAM,
MADISON, PAYETTE,
KOOTENAI, MINIDOKA,
SHOSHONE, BONNEVILLE, TWIN
FALLS
falls .... TWIN, SALMON,
AMERICAN, SHOSHONE
lake ...... MUD, BEAR, HAYDEN,
LOWELL, PRIEST, PAYETTE,
LUCKY PEAK, PEND OREILLE,
COEUR D'ALENE
main crop .... POTATOES
mountain .... POT, ALLAN,
WAUGH, MORMON, SADDLE,
CARIBOU, LOOKOUT, RAINBOW,
GREYLOCK, GOLDSTONE, TWIN
PEAKS
national park .... NEZ PERCE
pass .... LOLO, LOST TRAIL
peak .... RYAN, BORAH,
MEADE, BADGER, BANNOCK,
DIAMOND
range .... BITTERROOT
river .... RED, PACK, RAFT,
MALAD, MOYIE, SNAKE,
LOCHSA, SALMON, SELWAY
state bird .... BLUEBIRD
state flower .... SYRINGA
state motto .... ESTO PERPETUA
state nickname .... GEM
idea .... FANCY, IMAGE, NOESIS,
NOTION, INKLING,
CONCEPT(ION), OPINION,
THOUGHT, IMPRESSION
bright .... BRAINSTORM
combining form .... IDEO
main/dominant .... MOTIF
utopian .... BUBBLE
ideal .... HERO, MODEL, PARAGON,
PERFECT, UTOPIAN,
FAULTLESS, CONCEPTUAL
state .... OCEANA, UTOPIA
idealist .... ANIMIST, DREAMER,
VISIONARY
idealize .... DEIFY, OVERRATE,
RHAPSODIZE
ideals of citizenship ...... CIVISM
ideas, sentimental .... CORN
worthless .... BILGE
ideate .... FANCY, THINK,
IMAGINE, CONCEIVE
idee fixe .... OBSESSION
idem .... (THE)SAME
identical ...... ONE, ALIKE, EQUAL,
(SELF)SAME

combining form .... EQUI
item/counterpart .... TWIN
identification, means of
.... BADGE, BRAND, CHECK,
LABEL, NOTCH, MARKER,
(DOG)TAG, DRIVER'S LICENSE
identify .... NAME, EARMARK,
DIAGNOSE, RECOGNIZE
identifying marks ...... STIGMATA
identity .... ONENESS, ONESELF,
SELF(NESS), PERSONALITY,
INDIVIDUALITY
of origin .... ISOGENY
word .... NEE
ideologist .... DREAMER,
THEORIST, VISIONARY
ideology .... ISM, DOGMA,
THEORY, DOCTRINE, PRINCIPLE
Ides, date before .... NONES
of March victim .... CAESAR
idiocy .... FOLLY, AMENTIA,
ANOESIA, FATUITY,
CRETINISM, STUPIDITY
idiom .... CANT, ARGOT, SLANG,
PHRASE, DIALECT, LANGUAGE,
LOCUTION
idiosyncrasy .... ODDITY,
PECULIARITY, INDIVIDUALISM
idiot .... OAF, AMENT, MORON,
CRETIN, NITWIT, DULLARD,
IMBECILE, SIMPLETON
idle ...... LAZE, LAZY, LOAF, VAIN,
FUTILE, LOITER, OTIANT,
OTIOSE, VACANT, USELESS,
BASELESS, INACTIVE,
POINTLESS
talk .... GAB, GAS, GOSSIP,
PATTER, CHITCHAT
idleness .... SLOTH, LAZINESS,
INDOLENCE
idler .... BUM, DRONE, LOAFER,
LOUNGER, ROUNDER,
LAZYBONES
idol .... GOD, BAAL, ICON, LION,
IMAGE, EFFIGY, EIDOLON,
CELEBRITY
Chinese .... JOSS
social .... LION
worshiper .... PAGAN
idolater .... PAGAN, ADORER
object of .... TOTEM
idolatry .... SUTTEE, ANIMISM,
DEMONISM
idolism .... SOPHISM
idolize .... ADORE, ADMIRE,
WORSHIP
Idum(a)ea .... EDOM
idyl(l) .... POEM, ECLOGUE,
PASTORAL
idyllic .... POETIC, BUCOLIC,
PASTORAL

i.e. .... ID EST, THAT IS
if .... PROVIDED, CONDITION,
SUPPOSITION
not .... ELSE, NISI, UNLESS
igneous .... PLUTONIC
rock .... BOSS, BASALT,
DIABASE
ignis fatuus ...... DELUSION, WILL-
O'-THE-WISP
ignite .... BURN, FIRE, LIGHT,
EXCITE, KINDLE
ignited substance .... SPARK
igniter .... FUSE, DETONATOR
ignoble .... LOW, BASE, VILE,
MEAN, HUMBLE
ignominious ...... SHADY, SORDID,
SHAMEFUL, DEGRADING,
DISGRACEFUL
ignominy .... SHAME, INFAMY,
DISGRACE
ignoramus .... DUMMY, DUNCE,
NITWIT, KNOW-NOTHING,
SIMPLE SIMON
ignorance .... BLINDNESS,
INNOCENCE, STUPIDITY
ignorant ...... WITLESS, UNAWARE,
NESCIENT, ILLITERATE,
UNLETTERED, UNSCHOOLED
ignore .... CUT, OMIT, SNUB,
ELIDE, NEGLECT, OVERLOOK,
DISREGARD
Igraine's husband .... UTHER
iguana .... GOANNA, LIZARD
Il Trovatore gypsy ...... MANRICO
ileus .... COLIC
Iliad author .... HOMER
character .... AJAX, HECTOR,
CALCHAS, STENTOR, ACHILLES
nephew .... MEGES
Ilion .... TROY
ilium .... HIPBONE
ilk .... KIND, SORT, BREED, CLASS,
FAMILY, STRIPE
ill .... BAD, EVIL, SICK, QUEER,
UNWELL, ADVERSE,
INDISPOSED
advised .... UNWISE
at ease .... RESTIVE
bred .... BOOR, LOUT, RUDE,
IMPOLITE
defined .... VAGUE
disposed .... HOSTILE
fated .... DOOMED, UNLUCKY,
STAR-CROSSED
favored .... UGLY
humor .... BILE
humored .... CROSS, SULLEN
mannered .... RUDE, COARSE,
CADDISH, LOW-BRED
mannered child .... BRAT
prefix .... MAL

temper .... PET, BILE, SPLEEN
tempered .... CROSS, SURLY,
CRANKY, SULLEN, PEEVISH,
WASPISH
tempered, extremely .... AS
UGLY AS A BEAR
tempered one .... TARTAR
tempered person
.... CURMUDGEON
treatment .... ABUSE, CRUELTY,
MANHANDLING
will ...... HATE, SPITE, ANIMUS,
ENMITY, GRUDGE, HATRED,
MALICE, RANCOR, DISLIKE
illegal .... FOUL, ILLICIT,
UNLAWFUL, CONTRABAND
liquor .... BOOTLEG
slang .... HOT
illegally produced chemicals
.... DESIGNER DRUGS
illegible .... UNREADABLE
illegitimate .... BASTARD,
ILLEGAL, MISBEGOT(TEN)
illicit .... SECRET, CLANDESTINE
Illinois capital .... SPRINGFIELD
city/town .... ZION, ALTON,
CAIRO, ELGIN, PEKIN, AURORA,
DEKALB, JOLIET, MOLINE,
NORMAL, PEORIA, QUINCY,
SKOKIE, URBANA, CHICAGO,
DECATUR, LANSING, LINCOLN,
LOMBARD, WHEATON,
DANVILLE, EVANSTON,
KANKAKEE, ROCKFORD,
WAUKEGAN, WHEELING,
WILMETTE, BELVIDERE,
CHAMPAIGN, GALESBURG,
BELLEVILLE, DES PLAINES,
LOUISVILLE
college .... SHIMER
county .... COOK, KANE, KNOX,
LAKE, OGLE, WILL, ADAMS,
HENRY, MACON, BUREAU,
DUPAGE, FULTON, MARION,
MORGAN, PEORIA, JACKSON,
KENDALL, LA SALLE,
MADISON, WHITESIDE,
WINNEBAGO, WILLIAMSON,
ROCK ISLAND
greatest son .... LINCOLN
historic site .... TIME MUSEUM,
LINCOLN COURTROOM, ROCK
ISLAND ARSENAL
lake ..... FOX, REND, CALUMET,
CARLYLE, MICHIGAN,
SHELBYVILLE, CRAB ORCHARD
river .... OHIO, PLUM, ROCK,
SPOON, SALINE, WABASH,
ILLINOIS, BIG MUDDY,
MACKINAW, MACOUPIN,
SANGAMON, KASKASKIA, BIG

BUREAU, MISSISSIPPI
state bird .... CARDINAL
state flower .... NATIVE VIOLET
state motto .... NATIONAL
UNION
state nickname .... PRAIRIE,
LAND OF LINCOLN
state tree .... OAK
university .... DE PAUL,
BRADLEY, ROOSEVELT,
SANGAMON STATE
illiterate .... IGNORANT,
UNEDUCATED, UNLETTERED
illness .... MALADY, DISEASE
feign .... MALINGER
illume .... LIGHT
illuminate .... LIGHT(UP),
ELUCIDATE, ENLIGHTEN
in a certain way
.... TORCHLIGHT
illumination .... LIGHT
unit .... LUX
illusion .... FANCY, TULLE,
MIRAGE, CHIMERA, FANTASY,
DELUSION
illusionist, kind of .... MAGICIAN
illustrate .... CITE, DRAW,
EXPLAIN, PICTURE
illustration .... GRAPH, SAMPLE,
DIAGRAM, DRAWING,
EXAMPLE
illustrious .... NOTED, FAMOUS,
EMINENT, CELEBRATED
illy .... BADLY, POORLY
image .... ICON, EIKON, EFFIGY,
STATUE, (E)IDOLON, REPLICA,
LIKENESS
deceptive .... CHIMERA,
ILLUSION
destroyer .... ICONOCLAST
mental .... IDEA, RECEPT,
CONCEPT(ION)
prefix .... EIDO
imagery .... STATUES
imaginary ...... FECUND, UNREAL,
FICTIVE, FANCIFUL, MYTHICAL
ailment .... CRUD
terrestrial circle ...... EQUATOR
imagination .... IDEA, MYTH,
DREAM, FANCY, NOTION,
VISION, INVENTION
imagine .... WEEN, FANCY, GUESS,
CREATE, IDEATE, INVENT,
SUPPOSE, SURMISE, CONCEIVE
imagist .... POET, DREAMER
imam .... CALIPH, PRIEST
imaret .... INN, SERAI
imbalance .... DISPARITY
imbecile .... FOOL, AMENT, ANILE,
MORON, CRETIN, DOTARD,
STUPID

imbecility .... IDIOCY, FATUITY

imbibe .... BIB, SIP, DRINK, ABSORB, INHALE

imbiber .... SOT, WINO, DRUNK, BARFLY, TIPPLER

imbricate .... OVERLAP

imbricated .... TILED

imbroglio ...... PLOT, CONFUSION, ENTANGLEMENT

imbrue .... WET, SOAK, STEEP

imbue .... DYE, TINCT, INFUSE, INGRAIN, INSPIRE, PERVADE, PERMEATE

imitate .... APE, COPY, ECHO, MIME, MATCH, MIMIC, FOLLOW, DUPLICATE

Niobe .... CRY

the Cheshire cat .... GRIN

imitation .... COPY, SHAM, BOGUS, PARODY, FORGERY, MIMESIS, MIMICRY, COUNTERFEIT

gem .... PASTE

ludicrous .... TRAVESTY, CARICATURE

imitative .... APISH, MIMETIC

animal .... APE, MONKEY

imitativeness .... APERY

imitator ...... APER, ECHO, MIMIC, FORGER, MONKEY, PARROT

immaculate .... PURE, CLEAN, CHASTE, SINLESS, INNOCENT, PRISTINE, SPOTLESS, UNSOILED, UNTOUCHED

immanent ...... INNATE, INHERENT

immaterial .... TRIVIAL, IRRELEVANT

immature .... RAW, GREEN, YOUNG, CALLOW, UNRIPE

immeasurable .... VAST, BOUNDLESS, LIMITLESS

immediate .... FIRST, DIRECT, PROMPT, CLOSE(ST), NEAR(EST), INSTANT, PRESENT, ADJACENT

immediately ...... NOW, AT ONCE, PROMPTLY, FORTHWITH, AS SOON AS, INSTANTLY

available .... READY

slang .... PDQ

immense .... HUGE, VAST, GREAT, ENORM(OUS), INFINITE, LIMITLESS

enjoyment .... WHALE OF A TIME

immensity .... INFINITY, VASTNESS

immerse .... DIP, DUCK, DUNK, DOUSE, ABSORB, PLUNGE, BAPTIZE, ENGROSS, SUBMERGE

in fluid .... BATHE

immersed .... RAPT, ABSORBED

immersion .... BAPTISM

immigrant .... ALIEN, SETTLER

illegal .... WETBACK

newly arrived .... GRIFFIN, NEWCOMER, GREENHORN

status .... ALIENAGE

immigrants, island of ...... ELLIS

mid-19th century ..... SCOTCH-IRISH

immobile ...... FIRM, FIXED, STILL, SESSILE, MOTIONLESS

immoderate .... UNDUE, EXCESSIVE

immodest .... BOLD, BRAZEN, FORWARD, INDECENT, IMPUDENT

immolate .... SACRIFICE

immoral .... LEWD, WANTON, WICKED, OBSCENE, INDECENT

immorality .... VICE

immortal .... DIVINE, GODLIKE, ENDURING, DEATHLESS

immovable ...... SET, FIRM, FIXED, IMPASSIVE, STATIONARY

immune ...... EXEMPT, PROTECTED

render .... INOCULATE, VACCINATE

immunity .... EXEMPTION, PROTECTION

kind of .... DIPLOMATIC

immunization .... SHOT

method .... INOCULATION

immunizing substance
.... SERUM, VACCINE, ANTITOXIN

immure .... CONFINE, SHUT UP, ISOLATE, SECLUDE, IMPRISON

immutable .... FIRM, ETERNAL, CHANGELESS, UNCHANGING

imp ...... ELF, BRAT, PUCK, CHILD, DEMON, DEVIL, SPRITE

impact .... DINT, PACK, SLAM, FORCE, SHOCK, TOUCH, CONTACT, COLLISION

main .... BRUNT

impair .... MAR, HARM, SPOIL, DAMAGE, INJURE, WEAKEN, VITIATE

impairment .... INJURY

speech .... DYSPHASIA

impale .... SPIT, FENCE IN, PIERCE, TRANSFIX

impalpable .... SUBTLE

impart .... GIVE, LEND, TELL, SHARE, BESTOW, CONVEY, REVEAL, DIVULGE, DISCLOSE, COMMUNICATE

knowledge .... TEACH

impartial .... FAIR, JUST, UNBIASED, EVEN(HANDED)

impasse .... HALT, DEADLOCK, STANDOFF, STALEMATE, BLIND ALLEY

impassioned .... FIERY, ARDENT

impassive .... CALM, SERENE, STOLID, STOIC(AL), PHLEGMATIC

impasto .... PAINTING

impatience .... EAGERNESS

impatiens .... JEWELWEED, TOUCH-ME-NOT

impatient .... EAGER, ANXIOUS, RESTIVE

impeach .... ACCUSE, CHARGE, IMPUGN, INDICT, ARRAIGN, DISCREDIT

impeccable .... FLAWLESS, BLAMELESS, FAULTLESS

impecunious .... POOR, BROKE

impede .... BLOCK, DELAY, HAMPER, HINDER, RETARD, STYMIE, OBSTRUCT

legally .... ESTOP

impediment ...... HITCH, BARRIER, OBSTACLE, HINDRANCE

speech .... LISP, STAMMER, STUTTER

impedimenta .... BAGGAGE

impel .... MOVE, PUSH, URGE, DRIVE, FORCE, COMPEL, INCITE, PROPEL, ACTUATE, MOTIVATE, CONSTRAIN

impending .... IMMINENT

impenetrable .... DENSE, SOLID, IMPERVIOUS

impennate bird .... PENGUIN

imperative .... URGENT, NECESSARY, COMPELLING, COMPULSORY

imperator .... EMPEROR

imperceptible .... MINUTE, UNSEEN, INVISIBLE

imperfect .... CRUDE, FAULTY, FLAWED, CRACKED, UNSOUND

prefix .... ATELO

imperfection .... FLAW, VICE, FAULT, DEFECT, BLEMISH, FAILING, SHORTCOMING

imperial .... BEARD, REGAL, GOATEE, MAJESTIC

color .... PURPLE

decree .... RESCRIPT

domain .... EMPIRE, EMPERY

imperil .... ENDANGER, JEOPARDIZE

imperious .... URGENT, ARROGANT, MAGISTRAL

imperishable .... IMMORTAL

impersonal .... FAIR, DISTANT, REMOVED, DETACHED, OBJECTIVE

impersonate .... APE, MIMIC, EMBODY, IMITATE

impersonator .... ACTOR, IMPOSTOR

impertinence .... IMPUDENCE, INSOLENCE

impertinent .... PERT, SASSY, SAUCY, FLIP(PANT), IMPUDENT, INSOLENT, MALAPERT

one .... SNIP

talk .... LIP, SASS

impetuous .... HOT, RASH, BRASH, HASTY, TEARING, IMPULSIVE

too .... OVERRASH

impetus .... DRIVE, FORCE, IMPULSE, MOMENTUM

impi ...... ZULU, KAFFIR, WARRIOR

impiety .... SIN, APOSTASY, BLASPHEMY, PROFANITY

impinge .... ENCROACH, TRESPASS

impious .... GODLESS, PROFANE, UNCTUOUS

impish .... ELFISH, ELVISH, DEVILISH, MISCHIEVOUS

implacable .... MORTAL, PITILESS, VENGEFUL, RELENTLESS

implant .... FIX, EMBED, GRAFT, INSTILL, INCULCATE

deeply .... (EN)ROOT

implement .... TOOL, ENFORCE, DEVICE, EXECUTE, FULFILL, UTENSIL

hay spreading .... MULCHER

kitchen .... UTENSIL

pounding/crushing ..... PESTLE

threshing .... FLAIL

implicate ...... CONNECT, INCLUDE, INVOLVE, INCRIMINATE

implication .... ALLUSION, INNUENDO, OVERTONE

implicit .... TACIT, IMPLIED, ABSOLUTE, INHERENT

implied .... TACIT, IMPLICIT

implore .... BEG, PRAY, PLEAD, BESEECH, ENTREAT

imply .... HINT, ENTAIL, CONNOTE, SUGGEST, INTIMATE

impolite .... RUDE, ILL-MANNERED

impolitic .... UNWISE, TACTLESS

import ...... DRIFT, SENSE, TENOR, BRING IN, MEANING

tax .... TARIFF

important .... KEY, MAJOR, PRIME, VITAL, ESSENTIAL

celestial layer .... OZONE

document .... WILL, CONTRACT

U.S. military base ...... THULE

importance ...... VALUE, WEIGHT, ESSENCE, DISTINCTION

importune .... URGE, PRAY, PLEAD, PRESS, BESEECH, ENTREAT

importunist .... ASKER

impose .... FOB, LEVY, FOIST, FORCE, ENTAIL, PALM OFF, INFLICT

imposing .... EPIC, NOBLE, AUGUST, MAGNIFIC, GRAND(IOSE), DIGNIFIED, IMPRESSIVE

imposition .... BOTHER, NUISANCE, INTRUSION

impossible task? .... MISSION

impost .... TAX, DUTY, LEVY

impostor .... SHAM, CHEAT, FAKER, FRAUD, GOUGE, QUACK, HUMBUG, PHON(E)Y

imposture .... SHAM, FRAUD, PRETENSE, DECEPTION

impotent .... INEPT, UNABLE, STERILE, HELPLESS

impound .... POIND, SEIZE, CONFISCATE

impractical one .... DREAMER, IDEALIST

theorist .... DOCTRINAIRE

imprecation .... OATH, CURSE, EXPLETIVE

impregnable .... FIRM, INVINCIBLE

impregnate .... FILL, SOAK, INFUSE, SATURATE, FECUNDATE, FERTILIZE, POLLINATE

impresario .... PROMOTER, ENTREPRENEUR

Sol .... HUROK

impress .... DENT, LEVY, MARK, DRAFT, STAMP, AFFECT, COMPEL, (IM)PRINT

deeply .... ENGRAVE

impression .... IDEA, MARK, STAMP, EFFECT, FEELING, IMPRINT, INKLING, OPINION, PRINT(ING)

on coin .... MINTAGE

trial .... PROOF

impressionist painter .... DEGAS, MANET, MONET, RENOIR

impressive .... MOVING, AWESOME

imprest .... LENT, LOAN, (CASH)ADVANCE

imprimatur .... LICENSE, APPROVAL, SANCTION

imprint ...... ETCH, MARK, PRESS, STAMP

imprison .... CAGE, JAIL, (IM)MURE, CONFINE, INCARCERATE

improbable .... DOUBTFUL, UNLIKELY

impromptu .... OFFHAND, EXTEMPORE, IMPROVISED

improper .... AMISS, UNDUE, WRONG, RISQUE, INDECENT, UNFIT(TING), UNSEEMLY, UNBECOMING

improperly .... UNDULY

impropriety .... MISCONDUCT, MISBEHAVIOR

improve .... AMEND, EMEND, BETTER, ADVANCE, FORWARD, REMODEL, AMELIORATE

improvisation on stage .... AD LIB, ASIDE

improvise .... VAMP, AD LIB, MAKE-DO, INVENT, CONTRIVE

improvised .... OFFHAND, IMPROMPTU

imprudent .... RASH, BRASSY, CARELESS, INDISCREET

impudence .... LIP, GALL, SASS, BRASS, CHEEK, NERVE, SAUCE, INSOLENCE

impudent ...... ARCH, BOLD, PERT, RUDE, BRASH, FRESH, SASSY, SAUCY, SNOTTY, FORWARD, MALAPERT

impugn .... DENY, ASPERSE, CHALLENGE, CRITICIZE

impulse .... PROD, PUSH, URGE, FORCE, SHOVE, MOTIVE, THRUST, IMPETUS

to steal .... KLEPTOMANIA

impulsive ...... RASH, IMPETUOUS, UNGUARDED, CAPRICIOUS

impunity .... EXEMPTION

impure .... BAWDY, DIRTY, MIXED, AMORAL, DEFILED, UNCLEAN, UNCHASTE

impurity .... DROSS, FILTH, LEWDNESS, OBSCENITY

impute .... CHARGE, ASCRIBE, ATTRIBUTE

in ...... AT, WITH, AMONG, AMIDST, AT HOME, INSIDE, ENCLOSE

a body/group .... EN MASSE

brown study .... RAPT, DAYDREAMING

conflict .... AT WAR

correct way .... RIGHTLY

——— (excited) .... STEW

frenzy .... AMOK

group of .... AMONG, ALTOGETHER

headlong manner .... IMPULSIVELY

heedful way .... ATTENTIVELY

hurry .... POSTHASTE

jiffy .... SOON

lethargic way .... SLEEPILY

manner of speaking .... SO TO SAY

Milquetoast manner .... TIMOROUSLY
minute .... ANON
natty way .... SNAPPILY
quandary .... UP A TREE
reversed situation .... SHOE IS ON THE OTHER FOOT
ruddy way .... REDLY
saucy way .... PERTLY
tough spot .... OUT ON A LIMB
while .... LATER
abundance .... GALORE, TEEMING
accord .... EN RAPPORT
accordance with .... ALA, PURSUANT
addition .... TOO, ALSO, MOREOVER
agreement .... UNITED
an instant .... MOMENTARILY
and out .... TIDE
any case/any way .... EVER, AT ALL, ANYHOW
arrears .... OWING
as-much-as .... SINCE
bad taste .... RANK, COARSE
better spirits .... CHEERIER
case .... LEST
cheek, _____ .... TONGUE
circulation .... ABOUT, ABROAD
close cooperation .... HAND IN GLOVE
clover .... PROSPEROUS
confusion .... AT SIXES AND SEVENS
confusion, to a GI ...... SNAFU
due manner ..... DULY, TRULY, REALLY, ACCORDINGLY
fact .... DE FACTO
favor of .... FOR, PRO
front .... AHEAD
full measure .... ENTIRELY
good time .... SOON, EARLY
high dudgeon .... IRED
high spirits .... EBULLIENT
hoc signo _____ .... VINCES
_____ (in its natural place) .... SITU
like him? .... FLYNN
line .... AROW, APLUMB
love .... GAGA, INFATUATED
love with .... GONE ON
motion ...... ASTIR, UNDERWAY
name only .... NOMINAL, TITULAR
need of irrigation .... ARID
no key .... ATONAL
no manner .... NOWISE
no way .... NOHOW
on .... AWARE

one's ear, _____ .... PUT A BUG
one's element .... AT HOME
one's interest .... FOR
original position .... SITU
out .... PHASE
place of .... FOR, ELSE, LIEU, VICE, (IN)STEAD
preference to .... OVER
_____ (programmed) .... A RUT
progress .... CURRENT, (ON)GOING
re .... ANENT, CONCERNING
reserve .... ON ICE
row .... ALINED, ALIGNED
seventh heaven .... THRILLED
_____ (so to speak) .... A SENSE
somber style .... SADLY
status quo .... AS IS
stock .... ON HAND
succession .... ENSUITE
that case .... THEN
that respect .... THEREIN
the bag .... ON ICE
calaboose .... JAILED
capacity of .... QUA
center .... AMID
course of .... DURING
doghouse .... BAN, RIFT
dumps .... BLUE
end .... FINALLY, EVENTUALLY, ULTIMATELY
flesh .... LIVE
future .... LATER
know .... HIP
manner of a Dutch uncle .... SEVERELY
midst of .... AMONG
open .... OUTSIDE
past .... AGO
_____ (popular) .... SWIM
sack .... ABED
same category .... SUCH
same community .... SYNOETIC
same place .... IBID(EM)
slightest degree ...... AT ALL
time following .... WHEREAFTER
time .... EVENTUALLY
time, musically .... ATEMPO
want .... NEEDY
with .... AMID
in, _____ (be pushy) ...... MUSCLE
(contribute) .... CHIP
Ina, actress .... CLAIRE
inability .... IMPOTENCE
inaccessible ...... ALOOF, DISTANT
inaccurate .... WRONG,

MISLEADING
inaction .... INERTIA, IDLENESS
inactive ...... IDLE, INERT, ASLEEP, LATENT, STATIC, DORMANT, PASSIVE, RETIRED
inactivity ...... LULL, DORMANCY, LOTUSLAND, STAGNATION
inadequate .... THIN, SCANTY, LACKING, NOT ENOUGH
inadvertence .... OVERSIGHT
inamorata .... MISTRESS, SWEETHEART
inane .... EMPTY, INEPT, SILLY, FATUOUS, FOOLISH, PUERILE, VACUOUS
inanimate .... DEAD, DULL, LIFELESS, SPIRITLESS
inanity .... VACUITY
inappropriate .... IMPROPER, UNBECOMING
inapt ...... UNFITTING, UNSUITABLE
inarm .... EMBRACE
inarticulate .... DUMB, MUTE, APHONIC, UNSPOKEN, VOICELESS
inasmuch .... SINCE, BECAUSE
inattention .... NEGLECT, OVERSIGHT
inattentive .... DEAF, HEEDLESS
inaugurate .... OPEN, INDUCT, INSTALL
inauspicious .... ILL, UNLUCKY, UNTIMELY, ILL-OMENED
inauthentic .... SPURIOUS
inborn .... INBRED, INNATE, NATIVE, CONNATE, NATURAL, INHERENT
incalculable .... VAST, UNTOLD
Incan .... QUECHUA(N), PERUVIAN
empire capital .... CUSCO
king .... HUASCAR, ATABALIPA, ATAHUALPA
incandescence .... GLOW
incandescent .... RED-HOT, GLOWING, WHITE-HOT
incantation .... MAGIC, SPELL, SORCERY, CHANTING
incapable .... UNABLE
incapacitate ...... LAME, DISABLE, DISQUALIFY
incarcerate .... JAIL, CONFINE, IMPRISON
incarnate .... RED, FORM, ROSY, SHAPE, EMBODY
incarnation .... EMBODIMENT
of a god .... AVATAR
of Vishnu .... RAMA
incendiary .... FIREBUG, AGITATOR, ARSONIST, PYROMANIAC
incense .... GUM, IRK, ANGER,

ENRAGE, MASTIC, STACTE, BENZOIN, PERFUME, OLIBANUM, SANDARAC burner .... THURIBLE
incensed .... IRATE, WROTH
incentive .... SPUR, MOTIVE, IMPULSE, STIMULUS, INDUCEMENT
inception .... START, ORIGIN
incertitude .... DOUBT
incessant .... CONTINUAL
inch .... BIT, HILL, CRAWL, CREEP, ISLAND, TRIFLE
.0004 of an .... HAIR
.001 of an .... MIL
$^1/_{12}$ .... LINE
inches, eighteen .... CUBIT
forty-five .... ELL
nine .... SPAN
thirty .... PACE, STEP
twelve .... FOOT
incident .... EVENT, EPISODE
incidental ...... BYE, ODD, MINOR, CASUAL, CHANCE, PASSING
excursion .... SIDETRIP
in music .... GRACE NOTE
incinerate .... CREMATE, BURN(UP)
incinerator .... FURNACE, CREMATORY
incipient .... INITIAL
incise ...... CUT, CARVE, ENGRAVE
incision .... CUT, GASH
incisive ...... KEEN, ACUTE, SHARP, TRENCHANT
incisor .... TOOTH
incite .... GOAD, SPUR, EGG ON, EXHORT, FOMENT, INDUCE, AGITATE, INSTIGATE
inciter .... EGGER, AGITATOR, INSTIGATOR
incivility .... RUDENESS
inclement .... HARSH, SEVERE, STORMY, PITILESS
inclination .... GRADE, SLANT, SLOPE, TASTE, TREND, LEAN(ING), MINDSET
to laugh .... RISIBILITY
incline .... CANT, LEAN, SWAY, TEND, GRADE, SLANT, SLOPE
downward .... DIP
inclined ...... APT, ALIST, ASWAY, PRONE, MINDED, WILLING, OBLIQUE, DISPOSED
chute/trough .... FLUME
walk .... RAMP
include .... CONTAIN, EMBRACE, INVOLVE, COMPRISE
including everything
.... OVERALL
inclusive .... ENTIRE, GENERIC

incognito .... DISGUISE
incoherent .... RAMBLING, DISJOINTED
income .... USANCE, ANNUITY, EARNING, REVENUE
type of ..... RENTAL, ROYALTY, INTEREST, DIVIDENDS
incommode .... BOTHER, PUT OUT
incomparable .... PEERLESS, MATCHLESS
incomplete .... SHY, LACKING
incomprehensible .... GREE
inconclusive .... DOUBTFUL, UNCERTAIN
incongruous .... UNFIT
inconsequential .... TRIVIAL
inconsiderate .... TACTLESS, THOUGHTLESS
inconstant ...... FICKLE, MUTABLE, UNSTABLE, VOLATILE, CAPRICIOUS
inconvenience .... BOTHER, TROUBLE, INCOMMODE
incorporate .... MIX, MERGE, EMBODY, INCLUDE
incorporeal right .... PATENT, COPYRIGHT
incorrect .... OFF, WRONG, FAULTY, UNTRUE, IMPROPER, ERRONEOUS, INACCURATE
bite .... MALOCCLUSION
epithet/naming ...... MISNOMER
incorruptible .... HONEST, STRAIGHT
increase .... ADD, GROW, ACCRETE, AUGMENT, ENLARGE, MULTIPLY
bet on .... RAISE
money in circulation
.... REFLATE
to the highest degree
.... MAXIMIZE
incredible .... ABSURD, UNBELIEVABLE
incredulity .... DOUBT, UNBELIEF, SKEPTICISM
cry of .... WHAT, OH NO
incredulous .... SKEPTICAL
increment .... GAIN, ACCRUAL
incriminate .... CONNECT, INVOLVE, IMPLICATE
incrustation .... RIME, SCAB
incubate ...... SIT, BREED, BROOD, HATCH
incubator .... HATCHERY
incubus .... DEMON, BURDEN, SPIRIT, NIGHTMARE
inculcate .... IMBUE, IMPRESS, INSTIL(L)
incumbency .... TENURE
incumbent .... OFFICEHOLDER

incur .... RUN, ACQUIRE
incursion .... RAID, FORAY, INROAD, INVASION
incus .... ANVIL
indebted .... LIABLE, BEHOLDEN TO
indebtedness .... DEBT, OBLIGATION
certification of .... DEBENTURE
indecency .... FILTH
indecent ...... FOUL, LEWD, RACY, RANK, COARSE, RISQUE, IMMORAL, OBSCENE, OFF-COLOR, IMMODEST
indecision .... HESITATION, VACILLATION
indecisive .... WAVERING, CHANGEABLE
indecorous .... UNSEEMLY
indeed .... TRULY, REALLY, IN FACT, FORSOOTH, CERTAINLY
indefatigable ...... AVID, UNTIRING
indefensible .... UNTENABLE
indefinite .... HAZY, VAGUE, UNSURE, OBSCURE, NEBULOUS, NUBILOUS, AMBIGUOUS
amount .... ANY, SOME
article .... AN
person .... ANYBODY
pronoun .... (ANY)ONE
indelible .... LASTING
indelicate .... CRASS, CRUDE, GROSS, ROUGH, COARSE
indemnify .... PAY, REDEEM, REIMBURSE
indemnity .... SECURITY
indent .... NOTCH, IMPRESS
indentation ...... CUT, JAG, DINGE, NOTCH, MARGIN, SET IN, CRENELET
on a blade .... CHOIL
on glass bottle .... KICK
independent .... FREE
an .... LONER, MUGWUMP, LONE WOLF
island country .... MALTA, CYPRESS
indescribable .... INEFFABLE, EXTRAORDINARY
indestructible .... IMMORTAL, INDELIBLE
indeterminate .... VAGUE
in botany .... RACEMOSE
index .... LIST, MARK, SIGN, TABLE, CATALOG, POINTER, INDICATOR, FOREFINGER
sign in printing .... FIST
India(n) .... TAMIL, BHARAT, HINDUSTAN
aborigine .... BENGALI

373

acrobat .... NAT

alcoholic drink .... ARRACK

animal .... ZEBU, DHOLE

antelope .... CHIRU, SASIN, NILG(H)AI, NILG(H)AU

army officer .... JEMADAR

army servant .... LASCAR

artilleryman .... LASCAR

astrologer .... JOSHI

attendant .... AYAH, PEON

audience .... DURBAR

banker .... SARAF, SHROFF, SOUCAR

bay .... BACK

bear .... BALOO

bearer .... SIRDAR

Bihar capital .... PATNA

bird .... KOEL, RAYA, SARUS, SHAMA, ARGALA, JACANA, MARABOU, AMADAVAT

bison ..... GAUR, GAYAL, TSINE

boat .... DONGA, DUNGA

bodice .... CHOLI

bond .... ANDI

boycott .... SWADESHI

bread/cake .... CHAPATI

bride's neckwear .... TALIS

buck .... SASIN

Buddhist gateway .... TORAN

buffalo .... ARNA, ARNEE

building .... MAHAL

bulbul .... KALA

bush .... KANHER

butter .... GHEE

calico .... SAL(I)OO

camel .... CONT

canoe .... TANEE

cap .... TOPI, TOPEE

cape .... DIVI, COMORIN

capital .... (NEW)DELHI

capital, summer .... SIMLA

carpet .... AGRA

carriage .... EKKA, RATH, TONGA, GHARRY

cashmere .... ULWAN

caste .... JAT, MEO, SHIR, GADDI, MAL(I), LOHANA, PARIAH, SUDRA, RAJPUT

caste mark .... TILKA

caterpillar .... SUGA

cattle .... GAUR, GOUR, ZEBU, BRAHMA

cavalryman .... SOWAR

chamois .... SARAU

channel ..... COCO, GREAT, TEN DEGREE

chief .... MIR, RAJA(H), SIRDAR

church .... SAMAJ

cigarette .... BIRI

city/town .... AGRA, GAYA, AJMER, AKOLA, DELHI, JAMMU,

PATNA, SAGAR, SALEM, SIMLA, SURAT, THANA, AMBALA, BARODA, BHILAI, BHOPAL, BOMBAY, DUMDUM, HOWRAH, IMPHAL, INDORE, JAIPUR, JHANSI, KANPUR, MADRAS, MEERUT, MYSORE, NAGPUR, RAIPUR, RAJKOT, ROHTAK, ALIGARH, ASANSOL, BELGAUM, BENARES, BIKANER, CALICUT, DHANBAD, GAUHATI, GWALIOR, JODHPUR, KURNOOL, LUCKNOW, MADURAI, PATIALA, VELLORE, AMRITSAR, BAREILLY, BHATPARA, CALCUTTA, DURGAPUR, JABALPUR, JAMNAGAR, LUDHIANA, SRINAGAR, BADODARA, VARANASI, WARANGAL, AHMADABAD, ALLAHABAD, BANGALORE, BHAVNAGAR, HYDERABAD, JULLUNDAR, KOZHIKODE, MORADABAD, CHANDIGARH

civet .... ZIBET(H)

clerk .... BABU, BABOO

cloth .... SALU, SURAT, ULWAN, SAL(L)OO

cloth strip .... PATA

coast .... MALABAR

coin .... PI(E), ANNA, FELS, HOON, PICE, FANAM, MOHUR, RUPEE

combining form .... INDO

condiment .... CURCUMA

corporal .... NAIK

cot .... CHARPOY

cow .... GAEKWAR

crocodile .... GAVIAL, MUGGAR, MUGGER

curtain .... PURDAH

custom .... DASTUR

dancing girl .... BAYADEER, BAYADERE

deer .... AXIS, CHITAL, SAMBAR

desert .... THAR, GREAT INDIAN

devil's tree .... DITA

dialect .... PUSHTU

diamond cutting center .... GOLCONDA

diamond, famous .... KOHINUR, KOHINOOR

disciple .... CHELA

district .... DIU, GOA, AGRA, DAMAN, MALABAR

division .... OUDH

dog .... DHOLE, KOLSUN

dormitory .... GHOTUL

drama .... NATAKA

drink .... SOMA

drug .... BHANG

dugout .... DUNGA

dust storm .... PEESASH

elephant .... HATHI

elephant driver .... MAHOUT

emperor .... ASOKA, BABER

empress of .... VICTORIA

entertainment .... TAMASHA

epic .... RAMAYANA

estate, inherited .... TALUK

Eurasian in .... SAHIB, FERINGI, FERINGHEE

European in .... MEMSAHIB

extra pay .... BATTA

falcon .... BAS(A)RA, SHAHEEN, SHASHIN

fan .... PUNKA(H)

farmer .... MEO, RYOT

festival .... DEWALI

flute .... PUNGI, MATALAN

footman .... PEON

footstool .... MORA

founder .... IVAN

fowl .... BRAHMA

fruit .... BEL

game .... PACHISI

garment/garb ..... SARI, DHOTI, KURTA, SAREE, BANIAN

gazelle .... CHIKARA

ghost .... BUHT

girl leader .... BELOSA

goat, wild .... TAHR

goddess .... KALI

gorge .... TANGI

gossip .... GUP

government estates ..... AMANI

granary .... GOLA, GUNJ, GUNGE

grant .... ENAM

greeting .... NAMASTE

groom .... SICE, SYCE

guerrilla band .... TAMIL TIGERS

guide .... SHIKAREE

guitar .... VINA

gulf .... KUTCH, CAMBAY, MANNAR

gully .... NULLAH

guru .... MAHARISHI

harem .... ZENANA

harvest .... RAB(B)I

hawk .... BADIUS, SHIKRA

headman .... PATEL, MOKADDAM

helmet/hat .... TOPI, TOPEE

hemp ..... KEF, KEEF, B(H)ANG, GANJA, RAMIE

hemp shrub ..... PUA, POOA(H)

hill .... GARO

hill dweller .... DOGRA

hills .... ABOT, MIRI, KHASI, MISHMI

hog deer .... AXIS, ATLAS
holy city ..... NASIK, BENARES,
    HARDWAR
holy man .... YOGI, FAKIR,
    SADHU
home rule .... SWARAJ
hunt(er) .... SHIKAR(I),
    SHIKAREE
hut .... BARI
inheritance .... TALUK
instrument .... SITAR
island .... AMINI, PITTI,
    AGATTI, KADMAT, KILTAN,
    ANDAMAN, ANDROTH,
    BUTCHER, CHETLAT, KALPENI,
    MINICOY, NICOBAR, AMINDIRI,
    SALSETTE, NANCOWRY,
    ELEPHANTA
island group .... AMINDIVI,
    CANNANORE, LACCADIVE
islands near .... MALDIVES
jacket .... KOLA
Jesuit in .... PAULIST
jungle .... SHOLA
kingdom .... NEPAL
knife .... DAO
laborer .... PALLI
lace .... GOTA
lady .... BIBI, BEGUM,
    MEMSAHIB
lake .... CHILKA, COLAIR,
    PERIYAR, PULICAT, SAMBHAR
land grant .... SASAN
land grant tenant
    .... ENAMDAR
landing place .... GHAT
landowner .... ZAMINDAR
language .... URDU, HINDI,
    BIHARI, BENGALI, ASSAMESE,
    GUJARATI, SANSKRIT
leguminous plant .... GUAR
levee .... DURBAR
license .... CHOP
licorice .... ABRIN
lieutenant governor .... NAIB
litter .... DOLY, DOOLEE,
    MUNCHEEL
litter bearer .... SIRDAR
loam .... REGUR
loincloth .... LUNGI, LUNGEE
low class .... BHAT
lunch .... TIFFIN
lute .... SITAR
mahogany .... TOON
maid .... AYAH
mail .... DA(W)K
marijuana .... GANJA
market .... GUNGE, PASAR
master .... MIAN, SAHIB
master: var. .... SAHEB
matting .... TATTA

meal .... AT(T)A
measure of distance ...... GUZ,
    KOS
Menon of .... KRISHNA
merchant .... SOUDAGUR
midwife .... DHAI
military caste .... RAJPUT
millet .... JOAR, CHENA,
    DURRA, DOURA(H)
minstrel .... BHAT
mistress .... MEMSAHIB
Mogul dynasty founder
    .... BABAR, BABER, BABUR
monetary unit ..... LAC, LAKH,
    RUPEE
money lender .... MAHAJAN
monkey .... RHESUS,
    WANDEROO
Moslem .... SWAT
mountain .... ABIL, KAMET,
    DAPSANG, NILGIRI, NANDA
    DEVI, KANCHENJUNGA
mountain chain .... GHATS,
    ZASKAR, MUSTAGH,
    HIMALAYA, KARAKORAM,
    HINDU KUSH
mountain pass .... GHA(U)T.
    SHIPKI
mulberry .... (A)AL, ACH
murder .... THUGGEE
musical instrument ...... VINA,
    RUANA, SAROD, SARON
muslin .... DOREA, GURRAH
mystic .... GURU
Naga capital .... KOHIMA
narcotic ..... BHANG, HASHHISH
national mourning .... HARTAL
native .... BENGALI
Negro .... HUBSHI
novice .... CHELA
nurse .... AMAH, AYAH
Occidental in .... GRIFFIN
official .... DEWAN, NAZIR
oil tree .... BEN
ox .... GAUR
pageant .... TAMASHA
pagoda .... CHORTEN
palanquin .... PALKEE
parliament .... LOK SABHA
part of .... DECCAN
paymaster .... BUXY
pea .... DAL
peasant .... RYOT
peninsula .... HINDUSTAN
permit .... CHOP
physicist .... BOSE, RAMAN
pigeon .... TRERON
poison .... BIKH, BISH
police station .... THANA
policeman .... PEON, SEPOY
political party .... CONGRESS,

    BHARATIYA JANATA
political protest .... HARTAL
Portuguese district .... DAMAO
powder .... ABIR
prayerlike gesture
    .... NAMASTE
president .... PRASAD, ZIA
    ULHAQ
priest .... SHAMAN
priest's garment .... DHOTI
prime minister .... NEHRU,
    (RAJIV)GANDHI,
    (INDIRA)GANDHI, SHASTRI
prince .... (MAHA)RAJA(H)
princess/queen .... RANI,
    BEGUM, RANEE, MAHARANI
property .... DHAN
protectorate .... SIKKIM
province .... PUNJAB
quilt .... RESAI
race .... JAT, TAMIL
rat .... BANDICOOT
reception (hall) .... DURBAR
region ..... CANARA, MALABAR,
    CARNATIC
religious fanatic .... THUG
religious sect .... SAMAJ
republic .... BHARAT
resort .... SIMLA
rice .... BORO
rich man .... NABOB
rifle pit .... SANGAR
river .... INDUS, JUMNA,
    CHENAB, GANGES, JHELUM,
    KAVERI, SUTLEJ, CHAMBAL,
    DAMODAR, GHAGHRA,
    HOOGHLY, NARMADA,
    GODAVARI, MAHANADI,
    TUNGABHADRA
road .... PRAYA
robber .... THUG, DACOIT
rope dancer .... NAT
rubber .... CAOUTCHOUC
rug .... DRUGGET
rule .... RAJ
ruler .... RAO, NABOB, NAWAB,
    NIZAM, RAJA(H)
sacred city .... NASIK,
    BENARES, HARDWAR
sacred lore .... VEDA
sacrificial victim .... TRAGA
sailor .... LASCAR
salute .... NAMASTE
salvation .... MOKSHA
scholar .... PANDIT, PUNDIT
screen .... TATTY, PURDAH
seal .... CHOP
seaport .... SURAT
servant .... AMAH, AYAH,
    MATY, HAM(M)AL, HAMAUL,
    SIRDAR

shawl .... SHABO, CHUDDAR

sheep .... SHA, SNA, URIAL, OORIAL

shell money .... ULO

shirt .... BANIAN

show .... TAMASHA

shrine .... DAGOBA

shrub .... ODAL, MADAR

silk .... ERI, MUGA, ROMAL, RUMAL, CABECA

silk cloth .... PONGEE

sir .... SAHIB

skipper .... SERANG

snake .... COBRA, KRAIT, BONGAR, DABOIA, KATUKA

snake fighter ..... MONGOOS(E)

soldier .... PEON, SEPOY, GURKHA

songbird .... KOEL, SHAMA

sovereignty .... RAJ

spittoon .... PIGDAN

stairs .... GHAT

stamp .... CHOP

state .... GOA, ASSAM, BIHAR, JAMMU, KERALA, ORISSA, PUNJAB, SIKKIM, GUJARAT, HARYANA, KASHMIR, MANIPUR, TRIPURA, NAGALAND, KARNATAKA, TAMIL NADU, WEST BENGAL

state capital .... PATNA, IMPHAL, MERCARA, CALCUTTA

state revenue lands ..... AMANI

statesman .... NEHRU

stone .... LINGAM

storehouse .... GOLA

strait .... PALK

sugar .... GUR

sugar, coarse .... RAAB

tax collector .... ZAMINDAR

tax collection area ...... TALUK

tea .... ASSAM, PEKOE, NILGIRI, DARJEELING

teacher .... GURU

temple girl .... BAYADERE

tenant .... ENAMDAR

term of address .... BIBI, SAHIB

territory .... DIU, GOA, DADRA, DAMAN, DELHI, ANDAMAN, MIZORAM, NICOBAR, CHANDIGARH

title .... AGA, NAWAB, RAJA(H), SAHIB

title of respect .... SAHIB, S(H)RI, SHREE, HUZOOR, PANDIT

tower .... MINAR, SHIKARA

tracker .... PUGGE, PUGGI

tree .... BEL, DAR, ENG, SAJ, SAL, AMLA, AMLI, AMRA, MYXA, NEEM, GORAN, PIPAL, BANYAN, BAOBAB, RAMTIL, CHAMPAC, CHAMPAK, MARGOSA, PALMYRA

tree bark .... NIEPA

tribal community .... MURIA

tribesman .... NAGA, KHOND

turban ..... PUGGRY, PUG(G)REE

turban cloth .... LUNGI, LUNGEE

twilled cotton .... SALU, SALOO

two-wheeled carriage .... TONGA

umbrella .... CHATTA

valley .... DHOON

veranda .... PYAL

vessel ...... LOTA(H), PATAMAR

viceroy .... CURZON, MOUNTBATTEN

village .... ABADI

violin .... RUANA, SAROD

warrior .... SINGH, GURKHA

watchman .... MINA

water carrier .... BHEESTIE

wayside stop .... PARAO

weight .... SER, PICE, TOLA, MAUND, POLLAM, RAT(TI), CHITTAK

Westerner in .... GRIFFIN

wheat .... SUJI

wild cat .... CHAUS

wild dog .... DHOLE, BUANSU

wild hog .... BABIRUSA

woman's house .... ZENANA

woman's shaw .... CHADOR, CHUDDAR, CHUDDER

xylophone .... SARON

yellow .... P(I)URI, PURREE

Indian/Native American

.... SAC, UTE, CREE, ERIE, HOPI, OTOE, INCA(N), KIOWA, MAYAN, SIOUX, APACHE, MOHAWK, ONEIDA, PEQUOT, AMERIND, REDSKIN, CHIPPEWA, DELAWARE, IROQUOIS, SEMINOLE

Alabama .... CREEK

Alaska .... ALEUT, TLINGIT, TLINKIT

Aleutian island .... AKKHAS

Algonquian .... FOX, SAC, CREE, SAUK, MICMAC, PEQUOT, SANNUP, MAHICAN, MOHEGAN, MOHICAN, OJIBWA(Y), ARAPAHO(E), CHIPPEWA, DELAWARE, KICKAPOO

Antilles .... CARIB

Argentine .... ARAUCAN

Arikara .... REE

Arizona .... HOPI, PIMA, YUMA, APACHE, NAVAJO, PAPAGO

arrow poison .... CURARE

ascetic .... YOGI

Athapascan .... DENE, TAKU, APACHE, NAVAHO, NAVAJO

ax .... HATCHET, TOMAHAWK

baby .... PAPOOSE

ball game .... LACROSSE

bead money .... WAMPUN

bean .... CATALPA

blanket .... MACKINAW

boat .... CANOE

Bolivia .... MOXO, OTUKE, AYMARA, CHARCA, MAROPA

brave, young ..... TENDERFOOT

bread .... TUCKAHOE

British Honduras .... MAYA

cereal grass, East .... RAGGI

ceremony/conference .... POWWOW

challenge sign .... SCALP LOCK

chickpea .... GRAM

chief .... LOGAN, SACHEM, COCHISE, PONTIAC, GERONIMO, HIAWATHA, POWHATAN, SAGAMORE, TECUMSEH, MASSASOIT

Chile .... ARAUCAN

communal home .... LONG HOUSE

corn .... ZEA, SAMP, KANGA, FLINT, MAIZE, MEALY, MANDAN, NUBBIN, MEALIES, TEOSINTE

cotton .... SURAT

council hall .... LONG HOUSE

council room .... KIVA

Creek .... ALABAMA, MUSKHOGEAN

dwelling .... HOGAN, LODGE, TEPEE, WIGWAM, WI(C)KIUP

empire of 1500 A.D. .... INCA

Eskimo .... AMERIND

feast .... POTLATCH

female .... PURIS, MAHALY

fetish .... TOTEM

food .... PEMICAN

footwear .... MOCCASIN

for whom a sea was named .... CARIB

gardener .... MALI

gathering .... POWWOW

Georgia .... CREEK

Gila River .... PIMA

girl in poem .... MINNEHAHA

god .... MANITOU

great spirit .... MANITU, MANITO(U)

greeting .... HOW, NETOP

halfbreed .... METIF(F)

headdress .... WAR BONNET

hero in poem .... HIAWATHA

horse .... PONY, PINTO, CAYUSE, PAWNEE, MUSTANG

hut ..... HOGAN, LODGE, TEPEE, WI(C)KIUP

Illinois .... KICKAPOO

intoxicant .... BHANG

Iowa .... SAC, SAUK

Kansas .... PANI, PAWNEE

Lake Erie .... CHIPPEWA

macaque .... RHESUS

maize .... CORN

male, married .... SANNUP

Manitoba .... CREE

matting .... TAT

medicine man .... POWWOW, SITTING BULL

memorial post ..... XAT, XYST, TOTEM

mestizo .... GRIFF(E), METIF(F), HALF-BREED

Michigan .... SAC, SAUK

Missouri .... MANDAN

mixed blood .... METIF(F), METISSE, HALF-BREED

moccasin .... PAC

money .... PIMAN, PEAG(E), WAMPUM, SE(A)WANT(T)

mystic symbol .... SWASTIKA

Negro .... ZAMBO

nomadic .... APACHE

North Dakota .... PAWNEE, CADDOAN, CHIPPEWA

Ocean arm .... RED SEA

Ocean continent ...... LEMURIA

Ocean vessel .... DHOW

palm .... TALIPOT

Panama .... CUNA

pea .... DAL

Penutian .... CHINUK, CHINOOK

pierced nose .... NEZ PERCE

pipe .... CALUMET

poet .... TAGORE

poison .... CURARE

pole .... TOTEM

pony .... TAT, PINTO, CAYUSE

porridge .... SAMP

prairie .... KAW

prayer stick .... BAHO, PAHO

priest .... POWWOW

princess .... POCAHONTAS

Pueblo .... HOPI, TANO, ZUNI

room for religious service .... KIVA

Salishan .... TULALIP, FLATHEAD

seafaring .... TLINGIT

sled dog .... HUSKY

sledge .... TRAVOIS(E)

slipper .... MOCCASIN

spirit .... MANITOU

supplanted by Incan .... AYMARA

tepee .... LODGE, WIGWAM

tent .... TE(E)PEE, LODGE, WIGWAM

tree .... MEE

trophy .... SCALP

unit of money .... PIMAN

Uto-Aztecan .... YAQUI

village .... PUEBLO

wampum .... SE(A)WAN(T)

war cry .... WHOOP

war trophy .... SCALP

warrior .... BRAVE

weapon .... TOMAHAWK

Western .... UTE, HOPI, OTO(E), ZUNI

whisky to an .... FIREWATER

white man to an .... PALEFACE

wife .... SQUAW

wigwam ...... LODGE, TE(E)PEE

winter festival .... POTLATCH

woman .... SQUAW

yell .... WHOOP

"yes" of .... UGH

young ...... BUCK, TENDERFOOT

Indiana capital .... INDIANAPOLIS

city/town .... GARY, PERU, PAOLI, SALEM, VEVAY, GOSHEN, KOKOMO, MARION, MUNCIE, SHOALS, TIPTON, WABASH, WARSAW, ELKHART, HAMMOND, LEBANON, SPENCER, WINAMAC, ANDERSON, COLUMBUS, RICHMOND, FORT WAYNE, FRANKFORT, LAFAYETTE, SOUTH BEND, VINCENNES, EVANSVILLE, GREENSBURG, TERRA HAUTE, BLOOMINGTON

county ..... CASS, KNOX, LAKE, ALLEN, BOONE, CLARK, FLOYD, GRANT, HENRY, WAYNE, DE KALB, DUBOIS, GIBSON, HOWARD, MARION, MONROE, MORGAN, PORTER, ELKHART, HANCOCK, JOHNSON, LA PORTE, MADISON, DELAWARE, MANILTON, HENDRICKS, KOSCIUSKO, TIPPECANOE, VANDERBURGH

creek .... WILDCAT

lake .... LEMON, MONROE, SHAPER, FREEMAN, WAWASEE, MICHIGAN, SALAMONIE, MAXINKUCKEE, MISSISSINEWA

native .... HOOSIER

recreation site .... SANTA CLAUS LAND, CLIFTY FALLS PARK, INDIANAPOLIS MOTOR SPEEDWAY

river .... EEL, FAWN, OHIO, WHITE, MAUMEE, PATOKA, WABASH, (BIG) BLUE, (LITTLE) ELKHART, TIPPECANOE

state bird .... CARDINAL

state flower .... PEONY

state motto .... CROSSROADS OF AMERICA

state nickname .... HOOSIER

state tree .... TULIP

university .... BUTLER, PURDUE, BALL STATE, NOTRE DAME

village, famed .... SANTA CLAUS

Indic dialect .... PALI

indicate .... SHOW, POINT, EVINCE, SIGNIFY, INTIMATE

indication(s) .... SIGNS, INDICIA

slight .... INKLING

indicator .... CLUE, DIAL, SIGN, ARROW, GAUGE, INDEX, POINTER, REGISTER

air pressure .... BAROMETER

airport .... WINDSOCK

wind .... VANE

indicatory statement .... X MARKS THE SPOT

indict .... ACCUSE, CHARGE, ARRAIGN, IMPEACH

indictment .... CHARGE

indifference .... APATHY, LETHARGY

indifferent .... COLD, COOL, SOSO, ALOOF, TEPID, LANGUID, DETACHED, LISTLESS, APATHETIC, UNCONCERNED

to hardship .... STOIC(AL)

indigence .... NEED, WANT, PENURY, POVERTY

indigenous .... INBORN, INNATE, NATIVE, EDAPHIC, ENDEMIC, INHERENT

indigent .... POOR, NEEDY, DESTITUTE

indigestion .... APEPSIA, DYSPEPSIA

indignant .... ANGRY, IRATE, WROTH

indignation .... IRE, ANGER, SCORN, WRATH, RESENTMENT

indignity .... INSULT, SLIGHT, AFFRONT, HUMILIATION

indigo .... DYE, ANIL, BLUE

bale of .... SEROON

berry .... RANDIA

blue .... INDIGOTIN

compound .... ISATIN

derivative .... INDOL(E), ISATIN, KETOLE

forming substance
.... INDICAN
plant .... ANIL
wild .... BAPTISIA
indirect .... IMPLIED, OBLIQUE,
DEVIATING, ROUNDABOUT
expression .... AMBAGE,
PERIPHRASE, PERIPHRASIS
indiscreet .... UNWISE, RECKLESS,
IMPRUDENT
indiscretion .... SLIP, FOLLY,
PECCADILLO
indiscriminate .... SWEEPING,
EXTENSIVE, WHOLESALE
indispensable .... VITAL,
ESSENTIAL, NECESSARY
one .... KEYMAN
indisposed .... ILL, SICK, AVERSE,
UNWILLING
indisposition .... PIP, AILMENT,
MALAISE, AVERSION
indisputable .... ABSOLUTE,
APOD(E)ICTIC,
UNQUESTIONING
indistinct ...... DIM, HAZY, FAINT,
FOGGY, VAGUE, BLURRY,
UNCLEAR, OBSCURE
indite ...... PEN, WRITE, COMPOSE,
INSCRIBE
individual .... ONE, SELF, SOLE,
PARTY, PERSON, SINGLE,
PARTICULAR
combining form .... IDIO
performance .... SOLO
individualism .... EGOISM
Indo-China, part of .... LAOS,
BURMA, MALAYA, VIETNAM,
CAMBODIA, THAILAND
Chinese .... LAO, TAI, SHAN
European .... ARYAN, CROAT
European language
.... AVESTAN, HITTITE
indoctrinate .... BRIEF, IMBUE,
TEACH, INSTILL, INSTRUCT,
BRAINWASH, INCULCATE
indolence .... SLOTH, INERTIA,
IDLENESS, LAZINESS
indolent ...... IDLE, LAZY, OTIOSE,
SUPINE, LISTLESS, SLOTHFUL
indomitable .... INVINCIBLE,
UNBEATABLE
Indonesia .... EAST INDIES
capital of .... JAKARTA
Indonesian .... ATTA, DYAK,
BATTAK, LAMPONG
archipelago ...... RIAU, MALAY,
LINGGA, BANGGAI, KARIMATA
bay .... BERAU, SEBUKU,
GEELVINK
bird .... BULBUL, PEAFOWL
cape .... VALS, NGUNJU,

PERKAM, SELATAN, JAMBUAIR,
JAMURSBA
city/town ...... AMBON, BOGOR,
MEDAN, SOLOK, TEGAL,
BINJAI, BLITAR, (D)JAMBI,
KEDIRI, MADIUN, MALANG,
MANADO, PADANG, BANDUNG,
BATAVIA, CILICAP, CIREBON,
SIBOLGA, BENGKULU,
MAKASSAR, SEMARANG,
SURABAYA, GORONTALO,
PONTIANAK, SURAKARTA
gibbon .... LAR
gulf .... BONE, TOLO, TOMINI
island .... WE, BALI, BIAK,
BURU, JAVA, LAUT, MUNA,
NIAS, ROTI, SIAU, BABAR,
KALAO, KISAR, SUMBA,
WAKDE, WETAR, YAPEN,
BANGKA, BORNEO, BUTUNG,
FLORES, JEMAJA, KOMODO,
LINGGA, LOMBOK, MADURA,
MISOOL, PANTAR, RAKATA,
TIDORE, WAIGEO, CELEBES,
ENGGANO, KABAENA,
KANGEAN, NUMFOOR,
SELAYOR, SUMATRA,
SULAWESI, GREAT KAI,
HALMAHERA, WANGIWANGI
islands .... ARU, OBI, BATU,
EWAB, SAWU, SULA, MAPIA,
BANYAK, NATUNA, TALAUD,
ANAMBAS, SANGIHE,
MOLUCCAS, TAMBELAN,
TANIMBAR
knife .... PARANG
lake .... TOBA
language ..... MALAY, BAHASA,
PAPUAN, JAVANESE,
MADURESE, SUDANESE
monetary unit .... RUPIAH
mountain .... RAYA, LEUSER,
SEMERU, SIAMET, KERINCI,
PUNCAK JAYA
mountains .... MAOKE,
MULLER, BARISAN, SCHWANER
news agency .... ANTARA
ox .... BANTENG
peninsula .... DOBERAI
premier .... HATTA
president .... SUHARTO,
SUKARNO
puppeteer .... (TO)DALANG
region ..... TIMOR, IRIAN JAYA,
KALIMANTAN
rhino .... BADAK
river ..... MUSI, DIGUL, ROKAN,
BARITO, KAPUAS, TARIKU,
MAHAKAM, MAMBERAMO
sea .... JAVA, SAWU, BANDA,
TIMOR, FLORES, ARATURA,

CELEBES, MOLUCCA
strait .... MULI, OMBAI, SUMBA,
SUNDA, MALACCA, SIBERUT,
MAKASSAR
volcano .... AGUNG, TAMBORA,
KRAKATAO
xylophone .... GENDER,
GAMBANG
indoors weather ...... RAINY DAY
indorse .... ATTEST, APPROVE,
SUPPORT, SANCTION
indri .... LEMUR
indubitable .... SURE, CERTAIN,
EVIDENT, DOUBTLESS
induce .... LEAD, URGE, CAUSE,
PREVAIL, PERSUADE
love .... ENDEAR
to perjury .... SUBORN
inducement .... MOTIVE,
INCENTIVE
induct .... INSTALL, INITIATE
inductance, measure of
.... HENRY
induction rite .... INAUGURAL
indulge .... PET, BABY, SPOIL,
HUMOR, CODDLE, PAMPER,
GRATIFY, SATISFY
in happy talk .... BILL AND
COO
indulgence .... FAVOR, MERCY,
LENIENCY, PATIENCE
indulgent .... KIND, LENIENT,
TOLERANT, EASYGOING
Indus .... CONSTELLATION
River tributary .... SUTLEJ
tribesman .... GOR
industrial .... TRADING,
COMMERCIAL, MERCANTILE
activity, at times
.... ACCELERATION
giant .... TYCOON, MAGNATE
spy .... KEEK
Industrial Workers of the
World member ...... WOBBLY
industrialist .... BARON, TYCOON,
MAGNATE, FINANCIER
of a sort .... ANT
industrious .... BUSY, ACTIVE,
OPEROSE, DILIGENT,
ASSIDUOUS
industry .... LABOR, TRADE,
COMMERCE, MARKETING
inebriate .... SOT, TOPER,
DRUNK(ARD)
inedible .... UNEATABLE
inefficient .... INEPT, UNABLE
inelastic .... RIGID, STIFF,
INFLEXIBLE
inelegant .... CRUDE, CLUMSY,
COARSE, AWKWARD
ineligible .... UNFIT, UNQUALIFIED

ineluctable .... DOOM, FATE, CERTAIN, DEFINITE, INEVITABLE

inept .... UNFIT, ABSURD, CLUMSY, AWKWARD, FOOLISH, PUERILE

inerrant ...... PRECISE, UNERRING, INFALLIBLE

inert .... DULL, SLOW, LATENT, SUPINE, TORPID, AT REST, NEUTRAL, INACTIVE

gas .... NEON, FREON

inertia .... LETHARGY

inescapable .... SURE, INEVITABLE

responsibility .... TAXES

inestimable .... PRICELESS

inevitable .... DUE, FATED, BINDING, CERTAIN, DESTINED

inexact .... VAGUE, WRONG, ERRONEOUS, UNSPECIFIED

inexcitable .... COOLHEADED, COLDBLOODED

inexcusable .... UNFORGIVABLE

inexhaustible .... ENDLESS

inexorable .... HARD, STERN, UNYIELDING

inexperienced .... RAW, GREEN, NAIVE

infamous .... VICIOUS, NOTORIOUS, SCANDALOUS

infanticide .... HEROD

infamy .... ODIUM, SHAME, SCANDAL, ATROCITY, DISGRACE, NOTORIETY

infancy .... BABYHOOD, MINORITY

to puberty .... CHILDHOOD

infant .... TOT, BABE, BABY, BAIRN, CHILD, CHRISOM

Cupid .... AMOR

doctor of .... PEDIATRIST

room of .... NURSERY

infanta .... PRINCESS

infante .... PRINCE

infantile .... CHILDISH

paralysis ...... POLIO(MYELITIS)

infantryman .... DOGFACE, DOUGHBOY, (FOOT)SOLDIER

mounted .... DRAGOON

infantrymen's formation
.... PHALANX

infatuate .... BESET, CHARM, ENAMOR, OBSESS

infatuated .... GAGA, FOOLISH, ENAMORED

infatuation .... RAVE, CRUSH, PASSION, FONDNESS

infect ...... IMBUE, TAINT, AFFECT, CORRUPT, CONTAMINATE

infected .... MORBID, TAINTED, DISEASED

infection .... TAINT, VIRUS, DISEASE

causing .... SEPTIC

source .... NIDUS

infectious .... CATCHING, CONTAGIOUS

infecund .... BARREN, STERILE

infer .... IMPLY, DEDUCE, GATHER, PRESUME, CONCLUDE

inference .... ILLATION, DEDUCTION, ASSUMPTION, CONCLUSION

inferior .... SAD, POOR, LOUSY, MINOR, PETTY, LOW(ER), LESS(ER), SHODDY, MEDIOCRE, SECOND-RATE, SUBORDINATE

diamond .... BORT

horse .... NAG, TIT, PLATER

lawyer .... SHYSTER, PETTIFOGGER

performer .... BUSHLEAGUER

poet .... RIMESTER, POETASTER, RHYMESTER, VERSIFIER

slang .... SECOND-STRINGER

to .... UNDER

whisky .... REDEYE

writer .... HACK

infernal .... HATEFUL, HELLISH, SATANIC, DEVILISH, FIENDISH, DIABOLICAL

machine .... BOMB

region .... AVERNUS

inferno ...... HELL, ABYSS, HADES, GEHENNA

infertile .... BARREN

infertility .... STERILITY

infest .... SWARM, OVERRUN

infidel .... PAGAN, ATHEIST, HEATHEN, SARACEN

infidelity .... ADULTERY, BETRAYAL

infield cover .... TARP

infielder .... BASEMAN, SHORTSTOP

infiltrate .... ENTER, FILTER, PENETRATE

infiltration .... SEEPAGE

infinite .... VAST, ENDLESS, ETERNAL, IMMENSE, BOUNDLESS

infinitesimal .... TINY, MINUTE

infinity .... ETERNITY

infirm .... LAME, WEAK, ANILE, FEEBLE, SENILE, DECREPIT, UNSTABLE

infirmary .... CLINIC, HOSPITAL, DISPENSARY

infirmity .... FAULT, DEFECT, FRAILTY, WEAKNESS

inflame .... FAN, FIRE, ENRAGE, EXCITE, IGNITE, KINDLE, MADDEN

with love .... ENAMOR

inflammable ...... FIERY, PICEOUS, BURNABLE

material .... PUNK, AMADOU, TINDER, ACETONE

inflammation .... ANGINA, REDNESS, SWELLING

bone .... OSTEITIS, ARTHRITIS

bone marrow .... MYELITIS

glandular .... ADENITIS

intestinal .... COLITIS, ENTERITIS

iris .... IRITIS, UVEITIS

respiratory passages
.... CROUP

suffix .... ITIS

throat .... CATARRH

udders of cow .... GARGET

urinary bladder .... CYSTITIS

inflate ...... PUFF, SWELL, AERATE, DILATE, EXPAND, DISTEND

inflated .... TUMID, TURGID, BLOATED, POMPOUS, SWOLLEN

condition .... TYMPANY

inflect .... BEND, TURN, CURVE, MODULATE

inflection .... TONE, CADENCE

inflexible .... SET, DOUR, FIRM, IRON, FIXED, RIGID, STERN, STIFF, STONY, ADAMANT, OBDURATE, STUBBORN, UNBENDING

inflict ...... DEAL, WREAK, IMPOSE

inflorescence ...... CYME, WHORL, RACEME, FLOWERING, BLOSSOMING

type of .... SPIKE, UMBEL, CATKIN, SPADIX

influence ...... DRAG, HEFT, HOLD, MOLD, PULL, SWAY, CLOUT, IMPEL, POWER, AFFECT, EFFECT, INDUCE, WEIGHT, PRESSURE

influential ...... POTENT, WEIGHTY, POWERFUL, EFFECTIVE, PRESTIGIOUS

influenza .... FLU, CORYZA, GRIPPE, CATARRH

influx .... INFLOW, ARRIVAL

of settlers .... IMMIGRATION

inform .... TELL, WARN, ALERT, TEACH, ADVISE, CONVEY, NOTIFY, REPORT, APPRISE, ACQUAINT,

against .... BETRAY, DELATE

slang .... RAT, SING, SQUEAL

informal .... CASUAL

party .... BARBECUE

talk .... CHAT, CAUSERIE

informant .... APPRISER, REPORTER, NEWSCASTER, STOOL PIGEON

information .... DATA, NEWS,

WORD, AVISO, FACTS, ADVICE, LEARNING, KNOWLEDGE, INTELLIGENCE
bit of .... ITEM
file .... DOSSIER
in law .... ACCUSATION
slang .... DOPE, INFO, LOW-DOWN
informative .... NEWSY, EXPLICIT, REPORTED, FACT-FULL, INSTRUCTIVE
informed ...... HEP, HIP, WISE, ON TO, AWARE, CONVERSANT, KNOWLEDGEABLE
informer .... RAT, SPY, FINK, NARK, BIRDIE, SNITCH, TIPSTER, REPORTER, SQUEALER, TATTLETALE, STOOL PIGEON
turn .... SING, PEACH, STOOL, SQUEAL, DOUBLE-CROSS
infract .... VIOLATE
infraction .... VIOLATION
infrequency .... RARENESS
infrequent .... RARE, SCARCE, SELDOM
infrequently ...... ONCE OR TWICE
infringe .... BREAK, VIOLATE, ENCROACH, TRESPASS
infringement, copyright/patent
.... PIRACY
infuriate .... RILE, ANGER, PEEVE, ENRAGE, INCITE, MADDEN
infuse .... FILL, SOAK, IMBUE, STEEP, TINGE, IMPART, INSTILL
infusion .... TEA, TINCTURE
infusoria .... PROTOZOA
ingenious ...... CLEVER, D(A)EDAL, ORIGINAL, INVENTIVE
ingenue .... ACTRESS, STARLET
ingenuity .... WIT, SKILL, CLEVERNESS
ingenuous .... OPEN, FRANK, NAIVE, NOBLE, CANDID, SIMPLE, ARTLESS, INNOCENT, GUILELESS
ingest .... EAT, SWALLOW
ingle .... BLAZE, FIRE(PLACE)
ingot .... BAR, PIG, BULLION
silver .... SYCEE
zinc .... SPELTER
ingrain .... DYE, IMBUE, INFUSE
ingrained .... DEEP-SEATED
ingratiate .... INSINUATE
ingratiating .... WINNING, CHARMING
ingredient .... CONTENT, ELEMENT, COMPONENT
ingress .... ENTRY, ACCESS, ENTRANCE

ingrown .... EMBEDDED
inhabit ...... LIVE, DWELL, PEOPLE, RESIDE, SETTLE
inhabitant .... INMATE, CIT(IZEN), DENIZEN, RESIDENT
castle's .... CASTELLAN
suffix .... ITE
inhabited .... PEOPLED
inhabiting the shore
.... LIMICOLINE
inhalant .... VICKS
inhale .... DRAW, SUCK, BREATHE, INSPIRE, RESPIRE
sharply .... SNIFF
inhere .... DWELL IN, CLEAVE, (TO) STICK
inherence .... PRESENCE, IMMANENCE
inherent .... BASIC, INBORN, INNATE, NATIVE, IMMANENT, INTRINSIC, INDIGENOUS
inherit ...... COME INTO, RECEIVE, SUCCEED
inheritance .... LEGACY, BEQUEST, HERITAGE, PATRIMONY
law .... SALIC
tax .... DEATH DUTY
unit of .... GENE
inheritor .... HEIR, DEVISEE, LEGATEE, RECIPIENT
inhibit .... BAR, CHECK, ENJOIN, FORBID, HAMPER, PROHIBIT, RESTRAIN, SUPPRESS, WITHHOLD
as appetite .... CURB
inhospitable .... HOSTILE
inhuman .... CRUEL, BRUTAL, SAVAGE, BESTIAL
inhume .... BURY, INTER
inimical ...... ADVERSE, COUNTER, HOSTILE, CONTRARY, UNFRIENDLY
inimitable .... PEERLESS, MATCHLESS
iniquitous .... EVIL, UNJUST, WICKED
iniquity .... SIN, EVIL, VICE, CRIME, INJUSTICE, WICKEDNESS
initial .... FIRST, INCEPTIVE
ornamental .... PARAPH
initials .... MONOGRAM
woven together .... CIPHER
initiate .... HAZE, OPEN, ADMIT, BEGIN, FOUND, START, INDUCT, INSTITUTE, INTRODUCE
initiative .... LEAD, ENTERPRISE
inject .... INSERT, INOCULATE
injection ...... SHOT, INOCULATION
set .... SYRETTE

injudicious .... UNWISE
injunction .... ORDER, COMMAND, MANDATE, ENJOINING
injure .... MAR, HARM, HURT, MAIM, ABUSE, SPOIL, WRONG, DAMAGE, IMPAIR, SCATHE
injurious .... TOXIC, NOISOME, HARMFUL, NOXIOUS
injury .... HARM, WOUND, DAMAGE, TRAUMA, OFFENSE
compensation for
.... DAMAGES, SOLATIUM
mark .... SCAR
injustice .... BIAS, WRONG, INJURY, INEQUITY, PREJUDICE
ink .... DAUB, SIGN, BLACKEN
fish .... CUTTLE
ingredient .... TANNIN
spreader ...... BRAYER, ROLLER
inker .... PAD, DABBER, ROLLER
inkle .... TAPE, YARN, THREAD
inkling .... HINT, IDEA, NOTION, SUSPICION, INDICATION
inky .... DARK, BLACK
inlaid work .... BUHL, MOSAIC, NIELLO, TARSIA, PARQUETRY
inland .... INTERIOR
body of water .... LAKE
sea .... ARAL, CASPIAN
inlay .... INSET, INSERT, FILLING
material .... TILE, NIELLO
inlet .... ARM, BAY, RIA, COVE, BAYOU, BIGHT, CREEK, FIORD, FIRTH, ESTUARY
shallow .... LAGOON
inmate ...... OCCUPANT, PRISONER
inmost .... DEEPEST
nature .... ESSENCE
part .... CORE, HEART
inn .... PUB, KHAN, SERAI, TAMBO, HOSTEL, IMARET, TAVERN, AUBERGE, HOSPICE, LODGING, POTHOUSE, ROADHOUSE
Canterbury Tales' .... TABARD
roadside .... MOTEL
worker ..... POTBOY, BARMAID, TAPSTER
innards .... GUTS, NUMBLES, VISCERA, ENTRAILS
innate .... INBORN, INBRED, NATIVE, NATURAL, INHERENT, CONGENITAL
inner .... BEN, ENTAL, INSIDE, INWARD, INTERNAL
bark .... BAST
circle .... CADRE
combining form .... ENTO
man .... SOUL, PALATE, STOMACH
part .... INTERIOR

wheel member

.... (ROTARY)ANN

Inner Mongolian province

...... JEHOL, CHAHAR, NINGSIA

Innisfail ...... EIRE, ERIN, IRELAND

innkeeper .... (H)OSTLER,

PADRONE, HOST(ELER),

BONIFACE, LANDLORD,

PUBLICAN

wife of .... HOSTESS

innocence .... BLUET, PURITY,

NAIVETE, SIMPLICITY

innocent .... FOOL, NAIF, PURE,

NAIVE, SIMPLE, ARTLESS,

IGNORANT, DEWEY-EYED,

GUILTLESS

bystander .... WITNESS

in the woods .... BABE

Innocents' Day ...... CHILDERMAS

innocuous .... HARMLESS

innominate bone .... ILIUM,

PUBIS, HIPBONE

innovation .... CHANGE

innovative .... NEW

Innsbruck native, e.g.

.... TYROLEAN

innuendo .... HINT, SLUR,

ALLUSION, ASPERSION,

INSINUATION

innumerable ...... MANY, MYRIAD,

UNTOLD, COUNTLESS

Innuit's home .... IGLU, IGLOO

inoculation .... SHOT, SERUM,

VACCINE

inoculate .... INFECT, INJECT,

IMMUNIZE, VARIOLATE

Inonu, Turkish president

.... ISMET

inopportune .... ILL-TIMED,

UNTIMELY

inordinate .... UNDUE, EXCESSIVE

inordinately .... OVERLY

Ino's husband .... ATHAMAS

input, computer's .... DATA

inquest .... ASSIZE, INQUIRY,

INVESTIGATION

official .... CORONER

inquiry .... QUERY, REQUEST,

QUESTION, EXAMINATION

inquisition .... PROBE, INQUIRY,

HOLY OFFICE

inquisitive ...... NOS(E)Y, PRYING,

SNOOPY, CURIOUS

inroad .... RAID, INVASION

in's term .... TENURE

insane .... MAD, BUGS, DAFT,

BATTY, CRAZY, FOOLISH,

DEMENTED, SENSELESS

asylum .... BUGHOUSE,

MADHOUSE, NUTHOUSE

make .... DEMENT, DERANGE

person .... NUT, MADMAN,

LUNATIC, ODDBALL

slang .... LOCO, NUTTY,

PSYCHO, BONKERS

insanity .... MANIA, LUNACY,

MADNESS, DEMENTIA,

PARANOIA, PSYCHOSIS

insatiable .... VORACIOUS

inscribe .... MARK, WRITE,

ENROLL, ENGRAVE, DEDICATE

inscribed slab .... STELA

inscription ...... RUNE, GRAFFITO,

LETTERING, DEDICATION

bookplate .... EX LIBRIS

on book .... ENVOY,

COLOPHON

on coin ..... LEGEND, EXERGUE

on Unknown Soldier's tomb

.... KNOWN BUT TO GOD

tomb's .... EPITAPH

inscrutable .... ABSTRUSE,

ENIGMATIC, MYSTERIOUS

expression .... DEADPAN,

IMPASSIVE, POKERFACE

one .... SPHINX

insect .... BEE, BUG, FLY, NIT,

MITE, TICK, WASP, APHID,

THRIP, BEETLE, COCCID,

COOTIE, EARWIG, SPIDER,

ANTLION, CHALCID, MOSQUITO

adult .... IMAGO

appendage .... ENDITE

back of .... NOTUM

blood-sucking ..... FLEA, TICK,

LOUSE, MIDGE, BEDBUG,

CONENOSE

bodies, dried .... KERMES

carnival .... FLEA

colonists .... ANTS, BEES

combining form .... ENTOMO

cotton-eating .... WEEVIL

dipterous ..... GNAT, MOSQUITO

disease caused by .... DENGUE,

MALARIA, YELLOW FEVER

eating animal .... MOLE,

SHREW, DESMAN, TENREC,

TENDRAC, AARDVARK,

HEDGEHOG

egg .... NIT, OOTHECA

exudation .... LAC

eyes .... OCELLI

feeding ant .... KELEP

feeler ...... PALP(US), ANTENNA

flylike .... CICADA, CICALA

form between molts

.... INSTAR

guest of another .... INQUILINE

hard covering .... CHITIN

immature/pre-adult ...... PUPA,

LARVA

jaw .... MANDIBLE

larva .... GRUB, MAGGOT

leaping .... FLEA, LOCUST,

CRICKET, GRASSHOPPER

leg part .... TARSUS

leg segment .... COXA

lepidopterous .... MOTH,

BUTTERFLY

life stage .... EGG, PUPA,

IMAGO, LARVA, INSTAR,

MAGGOT

limb .... PROLOG

lip .... LABIUM, LABRUM

migratory .... LOCUST

molting .... ECDYSIS

nest .... NIDUS

noisy .... CICADA

order of ...... ACARID, LOCUST,

DIPTERA

part of .... COXA, HEAD, WING,

ACRON, CLAVA, NOTUM,

TARSUS, THORAX, ABDOMEN

scale .... COCCID

segment .... SOMITE, TELSON

slim-waisted .... WASP

smelly .... STINK BUG

social .... ANT, BEE

sound .... HUM, BUZZ, CHIRP,

CHIRR, DRONE, STRIDOR

stick .... EMESA

stinger of .... DART

stinging ..... BEE, GNAT, WASP,

GADFLY, HORNET

sucking .... SAPPER

sucking organ .... PROBOSCIS

trap .... WEB

tree .... KATYDID

tropical .... LANTERN FLY

wing cover .... ELYTRON

wing spot .... ISLE

winged ...... BEE, GNAT, WASP,

HORNET, MOSQUITO,

COCKROACH, GRASSHOPPER

wingless .... APTERA

with incomplete

metamorphosis

.... NYMPH

young .... NIT

insecticide .... DDT, PESTICIDE

insectivore .... MOLE, SHREW,

VIREO, DESMAN, TENREC,

HEDGEHOG

insects, kind of .... LACEWING

moving mass of .... SWARM

pertaining to .... ENTOMIC

insecure .... RISKY, UNSAFE,

UNSURE, UNSTABLE

inseminate .... IMPREGNATE

insensate .... COLD, STUPID,

FOOLISH, UNFEELING

insensibility .... COMA

insensible .... NUMB, STOIC,

IMPASSIVE, UNFEELING
insensitive .... CRASS, CALLOUS
inseparables .... CRONIES
insert .... IMMIT, INSET, PUT IN,
INGRAFT, INTROMIT,
INTRODUCE
slyly .... FOIST
insertion .... INLAY, INSET,
PENETRATION, INTRODUCTION,
AD(VERTISEMENT)
sign/mark .... CARET
inset .... INLAY, PANEL, INSERT
inside .... SECRET, WITHIN,
INDOOR(S), INTERIOR,
INTERNAL
combining form .... INTRA
out, turn .... EVERT
insidious ...... SLY, WILY, CRAFTY,
SHREWD, CUNNING,
DECEITFUL
insight .... KEY, ACUMEN,
INTUITION
insignia .... BADGE, CROWN,
EMBLEM, REGALIA, SCEPTER
corporate .... LOGO
saint's .... HALO
insignificant .... PUNY, MINOR,
PETTY, SMALL, PALTRY,
TRIVIAL, WORTHLESS
insincere .... UNTRUE, TWO-
FACED, HYPOCRITICAL
insinuate ...... HINT, FOIST, IMPLY,
SUGGEST, INTIMATE
insinuation .... HINT, INNUENDO
insipid .... DRY, DULL, FLAT,
BANAL, HOHUM, STALE,
VAPID, JEJUNE, PROSAIC,
LIFELESS, TASTELESS, WISHY-
WASHY
insist ...... URGE, PRESS, DEMAND,
MAINTAIN
insolation .... SUNSTROKE,
HEATSTROKE
insolence .... AIRS, HUBRIS,
DEFIANCE, ARROGANCE,
IMPUDENCE
insolent .... COCKY, SAUCY,
SASSY, UPPITY, HAUGHTY
insolvent .... BANKRUPT
insomnia .... VIGILANCE,
WAKEFULNESS, TROUBLE
SLEEPING
cause of .... WORRY,
DEPRESSION
insouciant .... CALM, COOL,
CAREFREE
inspan .... YOKE, HARNESS
inspect .... EYE, PRY, SCAN,
EXAMINE, SCRUTINIZE
before burglarizing .... CASE
closely .... PORE

thoroughly .... TAKE A GOOD
LOOK
inspection .... REVIEW, SURVEY,
PERUSAL, SCRUTINY
kind of ..... OCULAR, CUSTOMS
inspector .... EXAMINER,
OVERSEER, OVERLOOKER
inspiration .... IDEA, AFFLATUS,
INHALING
inspire .... SPUR, STIR, CAUSE,
IMBUE, AROUSE, EXCITE,
INHALE, UPLIFT, ANIMATE,
BREATHE, ENLIVEN,
INFLUENCE
affection .... ENDEAR
confidence .... ASSURE,
CONVINCE
inspired .... FIRED, DEMONIC
instability .... SHAKINESS,
INSECURITY, UNCERTAINTY
install .... FIX, SEAT, SET UP,
INDUCT, INVEST, ESTABLISH
installment .... PAYMENT PLAN
instance .... CASE, BEHEST,
EXAMPLE, OCCASION
of ostentatious display
.... SPLASH
instant .... WINK, TIME, HASTY,
JIFFY, QUICK, TRICE, ABRUPT,
MOMENT, SUDDEN, URGENT,
PRESSING, IMMEDIATE
instantly .... RIGHT NOW, QUICK
AS A WINK
instead .... ELSE, VICE, IN LIEU
(OF), RATHER
instigate .... EGG, ABET, SPUR,
URGE, CAUSE, FOMENT,
INCITE, INDUCE, PROMPT,
PROVOKE, INITIATE
instigation .... AROUSAL,
INSTANCE, PROVOCATION
instigator, kind of ...... PLOTTER,
AGITATOR, DEMAGOGUE,
PROVOCATEUR
instill .... IMPART, INFUSE,
INCULCATE
instinct .... BENT, GIFT, KNACK,
TALENT, IMPULSE
institute .... BEGIN, FOUND, SET
UP, START, SCHOOL,
COMMENCE, INITIATE,
ORGANIZE
institution ...... CHURCH, SCHOOL,
COLLEGE, SOCIETY,
FOUNDATION
instruct .... BRIEF, COACH, EDIFY,
TEACH, TRAIN, TUTOR, DIRECT
instruction .... ORDER, ADVICE,
LESSON, TUITION, TEACHING,
TRAINING, TUTELAGE,
TUTORSHIP

art of .... DIDACTICS
component .... STEP
editor's .... STET
to reader .... PTO
instructor .... COACH, TUTOR,
MENTOR, TEACHER,
PEDAGOGUE
instrument .... DEED, TOOL,
AGENT, MEANS, AGENCY,
DEVICE, IMPLEMENT
board .... PANEL
boring .... AUGUR, GIMLET,
JUMPER
carillon .... BELL
Casal's .... CELLO
denoting an: suffix .... TRON
in law .... DEED, CONTRACT,
DOCUMENT
measuring .... OCTANT
nautical .... SECTANT
panel, auto .... DASHBOARD
shaped like a stringed
.... LYRATE
stringed musical .... UKE,
KOTO, LUTE, LYRE, BANJO,
REBEC, VIOLA, GUITAR,
VIOLIN, CITTERN, SAMISEN,
MANDOLIN
toothed .... COMB
torture .... RACK, WHEEL,
STRAPPADO
instrumental composition
.... SONATA
introduction .... INTRADA
instrumentality .... HAND,
MEANS, AGENCY, MEDIUM,
VEHICLE
instruments .... MEDIA
for all .... TUTTI
insubordinate .... MUTINOUS,
DISOBEDIENT
insubstantial .... FLIMSY, FROTHY,
NOMINAL
insufferable .... AGONIZING,
UNBEARABLE, INTOLERABLE
insufficient .... MEAGER, SCANTY,
SKIMPY, LACKING, WANTING,
INADEQUATE
slang .... SHY OF
insular ...... DETACHED, ISOLATED,
NARROW-MINDED
insulate .... COVER, ENISLE,
DETACH, SHIELD, ISOLATE,
SET APART, SEGREGATE
insulating material .... KERITE,
BAGASSE, CELOTEX, OKONITE,
ASBESTOS
insulin discoverer .... BEST,
BANTING
disease treated with
.... DIABETES

insult .... SLAP, SLUR, OFFEND, AFFRONT, OUTRAGE, INDIGNITY

insurance agent .... UNDERWRITER

contract .... POLICY

protection .... COVERAGE

term .... RISK, POLICY, ANNUITY, TONTINE, ENDOWMENT

insure .... SECURE, GUARANTEE, SEE TO IT, UNDERWRITE

insurer ...... SURETY, GUARANTOR, UNDERWRITER

insurgence .... UPRISING, INSURRECTION

insurgent .... REBEL, RISER, MUTINEER, REVOLTER

insurrection .... REVOLT, UPRISING, REBELLION

intact .... WHOLE, COMPLETE

intaglio .... DIE, GEM, ENGRAVE

opposite of .... CAMEO

intangible ...... VAGUE, ABSTRACT

asset .... GOOD WILL, PRESTIGE

intarsia .... MOSAIC

integer ...... UNIT, WHOLE, ENTITY

odd .... GNOMEN

integral .... WHOLE, ENTIRE, COMPOSITE, ESSENTIAL

integrate .... FUSE, BLEND, UNIFY

integrity .... HONOR, VIRTUE, HONESTY, SINCERITY

integument .... ARIL, COAT, DERM, HIDE, HUSK, RIND, SKIN, SHELL, TESTA

intellect ...... MIND, BRAIN, LOGIC, SENSES, MENTALITY, INTELLIGENCE

of the .... NOETIC

intellectual ...... MENTAL, NOETIC, EGGHEAD, HIGHBROW, RATIONAL, INTELLIGENT

intellectuals, collectively .... CLERISY

intelligence .... WIT, MIND, NEWS, SENSE, ACUMEN, BRAINS, REPORT, TALENT, TIDINGS, CAPACITY, INTELLECT, KNOWLEDGE, INFORMATION

intelligent .... KEEN, SHARP, SMART, ASTUTE, BRAINY, BRIGHT, CLEVER, SENSIBLE, BRILLIANT, QUICK-WITTED

intelligentsia .... LITERATI, INTELLECTUALS

intelligible .... CLEAR, LUCID, OBVIOUS, UNDERSTANDABLE

intemperance .... EXCESS, REVELRY, CAROUSAL, DEBAUCHERY

intemperate .... WILD, RAKISH, SEVERE, VIOLENT, EXCESSIVE

intend ...... AIM, MEAN, PLAN(TO), ENDEAVOR, CONTEMPLATE

intended .... MEANT, PROPOSED

colloquial .... FIANCE(E), BETROTHED

intense .... DEEP, KEEN, ACUTE, SHARP, VIVID, ARDENT, STRONG

dislike .... HATRED

emotion .... PASSION

enthusiasm .... FANATICISM

excitement .... THRILL

rage .... FUROR

suffering ..... AGONY, ANGUISH

surprise .... SHOCK

intensify .... DEEPEN, ENHANCE, HEIGHTEN

intensity .... DEPTH, STRENGTH

intensive .... ALL-OUT

intent .... SET, EAGER, OBJECT, EARNEST, PURPOSE, SINCERE, ENGROSSED, DETERMINED

intention .... AIM, END, GOAL, PLAN, POINT, DESIRE, PURPOSE, OBJECT(IVE)

intentional .... PLANNED, WILLFUL, VOLUNTARY, DELIBERATE

inter .... BURY, INURN, ENTOMB, INHUME

companion of ..... ALIA, ALIOS

intercede .... MEDIATE, ARBITRATE, INTERPOSE, INTERVENE

intercept .... STOP, CATCH, HINDER, CUT OFF

intercessor ...... BISHOP, PLEADER, ADVOCATE, MEDIATOR, PARACLETE

interchange .... SWAP, TRADE, BARTER, EXCHANGE, ALTERNATE

intercom .... TALKBACK

interconnected ...... INTERLINKED

chain .... NETWORK

interdict .... BAN, VETO, (DE)BAR, ENJOIN, FORBID, PROHIBIT, RESTRAIN, PROSCRIBE

interest ...... WEAL, ZEAL, CLAIM, PIQUE, RIGHT, SHARE, STAKE, AFFECT, BEHALF, PROFIT, USANCE, BENEFIT, CONCERN, WELFARE

excessive .... MANIA, USURY

Dr. Rhine's .... ESP

interested .... CONCERNED, FASCINATED

interfere .... BUTT IN, MEDDLE, MOLEST, INTERPOSE,

INTERVENE

interference .... STATIC, JAMMING, HINDRANCE

interim .... INTERVAL, MEANTIME, MEANWHILE, TEMPORARY

interior .... INNER, MIDST, INLAND, INSIDE, INWARD

interject .... INSERT, INTERPOSE

interjection .... GEE, EGAD, GOSH, HECK, OUTCRY, EXPRESSION, EXCLAMATION

of surprise .... GOLLY

psalmic .... SELAH

to attract attention .... HIST

interlace .... BRAID, TWINE, WEAVE, PLEACH

interlock .... LINK, MESH

interlope(r) .... MEDDLE(R), INTRUDE(R), TRESPASS(ER)

interlude .... VERSET, EPISODE, INTERVAL, OVERTURE

intermediary .... AGENCY, MEDIUM, ARBITER, REFEREE, GO-BETWEEN, MIDDLEMAN

intermediate .... MESNE, MEDIAN, MIDDLE, HALFWAY

interment .... BURIAL

intermezzo .... INTERLUDE

interminable .... ENDLESS, LASTING, CEASELESS

intermingle .... MIX, BLEND

intermission ...... PAUSE, RECESS, ENTR'ACTE, INTERVAL, INTERLUDE

intermit .... DEFER, SUSPEND

intermittent .... FITFUL, OFF AND ON, PERIODIC, RECURRENT, SPASMODIC

intermix .... BLEND

intern .... HOLD, DETAIN, DOCTOR, CONFINE

internal .... INNER, INWARD, DOMESTIC, INTERIOR, INTRINSIC

organs .... VITALS, VISCERA

prefix .... ENTO

internally .... WITHIN

international .... GLOBAL, UNIVERSAL, WORLDWIDE

agreement ...... PACT, TREATY, ENTENTE

business combine ...... CARTEL

exhibition .... EXPOSITION

language .... RO, IDO, VOLAPUK, ESPERANTO

river .... ODER

sports .... OLYMPICS

writers' group .... PEN

International Workers Day .... MAYDAY

Internationale author

.... POTTIER

internecine .... DEADLY

interoffice note .... MEMO

interpolate .... INSERT

interpose .... INSERT, MEDDLE,
 MEDIATE, INTERCEPT,
 INTERRUPT, INTERVENE,
 INTRODUCE

interpret .... READ, RENDER,
 EXPLAIN, CONSTRUE,
 TRANSLATE

dreams .... REDE

interpretation .... READING,
 RENDITION, EXPLANATION,
 TRANSLATION

false .... WRENCH

interpretative ...... EXPLANATORY

interpreter .... EXEGETE,
 TRANSLATOR

of sacred mysteries

.... HIEROPHANT

travelers' .... DRAGOMAN

interregnum .... INTERVAL

interrogate .... ASK, QUIZ,
 EXAMINE, QUESTION

interrogation mark .... EROTEME

interrogative word, usually

.... HOW, WHO, WHAT, WHEN,
 WHERE, WHICH

interrogator .... PROBER,
 QUERIST, INQUIRER

interrogatory, old style

.... EROTETIC

interrupt .... CUT IN, CUT OFF,
 SUSPEND, BREAK INTO

interruption ...... BREAK, OUTAGE

intersect .... CUT, JOIN, MEET,
 CROSS

intersecting .... CRISSCROSSING

lines .... SECANTS

interstice ...... PORE, SLIT, CHINK,
 AREOLA, CREVICE

intertwine .... LACE, WEAVE,
 PLEACH, TANGLE

interval ...... GAP, BREAK, HIATUS,
 LACUNA, CAESURA, INTERIM,
 INTERLUDE, PARENTHESIS

intervene .... MEDDLE, BUTT IN,
 INTERFERE, INTERPOSE

intervening ...... MESNE, BETWEEN

intervention .... MEDIATION,
 INTERFERENCE

interweave .... PLAT, BLEND,
 PLAIT, RADDLE, SPLICE,
 ENTWINE, (INTER)LACE

interwoven .... LACED, NETTED,
 RETICULAR

intestinal .... ENTERIC

deposit .... BEZOAR

griping .... CRAMPS

not .... PARENTERAL

pains .... COLIC, CRAMPS

parasite .... ASCARIS,
 PINWORM, HOOKWORM,
 NEMATODE, TAPEWORM,
 TRICHINA, TRICHURIS

pouch .... C(A)ECUM

intestine(s) .... GUTS, COLON,
 BOWEL(S), VISCERA, ENTRAILS

combining form .... ENTERO

inflammation of .... COLITIS,
 ENTERITIS

membrane .... CAUL

of the .... ALVINE, ENTERIC

part .... COLON, ILEUM,
 ENTERON, DUODENUM

prefix .... COLI

process, hairlike .... VILLUS

intimate ...... HINT, NEAR, CLOSE,
 CRONY, IMPLY, FRIEND,
 PRIVATE, SUGGEST

wear ..... PANTY, SLIP-IN, STEP-
 IN(S)

intimation .... CUE, HINT, NOTICE,
 INKLING

intimidate .... COW, BULLY,
 DAUNT, COERCE, (OVER)AWE,
 FRIGHTEN, BAMBOOZLE

intolerable .... UNBEARABLE,
 UNENDURABLE

intolerance .... BIAS, BIGOTRY

intolerant .... BIGOTED,
 IMPATIENT

person .... BIGOT, ZEALOT

intone .... SING, CHANT, RECITE

intort .... COIL, CURL, TWINE,
 TWIST

intoxicant .... GIN, RUM, GROG,
 SOMA, LIQUOR, WHISKY

intoxicate .... ELATE, SOUSE,
 EXCITE, INEBRIATE

intoxicated .... LIT, FRIED, NAPPY,
 GROGGY, LOADED, POTTED,
 SOUSED, STEWED, DRUNK(EN),
 PLASTERED

intoxicating .... HEADY

effect .... KICK

intractable .... WILD, UNRULY,
 RESTIVE, FRACTIOUS,
 STUBBORN

intransigent .... STUBBORN,
 IRRECONCILABLE,
 UNCOMPROMISING

intrepid .... BOLD, BRAVE,
 DARING, FEARLESS

intrepidity .... GUTS, NERVE,
 VALOR, COURAGE

intricacy .... COMPLEXITY

intricate .... MAZY, KNOTTY,
 TRICKY, DA(E)DAL, COMPLEX,
 KNOTTED, INVOLUTE,

INVOLVED, COMPLICATED

knot .... GORDIAN

points/plots, etc. .... NODI

intrigue .... PLOT, AMOUR, CABAL,
 AFFAIR, SCHEME, SPYING,
 PERPLEX, ESPIONAGE,
 CONSPIRACY

intriguer .... SCHEMER

intrinsic .... REAL, TRUE,
 NATURAL, INHERENT,
 INTERNAL, ESSENTIAL

intrinsically .... PER SE

introduce .... OPEN, BEGIN,
 USHER, BROACH, INDUCT,
 INFUSE, INSERT, IMMIT,
 LAUNCH, PRESENT, INITIATE,
 INSTITUTE, INTERJECT

something new ...... INNOVATE

introducer, kind of .... EMCEE,
 TOASTMASTER

introduction .... PROEM, PREFACE,
 PRELUDE, FOREWORD,
 PRESENTATION

musical .... OVERTURE

to constitution .... PREAMBLE

to play .... PROLOGUE

to society .... DEBUT

introductory .... INITIAL,
 EXORDIAL, PREFATORY

remark .... PREFACE,
 FOREWORD

introit .... HYMN, PSALM

intromit .... ADMIT, ENTER, LET
 IN, INSERT

intrude .... BUTT IN, INVADE,
 ENCROACH, OVERSTEP,
 TRESPASS

intrusive .... MEDDLESOME,
 INTERFERING

intuition .... ESP, HUNCH, INSIGHT,
 INSTINCT, SIXTH SENSE

intuitive .... NOUMENAL,
 INSTINCTIVE

intumesce .... SWELL, BUBBLE,
 EXPAND, ENLARGE

inulin .... ALANTIN

inundate .... SWAMP, FLOOD,
 DELUGE, OVERFLOW,
 OVERWHELM

inundation .... FLOOD, DELUGE,
 SPATHE, OVERFLOW

inure .... HARDEN, TOUGHEN,
 ACCUSTOM, HABITUATE

inurn .... BURY, INTER, ENTOMB

inutile .... IDLE, USELESS

invade .... RAID, ENTER, ASSAIL,
 ATTACK, INTRUDE, VIOLATE,
 TRESPASS

invader of Rome .... GOTH

invaders' foothold

.... BEACHHEAD

invalid .... NULL, SICK, VOID, WEAK, INFIRM, SICKLY, UNWELL, PATIENT, NUGATORY
invalidate .... VOID, ANNUL, OUTLAW, NULLIFY, VITIATE
invaluable .... DEAR, COSTLY, PRECIOUS, PRICELESS
invariable .... FIXED, STEADY, UNIFORM, CONSTANT
invariably .... ALWAYS
invasion .... RAID, INROAD, TRESPASS, INCURSION, INTRUSION, INFRINGEMENT
beach of World War II .... OMAHA
craft .... LST
invective .... ABUSE, CURSE
inveigh .... RAIL, CENSURE, DENOUNCE
inveigle ...... COAX, LURE, TEMPT, TRICK, CAJOLE, ENTICE, ATTRACT, ENSNARE
invent .... CREATE, DESIGN, DEVISE, CONCOCT, IMAGINE, CONTRIVE, FABRICATE, ORIGINATE
new word .... COIN, NEOLOGIZE
invention .... DEVICE, COINAGE, FICTION, FIGMENT, CREATION, FALSEHOOD, INGENUITY, BRAINCHILD, FABRICATION
kind of .... LIE
of Arthur Wynne: 1913 .... CROSSWORD PUZZLE
start of an .... IDEA
inventor .... CREATOR, DEVISER, ARTIFICER
airplane .... WRIGHT BROTHERS
automobile .... DAIMLER
basketball .... NAISMITH
camera .... EASTMAN
computer .... BABBAGE
cordite, (co-) .... ABEL
cotton gin .... WHITNEY
crossword puzzle .... (ARTHUR) WYNNE
cylinder lock .... YALE
dynamite .... NOBEL
dynamo .... GRAMME, FARADAY
elevator .... OTIS
escape-lung .... MOMSEN
fountain pen .... WATERMAN
harp .... JUBAL
incandescent lamp ..... EDISON
kinetoscope .... EDISON
machine gun .... GATLING
microphone/phonograph .... EDISON
motor .... TESLA

new words .... NEOLOGIST
postage meter ..... PITNEY AND BOWES
Preparation H hemorrhoid treatment .... SPERTI
protection of .... PATENT
radar .... TUVE, BREIT
radio .... MARCONI
revolver .... COLT
root beer ..... (CHARLES) HIRES
safety lamp .... DAVY
sewing machine .... HOWE
sign language .... EPEE
steam engine .... WATT
steamboat .... FITCH, FULTON
steel plow .... DEERE
tank (military) .... SWINTON
telegraph .... MORSE
telephone .... BELL
thermometer .... GALILEI
tractor .... HOLT
transistor .... BARDEEN, BRATTAN, SHOCKLEY
typewriter .... SHOLES
Velcro .... DE MESTRAL
wireless telegraphy .... MARCONI
inventory .... LIST, STOCK, STORE, TALLY, CATALOG(UE)
official .... INDENTURE
Inverness .... CAPE, OVERCOAT
native .... SCOT
inverse .... OPPOSITE
inversion .... REVERSAL
invert .... REVERSE, HOMOSEXUAL
invertebrate .... SPINELESS
animal .... POLYP
covering of .... TEST, SHELL
invest .... DON, ADORN, COVER, ENDOW, ENDUE, CLOTHE, ORDAIN, BESIEGE, ENVELOP, INSTALL, SURROUND, BELEAGUER
investigate .... PROBE, SEARCH, EXAMINE, EXPLORE, SCRUTINIZE
for security reasons .... SCREEN
investigation .... PROBE, HEARING, INQUEST, ANALYSIS, RESEARCH, SCRUTINY
investigator .... PROBER, TRACER, EXAMINER, INQUISITOR
investiture .... VESTURE, INDUCTION, INSTALLATION
investment .... SIEGE, CAPITAL, COVERING, GRUBSTAKE
kind of .... BLUE CHIPS
investor .... CAPITALIST
list/securities of .... PORTFOLIO
quest of? .... BLUE CHIP

COMPANY
inveterate .... CHRONIC, HABITUAL, OBSTINATE, DEEP-ROOTED
invigorate .... BRACE, ANIMATE, ENLIVEN
invigorating .... CRISP, TONIC, BRACING
invincible .... UNDAUNTED, INDOMITABLE, UNCONQUERABLE
inviolable .... SACRED, SACROSANCT
inviolate ...... SACRED, UNBROKEN
invisible .... APHAN, UNSEEN
emanation .... AURA
Invisible Man author .... WELLS
invitation .... BID, CARD
letters .... RSVP
invite .... ASK, BEG, BID, CALL, LURE, TEMPT, SUMMON, REQUEST
inviting ...... ENTICING, TEMPTING
invocation .... PRAYER, INCANTATION
opening .... AGNUS DEI
invoke .... BEG, PRAY, PLEAD, BESEECH, CONJURE, ENTREAT, IMPLORE
involuntary .... AUTOMATIC, ACCIDENTAL, INSTINCTIVE
action .... REFLEX
involute .... ROLLED UP
involve .... IMPLY, ENTAIL, EMBROIL, INCLUDE, REQUIRE, ENTANGLE, IMPLICATE, COMPLICATE
involved .... COMPLEX, INVOLUTE, INTRICATE, IMPLICATED
involving effort .... OPEROSE
invulnerable .... IMMUNE, IMPERVIOUS, UNASSAILABLE
inward .... ENTAD, INTERNAL
Io, lover of .... ZEUS
rival of .... HERA
watcher of .... ARGUS
iodine antiseptic .... IODOL, IATROL
source .... KELP
Iolanthe .... PERI
ion, negative .... ANION
positive .... CATION
Ionian gulf .... ARTA, PATRAS
island .... KAI, LAUT, CORFU, LET(T)I, PAXOS, ZANTE, CERIGO, ITHACA, CORCYRA
Ionic capital's volute ...... HELIX
iota ...... BIT, DAB, DOT, JOT, WEE, DROP, HAIR, MITE, MOTE, WHIT, FLECK, SPECK, LITTLE, TITTLE

I.O.U. .... CHIT, NOTE
part of .... I, OWE, YOU
Iowa capital .... DES MOINES
city/town .... SAC, ADEL,
AMES, IOWA, TAMA, MASON,
ONAWA, OSAGE, SIOUX,
KEOKUK, NEWTON, ORANGE,
RED OAK, SIBLEY, TIPTON,
TOLEDO, CHARLES, CLINTON,
DECORAH, DUBUQUE,
OSCEOLA, OTTUMWA,
WAPELLO, WAVERLY,
ATLANTIC, WATERLOO,
DAVENPORT, FORT DODGE,
MUSCATINE, OSKALOOSA,
BURLINGTON, POCAHONTAS,
CEDAR RAPIDS,
MARSHALLTOWN, COUNCIL
BLUFFS
college .... COE, DORDT,
LORAS, CORNELL, WESTMAR,
VENNARD, GRINNELL,
GRACELAND
colony/co-op society
.... AMANA
county .... LEE, LINN, TAMA,
ADAIR, ADAMS, BOONE, SCOTT,
SIOUX, STORY, BENTON,
BREMER, DALLAS, HARDIN,
JASPER, MARION, CLAYTON,
FAYETTE, KOSSUTH,
PLYMOUTH, WOODBURY,
BLACK HAWK, DES MOINES
floating casino ..... PRESIDENT,
DIAMOND LADY, EMERALD
LADY
lake .... EAGLE, STORM, SPIRIT,
RATHBUN, TRUMBULL
Mississippi River town
...... DAVENPORT, BETTENDORE,
FORT MADISON
native .... HAWKEYE
recreation site .... WONDER
CAVE, CHILDREN'S MUSEUM
religious society .... AMANA
river .... BOYER, CEDAR,
SKUNK, RACCOON, MISSOURI,
THOMPSON, MISSISSIPPI
state bird .... GOLDFINCH
state flower .... CAROLINA
ROSE
state nickname .... HAWKEYE
university .... IOWA, DRAKE,
DUBUQUE
ipecac .... EVEA, MADDER
product .... EMETINE
Iphigenia's brother ..... ORESTES
sister .... ELECTRA
ipse ____ .... DIXIT
ipsissima .... VERBA
ipso ____ .... JURE, FACTO

IQ, part of .... QUOTIENT,
INTELLIGENCE
society member .... MENSA
iracund .... TESTY, CHOLERIC,
IRASCIBLE
irade .... DECREE
Iran .... PERSIA
Iranian .... KURD, TUDAH,
PERSIAN, SOGDIAN
angel .... MAH
bird .... BULBUL
cape .... KUH
capital .... TEH(E)RAN
carpet .... KALI, HAMADAN
chief .... MIR
city/town .... BAM, QOM, QUM,
REY, AHAR, AMOL, ARAK,
BAFT, EVAZ, EZNA, FASA,
YEZD, ABHAR, AHVAZ, BABOL,
KARAJ, KHVOY, RASHT, RESHT,
SAVEH, URMIA, ZABOL,
ABADAN, DIZFUL, DUZDAB,
ENZELI, GORGAN, JAHROM,
KASHAN, KAZVIN, MESHED,
MIANEH, NEYRIZ, SEMNAN,
SHIRAZ, SINNEH, TABRIZ,
ZANJAN, ZENJAN, ARDABIL,
BIRJAND, BUSHEHR, ESFAHAN,
HAMADAN, ISFAHAN,
MAHABAD, MASHHAD,
PAHLEVI, TAJRISH, ZAHEDAN,
BORUJERD, MARAGHEH,
SHAHREZA
coin .... KRAN, LARI, RIAL,
P(O)UL, DARIC, DINAR, MOHUR
coin, old .... TOMAN, STATER
communist party .... TUDEH
desert .... LUT, KAVIR
empress .... FARAH(DIBA)
evil spirit .... AHRIMAN
fairy .... PERI
gate .... DAR
gazelle .... CORA
governor .... SATRAP
gulf .... OMAN, PERSIAN
hero .... YIMA, RUSTAM
in Russia .... TA(D)JIK
island .... ARABI, FARSI,
KHARK, QESHM
lake .... TASHK, URMIA,
NAMAKSAR
language .... ARYAN, PAMIR,
AFGHAN, GALCHA, PASHTO,
PUSHTU, AVESTAN, KURDISH,
PAHLAVI, PERSIAN,
AZERBAIJANI
lower house .... MAJLIS
measure .... GAZ, GEZ, GUZ,
ZAR, ZER
monetary unit .... RIAL
moon .... MAHI

mountain .... NEZWAR, SIAH
KUH, DAMAVAND, DEMAVEND
mountain range .... ELBURZ,
ZAGROS
mystic .... SUFI
official .... KHAN
oil center .... ABADAN
poet .... OMAR
port .... ABADAN
premier ..... ZAHEDI, HOVEIDA,
RAZMARA, MOSSADEGH
province .... FARS, GILAN,
KERMAN, BUSHEHR, ISFAHAN,
KHORASAN, HORMOZGAN,
KORDESTAN, AZERBAIJAN
queen .... SORAYA
region .... MAKRAN, LARISTAN,
BALUCHSITAN
religion .... ISLAM
river .... DEZ, ARAS, SHUR,
ARAKS, KARUN, SILUP, TALAB,
BAMPUR, GORGAN, KURANG,
MEHRAN, ZILBIR, SHELAGH,
SAFID RUD
rug .... SENNA, KURDISTAN
ruins .... SUSA, BEHISTUN,
PERSEPOLIS
ruler .... SHAH, PAHLEVI
sacred cord .... KUSTI
sacred writings .... AVESTI
screen .... PARDAH, PURDAH
shah .... PAHLEVI
sir .... AZAM
tiara .... CIDARIS
tile .... KAS(H)I
trading center .... ISPAHA
Turk .... SART
water vessel .... AFTABA
water wheel .... NORIA
weight .... SER, MAUND
Iraq .... MESOPOTAMIA
capital .... BAG(H)DAD
city/town ...... A'NA, FAO, HAI,
HIT, KUT, AMARA, BASRA,
DOHUK, ERBIL, HILLA, MOSUL,
ZAKHO, ARBELA, KIRKUK,
RAMADI, SAMAWA, SHATRA,
TIKRIT, SAMARRA
desert .... SYRIAN
district .... AMARA
gnostic .... MANDEAN
king .... FAISAL GHAZI
lake .... HOR SANIYA
language ..... ARABIC, KURDISH
monetary unit .... DINAR
mountain .... ANEIZA, HAJI
IBRAHIM
palace .... QASR
president .... ARIF, HUSSEIN
prime minister .... YAHYA
province .... AMARA

river ..... ZAB, ADHAIM, TIGRIS,
EUPHRATES
ruins .... UR, BABYLON,
NINEVEH
seaport .... BASRA, MOSQUES
irascible .... BRASH, CROSS,
TESTY, IRACUND, IRRITABLE
irate .... MAD, ANGRY, WROTH,
FUMING, BOILING, INCENSED
colloquial .... TEED OFF
IRBM, part of .... RANGE,
MISSILE, BALLISTIC,
INTERMEDIATE
ire .... FURY, RAGE, ANGER, PIQUE,
CHOLER, UMBRAGE,
DISPLEASURE
Ireland .... EIRE, ERIN, ERSE,
IERNA, IRENA, EIRANN,
HIBERNIA, IRISH FREE STATE
bay .... CLEW, INVER, SLIGO,
BANTRY, DINGLE, GALWAY,
ROSSES, TRALEE, DONEGAL,
WEXFORD, YOUGHAI,
BLACKSOD
canal .... GRAND, ROYAL
cape .... CLEAR
capital .... DUBLIN
city/town .... BRAY, CORK,
ENNIS, MALIN, SLIGO,
CARLOW, GALWAY, TRALEE,
CLONMEL, DUNDALK,
THURLES, WEXFORD,
DROGHEDA, LIMERICK,
TIPPERARY, WATERFORD
county ..... CORK, LEIX, MAYO,
CAVAN, CLARE, KERRY,
MEATH, SLIGO, CARLOW,
DUBLIN, GALWAY, OFFALY,
KILDARE, KILKENNY,
MONAGHAN, LIMERICK,
TIPPERARY
_____ Eireann of .... DAIL
emblem of .... SHAMROCK
fairy folk .... SHEE,
LEPRECHAUN
island .... ARAN, OMEY, OWEY,
TORY, ACHILL, DURSEY,
LAMBAY, GORUMNA, SHERKIN,
THE BULL, VALENTIA
mountain .... ERRIGAL, NEPHIN,
KIPPURE, THE PAPS,
MWEELREA, CARRANTUOHILL
patron saint .... BRIGID,
PATRICK
president .... (MARY)
ROBINSON
river .... DEE, LEE, MOY,
DEEL(E), BANN, ERNE, FINN,
INNY, NORE, SUCK, SUIR,
AWBEG, BOYNE, FEALE,
GLYDE, LAUNE, MAINE,

OVOCA, BARROW, BROSNA,
LIFFEY, MAIGUE, SLANEY
settlers in .... OSTMEN
Spenser's .... IRENA
town in ancient .... TARA
Ireland, North bay .... RED,
DUNDRUM
capital .... BELFAST
city/town .... KESH, LARNE,
NEWRY, OMAGH, ARMAGH,
ANTRIM, BANGOR, COMBER,
LISBURN, STRABANE,
COLERAINE, COOKSTOWN,
CRAIGAVON, DUNGANNON,
HOLLYWOOD, LONDONDERRY
district .... ARDS, DOWN,
LARNE, MOYLE, ANTRIM,
BELFAST, LIMAVADY
island .... RATHLIN
lake .... ERNE, NEAGH
mountain .... DIVIS, SLIEVE
DONARD
mountain range .... MOURNE,
SPERRIN
river .... ROE, BANN, LAGAN
Irene .... PAX
actress .... RICH, DUNNE
parent of .... ZEUS, THEMIS
irenic .... DOVISH, SERENE,
PACIFIC
Irian .... PAPUA
iridescence .... LUSTER, RAINBOW,
OPALESCENCE
iridescent ...... NACRY, LUSTROUS,
NACREOUS, PAVONINE,
OPALESCENT, RAINBOWLIKE
gem .... OPAL
iris .... EYE, IXIA, CROCUS,
ORRICE, GODDESS, RAINBOW,
(BLUE) FLAG, FLEUR-DE-LIS
combining form .... IRIDO
inflammation of .... IRITIS,
UVEITIS
layer of .... UVEA
plant .... FLAG, ORRIS,
FREESIA, TILEROOT
plural of .... IRIDES
root .... ORRIS
Irish ...... ERSE, CELTIC, MILESIAN,
HIBERNIAN
accent .... BROGUE
alas .... OCHONE
alphabet .... OGUM, OG(H)AM
assembly .... DAIL
assessment .... CESS
battle cry .... ABU, SLOGAN
beauty: legendary .... EMER
buxom .... SONSIE
capital, former .... TARA
castle .... TARA
cattle .... KERRY

cheese .... KEBBOK
chisel .... CELT
church .... KIL
clan .... SEPT, SIOL
clansman .... AIRE
club/cudgel .... ALPEEN,
SHILLALA, SHILLELAH
coin, fake .... RAP
colloquial .... TEMPER
composer .... BALFE
county in Connacht
.... LEITRIM
dagger .... DHU, SKENE
dandy .... BUCKEEN
dialect .... OGHAM
dirge .... KEEN
doctor .... OLLAM
dissident .... FENIAN
district .... BIRR
dramatist .... SHAW, BEHAN,
YEATS, O'CASEY, STEELE
emblem .... SHAMROCK
endearment term .... MACHREE
epic .... TANA
exclamation .... ARU, AROO,
ARRA(H)
export .... LINEN
fairy .... SHEE, LEPRECHAUN
family .... CINEL
farmer .... SAER, COTTAR,
COTTIER
fish .... POLLAN
fishing boat .... HOOKER
folklore character .... LIMER
fortification .... LIS
freebooter .... RAPPAREE
freeman .... AIRE
fuel .... PEAT
Gaelic .... ERSE
garment .... INAR, LENN
general .... SHEA
girdle .... CRISS
girl .... LASSIE, COLLEEN
god .... LER, DAGDA
god of poetry .... OGMA
handsome .... SONSY, SONSIE
hero .... FINN, RORY, FIONN,
FENIAN, FERGUS
heroine .... EMER
hill .... INCH
historian .... LECKY
hockey .... HURLING
hood .... COCHULL
initials .... IRA
island group .... ARANN
jargon .... SHELTA
John .... EOIN, SEAN
king .... AED, BORU, ENNA,
BRIAN
kingdom .... MUNSTER
laborers .... AIRE

lake .... LOCH
lake dwelling .... CRANNOG
lament .... KEEN, WIRRA,
    CORONACH
landholding system
    .... RUNDALE
legendary imp .... PUCA
legislature .... DAIL, EIREANN
lighthouse rock .... FASTNET
limestone .... CALP
lord .... TANIST
love .... GRA
Lowlander .... SASSENACH
luck .... CESS
lucky .... SONSY, SONSIE
moss .... CARRAG(H)EEN
mother of song ...... MACHREE
musical festival .... FEIS
musical instrument ...... CRUT,
    TIMPAN
negative .... SORRA
novelist .... REID, SHAW,
    BEHAN, MOORE, WILDE
outlaw .... PAPIST
Papist .... TORY
partisans .... ORANGES
party .... SINN FEIN
patriot .... EMMET, PARNELL
patriotic group .... IRA
patron saint .... BRIGID,
    PATRICK
peasant ...... KERN(E), COTTAR,
    COTTIER
pipe (tobacco) .... DUDEEN
playwright ...... SHAW, MOORE,
    O'CASEY
poet .... COLUM, JOYCE, WILDE,
    YEATS
policeman .... PEELER
port .... SLIGO
potato .... YAM
pretender .... BUCKEEN
priest .... DRUID
prime minister .... LYNCH,
    LEMASS, DE VALERA
princess .... ISEULT, ISOLDE,
    DEIRDRE
proprietor .... TANIST
province .... ULSTER,
    MUNSTER, LEINSTER,
    CONNAUGHT
rascal/scamp .... SPALPEEN
rebel .... FENIAN, FIANNA
regret .... OCH
river .... BUSH, DERG, NORE,
    SUIR, BOYNE, CAVAN, FOYLE,
    LAGAN, SHANNON
saint .... AIDAN, PATRICK
saloon .... SHEBEEN
Saxon .... SASSENACH
sea god .... LER

seaport .... COBH, CORK,
    DUBLIN, TRALEE, BELFAST,
    LIMERICK
secret organization .... IRA,
    MOLLY MAGUIRES
secret society member
    .... ORANGEMAN
shield .... SCIATH
shillaly .... LAH
shoe .... BROGUE
slang .... MICK
smack .... HOOKER
society .... AOH, FEINN
soldier .... KERN(E), RAPPAREE,
    GALLOGLASS
song .... RANN
sorrow .... WIRRA
spirit .... BANSHEE
sprite .... SHEE
steward .... ERENACH
sweetheart .... GRA
symbol .... DEIRDRE
tax .... CESS
tenant .... SAER
tobacco pouch ..... SPLEUCHAN
tribe .... SEPT, SIOL, CINEL
Ulster County .... DOWN
verse .... RANN
wail .... KEEN
warrior .... FENIAN
whiskey .... POT(H)EEN
white .... BAWN
woman revolutionary
    .... GONNE
writing, old .... OGAM
young man .... BUCKEEN
Irishman .... PAT, CELT, HARP,
    MICK, PADDY, TEAGUE,
    MILESIAN, HIBERNIAN
irk ...... VEX, GALL, TIRE, ANNOY,
    BOTHER, NETTLE, DISGUST,
    IRRITATE
irksome .... TEDIOUS, TIRESOME
iron .... PRESS, FERRUM, MANGLE,
    SMOOTH, FERRITE
alloy .... STEEL
bar .... BLOOM, JOINTER
chancellor .... BISMARK
coated .... TERNE
collar .... GARROTE
combining form ...... SIDER(O)
horse .... LOCOMOTIVE
in golf .... CLUB, MASHIE,
    DRIVER, NIBLICK
lung .... RESPIRATOR
meteorite .... SIDERITE
number one .... CLEEK
ore .... TURGITE, HEMATITE,
    LIMONITE, SIDERITE,
    TACONITE, MAGNETITE
ore area .... SAAR

out .... RECTIFY, SMOOTHEN,
    STRAIGHTEN
oxide .... RED RUST,
    MAGNETITE
oxide powder .... CROCUS
pertaining to .... FERRIC
pig .... SPIEGEL
prefix .... FERRO
ready for rolling .... LARGET
sheet .... TERNEPLATE
sulfide .... PYRITE
symbol for .... FE
ironbark .... EUCALYPTUS
ironclad ...... ARMORED, MONITOR,
    WARSHIP, MERRIMAC,
    FOOLPROOF, UNBREAKABLE
ironer .... MANGLE
ironic(al) .... SARCASTIC,
    SATIRIC(AL)
writing .... LAMPOON
irons ...... GYVE, CHAINS, FETTERS,
    SHACKLES
Ironsides .... CROMWELL
ironwood .... ACLE, TITI, COLIMA,
    HORNBEAM
ironworks .... SMELTERY
irony .... SATIRE, MOCKERY,
    SARCASM, RIDICULE
Iroquoian .... ERIE, HURON,
    MINGO, CAYUGA, MOHAWK,
    ONEIDA, SENECA, WYANDOT,
    CHEROKEE, ONONDAGA,
    TUSCARORA
irrational .... INANE, ABSURD,
    BRUTISH, W(H)ACKY,
    SENSELESS
fear .... PHOBIA
number .... SURD
Irrawaddy tributary
    .... CHINDWIN
irreconcilable .... CONFLICTING,
    INCOMPATIBLE
irredenta .... UNREDEEMED
irregular .... EROSE, FITFUL,
    SPOTTY, UNEVEN, ERRATIC,
    ABNORMAL, ATYPIC(AL),
    SPORADIC, VARIABLE,
    ANOMALOUS, DESULTORY,
    DISORDERLY
in shape .... BAROQUE
irregularity .... ANOMALY
irreligious .... PAGAN, UNHOLY,
    GODLESS, IMPIOUS, PROFANE,
    AGNOSTIC, ATHEISTIC
irreparable .... HOPELESS
irrepressible ...... SAUCY, ELATED,
    CHEERY, UNRULY
irreproachable .... BLAMELESS,
    FAULTLESS, ABOVEBOARD,
    IMPECCABLE
irresistible .... COMPELLING,

OVERPOWERING
irresolute .... FICKLE, HESITANT
irrespective .... REGARDLESS
irreverence .... DISRESPECT
irrevocable .... FINAL, ABSOLUTE,
UNALTERABLE
irrigate .... FLUSH, WATER
irrigation ditch .... SLUICE,
ACEQUIA
irritability .... ERETHISM
irritable .... EDGY, CROSS,
BITCHY, TESTY, CRANKY,
GRUMPY, TOUCHY, TE(T)CHY,
IRACUND, IRASCIBLE,
SPLENETIC
person .... CRANK, GROUCH,
TARTAR, CURMUDGEON
irritant .... PEST
irritate .... IRK, VEX, GALL, ITCH,
RASP, RILE, ANNOY, CHAFE,
GRATE, PEEVE, PIQUE, TEASE,
GRAVEL, NEEDLE, NETTLE,
RANKLE, PROVOKE,
EXASPERATE
irritation .... ITCH, PIQUE,
ANNOYANCE
is .... EXISTS
able .... CAN
aswarm .... TEEMS
beholden .... OWES
evicted ..... WALKS THE PLANK
green about the gills ...... AILS
in accord .... JIBES
interested .... CARES
nosy .... SNOOPS
obligated .... OWES
short .... NEEDS
too fond .... DOTES
Isaac .... PATRIARCH
father of .... ABRAM,
ABRAHAM
father-in-law of .... BETHUEL
(half) brother of ...... ISHMAEL
mother of .... SARAH, SARAI
son of ..... EDOM, ESAU, JACOB
wife of .... REBECCA, REBEKAH
Isadora, dancer .... DUNCAN
Isagoge .... INTRODUCTION
Isaye's pupil .... MENUHIN
Iscariot .... JUDAS, TRAITOR
ischemia .... ANEMIA
Iseult .... ISOLDE
husband of .... MARK
love of .... TRISTAN,
TRIST(R)AM
Ishmael .... PARIAH, OUTCAST
daughter of .... MAHALATH
father of .... ABRAM,
ABRAHAM
(half) brother of .... ISAAC
mother of .... HAGAR

son of .... TEMA, DUMAH,
HADAD, JETUR, KEDAR,
MASSA, ABDEEL, MIBSAM,
MISHMA, KEDEMAH, NAPHISH,
NEBALOTH
Isidore, diminutive of .... IZZY
isinglass .... AGAR, MICA,
CARLOCK, GELATIN
Isis' brother/husband .... OSIRIS
sister .... NEPHTHYS
Islam adherent .... MOSLEM,
MUSLEM, MUSLIM
canonical law .... SHARIA
convert .... ANSAR, MURED
founder/prophet
.... MOHAMMED
holy city .... MECCA
pilgrimage place .... CAABA
school .... MADARA
supreme deity .... ALLAH
Islamic teacher .... ALIM,
MULLAH
island .... AIT, ALT, CAY, ISLE
at earth's center .... MERU
between two rivers
.... MESOPOTAMIA
British, in the South Atlantic
.... ASCENSION
Canadian .... BANKS, DEVON,
BAFFIN, VICTORIA, ELLESMERE,
NEWFOUNDLAND
Caroline .... YAP, TRUK
coral .... CAY, ATOLL
empire .... JAPAN
enchanted .... BALI
famed for giant lizards
.... KOMODO
in a lake .... HOLM
in Indian Ocean ...... REUNION
in the Aegean Sea ...... SAMOS
in the Malay Archipelago
.... TIMOR
in the South Pacific
.... EASTER
isolated .... INCH
King Minos's .... CRETE
largest in the Pacific ...... NEW
GUINEA
largest in Tuscan
Archipelago .... ELBA
legendary .... ATLANTIS
low .... KEY
Mediterranean .... CORSICA
mythical .... NAXOS
near bigger one .... CALF
North Pacific .... WAKE
of immigrants .... ELLIS
of lepers .... MOLOKAI
of song .... BALI, CAPRI,
HAWAII, TAHITI
off Cape Cod .... MARTHA'S

VINEYARD
off Venezuela .... ARUBA
river .... AIT, EYOT, HOLM
small ..... AIT, CAY, KEY, ISLE,
ISLET
to-mainland sandbars
.... TOMBOLOS
USSR .... SAKHALIN, NOVAYA-
ZEMLYA
west of New Guinea .... AROE
"Wonder Woman's"
.... PARADISE
world's largest .... GREENLAND
world's second largest
.... NEW GUINEA
world's third largest
.... BORNEO
Island, Beautiful .... FORMOSA
islands, group of
.... ARCHIPELAGO
of Langerhans secretion
.... INSULIN
off Ecuador .... GALAPAGOS
isle .... AIT, KEY, EYOT
Apia's .... UPOLU
Isle of Man capital ...... DOUGLAS
of Man judge .... DEEMSTER
of Wight channel ...... SOLENT
of Wight town .... COWES
islet .... AIT, ALT, CAY, KEY,
HOLM
ism .... DOXY, DOGMA, TENET,
BELIEF, SYSTEM, THEORY,
DOCTRINE
isolate .... ENISLE, IMMURE,
SECLUDE, INSULATE, SET
APART, SEGREGATE
oneself .... HOLE UP
isolated .... (A)LONE,
QUARANTINED
isolation .... SOLITUDE
isolationist .... LONER
Isolde .... ISEULT
love of .... TRISTAN, TRISTRAM
isomer .... MALEIC, METAMER
isometric .... CUBIC
isopod .... CRUSTACEAN
isopyre .... OPAL
Israel(i) .... SION, ZION, JACOB
a first name in .... MOSHE
airline .... ELAL
ancient capital .... SAMARIA
ancient city .... TIRZAH,
SAMARIA
battle site .... ESDRAELON
camp .... ETHAM
cape .... CARMEL
capital .... JERUSALEM
city/town .... LOD, ACRE,
ARAD, AFULA, EILAT, HAIFA,
HOLON, LYDDA, RAMLA,

SAFAD, YEHUD, ZEFAT, DIMONA, HADERA, REHOBOT, TEL AVIV (JAFFA), ASHQELON, NAZARETH, BEERSHEBA
coin ..... MIL, SHEKEL, AGOROT
dance .... HORA(H)
defense line .... BARLEV
desert .... NEGEV
district .... HAIFA, CENTRAL, TEL-AVIV, NORTHERN, SOUTHERN, JERUSALEM
farm .... KIBBUTZ
first king .... SAUL
first president .... WEIZMANN
foreign minister .... EBAN
general .... DAYAN
hero .... GIDEON
high priest .... ELI
king .... AHAB, ELAH, JEHU, JORAM, OMRI, DAVID, NADAB, PEKAH, ZIMRI, BAASHA, HOSHEA, AHAZIAH, JEHOASH, JEHORAM, MENAHEM, SHALLUM, SOLOMON, JEHOASH, JEHOAHAZ, JEROBOAM, PEKAHIAH, ZECHARIAH
lake .... HULEH, TIBERIAS
language ..... ARABIC, HEBREW
legislature .... KNESSET
member of a collective farm
.... KIBBUTZNIK
monetary unit .... SHEKEL
mountain ...... RAMON, TABOR, CARMEL, MEIRON
native .... SABRA
peace .... SHALOM
plain .... SHARON, JEZREEL, ESDRAELON
political party .... MAPAM
port .... ACRE, ELATH, HAIFA, JAFFA
president ..... BENZVI, SHAZAR, WEIZMANN
prime minister
.... (GOLDA)MEIR, RABIN, ESHKOL, SHAMIR, BEN GURION
prophet of .... ELIAS, ELIJAH, ELISHA
region .... NEGEV, GALILEE, JUDAEA
river .... BESOR, JORDAN, QISHON, YARMUK, YARQON
seaport .... JAFFA, JOPPA
statesman .... EBAN
strip .... GAZA
Israel's border, part of
.... DEAD SEA
Israelite ...... SION, ZION, DANITE, HEBREW, JEW(ISH)
judge .... ELON
king .... DAVID

land in Egypt .... GOSHEN
leader .... JOSUE, JOSHUA
paid curser .... BALAAM
strong man .... SAMSON
tribe .... JUDAH, REUBEN, SIMEON, EPHRAIM, ZEBULUN, BENJAMIN, ISSACHAR, DAN, GAD, LEVI, AS(H)ER, MANASSEH, NAPHTALI
Israelites, biblical ...... HERITAGE
issei's kin, of a sort .... KIBEI, NISEI
issue .... EMIT, EXIT, ARISE, CHILD, POINT, EMERGE, OUTLET, RESULT, UPSHOT, EDITION, DEAL OUT, OUTCOME, OUTFLOW, PROGENY, PUBLISH, QUESTION, OFFSPRING
forth .... EMANATE
minor point of
.... TECHNICALITY
take .... DIFFER, DISAGREE
issuing .... COMING, EMERGING
in rays .... RADIAL
Istanbul .... STAMBOUL, BYZANTIUM, CONSTANTINOPLE
foreign quarter .... PERA, FANAR, BEYOGLU
founder .... BYSAS
inn .... SERAI, IMARET
section .... BEYOGLU, SCUTARI, USKUDAR, STAMBOUL
suburb .... GALATA
isthmus .... KRA, BALK, NECK, PANAMA, STRAIT
Corinth .... MEGARIS
Panama .... DARIEN
istle .... PITA, PITO, FIBER
ita .... NEGRITO
itacolumite .... SANDSTONE
it came after fingers .... FORK
deserts a sinking ship .... RAT
doesn't pay .... CRIME
followed the ragtime review
.... HONKY TONK SHOW
has rich taste and aroma
.... PORT
has 32 men .... CHESS SET
is better to be born lucky
than _____ .... RICH
is legal .... LICET
is silent, in music .... TACET
is so .... AMEN
is what you make it .... LIFE
precedes rank .... NAME
reads same both ways
.... PALINDROME
takes two .... TANGO
Italian .... LATIN, ROMAN, PICENE, SABINE
actress .... DUSE, LOREN,

ANGELI, MAGNANI, LOLLOBRIGIDA
adventurer .... CASANOVA
all at once .... SUBITO
anatomist .... FALOPIUS
ancient .... OSCAN, ROMAN, PICENE, SABINE
ancient city .... CAPUA, CANNAE
anew .... DE NOVO
archipelago .... TUSCAN
art period .... SEICENTO, TRECENTO
astronomer .... GALILEO
author .... DANTE, PETRARCH
baby .... BAMBINO
baked shrimp .... SCAMPI
bandit .... CACO, BRIGANTE
bathhouse .... BAGNIO
beings .... ENTES
bell .... CAMPANA
bell town .... ATRI
bonfire .... FALO
bowl .... TAZZA
bread .... PANE
breed of cattle .... MODICA, PADOLIAN
business place .... BANCA
cape .... CIRCEO, VATICANO, CARBONARA
capital .... ROMA, ROME
car .... FIAT
cathedral .... DUOMO
cathedral city .... MILAN
Celt .... SENONE
cheer .... VIVA
cheese .... GRANA, ROMANO, FONTINA, RICOTTA, BEL PAESE, PARMESAN, PROVOLONE, GORGONZOLA, MOZZARELLA
chest .... CASSO(NE)
chief .... DUCE
city/town .... ASTI, ATRI, BARI, CIRO, ELEA, ITRI, LODI, MEDA, POLA, FORIL, GENOA, LECCE, LUCCA, MASSA, MILAN, MONZA, OSTIA, PADUA, PARMA, PAVIA, PRATO, SIENA, TURIN, TERNI, UDINE, ANCONA, CASAL(E), FOGGIA, LATINA, MANTUA, MESTRE, MODENA, NAPLES, NAPOLI, NOVARA, PESARO, RAGUSA, RIMINI, SAVONA, TIVOLI, TORINO, TRENTO, VARESE, VENICE, VERONA, BERGAMO, BOLOGNA, CARRARA, CASSINO, CATANIA, FIRENZE, GORIZIA, LIVORNA, MARSALA, MESSINA, PALERMO, RAVENNA, SALERNO, TRIESTE, SAN REMO, TRAPANI, VENEZIA,

BRINDISI, CAGLIARI, FLORENCE, MOLFETTA, PIACENZA, SIRACUSA
civil government .... QUIRINAL
coin .... LIRA, LIRE, SCUDO, SOLDI, SOLDO, SEQUIN, ZECHIN, ZECCHINO, TESTON(E), CENTESIMO
coin, medieval .... TARI
comedy character .... PANTALOON, SCARAMOUCH(E)
commune .... ALBA, ASTI, IESI, ESTE, MEDA, ASOLA, TRIEA
composer .... GUIDO, LULLY, TOSTI, VERDI, MENOTTI, PUCCINI, ROSSINI, MASCAGNI, PAGANINI, SCARLATTI
condiment .... TAMARA
conductor .... MANTOVANI, TOSCANINI
country, ancient .... LATIUM, ETRURIA
countryside .... CAMPAGNA
craftsmanship .... ARTE
cup .... TAZZA
cupid .... AMORINO, AMORETTO
customs house .... DOGANA
dance .... PAVIN, VOLTA, PAVAN(E), CALATA, SALTARELLO, TARANTELLA
dear .... CARA, CARO
department .... APULIA, EMILIA, UMBRIA, LIGURIA, LUCANIA, CALABRIA, LOMBARDY, PIEDMONT
dessert ..... SPUMONE, SPUMONI
"Detroit" .... TURIN
dialect .... LIGURIAN
dictator .... MUSSO(LINI)
dish .... PASTA, PIZZA, RISOTTO
dish, veal .... OSSO BUCO
Do Not Touch .... NON TOCCARE
dough .... PASTA
dramatist .... ALFIERI
drink .... BEVERE
dry .... SECCO
duchy .... PARMA
dynasty .... SAVOY
eight .... OTTO
enclave, Swiss .... CAMPIONE
enough .... BASTA
evening .... SERA
express train .... RAPIDO
faction .... NERI, BIANCHI
fair lady .... BELLA DONNA
family ..... ASTI, ESTE, CENCI, DORIA, DONATI, MEDICI
farewell .... ADDIO
feast .... FESTA, FESTINO

festival .... RIDOTTO
field .... CAMPO
fig .... FICO
film beauty .... SOPHIA LOREN, GINA LOLLOBRIGIDA
first .... PRIMO
flower .... FIORE
fortress .... ROCA
fountain, famous .... TREVI
gallery .... UFFIZI
game .... MORA, BOCCE
gangster .... DUMINI
gentleman ..... SER, SIGNOR(E), SIGNORINO
good .... BENE
good morning .... BUON GIORNO
good-bye .... ADDIO
goose .... OCA
governor .... PODESTA
greedy .... ESOSO
Greek city .... ELEA, PESTO
Greek colony .... ELEA
guessing game .... MORA
gulf .... GAETA, GENOA, OROSEI, VENICE, SALERNO, TARANTO, TRIESTE, ORISTANO, SQUILLACE
gypsy .... ZINGABI
hair .... PELO
hamlet .... BORGO, CASAL(E)
hammer .... MARTELLO
hand .... MANO
harbor .... PORTO
harlequin .... ZANNI
harp .... ARPA
hat .... LEGHORN
hate .... ODIO
headland .... SCILLA
heir .... EREDE
helmet .... ELME
historian .... CANTU
holiday .... FESTA, FESTE
house .... CASA
hymn .... INNO
innkeeper ...... OSTE, PADRONE
island .... ELBA, CAPRI, PONZA, GIGLIO, ISCHIA, LINOSA, LIPARI, SALINA, SICILY, USTICA, ALICUDI, ASINARA, CAPRAIA, GORGONA, LEVANZO, PANAREA, PIANOSA, VULCANO, FILICUDI, SARDINIA, FAVIGNANA, GIANNUTRI, LAMPEDUSA, MARETTIMO, SAN PIETRO, STROMBOLI, MONTECRISTO, VENTOTENE, PANTELLERIA
islander .... SARD
islands .... EGADI, LIPARI, PELAGIE, PONTINE, TREMITI

judge .... PODESTA
king .... EMMANUEL, HUMBERT(O)
kiss .... BACIO
know-nothing .... NESCI
labor contractor ...... PADRONE
lady/madam .... DONNA, SIGNORA, SIGNORINA
lake .... COMO, LAGO, VICO, GARDA, ALBANO, AVERNO, BOLSENA, MAGGIORE, BRACCIANO, TRASIMENO
language .... LADIN, OSCAN, TUSCAN
leader .... RAS, DUCE, MUSSO(LINI)
little .... POCO
love .... AMORE
lover .... AMOROSO
magistrate ..... DOGE, PODESTA
man .... SIGNOR(E)
marble .... CIPOLIN, CAR(R)ARA
marshy land .... MAREMMA, PONTINE
mayor .... PODESTA
measure .... CANNA, PALMO, PUNTO, MIGLIO, BRACCIO
meat balls .... RAVIOLI
milk .... LATTE
millet ..... BUDA, MOHA, TENAI
miss .... SIGNORINA
mister .... SIGNOR
monetary unit .... LIRA
monk's title .... FRA
mother .... MADRE
mountain .... CAVO, ROSA, VISO, BLANC, CENIS, CHIANTI, MARMOLADA, GENNARGENTU, GRAN PARADISO
movie director .... (DE)SICCA
music .... TARANTELLA
musical instrument .... ARPA
musical suite .... PARTITA
musical theme .... TEMA
musical theorist .... GUIDO
muslin .... MUSSOLINO
name for Florence .... FIRENZE
name for Italy .... ITALIA
nationalist .... MAZZINI
naval base .... POLA, TARANTO, BRINDISI
night .... SERA
nine .... NOVE
noble family .... ESTE
noblewoman .... MARQUIS, CONTESSA, MARCHESA, MARCHESE, MARCHIONESS
not only .... NONCHE
novelist .... MANZONI
one .... UNO
opera .... AIDA, NORMA, TOSCA

opera house .... SCALA
opera singer .... AMATO,
GIGLI, PATTI, PINZA, CARUSO,
CORELLI, TEBALDI, ALDANESE
painter ...... RENI, LIPPI, ROSSI,
SPADA, VINCI, ANDREA,
GIOTTO, TITIAN, VASARI,
RAPHAEL
pass .... BRENNER, GREAT
SAINT BERNARD
patriot .... CAVOUR, MAZZINI,
GARIBALDI
patriotic organization
.... CARBONARI
peak .... CIMA, BERNINA,
MARMOLADA
people .... OSCAN, SARDS,
SABINES
philosopher ...... DION, BRUNO,
(BENEDETTO) CROCE
physicist .... ROSSI, VOLTA,
GALILEO, MARCONI
pie .... PIZZA
plague .... PELLAGRA
plain .... CAMPAGNA
plateau .... SILA
poet .... REDI, DANTE, TASSO,
ARIOSTO, MANZONI, LEOPARDI,
PETRARCH
police .... CARABINIERI
political party member
.... GUELF, GUELPH
porridge .... POLENTA
port ...... BARI, GENOA, MILAN,
OSTIA, TRIESTE, SORRENTO
pottery ..... FAENZA, MAJOLICA
premier .... MORO, PARRI,
RUMOR, CAVOUR, CRISPI,
ORLANDO
president .... LEONE
prima donna .... TEBALDI
province .... ASTI, BARI, COMO,
PISA, ROME, GENOA, FORIL,
LECCE, MILAN, PADUA, PAVIA,
SIENA, TURIN, UDINE, ANCONA,
FOGGIA, MANTUA, MODENA,
NAPLES, TRENTO, VENICE,
VARESE, VERONA, AVELINO,
BERGAMO, BOLOGNA, BRESCIA,
CASERTA, CATANIA, MESSINA,
PALERMO, PERUGIA, SALERNO,
TARANTO, TRIESTE, VICENZA,
CAGLIARI, FLORENCE,
ALESSANDRIA
public square .... PIAZZA
range .... CARNIC, GRAIAN,
JULIAN, ORTLES, OTZTAL,
PENNINE, MARITIME,
APENNINES
region .... APULIA, LATIUM,
MARCHE, SICILY, UMBRIA,

VENETO, ABRUZZI, LIGURIA,
TUSCANY, CALABRIA,
CAMPANIA, LOMBARDY,
PIEDMONT, SARDINIA,
TRENTINO
republic .... GENOA
resort ...... COMO, LIDO, CAPRI,
AGNONE, SAN REMO,
SORRENTO
restaurant .... PIZZERIA
river .... PO, ADDA, ARNO,
NERA, ADIGE, OGLIO, PIAVE,
SALSO, TIBER, MINCIO,
PANARO, TANARO, LIVENZA,
METAURO, OMBRONE, TREBBIA,
VOLTURNO, DORA BALTEA,
DORA RIPARIA
road .... RADA, STRADA
Romance language ...... LADIN
ruins .... POMPEII
saddle .... SELLA
sausage .... SALAMI
sculptor .... DUPRE, LEONI,
CANOVA, PISANO, CELLINI
sea .... IONIAN, ADRIATIC,
LIGURIAN, TYRRHENIAN
seacoast .... MARINA
seaport .... POLA, GENOA,
TRANI, GENOVA, NAPLES,
VENICE, PALERMO, SALERNO,
SAN REMO, TRIESTE, (LA)
SPEZIA
seashore .... RIVA
seasoning mixture
.... TAMARA
secret society .... MAFIA,
CAMORRA, CARBONARI
ship .... POLACCA
shrimp dish .... SCAMPI
sign .... SEGNO
silk .... SETA
sir .... SIGNOR(E)
sky .... CIELO
slang .... GUINEA
small .... PICCOLO
somewhat .... POCO
song .... CANZONE
soup .... MINESTRONE
spa .... ABANO, AGNONE
spider .... TARANTULA
strait .... SICILY, MESSINA,
OTRANTO, BONIFACIO
street .... VIA, CALLE, CORSO
supper .... CENA
tender .... PIA
tenor .... CARUSO, SCHIPA,
CORELLI
that .... CHE
the .... GLI
three .... TRE
time .... TEMPO

title .... CONTE, DONNA,
MARCHE, SIGNOR, MARQUIS,
CONTESSA
tobacco .... CAPORALE
today .... OGGI
tractor .... PICCOLINO
tribe .... SABINE
under .... SOTTO
valley .... SACCO
vase .... TAZZA
verse .... RANN
violin .... AMATI, CREMONA,
STRAD(IVARIUS)
violin maker .... AMATI,
GUARNERI, STRADIVARI
violinist .... TARTINI, PAGANINI
voice .... VOCE
volcano .... ETNA, VESUVIUS,
STROMBOLI
waterway .... CANALE
we .... NOI
weight .... LIBRA, ONCIA,
DENARO, SALM(A)
well .... BENE
what .... CHE
what will be, will be ...... CHE
SARA SARA
wind .... ANDAR, SOVER,
SIROC(CO)
wine .... ASTI, FALERNO
wine, white .... SOAVE
wine measure ..... ASTI, ORNA,
ORNE
winter .... INVERNO
woman's title .... MADONNA
woods .... PINETOS
woodwork .... TARSIA
you .... TU, VOI
Italic type inventor
.... MANUTIUS
Italy .... AUSONIA, HESPERIA
itch .... RIFF, URGE, CRAVE,
MANGE, PSORA, DESIRE,
SCABIES, BURN(ING),
PRURITUS, HANKER(ING)
barber's .... SYCOSIS
item .... PART, UNIT, ENTRY,
PIECE, THING, DETAIL,
ARTICLE, PARTICULAR
black ink .... CREDIT
checkroom .... HAT, COAT,
WRAP
to be weighed .... ANCHOR
itemize .... LIST
itemized list .... ROSTER
items in first-aid procedures
.... EMETICS
iterate .... ECHO, HARP, REPEAT,
RETELL
Ithunn .... IDUN
itinerant .... HOBO, TRAMP,

DRIFTER, NOMADIC, VAGRANT, TRAVELER, TRAVELING

vendor .... PEDDLER

itinerary .... ROUTE, COURSE, CIRCUIT, ROADBOOK, CHECKLIST, GUIDEBOOK

itinerate .... TRAVEL

it's been said .... UTTERANCE

how you play the game .... WIN OR LOSE

often clipped .... COUPON

often the limit .... SKY

on the barrelhead .... CASH

sometimes due .... POSTAGE

to the left of the Rive Droite .... SEINE

itself .... PER SE

itty-bitty .... TEENSY

iva .... YELLOW BUGLE

Ivanhoe author .... SCOTT

character .... BOUEF, CRONE, GURTH, ISAAC, WAMBA,

CEDRIC, ROWENA, ULRICA

weapon of .... LANCE

Ives, actor .... BURL

partner of .... CURRIER

ivied .... VINY

ivories .... DICE, KEYS, TEETH

ivorine .... WHITE

ivory .... TUSH, TUSK, DENTINE

____ .... TOWER

animal with .... WALRUS, WARTHOG, ELEPHANT

Latin .... EBUR

like .... DENTINE

source .... TUSK, NARWHAL, ELEPHANT

synthetic .... IVORIDE

tickler .... PIANIST

time-beaters .... CASTANETS

tower .... HIDEOUT, RETREAT, HIDEAWAY

Ivory Coast capital .... YAMOUSSOUKRO

city/town .... DIVO, DALOA, BOUAKE, GAGNOA, ABIDJAN, KORHOGO, PORT-BOUET

gulf .... GUINEA

lagoon .... ABY, EBRIE

lake .... KOSSOU

president .... HOUPHOUET-BOIGNY

river .... BAGOE, COMOE, BAOULE, CAVALLY

ivy .... VINE, CLIMBER

clump .... TOD

family .... GINSENG

kind of .... POISON, GROUND

leaguers .... ELIS

of the .... HEDERAL

Iwo ____ .... JIMA

Jima mount .... SURIBACHI

ixia .... IRIS

Ixion offspring .... CENTAUR

ixtle .... PITA, ISTLE

Izmir .... SMYRNA

J

J in physics .... JOULE

letter .... JAY

ja .... YES

jab ...... DIG, BLOW, POKE, PUNCH, THRUST

jabber .... YAP, PRATE, BABBLE, GABBLE, GIBBER(ISH), CHATTER, SPUTTER

jack .... BAR, MUG, NOB, MULE, BOWER, CLOWN, HOIST, KNAVE, TORCH, DONKEY, FELLOW, OPENER, RABBIT, SAILOR, SALMON

in cribbage .... NOB

in-the-pulpit ..... ARAD, ARUM, AROID, WAKEROBIN

of-all-trades .... TINKER

of clubs .... PAM

part of .... DETENT

pudding .... FOOL, BUFFOON

rabbit .... HARE

slang .... MONEY

tree .... JACA

up .... HIKE, RAISE

Jack .... LORD, PARR, WEBB, OAKIE, BENNY, CARTER

and ____ .... JILL

Benny's stock in trade .... GAGS, VIOLIN

Horner's prize .... PIE

Ketch .... HANGMAN

Leonard's forte .... INSULT

Nasty .... SNEAK

Sprat's favorite .... LEAN

jackal .... DIEB, KOLA, THOS, CHEAT(ER), (WILD)DOG, SWINDLER, SCAVENGER

headed deity .... ANUBIS

jackanapes .... IMP, MONKEY, UPSTART

jackass .... DOLT, FOOL, DONKEY, NITWIT

and mare offspring ...... MULE

rarely one .... WISE GUY, SMART ALECK

jackdaw .... DAW

bird like .... CROW

jacket .... ETON, JUPE, RIND, SACK, SKIN, GREGO, PARKA, ANORAK, BOLERO, CASING, JERKIN, REEFER, COAT(EE), SACQUE, NORFOLK, SPENCER, WRAPPER, ROUNDABOUT

ad on book .... BLURB

Arctic .... ANORAK

armor .... ACTON, GIPON, JUPON

children's .... PALETOT

cowboy's .... CHAQUETA

dinner .... TUX(EDO)

fur .... PARKA

life-saving .... MAE WEST

mail .... HAUBERK, HABERGEON

outer ..... WAMPUS, WAM(M)US

sailor's .... PEACOAT

sleeveless/short .... VEST, BOLERO, TABARD, WAISTCOAT

sports .... WINDBREAKER

women's .... JUPE, JUPON, PALETOT, CAMISOLE

woolen .... CARDIGAN, LUMBERJACK

jackfish .... PIKE

Jackie's predecessor .... MAMIE

successor .... LADY BIRD

Jacks or better .... OPENER

jacksnipe .... SANDPIPER

Jackson, Andrew ...... ANDY, OLD HICKORY

follower of President .... JACKSONIAN

general .... STONEWALL

Jacob .... ISRAEL

burial place of .... MACHPELAH

daughter of .... DINAH

diminutive of .... JACK, JAKE

father of .... ISAAC

father-in-law of .... LABAN

grandfather of .... ABRAHAM

grandson of .... EPHRAIM, MANASSEH

in French .... JACQUES

mother of .... REBECCA, REBEKAH

son of .... DAN, GAD, LEVI, ASHER, JUDAH, JOSEPH, REUBEN, SIMEON, ZEBULUN, BENJAMIN, ISSACHAR, NAPHTABI

twin brother of .... EDOM, ESAU

variant of .... JAMES
wife of .... LEAH, RACHEL
Jacobin .... FRIAR, PIGEON,
      RADICAL, DOMINICAN
Jacob's sword .... IRIS
jaconet .... COTTON, NAINSOOK
jade .... NAG, TIT, MARE, SLUT,
      TIRE, YAUD, GREEN, HUSSY,
      STONE, WEARY, WOMAN,
      HARASS, MURRHINE,
      NEPHRITE, ROSINANTE
jaded .... BLASE
jaeger .... SKUA, ALLAN, SHOOI,
      TEASER, SEABIRD
Jael's husband .... HEBER
victim .... SISERA
weapon .... TENT PEG
Jaffa .... JOPPA
home of .... ISRAEL
jag .... BUN, BARB, PINK, SNAG,
      TEAR, NOTCH, SPREE
jaga .... BANTU
jager .... RIFLEMAN
jagged ...... CLEFT, EROSE, ROUGH,
      RAGGED, NOTCHED, SERRATED
jaguar ...... CAR, TIGER, PANTHER
jaguarundi .... EYRA
Jahve(h) .... JEHOVAH
jai-alai .... PELOTA
cheer .... OLE
court .... FRONTON
game like .... HANDBALL
player .... PELOTARI
racquet .... CESTA
stroke .... REBOTE
jail .... PEN, CAGE, CELL, COOP,
      GAOL, QUOD, LIMBO, LOCK
      UP, (IM)PRISON, BRIDEWELL
official ...... WARDEN, WARDER
slang .... JUG, STIR, POK(E)Y,
      COOLER, CLINK(ER), SLAMMER,
      CALABOOSE
jailbird .... INMATE, CONVICT,
      PRISONER, LAWBREAKER
jailer .... GAOLER, WARDEN,
      PROVOST, TURNKEY
Jakarta .... BATAVIA
jakes .... PRIVY, TOILET
jalopy .... CRATE, HOTROD
jalousie .... BLIND, SHADE,
      SCREEN
jam .... CRAM, BLOCK, CROWD,
      SHOVE, WEDGE, SQUEEZE,
      PRESERVES, CONGESTION
colloquial .... FIX, SPOT,
      PINCH, PREDICAMENT
every which way
      .... GRIDLOCK
like preparation .... JELLY
material .... CURRANT
Jamaican bay .... MONTEGO

bird .... TODY, GRACKLE,
      TINKLING
capital .... KINGSTON
export .... RUM
grackle .... TINKLING
island .... CAYMAN
peak .... BLUE MOUNTAIN
witchcraft .... OBEAH
jamb(e) .... (SIDE)POST
James Bond's creator
      .... FLEMING
direction to .... HOME
father of disciple ..... ZEBEDEE
the outlaw .... JESSE
the Second supporter
      .... JACOBITE
Watson topic .... DOUBLE
      HELIX
Jamshid's subjects .... PERIS
Jane, mate of .... TARZAN
singer .... FROMAN
jangle .... BICKER, QUARREL
Janis, pop singer .... JOPLIN
janitor .... SUPER, PORTER,
      SEXTON, DOORMAN,
      CONCIERGE
Janus, like .... TWO-FACED
Japan .... NIHON, ENAMEL,
      NIPPON, CIPANGO, LACQUER,
      VARNISH, ZIPANGU
foreigner in .... GAIJIN
Japanese .... NIPPONESE
a walk .... SANPO
abacus .... SORABAN
aborigine .... AINO, AINU
about .... GORO
admiral .... ITO, OKA, TOGO,
      OKADA, UGAKI, NAGANO,
      NOMURA, OIKAWA, SUZUKI,
      TOYODA, SHIMADA,
      YAMAMOTO
adviser .... GENRO
again .... MO ICHIDO
airplane .... HIKOOKI
airport .... HIKOJO, HIKOOZYOO
alien to a .... GAIJIN
all .... ZENBU
alone .... HITORIDE
always .... ITSUMO
A.M. (morning) .... GOZEN
American .... ISSEI, KIBEI,
      NIS(S)EI, SANSEI
ant .... ARI
anthem .... KIMIGAYO
apple .... RINGO
apricot .... UME, ANSU
April .... SHIGATSU, YONGATSU
arm .... UDE
army reserve .... HOJU
ash/gray .... HAIIRO
assets .... ZAISAN

August .... HACHIGATSU
aunt .... OBA, OBASAN
automobile .... ZIDOOSYA
automobile manufacturer
      .... HONDA, DATSUN, NISSAN,
      TOYOTA, SUZUKI, MITSUBISHI
autumn/fall .... AKI
back .... USIRO, SENAKA
bad .... DAME, WARUI
badge/crest .... (KIRI)MON
bag .... KABANG
baggage .... NIMOTU
bamboo craft .... TAKESEIHIN
bamboo shoot ...... TAKENOKO
banjo .... SAMISEN
bank .... GINKO(O)
barber .... RIYOOSHI
baron .... HAN
bathroom .... HUROBA
battle cry/cheer .... BANZAI
bay .... ISE, MUTSU, OSAKA,
      TOKYO, ATSUMI, SAGAMI,
      TOYAMA, WAKASA, UCHIURA,
      ISHIKARI, KAGOSHIMA
bean sprout .... MOYASHI
beans, all kinds .... MAME
beautician .... BIYOOSHI
beauty salon .... BIYOIN
bed .... BETTO, SINDAI
beef .... GYUUNIKU
beer .... ASAHI, BIIRU,
      SAPPORO
before/front .... MAE
begin .... HAJIMERU
bell .... BERU
beriberi .... KAKKE
beside .... YOKO
big .... OKI(I)
bird .... KOTORI
birthday .... TANJOO BI
bitter .... NIGAI
black .... KURO(I)
black tea .... KOOTYA
blue .... AO(I)
board game .... GOBAN(G)
body .... KARADA
book .... HON
bookshelf .... HONDANA
bookstore .... HONYA
box .... HAKO
branch .... EDA
brazier .... HIBACHI
bread .... PAN
bream .... TAI
bride .... HANAYOME
bridegroom .... HANAMUKO
brother .... ANI, OTOOTO
brother or sister ...... KYOODAI
brown .... CHAIRO
Buddha .... AMIDA
Buddhism .... ZEN

Buddhist festival .... BON
Buddhist monastery ...... TERA
bug/worm .... MUSHI
building .... TATEMONO
bull/cow .... USI
bullet train .... SHINKANSEN
bus .... BASU
butter .... BATA
buy .... KAU, KATTE
cabbage .... KYABETSU
camellia .... JAPONICA
cape .... IRO, OMA, DAIO,
ERIMO, INUBO, KAMUI, NYUDO,
TAPPI, NOJIMA, SHIONO,
MOTSUTA, SHIRIYA
capital .... TOKIO, TOKYO,
YED(D)O
capital, former .... NARA,
KYOTO
capital, old: var. .... KIOTO
car .... KURUMA
carriage .... RICKSHA(W)
carrot .... NINJIN
caste .... SAMURAI
cat .... NEKO
cedar .... SUGI
center of city .... TOSHIN
chair .... ISU
channel .... KII
cheap .... YASUI
cheese .... CHIIZU
cheerleader .... OENDAN
cherry .... SAKURANBO
cherry blossoms .... SAKURA
Cherry Society .... SAKURAKAI
chest .... MUNE
chest of drawers .... TANSU
chestnut .... KURI
chicken .... TORI
chicken dish .... YAKATORI
child/children .... KODOMO
chinaware .... IMARI, KUTANI
chopstick .... HAS(H)I
church .... TERA
cigarette .... TABAKO
circle .... MARU
city/town .... ISE, ITO, ODA,
TSU, UBE, UJI, YAO, FUJI, GIFU,
GOBO, HINO, HOFU, KOBE,
KOFU, MITO, MOJI, NAHA,
NARA, SOKA, UEDA, YONO,
ATAMI, BEPPU, CHIBA, CHOFU,
DAITO, FUCHI, FUKUE, ITAMI,
IZUMI, IWAKI, KOCHI, OSAKA,
OTARU, SAKAI, SUITA, URAWA,
ZUSHI, AKASHI, AOMORI,
ATSUGI, HADANO, HIMEJI,
JOETSU, KADOMA, NAGOYA,
SASEBO, SENDAI, TOYAMA,
TOYOTA, YAMATO, FUKUOKA,
HITACHI, IBARAKI, KASHIWA,

MACHIDA, MORIOKA, NIIGATA,
ODAWARA, OKAYAMA,
SAPPORO, SHIMIZU, ICHIHARA,
HACHIOJI, FUKUYAMA,
ICHIKAWA, KAWASAKI,
NAGASAKI, SHIZUOKA,
WAKAYAMA, YAMAGATA,
YOKOHAMA, AMAGASAKI,
HACHINOHE, HIROSHIMA,
KAGOSHIMA, MATSUMOTO,
MATSUYAMA
clam .... ASARI
clan ...... GEN, HEI, TOKUGAWA
clap/applaud .... KASSAI
climate .... KIKOO
clock/watch .... TOKEE
clogs .... GETA
close .... SIMARU
cloth for wrapping objects
.... FUROSHIKI
cloudy .... KUMORI
clover .... HAGI
coin .... RIN, SEN, YEN,
OBAN(G), ITZEBU
cold .... SAMUI
come .... KIMASU
commoner .... HEIMIN
company boss .... SHACHOO
compete .... SERU
confection .... AME
Consulate .... RYOOZIKAN
contract .... KEIYAKU
conveyance .... KAGO
coffee .... KOOHI
cook .... RYOORI
cookie/cake .... OKASI
cool .... SUZUSHII
couch/sofa .... NAGAISU
councilor .... KARO
courage .... YUUKI
court .... DAIRI
cousin ...... ITOKO, OITOKOSAN
cover/lid .... FUTA
crash (suicide) pilot
.... KAMIKAZE
Crown Prince .... NARUHITO
cucumber .... KYURI
customer/guest .... KYAKU
cut .... KITTA
dancing girl .... GEISHA
date/plum .... UME
daughter .... MUSUME(SAN)
December .... ZYUUNIGATSU
decreased .... HETTA
deer .... SIKA
deity .... AMIDA, AMITA
delicious .... OISII
dentist .... HAISHA
department store ..... DEPAATO
diary .... NISSHI
dictionary .... ZIBIKI

difficult .... MUZUKASI
dining room .... SYOKUDOO
dish .... SUSHI, TEMPURA,
SUKIYAKI, TERIYAKI,
YAKATORI, SHABU-SHABU
divine wind .... KAMIKAZE
divorce .... RIKON
doctor .... ISHA
dog .... INU
door .... TO
drama .... NOH, KABUKI,
NOGAKU
drink .... NOMI(MASU)
drugstore .... KUSURIYA
ear .... MIMI
earthquake .... JISHIN
earthquake, 1923 .... KANTO
easy .... YASAI
eat .... TABERU
egg .... TAMAGO
eggplant .... NASU
eight .... HATI, HACHI
electric light .... DENKI
embassy .... TAISIKAN
emperor .... JIMMU, JINMU,
TENNO, MIKADO, AKIHITO,
HIROHITO, MUTSUHITO,
YOSHIHITO
emperor's reign .... MEIJI,
SHOWA, TAISHO
Empire .... EDO
Empress .... NAGAKO, MICHIKO
empty hand .... KARATE
English language .... EEGO
Englishman .... IGIRISUZIN
engraver .... HOKUSAI
Enlightened Peace era
.... MEEZI, MEIJI
ethnic group .... AINU
everyday .... MAINITI,
MAINICHI
everyone .... MINNA
expectation .... OPE
expensive .... TAKAI
eye .... ME
eyebrow .... MAYUGE
face .... KAO
family .... KAZOKU
father .... TITI, OTOOSAN
February .... NIGATSU
fighter plane .... ZERO
finger .... YUBI
fine .... KEKKO
fire .... KASAI
fish .... SAKANA
fish gill .... ERA
fishworm .... ANISAKIS
five .... GO
flag .... RISING SUN
flower/nose .... HANA

flower arrangement .... IKEBANA
foreign language .... GAIKOKUGO
foreign ministry .... GAIMUSHO
four .... S(H)I
fork .... HOOKU
France .... HURANSU
Frenchman .... HURANSUZIN
Friday .... KINYOOBI
friend .... TOMODATI, TOMODACHI
fruit(s) .... KUDAMONO
game .... GOBAN(G)
game, ancient .... KEMARI
garlic .... NINNIKU
garment .... KIMONO
gateway .... TORII
general ..... MUTO, NOGI, TOJO, ANAMI, ARAKI, KOISO, SAKAI, UMEZU, KAWABE, TANABE, TANAKA, OKAMURA, TOMINAGA, KAWASHIMA, YAMASHITA
generalissimo .... SHOGUN
German .... DOITUZIN
German language .... DOITUGO
gift .... OMIYAGE
give .... YARU
go .... IKU, IKIMASU
goat .... YAGI
god .... KAMI, EBISU, HOTEI
goldfish .... FUNA
good .... YOROSI
good afternoon .... KONNITI-WA, KONNICHIWA
good evening ..... KONBAN-WA
good morning .... OHAYOO
good night .... OYASUMI-NASAI
goodbye .... SAYONARA
government system .... SHOGUNATE
grandchild .... MAGO
grandfather ...... SOHU, OZISAN
grandmother .... SOBU, OBAASAN
grape .... BUDOO
graveyard tombstone .... HAKA
green .... MIDORI
grill .... HIBACHI
guitar .... KOTO, SAMISEN
hand .... TE
hang .... KAKERU
Happy Birthday ..... TANJOOBI OMEDETOO
head .... ATAMA
healthy .... GENKI
Hello (on the telephone) .... MOSIMOSI
herb .... UDO

here .... KOKO
Hey there!/Say! .... ANONE
highest point .... (MOUNT) FUJI
hill/slope .... SAKA
hometown .... FURUSATO
horse .... UMA
hospital .... BYOOIN
hot .... ATSUI
house/home ...... UCHI, OTAKU
husband .... SYUZIN, GOSYUZIN
I/me .... WATASHI, WATAKUSHI
ice .... KOORI
jacket .... SEBIRO
January .... ICHIGATSU
July .... SHICHIGATSU
June .... ROKUGATSU
key .... KAGI
kind of fish .... AYU, TAI, FUGU, GOURAMI, TILAPIA
kitchen .... DAIDOKORO
knife .... NAIHU
immigrant .... ISSEI
imperial badge .... KIRIMON
important/valuable .... DAIZI
industrial family .... MITSUI, YASUDA, TOYODA, ZAIBATSU
inland sea .... SETO, NAIKAI
island .... AWA, IKI, IWO, NII, DOGO, HAHA, KUME, MUKO, SADO, TOBI, YAKU, AWAJI, IHEYA, KIKAI, YORON, CHICHI, MIYAKO, TANEGA, TARAMA, KUCHINO, NISHINO, OKINAWA, RISHIRI, ISHIGAKI
island, main .... HONSHU, KYUSHU, SHIKOKU, HOKKAIDO
island group .... IZU, GOTO, AMAMI, BONIN, DOZEN, KERAMA, RYUKYU, HABOMAI, KOSHIKI, YAEYAMA, VOLCANO
lagoon .... HACHIRO, KASUMIGA
lake .... BIWA, TOYA, TAZAWA, TOWADA, KUTCHARO, INAWASHIRO
language .... NIHONGO, NIPPONGO
lawyer .... BENGOSHI
left .... HIDARI
lightning .... INAZUMA
lily .... AURATUM
lips .... KUTIBIRU
litter .... NORIMONO
little .... SUKOSI
lobster .... ISEEBI
lord .... DAIMIO
lute .... BIWA
magazine .... ZASSI
man .... OTOKO
many/much .... TAKUSAN
map .... TIZU

March .... SANGATSU
marriage .... KEKKON
marriage ceremony .... KEKKON SHIKI
May .... GOGATSU
meaning of sayonara .... SO BE IT
measure ...... BU, MO, RI, CHO, RIN, SHO, HIRO, SHAKU
meat .... NIKU
medicine .... KUSURI
midnight .... MAYONAKA
military caste .... SAMURAI
military code .... BUSHIDO
military governor ..... SHOGUN
military police organization .... KEMPEITAI
military service .... YOBI
milk (cow's) .... GYUUNYUU
milk (mother's) .... BONYUU
mint .... HAKKA
monastery .... TERA
Monday .... GETSUYOOBI
money .... SEN, YEN, OKANE
monk .... BONZE
monopolies .... ZAIBATSU
morning .... ASA
mother .... HAHA, OKAASAN
mountain .... ASO, ZAO, HAKU, KUJU, FUJI(YAMA), NASU, ASAHI, ASAMA, IWAKI, IWATE, UNZEN, BANDAI, CHOKAI, GASSEN, HAKKEN, HODAKA, KARIBA, KOMAGA, NANTAI, ONTAKE, TESHIO, SHIRANE, DAIMANJI
mouth .... KUTI
movie .... EIGA
movie theater .... EIGAKAN
mushroom .... SHIITAKE
musical instrument ...... KOTO, SAMISEN
mystic symbol .... SWASTIKA
nail (finger, toe) .... TSUME
name .... NAMAE
national park .... ASO, AKAN, NIKKO, SAIKAI, HAKUSAN, DAISEN-OKI, BANDAI-ASAHI
naval base .... KURE, SASEBO
near .... CHIKAI
neck .... KUBI
nephew .... OI, OIGOSAN
new .... ATARASHI
news agency .... JIJI, DOMEI, KYODO
newspaper .... SINBUN, SHIMBUN, YOMIURI, MAINICHI
next door .... TONARI
niece .... MEI, MEIGOSAN
night/nighttime .... BAN, YORU

nine .... KU, KYU
no .... IIE
nobility .... SAMURAI,
                       HATAMOTO
nobleman .... KAMI, KUGE,
                DAIMIO, DAIMYO
nobody .... DARE MO
noodle shop .... SOBAYA
noodles .... SOBA, UDON
north .... KITA
number .... BANGOO
nurse .... KANGOFU
October .... JUGATSU
office .... KAISYA, ZIMUSYO
old .... HURUI
one .... ICHI
one-way .... KATAMITI
onion .... TAMANEGI
only .... DAKE
open .... AKERU
opera .... YUZURU
orange (color) .... DAIDAIIRO
out of order .... KOSYOO
outcast/outlaw .... YETA,
                          RONIN
outer garment .... MINO,
                HAORI, KIMONO
outside .... SOTO
over there .... ASOKO
pagoda .... TAA
painter .... HIROSHIGE
painting school .... KANO,
           TOSA, SHIJO, SESSHU
palanquin .... KAGO,
                  NORIMONO
paper art .... ORIGAMI
park .... KOOEN
parliament .... DIET
paste .... AME
pay .... HARAU
peach .... MOMO
pear .... NASHI
pearl .... SHINJU
pencil .... ENPIT(S)U
peninsula ..... IZU, OGA, NOTO,
               MIURA, OSUMI
people .... NIHONGIN,
                NIPPONGIN
persimmon .... KAKI
pine .... MATSU
pink .... MOMOIRU
"Pittsburg" .... YAWATA
plant .... UDO, AUCUBA
play .... NOH, KABUKI
play musical instrument
                    HIKIMASU
please .... DO(O)ZO, KUDASAI
plum .... KAKI, KELSEY,
                    SUMOMO
plumlike fruit .... LOQUAT
P.M. (afternoon) .... GOGO

poem .... HAIKU
point .... ESAN, SOYA, SUZU,
          MUROTO, NOSAPPU
policeman .... KEIKAN
porgy .... TAI
pork .... BUTANIKU
porter .... AKABOO
postcard .... HAGAKI
potato .... JAGAIMO
pottery ...... AWATA, SATSUMA,
                YAKIMONO
prefecture .... MIE, GIFU,
     NARA, OITA, SAGA, AKITA,
     KYOTO, OSAKA, SHIGA,
     TOKYO, MIYAGI, NAGANO,
     TOYAMA, FUKUOKA,
     OKAYAMA, OKINAWA,
     HOKKAIDO, YAMAGUCHI
premier .... SATO, TOJO,
    IKEDA, KAIFU, KISHI, OKADA,
    INUKAI, KONOYE, TANAKA,
               NAKASONE
pretty .... KIREI, KIREE
primitive .... AINO
prune .... SUMOMO
pumpkin .... KABOCHA
puppet emperor of .... PU-YI
puppet show .... BUNRAKU
quietly .... SOTTO
rabbit .... USAGI
radish, pickled .... TAKUWAN
radish, white .... DAIKON
rain .... AME
raincoat .... MINO
raisin .... HOSHIBUDOO
raw fish .... SASIMI, SASHIMI
read .... YOMU
red .... AKAI
religion .... BUDDHISM,
                SHINTOISM
religious dance .... NO
resort .... NIKKO, HAKONE
rest .... YASUMU
restaurant .... RYOORIYA
rice, cooked .... GOHAN
rice, uncooked .... KOME
rice-straw floor mat
                    TATAMI
rice wine .... SAKE
rice with fish, seaweed, etc.
                    SUSHI
right .... MIGI
river ...... ARA, EDO, INA, ONO,
    FUJI, KINO, MUKO, NAKA,
    OANI, TAMA, TONE, YODO,
    AGANO, OMONO, MOGAMI,
    OBITSU, SAGAMI, TOKACHI,
     YOSHINO, KITAKAMI
robe .... KIMONO
room .... HEYA
room divider .... SHOVI

rude .... SITUREE
sake-like wine .... SHOCHU
salmon .... MASU
salesgirl .... URIKO
salt .... SIO
salty .... KARAI
same .... ONAZI
samurai warlord .... BUSHI
samurai's code .... BUSHIDO
sandals .... ZORI
sash .... OBI
Saturday .... DOYOOBI
school .... GAKKO
screen .... BYOBU, SHOVI
script .... KANA
scroll .... KAKEMONO
sculptress .... (YOKO)ONO
sea .... IYO, SUO, HARIMA,
           SAGAMI, OKHOTSK
seal, business .... HANKO
seaport .... KOBE, KURE,
    OMUTA, OTARU, SAKATA,
    TOYAMA, YAWATAH,
    NAGASAKI, YOKOHAMA
seaweed .... KAISOO
secretary .... HISHO
sect .... ZEN
see .... MIRU, MITE
self-defense forces ...... JIEITAI
self-defense system ...... JUDO,
    KARATE, JUJITSU, JUJUTSU
September .... KUGATSU
sesame seed .... GOMA
sesame oil .... GOMA-ABURA
seven .... NANA, SHICHI
ship .... HUNE, MARU
shoe .... GETA
shoot, edible .... UDO
short .... MIJIKAI
shoulder .... KATA
show .... KABUKI
shrimp .... EBI
shrine .... JINJA, JINGUU,
            OYAMA-ZUMI
sick .... BYOOKI
sightseeing .... KEMBUTSU
sister .... ANE, IMOOTO
six .... ROKU
sky .... SORA
slang .... NIP
sleep .... NERU
slow .... OSOI
small .... TISAI, CHIISAI
snake .... HEBI
snow .... YUKI
soap .... SEKKEN
social reformer .... KAGAWA
sock .... TABI, TABO
sometimes .... TOKIDOKI
son .... MUSUKO
song .... UTA

sour .... SUPPAI
soy sauce .... SYOOYU
spicy .... KARAI
spirit .... GANBARO
spoon .... SUPUUN
spring .... HARU
spruce .... YEDDO
squid .... IKA
stamp .... HANKO, KITTE
statesman .... ITO, GENRO,
                                     TANAKA
station .... EKI
stew .... CHANKO
stomach .... ONAKA
stop .... YAMERU
stove .... RENZI
straggler .... YOKOI,
                       (HIROO)ONADA
strait .... BUNGO, OSUMI,
    NEMURO, TSUGARU, TSUSHIMA
straw mat .... TATAMI
strawberry .... ITIGO, ICHIGO
street, famed .... GINZA
strong .... KOI
student .... GAKUSEI
study .... BENKYOO
style of painting .... KANO
subject .... GAKKA
subway .... TIKATETU
sugar .... SATO
suicide .... SEPPUKU,
          HARAKIRI, HARIKARI
suicide attack .... KAMIKAZE
summer .... NATSU
Sunday .... NICHIYOOBI
sun tree .... HINOKI
sweet .... AMAI
sword .... KATANA
syndicate .... ZAIBATSU
talk/speak .... HANASU
tea .... CHA, OTYA
tea, green .... OCHA
teach .... OSHIERU
teacher .... SENSEI
telephone .... DENWA
television .... TEREBI
temple .... PAGODA
ten .... JU, ZYUU
10,000 years .... BANZAI
thank you .... ARIGATO
that .... SORE
there .... SOKO
this .... KORE
three .... SAN
throat .... NODO
thunder .... KAMINARI
Thursday .... MOKUYOOBI
ticket .... KIPPU
tidal wave .... TSUNAMI
tiger .... TORA
today .... KYOO

together .... ISSYO
toilet .... BENZYO, OTEARAI
tomorrow .... ASHITA
tongue .... SHITA
tooth .... HA
town .... TOI, MACHI
train .... KISYA
travel .... RYOKO
tree .... KIRI, SUGI, GINGKO,
                HINOKI, LOQUAT
true .... HONTOO
Tuesday .... KAYOOBI
two .... NI
typhoon .... TAIFUU
umbrella .... AMA-GASA
uncle .... OJI, OJISAN
understand .... WAKARU,
                    WAKARIMASU
university .... DAIGAKU
US 3rd-generation ..... SANSEI
useless .... DAME
usually .... TAITEE, TAITEI
vacation .... YASUMI
varnish .... RHUS
vegetable .... YASAI
vegetable/fruit store
                         YAOYA
vehicle, drawn .... RICKSHA
verse .... HAIKU, HOKKU
very .... TOTEMO
village .... MURA
violet/purple .... MURASAKI
volcano .... UNZEN, ASOSAN,
      FUJI(YAMA), ASAMA(YAMA)
wait .... MATSU, MATTE,
                   MACHIMASU
walk .... ARUKU
walking stick .... WHANGEE
warehouse .... HONG
warm .... ATTAKAI
warplane .... ZERO
warrior .... SAMURAI
water, cold .... MIZU
water, hot .... OYU
watermelon .... SUIKA
way of the warrior
                       BUSHIDO
weather .... TENKOO
weather, good .... TENKI
Wednesday .... SUIYOOBI
week .... SYUUKAN
weight .... MO, RIN, SHI,
                        CATTY
west .... NISHI
what .... NANI
what time .... NANJI
where .... DOKO
which .... DORE
whisky .... NIKKA, SUNTORY
white .... SHIROI
who .... DARE

wife .... KANAI, OKUSAN
wind .... MONSOON
window .... MADO
wine .... SAKE, SHOCHU
winter .... FUYU
wisteria .... FUJI
woman .... ONNA
wood oil .... TUNG
wooden shoes .... GETA
work .... SIGOTO
wrestler's foot exercise
                         SHIKO
wrestling .... SUMO
write .... KAKU, KAITE
writer .... KAGAWA
writing ...... KANA, KATAKANA
year .... NEN
yeast .... KOJI
yellow .... KIIROI
yes .... HAI
yesterday .... KINO
you .... ANATA
young .... WAKAI
zaibatsu (family business
      combines) .... MITSUI,
        YASUDA, SUMITOMO
zero .... REI, MARU
zither .... KOTO
jape ...... FOOL, GIBE, JEER, JOKE,
                 MOCK, TRICK
japery .... RIBALDRY
Japheth's brother .... HAM, SHEM
    father .... NOAH
japonica .... SHRUB, QUINCE,
                 CAMELLIA
jar .... JOG, JUG, URN, EWER,
    JOLT, OLLA, BANGA, CLASH,
    CROCK, CRUSE, GRATE,
    SHAKE, SHOCK, STEEN,
    GOGLET, HYDRIA, RATTLE,
    AMPHORA, GURGLET,
    HUMIDOR, TERRINE, VIBRATE
    bell-shaped .... CLOCHE
    druggist's .... GALLIPOT
    earlike projection .... LUG
    porcelain .... POTICHE
jara .... PALM
jardiniere .... POT, URN, BOWL,
                 VASE, STAND
jarfly .... CICADA
jargon ...... CANT, ARGOT, LINGO,
    SLANG, DRIVEL, PATOIS,
    PATTER, SHELTA, ZIRCON,
    DIALECT, GIBBERISH,
    ABRACADABRA
jarl .... NOBLEMAN, CHIEFTAIN
jasmine .... BELA, JESSAMY,
    GARDENIA, JESSAMINE
Jason, father of .... AESON
    men of .... ARGONAUTS
    quest of .... GOLDEN FLEECE

ship of .... ARGO
sorceress who helped
.... MEDEA
uncle of .... PELIAS
wife of .... MEDEA, CREUSA
jasper .... MICA, PARK, QUARTZ
jaundice .... HATE, RANCOR,
ICTERUS, PREJUDICE
cause of .... ENVY, JEALOUSY
relating to .... ICTERIC
jaundiced .... BIASED, YELLOW
eye .... JEALOUSY
jaunt .... SALLY, EXCURSION,
ESCAPADE, (SIDE)TRIP
jaunty .... GAY, AIRY, CHIC,
COCKY, PERKY, SMART,
DAPPER, MODISH, RAKISH,
SPRUCE, STYLISH, DEBONAIR
Java .... HOOD, COFFEE, ISLAND,
CHICKEN
capital of .... JAKARTA
island .... MADURA
Javanese .... SUNDANESE,
INDONESIAN
almond .... KANARI
animal .... TELEDU
bat .... KALON
carriage .... SADO
city .... KEDIRI, MALANG,
MADIUN, BANDUNG,
SEMARANG, SURABAYA
civet .... DEDES, RASSE
cotton .... KAPOK
language .... KAVI, KAWI
man .... PITHECANTHROPUS
measure .... PALEN
mountain .... AMAT
ox .... BANTENG
pepper .... CUBEB
plum .... JAMAN, LOMBOY,
JAMBOOL
port .... TEGAL
rhinoceros .... BADAK
silk .... IKAT
skunk .... TELEDU
tree .... UPAS, KAPOK,
ANTIAR(IN)
upas .... ANTIAR
village .... DESSA
volcano .... GEDE, RAUNG,
SEMERU
weight ..... AMAT, HOEN, TALI,
WANG, PICUL
javelin ...... DART, LANCE, SHAFT,
SPEAR, JER(R)ID, ASSEGAI,
HARPOON, HURLBAT,
JER(R)EED
throwing device .... AMENTA
jaw ...... MAW, CHAP, CHAT, CHOP,
JOWL, MANDIBLE
angle of .... GONION

combining form
.... GNATHOUS
cover .... GUM(S)
device with .... VISE
flesh .... GILL
lower .... CHIN, GONION,
MANDIBLE
muscle .... MASSETER
of the .... GNATHIC
slang .... TALK, SCOLD
upper .... MAXILLA
without .... AGNATHIC
jawbone .... JOWL, MAXILLA
jawbreaker .... CANDY
in boxing .... HAYMAKER
jay .... PIE, CROW, JACKSON,
CHATTERBOX
bird like a .... MOTMOT
talk .... CHATTER
Jayhawk state .... KANSAS
Jayne's man .... STEVE
jazerant .... ARMOR
jazz .... BOP, BLUES, SWING,
(BE)POP, RAG(TIME),
BOOGIEWOOGIE
composer .... (DUKE)
ELLINGTON
dance .... SHIMMY
ensemble/group .... COMBO
fan .... HEPCAT, JITTERBUG
fan jargon .... JIVE
form .... BOP
music .... SWING
singing .... SCAT
slang .... NONSENSE
style of .... DIXIELAND
time .... STOMP
Jazzman Getz .... STAN
jealous ...... ENVIOUS, JAUNDICED,
GREEN(EYED)
jeans .... LEVIS, DENIMS,
OVERALLS, TROUSERS
material .... DENIM
Jebel Musa .... MOUNTAIN OF
MOSES
believed to be .... MOUNT
SINAI
jeep .... PEEP
jeer .... BOO, GIBE, HOOT, JAPE,
JEST, JIBE, MOCK, FLOUT,
SCOFF, SNEER, TAUNT,
DERIDE, CATCALL, SARCASM
jeers .... TACKLE
Jeeves, boss of .... BERTIE
WOOSTER
creator of .... WODEHOUSE
position of .... BUTLER
Jefferson's (President) home
.... MONTICELLO
Jeffries, prize-fighter .... JIM
Jehovah .... GOD, JAH, YAHVE(H),

YAHWE(H), (THE)LORD
prophet of .... ELIAS
Jehovah's Witnesses founder
.... RUSSELL
jejune .... DRY, ARID, DULL, FLAT,
BANAL, STALE, BARREN,
INSIPID
Jekyll's (Dr.) alter ego
.... (MR.)HYDE
jell .... SET, CONGEAL, SOLIDIFY
jellied gasoline .... NAPALM
jelly .... JAM, ASPIC, SPREAD,
DESSERT, PRESERVES
animal .... GELATINE
delicacy/clear .... ASPIC
doughnut .... BISMARK
fruit .... JAM, GUAVA
like substance .... GEL,
COLLOID, GELATIN
material .... CURRANT
petroleum .... VASELINE
vegetable .... PECTIN
jellybean .... CANDY
jellyfish .... MEDUSA, ACALEPH,
AURELIA, HYDROZOAN, SEA
NETTLE
disk .... PILEUS
stinging cell ..... NEMATOCYST
jellyroll .... CAKE
jennet .... ASS, HORSE, DONKEY
Jenny, singer .... LIND, WREN
jeopardize .... RISK, IMPERIL,
ENDANGER
jeopardy .... RISK, PERIL,
DANGER, HAZARD
jerboa .... RODENT, GERBIL(LE)
jeremiad .... WOE, TALE,
LAMENT(ATION)
Jeremiah's scribe .... BARUCH
Jericho's betrayer .... RAHAB
jerk .... BOB, BEEF, FLIP, JUMP,
MEAT, PULL, SNAP, YANK,
HITCH, TWEAK, TWIST,
TWITCH, SODA MAN
jerkin .... COAT, VEST, JACKET
Jerry .... HUN, GERMAN
actor-comedian .... LEWIS
Jersey .... CLOTH, SHIRT, CATTLE,
SINGLET, SWEATER
Jerusalem .... ARIEL, SALEM,
(HOLY)CITY
artichoke .... GIRASOL(E)
captor of .... SALADIN
hill/mount .... SION, ZION
mosque .... OMAR
oak .... AMBROSE
pool .... BETHESDA
ridge .... OLIVET
spring .... SILOAM
stream .... KEDRON
theater .... KHAN

thorn tree .... RETAMA
Jespersen's language .... IDO
jess .... LEASH, STRAP
user of .... FALCON(ER)
jest .... GAG, PUN, WIT, JAPE, JEER,
JIBE, JOKE, MOCK, QUIP,
SALLY, BANTER, TRIFLE,
BADINAGE, RAILLERY
jester .... WAG, FOOL, MIME,
ZANY, CLOWN, JOKER,
GAGMAN, BUFFOON, GOLIARD,
COMEDIAN
cap of .... COXCOMB,
COCKSCOMB
garment of .... MOTLEY
Jesuit .... CASUIST, SCHEMER
order founder .... LOYOLA
saint .... REGIS
Jesus .... LOGOS, SAVIO(U)R
agony and suffering
.... PASSION
betrayer of .... JUDAS ISCARIOT
birthplace of .... BETHLEHEM
Christ, _____ .... SUPERSTAR
life's event .... MYSTERY
monogram .... IHS
of _____ .... NAZARETH
sayings of .... LOGIA
jet .... EBON(Y), GUSH, SPEW,
BLACK, RAVEN, SPOUT,
SPRAY, SPURT, NOZZLE,
SQUIRT, STREAM, LIGNITE
boom .... SONIC
engine .... TURBO PROP
engine housing .... POD
fast .... SST
follower .... SET
plane .... SABRE
jetsam .... LAGAN, LIGAN,
LAGEND, JETTISON
jettison .... JETSAM, DISCARD
jetty .... MOLE, PIER, BLACK,
WHARF, STARLING
jeu .... GAME
de mots .... PUN
Jew ...... TOBIT, HEBREW, JUDEAN,
SEMITE, ISRAELITE
born in Israel .... SABRA
legendary .... GOLEM
not a .... GOI, GOY(IM),
GENTILE
pseudo-Christian
.... MARRANO
Shakespearean .... TUBAL
jewel .... GEM, NAIF, OPAL, BIJOU,
STONE, TRINKET, BRILLIANT
Biblical .... BDELLIUM
colorful .... RED CORAL
setting .... PAVE, BEZEL,
MOUNT(ING)
jeweler's glass .... LOUPE

weight/unit ..... CARAT, KARAT
jewelry .... ICE, QUOIN, JEWELS,
BIJOUTERIE
artificial .... PASTE, STRASS
expert .... LAPIDARY,
APPRAISER, GEMOLOGIST
item .... PIN, TIARA, BROOCH,
DIADEM, (EAR)RING, PENDANT,
TRINKET, BRACELET,
NECKLACE
making material .... GEM,
TOPAZ, ORMOLU, OROIDE,
TOMBAC(K), AMETHYST,
CORUNDUM
set of .... PARURE
jewels, adorn with .... BEGEM
collectively .... JEWELRY
jewelweed .... CELANDINE,
IMPATIENS
Jewett, writer .... SARAH
jewfish ...... BASS, MERO, TARPON
Jewish .... HEBREW, JUDAIC,
JUDEAN, YIDDISH
ascetic .... ESSENE
benediction .... SHEMA
bread .... MATZOS, CHALLAH,
MATZOTH
bread roll .... BAGEL
breastplate gem .... LIGURE,
SARDIUS
bride .... KALLAH
calendar month ...... AB, ABIB,
ADAR, ELUL, IYAR, (ZIF),
NISAN, SIVAN, TEBET, KISLEV,
SHEBAT, TAMMUZ, TISHRI,
CHESHVAN
cantor .... CHAZ(Z)AN
Christians .... DIASPORA
cleric .... RABBI
commentaries on Scriptures
.... MIDRASH
court .... SANHEDRIN
day .... YOM
Day of Atonement .... YOM
KIPPUR
day of preparation ..... FRIDAY
demon .... ASMODEUS
Feast of Lots .... PURIM
festival .... PURIM, SEDER
Festival of Tabernacles
.... SUCCOTH, SUKKOTH
high priest .... ELI, EZRA
holiday .... PURIM, PESACH,
SUCCOS, PASSOVER, YOM
KIPPUR
Holy of Holies .... ORACLE
language .... HEBREW, YIDDISH
law .... TORAH, TALMUD
liturgy's first word ..... SHEMA
marriage broker
.... SCHATCHEN

measure .... SEAH
month, extra .... VEADAR
New Year .... ROSH
HASHANAH, ROSH HASHONA
pancake .... LATKE
Passover .... PESACH
"penicillin" .... CHICKEN SOUP
Pentecost .... SABUOTH
people ...... SION, ZION, ISRAEL
philosophy .... CABALA
prayer book .... MAHZOR,
SIDDUR
priest's girdle .... ABNET
priest's vestment .... EPHOD
quarter .... GHETTO
ram's horn .... SHOFAR
religion .... JUDAISM
religious party composed of
priests .... SADDUCEES
religious party during the
times of Jesus
.... PHARISEES
religious service .... HALLEL
scarf .... TALLIT(H)
scholar .... RAB(BI)
school .... CHEDER, YESHIVA
scribe .... MASORITE
sect member .... PHARISEE,
SADDUCEE
seminary .... YESHIVA
seventh day of week
.... SABBATH
skullcap .... YAMILKE,
YARMELKE, YARMULKE
slang .... YIDDISH
spices .... STACTES
teacher .... RAB(BI), SCRIBE
temple builder .... MICAH,
SOLOMON
title of honor .... RAB, GAON
trumpet ..... SHOFAR, SHOPHAR
undergarment .... TALLITH
vestment .... EPHOD
weight .... OMER, GERAH
Jews' dispersion .... DIASPORA
cloak .... GABARDINE
evensong .... MINHAN
harp .... CREMBALUM
massacre .... POGROM
of the .... JUDAIC
savior .... MORDECAI
section of city .... GHETTO
Jezebel .... VIRAGO
describing .... EVIL, WICKED
husband of .... AHAB
victim of .... NABOTH
jib .... SHY, BALK, BOOM, SAIL,
SPAR, SIDLE, START
jibe .... FIT, RIB, JEST, JEER,
AGREE, SCOFF, TAUNT
jiffy .... TRICE, MOMENT, SECOND,

jig .... INSTANT, DANCE, GIGUE, FISHHOOK
jigger ...... CUP, FLEA, SAIL, SHOT, TICK, CHIGOE, TACKLE
jiggle .... JERK, ROCK, TEETER
jihad .... CRUSADE, HOLY WAR
jill .... GIRL, SWEETHEART
jilt ...... DUMP, REJECT, BOOT OUT, CAST OFF
jilted .... SENT PACKING, GIVEN THE AIR
Jim Crow .... NEGRO
jimjams .... JITTERS
jimmy .... PRY, JACK, LEVER, (CROW)BAR
Jimmy, pantomimist .... SAVO
tennis player .... CONNORS
jimson ...... DATURA, STINKWEED, THORN APPLE
jingal .... CANNON, MUSKET
jingle .... CLINK, DITTY, VERSE, TINKLE, DOGGEREL
jingo .... RADICAL, WARRIOR, CHAUVINIST, MILITARIST
jingoism .... MILITARISM
jinks .... PRANKS, HORSEPLAY
jinn(i) .... DEMON, GENIE
jinrikisha .... RICKSHA(W)
Jinsen .... CHEMULPHO
jinx .... HEX, CURSE, HOODOO, BAD LUCK, EVIL EYE
personification of .... JONAH
slang .... WHAMMY
jipjapa hat .... PANAMA
jitney .... BUS, NICKEL
jitter .... FIDGET, TWITCH
jitters .... NERVES, DITHERS, HYSTERIA, NERVOUSNESS
the .... CREEPS, SHAKES, FIDGETS, JIMJAMS, WILLIES, (BIG)SCARE, HEEBIE-JEEBIES
jittery .... EDGY, JUMPY, ON EDGE, SCARED, NERVOUS
jiujutsu .... JUDO
jivatma .... EGO, ATMAN
jive .... JAZZ
Joan of Arc .... PUCELLE
_____ of Orleans .... MAID
scene of triumph .... ORLEANS
job ...... DUTY, LINE, POST, STINT, TASK, WORK, CHARE, CHORE, CALLING, POSITION, OCCUPATION
at Disney Studios .... ANIMATING
choice .... PLUM
do inferior .... SCAMP
easy .... SNAP, SINECURE
opening .... VACANCY
permanence .... TENURE
Job's comforter .... BILDAD,

ELIHU, ZOPHAR
jockey ...... CHEAT, RACER, RIDER, TRICK, MANEUVER
aid of .... CROP
famous .... AVILA, BAEZA, SANDE, SLOAN, ARCARO, BROOKS, DODSON, CAUTHEN, CRUGUET, HARTACK, MEHRTENS, TURCOTTE, SHOEMAKER
uniform .... SILKS, COLORS
woman .... CRUMP, RUBIN, KUSNER
jocko .... CHIMP, MONKEY
jocose .... DROLL, MERRY, WITTY, PLAYFUL, FACETIOUS
jocular .... WITTY, JESTING, WAGGISH, HUMOROUS, FACETIOUS
jocund .... GAY, AIRY, GENIAL
Jodhpur .... MARWAR
jodhpurs .... BREECHES
joe .... SWEETHEART
Joel's follower .... AMOS
joey .... PAL, KANGAROO
jog .... TROT, AMBLE, SHAKE, JIGGLE, REMIND
jogging suits .... SWEATS
John .... AGAR, DALY, DREW, ALDEN, KEATS, LOCKE, PAYNE, SAXON, WAYNE, CALVIN, LENNON, GILBERT, IRELAND, BARRYMORE
Birch society founder .... WELCH
Brown's Body author .... BENET
Bull .... ENGLAND, ENGLISHMAN
Dory .... FISH
Dos _____ .... PASSOS
Dos Passos novel .... MANHATTAN TRANSFER
father of disciple ..... ZEBEDEE
Hancock .... SIGNATURE
Irish .... IAN
_____ Jones .... PAUL
Paul's land .... POL
Silver's forte .... SKULDUGGERY
Smith's savior .... POCAHONTAS
the Baptist's father .... ZECHARIAH
the Baptist's mother .... ELIZABETH
unknown .... DOE
johnnie .... BOY, FOP, MAN, DANDY, LOTHARIO
Johnny .... CASH, CARSON
johnny jumper .... PANSY,

VIOLET
johnnycake .... PONE, CORNBREAD
Johnson (Mrs.), hunter ...... OSA
U.S. President .... ANDREW, LYNDON
joie de vivre .... ELAN
join ...... ADD, ABUT, LINK, MELD, WELD, YOKE, ENTER, MERGE, UNITE, ENROLL, FASTEN, RABBET, SOLDER, SPLICE, COMBINE, CONNECT, MORTISE, COALESCE
a cause .... ENLIST
corners .... MITER, MITRE
in the chorus .... SING
in wedlock .... MARRY
the colors .... ENLIST
together .... FUSE
joiner .... ENLISTEE, FOLLOWER
joint ...... HIP, KNEE, LINK, SEAM, ANKLE, ELBOW, NEXUS, TENON, RABBET, TOGGLE, JUNCTURE
arm's .... ELBOW, WRIST
carpenter's .... MITER, MITRE
cavity .... BURSA
deposit .... TOPHUS
door's .... HINGE
finger .... KNUCKLE
fluid .... SEROSITY
grass .... CULM
out of .... DISLOCATED
overlapping .... SHIPLAP
part .... TENON, TISSUE, CARTILAGE, LIGAMENTS
partial dislocation of .... SUBLUXATION
piping/tubing .... ELL
put out of .... LUXATE, DISLOCATE
rheumatic pain ...... LUMBAGO, ARTHRITIS
slang .... DIVE, REEFER, SALOON, RESTAURANT
stem .... NODE
tighten .... STEM
type of .... HINGE, PIVOT, ELLIPSOIDAL, BALL AND SOCKET
jointly .... TOGETHER, HAND IN HAND
joist .... BEAM
joke .... GAG, KID, PUN, RIB, DIDO, HOAX, JAPE, JEST, JOSH, QUIP, TWIT, PRANK, SALLY, SPOOF, WAGGERY, WISECRACK, WITTICISM
joker ...... GAG, WAG, WIT, CARD, FLOP, CLOWN, CUTUP, JESTER, BUFFOON, FARCEUR
in a bill, etc. .... RIDER

jollity .... FUN, MIRTH, GAIETY
jolly .... GAY, BOAT, YAWL,
    MERRY, SKIFF, JOVIAL,
    JOYOUS, CONVIVIAL
  season .... YULE
Jolson, Al .... ASA
jolt ...... JAR, BUMP, JERK, SHAKE,
    SHOCK, SURPRISE
Jonah (Jonas) .... PROPHET
  to all people .... JINX, BAD
    LUCK
Jonas, polio vaccine developer
  .... SALK
Jonathan .... APPLE
  brother of .... ABINADAB,
    MALCHISHUA
  father of .... SAUL
Jones, bandleader .... SPIKE
  spirit of sea .... DAVY
jongleur .... MINSTREL
jonquil .... NARCISSUS
Joplin, pop singer .... JANIS
Jordan .... POT, EDOM, MOAB,
    RIVER, KINGDOM
  capital of .... AMMAN
  city/town .... AJLUN, AQABA,
    IRBID, PETRA, JARASH, ES
    SALT, MADABA, NABLUS, EL
    KARAK, EZ ZARKA
  gulf .... AQABA
  king .... HUSSEIN
  language .... ARABIC
  monetary unit .... DINAR
  mountain .... EBAL, NEBO,
    RAMM, GILEAD
  peninsula .... EL LISAN
  port .... AQABA
  river .... ZARQA, JORDAN
  ruins .... PETRA
  sea .... DEAD
  valley .... GHOR
Joseph .... HABIT
  brother of .... BENJAMIN
  Egyptian master of
  .... POTIPHAR
  Egyptian name of
  .... ZAPENATH PANEAH
  father of .... JACOB, ISRAEL
  grandson of ...... EZER, ELEAD,
    ASRIEL, BERIAH, MACHIR
  hometown of .... ARIMATHEA
  mother of .... RACHEL
  of Nazareth's wife ...... MARY
  wife of .... ASENATH
josh .... KID, RAG, RIB, JEST,
    TEASE, BANTER
Joshua, father of .... NUN
  people of .... ISRAELITES
  predecessor of .... MOSES
  tree .... YUCCA
Josip Broz .... TITO, DICTATOR

joss .... IDOL
  house .... TEMPLE
jostle .... ELBOW, NUDGE, HUSTLE,
    SHOVE, BUFFET
jot .... BIT, IOTA, MITE, MOTE,
    NOTE, WHIT, MINIM, POINT,
    SPECK, TITTLE, PARTICLE
jota .... DANCE
jotting .... MEMO, NOTE
Jotun(n) .... GIANT
joule, part of .... ERG
jounce .... JOLT, SHAKE
journal .... DIARY, ANNALS,
    RECORD, DAYBOOK,
    LOGBOOK, MAGAZINE,
    REGISTER, NEWSPAPER
journalism .... PRESS, FOURTH
    ESTATE
journalist .... EDITOR, SCRIBE,
    DIARIST, NEWSMAN,
    REPORTER, PUBLICIST,
    NEWSPAPERMAN
  abolitionist 1852 ..... REDPATH
  budding .... CUB, COPYBOY
  kind of .... LEGMAN, STRINGER
  Runyon .... DAMON
journey .... TREK, TRIP, TOUR,
    JUNKET, SAFARI, TRAVEL
  end of .... HOMESTRETCH
  extended .... ODYSSEY
  for adventure .... QUEST
  forced .... EXODUS, FLIGHT,
    HEGIRA
  man .... TRAVEL AGENT
  of a .... VIATIC(AL)
  of solon abroad .... JUNKET
  over snow .... MUSH
  part of/stage of .... LEG
  stopping place ..... INN, OASIS,
    SERAI, STAGE, IMARET
  to shrine .... PILGRIMAGE
  water .... VOYAGE, PASSAGE
journeyman .... JOBBER, WORKER
joust .... BOUT, TILT, COMBAT,
    TOURNEY, TOURNAMENT
jousting arena .... LISTS
Jove .... JUPITER
jovial .... GAY, JOLLY, MERRY,
    GENIAL, CORDIAL
  friar .... TUCK
jowl .... CHAP, CHOP, CHEEK,
    DEWLAP, WATTLE, JAW(BONE)
joy .... GLEE, BLISS, DELIGHT,
    ECSTASY, ELATION, RAPTURE
  ride, of a sort .... SPIN
  song of .... CAROL, P(A)EAN
Joy Adamson's pet .... ELSA
joyful in triumph ...... JUBILANT
joyous .... GAY, GLAD, MERRY,
    RIANT, BLITHE, FESTAL,
    FESTIVE

jube .... LOFT, GALLERY
jubilee .... ANNIVERSARY
juca .... MANIOC, CASSAVA
Judah, brother of .... LEVI,
    REUBEN, SIMEON, ZEBULUN,
    ISSACHAR
  capital of .... JERUSALEM
  city of .... HEBRON, ADAR,
    AMAN, ENAM, LACHISH, BEER-
    SHEBA
  daughter-in-law of ..... TAMAR
  father of .... JACOB, ISRAEL
  governor of .... GEDALIAH
  king of ..... ASA, AHAZ, AMON,
    JOASH, ABIJAM, JOSIAH,
    JOTHAM, UZZIAH, AHAZIAH,
    ZEDEKIAH, AMAZIAH,
    JEHORAM, HEZEKIAH,
    JEHOAHAZ, MANASSEH,
    REHOBOAM, JEHOIACHIN,
    JEHOSHAPHAT
  mother of .... LEAH
  queen of .... ATHALIAH
  ruling dynasty of ..... DAVIDIC
  sister of .... DINAH
  son of .... ER, ONAN, PEREZ,
    ZERAH, SHELAH
  tree of .... REDBUD
  vassal state of .... EDOM
  wife of .... BATHSHUA
Judaism .... HEBRAISM
  convert to .... GER
  hymn of praise .... KADDISH
  of/pertaining to .... JUDAIC
  scriptures .... TORA(H)
Judas .... APOSTLE, BETRAYER
  _____ .... ISCARIOT,
    BARSABBAS, MACCABEUS
  brother of .... JAMES, JESUS,
    SIMON
  Iscariot's death place
  .... FIELD OF BLOOD
  motive for betrayal
  .... GREED, THIRTY PIECES
    SILVER
  replacement .... MATTHIAS
  symbol of treachery
  .... (DEADLY) KISS
  Maccabeus' brother .... JOHN,
    SIMON, ELEAZAR, JONATHAN
  father .... MATTATHIAS
  or _____, apostle of Jesus
  .... THADDAEUS
  tree .... REDBUD
Judea procurator .... PILATE
  vale .... ELAH
judge .... TRY, DEEM, (A)EDILE,
    CRITIC, UMPIRE, ARBITER,
    REFEREE, DELIVERER,
    ARBITRATOR
  biblical .... ELI, EHUD, ELON,

JAIR, TOLA, ABDON, IBZAN, GIDEON, SAMSON, DEBORAH, OTHNIEL, SHAMGAR, JEPHTHAH
court .... TRIER
of lower world .... MINOS, AEACUS
quality/worth .... APPRAISE
judge's assistant .... ASSESSOR
bench .... BANC, TRIBUNAL
challenge .... RECUSE
chamber .... CAMERA
decision .... VERDICT, SENTENCE
lower rank .... PUISNE
order .... WRIT, SUBPOENA, INJUNCTION
robe .... GOWN
room .... CHAMBER
seat .... BANC, BENCH
symbol of authority .... MACE, GAVEL
judges, collectively .... BENCH, JUDICIARY
Rabelais' satirical term for .... FURRY LAWCATS
said of .... PUISNE
judgment .... DOOM, VIEW, ARRET, AWARD, SENSE, DECREE, RULING, FINDING, OPINION, VERDICT, DECISION, SENTENCE
against property .... IN REM
suspension of .... EPOCHE
Judgment Day ...... DOOM(SDAY)
judicial assembly .... COURT
inquiry .... INQUEST
mallet .... GAVEL
opinions .... DICTA
order .... WRIT
wear .... ROBE
writ of execution .... ELEGIT
judicious .... WISE, SOUND, POLITIC, PRUDENT
Judith, the _____ supreme heroine .... APOCRYPHA'S
victim of .... HOLOFERNES
judo .... JUJITSU
Judy's husband .... PUNCH
jug .... URN, EWER, TOBY, BOTTLE, FLAGON, RANTER, PITCHER, THERMOS
slang .... JAIL
jugal .... MALAR
Juggernaut .... KRISHNA
incarnation .... VISHNU
juggle .... RIG, MANIPULATE
juggler .... CHEATER, MANIPULATOR
juice .... JUS, SAP, MUST, RHOB, STUM, FLUID, LIQUID, ESSENCE

meat .... GRAVY, DRIPPING
plant/tree .... SAP, LATEX, MANNA, CHICLE
slang .... GAS, OIL, ELECTRICITY
juicy .... RACY, RICH, MOIST, TASTY, SUCCULENT
Juilliard school degree .... DMUS
specialty .... MUSIC
jujitsu/jiujutsu .... JUDO
juju .... CHARM, TABOO, FETISH
jujube .... BER, ELB, JELLY, LOZENGE
jukebox .... PHONOGRAPH
julep .... DRINK
ingredient .... MINT, SYRUP, BRANDY
Jules Verne's captain .... NEMO
vessel .... NAUTILUS
Julia Ward .... HOWE
Juliana's (Queen) domain .... NETHERLANDS
house .... ORANGE
mother .... WILHELMINA
people .... DUTCH
spouse .... BERNHARD
julienne .... SOUP
cut .... (THIN) STRIPS
Juliet's confessor .... (FRIAR) LAURENCE
cousin .... TYBALT
family (name) .... CAPULET
love .... ROMEO
suitor .... PARIS
July 15, Roman calendar .... IDES, IDUS, IDIBUS
4th day .... INDEPENDENCE
7th day of ..... NONAS, NONES, NONIS
jumble .... MIX, HASH, MESS, COOKY, LITTER, MEDLEY, MUDDLE, CLUTTER, MISHMASH
jumbled type .... PI(E)
jumbo .... HUGE, LARGE, ELEPHANT
jump ...... BOB, HOP, BUCK, JERK, LEAP, SKIP, BOUND, START, VAULT, BOUNCE, SPRING
about .... FRISK, PRANCE
ahead, a .... ONE UP
in music .... SALTO
playful .... CAPER, FRISK, CAVORT, PRANCE
the track .... DERAIL
jumper ...... PAWL, SLED, BLOUSE, JACKET, ROMPER
accessory of .... POLE
jumping .... LEAPING, SALTANT
amphibian .... FROG, TOAD
animal .... GOAT, JERBOA, KANGAROO

dance .... JIG
insect .... FLEA, LOCUST, GRASSHOPPER
stick .... POGO
jumpy ...... EDGY, TENSE, JITTERY, NERVOUS, SKITTISH
junco .... FINCH, SNOWBIRD
junction .... UNION, MEETING, CROSSING
line .... SEAM
juncture ...... JOINT, POINT, CRISIS
June bug .... DOR, BEETLE, FIGEATER
event ..... WEDDING, MARRIAGE
14, in America ...... FLAG DAY
honorees .... DADS
promise .... I DO
6, 1944 .... D-DAY
13, Roman calendar ...... IDES
21 .... SOLSTICE
juneberry .... SHADBUSH
jungfrau .... ALPS
jungle .... WILDERNESS
fever .... MALARIA
hero .... TARZAN
Jungle Book's wolf .... AKELA
Jungles a la Kipling ...... RUKHS
junior .... CADET, PUISNE, YOUNGER
leaguer .... DEB
juniper .... CADE, EZEL, CEDAR, GORSE, RETEM, SHRUB, SAVIN(E), HACKMATAK
junk .... BOAT, SCRAP, STUFF, TRASH, DISCARD, RUBBISH
jalopy .... CRATE
part .... SAIL
junker .... GERMAN, PRUSSIAN
junket .... FEAST, PICNIC, JOURNEY, EXCURSION
junkie ...... ADDICT, (DOPE) FIEND
junkman .... SCRAPPER
Juno .... HERA, GODDESS
husband of .... JUPITER
messenger of .... IRIS
junta .... GROUP, CLIQUE, COUNCIL, ASSEMBLY
junto .... CABAL, CLIQUE
Jupiter .... JOVE, ZEUS, PLANET
consort of .... HERA, JUNO
daughter .... HEBE, MINERVA
has twelve .... MOONS
moon of .... IO, EUROPA, CALLISTO, GANYMEDE
mother of .... OPS
nurse of .... GOAT
son of .... ARCAS, CASTER, HERMES, TANTALUS, HEPHAETUS
temple .... CAPITOL
jupon .... TUNIC, JACKET

Jurassic, strata below ...... TRIAS
system strata .... LIAS
jurisdiction .... SOC, SOKE,
VENUE, DOMAIN, SPHERE,
CONTROL, BAILIWICK
bishop's .... SEE
jurisprudence .... LAW
jurist .... HAND, JUDGE, TANEY
juror ...... TALESMAN, VENIREMAN
challenge a .... RECUSE
guard of .... BAILIFF
jurors, collectively .... PANEL
one of the .... POLL
jury .... PANEL
finding of .... VERDICT
fixer .... SUBORNER
head .... FOREMAN
illegally influence
.... EMBRACE
kind of .... PETIT, GRAND
member .... TALESMAN
-rig .... IMPROVISE
-rigged .... MAKESHIFT
summons to .... VENIRE
jus .... LAW, GRAVE, JUICE
just .... FAIR, ONLY, LEGAL,
MORAL, VALID, BARELY,

HONEST, SIMPLY, UPRIGHT,
EQUITABLE, IMPARTIAL,
RIGHTEOUS
a touch .... TRACE
as said .... SIC
average .... SO-SO
beginning .... INCIPIENT
begun .... INCHOATE
clear of bottom .... ATRIP,
AWEIGH
right .... JAKE
think! .... IMAGINE
justice .... EQUITY, FAIRNESS,
JUSTNESS, RIGHTNESS
colloquial .... SQUARE DEAL
symbol .... SCALE(S)
U.S. Supreme Court ...... JAY,
TAFT, BLACK, CHASE, STONE,
TANEY, WHITE, FORTAS,
HUGHES, SCALIA, SOUTER,
THOMAS, VINSON, WARREN,
CARDOZO, KENNEDY, STEVENS,
STEWART, MARSHALL,
BLACKMUN, O'CONNOR,
REHNQUIST
justification .... EXCUSE, REASON,
DEFENSE

justify .... ACQUIT, EXCUSE,
ABSOLVE, WARRANT,
VINDICATE, RATIONALIZE
jut .... ABUT, PROJECT, OVERHANG,
PROTRUDE, STICK OUT
jute .... FIBER, PLANT, BALINE
chief .... HENGIST
cloth .... GUNNY
product .... MAT, ROPE,
BURLAP, (GUNNY)SACK
refuse .... TOW, HURDS
Jutland seaport .... AARHUS
Jutlander .... DANE
jutting land .... CAPE, NESS,
HEADLAND, PROMONTORY
rock .... TOR, CRAG
jutty .... MOLE, PIER, JETTY
Juvenal .... POET, SATIRIST
juvenile .... CHILD, IMMATURE,
YOUTHFUL, INFANTILE,
YOUNG(STER)
book heroine .... OZMA
hero .... ROLLO
story writer .... MILNE, OUIDA,
RAMEE, SEUSS
juxtapose .... NEIGHBOR

K

K, Greek .... KAPPA
Hebrew .... KAPH
in a sequence .... ELEVENTH
assaying .... CARAT
chemistry .... POTASSIUM
chess .... KING
electricity .... CAPACITY
mathematics .... CONSTANT
meteorology .... SMOKE
nautical usage .... KNOT
kabobs .... (ROAST) MEAT
kaddish .... HYMN, PRAYER
kadi .... JUDGE, MAGISTRATE
Kaffir .... CORN, BANTU, FODDER,
INFIDEL, SORGHUM
language .... XOSA
tribe .... ZULU
war club .... KIRI
warriors .... IMPI
kaftan .... ROBE
kago .... LITTER, PALANQUIN
kail .... COLE, KALE
Kailasa temple .... ELLORA
kailyard .... GARDEN
kaiser .... EMPEROR, WILHELM
Biblical .... NOAH
kaka(po) .... PARROT
Kalahari .... DESERT, PLATEAU

nomad .... BUSHMAN
kale .... BROTH, GREENS,
CABBAGE, COLLARD,
BORECOLE, BROCCOLI,
COLE(WORT)
slang .... MONEY
Kalinin .... TVER
kalinite .... ALUM
Kallikaks, the .... JUKES
kalmuck ...... ELEUT(H), MONGOL
kalong .... BAT
kalpak .... CAP
kamerad .... COMRADE
kamsin .... WIND
kanaka .... HAWAIIAN
kanari .... ALMOND
kangaroo .... ROO, JUMPER,
WOLABA, WOLARU, WALLABY,
WALLAROO
court .... MOCK COURT
describing a .... MARSUPIAL
male .... BOOMER
pouch .... MARSUPIUM
rat .... POTOROO
reddish-gray .... EURO
young .... JOEY
Kansan .... JAYHAWKER
famous .... EISENHOWER

Kansas, capital of .... TOPEKA
city/town .... GOVE, HAYS,
DODGE, PRATT, GARDEN,
KANSAS, OAKLEY, OTTAWA,
SALINA, SENECA, ABILENE,
CHANUTE, EMPORIA, LIBERAL,
RUSSELL, SHAWNEE, WICHITA,
ARKANSAS, EL DORADO,
LAWRENCE, CONCORDIA,
MANHATTAN, PITTSBURG,
GREAT BEND, LEAVENWORTH
college .... TABOR, BETHEL,
BETHANY, MARYMOUNT,
MCPHERSON
county ..... FORD, GOVE, RENO,
ALLEN, ELLIS, GEARY, OSAGE,
ROOKS, BARTON, BUTLER,
COWLEY, FINNEY, HARVEY,
SALINE, SUMNER, BOURBON,
DOUGLAS, JOHNSON, LABETTE,
ATCHISON, CRAWFORD,
SEDGWICK, DICKINSON,
MCPHERSON, WYANDOTTE,
LEAVENWORTH
historic site .... EISENHOWER
CENTER, LITTLE HOUSE ON
THE PRAIRIE
lake .... PERRY, POMONA,

WILSON, MILFORD, TORONTO, KANAPOLIS
mountain .... SUNFLOWER
native .... JAYHAWKER
output .... WHEAT
river .... ELK, FALL, OSAGE, KANSAS, PAWNEE, SOLOMON, ARKANSAS, MISSOURI
state bird .... MEADOWLARK
state flower .... SUNFLOWER
state nickname .... JAYHAWKER, SUNFLOWER
state tree .... COTTONWOOD
university .... BAKER, OTTAWA, FRIENDS, WASHBURN
kaolin(e) .... CLAY
Kapek drama .... RUR
kapok .... CEIBA, COTTON
kaput .... FINI, LOST, RUINED, DONE FOR, DEFEATED
Karachi is its capital .... SIND
Karafuto .... SAKHALIN
karakul .... FUR, OVINE, SHEEP
Karelian .... FINN
lake .... SEG, LADOGA
Karenina, ____ .... ANNA
Karloff, actor .... BORIS
Karlovasi citizen .... SAMIAN
Karlovy Vary .... CARLSBAD
karma .... FATE, DESTINY
Karnak city .... THEBES
Kashmir, capital of .... SRINAGAR
claimant of .... INDIA, PAKISTAN
district .... LADAKH
pagoda .... CHORTEN
river .... JHELUM
wool .... CASHMERE
Katanga leader .... TSHOMBE
Katherine, diminutive of .... KAY, KATE, KIT(TY)
Katmandu is capital of .... NEPAL
native .... NEPALI
kauri .... GUM, PINE, RESIN
kava .... SHRUB, PEPPER
Kay Kyser's Kabibble .... ISH
kayak .... CANOE, UMIAK
kayo .... KNOCKOUT
Kazan, movieman .... ELIA
kea .... PARROT
favorite prey of .... SHEEP
Keats .... ODIST
Keats' concern .... URN
name by Shelley ..... ADONAIS
poem .... LAMIA
kedge .... ANCHOR
keek .... SPY, PEEP
keel ...... LIST, SHIP, TILT, BARGE, CAREEN, RUDDLE, LIGHTER
like structure .... CARINA

over ..... UPSET, CAPSIZE, TURN OVER
part .... SKEG
shaped .... CARINATE
without .... RATITE
Keeling Islands .... COCOS
keen .... WAIL, ACUTE, DIRGE, EAGER, SHARP, SMART, ASTUTE, SHREWD, SUBTLE, CUTTING, PUNGENT, INCISIVE, PERCEPTIVE
eyed animal .... CAT, LYNX
keenly perceptive .... SHARP-EYED
keenness .... EDGE, ACUITY
of mind .... ACUMEN
keep .... FORT, HAVE, SAVE, TEND, CASTLE, DETAIN, DONJON, RETAIN, CUSTODY, POSSESS, RESERVE, (WITH)HOLD, LIVELIHOOD
an eye on .... WATCH
at it .... PERSIST, PERSEVERE
company .... HOBNOB, CONSORT
from .... AVOID, DETER
from flying .... GROUND
going .... RUN ON, CONTINUE
house for oneself .... BACH
in mind .... CHERISH
in touch .... WRITE
off .... BAR
one's fingers crossed .... HOPE
out .... BAN, OMIT, (DE)BAR, EXCLUDE
score .... TALLY
secret .... SIT ON
under close observation .... TAIL
under ____ (conceal) .... ONE'S HAT
keeper .... JAILER, GUARD(IAN), CARETAKER, CUSTODIAN, PROTECTOR
concern of .... ZOO
forest .... RANGER, WARDEN
game .... WARDEN
jail .... WARDEN, TURNKEY
museum .... CURATOR
keepers, usually .... FINDERS
keeping .... CARE, CUSTODY
keepsake .... RELIC, TOKEN, MEMENTO, SOUVENIR
keeve .... TUB, VAT, KEIR
kef .... HEMP, NARCOTIC
Kefauver, senator .... ESTES
keg .... TUN, VAT, CADE, CASK, BARREL, FIRKIN
of beer .... GROWLER
open a .... UNHEAD
stopper .... BUNG

water .... BREAKER
kegler .... BOWLER
Keijo .... SEOUL
keir .... VAT
keitloa .... RHINO(CEROS)
Kelantan capital .... KOTA BHARU
kelep .... ANT
Keller, Miss .... HELEN
teacher of .... SULLIVAN
Kelly, performer .... GENE, PATSY, EMMETT
kelp .... ASH, VARIC, WRACK, SEAWEED
derivative .... IODINE
Kemal, Turkish leader .... ATATURK
Kemble, actress .... FANNY
ken .... SEE, LORE, SIGHT, DESCRY, RECOGNIZE
kench .... BIN, BOX
Kenilworth heroine .... AMY
Kennedy Space Center site .... (CAPE) CANAVERAL
kennel ...... PACK, DRAIN, SEWER, GUTTER, DOGHOUSE
sound .... YIP, BARK, HOWL, YELP
keno, game like .... BEANO, BINGO, LOTTO
Kent county seat ...... MAIDSTONE
resort/seaport .... MARGATE
Kentuckian .... LINCOLN
Kentucky capital ...... FRANKFORT
city/town .... ALBANY, BENTON, MURRAY, ASHLAND, PADUCAH, DANVILLE, FORT KNOX, RICHMOND, COVINGTON, HENDERSON, LEXINGTON, GEORGETOWN, LOUISVILLE, BOWLING GREEN, INDEPENDENCE
college .... BEREA, ASBURY, BRESCIA, BELLARMINE
county ..... BELL, BOYD, HART, KNOX, OWEN, PIKE, TODD, BOONE, CLARK, FLOYD, KNOTT, PERRY, BARREN, CARTER, GRAVES, HARDIN, HARLAN, KENTON, LAUREL, WARREN, BULLITT, DAVIESS, FAYETTE, GREENUP, HOPKINS, LETCHER, MADISON, PULASKI, WHITLEY, CAMPBELL, JEFFERSON, MCCRACKEN
Derby winner:
1948 .... CITATION
1955 .... SWAPS
1956 .... NEEDLES
1959 .... TOMY LEE
1965 .... LUCKY DEBONAIR

1973 .... SECRETARIAT
1978 .... AFFIRMED
1980 .... GENUINE RISK
1982 .... GATO DEL SOL
1983 .... SUNNY'S HALO
1984 .... SWALE
Derby winning jockey
.... ERB, YORK, AVILA,
ARCARO, CAUTHEN, VASQUEZ,
TURCOTTE, SHOEMAKER,
DELAHOUSSAYE
event .... DERBY
explorer .... BOONE, JOLIET
honorary title .... COLONEL
lake .... DEWEY, NOLIN,
BARKLEY, BUCKHORN,
FISHTRAP
mountain .... PINE, BLACK
personage .... COLONEL
pride of .... HORSES
river ..... DIX, MUD, RED, OHIO,
POND, SALT, GREEN, BARREN,
CHAPLIN, TENNESSEE,
MISSISSIPPI
state bird .... CARDINAL
state flower .... GOLDENROD
state nickname .... BLUEGRASS
tobacco .... BURLEY
tourist attraction
.... MAMMOTH CAVE, DANIEL
BOONE'S GRAVE, KENTUCKY
DERBY MUSEUM, MARY TODD
LINCOLN HOME
tree .... CHICOT
university .... LOUISVILLE,
MURRAY STATE
Kenya bay ...... WINAM, FORMOSA
capital .... NAIROBI
city/town .... LAMU, THIKA,
KISUMU, KITALE, ELDORET,
MALINDI, MOMBASA, NANYUKI
distance runner .... JIPCHO
freedom .... UHURU
gulf .... KAVIRONDO
island .... PATTA
lake .... NATRON, RUDOLF,
VICTORIA
language .... BANTU, HINDU,
KAMBA, SWAHILI
mascot .... AHMED
monetary unit .... SHILLING
mountain .... ELGON, KENYA
Olympic champ .... TEMU,
KEINO, BIWOTT
president .... (JOMO)
KENYATTA, (DANIEL)ARAP MOI
river .... DAUA, TANA, GALANA
seaport .... MOMBASA
secret society .... MAUMAU
Keos .... ZEA
kepi .... CAP

Kepler, astronomer
.... JOHANNES
keratinous .... HORNY
formation .... HAIR, NAIL
keratosis .... WART
kerchief .... CURCH, SCARF,
MADRAS, BANDAN(N)A,
BABUSHKA
kerf .... NOTCH, CUT(TING)
kermes .... DYE, OAK
kermess .... FAIR, CARNIVAL
Kern show .... SUNNY
kernel ...... PIT, CORE, GIST, PITH,
SEED, GRAIN, HEART, BARREL,
ESSENCE, NUCLEUS,
NUT(MEAT)
combining form .... CARYO,
KARYO
kerosene .... OIL
source of .... COAL,
PETROLEUM
Kerry .... CATTLE, COUNTY
blue .... TERRIER
kestrel .... FALCON, WINDHOVER
ketch .... JACK, SHIP, YAWL
Levantine .... SAIC
ketchup .... SAUCE, CATSUP
ketone .... IRONE, CARONE,
ACETONE, BUTYRONE
Kett, comic strip's .... ETTA
kettle .... BILLY, BOILER,
POT(HOLE), CA(U)LDRON
handle .... BAIL
in the South .... SIROP
part of .... SNOUT
repairer .... TINKER
stand .... TRIVET
kettledrum ...... TIMBAL, TIMPANI,
AT(T)ABAL, TIMPANO
player .... TIMPANIST
kevel .... PEG, CLEAT
key .... CAY, PIN, BOLT, CLEW,
CODE, REEF, TONE, ISLE(T),
PITCH, WEDGE, ANSWER,
CLAVIS, COTTER, ISLAND,
OPENER, SOLUTION
blade of .... WEB
emergency .... PICK
fruit .... SAMARA
notch .... WARD
part .... BIT, PIN, STEM
pertaining to .... TONAL
repairer .... LOCKSMITH
shaped .... URDE, CLECHE
sight over Ft. McHenry
.... THE ROCKETS RED GLARE
signature in music .... FLAT,
SHARP
telegraph .... TAPPER
up .... EXCITE
keyboard .... CLAVIER

instrument (musical)
.... ORGAN, PIANO, SPINET,
CELESTA, CELESTE, CLAVIER,
MELODEON, VIRGINAL
machine .... TELEX,
COMPUTER, LINO(TYPE),
TELETYPE, TYPEWRITER
shaped .... URDE
keyed up .... AGOG, EAGER,
TENSE, EXCITED
keyhole guard .... TAPPET
ridge .... WARD
keynote .... THEME, TONIC
sign .... ISON
keystone .... WEDGE, SAGITTA,
SUPPORT
characters .... COPS
prop .... PIE
Keystone State .... PENNSYLVANIA
State founder .... PENN
keyway .... SLOT
Khachaturian, composer
.... ARAM
khaki color .... DUN
khamsin .... WIND
khan ...... AGA, ALI, INN, CHAM
Khartoum is capital of
.... SUDAN
Khayyam .... OMAR, POET,
TENTMAKER
birthplace .... NISHAPUR
khedive's estate .... DAIRA
Khmer .... CAMBODIAN
temple .... ANGKOR VAT
Khomeni's land .... IRAN
Khrushchev, USSR premier
.... NIKITA
Khufu .... CHEOPS
Kiang .... ONAGER
Kibbee, actor .... GUY
kibbutz .... SETTLEMENT
kibe .... CHILBLAIN
kibitz .... BUTT IN, HORN IN,
MEDDLE, COMMENT
kibitzer .... MEDDLER, ONLOOKER
kibosh .... VETO, SCRAG,
SQUELCH, NONSENSE
kick .... BOOT, GRIPE, KEVEL,
SPURN, STAMP, RECOIL,
THRILL, GRUMBLE,
COMPLAIN(T)
around .... STUDY, ANALYZE
in ...... DIE, PAY, CROAK, PONY
UP
in football .... HACK, PUNT
off .... DIE, BEGIN, START
off device .... TEE
out .... OUST, REMOVE,
DISCARD
up one's heels .... CAVORT
Kickapoo .... INDIAN

kickback .... CUT, BRIBE, PAYOLA, REFUND, REBATE, BACKFIRE
kickup .... ROW, FUSS
kid .... LAD, RIB, GOAT, JOKE, JIVE, JOSH, SUEDE, BANTER, DECEIVE, LEATHER, YOUNGER, ANTELOPE, (Y)EARLING
colloquial .... CHILD
neglected .... RAGAMUFFIN
sailor's .... TUB
slang .... FOOL, TEASE
Kidd, Captain .... PIRATE
kidnap .... SEIZE, ABDUCT, SNATCH, SHANGHAI, SPIRIT AWAY
kidney ...... SORT, GLAND, ORGAN
bean .... BON, PHASEL, HARICOT
combining form .... RENI, RENO, NEPHRO
concretion .... GRAVEL
condition .... NEPHRISM
disease .... NEPHROPATHY
duct .... URETER
of the .... RENAL, NEPHRIC
protein .... RENIN
shaped .... RENIFORM
stone .... JADE, NEPHRITE
kid's tummy .... BREADBASKET
kidskin parchment ...... VELLUM
kier .... VAT
Kierkegaard .... SOREN
Kilauea, goddess of .... PELE
kilderkin .... CASK, BARREL
Kilimanjaro peak .... KIBO
kill .... DO IN, RUIN, SLAY, PURGE, CANCEL, POISON, BUTCHER, DESTROY, DISPATCH, LIQUIDATE, ANNIHILATE
bill .... VETO
by drowning .... NOYADE
by hanging .... STRING UP
by mob action .... LYNCH
by stoning .... LAPIDATE
by suffocation .... BURKE
in printing .... DELE(TE)
in tennis .... SMASH
legally .... EXECUTE
time .... FOOL AROUND
unlawfully .... MURDER, ASSASSINATE
Killarney land .... ERIN
killer .... THUG, SLAYER, MURDERER, CUTTHROAT
hired .... BRAVO, HITMAN, ASSASSIN
of a god .... DEICIDE
political .... ASSASSIN
whale .... NAMU, ORC(A), DOLPHIN, GRAMPUS
killick .... ANCHOR

killing .... FATAL, DEADLY, CARNAGE, SLAUGHTER, STARVATION, ASPHYXIATION
mass .... PURGE, BATTUE, POGROM, CARNAGE, BUTCHERY, GENOCIDE, MASSACRE, ANNIHILATION
mercy .... EUTHANASIA
of a baby .... INFANTICIDE
of a fetus in the womb .... ABORTICIDE
of a king .... REGICIDE
of old men .... SENICIDE
one's mother .... MATRICIDE
one's parent .... PARRICIDE
one's relatives .... FRATRICIDE
oneself intentionally .... SUICIDE
slang .... HIT, SMASH, SUCCESS
killjoy .... DAMPER, SPOILSPORT, WET BLANKET
Kilmer poem .... TREES
poet .... JOYCE
kiln .... O(A)ST, LEER, OVEN, DRIER, DRYER, STOVE, TILER(Y), FURNACE
type of .... SCOVE
kilograms, 100 .... CENTAL, CENTNER, QUINTAL
1,000 .... MILLIER
kiloliter .... STERE
kilt .... TUCK, PLEAT, SKIRT, FILIBEG, PHILIBEG
undergarment .... TREWS
kilter .... ORDER
kiltie .... SCOT(SMAN)
Kim .... NOVAK, O'HARA, HUNTER
friend of .... LAMA
kimono .... ROBE, DRESSING GOWN
sash .... OBI
kin .... SIB(S), FOLKS, FAMILY, SIBLINGS, RELATED, RELATIVE(S), (BLOOD)RELATION
of ave. .... RD.
of rho .... CHI
to Eureka! .... AHA
kind ...... ILK, RACE, SORT, CLASS, GENUS, BENIGN, GENTLE, SPECIES, VARIETY
in .... GOODS, PRODUCE
of .... ALMOST, SOMEWHAT
a .... ALIKE, MEDIOCRE
acid .... FOLIC
act .... RIOT
agent .... UNDERCOVER
athletic event .... INTERCOLLEGIATE
azole .... IMID
badge .... MERIT

bank ...... LEFT, NOTE, ROLL, MONEY, RIVER
bee .... DRONE, HONEY, QUEEN
blow .... RABBIT PUNCH, BELOW THE BELT
blue .... SKY, BABY, NAVY, POWDER
board or box .... IDIOT
board or trap .... CLAP
body .... STUDENT
book .... (TELE)PHONE
bracelet ...... CHARM, TENNIS
brush or comb .... HAIR
buffalo .... CAPE
cake .... SHORT, GRIDDLE, WEDDING
candy .... CANE, LIFESAVER
case or flight .... TEST
cat .... FAT
chair .... EASY, LOUNGE, ELECTRIC, RECLINING
chest .... HOPE
circle .... INNER
clam .... STEAMER
club .... GLEE, GOLF
cry .... FAR
curve .... ESS
cut .... SHORT
daisy .... SHASTA
dancer .... GOGO, HULA
deck .... ORLOP
deer .... DOE, ROE, AXIS
derby .... ROLLER, KENTUCKY
dome .... GEODESIC
dope .... INSIDE
down .... EIDER
dream .... PIPE
driver .... PILE
energy .... SOLAR
engine .... DIESEL
father/mother .... STEP
fist .... IRON
flour or flower .... CORN
food/music .... SOUL
frost .... HOAR
garden .... BOTANICAL, ZOOLOGICAL
gazelle .... ARIEL
glass .... SHOT, STAINED, MAGNIFYING
goat .... SCAPE
goose .... SOLAN
gravure .... ROTO
gun .... RIOT, SHOT
hand or rags .... GLAD
happy .... SLAP
hydrometer ..... GRAVIMETER
introducer .... EMCEE, TOASTMASTER

institution .... PENAL
job .... DESK, PART-TIME
joint .... CLIP
landing .... CRASH
lark .... MUD
leave .... SICK, SHORE,
    MATERNITY
lens .... ZOOM, CONTACT
life some lead ..... CHARMED
light .... SEARCH
lily .... CALLA, TIGER
lounge .... VIP, COCKTAIL
machine .... SLOT
man .... YES, INNER
market .... BEAR, STOCK
meal .... OAT
meat .... LEAN, CHOICE
miss .... NEAR
money ..... GREASE, EARNEST
moss .... PEAT
moth .... LUNA
music .... POP, JAZZ, ROCK,
    CLASSICAL
nail .... HOB
numeral ..... ROMAN, ARABIC
opera .... SOAP, HORSE
orange .... NAVEL, OSAGE,
    TANGERINE
out .... INSIDE
page .... BLEED, FRONT
party .... HEN, TEA,
    SLUMBER, POLITICAL
peeve .... PET
piano or soprano ..... MEZZO
pigeon .... STOOL, HOMING
plane .... JET, MONO
plant .... EGG
plasm .... ECTO
poker .... STUD
police dog .... ALSATIAN,
    GERMAN SHEPHERD
pool or vehicle .... MOTOR
post .... GOAL
processing .... DATA
production .... INDUSTRIAL
progression .... GEOMETRIC
race .... DRAG, HORSE
race horse .... MILER
ranch .... DUDE
road .... RAIL
rocket .... RETRO
rubber .... BAND, INDIA
rule .... GAG
rumor .... IDLE
sale .... TAG, FIRE, WHITE,
GARAGE, SURPLUS, BARGAIN,
    CLEARANCE
salt .... TABLE, SAILOR
salt or wit .... ATTIC
service .... LIP
shark .... LOAN, NURSE

sheet .... TEAR, WORK
show .... GAME, TALK,
    COMEDY, ONE-MAN
shutout .... NO-HIT
sight .... HIND
skirt .... MIDI, MINI, A-LINE
soda .... POP, SAL
sole .... DOVER
space or plane .... AERO
squirrel .... TANA
sticks .... CHOP
stock .... PREFERRED, BLUE
    CHIP
stool .... TOAD
story .... SOB
suit .... PINSTRIPE
sync .... LIP
table .... POOL, STEAM
tax .... SALES, STATE,
    INCOME, PROPERTY
terrier .... CAIRN
this/that .... LIKE, SUCH
ticket .... FREE, MEAL,
    TRAFFIC, SPEEDING
tide .... LOW, HIGH, NEAP
tire .... RECAP, SPARE
triangle .... LOVE, SCALENE
type .... PICA, ELITE
wave .... TIDAL
wax .... SEALING
well .... INK, WISHING
will .... IRON, LAST
word .... NONCE
kindergarten ...... CLASS, SCHOOL
activity .... GAME, EXERCISE
pioneer .... FROEBEL
kindergartner .... LEARNER
kindle .... BURN, FIRE, LUNT,
TIND, LIGHT, ROUSE, SPUNK,
    EXCITE, IGNITE
kindled .... LIT
kindling .... PUNK, WOOD,
    AMADOU
kindly .... WARM, BENIGN,
    GENIAL, GRACIOUS
kindness .... GRACE, LENITY,
    GOOD WILL
kindred ...... SIB, TIE, AKIN, KITH,
BLOOD, ALLIED, FAMILY,
COGNATE, KINSHIP, RELATIVES
kine .... COWS, CATTLE
king .... REX, ROI, SIRE, RULER,
    MONARCH, PADISHAH,
    SOVEREIGN
and jack .... TENACE
Ammonite .... HANUN,
    NAHASH
beater/topper .... ACE
biblical ...... MAGUS, MAGI(PL.)
changed to mountain
    .... ATLAS

Cobra .... HAMADRYAD
crab .... LIMULUS, LIMULOID
do-nothing .... ROI FAINEANT
Egyptian .... PHARAOH
fairyland .... OBERON
Iranian .... SHAH
killer .... REGICIDE
maned .... LION
Midian .... EVI, HUR, REBA
morning reception of
    .... LEVER
of a .... REGAL, ROYAL
of Admah .... SHINAB
Amalek .... AGAG
Arcadia .... LYCAON
Argos .... DANAUS
Assyria .... PUL
Athens .... CODRUS, THESEUS
Attica .... CECROPS
Babylon .... SELEACUS,
    HAMMURABI
Bashan .... OG
beasts .... LION
Bela .... ZOAR
Belgium .... BAUDOIN,
    LEOPOLD
birds .... EAGLE
blues .... (B.B.) KING
Bohemia .... WENZEL
Britain .... LUR, LEAR,
UTHER, ARTHUR, ARTEGAL,
    BELINUS
Bulgaria .... BORIS
Burgundy .... GUNTHER
Bythinia .... NICOMEDES
Colon .... GASPAR
Corinth .... POLYBUS
Crete .... MINOS
Crete, legendary
    .... IDOMENEUS
Cyprus .... PYGMALION
Damascus .... ARETUS
Denmark .... VALDEMAR,
    WALDEMAR
dwarfs .... ALBERICH
Egypt .... FUAD, FAROUK
Elam .... CHEDORLAOMER
Ellasar .... ARIOCH
elves .... ERLKING
England .... HENRY,
    EDWARD, STEPHEN,
    ETHELRED
England and Denmark
    .... CNUT, KNUT
England and Northern
    Ireland .... GEORGE VI
England, the Conqueror
    .... WILLIAM
England, the first
    Plantagenet
    .... HENRY II

England, the last Plantagenet .... RICHARD III
England, the Lion-Hearted .... RICHARD I
England who abdicated in 1936 .... EDWARD VIII
Ethiopia .... CEPHEUS
fairies .... OBERON
Franks .... PEPIN
Gath .... ACHISH
Gerar .... ABIMELECH
"glitz" ..... WAYNE NEWTON
Goiim .... TIDAL
Gomorrah .... BIRSHA
"golden touch" .... MIDAS
hobbies, alleged .... PHILATELY
Huns .... ATLI, ETZEL, ATTILA
Ioclus .... AESON
Iran .... XERXES
Israel (see **Israel(i)**, king)
Israel, first .... SAUL
Israel, last .... HOSHEA
Jews .... HEROD
Judah/Judea (see **Judah,** king)
Judah, last .... ZEDEKIAH
Kent .... ETHELBERT
Langobards .... ALBOIN
Ligurians .... CYGNUS
Lydia .... CROESUS
Moab .... EGLON
Mycenae .... ATREUS
Myrmidons .... PELEUS
Naples .... MURAT
Norway .... OLAF, OLAV, HAAKON
Numidia .... MASINISSA
Peris .... JAMSHID
Persia .... CYRUS, DARIUS, XERXES
Phrygia ..... MIDAS, GORDIUS
Prussia .... WILHELM
"rock and roll" .... ELVIS PRESLEY
Rome .... TARQUIN
Salem .... MELCHIZEDEK
Scotland .... BRUCE
Siam .... ANANDA, MONGKUT
Siam's friend .... ANNA
Sodom .... BERA
Spain .... REY, JUAN, ALFONSO
Sparta .... LEONIDAS, MENELAUS
"swing" .... GOODMAN
Syria .... HAZAL
the blind ..... MAN WITH ONE EYE

Thebes .... CREON, LAIUS
Thessaly .... PELIAS, ADMETUS
Thrace .... TEREUS
Troy .... PRIAM
Tyre .... HIRAM
Visogoths .... ALARIC
Volsunga .... ATLI
Zeboiim .... SHEMEBER
Zulus .... CETEWAYO
sculptor .... PYGMALION
snake .... COBRA
with ass's ears .... MIDAS
with eternal thirst, hunger .... TANTALUS
King Arthur's birthplace .... TINTAGEL HEAD
Arthur's capital/court .... CAMELOT
death place .... CAMLAN
father .... UTHER
fictitious visitor ..... YANKEE
fool/jester .... DAGONET
foster brother .... KAY
knight ..... GARETH, GAWAIN, MODRED, GALAHAD, LANCELOT
knights .... ROUNDTABLE
lance .... RON(E)
magician .... MERLIN
mother ...... IGERNA, IGERNE, IGRAINE
nephew .... KAY, GARETH, GAWAIN, MO(R)DRED
place .... ASTOLAT
queen .... GUINEVERE
realm .... BRITAIN
resting place .... AVALON
seneschal .... KAY
shield name .... PRIDWIN
step-sister .... MORGAN(LE FAY)
sword .... EXCALIBUR
writer on .... PYLE
Canute's consort .... EMMA
Cole .... NAT, OLD
David's brother .... ELIAB, SHAMMAH, ABINADAB
captain/commander .... JOAB, AMASA
city .... ZION
daughter .... TAMAR
father .... JESSE
kingdom .... JUDAH, HEBRON, ISRAEL
priest .... IRA, ZADOK, ABIATHAR
rebellious son ...... ABSALOM
rebuker .... NATHAN
son .... AMNON, ABSALOM, CHILEAB, ITHREAM,

SOLOMON, ADONIJAH, SHEPHATIAH
trusted friend .... HUSHAI, JONATHAN
victim slain with sling .... GOLIATH
wife .... EGLAH, MICHAL, ABIGAIL, AHINOAM, HAGGITH, BATHSHEBA
Ferdinand .... BOMBA
Hadad's land .... EDOM
Henry VI author .... SHAKESPEARE
John's nickname .... LACKLAND
Kong .... GORILLA
Lear's daughter .... REGAN, GONERIL, CORDELIA
dog .... TRAY
Saul's ancestral tribe .... BENJAMIN
critic .... SAMUEL
daughter .... MERAB, MICHAL
deathplace .... (MOUNT) GILBOA
father .... KISH
general .... ABNER
grandfather .... NER
grandson .... MEPHIBOSETH
kingdom .... ISRAEL
servant .... ZIBA
shepherd .... DOEG
son .... ABINADAB, JONATHAN, ESHBAAL, MALCHISHUA, ISHBOSHETH
successor .... DAVID
wife/concubine .... RIZPAH
Solomon's brother .... ADONIJAH
daughter .... TAPHATH
father .... DAVID
land .... OPHIR
mines location .... ELATH, TIMNAH VALLEY
mother .... BATHSHEBA
sayings .... MAXIMS, PROVERBS
son .... MENELIK, REHOBOAM
kingcup .... MARIGOLD
kingdom .... REALM, DOMAIN, EMPIRE, MONARCHY
African .... NUBIA, NUMIDIA
ancient .... EDOM, ELAM, IDUMEA, CROATIA, MACEDONIA
Asiatic .... SIAM, KOREA, NEPAL, SIKKIM, THAILAND
Caspian .... PARTHIA
cause of loss of .... NAIL, HORSE
come ..... HEAVEN, HEREAFTER
kind of .... PLANT, ANIMAL,

409

kingfish .... BARB, CERO, HAKU, OPAH, SIERRA, PINTADO, WHITING

kingfisher .... HALCYON, KOOKABURRA

kingfisher's kin .... MOTMOT

kingly .... NOBLE, REGAL, ROYAL, AUGUST, LEONINE, MAJESTIC

authority/power .... DIADEM

king's chamber .... CAMARILLA

clover .... MELILOT

color .... PURPLE, ORPIMENT

evil .... SCROFULA

robe .... DALMATIC

rod .... WARDER

steward .... CHAMBERLAIN

symbol .... ORB, MOUND

symbol of authority .... SCEPTER

King's Peak range .... UINTA

kingship ...... MAJESTY, ROYALTY

kingsman's domain: var. .... BARONI

kink .... CURL, KNOT, WHIM, CRICK, QUIRK, SNARL, TWIST, BUCKLE, CROTCHET

thread .... BURL

kinkajou .... POTT(O), MAMMAL

kinky .... CURLY

kino .... GUM, ASTRINGENT

kinsfolk .... FAMILY, RELATIVES

kinship .... ENATION, AFFINITY

kinsman .... SIB, RELATIVE

kiosk ...... PAVILION, BANDSTAND, NEWSSTAND

kip .... BED, ROOMING HOUSE

Kipling's birthplace ...... BOMBAY

character .... KIM

children's fable .... THE JUNGLE BOOK

heroine .... MAISIE

mother .... ALICE

novel .... KIM

poem .... RECESSIONAL

Shere Khan .... TIGER

title .... SAHIB

wife .... CAROLINE

wolf .... AKELA

Kirghiz .... KAZAK(H), MONGOL

mountains .... ALAI

tent .... YURT

kirk .... CHURCH

Kirk, actor .... DOUGLAS

kirtle .... COAT, SKIRT, TUNIC

Kish's father .... NER

son .... SAUL

kismet .... FATE, DESTINY

kiss .... BUSS, PECK, CANDY, SMACK, TOUCH, CARESS, OSCULATE, SUGARPLUM

and _____ .... TELL

Kiss sculptor .... RODIN

Kissel and Opel .... CARS

kisser: sl. ...... FACE, LIPS, MOUTH

kissing cousins .... KIN

game .... POST OFFICE

kist .... BOX, CHEST, LOCKER

kit .... LOT, SET, TUB, GEAR, PACK, BUCKET, OUTFIT

and _____ .... CABOODLE

kitchen .... GALLEY, COOKERY, CUISINE, SCULLERY

chief .... CHEF

feature .... OVEN, MIXER, RANGE, TOASTER

garden .... OLITORY

help .... SCULLION

of the .... CULINARY

police for short .... KP

ship's .... GALLEY

specialty .... AROMA

tool ...... CORER, DICER, KNIFE, LADLE, SIEVE, GRATER, MASHER

waste .... SLOPS

wear .... APRON

kitchener .... RANGE, STOVE

Kitchener, statesman .... HORATIO

kitchenware .... PANS, POTS, SKILLET, UTENSILS

kite .... BIRD, HAWK, SOAR, GLED(E), MILAN, ROGUE, ELANET, FALCON, SHARPER

kith and kin .... RELATIVES

kitsch .... TRASH

kittenish .... FRISKY, PLAYFUL

kittens: colloq. .... HYSTERICS

kittiwake .... ANNET, SEA GULL

kitty .... CAT, POT, ANTE, POOL, WIDOW, STAKES

in gambling game .... POT

kiva .... ROOM, DWELLING

kiwi .... MOA, ROA, APTERYX

klaxon .... HORN

kleptomaniac .... THIEF, FILCHER, SHOPLIFTER

Klingsor .... MAGICIAN

Klondike road .... ALCAN

kloop .... GORGE, VALLEY

knack .... ART, FLAIR, SKILL, TRICK, TALENT, TRINKET, APTITUDE, INSTINCT, DEXTERITY

knap .... RAP, BITE, HILL, SNAP, SUMMIT

knapsack ...... KIT, PACK, BINDLE, MOCHILA, (DUFFLE)BAG, HAVERSACK

knar .... KNOT

knarl .... NODE

knave ...... CHURL, LOREL, LOSEL, ROGUE, SCAMP, RASCAL, VARLET

in cribbage .... NOBS

in euchre .... BOWER

of clubs .... PAM

playing cards' .... JACK

knead .... ELT, MOLD, PRESS, MASSAGE

kneading material .... CLAY, DOUGH

knee .... GENU, JOINT

ailment .... GONAGRA

bend the .... GENUFLECT

bone .... DIB

inflammation .... GONITIS

joint ....;...... HOCK, KNUCKLE

tendon .... HAMSTRING

kneecap .... ROTULA, PATELLA

kneel .... KOWTOW, GENUFLECT

kneeling desk .... PRIE DIEU

knell .... OMEN, RING, TOLL

knickerbocker(s) ...... TROUSERS, NEWYORKER, PLUSFOURS

knickknack .... TOY, GAUD, BAUBLE, DOODAD, GEWGAW, NOTION, TRIFLE, NOVELTY, TRINKET, GIMCRACK, BRIC-A-BRAC

Knievel .... EVEL

knife .... BOLO, SHIV, SNEE, STAB, BLADE, BOWIE, DAGGER, MACHET(T)E

combining form .... DORI

dealer .... CUTLER

handle .... HAFT

Hindu .... KURRI

Irish .... SKEAN

kind of .... FAN, PEN, BOWIE, TRENCH, TRIVET, CARVING

large .... COUTEAU

Malay .... PARANG

Maori .... PATU

Moro .... KRIS

sharpener .... STEEL

surgical .... CATLIN, LANCET, SCALPEL

tosser .... JUGGLER

Turkish .... YATAGHAN

knight .... SIR, NOBLE, BAYARD, RITTER, PALADIN, TEMPLAR, CAVALIER, CHAMPION

arena of the .... LISTS

armor bearer of ...... ARMIGER

armorless .... BARESARK

attendant .... PAGE, SQUIRE, DONZEL, ARMIGER

challenge .... GAGE

cloak of .... TABARD

Crusader .... TEMPLAR

ensign .... PENNON

errand of a .... QUEST
errant .... PALADIN
fratricidal .... BALIN
fight of a .... TILT, JOUST,
TOURNEY
groom of .... COISTREL
in chess .... HORSE
lance target .... QUINTAIN
of the road ...... HOBO, TRAMP
of the Round Table .... KAY,
BORS, BORT, BALAN, BALIN,
GARETH, GAWAIN, GALAHAD,
GERAINT, MO(R)DRED,
MORGA(I)N, PELLEAS, TRISTAN,
BEDIVERE, LANCELOT,
PERCIVAL, TRISTRAM
page of .... VARLET
pledge .... GAGE
self-styled .... HOBO
Templar .... MASON
vocation .... CHIVALRY
weapon of .... LANCE
wife of .... DAME
knightliness .... CHIVALRY
knightly .... BRAVE, NOBLE,
HEROIC, GALLANT
quest .... ERRANTRY
knights collectively
.... KNIGHTHOOD
knit .... JOIN, SEAM, PURSE, UNITE,
WEAVE, COUPLE, PUCKER,
INTERLOCK
goods .... LISLE
knitted goods dealer ...... HOSIER
knitter .... PURLER
problem of .... SLEEVES
knitting .... BROCADE, CROCHET
machine guide .... SLEY
stitch .... PURL
knob .... HILL, KNOP, NODE, STUD,
UMBO, KNOLL, KNURL,
FINIAL, HANDLE, NUB(BLE)
like .... NOPAL
ornamental .... BOSS, STUD
knobbed .... NODOSE, TOROSE
knobby .... HILLY, NUBB(L)Y,
TOROSE, STUDDED, TUBEROSE,
TUBEROUS
knock .... HIT, PAN, RAP, TAP,
BLOW, BUMP, POUND, SWIPE,
STRIKE, CRITICIZE
about .... ROAM, ABUSE,
HUSTLE, ROUGH UP
down .... DASH, FLOOR,
DAMPEN, FLATTEN,
DISCOURAGE
it off .... STOP
kneed .... VALGUS, WOBBLY,
BOWLEGGED
light .... RAP, TAP
on wood .... HOPE

out .... KO, KAYO, STUN,
CANCEL, DELETE, DEFEAT
knockabout .... YACHT
knocked down, as in equipment,
etc. .... UNASSEMBLED
for ... . A LOOP
knocker .... CRITIC, NAGGER,
RAPPER, FAULTFINDER
knockout .... STUNNER
blow ...... HAYMAKER, SUNDAY
PUNCH
knoll .... KNAP, TOFT, MOUND,
HILLOCK, HUMMOCK
Knossos .... CRETE
knot .... BOW, TIE, BIND, BOND,
KNUR, LUMP, NODE, SNAG,
TUFT, HITCH, JOINT, NODUS,
SNARL, FASTEN, NODULE,
COCKADE, (EN)TANGLE,
PROBLEM, SANDPIPER
fiber .... NEP, NOIL
hair .... BUN, NOIL, CHIGNON
kind of .... LOOP, REEF,
GRANNY, BOWLINE, LANYARD,
OVERHAND, CAT'S-PAW,
TREFOIL, SHEEPSHANK,
MAGNUS HITCH
loose .... GRANNY
nautical .... (SEA)MILE
necktie .... WINDSOR
rope .... CLINCH
running .... NOOSE
silk/wool .... NOIL
thread .... BURL
tied by King Midas
.... GORDIAN
tree .... GNARL
wood ...... BURL, KNAR, KNOR,
GNARL
yarn .... SKEIN
knots, full of .... NODOUS
knotted .... NODED, NODATED,
TANGLED, INTRICATE
knotty .... NODOSE, NODOUS,
PUZZLING
knotweed .... ALLSEEDS,
PERSICARY
knout .... FLOG, WHIP
know ...... KEN, AWARE, FATHOM,
DISCERN, UNDERSTAND
all: colloq. .... QUIDNUNC,
WISEACRE, SMART ALECK
beforehand .... FORESEE
by observation .... PERCEIVE
come to .... LEARN, REALIZE
in a way .... KEN
in one's bones .... FEEL
it-all .... BOASTER, EGOTIST,
WISEGUY, WISEACRE
long ago/archaic .... WOT
nothing .... AGNOSTIC,

IGNORANT
the ___ and outs .... INS
know-how .... SKILL, EXPERTISE
slang .... SAVVY
know-nothing .... DUNCE,
GREENHORN, IGNORAMUS
knowing .... HEP, HIP, WISE,
CLEVER, SCIENT, SHREWD,
GNOSTIC, COGNIZANT,
CONSCIOUS
knowledge ...... KEN, KITH, LORE,
NOESIS, THEORY, WISDOM,
AWARENESS, EXPERTISE,
INFORMATION
branch of .... OLOGY
intuitive .... INSIGHT
lack of .... IGNORANCE
means to .... ORGANON
of .... GNOSTIC
spiritual .... GNOSIS
surface .... SCIOLISM
universal .... PANSOPHY
vague ..... INKLING, SUSPICION,
IMPRESSION
knowledgeable .... HEP, HIP,
WISE, SKILLED, LEARNED,
SAPIENT, EDUCATED,
INFORMED, WELL-READ,
INTELLIGENT
about .... UP ON
known .... RECOGNIZED
as .... YCLEPT, YCLEPED
knuckle .... (FINGER)JOINT
down under ...... OBEY, YIELD,
COMPLY, GIVE IN
knucklebone .... BIB, KNOB
knucklehead .... FOOL,
THICKSKULL
knurl .... KNOB, KNOT, RIDGE
KO: sl. .... KNOCKOUT, PUT TO
SLEEP
koa .... ACACIA
koala .... BEAR
kobold .... GNOME, NIS(SE),
GOBLIN, SPRITE, BROWNIE
Kodak .... CAMERA
koel .... CUCKOO
Kohinoor .... DIAMOND,
(CROWN)JEWEL
kohl .... COSMETIC
Kohler, psychologist
.... WOLFGANG
kohl .... COSMETIC
Kohler, psychologist
.... WOLFGANG
kohlrabi .... CABBAGE
kok-sagyz .... DANDELION
Kok's (Adam) settlers
.... GRIQUA
Koko's weapon .... SNEE
kola .... NUT

nut content .... CAFFEIN(E)
kolinsky .... FUR, MINK
kon-tiki .... RAFT
kook .... CUCKOO
kookaburra .... KINGFISHER
kooky ...... CRAZY, LOOPY, SILLY,
ECCENTRIC
kop .... HILL, MOUNTAIN
kopje .... HILL(OCK)
kor .... HOMER
Koran chapter .... SURO, SURA(H),
ALCORAN
interpreter .... ULEMA
memorizer .... HAFIZ
paradise bridge .... AL SIRAT
scholar .... ULEMA
supplement to the ...... SHIITE,
SUNNA(H)
teacher of .... ALFAQUI
Korea .... CHOSEN
founder of .... TANGUN
Korean, North bay .... CHUNGSAN
capital .... PYONGYANG
city/town .... IWON, HAEJU,
NAJIN, NAMPO, ONSONG,
WONSAN, HAMHUNG,
KAESONG, SINUIJI, CHONGJIN,
PANMUNJON
mountain .... SASU, TUUN,
BAKTU, KOMDOK, KWANMO,
PAEKTU, KUMGANG
river .... YALU, TUMEN,
TAEDONG
sea .... JAPAN, YELLOW
seaport .... WONSAN
South bay .... KANGHWA
capital .... KEIJO, SEOUL
city/town .... IRI, MUJU,
YOSU, CHEJU, KIMJE, MASAN,
MOKPO, PUSAN, SUWON,
TAEGU, ULSAN, WONJU,
ANDONG, CHINJU, INCHON,
KIMHAE, KOHUNG, KUNSAN,
NONSAN, POHANG, TAEJON,
YANGGU, CHECHON,
CHINHAE, CHONGJU
island .... SO, KOJE, CHEJU,
DAGELET
mountain ...... CHIRI, HALLA,

SORAK, KEBANG
river .... HAN, KUM, NAKTONG
sea .... JAPAN
seaport .... YOSU, PUSAN,
INCHON
strait .... CHEJU
coin .... WON
dynasty/kingdom .... SILLA
honorable man of justice
.... YOLSA
martial art .... TAE KWON DO
monetary unit .... WON, HWAN
president .... PARK, RHEE, ROH
TAE-WOO
religion .... BUDDHISM,
CONFUCIANISM
soldier .... ROK
statesman .... TOO SUN CHOI
stockade .... JKOJE
true faith .... AL SIRAT
weight .... KON
woman's blouse .... CHIMA
woman's skirt .... CHOGORI
Korina wood .... AFARA
koruna, 1/100 of .... HELLER
kosher .... FIT, CLEAN, PROPER
opposed to .... TREF
Kosygin, Russian premier
.... ALEKSEI
Kotabaru .... HOLLANDIA
Koussevitsky .... SERGE
kowtow .... BOW, HOMAGE,
SCRAPE, RESPECT,
SALUTATION
slang .... BOOTLICK
kraal .... PEN, VILLAGE
Kraft .... WRAPPING PAPER
krait .... ADDER
kraken .... MONSTER
Kreisler, violinist .... FRITZ
Kremlin .... CITADEL
Kreuger .... IVAR
Kriemhild's husband .... ETZEL,
ATTILA, SIEGFRIED
kris .... CREESE, DAGGER
Kriss Kringle .... SANTA (CLAUS)
krona .... CROWN
Kronos' wife .... RHEA
Kronstadt .... PORT, BRASOV

Kruger, Transvaal president
.... OOM PAUL
Krypton symbol .... KR
Ku Klux Klan official
.... KLEAGLE
Kublai Khan dynasty ...... YUAN
kudos ...... FAME, GLORY, CREDIT,
PRAISE, PRESTIGE
kudu .... KOODOO, ANTELOPE
Kukla's pal .... OLLIE
Kuklapolitan hostess .... FRAN
kulak .... FARMER
Kumasi is capital of .... ASHANTI
is in .... GHANA
Kung Fu-tse .... CONFUCIUS
Kuomintang .... YUAN
founder .... SUN YAT-SEN
leader .... CHIANG KAI-SHEK
Kurdistan .... RUG
Kuril(e) island .... URUP, ITURUP,
ETOROFU, KUNASHIRI,
PARAMUSHIR
Kuwait .... SHEIKDOM
capital .... AL KUWAIT
city/town .... MINA SAUD,
MINA AL AHMADI
export .... OIL
gulf .... PERSIAN
island .... BUBIYAN
language .... ARABIC
monetary unit .... DINAR
religion .... ISLAM
kvass .... BEER
Kwangchow .... CANTON
Kwangsi capital .... NANNING
Kwantung capital .... CANTON
city .... SWATOW
seaport .... DAIREN
kwashiorkor .... MALNUTRITION
Kymric .... WELSH
kyphos .... HUMP
kyphosis .... HUMPBACK
Kyser, bandleader .... KAY
Kyushu base .... SASEBO
city/town .... OITA, SAGA,
BEPPU, KURUME, NOBEOKA,
KUMAMOTO, MIYAZAKI,
NAGASAKI, KAGOSHIMA
volcano .... ASO(SAN)

L

L, Greek .... LAMBDA
in geodesy .... LONGITUDE
letter .... EL, ELL
shaped .... ELL
La Boheme character .... MIMI,
MUSETTA, RODOLPHO
composer .... (GIACOMO)

PUCCINI
La Gioconda .... MONA LISA
painter .... (LEONARDO) DA
VINCI
La Guardia, Mayor
.... FIORELLO
La in chemistry .... LANTHANUM

La Perichole composer
.... (JACQUES) OFFENBACH
La Rochefoucauld's forte
.... MAXIMS
La Salle's lieutenant ...... TONTY
La Traviata heroine
.... VIOLETTA

La Valse composer
.... (MAURICE) RAVEL
laager .... CAMP
Laban's daughter .... LEAH,
RACHEL
sister .... REBEKAH
son-in-law .... JACOB
labarum .... STANDARD
labdanum .... RESIN
Labe .... ELBE
labefaction .... DOWNFALL
label ...... TAB, TAG, MARK, NAME,
BRAND, STAMP, TALLY,
DOCKET, FILLET, LAPPET,
PASTER, STICKER, DESCRIBE,
CLASSIFICATION
anew .... RETAG
labellum .... LIP, PETAL
flower with .... ORCHID
labia .... LIPS
minora .... NYMPHA(E)
labial .... (ORGAN)PIPE
labiate .... LIPPED
labile .... SKIMMING, UNSTABLE
labium .... LIP, LABELLUM
labor .... MOIL, TASK, TOIL,
WORK, EFFORT, STRIVE,
TRAVAIL, CHILDBIRTH,
PARTURITION
group .... UNION
leader .... GREEN, HOFFA,
LEWIS, MEANY, REUTHER,
PETRILLO
omnia _____ .... VINCIT
organization, international
.... ILO
resources .... MANPOWER
-saving device ...... APPLIANCE
spy recruiter .... HOOKER
strike placard carrier
.... PICKET
strikebreaker .... RAT, SCAB
throes, pains .... TRAVAIL
union .... AFL, CIO, ARTEL,
ILGWU
union branch .... LOCAL
union negotiation
.... COLLECTIVE BARGAINING
unionist .... NEGOTIATOR
laboratory burner .... ETNA,
BUNSEN
need .... ACIDS, OLEATES, TEST
TUBES
salt .... BORATE
specimen .... CELL
substance .... ACID
utensil .... RETORT
worker .... TESTER
labored .... HEAVY, FORCED,
OPEROSE
breath .... GASP, PANT

laborer .... HAND, PEON, SERF,
TOTY, NAVVY, PROLE,
COOLIE, SEGGON, WORKER,
BRACERO
day .... PEON
migratory .... OKIE
Spanish .... PEON, OBRERO,
TRABAJADOR
transient .... CASUAL,
FLOATER, MIGRANT,
ROUSTABOUT
unskilled .... NAVVY, BOHUNK,
AMATEUR
laborious .... ARDUOUS,
TOILSOME, STRENUOUS
Labrador .... PENINSULA
retriever .... HUNTING DOG
tea .... LEDUM
labrum .... LIP
laburnum .... SHRUB, PEA TREE
labyrinth .... MAZE, MEANDER
builder of .... DAEDALUS
dweller .... MINOTAUR
inflammation of
.... LABYRINTHITIS
site of, in human body
.... EAR
labyrinthine .... DAEDAL,
COMPLEX, INTRICATE
lace .... GIN, VAL, BEAT, LASH,
WHIP, ADORN, BRAID, FILET,
SNARE, EDGING, THRASH,
GUIPURE, MACRAME,
MALINES, NETTING, TATTING,
FILIGREE, EMBROIDER
beer .... NEEDLE
cape .... MANTILLA
collar .... BERTHA
edging .... FRILL
frilled .... R(O)UCHE
metal tip .... TAG, A(I)GLET
opening .... EYELET
pattern .... TOILE
shoe/sandal .... LATCHET
thread .... MACRAME
three-cornered .... FICHU
trimming .... FRILL, JABOT
Lacedaemon .... SPARTA
lacerate .... CUT, RIP, REND, TEAR,
WOUND, HARROW, MANGLE
lacert(il)ian .... GECKO, LIZARD
lacet .... BRAID
Lachesis .... FATE, GODDESS
companion of .... CLOTHO,
ATROPOS
lachrymose .... TEARY, WEEPY,
TEARFUL
lady .... NIOBE
lacing .... CORD, BRAID, BEATING,
TRIMMING
lack .... NEED, WANT, DEARTH,

REQUIRE, SHORTAGE,
DEFICIENCY
desire .... INAPPETENCE
of bladder control .... BED-
WETTING
information ..... IGNORANCE,
NESCIENCE
interest ..... ENNUI, BOREDOM
mental vigor .... CACHEXIA
oxygen .... SUFFOCATION
stress .... ATONY
vital energy .... ATONIA
lackadaisical .... BLASE,
INDOLENT, LANGUID,
LISTLESS, EASYGOING,
NONCHALANT, SPIRITLESS
"Lackaday!" .... ALAS
lackey .... SLAVE, TOADY,
FLUNK(E)Y, FOOTMAN,
SERVANT, FOLLOWER,
ATTENDANT
uniform of .... LIVERY
lacking .... SHY, SANS, ABSENT,
(DE)VOID, IN NEED, SHORT
OF, WANTING, DEFICIENT,
INCOMPLETE
courage .... CRAVEN
enthusiasm .... LUKEWARM
firmness .... LIMP
grace .... CRUDE, CLUMSY,
GAUCHE, AWKWARD
in symmetry .... LOPSIDED
one of "these three"
.... UNCHARITABLE
refinement ...... CRUDE, GROSS,
COARSE, INCONDITE
reverence .... IMPIOUS
the power .... UNABLE
lackluster .... DULL, DRAB
Laconia is capital of ...... SPARTA
people of .... SPARTAN(S)
laconic ...... BRIEF, PITHY, SHORT,
TERSE, CONCISE
answer .... UGH
person .... INDIAN
lacquer .... LAC, DUCO, JAPAN,
ENAMEL, VARNISH
lacquered metalware .... TOLE
lacs, 100 .... CRORE
lactary .... DAIRY
lactase .... ENZYME
lactate .... SUCKLE
lacteal/lactescent .... MILKY
lactose .... SUGAR
lactulose .... LAXATIVE
lacuna .... GAP, SPACE, HIATUS
lad .... SONNY, YOUTH, SHAVER,
STRIPLING, YOUNGSTER
lad's pursuit .... LASS
ladanum .... RESIN
Ladd western .... SHANE

ladder .... SCALE, SCALADE
   back .... SLAT
   kind of .... STEP, FOLDING,
      GANGWAY, EXTENSION
   part .... RUNG, STEP, SPOKE,
      STAVE, RUNDLE
   used to flee a burning
      building ...... FIRE ESCAPE
lade ...... DIP, BAIL, LOAD, LADLE,
      BURDEN
ladida .... FLOSSY, FOP(PISH)
ladies' man .... SHEIK(H),
      PHILANDERER
ladies with a common
   background .... DAR
Ladin .... ROMANSH
Ladino .... DIALECT, MESTIZO
ladle .... DIP, BAIL, BOWL, SCOOP,
      SPOON, DIPPER
   pour with .... LAVE
   spout .... GEAT
ladrone .... THIEF, BANDIT,
      ROBBER
Ladrone Island(s) .... GUAM,
      MARIANAS
lady .... BIBI, DAME, MADAM,
      WIFE, FEMALE, MISTRESS
   fair .... ROWENA
   killer: sl. .... DON JUAN,
      CASANOVA
   Private Lives .... AMANDA
   silk habit .... PELISSE
Lady Churchill .... CLEMENTINE
   Godiva, he saw .... PEEPING
      TOM
   Godiva's husband .... LEOFRIC
   Hamilton .... EMMA
   of the Lake .... ELLEN, NIMUE,
      VIVIAN
ladybird .... BEETLE, VEDALIA
ladybug .... BEETLE
ladyfinger .... COOKY, COOKIE
ladyfish .... 10-POUNDERS, TEN-
      POUNDERS
ladylike .... FEMININE, WELL-BRED
lady's maid .... ABIGAIL,
      SOUBRETTE
   slipper .... ORCHID
   smock .... CRESS
Laertes' sister .... OPHELIA
   son .... ODYSSEUS
lag .... DRAG, IDLE, DALLY,
      DELAY, STAVE, TARRY, TRAIL,
      FALTER, LINGER, LOITER
lagan .... JETSAM, FLOTSAM
lager .... BEER, CAMP
Lagerlof .... SELMA
laggard .... BACKWARD, LOITERER,
      SLOWFOOT
lagn(i)appe .... PRESENT,
      GRATUITY

lagomorph .... HARE, PIKA,
      RABBIT, RODENT
lagoon .... HAFF, LAKE, POND,
      LIMAN
   islands .... ELLICE
   site of .... ATOLL
lah-de-dah one .... SNOOT
Lahr, comedian .... BERT
laic .... CIVIL, LAY(MAN),
      SECULAR, TEMPORAL
lair .... DEN, CAVE, HAUNT,
      COVERT, HANGOUT
laity .... LAYMEN, BRETHREN
Laius's son .... OEDIPUS
lake .... LOCH, MERE, POND, POOL,
      LAGOON, SALINA
   African .... CHAD, TANA,
      NYASSA, VICTORIA
   artificial .... RESERVOIR
   basin .... PLAYA
   bird .... LOON
   city .... ERIE
   fish .... POLLAN
   fourth largest in the world
      .... ARAL
   island in a .... HOLM
   largest in U.S. .... SUPERIOR
   mountain .... TARN
   of Constance .... BODENSEE
   on California-Nevada border
      .... TAHOE
   outlet .... BAYOU
   poet ..... SOUTHEY, COLERIDGE,
      WORDSWORTH
   resort .... TAHOE
   second largest in the world
      .... SUPERIOR
   spooky-sounding .... ERIE
   third largest in the world
      .... VICTORIA
   trout .... POGY
   world's highest .... TITICACA
   world's largest .... CASPIAN
      SEA
   world's lowest .... DEAD SEA
Lake Chad tributary .... SHARI
   Erie city .... LORAIN
   Erie hero .... PERRY
   Erie port .... TOLEDO
   Erie tributary .... MAUMEE
   Geneva .... LEMAN
   Great .... ERIE, HURON,
      ONTARIO, MICHIGAN, SUPERIOR
   Maggiore town .... LOCARNO
   Michigan city .... GARY,
      KENOSHA, MILWAUKEE
lakes, study of .... LIMNOLOGY
Lal Bahadur .... SHASTRI
lalique .... GLASS
lallation .... LAMBDACISM
Lalo, composer .... EDOUARD

lam .... BEAT, FLEE, FLOG,
      ESCAPE, FLIGHT, THRASH,
      VAMO(O)SE
lama .... MONK, TESHU, PRIEST
   chief .... BLAMA, DALAI
lamasery .... MONASTERY
lamb .... (Y)EAN, CHILD, SHEEP,
      COSSET, FATLING, (Y)EANLING
   breast .... CARRE
   fur .... KARAKUL
   hide .... KIP
   holy .... AGNUS
   leg of .... GIGOT
   like a .... MEEK, TIMID
   mother of .... EWE
   pet .... CADE, COSSET
   skin .... BUDGE
Lamb, Charles .... ELIA
lambast(e) ...... HIT, BEAT, SCOLD
lambda in Hebrew .... LAMED(H)
lambent .... GLOWING
lambkin .... CHILD
lamblike .... MEEK, GENTLE
lambrequin .... DRAPERY
lambskin .... BUDGE, VELLUM
lame .... HALT, MAIM, WEAK,
      HALTING, CRIPPLE(D),
      DISABLE(D), SPAVINED
lamebrain .... NIT, SAP, SIMP,
      NINNY
Lamech, daughter of .... NAAMAH
   father of .... METHUSELAH
   son of .... NOAH, JABAL,
      JUBAL, TUBAL CAIN
   wife of .... ADAH, ZILLAH
lamed(h) .... ELL, LAMBDA
lamellibranch .... CLAM, OYSTER,
      MOLLUSK
lamellirostral bird .... DUCK,
      SWAN, GOOSE
lament .... RUE, DIRGE, ELEGY,
      MOURN, (BE)MOAN, (BE)WAIL,
      GRIEVE, REGRET, (RE)PINE,
      DEPLORE, ELEGIZE
lamentation .... PLAINT, WAILING,
      WEEPING, JEREMIAD,
      MOURNING
lamenting .... TEARFUL, UNHAPPY,
      MOURNFUL, PLAINTIVE
lamia .... WITCH, VAMPIRE,
      DEMON(ESS), SORCERESS
lamina .... PLY, LEAF, FLAKE,
      LAYER, PLATE, SCALE, SHEET,
      STRATUM
laminated .... LAYERED
   material .... PLYWOOD
   rock .... SHALE
lamination .... PLY, LAYER,
      OVERLAY
lammergeier .... VULTURE
lamp .... GAS, JET, BULB, ETNA,

GLIM, TORCH, ARGAND,
GEORDIE, LANTERN, LUCERNA,
GOOSENECK, LUMINAIRE
black .... SOOT
cord/tape .... WICK
for signals .... ALDIS
fuel .... KEROSENE
holder .... CRESSET
lighter .... SPILL, TAPER
miner's .... DAVY
oil .... LAMPION, LUCIGEN
poetic .... SUN, MOON, STAR
Lamp Lady .... (FLORENCE)
NIGHTINGALE
lampblack .... SOOT, GRIME
lampoon ...... SKIT, SPOOF, SQUIB,
SATIRE, RIDICULE,
CARICATURE, PASQUINADE
lamprey .... EEL, CYCLOSTOME
lanai .... PORCH
lanate .... WOOL(L)Y
Lancashire city .... WIGAN
county seat .... LANCASTER
seaport .... LIVERPOOL,
MANCHESTER
Lancaster, actor .... BURT
lance .... CUT, DART, PIKE, SHAFT,
SPEAR, PIERCE, JAVELIN,
(SEA)FISH
barb .... FLUKE
flag of .... BANDEROL(E)
part .... REST, MORNE
Lancelot .... KNIGHT
liege of .... ARTHUR
love of .... ELAINE
mistress of .... GUINEVERE
uncle of .... BORS
lancer .... U(H)LAN, HUSSAR
lancers .... DANCE, QUADRILLE
lancet .... FLEAM, KNIFE, SCALPEL,
PHLEBOTOME
point .... NEB
Lanchester, actress .... ELSA
lancinate .... PIERCE, CRUCIFY,
LACERATE
land .... SOIL, CATCH, EARTH,
TERRA, TRACT, ALIGHT,
DEBARK, ESTATE, GROUND,
REGION, COUNTRY, TERRENE,
DISEMBARK
adjoining port .... ONSHORE
along river .... HOLM,
BOTTOMS, INTERVALE
and sea fighter .... MARINE
barren .... GALL, WASTE,
DESERT
based .... ONSHORE
biblical, rich in gold
.... OPHIR
border .... RAND
Cardiff's .... WALES

cattail .... MARSH
church .... CLOSE, GLEBE
close .... GARTH
conveyance .... DEED
cultivated ...... ARADA, ARADO,
TILTH, TILLAGE
disputed .... MARCH
division .... PLOT
east of Eden .... NOD
eroded .... PENEPLAIN
fill area .... DUMP
grant .... HOMESTEAD
grassy .... DOWN, VELDT
held in fee simple .... ALOD,
ODAL
holder .... THANE, THEGN
holdings record .... TERRIER
in general .... REAL ESTATE
irrigated to excess .... WATER-
SICK
like arable .... OPEN FIELD
Machu Picchu .... PERU
marshy .... MAREMMA
meadow .... LEA
measure .... AR(E), ACRE,
RO(O)D, HECTARE
mine .... CLAYMORE
moist area .... SWALE
of dwarfs .... LILIPUT
leprechauns .... EIRE
Lincoln .... ILLINOIS
plenty .... GOSHEN
romance .... ARDEN
shrubs, etc. .... BARRENS
sleep .... NOD
song .... ARABY
10,000 lakes ..... MINNESOTA
the massage .... SWEDEN
the shamrock .... IRELAND
on the Mekong .... LAOS
ownership, restricted .... FEE
TAIL
ownership, unrestricted
.... FEE SIMPLE
pertaining to .... AGRARIAN,
GEOPONIC
piece of .... LOT, PLAT,
PARCEL
pledged as security
.... WADSET
point of .... CAPE,
PROMONTORY
point of low .... SPIT
promised .... CANAAN
reverting to the state
.... ESCHEAT
reclaimed .... POLDER, INNINGS
rental .... FEU
strip of .... NECK
tenure .... LEASEHOLD
tenure system .... SOCAGE

title .... PATENT
triangular piece .... GORE,
DELTA
valued for taxes .... CADASTRE
west of Nod .... EDEN
wet .... MARSH, SWAMP,
MAREMMA
with heaviest rainfall
.... ASSAM
landau .... CARRIAGE,
AUTOMOBILE
landed .... ALIT, PRAEDIAL
estate .... MANOR, DOMAIN
property .... ESTATE
proprietor .... ESQUIRE
landfall .... ISLE
biblical .... ARARAT
landgrave .... COUNT
landing field/ground, aircraft
.... STRIP, RUNWAY, AIRDROME
place ...... DOCK, GHAT, PIER,
QUAI, QUAY, JETTY, LEVEE,
WHARF, TARMAC, AIRPORT,
HELIPORT
place of the Ark .... ARARAT
Landis, baseball czar
.... KENESAW
landloper ...... TRAMP, VAGRANT,
SUNDOWNER
landloping .... ERRANT, ROAMING
landlord .... HOST, LAIRD, OWNER,
BONIFACE
landmark .... CAIRN, SENAL,
MONUMENT, MOUNTAIN,
MILESTONE
landowner .... LAIRD
landscape .... PAYSAGE,
SCENE(RY)
landslide .... RUNAWAY,
AVALANCHE
landsman .... SAILOR
landtag .... DIET, ASSEMBLY
lane .... PATH, ALLEY, TRACK,
COURSE, STREET
Lange, actress .... HOPE
Langtry, actress .... LILY
language ...... LIP, IDIOM, SPEECH,
TONGUE, DIALECT, DICTION,
PARLANCE
artificial .... RO, IDO,
VOLAPUK, ESPERANTO
beggars' .... ARGOT, LINGO
classical .... GREEK, LATIN
dead .... LATIN
dialect .... IDIOM, LINGO
difficulty of understanding
.... DYSPHASIA
Hebrew's sister .... ARAMAIC
hybrid .... JARGON, LINGUA
FRANCA
kind of .... SIGN, GESTURE

mixed .... PIDGIN
of .... LINGUAL, LINGUISTIC
of the soul, so-called
.... MUSIC
of the street ...... CANT, SLANG
ordinary .... PROSE, DIALECT
origin idea .... BOW-WOW
                     THEORY
our .... MOTHER TONGUE
pretentious .... CLAPTRAP
Romance ...... LADIN, FRENCH,
   CATALAN, ITALIAN, SPANISH,
   ROMANIAN, PROVENCAL,
             PORTUGUESE
science of .... LINGUISTICS
thieves' .... ARGOT, FLASH
used by Egyptian natives
.... COPTIC
using click sound .... NAMA
Visogoths' .... GOTHIC
languages, he speaks/writes
  several .... LINGUIST,
                 POLYGLOT
Languedoc's capital
                  TOULOUSE
languid .... WAN, DULL, WEAK,
   SLOW, WEARY, DREAMY,
   FEEBLE, DROOPING, LISTLESS
languish .... FADE, FAIL, FLAG,
   DROOP, SWOON, WASTE,
            PINE(AWAY)
languor .... BLUES, ENNUI,
   DULLNESS, LETHARGY,
   HEAVINESS, LASSITUDE,
            STILLNESS
langur .... MAHA, MONKEY,
   SIMPAI, WANDEROO
laniard .... CORD
laniary .... CANINE
Lanier, poet .... SIDNEY
lank(y) ...... BONY, LEAN, GAUNT,
   GANGLY, SLENDER, SPINDLING
lanner(et) .... FALCON
lanose .... WOOL(L)Y
Lansbury, actress .... ANGELA
  role .... MAME
lantana .... MAJORANA
lantern .... LAMP, CRESSET
  feast .... BON
Lantsang .... MEKONG
lanugo .... DOWN, HAIR
lanyard .... CORD, ROPE, THONG
Lanza, singer .... MARIO
Laodicea .... LATAKIA
Laomedon's kingdom ...... TROY
  son .... PRIAM
Laos .... KINGDOM
  capital ...... VIENTIANE, LUANG
              PRABANG
  city/town ...... PAKXE, PHIAFAI,
             KHAMKEUT

fortress town .... NAM BAC
king of .... VATHANA
language .... FRENCH,
              LAO(TIAN)
monetary unit .... KIP
mountain .... PHOU BIA
plain .... JARS
rebels .... PATHET LAO
river .... MEKONG, SE KHONG
lap .... LICK, RACE, WRAP,
   (EN)FOLD, CIRCUIT
  dog .... PET, POM
  of luxury .... EASY STREET
  robe .... RUG
lapel .... FLAP, FOLD, REVER(S)
  stiffener .... WIGAN
  thing on .... BOUTONNIERE
lapidary .... ENGRAVER,
  JEWEL(L)ER, GEM-CUTTER
  instrument of .... ENTAL
lapidify .... PETRIFY
lapillus .... ROCK
lapin .... FUR, RABBIT
lapis .... STONE
  lazuli .... AZURE-BLUE
Laplander .... LAPP
  sledge of .... PULK(H)A
lapper .... CAT, DOG
lappet .... FLAP, FOLD, LOBE,
  LABEL, DEWLAP, WATTLE
lapse .... FALL, ERR(OR), FAULT,
  SLIP(UP), MISSTEP, PASS(AGE),
  INTERVAL, OVERSIGHT
lapwing ...... BIRD, WEEP, PEWEE,
  PEWIT, PLOVER, TREUTERO
lar .... SPIRIT
larboard .... APORT, PORT(SIDE)
larceny .... THEFT
  kind of .... GRAND, PETTY
larch .... PINE, TREE, SPRUCE,
            TAMARAC(K)
lard .... FAT, OIL, ENRICH,
  GREASE, GARNISH
  tub for .... FIRKIN
larder .... PANTRY, SPENCE,
  BUTTERY, CUPBOARD,
          PROVISIONS
Lardner, humorist .... RING
large .... BIG, HUGE, IMMENSE,
  MAN-SIZE, OUTSIZE, SIZABLE
  amount .... SLEW, SCADS,
           OODLES
  animal/person .... JUMBO
  artery .... AORTA
  as a sum .... TIDY
  at .... FREE, LOOSE, ABROAD
  bag .... CARRY-ALL
  book .... TOME
  bulrush .... TULE
  butte .... MESA
  cask .... TUN

channel .... ARTERY
exceedingly .... ENORMOUS
extra .... MAXI
extraordinarily ...... COLOSSAL,
             GIGANTIC
grasshopper .... KATYDID
heap .... MOUNTAIN
heavy lifting machine
.... WHOOPING CRANE
in scope/size .... AMPLE,
            SPACIOUS
kettle .... CALDRON
prefix .... MEGA, MACRO,
            MAGNI
quantity .... RUCK
scale .... EXTENSIVE,
            MASS(IVE)
wave .... SURGE
woody plant .... TREE
largely .... MAINLY, GREATLY,
  (PRETTY) MUCH
largeness .... SIZE, SCOPE, EXTENT
largess(e) .... GIFT(S), BOUNTY,
          GRATUITY
largest continent .... ASIA
  inland body of water
  .... CASPIAN
  island .... GREENLAND
  lake in the world ..... CASPIAN
            SEA
  lake in U.S. .... SUPERIOR
  land mass .... EURASIA
  ocean .... PACIFIC
  of seven .... ASIA
  planet .... JUPITER
lariat .... ROPE, LASSO, REATA,
            RIATA
  eye of .... HONDA, HONDO
  loop .... NOOSE
larine bird .... GULL
lark .... PIPIT, PRANK, SPREE,
  FROLIC, HURDLE, WAGTAIL,
  LAVEROCK, SONGBIRD,
         ADVENTURE
  genus .... ALAUDA
larkspur ...... PLANT, DELPHINIUM
larrigan .... MOCCASIN
larrup .... BEAT, FLOG, WHIP,
           THRASH
larva .... LOA, BOT(T), GRUB,
           MAGGOT
  butterfly .... CATERPILLAR
  beetle's .... GRUB, WOLF,
          CADELLE
  botfly .... WABBLE
  final stage of .... CHRYSALIS
  flea's .... CHIGOE, CHIGGER
  fly .... GENTLE
  frog's .... TADPOLE
  mite's .... JIGGER, LEPTUS
  moth's .... WOLF, EGGER

non-feeding stage of ..... PUPA
of antlion .... DOODLEBUG
of horsefly .... BOT
of tapeworm .... COENURUS
of trematode .... CERCARIA
weevil's .... GRUGRU
laryngeal sound .... AHEM
larynx .... VOICE BOX
rod for clearing ...... PROBANG
lasagna .... PASTA, MACARONI
lascar .... SAILOR
lascivious .... LEWD, WANTON,
LUSTFUL, UNCHASTE
laser inventor .... TOWNEE
lash .... TIE, BIND, DASH, FLOG,
WALE, WHIP, QUIRT, SMITE,
FASTEN, REBUKE, SPLICE,
SWITCH, SCOURGE
with words .... BLISTER
lashing .... ROPE, REBUKE,
SCOLDING, WHIPPING
lass .... GIRL, MISS, MAID(EN),
SERVANT, SWEETHEART
lassie .... GIRL, COLLEEN,
SWEETHEART
Lassie of the movies ...... COLLIE
lassitude .... LANGUOR,
LETHARGY, TIREDNESS,
WEARINESS
lasso .... ROPE, NOOSE, REATA,
RIATA, LARIAT
lassoer .... ROPER
last .... END, FINAL, OMEGA,
ENDURE, NEWEST, ENDMOST,
HINDMOST, REARMOST,
ULTIMATE
act .... FINALE
but one .... PENULT(IMATE)
chance drink .... REDEYE
chance of ____ .... MONTANA
Czarina's adviser
.... RASPUTIN
mentioned of two ...... LATTER
Mohican .... UNCAS
month .... ULTIMO
of a familiar hebdomad
.... SATURDAY
of the ____ .... BIG TIME
SPENDERS
rite .... WAKE
syllable of word .... ULTIMA
three words spoken by Jesus
Christ ...... IT IS FINISHED
will and ____ .... TESTAMENT
word in a famous
palindrome .... ELBA
word of comedian
.... PUNCHLINE
word, usually .... AMEN
Last Days of Pompeii heroine
.... IONE

Judgment .... DOOMSDAY
Supper .... CENA
Supper cup .... GRAIL
lasting .... DURABLE, LIFELONG,
PERMANENT
forever .... AGE-LONG
mark .... SCAR
lastly .... ENFIN, FINALLY
Latakia ...... TOBACCO, LAODICEA
latch .... HOOK, LASKET,
FASTEN(ING), (SPRING)LOCK
latchet .... TAP, LACE(T), STRAP
late .... NEO, DEAD, SLOW, TARDY,
FORMER, BELATED, OVERDUE
arrival .... STANDEE
bloomer .... ASTER
fetal death .... STILLBIRTH
lateen .... SAIL, DHOW, VESSEL
rigged vessel .... CARAVEL
latent .... HIDDEN, DORMANT,
POTENTIAL, QUIESCENT
later .... AFTER, TARDIER
poet .... ANON
lateral .... SIDEWAYS, SIDEWISE
opposed to .... MEDIAL
laterally ...... SIDELONG, SIDEWISE
laterite .... CLAY
latest .... LAST, NEWEST,
CURRENT, PRESENT
combining form .... NEO,
CENE
thing .... FAD, CRAZE, FASHION
latex, plant's .... MILK
plural of .... LATICES
source of .... POPPY,
MILKWEED, RUBBER TREE
trees' coagulated .... GUTTA
lath .... RAIL, RAKE, SLAT, SPALE,
SPLINE, SPLINT
lathe clamp .... CHUCK
operator .... TURNER
spindle .... MANDRIL
lather .... FOAM, SCUM, SUDS,
CREAM, FROTH, SPUME,
SWEAT
latherer .... SOAPER
lathery .... SOAPY, SPUMY, SUDSY
lathing shop .... TURNERY
Latin .... ROMAN, ITALIAN,
LANGUAGE, SPANIARD
a slip of the tongue
.... LAPSUS LINGUAE
abbot .... ABBAS
above .... SUPRA
accusation of treachery
.... ETTU
actual being .... ESSE
after .... POST
after the deed .... EX POST
FACTO
aged: abbr. .... AET

alas .... VAE, (E)HEU
all .... TOTO
alone .... SOLUS
also .... ETIAM
always .... SEMPER
always faithful .... SEMPER
FIDELIS
am present .... AD SUM
America, foreigner in
.... GRINGO
American country .... PERU,
CHILE, BELIZE, BRAZIL,
GUYANA, MEXICO, PANAMA,
BAHAMAS, JAMAICA,
HONDURAS, PARAGUAY,
ARGENTINA, GUATEMALA,
NICARAGUA, COSTA RICA, EL
SALVADOR
American measure .... LINO,
MOIO, VARA
and .... ET
and others .... ET AL(II)
anger .... IRA
ankles .... TALI
Arable land .... AGER
art .... ARS
artificially maintained .... IN
VITRO
as above .... UBI SUPRA
at first sight .... PRIMA FACIE
at approximately .... CIRCA
at the age of .... AET
at the point of death .... IN
EXTREMIS
atmosphere .... AER
author's abbreviation ..... IBID
band/sash .... FASCIA
bear ..... URSA, URSUS, URSULA
before .... ANTE, PRAE
behold .... ECCE
being .... ESSE
belts .... CESTI
between .... INTER
bird .... AVIS
bird, rare .... RARA AVIS
black .... ATRA
blessed .... BEATA
blind .... CAECUM
book .... LIBER
born .... NATUS
both .... AMBI
bronze .... AES
brother .... FRATER
bug .... CIMEX
but .... SED
by itself .... PER SE
by right of office .... EX
OFFICIO
by the day .... PER DIEM
by the head .... PER CAPITA
by the year .... PER ANNUM

catch-all: abbr. .... ET AL
charity .... CARITAS
city .... URB(I)S
clan .... GENS
copper .... CUPRUM
countryside .... RUS
dagger man .... SICARIUS
day .... DIEM, DIES
day of wrath .... DIES IRAE
defendants .... REI
discourse .... SERMO
dog .... CANIS
duct .... VAS
dumbfounded ...... NONPLUSED
ear .... AURIS
earth/land .... TERRA
earth exhalation ...... MEPHITIS
egg .... OVA, OVUM
either .... AUT
epic .... AENEID
equal .... PAR
error .... LAPSUS
everywhere .... UBIQUE
evil .... MALA, MALUM
existing condition ...... STATUS
QUO
farewell .... VALE
fate .... NONA
field(s) .... AGER, AGRI
fillet .... FASCIA
fire .... IGNIS
first among equals ..... PRIMUS
INTER PARES
fish .... PISCES
fisherman .... PISCATOR
flag .... LABARUM
fly .... MUSCA
for .... PRO
for example .... EXEMPLI
GRATIA
for the good .... PRO BONO
for the time being .... PRO
TEMPORE
force/strength .... VIS
friend .... AMICUS
friend of the court .... AMICUS
CURIAE
from himself .... DESE
from one side only .... EX
PARTE
from the seat of authority
.... EX CATHEDRA
gentle .... LENIS
go .... ITE
God .... DEUS
God willing ..... DEO VOLENTE
goddess .... DEA
gold .... AURUM
good .... BONUM
grape .... UVA
great .... MAGNA, MAGNUS

gums .... GINGIVA
he .... ILLE, IPSE
he loves .... AMAT
he was .... ERAT
head .... CAPUT
headband .... VITTA
health .... SANITAS
heat .... CALOR
hence .... ERGO
high .... ALTA
highest .... SUMMA
himself .... IPSE
holidays .... FERIA
holy .... SANCTUS
honey .... MEL
hour .... HORA
house .... DOMUS
however .... SED
hut .... TABERNA
I love .... AMO
I know .... SCIO
in good faith .... BONA FIDE
in passing .... OBITER
in the beginning .... INITIO
in the matter of .... INRE
in what manner .... QUO
MODO
is .... EST
itself .... IPSO
knee .... GENU
ladder .... SCALA
lamb .... AGNUS
laughter .... RISUS
law .... JUS, LEX, JURA
leave of absence .... ABSIT
leisure .... OTIUM
let buyer beware .... CAVEAT
EMPTOR
letter .... LITTERA
light .... LUX, LUMEN
likewise .... SIMUL
localities .... LOCI
long .... LONGUS
magpie .... PICA
man .... VIR, HOMO
mass .... MISSA
mass, sung .... MISSA
CANTATA
masterpiece .... MAGNUM OPUS
members .... SOCII
mine .... MEUM
mint .... MONETA
month .... MENSIS
moon .... LUNA
mountain .... MONS
mouths .... ORA
name/title .... NOMEN
needle .... ACUS
net .... RETE
nine .... NONUS
nobody .... NEMO

not .... NON
not final .... NISI
note well .... NOTA BENE
now .... NONC
number .... UNUS
observe .... NOTA
of age .... AET
of anger .... IRAE
onion .... CEPA
order .... ORDO
other .... ALIA
other self .... ALTER EGO
otherwise .... ALITER
our .... NOSTER
Our Father ...... PATER NOSTER
peace .... PAX
peace-making .... PACIFUS
peacock .... PAVO
people .... POPULI
person, unacceptable/
unwelcome ...... PERSONA
NON GRATA
place(s) .... LOCI, LOCUS
pleasant .... AMOENUS
plume .... PINNACULUM
poet .... OVID
power/strength .... VIS
"Prayer and Work" .... ORA
ET LABORA
pray(ing) .... ORA(NS)
proper .... DECOROUS
proportionately ...... PRO RATA
provided that .... PROVISO
QUOD
Quarters dwellers .... ARTISTS,
STUDENTS
Quarters site .... PARIS
quickly .... CITO
ritual .... RITUS
sailor .... NAUTA
same .... IDEM
sands .... ARENAE
secretly .... SUB ROSA
see .... VIDE
shed .... TABERNA
ship .... NAVIS
sister .... SOROR
skin .... CUTIS
snow .... NIVIS
soft .... LENIS
solid ground ..... TERRA FIRMA
something in return/
something for something
.... QUID PRO QUO
son .... FILIUS
speed .... CELERITAS
star(s) .... ASTRA, STELLA
stone .... LAPIS
table .... MENSA
thank God .... DEO GRATIAS
that is .... ID EST

the Lord's Prayer .... PATER NOSTER
then .... TUNC
therefore .... ERGO
thing .... RES
this .... HIC, HOC
thread .... FILUM
throat .... GULA
throughout .... PASSIM
thus .... ITA, SIC
tile .... TEGULA
time .... TEMPUS, TEMPORA
time flies .... TEMPUS FUGIT
to a sickening degree ...... AD NAUSEAM
  be evident .... PATERE
  be pleasing .... COMPLACERE
  close .... CLAUDERE
  destroy .... PERIMERE
  go astray .... ABERRARE
  make .... FACERE
  make worse .... PEJORARE
  pour .... FUNDERE
  predict .... SAGIRE
  rule .... REGERE, REGNARE
  run ahead ..... PRAECURRERE
toad .... BUFO
total .... SUMMA
twice .... BIS
under .... SUB
under consideration .... SUB JUDICE
unless .... NISI
vegetable .... OLER
voice .... VOX
voice of the people .... VOX POPULI
wasp .... VESPA
waste away .... TABERE
water .... AQUA
wax .... CERA
way of working .... MODUS OPERANDI
we .... NOS
weight .... PONDUS
well .... BENE
wheel .... ROTA
where .... UBI
wife .... UXOR
within .... INTRA
without .... SINE
without setting a day ..... SINE DIE
without which there is nothing .... SINE QUA NON
wolf .... LUPUS
wool .... LANA
yawn .... HIARE
year(s) .... ANNI, ANNO, ANNUS
latite .... LAVA

latitude .... SCOPE, WIDTH, EXTENT, LEEWAY, BREADTH
latitudinarian .... DEMOCRAT
Latium, ancient people of
  .... VOLSCI
Latona .... LETO
  progeny of ..... DIANA, APOLLO
latrine .... PRIVY, TOILET
Latter-day Saint .... MORMON
lattice .... GRILLE, SCREEN, TRELLIS, ESPALIER
latticework .... PERGOLA, TRELLIS, ESPALIER
Latvian .... LETT(IC), LETTISH
  capital .... RIGA
  city/town .... SALDUS, JELGAVA, LIEPAJA, REZEKNE, VENTSPILS, DAUGAVPILS
  coin .... LAT
  gulf .... RIGA
  lake .... LUBANA
  monetary unit .... LAT(U)
  river .... DVINA, GAUJA, VENTA
  seaport .... RIGA, LIEPAJA
  state, ancient .... LIVONIA, COURLAND
laud .... HYMN, EXALT, EXTOL, PRAISE, GLORIFY
  publicly .... SING ONE'S PRAISES
laudable .... DESERVING, EXEMPLARY, COMMENDABLE, (PRAISE)WORTHY
laudanum .... RESIN
laudation .... EULOGY, PRAISE
laudatory .... PRAISING, EULOGISTIC
laugh .... BRAY, ROAR, FLEER, TE-HEE, CACKLE, DERIDE, GIGGLE, GUFFAW, HAW-HAW, HEEHAW, NICKER, TITTER, CHORTLE, CHUCKLE, SNICKER
  able to .... RISIBLE
  at .... MOCK, RIDICULE
  down .... SILENCE, EMBARRASS
  loudly .... ROAR
  off .... SCORN, REJECT
  too much .... CACHINNATE
laughable .... DROLL, FUNNY, ABSURD, AMUSING, COMICAL, RISIBLE, HUMOROUS
laughing .... RIANT, RIDENT
  gas .... NITROUS OXIDE
laughingstock .... BUTT
laughs, he never .... AGELAST
laughter. See also laugh
  causing .... RISIBLE
  measure of .... GALES
  pertaining to .... GELASTIC
  sound of .... PEAL
la(u)nce .... EEL

Launcelot the clown ...... GOBBO
Launce's dog .... CRAB
launch .... HURL, BEGIN, START, SEND OFF, DISCHARGE, MOTORBOAT
  Malay .... LANCA
  Spanish/Portuguese
  .... LANCHA
launder .... WASH
laundry equipment ...... SETTUBS
  frame .... AIRER
"Laura" of movie fame
  .... GENE TIERNEY
lauraceous tree .... LAUREL, NUTMEG, AVOCADO, CAMPHOR
laurel .... BAY, IVY, TREE, SHRUB, AZALEA, CAJEPUT
  bark .... COTO
  bay .... MAGNOLIA
  family .... HEALTH, KALMIA
  mountain .... BUSH, CALICO
  woven sprigs .... LAUREATE
Laurel, actor .... STAN
laurels ...... FAME, HONOR, KUDOS
Lausanne canton .... VAUD
lava .... ASH, MAGMA, COULEE, LATITE, TAXITE, OBSIDIAN
  cinder .... SCORIA
  cooled .... AA
  fine .... ASH
  fragment .... LAPILLUS
  lava .... LOINCLOTH
  pieces of .... SLAG, SCORIA
lavabo .... BASIN, TOWEL, LAVATORY, WASHBOWL
lavage .... WASHING
lavalier(e) .... PENDANT
lavatory .... BASIN, LAVABO, RESTROOM, (WASH)BOWL
lave ...... DIP, FLOW, POUR, WASH, BATHE, ABSTERGE
lavender .... MINT, ASPIC, PURPLE
  product .... OIL, PERFUME
laver .... FONT, BASIN, SEAWEED
lavish .... ORNATE, WANTON, LIBERAL, PROFUSE, GENEROUS, PRODIGAL, UNSPARING, UNSTINTED
law .... ACT, JUS, LEX, CODE, RULE, CANON, EDICT, STATUTE, ORDINANCE
  abstract .... JUS
  and order .... PEACE
  and order, GIs' .... MPS
  break the .... BREACH, INFRACT, VIOLATE
  breaker .... FELON, SINNER, CRIMINAL, JAILBIRD
  court .... BENCH, FORUM
  courts of .... JUDICIARY
  degree .... LLB

denying throne to women .... SALIC

expert .... JURIST

fictitious name in .... (JANE)DOE, (JOHN)DOE

imperial .... UKASE

intervening .... MESNE

kind of .... COMMON, STATUTE, (UN)WRITTEN

like for like .... TALION

municipal .... ORDINANCE

not enforced ..... DEAD LETTER

of the Middle Ages .... CURFEW

of the place .... LEX, LOCI

offenses against .... MALA

pertaining to .... JURAL, LEGAL, CANONIC, FORENSIC

points in .... LIS, RES

the .... POLICE(MAN)

unwritten .... COMMON

volume .... CODEX

Law in physics .... JOULE'S

of Moses .... TORAH, PENTATEUCH

of Moses book .... EXODUS, GENESIS, NUMBERS

lawful .... JUST, LEGAL, LICIT, VALID, LEGITIMATE

lawgiver .... MOSES, SOLON

lawless .... UNRULY, CRIMINAL, MUTINOUS, LICENTIOUS

lawlessness .... ANARCHY, LICENSE, VIOLENCE

lawmaker .... SOLON, SENATOR, LEGISLATOR

lawmaking .... LEGISLATION

lawman .... MARSHAL, OFFICER, SHERIFF, POLICEMAN

badge .... STAR

slang .... COP(PER), JOHN LAW, THE FUZZ

lawn .... GLADE, BATISTE, CAMBRIC, GRASS PLOT

pest .... MOLE

tool .... EDGER, MOWER

Lawrence of _____ .... ARABIA

laws, body of .... CODE, PANDECTS, DECALOG(UE)

describing some ..... ARCHAIC, DEAD LETTER

what some lack .... TEETH

lawsuit .... CASE, ACTION, DISPUTE, LITIGATION

expenses .... COSTS

grounds .... GIST

of a sort .... TEST CASE

party to a .... SUER, CLAIMANT, LITIGANT, DEFENDANT, LITIGATOR, PLAINTIFF

lawsuits, habitual ...... BARRATRY

prone to .... LITIGIOUS

lawyer .... LEGIST, ADVISER, COUNSEL(OR), ADVOCATE, ATTORNEY, LEGALIST, BARRISTER, SOLICITOR

cap of .... COIF

fee of .... RETAINER

inferior .... PETTIFOGGER

of fiction .... TUTT, MASON

profession of .... BAR

slang .... LIP, MOUTHPIECE

unscrupulous .... SHYSTER

woman .... PORTIA

word of .... HEREOF, WHEREFORE, HERETOFORE

lawyers' bag .... BRIEFCASE

body .... BAR

bible .... BLACKSTONE

concern .... CASE, BRIEF, TRIAL, HEARING, EVIDENCE

degree .... LLB

patron saint .... IVES

lax .... WEAK, LOOSE, SLACK, CARELESS, DISORDERLY

laxative .... ALOIN, CASSIA, PHYSIC, APERIENT, MAGNESIA, CATHARTIC, PURGATIVE

lay .... SET, LAIC, POEM, SONG, DITTY, PLACE, BALLAD, MELODY, DEPOSIT, RECLINE, SECULAR, LOUNGE LIZARD

aside .... PEND, SAVE, TABLE

away .... SAVE

by .... HOARD

down .... BET, WAGER

down arms .... SURRENDER, CAPITULATE

figure .... DUMMY, PUPPET

into .... BEAT, LASH, SCOLD

it on .... FLATTER, EXAGGERATE

off .... STOP, CEASE, DISCHARGE

open .... EXPOSE

siege .... INVEST

to rest .... BURY

up .... PILE, HOARD

waste .... RAVAGE, DEVASTATE

layer ...... PLY, COAT, FOLD, TIER, LAMINA, PATINA, VENEER, STRATUM

feathered .... HEN, BIRD

of iris .... UVEA

layered .... SCUMMY, LAMINAR, FOLIATED, TUNICATE

layette, part of .... BOOTEE

layman .... LAIC, AMATEUR

layout .... FORMAT, MAKE-UP

lazar .... LEPER, BEGGAR

Lazarus .... LEPER, BEGGAR

friend of .... JESUS

hometown of .... BETHANY

poet and essayist .... EMMA

sister of .... MARY, MARTHA

laze .... LOAF, GOOF OFF, LOUNGE

laziness .... SLOTH, INDOLENCE

lazuli, ... LAPIS

lazy .... IDLE, SLOW, OTIOSE, INDOLENT, SLOTHFUL

and Hayward .... SUSANS

fellow .... DRONE, IDLER, LOAFER, DEADBEAT, NE'ER-DO-WELL

Susan .... TRAY, TURNTABLE

lazybones .... BUM, DRONE, IDLER, LOAFER

Le Gallienne, actress .... EVA

lea .... MEAD(OW), PASTURE

leach .... BLEED, EXTRACT, LIXIVIATE

lead ...... CUE, CLUE, HEAD, HINT, OPEN, GUIDE, PILOT, BULLET, DIRECT, GALENA, PROMPT, CONDUCT, PLUMBUM

a passive existence .... VEGETATE

astray ...... DECEIVE, MISGUIDE, MISDIRECT

black .... GRAPHITE, PLUMBAGO

glass .... PASTE, STRASS

in alchemy .... SATURN

in chemistry .... PB

off .... BEGIN

on .... LURE, DIRECT, ENTICE

ore of .... GALENA

oxide .... LITHARGE

pellets .... SHOT

-pipe cinch .... SNAP

poisoning .... PLUMBISM

red .... MINIUM

rope .... LONGE

shot .... PELLET

up to .... PAVE (THE WAY)

white .... CERUSE

writing tool .... PENCIL

leaden .... HEAVY, GLOOMY, SOMBER

leader .... HEAD, CHIEF, GUIDE, OVERMAN, COMMANDER, CONDUCTOR, DOWNSPOUT

Argonauts' .... JASON

chorus .... CANTOR

of the Green Mountain Boys .... ALLEN

sheep .... BELLWETHER

leadership .... GUIDANCE, HIGH COMMAND

quality, special ...... CHARISMA

leading ...... MAIN, AHEAD, CHIEF, STELLAR, FOREMOST,

PRINCIPAL, UP ON THE LINKS
actor/actress .... STAR
bid .... OPENER
leaf .... PAGE, FROND, LAMINA,
SPATHE, LAMELLA
aperture .... STOMA(TA)
attachment .... STEM, TWIG,
STIPEL, PETIOLE
beverage .... TEA
book .... PAGE, FOLIO
bud .... GEMMA
central vein .... MIDRIB
combining form ..... PHYLL(O)
cutter .... ANT, ATTA
disease .... RUST, MOSAIC
division .... PALMATE, PINNATE
drug .... HEMP, HASHISH,
MARIJUANA
floating .... PAD
flower .... BRACT, SEPAL
fodder .... RAPE
front side of .... RECTO
grass .... BLADE
lily .... PAD
metal .... FOIL
miner beetle .... HISPA
modified .... BRACT, PALEA,
CARPEL, PISTIL
part .... VEIN, BLADE, STALK,
(MID)RIB, STIPLE, PETIOLE
pores .... STOMA
rib .... VEIN, NERVURE
shape .... OVAL, LINEAR,
OBLONG, DELTOID, CUNEATE,
PELTATE
side of .... RECTO, VERSO
stalk .... PETIOLE
through book .... RIFFLE
tip .... MUCRO
tobacco .... CAVENDISH
vein .... RIB, NERVURE
leafage .... FOLIAGE
leafless plant .... CACTUS
leaflet .... PINNA, PINNULE,
HANDBILL, THROWAWAY
leafstalk .... CHARD, PETIOLE
leafy .... FOLIOSE
shelter .... BOWER
spot .... TREE-TOP
league .... BUND, ALLIANCE,
COALITION
in .... JOINT, ALLIED
merchants' .... HANSE
Leah's daughter .... DINAH
father .... LABAN
husband .... JACOB, ISRAEL
maid .... ZILPAH
sister .... RACHEL
son ...... LEVI, JUDAH, REUBEN,
SIMEON, ZEBULUN, ISSACHAR
leak .... LET, DRIP, OOZE, SEEP

leakage .... ESCAPE
leakproofing item .... GASKET
leal .... TRUE, LOYAL
lean .... BONY, CANT, LANK(Y),
LIST, SLIM, TEND, THIN, TILT,
GAUNT, SLANT, SPARE,
MEAGER, SKINNY, INCLINE,
SCRAGGY
and sinewy .... WIRY
as a ship .... ALIST
into .... CAREEN
on .... COMPEL, PRESS(URE)
pocket .... POOR,
IMPOVERISHED
sideways .... TIP, TILT, CAREEN
toward .... PREFER
Leander's love .... HERO
leaning .... BENT, OBLIQUE,
PENCHANT, INCLINATION
tower of ____ .... PISA
leanto .... HUT, SHED, SHACK
leap .... HOP, DIVE, JUMP, LOUP,
BOUND, LUNGE, SPANG,
VAULT, BOUNCE, POUNCE,
SPRING
ballet .... ENTRECHAT
over .... SKIP, CLEAR
playful .... CAPER, CAVORT,
GAMBOL
year .... BISSEXTILE
year gainer .... FEBRUARY
leaping .... SALIENT, SALTANT
amphibian .... TOAD
Lear, daughter of .... REGAN,
GONERIL, CORDELIA
dog of .... TRAY
learn ...... HEAR, KNOW, UNEARTH,
DISCOVER, ASCERTAIN
by heart .... MEMORIZE
superficially .... SMATTER
learned .... WISE, ERUDITE,
LETTERED, LITERATE
man .... SAGE, PANDIT(A),
PEDANT, PUNDIT, SAVANT,
SCHOLAR, INTELLECTUAL
people .... CLERISY, LITERATI
learning .... WISDOM, CULTURE,
ERUDITION, KNOWLEDGE
branch of .... OLOGY
shallow .... SCIOLISM
traditional .... LORE
lease .... LET, RENT, REMISE,
CHARTER, CONTRACT
grant .... DEMISE
leaseholder .... LESSEE
leash ...... CURB, JESS, REIN, ROPE,
BRACE, LONGE, THONG,
TETHER, CONTROL
hound .... LIMER
ring .... TERRET
least .... FEWEST, MINIMUM,

SMALLEST, SLIGHTEST
abrasive .... MILDEST
amount .... WHIT
costly .... LOWEST
kempt .... SEEDIEST
likely .... LAST, MINIMAL
leastwise .... ANYWAY
leather .... KID, CALF, SUEDE
armor .... GAMBESON
bag .... POUCH
band .... STROP
bookbinding .... SKIVER
bottle .... MATARA
convert into .... TAN, TAW
cutter .... SKIVER
factory .... TANNERY
fine .... VELLUM
flask .... OLPE, MATARA
glove .... KID, NAPA, MOCHA,
SUEDE, MITTEN
heel (shoe) .... RAND
jacket .... JERKIN
kind of .... ELK, KIP, CALF,
NAPA, ROAN, MOCHA, LEVANT,
OXHIDE, CHAMOIS, COWHIDE,
MOROCCO, SHAGREEN
like .... CORIACEOUS
maker .... TANNER
napped .... SUEDE
pouch .... SPORRAN
prepare .... TAN, TAW
saddle .... MOCHILA
sheepskin .... ROAN, SKIVER
shoe repair .... FOXING
soft ...... NAPA, ROAN, MOCHA,
SUEDE, CHAMOIS
softener .... DUBBIN(G)
strap .... THONG
strip .... RAND, WELT, STRAP,
THONG
thong .... BRAIL
worker .... TANNER
leatherback .... TURTLE
leatherette .... MOROCCO
leatherfish .... LIJA
leatherneck ...... GYRENE, MARINE
leave .... QUIT, EXEAT, COMMIT,
DEPART, DESERT, PERMIT,
VACATE, SET OUT, VAMOOSE,
ENTRUST, FORSAKE,
BEQUEATH, PERMISSION
a margin .... INDENT
a Pullman .... DETRAIN
behind .... ABANDON
hurriedly .... LAM, DECAMP,
SKIDDOO, HIGHTAIL
kind of .... MATERNITY,
SABBATICAL
military .... FURLOUGH
of absence .... VACATION
off .... STOP, CEASE, DESIST

out .... BAN, OMIT, ELIDE, EXCEPT, IGNORE, EXCLUDE
port .... SAIL, OUTSTAND
secretly and suddenly .... DECAMP, ABSCOND
stage .... EXIT, EXEUNT
taking .... ADIEU, CONGE, PARTING, FAREWELL
the job .... QUIT, RETIRE
leaven .... BARM, YEAST, (EN)ZYME, SOURDOUGH
leaves .... PAGES, FOLIAGE
circular arrangement of .... VERTICIL
cluster .... ROSETTE
collectively .... FOLIAGE
covered with .... FOLIOSE
fragrant .... THYME
laxative .... SENNA
seasoning .... THYME, BAY, LAUREL
vegetable .... SLAW
leaving(s) .... ORTS, CHAFF, DRAFF, DREGS, WASTE, REFUSE, RESIDUE, REMNANTS
pick up .... GLEAN
Lebanon capital .... BEIRUT
city/town .... TYRE, ALEIH, SAIDA, ZAHLE, BATRUN, HERMIL, BAALBEK, TRIPOLI
language .... ARABIC
monetary unit .... POUND
native .... LEVANTINE
president .... HELOU, (ELIAS) HRAWI
river .... LITANI
seaport .... TYRE, SAIDA, TRIPOLI
Sur of, formerly .... TYRE
Valley river .... ORONTES
lecher .... ROUE, SATYR, DEBAUCHEE
lecherous .... RANDY, LUSTFUL, SENSUAL
look .... LEER
lectern .... AMBO, STAND, PULPIT, (READING) DESK
lection .... READING
lector .... READER, LECTURER, PREACHER
lecture .... TALK, SERMON, DISCOURSE, SCOLD(ING)
hall .... LYCEUM
lecturer .... DOCENT, READER, (PRE)LECTOR
Leda's daughter .... HELEN
husband .... TYNDAREUS
lover .... SWAN, ZEUS
son .... CASTOR, POLLUX
ledge .... LODE, SILL, RIDGE, BERM(E), SHELF

altar .... RETABLE
ledger entry .... LOSS, RENT, DEBIT, CREDIT, INCOME, EXPENSE, INTEREST
lee .... SHELTER, PROTECTION
Lee, horse of R. E. .... TRAVELER
opposed to .... STOSS, WEATHER, WINDWARD
leech .... HEAL, WORM, BLEED(ER), ANNELID, PARASITE, PHYSICIAN, BLOODSUCKER
leek ...... BULB, ALLIUM, SCALLION
relation .... ONION, GARLIC, SHALLOT
leer .... EYE, MOCK, OGLE, SCOFF, SMIRK, SNEER, STARE
leery .... WARY, DUBIOUS, GUARDED, SUSPICIOUS
lees ...... DRAFF, DREGS, GROUNDS, RESIDUE, SEDIMENT
leet .... COURT
Leeward islands .... NEVIS, ANTIGUA, ST. KITTS, MONTSERRAT
leeway .... SAG, ROOM, SPACE, MARGIN, LATITUDE
left .... WENT, NEAR(SIDE), DEPARTED, LARBOARD, PORT(SIDE)
aground .... NEAPED, BEACHED, STRANDED
combining form .... L(A)EVO
hand .... LEVO, SINISTER
hand of page .... VERSO
handed .... LEFTY, CLUMSY, DUBIOUS, SOUTHPAW, INSINCERE
on the .... NIGH
on the table .... UNEATEN
political .... RADICAL
turn .... HAW
unharmed .... SPARED
leftist ...... RED, LIBERAL, RADICAL
leftover .... END, ORT, SCRAP, MORSEL, REMNANT, SURPLUS
lefty .... SOUTHPAW
leg ...... PIN, LIMB, PROP, GAMB(E), SHANK
calf, of the .... SURAL
colloquial .... GAM, PEG, PIN, STUMP
covering .... PUTTY, GAITER, PEDULE, PUTTEE, LEGGINGS
fleshy part .... CALF
fowl's .... DRUMSTICK
front of .... SHIN
from hip joint to knee .... FEMUR
from knee to ankle ...... CRUS, SHANK
hinge .... KNEE

in heraldry .... GAMB
irons .... NIPPERS
joint .... HOCK, KNEE, ANKLE
journey's .... TREK
mutton .... AVINE, GIGOT
part .... HAM, CALF, CRUS, SHIN, FEMUR, SHANK, TIBIA, CONDYLES
pertaining to .... SURAL, CRURAL
shake a .... HURRY
support .... SPLINT
thigh .... FEMUR
vein .... SAPHENA
wooden .... STUMP
legacy .... GIFT, BEQUEST, PATRIMONY, INHERITANCE
receiver of .... HEIR(ESS), LEGATEE
legal .... JURAL, LICET, LICIT, VALID, LAWFUL, LEGITIMATE
abstract .... PRECIS
action .... RES, CASE, (LAW)SUIT, REPLEVIN, LITIGATION
arrest .... CAPTION
attachment .... LIEN
charge .... FEE
claim .... LIEN, DEMAND
code .... PANDECT
contestant .... LITIGANT
defense .... ALIBI
delay .... MORA, STAY
fee .... DUE, RETAINER
hearing .... OYER, TRIAL
instrument .... DEED
minority .... NONAGE
notice .... MONITION
offense .... CRIME, DELIT, DELICT
order .... WRIT
paper .... DEED
plea .... DEMURRER
point .... RES
possession .... SIESIN, SEIZIN
profession .... BAR, LAW
record .... ACTA, ESTREAT
redress .... REMEDY
right .... DROIT
site .... VENUE
substitute .... SURROGATE
summons .... SUBPOENA
tender .... MONEY
warning .... CAVEAT
wrong .... TORT
legalism in relation ...... NOMISM
legalize .... SIGN, ENACT
legally bound .... LIABLE
competent ..... SANE, SUI JURIS
legate .... ENVOY, AMBASSADOR
Papal .... NUNCIO

legatee .... HEIR, INHERITOR
legation .... EMBASSY, MISSION
legato, opposed to .... STACCATO
legator .... TESTATOR
legend .... MYTH, SAGA, TALE,
FABLE, MOTTO, STORY, TITLE,
CAPTION, INSCRIPTION
legendary .... EPIC, STORIED,
FABULOUS, FICTITIOUS
bird .... ROC, HALCYON
talespinner .... BARON
MUNCHAUSEN
leger .... LIGHT
legerdemain ...... MAGIC, TRICKS,
HOCUS-POCUS, SLEIGHT OF
HAND
leges, singular of .... LEX
legging(s) .... GAITER, PUTTEE
Leghorn ...... HAT, HEN, CHICKEN,
LIVORNO
legible .... READABLE
legion .... ARMY, HORDE,
MULTITUDE
unit .... COHORT, MANIPLE
legionary ant .... ECITON
Legionnaires' disease
.... PNEUMONIA
bacterium genus
.... LEGIONELLA
legislate .... ENACT
legislative body .... DAIL, DIET,
HOUSE, CORTES, SENATE,
COUNCIL, ASSEMBLY,
CONGRESS, PARLIAMENT
building .... CAPITOL
legislator .... SOLON, SENATOR,
LAWMAKER
legislature .... HOUSE, SENATE,
ASSEMBLY, CHAMBER,
COUNCIL
Canada .... PARLIAMENT
Denmark .... FOLKETING
Germany .... BUNDESTAG,
VOLKSHAMMER
Great Britain ..... PARLIAMENT
Ireland .... DAIL (EIREAN)
Israel .... KNESSET
Japan .... DIET
lameduck .... RUMP
Norway .... STORTING
Poland .... SEJM
Spain .... CORTES
Sweden .... RIKSDAG
United States .... CONGRESS
legist .... LAWYER
legit: sl. .... STAGE, THEATER
legitimate .... LEGAL, LICIT,
VALID, LAWFUL, ALLOWED
legless amphibian .... CAECILIAN
legree .... MASTER, OVERSEER
fictional .... SIMON

legume ...... PEA, POD, SOY, BEAN,
SEED, PLANT, PULSE, LENTIL,
LOMENT
Lehar, composer .... FRANZ
specialty .... OPERETTA
Lehmann, soprano .... LILLI,
LOTTE
lehua .... TREE, MYRTLE
lei .... WREATH, GARLAND
singular .... LEU
leister .... SPEAR, TRIDENT
leisure .... EASE, OTIOSE, FREE
TIME
leisurely .... EASY, RELAXED,
SLOW(LY), UNHURRIED
leman .... LOVER, MISTRESS
Lemberg .... LWOW, LVOV
lemming .... RAT, RODENT
destiny .... SUICIDE
kin .... VOLE
lemon .... FRUIT, CITRUS
juice squeezer .... REAMER
juice vitamin .... CITRIN
like fruit .... LIME, CITRON
peel .... RELISH
yellow ...... CITRINE, CITREOUS
lemons, of .... CITRIC
lemur .... INDRI, LORIS, POTTO,
AYEAYE, MACACO, MONKEY,
SIFAKA
flying .... COLUGO, GALAGO
kin of .... TARSIER
Lemuria .... CONTINENT
Lena, singer .... HORNE
tributary .... ALDAN
lenard .... LINNET
Lenape .... INDIAN
lend .... IMPART, LET OUT,
ADVANCE
an ear .... LISTEN
words with .... AN EAR, A
HAND
length .... EXTENT
abbreviation .... LGTH
finger to elbow .... CUBIT
having .... LINEAR
of day's march .... ETAPE
times width product ..... AREA
unit .... MIL, YARD, METER,
MICRON
lengthen .... EKE, EXTEND,
DISTEND, PROLONG, STRETCH,
ELONGATE, PROTRACT
lengthening of a short syllable
.... ECTASIS
lengthwise .... LONGWAYS
lengthy .... LONG, PROLIX, DRAWN
OUT, EXTENDED
lenient .... MILD, GENTLE,
AUDIENT, CLEMENT, MERCIFUL
Lenin, premier .... NIKOLAI

(ULIANOV)
Leningrad river .... NEVA
lenis ...... MILD, SOFT, SMOOTH
opposed to .... FORTIS
lenitive .... SOOTHING
lenity .... MILDNESS
leno .... WEAVE, FABRIC
lens .... MENISCUS, REFRACTOR
hand .... READER
kind of ..... CONVEX, CONCAVE
man .... PHOTOGRAPHER
of the eye .... CORNEA,
CRYSTALLINE LENS
opacification of the eye
.... CATARACT
plastic prosthesis ..... IMPLANT
shaped .... LENTOID
type of .... TORIC, MENISCUS
lent .... IMPREST
Lent, 4th Sunday in .... LAETARE
observance .... FASTING
revelry before .... CARNIVAL
lentigo .... FRECKLE
lentil .... PEA, SEED, PLANT,
PULSE, LEGUME
l'envoi .... VERSE, STANZA,
DEDICATION, POSTSCRIPT,
INSCRIPTION
Leonard's (Jack) forte
.... INSULT
Leonardo da ____ .... VINCI
Vinci's famous painting
...... MONA LISA, LA GIOCONDA
Vinci's masterpiece .... THE
LAST SUPPER
Leoncavallo, opera by ...... ZAZA,
PAGLIACCI
Leonidas' country .... SPARTA
scene of defeat
.... THERMOPYLAE
leopard .... CAT, OUNCE, OCELOT,
PANTHER
like animal .... JAGUAR
of old .... PARD
pet .... CHEETAH
young .... WHELP
leotard .... TIGHTS
leper .... LAZAR, PARIAH,
LAZARUS, OUTCAST
colony .... LEPROSARIUM
hospital .... SPITAL
patron saint of .... GILES
lepidolite .... MICA
lepidopteron .... MOTH
lepidate .... FLAKY, SCALY,
SCURFY
Lepontine Alps peak ...... LEONE
leporid (leporine) animal
.... HARE, RABBIT
leprechaun .... ELF, FAIRY,
GOBLIN

423

like .... ELFIN
leprosy .... LEPRA, HANSEN'S
                DISEASE
leprous .... UNCLEAN
    beggar .... LAZAR(US)
leptons, 100 .... DRACHMA
leptus .... MITE, LARVA
lepus .... HARE, CONSTELLATION
lerot .... DORMOUSE
Les Miserables author ...... HUGO
    character .... JAVERT, FANTINE,
                VALJEAN
Lesage, novelist ...... RENE, ALAIN
lesbian .... EROTIC, SAPPHO,
            HOMOSEXUAL
    ,
Lesbos .... MYTILENE
    poet .... ARION, SAPPHO,
         ALCAEUS, LESCHES
lese majeste .... TREASON
lesion .... HURT, SORE, WART,
      WOUND, DAMAGE, INJURY,
             INFECTION
Lesotho's capital .... MASERU
    city/town .... LERIBE,
              MAFETENG
    former name ..... BASUTOLAND
    language .... SESOTHO
    monetary unit .... LOTI,
              LISENTE
less .... BELOW, MINOR, MINUS,
    UNDER, FEW(ER), SMALLER
    appealing .... STALER
    colorful .... PALER
    degree/extent .... SCALED-
             DOWN
    experienced .... RAWER,
             GREENER
    feral/ferine .... TAMER
    hearty .... WEAKER
    in music .... MENO
    in quantity/value .... LOWER
    quality .... INFERIOR
    restrictive .... LOOSER
    ripe .... GREENER
    sufficient .... SHORTER
    sweet .... TARTER
    zany .... SANER
lessee .... RENTER, TENANT
lessen .... EASE, THIN, (A)BATE,
    TAPER, MINIFY, REDUCE,
    DECREASE, DIMINISH,
    MINIMIZE, MITIGATE,
          DISPARAGE
lesser .... MINOR, SMALLER
Lesser Antilles islands
    .... LEEWARD
    Bear .... URSA (MINOR)
lesson .... EXERCISE, ASSIGNMENT,
         INSTRUCTION
    from fable .... MORAL
    music .... ETUDE

lessor .... LANDLORD
let .... RENT, ALLOW, LEASE,
    ASSIGN, PERMIT, SUFFER,
         HIRE(OUT)
    fall .... DROP
    go .... FIRE, LOOSE(N),
             RELEASE
    in .... ADMIT, WELCOME,
             INTROMIT
    it go .... FORGET, IGNORE
    it stand .... STA, STET
    on .... ACT, HINT, PRETEND
    out .... EMIT, TELL, DISMISS,
        DIVULGE, RELEASE
    _____ rest, said Adam .... EVE
    sink .... VAIL
    up .... EASE, ABATE, CEASE,
    RELAX, SLACKEN, RELENT(ED)
letdown ...... BLOW, ANTICLIMAX,
        DISAPPOINTMENT
lethal .... FATAL, DEADLY
lethargic .... DULL, INERT,
    TORPID, COMATOSE, SLUGGISH
    sleep .... SOPOR
lethargy .... COMA, APATHY,
    TORPOR, STUPOR, INERTIA,
    LANGUOR, INERTNESS,
         LASSITUDE
Lethe .... RIVER, OBLIVION
Leto .... LATONA
    daughter of .... DIANA,
             ARTEMIS
    son of .... APOLLO
Lett .... BALT, LATVIAN, LIVONIAN
letter .... BREVE, EPISTLE,
    MESSAGE, MISSIVE, CREDENCE
    addition/afterthought .... (P)PS
    airmail .... AEROGRAM
    beginning a word ...... INITIAL
    bishop's .... PASTORAL
    capital, in printing ...... UPPER
             CASE
    carrier .... COURIER, MAILMAN,
            POSTMAN
    cross stroke .... SERIF
    cut off last .... APOCOPE
    large .... UNCIAL, CAPITAL,
           MAJUSCULE
    main stroke .... STEM
    of challenge .... CARTEL
    of credence .... CREDENTIAL
    official .... BULL
    opener .... SIR, MADAM,
            CENSOR
    Papal .... BULL
    representing a word
    .... LOGOGRAM
    resignation .... DEMIT
    short .... LINE, MEMO, NOTE,
           MISSIVE

small, in printing
    .... MINISCULE, LOWER CASE
    to _____ .... GARCIA
    to host .... GRACENOTE,
       BREAD-AND-BUTTER
    to the ...... EXACTLY, LITERAL,
           PRECISELY
lettered .... LEARNED, EDUCATED,
           LITERATE
letterhead detail .... TELEX,
    ADDRESS, TELEPHONE
letterpress .... TEXT
letters .... MAIL, LITERATURE
    and curves .... ESSES
    collection/delivery of
    .... MAIL, PAPERS
    Crucifixion .... INRI
    men of .... LITERATE,
    SCHOLARS, INTELLECTUALS
    slanting up .... ITALICS
    to the stars .... FAN MAIL
    woven in design
    .... MONOGRAM
lettuce .... COS, BIBB, SALAD,
        MINION, ROMAINE
    slang .... (PAPER)MONEY
letup .... LULL, PAUSE, RESPITE,
    ABATEMENT, SLACKENING
leukemia .... TUMOR, CANCER
    type of .... ACUTE, CHRONIC
Levant or Hammerstein
    .... OSCAR
Levantine .... SHIP, SILK
    garment .... GREGO, CAFTAN
    ketch ..... SAIC, XEBEC, SETTEE
    land .... ISRAEL
    port .... ACRE, ELATH
    region .... SYRIA, LEBANON,
          PALESTINE
levee .... DIKE, QUAY, DURBAR,
    RECEPTION, EMBANKMENT
level ...... AIM, EVEN, RASE, RAZE,
    EQUAL, GRADE, PLANE,
    HEIGHT, SMOOTH, LAY LOW,
    FLAT(TEN), ALTITUDE,
         DEMOLISH
    combining form .... PLANI
    headed .... RATIONAL,
          SENSIBLE
    on the .... FAIR, HONEST
leveling slip .... SHIM
lever ...... LAM, PRY, PRISE, SWIPE,
    PEAV(E)Y, SAMSON,
        (CROW)BAR
    cam-activated .... TAPPET
    foot .... PEDAL, TREADLE
leveret .... HARE
leviathan .... HUGE, WHALE,
         MONSTER
Leviathan, author of .... HOBBES
Levis .... TROUSERS, OVERALLS

Levi's father .... JACOB
mother .... LEAH
levitate .... RISE, SOAR, FLOAT
levity .... FRIVOLITY
levy .... TAX, CESS, FINE, TOLL,
DRAFT, TITHE, ASSESS,
ENLIST, IMPOSE, IMPOST,
MUSTER, COLLECT, IMPRESS
Lew Wallace hero ...... (BEN)HUR
lewd .... LUSTFUL, UNCHASTE
Lewis Carroll character
.... ALICE, SNARK,
MADHATTER
companion-explorer
.... CLARK
Gantry of Sinclair ...... ELMER
lex .... LAW
lexicographer .... ROGET,
WORDMAN, COMPILER
lexicon .... VOCABULARY
Leyte, capital of .... TACLOBAN
Lhasa holy man .... (DALAI)LAMA
is capital of .... TIBET
liability .... DEBT, DUTY,
HANDICAP, OBLIGATION
opposed to .... ASSET
liable .... APT, OPEN (TO), BOUND,
LIKELY, SUBJECT
to punishment .... PENAL
liaison .... LINK, AMOUR, GO-
BETWEEN, LINKING (UP),
LOVE AFFAIR
officer .... COORDINATOR
liana .... CIPO, SIPO, VIBURNUM
liang .... TAEL, WEIGHT
liar .... CHEAT, DENIER, FIBBER,
ANANIAS, FIBSTER, SAPPHIRA,
DISSEMBLER, PREVARICATOR
lias .... ROCK
libation .... DRINK
libel .... MUD, DEFAME, MALIGN,
CALUMNY, SLANDER,
ROORBACK
libelous .... DEFAMATORY
liber .... BOOK
liberal ...... FREE, AMPLE, LAVISH,
PROFUSE, GENEROUS,
RECEPTIVE
of others' beliefs, views
...... TOLERANT, BROADMINDED
political ...... LEFTIST, RADICAL
Liberal Arts subject ...... LOGIC,
HISTORY, RHETORIC,
LITERATURE, PHILOSOPHY
liberate .... FREE, RANSOM,
REDEEM, MANUMIT, RELEASE
liberator .... FREER
Liberian cape .... PALMAS
capital .... MONROVIA
city/town .... HARBEL, HARPER,
BUCHANAN, TUBMANBURG

coast .... KRU
ethnic group .... GIO, MANO
language .... VAI, BASSA
monetary unit .... DOLLAR
native .... VAI, TOM
president .... DOE, TUBMAN
river .... MANO, CESTOS
tribe .... KRA, KRU, GOLA,
GORA, KRAHN
"Uncle Shad" .... TUBMAN
libertine .... RAKE, ROUE,
SKEPTIC, DEBAUCHEE
liberty .... FREEDOM
abuse of .... LICENSE
Liberty Island .... BEDLOE'S
libidinous .... LEWD, LUSTFUL
libido .... SEXUAL DESIRE
librarian's bugaboo ...... ERRATA
concern .... ANA
stamp .... DATER
library .... BIBLIOTHECA
collection .... ANA
newspaper .... MORGUE
reading place .... CARREL(L)
supervisor .... CURATOR
librate .... HOVER, POISE
libretto .... BOOK, TEXT, WORDS
Libyan capital (joint) .... TRIPOLI,
BENGHAZI
city/town .... HOMS, BARCE,
DERNA, SEBHA, ZAWIA,
TOBRUK, ZLITEN, GHARIAN,
TARHUNA
desert .... SAHARA, TIBESTI
gulf .... BOMBA, SIDRA
king .... IDRIS
language ...... ARABIC, BERBER
monetary unit .... DINAR
port .... TRIPOLI
strongman .... GADAFFI
lice .... VERMIN
infested .... LOUSY
of .... PEDICULAR
license .... PATENT, PERMIT,
FREEDOM, LIBERTY,
AUTHORITY, FRANCHISE
licentious .... LEWD
licet .... LEGAL, VALID
lichee .... NUT, LITCHI
lichen .... ALGA, MOSS, ARCHIL,
FUNGUS, RATMARA, PARELLA,
EPIPHYTE, LUNGWORT
bearded .... USNEA
genus .... EVERNIA
product .... LITMUS
licit .... LEGAL, VALID, LAWFUL,
PERMITTED
lick .... LAP, BEAT, BLOW, CLIP,
WHIP, TASTE, DEFEAT,
THRASH, VANQUISH
lollipop .... SUCK

of hope .... GLEAM
of interest .... SPARK
licking .... HIDING, BEATING,
DRUBBING, WALLOPING
lickspittle .... TOADY, FLATTERER
licorice .... PEA, ABRIN
flavoring .... ANISE
seed .... GOONCH
lid .... CAP, TOP, CASE, COVER,
STOPPER
colloquial .... CURB,
RESTRAINT
lido .... BEACH, COAST, SHORE
lie .... FIB, FLAM, LIGE, REST,
TALE, SPRAWL, PERJURE,
RECLINE, STRETCH,
FABRICATE, FALSEHOOD,
PREVARICATE, MENDACITY
adjacent to .... ABUT
anchored .... MOORED
at anchor .... RIDE
big: colloq. .... WHOPPER
describing one .... WHITE
detector .... POLYGRAPH
in warmth .... BASK
Lie, U.N. Secretary General
.... TRYGVE
Liechtenstein capital ...... VADUZ
city/town .... SCHAAN, TRIESEN
king .... JOSEF II
language .... GERMAN
monetary unit .... FRANC
mountain .... GRAUSPITZ
peak .... FALKAIS
river .... RHINE
lied .... LILT, SONG, LYRIC
lief .... GLADLY, BELOVED,
WILLING(LY)
Liege ...... LORD, LOYAL, VASSAL,
SUBJECT, FAITHFUL,
SOVEREIGN
liegeman .... VASSAL
lien .... CLAIM
lierne .... RIB
lieu .... PLACE, STEAD
lieutenant .... AIDE, DEPUTY
command of .... PLATOON
slang .... LOOIE, LOOEY,
SHAVETAIL
life .... DAYS, BEING, BIOTA,
BREATH, EXISTENCE
account of one's .... MEMOIRS,
BIOGRAPHY
building block: abbr. ..... DNA
expectancy calculation, of
.... ACTUARIAL
history .... PAST
insurance .... TONTINE
Latin .... VITA, ANIMA
long .... LONGEVITY
of _____ .... RILEY

of Riley .... EASE
of the party .... CUTUP
pertaining to .... BIOTIC(AL)
plant and animal .... BIOTA
prefix .... BIO
preserver .... MAE WEST
preserver stuffing .... KAPOK
principle .... ATMAN, SPIRIT
raft .... BALSA
regional bird .... ORNIS,
AVIFAUNA
saving fluid .... PLASMA
size, larger than .... HEROIC
story .... BIO(GRAPHY)
without .... AMORT, AZOIC
work .... CAREER

lifeless .... ARID, DEAD, DULL,
AMORT, AZOIC, INERT, VAPID,
LISTLESS
lifelike .... NATURAL
lifesaver .... LIFEGUARD
lifetime .... AGE, DAYS
lift .... PERK, BOOST, EXALT,
HOIST, RAISE, STEAL, HOLD
UP, ELEVATE, UPRAISE
British .... ELEVATOR'
colloquial .... PLAGIARIZE
up .... REAR
lifting implement .... TONG(S)
muscle ..... ERECTOR, LEVATOR
ligament .... TAENIA, TENDON
combining form .... DESMO
twist a .... SPRAIN
ligan .... JETSAM, FLOTSAM
ligate .... BANDAGE
ligature .... TIE, BOND, TAENIA,
THREAD
Ligea and Parthenope
.... SIRENS
light ...... UMA, AIRY, FAIR, GLIM,
LAMP, MILD, NEON, KLIEG,
LEGER, TAPER, ILLUME,
SLEAZY, WHERRY, (IL)LUMINE
amplifier/amplification
.... LASER
around sun .... AUREOLA
blinding .... GLARE
bright .... NEON
bulb element .... ARGON
burning .... TORCH, CRESSET
celestial .... HALO, CORONA,
NIMBUS
circle .... HALO, CORONA,
NIMB(US), AUREOLA, AUREOLE
contact, in billiards .... KISS
entertainment .... REVUE
flippant .... AIRY
footed .... SPRY, NIMBLE
game luring .... JACK
gas .... ETHER
giving device .... LAMP,

TORCH, LANTERN
giving substance
.... PHOSPHOR
guiding .... BEACON
Horse Harry .... LEE
line .... RAY
manufacturing, room for
.... LOFT
measure .... LUMENS
of morning, the .... AURORA
opera .... OPERETTA
period .... DAY
perfume .... ROSEWATER
pertaining to .... PHOTIC
put out .... DOUSE
reflecting .... RELUCENT
refractor .... PRISM
ring of .... CORONA
science of .... OPTICS, PHOTICS
source of .... SUN, LAMP
sudden .... FLARE
the brandy .... FLAME
touch .... PAT, TAP
type of ...... ARC, NEON, KLIEG
unit .... LUX, PYR, PHOT,
LUMEN, HEFNER
with glass chimney
.... HURRICANE LAMP
without .... APHOTIC
lighted: poetic .... LITTEN
viewing instrument
.... ENDOSCOPE
lighten .... EASE, FLASH, BLEACH,
WHITEN, RELIEVE, BRIGHTEN
lighter .... HOY, BOAT, KEEL,
SCOW, BARGE
lamp .... SPILL
than-air craft .... AEROSTAT
lightfingered person .... DIP,
PICKPOCKET
lightheaded .... DIZZY, GIDDY,
SILLY, FLIGHTY, FRIVOLOUS
lighthearted .... GAY, AIRY,
LIVELY, CAREFREE
lighthouse .... FANAL, PHARE,
BEACON, PHAROS
lighting fixture .... SCONCE
means of .... SPILL
lightly .... AIRILY, EASILY
lightning .... FLASH, LEVIN,
FIREBALL
bug .... FIREFLY
flash of .... BOLT
rod .... ARRESTER
without thunder ...... WILDFIRE
lights .... LUCES, LUNGS
out signal .... TAPS, CURFEW
lightsome ...... GAY, AIRY, PERKY,
BRIGHT, NIMBLE
lignaloes .... ALOES
ligneous .... WOODY, XYLOID

lignite .... JET, (CHAR)COAL
ligule .... COROLLA
ligure .... STONE, JACINTH
Ligurian Sea city .... GENOA,
LEGHORN, LIVORNO, LA
SPEZIA
like .... AS, AKIN, COPY, SAME,
ALIKE, ENJOY, EQUAL, RELISH,
SUCH AS, COGNATE, SIMILAR,
RESEMBLING
a bachelor dinner .... STAG
bug in a rug .... SNUG
fifth wheel .... USELESS
gray day .... DREAR
kepi .... VISORED
kitten .... CUTE
knight .... ARMORED
machine .... GEARED
malt drink .... ALY
pampa .... GRASSY
parabola .... ARCED
pig out of mud
.... DISGRUNTLED
pindaric .... ODIC
rosebush .... THORNY
slender candle ...... TAPERED
smart aleck .... SASSY
switch-hitter
.... AMBIDEXTROUS
triangle .... DELTAIC
turnpike .... LANED
wallflower .... MANLESS
widow .... LORN
an acrobat .... AGILE
an angry babe? .... UP IN
ARMS
an angry cleric? .... HOT
UNDER THE COLLAR
an angry perfumer?
.... INCENSED
an X-rated film .... STEAMY
angry Captain Kangaroo?
.... HOPPING MAD
angry Clara Bow? ...... FIT TO
BE TIED
angry Ma Kettle? ..... BOILING
OVER
angry Mr. Burns? .... ALL
FIRED UP
basil or mint .... AROMATIC
bear .... URSINE
better .... PREFER
Caesar's Gallia ..... TRISECTED
Cassius' look .... LEAN
clockwork .... REGULAR
combining form ...... INE, OID,
HOME(O)
D.C. agencies .... FEDERAL
Don Juan's affairs
.... AMATORY

fields on the other side of
the fence .... GREENER
fine brandy .... AGED
flea market goods
.... SECOND-HAND
flotsam and jetsam .... ADRIFT
Halloween .... LURID
hotcakes, ____ .... SELLING
Humpty-Dumpty .... OVATE
Iago's purse .... TRASHY
iambic pentameter .... CADENT
many modern people
.... NEUROTIC
many of these items
.... HOMONYMIC
marl .... CLAYEY
Mary Lou .... AGILE
measles, mumps, etc.
.... VIRAL
Mercury's feet .... ALAR
Methuselah .... OLD
Milquetoast .... TIMID
new .... MINT
____ of bricks .... A TON
poetic justice .... IRONIC
quidnuncs .... NOSY
Rizzuto's cow? .... HOLY
Savalas .... BALD
sheep .... OVINE
Shelley's works .... LYRICAL
snakes .... APOD(AL)
snow or sugar ...... GRANULAR
some ale .... ON TAP
Bach music .... FUGAL
clothes .... SPORTY
eggs .... BAD
gowns .... DRAPED
horns .... TINNY
lagoons .... SHOALY
leaves .... LOBED
mortgages .... ASSUMABLE
paths .... BEATEN
pickles .... SOUR
poetry .... EROTIC
silk .... OILED
silver .... PLATED
soldiers .... AT WAR
stares .... ICY
talkers .... GLIB
tournaments .... OPEN
tricks .... DIRTY
walls .... IVED
weather .... NASTY
Standardbreds .... GAITED
teammates .... ALLIED
the best laugh .... LAST
depths .... LOWERMOST
duckling .... UGLY
18th amendment
.... REPEALED
Gobi .... ARID

infantry .... ON FOOT
market, at times .... BULLISH
otary .... EARED
Pisa Tower .... ATILT
Roman Forum .... RUINED
top of Fuji .... SNOWY
worker bee .... NEUTER
Willie Winkle .... WEE
wing .... PTERIC
likelihood .... CHANCE
likely .... APT, PRONE, LIABLE,
SEEMLY, PROBABLE
likeminded .... ONE
liken .... COMPARE
likeness ...... ICON, GUISE, IMAGE,
EFFIGY, SIMILARITY,
(RE)SEMBLANCE
bad .... CARICATURE
show .... MIRROR
likewise .... TOO, ALSO, DITTO,
BESIDES, MOREOVER
not .... NOR
liking ...... FANCY, GUSTO, TASTE,
PALATE, FONDNESS,
PENCHANT, PREFERENCE
lilac .... SHRUB, SYRINGA
Lili .... ST CYR, MARLENE
Liliom .... CAROUSEL
lilith .... DEMON, WITCH, VAMPIRE
Lilith, husband of .... ADAM
Lillie, Miss ...... PEEL, BEA(TRICE)
Lilliputian .... TINY, SMALL,
MIDGET, DWARF(ISH)
hallmark .... TININESS
republic .... SAN MARINO
lilt .... SONG, SWING, RHYTHM
lily .... LIS, LYS, ALOE, ARUM,
ARAD, IXIA, SEGO, CALLA,
LOTUS, ONION, TULIP, YUCCA
African .... ALOE
arum .... CALLA
bulb .... SQUILL
butterfly .... SEGO, MARIPOSA
leaf .... PAD
Lille .... LIS
livered .... CHICKEN,
COWARDLY
origin of .... BULB
palm .... TI
plant .... ALOE, CAMAS(S),
CAMMAS
relative .... ONION
sand .... SOAPROOT
shaped .... CRINOID
white .... PURE
Lily, Maid of Astolat .... ELAINE
Lima, money in .... SOL
limax/limacis .... SLUG
limb .... ARM, FIN, LEG, WING,
BOUGH, BRANCH, MEMBER
joint .... KNEE, ELBOW

muscle .... FLEXOR, LEVATOR
limber .... SPRY, AGILE, LITHE,
PLIANT, SUPPLE, LISSOM(E)
limbo .... JAIL, DANCE, PRISON,
NOWHERE
Limburg(er) .... CHEESE
lime .... CALX, CATCH, FRUIT,
CEMENT, CITRON, LINDEN
bush .... SNARE
combining form .... CALCI
fruit like .... CITRON
harden with .... CALCIFY
powder .... CONITE, KONITE
product .... CALCIC, APATITE
tree ..... TEIL, LINDEN, TUPELO,
BASS(WOOD)
limelight .... PUBLICITY,
SPOTLIGHT
limen .... THRESHOLD
limerick man .... LEAR
limes .... BORDER, DEFENSES
limestone ...... CALP, LIAS, MALM,
TUFA, CHALK, OOLITE,
CALCITE, DOLOMITE, PISOLITE
limey .... BRITON, SAILOR,
SOLDIER, ENGLISHMAN
limicoline bird .... SNIPE,
CURLEW, PLOVER, SANDPIPER
limit ...... FIX, CURB, METE, PALE,
SPAN, MARGIN, CONFINE,
BOUND(ARY), RESTRICT
limitation to inheritance
.... TAIL
limited .... SCANT, FINITE,
NARROW, SMALL SCALE
limitless .... VAST, IMMENSE,
INFINITE, BOUNDLESS
limits .... BOUNDS
limn .... DRAW, PAINT, DEPICT,
SKETCH, PORTRAY, DESCRIBE,
DELINEATE
Limoges .... PORCELAIN
limousine .... AUTO, SEDAN
limp ...... LAX, DRAG, HALT, SOFT,
HITCH, FLABBY, FLIMSY,
HOBBLE, WILTED, FLACCID,
DROOPING
went .... SAGGED
limpet .... LAMPREY, SHELLFISH
limpid .... CLEAR, PELLUCID
linage .... ALIGNMENT
linchpin .... FORELOCK
Lincoln Center offering
.... OPERA
Lincoln's assassin .... (JOHN
WILKES) BOOTH
burial place .... SPRINGFIELD
hat .... STOVEPIPE
sobriquet .... (HONEST) ABE,
RAILSPLITTER
son .... ROBERT, WILLIE

wife .... (MARY) TODD
Lind, soprano .... JENNY
sobriquet .... NIGHTINGALE
Lindbergh, a .... ANNE, CHARLES
prize money, donor of
.... ORTEIG
Lindbergh's flight .... SOLO
nickname .... LUCKY LINDY
linden .... TEIL
tree .... LIME, LINN, BASSWOOD
Lindsay, poet .... VACHEL
line .... ROW, CEIL, CORD, FILE,
RANK, REIN, ROPE, WIRE,
QUEUE, ROUTE, SERIF, TRADE,
CORDON, PATTER, STRING,
VECTOR, BUSINESS
ancestral .... LINEAGE
ancient boundary ...... ULTIMA
THULE
barometric .... ISOBAR
battle .... FRONT
bottom .... NET
cut .... SLIT
cutting .... SECANT
draw the .... LIMIT
family .... TREE, BLOOD,
ANCESTRY
fine .... SERIF, STRIA
imaginary .... VECTOR
in .... AROW
in prosody .... STICH
in trigonometry .... SINE,
SECANT, TANGENT
intersecting .... SECANT,
VECTOR
nautical ...... EARING, MARLINE
of action .... DEMARCHE
cliffs .... SCARP
David Brinkley
.... GOODNIGHT CHET
Ed McMahon .... HERE'S
JOHNNY
Gordon Hathaway ...... HIHO
STEVERINO
Jackie Gleason .... HOW
SWEET IT IS
Sgt. Friday .... JUST THE
FACTS
Steve McGarret .... BOOK
'EM DANNO
pertaining to .... LINEAL,
LINEAR
reference .... AXIS
threadlike .... STRIA
through a terret .... REIN
toe the .... OBEY, CONFORM
up .... ARRAY
waiting .... QUEUE
with bricks .... REVET
with stone .... STEAN(E)
without angle .... AGONE

lineage .... BLOOD, STOCK,
FAMILY, STRAIN, DESCENT,
ANCESTRY, PEDIGREE,
GENEALOGY
lined .... RULED, STRIATE(D)
linen .... CREA, CRASH, TOILE,
FLAXEN, NAPERY, BATISTE,
HOLLAND, LINGERIE,
STATIONERY
and wool cloth .... LINSEY
bookbinding .... BUCKRAM
closet item ..... SHEET, TOWEL,
NAPKIN
cloth .... DUCK, SEERSUCKER
coarse .... DOWLAS, DRABBET
fabric .... CRASH, SCRIM,
VELOUR(S)
fiber .... FLAX
fine .... LAWN, TOILE, DAMASK,
BATISTE, CAMBRIC
measure .... CUT
plant .... FLAXEN
room .... EWERY
scraped/softened .... LINT
sheer .... LAWN, TOILE
tape .... INKLE
transparent .... LAWN, TOILE
liner .... VESSEL, STEAMER,
(STEAM)SHIP
cheapest quarters of
.... STEERAGE
lines on map .... HACHURE
on optical lens .... RETICLE
ling .... BURBOT
linger .... LAG, WAIT, DALLY,
DELAY, DWELL, HOVER,
TARRY, LOITER
lingerie ...... SLIP, LINEN, UNDIES,
UNDERWEAR
lingering luminescence
.... AFTERGLOW
lingo ...... CANT, JARGON, PATOIS,
DIALECT, LANGUAGE
slang .... JIVE
lingua .... TONGUE
linguini .... PASTA
linguist .... POLYGLOT
linguistics branch .... SYNTAX,
SEMANTICS
liniment .... ARNICA, LOTION
linin .... CATHARTIC
lining .... GASKET, BUCKRAM,
BUSHING
link ...... TIE, JOIN(T), LOOP, RING,
YOKE, CHAIN, NEXUS,
ATTACH, CONNECT, CATENATE
consaguine .... BLOOD TIE
firmly .... KNIT
train cars .... COUPLE
linked series ...... CHAIN, CATENA
Linkletter, TV man .... ART

links ..... CAT(ENA), GOLF COURSE
connect in series
.... CATENATE
feat .... HOLE-IN-ONE
former fan club of the
.... ARNIE'S ARMY
locale .... TEE
man .... CADDY, CADDIE
number .... PAR
teacher .... PRO
linn .... POOL, LINDEN, RAVINE,
CASCADE, WATERFALL
linnet .... FINCH, SONGBIRD
linotypist .... COMPOSITOR,
TYPESETTER
linseed oil, hardened
.... LINOLEUM
mixture .... MEGILP(H)
refuse .... MILKCAKE
source .... FLAX
lint ...... NAP, FLAX, FUZZ, GAUZE,
FIBER, FLUFF, LINEN
lintel .... TRANSOM, CROSSPIECE
counterpart of .... SILL
linty .... FUZZY, FLUFFY
lion .... CAT, LEO, HERO, IDOL,
SIMBA, FELINE, CELEBRITY
biblical .... ARI
communication of .... ROAR
den of .... LAIR
female .... LIONESS
feminizes .... ESS
group .... PRIDE
mountain ...... PUMA, COUGAR,
PANTHER
neck hair .... MANE
portrayer .... LAHR
pride of .... MANE, CREST
young of .... CUB, WHELP,
LIONET
Lion of God .... ARIEL
of Judah .... SELASSIE
lioness of story/movie ..... ELSA
Lionhearted, the ...... RICHARD I
lip ...... EDGE, KISS, SASS, FLANGE,
LABIAL, LABIUM, LABRUM
adornment .... LABRET, PELELE
combining form .... CHIL(O)
cup's .... BRIM
service, of sorts
.... HYPOCRISY, MALARK(E)Y,
MOUTH TO MOUTH
slang .... INSOLENCE
touch with .... OSCULATE
lipase .... ENZYME
lipoma .... TUMOR
lipped .... LABIATE
Lippi, painter .... FILIPPO
lips .... LABIA, LABRA, KISSER
combining form .... LABIO
of the .... LABIAL

lipstick .... ROUGE, POMADE
liquefied .... FUSIL(E)
liquefy .... FUSE, MELT, THAW
   opposed to .... SOLIDIFY
liqueur .... CREME, COGNAC,
   CORDIAL, CURACAO, RATAFIA,
                ABSINTH(E)
   sweet .... CREME, GENEPI,
       CURACAO, ANISETTE,
           MARASCHINO
liquid .... CLEAR, FLUID, SMOOTH,
       AQUATIC, FLOWING
   assets .... CASH
   body tissue .... LYMPH
   change into .... LIQUEFY
   fatty oil .... OLEIN
   food .... SOUP, BROTH
   hydrocarbon .... OCTANE
   in pharmacy .... AQUA
   made .... FUSIL(E)
   measure .... TUN, GILL, PINT,
   LITER, MINIM, OUNCE, QUART,
   BARREL, GALLON, HOGSHEAD
   measuring device ...... JIGGER,
      DROPPER, DOSIMETER
   opposite .... SOLID
   oxygen .... LOX
   pickling .... BRINE, SOUSE
   rock .... MAGMA
   sour .... ALEGAR
   waste .... SLOPS
liquidate .... PAY, CASH, KILL,
   SETTLE, DISPOSE (OF)
liquidity concern .... BOTTOM-
                  LINE
liquor .... ALE, GIN, RUM, RYE,
   TAP, GROG, MEAD, CREME,
   DRINK, JUICE, MASTIC,
   POTTLE, WHISKY, BITTERS,
   ANISETTE, POTATION
   alcoholic .... LUSH, MESCAL
   bad .... BOUSE, BOWSE
   bitter .... ABSINTH(E)
   bootleg .... ROTGUT
   bottle .... MAGNUM
   cheap .... SLIPSLOP
   colloquial .... BOOZE
   dram of .... TOT
   drink .... DRAM, TIFF
   drugged .... MICKEY (FINN)
   follower .... CHASER
   fruit juice .... BRANDY
   glass .... SNIFTER
   leftover .... HEELTAP
   loss through leakage, etc.
   .... ULLAGE
   malt .... ALE, STOUT
   measure ...... NIP, DRAM, GILL,
   PINT, JIGGER, NOGGIN
   pick-me-up .... STIM
   sap .... NIPA

sugarcane .... TAF(F)IA
tonic .... BITTERS
lira, 1/20 of .... SOLDO
liripipe .... TIPPET
Lisbon river .... TAGUS
Lisle ...... LILLE, FABRIC, GLOVES,
   THREAD, STOCKINGS
lissom(e) .... LITHE, LIMBER,
   NIMBLE, SUPPLE, SVELTE
list .... TIP, CANT, HEEL, LEAN,
   ROLL, TILT, INDEX, SLATE,
   TABLE, CAREEN, ITEMIZE,
   CATALOG(UE), CALENDAR,
   REGISTER, TABULATE,
          INVENTORY
   actors' .... CAST
   business meeting ..... AGENDA
   candidates' ..... SLATE, TICKET
   of bonds, stocks
   .... PORTFOLIO
   of persons .... ROLL, ROSTER
   of the dead .... BEADROLL
   of things to be done
   .... AGENDA
   particulars .... ITEMS
   team players' .... LINEUP
listen .... HEAR, HEED, HIST,
   HARK(EN), HEARKEN,
         EAVESDROP
listener .... EAR, AUDITOR
   surreptitious .... BUGGER,
        EAVESDROPPER
listening .... AUDIENT
   device .... BUG, MONITOR
   post, usually .... EMBASSY
lister .... PLOW
listing .... TABLE, CATALOG,
          TABULATION
listless .... LANGUID, SPIRITLESS
listlessness .... ENNUI, APATHY
lists .... ROLLS, ARENA, TILTS
Liszt, pianist .... FRANZ
lit .... LANDED, ALIGHTED
   up .... SMILED
litany .... PRAYER
litchi .... NUT, TREE, LICHEE
literal .... REAL, EXACT, PLAIN,
   PROSAIC, TEXTUAL,
   ACCURATE, WORD-FOR-WORD
   quotation sign of .... SIC
   translation .... METAPHRASE
literally .... LITERATIM,
   PRECISELY, VIRTUALLY
literary ...... LEARNED, LETTERED,
         SCHOLARLY
   bits .... ANA, ANALECTA
   collection .... ANA,
        MISCELLANEA
   criticism .... REVIEW, CRITIQUE
   drudge .... GRUB, HACK
   extracts .... ANALECTA,

        ANALECTS
   form ...... POEM, ESSAY, VERSE
   grouping .... ODE
   hack .... GRUB
   initials .... GBS, RLS
   light .... WRITER
   patchwork .... CENTO
   quotation brief .... SNIPPET
   review .... CRITIQUE
   society .... LYCEUM
   style .... PEN, RACOCO
   work, inferior .... SCRIBBLE,
        POTBOILER
literate ...... LEARNED, CULTURED,
        LETTERED
literati .... MEN OF LETTERS
literature .... WRITINGS
lithe .... SLIM, AGILE, LIMBER,
   SUPPLE, SVELTE, LISSOM(E),
     SYLPHIC, FLEXIBLE
lithograph .... PRINT, CHROMO
lithology, subject of .... ROCKS
Lithuanian .... BALT, LETT
   capital .... VILNA, VILNIUS
   city/town .... KAUNAS,
   PLUNGE, TELSIAI, TAURAGE,
   KAPSUKAS, KLAIPEDA,
   KURSENAI, SIAULIAI
   coin .... LIT(AS), RUBLE
   president .... LANDSBERGIS
   river .... NIEMEN, VILIYA
   seaport .... MEMEL
litigant .... SUER, DEFENDANT,
   CONTESTANT, COMPLAINANT
litigate .... SUE
litigation .... LAWSUIT
litigious .... QUARRELSOME
   people .... SUERS
litotes .... MEIOSIS
litter .... BIER, FALL, MESS,
   MULCH, STREW, COFFIN,
   JUMBLE, CLUTTER, RUBBISH,
   SCATTER, OFFSPRING,
   PALANQUIN, STRETCHER
   bearer .... CAT, DOG, PIG
   last-born .... WALLYDRAG
   of pigs .... FARROW
little ...... WEE, POCO, PUNY, TINY,
   BRIEF, SMALL, YOUNG,
   MINUTE, PALTRY, TRIVIAL
   at a time, drink a .... SIP
   bird .... HUMMINGBIRD
   bit .... FIG, CRUMB, MORSEL
   bits .... SOUPCONS
   by little .... SLOWLY,
        PIECEMEAL
   combining form .... MICR(O)
   darling .... ANGEL
   Elizabeth .... BESS
   fellow .... BUB
   fib .... WHITE LIE

finger .... PINKIE
fragments .... FLINDERS
grimace .... MOUE
hours .... SEXT, TIERCE
island .... AIT
moon, old style .... LUNET
one .... SHAVER
ones: suffix .... ULI
piece of wood/stone ..... CHIP
spot/speck .... DOT, PINPOINT
Theresa .... TESSIE
umbrella .... PARASOL
Little Bear .... KOALA, URSA
MINOR
Big Horn protagonist
.... CUSTER, SITTING BULL
Boot .... KALIGULA
Boy Blue author .... FIELD
Boy Blue painter .... MONET
Caesar .... CAESARION
Corporal .... NAPOLEON
Flower, mayor .... LA
GUARDIA
Fox .... VULPECULA
Iodine cartoonist .... HATLO
Leaguer .... PEEWEE
Miss Muffet's food ..... WHEY
Orphan Annie creator
.... (JAMES WHITCOMB) RILEY
Russia .... UKRAINE
_____, Stowe character
.... EVA
Tibet .... LADAKH
littleneck .... CLAM, QUAHOG
littlest .... TINIEST
of the litter .... RUNT
littoral .... SHORE, COAST(AL)
stretch .... STRAND
litu, singular of .... LITAS
liturgical singer .... CANTOR
liturgy .... MASS, RITE, RITUAL
litus .... SERF
Litvinov, Russ, statesman
.... MAXIM
livable .... HABITABLE,
TENANTABLE
live .... ABIDE, DWELL, EXIST,
RESIDE, BREATHE, INHABIT,
SUBSIST, SURVIVE
a life of passivity
.... VEGETATE
able to .... VIABLE
alone .... BACH
coal .... EMBER
it _____ .... UP
it up .... HAVE A BALL
on bare essentials ...... ROUGH
IT
or die .... SINK OR SWIM
together .... COHABIT

under false pretenses
.... MASQUERADE
wire: colloq. .... HUSTLER, GO-
GETTER, POWERHOUSE
livelihood .... JOB, MEANS, LIVING,
(UP)KEEP, SUPPORT, (DAILY)
BREAD
liveliness .... PEP, VIVACITY
livelong .... WHOLE, ENTIRE
lively .... GAY, SPRY, AGILE,
BRISK, PE(A)RT, PERKY,
ACTIVE, ANIMATED, SPIRITED,
VIVACIOUS, SPRIGHTLY
air .... LILT
intelligence .... ESPRIT
music .... VIVO, ANIMATO
party .... BASH
liven .... CHEER (UP)
liver .... HEPAR
collection of pus in the
.... ABSCESS
diagnostic test .... BIOPSY
disease .... CIRRHOSIS
disease, sign of ...... JAUNDICE
inflammation .... HEPATITIS
is body's _____ factory
.... CHEMICAL
is supposed seat of
.... DESIRE, EMOTION
part ...... CELL, DUCT, ARTERY,
LOBULE, PORTAL VEIN,
HEPATIC VEIN
pertaining to .... HEPATIC
replacement of diseased
.... TRANSPLANT
secretion .... BILE, GALL
shape .... CONE
tumor .... HEPATOMA
livered, yellow .... COWARDLY
liverish .... CROSS, BILIOUS
liverwort .... HEPATICA,
BRYOPHYTE
genus .... RICCIA
liverwurst .... SAUSAGE
livery .... STABLE, UNIFORM
wearer of .... LACKEY,
FLUNK(E)Y, SERVANT
livestock .... COWS, CATTLE,
STEERS
bacterial infection
.... ANTHRAX
disease .... NAGANA
farm .... RANCH
round up .... WRANGLE
livid .... WAN, PALE, ASHEN,
PALLID, DISCOLORED, BLACK-
AND-BLUE
living .... ALIVE, BEING, QUICK,
EXTANT, ANIMATE, EXISTING,
LIVELIHOOD
capable of .... VIABLE

corpse .... ZOMBI(E)
matter .... PROTOPLASM
on land or in water
.... AMPHIBIAN
on river bank .... RIPARIAN
picture .... VIVANT, TABLEAU
prefix .... LIVI, VIVI
room .... SALA, PARLOR
Livonian ...... LETT, ESTH(ONIAN)
Livorno .... LEGHORN
lixivium .... LYE, LEACH
lizard ...... EFT, UTA, ADDA, GILA,
NEWT, SEPS, URAN, AGAMA,
ANOLE, ANOLI, GECKO,
GUANA, SKINK, SWIFT,
VARAN, IGUANA, MOLOCH,
MONITOR, SAURIAN, BASILISK,
CHAMELEON, LACERT(IL)AN
chameleon-like .... ANOLI
color-changing/starred
.... AGAMA, CHAMELEON
combining form .... SAURO,
SAURUS
genus .... UMA, AGAMA
like .... SAURIAN
wall/nocturnal .... GECKO
Lizette of poetry .... REESE
llama .... PACO, ALPACA, VICUNA,
RUMINANT
habitat .... ANDES
relative ...... CAMEL, GUANACO
llanero .... GAUCHO
llanero's weapon .... BOLA
llano .... PLAIN, STEPPE
LLB holder .... ATTY
lo .... SEE, ECCE, LOOK, BEHOLD
companion of .... BEHOLD
loa .... LARVA
loach .... CARP, SMERLIN
load .... FILL, LADE, ONUS,
CARGO, BURDEN, FREIGHT,
ENCUMBER, SHIPMENT
a gun .... CHARGE
transported .... HAUL
loaded .... LADEN, FRAUGHT,
WEIGHTED
carrier .... CARFUL
slang .... RICH, DRUNK,
STINKO, MONEYED, WEALTHY,
IN THE MONEY
loadstone/lodestone
.... MAGNET(ITE)
loaf .... IDLE, LOLL, BREAD,
LOITER, LOUNGE, GOLDBRICK,
TAKE IT EASY
white bread .... MANCHET
loafer .... BUM, SHOE, DRONE,
IDLER, LOUNGER
loafing .... FLANERIE
loam .... DIRT, MALM, MARL, SOIL,
EARTH, LOESS

loan .... PREST
  ask for a .... BRACE, TOUCH
  of money .... IMPREST
  note: colloq. .... IOU
  privilege .... CREDIT
  shark .... USURER, SHYLOCK
loath .... AVERSE, HOSTILE,
  RELUCTANT, UNWILLING
loathe ...... HATE, ABHOR, DETEST,
  ABOMINATE
loathsome .... FOUL, VILE,
  ABHORRENT, REPULSIVE,
  DETESTABLE
lob .... COP, LOP, LOFT
lobby ...... HALL, FOYER, LOUNGE,
  ANTEROOM, VESTIBULE
lobbyist .... RAINMAKER
lobbyists? .... THIRD HOUSES
lobe .... LAPPET
  ear .... EARLOP
  whale tail's .... FLUKE
lobelia .... CAMAS(S)
loblolly ...... PINE, BROTH, GRUEL,
  PUDDLE
lobo .... WOLF
lobster .... MACRURAN,
  CRUSTACEAN
  claw .... CHELA, NIPPER,
  PINCER
  coral .... ROE
  egg(s) .... BERRY, SPAWN
  feeler of .... ANTENNA,
  PALP(US)
  part of a .... CHELA, TELSON,
  THORAX
  protective cover .... MAIL
  spawn of .... CORAL
  trap for .... POT
local .... BRANCH, NATIVE,
  REGION, CHAPTER, TOPICAL,
  VICINAL, WAY TRAIN
  boy .... NATIVE SON
  hero .... THE TOAST OF THE
  TOWN
locale .... SITE, PLACE, SCENE,
  VENUE, LOCALITY
  for the indecisive .... FENCE
  landlubbers' .... ASHORE
  links' .... TEE
  Omsk's .... SIBERIA
locality .... AREA, SPOT, LOCUS,
  PLACE, SITUS, VENUE
  restricted to a .... ENDEMIC,
  INDIGENOUS
locate .... BASE, FIND, SPOT,
  PLACE, SETTLE, MARK OFF,
  SITUATE
locating system .... RADAR
location .... SITE, SPOT, POSITION,
  PLACE(MENT), SITUATION
  person's .... WHEREABOUTS

loch .... BAY, LAKE, POND,
  LOMOND
loci, singular of .... LOCUS
lock .... CURL, CLOSE, TRESS,
  COTTER, DETENT, FASTEN,
  SECURE, CONFINE, RINGLET
  brand .... ACE, YALE
  hair .... TAG, CURL, TRESS,
  RINGLET
  mechanism .... DETENT
  part .... BOLT, STUMP, DETENT,
  TUMBLER, CYLINDER
  stock, and barrel .... ENTIRE
  up .... JAIL
locker .... KIST, AMBRY, CHEST,
  CLOSET, COMPARTMENT
locket's content .... PICTURE
lockjaw .... TETANUS, TRISMUS
lockup .... JUG, PEN, JAIL, STIR,
  CALABOOSE
loco .... CRAZY, LOONY,
  DEMENTED
locofoco .... CIGAR, MATCH
locomotive .... DOLLY, DUMMY,
  MOGUL, DINKEY, SWITCHER,
  IRON HORSE
  coal car .... TENDER
  cowcatcher .... FENDER
  driver .... ENGINEER
  driver's place .... CAB
  sound .... CHOO, CHUFF
  stopping place ..... TANKTOWN
locus .... PLACE, POINT
locust ...... TREE, CICADA, CICALA,
  INSECT
  kin .... CRICKET
  tree .... CAROB, ACACIA
locution .... WORD, IDIOM,
  PHRASE, EXPRESSION
lode .... REEF, VEIN
  cavity .... VUG(G), VUGH
lodestar .... POLARIS, GUIDING
  STAR
lodge .... HUT, BOARD, HOUSE,
  BILLET, CHAPTER, QUARTER
  Indian .... TENT, TEPEE,
  WIGWAM
  member .... ELK, MASON
lodger .... GUEST, ROOMER
  temporary .... TRANSIENT
lodging .... ABODE, ROOST,
  QUARTERS
  house .... INN, HOTEL,
  HOSTEL(RY)
  house bed .... DOSS
loess .... LOAM
Lofgren, guitarist .... NILS
loft .... LOB, ATTIC, GARRET,
  GALLERY, MANSARD
lofty .... HIGH, GRAND, NOBLE,
  SKYEY, SUBLIME

  dwelling .... AERY, AERIE
log .... DIARY, RECORD, TIMBER
  barrier .... BOOM
  float .... RAFT, CATAMARAN
  holder .... CANT HOOK
  house/structure .... CABIN
  measure .... SCALAGE
  roller .... DECKER
  rolling contest .... ROLEO
  sling .... PARBUCKLE
  spin a .... BIRL
  splitter .... WEDGE
  splitting wedge .... FROE
  turner .... PEAV(E)Y
loganberry .... BRAMBLE
logarithm inventor .... NAPIER
  unit .... BEL
loge .... BOX, STALL
logger .... LUMBERJACK,
  WOODCUTTER
  boots of .... PACS
  sled of .... TODE, GO-DEVIL,
  TRAVOIS
loggerhead .... DUNCE, TURTLE
loggia .... ARCADE, GALLERY,
  PORTICO
logia .... MAXIMS, SAYINGS
logic .... REASONING
  deductive .... SYLLOGISM
  premise .... SUMPTION
logical .... WISE, SOUND,
  RATIONAL
  argument .... SYLLOGISM
logistic .... ARITHMETIC
logistics, concern of ...... SUPPLY,
  QUARTERS
logograph .... ANAGRAM, WORD
  PUZZLE
Logos .... WORD
logroller .... BIRLER, DECKER,
  POLITICIAN
logrolling .... BIRLING, EXCHANGE,
  LOBBYING, SWAPPING
  political booty of .... PORK
  (BARREL)
  subject .... BILL
logs floating in mass .... DRIVE
  passage down slope
  .... FLUME, SLUICE
  pile of .... ROLLWAY
Lohengrin's bride .... ELSA
  composer .... WAGNER
  father .... PARSIFAL
loin .... RACK, BEEFCUT
  combining form ...... LUMB(O)
  muscle .... PSOAS
  section .... GRISKIN
loincloth .... MALO, MARO, DHOTI,
  LUNGEE, SARONG, G-STRING,
  LAVA-LAVA
loins .... HIPS

pertaining to the ...... LUMBAR
Loire River city .... BLOIS,
    NANTES, ORLEANS
loiter .... LAG, IDLE, LOAF, DALLY,
    TARRY, DAWDLE, LINGER,
    LOUNGE, SAUNTER
loiterer .... IDLER, LAGGARD
Loki's daughter .... HEL(A)
  son .... NARE
  victim .... BALDER
  wife .... SIGYN
loll ...... LOP, HANG, LAZE, DROOP,
    LOUNGE
Lollander .... DANE
lollapaloosa .... LULU
lollipop .... CANDY, SUCKER
Lollobrigida, actress .... GINA
Lombard capital .... PAVIA
Lombardy capital .... MILAN
  city .... PAVIA
  ruler .... ALBOIN
Lombok neighbor .... BALI
loment .... LEGUME
London, ancient name of
  .... AGUSTA
  art gallery ..... TATE, SOTHEBY
  barrister .... TEMPLAR
  borough .... CHELSEA,
    LAMBETH, BATTERSEA,
    GREENWICH, WESTMINSTER
  botanical gardens .... KEW
  cleaning woman .... CHAR
  club .... KITCAT
  dessert, in .... AFTERS
  dialect/language ..... COCKNEY
  district .... SOHO, ADELPHI,
    CHELSEA, LAMBETH, MAYFAIR,
    LIMEHOUSE
  famous Guildhall effigy
  .... GOG
  fashionable section
  .... MAYFAIR, BELGRAVIA
  foreign quarter .... SOHO
  hawker .... MUN, COSTER
  hooligan .... SPIV
  horse market
  .... TATTERSALL'S
  landmark ...... TOWER, BRIDGE,
    BIG BEN, OLD VIC, MARBLE
    ARCH
  mental hospital .... BEDLAM
  native .... COCKNEY
  park .... HYDE
  people movers .... TRAMS
  policeman .... BOBBY
  prison .... NEWGATE
  river .... THAMES
  royal palace in
  .... BUCKINGHAM
  royal stables .... MEWS
  ruffian .... MOHOCK

ship of Jack .... SNARK
statue ...... GOG, EROS, MAGOG
street ...... BOND, SOHO, FLEET,
    REGENT, STRAND, DOWNING,
    LOMBARD, PALLMALL
streetcar .... TRAM
student of law .... TEMPLAR
suburb .... KEW, EALING,
    WEMBLEY
subway .... TUBE
theatre .... DRURY LANE
underwriters .... LLOYD'S
upperclass neighborhood
  .... GROSVENOR SQUARE
West End .... SOHO
writer .... JACK
Londoner .... COCKNEY
lone .... SOLE, SOLO, SINGLE,
    SOLITARY
Lone Ranger's pal .... TONTO
  Star State .... TEXAS
loneliness .... MELANCHOLIA
  kind of .... NOSTALGIA
lonely .... LORN, DESOLATE,
    SOLITARY
loner, kind of .... HERMIT,
    MUGWUMP
lonesome ...... LONELY, DESOLATE
long .... LENGTHY, EXTENDED,
    FAR-GOING, EXTENSIVE
  ago .... WAY BACK, OLDEN
    TIMES
  and lean .... LANK
  before .... SOON
  distance .... (TELE)PHONE CALL
  distance contest
  .... MARATHON
  drawn .... PROLONGED
  established .... ROOTED,
    CUSTOMARY
  face .... SCOWL
  faced ..... SAD, GLUM, SERIOUS
  fish .... EEL, GAR
  for .... ACHE, PINE, CRAVE,
    YEARN, ASPIRE, HANKER
  journey .... TREK, ODYSSEY
  lasting .... DURABLE
  life .... LONGEVITY
  limbed .... LANKY, LEGGY
  live! .... VIVA, VIVE
  lived .... AGED, HARDY,
    ANCIENT
  necked animal .... GIRAFFE
  period .... EON
  range .... APOGEE
  seat .... BENCH, SETTEE
  shot ...... GAMBLE, CHANCE HIT
  shot race horse .... PLATER,
    SLEEPER
  suffering .... STOIC, PATIENT,
    TOLERANT, FORGIVING

  winded .... GABBY, WORDY,
    PROLIX, TEDIOUS, VERBOSE,
    TALKATIVE
Long Island county .... KINGS,
    NASSAU, QUEENS, SUFFOLK
  racetrack .... BELMONT
longanimity .... PATIENCE,
    ENDURANCE, WAITING GAME
longeron .... SPAR
longevity .... AGE, LIFETIME, LONG
    LIFE, SURVIVAL
longest-running Broadway
  show:
  first .... A CHORUS LINE
  second .... OH! CALCUTTA
  third .... CATS
Longfellow bell town .... ATRI
  poet .... HENRY WADSWORTH
  wife of .... FANNY
longhair .... HIGHBROW
longhand .... WRITTEN,
    HANDWRITING, SCRIPT, IN
    ONE'S OWN HAND
longhorn .... CATTLE
longing .... YEN, CRAVING,
    YEARNING
longshoreman .... DECKER,
    LUMPER, STEVEDORE
longshot hopeful .... DARK HORSE
  winner .... SLEEPER
lonicera .... HONEYSUCKLE
loo .... PAM, CARD GAME
looby .... LOUT, LUBBER
looey/looie .... LIEUTENANT
  aide of .... SARGE
loofah .... SPONGE
look .... EYE, PRY, SEE, GAPE,
    GAZE, MIEN, PEER, SEEK,
    SEEM, APPEAR, ASPECT,
    BEHOLD, GANDER, GLANCE,
    SEARCH
  after .... TEND
  alike .... RINGER
  amorous .... OGLE
  angry .... GLARE
  askance .... LEER
  at/over .... EXAMINE, INSPECT
  back .... RECALL
  ____ (be alert) .... ALIVE
  coldly upon ..... SNUB, REBUFF
  fixedly/intently .... STARE
  forward to .... EXPECT
  frowning .... LOUR, SCOWL,
    (G)LOWER
  in .... ENTER, VISIT
  into .... PROBE, EXPLORE
  into the mirror? .... MEET
    FACE TO FACE
  over quickly .... PEEK, SCAN,
    GLANCE
  over: sl. .... CASE

scornful/nasty .... SNEER
sullen .... POUT
the other way .... IGNORE,
      LIVE AND LET LIVE
threatening .... LOWER
up to .... ADORE, REVERE,
      IDOLIZE, RESPECT
looker-on .... WITNESS, OBSERVER,
      BYSTANDER, SPECTATOR
looking glass .... MIRROR
lookout .... GUARD, SPOTTER,
      WATCHER, OBSERVER
alert .... ARGUS
nautical .... CROW'S NEST
post .... WATCH TOWER
loom .... WEAVE, APPEAR, TAKE
      SHAPE
bar .... EASER
frame .... BATTEN
part .... PIRN, REED, SLEY,
      WARP, EASER, BATTEN,
      HEDDLE, SHUTTLE, TREADLE
loon .... DOLT, LOUT, DIVER,
      GREBE, (DIVING)BIRD
loony .... DAFT, CRAZY, DEMENTED
loop .... TAG, RING, BRIDE, NOOSE,
      TERRY, EYE(LET), CIRCUIT,
      GROMMET
edging .... PICOT
in electricity .... CIRCUIT
in lariat .... HONDOO
on boot/garment .... TAG,
      STRAP
running .... NOOSE
small .... TAGLET
looper .... WORM, LARVA
loophole .... CHINK, JOKER,
      M(E)USE, ESCAPE, EYELET
Loos, writer .... ANITA
loose .... FREE, (RE)LAX, AT
      LARGE, INEXACT, RELEASE,
      UNBOUND
change .... CENTS, COINS
end .... TAGRAG
let .... RELEASE
sleeve .... RAGLAN
turn .... FREE, RELEASE
loosen .... EASE, UNDO, RELAX,
      UNTIE, RELEASE, SLACKEN
loot .... HAUL, SWAG, BOOTY,
      RIFLE, SPOILS, DESPOIL,
      PILLAGE, PLUNDER,
      (RAN)SACK
lop ...... CHOP, HANG, LOLL, POLL,
      SNED, SNIP, TRIM, PRUNE, CUT
      OFF, SNATHE
lope .... CANTER
Lopez of Hullabaloo .... TRINI
loppy .... LIMP, SAGGING,
      DROOPING
lopsided .... ALOP, ALIST, ASKEW,

      UNEVEN, UNEQUAL
loquacious .... GABBY, CHATTY,
      GOSSIPY, VOLUBLE,
      GARRULOUS, TALKATIVE
loquacity/loquaciousness
      .... GARRULITY, VERBOSITY
Loran, part of .... LONG, RANGE,
      NAVIGATION
lord .... EARL, PEER, RULE,
      BARON, LIEGE, RULER,
      ADONAI, BISHOP, MASTER,
      MARQUIS, SEIGNOR,
      DOMINEER, NOBLEMAN,
      VISCOUNT
companion of .... MASTER
wife of .... LADY
Lord Greystoke .... TARZAN
Marmion's horse .... BEVIS
of Hosts .... GOD, JEHOVAH
the .... GOD
lord's land ...... MANOR, DEMESNE
manor .... DEMESNE
Lord's Day .... SUNDAY
Prayer, first word(s) .... OUR
      FATHER, PATERNOSTER
Supper .... EUCHARIST
lordly .... NOBLE, HAUGHTY,
      ARROGANT, DIGNIFIED,
      OVERBEARING
lordship .... RULE, DOMINION,
      SEIGNIORY
lore .... WISDOM, LEARNING,
      ERUDITION, KNOWLEDGE
Lorelei .... SIREN, LURLEI
golden possession of
      .... COMB
river .... RHINE
victims .... SAILORS, MARINERS
Lorenz, ethologist .... KONRAD
Loretta Young role ...... RAMONA
lorgnette .... OPERA GLASS
lorgnon ...... MONOCLE, PINCENEZ
lorica .... SHELL, LORLEA,
      CUIRASS, CARAPACE,
      CORSELET
lorikeet .... LORY, PARROT
loris .... LEMUR
lorn .... BEREFT, DESOLATE,
      FORSAKEN
Lorna _____ .... DOONE
Doone author ..... BLACKMORE
Doone character .... TOM,
      ALAN, RIDD, LORNA
Doone rescuer .... RIDD
lorry .... TRUCK, WAGON
lory .... PARROT, LORIKEET
Lortzing's opera .... UNDINE
Los Angeles baseball team
      .... DODGERS
Angeles basketball team
      .... LAKERS, CLIPPERS

Angeles campus .... UCLA
Angeles football team
      .... RAMS, RAIDERS
Angeles mayor .... BRADLEY
_____ (atomic energy
      worksite) .... ALAMOS
Troyens .... THE TROJANS
lose .... MISS, WASTE, MISLAY,
      FORFEIT, MISPLACE,
      SQUANDER
ardor .... PALL
color ...... FADE, PALE, WHITEN
flavor .... PALL
footing .... SLIP, SLIDE
heart .... DESPAIR
one's head .... PANIC
purposely .... THROW
sweetness .... SOUR
traction .... SKID
weight .... DIET, SLENDERIZE
whiteness .... YELLOW
loser .... VICTIM, ALSO-RAN,
      PESSIMIST
attitude of .... FED-UP
poor/bad .... CRYBABY,
      SOREHEAD, SOURPUSS
to St. George .... DRAGON
to Ulysses S. Grant
      .... ROBERT E. LEE
loss .... DAMAGE, DEFEAT,
      PERDITION, FORFEITURE,
      DEPRIVATION
at a .... BAFFLED, PUZZLED,
      DISMAYED
from container .... LEAKAGE,
      SPILLAGE
gambling, ultimate .... (ONE'S)
      SHIRT
of ability to express thought
      .... ASEMIA
appetite .... ANOREXIA
consciousness ...... SYNCOPE,
      FAINTING
energy/strength
      .... ASTHENIA
feeling .... NUMBNESS
hair .... ALOPECIA
hope .... DESPERATION
memory .... AMNESIA
mental power ..... DEMENTIA
reading ability .... ALEXIA
smell .... ANOSMIA
speech ...... ALALIA, APHASIA
voice .... APHONIA,
      LARYNGITIS
will power .... AB(O)ULIA
writing ability .... AGRAPHIA
unexpected .... UPSET
lost ...... GONE, MISLAID, MISSING,
      ENGROSSED
animal .... STRAY

animal, in law .... ESTRAY
chord's hideout .... ORGAN
chord's sound .... AMEN
often, figuratively .... SHIRT
Lost Cause hero .... LEE
Horizon author .... HILTON
Horizon site .... SHANGRI-LA
lot .... DOOM, FATE, PLOT, RAFT,
SLEW, SLUE, BUNCH, SHARE,
PARCEL, DESTINY, FORTUNE,
PORTION, CABOODLE
Lot, city of .... ZOAR
father of .... HARAN
uncle of .... NAHOR, ABRAHAM
sister of .... MILCAH
son of .... MOAB, BENAMMI
Lothario .... RAKE, SEDUCER
Loti, Pierre .... VIAUD
lotion .... COLOGNE, CALAMINE,
OINTMENT, FRESHENER
lots .... MUCH, PLENTY, REALTY
divination by .... SORTILEGE
of dog .... POMP
of something .... HEAP, PILE
Lots, feast of .... PURIM
lottery .... GAME, CHANCE,
DRAWING, TOMBOLA,
SWEEPSTAKES
kin .... KENO, BINGO, LOTTO,
RAFFLE, NUMBERS
ticket .... BLANK
winning .... TERN
lotto kin .... KENO, BINGO
lotus .... HERB, SHRUB, NELUMBO,
WATER LILY
tree .... SADR, JUJUBE
loud ...... NOISY, SHOWY, FLASHY,
SHRILL, CLAMOROUS
clamor .... OUTCRY
colloquial .... VULGAR,
DEMANDING, UNREFINED
extremely/very .... DEAFENING,
STENTORIAN, EARSPLITTING
in music .... FFF, FORTE
noise .... CLAP
speaker .... WOOFER, MONITOR,
TWEETER, AMPLIFIER
loudmouthed .... BLATANT,
BOISTEROUS
person .... STENTOR, THERSITES
lough .... LAKE
Louis of trumpet fame .... PRIMA
the _____, Benedictine Order
advocate .... PIOUS
VII's wife .... ELEANOR
XIII's minister ...... RICHELIEU
XVI's wife .... MARIE
ANTOINETTE
Louisville event .... DERBY
Louisiana bay .... DRUM, EAST,
ELOI, BOUDREAU, BARATARIA

boat .... BATEAU
capital .... BATON ROUGE
city/town .... GRETNA,
KENNER, MONROE, RUSTON,
BOSSIER, LAFAYETTE, NEW
IBERIA, ALEXANDRIA, LAKE
CHARLES, NEW ORLEANS,
SHREVEPORT
county .... PARISH
dialect .... CREOLE
farmer .... HABITAN(T)
island .... BIRD, MARSH,
TIMBALIER
lake .... MUD, IATT, GRAND,
WHITE, VERNON, VERRET,
MAUREPAS, PONTCHARTRAIN
land measure .... ARPENT
mountain .... DRISKILL
native .... CAJUN, CAIJAN,
CREOLE, ACADIAN
patois .... GUMBO, CREOLE
parish .... WINN, CADDO,
ACADIA, VERNON, BOSSIER,
ORLEANS, RAPIDES,
CALCASIEU, JEFFERSON,
LAFAYETTE, LIVINGSTON
river .... AMITE, PEARL, LITTLE,
SABINE, TENSAS, MISSISSIPPI
state bird .... (BROWN)
PELICAN
state flower .... MAGNOLIA
(GRANDIFLORA)
state nickname .... PELICAN
tobacco .... PERIQUE
university .... LOYOLA,
TULANE, XAVIER, DILLARD,
MCNEESE, GRAMBLING
lounge .... LAZE, LOAF, LOLL,
SOFA, COUCH, DIVAN, LOBBY,
LOITER, SETTEE
lounger .... IDLER, LOAFER
lounging suit .... PAJAMAS
loup .... (HALF)MASK
garou .... WEREWOLF
lour .... FROWN, LOWER, SCOWL
Lourdes miracle .... CURE
visitor .... PILGRIM
louse .... NIT, RAT, APHID, COOTIE,
INSECT, SLATER, PARASITE
plural of .... LICE
up .... BOTCH, SPOIL, BUNGLE
lousy .... MEAN, POOR, DIRTY,
ROTTEN, WICKED, INFERIOR,
DISGUSTING
lout .... APE, HOB, OAF, BOOR,
CLOD, HICK, LOON, LOOBY,
BUMPKIN
louver .... SLAT, WINDOW,
TURRET, LANTERN, TRANSOM,
VENETIAN BLIND
lovage .... PARSLEY

love .... WOO, AMO(R), DOTE,
DESIRE, HEART, ENAMOR,
LIKING, DEVOTION, FONDNESS,
AFFECTION, SWEETHEART
according to George
Macdonald ..... THE LORD
AND THE SLAVE OF ALL
affair .... AMOUR, LIAISON,
ROMANCE, INTRIGUE
Bassanio's .... PORTIA
feast .... AGAPE
foolish .... INFATUATION
full of .... EROTIC, AMATIVE
in .... SMITTEN, ENAMORED
in tennis .... ZERO
kind of .... PUPPY
knot .... AMORET
letter: Fr. .... BILLET-DOUX
lies-bleeding .... AMARANTH
lightly .... PHILANDER
make .... WOO, COURT,
INTIMACY, BILL AND COO
note/letter .... VALENTINE
of country .... PATRIOTISM
of fine arts .... VIRTU
potion .... PHILTER
seat .... SOFA
set, in tennis .... SIX-ZERO
song ..... SERENADE, SERENATA
story .... ROMANCE
unwisely/foolishly .... DOTE
lovebird .... LOVER, PARROT
lovelier than poems .... TREES
lovelock .... CURL
lover .... BEAU, FLAME, LEMAN,
ROMEO, SPARK, SWAIN,
WOOER, ADORER, BELOVED,
PARAMOUR
boy .... WOLF, AMORIST,
LOTHARIO
silly .... SPOONER
lovers' lane frequenters
.... TRYSTERS, LOVEBIRDS
meeting .... TRYST
nemesis .... GREEN-EYED
MONSTER
loving .... FOND, ARDENT, DOTING,
EROTIC, TENDER, AMATIVE,
AMATORY, AMOROUS,
DEVOTED, AFFECTIONATE
combining form .... PHILE
couple, famous .... ROMEO
AND JULIET, SAMSON AND
DELILAH, TRISTAN AND
ISOLDE, ABELARD AND
HELOISE, ANTONY AND
CLEOPATRA
cup .... TIG, TROPHY
low .... MOO, BASE, ORRA, VILE,
WEAK, HUMBLE, MENIAL,
SCURVY, VULGAR, INFERIOR

blow .... SMEAR
brow .... PLEBEIAN
comedy .... FARCE,
   BURLESQUE, HORSEPLAY,
   SLAPSTICK
country .... BELGIUM
down: colloq. ...... DIRT, DOPE,
   MEAN, FACTS, DESPICABLE,
   INFO(RMATION)
lay .... HIDE
necked .... DECOLLETE
swinger of hymns
   .... CHARIOT
lowan .... LEIPOA, MALLEE
lowbred .... BASE, CRUDE,
   COARSE, VULGAR
lowbrow .... CRASS
Lowe, aeronaut .... THADDEUS
20,000 cubic foot balloon of
   .... ENTERPRISE
wife of .... LEONTINE
Lowell, astronomer .... PERCIVAL
fascination of .... MARS
observatory site of
   .... FLAGSTAFF
protege of .... (ROBERT)
   GODDARD
Lowell, poet .... AMY, ROBERT
lower .... DIP, LOUR, VAIL, ABASE,
   BASER, DEMIT, FROWN,
   SCOWL, DEBASE, DEMOTE,
   GLOWER, NETHER, REDUCE,
   DEGRADE
classman .... FRESHMAN
in rank .... JUNIOR, PUISNE
on one side .... LOPSIDED
Lower California capital
   .... LAPAZ, MEXICALI
World .... DIS, HELL, HADES,
   EARTH, SHEOL
World gods .... MANES
lowering .... CLOUDY, FROWNING,
   OVERCAST
lowest .... LAST, LEAST, MEANEST,
   LOWERMOST
animal life .... AM(O)EBA
deck .... ORLOP
form of wit .... PUN
part .... BOTTOM
point .... NADIR, BOTTOM,
   NETHERMOST
possible cost .... ROCK-
   BOTTOM PRICE
lowland .... HOLM, PLAIN
Lowlander .... SASSENACH
lowly .... MEEK, HUMBLE
lox .... OXYGEN, SALMON
loxia .... WRYNECK
loyal .... LEAL, DEVOTED,
   STA(U)NCH, FAITHFUL
countryman .... PATRIOT

friend .... DAMON, ACHATES
wife .... PENELOPE
loyalty .... TROTH, FEALTY,
   HOMAGE, FIDELITY,
   ALLEGIANCE
lozenge .... CANDY, RHOMB,
   CACHOU, JUJUBE, MASCLE,
   TROCHE, CATECHU, DIAMOND,
   COUGH DROP, PASTIL(LE),
   PEPPERMINT
LP .... LONG PLAY(ING)
LSD source .... ERGOT
term ..... ACID, TRIP, TURN ON,
   MICRODOT
Luanda is capital of .... ANGOLA
luau .... FEAST
dish .... POI
lubber .... OAF, LOOBY, SAILOR
word of .... AVAST
lube .... OIL, LUBRICANT
Lublin extermination camp
   .... MAIDENEK
lubricant .... OIL, DOPE, LUBE,
   CASTOR, GREASE, UNGUENT,
   VASELINE
lubricate .... OIL, GREASE,
   MOISTURIZE
Lucan's work .... PHARSALIA
luce .... FISH, PIKE
Luce (Clare Booth) estate
   .... HALENAIA
play .... THE WOMEN
lucent .... SHINING
Lucern(e) .... LAKE, MEDIC,
   CANTON, FODDER, ALFALFA
luces .... LIGHTS
singular of .... LUX
Lucia de Lammermoor
  composer .... (GAETANO)
   DONIZETTI
Lucian the _____ .... SKEPTIC
Luciano, Mafia chieftain
   .... CHARLES
sobriquet .... LUCKY
   (LUCIANO)
lucid .... SANE, CLEAR, BRIGHT,
   LIMPID, SHINING, RATIONAL
lucida .... STAR
lucidity .... SANITY, CLARITY,
   CLEARNESS
Lucifer .... DEVIL, MATCH, SATAN
poetic .... VENUS
lucite .... RESIN
luck .... HAP, LOT, FATE, CHANCE,
   FORTUNE, FORTUITY
bad .... CESS, JINX, DEUCE,
   HOODOO, WANION
Luck of Roaring Camp author
   .... HARTE
luckily .... HAPLY, TIMELY
luckless .... STAR-CROSSED

lucky .... CANNY, WITCH,
   FORTUNATE
number .... SEVEN
piece/thing .... CHARM,
   AMULET, HORSESHOE,
   RABBIT'S FOOT
stroke .... FLUKE
lucrative .... PAYING, GAINFUL,
   PROFITABLE
lucre .... GAIN, PELF, MONEY,
   RICHES, WEALTH
infamous connotation for
   .... FILTHY
Lucrezia, poisoner .... BORGIA
brother of .... JUAN, JOFRE,
   CESARE
father of .... RODRIGO
father's title of .... POPE
   ALEXANDER VI
husband of .... DUKE OF
   FERRARA, (GIOVANNI) SFORZA
lucule .... SUNSPOT
luculent .... CLEAR, LUCID
Lucy's TV friend .... ETHEL
ludicrous .... ABSURD, COMIC(AL),
   FARCICAL, RIDICULOUS
Ludwig, biographer .... EMIL
lues .... SYPHILIS
Luftwaffe bomber .... STUKA
leader .... GOERING
lug .... EAR, TOW, DRAG, HAUL,
   PULL, CARRY
luge .... SLED
luggage .... TAN, BAGS, TRAPS,
   BAGGAGE
adjunct .... STRAP
carrier .... PORTER
item .... TRUNK, VALISE,
   SUITCASE
lugger ...... BOAT, TOTER, FALCON,
   VESSEL
lugubrious .... SAD, DISMAL,
   DOLEFUL, MOURNFUL
lugworm .... ANNELID
Luik .... LIEGE
Luke .... EVANGELIST
lukewarm .... TEPID, INDIFFERENT
lull .... CALM, HUSH, ALLAY,
   QUIET, SOOTHE, RESPITE
lullaby .... (CRADLE) SONG
lulu: sl. ...... ONER, WHIZ, BEAUT,
   KNOCKOUT
lumbago .... BACKACHE,
   RHEUMATISM
lumber .... WOOD, BOARDS,
   RUMBLE, CLUTTER
British .... TIMBER
dressing machine .... TRIMMER
factory .... SAWMILL
marker .... KEEL
lumberjack ..... JACKET, LOGGER,

SAWYER, WOODCUTTER
blanket of .... MACKINAW
climbing iron of .... SPUR
warning cry of .... TIMBER
lumberman ...... HEWER, LOGGER, SAWYER, GIRDLER
boot of .... PAC, LARRIGAN
hook of .... PEAV(E)Y
sled of .... TRAVOIS
tool of .... AXE, SAW, ADZE
lumen .... LUX
luminaire .... LAMP
luminal ...... HYPNOTIC, SEDATIVE
luminary .... SUN, MOON, STAR
luminous .... BRIGHT, RADIANT
lummox ...... LOON, LOUT, DUNCE, LOOBY, LUBBER, DUMBBELL, LUNKHEAD
lump .... WAD, WEN, BLOB, BURL, CLOT, HUNK, KNOT, MASS, NODE, HUNCH, DOMINO, GOB(BET), NODULE, NUB(BIN), NUBBLE, NUGGET, SWELLING, COLLECTION
butter .... PAT
of earth/clay .... CLOD
round, small ..... KNOB, BOLUS
lumper ...... DOCKER, STEVEDORE
Lumumba, Congo premier .... PATRICE
Luna .... MOON, SELENE
in alchemy .... SILVER
lunacy .... MANIA, MADNESS, INSANITY
lunar .... PALE, ROUND, PALLID, MOON-SHAPED
crater .... LINNE
month .... MOON
phenomenon .... ECLIPSE
spaceship .... APOLLO
super bowl .... CRATER
lunatic .... INSANE, MADMAN, MANIAC
lunch(eon) .... BITE, MEAL, SNACK, TIFFIN, REFLECTION
lune .... LEASH
lung air passages .... BRONCHI
air sacs .... ALVEOLI
cancer, main cause of .... (CIGARETTE) SMOKING
disease .... TB, CANCER, PHTHISIS, EMPHYSEMA, SILICOSIS, BRONCHITIS, CONSUMPTION
function .... RESPIRATION
inflammation of the .... PNEUMONIA
location .... RIB CAGE
membrane .... PLEURA
of the .... LOBAR
prefix .... PNEU

pus-filled cavity .... VOMICA
sound .... RALE, WHEEZE
surgery .... LOBECTOMY
lunge .... FOIN, LEAP, LONGE, THRUST, PASSADO
lungee/lungi .... LOINCLOTH
lungfish .... DIPNOAN, MUDFISH
lungs used as food .... LIGHTS
lungwort .... LICHEN
lunkhead ...... ASS, LOON, DUNCE, LUMMOX, DUMBBELL
lunt .... MATCH, SMOKE, TORCH, KINDLE
lunule .... HALFMOON
Lupercus .... FAUNUS
Lupescu .... MAGDA
Lupin, thief .... ARSENE
lupine .... WOLFISH, WOLFLIKE
animal .... WOLF
Lupino, actress .... IDA
Lupus .... WOLF
lurch .... LURK, ROLL, SWAY, PITCH, CAREEN, STUMBLE
forward: naut. .... SCEND
lurcher .... DOG, POACHER
lure .... FLY, BAIT, DECOY, TEMPT, ENTICE, INDUCE, SEDUCE, TREPAN, ATTRACT, BEGUILE, SPINNER, INVEIGLE
workers .... PIRATE
lurer .... SIREN, SEDUCER, TEMPTRESS
lurid .... RED, VIVID, GARISH, GLARING, GLOWING, SINISTER
lurk .... PROWL, SKULK, SNEAK
lurker .... CREEPER, PROWLER, STALKER
among coral reefs ..... MORAY
Lurlei .... SIREN, LORELEI
luscious .... SWEET, TASTY, CLOYING, DELICIOUS
lush .... JUICY, LUXURIANT
slang .... BARFLY
Lusitania, now .... PORTUGAL
lust .... DESIRE, APPETITE
luster .... NAIF, GLAZE, GLORY, GLOSS, SHEEN, SHINE, POLISH, REFLECT, RADIANCE
lusterless ...... WAN, DRAB, DULL, MAT(TE)
lustful .... LEWD, RANDY, CARNAL, SENSUAL
lustrous .... NITID, SILKY, GLOSSY, SATINY, RADIANT, SHINING, BRILLIANT
lusty .... HEARTY, ROBUST, STRONG, STURDY, VIGOROUS
lute .... CLAY, SEAL, CEMENT, INSTRUMENT
obsolete .... THEORBO
relative .... ASOR, BANJO,

GUITAR, UKELELE, MANDOLIN
Lutetia .... PARIS
Luther, theologian .... MARTIN
Lutheran .... PROTESTANT
luthern .... DORMER, WINDOW
luting .... SEAL, CEMENT
lux .... LIGHT, LUMEN
luxe .... ELEGANCE, RICHNESS
Luxemb(o)urg capital .... LUXEMBOURG
city/town .... MAMER, PETANGE, REMICHT, DUDELANGET
language .... FRENCH, GERMAN
monetary unit .... FRANC
mountains .... EISLING
plateau .... ARDENNES
river .... OUR, CLERF, MOSEL, SAUER, ALZETTE
steel center .... ESCH
Luxor's neighbor .... KARNAK
luxuriant ...... LUSH, RANK, RICH, FERTILE, PROFUSE
luxuriate .... BASK, WALLOW
luxurious ...... POSH, RICH, TONY, PLUSH
sedan .... LIMO(USINE)
luxury .... EASE, MILK AND HONEY
lover ..... LUCULLUS, SYBARITE
Luzon battlesite .... BATAAN, MANILA BAY, CORREGIDOR
bay .... BALER, DASOL, LAMON, SUBIC, BANGUI, MANILA, BALAYAN, PALANAN, TAYABAS
channel .... BABUYAN
city/town .... IBA, DAET, AGOO, LIPA, NAGA, BALER, LAOAG, PASAY, VIGAN, APARRI, BAGUIO, BONTOC, CAVITE, LUCENA, MAKATI, MANILA, QUEZON, TARLAC, ANGELES, BANGUED, DAGUPAN, LEGAZPI, MALOLOS, CALOOCAN, OLONGAPO, TAGAYTAY, NAGUILIAN, LOS BANOS, SAN FERNANDO
falls .... PAGSANJAN
gulf .... LINGAYEN
island .... VERDE, LUBANG, ALABAT, BABUYAN, POLILLO, CAMIGUIN, CORREGIDOR
lake .... TAAL, LAGUNA DE BAY
mountain .... LABO, PULOG, ARAYAT, ISAROG, PASCAN, BANAHAO, CARBALLO, ZAMBALES, SANTO TOMAS
mountain capital .... BAGUIO
mountain people ...... IGOROTS

mountain range .... CORDILLERA, SIERRA MADRE
native .... AETA, ILOCANO, NEGRITO, TAGALOG, BICOLANO, PAMPANGO, ZAMBALENO
peninsula .... BICOL, BONDOC
province .... ABRA, ALBAY, RIZAL, BATAAN, CAVITE, LAGUNA, QUEZON, TARLAC, BULACAN, CAGAYAN, ISABELA, LA UNION, BATANGAS, PAMPANGA, SORSOGON, ZAMBALES, ILOCOS SUR, ILOCOS NORTE, PANGASINAN, NUEVA ECIJA
river .... ABRA, CAGAYAN
volcano .... TAAL, CAGUA, MAYON, PINATUBO
walled city .... INTRAMUROS
water buffalo .... CARABAO
wild buffalo .... TAMARAU
wonder attraction .... RICE TERRACES
Lwow .... LEMBERG
LXW .... AREA
lycanthrope .... WEREWOLF
lycee .... (SECONDARY) SCHOOL

lyceum .... LECTURE HALL
Lycian city .... MYRA
king .... SARPEDON
leader .... PANDARUS
lycra .... SPANDEX
Lydia, capital of .... SARDIS
Lydian .... GENTLE, SENSUAL, EFFEMINATE, VOLUPTUOUS
king .... CROESUS
language .... ANATOLIC
lye .... BUCK, CAUSTIC, LIXIVIUM
soak in .... BATE, BUCK
source of .... (WOOD)ASHES
lying .... FALSE, DISHONEST
downward .... PRONE, ACUMBENT, PRONATED
on one's back .... SUPINE
under oath .... PERJURY
lymph .... HUMOR, SERUM
and fats .... CHYLE
gland swelling .... BUBO
vessel .... VARIX
lymphatic .... PLASMIC
lymphoid tissue back of mouth .... TONSIL
lynching, end of .... HANGING
lynx .... PISHU, BOBCAT, CARACAL, WILDCAT

fur .... CARACAL
of a .... LYNCEAN
Lyra .... HARP
lyre .... HARP, TRIGON
like instrument .... ASOR, CITHARA, SACKBUT
shaped .... LYRATE
lyrebird .... MENURA
lyric .... ALBA, LIED, MELIC, SONGLIKE
muse .... ERATO
poem ...... ODE, HYMN, ELEGY, EPODE, MELIC, RONDEL, SONNET, CANZONE, RONDEAU
poet .... ODIST, LYRIST, SAPPHO, MINSTREL
solo .... MONODY
lyrical .... ODIC
lyricist David .... HAL
noted .... HAMMERSTEIN
lyrics of opera .... LIBRETTO
Lysander's love .... HERMIA
lysin .... ANTIBODY
lysol .... ANTISEPTIC, DISINFECTANT
constituent .... SOAP, CRESOL
lytta .... WORM
Lytton heroine .... IONE

M

M .... MU, EM(MA)
ma .... MA(M)MA, MOTHER
chere .... MY DEAR
Maas .... MEUSE
mabolo .... PLUM
macabre ...... GRIM, EERIE, LURID, WEIRD, MORBID, GHASTLY, GRUESOME
part of a title .... DANSE
macaco .... LEMUR, MONKEY
macadam .... ROAD, STONES
material .... TAR, ASPHALT
Macao coin .... AVO
island .... TAIPA, COLOANE
MacArthur, general .... ARTHUR, DOUGLAS
title .... SCAP
macaque .... KRA, MONKEY, RHESUS, WANDEROO
macaroni .... DANDY, PASTA
ingredient .... DURUM, SEMOLINA
strip ...... LASAGNA, SPAGHETTI
macaroon .... COOKY, BISCUIT, RATAFIA
Macassar .... MALAYAN

macaw .... PARROT, ARA(RA), MARACAN
Macbeth bailiwick .... GLAMIS
character .... ROSS, BANQUO, DUNCAN, HECATE, MACDUFF
has three .... CRONES
maccaboy .... SNUFF
MacDonald's co-star .... (NELSON) EDDY
mace .... CLUB, MAUL, SPICE, STAFF, STICK
bearer .... BEADLE
reed .... DOD
royal .... SCEPTRE
source of .... NUTMEG
wielder .... KNIGHT
macedoine .... SALAD, MEDLEY
Macedonia capital .... SKOPJE
capital, ancient .... PELLA
city/town .... STIP, BEREA, DEBAR, BEROVO, PRILEP, TETOVO, EDHESSA
region .... PIERIA
seaport .... SALONIKA
macer .... BEADLE
macerate .... RET, SOAK, STEEP,

SOFTEN, WASTE AWAY
Mach, physicist .... ERNST
machete ...... BOLO, KNIFE, PANGA
Machiavelli .... NICCOLO
Machiavellian .... CRAFTY
machina, _____ .... DEUS EX
machinate .... PLAN, PLOT, DEVISE, SCHEME
machination .... PLOT, CABAL, DESIGN, SCHEME, ARTIFICE, INTRIGUE
machine .... TOOL, MOTOR, DEVICE, ENGINE, GADGET, MECHANISM
cloth smoothing .... MANGLE
crushing .... MILL, PRESS
cutting .... CROPPER
device .... GLAND
duplicating .... RONEO, XEROX, MIMEOGRAPH
finishing .... EDGER
flying .... GLIDER, AIRCRAFT, AIR BALLOON
grinding .... MILL
gun .... BREN, STEN, MAXIM, POM POM, GATLING

gunned .... STRAFED
gunner's post .... NEST
nap-raising .... TEASEL(LER)
ore-dressing .... VANNER
part .... CAM, COG, GEAR,
PAWL, CRANK, ROTOR, VALVE,
PISTON, SOLENOID
political .... PARTY
printing .... PRESS
remote-controlled,
mechanical .... ROBOT
repairer .... MECHANIC,
TECHNICIAN
road-building .... GRADER
seed-bed preparation
.... COMPACTER
shearing .... CROPPER
stock quotation .... TICK
tool .... LATHE
weaving .... LOOM
wood-turning .... LATHE
machinist's gauge
.... MICROMETER
groove .... TSLOT
macho .... VIRILE,
ULTRAMASCULINE
match .... DUEL
machree .... MY HEART
Mack, of baseball .... CONNIE
Mackenzie tributary ...... LIARD
mackerel ...... FISH, TUNA, SARDA,
TUNNY, BONITO, SAUREL,
ALBACORE
cured .... BLOATER
like fish .... CERO, SCAD,
TUNNY, BESHOW, SIERRA,
TINKER, CAVALLA, PINTADO,
PLAINTAIL
net .... SPILLER
of the .... SCOMBROID
type .... ATKA
young .... SPIKE, TINKER
Mackinaw .... BOAT, COAT,
BLANKET
trout .... NAMAYCUSH
Mackintosh .... RAINCOAT
mackle ...... BLOT, BLUR, MACULE
MacLeish, poet .... ARCHIBALD
MacMahon, actress .... ALINE
macrocosm .... WORLD, UNIVERSE
macula .... SPOT
maculate .... SPOT, STAIN,
BLOTCH, DEFILE, BLEMISH,
SPECKLE
macule .... BLOT, BLUR, SLUR
mad .... SORE, ANGRY, CRAZY,
IRATE, RABID, INSANE,
FRANTIC, FURIOUS, FRENETIC,
FRENZIED, SENSELESS
about .... FOND OF
Anthony _____ .... WAYNE

monk .... RASPUTIN
scientist of Cairo .... ALHAZEN
Madagascar animal ...... LEMUR,
TEMEE, AYEAYE, TENREC
capital .... ANTANANARIVO
city/town .... TOLIARA,
ANTALAHA, MORONDAVA
civet .... FOSSA
fiber .... RAFFIA
lemur .... AYEAYE, INDRI(S)
native .... HOVA
river .... MANGOKY
tribe .... HOVA, MALAGASY
madam .... LADY, WOMAN,
MILADY, MISTRESS
Italian .... MADONNA
Madama Butterfly composer
.... (GIACOMO) PUCCINI
lover .... (B.F.) PINKERTON
name of .... CIO-CIO(SAN)
Madame .... MRS.
Du Barry's enemy ...... MARIE
ANTOINETTE
Karenina .... ANNA
Spanish .... SRA, SENORA
madcap .... RASH, HOTSPUR,
RECKLESS, IMPULSIVE
madden .... ANGER, ENRAGE,
INCENSE
madder .... DYE, EVEA, VINE,
PLANT, RUBIA, COFFEE,
IPECAC, CRIMSON, GARDENIA,
ALIZARIN(E)
made of wood .... XYLOID
reference to .... ALLUDED
to-order .... CUSTOM-BUILT
tracks .... SPED
up .... FALSE, INVENTED,
IMAGINED, COSMETIZED,
FABRICATED
Made in America author
.... (SAM) WALTON
Madeira .... WINE, RIVER, ISLAND
capital .... FUNCHAL
Island wind .... LESTE
wine .... TINTA
mademoiselle .... GIRL, LADY,
MISS, WOMAN
abbreviation .... MLLE
madhouse .... BABEL, CHAOS,
BEDLAM, ASYLUM
Madison Ave. people .... ADMEN
madman .... MANIAC, LUNATIC
madness ...... FURY, RAGE, FOLLY,
MANIA, FRENZY, IDIOCY,
LUNACY, RABIES, DEMENTIA
fits of .... LUNES
pertaining to .... MANIC
Madonna .... MARY
madras .... CLOTH, KERCHIEF

Madras city ...... SALEM, CALICUT
state .... COCHIN
weight .... SER, POLLAM
madre .... MOTHER
madrepore .... CORAL
formation .... REEF, ATOLL
Madrid boulevard/park/
museum .... PRADO
madrigal .... GLEE, POEM, SONG
syllables .... FALA
Madrileno .... SPANIARD
madwort .... SHRUB, ALYSSUM
Mae West .... LIFEBELT
maelstrom .... WHIRLPOOL
maenad ...... NYMPH, BACCHANTE
maestro .... MASTER, TEACHER,
COMPOSER, CONDUCTOR
Mafeking native .... BOER
Maffei work .... MEROPE
maf(f)ia .... BLACK HAND
chief .... CAPO
nemesis of .... FEDS, NARCO
surveyor .... CASER
Mafioso .... RACKETEER
magazine .... DEPOT, ARMORY,
JOURNAL, WAREHOUSE,
PERIODICAL, STORE(HOUSE)
a computer .... BYTE
a feminist .... MS
a sports .... GOLF, TENNIS
a weekly news .... TIME
classy .... SLICK
content .... AMMO,
MUNITION(S)
inferior .... PULP
output .... ISSUE
type ..... NEWS, GIRLIE, SPORTS
VIP .... EDITOR
work .... JOURNALISM
Magdalen scholar .... DEMY
mage .... WIZARD, MAGICIAN
Magellan .... FERDINAND
discovery of: 1521
.... PHILIPPINES
ship of .... SANTIAGO,
TRINIDAD, VICTORIA
magenta .... DYE, RED, FUCHSIN
maggot .... BOT(T), GRUB, MAWK,
WHIM, LARVA, NOTION
Magi .... MAGUS, GASPAR,
MELCHIOR, BALTHASAR
"guide" .... STAR
magic .... ART, JUJU, RUNE,
OBEAH, GRAMARY, THEURGY,
WIZARDRY
black .... VOODOO, SORCERY,
WITCHCRAFT
charm .... AMULET
formula .... ABRACADABRA
hammer, owner of .... THOR
horse .... BAYARD

incantation .... RUNE
lamp finder .... ALADDIN
potion .... PHILTER
practice .... CONJURE
sign .... SIGIL
spell .... CANTRIP,
CONJURATION
symbol .... WAND, PENTACLE
word .... SESAME

Magic Mountain author
.... MANN

magical .... RUNIC, HERMETIC,
MYSTICAL, ENCHANTING
conveyance .... CARPET
herb .... MOLY
piece .... CHARM, AMULET

magician .... MAGE, MAGUS,
MAGI(AN), MERLIN, SHAMAN,
WIZARD, HOUDINI, WARLOCK,
CONJURER, KLINGSOR,
SORCERER
assistants of .... FAMULI
device of .... GIMMICK
illusion of .... LEVITATION
of iron .... (ALEXANDER
GUSTAV)EIFFEL
rod of .... STAFF
skill of .... LEGERDEMAIN
talk of .... PATTER
tricks of .... HOCUS-POCUS
word of .... PRESTO

Maginot line, opposed to
.... LIMES, SIEGFRIED

magisterial .... POMPOUS,
ARBITRARY, MASTERFUL

magistral .... IMPERIOUS

magistrate .... JUDGE, JUSTICE
civil .... SYNDIC
Spanish .... JUEZ, ALCALDE
town .... REEVE

magnanimous .... GENEROUS

magnate .... BARON, MOGUL,
NABOB, BIGWIG, TYCOON

magnesia .... ANTACID, LAXATIVE

magnesium silicate .... TALC

magnet .... LOADSTONE,
LODESTONE
alloy .... ALNICO
end .... POLE

magnetic .... ELECTRIC,
MESMERIC, ATTRACTIVE
direction .... NORTH, SOUTH
flux, unit of .... WEBER,
MAXWELL
force .... OD, ODYL(E)
resistance .... RELUCTANCE

magnetism .... ALLURE, GRAVITY,
MESMERISM, ATTRACTION

magnetite .... LODESTAR,
LOADSTONE

magnetize .... SWAY, CHARM,

ATTRACT, INFLUENCE

magneto .... DYNAMO

magnific ...... POMPOUS, IMPOSING

magnificat .... HYMN, POEM, SONG

magnificence .... DASH, POMP,
GLORY, STATE, SPLASH,
GLITTER, GRANDEUR,
SPLENDOR

magnificent .... GRAND, PROUD,
SUPERB, STATELY
array .... PANOPLY

magnify .... LAUD, EXALT,
AUGMENT, ENLARGE

magnifying instrument
.... TELESCOPE, MICROSCOPE

magnitude .... BULK, SIZE,
RANGE, EXTENT

magnolia .... SHRUB, FLOWER,
SWEET BAY

Magnolia State .... MISSISSIPPI

magnum .... BOTTLE
opus ...... WORK, MASTERPIECE

magpie ...... CROW, MAG(G), PICA,
PIET
kin .... JAY

maguey ...... ALOE, AGAVE, FIBER

magus .... SEER, MAGICIAN,
SORCERER

Magyar .... HUNGARIAN

maharaja's wife ...... MAHARANI,
MAHARANEE

Mahatma, famous .... GANDHI

Mahdi follower .... DERVISH
victim .... GORDON

Mahican .... MOHEGAN

mahjongg piece .... TILE
wind ...... EAST, WEST, NORTH,
SOUTH

mahogany .... TOON, TREE,
CAOBA, NARRA, BAYWOOD,
(HARD)WOOD
color .... REDDISH-BROWN
family .... MELIACEAE
of the .... MELIACEOUS
pine .... TOTARA

Mahomet .... PROPHET,
MOHAMMED
burial place of .... MEDINA

Mahren .... MORAVIA

Maia .... MAY, PLEIADE

maid .... GIRL, LASS, FILLE,
WENCH, VIRGIN, DOMESTIC
lady's .... ABIGAIL
old .... TABBY, SPINSTER
servant .... BONNE, SOUBRETTE

Maid of Astolat .... ELAINE
of Orleans .... JOAN OF ARC

maiden .... NEW, LASS, FIRST,
FRESH, NYMPH, SYLPH,
DAMSEL, VIRGIN, COLLEEN,
DAMOSEL, GUILLOTINE

appearance .... DEBUT,
INITIATION
changed to heifer .... IO
changed to spider by Athena
.... ARACHNE
in Song of Solomon
.... SHULAMITE
name .... NEE

maidenhair .... FERN, GINKO

maidenhead .... HYMEN,
VIRGINITY

maidenly .... GENTLE, MODEST,
GIRLISH, VIRGINAL

mail .... DA(U)K, DAWK, POST,
SEND, ARMOR, LETTERS
bag .... POUCH
boat .... PACKET
carrier .... POSTMAN, PONY
EXPRESS
coat of .... ARMOR, BYRNIE,
HAUBERK
examine .... CENSOR
India .... DA(W)K
mark .... STAMP, CACHET,
INDICIA
pertaining to .... POSTAL
route .... RFD
type of/unwanted .... JUNK

Mailer, author .... NORMAN

mailing charge .... POSTAGE
right .... FRANK

mailman .... POSTMAN, LETTER
CARRIER

maim .... LAME, MANGLE,
CRIPPLE, DISABLE, DISFIGURE

main .... DUCT, CHIEF, FORCE,
POWER, LEADING, FOREMOST,
PRINCIPAL
action of drama .... EPITASIS
body .... TRUNK
bounding .... SEA, OCEAN
course/dish .... ENTREE
line of motion .... AXIS
point .... NUB, CRUX, GIST
road .... PIKE
stress .... BRUNT, ACCENT
trunk .... AORTA

Main Street attractions
.... STORES

Maine admiral .... SIGSBEE
bay .... CASCO, MACHIAS
cape .... SMALL
capital .... AUGUSTA
city/town .... BATH, MILO,
PERU, YORK, ORONO, PARIS,
AUBURN, BANGOR, CAMDEN,
LISBON, MEXICO, BELFAST,
HAMPDEN, MADISON,
FREEPORT, LEWISTON,
PORTLAND, KENNEBUNKPORT
college .... BATES, COLBY,

NASSON, BOWDOIN
college town .... ORONO
county .... KNOX, YORK,
    WALDO, OXFORD, HANCOCK,
    LINCOLN, SOMERSET,
    PENOBSCOT
game .... ELK
island .... HAUT, CROSS, GREEN
lake .... BOG, LONG, ROWE,
    WEBB, EAGLE, ONAWA,
    SEBAGO, SPIDER
Maritime Academy site
    .... CASTINE
mountain .... ABRAHAM,
    KATAHDIN
native .... DOWN-EASTER
peak .... KATAHDIN
river .... DEAD, FISH, SACO,
    ELLIS, SANDY, SWIFT
state bird .... CHICKADEE
state flower .... PINE CONE
state motto .... DIRIGO, I
    GUIDE, I DIRECT
state nickname ...... PINE TREE
state symbol .... PINE
trout .... OQUASSA
university site .... AUGUSTA,
    MACHIAS
Mainland .... POMONA
mainly .... MOSTLY, CHIEFLY,
    LARGELY
mainspring .... INCENTIVE,
    MOTIVATION
maintain .... KEEP, CLAIM,
    AFFIRM, ASSERT, DEFEND,
    CARRY ON, (UP)HOLD,
    CONTINUE, PRESERVE
maintenance .... UPKEEP,
    SUPPORT, LIVELIHOOD
divorcee's .... ALIMONY
Mainz .... MAYENCE
maison de sante .... HOSPITAL,
    SANITARIUM
maitre d'hotel .... BUTLER,
    STEWARD, MAJOR-DOMO,
    HEADWAITER
maize ...... CORN, MEALY, CEREAL,
    MEALIE, YELLOW
Maja painter .... GOYA
majestic .... EPIC, GRAND, NOBLE,
    REGAL, AUGUST, KINGLY,
    STATELY, IMPERIAL
majesty ...... DIGNITY, GRANDEUR,
    NOBILITY, SOVEREIGNTY
majolica .... POTTERY
major .... MAIN, CHIEF, OF AGE,
    GREATER, SPECIALTY
domo .... BUTLER, STEWARD,
    SENESCHAL
ending/chaser .... ETTE
follower .... DOMO

in .... SPECIALIZE
or minor .... URSA
premise .... SUMPTION
suit, in bridge .... HEARTS,
    SPADES
Major Barbara author .... SHAW
Majorca .... ISLAND, MAJOLICA
    MALLORCA
city/port .... PALMA
sister island .... MINORCA
majority .... AGE, BULK, MOST,
    PLURALITY, SENIORITY
age .... ADULTHOOD
majuscule .... UNCIAL, CAPITAL
make .... BRAND, BUILD, STYLE,
    CREATE, DEVISE, FASHION
a _____ at .... STAB
boo-boo .... ERR
cast .... PLASTER
catty remark .... MEOW
chair seat .... CANE
connection .... TIE TO
deal .... COMPROMISE
dent .... IMPRESS
face .... APE, POUT
fuss .... CLAMOR
hash of .... BOTCH UP
hole in one .... ACE
hook shot .... SINK
killing ...... WIN, SCORE, HIT-
    THE-JACKPOT
living .... EARN
mountain out of a molehill
    .... EXAGGERATE
movement .... GESTURE
new shade .... DYE
_____ of (bungle) ...... HASH
point of .... FIX, SETTLE
rustling sound .... SOUGH
scene .... GUSH, RANT, RAVE,
    EMOTE
show of .... SHAM, FEIGN,
    PRETEND
slip .... ERR
adherent .... PASTE
advances .... SOLICIT,
    OVERTURE, PROPOSITION
airtight .... LUTE, SEAL
allowance for .... IGNORE,
    DISCOUNT, OVERLOOK
amends .... ATONE
an appearance .... EMERGE
an impression .... AFFECT,
    RANKLE, PENETRATE
an incised mark .... RASE
an incursion .... RAID
angry .... ROIL
as profit .... CLEAR
askew .... TILT
available, as time ..... FREE UP
believe ..... ACT, SHAM, FEIGN,

FANTASY, MIMETIC, PRETEND,
    PRETENSE
beloved .... ENDEAR
black .... NEGRIFY
capital of .... EXPLOIT
certain .... ENSURE, INSURE
choice .... OPT
clear .... EXPLAIN
cloth .... WEAVE
complicated .... ENTANGLE
contact with .... ABUT
crackling sounds
    .... CREPITATE
cross sign .... SAIN
crystal clear .... SPELL OUT
dainty .... PRETTIFY
do .... EKE, MANAGE
dry .... PARCH
ends meet .... ECONOMIZE
even .... TRUE
expressive gestures with
    hands .... GESTICULATE
eyes at .... OGLE, FLIRT
fast .... BELAY, SECURE,
    TIGHTEN
fiendish .... DIABOLIZE
flawless .... PERFECT
full again .... REFILL
fun of .... RIB, MOCK, TWIT,
    DERIDE, RIDICULE
gentle .... HUMANIZE
good .... SUCCEED,
    COMPENSATE
happy .... ELATE
haste .... HIE, RUSH, HURRY
hay while the sun shines
    .... TAKE ADVANTAGE OF
headway .... ADVANCE,
    PROGRESS
headway against .... STEM
hit .... CLICK
indistinct .... DIM, BLOT, BLUR,
    SMEAR
inquiry .... ASK, QUESTION
inroads .... ADVANCE,
    ENCROACH, INFRINGE
insane .... DEMENT, DERANGE
into law .... ENACT, LEGISLATE
into leather .... TAN, TAW
intricate .... COMPLICATE
iridescent .... OPALIZE
it .... ARRIVE, ACHIEVE,
    SUCCEED
keen .... HONE
known .... AIR, REVEAL,
    DIVULGE, DISCLOSE,
    ADVERTISE, PUT ON THE MAP
lace .... TAT
less ...... DECREASE, (DI)MINISH
less distinct .... DIM
less volatile .... DEFUSE

level .... EVEN, TRUE, PLANE
light fainter .... BEDIM
light of .... DISREGARD
like ..... APE, MIMIC, EMULATE,
IMITATE
love .... PET, WOO, SPOON,
COHABIT, BILL AND COO
member .... JOIN, ENROLL
merry .... CHEER, REVEL
mistake .... ERR
money .... GAIN, PROFIT,
STRIKE-IT-RICH
more complex .... MUDDLE,
MYSTIFY, COMPLICATE
nervous ...... EXCITE, AGITATE,
RUFFLE, FLUSTER, STARTLE
night noises .... SNORE
no bones about .... STAND
FAST, STICK TO ONE'S GUNS
notch .... SERRATE
obscure .... BEDIM
one's day .... ELATE
one's mark .... SHINE
one's point .... PUTS ACROSS
one's way .... GO, COPE, WEND
oneself comfortable ...... COSE
oneself heard .... SPEAK UP
out .... ESPY, FARE, SPOT,
PROVE, DESCRY, DISCERN
out artist .... WOLF, SEDUCER
out the meaning ..... DECIPHER
over .... REDO, CHANGE,
REVAMP, CONVERT, REBUILD,
RENOVATE
peace .... MEDIATE, REUNITE,
RECONCILE
picots .... TAT
points .... SCORE
position secure .... CONFIRM,
FORTIFY, ENTRENCH
possible .... ALLOW, ENABLE,
PERMIT
prismatic .... IRIDIZE
public .... AIR, BARE,
ANNOUNCE, DISCLOSE
quiet .... MUTE, (S)HUSH,
MUFFLE
ragged .... FRAY, FRAZZLE
ready/receptive .... PRIME,
PREPARE
reparation .... ATONE
resentful .... VEX, INCENSE,
EMBITTER
road repairs .... RETAR
room .... MOVE OVER
rough .... COARSEN,
GRANULATE
safe .... SECURE
scholarly corrections
.... EMEND
selection .... OPT, PICK,

CHOOSE
sense ..... ADD UP, BE LOGICAL
sleek .... PREEN, GREASE,
LUBRICATE
smooth .... PREEN, PACIFY,
POLISH, SLICKEN
sound of boisterous laughter
.... CACHINNATE
strong .... STEEL
stupid/dull .... HEBETATE
suitable .... ADAPT
superficially attractive
.... WINDOW-DRESS
sure of .... SEE TO IT
the best of it .... ACCEPT, LIVE
WITH IT
the grade .... MANAGE,
CONTRIVE
the most of .... EXPLOIT
the scene .... COME, JOIN, GO
TO, ARRIVE
thread .... SPIN
unfriendly .... ALIENATE,
DISAFFECT, ANTAGONIZE
unintelligible .... GARBLE,
JUMBLE
unnecessary .... EXCLUDE,
OBVIATE
up .... FORM, INVENT, LAYOUT,
COMPOSE, RECONCILE
up for .... ATONE
up ground .... GAIN ON
up one's mind .... DECIDE
up to .... REPAY, BEFRIEND
use of .... AVAIL, EMPLOY,
UTILIZE
vinegary .... SOUR
watertight .... CALK
waves .... OBJECT, PROTEST,
DISAGREE
whole .... HEAL, MEND,
COMPLEMENT
young .... REJUVENATE
maker .... DOER, SIGNER,
CREATOR, PRODUCER
of cask and tub .... COOPER
makeshift .... STOPGAP,
SUBSTITUTE
makeup .... FORM, NATURE,
COMPOSITION
delta's .... SILT
material ..... ROUGE, PANCAKE,
MASCARA, LIPSTICK,
COSMETICS, FOUNDATION
newspaper .... FORMAT,
LAYOUT
maki .... LEMUR
mako .... SHARK
mal de mer .... SEASICKNESS
Malabar monkey .... WANDEROO
Malacca .... CANE, STRAIT

malachite .... BICE, VERDITER
maladroit .... INEPT, CLUMSY,
AWKWARD
malady .... AILMENT, DISEASE,
ILLNESS, SICKNESS
Malaga .... WINE, GRAPE
Malagasy ethnic group
.... MERINA
president .... TSIRANANA
malaise .... DISCOMFORT
malanders .... ECZEMA
malapert .... BOLD, SAUCY,
IMPUDENT
Malaprop's (Mrs.) creator
.... SHERIDAN
malapropos .... IMPROPER,
UNTIMELY, INOPPORTUNE,
INAPPROPRIATE
malar .... CHEEKBONE
coloring .... FLUSH
malaria ..... MIASM(A), QUARTAN,
PALUDISM
carrier .... MOSQUITO,
ANOPHELES
characteristic/symptom
.... AGUE, FEVER, CHILLS,
RIGORS, SHAKING
drug treatment .... ATEBRIN,
QUININE, ATABRINE,
CHLOROQUINE
parasite .... PLASMODIA
malark(e)y .... HOKUM, BALONEY,
BUNCOMBE, NONSENSE, LIP
SERVICE
Malawi .... NYASALAND
capital .... LILONGWE
city/town .... DEDZA, ZOMBA,
NSANJE, KARONGA, BLANTYRE
lake .... NYASA, CHILWA
language .... YAO, BANTU,
NGONI, TONGA
money .... KWACHA
mountains .... MULANJE
president .... BANDA
river .... SHIRE
Malay ape .... LAR, MIAS
apple .... OHIA
archipelago .... INDONESIA
beverage .... TAFIA
canoe .... PRAH, PRAO, PRAU,
PROA
chief .... DATO, DATU
cloth .... BAT(T)IK
coin .... ORA, TRA(H),
TAMPANG
crane .... SARUS
dagger .... CRIS, KRIS, CREESE
dish .... SATAY
dress .... PAREUS, SARONG
dyeing .... BAT(T)IK

441

English trade language
.... BECHE-DE-MER
fiber .... TERAP
fruit/nut .... KANARI
gibbon .... LAR
island .... JAVA, SABAH,
    TIMOR, BORNEO, SUMATRA
isthmus .... KRA
jacket .... BAJU
knife .... PARANG
law .... ADAT
leather .... KULIT
"man of the woods"
.... ORANGUTAN
measure .... PAU
mountain .... TAHAN
negrito .... ITA, A(E)TA
nervous disease .... LATA
palm .... ARECA, ARENG,
    BETEL, GEBANG, GOMUTI
Peninsula city .... KUALA
    LAMPUR
puppeteer .... (TO)DALANG
rattan .... SEGA
sea cucumber .... TRIPANG,
    TERIPANG
seaweed product
.... AGAR(AGAR)
shadow play .... WAYANG
sir .... TUAN
state .... KEDAH, JOHOR(E),
    PERAK, MELAKA, PAHANG,
    PENANG, PERLIS, KELANTAN,
    SELANGOR, TERENGGANU
station .... STESHEN
telephone .... TALIPON
tic .... LATA
title .... TUAN
tree ..... UPAS, TERAP, DURIAN,
    RAMBUTAN
tribe .... ARIPAS
tribesman .... MACASSAR
ungulate .... TAPIR
verse form .... PANTUN
village .... KAMPONG
warehouse .... GODON
warrior .... KURIPAN
weapon .... PARANG
weight .... KATI, CADDY
wild ox .... BANTENG
xylophone .... GAMBANG
yam .... UBI
Malayan .... TAGALOG
Malaysia capital .... KUALA
    LAMPUR
city/town .... IPOH, MUAR,
    PEKAN, KELANG, BENTONG,
    KELUANG, KUANTAN,
    MALACCA, SEREMBAN
crocodile .... MUGGER
flower .... GUMAMELA,

HIBISCUS
flying bat .... KALONG
language ...... DAYAK, MALAY,
    TAMIL
master .... TUAN
monetary unit .... RINGGIT
mountain .... KINABALU
palm .... SAGO
plant .... RAFFLESIA
prime minister .... RAHMAN
river .... JOHOR, PULAI,
    PAHANG
seaport ..... MALACCA, GEORGE
    TOWN
shadow play .... WAYANG
state .... SABAH, MALAYA,
    SARAWAK
title for man .... TUN
title for woman ..... TOH PUAN
malcontent .... REB(EL),
    GRUMBLER, DISSIDENT,
    REBELLIOUS
Maldive Islands ...... SULTANATE
capital .... MALE
prime minister .... NASIR
sultan .... FARID DIDI
male .... HE, BOY, MANLY,
    MISTER, VIRILE, MASCULINE
animal ...... RAM, BOAR, BUCK,
    BULL, JACK, STAG
ant .... ANER
bee .... DRONE
brant/goose .... GANDER
cat .... GIB, TOM
cattle .... OX, BULL, STEER
chicken .... COCK, CAPON,
    ROOSTER
deer .... BUCK, HART, STAG,
    PRICKET, ROEBUCK
donkey .... JACKASS
duck .... DRAKE
elk/elephant .... BULL
figure of column
.... TELAMON, ATLANTES
goat .... BILLYGOAT
hog/swine .... BOAR
horse .... STALLION
horse, castrated .... GELDING
human, castrated ..... EUNUCH
line of family ...... SPEAR SIDE
presumptuous: sl. ..... MASHER
servant ..... BOY, MAN, KNAVE,
    VALET, LACKEY
sex hormone .... ANDROGEN
sheep .... RAM, TUP, WETHER
slang .... GUY
swan .... COB
turkey .... TOM
virile .... HE-MAN
young .... BUCK
maledict .... ACCURSED

malediction .... CURSE, MALISON,
    SLANDER, ANATHEMA,
    DAMNATION
malefaction .... CRIME, GUILT
malefactor ...... FELON, CRIMINAL,
    EVILDOER
malefic .... EVIL, HARMFUL
malemute .... DOG, HUSKY
malevolence .... MALICE, ILL WILL
malevolent .... EVIL, FELL,
    VICIOUS, SPITEFUL, MALICIOUS
malfeasance .... MISCONDUCT
malformed .... MISSHAPEN
human .... HUNCHBACK
Mali capital .... BAMAKO
city/town ...... GAO, SAN, KATI,
    KITA, KAYES, MOPTI, SEGOU,
    SIKASSO, TIMBUKTU
desert .... CHECH, SAHARA
ethnic group .... PEULS,
    MARKAS, BAMBARA, TOUAREG,
    MALINKES
lake .... DEBO
language ...... FULANI, SENUFU,
    BAMBARA
monetary unit .... FRANC
mountains .... HOMBORI
president .... (MODIBO)KEITA
region .... SUDAN
river .... BANI, NIGER, SENEGAL
malic acid salt .... MALATE
malice .... ENVY, SPITE, VENOM,
    GRUDGE, RANCOR, SPLEEN,
    ILL WILL
malicious .... CATTY, NASTY,
    VICIOUS, SPITEFUL,
    VINDICTIVE
burning .... ARSON
destruction .... SABOTAGE
malign .... ABUSE, LIBEL, DEFAME,
    REVILE, VILIFY, ASPERSE,
    SLANDER, TRADUCE
malignant .... EVIL, HARMFUL,
    VICIOUS, VIRULENT
opposite of .... BENIGN
skin cancer .... MELANOMA
spirit .... KER
tumor .... CANCER
Malines .... LACE, MECHLIN
malinger .... SHIRK, SKULK
malingerer .... DODGER
malison ...... CURSE, MALEDICTION
malkin .... CAT, MOP, HARE,
    DOWDY, SCARECROW
mall .... LANE, WALK, ALLEE,
    ALLEY, AVENUE, PROMENADE,
    SHOPPING CENTER
mallard ...... DRAKE, (WILD)DUCK
malleable .... SOFT, DUCTILE,
    PLIABLE, TENSILE, AMENABLE
malleate .... POUND

mallemuck ...... FULMAR, PETREL, ALBATROSS
mallet .... TUP, MAUL, GAVEL, MADGE, BEETLE, HAMMER, PESTLE
finger .... INJURY
game played with .... POLO, CROQUET
striking part of .... TUP
toe .... DEFORMITY
malleus .... HAMMER
Mallorca .... MAJORCA
area of .... MURO
mallow ...... OKRA, SIDA, ALTHEA, COTTON, HIBISCUS, (HOLLY)HOCK
malm .... LOAM, MARL, LIMESTONE
Malmo man .... SWEDE
malmsey .... WINE, GRAPE, MADEIRA, MALVOISIE
grape .... MALVASIA
Malo les _____ .... BAINS
malodorous ...... FETID, STINKING
malt .... BARLEY, LIQUOR
liquor .... ALE, BEER, STOUT, PORTER
liquor's yeast .... BARM
product .... ALE, BEER, ALEGAR, VINEGAR
strainer: var. .... STROM
sugar .... MALTOSE
Malta capital .... VALETTA
city/town .... SILEMA, VICTORIA
coin, old .... TARI
defender .... GORT
island .... GOZO, COMINO
monetary unit .... POUND
wind .... GREGALE
Maltese .... CAT, DOG, CROSS
maltha .... TAR, CEMENT, BITUMEN, OZOCERITE
maltose .... SUGAR
maltreat(ment) .... ABUSE
malvasia .... GRAPE
product .... MALMSEY
mama .... MAW, MOM, MOTHER
Mama _____ **Elliot** .... CASS
mamba .... COBRA, ELAPINE
mambo .... RIFF, DANCE
mameluke .... SLAVE
Mamie's maiden name .... DOUD
mammal .... COATI, PRIMATE, SUCKLER
antlered .... DEER
aquatic/marine .... MINK, SEAL, OTTER, WHALE, DESMAN, DUGONG, SEACOW, DOLPHIN, MANATEE, PORPOISE
"armored" .... ARMADILLO

egg-laying .... DUCKBILL, PLATYPUS
extinct .... MASTODON
flesh-eating ...... MINK, OTTER, RATEL, WEASEL
fur .... PELAGE
furry .... SEAL
hoglike .... TAPIR
lowest order .... MONOTREME
musteline ...... RATEL, MARTEN
nocturnal .... RAT, LEMUR
plant-eating ..... RHINO(CEROS)
ring-tailed .... RACCOON
snouted .... DESMAN, DOLPHIN, PORPOISE
swift .... HARE
two-handed .... BIMANE
water-loving .... OTTER
mammals, of certain .... MUSTELINE, NOCTURNAL
mammary gland .... UDDER
inflammation .... MASTITIS
mammee ...... MAMEY, SAPODILLA
mammet ...... DOLL, IDOL, PUPPET
mammilla .... TEAT, NIPPLE
mammoth ...... HUGE, ELEPHANT, ENORMOUS, GIGANTIC
like animal .... MASTODON
mammy .... MOTHER
man. See also **person/fellow** .... GUY, RUN, MALE, BIPED, BRACE, STAFF, FELLER, GEEZER, HOMBRE, PERSON, FORTIFY, HUSBAND, OPERATE, PRIMATE, SERVANT, HOMO SAPIENS
ancestor of modern .... CRO-MAGNON(MAN)
and wife up to no good .... PARTNERS IN CRIME
"April Love" ...... PAT BOONE
at home .... BATTER
B.C. .... ADAM
"blushing crows" .... SPOONER
chimney .... SWEEP
country, old .... GAFFER, GAMMER
dashing, gay .... SPARK
dissolute .... ROUE
eater .... LAMIA, SHARK, CANNIBAL
elderly .... FOGY, CRONE, DOTARD
farm-implement .... DEERE
Friday .... SERVANT, FOLLOWER
from Columbus .... OHIOAN
from Punjab .... JAT
from Susa .... ELAMITE
from "U.N.C.L.E." ..... SOLO

Genesis .... ONAN
gentleman's .... VALET
gridiron .... END, CENTER, (NOSE) TACKLE, RECEIVER, LINEBACKER QUARTERBACK
handsome .... ADONIS, APOLLO
handy .... FACTOTUM
Hang Ten .... SURFER
hideous .... OGRE
in a cast .... ACTOR
in the street .... COMMONER
in the van .... NEO
itinerant .... HOBO
kind of .... YES, STRAW
lanky .... BEANPOLE
lecherous .... SATYR
like .... ANDROID
little .... MANIKIN
-made ornament ..... ARTIFACT
mean .... CAITIFF
nautical .... TAR, SALT, SAILOR, MARINE(R)
of action .... DOER, GO-GETTER
brass .... TALOS
circa 1100, learned .... OMAR THE TENTMAKER
figures .... CPA, AUDITOR
Galilee .... JESUS
God .... RABBI, SAINT, BISHOP, HERMIT, PRIEST
learning .... PUNDIT, SAVANT
letters .... POET, SAVANT, SCHOLAR, LITTERATEUR
Nod .... CAIN
Shelah .... METHUSELAH
song Carmichael ..... HOAGY
the hour .... HERO, CHAMPION
the world .... SLICKER, GLOBETROTTER
old .... GAFFER, GEEZER, SENIOR, GRAYBEARD
on a beat .... COP, REPORTER
on the lam .... FLEER
patient .... JOB
piano .... TUNER
Prize .... NOBEL
recently married .... BENEDICT
rubber .... GOODYEAR
single .... BACHELOR
strong .... ATLAS, SAMSON
tax .... ASSESSOR
"the" .... STAN
thin .... SLAT(S), BEANPOLE
ticker-tape .... STOCKBROKER
to a .... ALL, EVERYONE
unmarried .... SINGLE, BACHELOR, CELIBATE, SPOUSELESS
vat .... DYER

"What's it all about"
.... ALFIE
wise .... SOLON, NESTOR
with "a little list" .... KOKO
without a country ..... NOLAN,
STATELESS
who annoys women
.... MASHER
who spilled the salt ..... JUDAS
young, gay .... SPARK
Man of a Thousand Faces
.... CHANEY
O'War, e.g. .... STEED
manacle .... FETTER, HAMPER,
SHACKLE, HANDCUFF
manage ...... RUN, GET BY, WIELD,
DIRECT, HANDLE, OPERATE,
CONTRIVE, ADMINISTER
frugally ...... NURSE, HUSBAND,
CONSERVE
to get by .... EKE
to live .... SCRAPE, SURVIVE
manageable .... RULY, TAME,
DOCILE, WIELDY, TRACTABLE
manager .... GERENT, SYNDIC,
HANDLER, STEWARD,
DIRECTOR, OPERATOR
opera .... IMPRESARIO
Managua is capital of
.... NICARAGUA
manakin .... BIRD, DWARF,
MODEL
mañana .... LATER, TOMORROW
Manassas Mauler
.... (JACK)DEMPSEY
Manasseh's brother ...... EPHRAIM
father .... JOSEPH
grandfather .... JACOB
grandson .... GILEAD
mother .... ASENATH
son .... ASRIEL, MACHIR
manatee .... DUGONG, COWFISH,
SEA COW, HALICORE,
SIRENIAN
manchet .... BREAD
Manchu .... TUNGUS, MONGOLIAN
dynasty .... TA CH'ING
dynasty, revolt against
.... TAIPING
Manchukuo .... MANCHURIA
emperor of .... PU-YI
Manchuria capital .... MUKDEN
city/town .... JEHOL, DAIREN,
TALIEN, CHENGTEN
port of .... ANTUNG, HARBIN
river .... SUNGARI
seaport of .... DAIREN
manciple .... SLAVE, STEWARD
mandamus .... WRIT, ORDER
mandarin .... COAT, DUCK,
ORANGE, BRAHMIN,

TANGERINE
Mandarin, residence of
.... YAMEN
tea .... CHA
mandate .... ORDER, BEHEST,
COMMAND, COMMISSION
mandatory .... BINDING,
COMPULSORY, OBLIGATORY
mandible .... JAW, BEAK
Mandingo .... NEGRO
mandolin strumming piece
.... PLECTRUM
mandrake .... MAY APPLE,
MANDRAGORA
mandrel .... LATHE, SPINDLE
mandrill .... APE, BABOON
manducate .... CHEW, MASTICATE
mane .... JUBA, CREST
maned .... JUBATE, LEONINE
king .... LION
manege .... HORSEMANSHIP
manes .... SOUL
Manet, famed impressionist
artist .... EDOUARD
portraitist of .... DEGAS
maneuver .... PLOY, TRICK,
JOCKEY, ARTIFICE,
STRATAGEM
manganese spar ...... RHODONITE
mange .... SCAB(IES)
cause of .... MITE
loss caused by .... HAIR
mangel .... BEET
manger .... BIN, CRIB, RACK,
STALL, CRATCH, TROUGH
mangle .... MAR, IRON, GARBLE,
HACKLE, HAGGLE, CALENDER,
LACERATE, MUTILATE,
DISFIGURE
mangler ...... IRONER, MUTILATOR
mango .... FRUIT, MUSKMELON
wild .... DIKA
mangonel kin .... CATAPULT
mangy ...... MEAN, ITCHY, SCALY,
SCABBY, SCURFY, SCURVY,
SORDID, SQUALID, SCABROUS
manhandle .... MAUL, TITLE
Manhattan, former name
.... MANAHATIN
hotel .... PLAZA, HILTON,
CHELSEA, WALDORF,
WARWICK, AMERICANA,
DELMONICO'S
in Algonquian .... HILL
ISLAND
purchaser .... (PETER)MINUIT
seller .... SEYSEYS
manhunters' group .... POSSE
mania .... RAGE, CRAZE,
DELIRIUM, DISORDER,
OBSESSION

for dancing .... TARANTISM
with mild symptoms
.... HYPOMANIA
maniac .... MADMAN, LUNATIC
maniacal .... MAD, RAVING,
FRENZIED
manifest .... LIST, OPEN, SHOW,
CLEAR, OVERT, PLAIN, PROVE,
ATTEST, EVINCE, PATENT,
REVEAL, EVIDENT, OBVIOUS,
SIGNIFY, TESTIFY WAYBILL,
APPARENT
disdain .... SNEER
manifesto .... CREDO, EDICT,
STATEMENT, DECLARATION
manifold .... COPIED, VARIED,
DIVERSE, MULTIPLE
manihot .... MANIOC, CASSAVA
manikin .... DUMMY, DWARF,
MODEL
Manila .... BAY, CITY, HEMP,
ROPE, CIGAR, PAPER
Acapulco trading ship
.... GALLEON
Bay hero .... DEWEY
Bay island .... CORREGIDOR
is capital of .... PHILIPPINES
to the Filipinos .... MAYNILA
walled city in .... INTRAMUROS
manioc ...... JUCA, YUCA, STARCH,
CASSAVA, MANIHOT
maniple .... FANO(N), ORALE
maniples, three .... COHORT
manipulate ...... RIG, USE, WIELD,
HANDLE, JUGGLE, TAMPER,
CONTROL, EXPLOIT,
MANEUVER
manipulator ...... USER, SCHEMER
Manipur capital .... IMPHAL
Manitoba capital ...... WINNEPEG
mankind .... HUMANITY
manly .... VIRILE, MASCULINE
Mann .... HORACE, THOMAS
daughter of .... ERIKA
manna .... BOON, FOOD, LERP,
GODSEND, BLESSING,
SUSTENANCE
mannequin ...... DUMMY, MODEL,
STATUE, FIGURINE
manner .... AIR, WAY, MIEN,
MODE, SORT, HABIT, METHOD,
BEARING, FASHION, BEHAVIOR
of dress .... GUISE
of running .... JOG, LOPE,
TROT, CANTER
of speaking .... DICTION
of walking ..... GAIT, WADDLE,
SWAGGER
mannerism .... POSE, QUIRK,
STYLE
mannerly .... CIVIL, POLITE,

COURTEOUS
manners .... MORES, CONDUCT, ETIQUETTE
expert .... EMILY POST
study of .... ETHOLOGY
mannish .... ANDRIC, VIRILE, MASCULINE
manor .... ESTATE, DEMESNE, MANSION
manorial court .... LEET
manpower .... WORKING FORCE
manque .... FAILED, USELESS, DEFECTIVE
manrope .... HANDRAIL
man's castle .... HOME
mansard .... ROOF, ATTIC, GARRET
manse .... PARSONAGE
manservant ...... VALET, LACKEY, YEOMAN, FLUNK(E)Y, FOOTBOY
mansion .... DOME, HOUSE, MANOR, VILLA, CASTLE
spirit .... ATUA
manslaughter .... HOMICIDE
premeditated .... MURDER
mansuetude .... TAMENESS, GENTLENESS
manta .... RAY, CAPE, SHAWL, BLANKET, DEVILFISH
manteau .... CLOAK, MANTLE
mantel ...... LEDGE, SHELF, LINTEL
band .... FRIEZE
mantelet .... CAPE, CLOAK, SCREEN, SHELTER
mantilla ...... CAPE, VEIL, CLOAK, SCARF
user .... SEÑORA, SEÑORITA
mantis, ____ .... PRAYING
crab/shrimp .... SQUILLA
mantle .... CAPE, COPE, CLOAK, COVER, FROCK
armor .... TABARD
Mantuan, the .... VIRGIL
manual .... HAND(BOOK), TEXTBOOK, GUIDEBOOK
art .... CRAFT
training .... SLOID, SLOYD
workers, all .... LABOR
manufacture ...... MAKE, INVENT, CONCOCT, PRODUCE, FABRICATE
manufacturing left-overs
.... SHORTS
manumit .... FREE, LIBERATE, EMANCIPATE
manure .... DUNG, MUCK, GUANO, ORDURE, FERTILIZER
manuscript .... MS., SCREED, SCRIPT, SCROLL, (HAND)WRITTEN

copier .... SCRIBE
leaf of .... FOLIO
to be set in type .... COPY
volume .... CODEX
manx .... CAT, CELT, GAEL
many ...... LOTS, LOADS, MYRIAD, SCORES, UMPTEEN, MANIFOLD, NUMEROUS, COUNTLESS
a time .... OFT(EN)
centuries .... EON
combining form .... POLY, MYRIA
headed serpent .... HYDRA
sided .... VERSATILE
manyplies .... OMASUM
Mao Tse ____ .... TUNG
daughter of .... LI-NA, MAU-MAU
wife .... CHIANG CHING
Maori canoe .... WAKA
clan .... HAPU
club .... MARREE
food .... KAI
human flesh .... LONG PIG
parrot .... TUI
raft .... MOKI
tattoo .... MOKO
throwing stick
.... BOOMERANG
village .... KAIK(A)
wages .... UTU
weapon .... PATU
wood .... RATA
map .... PLAN, PLAT, CARTE, CHART, GRAPH, ORRERY
book .... ATLAS
city .... PLAT
extra in a/feature .... INSET
giant .... ASIA
line(s) .... ISOBAR, HACHURE, ISOTHERE
maker .... MERCATOR
maker's abbreviation .... RD, ISL, RTE
maker's machine
.... OROGRAPH
marker .... PUSHPIN
mini .... INSET
of lines .... CARTOGRAM
slang .... FACE
maple .... ACER, TREE, WOOD, SIRUP, SUGAR, BOX ELDER
leaf land .... CANADA
seed .... SAMARA
tree .... SYCAMORE
Maputo, once .... LOURENCO MARQUES
maquis .... GUER(R)ILLA
mar .... SCAR, SPOIL, DAMAGE, DEFACE, IMPAIR, INJURE, BLEMISH, DISFIGURE

marabou .... STORK, ARGALA
marabout .... TOMB, HERMIT, HOLY MAN
maraca .... RATTLE
marasca .... CHERRY
product .... CORDIAL
marasmus .... WASTING, MALNUTRITION
Marat (Jean), killer of
.... CORDAY
marathon .... NONSTOP, (FOOT)RACE
talker .... CHATTERBOX
Marathon, victor at
.... MILTIADES
maraud .... RAID, FORAY, PILLAGE, PLUNDER
marauder .... PIRATE, RAIDER
marble .... MIB, TAW, AGATE, AGGIE, ALLEY, RANCE, MIG(GLE), CALCITE, CARRARA, CIPOLIN, SHOOTER, DOLOMITE, LIMESTONE
bone disease
.... OSTEOPOROSIS
colorful .... AGATE
designating a white
.... PARIAN
flooring .... TERRAZO
game ..... TAW, MIGS, MIGGLES
glass .... TESSERA
imitation .... SCAGLIOLA
like/of .... MARMOREAL
players' line .... TAW
screen .... JALEE
stone like .... SODALITE
worker's tool .... BURIN
marc .... BRANDY, REFUSE
marceau .... MIME
marcel .... HAIRDRESSER
march .... FILE, HIKE, WALK, BORDER, ADVANCE, FRONTIER, PROGRESS, BORDERLAND
day's .... ETAPE
in a group .... TROOP
organized .... PARADE
style .... TRAMP, GOOSE-STEP
March date .... IDES
of Dimes advocate
.... (FRANKLIN DELANO) ROOSEVELT
of Dimes fund-raising cause
.... POLIO
marches, king of .... SOUSA
marchioness .... LADY, MARQUISE
Marciano, ____ .... ROCKY
Marco, traveler .... POLO
Polo's father .... NICCOLO
Polo's nationality
.... VENETIAN
Polo's uncle .... MAFFEO

Marconi .... GUGLIELMO
marconigram .... RADIOGRAM
Mardi Gras .... GALA, CARNIVAL,
　　　　　　　　　　FESTIVAL
　day .... TUESDAY
　follower .... LENT
　king .... REX
　scene of .... PARIS, NEW
　　　　　　　　　　ORLEANS
mare .... SEA, JADE, HORSE
　milk of .... KUMISS
　nostrum .... OUR SEA,
　　　　　　　　　MEDITERRANEAN
　tail of .... CLOUD
　young .... FILLY
Margaret, diminutive of
　.... MEG, PEG, MADGE, GRETA,
　　　　MARGE, PEGGY, MAGGIE
margarin(e) .... OLEO
margarite .... PEARL
margay .... CAT, OCELOT
marge .... EDGE, BORDER
Marge Schott's boys .... REDS
margin .... LIP, EDGE, RAND,
　BRINK, LIMIT, MARGE, VERGE,
　　　　　BORDER, LEEWAY
　narrow .... NECK
marginal note .... APOSTIL(LE)
　notes of Old Testament
　............................... MASORA(H)
marguerite .... DAISY
Maria .... LING
　queen of Spain .... CRISTINA
　soprano .... CALLAS
Marian, contralto .... ANDERSON
Marianas Island .... GUAM,
　ROTA, PAGAN, SAIPAN,
　TINIAN, AGRIHAN, LADRONES
Marie Antoinette .... REINE
　Antoinette's husband
　.............................. LOUIS XVI
　Antoinette's palace
　................................... TRIANON
　de _____, Queen Eleanor's
　　　daughter ..... CHAMPAGNE
　Dressler role .... TILLIE
　Wilson role .... IRMA
marigold .... ASTER, CAPER,
　　　　COWSLIP, KINGCUP
marijuana ...... POT, HEMP, WEED,
　GANJA(H), GRASS, HASHISH,
　　　　　　　　NARCOTIC
　cigarette .... REEFER
　cigarette butt .... ROACH
　cigarette holder .... ROACH
　　　　　　　　　　CLIP
　form of .... HASH
　smoker .... POTHEAD
marimba-like instrument
　............................ XYLOPHONE
marina .... DOCK, BASIN, HARBOR

marinade .... SALT, WINE, BRINE,
　　　PICKLE, VINEGAR
marinate .... CORN, PICKLE
marine .... FLEET, NAVAL,
　GYRENE, OCEANIC, MARITIME,
　NAUTICAL, LEATHERNECK
　gastropod .... WHELK
　glow .... SEAFIRE
　plant .... SEAWEED
　plant cast ashore .... WRACK
　plant group .... BENTHOS
　worm .... NEMERTEAN
mariner .... GOB, SAILOR,
　SEAMAN, JACK-TAR
　colloquial .... TAR, SALT
　fictional .... AHAB
　victim of .... ALBATROSS
Marion, actress .... DAVIES
marionette ...... DOLL(Y), PUPPET
mariposa flower ...... LILY, TULIP
marital .... WEDDED, NUPTIAL,
　　　　　　　　　SPOUSAL
　bliss .... HONEYMOON
　separation .... DIVORCE
marjoram .... HERB, MINT,
　ORIGAN, OREGANO
mark .... SCAR, SIGN, BRAND,
　GRADE, STAIN, TOKEN,
　DENOTE, MACRON, VESTIGE,
　　　　　　IMPRESSION
　aimed at .... TARGET,
　　　　　　　　COCKSHY
　authentication .... SEAL,
　　　　　　　　CACHET
　bad conduct .... DEMERIT
　black .... STIGMA
　cattle .... BRAND
　critical .... OBELUS
　diacritical .... BREVE, CARET,
　TILDE, ABLAUT, ACCENT,
　UMLAUT, CEDILLA
　dirty ...... BLOT, SMUT, SMEAR,
　　　SMUDGE, SMUTCH
　down .... NOTE, RECORD
　footnote .... STAR, DAGGER,
　OBELISK, ASTERISK
　for a Spanish n .... TILDE
　for identification .... MOLE,
　BRAND, LABEL, DAGGER,
　　　　　　　　DOGTAG
　give-away .... TREAD
　kind of .... DOT, DENT, LINE,
　SPOT, COMMA, STAIN, BRUISE,
　PERIOD, BLEMISH, SCRATCH
　missile's .... TARGET
　of bondage ...... YOKE, BRAND
　of disgrace .... BRAND,
　　　　　　　　STIGMA
　of omission ...... DELE, CARET,
　　　　　　　　ELLIPSIS
　one hundredth of .... PFENIG

　over consonant .... HACEK
　over syllable .... BREVE
　over vowel .... BREVE, TILDE,
　MACRON, UMLAUT
　passing .... CEE
　possessive .... APOSTROPHE
　postal .... STAMP, CACHET
　proofreader's ...... DELE, STET,
　　　　　　　　CARET
　question .... QUERY
　reference ...... OBELI, DAGGER,
　DIESIS, OBELUS, ASTERISK
　road .... MEDIAN
　skin .... MOLE, NEVUS, TATTOO
　up .... HIKE, RAISE
　what come to the .... TOES
　with spots .... DOT, DAPPLE,
　MOTTLE, SPECKLE
Mark Antony's lover
　............................. CLEOPATRA
　Antony's wife .... OCTAVIA
　VI .... TANK, TIGER
　Twain .... CLEMENS
　Twain's embarrassing
　　　affliction .... SADDLE
　　　　　　　　　SORES
　Twain's patent .... SCRAPBOOK
markdown .... DISCOUNT
marked .... OBVIOUS, DISTINCT
　by inactivity .... DULL
　by morbid displacement of
　　　parts: med. .... ECTOPIC
marker .... IOU, PEG, TAG, LABEL,
　STELE, SCORER, MONUMENT
　air-race .... PYLON
　boundary .... STAKER
　channel .... BUOY
　grave .... BARROW
　slang .... IOU, PLEDGE
　stone .... CAIRN, STELA
market .... MART, SELL, SHOP,
　VEND, STORE, BAZA(A)R,
　OUTLET, ADVERTISE
　bid .... QUOTATION
　index .... DOW
　place .... SOUK, AGORA,
　FORUM, PLAZA, RIALTO,
　　　　　　　　EMPORIUM
　stock .... CURB, EXCHANGE
marksman .... SHOT, SHOOTIST,
　　　　　　　SHARPSHOOTER
　hangout ...... RANGE, GALLERY
　hidden .... SNIPER
　hired .... ASSASSIN
　target of .... BULL'S-EYE
marl .... MALM, EARTH, STRATUM
marlin .... GAMEFISH
　colorful variety .... BLUE
　kin ...... SAILFISH, SPEARFISH
marlinspike .... FID
marmalade .... JAM, PRESERVE,

CONFECTION
material .... PEEL, RIND
tree .... CHICO, MAMEY,
MAMMEE, SAPOTA, SAPODILLA
Marmion hero .... LOCHINVAR
marmoreal .... MARBLELIKE
marmoset .... MICO, MONKEY,
TAMARIN
marmot .... RODENT, WHISTLER,
PRAIRIE DOG
Marner, _____ .... SILAS
Maroc .... MOROCCO
maroon .... LOAF, SLAVE, ENISLE,
STRAND, ISOLATE, CHESTNUT
Marpessa's abductor .... IDAS
Marquand's sleuth
.... (MR.)MOTO
marque .... REPRISAL
marquee .... TENT, AWNING,
CANOPY, LIGHTS, POSTER,
SHELTER
marquetry .... MOSAIC
material .... TILE, WOOD,
IVORY, PARQUET
Marquette, explorer .... PERE,
JACQUES
marquis .... BARON
Marquis, humorist .... DON
marquise .... RING, GEM CUT,
MARQUEE
marred .... UGLY
marriage .... UNION, WEDDING,
WEDLOCK, ALLIANCE,
NUPTIALS, MATRIMONY
bond .... KNOT
broker .... SCHATCHEN,
MATCHMAKER
contract .... HANDFAST
dowry .... DOT
gift .... DOWRY
god of .... HYMEN
goddess of .... HERA, FRIGG
hater of .... MISOGAMIST
kind of .... BIGAMY,
MONOGAMY, MORGANATIC,
CONVENIENCE
notice .... BAN(N)S
outside the tribe .... EXOGAMY
pertaining to .... MARITAL
second .... DIGAMY
settlement .... DOS, DOWRY
unsuitable .... MISALLIANCE
vow .... TROTH
with one of lesser status
.... MESALLIANCE
within the tribe
.... ENDOGAMY
without ceremonial rites
.... COMMON-LAW
marriageable .... NUBILE
married .... MATED, CONJUGAL

couple .... MAN AND WIFE
e.g. .... IN DOUBLE HARNESS
marron .... CHESTNUT
marrow .... PITH, ESSENCE,
MEDULLA
bone .... TISSUE
fat .... PEA
kind of bone .... RED, YELLOW
marry .... WED, WIVE, ADOPT,
HITCH, UNITE, ESPOUSE, TIE
THE KNOT
again .... REMATE
on the run .... ELOPE
Mars .... WAR, ARES, PLANET
combining form .... AREO
in alchemy .... IRON
moon of ...... DEIMOS, PHOBOS
of .... MARTIAN
sister of .... BELLONA
son of .... REMUS
Marseillaise composer
.... (DE)LISLE
marsh .... BOG, FEN, MOOR, OOZE,
QUAG, SLUE, VLEI, LERNA,
SWAMP, MORASS, MUSKEG,
SALINA, SLOUGH, WETLAND
danger spot .... QUAGMIRE
elder .... IVA, RAGWEED,
GUELDER-ROSE
fever .... AGUE, HELODES
gas .... METHANE
grass .... REED, SEDGE
hen .... COOT, RAIL
hollow .... SWALE
marigold ...... CAPER, COWSLIP
plant .... TULE, FESCUE,
BULRUSH, CATTAIL
salt .... SALINA
shrub, fragrant .... GALE
marshal .... ARRAY, GUIDE,
ARRANGE, OFFICER, SHERIFF,
ASSEMBLE
badge of .... STAR
famous ...... NEY, FOCH, GORT,
PETAIN, ROMMEL,
MONTGOMERY
Marshall Islands group/chain
.... RALIK, RATAK
island .... ARNO, KILI, MILI,
AILUK, BIKAR, WOTJE, BIKINI,
JALUIT, MAJURO, NAMORIK,
ENIWETOK, MALOELAP,
RONGELAP, KWAJALEIN
marshmallow .... CANDY,
CONFECTION
marshy .... BOGGY, FENNY,
PALUDAL, PALUDIC, PALUDINE
fertile land .... MAREMMA
hollow area .... SWALE
inlet/outlet .... BAYOU
tract .... FEN

marsupial .... TAIT, KOALA,
WOMBAT, DASYURE,
(O)POSSUM, KANGAROO,
BANDICOOT, PHALANGER
mart .... SHOP, STORE, BAZAAR,
MARKET, EMPORIUM
Marta, actress .... TOREN
Martell .... COGNAC
marten .... SABLE, MAMMAL
describing a .... MUSTELINE
fur .... BAUM
like animal .... MINK, WEASEL,
POLECAT
Martha Finley's heroine
.... ELSIE
J. Burke .... CALAMITY JANE
martial .... WARLIKE, MILITARY
martin .... BIRD, MARTLET,
SWALLOW
Martin Chuzzlewit character
.... GAMP, SAIREY
Luther King .... MLK
biography author
.... (DAVID)GARROW
biography title ...... BEARING
THE CROSS
memorable words from I
HAVE A DREAM
1964 award received by
.... NOBEL PEACE PRIZE
philosophy preached by
.... NON-VIOLENCE
martinet .... RAMROD, TYRANT,
DISCIPLINARIAN
martini .... COCKTAIL
extra/fruit .... OLIVE
ingredient ..... GIN, VERMOUTH
with a pickled onion
.... GIBSON
Martinique capital ...... FORT-DE-
FRANCE
landmark .... PELEE
music .... BEGUINE
river .... LEZARDE, LORRAINE
volcano .... (MONT) PELEE
Martinmas to X'mas
.... ADVENT
martlet .... MARTIN
marvel .... WONDER, MIRACLE,
PRODIGY
of-Peru .... FOUR-O'CLOCK
marvelous .... SPLENDID,
WONDROUS, MIRACULOUS
Marwar .... JODHPUR
Marx .... KARL, CHICO, HARPO,
ZEPPO, GROUCHO
Brothers' film .... HORSE
FEATHERS
co-worker of .... ENGELS
Marxian, a .... LENINIST
Marxism .... COMMUNISM,

SOCIALISM

Mary .... URE, ASTOR, TYLER

MOORE

Catholic queen of _____

.... SCOTS

form of: French .... MARIE

Greek .... MARIAM,

MARIAMNE

Hebrew .... MIRIAM

Italian/Spanish .... MARIA

healed of evil spirits by

Jesus .... MAGDALENE

Magdalene's home

.... MAGDALA

mother of Jesus .... MADONNA

picture of .... MADONNA

Maryland bay .... FISHING,

CHESAPEAKE

capital .... ANNAPOLIS

city/town .... ESSEX, EASTON,

ELKTON, TOWSON, DUNDALK,

ODENTON, ABERDEEN,

BETHESDA, ROSEDALE,

BALTIMORE, CAMBRIDGE,

ROCKVILLE, SALISBURY, SOUTH

GATE, CUMBERLAND, GLEN

BURNIE, HAGERSTOWN

college .... HOOD, LOYOLA,

GOUCHER, BOWIE STATE

county .... CECIL, HOWARD,

CARROLL, CHARLES, HARFORD,

ALLEGANY, WICOMICO,

BALTIMORE, FREDERICK,

MONTGOMERY, WASHINGTON

founder .... CALVERT

island .... KENT, SMITH,

POOLES, POPLAR

lake .... LIBERTY

mountain .... BACKBONE

river ..... ELK, HONGA, SEVERN,

POTOMAC, GUNPOWDER

state bird .... BALTIMORE

ORIOLE

state flower .... BLACK-EYED

SUSAN

state nickname ...... FREE, OLD

LINE

swamp .... POCOSON

symbol .... ORIOLE

tree .... OAK

U.S. Air Force Base

.... ANDREWS

U.S. Naval Academy

.... ANNAPOLIS

university .... MORGAN,

TOWSON, JOHNS HOPKINS

Mascagni, composer ...... PIETRO

opera .... IRIS

mascara .... COSMETIC

mascle .... LOZENGE

mascot .... PET

masculine .... MALE, MAN(LY),

VIRILE, MANNISH

Masefield, poet .... JOHN

work .... ODTAA

mash .... PAP, CRUSH, BATTER

masjid .... MOSK, MOSQUE

mask .... HIDE, LOUP, COVER,

VISOR, HELMET, MASQUE,

SCREEN, VIZARD, CONCEAL,

DISGUISE, PRETENSE

as of disguise .... VISOR,

FALSE FACE

half .... LOUP, DOMINO

lacy .... VEIL

wearer .... MUMMER,

MASQUER, KLANSMAN

maskalonge .... FISH, PIKE

masked .... DISGUISED

as in drama .... PORTRAY,

PERSONATE

ball .... MASQUE, MASQUERADE

masochism .... SADISM

mason .... STONECUTTER

bench .... BANKER

chisel of ..... BROACH, TOOLER

companion of .... DIXON

hammer of .... GAVEL

mortar board/holder .... HAWK

need of .... STONE

masonry .... BRICKWORK,

STONEWORK

broken pieces .... RUBBLE

leveling piece/wedge ..... SHIM

masque ...... BALL, MASK, COMUS,

MASQUERADE

masquerade ...... BALL, MUM(M),

DANCE, PARADE, DISGUISE

costume ..... DOMINO, MOTLEY

mass .... WAD, CLOT, LUMP,

MUSH, BOLUS, GOB(BET),

SQUASH, LITURGY, ASSEMBLE,

MAJORITY

book .... MISSAL

for the dead .... REQUIEM

killing .... BATTUE, POGROM,

CARNAGE, MASSACRE

media .... TV, RADIO,

NEWSPAPER(S)

meeting .... RALLY

movement .... EXODUS,

STAMPEDE, MIGRATION

of bacteria .... CLUMP

of dusts, etc. .... FOG

part of religious .... KYRIE,

GLORIA, GOSPEL, HOMILY,

SANCTUS

production .... VOLUME

Massachusetts bay ...... BOSTON,

QUINCY, BUZZARDS,

PLYMOUTH

cape .... ANN, COD, POGE

capital .... BOSTON

city/town .... AVON, AYER,

GILL, HULL, LYNN, ACTON,

ADAMS, ATHOL, DOVER,

SALEM, CANTON, DEDHAM,

GROTON, LOWELL, MALDEN,

NEWTON, REVERE, WOBURN,

AMHERST, ANDOVER,

BELMONT, CHELSEA, EVERETT,

HOLYOKE, MEDFORD,

MELROSE, METHUEN,

NORWOOD, TAUNTON,

WALTHAM, BROCKTON,

CHICOPEE, LAWRENCE,

PLYMOUTH, ARLINGTON,

BRAINTREE, CAMBRIDGE,

WORCESTER, FRAMINGHAM,

SPRINGFIELD

college .... REGIS, SMITH,

GORDON, LESLEY, BENTLEY,

EMERSON, HELLENIC, HOLY

CROSS, RADCLIFFE

college of music in Boston

.... BERKLEE

county .... DUKES, ESSEX,

BRISTOL, HAMPDEN, NORFOLK,

SUFFOLK, FRANKLIN,

PLYMOUTH, BERKSHIRE,

HAMPSHIRE, MIDDLESEX,

NANTUCKET, WORCESTER,

BARNSTABLE

famous hall .... FANEUIL

gulf .... MAINE

island .... LONG, PASQUE,

CUTTYHUNK, NANTUCKET,

CHAPPAQUIDDICK, MARTHA'S

VINEYARD

lake .... BUEL, ONOTA, MYSTIC,

SILVER, ASHMERE, WEBSTER

mountain .... TOM, TOBY,

GRACE, GREYLOCK

river ...... MILL, NORTH, SWIFT,

AGAWAM, HOOSIC, MANHAN,

MYSTIC, NASHUA, WHITMAN,

CHICOPEE, DEERFIELD,

QUINEBAUG

state bird .... CHICKADEE

state flower .... TRAILING

ARBUTUS

state nickname .... BAY, OLD

COLONY

state tree .... ELM

tourist attraction .... FRANKLIN

PARK ZOO, PAUL REVERE

HOUSE, DINOSAUR FOOTPRINTS,

NEW ENGLAND AQUARIUM

university .... TUFTS,

HARVARD, SUFFOLK

massacre ...... POGROM, CARNAGE,

SLAUGHTER

massage ...... KNEAD, RUB(DOWN),

SHAMPOO
massager .... MASSEUR, MASSEUSE
Massenet, composer .... JULES
opera by .... MANON, THAIS
masses, the .... PLEBS, PEOPLE,
HOI POLLOI, MULTITUDE
masseur ...... RUBBER, MASSAGER
Massey, performer .... ILONA,
RAYMOND
Massine, dancer .... LEONIDE
massive .... HUGE, BULKY, HEAVY,
SOLID, MASSY, MAMMOTH,
IMPOSING, PONDEROUS
mast .... POLE, SPAR, ACORNS,
BEECHNUTS, (CHEST)NUTS
iron band of .... TRUSS
platform .... LOOKOUT,
MAINTOP, CROW'S NEST
support .... BIBB
master .... BOY, DAN, DOM, MAIN,
CHIEF, SAHIB, SUBDUE,
CONTROL, EFFENDI
builder .... ARCHITECT
cruel .... LEGREE
in any art/music ..... MAESTRO
of a battle .... CONQUEROR
of a situation .... VICTOR,
WINNER
of ceremonies ..... MC, EMCEE,
COMPERE
of household .... GOODMAN
of suspense .... HITCHCOCK
of syllogism .... SOCRATES
pertaining to a .... HERILE
race ideology .... HERRENVOLK
stroke .... COUP
workman .... ARTIST,
FOREMAN, OVERSEER,
CRAFTSMAN
masterfully ...... ABLY, EXPERTLY,
SKILLFULLY
mastermind .... PLAN(NER),
DIRECTOR
masterpiece .... MAGNUM OPUS,
CHEF-D-OEUVRE
Bernini's .... ST. PETER'S
CHURCH
Leonardo da Vinci's
.... MONA LISA, THE LAST
SUPPER
marble .... TAJ MAHAL
mastery .... GRIP, SWAY, SKILL,
CONTROL, UPPER HAND
masthead .... LOOKOUT
mastic .... RESIN, CEMENT, LIQUOR
tree .... ACOMA
masticate .... CHEW, GRIND,
CRUNCH, MANDUCATE
mastication product .... CUD
mastiff .... ALAN, BULLDOG,
(WATCH)DOG

mat ...... PAD, DULL, SHAG, DOILY,
SNARL, CARPET, MATRIX,
CUSHION
leaf .... YAPA
making material .... BAST,
REED, RUSH, VETIVER
sleeping .... PETATE
Mata Hari .... SPY
Matabele .... ZULU
matador ...... TORERO, TOREADOR,
BULLFIGHTER
dart of .... BANDERILLA
garment of .... CAPE
opponent of .... BULL, TORO
passes .... FAENA
queue of .... COLETA
red cloth of .... MULETA
sweet sounds to a .... OLES
sword of .... ESTOQUE
match .... FIT, PIT, LUNT, MATE,
PAIR, SUIT, EQUAL, TALLY,
CONTEST, MARRIAGE,
PARALLEL, VESUVIAN
boxing .... BOUT, SETTO
cockfighting .... MAIN
friction .... FUSEE, FUZEE,
LUCIFER, LOCOFOCO
in dice .... MAIN
stick .... LINSTOCK
tycoon .... KREUGER
wax/wooden .... VESTA
matching pair .... SET
piece .... MATE
matchless .... SOLE, PEERLESS,
UNEQUALED, INIMITABLE
matchmaker .... SHADCHEN,
SCHATCHEN
craft of: biblical .... ARK
indefatigable ...... EROS, CUPID
matchwood .... SPLINTERS
mate .... TEA, WIFE, HOLLY,
MARRY, MATCH, COUPLE,
FELLOW, SPOUSE, CONSORT,
(SLEEPING)PARTNER
ship's .... BOATSWAIN
mated .... YOKED, WEDDED,
COUPLED
mateless .... AZYGOUS
mater .... MOTHER
dolorosa .... VIRGIN MARY
material .... DATA, METAL, VITAL,
GOODS, MATTER, CONTENT,
SENSUAL, WORSTED,
PHYSICAL, ESSENTIAL,
PERTINENT, SUBSTANCE
bat .... ASH
carton .... CARDBOARD
court .... EVIDENCE
curtain .... VOILE, BAMBOO
for hut building .... GRASS
inner surface ...... PAD, LINING

inorganic .... METAL
tablecloth .... DAMASK
materialize .... SHOW, OCCUR,
APPEAR, REALIZE
materiel .... MUNITIONS
maternal .... MOTHERLY
relationship .... ENATION
maternally related .... ENATE
maternity .... MOTHERHOOD
hospital .... LYING-IN
matgrass .... NARD, MARRAM
mathematical .... EXACT,
PRECISE, ACCURATE
arbitrary number .... RADIX
arc .... RADIAN
figure .... CONE, DIAGRAM
function .... (CO)SINE,
LOGARITHM
instrument .... VERNIER,
COMPUTER, CALCULATOR
line .... VECTOR
proposition .... THEOREM
ration .... SINE
symbol ..... DOT, DIGIT, POINT,
FACIEND, OPERAND
term .... COSH, ROOT, SURD,
(CO)SINE, FACIENT, CONSTANT
mathematician .... GAUSS,
EUCLID, NEWTON, PASCAL,
PTOLEMY, GEODETE,
DESCARTES, ARCHIMEDES
mathematics .... COMPUTATION
certain theorem in
.... BINOMIAL
subject .... ALGEBRA,
CALCULUS, GEOMETRY,
ARITHMETIC
there are two in .... EMS
**Matilda of ____, Henry I's
daughter** .... ANJOU
Matilda, Queen of ____
.... ENGLAND
husband of .... WILLIAM(THE
CONQUEROR)
work of .... BAYEUX TAPESTRY
matin .... AUBADE
canticle .... VENITE
of .... MORNING, DAYBREAK
matinee .... LEVEE, SOIREE,
RECEPTION, PERFORMANCE
idol of old ..... BOYER, GABLE,
BARRYMORE, VALENTINO
Matlock's forte .... DEFENSE
matrass .... FLASK, BOLTHEAD
matriarch .... MATRON, DOWAGER
of "Dallas" .... ELLIE
matriculate .... ENTER, ENROL(L),
REGISTER
matriculation fee .... TUITION
matrimonial .... MARITAL,
NUPTIAL, CONJUGAL

matrimony .... MARRIAGE

matrix .... DIE, MAT, CAST, WOMB, MODEL, MO(U)LD, GANG(UE), PATTERN

matron .... DAME, WIFE, WIDOW

matronly ...... SEDATE, DIGNIFIED

matted .... CESPITOSE

matter .... STUFF, CONTENT, ELEMENT, SUBSTANCE

arcane .... SECRET

business .... AFFAIR, INTEREST, COMMERCE

classification of .... ANIMAL, MINERAL, ORGANIC, VEGETABLE

in law .... RES

of course .... ROUTINE

of fact .... CASUAL, LITERAL, PROSAIC, PRACTICAL

of law .... CASE

of opinion .... MOOT, DEBATABLE

printed .... CALENDAR, CIRCULAR, NEWSPAPER

written .... DRAFT, LETTER, MANUSCRIPT

Matterhorn .... MOUNTAIN, MONT CERVIN

matters of faith .... CREDENDA

Matthew .... APOSTLE, EVANGELIST

alternate name of .... LEVI

hometown of ...... CAPERNAUM

job of .... TAX COLLECTOR

symbol of .... WINGED MAN

mattock .... HACK, PICK(AX), TWIBIL(L)

mattress .... FUTON, PALLET, PAILLASSE

case/cover .... TICK, BEDDING

stuffing material .... CEIBA, FLOCK, KAPOK

maturation .... AGING, MEIOSIS

mature .... AGE, ADULT, RIPEN, EVOLVE, FULL-GROWN, DEVELOP(ED)

note .... DUE, PAYABLE

Mau Mau land .... KENYA

maud .... RUG, WRAP, PLAID, SHAWL

wearer of .... SHEPHERD

maudlin .... MUSHY, SOBBY, TEARY, WEEPY, TEARFUL, SENTIMENTAL

sentiment .... MUSH

Maugham heroine .... SADIE (THOMPSON)

play .... RAIN

Maui volcano .... HALEAKALA

maul .... CLUB, MACE, BEETLE, BRUISE, HAMMER, MALLET, MANGLE, CLOBBER

mauler .... BOXER, WRESTLER

Maumee River city ...... TOLEDO

maumet ...... DOLL, IDOL, PUPPET

Mauna Loa crater .... KILAUEA

volcano .... KEA, LOA

maund .... BASKET, HAMPER

Mauriac, novelist ...... FRANCOIS

Maurois, novelist .... ANDRE, HERZOG

work on George Sand .... LELIA

work on Shelley .... ARIEL

Mauritania bay .... ARGUIN, LEVRIER

cape .... BLANC, MIRIK

capital .... NOUAKCHOTT

city/town .... ALEG, ATAR, BOGUE, KAEDI, KIFFA, ROSSO, ZOUIRAT

desert .... IGUIDI, SAHARA

ethnic group .... MOOR, NEGRO, BERBER

island .... TIDRA

language .... WOLOF, ARABIC

money .... KHOMS, OUGIYA

president .... DADDAH

river .... SENEGAL

Mauritius capital .... PORT LOUIS

islands .... MASCARENE

monetary unit .... RUPEE

Mauser .... RIFLE, PISTOL

mausoleum .... TOMB, GRAVE, VAULT, SHRINE, SEPULCHER

Buddhist .... TOPE, STUPA

Egyptian .... MASTABA, PYRAMID

India .... TAJ MAHAL

pertaining to/of .... MAUSOLEAN

mauve .... DYE, MALLOW, PURPLE, PIGMENT

maverick ...... CALF, WAIF, DOGIE, LONER, REBEL

Texas rancher .... SAM

mavis .... BIRD, THRUSH

maw .... CRAW, CROP, GULLET, THROAT, ABDOMEN, STOMACH

mawkish .... SOUPY, MAUDLIN, BATHETIC, NAUSEOUS, SPOON(E)Y, SICKENING, SENTIMENTAL

max., opposite of .... MIN

Max, the boxer .... BAER

maxilla .... JAW BONE, UPPER JAW

disorder .... SINUSITIS

segment of .... STIPES

maxim .... SAW, REDE, ADAGE, AXIOM, GNOME, MORAL, MOTTO, TENET, BYWORD, SAYING, TRUISM, SLOGAN, FORMULA, PRECEPT, PROVERB, APHORISM, PRINCIPLE

Maxim, inventor .... HUDSON, HIRAM STEVENS

invention of .... EXPLOSIVES, (MACHINE)GUN

maxims, collection of ...... SUTRA

religious leader's .... LOGIA

maximum .... MOST, UTMOST, HIGHEST, SUPREME

penalty .... EXECUTION, THE CHAIR

Maxwell .... ELSA, WEBER

Anderson play .... SATURDAY'S CHILDREN

may .... CAN, PRIME, HEYDAY, MAIDEN, SPRINGTIME

apple .... MANDRAKE

fly .... DUN, DRAKE

May Day .... BELTANE

Day celebration, subject of .... ARMED FORCES

Day folk dance .... MORRIS

fifteen .... IDES

first .... BELTANE

tree .... HAWTHORN

VIPs .... MOTHERS

Maya .... DEVI, SAKTI, INDIAN

consort of .... SIVA

Mayan .... INDIAN

city .... UXMAL

maybe .... MAYHAP, PERHAPS, POSSIBLY, PERCHANCE

Mayday .... SOS, SIGNAL, M'AIDEZ

Mayence .... MAINZ

mayflower .... ARBUTUS, ANEMONE, COWSLIP, HAWTHORN, MARIGOLD

Mayflower passengers .... PILGRIMS

mayhem .... MAIMING, CRIPPLING, MUTILATION

mayor .... BURGOMASTER

domain of .... CITY, TOWN

term of office of .... MAYORALTY

title: sl. .... HIZZONER

Mayotte capital .... DZAOUDZI

Mays' one-time job .... GIANT

mazard ...... FACE, HEAD, MAZER, SKULL

Mazarin, statesman .... JULES

maze ...... DAZE, ADDLE, STUPEFY, JUNGLE, NETWORK, LABYRINTH

exit aid .... CLEW

mazer .... CUP, BOWL, GOBLET

mazurka .... DANCE, POLKA

mazzard .... CHERRY

MC .... EMCEE, TOASTMASTER

asset of .... WIT

McAuliffe's historic reply:
12/23/44 .... NUTS
McCambridge, actress
.... MERCEDES
McCoy, the real .... GENUINE
McCrea, the actor .... JOEL
McDonald's franchise chain
creator .... RAY KROC
McGuffey's volume ...... READER
McIntosh .... (RED) APPLE
McLaglen's role .... INFORMER
McMahon, Carson's
announcer .... ED
drawn-out word of ..... HERE'S
McPherson, evangelist .... AIMEE
MD .... DOC(TOR), PHYSICIAN
M.D. Zaharias .... BABE
me .... EGO, (ONE)SELF
_____ and I .... MYSELF
thinker .... EGOIST
mead .... LEA, HYDROMEL
meadow .... LEA, PASTURE,
GRASSLAND
barley .... RIE
bird .... LARK, BOBOLINK
grass .... POA, FESCUE
mouse .... VOLE
poetic .... MEAD
rue .... CROWFOOT
Meadowlands event .... TROT
meadowlike .... GRASSY
meager .... BARE, LEAN, POOR,
THIN, GAUNT, SPARE, LENTEN,
SCANT(Y), SLIGHT, SPARSE,
SPARING, MARGINAL
meal .... BRAN, CHOW, CORN,
FARE, FEED, FOOD, MASH,
FLOUR, GRIST, LUNCH, SNACK,
FARINA, PINOLE, REPAST,
SPREAD, SUPPER, COLLATION,
REFECTION
boiled in milk .... MUSH
coarse .... SAMP, GRITS,
GROUT, GROATS, HOMINY
corn .... SAMP, HOMINY
end's serving .... DESSERT
family .... POTLUCK
field .... K-RATION
main course .... ENTREE
noon .... LUNCH(EON)
oat/wheat .... GROATS
table .... BOARD
mealies .... CORN, MAIZE
meals .... EATS, BOARD
complete .... TABLES D'HOTE
mealy .... PALE, SPOTTY,
POWDERY, FARINOSE
mealymouth .... HYPOCRITE
mealymouthed .... OILY,
EVASIVE, UNCTUOUS,
INSINCERE

mean .... LOW, BASE, EVIL,
CATTY, CRUEL, IMPLY, INFER,
NASTY, PETTY, SNIDE,
DENOTE, HUMBLE, INTEND,
MEDIUM, PALTRY, SORDID,
STINGY, TYPIFY, AVERAGE,
CAITIFF, IGNOBLE, LOW-
DOWN, MISERLY, PITIFUL,
SIGNIFY, VICIOUS, INFERIOR,
TWO-PENNY
abode .... HOVEL
person .... CAITIFF
meander .... ROAM, ROVE, STRAY,
RAMBLE, WANDER
meandering .... FLOWING,
WINDING, LABYRINTHINE
meanie .... OGRE, BULLY, GORILLA
meaning .... AIM, GIST, SENSE,
IMPORT, INTENT, PURPOSE,
PURPORT, SIGNIFICANCE
ambiguous in .... CRYPTIC
meaningful .... PITHY, LITERAL,
ARTICULATE, EXPRESS(IVE)
meaningless .... IDLE, FUTILE,
AIMLESS, SENSELESS
means .... WAY, DINT, TOOL,
AGENCY, ASSETS, AVENUE,
METHOD, RICHES, WEALTH,
RESOURCES
by all .... CERTAINLY, OF
COURSE
by any .... SOMEHOW
of entry .... DOOR, GATE,
PORTAL, INGRESS
of escape .... LOOPHOLE
of living .... LIVELIHOOD
of propulsion .... OARS
of surmounting .... STILE
meant .... VOLUNTARY,
INTENTIONAL
meantime .... WHILST, INTERIM
measles .... ROSEOLA, RUBELLA,
RUBEOLA
characteristic .... RED RASH
symptom .... COUGH, FEVER,
SORE EYES
measly .... PUNY, PETTY, SCANTY,
TWO-BIT, MISERLY
measure .... LAW, BILL, FOOT,
INCH, METE, POLE, SPAN,
STEP, YARD, INDEX, GAUGE,
LITER, AMOUNT, BUSHEL,
EXTENT, CRITERION
cloth .... ELL
combining form .... METRO
depth .... FATHOM
distance ...... MILE, KILOMETER
dry .... CORD, PECK, ROTL,
BARREL, BASKET, BUSHEL
for oil .... KULA
grain .... PECK, BUSHEL

land .... AR(E), ACRE, MORGEN,
HECTARE
length .... ELL, ROD, FOOT,
MILE, STEP, YARD, CUBIT,
METER
liquid .... TUN, DRAM, GILL,
PINT, LITER, OUNCE, QUART,
GALLON, TIERCE
medicine .... DOSE
nautical .... KNOT
of .... MENSURAL
astronomical distance
.... PARSEC, SECPAR
capacity .... TUN, CASK,
GILL, PECK, PINT, LITER,
QUART, STERE, BARREL,
BUSHEL, GALLON
earth .... GEODESY
length, ancient .... ELL,
CUBIT
length: naut. .... CABLE
stone .... PERCH
wood .... CORD
work .... ERGON
paper .... REAM, QUIRE
poetry .... SCAN
speed .... KNOT
type .... EM, EN
up to .... EQUAL
weight .... GRAM, KILO,
CARAT, GRAIN, OUNCE,
POUND, METAGE
wine .... BUTT
yard .... VERGE
measured .... TIMED, GAUGED
medicine .... DOSE, DOSAGE
measurement .... METERAGE,
DIMENSION(S), MENSURATION
content/weight .... METAGE
measurer .... METER, GAUGER
lung capacity ...... SPIROMETER
measuring instrument .... METER,
GA(U)GE, STADIA, SEXTANT,
TRANSIT, CAL(L)IPER
standard .... YARDSTICK
stick .... ROD, RULE
worm .... LARVA, LOOPER
meat .... BEEF, FOOD, PITH, PORK,
VEAL, FLESH, STEAK, TRIPE,
KERNEL, MUTTON, ESSENCE,
VENISON, SUBSTANCE
and vegetable dish .... HASH,
OLLA, RAGOUT, CASSEROLE
carving board .... TRENCHER
cooking method .... FRYING,
BOILING, STEWING, BRAISING,
BROILING, GRILLING,
ROASTING, ROTISSERIE
covering/coating .... GLAZE
cured .... HAM
cut ...... HAM, RIB, CHOP, LOIN,

RUMP, CARVE, CHUCK, FLANK, STEAK, FIL(L)ET, BRISKET, ICEBONE

dish .... LOAF, STEW, CURRY, RAVIOLI, RISSOLE, HAMBURGER, STROGANOFF, WELLINGTON, BOURGUIGNON, YANKEE POT ROAST

dried .... JERK(Y), BILTONG, CHARQUI, PEM(M)ICAN

dried coconut .... COPRA

eater .... CARNIVORE

hard, salted .... JUNK

jelly .... ASPIC

juice .... GRAVY

kind/grade of .... PRIME, CHOICE, SELECT

leg .... CUTLET

paste .... PATE, PEM(M)ICAN

pie .... PATE, PASTY, RISSOLE

piece ..... COLP, CUBE, CHUNK, STRIP, COLLOP, FIL(L)ET

preserved, pickled .... CORNED BEEF, SALMAGUNDI

rib .... CUTLET

roast .... BAR, CABOBS, KEBABS, KABOBS, FRICANDO

roasting device .... SPIT, GRILL, BROACH, SKEWER, BUCCANEER

roll .... RISSOLE, ROULADE

sauce, type of .... MINT, RAISIN, AU JUS, BARBECUE, MUSHROOM, BEARNAISE, CRANBERRY, BORDELAISE

seller ...... BUTCHER, KNACKER

shop .... SHAMBLES, ROTISSERIE, DELI(CATESSEN)

skewered .... CABOB, KABOB, KEBAB

smoked .... HAM, BACON

spiced ...... SALAMI, BOLOGNA, SAUSAGE

spread .... PATE

stew .... OLLA, RAGOUT, GOULASH, HARICOT, MILANESE, FRICASSEE

strips .... BILTONG

stuffed .... SAUSAGE

tenderizer .... PAPAIN

tenderizing, mechanical .... GRINDING

you cannot identify .... MYSTERY(MEAT)

meatball .... PINDA, RISSOLE

meatman .... BUTCHER

meatus .... DUCT, CANAL, PASSAGE(WAY)

meaty .... HEFTY, PITHY, STOUT, FLESHY

Mecca black stone location .... KIBLAH

chief magistrate .... SHERIF

pilgrimage .... HADJ

pilgrim's dress .... IHRAM

shrine .... CAABA, KAABA

son of .... MAHOMET, MOHAMMED

to Medina journey .... HEGIRA, HEJIRA

Meccawee, e.g. .... ASIAN

mechanic .... RESETTER, REPAIRMAN

military .... ARTIFICER

wear of .... COVERALLS

mechanical .... POWERED, AUTOMATIC, INVOLUNTARY, SPONTANEOUS

bar .... LEVER

contrivance .... DEVICE, GADGET

game .... PINBALL

man .... ROBOT, AUTOMATON

method/routine .... ROTE

mechanically repetitious .... SINGSONG

mechanics .... DYNAMICS, WORKINGS

Mechlin .... LACE, MALINES

medal ...... AWARD, BADGE, PRIZE

back of .... VERSO

face of .... OBVERSE

present .... DECORATE

space .... EXERGUE

Medal of Honor, only woman awardee .... MARY WALKER

symbol of _____ ...... HEROISM

medallion .... CAMEO

medals collector .... NUMISMATIST

of .... NUMISMATIC

meddle ...... PRY, MELL, BUTT IN, TAMPER, INTRUDE, INTERFERE, INTERLOPE, INTERVENE

meddler .... GREMLIN, BUSYBODY, KIBITZER

meddlesome .... CURIOUS, OFFICIOUS, INTERFERING

man .... PAUL PRY

Medea .... SORCERESS

consort of .... JASON

father of .... AEETES

victim of ...... CREON, CREUSA, GLAUCE

Medean king .... CAMBYSES

Medes' language .... AVESTAN

media, part of mass ...... PRESS, RADIO, TELEVISION

medial .... MIDDLE, AVERAGE, MIDDLING, MEDIOCRE

median .... MEAN, MESAL, MIDST, MESNE, CENTER, MESIAL, MIDDLE, AVERAGE, MIDMOST

priests .... MAGI

mediate .... ARBITRATE, INTERCEDE, RECONCILE, CONCILIATE

mediation .... PARLEY, ARBITRATION

mediator ...... ARBITER, REFEREE, GO-BETWEEN, INTERCESSOR

medic .... DOC, HEALER, ALFALFA, SURGEON, CORPMAN, THERAPIST

medic's sorting process .... TRIAGE

medicable .... CURABLE, CURATIVE

medical .... IATRIC, CLINICAL, CURATIVE

abbreviation DX, meaning of .... DIAGNOSIS

abbreviation PX, meaning of .... PROGNOSIS

assistant .... INTERN(E)

beam .... X-RAY

combining form .... IATRO

examiner .... CORONER

group .... AMA

instrument .... PROBE, FORCEPS, SCALPEL, SYRINGE, CATHETER, STETHOSCOPE, THERMOMETER

patient .... CASE

profession symbol .... CADUCEUS

student .... MEDIC(O), INTERN(E)

suffix .... OMA, EMIA, ITIS

tool, obsolete .... LEECH

treatment .... THERAPY

treatment: comb. form .... IATRY

medicate ...... CURE, HEAL, TREAT

medicated candy .... LOZENGE, SUCRETS, COUGH DROP

cloth .... STUPE

liquid .... LOTION

medication .... DRUG, REGIMEN, THERAPY, TREATMENT

Medici, ruler of Florence .... LORENZO

brother of .... GIULIANO

grandfather of .... COSIMO

father of .... PIERO

rival family of .... PAZZI, ALBIZZI

sobriquet of .... THE MAGNIFICENT

medicinal .... LATRIC, HEALING

bark .... COTO, PEREIRA, CINCHONA, VIBURNUM

cigarette .... CUBEB

fluid .... SERUM
herb ..... ALOE, SENNA, ARNICA
lozenge .... TROCHE
root ...... ARTAR, JALAP, ORRIS,
       GINSENG
shrub .... ALEM
medicine .... CURE, DRUG,
       REMEDY
branch of .... SURGERY,
 NEUROLOGY, GYNECOLOGY,
 OBSTETRICS, PEDIATRICS,
 PSYCHIATRY, DERMATOLOGY
chest ....:......... CABINET
cure-all .... ELIXIR, PANACEA
dropper .... PIPETTE
giver .... DOSER
liquid .... DROPS
man .... QUACK, SHAMAN,
 ANGEKOK, MAGICIAN,
 MUMBOJUMBO,
 (WITCH)DOCTOR
man, Sioux ...... SITTING BULL
measure .... DOSE, DOSAGE
mock .... PLACEBO
obsolete .... LEECHCRAFT
patent/quack .... NOSTRUM
pertaining to .... IATRIC
vomit .... EMETIC
Medicine Lodge _____ of 1867
 .... TREATY
medieval catapult .... ONAGER,
 MANGONEL, TREBUCHET
coat .... GAMBESON
collar .... RABATO
emperor .... OTTO,
 CHARLEMAGNE, JUSTINIAN I,
 FREDERICK II
empire .... AZTEC, PERSIA,
 ARMENIA, TREBIZOND,
 CAROLINGIAN
empire held together with
  string .... INCA
empress .... THEODORA
feudal vassal .... VAVASOR
folk hero, a ..... HSUAN-TSANG
galley .... AESC, BIREME,
       GALIOT
helmet .... ARMET
judicial council .... CURIA
knight .... PENNON
land under the lord's control
 .... DEMESNE
latitude-measuring device
 .... KAMAL
man-eating race .... TAFUR
musical instrument ...... LUTE,
 LYRE, ROT(T)E, REBEC(K)
musician .... MINSTREL,
      TROUBADOUR
plague ...... THE BLACK DEATH
ruler .... KING ALFRED, KING

 HAROLD, GENGHIS KHAN
servant .... SEWER
shield .... ECU, PAVIS
sport .... TILT, TOURNEY,
 JOUST(ING), TOURNAMENTS,
 CHARIOT-RACING
stable boss .... AVENER
sultan of Egypt .... SALADIN
Teutonic estate .... ODAL
tool .... AX, KNIFE
town .... BOURG
trading vessel ..... NEF, KNORR
tribe .... MONGOL
war engine .... BOAR,
       TREBUCHET
warrior .... TAFUR, VIKING
warship .... DROMON
weapon .... MACE, SPEAR,
 SWORD, HARPOON, LONGBOW
wind instrument ..... SACKBUT
mediocre .... SO-SO, AVERAGE,
 INFERIOR, MIDDLING,
      ORDINARY
meditate ...... MULL, MUSE, PORE,
 PONDER, REFLECT
moodily .... BROOD
meditative .... MUSING, PENSIVE
Mediterranean .... INLAND
bush .... CAPER
city .... ORAN
country .... MALTA, TUNISIA
fish .... OMBER
galley ...... BIREME, GAL(L)IOT,
       TRIREME
grass .... DISS
gulf .... TUNIS, TARANTO
island .... ELBA, GOZO, LIDO,
 RODI, CAPRI, CRETE, MALTA,
 SICILY, CORSICA, SARDINIA
pirate .... XEBEC
plant .... ANISE, MANDRAKE,
      TURNSOLE
principality .... MONACO
regions .... LEVANT
resort .... LIDO, NICE, MENTON,
       RIVIERA
river to the .... EBRO, NILE,
       RHONE
seaport .... TETUAN, TOULON,
 TRIPOLI, PORT SAID
ship .... SAIC, SETEE, XEBEC,
 LATEEN, TARTAN, ZEBEC(K),
 FELUCCA, POLACRE
ship master .... PADRONE
shrub .... TAMARISK,
      LAURUSTINE
trading ship .... PADRONE
tributary .... TIBER, TEVERE,
      ORONTES
volcanic island .... LIPARI
warship .... BIREME, TRIREME

wind .... SOLANO, MISTRAL,
 PTESIAN, SIROCCO, LEVANTER
medium .... TOOL, AGENT,
 MEAN(S), AGENCY, CENTER,
 MIDDLE, AVERAGE, VEHICLE
advertising .... PRESS, RADIO,
 MAGAZINE, NEWSPAPER,
 BILLBOARDS, SKYWRITING,
 TELEVISION, DIRECT MAIL
artist's ...... OIL, CLAY, STONE,
 MUSIC, PIANO, BRONZE,
 CANVAS, VIOLIN, PAINTING
exchange .... MONEY,
      CURRENCY
in music .... MEZZO
response of a .... ORACLE
session with a .... SEANCE
spiritualistic .... PSYCHIC
medley .... OLIO, CENTO, JUMBLE,
 FARRAGO, MELANGE,
 MIXTURE, VARIETY, FANTASIA,
 POSTICHE, MACEDOINE,
 POTPOURRI, HODGEPODGE
of skits .... REVUE
race .... RELAY
medrick .... TERN
medulla .... PITH, MARROW
Medusa .... GORGON, JELLYFISH
hair of .... SNAKE(S)
sister of ..... STHENO, EURYALE
slayer of .... PERSEUS
medusan .... JELLYFISH
meed .... REWARD, RECOMPENSE
meek .... LOWLY, HUMBLE,
      PATIENT
meekness .... LOWNESS
meerschaum ...... PIPE, SEAFOAM
meet .... SIT, FACE, GREET,
 MATCH, OPPOSE, CONVENE,
 FIT(TING), WELCOME,
 ASSEMBLE, CONFRONT,
 RENDEZVOUS
a poker bet .... SEE
companion of .... PROPER
halfway .... COMPROMISE, GIVE
 AND TAKE, SPLIT THE
      DIFFERENCE
the day .... ARISE
the eye .... APPEAR, EMERGE
with fortitude .... BREAST
meeting .... BEE, DATE, RALLY,
 SYNOD, CAUCUS, HUDDLE,
 SESSION, ASSEMBLY,
      CONGRESS
atmosphere of a .... TENOR
full attendance .... PLENARY
lovers'/secret .... TRYST
necessity .... AGENDA
of minds .... AGREEMENT
place of ''Big Three''
 .... YALTA, POTSDAM,

point .... JUNCTION CASABLANCA

room .... CAMARILLA

to discuss particular topics

.... SYMPOSIUM

to elect Pope .... CONCLAVE

mega .... MILLION

megalomania .... DELUSION

megapod .... MALEO, LEIPOA

megalith .... STONE, MENHIR

megaphone .... AMPLIFIER, LOUDSPEAKER

megrim(s) .... WHIM, VERTIGO, HEADACHE, MIGRAINE

Mehitabel .... CAT

Mehta, conductor .... ZUBIN

Meiji emperor .... MUTSUHITO

Mein Kampf author ...... HITLER

meiosis .... LITOTES

Meir, Israeli prime minister

.... GOLDA

Mekong .... LANTSANG

Mel .... HONEY

actor .... FERRER, GIBSON

baseballer .... OTT

singer .... TORME

melancholia .... HYP, GLOOM, DEPRESSION

melancholic spell .... HUMP

melancholy .... BLUE, DREAR, GLOOMY, HIPPED, SOMBER, PENSIVE, SAD(NESS), DEJECTED

fit of .... HYP(S), HUMP, HYPOCHONDRIA

Melanesian islands .... FIJI, SOLOMON, ADMIRALTY

native .... FIJIAN

melange .... OLIO, MIXTURE, HODGEPODGE

melanin .... PIGMENT

melanite .... GARNET

melanoma .... TUMOR

Melba, soprano .... NELLIE

Melchior, tenor .... LAURITZ

meld .... FUSE, BLEND, MERGE, UNITE

Meleager .... ARGONAUT

father of .... OENEUS

mother of .... ALTHEA

melee .... RIOT, BRAWL, MIX-UP, (AF)FRAY, HASSLE, RUCKUS, RUMBLE, SCUFFLE, SKIRMISH, TURMOIL, FREE-FOR-ALL

melic .... LYRIC

melicocca .... GENIP

Melissa, singer ...... MANCHESTER

mellow .... SOFT, RIPE(N), LOAMY, TIPSY, MATURE

melodeon .... ORGAN, ACCORDION

melodic .... ARIOSE, ARIOSO, LYRICAL

melodious .... ARIOSE, ARIOSO, DULCET, LILTING, MUSICAL, ORPHEAN, CANOROUS

melodrama .... SHOCKER, THRILLER

melodramatic .... HISTRIONIC

melody .... AIR, LAY, ARIA, SONG, TUNE, STRAIN, ARIETTA, CAVATINA

meloid .... BEETLE

melon .... PEPO, GOURD, CAS(S)ABA, HONEYDEW, CANTALOUP(E)

dessert .... BOMB

pear .... PEPINO

slang .... PROFITS

Melpomene .... MUSE

melt .... FUSE, THAW, SOFTEN, LIQUEFY, DISSOLVE

into mold .... FOUND

ore .... SMELT

melted .... FUSIL(E)

melting pot .... AMERICA, CRUCIBLE

Melville .... HERMAN

character .... AHAB, BUDD, WHALE, MOBY DICK

novel ..... OMOO, TYPEE, MOBY DICK

protagonist .... AHAB

member .... ARM, LEG, LIMB, PART, ORGAN, AFFILIATE

academy .... FELLOW

Aesir .... TYR, LOKI, ODIN

club .... ELK, LION, JAYCEE, ROTARIAN

fraternity .... BROTHER

of a law firm .... ASSOCIATE

of an old English sect

.... SHAKER

of the ''woodpile'' .... BAT

sorority .... SISTER

membership .... BODY, SEAT, MEMBERS, INCLUSION, AFFILIATION

fee .... DUES

grass roots .... RANK AND FILE

membrane .... PIA, WEB, TELA, VELUM, TISSUE, VELAMEN, COVERING, PELLICLE

abdominal cavity

.... PERITONEUM

animal eye .... TAPETUM

bird's beak .... CERE

brain .... MENINGES

combining form .... HYMEN(O)

ear .... EARDRUM

ear: descriptive ...... TYMPANIC

embryo's sac .... AMNION

enclosing .... CAUL

eye .... IRIS, UVEA, CORNEA

eyeball .... SCLERA

fetus .... CAUL, CHORION

nictitating .... HAW

uniting toes .... WEB(BING)

web-like .... TELA

Memel River city .... TILSIT

memento .... PRIZE, RELIC, TOKEN, TROPHY, KEEPSAKE, SOUVENIR, REMEMBRANCE

album .... SCRAPBOOK

Memnon, killer of ...... ACHILLES

memo .... CHIT, NOTE

memoir .... BIOGRAPHY, MONOGRAPH, REMINISCENCE

memorabilia .... ANA

memorable .... NOTABLE, SPECIAL, STRIKING

period .... ERA, EPOCH

memoranda .... ITEMS

memorandum .... CHIT, NOTE, BRIEF, RECORD, MINUTES

pad .... TICKLER

memorial .... TOMB, CAIRN, SHRINE, STATUE, TROPHY, MONUMENT

ancient .... DOLMEN, CROMLECH

of a sort .... PETITION

post .... XAT, XYST, TOTEM, COLUMN, PILLAR

memory .... ROTE, RETENTION, RECOLLECTION

book .... ALBUM, DIARY, MEMOIR

loss of .... AMNESIA

of .... MNESIC, MNEMONIC

Memphis god .... PTAH

high priest .... RANOFER

river .... NILE

ruler .... PHARAOH

men in blue .... UMP(IRES)

of letters .... LITERATI

menace .... BULLY, DANGER, THREAT(EN)

menacing .... DIRE, ALARMING, MINATORY, MINACIOUS

menad .... NYMPH, BACCHANTE

menage .... DOMICILE, HOUSEHOLD, HUSBANDRY, HOUSEKEEPING

menagerie .... ZOO

mend .... FIX, DARN, PATCH, COBBLE, REPAIR, CORRECT, IMPROVE

a seam .... RESEW

in tailoring .... BUSHEL

mendacious .... FALSE, LYING

mendacity .... LIE, FALSEHOOD

Mendel, botanist .... GREGOR
　forte of .... GENETICS,
　　　　　　　　　　HEREDITY
Mendelssohn .... FELIX
mender ...... REPAIRER, RESTORER
　pots/pans .... TINKER
　shoe .... COBBLER
　socks/tear .... DARNER
mendicant ...... BEGGAR, PAUPER,
　　　　　　　　　　BEGGING
　kind of .... FRIAR
Menelaus' brother
　.......................... AGAMEMNON
　daughter .... HERMIONE
　father .... ATREUS
　wife .... HELEN
menhaden .... FISH, POGY,
　HERRING, OLDWIFE, WHITING,
　　　　　　　　　GREENTAIL
menhir .... MEGALITH
menial .... VARLET, SERVANT,
　　　　　SERVILE, DOMESTIC
meninges .... MEMBRANES
　inflammation .... MENINGITIS
　innermost .... PIA MATER
　middle layer .... ARACHNOID
　　　　　　　　　　MATER
　outermost layer .... DURA
　　　　　　　　　　MATER
　tumor .... MENINGIOMA
meniscus .... DISK, LENS,
　　　　　　　　　CARTILAGE
　plural of .... MENISCI
　shape .... CRESCENT
　site of .... JAW JOINT, KNEE
　　JOINT, WRIST JOINT
Menlo Park initials .... TAE
　invention of Edison at
　.......................... PHONOGRAPH,
　　INCANDESCENT BULB
　inventor/man
　.................... (THOMAS)EDISON
　inventor's sobriquet
　....... WIZARD OF MENLO PARK
Mennonite .... AMISH
　founder .... MENNO
menopause .... CLIMACTERIC
　symptoms .... HOT FLASHES
Menotti .... GIAN-CARLO
　heroine .... AMELIA
men's affair/party .... STAG,
　　　　　　　　　　SMOKER
　organization .... YMCA
mensal .... MONTHLY
mental .... NOETIC, PHRENIC
　attic .... MIND
　bias .... WARP
　communication .... TELEPATHY
　condition .... LUNACY,
　　MADNESS, DEMENTIA
　deficiency .... IDIOCY,

AMENTIA, MONGOLISM
　discipline .... YOGA
　disorder .... NEUROSIS,
　PARANOIA, DISTEMPER
　disposition .... HUMOR
　drug .... METRAZOL
　hospital .... BEDLAM,
　BUGHOUSE, MADHOUSE,
　　　　　　　　NUTHOUSE
　illnesses, category of
　............ NEUROSES, PSYCHOSES
　patient .... LUNATIC,
　BEDLAMITE, PSYCHO(PATH)
　perception .... KEN
　picture .... FANCY, IMAGE,
　VISTA, RECEPT, VISION,
　CONCEPT, FANTASM
　position .... VIEWPOINT
　reservation .... SALVO
　state .... MOOD, MORALE,
　　　　　　　DISPOSITION
　telepathy .... MIND READING
　telepathy: abbr. .... ESP
　view .... OUTLOOK
mentality .... MIND, ATTITUDE
mentally alert .... ACUTE
　deficient person .... IDIOT,
　MORON, IMBECILE
　ill .... PARANOID, DISTURBED,
　　　　　　　PSYCHOTIC
　retarded .... HALF-WITTED
　sound .... SANE, LUCID,
　　　　　　COMPETENT
　wandering .... DELIRIOUS
mention .... CITE, NAME, ALLUDE,
　SPECIFY, REFER(ENCE)
mentor .... COACH, ADVISER,
　　　　　　　　TEACHER
　of Luke Skywalker ...... YODA
menu .... CARTE, BILL(OF FARE)
　item .... ENTREE
Menuet .... DANSE
Menuhin, violinist .... YEHUDI
　teacher of .... ENESCO
Mephisto(pheles), debtor of
　............................. FAUST(US)
mephitic .... NOXIOUS, POISONOUS
mephitis .... DAMP, MIASMA,
　　　　　　　　STENCH
mercantile .... COMMERCIAL
　paper .... CHECK, DRAFT
Mercator .... MAPMAKER,
　GEOGRAPHER, CARTOGRAPHER
　work .... ATLAS
mercenary .... VENAL, GREEDY,
　SORDID, HIRELING,
　　　　　　　POTHUNTER
　soldier .... HESSIAN, SWISSER
mercer .... DRAPER
mercery .... TEXTILES
merchandise .... GOODS, WARE(S)

merchant .... COSTER, DEALER,
　TRADER, RETAILER
　fleet captain ...... COMMODORE
　ship .... ARGOSY, TRADER
　ship, India-England
　.............................. INDIAMAN
　U.S. fur .... ASTOR
Merchant of Venice character
　........ GOBBO, TUBAL, PORTIA,
　ANTONIO, JESSICA, NERISSA,
　SALERIO, SHYLOCK, SOLANIO,
　　　　　　　BASSANIO
merchantman .... SHIP
merchants, guild of .... HANSE
merci .... THANKS
merciful .... HUMANE, LENIENT
　be .... SPARE
merciless .... GRIM, CRUEL
Mercouri, actress .... MELINA
mercurial .... FICKLE, VOLATILE
mercuric chloride .... CALOMEL
　sulfide .... CINNABAR,
　　　　　　　VERMILION
mercury .... QUICKSILVER
　in chemistry .... HG
　ore .... CINNABAR
Mercury .... AZOTH, HERMES,
　　　　　　　MESSENGER
　cap of .... PETASUS
　shoes of .... TALARIA
　staff of .... CADUCEUS
mercy .... GRACE, LENITY,
　CHARITY, CLEMENCY,
　HUMANITY, COMPASSION
　grant .... SPARE
　in military usage .... QUARTER
　killing .... EUTHANASIA
mere .... LAKE, ONLY, POND,
　MARSH, SHEER, SIMPLE,
　　　　　　　BOUNDARY
　nonsense .... FALDERAL
　nothing .... FIDDLESTICK
merely .... JUST, ONLY, SIMPLY
merganser .... DUCK, SMEE,
　SMEW, HARLE, GOOSANDER
merge .... FUSE, MELD, BLEND,
　UNITE, ABSORB
merger .... FUSION, COMBINE,
　AMALGAMATION
Merida is capital of
　.............................. YUCATAN
meridian .... NOON, ZENITH
merino .... WOOL, YARN, SHEEP
merit .... EARN, VALUE, WORTH,
　DESERT, VIRTUE, DESERVE
　anew .... RE-EARN
Merkel, actress .... UNA
merl(e) .... BLACKBIRD
Merle, actress .... OBERON
merlin .... FALCON, PIGEON HAWK
Merlin .... SEER, MAGICIAN

forte of .... MAGIC
mistress of .... VIVIAN
Merovingian king .... CLOVIS
Merrimac(k) .... (UNION)FRIGATE,
    IRONCLAD WARSHIP
adversary of .... MONITOR
rechristened name of
.... VIRGINIA
merriment .... GLEE, FROLIC,
    GAIETY
merry .... GAY, JOLLY, FESTAL,
    JOCOSE, FESTIVE, MIRTHFUL
go-round .... WHIRL,
    TURNABOUT, CAR(R)OUSEL,
    WHIRLIGIG
maker .... REVEL(L)ER
making time .... CARNIVAL,
    FESTIVAL
monarch .... COLE
Merry Andrew .... MIME, CLOWN,
    JESTER, BUFFOON
Widow composer .... LEHAR
mesa .... BUTTE, PLATEAU,
    TABLELAND
Mesabi output .... ORE
Range locale ...... MINNESOTA
mescal .... AGAVE, CACTUS,
    LIQUOR, PEYOTE
mesh .... WEB, ENGAGE, TISSUE,
    NETTING, NET(WORK),
    ENTANGLE, INTERLOCK,
    SCREENING
meshed .... GEARED, SHRINE
fabric .... NET, LACE
Meshed is in _____ .... IRAN
mesmeric .... HYPNOTIC,
    MAGNETIC
force .... OD
mesmerist .... HYPNOTIST
mesne .... MIDDLE, INTERMEDIATE
Mesopotamia .... IRAK, IRAQ
boat .... GUFA
city ..... URFA, EDESSA, NIPPUR
region .... SUMER
wind .... SHAMAL
mesquit(e) .... ALGARROBA
mess .... CHOW, FOOD, HASH,
    MEAL, MUSS, BOTCH, SNAFU,
    JUMBLE, MUDDLE, PUTTER
up .... ERR, SLIP
message .... WORD, REPORT,
    DISPATCH
Messala, enemy of .... (BEN)HUR
messenger .... PAGE, HERALD,
    COURIER, HARBINGER
messer-upper .... LITTERBUG
Messiah .... JESUS, CHRIST,
    SAVIOR, DELIVERER
composer .... HANDEL
Messina rock .... SCYLLA
Messrs. ...... MISTERS, MESSIEURS

messuage ...... TOFT, HOMESTEAD
messy .... DIRTY, SLOPPY, UNTIDY,
    DISORDERLY
Mesta, _____ .... PERLE
mestizo .... CHOLO, METIS, LADINO
metabolism .... BASAL,
    METASTASIS
process .... ANABOLISM,
    CATABOLISM
metal ...... TIN, IRON, LEAD, ZINC,
    ALUMINUM, CASTIRON
alloy .... BRASS, STEEL,
    BRONZE, MONEL(L), NIELLO,
    SOLDER
assaying vessel .... TEST,
    CUPEL
band .... COLLET
bar .... FID, INGOT, OFFSET
barracks .... QUONSETS
block .... DIE
casting(s) .... PIG, INGOT,
    FOUNDRY
coat with .... PLATE, TERNE
coating .... RUST, PATINA
comb .... CARD
covering of an airplane
.... SKIN
cutting tool .... HACKSAW
disk .... MEDAL, PATEN,
    SEQUIN, MEDALLION
dross .... SLAG
fastener .... TNUT, RIVET,
    U-BOLT
filings .... LEMEL
for coinage .... FLAN,
    PLANCHET
hard .... COBALT
hard-tipped end .... TAG
heavy .... LEAD
japanned .... TOLE
lightest .... LITHIUM
line of type .... SLUG
lining .... BUSH(ING)
marker .... DIE, STAMP, SWAGE
mixture .... ALLOY
patching .... SOLDER
peg/pin .... BOLT, SPILL,
    GUDGEON
piece .... SHIM
plate .... PATEN, PATIN(A)
plate, cut .... TREPAN
refine .... SMELT
refuse .... SCUM, SLAG, DROSS,
    SCORIA
ring .... BEE, GROMMET
rod .... BOLT
rod, thin .... WIRE
shaper ..... DIE, LATHE, STAMP,
    SWAGE
shavings .... WOOL
sheet cutter .... SHEAR

sheet of .... FOIL, LAMINA,
    LATTEN, TAGGERS
suit .... MAIL, ARMOR,
    HAUBERK
thread .... LAME, WIRE
used for trays .... TOLE
waste ...... CALX, SLAG, SPRUE,
    CALCES
welding .... SOLDER
worker .... SMITH, WELDER
works .... SMITHY, FOUNDRY
Metalious novelist .... GRACE
work .... PEYTON PLACE
metallic oxidation .... RUST
rock .... ORE
sulfide .... PYRITE
wire .... LAME
metalware, enameled .... TOLE
metalworker .... WELDER,
    RIVETER, (TIN)SMITH
metamorphose .... TRANSFORM
Metamorphoses author ...... OVID
character .... THISBE
metamorphosis ...... METASTASIS
metaphor .... TROPE, SIMILE,
    ANALOGY, COMPARISON
incorrect use of/mixed
.... CATACHRESIS
metaphorical .... FIGURATIVE,
    ALLEGORICAL
metaphrase .... TRANSLATE
metaphysical .... SUBTLE,
    ABSTRACT, ABSTRUSE,
    ESOTERIC
poet .... DONNE, COWLEY
metastasis .... METABOLISM
metathesis .... INTERCHANGE
metazoan stage .... BLASTULA
mete .... DOLE, GIVE, ALLOT,
    LIMIT, MEASURE, BOUNDARY,
    APPORTION
meteor .... HAIL, STAR, FIREBALL,
    FALLING STAR, SHOOTING
    STAR
exploding/fiery .... BOLIS,
    BOLIDE
train of .... TAIL
visible during August
.... PERSEIDS
visible during November
.... LEONIDS
meteoric .... FLEET, SWIFT,
    BLAZING, DAZZLING,
    FLASHING
shower ...... LEONIDS, PERSEIDS
meteorite .... TEKTITE, AEROLITE,
    SIDERITE
meteorological line .... ISOBAR
prefix .... STRATO
meteorologist's concern
.... CLIMATE, WEATHER

instrument .... ACTINOMETER
meter .... RHYTHM, CADENCE
cubic .... STERE
face of .... DIAL
millionth part .... MICRON,
MIKRON
meters, 25.293 square .... POLE
100 square .... AR(E)
1000 square .... DECARE
10,000 square .... HECTARE
methane .... PARAFFIN
metheglin .... MEAD, LIQUOR
material .... HONEY
method ...... WAY, MODE, MODUS,
MANNER, SYST(EM), PROCESS,
PROCEDURE, TECHNIQUE
methodical .... FORMAL,
ORDERLY, SYSTEMATIC
Methodism founder ...... WESLEY
Methodist Church, of the
.... WESLEYAN
preacher .... ROUNDER
Methuselah's fame .... AGE
father .... ENOCH
grandson .... NOAH
meticulous .... FUSSY, FINICAL,
PRECISE, EXACTING,
PARTICULAR
metier .... FORTE, TRADE,
VOCATION, SPECIALTY
metif(f) ...... MESTEE, HALFBREED
metis .... MULATTO
metopic .... FRONTAL
metric measure .... AR(E), GRAM,
KILO, LITER, METER, STERE,
DECIARE, HECTARE
ton .... MILLIER
metrical accent/beat .... ICTUS
composition ..... POEM, VERSE,
POETRY
foot .... DACTYL, IAMB(US),
ANAPEST, PYRRHIC, TROCHEE,
TRIBRACH, CHORIAMB(US)
time unit .... MORA
metrician .... POET
metrify .... VERSIFY
metro .... SUBWAY
metropolis .... SEE, CITY, SEAT,
CAPITAL
metropolitan .... URBAN, EPARCH,
OPPIDAN, (ARCH)BISHOP
Metropolitan Opera man
.... BING
Mets' home .... SHEA
mettle .... ARDOR, PLUCK, SPUNK,
SPIRIT, COURAGE
mettlesome .... BRAVE, SPUNKY
Metz's river .... MOSELLE
Meuse .... MAAS, LESSE
River city .... SEDAN
mew .... DEN, BARN, CAGE, MOLT,

SHED, GARAGE, STABLE,
(SEA)GULL
mewl ...... MEOW, MIAOW, WHINE,
WHIMPER
Mexican .... NAHUATL
agave .... PULQUE
American to a .... GRINGO,
YANQUI
ancient .... MAYAN
bandit ..... BANDIDO, LADRONE
basket grass .... ISTLE
battlesite .... BUENAVISTA
bay .... LA PAZ, CHAMELA,
BALLENAS, BANDERAS,
CAMPECHE
bean .... FRIJOL(E)
bean beetle .... LADYBUG
beverage .... OCTLI, MESCAL,
PULQUE, TEQUILA
beverage seed .... CHIA
bird .... VERDIN, TINAMOU
blanket .... SERAPE
bread/cake .... TORTILLA
cab .... ARANA
cape .... FALSO, LOBOS,
CATOCHE
capital .... MEXICO CITY
cat .... EYRA, MARGAY
Christmas pot for children
.... PIÑATA
city/town .... LERDO, MANTE,
CANCUN, CELAYA, COLIMA,
JALAPA, JUAREZ, LAREDO,
MADERO, MERIDA, OAXACA,
CORDOBA, MORELIA,
OBREGON, ORIZABA, PACHUCA,
TAMPICO, TIJUANA, TORREON,
ACAPULCO, CAMPECHE,
CULIACAN, ENSENADA,
MAZATLAN, VICTORIA,
ZARAGOZA, MONTERREY,
GUADALAJARA
coin .... PESO, AZTECA,
CENTAVO
coin, small old .... TLACO
conqueror
.... (HERNAN)CORTES
corn mush .... AMOLE
dance .... BAILE, RASPA
dish .... CHILI, TACOS,
TAMALE, ENCHILADA
district .... TEQUILA
dog .... CHIHUAHUA
dollar .... PESO
emperor .... MONTEZUMA,
MAXIMILIAN
farm worker .... PEON
fiber plant .... PITA, DATIL,
ISTLE, IXTLE, SISAL
gopher .... TUZA
grass .... OTATE, TUCAN,

ZACATON, TEOSINTE
grinding stone .... METATE
gulf ...... MEXICO, CALIFORNIA,
TEHUANTEPEC
handyman .... MOZO
hill .... CERRO
hut .... JACAL
Indian .... PIMA, SERI, TECA,
ZUNI, WABI, ALAIS, AZTEC,
LIPAN, MAYAN, OLMEC,
OPATA, OTOMI, SERIA, YAQUI,
APACHE, TOLTEC
Indian craft .... OJOS
island .... PEREZ, CARMEN,
CEDROS, CLARION, SOCORRO,
TIBURON, MONSERRATE
laborer .... PEON, BRACERO
lagoon .... MADRE, TERMINOS
lake .... GUZMAN, BACALAR,
CHAPALA
liquor .... MESCAL, PULQUE,
TEQUILA
man .... HOMBRE
manor .... CASA
mat .... PETATE
measure .... VARA, CARGA,
LABOR, LEGUA, LINEA, SITIO,
FANEGA, PULGADA
migrant .... WETBACK
monetary unit .... PESO
mountain .... ORIZABA,
CITLALTEPETL
mountain range .... BURRO,
SIERRA MADRE
mullet .... BOBO, LISITA
muralist .... OROZCO, RIVERA
musical instrument .... CLARIN
muzhik .... PEON
native .... AZTEC, MAYA(N)
noble .... HIDALGO
onyx .... TECALI
peasant .... PEON
peninsula .... YUCATAN
persimmon .... CHAPOTE
plant .... CHIA, AGAVE, AMOLE,
DATIL, JALAP, SOTOL, CACTUS,
MESCAL, PULQUE
policeman .... RURALES
president .... DIAZ, ORDAZ,
ALEMAN, CALLES, HUERTA,
JUAREZ, MATEOS, CAMACHO,
OBREGON, ZEDILLO,
CARDENAS, PORTILLO
pyramid .... TEOCALLI
race .... MAYA, AZTEC, TOLTEC
reed .... OTATE
resin tree .... DRAGO
resort .... TAOS, CANCUN
revolutionary .... PANCHO
VILLA
river ..... TULA, BABIA, HONDO,

NAZAS, RAMOS, VERDE,
YAQUI, ATOYAC, BALSAS,
BLANCO, COYUCA, FUERTE,
GRANDE, PANUCO, SONORA,
URIQUE, CONCHOS, SABINAS,
RIO BRAVO, COLORADO
robber .... BANDIDO
rodent .... TUCAN
scarf .... TAPALO
seaport .... TAMPICO,
ACAPULCO, MATAMOROS
shawl .... SERAPE
"spitfire" .... (LUPE)VELEZ
state .... MEXICO, OAXACA,
PUEBLA, SONORA, CHIAPAS,
DURANGO, HIDALGO, JALISCO,
SINALOA, TABASCO, YUCATAN,
COAHUILA, GUERRERO,
VERACRUZ, CHIHUAHUA,
MICHOACAN, NUEVO LEON,
ZACATECAS, GUANAJUATO
state capital .... LA PAZ, TEPIC,
COLIMA, JALAPA, OAXACA,
PUEBLA, TOLUCA, DURANGO,
MORELIA, CULIACAN,
MEXICALI, SALTILLO,
VICTORIA, CUERNAVACA,
HERMOSILLO, GUADALAJARA
sugar ..... PANOCHA, PANOCHE,
PENUCHE
tea .... APASOTE
temple .... TEOCALLI
tennis star .... OSUNA
thong .... ROMAL
timber tree .... EBANO
tree .... ULE, ABETO, DRAGO,
RETAMA, GUAYULE,
MESQUIT(E), AHUEHUETE
volcano .... ORIZABA,
PARICUTIN
weight .... ONZA, LIBRA,
ARROBA, QUINTAL
wood .... LINOLOA
Mexico City district
.... TACUBAYA
empress of .... CARLO(T)TA
watercourse in .... RIO
Meyerbeer ...... JAKOB, GIACOMO
opera by .... L'AFRICAINE
mezzanine .... ENTRESOL
mezzo .... MEDIUM, MIDWAY,
HALFWAY, MODERATE,
SOMEWHAT
Marilyn .... HORNE
MGM trademark .... THE LION'S
ROAR
mho, reciprocal of .... OHM
miasma .... METHANE
disease .... MALARIA
mib .... MARBLE
mica .... TALC, BIOTITE, MINERAL,

NACRITE, SILICATE, ISINGLASS,
MUSCOVITE
Micah .... PROPHET
Micawber, Dickens' .... WILKINS
mice .... VERMIN
of .... MURINE
Michael .... (ARCH)ANGEL
Michaelmas daisy .... ASTER
Michelangelo's birthplace
.... CAPRESE
trio, one of a .... PIETA
Michel's follower .... ANGELO
Michener .... JAMES
novel .... HAWAII, IBERIA
Michigan bay .... GREEN, HURON,
MISERY, AU-TRAIN
capital .... LANSING
city/town .... HART, HOLT,
NOVI, TROY, YALE, FLINT,
IONIA, MASON, GARDEN,
MONROE, TAYLOR, WARREN,
DETROIT, JACKSON, LINCOLN,
LIVONIA, MIDLAND, PONTIAC,
PORTAGE, ROMULUS, SAGINAW,
TRENTON, WYOMING, ANN
ARBOR, DEARBORN, FERNDALE,
MUSKEGON, KALAMAZOO,
MARQUETTE
college .... ALMA, HOPE,
MERCY, JORDAN, AQUINAS,
FERRIS STATE, CONCORDIA,
JOHN WESLEY
county .... BAY, CASS, KENT,
LAKE, BARRY, CLARE, DELTA,
EATON, IONIA, IOSCO, WAYNE,
INGHAM, MACOMB, MONROE,
OTTAWA, ALLEGAN, BERRIEN,
CALHOUN, GENESEE, LENAWEE,
MIDLAND, OAKLAND,
SAGINAW, TUSCOLA,
WEXFORD, ISABELLA
island .... SUGAR, GARDEN,
MANITOU, POVERTY,
DRUMMOND
lake .... ELK, GUN, BURT, ERIE,
GLEN, CEDAR, PERCH, TAWAS,
BEAVER, OTSEGO, PLATTE,
MICHIGAN, PARADISE,
SUPERIOR
lake city .... MUSKEGON,
MILWAUKEE
lake port .... RACINE
mountain .... CURWOOD
river .... CASS, DEAD, FORD,
FLINT, PAINT, RIFLE, PIGEON,
RABBIT, PRAIRIE, SAGINAW
state bird .... ROBIN
state flower .... APPLE
BLOSSOM
state nickname .... WOLVERINE
tourist site ..... DOW GARDENS,

PIONEER VILLAGE
university .... ANDREWS,
DETROIT, DEARBORN, WAYNE
STATE, MICHIGAN STATE
Mick, Rolling Stones'
.... JAGGER
Mickey .... FINN, MOUSE,
ROONEY
Mickey's friend .... MINNIE
micra, singular of .... MICRON
microbe .... GERM, VIRUS,
PATHOGEN, BACTERIUM
microcosm .... MAN, WORLD,
SMALL WORLD, UNIVERSE
Micronesia island .... MOEN,
TRUK, NAURU, KOSRAE,
PONAPE, POHNPEI
microorganism(s) .... AM(O)EBA,
BACTERIA, PROTOZOA
microphone .... MIKE
microscope glass plate .... SLIDE
microscopic .... MINUTE
Midas' touch product ...... GOLD
midday .... NOON
middle .... HUB, CORE, MESNE,
MIDST, WAIST, CENTER,
MEDIAL, MEDIAN, MESIAL,
CENTRAL
class ..... COMMON, ORDINARY,
BOURGEOISE
combining form .... MEDI(O)
ear .... DRUM, TYMPANUM
in law .... MESNE
kingdom .... CHINA
name in mysteries ...... CONAN
name of:
Alexander Bell, inventor
.... GRAHAM
Alvah Roebuck, Sears'
partner .... CURTIS
Amadeo Giannini, owner
of Bank of America
.... PETER
Anne Royall, first woman
editor .... NEWPORT
Dwight Eisenhower
.... DAVID
Edgar Poe, poet .... ALLAN
Francis Key, The Star-
Spangled Banner
writer .... SCOTT
Franklin Roosevelt
.... DELANO
George Bush .... HERBERT
WALKER
Gerald Ford .... RUDOLPH
Harriet Stowe, author
.... BEECHER
Henry Beecher, preacher-
abolitionist .... WARD

Henry Longfellow, poet .... WADSWORTH
Howard Hughes, billionaire .... ROBARD
James Carter .... EARL
James Garfield .... ABRAM
James Polk .... KNOX
John Adams .... QUINCY
John Astor, fur trader .... JACOB
John Booth, assassin .... WILKES
John Coolidge .... CALVIN
John Kellogg, cereal
 company founder .... HARVEY
John Kennedy .... FITZGERALD
Lyndon Johnson ...... BAINES
Ralph Emerson, poet .... WALDO
Richard Nixon ..... MILHOUS
Richard Sears of mail-
 order business .... WARREN
Ronald Reagan ...... WILSON
Thomas Edison, inventor .... ALVA
Thomas Jackson, nicknamed
 "Stonewall" .... JONATHAN
Ulysses Grant .... SIMPSON
Walt Disney .... ELIAS
William Hearst, newspaper
 tycoon .... RANDOLPH
William Taft .... HOWARD
of the roader .... NEUTRAL
part .... CORE, DEEP
toward the .... MESAD
Middle Ages empire .... INCA,
 MALI, ASIAN, AZTEC, CHIMU,
 ROMAN, MONGOL, ANGEVIN,
 BYZANTINE
of the .... MEDIEVAL
middlebreaker .... LISTER
middleman ...... AGENT, BROKER,
 RETAILER, GO-BETWEEN
middling .... PORK, SOSO,
 MEDIUM, AVERAGE,
 MEDIOCRE, ORDINARY
middy .... BLOUSE, MIDSHIPMAN
Midgard .... EARTH
to Asgard .... BIFROST
midge .... FLY, GNAT, DWARF,
 BANTAM, MIDGET, PUNKIE
midget .... DWARF, PYGMY,
 MINIATURE
slang .... SHRIMP
Midianite king .... EVI, HUR,
 REBA
midland .... INTERIOR

dialects .... MERCIAN
mid-May or mid-July .... IDES
midmost .... CENTER, MIDDLE
midnight .... WITCHING HOUR
assembly of witches .... SABBAT
sun, land of .... NORWAY
midriff .... DIAPHRAGM
midshipman .... MIDDY, PLEBE,
 REEFER
Midsummer Night's Dream
character ...... PUCK, HERMIA,
 OBERON, THISBE, TITANIA
tinker .... SNOUT
midterm event .... EXAM(S)
midway .... HALFWAY
features .... SIDESHOWS
Midway Islands discoverer .... BROOKS
midweek .... WEDNESDAY
midwifery .... TOCOLOGY,
 OBSTETRICS
mien .... AIR, LOOK, ASPECT,
 MANNER, BEARING,
 APPEARANCE
miff .... HUFF, TIFF, ANNOY,
 OFFEND
miggle .... TAW, MIBS, MIGS,
 MARBLE
might ...... FORCE, POWER, VIGOR,
 ENERGY, POTENCY, STRENGTH
and _____ .... MAIN
mightily .... AMAIN
mighty .... VERY, GREAT, POTENT,
 STRONG, POWERFUL, PUISSANT
batsman .... MAYS, RUTH,
 AARON, CASEY
implement .... PEN
mite .... ATOM
symbol .... OAK
mignon .... DAINTY, PRETTY,
 DELICATE
mignonette .... WELD, WOLD,
 PLANT, RESEDA
migraine .... MEGRIM, HEADACHE
type of .... COMMON,
 CLASSICAL
migrant .... ROVER, TREKKER
farm worker .... OKIE
slang .... WETBACK
migrate .... MOVE, TREK
migration .... TREK, EXODUS
migratory .... ROVING, NOMADIC,
 PEREGRINE, WANDERING
bird .... TERN, KUTSARA,
 WI(D)GEON, SHOVELER
creature ..... LOCUST, LEMMING
worker ...... HOBO, JOAD, OKIE,
 PEON, ARKIE, BRACERO,
 WETBACK
Mikado .... OPERA, EMPEROR

character ..... KOKO, YUM YUM
court of .... DAIRI, DAIRO
mike .... LOAF, MICROPHONE
man .... EMCEE
Mike's friend .... PAT
Mikhaelovitch ally .... CROAT
milady's concern .... DIET,
 FIGURE, HAIRDO, WEIGHT,
 WAISTLINE
Milan operahouse .... (LA)SCALA
mild .... SOFT, WEAK, BALMY,
 BLAND, GENTLE, PLACID,
 LENIENT, MODERATE,
 TEMPERATE
drink .... CHASER
oath .... GEE, DRAT, EGAD,
 GOSH
smoke .... CLARO
mildew ...... MOLD, RUST, BLIGHT,
 FUNGUS
mile, nautical .... KNOT
1/8 of .... FURLONG
1/3 of LI
Miled, son of .... EBER
Milesian .... IRISH
milestone .... EVENT, HERMA,
 STELE, PILLAR, LANDMARK,
 PROGRESS
milfoil .... PLANT, YARROW
miliaria ...... HEAT RASH, PRICKLY
 HEAT
milieu .... CLIMATE, ENVIRON,
 AMBIENCE
militant .... WARLIKE, ACTIVIST,
 FIGHTING, COMBATANT,
 COMBATIVE
militarist .... JINGO
military .... ARMY, MARTIAL,
 SOLDIERLY, ARMED FORCES
abode .... CAMP
academy site .... WEST POINT
acronym .... AWOL
address .... APO, FPO
assistant .... AIDE
banner .... STANDARD
blockade .... SIEGE
cap .... KEPI, BUSBY, SHAKO,
 HAVELOCK, PERSHING
ceremony .... REVIEW
coat .... TUNIC
decoration .... DSC, BATTLE
 STAR, MEDAL OF HONOR
depot .... ARMORY, ARSENAL,
 MAGAZINE
engineer .... PIONEER,
 PONTONIER
equipment .... HARDWARE
exercises .... WAR GAMES
felony .... AWOL
force .... MILITIA, AIR POWER
formation .... PHALANX

greeting .... SALUTE
group ..... UNIT, NAVY, CORPS,
DIVISION
guardhouse .... BRIG
landing point ...... BEACHHEAD
meal .... MESS, K-RATION
messenger .... ESTAFET
movement .... MARCH,
MANEUVER, DEPLOYMENT
music .... TAPS
officer .... BRASSHAT
operations .... WARFARE
police .... MP, REDCAP
post ..... BASE, FORT, STATION,
GARRISON, PRESIDIO
prisoner .... POW
rank, temporary .... BREVET
roll .... MUSTER
salute .... SALVO
school site .... ANNAPOLIS,
WEST POINT
signal for parley/retreat
.... CHAMADE
station .... GARRISON
store .... PX, CANTEEN,
(POST)EXCHANGE
storehouse .... DEPOT, ETAPE,
ARMORY, ARSENAL, MAGAZINE
student .... CADET, PLEBE
supplies .... MUNITIONS
truck .... AMTRAC, CAMION,
CARRIER
unit .... CADRE, SQUAD,
COMPANY, PLATOON
weapons .... ORDNANCE
militate .... OPERATE, FUNCTION
militia .... RESERVES, SOLDIERY,
(CITIZEN)ARMY
member .... RESERVIST
milk .... LAC, SUCK, BLEED,
EXTRACT, LACTOSE,
EMULSION
animal's .... K(O)UMISS
beverage .... SHAKE
coagulated part .... CURD
coagulating enzyme
.... RENNIN
combining form .... LACT(O)
constituent .... CASEIN
curd .... CASEIN
curdler .... RENNET, RENNIN
farm .... DAIRY, LACTARY
fermented .... K(O)UMISS
food from .... YOG(H)URT
from .... LACTIC
giving .... MILCH
gland .... MAMMA
kind of .... SKIM, FRESH,
CONDENSED, EVAPORATED
like .... LACTEOUS
not giving .... YELD

of magnesia .... LAXATIVE
part of .... CURD, WHEY,
SERUM, CASEIN, PLASMA,
LECITHIN
pertaining to .... LACTIC,
LACTARY, LACTEAL
product, cultured ...... YOGURT
protein .... CASEIN
secrete .... LACTATE
separator .... CENTRIFUGE
shake .... FRAPPE
sickness .... SHAKES
sour .... CURD, CLABBER
source .... COW, GOAT,
COCONUT, COCOANUT
store .... DAIRY
teeth .... FIRST TEETH
with .... AU LAIT
milker's seat .... STOOL
milkfish .... AWA, SABALO,
TARPON
milkless .... YELD
milksop .... SISSY, MOLLYCODDLE
milkweed .... SOMA, SPURGE,
ANGLEPOD, STAPELIA
juice .... LATEX
milkwort .... SENEGA
milky .... LACTEAL, LACTEOUS
liquid .... LATEX
Milky Way .... GALAXY
area .... COALSACK
of the .... GALACTIC
shape .... SPIRAL
mill .... FACTORY, GRIND(ER)
dam .... WEIR
hand .... MANO, QUERN
owner's fee .... MULTURE
Millay, Edna _____ .... ST.
VINCENT
millenium .... GOLDEN AGE
millepore .... CORAL
miller .... MOTH
fee of .... MULTURE
who dances .... ANN
Miller's salesman .... LOMAN
millet ...... DURRA, GRAIN, GRASS,
HIRSE, PEARL, DOURA(H)
sorghum-like .... MILO
milliard .... BILLION
milliner .... HATTER
millinery .... HATS, HEADDRESSES
worker .... FACER
milling charge .... TOLL,
MULTURE, THIRLAGE
refuse .... TAILING
millimeter, 1/1,000 of a
.... MICRON, MIKRON
million electron volts .... MEV
hardest to earn .... FIRST
times: comb. form .... MEGA

ton explosive force
.... MEGATON
millions of years .... EON
millipede .... MYRIAPOD,
WIREWORM, ARTHROPOD
it has plenty of .... LEGS
millpond .... DAM, DIKE
Mills bomb .... GRENADE
millstone .... BUHR, BURDEN
part .... INK, RYND
Milne character .... PIM
readers .... CHILDREN
Milo .... MELOS, SORGHUM
milord .... NOBLEMAN
Milquetoast .... CASPAR
creator of .... WEBSTER
milt .... ROE, SPLEEN
mime ...... APERY, CLOWN, MIMIC,
JESTER, BUFFOON, IMITATE
mimeograph .... STENCIL,
DUPLICATE
mimesis .... IMITATION
mimetic .... APISH, IMITATIVE
mimic .... APE(Y), COPY, MIME,
MOCK, IMITATE, IMITATIVE,
SIMULATE(D)
female .... MIMA
mimicking .... APERY
mimicry ...... MIMESIS, IMITATION
mimosa .... HERB, SHRUB,
ACACIA, SOAPBARK
descriptive word for
.... SHRINKING
mina .... STARLING
minaret .... TOWER
caller from a .... MUEZZIN
place of .... MOSQUE
mince .... CHOP, DICE, HASH
minced meat .... RISSOLE
oath .... GAD, GEE, DRAT,
EGAD, HECK
mincing bite .... NIBBLE
mind .... CARE, HEED, MOOD,
NOUS, OBEY, TEND, BELIEF,
PSYCHE, REASON, OPINION,
MENTALITY, LOOK AFTER
bear in .... REMEMBER
-boggling ...... BREATH-TAKING
call to .... RECALL, RECOLLECT
drug .... LSD, SEDATIVE,
MESCALINE, AMPHETAMINE
of the .... MENTAL, PHRENIC
part of the .... ID, EGO,
SUPEREGO
to-mind communication
.... TELEPATHY
Mindanao bay .... MAYO,
BUTUAN, ILIGAN, ILLANA,
LANUZA, LIANGA, PUJADA,
MACAJALAR
city .... DAVAO, BUTUAN,

ILIGAN, OROQUIETA, ZAMBOANGA, CAGAYAN DE ORO

gulf .... MORO, DAVAO

inhabitant .... MOSLEM, MUSLIM

lake .... LANAO, MAINIT

province .... DAVAO, LANAO, AGUSAN, SURIGAO, BUKIDNON, COTABATO, ZAMBOANGA

river .... AGUSAN, PULANGI

volcano .... APO, RAGANG

mindful .... ALERT, AWARE, CAREFUL, CAUTIOUS

mindless .... DUMB, HEEDLESS

followers .... SHEEP

one .... IDIOT

mine .... DIG, PIT, SOURCE, TUNNEL, EXCAVATE, EXPLOSIVE

arch .... OVERCAST

car .... TRAM, HUTCH

ceiling .... ASTEL

channel .... TAILRACE

claim .... STAKE

entrance/access .... ADIT

excavation .... STOPE

gas .... DAMP, MEPHITIS

kind of .... COAL, GOLD, NICKEL, SILVER, DIAMOND

layer .... SAPPER

partition .... SOLLAR

passage .... STULM, WINZE

pit/pool .... SUMP, STOPE, ARROYO

prop .... NOG, SPRAG, STULL

refuse/waste .... ATTLE, MULLOCK, TAILING

remover .... SWEEPER

rich .... BONANZA

shaft .... WINZE, ARROYO, DOWNCAST

sieve .... JIG(GER)

step .... LOB

thrower .... MORTAR

timber .... STULL

truck .... CORF, HUTCH

tunnel .... ADIT, STOPE

vein .... LODE

wall .... ASTEL

winch .... WHIM

Mineo, ——— .... SAL

miner .... PITMAN, SAPPER, COLLIER, DRILLER, EXCAVATOR, GOLDDIGGER

disease of .... SILICOSIS

safety lamp of .... DAVY

mineral .... ORE, TALC, SPALT, TOPAZ, TRONA, BARITE, GYPSUM, PINITE, PYRITE, QUARTZ, SPINEL, APATITE,

CALCITE, DIAMOND, EPIDOTE, LEUCITE, URALITE, SERPENTINE

black .... COAL, GRAPHITE

black crystalline .... SPINEL(LE)

blue .... IOLITE, LAZULITE

concretion .... CALCULUS

crystalline .... MICA, SPAR, FELDSPAR

deposit .... BED, LODE, VEIN, PLACER, SINTER

essential to health .... IRON, ZINC, SODIUM, CALCIUM, MAGNESIUM, POTASSIUM, PHOSPOROUS

glassy .... SILICA

hardest .... DIAMOND

in quartz .... SILICA

jelly .... VASELINE, PETROLEUM

luster of .... SCHILLER

lustrous .... SPAR, RUTILE

mixture .... MAGMA

oil .... KEROSENE

radioactive .... CARNOTITE

salt .... ALUM

softest/soapy .... TALC

spot in a .... MACLE

spring .... SPA

water .... VICHY, SELTZER

wax .... OZOCERITE

worthless .... GANGUE

miners' group .... MFD, UMW

Minerva .... ATHENA, AZALEA, GODDESS

shield of .... (A)EGIS

minestrone .... SOUP, TUREEN

minesweeper .... TRAWLER, PARAVANE

Ming .... PORCELAIN

mingle .... MIX, JOIN, MELL, BLEND, ASSOCIATE

as vapor .... COALESCE

mini .... MINIMAL, MINISCULE, VERY SHORT, VERY SMALL

swallow .... SIP

miniature .... MODEL, SMALL, PORTRAIT, DIMINUTIVE

aquarium .... BOWL, TANK

garden .... TERRARIUM

tree .... BONSAI

minify .... REDUCE

opposed to .... MAGNIFY

minikin .... DOLL, PEEWEE, DARLING, SNIPPET

minim .... DASH, DROP, TINIEST, SMALLEST

in music .... HALF NOTE

minimal .... LEAST

minimize .... LESSEN

minimum .... LEAST, LOWEST,

SMALLEST

as a .... NO LESS

mining bar/chisel .... GAD

basket .... CORF

bed of ore .... REEF

claim .... STAKE

kind of .... PLACER

nail .... SPAD

trough .... HUTCH

minion .... TYPE, FAVORITE, FOLLOWER, MISTRESS

of the law .... POLICEMAN

minister .... CATER, SERVE, CURATE, (AT)TEND, PASTOR, VIZIER, CLERGYMAN

assistant of .... DEACON

home of .... MANSE, RECTORY, PARSONAGE

title of .... REVEREND

ministry .... CLERGY, PULPIT

admit to the .... ORDAIN

miniver .... FUR, ERMINE

mink .... FUR, MAMMAL

kin of .... OTTER, SKUNK

Minnehaha's love .... HIAWATHA

minnesinger .... MINSTREL

Minnesota bay .... MUSKEG

capital .... ST. PAUL

city/town .... ADA, ELY, MORA, ANOKA, AUSTIN, BLAINE, DULUTH, WADENA, WILMAR, WINONA, FRIDLEY, HIBBING, HOPKINS, MANKATO, RED WING, BRAINERD, FAIRMONT, MOORHEAD, ROCHESTER, TWIN LAKES, ALEXANDRIA, COON RAPIDS, MINNETONKA, MINNEAPOLIS

county ...... CASS, CLAY, LAKE, LYON, POLK, RICE, ANOKA, MOWER, CARVER, DAKOTA, ITASCA, RAMSEY, WINONA, WRIGHT, GOODHUE, OLMSTEAD, STEARNS, FREEBORN, HENNEPIN, KANDIYOHI, OTTER TAIL, SAINT LOUIS

lake .... MUD, RED, CASS, DEER, GULL, LONG, NETT, RENO, RICE, EMILY, HERON, LEECH, RAINY, TROUT, WOODS, ITASCA, SUPERIOR

mountain .... EAGLE

native .... GOPHER

river .... MUD, RUM, COBB, CROW, HILL, LEAF, PIKE, ROCK, ROOT, CEDAR, MAPLE, SAUK, RAPID, SHELL, SNAKE, ZUMBRO, PELICAN, MUSTINKA, PARTRIDGE, WHITEFACE, MISSISSIPPI state bird .... LOON

state flower .... SHOWY LADY SLIPPER

state nickname .... GOPHER, NORTH STAR

tourist site ...... BELL MUSEUM, ZOOLOGICAL GARDEN

university .... HAMLINE, MANKATO STATE, MOORHEAD STATE

minnow .... MINNY, SHINER, GUDGEON, MOONFISH

minor .... PETTY, YOUTH, LESS(ER), INFERIOR, UNDER-AGE

details .... MINUTIAE

in law .... PETIT, PUPIL

offense .... MISDEMEANOR

suit .... CLUBS, DIAMONDS

Minorca .... ISLAND, CHICKEN

sister island .... MAJORCA

minoress .... CLARE

Minorite ...... FRIAR, FRANCISCAN

minority .... NONAGE, PUPILAGE

group's persecution .... POGROM

Minos' co-judge .... AEACUS

daughter .... ARIADNE

kingdom .... CRETE

monster .... MINOTAUR

parent .... ZEUS, EUROPA

structure .... LABYRINTH

wife .... PASIPHAE

Minotaur's dwelling .... LABYRINTH

killer .... THESEUS

minster ...... CHURCH, CATHEDRAL

minstrel .... BARD, RIMER, SKALD, MUSICIAN, TROUBADOUR, (MINNE)SINGER

musical instrument ...... HARP, LUTE

show end man .... BONES

wandering .... GLEEMAN, GOLIARD, JONGLEUR

mint .... COIN, HERB, SAGE, BASIL, CANDY, CLARY, PLANT, STAMP, THYME, CATNIP, HYSSOP, INVENT, SAVORY, DITTANY, MONARDA, OREGANO, MARJORAM, FABRICATE

charge .... BRASSAGE

drink .... JULEP

genus .... MENTHA

product .... COIN(S), SPECIE

mintage .... COINAGE

minuet .... DANCE

Minuit's bargain .... MANHATTAN

minus .... LESS, WITHOUT, NEGATIVE

minuscule .... DROP, TINY, SMALL, MINUTE

minute .... WEE, NOTE, TINY, PETTY, SMALL, MOMENT, INSTANT, MINUSCULE

combining form .... MICRO

distinction .... NICETY

organism .... GERM, AM(O)EBA, MICROBE

orifice .... PORE, STOMA

quantity .... MITE

minutiae .... TRIVIA, DETAILS

minutes .... ACTA, RECORD

15 .... QUARTER

minx .... GIRL, JADE, TART, HUSSY, MALAPERT

play the .... FLIRT

miracle .... MARVEL, WONDER

bread/food .... MANNA

scene of .... CANA, LOURDES

worker .... THAUMATURGE

miraculous .... MARVELOUS, WONDERFUL, SUPERNATURAL

mirage .... VISION, DELUSION, ILLUSION

in Arabia .... SERAB

mire ...... BOG, MUD, MUCK, OOZE, EMBOG, SLUSH

Miriam's brother .... AARON, MOSES

mirror .... CRYSTAL, REFLECT(OR), (LOOKING)GLASS

tinfoil of .... TAIN

mirth ...... GLEE, GAIETY, JOLLITY, HILARITY, MERRIMENT

provoker .... SCREAM

miry .... OOZY, BOGGY, MUDDY

misadventure .... MISHAP, BAD LUCK, ACCIDENT

misalliance .... MISMATCH

misanthrope .... (MAN)HATER

of sorts .... CYNIC, LONER

misbegotten .... BASTARD

misbehavior .... MISCONDUCT

miscalculate .... ERR, GOOF, MISJUDGE

miscarriage .... ABORTION

miscarry .... FAIL, ABORT

miscellanea .... ANA, MISCELLANY

miscellaneous .... MIXED, VARIED, SUNDRY, ASSORTED

miscellany .... ANA, OLIO, MEDLEY, MELANGE, MIXTURE, POTPOURRI, ODDS AND ENDS

mischief .... HOB, DIDO, HARM, PRANK, TRICK, INJURY, TROUBLE, DEVILTRY

maker .... IMP, ERIS, LOKI, PEST, PUCK, DEVIL, SCAMP, PLOTTER, INTRIGUER, PRANKSTER

mischievous .... PESKY, IMPISH, NAUGHTY, PUCKISH, ROGUISH, DEVILISH, PRANKISH

misconduct .... IMPROPRIETY

miscreant .... INFIDEL, HERETIC, VILLAIN, CRIMINAL

miscue .... ERROR, MISTAKE

misdeed .... SIN, CRIME, FAULT

misdemeanor .... CRIME, DELICT, OFFENSE, INFRACTION, MISCONDUCT

misdoing .... ERRING

mise .... PACT, AGREEMENT

miser .... HUNKS, WRETCH, HOARDER, NIGGARD, TIGHTWAD, SKINFLINT

of fiction .... MARNER, SCROOGE

miserable .... MEAN, ABJECT, PALTRY, FORLORN, PITIABLE, WRETCHED

misericord .... DAGGER

miserly .... TIGHT, GREEDY, SORDID, STINGY, CRIPPLE, NIGGARDLY, PENURIOUS

person .... NIGGARD, TIGHTWAD, SKINFLINT

misery .... WOE, PAIN, AGONY, DOLOR, GRIEF, DISTRESS

misfire .... FAIL, FIZZLE

misfortune .... WOE, MISHAP, CALAMITY, ADVERSITY

misgiving .... FEAR, DOUBT, QUALM, SCRUPLE, PREMONITION

misguided .... MISLED

mishandle ...... ABUSE, MALTREAT

mishap ...... BAD LUCK, ACCIDENT

on Broadway .... FLOP

mishmash .... MESS, OLIO, JUMBLE, FARRAGO, MELANGE, HODGEPODGE

Mishnah .... TALMUD, TEACHINGS

section .... ABOT

misinform .... MISLEAD, MISDIRECT

misjudge .... ERR, MISDEEM

mislay .... LOSE, MISPLACE

misle .... MIST, MIZZLE, DRIZZLE

mislead .... DELUDE, DECEIVE

misleading appearance .... FACADE

clue .... RED HERRING

mismanage .... BOTCH, BUNGLE

mismatch .... MISFIT, MISALLIANCE

misogynist .... WOMAN-HATER

misplace .... LOSE, MISLAY, DERANGE

misrepresent .... (BE)LIE, COLOR, GARBLE, DISTORT

miss .... GIRL, LADY, LOSE, NEED, OMIT, SKIP, WANT, AVOID, ESCAPE, MISLAY, OVERLOOK

a catch .... MUFF
archaic .... SPINSTER
contrary .... MARI
intentionally .... BALK
the bus .... FAIL

Miss America, first: 1921 .... MARGARET GORMAN

America pageant emcee .... BERT PARKS
Bagnold .... ENID
Barrett, Hollywood's .... RONA
_____: Bleak House character .... FLITE
Bryant .... ANITA
Cantrell .... LANA
Cilento .... DIANE
Claire .... INA
Davis .... BETTE
Diller .... PHYLLIS
Dinsmore .... ELSIE
D'Urberville .... TESS
Gam .... RITA
Garson .... GREER
Hagen .... UTA
Haver .... JUNE
Hayworth .... RITA
Horne .... LENA
Kett .... ETTA
Le Gallienne .... EVA
Lollobrigida .... GINA
Loren .... SOPHIA
Lupino .... IDA
Miles .... VERA
Moreno .... RITA
Munson .... ONA
O'Grady .... ROSIE
Oyl .... OLIVE
Piggy's cry .... MOI
Reese .... DELLA
St. John .... JILL
Street .... DELLA
Taylor .... ELIZABETH
Verdugo .... ELENA
West .... MAE
Woodhouse .... EMMA

Missa Solemnis composer .... BEETHOVEN

missal .... PRAYERBOOK
missel .... THRUSH
misshape ...... DEFORM, CONTORT, DISTORT
missile .... BOLT, DART, MIRV, ARROW, LANCE, SHAFT, SHELL, SPEAR, BULLET, ROCKET, GRENADE, PROJECTILE, TRAJECTILE

acronym .... ABM, ASM, SAM, SSM, ICBM, IRBM, XAAM
anti-missile .... PATRIOT
anti-ship .... EXOCET
detecting device .... RADAR
guided .... SAM, IRBM, NIKE, SCUD, TALOS, ROCKET
launching .... BLAST OFF
part of .... WARHEAD
pit/housing .... SILO
tip of .... WARNOSE
type .... BALLISTIC
whaler's .... HARPOON

missing .... LOST, ABSENT, LACKING, OMITTED
link? .... APEMAN

mission .... TASK, ERRAND, CALLING, EMBASSY
to remember .... ALAMO

missionary .... APOSTLE, EVANGELIST

Mississippi capital .... JACKSON
city/town .... PEARL, YAZOO, BILOXI, LAUREL, TUPELO, GRENADA, NATCHEZ, COLUMBUS, GULFPORT, MERIDIAN, VICKSBURG, PASCAGOULA, HATTIESBURG
college .... BELHAVEN, MILLSAPS
county .... LEE, CLAY, PIKE, ADAMS, HINDS, JONES, LAMAR, YAZOO, ALCORN, DE SOTO, MONROE, RANKIN, WARREN, COAHOMA, FORREST, JACKSON, LEFLORE, LINCOLN, LOWNDES, MADISON, LAFAYETTE, SUNFLOWER
explorer ...... JOLIET, HENNEPIN
Indian .... TIOU, BILOXI
island .... CAT, HORN
lake .... ENID, SARDIS, TCHULA, PICKWICK
mountain .... WOODALL
river .... LEAF, WOLF, AMITE, PEARL, SKUNA, YAZOO, STRONG, NOXUBEE, MISSISSIPPI, YOCKANOOKANY
state bird .... MOCKINGBIRD
state flower .... MAGNOLIA
state nickname .... BAYOU, MAGNOLIA
steamboater .... RIVERMAN
tourist site .... GOVERNOR'S MANSION, OLD CAPITOL MUSEUM
university ...... JACKSON STATE
U.S. Air Force Base .... KESSLER, COLUMBUS

U.S. Naval Air Station .... MERIDIAN

Mississippian, any .... TADPOLE
missive .... LETTER, MESSAGE
Missouri capital .... JEFFERSON CITY
caverns .... MERAMEC
city/town .... AVA, LAMAR, MACON, MILAN, FULTON, JOPLIN, KANSAS, WARSAW, CLINTON, MEMPHIS, RAYTOWN, SEDALIA, CARTHAGE, HANNIBAL, CRESTWOOD, GLADSTONE, FLORISSANT, SAINT LOUIS, SPRINGFIELD, INDEPENDENCE
college .... AVILA, DRURY, LOGAN, TARKIO, COLUMBIA, ROCKHURST, FONTBONNE, MARYVILLE
county .... RAY, CASS, CLAY, COLE, DADE, HOLT, IRON, KNOX, LINN, PIKE, POLK, ADAIR, BOONE, SCOTT, TEXAS, BUTLER, GREENE, JASPER, MARION, MILLER, NEWTON, PETTIS, PHELPS, PLATTE, DUNKLIN, JACKSON
guerrilla .... JAWHAWKER
lake .... OZARKS, NORFOLK, TANEYCOMO, WAPPAPELLO
mountain .... TAUM SAUK
notable .... TRUMAN, PERSHING
plateau .... OZARK
river .... KAW, SAC, GRAND, OSAGE, PLATTE, MERAMEC, MISSOURI, MISSISSIPPI
state bird .... BLUEBIRD
state flower .... HAWTHORN
state nickname .... SHOW ME
state tree .... DOGWOOD
tourist attraction .... RIVERBOATS, WORLDS OF FUN, BOTANICAL GARDEN, MARK TWAIN MUSEUM
tributary .... PLATTE
university .... LINCOLN, ST. LOUIS, WASHINGTON
U.S. Air Force Base .... WHITEMAN, RICHARDS GEBAUR

misspelling .... CACOGRAPHY
misspend ...... WASTE, SQUANDER
misstep .... SLIP, TRIP, ERROR, FAUX PAS
missy: colloq. .... GIRL
mist .... FOG, HAZE, SMOG, BRUME, GAUZE, MISLE, VAPOR, SEREIN
rain like .... DRIZZLE

mistake .... SLIP, TRIP, BONER,

ERROR, FAULT, LAPSE, MISCUE, BLUNDER, OMISSION, SOLECISM
in conduct .... FAUX PAS
in printing .... ERRATUM
mistaken .... WRONG, ERRONEOUS, INCORRECT
mister .... SIR, HERR, SENOR, SIGNOR, MONSIEUR
mistle thrush .... MAVIS
mistral .... WIND
Mistral, poet .... FREDERIC
mistreat .... ABUSE
mistress ...... MRS., MOLL, LEMAN, MADAM, MINION, MISSIS, MISSUS, PARAMOUR, INAMORATA
mistrial, one cause of
.... TECHNICALITY
mistrust .... DOUBT, SUSPICION
misty .... BRUMOUS, NEBULOUS
rain .... SEREIN, MIZZLE
misunderstanding .... ODDS, QUARREL, DISPARITY, IMBROGLIO
misuse .... ABUSE, WASTE, MISTREAT
of words .... MALAPROPISM
Mitchell (Helen) singer
.... MELBA, NELLIE
mite .... MOTE, TICK, ATOMY, ACARID, ACARUS, SPIDER
larva .... CHIGOE, JIGGER, LEPTUS, CHIGGER
miter .... TIARA, HEADBAND, BISHOPRIC, HEADDRESS
mitigate .... EASE, ALLAY, LESSEN, SOFTEN, TEMPER, ASSUAGE, MODERATE, EXTENUATE
mitosis, stage of .... ANAPHASE
mitt .... PAW, GLOVE
slang .... HAND
mitten .... GLOVE
mitzvah .... PRECEPT, BLESSING, COMMANDMENT
mix .... FUSE, STIR, ADDLE, BLEND, MERGE, JUMBLE, MINGLE, INFUSE, COMBINE, COALESCE
archaic .... MELL
dough .... KNEAD
up ...... FIGHT, SNAFU, GARBLE, TANGLE, EMBROIL, COMPOUND
with .... ASSOCIATE, (INTER)MINGLE
mixed, capable of being
.... MISCIBLE
language .... JARGON, PIDGIN
type .... PI
variety .... HYBRID, CROSS-BRED

mixer, drink ...... SODA, SHAKER, BARTENDER
mixing implement .... AGITATOR
mixture ...... HASH, OLIO, BLEND, AMALGAM, FARRAGO, MELANGE, COMPOUND, (MISH)MASH, POTPOURRI, HODGEPODGE
flour, milk, etc. .... BATTER
musical .... MEDLEY
Mizar .... ALCOR
Mize, ballplayer .... BIG JAWN
mizzen .... SAIL
mizzle .... RAIN, DRIZZLE
Mme. Bovary .... EMMA
Chian Kai-shek, nee
.... SOONG
mnemonic routine .... ROTE
subject .... MEMORY
Mnemosyne's daughter(s)
.... MUSE(S)
concern .... MEMORY
moa .... RATITE
relative .... KIWI, APTERYX
Moab .... KINGDOM
father of .... LOT
giant .... EMIM, ZUZIM
king .... MESHA
mountain .... NEBO
Moabite stone, name on
.... AMRI
moan .... (BE)WAIL, LAMENT, BELLYACHE
moat .... DITCH, FOSS(E)
structure surrounded by
.... CASTLE
mob ...... GANG, CROWD, BOODLE, RABBLE, THRONG, CANAILLE, HOI POLLOI, RIFFRAFF
scene .... RIOT
mobile .... FREE, LOOSE, MOVABLE, FLEXIBLE
hospital .... AMBULANCE
mobilize .... MUSTER, ORGANIZE
mobster .... GOON, PUNK, GANGSTER, RACKETEER
girl .... MOLL
Moby Dick .... PELEG, WHALE
author of .... MELVILLE
foe/hunter of .... AHAB
moccasin .... PAC, SNAKE, FLOWER, LOAFER, SLIPPER, LARRIGAN
mocha .... COFFEE, LEATHER
mochila .... KNAPSACK
mock ...... APE, DEFY, FAKE, GIBE, JAPE, JEER, JEST, JIBE, TWIT, FLEER, FLOUT, MIMIC, SCOFF, SNEER, TAUNT, DERIDE, IMITATE, RIDICULE
attack .... FEINT

orange .... SHRUB, SERINGA, SYRINGA
sea battle .... NAUMACHY
sun .... PARHELION
up ...... COPY, DUMMY, MODEL, REPLICA
mocker .... MIME, MIMIC, DERIDER
mockery ...... JOKE, SHAM, FARCE, DERISION, TRAVESTY, BURLESQUE
mod .... TRENDY
modal .... CONDITIONAL
mode .... FAD, WAY, STYLE, VOGUE, METHOD, FASHION
model .... COPY, POSE, TYPE, DESIGN, MOCK-UP, SIT(TER), EXAMPLE, MANIKIN, PATTERN, EXEMPLAR, PARADIGM, STANDARD
artist's .... NUDE
of a planned building
.... MAQUETTE
of perfection .... IDEAL, PARAGON
original .... ARCHETYPE, PROTOTYPE
small .... MINIATURE
Model T .... TIN LIZZIE
moderate .... DRY, MILD, (A)BATE, SOBER, TEMPER, ABSTAIN, LENIENT, PRESIDE, MITIGATE, RESTRAIN
in music .... MEZZO
in politics .... MIDDLE-OF-THE-ROAD
moderation .... SOBRIETY, TEMPERANCE, SELF-CONTROL
modern ...... NEO, NEW, LATE(ST), RECENT, UP-TO-DATE
city sight .... SKYSCRAPER, TRAFFIC JAM
person .... NEOTERIC
Modernismo's Ruben .... DARIO
modernist .... NEO
modernize ...... RETOOL, UPDATE, RENOVATE
modest .... COY, SHY, LOWLY, TIMID, DECENT, DEMURE, FRUGAL, HUMBLE, SIMPLE, BASHFUL, RESERVED
modicum .... BIT, DAB
modifier ...... ADVERB, ADJECTIVE
modify .... VARY, ALTER, AMEND, LIMIT, CHANGE, QUALIFY
modish .... CHIC, SMART, DRESSY, STYLISH, FASHIONABLE
modiste .... COUTURIER, DRESSMAKER
modulate .... ADAPT, ADJUST, ATTUNE, (IN)TONE
modulation .... CADENCE

module .... UNIT
modus operandi ...... PROCEDURE
   vivendi .... COMPROMISE
Moffo, singer .... ANNA
mogul .... RULER, AUTOCRAT,
                  LOCOMOTIVE
   slang .... VIP, BIGWIG
Mogul ...... NABOB, MONGOL(IAN)
   emperor .... AKBAR, BABAR,
         BABER, BABUR, JEHAN,
                 HUMAYUN
   ruler .... NAWAB
mohair .... FABRIC, MOREEN
   source of .... ANGORA
Mohammed .... MAHOMET,
       MAHOUND, PROPHET
   birthplace of .... MECCA
   burial place of .... MEDINA
   daughter of .... FATIMA
   descendant of .... SEID, SAYID,
                  SHERIF
   flight of .... HEGIRA, HEJIRA
   follower of .... ISLAM,
         MOSLEM, MUSLIM
   opus .... KORAN
   religion founded by
     .... ISLAM, MOSLEM
   sister of .... JINNAH
   son-in-law .... ALI
   successor of .... CALIF,
        CALIPH, K(H)ALIF
   wife of ...... AISHA, AYESHA(H)
Mohammedan .... ISLAMIC,
               ISLAMITE
   angel .... AZRAIL
   beggar/ascetic .... FAKIR
   bible .... KORAN, ALCORAN
   bier .... TABUT
   blacksmith .... LOHAR
   call to prayer ..... ADAN, AZAN
   canonical law .... SHARIA
   cup .... LOTAH
   demon .... JENNI(E)
   devil .... EBLIS, SHAITAN,
                SHEITAN
   fasting period .... ASHURA,
              RAMADAN
   festival .... BAIRAM
   god .... ALLAH
   hermit/monk .... SANTON
   holy war .... JEHAD, JIHAD
   infidel .... KAFIR
   inn .... IMARET, CARAVANSARY
   judge/magistrate .... CADI
   law .... SUNNA(H)
   leader .... IMAM, MAHDI
   Malay .... MORO
   messiah .... MAHDI
   month .... RABIA, RAJAB,
       SAFAR, JUMADA, SHABAN,
              RAMADAN

mystic .... SUFI, SUNNITE
mysticism .... SUFISM
noble ...... AMIR, EMIR, AMEER,
         EMEER, SHERIF
nymph .... HOURI
orthodox .... SUNNITE
prayer hour .... AZAN
priest .... IMAM
prince's title .... NAWAB
principle .... IJMA
religion .... ISLAM
ruler .... AMIR, AMEER,
        CALIPH, SULTAN
ruler's decree .... IRADE
saint .... PIR
salutation .... SALAAM
scholars .... ULEMA
sect member ...... SUFI, SHIAH,
      SHIITE, SUNNITE
shrine .... KAABA
slave .... MAMELUKE
teacher .... MOLLAH, MULLA(H)
title .... AGA, AMIR, EMIR,
     EMEER, NAWAB, CALIPH,
              SAY(Y)ID
unbeliever .... KAF(F)IR
uncle .... ABBAS
veil .... YASHMAC, YASHMAK
woman's clothing .... ISAR
Mohave .... YUMA(N)
Mohawk .... RIVER, INDIAN
   chief .... BRANT, HIAWATHA
   city on the .... UTICA
mohur, ¹/₁₅ of .... RUPEE
moiety .... CLAN, HALF, PART,
       SHARE, PORTION
moil .... DRUDGE(RY), COMMOTION
   and _____ .... TOIL
moire .... SILK, TABBY, FABRIC,
            TAFFETA
moist .... WET, DAMP, DANK,
      DEWY, HUMID, RORIC
   to the touch .... CLAMMY
moisten .... WET, SOAK, WASH,
   (BE)DEW, WATER, DAMPEN,
       SPONGE, SPLASH
   and rub with oil
      .... EMBROCATE
   as flax .... RET
moisture .... WETNESS, DAMPNESS
   combining form ...... HYGR(O)
   condensed .... DEW, FOG, MIST
moke .... NAG, DOLT, IDIOT,
             DONKEY
molar .... TOOTH, CHOPPER,
             GRINDER
molasses .... SYRUP, TREACLE
   beverage .... RUM, TAFIA,
             ARRACK
   candy .... TAFFY, TOFFEE
   source .... SORGO

molave .... TREE, WOOD, VITEX
mold .... CAST, COPY, FORM,
   MUST, DECAY, KNEAD, SHAPE,
   FUNGUS, MATRIX, MILDEW,
             MOULAGE
   core .... NOWEL
   opening for molten metal
   .... GIT, GEAT, SPRUE
   product .... CASTING
Moldavia, capital of .... KISHINEV
   town .... JASSY
molder .... DIE, DECAY, STAMP
molding .... CYMA, CONGE,
   BORDER, EDGING, FILLET,
       REGLET, TRINGLE
   building's .... CORNICE
   concave .... COVE, COVING,
             SCOTIA
   convex .... OVOLO, TORUS,
      REEDING, BAGUET(TE)
   curved .... NEBULE
   edge .... ARRIS
   egg-shaped .... OVOLO
   material .... ORMOLU
   ogee .... TALON
   rounded .... REED, TORUS
   S-shaped .... OGEE
   square .... LISTEL
   wall .... CORNICE
moldy .... HOAR, FUSTY, MUCID,
           MUSTY, STALE
mole .... NOSE, PIER, QUAY, STAR,
   JUTTY, TAUPE, N(A)EVUS,
   HARBOR, MAMMAL, FRECKLE,
      LENTIGO, PLATYPUS
   animal resembling
   .... DESMAN
molecular film .... MONOLAYER
   makeup .... ATOMS
molecule .... PARTICLE
   component ..... ATOM, (AN)ION
   genetic .... DNA
molehill .... TRIFLE, ANTHILL
molest .... VEX, HARM, ABUSE,
   ANNOY, HARASS, INJURE,
   PESTER, DISTURB, TROUBLE
Moliere character ...... ALCESTE,
           TARTUF(FE)
Moll Flanders author .... DEFOE
mollifier, baby's .... THUMB,
   SUCKER, RATTLE(R), PACIFIER
mollify ...... CALM, TAME, PACIFY,
   SOFTEN, SOOTHE, APPEASE,
           PLACATE
moll's friend .... GOON,
   MOBSTER, GANGSTER
mollusca .... SLUG
mollusk ...... CLAM, SLUG, HELIX,
   MUREX, SNAIL, SQUID,
   WHELK, CHITON, COCKLE,
   LIMPET, MUSSEL, OYSTER,

TRITON, ABALONE, OCTOPUS, SCALLOP, NAUTILUS, RETEPORE

beaked .... SQUID, OCTOPUS, CUTTLEFISH

bivalve .... CLAM, CHAMA, MUSSEL, PIDDOCK

borer .... TEREDO, SHIPWORM

cephalopod .... NAUTILUS

egg(s) of .... OOTHECA

genus .... MUREX, OLIVA

gills .... CERATA

product .... PEARL

shell .... CONCH, COWRY, COWRIE

spiral-shaped .... SNAIL

study of .... CONCHOLOGY

sucking organ .... PROBOSCIS

teeth .... RADULA

tentacled ...... SQUID, OCTOPUS

two-gilled .... SPIRULA

molly .... FISH

where seen usually .... AQUARIUM

mollycoddle .... PET, SPOIL, PAMPER, MILKSOP

Molnar, dramatist .... FERENC

work .... LILIOM

Moloch .... GOD, LIZARD

sacrificial site .... TOPHET

Molotov .... PERM

cocktail .... BOMB, GRENADE

molt ...... MEW, SHED, CAST(OFF), EXUVIA(T)E, SLOUGH(OFF)

molten .... FUSED, MELTED, LIQUEFIED

discharge .... LAVA

rock .... LAVA, MAGMA

waste .... SCUM, DROSS, SPRUE, SCORIA

Molucca island .... BANDA, CERAM, GILOLO, SERANG, TERNATE

moly .... GARLIC

mom .... MOTHER

title of .... MRS

moment .... SEC, TICK, JIFF(Y), FLASH, POINT, TRICE, INSTANT, IMPORT(ANCE)

of truth .... CRISIS

momentarily ...... SOON, SHORTLY

momentous .... HISTORIC, SOLEMN, NOTABLE

momentum .... FORCE, SPEED, THRUST, IMPETUS

Mona Lisa .... PORTRAIT, (LA)GIOCONDA

painter .... DA VINCI

smile of .... CRYPTIC, ENIGMATIC

Monaco's first Grimaldi .... LANFRANCO THE SPITEFUL

First Lady (deceased) .... PRINCESS GRACE

former ruling enclave .... GENOESE

language .... FRENCH

monarch .... RANIER

monetary unit .... FRANC

playground ...... MONTE CARLO

prince .... ALBERT

princess .... GRACE, CAROLINE, STEPHANIE

Princess Caroline's child .... ANDREA, PIERRE, CHARLOTTE

Princess Caroline's husband .... JUNOT, CASIRAGHI

ruling family .... GRIMALDI

monad .... ATOM, UNIT, ELEMENT, MICROCOSM

monarch .... REX, REY, ROI, CZAR, KING, SHAH, TSAR, RULER, KAISER, EMPEROR, BUTTERFLY, POTENTATE, SOVEREIGN

golden ball of .... MOUND

monarchist .... ROYALIST

monarchy, type of ...... CZARISM, LIMITED, TYRANNY, DESPOTISM, DICTATORSHIP, ABSOLUTISM

monarda .... BERGAMOT

monastery .... ABBEY, LAURA, FRIARY, PRIORY, CONVENT, HOSPICE, NUNNERY, CLOISTER, LAMASERY, HERMITAGE

church of .... MINSTER

dining hall .... FRATER

head of .... ABBOT, PRIOR, MANDRA, HEGUMEN

island .... IONA

resident .... MONK, CENOBITE

room .... CELL, LAVABO

monastic .... MONK, OBLATE, ASCETIC, MONACHAL

brother .... FRA

haircut .... TONSURE

monasticism .... MONKHOOD, FRIARHOOD

monde .... WORLD, SOCIETY

Monegasque land .... MONACO

Monet, painter .... CLAUDE

monetary ...... FISCAL, FINANCIAL, PECUNIARY

craving .... YEN

money ...... CASH, FUND(S), GOLD, BILLS, COIN(S), COWRY, LUCRE, SILVER, SPENSE, TENDER, CAPITAL, CURRENCY, BANKNOTES, FINANCIAL

CONSIDERATIONS

advance .... ARLES, EARNEST, IMPREST

assessed .... SCOT

at interest .... LOAN

bead .... PEAG(E), WAMPUN

box .... ARCA, KIST, TILL

bribe .... FUND, SOAP, SLUSH, GREASE

certificate .... BOND, SCRIP, TENDER

changer ...... SHROFF, CAMBIST

coin .... MINT

coined .... SPECIE

counterfeit .... SLUG

"dirty" .... FILTHY LUCRE

drawer for .... TILL

earnest .... ARLES, TOKEN, ADVANCE

exchange fee .... AGIO

fishhook .... LARI(N)

for political purposes ..... LUG

from public office .... PAP

handler .... TELLER, CASHIER

hoard .... DEPOSITORY

in reserve .... NEST EGG

in the bank .... ASSET

legalize as .... MONETIZE

lender .... USURER, SHYLOCK

make .... ENRICH, PROFIT

-making .... LUCRATIVE, PROFITABLE

market .... BOURSE

of account .... ORA

on hand .... CASH

player .... PRO

political patronage .... PAP

premium .... AGIO

ready .... CASH, FUND

receiver .... PAYEE

roll of .... WAD, ROULEAU

slang .... TIN, DUST, GELT, JACK, KALE, ROLL, BREAD, BEANS, BUCKS, CHIPS, DOUGH, MOOLA, SUGAR, BOODLE, BUNDLE, MAZUMA, SHEKEL, TENNER, WAMPUN, CABBAGE, LETTUCE, SCRATCH

small amount .... PITTANCE

stone .... FEI

substitute .... SCRIP, COUPON

temporary paper .... SCRIP

token .... ARLES, ADVANCE, EARNEST

tray .... TILL

voucher .... CHIT

moneybags .... 1000000AIRE, ZILLIONAIRE

moneyed .... RICH, OPULENT WEALTHY, AFFLUENT, WELL-TO-DO

slang .... LOADED
monger .... DEALER, TRADER
Mongol .... MOGUL, BURIAT,
    ELEUT(H), ESKIMO, INDIAN,
    TA(R)TAR, ASIATIC
conqueror .... TAMERLANE,
    TIMURLENK, GENGHIS(KHAN)
emperor .... KUBLAI KHAN
Mongolian .... KALMYK, TUNGUS,
    KALMUCK
capital ..... URGA, ULAN BATOR
conqueror .... KUBLAI,
    GENGHIS(KHAN)
desert .... GOBI, SHAMO
dynasty .... YUAN
lake .... NOR
monetary unit .... TUGRIK
monk .... LAMA
priest .... LAMA, SHAMAN
river .... TES
tent .... YURT
tribesman .... BURYAT
weight .... LAN
mongolism .... IDIOCY, DOWN'S
    SYNDROME
Mongoloid ...... LAI, LAPP, SHAN,
    TURK, DURBAN, SHAR(R)A
mongoos(e) .... URVA,
    ICHNEUMON
prey of .... RAT, COBRA,
    SNAKE
mongrel .... CUR, DOG, MUTT,
    TYKE, MIXED, STRAY, HYBRID
relative .... SURICATE
mongst .... MIDST
moni(c)ker .... (NICK)NAME
monition .... NOTICE, CAUTION,
    SUMMONS, WARNING
monitor .... CHECK, WATCH,
    CENSOR, LIZARD, WARSHIP,
    IRONCLAD, REMINDER,
    SUPERVISE
builder of the .... ERICSSON
foe of the .... MERRIMAC(K)
lizard .... URAN
skeptics' nickname of the
    .... ERICSSON'S FOLLY
monk .... FRA, ABBE, BEDE, LAMA,
    BONZE, FRIAR, PRIOR,
    SANTON, VOTARY, BROTHER,
    CALOYER, EREMITE, RECLUSE,
    CENOBITE, CAPUCHIN,
    TALAPOIN, CARMELITE
Buddhist .... BONZE, AR(A)HAT
cloak of .... COWL
ever silent .... TRAPPIST
habit .... FROCK
head .... ABBOT
head cover .... COWL, HOOD,
    AMICE, CAPOUCH, CAPUCHE
hermit .... ANCHORET

room of .... CELL
settlement .... SCETE
monkey .... APE, RAM, SAI, FOOL,
    MONA, TOTA, ZATI, JOCKO,
    MIMIC, HOWLER, LANGUR,
    NISNAS, RHESUS, SIMIAN,
    TRIFLE, VERVET, MACAQUE,
    PRIMATE, TAMARIN, TARSIER,
    CAPUCHIN, MARMOSET,
    TALAPOIN, WANDEROO
arboreal ...... SIME, TITI, TOTO,
    POTTO, GRIVET, TARSIER
astronaut .... BONNY
bearded .... ENTELLUS
bonnet .... SATI, TOQUE
bread .... TREE, FRUIT, BAOBAB
business .... MISCHIEF, HURDY-
    GURDY, FOOLISHNESS
capuchin .... SAI, SAPAJOU
crab-eating .... KRA
flower .... FIGWORT
green .... GRIVET, GUENON,
    VERVET
howling .... MONO, ARABA,
    STENTOR
nocturnal cousin of .... LEMUR
proboscis .... NOSEAPE
puzzle .... TREE, PINON
red .... PATAS
sacred .... RHESUS
space traveler .... BONNY,
    ASTROMONK
spider .... QUATA, ATELES
squirrel .... SAMIRI
suit .... JACKET, UNIFORM
tailless .... APE
wrench part .... JAW
monkeyshine .... DIDO, JOKE,
    PRANK, MISCHIEF
monkish .... MONASTIC
title .... DOM
monkshood .... ATIS, ATEES,
    ACONITE, WOLFSBANE
monocle .... LORGNON, EYEGLASS
monogram .... CIPHER, INITIALS
monograph .... ESSAY, PAPER,
    MEMOIR, THESIS, TREATISE
monolith .... COLUMN, DOLMEN,
    MENHIR, PILLAR, OBELISK
inscribed .... STELE
monologue .... SOLILOQUY
monologuist .... ENTERTAINER,
    SOLILOQUIST
monomania .... CRAZE,
    OBSESSION
monopolize .... CORNER, ENGROSS
monopoly .... POOL, TRUST,
    CARTEL, CORNERING,
    SYNDICATE
grant .... PATENT
maneuver .... COEMPTION

monosaccharide .... OSE, SUGAR,
    GLUCOSE, PENTOSE
monoski .... SLED
monosodium glutamate .... MSG,
    AJINOMOTO
monotone .... DRONE
monotonous .... DRAB, FLAT,
    DREARY, HUMDRUM, TEDIOUS,
    SINGSONG
routine .... RUT
talk .... DRONE
monotony .... TEDIUM
Monroe _____ .... DOCTRINE
actress .... MARILYN
poet .... HARRIET
mons _____ .... PUBIS, VENERIS
Mon's language .... PEGU
monsieur .... MR, SIR, MISTER,
    (GENTLE)MAN
monsoon .... (TRADE)WIND
weather .... RAINS, RAINY
monster .... GILA, BOGIE, DEMON,
    FREAK, GIANT, CENTAUR,
    UNICORN, CERBERUS,
    TERATISM, MONSTROSITY
combining form .... TERAT(O)
fabulous ..... HARPY, CHIMERA,
    BASILISK, MINOTAUR,
    COCKATRICE
fairy tale .... OGRE
female .... HARPY, GORGON,
    MEDUSA, SCYLLA, CHIMERA,
    CHARYBDIS
fire-breathing .... DRAGON,
    CHIMERA
half man-half bull
    .... MINOTAUR
half woman-half bird
    .... HARPY
half woman-half serpent
    .... LAMIA
hundred-eyed .... ARGUS
killed by Hercules .... GERYON
many-headed .... HYDRA
mythical ...... HARPY, DRAGON,
    SPHINX, CENTAUR, CHIMERA,
    GRIFFIN, GRYPHON, MINOTAUR,
    CHARYBDIS, HIPPOGRIFF
resembling a .... TERATOID
sea .... WHALE, KRAKEN
slain by Beowulf .... GRENDEL
winged .... GERYON
with lion's body and
    woman's head .... SPHINX
with snakes for hair
    .... GORGON, MEDUSA
monstrosity .... FREAK, MONSTER,
    TERATISM
monstrous .... HUGE, HIDEOUS,
    ENORMOUS, FIENDISH,
    HORRIBLE, TERATOID,

467

Mont Cervin .... MATTERHORN

montage .... ASSEMBLAGE

Montague Barstow .... ORCZY

    scion of .... ROMEO

Montana capital .... HELENA

    city/town .... BAKER, BUTTE,

    MALTA, DILLON, SIDNEY,

    WIBAUX, BOULDER, WINNETT,

    BILLINGS, MISSOULA,

    KALISPELL, GREAT FALLS,

    LIVINGSTON

    college .... CARROLL

    county ...... HILL, LAKE, PARK,

    BLAINE, CARTER, CUSTER,

    CASCADE, LINCOLN, RAVALLI,

    FLATHEAD, GALLATIN,

    MISSOULA, YELLOWSTONE

    Indian .... CREE, CROW

    lake .... BIG, SWAN, ENNIS,

    ASHLEY, HELENA, HOLTER,

    BIGHORN, FLATHEAD,

    MEDICINE, EARTHQUAKE

    motto ..... ORO Y PLATA, GOLD

    AND SILVER

    mountain .... ALLEN, SHEEP,

    SPHINX, GRANITE, JACKSON,

    STIMSON, HURRICANE

    mountain range .... CABINET,

    PURCELL

    national park .... GLACIER,

    YELLOWSTONE

    river .... SUN, MILK, RUBY,

    TETON, JUDITH, MARIAS,

    POPLAR, POWDER, BIGHORN,

    MADISON, MISSOURI, LITTLE

    HORN

    state bird .... MEADOWLARK

    state flower .... BITTERROOT

    state nickname ...... BONANZA,

    MOUNTAIN, TREASURE

    U.S. Air Force Base

    .... MALMSTROM

Monte Carlo location

    .... MONACO

Monte Cristo author ...... DUMAS

    castle .... D'IF

    hero .... DANTES

Montenegro capital, former

    .... CETINJE

    city/town .... KOTOR, NIKSIC,

    KOLASIN, TITOGRAD

    lake .... SCUTARI

    mountain .... BOBOTOV KUK

    port .... BAR, ULCINJ

montero .... CAP

Montez, dancer .... LOLA

Montezuma's conqueror

    .... CORTES

    revenge .... CHOLERA,

    DIARRHEA

    ATROCIOUS

Montgomery is capital of

    .... ALABAMA

month after Ab/Av .... ELUL

    Black History .... FEBRUARY

    Eliot's "cruellest" ...... APRIL

    excess of calendar over lunar

    .... EPACT

    first day .... KALENDS,

    CALEND(I)S

    last .... ULT(IMO)

    of proposed calendar

    .... NIVOSE

    shower .... APRIL

    the present, for short ..... INST

monthly .... MENSAL, MENSES,

    MENSTRUAL, PERIODICAL

Montreal fair .... EXPO

monument .... CAIRN, STELE,

    DOLMEN, MENHIR, PILLAR,

    STATUE, CENOTAPH,

    (CROM)LECH, MEMORIAL

    inscription .... EPIGRAPH

    upright .... STELE

monumental .... COLOSSAL

moo .... LOW

    juice .... MILK

mooch .... BEG, LOAF, CADGE,

    SKULK, SNEAK, STEAL,

    BORROW, LOITER, PILFER,

    SPONGE

    slang .... BUM

mood .... HUMOR, MORALE,

    TEMPER, SPIRIT(S),

    DISPOSITION

moody .... GLUM, TESTY,

    GLOOMY, SULLEN, PEEVISH,

    VARIABLE, DEPRESSED

Moog feat .... SAVE

moola ...... KALE, DOUGH, MONEY

moon .... ORB, LUNI, MONTH,

    LUMINARY, SATELLITE

    age of new, Jan. 1st

    .... EPACT

    apogee/perigree .... APSIS

    between half and full

    .... GIBBOUS

    crater .... TYCHO, COLOMBO

    dark area on .... MARE

    first on .... ARMSTRONG

    flower .... ACHETE

    goddess .... LUNA, HECATE,

    HEKATE, PHOEBE, SELENE,

    CYNTHIA, ARTEMIS, ASTARTE

    goddess, virgin .... DIANA

    half .... DEMILUNE

    horn .... CUSP

    inhabitant .... LUNARIAN

    mountain .... PYRENESS

    of delight .... HONEY

    of Saturn .... TITAN

    of song .... PAPER

    of the .... LUNAR, SELENIC

    orbit closest to .... PERILUNE

    orbiter .... ROOSA, YOUNG,

    APOLLO, BORMAN, GORDON,

    LOVELL, WORDEN, COLLINS

    personified .... LUNA

    phase .... GIBBOUS

    point .... APOGEE, PERIGREE

    sea .... RAINS, CRISES, NECTAR,

    SERENITY

    shadow .... UMBRA

    shaped ..... LUNATE, CRESCENT

    trench/valley .... RILL(E)

    vehicle .... LEM, ROVER

    walker .... DUKE, IRWIN,

    SCOTT, ALDRIN, CERNAN,

    CONRAD, SHEPARD, SHIMITT,

    ARMSTRONG

    watcher .... ASTROLOGER

mooncalf .... FOOL, IDIOT,

    IMBECILE

moonling, fictional .... SQUAPS

moonshine .... WHISKY, BOOTLEG,

    FUSTIAN, HOME BREW,

    NONSENSE

    apparatus .... STILL

    slang .... BOOZE, HUMBUG,

    HOGWASH

moonshiner .... BOOTLEGGER

    worry of .... RAID

moonstone ...... OPAL, ADULARIA,

    FELDSPAR

moonstruck .... DAFT, CRAZED,

    LUNATIC

moonwort .... FERN, LUNARIA

moor .... FEN, BENT, BRAE, DOCK,

    FELL, HEATH, LANDE,

    ANCHOR, FASTEN, MOSLEM,

    SECURE, MORISCO

    fowl .... GROUSE, GORCOCK

    grass .... NARD

    grouse .... GORHEN

    hen .... GROUSE, GALLINULE

Moore, actress .... DEMI

mooring .... WHARF

    buoy/spar .... DOLPHIN

    fee .... WHARFAGE

    place ...... DOCK, PORT, BERTH,

    MARINA

Moorish .... MORESQUE,

    MORISCAN

    cloak .... BURNOUS

    coin .... MARAVEDI

    drum/tabor .... AT(T)ABAL

    fabric .... TIRAZ

    garment .... JUPON

    king of Granada ...... BOABDIL

    palace/fortress .... ALCAZAR,

    ALHAMBRA

    sailboat .... SAPIT

moose .... ELK, DEER, ALCES

feeding place .... YARD
kin .... CARIBOU, REINDEER
male .... BULL
pouch .... BEL
territory .... MAINE
moot .... SUSPECT, ASSEMBLY,
    CONTESTED, DEBATABLE
mop .... RUB, SWAB, WASH, WIPE,
    MALKIN, MAUKIN, GRIMACE
mope .... FRET, MOON, POUT,
    SULK, BROOD
moppet .... TAD, DOLL, GIRL,
    CHILD, (SMALL)FRY
Moqui .... HOPI
moraine .... ESKER
moral ...... JUST, MAXIM, DECENT,
    LESSON, ETHICAL, UPRIGHT,
    VIRTUOUS, RIGHTEOUS
allegorical story with
    .... FABLE, APOLOGUE
decay .... ROT, CORRUPTION
distinction ...... RIGHT, WRONG
fault .... VICE
lapse .... SIN
law .... DECALOG(UE)
obligation .... DUTY
philosophy/principle
    .... ETHICS
poem .... DIT
slip .... LAPSE
talk .... HOMILY, SERMON
teachings .... PRECEPTS
weakness .... FRAILTY
morale ...... MOOD, CHEER, FAITH,
    NERVE, SPIRIT, TEMPER,
    COURAGE
morality .... ETHICS, VIRTUE,
    ETHICALITY
talk .... HOMILY, SERMON
moralized tale .... EXEMPLUM
morally corrupt .... VENAL,
    ROTTEN
instructive .... DIDACTIC
weak .... FRAIL
morals, pertaining to ...... ETHICS
supervisor .... CENSOR
morass ...... BOG, FEN, MARSH,
    SLACK, SWAMP, QUAGMIRE
moratorium .... GRACE
Moravia .... MAHREN
capital .... BRNO
moray .... EEL, ELGIN, CONGER
morbid .... GLOOMY, GRISLY,
    DISEASED, GRUESOME
morbilli .... MEASLES
morceau .... BIT, MORSEL,
    FRAGMENT
mordant .... ACID, ACRID, BITING,
    CUTTING, EROSIVE, SARCASTIC
more .... ELSE, PLUS, ADDED,
    AGAIN, BESIDE(S), FURTHER,

ADDITIONAL
accurate/agreeable .... NICER
acute .... KEENER, SMARTER
aloof .... ICIER
ancient .... OLDER
attractive .... CUTER
bashful .... SHIER
Bohemian .... ARTIER
comely .... PRETTIER
comfortable .... EASIER
compendious .... TERSER
crafty .... SLYER
cry for .... ENCORE
delicate .... FINER, AIRIER,
    DAINTIER
distressed .... NEEDIER
docile .... TAMER
domineering .... BOSSIER
eccentric .... ODDER
efficient .... ABLER
elegant .... FINER
energetic .... SPRIER
frequent .... OFTENER
frugal .... SPARER
gentle .... MILDER
gentle creature of mythology
    .... UNICORN
grating .... RASPIER
greedy .... THIRSTIER
hideous .... UGLIER
in music .... PIU
ineffectual .... LAMER
inexplicable .... EERIER
infrequent/unusual ...... RARER
laid-back .... MELLOWER
lawnlike .... GRASSIER
likely to be plucked ..... RIPER
malicious .... CATTIER
melodious .... AIRIER
normal .... SANER
or less .... ABOUT, SOMEWHAT,
    APPROXIMATE(LY)
orderly .... NEATER
peevish .... CRABBIER
perspicacious .... SAGER
pleasing .... NICER
positive .... SURER
precious .... DEARER
precipitous .... STEEPER
prevalent .... RIFER
primitive .... RUDER
rational/reasonable ...... SANER
restless .... ANTSIER
savory .... TASTIER
secret .... INNER
secure .... SAFER
shoddy .... SEEDIER
spherical .... ROUNDER
stylish: slang .... CLASSIER
tender .... SORER
than a few .... MANY

than eager .... AGOG
than enough .... AMPLE,
    PLENTY, OVERDOSE
than one/once .... SEVERAL,
    MULTIPLE
than unpleasant .... RUDE
unctuous .... OILIER
unfeeling .... STERNER
unusual .... ODDER
vulgar .... RAWER
wary .... LEERIER
willing .... READIER
moreen .... TABBY, FABRIC
morel .... MUSHROOM,
    NIGHTSHADE
morello .... CHERRY
moreover .... AND, TOO, ALSO,
    ELSE, BESIDES, LIKEWISE,
    FURTHER(MORE)
morepork .... RURU
mores .... CULTURE, CUSTOMS,
    FOLKWAYS
Moresque .... MOORISH
Morgan ...... TROTTER, STALLION,
    BUCCANEER
actress .... FAIRCHILD
Morgana, _____ .... FATA
morganite .... BERYL
Morgiana's master .... ALI BABA
morgue .... LIBRARY, MORTUARY,
    DEADHOUSE
Moriarty's foe .... HOLMES
moribund .... DYING
moringa .... BEN
morion .... HELMET, QUARTZ
Morisco .... MOOR
Mormon .... DANITE
Church founder .... SMITH
leader, U.S.
    .... (BRIGHAM)YOUNG
not a .... GENTILE
priest .... ELDER
sacred instrument .... URIM
morning .... A.M., EOS, DAWN,
    MATIN, AURORA, MORROW,
    DAYBREAK
-after retribution
    .... HANGOVER
canticle .... VENITE
delivery .... MAIL, MILK,
    (NEWS)PAPER
early .... SMALL HOURS
glory .... IPOMEA, SUNRISE
music .... MATIN, AUBADE
nuisance .... ALARM
of .... MATIN(AL)
poetic .... MORN
prayer .... MATINS
reception .... LEVEE
song .... ALBA, MATIN,
    AUBADE, MATTINS

star .... VENUS, SATURN,
PHOSPHOR

Moro cannon .... LANTAKA

chief .... DATO, DATU

Italian premier .... ALDO

priest .... PANDITA

sailboat .... VINTA

tribesman: var. .... ILANO

Moroccan .... MOOR, RIFF,
BERBER

wife .... SHERIFA

Morocco ...... KINGDOM, LEATHER

cape .... SIM, JUBY, RHIR

capital .... RABAT

city/town ...... FEZ, SAFI, SALE,
TAZA, NADOR, OUJDA, AGADIR,
FEDALA, MEKNES, SETTAT,
KENITRA, LARACHE, TANGIER,
MARRAKECH, CASABLANCA

coin .... RIAL

district .... RIFF

French name .... MAROC

hat .... FEZ

hilly region .... ERRIF

international zone .... TANGIER

king .... HASSAN

language ...... ARABIC, FRENCH

monetary unit .... DIRHAM

mountain .... JEBEL MUSA,
JEBEL TOUBKAL

mountains .... BANI, ATLAS,
SARHRO

native ..... MOOR, RIFF, BERBER

prime minister .... (AZEDDINE)
LARAKI

region .... RIF, TAFILET

river .... SEBOU, MOULOUYA

ruler .... HASSAN, SULTAN

seaport .... CEUTA, RABAT,
AGADIR, TETUAN, MOGADOR,
TANGIER, CASABLANCA

soldier .... ASKAR

moron ...... AMENT, IDIOT, NITWIT,
IMBECILE, SIMPLETON

morose .... SAD, BLUE, DOUR,
GLUM, MOODY, MOPEY,
SULKY, SURLY, GLOOMY,
SULLEN

Morpheus, god of ____
.... DREAMS

father of .... HYPNOS

morphine drug .... METHADONE

refined .... HEROIN

morro .... BLUFF, HILL(OCK)

morrow ...... MORNING, NEXT DAY

Morse code symbol .... DASH

code word .... DIT

invention .... TELEGRAPH

recourse .... SOS

morsel .... BIT(E), ORT, DISH,
CRUMB, PIECE, SCRAP, TIDBIT,

MORCEAU

mort .... DEAD, DEATH

mortal .... FATAL, HUMAN,
DEADLY, LETHAL, PERSON,
IMPLACABLE

remains .... DUST, CORPSE,
CADAVER

mortality .... DEATH(RATE)

mortar .... BOWL, COMPO,
CANNON, CEMENT, PLASTER

and ____ .... PESTLE

crush in a .... BRAY

for filling .... GROUT

mixer/beater .... RAB

patch with .... SLUSH

tray .... HOD

mortarboard .... CAP, HAWK

part .... TASSEL

mortgage ...... DEED, LIEN, LOAN,
PLEDGE, WADSET

mortgagee .... LIENOR

mortician .... UNDERTAKER

mortification .... SHAME,
CHAGRIN, GANGRENE,
VEXATION

mortify .... ABASH, SHAME,
EMBARRASS, HUMILIATE

Mortimer, the dummy
.... SNERD

mortise .... JOIN, FASTEN

counterpart of a .... TENON

mortuary .... MORGUE, CHARNEL,
CREMATORY, CINERARIUM

carriage/vehicle .... HEARSE

mosaic .... INLAY, COLLAGE

gold .... ORMOLU

law .... TORA(H)

material .... TILE, SMALTO,
TESSERA

work .... INTARSIA, TESSERAE

Moscow .... MOSKVA

chief rabbi .... LEVIN

citadel .... KREMLIN

square .... PUSHKIN

turndown .... NYET

Moselle .... WINE

city on .... METZ, TRIER,
TREVES

tributary .... SAAR

Moses .... LEADER, LAWGIVER

brother of .... AARON

father of .... AMRAM

father-in-law of .... JETHRO

mount/death place of
.... NEBO

saw Canaan there .... NEBO,
PISGAH

sister of .... MIRIAM

spy/scout of .... CALEB, NAHBI,
JOSHUA

successor of .... JOSUE,

JOSHUA

wife of .... ZIPPORAH

mosey: sl. .... MOVE, AMBLE,
STROLL, SHUFFLE

Moslem. See also **Muslim**

.... BERBER, MUSLIM, PATHAN,
PAYNIM, ISLAM(IC), SARACEN,
MUSSULMAN, MOHAMMEDAN

angel .... ISRAFIL

beggar .... FAKIR, DERVISH

brass .... AGAS

bridge to paradise .... ALSIRAT

caliph .... OMMIAD

call to prayer ..... ADAN, AZAN

cap .... FEZ, TARBOOSH

chief .... REIS

Christian to a .... GIAOUR

chronicle .... SARSILA, TARSILA

coin .... DINAR

college .... ULEMA

converts .... ANSAR

devil/Satan .... EBLIS

doctor .... HAKIM, HAKEEM

drinking cup .... LOTAH

Egyptian .... FULA(H)

fasting period .... RAMADAN,
RAMAZAN

festival .... BAIRAM

garment .... IZAR, JUBBAH

governor .... HAKIM

head .... RAIS, REIS

headgear .... FEZ, TAJ,
TARBUSH, TARBOOSH

hermit .... SANTON, MARABOUT

hero .... GHAZI

holy book .... KORAN

holy city ...... MECCA, MEDINA,
KAIROUAN

holy man .... IMAM,
MARABOUT

holy war .... JEHAD, JIHAD

idol .... MAUMET

interpreter of religious laws
..... MUFTI, MOLLAH, MULLA(H)

judge .... CADI, CAZI, KADI,
KAZI, HAKIM

lady .... BEGUM

language .... URDU

law .... SUNNA(H)

lawyer .... MUFTI

leader .... AGA, IMA(U)M,
CALIPH

marketplace .... SOUK

marriage .... MUTA

measure .... ARDEB

mendicant ..... FAKIR, DERVISH

messiah .... MAHDI

minister .... VIZI(E)R

monk .... SANTON

month .... RABIA, RAJAB,
SAFAR, JUMADA, SHABAN,

RAMADAN, RAMAZAN
mosque .... MASJID, MUSJID
mystic .... SUNI
noble .... EMIR, AMEER,
EMEER, SHERIF
nomad .... KURD
non .... RAIA, GIAOU, RAYAH,
KAF(F)IR
nymph .... HOURI
official .... HAJIB
people .... PATHAN
pilgrim .... HA(D)JI, IHRAM
pilgrimage .... HADJ
pilgrim's costume .... IHRAM
place for prayer .... MOSQUE
prayer .... SALAT
prayer caller .... MUEZZIN
prayer's direction ...... KAABA,
KIBLAH
priest .... IMA(U)M
prince .... AMIR, EMIR, AMEER,
EMEER, NAWAB
princess .... BEGUM
principle .... IJMA
prophet .... MAHDI
religion .... ISLAM
religious brotherhood
.... SENUS(S)I
religious duty .... HADJ
rosary .... TASBIH
ruler .... CALIF, HAKIM,
CALIPH, SULTAN
sacred book .... KORAN
saint .... PIR, SANTON
scholar(s) .... ULEM(A)
school .... MADRASA
sect adherent .... BAHAI
sect member .... SUFI,
WAHABI, SUNNITE, WAHABEE
shrine .... CAABA, KAABA,
MESHED
slave .... MAMELUKE
spirit ...... JIN(N), GENIE, GENII,
JINN(I), JINNEE
sword .... SCIMITAR,
(Y)ATAGHAN
teacher .... ALIM, MOLLAH,
MULLA(H)
temple .... MOSQUE
title .... AGA, HADJI, HAFIZ,
MAHDI, MOLLA, MULLA(H),
SHERIF
title of respect .... AG(H)A,
SYED, NAWAB, SA(I)YID
tomb .... TABUT
tribe .... BASHKIR
tunic .... JAMA(H)
Turkestan .... SALAR
Turko-Tartar .... BASHKIR
viceroy .... NABOB, NAWAB
weight .... ROTL

Moslems collectively .... ISLAM
mosque .... MOSK, MASJID,
MUSJID, TEMPLE
tower .... JAMI, MINARET
mosquito .... CULICID, SKEETER,
STEGOMYIA
bite injection .... ALLERGEN
carried disease .... DENGUE,
MALARIA
dangerous .... AEDES, CULEX,
ANOPHELES
genus/species .... AEDES,
CULEX
hawk .... DRAGONFLY
larva .... W(R)IGGLER
yellow fever .... STEGOMYIA
moss .... LICHEN, EPIPHYTE,
BRYOPHYTE, CARRAGEEN
filaments .... RHIZOID
shade of green .... BLUE
mossbunker .... POGY, MENHADEN
mosstrooper .... RAIDER,
MARAUDER
most .... GREATEST
aged .... OLDEST
ancient .... HOARIEST
appropriate .... APTEST
ashen .... PALEST
barren .... DRIEST
base .... MEANEST
calamitous .... DIREST
cerulean .... BLUEST
cherished/precious
.... DEAREST
costly ..... DEAREST, PRICELESS
desirable .... BEST
dictatorial .... BOSSIEST
difficult to find .... RAREST
dignified .... STATELIEST
disagreeable .... MEAN AS CAN
BE
distinctive ..... FINEST, RAREST
doubtful .... IFFIEST
elegant .... FINEST
eligible bachelor .... CATCH
enraged .... SOREST
extensive .... WIDEST
famous of the Black Hills
.... MOUNT RUSHMORE
fascinating game .... CHESS
fit/healthy .... HALEST
haunting .... EERIEST
indigent .... POOREST
important .... ARCH
insignificant .... LEAST
ironic .... WRIEST
joyful .... MERRIEST
like a leopard .... SPOTTIEST
likely .... PROBABLY,
DOUBTLESS
obscure .... VAGUEST

orderly .... NEATEST
peculiar .... ODDEST
populous city in Western
Hemisphere
.... MEXICO(CITY)
populous country .... CHINA
rational .... SANEST
robust .... HARDIEST
savage .... WILDEST
sensible .... SANEST
sordid .... BASEST
spare .... LEANEST
unpleasant/unsatisfactory
.... WORST
vague .... PALEST
valuable possession .... LIFE
vile .... DIRTIEST
weighty .... GRAVEST
mostly ...... CHIEFLY, PRINCIPALLY
mot .... REPARTEE, WITTICISM
mote .... SPECK
motel .... INN
motet .... SONG, ANTHEM
moth .... IO, LUNA, EGGER, GYPSY,
MILLER, AGLOOSA, ARRINDA,
BOMBYCID, CECROPIA,
FORESTER
clothes .... TINEA
destroying apples
.... CODLIN(G)
kin .... BUTTERFLY
larva .... LOOPER
night-flying .... NOCTUID
proboscis .... LINGUA
repellent .... CAMPHOR
wing spot .... FENESTRA
mother .... MATER, MATRON,
PARENT
colloquial ..... MAMA, MOM(S),
MAMMA, MAMMY, MOMMY,
MOMSY
combining form/prefix
.... MATRI
country .... HOMELAND
famous .... MARY
-in-law, biblical .... NAOMI
killing of one's .... MATRICIDE
kind of .... DEN
Little Lord Fauntleroy's
.... DEAREST
of a four-legged animal
.... DAM
of gods .... RHEA, CYBELE
of Gracchi .... CORNELIA
of Hippothous .... ALOPE
of pearl .... NACRE
of quintets .... ZAHRA
of several children
.... MULTIPARA
superior .... ABBESS
tongue .... VERNACULAR

who rules .... MATRIARCH
wit .... COMMON SENSE
Mother Cary's chicken
.... PETREL
Earth .... GAEA
Goose creator .... PERRAULT
Hubbard .... CRONE
Hubbard's quest .... BONE
_____, Nobel laureate
.... TERESA
of Cities .... KIEV
of God .... VIRGIN MARY
motherhood .... MATERNITY
motherly .... MATERNAL
motif .... IDEA, THEME, TOPIC,
CONCEPT, FEATURE, SUBJECT
motion .... FLUX, SIGNAL,
GESTURE, MOVEMENT,
PROPOSAL
downward .... DESCENT
in .... MOVING, TRANSIT,
TRAVELING
neurotic .... TIC
pertaining to .... KINETIC
picture .... FILM, MOVIE,
CINEMA, FLICKER
picture first prints ..... RUSHES
producing .... MOTILE
rolling/swelling .... SURGE
motionless .... FIXED, INERT,
STILL
motivate .... IMPEL, INCITE,
INDUCE, PROMPT, INSPIRE
motivation .... CAUSE, IMPETUS,
INFLUENCE, MAINSPRING
motive .... GOAD, SPUR, CAUSE,
DESIGN, GROUND, REASON,
PURPOSE, KEYSTONE,
INCENTIVE, INTENTION,
ENTICEMENT, INDUCEMENT
power .... STEAM
motley .... COLORFUL,
VARICOLORED,
KALEIDOSCOPIC
motor .... ENGINE, TURBINE
speed .... RPM
speed up .... REV, RACE
vehicle frame .... CHASSIS
motorbike .... MOPED
motorcycle .... SCOOTER
extra .... SIDECAR
Motown .... DETROIT
mistake .... EDSEL
squad .... LIONS
mott(e) .... GROVE
mottle .... SPOT, BLOTCH, DAPPLE,
STREAK
mottled .... PIED, PINTO, DAPPLED,
PIEBALD, SPOTTED
gray .... GRISEOUS
motto .... SAW, ADAGE, GNOME,

MAXIM, DEVICE, SAYING,
SLOGAN, PRECEPT,
CATCHWORD
in a book .... EPIGRAPH
in a ring .... POSY
moue .... POUT, GRIMACE
mouflon .... SHEEP
mould .... FORM, KNEAD, MATRIX,
FASHION
moulin .... SHAFT
mound .... DUNE, HEAP, HILL,
HUMP, PILE, TELL, TERP,
AGGER, ESKER, GLOBE,
KNOLL, RAISE, BARROW,
HILLOCK, HUMMOCK
domelike .... STUPA
formed by wind .... DOWN
golfer's .... TEE
Goose .... GOSSAGE
of burrowing animal
.... MOLEHILL
of sand/gravel .... ESKAR,
ESKER, RIDGE
mount .... FIX, SET, HILL, POST,
RISE, CLIMB, HORSE, PLACE,
ASCEND, MOUNTAIN
Balaam's .... ASS
by ladder .... SCALE,
ESCALADE
Mount Hood's range
.... CASCADES
of Olives .... OLIVET
Rushmore location .... SOUTH
DAKOTA
portrait carved on
.... LINCOLN, JEFFERSON,
WASHINGTON,
(THEODORE)ROOSEVELT
sculptor
.... (GUTZON)BORGLUM
mountain .... KOP, HEAP, PILE,
BUTTE, MOUND, MOUNT,
BARROW, ELEVATION
antelope .... KLIPSPRINGER
Apollo's .... PARNASSUS
ash .... SORB, ROWAN
base .... PIEDMONT
biblical .... NEBO, ZION,
HOREB, SINAI, ARARAT
cat .... PUMA, COUGAR
chain .... RANGE, SIERRA
climber .... ALPINIST
climber's aid .... PITON,
CRAMPON
climber's slide .... GLISSADE
climber's staff
.... ALPENSTOCK
combining form .... ORO,
OREOS
crest .... SPUR, ARETE
feature ...... TOR, SPUR, ARETE,

CRATER, SNOWCAP
formation .... OROGENY
goat .... IBEX, TAHR, GORAL
gorge/gully .... COULOIR
group .... RANGE
high .... ALP
highest .... EVEREST
lake .... TARN
legendary .... MERU
lion .... PUMA, COUGAR,
PAINTER, PANTHER
main mass .... MASSIF
nymph .... OREAD
of China, sacred .... OMEI
of the Muses .... PARNASSUS
pass .... COL, GAP, GHAT,
DEFILE
peak .... BEN, CIMA, CONE,
HORN
pool .... TARN
range .... ANDES, SIERRA,
CORDILLERA
ridge .... ARETE, SIERRA,
SAWBACK
road peril ...... HAIRPIN CURVE
road's bend .... LOOP
rocky .... TETON
rubble .... SCREE
sheep ...... BIGHORN, MOUFLON
sickness .... PUNA, VETA
slope .... VERSANT
small .... MONTICULE
spur .... ARETE
stem for .... OREO
sunrise .... ALPENGLOW
top .... PEAK
top cover .... ICECAP,
SNOWCAP
trail marker .... KARN
valley .... GLEN
way .... TUNNEL
Mountain State .... MONTANA
mountaineer .... SHERPA,
CLIMBER, ALPINIST, HILLBILLY
mountainous .... LOFTY, CRAGGY,
RUGGED
mountains between France and
Switzerland .... JURA
formation of .... OROGENY
study of .... OROLOGY,
OROGRAPHY
mountebank .... QUACK, EMPIRIC,
CHARLATAN
mounted .... ASTRIDE
policeman .... MARSHAL,
CONSTABLE
rider ...... JOCKEY, EQUESTRIAN
sentinel .... VEDETTE
traveler ...... RIDER, HORSEMAN
Mountie .... POLICE, TROOPER
outfit of .... RCMP

mourn .... RUE, (BE)WAIL, GRIEVE, LAMENT
in sympathy .... CONDOLE
mourner .... LAMENTER
hired .... MUTE, WEEPER
mournful .... SAD, DREARY, GLOOMY, GRIEVOUS
piece .... DIRGE
mourning band .... CRAPE, CREPE, WEEDS
clothes .... WEEDS, SABLES, BOMBASINE, SACKCLOTH
silk .... ALMA
song .... DIRGE
mouse .... RODENT, BLACKEYE
bird .... COLY
deer .... NAPUS, CHEVROTAIN
genus .... MUS
he's not one .... MAN
like animal .... VOLE, SHREW
meadow/field .... VOLE
relative .... JERBOA, GERBIL(LE)
mouser .... OWL
mousseline .... MUSLIN
mousy .... DRAB, QUIET, TIMID
mouth .... OS, LIPS, INLET, STOMA, DECLAIM, OPENING, ORIFICE, ENTRANCE
and lower cheeks .... CHOPS
away from .... ABORAL
by word of ..... ORAL, VERBAL
combining form .... ORI, STOMA, STOM(E)
disease .... APHTHA
disorder .... ULCER, CANDIDIASIS
gag .... MUZZLE
gaping .... RICTUS
Latin .... OS, ORIS
of the .... ORAL, BUCCAL, OSCULAR, STOMATIC
off .... SASS
organ ..... (BAG)PIPE, OCARINA, HARMONICA
part .... GUMS, LIPS, TEETH, PALATE, TONGUE
pertaining to .... BUCCAL
river .... DELTA, FRITH, ESTUARY
roof .... PALATE
slang .... MUG, YAP, PUSS, TRAP, KISSER
strap .... MUZZLE
thru the .... ORAL
to pharynx passage
.... FAUCES
toward the .... ORAD
ulcerous condition .... NOMA
volcano .... CRATER
wash .... GARGLE, LISTERINE

-watering .... TEMPTING, APPETIZING
mouthed, loud ...... STENTOR(IAN)
open- .... AGAPE
mouthful .... BITE, GOBBET
small .... MORSEL
mouthlike .... MANDIBULAR
entrance .... OSTIUM
mouthpiece .... REED, BOCAL, NOZZLE, SPOKESMAN
slang .... LAWYER
mouths .... ORA
mouthy .... GASSY, WINDY, BOMBASTIC
mouton .... FUR
movable .... MOBILE, PORTABLE
defense structure
.... BASTIL(LE)
mountain .... OSSA
part of tabletop .... LEAF
shelter in siege .... CAT
support .... TRESTLE
move .... ACT, STIR, BUDGE, (A)ROUSE, IMPEL, SHIFT, TOUCH, AFFECT, PROMPT, PROPOSE
able to .... MOTILE
ahead steadily .... BORE
aimlessly .... MAUNDER
along .... PROD, MOSEY, SASHAY
at a certain marching
cadence .... DOUBLE-TIME
back .... RECEDE, REGRESS, RETREAT
back and forth .... DIDDLE, SEESAW, SHUTTLE
camera .... PAN
carefully .... EASE
clumsily .... BARGE, LUMBER
confusedly .... MILL
crabwise .... SIDLE
easily .... SLIDE
furtively .... LURK, PROWL, SKULK, SLINK, SNEAK
gently .... LAP
heavily .... LUMP, LUMBER
in a smooth motion
.... UNDULATE
in a stream .... FLOW
in and out .... WEAVE
in opposition .... RETROACT
it! .... STEP ON IT, ON THE DOUBLE
merrily .... DANCE
on .... RESETTLE
on wheels .... ROLL
shakily .... DODDER
sidewise ...... JIB, EDGE, SKEW, SLUE, SIDLE
slowly .... INCH, WORM,

CRAWL, CREEP
smoothly .... SLIDE
swiftly .... DART, FLIT, SCUD, SPEED
to a new job .... RELOCATE
toward .... GRAVITATE
unfair .... FOUL
unsteadily: var. .... WABBLE
up .... RISE
wary .... FEELER
without power .... GLIDE
movement .... ACTION, MOTION, CRUSADE, GESTURE, ACTIVITY
ballet .... ENTRECHAT
deceptive .... FEINT
in music ...... TEMPO, RHYTHM
in prosody .... CADENCE
of goods .... FREIGHT
of organism .... TAXIS
of the sea .... TIDE
mover, slow .... SNAIL, TURTLE
movie .... CINEMA, PHOTOPLAY, MOTION PICTURE
award .... OSCAR
camera platform .... DOLLY
cartoon producer ...... BAKSHI, DISNEY
combining form .... CINE
director's command .... CUT, ACTION
fade-out .... THE END
fare .... COMEDY, CARTOON, MUSICAL, MYSTERY, WESTERN, MELODRAMA
film, 1000 ft. .... REEL
full length .... FEATURE
immortal star .... VALENTINO
last word of a .... END
low budget .... QUICKIE
ma and pa .... KETTLES
operator/theater owner
.... EXHIBITOR
part .... LEAD, ROLE, HEAVY, INGENUE
projector .... BIOSCOPE
role, minor .... CAMEO
role, small .... BIT, EXTRA
script .... SCENARIO
short ..... CARTOON, NEWSREEL
shot .... CLINCH, CLOSE-UP
studio worker .... GRIP, STAGEHAND
theater, oldtime
.... NICKELODEON
with sound .... TALKIE
moving .... MOTILE, AMBULANT, ELOQUENT, PATHETIC, POIGNANT, STIRRING, TOUCHING, AFFECTING, IMPRESSIVE
combining form .... KINETO

staircase .... ESCALATOR
vehicle .... VAN
mow .... CLIP, DESS, MATH, REAP,
CUT DOWN, DESTROY,
GRIMACE, (HAY)LOFT,
HAYSTACK
Mowgli, friend of .... BALU,
BEAR, AKELA, BALOO
tiger of .... SHERE KHAN
mowing implement ...... MOWER,
REAPER, SCYTHE, SICKLE
Mowrer, Edgar _____ .... ANSEL
moxa .... PLANT, CAUTERY
moxie .... NERVE
Mozambique bay .... DELAGOA
cape .... DELGADO
capital .... MAPUTO
city/town .... BEIRA, LUMBO,
LURIO, MABOTE, MANDIE,
MUCOJO, CHIBUTO, MACHAZE,
MUALAMA
island .... ANGOCHE
lake .... NYASA, CHILWA
language .... MAKUA, SHONA,
THONGA
monetary unit .... METICAL
mountain .... BINGA
native .... YAO, BANTU
port .... BEIRA
river ..... SAVE, LURIO, MAZOE,
SHIRE, ROVUMA, LIMPOPO,
LUGENDA, ZAMBEZI, OLIFANTS
Mozart .... WOLFGANG
opera .... FIGARO, SERAGLIO,
MAGIC FLUTE, DON GIOVANNI,
COSI FAN TUTTI
Mozart's city .... SALZBURG
mozetta .... CAPE
wearer of .... POPE
Mr. "Blackwell" .... (RICHARD
SYLVAN)SELZER
Borgnine .... ERNEST
Brinkley, for short .... DAVE
Brubeck .... DAVE
Cassini .... OLEG
Catastrophe, sobriquet
.... TRIPP
Chaney .... LON
Connery .... SEAN
Cupid .... DAN
Duck .... DONALD
Europe, sobriquet .... MONNET
Foxx .... REDD
Greer, of track fame .... ROSIE
Hirt .... AL
Hodges .... GIL
Houston .... SAM
Marner .... SILAS
O'Casey .... SEAN
Onassis .... ARI
Preminger .... OTTO

Preston .... CHARLES
Previn .... ANDRE
Roberts on Broadway creator
.... (HENRY)FONDA
Sevareid .... ERIC
Sinatra .... FRANK
Slaughter .... ENOS
Sparks .... NED
T's group .... A-TEAM
"Tambourine Man" group
.... BYRDS
Ulyanov .... LENIN
Vidal .... GORE
Ziegfeld, to friends .... FLO
Mrs. .... MADAM(E), MISTRESS
Bogart .... (LAUREN)BACALL
Chaplain .... OONA
Copperfield .... DORA
Grundy .... PRUDE, SNOOPER
Hoover .... LOU
"Machine Gun Kelly"
.... KATHRYN SHANNON
Montagu Barstow .... ORCZY
Sairey .... GAMP
Tanqueray's creator
.... PINERO
Walter Findlay .... MAUDE
Ms. .... MRS, MISS, MIZZ,
MANUSCRIPT
Adams .... EDIE
Adoree .... RENEE
Claire .... INA
Lee .... PEGGY
LeShan .... EDA
Lillie, to friends .... BEA
Ono .... YOKO
Robson .... FLORA
MS .... MULTIPLE SCLEROSIS
much ...... LOT(S), MANY, AMPLE,
SLEWS, PLENTY, COPIOUS,
PROFUSE
combining form .... ERI
in music .... MOLTO
traveled .... BEATEN
mucid .... MOLDY, MUSTY
mucilage ...... GUM, GLUE, PASTE,
ARABIN, ADHESIVE
muck .... DIRT, MIRE, FILTH,
MANURE
mucker .... CAD
muckworm .... MISER
mucous: comb. form .... MYX(O)
membrane disease ..... LUPUS
fold .... PLICA
inflammation .... CATARRH
secretion .... MUCIN
watery discharge ..... RHEUM
mud .... MIRE, MUCK, OOZE, SILT,
LIBEL, SALSE, SLIME, SLUSH,
PELOID, SLUDGE, SLANDER
bath .... WALLOW

dauber .... WASP
hen .... COOT, RAIL,
GALLINULE
viscous .... SLIME
mudcap .... ADOBE
mudder or bangtail .... RACER
muddle ...... MESS, ADDLE, SNAFU,
BUNGLE, FIASCO, JUMBLE,
MIX UP, CONFUSE, FLUSTER
muddled .... DAZED, DIZZY,
GIDDY, WOOZY, STUPID
muddlehead .... ADDLEPATE
muddy .... DINGY, ROILY,
DAGGLE, SLOPPY, SLUDGY,
TURBID
mudfish .... BOWFIN, DIPNOAN
mudguard .... FENDER
mudhole .... WALLOW, LOBLOLLY
mudslinger .... MUCKRAKER
lawsuit .... LIBEL
mudworm .... IPO
muezzin .... CRIER
call of .... AZAN
place of .... MINARET
muff .... BOTCH, FUMBLE,
BUNGLE(R)
muffin ...... BUN, COB, GEM, ROLL,
BREAD, POPOVER
muffle .... MUTE, OVEN, WRAP,
DEADEN, STIFLE
muffler .... SCARF, NECKWEAR,
SILENCER
mufti .... ULEMA
slang .... CIV(V)IES
mug .... CUP, TOBY, MUNGO,
STEIN, NOGGIN, SEIDEL,
TANKARD
leather .... JACK
man-shaped .... TOBY
material .... PEWTER
slang .... FACE, KISSER,
ATTACK, HOLD UP, ASSAULT
mugger .... GOA, ACTOR, ROBBER,
HOODLUM, CROC(ODILE)
nemesis of .... COP
muggins .... DUPE, FOOL, DOMINO,
CARD GAME
muggy .... DANK, HUMID, STICKY,
SULTRY
mugwump .... REPUBLICAN
Muhammad Ali
.... (CASSIUS)CLAY
Muhammadan deity ...... ALLAH
Mukden is capital of
.... MANCHURIA
mulatto .... METIS, CREOLE,
GRIFF(E), GRIQUA
mulberry ...... AAL, TREE, FUSTIC,
MURREY, SYCAMINE
bark .... TAPA
tree genus .... MORUS,

CECROPIA

mulct .... BILK, FINE, AMERCE, DEFRAUD, PENALIZE
mule .... HINNY, HYBRID, SLIPPER, PIGHEAD, TRACTOR, SHAVETAIL
cry .... BRAY
driver .... SKINNER
female .... MARE
of songdom .... SAL
on the Erie Canal .... SAL
pack .... BURRO, SUMPTER
parent .... MARE, DONKEY
young .... FOAL
muliebrity .... WOMANHOOD
mulish .... STUBBORN, OBSTINATE, PIGHEADED
mull ...... THINK, FLAVOR, MUSLIN, PONDER, REFLECT, SWEETEN, COGITATE, CONSIDER
in a way .... DEBATE
mulla(h) .... TEACHER
mulle(i)n .... PLANT, FIGWORT, FOXGLOVE
muller .... PESTLE, GRINDER
mullet .... LIZA, (GOAT)FISH
mulley .... POLLED COW
mulligan .... HASH, STEW
connoisseur .... HOBO
mulligatawny, for one ...... SOUP
mulligrubs .... COLIC
multifarious ...... MANY, VARIED, DIVERSE, MANIFOLD
multiped(e) arthropod
.... CENTIPEDE
multiple .... MANIFOLD, NUMEROUS
multiplicand .... FACIEND
multiplication ...... PROCREATION
result .... PRODUCT
multiply itself .... SQUARE
multitude .... ARMY, HOST, CROWD, HORDE, SWARM, GALAXY, LEGION, MYRIAD, SCORES, THRONG
colloquial .... PILES, RAFTS, SCADS
multitudinous ...... MANY, LARGE, CROWDED, MANIFOLD, NUMEROUS
mum .... ALE, BEER, MOTHER, SILENT, DEODORANT, CHRYSANTHEMUM
is the ____ .... WORD
mumble .... CHEW, MUMP, MURMUR, MUTTER
mumbojumbo .... IDOL, SPELL, FETISH, GIBBERISH, MEDICINE MAN
mummer .... ACTOR, GUISER, MASKER, PARADER,

PANTOMIMIST

mummify .... DRY, SHRIVEL, PRESERVE
mummy .... CORPSE
cloth .... BYSSUS
mump .... MUMBLE, MUTTER
slang .... BEG, CHEAT
mumps .... PAROTITIS
munch .... BITE, CHEW, CHAMP, CRUNCH, NIBBLE
Munchausen specialty .... YARNS
tales collector .... RASPE
title of .... BARON
Munchen .... MUNICH
mundane ...... CARNAL, EARTHLY, WORLDLY, TEMPORAL
mundungo .... TOBACCO
Mundy work .... OM
Munich .... MUNCHEN
municipal .... URBAN
building .... CITY HALL, COURTHOUSE
council member
.... ALDERMAN
tax .... OCTROI
municipality .... CITY, TOWN, PUEBLO
munificent ...... LAVISH, PROFUSE, GENEROUS
munitions .... ARMS
manufacturer .... KRUPP, SKODA
storehouse .... ARSENAL
Munro, H. H. .... SAKI
Munsel, singer .... PATRICE
Munster seaport .... CORK
mural .... PAINTING, WALL-LIKE
or state .... INTRA
painter .... (DIEGO)RIVERA
Murat .... JOACHIM
murder .... KILL, SLAY, BUMP OFF, HOMICIDE
by drowning .... NOYADE
by suffocation .... BURKE
king's .... REGICIDE
victim, first .... ABEL
murdered .... SLAIN
murderer .... KILLER, BUTCHER, ASSASSIN, MANSLAYER
biblical .... CAIN
murderous frenzy .... AMOK, BERSERK
murex .... WHELK
murid .... RAT, DISCIPLE
murine .... MICE, RATS, RODENT
murk .... DIM, DUSK, HAZE, GLOOM, DARK(NESS)
murky .... VAGUE, CLOUDY, OBSCURE
murmur .... HUM, CURR, PURL, MUMBLE, MUTTER, WHISPER

cat's .... PURR
dove's .... COO
fondly .... COO
wind's .... SOUGH
murmuring sound .... SUSSURUS
murphy ...... BED, TATER, POTATO
murre .... AUK, GUILLEMOT
murrey .... MULBERRY
musaceous plant .... BANANA
musca .... FLY
Muscat .... WINE, GRAPE
and ____ .... OMAN
lover .... WINO
natives .... OMANI
muscatel .... WINE
muscle .... BRAWN, SINEW, BICEPS, TENSOR, TISSUE, LEVATOR, TRICEPS
arm .... BICEPS, DELTOID
attachment .... TENDON
bending .... FLEXOR
builder .... STEROID
buttocks .... GLUTEUS
combining form .... MY(O)
contraction .... TIC, SPASM, CRAMPS
infection .... GANGRENE
injury .... TEAR, SPRAIN
jaw .... MASSETER
like .... MYOID
loin .... PSOAS
movement .... CONTRACTION
of .... SARCOUS
pain .... MYALGIA
part of .... HEAD, CELLS, FIBERS, T(A)ENIA, MYOFIBRIL
protein .... ACTIN
spasm(s) .... CRICK, CLONOS, CRAMP(S)
tension .... TONUS
type .... SMOOTH, CARDIAC, SKELETAL
muscles .... BRAWN, THEWS
science of .... MYOLOGY
wasting of .... DYSTROPHY
Muscovite .... MICA, GRANITE, RUSSIAN, SERICITE
Muscovy .... DUCK, RUSSIAN
duck .... PATO
muscular .... BURLY, THEWY, BRAWNY, TOROSE
contraction .... TIC, CRAMP
contraction, childbearing
.... LABOR
disorder .... MYASTHENIA
elasticity .... TONUS
impotence .... ATAXIA
tissue tumor .... MYOMA
muscularity .... BRAWN, BEEF(INESS)
muse .... MULL, PIERIS, PONDER,

475

(DAY)DREAM, MEDITATE, MEDITATION

Muse, astronomy .... URANIA

chief .... CALLIOPE

comedy .... THALIA

dance .... TERPSICHORE

eloquence .... CALLIOPE

history .... CLIO

love .... ERATO

memory .... MNEME

music .... EUTERPE

poetry .... ERATO, THALIA, EUTERPE, CALLIOPE

sacred song .... POLYMNIA, POLYHYMNIA

tragedy .... MELPOMENE

Muses' domain .... AONIA, PARNASSUS

fountain .... HIPPOCRENE

home .... HELICON

mountain .... HELICON, PARNASSUS

of the .... PIERIAN

one of the .... CLIO, ERATO, THALIA, URANIA, EUTERPE, CALLIOPE, PIERIDES, POLYMNIA, MELPOMENE

place of worship .... PIERIA

spring of the .... CASTALIA

musette .... OBOE, BAGPIPE

museum .... GALLERY

custodian .... CURATOR

mush .... GOO, PAP, SAMP, ATOLE, JOURNEY, POTTAGE, PORRIDGE

slang .... CORN

mushroom .... MOREL, MORIL, AGÀRIC, FUNGUS, AMANITA, TOADSTOOL, DEATH CUP, CHAMPIGNON

alkaloid .... MUSCARIN(E)

cap .... PILEUS

cap's part .... LAMELLA

covering .... VOLVA

immature .... BUTTON

umbrella .... MITRA

underground .... TRUFFLE

mushy .... SOFT, PAPPY, SENTIMENTAL

Musial .... STAN, THE MAN

music .... AIR, LAY, TUNE, MELODY, HARMONY, HARMONICS

adapter .... ARRANGER

aftersong .... EPODE

as is .... STA

canto .... PASSUS

change in .... MUTA

clef .... TREBLE

composition .... FUGUE, RONDO, RONDEAU

concluding .... CODA

country/folk .... BALLAD, BLUEGRASS

cradlesong/nursery .... LULLABY

drama set to .... OPERA

first part .... PRIMO

for a movie .... SCORE

for nine .... NONET

grace note .... SANGLOT

hall .... GAFF, ODEA, ODEON, ODEUM, THEATER

high in .... ALT

high part .... TREBLE

interval in .... OCTAVE, TRITONE

lead in .... PRESA

leap in .... SALTO

lively .... GALOP, GIACOSO

lumberman's? ..... LOGARITHM

major in .... DUR

major scale .... GAMUT

mark in .... SLUR, SEGNO

measured beat .... MOTO, PULSE, TEMPO

melodious .... ARIOSO

military .... MARCH

modern .... BOP

modern type .... RAP

mournful .... DIRGE

mute .... SORDINO

night .... NOCTURNE, SERENADE

played on bells .... CHIMB, CHIMES, CARILLON

portamento .... GLIDE

rate of speed .... LENTO, TEMPO, ALLEGRO, ANDANTE

sacred .... CHORAL(E)

sentimental .... CORN, SCHMALTZ

sign .... PRESA, SEGNO

silent: direction .... TACET

slow in .... LARGO, LENTO, TARDO, ANDANTE

slow movement .... ADAGIO

soft in .... DOLCE, PIANO

solo .... ETUDE

solo, opposed to .... TUTTI

source .... TAPEDECK

stately .... LARGO, MINUET

sustained .... TENUTO

swing .... JIVE

symbol .... REST

syncopated .... RAG(TIME)

teacher .... MAESTRO

tempo .... LENTO, PRESTO, ALLEGRO, ANDANTE

term in .... MAJOR, MINOR

theme .... MOTIF, MOTIVE

throughout .... SEMPRE

timing device ..... METRONOME

together in .... ADUE

twice in .... BIS

unaccented/upbeat .... ARSIS

whole note .... SEMIBREVE

musical .... MELIC, LYRIC(AL), CANOROUS, MELODIOUS

accompaniment .... OB(B)LIGATO

Aquarian .... HAIR

beginning .... INTRO

bells .... CHIMES, CARILLON

character ..... KEY, CLEF, REST, SHARP

chord .... TRIAD, CATGUT

comedy .... REVUE, PARODY

composition ..... OPUS, FUGUE, MOTET, OPERA, PIECE, RONDO, SUITE, ARIOSO, MINUET, SONATA, CANTATA, CONCERTO, NOCTURNE, ORATORIO, SERENADE, SERENATA, SYMPHONY

direction .... PPP, STA, POCO, SOLI, LARGO, MOLTO, PRESA, TACET

disability .... AMUSIA

Domino .... FATS

drama .... OPERA

ending/closing .... CODA

entertainer .... MINSTREL

excerpt .... MORCEAU

exercise .... ETUDE

family .... TRAPPS

flourish .... CADENZA, FANFARE

group .... BAND, DUET, TRIO, CHOIR, COMBO, OCTET, CHORUS, MAZURKA, QUARTET, GLEE CLUB

half step .... SEMITONE

horn, comic .... BAZOOKA

interval .... REST, OCTAVE, TRITONE

instruction ..... LARGO, LENTO, FORTISSIMO, PIANISSIMO

instrument .... LUTE, LYRE, OBOE, REED, FLUTE, PIANO, ROTTE, SITAR, CORNET, GUITAR, SPINET, VIOL(IN), BASSOON, CITHERN, OCARINA, CALLIOPE, CLARINET, MANDOLIN, SAXOPHONE

brasswind .... BUGLE, CORNET, TRUMPET, TROMBONE

fingerboard .... VINA

fipple flute .... FLAGEOLET

guitar-like ...... LUTE, BANJO, GITTERN, UKULELE, MANDOLIN

harp-like .... SAMBUKE

inventor .... JUBAL
keyboard ..... ORGAN, PIANO,
  SPINET, CELESTA, CLAVIER,
              CALLIOPE
lute, obsolete .... THEORBO
lyre-like .... CITHARA
muffler .... MUTE
organ-like .... CALLIOPE
player ..... FLUTIST, HARPIST,
  PIANIST(E), GUITARIST,
  TRUMPETER, VIOLINIST
range of .... DIAPASON
string .... CHORD, CATGUT
stringed .... ASOR, LUTE,
  LYRE, ROTE, VINA, VIOL,
  BANJO, REBEC, VIOLA,
  CITOLE, GUITAR, VIOLIN,
  ZITHER, BANDORE,
  CITHER(N), CLAVIER,
  SAMBUKE, SAMISEN,
  UKULELE, DULCIMER,
          MANDOLIN
tone changer .... PEDAL
toy .... KAZOO
violin-like ...... VIOL, CELLO,
  VIOLA, REBEC(K)
wind .... REED, TUBA, FLUTE,
  ORGAN, OCARINA, CLARINET,
  FLAGEOLET, SAXOPHONE
instruments, collectively
.... BRASS, TRAPS, WINDS,
  STRINGS, PERCUSSION
introduction .... OVERTURE
key .... B FLAT, E FLAT
keys .... CLEFS
lines .... STEM, STAFF
medley .... OLIO, CENTO,
  PASTICHE, PASTICCIO
movement .... SCHERZO
notation ..... REST, TABLATURE
org. .... ASCAP
ornament .... ROULADE
part .... CODA
passage .... PRESTO, BRAVURA,
  CADENZA, MORCEAU
performance .... REVUE,
  CONCERT, RECITAL
phrase .... LEITMOTIF
pipe .... OAT, OBOE, REED,
  FLUTE, CLARINET, FLAGEOLET
play .... OPERETTA
range .... GAMUT
river .... DANUBE
scale .... SOLFA
short interlude .... VERSET
show that fails .... TURKEY
sign .... DOT, CLEF, ISON,
  REST, PRESA, SEGNO, SHARP
signature .... THEME
sound .... TONE, CHIME

sounds, science of
.... HARMONICS
study .... ETUDE
suite .... PARTITA
syllable .... DO, RE, MI, FA,
  SOL, LA, TI
symbol .... CLEF, SHARP
transition .... SEGUE
trill .... TREMOLO, VIBRATO
work .... OPUS, RHAPSODY
musicale .... CONCERT, SYMPHONY
musically together .... ADUE
musician .... FIFER, JUBAL,
  BUGLER, HARPER, OBOIST,
  CELLIST, DRUMMER, FIDDLER,
  FLUTIST, HARPIST, ORPHEUS,
  PIANIST, ARRANGER,
  COMPOSER, ORGANIST,
  HARMONIST, VIOLINIST
Hamelin .... PIPER
musicians' patron .... CECILIA
musing .... REVERIE, MEDITATION,
  REFLECTION
musk cat .... CIVET
product .... PERFUME
smell .... MOSCHATE
muskeg .... BOG, MARSH
muskellunge .... PIKE
musket .... GUN, DRAGON,
  GINGAL(L), JINGAL, CULVERIN
musketeer of fiction ...... ATHOS,
  ARAMIS, PORTHOS,
  D'ARTAGNAN
muskmelon ...... MANGO, ATIMON,
  CASABA, CANTALOUPE
muskrat kin .... VOLE
Muslim. See also Moslem
.... SENUSI, MUSSULMAN
ascetic ...... WHIRLING DERVISH
branch .... SHIAH
cap .... TAJ, KOPIA
chronicle .... TARSILA
court .... AGAMA
faith .... ISLAM
fasting month .... RAMADAN
group .... ULAMA
maid .... HOURI
prayers, part of .... RAKA
queen in India .... BEGUM
religious person .... IMAM,
  HADJI, HATIB, PAKIL
sacred city .... MECCA
muslin ...... MULL, ADATI, MOSAL,
  SHELA, BATISTE, NAINSOOK,
  TARLETAN
bag .... TILLOT
gauze .... TIFFANY
striped .... DORIA
very fine .... ORGANDY
muss .... ROW, MESS, CREASE,

  MUDDLE, RUMPLE, TANGLE,
  TOUSLE, DISHEVEL, DISORDER
mussel .... UNIO, MOLLUSK
product .... PEARL
Mussolini .... BENITO
nickname .... MUSSO
son-in-law .... CIANO
title of .... (IL)DUCE
Mussulman .... MOSLEM,
  SARACEN
must .... ALBA, MAUN, MOLD,
  SAPA, STUM, WINE, BOUND,
  JUICE, OUGHT, MILDEW,
  SHOULD
elephant's .... FRENZY
mustache ...... BEARD, WHISKERS,
  HANDLE BAR
Mustafa Kemal _____
.... ATATURK
mustang .... PONY, HORSE,
  BRONCO
mustard .... WEED, WOAD, CRESS,
  RADISH, TURNIP, CHARLOCK,
  CONDIMENT, SEASONING
application .... POULTICE
container .... CASTER
counterpart of .... CRESS
gas .... YPERITE, VESICANT
plaster .... SINAPISM
pod .... SILIQUE
mustee .... MESTIZO, OCTOROON
musteline animal .... MINK,
  OTTER, RATEL, MARTEN,
  WEASEL, POLECAT,
  WOLVERINE
muster .... CALL, LEVY, LIST,
  POLL, ROLL, GATHER,
  SUMMON, COLLECT,
  ASSEMBLE, MOBILIZE
in .... ENLIST
out .... DISBAND
musty .... DULL, HOAR, RANK,
  FETID, FUSTY, MOLDY, MUCID,
  STALE, TRITE, RANCID
mutable .... FICKLE, VOLATILE
mutate .... VARY, CHANGE
mutation .... CHANGE,
  EVOLUTION, SALTATION
in linguistics .... UMLAUT
mute .... MUM, DUMB, SURD,
  DUMMY, DEADEN, MUFFLE,
  SILENT, VOICELESS
become .... CLAM UP
consonant .... LENE
for trumpet .... SOURDINE
mutilate .... MAR, MAIM, DAMAGE,
  DEFACE, DEFORM, MANGLE,
  CRIPPLE, DISFIGURE
mutineer .... REBEL
mutiny .... RISE, REVOLT,

UPRISING, REBELLION
Mutsuhito's realm .... JAPAN
reign .... MEIJI
son .... HIROHITO
mutt .... CUR, DOG, POOCH,
MONGREL
mutter .... GROWL, MUMBLE,
MURMUR, GRUMBLE,
COMPLAIN
mutton .... SHEEP, (RED)MEAT
bird .... OII
chop .... CABOBS
chops .... WHISKERS,
BURNSIDES, SIDEBURNS
cut .... SADDLE
fish .... SAMA, EELPOUT
leg of .... GIGOT
neck .... SCRAG
soup .... SCOTCH BROTH
stew .... HARICOT
muttonhead .... DOLT, DUNCE
mutual .... JOINT, COMMON,
COMBINED, RECIPROCAL
muzhik .... PEASANT
muzzle .... GAG, NOSE, SNOUT,
SILENCE
loader .... RAMROD
muzzy .... DAZED, DRUNK,
SOUSED, MUDDLED
my faith .... MA FOI
fault .... MEA CULPA
heart, literally .... MACHREE
"kingdom for a _____"
.... HORSE
"my dear Watson, _____"
.... ELEMENTARY
My Fair Lady author .... SHAW,
LOWEW
Gal _____ .... SAL
Sweetness .... NAOMI
Myanmar neighbor .... LAOS
myna(h) .... BIRD
kin of .... STARLING
Mynheer .... SIR, DUTCHMAN
myopic .... NEARSIGHTED,
SHORTSIGHTED
Myra Breckinridge personified
.... (RAQUEL)WELCH

pianist .... HESS
myriad ..... TEEMING, COUNTLESS,
MULTITUDE, TEN THOUSAND
myriapod .... CENTIPEDE,
MILLIPEDE
segment .... SOMITE, TELSON
myrmicid .... ANT
Myrmidon .... ADHERENT,
FOLLOWER
Myrna, actress .... LOY
myrrh .... CICELY
myrtle .... SHRUB, GUAVA,
CAJEPUT, CAJUPUT,
PERIWINKLE
berry .... ALLSPICE
Mysore capital .... BANGALORE
mysterious .... RUNIC, WEIRD,
ARCANE, OCCULT, SECRET,
CRYPTIC, MYSTIC(AL),
ESOTERIC, ENIGMATIC
object .... UFO
mystery .... RUNE, PUZZLE,
RIDDLE, ENIGMA, SECRET,
ARCANUM, SECRECY
solve one .... UNRAVEL
story ..... MAIGRET, WHODUNIT
writer's award .... EDGAR
mystic .... YOGA, YOGI, ESSENE,
EPOPT(IC), HIDDEN, OCCULT,
SUFIST, CABALIST, ESOTERIC
art .... MAGIC, CABALA,
VOODOO, ALCHEMY, SORCERY,
ASTROLOGY
cry .... OM, EVOE
number .... SEVEN
practice .... YOGA
writing .... RUNE
mystical ...... OCCULT, ENIGMATIC
biblical word .... SELAH
British chronicle .... BRUT
doctrine .... CAB(B)ALA,
KABALA
interpretation .... ANAGOGE
mystify .... HOAX, BAFFLE,
PUZZLE, PERPLEX, BEWILDER,
CONFOUND, OBFUSCATE
mystique .... AURA, MAGIC,
CHARISMA

myth ...... FABLE, STORY, LEGEND
mythical ...... UNREAL, FABULOUS,
FICTIONAL, IMAGINARY,
LEGENDARY
animal .... GRIFFIN, GRIFFON,
GRYPHON
antelope .... YALE
beast .... DRAGON
being .... CENTAUR
bird .... ROC
character .... MOTHER GOOSE
ferryman .... CHARON
flyer .... ICARUS
giant ...... YMER, YMIR, JOTUN,
FAFNIR, CYCLOPS
hero .... EGIL(E)
horse/steed .... PEGASUS,
UNICORN
hunter .... ORION
island/continent ...... ATLANTIS
king .... ATLI, OLAF, MIDAS
lance .... RON
land .... LEMURIA
maiden .... IO, DANAE
man of brass .... TALOS
monster ...... DRAGON, SPHINX,
CHIMERA, GRIFFIN, MINOTAUR
mountain .... OSSA, HELICON,
PARNASSUS
musician .... ORPHEUS
river .... STYX
serpent .... APEPI, MIDGARD
sisters .... GORGONS
symbol of purity ..... UNICORN
trio .... FATES, GORGONS
watchdog .... GARM, CERBERUS
wolf .... FENRIR
woman .... IDUN
mythicize .... ALLEGORIZE
mythmaker .... FABULIST
mythologist .... MULLER
mythology ...... LEGEND, MYTHOS,
FOLKLORE
mythomania ...... LYING, FIBBERY
mythomaniac .... LIAR, ANANIAS,
MUNCHAUSEN
Mytilene .... LESBOS
myxoma .... TUMOR

N, Greek .... NU
Hebrew .... NUN
in physics .... NEUTRON
letter .... EN
'n' calls, _____ .... PUTS
N.B. .... NOTA BENE
Na .... SODIUM

nab .... BAG, GRAB, SNAG, CATCH,
SEIZE, ARREST, COLLAR,
CORNER, SNATCH, CAPTURE
Nabal's wife .... ABIGAIL
nabob .... DIVES, NAWAB
Nabokov, author .... VLADIMIR
heroine .... IDA

nacelle .... CAR, BASKET,
FUSELAGE
NaCl .... SALT
nacre .... SHELLFISH, MOTHER-OF-
PEARL
nacreous .... LUSTROUS
Nader .... RALPH

nadir .... DEPTHS, LOW POINT
   opposite of .... ZENITH
nag .... TIT, PONY, RIDE, URGE,
   ANNOY, HORSE, SCOLD,
   SHREW, TEASE, BADGER,
   HECTOR, PESTER, PLAGUE,
   VIRAGO, HENPECK,
   TERMAGANT
   slang .... HOSS
naga .... COBRA, SNAKE
nagana disease carrier
   .... TSETSE
nagger .... SHREW, GRIPER,
   VIRAGO, TERMAGANT
Nagoya bay .... ISE
Naha is capital of ...... OKINAWA
nahoor ...... SNA, SHEEP, BHARAL
Nahor's brother .... ABRAM,
   HARAN, ABRAHAM
   concubine .... REUMAH
   son .... UZ, BUZ, HAZO,
   GAHAM, TERAH, CHESED,
   KEMUEL, BETHUEL, JIDLAPH,
   PILDASH
   wife .... MILCAH
naiad .... NYMPH, OREAD
naid .... WORM
nail .... FIX, PIN, BRAD, CLAW,
   SPAD, TACK, CATCH, SPIKE,
   SPRIG, TACH(E), FASTEN,
   SECURE, TENTER
   board .... EMERY
   finishing/thin .... BRAD
   half-moon shape in the
   .... LUNULA
   having .... UNGUAL
   part of the .... BED, PLATE,
   LUNULA, CUTICLE
   polish .... CUTEX, ENAMEL
   puller .... CLAW
   shoemaker's .... SPARABLE
   short .... TACK
   short, thick .... STUB
   slang .... CIGARETTE
   slantingly .... TOE
   substance .... KERATIN
   3-inch .... TENPENNY
   unit of weight .... KEG
   wooden .... PEG
nailhead .... STUD
nainsook .... COTTON, MUSLIN
naive .... NAIF, GREEN, SIMPLE,
   ARTLESS, INNOCENT,
   CHILDLIKE, GUILELESS,
   INGENUOUS
   girl .... INGENUE
   one .... BABE
naivete .... INNOCENCE
naked .... BARE, NUDE, PLAIN,
   STARK, UNCLAD, EXPOSED
   in law .... INVALID

namaycush .... TOGUE, TROUT
namby-pamby ...... SILLY, VAPID,
   INSIPID, WISHY-WASHY
   person .... PHILIPS
name .... DUB, CITE, FAME, TERM,
   LABEL, (EN)TITLE, APPOINT,
   EPITHET, MENTION,
   COGNOMEN, IDENTIFY,
   MONICKER, NOMINATE,
   DESIGNATE, REPUTATION
   aristocratic .... PATRICK
   assumed .... ALIAS, INCOG,
   PSEUDONYM, SOBRIQUET
   bad .... CACONYM
   characteristic .... EPITHET,
   SOBRIQUET
   claimed by Naomi .... MARA
   derivation of .... EPONYM
   divine .... AMBROSE
   dropper .... SNOB
   fake .... ALIAS
   false .... ANONYM
   heavenly .... CELESTE
   lively .... VIVIAN
meaning beauty .... ADA
   bee .... DEBORAH
   bitter .... MARA
   breath .... ABEL
   bright .... BERTA
   champion .... NEAL
   comfort .... NOAH
   daughter .... INGA
   ewe .... RACHEL
   flaxen-haired .... LINUS
   girl .... COLLEEN
   God's protector .... ANSEL
   great fame .... ELMER
   healer .... ASA
   high .... ELI
   holy .... OLGA
   life/life-giving .... EVA
   little .... ETTA
   merry .... HILARY
   moon goddess .... DELIA
   mortal man .... ENOS
   noble .... PATRICK
   peace .... IRENE
   pleasure .... EDNA
   princess .... SARA
   rose .... RHODA
   sad .... DOLORES
   serving .... OBED
   spring born .... VERNA
   "the harvester" .... TESS
   twins .... THOMAS
   wild cow/weary .... LEAH
of A-bomb dropped in
   Hiroshima .... LITTLE
   BOY
   A-bomb dropped in
   Nagasaki ...... FAT MAN

   eight popes .... URBAN
   Jesse James' wife and
   mother .... ZERELDA
   Oz canine .... TOTO
   thing, etc. .... NOUN
   on a green stamp .... EIRE
   on envelope .... ADDRESSEE
   plate .... FACIA
   shaggy dog's .... RAGS
   slang .... HANDLE, MONI(C)KER
   substitute .... DINGUS
   to remember .... MAINE
named .... CITED, YCLEPT,
   YCLEPED, APPOINTED,
   IDENTIFIED
nameless .... UNKNOWN,
   ANONYMOUS
   person .... ANONYM
namely .... VIZ, TO WIT, SILICET
names list .... BEADROLL
namesake .... EPONYM, HOMONYM
   La Douce .... IRMA
   of Chinese leader .... MAO
nana .... AMAH, NANNY, NURSE
Nancy .... NARCISSUS
nankin .... BUFF, COTTON
nanny .... (DRY)NURSE
   vehicle of .... PRAM, BUGGY,
   STROLLER
Naomi .... MARA
   daughter-in-law .... RUTH
naos .... CELLA, TEMPLE
nap ...... DOZE, PILE, SHAG, SLEEP,
   SIESTA, SNOOZE, FORTY
   WINKS
   Brit. .... KIP
   raising device ...... GIG, CARD,
   TEASEL, TEAZEL
   shearer .... CROPPER
napalm inventor .... FIESER
nape .... PALL, NUCHA, NUQUE,
   SCRAG, SCRUFF
napery .... DAMASK, LINENS,
   DOILIES, NAPKINS
napkin .... BIB, DOILY, DIAPER,
   NAPERY, SERVIETTE
Naples .... NAPOLI
   beggar .... LAZZARONE
   island .... CAPRI
   king of .... MURAT
   lake near .... AVERNUS
   native of .... NEOPOLITAN
Napoleon ..... CARD, COIN, GAME,
   PASTRY
   birthplace of .... AJACCIO
   brother of ..... JEROME, LUCIEN
   conqueror of .... KUTUZOV,
   WELLINGTON
   downfall of .... WATERLOO
   game like .... PAM
   general .... RAPP, KLEBER

isle identified with .... ELBA,
HELENA, CORSICA
marshal of .... NEY, MURAT
scene of defeat .... WATERLOO
scene of victory .... JENA,
LODI, WAGRAM, MARENGO,
AUSTERLITZ
sister of .... ELISA, CAROLINE
wife of .... JOSEPHINE
Napoleonic marshal .... NEY,
MURAT
victory site: 1796 .... LODI
Napoli .... NAPLES
napped, as fabrics .... FRIEZED
nappy .... ALE, DOWNY, HAIRY,
WOOLLY, FOAMING
narcissism .... SELF-LOVE
narcissus .... NANCY, FLOWER,
JONQUIL, DAFFODIL
Narcissus .... EGOIST
composer .... NEVIN
love of .... SELF
nymph who loved .... ECHO
narcosis .... SLEEP, STUPOR
narcotic .... DOPE, DRUG, JUNK,
OPIUM, HEROIN, OPIATE,
ANODYNE, COCAINE, CODEINE,
HASHISH, MORPHINE,
SEDATIVE
beechnut .... FAGINE
cigarette .... KEF, REEFER,
MARIJUANA
dreamy tranquility .... KEF
drug, inject .... MAINLINE
plant ..... CUCA, HEMP, K(H)AT,
BHANG, DUTRA, POPPY,
MANDRAKE, MARIJUANA
slang .... POT, ACID, COKE,
JUNK, SNOW
under influence of .... HIGH,
DOPEY, STONED
user .... DOPER, FIEND, ADDICT,
JUNKIE, SMOKER, POTHEAD,
SNOWBIRD
nard .... SALVE, OINTMENT
nares .... NOSTRILS
narghile .... PIPE, HOOKA(H)
narial .... RHINAL
narine .... NASAL
nark .... SPY, AGENT, INFORMER
Narragansett vegetable dish
.... SUCCOTASH
narrate .... TELL, RECITE, RELATE,
REPORT, RECOUNT
narrative .... SAGA, TALE, CONTE,
STORY, ACCOUNT, NOVELLA,
RECITAL
poem .... LAY, EPIC, EPOS,
ILIAD, BEOWULF, ODYSSEY
narrator .... RELATOR
narrow ...... CLOSE, LIMIT, TAPER,

ANGUST, STRAIT(EN)
combining form .... STENO
escape .... CLOSE CALL
gash .... SLIT
minded .... PETTY, BIASED,
BIGOTED, PEDANTIC
opening .... SLOT
pew .... SLIP
point of land .... SPIT
street .... LANE, ALLEY
narrowed .... STENOSED
narrowing of a passage
.... STENOSIS
narrows .... SOUND, STRAIT
narwhal .... WHALE, CETACEAN
nary .... NO, NOT ANY
NASA effort .... MOONSHOT
nasal .... NARINE, RHINAL
catarrh .... CORYZA
cavity .... NARE
intonation .... TWANG
mucous .... SNOT, SNIVEL
passage .... NARES, NOSTRIL
nascency .... BIRTH, ORIGIN,
GENESIS, BEGINNING,
FORMATION
Nash, humorist .... OGDEN
Nasser .... GAMAL(ABDEL)
nasty .... FOUL, MEAN, FILTHY,
OBSCENE, ILL-TEMPERED
type .... DASTARD
Nat and Natalie .... COLE
natal .... INNATE, NATIVE
day .... BIRTHDAY
natant ...... FLOATING, SWIMMING
natatorium .... POOL
Nathan, George _____ ...... JEAN
nation .... STATE, PEOPLE,
COUNTRY
massacre of .... GENOCIDE
"of shopkeepers"
.... ENGLAND
Nation, temperance leader
.... CARRY
national .... CITIZEN, FEDERAL
character .... ETHOS
hymn .... ANTHEM
National Guard .... MILITIA
nations, alliance of .... AXIS
native .... SON, NATAL, INBORN,
ENDEMIC, NATURAL,
INHERENT, ABORIGINE,
INDIGENOUS
ability .... GIFT, TALENT,
APTITUDE
agent .... COMPRADOR
animal/plant .... INDIGENE
chief .... DATU, CACIQUE
inhabitant .... DENIZEN
policeman .... SEPOY
ruler .... NIZAM

salt .... HALITE
suffix .... ITE
Native American. See **Indian/
Native American**
nativity .... BIRTH
NATO .... ALLIANCE
natty .... CHIC, TRIM, SHARP,
SMART, SPRUCE
natural .... REAL, WILD, PLAIN,
INBORN, INNATE, NORMAL,
SIMPLE, UNPOSED
ability .... GIFT, FLAIR, KNACK,
GENUIS, TALENT, APTITUDE
abode .... HABITAT
endowment .... TALENT
flier .... BIRD
inclination .... PROPENSITY
pigment .... OCHRE
naturalist .... MUIR, BEEBE,
DARWIN, ANDREWS, ANIMIST,
AUDUBON, BURBANK,
BIOLOGIST, COMSTOCK,
ECOLOGIST
prefix .... ECO
naturalize ...... ADOPT, CONVERT,
AFFILIATE
naturally .... OF COURSE
nature .... KIND, SORT, TYPE,
ESSENCE, CREATION,
CHARACTER
group .... EPA
nature's soil builder
.... EARTHWORM
naught .... NIL, ZERO, NOTHING
bring to .... UNDO, VOID,
CANCEL, NULLIFY
naughty .... IMPISH, OBSCENE,
WAYWARD, MISCHIEVOUS
-naughty .... NO-NO
nausea .... PALL, QUALM,
WAMBLE, DISGUST, AVERSION
affected with .... QUEASY
nauseate .... REVOLT, SICKEN
Nausicaa's discovery
.... ODYSSEUS
father .... ALCINOUS
nautical .... NAVAL, MARINE,
OCEANIC, MARITIME
call .... AHOY
chain .... TYE
command/cry .... ALEE, AVAST
cry: var. .... OHOY
dick .... DEADEYE
fly .... BURGEE
Halt! .... AVAST
mile .... KNOT
rope .... HAWSER, NETTLE,
MARLINE, RATLINE
term .... AYE, ALEE, ATRY,
ABAFT, ABEAM, AFORE,
ASTERN, AWEATHER, PORTSIDE

time: abbr. .... GST
nautilus .... MOLLUSK, ARGONAUT
Nautilus, commander of
.... NEMO
Navaho .... INDIAN
hut .... HOGAN
naval .... MARINE, MARITIME,
NAUTICAL
academy .... ANNAPOLIS
cadet ...... MIDDY, MIDSHIPMAN
commander .... ADMIRAL,
CAPTAIN, SKIPPER
detection method .... SONAR
force .... FLEET, ARMADA
hero .... DEWEY, NELSON,
FARRAGUT
officer .... MATE, ENSIGN,
YEOMAN
pass of a sort .... NAVICERT
title .... ADMIRAL, COMMODORE
unit .... FLOTILLA
unit list/roll .... MUSTER
vessel .... UBOAT, TENDER,
CRUISER, FLATTOP, WARSHIP,
CORVETTE, DESTROYER
Naval Reserve woman .... WAVE
nave .... HUB
navel .... UMBILICUS
of Sicily .... ENNA
point .... NOMBRIL
navigate .... SAIL, STEER, AVIATE,
CRUISE
navigation detecting systems
.... LORAN, SONAR, SHORAN
device .... RACON
hazard .... REEF
navigator .... COOK, ERIC, NAVVY,
BAFFIN, BERING, TASMAN,
MAGELLAN
Navigators Island .... SAMOA
navvy .... LABORER
navy .... FLEET, WARSHIPS, SEA
FORCE
bed .... SACK
color .... BLUE
engineer .... SEABEE
group ...... ARMADA, FLOTILLA,
SQUADRON, TASKFORCE
man .... CPO, MATE, SEABEE
mascot of .... GOAT
pharmacist .... CORPSMAN
ration .... HARDTACK
recruit .... BOOT
scout boat .... VEDETTE
nawab .... NABOB, TITLE
nay .... NO, VOTE, DENIAL
naysayer .... DENIER
Nazarene .... JESUS
Nazarite, he was one
.... SAMSON
Nazi .... FASCIST, HITLERITE

airforce .... LUFTWAFFE
collaborator .... LAVAL,
QUISLING
concentration camp
.... BELSEN, DACHAU
defector .... HESS
district .... GAU
district leader .... GAULEITER
emblem .... FYLFOT, SWASTIKA
greeting .... HEIL
ideology .... HERRENVOLK
leader .... LEY, HESS, HITLER,
FUEHRER, GOERING, HIMMLER,
GOEBBELS
organization, U.S. .... BUND
salute .... HEIL HITLER
state police .... GESTAPO
Nazimova, actress .... ALLA
NB, part of .... NOTA, BENE
NBA all time record holder:
for assists .... EARVIN
"MAGIC" JOHNSON, JOHN
STOCKTON
for points ...... KAREEM ABDUL
JABBAR
for rebounds .... WILT
CHAMBERLAIN
NCO .... SARGE, CORPORAL,
SERGEANT
Ne ___ ultra (acme) ...... PLUS
neap .... TIDE
near .... NIGH, ABOUT, CLOSE,
APPROACH, FRIENDLY,
INTIMATE
solution .... HOT
the ankle .... TARSAL
where the action is
.... RINGSIDE
Near East country .... EGYPT,
SYRIA, ISRAEL, JORDAN,
TURKEY, LEBANON
nearby .... CLOSE, HANDY,
AROUND, BESIDE, A STONE'S
THROW AWAY
poetically .... ANIGH
nearest .... NEXT, NIGHEST,
IMMEDIATE
nearly .... ALL BUT, ALMOST, NOT
QUITE
nearsighted .... MYOPIC
person .... MYOPE
nearsightedness .... MYOPIA
neat ...... CHIC, PURE, TIDY, TRIG,
TRIM, CLEAN, NATTY, SLEEK,
ADROIT, SOIGNE, SPIFFY,
SPRUCE
neb .... TIP, BEAK, BILL, NOSE,
SNOUT
Nebraska capital .... LINCOLN
city/town .... ORD, ALMA,
YORK, BLAIR, OMAHA, PONCA,

SIDNEY, CHADRON, FREMONT,
KEARNEY, BEATRICE,
COLUMBUS, HASTINGS, WEST
POINT, SCOTTSBLUFF
college ..... DOANE, BELLEVUE,
HASTINGS
county ..... BOYD, CASS, CLAY,
GAGE, HALL, HOLT, KNOX,
OTOE, POLK, YORK, ADAMS,
DODGE, SARPY, DAKOTA,
DAWSON, PLATTE, SEWARD,
DOUGLAS
dam .... KINGSLEY
Indian .... OTOE, KIOWA,
PONCA, OMAHA, PAWNEE
lake .... DADS, MOON, SWAN,
ALICE, SWANSON, CRESCENT
river ...... LOUP, CEDAR, SNAKE,
WHITE, DISMAL, NEMAHA,
PLATTE, COLAMUS, ELKHORN,
MISSOURI
state bird .... MEADOWLARK
state flower .... GOLDENROD
state nickname
.... CORNHUSKER
tourist attraction .... BOYS
TOWN, PIONEER VILLAGE
U.S. Air Force Base
.... OFFUT
university .... WESLEYAN
nebulous .... HAZY, MISTY,
VAGUE, CLOUDY, OBSCURE,
UNCLEAR, INDEFINITE
necessaries .... ESTOVERS
necessarily .... PERFORCE,
INEVITABLY
necessary .... MUST, VITAL,
URGENT, NEEDFUL, PRESSING,
REQUIRED, ESSENTIAL,
REQUISITE
necessitate ...... COMPEL, ENTAIL,
OBLIGE, REQUIRE
necessity ...... FATE, NEED, WANT,
DEMAND, URGENCY,
COMPULSION
neck .... PET, KISS, SCRAG, SPOON,
CARESS, CERVIX, GULLET,
STRAIT, CHANNEL
and shoulder covering
.... SHAWL, TUCKER
animal with long ...... GIRAFFE
armor .... GORGET
artery .... CAROTID
back of .... NAPE, NUCHA,
CERVIX, SCRUFF
covering .... MANE, RUFF
cramp .... CRICK
ligament .... PAXWAX
of beef .... CLOD
of land .... SPIT, ISTHMUS
of the ..... JUGULAR, CERVICAL

pain .... CRICK
part of horse .... WITHERS
piece .... BOA, TIE, FICHU,
SCARF, STOLE, COLLAR,
CRAVAT
scarf .... ASCOT, TIPPET
slang .... SMOOCH
neckerchief .... SCARF
necklace .... BEAD, STRAND,
STRING, TORQUE, CHAPLET,
RIVIERE, CARCANET
appendage .... LOCKET,
PENDANT, LAVALIER
colloquial .... CHOKER
ornament .... LAVALIER(E)
neckline, low .... DECOLLETE
shape .... VEE
necktie .... BOW, ASCOT, SCARF,
CHOKER, CRAVAT
ornament .... STICKPIN
party .... HANGING
neckwear .... RUFF, COLLAR,
MUFFLER
necrology .... OBIT(UARY)
necromancer .... DIVINER,
SORCERER
necromancy .... SORCERY,
(BLACK)MAGIC
necropolis .... CEMETERY,
GRAVEYARD
necropsy .... AUTOPSY, POST
MORTEM
nectar .... DRINK, BEVERAGE,
HONEY(DEW)
of the gods .... AMBROSIA
product .... HONEY
nectarine .... PEACH
nee .... BORN
need .... LACK, WANT, DESIRE,
EXIGENCY, REQUISITE
needle .... GOAD, PROD, PRICK,
TEASE, BODKIN, HECKLE,
POINTER, PROVOKE,
INDICATOR
bug .... NEPA
case .... ETUI, ETWEE
combining form .... ACU
crystal like .... ACICULA
etching .... STYLE
hole .... EYE
pushing disk .... PALM
shaped ...... ACUATE, ACERATE,
ACEROSE, ACIFORM, SPICULE
needlefish .... GAR, PIPEFISH
needlewoman .... SEAMSTRESS,
SEMPSTRESS
needlework .... SEWING,
KNITTING, EMBROIDERY
beginner's .... SAMPLER
loop .... BRIDE
needy .... POOR, INDIGENT,

DESTITUTE, PENNILESS
ne'er-do-well .... DRIFTER,
WASTREL
nefarious .... EVIL, WICKED,
VICIOUS
Nefertiti's husband .... PHARAOH
negate .... VOID, ANNUL, BELIE,
CANCEL, NULLIFY,
COUNTERACT
negation .... DENIAL, NULLITY
act of .... VETO
polite .... NO SIR
negative .... NO, MINUS
conjunction .... NOT
connective .... NOR, NEITHER
emphatic .... NEVER
ion .... ANION
opposite of .... POSITIVE,
AFFIRMATIVE
outcome .... NIL
particle .... ION
photo .... FILM
prefix .... NON
slangy .... NAW, NIX, NOPE, NO
DICE, NO SOAP
terminal .... CATHODE
vote .... NAY, NYET
neglect .... MISS, OMIT, SKIP,
SHIRK, FORGET, IGNORE,
OMISSION, OVERLOOK,
OVERSIGHT
neglected .... ABANDONED
neglectful .... LAX, SLACK,
REMISS, DERELICT
negligee .... (NIGHT)GOWN,
PEIGNOR
negligent .... LAX, REMISS,
CARELESS, DERELICT,
DELINQUENT
negligible .... SLIGHT, TRIVIAL,
TRIFLING
amount .... PEANUTS
negotiable .... WORKABLE
negotiate .... DEAL, TREAT,
HANDLE, PARLEY, ARRANGE,
BARGAIN, DISCUSS, TRANSACT
Negri of films .... POLA
Negrillo .... BUSHMAN
negus, Ethiopia's
.... (HAILE)SELASSIE
Nehru .... JAWAHARLAL
neigh .... (W)HINNY, (S)NICKER
neighborhood ...... AREA, VENUE,
REGION, PURLIEU, LOCALITY,
VICINAGE, VICINITY,
COMMUNITY
neighboring .... NEXT, NEARBY,
ADJACENT, ADJOINING
neighbor's gathering .... BEE
neither, companion of .... NOR
moral or immoral .... AMORAL

right or left .... MIDDLE OF
THE ROAD
Nejd, capital of .... RIYADH
robe .... ABA
Nejdi .... ARAB
Nellie, journalist .... BLY
Nelson, Admiral .... HORATIO
victory scene ...... TRAFALGAR
"Nelson's blood" .... RUM, GROG
nelumbo .... LOTUS
nemathelminth .... (HOOK)WORM
nematode .... ASCARID, PINWORM,
(HOOK)WORM, ROUNDWORM
nembutal .... HYPNOTIC, SEDATIVE
nemesis .... BANE, CURSE,
PLAGUE, AVENGER, GODDESS
Nitti's .... NESS
neon .... LIGHT
neophyte .... TYRO, NOVICE,
AMATEUR, CONVERT,
TRAINEE, BEGINNER
Neopolitan secret society
.... CAMORRA
neoteric .... NEW, MODERN,
RECENT
Nepal capital .... KAT(H)MANDU
city/town .... JUMLA,
MUSTANG, PYUTHAN,
SALLYAN, LALITPUR,
BHAKTAPUR
coin .... MOHAR
inhabitant .... KHA, MAGAR,
NEWAR, GURKHA, GURUNG
king .... PRITHWI, BIRENDRA,
MAHENDRA
language .... THARU, NEPALI,
BHUTIA, NEWARI
monetary unit .... RUPEE
Mongoloid .... LAI, RAIS
mountain .... LHOTSE,
EVEREST, ANNAPURNA
mountaineers .... SHERPAS
neighbor .... CHINA, INDIA,
TIBET
panda .... WAH
peak .... API
people .... GURKHA
premier .... KOIRALA
river .... BHERI
sect .... ACHAR(A)
warrior .... GURKHA, RAJPUT
wild goat .... TAHR
Nephele, daughter of ...... HELLE
nephrite .... JADE
nephritic .... RENAL
nepotism .... FAVORITISM
beneficiary of .... RELATIVE
subject of .... EMPLOYMENT
nepotists, first .... PRELATES
beneficiaries .... NEPHEWS
Neptune .... LER, PLANET,

discoverer of .... GALLE

scepter of .... TRIDENT

son of .... TRITON

nerd .... DRIP

nereid .... THETIS, (SEA)NYMPH, AMPHITRITE

Nereus' daughter .... NEREID, THETIS

wife .... DORIS

Nero .... DESPOT, EMPEROR

band leader .... PETER

mother of .... AGRIPPINA

start of his reign LIV

teacher of .... SENECA

wife of ..... OCTAVIA, POPPAEA

Wolfe's creator .... STOUT

neroli .... OIL

nerve .... GRIT, PLUCK, SINEW, TENDON, COURAGE, BOLDNESS, TEMERITY

cell .... NEURON(E)

cell branch .... DENDRON

cell process .... AXON, NEURITE, DENDRITE

colloquial .... FACE, GALL, GUTS, BRASS, CHEEK, CRUST, AUDACITY

combining form .... NEUR(O)

fiber, sheath of .... MYELIN

fibers, bundle of .... TRACT, PEDUNCLE

inflammation .... NEURITIS

injury .... NEURAPRAXIA

layer .... ALVEUS

network .... RETE, RETIA

of a .... NEURAL

pain .... NEURALGIA

passage for .... HILUM

sensory .... AFFERENT, EFFERENT

substance .... ALBA

tonic .... NERVINE, SEDATIVE

(w)racking .... TRYING, JARRING

nerves ...... FIT, JITTERS, HYSTERIA

network of .... PLEXUS

pertaining to .... NEURO, NEURAL, NERVINE

nervous .... EDGY, TENSE, FEARFUL, JITTERY, SKITTISH, TIMOROUS

condition .... NEURALGIA

disease .... NEURITIS, TARANTISM

disorder .... TIC, CHOREA, NEUROSIS, PARALYSIS

feeling .... JIMJAMS, JITTERS

seizure .... PANIC, FRENZY, ANEURIA, JITTERS, EPILEPSY

state .... TIZZY

strain .... TENSION

twitch .... TIC

nervy .... BOLD, BRASH, GUTSY

nescient .... AGNOSTIC, IGNORANT, INNOCENT

ness .... CAPE, HEADLAND

Nessus .... CENTAUR

slayer of .... HERCULES

nest .... DEN, NIDE, HAUNT, NIDUS, RESORT, RETREAT

ant's ..... ANTHILL, FORMICARY

bird of prey's/eagle's ...... AERY, EYRY, AERIE, EYRIE

build a .... NIDIFY

egg .... MONEY, SAVINGS

mare's .... HOAX

of eggs .... CLUTCH

on a cliff .... EYRIE

nested boxes .... INRO

nestle .... CUDDLE, NUZZLE, SETTLE, SHELTER, SNUGGLE

nestling .... EYAS, OWLET, POULT, SQUAB, EAGLET

noise of .... CHIRP

Nestor .... SAGE, WISE MAN, COUNSELOR

relative of .... SOLOMON

net ...... GIN, GAIN, MESH, CLEAR, FILET, TULLE, (EN)TRAP, SAGENE, BALANCE, (EN)SNARE, RETICLE, LEFT-OVER

fishing .... SEINE, TRAWL, TRAMMEL

like a .... RETIFORM

making of .... RETIARY

ornamental .... FRET

silk .... MALINE(S)

trapping .... TOIL

nether ...... DOWN, LOWER, UNDER

world .... HELL, HADES

world deity .... DIS, CORA, KORE, LOKI, MINOS, ORCUS, CHARON

Netherlands. See also **Dutch**
.... HOLLAND

anatomist .... RAU

Antilles capital
.... WILLEMSTAD

Antilles island .... SABA, ARUBA, BONAIRE, CURACAO

bay .... DOLLARD

canal .... ORANGE, WILLEMS

capital .... AMSTERDAM, THE HAGUE

cheese market .... EDAM

city/town .... EDE, BREDA, DELFT, EMMEN, GOUDA, VENLO, ZEIST, ARNHEM, LEIDEN, ZWOLLE, HAARLEM, TILBURG, UTRECHT, ZAANDAM,

FLUSHING, NIJMEGEN, APELDOORN, DORDRECHT, EINDHOVEN, GRONINGEN, HILVERSUM, ROTTERDAM

coin .... RYDER, GULDEN, GUILDER

colonist .... BOER

commune .... EDE, EPE

cupboard .... KAS

duchy .... BRABANT

fair/carnival .... KERMIS, KERMESS

island .... TEXEI GOEREE, GRIEND, MARKEN, VOORNE, AMELAND

lake .... IJSSELMEER, SLOTERMEER

language .... DUTCH

measure ...... ROEDE, MORGEN, STREEP

monetary unit .... GUILDER

mountain .... VAALSERBERG

premier .... (DE)JONG, ZIJLSTRA

province .... DRENTHE, LIMBURG, UTRECHT, ZEELAND, FLEVOLAND, FRIESLAND, GRONINGEN, GELDERLAND

queen of .... JULIANA, WILHELMINA

queen's consort .... BERNHARD

river .... LEK, EEMS, MAAS, MARK, ROER, WAAL, HUNSE, IJSSEL, MEUSE, REGGE, RHINE, VECHT, DOMMEL

ruling family .... NASSAU

seaport .... ROTTERDAM

tulip center .... HAARLEM

weight .... ONS, WIGT(JE)

youth gangs .... PROVOS

nethermost .... LOWEST

nettle .... BUG, VEX, WEED, ANNOY, STING, RUFFLE, IRRITATE

Latin .... URTICA

plant .... RAMEE, RAMIE

rash .... HIVES, UREDO, URTICARIA

sting .... URTICATE

network .... WEB, LACE, MAZE, MESH, RETE, RETIA, HOOKUP, PLEXUS, TISSUE, LATTICE, NETTING, TRELLIS

neuralgic pain .... HEMIALGIA

neurasthenia .... NEUROSIS, MELANCHOLIA

neuron, part of .... AXON, DENDRITE

type of .... MOTO, INTER, SENSORY

neurons' contact point
.... SYNAPSE
neurotic .... NEURAL, PSYCHIC
disorder .... ANXIETY,
DEPRESSION
neuter .... GENDER, ASEXUAL
verbal noun .... GERUND
neutral .... ALOOF, MUGWUMP,
INDIFFERENT, NONPARTISAN
ground .... FENCE
neutralize .... ANNUL, CANCEL,
NEGATE, OFFSET, NULLIFY,
COUNTERACT
magnetic field .... DEGAUSS
Nevada capital ...... CARSON CITY
city/town .... ELY, ELKO,
RENO, SPARKS, LAS VEGAS,
LOVELOCK, BOULDER CITY,
HENDERSON, SUNRISE MANOR,
PARADISE VALLEY
county .... NYE, ELKO, LYON,
CLARK, WASHOE, DOUGLAS,
ESMERALDA, CARSON CITY
dam .... DAVIS, HOOVER
desert ..... TULE, BLACK ROCK,
SMOKE CREEK
desert event .... A-TEST
Indian .... PAIUTE
lake ...... MEAD, RUBY, TAHOE,
CARSON, MOHAVE, MASSACRE
mountain .... BIG, LONE,
CEDAR, TABLE, BERLIN,
POTOSI, TIMBER
mountain range .... BUTTE,
MUDDY, SNAKE, MORMON,
VIRGIN
peak .... PIPER, VIRGIN,
BOUNDARY
river ..... KINGS, QUINN, REESE,
WHITE, OWYHEE, TRUCKEE
state bird .... BLUEBIRD
state flower .... SAGEBRUSH
state nickname .... SILVER,
SAGEBRUSH
state tree .... PINON
tourist attraction .... RENO,
TAHOE, LAS VEGAS, HOOVER
DAM
U.S. Air Force Base
.... NELLIS
valley .... SPRING, CRESCENT,
BIG SMOKY, LITTLE SMOKY
neve .... ICE, FIRN, SNOW
never ...... NOT EVER, AT NO TIME
ending .... ETERNAL
mind! .... SKIP IT
say die .... GO FOR BROKE
nevertheless ..... BUT, YET, STILL,
ANYHOW, ANYWAY, HOWEVER
Nevin's song .... ROSARY,
NARCISSUS

nevus .... MOLE, FRECKLE,
LENTIGO, BIRTHMARK
main type of .... VASCULAR,
MELANOCYTIC
new .... RAW, CENE, LATE, FRESH,
GREEN, NOVEL, YOUNG,
MODERN, RECENT, UNUSED,
CURRENT, FOREIGN, STRANGE,
NEO(TERIC)
deal .... RETRADE
combining form .... NEO
New Britain city .... RABAUL
Caledonia capital ..... NOUMEA
Deal agency .... NRA, TVA
Deal president .... FDR,
ROOSEVELT
England boat .... SHARPIE
England state .... MAINE,
VERMONT, CONNECTICUT,
RHODE ISLAND,
MASSACHUSETTS, NEW
HAMPSHIRE
Englander .... YANK(EE),
DOWN EASTER
Guinea .... PAPUA
bay .... MILNE
brain disease .... KURU
capital .... PORT MORESBY
city/town .... LAE, WEWAK,
GOROKA, MADANG
gulf .... HUON
hog .... BENE
island .... ARU, LONG,
KARKAR, MISIMA, ROSSEL,
TAGULA, WOODLARK
lodge .... YEU
monetary unit .... KINA
native .... ASMAT, KARON,
PAPUAN
pole .... BIS
port .... LAE, DARU
river .... FLY, RAMU, SEPIK
strait .... TORRES, DAMPIER
Hampshire
capital .... CONCORD
city/town .... DERRY, DOVER,
KEENE, SALEM, BERLIN,
DURHAM, EXETER, HUDSON,
NASHUA, PELHAM, TILTON,
AMHERST, HAMPTON,
LACONIA, ROCHESTER,
MANCHESTER, PORTSMOUTH,
LONDONDERRY
county .... COOS, BELKNAP,
GRAFTON, MERRIMACK,
STRAFFORD
dam .... MOORE, WILDER,
EVERETT
island .... WHITE
lake .... BOW, CONWAY,
MASCOMA, OSSIPEE,

SUNAPEE, NUBANUSIT
mountain .... TOM, BLUE,
BOND, CUBE, LONG, RICE,
ADAMS, CABOT, CANNON,
SANDWICH, WHITEFACE
river .... MAD, COLD, GALE,
PINE, SACO, BAKER, ELLIS,
SUGAR
state bird ...... PURPLE FINCH
state college .... KEENE,
PLYMOUTH
state flower .... PURPLE
LILAC
state nickname ...... GRANITE
U.S. Air Force Base
.... PEASE
Haven blue .... YALE
Hebrides
capital .... VILA
island .... TANA
Jersey bay .... NEWARK,
RARITAN, BARNEGAT,
DELAWARE
cape .... MAY
capital .... TRENTON
city/town .... LODI, WALL,
BRICK, UNION, CAMDEN,
EDISON, HAZLET, JERSEY,
LINDEN, LEONIA, NEWARK,
NUTLEY, ORANGE, RAHWAY,
BAYONNE, HOBOKEN,
PARAMUS, PASSAIC,
TEANECK, WYCKOFF,
GARFIELD, ATLANTIC,
PATERSON, ELIZABETH,
LAKEHURST, HACKENSACK,
MONTCLAIR, LIVINGSTON,
RUTHERFORD
college .... CALDWELL,
FELICIAN, DON BOSCO
colonizer .... PATROON
county .... ESSEX, OCEAN,
SALEM, UNION, BERGEN,
CAMDEN, HUDSON, MERCER,
MORRIS, SUSSEX, PASSAIC,
ATLANTIC, SOMERSET,
CUMBERLAND
island .... LONG BEACH
lake .... BUDD, ECHO, UNION,
MOHAWK, OWASSA, TAPPAN,
CULVERS, POMPTON,
WAWAYANDA
mountain .... HIGH POINT
resort .... LONG BRANCH
river .... TOMS, SALEM,
HUDSON, OSWEGO, RAMAPO,
SADDLE, MULLICA, PASSAIC,
PEQUEST, RARITAN,
COHANSEY, DELAWARE,
NAVESINK, TUCKAHOE
state bird .... GOLDFINCH

state college ..... MONTCLAIR
state flower .... BOGBICE
VIOLET
state nickname ...... GARDEN
tourist site .... LIBERTY
VILLAGE, WATERLOO
VILLAGE, ATLANTIC CITY
BOARDWALK
university .... DREW,
PRINCETON

Mexico
artists' colony .... TAOS
canyon ..... CHACO, CHIVATO
capital .... SANTA FE
caverns .... CARLSBAD
city/town .... TAOS, ZUNI,
HOBBS, RATON, CLOVIS,
SILVER, ROSWELL, SOCORRO,
CARLSBAD, LAS CRUCES,
FARMINGTON, ALAMOGORDO,
ALBUQUERQUE
colonizer .... ONATE
county .... LEA, EDDY, TAOS,
CURRY, OTERO, CHAVES,
DONA ANA, SAN JUAN,
SANDOVAL, VALENCIA, LOS
ALAMOS, BERNALILLO
Indian .... SIA, UTE, PIRO,
TANO, TEWA, ZUNI, APACHE,
NAVAHO, NAVAJO, PUEBLO,
MESCALERO
Indian pueblo .... ACOMA
lake .... SALT, SUMNER,
BOULDER, CONCHAS, RED
BLUFF
mountain .... BLACK,
GROUSE, TAYLOR, WHEELER
resort .... TAOS
river ..... GILA, ZUNI, CHACO,
PECOS, ANIMAS, PUERCO,
CIMARRON, RIO GRANDE
state bird .... ROADRUNNER
state flower .... YUCCA
state nickname
.... SUNSHINE, LAND OF
ENCHANTMENT
state tree .... PINON
university .... HIGHLANDS

Orleans
festival .... MARDI GRAS
institution .... TULANE
music .... RAGTIME
native .... CREOLE
nickname of .... CRESCENT
CITY
pro .... SAINT
South Wales capital
.... SYDNEY
Testament book .... ACTS,
JOHN, JUDE, LUKE, JAMES,
MARK, PETER, TITUS, ROMANS,

MATTHEW, TIMOTHY,
EPHESIANS, REVELATION
gospel .... JOHN, LUKE,
MARK, MATTHEW
hell .... GEHENNA
in Syriac .... PESHITO
language of .... GREEK,
KOINE
longest book in the ..... LUKE
measure of capacity
.... COR, POT, BATH, SEAH,
QUART, BUSHEL
measure of length ..... MILE,
CUBIT, FATHOM, FURLONG
middle book in the
.... THESSALONIANS
oldest complete copy of
the .... CODEX SINAITICUS
shortest book in the .... JOHN
weight .... MINA, LIBRA,
TALENT
Year's Day sight .... FLOATS
York
bay ..... PECONIC, GARDINERS
capital .... ALBANY
city/town .... ROME, TROY,
OLEAN, UTICA, AUBURN,
CARMEL, ELMIRA, ITHACA,
NASSAU, ONEIDA, OSWEGO,
BUFFALO, YONKERS, DEER
PARK, LOCKPORT, OSSINING,
SYRACUSE, JAMESTOWN,
NEW YORK, OCEANSIDE,
ROCHESTER, BINGHAMTON,
GLENS FALLS, HICKSVILLE,
MOUNT VERNON, NEW
ROCHELLE, WHITE PLAINS
college .... BARD, IONA,
VASSAR, DOWLING,
LADYCLIFF, MARYMOUNT
college town .... ITHACA
colonizer .... PATROON
county .... ERIE, BRONX,
ESSEX, KINGS, TIOGA,
YATES, ALBANY, GREENE,
MONROE, NASSAU, ONEIDA,
ORANGE, OSWEGO, QUEENS,
ULSTER, NEW YORK,
STEUBEN, SUFFOLK,
ONONDAGA, SARATOGA,
WESTCHESTER
creek .... CONEWANGO
division .... BORO(UGH)
falls .... NIAGARA
fictitious name .... JUKES
Indian .... ERIE, CAYUGA,
ONEIDA, SENECA
Institute .... PRATT
Institute of Technology
.... ROCHESTER
island .... LONG, PLUM,

ELLIS, GRAND, STONY,
GALLOO, STATEN, FISHERS,
SHELTER, VALCOUR,
GARDINERS, GRENADIER,
MANHATTAN
islands .... THOUSAND
lake .... ERIE, LILA, BRANT,
TITUS, CAYUGA, ONEIDA,
KEUKA, PLACID, SENECA,
SILVER, TUPPER, HEMLOCK,
ONTARIO, SARANAC,
SARATOGA, CHAMPLAIN,
BONAPARTE
Military Academy/post
.... WEST POINT
motto .... EXCELSIOR, EVER
UPWARD
mountain ..... MARCY, SLIDE,
HUNTER, HAYSTACK,
SKYLIGHT, WHITEFISH
mountains .... CATSKILL,
ADIRONDACK
newspaper .... TIMES
newspaper founder
.... GREELEY
old name .... NEW ORANGE
planetarium .... HAYDEN
repertory company ...... APA
reservoir .... KENSICO
resort .... LAKE PLACID
river .... DEER, BLACK,
GRASS, MOOSE, BEAVER,
HUDSON, MOHAWK, OSWEGO,
SALMON, SENECA, GENESEE,
NIAGARA, SARANAC,
CHENANGO, COHOCTON,
DELAWARE, UNADILLA,
WALLKILL
state bird .... BLUEBIRD
state flower .... ROSE
state nickname .... EMPIRE
state penitentiary .... SING
SING
team .... JETS, METS, GIANTS,
KNICKS, YANKEES
time zone .... EST
tourist attraction ...... BRONX
ZOO, WALL STREET, TIMES
SQUARE, NIAGARA FALLS,
STATUE OF LIBERTY, EMPIRE
STATE BUILDING
university .... ADELPHI,
CORNELL, FORDHAM,
HOFSTRA, COLUMBIA,
ROCHESTER, ROCKEFELLER
village .... NYACK,
GREENWICH
New York City borough
.... BRONX, QUEENS,
BROOKLYN, STATEN ISLAND,
MANHATTAN

modernism showplace of .... MOMA, MUSEUM OF MODERN ART

nickname .... THE BIG APPLE

political machine .... TAMMANY

prison .... TOMBS

section .... HARLEM

street .... BOWERY

subway .... BMT, IND, IRT

New Yorker .... GOTHAMITE, MANHATTANITE, KNICKERBOCKER

cartoonist .... STEIG

New Zealand aborigine .... MAORI

author .... MARSH

bay .... BREAM, HAWKE, CLOUDY, GOLDEN, TASMAN

bird ..... MOA, TUI, KIWI, MIRO, PEHO, RURU, WEKA, LOWAN, APTERYX, MOREPORK, NOTORNIS

cape .... BRETT, EGMONT, REINGA, FAREWELL, KIDNAPPERS

capital .... WELLINGTON

caterpillar .... WERI, AWETO

cattail .... RAUPO

city/town ..... NAPIER, NELSON, DUNEDIN, ROTORUA, AUCKLAND, HASTINGS, TAKAPUNA, TAURANGA, WANGANUI, WHANGAREL

corn .... KANGA

demon .... TAIPO

discoverer .... TASMAN

explorer .... COOK

extinct bird .... MOA

firth .... THAMES

fish .... IHI, HIKU

gorge .... OTIRA

gulf .... HAURAKI

harbor .... OTAGO, KAIPARA, MANUKAU

hen .... WEKAS

island .... PITT, RUAPUKE, STEWART, WAIHEKE

islands .... CHATHAM, MERCURY

lake .... TAUPO, PUKAKI, TEKAPO, WANAKA, ROTORUA, WAKATIPU

language ...... MAORI, ENGLISH

locust .... WETA

mollusk .... PIPI

monetary unit .... DOLLAR

morepork .... PEHO, RURU

mountain .... UNA, COOK, OWEN, EGMONT, TASMAN, WHITCOMBE

mountain climber .... HILLARY

mulberry .... AUTE

native .... M(A)ORI

owl .... RURU

palm .... NIKAU

parrot .... KEA, KAKA, KAKAPO

peninsula .... BANKS, MAHIA, OTAGO, COROMANDEL

pigeon .... KUKU

pine ...... RIMU, KAURI, KAURY

plant .... KARO

prime minister .... KIRK, BOLGER, COATES, WHITLAM

raft .... MOKI

river .... HUTT, WAIPA, BULLER, CLUTHA, RAKAIA, WAIRAU, WAIKATO

sandalwood .... MAIRE

seaport .... AUCKLAND, WELLINGTON

shark .... MAKO

shrub .... KARO, TUTU, RAMARAMA

smelt .... INANGA

soldier .... ANZAC

strait .... COOK, FOVEAUX

tree .... AKE, AUTE, GOAI, KOPI, MIRO, PUKA, PELU, RATA, TORU, WHAU, HINO(U), HINAU, MAIRE, NAPAU, TARATA, TATARA, TOTARA, KAIKAKA

tribe .... RINGATU

vine .... AKA

volcano .... RUAPEHU

wages .... UTU

war club .... MERI

weapon .... PATU

wild hog .... BENE

wineberry .... MAKO

wood hen .... WEKA

newborn .... INFANT, NEONATE, YEANLING

Newcastle product .... COAL

river .... TYNE

newcomer .... ROOKIE, STRANGER, GREENHORN, TENDERFOOT

flock .... KID, LAMB

in January .... YEAR

newel .... POST

Newfoundland airport .... GANDER

bay ...... HARE, BONNE, SHOAL, CANADA, ESPOIR, SAGLEK, HOLYROOD, BONAVISTA

cape .... RAY, PINE, RACE, BAULD, CHIDLEY, ANGUILLE, TERRITOK

capital .... ST. JOHN'S

city/town .... GANDER, WABANA, KILBRIDE,

LABRADOR, CARBONEAR, GRAND FALLS, MOUNT PEARL, CORNER BROOK

cod-fisher .... BANKER

falls .... CHURCHILL

fishing grounds .... BANKS

floating ice .... GROWLER

Indian .... MICMAC

island .... RED, BELL, FOGO, GLOVER, GROAIS

lake ...... DYKE, LONG, GRAND, MEALY, GANDER, VICTORIA

mountain .... CIRQUE, THORESBY, GROS MORNE

mountains .... TORNGAT, KAUMAJET

national park ..... TERRA NOVA

peninsula .... AVALON

river .... EAGLE, GOOSE, ALEXIS, BRANCH, PINWARE, SALMONIER

sea .... LABRADOR

seal hunter .... SWILER

strait .... CABOT, BELLE ISLE

tea .... SWITCHEL

newfangled .... BRAND-NEW

newly .... AFRESH

newlywed .... BRIDE(GROOM), BENEDICT, HONEYMOONER

serenade to .... SHIVAREE

newness .... NOVELTY

news ...... WORD, ADVICE, REPORT, TIDINGS, INFORMATION

agency .... AP, INS, UPI, JIJI, TASS, ANETA, DOMEI, HAVAS, KYODO, CETEKA, REUTERS, WIRE SERVICE

aid .... NOSE

beat .... SCOOP

bit .... ITEM

commentator .... KALB, DOWNS, SHAW, BROKAW, DUNPHY, KOPPEL, RATHER, HUNTLEY, BRINKLEY, CRONKITE, JENNINGS, LAWRENCE

flash/brief .... ITEM

item .... OBIT, REPORT

last minute ..... BREAK, FLASH, FUDGE

medium .... RADIO, RUMOR, GOSSIP, BULLETIN, GRAPEVINE

report .... FLASH, BULLETIN

source .... PIPELINE

summary .... WRAP-UP

newsboy's territory .... ROUTE

wheels .... BIKE

newscast .... TELECAST, BROADCAST

newsletter .... BULLETIN, CIRCULAR

newsman .... ANCHOR, SCRIBE, REPORTER, JOURNALIST
newsmonger .... GOSSIP, TATTLER
newspaper .... DAILY, SHEET, WEEKLY, GAZETTE, JOURNAL, TABLOID
bit .... ITEM, FILLER
columnist .... CAEN, ALSOP, RESTON, WINCHELL
extra leaf .... INSERT
facing pages .... SPREAD
feature .... ESSAY, SCOOP, COLUMN, COMICS, ARTICLE, SPORTS, HEADLINE, EDITORIAL, ROTO(GRAVURE), CROSSWORD PUZZLE
headline .... BANNER, STREAMER
item .... FILLER
issue .... EXTRA, EDITION, STARFINAL
makeup ...... FORMAT, LAYOUT
name, for short .... TRIB
notice .... OBIT
official ..... EDITOR, REDACTOR
page insert .... FUDGE
paid circulation .... SUBSCRIPTION
section ..... ROTO, SUPPLEMENT
slang .... RAG
VIP .... EDITOR
work .... JOURNALISM
Newspaper Days author .... MENCKEN
newspaperman ...... CUB, SCRIBE, PRESSMAN, REPORTER, COLUMNIST, INKSLINGER, JOURNALIST
archaic .... GAZETTEER
feat of .... BEAT, SCOOP
report of .... COPY, STORY, DISPATCH
reporting from a distant place .... CORRESPONDENT
source of .... CONTACT, INFORMER, PIPELINE
territory of .... BEAT
newspapers and networks .... MEDIA
in general .... PRESS
newsprint .... PAPER
roll of .... WEB
newsstand .... KIOSK
newt .... EFT, SWIFT, TRITON, SALAMANDER
Newton, mathematician .... ISAAC
next .... THEN, AFTER, LATER, BESIDE, ENSUING, NEAREST
best thing to a strike .... SPARE

door resident .... NEIGHBOR
in musical directions .... POI
to last .... PENULT(IMATE)
year's alumni .... SENIORS
nexus ...... TIE, LINK, CONNECTION
Ney, Marshal .... MICHEL
Nez Perce .... INDIAN
Niagara .... FALLS
falls .... HORSESHOE
greatest drawing card of .... BLONDIN ROPEWALK
or a range .... CASCADE
nib .... END, BEAK, BILL, POINT, PRONG
nibble .... BIT, EAT, NIP, BITE, CHEW, GNAW, KNAP, PECK, SNACK, BROWSE, MORSEL
Nibelung .... DWARFS
guard .... FAFNIR
leader .... ALBERICH
Nibelungenlied king .... ETZEL
knight .... HILDEBRAND
niblick .... IRON, (GOLF)CLUB
Nicaragua bay .... SALINAS
capital .... MANAGUA
cays .... KING, TYRA, PEARL
city/town .... LEON, RIVAS, ESTELL, MASAYA, GRANADA, JINOTEPE, CHINANDEGA
coin .... CENTAVO, CORDOBA
gulf .... FONSECA
island .... OMETEPE, ZAPATERA, GREAT CORN, LITTLE CORN
lake .... MANAGUA
language .... SPANISH
measure ...... SUERTE, ESTAJAL
monetary unit .... CORDOBA
mountain .... MOCOTON
mountains .... HUAPI
point .... GORDA, MONKEY
president .... ORTEGA, SAMOZA, CHAMORRO
river ...... COCO, TUMA, WAWA, GRANDE, WASPUK, SAN JUAN, KUKALAYA, ESCONDIDO
nice .... FINE, NEAT, DAINTY, PRETTY, PROPER, FINICAL, REFINED, DELICATE, PLEASING
discernment .... ACUMEN, INSIGHT
figure .... SVELTE, LISSOM(E)
guy .... TRUMP
Nelly .... PRIG, PRUDE
nicely .... KINDLY, ROYALLY
nicety .... AMENITY, DELICACY, SUBTLETY
niche .... APSE, NOOK, SLOT, AMBRY, ALCOVE, CORNER, RECESS, TABERNACLE
nick .... CUT, JAG, CHIP, DENT, CHEAT, GOUGE, NOTCH,

SCORE, TALLY, ARREST
Nick, actor .... ADAMS, NOLTE
Charles's dog .... ASTA
Old .... DEVIL, SATAN
the detective .... CARTER
nickel .... COIN, FIVE CENTS
alloy .... INVAR
like metal .... MONEL
slang .... JITNEY
nickname .... AGNAME, AGNOMEN, COGNOMEN, MONI(C)KER, DIMINUTIVE, SO(U)BRIQUET
Amelia Earhart's .... LADY LINDY
Attila the Hun's .... FLAGELLUM DEI
Belle Starr's .... BANDIT QUEEN
Casal's .... ROSIE
Charles Lindbergh's .... LUCKY LINDY
city of witches .... SALEM
feminine/masculine .... LOU
for Detroit .... MOTOWN
General Arnold's .... HAP
General Schwarzkopf's .... STORMIN' NORMAN
Joan of Arc's .... MAID OF ORLEANS
Joan of Arc of the Confederacy .... BELLE BOYD
Martha Jane Canary's .... CALAMITY JANE
Martin's .... DINO
Mrs. Lyndon B. Johnson's .... LADY BIRD
Mrs. James Madison .... DOLLEY
Mrs. Rutherford B. Hayes .... LEMONADE LUCY
of Edward Teach .... BLACKBEARD
of the Beatles .... THE FAB FOUR
of U.S. President
Eisenhower, Dwight ..... IKE
Garfield, James .... THE PREACHER
Harrison, Benjamin .... LITTLE BEN
Jackson, Andrew .... OLD HICKORY
Jefferson, Thomas ..... LONG TOM
Lincoln, Abraham .... OLD ABE
Roosevelt, Franklin ..... NEW DEALER

Roosevelt, Theodore
.... TEDDY BEAR, ROUGH
RIDER
Taylor, Zachary .... OLD
ROUGH-AND-READY
Washington, George .... OLD
FOX
Wilson, Woodrow
.... WOODY
Thomas J. Jackson's
.... STONEWALL JACKSON
Wizard of Menlo Park
.... EDISON
Nicosia is capital of ...... CYPRUS
nicotine .... TAR
acid .... NIACIN
nictate/nictitate ...... WINK, BLINK
nide/nidus .... NEST
Niemen .... MEMEL, NEMAN
river .... RUSS
Nietzsche .... FRIEDRICH
nieve .... FIST, HAND
nifty .... SMART, STYLISH
Niger capital .... NIAMEY
city/town .... GAYA, TERA,
AGADES, ILLELA, TAHOUA,
ZINDER
desert .... SAHARA, TENERE
lake .... CHAD
language ...... HAUSA, DJERMA,
FULANI, SONGHAI
monetary unit .... FRANC
mountain .... BANGUEZANE
people .... IJO, PEUL, HAUSA,
TOUAREG
president .... DIORI
river mouth .... NUN
Nigerian capital .... LAGOS
city/town .... ABA, ADO, EDE,
IFE, IWO, OYO, KANO, BENIN,
ENUGU, ZARIA, IBADAN,
ILESHA, ILORIN, ISEYIN,
KADUNA, CALABAR, KATSINA,
ONITSHA, OSHOGBO,
ABEOKUTA, OGBOMOSHO
gulf .... GUINEA
island .... FOGE
king of Asaba
.... (JOSEPH)EDOZIEN
lake .... CHAD
language .... EDO, IBO, TIV,
HAUSA, FULANI, KANURI,
YORUBA
monetary unit .... NAIRA
mountain .... DIMLANG
native .... ARO, EDO, IBO,
BENI(N), HAUS(S)A
region .... SUDAN
river ...... OSSE, BENUE, CROSS,
DONGA, KEBBI, NIGER,
KADUNA, SOKOTO

seaport .... BONNY, LAGOS
state .... IMO, OYO, KANO,
OGUN, ONDO, BENUE, BORNO,
KUARA, LAGOS, NIGER,
BAUCHI, BENDEL, KADUNA,
RIVERS, SOKOTO, ANAMBRA,
GONGOLA
tribal chief .... OBA
tribe .... ARO, EDO, IBO, BINI,
EBOE, EKOI, BENIN, HAUSA,
FULANI, YORUBA
niggard .... CHURL, MISER,
STINGY, SKINFLINT
niggardly .... FEW, MEAGER,
SCANTY, MISERLY, STINGILY
night .... EVENING, DARK(NESS),
EVENTIDE
attack .... CAMISADO
bash .... SOIREE
before .... EVE
clothes .... NIGHTY, NIGHTIE,
PAJAMAS
club .... BOITE, BISTRO,
CABARET, ROADHOUSE
combining form .... NOCT(I)
flyer .... BAT, OWL, MOTH,
FIREFLY
letter .... TELEGRAM
lights .... NEONS
noise-maker .... ALLEYCAT
nuisance .... SNORER
of the .... NOCTURNAL
nightcap .... DRINK
nightfall .... DUSK
occurring at .... ACRONICAL,
ACRONYCAL
nighthawk .... BULLBAT,
GOATSUCKER
nightingale ...... BULBUL, THRUSH,
PHILOMEL, SONGBIRD
note of .... JUG
so-called .... (JENNY)LIND
nightjar .... BIRD, POTOO,
GOATSUCKER
nightmare .... DREAM, INCUBUS
demon .... MARA
kicker's .... BLOCKED
nightrider .... TERRORIST,
VIGILANTE
nightshade .... MOREL, MORIL,
PLANT, DATURA, HENBANE,
PETUNIA, SOLANUM,
MANDRAKE, BELLADONNA
nightstick .... CLUB, BILLY,
TRUNCHEON
user .... COP, POLICE(MAN)
nightwalk .... PROWL, TIPPYTOE
nightwalker .... THIEF,
NOCTAMBULIST
nihil .... NOTHING
nihilist .... CYNIC, PESSIMIST

Nihon .... JAPAN
Nike .... ATHENA, VICTORIA
nil .... NULL, ZILCH, NOTHING
Nile .... HAPI, NILUS
bird .... IBIS
boat .... BARIS, DAHABEAH
catfish .... BAGRE
city ...... SAIS, ASWAN, MEROE,
TANIS, TANTA, THEBES,
KHARTOUM, OMDURMAN
dam .... ASWAN
feature .... DELTA
feeder of Blue
.... (LAKE)TANA
feeder of White
.... (LAKE)VICTORIA
goddess .... ISIS
has one .... DELTA
island .... RODA
native .... NILOT
negro .... JUR, SUK
of the .... NILOTIC
plant .... PAPYRUS
queen .... CLEO(PATRA)
reeds/weeds .... SUDD
sailboat .... CANGIA
ship's captain .... RAIS, REIS
source of .... T(S)ANA, BLUE
NILE, WHITE NILE
town .... LUXOR, ROSETTA
village on the .... KARNAK
Nilgiri .... TEA, BADAGA
nim .... STEAL
nimble .... YAR, DEFT, SPRY,
AGILE, ALERT, LIGHT, QUICK,
ADROIT, LIVELY, VOLANT,
LISSOM(E)
nimbus ...... AURA, HALO, CLOUD,
GLORIA, AUREOLA
nimiety .... EXCESS, PLEONASM
Nimitz, admiral .... CHESTER
Nimrod .... HUNTER
city of .... ACCAD
parent of .... CUSH
nincompoop .... DOLT, FOOL,
IDIOT, NITWIT, SOFTHEAD,
SIMPLETON
nine: comb. form .... ENNE
days' devotion .... NOVENA
group of .... ENNEAD
"ladies" .... MUSES
number .... ENNEA
part opus .... NONET
sided plane .... NONAGON,
ENNEAGON
team of .... BASEBALL
ninefold .... NENARY
ninepins .... GAME, SKITTLE
ninesome .... NONET
nineteen XIX
nineteenth hole: colloq. .... BAR,

CLUBHOUSE, LOCKER ROOM
Nineveh founder .... NINUS
ninny .... ASS, DOLT, FOOL,
DUNCE, IDIOT, SIMPLETON
ninnyhammer .... ASS
ninth day before ides .... NONES
Ninus .... NINEVEH
Niobe, brother of .... PELOPS
fate of .... STONE
father of .... TANTALUS
husband of .... AMPHION
Niobean .... WEEPY, WEEPING
nip .... CUT, SIP, BITE, DRAM,
PECK, DRINK, PINCH, SEVER,
BLIGHT, SHORTEN
and tuck .... CLOSE, NECK AND
NECK
in the bud .... CHECK
slang .... CATCH, STEAL,
JAPANESE
nipa .... PALM, AT(T)AP
liquor .... TUBA
nipper .... CLAW, PLIERS,
FORCEPS, PINCERS, TWEEZERS
nippers .... HANDCUFFS, LEG
IRONS
Nipper's co. .... RCA
nipping .... SHARP, BITING
nipple .... DUG, PAP, TIT, TEAT,
PAPILLA, MAMMILLA
abnormal .... INVERTED
baby's toy .... PACIFIER
benign swelling of the
.... PAPILLOMA
disorder .... CYST, CANCER,
MASTITIS
inflammation .... THELITIS
shaped like a .... MASTOID
Nippon .... JAPAN
nippy ...... SHARP, BITING, NIMBLE
nirvana .... BLISS, HEAVEN,
OBLIVION
nis .... KOBOLD
Nishapur's famous son
.... OMAR(KHAYYAM)
nisi .... UNLESS
Nissen hut .... PREFAB
nit .... EGG, LOUSE, INSECT
niter .... SALT, NITRATE,
SALTPETER
nitid .... SHINY
niton .... RADON
nitpick .... CAVIL, QUIBBLE
nitpicker .... FAULT-FINDER
nitrate .... SALT, ESTER, NITER,
SALTPETER, FERTILIZER
drugs .... VASODILATOR
nitric .... AZOTIC
acid .... AQUA FORTIS
nitrogen .... AZOTE, NONMETAL
atmospheric .... GAS

containing .... AZO(TIC)
describing atmospheric
.... ODORLESS, COLORLESS
nitroglycerin(e) .... TNT,
CORDITE, MELINITE,
GLONOIN(E)
nitrous oxide ...... LAUGHING GAS
nitty-gritty .... BRASS TACKS
nitwit ...... FOOL, BOOB(Y), IDIOT,
MORON, DIMWIT, JACKASS,
LAMEBRAIN
Niven, actor .... DAVID
niveous .... SNOWY, SNOWLIKE
nix(ie) .... FAIRY, KELPIE, NEGATE,
REFUSE, SPRITE
slang .... NO, NAY, NOPE, NO
SIREE, NOT AT ALL
Nixon "bete noir" .... TAPES
Nizam .... NABOB
domain .... HYDERABAD
Njorth .... VANIR
child of .... FREY(A), FREYJA
no .... NAY, NOT-SO, NOWISE,
NEGATIVE
doubt .... CERTAINLY
gentleman he ...... CAD, BOOR,
LOUT, BRUTE
he-man .... SISSY
longer ahead .... OVERTAKEN
longer existing .... DEAD,
EXTINCT
longer recumbent .... RISEN
more ...... DEFUNCT, OBSOLETE
more! .... ENOUGH
more room .... FULL
more than .... MERE, ONLY
-no .... DONT
____ (nothing doing)
.... WAY, DICE
one .... NONE, NOBODY
rod sparer .... SWITCHER
sailor he .... LANDLUBBER
seats available sign .... SRO
slang .... FAT CHANCE, IN A
PIG'S EYE
slangy .... NIX, NAW, NOPE
-sweat state .... EASE
vote .... NAY
Noah, boat of .... ARK
father of .... LAMECH
grandson of .... ARAM
landing place of .... ARARAT
pertaining to .... NOETIC
son of .... HAM, SHEM,
JAPHETH
nob .... HEAD, JACK
nobby .... CHIC, STYLISH, FIRST-
RATE
Nobel, industrialist .... ALFRED
invention of .... DYNAMITE
laureate .... UREY

Prize decliner .... SARTRE,
PASTERNAK
Prize winner:
chemistry .... HAHN, UREY,
ADLER, CURIE, BAEYER,
SANGER, WERNER, PAULING,
SEABORG
literature .... MANN, SHAW,
CAMUS, ELIOT, SACHS,
JENSEN, SARTRE, BRODSKY,
FAULKNER, GORDIMER,
CHURCHILL, PASTERNAK,
STEINBECK
medicine .... KOCH, GOLGI,
KREBS, LYNEN, MINOT,
BURNET, ECCLES, RICHET
peace ...... ORR, KING, MOTT,
LANGE, BUNCHE, DUNANT,
WILSON, GORBACHEV,
SCHWEITZER
physics .... BOHR, RABI,
TAMM, YANG, BRAUN,
CURIE, DALEN, FERMI,
RAMAN
nobility .... PEERS, PEERAGE,
ROYALTY, GRANDEUR,
NOBLESSE, BLUE BLOOD,
ARISTOCRACY
rank below .... GENTRY
noble .... PEER, GRAND, LOFTY,
KINGLY, GALLANT, STATELY,
SUBLIME, MAJESTIC,
PATRICIAN
birth .... EUGENY, HIGHBORN
obsolete .... ATHEL
nobleman ...... DUKE, EARL, JARL,
LORD, PEER, BARON, COUNT,
THANE, KNIGHT, MILORD,
PRINCE, GRANDEE, HIDALGO,
MARQUIS, MAGNIFICO
noblewoman ...... LADY, MILADY,
DUCHESS, PEERESS, CONTESSA,
COUNTESS, MARCHESA,
MARCHIONESS
nobody .... NONE, NO ONE,
NONENTITY
nocent .... GUILTY, HURTFUL
nock .... NOTCH
noctambulist .... SLEEPWALKER
nocturnal .... NIGHT(LY)
bird .... OWL, KAKAPO
creature .... BAT, COON,
LEMUR, RATEL, TAPIR,
JACKAL, WEASEL, (O)POSSUM,
RAC(C)OON, TARSIER
sawyer .... SNORER
nocturne .... SERENADE
nod .... BOW, BECK, DOZE,
DROWSE, NUTATE
auction .... BID
Nod, land of .... SLEEP

489

nodding .... NUTANT
noddle .... GULL, HEAD, PATE
noddy .... FOOL, SIMPLETON
node .... KNOB, KNOT, FOCUS,
    GNARL, JOINT, DILEMMA,
    SWELLING
  abnormal .... NODULE
nodular .... LUMPY, KNOTTY,
    NODOSE, GNARLED, STUDDED
nodule .... KNOT, LUMP, JOINT
  tone's .... GEODE
noel .... CAROL, CHRISTMAS
Noel Coward's song .... NINA
noesis .... PERCEPTION
noetic .... SCHOLAR
nog .... ALE, PIN, BRICK
noggin .... CUP, MUG, GILL, HEAD,
    PATE
noise .... DIN, FLAP, BRUIT,
    SOUND, CLAMOR, HUBBUB,
    RACKET, (UP)ROAR, STRIDOR
  activity .... ADO
  of revelers .... RIOT
  resounding .... BAM
  surf .... ROTE
noiseless .... QUIET, STILL, SILENT,
    CATLIKE
noisome .... FETID, HARMFUL,
    NOXIOUS, STINKING
noisy .... LOUD, BLATANT,
    CLAMANT, CLAMOROUS,
    CACOPHONOUS
  bird .... JAY, (MAG)PIE
  merry-making .... REVELRY,
    CAROUSAL
  revelry .... JAMBOREE
nom de plume. See also pen
  name .... PEN NAME,
    PSEUDONYM
nomad .... GYPSY, ROVER, TRAMP,
    ROAMER, WANDERER,
    ITINERANT
  desert ...... ARAB, KURD, SLEB,
    BEDOUIN, BUSHMAN
  Northern .... LAPP
nomadic .... ITINERANT,
    WANDERING
nominal .... SMALL, TOKEN,
    SLIGHT, TITULAR
  value .... PAR
nominate .... CALL, NAME,
    APPOINT, DESIGNATE
nomination .... NAMING,
    APPOINTMENT
nominee .... CANDIDATE,
    APPOINTEE
non-accidental injury .... CHILD
    ABUSE
  believer .... PAGAN, ATHEIST,
    INFIDEL, AGNOSTIC
  Christian .... PAGAN, PAYNIM

clergy .... LAITY
member .... MAVERICK,
    OUTSIDER
payer, proverbially ...... CRIME
paying activity .... CRIME
paying one .... DEADBEAT
professional .... LAY, LAIC,
    AMATEUR
union place .... OPEN SHOP
workers .... LILIES
nonage .... MINORITY
nonce .... MEANTIME, MEANWHILE
noncom .... CPL, NCO, SARGE,
    SERGEANT
nonchalant .... COOL, CASUAL,
    INSOUCIANT, INDIFFERENT
nonconformist .... REB(EL),
    HERETIC, SECTARY,
    MAVERICK, RECUSANT,
    DISSIDENT, DISSENTER
nondescript .... ODD, PLAIN,
    COMMON, ORDINARY
none .... NARY, NO ONE, NOT ANY,
    NOTHING
nonentity .... CIPHER, NOBODY,
    STRAWMAN, UNPERSON
nonesuch .... ONER, APPLE,
    RARITY, PARAGON, NONPAREIL
nonmetallic element ...... BORON,
    IODINE, SILICON, ASTATINE,
    FLUORINE
nonpareil .... SUPREME, UNEQUAL,
    NON(E)SUCH, MATCHLESS,
    PEERLESS, UNRIVALED
nonpartisan .... NEUTRAL,
    INDEPENDENT
nonplus .... STUMP, BAFFLE,
    PUZZLE, CONFUSE, MYSTIFY,
    PERPLEX, SQUELCH
nonprofit organization
  .... FOUNDATION
nonsense .... BAH, BLAH, BOSH,
    BULL, BUNK, TOSH, BILGE,
    FOLLY, FUDGE, HOKUM,
    HOOEY, PRATE, TRASH,
    DRIVEL, SLAVER, BALONEY,
    BLATHER, RUBBISH, TWADDLE,
    FALDEROL, FLIMFLAM,
    FOLDEROL, MALARK(E)Y,
    (TOMMY)ROT, TRUMPERY,
    ABSURDITY, POPPYCOCK,
    SILLINESS, RIG(A)MAROLE
deceitful .... GAMMON
high-sounding .... FUSTIAN
singing .... SCAT
nonsensical .... INANE, SILLY,
    ABSURD, FOOLISH,
    RIDICULOUS
creature .... GOOF, GOOP, NOIO,
    SMOO, SNARK
nonspiritual .... MATERIAL

nonstick pan spray .... PAM
nonstop .... MARATHON,
    CONTINUOUS
noodle .... FOOL, HEAD, PASTA,
    FARFEL, FERFEL
  dish .... CHOW MEIN
nook .... DEN, NICHE, (AL)COVE,
    CORNER, RECESS, RETREAT
  and _____ .... CORNER,
    CRANNY
noon .... MIDDAY, MERIDIAN
  rest .... SIESTA
noose .... LOOP, TRAP, HALTER,
    (EN)SNARE
  trap .... SPRINGE
nope .... NO, NIX
  opposite of .... YEP
Nordic .... ARYAN, CAUCASIAN,
    TEUTON(IC)
Norfolk .... JACKET
Norge .... NORWAY
noria .... (WATER)WHEEL
norm .... RULE, MODEL, AVERAGE,
    PATTERN, STANDARD,
    CRITERION
Norma .... RAE
  actress .... SHEARER
normal .... PAR, MEAN, USUAL,
    AVERAGE, NATURAL,
    REGULAR, TYPICAL, ORDINARY
  breathing .... EUPN(O)EA
Norman .... LEAR, MAILER
  crusader .... TANCRED
  Vincent _____ .... PEALE
Normand, actress .... MABEL
Normandy capital .... ROUEN
  conqueror of .... ROLLO
  department .... EURE, ORNE,
    MANCHE
  duke of .... HROLF, ROLLO
  liqueur .... BENEDICTINE
Norn .... URTH, SKULD, GODDESS,
    VERTHANDI
Norse .... LANGUAGE,
    SCANDINAVIAN
  Adam .... ASKR
  chieftain .... JARL, ROLLO
  deity .... EIR, ODIN, THOR
  destiny .... NORN
  dwarf .... ANDVARI
  earth: myth .... MIDGARD
  epic .... EDDA
  explorer .... ERIC, ERICSSON
  galley .... AESC
  giant .... ATLI, EGIL, WATE,
    YMER, (H)YMIR, MIMIR,
    TROLL, FAFNIR, JOTUN(N)
  giantess .... GROA, NORN
  goat .... HEIDRUN
  god ...... LOK, TYR, ULL, FREY,
    LOKI, ODIN, THOR, VALI,

AEGER, AEGIR, AESIR, BRAGI, DONAR, HODER, HODUR, VANIR, BALDER, HOENIR, FORSETI, HEIMDALL

goddess .... EIR, SIF, HEL(A), IDUN, NORN, RANA, URTH, WYRD, FREYA, FRIGG(A), ITHUN(N), MOIRA, SKULD, VERTHANDI

gods, king of .... ODIN, WODEN

hall of heroes .... VALHALLA

hero .... OLAF, EGIL(L)

home of gods .... ASGARD

king .... ATLI, OLAF

land holding .... ODAL

letter/lore .... RUNE

minstrel .... SCALD

name .... LARS

navigator .... ERIC

Nibelung dwarf ...... ALBERICH

patron saint .... OLAF

plateau .... FJELD

poet .... SCALD, SKALD

poetry .... EDDA, RUNE(S)

race of gods .... VANIR

rainbow bridge .... BIFROST

river .... KLAR

saga/heroic work .... EDDA

underworld .... HEL

viking .... ROLLO

watchdog .... GARM

watchman of Asgard .... HEIMDALL

wolf .... FENRIR

woman, first .... EMBLA

Norseman .... VIKING

of the .... RUNIC

North African bread wafer .... ABRET

city .... ALGIERS

garment .... HAIK

garment, shirtlike .... TOB

region .... SUDAN

seaport .... ORAN

sheep .... AOUDAD

wind .... LESTE

North Atlantic alliance: abbr. .... NATO

fish .... LING, BURBOT, CAP(E)LIN, MACKEREL

North Borneo .... SABAH

North Carolina bay .... ONSLOW, RALEIGH

cape .... FEAR, LOOKOUT, HATTERAS

capital .... RALEIGH

city/town .... BOONE, DURHAM, CONCORD, HICKORY, GASTONIA, ASHEVILLE, CHARLOTTE, HIGH POINT,

SALISBURY, BURLINGTON, GREENSBORO, WILMINGTON

college .... ELON, BENNETT, CAMPBELL, GUILFORD, JOHN WESLEY, LIVINGSTONE, GARDNER-WEBB, LENOIR-RHYNE

county .... LEE, ASHE, CLAY, DARE, HOKE, HYDE, NASH, PITT, POLK, MOORE, ROWAN, SURRY, UNION, DURHAM, ONSLOW, ORANGE, CATAWBA, FORSYTH, ROBESON, WATAUGA, BUNCOMBE, DAVIDSON, RANDOLPH

island .... ASHE, BODIE, OCRACOKE

lake .... LONG, PUNGO, THORPE, CATFISH, WACCAMAW, ALLIGATOR

mountain .... GUYOT, MITCHELL

native .... TARHEEL

resort town .... TRYON

river .... DAN, HAW, TAR, NEUSE, ROCKY, TRENT, CHOWAN, PEE DEE

state bird .... CARDINAL

state flower .... DOGWOOD

state nickname .... TARHEEL, OLD NORTH

tourist attraction .... OLD SALEM, TRYON PALACE, ZOOLOGICAL PARK

university ...... DUKE, CENTRAL

North Dakota capital .... BISMARCK

city/town .... FARGO, MINOT, MANDAN, JAMESTOWN, WILLISTON, GRAND FORKS

college .... MARY

county .... CASS, DUNN, WARD, STARK, WALSH, BARNES, MCLEAN, MORTON, RAMSEY, PEMBINA, BURLEIGH

lake .... FAN, VAN, ETTA, TURTLE, DARLING

mining town .... ZAP

mountain .... WHITE BUTTE

river .... ELM, GREEN, HEART, FOREST, TONGUE

state bird .... MEADOWLARK

state flower ...... WILD PRAIRIE ROSE

state nickname .... SIOUX, FLICKERTAIL

tourist attraction ..... FRONTIER VILLAGE

tree .... BLACK HILLS SPRUCE

North Pole discoverer .... PEARY

North Sea feeder .... YSER

port .... KIEL, EMDEN, BERGEN, BREMEN

serpent .... KRAKEN

tributary .... TAY, ELBE, MAAS, TEES, TYNE, YSER, MEUSE, RHINE, WESER, THAMES, SCHELDE

water .... KATTEGAT

North Star .... POLARIS, LODESTAR

northern .... BOREAL

constellation .... BOOTES

diver .... LOON

sea bird .... SKUA, JAEGER, PUFFIN

Northern Bear .... RUSSIA

Cross .... CYGNUS

Rhodesia .... ZAMBIA

Spy .... (WINTER)APPLE

Northerner .... YANKEE, COPPERHEAD

Northampton landmark .... MT. TOM

Northman .... THULE, NORMAN, NORSE(MAN)

Northumberland river ...... ALN, TYNE

Norway. See also **Norse; Norwegian** .... NORGE

betrayer of .... QUISLING

in Norway .... NORGE

Norwegian. See also **Norse** .... NORSE(MAN)

bay ..... FROHAVET, LOPPHAVET

cape .... LINDESNES

capital .... OSLO

city/town .... MO, BODO, MOSS, HAMAR, MOLDE, SKIEN, BERGEN, LARVIK, NARVIK, TROMSO, ALESUND, DRAMMEN, HARSTAD, SANDNES, LYSAKERT, TONSBERG, HAUGESUND, PORSGRUNN, SARPSBORG, STAVANGER, TRONDHEIM

coin .... ORA, ORE, KRONA

composer .... GRIEG, OLSEN

county .... OSLO, TROMS, OPPLAND, AKERSHUS, BUSKERUD, FINNMARK, NORDLAND, ROGALAND, TELEMARK

dramatist .... IBSEN

explorer .... NANSEN, AMUNDSEN

fish .... LING, BURBOT

fjord .... RANA, FOLDA

goblin .... NIS(SE), KOBOLD

inlet .... FIORD, FJORD

island .... LEKA, VEGA, DONNA, HITRA, HOPEN, SENJA, SMOLA,

491

ALSTEN, ANDOYA, LANGOY, SOROYA, VAEROY, VANNOY, KVALOYA
island off .... ANDO
islands .... VIKNA, LOFOTEN, SVALBARD
king ..... OLAF, OLAV, HAAKON
lake .... VAGAVATN, FEMUNDSJO, TYRIFJORD
language .... SAMISK, RIKSMAAL, LANDSMAAL
measure .... FOT, MAL, ALEN, MORGEN, SKIEPPE
monetary unit .... KRONE
mountain .... SULITJELMA, GLITTERTINDEN
mountains .... KJOLEN
native .... LAPP, LAPLANDER
noble .... JARL
novelist .... NOJER, HAMSUN
parliament .... LAGT(H)ING, STORT(H)ING
peninsula .... LISTA
poetry .... EDDA
port .... HAMMERFEST
region .... LAPLAND
river ...... OTRA, TANA, LAGEN, RAUMA, TOKKE, NAMSEN, BARDUELV, PASVIKELV
saint .... OLAF
sea monster .... KRAKEN
seaport .... BERGEN, STAVANGER, TRONDHEIM, HAMMERFEST
sight .... FIORD
soprano .... FLAGSTAD
statesman .... LIE
territorial subdivision .... AMT
The People's King .... FOLKEKONGEN
toast .... SKOAL
traitor .... QUISLING
weight .... LOD, MARK, PUND
writer .... IBSEN, NOJER
warship .... WASA
nose .... NEB, PRY, BEAK, CONK, SCENT, SMELL, SNIFF, SNOOP, SNOUT, SPOUT, MUZZLE, NOZZLE, PROBOSCIS
ailment ..... CORYZA, CATARRH
allergy .... HAY FEVER
bone .... VOMER
combining form .... NASI, RHIN(O)
counting .... POLL, CENSUS
describing one ..... PUG, SNUB, ROMAN, SHARP, SIMOUS, TILTED, AQUILINE
discharge .... RHEUM
dive .... PLUNGE
elephant's .... TRUNK

inflammation .... RHINITIS
Latin .... NASUS
long .... SNOUT, PROBOSCIS
obstruction .... POLYP
of the .... NASAL, NARIAL, RHINAL
opening .... NARE, NARIS, NOSTRIL
person with famous .... DURANTE, CYRANO(BERGERAC)
point on .... ALARE
reshaping .... RHINOPLASTY
slang ..... SPY, SNOOT, NOZZLE, INFORMER, SCHNOZZLE
nosebag contents .... OATS
nosebleed .... EPISTAXIS
nosegay .... POSY, BOUQUET, CORSAGE
nos(e)y .... PRYING, SNOOPY, CURIOUS, MEDDLESOME, INQUISITIVE
animal .... TAPIR
one .... SPIER, SNOOPER
person .... PEEPING TOM, EAVESDROPPER
Nosey Parker .... MEDDLER
nosferatu .... (THE)UNDEAD
nosh .... EAT, NIBBLE
nostalgia .... PATHOS, REGRET, LONGING, NOSTOMANIA, HOMESICKNESS
noster, _____ .... PATER
nostology .... GERIATRICS
subject of .... OLD AGE
nostomania .... NOSTALGIA, HOMESICKNESS
Nostradamus .... SEER, ASTROLOGER
nostril .... NARE
hairs .... VIBRISSA
of the .... NARIAL, NARINE
nostrum .... REMEDY, PANACEA
not .... NEGATIVE, NOTHINGNESS
a person/a (living) soul .... NO ONE
a quarternary .... TRIAD
a whit .... NONE
absent .... HERE
absolutely .... NO WAY
absolved .... UNVINDICATED
adequate .... SCANTY
allowed apostles .... FOOD, MONEY
an easy catch .... EEL
any/one .... NARY, NONE
appropriate .... INAPT, INEPT, UNFIT, IMPROPER
as common .... RARER
as dotty .... SANER
as lovely as a tree .... A POEM

as many .... FEWER
as tight .... LOOSER
at all .... NOWISE
at home .... OUT, AWAY, ABROAD
aweather .... ALEE
barefoot .... SHOD
belligerent .... IRENIC
cautious .... RASH, RECKLESS
completed .... UNDONE
complex .... EASY, SIMPLE
compulsory .... ELECTIVE, OPTIONAL
conforming .... IRREGULAR
copy .... ORIGINAL
divided .... WHOLE, UNITED
ecclesiastic .... LAIC
even .... EROSE
even once/even sometimes .... NEVER
feral .... TAME
final: law .... NISI
fitting .... UNAPT
fixed .... UNRESTORED
flat .... HILLED
for .... AGAINST
for bargain hunters .... DEAR
forbidden .... ALLOWED
fresh .... STALE
friendly .... ICY
gained .... LOST
gross .... NET
guaranteed .... RISKY
harsh .... LENIENT
hep .... SQUARE
here .... THERE
hollow .... SOLID
identified .... UNKNOWN
idle .... BUSY, IN USE
illuminated .... UNLIT
in a whisper .... ALOUD
in any way .... NEVER
in cipher .... UNCODED
in house .... OUTSIDE
in jail anyway .... LOOSE, AT LARGE
indisputably .... ARGUABLY
jerky .... EVEN
just a note .... LONG LETTER
kindled .... UNLIT
knowing which way to turn .... UNSURE
level or flat .... UNEVEN
live .... TAPED
long .... BRIEF
make sense .... TALK IN RIDDLES
many .... FEW
mature .... GREEN
mounted .... UNSET
moving .... INERT, STILL,

STATIC

nearly settled .... UP IN THE
                                    AIR

_____ (no way) .... AT ALL

now .... LATER

of this world ..... SUPERLUNAR

on your life! ..... NOPE, NO SIR

one or the other .... NEITHER

pawned .... UNGAGED

permanent .... PROTEM

planned ..... CASUAL, RANDOM,
                          HAPHAZARD

poetry .... PROSE

precise .... INEXACT

prefix of .... DIS, MIS, NON

pronounced .... ELIDED,
                              UNSPOKEN

pungent .... UNSPICY

ready .... ILL-PREPARED

refined .... COARSE, VULGAR

seldom .... OFT

severe .... MILD

showing any wear .... GOOD
                             AS NEW

skillful .... UNAPT

so hot .... TEPID

so shaky .... STEADIER

_____ (so-so) .... SO HOT

speaking .... MUM, MUTE

straight .... ALOP

the Occident .... ORIENT

the original color .... DYED

the real reason .... PRETEXT

to weather: naut. .... ALEE

too many .... SOME

up and about .... ABED

up to standard ..... IRREGULAR

us .... THEM, OTHERS

violent .... GENTLE

warranted .... UNCALLED FOR

well-reasoned: colloq.
         .... HALF-BAKED

with it, they're ..... OUTSIDERS

working .... IDLE, ON THE
             BLINK, OUT OF ORDER

written, as a will
         .... NUNCUPATIVE

yet mature .... YOUTHFUL

youthful .... PASSE

nota bene .... NOTE WELL

notable .... VIP, UNCO, FAMOUS,
         SIGNAL, EMINENT, STRIKING

act .... DEED, FEAT, GEST(E),
                 EXPLOIT, HEROISM

one .... STANDOUT

personage .... VIP, HERO, LION,
                 STAR, CELEBRITY

notarize .... ATTEST, CERTIFY

notary .... SCRIVENER

notation .... NOTE, ENTRY,
                            COMMENT

notch .... GAP, JAG, PEG, MARK,
         NICK, SCORE, TALLY, DEGREE,
                 (IN)DENT, RECORD

edged .... SERRATE

key .... WARD

made by ax/saw .... KERF

notched .... EROSE, CRENATE,
                 DENTATE, SERRATE

bar .... RATCH

part .... JOG

wheel .... RATCHET

note .... FAME, HEED, MARK,
         TONE, BILLET, LETTER,
         REMARK, MISSIVE, OBSERVE,
                          EMINENCE

an eighth .... QUAVER

explanatory .... POSTIL

Guido's .... GAMUT

half .... MINIM

highest .... ELA

marginal .... (A)POSTIL

musical .... THESIS

part of .... STEM

promissory .... IOU

short .... CHIT, LINE, MEMO

stem of .... TAIL

well .... NOTA BENE

notebook .... CAHIER

noted .... FAMOUS, EMINENT,
                          RENOWNED

noteworthy .... EMINENT,
                 NOTABLE, SPECIAL,
                          EXCEPTIONAL

nothing .... NIL, NONE, ZERO,
         BLANK, NIHIL, NAUGHT,
                          NOUGHT

but .... ONLY, MERELY

doing! .... NO, NO DICE, NO
                               SOAP

else than .... MERE

for .... FREE, GRATIS

in tennis .... LOVE

more or less .... MERE

slang .... NAPOO, ZILCH

to be worried about .... NOT
                          REAL BAD

notice .... AD, SEE, HEED, SIGN,
         ADVICE, DETECT, REGARD,
         REVIEW, BILLING, DISCERN,
         OBSERVE, WARNING, PERCEIVE

for display in a public place
         .... POSTER, PLACARD

of payment due .... PROMPT

official .... BULLETIN,
                               MONITION

to desist .... CAVEAT

noticeable ...... EVIDENT, VISIBLE,
                          CONSPICUOUS

notification .... AVISO, ADVICE

sort of .... THREAT

notify .... TELL, WARN, BRIEF,

ADVISE, INFORM, APPRISE,
                          ACQUAINT

notion .... IDEA, VIEW, WHIM,
         CURIO, FANCY, BELIEF,
         DESIRE, CAPRICE, INKLING,
                 OPINION, THOUGHT

commonplace .... BROMIDE

counter item .... THREAD,
         SHOELACE, SAFETY PIN

fallacious .... IDOLISM

foolish .... MOONSHINE

notions .... ARTICLES

notorlety .... FAME, ECLAT,
         REPUTE, BLATANCY,
                          PUBLICITY

notorious .... ARRANT, FLAGRANT,
         INFAMOUS, TALK OF THE
                               TOWN

notornis relative ...... COOT, RAIL

Notre Dame .... OUR LADY,
                          CATHEDRAL

bench .... PEW

coach .... ARA, ROCKNE

notwithstanding .... THO, YET,
         EVEN, STILL, MAUGRE,
         DESPITE, HOWEVER,
                 (AL)THOUGH

nougat .... CANDY, CONFECTION

nought .... ZERO, CIPHER,
                 NOTHING, USELESS

bring to .... VOID, NULLIFY

nomenal .... INTUITIVE

noun .... SUBSTANTIVE

form .... CASE

kind of ...... APTOTE, TRIPTOTE

modifier .... ADJECTIVE

of common gender
         .... EPICENE

suffix ...... AST, ENT, ERY, FER,
         ICS, IER, ISE, IST, ITE, ULA,
         ULE, ENCE, ITIS, TUDE, ATION

verbal .... GERUND

nourish .... FEED, FOSTER,
         NURTURE, SUPPORT, SUSTAIN

nourishing .... ALIBLE, NUTRIENT,
         ALIMENTAL, ALIMENTARY,
                          NUTRITIOUS

nourishment .... FOOD, ALIMENT,
         PABULUM, NUTRIMENT,
         NUTRITION, SUSTENANCE

baby's .... PAP, MILK

nous .... MIND, REASON,
                          INTELLECT

nouveau or theater .... ART

riche .... PARVENU, UPSTART,
                 NEWLY RICH

nova .... STAR

Nova Scotia(n) .... ACADIA(N),
                          BLUENOSE

basin .... MINAS, ANNAPOLIS

bay .... ASPY, CLAM, MIRA,

FUNDY, SCOTS, SHOAL, VERTE, FORCHU, JORDAN, MAHONE, GABARUS, ADVOCATE, CHIGNECTO

cape ..... JOHN, ARGOS, CANSO, CLIFF, PERCE, SABLE, SMOKY, SPLIT, BRETON, GEORGE, LINZEE, MORIEN, DAUPHIN

capital .... HALIFAX

city/town .... DIGBY, TRURO, PICTOU, SYDNEY, AMHERST, WINDSOR, YARMOUTH, DARTMOUTH, LIVERPOOL

county .... DIGBY, HANTS, KINGS, PICTOU, QUEENS, HALIFAX, COLCHESTER

harbor .... COLE, MABOU, CODDLE, HALIFAX

island .... MUD, OAK, BRIER, CROSS, GOOSE, HAUTE, SOBER, ANDREW, BARREN, MADAME, TUSKET, CARIBOU, LISCOMB, CHETICAMP, CAPE BRETON

lake .... OCEAN, FISHER, GEORGE, JORDAN, MOLEGA, TUPPER, BRAS D'OR, GASPEREAU, ROSSIGNOL, LOCH LOMOND

mountain .... NUTTBY, DALHOUSIE

river .... AVON, GOLD, MIRA, OHIO, MERSEY, SALMON, TUSKET, BADDECK, CARLETON, KENNETCOOK

seaport .... TRURO

strait .... CANSO

village .... GRAND PRE

Novarro, actor .... RAMON

movie role .... BEN HUR

novel .... NEW, BOOK, EPIC, RARE, FRESH, PROSE, STORY, ROMANCE, SIMENON, STRANGE, UNUSUAL

by Bronte .... JANE EYRE

Edna Ferber .... SO BIG

Felix Salten .... BAMBI

Fielding .... AMELIA

H. Rider Haggard .... SHE

Helen Hunt Jackson .... RAMONA

Hugo .... LES MISERABLES

James Clavell .... SHOGUN

Jane Austen .... EMMA

Nabokov .... ADA

Uris .... TOPAZ

Isaac Singer's last .... SCUM

novelist Anatole .... FRANCE

aptly named .... READE

Bernard .... MALAMUD

Dunn .... OLAV

Eugene .... SUE

Felix .... SALTEN

Ferber .... EDNA

Hobson .... LAURA

Hunter .... EVAN

Michael .... ARLEN

Nevil .... SHUTE

Norman .... MAILER

romance .... (VICTORIA)HOLT

Stephen .... CRANE

Willa .... CATHER

novella .... NARRATIVE

Novello .... IVOR

novelty .... FAD, CHANGE, NEWNESS, TRINKET, GIMCRACK, BRIC-A-BRAC

November 11 .... MARTINMAS

event .... VETERANS' DAY

13, Roman date .... IDES

novena .... NINE, DEVOTIONS

novice .... CUB, TIRO, TYRO, ACOLYTE, AMATEUR, BEGINNER, NEOPHYTE, GREENHORN, APPRENTICE, TENDERFOOT

novitiate .... NOVICE, TRAINEE, NEOPHYTE

novocaine .... ANESTHETIC

Novotna .... JARMILA

tennis star .... JANA

now .... TODAY, AT ONCE, IMMEDIATELY

nowadays .... PRESENTLY, AT PRESENT

noway .... NOWISE, NOT AT ALL

nowhere place .... LIMBO

nowt .... OXEN, CATTLE

Nox .... NYX, GODDESS

brother of .... EREBUS

husband of .... CHAOS

is goddess of .... NIGHT

noxious .... EVIL, NOCENT, BANEFUL, HARMFUL, MIASMIC, NOISOME, MEPHITIC, PERNICIOUS

air/effluvium .... MIASMA, MALARIA

vapor .... FUME, REEK

Noyes, poet .... ALFRED

nozzle .... JET, NOSE, ROSE, SNOUT, SPOUT

furnace .... TUYERE

thing with .... HOSE, PIPE, TEAPOT, BELLOWS

nuance .... SHADE, VARIATION

nub ...... CORE, GIST, KNOB, LUMP, PITH, SNAG

nubbin ...... CORN, LUMP, BUTTON

nubble .... KNOB, KNOT, LUMP

nubby .... STUDDED

nubia .... WRAP

Nubian .... NEGRO(ID)

harp .... NANGA

nubile .... RIPE, ADULT, OF AGE, MATURE, MARRIAGEABLE

nubilous .... FOGGY, MISTY, CLOUDY, OBSCURE, VAPOROUS

nucha .... NAPE, SCRUFF

nuclear device .... REACTOR

division in germ cells .... MEIOSIS

missile .... ICBM, MIRV, A-BOMB, H-BOMB

scientist .... BRAUN

nucleic acid: abbr. .... DNA

nucleus .... CORE, HEART, CENTER, KERNEL

atom's .... PROTON, DEUT(E)RON

cell .... MESOPLAST

military unit's .... CADRE

nude ...... BARE, NAKED, UNCLAD, EXPOSED, UNCLOTHED

nudge .... JOG, POKE, PROD, PUSH, ELBOW, JOSTLE

nudist .... ADAMITE, GYMNOSOPHIST, CLOTHESTROPHOBIAC

Nuevo Leon capital .... MONTERREY

nugatory .... FUTILE, INVALID, USELESS, HELPLESS

nugget .... HUNK, LUMP, SLUG

nuisance .... BANE, BORE, BOTHER, PLAGUE, TROUBLE, ANNOYANCE

colloquial .... PEST, TERROR

insect .... GNAT

null .... NIL, VOID, INVALID

nullah .... GORGE, GULLY, RAVINE, WATERCOURSE

nullify .... VETO, VOID, UNDO, ANNUL, ABJURE, CANCEL, NEGATE, REPEAL, REVOKE, RESCIND, RETRACT, ABROGATE, OVERRIDE, INVALIDATE

nulliparous .... BARREN

nullipore .... SEAWEED

numb .... DAZED, TORPID, DEADEN(ED), DRUGGED, SHOCKED, UNFEELING, INSENSIBLE, NARCOTIZED

number .... COUNT, TALLY, CIPHER, FIGURE, SYMBOL, ENUMERATE

added .... ADDEND

after due .... TRE

astronomic .... GOOGOL

before sette .... SEI

biggest/greatest .... MOST

countless ...... HORDE, SWARM, MYRIAD

dividing evenly .... ALIQUOT
8 iron .... NIBLICK
5 iron .... MASHY, MASHIE
in Brooklyn .... TREE
indefinite .... SEVERAL
irrational .... SURD
large .... MANY, RAFF, RAFT,
    SLEW, LEGION, MULTITUDE
leaves of book .... FOLIATE
less than ten .... DIGIT
lonely .... ONE
lost .... TOLL, CASUALTY
magazine .... ISSUE
of a crowd .... THREE
of deadly sins .... SEVEN
of Sinbad's voyages
    .... SEVEN
of tails on a cat .... NINE
of winks in a short nap
    .... FORTY
page .... FOLIO
part of .... FRACTION
whole .... INTEGER
numbers .... BOOK, QUANTITY
game .... KENO, LOTTO,
    LOTTERY
racket .... POLICY GAME
specialist .... BOOKIE
numbfish .... TORPEDO,
    (ELECTRIC)RAY
numbles .... INNARDS
numen .... SPIRIT, DIVINITY
numerate .... READ, TELL, COUNT,
    TALLY, NUMBER
numerical ending .... ETH
numerous .... MANY, THICK,
    MYRIAD, PLENTY, MANIFOLD
combining form .... MYRIA
Numidian crane ...... DEMOISELLE
king .... MASINISSA
town .... ZAMA
numismatist .... COLLECTOR
concern of ..... COINS, MEDALS
numskull .... DOLT, DUNCE,
    MORON, NITWIT, MEATHEAD,
    BLOCKHEAD, DUNDERHEAD
nun .... SMEW, CLARE, MONASA,
    PIGEON, SISTER, VESTAL,
    VIRGIN, VOTARY, TITMOUSE,
    CARMELITE
abode of .... CONVENT,
    MONASTERY
dress of .... HABIT
head covering .... WIMPLE
moth .... TUSSOCK
throat cover .... BARB
nunbird .... MONASE
nuncio ...... LEGATE, AMBASSADOR
nuncupative .... ORAL, VERBAL,
    UNWRITTEN
nunnery .... ABBEY, PRIORY,

CONVENT, CLOISTER
head of a .... ABBESS,
    PRIORESS, SUPERIOR
nuns, of .... MONASTIC
nuptial(s) .... BRIDAL, SPOUSAL,
    WEDDING, HYMENEAL,
    MARRIAGE, CONNUBIAL
agreement .... I DO
participant .... BESTMAN,
    SPONSOR, BRIDESMAID,
    RINGBEARER
principal .... BRIDE(GROOM)
yes/pledge .... I DO
nuque .... NAPE, SCRUFF
Nuremberg war crimes
    defendant ...... HESS, KEITEL,
    GOERING, RIBBENTROP
nurse .... AMAH, AYAH, CARE,
    NANA, TEND, NANNY, SERVE,
    FOSTER, SUCKLE(R),
    ATTENDANT
head covering of .... WIMPLE
instrument of
    .... THERMOMETER
part-time .... SITTER
nursery ...... ASYLUM, HOTHOUSE,
    PLAYROOM, GREENHOUSE
bete noire .... CROUP
furniture ...... CRIB, PLAYPEN,
    BASSINET, ROCKING CHAIR
public/day .... CRECHE
rhyme character .... GILES,
    SPRAT
rhyme eloper .... SPOON
rhyme home .... SHOE
rhyme Miss .... MUFFET
rhyme opening words
    .... PAT-A-CAKE
song .... LULLABY
VIP .... BABY
word .... DADA, MAMA, TATA
worker .... (BABY)SITTER
nurture .... FEED, FOOD, REAR,
    BREED, TRAIN, FOSTER,
    CHERISH, NOURISH, SUSTAIN
nut .... COCO, KOLA, PARA, PILI,
    SEED, ACORN, BEECH, BETEL,
    PECAN, PINON, TRYMA,
    ALMOND, BRAZIL, CASHEW,
    LICHEE, LI(T)CHI, HICKORY
combining form .... NUCI,
    CARYO, KARYO
confection .... NOUGAT,
    PRALINE, MARZIPAN
covering .... HUSK, SHELL
kidney-shaped .... CASHEW,
    KASHEW
meat .... KERNEL
off one's .... CRAZY, INSANE
slang .... HEAD, KOOK, CRANK,
    FOOLISH, ECCENTRIC

three-sided .... BRAZIL
tonic/used in beverages
    .... KOLA
turner .... WRENCH, SPANNER
nutant .... NODDING, DROOPING
nutcracker .... BIRD, CROW,
    PECKER
nuthatch .... CREEPER, TITMOUSE,
    NUTCRACKER
genus .... SITTA
nutlet .... PIT, STONE, PYRENE
nutmeg ...... MACE, SPICE, KERNEL
nutria .... FUR, COYPU, RODENT
animal like .... BEAVER
nutriment .... FOOD, ALIMENT,
    NUTRIENT
nutrition, of .... TROPHIC
study of .... DIETETICS
nutritionist .... DIETICIAN,
    DIETITIAN
nutritive .... ALIBLE
nuts .... FOOL, GAGA, BATTY,
    CRAZY, QUEER, ENTHUSIASTIC
about .... FOND OF
collectively .... MAST
counterparts of .... BOLTS
pertaining to .... NUCAL
nutshell .... DIGEST, CAPSULE,
    OUTLINE, SYNOPSIS
nutty ...... CRAZY, MEATY, QUEER,
    GAGA, CUCKOO, BONKERS,
    FOOLISH, HAYWIRE, OFF
    ONE'S ROCKER
nux vomica .... SEED, PLANT
product .... STRYCHNIN(E)
nuzzle .... RUB, NOSE, PUSH,
    CUDDLE, NESTLE, SNUGGLE
Nyasaland .... MALAWI
capital .... LILONGWE
president .... BANDA
nylon .... HOSE, FIBER, THREAD,
    BRISTLE
flow of .... RUN, SNAG
thread weight of .... DENIER
nylons .... HOSE, SHEERS,
    HOSIERY, STOCKINGS
nymph ...... PUPA, AEGLE, HOURI,
    LARVA, SYLPH, WOMAN,
    DAPHNE, EGERIA, HESTIA,
    MAENAD, MAIDEN, OENONE,
    ONDINE, SYRINX, OCEANID,
    SALMACIS
changed into bear
    .... CALLISTO
changed into laurel tree
    .... DAPHNE
changed into a rock ..... ECHO
changed into a stream
    .... ARETHUSA
fountain .... NAIAD

guards .... HESPERIDES
mountain .... OREAD
pursuer of .... SATYR
river .... NAIS, NAIAD
sea .... SIREN, NEREID,
NEMERTES
tree .... (HAMA)DRYAD
water .... APAS
nymphet .... LOLITA
nymphs, father of 50 .... NEREUS
fountain .... CAMENAE
nyssa .... TUPELO
Nyx .... NOX
daughter of .... ERIS
is goddess of .... NIGHT

O

O .... ZERO, CIPHER, EXCLAMATION
Greek .... OMEGA, OMICRON
in chemistry .... OXYGEN
in pharmacy .... PINT
in physics .... OHM
O gosh! .... O GEE
oaf .... BOOR, DOLT, GAWK, LOUT,
RUBE, DUNCE, RUSTIC,
DEADHEAD, DULLHEAD
variant of .... OUPHE
Oahu city .... HONOLULU
oak .... HOLM, ILEX, TREE, WOOD,
ALDER, EMORY, ROBLE,
ROBUR, CERRIS, DURMAS,
ENCINA
bark .... TAN, CRUT, EMORY
British slang .... DOOR
evergreen .... ILEX, ENCINA
fruit .... MAST, ACORN,
CAMATA
genus .... QUERCUS
moss .... EVERNIA
starter .... ACORN
thicket of evergreen
.... CHAPARRAL
Oak Ridge work .... NUCLEAR
Oakley, rifle expert .... ANNIE
slang .... PASS
oakum .... FIBER
seal with .... CA(U)LK
oar ...... BLADE, ROW(ER), SCULL,
SPOON, SWEEP, PADDLE,
PROPEL
blade .... PALM, WASH
fulcrum/lock .... THOLE
part of .... LOOM, PEEL
shaped .... REMIPED
oarlock support .... POPPET
oars, row of .... BANK
oarsman .... ROWER, STROKE,
SCULLER
oasis .... WADI, WADY, DOUMA,
SPRING
fruit .... DATES
sight .... DATE PALM
oast .... KILN, OVEN
oat .... REED, GRASS, CEREAL
burner .... NAG
genus .... AVENA
rental .... AVENAGE

oatcake .... CAPER
oater .... HORSE OPERA
locale .... SALOON
Oates, Popish Plot's .... TITUS
oath .... VOW, CURSE, PLEDGE,
PLIGHT, EXPLETIVE,
PROFANITY
breaking of .... PERJURY
mild .... DRAT, EGAD, GOSH,
HECK, ZOUNDS
take .... SWEAR, PROMISE
taker .... JURANT
testify under .... DEPOSE
oatmeal .... PORRIDGE
cake .... PONE, SCONE
porridge .... BURGOO,
STIRABOUT
oats .... FEED, AVENA
hulled, cracked .... GROATS
Oaxaca is in .... MEXICO
Ob river is in .... SIBERIA
Obadiah .... ABDIAS, PROPHET
obdurate .... FIRM, DOGGED,
MULISH, ADAMANT,
STUBBORN, OBSTINATE,
BULLHEADED, INFLEXIBLE
obeah .... CHARM, MAGIC, FETISH,
TALISMAN, WITCHCRAFT
obedience .... DEFERENCE,
COMPLIANCE, SUBMISSION
obedient .... LOYAL, DOCILE,
DUTIFUL, AMENABLE,
COMPLIANT, HENPECKED,
TRACTABLE
obeisance .... BOW, CONGE(E),
CURTSY, HOMAGE, KOWTOW,
SALAAM, DEFERENCE
obelisk .... PYLON, SHAFT,
NEEDLE, OBELUS, PILLAR,
MONOLITH
obelus .... MARK, DAGGER,
OBELISK
Oberammergau is in
.... BAVARIA
religious play .... PASSION
Oberon .... KING, FAIRY
actress .... MERLE
domain of .... FAIRYLAND
wife of .... TITANIA
obese .... FAT, PLUMP, PUDGY,

PUFFY, PURSY, STOUT,
FLESHY, PORTLY, ROTUND,
ADIPOSE, BLUBBERY,
LIPAROUS, CORPULENT
obesity .... FATNESS, LIPOSIS,
ADIPOSIS
medical syndrome
.... PICKWICKIAN
obey .... HEED, MIND, COMPLY,
FOLLOW, SUBMIT, FULFILL,
CARRY OUT
obfuscate ...... DARKEN, CONFUSE,
OBSCURE, STUPEFY, BEWILDER
obi .... SASH, CHARM, MAGIC,
OBEAH, FETISH, TALISMAN
obiter dictum .... ASIDE,
REMARK, COMMENT
obit(uary) .... MEMORIAL,
NECROLOGY, (DEATH)NOTICE
words .... IN MEMORIAM
object ...... AIM, END, GOAL, ITEM,
KICK, MIND, DEMUR, THING,
INTENT, OPPOSE, RESIST,
TARGET, DISSENT, PROTEST,
PURPOSE, REMONSTRATE
art .... CURIO, BIBELOT
of infatuation .... IDOL
of manipulation .... PUPPET,
MARIONETTE
of pursuit ...... GAME, QUARRY
objecting fan .... BOOER
objection .... KICK, CAVIL,
BARRIER, PROTEST, QUARREL,
DEMURRER, OPPOSITION
objectionable .... CULPABLE,
OFFENSIVE, UNDESIRABLE
gray .... TATTLETALE
objective .... AIM, GOAL, REAL,
ACTUAL, TARGET, PURPOSE,
DETACHED, UNBIASED
objector .... REBEL, OPPOSER,
DISSENTER, DISSIDENT
objet d'art .... VASE, VIRTU,
FIGURINE
collector .... VIRTUOSO
objurgate .... CHIDE, BERATE,
REBUKE, REPROVE, UPBRAID
oblate .... NUN, MONK, ASCETIC
oblation ...... OFFERING, SACRIFICE
obligate .... OWE, BIND

obligated .... BEHOLDEN, INDEBTED
obligation ...... DUE, BOND, DEBT, DUTY, ONUS, BURDEN, PROMISE
abbr. .... IOU
evade an .... WELSH
obligatory .... BINDING, BOUNDEN
oblige .... FORCE, ASSIST, COMPEL, PLEASE, GRATIFY, CONSTRAIN
obliging .... HELPFUL, ACCOMMODATING
oblique .... AWRY, CANT, SKEW, ASLANT, EVASIVE, INCLINED, INDIRECT
glance .... SQUINT
line .... BIAS
obliquely .... ASKANCE, SIDEWAYS, SIDEWISE
obliterate .... RAZE, ERASE, DEFACE, EFFACE, BLOT OUT, DESTROY, EXPUNGE, SPONGE OUT
obliteration .... ERASURE, ERASEMENT
oblivion .... LETHE, PARDON, FORGETFULNESS
drug of .... NEPENTHE
place of .... LIMBO
river of .... LETHE
oblivious .... HEEDLESS, FORGETFUL
oblong .... ELONGATED
obloquy .... INFAMY, CENSURE
obnoxious .... GROSS, ODIOUS, HATEFUL, OFFENSIVE, REPULSIVE, TASTELESS, UNPLEASANT
one .... PILL, CREEP
oboe .... REED, WIND, WOOD, SHAWN, BASSOON, HAUTBOY, BOMBARDON
oboli, six .... DRACHMA
obol(us) .... COIN
Obote, Uganda president
.... APOLO
Obregon, Mex. president
.... ALVARO
obscene .... RAW, FOUL, LEWD, DIRTY, GROSS, COARSE, FILTHY, SMUTTY, NAUGHTY, INDECENT, REPULSIVE
language .... BAWDRY, RIBALDRY
pictures/writings
.... PORNO(GRAPHY)
obscure .... DIM, DARK, DUSKY, FOG(GY), MURKY, VAGUE, GLOOMY, HIDDEN, CRYPTIC, ECLIPSE, SHADOWY, NUBILOUS, OBFUSCATE

by smearing .... BLUR
obscurity .... ANONYMITY
obsequies .... EXEQUY
obsequious .... ABJECT, FAWNING, SERVILE
observance .... RITE, RULE, CUSTOM, PRACTICE
for a dead .... WAKE
of formalities .... PUNCTILIO
of official precedence
.... PROTOCOL
observant .... ALERT, VIGILANT, WATCHFUL, ATTENTIVE
observation .... ESPIAL, NOTICE, REMARK, COMMENT, ASSERTION
car feature .... BLISTER
irrelevant .... POINTLESS REMARK
to little star .... TWINKLE TWINKLE
work .... SURVEY, RECONNAISSANCE
observatory, California
.... PALOMAR
concern of an .... MOON, STARS, PLANETS, WEATHER
observe .... EYE, SEE, NOTE, OBEY, ABIDE, NOTICE, REMARK, DISCERN, CELEBRATE
secretly .... SPY, STALK
Yom Kippur .... FAST
observer .... LOOKOUT, WATCHER, EYEWITNESS
forward .... SCOUT
obsess .... BESET, HAUNT, HARASS, PREOCCUPY
obsessed .... HIPPED, RIDDEN
stubbornly .... HELLBENT
obsession .... FIXE, IDEE, FIXATION, (MONO)MANIA
obsidian .... LAVA, ROCK, PERLITE, TEKTITE
obsolescence .... DISUSE
obsolete ...... OLD, DATED, PASSE, ARCHAIC, DISUSED, EXTINCT, OUTMODED, OUT OF DATE, DISCARDED, OLD-FASHIONED
auto .... PEERLESS
seat .... SEDE
obstacle .... BAR, SNAG, CRIMP, HITCH, HURDLE, BARRIER, HINDRANCE, IMPEDIMENT
course .... GANTLET
unexpected .... SNAG
obstinate .... DOUR, DOGGED, MULISH, ORNERY, WILLFUL, CONTRARY, RESOLUTE, STUBBORN, PIGHEADED, UNBENDING, BULLHEADED, HARD(HEADED)

obstreperous .... NOISY, UNRULY, RIOTOUS, BOISTEROUS, VOCIFEROUS
obstruct .... BAR, DAM, CLOG, BLOCK, CHECK, CHOKE, HINDER, IMPEDE, RETARD, STOP UP, BARRICADE
obstruction .... BARRIER, OBSTACLE, HINDRANCE
obstructionist's trick
.... FILIBUSTER
obtain .... GET, WIN, EARN, GAIN, DERIVE, SECURE, ACQUIRE, PREVAIL, PROCURE
fresh energy .... REVIVE
obtainable .... AVAILABLE, ATTAINABLE
obtrude .... EJECT, MEDDLE, INTRUDE
obtund .... DULL, BLUNT, DEADEN
obtuse .... DULL, BLUNT, DENSE
opposite of .... ACUTE
obverse .... FRONT, COUNTERPART
opposite of .... VERSO, REVERSE
obviate .... PREVENT
obvious .... PLAIN, PATENT, EVIDENT, PALPABLE, UNSUBTLE, OPEN AND SHUT
not .... SUBTLE, SUBTILE
oca .... OXALIS
ocarina .... SWEET POTATO
O'Casey, dramatist .... SEAN
occasion .... TIME, CAUSE, EVENT, NONCE, HAPPENING
occasional .... RARE, CASUAL, SPORADIC, IRREGULAR, INCIDENTAL
occasionally .... RARELY, SOMETIMES, NOW AND THEN
occident .... WEST
opposite of .... ORIENT
occidental .... PONENT, WESTERN, HESPERIAN
occipital protuberances .... INIA
occlude ...... SHUT, BLOCK, CLOSE, ABSORB
occlusion .... SHUTDOWN
occult .... HIDDEN, MYSTIC, ORPHIC, SECRET, CRYPTIC, ESOTERIC, MYSTERIOUS
art .... MAGIC, ALCHEMY, ASTROLOGY
knowledge .... GRAMARY(E)
philosophy .... CABALA
occultism .... MAGIC, KABALA, CAB(B)ALA
occupancy .... TERM, TENANCY
occupant .... INMATE, TENANT, HABITANT
occupation .... WORK, TRADE,

METIER, TENURE, CALL(ING), PURSUIT, PROFESSION
occupied .... BUSY, ENGROSSED
occupy .... USE, FILL, EMPLOY, ENGAGE, INVEST, LIVE IN, POSSESS
attention .... ENGROSS
occur .... PASS, EXIST, LIGHT, BEFALL, BETIDE, HAPPEN
again .... RECUR, REPEAT
at the same time .... COINCIDE
irregularly .... SPORADIC
once a year .... ANNUAL(LY)
occurrence .... CASE, EVENT, EPISODE, INCIDENT, OCCASION, HAPPENING
degree of .... INCIDENCE
occurring at intervals
.... SEASONALLY
every 8th day .... OCTAN
5th day .... QUINTAN
4th day .... QUARTAN
3rd day .... TERTIAN
two years .... BIENNIAL
together .... SIMULTANEOUS
ocean .... SEA, DEEP, MAIN, BRINE, ARCTIC, INDIAN, EXPANSE, PACIFIC, ATLANTIC, ANTARCTIC
current .... UNDERTOW
denizen, inflatable .... PUFF FISH
depression .... DEEP
greyhound .... LINER, STEAMSHIP
largest and deepest
.... PACIFIC
route .... LANE
Oceania island .... MELANESIA, POLYNESIA, MICRONESIA
oceanic .... VAST, PELAGIC
oceanid .... NYMPH
Oceanus .... GOD, TITAN
ocellus .... SPOT, EYE(LET)
ocelot .... CAT
cat-like .... MARGAY
ocher .... SIL, CLAY, YELLOW, PIGMENT
red .... TIVER, RADDLE, REDDLE, RUBRIC
ochre .... ALMAGRA
Ochs, publisher .... ADOLPH
folksinger .... PHIL
octan .... FEVER
octave .... UTAS, EIGHT
Octavia's husband ...... ANTONY
octet(te) .... EIGHT
October 15 .... IDES
Revolution leader .... LENIN, TROTSKY
octogenarian .... DOTARD

age of .... EIGHTIES
octopus .... SQUID, POULPE, MOLLUSK, OCTOPOD, DEVILFISH
arm of .... TENTACLE
octoroon .... METIS, MESTEE, MUSTEE
octroi .... TAX
octuple .... EIGHTFOLD
ocular .... LENS, VISUAL, OPTIC(AL), EYESIGHT
oculist's concern .... EYE
Ocypete .... HARPY
od, manifestation of
.... HYPNOTISM, MAGNETISM
odalisque ...... SLAVE, CONCUBINE
place of .... ADA, IDA, ODA
odd .... RUM, DROLL, EXTRA, QUEER, QUAINT, AZYGOUS, STRANGE, PECULIAR, SINGULAR, ANOMALOUS, ECCENTRIC
job .... CHAR(E), CHORE
job man .... JACK
mannerism/trait .... QUIRK
slang .... BATTY, SCREWY
oddity .... FREAK, QUIRK, VAGARY, QUEERNESS
odds .... CHANCES, ADVANTAGE
and ends ...... JOBLOT, SCRAPS, REMNANTS, RUMMAGE, ETCETERAS
ode .... HYMN, POEM
division of .... STROPHE
odeon .... HALL, THEATRE
Oder, city on the .... BRESLAU, STETTIN
tributary .... WARTHE
odeum .... HALL
odiferous .... AREEK
Odin .... GOD, WODEN, WOTAN
concern of .... WAR, DEAD
horse of .... SLEIPNER
maiden of .... VALKYR(IE)
parent of .... BOR
son of .... TIU, TYR, THOR, VALI, BALDER
victim of .... YMIR
wife of .... FRIA, JORD, FRIGG(A)
wolf of .... GERE, GERI
odious .... HATEFUL, HEINOUS, OFFENSIVE, REPUGNANT, REPULSIVE, DETESTABLE, DISGUSTING
odium .... HATE, HATRED, INFAMY, DISGRACE, APPROBIUM
odometer .... TAXIMETER
odontoid .... TOOTHLIKE
odontology .... DENTISTRY

subject of .... TEETH
odor .... FUME, NOSE, AROMA, SCENT, SMELL, TRAIL, BOUQUET, FRAGRANCE
disagreeable .... STINK, F(O)ETOR, STENCH
musty .... FUNK
pleasant .... INCENSE, PERFUME, FRAGRANCE
odorless .... AOSMIC
odorous ...... FETID, OLENT, SPICY, PUNGENT, AROMATIC, FRAGRANT, REDOLENT, OLFACTORY
Odysseus .... KING, ULYSSES
captor of .... POLYPHEMUS
father of .... LAERTES
monstrous beings encountered by
.... LAESTRYGON OGRES
nephew of .... MEGES
protection against Circe
.... MOLY
realm of .... ITHACA
to Cyclops .... NOMAN
wife of .... PENELOPE
odyssey .... QUEST, VOYAGE, JOURNEY, WANDERING, PILGRIMAGE
Odyssey .... POEM
author of .... HOMER
beggar of .... IRUS
enchantress in .... CIRCE
nymph .... CALYPSO
queen in .... PENELOPE
Oedipus daughter ...... ANTIGONE
father .... LAIUS
mother .... JOCASTA
son .... ETEOCLES, POLYNICES
wife of .... JOCASTA
oenologist's concern .... YEAR
need .... YEAST
oenology, subject of .... WINES
Oenone .... NYMPH
husband of .... PARIS
rival of .... HELEN
of .... BY, FROM, HAVE, WITH, ABOUT
a biological partition
.... SEPTAL
a great poet .... KEATSIAN
a killing: comb. form
.... CIDAL
a metallic element
.... EUROPIC
a reign .... REGIME, REGNAL
a target spot .... FOCAL
a time period .... ERAL
a verse .... ODIC
an age/epoch .... ERAL
any kind .... SO EVER

Attica .... IONIC
course: sl. .... NATCH
distinction .... NOTABLE
each .... PER
flight .... AERO
grandparents .... AVAL
greater size .... LONGER
inferior quality .... BUM
Lamb's writings .... ELIAN
lunar stages .... PHASIC
melody/pitch .... TONAL
mysterious meaning .... RUNIC
no _____ .... USE, MOMENT,
.... ACCOUNT
old age .... GERIATRICS
poetic feet .... ANAPAESTIC
roses, _____ .... ATTAR
seers .... VATIC
sight .... OPTIC
sound mind .... SANE
substance .... MEATY
summer .... ESTIVAL
the cheekbone .... MALAR
the dawn .... EOAN
the kidneys .... RENAL
the mind .... PSYCH
the source or origin
.... PARENTAL
the tail .... CAUDAL
the world .... MUNDANE
this planet .... EARTHLY
thread .... FILAR
Of _____ **and the River** ...... TIME
Mice and Men author
.... STEINBECK
Mice and Men character
.... LENNIE
off .... AGEE, AWAY, GONE,
WRONG, ABSENT, IN ERROR
-base, slightly .... LOONY
-color .... RACY, DIRTY,
RISQUE, OBSCENE
-key .... FLAT
nautical .... SEAWARD
one's rocker .... LOCO
the beaten path .... AMISS
the mark/track .... AMISS
the regimen .... EX-DIET
-the-streets signal ..... CURFEW
-white .... ECRU
off, _____ (get along) ...... HIT IT
(go away) .... BUZZ
(irate) .... TEED
offal .... WASTE, REFUSE,
GARBAGE
offbeat ...... ODD, KOOKY, WACKY,
WEIRD, UNUSUAL
Offenbach, composer
.... JACQUES
offend .... VEX, HARM, HUFF,
HURT, MIFF, ANGER, PIQUE,

UPSET, WRONG, INSULT,
SLIGHT, AFFRONT, MORTIFY,
OUTRAGE, DISPLEASE
offender .... CULPRIT
offense .... SIN, CRIME, FELONY,
OUTRAGE, UMBRAGE,
RESENTMENT
against law .... MALA
in law .... DELICT
offensive .... UGLY, ATTACK,
ODIOUS, FULSOME, NOISOME,
UNSAVORY, REPULSIVE
for quick victory
.... BLITZ(KRIEG)
to morals .... OBSCENE,
IMPROPER, INDECENT
offer .... BID, EXTEND, TENDER,
PRESENT, PROFFER, PROPOSE,
PROPOSAL, SUGGEST(ION)
final .... ULTIMATUM
in sacrifice .... IMMOLATE
introductory .... OVERTURE
of one's free will
.... VOLUNTEER
offering .... GIFT, TRIBUTE,
DONATION, OBLATION,
SACRIFICE, CONTRIBUTION
at a wedding ..... RING-FINGER
to God .... CORBAN
widow's .... MITE
offhand .... CURT, ABRUPT,
CASUAL, INFORMAL,
SLAPDASH, EXTEMPORE,
IMPROMPTU
office .... JOB, DUTY, POST, RANK,
ROLE, SERVICE, FUNCTION,
POSITION
bigwig .... BOSS
boss .... MANAGER
holder ...... IN, INCUMBENT
of the Dead: Eccles .... DIRGE
remove from .... OUST,
DEPOSE, RECALL
wall sign .... THINK
worker, for short .... STENO
officer .... DIRECTOR, CONSTABLE,
POLICEMAN, PRESIDENT
abbey .... ABBOT
abbreviation .... LT, ADM, COL,
GEN, MAJ, NCO, CAPT, LIEUT
assistant to an .... AIDE,
DEPUTY
church .... ELDER, BISHOP,
DEACON, PRIEST, SEXTON,
MINISTER, PRESBYTER
court .... BAILIFF
Customs .... EXAMINER
IRS .... AGENT, COLLECTOR
kind of ...... TRUANT, FINANCE,
WARRANT
medical .... CORONER

military ...... MAJOR, ADMIRAL,
CAPTAIN, COLONEL, GENERAL,
LIEUTENANT
national chief law
.... ATTORNEY GENERAL
police .... CHIEF, INSPECTOR
school .... DEAN, PRINCIPAL,
REGISTRAR
officer's insignia .... BAR, EAGLE,
INSIGNE
official .... FORMAL, OFFICER,
DIGNITARY, AUTHORIZED,
BUREAUCRAT
approval .... IMPRIMATUR
course .... CHANNEL(S)
decree .... EDICT, IRADE,
UKASE, RESCRIPT
denial .... DEMENTI
elected .... POLITICIAN
family, President's
.... CABINET
list .... CANON
paper container .... POUCH,
HAMPER, HANAPER
proceedings .... ACTA
residence, U.S. President's
.... WHITE HOUSE
routine .... RED TAPE
seal .... SIGNET
self-important .... BASHAW,
PANJANDRUM
snafu .... RED TAPE
statement .... BULLETIN,
COMMUNIQUE
officialdom .... BUREAUCRACY
officiate .... DIRECT, PRESIDE
officious .... BOSSY, PUSHY,
PUSHING, PRAGMATIC,
GRATUITOUS, MEDDLESOME
offish .... ALOOF
offset .... SPUR, BRANCH,
BALANCE, (OFF)SHOOT,
COMPENSATE, NEUTRALIZE
offshoot ...... STEM, ISSUE, SCION,
BRANCH
offshore .... SEAWARD
O'Flaherty, author .... LIAM
offspring .... ISSUE, PRODUCT,
PROGENY, CHILD(REN)
in womb .... FETUS
oft .... OFTEN
often .... FREQUENTLY, AGAIN AND
AGAIN
plastered .... PARIS
Ogasawara island .... BONIN
Ogden .... NASH
ogee .... MOLDING
molding .... TALON
ogle ...... EYE, GAZE, LEER, LOOK,
STARE, GLAD EYE, OEILLADE
ogler .... EYER, STARER

Ogpu .... GAYPAY-OO

   predecessor of .... CHEKA

ogre .... BOGY, BEAST, DEMON,

   FIEND, GIANT, BUGABOO,

   MONSTER, BLUNDERBORE

Oh, what a girl .... SUSIE

O'Hara's manse .... TARA

Ohio bay .... MAUMEE, SANDUSKY

   capital .... COLUMBUS

   city/town .... KENT, LIMA,

   TROY, AKRON, BEREA, PARMA,

   XENIA, CANTON, DAYTON,

   ELYRIA, LORAIN, MARION,

   NEWARK, TIFFIN, TOLEDO,

   WARREN, FINDLAY, WOOSTER,

   HAMILTON, CLEVELAND,

   CINCINNATI, SPRINGFIELD

   college .... DYKE, HIRAM,

   WALSH, KENYON, MALONE,

   EDGECLIFF, NOTRE DAME,

   HEIDELBERG

   college town .... WOOSTER

   county .... ERIE, WOOD, ALLEN,

   CLARK, LUCAS, STARK,

   WAYNE, ATHENS, BUTLER,

   GREENE, LORAIN, MARION,

   MEDINA, SCIOTO, SUMMIT,

   WARREN, BELMONT, PORTAGE,

   CUYAHOGA, TRUMBULL

   lake ...... ERIE, DOVER, BERLIN,

   DILLON, INDIAN, BUCKEYE,

   LORAMIE, DELAWARE,

   PIEDMONT

   native .... BUCKEYE

   oil corporation, one time

   .... ESSO

   river .... MAD, OHIO, BLACK,

   GRAND, HURON, MIAMI,

   ROCKY, SCIOTO, TIFFIN,

   WABASH

   river city .... BELLAIRE

   state bird .... CARDINAL

   state flower .... SCARLET

   CARNATION

   state nickname .... BUCKEYE

   tourist attraction .... SEA

   WORLD, TAFT MUSEUM,

   CINCINNATI ZOO

   university .... KENT, TIFFIN,

   TOLEDO, XAVIER, CAPITAL,

   DENISON, FRANKLIN,

   WESLEYAN

Ohm, physicist .... GEORG

oikologist .... HOUSEKEEPER

oil .... LUBE, TUNG, BENNE, BRIBE,

   IRONE, ACEITE, ANOINT,

   SAFROL(E), PAINTING,

   LUBRICATE, LUBRICANT

   antiseptic .... CARVACROL

   aromatic ...... ATTAR, BALSAM,

   LAVENDER

   baptismal .... CHRISM

   bottle .... CRUET, CRUSE,

   CASTOR, AMPULLA

   burner .... LAMP, CRAMMER,

   CRESSET

   butter .... GHEE

   colloquial .... FLATTER(Y)

   combining form .... OLEO

   consecrated .... CHRISM

   container .... DRUM, CRUSE

   countries, for short .... OPEC

   country .... IRAQ, IRAN,

   KUWAIT, SAUDI ARABIA

   driller .... WILDCATTER

   essential .... ESSENCE

   flower .... ATTAR, NEROLI

   fragrant .... NARD, ATTAR

   fruit rind .... BERGAMOT

   lubricating .... LUBE

   of/obtained from .... OLEIC

   painting .... CANVAS

   painting board .... PANEL

   perfume-making .... BEN,

   ATTAR, BERGAMOT

   plant .... RAMTIL, PATCHOULI

   refining waste .... SLUDGE

   rub with .... ANOINT

   seed .... TIL, POON, RAPE,

   BEN(NE), RAMTIL, SESAME

   ship .... TANKER

   skin .... SEBUM

   solvent .... ACETONE

   source ..... COD, OLIVE, SHALE,

   PEANUT, BLUBBER

   tree .... EBO(E), TUNG

   well .... GASSER, GUSHER

   well adjunct .... RIG

oilbird .... GUACHARO

oiler .... SHIP, TANKER

oilstone .... HONE

oily .... FATTY, SLEEK, SLICK,

   SOAPY, GREASY, SMOOTH,

   PINGUID, SLIPPERY,

   UNCTUOUS, SEBACEOUS

   hydrocarbon in petroleum

   .... CETANE

ointment .... BALM, NARD, SALVE,

   POMADE, CALAMINE,

   VASELINE

   base for .... LANOLIN(E)

Oise tributary .... AISNE

Ojibway .... INDIAN, CHIPPEWA

OK .... GO, ROGER, CORRECT, ALL

   RIGHT, APPROVAL

Oka city .... OREL

okapi relative .... GIRAFFE

Okie is from .... OKLAHOMA

Okinawa capital .... NAHA

Oklahoma capital .... OKLAHOMA

   CITY

   city/town ...... ADA, JAY, ENID,

   ALTUS, MOORE, PONCA,

   TULSA, YUKON, DUNCAN,

   EDMOND, LAWTON, NORMAN,

   ARDMORE, BETHANY,

   CATOOSA, GUTHRIE, SHAWNEE,

   WAGONER, MUSKOGEE,

   CHICKASHA

   college .... CHRISTIAN

   county .... KAY, BRYAN,

   CADDO, CREEK, GRADY,

   OSAGE, PAYNE, TULSA,

   CARTER, JACKSON, CANADIAN,

   CHEROKEE, COMANCHE,

   SEMINOLE

   cowboy hero .... CURLY

   falls .... TURNER

   fish hatchery site

   .... MEDICINE PARK

   hiding place of outlaws, once

   .... DEVIL'S DEN

   Indian ...... SAC, SAUK, CREEK,

   KIOWA, PONCA, APACHE,

   PAWNEE, ARAPAHO,

   CHEROKEE, COMANCHE

   Indian Cheyenne chief

   .... BLACK KETTLE

   Indian Comanche chief

   .... QUANAH PARKER

   lake .... KAW, HUGO, EUCHA,

   HULAH, CANTON, TEXOMA,

   WISTER, KEYSTONE,

   LAWTONKA

   largest fishing lake ..... ELMER

   THOMAS

   migratory worker .... OKIE

   mountain .... OZARK, SCOTT,

   PICHOT, BLACK MESA

   mountains .... QUARTZ,

   WICHITA

   national park .... PLATT

   native .... OKIE, SOONER

   part of .... PANHANDLE

   refuge for crows .... FORT

   COBB

   river .... RED, BLUE, CANEY,

   POTEAU, WASHITA, CIMARRON,

   ILLINOIS

   state bird .... FLYCATCHER

   state flower .... MISTLETOE

   state nickname .... SOONER

   state park ..... LITTLE SAHARA,

   RED ROCK CANYON

   tourist attraction ...... COWBOY

   HALL OF FAME, WILL ROGERS

   MEMORIAL

   university .... CAMERON,

   PHILLIPS, ORAL ROBERTS,

   PANHANDLE STATE

okra .... POD, SOUP, BENDY,

   GUMBO, PLANT, MALLOW

old ...... AGED, AULD, GRAY, WISE,

WORN, YORE, DATED, PASSE, STALE, SENILE, ANCIENT, ANTIQUE, ARCHAIC
age .... SENILITY
campaigner .... VET, WARHORSE
car .... REO
car's noise .... RATTLE
chaise longue .... DAYBED
"chap" preceder .... I SAY
country .... MOTHERLAND, NATIVE LAND
enough .... OF AGE
exclamation .... FIE
fashion .... COCKTAIL
fashioned .... DATED, FUSTY, PASSE, DEMODE, SQUARE
growing .... AGING, SENESCENT
hand .... PRO, EXPERT, STAGER, VET(ERAN)
hat .... RATED, STALE
heater .... ETNA
lady: sl. .... WIFE, MOTHER
landowner .... LORD
maid .... SPINSTER
man .... BOSS, FATHER, GAFFER, GEEZER, HUSBAND
movies .... SILENTS
novel price .... DIME
one .... CRONE
pen .... QUILL
pies .... SPOILED ROTTEN
refrain .... FALA
salt .... SAILOR
saying .... SAW
structure .... RUNE
things, done over
.... RETREADS
time auto .... MERCER
time flour container
.... BARREL
time zither .... ASOR
very .... HOARY
wheeze .... ADAGE
woman/witch .... HAG, GAMMER
Old Dominion .... VIRGINIA
English letters .... EDHS
Faithful .... GEYSER
Faithful's activity
.... SPURTING
Faithful's locale
.... YELLOWSTONE PARK
Glory .... FLAG, STARS AND STRIPES
Harry .... DEVIL, SATAN
Hickory .... (ANDREW) JACKSON
Nick .... SATAN
_____: NY historic shrine
.... FORT NIAGARA

Saxon poem .... HELIAND
Scratch .... DEVIL, SATAN
Sod .... ERIN
Testament aboriginal giant
.... ANAK
addenda .... APOCRYPHA
book .... JOB, NEH, AMOS, EZRA, JOEL, RUTH, KINGS, HOSEA, JONAH, MICAH, NAHUM, DANIEL, ESTHER, EXODUS, HAGGAI, ISAIAH, JOSHUA, JUDGES, PSALMS, SAMUEL, EZEKIEL, GENESIS, MALACHI, NUMBERS, OBADIAH, JEREMIAH, NEHEMIAH, PROVERBS, LEVITICUS, CHRONICLES, DEUTERONOMY, LAMENTATIONS, ECCLESIASTES
first five books of the
.... PENTATEUCH
Greek translation of the
.... SEPTUAGINT
in Syriac .... PESHITO, PESHITTA
language .... HEBREW
longest book in the
.... PSALMS
marginal notes
.... MASORA(H)
measure of capacity .... HIN, KAB, LOG, BATH, OMER, EPHAH, HOMER, LETHECH
measure of length ..... SPAN, CUBIT, FINGER, HANDBREATH
middle book .... PROVERBS
Origen's .... HEXAPLA
scribe .... EZRA
shortest book in the
.... OBADIAH
weight .... BEKA, MINA, GERAH, SHEKEL, TALENT
wisdom book of the .... JOB, PROVERBS, ECCLESIASTES
writer .... ELOHIST
"Tin Lizzie" .... CRATE
West schoolteacher ..... MARM
World falcons .... SAKERS
lizard .... SEPS, AGAMA
rulers .... ROMANS
sedge .... GALINGALE
swan .... WHOOPER
olden .... ANCIENT
older .... SENIOR
people, discrimination against .... AGEISM
people, discriminator against
.... AGEIST
oldest continent .... AUSTRALIA
member .... DEAN

person in the Bible
.... METHUSELAH
son .... HEIR, SCION
street in L.A. .... OLVERA
U.S. national park
.... YELLOWSTONE
oldfangled .... PASSE, OLD-HAT
oldtimer .... VET(ERAN)
oldwife .... MENHADEN, TRIGGERFISH
Ole, Norwegian composer
.... OLSEN
oleaceous tree .... ASH, LILAC, OLIVE, FORSYTHIA
oleaginous .... OILY, GREASY
oleander .... SHRUB, ROSEBAY
oleate .... SALT, ESTER
olefine .... ALKENE
olent .... FRAGRANT
oleo .... SPREAD, MARGARINE
oleoresin .... TOLU, ANIME, ELEMI, BALSAM
olfactory organ .... NOSE
stimulant .... ODOR
olibanum .... INCENSE
olio .... MESS, OLLA, STEW, MEDLEY, MELANGE, HODGEPODGE, MISCELLANY, SALMAGUNDI
olive .... TREE, RELISH, WREATH, OLEA(STER)
branch offering .... PEACE
genus .... OLEA
pimiento-stuffed .... PIMOLA
refuse .... BAGASSE
wild .... OLEASTER
Oliver .... NORTH, TWIST
composer .... BART
Twist author .... DICKENS
Twist character .... ROSE, TOBY, FAGIN, NANCY, SALLY, SIKES, BUMBLE, DODGER
Oliver's request .... MORE
Olivia's clown .... FESTE
olivine .... GARNET, PERIDOT
olla .... JAR, JUG, POT, STEW
ollapodrida .... HASH, OLIO, STEW, MEDLEY, ASSORTMENT
Ollie's friend .... FRAN
oloroso .... SHERRY
Olympian .... GOD, EROS, ATHLETE, EXALTED, GODLIKE, MAJESTIC, CELESTIAL
chief .... ZEUS
cupbearer .... GANYMEDE
queen .... HERA
reckless .... ATE
Olympic giant .... TITAN
gofer .... HEBE
name .... ATHENA

Olympic games site: first
.... ELIS
1912 .... STOCKHOLM
1928 .... AMSTERDAM
1956 .... MELBOURNE
1992 .... BARCELONA
Olympics ...... ATHLETIC CONTEST
Number 1 award .... GOLD
MEDAL
Number 2 award .... SILVER
MEDAL
Number 3 award .... BRONZE
MEDAL
Olympus .... SKY, MOUNT,
HEAVEN
mountain .... OSSA, PELION
Oman bay .... SAUQIRA
cape .... HADD, JIBSH
capital .... MASQAT, MUSCAT
city/town .... MATRAH, SALALA
gulf .... MASIRAN
language .... ARABIC
money .... RIAL
sultan .... TAIMUR
Omar, actor .... SHARIF
general .... BRADLEY
Khayyam's birthplace
.... NISHAPUR
country .... IRAN
work .... RUBAIYAT
omasum .... MANYPLIES
omber ...... HOMBRE, CARD GAME
omber, trump in .... MANILLA
omega .... END
antithesis of .... ALPHA
omelet(te) .... EGG DISH
omen .... SIGN, AUGUR(Y),
AUSPICE, PORTENT, PRESAGE,
PRECURSOR
death's .... KNELL
omentum .... CAUL
omers, ten .... EPHA
Omicron (variable star) .... CETI
ominous .... GRAVE, BODEFUL,
FATEFUL, MENACING,
SINISTER, PORTENTOUS
omission .... CUT, EVASION,
NEGLECT, OVERSIGHT
sign of .... CARET
syllable .... APOCOPE
vowel .... ELISION
word .... ELLIPSIS
omit .... DROP, MISS, SKIP,
DELETE, EXCEPT, EXCLUDE,
NEGLECT, LEAVE OUT,
PRETERMIT
a syllable .... ELIDE
omnia vincit _____ .... AMOR
omnibus .... BUS, COACH,
READER, COLLECTION, ALL-
EMBRACING

omnipotent .... ALMIGHTY
omnipresent .... IMMANENT,
UBIQUITOUS
omnivorous animal .... SWINE
Omphale's domain .... LYDIA
servant .... HERCULES
Omri's son .... AHAB
on .... AT, ATOP, UPON, ABOUT,
ABOVE, ONWARD, FORWARD
a bunt .... SACRIFICE
a grand scale ..... WORLDWIDE
a miscue .... ERROR
a par with .... EVEN, BESIDE
a ship's left side .... APORT
a ship's right side ...... ABEAM
a voyage .... ASEA
_____ (active) .... THE GO
and on .... ALWAYS,
(FOR)EVER
call .... READY
dit .... RUMOR, GOSSIP
edge .... TENSE, KEYED UP
every side .... ABOUT
guard .... ALERT
horseback .... ASTRIDE
land .... ASHORE
one's toes .... ALERT, ALIVE
one's uppers .... POOR
pins and needles .... EAGER,
TENSE, NERVOUS
tap .... NEXT
the _____ (at odds) .... OUTS
ball .... ALERT, SHARP
blue/briny/coral .... ASEA
crest .... ATOP
face of document .... EX
FACIE
go .... BUSY
heights .... ATOP
_____ (honest) .... LEVEL
house .... FREEBIE
house, in a way .... RENT-
FREE
left: comb. form .... LEVO
line .... AT STAKE
main .... ASEA
make .... SOCIAL-CLIMBING
mend .... IMPROVING
move .... ASTIR
other hand .... AGAIN
road .... AWAY
rocks .... ICED, AGROUND,
FAILED, BUSTED, RUINED,
WRECKED
sheltered side .... ALEE
side .... MORE
spot .... TREED, CORNERED
up and up .... LEGIT
warpath .... IRATE
way .... OFF, BOUND, EN
ROUTE, PREGNANT, IN

TRANSIT
this earth .... HERE
time .... SHARP, PROMPT,
PUNCTUALLY
to .... HEP, AWARE
two occasions .... TWICE
_____ (very busy) .... GO
windward side .... LEE,
AWEATHER
your way! .... GIT, SCAT,
SCRAM
on, _____ **(gather facts)** .... READ
UP
on the donkey, _____ .... PIN A
TAIL
onager .... ASS, DONKEY,
CATAPULT
Onassis, (A) nickname of
.... ARI, DADDY-O
yacht of .... CHRISTINA
once .... ANES, WHILOM, ONE
TIME, QUONDAM,
FORMER(LY), ERST(WHILE)
all at .... SUDDENLY
around Sol .... YEAR
around (the track) .... LAP
called .... NEE
called Ptolemais .... ACRE
more .... AGAIN, AFRESH,
ENCORE
once-over ...... GLANCE, SCRUTINY
oncoming .... IMPENDING,
APPROACHING
one .... ACE, EACH, SAME, UNIT,
SINGLE, UNITED, UNDIVIDED
against .... ANTI
and only .... SOLE
and the other .... BOTH
-armed bandit: sl. .... SLOT
MACHINE
base hit .... SINGLE
behind another .... TANDEM
billionth .... NANO
bottled up .... GENIE
bringing a case .... SUER
-celled creature ...... STENTOR,
AM(O)EBA, PROTOZOA,
INFUSORIA
combining form .... UNI,
MONO
eighth of dollar .... BIT
Eve had three .... FACES
-eyed .... MONOCULAR
-eyed giant .... CYCLOPS
-footed .... UNIPED
fourth of an anna .... PICE
headed for defeat .... GONER
hopelessly behind the times
.... DODO
-horned animal .... RHINO,
UNICORN

-horned fish .... UNIE
horse .... PETTY
horse town .... PODUNK
horse vehicle .... SHAY
hundred: comb. form
.... HECTO
hundred kopecks .... RUBLE
hundred percent .... WHOLE,
ENTIRE
hundred thousand in India
.... LAC
hundred years .... CENTURY,
CENTENARY
in line .... STANDER
kind of horse .... IRON,
WOODEN, ARABIAN
kind of pen .... POISON
kind of steer .... BUM
-legged .... UNIPOD
liner .... GAG
more .... ANOTHER
more than septi- .... OCTA
more time .... AGAIN
next to the last .... PENULT
of a cold weather pair
.... EARMUFF
a famous five .... QUINT
a friendly pair .... DAMON,
PYTHIAS
a trio .... TOM, DICK, HARRY,
CALM, COOL, COLLECTED,
ATHOS, ARAMIS, PORTHOS
Columbus' ships .... NIÑA,
PINTA, SANTA MARIA
eighteen .... HOLE
nine .... MUSE
of the Bowls .... SUN, HULA,
ROSE, GATOR, FIESTA, SUPER,
ORANGE
Carolines .... YAP, MOEN,
TRUK, BELAU, PALAU,
ULITHI, PELELIU
Cartrights .... BEN, HOSS,
LITTLE JOE
elite ..... SOCIAL REGISTERITE
Great Lakes ...... LAKE ERIE,
LAKE HURON, LAKE
ONTARIO, LAKE MICHIGAN,
LAKE SUPERIOR
towels .... HIS, HERS
Trimurti .... SIVA, VISHNU,
BRAHMA
of two .... EITHER
on the payroll .... EARNER
or another .... ANY
out on bond .... BAILEE
pound sterling .... QUID
recently hatched ..... NESTLING
result of thinking .... PLAN
sending an overseas message
.... CABLER

sergeant's .... HUP
showing promise .... COMER
sided .... ROUT, BIASED,
PARTIAL, EX PARTE,
UNILATERAL
spot .... ACE
square meter .... CENT(I)ARE
tenth are .... DECIARE
tenth of annual income
.... TITHE
thing .... UNIT
thousand .... MIL
time .... EARLIER
-time St. Petersburg residents
.... TSARS
-track mind .... MONOMANIA
type of photograph .... X-RAY,
GLOSSY
way of breaking glass
.... SHOOTING PANES
-way sign .... ARROW
way to go for dinner
.... DUTCH
way to ride .... ASTRIDE
way to stand .... PAT
who: suffix .... STER
acquires .... ASSUMER
catches sight of
.... DESCRIER
dodges .... EVADER
enjoys .... SAVORER
entertains .... HOST
goes in haste .... HIER
incites .... URGER
is being quizzed ..... TESTEE
is being tutored .... TUTEE
is quoted .... CITEE
makes a statement
.... RESOLUTIONER
practices witchcraft
.... SORCERER, SORCERESS
transfers property
.... ALIENOR
walks in water .... WADER
watches .... SPIER
worships only one god
.... MONOLATER
with a bright future
.... COMER
with a foreign accent
.... XENOEPIST
with a taxing job
.... ASSESSOR
with dependents
.... BREADWINNER
within the playing field
.... ONSIDER
one's betrothed .... FIANCE(E)
dialect .... IDIOLECT
own: comb. form .... IDIO

personal mannerism
.... IDIOSYNCRASY
public .... AUDIENCE,
FOLLOWING
strong point .... FORTE
Oneida .... INDIAN, IROQUOIS
O'Neill, playwright ...... EUGENE
character .... ANNA, NINA,
ORIN
daughter .... OONA
field of .... DRAMA
son-in-law
.... (CHARLIE)CHAPLIN
oneness .... UNITY, IDENTITY,
SAMENESS
oner .... LULU, LONER
onerous .... DIFFICULT,
BURDENSOME, OPPRESSIVE
ones here .... THESE
onion .... BULB, CEPA, LEEK,
CIBOL, ALLIUM, SHALLOT,
ESCHALOT, SCALLION
plant .... CHIVE
sea .... SQUILL
onions, prepared with
.... LYONNAISE
onionskin .... PAPER
onlooker .... BYSTANDER,
WITNESS, SPECTATOR
only .... BUT, LONE, MERE(LY),
SIMPLY, SINGLY, SOLE(LY)
onomatopoeia .... ECHOISM
onomatopoeic .... ECHOIC,
IMITATIVE
Onondaga .... LAKE, INDIAN,
IROQUOIS
onrush .... BIRR, DASH, FLOW,
STAMPEDE
onset .... START, ATTACK,
ASSAULT, APPROACH,
OUTBREAK, BEGINNING
onslaught .... RUSH, DRIVE,
ONSET, ATTACK, CHARGE,
THRUST, ASSAULT, OFFENSIVE
Ontario .... LAKE, PROVINCE
bay .... SOUTH, GEORGIAN
canal .... WELLAND
cape .... HURD, CROKER
capital .... TORONTO
city/town .... BARRIE, LONDON,
SUDBURY, TRENTON, WINDSOR,
BRAMPTON, HAMILTON,
KINGSTON, WATERLOO,
BRANTFORD, CAMBRIDGE,
ETOBICOKE, KITCHENER,
BURLINGTON, SCARBOROUGH
island .... PARRY, BARRIE,
AMHERST, WALPOLE,
COCKBURN, CHRISTIAN,
FLOWERPOT
lake .... DORE, ERIE, RICE,

SEUL, HURON, RAINY, WOODS, RIDEAU, SIMCOE, NIPIGON, PANACHE, SUPERIOR, NIPISSING, SAINT CLAIR
mountain .... OGIDAKI
river .... DON, GRAND, HUMBER, OTTAWA, SEVERN, ABITIBI, NIAGARA, MISSINAIBI
onto .... HEP, AWARE, WISE TO, COGNIZANT, CONVERSANT
onus .... DUTY, LOAD, TASK, BURDEN, CHARGE, OBLIGATION
onward .... AHEAD, FORTH, ADVANCING
onyx .... GEM, AGATE, NICOLO
007 .... JAMES BOND
antagonist of (in a '64 film) .... GOLDFINGER
creator .... IAN FLEMING
portrayer ..... MOORE, DALTON, BROSNAN, CONNERY, LAZENBY
oocyte .... EGG, GAMETE
oodles .... HEAP, LOTS, MANY, RAFTS, SCADS, SLEWS
oolite .... LIMESTONE
oology subject ...... (BIRD'S)EGGS
oolong .... TEA
Oom Paul .... KRUGER
oomiak .... CANOE, KAYAK
oomph .... VIGOR, SEX APPEAL
oorial .... SHA
oosperm .... ZYGOTE
ootheca .... OVISAC, EGG CASE
ooze .... BOG, MUD, DRIP, FLOW, LEAK, MIRE, SEEP, EXUDE, GLEET, MARSH, SLIME, SWEAT, FILTER, SLUDGE, EXUDATE, PERMEATE, SEDIMENT
oozy .... MIRY, SOFT, SLIMY, SLUDGY, SLOUGHY
opacate .... DIM
opah .... SOKO, (MOON)FISH
opal .... GEM, PITCH, RESIN, SILICA, HYALITE, ISOPYRE, CACHOLONG
fire .... GIRASOL(E), GIROSOL
opalescent .... IRIDESCENT
opaline .... GLASS
opaque ...... DARK, DULL, OBTUSE, OBSCURE
OPEC .... CARTEL
open .... BARE, FREE, UNDO, CLEAR, FRANK, OVERT, START, CANDID, EXPOSE(D), PUBLIC, UNFOLD, UNLOCK, UNSEAL(ED), LIBERAL, DISCLOSE, GENEROUS
air ..... ALFRESCO, OUTDOOR(S)
and shut .... CLEAR, SIMPLE,

EVIDENT, OBVIOUS
car .... PHAETON
country .... VELDT
-eyed ...... AWARE, WATCHFUL, OBSERVANT
-handed ...... GIVING, LIBERAL, GENEROUS
-hearted .... FRANK, CANDID, GENIAL, CORDIAL
in a way .... UNBOLT
-minded .... AMENABLE, RECEPTIVE
-mouthed .... AGOG, AGAPE
partly .... AJAR
sea .... MAIN
sesame .... PASSWORD
the bottle .... UNCAP
to attack .... VULNERABLE
to view .... OVERT
up .... UNDO
widely .... GAPE
opener .... KEY, CLAVIS
opening .... GAP, GATE, HOLE, PORE, SLIT, SLOT, MOUTH, CHANCE, ORIFICE, VACANCY, APERTURE, LOOPHOLE
in chess .... GAMBIT
small .... PORE, CRANNY, FORAMEN, ORIFICE, OSTIOLE
openings, in zoology .... STOMATA
opera .... AIDA, FAUST, MANON, NORMA, THAIS, TOSCA, CARMEN, ERNANI, MIKADO, RIENZI, SALOME, FIDELIO, LA BOHEME
box .... LOGE
by Gershwin .... PORGY AND BESS
Gounod .... ROMEO ET JULIETTE
Handel .... NERO, SERSE
Humperdinck .... HANSEL AND GRETEL
Massenet .... THAIS
Puccini .... TOSCA, TURANDOT, LA BOHEME, MADAMA BUTTERFLY
Rossini .... WILLIAM TELL, THE BARBER OF SEVILLE
Salieri .... A TAR
Smetana ...... THE BARTERED BRIDE
Strauss .... SALOME
Verdi .... ERNANI, RIGOLETTO
Von Weber .... OBERON
Wagner .... LOHENGRIN, GOTTERDAMMERUNG, TRISTAN UND ISOLDE
comic .... BUFFO, BOUFFE

company director/manager .... IMPRESARIO
composer .... BIZET, VERDI, HANDEL, GOUNOD, MOZART, WAGNER, MENOTTI, PUCCINI, ROSSINI, SMETANA, STRAUSS, MASSENET, HUMPERDINCK
describing an .... SOAP, COMIC, HORSE, LIGHT, BALLET
glass .... LORGNETTE
hat .... GIBUS, TOPPER
heroine ...... AIDA, ELSA, MIMI, LUCIA, SENTA, GRETEL, ISOLDE, PAMINA, ARIADNE, CIO CIO SAN
highlight .... ARIA
horse .... OATER
house .... MET, (LA)SCALA
singer .... ALDA, PONS, EAMES, HORNE, MELBA, PINZA, PRICE, CALLAS, GARDEN, PETERS, STEBER, TUCKER, CABALLE, CORELLI, DOMINGO, NILSSON, STEVENS, TEBALDI, CHALIAPIN
solo .... ARIA, CAVATINA
star .... DIVA, PRIMA DONNA
text of .... LIBRETTO
operate .... ACT, RUN, USE, TEND, WORK, MANAGE, CONDUCT
against .... MILITATE
on .... TREAT, INFLUENCE
operatic character .... BUFFO
impresario, 1843–89 ..... ROSA
prince .... IGOR
slave .... AIDA
solo .... ARIA
operation .... ACTION, PROCESS, PROJECT
operative .... SPY, AGENT, WORKING, DETECTIVE, EFFECTIVE
operator .... AGENT, HANDLER
operculum .... LID, FLAP
operetta composer .... FRIML, LEHAR, STRAUS, HERBERT, ROMBERG, STRAUSS, OFFENBACH
Herbert's .... NAUGHTY MARIETTA
Lehar's .... THE MERRY WIDOW
Offenbach's .... LA PERICHOLE
Romberg's .... THE STUDENT PRINCE
singer .... MOFFO, SILLS, FRANCHI
Straus' .... THE CHOCOLATE SOLDIER
Strauss' .... DIE FLEDERMAUS
operose ...... ARDUOUS, ONEROUS, DIFFICULT, LABORIOUS
Ophelia's love .... HAMLET

ophidian .... ASP, COBRA, SNAKE, REPTILE, SERPENT
Ophir's wealth .... GOLD
ophthalmologist .... OCULIST
ophthalmology, subject of
.... EYE, SIGHT, VISION
opiate .... SEDATIVE, ANALGESIC
opine .... THINK, BELIEVE, SUPPOSE
opinion .... IDEA, VIEW, TENET, ADVICE, BELIEF, NOTION, THEORY, THOUGHT, VERDICT, JUDGMENT, SENTIMENT, CONVICTION, IMPRESSION, PERSUASION
barometer .... GALLUP POLL
general .... CONSENSUS
having opposite .... POLES APART
man .... POLLSTER, POLL-TAKER
opposing .... HERESY
united in .... AGREEING, CONSENTIENT
opinionated .... BIASED, BIGOTED, DOGMATIC
speaker .... DOGMATIZER
opium .... DRUG, NARCOTIC
addict .... USER, DOPER, JUNKY, JUNKIE, NOSCAPINE, (DOPE)FIEND
alkaloid ...... CODEA, CODEINE, MORPHINE, PAPAVARINE
seed .... MAW
seller .... PUSHER
source .... POPPY
tincture of .... LA(U)DANUM
traffic center .... TACHILEK
opossum .... QUICA, YAPO(C)K, MARSUPIAL
place of young .... POUCH
play .... DEAD, FEIGN
oppidan .... URBAN
opponent ...... FOE, ANTI, ENEMY, ADVERSARY, ANTAGONIST
of change .... DIEHARD
opportune .... APT, TIMELY, APROPOS, FORTUITOUS, WELL-TIMED, PROPITIOUS, SEASONABLE
opportunist .... EXPLOITER, TIME-SERVER
opportunity .... CHANCE, OPENING, OCCASION
oppose .... DARE, DEFY, DENY, FACE, FOIL, CROSS, REPEL, HINDER, OBJECT, REPUGN, RESIST, COUNTER(ACT), PROTEST, DISAGREE, WITHSTAND

opposed .... ANTI, AVERSE, AGAINST, CONTRARY
opposing .... RIVAL
opposite ...... FORNENT, REVERSE, VIS-A-VIS, ANTIPODE, CONTRAST, CONTRARY, ANTITHESIS, ANTITHETIC
Adam's .... LAST MAN
belief .... HERESY
directly ..... HEAD-ON, INVERSE
exact .... ANTIPODE
extremity .... POLE
number .... COUNTERPART
of what's expected ..... IRONIC
prefix .... ANTI
opposition .... FOE, RIVAL, DEFIANCE, ANTIPATHY, HOSTILITY, RESISTANCE, COMPETITION
abrupt show of ...... WALKOUT
act of .... STRIKE, BOYCOTT
in .... CON, ANTI, AGAINST
party .... MINORITY
oppress .... CRUSH, GRIPE, BURDEN, MISTREAT, PERSECUTE, TYRANNIZE
oppressive ...... CRUEL, ONEROUS, TYRANNICAL
anything .... INCUBUS
oppressor .... BULLY, TYRANT
opprobrious .... ABUSIVE, MALICIOUS, DEROGATORY
opprobrium .... ODIUM, SCORN, SHAME, INFAMY, DISGRACE
oppugn .... OPPOSE, DISPUTE, CRITICIZE, CONTROVERT
Opryland's Wagoner .... PORTER
Ops .... RHEA, GODDESS
concern of .... HARVEST
daughter of .... CERES
husband of .... SATURN
opt .... CHOOSE, DECIDE, SELECT
optic .... EYE
branch of .... CATOPTRICS
optical .... OCULAR, VISUAL
aid .... LENSES, GLASSES, LORGNON, MONOCLE, PINCENEZ, LORGNETTE, BINOCULARS
glass .... LENS, SPECS, CONTACT
illusion .... MIRAGE
instrument .... VIEWER, ALIDADE, PERISCOPE, TELESCOPE, MICROSCOPE
instrument lines .... RETICLE
optician .... OPTOMETRIST
Optics author .... NEWTON
optimism .... HOPE, TRUST, ENTHUSIASM
optimistic .... ROSY, UPBEAT,

HOPEFUL, ROSEATE, SANGUINE, CONFIDENT, EXPECTANT
optimum .... BEST, PRIME, CHOICE
option ...... VOTE, RIGHT, CHOICE, PREFERENCE, ALTERNATIVE
optional .... ELECTIVE
opulent .... RICH, WEALTHY, ABUNDANT
opuntia .... TUNA, CACTUS
opus .... WORK, OPERA, SYMPHONY, COMPOSITION
plural of .... OPERA
oquassa .... TROUT
or .... GOLD, YELLOW, CONJUNCTION
ora .... COIN, MOUTHS
orach(e) .... SPINACH, GOOSEFOOT
oracle .... SEER, AUGUR, DELOS, PROPHET, HOLY OF HOLIES
giver .... FAUNUS
seat .... DODONA
site of .... DELPHI
woman .... SYBIL, SIBYL
oracular .... VATIC, ORPHIC, PROPHETIC, SYBILLINE
oral .... VOCAL, SPOKEN, VERBAL, STOMATIC, UNWRITTEN
pledge .... WORD, PAROLE
orale .... FANON
orally .... PAROL, VIVA VOCE
Oran is in .... ALGERIA
orange .... CITRUS, TANGELO, MANDARIN, TANGERINE
flower oil .... NEROLI
genus .... CITRUS
inedible .... OSAGE
juice squeezer .... REAMER
mock .... SYRINGA
of an .... CITRIC
peel .... ZEST
pekoe .... TEA
preserve .... MARMALADE
red chalcedony .... SARD
seed .... PIP
skin .... RIND
variety/type .... NAVEL, MICHAEL, VALENCIA
yellow ...... CROCUS, LUTEOUS, SAFFRON
Orange River tributary
.... VAAL
orangewood .... HEDGE
orangutan .... APE, MIAS
habitat ...... BORNEO, SUMATRA
orate .... MOUTH, DECLAIM, PERORATE, SPEECHIFY
oration .... SPEECH, ADDRESS, DISCOURSE
orator ...... OTIS, BRYAN, CICERO, RHETOR, SPEAKER

505

in law .... PLAINTIFF,
PETITIONER
oratorio lyrics .... LIBRETTO
part of .... ARIA, DUET, TRIO,
CAVATINA
oratory .... CHAPEL, CHANTRY,
ELOQUENCE
fathers, founder of .... NERI
master of .... RHETOR
orb ...... EYE, SUN, MOON, GLOBE,
SPHERE
orbit .... PATH, REALM, SCOPE,
TRACK, CIRCUIT, EYE SOCKET
heavenly body's .... CYCLE
perigee of .... NADIR
orbital point .... APSE, APSIS,
APOGEE, PERIGEE
orc .... WHALE, GRAMPUS
kind of .... DOLPHIN
orchard .... GROVE, GARDEN
orchal .... LICHEN
orchestra .... BAND, PARQUET,
SYMPHONY
circle .... PARTERRE
conductor/leader .... MACE,
SHAW, BOULT, CUGAT, GOULD,
JAMES, LEWIS, MEHTA, SANTI,
DUCHIN, PREVIN, VALLEE,
FIEDLER, ORMANDY, FERRARIS,
GERHARDT, WILLIAMS,
LEINSDORF, STOKOWSKI,
HAMMERSTEIN
platform .... BANDSTAND
section .... BRASS, REEDS,
TRAPS, WINDS, STRINGS,
PERCUSSION
space for .... PIT
theater's .... GROUND FLOOR
orchestral exclamation point
.... CYMBAL
orchestrate .... ARRANGE
orchid .... SATYR, DICHEA,
FLOWER, POGONIA, EPIPHYTE,
BUTTERFLY, PUTTYROOT
as food .... SALEP
climbing .... VANILLA
genus .... DISA, ORCHIS
third petal of .... LIP
tuber .... SALEP
orchil .... DYE, LICHEN
Orcus .... DIS, HADES, PLUTO
ordain .... ENACT, FROCK, ORDER,
DECREE, INVEST, APPOINT,
PRESCRIBE
ordeal .... TEST, CROSS, TRIAL,
CRUCIBLE, HARDSHIP,
TRIBULATION
order ...... BID, HEST, KIND, SORT,
CLASS, LODGE, DEMAND,
DIRECT(ION), METHOD, SERIES,
SYSTEM, COMMAND,

MANDATE, CATEGORY,
PRESCRIBE, COMMISSION,
INSTRUCT(ION)
back .... REMAND
good .... EUTAXY
marching .... FALL IN
of animals .... INI
to cease .... RESTRAINER
Order of the Garter
.... KNIGHTHOOD
ordered, old style .... BADE
orderly .... AIDE, NEAT, TIDY,
TRIM, SPRUCE, REGULAR,
ATTENDANT, METHODICAL,
SYSTEMATIC
arrangement .... PLAN
ordinal .... NUMBER
number .... FIRST, SECOND,
THIRD, FOURTH, FIFTH
suffix .... (E)TH
ordinance .... LAW, EDICT,
STATUTE, REGULATION
ordinary .... SO-SO, USUAL,
COMMON, MEDIAL, MEDIUM,
NORMAL, TAVERN, AVERAGE,
MILL-RUN, REGULAR,
ROUTINE, CHAPLAIN,
MEDIOCRE, MIDDLING,
CUSTOMARY
ordnance .... GUNS, ARMOR,
CANNON, WEAPONRY,
ARTILLERY
ordure .... DUNG, FILTH, MANURE
ore .... MINERAL
analyze .... ASSAY
bearing rock layer .... LEDGE
bed of .... REEF
crushing machine .... STAMP
deposit .... LODE, POCKET
digger .... MINER
extract/refine .... SMELT
iron .... OCHER, OCHRE
layer .... SEAM, STOPE
lead .... GALENA
refiner .... SMELTER
screening sieve ...... TROMMEL
shovel for washing .... VAN
smelting product .... SPEISS
truck/wagon .... CORF
vein .... LODE, STREAK
washing container .... PAN
washing device .... DOLLY
worthless .... MATTE
oread .... NAIAD, NYMPH
oregano .... MINT, PLANT,
MARJORAM
Oregon bay .... TILLAMOOK,
WINCHESTER
beach ...... NYE, GOLD, AGATE,
SECCHI, CRESCENT
cape .... ARAGO, BLANCO,

FALCON, MEARES, LOOKOUT,
PERPETUA, SEBASTIAN
capital .... SALEM
city/town .... BEND, ALOHA,
ALBANY, DALLAS, EUGENE,
KEIZER, TIGARD, KIWANDA,
ASHLAND, ASTORIA, GRESHAM,
LEBANON, LINCOLN, MEDFORD,
NEWPORT, ALTAMONT,
PORTLAND, ROSEBURG,
WOODBURN, BEAVERTON,
CORVALLIS, HILLSBORO,
GRANTS PASS
college .... REED
county ..... COOS, LAKE, LANE,
LINN, POLK, BAKER, CURRY,
GRANT, UNION, WASCO,
BENTON, MARION, DOUGLAS,
KLAMATH, YAMHILL,
CLACKAMAS, JOSEPHINE
dam .... OXBOW, MCNARY,
OWYHEE, THE DALLES,
BONNEVILLE, HELLS CANYON
falls .... MUNSON, PUNCHBOWL,
STEAMBOAT
Indian .... COOS, KUSAN,
MODOC, YANAN, CAYUSE,
CHINOOK, NEZ PERCE
island .... WIZARD
lake .... HART, LAVA, LOST,
ABERT, ASPEN, DAVIS, GUANO,
WALDO, ALVORD, CRATER,
CULTUS, DORENA, EWAUNA,
HARNEY, SILVER, SPARKS,
SUMMER, TUMTUM, DETROIT,
DIAMOND, PAULINA,
WALLOWA, FOURMILE,
UMATILLA
mountain .... HART, HOOD,
STEENS, THIELSEN,
MCLOUGHLIN
mountain, twin-peaked
.... SADDLE
mountain range .... BLUE,
OWYHEE, PUEBLO, CASCADE,
KLAMATH, WALLOWA,
SISKIYOU
Myrtle Grove site
.... MILLICOMA
National forest .... SIUSLAW
National memorial to Lewis
and Clark .... FORT
CLATSOP
National park .... CRATER
LAKE
National wildlife refuge
.... MALHEUR
river .... COOS, HOOD, ALSEA,
BURNT, ROGUE, SMITH, SNAKE,
SYCAN, WHITE, CHETCO,
UMPQUA, NEHALEM, SPRAGUE,

MALHEUR, COLUMBIA, ILLINOIS, CALAPOOIA, DESCHUTES, WALLA-WALLA, WILLAMETTE
seaport .... ASTORIA
state bird .... MEADOWLARK
state flower .... (OREGON)GRAPE
state nickname .... BEAVER, SUNSET
state park .... ECOLA, SMITH ROCKS, SILVER CREEK
state university .... EUGENE, CORVALLIS
Trail users .... PIONEERS, SETTLERS
underwater marine science center site .... YAQUINA BAY
village, once upon a time .... BAY OCEAN
volcano that exploded and collapsed .... MOUNT MAZAMA

Orestes, parent of .... AGAMEMNON
sister of .... ELECTRA
wife of .... HERMIONE
orfe .... IDE
org. .... ASSN, SYST
ecological .... EPA, STE
for doctors .... AMA
for sharp students .... NHS
for teachers .... NEA
organ .... MEANS, VEHICLE, BOMBARDON, HARMONIUM, INSTRUMENT, PERIODICAL
atrophied .... VESTIGE
barrel .... HURDY-GURDY
connecting tissue .... PONS
device .... PIPE, REED, STOP, TREMOLO
falling of .... PTOSIS, PROLAPSE
grinder's assistant .... MONKEY
keyboard .... CLAVIER, MELODEON, ACCORDION, HARMONIUM
loft .... GALLERY
matrix of .... STROMA
mouth .... HARMONICA
of flight .... WING
of speech .... TONGUE
outgrowth .... APPENDIX
part .... PIPE, REED, STOP, PALLET, CONSOLE
pipe .... FLUE, REED, LABIAL, MONTRE
pipe plug .... TAMPION
place in church .... LOFT,

GALLERY
point/tip .... MUCRO
seed-bearing .... PISTIL
stop .... SEXT, TUBA, DOLCE, FLUTE, GAMBE, VIOLA, DULCET, MONTRE, OCTAVE, BASSOON, BOURDON, CELESTA, MELODIA, TREMOLO, VIOLONE, BOMBARDE, DIAPASON, DULCIANA
touch .... BARBEL, PALP(US)
transplantation pioneer .... BARNARD, DEBAKEY
vital .... EYE, LUNG, HEART, LIVER, KIDNEY
voice .... LARYNX
organic .... INBORN, INHERENT
body .... ZOOID
compound .... ENOL, AMINE
law .... CHARTER, CONSTITUTION
substance of .... MEDULLA
organism .... MONAD, MONAS, PLANT, ANIMAL
animal .... ZOOID
ductless .... SPLEEN
life cycle of .... ONTOGENY
living on another .... PARASITE
mode of formation .... MORPHOSIS
one-celled .... AM(O)EBA, PARAMECIUM
reaction to stimulus ..... TAXIS
requiring no air .... ANAEROBE
sea .... NEKTON
with parasite .... HOST
organist .... BACH, BIGGS
organization .... CLUB, CADRE, SETUP, UNION, OUTFIT, COMPANY, STRUCTURE
organize .... FORM, SET UP, ARRANGE, ESTABLISH, SYSTEMATIZE
organized movement ...... DRIVE, CRUSADE, CAMPAIGN
orgeat .... SIRUP
orgy .... BASH, BINGE, SPREE, REVELRY, CAROUSAL
oribi .... ANTELOPE
oriel .... NOOK, ALCOVE, (BAY)WINDOW
part .... PANE
orient .... ASIA, ADAPT, PEARL, ADJUST, (FAR)EAST
Oriental .... ASIAN, ASIATIC, EASTERN, CHINESE, JAPANESE
banker .... SHROFF
beverage .... CHA, TEA
bow .... SALAAM
cloth .... CAMLET
coin ..... RIN, SEN, ANNA, PICE,

TAEL, DINAR
decree .... FIRMAN
destiny .... KISMET
drink .... SAKE, TUBA, ARRACK
dwelling .... DAR
gate .... TORII
greeting .... SALAAM
inn ...... KHAN, SERAI, IMARET, CARAVANSARY
laborer .... COOLIE, SACADA
litter .... KAGO, DOOLEE, PALANQUIN
market .... SOOK, SOUK
martial art ...... JUDO, KARATE, JUJITSU, TAI CHI
money-changer .... SHROFF
name .... ALI, OMAR
nurse .... AMA(H), AYAH, EYAH
opposite of .... WESTERN, OCCIDENTAL
palanquin .... DOOLEE
porter .... HAMAL, HAMAUL
potentate .... AGA
prince .... EMIR, AMEER
prison .... BAGNIO
punishment .... BASTINADO
rice dish .... PILAU, PILAF(F)
rug .... USHAK
ruler .... KHAN, SHAH, NAWAB, RAJAH, SULTAN
salute .... KOWTOW, SALAAM
sash .... OBI
seed .... SESAME
ship .... GRAB
sword .... SCIMITAR
taxi .... RICKSHA
title .... BABA, RAJAH
trousers ..... AJAMAS, PYJAMAS
weight .... ROTL, TAEL, CATTY, PICUL
wind .... MONSOON
orientate .... ADJUST, FAMILIARIZE
orientation of sorts .... BRIEFING
orifice .... HOLE, PORE, VENT, MOUTH, STOMA, OUTLET, OPENING, OSTIOLE, SPIRACLE
Origen, for one ...... THEOLOGIAN
origin .... GERM, ROOT, SEED, BIRTH, CAUSE, FATHER, SOURCE, GENESIS, LINEAGE, BEGINNING, PARENT(AGE)
of the .... GENETIC
original .... NEW, FIRST, FRESH, NOVEL, NATIVE, INITIAL, EARLIEST, PRISTINE, AUTHENTIC
name of Camp David .... SHANGRI-LA
native .... ABORIGINE
settler .... PIONEER
sin .... DISOBEDIENCE

507

sin site .... EDEN
sinner .... EVE, ADAM
Yellow Rose of Texas
.... EMILY MORGAN
words .... TEXT
originally .... ERST, INITIALLY
the ninth hour .... NOON
originate .... (A)RISE, BEGIN,
FOUND, START, CREATE,
DERIVE, INVENT
originator ...... AUTHOR, FATHER,
CREATOR, INVENTOR
Orinoco River tributary
.... ARO, APURE
oriole .... BIRD, PIROL, LORIOT,
FIREBIRD, HANGBIRD,
HANGNEST, TROUPIAL,
GOLDENROBIN
genus .... ICTERUS
kin of .... STARLING
Orion .... HUNTER, ALGEBAR
lover/killer of .... DIANA
star .... RIGEL, BETELGEUSE
orison(s) .... PRAYER
Orkney county seat
.... KIRKWALL
fishing waters .... HAAF
inlet .... VOE
island .... POMONA
islands channel .... SCAPA
FLOW
Orlando .... ROLAND
servant of .... ADAM
Orleans heroine .... JOAN OF ARC
orlon .... FIBER, FABRIC
orlop .... DECK
ormer .... (EAR)SHELL
ormolu ...... ALLOY, GOLD MOSAIC
ornament .... ADORN(MENT),
DECOR(ATE), EMBOSS,
SPANGLE, BEAUTIFY,
DECORATION
by engraving .... CHASE
cheap .... GAUD, BAUBLE,
GEWGAW, TRINKET
dangling .... MOBILE
drop-like .... GUTTA
metal .... ETCH, CHASE,
EMBOSS, ENGRAVE
metal collar .... TORQUE
showy .... GAUD, BAUBLE,
GEWGAW, BIJOU(TERIE)
silverware .... CHASE
ornamental .... ARTY, FANCY,
ARTISTIC, DECORATIVE
accessories .... TRAPPINGS
article .... TRINKET, GIMCRACK,
KNICKKNACK
band/belt .... SASH
border .... DADO
button/knob .... STUD

clasp .... CHATELAINE
cloth headband .... DIADEM
collar ...... TORQUE, CARCANET
design .... LACE
dish .... EPERGNE
feathers .... PLUME
garden area .... PARTERRE
lacework of gold and silver
wire .... FILIGREE
lacing .... PICOT
metal foil .... TINSEL
needlework .... EMBROIDERY
network .... FRET
pin .... AGLET, BROOCH
plasterwork .... PARGET
shrub .... HENNA
tuft of cords .... TASSEL
tuft of silk .... POMPON
vessel .... VASE
work .... TRACERY
ornate .... FANCY, SHOWY,
FLORID, PURPLE, AUREATE,
BAROQUE, ELEGANT,
ARABESQUE, ELABORATE
plastering .... CEIL
ornery .... MEAN, TESTY, MULISH,
STUBBORN, OBSTINATE,
QUARRELSOME
person .... CURMUDGEON
ornis .... BIRDS, AVIFAUNA
ornithologist .... AUDUBON
ornithology subject of .... BIRDS
oro .... GOLD
de _____ .... PLATA
oroide .... ALLOY
orology subject .... MOUNTAINS
orotund .... ROUND, SHOWY,
POMPOUS, RESONANT,
BOMBASTIC
orphan .... WAIF
Jane's family .... EYRES,
EYRIA
orphanage .... ASYLUM
Orpheus, for one .... MUSICIAN
instrument of .... LYRE
wife of .... EURYDICE
orphic .... MYSTIC, OCCULT,
ORACULAR
orpiment .... PIGMENT
orpin(e) .... STONECROP
orra .... ODD, EXTRA
orrery .... PLANETARIUM
orris/orrice .... IRIS, PLANT
Orsino's (duke) wife ...... VIOLA
Orson, actor .... WELLES
daughter of .... REBECCA,
BEATRICE
wife of .... RITA, PAOLA,
VIRGINIA
ort ...... CRUMB, SCRAP, REMNANT,
FRAGMENT, LEFTOVER

of a sort .... CRUST
orthodox .... PROPER,
CONVENTIONAL
Orthodox, Eastern Church
diocese .... EPARCHY
orthographer .... SPELLER
orthopedist's concern .... BONES
orthopteron .... INSECT, CRICKET,
COCKROACH
ortolan .... SORA, BUNTING,
BOBOLINK
Orwell's Farm .... ANIMAL
oryx .... GEMSBOK, ANTELOPE
os .... BONE, ESKER, MOUTH,
OPENING
Osage .... SIOUX, INDIAN
Osaka Bay port .... KOBE
location of .... HONSHU
Oscar .... AWARD, STATUETTE
film: 1928 .... WINGS
1932 .... GRAND HOTEL
1933 .... CAVALCADE
1943 .... CASABLANCA
1968 .... OLIVER
1970 .... PATTON
1976 .... ROCKY
1977 .... ANNIE HALL
1984 .... AMADEUS
1986 .... PLATOON
1993 .... PHILADELPHIA
1994 .... FORREST GUMP
kin of .... EMMY, TONY
1952 winner .... HUMPHREY
BOGART
1960 winner .... ELIZABETH
TAYLOR
1991 winner ..... JODIE FOSTER
1993 winner .... TOM HANKS
1994 winner .... TOM HANKS
Osceola's tribe .... SEMINOLE
oscillate ...... WAG, SWAY, WAVE,
SWING, LIBRATE, VIBRATE
oscillating .... PENDULAR
device .... ELECTRIC FAN
oscillation transformer
.... JIGGER
oscine .... CHAT, CROW, LARK,
FINCH, SHRIKE, BUNTING,
TANAGER
oscitancy .... APATHY, STUPOR,
DROWSINESS
oscitate .... GAPE, YAWN
osculate .... BUSS, KISS, SMACK,
TOUCH
osculation .... KISS(ING), CONTACT
osier .... ROD, WAND, SALLOW,
WILLOW, DOGWOOD
twig .... WITHE
Osiris' brother .... SET, SETH
crown .... ATEF
domain .... AMENTI

emblem .... APIS
father .... GEB, KEB, SEB
mother .... NUT
sister .... ISIS
son .... HORUS, ANUBIS
wife .... ISIS
Oslo .... CHRISTIANIA
Osman sobriquet .... CONQUEROR
empire founded by
.... OTTOMAN
Osmanli .... TURK, OTTOMAN
osmosis, e.g. .... DIFFUSION
osmund .... FERN
osprey .... HAWK, OSSIFRAGE
O.S.S.'s successor .... CIA
Ossa's companion .... PELION
osseous .... BONY, OSTEAL
ossicle .... BONELET, (EAR)BONE
ossifrage .... HAWK, OSPREY,
LAMMERGEIER
Ossining institution .... SING
SING
ossuary .... URN, VAULT
content of .... BONES
ostensible .... SEEMING, APPARENT
ostentation .... POMP, GLOSS,
PARADE, DISPLAY, SPLURGE,
SHOWINESS, EXHIBITION
ostentatious .... ARTY, GAUDY,
SHOWY, POMPOUS,
PRETENTIOUS
display: colloq. .... RITZ
show .... POMP, PARADE
osteo: comb. form .... BONE(S)
osteoid .... BONE-LIKE
osteoma .... TUMOR
Osterreich .... AUSTRIA
ostiary .... GUARD
ostiole .... PORE, STOMA, OPENING,
ORIFICE
ostler .... STABLEMAN
ostracism ...... EXILE, EXCLUSION,
REJECTION
ostracize .... BAR, EXILE, BANISH,
REJECT, EXCLUDE, SHUT OUT
ostrich ...... RHEA, NANDU, RATITE
bird like .... EM(E)U,
CASSOWARY
kin of .... TINAMOU
Oswego .... TEA
tea .... BEE BALM, MONARDA
Otaheite .... TAHITI
otalgia .... EARACHE
otary .... SEAL
like an .... EARED
Ot(h)ello .... MOOR, OPERA,
TRAGEDY
author .... SHAKESPEARE
opera composer .... VERDI
tormentor of .... IAGO
wife of .... DESDEMONA

other .... ELSE, ALTERNATE,
DIFFERENT, ADDITIONAL
comb. form .... ALLO,
HETER(O)
"____, other rooms":
Capote .... VOICES
than .... APART FROM
others, and .... ET AL, REST
otherwise .... THAN, (OR)ELSE
otic .... AURAL, AUDITORY
otiose .... IDLE, VAIN, FUTILE,
STERILE, USELESS, INDOLENT
Otis (Cornelia) .... SKINNER
otitis externa .... SWIMMER'S EAR
otological subject .... EAR
otologist .... AURIST
concern of .... EAR(ACHE)
Ott .... MASTER, MEL(VIN)
Ottawa .... INDIAN, ALGONQUIN
Ottawan chief .... PONTIAC
otter .... FUR, MAMMAL,
PARAVANE, BROADTAIL
genus .... LUTRA
relative of .... MINK, SKUNK,
WEASEL
Otto .... GRAHAM, PREMINGER
ottoman ...... POUF, SILK, COUCH,
DIVAN, (FOOT)STOOL
Ottoman .... TURK, OTHMAN
court/government .... PORTE
emperor .... SELIM
Empire founder .... OSMAN
non-Moslem .... RAIA
official .... PASHA
standard .... ALEM
sultan .... MURAD, SULEIMAN
oubliette .... PRISON, DUNGEON
ouch .... CLASP, BROOCH, BUCKLE
ought ...... ZERO, AT ALL, CIPHER,
NAUGHT
oui .... YES
ouija equipment .... BOARD,
PLANCHETTE
ounce .... ONS, WEIGHT,
(SNOW)LEOPARD
ouph(e) .... ELF, GOBLIN
our pilots .... USAF
times .... TWENTIETH CENTURY
Our Lady .... MARY, NOTRE DAME
"Miss Brooks" .... EVE
ARDEN
oust .... EJECT, EVICT, EXPEL,
BOUNCE, DEPOSE, REMOVE,
FORCE OUT
ouster .... EVICTOR, EVICTION,
DISMISSAL
out .... AWAY, BEGONE, NOT IN,
OUTSIDE, WITHOUT, EXTERNAL
-and-out .... RANK, GROSS,
SHEER, UTTER, ARRANT,
ABSOLUTE, COMPLETE,

CONFIRMED, DOWNRIGHT
in ____ (stranded) .... LEFT
FIELD
in the open .... OVERT
of .... FROM, BEYOND
bounds .... OFF-LIMITS
date .... DEMODE
gear .... CRANKY
harmony .... AJAR
line .... ASKEW
order ...... BROKEN, HAYWIRE
place .... INAPT, INEPT,
MISLAID, UNSEEMLY
practice .... RUSTY, STIFF
reach .... UNTOUCHABLE
sight .... PERDU(E),
CONCEALED
sort(s) ..... MOODY, GRUMPY,
CAUSTIC, INDISPOSED
the blue .... ABRUPTLY,
SUDDENLY
the ordinary .... RARE,
UNIQUE, UNUSUAL,
DIFFERENT
the way .... REMOTE,
SECLUDED
the wind .... ALEE
town play opening
.... PREVIEW
on a limb .... IN A JAM
slang .... ALIBI, EXCUSE
way .... EXIT, EGRESS
out, ____ (betray one's cause)
.... SELL
(serve) .... DISH
outage .... BREAK, INTERVAL,
INTERRUPTION
outbreak .... RASH, RIOT,
ERUPTION, OCCURRENCE
outbuilding .... BARN, SHED,
GARAGE
outburst .... GUST, STORM,
TIRADE, FLAREUP, TANTRUM,
ERUPTION
uncontrolled .... HYSTERIA
outcast .... EXILE, PARIAH,
WRETCH, OUTLAW, DERELICT
Biblical .... HAGAR,
ISHMAEL(ITE)
of a sort .... LEPER
outclass .... BEST, EXCEL, SURPASS
outcome ...... END, ISSUE, EFFECT,
RESULT, UPSHOT, AFTERMATH
outcropping .... BASSET
outcry .... SHOUT, CLAMOR,
DIRDUM, UPROAR, PROTEST,
OBJECTION
outdated .... PASSE
outdo .... CAP, TOP, BEAT, EXCEL,
EXCEED, SURPASS
outdoor .... ABROAD, OPEN-AIR,

ALFRESCO

bench .... EXEDRA

party .... FETE, PICNIC,
BARBECUE

stairs .... PERRON

theatre .... DRIVE-IN

time .... SUMMER

outer .... ECTAL, EXTERIOR,
EXTERNAL

covering .... COAT, HUSK,
RIND, SKIN, WRAP, CRUST,
SHELL, TESTA, COCOON

edge .... LIP, RIM, PERIMETER

garment .... ROBE, WRAP,
DOLMAN, JACKET, KIMONO,
PALETOT, SURTOUT,
(OVER)COAT

layer of cells .... ECTODERM

space explorer
.... ASTRONAUT, COSMONAUT

space visitor .... ET

outfit ...... RIG, GARB, GEAR, SUIT,
UNIT, GETUP, TURN-OUT,
CAPARISON

bride's .... TROUSSEAU

matching .... ENSEMBLE

to .... ACCOUTER

outflank .... OUTWIT, THWART

outflow .... EFFLUX, ESCAPE

outgo .... EXPENDITURE

or income .... RENT

outgoing .... SOCIABLE,
GREGARIOUS

outgrowth .... RESULT, OFFSHOOT

outhouse .... PRIVY

outing .... TRIP, AIRING, PICNIC,
CLAMBAKE, EXCURSION

outlander ...... ALIEN, STRANGER,
FOREIGNER

outlandish .... ALIEN, ABSURD,
BIZARRE, STRANGE, PECULIAR,
FANTASTIC, GROTESQUE

outlast .... OUTLIVE, OUTWEAR,
SURVIVE

outlaw .... BAN, BANDIT, BRIGAND,
CRIMINAL, FUGITIVE,
DESPERADO, PROSCRIBE,
HIGHWAYMAN

outlay .... COST, FUND

outlet .... EXIT, VENT, AGENCY,
MARKET, PASSAGE

outline .... DRAW, SCHEMA,
SKETCH, PROFILE, SUMMARY,
ADUMBRATE, DELINEATE

sharply .... LIMN

outlive .... SURVIVE

outlook .... VISTA, PROSPECT,
VIEW(POINT), EXPECTATION

outlying .... REMOTE, OFF-CENTER

district .... SUBURB, PURLIEU

outmoded .... PASSE, DESUETE,

HORSE AND BUGGY

outpost guard .... PICKET, SENTRY

of an empire .... COLONY

outpouring .... SPATE, TORRENT

output .... YIELD, HARVEST,
PRODUCT(ION)

outrage .... INSULT, OFFEND,
OFFENSE, SCANDAL, ATROCITY

outrageous .... DAMNED, HEINOUS,
DAMNABLE, FLAGRANT,
SHOCKING, ATROCIOUS,
MONSTROUS

wickedness .... VILLAINY

outre .... BIZARRE, ECCENTRIC

outrigger ...... PRAO, PRAU, PROA,
CANOE

outright .... TOTAL, WHOLE, AT
ONCE, OPENLY, COMPLETE

outset .... START, BEGINNING,
INCEPTION

outshine .... EXCEL, ECLIPSE

outside: prefix .... ECTO

outsider .... ALIEN, STRANGER,
NON-MEMBER

outsize .... HUGE, LARGE

outskirts ...... SUBURBS, ENVIRONS

outsmart .... OUTWIT

outspoken .... LOUD, OPEN,
BLUNT, BRASH, FRANK,
CANDID, ARTICULATE

outstand .... SAIL, ENDURE

outstanding .... DUE, OWING,
UNPAID, NOTABLE, STELLAR,
(E)SPECIAL, PROMINENT,
UNSETTLED, EXCEPTIONAL

example: sl. .... BEAUT

person .... ONER

outstretched .... PRONE,
EXTENDED

outstrip .... BEST, EXCEL, OUTDO,
OUTRUN, SURPASS

outward .... ECTAD, OUTER,
VISIBLE, EXTERIOR, EXTERNAL

outwit .... FOIL, EUCHRE,
OUTSMART, OVERCOME,
FRUSTRATE

ouzel .... THRUSH, BLACKBIRD

water .... PIET

ova .... EGGS

oval .... EGG-SHAPED,
ELLIPSOIDAL, ELLIPTIC(AL)

figure .... ELLIPSE

-Office related
.... PRESIDENTIAL

ovary .... GONAD

inflammation .... OOPHORITIS

malignant growth ..... CANCER

production .... OVUM,
HORMONE

wall .... EPICARP, ENDOCARP,
PERICARP

ovate .... EGG-SHAPED

ovation .... PLAUDIT, APPLAUSE

oven ...... KILN, LEER, LEHR, OAST,
MUFFLE, FURNACE

part of .... RACK, BROILER

portable .... BAKER

quick-cooking .... MICROWAVE

var. .... OST

over .... ATOP, DONE, UPON,
ABOVE, AGAIN, ENDED,
ACROSS, BEYOND, SURPLUS,
FINISHED, MORE THAN

a ____ .... BARREL

and above .... EXTRA, IN
EXCESS OF

and over .... OFTEN

combining form .... SUR,
HYPER, SUPER, SUPRA

expose film .... SOLARIZE

one's head .... DEEP, TOUGH

the hill: colloq. .... AWOL

there: poetic .... YON(DER)

over, ____ **(capsize)** .... KEEL

Over There songwriter
.... COHAN

overabundance .... PLETHORA

overact .... EMOTE, HAM(FAT)

overacting .... HISTRIONIC

overage .... EXTRA, EXCESS,
SURPLUS

overall .... BLANKET, ALTOGETHER

overalls ...... FROCK, JEANS, LEVIS,
SMOCK, DUNGAREES

overawe .... COW, DAUNT,
SUBDUE, BUFFALO, IMPRESS

overbearing .... BOSSY, PROUD,
LORDLY, ARROGANT,
CAVALIER, IMPERIOUS,
DOMINEERING

overcast .... SEW, DARK, CLOUDY,
GLOOMY, LOWERING

overcharge .... CHEAT, GOUGE,
HOLD UP, FLEECE

for tickets .... SCALP

slang .... SOAK

overcoat .... BENNY, CAPOTE,
RAGLAN, ULSTER, PALETOT,
SURTOUT, INVERNESS

double-breasted
.... REDINGOTE

overcome .... WIN, BEAT, BEST,
DEFEAT, MASTER, SUBDUE,
CONQUER, SURMOUNT,
OVERWHELM

difficulties .... COPE

overconcern with oneself
.... EGOMANIA

overconfident .... COCKSURE

overcrowd .... CONGEST

overdo .... EXHAUST, EXAGGERATE

overdresser .... DUDE

overdue .... LATE, TARDY, BELATED
instalment .... ARREAR
overeat .... GORMANDIZE
overfed .... GROSS
overflow .... FLOOD, SPATE, SPILL, DELUGE, RUN OVER
overflowing .... INUNDANT
overhang .... JUT, BEETLE, LAPPET, PROJECT
overhaul .... REDO, GAIN ON, REPAIR, OVERTAKE
overhead .... ABOVE, ALOFT, COSTS, UPKEEP
conveyor's car .... TRAM
item .... RENT, WAGES
overheat .... PARBOIL
overheated .... FEBRILE
overindulge .... GLUT, SATE
overindulgence .... ORGY, EXCESS
overjoy .... ELATE, DELIGHT
overlaid .... APPLIQUED
overlap .... IMBRICATE, EXTEND(OVER)
overlapping .... EQUITANT
overlay .... CEIL, PAVE
overlook .... MISS, IGNORE, CONDONE, NEGLECT, PRETERMIT, SUPERVISE
overlord .... BAN, LIEGE
overly .... TOO MUCH
overman .... ARBITER, REFEREE
overnice .... FINICAL, FINICKY, PRECISE
overpass .... SPAN, BRIDGE, EXCEED
overpower .... BEAT, MASTER, SUBDUE, CONQUER
overproud ...... LOFTY, TOO VAIN
override .... NULLIFY
overrule .... VETO, ANNUL, CANCEL, RESCIND, SET ASIDE, COUNTERMAND
overrun .... SWARM, INFEST, INVADE
overseas .... ABROAD, FOREIGN
oversee .... STEER, WATCH, DIRECT, MANAGE, SURVEY, SUPERVISE, SUPERINTEND
overseer .... BOSS, LEGREE, REEVE, BAILIFF, MANAGER, SUPERVISOR, TASKMASTER
overshadow .... DIM, ECLIPSE, OBSCURE, DOMINATE
overshoe .... BOOT, ARCTIC, PATTEN, ZIPPER, GALOSH(E), RUBBERS
overshoes, rubber .... GUMS
oversight .... ERROR, LAPSE, SLIP(UP), MISTAKE, OMISSION
oversize .... HUGE, LARGE

overstate .... EXAGGERATE
overstrung .... TAUT, TENSE, JITTERY
oversupply .... SATE
overt .... OPEN, PUBLIC
overtake .... CATCH UP, PASS(BY), OVERHAUL
overtax .... STRAIN
overthrow .... DOWN, RUIN, UPSET, DEPOSE, TOPPLE, UNSEAT, CONQUER, OVERCOME
overtone .... HINT, IMPLICATION
overtrained .... STALE
overture .... BID, OFFER, PRELUDE, PROPOSAL
overturn .... UPEND, UPSET, CAPSIZE, TIP OVER
overweening .... ARROGANT
overweight .... HIPPY, OBESE
overwhelm .... CRUSH, DEFEAT, SWAMP, DELUGE
overwhelming .... DAMNING, COMPELLING, OVERPOWERING
defeat .... SHUTOUT, NO-CONTEST
desire .... ESTRUS
emotion .... PASSION
terror .... PANIC
overworked .... STALE
overwrought .... ORNATE, FRANTIC, NERVOUS, FATIGUED
Ovid .... NASO
wife of .... UXOR
work of .... AMORES, METAMORPHOSES
oviform .... OVATE, OVOID
ovine .... SHEEP(LIKE)
ovisac .... OOTHECA
ovoid .... OVATE, OVIFORM
ovolo .... THUMB, MOLDING
ovule .... EGG, SEED, EMBRYO
center of .... NUCELLUS
covering .... PRIMINE
ovum .... EGG
content .... YOLK
owing .... DUE, INDEBT, UNPAID, BEHOLDEN
monies .... ARREARS
owl .... BUBO, MOMO, RURU, UTUM, KAKAPO
barn .... MADGE
leg feathers .... FLAG
-like .... STRIGINE
like an .... WISE
shipmate of .... PUSSY
sound .... HOOT, WHOOP
young .... OWLET
Owl and Pussycat author .... LEAR
owlish appearance .... SOLEMN

own .... HAVE, HOLD, ADMIT, CONFESS, POSSESS, RECOGNIZE
owner .... LANDLORD, POSSESSOR, PROPRIETOR, TITLEHOLDER
ownership ...... TITLE, POSSESSION
yield .... CEDE, QUITCLAIM
ox .... YAK, BEEF, ANOA, GAUR, REEM, BISON, GAYAL, STEER, BOVINE, BANTENG, BUFFALO, BULL(OCK)
command to .... GEE, HAW
disease .... GRAPE
extinct .... URUS, AUROCHS
eyed goddess .... HERA
hornless .... POLLARD
joint .... HOUGH
like .... BOVINE
like animal .... ZEBU
meat, dried .... BILTONG
stomach .... TRIPE
strap .... REIM, RIEM
tuberculosis .... GRAPE
young .... STIRK
oxalis .... OCA
oxen .... KINE, NOWT
stall .... CRIB
oxeye .... DAISY, PLANT, DUNLIN
oxford .... SHOE, BROGAN, COTTON
Oxford bell .... GREAT TOM
college .... BALLIOL
fellow .... DON
grad .... AUNT
movement leader .... KEBLE, BUCHMAN
officer .... BEADLE, BEDEL(L)
scholar .... DON, DEMY
Thames at .... ISIS
University Day ...... ENCAENIA
University fine .... SCONCE
University student .... OXONIAN
oxheart .... CHERRY, CABBAGE
oxide .... CALX
cobalt .... ZAFFER
lead .... LITHARGE, MASSICOT
oxidize .... RUST, CALCINE
oxlip ...... PLANT, PRIMROSE, FIVE-FINGER
oxpecker .... STARLING
oxter .... ARMPIT
oxtongue .... PLANT, BUGLOSS
oxygen .... OZONE
compound .... OXIDE
lack .... ANOXIA
liquid .... LOX
oyes .... HEAR(YE), ATTENTION
oyster .... BAY, BIVALVE, MOLLUSK, SCALLOP, BLUEPOINT
bed .... LAYER
bed material .... CULCH,

CULTCH
fish .... TAUTOG
gatherer .... TONGMAN
joint .... HINGE
killing snail .... DRILL
order .... RAW
plant ...... SALSIFY, LUNGWORT
product .... NACRE, PEARL
shell .... TEST, SHUCK
spawn .... SPAT, CULTCH
species .... MOLLUSCA

young .... SPAT
Oz books illustrator .... NEILL
creator of .... BAUM
Ozarks' animal .... DEER,
BOBCAT, RABBIT, CRITTER,
OPOSSUM, RACCOON,
SQUIRREL
bird .... OWL, QUAIL,
(BLUE)HERON, WOODPECKER,
WILD TURKEY,
WHIPPOORWILL

fish ..... TROUT, BLUEGILL, RED
BASS
most famous fighting fish
.... SMALLMOUTH BASS
river .... CURRENT, JACKS FORK
wildflower .... IPECAC,
PRIMROSE, HORSEMINT,
GOAT'S RUE, PEPPERMINT,
BEGGAR-TICKS, BLAZING STAR
ozocerite .... WAX, MALTHA
ozone .... AIR, OXYGEN, BLUE GAS

P

P .... PI, PEE, PEH, RHO
38 .... (WAR)PLANE, LIGHTNING
pa .... NOTE, DADDY, FATHER
pabulum .... FOOD, CEREAL,
PABLUM, SUSTENANCE
pac .... BOOT, LARRIGAN
paca ...... CAVY, AGOUTI, RODENT
pace .... GAIT, RATE, STEP, WALK,
SPEED, TEMPO, STRIDE
kind of .... RUN, LOPE, TROT,
AMBLE, SPRINT
setter .... LEADER
Pacelli, Eugenio .... POPE, PIUS
XII
pachyderm .... ELEPHANT,
RHINO(CEROS),
HIPPO(POTAMUS)
trap .... KEDDAH, KHEDAH
Pacific ...... CALM, OCEAN, IRENIC,
PEACEFUL, TRANQUIL
Antarctic arm of the ..... ROSS
SEA
archipelago .... SULU,
BISMARCK
battlesite .... GUAM, SAIPAN,
WAKE ISLAND
coast evergreen .... MADRONA,
REDWOOD, SEQUOIA
coast peak .... LASSEN
discoverer .... BALBOA
island .... YAP, GUAM, MOEN,
ROTA, TRUK, WAKE, BELAU,
EFATE, MANUS, PAGAN,
PALAU, TANNA, UPOLU,
AMBRYM, KOSRAE, MAJURO,
MIDWAY, MOOREA, SAIPAN,
TAHITI, TINIAN, PELELIU,
POHNPEI, TUTUILA,
ADMIRALTY, VITI LEVU,
BABELTHUAP, NEW GUINEA,
VANUA LEVU, NEW BRITAIN,
NEW CALEDONIA
island group .... COOK, FIJI,
LINE, BONIN, SAMOA,

AUSTRAL, GILBERT, LOYALTY,
SOLOMON, VOLCANO,
CAROLINE, HAWAIIAN,
MARIANAS, MARSHALL,
SENYAVIN, MARQUESAS,
MICRONESIA
pact .... SEATO
shrub .... SALAL
pacifier .... SOP, NIPPLE,
APPEASER, (TEETHING)RING
pacifist: colloq. .... DOVE
pacify .... ALLAY, SOOTHE,
APPEASE, MOLLIFY, PLACATE,
CONCILIATE
pack .... WAD, CRAM, GANG,
LOAD, MASS, STOW, TAMP,
CROWD, GROUP, PRESS,
TRUSS, BUNDLE, (EM)BALE,
FARDEL, COLLECTION
animal ..... ASS, MULE, BURRO,
CAMEL, LLAMA, DONKEY,
SUMPTER
animal basket .... DOSSER,
PANNIER
animal cover .... MANTA
dishonestly .... DEACON
down .... TAMP
girth .... CINCH
led by Sinatra and Martin
.... RAT
mule .... SUMPTER
of _____ .... LIES
of cards .... DECK
of dogs .... KENNEL, CANAILLE
of pups .... LITTER
rat .... HOARDER
package .... BOX, BALE, CASE,
WRAP, BUNDLE, CARTON,
CEROON, PARCEL
packer .... CASER, CANNER
packet .... BOAT, DECK, ROLL,
BUNDLE, PARCEL
boat .... PAQUEBOAT
packing .... BUFFER, FILLER,

CANNING, STUFFING
box .... CRATE
house .... CANNERY
packman .... PEDDLER
packsack .... KYACK
packsaddle .... APAREJO
pact .... MISE, TREATY, COMPACT,
COVENANT, AGREEMENT
Atlantic .... NATO
pad .... MAT, ROAD, WALK, STUFF,
BUFFER, PILLOW, SADDLE,
TABLET, CUSHION, ENLARGE,
FOOT(PRINT), HIGHWAYMAN
expense account .... INFLATE
gauze .... SPONGE
hippie's .... BED, COMMUNE
ink .... DABBER
medicated cloth .... COMPRESS
of hay .... WASE
portable .... TENT
powder .... PUFF, SACHET
silk .... VELURE
slang .... BED, FLAT, JOINT,
CONDO, APARTMENT
padded cell inmate .... MADMAN,
PRISONER
item .... DASHBOARD
padding .... WAD, DOWN, FELT,
EXTRA, KAPOK, STRAW,
COTTON, CUSHION, ADDITIONS
paddle .... BAT, OAR, ROW,
SCULL, SPANK, SPOON,
PROPEL
pingpong .... BAT, RACKET
paddlefish .... GANOID, SPOONBILL
paddock ...... FROG, PARK, TOAD,
FIELD, ENCLOSURE
parent .... MARE
paddy .... RICE(FIELD)
wagon .... BLACK MARIA
Paddy .... IRISH(MAN)
paddywack .... RAGE, BEATING
Paderewski ...... IGNACE, PIANIST
padina .... ALGAE

padishah .... KING, SULTAN, EMPEROR
padlock .... CLOSE
padnag .... HORSE
padre .... FATHER, PRIEST, CHAPLAIN
padrone .... MASTER, PATRON, INNKEEPER
Padua, Katherina of ...... SHREW
paean .... HYMN, SONG
paella .... STEWS
pagan .... ETHNIC, PAYNIM, GENTILE, HEATHEN, INFIDEL, IDOLATOR, NON-MOSLEM
god .... ODIN
pagan's forte .... IDOL
Paganini, violinist .... NICOLO
page .... CALL, LEAF, FOLIO, RECORD, SUMMON, BELL-BOY, (FOOT)BOY, SERVANT, ATTENDANT
boy .... BUTTONS
left hand .... VERSO
ledger .... FOLIO
lines on .... LINAGE
number .... FOLIO
ornamental design .... VIGNETTE
person served by .... NOBLE, KNIGHT, SENATOR
place of employment .... HOTEL, CONGRESS
right hand .... RECTO
size .... OCTAVO
slang .... BUTTONS
title .... RUBRIC
Page, singer .... PATTI
pageant .... POMP, SHOW, PARADE, SPECTACLE, EXHIBITION
pageantry .... SHOW, DISPLAY, SPLENDOR, SPECTACLE
pages .... RECORD
of history .... ANNALS, CHRONICLES
set of 24 .... QUIRE
Paget, actress .... DEBRA
Pagliacci character .... BEPPO, CANIO, NEDDA, TONIO, SILVIO
word .... RIDI
Pago Pago is in .... SAMOA, TUTUILA
pagoda .... TAA, TEMPLE
pagurian .... CRAB
pah .... TUT, POOH
paid .... HIRED, BRIBED, SETTLED, RETAINED, DISBURSED
athlete .... PRO
witness .... PERJURER
pail .... SKEEL, STOUP, BUCKET, PIGGIN, CANNIKIN
paillasse .... MATTRESS

paillette .... SPANGLE
pain ...... AIL, ACHE, HURT, PANG, AGONY, THROE, TWINGE, ANXIETY, PENALTY, DISTRESS, OFFEND
abdominal ..... COLIC, TUMMY-ACHE
common description of .... ACHING, BURNING, GNAWING, GRIPPING, THROBBING
emotional .... PANG
in the neck .... CRICK
in the side .... STITCH
minor .... FLEABITE
muscle .... CRAMP
non-drug treatment of ..... ICE PACK, MASSAGE, POULTICE, ACUPUNCTURE
of jealousy .... HEARTACHE, HEARTBURN
sharp .... ACHE, TWINGE
undergo ...... SUFFER, AGONIZE
painful ...... ACHY, SORE, BITTER, WOEFUL, HURTING, IRKSOME
urination .... DYSURIA
painkiller .... TONIC, OPIATE, ANODYNE, CODEINE, DEMEROL, NARCOTIC, SEDATIVE, ANALGESIC, PAREGORIC, ANESTHESIA
painless .... NUMB, UNFELT, ANESTHETIC
puller .... DENTIST
pains, great .... CARE, EFFORT
partner of .... ACHES
painstaking .... CAREFUL, DILIGENT, ELABORATE
paint .... LIMN, ADORN, COLOR, ROUGE, STAIN, DEPICT, ENAMEL, PIGMENT, PORTRAY, STIPPLE, VARNISH, LIPSTICK
badly .... DAUB
drier .... JAPAN
face .... FARD, ROUGE, COSMETIC
factory employee .... TONER
finishing oil .... TUNG
first coat of .... BASE, PRIMING
grinder .... MULLER
in dots .... STIPPLE
ingredient .... TUNG, BARITE
laid on thickly .... IMPASTO
layer .... COAT
remover .... ACETONE
spreader .... SPATULA
wall .... PARGET
painter .... DALI, GOYA, MIRO, DEGAS, HOMER, MANET, MONET, COROT, ARTIST, COUGAR, LIMNER, RUBENS,

TITIAN, CEZANNE, PANTHER, PICASSO, VAN GOGH, STIPPLER, REMBRANDT
Chagall .... MARC
designating one .... SUNDAY
Dutch genre .... STEEN
early Venetian .... BELLINI
eccentric .... DALI
Guido .... RENI
handrest of .... MAULSTICK
impressionist .... MANET
limp-watch .... DALI
mediocre .... DAUBER
medium of .... GESSO
of American Indians .... CATLIN
animals .... BONHEUR, LANDSEER
Fish Magic .... KLEE
Little Boy Blue .... MONET
Mona Lisa .... DA VINCI
Olympia .... MANET
presidents .... STUART
Street Scene .... SOYER
The Last Supper .... DA VINCI
oil of .... MEGILP
who illustrated Dante's works .... DORE
painting .... OIL, CANVAS, IMPASTO, PORTRAIT, SEASCAPE, LANDSCAPE
board .... PALLET, PALETTE
cult .... DADA(ISM)
form of expression .... OP ART
genre .... CUBISTIC, ABSTRACT, ORIENTAL
material .... DYE, ROUGE, CANVAS, PIGMENT, COSMETIC
medium .... OIL, PASTE, WATER COLOR
on a board .... PANEL
on ceiling .... MURAL
plaster .... SECCO, FRESCO
plasterlike surface for .... GESSO
religious .... ICON
small .... MINIATURE
stand .... EASEL
style .... GENRE, SESSHU, CLASSIC, DADAIST, ABSTRACT
technique ...... SECCO, FRESCO, IMPASTO, TEMPERA
tool .... BRUSH, ROLLER, SPRAY GUN
wall .... MURAL
water color .... AQUARELLE
paintings, collection of .... GALLERY
pair ...... DUO, TWO, DUAD, DUET, DYAD, MATE, SPAN, TEAM,

YOKE, BRACE, COUPLE

dos-a-dos ...... ACES BACK-TO-
BACK

harnessed .... YOKE

one of a .... MATE, MATCH

paired .... GEMEL, MATED,
JUGATE, TEAMED, COUPLED,
MATCHED

paisley .... SHAWL

Paiute .... INDIAN

pajamas .... TROUSERS

Pakistan cape .... RAS MUARI

capital .... ISLAMABAD

city/town .... BANNU, KASUR,
KOHAT, CHAGAI, JHELUM,
LAHORE, MARDAN, MULTAN,
QUETTA, SUKHUR, KARACHI,
LARKANA, SAHIWAL, SIALKOT,
LYALLPUR, PESHAWAR,
HYDERABAD, RAWALPINDI

coin .... ANNA, PICE

disputed land .... KASHMIR

language .... URDU, HINDI,
PUSHTU, SINDHI, BALUCHI,
BENGALI, PUNJABI

monetary unit .... RUPEE

mountain .... TIRICH MIR

mountain range .... HINDU
KUSH

native .... SIKH, PATHAN,
BENGALI

port .... KARACHI

president .... AYUB, MIRZA,
JINNAH

province .... SIND, PUNJAB,
BALUCHISTAN

region .... SWAT

river .... RAVI, ZHOB, INDUS,
KONAR, TALAB, CHENAB,
JHELUM, SUTLEJ

sea .... ARABIAN

spiritual guide of .... PIR

Pakistani .... SIKH, PATHAN

U.N. president .... SHAHI

pal .... CHUM, BUDDY, CULLY,
HOBNOB

Joey author .... O'HARA

palace .... COURT, CHATEAU,
MANSION, EL PARDO,
VATICAN, SERAGLIO,
TUILERIES, BUCKINGHAM,
MALACAÑANG

of a .... PALATIAL, PALATINE

resident .... KING, QUEEN,
BISHOP, PRINCE(SS), EMPEROR,
PRESIDENT

paladin .... PEER, KNIGHT,
CHAMPION

paladins, Charlemagne's 12
.... DOUZEPERS

palanquin .... JAUN, KAGO,

DOOLEE, LITTER

bearer .... SIRDAR, HAMA(U)L

palatable .... SAPID, TASTY,
SAVORY, AGREEABLE,
FLAVORFUL, TOOTHSOME

palate .... TASTE, UVULA, LIKING

covering .... VELUM

palatial .... STATELY

Palatinate .... PFALZ

palatine .... CAPE, ROYAL

Palau Islands ...... BELAU, PELEW

palaver ...... CHAT, TALK, PARLEY,
CHATTER, FLATTER(Y),
CONFERENCE

pale .... DIM, WAN, ASHEN, FAINT,
FENCE, LIVID, STAKE,
BLANCH, FEEBLE, PALLID,
PICKET, SALLOW, ORDINARY,
WHITE(FACED)

tan .... ECRU

yellow .... FLAXEN

palea .... FOLD, BRACT, SCALE,
DEWLAP

paleface .... AMERICAN,
WHITE(MAN)

paleness .... PALLOR

Paleolithic Age division
.... CHELLEAN

paleontologist Hutchinson
.... HOWARD

paler than citrine .... GREEN

Palermo is in ____ .... SICILY

Palestine .... CANAAN, ISRAEL,
HOLY LAND

animal .... DAMAN

capital .... JERUSALEM

city/town .... ACRE, CANA,
GAZA, HAIFA, SILOH, HEBRON,
MEGIDDO, SAMARIA,
CAPERNAUM

coin .... MIL

district .... DECAPOLIS

division .... GILEAD, PERAEA,
GALILEE

guerrilla .... FEDAYEEN

guerrilla leader .... ARAFAT

guerrilla outfit .... EL FATAH

kingdom .... SAMARIA

mountain .... EBAL, NEBO,
CARMEL, GILEAD

plain .... SHARON

port .... ACRE, HAIFA, JAFFA

tiger cub .... ASHBAL

tribesman .... ADANITE

village .... BETHEL

palestra .... SCHOOL, GYMNASIUM

trainee .... WRESTLER

paletot .... JACKET, OVERCOAT,
GREATCOAT

palette .... BOARD, COLORS

knife .... SPATULA

palfrey .... (SADDLE)HORSE

palimpsest .... TABLET,
PARCHMENT

palindrome .... ANAGRAM,
ACROSTIC, WORDPLAY

a ladylike .... MADAM

for father .... DAD, ABBA

for mother .... MOM

for sheep, female .... EWE

palindromic before .... ERE

name .... ANA, AVA, EVE, BOB,
NAN, TUT, OTTO

pop quartet .... ABBA

time .... NOON

word .... BIB, BOB, DAD, DID,
EKE, ERE, EWE, EYE, GAG,
KAYAK, GIG, MOM, MUM, NUN,
PAP, PUP, TIT, TAT, ABBA,
MADAM

paling .... FENCING

palisade .... BAIL, FENCE,
ESPALIER

composition of .... STAKES

pall .... BORE, CLOY, SATE,
CLOAK, WEARY, DISGUST,
SATIATE

Palladium of Rome .... ANCILE

Pallas .... ATHENA, ASTEROID

statue .... PALLADIUM

pallbearer .... MOURNER

pallet .... BED, PATE, PAWL,
CLICK, PALETTE, MATTRESS,
PLATFORM

palliate .... EASE, SALVE, EXCUSE,
SOOTHE, TEMPER, RELIEVE,
MITIGATE, ALLEVIATE,
EXTENUATE

palliative .... OPIATE, REMEDY,
BROMIDE, SEDATIVE

treatment .... THERAPY

pallid .... WAN, PALE, FAINT,
WHITE, SALLOW

pallor .... WANNESS, PALENESS

palm .... ENG, COCO, D(O)UM,
JARA, NIPA, SAGO, TREE,
ASSAI, NIKAU, PRIZE, COHUNE,
GOMUTI, GRIGRI, COQUITO,
TALIPOT, TRIUMPH, VICTORY

Asiatic .... NIPA, BETEL,
CALAMI, PALMYRA

betel .... ARECA, BONGA

Brazilian .... ASSAI, JUPATI,
BABASSU, CARNAUBA

cabbage .... PALMETTO

climbing .... RATTAN

drink .... NIPA, TUBA, ASSAI,
TODDY

fiber .... DOH, BURI, DATIL,
GOMUTI, RAFFIA

fruit .... DATE, DOUM, SASA,
COCONUT

grease the .... BRIBE, CORRUPT
leaf ..... OLA, PAN, ATAP, NIPA, FROND
leaf fan .... PUNKA(H), TALIPOT
leaf mat .... YAPA, PETATE
leaf's symbol .... TRIUMPH, VICTORY
leaves, plaited .... SENNIT
like plant .... CYCAD, ZAMIA
liquor .... BINO, NIPA, TODDY
Madagascar .... RAFFIA
Malayan .... ARENG, GOMUTI
muscle .... LUMBRICALIS
nipa .... AT(T)AP
nut .... COCO
of the hand .... VOLAR, THENAR
off .... FOB, FOIST, IMPOSE
pest .... GRUGRU
pith product .... SAGO
plant resembling .... CYCAD
raised part of .... MOUNT
reader .... PALMIST, CHIROMANCER
sap liquor .... NIPA, TODDY
showy fan .... TALIPOT
shrub like .... ZAMIA
starch .... SAGO
stem .... CANE, CAUDEX, RAT(T)AN
stroke on the .... PANDY
sugar .... JAGGERY
tree .... DATE, DOUM, SAGO, ARENG, ROYAL, TODDY, GRIGRI, RAFFIA, CALAMUS, PALMYRA, TALIPOT, PALMETTO
tree bud .... CABBAGE
wax .... CARNAUBA
wine .... TUBA, TAREE, TODDY, GOMUTI
Palma capital .... SANTA CRUZ
palmate .... WEB-FOOTED
palmer .... PILGRIM
need of .... DRIVER
palmetto .... SABAL, SERENOA
palmist .... FORTUNE-TELLER
interests of .... LINES
palmistry .... CHIROMANCY
Palmyra .... TADMOR
leaf .... TAL, OLA(Y)
leaf fan .... PUNKA(H)
queen of .... ZENOBIA
palomino .... HORSE, EQUINE
palp(us) .... FEELER, ANTENNA
palpable .... CLEAR, PLAIN, EVIDENT, OBVIOUS, MANIFEST, TANGIBLE
palpate .... FEEL
palpitate .... BEAT, THROB, QUIVER, FLUTTER, PULSATE,

TREMBLE, VIBRATE
palpitation .... BEATING, SALTATION, THROB(BING)
cause of heart .... ARRHYTHMIA
palsied .... SHAKING
palsy .... PARALYZE, PARALYSIS
kind of .... ERB'S, BELL'S, CEREBRAL
palter .... LIE, TRIFLE, QUIBBLE
paltry ...... MEAN, PETTY, SMALL, MEAGER, TRIVIAL, PICAYUNE, TRIFLING, WORTHLESS
paludal .... BOGGY, MARSHY, SWAMPY
paludism .... MALARIA
pam .... GAME, JACK
game like .... NAPOLEON
Pamir .... GALCHA
pampas .... PLAIN
country of .... ARGENTINA
native .... GAUCHO
weapon .... BOLAS
pamper .... PET, GLUT, HUMOR, SPOIL, COSHER, COSSET, FONDLE, GRATIFY, INDULGE, (MOLLY)CODDLE
pampero .... WIND
pamphlet .... TRACT, MANUAL, BROCHURE, FLYSHEET, TREATISE
of poems .... CHAPBOOK
unstitched .... FOLDER
Pamplona animal .... TORO
pan .... POT, DISH, KETTLE, ROTATE, GRIDDLE, (ICE)FLOE, SKILLET
oil .... SUMP
out .... SUCCEED
perforated .... COLANDER
slang .... RIB, FACE, ROAST, CRITICIZE
small .... PATELLA, PANNIKIN
warming .... CALEFACTORY
Pan .... GOD, FAUNUS
concern of .... FLOCKS, SHEPHERDS
panacea .... CURE, ELIXIR, REMEDY, CURE-ALL, NOSTRUM, MEDICINE, CATHOLICON
panache .... PLUME, VERVE, APLOMB, ECLAT, ELEGANCE, FLAMBOYANCE
Panama .... HAT, GULF, CANAL, DARIEN, ISTHMUS
archipelago .... PERLAS
bay .... PARITA
boxing champ .... DURAN
Canal locks .... GATUN, MIRAFLORES

cape .... PUNTA BURICA
capital .... PANAMA
city/town .... NATA, SONA, ANTON, COLON, DAVID, GATUN, TOCUMEN, PENONOME, SANTIAGO, AGUADULCE, LA CHORRERA
coin/explorer .... BALBOA
gulf .... PANAMA, MONTIJO, SAN BLAS, CHIRIQUI, MOSQUITOS
hat material .... JIPIJAPA
island ..... REY, COIBA, COLON, CEBACO, PARIDA, TABOGA, JICARON
island group .... SECAS, LADRONES, CONTRERAS
lagoon .... CHIRIQUI
lake .... GATUN
monetary unit .... BALBOA
mountain .... PANDO, BREWSTER, SANTIAGO
mountain range .... DARIEN, SAN BLAS, TABASARA
peninsula .... AZUERO, VALIENTE
port .... COLON
president .... ROBLES
river .... CHEPO, CHAGRES, CHUCUNAQUE
tree .... COPA, CATIVO
Panamanian jockey .... ICAZA
leader .... NORIEGA
panatella .... CIGAR
Panay city .... ILOILO
native/negrito .... ATI
pancake .... FRITTER, FLAPJACK
flaming French .... CREPE SUZETTE
mix .... BATTER
turner .... SPATULA
Pancake Tuesday .... MARDI GRAS
pancreas .... GLAND, SWEETBREAD
disorder .... CANCER, DIABETES
enzyme produced by ..... LIPASE, AMYLASE, TRYPSIN
inflammation .... PANCREATITIS
injury .... TRAUMA
part of .... DUCT, HEAD, TAIL
secretion .... INSULIN, GLUCAGON
panda .... WAH, BEARCAT
anamial resembling the .... RACCOON
pandanus ...... TREE, SCREW PINE
pandects .... LEGAL CODE
pandemic .... GENERAL, PREVALENT, WIDESPREAD
pandemonium .... DIN, HELL,

CHAOS, NOISE, BEDLAM, DISORDER, CONFUSION

pander .... PIMP, CATER, PROCURER

Pandora .... BANDORE

pandowdy .... PUDDING, APPLE PIE

pane .... QUARREL, ROUNDEL

panegyric .... ELOGE, EULOGY, PRAISE, TRIBUTE, ENCOMIUM, LAUDATION

panegyrist .... EULOGIST, ENCOMIAST

panel ...... JURY, JURORS, SADDLE, VENIRE

sunken .... COFFER

panelist .... CERF, JUROR

panes, frame for .... SASH

panfry .... SAUTE

pang .... ACHE, PAIN, AGONY, DOLOR, THROE, TWINGE

Pangloss' pupil .... CANDIDE

pangolin .... MANIS, ANTEATER

pangs of childbirth ...... THROES

panhandle .... BEG

panhandler .... BEGGAR

panic .... FEAR, ALARM, GRASS, SCARE, BUTTON, FRIGHT, MILLET, TERROR

result of .... STAMPEDE, HYSTERICS

slang .... DELIGHT

panicky .... EDGY, FUNKY

panicle .... RACEME, CLUSTER

panoply .... ARRAY, REGALIA

panorama .... VIEW, SCENE, VISTA

Panpipe .... SYRINX

pansy .... PENSE, VIOLA, HEARTSEASE

slang .... QUEER

pant .... GASP, HUFF, PUFF, HEAVE, THROB, PULSATE

Pantagruel .... GIANT

companion/friend of .... PANURGE

father of .... GARGANTUA

grandmother of .... GARGAMELLE

mother of .... BADEBEC

pantalets .... DRAWERS

pantaloons .... TROUSERS

Pantelleria .... COSYRA

pantheon .... TOMB, TEMPLE

member .... GOD

panther .... PARD, PUMA, COUGAR, JAGUAR, LEOPARD, PAINTER

panties .... DRAWERS, UNDERPANTS

panting .... PUFFY, GASPING, HYPERPNEA

pantomime .... SAVO, MIMIST

game .... CHARADE

pantry .... AMBRY, EWERY, CLOSET, LARDER, SPENCE, SPENSE, BUTTERY, CUPBOARD

pants .... JEANS, LEVIS, SLACKS, DRAWERS, TROUSERS

baby's .... SOAKERS

pantywaist ...... SISSY, WEAKLING

Panza squire .... SANCHO

panzer .... ARMORED

pap .... MASH, PULP, TEAT, NIPPLE

papa ...... PA, PAW, POP, DAD(DY), FATHER

Papa .... ERNEST

Papa's Lady Ashley .... BRETT

papal. See also **Pope**

.... APOSTOLIC

ambassador .... LEGATE, NUNCIO

book of decrees .... DECRETALE

cape/veil .... FANO(N), FANUM, ORALE, FANNEL, MOZ(Z)ETTA

chamberlain ...... CAMERLINGO

court .... SEE, CURIA

decree .... BULL, DECRETAL, RESCRIPT

envoy, special .... ABLEGATE

letter .... TOME, BREVE, BULL(A), ENCYCLICAL

order .... RESCRIPT

palace .... VATICAN

seal .... BULI(A)

skullcap .... ZUCCHETTO

papaveraceous plant ...... POPPY

papaverine .... VASODILATOR

papaw .... PAPAYA

papaya .... PA(W)PAW

enzyme .... PAPAIN

Papeete's location .... TAHITI

paper .... DAILY, ESSAY, SHEET, TRACT, PAPIER, THESIS, JOURNAL, WRAPPER, WRITING, TREATISE, MONOGRAPH

ancient .... PAPYRUS

candy holder .... CORNET

cutter ..... SLITTER, GUILLOTINE

damaged .... CASSE, RETREE

fastener .... CLIP, STAPLER

filler .... KAOLIN(E)

gummed .... PASTER

holder .... FOLDER

kind of ..... TAR, BOND, CREPE, LINEN, MANILA, TISSUE, PAPYRUS, FOOLSCAP

legal size pad .... FOOLSCAP

making material .... PULP, ESPARTO, CELLULOSE

manufacturer's technique .... PLATEGLAZING

match .... SPILL

measure .... REAM, QUIRE, BUNDLE

money ...... BILL, NOTE, SCRIP, LETTUCE

nautilus .... MOLLUSK

official .... DOCUMENT

roll of .... BOLT

scrap of, sometimes .... TREATY

seller .... NEWSBOY, STATIONER

shell .... MARRON

size .... CAP, DEMY, POST, POTT, ATLAS, CROWN, FOLIO, ROYAL, FOOLSCAP, IMPERIAL

small town .... WEEKLY

spoiled .... SALLE, CASS(I)E, RETREE

sugar holder .... CORNET

untrimmed edge .... DECKLE

used for newspapers .... NEWSPRINT

waterproofing substance .... PARAFFIN

white .... REPORT

wrapping .... KRAFT

writing .... FOOLSCAP, STATIONERY

yellow .... MANILLA

papers .... WRITINGS, CREDENTIALS

papilla .... NIPPLE

papilloma .... CORN, WART, TUMOR

papillon .... SPANIEL

papillote .... CURLPAPER

pappy ...... PAPA, DADDY, MUSHY

paprika .... PIMIENTO, CONDIMENT

vitamin .... CITRIN

Papua .... IRIAN

papule .... ACNE, PIMPLE, BLISTER

papyrus .... SEDGE, BULRUSH

par .... EQUAL, LEVEL, NORMAL, AVERAGE, STANDARD

avion .... (BY)AIR MAIL

one over, in golf .... BOGEY

one under, in golf ...... BIRDIE

two under, in golf ...... EAGLE

Para, capital of .... BELEM

parable .... FABLE, STORY, ALLEGORY, APOLOGUE

parabolic .... ALLEGORICAL

Paracelsus' remedy .... AZOTH

parachute .... PARAFOIL

gear .... HARNESS

jumper .... STUNTMAN, PARAMEDIC, PARATROOPER

release device .... RIP CORD

shape of .... UMBRELLA

paraclete .... PLEADER, ADVOCATE, HOLY SPIRIT

parade .... MARCH, STRUT, FLAUNT, DISPLAY, SHOW(OFF), CAVALCADE, PROMENADE
church .... PROCESSION
feature .... FLOAT
march .... GOOSESTEP
military .... REVIEW
of cars .... MOTORCADE
official .... MARSHAL
prefix .... CADE
parader .... MODEL, MUMMER
paradigm ...... MODEL, EXAMPLE, PATTERN
Paradise .... EDEN, HEAVEN, UTOPIA, ELYSIUM
Arthurian .... AVALON
imaginary .... SHANGRILA
Lost character .... EVE, ADAM, (ITH)URIEL
paraffin .... WAX
parafoil .... PARACHUTE
paragon .... IDEAL, MODEL, PATTERN, NON(E)SUCH
paragonite .... MICA
paragraph .... ITEM, NOTE, CLAUSE
Paraguay capital .... ASUNCION
city/town .... LUQUE, PILAR, LAMBARE, CONCEPCION, VILLARRICA, SAN LORENZO, ENCARNACION
department .... CHACO, GUAIRA, ITAPUA, AMAMBAY, CAAZAPA, BOQUERON, MISIONES
explorer of .... CABOT
falls .... IGUAZU
lagoon .... VERA
language .... GUARANI, SPANISH
measure ..... PIE, LINO, LEGUA, CORDEL, CUADRA
monetary unit .... GUARANI
mountain .... CHOVORECA
plains .... GRAN CHACO
river .... APA, NEGRO, VERDE, ACARAY, MONDAY, TIMANE, CONFUSO, PILCOMAYO, ALTO PARANA
tea .... MATE, YERBA
territory .... CHACO
wood .... QUEBRACHO
parakeet .... BUDGIE, PARROT, BUDGERIGAR
parallel .... EQUAL, MATCH, COUNTERPART
parallelogram .... DIAMOND, RHOMB(US), RHOMBOID, RECTANGLE
remains of a .... GNOMON
paralysis .... PALSY, PTOSIS, STROKE, PARESIS, HEMIPLEGIA
combining form .... PLEGY, PLEGIA
infantile .... POLIO
paralyze .... NUMB, PALSY, SHOCK
Paramaribo is capital of
.... SURINAM
paramo .... PLAIN
paramount ...... CHIEF, SUPREME, DOMINANT, FOREMOST
paramour .... LEMAN, LOVER, MINION, MISTRESS, INAMORATA, SWEETHEART
paranymph .... BEST MAN, BRIDESMAID
parapet .... WALL, RAILING, BRATTICE
opening .... EMBRASURE
part .... MERLON
paraphernalia .... GEAR, OUTFIT, EQUIPMENT, TRAPPINGS, BELONGINGS
paraphrase .... RESTATE, REWORD(ING)
paraplegic .... CRIPPLE, PARALYTIC
paraquet .... PARROT
parasite .... FLEA, LEECH, TOADY, MOOCHER, SPONGE(R), HANGER-ON, TRENCHER, SYCOPHANT
blood .... TRYP
feeder of .... HOST
fish .... REMORA
intestinal .... HELMINTH, TAPEWORM
living inside plant/animal .... ENTEZOON, ENTOPHYTE
outside body .... EPIZOON
plant ..... BINE, APHID, LICHEN, MISTLETOE
root .... PINESAP
parasite's find .... HOST, MEAL TICKET
parasitic insect ...... FLEA, GNAT, LICE, MITE, APHID, LOUSE, ACARID, CHIGOE, CHIGGER, MOSQUITO
plant .... DODDER, ORCHID
worm .... FLUKE, LEECH, NEMATODE, TRICHINA, TREMATODE
parasol .... SUNSHADE, UMBRELLA
ant .... ATTA
paratrooper's cry .... GERONIMO
paravane .... OTTER
parboil .... SCALD, OVERHEAT
Parcae .... FATES
parcel .... LOT, PLAT, BUNCH, BUNDLE, PACK(ET), PACKAGE, (AP)PORTION
out .... METE, ALLOT
parch .... DRY, HEAT, TORREFY, TORRIFY, DESICCATE
parched .... DRY, ARID, ADUST, THIRSTY, ANHYDROUS
parchment .... FOREL, VELLUM, DIPLOMA, KIDSKIN, PAPYRUS, SHEEPSKIN
inscribed .... PALIMPSEST
roll .... PELL, SCROLL
pard .... PANTHER, PARTNER, COMPANION
pardon .... REMIT, SPARE, ASSOIL, EXCUSE, ABSOLVE, CONDONE, FORGIVE, OVERLOOK, INDULGENCE
archaic .... ASSOIL
general .... AMNESTY
pardonable .... VENIAL, EXCUSABLE
pare .... CUT, PEEL, SKIN, TRIM, SHAVE, SKIVE, REDUCE, WHITTLE
paregoric .... SEDATIVE
parent .... DAM, SIRE, MATER, PATER, FATHER, MOTHER, SOURCE, ANCESTOR
parentage .... BIRTH, ORIGIN, ANCESTRY, PATERNITY
parenthesis .... EPISODE, INTERLUDE
parenthetical remark ...... ASIDE
paresis .... PARALYSIS
paretic .... PARALYTIC
pareu .... SKIRT
parfait .... DESSERT
parhelic circle's halo
.... SUNDOG
parhelion .... SUNDOG, (MOCK)SUN
pari ____ (side by side)
.... PASSU
pariah .... EXILE, LEPER, WRETCH, OUTCAST
paries .... WALL
parietal .... SOMATIC
Paris .... PAREE, LUTETIA
airport near .... ORLY
ancient royal palace
.... LOUVRE
artists' quarter
.... MONTMARTRE
beloved of .... HELEN
brother of .... HECTOR, TROILUS
cathedral .... NOTRE DAME
chief of police .... PREFECT
church of Sainte-Geneviève
.... PANTHEON
district in .... AUTEUIL
express train .... RAPIDE

517

famous avenue .... CHAMPS ELYSEES
famous iron structure .... EIFFEL TOWER
father of .... PRIAM
Gothic architecture ..... NOTRE DAME
green .... POISON
mother of .... HECUBA
museum .... CLUNY, LOUVRE
native .... PARISIAN
palace .... TUILERIES
patron saint .... GENEVIEVE
police department .... LA SURETE
police inspector, fictional .... MAIGRET
police station .... COMMISSARIAT
rival of .... ROMEO
river .... SEINE
section .... MONTMARTRE
sister of .... CASSANDRA
stock exchange .... BOURSE
suburb .... ISSY, VITRY, CLICHY, DRANCY, SEVRES, NEUILLY, MONTREUIL
subway .... METRO
thug .... APACHE
tube .... METRO
university .... SORBONNE
victim of .... ACHILLES
war caused by .... TROJAN
weapon of .... ARROW
wife of .... OENONE
woman kidnapped by .... HELEN
parish .... CONGREGATION
head of .... PARSON, PASTOR, RECTOR
official .... OVERSEER
Parisienne .... FEMME
parity .... PAR, EQUALITY
park .... SQUARE, DEPOSIT, STADIUM
fence/wall .... HAHA
parka .... SHIRT, ANORAK, JACKET
parker's watchdog .... METERMAID
Parkinson's disease .... PALSY
characteristic of ...... TREMOR, WEAKNESS, STIFFNESS, TREMBLING
drug for .... L-DOPA, LEVODOPA
patient's deficiency .... DOPAMINE
parlance .... IDIOM, SPEECH, LANGUAGE
parlay ...... BET, WAGER, EXPLOIT
parley .... TALK, TREAT,

POWWOW, PALAVER, CONVERSE, NEGOTIATE, CONFER(ENCE), DISCUSSION
signal .... CHAMADE
parliament .... DIET, SEJM, LEGISLATURE
figure .... LORD
report .... CAHIER, HANSARD
parliamentary move .... CLOSURE, CLOTURE
parlor .... BEN, DEN, SALA, SHOP, SALO(O)N, LIVING-ROOM
instrument .... PIANO
kind of ...... BEAUTY, FUNERAL
Parnassus dweller .... MUSE
spring .... CASTALIA
parochial .... LOCAL, NARROW, INSULAR, LIMITED, EXCLUSIVE, PROVINCIAL
parodist .... APER, IMITATOR
parody .... SKIT, COMEDY, SATIRE, BURLESQUE, CARICATURE
parol(e) .... ORAL, PROMISE, (PASS)WORD
paronomasia .... PUN
parotitis .... MUMPS
paroxysm .... FIT, SPASM, ATTACK, SEIZURE, OUTBURST, CONVULSION
parquet .... FLOORING, ORCHESTRA
circle .... PARTERRE
parr .... SALMON
parrot ...... KEA, ECHO(ER), JAKO, KAKA, LORO, LORY, VASA, ARA(RA), BUGIE, MACAW, POLLY, AMAZON, KAKAPO, REPEAT, IMITATE, COCKATOO, LORIKEET, PARAKEET, POPINJAY
cry of .... SQUAWK
Dr. Doolittle's ...... POLYNESIA
fever .... PSITTACOSIS
fish ..... LORO, LANIA, COTORO, SCARID, SHANNY
hawk .... HIA
like .... ARINE
parry .... FEND, VOID, WARD, EVADE, FENCE, DEFLECT
fencing .... SEPTIME
parse .... ANALYZE
Parsee .... ZOROASTRIAN
priest .... MOBED
sacred writings .... AVESTA
parsees, e.g. .... SECT
Parsi ''baptismal'' rite .... NAVJOT
fried rice .... PULLAO
language .... GUJARATI
platform for dead bodies .... TOWER OF SILENCE

undershirt .... SUDRA
Parsifal composer .... WAGNER
magician .... KLINGSOR
person healed by .... AMFORTAS
priest .... MOBED
son of .... LOHENGRIN
woman in .... KUNDRY
parsimonious ...... CLOSE, TIGHT, SHABBY, STINGY, MISERLY, PIDDLING, NIGGARDLY
parsley .... DILL, CICELY, LOVAGE, GARNISH, POTHERB, SANICLE
parsnip .... PLANT
parson .... PASTOR, MINISTER, SKYPILOT, CLERGYMAN
assistant of .... CURATE
bird .... POE, TUI, KOKO
concern of a .... PARISH
parsonage .... MANSE, RECTORY
part .... DUTY, ROLE, LEAVE, PIECE, SHARE, SEVER, DIVIDE, PARCEL, PORTION, SECTION, SEGMENT, SEPARATE
eagle-part lion .... GRIFFIN
main .... KEYSTONE
of a book .... COVER, CHAPTER
a chopper .... ROTOR
a document .... CLAUSE, ARTICLE
a garment .... YOKE
A.M. .... ANTE, MERIDIEM
a maison .... SALLE
a seafood platter .... CRAB, SHRIMP, SCALLOP, FISHCAKES
a shoe .... SOLE, TONGUE
a sound system .... COMPONENT
a worm's body .... SOMITE
a yard .... FOOT
an axel .... LINCHPIN
an impeller .... ROTOR BLADE
an ounce .... DRAM
chromosome .... GENE
C.O.D. .... ON, CASH, DELIVERY
Israel and Jordan .... PALESTINE
P.M. .... POST, MERIDIEM
Q.E.D. .... ERAT, QUOD, DEMONSTRANDUM
Q.I.D. .... IN, DIE, QUATER
some street scenes .... GASLAMP
speech .... (AD)VERB, (PRO)NOUN, ADJECTIVE
the ear .... ANVIL, CANAL, PINNA, HAMMER, COCHLEA, EARDRUM, STIRRUP,

VESTIBULE, EUSTACHIAN TUBE
the eye .... IRIS, PUPIL, CORNEA, RETINA, SCLERA, SOCKET
the ionosphere .... E-REGION, D-REGION, F-REGION
the scheme .... IN ON
the street scene .... ALLEYCAT
TLC .... CARE, LOVING, TENDER
payment .... DEPOSIT, INSTALMENT
proportional .... QUOTA
remaining .... REMNANT
song .... GLEE, MADRIGAL
stage .... ROLE
that separates .... SEPTUM, DIVIDER
partake ...... EAT, SHARE, RECEIVE
parted .... SPLIT, DIVIDED
Parthenon .... TEMPLE
designer .... ICTINUS
sculptor of .... PHIDIAS
site .... ATHENS, ACROPOLIS
Parthenope .... SIREN
intended victim of .... ULYSSES
partial .... BIASED, ONE-SIDED, PREJUDICED
partiality .... BIAS, LIKING, FONDNESS, PREJUDICE
participant .... PLAYER, ENTRANT, PARTAKER
in a beauty pageant .... CONTESTANT
in a confidence game .... SHILL, SWINDLER
in a fight with deadly weapon .... DUELIST, DUELLER
in a quarrel .... FEUDIST
participate .... SHARE, SIT IN, ENTER INTO, PARTAKE, COOPERATE
particle ...... BIT, JOT, IOTA, MITE, MOTE, WHIT, FLECK, SHRED, SPECK, TITTLE, GRANULE, SCINTILLA
accelerator .... BETATRON, CYCLOTRON
atom .... PROTON, NEUTRON
beam .... DEATH RAY
glowing .... SPARK(LE)
in space .... COSMIC DUST
particular .... ITEM, FUSSY, DETAIL(ED), EXACT(ING), FINICAL, PRECISE, SPECIAL, DISTINCT, SPECIFIC, FASTIDIOUS

moment .... JUNCTURE
particularize .... DETAIL, ITEMIZE, SPECIFY
parties, fast round of .... WHIRL
parting .... FAREWELL
partisan .... MAQUI, ZEALOT, DEVOTEE, FANATIC, ADHERENT, FOLLOWER, FACTIONAL, GUERRILLA
combining form .... CRAT
partita .... SUITE
partition .... WALL, SCREEN, SEPTUM, DIVIDE(R), DIVISION, (AP)PORTION
partlet .... HEN, RUFF, BIDDY, COLLAR
partly .... SOMEWHAT
open .... AJAR
prefix .... SEMI
partner ...... SHARER, CO-OWNER, TEAMMATE, ASSOCIATE
bill's .... COO
Chase's (coffee) ..... SANBORN
cry's .... HUE
in crime .... ACCOMPLICE
itsy's .... BITSY
marriage .... MATE, SPOUSE
of bounds .... LEAPS
rod's .... REEL
slang .... PARD
partnership .... CAHOOTS, ALLIANCE
partridge ...... BIRD, KYAH, YUTU, QUAIL, TITAR, GROUSE, SEESEE, TINAMOU, PHEASANT, FRANCOLIN
call .... JUCK
parturition .... LABOR, BIRTHING, DELIVERY, CHILDBIRTH
party .... TEA, BASH, GROUP, CLIQUE, PERSON, SOCIAL, SOIREE, FACTION, SHINDIG, GATHERING, MERRIMENT
afternoon .... TEA
beach .... CLAMBAKE
boisterous, noisy .... JAMBOREE
dance .... BALL
declaration .... MANIFESTO
didoes .... HIGHJINKS
disciplinarian .... WHIP
drinking .... WASSAIL, CAROUSAL
festive .... GALA
for bride-to-be .... SHOWER
giver .... MESTA, HOST(ESS)
goer .... GUEST
kind of .... HEN, TEA, STAG, BRIDAL, PAJAMA, SOCIAL, SHOWER, SEND-OFF, CAROUSAL, DESPEDIDA,

POLITICAL
member .... JOINER
organization .... FACTION, MACHINE
pooper .... FLAT-TIRE
slang .... BLOWOUT
stags .... SINGLES
wild .... ORGY
with speeches, formal .... BANQUET
withdraw from .... BOLT
parvenu .... UPSTART, SNOB(BISH), PRETENDER, (SOCIAL)CLIMBER
parvis .... COURT, PORTICO, COLONNADE
pas .... STEP, DANCE
de Calais .... DOVER
Pascal, Fr. mathematician .... BLAISE
Pasch .... EASTER, PASSOVER
paschal lamb .... JESUS
pasha .... DEY, DOWLAH
Pasiphae's husband .... MINOS
island .... CRETE
son .... MINOTAUR
son, killer of .... THESEUS
pasquinade .... SQUIB, SATIRE, LAMPOON
pass .... END, GAP, ABRA, GHAT, GO BY, GORGE, OCCUR, ELAPSE, KHYBEE, STRAIT, ADVANCE, BRENNER, PROCEED, NACIVERT
away .... DIE, (E)LAPSE
between peaks .... COL
come to .... OCCUR, HAPPEN, TRANSPIRE
downward .... SWOOP
football .... LATERAL
for .... IMPERSONATE
holder .... DEADHEAD
in/through .... REEVE
in sports .... BYE
judgment .... RULE
let it .... ALLOW, TOLERATE
lightly .... FLIT, FLUTTER
matador's .... FAENA
mountain .... COL, GHAT, DEFILE
off .... FOB, PALM, FOIST
on .... RELAY
out .... FAINT, SWOON
over .... OMIT, SKIM, SKIP, ELIDE, IGNORE, TRANSIT
over lightly .... SCAN
pretty .... FIX, JAM
slang .... ANNIE OAKLEY
tongue over .... LAP, LICK
up .... LET GO, REJECT
passable .... FAIR, SOSO, TOLERABLE, ACCEPTABLE

passado .... LUNGE, THRUST
passage .... WAY, PATH, ROAD,
VENT, AISLE(S), TRAVEL,
VOYAGE, OPENING, CORRIDOR,
CROSSING, TRANSIT(ION)
between cliffs .... GAT, DEFILE
between house and garage
.... BREEZEWAY
between train cars
.... VESTIBULE
body .... MEATUS
closed at one end
.... IMPASSE, DEAD-END,
BLIND-ALLEY
covered .... SLYPE, ARCADE
in(to) .... ENTRY, ENTRANCE
means of ...... DUCT, CHANNEL
mine .... ADIT
mouth to anus .... ENTERO
organ .... LUMEN
out .... EXIT
performed by all .... TUTTI
sloping .... RAMP
smoke .... STACK, FUNNEL,
CHIMNEY
passageway .... DUCT, HALL,
RAMP, AISLE, ALLEY, CANAL,
SLYPE, ARCADE, CATWALK,
CHANNEL, CORRIDOR,
GANGPLANK
covered .... ARCADE
underground .... SAP, TUBE,
BURROW, SUBWAY, TUNNEL
passe .... PAST, DATED, OBSOLETE,
OLD-HAT, OUT-OF-DATE,
OUTMODED
barber treatment .... SINGE
passed .... ADOPTED, CARRIED,
APPROVED, QUALIFIED
passenger .... FARE, RIDER,
COMMUTER, TRAVELER
boat on a regular schedule
.... PACKET
kind of .... CHANCE, TENDER,
STEERAGE, STOW-AWAY
passerine .... SPARROW
passing .... DEATH, CASUAL,
CURSORY, FLEETING,
MOMENTARY, TRANSIENT
fancy .... FAD, WHIM
over .... LABILE
passion .... FIRE, FURY, HEAT,
LOVE, LUST, RAGE, ZEAL,
ANGER, ARDOR, FLAME,
DESIRE, FERVOR, EMOTION,
FEELING
for big things
.... MEGALOMANIA
fruit .... MAYPOP, GRANADILLA
passionate .... ARDENT, TORRID,
AMOROUS, EMOTIVE,

FERVENT, INTENSE, IRASCIBLE
passionflower .... MAYPOP
passive .... INERT, QUIET, PATHIC,
DORMANT, PATIENT, INACTIVE
resistance exponent
.... GANDHI
Passover .... PASCH(AL), SEDER,
PESACH
bread .... MATZOS, MATZOTH
feast, according to Matthew,
Mark and Luke .... THE
LAST SUPPER
festival: var. .... PESAH
Hebrew word for ...... PESACH
meal .... SEDAR
month .... NISAN
of the .... PASCHAL
sacrificial animal .... LAMB
passport .... SAFE-CONDUCT
endorsement .... VISA, VISE
password .... PAROLE, SIBBOLETH,
OPEN SESAME, COUNTERSIGN
past ...... EX, AGO, WAS, YORE, OF
OLD, SINCE, BEHIND, BEYOND,
BYGONE, GONE BY, HAS-BEEN,
PRETERITE
middle age .... ELDERLY
of yore .... AGONE
recovery .... GONER
pasta dish .... LASAGNA, RAVIOLI,
CANNELONI
ingredient .... DOUGH,
SEMOLINA, DURUM WHEAT
long ..... LINGUINE, SPAGHETTI,
FETTUCCINE
manufacturer, first in U.S.
.... (ANTOINE)ZEREGA
sauce for .... MEAT, PESTO,
CHEESE, MARINARA
short .... ZITI, MACARONI,
MANICOTTI, CAPPELLETTI
paste .... HIT, PAP, BLOW, GLUE,
MASH, DOUGH, PUNCH, STICK,
BINDER, FASTEN, ADHESIVE,
MUCILAGE
clay .... PATE
food .... POI, PEM(M)ICAN
jewelry .... STRASS
slang .... SLUG, WALLOP
pasteboard .... FAKE, PHONY,
TICKET, BRISTOL,
(PLAYING)CARD
container .... CARTON
pastel .... DYE, PALE, WOAD,
TINT(ED), LIGHT, CRAYON,
DRAWING, DELICATE,
PASTILLE
Pasternak heroine .... LARA
Pasteur treatment, object of
.... RABIES
pasteurize .... STERILIZE

pasticcio .... CENTO, MEDLEY,
PASTICHE, POTPOURRI
pastiche .... MEDLEY, POTPOURRI,
HODGEPODGE
pastille .... CACHOU, TABLET,
LOZENGE
pastime .... PLAY, HOBBY, SPORT,
AMUSEMENT, DIVERSION,
RECREATION
St. Andrew's .... GOLF
pastor .... PARSON, PRIEST,
DOMINIE, MINISTER,
SHEPHERD, CLERGYMAN
pastoral .... RURAL, RUSTIC,
BUCOLIC, CROSIER, IDYLLIC,
ARCADIAN
god .... PAN, FAUNUS
melody .... MUSETTE
pipe .... OAT, REED
place .... ARCADIA
sound .... LOW, MOO, BLEAT,
CANTATA
staff .... PEDA, CROSIER
pastrami .... BEEF
pastry .... PIE, CAKE, FLAN,
TORTE, ECLAIR, STRUDEL,
TART(LET)
cook/chef .... ICER, BAKER
fried .... TIMBALE
shell ...... PUFF, CRUST, ECLAIR
tool .... BRUSH, WHEEL,
BLENDER, SCRAPER, ROLLING
PIN
type of .... PUFF, FLAKY, PLAIN
pasture .... LEA, GRASS, GRAZE
for pay .... AGIST
grass .... GRAMA, REDTOP,
SACATON
land .... LEA, LLANO, RANCH,
RANGE, ESTANCIA
pasty .... DOUGHY, (MEAT)PIE
substance for cloth filler
.... SIZE
pat .... APT, DAB, RAP, TAP,
TOUCH, CARESS, STRIKE,
STROKE, TIMELY, FITTING,
OPPORTUNE
Patagonia is in .... CHILE,
ARGENTINA
Patagonian .... INDIAN,
TEHUELCHE
rodent .... CAVY, MARA
patch .... DARN, PLOT, SPOT,
VAMP, PIECE, SCRAP, COBBLE,
REPAIR, REMNANT
up .... MEND, REVAMP, SETTLE,
TINKER, RECONCILE
Patch, famous trotter .... DAN
patchouli .... MINT, PLANT
patchwork .... VAMP, CENTO,
QUILT, JUMBLE, MOSAIC

pate .... HEAD, PASTE, NODDLE

  de foie _____ .... GRAS

patella .... PAN, ROTULA,

  KNEECAP, KNEEPAN

paten .... ARCA, DISC, HOST,

  PLATE, PATIN(A)

patent .... OPEN, PLAIN, TITLE,

  EVIDENT, LICENSE, OBVIOUS,

  MANIFEST

  basis .... IDEA

patentee, usually .... INVENTOR

pater .... FATHER, OLD MAN

  companion of .... NOSTER,

  FAMILIA

paternal .... FATHERLY

paternity .... ORIGIN, PARENTAGE,

  FATHERHOOD

paternoster ...... PRAYER, ROSARY

path .... WAY, LANE, ROAD,

  WALK, ORBIT, ROUTE, TRACK,

  TRAIL, COURSE, FOOTWAY

  finder .... SCOUT, PIONEER,

  TRAILBLAZER

  heavenly .... ORBIT

  like some .... BEATEN

  winding .... AMBAGE

Pathan .... MOSLEM, PAKISTANI

Pathet _____, **Communist**

  group .... LAO

pathetic .... SAD, MOVING, TEARY,

  PITIFUL, TOUCHING

pathogen .... GERM, VIRUS,

  MICROBE

pathological .... MORBID

  subject .... DISEASE

pathos .... POIGNANCY,

  SENTIMENT, SUFFERING

  false .... BATHOS

  opposite of .... ETHOS

patience .... LENIENCY, STOICISM,

  ENDURANCE, SOLITAIRE

patient .... CASE, STEADY,

  INVALID, TOLERANT,

  FORBEARING

  man .... JOB, STOIC

patina .... FILM, VERD, CRUST,

  PATEN, PLATE, ANTIQUE,

  COATING, VERDIGRIS

patio .... TERRACE, VERANDA,

  COURT(YARD)

patisserie .... BAKERY, PASTRY

  SHOP

patois .... GUMBO, SLANG, SPEECH,

  DIALECT, LANGUAGE

patriarch .... ELDER, PATER,

  BISHOP, FATHER, LEADER

  biblical, antediluvian

  .... NOAH, SETH, LAMECH,

  METHUSELAH

  biblical, postdiluvian

  .... ISAAC, JACOB, ABRAHAM

patrician .... NOBLE,

  ARISTOCRAT(IC)

patrimony ...... ESTATE, HERITAGE

patriot, kind of .... JINGO,

  CHAUVINIST, NATIONALIST

  of '76 .... PAINE

  target of a .... SCUD

patriotism, fanatical

  .... JINGOISM, CHAUVINISM

patrol .... SCOUT, RECONNOITER

  wagon .... BLACK MARIA

patrolman .... (BEAT)COP,

  POLICEMAN

patron .... SAINT, BACKER,

  PADRONE, SPONSOR,

  CUSTOMER, PROTECTOR,

  BENEFACTOR

  animals' .... PAN, FAUNUS

  art .... MASCENAS

  Broadway .... ANGEL

  largesse of a .... PENSION

  literature .... MAECENAS

  mariners' .... ELMO

  music .... CECILIA

  sailors' .... ELMO, NICHOLAS

  saint of Cornish parishes

  .... COLIN

  saint of Ireland .... PATRICK

  saint of Russia ...... NICHOLAS

  saint of shoemakers

  .... CRISPIN

  youth's .... NICHOLAS

patronage .... FAVOR, (A)EGIS,

  SUPPORT, AUSPICES,

  CLIENTELE, SPONSORSHIP

  solicitor .... RUNNER

patronize .... ENDORSE, SPONSOR,

  SUPPORT

patronizing .... HOITY-TOITY

patrons, collectively

  .... CLIENTELE

Patrons of Husbandry

  association .... GRANGE

patsy .... SAP, FALLGUY,

  SCAPEGOAT

patten .... CLOG, SANDAL,

  CHOPINE, OVERSHOE

patter .... CANT, TALK, TAPS,

  BICKER, JABBER, JARGON,

  CHATTER

pattern .... MOLD, IDEAL, MODEL,

  DESIGN, FORMAT, DIAGRAM,

  PARADIGM, TEMPLATE

  of flow movement ..... TREND,

  RHYTHM

  of human behavior

  .... CULTURE

Patti, singer .... ADELINA

patty .... PIE, CAKE

paucity .... DEARTH, FEWNESS,

  SCARCITY

Paul, actor .... MUNI, NEWMAN

  Bunyan .... LUMBERJACK

  Bunyan's ox .... BABE

  companion of .... TITUS

  pry .... SNOOP(ER)

  Reubens, performer .... PEE

  WEE HERMAN

  singer .... ANKA, ROBESON,

  MCCARTNEY

paunch .... RUMEN, ABDOMEN,

  STOMACH, (POT)BELLY, BAY

  WINDOW

paunchy .... FAT, BLOATED,

  POTBELLIED

pauper .... BEGGAR

paupers' place .... POORHOUSE

pause .... LULL, REST, STOP,

  BREAK, LET UP, RESPITE,

  HESITATE

  in music .... FERMETA

  in prosody .... C(A)ESURA

  indicator/sign .... COMMA

  momentary .... LAPSE

  vocalized .... ER

pave .... TAR, COAT, COVER,

  COBBLE, ASPHALT, OVERLAY

pavement .... ROAD, CEMENT,

  CONCRETE, FLAGGING,

  (SIDE)WALK

  pounder .... BEAT COP,

  PATROLMAN

  walker .... PEDESTRIAN

paver .... PAVIOR

  mallet of .... TUP

  of a sort .... PIONEER

pavid .... TIMID, AFRAID, FEARFUL

pavilion .... TENT, KIOSK,

  GALLERY, MARQUEE,

  BELVEDERE, SUMMERHOUSE

paving material .... TAR, SETT,

  SLAB, TILE, BRICKS, CEMENT,

  ASPHALT, MACADAM,

  FLAGSTONE

Pavlova, ballet dancer .... ANNA

pavo .... PEACOCK

pavonine .... IRIDESCENT

paw .... PUD, FOOT, GAUM, HAND,

  MAUL, PAPA, TOUCH, FATHER,

  HANDLE, OLD MAN

pawl .... BOLT, CLICK, DETENT,

  PALLET, RATCHET, TRIPPER

pawn .... DUPE, GAGE, HOCK,

  TOOL, SPOUT, STAKE, WAGER,

  PLEDGE, HOSTAGE, CHESSMAN

  queened .... FERS

  receipt .... TICKET

  slang .... HOCK

  superior of .... PIECE

pawnbroker ...... (MONEY)LENDER

  shop of .... SPOUT

  slang .... UNCLE

Pawnee .... CHAUI, INDIAN
pawnshop: sl. .... SPOUT
pawpaw .... PAPAYA, CLASPED
        HANDS
pax .... PEACE, GODDESS
pay ...... FEE, QUIT, WAGE, CLEAR,
   REMIT, DEFRAY, SALARY,
   SETTLE, STIPEND, LIQUIDATE
  as-you-go taxer .... RUML
  attention .... CARE, HEED,
         LISTEN
  back .... REIMBURSE
  boost .... RAISE
  for .... FOOT(THE BILL)
  for injury .... DAMAGES
  for loss .... INDEMNIFY
  heed .... MIND
  homage/respect .... HONOR
  load .... CARGO
  one's share .... ANTE
  off .... RECKONING
  something additional to
   .... PERQUISITE
  up .... ANTE, PONY, KICK IN,
      COME ACROSS
payable ....:...... DUE
paying guest .... BOARDER
paymaster .... PURSER, CASHIER
payment, advance .... ANTES,
     HERIOT, HANDSEL
  back .... REBATE
  behind in .... ARREAR(S)
  call for .... DUN
  forced .... LEVY, EXACTION
  plan .... LAYAWAY
  to atone for killing
   .... WER(E)GILD, BLOOD MONEY
  token .... ARLES, HANDSEL
paynim .... PAGAN, MOSLEM,
        HEATHEN
payola .... BRIBE
PB in chemistry .... LEAD,
        PLUMBUM
PBX .... SWITCHBOARD
P.D.Q. .... ASAP
  part of .... PRETTY, DAMN,
         QUICK
pea .... PEASE, SENNA, LEGUME,
        LICORICE
  covering .... POD
  heath .... CARMELE
  pod .... PEASECOD
  pod, removal of ..... SHELLING
  relative .... REDBUD, BLACK
        LOCUST
  seed .... PULSE
  soup .... FOG
  stalk/stem .... HA(U)LM
  tree .... AGATI, LABURNUM
peabody bird .... SPARROW
peabrain .... NITWIT

relative .... IDIOT
peace .... CALM, AMITY, GRITH,
   QUIET, SHALOM, CONCORD,
   HARMONY, SERENITY
  agreement .... TREATY
  branch of .... OLIVE
  keep the .... POLICE
  offering .... GIFT, SACRIFICE
  officer ...... MARSHAL, SHERIFF,
   CONSTABLE, POLICEMAN
  pipe .... CALUMET
  symbol of .... DOVE
Peace Prize winner .... ORR,
   KING, MOTT, ROOT, LANGE,
   BUNCHE, DUNANT, WILSON,
       GORBACHEV
peaceable .... IRENIC, HENOTIC
peaceful .... CALM, IRENIC(AL),
   SERENE, HALCYON, PACIFIC
  period .... CALM, TRUCE,
       CEASE-FIRE
  person .... PACIFICO
peacemaker .... SOOTHER,
   MEDIATOR, PACIFIER,
       ARBITRATOR
  slang .... COLT
peach .... PAVY, TREE, FRUIT,
   BRANDY, VICTORINE
  fuzzless .... NECTARINE
  kind of ...... CLING, FREESTONE
  peel .... EPICARP, EXOCARP
  slang .... RAT, SING, BEAUT,
   BETRAY, SNITCH, SQUEAL
  state .... GEORGIA
  stone .... PIT, NUTLET,
       PUTAMEN
peachy .... FUZZY
peacoat .... JACKET
peacock .... MAO, BIRD, PAON,
   PAVO, PEAFOWL
  bird resembling .... ARGUS
  butterfly .... IO
  feather's spot .... OCELLUS
  female .... PEAHEN
  fish .... WRASSE
  genus .... PAVO
  like a .... VAIN
  neck feathers .... HACKLE,
       PLUMAGE
  of a .... PAVONINE
  ore .... BORNITE
  symbol of the .... VANITY
  walk .... STRUT
peacockish .... PROUD
peag(e) .... WAMPUM
peak .... ALP, TOP, TOR, CRAG,
   FADE, PEEP, CREST, CROWN,
   DROOP, PITON, HEIGHT,
   SUMMIT, MAXIMUM
  of rock .... AIGUILLE
  volcano's .... CONE

peaked .... TOPPED, POINTED
peal .... CLAP, RING, TOLL, CHIME,
   (RE)SOUND, CARILLON
peanut .... MANI, GOOBER
pear .... BOSC, POME, TREE,
   ANJOU, FRUIT, NOPAL,
   SECKEL, BARTLETT,
   JARGONEL(LE)
  family .... ROSE
  juice drink .... PERRY
  prickly .... TUNA, NOPAL,
   CACTUS, OPUNTIA
  prince's .... BERGAMOT
  seed .... PYRENE
  shaped ..... PEG-TOP, PYRIFORM
  shaped fruit .... FIG,
   AVOCADO, SHADDOCK
  winter .... BOSC
pearl .... GEM, BEAD, PURL,
   OLIVET, MARGARITE
  biblical .... BDELLIUM
  high quality .... ORIENT
  imitation .... OLIVET
  mother of .... NACRE
  producer .... NACRE, OYSTER,
       MOLLUSK
  quality of a .... LUSTER
Pearl .... MINNIE
  Buck heroine .... OLAN
  Harbor is in .... OAHU
  Mosque city .... AGRA
  novelist .... BUCK
  River .... CHU-KIANG
  singer .... BAILEY
  site perfidiously bombed:
   1941 .... HARBOR
pearlweed .... SAGINA
pearly ...... LUSTROUS, NACREOUS
pearmain .... APPLE
Pearson, Canadian premier
   .... LESTER
peart .... PERT, CLEVER, LIVELY
Peary's discovery .... NORTH
        POLE
peas and beans .... LEGUMES
  variety .... SNOW, CHICK,
      SUGAR(SNAP)
peasant ...... TAO, BOOR, CARL(E),
   HIND, PEON, RYOT, SERF,
   CEORL, CHURL, COTTAR,
   FARMER, FELLAH, KASAMA,
   MUZHIK, RUSTIC, TILLER,
   LABORER, VILLEIN,
       CAMPESINO
  farmer .... CROFTER
peasants' revolt .... JACQUERIE
pease .... PEAS
peat .... FUEL, TURF
  bog .... MOSS
  land .... TURBARY
  moss .... SPHAGNUM

spade .... SLADE
peav(e)y .... CANTHOOK
pebble .... SCREE, STONE, NUGGET,
QUARTZ
pecan ...... NUT, NOGAL, HICKORY
peccadillo .... SIN, FAULT
peccant .... SINFUL, SINNING
peccary .... BOAR, JAVALI
peck .... DAB, NAG, NIP, TAP,
BITE, KISS, PICK, NIBBLE
e.g. .... DRY MEASURE
¼ of .... QUARTERN
pecker .... PICK
pecks, 4 .... BUSHEL
peculate .... EMBEZZLE
peculiar .... ODD, QUEER,
SCREWY, UNIQUE, SPECIAL,
STRANGE, UNUSUAL,
SINGULAR
to locality .... ENDEMIC
peculiarity .... TRAIT, ODDITY,
ANOMALY
pecuniary .... MONETARY,
FINANCIAL
affairs .... FINANCES
pedagogical .... ACADEMIC,
SCHOLASTIC
pedagogue .... TUTOR, TEACHER
pedagogy .... TEACHING,
DIDACTICS
pedal ...... TREADLE, (FOOT)LEVER
decade .... TOES
digit .... TOE
pedant .... TUTOR, SCHOLAR,
TEACHER, EDUCATOR
pedantic .... BOOKISH, ACADEMIC,
DIDACTIC
pedate .... FOOTED, FOOTLIKE
peddle .... HAWK, SELL, VEND
peddler .... COSTER, DUFFER,
HAWKER, PEDLAR, PUSHER,
VENDOR, CHAPMAN,
PACKMAN, HUCKSTER
confederate of .... SHILL
vehicle of .... PUSHCART
pederasty .... SODOMY
boy used in .... CATAMITE
pedestal .... BASE, SUPPORT
part of .... DADO, SOCLE,
PLINTH
put on a ..... IDOLIZE, WORSHIP
pedestrian .... DULL, WALKER,
STROLLER, PROSAIC, WALKING
pediatrist's concern .... INFANTS
pedicel .... RAY, STEM, STALK,
PEDUNCLE
without .... SESSILE
pedicular .... LOUSY
pediculosis .... LOUSE
INFESTATION
problem .... LICE

pedicure, subject of
.... TOENAILS
pedidigitally misaligned
.... PIGEON-TOED
pedigree .... DESCENT, LINEAGE,
ANCESTRY, GENEALOGY
pedro ...... SEVEN UP, CARD GAME
peduncle .... STEM, SCAPE, STALK,
STIPE(S), PEDICEL, PEDICLE,
PETIOLE
without .... SESSILE
Pee Dee .... RIVER, YADKIN
Pee Wee of baseball .... REESE
peek .... LOOK, PEEP, PEER,
GLANCE
peel ...... BARE, FLAY, PARE, RIND,
SHED, SKIN, TRIM, STRIP,
TOWER, EPICARP, UNDRESS
for flavoring .... ZEST
skin off .... EXCORIATE
peen, tool with .... HAMMER
peep .... PRY, SPY, KEEK, LOOK,
PEEK, PEER, PULE, CHEEP,
CHIRP, GLIMPSE
military slang .... JEEP
show .... RAREE
peeper ...... EYE, PRY, TOM, FROG,
CHICK, SNOOP(ER), NESTLING
peephole .... EYELET, KEYHOLE
Peeping Tom .... PEEKER,
VOYEUR
saw her .... GODIVA
peer .... DUKE, EARL, LOOK, LORD,
PEEP, BARON, EQUAL, NOBLE,
SQUINT, MARQUIS, PALADIN,
VISCOUNT, ARISTOCRAT
domain of .... EARLDOM
Peer Gynt author .... IBSEN
character .... ASE, ANITRA
composer .... GRIEG
peerage .... NOBILITY
Peerce, operatic singer ...... JAN
peeress .... LADY, DUCHESS,
BARONESS, MARQUISE
peerless .... MATCHLESS,
NONPAREIL, UNRIVALED
peetweet .... SANDPIPER
peeve .... IRK, PIQUE, GRUDGE,
NETTLE, IRRITATE,
ANNOY(ANCE)
peevish .... PET, SOUR, CROSS,
MOODY, TESTY, TE(T)CHY,
CRANKY, GRUMPY, TOUCHY,
FRETFUL, PETULANT,
IRRITABLE, SPLENETIC
peewee ...... RUNT, CHILD, DWARF,
LAPWING, SMALL FRY
peg .... HOB, NOG, PIN, BOLT,
PLUG, STEP, DOWEL, KEVEL,
SPILL, STAKE, THOLE, SPIGOT,
TRE(E)NAIL

and rings game .... QUOITS
colloquial .... LEG, FOOT,
TOOTH
golf .... TEE
joining timbers ...... TRUNNEL,
TRE(E)NAIL
mountaineer's .... PITON
pega .... REMORA
Pegasus .... HORSE, STEED
part of .... STAR
Peggy .... MARGARET
pegs, set of .... SPILIKIN
Pegu capital .... RANGOON
ironwood .... ACLE
peignor .... ROBE, NEGLIGEE
Peiping .... PEKING
pejorative .... DISPARAGING
pekan .... WEASEL, WEJACK
pekin .... SILK, SATIN
Peking .... PEIPING
Pekingese .... DOG
pekoe .... TEA
pelage .... FUR, HAIR
pelagic .... MARINE, OCEANIC
Pele, football star .... EDSON,
NEGRAO
Peleg's father .... EBER
son .... REU
pelerine .... CAPE
Peleus, son of .... ACHILLES
wife of .... THETIS
Pelew .... PALAU
pelf .... BOOTY, WEALTH
Pelias' nephew .... JASON
son .... ACASTUS
Pelides .... ACHILLES
Pelion, companion of .... OSSA
pelisse .... COAT, CLOAK
pelite .... SHALE
pellagra treatment .... NIACIN
pellet .... BALL, SHOT, BULLET,
PEBBLE, MISSILE
of medicine .... PILL, PILULE,
TABLET, CAPSULE
pellmell .... JUMBLED, HEADLONG,
DISORDER(LY), HELTER-
SKELTER
pellucid .... CLEAR, SHEER, LIMPID
peloid .... MUD
Pelop's father .... TANTALUS
son .... ATREUS, THYESTES
Peloponnesus city .... MESSENE
country .... LACONIA
promontory .... MATAPAN
seaport .... PATRAS
pelota .... JAI ALAI
basket .... CESTA
court .... FRONTON
player .... PELOTARI
pelt .... FUR, BEAT, CAST, FELL,
HIDE, SKIN, POUND, STONE,

PEPPER, BOMBARD
pelter .... STONER
peltry .... FURS, SKINS
pelvic .... ILIAC, PUBIC
bones .... ILIA, SACRA
pemmican .... MEAT
pen ...... COOP, COTE, JAIL, YARD,
STIR, HUTCH, KRAAL, QUILL,
WRITE(R), CORRAL, INDITE,
PRISON, BALLPOINT,
ENCLOSURE
name (see also **pseudonym**)
.... NOM DE PLUME
pig .... STY
point .... NEB, NIB, STUB
up .... CONFINE
variant .... CRAAL
penal .... PUNITIVE
penalize .... FINE, PUNISH
penalty .... FINE, FORFEIT,
HANDICAP, PUNISHMENT
penance .... FASTING,
ATONEMENT, PUNISHMENT
penates .... LARES
pence .... COPPERS
penchant ...... YEN, FLAIR, TASTE,
DESIRE, LIKING, LEANING,
FONDNESS, INCLINATION
pencil .... STYLUS
lead .... GRAPHITE
well-used .... STUB
pend .... HANG
pendant .... FOB, LOCKET, TASSEL,
EARRING, GIRANDOLE,
LAVALIER(E)
pendent .... HANGING, PENSILE,
SUSPENDED
pending .... UNTIL, DURING,
DEPENDENT, UNDECIDED
pendulous ...... LOOSE, HANGING,
PENSILE, SWINGING
pendulum, device with inverted
.... METRONOME
weight .... BOB
Penelope .... WEAVER
father of .... ICARIUS
husband of .... ULYSSES,
ODYSSEUS
son of .... TELEMACHUS
penetrable .... PERVIOUS
penetralia .... SECRETS
penetrate .... BORE, GORE, ENTER,
IMBUE, REACH, INVADE,
PIERCE, PERMEATE,
PERFORATE
penetrating .... DEEP, KEEN,
ACUTE, SHARP, ASTUTE,
PUNGENT, INCISIVE
penetration .... INSIGHT,
INVASION, INTRUSION
open to .... PERMEABLE

penetron .... MESON
pengo replacement .... FORINT
penguin .... AUK, BIRD, JOHNNY
breeding place .... ROOKERY
describing a .... IMPENNATE
peninsula .... KOLA, NECK, GASPE,
MALAY, SINAI, BONDOC,
IBERIA, ISTRIA, KOWLOON,
LABRADOR, KAMCHATKA,
CHERSONESE, PROJECTION
penitence ...... REGRET, REMORSE,
CONTRITION, REPENTANCE
penitent .... SORRY, CONTRITE,
REPENTANT, REMORSEFUL
wear of .... SACKCLOTH,
SANBENITO
Penitentes .... CULT,
BROTHERHOOD
aim of .... PENANCE,
ATONEMENT
practice .... SELF-
FLAGELLATION
sacred holiday .... GOOD
FRIDAY
two-wheeled vehicle of
.... DEATH CART
penitential period .... LENT
penitentiary .... PRISON
penman .... AUTHOR, SCRIBE,
WRITER, CHIROGRAPHER
penmanship .... SCRIPT,
HANDWRITING, CHIROGRAPHY
Penn, actor .... SEAN
William .... QUAKER
penna .... FEATHER
pennant .... FLAG, BANNER,
BURGEE, ENSIGN, PENNON,
STREAMER
pennies .... PENCE
penniless .... POOR, NEEDY,
BANKRUPT, INDIGENT,
(FLAT)BROKE
Pennine Alps peak .... ROSA
pennon ...... FLAG, WING, ENSIGN,
PINION, PENNANT
Pennsylvania capital
.... HARRISBURG
city/town .... ONO, ERIE, YORK,
EASTON, SHARON, ALTOONA,
BRISTOL, CHESTER, HANOVER,
HERSHEY, INDIANA, LEBANON,
READING, SUNBURY, SWATARA,
BRADFORD, HAZLETON,
KINGSTON, SCRANTON,
ALLENTOWN, BETHLEHEM,
HAVERFORD, LANCASTER,
LEVITTOWN, NEW CASTLE,
PITTSBURGH, UPPER DARBY,
SPRINGFIELD, WILKES-BARRE,
PHILADELPHIA
college .... YORK, CARLOW,

WILSON, CHEYNEY, WESLEYAN,
HAVERFORD, GETTYSBURG,
POINT PARK, SETON HILL,
HOLY FAMILY, SWARTHMORE,
GWYNEDD-MERCY
county .... ELK, ERIE, ETNA,
KANE, KNOX, TROY, YORK,
BERKS, BLAIR, BUCKS,
BUTLER, LEHIGH, MERCER,
PLAINS, CAMBRIA, DAUPHIN,
FAYETTE, LEBANON, LUZERNE,
DELAWARE, LAWRENCE,
LYCOMING, ALLEGHENY,
LANCASTER
"Dutch" .... GERMAN
SETTLERS
founder .... (WILLIAM)PENN
Institute of Music ...... CURTIS
insurrection, cause of
.... WHISKY
island .... LITTLE TINICUM
lake .... ERIE, ARTHUR,
GLENDALE, WALLENPAUPACK
line .... READING RAILROAD
mountain .... BLUE, DAVIS,
NORTH, SOUTH, ARARAT, BLUE
KNOB, TUSCARORA
mountain range .... POCONO,
ALLEGHENY, APPALACHIAN
newspaper .... PACKET,
GAZETTE
port .... ERIE
river .... OHIO, TIOGA, BEAVER,
LEHIGH, CLARION, JUNIATA,
DELAWARE, ALLEGHENY,
CONEMAUGH
sect .... AMISH
state bird .... GROUSE
state flower .... MOUNTAIN
LAUREL
State House .... INDEPENDENCE
HALL
State House bell ...... LIBERTY
BELL
state nickname ...... KEYSTONE
state park .... PYMATUNING,
PRESQUE ISLE
state tree .... HEMLOCK
university .... DREXEL, LEHIGH,
TEMPLE, LINCOLN, BUCKNELL,
DUQUESNE, VILLANOVA,
PITTSBURGH, CARNEGIE-
MELLON
penny ...... COIN, GROAT, COPPER,
SALTEE, (RED)CENT
a-liner .... (HACK)WRITER,
SCRIBBLER
candy .... LICORICE
pincher .... TIGHTWAD
wise .... FRUGAL, THRIFTY
Penologist Lewis E. .... LAWES

penpoint .... NEB, NIB, STUB
Penrod's pal .... SAM
pensile .... HANGING, PENDENT
pension .... ANNUITY, STIPEND,
SUBSIDY
pensionary ...... PUPPET, HIRELING
pensive .... SAD, MEDITATIVE
penstock .... SLUICE, TROUGH
pent(up) ...... PENNED, GUARDED,
CONFINED, SUPPRESSED
pentacle .... STAR, SYMBOL,
PENTAGRAM
pentad .... FIVE, QUINTET
pentagram .... PENTACLE
Pentateuch .... TORA(H)
lesson read from .... PARASHAH
Pentecost .... WHITSUNDAY,
ASCENSION DAY
penthouse .... AERIE, LEANTO,
APARTMENT
pentose .... SUGAR, ARABINOSE
penurious .... POOR, STINGY,
MISERLY
one .... MISER
penury ...... POVERTY, INDIGENCE
peon .... SERF, LABORER
peony .... MOUTAN
flower .... PIP
people .... FOLK, RACE, DEMOS,
LAITY, NATION, PUBLIC,
MANKIND, MORTALS, NATIVES,
CITIZENS, HUMANITY,
POPULATE
angry .... FUMERS
biased .... OPINIONISTS
characteristics of .... ETHOS
common .... PLEBE, MASSES,
HOI POLOI, POPULACE
full of .... POPULOUS
in a legation .... DIPLOMATIC
CORPS
in second childhood
.... DOTARDS
insignificant .... NOBODIES,
SMALL FRY
mass killing of .... NOYADE,
POGROM, GENOCIDE,
HOLOCAUST
of all the .... PANDEMIC
of great interest ...... USURERS,
SHYLOCKS, LOAN SHARKS
of high social standing
.... GENTRY
on the move .... GOERS
prehistoric .... PELASGI(AN)
primitive .... SAVAGES
violent .... TARTARS
worthless .... RIFFRAFF
young .... TEENS
pep .... VIM, DASH, ZEST, ZING,
SNAP, VERVE, VIGOR, ENERGY

drug .... ELAVIL, TRIAVIL
pill .... DMT, LSD, STP
talk .... HYPE
peplos .... SCARF, SHAWL, PEPLUM
peplum .... SKIRT, PEPLOS
pepo .... GOURD, MELON, SQUASH,
PUMPKIN
pepoaza .... WHISTLING BIRD
habitat .... ARGENTINA
pepper .... ARA, BEAT, KAVA,
PELT, BETEL, SPICE, RIDDLE,
SEASON, STRAFE, CAYENNE,
CHILI(ES), CAPSICUM,
PIM(I)ENTO, SPRINKLE,
CONDIMENT
and-salt .... GRAY, MOTTLED,
SPOTTED
berry .... CUBEB
beverage .... KAVA
fruit .... CHILI, PAPRIKA
grinder .... MILL
hottest .... CAYENNE
mild, sweet .... PIMENTO
mildest variety of .... WHITE
picker .... PIPER
plant .... KAVA, BETEL,
PAPRIKA
pod .... CHILI
pot .... STEW
sauce .... TABASCO
shrike .... VIREO(NINAE)
shrub ...... CAVA, KAVA, KAWA
slang .... VIM, ZIP
variety .... BELL, BLACK, CHILI,
WHITE, JALAPENO
pepperidge .... TUPELO
peppermint .... OIL, CANDY,
PLANT, LOZENGE
camphor/oil product
.... MENTHOL
peppery .... HOT, FIERY, SHARP,
SPICY, TESTY, SPUNKY,
PUNGENT, IRRITABLE
peppy .... BRISK, SPIRITED
pepsin .... ENZYME
Pepys, Samuel .... DIARIST
Pequod .... WHALER, WHALEBOAT
captain of .... AHAB
quest of .... WHALE, MOBY
DICK
per ...... BY, VIA, EACH, THROUGH
annum .... ANNUALLY
diem .... DAILY
hundred .... PER CENT
pro. .... BY PROXY
se .... BY ITSELF
Pera .... BEYOGLU
peradventure .... MAYBE,
PERHAPS, POSSIBLY
perambulate .... WALK, STROLL
perambulator ...... PRAM, BUGGY

percale .... COTTON
perceive .... SEE, HEAR, KNOW,
NOTE, GRASP, SENSE, NOTICE,
DISCERN, OBSERVE
percentage .... FEE, PORTION
perceptible ...... TACTILE, VISIBLE,
PALPABLE, SENSIBLE,
TANGIBLE
perception .... EAR, GRASP,
NOESIS, INSIGHT, COGNITION
false .... HALLUCINATION
perceptive .... KEEN, ACUTE,
AWARE, KNOWING
perch .... SIT, FISH, REST, SEAT,
ROOST, RUFF(E), ALIGHT,
SAUGER, SETTLE, PERCOID
chance-taker's .... LIMB
fish like ..... ANABAS, DARTER,
CABRILLA
high .... AERY, AERIE
perchance ...... MAYBE, MAYHAP,
PERHAPS, POSSIBLY
percheron .... HORSE, TROTTER
repast of .... OATS
percoid .... FISH, PERCH
percolate ...... BREW, DRIP, OOZE,
PERK, SEEP, DRAIN, LEACH,
FILTER, TRICKLE, PERMEATE
percolator .... BREWER,
COFFEEPOT
percuss .... RAP
percussion .... SHOCK, IMPACT
cap .... PRIMER
hammer ...... PLEXOR, PLESSOR
instrument .... BELL, DRUM,
PIANO, TRAPS, MARACA,
CYMBALS
section .... TRAPS
Percy, Sir Henry .... HOTSPUR
perdition .... PIT, FALL, HELL,
LOSS, RUIN, DAMNATION
perdu(e) .... HIDDEN, CONCEALED
perdurable .... PERPETUAL
perdure .... LAST
pere .... FATHER, SENIOR
peregrinate .... TRAVEL, JOURNEY
peregrinator .... PILGRIM,
TRAVELER
peregrine .... ALIEN, FALCON,
FOREIGN, MIGRATORY
falcon .... T(I)ERCEL
falcon relative .... MILVAGO,
CARACARA
peremptory ...... FINAL, BINDING,
ABSOLUTE, DECISIVE,
DOGMATIC, ARBITRARY,
IMPERIOUS
perennial .... LASTING, PERPETUAL
plant .... DAHLIA, EVERGREEN
Presidential hopeful
.... STASSEN

perfect .... PURE, EXACT, IDEAL, MODEL, SOUND, UTTER, REFINE, PRECISE, ACCURATE, FLAWLESS, FAULTLESS, CONSUMMATE
blessedness .... NIRVANA
diamond .... PARAGON
shot .... ACE
perfection .... EXCELLENCE
model of .... PARAGON, PRECISION, MASTERPIECE
standard of .... IDEAL
perfectionist .... STICKLER
perfectly .... FULLY
perfecto .... CIGAR
perfidious ...... SHIFTY, FAITHLESS
perfidy .... BETRAYAL, TREACHERY
perforate .... BORE, DRILL, PINK(Y), PUNCH, PIERCE, PINKIE, RIDDLE, PUNCTURE
perforated .... FENESTRATE
utensil .... SIEVE, COLANDER, STRAINER
perforator .... PUNCHEON
perforation .... HOLE, PUNCH
perforce .... NECESSARILY
perform ...... DO, (EN)ACT, PLAY, WORK, EFFECT, RENDER, EXECUTE, FULFILL
in unison .... ACT AS ONE
with restraint .... UNDERACT
performance ...... SHOW, ACTION, RENDITION, EXHIBITION
balance-beam .... GYMNASTICS
between acts .... INTERLUDE
by king's comedians .... JESTING
in person .... LIVE
kind of .... MIMING, REPEAT
musical ..... CONCERT, RECITAL
thrilling .... STUNTS
performer .... DOER, ACTOR, PLAYER, ARTIST(E), TROUPER, PRETENDER, ENTERTAINER
actuated by wires ...... PUPPET, MARIONETTE
aquatic .... SEAL, DOLPHIN
kind of .... MAGICIAN, MUSICIAN
stock of .... REPERTORY, REPERTOIRE
performers, group of ...... CAST, TROUPE
perfume .... AROMA, A(T)TAR, SCENT, BOUQUET, ESSENCE, (IN)CENSE, FRAGRANCE
bag/pad .... SATCHET
base .... MUSK, ATTAR
box/case .... POMANDER
flask .... FLACON
making substance .... MUSK,

ATTAR, IRONE, MYRRH, ORRIS, IONONE, ORRICE, SAFROL(E), BERGAMOT, AMBERGRIS, VERDIGRIS
oil .... BEN, ATTAR, NEROLI, CITRONELLA
perfumed .... SCENTED, FRAGRANT, SWEET(SMELLING)
perfumer .... ATOMIZER
perfunctory .... CARELESS, SUPERFICIAL
Pergamum physician ...... GALEN
pergola .... ARBOR, ARCADE, GAZEBO
perhaps .... HAPLY, MAYBE, MAYHAP, POSSIBLY, PERCHANCE
peri .... ELF, FAIRY
cousin .... NISSE
meaning of: as prefix .... AROUND
Periander's wife .... MELISSA
perianth .... CALYX, PETAL
periapt .... AMULET
pericarp .... SEEDCASE
Pericles' mistress .... ASPASIA
peridot ...... OLIVINE, CHRYSOLITE
peril ...... RISK, DANGER, HAZARD, MENACE, JEOPARDY
perimeter .... BORDER, BOUNDARY
perinatologist ...... OBSTETRICIAN
period ...... AGE, DOT, ERA, STOP, TERM, CYCLE, EPACT, POINT, SPELL, STAGE, DURATION, (LIFE)TIME, SENTENCE
academic .... SEMESTER
break .... RECESS
brief .... SEC, SNAP, SPELL, MOMENT, SNATCH
dormant .... HIBERNATION
dull/slow .... SLACK
economic .... SLUMP, RECESSION
endless .... ETERNITY
extension .... GRACE
fast(ing) .... LENT
geological .... JURA(SSIC), ERIAN, UINTA, EOCENE, MIOCENE, SILURIAN
holding/occupancy ...... TERM, TENURE
inactive .... LULL, REST, RESPITE, DORMANCY, VEGETATION
leisure .... HOLIDAY, VACATION
of authorized delay .... MORATORIUM
decline .... SUNSET
existence .... LIFE
grief .... MOURNING

maturation, hopefully .... TEENS
100 years .... CENTURY
peace and prosperity .... MILLENNIUM
rest .... SABBATH
satellites .... SPACE AGE
seclusion .... RETREAT
sunlight .... DAYTIME
ten years .... DECADE
time .... AGE, DAY, ERA, (A)EON, HOUR, WEEK, YEAR, EPOCH, MONTH, DECADE, MINUTE, SECOND, CENTURY
twenty years .... SCORE
unemployment .... LAYOFF
vigil .... WAKE
year .... SEASON
quiet .... CALM, LULL
short .... SNAP, SPELL
significant .... ERA
temporary .... INTERIM
trial .... PROBATION
two-week .... FORTNIGHT
unbroken .... STRETCH
woman's .... MENSES
periodic .... ETESIAN, REGULAR, SEASONAL, RECURRENT
periodical .... WEEKLY, GAZETTE, JOURNAL, MONTHLY, MAG(AZINE)
employee .... REPORTER
periodontal disease .... GINGIVITIS
peripatetic .... WALKER, ITINERANT, PEDESTRIAN
peripheral .... OUTER, DISTAL, EXTERNAL
periphery .... RIM, AMBIT, ENVIRONS, PERIMETER
periphrasis .... AMBAGE
periphrastic .... VERBOSE
perique .... TOBACCO
periscope trail ....WAKE, FEATHER
perish .... DIE, END, EXPIRE
perissodactyl ungulate .... TAPIR
peristyle ...... COURT, COLONNADE
peritoneum .... MEMBRANE
fold .... OMENTUM
periwig .... PERUKE
periwinkle .... SHELL, SNAIL, MUSSEL, MYRTLE
perjure .... LIE
perjury, induce to commit .... SUBORN
perk .... LIFT, RAISE, BUBBLE
perky .... GAY, SAUCY, JAUNTY, SPIRITED
Perle, society hostess ...... MESTA
perlite .... ROCK, OBSIDIAN
permanence .... FIXITY

permanent .... FIXED, LASTING, STABLE, INDELIBLE, PERPETUAL
calling .... CAREER
permeable .... PERVIOUS
permeate .... OOZE, IMBUE, DIFFUSE, PERVADE, PENETRATE
permissible .... ALLOWABLE
permission .... GRACE, LEAVE, CONSENT, LICENSE, FURLOUGH
authorized .... SANCTION
to enter .... ENTREE
permissive .... LENIENT, ALLOWING, INDULGENT
permit ...... LET, FIAT, PASS, VISA, ALLOW, GRANT, LEAVE, CEDULA, LICENSE, WARRANT, SANCTION, AUTHORIZE
reluctantly .... BEAR, BROOK, ENDURE, SUFFER, TOLERATE
to leave .... EXCUSE
permitted .... LEGAL, LICIT, LAWFUL
permutation .... CHANGE
permute ...... ALTER, REARRANGE
Pernambuco .... RECIFE
pernicious .... EVIL, FATAL, DEADLY, WICKED, BANEFUL, HARMFUL, NOISOME, NOXIOUS, VICIOUS
per(s)nickety .... FUSSY, FASTIDIOUS
Peron's lady .... EVA, EVITA, ISABEL
slogan .... CUMPLE
perorate ...... ORATE, HARANGUE, SPEECHIFY
peroration .... EPILOGUE
perpend .... PONDER
perpendicular .... SINE, ERECT, PLUMB, UPRIGHT, VERTICAL, STRAIGHT UP
perpetrate .... DO(TO), COMMIT
perpetual .... ENDLESS, ETERNAL, LASTING, CONSTANT, INFINITE, INCESSANT, PERMANENT
perpetually .... ALWAYS, (FOR)EVER
perpetuate .... PRESERVE, ETERNALIZE
perpetuity .... ETERNITY, INFINITY
perplex .... ELUDE, STUMP, BAFFLE, PUZZLE, CONFUSE, FLUMMOX, MYSTIFY, NONPLUS, INTRIGUE
perplexed .... IN A DILEMMA
perquisite .... TIP, BONUS, REWARD, APPANAGE, GRATUITY
slang .... PERK

perron .... STAIRCASE
Perry, lawyer of fiction .... MASON
singer .... COMO
perse .... BLUE
persecute .... ABUSE, ANNOY, HOUND, HARASS, OPPRESS, MALTREAT
persecution .... DOGGING, TORMENT, TORTURE
complex .... PARANOIA
of minority group .... POGROM
victim of .... JEW, MARTYR
persecutor .... PLAGUER, OPPRESSOR, TORMENTOR
Perseid .... METEOR
Persephone .... CORA, PROSERPINA
husband/abductor of .... HADES, PLUTO
parent of .... ZEUS, DEMETER
Perseus, daughter of ...... PERSEIS
mother of .... DANAE
victim of .... MEDUSA
wife of .... ANDROMEDA
perseverance .... PATIENCE, TENACITY
slang .... GUT
perseverant ones .... STAYERS
persevere .... KEEP ON, PERSIST, STICK TO IT
Pershing's command .... AEF
Persia .... IRAN
conqueror of .... CYRUS
Persian .... MEDE, ELAMITE, PAHLAVI, IRANI(AN), PARTHIAN
ally .... MEDE
almond .... BADAM
angel .... MAH
apartment .... ZENANA
bird .... BULBUL
blinds .... PERSIENNES
capital ..... ESFAHAN, ISFAHAN, PERSEPOLIS
carpet/rug .... KALI, SENNA, HAMADAN
city .... ERBIL, ARBELA, TABRIZ, TEH(E)RAN
coin .... PUL, ASAR, POUL, DARIC, DINAR, TOMAN, STATER, ASHRAFI, PAHLAVI
dance .... SARABAND
deity, supreme .... ORMAZD
dynasty ...... SELJUK, SASSANID
elf .... PERI
emigree .... PARSI, PARSEE
empire founder .... CYRUS
evil spirit .... AHRIMAN
fairy .... ELF, PERI
father .... BABA

fire worshipper .... PARSI
Gate of Faith .... BAB
god of light .... MITHRA(S)
governor .... SATRAP
Gulf region .... CHALDEA
Gulf sight .... OILER
gypsy .... SISECH
hemp .... KANAB
hook money .... LARI
inn .... SARAI, SERAI
javelin .... JERID
judge .... CADI
king .... CYRUS, DARIUS, CAMBYSES, (ARTA)XERXES
king of peris .... JAMSHID
language .... ZEND, PASHTO, AVESTAN, KURDISH, PAHLAVI
lynx .... CARACAL
measure .... PARASANG
monk .... DERVISH
mystic .... SUFI
native .... LUR, MEDE
nightingale .... BULBUL
official .... HAMAN
pal .... MEDE
people .... MEDES, ELAMITES
perfume .... ATAR
pixie .... PERI
poet .... SADI, HAFIZ, FIRD(A)USI, OMAR(KHAYYAM)
potentate .... SHAH
pottery .... GOMBROON
priestly caste .... MAGI
prince .... SATRAP
prophet .... MANI, MANES
pungent .... TEZ
refugee .... PARSI, PARSEE
religion .... BABISM, MITHRAISM
rice dish .... PILAU, PILAW
ruler .... SHAH, DARIUS, SULTAN, XERXES
sect .... BABI(SM)
screen/veil .... PARDAH
servant .... BACHA
spinel .... BALAS
sprite .... PERI
symbol .... SWASTIKA
teacher .... MULLA(H)
tiger .... SHER
title .... BAB, AZAM, KHAN, SHAH, MIR(ZA)
water wheel .... NORIA
weight .... SER, ABBAS
writings .... (ZEND)AVESTA
persicary .... KNOTWEED
persiennes ...... BLINDS, SHUTTERS
persiflage .... BANTER, BADINAGE, RAILLERY
persimmon(s) .... FRUIT
family .... EBONY

kind of .... ORIENTAL, AMERICAN, JAPANESE, DATE-PLUM
Oriental/Japanese .... KAKI
shape of .... EGG, ROUND
persist ...... PLOD, ENDURE, INSIST, KEEP ON, CONTINUE, PERSEVERE
persistence .... TENACITY
persistent .... DOGGED, STUBBORN, CONTINUED, TENACIOUS
assault/attack .... SIEGE
is .... LEAVES NO STONE UNTURNED
person ...... EGG, MAN, ONE, SELF, BEING, CHILD, WIGHT, WOMAN, FELLOW, INDIVIDUAL
abject .... WORM, WRETCH
actively modern ...... SWINGER
African American–Native American .... GRIFF(E)
an idle ...... SCOBBER LOTCHER
Anglo–Native American .... WALLA(H)
angry/disgruntled .... SOREHEAD
annoying .... CUSS, PEST, HUNKS
argumentative .... POLEMIST
ark .... NOAH, SHEM
at least 100 years old .... CENTENARIAN
authorized to practice profession .... LICENTIATE
awkward ..... DUFFER, FOOZLE, GALOOT
bad luck .... JONAH, JONAS, HOODOO
beastly .... YAHOO
between ages of 60 and 70 .... SEXAGENARIAN
between ages of 80 and 90 .... OCTOGENARIAN
boastful .... GASCON
boorish .... GOOP, LOUT
burdensome/useless .... DEADWOOD
callow .... CALF
clumsy .... DUB, OAF, HULK, LOON, SLOB, SWAB, CHUMP, JUMBO, LUBBER, LUMMOX, CHUKKER
coarse .... MUG, BOOR, LOUT, OGRE, RUBE, MUCKER, SAVAGE
colorless .... ALBINO
common .... PLEBEIAN
complaining .... CRAB, CRANK, GROUCH, GROUSE, WHINER, CRYBABY
contemptible .... CAD, CUR,

RAT, SNOT, TOAD, WORM, LOUSE, SKUNK, SWINE, BUGGER, INSECT, ROTTER, STINKER, SCOUNDREL
cowardly .... CUR, SISSY, CAITIFF, POLTROON
cunning .... FOX, WEASEL
dangerous .... DESPERADO
dark-skinned .... NEGRO
deceitful .... KNAVE
defeated in a contest .... ALSO-RAN
demented .... NUT, LOCO, LOONY, MORON, CRACKPOT
destructive ...... HUN, VANDAL, ARSONIST
diabolical ..... FIEND, HELLION, MEPHISTO
disorderly .... LARRIKIN
dissolute .... RIP, RAKE
drunken .... LUSH, STIFF, HELLBENDER
dull .... BORE, JERK, LUMP, MOKE, DUNCE, FOOZLE, LURDAN(E), DULLARD, PLODDER
easily cheated ..... DUPE, GULL
easily seduced .... PUSHOVER
eccentric .... NUT, JERK, KOOK, CRANK
eminent .... VIP, NOTABLE, LUMINARY
energetic .... DYNAMO, HUSTLER, LIVEWIRE
engaged to be married .... FIANCE(E)
entertaining .... SCREAM
evil .... THUG, DEMON, YAHOO, CAITIFF, HOODLUM, HOOLIGAN, MISCREANT
excessively formal .... PRIG, PRUDE, STIFF
extraordinary .... ONER, PRODIGY
famous .... NOTABLE, CELEBRITY
feeble-minded .... AMENT, IDIOT, MORON
fiendish .... HELLKITE
fine/nice .... BRICK, TRUMP
fleeing from justice .... FUGITIVE
fond of fighting ..... HOTHEAD, SCRAPPER
foolish .... FOP, JAY, COOT, GOOF, BOOB(Y), BUFFOON
foppish .... LADIDA
formal .... STICKLER, CONFORMIST
frenzied .... AMOK, AMUCK, BERSERK(ER)

fuzzy .... FUDDY-DUDDY, HOITY-TOITY
gifted .... WHIZ, GENIUS, TALENT, WIZARD
greedy .... HOG, PIG, KITE, HARPY, VULTURE
guilty of a crime .... FELON, LAWBREAKER
gullible .... BABE, DUPE, SUCKER
handsome .... ADONIS, LOOKER
head of .... COSTARD
high in society .... NOB
high-born .... NOBLE
high-ranking .... MAGNIFICO
holy .... MAHATMA
hotheaded .... HOTSPUR
humorous .... WAG, CLOWN, JESTER, WISECRACKER
ill-humored .... GROUCH, SOREHEAD
ill-mannered ...... BOOR, CRAB, GOOP, LOUT, YAHOO
important .... VIP, NIBS, MOGUL, BASHAW, BIGWIG, MAGNATE, (BIG)WHEEL, DIGNITARY, MAGNIFICO
impractical .... DREAMER, FANTAST, IDEALIST, VISIONARY
impudent .... HUSSY, UPSTART, MALAPERT
impulsive .... MADCAP
inquisitive .... SNOOP, MOUSER, BUSYBODY
insane .... LUNATIC, PSYCHO(PATH)
insignificant ..... SNIP, SHRIMP, SQUIRT, NONENTITY
intellectual .... NOETIC, PUNDIT, SAVANT, EGGHEAD, SCHOLAR
irresponsible .... FLIBBERTIGIBBET
lazy .... POKE, DRONE, IDLER, LOAFER, LURDAN(E)
learned .... SAGE, ORACLE, PUNDIT, SAVANT, SCHOLAR, SOPHIST
lively .... GRIG
living by his wits .... SPIV
living in town .... OPPIDAN
loud-voiced .... STENTOR, THERSITES
lovable .... DOLL
maladjusted .... MISFIT
matchless/unique .... ONER
mean ..... CAD, LOUSE, CAITIFF
meddling .... BUTTINSKY
mentally deficient .... IDIOT, MORON, IMBECILE, SIMPLETON
mischievous .... SCAMP,

HELLION

miserly .... CHURL, NIGGARD, TIGHTWAD, SKINFLINT

mix-blooded .... METIS, CREOLE, GRIFF(E), LADINO, MESTEE, METIF(F), MUSTEE, MESTIZO, MULATTO, HALF-CASTE

modern .... NEOTERIC

much-admired .... PIP(PIN)

mythical .... SANDMAN

naive .... BABE, GREENHORN

name of .... HANDLE, MONICKER

nameless .... ANONYM

nearsighted .... MYOPE

noble born .... CHILDE

obnoxious .... CAD, FINK, SNOB, HUNKS

obstinate .... ASS, MULE

odd .... QUEER, ECCENTRIC

of great courage .... LION

of great energy .... DEMON

of prominence .... NABOB

of recognized excellence .... CRACKERJACK

of unbalanced mind .... MATTOID

old-fashioned .... FOG(E)Y, FOSSIL, MOSSBACK

optimistic .... POLLYANNA

out of place .... ESTRAY

overnice .... PRIG

overweight .... FATSO

pale-looking .... WHEYFACE

panel .... JUROR

partly paralyzed .... PARETIC

pedantic .... PRIG

pleasure-loving .... SPORT

pledged .... HOSTAGE, BETROTHED

poor .... BEGGAR, PAUPER

popular ..... HERO, LION, STAR, CELEBRITY

powerful .... GIANT, MOGUL, TITAN, PARAMOUNT, POTENTATE

pretending to knowledge .... SCIOLIST

prominent: sl. .... WHEEL

promising .... COMER

prone to argue .... POLEMIC, POLEMIST

prying .... SPY, GOSSIP, MOUSER, SNOOPER, BUSYBODY, DETECTIVE

pugnacious .... BANTAM, SCRAPPER

punctilious .... PRIG

puritanical .... BLUENOSE

quarrelsome .... SCRAPPER

queer ...... NUT, DUCK, CRANK, GOOSE, CODGER, ODDBALL, CHARACTER

quick-tempered .... HOTSPUR

rebellious .... DISSIDENT, MALCONTENT

reckless .... MADCAP, HOTSPUR, PLUNGER, DAREDEVIL

resembling another .... RINGER

rich/wealthy .... NABOB, FAT CAT, CROESUS, MONEYBAGS, PLUTOCRAT, CAPITALIST

rough .... MUG, LARRIKIN

saucy .... MALAPERT

savage .... HUN, BRUTE, VANDAL, BARBARIAN

second .... YOU

self-centered .... EGOIST, EGOTIST, EGOMANIAC

self-important .... NIBS, BASHAW

servile .... TOADY, MINION, FLUNK(E)Y, SPANIEL

short, fat .... SQUAB, DUMPLING

silly .... GOOF, GOOP, KOOK, GOOSE, PINHEAD, TOMFOOL

simple, country .... BUMPKIN

slow-moving ..... POKE, SNAIL, DAWDLER, LAGGARD

sly .... FOX, SNEAK, WEASEL, SHYSTER

small/undersized .... BUB, RUNT, AGATE, DWARF, PYGMY, BANTAM, INSECT, MIDGE(T), SHRIMP, SQUIRT, SNIP(PET), HALFPINT, PIPSQUEAK, LILLIPUTIAN

stateless .... REFUGEE

stingy .... HUNKS, MISER, NIGGARD, SKINFLINT

stubborn .... ASS, MULE

stupid .... NIT, OAF, SAP, DOLT, DOPE, GABY, LOON, MOKE, MUTT, SLOB, NINNY, BOOB(Y), SCHMO, DIMWIT, DUFFER, LUMMOX, ZOMBI(E), CHUKKER, DULLARD, JACKASS, PINHEAD, DUMBBELL, LUNKHEAD, NUMSKULL, SOFTHEAD, LAMEBRAIN, SIMPLETON, DUNDERHEAD, MUTTONHEAD

stylish .... FOP, DUDE, SWELL

surly .... HUNKS

sweet-faced .... CHERUB

sworn legally .... JURAT

syphilitic .... LUETIC

talkative ..... GABBER, MAGPIE, (POPIN)JAY, CHATTERBOX

tall, lean: colloq.

.... BEANPOLE, LONGLEGS

terrible-tempered ...... TARTAR

third .... HE, IT, SHE, THEY

timid ..... LAMB, MOUSE, SISSY

tireless .... DYNAMO

tiresome .... PILL

tongue of .... CLAPPER

tricky .... FOX, SHYSTER, SLICKER

tuberculous .... LUNGER, CONSUMPTIVE

ugly .... GOON, HOOD, OGRE, FRIGHT, GALOOT, ZOMBI(E), GORILLA, GOLLIWOG, SOURPUSS

under patronage .... WARD, PROTEGE

ungrateful .... INGRATE

unhappy .... WRETCH

unprincipled .... ROGUE, SCAMP, SCALAWAG, SCAPEGRACE

unreasonable .... MISOLOGIST

unsophisticated, country .... HICK, YOKEL, RUSTIC, HAYSEED

untidy .... SLOB

unwanted .... LEPER, PARIAH, OUTCAST, PERSONA NON GRATA

used as tool .... PAWN, DUMMY, FRONT, PUPPET, STOOGE, SCAPEGOAT

utterly foolish .... IDIOT

vain ...... PEACOCK, NARCISSIST

very funny .... RIOT

violent, lawless .... RUFFIAN, ROUGHNECK, TERRORIST

vulgar .... CAD, BOOR, LOUT, MUCKER

waist measure of .... GIRTH

weak .... WIMP, NAMBY-PAMBY

white .... CAUCASIAN

who acts as prostitute's agent .... PIMP, PROCURER

who avoids obligation .... SLACKER

who betrays .... RAT, TRAITOR, SQUEALER

who browbeats .... THUG, BULLY, CUTTHROAT

who defrauds .... SWINDLER

who has great skill .... DEMON, GENIUS

who makes kids sleepy .... SANDMAN

who never laughs .... AGELAST, DEADPAN, POKERFACE

who sells on installment .... TALLYMAN wicked .... FIEND, MONSTER, VILLAIN, SCOUNDREL

wise .... GURU, SAGE, SEER, SOLON, SAVANT, MAHATMA

with free ticket .... DEADHEAD, DEADBEAT

with unsatiable thirst .... TANTALUS

with the same name as another .... NAMESAKE

withered, thin .... MUMMY

without melanin pigment .... ALBINO

wonderfully dull .... COLOSSAL BORE

working off a debt .... PEON

worthless .... BUM, LOSEL, CADGER, VAGRANT, RAKE, WASTREL

young .... CALF, SLIP, LAMBKIN, WHIFFET, TEENAGER

persona non grata, designating a .... UNWANTED, UNDESIRABLE, UNACCEPTABLE

personable ...... COMELY, GENIAL, CHARMING, HANDSOME

personage .... NIBS, BIGWIG, NOTABLE, DIGNITARY, MAGNIFICO

personal .... OWN, PRIVATE, CORPORAL, INTIMATE, INDIVIDUAL

appearance .... MIEN, BEARING, PRESENCE

aura ..... CHARISMA, MYSTIQUE

belongings .... TRAPS

characteristic .... TRAIT

charm .... CHARISMA

combining form .... IDIO

effects .... DUNNAGE

well-being .... COMFORT, WELFARE, CONVENIENCE

personality .... EGO, SELF, PRESENCE, CHARACTER

test .... RORSCHACH

personate .... PORTRAY, REPRESENT

personator .... IMPOSTOR

personified .... INCARNATE

personify .... EMBODY, TYPIFY, SYMBOLIZE

personnel .... CREW, STAFF, WORKERS, EMPLOYE(E)S

concern .... ABSENTEEISM

perspective .... ANGLE, VISTA, ASPECT, OUTLOOK, STANDPOINT, (POINT OF)VIEW

perspicacious .... KEEN, ACUTE, SHREWD

perspicacity .... ACUMEN, INSIGHT

perspicuous .... CLEAR, LUCID, LIMPID

perspiration ...... SUDOR, SWEAT, EGESTA, HIDROSIS

stimulator .... BONESET

perspire .... EGEST, SWEAT

profusely .... SWELTER

persuade .... COAX, URGE, INDUCE, WORK ON, CONVINCE, PREVAIL ON

by giving reasons .... ARGUE

persuasible .... DOCILE, AMENABLE

persuasion .... PLEA, BELIEF, CONVICTION, INSISTENCE

art of .... SOFT SELL

persuasive .... COGENT, CONVINCING

pert ...... ARCH, BOLD, FLIP(PANT), BRASH, SASSY, SAUCY, FORWARD, IMPUDENT

girl .... CHIT, MINX

language .... SASS

pertain .... REFER, BELONG, RELATE

pertaining .... APROPOS, RELATIVE, INVOLVING, REFERRING

to a certain pope .... SISTINE

to a nonmetallic element .... SELENIC

to 4th century Franks .... SALIC

Perth river .... TAY

pertinacious .... FIRM, STUBBORN

pertinence .... BEARING, RELEVANCE

pertinent .... APT, GERMANE, RELEVANT

perturb .... ALARM, UPSET, RUFFLE, AGITATE, DISTURB, DISTRESS

perturbation .... FEEZE

pertussis ...... (WHOOPING)COUGH

Peru, capital of .... LIMA

conqueror of .... PIZARRO

peruke .... HAIR, PERI(WIG)

peruse .... CON, READ, SCAN, STUDY, EXAMINE, SCRUTINIZE

Peruvian .... INCA(N), LIMAN

animal .... LLAMA, ALPACA, VICUNA

austerity program .... FUJISHOCK

bark/tree .... CINCHONA

bay .... PAITA, PISCO, SECHURA

beef .... CHARQUI

bird .... YUTU, TINAMOU

cape .... BLANCO

carrot .... APIO

city/town .... ICA, ILO, JAEN, PUNO, CUSCO, PISCO, PIURA, TACNA, CALLAO, TALARA, TUMBES, SULLANA, AREQUIPA, AYACUCHO, PUCALLPA, TRUJILLO

coin .... SOL, LIBRA, DINERO, PESETA

current .... EL NINO

dance .... CUECA

department .... ICA, LIMA, PUNO, JUNIN, PIURA, TACNA, ANCASH

falcon .... ALETO

first ambassador to the Soviet Union .... DE CUELLAR

fox .... ATOC

goddess .... MAMA

hill .... LOMA, MEDANO

Indian ...... ANDE, CANO, INCA, PANA, COLLA, AYMARA, CHANCA, CHUNCHO, QUECHUA

inn .... TAMBO

island .... CHINCHA, SAN GALLAN, INDEPENDENCIA

king .... INCA, ATABALIPA, ATAHUALPA

lake .... JUNIN, TITICACA

language .... AYMARA, QUECHUA, SPANISH

monetary unit .... SOL

mountain .... EL MISTI, COROPUNA, HUASCARAN, SALCANTAY

mountain range .... ANDES

peninsula .... PARACAS

plant .... OCA, TOLA

plateau .... TABLAZO

port .... CALLAO

president .... BELAUNDE, FUJIMORI

recording device .... QUIPU

river .... ENE, ICA, MANU, MAYO, NAPO, SAMA, ACARI, CASMA, JURUA, NANAY, PURUS, RIMAC, SANTA, TIGRE, VITOR, GRANDE, MORONA, PAMPAS, PERENE, PICHIS, TUMBES, YAGUAS, YAVARI, MANTARO, MARANON, UCAYALI, APURIMAC

singer .... SUMAC

tanager .... YENI

tobacco .... SANA

volcano .... MISTI, OMATE

wind .... PUNA, SURES

pervade .... FILL, IMBUE, DIFFUSE, PERMEATE

pervasive .... SUFFUSIVE

quality .... ODOR

perverse .... WRY, WICKED, CONTRARY, UNTOWARD, DIFFICULT

attitude .... CONTRARINESS
pervert .... WARP, TWIST, DEBASE,
   GARBLE, MISUSE, CORRUPT,
   DISTORT, MISLEAD, VITIATE
pervious .... PERMEABLE
Pesach .... PASSOVER
Pescadores .... HOKO GUNTO
pesky .... IRKSOME, ANNOYING,
   MISCHIEVOUS
peso .... DURO
   $1/100$ of ..... CENTAVO, CENTIMO
pessimist .... CYNIC, KILLJOY,
   WORRIER
   opposite of .... OPTIMIST
   slang .... CRAPEHANGER
pessimistic .... GLOOMY, CYNICAL,
   NEGATIVE, DEFEATIST
pest .... IMP, BANE, BORE, PLAGUE,
   VERMIN, NUISANCE
   colloquial .... TERROR
   in a pool .... SPATTERER
   problem .... TROUBLER
pester .... DUN, NAG, VEX,
   ANNOY, HARRY, TEASE,
   BADGER, BOTHER, HARASS,
   HECTOR
pesticide .... DDT, BUG BOMB
   controversial .... ALAR
pestiferous .... NOXIOUS
pestilence ...... PLAGUE, MURRAIN,
   SCOURGE, EPIDEMIC
pestle .... BRAY, BEETLE, MULLER,
   POUNDER
   companion of .... MORTAR
pet .... SULK, CODDLE, COSSET,
   DANDLE, FONDLE, DARLING,
   FAVORITE
   lamb .... CADE, COSSET
   name .... NICKNAME,
   SOBRIQUET
   of the wicked witch
   .... BLACK CAT
Petain, Marshall .... HENRI
petal .... LEAF, LABELLUM
   base .... UNGUIS
   protuberance .... CALCAR
petals, arrangement of
   .... WHORL, ROSETTE
   without .... APETALOUS
petard .... FIRECRACKER
petasus .... CUPALO, (WINGED)HAT
petcock .... VALVE, FAUCET
Pete of baseball fame ...... ROSE
peter .... WANE, DWINDLE
   out .... END, EXPIRE, PERISH,
   COLLAPSE
Peter, actor .... FALK, FONDA,
   LORRE, O'TOOLE, USTINOV
   Bull's subject .... TEDDIES,
   TEDDYBEAR
   Falk role .... COLUMBO

Pan's author .... BARRIE
   captain .... HOOK
   dog .... NANA
   loss .... SHADOW
   opponents .... PIRATES
   pal .... WENDY
   pirate .... SMEE
   the Great's wife ...... EUDOXIA
Peter's tribute to Pope
   .... PENCE
petiole .... STIPE, PEDUNCLE,
   (LEAF)STALK
petit .... PETTY
   mal .... EPILEPSY
petite .... TINY, SMALL,
   DIMINUTIVE
petition .... ASK, SUE, PLEA, SUIT,
   APPLY, APPEAL, PRAY(ER),
   IMPLORE, REQUEST, SOLICIT,
   ENTREATY
petitioner, in law .... ORATOR
petits fours .... CAKES
Petrarch's lady .... LAURA
petrel ...... TITI, FULMAR, STINKER,
   MALLEMUCK
   describing one .... STORMY
   Leach's storm
   .... OCEANODROMA
   relative .... FULMAR, PUFFIN
   resembling diving .... AUK
   white-faced storm
   .... PELAGODROMA
   Wilson's storm .... OCEANITES
petrified ...... FROZEN, APPALLED,
   TERRIFIED
   goddess .... NIOBE
   substance .... COAL, FOSSIL
Petrified Forest site .... ARIZONA
petrify ...... STUN, SHOCK, HARDEN,
   DEADEN, CALCIFY, STUPEFY,
   PARALYZE, FOSSILIZE
Petrograd .... LENINGRAD
petrol .... GAS(OLINE)
petrolatum .... VASELINE
petroleum jelly .... PARAFFIN,
   VASELINE, PETROLATUM
   product .... COKE, PITCH,
   BUTANE, OILTAR, BENZENE,
   BITUMEN, NAPHTHA, PROPENE,
   CYMOGENE, GASOLINE,
   KEROSENE, LIGROIN(E),
   PARAFFIN
   solvent .... OCTANE
   tanker .... OILER
Petrosian, chess champ
   .... TIGRAN
Petrova, actress .... OLGA
petticoat .... GIRL, WOMAN,
   BALMORAL, CAMISOLE,
   (HALF)SLIP, (UNDER)SKIRT
   material .... CRINOLINE

pettifogger .... SHYSTER
petting .... CARESSING
pettish .... CROSS, FRETFUL,
   PEEVISH
pettitoes .... FEET, TOES
petty .... MEAN, MINOR, SMALL,
   PALTRY, TRIVIAL, FIDDLING,
   PICAYUNE, TRIFLING
   fault .... PECCADILLO
   officer .... MATE, BOSUN,
   YEOMAN
Petula, singer .... CLARK
petulance .... PEEVISHNESS,
   PETTISHNESS
petulant .... CROSS, SHORT,
   TESTY, FRETFUL, PEEVISH,
   WASPISH, IRRITABLE, HOITY-
   TOITY
petunia .... NIGHTSHADE
pew .... SLIP, STALL, BENCHES
   end carving .... POPPYHEAD
pewee .... PEWIT, PHOEBE,
   FLYCATCHER
pewit ...... GULL, PEWEE, PHOEBE,
   LAPWING
pewter .... TRIFLE
peyote .... CACTUS, MESCAL
   product .... MESCALINE
Peyton Place author
   .... METALIOUS
pfennig, $1/2$ of .... HELLER
   100 .... MARK
pH is measure of .... ACIDITY,
   ALKALINITY
   result of high .... ALKALOSIS
   result of low .... ACIDOSIS
   7 of body fluids
   .... NEUTRALITY
Phaedra's husband ...... THESEUS
   parent .... MINOS
Phaedrus' forte .... FABLES
phagocyte .... CELL
   "free" .... MONOCYTE,
   GRANULOCYTE
   locale .... BLOOD, LUNGS,
   SPLEEN, ALVEOLI
phalanger .... ARIEL, TAPOA
phantasm .... GHOST, VAPOR,
   EIDOLON, SPECTER
phantasmal .... EERIE
phantom .... GHOST, SPIRIT,
   (E)IDOLON, SPECTER,
   ILLUSION, APPARITION
Pharaoh .... SETI, CHEOPS,
   RAM(E)SES
   residence .... MEMPHIS
pharmacist .... DRUGGIST
   obsolete term .... APOTHECARY
pharmacology subject .... DRUGS
pharmacy .... DRUGSTORE
pharos ...... BEACON, LIGHTHOUSE

builder .... SOSTRATOS
pharynx .... TUBE, THROAT, PASSAGE
   inflammation .... PHARYNGITIS, SORE THROAT
   part of .... OROPHARYNX, NASOPHARYNX, LARYNGOPHARYNX
phase .... FORM, PART, SIDE, ANGLE, FACET, STAGE, STATE, ASPECT
Ph.D. applicant .... TESTEE
pheasant .... CHIR, MONAL, POULT, GROUSE, LEIPOA, RING-NECK, TRAGOPAN
   brood .... NYE, NID(E)
   Elliot's .... SYRMATICUS
   family .... NUMIDIDAE, PHASIANIDAE
   genus .... PAVO, PHASIANUS, ARGUS(IANUS)
   nest .... NIDE
   relative .... QUAIL, FRANCOLIN, PARTRIDGE
   Swinhol's .... LOPHURA
phenazopyridine ...... PAINKILLER
phenobarbital .... LUMINOL, SEDATIVE
   effect .... DIZZINESS, DROWSINESS
phenomenon .... EVENT, HAPPENING
phial .... VIAL, BOTTLE
philabeg .... KILT
philanderer: sl. .... WOLF, PLAYBOY, CASANOVA
philanthropic .... GENEROUS, ALTRUISTIC, CHARITABLE
philatelist's delight .... STAMP
Philip II's kingdom .... MACEDON
   naval fleet .... ARMADA
   son .... ALEXANDER(THE GREAT)
   wife .... OLYMPIAS, CLEOPATRA
Philip IV's enemies .... TEMPLARS
philippic .... SCREED, TIRADE, ORATION, DIATRIBE, HARANGUE, INVECTIVE
Philippine(s) abbot ...... MONGHE
   abode .... TAHANAN
   aborigine .... ATA, ATI, ITA, AETA, NEGRITO
   abyss .... BANGIN
   accident .... SAKUNA
   ace .... ALAS
   act .... GAWA
   activity/affair .... GAWAIN
   actor/actress .... BITUIN, ARTISTA
   adage .... KAWIKAAN

advantage .... BENTAHA
advice .... PAYO
afternoon .... HAPON
age .... TANDA, GULANG
aid .... ABULOY, TULONG
all .... LAHAT
alligator .... BUWAYA
ally .... ALYADO
almond .... PILI
alum .... TAWAS
American base (erstwhile) .... CLARK, SUBIC, CAVITE, OLONGAPO, SANGLEY POINT
amulet .... ANTING-ANTING
anchovy .... DILIS
anger .... GALIT
animal .... HAYOP, CARABAO, TAMARAW, TARSIER
answer .... SAGOT
ant .... LANGGAM
antidote .... LUNAS
ape .... BAKULAW, ORANG-UTAN
apostle .... ALAGAD
apple .... MANSANAS
archipelago .... SULU
ash .... ABO
aunt .... ALE, TIYA
baby .... BATA, SANGGOL
badge .... TSAPA
bag .... SUPOT
bakery .... PANADERYA
bamboo dance .... TINIKLING
barge .... CASCO, KASKO
barracks .... KUARTEL
bat .... PANIKI
battlesite, WW II .... BATAAN, CORREGIDOR
bay .... BALER, HONDA, ORMOC, SUBIC, ILIGAN, BALAYAN, TAYABAS
bear .... OSO
bell .... KAMPANA
bet .... TAYA, PUSTA
binoculars .... LARGABISTA
bird .... IBON, KULASISI
birthmark .... BALAT
blanket .... KUMOT
boat .... BATEL, BANGKA
book .... AKLAT, LIBRO
boss .... AMO
boy .... TOTOY
bread .... TINAPAY
breadfruit .... RIMA
brook .... BATIS
broom .... WALIS
brother/sister .... KAPATID
bucket .... TIMBA
buffalo .... CARABAO, KALABAW, TAMARAW, TIMARAU

bullet .... BALA
cabbage .... REPOLYO
cage .... HAWLA
can .... LATA
cannon .... LANTAKA
canoe .... BANCA
cape .... MAYO, LAMON, ENGAÑO, ILLANA, LIANGA, PUJADA, BOLINAO
capital .... MANILA, QUEZON CITY
cat .... PUSA
Catholic cardinal .... SIN, SANTOS
chair .... SILYA, UPUAN
channel ...... BASHI, MAQUEDA, BALINTANG, JINTOTOLO
charcoal .... ULING
cheer .... MABUHAY
chicken .... MANOK
chief .... HEPE
child .... ANAK, BATA
Chinese invader .... LIMAHONG
church ... IGLESIA, SIMBAHAN
cinema .... PELIKULA
circle .... BILOG
citizen ...... TAGALOG, PILIPINO
city/town .... IBA, BOAC, CEBU, JOLO, LIPA, NAGA, DAVAO, LAOAG, VIGAN, APARRI, BAGUIO, BONTOC, BUTUAN, CAVITE, ILAGAN, ILIGAN, ILOILO, LUCENA, MAKATI, TARLAC, ANGELES, BACOLOD, BALANGA, BANGUED, CALAMBA, DAGUPAN, LEGAZPI, MALOLOS, BATANGAS, CALBAYOG, COTABATO, LINGAYEN, OLONGAPO, TACLOBAN, ZAMBOANGA, CABANATUAN, TAGBILARAN, NAGUILIAN, SAN FERNANDO
civet .... MUSANG
clam .... TULYA
client .... SUKI
clock/watch .... RELOS
cloud .... ULAP
clown .... BUBO
cobbler .... SAPATERO
cockfight .... SABONG
coconut .... NIOG
   kind of .... MACAPUNO
   meat .... COPRA
   toddy .... TUBA
   young .... BUKO
coin .... PESO, BARYA, PESETA, SALAPI, CENTAVO, CENTIMO
condiment/spice .... REKADO
Congress .... KAPULUNGAN
contest .... TIMPALAK
contribution .... AMBAG

convict .... BILANGGO
cop .... PULIS
cork .... TAPON
corn .... MAIS
cotton .... BULAK
cough .... UBO
country .... BAYAN
court .... HUSGADO
cousin .... PINSAN
cow .... BAKA
coward .... DUWAG
cross .... KRUS
crow .... UWAK
dagger .... DAGA, PUNYAL,
BALISONG
dart .... PANA
day .... ARAW
dead .... PATAY
deaf .... BINGI
debt .... UTANG
decision .... PASIYA
decoy .... PAIN
decree .... BATAS
deer .... USA
depot .... BODEGA
devil .... DIABLO, DIMONYO
dew .... HAMOG
dialect .... WIKA, BICOL,
IBANAG, ILONGO, ILOCANO,
VISAYA, TAGAL(OG),
PAMPANGO, PANGASINAN,
WARAY-WARAY
diaper .... LAMPIN
discoverer of .... MAGELLAN
dissident .... HUK
dog .... ASO
door .... PINTO
dove .... KALAPATI
drama .... DULA
dress .... DAMIT
drink .... ALAK, BASI, TUBA,
VINO, CERVEZA, LUMBANOG
drum .... TAMBOL
duck .... BIBI, ITIK, PATO
dwarf .... AETA, UNANO,
NEGRITO
eagle .... AGILA
ear .... TAINGA
earth .... LUPA, MUNDO
east .... SILANGAN
eel .... IGAT
egg .... ITLOG
eggplant .... TALONG
ego .... AKO, SARILI
election .... HALALAN
error/mistake .... MALI
evening .... GABI
eye .... MATA
fabric .... PINA, JUSI, TELA,
RAMIE
fad .... USO, MODA

fairy .... DIWATA
falls .... PAGSANJAN
famous .... BANTUG
fan .... ABANIKO
farewell .... PAALAM
farm .... BUKID
farmer .... KASAMA,
MAGSASAKA
fat .... TABA
father ...... AMA, PAPA, PADRE,
TATAY
fear .... TAKOT
fee/rent .... UPA
fence .... BAKOD
fern .... PAKO
fetish .... ANITO
fever .... LAGNAT
fiber .... HEMP, JUSI, PINA,
ABACA, BUNTAL, MAGUEY
fish .... ISDA, DALAG, BACOCO,
BANGUS, TILAPIA, TULINGAN,
GALONGGONG
dried .... TUYO
sauce .... PATIS
smoked .... TINAPA
flag .... BANDERA, WATAWAT
flood .... BAHA
floor .... SAHIG, PALAPAG
flour .... ARINA
flower .... BULAKLAK
follower .... KAMPON
food .... PAGKAIN
staple ..... CORN, RICE, BIGAS
fool .... ULOL
foot .... PAA, PIYE
forefather .... NINUNO
forest .... GUBAT
fork .... TENEDOR
fort .... KUTA, COTTA
free .... LIBRE, MALAYA
freedom .... KALAYAAN
fruit .... BUNGA, PRUTAS
fruit tree .... CHICO, DUHAT,
GUAVA, DURIAN, LANGKA,
MANGGA, SANTOL, LANZONES,
SAMPALOK, TAMARIND
funeral .... LIBING
gag/joke .... BIRO
garbage .... BASURA
garlic .... BAWANG
gift .... REGALO
ginger .... LUYA
God .... DI(Y)OS
gold .... GINTO
goon .... MATON
grapes .... UBAS
grapefruit .... SUHA
grass .... DAMO, COGON,
SAKATE, TALAHIB
guard .... BANTAY
guava .... BAYABAS

guess .... HULA
guest/visitor .... BISITA
gulf .... MORO, DAVAO, LEYTE,
RAGAY, LAGONOY, LINGAYEN
hammock .... DUYAN
hand .... KAMAY
hardwood .... IPIL, NARRA,
YAKAL, MOLAVE
hat .... GORA, SOMBRERO
hawk .... LAWIN
head .... ULO
heart .... PUSO
heaven .... GLORIA
heir .... EREDERO
hell .... IMPI(Y)ERNO
hemp .... ABACA, ABAKA
hero .... BIDA, BAYANI
hero, national .... RIZAL,
MABINI, BONIFACIO,
AGUINALDO, LAPU-LAPU, ABAD
SANTOS
highest peak .... MOUNT APO
hobgoblin .... DWENDE
horse .... KABAYO
-drawn vehicle ...... CALESA,
CARRETELA, CARROMATA
hot springs .... ASIN, LOS
BANOS
house .... BAHAY
hunchback .... KUBA
ice .... YELO
income .... KITA
island .... CEBU, CUYO, BOHOL,
CORON, LEYTE, LUZON,
PANAY, SAMAR, CULION,
MACTAN, NEGROS, BABUYAN,
BASILAN, MASBATE, MINDORO,
PALAWAN, ROMBLON,
MINDANAO, TAWI-TAWI,
CORREGIDOR
island group .... BATAN,
SIBUTU, TURTLE, CAMOTES,
LAPARAN, SAMALES,
CALAMIAN
jackfruit .... LANGKA
jail .... KARSEL
jar .... BANGA
jewelry .... ALAHAS
jockey .... HINETE
juror .... HURADO
kettle .... KALDERO
key .... SUSI
kiss .... HALIK
kitchen .... KUSINA
knee .... TUHOD
knife .... BOLO, ITAK,
KUTSILYO
lake .... TAAL, LANAO,
LAGUNA DE BAY
lamb .... KORDERO
language .... ENGLISH,

Philippine(s)

TAGALOG, PILIPINO

lantern .... PAROL
law .... BATAS
lawyer .... ABOGADO
leech .... LINTA
lemon .... CALAMANSI
Lent .... KUWARESMA
leper colony .... TALA, CULION
library .... AKLATAN
light .... ILAW
lime .... DAYAP
lip .... LABI
liver .... ATAY
luck .... SUWERTE
lungs .... BAGA
mahogany .... NARRA,
KAMAGONG
maid .... ALILA, DALAGA
mail .... KOREO
box .... BUSON
carrier .... KARTERO
man/male .... LALAKI
mate/spouse .... ASAWA
mayor .... ALKALDE
measure .... CAVAN, CHUPA,
GANTA, SALOP
meat .... KARNE
dried, salted .... TAPA
medicine .... GAMOT
mendicant .... PULUBE
mental institution
.... MANDALUYONG
mermaid .... SIRENA
midwife .... HILOT
miracle ...... HIMALA, MILAGRO
mirror .... SALAMIN
monetary unit .... PESO
money .... KUWARTA
monkey .... UNGGOY
moon .... BUWAN
morning .... UMAGA
Moro boat .... LIPA, VINTA,
KUMPIT
chief .... DATO, DATU
Moslem .... MORO, MUSLIM,
MARANAW
mosquito .... LAMOK
moss .... LUMOT
mother .... INA, NANAY
mountain .... APO, PULOG,
HALCON, BANAHAW,
CANLAON, ARAYAT,
ZAMBALES, CABALASAN,
MALINDANG, SANTO TOMAS,
SIERRA MADRE, DIWATA,
CORDILLERA
mouse .... DAGA
municipality/town ..... BAYAN,
PUEBLO, MUNISIPYO
mystery/puzzle .... HIWAGA
myth .... ALAMAT

namesake .... TUKAYO
nation .... BANSA
national park .... LUNETA,
MOUNT APO
native .... MORO, IGOROT,
DUMAGAT, TAGALOG
naval base ...... SUBIC, CAVITE,
OLONGAPO
negrito .... ATA, ITA, AETA
news .... BALITA
newspaper .... DIARYO
no .... HINDI
none/nothing .... WALA
north .... NORTE, HILAGA
number ...... BILANG, NUMERO
one .... ISA
two .... DALAWA
three .... TATLO
four .... APAT
five .... LIMA
six .... ANIM
seven .... PITO
eight .... WALO
nine .... SIYAM
ten .... SAMPU
nut .... PILI
oil .... ACIETE, LANGIS
omelet .... TORTA
omen .... BABALA
orange .... KAHEL
oven .... HURNO
overseer .... KATIWALA
ox .... TORO
oyster .... TALABA
pail .... TIMBA
palace .... MALACANANG
palm .... PALAD
palm tree .... NIPA, ANAHAW
parent .... MAGULANG
parrot .... LORO
partridge .... PUGO
passenger .... SAKAY
peacock .... PABOREAL
peanut .... MANI
pear .... PERAS
peasant .... KASAMA
pencil .... LAPIS
person .... TAO
plum .... DUHAT
poem .... TULA
poison .... LASON
Pope .... PAPA
port .... CEBU, MANILA
president ...... ROXAS, AQUINO,
GARCIA, LAUREL, MARCOS,
RAMOS, OSMENA, QUIRINO,
MACAPAGAL, QUEZON,
MAGSAYSAY
prison .... MUNTINGLUPA
province .... ABRA, CEBU,
SULU, ALBAY, BOHOL, CAPIZ,

DAVAO, LANAO, LEYTE, RIZAL,
SAMAR, AGUSAN, BATAAN,
CAVITE, ILOILO, LAGUNA,
NEGROS, QUEZON, TARLAC,
BULACAN, CAGAYAN, ISABELA,
LA UNION, MASBATE,
MINDORO, PALAWAN,
ROMBLON, SURIGAO,
BATANGAS, COTABATO,
MOUNTAIN, PAMPANGA,
ILOCOS SUR, PANGASINAN,
ILOCOS NORTE
public transportation ...... BUS,
JITNEY, JEEPNEY
pugilist .... ELORDE
race driver .... MARCELO
rain .... ULAN
raincoat .... KAPOTE
raisin .... PASAS
rattan .... YANTOK
rebel .... HUK, KATIPUNAN,
INSURRECTO
resort .... TAGAYTAY
rice .... BIGAS, PALAY
variety .... MACAN, WAGWAG
ring .... SINGSING
river .... AGNO, ILOG, CHICO,
PASIG, AGUSAN, APARRI,
CAGAYAN, PULANGI,
MINDANAO
sailboat .... BATEL, PARAW,
VINTA
salt .... ASIN
sapodilla .... CHICO
sash .... BIGKIS
sausage .... LONGGANISA
scavenger .... BASURERO
Scriptures .... BIBLIA
sea ...... SULU, BOHOL, DAGAT,
SAMAR, CAMOTES, CELEBES,
SIBUYAN, VISAYAN
seaman .... MARINERO
servant .... ALILA, UTUSAN
shadow .... ANINO
sharecropper .... KASAMA
sheep .... TUPA, KARNERO
ship .... BAPOR, BARKO
shoes .... SAPATOS
shovel .... PALA
shrimp .... HIPON
silk .... SEDA
silver .... PILAK
sin .... SALA
sir .... GINOO
skirt .... SAYA, PALDA
sky .... LANGIT
slave/serf ..... ALIPIN, BUSABOS
snafu .... GULO
snail .... SUSO
snake .... AHAS
snob .... HAMBOG

soap .... SABON
society .... LIPUNAN
song .... AWIT, KANTA
soup .... CALDO, SABAW,
SOPAS
south .... SUR, TIMOG
souvenir .... ALAALA
soy sauce .... TOYO
specter .... MULTO, IMPAKTO
spider .... GAGAMBA
spinach .... TALINUM
spleen .... LAPAY
sponsor .... NINANG, NINONG,
MADRINA, PADRINO
spy .... TIKTIK
squid .... PUSIT
stateroom .... KAMAROTE
statesman .... RECTO, OSMENA,
QUEZON, ROMULO
stew .... NILAGA
stone .... BATO
story .... KUWENTO
strait .... LUZON, TANON,
TABLAS, MINDORO
street .... KALYE
suet .... SEBO
sugar .... ASUKAL
suitcase .... MALETA
sultanate .... SULU
summer capital .... BAGUIO
sun .... ARAW
sweet potato .... CAMOTE
sword .... SABLE
table .... MESA
tail .... BUNTOT
tailor .... SASTRE
taro .... GABI
tea .... CHA, TSA(A)
teacher .... MAESTRA,
MAESTRO
tear(drop) .... LUHA
tempest .... UNOS
termite .... ANAY
thatch .... ATIP, NIPA, COGON
theater .... DULAAN
thief .... TULISAN
thimble .... DEDAL
thread .... SINULID
tick .... PULGAS
tiff .... AWAY, LABAN
tomato .... KAMATIS
tongs .... SIPIT
tongue .... DILA
tooth .... NGIPIN
tree .... DAO, IPIL, ABETO,
LIGAS, YAKAL, ACACIA,
LANETE, MOLAVE, SAMPALOK
tribe .... ATI, LIPI
tribesman .... BADJAO, IGOROT,
TAUSUG, KALINGA, MARANAW,
NEGRITO, TINGGIAN

tripe .... GOTO
trousers .... PANTALON
turnip .... SINGKAMAS
turtle .... PAGONG
twins .... KAMBAL
typhoon .... BAGYO
uncle .... TIYO, AMAIN
vagrant .... LAGALAG
vegetable .... GULAY
village .... BARYO, NAYON,
SITIO
vinegar .... SUKA
volcano .... APO, TAAL,
MAYON, CANLAON, PINATUBO,
HIBOK-HIBOK
walkout .... WELGA
wall .... PADER
"walled city"
.... INTRAMUROS
water .... TUBIG
buffalo .... CARABAO
chestnut .... APULID
melon .... PAKWAN
well .... BALON
weapon .... BOLO, KRIS,
ARMAS, SANDATA, KAMPILAN
weasel .... MUSANG
weed .... DAMO
week day: Sunday
.... LINGGO, DOMINGO
Monday .... LUNES
Tuesday .... MARTES
Wednesday
.... MI(Y)ERKOLES
Thursday .... HUWEBES
Friday .... BI(Y)ERNES
Saturday .... SABADO
weight .... KILO, FARDO,
PICUL, QUINTAL, TONELADA
west .... KANLURAN
wheel .... GULONG
whip .... LATIKO
widow .... BIYUDA
wig .... PELUKA
wind .... HANGIN
wish .... NAIS
witch .... BRUHA
witness .... TESTIGO
wolf .... LOBO
woman/female .... BABAE
word .... SALITA
work .... TRABAHO
worm .... BULATE
yam .... UBI, GABI, TUGI
year .... TAON
yes .... OO, OHO, OPO
youth .... KABATAAN
zone .... POOK
philistine .... BABBIT
Philistine city .... GATH, GAYA,
GAZA

giant .... GOLIATH
Philo, dick .... VANCE
philology .... LINGUISTICS
philomel .... NIGHTINGALE
Philomela, sister of ...... PROCNE
philosopher .... HUME, KANT,
SAGE, ZENO, CYNIC, HEGEL,
LOCKE, PLATO, SKEPTIC,
SPINAGE
great .... PLATO, THALES,
ARISTOTLE, LEUCIPPUS,
DEMOCRITUS, EMPEDOCLES
"laughing" .... DEMOCRITUS
scientist .... THALES
stone of .... ELIXIR
philosophy ...... EGOISM, MONISM
abstract beings, in .... ENTIA
philter .... CHARM, POTION
phlebotome .... FLEAM, LANCET
phlegm is one .... HUMOR
phlegmatic .... COOL, DULL,
SLUGGISH, IMPASSIVE
phloem .... BARK, BAST, TISSUE
phlogistic .... INFLAMMATORY
phlogosis .... ERYSIPELAS
phobia .... FEAR, AGORA, HATRED
phocid .... SEAL
Phoebe .... MOON, DIANA, PEWEE,
PEWIT, SELENE, ARTEMIS,
GODDESS
Phoebus .... SOL, SUN, APOLLO
Phoenician capital .... TYRE,
SIDON
god .... BAAL, DAGON,
MOLOCH
goddess .... ASTARTE
princess .... EUROPA
Phoenix .... BENU
phone and zip .... CODES
call .... BUZZ, RING
cubicle .... BOOTH
emergency .... HOTLINE
system .... INTERCOM
system, part of
.... TRUNKLINES
phonetic .... ORAL, VOCAL,
SPOKEN
elision .... SLUR
phonetics, smooth .... LENE
phonics .... ACOUSTICS
phonograph .... VICTROLA,
GRAMAPHONE
needle .... STYLE, STYLUS
record .... DISC, PLATTER,
LONG-PLAY
record mold .... MASTER
with coin slot .... JUKE BOX
phony .... FAKE, SHAM, FLASE,
POSEUR, IMPOSTOR, SPURIOUS,
CHARLATAN
phosphate .... APATITE

photo ...... MUG, PIX, SHOT, SNAP, PIC(TURE)
finish .... STAT, DEAD HEAT
finishes .... GRAPHS, SYNTHESIS
light .... STROBE
solution .... HYPO, REDUCER
photocopy .... STAT
photograph .... FILM, SHOT, SNAP, PRINT, STILL, PICTURE
book .... ALBUM
enlarge a .... BLOW UP
photographer .... CAMERIST, SHUTTERBUG, SNAPSHOOTER
Adams .... ANSEL
fixing agent .... HYPO
Morath .... INGE
place of .... DARKROOM
test print of .... PROOF
word of .... SMILE, CHEESE
photographic camera .... CANON, KODAK, LEICA, REFLEX, BROWNIE, GRAFLEX, MINOLTA, OLYMPUS, POLAROID
equipment .... LENS, TIMER, CAMERA, FINDER, TRIPOD, SHUTTER, ENLARGER, FLASHGUN, FLASHBULB
prints, certain .... ROTOGRAPHS
result .... PICTURE, SNAPSHOT
solution .... HYPO, FIXER, TONER, REDUCER, DEVELOPER
photographs pieced together .... MOSAIC, MONTAGE
photography ...... ARTS, PICTURE-TAKING
word .... FOCAL
photoplay .... MOVIE, MOTION PICTURE
phrase .... CLAUSE, LOCUTION, EXPRESSION
applying to a celebrity ...... IN THE NEWS
dictator's .... IN RE
figuratively ..... SO TO SAY, AS IT WERE, IN A SENSE, SO TO SPEAK
in law .... IN REM
in liturgy .... PARSE
in song .... REFRAIN
listener's .... I SEE
meaning "about" ...... OR SO, MORE OR LESS
meaning "concerning" .... IN RE
on many dietary foods ...... FAT FREE, LESS SALT, ALL NATURAL, NO CHOLESTEROL
phraseology .... DICTION, WORDING, EXPRESSION
phratry .... CLAN, PHYLE

phrenetic .... WILD, INSANE, EXCITED, FANATIC, FRENZIED
phrenic .... MENTAL, NOETIC
phrenitis .... DELIRIUM
Phrygian king .... MIDAS
lunar god .... MEN
slave .... AESOP
phthisis .... CONSUMPTION, TUBERCULOSIS
phylactery .... CHARM, REMINDER
phyletic .... RACIAL, TRIBAL
Phyllis/Phillis .... SWEETHEART
phylloid .... LEAFLIKE
physic .... APERIENT, LAXATIVE, CATHARTIC, PURGATIVE
physical .... SOMAL, BODILY, NATURAL, SOMATIC, MATERIAL, ANATOMICAL
dimension ..... WIDTH, HEIGHT, LENGTH
direction .... UP AND DOWN, BACK AND FORTH, LEFT AND RIGHT
discomfort .... DYSPHORIA
examination .... CHECKUP
science .... GEOLOGY, PHYSICS, ASTRONOMY, CHEMISTRY
therapy, kind of ..... MASSAGE, EXERCISE, HEAT TREATMENT
vigor .... ENERGY, VITALITY
physician ...... MD, MAYO, GALEN, DOC(TOR), LISTER, MEDIC(O), MESMER, SURGEON
former .... LEECH
second century AD .... GALEN
symbol .... CADUCEUS
physicist ...... OHM, HAHN, MACH, RABI, BOYLE, CURIE, FERMI, AMPERE, EINSTEIN
physics, branch of .... OPTICS, STATICS, DYNAMICS, KINETICS, ACOUSTICS, MECHANICS
Nobelist .... RABI, CURIE, BRAUN, FERMI, RAMAN
preceder .... NNE
physiognomy .... FACE
phytology .... BOTANY
pi ...... MIX UP, JUMBLE, MIXTURE
follower .... RHO
piacular .... SINFUL, WICKED, ATONING, EXPIATORY
pianist .... ANDA, HESS, ITURBI, LEVANT, CLIBURN, LIBERACE
Claudio from Chile .... ARRAU
kind of .... CONCERT
White House .... NIXON, TRUMAN
piano .... SOFT(LY), SPINET
favorite .... NOLA
forerunner .... CLAVICHORD

grand .... BABY, PARLOR, CONCERT
in music .... SOFT
key .... IVORY
keyboard .... CLAVIER
skill in playing the .... PIANISM
small, upright .... PIANETTE
pianolike instrument .... SPINET, CELESTA, CLAVICHORD
piaster, 1/120 **of** .... ASPER
piazza .... PORCH, ARCADE, SQUARE, GALLERY, PORTICO, VERANDA(H)
pibroch instrument ...... BAGPIPE
pica .... TYPE
picador's prey ...... BULL, TORO
picaresque .... ROGUISH
character .... VAGABOND
picaroon .... ROGUE, THIEF, PIRATE, ADVENTURER
Picasso, painter .... PABLO
picayune .... CHEAP, PETTY, PALTRY, TRIVIAL, TRIFLING
Piccadilly Circus figure .... EROS
piccolo .... FLUTE
pick .... BEST, CULL, ELITE, GLEAN, PLUCK, CHOOSE, NIBBLE, PECKER, SELECT, CHOICE(ST), MANDREL, MATTOCK
at .... NAG, FINGER
-me-up .... TONIC
on .... ANNOY, TEASE
over .... CULL
the .... ELITE
up .... LEARN, IMPROVE
up the pieces .... RECOVER
pickax .... GURLET, MATTOCK
Pickens of films .... SLIM
pickerel .... PIKE
amphibian .... GREEN FROG
weed .... HERB
picket .... PALE, POST, FENCE, GUARD, STAKE, PATROL, TETHER, STRIKER
station of a .... OUTPOST
pickiness .... CHOOSINESS
pickings .... SCRAPS, SPOILS
pickle ...... FIX, JAM, ALEC, CORN, DILL, MESS, ACHAR, BRINE, SOUSE, GHERKIN, MARINADE
pickled ...... TREATED, PRESERVED
food/meat .... SOUSE
pepper picker .... PETER
slang .... DRUNK, INTOXICATED
pickles .... RELISH
pickling solution .... BRINE, SOUSE, MARINADE
picklock .... THIEF, BURGLAR
pickpocket .... DIP, PRIG,

CUTPURSE
trainer .... FAGIN
working place of ..... CROWDS
picky .... CHOOSY, PARTICULAR
picnic ...... EAT, JUNKET, OUTING,
COOKOUT, CLAMBAKE
area .... GROVE
author of .... INGE
game .... HORSESHOES,
VOLLEYBALL
visitor .... ANT
picot .... PURL
picotee .... CARNATION
pictograph .... (HIERO)GLYPH
pictorial .... VIVID, GRAPHIC,
ILLUSTRATED
picture ...... IMAGE, PHOTO, PRINT,
SLIDE, STILL, SCENE(RY),
DEPICT, SKETCH, DRAWING,
IMAGINE, REFLECT, TABLEAU,
LIKENESS, PAINTING
composite .... MONTAGE
frame .... EASEL
girl .... PIN-UP, CHEESECAKE
in words .... DESCRIBE,
DELINEATE
life .... STILL
moving .... FILM, MOVIE,
CINEMA
of many images ..... MONTAGE
of the Last Supper .... CENA
person's .... PORTRAIT
pertaining to a .... ICONIC
poorly painted .... DAUB
puzzle .... REBUS
section .... ROTO
show .... MOVIE, CINEMA
tube .... KINESCOPE
wall .... MURAL
picturesque .... VIVID, QUAINT,
SCENIC, GRAPHIC, IDYLLIC,
STRIKING
piddle .... DABBLE, TRIFLE,
URINATE
piddling .... PETTY, USELESS
pidgin .... JARGON, CHINOOK
pie .... PATE, TART, PASTY, PATTY,
JUMBLE, PASTRY, COBBLER,
DUMPLING
baker .... OVEN
covering .... CRUST, MERINGUE
cracker .... GRAHAM
cut, shape of .... WEDGE
deer's vitals .... HUMBLE
eyed .... DRUNK
faced .... MOONFACED
filling .... APPLE, PECAN,
PEACH, RAISIN, CHERRY,
MINCEMEAT
piebald .... PIED, HORSE, PINTO,
CALICO, DAPPLED

piece ...... BIT, CHIP, HUNK, PART,
CHUNK, SCRAP, SLICE,
CANTLE, COLLOP, MORSEL,
SLIVER, PORTION, FRAGMENT,
SPLINTER
burlesque .... SKIT
de resistance .... ENTREE,
MAIN EVENT
of cake .... A CINCH
candy .... DROP
eight .... REAL
evidence .... CLUE
marble .... SLAB
news .... ITEM
one's mind .... SCOLDING
soap .... CAKE
the rock .... SLAB
turf .... SOD, DIVOT
wood .... PANEL, SPLAT
together .... PATCH
worker .... JOBBER
piecemeal .... GRADUALLY,
PARTIALLY, BIT BY BIT,
SEPARATELY
piecen .... SPLICE
pieces, go to .... COLLAPSE
pied .... MOTTLED, PIEBALD,
SPOTTED, VARIEGATED
-a-terre .... LODGING,
FOOTHOLD
Pied Piper .... MAGICIAN
Piper's river .... WESER
Piper's town .... HAMELIN
Piedmont .... PIEMONTE
city .... OSTI, TRINO, TURIN
native of .... PIEDMONTESE
ruling family .... SAVOY,
SAVOIE
village .... MARENGO
pieplant .... RHUBARB
pier .... ANTA, DOCK, MOLE,
QUAY, SLIP, JETTY, JUTTY,
WHARF, LANDING, PILASTER
architectural .... ANTA
glass .... MIRROR
landing .... DOCK, JETTY
rectangular .... ANTA
space .... SLIP
support .... PILES, COLUMNS
pierce .... BORE, GORE, STAB,
CHILL, DRILL, LANCE, GRIDE,
GOUGE, PRICK, PUNCH, SPEAR,
THIRL, WOUND, IMPALE,
THRUST, PUNCTURE,
PENETRATE
piercing .... KEEN, ACUTE, SHARP,
BITING, SHRILL, CUTTING,
CHILLING, INCISIVE
pieridine .... BUTTERFLY
Pierre .... PETER, PIETRO
piers, space between .... SLIP

piet .... OUSEL, OUZEL, MAGPIE
pietist .... DEVOTEE
piety .... FAITH, BELIEF,
DEVOTION, HOLINESS
exaggerated .... PIETISM
piffle .... GAS, ROT, WIND, HOKUM,
HOGWASH, TWADDLE
pig .... HOG, SOW, PORK(ER),
DUROC, SHOTE, SWINE,
GRUNTER, JACOBIN
animal like .... PECCARY
castrated .... BARROW
disease .... BULLNOSE
80 to 189 lbs. weight
.... SHOAT
famous ...... ARNOLD, BIG RED,
LOUISA, WILBUR, SALOMEY,
NAPOLEON, PORKY PIG, MISS
PIGGY
feature .... SNOUT
feet of .... TROTTERS
female .... SOW, GILT
female that has given birth
.... FARROWED
51 to 79 lbs. weight
.... FEEDER
for slaughter .... FATLING
intestines .... CHITTERLINGS
iron .... INGOT
like a .... PIGGISH
litter .... FARROW
little .... PIGGY, PIGLET
male .... BOAR
nursing .... PIGLET
190 to 240 lbs. weight
.... MARKET
out .... OVEREAT
pen/paddock .... STY
slang .... SLOB, GLUTTON
vital organs .... HA(R)SLET
wild .... BOAR
young .... ELT, GILT, GRICE,
SHOAT, SHOTE, PIGLET,
WEANER
pig's eye, in a .... NEVER
pigboat .... SUBMARINE
pigeon .... NUN, BARB, DOVE,
RUFF, PIPER, CULVER, PIDGIN,
POUTER, TURBIT, FANTAIL,
TUMBLER
_____ .... TOED
call .... COO
carrier .... HOMING
crested .... TRUMPETER
hawk .... MERLIN
house .... (DOVE)COTE,
COLUMBARY
ID tag .... LEGBAND
neck feathers .... HACKLE
pea .... DAL
slang .... DUPE, PUSHOVER

tumbler .... ROLLER
walk like .... TOE IN
wood .... CUSHAT, RINGDOVE
young .... PIPER, SQUAB
pigeonhole .... SHELVE,
CUBBYHOLE
pigfish .... GRUNTER
piggery .... STY
piggin .... PAIL, PIPKIN
piggish .... FILTHY
piggyback .... PICKABACK
pigheaded .... STUBBORN,
OBSTINATE
piglet .... GILT
pigment .... DYE, BICE, COLOR,
SMALT, STAIN, UMBER,
ZAFFER, ZAFFRE, ETIOLIN,
GAMBOGE, STAINER,
CINNABAR, ORPIMENT
absence of .... ALBINISM,
ALPHOSIS, LEUCODERMA
black .... MELANIN
blood's .... HEMACHROME
bluish green .... VIRIDIAN
brown .... SEPIA, UMBER,
BISTER, BISTRE, SIENNA
calico printing .... CANARIN
coal tar ...... MAUVE, MADDER,
ANILIN(E), ALIZARIN
cuttlefish .... SEPIA
grayish-blue/green .... BICE
red .... CARMINE, CINNABAR,
VERMILION
reddish brown .... SIENNA
skin tissue .... MELANIN
soot .... BISTER, BISTRE,
LAMPBLACK
without .... ALBINO
yellow .... OCHER, OCHRE,
ETIOLIN, FLAVIN(E), RETINENE,
QUERCETIN
pigmentation .... DISCOLORATION
comb. form .... CHROMAT(O)
dark .... MELANISM
pigmy. See **pygmy**
pignus .... PAWN, PLEDGE,
CONTRACT
pigpen .... STY
sound .... OINK, GRUNT(LE),
SQUEAL
pigs' feet .... PETTITOES
litter .... TEAM, FARROW
pigskin .... SADDLE, FOOTBALL
pounce .... TACKLE
pigsticker .... POCKETKNIFE
pigtail .... CUE, BRAID, PLAIT,
QUEUE, COLETA, TOBACCO
pigweed .... AMARANTH
pika .... CONY, HARE, LAGOMORPH
pike .... FISH, GATE, PICK,
LUCE(T), PIERCE, MOUNTAIN,

PICKEREL, SPONTOON, TOLL
ROAD, SPEARHEAD
collection .... TOLL
full-grown .... LUCE
like fish .... GAR, ROBALO,
ARAPAIMA
perch .... SAUGER
piked .... PEAKED, POINTED
piker: sl. .... MISER, TIGHTWAD,
CHEAPSKATE
pilaster ...... ANTA, PIER, ALETTE,
COLUMN
groove .... STRIA
top of .... CAPITAL
Pilate .... PONTIUS
realm of .... JUDEA
pilau/pilaw .... PILAF(F)
pilchard .... FUMADO, HERRING,
PILCHER, SARDINE
pilcher .... SCABBARD
pile ...... NAP, HEAP, LOAD, MASS,
RICK, HOARD, SPILE, STACK,
EDIFICE, BUILDING,
CONGERIES, STRUCTURE
driver .... RAM, TUP, MAUL,
OLIVER
fabric .... NAP
hay .... MOW, RICK, STACK
on .... RUN UP
slang .... MONEY, FORTUNE
up .... AMASS
pileous .... HAIRY
piles .... HEMORRHOIDS
pileus .... (SKULL)CAP
pilewort .... CELANDINE
pilfer .... COP, ROB, FILCH, MICHE,
MOOCH, STEAL, SWIPE,
THIEVE, SHOPLIFT
pilferage .... THEFT
pilferer .... THIEF
pilgrim .... ALDEN, IHRAM,
PALMER, DEVOTEE, PIONEER,
WANDERER, WAYFARER,
SOJOURNER
badge of .... SCALLOP
bottle of .... COSTREL
destination of .... ROME,
MECCA, SHRINE, JERUSALEM
Fathers .... SETTLERS
garment of .... IHRAM
leaders ..... JOHN SMITH, MILES
STANDISH
protector .... TEMPLAR,
CRUSADER
pilgrimage .... HADJ
pilgrims, Indian friend of
...... MASSASOIT, WAMPANOAG
settlement .... PLYMOUTH
ship of .... MAYFLOWER
traveling together
.... CARAVAN

Pilgrim's Progress author
.... BUNYAN
pill .... BOLUS, DRAGEE, PELLET,
PILULE, TABLET, CAPSULE
kind of: sl. .... UPPER,
DOWNER
like a .... PILULAR
slang .... BORE, GOOFBALL
vet's/big .... BOLUS
pillage .... LOOT, SACK, FORAY,
HARRY, RIFLE, SPOIL, STRIP,
MARAUD, RAPINE, RAVAGE,
PLUNDER
pillar ...... LAT, PIER, POST, STELE,
COLUMN, OBELISK, SUPPORT,
MAINSTAY, MONUMENT
combining form .... STYL
of ____ .... FIRE, SMOKE,
STELAR, STRENGTH
of Hercules .... GIBRALTAR,
JEBEL MUSA
projecting ring .... CINCTURE
sitter .... STYLITE
support .... PEDESTAL
tapering .... OBELISK
top inhabitant .... STYLITE
top of .... IMPOST
with figure .... TELAMON,
ATLANTES, CARYATID
writing on .... GRAFFITO
pillbox .... HAT
pillory .... YOKE, CANGUE,
GIBBET, STOCKS
pillow .... PAD, BOLSTER,
CUSHION, HEADREST
covering .... SLIP, TICK
covers .... SHAM
fight .... ROMP
slip .... CASE
stuffing .... CEIBA, KAPOK,
COTTON, FEATHERS
pilose .... HAIRY, HIRSUTE
pilot .... LEAD, FLYER, GUIDE,
AVIATOR, CONDUCT,
HELMSMAN, STEER(SMAN)
biscuit .... CRACKER,
HARDTACK
cow .... PINTANO
fish .... REMORA
lifesaver for .... CHUTE,
PARAFOIL
milieu of .... SKY
place of .... COCKPIT
stove .... SWITCH
student .... CADET
test flight .... SOLO
wear of .... WINGS
pilotless plane .... DRONE, GLIDER
piloua .... HAIRY
Pilsudski, president .... JOSEF
pilule .... PILL

pilum .... SPEAR
Pima .... COTTON, INDIAN
pimento .... (ALL)SPICE
   spread .... CHEESE
pimiento .... PEPPER, RELISH,
                        PAPRIKA
pimola .... OLIVE
pimp ...... PANDER(ER), PROCURER
   occupation of .... PIMPERY
pimpernel .... PRIMROSE
pimple .... BOIL, POCK, WHEAL,
     WHELK, PAPULE, BLEMISH,
        PUSTULE, CARBUNCLE
   scar .... POCK
pin .... FID, NOG, PEG, ACUS,
     BOLT, COAG, LILL, NAIL,
     TACK, BADGE, DOWEL, RIVET,
     BODKIN, BROOCH, COTTER,
     FASTEN, TOGGLE, TRIFLE,
              FASTENER
   buckle's .... TONGUE
   colloquial .... LEG
   cotter .... KEY
   down .... BIND, HOLD, NAIL
   firing .... TIGE
   flatheaded .... TACK
   gunwale/oar .... THOLE
   in bowling .... CLUB
   meat-cooking .... SPIT,
        BROACH, SKEWER
   metal .... RIVET
   money .... ALLOWANCE
   pivot .... PINTLE
   -up .... CHEESECAKE
pina .... PINEAPPLE
pinaceous tree .... FIR, PINE,
                  CEDAR
pinafore .... SLIP, TIER, APRON,
      DICKEY, SAVE-ALL
   initials for .... HMS
pinball worry .... TILT
pince-nez .... LORGNON,
           EYEGLASSES
pincer ...... CLAW, CHELA, TONGS,
     NIPPER, PLIERS, FORCEPS,
       GRIPPER, TWEEZER
   movement, in a way .... SIEGE
pinch ...... NIP, BITE, HURT, RAID,
     CRAMP, FILCH, GRIPE, PUGIL,
     STEAL, ARREST, STRESS,
     SQUEEZE, DISTRESS
   and twist .... TWEAK
   hit .... SUBSTITUTE
   in a .... HARDSHIP
   of something .... BIT, DASH
pincher .... TWEAKER
pindaric .... ODE, EPODE
pine .... LONG, MOPE, CEDAR,
     CRAVE, KAURI, KAURY,
     OCOTE, PINON, WASTE,
     YEARN, CONIFER, LANGUISH,

     LOBLOLLY, PONDEROSA
   board/wood .... DEAL
   cone .... STROBILE
   disease .... RUST, BLISTER
   fruit .... CONE
   leaves .... NEEDLES
   nut/seed .... PINON
   Pacific .... HALA
   product/ooze .... RESIN,
                GALIPOT
   resin .... DAMMER
   siskin .... FINCH
   tar extract .... RETENE
   tree, kind of .... CHIR
   wild .... PINASTER
Pine Tree State .... MAINE
pineapple .... PINA, ANANA
   plantation .... PINERY
   slang .... BOMB,
         (HAND)GRENADE
   topknot .... COMA
pinfold .... POUND
ping pong .... TABLE TENNIS
   racket .... BAT, PADDLE
pinguid .... FAT, OILY, GREASY,
     FERTILE, UNCTUOUS
pinion .... WING, PENNON,
     FEATHER, SHACKLE,
          COGWHEEL
pink .... SHIP, STAB, PRICK,
     RADICAL, FOXHUNTER
   become .... PINKEN
   color/shade ...... ROSY, CORAL,
     DAMASK, SALMON
   lady .... COCKTAIL
   turn .... BLUSH
Pinkerton .... DETECTIVE,
        PRIVATE EYE
pinkie .... SHIP, FINGER
pinkish red skin blemish
   .... STORK BITE, SALMON
           PATCHES
Pinkster .... WHITSUNTIDE
   flower .... AZALEA
pinna .... EAR, FIN, WING,
   AURICLE, FEATHER, LEAFLET
pinnace .... BOAT
pinnacle .... ACME, PEAK, CROWN,
       SPIRE, SUMMIT
   of ice .... SERAC
pinnae .... FINS
pinner .... HEADDRESS
pinniped ...... SEAL, WALRUS, SEA
               LION
   feet of .... FLIPPERS
pinnule .... LEAFLET
pinny .... PINAFORE
pinochle .... (CARD)GAME
   action .... MELD
   deck, card not in .... TREY,
     DEUCE, CINQUE, QUATRE

   game like .... BEZIQUE
   lowest cards .... NINES
   score .... DIX
   term .... DIX, MELD, KITTY
pinole .... FLOUR
pinon .... NUT, PINE
pinpoint .... DOT, LOCATE
pins and needles .... PARESTHESIA
   or pence .... TEN
pinscher .... DOG, DOBERMAN
pint, ¼ .... NOGGIN, QUARTERN
½ .... SPLIT
pintado .... CERO, SIERRA,
            KINGFISH
pintail .... DUCK, SMEE, GROUSE
pintano .... FISH, COWPILOT
pintle .... PIN, BOLT
pinto .... PONY, MOTTLED,
     PIEBALD, SPOTTED
pinweeds .... LECHEA
pinwheel, noisy action of
   .... WHIRRING
pinworm ...... ASCARID, ASCARIS
Pinza, operatic singer .... EZIO
Pinzon's caravel .... PINTA
pioneer .... PAVER, PLANTER,
            SETTLER
   farm implement .... DEERE
pious .... GODLY, DEVOUT,
   SACRED, SAINTLY, RELIGIOUS
   feeling .... PIETISM
   person .... PIETIST
pip .... HIT, PEEP, ROUP, SEED,
          SPOT, CHIRP
pipa .... TOAD
pipal .... (BO)TREE, FIG TREE
pipe .... FLUE, HUB(B), TUBE,
     BRIAR, BRIER, CHALAM,
     DUDEEN, CALUMET, WHISTLE
   air .... VENTIDUCT
   bending tool .... HICKEY
   bowl leaving .... DOTTEL,
            DOTTLE
   collar of .... FLANGE
   curve of .... OFFSET
   down .... SHUT UP
   fitting .... TEE
   Irish .... DUDEEN
   joint .... ELL
   joint ring .... GASKET
   line .... SOURCE, CONTACT
   musical .... OAT, FIFE, FLUTE
   nozzled .... HOSE
   oriental .... REED, HOOKAH,
          NARG(H)ILE
   part .... BOWL, STEM
   peace .... CALUMET
   player .... FLUTIST
   principal .... MAIN
   run-off .... DRAIN
   shape .... BULLDOG, FULL-BENT

shaped .... TUBULAR
shepherd's .... OAT, REED,
                              LARIGOT
small .... TUBULE, PIPETTE
smoke .... TEWEL, HOOKAH,
               CALUMET, NARGILE
smoker, at times .... TAMPER
steam .... RISER
tobacco .... CHIBOUK
tobacco bag .... POUCH
up .... SAY, SPEAK
pipefish .... GAR
pipelike .... TUBATE
piper .... TRILLER
   actress .... LAURIE
piping ...... FOLD, REEDY, SHRILL,
     HISSING, SIZZLING, TRIMMING
   bird .... PLOVER
   hot .... BOILING
   joint .... ELL
pipit .... (TIT)LARK
pipkin .... POT, PIGGIN
pippin .... SEED, APPLE
pipsqueak .... SNIP
pipy .... SHRILL
piquancy .... NIP, ZEST
piquant .... RACY, SALTY, SHARP,
    SPICY, BITING, PUNGENT,
                     STINGING
pique .... VEX, PEEVE, STING,
    EXCITE, FABRIC, NETTLE,
    OFFEND, OFFENSE, PROVOKE,
              RESENTMENT
piqued .... IRATE
piracy .... ROBBERY
   literary .... PLAGIARY,
                  PLAGIARISM
piragua .... BOAT, CANOE,
                  PIROGUE
Pirandello .... LUIGI
piranha .... FISH, CARIBE, PIRAYA
pirate .... XEBEC, SEA-RAT,
    CORSAIR, SEAWOLF,
    (SEA)ROVER, MARAUDER,
    PICAROON, PRIVATEER,
              FREEBOOTER
   arm .... CUTLASS
   famed .... KIDD, DRAKE,
    MORGAN, ROGERS, CORNISH,
              BLACKBEARD
   flag .... (JOLLY)ROGER
   literary .... PLAGIARIST
   ship .... FRIGATE, PICAROON,
    PRIVATEER, BRIGANTINE
   state .... TUNISIA
pirn .... SPOOL, BOBBIN
pirogue .... CANOE, PIRAGUA
Pisa feature .... TOWER
   river .... ARNO
Pisan .... ITALIAN
piscatorial abode ...... AQUARIUM

Pisces .... FISH(ES)
piscine egg .... ROE
   lore name .... WALTON
Pisgah's biblical climber
    .... MOSES
   summit .... NEBO
pishu .... LYNX
pismire .... ANT, EMMET
pisolite .... LIMESTONE
piss .... URINE, URINATE
Pissarro, Fr. painter
    .... CAMILLE
pistachio .... NUT, CASHEW
pistil, part of ...... OVARY, STIPE,
    STYLE, CARPEL, STIGMA
pistol .... DAG(G), LUGER,
    MAUSER, ZIP GUN, FIREARM,
    HANDGUN, (SIDE)ARM,
    REPEATER, REVOLVER,
    AUTOMATIC, DERRINGER
   case .... HOLSTER
   chamber .... MAGAZINE
   slang .... GAT, ROD, HEATER,
    EQUALIZER, PEACEMAKER
pistole .... COIN
piston .... VALVE, PLUNGER
pit .... GAP, HOLE, HELL, SCAR,
    SEED, TRAP, WELL, ABYSS,
    ARENA, FOVEA, GRAVE,
    SNARE, STONE, ARROYO,
    CAVITY, CRATER, POTHOLE,
             POCK(MARK)
   bottomless ...... ABYSS, CHASM
   for draining or storing
    liquids .... SUMP
   in anatomy .... FOSSA
   mine .... SUMP
   peach/plum .... PUTAMEN,
                 ENDOCARP
   theater .... PARQUET
pita .... AGAVE, FIBER, BROCKET
pitch .... KEY, SHY, TAR, CANT,
    CAST, HURL, REEL, ROLL,
    SWAY, TOSS, ERECT, FLING,
    LURCH, RESIN, SET UP,
    THROW, ENCAMP, PLUNGE,
    ASPHALT(UM), BITUMEN
   a complete game .... GO THE
                   ROUTE
   black .... PICEOUS
   in .... CONTRIBUTE
   in golf .... CHIP, LOFT
   indicator .... CLEF
   musical .... DIAPASON
   salesman's .... LINE, PLUG,
             SPIEL, PATTER
   uncompleted .... BALK
pitchblende ingredient
    .... URANIUM
pitcher .... JUG, EWER, OLLA,
    TOBY, CARAFE, HURLER,

    TOSSER, THROWER
   and catcher .... BATTERY
   aspiration of .... NO HIT
   crime of .... BALK
   goal of .... OUTS
   Gooden .... DWIGHT
   Hershiser .... OREL
   Koufax .... SANDY
   leaf .... ASCIDIUM
   left-handed .... SOUTHPAW
   Marichal .... JUAN
   Perry .... GAYLORD
   pitch of .... CURVE, TWIRL,
    SLIDER, SPITTER, BEANBALL,
    KNUCKLER, SPITBALL,
             KNUCKLE BALL
   plant ...... EVE'S CUP, FLYTRAP
   plate of the .... BOX, SLAB,
                  MOUND
   preparatory motion of
    .... WINDUP
   relief .... FIREMAN
   Ryan .... NOLAN
   Seavers .... TOM
   stat. .... ERA
   Welch .... BOB
pitching niblick ...... IRON, GOLF
                    CLUB
pitchman .... HAWKER
pitchy .... DARK, BLACK
piteous .... PITIFUL, PATHETIC
pitfall .... GIN, SNAG, TRAP, SNARE
pith ...... CORE, GIST, MEAT, PULP,
    MARROW, MEDULIA,
              SUBSTANCE
Pithecan-thropine .... APEMAN
Pithecanthropus erectus
    .... JAVA MAN
pithecoid .... SIMIAN
pithless .... WEAK
pithy .... TERSE, CONCISE,
   LACONIC, POINTED, FORCEFUL
pitiable .... MEAN, PALTRY,
                DEPLORABLE
pitiful .... MEAN, PITEOUS,
    PATHETIC, WRETCHED
pitiless .... CRUEL, RUTHLESS
pitman .... MINER
pittance .... BIT, ALMS, DOLE,
    STIPEND, ALLOWANCE
pitted .... STONED, FOVEATE
pitter-patter .... PITAPAT,
                DRUMBEAT
Pittsburgh rooter .... PIRATE FAN
pituitary hormone .... PROLACTIN
   secretion .... MUCUS,
              HORMONE
pity .... MERCY, SYMPATHY,
             COMPASSION
pivot .... SLUE, TURN, HINGE,
    WHEEL, PINTLE, STATOR,

SWIVEL

on one's _____ .... HEEL

pivotal .... CRUCIAL, CARDINAL

pixilated .... DRUNK, LOOPY,
    BEMUSED, BEDEVILED,
    POSSESSED

pixy .... ELF, IMP, FAIRY, SPRITE

pixyish .... ELFIN, IMPISH

Pizzaro's conquest .... PERU

pizzicato .... PLUCKED

placard .... BILL, SIGN, POSTER

placate .... PACIFY, SOOTHE,
    APPEASE, MOLLIFY

colloquial .... BUTTER UP

placatory .... CONCILIATORY

place .... PUT, SET, LIEU, RANK,
    ROOM, SITE, SPOT, LOCUS,
    POINT, SPACE, STEAD,
    LOCALE, REGION, APPOINT,
    LOCATION, POSITION,
    PREMISES, STANDING

accurately .... TRUE

apart .... ENISLE, ISOLATE,
    SEGREGATE

between .... INTERPOSE

Blue Ribbon .... FIRST

busy .... HIVE

camping .... ETAPE, BIVOUAC

city's .... PLAZA, SQUARE

dancing ..... CASINO, CABARET,
    BALLROOM

down under .... CELLAR,
    BASEMENT

drafty .... BARN

first .... EDEN

for a coin .... SLOT

a dance .... BARN

a hero .... DELI

a padlock .... HASP

a pigskin .... GRID

aging .... VAT

bargains .... FLEA MARKET

bric-a-brac .... ETAGERE

clinging things .... VINERY

coal .... BIN

eggs .... NEST

eleves .... ECOLE

exes .... RENO

fans .... ARENA, STADIUM

outerwear .... CLOAKROOM

races .... OVAL

relics .... SEPULCHER

rubbish .... DUMP

tankers: abbr. .... SPT

trees .... ARBOR

"trois" .... MENAGE

white water .... RAPIDS

for: suffix .... ORIA

gambling .... CASINO

hiding .... DEN, MEW, LAIR,
    CACHE, HANGOUT, HIDEOUT

ideal .... UTOPIA

in a wall .... NICHE

an envelope .... ENCLOSE

office .... INSTALL

proximity/next to .... APPOSE

inside .... INSERT

like Camp David ..... RETREAT

mat .... DOILY

meeting .... TRYST,
    RENDEZVOUS

of .... LIEU, STEAD

abode .... HOME, HOUSE,
    DWELLING, RESIDENCE

accused in court .... DOCK

agony .... GOLGOTHA

confusion/noise

.... MADHOUSE

honor .... PEDESTAL,
    HEADTABLE

oblivion .... LIMBO

offering .... PARATORIUM

penitence .... CANOSSA

rapid growth .... HOTBED

refreshment .... OASIS

religious seclusion

.... ABBEY, PRIORY,
    CONVENT, CLOISTER,
    NUNNERY, MONASTERY

reputed fabulous wealth

.... ELDORADO

safety .... HAVEN, ASYLUM,
    (ASYLA-PL.), HARBOR,
    REFUGE, SANCTUARY

torment .... GEHENNA

trial .... VENUE

worship .... ALTAR

out of .... ILL-TIMED

pea .... POD

resting .... PARK BENCH

rough .... SEAM

secret/secluded ..... DEN, MEW,
    NOOK, HIDEOUT, RETREAT

set in .... POSIT, SITUATE

side by side .... COLLOCATE

snugly .... ENSCONCE

stopping .... HOSTEL

storage ..... CRIB, SILO, CACHE,
    DEPOT, CELLAR, CLOSET,
    WAREHOUSE

take .... OCCUR, HAPPEN,
    TRANSPIRE

that has had its dey .... TUNIS,
    TRIPOLI

to caulk .... SEAM

lie, bad ...... WITNESS STAND

remember .... ALAMO

see stars .... PLANETARIUM

stand on .... POU STO

trading .... MART, MARKET,
    EXCHANGE

under water .... IMMERSE,

SUBMERGE

where an artist starves

.... ATTIC

beer is served ...... TAPROOM

bones meet .... JOINT

placid ...... CALM, QUIET, SERENE,
    PEACEFUL, TRANQUIL,
    IMPASSIVE

placket .... POCKET

plagiarism .... CRIB, PIRACY

plagiarist .... THIEF

plagiarize ...... CRIB, LIFT, STEAL,
    PIRATE

plagiarized phrase

.... PEACOCK'S FEATHER

plague ...... VEX, ANNOY, HARRY,
    TEASE, HARASS, HECTOR,
    PEST(ER), WANION, MURRAIN,
    SCOURGE, TORMENT,
    CALAMITY, NUISANCE

plagued .... BESET

plagues, one of the .... LOCUST

plaice .... SOLE, (FLAT)FISH,
    FLOUNDER

plaid .... MAUD, TARTAN

plaidman .... TARTAN,
    HIGHLANDER

plain .... BARE, FLAT, MERE,
    OPEN, CAMPO, CLEAR, LEVEL,
    LLANO, HOMELY, PATENT,
    SIMPLE, EVIDENT, OBVIOUS,
    CAMPAGNA, PALPABLE

barren, high .... PARAMO

dweller .... GAUCHO, LLANERO,
    LOWLANDER

grassy .... CAMPO, LLANO,
    VELD(T), PRAIRIE, SAVANNA(H)

high ..... MESA, WOLD, WEALD,
    PARAMO

hill on a .... BUTTE

ingenuous .... GUILELESS

one .... JANE

spoken .... BLUNT, FRANK,
    CANDID

treeless .... WOLD, VELD(T),
    PAMPAS, PARAMO, STEPPE,
    TUNDRA, SAVANNA(H)

vast arid .... STEPPE

Plains, _____ .... DES

Indian .... KIOWA, PAWNEE

plainsman .... WESTERNER

plaint ...... GRIPE, LAMENT(ATION)

plaintiff .... SUER, USEE, ORATOR,
    SUITOR, ACCUSER, LITIGANT,
    DEMANDANT, COMPLAINANT

answer of .... REPLICATION

list of wrongs .... LIBEL

withdrawal of case

.... NONSUIT

plaintive .... SAD, FRETFUL,

WISTFUL, MOURNFUL

plait ...... PLY, PLAT, PLEX, BRAID, PLEAT, QUEUE, TRESS, PLEACH, WIMPLE, PIGTAIL

plaited .... BRAIDED, PLICATE

gass/leaves .... SENNIT

trimming .... RUCHE

plan ...... AIM, MAP, PLAT, DRAFT, ETTLE, DESIGN, INTEND, SCHEMA, SCHEME, SKETCH, OUTLINE, PROJECT

artful .... MACHINATION

for a proposed journey .... ITINERARY

for deceiving enemy in war .... STRATAGEM

of action .... IDEA, DEVICE

secretly to commit a crime .... PLOT, CONNIVE, CONSPIRE

spoiler .... MARPLOT

townsite .... PLAT

planch(e) .... BOARD, FLOOR

plancher .... PALLET

plane .... EVEN, FLAT, GLIDE, GRADE, LEVEL, SMOOTH, AIRFOIL, SURFACE

controversial .... SST

curve .... ELLIPSE

inclined .... RAMP

instruments on .... ALTIMETERS

lane .... RUNWAY

smoothing .... TROWEL

swift .... SST

10-sided .... DECAGON

tree .... CHINAR, PLATAN

war .... MIG, SPAD, ZERO, STUKA, NAPIER, SABREJET, SPITFIRE, SUPERFORT

planet ...... MARS, EARTH, PLUTO, VENUS, PALLAS, SATURN, URANUS, JUPITER, MERCURY, NEPTUNE

fastest .... MERCURY

largest .... JUPITER

minor .... ASTEROID

Mork's .... ORK

most brilliant .... VENUS

movement of .... LIBATION

red-colored .... MARS

ringed .... SATURN

satellite .... MOON, RHEA, DIONE, MIMAS, DEIMOS, HESTIA, NEREID, PHOBAS, UMBRIEL

secondary .... MOON

shadow of .... (PEN)UMBRA

smallest .... MERCURY

planetoid .... ASTEROID

planetarium .... ORRERY

plank .... DECK, BOARD, SLATE,

POLICY, FLOORING, PRINCIPLE

curve of .... SNY

or way .... GANG

planks above keel .... DEADWOOD

planoblast .... JELLYFISH

plant. See also **shrub** .... SOW, HERB, MILL, TREE, WORT, AROID, BUGLE, ORACH, SHRUB, STOCK, CLOVER, HYSSOP, FACTORY, FREESIA, PLANTAIN

a tap .... BUG

aconite .... MONKSWOOD, WOLFSBANE

agave .... PITA

air ..... MOSS, LICHEN, ORCHID, EPIPHYTE

Alpine .... BISTORT, EDELWEISS

amaranth .... COCKSCOMB

amaryllis .... CRINUM, EUCHARIS

and animal life .....BIOS, BIOTA

appendage .... STIPEL, STIPULE, TENDRIL

arum family ..... JACK-IN-THE-PULPIT

Asiatic .... RAMIE

axis ..... STEM, STALK, CAUDEX

banana .... ABACA, CANNA, PLANTAIN

base .... CAUDEX, CAULIS

beetle .... SCARAB, ROSEBUG, (COCK)CHAFER

biblical .... TARE, HYSSOP

bitter .... RUE

blue-flowered .... BLUET, LUPINE

body .... THALLUS

branch .... TWIG, SPRAY, SPRIG

breathing pore .... STOMA

broom .... SPART

bud .... (S)CION

bug .... CHINCH

bulb .... SEGO, GARLIC, SQUILL, JONQUIL, ATAMASCO, NARCISSUS

bursting .... PUFFBALL

cabbage-like .... KALE

cactus .... CEREUS, MESCAL, SAGUARO

capsule .... POD

carbohydrate ..... PENTOSAN(E)

carrot family ...... DILL, ANISE, CONIUM, CUM(M)IN, ERINGO, ERYNGO, CHERVIL, COWBANE, HEMLOCK, CORIANDER

celery family .... CARROT

century .... ALOE, AGAVE, MAGUEY

chili .... CAPSICUM

classification .... LINNEAN

climbing .... YAM, VINE, LIANA, LIANE, RATTAN, RUNNER, SCAMMONY

clinging part of .... TENDRIL

cloverlike ..... MEDIC, MELILOT

composite family .... ASTER, DAISY, COSMOS, DAHLIA, YARROW, MILFOIL, COREOPSIS, DANDELION, SUNFLOWER

covering .... PEAT, TUNIC, ARMATURE

creeping ...... PYXIE, IPOMOEA, GROUNDLING, PERIWINKLE

crow family .... COLUMBINE, HELLEBORE

crowfoot family .... HEPATICA, MOUSETAIL

cruciferous .... CRESS, MUSTARD

cutting .... SLIP

cycad family .... COONTIE

cyperaceous .... SEDGE

daisylike .... OXEYE

decay .... ROT, NECROSIS

delicate .... FERN, MOSS

disease ..... BLET, BUNT, CURL, ESCA, GALL, RUST, SCAB, SMUT, WILT, BRAND, ERGOT, SCALD, BLIGHT, CANKER, MILDEW, MOSAIC, YELLOW, ERINOSE, ICTERUS, (BLACK)ROT, CLUBROOT, NECROSIS, PSOROSIS

dry climate .... CACTUS, XEROPHYTE

dwarf .... ALYSSUM

dye .... ANIL

eating animal .... HERBIVORE

eating aquatic mammal .... DUGONG, MANATEE

emetic .... IPECAC

environment .... HABITAT

experimental garden .... NURSERY

exudation .... GUM, LAC, COPAL, RESIN

feature .... STOLON

fiber .... FLAX, HEMP, JUSI, PITA, SUNN, ABACA, AGAVE, ISTLE, RAMIE, SISAL, MAGUEY

figwort .... COLLINSIA

firmly .... EMBED

floating .... LOTUS, WATER LILY

flowering .... ROSE, CALLA, ORCHID, RHODORA, ACANTHUS

flowerless .... FERN, LICHEN, LYCOPOD

fluid .... SAP, MILK, LATEX

fodder .... VETCH, LENTIL,

forage .... GUAR
form, habitat .... ECAD
fossil .... CALAMITE,
                HORSETAIL
foundation .... TAPROOT
fragrant .... ANISE, BASIL,
    THYME, HYSSOP, ANGELICA,
      CAMOMILE, MARJORAM,
    TARRAGON, (SPEAR)MINT
fungus .... ERGOT
garden .... ORACH(E)
gentian .... CENTAURY
genus .... ARUM, AGAVE,
                ERINGO
geranium .... ALFILARIA
ginger family .... CURCUMA,
                TURMERIC
goosefoot .... BEET, SPINACH
gourd .... CANTALOUPE,
           (MUSK)MELON
gout medicine .... GUACO
grass .... AVENA
grasslike .... RUSH
growing from inside
    .... ENDOGEN
growing in solutions, science
    of .... HYDROPHONICS
growing within another
    .... ENDOPHYTE, ENTOPHYTE
growth on a .... GALL
gumbo .... OKRA
hair .... VILLUS
hairlike growth .... BRISTLE,
      PRICKLE, TRICHOME
hairy-leafed .... ANCHUSA
heath .... ERICA, AZALEA,
                LAUREL
hemp .... CANNABIS
herbaceous .... LOBELIA,
                PLANTAIN
honeysuckle family ..... ELDER
insect/louse ...... APHID, APHIS,
                SCALE
insect-catching .... FLYTRAP
insect-eating .... CARNIVORE
iris family .... IXIA, ORRIS,
                CROCUS
juice .... SAP, MILK
kind of .... ANNUAL
kingdom part .... PHYLUM
leaf, poisonous .... JABORANDI
leguminous .... PEA, GUAR,
          DERRIS, LENTIL
lice genus .... APHIS
life .... FLORA, VEGETATION
lilaceous .... LEEK, SEGO,
           ONION, TULIP
lily family .... ALOE, LEEK,
    LOTUS, ONION, YUCCA,
    ALLIUM, CAMAS(S), GARLIC,

SAINFOIN
NERINE, SQUILL, ASPHODEL,
    HELLEBORE, SABADILLA
madder .... CHAY, BLUET,
    COFFEE, IPECAC, CINCHONA,
    GARDENIA, HOUSTONIA
male .... MAS
mallow family .... HIBISCUS,
    HOLLYHOCK, CHECKERBLOOM
marsh .... CATTAIL
material spread around
    .... MULCH
matter, decaying .... PEAT
meadow .... INNOCENCE
medicinal .... RUE, ALOE,
    HERB, SENNA, TANSY, URENA,
    ARNICA, IPECAC, SIMPLE,
    SPURGE, BONESET, GENTIAN,
    LOBELIA, PENNY ROYAL
menthaceous .... OREGANO
milkweed family .... STAPELIA
milkwort family .... SENEGA
milky liquid .... LATEX
mint family .... SAGE, BASIL,
    BUGLE, CLARY, THYME,
    BETONY, CATNIP, COLEUS,
    HENBIT, HYSSOP, SALVIA,
    DITTANY, MONARDA,
    OREGANO, BERGAMOT,
    LAVENDER, MARJORAM,
    ROSEMARY, GERMANDER,
    PATCHOULI, FRAXINELLA
moor .... HEATHER
mosslike .... LICHEN,
    LIVERWORT, TILLANDSIA
mulberry .... CONTRAYERVA
mushroom-like .... PUFFBALL
mustard .... COLE, KALE, RAPE,
    WOAD, CRESS, STOCK, RADISH,
    ALYSSUM, CABBAGE,
    MADWORT, CHARLOCK,
                CRUCIFER
narcotic .... HEMP, POPPY,
    HASHISH, MARIJUANA
nettle family .... HEMP,
                PELLITORY
nightshade family .... POTATO,
    PETUNIA, SOLANUM, TOBACCO
non-flowering .... FERN
not native .... EXOTIC
noxious .... WEED, TARE
odorous .... BUGBANE
oil .... RAPE, BENNE, RAMTIL
one-celled .... PROTIST
onion family .... CHIVE
onion-like .... CEPA
ornamental .... CLARY,
                BEGONIA
palmlike .... CYCAD
parasite .... APHID, BLIGHT,
                LICHEN
parasitic ..... DODDER, ORCHID,

MISTLETOE
parsley family .... CICELY,
                SANICLE
pea family .... DHAL, GRAM,
    SENNA, VETCH, INDIGO,
    LEGUME, LUPINE, ALFALFA,
    LENTIGO, LICORICE,
    LOCOWEED, COCKSHEAD
pepper .... KAVA, BETEL,
    CAYENNE, CAPSICUM
perennial .... IRIS, OXLIP,
    SEDUM, THYME, CROCUS,
    DAHLIA, DOGBANE,
           COLUMBINE
pest .... CHINCH
phlox family .... JACOB'S
                LADDER
pink .... CAMPO, CAMPION,
    DIANTHUS, CARNATION
pith .... PULP
pithy .... SOLA
poisonous ..... LOCO, ACONITE,
    HEMLOCK, HENBANE,
          WOLFSBANE
poppy family ..... BLOODROOT,
    CELANDINE, CHICALOTE
pore .... STOMA, LENTICEL
potato family .... DATURA
potherb .... ORACHE
prickly .... BRIER, CACTUS,
    NETTLE, TEASEL, BRAMBLE,
           THISTLE
primrose family .... OXLIP,
    COWSLIP, FUCHSIA,
    CYCLAMEN, MARIGOLD
ragweed .... BURDOCK,
          COCKLEBUR
ramie .... RHEA
receptacle .... TORUS
red-sapped .... BLOODROOT
reedlike, sweet-smelling
    .... CALAMUS
rheumatism medicine
    .... GUACO
rock .... MOSS, LICHEN,
    STONECROP, LITHOPHYTE
Rocky Mountain .... PINON
root .... EDDO, RADIX
edible ..... MANIOC, CASSAVA
fragrant .... ORRIS
ointment .... NARD
purgative .... JALAP
rose family .... AVENS,
    BENNET, BURNET, DROPWORT,
    SHADBUSH, CINQUEFOIL, FIVE-
    FINGER, POTENTILLA
rudimentary .... EMBRYO
rue family .... LIME, LEMON,
            ORANGE
runner .... STOLON
rushlike .... SEDGE

sacred .... RAGTREE

salad .... ENDIVE, CHICORY,
(WATER)CRESS

salty soil .... HALOPHYTE

saxifrage .... MITERWORT

scale .... PALEA, SQUAMA

sea .... ENALID

sea animal resembling
.... SPONGE

sea-bottom .... BENTHOS

secretion .... GUM, RESIN

sedge .... PAPYRUS

seed .... HERB

seed case .... POD

seed yielding oil .... BENNE,
SESAME

seedless .... FERN

sensitive .... MIMOSA

sesame .... TIL, TEEL

shoot .... LAYER, (S)CION,
SPRIG

shoots .... ASPARAGUS

single-seeded .... PSORALEA

slang ..... TRAP, DECOY, TRICK,
SWINDLE

smelly .... RUE, TANSY,
YARROW, BUGBANE, BURDOCK,
FIGWORT, HENBANE, MILFOIL,
MULLE(I)N, RAFFLESIA,
STINKWEED

soap .... AMOLE

spiny .... CACTUS

sprout .... SPIRE

stalk .... STEM, SPIRE,
HA(U)LM, CAULIS

stand .... JARDINIERE

starch .... CORN, TARO,
MANIOC, POTATO, CASSAVA

stem .... AXIS, BINE, CORM,
HA(U)LM, CAUDEX, CAULIS

stem joint .... NODE

stem spongy center .... PITH,
MEDULLA

stinging .... NETTLE

stunted .... SCRAG

stunter .... HERBICIDE

suckers .... APHID

sun-turning .... HELIOTROPE

swamp ..... COWSLIP, DIONAEA,
MARIGOLD

swelling on .... BLEB

syrup-yielding .... SORGHUM

tendril .... CIRRUS

thistlelike .... ARTICHOKE

thorny .... ROSE, BRIAR, BRIER,
BRAMBLE, WAIT-A-BIT

threadlike part .... TENDRIL

tissue .... XYLEM

tissue cavity .... LOCULUS

trained to grow flat
.... ESPALIER

trifoliate .... SHAMROCK

tropical ..... UDO, PALM, TARO,
CYCAD, BANANA, CLEOME,
PAPAYA, RAMTIL, CASSAVA,
LANTANA, QUASSIA,
MANGROVE, PLANTAIN

trumpet .... BIGNONIA

tumor .... GALL

twining .... IPOMOEA

underwater .... BENTHOS,
HORNWORT

used in religious ceremonies
.... HYSSOP

vegetable .... CELERY,
TOMATO, ARTICHOKE,
CAULIFLOWER

verbena family .... VERVAIN

violet family .... PANSY

water ...... ALGA(E), FANWORT,
PAPYRUS, SEAWEED,
HYDROPHYTE

with aromatic seeds
.... ANISE, CUMIN

bulblike root .... TUBEROSE

edible root .... SKIRRET

edible stalk .... CARDOON

fragrant root .... ORRIS

fragrant seed .... ANISE

fruit .... BEARER

heart-shaped flowers
.... DICENTRA

no seeds .... FERN

perennial stem ..... ACROGEN

pungent pods ...... CAPSICUM

sun-turning flowers
.... TURNSOLE, HELIOTROPE

trumpet-shaped flower
.... SEGO, BIGNONIA

underground buds
.... GEOPHYTE

woody .... BUSH

woody tissue .... XYLEM

yielding fruit .... BEARER

yielding hashish .... CANNABIS

young .... SAPLING

yuccalike .... SOTOL

Plantae's counterpart
.... ANIWALIA

plantain .... WEED, RIBWORT,
FLEAWORT

fruit .... BANANA

spike .... CHAT

plantation ...... BOWERY, COLONY,
ESTATE, HACIENDA

boss of yore .... MASSA

cacti .... NOPALRIE

coffee .... FINCA

fictional .... TARA

kind of .... COFFEE, COTTON,
RUBBER, SUGAR CANE

Scarlett O'Hara's .... TARA

planter .... SOWER, SEEDER,
PIONEER, COLONIST

planting tool .... DIBBLE, SEEDER

plantlike animal .... CORAL,
SPONGE, ZOOPHYTE

plants, book on .... HERBAL

collector of .... HERBALIST

of .... VEGETAL

scourge of .... BLIGHT,
LOCUSTS

stand for .... JARDINIERE

study of .... PHYTOLOGY

where sold .... NURSERY

plantsman .... FLORIST

plaque .... BADGE, BROOCH,
TABLET

relative of a .... MEDAL

plash .... POOL, PUDDLE

plasma .... WHEY, QUARTZ,
PROTOPLASM

plaster .... DAUB, COMPO, COVER,
GROUT, SMEAR, PARGET,
STUCCO, OVERLAY

bandage .... SPICA

cement .... PUTTY

cover with .... CEIL

first coat .... RENDER

for broken limb .... CAST

mustard .... SINAPISM

of _____ .... PARIS

of Paris .... YESO, GESSO,
GYPSUM, STUCCO, HYDRATE

smoothing tool .... TROWEL

wall .... STUCCO

plastered: sl. .... DRUNK

plasterwork .... PARGET,
SCAGLIOLA

plastic .... VINYL, FICTILE,
PLIABLE, STYRENE, FLEXIBLE,
NEOPRENE

art .... CERAMICS, MODELING,
SCULPTURE

clay .... PUG

material .... LIGNIN, LUCITE,
MORTAR, FORMICA

synthetic .... BUNA, NYLON,
LUCITE, FORMICA, BAKELITE

wrap .... SARAN

plastid .... CELL

plastron .... DICKEY,
BREASTPLATE, SHIRT FRONT

plat .... MAP, PLAN, BRAID,
CHART, PLAIT

Plata river city ...... MONTEVIDEO

plate ...... COAT, DISC, DISH, DISK,
PATIN(A), SCUTE, SHARD,
LAMINA, LAMELLA, OVERLAY,
PLATTER

armor .... TASSE

baseball .... (HOME)BASE

battery .... GRID

bony/horny .... SCUTE, SCUTUM
dental .... BRIDGEWORK, FALSE TEETH
Eucharist .... PATEN
hot .... STOVE
hurler's .... DISCUS
metal .... LAME
metal cooking .... GRIDDLE
metallic .... PATEN
ship-shaped .... NEF
with brass .... BRAZE
with zinc .... GALVANIZE
plateau ...... MESA, PUNA, KAROO, DEGREE, ALTIPLANO, TABLELAND
top cover .... ICECAP
plated .... COATED, ARMORED
platelet .... SCUTUM
platelike organ .... LAMELLA
platen .... ROLLER
plater .... NAG, HORSE
platform .... BEMA, ARENA, DOLLY, STAGE, STOOP, SOLLAR, BALCONY, ESTRADE, GALLERY
ancient .... SOLEA
article .... PLANK
car .... FLATCAR
election .... HUSTINGS
engineroom .... CATWALK
floating .... RAFT
food-drying .... FLAKE
for execution .... SCAFFOLD
fort's gun .... BARBETTE
kind of .... SKID, ALTAR, HUSTINGS, POLITICAL
on wheels .... TRUCK
painter's .... SCAFFOLD
politician's .... STUMP, HUSTINGS
portable .... PALLET
principle .... PLANK
raised .... DAIS, STAND, PODIUM, PULPIT, TRIBUNE
revolving .... TURNTABLE
ship's .... DECK, MAINTOP, CROW'S NEST
speaker's .... ROSTRUM, TRIBUNE
streetcar .... VESTIBULE
platina .... PLATINUM
platinum .... ORE, PLATINA
-blonde actress .... HARLOW
symbol .... PT
platitude .... MAXIM, CLICHE, TRUISM, BROMIDE
platitudinous .... DULL, STALE, TRITE
platoon leader .... LIEUTENANT
unit .... SQUAD

Platoon director .... STONE
Plato's dialogue .... ION
school .... ACADEME
work .... CRITO, PHAEDO, APOLOGY, REPUBLIC, DIALOGUES, SYMPOSIUM
platter .... DISC, DISH, TRAY, PLATE, RECORD, SALVER, (HOME)BASE, TRENCHER
platyhelminth .... FLUKE, FLATWORM, PLANARIAN, TREMATODE
platypus .... DUCKBILL
plaudit .... PRAISE, ACCLAIM, OVATION, APPLAUSE
plausible ...... CREDIBLE, SPECIOUS
play ...... ACT, FUN, TOY, BET(ON), GAME, IDLE, LARK, DALLY, FRISK, SPORT, FROLIC, GAMBLE, GAMBOL, TRIFLE, COMPETE, PERFORM, RECREATE, (MELO)DRAMA
a part .... PERSONATE
a role .... EMOTE
actors in a .... CAST, PERSONAE
amateurs' .... DRAMATICS
around .... GAD
at love .... DALLY, FLIRT
award-winning .... STATE OF THE UNION, DEATH OF A SALESMAN, THE SKIN OF OUR TEETH, THE TIME OF YOUR LIFE
backer of .... ANGEL
between acts .... INTERLUDE
bridge .... FINESSE
by ear .... AD LIB, IMPROVISE
dilemma in a .... NODE, NODUS
direction .... ENTER, ACTION
down .... MINIMIZE
famous morality .... EVERYMAN
fast and loose .... DALLY, TRIFLE
first performance .... PREMIERE
for one actor ..... MONOLOGUE
for stakes .... GAMBLE
grandstand .... STUNT
heroine .... PREMIERE
host .... TREAT
introduction .... PROLOGUE
joke on .... RAG
on words .... PUN, QUIBBLE
orchestral reeds .... BLOW SAXOPHONES
part in a .... BIT, ROLE
part of a .... ACT, ACT I, ACT II, ACT IV, ACT III, SCENE

possum .... DEAD, FEIGN, PRETEND
silent .... PANTOMINE
successful .... HIT
the beau .... GALLIVANT
the game ..... FIT IN, CONFORM
the lead .... STAR
the violin .... FIDDLE
tricks on .... JAPE
truant .... MICHE
unsuccessful .... BOMB, TURKEY
up .... ADVERTISE
up to .... BUTTER, SOFT-SOAP
with fire .... DARE, RISK, GAMBLE
wrong card .... RENIG
playa .... BASIN, BEACH, SHORE
playboy .... GADABOUT, SENSUALIST, MAN-ABOUT-TOWN
Playboy bunny .... HOSTESS
Club founder .... HEFNER
player .... ACTOR, MUMMER, ACTRESS, GAMBLER, THESPIAN, COMPETITOR, CONTESTANT
at dealer's right .... PONE
baseball .... BATTER, BASEMAN, CATCHER, PITCHER, SHORTSTOP, INFIELDER, OUTFIELDER
basketball .... GUARD, CENTER, FORWARD
contest .... VIER, DUELIST, ENTRANT
football .... END, CENTER, TACKLE, FULLBACK, HALFBACK, QUARTERBACK
fraudulently substituted in a competition .... RINGER
incompetent .... DUB, PALOOKA
links .... GOLFER
match .... RIVAL
music .... SINGER, DRUMMER, FLUTIST, PIANIST, MINSTREL, INSTRUMENTALIST
performing arts ...... ARTIST(E)
piano .... NICKELODEON
sports .... JOCK, BOXER, ATHLETE, PUGILIST, PRIZEFIGHTER
unwilling to sign contract .... HOLDOUT
who cuts the cards .... PONE
with lowest score .... BOOBY
players' position .... LINEUP
playful .... MERRY, FRISKY, JOCOSE, PRANKISH, SKITTISH, SPORTIVE, KITTENISH

545

playground .... OVAL, PARK, ARENA, FIELD, SANDLOT
baseball .... DIAMOND
basketball/tennis .... COURT
billiard .... PARLOR, POOL HALL
boxing .... RING, CANVAS
football .... GRIDIRON
golf .... LINKS, COURSE
item .... SLIDE, SWING
skating .... RINK
playing card(s) extra .... JOKER
shuffle .... RIFFLE
spot .... PIP
suit .... CLUBS, HEARTS, SPADES, DIAMONDS
playing field .... OVAL, PARK, ARENA, DIAMOND, GRIDIRON
playlet .... SKIT, SKETCH
playroom .... NURSERY
plays collectively .... DRAMA
performed by amateurs .... DRAMATICS
plaything .... TOY, PAWN, BAUBLE, TRIFLE, TRINKET
playwright .... DRAMATIST
ploy of .... ASIDE
Williams .... EMLYN
plaza .... MART, MARKET, SQUARE
plea .... APPEAL, EXCUSE, PRAYER, REQUEST, ENTREATY, PETITION, ALLEGATION
bargain .... NEGOTIATE
for dismissal .... DEMURRER
pleach .... PLAIT, (INTER)LACE, INTERTWINE
plead ...... BEG, SUE, PRAY, URGE, ARGUE, STATE, ALLEGE, APPEAL, ENTREAT, IMPLORE
in law .... SHOW
in protest .... REMONSTRATE
pleader .... ADVOCATE, PARACLETE
pleading, act of .... SUIT
pleasant .... GAY, NICE, MERRY, GENIAL, AFFABLE, AMIABLE, FRIENDLY, AGREEABLE, ENJOYABLE
and cheerful .... ALL SMILES
existence .... LIFE OF EASE
place .... SUNNY SIDE OF THE STREET
weather .... SUNNY
Pleasant Island .... NAURU
pleasantries .... AMENITIES, CIVILITIES
pleasantry .... WIT, JOKE, BANTER
please ...... SUIT, ELATE, DELIGHT, GLADDEN, GRATIFY, INDULGE, PRITHEE, SATISFY
pleased .... GLAD, HAPPY,

THRILLED, CONTENTED
pleasing .... NICE, ROSEATE, PLEASANT, AGREEABLE
pleasure .... JOY, WILL, WISH, BLISS, GRACE, CHOICE, LIKING, RELISH, COMFORT, DELIGHT, ECSTASY, ENJOYMENT
boat .... BARGE, YACHT, CRUISER
carriage .... SURREY
craft harbor .... MARINA
ground .... RESORT, PLEASANCE
pursuit of .... HEDONISM
seeker .... PLAYBOY, HEDONIST, PLAYGIRL, SYBARITE
slang .... KICKS
trip .... JUNKET, OUTING
voyage .... CRUISE
pleat .... FOLD, PLAIT, SHIRR, CREASE, GATHER, RUFFLE, PLICATE
pleated .... PLICATE
pleating .... GOFFER, GAUFFER
plebe .... FROSH, FRESHMAN
plebeian .... COARSE, COMMON, VULGAR, ILL-BRED
plebiscite .... REFERENDUM
plebs .... MASSES
plectron .... PLECTRUM
plectrum .... PICK, QUILL, PLECTRON
pledge .... VOW, BOND, GAGE, HEST, OATH, PAWN, WORD, SWEAR, TOAST, TOKEN, ENGAGE, PAROLE, PIGNUS, PLIGHT, DEPOSIT, EARNEST, HOSTAGE, PROMISE, SPONSION
slang .... HOCK
pledged .... BOUND, SWORN
pledget .... WAD, SWAB, DOSSIL, DRESSING
pledgor .... PAWNER
Pleiades, eldest of the ...... MAIA
one of the ...... MAIA, MEROPE, ALCYONE, CELAENO, ELECTRA, STEROPE, TAYGETA
parent of ...... ATLAS, PLEIONE
Pleione's daughter .... MAIA, PLEIAD, STEROPE, TAYGETA
husband .... ATLAS
plenary .... FULL, ABSOLUTE, COMPLETE
plenipotentiary .... FULL, ENVOY, PLENARY, AMBASSADOR
plenitude .... FULLNESS
plenteous .... COPIOUS, ABUNDANT
plentiful .... FULL, RIFE, AMPLE, COPIOUS, REPLETE,

ABUNDANT, BOUNTIFUL
plenty .... ENOW, AMPLE, ENOUGH, WEALTH, OPULENCE
plenum .... FULL(NESS)
opposite of .... VACUUM
pleon .... TELSON
pleonasm .... NIMIETY, TAUTOLOGY, VERBOSITY, REDUNDANCY
pleonastic .... REDUNDANT
plessor .... HAMMER, PLEXOR
plethora .... EXCESS
plexor .... PLESSOR
plexus .... RETE, RETIA, NETWORK
pliable .... PLIANT, PLASTIC, SUPPLE, FLEXIBLE, MALLEABLE
plice .... FOLD
pliers .... CLAMP, PINC(H)ERS
plight .... ENGAGE, PLEDGE, BETROTH, DILEMMA, TROUBLE, CONDITION, SITUATION
plinth .... BASE, ORLO, BLOCK, SOCLE
PLO leader ...... (YASSER)ARAFAT
plod ...... SLOG, STEP, TOIL, WALK, DRUDGE, TRUDGE, PERSIST
plop .... DROP, PLUMP
plot .... LOT, MAP, DRAW, PLAN, PLAT, CABAL, CHART, FIELD, PATCH, SCHEME, DIAGRAM, OUTLINE, CONSPITE, INTRIGUE, MACHINATE, CONSPIRACY
of story/play .... NODE, SCENARIO
plottage .... AREA
plotter .... CABAL, SCHEMER, INTRIGANT(E), INTRIGUER, MACHINATOR
plotters group .... CABAL
plough .... PLOW
ploughshare .... CO(U)LTER
plover .... PEWIT, STILT, LAPWING, DOTT(E)REL, KILLDEER, SURFBIRD, SANDPIPER
bird like .... TURNIX
kin of ...... BUSTARD, COURSER
plow .... DIG, ROVE, TILL, TURN, BREAK, LIST(ER), FURROW, PLOUGH
blade .... SHARE, CO(U)LTER
land .... ARABLE
part .... SOLE, SHARE, SLADE, CLEVIS, SHE(A)TH
pullers .... OXEN
through .... WADE
plowed land .... ERD, ARADO, FURROW
plowman .... RUSTIC, TILLER
shoe of .... CLODHOPPER

plowshare part ...... MOLDBOARD
ploy .... RUSE, MANEUVER,
STRATEGY, STRATAGEM
business .... MERGER
pluck ...... TUG, GRIT, GUTS, PICK,
NERVE, SPUNK, STRUM,
AVULSE, TWANG, VALOR,
SPIRIT, TWEEZE, COURAGE,
DEPLUME, PULL(OUT),
STAMINA, SWINDLE,
FORTITUDE
slang .... FLEECE
plucky .... GAME, BRAVE, SPUNKY
plug .... NAG, TAP, WAD, BUNG,
CORK, PLOD, QUID, SLOG,
DOWEL, SHOOT, SPILE,
DOSSIL, PLATER, SPIGOT, STOP
UP, PLUNGER, STOPPER,
PUBLICIZE, ADVERTISEMENT
absorbent .... TAMPON
colloquial .... LINE, PITCH
for wound .... DOSSIL, TAMPON
gun .... TAMPION, TOMPION
in radio/TV .... COMMERCIAL
of dirt .... COMEDO
slang .... BLURB, PROMO,
COMMEND
tobacco .... PERIQUE
ugly .... GOON, HOOD, THUG,
ROWDY, TOUGH, TERROR,
RUFFIAN, GANGSTER
wind instrument .... FIPPLE
with a spigot .... SPILE
plugger, kind of .... BARKER,
PRESS AGENT
plum .... GAGE, KAKI, SLOE,
DRUPE, FRUIT, PRIZE, RAISIN,
TROPHY, FREESTONE
brandy .... SLIVOVITZ
cake .... BABA, PUDDING
color .... PURPLE, VIOLET,
LAVENDER
common .... GRAVY TRAIN
disease .... BLACKKNOT,
BLACKRUST
family .... ROSE
fleshy part of .... MESOCARP
fruit like .... LOQUAT,
PERSIMMON
Java .... LOMBOY
pit of .... PUTAMEN, ENDOCARP
powdery coating .... BLOOM
small .... DAMSON,
DAMASCENE
stone .... NUTLET
variety .... GREENGAGE
wild .... SLOE, BULLACE
plumage .... DOWN, PLUME,
FEATHERS
plumb ...... ERECT, PROBE, SOUND,
FATHOM, VERTICAL

bob .... PLUMMET
colloquial .... WHOLLY,
UTTERLY, ENTIRELY,
DOWNRIGHT
plumbago .... LEAD, GRAPHITE
plumbeous .... LEADEN
plumber .... (GAS)FITTER,
PIPEFITTER
concern of .... AIRTRAP
helper of .... PLUNGER
tool of .... SNAKE, WRENCH
plumbing device .... ELL, PIPING,
TUBING
plumbum .... LEAD
plume ...... DOWN, CREST, EGRET,
QUILL, AIGRET, FEATHER,
MARABOU, PLUMAGE
helmet .... PANACHE
heron's .... AIGRET(TE)
plummet .... DROP, FALL, PLUMB,
PLUNGE
plumose .... FEATHERED
plump .... FAT, PLOP, BUXOM,
FUBSY, PLUNK, PUDGY,
ROUND, STOUT, CHUBBY,
BLUNT(LY), ROTUND
and short .... ROLY-POLY
plumule .... BUD, FEATHER,
PLUMELET
plunder .... ROB, LOOT, PREY,
PROG, SWAG, BOOTY, FORAY,
HARRY, RIFLE, STEAL, STRIP,
FORAGE, MARAUD, RAPINE,
RAVAGE, (DE)SPOIL, PILLAGE,
(RAN)SACK
archaic .... REAVE
search for .... RAVEN, RAVIN
plunderer .... LOOTER, RAPPAREE,
FREEBOOTER
plunge .... DIP, DIVE, DROP, FALL,
SWIM, FLING, LUNGE
headlong .... PITCH
into a liquid .... DUNK, DOUSE,
SOUSE, IMMERSE
plunger .... DIVER, DASHER,
PISTON, GAMBLER
plunk .... BLOW, PLUCK, PLUMP,
STRUM
slang .... DOLLAR
sound .... THUD, TWANG
plural marriage ...... POLYGAMY,
POLYANDRY
plurality .... MAJORITY
plus .... AND, ADDED, EXTRA
fours .... KNICKERS
value .... ASSET
plush .... POSH, SWANKY,
LUXURIOUS
cloth like .... BOLIVIA
fabric .... SILK, WOOL
Plutarch's forte ...... BIOGRAPHY

Pluto ...... DIS, DOG, GOD, HADES,
ORCUS, PLANET
domain of .... HELL, HADES,
SHEOL, INFERNO, LOWER
WORLD
wife of .... PERSEPHONE,
PROSERPINE
plutocrat .... NABOB, CROESUS
plutonic .... IGNEOUS
pluvial .... RAINY, SOPPY
ply .... FOLD, URGE, WORK, EXERT,
LAYER, TWIST, HANDLE,
THICKNESS, LAMINATION
plywood layer .... VENEER
Plymouth Colony governor
.... CARVER, WINSLOW,
BRADFORD
Rock figure .... PILGRIM
FATHER
Rock locale
.... MASSACHUSETTS
pneuma .... SOUL, SPIRIT, HOLY
SPIRIT
pneumatic .... AERY, AIRY,
AERIAL
pneumatics .... AERODYNAMICS
pneumogastric nerve ...... VAGUS
Po, city on the .... TURIN, TORINO
river .... PADUS, ERIDANUS
tributary .... ADDA, TESSIN,
TICINO, TREBBIA
valley tribesman .... LOMBARD
poach .... MIX, BOIL, COOK, FILCH,
SHIRR, STEAL, PILFER,
TRAMPLE, TRESPASS
eggs .... CODDLE
poacher .... THIEF, FILCHER,
LURCHER
dog of .... LURCHER
poachy .... SOGGY, SODDEN
Pocahontas' adapted Christian
name .... REBECCA
father .... POWHATAN
half sister .... MATACHANNA
husband .... (JOHN)ROLFE
sister .... CLEOPATRA
son .... THOMAS(ROLFE)
pochard .... DUCK, SMEE
kin of ..... REDHEAD, WIDGEON
pochette .... KIT
pock .... PIT, SCAR, PIMPLE,
PUSTULE
pocket .... BAG, BIN, FOB, HIDE,
POKE, SACK, TAKE, POUCH,
CAVITY, PLACKET
billiards .... POOL
bread .... PITA
contents .... KEYS, COINS
fuzz .... LINT
money .... CASH
shape of .... U-CUT

size .... SMALL
pocketbook ...... PURSE, WALLET,
BILLFOLD
pockmark .... PIT, SCAR
poco .... LITTLE
pod .... GAM, ARIL, BOLL, HULL,
HUSK, BENDY, FLOCK, POUCH,
SHELL, SHUCK, CHIL(L)I,
ACHENE, COCOON, GROOVE,
LEGUME, SCHOOL, CAPSULE,
CYPSELA, SEEDCASE
edible .... OCRA, OKRA
fodder .... CAROB
gastric stimulant .... CAPSICUM
like fruit bearers .... CAROB,
CATALPA
mustard plant .... SILIQUE
tree .... LOCUST
podagra .... GOUT
podesta .... JUDGE, MAYOR,
GOVERNOR
podium .... DAIS, PLATFORM
Poe, _____ Allan .... EDGAR
bird .... RAVEN
character .... PYM
foster father of .... ALLAN
girl in poem/heroine
.... LENORE, ANNABEL(LEE)
gold bug .... SCARAB
work of .... RAVEN,
TAMERLANE
poem ...... LAI, ODE, RUNE, VERSE,
BALLAD(E), RONDEL, SESTINA,
VIRELAY, PALINODE
by Frost .... FIRE AND ICE
Homer .... ILIAD, ODYSSEY
Kilmer .... TREES
Poe .... THE RAVEN
concluding stanza ..... ENVOY,
(L)ENVOI
dirgelike .... REQUIEM
division .... FIT, CANTO,
FYTTE, STANZA
epic .... EPOS, EPODE, ILIAD,
EPOPEE, ODYSSEY
for singing .... LAY
four-line .... QUATRAIN
14-line .... SONNET
handed down orally ...... EPOS
heroic .... EPIC, EPOS
Icelandic .... EDDA
introduction to a
.... PROLOGUE
love .... MADRIGAL
lyric ..... ODE, EPODE, RONDEL,
CANZONE, RONDEAU,
MADRIGAL
mourning .... MONODY
mystical .... RUNE
narrative .... LAY, EPIC,
IDYL(L), ILIAD, ODYSSEY

nonsense .... LIMERICK
of lament .... ELEGY
of praise .... MAGNIFICAT
of rural life .... GEORGIC
one-line .... MONOSTICH
oral .... EPOS
part of .... CANTO, PASSUS,
STANZA, STROPHE
pastoral ..... IDYL(L), BUCOLIC,
ECLOGUE, GEORGIC
play's .... EPILOGUE,
PROLOGUE
popular .... ILIAD, TREES,
ODYSSEY, THE RAVEN
postscript .... (L)ENVOI,
(L)ENVOY
sacred .... PSALM
said at play's end
.... EPILOGUE
satirical/witty .... IAMBIC,
EPIGRAM
set to music .... ORATORIO
short .... VIRELAY,
TELESTIC(H), VILLANELLE
with six six-line stanzas
.... SESTINA
poems collection .... GARLAND,
ANTHOLOGY
poet .... BARD, ODIST, LYRIST,
RHYMER, ELEGIST, METRIST,
MINSTREL, TROUBADOUR,
MINNESINGER
Civil Elegies .... LEE
inferior .... RIMER, RHYMER,
RHYMESTER, POETASTER,
SONNETEER, VERSIFIER
inspiration of .... MUSE
of a .... HOMERIC
old English .... SCOP
singer .... BARD, MINSTREL
unknown .... ANON
Poet and Peasant composer
.... (VON)SUPPE
poetaster .... POETLING, VERSIFIER
activity of .... RIMING
poetess .... LOWELL, MILLAY,
PARKER, SAPPHO, SEXTON,
TEASDALE
poetic dusk .... EVE
foot .... DACTYL, IAMB(US),
SPONDEE, TROCHEE, CHORIAMB
inspiration .... PEGASUS
measure .... METER
pronoun .... THEE, THOU,
THINE
pugilist .... ALI
retraction .... PALINODE
trio .... NOD
verb .... DOST, HAST, HATH
poetry .... POESY, BALLADRY
ancient reciter of .... BARD

epic .... EPOPEE
incomplete line of
.... HEMISTICH
line of .... STICH
muse of .... ERATO, THALIA,
CALLIOPE
of .... LYRIC, MELIC, HEROIC
short excerpt .... MORCEAU
poets, collectively .... PARNASSUS
pogonia .... ORCHID
pogonip .... FOG
Pogo's friend .... OWL
pogrom .... CARNAGE, KILLING,
MASSACRE, SLAUGHTER
pogy .... FISH, MENHADEN
poi source .... TARO
poignancy .... PATHOS
poignant ...... KEEN, TART, SHARP,
BITING, MOVING, PAINFUL,
PIQUANT, PIERCING, TOUCHING
poignard .... DAGGER
poilu .... SOLDIER
poind .... SEIZE, IMPOUND,
DISTRAINT
point .... AIM, DOT, END, JOT, NIB,
PIN, TIP, CAPE, CUSP, PEAK,
SPOT, ISSUE, PRICK, PRONG,
PUNTO, SPECK, OBJECT,
PERIOD
antler's .... SNAG
beside the .... UNRELATED,
IRRELEVANT
barbed .... FLUE
blank .... BLUNT, PLAIN,
DIRECT, STRAIGHT
central .... CRUX, FOCUS
compass .... AIRT(H), RHUMB
culmination .... SOLSTICE
deep under the ocean floor
.... MOHO
earthquake's starting
.... FOCUS
ending in a .... MUCRONATE
essential .... CRUX
farthest ...... APOGEE, SOLSTICE
having ..... ACUATE, HEBETATE
highest .... ACME, APEX, PEAK,
CLIMAX, SUMMIT, ZENITH
in/to the .... APT, PERTINENT
in game .... SCORE
in law .... RES
joint .... JUNCTURE
land .... CAPE, NESS, SPIT,
PROMONTORY
lowest .... ZERO, NADIR
magnet .... POLE
make a .... SCORE
meeting .... FOCUS
of a curve .... ACNODE
concentration .... NODE
debate .... ISSUE

difference .... LIMEN
land .... MORRO
law: sl. .... BUTTON
time ..... INSTANT, JUNCTURE
view .... ANGLE, SLANT,
          BELIEF, OPINION
on the skull .... INION
orbital .... APSIS, APOGEE
out .... SIGNIFY, INDICATE
pen .... NEB, NIB, TIP
spear .... GAD, PIKE
starting .... POST
turning .... HINGE, PIVOT
won .... GOAL, SCORE
won by a single stroke
.... ACE
pointed ...... KEEN, PIKED, SHARP,
     TERSE, ACUATE, BARBED,
     PEAKED, CONICAL, TAPERED,
         INCISIVE, TAPERING
arch ...... OGEE, OGIVE, GOTHIC
dull .... ACUATE, HEBETATE
end .... CUSP
missile .... BOLT, DART,
     LANCE, SPEAR, HARPOON
stick .... GOAD
weapon ...... STYLET, STILETTO
pointer .... DIAL, HAND, SIGN,
     VANE, WAND, AIMER, ARROW,
     INDEX, (GUN)DOG, SETTER,
         INDICATOR, RETRIEVER,
              HUNTING DOG
colloquial ..... TIP, CLUE, HINT,
          GUIDE, DIRECT
dial's .... STYLE
printer's .... FIST
sundial .... GNOMON
teacher's .... FESCUE
pointing out .... INDICANT
pointless .... DULL, BLUNT, INANE,
     SILLY, USELESS, FECKLESS,
     SENSELESS, MEANINGLESS
poise ...... CALM, HOVER, APLOMB,
     BALANCE, BEARING, DIGNITY,
     LIBRATE, SUSPEND, CARRIAGE,
     PRESENCE, COMPOSURE,
              STABILITY
poised .... (COCK)SURE
poison .... BANE, DRUG, GALL,
     KILL, TAINT, TOXIN, VENOM,
     DATURA, ARSENIC, CORRUPT,
     TOXICANT, TOXICITY
antidote .... TREACLE,
     THERIACA, MITHRIDATE
archaic .... VIRUS
arrow .... INEE, UPAS, CURARE,
     (C)URARI, OURARI
castor bean .... RICIN
caused by .... TOXIC
deadly ...... ARSENIC, CYANIDE,
          STRYCHNIN(E)

food .... BOTULIN
gas .... MUSTARD, LEWISITE
hemlock .... BENNET,
          CONIN(E), CONIUM
ivy .... SUMAC
ivy aftermath .... ITCH, RASH
label for .... SKULL AND
          CROSSBONES
remedy for .... TREACLE
snake .... VENOM, VIRUS
weed .... LOCO, CONIUM,
              HEMLOCK
poisoned .... SEPTIC, PECCANT
poisoner, alleged .... BORGIA
poisoning .... KILLING, BOTULISM,
              TOXICATION
blood .... TOXEMIA
poisonous .... DEADLY, NOCUOUS,
     NOXIOUS, MEPHITIC,
     TOXIC(ANT), VENOMOUS,
     VIPERINE, VIRULENT
air .... MIASMA, MALARIA
alkaloid .... CONINE,
     TROPIN(E), NICOTINE,
              STRYCHNINE
bark .... UPAS, SASSY
compound .... TOXIN(E),
     PHENOL, CYANIDE
element ..... ARSENO, ARSENIC,
              MERCURY
fungus/mushroom
.... AMANITA
liquor .... ROTGUT
lizard .... GILA
oil .... TUNG
plant .... UPAS, ERGOT,
     CONIUM, DATURA, ACONITE,
     HEMLOCK, HENBANE,
     FOXGLOVE, LARKSPUR,
     MANDRAKE, MAY APPLE, NUX
     VOMICA, BELLADONNA,
              NIGHTSHADE
protein .... RICIN(E)
resin .... CANNABIN
seed .... CALABAR
shrub .... OLEANDER
snake ..... ASP, ADDER, COBRA,
     KRAIT, VIPER, BUSHMASTER,
     COPPERHEAD, FER-DE-LANCE
spider .... TARANTULA
substance ..... OPIUM, COCAINE
tint .... RED DYE
vine .... IVY, BITTERSWEET
weed .... LOCO, HEMLOCK
poitrel .... ARMOR
pokal .... GOBLET
poke .... BAG, DUB, HIT, JAB, JOG,
     PRY, GOAD, PROD, PUSH,
     PUNCH, BONNET, MEDDLE,
     POCKET, THRUST, DAWDLE(R),
              INTRUDE

around .... ROOT
with elbow .... NUDGE
poker .... ROD, STOKER, CARD
              GAME
aces and eights in .... DEAD
          MAN'S HAND
bet .... RAISE
chips .... STACK
counter .... DIB, CHIP
deal .... DRAW, STUD
faced comedian .... KEATON
game like .... BRAG
hand .... PAIR, TRIO, STRAIGHT,
     FULL HOUSE, (ROYAL)FLUSH
holding .... ACE HIGH
kind of .... LIARS
move .... FOLD, RAISE
player .... FOURFLUSHER
stake .... POT, ANTE, KITTY
term .... ANTE, FOLD, HOLD,
     RAISE, KICKER, PIGEON,
              BOBTAIL
to call in .... SEE
variety of .... DRAW, STUD
pokerface .... DEADPAN
pokeweed .... POCAN, INKBERRY
pok(e)y .... DULL, SLOW, STIR,
          DOWDY, STUFFY
slang .... JAIL, SLAMMER
Pola .... PULA
movie actress .... NEGRI
Poland .... POLSKA, POLONIA,
              SARMATIA
capital of .... WARSAW
dictator .... GOMULKA
Mrs. in .... PANI
native of .... POLE, SLAV,
              POLACK
polar .... ICY, COLD, FRIGID,
     EXTREME, ENDMOST,
     MAGNETIC, OPPOSITE
cover .... ICECAP
Polaris .... POLESTAR, NORTH
              STAR
polarize .... SPLIT, OPPOSE
pole .... HUB, ROD, AXIS, BEAM,
     MAST, POST, PUNT, SLAV,
     CABER, PIVOT, SHAFT, STAFF,
     STICK, STILT, THILL
battery .... ANODE, CATHODE
boat .... QUANT
carriage .... SHAFT
curtain/fishing .... ROD
fir .... UFER
forked .... NEAP
in Gaelic game .... CABER
memorial .... XAT
metal cap .... SHOE
positive .... ANODE
propelled watercraft ..... PUNT,
     CASCO, GONDOLA

549

symbolic .... TOTEM
to pole .... AXIAL
tribal .... TOTEM
vertical .... MAST
wagon/vehicle .... SHAFT,
    THILL
with decoy bird .... STOOL
with footrest .... STILT
wooden .... TREE
poleax(e) ...... HALBERD, HALBERT
polecat .... SKUNK, MUSANG,
    FITCHEW, FITCH(ET),
    FOUMART, STINKER,
    CARNIVORE
animal like .... FERRET,
    WEASEL, ZORIL(A)
polehorse .... POLER
poleman ...... LOGGER, SURVEYOR
polemic .... MOOT, ARGUER,
    ARGUMENT, DEBATABLE,
    CONTROVERSIAL
polemics .... DEBATE, DISPUTE
polenta .... PORRIDGE
poler .... HORSE, OARSMAN,
    GONDOLIER
poles apart .... OPPOSITE
walking .... STILTS
polestar .... GUIDE, MAGNET,
    POLARIS, NORTH STAR
poley .... HORNLESS
police .... PATROL, PROTECT,
    (SAFE)GUARD, CARABINIERI,
    CONSTABULARY
action .... RAID, ARREST
concern .... RIOT, CRIME,
    THEFT, MURDER, BURGLARY
inspector, fictional
    .... MAIGRET
line .... CORDON
military .... MP, REDCAP
perusal .... LINEUP
procedure .... DRAGNET
record book .... BLOTTER
record, letters in .... AKA
state .... TROOPER
test ...... PARAFFIN, POLYGRAPH
vehicle .... WAGON, BLACK
    MARIA
policeman .... BOBBY, MINION,
    REDCAP, MARSHAL, OFFICER,
    SHERIFF, TROOPER, ZAPTIAH,
    BLUECOAT, GENDARME,
    CONSTABLE, DETECTIVE
a native .... PEON
baton/club of .... MACE,
    BILLY, STICK, TRUNCHEON
mounted .... TROOPER
of lowest rank .... PATROLMAN
slang ..... PIG, COP(PER), BULL,
    DICK, PEELER, JOHN LAW, THE
    FUZZ, FLATFOOT

policewoman .... MATRON
policy .... PLAN, CONDUCT,
    WISDOM, PLATFORM,
    STRATEGY, PRINCIPLE(S),
    MANAGEMENT
insurance .... CONTRACT
polio .... INFANTILE PARALYSIS
research, noted name in
    .... SABIN
treatment method .... KENNY
vaccine man .... SALK
vaccine, type of .... IPV, OPV
polish .... RUB, WAX, BUFF, SAND,
    GLAZE, GLOSS, GRACE, POISE,
    SCOUR, SCRUB, SHEEN, SHINE,
    SLEEK, FINISH, LUSTER,
    LUSTRE, REFINE, VENEER,
    BURNISH, FURBISH, PERFECT,
    BRIGHTEN, LEVIGATE
by friction .... RUB, BURNISH
by hammering .... PLANISH
friend of .... SPIT
up .... EDIT, IMPROVE
Polish bay .... POMERANIAN
carriage .... BRITSKA
city/town .... ELK, KOLO,
    LODZ, NYSA, PISZ, ZARY,
    BREST, BRZEG, BYTOM,
    CHELM, OPOLE, RADOM,
    TORUN, TYCHY, CRACOW,
    DANZIG, ELBING, ELBLAG,
    GDANSK, GDYNIA, KALISZ,
    KIELCE, KOSLIN, KRAKOW,
    LUBLIN, OPPELN, POZNAN,
    RYBNIK, TARNOW, BRESLAU,
    CHORZOW, LEGNICA, STETTIN,
    WROCLAW, GLEIWITZ,
    KATOWICE, SZCZECIN,
    LANDSBERG, WALDENBURG
coin .... DUCAT, GROSZ,
    MARKA
commander .... BOR, HETMA,
    ANDERS
dance .... MAZURKA,
    POLONAISE
dictator .... GOMULKA,
    PILSUDSKI
diet member .... MAGNATE
dress .... POLONAISE
gulf .... DANZIG, GDANSK
island .... UZNAM, WOLIN
king .... CONTI, SOBIESKI
lake .... MAMRY, SNIARDWY
legislator .... MAGNATE
marshy region .... PRIPET
measure ..... CAL, MILA, LINJA,
    MORG(A), SAZEN, STOPA,
    KORZEC, KUARTA
monetary unit .... ZLOTY
mountain .... RYSY
mountain range .... BESKIDS,

    SUDETEN, HIGH TATRA
music .... MAZURKA,
    POLONAISE
parliament .... SEJM
peninsula .... HEL
physicist .... CURIE
pianist .... CHOPIN,
    PADEREWSKI, RUBINSTEIN
port .... DANZIG, GDANSK,
    GDYNIA
premier .... SIKORSKI,
    PILSUDSKI, PADEREWSKI
president .... PILSUDSKI,
    (LECH)WALESA
province .... LODZ, OPOLE,
    CRACOW, GDANSK, KIELCE,
    LUBLIN, POZNAN, WARSAW,
    BIELSKO, WROCLAW
region .... WARMIA, MASURIA
river .... BUG, SAN, BRDA,
    GWDA, LYNA, ODER, WKRA,
    NAREW, NOTEC, SERET,
    WARTA, NEISSE, PILICA,
    PRIPET, PROSNA, WIEPRZ,
    BRYNICA, DUNAJEC, VISTULA
sea .... BALTIC
seaport .... DANZIG, GDANSK
slang .... POLACK
soldier .... UHLAN
soup .... ZUPA
title of address .... PANI
weight ..... LUT, FUNT, UNCYA,
    KAMIAN, SKRUPUL
polished .... SLEEK, SUAVE,
    GLOSSY, POLITE, URBANE,
    ELEGANT, REFINED, CULTURED
polishing material .... WAX,
    BUFF, EMERY, RABAT,
    CROCUS, LUSTER, PUMICE,
    RUBIGO, ABRASIVE
polite .... CIVIL, URBANE,
    CORRECT, GENTEEL, REFINED,
    GRACIOUS, MANNERLY,
    POLISHED, WELL-BRED,
    COURTEOUS
act .... CIVILITY
society .... BON TON
politic .... WARY, WISE, CRAFTY,
    SHREWD, PRUDENT, TACTFUL,
    DISCREET, EXPEDIENT,
    DIPLOMATIC
political .... CIVIC, CIVIL,
    OFFICIAL, BUREAUCRATIC,
    GOVERNMENTAL
casualty .... LAMEDUCK
division .... HUNDRED
faction/group .... BLOC, RUMP,
    JUNTA
favor .... PLUM
gathering .... CAUCUS,
    POWWOW

henchman ...... (WARD)HEELER
line-up .... SLATE
organization ..... PARTY, STATE
patronage .... PAP,
                   PORK(BARREL)
policy .... PARTYLINE
radical .... JACOBIN
rostrum .... STUMP
science .... CIVICS, POLITICS,
               GOVERNMENT
spoils ..... MELON, PATRONAGE
system .... REGIME
weight .... CLOUT
politician ...... HEELER, DIPLOMAT,
      POLITICO, STRATEGIST
not reelected .... LAMEDUCK
politics of a .... LEFT, RIGHT,
      CENTER, LIBERAL,
      CONSERVATIVE
unattached .... MAVERICK,
      INDEPENDENT
politicians' stock in trade
      .... HANDSHAKES
polity .... STATE
polka-like dance .... REDOWA,
      MAZURKA
poll .... CUT, TOP, CLIP, CROP,
      HEAD, PATE, VOTE, COUNT,
      JUROR, SKULL, BALLOT,
      SURVEY, REGISTER,
      TABULATE, CANVASS(ING)
taker .... ROPER, GALLUP,
      HARRIS
pollack .... SEY, GADID, COALFISH
relative .... COD, HADDOCK
pollard .... OX, DEER, GOAT,
      SHEEP
polled .... MUL(L)EY, HORNLESS,
      CANVASSED
pollen .... DUST, FLOUR, POWDER,
      MICROSPORES
bearing organ .... STAMEN
brush .... SCOPA
grains, body of ..... POLLINIUM
sac .... ANTHER
pollex ...... BIG TOE, DIGIT, THUMB
pollinate .... FERTILIZE
pollinator .... BEE
polling place .... BOOTH
pollinosis .... HAYFEVER
polliwog .... TADPOLE
pollock .... CODFISH
pollster .... ROPER, GALLUP,
      HARRIS, POLL TAKER
pollute .... SOIL, DIRTY, SULLY,
      TAINT, BEFOUL, DEFILE,
      CONTAMINATE
polluted .... IMPURE, UNCLEAN,
      CORRUPTED
Pollux and Castor .... ANAX,
      TWINS, GEMINI, DIOSCURI

father of .... ZEUS
mother of .... LEDA
twin brother of .... CASTOR
Pollyanna, for example
      .... OPTIMIST
pollywog .... FROG, TADPOLE
polo play period .... CHUKKAR,
      CHUKKER
player .... POLOIST
requirement .... HORSE,
      MALLET, WOODEN BALL
stick .... MALLET
team .... FOUR
Polo, Venetian traveler .... MARCO
Polonius' daughter .... OPHELIA
servant .... REYNALDO
son .... LAERTES
Polska .... POLAND
poltergeist .... GHOST, SPIRIT
poltroon .... CAD, COWARD,
      CRAVEN, CAITIFF, DASTARD
polyanthus ...... OXLIP, PRIMROSE,
      NARCISSUS
polygamy .... HAREM
polyglot .... LINGUIST
polygon .... ISAGON, HEXAGON,
      NONAGON, TETRAGON
kind of .... ISOSCELES
      TRIANGLE
polygraph .... LIE DETECTOR
they swear by the .... POLICE
Polynesian ...... MAORI, KANAKA,
      SAMOAN, NUKUORO,
      HAWAIIAN, TAHITIAN
apparel .... GRASS SKIRT
apple .... HEVI
baking pit .... UMU
beverage .... KAVA, KAWA
chestnut .... RATA
cloth .... TAPA
dress .... MALO
god .... ATUA, PELE, TANE
herb .... PIA
hero .... MAUI
human body (cannibals'
      food) .... LONG PIG
island .... FIJI, SAMOA, TONGA,
      HAWAII, TAHITI, TOKELAU,
      PITCAIRN, MARQUESAS
kingdom .... TONGA
language .... TONGAN
loincloth .... PARAE
louse .... KUTU
mound .... AHU
mulberry bark .... TAPA
oven .... UMU
sky .... LANGI
spirit .... ATUA
supernatural force .... MANA
tree .... IPIL
wages .... UTU

yam .... UBE, UBI
polyp .... CORAL, HYDRA, SEA
      PEN, HYDROZOAN, SEA
      ANEMONE
colony .... CORAL
like a .... HYDROID
Polyphemus ...... MOTH, CYCLOPS
captive .... ULYSSES, ODYSSEUS
polypody .... FERN
Polyxena's father .... PRIAM
mother .... HECUBA
slain bridegroom .... ACHILLES
polyzoan ...... HYDRA, POLYP, SEA
      PEN, BRYOZOAN, SEA
      ANEMONE
Pom's pal .... PEKE
pomace .... (FRUIT)PULP
pomaceous fruit .... POME,
      APPLE, HAWTHORN
pomade .... POMATUM, COSMETIC,
      OINTMENT, BANDOLINE
pomatum .... POMADE
pome .... PEAR, APPLE, QUINCE
disease .... BROWN ROT
like fruit .... AZAROLE
pomegranate .... BERRY
flower .... BALUSTER
syrup .... GRENADINE
pomelo .... SUHA, SHADDOCK,
      GRAPEFRUIT
Pomeranian .... SPITZ DOG
pommel ...... BEAT, KNOB, STRIKE
pomp .... SHOW, GLITTER,
      FLOURISH, DISPLAY,
      GRANDEUR, SPLENDOR,
      PAGEANTRY
empty .... PAGEANT
Pomp and Circumstance
composer .... ELGAR
pompadour .... HAIRDO, POISSON
base/pad .... RAT
Pompadour, paramour of
      Marquise de .... LOUIS XV
pompano .... SAUREL, ALEWIFE,
      CARANGOID
Pompey's scene of defeat
      .... THAPSUS
pompom .... CANNON, MACHINE
      GUN
fire .... FLAK, ACK-ACK
pompon ...... DAHLIA, ORNAMENT,
      (CHRYSANTHE)MUM
pomposity .... WIND
pompous .... VAIN, TUMID,
      TURGID, OROTUND, STATELY,
      MAGNIFIC, BOMBASTIC,
      GRANDIOSE, HIGHFALUTIN
slang .... GASSY
speech .... BOMBAST
walk .... STRUT, SWAGGER
Ponca .... SIOUX, SIOUAN

Ponce de Leon's discovery
.... FLORIDA
quest ..... FOUNTAIN OF YOUTH
Ponchielli opera .... (LA)
GIOCONDA
poncho .... CLOAK, RAINCOAT
pond .... LAKE, MERE, POOL,
TARN, LAGOON, LAGUNE,
SALINA, WATER HOLE
kind of .... FISH, MILL, STEW
plumed dweller .... EGRET
ponder .... MULL, MUSE, PORE,
THINK, WEIGH, PERPEND,
REFLECT, CONSIDER,
MEDITATE, RUMINATE
ponderer .... MUSER
ponderosa .... PINE
ponderous .... BULKY, HEAVY,
MASSIVE, WEIGHTY, DULL
AND LABORED, HUGE AND
AWKWARD
ponds, study of ...... LIMNOLOGY
pone .... LOAF, BREAD
poniard .... DAGGER
Pons, operatic singer .... LILY
pontiff .... POPE, BISHOP,
PONTIFEX, HIGH PRIEST
pontifical .... PAPAL, EPISCOPAL
pontil .... PUNTY, POINT
Pontius, Roman governor
.... PILATE
pontlevis .... DRAWBRIDGE
pontoon .... RAFT, BARGE, FLOAT,
BRIDGE, CAISSON
pony .... NAG, CRIB, HORSE,
PINTO, BRONCO, CAYUSE,
SHELTY, SHELTIE
tail .... HAIRDO
up .... PAY, ANTE
pooch .... DOG
poodle .... DOG, BARBET
pooh .... TIRE, EXHAUST,
EXCLAMATION
pooh .... DISMISS, DISREGARD
Pooh's creator .... MILNE
friend .... ROO
pool ...... POT, CARR, LINN, MERE,
POND, PLASH, PUDDLE,
MONOPOLY, BILLIARDS,
WATER HOLE
artificial .... TANK
ball .... RINGER
bettors' .... POT, KITTY
business firms' .... TRUST,
MONOPOLY
member .... STENO, TYPIST
mine .... SUMP
mountain .... TARN
pouch .... POCKET
rod .... CUE
shallow .... PLASH, PUDDLE

triangle .... RACK
waterfall .... LINN
poon .... DILO, TREE, DOMBA,
TELUGU
poop out .... TIRE, WEAKEN
pooped .... SPENT, EXHAUSTED
slang .... BEAT, BUSHED
poor .... LEAN, NEEDY, PALTRY,
SHABBY, INDIGENT, INFERIOR,
DESTITUTE, PENNILESS
person .... PAUPER
player .... DUB, HAM
slang .... LOUSY
sport .... SOREHEAD
poorhouse .... HOSPICE
poorly ILL
born .... LOWBRED
done literary work
.... INCONDITE
lit .... DIM
pop ...... BANG, SHOT, SLAP, SNAP,
SODA, BURST, CRACK, SHOOT,
SMACK, FATHER, EXPLODE
art .... FUNK
conductor .... WHITEMAN
singer .... ANKA, JOPLIN,
MADONNA
the question .... PROPOSE
Pope. See also **Papal** .... LEO,
JOHN, PAUL, PIUS, URBAN,
VICAR, ADRIAN, PONTIFF,
PRIMATE
cape of .... MOZ(Z)ETTA
cathedral of the ...... LATERAN
collar of the .... ORALE
crown of the .... TIARA
decree of the .... BULL,
DECRETAL, RESCRIPT
envoy .... (AB)LEGATE
first .... PETER
headdress of .... MITER, MITRE
meeting to elect
.... CONCLAVE
of Video .... SULLIVAN
palace of .... VATICAN
pertaining to the .... PAPAL
see of the .... ROME
tenure of the .... PAPACY
the .... PAPA
title of .... HOLINESS, HOLY
FATHER
vestment of .... FANO(N),
FANUM
Pope's (Alexander) love
.... GONNE
popes collectively .... PAPACY
Popeye, rival of .... BRUTO
sweetheart of ..... OLIVE (OYL)
the _____ .... SAILOR (MAN)
popinjay .... FOP, PARROT,
WOODPECKER

poplar .... ABELE, ALAMO, ASPEN,
LIARD, COTTONWOOD
balsam .... TACMAHACK
glucoside from .... SALICIN
spike .... AMENT, CATKIN
white .... ABELE
poplin .... FABRIC
popover .... MUFFIN
Poppaea, Nero's wife .... SABINA
popping the eyes .... OGLING
poppy .... OPIUM, PAPAVER,
CELANDINE, CHICALOTE,
BLOODROOT, SANGUINARIA
genus .... PAPAVER
juice extract .... OPIUM
prickly .... CHICALOTE
sap .... LATEX
seed .... MAW
poppycock ...... ROT, BOSH, BULL,
BUNK, CRAP, BALONEY,
HOGWASH, MALARKEY,
NONSENSE
populace .... DEMOS, PLEBS,
MASSES, PEOPLE
popular .... COMMON, FAMOUS,
ADMIRED, CURRENT, DEMOTIC,
VULGATE, ACCEPTED,
EXOTERIC, ENCHORIAL,
PREVALENT, WELL-LIKED,
PREVAILING
beauty .... BELLE
no more .... HAS-BEEN
opinion .... CONSENSUS
parlance .... SLANG
social figure .... LION, STAR,
CELEBRITY
success .... HIT
popularity .... FAME
populate .... PEOPLE, INHABIT
population .... PEOPLE,
DWELLERS, POPULACE,
CITIZENRY, INHABITANTS
count .... CENSUS
populous .... CROWDED
Poquelin, Fr. writer .... MOLIERE
porbeagle .... SHARK
porcelain .... MING, CHINA,
SPODE, SEVRES, CELADON,
FAIENCE, LIMOGES, FIGULINE,
EARTHENWARE
art of making .... CERAMICS
clay .... PATE, CHINA,
KAOLIN(E)
fine .... MING, CHINA
of/relating to .... CERAMIC
worker .... POTTER
porch ...... STOA, LAN(A)I, STOOP,
PARVIS, PIAZZA, BALCONY,
GALILEE, GALLERY, PORTICO,
VERANDA(H)
church .... GALILEE

seat .... GLIDER
porcine animal .... HOG, PIG
  disease .... BULLNOSE
porcupine .... HEDGEHOG
  anteater .... ECHIDNA
  Canadian .... URSON
  spine .... QUILL
pore .... CON, READ, STUDY,
  PERUSE, PONDER, CHANNEL,
  FORAMEN, OPENING, OSTIOLE,
  MEDITATE
  breathing .... STOMA
  plant .... STOMA, LENTICEL
pores, block the .... OPPILATE
  having .... PORIFEROUS
porgy .... TAI, SCUP, BREAM,
  PARGO, (PIN)FISH, SPAROID
poriferan .... SPONGE
pork .... HOG, PIG, LARDO(O)N
  chops on the hoof .... HOG
  cut .... HAM, CHOP, LOIN,
  BACON, ROAST, SHANK,
  SPARERIBS
  loin .... GRISKIN
  pie .... HAT
  sausage .... BOLOGNA
  shoulder .... CALA
porker ...... ELT, HOG, PIG, SWINE
porkfish .... SISI
porky .... FAT
pornographic .... LEWD, DIRTY,
  SMUTTY, OBSCENE,
  SALACIOUS
  slang .... BLUE
porous .... LEAKY, LEACHY
porpoise .... INIA, SEA HOG,
  DOLPHIN, HOGFISH, CETACEAN
porridge .... MUSH, SAMP, ATOLE,
  BROSE, GROUT, GRUEL,
  BURGOO, OATMEAL, POLENTA,
  POTTAGE, STIRABOUT
  bowl .... PORRINGER
  oat husks .... SOWENS
Porsena, king .... LARS
  Tarquin's .... AVENGER
port .... WINE, HAVEN, HARBOR,
  GATE(WAY), LARBOARD,
  ANCHORAGE
  ancient .... TYRE
  facilities .... WHARFAGE
portable .... MOVABLE
  bridge .... BAILEY, PONTOON
  chair .... SEDAN
  float .... PONTOON
  hut .... QUONSET
  kitchen cart .... CHUCK
  WAGON
  lamp .... LANTERN
  light .... TORCH
  linens .... HANKIES
  oven .... BAKER

sanctuary .... TABERNACLE
serving stand .... DUMB
  WAITER
shelter .... TENT
stove .... CHAUFFER
portal .... GATE, DOOR(WAY),
  ENTRY, POSTERN, ENTRANCE
portamento .... GLIDE
portance ...... BEARING, CONDUCT,
  CARRIAGE
portas .... BREVIARY
portcullis .... BAR, GRATE, HERSE,
  GRATING
portend .... MEAN, WARN, AUGUR,
  PRESAGE, SIGNIFY,
  (FORE)BODE, FORESHADOW
portent .... OMEN, SIGN, MARVEL,
  WONDER, PRODIGY, WARNING
portentous .... AMAZING,
  OMINOUS, SINISTER
porter ...... ALE, BEER, HAMA(U)L,
  REDCAP, CARRIER, DOORMAN,
  JANITOR, CONCIERGE,
  GATEKEEPER
  brew like .... STOUT
  musical .... ROSALIE
Porter, songwriter .... COLE
porterhouse .... BEEF, STEAK,
  T-BONE
portfolio .... OFFICE, HOLDINGS,
  BRIEFCASE, SECURITIES,
  ATTACHE CASE
porthole .... PEEPHOLE,
  EMBRASURE
Portia .... LAWYER
  maid of .... NERISSA
portico .... STOA, PORCH, ARCADE,
  LOGGIA, PARVIS, PIAZZA,
  PROSTYLE, COLONNADE,
  VERANDA(H)
portion ...... BIT, DUE, LOT, FATE,
  PART, SHARE, DIVIDE,
  DESTINY, ALLOTMENT
  book .... CHAPTER, SECTION
  marriage .... DOWER, DOWRY
  meal .... HELPING, SERVING
  of food .... MORSEL
  out .... DEAL, DOLE, METE
  slang .... DIVVY
  slight .... WISP
  tiny .... MINIM, MODICUM
portly .... FAT, BULKY, OBESE,
  STOUT, FLESHY, STATELY,
  IMPOSING
portmanteau .... TRUNK, VALISE,
  SUITCASE
Porto Rico. See **Puerto Rico**
portrait .... EFFIGY, SKETCH,
  PICTURE
on U.S. currency:
  $1 .... WASHINGTON

$2 .... JEFFERSON
$5 .... LINCOLN
$10 .... HAMILTON
$20 .... JACKSON
$50 .... GRANT
$100 .... FRANKLIN
self .... PAINTING
portray .... LIMN, ENACT, DEPICT,
  PICTURE, DESCRIBE,
  REHEARSE, DELINEATE,
  PERSONATE, REPRESENT
  verbally .... DESCRIBE
portrayer .... ACTOR, PLAYER,
  DEPICTER, PERFORMER
  of Cohan: 1942 .... CAGNEY
portside .... LEFT
Portugal .... LUSITANIA
  capital of .... LISBON
Portuguese bay .... SETUBAL
  cape ...... ROCA, ESPICHEL, SAO
  VINCENT
  city/town .... FARO, MIRA,
  OVAR, ALGES, BELEM, BRAGA,
  EVORA, LAGOS, PORTO, VISEU,
  ALMADA, AVEIRO, LISBON,
  OPORTO, QUELUZ, SINTRA,
  AMADORA, BENFICA, COIMBRA,
  COVILHA, ESTORIL, FUNCHAL,
  MONTIJO, OLIVAIS, SETUBAL,
  BARREIRO, CAPARICA,
  ODIVELAS, SANTAREM,
  CARNAXIDE, MOSCAVIDE
  coin ...... REI, DOBRA, ESCUDO,
  CENTAVO, CRUSADO, MOIDORE,
  JOHANNES
  colony/territory .... MACAO,
  MACAU, TIMOR, ANGOLA, SAO
  TOME, CAPE VERDE,
  MOZAMBIQUE
  colony, former .... GOA
  dictator .... SALAZAR
  district .... BEJA, FARO,
  BRAGA, EVORA, PORTO, VISEU,
  AVEIRO, GUARDA, LEIRIA,
  LISBON, OPORTO, SETUBAL,
  SANTAREM, VILA REAL
  folk song .... FADO
  former colony in SE Africa
  .... MOZAMBIQUE
  gentleman .... SENHOR
  governess .... AIA
  Guinea capital .... BISSAU
  India district .... DAMAO
  Indian ..... FERINGI, FERINGHEE
  island .... PORTO SANTO
  islands ...... AZORES, MADEIRA,
  DESERTAS, TERCIERA
  lady .... DONA
  legislature .... CORTES
  measure ..... PE, VARA, BRACA,
  LEGOA, MILHA, COVADO

553

molasses .... MELACO
monetary unit .... ESCUDO
mountain .... MONSANTO,
    MALHAO DA ESTRELA
mountain ranges .... SERRAS
mountains ..... OSSA, ESTRELA,
    MONCHIQUE
navigator .... DIAZ, (DA)
    GAMA, MAGELLAN
nobleman .... GRANDEE
novelist .... ECA DE QUEIROZ
poet .... CAMOE(N)S
port .... LISBON, SETUBAL
premier .... SALAZAR,
    CAETANO
river .... LIMA, MIRA, SADO,
    TEJO, DUORO, MINHO, TAGUS,
    TAMEGA, MONDEGO,
    XARRAMA, GUADIANA
sail .... LATEEN
saint .... SAO
seaport .... LISBON, OPORTO
ship .... CARVEL, CARAVEL(LE)
Timor capital .... DILI
title ..... DOM, DONNA, SENHOR
weight .... GRAO, ONCA,
    LIBRA, ARROBA, QUILATE,
    QUINTAL
West Africa .... ANGOLA
wine .... PORTO, MADEIRA
yard .... VARA
pose .... SIT, QUIZ, PUZZLE,
    INQUIRE, POSTURE, PROPOSE,
    ATTITUDE, PRETENSE,
    PROPOUND, MANNERISM
as .... (EN)ACT, PRETEND
Poseidon .... GOD, NEPTUNE
attendant of .... PROTEUS
brother of .... ZEUS
father of .... CRONUS
mother of .... RHEA
realm of .... SEA
scepter .... TRIDENT
sister of .... HERA, HESTIA,
    DEMETER
son of .... TRITON
wife of .... AMPHITRITE
Posen .... POZNAN
poser .... FACER, MODEL, ENIGMA,
    POSEUR, RIDDLE, SITTER,
    TEASER, PROBLEM, IMPOSTOR
posh .... CHIC, RITZY, ELEGANT,
    LUXURIOUS
Posidonius' contemporary
    .... GEMINUS
invention .... (RHODES)
    CALCULATOR
posit .... PUT, PLACE, ASSERT,
    ASSUME, SET (FORTH),
    SITUATE, POSTULATE
position .... LAY, LIE, JOB, SET,

RANK, ROLE, SITE, SPOT,
    SITUS, STAND, OFFICE,
    STANCE, STATUS, STATION,
    ATTITUDE, LOCATION,
    POST(URE), PLACE(MENT),
    SITUATION, (VIEW)POINT
a difficult .... FIX
anchor .... ATRIP
change .... MOVE
jockey for .... MANEUVER
of a part, abnormal
    .... ECTOPIA
of abused pinball machine
    .... ATILT
of authority .... IN THE
    SADDLE
of the arms, in ballet
    .... ENBAS
secure .... FOOTING, FOOTHOLD
positive .... FIRM, PLUS, SURE,
    UTTER, CERTAIN, DECIDED,
    EXPRESS, GENUINE, PRECISE,
    ABSOLUTE, DEFINITE,
    EMPHATIC, SPECIFIC, OUT-
    AND-OUT
answer .... AYE, YEA, YES
electrode/pole .... ANODE
sign .... PLUS
terminal of a battery
    .... CATHODE
positively .... QUITE, TRULY,
    REALLY, EXACTLY
charged electrode .... ANODE
positivism .... COMTISM,
    ASSURANCE, CERTAINTY,
    DOGMATISM
originator .... COMTE
posse .... BAND, DETAIL,
    SEARCHERS
possess .... OWN, HAVE, HOLD,
    ENJOY, OCCUPY, DOMINATE
possessed .... MAD, CRAZED,
    CHARMED, BEWITCHED
possession(s) ...... ASSET, ESTATE,
    WEALTH, PROPERTY,
    OWNERSHIP
in actual: law .... MANUAL,
    SEISIN
possessive .... GREEDY, SELFISH
possessor .... OWNER, HOLDER
posset .... DRINK, BEVERAGE
possible .... LATENT, FEASIBLE,
    PROBABLE, POTENTIAL
possibly .... MAYBE, LIKELY,
    PERHAPS
possum .... COON
play .... FEIGN, PRETEND
post .... JOB, DA(W)K, MAIL, POLE,
    STOB, STUD, ENTER, PLACE,
    STAKE, ASSIGN, INFORM,
    MARKER, PILLAR, BOLLARD,

PUBLISH, STATION, GARRISON,
    POSITION
box device .... US MAIL
boy .... COURIER
chaise .... COACH, CARRIAGE
doorway .... JAMB(E)
exchange .... PX, STORE,
    CANTEEN
memorial .... XAT
mortem .... AUTOPSY,
    INQUEST, NECROPSY
mortem conductor
    .... CORONER, AUTOPSIST
office bank .... GIRO
staircase .... NEWEL
window frame .... JAMB(E)
wooden framework
    .... PUNCHEON
postage stamp country .... SAN
    MARINO
sticker .... STAMP
postal stamp .... CACHET
system .... MAIL
poster .... PLACARD, STICKER,
    BILL(BOARD)
posterior ..... HIND, REAR, LATER,
    DORSAL, RETRAL, BUTTOCK
opposed to .... PRIOR,
    ANTERIOR
posterity .... FUTURE, SEQUEL
postern .... BACKDOOR,
    (BACK)GATE, ENTRANCE
postfree mail .... FRANK
posthaste .... SWIFTLY
posthumous .... AFTERDEATH
postiche ...... WIG, FALSE, TOUPEE,
    PRETENSE, ARTIFICIAL
postmark .... CACHET, IMPRINT
substitute .... INDICIA
postmeridian .... PM, AFTERNOON
"post office" delivery .... KISS
postpone .... WAIT, DEFER,
    DELAY, TABLE, SHELVE, PUT
    OFF, ADJOURN, SUSPEND, PUT
    ON ICE
postponement .... STAY, STOP,
    RAIN CHECK
postponing, in law
    .... MORATORY
postrider .... COURIER
postscript .... ADDITION,
    AFTERTHOUGHT
of poem ..... LENVOY, LIENVOI
postulant .... CANDIDATE,
    PETITIONER
postulate .... AXIOM, CLAIM,
    POSIT, ASSUME, THESIS,
    PREMISE, PRESUME, THEORIZE
posture .... MOOD, POSE, STANCE,
    BEARING, ATTITUDE,
    CARRIAGE, POSITION

posy .... SPRAY, FLOWER, BOUQUET, CORSAGE, NOSEGAY

pot ...... PAN, OLLA, POOL, CROCK, KITTY, SHOOT, ALUDEL, KETTLE, SKILLET

au-feu .... (BEEF) STEW

coffee .... URN

earthenware .... CROCK, PIPKIN

go to .... ROT, GO BAD, DECLINE, FALL OFF, DETERIORATE

handle .... BAIL

herb .... CLARY

holder .... COSY, MITT

kind of ...... FLOWER, LOBSTER

marigold .... CALENDULA

mender .... TINKER

ornamental .... JARDINIERE

slang .... MARIJUANA

small .... CRUSE, PIPKIN

stand .... TRIVET

tea .... SAMOVAR

user .... ADDICT, HIPPIE

user's feeling .... HIGH

water .... LOTA(H)

potable .... DRINKABLE

potage .... SOUP, BROTH

potash and saltpeter .... NITRES

source .... SUINT

potassium .... ALUM

bitartrate .... TARTAR

carbonate .... POTASH

chloride .... MURIATE, SYLVITE

nitrate .... NITER, SALTPETER

potation .... DRAFT, DRINK, LAGER, LIQUOR

potato .... OCA, SPUD, IDAHO, TATER, TUBER

bud .... EYE

bug .... BEETLE

disease .... CURL, BLIGHT

flour/meal .... FARINA

fried .... CHIP

scraper .... PARER

skin .... JACKET

slang .... MURPHY

starch .... FARINA

sweet ...... OCA, YAM, BATATA, CAMOTE

potatoes with fried onions
.... LYONNAISE

potbellied .... BLOATED, PAUNCHY, PAUNCHED

potbelly .... PAUNCH, BAY WINDOW

potboiler .... LITERARY HACK

poteen/potheen .... WHISK(E)Y

potency .... VIS, POWER, VIGOR, STRENGTH

potent .... STRONG, VIRILE, (CAP)ABLE, EFFECTIVE

potable .... BOILERMAKER

potentate .... KING, RULER, PRINCE, MONARCH, (MAJA)RAJAH, SOVEREIGN

potential ...... LATENT, CAPACITY, POSSIBLE, PROMISING

difference .... TENSION

energy .... ERGAL

mutiny .... UNREST

potentilla ...... ROSE, CINQUEFOIL, FIVE-FINGER

pothead ...... ADDICT, MARIJUANA SMOKER

pother .... ADO, FUSS, STIR, WORRY, BUSTLE, UPROAR

potherb .... CLARY, CHIVES, PARSLEY

pothole ...... PIT, CAVE, MUDHOLE

potholer .... SPELUNKER

pothook .... SCRAWL

user .... STENO

pothouse .... INN, TAVERN, ALEHOUSE

potiche .... JAR, VASE

potion .... DOSE, DRAFT, DRINK, LIBATION, NEPENTHE

love .... PHILTER, PHILTRE

mesmeric .... OPIATE, MANDRAGORA

sleep-inducer .... NARCOTIC

potlatch .... GIFT, FEAST, FESTIVAL

potman .... WAITER

potoo .... NIGHTJAR, GOATSUCKER

potpie .... STEW, MEAT-PIE

potpourri .... OLIO, STEW, MEDLEY, MIXTURE, ANTHOLOGY, HODGEPODGE, SALMAGUNDI

scented .... SACHET, POMANDER

Potsdam conference member
...... ATTLEE, STALIN, TRUMAN

potsherd .... CROCK, SHARD

potshot .... SNIPE

potsy .... HOPSCOTCH

need .... PEBBLE

pottage .... SOUP, STEW, BROSE, PORRIDGE, HODGEPODGE

potted .... DRUNK, SMASHED

potter .... DOODLE, PIDDLE, CERAMIST

potter's clay .... PATE, ARGIL, SAGGER, SEGGAR

field .... CEMETERY, GRAVEYARD

field of Judas .... ACELDAMA

ore .... GALENA

tool .... PALLET

wheel .... LATHE

pottery .... BASALT, FAIENCE,

CERAMICS, DELFT(WARE), FIGULINE, GOMBROON, MAJOLICA, (EARTHEN)WARE

art of making .... CERAMICS

before glazing .... BISCUIT

clay .... PATE, ARGIL, KAOLIN

enameled, glazed
.... MAJOLICA

finest type of .... PORCELAIN

fragment .... CROCK, SHARD, SHERD

glaze on .... REFLET

glazed .... DELFT(WARE)

glazing material .... GALENA

making device .... SAGGER

of/relating to .... CERAMIC, FICTILE

speckled .... GRANITEWARE

unglazed, black .... BASALT

white .... GOMBROON

pottle .... BASKET, TANKARD

potto .... LEMUR, KINKAJOU

potty .... JOHN, BATTY, FLAKY, KOOKY, NUTTY, PETTY, TOILET, TRIVIAL

plan .... CRACKBRAINED SCHEME

pouch .... BAG, POD, SAC, BURSA, CECUM, PURSE, POCKET, SPORRAN, SPLEUCHAN

intestinal .... C(A)ECUM

like a .... SACCATE, MARSUPIAL

pouched animal ...... KANGAROO

pouchy .... BAGGY

pouf .... OTTOMAN, HEADDRESS

poulard ...... HEN, FRYER, PULLET

poule .... PROSTITUTE

poult .... PULLET, CHICKEN

poultice ...... PLASTER, DRESSING, CATAPLASM, APPLICATION

poultry .... DUCKS, FOWLS, GEESE, TURKEYS, CHICKENS

breeding place .... HENNERY

disease .... PIP, POX, ROUP, GAPES

man .... POULTER(ER)

pen .... COOP, HUTCH

shelter .... HENNERY, HENHOUSE

shelter, heated .... BROODER

pounce ..... CLAW, SWOOP, TALON

pound .... HIT, PEN, SOV, BEAT, BLOW, BRAY, QUID, TAMP, THUD, CRUSH, LIBRA, THROB, THUMP, CORRAL, KENNEL, MALLEATE, ENCLOSURE, PULVERIZE

dog .... MONGREL

down .... TAMP

dweller .... STRAY

-foolish .... WASTEFUL
fraction .... OUNCE
out .... FLATTEN
put in a .... IMPOUND,
    IMPRISON
sterling, one .... QUID,
    SOVEREIGN
Pound, educator .... ROSCOE
poet .... EZRA (LOOMIS)
pounder .... WAVE, CANNON,
    TAMPER
of the pavement ...... JOBLESS,
    JOB-SEEKER
pounding implement .... GAVEL,
    HAMMER, MALLET, PESTLE
pounds, 100 .... CENTAL,
    CENTNER
2,000 .... NET TON, SHORT TON
2,240 .... LONG TON
pour .... FLOW, GUSH, RAIN,
    TEEM, SERVE, SPOUT, SWARM,
    DECANT, EFFUSE, SQUIRT
forth .... EMIT, GUSH, WELL
metal into mold .... CAST,
    FOUND
out swiftly .... SWOOSH
pourboire .... TIP, GRATUITY
pouring hole .... SPRUE
on water in baptism
    .... AFFUSION
pourpoint .... JUPON, TUNIC,
    DOUBLET
pout .... MOPE, MOUE, SULK,
    (CAT)FISH, GRIMACE
pouter .... PIGEON
pouting spell .... MAD
poverty .... LACK, NEED, WANT,
    DEARTH, PENURY, PAUCITY,
    SCARCITY, INDIGENCE
stricken .... POOR, BROKE,
    NEEDY, HARD-UP, BANKRUPT,
    DESTITUTE, PENNILESS
pow .... HEAD, POLL
powder .... DUST, MEAL, TALC,
    CRUSH, PICRA, POUNCE,
    SPRINKLE, PULVERIZE
burn to/by heat .... CALCINE
clothes scenting .... SACHET
crush/pound into .... BRAY,
    GRIND
dried fly .... CANTHARIDES
explosive .... TETRYL, CORDITE
flower .... POLLEN
grind into fine .... LEVIGATE,
    TRITURATE
insect .... PYRETHRUM
kind of .... GUN, BATH, FACE
perfumed .... SACHET
polishing .... ROUGE
room ...... LOUNGE, LAVATORY
skin .... TALC(UM)

stain removing .... PUMICE
powdered tobacco .... SNUFF
powdery .... DUSTY, MEALY,
    CRUMBLY, FRIABLE
power .... VIS, DINT, SWAY,
    DYNAS, FORCE, MIGHT,
    VIGOR, ENERGY, ABILITY,
    CONTROL, POTENCY,
    CAPACITY, STRENGTH,
    AUTHORITY, PUISSANCE
colloquial ..... STEAM, MUSCLE
failure .... OUTAGE
kind of .... SOLAR, STEAM,
    ATOMIC, MOTIVE, ELECTRIC
loom inventor
    .... CARTWRIGHT
of attorney .... AUTHORIZATION
of divination: abbr. .... ESP
producer .... DYNAMO
source of .... SUN, FUEL
symbol of .... FASCES
theoretical .... OD(YL)
to affect others ..... INFLUENCE
to survive .... VITALITY
unit .... VOLT, WATT
will .... SELF-CONTROL
world .... USA, RUSSIA,
    AMERICA, ENGLAND
powerful .... POTENT, STRONG,
    DYNAMIC, (AL)MIGHTY,
    ELECTRIC, PUISSANT
beam .... LASER
powerless .... WEAK, IMPOTENT
Powers of Hollywood ...... MALA
Powhatan's daughter
    .... POCAHONTAS
powwow .... GATHERING,
    CONFERENCE, MEDICINE MAN
place .... TEPEE
political .... CONVENTION
Zuluans' .... INDABA
pox .... ACNE, PUSTULE,
    SMALLPOX, SYPHILIS
practicable .... UTILE, USABLE,
    USEFUL, FEASIBLE, OPERABLE,
    POSSIBLE, EXPEDIENT
practical .... SOUND, UTILE,
    USEFUL, LOGICAL, RATIONAL,
    SENSIBLE, WORKABLE,
    PRAGMATIC, REALISTIC
joke .... HOAX, JAPE, PRANK,
    TRICK
joker .... PRANKSTER
person .... REALIST
practically ...... ALMOST, NEARLY
practice .... DO, USE, DRILL,
    HABIT, USAGE, CUSTOM,
    MANNER, METHOD, PRAXIS,
    PERFORM, WORKOUT,
    EXERCISE, REHEARSE
common .... USAGE

composition .... ETUDE
dishonest .... RACKET
established .... USAGE,
    CUSTOM, PRAXIS
firearms with blanks ...... DRY
    RUN
game .... WORKOUT
one-upmanship .... PUT ON
    AIRS
performance .... REHEARSE
religious .... CULT
systematic .... EXERCISE
practiced .... DEFT, SKILLED,
    TRAINED, SEASONED
practicing economy .... AUSTERE,
    THRIFTY
practitioner ...... DOER, WORKER,
    OPERATOR, PERFORMER
Christian science ...... HEALER
medical .... DOCTOR,
    SURGEON, PHYSICIAN
pragmatic .... ACTIVE, DOGMATIC,
    OFFICIOUS, PRACTICAL
Prague .... PRAHA
castle .... HRADCANY
river .... VLTAVA
square .... WENCESLAS
prairie ...... MESA, LLANO, PLAIN,
    MEADOW, PAMPA(S),
    PLATEAU, SAVANNA,
    GRASSLAND
dog .... MARMOT
grove .... MOTT(E)
hen .... GROUSE
province .... ALBERTA,
    MANITOBA
soil .... GUMBO
squirrel .... GOPHER
vehicle .... SCHOONER
wolf .... COYOTE
Prairie State .... NEBRASKA
praise .... LAUD, TOUT, BLESS,
    ELOGE, EXALT, EXTOL,
    GRACE, KUDOS, EULOGY,
    GLORIA, HOMAGE, ACCLAIM,
    APPLAUD, COMMEND,
    GLORIFY, TRIBUTE,
    ENCOMIUM, EULOGIZE,
    PANEGYRIC
excessive .... IDOLIZING
expression of .... PLAUDIT,
    APPLAUSE
extravagantly .... HONOR,
    GLORIFY
insincerely/too much
    .... FLATTER
phrase of .... WELL DONE
sign of .... ACCOLADE
song of .... HYMN, CAROL,
    PAEAN
undue .... PUFF

praiseworthy .... LAUDABLE, DESERVING, EXEMPLARY
praline .... CANDY, CONFECTION
pram .... BUGGY, STROLLER, PERAMBULATOR
pusher ...... AMAH, NURSEMAID
prance .... CAPER, DANCE, STRUT, CAVORT, SWAGGER
prandial meal .... DINNER, SUPPER
prank .... DIDO, HOAX, JAPE, JEST, JOKE, LARK, ANTIC, CAPER, TRICK, FROLIC, CANTRIP, CAPRICE, DRESS UP, GAMBADO, ESCAPADE, MISCHIEF
reckless .... ESCAPADE
with lighted match .... HOTFOOT
pranks .... (HIGH)JINKS
full of .... PRANKISH
prankster .... JOKER, BUFFOON
prase .... QUARTZ, CHALCEDONY
prat: sl. .... BUTTOCKS
prate .... GAB, YAP, BLAB, BABBLE, TATTLE, CHATTER, PRATTLE
prattle .... BLAB, PRATE, BABBLE, JABBER, MURMUR, CHATTER
Pravda founder .... LENIN
prawn .... SCAMP, MACRURAN, CRUSTACEAN
praxis .... CUSTOM, PRACTICE
pray .... ASK, BEG, ORA, PLEAD, APPEAL, BESEECH, ENTREAT, IMPLORE
prayer .... AVE, BENE, PLEA, SUIT, GRACE, LITANY, NOVENA, ORISON, REQUEST, ENTREATY, PETITION, ROGATION
bead .... ROSARY
bones .... KNEES
book .... ORDO, HOURS, MISSAL, PRIMER, PORTAS(S), BREVIARY
desk .... PRIEDIEU
ending .... AMEN
evening .... VESPER
for another .... BEADSMAN, INTERCESSION
hour .... MATIN, VESPER
hour, Moslem .... AZAN
in gibberish .... GLOSSOLIA
last of the day .... COMPLIN(E)
meal .... GRACE
morning .... MATIN
nine-day .... NOVENA
of supplication ...... SUFFRAGE
offer a .... WORSHIP
protect by .... SAIN
rug .... ASAN

shawl .... TALLITH
short .... GRACE
wheel user .... LAMA, BUDDHIST
prayerful .... DEVOUT
prayers, endowment for .... CHANTRY
praying figure .... ORANT
Indians .... NATICKS
pre .... BEFORE, PRIOR TO
feast period .... EVE
war .... ANTEBELLUM
wedding surprise ...... SHOWER
preach .... EXHORT, LECTURE, ADVOCATE, SERMONIZE, EVANGELIZE
preacher .... PASTOR, HOMILIST, MINISTER, CLERGYMAN, PREDICANT, PULPITEER, EVANGELIST
circuit .... ROUNDER
pronouncement ...... MAN AND WIFE
talk of .... HOMILY, SERMON
traveling .... EVANGEL(IST), MISSIONARY
preachers collectively .... PULPIT
preaching .... SERMON, PREDICANT
Preakness winner: 1942 .... ALSAB
winning horse .... AFFIRMED, CITATION, WHIRLAWAY, COUNT FLEET, SECRETARIAT
winning jockey .... ARCARO, CAUTHEN, LONGDEN, TURCOTTE
precarious .... RISKY, UNSAFE, CRITICAL, INSECURE, UNCERTAIN
state .... TOUCH-AND-GO
precaution .... CARE, WARNING
precede .... HEAD, FOREGO, FORERUN
in time .... ANTEDATE
the fall .... PRIDE
precedence .... LEAD, PRIORITY
precedent .... PRIOR, FORMER, EXAMPLE
preceder .... PRECURSOR, FORERUNNER
of bravo .... ABLE
craftsy .... ARTSY
daisy .... UPSA, UPSY
geste .... BEAU
poly .... ROLY
puzzle .... JIGSAW
valorem .... AD
preceding ...... BEFORE, PREVIOUS, FOREGOING
all others .... FIRST, PIONEER,

FOREMOST
precentor .... CANTOR
precept ...... CODE, RULE, CANON, MAXIM, ORDER, DICTUM, APHORISM, DOCTRINE
Brahmanism .... SUTRA
in law .... WRIT, WARRANT
preceptor .... TUTOR, TEACHER
precepts, collection of .... SUTRA
precinct(s) .... AREA, WARD, DISTRICT, ENVIRONS, NEIGHBORHOOD
precious .... DEAR, RARE, ARRANT, COSTLY, WORTHY, BELOVED, VALUABLE
colloquial .... VERY, UTTER
stone .... GEM, JADE, ONYX, OPAL, RUBY, SARD, BERYL, JEWEL, TOPAZ, GARNET, DIAMOND, EMERALD, CABOCHON, SAPPHIRE, BRILLIANT
stone cutter .... LAPIDARY
precipice ...... CRAG, DROP, SCAR, BLUFF, CLIFF
precipitate .... FALL, RASH, CAUSE, HASTY, HEADY, ABRUPT, FOMENT, HASTEN, SUDDEN, HURRIED, BRING ON, CONDENSE, HEADLONG, IMPETUOUS, IMPULSIVE
precipitation .... DEW, HAIL, MIST, RAIN, RUSH, SNOW, HASTE, SLEET
prognosticator .... WEATHER MAN
precipitator .... REAGENT, CATALYST, CATALYZER
precipitous .... RASH, HASTY, SHEER, STEEP
rock .... CRAG, SCAR, BLUFF, CLIFF
precis .... DIGEST, RESUME, SUMMARY, ABSTRACT, SYNOPSIS
precise .... PRIM, EXACT, FORMAL, PRISSY, CORRECT, ACCURATE, DEFINITE, EXPLICIT, SPECIFIC, PARTICULAR
pace .... GOOSE-STEP
precisely .... EXACTLY
precision .... ACCURACY
preclude ...... BAR, CHECK, ESTOP, HINDER, INHIBIT, PREVENT, SHUT OUT
precocious .... ADVANCED
child .... PRODIGY
precognitive one .... SEER
precollege exam .... SAT
precook .... PARBOIL
precursor .... OMEN, HERALD,

HARBINGER, FORERUNNER
predator .... USURER, VAMPIRE, BLACKMAILER, BLOODSUCKER
predatory .... PREYING, RAVAGING, RAVENOUS, PREDACIOUS
bird .... OWL, EAGLE, HAWK, VULTURE
fish .... SHARK
mammal .... WOLF, WOLVERINE
worm .... LEECH
predecessor .... ANCESTOR, PRECURSOR
predestinate .... FOREDOOM
predestination .... FATE, DESTINY, ELECTION
predicament ...... FIX, JAM, MESS, PASS, SPOT, CORNER, CRISIS, PICKLE, PLIGHT, SCRAPE, DILEMMA, RATTRAP, QUANDARY
with no way out .... IMPASSE
predicant .... PREACHER
predicate .... BASE, ASSERT
predict .... AUGUR, PORTEND, (FORE)BODE, FORECAST, FORETELL, PROPHESY
prediction .... FORECAST, PROPHECY
predictor .... PALMIST, SEER(ESS), SORCERER, FORECASTER, PROPHET(ESS), WEATHERMAN
predilection .... BIAS, TASTE, LIKING, LEANING, FONDNESS, PREJUDICE, PARTIALITY, PREFERENCE
predisposed .... PRONE, READY, BIASED, PARTIAL, WILLING, INCLINED, PREPARED
predominant .... RULING, REGNANT
preeminent .... NOTABLE, RENOWNED
preempt .... COOPT, SEIZE, USURP, OCCUPY, APPROPRIATE
preen ...... GROOM, PRIMP, PRINK, DOLL UP, DRESS UP
prefab(ricated) .... NISSEN, QUONSET(HUT), READY-BUILT
preface ...... OPEN, BEGIN, PROEM, START, PRELUDE, FOREWORD, PREAMBLE, PROLOGUE, FRONTISPIECE, INTRODUCTION
prefatory note .... FOREWORD
prefect .... DEAN
prefer .... FAVOR, CHOOSE, SELECT, PRESENT
preferably .... RATHER
preference .... PICK, CHOICE, LIKING

prefix .... BEFORE
a place for .... ORY
about .... PERI
across .... TRANS
after .... META, POST
against .... ANTI, CONTRA
air .... ATMO
all .... OMNI
archaic .... PALES
aside from .... PARA
backward .... RETRO
bad .... MAL
before .... PRE, ANTE
between .... META, INTER
bigness .... MEGALO
black .... MELA
blood .... HEMO
both .... AMBI, AMPH
cast .... TELE
cold .... CYRO
decay .... SAPRO
distant .... TEL(E)
eight .... OCTA, OCT(O)
entire .... HOLO
equal .... ISO
external .... ECTO
false .... PSEUDO
far .... TEL(E)
farm .... AGRO
father .... PATRI
fire .... PYR(O)
fix .... TRANS
foreign .... XENO
front .... ANTERO
gaseous .... AER
glade/green .... EVER
gold .... AURI
half .... DEMI, HEMI, SEMI
hap .... MIS
inner .... ENTO
insect .... ENTOMO
intermediate .... MED
intestine .... COLI
kidney .... RENI
lateral .... UNI
many .... MULT(I)
mind .... PHREN
mountain .... ORO, OREO
nautics .... AERO
nine .... ENNEA
nomer .... MIS
nose .... NAS
not .... DIS, MIS, NON
numerical .... TRI, PENTA
numerical: var. .... DEK
outer .... EXO, ECT(O)
outside .... ECT
over .... SUPRA
partial .... DEMI
physician .... IATRO
plane .... AERO

pod .... TRI
rainbow .... IRID
recent .... CAENO
root .... RHIZO
scient .... OMNI
scope .... TELE, STETHO
single .... MONO
size .... DEMI
sphere .... ATMO, HEMI
syllable .... MONO
thought .... IDEO
thrice .... TER
through .... DIA
tooth .... DENTI
totally .... HOL
touch .... TAC
town .... TRE
under .... SUB
upon .... EPI
upward .... ANO
usage .... NOMO
where .... UBI
width .... LATI
wind .... ANEMO
with .... SYN
with cure and center .... EPI
within .... ENDO, INTRA, INTRO
wrong .... MIS
pregnable .... VULNERABLE
pregnancy ...... CYESIS, FETATION, GESTATION
complication .... MISCARRIAGE, PREMATURITY
discomfort .... NAUSEA, MORNING SICKNESS
false .... PSEUDOCYESIS
outside uterus .... ECTOPIC
pregnant .... GRAVID, FERTILE, CHILDING, ENCEINTE, ABOUNDING, EXPECTING
prehistoric .... ARCHAIC, PRIMITIVE
chisel .... CELT
combining form .... PALE(O)
human .... CAVEMAN
upright stone .... MENHIR
prejudge .... ASSUME, PRESUME
prejudice .... BIAS, HARM, COLOR, IMPERIL, OPINION, ENDANGER, PARTIALITY
prejudiced .... BIASED, PARTIAL
prejudicial .... HARMFUL, DAMAGING, INJURIOUS
prekindled .... PRELIT
prelate .... BISHOP, PRIMATE, CARDINAL
prelect .... LECTURE
preliminary .... PREFATORY
meeting .... CAUCUS
race .... HEAT

statement .... PREFACE,
FOREWORD, PREAMBLE
work .... PREPARATION
prelude .... PROEM, OPENING,
PREFACE, PROLOGUE,
OVERTURE
of fugue .... TOCCATA
premature .... EARLY, FORWARD,
UNTIMELY, INCOMPLETE
aging .... PROGERIA
as in action .... RASH
baby .... PREEMIE
development .... PRECOCITY
premeditate .... PLAN, PLOT,
SCHEME
premeditated .... PREPENSE,
DELIBERATE
killing .... MURDER
premier .... CHIEF, FIRST,
FOREMOST
premiere .... OPENING
Preminger, movie director
.... OTTO
premise .... BASIS, PREFACE,
PROPOSITION
premises, series of .... SORITES
premium .... FEE, AGIO, GIFT,
BONUS, PRIZE, BOUNTY,
REWARD
premonition .... HUNCH,
FOREBODING
Prentiss, actress .... PAULA
preoccupation .... FIXATION,
OBSESSION
with sex .... EROT(IC)ISM
preoccupied .... LOST, RAPT,
ABSTRACTED, ABSENT-MINDED
preoccupy .... ABSORB, OBSESS,
ENGROSS
preparation .... FORESIGHT,
READINESS
concrete .... FOUNDATION
prepare .... SET, ADAPT, GIRD(UP),
EQUIP, PRIME, READY, TRAIN,
FIT(OUT), DISPOSE, ARRANGE,
ACCUSTOM
copy .... EDIT, REDACT
by special treatment .... CURE,
PROCESS
for a play .... REHEARSE
action .... GIRD UP, LIMBER
UP, UNLIMBER
an exam .... BONE UP
conflict .... ARM
roasting .... LARD
the try-pot .... FLENSE
war .... DEPLOY, MOBILIZE
meat .... DRESS
the ground .... CULTIVATE
to solder .... START A
BLOWTORCH

prepared .... YARE, READY,
COACHED, GROOMED
as skins .... TAWED
for war ..... ARMED, ON ALERT
medicine ..... PRESCRIPTION
to take on fares
.... BOARDABLE
prepense .... AFORETHOUGHT
preponderant .... DOMINANT
preposition .... AT, BY, IN, ON,
TO, BUT, FOR, OUT, FROM,
INTO, ONTO, UNTO, UPON,
WITH, AFTER
prepossessing .... WINNING,
PLEASING, ATTRACTIVE
prepossession .... BIAS
preposterous .... ABSURD,
FOOLISH, SENSELESS,
RIDICULOUS
prerequisite .... MUST
prerogative ...... RIGHT, PRIVILEGE
king's .... REGALIA
presage .... BODE, OMEN, SIGN,
AUGUR(Y), PORTEND,
PORTENT, WARNING,
FORETELL, FORESHADOW
presbyter .... ELDER, PRIEST,
PRESTER, MINISTER
prescience .... FORESIGHT
prescind .... ISOLATE, SEGREGATE
prescribe .... LIMIT, ORDER,
ASSIGN, DIRECT, ORDAIN,
OUTLAW, DICTATE,
SET(DOWN)
prescribed .... THETIC
share .... STINT
prescript .... RULE, ORDER
prescription .... RECIPE, FORMULA
physician's .... INSTRUCTION
presence .... GHOST, SPIRIT,
COMPANY, APPEARANCE,
ATTENDANCE
of mind .... WIT
present .... BOON, GIFT, HERE,
SHOW, NONCE, SERVE, AT
HAND, BESTOW, TENDER,
DISPLAY, DONATION,
INTRODUCE
at .... NOW, TODAY
at birth .... CONGENITAL
charges against .... PREFER
good luck .... HANDSEL
time .... NONCE
to departing person .... FOY
with .... FURNISH
presentable .... PASSABLE
presentation .... GIFT, SHOW,
DEBUT, DISPLAY, EXHIBIT,
OFFERING, PERFORMANCE,
INTRODUCTION
presentiment .... HUNCH,

FOREBODING, PREMONITION
presently ...... NOW, ANON, SOON,
SHORTLY, NOWADAYS
preservative ...... BRINE, NITRATE,
VINEGAR
preserve .... CAN, DRY, JAM,
CORN, CURE, KEEP, SALT,
SASS, SAVE, JELLY, SMOKE,
PICKLE, RETAIN, MAINTAIN,
CONFITURE, MARMALADE,
PERPETUATE
by drying .... DESSICATE,
DEHYDRATE
game .... SANCTUARY
with salt .... CORN
with wax .... CERE
preserved dead body .... MUMMY
preshrink cloth .... SANFORIZE
preside .... DIRECT, MANAGE,
CONDUCT, MODERATE
at rural hops .... CALL BARN
DANCES
at tea .... POUR
over .... CHAIR
president, college .... PREXY
yacht club .... COMMODORE
presidential disapproval .... VETO
monogram ..... DDE, FDR, GRF,
HST, JEC, JFK, LBJ, RMN, RWR,
GHWB
nickname ...... ABE, CAL, BILL,
IKE, RON, ANDY, JACK, JERRY,
TEDDY, RONNIE
pet's name:
Bush .... FRED, MILLIE,
RANGER
Coolidge .... TIGER, ROB
ROY, BOUNDER, REBECCA
DDE .... TELEK, CAACIE
FDR .... FALA
Harrison .... SUKEY
Hayes .... DUKE, HECTOR,
NELLIE
Hoover .... KING TUT
Jackson .... POLL
Jefferson .... DICK
JFK .... WOLF, CHARLIE,
CLIPPER, SHANNON
LBJ .... HER, HIM, YUKI,
BLANCO
Nixon .... CHECKERS, KING
TIMAHOE
Reagan .... REX, LUCKY
Washington .... TIPLER,
SWEETLIPS, MADAME MOOSE
Wilson ..... OLD IKE, PUFFINS
reception .... LEVEE
presiding officer .... SPEAKER,
CHAIRMAN, MODERATOR,
PRINCIPAL
officer's vote .... CASTING

presidio .... FORT, GARRISON
press ...... BEG, HUG, CRAM, IRON,
PUSH, URGE, CROWD, CRUSH,
DRIVE, FORCE, WEDGE,
WRING, COMPEL, SMOOTH,
SQUASH, SQUEEZE, NEWS
MEDIA, JOURNALISM
a request .... DEMAND
agency (see **news agency**)
agent .... PUBLICIST,
JOURNALIST
agentry .... BALLYHOO,
PUBLICITY, PROPAGANDA
dough .... KNEAD
down .... TAMP
equipment .... LINOTYPE
for payment .... DUN
one's suit .... WOO
person .... PRINTER, REPORTER,
COMPOSITOR, PROOFREADER
presser .... IRONER, MANGLE
pressing .... URGENT, EXIGENT,
CRITICAL
iron .... GOOSE
need .... IRON
piece .... SADIRON
pressure .... FORCE, DURESS,
STRAIN, STRESS, DEMANDS,
URGENCY, INFLUENCE
gauge .... MANOMETER
group .... BLOC, LOBBY
measuring device .... GAUGE
prefix .... BARO
system .... HIGH
unit .... BARAD, BARIE
prest .... LOAN
prester .... PRIEST, PRESBYTER
prestidigitator .... MAGICIAN
prestige ...... FAME, NOTE, KUDOS,
RENOWN, REPUTE,
REPUTATION
presto .... QUICKLY
person who says .... MAGICIAN
Preston's milieu .... YUKON
presume ...... DARE, IMPLY, INFER,
ASSUME, SUPPOSE, VENTURE
presumption .... GUESS,
AUDACITY, TEMERITY,
INFERENCE
presumptive .... LIKELY,
PROBABLE, SUPPOSED,
ASSUMPTIVE
presumptuous ...... BOLD, BRASH,
FORWARD, ARROGANT,
INSOLENT
presuppose .... PREJUDGE
pretend .... ACT, FAKE, SHAM,
CLAIM, FEIGN, LET ON,
ALLEGE, PROFESS, SIMULATE,
DISSEMBLE, FANTASIZE,
MASQUERADE, (PUT ON AN)

ACT, PLAY A PART
pretended .... FALSE
courage .... BLUFF, BRAVADO
pretender .... SHAM, SNOB,
FAKER, FRAUD, USURPER,
ASPIRANT, CLAIMANT,
IMPOSTOR, IMPERSONATOR
to knowledge .... QUACK,
SCIOLIST, CHARLATAN
pretending .... MAKE BELIEVE
pretense .... ACT, AIR, RUSE,
SHAM, SHOW, CLAIM, FEINT,
GUISE, EXCUSE, PRETEXT
of virtue .... HYPOCRISY
transparent .... CHARADE
pretension .... AIR, BLUFF, CLAIM,
PRETEXT, ALLEGATION
pretentious ...... ARTY, POMPOUS,
ASSUMING, BOASTFUL
art .... KITSCH
preterition .... OMISSION
pretermit .... OMIT, NEGLECT,
OVERLOOK
pretext ...... PLEA, FRONT, COVER-
UP, EXCUSE, PRETENSE
for war .... CASUS BELLI
pretty .... FAIR, NICE, BONNY,
BONNIE, COMELY, LOVELY
and delicately formed
.... DAINTY, MIGNON
girl .... CUTEY
woman .... PERI
pretzel .... BISCUIT
Preussen .... PRUSSIA
prevail .... WIN, RULE, EXIST,
SUCCEED, TRIUMPH,
DOMINATE
on .... INDUCE, PERSUADE
prevalent .... RIFE, COMMON,
CURRENT, GENERAL,
RAMPANT, REGNANT,
PANDEMIC, PREVAILING,
WIDESPREAD
prevaricate .... LIE, PALTER,
QUIBBLE, EQUIVOCATE
prevarication .... LIE, FALSEHOOD
prevaricator .... LIAR
prevent .... BALK, STOP, AVERT,
BLOCK, CHECK, DETER,
HINDER, IMPEDE, THWART,
OBVIATE, WARD OFF,
PRECLUDE, FORESTALL,
FRUSTRATE
legally .... ESTOP
prevention .... STOPPAGE,
RESTRAINT
legal .... ESTOPPEL
preventive court order
.... INJUNCTION
medicine .... ANTIBIOTIC
preview .... TRY OUT, TRAILER

sneak .... SHOWING
Previn of music .... ANDRE
previous .... PRIOR, FORMER,
PRECEDING, ANTECEDENT
previously .... AFORE
mentioned .... AFORESAID
previse .... WARN, FORESEE,
FORECAST
prexy .... PRESIDENT
prey .... ROB, GAME, VICTIM,
QUARRY, PILLAGE, PLUNDER
bird of .... OWL, HAWK,
EAGLE, VULTURE
high sea .... PRIZE
insect of .... (PRAYING)
MANTIS
of cats .... MICE, BIRDS
on .... EAT, DUPE, KILL,
VICTIMIZE
search for .... HUNT, RAVEN,
RAVIN
Priam's daughter .... CREUSA,
CASSANDRA
domain .... TROY
father .... LAOMEDON
son .... PARIS, HECTOR,
TROILUS
son-in-law .... AENEAS
son who caused the Trojan
War .... PARIS
wife .... HECUBA
price .... FEE, COST, RATE, QUOTE,
VALUE, WORTH, AMOUNT,
CHARGE
cutting event .... SALE
go up in .... BULL
kind of .... FIXED, ASKING
list .... CATALOG(UE)
of ride .... FARE
slang .... ANTE, DAMAGE
priceless .... PRECIOUS
pricey .... EXPENSIVE
prick .... DOT, GOAD, PINK, PROD,
SPUR QUALM, STING, WOUND,
PIERCE, TINGLE, PUNCTURE
pricket .... BUCK, DEER,
CANDLESTICK
prickle .... BARB, BUR(R), SETA,
BRIAR, SPINE, STING, THORN,
TINGLE, ACULEUS, TRICHOME
prickly .... BURRY, SPINY,
BARBED, BRIERY, THORNY,
ECHINATE, SMARTING,
STINGING, TINGLING
bush .... ROSE, BRIAR, BRIER
heat .... RASH, LICHEN,
MILIARIA
pear .... TUNA, NOPAL,
CACTUS, OPUNTIA
seed coat .... BUR(R)
shrub .... BRAMBLE,

DEWBERRY, RASPBERRY

weed .... NETTLE

pride ...... AIRS, VANITY, CONCEIT,
RESERVE, ARROGANCE,
VAINGLORY, SELF-ESTEEM

according to Alexander Pope
.... NEVER FAILING VICE OF
FOOLS

disdainful .... HAUTEUR

lion's .... MANE, LITTER

member .... LION

ruffled .... PIQUE

priest .... FRA, CURE, CURATE,
FLAMEN, SHAMAN, CASSOCK,
PRESTER, MINISTER,
CLERGYMAN, PRESBYTER

armband .... FANON

army .... PADRE, CHAPLAIN

assistant of .... ACOLYTE,
SACRISTAN

authorized to hear
confessions
.... CONFESSOR

Buddhist .... LAMA

gift to a .... MORTUARY

high .... ELI, AARON, PONTIFF

house of a .... PRESBYTERY

Indian ...... SHAMAN, MEDICINE
MAN

Jewish .... RABBI(N)

neckpiece of .... AMICE

newly ordained ..... NEOPHYTE

office of .... CURACY,
MINISTRY

salaried .... VICAR

shaven head of .... TONSURE

skullcap .... ZUCCHETTO

title of respect .... FATHER,
REVEREND

vestment .... ALB, COPE,
ORALE, SURPLICE

priestess of Aphrodite ...... HERO

of Apollo .... PYTHIA

priestly .... AARONIC, HIERATIC,
SACERDOTAL

priests group of 20 .... FETIAL

prig .... PRUDE, THIEF, PEDANT,
PICKPOCKET, STUFFED-SHIRT

prill and cinnabar .... ORES

prim ...... NICE, DEMURE, FORMAL,
MODEST, PRISSY, PROPER,
PRUDISH, PRIGGISH

prima _____ .... FACIE,
BALLERINA

donna .... ALDA, DIVA, PONS,
MELBA, CALLAS, STEBER,
TEBALDI

primal .... FIRST, ORIGINAL

primary ...... MAIN, FIRST, CHIEF,
ORIGINAL, ULTIMATE,
PRINCIPAL

primate ...... APE, LEMUR, ORANG,
BABOON, BONOBO, GIBBON,
MONKEY, GORILLA, SIAMANG,
(ARCH)BISHOP

prime .... MAY, A-ONE, PICK,
CREAM, CHOICE, FINEST,
PREPARE, FIRST(RATE)

in music .... UNISON

minister .... PREMIER

mover .... LEADER

of life .... HEYDAY

primer .... READER, HORNBOOK,
(TEXT)BOOK

primitive .... OLD, WILD, BASIC,
CRUDE, ROUGH, ANCIENT,
BARBARIC, ABORIGINAL

combining form .... PALE(O)

fish .... COELACANTH

tribesman's ornament
.... LABRET

primogenitor .... ANCESTOR

primordial .... ORIGINAL

primp ...... GROOM, PREEN, PRINK,
PRUNE

primrose .... OXLIP, SPINK,
COWSLIP, FAIRYCUP

genus .... PRIMULA

prince .... RAS, KING, RAIA,
RULER, MONARCH, PRINCIPE

consort's wife .... QUEEN,
EMPRESS

ecclesiastical .... CARDINAL

Ethiopian .... RAS

in India .... RANA,
(MAHA)RAJAH

look-alike of .... PAUPER

Monaco's reigning
.... RAINIER

Moslem .... IMAM, NAWAB

of Broadway .... HAL

opera .... IGOR

the church .... CARDINAL

Wales .... CHARLES

royal, of England .... CHARLES

Prince Albert's (of England)
wife .... (QUEEN) VICTORIA

Charming's wife, fairy tale
.... CINDERELLA

Norodom, Cambodian
.... SIHANOUK

of Darkness .... SATAN

of Peace .... MESSIAH, JESUS
(CHRIST)

princeling .... SATRAP

princely .... NOBLE, REGAL,
ROYAL, LAVISH, LIBERAL,
GENEROUS

princess .... RANI, RANEE,
INFANTA, MAHARANI

disguised as a bull
.... EUROPA

loved by Zeus .... EUROPA

marble .... SODALITE

mythical .... INO

swift-footed .... ATALANTA

Princess Ida character .... GAMA

Princetonian .... COED

principal ...... ARCH, MAIN, CHIEF,
MAJOR, PREMIER, PRIMARY

actor .... LEAD, STAR

crop .... STAPLE

principality .... PRINCEDOM

principle .... LAW, CODE, RULE,
IDEAL, MAXIM, TENET,
THEORY, PRECEPT, DOCTRINE,
THEOREM, POSTULATE

first .... RUDIMENTS

main .... KEYSTONE

Principles of citizenship
.... CIVISM

of Scientific Management
author: 1911 ..... TAYLOR

princox .... FOP, COXCOMB

prink .... PREEN, PRIMP, PRUNE,
DECK OUT, DRESS UP

print .... COPY, STAMP, IMPOSE,
RUN OFF, ETCHING, PICTURE,
PUBLISH, IMPRESS(ION)

blurred/double .... MACKLE

direction .... STET

in red letters .... RUBRICATE

printed books, early
.... INCUNABULA

printer .... PRESSMAN, STONEMAN,
PUBLISHER, COMPOSITOR,
TYPESETTER

of first books in English
.... (WILLIAM) CAXTON

printer's aid .... GUIDE, INKER,
GRIPPER

apprentice/helper .... DEVIL

direction .... STET, RESET,
DELE(TE)

ink pad .... DABBER

ink spreader .... BRAYER

lock .... QUOIN

mark ..... DASH, CARET, TILDE,
DAGGER, DIESIS, ASTERISK

marking equipment ..... BEVEL

measure .... EM, EN, PICA

metal block for spacing
.... QUAD

metal mold .... MATRIX

metal roller .... PLATEN

pawl .... RATCHET(WHEEL)

proof .... GALLEY

roller .... BRAY

shop spirit .... RALPH

sign for special attention
.... FIST

star .... ASTERISK

printing .... ISSUE, EDITION

art/business of .... PRESS
assortment of type, one size
     and style .... FONT
capital letter in
    .... MAJUSCULE, UPPER CASE
error(s) ..... ERRATUM, ERRATA
establishment .... PRESS
form .... DIE, MAT, MOLD
method .... LITHOGRAPHY
modern method of ...... LASER
part of a letter .... FACE
plate .... STEREO(TYPE)
press, part of ..... BED, BEVEL,
    FRAME, GUIDE, INKER, QUOIN,
    BRAYER, PLATEN, REGLET,
    ROUNCE, FRISKET, GRIPPER
press, type of .... HAND,
    GALLEY, GRAVURE
process .... OFFSET, STENCIL,
    STEREOTYPY, LITHOGRAPHY,
    ROTOGRAVURE
second .... REISSUE
slanted type .... ITALICS
small letter in ...... MINISCULE,
    LOWER CASE, MINUSCULE
system for the blind
    .... BRAILLE
term .... STET, DELE(TE),
    RESET, STONE, CENTER, EM
    DASH, EN DASH, INDENT,
    INSERT, CLOSE UP, LIGATURE,
    LOGOTYPE
trial impression .... PROOF
type ...... PICA, ITALIC, SCRIPT,
    BOLDFACE, LIGHTFACE
part of .... BODY, FEET,
    NICK, STEM, BEARD, SERIF,
    GROOVE
-setting machine
    .... LINOTYPE
size ...... PICA, ELITE, MINION
style .... DORIC, ROMAN,
    GOTHIC, OLD ENGLISH
prior .... ELDER, FORMER,
    EARLIER, PREVIOUS
superior to a .... ABBOT
to .... BEFORE
priority .... PRECEDENCE
priory .... ABBEY, NUNNERY,
    MONASTERY
Priscilla's husband .... ALDEN
suitor .... (MILES) STANDISH
prism .... NICOL
prison .... PEN, CAGE, COOP,
    GAOL, JAIL, QUAD, QUOD,
    LIMBO, BRIDEWELL,
    BASTIL(L)E, PENITENTIARY
camp .... GULAG
cell .... HOLE
chaplain .... ORDINARY
colloquial/slang ..... CAN, JUG,

PEN, STIR, CLINK, POKEY,
    COOLER, LOCKUP, SLAMMER,
    BIG HOUSE, HOOSEGOW,
    CALABOZO, CALABOOSE
cubicle .... CELL
division .... WARD
employee .... GUARD, JAILER,
    WARDER, TURNKEY
federal .... ALCATRAZ, SING
    SING
for stray animals .... POUND
grounds .... BARRED YARD
guard: sl. .... SCREW
head of a .... WARDEN
in California .... SAN QUENTIN
    Devonshire .... DARTMOOR
    island of pelicans
    .... ALCATRAZ
    Kansas .... LEAVENWORTH
    London .... NEWGATE
    New York .... SING SING
    Paris .... BASTILLE
occupant .... FELON, INMATE,
    CONVICT, CRIMINAL
priest .... CHAPLAIN, ORDINARY
sentence .... RAP, STRETCH,
    PUNISHMENT
ship's .... BRIG, HULK
spy .... MOUTON
term .... RAP
underground .... DUNGEON
prisoner .... FELON, INMATE,
    TERMER, CAPTIVE, CONVICT,
    JAILBIRD
at bar .... CULPRIT
bond of .... BAIL, PAROLE
guard of .... BAILIFF
kind of .... LIFER, RAPIST,
    MURDERER
privileged .... TRUSTY
redeem a .... RANSOM
shackles of .... BILBO
prissy ...... PRIM, FUSSY, PRECISE,
    OVERNICE, EFFEMINATE
pristine .... NEW, PURE, FIRST,
    FRESH, PRIME, ORIGINAL,
    UNSPOILED
prithee ...... PLEASE, I PRAY THEE
privacy ...... SECRECY, ISOLATION,
    SECLUSION
private .... INNER, SECRET,
    INTIMATE, PERSONAL,
    SECLUDED, CONFIDENTIAL
apartment .... MAHAL
army .... PFC
entrance .... POSTERN
eye ...... TEC, DICK, DETECTIVE
eye task .... TAIL
information .... TIP
remarks .... ASIDES, AD LIBS
road .... DRIVEWAY

room .... DEN, MEW, LAIR,
    CLOSET
teacher .... COACH, TUTOR
wrong .... TORT
privateer .... KIDD, DRAKE,
    PIRATE, CORSAIR, FREEBOOT,
    SEA ROVER, BUCCANEER
privateering .... PIRACY
privation .... NEED, WANT,
    POVERTY
privilege .... FAVOR, RIGHT,
    OPTION, LICENSE
corporation's .... FRANCHISE
exclusive .... PATENT,
    COPYRIGHT
king's .... REGALITY
people's .... FREEDOM,
    LIBERTY
privileged .... EXEMPT(ED)
privileges, equality of
    .... ISONOMY
privy ...... JAKES, STOOL, CLOACA,
    HIDDEN, SECRET, LATRINE,
    PRIVATE, OUTHOUSE
council .... CAMARILLA
ones .... EPOPTS
to (the secret) .... IN ON,
    AWARE OF, INFORMED
prize .... PRY, AWARD, BOOTY,
    LEVER, STAKE, VALUE,
    ESTEEM, REWARD, TROPHY,
    CHERISH, TREASURE
award since 1917
    .... PULITZER
donor .... NOBEL, PULITZER
fighter ...... BOXER, PUG(ILIST),
    SLUGGER, RINGSTER,
    BEAKBUSTER
fighter's wear .... SILKS
fighting program .... CARD
kind of .... BOOBY
money .... PURSE
of a sort .... BRASS RING
winner .... CHAMPION,
    MEDALIST
pro .... FOR, EXPERT,
    PROFESSIONAL
bono ____ .... PUBLICO
tempore .... TEMPORARY
proa .... PRAU, CANOE
probability .... ODDS, CHANCE,
    LIKELIHOOD
probable .... LIKELY, ODDS-ON,
    POSSIBLE
probandi, ____ .... ONUS
probate court's concern
    .... WILLS, ESTATES
judge .... SURROGATE
probation .... TRIAL, TEST(ING)
probationer .... ROOKIE
probe .... DELVE, SEARCH,

surgical .... STYLET
EXPLORE

probity .... VIRTUE, DECENCY,
HONESTY, INTEGRITY

problem ...... CRUX, KNOT, TASK,
ISSUE, POSER, QUERY,
ENIGMA, PUZZLE, RIDDLE,
DILEMMA, TICKLER,
QUESTION, DIFFICULTY

airport .... NO SHOW

of scarcity ..... BLACK MARKET

problematic .... MOOT

proboscidian .... ELEPHANT,
MASTODON

proboscis .... (BANANA) NOSE,
SNOUT, TRUNK

butterfly's/moth's ...... LINGUA

insect .... HAUSTELLUM

procedure .... WAY, METHOD,
POLICY

proceed ...... GO ON, MOVE, ISSUE,
MARCH, ADVANCE, CONTINUE

at great speed .... HIGHBALL

laboriously .... WADE

without power .... COAST

proceedings .... ACTA, ACTS,
STEPS, MEASURES,
TRANSACTIONS

last part of .... TAG

legal .... LAWSUIT

proceeds ...... GAIN, ISSUE, YIELD,
INCOME, PROFIT, EARNINGS,
RECEIPTS

process .... COURSE, METHOD,
CONDUCT, PRACTICE,
TUBERCLE, APPENDAGE,
OUTGROWTH

fish .... BARBEL

in law .... SUIT, WRIT, (LEGAL)
ACTION, PROSECUTE

of decline .... DECADENCE

of knowing .... NOESIS,
COGNITION

server .... SHERIFF

steel-making .... BESSEMER

procession .... FILE, TRAIN,
PARADE, CORTEGE, RETINUE,
SEQUENCE, CAVALCADE

of cars .... MOTORCADE

official .... MARSHAL

staff .... VERGE

staff bearer .... VERGER

processional .... HYMN

prochein, in law .... NEAREST

proclaim .... CRY, SING, EXTOL,
STATE, HERALD, PRAISE,
DECLARE, ENOUNCE,
TRUMPET, ANNOUNCE,
BROADCAST

proclamation .... FIAT, EDICT,
BAN(N)S, UKASE, NOTICE,
BULLETIN, MANIFESTO

proclivity .... LEANING,
TENDENCY, INCLINATION

Procne's husband .... TEREUS

parent .... PANDION

sister .... PHILOMELA

transformation .... SWALLOW

procrastinate ...... DEFER, DELAY,
LINGER, NEGLECT, POSTPONE,
DILLY-DALLY

procreate .... BEGET, BREED,
PRODUCE

proctor .... AGENT

procumbent .... PRONE

procurator ...... PILATE, PROCTOR

procure .... BUY, GET, OBTAIN,
SECURE, ACQUIRE

procurer .... PIMP, PANDER

prod .... EGG(ON), DIG, JAB,
GOAD, POKE, URGE, DRIVE,
IMPEL, ROUSE, PUNCH, INCITE,
PIERCE, THRUST

prodder .... NEEDLER

elephant .... MAHOUT

prodigal .... LAVISH, WASTER,
SPENDER, PROFUSE, WASTREL,
WASTEFUL, ABUNDANT,
SPENDTHRIFT

one .... SON

prodigious .... HUGE, VAST,
AMAZING, IMMENSE,
ENORMOUS

prodigy .... MARVEL, WIZARD,
WONDER, MIRACLE, MONSTER

prodrome .... SYMPTOM

produce ...... BEAR, MAKE, BEGET,
BREED, CAUSE, FETCH,
HATCH, ISSUE, RAISE, YIELD,
CREATE, ENGENDER,
GENERATE

a musical .... COMPOSE

cloth .... WEAVE

colloquial .... FRUITS,
VEGETABLES

from raw materials
.... MANUFACTURE

proof .... SHOW

produced on earth's surface
.... EPIGENE

producer's favorite letters
.... SRO

producing abundantly
.... FRUITFUL, FERACIOUS

vinegar .... ACETIC

product ...... CROP, FRUIT, YIELD,
RESULT, OUTCOME, CREATION,
OFFSPRING, OUTGROWTH

for combustion .... SMOKE

of dexterity .... FEAT

of imagination .... FIGMENT

of wood distillation ...... PINE-
TAR

production .... OUTPUT

excess .... OVERRUN

sleeper's .... ZEES

productive .... RICH, FECUND,
FERTILE, CREATIVE, FRUITFUL,
PREGNANT, PROLIFIC,
THRIVING, FRUCTUOUS

source .... FONT, MINE

proem .... PREFACE, PRELUDE,
INTRODUCTION

prof. .... PROFESSOR

profanation .... SACRILEGE

profane ...... FOUL, VILE, DEBASE,
DEFILE, VULGAR, VIOLATE,
IMPIOUS, BLASPHEME,
DESECRATE

profanity ...... CURSING, CUSSING,
SWEARING

profess .... AVOW, CLAIM, AFFIRM,
ALLEGE, PURPORT

professed .... AVOWED,
PRETENDED

profession .... LINE, TRADE,
AVOWAL, CAREER, METIER,
CALLING, PURSUIT, VOCATION

"the oldest"
.... PROSTITUTION

professional .... PRO, EXPERT,
SKILLED

non .... LAY, LAIC, AMATEUR

professor .... DON, DOCENT,
TEACHER

assistant .... READER

proffer ...... GIVE, OFFER, EXTEND,
SUBMIT, TENDER, PRESENT

proficient .... APT, ABLE, DEFT,
ADEPT, EXPERT, SKILLED

profile .... BIO-DATA, SKETCH,
CONTOUR, OUTLINE, SIDE
VIEW, SILHOUETTE

profit .... BOOT, GAIN, AVAIL,
BENEFIT, IMPROVE, EARNINGS,
CASH IN ON, ADVANTAGE

addition .... EER

clear .... NET, VELVET

easy .... GRAVY

kind of extra .... PERQUISITE

sudden, great .... KILLING

profitable .... PAYING, GAINFUL,
FRUITFUL, LUCRATIVE

thing, in high finance
.... PLUM

profiteer .... LEECH, SCALPER

profits .... RETURNS, PROCEEDS

for distribution .... MELON

from lands, etc. .... ISSUE

profligate .... WASTEFUL,
DISSOLUTE

person .... ROUE, SPENDER

profound .... DEEP, ABYSS,

HEAVY, INTENSE
profundity .... DEPTH
profuse .... LUSH, LAVISH,
GENEROUS, PRODIGAL,
PLENTIFUL
profusion .... EXCESS,
ABUNDANCE
prog .... FORAGE, PLUNDER
progenitor .... PARENT, ANCESTOR
progeny ...... SEED, BREED, ISSUE,
SCION, CHILDREN, OFFSPRING
prognosis .... ASSESSMENT,
FORECAST(ING), INFORMED
GUESS
prognosticate .... AUGUR,
PREDICT, FORETELL,
PROPHESY
prognosticator .... SEER, DIVINER,
PROPHET, PREDICTOR,
FORECASTER
program .... CARD, PLAN, DRAFT,
AGENDA, OUTLINE, PLAYBILL,
SYLLABUS, PROSPECTUS
progress .... GAIN, COURSE,
STRIDE, ADVANCE,
IMPROVE(MENT)
in work .... HEADWAY
level .... GRADE
planned .... TELESIS
slowly .... CRAWL
progressing by tens .... DECIMAL
progressive loss of hearing
.... PRESBYCUSIS
Progressive of 1912
.... BULLMOOSE
prohibit .... BAN, DENY, TABU,
VETO, (DE)BAR, TABOO,
DISBAR, ENJOIN, FORBID,
HINDER, EXCLUDE, INHIBIT,
PREVENT, DISALLOW
prohibited .... TABU, BANNED,
ILLEGAL, TABOO(ED),
CONTRABAND
prohibition .... BAN, DONT, NO-
NO, TABU, TABOO, EMBARGO
opponents/foes .... WETS
trade .... EMBARGO
prohibitionist .... DRY
prohibitive .... RESTRICTIVE
price .... DEAR, COSTLY,
GOUGING
project .... JUT, HURL, IDEA,
PLAN, PITCH, THROW, DEVISE,
INTEND, SCHEME, PURPOSE,
ENDEAVOR, PROPOSAL,
PROTRUDE
projectile .... BALL, BOMB, SHELL,
BULLET, PELLET, ROCKET,
JAVELIN MISSILE
part of .... WARHEAD, WAR
NOSE

path of .... TRAJECTORY
projecting corner .... COIGN(E)
edge .... BRIM, EAVE
knob .... BOSS
part .... JOG, SOCLE
point .... NEB
rim .... FLANGE
projection .... EAR, FIN, JAG, JOB,
NOB, LOBE, SPUR, BULGE,
LEDGE, SHELF, SOCLE, TORUS,
EXTENSION
on horse collar .... HAME
projector .... VIEWER,
CINEMATOGRAPH
early motion-picture
.... VITASCOPE
old-fashioned term for
.... MAGIC LANTERN
room .... BOOTH
Prokofiev ballet: 1935
.... ROMEO AND JULIET
prolapse .... PTOSIS,
DISPLACEMENT
structure subject to .... DISK,
EYELID
prolegomenon .... FOREWORD
proletarian .... WORKER,
LABORER
proletariat .... WORKING CLASS
proliferate .... SPREAD, MULTIPLY
prolific .... FECUND, FERTILE,
FRUITFUL, INVENTIVE,
PRODUCTIVE
prolix .... WORDY, LENGTHY,
VERBOSE, DISCURSIVE, LONG-
WINDED
prolocutor .... CHAIRMAN,
SPOKESMAN, MOUTHPIECE
prologue reciter .... CHORUS
prolong .... HOLD, NURSE,
EXTEND, STRETCH, CONTINUE,
LENGTHEN, PROTRACT
prolonged dry weather
.... DROUGHT
oppression .... PERSECUTION
shortage of food .... FAMINE
suffering .... AGONY
torment .... HARASSMENT
prom .... HOP, BALL, DANCE
organizers .... JUNIORS
queen's date .... ESCORT
promenade .... BALL, MALL,
WALK, DANCE, MARCH,
PASEO, AVENUE, OUTING,
PARADE, STROLL, GALLERY,
ESPLANADE
along a coast .... FRONT
leisurely ..... STROLL, SAUNTER
ship's .... DECK
tree-lined .... ALAMEDA,
BOULEVARD

Prometheus' boon to man
.... FIRE
brother .... ATLAS
chastiser .... ZEUS
prominence .... EMINENCE,
EMPHASIS, PRESTIGE
between eyebrows
.... GLABELLA
give .... HIGHLIGHT, SPOTLIGHT
prominent .... CONVEX, MARKED,
RAISED, EMINENT, JUTTING,
NOTABLE, SALIENT,
IMPORTANT, NOTICEABLE,
PROTRUDING, CONSPICUOUS
promiscuous .... LAX, LOOSE,
MIXED, CASUAL, CONFUSED
woman .... COCOTTE
promise .... VOW, OATH, WORD,
TROTH, ASSURE, AVOWAL,
ENGAGE, PAROLE, PLEDGE,
SPONSION, GUARANTEE
broke a .... RENEGED
formal .... SPONSION
in marriage .... BETROTH
manufacturer's
...... WARRANT(Y), GUARANTEE
solemn .... VOW, OATH
to tell the truth .... SWEAR
Promised Land .... SION, ZION,
CANAAN
for immigrants .... AMERICA
promises, not always kept
.... PRE-ELECTION
promising ...... ROSY, BRIGHT, UP
AND COMING
one .... COMER
promissory note .... IOU
signer .... MAKER
promontory .... TOR, CAPE, NESS,
SKAW, SPIT, HEADLAND
promote .... AID, BOOST, RAISE,
FOSTER, ADVANCE, DIGNIFY,
ELEVATE, FURTHER, SUPPORT
vigorously .... BOOM
promoter .... FLACK, LOBBYIST,
IMPRESARIO, PRESS AGENT
promotion .... PUBLICITY,
ADVANCEMENT
advertising .... BUILDUP,
CAMPAIGN
sales .... MARKETING
prompt .... CUE, EGG, LEAD,
MOVE, URGE, YARE, EARLY,
QUICK, READY, RATH(E),
INCITE, INDUCE, PUNCTUAL
prompter .... CUER, TICKLER
promptly .... SOON, AT ONCE,
PRONTO
promulgate .... ISSUE, PUBLISH,
ADVOCATE, ANNOUNCE
prone .... APT, FLAT, LIKELY,

SUPINE, DISPOSED, INCLINED, PROSTRATE, RECUMBENT
proneness to anger .... BILE
pronephros .... KIDNEY
prong .... NIB, TIP, FANG, STAB, TINE, POINT, PIERCE
pronged thing .... FORK, HORN, RAKE, SPEAR, TOOTH, ANTLER, TRIDENT
pronounce .... SAY, JUDGE, SPEAK, UTTER, DECLARE, ARTICULATE
distinctly .... ENUNCIATE
imperfectly .... LAMBDACISM
indistinctly .... SLUR
pronounced .... GLARING, OBVIOUS, DISTINCT
by using the tongue
.... LINGUAL
pronouncement .... ORDER, DECREE, RULING, JUDGMENT, SENTENCE
pronto .... AT ONCE, QUICKLY, (RIGHT) NOW, INSTANTLY
pronunciamento ...... MANIFESTO
pronunciation .... UTTERANCE
aid .... BREVE
childlike .... LISP
nasal way of .... TWANG
of r like l .... LALLATION
pause .... HIATUS
poor .... CACOLOGY
prolonging the vowels
.... DRAWL
rough .... BURR
standard .... ORTHOEPY
study of .... PHONOLOGY
unit of .... SYLLABLE
proof .... COPY, TEST, BASIS, TRIAL, REASON, SAMPLE, EXHIBIT, DOCUMENT, EVIDENCE
burden of .... ONUS
kind of .... IRONCLAD
math .... QED
printing .... GALLEY
proofreader's mark ...... BF, LC, LD, LF, SP, TR, WF, ROM, CAPS, DELE, ITAL, STET, CARET
prop ...... GIB, BACK, BASE, STAY, BLOCK, BRACE, SHORE, STAFF, TRUSS, CRUTCH, HOLD UP, PILLAR, UPHOLD, SUPPORT, SUSTAIN, BUTTRESS
briefing .... GRAPH
"Hansel and Gretel"
.... OVEN
one-legged .... UNIPOD
propaganda .... BALLYHOO, PUBLICITY

propagate .... BREED, RAISE, SPREAD, PRODUCE, PUBLISH, GENERATE, INCREASE, MULTIPLY
propagator .... SOWER
propel .... OAR, PUSH, DRIVE, FORCE, IMPEL, SHOVE, SLING
a bayou boat .... POLE
with a pole .... PUNT
propeller .... BLADE, ROTOR, SCREW, DRIVER
driving force of .... THRUST
part of .... BLADE
propensity .... BENT, FLAIR, TALENT, APTITUDE, PENCHANT, TENDENCY, INCLINATION
proper .... FAIR, JUST, MEET, PRIM, RIGHT, DECENT, SEEMLY, APROPOS, CORRECT, FIT(TING), DECOROUS, SUITABLE, BEFITTING
code of precedence
.... PROTOCOL
order .... EUTAXY
slang .... KOSHER
properly .... DULY
property .... ASSETS, ESTATE, REALTY, WEALTH, CHATTEL, HOLDINGS, ATTRIBUTE, OWNERSHIP, POSSESSION
absolute .... AL(L)OD
act to regain .... REPLEVIN
captured at sea .... PRIZE
claim to/charge .... LIEN
delivery of .... LIVERY
endowed .... PATRIMONY
ill-gotten .... PELF, BOOTY, LUCRE
illegal detention of
.... DETINUE
landed .... ESTATE
law .... BONA
legally held ...... SEISIN, SEIZIN
lock .... LIEN
movie-making .... PROP
personal .... CHOSE, CHATTEL
reverted .... ESCHEAT
stationary .... PRAEDIAL
taken by conqueror .... SPOILS
transfer document ..... BILL OF SALE
transferee .... ALIENEE
transferor .... ALIENOR
willed to someone .... LEGACY
prophecy .... AUGURY, FORECAST, PREDICTION
by lots .... SORTILEGE
prophesy .... AUGUR, DIVINE, PORTEND, PREDICT, PRESAGE, FORECAST, FORETELL

prophet .... AMOS, JOEL, JOHN, SEER, HOSEA, JONAH, DANIEL, ELIJAH, ISAIAH, ORACLE, DIVINER, EZEKIEL, MICAIAH, JEREMIAH, PREDICTOR
anointed by Elijah ..... ELISHA
first biblical .... ABRAHAM
great .... MOSES
Moslem .... MOHAMMED
non-Israelite .... BALAAM
of disaster .... ALARMIST
prophetess .... ANNA, SIBYL, DEBORAH, SEERESS, PYTHONESS
discredited .... CASSANDRA
prophetic ...... MANTIC, FATEFUL, FATIDIC, ORACULAR, PYTHONIC, VATIC(AL), SYBILLINE, VATICINAL
prophets, book of the .... NEBI'IM
garb of the .... HAIR-SHIRT
prophylactic .... CONDOM, PROTECTIVE
propinquity .... KINSHIP, AFFINITY, NEARNESS, VICINITY, PROXIMITY
propitiate .... ATONE, PACIFY, APPEASE, MEDIATE
propitious .... TIMELY, GRACIOUS, FAVORABLE, OPPORTUNE, AUSPICIOUS
proponent .... BACKER, ADVOCATE, CHAMPION, PROPOSER, STALWART
of self-realization
.... ENERGIST
proportion .... PART, RATE, QUOTA, RATIO, SHARE, EXTENT, BALANCE, SYMMETRY, DIMENSION
proposal .... BID, PLAN, OFFER, MOTION, TENDER, REQUEST, OVERTURE, SUGGESTION
legislative .... BILL
tentative .... FEELER
propose .... MOVE
for office .... NOMINATE
proposed international language .... IDO, ESPERANTO
proposer .... MOVER
proposition .... PLAN, OFFER, THEORY, PREMISE, PROJECT, THEOREM, PROPOSAL, (HYPO)THESIS
secondary .... LEMMA
self-evident .... AXIOM
propound .... POSE, STATE, PROPOSE, SET FORTH
proprietor .... LORD, OWNER, MANAGER, TITLEHOLDER
propriety .... APTNESS, DECORUM,

propulsion .... PUSH, FLING, EJECTION

prorogue .... ADJOURN

prosaic ...... DULL, PLAIN, SOBER, LITERAL, UNPOETIC

proscribe .... BAN, EXILE, BANISH, FORBID, OUTLAW, CONDEMN, INTERDICT

prosecute ...... SUE, URGE, PRESS, CHARGE, INDICT, PURSUE, ARRAIGN, CARRY ON, FOLLOW UP

prosecuting attorney .... DA, FISCAL

proselyte .... CONVERT

Proserpina .... CORA, PERSEPHONE

husband of .... PLUTO

mother of .... CERES

proseuchae .... ORATORIES

prosit .... TOAST

prosody .... METRICS, SCANSION

verse .... STICH

prospect ...... HOPE, VIEW, SCENE, SIGHT, VISTA, SEARCH, OUTLOOK, PROMISE

A-one .... COMER

prospective ...... COMING, FUTURE, LIKELY, EXPECTED, IMMINENT

prospector .... MINER

advance to .... GRUBSTAKE

colloquial .... SOURDOUGH, FORTY-NINER

companion of .... MULE

helper of .... BURRO

quest of .... LODE

transportation of .... PACKHORSE

prospectus .... CATALOG, PROGRAM, BROCHURE

prosper .... GROW, BATTEN, FATTEN, THRIVE, BURGEON, SUCCEED, FLOURISH, MULTIPLY

prosperity .... BOOM, BONANZA

archaic .... WEAL

slang .... FAT CITY

Prospero's slave .... CALIBAN

sprite .... ARIEL

prosperous .... FAT, RICH, PALMY, WEALTHY, WELL-OFF, AFFLUENT, WELL-TO-DO, THRIVING

prostitute ...... DRAB, SLUT, TART, TRAMP, TRULL, WHORE, CHIPPY, HARLOT, TROLLOP, FILLE DE JOIE

biblical .... GOMER, RAHAB, MARY MAGDALENE

kind of .... COURTESAN

prostitution .... HARLOTRY, STREETWALKING, WHITE SLAVERY

house of .... BROTHEL, BORDELLO

prostrate .... FLAT, ABASE, PRONE, FALLEN, LAY LOW, SUPINE, LAID LOW, SUPINATE, POWERLESS, RECUMBENT

prosy ...... DULL, JEJUNE, PROSAIC, COMMON(PLACE)

protagonist .... HERO, STAR, RIVAL, LEADER, HEROINE, EXPONENT, CONTENDER

protean .... MULTIFORM

protect .... SAVE, POLICE, SCREEN, SECURE, SHIELD, SHELTER, (DE)FEND, PRESERVE, (SAFE)GUARD

from heat .... INSULATE

protection .... AID, CUSTODY, (A)EGIS, DEFENSE, PASS(PORT), SECURITY, TUTELAGE

against loss .... INSURANCE

means of .... MOAT, ARMOR, PAINT, QUILL, SPINE, HELMET, CAMOUFLAGE

palatial .... MOAT

racket .... EXTORTION

protective band, fencing .... BRACER

coloration .... DISGUISE

cover .... FOIL, ARMOR, CRATE, SHELL, HELMET, SCREEN, SHIELD, CAMOUFLAGE

protector .... KEEPER, PATRON, REGENT, DEFENDER, GUARDIAN

of auto .... GARAGE

of the President .... SECRET SERVICE

protectorate .... CONDOMINIUM, TRUST TERRITORY, TRUSTEESHIP

protege(e) .... WARD, PUPIL, CHARGE

proteid(e) .... AMINE, PROTEIN

protein .... AMINE, CASEIN, ENZYME, FIBRIN, RICIN(E), ALBUMIN, HISTONE, ALEURONE, GLOBULIN, PROTEID(E)

building acid .... AMINO

component of hemoglobin .... GLOBIN

egg yolk .... LECITHIN, VITELLIN

enzyme that digests .... PROTEASE

in muscles ..... ACTIN, MYOSIN

in tissue/bone .... MUCIN, COLLAGEN

insoluble ...... FIBRIN, KERATIN

milk .... CASEIN

soluble .... PEPTONE

type of .... LIPID, MUCIN, ALBUMIN, EDESTIN, ELASTIN, FIBROIN, KERATIN, PEPTIDE, SALMINE, LECITHIN, VITELLIN

white albuminoid ...... FIBROIN

proteose .... ALBUMOSE, ELASTOSE

protest .... ASSERT, OUTCRY, REFUSE, SQUAWK, DISSENT, COMPLAIN, (COM)PLAINT, OBJECT(ION)

Protestant .... BAPTIST, ANGLICAN, LUTHERAN, OBJECTOR, DISSENTER, METHODIST, NON-CATHOLIC

Anglo-Saxon .... WASP

non-conformist .... SECTARY

protocol .... CUSTOMS, PROCEDURES

proton .... ANLAGE

accelerator .... COSMOTRON

provide with a .... PROTONATE

protoplasm .... PLASMA, COLLOID

composing nucleus of a cell .... NUCLEOPLASM

granule in .... MICROSOME

of a cell .... CYTOPLASM

unit of .... PLASTID

prototype ...... DIE, MOLD, IDEAL, MODEL, EXAMPLE, PATTERN, EXEMPLAR, ORIGINAL, STANDARD

protozoan .... MONAD, AM(O)EBA, SPORE, EUGLENA, PROTIST

organ of locomotion .... FLAGELLUM

protract .... DRAG, DEFER, DELAY, EXTEND, PROLONG, STRETCH, LENGTHEN

protrude .... BULGE, EXSERT, JUT(OUT), PROJECT

protrusion of organ ...... HERNIA

of the eyeball .... PROPTOSIS

protuberance ...... EAR, JAG, JUT, NUB, HUMP, KNOB, LOBE, LUMP, NODE, SNAG, UMBO, BULGE, INION, VENTER, SWELLING

camel's back .... HUMP

protuberant .... CONVEX, TOROSE, TOROUS, BULGING

proud .... VAIN, BYRONIC, HAUGHTY, ARROGANT, BOASTFUL, SPIRITED, SUPERIOR, OVERBEARING

as a _____ .... PEACOCK

Proust, F., novelist ...... MARCEL

prove .... SHOW, TEST, CHECK,

FITNESS

TRY(OUT), VERIFY, CONFIRM, DEMONSTRATE
false .... BELIE, DEBUNK, REFUTE
successful .... PAN OUT
provenance .... ORIGIN, DERIVATION
Provençal love song .... ALBA
poet .... MISTRAL
provender ...... HAY, CORN, FEED, FOOD, OATS, GRAIN, FODDER, PROVISIONS
proverb ...... SAW, ADAGE, AXIOM, MAXIM, BY-WORD, SAYING, PARABLE, PRECEPT, APHORISM
proverbial blushers .... BRIDES
provide .... CATER, AFFORD, PURVEY, SUPPLY, FURNISH, STIPULATE
a crew .... MAN
food .... CATER
for .... SUPPORT
for oneself .... FEATHER ONE'S NEST
services .... RENDER
with a top .... ENCAP
with means .... ENABLE
with what is needed .... EQUIP, OUTFIT, ACCOUTER
provided .... IF, THOUGH
Providence .... LORD, HEAVEN, PRUDENCE, GOD(ALMIGHTY)
provident ...... FRUGAL, PRUDENT, THRIFTY, CAUTIOUS
providential .... LUCKY, FORTUNATE, AUSPICIOUS, HEAVEN-SENT
provider .... DONOR, ENDURER, BREADWINNER
province .... REGION, SPHERE, DISTRICT, TERRITORY
ruler of .... ETHNARCH, GOVERNOR
provincial .... LOCAL, RUSTIC, INSULAR, NARROW(-MINDED)
speech .... IDIOM, PATOIS, DIALECT
proving directly .... D(E)ICTIC
ground .... LAB(ORATORY)
provision ...... FARE, FEED, FOOD, CATES, LARDER, PROVISO, EATABLES, PLANNING, VICTUALS, CONDITION, GROCERIES, STIPULATION
search for .... FORAGE
storage for .... CELLAR
provisional .... IFFY, INTERIM, TEMPORARY, TENTATIVE
provisioner ...... GROCER, SUTLER, CATERER, PURVEYOR
proviso .... CLAUSE, CONDITION(S),

REQUIREMENT, STIPULATION
provisory .... SUBJECT, CONDITIONAL
provocation .... AFFRONT, VEXATION, INCITEMENT
with little .... AT THE DROP OF A HAT
provocative .... RACY, PIQUANT, EXCITING, INVITING, SEDUCTIVE, TANTALIZING
provoke .... IRE, VEX, BAIT, GOAD, RILE, STIR, ANGER, ANNOY, PIQUE, AROUSE, EXCITE, INCITE, NEEDLE, NETTLE, IRRITATE
provost .... JAILER
officer .... MARSHAL
prow .... BOW, BEAK, NOSE, FRONT
prowess .... SKILL, VALOR, ABILITY, COURAGE, HEROISM
prowl .... LURK, ROAM, ROVE, SKULK, SLINK, SNEAK
proximal .... NEXT, NEAREST
opposed to .... DISTAL
to the fingernail ..... KNUCKLE
to the hip joint .... KNEE
proximity .... NEARNESS
proxy .... AGENT, DEPUTY, SUBSTITUTE
prude .... PRIG
prudence .... CARE, TACT, DISCRETION, CAUTION, FORESIGHT
prudent .... WISE, CHARY, CAREFUL, HEEDFUL, CAUTIOUS, DISCREET, SENSIBLE
prudery-personified .... GRUNDY
prudish .... DEMURE, PRISSY
prune .... CUT, LOP, CLIP, PARE, PLUM, SNIP, TRIM, SHEAR, REMOVE
prunella .... TEXTILE
prurient .... LEWD, LUSTFUL
prurigo .... RASH
pruritus .... ITCHING
Prussian .... GERMAN, JUNKER
cavalryman .... U(H)LAN
city .... EMDEN, ESSEN, AACHEN
district .... STADE
land measure .... MORGEN
legislature .... LANDTAG
province .... SAXONY
resort .... EMS
river .... RUHR
seaport .... KIEL, EMDEN, STETTIN
prussiate .... CYANIDE
pry ...... LOOK, NOSE, PEEK, PEER,

SEEK, FORCE, JIMMY, LEVER, PRIZE, RAISE, CROWBAR, INSPECT, SNOOP(ER)
pryer .... BUSYBODY
prying .... NOSY, CURIOUS, INQUISITIVE
person .... SPY, SNOOP, GOSSIP, PEEPER, MEDDLER, PEEPING TOM
PS .... POSTSCRIPT
psalm .... HYMN, LAUD, SONG, MOTET, PAEAN, ANTHEM, CANTATA, CANTATE, CHORALE, INTROIT, CANTICLE
word .... SELAH
psalter .... PSALMBOOK
psalterium .... OMASUM, MANYPLIES
psaltery .... DULCIMER
plucker .... PLECTRUM
psammite .... SANDSTONE
pseudo .... FAKE, MOCK, SHAM, BOGUS, FALSE, PHONY, SPURIOUS, COUNTERFEIT
intellectual .... PUNDIT, SCIOLIST, CHARLATAN
pseudodementia ...... DEPRESSION
pseudogout .... ARTHRITIS
pseudologist .... LIAR
forte of .... LIES
pseudonym ...... ALIAS, ANONYM, BYNAME, PEN NAME, NICKNAME, INCOGNITO, SOBRIQUET, NOM DE PLUME
Arouet .... VOLTAIRE
Athorton .... LIN
Austen .... DAPSANG
Bronte .... (CURRER) BELL
Clemens .... (MARK) TWAIN
Dickens .... BOZ
Dodgson .... (LEWIS) CARROLL
Dudevant ...... (GEORGE) SAND
Evans, Mary Ann .... (GEORGE) ELIOT
Gardner, E.S. .... FAIR
Geisel, Theodor Seuss .... DR. SEUSS, THEO LESIEG
Goodman .... ADAM SMITH
Herzog ...... (ANDRE) MAUROIS
Josip Broz .... TITO
Lamb .... ELIA
Millay .... (NANCY) BOYD
Moir .... DELTA
Mrs. Humphrey .... RITA
Munro .... SAKI
Poquelin .... MOLIERE
Porter .... (O) HENRY
Pyeshkov, Aleksei .... (MAXIM) GORKI
Rabelais, Francois .... (ALCOFRIBAS) NASIER

Ramee, M. L. .... OUIDA
Rosegger .... PK
Stein .... (ALICE) TOKLAS
Thibault .... (ANATOLE) FRANCE
Ulyanov, Vladimir
.... (NICOLAI) LENIN
Viaud, L. M. ..... (PIERRE) LOTI
Wright .... (S.S.) VAN DINE
pshaw .... TUT, POOH
Psiloriti, Mount .... IDA
location of .... CRETE
psilosis .... SPRUE
psittacosis .... INFLUENZA
spreader .... PARROT, PIGEON
psoas .... LOIN, MUSCLE
disorder .... ABSCESS
location .... FEMUR, PELVIS
psora .... SCABIES
psoriasis .... ECZEMA, DERMATITIS
type of ..... DISCOID, GUTTATE, PUSTULAR
psychasthenia .... NEUROSIS
psyche .... MIND, SOUL, SPIRIT
Psyche, love of ...... EROS, CUPID
psyched up .... PRIMED
psychedelic experience ...... LSD
psyches, part of .... IDS, EGOS
psychiatrist .... ADLER, FREUD, MESMER, ANALYST, ALIENIST
concern of .... EGO
slang .... HEADSHRINKER
psychic ...... MENTAL, PREDICTOR, SPIRITUAL
disorder .... NEUROSIS
energy .... LIBIDO
person .... MEDIUM
power: abbr. .... ESP
psycho .... NEUROTIC
psychological .... MENTAL
jargon, trite
.... PSYCHOBABBLE
psychologist .... BINET, REICH, PAVLOV, PIAGET, WATSON
psychology, branch of
.... HEDONICS
psychopath .... MADMAN
psychopathic .... LOCO, SCHIZY
psychosis .... INSANITY
psychotic .... CRAZY, LUNATIC, PARANOID
Pt, in chemistry .... PLATINUM
ptarmigan .... RIPA, GROUSE
pteric .... ALAR
pteridophyte .... FERN, MOSS
pteris rootstock .... ROI
pterodactyl .... PTEROSAUR
pteropod .... CLIONE, MOLLUSK
pterygoid .... WINGLIKE
ptisan .... TEA, DRINK, TISANE, DECOCTION

Ptolemais, formerly .... ACRE
ptomaine, liquid .... CHOLINE
ptosis .... PROLAPSE
ptyalin .... ENZYME
pub .... BAR, INN, HOTEL, SALOON, TAVERN
missile .... DART
potion ...... ALE, BEER, PORTER
worker ..... BARMAID, TAPSTER
puberty .... MATURITY, NUBILITY, ADOLESCENCE
of .... HEBETIC
pubescence .... DOWN
public .... FREE, OPEN, CIVIC, KNOWN, OVERT, COMMON, PEOPLE, GENERAL, POPULAR, COMMUNAL, COMMUNITY
announcer .... CRIER
assistance .... WELFARE
auction .... VENDUE
baths .... THERMAE
disclosure .... EXPOSE
enemy .... CRIMINAL, GANGSTER, RACKETEER
funds, steal .... PECULATE
good .... COMMONWEAL
house .... BAR, INN, HOTEL, TAVERN
indignation .... FUROR
land .... AGER
life .... CAREER
notice .... AD, BULLETIN, PUBLICITY, SPOTLIGHT
opinion .... CONSENSUS
opinion-taker .... ROPER, GALLUP, HARRIS
outcries: sl. .... STINKS
press ...... THE FOURTH ESTATE
prosecutor .... DA, FISCAL
recreation spot .... PARK
square .... FORUM, PLAZA, PIAZZA
supervisor of accounts
.... COMPTROLLER
transportation .... BUS, TAXI(CAB), STREETCAR
utility .... GAS, POWER, WATER, TELEPHONE, ELECTRICITY, MAIL DELIVERY
walk .... ESPLANADE
welcome, enthusiastic
.... OVATION
worship, science of
.... LITURGIES
publican .... TAXER, TAXMAN, INNKEEPER, BARKEEP(ER)
publication .... BOOK, ORGAN, ARTICLE, GAZETTE, JOURNAL, TABLOID, BULLETIN, MAGAZINE, NEWS(PAPER), PERIODICAL

examiner .... CENSOR
publicist .... AUTHOR, WRITER, COLUMNIST, JOURNALIST, (PRESS)AGENT
publicity .... NOTICE, RECLAME, EXPOSURE, LIMELIGHT, NOTORIETY
exaggerated .... PUFFERY
ploy .... PRESS RELEASE
society .... MEDIA WORLD
publicize .... AIR, PLUG, VOICE, REPORT, ADVERTISE, CIRCULATE
publish .... AIR, EDIT, ISSUE, NOISE, PRINT, BLAZON, HERALD, PUT OUT, RELEASE, ANNOUNCE, PROCLAIM
publisher .... OCHS, VALK, MCKAY, FIELDS, HEARST, PUTNAM, MERRIAM, NEWHOUSE, SULZBERGER
publisher's announcement
.... BLURB
trademark .... COLOPHON
Puccini, composer ...... GIACOMO
heroine ...... MIMI, TOSCA, CIO-CIO SAN
opera .... MANON, TOSCA, LESCAUT, LA BOHEME, TURANDOT, MADAMA BUTTERFLY
puccoon .... DYE, BLOODROOT
puce .... PURPLE
puck .... ELF, IMP, DISK, SPRITE, (HOB)GOBLIN
pucka ...... GOOD, REAL, GENUINE
pucker .... FOLD, KNIT, POUT, RUCK, TUCK, PURSE, SHIRR, COCKLE, CREASE, CRINKLE, WRINKLE
puckered .... BULLATE, CORRUGATED
puckerel .... IMP
puckish .... ELFIN, IMPISH, DEVILISH, MISCHIEVOUS
pudding .... DUFF, MUSH, BURGOO, JUNKET, SPONGE, CUSTARD, DESSERT, SAUSAGE, PORRIDGE, ROLY-POLY
baked apple .... BROWN BETTY
in England .... TRIFLE
Indian .... CORNMEAL
ingredient .... MILK, SAGO, SUET, FLOUR, FRUIT, TAPIOCA, VANILLA, MOLASSES, SEMOLINA
kind of .... PLUM, RICE, CARROT, CHARLOTTE, CHOCOLATE, YORKSHIRE
sailor's/seaman's .... DUFF
puddle .... POOL, SLOP, SUMP,

MUDDY, SLUSH, WALLOW, PLASH(ET), LOBLOLLY
puddling tool .... RABBLE
pudency .... MODESTY
pudendum .... VULVA
pudgy ...... FAT, DUMPY, CHUBBY, STOCKY, ROLY-POLY
Pueblo .... TOWN, INDIAN, VILLAGE
council room .... KIVA
Indian .... HOPI, PIRO, TANO, ZUNI, MOQUI
Indian dwelling .... KIVA
puerile .... SILLY, YOUNG, FOOLISH, TRIVIAL, CHILDISH, IMMATURE, INFANTILE
passion .... PUPPY LOVE
Puerto Rico bay .... HONDA, JOBOS, SUCIA, ANASCO, RINCON, BOQUERON, MAYAGUEZ, AGUADILLA, GUAYANILLA
beverage .... MABI
cape .... ROJO
capital .... SAN JUAN
city/town ...... CAYEY, COAMO, LARES, PONCE, YAUCO, CAGUAS, CATANO, DORADO, MANATI, ARECIBO, BAYAMON, FAJARDO, GUAYAMA, HUMACAO, ISABELA, CAROLINA, MAYAGUEZ, VEGA ALTA, VEGA BAJA, LEVITTOWN, RIO GRANDE
conqueror .... MILES
discoverer of .... COLUMBUS
district .... PONCE, ARECIBO, BAYAMON, GUAYAMA, HUMACAO, SAN JUAN, MAYAGUEZ, AGUADILLA
governor ..... MUNOZ, ROMERO, ALBERTO, SANCHEZ, MAYAGUEZ, HERNANDEZ
island .... CULEBRA, VIEQUES
lake .... GUAYO, YAUCO, CARITE, GUANICA, CARRALZO, GUAYABAL, PATILLAS, CAONILLAS
language .... ENGLISH, SPANISH
measure .... CUERDA
monetary unit .... DOLLAR
mountain .... EL TORO, PIRATA, EL YUNQUE, GUILARTE
mountains ..... CAYEY, JAICOA, LUQUILLO
passage .... MONA, VIEQUES
porkfish .... SISI
river .... BAUTA, CAMUY, COAMO, LOIZA, NIGUA, PLATA, ANASCO, MANATI, YAQUEZ, TANAMA, ARECIBO, FAJARDO,

GUAYANES, JACAGUAS, CANOVANAS, CULEBRINAS
sea .... CARIBBEAN
seaport .... ARECIBO
puff .... PAD, BLOW, BRAG, FLAM, GASP, PANT, WAFF, WHIFF, BREATH, PRAISE, INFLATE, SWELL(ING)
adder .... SNAKE
at a cigarette .... DRAG
ball .... FUNGUS
bird .... BARBET, MONASA
headdress .... POUF
of wind .... GUST, FLATUS
out .... BOUFFANT
small .... WHIFFET
up .... BLOW, BLOAT, ELATE, SWELL, INFLATE
puffed .... BAGGY
puffer .... (GLOBE)FISH
puffin .... BIRD
kin of .... AUK
puffing .... BREATHLESS
puffy .... FAT, OBESE, BLOATED, PANTING, SWOLLEN
pug .... CLAY, BOXER, TRACK, TRAIL, (BULL)DOG, PAW(MARK), PUGILIST, FOOTPRINT
Puget Sound seaport
.... TACOMA
pugging .... CLAY, MORTAR, SAWDUST
puggree .... SCARF
pugh .... BAH, PAH, PISH, EXCLAMATION
pugilism ...... BOXING, FISTICUFFS
pugilist .... PUG, BOXER, FIGHTER, RINGSTER, BEAKBUSTER
aide, in practice ..... SPARRER, SPARRING PARTNER
arena .... RING
assistant of .... SECOND, HANDLER
encounter .... MILL
pants .... TRUNKS
pugnacious .... BELLICOSE, COMBATIVE, BELLIGERENT, QUARRELSOME
man .... BRUISER
puisne .... JUDGE, JUNIOR
puissant .... MIGHTY, STRONG
puke ...... SPIT, VOMIT, THROW UP
pukka .... REAL, GENUINE
pulchritude ...... CHARM, GRACE, BEAUTY
pulchritudinous .... BEAUTIFUL
one .... PIN-UP, VENUS
pule .... WHINE, WHIMPER
pulex .... FLEA

Pulitzer Prize author, 1984
.... GEISEL
author Tuchman's book
.... THE GUNS OF AUGUST
cartoonist, 1955 .... (DAN) FITZPATRICK
novelist, 1958 .... AGEE
poet .... (ROBERT) FROST
winning play .... HEIDI CHRONICLES, DRIVING MISS DAISY
work category .... MUSIC, JOURNALISM, LITERATURE
Pulj, former name of ...... POLA
pull .... DO, LUG, TOW, TUG, DRAG, DRAW, HAUL, JERK, MOVE, SWAY, PLUCK, GRAVITY, PERFORM, (RE)STRAIN
a fast one .... OUTWIT, OUTSMART
an oar .... CREW
apart .... PAN, RIP, REND, TEAR, SEPARATE, CRITICIZE
back ...... RETREAT, WITHDRAW
down .... RAZE, HUMBLE, REDUCE, DOWSE, DESTROY
for .... BACK, ROOT, CHEER
forcibly .... YANK, WRENCH
off .... DO, EFFECT, MANAGE, SUCCEED, ACCOMPLISH
one's leg .... FLATTER
one's punches .... HESITATE
out .... UPROOT, ABANDON
out by the root .... STUB
slang .... POWER, INFLUENCE
teeth .... EXTRACT
through .... RECOVER, SURVIVE
toward .... ATTRACT, MAGNETIZE
up .... HIKE, REIN, STOP
up stake .... LEAVE, DEPART
pullet .... HEN, POULARD
pulley .... WHEEL, ROLLER, SHEAVE, TACKLE, TRUCKLE
pullman .... BERTH, SLEEPER
pullover .... SHIRT, SWEATER
pullulate ...... BUD, TEEM, BREED, SWARM, GERMINATE
pulmonary disease ...... PHTHISIS
pulp .... PAP, CURD, MASH, MASS, MUSH, PITH, CHYME, PASTE
apple/fruit .... POMACE
grape .... RAPE
in mining .... SLIME
product .... PAPER
slang .... MAGAZINE
pulper ...... MASHER, MACERATOR
pulpit .... BEMA, DESK, ROSTRUM, MINISTRY, PLATFORM
early Christian .... UMBO

preachings .... SERMONS, HOMILIES
pulpiteer .... PREACHER
pulpy .... PAPPY, PASTY, PITHY, FLESHY
fruit .... FIG, UVA, DRUPE, GRAPE, MANGO, PEACH, CASABA, PAPAYA, AVOCADO, CANTALOUPE, POMEGRANATE
pulque .... AGAVE, MESCAL
pulsate ...... BEAT, DRUM, THROB, THRILL, QUIVER, VIBRATE, PALPITATE
pulsation .... PULSE, BEAT(ING), HEARTBEAT, THROB(BING), VIBRATION
pulse .... SEED, ARSIS, THROB, THUMP, SPHYGMUS, (HEART)BEAT
beat absence .... ACROTISM
combining form ..... SPHYGMO
instrument for measuring .... SPHYGMOMETER
kind of .... ECHO, TRIGGER
of the .... SPHYGMIC
plant .... PEA, (SOY)BEAN, VETCH, LENTIL
split .... DAL
pulverize ...... BRAY, MILL, MULL, CRUSH, GRIND, POUND, POWDER, ATOMIZE, CRUMBLE, LEVIGATE, TRITURATE
pulverized material .... DUST, POWDER
pulverizing device .... SPIDER
pulverulent .... DUSTY, POWDERY
puma .... CAT, FUR, COUGAR, PANTHER, CATAMOUNT, (MOUNTAIN) LION
pumice ...... ROCK, STONE, POLISH
source of .... LAVA
pummel .... BEAT, DRUB, PELT, BASTE, POUND, BATTER, THRASH, WALLOP, BELABOR
pump .... QUIZ, SHOE, GRILL, DRAW (OUT), INFLATE, INJECTOR, QUESTION, INTERROGATE
handle .... SWIPE
iron .... EXERCISE, WEIGHT-LIFT
kind of ...... RAM, LIFT, CHAIN, FORCE, SUCTION, PRESSURE
part .... RAM, VALVE, PISTON
plunger of .... RAM
pumpernickel .... BROT, BREAD
pumpkin .... PEPO, FRUIT, GOURD, MELON, SQUASH
"eater" .... PETER
pumpkinseed .... (SUN)FISH
pun .... JOKE, QUIP, GROANER, QUIBBLE, EQUIVOKE, WORDPLAY, PARONOMASIA
slang .... WISECRACK
puna .... PLATEAU
punch .... ADE, AWL, BOP, BOX, GAD, HIT, JAB, BLOW, POKE, PROD, DRINK, DOUSE, FORCE, STAMP, BUFFET, PIERCE, PUPPET, STRIKE, PUNCTURE, PERFORATE
bowl .... MONTEITH
drunk .... DAZED, DIZZY, PUNCHY
drunk boxer .... STUMBLE BUM
engraver's .... MATTOIR
in .... TIME IN, CLOCK IN
slang .... PASTE
weak .... TIFF
Punch and _____ .... JUDY
and Judy character .... PUPPET
and Judy dog .... TOBY
wife of .... JUDY
puncheon .... AWL, DIE, CASK, POST, TIMBER, PERFORATOR
punchinello .... CLOWN, BUFFOON
punchpoked ...... KNITTED SOCKS
punctate .... DOTTED, SPOTTED
punctation .... DOT
punctilio .... NICETY
punctilious .... PRIM, EXACT, FUSSY, FORMAL, SEVERE, STRICT, PRECISE, SCRUPULOUS
person .... PRIG, PRUDE
punctual .... EARLY, ON TIME, PROMPT, TIMELY, TO THE MINUTE
punctually .... IN GOOD TIME
punctuate .... MARK, POINT, INTERRUPT
punctuation mark .... DOT, COLA, COMMA, HYPHEN, PERIOD, BRACKETS, (SEMI)COLON, APOSTROPHE, PARENTHESES, QUESTION MARK, EXCLAMATION MARK
puncture .... JAB, HOLE, PRICK, PUNCH, PIERCE, DEFLATE, OPENING, PERFORATE
pundit .... SAGE, SAVANT, SCHOLAR, AUTHORITY
slang .... WISE GUY
pung .... SLED, SLEIGH, TOBOGGAN
pungent .... TEZ, KEEN, RACY, TART, ACERB, ACRID, SALTY, SHARP, SPICY, TANGY, ZESTY, BITING, STRONG, CAUSTIC, GINGERY, PEPPERY, PIQUANT
bulb ..... LEEK, ONION, GARLIC, SHALLOT, SCALLION
seasoning ..... CURRY, GINGER, PEPPER, CAYENNE, MUSTARD

Punic citizen ...... CARTHAGINIAN
War battlesite .... ZAMA
belligerent .... ROME, CARTHAGE
general .... SCIPIO
victor .... ROME
punish .... CANE, DOCK, FINE, FLOG, FRAP, LASH, WHIP, SPANK, STRAP, WREAK, AVENGE, BEAT UP, CHASTEN, CORRECT, CHASTISE, PENALIZE, CASTIGATE, DISCIPLINE
by depriving right to practice profession .... EXPEL, DISBAR
imposing fine .... AMERCE
lowering rank .... DEMOTE
retaliation .... REQUITE
cruelly ...... CRUCIFY, TORTURE
errant priest .... UNFROCK
severely .... SLATE
to correct .... CHASTEN, CHASTISE
punished: sl. .... GOT IT, WORKED OVER
punishing .... KILLING, CRUSHING, GRUELING
punishment .... RAP, FINE, EXILE, TALION, FORFEIT, PENALTY, REQUITAL, BASTINADO
capital ..... DEATH, EXECUTION, GAS CHAMBER, ELECTRIC CHAIR
convicted person's .... JUDGMENT, SENTENCE
divine .... PLAGUE
eye for an eye .... TALION
endless .... DAMNATION
instrument of ...... ROD, RACK, STICK, FERULE, STOCKS, GARROTE, PILLORY
of .... PENAL, PUNITIVE
retaliatory .... REVENGE, REPRISAL
unlawful .... LYNCHING
voluntary .... PENANCE
punitive .... PENAL, PUNITORY, INFLICTIVE
Punjab, capital (India) .... CHANDIGARH
capital (Pakistan) ...... LAHORE
city/town ..... SIMLA, AMBALA, PATIALA, SIALKOT, AMRITSAR, JULLUNDAR
native .... JAT, SIKH
warrior .... SIKH
punk .... AMADOU, TINDER, TOUCHWOOD
slang .... BUM, MUG, HOOD(LUM), (SNOTNOSE) KID

punka(h) .... FAN
punkie .... FLY, GNAT, MIDGE
punster .... WAG, WIT, COMIC,
JOKER
punt .... BET, QUANT, SCULL,
WAGER, GAMBLE, PROPEL,
(PLACE)KICK
punter .... BETTOR, KICKER
punty .... POINTIL
puny .... TINY, WEAK, FRAIL,
SMALL, SLIGHT, STUNTED
one .... RUNT
pup ...... CUB, DOG, SEAL, POOCH,
PUPPY, WHELP
pupa .... NYMPH, CHRYSALIS
covering of .... THECA,
COCOON
pupil .... TYRO, WARD, GRADER,
LEARNER, STUDENT, TRAINEE,
DISCIPLE
constrict the .... NARROW
constrictor .... PILOCARPINE
contraction of .... MYOSIS
dilatation of .... MYDRIASIS
dilate the .... WIDEN
dilator .... ATROPINE
organ with .... EYE
pupilage .... NONAGE
puppet .... DOLL, DUPE, PAWN,
TOOL, DUMMY, FIGURE,
MAMMET, MAUMET, VASSAL,
MANIKIN, HIRELING,
MARIONETTE, PENSIONARY
maker .... SARG
Mortimer .... SNERD
show .... GALANTY
show character .... JUDY,
PUNCH(INELLO)
show dog .... TOBY
puppeteer .... SARG
Lewis .... SHARI
puppy .... CUB, DOG, FOP, TAD,
WHELP, UPSTART
purblind .... MOLE-EYED
purchasable .... VENAL,
AVAILABLE
purchase .... BUY, ORDER,
ACQUIRE, PROCURE
or sale of office .... BARRATRY
purchaser ...... EMPTOR, VENDOR,
SHOPPER, CONSUMER
purdah .... VEIL, SCREEN,
ZENANA, CURTAIN
pure .... MERE, NEAT, CLEAN,
CLEAR, FRESH, SHEER, UTTER,
CHASTE, SIMPLE, VIRGIN,
GENUINE, PERFECT, SAINTLY,
ABSOLUTE, VIRTUOUS,
UNDEFILED
air .... OZONE
gold .... TWENTY FOUR CARATS

silver, almost .... STERLING
puree .... SOUP, GUMBO
purfle .... PURL, BORDER,
TRIMMING
purgation .... CATHARSIS
purgative .... JALAP, EMETIC,
PHYSIC, CALOMEL, APERIENT,
LAXATIVE, CASTOR OIL,
CATHARTIC, CLEANSING
bitter .... ALOIN
rectal .... ENEMA
purgatory .... HELL, LIMBO,
EREBUS
purge ...... RID, FLUX, KILL, SOIL,
WASH, ATONE, FLUSH, PHYSIC,
PURIFY, CLEANSE, ABSTERGE,
EXORCISE
purification .... CATHARSIS,
REFINEMENT
by holy water .... BAPTISM
purified .... CLEAR, REFINED,
DISTILLED
capable of being ...... FINABLE
purifier .... REFINERY
purify ...... WASH, CLEAN, CLEAR,
PURGE, FILTER, REFINE,
STRAIN, CLARIFY, CLEANSE,
DISTIL(L), DEPURATE,
SANCTIFY, SUBLIMATE
by distillation .... RECTIFY
by holy water .... BAPTIZE
Puritan .... BLUENOSE,
ROUNDHEAD
nickname .... CANTER
of a sort .... WOWSER
puritanical ...... STRICT, AUSTERE,
STRAITLACED
purity .... HONESTY, CHASTITY,
SANCTITY, CLEANNESS,
INNOCENCE, WHITENESS
purl .... RIB, EDDY, LOOP, REEL,
PEARL, SWIRL, TRILL, WHIRL,
FRINGE, GURGLE, MURMUR,
RIPPLE
purlieu .... HAUNT, LOCALE,
MILIEU, HANGOUT
purlieus .... BOUNDS, LIMITS,
CONFINES, ENVIRONS,
OUTSKIRTS
purloin .... ROB, FILCH, STEAL,
PILFER
purple .... MAUVE, REGAL, ROYAL,
ORNATE, AMETHYST,
IMPERIAL, LAVENDER,
AMARANTHINE
brown .... PUCE
medic .... ALFALFA
red .... CARMINE, CRIMSON,
FUCHSIA
shade .... PLUM, GRAPE, LILAC,
MAUVE, MODENA, ORCHID,

VIOLET, AMARANTH
Purple Heart ...... MEDAL, ORDER,
DECORATION
Rain star .... PRINCE
purplish red .... WINE, CLARET,
MURREY, MAGENTA,
MULBERRY
purport .... AVOW, CLAIM, SENSE,
TENOR, ALLEGE, IMPORT,
INTEND, OBJECT, MEANING,
PROFESS, INTENTION
purpose .... AIM, END, USE, GOAL,
PLAN, SAKE, VIEW, POINT,
DESIGN, INTENT(ION)
purposeful/purposive ...... TELIC,
DECIDED, WILLFUL, DECISIVE,
RESOLUTE
purr .... HUM, SING, SMILE
purse .... KNIT, BURSE, POUCH,
PRIZE, PUCKER, WALLET,
HANDBAG, SPORRAN,
WRINKLE, BILLFOLD,
FINANCES, MONEY(BAG),
RETICULE
purser .... BURSAR, CASHIER
purslane .... WEED
pursuant .... ACCORDING,
FOLLOWING
pursue .... DOG, HUNT, SEEK,
CHASE, COURT, HOUND,
TRAIL, FOLLOW, CARRY ON,
CONTINUE, GO AFTER, RUN
AFTER
a tort .... SUE
foxes .... HUNT
hares .... SNARE
pursuer .... HOUND, HUNTER,
PROSECUTOR
pursuit .... CHASE, QUEST,
CAREER, VENTURE,
ENDEAVOR, OCCUPATION
pursy .... FAT, OBESE, PUDGY,
PUCKERED
purulence .... PUS
purulent .... PYIC
purvey ...... GIVE, CATER, SUPPLY,
DELIVER, FURNISH, PROVIDE,
PROVISION
purveyor .... DONOR, SUTLER,
CATERER, PROVIDER
of the past .... ICEMAN
purview .... VISION, INSIGHT,
SCOPE (OF VISION)
pus .... MATTER, SANIES,
PURULENCE, SUPPURATION
accumulation .... EMPYEMA
cause formation of .... FESTER
collection in tissue
.... ABSCESS
filled cavity .... VOMICA
form .... FESTER, MATURATE,

SUPPURATE
formation of .... PYOSIS
forming organism
.... PNEUMOCOCCI,
STREPTOCOCCI
in the urine .... PYURIA
of .... PYIC, PYOID
substance .... PYIN
push .... URGE, ELBOW, FORCE,
IMPEL, NUDGE, PINCH, SHOVE,
CLIQUE, HUSTLE, JOSTLE,
PROPEL, THRUST, PRESS(URE)
along .... PLOD
colloquial ...... DRIVE, EFFORT,
ENTERPRISE
firmly .... RAM
forward .... MOVE, ADVANCE
in .... ENTER
off .... LEAVE, DEPART
on .... PROCEED, CONTINUE
with nose .... NUZZLE
pushcart operator ...... VENDER,
VENDOR, PEDDLER
pusher .... SHOVER, PEDDLER,
RACKETEER
commodity of .... LSD, POT,
DOPE, HEROIN, COCAINE,
NARCOTIC, MARIJUANA
pushing .... ARROGANT,
BUMPTIOUS, CONCEITED
pushover .... DUPE, SETUP,
SUCKER
pushy .... FORCEFUL, INSOLENT,
AGGRESSIVE
pusillanimous .... COWARDLY,
IRRESOLUTE
puss ...... CAT, FACE, GIRL, HARE,
MOUTH
pussy .... CAT, CATKIN
pussycat .... DOLL, TABBY, KITTEN
pussyfoot .... GUMSHOE
pustule .... BLAIN, BUBBLE,
FESTER, PIMPLE, BLISTER
caused by insect bite
.... WHEAL, WHELK
content .... PUS
eyelash .... STYE
on face and back .... ACNE
on neck .... MALANDERS
scar .... POCK
put .... FIX, LAY, SET, PUSH,
APPLY, DRIVE, IMPEL, PLACE,
PLANT, STATE, WAGER,
IMPOSE, EXPRESS
a blanket on .... COVER
a crew again .... REMAN
a watch on .... TIME
aside .... DAFF, DISCARD
aside: sl. .... STOW
at rest .... ALLAY
away .... KILL, STOW, STORE,

CONSUME
back .... REPOSIT, RESTORE
back in the microwave
.... REHEAT, REWARM
back on the payroll
.... REHIRE
by .... STASH
down .... ABASE, CRUSH,
PLUMP, DEMEAN, HUMBLE
down in writing .... INDITE,
RECORD
effort/forth .... EXERT,
PROPOSE
faith in .... TRUST(ED)
film in camera .... LOAD
forth a perplexing problem
.... POSE(D)
forward ..... PRESENT, PROPOSE
in .... ENTER, FOIST, INSERT,
INSTALL, INTROMIT
in a cask .... BARRELED
in a new voice .... REDUB
in irons .... FETTER, MANACLE,
SHACKLE
in jeopardy .... ENDANGER
in office .... ELECT
in the wrong pigeonhole
.... MISASSIGN
in writing .... RECORD, SET
DOWN
into a cipher .... ENCODE
into use anew .... RECYCLE
it there .... SHAKE
off .... DOFF, AVOID, DEFER,
DELAY, DODGE, EVADE, STALL,
DIVERT, POSTPONE
off position .... LUXATE
on .... DON, APPLY, COVER,
CLOTHE, SPREAD
on a ship .... LADE
on guard/notice .... WARN,
ALERT
on the block .... SELL,
AUCTION
on the Exchange .... LIST
one's foot down .... INSIST,
REFUSE, REJECT
out .... EMIT, OUST, EGEST,
DOUSE, EVICT, EXPEL,
QUENCH, DISMISS, PUBLISH,
INCOMMODE
out of office .... UNSEAT
right .... AMEND
side by side .... JUXTAPOSE
the kibosh on .... NIXED
to flight .... FEEZE, CHASED,
ROUT(ED)
to rights .... EMEND
to test .... ASSAYED
to work .... HARNESS

together .... MERGE, CREATE,
COMBINE, COMPILE, ASSEMBLE
together again .... RE-FORM
under restraint .... ARREST
up .... ANTE, POST, SHOW,
BUILD, ERECT, LODGE
up with .... BEAR, ABIDE(D),
ENDURE(D), TOLERATE(D)
upon .... BESET, IMPOSE,
INTRUDE
with force .... CAST, HURL,
FLING, THROW
putamen .... PIT, STONE
putative ...... ALLEGED, REPUTED,
PRESUMED, SUPPOSED
putdown .... INSULT
Put-in-Bay hero .... PERRY
Putnam, Revolutionary general
.... ISRAEL
put-on .... AIRS, HOAX, SHAM,
STAGE
putrefaction .... DECAY,
ROT(TING)
putrefy .... ROT, DECAY,
DECOMPOSE
putrescent .... ROTTING,
DECAYING
putrid ...... FOUL, RANK, ROTTEN,
CORRUPT, DECAYED, STINKING
putsch .... UPRISING, REBELLION
puttee .... PUTTY, GAITER,
LEGGING
putter .... CLUB, IDLE, LOAF,
DABBLE, DAWDLE, NIGGLE,
TINKER
puttier .... GLAZIER
putting area .... GREEN
putty .... CEMENT
knife .... SPATULA
puttyroot .... ORCHID
Putumayo river .... ICA
puzzle ...... POSER, REBUS, STUMP,
BAFFLE, ENIGMA, KITTLE,
RIDDLE, CONFUSE, DILEMMA,
MYSTIFY, NONPLUS, PERPLEX,
BEWILDER, QUESTION,
CONUNDRUM, DUM(B)FOUND
certain word .... ACROSTIC
inexplicable .... MYSTERY
like crossword .... SCRABBLE
picture .... JIGSAW
using anagrams
.... LOGOGRIPH
using clues .... CROSSWORD
word .... LOGOGRAPH
puzzled .... STUCK, STUMPED
puzzler .... CRUX, POSER
puzzler's problem, often
.... ERASURE
wish .... LEARN A WORD

puzzling .... ODD, BAFFLING, KNOTTING, ENIGMATIC
  mystery .... ENIGMA
  problem .... POSER
  thing .... CRUX
PX .... COMMISSARY, POST EXCHANGE
pygarg .... ADDAX
Pygmalion's creator .... SHAW
  statue/love .... GALATEA
pygmy .... RUNT, ATOMY, DWARF, MINIM, PIGMY, MIDGET, MANIKIN, HOMUNCULUS
  antelope .... ORIBI
Pyle, _____ .... GOMER
  newspaperman .... ERNIE
pylon ...... POST, TOWER, MARKER, GATEWAY, PYRAMID
Pylos king .... NESTOR
pyralidid .... MOTH
pyramid .... CONE, HEAP, PILE, STACK
  builder of largest .... KHUFU, CHEOPS
  builders .... EGYPTIANS
  dweller .... UNAS, DJOSER

pharaoh entombed in
  .... KHUFU, KHAFRE, MENKAURE
  site of .... EL GIZA
terraced .... ZIKURAT, ZIGGURAT
  truncated .... PYLON
Pyramid of the Sun site
  .... TENOCHTITLIN
  Step, builder of .... IMHOTEP
Pyramus' lover: myth .... THISBE
pyre .... PILE, BONFIRE
pyrene .... PIT, STONE, NUTLET
Pyrenees goat .... IBEX
  highest point .... ANETO, ANETHOU
  mammal .... DESMAN
  republic .... ANDORRA
pyretic .... FEVERISH
pyrexia .... FEVER
pyriform .... PEAR-SHAPED
pyrite .... FOOL'S GOLD
pyrogenic .... IGNEOUS
pyromaniac .... FIREBUG, ARSONIST, INCENDIARY
pyrope .... GARNET
pyrosis .... BRASH, HEARTBURN

pyrotechnics .... FIREWORKS
pyrrhic .... WAR DANCE
  like victory .... CADMEAN
  victory site .... ASCULUM
Pyrrhonism .... SKEPTICISM
Pythagoras birthplace .... SAMOS
  forte .... MATHEMATICS
Pythia .... ORACLE, PRIESTESS
  city of the .... DELPHI
  house of the .... APOLLO'S TEMPLE
  original .... VIRGIN
  purifying rite of the ..... BATH
  skeptic .... DAPHNITAS
Pythias' friend .... DAMON
python .... BOA, SNAKE, SERPENT, ANACONDA
  deity .... ZOMBI(E)
Python, killer of .... APOLLO
  shrine guarded by .... GE'S, GAEA'S
pythoness .... PRIESTESS, PROPHETESS, SOOTHSAYER
pythonic .... ORACULAR, PROPHETIC
pyx .... BOX, CIBORIUM
pyxis .... BOX, CASE, VASE

Q

Q, Greek .... KAPPA
  in chess .... QUEEN
Qatar's cape .... RAKAN
  capital .... DOHA
  city/town .... DUKHAN, UMM SAI'D
  gulf .... PERSIAN
  language .... ARABIC
  monetary unit .... RIYAL
QED, part of .... QUOD, ERAT, DEMONSTRANDUM
quack .... CRY, FAKER, CROCUS, IMPOSTOR, SCIOLIST, WISEACRE, CHARLATAN, DEMAGOGUE, EMPIRIC(IST), MOUNTEBANK
  crier .... DUCK
  doctor's aide .... TOADY, TOADEATER
  medicine ...... HERB, NOSTRUM
  method of a .... QUACKERY
quad .... JAIL, QUOD, PRISON
quadragesima .... LENT
quadragenarian .... FORTYISH
quadragesimal .... FORTY, LENTEN
quadrangle .... CAMPUS, SQUARE, TETRAGON, (COURT)YARD

quadrant .... ARC, FOURTH, ALTIMETER
  graduated edge of .... LIMB
quadrate .... AGREE, SQUARE, CONFORM, QUARTER, RECTANGLE, RECTANGULAR
quadrel .... TILE
quadriga .... CHARIOT
quadrille .... LANC(I)ERS, (SQUARE)DANCE
  card .... MATADOR
  second highest trump
  .... MANILLA
quadriplegia .... PARALYSIS
quadrivium, part of ...... MUSIC, GEOMETRY, ASTRONOMY
quadroon ...... HYBRID, MULATTO
quadrumane .... APE, BABOON, MONKEY, PRIMATE
quadruped .... ASS, CAMEL, HIPPO, RHINO, TAPIR, ZEBRA, DONKEY, MAMMAL, GIRAFFE, FOUR-FOOTED
quadruple .... FOURFOLD
quaff .... ALE, NOG, GULP, DRINK, SWILL, SWALLOW
  fall/rustic .... CIDER
  holiday .... NOG

quagga-like animal .... ZEBRA, DONKEY
quaggy .... MIRY, SOFT, BOGGY, FLABBY
quag(mire) .... BOG, FEN, MIRE, MORASS, DILEMMA, QUICKSAND
quahaug/quahog .... CLAM
  young .... LITTLENECK
quail .... BIRD, WILT, COLIN, COWER, WINCE, CRINGE, FLINCH, RECOIL, BOBWHITE, PARTRIDGE
  flock .... BEVY, COVEY
quaint .... ODD, ANTIQUE, CURIOUS, STRANGE, UNUSUAL, FANCIFUL, SINGULAR, OLD-FASHIONED
  humor .... DROLLERY
quake .... SHAKE, WAVER, QUIVER, SHIVER, TREMOR, SHUDDER, TEMBLOR, TREMBLE, EARTHQUAKE
Quaker .... FRIEND
  colonist .... PENN
  gray .... ACIER
  in a grove .... ASPEN
  ladies .... BLUETS

midweek of a ..... WEDNESDAY
pronoun of .... THEE
quaking tree ...... ASPEN, POPLAR
quaky .... SHAKY
qualification ...... SKILL, ABILITY,
PROVISO, CONDITION,
EXPERIENCE
qualified .... FIT, ABLE, CAPABLE,
LIMITED, COMPETENT
qualifier .... MODIFIER
qualify .... FIT, PASS, LIMIT,
ENTITLE, DESCRIBE, RESTRICT
qualifying word .... ADVERB,
ADJECTIVE
quality .... AURA, KIND, TONE,
GRADE, TRAIT, NATURE,
STATUS, CALIBER, FEATURE,
PROPERTY, ATTRIBUTE,
CHARACTER(ISTIC)
admirable .... GRIT
bad/poor .... BUM, PUNK,
LOUSY, INFERIOR
colloquial .... CLASS
distinctive/pervasive ..... AURA
distinguishing .... TRAIT
of being fleeting
.... TRANSIENCE
of high .... TONY, PLUSH
of sound .... TONE, TIMBRE
special .... (DE)LUXE
qualm .... PANG, DOUBT, NAUSEA,
REGRET, TWINGE, REMORSE,
SCRUPLE, MISGIVING,
UNEASINESS, COMPUNCTION
qualmish .... QUEER, QUEASY,
NAUSEOUS
quamash .... LILY, CAMAS(S)
quandary ...... PLIGHT, DILEMMA,
NONPLUS, STRAIT(S),
PREDICAMENT
Quandary Peak site
.... COLORADO
quant .... POLE, PUNT, PROPEL
quantify .... COUNT, MEASURE
quantity .... LOT, SUM, BULK,
DOSE, MASS, AUGHT, BATCH,
GRIST, AMOUNT, NUMBER,
PORTION
abundant .... SPATE
fixed .... UNIT
indefinite .... ANY, MANY,
SOME, HANDFUL, SEVERAL
large .... LOTS, RAFF, RAFT,
SLEW, BUSHEL
small .... BIT, DAB, DASH,
LICK, WHIT, SCRUPLE,
SMIDGEN, SCANTLING
Quantrill's men .... RAIDERS
quantum ...... AMOUNT, PORTION,
QUANTITY, MAGNETON,
PARTICLE

of heat energy .... PHOTON
of sound energy .... PHONON
quarantine ...... DETAIN, ISOLATE,
CORDON OFF, ISOLATION
building/ship .... LAZARETTO
signal .... YELLOW JACK
quarrel .... JAR, ROW, FEUD, FUSS,
MIFF, SPAT, TIFF, BRAWL,
BROIL, BRUSH, CLASH, FIGHT,
FLITE, RUN-IN, SCRAP,
(AF)FRAY, BICKER, FRACAS,
STRIFE, BRABBLE, DISPUTE,
RUCTION, WRANGLE,
CONFLICT, SQUABBLE,
ALTERCATION
quarreling ...... AT LOGGERHEADS
quarrelsome .... HOSTILE,
SCRAPPY, BELLICOSE,
COMBATIVE, LITIGIOUS,
PUGNACIOUS, BELLIGERENT
quarry .... PIT, GAME, MINE,
PREY, CATCH, DIG UP,
TARGET, VICTIM, EXCAVATE
output .... GRAVEL
quarrying tool .... TRAPAN,
TREPAN
quarryman .... STONECUTTER
quart(e) .... CARTE
quarter .... SPAN, LODGE, MERCY,
BILLET, CANTON, FOURTH,
LODGING, TWO BITS, DISTRICT
eagles .... OLD GOLD
note .... CROTCHET
of a circle .... QUADRANT
phase .... DIPHASE
round .... OVOLO
quartern .... GILL
quarters .... ABODE, ROOMS,
BILLET, BARRACKS, LODGINGS
slang .... DIGGINGS
quartet .... FOUR(SOME)
quarts, 4 .... GALLON
quartz .... CACO, ONYX, AGATE,
CHERT, FLINT, PRASE, SILEX,
TOPAZ, JASPER, MORION,
PLASMA, SILICA, CAT'S EYE,
CITRINE, CRYSTAL, RUBASSE,
SARD(INE), SINOPLE,
AMETHYST, SARDONYX,
CAIRNGORM, CARNELIAN,
AVENTURINE, CHALCEDONY,
CHRYSOPRASE
quartzite .... SANDSTONE
quash .... VOID, ANNUL, QUELL,
SQUELCH, SET ASIDE,
SUPPRESS
in law .... ABATE
quasi .... AS IF, SEEMINGLY
quass .... KVASS
quaternion .... TETRAD
quatrain .... POEM, STANZA

quaver .... SHAKE, TRILL,
TREMBLE, TREMOLO
quavery .... TREMULOUS
quay .... PIER, LEVEE, WHARF,
LANDING
quean .... JADE, MINX, SLUT,
HUSSY, PROSTITUTE
queasy .... QUALMISH,
NAUSEATED, FASTIDIOUS
Quebec acre .... ARPENT
bay .... HUDSON, CHALEUR
cape .... GASPE
capital .... QUEBEC
city/town .... HULL, LAVAL,
GRANBY, VERDUN, LA SALLE,
BROSSARD, GATINEAU,
JOLIETTE, MONTREAL,
JONQUIERE
dam .... MERCIER
gulf .... SAINT LAWRENCE
island .... ALMA, VERTE,
COUDRES, LIEVRES, ORLEANS
lake .... BROME, MINTO,
ALLARD, AYLMER, KIAMIKA,
BROMPTON, MEGANTIC,
CHAMPLAIN, TREMBLANT
mountain .... JACQUES-CARTIER
peninsula ...... GASPE, UNGAVA
river .... BELL, NORD, YORK,
DITTON, GEORGE, LIEVRE,
MATANE, MOISIE, OTTAWA,
FEUILLES, SAGUENAY
Quechuan .... INCA(N), INDIAN,
PERUVIAN
queen ...... REINA, RULER, REGINA
ace combination .... TENACE
beheaded .... ANTOINETTE
"City of the South"
.... SYDNEY
English .... ANNE, BESS,
VICTORIA, ELIZABETH
fairy .... MAB, UNA, TITANIA
Greek gods' .... HERA
it .... DOMINEER
legendary .... DIDO
Moslem .... BEGUM
nicknamed "The Catholic"
.... ISABELLA
of Aquitaine .... ELEANOR
daughter of .... MARIE
husband of .... HENRY II,
LOUIS VII
son of .... JOHN, RICHARD
of Calydon .... ALTHEA
of Crete .... PASIPHAE
husband of .... MINOS
offspring .... MINOTAUR
of gods ...... HERA, JUNO, SATI
of Ithaca .... PENELOPE
of Iceland ..... BRUN(N)HILD(E)
of Lydia .... OMPHALE

of Palmyra .... ZENOBIA
of scat .... ELLA
of spades in solo .... BASTA
of Spain, deposed
.... ISABELLA
of the Antilles .... CUBA
of the jungle .... SHEENA
of the Nile .... CLEO(PATRA)
of the nymphs .... MAB
of Thebes .... JOCASTA
Olympian .... HERA
Roman gods' .... JUNO
Sheba .... BALKIS
widowed .... DOWAGER
Queen Anne's lace
.... (WILD)CARROT
Charlotte Island Indian
.... HAIDA
Mab author .... SHELLEY
queening .... APPLE
queenly .... NOBLE, REGAL,
ROYAL, REGINAL, MAJESTIC
Queens .... BOROUGH
Queensland's bay .... ALBATROSS
capital .... BRISBANE
city/town .... CAIRNS, IPSWICH,
BUNDABERG, GLADSTONE,
REDCLIFFE, TOOWOOMBA,
TOWNSVILLE, ROCKHAMPTON
island .... BANKS
mountain .... BARTLE FRERE
river .... ARCHER, BALONNE
Queenstown .... COBH
queer .... ODD, RUM, FUNNY,
GIDDY, WEIRD, CRANKY,
BIZARRE, ERRATIC, STRANGE,
SINGULAR, ECCENTRIC
bird .... NUT, CRANK
notion .... KINK
person .... NUT, KOOK,
SCREWBALL
slang .... SHADY, SPOIL,
HOMOSEXUAL, COUNTERFEIT
quell .... END, ALLAY, CRUSH,
QUASH, QUIET, SUBDUE,
SUPPRESS
quelque chose .... TRIFLE
quench .... COOL, SATE, DOUSE,
SLAKE, PUT OUT, SATISFY,
EXTINGUISH
quercetin .... DYE, FLAVIN(E)
quercitron .... DYE, OAK
quercus genus .... OAKS
querist .... ASKER
quern .... MILL, GRINDER
querulous ...... FRETFUL, PEEVISH,
WHINING, PETULANT
query ...... ASK, DOUBT, INQUIRY,
QUESTION
quest .... AIM, GOAL, HUNT,
PROBE, DESIRE, SEARCH,

PURSUIT, SEEK(ING)
question .... ASK, POSE, QUIZ,
DOUBT, GRILL, ISSUE, POINT,
QUERY, DISPUTE, INQUIRY,
PROBLEM, CHALLENGE,
INTERROGATE
and answer teaching
.... CATECHESIS
baffling .... POSER, DILEMMA
of ownership .... WHOSE
questionable .... MOOT, FISHY,
SHADY, DUBIOUS, SUSPECT,
DOUBTFUL, DEBATABLE,
UNCERTAIN, SUSPICIOUS
questioning .... CURIOUS,
PROBING, ROGATORY
questionnaire ...... POLL, SURVEY
quetzal .... BIRD, TROGON
queue .... CUE, FILE, LINE, BRAID,
PLAIT, TRESS, (PIG)TAIL
torero's .... COLETA
Quezon, first Philippine
president .... MANUEL
wife of .... AURORA
quibble .... PUN, CARP, QUIP,
CAVIL, EVADE, PALTER,
EVASION, SHUFFLE
quick ...... APT, FAST, YARE, SPRY,
AGILE, ALERT, ALIVE, BRIEF,
BRISK, FLEET, HASTY, RAPID,
READY, SWIFT, PROMPT,
SNAPPY, VOLANT, PREGNANT
answer .... RIPOSTE
assets .... CASH
bread .... MUFFIN, BISCUIT
drink .... SNORT
in learning .... APT
look .... GLANCE, EYEBEAM,
ONCEOVER
response to helm .... YARE
sharp blow .... SLAP
tempered .... FIERY, SPUNKY,
IRACUND, HOT(HEADED),
IRASCIBLE
witted .... KEEN, ALERT,
SHARP, SMART, WITTY,
BRAINY, NIMBLE
witticism .... SALLY
quicken ...... STIR, HURRY, SPEED,
(A)ROUSE, HASTEN, REVIVE,
VIVIFY, ANIMATE, REFRESH,
ENERGIZE, ACCELERATE
quickie .... DRINK, MOVIE,
B-PICTURE
quickly .... ANON, FAST, SOON,
AMAIN, APACE, PRESTO,
PRONTO
in music .... SUBITO
slang .... PDQ
quicksand .... BOG, MIRE,

MORASS, SLOUGH, SYRT(IS),
PITFALL, (DEATH)TRAP
quickset .... SLIP, HEDGE,
CUTTING
quicksilver .... AZOTH, MERCURY,
VOLATILE, MERCURIAL
quid .... CUD, PLUG, POUND,
SOVEREIGN
pro quo .... TIT-FOR-TAT,
SUBSTITUTE
quiddle .... FUSS
quidnunc .... SNOOP, GOSSIP,
BUSYBODY
Quien ____? (Who knows?)
.... SABE
quiescent .... QUIET, STILL,
LATENT, DORMANT, INACTIVE
quiet .... MIM, MUM, CALM,
ALLAY, STILL, GENTLE,
HUSH(ED), PACIFY, SERENE,
SILENT, SILENCE, PEACEFUL,
STILLNESS
interval .... LULL
quietism, teacher of .... MOLINOS
quietude .... REST, ORDER, PEACE,
SILENCE, CALMNESS,
STILLNESS
quietus ...... RELEASE, ACQUITTAL,
DEATH(BLOW), DISCHARGE
quill .... PEN, REMEX, SPINE,
BARREL, PINION, CALAMUS,
FEATHER, PLECTRUM
driver .... WRITER
feathers ...... CALAMI, REMIGES
pig .... PORCUPINE
quillai .... SOAPBARK
quilt .... DUVET, CADDOW, STITCH,
BEDCOVER, BEDSPREAD,
COMFORT(ER), PATCHWORK
stuffing .... DUVETYN(E),
EIDERDOWN
quilting party .... BEE
**Quimby, ** .... HARRIET
occupation .... AVIATRIX
quince .... BEL, POME
quinia .... QUININ(E)
quinine, illness remedied by
.... MALARIA
source .... CINCHONA
water .... TONIC
quinnat salmon .... CHINOOK
quinsy .... TONSILLITIS
quintessence .... PITH, CREAM,
ELIXIR
quintuple .... FIVEFOLD
Quintuplet Altar site .... LA
VENTA
quintuplets .... DIONNE, FISHER
quip .... MOT, GIBE, JEST, JOKE,
SALLY, SNEER, RETORT,

QUIBBLE, (WISE)CRACK, WITTICISM
quipper Mort .... SAHL
quippish .... WITTY, SARCASTIC
quipus .... KNOTS
keepers of the ...... CAMAYOCS
system .... TALLYING
system, users of .... INCAS
quire .... PAPER
20 .... REAM
var. .... CHOIR
quirk .... JIBE, KINK, TURN, HABIT, SHIFT, TRICK, TWIST, ODDITY, STROKE, MANNERISM, PECULIARITY
quirky .... FLAKY, KINKY, DEVIANT, TWISTED
quisling .... TRAITOR, COLLABORATOR
fifth columnist .... VIDKUN
quit .... RID, FREE, STOP, CEASE, CLEAR, LEAVE, REPAY, DESIST, GIVE UP, RESIGN, RETIRE, ABANDON, DISCHARGE, RELINQUISH
quitch .... WEED, GRASS
quitclaim .... RELEASE, QUITTANCE
document .... DEED
quite .... ALL, VERY, TRULY, ENOUGH, REALLY, WHOLLY, UTTERLY, ENTIRELY, SOMEWHAT

Quito is capital of ...... ECUADOR
quits .... EVEN
quittance .... FREEDOM, PAYMENT, RECEIPT, REPRISAL
quitter .... LOSER, COWARD, AVOIDER, SHIRKER, WELSHER
quiver .... QUAKE, SHAKE, THRILL, TREMOR, FLUTTER, SHUDDER, TREMBLE, VIBRATE
content of .... ARROWS
quivering .... PALPITANT, FLUTTERING
tree .... ASPEN, POPLAR
Quixote's giant .... WINDMILL
horse .... ROSINANTE
love .... DULCINEA
squire .... SANCHO (PANZA)
title .... DON
quixotic .... ABSURD, FOOLISH, UTOPIAN, ROMANTIC, VISIONARY, WHIMSICAL, CHIVALROUS
quiz .... ASK, HOAX, JOKE, PROBE, TEASE, BANTER, QUESTION, EXAM(INATION)
kid .... PRODIGY
master .... MC, HOST, EMCEE
show .... JEOPARDY, FAMILY FEUD, PRESS YOUR LUCK
quizzical .... ODD, QUEER, COMICAL
quod .... JAIL, PRISON
quoddy .... SAILBOAT

quodlibet .... DEBATE, MEDLEY
quoin .... (B)LOCK, WEDGE, CORNER, KEYSTONE
var. .... COIN
quoit .... DISCUS, RINGER
quoits pin .... HOB, PEG
player ...... QUOITER, THROWER
target .... HOB, PEG, TEE
quomodo .... WAY, MEANS, MANNER
quondam .... ONCE, FORMER, WHILOM, ONETIME, ERSTWHILE
quonset hut .... PREFAB, BUILDING
British kind .... NISSEN
quorum .... PLENUM, MAJORITY
quota .... SHARE, PORTION, ALLOTMENT
quotation .... CITAL, PRICE, EXCERPT, EXTRACT, CITATION, REPETITION
ending speech/story .... TAG
opening chapter ..... EPIGRAPH
reader .... SPECULATOR, STOCKBROKER
quote .... CITE, REFER, ADDUCE, RECITE, REPEAT, ABSTRACT
quoth .... SAID, SPOKE
quotha .... INDEED
quotidian .... DAILY
quotient .... RATIO, RESULT, FRACTION

R

R, Greek .... RHO
Hebrew .... RESH
in chemistry .... RADICAL
in chess .... ROOK
in mathematics .... RATIO, RADIUS
pronunciation like L .... LALLATION
Ra .... SUN GOD
crown of .... ATEN
in chemistry .... RADIUM
symbol of .... SUNDISK
wife of .... MUT
raad .... CATFISH
Rabat is capital of .... MOROCCO
rabato .... RUFF, COLLAR
Rabbat Ammon .... AMMAN
rabbet .... JOINT, REBATE
rabbi .... AMORA, MASTER, TEACHER
seminary .... YESHIVA
teachings .... MISHNA(H)

rabbinical .... CHURCHLY, PASTORAL
early group .... AMORA
rabbit ...... CONY, HARE, ANGORA, RODENT, LEPORID, LAGOMORPH, COTTONTAIL
baby .... KID
breeding place .... WARREN
ears .... ANTENNA
family .... LEPORID
female .... DOE
fever .... TULAR(A)EMIA
foot .... CHARM, TALISMAN
fur .... CON(E)Y, LAPIN
fur hat .... CASTOR
hunting dog .... HARRIER
hybrid .... LEPORIDE
like rodent .... MARMOT
male .... BUCK
pen .... HUTCH
pet name .... BUNNY
rock .... HYRAX

tail of .... SCUT
variety .... LOP
young .... BUNNY
rabbitry .... HUTCH, WARREN
rabble .... MOB, SCUM, CROWD, RAGTAG, TRASH, DOGGERY, CANAILLE, (RIFF)RAFF
rouser .... RIOTER, INCITER, AGITATOR, DEMAGOGUE
the .... MASSES, POPULACE, HOI POLLOI
Rabelais, Fr. satirist .... FRANCOIS
Rabelaisian .... EARTHY
voracity .... GARGANTUAN APPETITE
rabid .... RAGING, FURIOUS, VIOLENT, ZEALOUS, FANATICAL
rabies .... LYSSA, MADNESS, HYDROPHOBIA

RCA trademark .... NIPPER
raccoon .... TREEBEAR
   tropical cousin of .... COATI,
              PANDA
race .... CLAN, FOLK, RUSH,
        SPEED, TRIBE, FAMILY,
        PEOPLE, STIRPS, CHANNEL,
        COMPETE, CONTEST, LINEAGE,
        MANKIND, PEDIGREE
   black .... NEGROID
   channel .... FLUME
   contestant .... ENTRY,
        ATHLETE, ENTRANT
   division .... HEAT, NEGROID,
        CAUCASIAN, MONGOLOID
   downhill .... SLALOM
   easily won .... RUNAWAY
   engine .... REV
   hotrods' .... DRAG
   kind of .... RAT, DERBY,
        HORSE, SWEEPS, REGATTA,
        MARATHON, STOCK-CAR,
        TROT(TING), SWEEPSTAKE(S)
   of dwarfs .... NIBELUNG
   official .... TIMER
   open to anyone ..... FREE-FOR-
        ALL
   pertaining to .... ETHNIC
   prelims .... HEATS
   short .... DASH, SPRINT
   start of .... BREAKAWAY
   sulky .... TROT
   track .... OVAL, PATH, TURF,
        CINDER, HIPPODROME
   track tout: Brit. .... SPIV
   water .... ARROYO
   white .... CAUCASIAN
   yellow .... MONGOLOID
racecourse/racetrack ...... OVAL,
   TURF, ARENA, TRACK, CIRCUS,
        HIPPODROME
   character .... TOUT, TIPSTER,
        DOPESTER
   circuit .... LAP
   combining form .... DROME
   cover .... TANBARK
   fence .... RAIL
   marker .... LANE, PYLON
   name/site of .... ASCOT,
        EPSOM, HIALEAH, JAMAICA,
        PIMLICO, SARATOGA
   official .... TIMER, STARTER
   performers .... HORSES
   section .... BEND, STRETCH
racehorse .... TROTTER
   disability .... SPAVIN,
        GLANDERS, STRINGHALT
   enclosure/exercise area
   .... PADDOCK
   inferior .... PLATER, SLEEPER
   kind of .... MUDDER, PLATER

winless .... MAIDEN
raceme .... CLUSTER, PANICLE
racer .... MILER, HOTROD,
        RUNNER, SPRINTER,
        TRACKMAN, (BLACK)SNAKE
   course of .... LANE
raceway .... CHANNEL
Rachel's father .... LABAN
   husband .... JACOB, ISRAEL
   maid .... BILHAH
   sister .... LEAH
   son .... JOSEPH, BENJAMIN
rachis .... STEM, SPINE, BACKBONE
rachitis .... RICKETS
Rachmaninoff, composer/
   pianist .... SERGEI
   title of .... MAESTRO
racial .... FAMILY, TRIBAL,
        ANCESTRAL
   division, of .... ETHNIC
   origin .... ETHNOGENY
Racine (Jean), Fr. poet
   .... BAPTISTE
   masterpiece .... PHEDRE
racing colors .... SILKS
   course .... CAREER,
        HIPPODROME
   program .... CARD, FORM
   sailboat .... MOTH
   scull .... WHERRY
racism .... BIGOTRY, PREJUDICE
   slang .... JIM CROW
racist .... BIGOT, HATER
rack .... GIN, FRAME, STAND,
        CLOUDS, STRESS, ANGUISH,
        TENSION, TORMENT, TORTURE,
        DISTRESS, UPHEAVAL,
        WRECKAGE
   corn .... CRIB
   display .... EASEL
   fodder .... CRIB, HACK,
        CRATCH
   food .... FLAKE
   for storing boxes .... RICK
   for storing hay/grain ..... BAY,
        BIN
   hat .... TREE
   horse's .... GAIT, PACE
   lay on the .... AGONIZE
   partner of .... RUIN
racket .... BAT, DIN, BABEL,
        NOISE, HUBBUB, PADDLE,
        RUMPUS, UPROAR, CAROUSE,
        REVEL(RY), SNOWSHOE
   hold on .... GRIP
   -shaped footwear
   .... SNOWSHOE
   slang .... LINE, BUSINESS,
        PROFESSION
   string .... CATGUT
racketeer .... HOODLUM, MOBSTER

rackets .... SQUASH, TENNIS
raconteur .... NARRATOR
   forte of ...... STORIES, STORIER,
        STORYTELLER, ANECDOTES
racy .... FRESH, SMART, SPICY,
        LIVELY, RISQUE, PIQUANT,
        PUNGENT, ZESTFUL, SPIRITED
Radames' love .... AIDA
radar device, for short .... TFR
   display .... SCAN
   image .... BLIP
   like device .... SONAR
   part of word .... RADIO,
        DETECTING, RANGING
   screen .... SCOPE
   screen flash .... BLIP
   sound .... BEEP, RACON
   system .... SHORAN
   transmitter .... BEACON
Radcliffe's sister .... VASSAR
raddle .... KNIT, OCHER, STICK,
        INTERWEAVE
Radek, Soviet writer .... KARL
Radha's consort .... KRISHNA
radian .... ARC
radiance .... GLORY, LIGHT,
        LUSTER, SPLENDOR,
        BRIGHTNESS, BRILLIANCE,
        REFULGENCE
radiant .... AGLOW, BRIGHT,
        BEAMING, GLOWING, SHINING,
        GLORIOUS, SPARKLING
   combining form .... HELI(O)
   energy .... RADIATION
   look .... BEAM
radiate .... BEAM, CAST, EMIT,
        SHINE, DIVERGE, TRANSMIT
radiation .... EMISSION, DIFFUSION
   measure .... ROENTGEN
radiator .... HEATER
   additive .... COOLANT
radical ...... BASIC, JINGO, REBEL,
        ULTRA, DRASTIC, EXTREME,
        JACOBIN, LEFTIST, FIREBRAND
   colloquial .... RED, PINK
   sign .... SQUARE ROOT
   slang .... COMMIE
   with valence of two ..... DYAD
radicle .... RADIX, ROOT(LET)
radio .... WIRELESS
   active shower .... FALLOUT
   ad .... COMMERCIAL
   aerial .... ANTENNA
   broadcasting outfit .... VOA
   cabinet .... CONSOLE
   control, kind of .... REMOTE
   converting device .... BALUN
   dash in .... DAH
   detector .... RADAR
   dial .... TUNER
   father of .... MARCONI

frequency band .... CHANNEL
gear .... AERIAL, ANTENNA
interference .... STATIC
news, brief .... FLASH
newscaster .... SWING,
    MURROW, CRONKITE, HEATTER
operator, amateur .... HAM
performer .... TALENT,
    NEWSCASTER
performer: sl. .... DEEJAY
person .... DISC JOCKEY
receiver .... SET, CRYSTAL,
    TRANSISTOR
reception disturbance
.... STATIC, STRAYS
signal .... BEEP
signal for aviators .... BEAM
signoff .... ROGER
station ID .... CALL LETTERS
term .... ROGER
transmitting antenna
.... RADIATOR
true inventor of
.... STUBBLEFIELD
tube .... GRID
TV, et al .... MEDIA
radio's Cronkite .... WALTER
Dallas .... STELLA
Murrow .... EDWARD
radioactive matter .... NITON,
    RADON, NOBELIUM,
    CARNOTITE
particles .... GEIGERS
radioactivity, measure of
.... CURIE
radiolocator .... RADAR
radiotelephony term ...... ROGER,
    TEN-FOUR
radium F .... POLONIUM
discoverer .... CURIE
disease treated with
.... CANCER
emanation .... NITON, RADON
source of .... URANITE,
    PITCHBLENDE
radius .... RAY, RANGE, SCOPE,
    SPOKE, EXTENT
radix .... BASE, ROOT, ETYMON,
    RADICLE
radon .... NITON
RAF, part of .... ROYAL, AIR,
    FORCE
raff .... TRASH, RABBLE
companion .... RIFF
raffish ...... LOW, CHEAP, FLASHY,
    TAWDRY, VULGAR,
    DISREPUTABLE
raffle .... LOTTO, LOTTERY
ticket .... BLANK
raft .... BALSA, BARGE, FLOAT,
    CATAMARAN

colloquial .... LOT,
    MULTITUDE, COLLECTION
component of .... LOGS,
    BOARDS, BARRELS
log .... CATAMARAN
rafter .... BEAM, SPAR, TIMBER
rag .... SCRAP, SCOLD, SHRED,
    SLATE, TATTER, REMNANT,
    CASTOFFS
baby .... DOLL
chew the ..... CHAT, CONVERSE
slang .... KID, RIB, BRAT, JOSH,
    MOCK, TEASE
ragamuffin .... WAIF,
    TATTERDEMALION
ragamuffinly .... RAGGED,
    SLOVENLY
rage .... FAD, IRE, BOIL, FUME,
    FURY, RAVE, ANGER, CRAZE,
    FUROR, STORM, VOGUE,
    WRATH, FRENZY, SPREAD,
    BLUSTER, FASHION, RAMPAGE
ragged .... HARSH, ROUGH,
    FRAYED, JAGGED, SHABBY,
    SHAGGY, UNEVEN, UNKEMPT,
    TATTERED
child, poor .... RAGAMUFFIN
plant .... ROBIN
raggee .... RAGI, GRASS
ragger .... TEASER
Raggedy doll .... ANDY, ANNE
raging .... RAMPANT, VIOLENT,
    RAMPAGING
raglan .... TOPCOAT, OVERCOAT
ragman/ragpicker ...... JUNKMAN
ragout .... HASH, STEW, SALMI,
    TUCKET, GOULASH, HARICOT
rags .... CLOTHES
Rags to Riches author
.... ALGER
ragtag .... RABBLE
ragtime .... JAZZ
ragweed .... IVA, AMBROSIA,
    COCKLEBUR
ragwort .... TANSY, JACOBY,
    GROUNDSEL
rah .... CHEER, HURRAH
opposite of .... HISS
raid ...... FORAY, ONSET, ATTACK,
    FORAGE, INROAD, INVADE,
    MARAUD, SORTIE, ASSAULT,
    INVASION, INCURSION
slang .... PINCH
raider .... UBOAT, RANGER,
    COMMANDO
rail .... BAR, BIRD, COOT, RANT,
    SORA, WEKA, CHIDE, CRAKE,
    FENCE, HERON, SCOFF, SCOLD,
    MUDHEN, ORTOLAN,
    COMPLAIN
bird like .... COURLAN

collar of .... FLANGE
kin of .... NOTORNIS
railer .... REVILER
railing .... FENCE, BALUSTRADE
bridge .... PARAPET
raillery .... BANTER, SATIRE,
    BADINAGE, RIDICULE,
    PERSIFLAGE
slang .... KIDDING
railroad ...... RAILWAY, TRAMLINE
baggage car .... VAN
bridge .... TRESTLE
car .... COACH, DINER,
    SMOKER, CABOOSE, PULLMAN,
    SLEEPER
car compartment .... DUPLEX
center .... YARD
colloquial ..... RUSH, EXPEDITE
crossing .... GATE
elevated .... EL, MONORAIL
engine .... LOCOMOTIVE
engine serviceman
.... HOSTLER
flare .... FUSEE, FUZEE
freight car .... GONDOLA
handcar .... VELOCIPEDE
industrial .... TAPLINE
line end .... TERMINUS
side track .... SPUR
siding .... TURN-OUT
signal .... HIGHBALL,
    SEMAPHORE
single track .... MONORAIL
slang .... FRAME
sleeping car .... WAGON-LIT
station .... DEPOT
stop for locomotives .... TANK
    TOWN
supply car .... TENDER
switch device .... FROG, SHUNT
tie .... SLEEPER
track section .... GANTLET
trunkline .... MAIN
underground .... METRO,
    SUBWAY
workers' vehicle .... HANDCAR
raiment .... DRESS, ATTIRE,
    APPAREL, CLOTHING
of the early wilds .... TIGER
    SKIN
rain .... FALL, HYET, BESTOW,
    FLURRY, LAVISH, SEREIN,
    SHOWER, (OUT)POUR,
    DOWNPOUR
briefly .... SPIT
combining form .... HYETO
forest .... SELVA
fine mist .... MIZZLE, SEREIN,
    DRIZZLE
formed by .... PLUVIAL
frozen/icy .... HAIL, SNOW,

SLEET gauge .... UDOMETER
heavy .... TORRENT
mist .... SCUD
or shine ..... COME WHAT MAY
sudden .... BRASH, SPATE, CLOUDBURST
sunset .... SEREIN
tree .... SAMAN, ZAMIA
Rain girl .... SADIE
setting .... SAMOA
rainbird .... CUCKOO, WOODPECKER
rainbow .... ARC(H), IRIS, METEOR, SPECTRUM
bridge .... BIFROST
combining form .... IRIDO
fish .... GUPPY
horse .... APPALOOSA
like colors, having ..... IRISED, PAVONINE, IRIDESCENT
trout .... STEELHEAD
raincheck .... STUB, TICKET
raincoat .... PONCHO, SLICKER, MACKINTOSH, TRENCH COAT
raindrops, frozen .... HAIL
Rainer, actress .... LUISE
Maria, Ger. poet .... RILKE
rainfall .... SHOWER, WETNESS, PRECIPITATION
heavy .... DELUGE
place of heaviest .... ASSAM
Rainier (Mount) site
.... TACOMA
Rainier's domain, Prince
.... MONACO
rainless .... ARID
rainmaker: sl. .... LOBBYIST
rainproof canvas ...... TARPAULIN
rainy .... WET, SOPPY, SLOPPY, PLUVIAL, SHOWERY, PLUVIOUS
season .... MONSOON
raise .... EAN, HIKE, REAR, STIR, BOOST, BREED, BUILD, ERECT, EXALT, HOIST, AROUSE, INCITE, MUSTER, PULL UP, (UP)LIFT, COLLECT, ELEVATE, NURTURE
a check .... KITE
goose pimples .... SCARE
in relief .... EMBOSS
in value .... ENDEAR
nap .... TEASE(L)
rents exorbitantly .... RACK
to third power .... CUBE
raised .... EMBOSSED
again .... RE-ELEVATED
road .... CAUSEWAY
raisin .... GRAPE, SULTANA
in pudding .... PLUM
raisins drink .... CORDIAL,

ROSOLIO
raison .... D'ETAT, D'ETRE
raj .... RULE
rajah's wife .... RANI, RANEE
Rajasthan's capital .... JAIPUR
rake .... COMB, ROUE, SCOUR, SLANT, GATHER, LECHER, SCRAPE, SEARCH, COLLECT, RANSACK, LOTHARIO, DEBAUCHEE, LIBERTINE
off: sl. .... BRIBE, PAYOFF, REBATE, KICKBACK, COMMISSION
with gunfire .... STRAFE, ENFILADE
rakish .... JAUNTY, DASHING, DISSOLUTE
man .... RAKEHELL
rale .... RATTLE, RHONCHUS
ralline bird .... RAIL
rally .... MOCK, ROUSE, TEASE, BANTER, MUSTER, REVIVE, COLLECT, MARSHAL, MEET(ING), RESURGE, ASSEMBLY, GATHERING
ram ...... TUP, BUMP, BUTT, CRAM, PUMP, TAMP, DRIVE, PRESS, POUND, SHEEP, STUFF, BATTER, THRUST
constellation .... ARIES
headed god .... AMMON
horn .... SHOFAR, SHOPHAR
kind of .... (BELL)WETHER
ship's .... BEAK
Rama .... KRISHNA
Ramachandra's wife .... SITA
Ramadan/Ramazan .... FASTING
ramage .... BOUGH
Ramayana character .... SITA, HANUMAN
ramble .... GAD, ROAM, ROVE, STRAY, STROLL, WANDER, MAUNDER, MEANDER, SAUNTER
rambler .... ROSE, NOMAD, ROVER, TRAMP, TRUANT
Rambouillet ...... (MERINO) SHEEP
rambunctious ...... WILD, ROWDY, UNRULY, BOISTEROUS, DISORDERLY, PUGNACIOUS
one .... TEARER
ramekin/ramequin .... DISH, HASH
Rameses/Ramses ...... MONARCH, PHARAOH
domain .... EGYPT
ramie .... HEMP, FIBER
ramification .... SPUR, BRANCH, RESULT, IN AND OUT, OFFSHOOT
ramify .... DIVIDE, SPREAD

ramjet .... ENGINE, ATHODYD
rammer .... BEAK, RAMROD
ramose .... BRANCHED
ramp .... RAGE, REAR, RUSH, TEAR, PITCH, SLANT, SLOPE, STAND, STORM, RUNWAY, INCLINE, PASSAGE, ROADWAY
rampage .... RAGE, FRACAS, FRENZY, TANTRUM, OUTBREAK, COMMOTION
rampaging person .... AMOK, BERSERK, JURAMENTADO
rampant .... LUSH, RIFE, EPIDEMIC, WIDESPREAD
rampart .... WALL, REDAN, BULWARK, PARAPET, RAVELIN, VALLATION, EMBANKMENT
rampion .... CAMPANULA, BELLFLOWER
ramrod .... POKER, RAMMER
ramshackle ...... SHAKY, RICKETY, RUN-DOWN
ramson .... ROOT, GARLIC
ramtil .... SESAME
ramus .... BRANCH
ran, also .... LOST, COMPETED
tan .... SPREE
rana .... FROG, RAJA, PRINCE
rance .... MARBLE
ranch .... FARM, GRAZE, (G)RANGE, ESTANCIA, HACIENDA, PLANTATION
event .... RODEO, ROUNDUP
hand .... COWBOY, COWPOKE
tyro .... DUDE
rancher ...... COWBOY, STOCKMAN
rancho .... HUT, RANCH
rancid ...... RANK, STALE, PUTRID, SMELLY, SPOILED, STINKING
rancor ...... GALL, SPITE, ENMITY, HATRED, MALICE, ILL WILL
rand ...... EDGE, BORDER, MARGIN
random .... CASUAL, CHANCE, AIMLESS, DESULTORY, HAPHAZARD, HIT-OR-MISS
archer .... CUPID
randy .... BAWDY, CRUDE, BEGGAR, COARSE, VULGAR, LUSTFUL
woman .... SHREW
range .... ROW, RANK, ROAM, SPAN, GAMUT, REACH, SCALE, SCOPE, STOVE, SWEEP, TRAIN, EXTENT, SERIES, CALIBER, COMPASS, LATITUDE, GRASSLAND
auditory .... EARSHOT
finder ...... STADIA, TELEMETER
mountain .... CHAIN, SIERRA
of emotion .... GAMUT
of hills .... RIDGE

of vision .... SCAN, SCOPE, EYESHOT, EYESIGHT
over .... SCOUR
Rocky Mountains ...... TETON, UINTA
sighting for .... ZERO
ranger .... WARDEN, SOLDIER, FORESTER
before 1972 .... SENATOR
concern of a .... FOREST
Rangoon is capital of .... BURMA
measure .... DHA
measure, distance .... TAUN
weight .... CATTY
rangy .... LANKY, SPARE
rani/ranee .... QUEEN
garb of .... SARI
husband of .... RAJA(H)
ranine .... FROGLIKE
rank ...... ROW, LINE, LUSH, TIER, CASTE, GRADE, GROSS, RANGE, REEKY, UTTER, ARRANT, COARSE, RANCID, STATUS, FERTILE, EMINENCE, FLAGRANT, INDECENT, POSITION, STANDING
above viscount .... EARL
and file .... RUCK, SOLDIERS, FOLLOWERS
having .... GENETIC
of lower .... JUNIOR, PUISNE
pulling .... BOSSY
rankle .... RILE, ROIL, FESTER
ranks .... ARMY
ransack .... LOOT, RAKE, RIFLE, SEARCH, PILLAGE, RUMMAGE
ransom .... REDEEM, RESCUE, BLOODMONEY
person held for .... HOSTAGE
rant ...... NAG, RAGE, RAIL, RAVE, BOAST, SCOLD, TIRADE, BLUSTER, BOMBAST, DECLAIM, HARANGUE
ranunculaceous plant .... PEONY, ANEMONE, LARKSPUR
ranunculus .... CROWFOOT, BUTTERCUP
rap .... BOP, BOX, TAP, BLOW, CUFF, KNAP, SWAT, BLAME, CLOUT, KNOCK, (TH)WACK, SENTENCE, PUNISHMENT
colloquial .... CHAT, CONVERSE
gently and firmly ..... PERCUSS
rapacious .... GREEDY, RAVENOUS, PREDATORY, VORACIOUS, AVARICIOUS
bird .... SHRIKE, VULTURE
fish .... PIRANHA
rapacity .... GREED, VORACITY
rape .... COLE, PULP, SEIZE, FODDER, RAVISH, SEDUCE, ASSAULT, CABBAGE, PLUNDER, VIOLATE
rapeseed .... COLZA
mass of crushed ..... OIL CAKE
rapid .... FAST, FLEET, HASTY, QUICK, SWIFT, SPEEDY
combining form .... TACHY
fire ...... STACCATO, FUSILLADE
in a stream .... RIPPLE
rapidity .... SPEED, VELOCITY
rapidly .... AMAIN, APACE
rapids ...... CHUTE, DELLS, DALLES
rapier .... EPEE, TUCK, BILBO, SWORD
rapine .... RAVIN, PILLAGE, PLUNDER
rapparee .... ROBBER, VAGABOND, PLUNDERER
rappee .... SNUFF
rapper .... DOOR KNOCKER
rapping .... TATTOO
rapport ...... ACCORD, HARMONY, AFFINITY, AGREEMENT, RELATION(SHIP)
heightened .... VIBES
rapscallion .... ROGUE, RASCAL
rapt .... INTENT, CHARMED, ABSORBED, ENGROSSED, ENTRANCED
raptorial bird .... OWL, HAWK, EAGLE, FALCON, VULTURE
rapture ...... JOY, BLISS, DELIGHT, ECSTASY, TRANSPORT
rapturous .... ECSTATIC
Rapunzel's specialty .... TRESSES
Raquel Welch's pet name .... BIRDLEGS
soubriquet .... SEX QUEEN
rara avis .... BIRD, ONER, RARITY
rare ...... ODD, RAW, THIN, SCANT, SCARCE, UNIQUE, TENUOUS, UNUSUAL, UNCOMMON, UNDERDONE
find .... ONE OF A KIND
rarebit .... RABBIT
raree .... (PEEP)SHOW
rarefy .... REFINE, THIN(OUT), ATTENUATE
rarely .... SELDOM
rareripe fruit .... PEACH
rarity .... ONER, TENUITY, SCARCITY, THINNESS
rascal .... CAD, IMP, YAP, KNAVE, ROGUE, SCAMP, VARLET, VILLAIN, SCALAWAG, SPALPEEN, SCOUNDREL, SCAPEGRACE
rascally .... BASE, MEAN, VILE, DISHONEST
rase .... RUIN, LEVEL, DESTROY
rash .... WILD, HASTY, HEADY, DARING, WANTON, MEASLES, ROSEOLA, ERUPTION, RECKLESS, EXANTHEMA, FOOLHARDY
person .... BRAVO, HOTSPUR, PLUNGER
rasher .... HAM, BACON
rashness .... FOLLY, TEMERITY
Rasmussen, Arctic explorer .... KNUD
rasorial .... GALLINACEOUS
bird .... HEN, CHICKEN
rasp .... RUB, FILE, CHAFE, GRATE, ABRADE, SCRAPE, IRRITATE
raspberry .... SASS, FRUIT, SHRUB, ACINUS
Raspe's character .... MUNCHAUSEN
Rasputin, Russian monk .... GRIGORI
raspy .... HUSKY, ROUGH, HOARSE, GRATING, ABRASIVE, IRRITABLE
rasse .... CIVET
rassle .... WRESTLE
rat .... VOLE, GNAWER, RODENT, VERMIN, APOSTATE
catcher .... MOUSER
colloquial .... SKUNK
domesticated .... GUINEA PIG
family .... MURIDAE
genus .... MUS
hair .... PAD
i.e. .... DESERTER
kind of .... MOLE
poison .... RATSBANE
race .... SCURRY, SCRAMBLE, STRUGGLE
rodent resembling ..... MOUSE, HAMSTER
slang .... LIAR, SNEAK, SQUEAL, TRAITOR, DESERTER, INFORMER, STOOL(PIGEON)
"Rat Pack" associate .... DAVIS, MARTIN
leader .... SINATRA
ratable .... TAXABLE
ratal .... ASSESSMENT
ratafia .... COOKY, CORDIAL, LIQUEUR, MACAROON
rataplan .... DRUMBEAT
ratchet .... PAWL, WHEEL, BOBBIN, DETENT, SPINDLE, SPROCKET
rate .... CHIDE, CLASS, JUDGE, MERIT, PRICE, RATIO, SCOLD, VALUE, WORTH, DEGREE, ESTEEM, DESERVE, PERCENT, APPRAISE, PROPORTION
at any .... ANYWAY
exchange .... AGIO
military .... GRADE

of mass to volume .... DENSITY

rated .... TAXED, RANKED, VALUED

ratel-like animal .... BADGER

Rathbone, actor .... BASIL

rathe .... EAGER, EARLY, QUICK, PROMPT

rather .... SOONER, SOMEWHAT, CERTAINLY, PREFERABLY

than .... ERE

Ratibor river .... ODER

ratification .... APPROVAL, SANCTION, AFFIRMATION

ratify ...... OK, OKAY, PASS, SEAL, APPROVE, ENDORSE, CONFIRM, SANCTION

rating .... MARK, RANK, CLASS, GRADE, SCORE, REPRIMAND

ratio .... RATE, QUOTIENT, PERCENTAGE, PROPORTION

phrase .... IS TO

ratiocinate .... REASON

ration .... METE, LIMIT, SHARE, DOLE OUT, RESTRICT, ALLOT(MENT), ALLOWANCE

rational .... SANE, LUCID, SOUND, LOGICAL, SENSIBLE, REASONABLE, CLEARHEADED

rationale .... BASIS, REASON, THEORY, COMMON SENSE, EXPLANATION

rationalize .... EXPLAIN

rations .... FOOD

bag .... HAVERSACK

ratite .... MOA, EM(E)U, RHEA, OSTRICH, CASSOWARY

ratoon .... SHOOT, SPROUT

rats, of .... MURINE

rattail .... GRENADIER

rattan .... CANE, PALM, REED, SEGA, BAMBOO

ratter .... DOG, STINKER, BETRAYER, DESERTER, QUISLING, SNITCHER

rattle .... JAR, RALE, CLACK, UPSET, BABBLE, MARACA, UPROAR, CHATTER, CLAPPER, CRACKLE, FLUSTER, SISTRUM, CREPITATE, DISCONCERT, NOISE(MAKER)

rattlebrain ...... ASS, FOOL, IDIOT, RATTLEPATE

rattlebrained .... SILLY, FRIVOLOUS, TALKATIVE

rattlesnake .... VIPER, CASCABEL, MASSASAUGA, SIDEWINDER

plantain .... ORCHID

without rattle ..... COPPERHEAD

rattletrap .... MOUTH, JALOPY

rattling .... CREPITANT

rattrap .... CAT, FIX, JAM, PREDICAMENT

ratwa .... MUNTJAC

raucous .... HARSH, HOARSE, GRATING

Raul's brother .... FIDEL

ravage .... RUIN, SACK, HAVOC, DESPOIL, PILLAGE, PLUNDER, DEVASTATE

rave .... RAGE, RANT, ROAR, TEAR, STORM

ravel .... FRAY, UNDO, SLEAVE, INVOLVE, UNTWIST, ENTANGLE, SEPARATE, UNTANGLE

stocking's .... RUN

Ravel, composer .... MAURICE

opera .... BOLERO, LA VALSE

ravelin .... REDAN, OUTWORK, FORTIFICATION

raveling .... LINT

raven .... CROW, PREY, CORBIE, DEVOUR, PLUNDER, BLACK(BIRD)

Barnaby Rudge's .... GRIP

constellation .... CORVUS

cry of .... CAW

like a/of a .... CORVINE

quote of .... NEVERMORE

ravenous .... GREEDY, HUNGRY, LUPINE, RAPACIOUS, VORACIOUS, GLUTTONOUS

ravin ...... PREY, RAPINE, PLUNDER

ravine .... GAP, DELL, GILL, GULF, LINN, OMB(E), WADI, WADY, CHINE, COOMB, FLUME, GORGE, GULCH, GULLY, NOTCH, CANYON, CLOUGH, COULEE, NULLAH, BARRANCA

raving .... EXCITED, NOTABLE, FRENZIED, DELIRIOUS

ravish .... RAPE, CHARM, SEDUCE, DELIGHT, ENCHANT, VIOLATE, ENTHRALL, ENRAPTURE

ravishment .... ECSTASY, RAPTURE

raw .... SORE, BAWDY, BLEAK, CRUDE, HARSH, UNCOOKED, UNTESTED

cotton .... LINT

deal .... WRONG, INJUSTICE

in the .... NUDE, NAKED

material .... STOCK, STUFF, STAPLE

recruit .... ROOKIE

slang .... UNFAIR

rawboned .... BONY, LEAN, GAUNT

Rawalpindi is capital of .... PAKISTAN

native of .... PAKISTANI

rawhide .... WHIP, PARFLECHE, LEATHERETTE

kind of .... SHAGREEN

whip ..... LASH, KNOUT, QUIRT, STRAP, THONG

ray .... BEAM, BETA, ALPHA, GAMMA, GLEAM, LASER, MANTA, PETAL, SKATE, TRACE, STRIPE, SAWFISH, STINGAREE, THORNBACK

eagle .... OBISPO

flower .... FLORET

from a satellite .... MOONBEAM

huge .... MANTA

kind of .... BETA, GAMMA, LASER

like part .... RADIUS

Ray, actor .... ALDO

rayah .... RAIA, NON-MOSLEM

Rayburn, Speaker .... SAM

rayless .... DARK, GLOOMY

Raymond or Ilona .... MASSEY

Raymonda ballet composer .... PETIPA

rayon ...... FIBER, FABRIC, JERSEY, ACETATE, TEXTILE, VISCOSE

cellulose acetate .... CELANESE

corded/ribbed .... REPP, REP(S), OTTOMAN

making material .... CELLULOSE

sheer .... VOILE

twilled .... SERGE

with knotty surface .... RATINE

raze .... ERASE, LEVEL, SHAVE, SCRAPE, DESTROY, DEMOLISH

razee .... SHIP

razer .... DESTROYER

razor .... SHAVE(R)

billed bird .... ALCA

clam .... SOLEN

seller .... CUTLER

sharpen(er) .... HONE, STROP

razorback .... HOG, FINBACK, (RORQUAL) WHALE

razz .... JEER, SASS, TEASE, DERIDE, HECKLE, RIDICULE

razzle-dazzle .... CONFUSE, BEWILDER, CONFUSION

Rb, in chemistry .... RUBIDIUM

RCA founder .... (DAVID) SARNOFF

part of .... RADIO, AMERICA, CORPORATION

re .... ABOUT, ANENT, REGARDING, CONCERNING

echoing .... REBOANT

Re in chemistry .... RHENIUM

rea .... TURMERIC

reach .... GAIN, PASS, SPAN,

GRASP, RANGE, TOUCH,
ARRIVE, ATTAIN, EXTEND,
FATHOM, LENGTH, ACHIEVE,
STRETCH

a conclusion .... DECIDE

reachable .... OBTAINABLE

reachless .... LOFTY,
UNATTAINABLE

react .... ANSWER, RESPOND,
REDOUND

reacting easily/readily
.... RESPONSIVE

reaction .... REPLY, IMPACT,
REFLEX, RESPONSE, TROPISM

angry .... RISE

challenging .... DEFIANCE

disapproving .... PROTEST

drowsy .... YAWN

of disgust .... REPULSION

of refusal .... REBUFF,
REJECTION

reverberating .... ECHO

to stimuli .... TROPISM

reactionary .... TORY, RIGHT(IST),
CONSERVATIVE

read .... CON, PORE, STUDY,
TEACH, PERUSE, CONSTRUE,
DECIPHER, FORETELL,
REGISTER, INTERPRET,
RENOUNCE, UNDERSTAND

all about it! .... NEWS

aloud .... RECITE

closely .... PORE(D)

cursorily .... SKIM

inability to .... ALEXIA

letter by letter .... SPELT

metrically .... SCAN

numbers .... NUMERATE

out of .... EXPEL, DISMISS

readable .... LEGIBLE

reader ...... BOOK, CRITIC, PRIMER,
PERUSER, RECITER, LECTURER

meter .... RECORDER

scripture .... LECTOR

readily .... EASILY, QUICKLY,
PROMPTLY, WILLINGLY

readiness .... EASE, ALACRITY

reading .... LECTION, PERUSAL,
RECORD(ING)

desk/stand .... AMBO,
LECTERN, PRIE-DIEU

disability .... DYSLEXIA

of Scriptures .... LECTION

reads alike forward or
backward .... PALINDROME

ready .... APT, SET, FAIN, KEEN,
OPEN, RIPE, WARE, YARE,
ALERT, HANDY, QUICK,
SHARP, LIKELY, MATURE,
POISED, PRIMED, PROMPT,
WILLING, INCLINED,

PREPARE(D), AVAILABLE

artillery .... UNLIMBER

at the bar .... ON TAP

for action .... ARMED

for bed .... SLEEPY

made .... STOCK, INSTANT

money .... CASH

to eat .... DONE

to swing .... AT BAT

Reagan, familiarly ...... RONNIE

real .... COIN, SURE, TRUE, PUCKA,
PUKKA, ACTUAL, CERTAIN,
FACTUAL, GENUINE,
CONCRETE, AUTHENTIC, SIMON
PURE

estate .... LAND, LOTS, REALTY

estate broker .... REALTOR

estate bugaboo .... TERMITES

plural of .... REIS

thing, the .... MCCOY

tidy .... APPLE-PIE ORDER

realgar ...... MINERAL, SANDARAC

realism .... VERITY

opposite of .... IDEALISM

realistic .... GRAPHIC, PRACTICAL,
DOWN-TO-EARTH

opposite of .... VISIONARY

reality .... FACT, TRUTH, VERITY

realize .... NET, GAIN, KNOW,
ATTAIN, OBTAIN, ACHIEVE,
IMAGINE, UNDERSTAND

really ...... QUITE, TRULY, INDEED,
SURELY, ACTUALLY,
ABSOLUTELY

realm .... CLIME, DOMAIN, EMPIRE,
REGION, SPHERE, DEMESNE,
KINGDOM, BAILIWICK

realty .... PROPERTY

bargain of New World
.... MANHATTAN ISLAND

ream .... ENLARGE

reamer .... BORER, BROACH,
ENLARGER

reams .... LOTS

reanimate .... REVIVE

reap .... MOW, GAIN, GATHER,
COLLECT, HARVEST

reaper .... MOWER

Reaper, Grim .... DEATH

reaping tool ...... SICKLE, SCYTHE,
TWIBIL(L)

reappearance .... RERUN

rear ...... AFT, END, GROW, RAMP,
RISE, BREED, BUILD, ERECT,
NURSE, RAISE, (BE)HIND,
SUCKLE, ARRIERE, REVERSE,
BACK(PART), BACKSIDE

colloquial .... FANNY

horse's .... PESADE

young bird .... FLEDGE

reared by hand .... CADE

rearmost .... LAST

rearrange .... PERMUTE

reason .... WHY, NOUS, ARGUE,
BASIS, CAUSE, LOGOS,
GROUND, MOTIVE, SANITY,
DISCUSS, JUSTIFY,
EXPLANATION, RATIOCINATE

against .... OPPUGN

deprive of .... DEMENT

for being .... END, RAISON
D'ETRE

for ill-will .... GRUDGE

with .... RIGHTLY

reasonable ...... FAIR, JUST, SANE,
SOUND, LOGICAL, RATIONAL,
SENSIBLE

reasoning, correct ...... LOGIC(AL)

false .... IDOLISM, SOPHISM

faulty .... SYLLOGISM,
PARALOGISM

subtle, difficult
.... METAPHYSICS

reata .... LASSO, NOOSE, LARIAT

reave ...... ROB, REND, TEAR, SEIZE

rebaptize .... RENAME

rebate .... RABBET, RAKE-OFF,
DISCOUNT, KICKBACK,
DEDUCTION

partial .... REFUND

rebec(k) .... FIDDLE, VIOLIN

Rebecca, diminutive of
.... REBA, BECKY

Rebekah's brother .... LABAN

father .... BETHUEL

husband .... ISAAC

niece .... LEAH, RACHEL

son .... ESAU, JACOB

rebel .... DEFY, DEFIER, RELUCT,
RESIST, RISE (UP), OPPOSE(R),
MUTINEER, RECUSANT,
REVOLT(ER), DISOBEY(ER),
DISSENTER, DISSIDENT,
INSURGENT, INSURRECTO,
MALCONTENT

angel .... BELIAL

rebellion .... MUTINY, REVOLT,
SEDITION, UPRISING,
INSURGENCE, REVOLUTION,
INSURRECTION

minor .... PUTSCH

rebellious .... BOLD, DARING,
UNRULY, DEFIANT, LAWLESS

rebelliously .... IN DEFIANCE OF

rebirth .... REVIVAL, UPSURGE,
REDEMPTION, RENAISSANCE

rebound .... DAP, CAROM, RECOIL,
RESILE, RICOCHET, BOUNCE
(BACK)

rebuff .... CUT, SLAP, SNUB,
CHECK, REPEL, SPURN,
REFUSE, REJECT, REPULSE

slang .... COLD-SHOULDER
rebuild .... RESTORE
rebuke ...... SLAP, CHIDE, BERATE,
DERIDE, CENSURE, REPROVE,
UPBRAID, REPREHEND,
REPRIMAND
obsolete .... REPRESS,
INCREPATE
old style .... SNEAP
rebus for example .... PUZZLE
rebut .... OPPOSE, REFUSE,
DISPROVE, CONTRADICT
rebuttal .... RETORT, REJOINDER
brat's .... SASS
colloquial .... CLINCHER
recalcitrant .... REBEL, MULISH,
UNRULY, DEFIANT, RENITENT,
STUBBORN, RESISTANT
recall .... ANNUL, CANCEL,
REPEAL, REVIVE, REVOKE,
RETRACT, REMEMBER,
WITHDRAW, RECOLLECT
recant .... ABJURE, DISAVOW,
RETRACT, RENOUNCE,
WITHDRAW
recantation .... DENIAL
recap .... GIST, RETREAD
recapitulate .... SUM UP, REPEAT,
RESTATE, SUMMARIZE
recapitulation .... REPRISE,
SUMMARY
recast .... REMOLD, REMODEL
recede .... EBB, WANE, DRAW
BACK, FALL BACK
receipt .... RECIPE, QUITTANCE,
ACKNOWLEDGMENT
receipts .... TAKE, INCOME,
PROCEEDS
receivable .... DUE
receive .... GET, HOLD, TAKE,
ADMIT, ABSORB, ACCEPT,
ACQUIRE
for work done .... EARN
information from ..... DEBRIEF
received, in radio .... ROGER
receiver .... PAYEE, ACCEPTER,
COLLECTOR, RECIPIENT,
TREASURER, BENEFICIARY
in baseball .... CATCHER
inheritance .... HEIR
insurance .... BENEFICIARY
stolen goods .... FENCE
trust property .... BAILEE,
TRUSTEE
receiving .... RECEPTION
callers .... IN, AT HOME
recent .... NEW, LATE, FRESH,
MODERN, NEOTERIC
arrival .... NEWCOMER
combining form .... NEO
recently .... ANEW, LATELY, OF

LATE, LATTERLY
receptacle .... BIN, BOX, CAN,
CASE, BASIN, CHEST, BASKET,
VESSEL, CONTAINER
flower .... VASE, TORUS
holy water .... FONT, STOUP
of a sort .... HOD
reception .... LEVEE, PARTY, AT
HOME, DURBAR, SOIREE,
WELCOME, ADMITTANCE
receptionist .... GREETER
receptive .... AMENABLE,
RESPONSIVE, OPEN(-MINDED)
receptor .... EAR, EYE, NOSE
recess .... NOOK, REST, BREAK,
NICHE, PAUSE, HOLLOW,
INTERIM, VACATION
recession ...... DECLINE, SETBACK,
RECEDING
business .... SLUMP,
SLOWDOWN
economic .... DEPRESSION,
UNEMPLOYMENT
recessional .... HYMN
recessionary ill .... LAYOFF
recherche .... RARE
Recife is capital of
.... PERNAMBUCO
recipe .... METHOD, REMEDY,
FORMULA, RECEIPT,
DIRECTIONS, PRESCRIPTION
recipient .... DONEE, PAYEE,
TAKER, ACCEPTER, ENDORSER,
RECEIVER
reciprocal .... MUTUAL
ohm .... MHO
reciprocate .... RETURN,
EXCHANGE, INTERCHANGE
recital .... STORY, ACCOUNT,
CONCERT, MUSICALE,
NARRATION, REHEARSAL
recitation .... STORY, READING,
RECITAL, NARRATIVE
recite .... RELATE, REPEAT,
NARRATE
item by item .... DETAIL
loudly .... DECLAIM, REHEARSE
main points briefly
.... SUMMARIZE,
RECAP(ITULATE)
mechanically .... PATTER
monotonously .... CHANT,
DRONE
reciter of literary works
.... READER
reck .... HEED
reckless .... RASH, WILD, DARING,
WANTON, CARELESS,
HEEDLESS, AUDACIOUS
courage .... DERRING-DO
person ..... MADCAP, HOTSPUR,

PLUNGER, DAREDEVIL
reckon .... COUNT, GUESS, JUDGE,
OPINE, THINK, COMPUTE,
SUPPOSE, CONSIDER, FIGURE
(UP), CALCULATE
long ago .... ARET
reckoning .... TAB, COUNT,
GUESS, TALLY, CALCULATION
reclaim .... REDEEM, REFORM,
RECOVER, RESTORE
reclaimed land .... POLDER
reclame .... PUBLICITY
reclinc ...... LAY, LIE, REST, LEAN
(ON), REPOSE
reclining .... RECUMBENT
recluse .... MONK, LONER, HERMIT,
ASCETIC, EREMITE, SOLITARY,
ANCHORESS, ANCHORITE,
SOLITAIRE, TROGLODYTE
recognition .... NOTICE,
GREETING, ADMISSION,
AWARENESS, COGNIZANCE
recognizance .... BOND, BADGE,
TOKEN, PLEDGE, OBLIGATION
recognize .... OWN, KNOW, ADMIT,
GREET, ACCEPT, SALUTE,
IDENTIFY, PERCEIVE
recoil .... KICK, COWER, QUAIL,
BOUNCE, CRINGE, RESILE,
SHRINK, REDOUND, RETREAT,
DRAW BACK, REACTION
recollect ...... RECALL, REMEMBER
recollection .... MEMORY,
ANAMNESIS, REMEMBRANCE,
REMINISCENCE
recolor .... DYE
recommend .... TOUT, URGE,
ADVISE, COMMIT, COUNSEL,
ENTRUST, SUGGEST
recommendation .... PLUG,
BOOST
recompense ...... REPAY, REWARD,
COMPENSATE
reconcile .... ATONE, ADJUST,
MAKE UP, SQUARE,
SYNCRETIZE
differences .... SETTLE,
COMPOSE, HARMONIZE
recondite .... DEEP, SECRET,
OBSCURE, ABSTRUSE,
PROFOUND
recondition .... OVERHAUL
reconnaissance .... SURVEY,
OBSERVATION
reconnoiter .... CASE, SCOUT,
SURVEY, EXPLORE
reconstruction .... PLASTIC
SURGERY
record .... TAB, ACTA, DISC, DISK,
FILE, HIGH, NOTE, POST, TAPE,
ANNAL, ENTER, ENTRY,

ENROLL, NOTATE, SET DOWN

Captain's/ship .... LOG

copy of .... ESTREAT

formal .... MINUTES,
DOCUMENT, REGISTER

historical .... ANNALS

of arrests/crime .... BLOTTER

of past events .... HISTORY

of travel .... ITINERARY

off the .... PRIVILEGED

personal .... DIARY, DOSSIER

police .... BLOTTER

recorded proceedings ...... ACTA

recorder .... CLERK, FLUTE,
STENO, TAPER, NOTARY,
HISTORIAN, REGISTRAR,
SECRETARY

recording device .... TAPE,
DATER, METER, TIMER

of chess moves ...... NOTATION

records, place for public
.... ARCHIVES

recount .... RECITE, RELATE,
(RE)TELL, NARRATE

recoup .... REGAIN, RECOVER, WIN
BACK, REIMBURSE

recourse .... REFUGE, RESORT

way of .... SUIT

recover .... RALLY, RECOUP,
REGAIN, RECLAIM, RETRIEVE,
RECUPERATE

from illness .... GET WELL,
CONVALESCE

one's spirit .... RALLY, PERK
(UP)

quickly .... BOUNCE BACK

recreant ...... CRAVEN, APOSTATE,
COWARD(LY), DISLOYAL,
TRAITOR(OUS)

recreate, as a movie .... REMAKE

recreation .... PLAY, SPORT,
PASTIME, AMUSEMENT,
DIVERSION

area .... PARK, BEACH

recrement .... DROSS, WASTE,
REFUSE

recrimination
.... COUNTERCHARGE

recruit .... MUSTER, NOVICE,
ROOKIE, DRAFT(EE),
ENLIST(EE), ENROLL(EE),
CONSCRIPT

conditioning site .... BOOT
CAMP

raw .... TENDERFOOT

rectangle/rectangular
.... QUADRATE

rectifier .... ADJUSTER

tube .... DIODE

rectify .... AMEND, ADJUST,
PURIFY, REFINE, REMEDY,

CORRECT

rectitude .... HONESTY, INTEGRITY

recto, opposed to .... VERSO

rector ....:......... PASTOR, PREFECT,
MINISTER

assistant of .... CURATE

dwelling of .... MANSE

recumbent .... LYING, PRONE,
LEANING, RESTING

recuperate .... RECOVER

recuperation .... RECOVERY

recur .... REPEAT, RETURN,
REVERT, COME BACK

recurrence .... RETURN,
REPETITION

recurrent seizures ...... EPILEPSY

recurring period .... CYCLE

women's .... MENSES

recuse .... REJECT, CHALLENGE

red .... RUBY, COLOR, CORAL,
CERISE, CHERRY, GARNET,
CRIMSON, RADICAL, RUBIOUS,
SCARLET, COMMUNIST

admiral .... BUTTERFLY

alert ...... VIGILANCE, WARNING
SIGNAL

and blue color .... PURPLE

apple .... DELICIOUS

berry .... HAW

bird ...... TANAGER, CARDINAL,
BULLFINCH

blood cell .... ERYTHROCYTE

blood cell content
.... HEMOGLOBIN

breasted bream .... SUNFISH

bright .... CERISE, SCARLET,
CARDINAL

brilliant .... SCARLET

carpet ...... (GRAND) WELCOME

cedar .... JUNIPER, SAVIN(E)

cent .... PENNY

corundum .... RUBY

country .... CHINA

deep .... RUBY, GARNET,
CARNATION

deer .... STAG(GARD),
STAGGART

dye ..... EOSIN, HENNA, AURINE

eye .... CONJUNCTIVITIS

eyed fish .... CARP, RUDD

faced .... FLUSHED

flag signal .... DANGER

fuchsia .... MAGENTA,
PURPLISH

haired .... CARROTY

hat .... BIRETTA

hat wearer .... CARDINAL

herring .... PLOY, RUSE,
TACTIC

hind .... CABRILLA

hue .... PINK, ROSE, BLOOD,

SCARLET

in heraldry .... GULES

in the .... LOSING, INDEBTED

ink indicator ... LOSS, DEFICIT

inscribed in .... RUBRIC

item .... DEBT

lattice .... INN, TAVERN

lead .... MINIUM

letter .... MEMORABLE

letter day .... HOLIDAY

light signal ..... STOP, DANGER

man .... (AMERICAN) INDIAN

meat .... BEEF, LAMB, PORK,
MUTTON

mineral .... GARNET, RUTILE

mud .... CLAY

ocher .... RADDLE, REDDLE,
RUBRIC, RUDDLE

osier .... DOGWOOD

pepper .... CAYENNE

pigment .... CHICA, ROSET,
CAROTENE

planet .... MARS

purplish .... CARMINE,
FUCHSIA, MAGENTA,
AMARANTH

shade .... CLARET, TOMATO,
CARNATION, STRAWBERRY

squirrel .... CHICKAREE

star .... MARS, ANTARES

stone .... RUBY, SARD

striped apple .... NORTHERN
SPY

suit .... HEARTS, DIAMONDS

wine .... CLARET

yellow .... ORANGE, TITIAN

Red Book author .... MAO

Cross' concern ..... CALAMITY,
DISASTER

Cross fund raiser ...... TAGGER

Desert .... NEFUD, NEFUF

Polled .... CATTLE

River .... SONGKOI

River city .... FARGO

Sea city .... JEDDA, JIDDA

Sea kingdom .... YEMEN

Sea peninsula .... ARABIA

Sea seaport .... MOCHA

Sea ship .... DHOW

Square figure .... LENIN

Square landmark ..... KREMLIN

redact .... EDIT, REVISE

redactor .... EDITOR

redbreast .... KNOT, BREAM,
ROBIN, SANDPIPER

redbug .... FLEA, CHIGGER

redcap .... TOTER, PORTER,
CARRIER, GOLDFINCH

redd .... TIDY-UP

redden ...... BLUSH, COLOR, FLUSH

reddish ...... PUCE, RUST, RUFOUS,

aromatic wood .... CEDAR
RUFESCENT
brown ..... BAY, ROAN, HAZEL,
AUBURN, MADDER, RUSSET,
SORREL, BURGUNDY,
CHESTNUT, CORDOVAN,
MAHOGANY, CHOCOLATE
brown wood .... MAPLE
fish .... MULLET
wood .... FIR
yellow .... AMBER, SANDY,
ORANGE, TITIAN, LUTEOUS,
TANGERINE
rede .... PLAN, TALE, STORY,
ADVISE, SCHEME, COUNSEL
redecorate .... READORN
redeem .... ATONE, RANSOM,
RESCUE, DELIVER, FULFILL,
RECOVER
Redeemer .... GOEL, SAVIOR,
JESUS CHRIST
redemption .... SALVATION
Redemptorist founder
.... LIGUORI
redeye .... RUDD, VIREO
redfin .... CARP, FISH
redhead ...... DUCK, CARROT TOP,
WOODPECKER
kin of ..... POCHARD, WIDGEON
redhot ...... NEW, FRESH, VIOLENT,
SCALDING, SIZZLING,
SPIRITED, INCANDESCENT
redingote .... OVERCOAT
redneck .... LOWBROW
redness, excessive .... ERYTHRISM
of skin .... RUBEFACTION
redo .... REVAMP
redolence .... ODOR, SCENT
redolent .... SCENTED, FRAGRANT,
SMELLING
redouble ...... (RE)ECHO, REFOLD,
REPEAT, INCREASE
redoubt .... BREASTWORK,
STRONGHOLD
redoubtable .... DREAD,
FEARSOME
redound .... REACT, RECOIL
redowa-like dance .... POLKA,
WALTZ
redpoll .... FINCH
redress .... REMEDY, CORRECT
redskin .... INDIAN
trophy of .... SCALP
redstart .... BIRD, WARBLER,
BRANTAIL
redtop .... GRASS
reduce .... CUT, DIET, PARE, SLIM,
THIN, ALLAY, LOWER, QUELL,
SLASH, DELETE, LESSEN,
SHRINK, SUBDUE, CONQUER,
CURTAIL, DECREASE, DIMINISH

expenses .... PARE
in rank .... DEMOTE
in value .... CHEAPEN,
DEPRECIATE
one's dignity .... DEGRADE,
HUMILIATE
one's weight .... SLENDERIZE
reduction .... CUTBACK
in biology .... MEIOSIS
redundance/redundancy
.... NIMIETY, SURFEIT,
SURPLUS, PLEONASM,
TAUTOLOGY
redundant .... WORDY,
EXCESS(IVE), PLEONASTIC,
REPETITIOUS, SUPERFLUOUS
reduplicate, in botany
.... VALVATE
redware .... SEAWEED
redwing .... THRUSH, SONGBIRD
redwood .... SEQUOIA
ree .... ARIKARA
reecho .... RESOUND
reechoing .... REBOANT
reed .... OAT, GRASS, STALK,
STRAW, RATTAN
bird .... BOBOLINK
buck .... BOHOR, NAGOR,
ANTELOPE
in architecture .... MOLDING
instrument with .... OBOE,
ORGAN, BASSOON, CLARINET,
SAXOPHONE
like .... FERULACEOUS
loom/weaver's .... SLEY
mace .... CATTAIL
poetic .... ARROW
Reed, surgeon/bacteriologist
.... WALTER
reeding .... GADROON, MOLDING
reedy .... SLIM, THIN, PIPING,
FRAGILE, SLENDER
reef .... KEY, BANK, LEDGE, RIDGE,
SHELF, SHOAL, SANDBAR
coral .... CAY, KEY
mining .... LODE, VEIN
reefer ...... COAT, MIDDY, JACKET,
MUFFLER, MIDSHIPMAN,
(MARIJUANA) CIGARETTE
prototype of .... JOINT
reek .... FUME, EXUDE, SMOKE,
STINK, VAPOR, STENCH
reel .... SPIN, SWAY, WIND, DANCE,
LURCH, SPOOL, SWIFT, SWING,
WHEEL, WHIRL, WINCE,
BOBBIN, TEETER, TOTTER,
WAMBLE, STAGGER, FALL
BACK
to hold skeins of silk
.... SWIFT
reeling appearance .... SWIM

of cocoon silk .... FILATURE
reem .... UNICORN
Reese, baseball player .... PEEWEE
Tears author .... LIZETTE
reeve ...... SLIP, PASS IN, THREAD,
BAILIFF, STEWARD, OVERSEER,
SANDPIPER
refection .... MEAL, LUNCH,
REPAST
refectory .... FRATER,
MESS(HALL), DINING HALL
refer .... POINT, ADVERT, ALLUDE,
ASSIGN, DIRECT, SUBMIT,
ASCRIBE, CONSULT
to .... CITE, VIDE
referee .... JUDGE, UMPIRE,
ARBITER, OVERMAN,
MODERATOR
for short .... REF, UMP
reference ...... REGARD, BEARING,
CONCERN, MENTION, RESPECT,
ALLUSION, PERTINENCE
book .... ATLAS, MANUAL,
ALMANAC, DIRECTORY,
DICTIONARY, ENCYCLOPEDIA
expertise .... CREDENTIAL(S)
mark ...... FIST, STAR, DAGGER,
DIESIS, OBELUS, ASTERISK,
PUNCTUATION
personal character
.... TESTIMONIAL
to a law .... CITATION
referendum .... PLEBESCITE
refine .... POLISH, PURIFY,
CLARIFY, CLEANSE, EDUCATE,
IMPROVE, PERFECT,
SUBLIMATE
by distillation .... RECTIFY
metal .... SMELT
refined .... GENTEEL, CULTURED
refinement ...... POLISH, CULTURE,
DELICACY, ELEGANCE,
GENTILITY
refiner .... SIEVE, TRIER, FILTER
refinery .... SMELTERY,
DISTILLERY
refining vessel .... CUPEL
refinish the floor .... SAND
reflect ...... MUSE, THINK, MIRROR,
PONDER, CONSIDER
exactly .... MIRROR, DUPLICATE
reflection .... IMAGE, BLAME,
MUSING, REFLEX, SHADOW,
LIKENESS, ASPERSION,
DISCREDIT
of a sound .... ECHO
reflective .... PENSIVE, WISTFUL
reflet .... LUSTER
reflex .... INSTINCT
refluent .... EBBING, REFLUX
reform .... BETTER, CHANGE,

CONVERT, CORRECT
reformatory .... PRISON, MAGDALENE
reformed .... TURNED OVER A NEW LEAF
reformer .... CRUSADER, MORALIST
Bohemian .... HUSS
Protestant .... CALVIN
religious .... LUTHER
social .... (JACOB) RIIS
refract .... BEND, DEFLECT
refractory ...... UNRULY, RESTIVE, STUBBORN, FRACTIOUS, OBSTINATE
refrain ...... CURB, MUSIC, VERSE, WHEEL, BURDEN, CHORUS, DESIST, PHRASE, ABSTAIN, FORBEAR, HOLD BACK, REPETEND
of a song .... BURDEN, CHORUS
short .... BOB
syllable .... TRA
refresh .... AIR, FAN, COOL, RENEW, REVIVE, ENLIVEN
with food/drink .... REFECT
refresher .... REMINDER
refreshing .... BALMY, BRISK, CRISPY, BRACING
drink .... LEMONADE
refreshment .... FOOD, DRINK, SNACK, REPAST, REFECTION
refrigerant .... ICE, FREON, ETHANE, CRYOGEN
refrigerate .... COOL, CHILL, FREEZE
refrigerator .... ICEBOX, FREEZER, FRIGIDAIRE
for short .... REEFER
gas .... FREON
kind of .... WALK-IN
Refrigerator, football player nicknamed .... PERRY
reft .... ROBBED
refuge .... HAVEN, ASYLUM, HARBOR, CITADEL, HOSPICE, RETREAT, SHELTER, SANCTUARY
refugee .... EMIGRE, ESCAPEE, EVACUEE, FUGITIVE
organization .... IRO
refulgent .... GLOWING, RADIANT, SHINING
refund .... REBATE, REIMBURSE, REPAY(MENT)
refurbish .... RENOVATE
refusal ...... NAY, DENIAL, OPTION, REJECTION
phrase .... NO WAY, NO DICE, NO SOAP
word .... NO, NAY, NEVER

refuse .... BALK, DENY, NILL, SCUM, OFFAL, SPURN, TRASH, WASTE, EJECTA, NAYSAY, REBUFF, REJECT, DECLINE, RUBBISH
brewery .... DRAFF, DREGS
cane .... BAGASSE
collectors .... ASHMEN
consent to .... VETO
grape .... MARC
metal .... SCUM, DROSS
nourishment .... FAST
table .... ORT, SCRAPS
to acknowledge .... DENY
to move .... STAY PUT
to talk: sl. .... CLAM UP
wine .... LEES
refusing to plead in court .... MUTE
refutation .... DISPROOF
refute .... REBUT, DISPUTE, DISPROVE
regain .... RECOUP, RECOVER
consciousness .... COME TO
regal .... ROYAL, KINGLY, QUEENLY, STATELY, MAJESTIC
regale .... FEAST, TREAT, ENTERTAIN
regalia .... TIARA, FINERY, EMBLEMS, INSIGNIA, DECORATIONS
king's .... CROWN, SCEPTER
Regan's father .... LEAR
sister .... GONERIL, CORDELIA
regard .... EYE, DEEM, GAZE, LOOK, NOTE, ESTEEM, CONCERN, OBSERVE, RESPECT, CONSIDER, REFERENCE
closely .... SCRUTINIZE
with terror .... DREAD
regarding .... IN RE, ABOUT, CONCERNING
regardless .... ANYHOW, CARELESS, HEEDLESS, NEGLIGENT
of circumstances ...... RAIN OR SHINE
regards .... EYES, ESTEEM, AFFECTION
regatta .... BOAT RACE
boat ..... SCULL, SHELL, YACHT
sights .... CATBOATS
Venetian .... GONDOLA RACE
regenerate .... RENEW
regent .... DEPUTY, INTERREX
of the sun .... URIEL
regentship .... REGENCY
Reggae relative .... SKA
regicide's victim .... KING
regime .... RULE, REIGN, GOVERNMENT

regimen .... DIET, COURSE, METHOD, SYSTEM
regiment commander .... COLONEL
part of .... BATTALION
regimental flag .... PENNON
Regin, son of .... SIGURD, SIEGFRIED
regina .... QUEEN(LY)
Regina, monastery .... LAUDIS
region .... AREA, ZONE, CLIME, PLACE, REALM, SPACE, DOMAIN, SPHERE, SECTION, VICINITY, TERRITORY
of shifting sands .... REG
regional .... LOCAL, SECTIONAL, TERRITORIAL
register ...... LIST, ENROL, ENTER, METER, (EN)ROLL, RECORD, ROSTER, EXPRESS, CALENDAR
death .... NECROLOGY
regma .... MAPLE, SCHIZOCARP
regnant .... RULING, REIGNING, PREVALENT
regorge .... VOMIT
regress .... RETURN
regret ...... RUE, MOURN, GRIEVE, REPENT, REPINE, DEPLORE, REMORSE, PENITENCE
regretful .... SORRY, CONTRITE
sounding garment .... SARI
regular .... EVEN, USUAL, NORMAL, PROPER, STABLE, STEADY, ORDERLY, UNIFORM, CONSTANT, HABITUAL, CUSTOMARY
method .... HABIT, PRACTICE
patronage .... CUSTOM
recurrence of beat .... RHYTHM
regulate .... FIX, RULE, ADJUST, DIRECT, MANAGE, CONTROL
regulation .... LAW, RULE, ORDER
regulator ...... VALVE, GOVERNOR
temperature .... CRYOSTAT
regurgitate .... SPEW, VOMIT
rehabilitate .... RESTORE, RECONDITION
rehash .... REVIEW, RECOUNT
rehearsal ...... RECITAL, PRACTICE, PROLUSION
kind of .... DRESS, DRYRUN
rehearse .... DRILL, TRAIN, RECITE, PRACTICE
quickly .... RUN OVER
Rehoboam's father .... SOLOMON
taskmaster .... ADORAM
Reich .... GERMANY
reign .... RULE, SWAY, GOVERN, REGIME, COMMAND, PREVAIL
of a family .... DYNASTY

reigning .... REGNANT

reimburse .... REPAY, REFUND, PAY BACK

rein .... CHECK, LEASH, CONTROL, RESTRAIN

draw .... STOP

reincarnation .... REBIRTH

reindeer .... CARIBOU

man/herder .... LAPP

reine's husband .... ROI

Reiner .... ROB, CARL

reinforce .... SUPPORT, STRENGTHEN

reinstate .... REVEST, RESTORE, REINSTALL

reiterate ...... HARP, REPEAT, SAY AGAIN

reject .... EJECT, REPEL, SPURN, VOMIT, ABJURE, REBUFF, REFUSE, DECLINE, DISCARD

a lover abruptly .... JILT

bill .... VETO

slang .... BRUSH OFF

rejoice .... ENJOY, EXULT, GLORY, REVEL, DELIGHT, GLADDEN

rejoin .... REPLY, ANSWER, RESPOND, REUNITE

rejoinder .... REPLY, RETORT, RESPONSE

rejuvenate .... RENEW, REFRESH

relapse .... FALL BACK, SLIP BACK, BACKSLIDE

relate .... TELL, REPORT, CONNECT, NARRATE, PERTAIN, RECOUNT

related .... AKIN, TOLD, ALLIED, COGNATE, GERMANE, CONNECTED

by blood .... SIB, KIN(DRED)

on father's side .... AGNATE, AGNATIC

on mother's side .... ENATE, ENATIVE

relating to backbones .... SPINAL

relation .... TIE, LINK, FAMILY, ACCOUNT, KINFOLK, KINSMAN, KIN(SHIP), RECITAL

relationship .... KINSHIP, AFFINITY, COGNATION, RELEVANCE, CONNECTION

sympathetic .... RAPPORT

relative .... SIB, COGNATE, KIN(FOLK), KINSMAN, RELEVANT, PERTINENT

by marriage .... AFFINE

for short .... SIS, BROD

of a grimace .... LEER

of a kickback .... SHAKEDOWN

of a sort .... IN-LAW

of OSS .... CIA

relatives, employment of
.... NEPOTISM

relator .... NARRATOR, COMPLAINANT

relax .... EASE, REST, ABATE, LOOSEN, RELENT, SOFTEN, UNBEND, SLACKEN, EASY DOES IT

relaxation .... REPOSE, AMUSEMENT, DIVERSION, RECREATION

relaxer .... OPIATE

relay .... AGENT, SHIFT, FORWARD, REMOUNT, TRANSMIT

release .... FREE, UNDO, CLEAR, LET GO, UNTIE, EXEMPT, LOOSEN, RELIEF, RELIEVE, LIBERATE, DISCHARGE, QUITCLAIM

air .... DEFLATE

claim .... REMISE, WAIVER

conditionally .... PAROLE

from sin .... CLEANSE

hold .... DROP

mass of ice .... CALVE

relegate .... EXILE, ASSIGN, BANISH, COMMIT, CONSIGN

relent ...... THAW, YIELD, SOFTEN, SUBMIT

relentless .... GRIM, HARSH, PITILESS

relevant .... APT, APROPOS, FITTING, GERMANE, RELATED, APPOSITE, PERTINENT, APPLICABLE

reliability .... SOUNDNESS

reliable .... SOLID, TRIED, TESTED, TRUSTY, DEPENDABLE, TRUSTWORTHY

reliance .... FAITH, TRUST, CREDENCE, DEPENDENCE

relic ...... CURIO, TOKEN, ANTIQUE, MEMENTO, SOUVENIR

sacred .... HALIDOM

relics .... RUINS

relict .... WIDOW, WIDOWED, SURVIVOR

relief .... AID, EASING, REMEDY, SOLACE, SUCCOR, COMFORT, RELEASE, RELIEVO, EASEMENT

emotional drug
.... TRANQUILIZER

from difficulty .... OASIS

medicinal .... PAINKILLER

provider .... RED CROSS

relieve .... RID, CURE, EASE, FREE, HELP, ALLAY, SOFTEN, SOOTHE, COMFORT, LIGHTEN, PALLIATE, ALLEVIATE

by talking .... ABREACT

thirst .... SLAKE, QUENCH

relievo .... RELIEF

religieuse .... NUN, SISTER

religieux .... MONK, PIOUS, OBLATE

religion .... CREED, FAITH, BELIEF, DOCTRINE

religionist .... DEIST, FANATIC

religious .... TRUE, GODLY, PIOUS, DIVINE, DEVOUT, STRICT, FAITHFUL, ORTHODOX, CANONICAL, SECTARIAN, GODFEARING, SCRUPULOUS, EVANGELICAL

beggar .... FAKIR, SERVITE

belief .... CREED

belief, antagonistic .... HERESY

blessing said over the wine
.... KIDDUSH

brotherhood .... ORDER, SODALITY

candidate .... POSTULANT

day of atonement, Jewish
.... YOM KIPPUR

denomination .... ISLAM, JUDAISM, BUDDHISM, HINDUISM, CATHOLICISM, UNITARIANISM, PROTESTANTISM

devotee .... FAKIR, ZEALOT

devotion .... NOVENA

dietary regulation, Judaism
.... KASHRUT(H)

emotion .... THEOPATHY

exclamation .... HOSANNA, ALLELUIA

expedition .... CRUSADE

group chief .... HIERARCH

holy day .... SABBATH, HANNUKAH, PASSOVER, ASCENSION

journey .... PILGRIMAGE

lay society .... SODALITY

leader .... POPE, PONTIFF, SHEPHERD

leader's saying .... LOGIA

lore .... HIEROLOGY

man .... LAMA, MONK, SAINT, PRIEST, SHAMAN

military order member
.... TEMPLAR

mysticism .... QUIETISM

observance .... FAST, LENT

offering .... OBLATION, SACRIFICE

order .... JESUIT, MARIST, TEMPLAR, URSULINE, DOMINICAN, FRANCISCAN

period .... LENT, EASTER, HANNUKAH

person .... OBLATE, THEIST, DEVOTEE, PIETIST, BELIEVER, EVANGELIST

rebel .... HERETIC

recluse .... EREMITE
reformer .... HUSS, KNOX,
LUTHER
rites, of .... SACRAL
ritual .... CULT
school head .... RECTOR
sect .... DENOMINATION
springtime holy day
.... PASSOVER
statue .... PIETA
vigil .... WATCH
war .... CRUSADE
worship, system of .... CULT
relinquish .... CEDE, DROP, LET
GO, WAIVE, YIELD, FOR(E)GO,
RESIGN, ABANDON, RELEASE,
PART WITH, RENOUNCE,
SURRENDER
slang .... DITCH
reliquary .... ARCA, CASKET,
SHRINE, SEPULCHER
relish .... ZEST, ACHAR, ENJOY,
GUSTO, SAPOR, SAUCE,
SAVOR, SPICE, TASTE,
FLAVOR, LIKING, RADISH,
CHUTNEE, CHUTNEY, PICKLES,
PLEASURE, CONDIMENT
fish egg .... CAVIAR(E)
meat juice .... ASPIC
the scene ,.......... FEAST ONE'S
EYES
relucent .... BRIGHT
reluct .... REVOLT
reluctant .... LO(A)TH, AVERSE,
HESITANT, UNWILLING
rely .... BANK ON, LEAN, TRUST,
RECKON, COUNT (ON),
DEPEND (ON)
relying on experience
.... EMPIRICAL
remain .... LAST, STAY, ABIDE,
ENDURE
balanced .... LIBRATE
close .... CLING
firm .... STAND (PAT)
in a fixed position .... STAY
PUT
undecided .... PEND, HANG
FIRE
remainder .... REST, EXCESS,
BALANCE, REMNANT, RESIDUE,
LEAVINGS, LEFT-OVER,
RESIDUAL, RESIDUUM
bolt of cloth .... REMNANT
cigarette .... BUTT
drunken binge ...... HANGOVER
of destruction .... DEBRIS
of partially burned wood
.... CINDER
of thorough burning .... ASH
pencil .... STUB

tree .... STUMP
remains ...... LEES, DREGS, RUINS,
TRACES, CADAVER, REMNANT,
SEDIMENT, VESTIGES
person's .... CORPSE
worthless .... CARCASS
remand .... RECALL, RETURN,
SEND BACK
remark .... NOTE, WORD, NOTICE,
EXPRESS, MENTION, OBSERVE,
REMARQUE, COMMENT(ARY)
clever .... NIFTY, SALLY, BON
MOT, (WISE)CRACK, WITTICISM
correct: sl. .... MOUTHFUL
cutting ... DIG, NIP, SARCASM
indirect, derogatory
.... INNUENDO
mocking .... JEST
nasty/pointed .... BARB
unfavorable .... BRICKBAT
remarkable .... UNCO, SIGNAL,
NOTABLE, UNUSUAL,
STRIKING, EXTRAORDINARY
remarkably bad ...... EGREGIOUS
Remarque, Ger. novelist
.... (ERICH) MARIA
Rembrandt, Dutch painter
.... VAN RIN, VAN RIJN
work .... TITUS, THE
ASCENSION
remedy .... CURE, HEAL, HELP,
TREAT, RECIPE, RELIEF,
REPAIR, CORRECT, REDRESS,
ANTIDOTE
any .... TREACLE
bacteria-fighting
.... ANTIBIOTIC, PENICILLIN,
TETRACYCLINE
cure-all .... ELIXIR, PANACEA
in coinage .... TOLERANCE
medicinal .... DRUG, POTION,
SIMPLES
preventive .... ANTITOXIN
quack .... NOSTRUM
secret .... ELIXIR, ARCANUM
soothing .... BALM, SALVE,
BALSAM, LOTION, UNGUENT,
LINIMENT, DEMULCENT
to counteract poison
.... ANTIDOTE
remember ...... RECALL, REMIND,
OBSERVE, RECOLLECT,
REMINISCE
remembrance .... TOKEN,
MEMORY, MEMENTO,
KEEPSAKE, SOUVENIR
remex .... FEATHER, OARSMAN
remiges .... FEATHERS
remind .... PROMPT
reminder .... MEMO, MEMENTO,
TICKLER, SOUVENIR

reminiscence .... MEMORY
reminiscent .... SUGGESTIVE
remiss .... LAX, SLACK, DERELICT,
NEGLIGENT, NEGLECTFUL
remission .... PARDON, RESPITE,
ABATEMENT, SUSPENSION
remit .... PAY, SEND, CANCEL,
PARDON, FORGIVE, SLACKEN
remnant .... RAG, DREG, SCRAP,
TRACE, (TAG) END, LEAVING,
ODDMENT, RESIDUE,
FRAGMENT, LEFT-OVER,
REMAINDER
remodel ...... RECAST, MODERNIZE
remo(u)lade .... SAUCE
remonstrance .... PROTEST,
COMPLAINT, OBJECTION
remonstrate ...... PLEAD, OBJECT,
PROTEST
remora .... PEGA, SUCKFISH
favorite host of .... SHARK
remorse .... PITY, GRIEF, REGRET,
QUALMS, PENITENCE,
COMPASSION, COMPUNCTION,
SELF-REPROACH
remorseful .... SORRY, ASHAMED,
CONTRITE, FEEL BADLY
remorseless .... CRUEL, CALLOUS,
PITILESS, MERCILESS,
UNTOUCHED
remote .... ALIEN, ALOOF, FAR
(OFF), SLIGHT, DISTANT,
SECLUDED, ULTERIOR
remount .... HORSE, RELAY
removable .... PORTABLE,
DETACHABLE
removal .... OUSTER, DISMISSAL,
ELIMINATION
as by killing ...... LIQUIDATION
of decayed tooth ..... PULLING,
EXTRACTION
diseased tissue ...... ERASION
rank, rights ..... DIVESTMENT
something undesirable
.... RIDDANCE
unwanted hair
.... ELECTROLYSIS
waste products from blood
.... DIALYSIS
surgical .... ABLATION
remove .... DELE, DOFF, KILL,
OUST, EJECT, EXPEL, DELETE,
DEPOSE, EXCISE, DISMISS,
TAKE OFF, DISPLACE,
ELIMINATE
as graffiti .... ERASE
as one's hat .... DOFF
bark .... DECORTICATE
by popular vote .... RECALL
clothes .... STRIP, UNDRESS

clothes from suitcase
.... UNPACK
feathers .... PLUCK
from grave .... DISINTER
from office/the throne
.... OUST, DEPOSE
grease .... DEFAT
grit .... DESAND
hair .... SHAVE
ice .... DEFROST
impurities ...... SMELT, FILTER,
REFINE, DISTILL, RECTIFY
in law .... ELOIN, ELOIGN
juice .... REAM, SQUEEZE
marks .... ERASE
scum .... SCOUR
stopple .... UNCORK
to a distance: law .... ELOIN
to another place .... TRANSFER
tumor .... EXCISE
waste from body ..... EXCRETE
water .... DEHYDRATE
removed .... APART, DISTANT
remunerate .... PAY, REWARD,
REIMBURSE, RECOMPENSE
remuneration .... PAY, WAGES,
INCOME, SALARY,
EMOLUMENT, COMPENSATION
remunerative .... PAYING,
GAINFUL, LUCRATIVE,
REWARDING
Remus' brother .... ROMULUS
parent .... MARS, RHEA
Renaissance .... REBIRTH,
REVIVAL
archetypal man .... DA VINCI
artist .... RAPHAEL
humanist .... ERASMUS
masterpiece .... MONA LISA,
THE LAST SUPPER
sword .... ESTOC
renal .... NEPHRIC, NEPHRITIC
Renard .... FOX
renascence .... REBIRTH,
RENEWAL, REVIVAL
rend .... CUT, RIP, PULL, RIVE,
TEAR, REAVE, SPLIT, CLEAVE
render .... DO, PAY, PUT, GIVE,
ACT (OUT), DEPICT, RECITE,
SUBMIT, DELIVER, FURNISH,
PERFORM, PRESENT,
CONSTRUE, HAND OVER,
TRANSLATE
a musical .... PERFORM
fluid .... FUSE, LIQUEFY
unclear .... BEFOG
rendezvous .... DATE, TRYST,
MEET(ING), APPOINTMENT
rocket .... AGENA
rendition .... VIEW, VERSION,
PERFORMANCE, TRANSLATION

renegade .... RAT, TRAITOR,
APOSTATE, DEFECTOR,
DESERTER, TURNCOAT
renege .... WELSH, BACK OUT,
DISAVOW, FINAGLE
renew .... REPEAT, RESUME,
REVIVE, REFRESH, RESTORE,
CONTINUE, RENOVATE,
REGENERATE
Reni, Ital. painter .... GUIDO
rennet .... RENNIN
Reno is in .... NEVADA
rival of .... LAS VEGAS, (LAKE)
TAHOE
Renoir, painter .... PIERRE
renounce .... DENY, ABJURE,
DISOWN, GIVE UP, RECANT,
REJECT, ABANDON, ABDICATE,
FORSWEAR, RELINQUISH
throne .... ABDICATE
renovate .... REDO, RENEW,
REPAIR, REVIVE, FRESHEN,
FURBISH
renown .... FAME, ECLAT, GLORY,
REPUTE, REPUTATION,
DISTINCTION
person of .... CELEBRITY
renowned .... FAMOUS
bridge master .... GOREN
rensselaerite .... TALC
rent .... GAP, LET, RIP, HIRE,
HOLE, SLIT, TEAR, RENTAL,
LEASE, SCHISM, PAYMENT
again .... RELET
asunder .... RIVEN
rente .... ANNUITY, REVENUE
renunciation .... WAIVER,
CESSATION, ABDICATION
reopen .... RESUME
reorganization .... REVAMP,
SHAKE-UP
rep .... FABRIC
repair .... GO, FIX, (A)MEND,
BETAKE, REMEDY, RESTORE
a coat .... RELINE
a green .... RESOD
a hole tear .... DARN
a threaded hole .... RETAP
loose paper .... REPASTE
shop .... GARAGE
repairman .... FIXER, MENDER,
COBBLER, MECHANIC,
TECHNICIAN
reparable .... MENDABLE
reparation .... AMENDS, REDRESS,
REPAIRS, ATONEMENT,
INDEMNITY
reparative .... MENDING
repartee .... MOT, QUIP, SALLY,
BANTER, RETORT, RIPOSTE,
DIALOGUE, REJOINDER

engage in .... FENCE
skilled in .... WITTY, CLEVER
repast ...... MEAL, SNACK, SPREAD,
REFECTION
repatriate .... RETURN, SEND
BACK
repay .... REFUND, REWARD,
REIMBURSE, RECOMPENSE
repeal .... ANNUL, CANCEL,
RECALL, REVOKE, ABOLISH,
NULLIFY, RE-SOUND,
ABROGATE
repeat .... BIS, ECHO, REDO,
RECUR, PARROT, RECITE,
(RE)ITERATE
gossip, secrets .... RETAIL
performance .... ENCORE
tiresomely .... HARP
repeatedly .... ANEW, OFT(EN),
AGAIN, FREQUENTLY
repeater .... ECHO, CLOCK, RIFLE,
WATCH, PARROT, PISTOL
repeating rifle inventor
.... MAUSER
repel ...... SPURN, REFUSE, REJECT,
RESIST, REPULSE
danger .... DEFEND
repellent .... REPULSIVE,
RESISTANT, WATERPROOF
repent ...... RUE, GRIEVE, REGRET,
CRAWLING, CREEPING,
APOLOGIZE
repentance .... REGRET, REMORSE,
ATTRITION, PENITENCE,
CONTRITION
repercussion .... ECHO, EFFECT,
IMPACT, RECOIL, RESULT,
REBOUND, REACTION
repertoire .... ACTS, STOCK,
ROUTINES
repertory .... STOCK, COLLECTION,
STORE(HOUSE)
repetend .... REFRAIN
repetition .... COPY, HARPING,
RECITATION, RECURRENCE,
DUPLICATION
in music .... REPRISE
mechanical .... ROTE
of a movie scene ...... RETAKE
performance .... ENCORE,
REPLAY
same sound, uninterrupted
.... MONOTONE
TV show .... RERUN
repine .... FRET, MOPE, GRIEVE,
COMPLAIN
replace .... RETURN, RESTORE,
SUCCEED, SUPPLANT
a performer .... SUBSTITUTE
a starter .... RELIEVE
replenish .... REFILL, RESTOCK

replevin .... BOND, PLEDGE, TROVER

replete .... FULL, STUFFED

repletion .... GLUT, SATIETY, FULLNESS

replica ...... COPY, CLONE, IMAGE, DOUBLE, DUPLICATE, FACSIMILE, REPRODUCTION

replicate .... FOLD, REPEAT

replication .... ECHO, FOLD, REPLY, ANSWER, COPY(ING), PARROT(ING), DUPLICATION

reply .... ANSWER, RETORT, RETURN, RESPOND, COMEBACK, RESPONSE, REJOIN(DER)

to a knock .... ENTER

repondez s'il vous plait .... RSVP

report .... SAY, NEWS, TALK, TELL, BLAST, BRUIT, NOISE, RUMOR, STATE, CAHIER, GOSSIP, ACCOUNT, HANSARD, HEARSAY, BULLETIN, DENOUNCE, BROADCAST

card entry .... MARK, GRADE

on policy and procedure .... CAHIER

slanderous .... SCANDAL

reportable infectious disease ...... AIDS, MALARIA, MEASLES, RUBELLA, SYPHILIS, GONORRHEA, DIPTHERIA, HEPATITIS, CHICKENPOX, TUBERCULOSIS

reporter .... CRIER, SCRIBE, NEWSMAN, COLUMNIST, NEWSHOUND, JOURNALIST

concern of .... BEAT, DATA, FACTS, SCOOP, ACCURACY, CONTACTS, DEADLINE

delight of .... BY-LINE

material of .... STORY

paper of .... FLIMSY

routine of .... LEGWORK

repose ...... LAY, LIE, CALM, REST, PEACE, RELAX, SLEEP, RECLINE, RESPITE, BREATHER

archaic .... RELY, ENTRUST

repository ...... BOX, SAFE, CHEST, VAULT, CLOSET, MUSEUM, CONFIDANT, SEPULCHER, WAREHOUSE

reprehend .... BLAME, REBUKE, CENSURE, REPROVE

reprehensible .... CENSURABLE, BLAMEWORTHY

represent .... ENACT, DENOTE, EMBODY, DEPICT, TYPIFY, EXHIBIT, PICTURE, PORTRAY, DESCRIBE, PERSONATE, DELINEATE, SYMBOLIZE, VISUALIZE, SUBSTITUTE

facts, information .... OUTLINE, ILLUSTRATE

graphically .... PLOT

representation ...... ICON, IMAGE, MIMESIS, ALLEGORY, LIKENESS, RENDITION, ALLEGATION

of heavenly bodies .... ORRERY

ridiculous .... TRAVESTY

representative .... AGENT, ENVOY, PROXY, SOLON, DEPUTY, TYPICAL, DELEGATE, AMBASSADOR, LEGISLATOR, DESCRIPTIVE

repress ...... CURB, CRUSH, QUELL, SIT ON, STIFLE, SUBDUE, SMOTHER, HOLD BACK, RESTRAIN

reprieve .... STAY, DELAY, GRACE, RESPITE, SUSPENSION, POSTPONEMENT

reprimand .... BAWL, SCOLD, RATING, REBUKE, CENSURE, REPROVE, ADMONISH

reprint .... REISSUE, REVISION

reprisal ...... REVENGE, REQUITAL, QUITTANCE, RETORSION, RETORTION, VENGEANCE, RETALIATION

obs. .... MARQUE

reprise .... ENCORE, REPEAT, SUMMARY, REPETITION

reproach .... TWIT, BLAME, CHIDE, REBUKE, CENSURE, REPROVE, UPBRAID

reproachful word .... FIE

reprobate .... RAKE, ROUE, ROGUE, SINNER, VICIOUS, DEPRAVED, SCOUNDREL

reproduce .... BREED, REFLECT, MULTIPLY, PROCREATE

reproduction .... COPY, FACSIMILE, DUPLICATION

reproductive .... FECUND, CREATIVE

agent/unit .... SPORE

cell .... GONAD, GAMETE

organ .... OVARY, TESTIS

reproof .... RATING, REBUKE, REPROACH, SCOLDING

reprove ...... RATE, CHIDE, SCOLD, REBUKE, CENSURE, UPBRAID, ADMONISH

reptant .... REPENT, CRAWLING, CREEPING

reptile .... SNAKE, LIZARD, TURTLE, SAURIAN, SERPENT, OPHIDIAN, ALLIGATOR, CROCODILE, LACERT(IL)IAN

carnivorous .... TUATARA

edible .... TERRAPIN

endangered ..... GREEN TURTLE

extinct .... PTEROSAUR

eye tissue .... PECTEN

footless .... APOD, SNAKE

fossil .... STEGOSAURUS

movement of .... CRAWL, CREEP, SLITHER

mythical .... SALAMANDER

Nile .... CROC

scale .... SCUTUM, PLATELET

reptiles, study of .... HERPETOLOGY

republic .... COUNTRY, DEMOCRACY

not quite one .... BANANA

of letters .... LITERATI

Republic author .... PLATO

Republican .... WHIG

mascot .... ELEPHANT

Mr., soubriquet .... TAFT

Party .... GOP

recalcitrant .... MUGWUMP

repudiate .... DENY, DISOWN, RECANT, REJECT, DISAVOW

repugnance .... HATE, DISGUST, DISLIKE, AVERSION, DISTASTE

repugnant .... HATEFUL, OFFENSIVE, REPULSIVE

repulse ...... SNUB, REPEL, SPURN, REBUFF, REFUSE, REJECT, DRIVE BACK

repulsion ...... DISLIKE, AVERSION, DISTASTE, REJECTION, ABHORRENCE

repulsive .... UGLY, COARSE, ODIOUS, MAWKISH, LOATHSOME, OFFENSIVE, REVOLTING, DISGUSTING

reputable .... NOTABLE, ESTEEMED, CREDIBLE, RESPECTABLE

reputation .... FAME, NAME, RENOWN, REPUTE, PRESTIGE, CHARACTER, DISTINCTION

repute .... ODOR, ESTEEM, REGARD, GOODWILL

reputed .... KNOWN, PUTATIVE, SUPPOSED

request ...... ASK, BEG, SUE, PRAY, SUIT, APPLY, PLEA(D), APPEAL, ENLIST, BESEECH, IMPLORE, ENTREAT(Y), INSTANCE, PETITION

requiem ...... HYMN, MASS, DIRGE

requiescat in _____ .... PACE

require ...... NEED, FORCE, ORDER, COMPEL, DEMAND, ENTAIL, OBLIGE, INVOLVE

requirement .... NEED, WANT,

NECESSITY, REQUISITE
unjust .... IMPOSITION
requisite .... NEED, REQUIRED,
ESSENTIAL
requite .... ATONE, (RE)PAY,
RETALIATE, COMPENSATE
reredos .... SCREEN, PARTITION
reroute .... DETOUR
rerun .... REPEAT, REPLAY,
RESHOW
rescind .... ANNUL, CANCEL,
RECALL, REPEAL, ABOLISH,
ABROGATE
rescript .... COPY, ORDER, DECREE
rescue .... SAVE, RANSOM,
REDEEM, RECLAIM, RECOVER,
SALVATION, DELIVER(ANCE)
research .... STUDY, EXPLORATION
center .... LAB(ORATORY)
reseau .... NETWORK
resect .... EXCISE
reseda .... MIGNONETTE
resemblance .... LIKENESS,
SIMILARITY
resent .... ENRAGE, OFFEND,
RANKLE, INCENSE
resentful .... SORE
resentment .... HATE, HUFF,
ANGER, PIQUE, DUDGEON,
OFFENSE, UMBRAGE, BAD
BLOOD, ANIMOSITY,
INDIGNATION
reservation, in law .... SALVO,
SAYING
without .... OUTRIGHT
reserve .... KEEP, CASH, STOCK,
STORE, RETAIN, BACKLOG,
DIGNITY, EARMARK, SILENCE,
SET ASIDE, RETICENCE
space .... BOOK
reserved ...... SHY, ALOOF, QUIET,
STAID, DISTANT, INDRAWN,
RETICENT, RETIRING,
TACITURN
reserves, armed forces
.... MILITIA
reservoir .... SUMP, STORE,
SOURCE, SUPPLY, CISTERN
overflow of .... SPILTH
reset gem .... REMOUNT
resettle .... MOVE
reside .... LIVE, ABIDE, DWELL,
LODGE
residence .... HOME, ABODE,
DOMICILE, DWELLING
king's .... CASTLE, PALACE
minister's .... MANSE,
RECTORY, PARSONAGE
papal .... VATICAN
place of .... ADDRESS
restricted .... HAREM

rural .... BOWER
slang .... DIGS
stately .... VILLA, PALACE,
MANSION
resident ...... DENIZEN, INHERENT,
(IN)HABITANT
aquarium .... TETRA
doctor .... INTERN(E)
residential blind alley .... CUL-
DE-SAC
street .... TERRACE
residual .... EXTRA, SURPLUS,
REMAINDER
residue .... ASH, DREG, LEES,
REST, SILT, BITTERN,
REMNANT, LEAVINGS, LEFT-
OVER, REMANENT, SEDIMENT,
SIFTINGS, REMAINDER
resign ...... QUIT, DEMIT, VACATE,
ABDICATE, STEP DOWN,
RELINQUISH
resignation .... PATIENCE,
DEMISSION, SURRENDER,
ABDICATION, SUBMISSION
resile .... REBOUND
resiliency .... BUOYANCY,
ELASTICITY
resilient .... SUPPLE, DUCTILE,
BUOYANT, ELASTIC, PLIABLE,
TENSILE, FLEXIBLE
resin .... GUM, TUPI, ALKYD,
AMBER, ANIME, COPAL,
KAURI, PITCH, ROSIN, SARAN,
COPALM, MASTIC, COPAIBA,
ASAFETIDA, ELATERITE,
LA(B)DANUM, SHELLAC(K)
aromatic .... COPAIBA
asphaltic .... BITUMEN
cathartic .... SCAMMONY
fossil .... AMBER, RETINITE
fragrant .... ELEMI, MYRRH,
FRANKINCENSE
gum .... COPAL, MYRRH,
MASTIC, GAMBOGE,
AMMONIAC, EDELLIUM,
RESINOID
hemp .... CHARAS, HASHISH
incense .... MYRRH, SANDARAC
perfume-making ...... BENZOIN
pine .... DAMMAR, DAMMER
poisonous .... CANNABIN
solvent for .... ETHER
sweet-smelling .... MYRRH
synthetic .... LUCITE, CATALIN,
BAKELITE, SILICONE
thermoplastic .... SARAN
tropical .... COPAL
used as paint drier ...... JAPAN
used to give glossy surface
.... VARNISH

used to rub on thread
.... WAX
varnish .... ANIME, COPAL,
DAMMAR, DAMMER
resinous juice .... LABDANUM
powder, hops .... LUPULIN
secretion .... LAC
resist .... BUCK, DEFY, FACE,
FEND, FIGHT, OPPOSE,
REPUGN, CONFRONT,
WITHSTAND
resistance .... REFUSAL, DEFIANCE,
FRICTION, OPPOSITION
fighter ..... EDES, ELAS, MAQUI,
ACTIVIST, PARTISAN,
GUERRILLA
labor union .... STRIKE,
WALKOUT
passive .... DISOBEDIENCE,
INSUBORDINATION
purchaser .... BOYCOTT
to authority .... MUTINY
resister .... REBEL, HOLDOUT,
STRIKER
resolute ...... FIRM, GRIM, STEADY,
DECISIVE, RESOLVED,
DETERMINED
resolve .... END, DECIDE,
ANALYZE, DETERMINE
resonance .... ECHO, RINGING,
SYNTONY, SONORITY,
VIBRANCY, VIBRATION
resonant ...... OROTUND, VIBRANT,
SONOROUS, REECHOING,
RESOUNDING
resort .... SPA, HAUNT, RECOURSE,
RESOURCE
city .... ASPEN, MIAMI,
HONOLULU
Riviera .... CANNES
resound .... BOOM, PEAL, RING,
CLANG, EXTOL, (RE)ECHO,
VIBRATE, REVERBERATE
resource(s) .... CASH, MEANS,
ASSETS, RESORT, WEALTH,
CAPITAL, EXPEDIENT
resourceful .... CUNNING,
INGENIOUS, VERSATILE,
QUICK-WITTED
respect .... HONOR, ESTEEM,
HOMAGE, REGARD, REVERE,
DEFERENCE
respectable .... DECENT
respectful .... OBEISANT,
REVERENT
Respighi, composer
.... OTTORINO
respiration .... EUPN(O)EA,
DYSPN(O)EA, BREATHING
combining form .... SPIRO
stimulant .... METRAZOL

respirator .... INHALER, GAS MASK, IRON LUNG, VENTILATOR

respiratory arrest .... ANOXIA

arrest consequence ..... COMA, BRAIN DAMAGE

disease .... ASTHMA, EMPHYSEMA, PNEUMONIA, BRONCHITIS

disease of horses ...... HEAVES

failure .... HYPOXIA

organ .... LUNG

rattle .... RALE

system, part of .... LUNG, ALVEOLI, TRACHEA, BRONCHUS, BRONCHIOLE

tract infection .... COLD, CROUP, SINUSITIS, LARYNGITIS

respire .... EXHALE, INHALE, BREATHE

respite ...... LULL, DELAY, GRACE, PAUSE, REPRIEVE

from conflict .... TRUCE

resplendent ...... GRAND, SHINING, DAZZLING, GORGEOUS, SPLENDID, BRILLIANT

respond .... REACT, REPLY, ANSWER, RETURN

response .... REPLY, ANSWER, REACTION

evokers .... STIMULI

responsibility .... DUTY, ONUS, LIABILITY, OBLIGATION

responsible .... LIABLE, RELIABLE, DEPENDABLE, ACCOUNTABLE

responsive .... RECEPTIVE, SENSITIVE

rest ...... EASE, SEAT, STOP, SLEEP, OTHERS, REPOSE, BALANCE, RECLINE, SUPPORT, REMAINDER

colloquial .... BREAK, PAUSE, BREATHER

eternal .... DEATH

in prosody .... C(A)ESURA

midday .... SIESTA

restaurant .... DINER, GRILL, BISTRO, EATERY, AUTOMAT, CABARET, CANTEEN, CAFE(TERIA)

bench .... BANQUETTE

compartment .... BOOTH

vehicle .... BUS

restauranteur Toots .... SHOR

restful .... QUIET, PEACEFUL, TRANQUIL

resting .... ABED, DORMANT

place of great men .... VALHALLA

restive .... EDGY, BALKY, UNEASY, UNRULY, FRETFUL, NERVOUS, RESTLESS, IMPATIENT

restless .... ITCHY, UNEASY, AGITATO, FRETFUL, RESTIVE, AGITATED, PERTURBED

seeker after fun .... GADABOUT

restock .... REPLENISH

restoration .... RENEWAL, REVIVAL, RENOVATION, REINSTATEMENT

restorative .... ANODYNE, CURATIVE, REMEDIAL

restore .... CURE, RENEW, REPAIR, RETURN, PUT BACK, REBUILD, RETROCEDE

energy .... REFRESH

to a good condition .... RENOVATE

to health .... HEAL, RECUPERATE

restrain .... CURB, HOLD, STAY, STEM, CHECK, DETER, BRIDLE, HINDER, CONTAIN, INHIBIT, HOLD BACK, SUPPRESS

freedom of expression .... SHACKLE

one's activity .... HOGTIE, MANACLE, HANDCUFF

restrainer .... LEASH, MUZZLE, TRAMMEL

restraint .... CURB, REIN, CONTROL, RESERVE, DISCIPLINE

kind of .... DETERRENT

of free speech .... GAG

restrict .... LIMIT, IMPEDE, CONFINE

restrictive .... LIMITING, EXCLUSIVE, HINDERING, RESTRAINING

over-garment .... STRAIT-JACKET

restroom .... LAVATORY, POWDER ROOM, (WATER)CLOSET

slang .... JOHN

result .... ENSUE, FRUIT, ISSUE, ANSWER, EFFECT, UPSHOT, OUTCOME, EVENTUATE

of extreme starvation .... CACHEXIA

old age .... SENILITY

thrift .... RICHES

worry .... LINES

resume .... RENEW, PRECIS, REOPEN, REPRISE, SUMMARY, ABSTRACT, CONTINUE, CURRICULUM VITAE

resurge .... RALLY, REVIVE

resurrect .... REVIVE, RESTORE

resurrection .... REVIVAL

he experienced .... JESUS, LAZARUS

resuscitate .... REVIVE

resuscitation .... ANABIOSIS

ret .... DAMP, SOAK, STEEP, MACERATE

retable .... SHELF

retail .... SELL, VEND, PEDDLE

business .... STAND

retailer .... CLERK, DEALER, VENDOR, PEDDLER, MERCHANT

retain .... OWN, HAVE, HOLD, KEEP, SAVE, RESERVE

retainer .... FEE, ADHERENT, FOLLOWER, ATTENDANT, DEPENDENT

retainers, body of .... RETINUE

retaining wall .... REVETMENT, EMBANKMENT

material ..... PILING, SANDBAGS

retake .... REFILM, RECAPTURE

retaliate .... AVENGE, REQUITE

retaliation ...... TALION, REVENGE, REPRISAL, RETORSION, RETORTION

in kind .... TIT-FOR-TAT, BLOW-FOR-BLOW, AN-EYE-FOR-AN-EYE

retard ...... SLOW, DELAY, HINDER, IMPEDE

retch .... GAG, KECK, VOMIT

rete .... PLEXUS, NETWORK

obs. var. .... RIET

retem .... JUNIPER

retention .... MEMORY

retentive .... TENACIOUS

retepore .... MOLLUSK

rethink .... REVIEW

retiarius .... GLADIATOR

retiary/reticular .... NETLIKE

reticence .... RESERVE

reticent .... SILENT, RESERVED, TACITURN

reticule ...... RETICLE, (HAND)BAG

reticulum .... NETWORK

retina, disease of the .... RETINOPATHY

inflammation .... RETINITIS

tear .... SPLIT

tumor/cancer .... RETINOBLASTOMA

retinue .... CREW, ROUT, MEINY, SUITE, TRAIN, ESCORT, MEINIE, CORTEGE, ENTOURAGE, RETAINERS

retire .... QUIT, REST, LEAVE, SLEEP, REMOVE, RESIGN, RETREAT, WITHDRAW

retired .... ABED, ASLEEP, EMERITUS, SECLUDED, TURNED IN

retiree .... GOLDENAGER

retirement association: abbr.
.... AARP

retiring .... SHY, MODEST, BASHFUL, RESERVED

retort .... QUIP, REPLY, SALLY, ALEMBIC, RIPOSTE, SQUELCH, REJOIN(DER), WITTICISM

retortion .... REPRISAL

retouch .... FIX

retract .... UNSAY, ABJURE, RECALL, RECANT, RENEGE, REVOKE, DISAVOW, WITHDRAW

a statement .... EAT ONE'S WORDS

retraction .... PALINODE

retral .... POSTERIOR

retread .... RECAP

retreat .... LAIR, NEST, ARBOR, STUDY, ASYLUM, ESCAPE, REFUGE, RETIRE, HIDEOUT, PULLOUT, SANCTUM, SHELTER, BACK DOWN, WITHDRAW, KATABASIS

cozy .... DEN, NOOK, ALCOVE

disorderly .... ROUT, FLIGHT

kind of .... CONVENT, NUNNERY, HERMITAGE, MONASTERY

shaded .... BOWER

signal .... CHAMADE

retrench .... LESSEN, REDUCE, CURTAIL, CUT DOWN, DECREASE, ECONOMIZE

retrenchment .... RAMPART

retribution .... AMENDS, REWARD, NEMESIS, REQUITAL, RESTITUTION

retributive justice .... NEMESIS

retrieve .... FETCH, MAKE UP, REGAIN, REVIVE, RECLAIM, RECOVER, RESTORE, SET RIGHT

fly balls .... SHAG

retriever ...... (GUN)DOG, SETTER, POINTER

retroactive .... BACK(WARD)

retrocede .... RESTORE

retrograde .... DECLINE, INVERSE, RELAPSE, REVERSE

retrogress ...... REVERT, DECLINE, BACKSLIDE, DEGENERATE

retrospect .... REVIEW

return ...... RECUR, REPLY, YIELD, GO BACK, REPORT, REVERT, REELECT, REPLACE, REQUITE, RESPOND, RESTORE, COME BACK, RESPONSE

as in performance ..... REPEAT

as in ticket .... ROUND-TRIP

in kind .... RECIPROCATE

of the Jews to Palestine: 538 B.C. .... RESTORATION

to soundness ...... HEAL, MEND

returns .... YIELD, PROFIT, REVENUE

Reuben sandwich meat
.... CORNED BEEF

Reuben's brother .... LEVI, JUDAH, SIMEON

father .... JACOB

grandfather ...... ISAAC, LABAN

mother .... LEAH

reunion .... GET-TOGETHER

kind of .... CLASS, FAMILY

with Brahma .... NIRVANA

Reunion capital .... ST. DENIS

city/town .... LE PORT, ST. PIERRE

mountain .... PITON DES NEIGES

Reu's son .... SERUG

rev .... RACE, SPEED, ACCELERATE

Reval .... TALLINN

revamp .... REDO, CHANGE, REVISE, SHAKE UP, RENOVATE, REORGANIZE

reveal .... BARE, SHOW, TELL, EXPOSE, DISPLAY, DIVULGE, EXHIBIT, DISCLOSE, MANIFEST

unknowingly .... BETRAY

revealing .... SEE-THROUGH

reveille .... ROUSE, SIGNAL, AWAKENING, (WAKE-UP) CALL

revel ...... ROMP, ENJOY, GAMBOL, CAROUSE, DELIGHT, ROISTER, CAROUSAL

revelation .... ORACLE, DISCLOSURE

revelations .... APOCALYPSE

revel(l)er .... CORYBANT, MERRYMAKER

exclamation of a .... WHOOPEE

revelry .... ORGY, RIOT, SPREE, FESTIVITY, SATURNALIA

revenant .... GHOST, EIDOLON

revenge .... AVENGE, TALION, RETALIATE, VENGEANCE

revenue .... NET, INCOME, PROFIT, EARNINGS, RECEIPTS

bishop's .... ANNAT

revenuers' target .... STILL

reverberate .... RECOIL, (RE)ECHO, REBOUND, REFLECT, RESOUND

revere .... ADORE, HONOR, ADMIRE, RESPECT, WORSHIP, VENERATE

reverence .... AWE, BOW, CURTSY, HOMAGE, WORSHIP, ADORATION, VENERATION

gesture of .... OBEISANCE

lacking .... IMPIOUS

reverie .... FANCY, MUSING, NOTION, FANTASY, (DAY)DREAM

revers .... LAPEL

reversal .... UPSET, SETBACK, ABOUT-FACE, ANNULMENT, TURNABOUT, VOLTE-FACE

combining form .... ALLO

reverse ...... BACK, UNDO, ANNUL, EVERT, INVERT, REVOKE, CONTRARY, OPPOSITE

a situation .... TURN THE TABLES

reversion .... RETURN

of property .... ESCHEAT

to primitive type .... ATAVISM, THROWBACK

revert .... RECUR, RETURN, REGRESS

revest .... REINSTATE

review .... REVUE, NOTICE, PARADE, REPORT, SURVEY, ACCOUNT, INSPECT, CRITIQUE, CRITICISM, CRITICIZE, EPICRISIS

adverse .... PAN

briefly .... RECAP

enthusiastic .... RAVE

for an exam hurriedly
.... CRAM

four-star .... RAVE

of marching troops
.... PARADE

one's thoughts .... RETHINK

reviewer .... CRITIC

revile ...... ABUSE, SCOLD, DERIDE, MALIGN, VILIFY, ASPERSE, BELITTLE, VILIPEND

revise .... EDIT, ALTER, AMEND, REHASH, CORRECT, REWRITE

revival .... REBIRTH, RENEWAL

revivalist .... EVANGELIST

revive .... RALLY, COME TO, PERK UP, RESURGE, RESUSCITATE

memory .... JOG, RECALL, REMIND, REFRESH

revocation .... REPEAL, ANNULMENT, NULLIFICATION

revoke .... ADEEM, ANNUL, RENIG, ABJURE, CANCEL, RECALL, RECANT, RENEGE, REPEAL, DISAVOW, RESCIND

revolt .... (A)RISE, MUTINY, DISGUST, SEDITION, UPRISING, REBEL(LION)

revolting .... HORRID, LOATHSOME, OFFENSIVE, REPULSIVE

revolution .... GYRE, TURN, CYCLE, ROTATION, COUP (D'ETAT), REBELLION

fighter .... MINUTEMAN
general of the .... ASHE,
GATES, ARNOLD, GREENE,
LINCOLN, SULLIVAN
statesman of the .... OTIS
revolutionary .... REBEL,
RADICAL, INSURGENT
Allen .... ETHAN
revolutionist .... REB(EL),
ANARCH(IST)
revolve .... ROLL, SPIN, TURN,
ORBIT, CIRCLE, GYRATE,
ROTATE
revolver .... GAT, ROD, COLT,
PISTOL, BULLDOG, HANDGUN,
REPEATER, AUTOMATIC
part .... COCK, LOCK, SEAR,
TRIGGER, CYLINDER
revolving part .... ROTOR
revue .... SHOW, REVIEW, FOLLIES,
VAUDEVILLE
revulsion ...... DISGUST, AVERSION
reward .... FEE, PAY, TIP, AWARD,
BONUS, PRIZE, ENRICH,
RETURN, GUERDON, PREMIUM
of a sort .... SOP, WAGES,
SALARY
slang .... PAYOFF
reword .... EDIT
rewrite .... REVISE
rewriting .... RESCRIPT
rex .... KING
Rex Stout's Wolfe .... NERO
Reynard .... FOX
Rey's consort .... REINA
RH factor .... RHESUS
rhabdomancy .... DOWSING,
DIVINATION
rhapsodic .... LYRIC
rhapsodical .... ECSTATIC
Rhapsody in Blue composer
.... (GEORGE) GERSHWIN
rhea .... EMU, OPS, NANDU,
CYBELE, OSTRICH
Rhea, husband of .... CRONUS
parent of .... GAEA, URANUS
progeny of .... HERA, ZEUS,
HADES, HESTIA, DEMETER,
POSEIDON
rheotrope .... COMMUTATOR
rhesus .... MONKEY, MACAQUE
rhetor .... ORATOR
rhetoric .... ORATORY
rhetorical .... FORENSIC
device .... ANAPHORA
figure .... LITOTES
rheum .... COLD, CATARRH,
RHINITIS
rheumatic pain .... LUMBAGO
person .... ACHER

rheumatism of back/loins
.... LUMBAGO, BACKACHE
of joints ...... GOUT, ARTHRITIS
remedy .... MOTRIN, ASPIRIN,
THERAPY
rhinal .... NASAL
Rhine .... RIJN, RHEIN, RIVER
branch .... WAAL
city on the .... KOLN, MAINZ,
WORMS, MAYENCE, MANNHEIM
siren .... LURLEI, LORELEI
tributary .... MAIN
wine .... HOCK, MOSELLE
rhinitis, allergic .... HAY FEVER
viral .... (COMMON) COLD,
SINUSITIS
rhino(ceros) .... CASH, ABADA,
MONEY, BORELE
feature .... HORN
for one .... PACHYDERM
one-horned .... BADAK
two-horned .... KEITLOA
rhinology subject .... NOSE
rhinoplasty .... NOSE JOB
object .... NOSE
rhizoid .... ROOTLIKE
rhizome .... STEM, TUBER,
STOLON, ROOTSTALK,
ROOT(STOCK)
rhizopod .... TESTACEAN
protozoan .... AMOEBA
rhizopus .... FUNGUS
Rhode Island bay
.... NARRAGANSETT
capital .... PROVIDENCE
city/town .... BRISTOL,
NEWPORT, WARWICK,
COVENTRY, CRANSTON,
TIVERTON, WESTERLY,
PAWTUCKET, BARRINGTON,
WOONSOCKET
college .... BRYANT,
PROVIDENCE, ROGER WILLIAMS
county .... KENT, BRISTOL,
NEWPORT, PROVIDENCE
founder .... (ROGER) WILLIAMS
island .... BLOCK, PRUDENCE,
CONANICUT
naval base .... NEWPORT
point .... SANDY, NOYES
rebel: 1842 .... DORR
red .... HEN, CHICKEN
river .... SAKONNET,
PAWCATUCK
state flower .... VIOLET
state nickname .... OCEAN,
LITTLE RHODY
tourist attraction .... TENNIS
HALL OF FAME
tree .... MAPLE
university .... BROWN

Rhodes .... RODI
ancient wonder ...... COLOSSUS
Rhodesia, new name of
.... ZIMBABWE
Northern .... ZAMBIA
port .... BEIRA
premier .... SMITH
tribe .... ILAS
rhododendron .... LAUREL,
ROSEBAY
kin of .... AZALEA
rhodolite .... GARNET
rhomb(us) .... LOZENGE,
PARALLELOGRAM
rhombencephalon .... HINDBRAIN
part .... PONS, CEREBELLUM
rhonchus .... RALE, SNORE,
RATTLE
Rhone tributary .... ISERE,
SAONE
rhubarb .... SCRAP, SET-TO,
HASSLE, ARGUMENT,
PIEPLANT, DISCUSSION
rhyme .... POESY, VERSE,
CRAMBO, CONCORD,
HARMONY
and reason .... SENSE
inferior .... DOGGEREL
scheme .... ABABA
rhymer/rhymester
.... POET(ASTER), VERSIFIER
rhyming .... CRAMBO
rhythm .... BEAT, LILT, TIME,
METER, METRE, SWING,
TEMPO, CADENCE, MEASURE
in verse .... METER
meter .... IONIC
method .... CONTRACEPTION
rhythmic .... PULSATING
flow .... CADENCE
rise and fall .... HEAVE
rhythmical accent .... ICTUS
ria .... INLET
rial .... COIN
rialto .... MART, BRIDGE, MARKET
riant .... GAY, BLITHE, SMILING,
CHEERFUL, LAUGHING
riata .... LARIAT
rib .... BONE, VEIN, COSTA, RIDGE
Adam's .... EVE, WIFE
colloquial .... KID, TWIT,
TEASE
cut, meat .... SPARERIB
disorder .... FRACTURE
in architecture .... LIERNE
leaf .... NERVURE
of a .... COSTAL
slang .... ROAST
ribald .... LOW, COARSE, VULGAR,
PROFANE
ribaldry .... JAPERY

riband .... RIBBON
ribbed .... KIDDED, RIDGED,
TEASED, COSTATE
as cloth .... WALED
ribbon .... BAND, BADGE, STRIP,
DECORATION
award .... CORDON
cutting, for example
.... CEREMONY
decorative .... RIBAND
document's .... LABEL
elastic .... GARTER
hair .... BANDEAU
knot .... COCKADE
like part .... T(A)ENIA
of cotton, etc. .... FERRET
paper .... TICKER TAPE
seal .... LABEL
trimming .... GALLOON
worsted .... CADDIS
woven .... BRAID
Ribbon, Blue .... FIRST PRIZE
ribbons .... SHREDS, TATTERS,
STREAMERS
ribwort .... PLANTAIN
Ricardo, actor .... MONTALBAN
rice .... GRAIN, GRASS, SEEDS,
PADDY, CEREAL
alcoholic drink .... BASI,
SAKE, ARRACK
boiled with meat .... PILAU,
PILAF(F)
cooked with gravy
.... RISOTTO
dessert .... PUDDING
dish, spicy ...... CURRY, PILAU,
PILAF(F)
field .... PADDY
husk .... BRAN
in the husk .... PADDY
nutritive substance .... STARCH
playwright .... ELMER
type of .... WILD, BROWN,
SWEET, WHITE, PARBOILED
riceball .... PINDA
ricebird ...... SPARROW, BOBOLINK
rich .... VIVID, FERTILE, OPULENT,
WEALTHY, AFFLUENT,
VALUABLE, WELL-TO-DO,
ABOUNDING, LUXURIANT,
LUXURIOUS, PLENTIFUL
oil country .... KUWAIT
person .... DIVES, MIDAS,
NABOB, TYCOON, CROESUS,
FINANCIER, MONEYBAG(S),
PLUTO(CRAT), CAPITALIST
slang .... LOADED
source .... LODE, MINE
streak .... LODE
the .... MONEYED
Richard I of England ...... LION-

HEARTED, COEUR DE LION
brother of .... JOHN
father of .... HENRY II
mother of .... ELEANOR
Richard, unknown .... ROE
riches .... PELF, LUCRE, MONEY,
ASSETS, WEALTH, FORTUNE,
OPULENCE, PROPERTY
antipode of .... RAGS
deified .... MAMMON
richest part .... FAT, CREAM
richly .... AMPLY, FULLY
mellow .... GOLDEN
richness .... LUXE, MEANS,
AFFLUENCE, PROSPERITY
Richter scale's concern
.... EARTHQUAKES
Richthofen's forte .... DOGFIGHT
ricin .... PROTEIN
rick .... PILE, STACK
Rickenbacker, American ace
.... EDDIE
rickets .... RACHITIS
feature .... BOWLEGS,
DEFORMITY
is deficiency of ____
.... VITAMIN D
rickety ...... WEAK, FRAIL, SHAKY,
FEEBLE, RACHITIC
rickey .... DRINK
ingredient .... GIN
Rickover, Adm. .... HYMAN
rickrack .... BRAID, TRIMMING
ricksha(w) .... JINRIKISHA
ricochet .... SKIP, BOUNCE,
CAR(R)OM, DEFLECT,
REBOUND
rictus .... GAPING, RINGENT
rid .... FREE, SHED, CLEAR,
RELIEVE, DISENCUMBER
of defect .... REAM
of false ideas .... DISABUSE
riddance .... RELEASE, SEVERANCE
ridden .... OBSESSED
riddle ...... POSER, SIEVE, ENIGMA,
PEPPER, PUZZLE, MYSTERY,
PROBLEM, CONUNDRUM,
PERFORATE
bandleader .... NELSON
picture .... REBUS
Ridd's heroine .... LORNA
(DOONE)
ride .... BAIT, ANNOY, DRIVE,
MOUNT, TEASE, HARASS,
TRAVEL
at full speed .... GALLOP
pay for .... FARE, PASSAGE
take for a .... KILL, DECEIVE
to hounds .... HUNT
rider .... FARE, JOKER, CLAUSE,
JOCKEY, CODICIL, ADDITION,

PASSENGER, EQUESTRIAN
for free .... DEADHEAD
1775 .... (PAUL) REVERE
ridge .... BACK, RAND, RUGA,
WALE, ARETE, CHINE, CREST,
ESKAR, RANGE, ARISTA,
CUESTA
between furrows .... LIST
between peaks .... SADDLE
glacial .... OSAR, ESKER,
DRUMLIN
having a .... RIDGY
like part .... KEEL, CARINA
of earth .... HOGBACK,
HORSEBACK
sand .... DENE, DUNE
sandy .... LANDE
saw-toothed .... SIERRA
ridgepole .... ROOFTREE
ridicule .... JEER, JEST, MOCK,
TWIT, ROAST, SCOFF, SCOUT,
TAUNT, DERIDE
expose to .... PILLORY
playfully .... KID
satirical .... LAMPOON
ridiculous .... INANE, ABSURD,
FOOLISH, DERISIVE,
GROTESQUE, LUDICROUS,
SARCASTIC
laugh .... SNICKER
look .... LEER
rite .... MUMMERY
riding boot .... JEMMY
breeches .... JODHPURS
costume .... HABIT
horse .... MOUNT, PALFREY,
ROADSTER
master .... TEACHER
place .... TRACK
school/academy .... MANEGE
whip .... CROP, QUIRT
Rienzi composer .... WAGNER
Ries, composer .... FERDINAND
rife .... CURRENT, PROFUSE,
TEEMING, PREVALENT,
PREVAILING, WIDESPREAD
Riff .... BERBER
riffle .... REEF, SHOAL, SHUFFLE
riffraff .... MOB, SCUM, TRASH,
RABBLE, DOGGERY, CANAILLE
rifle ...... GUN, ROB, PIECE, STEAL,
GARAND, MAUSER, CARBINE,
FIREARM, PILLAGE, PLUNDER,
RANSACK, REPEATER,
CHASSEPOT
automatic ..... BAR, BROWNING
bullet .... MINIE (BALL)
chamber .... MAGAZINE
light .... CARBINE
pin .... TIGE
position .... READY

rifleman .... YAGER, JA(E)GER
  rating of .... EXPERT,
    MARKSMAN, SHARPSHOOTER
rifler .... ROBBER
rift .... GAP, FLAW, BREAK, CLEFT,
    CRACK, SPLIT, BREACH,
    CREVICE, FISSURE, DISUNITY,
    SEPARATION
rig .... CART, GEAR, DRESS,
    ATTIRE, CLOTHE, FIT (OUT),
    OUTFIT, TACKLE, COSTUME,
    CARRIAGE, EQUIP(MENT),
    MANIPULATE
Riga gulf island .... OESEL
  native .... LATVIAN
rigatoni .... PASTA
Rigel .... STAR
rigger .... SCAFFOLD
rigging ...... GEAR, TACK, ROPING,
    TACKLE, EQUIPMENT
  part .... SPAR, MASTS, ROPES,
    SAILS, YARDS, CHAINS,
    SHROUDS
  type of .... LIFT, BRACE,
    SHROUD, BOWLINE, HALYARD,
    (BOOM)VANG, BACKROPES
Rigg's disease .... PYORRHEA
right ...... SOUND, TITLE, NORMAL,
    CURRENT, DEXTRAL, FITTING,
    LICENSE, REDRESS, STRAIGHT,
    SUITABLE, VIRTUOUS,
    PREROGATIVE
  a wrong .... REDRESS
  and wrong decider
  .... CASUIST
  angle gauge .... TRYSQUARE
  by .... PROPERLY
  combining form .... RECT(I)
  exclusive .... PATENT
  hand side .... DEXTER
  hand page .... RECTO
  hand side of ship or airplane
  .... STARBOARD
  hereditary .... UDAL
  in politics .... RIGHTIST,
    CONSERVATIVE
  in politics: extreme ..... TORY
  king's .... REGALITY
  legal .... DROIT, TITLE
  now .... AT ONCE, PRONTO,
    IMMEDIATELY
  of expression .... VOICE
  of holding .... TENURE
  of way .... EASEMENT
  on the .... OFF(SIDE)
  slang .... ROGER
  special .... CHARTER,
    FRANCHISE
  to choose .... OPTION
  to decide .... SAY-SO
  to enter .... ENTREE, INGRESS

  to mail free .... FRANK
  to ownership .... TITLE
  triangle ratio .... SINE
  turn .... GEE
  word .... MOTJUSTE
righteous .... JUST, MORAL,
    VIRTUOUS
rightfully .... DULY
righto .... YES, CERTAINLY
rights, equality of .... ISONOMY
  relating to .... JURAL
rigid ...... SET, FIRM, TAUT, STIFF,
    SEVERE, STRICT, AUSTERE,
    RIGOROUS
rigmarole .... BLATHER,
    NONSENSE
Rigoletto author .... VERDI
rigor .... HARDNESS, HARDSHIP,
    RIGIDITY, SEVERITY,
    STIFFNESS
  companion of .... MORTIS
rigorous .... HARSH, RIGID, STERN,
    STIFF, SEVERE, STRICT,
    PRECISE, DIFFICULT
Rigsdag, part of .... FOLKETING,
    LANDSTING
Riis, social reformer ...... JACOB
Rijeka .... FIUME
Rijn .... RHINE
rile .... IRK, VEX, ROIL, ANGER,
    IRRITATE
Riley, coach .... PAT
  of Knots Landing .... LARRY
Rilke, Ger. poet .... RAINER
rill ...... BROOK, FURROW, STREAM,
    TRENCH, VALLEY, RIVULET
rim .... LIP, BRIM, EDGE, BRINK,
    VERGE, BORDER, MARGIN
  cap's projecting .... VISOR
  cask's .... CHIME, CHINE
  rail/pipe's .... FLANGE
  roof's .... EAVE
  wheel .... FELLY, FELLOE
rime .... RHYME, (HOAR)FROST
rimer .... MINSTREL
rimple .... CREASE, WRINKLE
rimy .... FROSTY
Rinaldo's magic horse
    .... BAYARD, BAJARDO
rind .... BARK, PEEL, SKIN, CRUST,
    CORTEX, COATING, EPICARP,
    EXOCARP
  candied .... CITRON
ring .... RIM, SET, DING, GYRE,
    TOLL, ARENA, KNELL, CALL
    (UP), CIRQUE, CLIQUE,
    SIGNAL, ANNULET, RESOUND,
    (EN)CIRCLE
  again .... RETOLL
  around the collar
  .... NECKLINE

  around the sun/moon
  .... HALO
  bell .... PEAL, TOLL, CHIME,
    KNELL
  decision .... TKO, DRAW
  gem .... CAMEO
  give a ...... CALL, (TELE)PHONE
  harness .... TERRET
  jeweled .... MARQUISE
  master .... PUG, BOXER
  metal .... BEE
  mounting style .... TIFFANY
  neck .... PHEASANT
  of fiction .... LARDNER
  guards .... CORDON
  leaves .... INVOLUCEL,
    INVOLUCRE
  light .... HALO
  neck feathers .... RUFF,
    TORQUES
  rope .... GROMMET
  rubber .... GASKET
  virtue .... HALO
  out .... PEAL
  result .... TKO, DRAW,
    KNOCKOUT
  shaped .... ANNULAR
  shaped cake .... DOUGHNUT
  single gem of .... SOLITAIRE
  stone setting .... COLLET
  tailed animal .... COON
  up .... CALL, DIAL,
    (TELE)PHONE
  wedding .... BAND
ringdove .... CUSHAT
ringent .... GAPING, RICTUS
ringer .... QUOIT, POSEUR,
    HORSESHOE, LOOK-ALIKE
ringing, persistent ...... CLANGOR
  sound in ear .... TINNITUS
ringleader .... TROUBLE-MAKER
ringlet .... CURL, LOCK, TRESS
ringmaster .... MC, EMCEE,
    DIRECTOR
ringworm .... TINEA, SERPIGO
rinse .... LAVE, WASH
rinsings .... DREGS
rio .... RIVER
Rio _____ .... MUNI, BRAVO,
    NEGRO, GRANDE
  de _____ .... ORO, JANEIRO
  Grande, city on .... LAREDO
  Grande national park ...... BIG
    BEND
  Grande tributary .... PECOS
  Mister in .... SENHOR
  Muni city .... BATA
  seaport .... MATAMOROS
riot ...... HIT, ROW, ORGY, BRAWL,
    EMEUTE, FRACAS, HUBBUB,
    UPROAR, DISORDER

rioter .... BRAWLER, RABBLEROUSER
riotous .... WILD, NOISY, WANTON, DISSOLUTE, LUXURIANT, TURBULENT
rip .... CUT, REND, RIVE, TEAR, SPLIT, SEVERE
colloquial .... NAG, HORSE
into .... ATTACK
roaring .... NOISY, BOISTEROUS
Rip van Winkle author
.... IRVING
riparian .... RIVERINE
glitter .... SPARKLE ON THE WATERS
recess .... INLET
ripe ...... ADULT, READY, MATURE, MELLOW, DEVELOPED
ripen ...... AGE, MATURE, TEMPER
ripening agent .... AGER
early .... RATH(E), RARERIPE
ripoff .... SWINDLE
riposte .... MOT, RETORT, RETURN, THRUST
ripping .... FINE, SPLENDID, EXCELLENT
ripple .... LAP, PURL, RAPID, BABBLE, GURGLE, SPLASH, WAVE(LET), UNDULATION
riptide .... UNDERTOW
Ripuarian .... FRANK
ris de veau .... SWEETBREAD
rise .... HILL, LOOM, SOAR, GET UP, OCCUR, REBEL, SLOPE, STAND, ASCEND, APPEAR, ASCENT, REVOLT
again .... RESURGE
and fall .... WELTER, FLUCTUATE
and float in the air
.... LEVITATE
from the dead ...... RESURRECT
high .... SOAR
in the ground .... LIFT
of the tide .... FLOOD
with success .... PROSPER
Rise, soprano .... STEVENS
risibility .... MIRTH
risible .... FUNNY, AMUSING, LAUGHABLE, LUDICROUS
rising .... BOIL, MONTANT, ANABATIC, MOUNTING
risk .... SINK, PERIL, CHANCE, GAMBLE, HAZARD, JEOPARDY, (EN)DANGER
risky .... CHANCY
risque .... RACY, SEXY, DARING, OFF-COLOR, SCABROUS
rhyme .... LIMERICK
rissole .... MEATBALL
rite .... LITURGY, CEREMONY,

(HOLY) ORDERS
meaningless .... MUMBO-JUMBO
public worship .... LITURGY
washing .... LAVABO
ritual ...... FORMAL, LITURGIC(AL)
beads .... ROSARY
ceremony .... BAPTISM, MATRIMONY, CONFIRMATION
container .... CENSER, THURIBLE
greeting .... PAX
supper .... SEDER
symbol .... CROSS, CRUCIFIX
Ritz, Swiss hotelman ...... CESAR
ritzy .... POSH, TONY, PLUSH, SWANK, SWELL, CLASSY, ELEGANT, LUXURIOUS
auto .... LIMO
rivage .... BANK, COAST, SHORE
rival .... FOE, VIE, EQUAL, MATCH, COMPETE, EMULATE, OPPONENT, COMPETITOR, CONTESTANT
Las Vegas' .... RENO, TAHOE
rivalry .... EMULATION, COMPETITION
rive .... REND, TEAR, SPLIT, CLEAVE
riven .... RENT, TORN, SPLIT
river .... STREAM, WATERWAY, WATERCOURSE
Avignon's .... RHONE
bank .... RIPA, LEVEE
bank, of a .... RIPARIAN
barge .... GONDOLA
barrier .... BOOM, WEIR, BARRAGE
"beautiful" .... OHIO
bed .... CHANNEL
bed, dry .... WADI
bend .... OXBOW
Bern's .... AAR(E)
blindness ..... ONCHOCERCIASIS
blue, poetically .... DANUBE
boat .... BARGE, FERRY, PACKET, SAMPAN
bottom .... BED
branch .... ARM
Caen's .... ORNE
channel .... FAIRWAY
Chauny's .... OISE
cross a .... FERRY
crossed by Caesar
.... RUBICON
curve in .... BEN, BIGHT
dam .... WEIR
deep, still spot of .... POOL
deposit .... LOESS
duck .... TEAL, SHOVEL(L)ER
edge/embankment .... BANK,

DIKE, LEVEE
elbow .... BEND
falls .... SAULTS
famous .... AVON, NILE, AMAZON, DANUBE, RUBICON
Firenze's/Florence's ..... ARNO
Flanders .... YSER
flowing into Lake Rudolf
.... OMO
Frankfurt's .... ODER
Giza's .... NILE
horse .... HIPPO(POTAMUS)
in a Burns poem .... AFTON
in Central India .... PURNA
in the broads .... YARE
in the Hades .... LETHE
in Zaire .... UELE, CONGO
inlet .... BAYOU, SLOUGH
island/isle .... AIT, HOLM
land near ..... HOLM, BOTTOMS
landing .... GHAT, LEVEE
large .... NILE, AMAZON, YELLOW, YANGTZE, MISSOURI, MISSISSIPPI
longest .... NILE
Mexico .... RIO GRANDE
mouth .... BOCA, DELTA, ESTUARY, EMBOUCHURE
nymph .... NAIS, NAIAD
of song .... OHIO, AFTON, VOLGA, DANUBE, SWANEE
of wailing .... COCYTUS
or monster .... GILA
outlet .... BAYOU
Parisian .... SEINE
Pultusk's .... NAREV
rapid .... SAULT
Rheine's .... EMS
sacred .... ALPH, GANGES
sell down the .... BETRAY, DECEIVE
siren .... LORELEI
soil .... DELTA
source .... HEAD
South American .... NEGRO, PURUS, JAPURA, MADEIRA, ORINOCO, URUGUAY, PARAGUAY, PILCOMAYO
Stratford's .... AVON
through Belgium .... YSER
to the Baltic .... ODER
Caspian .... URAL
Congo .... UELE
Elbe .... EGER, ISER
Euphrates .... MURAT
Mediterranean .... NILE
North Sea .... YSER
Rhine .... (THE) RUHR
Seine .... OISE
Yellow Sea .... YALU

tributary of the James .... COW PASTURE (RIVER)
underworld .... STYX
U.S.A. ...... RED, OHIO, PECOS, SNAKE, TEXAS, BRAZOS, ARKANSAS, COLORADO, COLUMBIA, MISSOURI, MISSISSIPPI
U.S.S.R. .... DON, OKA, KAMA, LENA, URAL, VOLGA, ANGARA, KOLYMA, DNIEPER, PECHORA
valley .... DALE, STRATH
wade across .... FORD
widened part .... LAKE
winding of .... ESS
Yuma's .... GILA
River, Big .... MISSISSIPPI
Big Muddy .... MISSOURI
Rivera, Mex. painter ...... DIEGO
forte .... MURAL
riverine .... RIPARIAN
rivet ...... BOLT, FASTEN, HAMMER
holder .... DOLLY
washer of .... BURR
riveter, female .... ROSIE
Riviera beach .... PLAGE
port .... CANNES
resort .... NICE, CANNES
rivulet .... RILL, BROOK, ARROYO, RUNNEL, STREAM, RUN(D)LET
rix-dollar .... DALER
Riyadh is capital of the .... NEJD
Rizal, Filipino patriot ...... JOSE
Rizpah's husband .... SAUL
RMN, to friends .... DICK
Rn, in chemistry .... RADON
R.N. .... ROYAL NAVY, REGISTERED NURSE
roach ...... CARP, INSECT, SUNFISH, COCKROACH
movie producer .... HAL
road .... ITER, PATH, TRACK, TRAIL, COURSE, (HIGH)WAY, MACADAM, CAUSEWAY
agent .... HIGHWAYMAN
along embankment .... STAITH
Canada to Key West .... USI
character .... HOG, HOBO, TRAMP, JOGGER, (HITCH)HIKER
charge .... TOLL
contractor .... PAVER
curve .... ESS
descriptive of a ...... UNPAVED
fast .... SPEEDWAY
feature .... JOG
for locomotive .... RAILWAY
ledge/shoulder .... BERM(E)
map abbreviation .... RTE
of a .... VIATIC(AL)
on the .... ON TOUR, TRAVELING

pavement .... TELFORD
private .... DRIVEWAY
runner .... BIRD, COCK, CUCKOO, JOGGER
sign .... ESS, MILEPOST, MILESTONE
surface .... TAR, ASPHALT, MACADAM
toll .... (TURN)PIKE
treatment, winter .... GRIT
worker ...... NAVVY, CAMINERO
roadbed fill .... GRAVEL
roadblock .... BLOCKADE
border .... CHECKPOINT
roadhouse .... INN, TAVERN, NIGHTCLUB
roads scholar .... HOBO
roadside sign .... GAS, EATS, MOTEL, DETOUR, LODGING, REST AREA, SPEED LIMIT
weed .... DOG, FENNEL
roadster .... HORSE, RUNABOUT, TWO-SEATER
feature .... RUMBLE SEAT
roadway, sloping .... RAMP
roam .... GAD, ROVE, RANGE, STRAY, RAMBLE, STROLL, WANDER, MEANDER
roan ...... BAY, HORSE, SHEEPSKIN
color ..... CHESTNUT, REDDISH-BROWN
Roanoke bell .... COWSLIP
tributary .... DAN
roar ...... DIN, BAWL, BELL, BOOM, HOWL, ROLL, GROWL, NOISE, SHOUT, STORM, BELLOW, RUMBLE, THUNDER, LAUGHTER
roaring .... BRISK, NOISY, BOOMING
Roaring Twenties dance .... CHARLESTON
roast .... BAKE, HEAT, BROIL, BROWN, PARCH, PICNIC, BARBECUE, CRITICIZE
meat .... CABOBS, KABOBS
slang .... TEASE, RIDICULE
turner .... JACK
roaster .... PIG(LET), BROILER, CHICKEN
roasting device/tool .... PAN, OVEN, SPIT, GRILL, GRIDIRON, BUCCANEER
rob ...... CLIP, FLAY, LOOT, REAVE, RIFLE, STEAL, PLUNDER, PURLOIN
a house .... BURGLARIZE
a truck .... HIJACK
slang .... MUG
_____ to pay Paul .... PETER
Rob Roy author .... SCOTT

robalo .... FISH, SNOOK, PICKEREL
roband .... ROPE
robbed .... REFT, DEPRIVED, PILFERED, PURLOINED
robber ...... YEGG, THIEF, BANDIT, DACOIT, RIFLER, BANDIDO, BRIGAND, CATERAN, (FOOT)PAD, LADRONE, RAPPAREE, SPOLIATOR
bank ...... YEGG, SAFECRACKER
bird .... DAW, SKUA, SHOOI, JA(E)GER
cattle .... RUSTLER
den of .... LAIR, HIDEOUT
fond of crowds .... DIP, PICKPOCKET
highway .... BANDIT, HIJACKER
house .... BURGLAR
kind of .... BANK, HOUSE, TRAIN
sea .... PIRATE, CORSAIR, PRIVATEER
slang .... MUGGER
robbery .... THEFT, HOLD-UP, PIRACY, DACOITY, STICKUP
literary .... PLAGIARISM
Robbia, Ital. sculptor ...... LUCA DELLA, ANDRE DELLA
robe ...... TOGA, WRAP, VESTMENT, (DRESSING) GOWN
at-home/long-sleeved .... CAFTAN, KAFTAN
bishop's ...... CHIMAR, CHIMER
long .... TALAR
loose/woman's .... SIMAR, KIMONO
monk's .... FROCK
of office .... TOGA
plural ...... APPAREL, CLOTHES, COSTUME
robed .... VESTED
Robert, actor .... YOUNG, TAYLOR, REDFORD
American muralist .... REID
"Robert E. Lee" .... MISSISSIPPI RIVERBOAT
robin .... THRUSH, RUDDOCK, REDBREAST
Robin Goodfellow .... ELF, PUCK, FAIRY, SPRITE, HOBGOBLIN
Hood .... OUTLAW, DO-GOODER
Hood's companion .... (FRIAR) TUCK, WILL (SCARLET)
Forest .... SHERWOOD
sweetheart .... (MAID) MARIAN
weapon .... LONGBOW
Robinson, baseball coach .... FRANK
Crusoe's man .... FRIDAY

model .... SELKIRK
of baseball hall of fame
.... FRANK, BROOKS, JACKIE
Ray .... SUGAR
roble .... OAK, TREE, BEECH
roborant .... TONIC
robot .... GOLEM, PUPPET,
AUTOMATON
robots, play about .... RUR
robust ...... HALE, HARDY, HUSKY,
LUSTY, ROUGH, SOUND,
STOUT, WALLY, STURDY,
HEALTHY, MUSCULAR,
VIGOROUS
roc .... BIRD, SIMURG
passenger .... SIN(D)BAD
rocambole .... LEEK, ONION
rochet .... FROCK, SURPLICE,
VESTMENT
rock .... CRAG, SWAY, CANDY,
SHAKE, STONE, SWING,
GNEISS, JIGGLE, TEETER,
TOTTER, DOLOMITE,
GANISTER, PSEPHITE
above a plain .... MONODOCK
basaltic .... WHIN(STONE)
bass .... SUNFISH
black .... BASALT
boring tool .... TRAPAN,
TREPAN
bottom .... LOWEST
carving .... PETROGLYPH
cavity .... VUG(G), VUGH,
GEODE
combining form .... SAXI,
LITH(O), PETR(O)
colorful, glassy ...... FELDSPAR
conglomerate ..... GRAYWACKE
containing gem, fossil, etc.
.... MATRIC
crushed .... BALLAST
crystal .... QUARTZ
decomposed .... SAPROLITE
dug out .... FOSSIL
easily split .... SCHIST
ejected by volcano
.... LAPILLUS
eroded .... BOSS
face .... PRECIPICE
fine-grained ..... SHALE, SLATE
finely broken .... SAND
fluid .... LAVA
formation .... SIAL, TERRANE
formation at Colorado
Springs .... GARDEN OF
THE GODS
formed by geyser .... SINTER
fragment(s) ..... BRASH, SPALL,
DETRITUS
fragmental .... PSEPHITE
garden .... ROCKERY

granitelike .... GNEISS
green .... OPHITE, VERD
ANTIQUE
growths on ...... TRIPE, LICHEN
hard .... GRANITE
igneous .... TRAP, BASALT,
DIORITE, GRANITE, PICRITE,
SYENITE, PORPHYRY,
PEGMATITE, PHONOLITE,
PERIDOT(ITE)
in another rock ...... XENOLITE
isolated .... SCAR
jagged .... CRAG
like/of .... PETROUS
like fish roe .... OOLITE
mass .... HORST
metamorphic .... GNEISS
mica and quartz .... GREIN
molten .... MAGMA
mottled .... OPHITE
oil .... NAP(H)THA, PETROLEUM
pinnacle .... TOR, NEEDLE
plant .... MOSS
porous .... TUFA, TUFF,
TOPH(E)
projecting .... SCAR, LEDGE
rabbit .... HYRAX
ribbed .... FIRM, RIGID
road-making .... TRAP, BASALT
rose product ...... LA(B)DANUM
salt .... HALITE
salt money .... EMOL
sediments .... ELUVIA
sedimentary .... PELITE,
MUDSTONE
siliceous .... GANISTER
steep .... CLIFF
stratified .... SHALE
system .... TRIAS
volcanic .... LAVA, WACK,
BASALT, LATITE, PERLITE
weed .... FUCUS, SEA OAK
rockaway .... CARRIAGE
Rockefeller, John _____
.... DAVISON
one other .... EDSEL, NELSON
rocker .... CHAIR, SKATE, CRADLE
off one's: sl. .... CRAZY
rockery .... GARDEN
rocket ...... SOAR, AGENA, ASROC,
MISSILE, PROJECTILE
bomb .... TORPEDO
firing platform .... LAUNCHING
PAD
French-built .... ARIANE
fuel .... LOX, HYDRAZINE
gun/launcher .... BAZOOKA
load .... WARHEAD
part of .... CAPSULE,
(NOSE)CONE, JET ENGINE
propellant .... FUEL

to get astronaut back
.... RETRO
upper stage for a .... AGENA
rockfish .... BASS, RE(I)NA,
GROUPER, BOCACCIO,
YELLOWTAIL
rockfoil .... SAXIFRAGE
Rockies' range .... TETON, UINTA
Rockne, football coach
.... KNUTE
rocks at foot of cliff .... TALUS
bluish .... LIAS
living on .... SAXATILE,
SAXICOLINE
of the oldest .... ARCHEAN
on the ...... RUINED, BANKRUPT
pile of .... TALUS, DEBRIS
slang .... GEM, ICE, MONEY,
DIAMOND(S)
study of .... LITHOLOGY,
PETROLOGY
rockweed .... FUCUS, FUCOID
rocky .... HARD, WEAK, DIZZY,
SHAKY, STONY, CRAGGY,
RUGGED, UNSTEADY
cliff .... SCAR
hill/crag .... TOR
outcrop .... CRAG
pinnacle/ridge ...... TOR, SCAR,
ARETE
Rocky Mountain feature
.... CONTINENTAL DIVIDE
Mountain mammal .... ELK,
BADGER, COYOTE, MARMOT,
RED FOX, CHIPMUNK, MULE
DEER, SQUIRREL, BLACK BEAR,
GRIZZLY BEAR
Mountain sheep ...... BIGHORN
Mountain wind .... CHINOOK
Mountains .... ROCKIES
rococo .... FLORID, ORNATE,
BAROQUE, ARABESQUE
rod ...... BAR, POLE, TWIG, WAND,
PERCH, SHAFT, SHOOT, STAFF,
STICK, VERGE, HEATER,
TOGGLE, WATTLE, SCEPTER
biblical use ...... RACE, STOCK,
OFFSHOOT
billiards .... CUE
birds' .... PERCH
cap .... FERULE
connecting .... PITMAN
divination .... DOWSING,
RHABDOMANCY
emblematic .... CADUCEUS
king's/royal .... WARDER,
SCEPTER
mate of .... REEL
of authority ...... MACE, GAVEL
shaped .... BACILLAR,
VIRG(UL)ATE

slang .... GAT, GUN, PISTOL, REVOLVER
steadying .... GUY
twirling .... BATON
used for flogging/whipping .... CANE, SWITCH
walking .... CANE, STICK
Rod, actor .... STEIGER
tennis great .... LAVER
rodent .... RAT, CAVY, HARE, PIKA, CON(E)Y, MOUSE, BEAVER, RABBIT, GNAWING, LEPORID, SQUIRREL
albino .... WHITE MOUSE
aquatic ..... BEAVER, MUSKRAT
Belgian .... LEPORIDE
burrowing ...... VOLE, GOPHER, MARMOT, SUSLIK, CHIPMUNK, GERBIL(LE), VISCACHA
eight-toothed .... OCTODON
European .... CON(E)Y
fur .... BEAVER, RABBIT
genus .... MURIS, CASTOR
largest extant .... CAPYBARA
leaping .... JERBOA
nocturnal .... PACA
Patsy winner .... BEN
pet .... HAMSTER
poison .... RODENTICIDE
rapid .... SNOWSHOE RABBIT
short-eared .... AGOUTI
squirrel-like .... GOPHER, SUSLIK, CHIPMUNK, DORMOUSE
suicidal .... LEMMING
tailless/spotted .... PACA
that collects small particles .... PACKRAT
water .... COYPU, NUTRIA, MUSKRAT
Western .... PACKRAT
rodents' disease .... TULAR(A)EMIA
enemy .... RATTER
of .... MURINE
rodeo .... ROUNDUP
competitor .... COWBOY
skill .... LASSOING
Rodi .... RHODES
Rodin, Fr. sculptor .... AUGUSTE
work .... THINKER
rodomontade .... BOAST(ING), BRAG(GING)
Rodrigo Diaz de Bivar ...... (EL) CID
rods, 40 .... FURLONG
roe ...... OVA, DEER, MILT, CORAL, SPAWN, (FISH)EGGS
roebuck .... DEER
Roentgen's discovery ...... X-RAY
rogation .... PRAYER
rogatory .... QUESTIONING

roger .... OK, OVER, RIGHT, RECEIVED
Rogers .... ROY, CARL, WILL, KENNY, GINGER
religious freedom fighter .... JOHN
followers of ...... ROGERENES
Rogers' prop .... LASSO
Rogers St. John, _____
.... ADELA
rogue .... IMP, KITE, CHEAT, SCAMP, BEGGAR, RASCAL, PICAROON, SCOUNDREL, SCAPEGRACE
animal .... ELEPHANT
wandering .... TRAMP, VAGABOND
rogues, of .... PICARESQUE
gallery item .... MUG, ALIAS
roguish .... ARCH, PRANKISH, FUN-LOVING
Rohrer, humor hobbyist .... DICK
roil .... IRK, VEX, RILE, ANNOY, MUDDY, AGITATE, IRRITATE, DISPLEASE
roily ...... ANGRY, MUDDY, TURBID
roi's heir .... DAUPHIN
realm .... FRANCE
wife .... REINE
roister .... BULLY, REVEL, FROLIC, BLUSTER, SWAGGER
Roland's magic possession .... HORN, OLIVANT
role ...... JOB, DUTY, PART, OFFICE, PERSON, FUNCTION, CHARACTER
bit/without speech ...... WALK-ON
lead .... STAR
minor .... EXTRA
minor, well-defined .... CAMEO
movie .... HERO, LEAD, HEAVY, HEROINE, VILLAIN
roll .... BUN, CAKE, LIST, PEAL, PUSH, TOLL, WRAP, CHIRR, LURCH, SCONE, TRILL, ELAPSE, ENFOLD, MUFFIN, ROSTER, SCROLL, SLIP BY, BISCUIT, BRIOCHE, TRUNDLE, DRUMBEAT, REGISTER, CATALOG(UE)
about .... WALLOW, WELTER
along .... TRUNDLE
around .... ROTATE, REVOLVE
back .... REDUCE, REPULSE
call response .... HERE, PRESENT
from side to side, speedily .... CAREEN

hard .... BAGEL
of bills .... WAD
bread .... MANCHET
cloth .... BOLT
coins .... ROULEAU
paper .... WEB, BOLT
something, like ribbons, etc. .... ROULEAU
out .... SPREAD, FLATTEN
over ..... REINVEST, REFINANCE
parchment .... SCROLL
slang .... WAD, ROB, MONEY
the eyes .... GOGGLE
up .... FURL
up one's sleeves .... DIG IN
Rolland, Fr. novelist .... ROMAIN
rollback .... CUTBACK, REDUCTION
rolled backward .... REVOLUTE
roller .... WAVE, SKATE, WHEEL, WINCE, BRAYER, CANARY, PIGEON, RUNDLE, CYLINDER
coaster .... SWITCHBACK
of hardened steel .... MILL
on a typewriter .... PLATEN
printing .... BRAYER
rollick .... ROMP, CAPER, FRISK, GAMBOL
rollicking ...... LIVELY, CAREFREE
rolling fields, having ...... ACRED
prevent from .... TRIG
sound .... RUMBLE
stock .... LOCOMOTIVES
sudden .... LURCH
Rolling Stones member ...... WATTS, WYMAN, JAGGER
Rollo .... VIKING
rolltop .... DESK
rollway .... CHUTE
roly-poly .... DUMPY, PODGY, PUDGY, TUBBY, CHUBBY, PUDDING
person .... FATSO
rom .... GYPSY
romaine .... COS, LETTUCE
Romains, Fr. novelist ...... JULES
Roman .... LATIN, QUIRIS, ITALIAN, QUIRITES
actor's boot .... BUSKIN
administrator .... PATRICIAN
agreement .... PACTA
ancient, black marble .... NERO ANTICO
apostle .... NERI
assembly ..... FORUM, COMITIA
awning .... VELARIUM
basilica .... LATERAN
bathhouses .... THERMAE
bishop .... POPE
bottle .... AMPULLA
boxer's strap .... CESTUS

boxing-wrestling contest
.... PANCRATIUM
bronze .... AES
buckle .... FIBULA
building for musical
    performances ..... ODEUM
camps .... CASTRA
cap .... PILEUS
candle .... FIREWORK,
    FIRECRACKER
Catholic .... LATIN, PAPIST,
    ROMANIST
Catholic Church .... ROME,
    LATERAN
Catholic Church supreme
    head .... POPE
Catholic festival ...... LAMMAS
Catholic French ..... GALLICAN
censor .... CATO
census taker .... CENSOR
chariot .... ESSED
circus arena .... HIPPODROME
circus fighter .... GLADIATOR
citizens .... EQUITES
civil law digest .... PANDECT
civilian .... QUIRITE
clan .... GENS
clasp .... FIBULA
cloak .... SAGUM, ABOLLA,
    PALADUMENTA
coin .... AES, ASSES, SEMIS,
    AUREUS, BEZANT, DINDER,
    TRIENS, SOLIDUS, DENARIUS,
    SESTERCE
cold bath .... FRIGIDARIUM
cool room .... TEPIDARIUM
commander .... CENTURION
commoner .... PLEBEIAN
conspirator .... CASCA
corselet .... LORICA, LORLEA
court(s) .... ATRIUM, ATRIA
cuirass .... LORICA, LORLEA
date .... IDES, NONES
deity .... LAR
dictator .... SULLA
diviner .... AUSPEX
emperor .... NERO, OTHO,
    OTTO, CARUS, GALBA, NERVA,
    TITUS, CAESAR, PROBUS,
    TRAJAN, HADRIAN, AUGUSTUS,
    CALIGULA, CLAUDIUS,
    JUSTINIAN, VESPASIAN,
    THEODOSIUS, CONSTANTINE
emperor's bodyguard
.... PRETORIAN
decree .... RESCRIPT
standard .... LABARUM
Empire founder .... AUGUSTUS
Empire part .... GAUL,
    HISPANIA, BYZANTIUM
empress .... POPPAEA,

THEODORA
entrance court/hall .... ATRIUM
epigrammatist .... MARTIAL
estate .... LATIFUNDIUM
fable writer .... PHAEDRUS
farce .... MIME
farewell .... ADDIO
fates .... PARCAE
festival .... OPALIA,
    LUPERCAL(IA), SATURNALIA
fiddler .... NERO
foot soldiers .... VELITES
fountain, famed .... TREVI
frontier fortification ..... LIMES
galley .... BIREME, TRIREME
games .... LUDI
games official .... (A)EDILE
garment .... TOGA, STOLA,
    STOLE, TUNIC
general .... SULLA, TITUS,
    DRUSUS, MARIUS, SCIPIO,
    AGRIPPA, CASSIUS, AGRICOLA,
    LUCULLUS, BELASARIUS
general, defeated Attila
.... AETIUS
girdle .... CESTUS
girl traitor .... TARPEIA
gladiator .... RETIARIUS
god, agriculture .... PICUS,
    SATURN
chief .... JOVE, JUPITER
festivity .... COMUS
fire .... VULCAN
gates .... JANUS
Hades .... DIS, ORCUS, PLUTO
herds .... PAN
household ..... LAR, PENATES
lightning .... JUPITER
love .... AMOR, CUPID
lower world .... ORCUS,
    SERAPIS
night .... SOMNUS
pastoral .... FAUNUS,
    LUPERCUS
patron .... MERCURY
rain .... JUPITER PLUVIUS
sea .... NEPTUNE
season .... VERTUMNUS
sleep .... SOMNUS, MORPHEUS
sun .... SOL
tutelary .... LAR
underworld ...... DIS, ORCUS,
    PLUTO
war .... ARES, MARS,
    QUIRINUS
wind: east .... EURUS
    north .... BOREAS
    south .... NOTUS
    west .... ZEPHYR
wine .... BACCHUS
woods .... SYLVANUS

goddess .... DEA
agriculture .... OPS, CERES
beauty .... VENUS
birth .... PARCA, LUCINA,
    MATUTA
crops .... ANNONA
crossroads .... TRIVIA
dawn .... AURORA, MATUTA
earth .... TERRA, TELLUS
faith .... FIDES
fates .... PARCAE
fertility .... OPS, CERES,
    FAUNA, DEMETER
fields .... TERRA, TELLUS
fire .... VESTA
flowers .... FLORA
fountain .... FERONIA
fruits .... POMONA
harvest .... OPS
health .... SALUS
hearth .... VESTA
herds .... PALES
hope .... SPES
horses .... EPONA
hunting ...... DIANA, VACUNA
light .... LUCINA
love .... VENUS
marriage .... JUNO
moon .... LUNA, ARTEMIS,
    CYNTHIA
nether world .... CORA,
    PROSERPINA
night .... NOX
peace .... PAX
plenty .... OPS
sea .... MARE
summer .... AESTAS
vegetation .... CERES
virtue .... FIDES
war .... BELLONA, MINERVA
wisdom .... MINERVA
governor ...... LEGATE, PILATE,
    PROCONSUL
guard .... LICTOR
guardian spirits .... LARES,
    PENATES
Hades/hell .... AVERNUS
half boot .... CALIGA
hall .... OECUS, ATRIUM
harvest festival .... OPALIA
headband .... VITTA
helmet .... GALEA
highway .... VIA, ITER
hill .... (SEE **Rome**)
historian .... LIVY, NEPOS,
    TACITUS, SUETONIUS
holiday .... FERIA
hot bath .... CALDARIUM
hot room .... LACONICUM
household gods .... LARES,
    PENATES

jar .... AMPHORA
judge .... (A)EDILE,
    QU(A)ESTOR
lady .... DONNA
law .... LEX
lawmaker .... SENATOR
legion commander
.... TRIBUNE
leisure center .... BATH,
    AQUAE SULIS
list .... ALBE
lower world .... HADES, ORCUS
magistrate ..... EDILE, CENSOR,
    CONSUL, DUUMVIR, PR(A)ETOR,
    PREFECT, TRIBUNE
magistrate's symbol
.... FASCES
maiden traitor .... TARPEIA
marble .... CIPOLIN
masses .... PLEBS
matron's garment .... STOLE
meal .... CENA, GENA
measure .... URNA, CLIMA,
    CULEUS, DOLIUM
military unit .... COHORT,
    LEGION
monster: myth. .... LAMIA,
    TYPHON
month's first day .... CALENDS
name .... NOMEN
naturalist .... PLINY
noble .... PATRICIAN
nose .... NASUS
nothing .... NIHIL
nymph: myth. .... EGERIA,
    M(A)ENAD
officer for 10 men
.... DECURION
official .... EDILE, SATRAP,
    PREFECT
official with the fasces
.... LICTOR
Optimus Princeps ...... TRAJAN
orator .... CATO, CAESAR,
    CICERO
palace .... LATERAN
patriot .... RIENZI
patron of literature
.... MAECENAS
people .... SABINES
philosopher .... SENECA
physician, 1st century AD
.... CELSUS
physician, 2nd century
.... GALEN
physician's tool ...... FORCEPS,
    SCALPEL, (SURGICAL) SCISSORS
pin .... ACUS
plain .... CAMPAGNA
playwright .... TERRENCE
poet ...... OVID, CINNA, LUCAN,

VERGIL, VIRGIL, JUVENAL,
    LUCRETIUS
poet banished by Augustus
.... OVID
pontiff .... CAESAR
port .... OSTIA
portrait, wax .... IMAGO
pound .... LIBRA
priest .... AUGUR, AUSPEX,
    FLAMEN
procession .... TRIUMPH
province .... DACIA, MOESIA,
    NUMIDIA, PISIDIA, PANNONIA
public land .... AGER
racing course ..... HIPPODROME
revolt, leader of
.... SPARTACUS
river .... LETHE, TIBER
road .... VIA, ITER
road, famous .... APPIAN
robe .... TOGA, STOLA, STOLE
room(s) .... ATRIUM, ATRIA
royal standard .... LABARUM
secret cult .... BACCHUS
senator .... CATO, CICERO,
    PUBLIUS
Senate house .... CURIA
serf .... COLONA, COLONUS
shield(s) .... EGIS, SCUTA,
    SCUTUM, CLIPEUS
soldier ..... VELITE, LEGIONARY
soldier's covering
.... TESTUDO
soothsayer .... HARUSPEX
spirits .... LARES, MANES,
    LEMURES
standard .... LABARUM
stern .... CATO
street .... CORSO
tablet .... TESSERA
taxman .... PUBLICAN
temple .... NAOS, CELLA
theater awning ...... VELARIUM
theater's stage
.... PROSCENIUM
ticket/token .... TESSERA
tragedian .... SENECA
traitor's cliff .... TARPEIAN
treasurer .... QU(A)ESTOR
triumvir .... LEPIDUS
two-wheeled cart .... BIROTA
tyrant .... NERO
urn .... CAPANNA
vase .... PYXIS
vestment .... ROBE, TOGA
war trumpet .... TUBA
warrior .... GLADIATOR
way .... VIA
weapon .... SPEAR, SWORD,
    GLADIUS
weight .... AS, BES, LIBRA,

UNCIA, DUELLA, SCRUPLE,
    SEXTULA
writer .... LIVY, PLINY, VARRO,
    PLAUTUS, TERENCE, VEGETIUS
writing tablet .... DIPTYCH
romance .... WOO, COURT, NOVEL,
    FICTION, (LOVE) AFFAIR
icon .... FABIO
Romance language .... LADIN,
    FRENCH, CATALAN, ITALIAN,
    SPANISH, ROMANIAN,
    PROVENCAL
Romancero gitano poet
.... LORCA
Romania, etc. of yore ...... DACIA
president .... (ION) ILIESCU
prime minister .... (PETRE)
    ROMAN
Romanian. See **Rumanian**
Romanov, Russ. czar
.... MIKHAIL
Romansh .... LADIN
romantic .... DREAMY, POETIC,
    BYRONIC, FABULOUS,
    FANCIFUL, QUIXOTIC,
    FANTASTIC, VISIONARY,
    PICTURESQUE, SENTIMENTAL
Romany .... GYPSY
Rome .... ROMA, ETERNAL CITY
amphitheater .... COLOSSEUM
Beauty .... APPLE
conqueror of .... ALARIC
dominant building of ancient
.... (THE) FORUM
first emperor of .... AUGUSTUS
founder of .... ROMULUS
fountain of .... TREVI
grandeur of .... EMPIRE
is capital of .... ITALY
nemesis of .... NERO
"pest" of .... PAPPAGALLO
port .... OSTIA
rebel against .... SPARTACUS
river .... TIBER
saviors of, in 390 BC
.... GEESE
second king of .... NUMA
    POMPILIUS
Seven Hills, one of
.... CAELIAN, VIMINAL,
    AVENTINE, PALATINE,
    QUIRINAL, ESQUILINE,
    CAPITOLINE
unlucky, in ancient XIII
Romeo .... LOVER
and Juliet .... TRUE LOVERS
author .... SHAKESPEARE
character ..... ABRAM, PARIS,
    TYBALT, CAPULET, ESCALUS,
    LAWRENCE, MERCUTIO,
    MONTAGUE

enemy of .... TYBALT
father of .... MONTAGUE
kinsman of .... MERCUTIO
love of .... JULIET, ROSALINE
rival of .... PARIS
to Juliet .... SWEETHEART
Rommel, Ger. marshal
.... ERWIN
romp .... PLAY, CAPER, FRISK,
CAVORT, FROLIC, GAMBOL,
ROLLICK
rompers .... JUMPERS
Romulus .... QUIRINUS
brother of .... REMUS
conqueror of .... ODOACER
parent of .... MARS, RHEA
savior of .... (SHE) WOLF
Ronald, actor .... COLMAN,
REAGAN
U.S. president .... REAGAN
rondeau .... POEM, RONDO,
RO(U)NDEL
rondure .... CIRCLE, SPHERE
ronin .... OUTLAW, OUTCAST
rood .... CROSS, CRUCIFIX
roof .... DOME, CUPOLA, LEAN-TO,
CEILING, GAMBREL, MANSARD,
SHELTER, COVERING,
(HOUSE)TOP
arched .... VAULT
architectural style ...... GABLE,
CUPOLA, GAMBREL, MANSARD
coach's .... IMPERIAL
covering .... TILE, SLATE,
THATCH, SHINGLE
drain .... GUTTER
edge/overhang .... EAVE
feature .... EAVES
figuratively .... HOME, HOUSE
finial: arch. .... EPI
glass for admitting light
.... BULL'S-EYE
lantern .... LOUVER
of straw, palm leaves, etc.
.... THATCH
opening .... LUNET(TE),
SCUTTLE, SKYLIGHT
raise the .... COMPLAIN
raised border .... COAMING
rounded .... DOME, CUPOLA
sloped .... SHED, LEANTO
support .... SPRAG, TRUSS,
RAFTER, PURLIN(E)
timber .... RIDGEPOLE
top indicator .... VANE
trough .... GUTTER
two-sloped on two sides
.... GAMBREL
two-sloped on four sides
.... MANSARD
type of .... DOME, TILE, SLATE,

SHINGLE, THATCHED,
PENTHOUSE
window .... DORMER,
SKYLIGHT
woven work .... WATTLE
"Roof of the World" .... PAMIR,
TIBET
roofer .... SLATER
roofing material .... TILE, THATCH
slate .... RAG
slate trimmer .... ZAX
tile .... SLATE, PANTILE
roofless .... HOMELESS,
HYPETHRAL
rooflike covering .... CANOPY
rooftree .... HOME, SHELTER,
RIDGEPOLE
rook .... CROW, CHEAT, CASTLE,
SWINDLE(R)
cry of .... CAW
rookery .... SLUM, TENEMENT
inhabitant .... CROW, SEAL,
PENGUIN
rookie .... NOVICE, RECRUIT,
BEGINNER, NEWCOMER,
GREENHORN
room .... CELL, HALL, SALA,
CUDDY, LODGE, SALLE,
SPACE, STUDY, CLOSET,
LEEWAY, QUARTER, ROTUNDA
band, ornamental .... FRIEZE
beneath roof .... LOFT, ATTIC
conversation .... LOCUTORY
dressing .... BOUDOIR
for dance lessons .... STUDIO
harem .... ADA, ODA
hot bath .... CALDARIUM
inner .... BEN
Maison .... SALLE
perfumer .... INCENSE
private .... DEN, STUDY,
CLOSET, SANCTUM
Pueblo Indian .... KIVA
wine .... CELLAR
woman's sitting ...... BOUDOIR
roomer .... LODGER, BOARDER
rooming house .... KIP
housekeeper .... LANDLORD
rooms .... LODGINGS, QUARTERS
roomy .... AIRY, AMPLE, SPACIOUS
dress style .... TENT
roorback .... LIE, LIBEL, CANARD,
MUDSLINGING
roose .... PRAISE
Roosevelt, president .... FDR,
TEDDY, THEODORE, FRANKLIN
(DELANO)
Roosevelt's (F.D.) charity
.... MARCH OF DIMES
cottage in Warm Springs
.... LITTLE WHITE HOUSE

mother .... SARA
pet's name ..... FALA, BIG BOY
wife .... (ANNA) ELEANOR
roost .... SIT, BERTH, PERCH,
NEST(LE), SETTLE
rooster .... COCK, BANTAM,
CHANTICLEER
castrated .... CAPON
comb of .... CARUNCLE
cry of .... CROW
fattened .... CAPON
feathers of .... HACKLE
leg outgrowth .... SPUR
mate of .... HEN
young .... COCKEREL
root .... BASE, CORE, PLUG,
CAUSE, CHEER, RADIX,
ORIGIN, SOURCE, RHIZOME
aromatic ..... ORRICE, GINSENG
combining form .... RHIZ(O)
diuretic ....,.............. PAREIRA
dried .... RHATANY
dye .... CHAY, CHOY
edible .... YAM, EDDO, TARO,
MANIOC, POTATO, RADISH,
CASSAVA, PARSNIP,
GIRASOL(E)
emetic .... MANDRAKE
expectorant .... SENEGA
flavoring .... SARSAPARILLA
fleshy .... TUBER
for ..... HAIL, CHEER, ACCLAIM,
APPLAUD
for planting .... SLIP
fragrant .... ORRIS
garlic .... RAMSON(S)
growth .... TUBERCLE
hair .... FIBRIL, TRICHOME
medicinal .... GINSENG,
RHATANY
narcotic .... MANDRAKE
of the .... RADICAL
out: obs. .... ARACE
part of .... RADICLE
perfume making .... ORRIS,
ORRICE
purgative .... JALAP
relish/used for salads
.... RADISH
salad .... RAMPION, RAMSON(S)
seasoning .... TURMERIC
shoot .... SUCKER, TILLER
small .... RADICEL
stock .... GINGER
substance .... ZEDOARY
tip tissue .... MERISTEM
word .... ETYMON, RADICAL
Root, U.S. statesman ...... ELIHU
rooter .... FAN
rooting out .... EVULSION
rootlet .... RADICEL

rootlike .... RHIZOID
rootstalk .... GINGER, RHIZOME
rootstock .... PIP, ORIGIN, SOURCE,
RHIZOME
rope .... TIE, BIND, CORD, LINE,
CABLE, LASSO, TWIST,
FASTEN, MARLIN, STRAND
anchor .... CLEAT
and pulley block .... TACKLE
cattle catcher's .... BOLA
cord tied to .... MARLINE
cowboy's .... LASSO, RIATA,
LARIAT
dancer/walker
.... FUNAMBULIST
dancer's .... POY
fiber .... BAST, COIR, HEMP,
JUTE, ABACA, ISTLE, IXTLE,
SISAL, GOMUTI, MAGUEY
flag .... LANYARD
for cable's end .... MARLINE,
MARLING
for hanging ..... HEMP, NOOSE,
HALTER
for hoisting yards: naut.
.... TYE
for Tarzan .... LIANA
frayed end of .... FAG END
gaff to deck .... VANG
guiding .... GUY, LONGE,
LUNGE, DRAGLINE
guy .... VANG
horse trainer's .... LONGE
in .... LURE, ENTICE
knotted at end .... COLT
lead .... LONGE
loop .... LAP, FRAP, BIGHT
mooring .... PAINTER
old .... JUNK
part .... END, FIBER
pulling .... TUG
ship's .... GUY, TYE, STAY,
VANG, EARING, SHROUD,
LANYARD, PAINTER, RATLINE
steadying .... GUY, VANG
tether .... LARIAT
thin .... CORD, WIRE, STRING
thread a .... REEVE
towing .... CORDELLE
wire .... CABLE
roped .... LASSOED, TETHERED
Roper, Elmo .... POLLSTER
ropy .... GLUTINOUS
roque .... CROQUET
Roquefort .... CHEESE
rorqual .... WHALE, FINBACK,
RAZORBACK
Rosa, _____ (1929 song) .... NINA
odorata, descendant of
.... TEAROSE
rosaceous .... ROSY

plant .... PLUM, AGRIMONY,
STRAWBERRY
rosary .... BEADS, GARDEN,
CHAPLET, GARLAND
prayer .... AVE, HAIL MARY,
OUR FATHER, GLORIA PATRI,
PATER NOSTER
subject .... MYSTERY
Roscoe .... GAT
rose .... RHODA, DAMASK,
FLOWER, NOZZLE, PERFUME,
RAMBLER, ROSETTE
aborigine boxing champ
.... LIONEL
apple .... POMAROSA
bush .... SHADBLOW,
SASKATOON
extract .... ATTAR
garden .... ROSARY
hermosa .... PINK PEARL
mallow .... HIBISCUS,
HOLLYHOCK
moss .... PORTULACA
noble .... RYAL
plant .... AVENS
petal oil/perfume .... ATTAR
rash .... MEASLES, RUBELLA,
ROSEOLA
red spinel .... BALAS RUBY
straggling/climbing
.... RAMBLER
time .... JUNE, SPRING
tree .... RHODODENDRON
under the ...... SECRETLY, SUB
ROSA
wild .... BRIER, EGLANTINE
Rose Bowl players .... USC, UCLA
of Sharon .... ALTHEA
roseate .... ROSY, BRIGHT,
PROMISING
rosebay .... OLEANDER,
RHODODENDRON
rosebush .... SHRUB
feature .... BUD, THORN
fruit .... HIP
roseola .... RASH, MEASLES,
RUBELLA
Rose's love .... ABIE
rosette .... COCKADE
Rosie the _____ .... RIVETER
rosin .... FLUX, RESIN, ROZET
Rosinante .... JADE, HORSE
master of .... QUIXOTE
rosolio .... CORDIAL
Ross, flag-maker .... BETSY
U.S. woman governor
.... NELLIE
Rossetti, poet .... DANTE,
CHRISTINA
Rosshalde author .... HESSE

Rossini, composer
.... GIOACCHINO
hero of .... TELL
last opera of .... WILLIAM
TELL
work ...... OT(H)ELLO, WILLIAM
TELL, THE BARBER OF SEVILLE
Rossiya .... RUSSIA
roster .... LIST, ROTA, COUNT,
TALLY, RECORD, REGISTER,
ROLL CALL
rostrum .... BEAK, DAIS, STAGE,
PODIUM, PULPIT, LECTERN,
TRIBUNE, PLATFORM
rosy .... PINK(Y), RUDDY, BRIGHT,
BLUSHING, ROSACEOUS
fingered goddess ...... AURORA
rot .... RET, DECAY, SPOIL, WASTE,
PUTREFY, DECOMPOSE
slang .... BOSH, BALONEY,
RUBBISH, NONSENSE
rota .... LIST, COURT, ROUND,
WHEEL, AGENDA, ROSTER,
CLASSIS, ROUTINE
member .... AUDITOR
Rotarian, female .... ANN
rotate .... PAN, ROLL, SPIN, TURN,
TWIRL, WHEEL, WHIRL,
GYRATE, SWIVEL, REVOLVE
unevenly .... WOBBLE
rotating device .... CAM, AXIS,
AXLE, REEL, ROTOR, DASHER,
SPINDLE
firework .... GIRANDOLE
ride .... CAROUSEL, MERRY-GO-
ROUND
toy .... TOP, WHIRLIGIG
water .... WHIRLPOOL
wing craft .... GIRO
rotation ...... TURNING, GYRATION,
REVOLUTION
wind-operated .... WINDMILL
rotch(e) .... AUK, DOVEKEY,
DOVEKIE, GUILLEMOT
rote .... ROUTINE, PRACTICE
by .... MEMORY
rotenone source .... DERRIS
rotgut .... WHISKY
rotifer .... ANIMALCULE
rotisserie .... GRILL
pin .... SKEWER
rotl .... WEIGHT
plural of .... ARTAL
rotor .... STATOR
rotten .... BAD, FOUL, RANK,
ADDLE, FETID, NASTY,
PUTRID, CORRUPT, DECAYED,
SPOILED, TAINTED,
DISGUSTING
rottenstone .... TRIPOLI
rotund .... FAT, PLUMP, OBESE,

ROUND, STOUT, SONOROUS

roturier .... COMMONER

roue .... RAKE, RAKEHELL,
DEBAUCHEE, LIBERTINE

rouge .... PAINT, BLUSH-ON,
MAKEUP, COSMETICS

Rouge, _____ .... BATON, MOULIN

rough .... RUDE, CRUDE, HARSH,
COARSE, HUBBLY, JAGGED,
RAGGED, RUGGED, SHAGGY,
STORMY, UNEVEN, RIOTOUS,
SCRAGGY, VIOLENT, AGRESTIC

and disorderly .... LARRIKIN

and tumble .... HAYWIRE,
SLOVENLY, DISORDERLY,
TOPSY-TURVY, HELTER-
SKELTER

and tumble fight .... BRAWL,
MELEE

as in ride ..... BUMPY, JOLTING

boisterous activity
.... HORSEPLAY

cloth .... SHAG, DENIM, TERRY,
DUFFEL, DUFFLE

combining form .... TRACHY

edged .... EROSE

facial growth .... WHISKER

handler .... PAWER

in manner/speech .... BLUNT,
GRUFF, HARSH

make .... FRAY, FRET, RASP,
GRATE

outline .... DRAFT

skin .... SHAGREEN

sounding ...... RASPY, HOARSE,
RAUCOUS

water .... SEA

with small knobs
.... BLOTCHY, SCABROUS

roughage .... FIBER

roughen .... CHAP, FRAY, FRET,
RASP, RUFFLE

roughly .... ABOUT

roughneck .... BOOR, GOON,
HOOD, THUG, BULLY, ROWDY

roughness .... RIGOR, ASPERITY,
SEVERITY

roughshod, go .... TRAMPLE

rouleau .... ROLL

roulette color .... RED, BLACK

man .... CROUPIER

term .... BAS, NOIR, PASSE,
ROUGE, MANQUE

round ...... AMBIT, CYCLE, ORBED,
SALVO, COURSE, ANNULAR,
GLOBOID, CIRCULAR,
GLOBULAR, SPHERICAL

and plump .... CHUBBY

and round .... BY TURNS

clam .... QUAHOG

dance .... POLKA

figure .... ORB

filing desk .... RENT TABLE

make .... CIRCINATE

of applause .... PLAUDIT

of consecutive games
.... SERIES

of duty .... BEAT, TOUR

of play .... LAP, INNING

protuberance ..... KNOB, UMBO

shield, small .... TARGET

this is sometimes .... ROBIN

trip .... EXCURSION

tripper .... HOMER

up .... CORRAL, GATHER,
RUSTLE, COLLECT

watchman's .... TOUR

Round Table, central image of
.... ROSE

king .... ARTHUR

king's sword .... EXCALIBUR

knight .... KAY, BORS, BORT,
BALAN, BALIN, GARETH,
GAWAIN, GALAHAD, GERAINT,
MO(R)DRED, MORGA(I)N,
PELLEAS, TRISTAN, BEDIVERE,
LANCELOT, PARSIFAL,
PERCIVAL, TRISTRAM

roundabout .... JACKET, DEVIOUS,
INDIRECT, AMBAGIOUS,
CIRCUITOUS

expression .... AMBAGE,
PERIPHRASIS

way .... AMBAGE, DETOUR

rounded ...... ROTUND, FUSIFORM,
RINGSHAPE

and bulging .... GIBBOUS

edge .... NOSING

projection/protrusion
.... KNOB, LOBE

rounder ...... GUARD, DRUNKARD,
SENTINEL, WATCHMAN,
POLICEMAN

Roundhead .... PURITAN

roundly .... FULLY, SEVERELY

roundup ...... RODEO, GATHERING

roundworm .... ASCARID,
NEMATODE, PARASITE,
STRONGYL(E), LUMBRICALIS

disease .... ASCARIASIS,
FILARIASIS, TRICHINOSIS

roupy .... HUSKY, HOARSE

rouse .... HAUL, ROUST, WAKE(N),
EXCITE, INCITE, STIR (UP),
REVEILLE

rousing .... BRISK, BRACING,
STIRRING

Rousseau work/hero .... EMILE

roust ...... ROUT, STIR (UP), DRIVE
(OUT)

roustabout .... LUMPER, LABORER,
DECK HAND, STEVEDORE

rout .... MOB, RUCK, PANIC,
ROUST, DEFEAT, FLIGHT,
RABBLE, DEBACLE, STAMPEDE

in a way .... SKUNK

route .... RUN, WAY, PATH, ROAD,
TRACK, COURSE, FORWARD,
PASSAGE, ITINERARY

circuitous .... DETOUR

for excess water .... SPILLWAY

shortest .... BEELINE

to oblivion for defeated
candidates? .... SALT
RIVER

traveling .... ITINERARY

routine ..... ROTA, HABIT, ROT(T)E,
SYSTEM, HUMDRUM,
REGULAR, PRACTICE,
CUSTOMARY

dull .... RUT

monotonous .... GRIND

task .... CHARGE, CHORE

rove .... GAD, ROAM, RANGE,
RAMBLE, WANDER, MEANDER,
STRAGGLE

in search of plunder
.... FORAGE, MARAUD

rover ...... HOBO, NOMAD, PIRATE,
TARGET, VAGRANT,
WANDERER

roving .... CURSORY, RESTLESS,
WANDERING

band .... GANG

for adventure .... ERRANT

row .... OAR, FILE, LINE, TIER,
BRAWL, MELEE, NOISE, SCULL,
CLAMOR, KICK-UP, PADDLE,
RUCKUS, RUMPUS, SHINDY,
DISPUTE, QUARREL, SQUABBLE

form in a .... ALIGN, ALINE

of cut grass .... SWATH

of planted seeds .... DRILL

rowan .... ASH

rowboat ...... GIG, BANCA, CANOE,
COBLE, SKIFF, CAIQUE,
WHERRY, GONDOLA

racing .... GIG, SCULL, SHELL

warship's .... GALLEY

rowdy .... THUG, BULLY,
HOOD(LUM), LARRIKIN, PLUG-
UGLY, ROUGH(NECK)

one .... YAHOO

young .... HOOLIGAN

Rowe's (Nicholas) play ...... THE
FAIR PENITENT

rake .... LOTHARIO

rowed .... OARED

rowel .... SPUR, PRICK, WHEEL

rowen .... HAY, GRASS,
AFTERMATH

rower .... OAR(SMAN), GONDOLIER

seat of .... THWART

rowing contest .... REGATTA
rowlock .... THOLE, POPPET
Roxas, Philippine president
.... MANUEL
Roy Crane's captain .... EASY
Rogers' horse .... TRIGGER
royal ...... NOBLE, REGAL, AUGUST,
KINGLY, REGIUS, IMPERIAL,
MAJESTIC, PRINCELY
authority .... SCEPTER,
SCEPTRE
color .... PURPLE
council, Oriental .... DIVAN
court official
.... CHAMBERLAIN
crown .... TIARA, DIADEM,
CORONET
domain/realm .... EMPIRE,
CZARDOM, KINGDOM,
SULTANATE
flush, part of .... ACE, TEN,
JACK, KING, QUEEN
fur .... ERMINE
house .... YORK, TUDOR,
STUART, WINDSOR, HAPSBURG,
PLANTAGENET
initials .... HRH
palace .... COURT
residence .... PALACE,
BALMORAL, BUCKINGHAM
seat .... THRONE
staff .... ROD, SCEPTER
symbol ..... ORB, SEAL, SIGNET
title .... REY, ROY, DUKE,
EARL, EMIR, KING, SIRE, TSAR,
QUEEN, RAJAH, PRINCE,
SULTAN, CZAR(INA), DAUPHIN,
DUCHESS, EMPEROR, EMPRESS,
ESQUIRE, INFANTA,
BARON(ESS), COUNT(ESS),
MARQUESS, MARQUIS(E),
PRINCESS, VISCOUNT
treasury .... FISC
royalist .... TORY, CAVALIER,
MONARCHIST, IMPERIALIST
royalty .... NOBILITY, BLUE
BLOOD, ARISTOCRACY,
SOVEREIGNTY
payment .... DIVIDEND
RSVP, part of .... REPONDEZ,
S'IL, VOUS, PLAIT
rub .... BUFF, RASP, SAND, CHAFE,
GRATE, GRIND, SCOUR,
ABRADE, POLISH, MASSAGE
a-dub .... DRUMBEAT
against .... CHAFE
dry .... WIPE
off .... ABRADE
out ...... KILL, ERASE, MURDER,
SCRAPE, EXPUNGE
the wrong way .... RILE,

ANNOY, IRRITATE, DISPLEASE
to brightness .... POLISH,
FURBISH
with a file .... RASP
with nose .... NUZZLE
with oil/liniment
.... EMBROCATE
Rubaiyat author .... OMAR
(KHAYYAM)
rhyming .... ABBA
rubasse .... QUARTZ
rubber .... GUM, BUNA, PARA,
ERASER, EBONITE, GUAYULE,
MASSEUR, MASSEUSE,
MASSAGIST, CAOUTCHOUC
band .... ELASTIC
boot .... WADER
cement .... ADHESIVE
filler in .... KAOLIN(E)
game .... TIEBREAKER
game, first .... LEG
gas bubbles in liquid
.... FOAM
hard .... EBONITE, VULCANITE
necking vehicle .... STAGE
overshoe .... GUMSHOE
plant .... ULE, CAUCHO,
GUAYULE, MILKWEED
plant family .... MULBERRY
ring .... GASKET
roller .... SQUEEGEE
sap .... LATEX
sheeting .... PLIOFILM
shoe .... GALOSH(E),
GOLOSH(E)
slang .... CONDOM
stamp .... DATER, RATIFY,
APPROVE
stamp inker .... PAD
substance like .... GUTTA-
PERCHA
synthetic .... BUNA, BUTYLE,
CARIFLEX, NEOPRENE
synthetic material .... THIOKOL
synthetic polymer
.... SILICONE, ELASTOMER
thing made of .... BALL,
BAND, SHOE, TIRE, ERASER,
GASKET, SQUEEGEE
thread wound with cotton
.... LASTEX
tree ...... ULE, HEVEA, SERINGA
type of .... CEARA, INDIA,
CAUCHO, EBONITE, NITRILE,
KOROSEAL, VULCANITE
Rubber City .... AKRON
rubberneck .... GAWK, CRANE,
GAZE(R), SIGHTSEER
rubbers .... GUMSHOE, OVERSHOE,
GALOSHES, SNEAKERS
rubbery .... TOUGH, ELASTIC

rubbing ...... FRICTION, STROKING
liquid .... ALCOHOL
tool .... FILE
rubbish .... DUST, JUNK, RAFF,
DROSS, OFFAL, TRASH, TRIPE,
TRUCK, WASTE, DEBRIS,
LITTER, REFUSE, NONSENSE,
(TOMMY)ROT, TRUMPERY
collect .... SCAVENGE
mine .... STENT
pile .... DUMP
slang .... ROT
rubble ...... RUINS, SCREE, TRASH,
DEBRIS, LITTER, SHARDS
rubdown .... MASSAGE
rube .... HICK, YOKEL, RUSTIC
rubefacient ...... SALVE, PLASTER
rubella .... RASH, MEASLES,
RUBEOLA, ROSEOLA
rubellite .... TOURMALINE
rubeola .... MEASLES, RUBELLA
rubiaceous plant .... COFFEE,
IPECAC, CINCHONA, GARDENIA
Rubicon, he crossed the
.... CAESAR
rubicund .... ROSY, RUDDY,
FLORID, RED(DISH)
Rubinstein opera .... DEMONIO
pianist .... ANTON, ARTUR
rubious .... RED
ruble, 1/100 of a .... KOPE(C)K
rubric .... TITLE, HEADING,
RED(DISH)
ruby .... GEM, RED, STONE,
SARDIUS, CORUNDUM
spinel .... BALAS
ruche .... FRILL, TRIMMING
ruck .... FOLD, HEAP, SLEW,
STACK, CREASE, PUCKER,
WRINKLE
ruckus .... ROW, FRAY, BRAWL,
MELEE, HASSLE, RUMPUS,
UPROAR
ruction .... UPROAR, QUARREL
rudbeckia .... CONEFLOWER
rudd ...... CARP, FISH, VIREO, RED-
EYE
rudder .... HELM
guide with .... STEER
handle .... WHEEL, TILLER
ruddle .... KEEL
ruddock .... ROBIN
ruddy .... ROSY, FLORID,
FLUSH(ED), RED(DISH),
RUBICUND, SANGUINE
rude .... CRUDE, GROSS, GRUFF,
HARSH, ROUGH, SAUCY,
COARSE, RUGGED, BOORISH,
UNCIVIL, UNCOUTH, IMPOLITE,
INSOLENT
dwelling .... HUT, HOVEL

rudimentary .... INCHOATE, EMBRYONIC, VESTIGIAL, ELEMENTARY, ABECEDARIAN
rudiment(s) .... ABC, GERM, ROOT, FIRST, BASICS, EMBRYO, VESTIGE, ELEMENT(S), BEGINNING(S)
rue .... HERB, MOURN, BEMOAN, BEWAIL, GRIEVE, LAMENT, REGRET, REPENT, DEPLORE
plant .... LIME, LEMON, ORANGE
rueful .... SORRY, WOEFUL, ASHAMED, DOLEFUL, PITEOUS, PENITENT
ruff ...... COLLAR, FRAISE, PIGEON, SANDPIPER
female .... REE(VE)
in card game .... TRUMPING IN
turned down .... FALL
ruff(e) .... FISH, PERCH
ruffed .... UPSET, PIQUED, ABRISTLE
grouse .... PHEASANT, PARTRIDGE
ruffian ...... GOON, THUG, BRAVO, BULLY, ROWDY, HOODLUM, TOUGH(IE), HOOLIGAN, PLUG-UGLY, HIGHBINDER
ruffle .... VEX, RILE, FRILL, PLEAT, SHIRR, GATHER, RIPPLE, AGITATE, DERANGE, DISTURB, FLOUNCE, SHUFFLE, WRINKLE, FURBELOW, IRRITATE
rufous .... RUSTY, REDDISH
rug .... MAT, MAUD, CARPET, RUNNER, TOUPEE, WILTON, DRUGGET, COVERING, FOOTCLOTH
ruga ...... FOLD, CREASE, WRINKLE
rugate .... FOLDED, CREASED
rugby .... FOOTBALL
football .... RUGGER
formation .... SCRUM(MAGE)
play .... TRY
rival .... ETON
rugged .... RUDE, HARD(Y), HARSH, HILLY, ROUGH, STERN, CRAGGY, ROBUST, SEVERE, STORMY, STURDY, UNEVEN
rugger .... RUGBY
score .... TRY
rugose/rugous .... RIDGED, CORRUGATED
ruin .... BANE, RAZE, UNDO, CHAOS, HAVOC, SPOIL, DIDDLE, DESTROY, LOUSE UP, DOWNFALL, WRECK(AGE), PERDITION
irretrievably .... COOK ONE'S GOOSE
ruined: sl. .... KAPUT
ruinous .... TRAGIC, HARMFUL
ruins .... RELIC, DEBRIS, REMAINS
in .... RUN-DOWN
rule .... FIX, LAW, CODE, LINE, NORM, SWAY, AXIOM, HABIT, MAXIM, ORDER, REIGN, CUSTOM, DECIDE, GOVERN, SETTLE, SYSTEM, PRECEPT, REGIME(N), DECISION, STANDARD, CRITERION, PRESCRIPT, ADJUDICATE, REGULATION
as a .... USUALLY
book .... HOYLE, MANUAL
for rapid calculations .... SLIDE RULE
of conduct .... PRECEPT
of thumb basis ...... PRACTICE, EXPERIENCE
out .... OMIT, FORBID, EXCLUDE
ruler .... CZAR, EMIR, KING, TSAR, EMEER, QUEEN, RAJAH, FERULE, GERENT, PRINCE, REGENT, EMPEROR, MONARCH, GOVERNOR, POTENTATE
absolute .... SHAH, DESPOT, SHOGUN, TYRANT
amuser of a .... CLOWN, JESTER
ancient Egypt .... PHARAOH
Arab .... SHEIK(H)
cruel .... DESPOT
Ethiopian .... NEGUS
15th century Florentine .... LORENZO DEMEDICI
hereditary .... DYNAST
Indian .... SACHEM, CHIEF(TAIN)
length of a .... FOOT
Tatar .... KHAN
Tunisian .... BEY
who dusted his body with gold .... ELDORADO
wife of .... RANI, QUEEN, RANEE, REINA, CZARINA, EMPRESS, TSARINA
rules of conduct .... CODE
one kind of .... GROUND
Rules of Order author .... ROBERT
ruling ...... LINE, ORDER, DECREE, DECISION, REIGNING, GOVERNING, PREVALENT
party .... MAJORITY
rum .... LIQUOR, ROM(ANY), TAF(F)IA, BACARDI
dessert .... BABA
low grade .... TAF(F)IA
slang .... BAD, ODD, POOR, QUEER, STRANGE
source .... MOLASSES, SUGAR CANE
Rumania .... ROMANIA
once .... DACIA
Rumanian .... MAGYAR
capital .... BUCHAREST
city/town .... ARAD, BRAD, DEVA, IASI, BACAU, BUZAU, LUGOJ, ROMAN, SIBIU, TURDA, ZALAU, BRAILA, BRASOV, GALATI, MEDIAS, ORADEA, RESITA, TECUCI, TULCEA, PITESTI, FOCSANI, CRAIOVA, SLATINA, SUCEAVA, PLOIESTI, SATU MARE, CONSTANTA, TIMISOARA
coin .... BAN, LEI, LEU, LEY, BANI
composer .... ENESCO
district .... DOBRUJA
dramatist .... IONESCO
folk dance .... HORA
king .... CAROL, (MIHAI) MICHAEL
monetary unit .... LEU
mountain .... PELEAGA, PIETROSUL, MOLDOVEANUL
mountain range .... CARPATHIAN
native .... MAGYAR, MOLDAVIAN
part of .... WALACHIA
premier .... MAURER, ANTONESCU, CEAUSESCU
river .... JIU, OLT, PRUT, ARGES, BUZAU, JIJIA, MURES, SIRET, SOMES, TIMIS, BIRLAD, DANUBE
sea .... BLACK
rumba .... DANCE
exponent .... CUBAN, CUGAT
rumble .... BOOM, PEAL, ROAR, ROLL, BRAWL, GROWL, MELEE, FRACAS, LUMBER, FREE-FOR-ALL
seat .... DICKEY
rumbling .... THUNDER
rumdinger .... ONER
rumen .... CUD, GULLET, PAUNCH, STOMACH
of the .... RUMINAL
ruminant ...... PENSIVE, WISTFUL, CUD-CHEWING, MEDITATIVE
animal .... GNU, ROE, YAK, DEER, GOAT, IBEX, KUDU, ORYX, ZEBU, ADDAX, BISON, BONGO, CAMEL, ELAND, LLAMA, MOOSE, OKAPI, IMPALA, NILGAI, WAPITI,

BLESBOK, BUFFALO, GAZELLE, GIRAFFE, MUNTJAC, ANTELOPE, REEDBUCK

chew of .... CUD

stomach chamber ...... RUMEN, (AB)OMASUM, RETICULUM

ruminate .... CHEW, MUSE, PONDER, REFLECT, COGITATE, CONSIDER, MEDITATE

rummage .... COMB, GRUB, SEARCH, RANSACK, ODDS-AND-ENDS

sale .... BAZAAR

rummer .... CUP, GLASS

rummy .... GIN, ODD, QUEER, STRANGE, CARD GAME

bonus, sometimes .... ROODLES

game like .... COONCAN

slang .... SOT, TOPER, DRUNK(ARD)

strategy .... KNOCK

rumor .... BUZZ, TALK, BRUIT, NOISE, ONDIT, GOSSIP, REPORT, HEARSAY, GRAPEVINE

monger .... TATTLER, BUSYBODY

personified .... FAMA

rump .... ARSE, HIPS, CROUP, BREECH, FAG END, BUTT END, BUTTOCKS

Rumpelstiltskin .... DWARF

rumple ...... FOLD, MUSS, CREASE, TOUSLE, CRUMPLE, WRINKLE, DISHEVEL

rumpus .... ROW, STIR, POTHER, RACKET, RUCKUS, SHINDY, UPROAR, RUCTION, COMMOTION, DISTURBANCE

room .... GAMEROOM, PLAYROOM

rumrunner .... SMUGGLER, BOOTLEGGER

run .... ACT, HIE, PLY, FLOW, LEAK, LOPE, RACE, RILL, SCUD, TRIP, TROT, WORK, YARD, CREEP, INCUR, RAVEL, ROUTE, SCORE, SPEED, ELAPSE, EXTEND, HASTEN, SPREAD, TRAVEL, COMPETE, OPERATE, PUBLISH

about .... GAD

across .... MEET, ENCOUNTER

after .... CHASE, PURSUE

at full speed .... SPRINT

away .... BOLT, FLEE, ELOPE, DECAMP, ABSCOND

baseball .... HOME

colloquial .... STREAK

counter to .... BELIE

cricket .... BYE

down ..... OUTLINE, SUMMARY, NARRATIVE

in ...... BUST, ARREST, COLLAR, INSERT, INCLUDE

in haste ...... SCURRY, SCUTTLE

in the long .... EVENTUALLY, ULTIMATELY

in unbroken order .... SEQUENCE

of-the-mill ...... SO-SO, USUAL, COMMON, AVERAGE, ORDINARY

off .... PRINT

off, in a way .... ELOPE

off the tracks .... DERAIL

off with .... STEAL, ABDUCT, KIDNAP, SNATCH

out .... LAPSE

over .... SPILL, TRAVERSE

playfully .... SCAMPER

producer .... SNAG

swiftly .... DART

through .... REEVE, PIERCE, THRUST, PASS INTO

runabout .... ROADSTER

runagate .... RAT, DRIFTER, DESERTER, FUGITIVE, VAGABOND

runaround, (the) .... DELAYS, EVASION, EXCUSES, AVOIDANCE, PASSING-THE-BUCK

runaway .... FLEER, ELOPER, ESCAPEE, FUGITIVE

military .... AWOL, DESERTER

school .... TRUANT

slave .... MAROON

traitorous .... DEFECTOR

runcible spoon .... FORK

runcinate .... SAWTOOTHED

rundle .... RUNG

rundlet .... CASK, BARREL

rundown .... SEEDY, RICKETY, RAMSHACKLE

rune .... POEM, SONG, VERSE

rung .... STEP, SPOKE, STAVE, RUNDLE, CROSSBAR

runic alphabet .... FUTHARK

run-in .... TIFF, FIGHT, SCRAP, HASSLE, RHUBARB

runnel .... BROOK, RUNLET, CHANNEL, RIVULET

runner .... SKI, SKEE, AGENT, BLADE, RACER, SKATE, COURIER, SMUGGLER, SPRINTER, CONTENDER, ERRAND BOY, MESSENGER, (RACE)HORSE

botanical ...... SHOOT, STOLON, FLAGELLUM, SARMENTUM

Budd Schulberg's ...... SAMMY

corridor/floor .... MAT, RUG

foundry .... GATE, SPRUE

machine .... OPERATOR

table .... SCARF

-up .... SECOND

way of .... LANE

running .... EASY, LINEAR, MOVING, CURRENT, CURSIVE, FLOWING, MELTING, PASSING, CLIMBING, CREEPING, CONTINUOUS

knot .... NOOSE

nicely .... SPINNING LIKE A TOP

start .... EDGE

runt .... CHIT, DWARF, PYGMY, BANTAM

runway ...... PATH, RAMP, APRON, CHUTE, TRACK, CHANNEL, TROUGH, (AIR)STRIP

rupee, newly minted .... SICCA

weight of .... TOLA

rupees, 15 .... MOHUR

100,000 .... LAC

rupture ...... RIFT, BREAK, BURST, SPLIT, BREACH, HERNIA

support .... TRUSS

Rur characters .... ROBOTS

rural .... RUSTIC, BUCOLIC, AGRESTIC, ARCADIAN, GEOPONIC, PASTORAL

abode .... BOWER, VILLA, HACIENDA

building .... BARN

life, of .... PASTORAL

musical composition .... CANTATA, PASTORALE

one .... HICK, RUBE, YOKEL

opposed to .... URBAN

poem ..... ECLOGUE, PASTORAL

power initials .... REA

sound .... BAA, LOW, MOO, CROW, BLEAT

ruse .... DODGE, TRICK, GAMBIT, ARTIFICE, DECEPTION, STRATAGEM

rush .... HIE, RUN, DASH, RACE, DRIVE, HASTE, HURRY, PRESS, SCOOT, SPATE, SPEED, SURGE, HUSTLE, TORRENT, HIGHTAIL, ONSLAUGHT, SCRIMMAGE

an order .... EXPEDITE

furiously .... RAMP

grass .... CANE, REED, BAMBOO

headlong .... DIVE, PLUNGE, PRECIPITATE

hour .... GRIDLOCK

hour, usually .... NOON, FIVE (PM), NINE (AM)

line member (football) .... GUARD, CENTER, TACKLE

mass movement, panicked .... STAMPEDE
of air/wind ...... GUST, FLURRY
emotion .... THRILL, EXCITEMENT
sudden, strong rain .... FLASH FLOOD
water .... WASH, FLUSH, SWASH, SPLASH
words .... SPATE, TORRENT
plant .... BULRUSH, JONQUIL
strong onward .... BIRR, SURGE, ONRUSH
the opposing football passer .... BLITZ
travel period .... PEAK (SEASON)
upon .... CHARGE
violently .... RAMP(AGE)
with a .... QUICKLY
rushlight .... CANDLE
rusk .... CAKE, BREAD, BISCUIT, ZWIEBACK
Russ .... RUSSIAN
Russell, Miss .... GAIL, JANE, CONNIE, LILLIAN, ROSALIND
philosopher .... BERTRAND
russet .... APPLE, CLOTH, HOMELY, SIMPLE, (REDDISH-)BROWN, YELLOWISH-BROWN
Russia .... ROSSIYA, RUTHENIA, THE NORTHERN BEAR
former capital of .... PETROGRAD
former name of ..... MUSCOVY
founder of .... IVAN
Russian .... MUSCOVITE
administrative body .... ZEMSTVO
airline .... AEROFLOT
alcoholic drink .... KVASS, VODKA
America, capital of ...... SITKA
anarchist .... KROPOTKIN
antelope .... SAIGA
aristocrat .... BOYAR(D)
assembly .... RADA
astronaut .... LAIKA, TITOV, KOMAROV, POPOVICH, (YURI) GAGARIN
author/novelist .... GOGOL, GORKI, GORKY, TOLSTOI, TOLSTOY, (ALEKSANDR) SOLZHENITSYN
bag .... CYMKA
ballet dancer .... MASSINE, NUREYEV, (ANNA) PAVLOVA
bay .... OLENEK, GIZHIGA, PENZHINA
beer: var. .... QUAS
cape .... GOVENA, DEZHNEV, LOPATKA, NAVARIN, OZERNOY, CHELYUSKIN
capital .... MOSCOW
carriage .... TROIKA, DROS(H)KY, TARANTAS(S)
cart .... TELEGA
cathedral .... SOBOR
cereal .... EMMER
chalet .... DACHA
chess champion .... TAL, SMYSLOV, SPASSKY, ALEKHINE, BOTVINNIK, PETROSIAN
choreographer .... MASSINE
citadel .... KREMLIN
city/town .... UFA, BAKU, INTA, KIEV, LUGA, LVOV, MERV, OMSK, OREL, PERM, SUMY, TULA, BIYSK, BREST, CHITA, GOMEL, KAZAN, KIROV, KIZEL, KURSK, MINSK, NAVOI, PENZA, SEROV, TARTU, TOMSK, VILNA, ERIVAN, FRUNZE, GRODNO, KALUGA, KARSHI, KOVROV, KURGAN, ODESSA, RYAZAN, TAMBOV, URALSK, ACHINSK, ANGARSK, BARNAUL, BUKHARA, DONETSK, FERGANA, IRKUTSK, IVANOVO, KALININ, KHARKOV, KHERSON, LIPETSK, SARATOV, TALLINN, TBILISI, USTINOV, VOLOGDA, ZHDANOV, ANDROPOV, BELGOROD, CHIMKENT, DUSHANBE, TASHKENT, VLADIMIR, ARCHANGEL, ASTRAKHAN, CHERNIGOV, KARAGANDA, LENINAKAN, LENINGRAD, SAMARKAND, VOLGOGRAD, SEVASTOPOL, VLADIVOSTOK
coin ..... ALTIN, COPEC, RUBLE, KOPE(C)K, POLTINA, IMPERIAL, CHERVONETS
collective farm .... KOLKHOZ
comedian .... RAIKIN
community .... MIR
composer .... GLIERE, BORODIN, PROKOFIEV, STRAVINSKY, T(S)CHAIKOVSKY
cooperative .... ARTEL
Cossack .... TATAR
council .... DUMA, SOVIET
country estate .... DACHA
county .... OKRUG, OBLAST
dancer .... PAVLOVA, DANILOVA
dandelion .... KOK-SAGYZ
desert .... KARA-KUM, KYZL-KUM
diet .... DUMA
dramatist .... GOGOL

drink .... KVAS(S), QUASS, VODKA
dwelling/hut .... ISBA
edict .... UKASE
elite .... COSSACK
empress .... CZARINA, TSARINA
exile's place .... SIBERIA
farmer .... KULAK
fur .... CARACUL, KARAKUL
"Great" .... CATHERINE
great salt lake .... ELTON
greeting .... BEAR HUG
guitar .... BALALAIKA
guild .... ARTEL
gulf .... OB, RIGA, ANADYR, FINLAND, SAKHALIN, SHELEKHOV
hemp .... RINE, KONOPEL
holy city .... KIEV
holy picture .... ICON, IKON
hood .... BASHLYK
horse team .... TROIKA
horseman .... COSSACK
ibex .... TEK
imperial order .... UKASE
inland sea .... ARAL, AZOV
island .... AYON, URUP, BELYY, WIESE, BERING, PIONER, ETOROFU, HIIUMAA, WRANGEL, KOLGUYEV, SAAREMAA, SAKHALIN, BOLSHEVIK, PARAMUSHIR, GRAHAM BELL
island group .... KURIL, SHANTAR, NOVOYA ZEMLYA, KOMANDORSKIYE, SERGEYA KIROVA
James Bond .... ZAKHOV
lake .... ARAL, NEVA, ELTON, ILMEN, ONEGA, ALAKAL, BAYKAL, BELOYE, KHANKA, LADOGA, PEIPUS, TAYMYR, TENGIZ, IMANDRA, BALKHASH, ISSYK-KUL
language .... RUSS, TATAR, UEBEK, KAZAKH, KIRGIZ, SLAVIC, YIDDISH
leather .... YUFT, JUPTI
Little .... UKRAINIAN
log hut .... ISBA, ISPA
mammal .... DESMAN
marshal .... ZHUKOV, KUTUZOV
measure .... FUT, LOF, DUIM, FASS, VERST, ARSHIN, CHARKA, PALETZ, SAGENE, ARCHINE, BOTCHKA, VERCHOK
mister .... GOSPODIN
monarchy founder .... RURIK
monetary unit .... RUBLE
"mother of cities" .... KIEV
mountain .... ALAI, URAL, NARODNAYA

mountains ..... ALTAY, SAYAN, URALS, BAYKAL, ULUTAU, CAUCASUS
museum .... HERMITAGE
musical instrument .... BALALAIKA
name for Russia ...... ROSSIYA
negative/no .... NYET
news agency .... TASS, NOVOSTI
nurse .... BABA
oboe .... SZOPELKA
oil center .... BAKU
operatic singer ...... CHALIAPIN
painter .... CHAGALL
parliament .... D(O)UMA
peak ..... POBEDA, COMMUNISM
peasant .... KULAK, MUZHIK, MUZJIK
peasant cap .... ASKA
peasants' district .... VOLOST
peninsula .... GYDA, KOLA, KONI, KANIN, YAMAL, CRIMEA, TAYMYR, CHUKCHI, RYBACHIY
physiologist .... PAVLOV
pianist .... RACHMANN
plain .... STEPPE, TUNDRA
plane .... MIG, ILYUSHIN
poet .... PUSHKIN
port ...... ODESSA, SEVASTOPOL
pound .... POOD
praenomen .... IGOR
premier ...... STALIN, KOSYGIN, ANDROPOV, BREZHNEV, BULGANIN, MALENKOV, CHERNENKO, GORBACHEV, KHRUSHCHEV
president .... YELTSIN, SHVERNIK, GORBACHEV
prison .... ETAPE
range .... OLOY, GYDAN, URALS, ANADYR, KOLYMA, KORYAK, CHERSKIY
region .... MARI, SIBERIA
resort .... SOCHI, YALTA, ODESSA
revolutionary leader .... LENIN, KERENSKY, (LEON) TROTSKY
river .... OB, DON, ILI, OKA, PUR, TAZ, TYM, UDA, UFA, AMGA, AMUR, EMBA, KUMA, KURA, LENA, MAYA, NEVA, URAL, VAKH, YANA, ZEYA, ALDAN, AMGUN, ATREK, CHUNA, DVINA, ISHIM, KHETA, KOTUY, MEZEN, NADYM, ONEGA, TOBOL, TYUNG, VITIM, VOLGA, ANABAR, ANGARA, CHULYM, CHUNYA, DONETS, IRTYSH, KOLYMA, MARKHA,

MURGAB, OLEKMA, OMOLON, TAYMYR, USSURI, VILYUY, DNIEPER, PECHORA, PYASINA, YENISEY
ruler .... CZAR, TSAR
ruling family .... ROMANOV, ROMANOFF
saint .... OLGA
scarf .... BABUSHKA
sea .... ARAL, AZOV, KARA, BLACK, WHITE, BALTIC, BERING, LAPTEV, BARENTS, CASPIAN, OKHOTSK, SIBERIAN
seaport .... PETSAMO, PECHANGA, LENINGRAD
secret service .... KGB, MVD, NKVD, OGPU, CHEKA, GAY-PAY-OO
soup .... BORSCH
Soviet, rural .... VOLOST
spacecraft .... LUNA, LUNIK, SOYUZ, COSMOS, VOSTOK, YANTAR, SPUTNIK
squadron .... ESKADRA
strait .... LONG, TATAR, BERING, SANNIKOVA
stockade .... ETAPE
teapot/urn .... SAMOVAR
trade union .... ARTEL
vehicle .... TROIKA
villa .... DACHA
village .... MIR
violinist .... ELMAN, ZIMBALIST
wagon .... TELEGA
water barrier ...... ROGUN DAM
weight .... LOT, PUD, DOLA, FUNT, POOD, KAMIAN
wheat .... EMMER
whip .... KNOUT
windstorm .... BURAN
wolfhound .... ALAN, BORZOI
yes .... DA
youth organization .... KOMSOMOL

Russo-Japanese warship
.... MIKASA
rust .... ERODE, OXIDE, AERUGO, FUNGUS, CORRODE, OXIDIZE, VERDIGRIS
colored .... RUFOUS
fungus .... AECIA
life cycle of .... TELIAL
on bronze .... PATINA
plant .... FERRUGO
sorus .... TELIUM
rusted .... ATE
rustic .... HOB, CLOD, HICK, HIND, RUBE, RUDE, CHURL, RURAL, YOKEL, ARTLESS, AWKWARD, BUCOLIC, BOOR(ISH),

BUM(P)KIN, HAYSEED, ARCADIAN, GEOPONIC
lover/gallant .... SWAIN
musical instrument ...... OBOE, PIPE, REED, BASOON
peasant .... AGRESTIAN
pipe .... CORN, REED
quaff .... CIDER
rusticate .... COUNTRIFY
rustle .... STEAL, SWISH, CRINKLE, SUSURRATE
cattle .... ROUND UP
of silk skirt .... FROUFROU
up .... FORAGE, COLLECT
rustler .... ROBBER, (CATTLE) THIEF
object of .... CATTLE
rustling .... FROUFROU, SWISHING, SUSURRANT
sound .... SOUGH, SWISH, MURMUR, SUSURROUS
Rustum's son .... SOHRAB
rusty ...... STIFF, RUSTED, SHABBY, TIMEWORN, OUT-OF-PRACTICE
rut .... HEAT, RUCK, HABIT, TRACK, FURROW, GROOVE, ROUTINE, (BEATEN) PATH
rutabaga .... SWEDE, TURNIP
rutaceous plant .... RUE, LIME, LEMON, ORANGE
ruth .... PITY, GRIEF, SORROW
Ruth, baseball player .... BABE, GEORGE (HERMAN)
husband of .... BOAZ
mother-in-law of .... NAOMI
sister of .... EILEEN
son of .... OBED
Ruthenia .... RUSSIA
Ruthenian .... UKRAINIAN
ruthless .... CRUEL, GRUELING, PITILESS, MERCILESS
rutilate .... GLOW, GLEAM, GLITTER
rutty ...... HOT, IN HEAT, BURNING
Ruy Diaz de Bivar ...... (EL) CID
Rwanda capital .... KIGALI
city/town ..... BUTARE, GISENYI
lake .... KIVU
language .... SWAHILI
monetary unit .... FRANC
mountain .... KARISIMBI
neighbor .... BURUNDI
people .... HUTU
president .... KAYIBANDA
river .... RUZIZI
Rx .... RECIPE, REMEDY
is symbol for .... PRESCRIPTION
writer ..... GP, MEDIC, DOCTOR, PHYSICIAN

rye .... RIE, GRASS, GYPSY, CEREAL, WHISKY, GENTLEMAN
disease .... ERGOT, BLACKRUST
grass .... DARNEL
grass genus .... LOLIUM
gypsy .... ROMANO
liquor .... WHISK(E)Y
ryot .... PEASANT
Ryukyu island .... OKINAWA

S

S-curve .... ESS, OGEE
Greek .... SIGMA
Hebrew .... SIN
letter .... ESS
mark .... POTHOOK
shaped .... ESS, OGEE, SIGMATE, SIGMOID
shaped seat .... VIS-A-VIS, TETE-A-TETE
shaped worm .... ESS
sound .... HISS
Sa, in chemistry ...... SAMARIUM
Saar(land) capital
.... SAARBRUCKEN
Saarinen, architect .... EERO
Saba .... SHEBA
sabadilla alkaloid .... VERATRIA, VERATRIN(E)
Sabah .... NORTH BORNEO
bay .... LABUK
capital .... JESSELTON, KOTA KINABALU
city/town .... LAMAG, PAPAR, RAMAU, TAWAU, WESTON
mountain/peak .... KINABALU
seaport .... JESSELTON
Sabaist's object of worship
.... STARS
sabalo .... MILKFISH
Sabatini affair .... DUEL
novelist .... RAFAEL
sabbat .... MEETING
Sabbath ...... SUNDAY, SATURDAY
Sabbatical privilege .... REST, LEAVE, VACATION
saber .... SWORD, CUTLASS, SCIMITAR, YATAG(H)AN
sable ...... FUR, CAPE, FELT, PELT, BLACK, SKUNK, SOBOL, LEMMING, DARK(ENED), MUSTELINE
animal like .... MARTEN, WEASEL
fur .... ZIBEL(L)INE
imitation .... KOLINSKY
sablefish .... BESHOW
sabot ...... CLOG, DINGHY, PATTEN, (WOODEN)SHOE
sabotage .... RUIN, SPOIL, DESTROY, DISABLE, UNDERMINE, VANDALISM, SUBVERSION

perpetrator .... SABOTEUR
Sabrina river .... SEVERN
sabulous .... SANDY, GRITTY
sac ...... BAG, BLEB, CYST, ASCUS, BURSA, POUCH, INDIAN, POCKET, VENTER, VESICLE
air .... BLADDER
bubblelike/cavity-like
.... BLISTER
kangaroo .... MARSUPIUM
like a .... SACCULAR
-like organ .... STOMACH
organ(ism) .... THECA
pus-filled .... BOIL
seed .... POD, CASE, SILIQUE
small .... SACCULE
spore .... ASCUS
SAC, part of .... STRATEGIC, AIR, COMMAND
sacaton .... HAY, GRASS
saccate .... POUCHLIKE
saccharin .... SWEETENER
saccharine .... SWEET, SIRUPY, SUGARY, HONEYED
saccharize .... FERMENT
saccharose .... SUGAR, SUCROSE
saccule .... SAC, BOSS
sacerdotal .... HIERATIC, PRIESTLY
sachem .... CHIEF, SAGAMORE
sachet .... BAG, PAD, POWDER
Sachs, Ger. playwright .... HANS
trade of .... COBBLER
Sachsen .... SAXONY
sack .... BAG, BED, BASE, BUNK, LOOT, POKE, WINE, GUNNY, POUCH, JACKET, RAVAGE, SACQUE, PILLAGE, PLUNDER
hit the .... SLEEP, RETIRE
kind of .... SAD
making cloth .... OSNABURG
slang .... FIRE, DISCHARGE, DISMISS(AL)
sackbutlike instrument
.... LYRE, TROMBONE
sackcloth and _____ .... ASHES
symbol of .... REMORSE, MOURNING, PENITENCE
sacking .... JUTE, BURLAP, LOOTING
sacque .... SACK, JACKET
sacrament .... MASS, RITE, BAPTISM, PENANCE,

(HOLY)COMMUNION, EUCHARIST, MATRIMONY, CONFIRMATION
sacrarium ...... SHRINE, CHANCEL, SANCTUARY
sacred .... HOLY, PIOUS, SAINT, DIVINE, BLESSED, HALLOWED, INVIOLATE, VENERATED, INVIOLABLE, SACROSANCT, SANCTIFIED, CONSECRATED
beetle .... SCARAB
bird .... IBIS
book/tome ...... BIBLE, KORAN, ALCORAN
bull .... APIS, HAPI
chest .... ARCA, CIST
city .... MECCA, MEDINA, BENARES, LOURDES, JERUSALEM
combining form .... HIERO, HAGI(O)
container .... AMA, PYX, CIST
cord .... KUSTI
cow .... IDOL, UNTOUCHABLE
fig tree .... PIPAL
food .... MANNA
fountain .... HIPPOCRENE
hymn .... PSALM
image .... ICON, IKON, PIETA
language .... PALI, HEBREW, ARAMAIC
literature .... VEDA
make .... BLESS, HALLOW, SANCTIFY, CONSECRATE
melody .... CHORALE
music .... MOTET
object .... RELIC
ode .... HYMN
opposed to .... PROFANE, SECULAR
picture .... ICON
place .... CHURCH, SHRINE, TEMPLE, SANCTUM, SYNAGOGUE
plant .... RAGTREE
poem .... HYMN, PSALM
prohibition .... TABU, TABOO
relic .... HALIDOM
scriptures .... BIBLE, KORAN, ALCORAN
shield .... ANCILE
song .... MOTET, PSALM

things, traffic in .... SIMONY
tree .... PIPAL, BO(TREE)
wine vessel .... AMA
word .... OM, LOGOS
writer .... HAGIOGRAPHER
writing .... TORAH, AVESTA,
GOSPEL, TALMUD,
HAGGADA(H), MASORA(H),
SCRIPTURE

Sacred College member
.... CARDINAL
sacredness .... SANCTITY
sacrifice .... COST, LOSS, GIVE UP,
OBLATION, OFFERING
burning place of .... PILE
by killing .... IMMOLATE
god demanding .... MOLECH,
MOLOCH
human .... SUTTEE
object of .... HOMAGE,
ATONEMENT, EXPIATION,
APPEASEMENT
place of .... ALTAR
play, in baseball .... FLY,
BUNT
sacrificial animal .... LAMB
block/place/table .... ALTAR
fire .... IGNI
lamb, of a sort ...... FALL GUY
offering .... LAMB, HIERA,
IMMOLATION
rite .... LIBATION
sacrilege .... SIN, INFAMY,
IMPIETY, BLASPHEMY,
PROFANITY
sacrilegious .... IMPIOUS,
PROFANE, IRREVERENT
condition .... SCANDAL,
DESECRATION
sacrilegist .... RENEGADE,
BLASPHEMER
sacrist(an) .... SEXTON
sacristy .... VESTRY
sacrosanct .... HOLY, DIVINE,
SACRED, HALLOWED,
INVIOLABLE
slang .... LILY-WHITE
sacrum .... SPINAL BONE
of the .... SACRAL
pain in the .... SACRALGIA
sad .... BAD, GLUM, DISMAL,
DOLENT, GLOOMY, TRISTE,
DOLEFUL, UNHAPPY,
DEJECTED, DOLOROUS,
MELANCHOLY
colloquial .... BLUE, DOWN
sack .... BOLO
sack at dockside .... DEPORTEE
shack .... HOVEL
saddle .... PAD, HUMP, LOAD,
SEAT, PANEL, HARNESS

attachment .... HOLSTER
bag .... ALFORJA
band .... GIRTH
blanket .... TILPAH
block .... ANESTHESIA
bow/front part .... POMMEL
cloth .... MANTA, PANEL
colloquial .... PIGSKIN
cover for .... MOCHILA
footrest .... STIRRUP
gaiter/legging .... GAMBADO
girth .... CINCH
gun case .... HOLSTER
horse .... NAG, HACK, REMUDA,
PALFREY
lining .... PANEL
pack .... APAREJO
pad .... CORONA
part .... PAD, CINCH, GIRTH,
CANTLE, LATIGO, POMMEL,
STIRRUP
rear part .... CANTLE
seat behind .... PILLION
slang .... RIG
stirrup .... GAMBADO
strap .... CINCH, GIRTH
upon .... LOAD, ENCUMBER
with charges .... BLAME,
ACCUSE

Sadducee, opposite of
.... PHARISEE
Sadduceeism .... SKEPTICISM
sadhe .... TSADI
sadiron .... FLATIRON
sadism .... ABUSE,
MALTREATMENT
is derived from name
of _____ ..... MARQUIS DE
SADE
sadistic .... CRUEL, BRUTAL,
FIENDISH
activity .... BEATING,
BONDAGE, WHIPPING
sadness ...... WOE, DOLOR, GRIEF,
MISERY, PATHOS, SORROW,
ANGUISH, DESPAIR
expression of .... ALAS
slang .... BLUES, DUMPS
safari .... TREK, CARAVAN,
JOURNEY, EXPEDITION
safe .... CHEST, ON ICE, VAULT,
COFFER, SECURE, UNHURT,
UNHARMED, PROTECTED,
STRONGBOX
and _____ .... SOUND
conduct .... PASS, CONVOY,
ESCORT, PASSPORT
cracker .... YEGG(MAN)
safeblower ...... YEGG, PETERMAN
safeguard .... COVER, GUARD,
WATCH, CONVOY, DEFEND,

SHIELD, DEFENSE, PROTECT
safekeeping .... CARE, (A)EGIS,
CUSTODY, STORAGE,
TUTELAGE, PROTECTION
of public lands
.... RESERVATION-
PRESERVATION
safely .... WITHOUT RISK
safety .... SURETY, SECURITY
device .... ARMOR, CATCH,
VALVE, BUFFER, BUMPER,
FENDER, SCREEN, SHIELD
device, airplane
.... PARACHUTE
device, sea .... MAE WEST,
LIFE PRESERVER
lamp .... DAVY
place of .... HOME, HAVEN,
ASYLUM, HARBOR, REFUGE,
HOSPICE, SHELTER,
SANCTUARY
zone .... ISLAND
saffron .... CROCUS, YELLOW
family .... IRIS
use of .... DYE, COLORING,
SEASONING
safrol(e) .... OIL
sag ...... HANG, SINK, WARP, WILT,
CURVE, DROOP, SLUMP,
BUCKLE, SLOUCH, WEAKEN,
DECLINE
nautical .... DRIFT, LEEWAY,
LEEWARD
saga ...... EDDA, EPIC, TALE, ILIAD,
LEGEND
sagacious .... ASTUTE, SHREWD,
SAPIENT, DISCERNING,
PERCEPTIVE, WISE(AS AN
OWL)
sagacity .... WIT, ACUMEN,
WISDOM
sagamore .... SACHEM
Sagan, modern scholar .... CARL
sage ...... HERB, MINT, SEER, WISE,
SOLON, NESTOR, SAPIENT,
SCHOLAR
scarlet .... SALVIA
hen .... GROUSE
of Emporia .... WHITE
Sagebrush State .... NEVADA
sagger .... (FIRE)CLAY
Sagitta .... ARROW, KEYSTONE,
CONSTELLATION
sagittary .... CENTAUR
sago .... PALM, GOMUTI, STARCH
saguaro .... CACTUS
Sahara ...... DESERT, WASTELAND
fertile area .... FEZZAN
like the .... ARID
section .... ERG
wind .... LESTE

sahib .... SIR, MASTER
saiga .... ANTELOPE
Saigon Chinese district
.... CHOLON
new name of .... HO CHI MINH
sail ...... LUG, KITE, FLOAT, GLIDE,
CANVAS, CRUISE, JIGGER,
LATEEN, VOYAGE, SPANKER,
NAVIGATE
around the world
.... CIRCUMNAVIGATE
bellying part of .... BUNT
billowing .... SPINNAKER
close to the wind .... LUFF,
POINT
corner/attachment .... CLEW
edge of .... LUFF
fastener .... CLEW
for a sloop .... JIB
fore-and-aft .... MIZ(Z)EN,
SPANKER
free edge of .... LEECH
furl .... REEF
haul up .... TRICE
hoist .... CLUE UP
ice .... SCOOTER
into .... SCOLD, BERATE,
ASSAIL
kind of ...... JIB, MAIN, ROYAL,
LATEEN, SPANKER, TOPMAST,
FOREROYAL, TOPGALLANT
loop .... CRINGLE
near the wind .... LUFF
out to sea .... OUTSTAND
part of ..... BUNT, CLEW, FOOT,
HEAD, LUFF, MAST, REEF,
YARD, LEECH, EARING,
CRINGLE, BOLTROPE
poetic .... SHEET
reduce size of .... REEF
ring .... CRINGLE
rope .... TYE, HALYARD
specified distance .... LOG
square .... LUG
support .... MAST
tackle .... HALYARD
tapering cloth .... GORE
triangular .... JIB, LATEEN
tuck .... REEF
sailboat ...... BARK, DHOW, YAWL,
KETCH, SKIFF, SLOOP, SMACK,
VINTA, YACHT, BARQUE,
CAIQUE, KUMPIT, SAILER,
VESSEL, CRUISER, SCHOONER
sailed at Newport ...... YACHTED
sailer, 1492 .... PINTA, NINA,
SANTA MARIA
sailfish .... (BASKING) SHARK
kin of .... MARLIN
sailing, oblique .... LOXODROMICS
race .... REGATTA

raft .... BALSA, CATAMARAN
vessel .... YAWL, KETCH,
SLOOP, FRIGATE, GALLEON,
SCHOONER
sailor .... GOB, HAT, TAR, JACK,
SALT, LASCAR, SEAMAN,
MARINER, NAVYMAN,
SHIPMAN, DECK HAND,
SEAFARER
bed of .... HAMMOCK
clumsy .... LUBBER
contentious .... SEA LAWYER
drink of .... GROG
experienced .... SEADOG,
SHELLBACK
jersey .... FROCK
kidnap .... SHANGHAI
new, inexperienced
.... LUBBER, LANDSMAN
prospective .... MIDDY
sailor's bad luck .... JONAH,
JONAS
biscuit .... TACK
brew .... RUM
call .... AHOY
choice .... PORGY, PIGFISH
church .... BETHEL
cord .... LANIARD, LANYARD
dish .... SCOUSE
handicraft .... SCRIMSHAW
hat .... SOU(TH)WESTER
hello .... AHOY
jumper .... BLOUSE
leave .... FURLOUGH
mess tub .... KID
patron saint .... ELMO
patroness .... EULALIA
quarters .... FOCSLE,
FORECASTLE
rebellion .... MUTINY
social call .... GAM
sword .... CUTLAS(S)
underwear .... SKIVY
(work)song .... CHANTEY,
SHANT(E)Y
''yes'' .... AYE-AYE
sain .... BLESS, CROSS
saint. See also **patron** ...... HOLY,
SAN(TA), SACRED, BLESSED,
CANONIZE
celebrated on January 21st
.... AGNES
colloquial .... ANGEL
declare person a .... CANONIZE
early .... AUGUSTINE
first native-born American
.... SETON
homage to a .... DULIA
memorial of .... RELIC
sacred image of .... ICON,
(E)IKON

tomb of .... SHRINE
topper .... HALO
worshiper .... HAGIOLATER
Saint Andrew's Cross .... SATIRE,
SALTIER
Anthony's fire ..... ERYSIPELAS
Bernard .... DOG
Bernard monk's concern
.... TRAVELER, WAYFARER
Elmo's fire .... CORPOSANT
Joan character .... DAUPHIN
John's bread .... CAROB,
ALGAROBA
John's evil .... EPILEPSY
Laurent, fashion stylist
.... YVES
Patrick's Day celebrant
.... IRISH
Peter Gonzalez .... ELMO
Vitus' dance .... CHOREA
saintly .... PIOUS
saints, author of lives of
.... HAGIOGRAPHER
catalogue/list of .... CANON,
DIPTYCH, HAGIOLOGY
register .... MENOLOGY
rule by .... HAGIARCHY,
THEOCRACY, HAGIOCRACY
worship of .... HAGIOLATRY
Saint's day .... FIESTA
sake .... END, GOOD, WINE, CAUSE,
BEHALF, MOTIVE, REGARD,
ACCOUNT, BENEFIT, PURPOSE
source .... RICE
saker .... FALCON
Sakhalin .... KARAFUTO
Saki .... MUNRO
Sakti .... MAYA
sal volatile .... HARTSHORN
salaam .... BOW, GREETING,
OBEISANCE
salable .... VENDIBLE,
MARKETABLE
salacious .... LEWD, BAWDY,
RIBALD, LUSTFUL, OBSCENE
salad .... GREENS, (COLD)DISH,
(COLE)SLAW
days .... TEENS, YOUTH
dressing .... RANCH, ITALIAN,
REMO(U)LADE, MAYONNAISE,
BLUE CHEESE, VINAIGRETTE,
THOUSAND ISLAND
fruit .... AMBROSIA,
MACEDOINE
green .... UDO, CRESS(E),
ENDIVE, DANDELION
herb ...... DILL, CRESS, ENDIVE,
FENNEL, PARSLEY
kind of .... CHEF, CAESAR,
POTATO, TOSSED, WALDORF,
FOUR-BEAN

leaves ..... SPINACH, ESCAROLE, WATERCRESS, (ROMAINE)LETTUCE
molded .... ASPIC, JELLO
vegetable .... BEET, CELERY, RADISH, TOMATO, CABBAGE, CHICORY, SUCCORY, CUCUMBER, MUSHROOM, SCALLION, ASPARAGUS, BELL PEPPER
Saladin's foes .... CRUSADERS
salamander .... EFT, NEWT, POKER, AXOLTL, LIZARD, REPTILE, MUD PUPPY, WATER DOG, HELLBENDER
obsolete .... EVET
Salambria .... PENEUS
salami .... SAUSAGE
salary .... FEE, PAY, HIRE, SCREW, WAGE(S), STIPEND, EMOLUMENT, COMPENSATION
additional to .... BONUS, PERK, PERQUISITE
increase .... RAISE
limit .... CAP
payment other than .... FRINGE BENEFIT
sale ...... DEAL, BARTER, MARKET, BARGAIN, SELLING, VENDITION
incentive .... REBATE
kind of ..... CASH, FIRE, YARD, WHITE, GARAGE, AUCTION, RUMMAGE, CLEARANCE, INVENTORY
public .... VENDUE, AUCTION
proviso/term .... AS IS
Salem witchcraft trial judge .... SEWALL
salep .... TUBER
drink from .... SALOOP
source of .... ORCHID
saleratus .... BAKING SODA
sales caveat .... AS IS
promotion .... FREE SAMPLE, ADVERTISING
talk .... LINE, PITCH, SPIEL, PATTER
salesman .... CLERK, SELLER, DRUMMER
kind of .... PEDDLER, TRAVELING, AUCTIONEER, DOOR-TO-DOOR
salicaceous tree .... POPLAR, WILLOW
salicin .... GLUCOSIDE
saliferous .... SALTY, SALINE
salient .... LEAPING, NOTABLE, CAPERING, STRIKING, PROMINENT
points .... GIST
salientian .... FROG, TOAD

salina .... LAKE, POND, (SALT)MARSH, SALT PITS
saline .... SALTY, MARINAL
drop .... TEAR
solution .... BRINE
Salisbury steak ...... HAMBURGER
Salish .... INDIAN, FLATHEAD
saliva .... SPUTUM, SPIT(TLE)
content .... UREA, MUCIN, SALTS, SODIUM, ALBUMIN, AMYLASE, CHLORIDE
enzyme .... AMYLASE, PTYALIN
excessive secretion of .... PTYALISM
insufficient secretion of .... DRY MOUTH
resembling .... SIALOID
running from mouth .... DROOL, DRIVEL, SLAVER
wet/smear with .... SLOBBER
salix .... ITEA, OSIER, WILLOW
Salk, vaccine developer .... JONAS
salle .... HALL, ROOM
sallet .... HELMET
sallow .... WAN, PALE, MUDDY, OSIER, PASTY, PALLID, SICKLY, WILLOW, YELLOW
sally .... JEST, JOKE, QUIP, RAID, TRIP, FORAY, JAUNT, ISSUE, BANTER, RETORT, SORTIE, RIPOSTE, REPARTEE, OUTBURST, EXCURSION, WIT(TICISM)
forth .... RUSH OUT
Sally, actress .... FIELD
Lunn .... TEACAKE
with the fan .... RAND
salmacis .... NYMPH
salmagundi .... OLIO, JUMBLE, MEDLEY, MIXTURE, POTPOURRI, HODGEPODGE
salmi .... STEW
salmon .... COHO, JACK, MORT, HADDO, HOLIA, SPROD, ALEVIN, GRILSE, CHINOOK, CHINUCK, QUINNAT, SOCKEYE
color .... PINK
dog .... CHUM, KETA
eggs .... ROE
eggs relish .... CAVIAR(E)
female .... RAUN, BAGGIT
gristle .... GIB
hook .... GIB, KIP
humpback .... HADDO, HOLIA
male .... COCK, KIPPER
net .... MAUD
one year old .... BLUECAP
red .... SOCKEYE
running up river .... ANADROMOUS

salted .... LOX
trout .... HARDHEAD, NAMAYCUSH, STEELHEAD
variety ..... RED, PINK, PACIFIC, ATLANTIC
young .... PARR, SMOLT, GRILSE, SAMLET
salmonella .... BACTERIA
disease caused by .... TYPHOID FEVER, FOOD POISONING
salmonoid .... TROUT, NAMAYCUSH, STEELHEAD
Salome's mother .... HERODIAS
stepfather .... HEROD
salon .... HALL, SHOP, LEVEE, STUDIO, ATELIER, GALLERY, BALLROOM, SHOWROOM, DRAWING ROOM, (BEAUTY)PARLOR
service .... SET, PERM, TRIM
Salonika .... THERMA
saloon ...... BAR, PUB, DIVE, HALL, SEDAN, BISTRO, TAVERN, CANTINA, GINMILL, TAPROOM, DRAMSHOP, GROGGERY, GROGSHOP, HONKY-TONK, BARRELHOUSE
keeper .... PUBLICAN
slang .... OASIS
saloop .... DRINK
Salop .... SHROPSHIRE
salpa .... TUNICATE
salt .... SAL, TAR, WIT, NACL, BRINE, HUMOR, SOUSE, PICKLE, SAILOR, SEASON, PICRATE, SALINIZE
away ...... BANK, SAVE, STORE, INVEST
acid .... OLEATE
alkaline .... BORAX
bed .... VAT
bottle .... CRUET, CASTER, CASTOR, SHAKER
chemical .... ESTER
crystalline .... NITER, NITRE
deposit .... LICK
factory .... SALTERN
lake .... SINK
malic acid .... MALATE
marsh/pond .... SALINA
meat .... SALAMI
organic .... ESTER
person who makes or sells .... SALTER
pertaining to .... SALINE
pork .... SOWBELLY
preserve with .... CORN
resembling .... HALOID
rheum .... ECZEMA
rock .... HALITE
soluble .... SALAR

spring .... LICK, SALINA

tax .... GABELLE

tree .... ATLE, TAMARISK

water .... BRINE

saltant .... DANCING, JUMPING, LEAPING

saltation ...... BEATING, DANCING, LEAP(ING), MUTATION, PALPITATION

salted .... CORNED

saltpeter .... NITER, NITRE

salts, _____ .... EPSOM

saltworks .... SALINA, SALTERN

saltwort .... KALI, BARILLA

salty .... RACY, BRINY, SHARP, WITTY, CORNED, SALINE, PIQUANT, PUNGENT

salubrious .... SALUTARY, HEALTHFUL

Salus .... HYGEIA

concern of .... HEALTH, PROSPERITY

salutary .... TONIC, HEALTHY, HEALING, HEALTHFUL, WHOLESOME, BENEFICIAL, SALUBRIOUS

salutation .... AVE, BOW, HAIL, ALOHA, CURTSY, SALAAM, WELCOME, GREETING, RESPECTS

salute .... BOW, TIP, HAIL, KISS, GREET, CURTSY, WELCOME

flag .... DIP (COLORS)

gun/military .... SALVO

salvage .... SAVE, REDEEM, RESCUE, RECLAIM, RETRIEVE

salvation .... RESCUE, REDEMPTION, DELIVERANCE

Salvation Army founder
.... BOOTH

salve ...... OIL, BALM, HAIL, NARD, ANOINT, LOTION, POMADE, REMEDY, SOOTHE, ASSUAGE, PLASTER, UNGUENT, OINTMENT, DEMULCENT, EMOLLIENT

sacramental .... CHRISM

salver .... TRAY, WAITER

salvia .... SAGE

salvo .... BURST, EXCUSE, SALUTE, VOLLEY, EVASION, FANFARE, GUNFIRE, HEDGING, STRAFING, BROADSIDE, FUSILLADE

in law .... RESERVATION

Samantha, actress .... EGGAR

samara .... CHAT, KEY FRUIT

tree bearing .... ASH, ELM, MAPLE

Samaritan magician ...... MAGUS

sambar .... DEER, MAHA, RUSA

sambuke-like instrument
.... HARP

same .... IBID, IDEM, ALIKE, DITTO, EQUAL, SIMILAR, IDENTICAL

combining form .... ISO, HOMO

in value .... EQUIVALENT

sound, without variation
.... MONOTONOUS

Samedi .... SATURDAY

samiel .... SIMOOM

samisen-like instrument
.... BANJO

samite .... LAME

samlet .... PARR, SALMON

Sammy Cahn creation .... LYRIC

Samoa .... NAVIGATORS

Samoa, American bay
.... MASSACRE

cape .... TAPUTAPU

capital .... PAGO PAGO

island .... TUTUILA

Samoa, Western bay .... SAFATA, PALAULI

cape .... MULINU'U

capital .... APIA

city/town .... ASAU, SALA'ILUA, SATUPAITEA

island .... UPOLU, SAVAI'I

monetary unit .... TALA

mountain .... VAEA, SILISILI, VAAIFETU

seaport .... APIA

strait .... APOLIMA

Samoan .... POLYNESIAN

bird .... IAO

cloth .... TAPA

clothes .... PAREUS

costume .... PULETASI

council .... FONO

loincloth .... LAVA-LAVA

maiden .... TAUPO

mollusk .... ASI

owl .... LULU

waistcloth .... LAVA-LAVA

warrior .... TOA

samovar .... URN, TEAPOT

samp .... GRITS, HOMINY, (CORN)MEAL, PORRIDGE

sampan .... BOAT

samphire .... GLASSWORT

sample .... TEST, TASTE, TRIAL, EXAMPLE, PATTERN, SPECIMEN

cloth .... SWATCH

sampler .... TESTER, NEEDLEWORK

item .... MOTTO

Samson and Delilah composer
.... SAINT SAENS

Samson in Hebrew .... SHIMSHON

Samson's deathplace .... GAZA

father .... MANOAH

mistress .... DELILAH

mother .... ZORAH

tribe .... DAN

vulnerable part .... HAIR

weapon .... JAWBONE

Samuel .... PROPHET

Samuel's birthplace .... RAMAH

father .... ELKANAH

mother .... HANNAH

son .... ABIA

teacher .... ELI

samurai .... RONIN, WARRIOR

San .... SAINT

Antonio shrine .... ALAMO

_____ fault .... ANDREAS

Francisco .... FRISCO

Francisco's _____ Tower
.... COIT

_____ of Hearst fame
.... SIMEON

Marino mount .... TITANO

Marino rulers .... REGENTS

sana in corpore sano, _____
.... MENS

sanatory .... CURATIVE

sanbenito wearer .... HERETIC, PENITENT

Sancho Panza's master
.... (DON)QUIXOTE

sanctify .... BLESS, HALLOW, PURIFY, BEATIFY, GLORIFY, CONSECRATE

sanctimonious .... DEVOUT, PRUDISH, HYPOCRITICAL

colloquial .... GOODY-GOODY

sanction .... OK, LAW, AMEN, FIAT, ALLOW, DECREE, PERMIT, RATIFY, APPROVE, CONFIRM, ENDORSE, PENALTY, SUPPORT, APPROVAL, IMPRIMATUR

given by an Oriental ruler
.... FIRMAN

sanctioned .... LEGAL

sanctity .... PURITY, HOLINESS, GODLINESS

sanctuary .... BEMA, FANE, HAVEN, ASYLUM, CHURCH, REFUGE, TEMPLE, CHANCEL, SHELTER, HALIDOM(E)

animal/bird .... RESERVATION

portable .... TABERNACLE

sanctum .... DEN, STUDY, ADYTUM, OFFICE, RETREAT

sand .... GRIT, BEACH, GRAIN, SPECK, DESERT, POLISH, SILICA, SMOOTH, ABRASIVE, GRANULES

bank .... CAY, DUNE, SHOAL

bar .... REEF, SPIT, SHELF,

dab .... SHOAL, FLATFISH
deposit .... ESKER
dollar .... SEA URCHIN
eel .... LA(U)NCE
flea .... CHIGOE, CHIGGER
hill .... DENE, DUNE
lily .... SOAPROOT
lot game .... BASEBALL
living in .... ARENICOLOUS
mist .... BAI
mound .... DENE, DUNE
particles .... GRIT, SILT
ridge ...... DUNE, OSAR, ESKAR, ESKER
slang ..... GRIT, PLUCK, SPUNK, COURAGE
snake .... ERYX
trotter .... CAMEL
viper .... HOGNOSE
Sand, George .... DUPIN, DUDEVANT
sandal .... THONG, LOAFER, SLIPPER, HUARACHE, (OVER)SHOE
fastener .... LACET, LATCHET
wooden .... PATTEN
sandals, winged .... TALARIA
sandalwood ...... ALGUM, ALMUG, SANTAL, INCENSE, LABURNUM
Sandalwood Island .... SUMBA, SOEMBA
sandarac .... ARAR, RESIN, ALERSE, INCENSE, REALGAR
sandbank .... CAY, DUNE, SPIT
channel .... GAT
Sandburg, poet .... CARL
sander ...... POLISHER, SMOOTHER
sandglass .... HOURGLASS
what it tells .... TIME
sandhog .... DIGGER
sandpaper .... ABRASIVE
sandpiper .... REE, BIRD, RUFF, STILT, STINT, TEREK, DUNLIN, CURLEW, RED KNOT, TATTLER, JACKSNIPE, GREENSHANK, YELLOWLEGS
African .... RUFF
American .... PEEP
Arctic .... PECTORAL
beach .... SANDERLING
European .... STINT
female .... REEVE
gathering place of male
.... LEK
genus .... TRINGA, CALIDRIS, VANELLUS
long-beaked ..... SNIPE, TEREK, CURLEW, GODWIT, WOODCOCK
means of feeding ..... PROBING
relative .... SNIPE, PLOVER

short-beaked .... STINT, DOWITCHER
spotted .... PEETWEET
sands .... BEACH, MOMENTS
sandstone .... PAAR, BEREA, ARKOSE, PSAMMITE, ITACOLUMITE
formed from granite
.... ARKOSE
sandstorm .... SAMIEL, SIMOOM
sandwich .... INSERT, PUT BETWEEN
bread .... BUN, RYE, CROISSANT, PUMPERNICKEL
cookie .... OREO
Dagwood .... HERO, HOAGIE
filling .... EGG, HAM, TUNA, BACON, BURGER, CHEESE, SALAMI, WIENER, BOLOGNA
garnish .... ONION, LEMON, PICKLE, TOMATO
kind of ...... HOT, CLUB, COLD, POOR BOY, OPEN(-FACE)
underwater .... SUBMARINE
Sandwich Islands .... HAWAII
sandy .... GRITTY, ARENOSE, SABULOUS, SHIFTING, ARENACEOUS
color .... GINGER
mound .... DOWN
soil .... LOAM, LOESS
waste(land) .... DESERT
sane .... WISE, LUCID, SOBER, SOUND, NORMAL, RATIONAL, SENSIBLE, REASONABLE
colloquial .... ALL HERE
sanforize .... PRESHRINK
sang-froid .... CALM, COOL, POISE, APLOMB, COMPOSURE, INSOUCIANCE
Sangraal .... (HOLY)GRAIL
sanguinaria .... PLANT, POPPY, BLOODROOT
sanguinary .... GORY, BLOODY, SAVAGE, BLOODTHIRSTY
sanguine .... RUDDY, HOPEFUL, CHEERFUL, CONFIDENT, OPTIMISTIC
color .... RED, RUDDY, MURREY, CRIMSON
person .... OPTIMIST
Sanhedrin .... COURT, COUNCIL
sanicle .... PARSLEY
sanies .... PUS, DISCHARGE
sanitarium .... RESORT, RETREAT, HOSPITAL, SANATORIUM
building .... PAVILION
sanitary .... CLEAN, HYGIENIC
protection .... NAPKIN, TAMPON
sanity .... REASON, SENSES,

SOBRIETY
sannup ...... INDIAN, ALGONQUIAN
sans .... WITHOUT
culotte .... RADICAL, REVOLUTIONARY
doute .... SURE, CERTAINLY, DOUBTLESS
ethical standards ...... AMORAL
pareil .... PEERLESS
souci .... GAY, CASTLE, CAREFREE
Sans Souci site .... POTSDAM
Sanskrit .... INDIC, VEDIC
dialect .... PALI
epic .... RAMAYAMA
god .... VAYU, INDRA
god's elephant .... AIRAVATA
word meaning "kinsmen"
.... ARYAN
Santa .... HOLY, SAINT
_____ .... FE, CLAUS, ANITA, BARBARA
_____, Antonio Lopez de, Mexican leader against the Alamo .... ANNA
Claus .... NICK, KRISS KRINGLE
Claus' illustrator
.... (THOMAS) NAST
Claus' sled runner
.... REINDEER
Claus' vehicle .... SLED, SLEIGH
Claus' way .... CHIMNEY
Claus who first arrived in America: 17th century
.... (SAINT)NICHOLAS
_____, Columbus' flagship: 1492 .... MARIA
Fe _____ .... TRAIL
Severa .... PYRGI
stand-in of .... POP, PAPA, DAD(DY)
Santiago de Cuba .... ORIENTE
santon .... MONK, HERMIT
santonica .... WORMSEED, WORMWOOD
Santorini, former name of
.... THERA
Sao Salvador .... BAHIA
sap ...... DIG, DRAIN, FLUID, JUICE, VIGOR, SPIRIT, TRENCH, WEAKEN, EXHAUST, UNDERMINE
drain .... TAP, SPILE, SPOUT
flow of .... LACTESCENCE
poisonous .... UPAS
slang .... BOOB, DUPE, FOOL
the foundations of
.... DESTROY
tree .... MILK, UPAS, LATEX, BALATA, RUBBER

sapajou .... GRISON, MONKEY, CAPUCHIN
saphead .... BOOB, DOLT, DUPE, FOOL, DINGBAT, DING-A-LING
sapid .... TASTY, SAVORY, FLAVORY, TASTEFUL
sapience .... WISDOM, SAGACITY
sapient .... SAGE, WISE, KNOWING, LEARNED, DISCERNING
sapindaceous plant
.... SOAPBERRY
sapless .... DRY, INSIPID
sapling .... YOUTH, SPROUT, SEEDLING, YOUNGSTER
sapodilla .... PLUM, ACANA, CHICO, MAMEY, MAMMEE, SAPOTA, MARMALADE
saponaceous .... SOAPY
saponin .... GLUCOSIDE
sapor .... TANG, SAVOR, TASTE, FLAVOR, RELISH
saporous .... TASTY, SAVORY
sapota .... MARMALADE, SAPODILLA
sapped .... SPENT, DISABLED
sapper .... DIGGER, TRENCHER
Sapphira's husband .... ANANIAS
weakness .... LYING
sapphire ...... GEM, BLUE, STONE, CORUNDUM
sapphirine .... SPINEL
Sappho's home .... LESBOS
work .... POETRY
sappy .... JUICY
slang ..... INANE, INEPT, SILLY, FATUOUS, FOOLISH
saprophyte .... FUNGUS, PARASITE
sapsago .... CHEESE
sapsucker .... WOODPECKER
sapwood .... ALBURNUM
saraband .... DANCE
Saracen .... ARAB, MOOR, MOSLEM
foe of .... CRUSADER
holy man .... IMAM
leader .... SALADIN
Sarah .... MILES, BERNHARDT
diminutive of ...... SAL, SADIE, SALLY
handmaid of/slave of
.... HAGAR
husband of .... ABRAHAM
son of .... ISAAC
saran .... RESIN
Saratoga general .... GATES
Sarawak's rajah .... BROOKE
sarcasm .... GIBE, JEER, IRONY, SCORN, SATIRE, CONTEMPT, CYNICISM
sarcastic .... ACID, CAUSTIC, CYNICAL, MORDANT,

IRONIC(AL), SARDONIC, SCORNFUL, SATIRIC(AL), VITRIOLIC
sarcoma .... TUMOR, CANCER
bones .... OSTEO(SARCOMA), CHONDRO(SARCOMA)
skin .... KAPOSI'S
sarcophagus .... TOMB, COFFIN
sard .... CHALCEDONY
sardine .... LOUR, HERRING, PILCHARD
fish like .... BRISLING
——— like .... PACKED
local .... CAN
relative .... KIPPER
Sardinian cape .... TESTA, TEULADA, CARBONARA, SPARTIVENTO
capital .... CAGLIARI
city/town .... BOSA, BITTI, NUORO, SORSO, ARBOREA, SASSARI, CARBONIA, IGLESIAS
coin .... CARLINE
duchy .... SAVOIE
gulf .... OROSEI, ASINARA, CAGLIARI, ORISTANO
language .... CATALAN
mountain .... GENNARGENTU
neighbor island .... CORSICA
province ...... NUORO, SASSARI, CAGLIARI
river .... MANNU, TIRSO, COGHINAS
ruling family .... SAVOY
seaport .... BOSA
sheep .... MOUF(F)LON
strait .... BONIFACIO
sardius .... RUBY, SARD
sardonic .... CAUSTIC, TWISTED, DERISIVE, IRONIC(AL), SARCASTIC, SATIRIC(AL)
sardonyx product .... CAMEO
Sarg, U.S. puppeteer ...... TONY
sargasso .... SEAWEED, (GULF)WEED
sark .... SHIRT, CHEMISE
sarmentose plant
.... STRAWBERRY
sarong .... PAREUS, LOINCLOTH, WAISTCLOTH
Sarpedon's father .... ZEUS
killer .... PATROCLUS
mother .... EUROPA
sarsaparilla .... MEAD, SMILAX, GINSENG, BEVERAGE
sartor .... TAILOR
sash ...... OBI, BAND, BELT, TOBE, SCARF, GIRDLE, RIBBON, WAISTBAND, CUMMERBUND
door/window .... FRAME, CASING

pane holder .... SPRIG
sashay .... GAD, GLIDE
sasin .... BUCK, ANTELOPE
Saskatchewan capital .... REGINA
city/town .... MELFORT, TISDALE, WEYBURN, YORKTON, HUMBOLDT, ROSETOWN, MOOSE JAW, SASKATOON, PRINCE ALBERT
hills .... CYPRESS, PORCUPINE
lake .... CREE, DORE, TOBIN, MONTREAL, REINDEER, OLD WIVES, ATHABASCA
lakes .... QUILL, WHITESWAN
mountain .... MOOSE
river .... SWAN, MAKWA, MOSSY, TORCH, CARROT, GEIKIE, OLDMAN, POPLAR, MUDJATIK, SASKERAM, CHURCHILL, ASSINIBOIA
saskatoon .... SHADBLOW, (SHAD)BUSH, JUNEBERRY
Sasquatch .... BIG FOOT
sass ...... LIP, SAUCE, (BACK)TALK, RUDENESS, VEGETABLES
sassaby .... ANTELOPE
sassafras drink .... SALOOP, ROOT BEER
oil .... SAFROL(E)
Sassenach .... SAXON, LOWLANDER, ENGLISHMAN
Sassoon, poet .... SIEGFRIED
sassy .... RUDE, TREE, SAUCY, IMPUDENT
one .... SNIP
Satan .... DEIL, EVIL, DEMON, DEVIL, EBLIS, BELIAL, HORNIE, ABADDON, LUCIFER, OLD NICK, SHAITAN, APOLLYON, MEPHISTO, OLD HARRY, ARCHFIEND, BEELZEBUB
co-rebel of .... AZAZEL
satanic .... WICKED, DEVILISH, INFERNAL, DIABOLICAL
satchel .... ETUI, ETWEE, SCRIP, VALISE, (HAND)BAG, GRIP(SACK)
sate .... FILL, GLUT, GRATIFY, SATIATE, SATISFY, SURFEIT
sated .... BLASE
satellite .... MOON, PLANET, FOLLOWER, DEPENDENT
artificial .... ECHO, LUNA, NOVA, LUNIK, SOYUZ, APOLLO, GEMINI, HELIOS, OHSUMI, VOSTOK, MERCURY, PIONEER, SPUTNIK, EXPLORER, CHALLENGER
path of .... ORBIT
shadow of .... UMBRA

unmanned .... IRAS
satiate .... CLOY, FILL, GLUT, JADE, SATE, SLAKE, GRATIFY, SATISFY, SURFEIT
satin, adjective for .... SOFT, GLOSSY, SMOOTH
fabric .... SILK, NYLON, RAYON, CYPRUS, CYPRESS
fabric smooth like ..... PANNE, PONGEE, VELVET
flower .... LUNARIA
imitation .... SATEEN, SATINET(TE)
satiny .... SILKY, LUSTROUS
satire ...... WIT, IRONY, LAMPOON, MOCKERY, SARCASM, RIDICULE, PASQUINADE
satirical .... WRY, CAUSTIC, CUTTING, IRONIC(AL), SARCASTIC
work .... SKIT, PARODY, LAMPOON, BURLESQUE, CARICATURE
satirist .... JUVENAL
satirize .... LAMPOON, RIDICULE
in verse .... BERIME
satisfaction .... CONTENT, PAYMENT, PLEASURE, ATONEMENT, REPARATION
for a killing .... CRO
for injuries .... GREE, DAMAGES
satisfactory .... GOOD, JAKE, AMPLE, ADEQUATE
satisfied .... HAPPY
satisfy .... PAY, MEET, SOLVE, ANSWER, PLEASE, APPEASE, FULFILL, GRATIFY, PLACATE, MEASURE UP
every whim .... CATER
satisfying .... HUNKY, REWARDING
satrap .... RULER, TYRANT, GOVERNOR
saturate .... SOP, FILL, SOAK, IMBUE, STEEP, DRENCH, SEETHE
saturated state ...... WET, SOGGY, SOAKED, SODDEN
Saturday night special ...... GUN, PIECE, REVOLVER, AUTOMATIC
Saturn .... CRONUS, PLANET
ancient god and ruler of .... REPHAN
in alchemy .... LEAD
largest satellite .... TITAN
moon of .... DIONE
orbiters of .... RINGS
wife of .... OPS
saturnalia .... ORGY, REVELRY, CARNIVAL, FESTIVAL
saturniid .... MOTH

saturnine .... GLUM, GRAVE, GLOOMY, MOROSE, TACITURN
satyr .... FAUN, DEITY, LECHER, SILENUS, BUTTERFLY
deity resembling a .... SILENUS
Satyr, god attended by .... BACCHUS
staff of .... THYRSUS
Sau .... SAVA
sauce .... DIP, SOY, CHILI, CURRY, GRAVY, FLAVOR, MORNAY, RELISH, SEASON, SOUBISE, VELOUTE, DRESSING, MATELOTE, WORCESTER
and liqueurs .... CREMES
bean .... SOJA, SOY(A)
colloquial .... IMPUDENCE, INSOLENCE
dessert .... MINT, MELBA, CARAMEL, HOT FUDGE, CHOCOLATE, BUTTERSCOTCH
fish .... ALEC
flavoring material .... EGGS, MINT, WINE, LEMON, ONION, CAPERS, CHEESE
kind of ..... WHITE, BARBECUE, BECHAMEL, MUSHROOM, BEARNAISE, BORDELAISE, HOLLANDAISE
made with eggs and cheese .... MORNAY
made with onion puree .... SOUBISE
pepper .... TABASCO
slang .... LIQUOR
spicy .... REMO(U)LADE
thickener .... ROUX
tomato .... CATSUP, KETCHUP
white .... VELOUTE
saucepan .... POT, POSNET, CASSEROLE
saucer .... DISH, DISK, DISCUS
flying .... UFO
object likened to .... EYE
saucy .... ARCH, BOLD, CHIC, PERT, RUDE, BRASH, COCKY, PERKY, SASSY, SMART, FLIP(PANT), IMPUDENT, INSOLENT, IMPERTINENT
girl .... CHIT, MINX, MALAPERT
slang .... FRESH, BRASSY, CHEEKY
talk .... LIP
Saudi Arabian cape .... ABU-MAD, BARIDA, HATIBA, AL ASWAD, MISHAAB, SAFANIYA
capital .... RIYADH
city/town .... ABHA, HAIL, TAIF, HOFUF, JIDDA, JIZAN, MECCA, QIZAN, TEBUK,

DAMMAM, MEDINA, NAJRAN, BURAIDA, MUBARRAZ
coin .... QURSH, QURUSH
desert .... DAHANA, JAFURA, AR RIMAL, NEFUD(DAHI), BAHR ES SAFI, RUB AL KHALI
district .... MIDIAN
gulf .... AQABA, PERSIAN
inhabitant .... BEDOUIN
island .... TIRAN, FARASAN, MASHABI, SHAIBARA
language .... ARABIC
monetary unit .... RIYAL
mountain .... SUBH, SALMA, ANEIZA, ARAFAT
plateau .... ARMA, SUMMAN
port .... JIDDA
principality .... ASIR
province .... HE(D)JAZ
range .... TUWAIQ, HADHB DAWASIR
region .... TIHAMA
religion .... ISLAM
religious center .... MECCA, MEDINA
river, dry .... ARAR, RIMA, BISHA, RANYA, SIRHAN, DAWASIR
ruler .... KING, FEISAL, (IBN)SAUD
sea .... RED
state .... NEJD
strait .... TIRAN
sauger .... PERCH
Sauk .... SAC
Saul. See **King Saul**
Sault Ste. Marie canals .... SOO
sauna .... BATH(HOUSE)
saunter ...... GAIT, WALK, AMBLE, MOSEY, LOITER, STROLL
across street .... JAYWALK
saurel .... SCAD, SKATE
saurian .... LIZARD, REPTILE, DINOSAUR, ALLIGATOR, CROCODILE
sauropod .... DINOSAUR
saury .... SKIPPER, LIZARDFISH
sausage ...... PIG, WEENY, SALAMI, WEENIE, WEINER, BOLOGNA, PUDDING, SAVELOY, (LIVER)WURST, FRANKFURTER
cover .... INTESTINE
shaped .... ALLANTOID
saute .... FRY
sauterne .... WINE, YQUEM
savage .... HUN, FELL, WILD, ANGRY, CRUEL, FERAL, BRUTAL, FERINE, FIERCE, RUGGED, BESTIAL, UNTAMED, TERRIBLE, BARBARIAN, BARBAROUS, FEROCIOUS

beast .... BRUTE
state .... FERITY
Savage Island .... NIUE
savagery .... WILDNESS,
    BARBARISM, BARBARITY,
    BRUTALITY
savanna(h) .... PLAIN, GRASSLAND
plain like ..... LLANO, PAMPAS,
    STEPPE
savant .... SAGE, EXPERT, PANDIT,
    PUNDIT, SCHOLAR
save ...... BUT, KEEP, HOARD, LAY
    BY, SPARE, STORE, EXCEPT,
    REDEEM, RESCUE, BARRING,
    SALVAGE, PRESERVE,
    ECONOMIZE
all .... OVERALLS, PINAFORE
saveloy .... SAUSAGE
savin(e) .... CEDAR, JUNIPER
saving .... EXCEPT, FRUGAL,
    REDEEMING
clause .... SALVO, LOOPHOLE
in law .... EXCEPTION
savings .... FUNDS, ACCOUNT,
    NEST EGG, RESERVE(S)
and loan association
    .... BANK, (MONEY)LENDER
bank .... SAVE-ALL
investments .... BONDS,
    LEGALS, PORTFOLIO
savior .... RESCUER, REDEEMER,
    LIBERATOR, JESUS(CHRIST)
financial .... PATRON,
    BENEFACTOR
savoir-faire .... TACT, POISE,
    DIPLOMACY
Savonarola, Ital. reformer
    .... GIROLAMO
savor .... AROMA, ENJOY, EAT UP,
    SAPOR, SMELL, TASTE, TINGE,
    FLAVOR, RELISH, SEASON,
    DELIGHT IN, SMACK (THE
    LIPS)
savorless .... FLAT
savory .... MINT, SALTY, SAPID,
    SIPID, TASTY, YUMMY,
    DAINTY, PIQUANT, DELICIOUS,
    FLAVORFUL, PALATABLE,
    TOOTHSOME, APPETIZING
smell .... AROMA
savoy .... CABBAGE
Savoyard show(man) ...... RAREE
savvy ...... CRAFT, SENSE, WISDOM,
    KNOW-HOW,
    UNDERSTAND(ING)
slang .... SMARTS
saw ...... CUT, RASP, REDE, ADAGE,
    GRATE, MAXIM, MOTTO,
    SAYING, PROVERB
blade .... WEB
cut of .... KERF

kind of .... RIP, BUCK, HACK,
    HAND, EDGER, CIRCULAR
notch .... KERF
sawfish's .... SERRA
surgical ..... TREPAN, TREPHINE
toothed .... SERRATE
sawbones: sl. .... SURGEON
sawbuck: sl. .... TEN(SPOT)
sawdust .... COOM, SCOBS
sawfish .... RAY
snout .... SERRA
sawfly .... HORNTAIL
sawhorse .... BUCK, TRESTLE
sawing frame .... HORSE
sawtooth .... SERRA
ridge .... SIERRA
sawtoothed .... RUNCINATE
sawyer ...... BEETLE, WOODCUTTER
Sax Rohmer character
    .... DOCTOR FUMANCHU
Saxe _____ .... COBURG
Coburg and Gotha
    .... WINDSOR
saxhorn .... TUBA
saxifrage .... SESELI, ROCKFOIL
Saxon .... ENGLISH, SASSENACH
Saxony .... YARN, SACHSEN
capital of .... DRESDEN
city .... ERFURT
say .... AVER, TELL, MOUTH,
    SPEAK, STATE, UTTER,
    AFFIRM, ALLEGE, DICTUM,
    RECITE, REPORT, DECLARE,
    MENTION
again .... REPEAT, RESTATE
"cheese" .... SMILE
further .... ADD
it's so .... AVER, AVOW
over .... ITERATE
repetitiously ..... HARP, CHANT
something meaningful
    .... TALK SENSE
"There, there" ...... COMFORT
under oath .... VOW, SWEAR,
    DEPOSE, TESTIFY
what you _____ .... MEAN
sayid .... SAID, FATIMID
saying .... MOT, SAW, ADAGE,
    AXIOM, GNOME, MAXIM,
    MOTTO, DICTUM, EPIGRAM,
    PROVERB, APHORISM
common .... BYWORD
wise .... GNOME, MAXIM
sayings attributed to
    Jesus(Christ) .... LOGIA
Sb in chemistry .... STIBIUM,
    ANTIMONY
scab .... SORE, CRUST, MANGE,
    ESCHAR, BLACKLEG,
    SCOUNDREL
slang .... FINK

scabbard .... CASE, PILCHER,
    SHEATH(E)
plate .... CHAPE
what it sheathes .... BOLO,
    SWORD, DAGGER, BAYONET,
    SCIMITAR
scabby .... LOW, BASE, MEAN,
    MANGY, SCALY, SCURVY
scabies ...... ITCH, MANGE, PSORA,
    PSORIASIS, INFESTATION
treatment .... LINDANE
scabrous .... FLAKY, MANGY,
    SCALY, RISQUE, SCABBY, OFF-
    COLOR, SALACIOUS
scad .... SKATE, SAUREL
scads .... GOBS, LOTS, TONS,
    OODLES, PLENTY
scaffold .... STAGE, GIBBET,
    RIGGER, GALLOWS, PLATFORM
scaffolding timber .... PUTLOG
scalawag .... SCAMP, RASCAL
scald .... BOIL, BURN, HEAT, SEAR,
    SCORCH, SEETHE
scale .... GO UP, CLIMB, FLAKE,
    GAMUT, PLATE, RATIO,
    WEIGH, DEGREE, ESCHAR,
    LAMINA, CLAMBER, LAMELLA,
    ESCALADE, GRADUATION
animal/plant .... SQUAMA
chaffy .... PALEA
charges .... TARIFF
horny .... SCUTUM
insect's secretion .... LAC
measuring .... VERNIER
model .... MOCK-UP
musical .... GAMUT
pointer .... TONGUE
skin off .... BLANCH
weighing .... STEELYARD
scales .... BALANCE
covered with .... LEPIDOTE,
    SQUAMATE, SQUAMOSE,
    SQUAMOUS
kind of .... BEAM, SPRING,
    COUNTER, TORSION, PLATFORM
the .... LIBRA
scaling ladder .... SCALOSE
of wall .... ESCALADE
scall .... SCURF
scallion .... LEEK, ONION,
    SHALLOT
scallop .... PINK, QUIN, BADGE,
    CRENA, NOTCH, WHELK,
    MUSSEL, MOLLUSK,
    CRENULATE, PERIWINKLE,
    CRENEL(L)ATE, CRENULATION
scalloped ...... CRENATE, NOTCHED
scalp .... EPICRANIUM
colloquial .... ROB, FLAY,
    PEEL, SKIN, CHEAT, GOUGE,
    STRIP, DEFEAT, FLEECE,

disease .... FAVUS, SCALL

disorder .... LICE, DANDRUFF

infant's crusty patch on

.... CRADLE CAP

muscle .... EPICRANIUS

preparation .... TONIC

to an Indian .... TROPHY

tumor .... WEN

scalpel .... KNIFE, LANCET,

BISTOURY

scalper .... INDIAN, PROFITEER,

SPECULATOR

scaly .... LOW, BASE, MEAN,

FLAKY, MANGY, SCABBY,

SCURFY, LEPROSE, SCABROUS,

SQUAMATE, SQUARROSE

bark .... PSOROSIS

coating .... SCURF

combining form ...... LEPID(O)

Scamander .... MENDERES

scammony .... RESIN

scamp .... ROGUE, RASCAL,

SCALAWAG, SPALPEEN,

SCOUNDREL, SCAPEGRACE

scamper .... RUN, DASH, RACE,

SCUD, SKIP, SCOOT, SCURRY,

BRATTLE

scampi .... PRAWN

scan ...... STUDY, SWEEP, GLANCE,

RECITE, ANALYZE, SCRUTINIZE

type of .... CAT

scandal .... SHAME, GOSSIP,

INFAMY, SLANDER, OUTRAGE,

DISGRACE

scandalize .... SHOCK, APPALL,

DEFAME, INSULT, MALIGN,

OFFEND, OUTRAGE

scandalmonger .... GOSSIP(ER),

BACKBITER, TALEBEARER

scandalous .... LIBELOUS,

SHAMEFUL, SHOCKING,

OFFENSIVE

scandent plant .... VINE

Scandinavian .... DANE, FINN,

LAPP, SWEDE, NORDIC,

NORSE(MAN), NORTHMAN,

SQUAREHEAD

chieftain .... JARL, RURIK

coin .... ORE, KRONA, KRONE

collection of myths ...... EDDA

country .... NORWAY, SWEDEN,

DENMARK, ICELAND

equivalent of Lawrence

.... LARS

explorer .... ERIC

folklore being .... TROLL

giantess .... URTH, WYRD

goblin .... NIS

god .... LOKI, THOR, ALFADIR

goddess .... HEL

heaven: myth. .... ASGARD,

ASGARTH

legend .... EDDA, SAGA

legislature .... T(H)ING

measure .... ALN, FOT, REF,

TUM, ALEN, FAMN, LINJE

monster .... KRAKEN

musician .... SKALD

name .... ERIC, NILS, OLAF,

SVEN

nation .... GEATAS

navigator .... ERIC

pirate/sea rover .... VIKING

plateau .... FJELD

poem .... EDDA, RUNE

poet .... SKALD

race of gods: myth. ..... AESIR

settler .... VARANGIAN

territorial division .... AMT

war deity .... TYR

weight .... LOD, ORT, MARK,

PUND, STEN, UNTZ, NYLAST,

LISPUND

scant .... FEW, SHORT, STINT,

MEAGER, SLIGHT, SPARSE,

EXIGUOUS, INADEQUATE

scantling .... BEAM, STUD, TIMBER

scanty .... SHORT, SMALL,

MEAGER, SCARCE, SPARSE,

SPARING

scape .... STALK

bearing .... SCAPOSE

scapegoat .... BUTT, TOOL, PATSY,

VICTIM, FALL GUY, WHIPPING

BOY

scapegrace .... ROUE, ROGUE,

SCAMP, RASCAL

scaphoid .... BOAT-SHAPED

scapolite .... SILICATE, WERNERITE

scar ...... PIT, CRAG, FLAW, MARK,

POCK, CLIFF, NAVEL,

BLEMISH, CICATRIX,

CICATRICE

scarab .... CHARM, BEETLE

scaramouche .... RASCAL,

BRAGGART, POLTROON

Scaramouche author

.... SABATINI

scarce .... FEW, DEAR, RARE,

SCANTY, UNCOMMON

in rainy weather .... CAB, TAXI

scarcely .... BARELY, HARDLY

scarcity .... LACK, DEARTH,

RARITY, PAUCITY, SHORTAGE

scare .... FEAR, ALARM, PANIC,

STARTLE, FRIGHT(EN)

off .... STOP, DAUNT

slang .... SPOOK

suddenly .... STARTLE

up .... PRODUCE

scarebabe of a sort .... OGRE

scarecrow ...... MALKIN, MAUKIN,

MAWKIN, BUGABOO,

MONSTER, STRAWMAN,

JACKSTRAW

stuffing .... STRAW

with grotesque features

.... GARGOYLE

scared .... AFRAID, TERRIFIED

scaredy-cat .... SISSY, COWARD

scarehead .... BANNER, HEADLINE,

STREAMER

scaremonger .... ALARMIST,

TERRORIST

scarf .... HOOD, SASH, VEIL,

ASCOT, TAPALO, TIPPET,

FOULARD, MUFFLER, NECKTIE,

MANTILLA, (NEC)KERCHIEF

clerical .... STOLE, TIPPET

cloth .... LUNGI, LUNGEE

fluffy/long .... BOA

head .... BABUSHKA

pope's .... ORALE

shoulder .... SASH, STOLE

sun helmet .... PUGGRY,

PUG(G)REE

woman's .... BOA, STOLE,

PEPLOS, MANTILLA

Scarface .... (AL)CAPONE

scarfskin ...... CUTICLE, EPIDERMIS

scarlatina .... FEVER

scarlet .... RED

bird .... TANAGER

cloak .... CARDINAL

fever .... SCARLATINA

woman: sl. .... HOOKER

Scarlett O'Hara's home

.... TARA

scarp .... SLOPE, DECLIVITY

Scarpia's nemesis .... TOSCA

scarum, _____ .... HARUM

scary creature .... OGRE

scat .... GIT, TAX, SCRAM

scathe ...... HARM, HURT, SCORCH,

LAMBASTE

scathing .... SEARING

scatter .... SOW, SHED, STUD,

STREW, DISPEL, LITTER,

DISPERSE, SPRINKLE,

DISSIPATE

by blowing .... WINNOW

for lost scent .... CAST

grass .... TED

scatterbrained ...... DAFT, DAFFY,

DIZZY, GIDDY, FLIGHTY,

FRIVOLOUS

scattered ...... STREWN, STUDDED,

SPORADIC

scattergood .... WASTREL,

PRODIGAL, SPENDTHRIFT

scattering of Jews ...... DIASPORA

scaup .... DUCK, REDHEAD,

OVERCHARGE

GRAYBACK, SHUFFLER, CANVASBACK

scavenge .... PICK, HUNT, RANSACK, SCROUNGE

scavenger .... HYENA

cry of .... CAW

fish .... WRASSE

scenario .... TEXT, SCRIPT, OUTLINE, LIBRETTO

scend .... TOSS, HEAVE, PITCH, BILLOW

scene .... SITE, VIEW, VISTA, LOCALE, SETTING, TABLEAU, TANTRUM, OUTBURST, SPECTACLE

scenery .... VIEW, VISTA, DIORAMA, PICTURE, PANORAMA, LANDSCAPE

chewer: sl. .... HAM

mover .... PROP(MAN)

natural .... LANDSCAPE

sceneshifter .... GRIP

scenic .... STAGY, DRAMATIC, PICTURESQUE

peninsula .... GASPE

representation .... DIORAMA

view .... SCAPE, VISTA, PANORAMA

scent .... CLUE, NOSE, ODOR, AROMA, SMELL, TRACK, TRAIL, DETECT, PERFUME, FRAGRANCE

animal's .... FOIL

bag .... SACHET

kitchen .... AROMA, NIDOR

left by animal .... DRAG, SPOOR

of wine .... BOUQUET

subtle .... AURA

scented .... OLENT

water ...... BAY RUM, COLOGNE

scepter .... ROD, MACE, WAND, BATON, STAFF, FERULA, WARDER, TRIDENT

Schacht, Ger. financier .... HJALMAR

Scharre, mimist .... ROLF

schedule .... BOOK, LIST, PLAN, TIME, SLATE, AGENDA, DOCKET, RECORD, CALENDAR, REGISTER, CATALOGUE, INVENTORY, TIME-TABLE

Scheherazade's life-saver .... TALES

Scheldt .... ESCAUT

schema .... PLAN, DIAGRAM, OUTLINE

schematic .... ANALYTICAL

scheme .... PLAN, PLOT, CABAL, DESIGN, DEVICE, METHOD, SYSTEM, OUTLINE, PROJECT,

PURPOSE, INTRIGUE

fraudulent .... SCAM

utopian .... BUBBLE

scheming .... CRAFTY, TRICKY, CUNNING, DECEITFUL

Schick, pediatrician .... BELA

Schicklgruber's son .... (ADOLF)HITLER

schipperke .... DOG

schism .... RENT, RIFT, SECT, SPLIT, DISSENT, FACTION, DIVISION, CONCISION, SECESSION, SEPARATION

schist .... ROCK, SLATE

schistosome .... FLUKE

schizocarp .... MAPLE, REGMA

schizoid person .... LONER

schizophrenia .... SPLIT PERSONALITY

drug treatment .... CHLORPROMAZINE

schizophrenic syndrome .... CATATONIA

Schlesien .... SILESIA

Schleswig-Holstein capital .... KIEL

canal .... NORD-OSTSEE

schnapps .... GIN

schnauzer .... DOG, TERRIER, PINSCHER

Schneider, actress .... ROMY

schnozzle .... NOSE

Schnozzola .... DURANTE

scholar .... SAGE, CLERK, PUPIL, MASTER, PANDIT, PUNDIT, SAVANT, LEARNER, STUDENT, CLASSICIST

assistant/attendant .... FAMULUS

half .... DILETTANTE

inferior .... PEDANT

literary .... HARMONIST

Moslem .... ULEM

overstudying .... BOOKWORM

scholarly ...... ERUDITE, LEARNED, STUDIOUS

paper .... THESIS

people .... LITERATI

scholars' association .... ACADEMY

scholarship .... AWARD, BURSE, BURSARY, SUBSIDY, LEARNING, PEDANTRY, ERUDITION, PHILOLOGY, FELLOWSHIP

scholastic ...... BOOKISH, ERUDITE, ACADEMIC, DOGMATIC, PEDANT(IC), STUDIOUS, LETTERED, CURRICULAR, PROFESSORIAL

scholiast .... ANNOTATOR

school .... SECT, ECOLE, LEARN, LYCEE, TEACH, TRAIN, LYCEUM, ACADEME, ACADEMY, COLLEGE, EDUCATE, INSTITUTE, UNIVERSITY

assignment .... LESSON

athlete .... LETTERMAN

athlete: sl. .... HOTSHOT

banner .... PENNANT

book .... TEXT, PRIMER, READER

boy .... LAD, PUPIL

boy, new .... SCUM

charge for instruction .... TUITION

children's .... NURSERY, KINDERGARTEN

courses offered, collectively .... CURRICULUM

eastern .... YALE, VASSAR, CORNELL, HARVARD, MARYMOUNT, RADCLIFFE

for training horses .... MANEGE

girl .... COED

graduation ceremony .... COMMENCEMENT

grounds .... CAMPUS, QUADRANGLE

group .... PTA

headmaster .... RECTOR, PRINCIPAL

honor society .... ARISTA

kind of .... HIGH, MUSIC, NIGHT, PUBLIC, COLLEGE, DANCING, PRIVATE, MILITARY, SUMMER, SEMINARY, FINISHING, ELEMENTARY, VOCATIONAL, PREP(ARATORY)

of bees .... SWARM, COLONY

birds .... FLOCK

fish .... SHOAL

locusts .... CLOUD

seals .... POD

thought .... ISM, LOGIC, THEORY

whales .... GAM, POD

official .... DEAN, PROVOST, PRINCIPAL, SUPERINTENDENT

official in charge of records .... REGISTRAR

partisan .... POLEMIST

quitter .... DROPOUT

riding .... MANEGE

student, high/college .... JUNIOR, SENIOR, FRESHMAN, SOPHOMORE

studies leading to a degree .... COURSE

supervisor .... PROCTOR

teacher .... MASTER,
    PROFESSOR, INSTRUCTOR
teaching staff .... FACULTY
term .... SEMESTER
term, of a .... TRIMESTRIAL
that one attended .... ALMA
    MATER
treasurer .... BURSAR
young women's, private
    .... SEMINARY
schooled .... (WELL-)VERSED
schooling .... LEARNING,
    EDUCATION
schoolmaster .... PEDANT,
    DOMINIE, PROCTOR, SNAPPER,
    TEACHER, PEDAGOGUE,
    INSTRUCTOR
rod of .... FERULE
schooner ...... SHIP, SAILS, WAGON
three-masted .... TERN
schorl .... T(O)URMALINE
schottish, dance like ...... POLKA
Schranz, Austrian skier
    .... KARL
Schubert, composer .... FRANZ
classic .... AVE MARIA
Schumann, composer .... ROBERT
well-known song ...... WARUM
Schumann-Heink, singer
    .... ERNESTINE
Schwarzenegger .... ARNOLD
film .... THE TERMINATOR, THE
    RUNNING MAN, KINDERGARTEN
    COP
wife of .... MARIA (SHRIVER)
Schweiz .... SWITZERLAND
sciatic area .... HIP
science .... ART, OLOGY, SKILL,
    STUDY, TECHNICS,
    KNOWLEDGE
applied .... TECHNOLOGY
attempting to explain the
    brain .... CYBERNETICS
combining form .... TECHNO
electrical .... MAGNETICS,
    ENGINEERING
fiction writer .... VERNE,
    ASIMOV
natural .... PHYSICS
of boxing .... FISTICUFFS
causes .... ETIOLOGY
crop production
    .... AGRONOMY
deciphering documents
    .... DIPLOMATICS
earthquakes ..... SEISMOLOGY
fruit cultivation
    .... POMOLOGY
government .... POLITICS
heard sound .... ACOUSTIC(S)

human behavior
    .... PSYCHOLOGY
law-making .... NOMOLOGY
life history of cells
    .... CYTOLOGY
medicine .... IATROLOGY
motion .... DYNAMICS,
    KINETICS, KINEMATICS
mountains .... OROLOGY
musical sounds
    .... HARMONICS
origins .... ETIOLOGY
plants .... BOTANY
public worship
    .... LITURGICS
soils .... AGROLOGY
versification .... PROSODY
vital statistics
    .... DEMOGRAPHY
words .... SEMANTICS
on freezing points
    .... CRYOSCOPY
on races .... EUGENICS,
    EUTHENICS
system of principles .... LOGIC
scientific .... EXACT, SOUND,
    ACCURATE
quack .... EMPIRIC
research animal ...... HAMSTER
routine .... TEST
study of trees
    .... DENDROLOGY
sub .... SEA LAB
scientist .... EXPERT, SAVANT,
    STARGAZER, SPECIALIST
ancient, "most brilliant"
    .... ARCHIMEDES
of bathysphere fame
    .... BEEBE
of Cairo, "mad" .... ALHAZEN
Sci-fi .... SCIENCE-FICTION
award .... HUGO
type .... ANDROID
scilicet .... TO WIT, NAMELY
scimitar ...... SAX, SABER, SWORD,
    RAPIER
scincoid .... SKINK
scintilla .... BIT, IOTA, WHIT,
    SPARK, TRACE, PARTICLE
scintillate .... FLASH, SHINE,
    GLISTEN, GLITTER, SPARKLE,
    TWINKLE
sciolist .... QUACK, PEDANT,
    AMATEUR, CHARLATAN
scion .... BUD, SON, HEIR, SLIP,
    TWIG, GRAFT, SHOOT, SPRIG,
    SPROUT, OFFSPRING,
    DESCENDANT
Scipio, Roman general
    .... AFRICANUS
victim of .... CARTHAGE,

    HANNIBAL
scirrhus .... TUMOR, CANCER
scission .... FISSION, DIVISION
scissorbill .... SKIMMER
scissors .... CUTTER, CLIPPER
kind of .... SURGICAL
-like instrument .... NIPPER,
    SHEARS
scissortail .... FLYCATCHER
sciurine animal .... MARMOT,
    RODENT, SQUIRREL
sclera, inflammation of the
    .... SCLERITIS
location of the .... EYE
softening of the
    .... SCLEROMALACIA
sclerite .... SPICULE
scoff .... GIBE, GIRD, JEER, JIBE,
    MOCK, RAIL, TWIT, FLEER,
    FLOUT, SCORN, SNEER,
    TAUNT, DERIDE, DISDAIN,
    LAUGH(AT), RIDICULE
scofflaw .... CROOK, FELON
scold .... JAW, NAG, FLAY, RAIL,
    CHIDE, FLITE, (BE)RATE,
    DERIDE, REBUKE, REVILE,
    REPROVE, UPBRAID,
    LAMBASTE
severely .... BLISTER
scolder .... BITCH, CARPER,
    MAGPIE, NAG(GER), BERATER
scolding .... EARFUL, TONGUE-
    LASHING
lengthy .... LECTURE
scombroid .... MACKEREL
sconce .... HUT, FORT, HEAD,
    SHED, SKULL, BRAINS,
    HELMET, SCREEN, BRACKET,
    BULWARK, FORTIFY, PROTECT,
    SHELTER
scone .... BISCUIT, (TEA)CAKE
scoop .... BEAT, ROUT, GOUGE,
    LADLE, SPOON, DIPPER,
    DIG(OUT), DREDGE, SHOVEL,
    TROWEL
slang .... EXCLUSIVE
scoot .... GO, HIE, RUN, DART,
    DASH, EXIT, DECAMP, SCURRY
scooter .... SAILBOAT, MOTORBOAT
scop .... BARD, POET
scope .... AREA, AMBIT, FIELD,
    RANGE, SPACE, SWEEP,
    EXTENT, SPHERE, LATITUDE
limited .... LOCAL
of an act or bill ...... PURVIEW
of authority .... POWER
Scopes' counsel
    .... (CLARENCE)DARROW
prosecutor .... BRYAN
trial reason .... EVOLUTION
trial venue .... DAYTON

scopolamine .... NARCOTIC
   effect .... DROWSINESS
scopulate .... BRUSHLIKE
scorch .... BURN, CHAR, SEAR,
   SERE, PARCH, SCALD, SINGE,
   TOAST, SCATHE, WITHER,
   BLISTER, SHRIVEL, CRITICIZE
scorcher .... HOT DAY, SPEEDER
score .... TAB, DEBT, MARK,
   CHALK, NOTCH, TALLY,
   GRUDGE, RATING, REASON,
   RECORD, TWENTY, ACCOUNT,
   SCRATCH
scoreless .... NO GOAL
   hold .... BLANK
scoria .... AA, LAVA, SLAG, DROSS
scorn .... MOCK, SCOFF, SPURN,
   CONTEMN, DESPISE, DISDAIN,
   CONTEMPT, DERISION
scorpine .... HOGFISH
scorpion .... WHIP, SCOURGE,
   ARACHNID, VINEGARROON
   claw .... CHELA
   fish .... LAPON
   number of legs .... EIGHT
   pain caused by .... STING
   poison reservoir of .... TAIL
Scorpio's brightest star
   .... ANTARES
Scot .... TAX, GAEL, LEVY, KILTIE,
   SCOTCHMAN
Scotch .... CUT, MAIM, BLOCK,
   CRUSH, NOTCH, SCORE,
   WEDGE, HINDER, STIFLE,
   STINGY, WHISKY
   companion, sometimes
   .... SODA, WATER
   for one .... BROTH
   sheepdog .... SHELTIE
scoter .... COOT, DUCK, EIDER
Scotia .... MOLDING, SCOTLAND
Scotland .... SCOTIA
   ancient tongue of ...... GAELIC
   capital of .... EDINBURGH
   capital's poetic name
   .... EDINA
   largest lake of .... LOCH
   LOMOND
   legendary beast of
   .... LOCHNESS
   Roman name of
   .... CALEDONIA
scotoma .... BLIND SPOT
Scot's nickname .... MAC
Scotsman .... SANDY, BLUECAP
Scott, black .... DRED
   hero: 1812 war and Mexican
   war .... WINFIELD
   novel .... IVANHOE
   poem .... MARMION
Scottish .... CALEDONIAN

absent .... AWA
accuse .... DELATE
ache .... WARK, STOUND
active .... YAULD
ago .... SYNE
alas .... OCHONE
alder tree .... ARN
alderman .... BAILIE
ale/beer .... YILL, NAPPY
alley .... WYND
assembly signal .... SLOGAN
attempt .... ETTLE
attendant .... GILLY, GILLIE
awl .... ELSEN
awry .... AGL(E)Y
bagpipe music .... PIBROCH,
   CORONACH
bailiff .... REEVE
bank .... BRAE
barren .... YELD
barter .... TROKE
bay ...... LUCE, BROAD, ENARD,
   DUNNET, LAGGAN, WIGTOWN,
   GRUINARD, SINCLAIR'S
beef cut .... SEY
beg .... SORN
beggar .... RANDY
belly .... WAME
biscuit .... SCONE
blastie .... DWARF
blaze .... INGLE
blow .... BLAW, DEVEL
bold .... CROUSE
boor .... TYKE
bound .... STEND
boundary .... MEAR
box/chest .... KIST
boy .... LOON
brandy .... ATHOLE
breeches .... TREWS
broadsword .... CLAYMORE
brook .... SIKE
broth .... BREE, BROO
brow of hill .... SNAB
bucket .... STOOP, STOUP
burden .... BIRN
burn .... STREAM
bushel .... FOU
buxom .... SONSIE
cake .... SCONE, BANNOCK
canal ...... CALEDONIAN, FORTH
   AND CLYDE
cap/hat .... BALMORAL,
   GLENGARRY,
   TAM(-O-SHANTER)
cape .... WRATH, RUDH RE
cascade .... LINN
cat .... MALKIN
catch .... KEP
cattle .... NOWT
channel .... NORTH, SCAPA

   FLOW
charm .... CANTRIP
cheese .... KEBBOK
chemise .... SARK
child .... WEAN, BAIRN
church .... KIRK
churl .... CARLE
city/town .... AYR, PERTH,
   TROON, DUNDEE, IRVINE,
   AIRDRIE, FALKIRK, GLASGOW,
   PAISLEY, RENFREW, ABERDEEN,
   DUMFRIES, GREENOCK,
   HAMILTON, LARKHALL,
   STIRLING, DUMBARTON,
   EDINBURGH, INVERNESS,
   KIRKCALDY, SALTCOATS,
   LIVINGSTON
clan chief .... THANE
cleanser .... SAIP
clothe .... CLEAD
codfish .... GLASHAN
coin ..... DEMY, LION, BAUBEE,
   BAWBEE
comb .... KAME
congress .... MOD
corner .... NEUK
corpse .... LICH
countrified .... HODDEN
county .... AYR, BUTE, FIFE,
   ANGUS, PERTH, NAIRN,
   MORAY, BANFF, ARGYLL,
   LANARK, ORKNEY, BERWICK,
   KINROSS, PEEBLES, RENFREW,
   SELKIRK, ZETLAND, ABERDEEN,
   INVERNESS, MIDLOTHIAN
court officer .... MACER
cow .... RUNT, CRUMMIE
crab .... PARTAN
cravat .... OVERLAY
craw .... CRAG
crowd .... MEINY, MEINIE
cry of blame .... DIRDUM
cuckoo .... GOWK
cuddy .... FOOL, DONKEY
cup .... TASS
curlew .... WHAUP
cut .... SNEG
dagger .... SKEAN
dairymaid .... DEY
daisy .... GOWAN
darling .... DAUTIE
deception .... BROGUE
dell .... SLACK
devil .... DEIL, MOHOUND
dining room .... SPENCE
dirge .... CORONACH
dish .... HAGGIS
dismal .... OORIE
disordered .... UNRID
district ...... MAR, PARK, APPIN,
   ATHOL, COWAL, LEWIS,

623

LORNE, SLEAT, ARGYLL, ASSYNT, BUCHAN, HARRIS, MORVEN, ARDGOUR, BRAEMAR, CARRICK, GARIOCH, MOIDART, RANNOCH, BADENOCH, GALLOWAY, KNAPDALE, LOCHABER
do .... DAE
dog .... SEALYHAM
dolt .... GOWK, GOMERAL
donkey .... CUDDY
dramatist .... BARRIE
dwarf .... BLASTIE
ear .... LUG
earnest money .... ARLES
earth .... YIRD
else .... ENSE
empty .... TOOM
endure .... DREE
exchange .... NIFFER
explorer .... RAE
extent .... STENT
extra .... ORRA
eyes .... EEN
factor .... BAILIFF, STEWARD
fair .... TRYST
faithful .... LEAL
fall of rain .... ON-DING
falls .... SHIN
farm worker .... HIND, ORRAMAN
farmer .... COTTAR, COTTER, CROFTER
fellow .... WAT, CARL(E), CALLAN(T)
festivity .... KIRN
few .... WHEEN
fine/first-rate .... WALLY
fireplace .... INGLE
firth .... TAY, CLYDE, KYLE, FORTH, LORNE, MORAY, SOLWAY, DORNOCH, CROMARTY, PENTLAND
fold .... WIMPLE
fool .... GOMERAL
fox .... TOD
friend .... EME
game .... SHINTY
garment .... SARK
girl .... QUEAN, CUMMER, LASSIE
glimmer .... STIME
go .... GAE, GANG
goblet .... TASS
godmother .... CUMMER
goldsmith .... GED
good .... GUDE
good-for-nothing .... ORRA
gooseberry .... THAPRES
guillotine .... MAIDEN
gulf .... BISM

gypsy .... CAIRD
hag .... CARLINE
haggle .... PRIG
hamlet .... CLACHAN
handsome .... SONSY, SONSIE
hare .... MALKIN, MAUKIN
hawk .... ALLAN
head .... POW
headwear .... TAM
heath .... MUIR
heir .... TEIND
hellside hollow .... CORRIE
Highlander .... CELT, GAEL
hill .... DOD(D), INCH
hill(side) .... BRAE
hills .... OCHIL, LENNOX, SIDLAW, CHEVIOT, CUILLIN, MOORFOOT
historian .... HUME
hoe .... PADLE
holiday .... VACANCE
hut .... BOTHY
inlet .... GIO
inventor .... WATT
island .... HOY, RUM, BUTE, EDAY, EIGG, HOLY, IONA, JURA, MUCK, MULL, RONA, SEIL, SOAY, ULVA, UNST, WYRE, YELL, ARRAN, BARRA, CANNA, FOULA, GIGHA, ISLAY, LUING, SANDA, SCARP, SHONA, SWONA, TIREE, BURRAY, FETLAR, PABBAY, PLADDA, RAASAY, ROUSAY, STROMA, BERNERA, ERISKAY, GOMETRA, LISMORE, INCH(CAPE), MAINLAND, INCHKEITH
islands ..... ORKNEY, FLANNAN, HEBRIDES, SHETLAND
jackdaw .... KAE
jade .... YAUD
jail/prison .... TOLBOOTH
keen .... GLEG
kilt .... FILIBEG
kindle .... LUNT, TIND
kindred .... SIB
king .... BRUCE
kiss .... PREE
knowledge .... KENNING
laborer .... HIND
lake .... AWE, EIL, LIN, TAY, LOCH, EARN, NESS, SHIN, GARRY, LEVEN, LOCHY, LOYAL, MAREE, SHIEL, ARKAIG, ERICHT, LOMOND, QUOICH, KATRINE, RANNOCH
lake dwelling .... CRANNOG
land, flat .... LINKS
land tax .... CESS
landholder ...... LAIRD, THANE, THEGN

language .... ERSE, GAELIC, LALLAN(S)
lark .... LAVEROCK
legally excessive .... ENORM
light .... LICHT
list of candidates .... LEET
little .... SMA
lively .... CROUSE
locker .... KIST
long ago .... LANG SYNE
lord .... THANE
love .... LOE
lowland .... CARSE
lowlander .... SASSENACH
Lowlands .... LALLAN
lucky .... SONSIE
magic spell .... CANTRIP
magistrate .... BAILIE, PROVOST
marauder ...... CATERAN, MOSS TROOPER
mare .... MEER, YAUD
market .... TRYST
match .... LUNT
mathematician .... NEPER, NAPIER
Mayday .... BELTANE
measure .... CRAN, LIPPY, FIRLOT, CHALDER
miscellaneous .... ORRA
mist .... URE, DROW
money .... SILLER
more .... MAIR
mortgage .... WADSET
mountain .... BEN LUI, MORVEN, ASKIVAL, BATTOCK, BEN AVON, BEN MORE, BEN MHOR, CARN BAN, CLISHAM, MERRICK, BEN ALDER, BEN NEVIS, CARN EIGE, GOAT FELL, PEEL FELL, BEN LAWERS, LOCHNAGAR, BEN MACDHUI
mountains .... GRAMPIAN, CAIRNGORM, MONADHLIATH
much .... MICKLE, MUCKLE
mud .... GLAR
municipal official .... BAILIE
musical instrument
.... BAGPIPE
must .... MAUN
myself .... MASEL
national emblem .... THISTLE
native .... CELT, GAEL, CALEDONIAN
neck .... CRAG
negative .... NAE, DINNA
New Year's eve
.... HOGMANAY
nimble .... YAULD
no .... NAE
oatmeal dish .... BROSE

odd .... ORRA
once .... ANES
one .... AIN, ANE, YIN
otherwise .... ENSE
outcry of blame .... DIRDUM
own .... AIN, ANE
ox .... NOWT, RUNT
oxter .... ARMPIT
pail .... STOUP, COGGIE
pain .... WARK, STANG,
                                    STOUND
parlor .... BEN
pay for a killing .... CRO
peak .... NEVIS
peasant/tenant .... COTTAR,
                    COTTER, CROFTER
peep .... KEEK
peninsula .... RHINNS,
    KINTYRE, MACHERS, ROSS OF
                                    MULL
people driven from Great
        Britain .... PICT
pert .... CROUSE
philosopher .... HUME, CAIRD
physicist .... BAIRD
pig .... GRICE
pipe .... CUTTY
pirate/privateer .... KIDD
plaid .... MAUD, TARTAN
pleasant .... DOUCE
pocket .... POUCH
poet ..... HOGG, BURNS, EDINA,
                                DUNBAR
pole .... CABER
poll .... POW, HEAD
pool .... CARR, LINN
porridge .... BROSE, SOWENS
port .... OBAN
pottage .... BROSE
pouch .... SPORRAN,
                            SPLEUCHAN
praise .... ROOSE
prank .... CANTRIP
precipitation .... SNA
prefix to names .... MAC
presently .... NOO
pronunciation .... BURR
pudding .... SAUSAGE
puzzle .... KITTLE
rafter .... SILE
ragged .... DUDDY, DUDDIE
reef .... SKERRY
region .... FIFE, ORKNEY,
    BORDERS, CENTRAL, LOTHIAN,
    TAYSIDE, GRAMPIAN,
                                SHETLAND
relish .... GUST
require .... NEID
resort .... OBAN
river ...... AYR, DEE, DON, ESK,
    TAY, AVON, DOON, EARN,

EDEN, ISLA, LYON, NITH, OICH,
    SPEY, TYNE, ANNAN, ARDLE,
    CLYDE, FORTH, GLASS, NAIRN,
    NAVER, ORCHY, OYKEL,
    SPEAN, TEITH, TWEED, YTHAN,
    ALMOND, BEAULY, CARRON,
    TEVIOT, THURSO, YARROW,
    DEVERON, FINDHORN,
    MORISTON, STINCHAR
river land .... CARSE
rivulet .... RINDLE
robber .... CATERAN
robbery .... REIF
rock .... SKERRY
rock projection .... SNAB
rope .... WANTY
rosin .... ROZET
rowboat .... COBLE
rug .... MAUD
Satan .... DEIL, HORNIE
scholarship .... BURSE
schoolmaster .... DOMINIE
scold .... THREAP
scone .... FARL(E)
scratch .... RIT
sea .... HEBRIDES
seaport .... AYR, DUNDEE,
    ABERDEEN, GREENOCK
seize .... VANG
seldom .... SINDLE
self .... SEL
servant .... GILLY, GILLIE
sharp .... GLEG, SNELLY
shawl .... MAUD
shelter .... BIELD
shirt .... SARK
silver .... SILLER
simpleton .... GOWK
since .... SYNE
sister .... TITTY, TITTIE
skirt .... KILT
small/wee .... SMA
smart .... STOUND
smoke .... LUNT
snow .... SNA
snowfall .... ON-DING
soldier .... KERN(E)
spell .... CANTRIP
spirit .... BANSHEE
sponge .... SORN
squall .... BLEFFERT
stomach .... KYTE
stream .... BURN
stretch out .... STENT
student scholar .... BURSAR
stumble .... STOT
suffer .... DREE
supple .... WANDLE
sweetheart .... JO(E)
sword .... SKEAN, CLAYMORE
tap .... TUCK

tartan pattern ...... SETT, PLAID
taste .... GUST, PREE
tatter .... TAVER
tea cake .... SCONE
tedious .... DREE
tern .... TARRET
terrier .... SKYE, CAIRN,
                                SEALYHAM
theologian .... DUNS
thicket .... RONE
throat .... CRAG
thumb .... THOOM
tickle .... KITTLE
tinker .... CAIRD
toad .... TADE
tobacco pouch ..... SPLEUCHAN
toes .... TAES
topper .... TAM
torch .... LUNT
tower .... PEEL
town .... BUR(G)H
toy .... WALLY
trade .... TROKE
tribal payment .... CRO
trick .... BROGUE
trousers .... TREWS
true .... LEAL
turnip .... NEEP
tuyere .... TEW
twang .... TIRL
uncanny .... UNCO
uncle .... EAM, (Y)EME
underwear .... TREWS
urge .... ERT
vagabond .... WAFF
vagrant .... CAIRD
valley ...... SLACK, TROSSACHS,
                        STRATH(MORE)
vex .... FASH
vigor .... VIR
village .... REW
violet .... BLAVER
vulgar .... RANDY
walk .... GO
water spirit ..... KELPY, KELPIE
waterfall .... LYN, LIN(N)
wear under kilts .... TREWS
weeds .... WRACK
weighing machine ...... TRONE
weight ..... BOLL, DROP, TRONE
whether .... GIN
whirlpool .... WEEL
whiskey .... ATHOL(E),
    MOUNTAIN DEW, USQUEBAUGH
witch .... CARLINE
woman .... RANDY, CUMMER,
                            CARLINE
woman, unmarried ..... QUEAN
womb .... WAME
world .... WARL
worse .... WAUR

worthless .... WAUF
wrap .... MAUD
wrestle .... WARS(T)LE
yawn .... GANT
yell .... GOWL
scoundrel .... CAD, BASE, SCAB,
KNAVE, ROGUE, SCAMP,
BEGGAR, RASCAL, VARLET,
VILLAIN, DECEIVER,
REPROBATE
scour .... RUB, RAKE, SAND,
FLUSH, PURGE, SCRUB, SKIRR,
ABRADE, POLISH, SCRAPE,
SEARCH, CLEANSE, FURBISH,
LOOK OVER
scourer .... CATHARTIC
scourge .... BANE, BELT, FLAY,
FLOG, LASH, WHIP, CURSE,
SLASH, STRAP, PLAGUE,
PUNISH, TORMENT, SCORPION,
AFFLICTION
of clothing .... MOTH
of God .... ATTILA
of serge .... LINT
scouring rush .... HORSETAIL
scout ...... GUY, SPY, SCOFF, SPIER,
FELLOW, REJECT, SPOTTER,
DO-GOODER, OBSERVER,
RIDICULE, FORERUNNER,
TENDERFOOT, RECONNOITER
boat .... VEDETTE
group .... DEN, PACK, TROOP,
PATROL
scow .... BARGE, LIGHTER,
FLATBOAT
puller .... TOWBOAT,
TUG(BOAT)
scowl .... LOUR, MOUE, FROWN,
(G)LOWER, GRIMACE
scrabble .... PAW, DOODLE,
SCRAPE, SCRAWL
scrag ...... HANG, NECK, GARROTE,
THROTTLE
scraggly .... JAGGED, RAGGED,
UNKEMPT
scram ...... GIT, LAM, SCAT, SHOO,
BEAT IT, VAMO(O)SE, GET
LOST
scramble .... TEAR, CLIMB, MIX
UP, SWARM, JUMBLE, TUSSLE,
CLAMBER, RAT RACE,
SCUFFLE, STRUGGLE
in football .... RUN,
MANEUVER
scrambled .... PIED, GARBLED
scrannel ...... LEAN, THIN, SLIGHT,
SQUEAKY, SHRIVELED
scrap .... BIT, END, ORT, FIGHT,
PIECE, SHRED, MORSEL,
TATTER, DISCARD, JUNK(RAG),
ODDMENT, QUARREL,

ARGUMENT, FRACTION,
FRAGMENT, LEFTOVER
glass .... CULLET
hunt for .... SCAVENGE
of paper only, sometimes
.... PACT, TREATY
scrapbook .... ALBUM
scrape ...... FIX, RUB, RAKE, RASP,
BRUSH, GRATE, GRAZE, GRIDE,
GRIND, SCOUR, SCUFF, SHAVE,
ABRADE, PLIGHT, SCRATCH,
PREDICAMENT
along .... MANAGE, SURVIVE
bottom .... SCOUR, DREDGE
ground in golf .... SCLAFF
leaves off the grass ...... RAKE
together .... GATHER,
ASSEMBLE
scraped linen .... LINT
metal .... FILING
scraper, strings .... FIDDLER,
GUITARIST
water .... SQUEEGEE
scraping .... SHAVING
act of .... RASURE
scrapman .... JUNKMAN
scrapper .... BATTLER, FIGHTER
scrappy .... GAME, PATCHY,
SPOTTY, SKETCHY,
PUGNACIOUS
scraps ...... MEMENTOS, CLIPPINGS,
SOUVENIRS
literary .... ANA
scratch .... RUB, GASH, RAKE,
RASP, CHAFE, ERASE, GRATE,
DEFACE, REJECT, SCRAPE,
SCRAWL, LACERATE, SCRIBBLE
Scratch, Old .... DEVIL
scratching ground for food
.... RASORIAL
scratchy .... ITCHY
scrawl .... DOODLE, SCRIBBLE
scrawny .... BONY, LEAN, PUNY,
THIN, SCRAGGY
unkempt creature .... SCRAG
screak .... SCREECH
scream .... CRY, WAIL, YELL,
SHRIEK, SQUALL, SCREECH,
CATERWAUL
comics style .... EEK
screamer .... HEADLINE
black-necked .... CHAVARIA
crested .... TORQUATA
horned .... ANHIMA CORNUTA
scree ...... STONE, TALUS, PEBBLE,
RUBBLE
screech .... CRY, SCREAM, SHRIEK
screechy .... SHRILL
screed .... EDGING, SPEECH,
TIRADE, HARANGUE
screen .... HIDE, MASK, SIFT, VEIL,

BLIND, PAVIS, SHADE, GRILLE,
MOVIES, SCONCE, SHIELD,
SHROUD, CURTAIN, NETTING,
SECLUDE
altar/chancel .... REREDOS
bar .... MULLION
bulletproof .... MANT(E)LET
canvas .... PAVESADE
chimney .... BONNET
for concealment/protection
.... BLINDAGE
making material .... VETIVER
mesh .... SIEVE
wall .... PARTITION
wind .... PARAVENT
screening .... TESTING
screw .... JACK, TURN, MISER,
TWIST, SALARY, TIGHTEN,
PROP(ELLER)
part .... THREAD
pine tree .... PANDANUS
relative .... NAIL
slang .... JAILER
thread .... HELIX
threader .... CHASER
up .... FOUL UP, BOTCH UP
screwball .... PITCH
slang .... NUT
screwy .... ODD, CRAZY,
PECULIAR, ECCENTRIC
scribble .... DASH(OFF), WRITE,
DOODLE, SCRAWL
scribbler .... HACK
scribe .... CLERK, AUTHOR,
WRITER, PENMAN, SCRIVENER,
SECRETARY, AMANUENSIS
biblical .... BARUCH
scrimmage .... FIGHT, MELEE,
AFFRAY, TUSSLE
scrimp .... SKIMP, STINT, SCANTY,
ECONOMIZE
scrip .... BAG, LIST, WALLET,
SATCHEL, WRITING,
CERTIFICATE
script .... RONDE, SERTA,
DIALOGUE, LIBRETTO,
SCENARIO, PENMANSHIP,
HANDWRITING
scriptural ...... SACRED, BIBLICAL,
APOSTOLIC
analysis .... EXEGESIS
interpreter .... EXEGETE
scripture(s) .... BOOK, BIBLE,
ITALA, KORAN, SUTRA,
TORAH, ALCORAN
interpretation of ..... ANAGOGE
passage .... TEXT
reader .... LECTOR
scrivener .... NOTARY, SCRIBE,
COPYIST, AMANUENSIS
scrivener's palsy .... WRITER'S

CRAMP
scrobiculate .... PITTED
scrod .... CODFISH
scrofula .... STRUMA, KING'S EVIL
scroll ...... LIST, ROLL, MEMORIAL,
SCHEDULE
of Ionic capitals .... VOLUTE
shaped .... TURBINATE
tablet like .... CARTOUCH(E)
scromboid fish .... CERO
Scrooge .... EBEN, MISER
before reforming .... MEANIE
word .... BAH
scrouge .... CROWD, PRESS,
SQUEEZE
scrounge .... EKE, PILFER, SPONGE
scrub .... MOP, RUB, MEAN, POOR,
SWAB, BRUSH, SCOUR, SMALL
scrubber .... CHARWOMAN
scrubbing implement .... MOP
scruff .... NAPE, NUBIA, NUQUE
scrunch .... CHEW, CRUSH,
CRUMPLE
scruple .... DOUBT, QUALM,
MISGIVING
scrupulous .... EXACT, MORAL,
HONEST, CAREFUL, CORRECT,
FINICAL, PRECISE, UPRIGHT,
RELIGIOUS, METICULOUS,
PUNCTILIOUS
scrutinize .... CON, EYE, SEE,
SCAN, VIEW, PROBE, PERUSE,
EXAMINE, INSPECT
scrutiny .... SCAN, REVIEW,
SURVEY, PERUSAL,
INSPECTION
of financial records ..... AUDIT
Scuba enthusiast .... DIVER
fishing .... SPEARING
gear .... MASK, TANK,
SNORKLE
scud .... RUN, SKIM, GLIDE
Scud destroyer .... PATRIOT
scuff .... BRUSH, SCRAPE, SHUFFLE,
SLIPPER
mark .... SCAR
scuffle .... FRAY, BRAWL, FIGHT,
MELEE, FRACAS, STRIFE,
TUSSLE, SHUFFLE, STRUGGLE
scull .... OAR, ROW, SHELL,
PADDLE, PROPEL, WHERRY,
(RACING)BOAT
sculler .... OARER, BOATMAN,
OARSMAN
scullery, content of .... PANS,
POTS, DISHES, UTENSILS
equipment .... DISHWASHER
scullion .... WRETCH, SERVANT
sculpin .... BULLHEAD,
HARDHEAD, ROCKFISH, SEA
RAVEN

sculptor .... ARTIST, CARVER,
MOLDER, MODELER,
STATUARY, STONECUTTER
abstract .... CALDER
famous:
American
.... (GUTZON)BORGLUM,
(ALEXANDER)CALDER,
(DANIEL CHESTER) FRENCH
American (born in Ireland)
.... SAINT-GAUDENS
American (born in
Lithuania)
.... (JACQUES)LIPCHITZ
American (born in
Sweden)
.... (CARL)MILLES
Athenian .... PRAXITELES
British .... (HENRY)MOORE,
(JACOB)EPSTEIN
Florentine
.... (LORENZO)GHIBERTI,
(LUCA)DELLA ROBBIA
French .... (JEAN)ARP,
(AUGUSTE)RODIN,
(ARISTIDE)MAILLOL
Greek ...... SKIPAS, BRYAXIS,
LEOCARES, PH(E)IDIAS,
TIMOTHEOS
Italian .... DONATELLO,
MICHELANGELO,
(NICOLA)PISANO,
(BENVENUTO)CELLINI
Romanian ..... (CONSTANTIN)
BRANCUSI
Spanish .... (PABLO) PICASSO
Swiss .... (ALBERTO)
GIACOMETTI
framework of .... ARMATURE
of Mount Rushmore
.... BORGLUM
The Colossus of Rhodes
.... CHARES
The Statue of Zeus
.... PH(E)IDIAS
The Temple of Artemis
.... KING CROESUS
The Thinker .... RODIN
tool of .... BURIN, POINT,
PUNCH, TORCH, CHISEL,
GRAVER, ROCKER, STYLE(T),
CALIPER, SPATULA
woman .... SCULPTRESS
work of .... BUST, TORSO,
STABILE, STATUARY,
STATUE(TTE)
sculpture .... CARVING,
(PLASTIC)ARTS,
STONECUTTING
earliest .... STONE AGE
VENUSES

famous .... PIETA, PARTHENON,
THE PHAROS, MOUNT
RUSHMORE, STATUE OF
LIBERTY, GREAT WALL OF
CHINA, THE PYRAMIDS (OF
GIZA)
head to chest .... BUST
medium ..... GEM, WAX, CLAY,
WOOD, SHELL, STONE,
BRONZE, MARBLE, PLASTICINE,
TERRA COTTA
on gems .... GLYPTICS
on wood .... XYLOGRAPHY
piety personified in .... ORANT
style of .... GROTESQUE
sculptured ...... CARVED, CARVEN,
GRAVEN, MOLDED, GLYPHIC,
CHISELED
animal/person .... STATUE
design on a gem
.... GLYPTOGRAPH
gem/shell .... CAMEO
in low relief .... ANAGLYPH
oval ornament
.... MEDAL(LION)
work in metal .... TOREUTIC
scum .... SKIM, ALGAE, DROSS,
SPUME, REFUSE, PELLICLE
of society .... RIFF-RAFF
rid of .... SKIM, DESPUMATE
scup .... FISH, BREAM, PORGY,
BURGOO, SPAROID
kin of .... GRUNT, SNAPPER
scupper .... DRAIN
scuppernong .... WINE, GRAPE,
MUSCADINE
scurf .... SCALL, FURFUR,
DANDRUFF
scurfy .... FLAKY, MANGY,
SCABBY, LEPROSE, LEPIDOTE
scurrilous ...... COARSE, VULGAR,
ABUSIVE, OFFENSIVE, FOUL-
MOUTHED, THERSITICAL
scurry .... RUN, DART, DASH,
RACE, SCOOT, HASTEN,
SCAMPER, HIGHTAIL
scurvy .... LOW, MEAN, VILE,
NASTY, DISEASE
caused by deficiency of
_____ .... VITAMIN C
scut .... TAIL
work, describing ...... MENIAL,
ROUTINE, TEDIOUS
scutage .... TAX
Scutari .... LAKE, SHKODER,
USKUDAR
scutellate .... ROUND
scutter .... BUSTLE
scuttle ...... HOD, RUN, FLEE, PAIL,
SINK, SCOOP, BASKET,
BUCKET, ESCAPE, SCURRY,

627

DESTROY, SCAMPER, HATCHWAY

scuttlebutt .... RUMOR, GOSSIP, HEARSAY

scutum .... SHIELD, PLATELET

plural of .... SCUTA

Scylla .... ROCK

and Charybdis personification .... MONSTERS

whirlpool opposite .... CHARYBDIS

scye .... ARMHOLE

scyphozoan .... JELLYFISH

scythe bearer .... DEATH

cut, one stroke .... SWATH

handle .... NIB, SNEAD, SNATH(E)

sharpener .... STRICKLE

sweep of .... SWATH

sea .... DEEP, MAIN, MARE, WAVE, OCEAN, SWELL, BILLOW

anemone .... POLYP, ACTINIA

animal, fishlike .... LANCELET, AMPHIOXUS

arm .... BAY, GULF, LAKE, FIORD, FIRTH, FRITH, LOUGH, ESTUARY

bass .... JEWFISH

bat .... DEVILFISH

beast .... MOBY DICK

bird .... MEW, ERN(E), GULL, SHAG, SKUA, TERN, EIDER, NODDY, SCAUP, SOLAN, FULMAR, GANNET, PETREL, PUFFIN, SCOTER, KASTREL, ALBATROSS, CORMORANT

biscuit/bread .... HARDTACK

born goddess .... APHRODITE

borne .... AFLOAT

bottom .... BED, FLOOR

calf .... SEAL

coast .... SHORE, STRAND, LITTORAL

cock ..... PEG, VALVE, STOPPER

cow .... DUGONG, WALRUS, MANATEE, SIRENIAN, HIPPOPOTAMUS

creature, legendary .... MERMAN, MERMAID

cucumber .... TREPANG, HOLOTHURIAN

devil .... RAY, SHARK, OCTOPUS, ANGELFISH

disaster aid device ...... SOFAR

dog .... GOB, TAR, SEAL, SAILOR, MARINER

duck ...... COOT, EIDER, SCAUP, SCO(O)TER

eagle .... ERN(E), TERN, OSPREY

ear .... ABALONE

east of the Caspian ...... ARAL

elephant .... SEAL

fan .... CORAL

farer .... MAORI, SAILOR, MARINER, FISHERMAN

foam .... SPUME, MEERSCHAUM

fox .... SHARK

god .... LER, AEGIR, NEREUS, TRITON, NEPTUNE, PROTEUS, POSEIDON

grave .... LOCKER

greeting .... AHOY

gull .... MEW, COB(B), KITTIWAKE

heavy .... RACE

hog .... PORPOISE

holly .... ERINGO, ERYNGO

horse .... WALRUS, HIPPOCAMPUS

inhabitant: myth. .... MERMAN, MERMAID

inland .... ARAL

inlet .... RIA, FIORD, FJORD

jettison, temporary ..... LAGAN

lands beyond the .... OUTREMER

lawyer .... SAILOR

lettuce .... ULUA, LAVER

lily .... CRINOID

lion .... SEAL

marker .... DAN, BUOY

mew .... GULL

mile .... KNOT, NAUT

monster .... KRAKEN, LEVIATHAN

near the/on the ...... MARITIME

needle .... GAR(FISH)

nettle .... MEDUSA, ACALEPH, JELLYFISH

nymph .... NAIAD, SIREN, NEREID, THETIS, CALYPSO

of the .... NAVAL, MARINE, PELAGIC, MARITIME, NAUTICAL, THALASSIC

onion .... SQUILL(A)

pen .... POLYP

personified .... NEPTUNE

poetic .... FOAM

prefix .... MARI

put to .... SAIL

raven .... SCULPIN

robber .... PIRATE, CORSAIR, PICAROON, BUCCANEER, PRIVATEER

robin .... GURNARD

rock .... SKERRY

route .... LANE

rover .... PIRATE, SAILOR, JASON, SEAMAN, VIKING, MARINER, ARGONAUT

serpent .... ELAPS, OARFISH

shell .... MOLLUSK

shell, Pacific .... NETTED CONE

shell with curved edge .... SCALLOP

slug .... TREPANG

snail .... W(H)ELK

soldier .... MARINE, SAILOR

spot at .... ISLE(T)

spray .... SPINDRIFT

squirt ..... ASCIDIAN, TUNICATE

surface movement ...... LIPPER

swallow .... TERN, PETREL

swooper .... GULL

tangle .... SEAWEED

trip .... CRUISE

unicorn .... NARWHAL

urchin ...... ECHINUS, ECHINOID

wall .... JETTY, BREAKWATER

water .... BRINE

with many islands .... ARCHIPELAGO

wolf .... PIRATE, BLENNY

Seabee's concern .... HARBOR, AIRFIELD

seaboard .... COAST

seaflower .... POLYP, ANEMONE

seafood delicacy .... ORMER

seal .... DIE, BULLA, CLOSE, SIGIL, STAMP, CACHET, FASTEN, RATIFY, SECURE, SIGNET, INITIAL, PINNIPED, BLADDERNOSE

bottle/tube .... CAPSULE

Christmas .... STAMP

cut skin of .... FLENSE

eared .... OTARY, SEA LION

fur .... URSAL, SEECATCH

hooded .... BLADDERNOSE

hunter .... SWILER

kind of .... EARED, WAFER

large .... SEA LION

letter .... CACHET

male .... SEECATCH

off .... TRAP

point .... SIAMESE CAT

Pope's .... BULL

rawhide .... SHAGREEN

skin .... FUR, PELT

sound of .... BARK

tusked .... WALRUS

with lead .... PLUMB

young .... PUP, CALF, HARP

sealed completely ...... HERMETIC

sealer .... PUTTY, SWILER, CA(U)LKER

sealing agent .... LUTE

material .... GLUE, TAPE, PASTE, MUCILAGE, WAX(WAFER)

wax ingredient .... LAC

seals, breeding place of .... ROOKERY

flock of .... POD

pertaining to .... PHOCINE

sealskin .... SCULP

seam .... LINE, PURL, SCAR, JOINT, LAYER, RIDGE, FURROW, SUTURE, WRINKLE, JUNCTURE

fill up .... CALK

filling material .... TAR, OAKUM

tapered .... DART

seamaid .... NYMPH, SIREN(A), MERMAID

seaman .... GOB, TAR, SALT, JACKY, RATING, SAILOR, MARINER, SEAFARER

rating of .... ABLE

seamark .... DAN, BUOY, BEACON, PHAROS, LIGHTHOUSE

seamen's chapel .... BETHEL

seamstress .... SEWER, TAILOR, STITCHER, SEMPTRESS

seamy .... SHADY, SORDID

seance .... COUNCIL, MEETING, SESSION, SITTING, SPIRITUALISM

noise .... RAP

participant .... MEDIUM, SPIRITUALIST

recording device .... OUIJA

seaplane .... AEROBOAT, FLYING BOAT

stabilizer .... SPONSON

sear .... BURN, SERE, BRAND, BROWN, DRY(UP), PARCH, SINGE, BRAISE, HARDEN, SCATHE, SCORCH, WITHER

search .... HUNT, SEEK, TEST, DELVE, GROPE, PROBE, QUEST, FERRET, FORAGE, EXPLORE, LOOK FOR, RANSACK, RUMMAGE

deeply .... DREDGE

diligently .... SCOUR

for food .... FORAGE

for Holy Grail .... QUEST

for mineral .... PROSPECT

for talent .... SCOUT

party of a sort .... POSSE

person's person .... FRISK

steadily .... MOUSE

thoroughly .... COMB

with divining rod .... DOWSE

with "out" .... FERRET

searching .... KEEN, SHARP, PENETRATING

Seas predecessor .... SEVEN

seashore .... BEACH, COAST, STRAND, WATERFRONT

of the .... LITTORAL

seasickness ...... NAUSEA, MAL DE MER, MOTION SICKNESS

seaside strip .... BOARDWALK

structure .... WHARF

season .... AGE, CORN, CURE, FALL, SALT, TIME, IMBUE, INURE, SPICE, SPELL, FLAVOR, HARDEN, PERIOD, SPRING, SUMMER, TEMPER, WINTER

in .... AVAILABLE

dry .... SUMMER

rainy .... MONSOON

yield of .... VINTAGE

seasonable .... TIMELY, SUITABLE, OPPORTUNE

seasonal .... PERIODIC

employees .... SANTAS

observation .... VERNAL EQUINOX, AUTUMNAL EQUINOX

phenomenon .... SUMMER SOLSTICE, WINTER SOLSTICE, DAYLIGHT LESSENS

symbol .... SNOW, HOLLY, PUMPKIN, SWALLOW

time ..... FALL, LENT, AUTUMN, EASTER, SPRING, SUMMER, WINTER, CHRISTMAS

seasoned .... TRIED, MATURE, MELLOW, SOFTENED, TEMPERED

seasoning .... SAGE, SALT, HERBS, ONION, GARLIC, SPICES, MUSTARD, CONDIMENT

leaf .... BAY, LAUREL

pod .... CHILI

seasons .... HORAE

four .... YEAR

seat .... SITE, SOFA, BENCH, CHAIR, PERCH, STOOL, CENTER, CHAISE, GRADIN, SEDILE, SETTEE, INSTALL, OTTOMAN, VIS-A-VIS

bishop's ...... SEE, METROPOLIS

chair's .... BOTTOM

coach .... DICKY

colloquial .... RUMP, BUTTOCKS

for a judge .... BANC

high .... ROOST

mobile .... WHEELCHAIR

of a sort .... SADDLE

of early Irish kings ...... TARA

of government .... CAPITAL

of judgment .... TRIBUNAL

of power .... THRONE

on camel/elephant .... HOUDAH, HOWDAH

royal .... THRONE

seating area, at times ...... AISLE

SEATO .... TREATY

seats, church .... PEW, SEDILIA

seawall .... JETTY, BREAKWATER

se(a)wan .... WAMPUM

seaward .... OFF

away from the wind .... LEEWARD

toward the wind .... WINDWARD

seaweed .... AGAR, ALGA(E), KELP, FUCUS, LAVER, VAREC, MOSS, FUCOID, LICHEN, TANGLE, REDWARE, GULFWEED, SARGOSSO, SEA LETTUCE, NULLIPORE, SARGASSUM

edible ..... AGAR, LIMU, DULSE, LAVER, TANGLE, CARRAG(H)EEN

extract/product .... AGAR(AGAR)

genus .... ALARIA

leaflike part .... FROND

red .... FUCUS

red-purplish .... CARRAG(H)EEN

soda ash .... BARILLA

washed ashore .... WRACK, SEAWARE

with fluted ribbonlike blades .... LAMINARIA

seaworm .... SAO, LURG

seaworthy .... BOLD, SNUG, STURDY, STA(U)NCH, WATERTIGHT

sebaceous .... OILY, FATTY

glands secretion .... SEBUM

glands disorder .... SEBORRHEA

matter .... FAT, TALLOW

sec .... DRY, BRUT, INSTANT

secant .... CROSSED, CROSSING, DIAGONAL, INTERSECTING

secede .... BOLT, SEPARATE, WITHDRAW

secern .... SECRETE, SEPARATE, DISTINGUISH

secessionist .... BOLTER, APOSTATE, SEPARATIST

Seckel .... PEAR

seclude .... IMMURE, RETIRE, SCREEN, CONFINE, ISOLATE

secluded .... REMOTE, PRIVATE, SHUT OFF, HERMITIC, ISOLATED, SEQUESTERED

religious place .... CONVENT, CLOISTER

safe, quiet place ...... RETREAT

spot .... DEN, NOOK

valley .... GLEN

seclusion .... PRIVACY, SOLITUDE, (H)ERMITISM, ISOLATION, QUARANTINE

second .... ABET, AID(E), JIFFY,

TRICE, BACK(ER), MOMENT, INSTANT, STAND-IN, ASSISTANT

as of time to wink .... TWINKLING

best .... RUNNER-UP

brightest star .... BETA

childhood .... DOTAGE, SENILITY

estate .... NOBILITY

growth crop .... ROWEN

-guess .... ANTICIPATE

lieutenant: sl. .... SHAVETAIL

look .... REVIEW, RECHECK

mentioned .... LATTER

nature .... HABIT, CUSTOM

of two .... LATTER

person .... YOU

placer ..... ALSO-RAN, RUNNER-UP

-rate .... LESSER, INFERIOR, MEDIOCRE

self .... ALTER EGO

sight .... INTUITION

smallest sovereign state .... MONACO

story man .... BURGLAR

string .... RELIEF, RESERVE, SUB(STITUTE), BENCH-WARMER

team .... SCRUB

thought ...... CHANGE OF MIND, MISGIVING

to first, sometimes .... DOUBLE-PLAY

to none .... FIRST, UNIQUE, PEERLESS, MATCHLESS

secondary .... BYE, MINOR, INFERIOR, RESULTANT

disease .... METASTASIS

secondhand .... OLD, USED, WORN, HEARSAY, INDIRECT

dealer ..... RAGMAN, JUNKMAN, SCRAPMAN

secque .... SHOE

secrecy .... PRIVACY, COVERTNESS, CONFIDENTIALITY

fraudulent .... DECEPTION

of identity .... INCOGNITO

of withholding name .... ANONYMITY

secret ...... INNER, PRIVY, ARCANE, COVERT, HIDDEN, OCCULT, ARCANUM, CRYPTIC, MYSTERY, VEILED, PRIVATE, UNDERHAND

action .... PROWL, STEALTH, STALKING

adviser's group .... CAMARILLA

agent .... SPY, OPERATIVE

agent's work .... ESPIONAGE

colloquial .... HUSH-HUSH

date .... TRYST

device/plan .... STRATAGEM, SUBTERFUGE

discussion .... HUDDLE

file on a person .... DOSSIER

government information/ reports, designation of .... CLASSIFIED

identity .... INCOGNITO

meaning, having a .... RUNIC

meeting .... CONCLAVE

most .... TOP, INMOST, RESTRICTED

murder, e.g. ..... DARK HIDDEN ACT

place .... HIDEOUT, RETREAT, SANCTUM

remedy .... ELIXIR

service .... INTELLIGENCE

society .... BUND, PORO, TONG, MAF(F)IA, CAMORRA, BLACKHAND, KU KLUX KLAN (KKK)

watch ...... SPYING, ESPIONAGE, SURVEILLANCE

writing .... CODE

secretary .... DESK, CLERK, STENO, AMANUENSIS, ESCRITOIRE

abbreviation .... SECY

bird .... SERPENTARIUS

bird's prey .... SNAKES, INSECTS, RODENTS

Ollie's document-shredding .... (FAWN) HALL

public .... SCRIBE

secrete .... HIDE, MASK, CACHE, STASH, SECERN, CONCEAL

secretion .... SAP, BILE, LATEX, MUCUS, SUDOR, SWEAT, SALIVA, CHALONE, EXUDATION

cells/glands .... MUCUS, SEBUM, ENZYMES, HORMONES

liver .... BILE

secretive ...... SLY, DARK, SHIFTY, EVASIVE, FURTIVE, RETICENT, STEALTHY, CLOSE (-MOUTHED)

secretly ...... SLYLY, SUBROSA, ON THE SLY, UNDERHAND

secrets .... PENETRALIA, SKELETONS IN THE CLOSET

sect .... CULT, PARTY, SCHOOL, FACTION, FOLLOWING, DENOMINATION

early Christian .... DOCETAE

sectarian .... BIGOTED, APOSTATE, PARTISAN, FACTIONAL

sectary .... DISSENTER, NON-

CONFORMIST

section .... LEG, PART, GROUP, PORTION, SEGMENT, DIVISION

book .... INDEX, CHAPTER, GLOSSARY

city .... ZONE

of a country .... REGION

secular .... LAY, LAIC(AL), EARTHLY, MUNDANE, WORLDLY, TEMPORAL

secund .... UNILATERAL

secundine .... AFTERBIRTH

secure .... GET, FIRM, HOLD, MOOR, NAIL, SAFE, SNUG, SURE, BELAY, GUARD, ANCHOR, FAST(EN), INSURE, STABLE, ACQUIRE

a door again .... REBOLT

a sail .... TRICE

place .... FORT, VAULT, FASTNESS, SANCTUARY, STRONGHOLD

tightly .... TRUSS

security ...... BOND, GAGE, GRITH, PLEDGE, SAFETY, SURETY, WARRANTY, GUARANTEE, SAFEGUARD, PROTECTION

against loss .... INSURANCE

for payment .... BOND, LIEN, COLLATERAL

interest .... LIEN

money, binding .... DEPOSIT, EARNEST

object .... TOY, BLANKET

on property .... TITLE DEED

sedan .... CHAIR, (CLOSED)CAR, LIMOUSINE, AUTOMOBILE

sedate .... CALM, GRAVE, QUIET, SOBER, STAID, DEMURE, SERENE, SERIOUS, COMPOSED

sedation .... CALMNESS

sedative .... DRUG, OPIATE, AMYTAL, ANODYNE, BROMIDE, CALMANT, CODEIN(E), DEMEROL, LUMINAL, BARBITAL, HYPNOTIC, NARCOTIC, URETHAN(E), PAINKILLER

sedentary ...... PASSIVE, INACTIVE

Seder, event commemorated by .... EXODUS

sedge .... REEDS

clump .... TUSSOCK

sediment .... LEES, OOZE, SILT, DRAFF, DREGS, FOOTS, GROUT, MAGMA, SLUDGE, RESIDUE

sedimentary .... RESIDUAL

deposit layer .... VARVE

sedition .... TREASON, INSURGENCE

seduce .... LURE, TEMPT, BETRAY, ENAMOR, ENTICE, DEBAUCH, MISLEAD, PERSUADE
seducer .... VAMP, SIREN, LECHER, ENTICER, CASANOVA, LOTHARIO, DON JUAN, PHILANDERER
seductive .... WINNING, ALLURING, CHARMING, BEGUILING
sedulous .... BUSY, DILIGENT, ASSIDUOUS, INDUSTRIOUS
sedum .... STONECROP
see ...... ESPY, MEET, NOTE, VIEW, VISIT, BEHOLD, DESCRY, DISCERN, OBSERVE, WITNESS, PERCEIVE, COMPREHEND
bishop's .... DIOCESE, METROPOLIS
head of a .... BISHOP
slow to .... PURBLIND
socially .... DATE
See! .... LO AND BEHOLD
seed .... SOW, BEAN, CORN, GERM, CAUSE, GRAIN, OVULE, SPERM, ORIGIN, PIP(PIN)
again .... REGROW
aromatic .... TONKA, CUM(M)IN, GUAIAC, ANISE(ED)
bearing organ .... PISTIL
bud .... PLUMULE
case .... POD, BUR(R), CYPSELA
coat .... ARIL, BRAN, HULL, HUSK, TESTA, TEG(U)MEN
combining form .... SPERM, SPERMAT(O)
container ...... PIT, POD, STONE
cover, false .... ARILLODE
edible .... PEA, BEAN, CORN, GRAIN, PINON, PULSE, LENTIL, SOYBEAN, PISTACHIO
flavoring .... ANISE, CUM(M)IN, CARAWAY
food .... PEA, SOY, BEAN, LEGUME, LENTIL, SESAME, COQUITO
hole-making tool .... DIBBLE
immature .... OVULE
integument/covering ..... ARIL, BRAN, HUSK
leaf .... COTYLEDON
lense-shaped .... LENTIGO
like .... SEMINAL
oil-yielding .... TILL, BENNE, SESAME, GINGELI, GINGILI, CHAULMOOGRA
one-celled .... CARPEL
oyster .... SPAT
pear/orange .... PIP
plant .... HERB, EXOGEN
plant dust .... POLLEN
pod .... CYPSELA

poisonous .... NUX VOMICA
prematurely produce ..... BOLT
remove .... GIN, RIPPLE
remover .... GIN, RIPPLER
rudimentary .... OVULE
scar(s) .... HILUM, HILA
spice ..... NUTMEG, CARDAMON
stalk .... FUNICULUS
strong-smelling ..... CARAWAY
vessel .... BUR, POD, SILICLE, CAPSULE, PERICARP
wings .... ALAE
seeded .... SOWN
seedless .... AGAMOUS
plant .... FERN
seedling .... SAPLING
seeds: comb. form .... CARPO
row of planted .... DRILL
study of .... CARPOLOGY
seed(s)man .... SOWER
seedy .... TACKY, SHABBY, RUNDOWN, RAMSHACKLE
seeing .... SIGHT, VISION
eye dog .... GUIDE
seek .... TRY, HUNT, PURSUE, ATTEMPT, EXPLORE, REQUEST, ENDEAVOR, SEARCH(FOR)
information .... INQUIRE
pleadingly/earnestly
.... SOLICIT
to accomplish a goal
.... ASPIRE
seel .... BLIND, HOODWINK, STITCH UP
seeled bird .... HAWK, FALCON
seely .... POOR, FRAIL, TRIFLING
seem .... LOOK, APPEAR, RESEMBLE
seeming .... SHOW, QUASI, EVIDENT, OUTWARD, APPARENT, OSTENSIBLE
seemingly .... QUASI
endless .... VAST
true .... PLAUSIBLE
seemliness .... DECENCY, DECORUM, PROPRIETY
seemly ...... FAIR, MEET, COMELY, DECENT, PROPER, FITTING, BECOMING, DECOROUS, SUITABLE
seen, can be .... VISIBLE, DISCERNIBLE, MATERIALIZE, PERCEPTIBLE
seep .... DRIP, LEAK, OOZE, EXUDE, TRICKLE, PERMEATE, PERCOLATE
seer .... ORACLE, PROPHET, ARUSPEX, SOOTHSAYER
stock in trade of .... OMENS
woman .... SIBYL, SEERESS, CASSANDRA, PROPHETESS

seersucker .... LINEN, FABRIC
characteristic of ..... CRINKLED
seesaw .... WAG, FLAP, TILT, WAVER, TESTER, BASCULE, CROSSRUFF, VACILLATE, TEETER (-TOTTER)
seethe .... BOIL, SOAK, STEW, STEEP, BUBBLE, SIMMER, AGITATE, FERMENT
seething .... ABOIL, ANGRY, FUMING, EBULLIENT
segment .... PART, SLICE, BRANCH, MEMBER, SECTOR, PORTION, SECTION, DIVISION
of crustacean .... TELSON
sego .... LILY, PLANT
segregate .... SEVER, DIVIDE, EXCLUDE, ISOLATE, SECLUDE, SET APART, SEPARATE
segregation, racial
.... APARTHEID, DISCRIMINATION
seidel .... MUG
seigneur .... LORD, NOBLE
Seine .... NET, RIVER
city on the .... ROUEN, TROYES
tributary .... EURE, OISE, MARNE
Seinfeld character .... ELAINE
seism .... EARTHQUAKE
seismograph subject .... QUAKE, TREMOR, TEMBLOR
seize .... NAB, GRAB, LASH, TAKE, GRASP, ARREST, ATTACK, CLUTCH, COLLAR, CAPTURE, CONFISCATE
first .... PREEMPT
for debt .... GARNISH, DISTRAIN
for official use
.... COMMANDEER
in law .... LEVY
power, etc. .... USURP
property as security
.... SEQUESTER
seizure ...... FIT, ATTACK, STROKE, CAPTURE, CONVULSION, CONFISCATION
recurrent .... EPILEPSY
type of .... PARTIAL, GRAND MAL, PETIT MAL
selachian .... RAY, SHARK, DOGFISH
Selassie, Emperor .... HAILE
country of .... ETHIOPIA
sobriquet of .... LION OF JUDAH
seldom .... RARELY
select .... OPT, CULL, WALE, ELECT, CHOOSE, PICK(ED), PREFER

631

by elimination .... SCREEN
group .... ELITE, EXCLUSIVE
selectee .... DRAFTEE, RECRUIT,
INDUCTEE
selection .... CHOICE, OPTION,
PREFERENCE
of one out of two
possibilities
.... ALTERNATIVE
selective service .... DRAFT
Selene ...... LUNA, MOON, HECATE,
ARTEMIS
love of .... ENDYMION
selenite .... GYPSUM
self .... I, EGO, BEING,
PERSONA(LITY)
addressed item ...... ENVELOPE
assertive person .... WISE GUY,
SMART ALEC(K)
assurance ...... POISE, APLOMB,
CONFIDENCE
centered .... SELFISH,
EGOCENTRIC
combining form .... AUTO
conceit .... PRIDE, EGOISM,
VANITY, EGOTISM
conceited person .... EGOIST,
EGOTIST
confidence .... PANACHE
confident .... COCKY, PROUD,
POISED, ASSURED, (COCK)SURE
conscious .... COY, SHY,
TIMID, DEMURE, AWKWARD
contained .... INDEPENDENT
control, power of .... WILL
cremation .... SUTTEE
defense art ..... JUDO, KARATE,
JUJITSU, JUJUTSU
denial .... SACRIFICE
denying .... MONASTIC
destruction .... SUICIDE,
IMMOLATION
determination ...... FREE WILL,
AUTOMATION
esteem .... PRIDE, EGOISM,
VANITY
evident .... AXIOMATIC
explanatory .... CLEAR,
OBVIOUS
fertilization .... ORTHOGAMY
governing .... AUTONOMOUS
government .... HOME RULE
immolation .... SUICIDE
importance .... VANITY,
POMPOSITY
important ..... VAIN, POMPOUS,
ARROGANT, BUMBLING,
BUMPTIOUS, OVERPROUD
important person .... NIBS,
EGOIST, EGOTIST
love .... NARC(ISS)ISM

possessed .... CALM, COOL,
COMPOSED
possession .... APLOMB
propelled .... AUTOMOTIVE
protection .... DEFENSE
reliant .... DEPENDABLE
reproach .... REMORSE,
REPENTANCE
restraint .... MODERATION,
TEMPERANCE
righteous .... SMUG
sacrificing .... DEDICATED,
UNSELFISH
salesman .... EGOTIST
satisfied .... SMUG,
COMPLACENT
service .... PUMP YOUR GAS,
FIX YOUR OWN PLATE
serving .... GREEDY, SELFISH
winding .... AUTOMATIC
selfheal .... SANICLE
selfish .... MEAN, VENAL,
WORLDLY, SELF-CENTERED
one .... EGOIST
sell .... DEAL, DUPE, HAWK, VEND,
OFFER, TRADE, BARTER,
MARKET, PEDDLE, AUCTION,
DISPOSE OF
for ..... BRING, FETCH, REALIZE
out .... BETRAY
short .... BELITTLE,
DOWNGRADE
tickets illegally .... SCALP
seller .... COSTER, DEALER,
VENDOR, PEDDLER,
MERCHANT, RETAILER
on installment ...... TALLYMAN
sellout .... HIT, SMASH,
CLEARANCE
sign .... SRO
Selm .... LAGERLOF
selvage .... HEM, LIST, BORDER
semantics, concern of
.... MEANING
semasiology .... SEMANTICS
semblance .... COPY, GUISE,
IMAGE, ASPECT, LIKENESS,
PRETENSE
seme .... DOTTED
Semele's father .... CADMUS
son .... DIONYSUS
semester .... TERM, HALF-YEAR
seminar .... SYMPOSIUM,
DISCUSSION
Seminole chief .... OSCEOLA
semiology, subject of ...... SIGNS,
SYMPTOMS
Semiramis' husband .... NINUS
kingdom .... BABYLON
semisolid substance .... GELATIN
Semite .... JEW, ARAB, HEBREW,

BABYLONIAN, PHOENICIAN
god .... STERAPH
Semitic language .... PUNIC,
ARABIC, HEBREW, ARAMAIC,
AMHARIC
people .... CHALDEAN,
BABYLONIAN
tribe .... AMMON
vampire .... LILITH
semolina .... MEAL
"Semper Fidelis" .... ALWAYS
FAITHFUL
composer .... SOUSA
is U.S. Marine Corps' ____
.... MOTTO
Semple McPherson, ____
.... AIMEE
sempstress ...... SEWER, STITCHER,
SEAMSTRESS
sen, 1/10 of a .... RIN
senate .... ASSEMBLY,
LEGISLATURE
gofer .... PAGE
house .... CURIA
senator .... SOLON, LAWMAKER,
LEGISLATOR
send .... DRIVE, REMIT, FORWARD,
DISPATCH, TRANSMIT
abroad .... EXPORT
another message .... REWIRE
as signals .... EMIT
back .... REMIT, RETURN,
REMAND, REPATRIATE
flying .... ROUT
for .... SUMMON
forth .... EMIT
out .... ISSUE, DESPATCH,
DISPATCH
packing .... OUST, DRIVE,
DISMISS
up supplications ...... PRAY TO
send-off .... FAREWELL
Seneca .... CAYUGA, INDIAN,
IROQUOIAN
senega .... MILKWORT
Senegal cape .... VERDE
capital .... DAKAR
city/town .... KOLDA, LOUGA,
M'BOUR, THIES, KAOLACK,
DIOURBEL, SAINT-LOUIS,
ZIGUINCHOR
ethnic group .... PEUL, WOLOF,
SERERE
language .... MENDE, WOLOF,
FRENCH, FULANI, MANDINGO
monetary unit .... FRANC
president .... SENGHOR
region .... FERIO
river .... FALEME, GAMBIA,
SENEGAL, CASAMANCE
senescent .... AGING

seneschal ...... KAY, MAJOR-DOMO
senhor .... MR., SIR, (GENTLE)MAN
senile .... AGED, DOITED, ELDERLY
senility .... DOTAGE, OLD AGE
senior .... OLDER, ELDER, SUPERIOR
citizen .... RETIREE, OLD-TIMER
class publication ..... ANNUAL, YEARBOOK
member of group .... DEAN, DOYEN
seniority .... RANK, PRIORITY, PRECEDENCE
senna ...... PEA, PLANT, LAXATIVE
family .... LEGUME
source of .... CASSIA
sennet .... FLOURISH
sennight .... WEEK
señor ...... MR., SIR, (GENTLE)MAN
señora .... MRS., LADY, MADAM
señorita .... LADY, MISS
sensate ...... ESTHESIA, CONSCIOUS
sensation .... HIT, FEELING, EXCITEMENT, IMPRESSION, PERCEPTION
abnormal ..... PAIN, NUMBNESS
of touch .... THRILL
pins and needles .... TINGLING
that does not involve thought
.... SENTIENCE
sensational ...... LURID, EXCITING, SHOCKING, STARTLING, THRILLING
sensationalism .... PUFFERY, BALLYHOO, MELODRAMATICS
sense .... SIGHT, SMELL, TASTE, TOUCH, INTUIT, VISION, FEEL(ING), HEARING, MEANING, PERCEIVE, SAPIENCE, FEEL IN ONE'S BONES
of hearing disorder
.... DEAFNESS, TINNITUS
of sight .... OPTIC
of smell .... OLFACTION
of smell disturbance
.... ANOSMIA
of taste .... GUSTATION
organ .... EAR, EYE, NOSE, FEELER, PALP(US), ANTENNA, RECEPTOR, TASTE BUD
sixth .... ESP, INTUITION
sound .... LOGIC
senseless ...... MAD, INANE, INEPT, SILLY, ABSURD, STUPID, WANTON, UNWISE, FATUOUS, FOOLISH, IRRATIONAL, UNCONSCIOUS
senses, one of the .... SIGHT, SMELL, TASTE, TOUCH, VISION, HEARING, INTUITION

the five .... SENSORIUM
sensible .... KEEN, SANE, WISE, ACUTE, ALERT, AWARE, VIVID, PASSIBLE, RATIONAL, REASONABLE, LEVEL-HEADED
sensitive .... RAW, SORE, ALERT, AWARE, TENSE, PLIANT, TENDER, TE(T)CHY, TOUCHY, SENTIENT, CONSCIOUS
extremely .... TICKLISH
favorably .... RECEPTIVE
plant .... MIMOSA
sensitivity .... ERETHISM
to dust or pollen ..... ALLERGY
to strong light
.... PHOTOPHOBIA
sensual .... LEWD, CARNAL, LYDIAN, LUSTFUL, SYBARITIC
sensualist .... SYBARITE, LIBERTINE
sensuous .... EMOTIONAL, EPICURIAN, VOLUPTUOUS
sentence .... DOOM, OPINION, DECISION, JUDGMENT, STATEMENT, EXPRESSION
break down .... PARSE
mark .... COLON, COMMA, PERIOD
part ...... NOUN, VERB, PHRASE, SUBJECT, PREDICATE
reading same backward
.... PALINDROME
slang .... RAP
structure .... SYNTAX
sententious .... CURT, PITHY, LACONIC, POINTED, MORALISTIC
sentient .... ALIVE, FEELING, CONSCIOUS
sentiment .... BELIEF, EMOTION, FEELING, OPINION, PASSION, ATTITUDE, FONDNESS
sentimental .... GUSHY, MUSHY, SOPPY, SPOONY, MAUDLIN, MAWKISH, ROMANTIC, EMOTIONAL, NAMBY-PAMBY
sentimentalism .... SCHMALTZ
sentimentality, kind of
.... BEERY, NOSTALGIA
slang .... CORN, MUSH
sentinel .... GUARD, PICKET, SENTRY, WATCH(DOG)
mounted .... LOOKOUT, VEDETTE, VIDETTE
sentry .... GUARD, WATCH, BIVOUAC, SENTINEL
box .... BOOTH
challenge of .... WHO GOES THERE
challenge of French .... QUI VA LA

order of .... HALT
Seoul .... KEIJO
sepal .... LEAF, CALYX
separate ...... PART, SORT, SEVER, SPLIT, DETACH, DIVIDE, SECEDE, SECERN, ISOLATE, SEVERAL, ALIENATE, DISCRETE, DISTINCT, DISUNITE, INSULATE, SET APART, SEGREGATE
checks .... DUTCH TREAT
coarse from fine particles
.... SIFT
forcibly .... REND, SUNDER, WRENCH
from military service
.... DISCHARGE
in botany .... SOLUTE
into filaments .... SLEAVE
into parts .... DISMEMBER
metal from ore .... EXTRACT
threads .... RAVEL
useless undesirables ..... WEED OUT
separately .... APART
separation .... SCHISM, BREAK(-UP), DIVORCE, PARTING, SPLIT-UP, AVULSION, ISOLATION, SECESSION
center .... RENO
from employment
.... SEVERANCE
in chemistry .... DIALYSIS
separatist .... DISSENTER, NON-CONFORMIST
separator .... WALL, SEPTUM, BARRIER
of two continents ...... BERING STRAIT
Sephardic dialect .... LADINO
Sephardim .... JEWS
sepia .... DUN, PIGMENT, BROWNISH, CUTTLEFISH, (REDDISH-)BROWN
sepiolite .... MEERSCHAUM
seppuku .... SUICIDE, HARAKIRI
seps .... SKINK, SNAKE
sept .... CLAN, TRIBE
septal defect .... HOLE IN THE HEART
type of .... ATRIAL, VENTRICULAR
September 13, Roman
calendar .... IDES
septic .... POISONED, INFECTIVE
tank .... CESSPOOL
septicemia .... SEPSIS, BLOOD POISONING
consequence of .... SEPTIC SHOCK
septime .... PARRY

633

septum .... WALL, PARTITION
nasal .... CARTILAGE
septuple .... SEVENFOLD
sepulcher .... BURY, TOMB,
CRYPT, GRAVE, VAULT,
RELIQUARY, SEPULTURE
sepulchral ...... DISMAL, GLOOMY,
FUNEREAL, TOMBLIKE
sepulture .... BURIAL, SHRINE,
INTERMENT, MAUSOLEUM
pharaohs' .... PYRAMIDS
sequel .... EFFECT, UPSHOT,
OUTCOME, AFTERMATH,
CONTINUATION
sequence .... RUN, ORDER,
SEQUEL, SERIES, SUCCESSION
sequester .... SEIZE, ENISLE,
CONFINE, ISOLATE, SECLUDE,
SEPARATE, SET APART,
SEGREGATE, CONFISCATE
sequestered .... RETIRED,
ISOLATED, SECLUDED,
CLOISTERED
sequin ...... SPANGLE, ZECCHIN(O)
sequoia .... REDWOOD
seraglio .... HAREM, SERAI,
PALACE, ZENANA
segment .... ODA
serai .... INN, KHAN, IMARET,
SERAGLIO, CARAVANSARY
Serang .... CERAM
serape .... SHAWL, BLANKET
seraph .... ANGEL, CHERUB
seraphic .... ANGELIC
Serapis' temple .... SERAPEUM
site of .... ALEXANDRIA
Serb .... SLAV
Serbian former capital .... NIS
guerrilla .... CHETNIK
language .... BALKAN
measure .... RIF
sere ...... DRY, DRIED, WITHER(ED)
serein .... RAIN
serenade .... WOO, COURT,
NOCTURNE, SERENATA,
ENTERTAIN
mock .... SHIVAREE,
CHARIVARI
the moon .... BAY
serendipity .... GOOD LUCK
serene ...... CALM, QUIET, PLACID,
EQUABLE, COMPOSED,
TRANQUIL, IMPASSIVE
serenity .... PEACE, REPOSE,
CALMNESS
serf .... ESNE, HELOT, LITUS,
SLAVE, THRALL, BONDMAN,
VILLEIN
female .... NEIF
liberate a .... MANUMIT
serfdom ...... BONDAGE, HELOTRY,

SLAVERY
sergeant .... NCO, SARGE,
NONCOM, TOPKICK
at-law's cap .... BIGGIN
fish .... COBIA, ROBALO
slang .... GUNNY
serial .... EPISODIC
seric .... SILKEN
sericeous .... DOWNY, SILKY
series .... RUN, SET, CYCLE,
STRING, SEQUENCE,
SUCCESSION
of columns .... COLONNADE
of links .... CHAIN
of six .... HEXAD
of stairs .... FLIGHT
of steps .... SCALE
of trouble .... GA(U)NTLET
serin .... FINCH
serious ...... GRIM, GRAVE, SOBER,
SEDATE, SOLEMN, SOMBER,
EARNEST, LIFE AND DEATH,
ALARMING, CRITICAL
reserved .... STAID
sermon .... HOMILY, SPEECH,
LECTURE, DISCOURSE
sermonize .... PREACH
sermons, study of
.... HOMILETICS
serous .... WATERY
membrane .... PERITONEUM
serow .... JAGIA, ANTELOPE
serpent .... ASP, BOA, SEPS,
(A)BOMA, ELAPS, SATAN,
SNAKE, VIPER, DRAGON,
BASILISK, OPHIDIAN,
COCKATRICE
fabulous and deadly
.... COCKATRICE
harmless .... GARTER SNAKE
like a .... OPHIDIAN
monster .... ELOPS, HYDRA,
LAMIA
nine-headed .... HYDRA
slain by Apollo .... PYTHON
symbol of royalty .... ASP
worship .... OPHISM,
OPHIOLATRY
worshiping group, of a
.... OPHITIC
Serpent Mound site .... OHIO
serpentine .... WILY, COILED,
OPHITE, CUNNING, SINUOUS,
WINDING, OPHIDIAN,
SLITHERY, VENOMOUS,
REPTILIAN
Serpico author .... MAAS
serpigo .... RINGWORM
serranoid fish .... REDHIND,
CABRILLA
serrated .... JAGGED, SCALLOPED,

SAW-TOOTHED
serried .... DENSE, PACKED,
COMPACT
serum .... WHEY, ANTITOXIN
serval .... WILDCAT
servant .... HIND, MAID, GILLY,
SLAVE, (BAT)MAN, GILLIE,
HELP(ER), MENIAL, DOMESTIC,
SERVITOR, ANCILLARY,
ATTENDANT
airplane/ship ...... ATTENDANT,
STEWARD(ESS)
all-around .... FACTOTUM
boy .... PAGE, GARCON,
GROOM, GOSSOON
college .... GYP
devoted .... FRIDAY
female .... MAID, WENCH,
SLAVEY, HANDMAID(EN)
feudal .... SERF, BONDMAN,
SERGEANT
head .... BUTLER, STEWARD,
MAJORDOMO
hospital .... ORDERLY
hotel .... BELLBOY, BELLMAN
house of .... LODGE, QUARTERS
household .... COOK,
FOOTMAN, CHARWOMAN,
LAUNDRESS
kitchen .... SCULLION
lady's .... MAID, ABIGAIL
liveried .... FLUNKY, LACKEY
male .... PAGE, GROOM,
BUTLER, LACKEY, SQUIRE,
HENCHMAN
office .... ERRAND BOY,
MESSENGER, ERRAND GIRL
personal ..... VALET, EQUERRY,
HANDMAID(EN)
royal .... EQUERRY, LADY-IN-
WAITING
seat in carriage .... RUMBLE
stable .... GROOM, HOSTLER
uniformed .... CHASSEUR
serve .... AID, AVAIL, (AT)TEND,
ASSIST, SUPPLY, DELIVER,
FURTHER, SATISFY, SUFFICE
flawless .... ACE
food .... CATER, WAIT ON
leftovers .... REHEAT
server .... TRAY, SALVER, WAITER,
WAITRESS, ATTENDANT
alcoholic drinks
.... BARTENDER
counter .... SODA JERK
drive-in restaurant .... CARHOP
service .... AID, USE, HELP, MASS,
WORK, UTILITY, FUNCTION,
RITE, VIGIL, SERVITUDE,
EMPLOYMENT

attendants, accompanying .... CORTEGE, RETINUE

charge .... TIP, GRATUITY

club .... LIONS, JAYCEE, ROTARY, KIWANIS

club, military .... USO

military .... DUTY

stripe, military .... HASH MARK

tree .... SORB, SHADBUSH

serviceable .... HANDY, UTILE, USABLE, USEFUL, HELPFUL, EXPEDIENT, CONVENIENT

serviceman .... SOLDIER, REPAIRMAN, TECHNICIAN, TROUBLE-SHOOTER

services, one of the .... ARMY, NAVY, AIR FORCE, COAST GUARD, MARINE CORPS, NATIONAL GUARD

serviette .... NAPKIN

servile .... BASE, MEAN, TAME, ABJECT, MENIAL, PLIANT, FAWNING, SLAVISH, CRINGING

one .... YESMAN

serving .... HELPING, PORTION

boy .... KNAVE

girl .... MAID

man .... POTMAN

stand .... DUMB WAITER

to delay .... DETERRENT

servite .... MENDICANT

servitor .... SERVANT, ADHERENT, FOLLOWER, ATTENDANT

servitude .... YOKE, BONDAGE, PEONAGE, SERFDOM, SLAVERY, SUBJECTION

symbol of .... YOKE

sesame .... TIL, TEEL, BENNE, SEMSEM, GINGILI

grass .... GAMA

oil .... BENI, GINGILI

seed .... GENGELI, GINGILI, GINGELLY

sess .... TAX

sessile .... IMMOBILE

session .... TERM, PERIOD, HEARING, MEETING, SITTING, ASSEMBLY

diamond practice .... PEPPER GAME

discontinue ..... ADJOURN, SINE DIE, PROROGUE

spirited .... SEANCE

sestet .... SEXTET(TE)

set .... FIX, KIT, LAY, PUT, JELL, POST, SEAT, WANE, BATCH, EMBED, GROUP, MOUNT, PLANT, CLIQUE, HARDEN, RECORD, ARRANGE, COTERIE, SCENERY, REGULATE,

RESOLUTE, ESTABLISH, PRESCRIBE, COLLECTION

a course .... NAVIGATE(D)

afire .... IGNITE

afloat .... LAUNCH

against .... PIT

all .... READY, PREPARED

apart .... ISOLATE, RESERVE, SEPARATE, SEGREGATE

as the sun .... SINK, DECLINE

aside .... PEND, ANNUL, DEFER, QUASH, SPARE, REJECT, DISCARD, EARMARK

back .... PULL, RECESS, RETARD

down .... LAY, PUT, RECORD

down as a fact .... POSIT

firmly .... INFIX

forth .... START, STATE, THETIC

free .... CLEAR, ACQUIT, DELIVER, RELEASE, UNLOOSE, LIBERATE, EXTRICATE

in competition ..... PIT, MATCH

in motion .... AROUSE, EXCITE, STIR UP, ACTIVATE

in operation .... START, LAUNCH

in type .... COMPOSE

into a groove .... DADO

of clothes .... SUIT, OUTFIT, COSTUME

nine .... ENNEAD

players .... TEAM

rules .... CODE

steps .... STILE

three .... TERNION

tools .... KIT

off .... EXPLODE, DETONATE

on .... SIC ON, INCITE

on end .... UPEND

on fire .... IGNITE, KINDLE

on horse .... MOUNT

out .... GO, PLAN, BEGIN, LEAVE, DEFINE, DEPART

playing cards ...... DECK, PACK

right .... ALIGN, AMEND, ADJUST, REPAIR, CORRECT

sail .... CAST OFF

since the 40's .... TV

straight .... ALIGN, UNBEND, RECTIFY

system .... ROTE

tables .... BUS

thickly .... STUD

up .... ERECT, FOUND, PITCH, ESTABLISH

up in advance ..... PRO FORMA

upon .... SIC, AMBUSH, ATTACK

value on .... PRICE, APPRAISE

seta .... CHAETA, BRISTLE

setback ...... EDDY, DELAY, UPSET,

HOLDUP, RELAPSE, REVERSE, REVERSAL

Seth's brother .... ABEL, CAIN

father .... ADAM

mother .... EVE

son .... ENOS(H)

Seti I .... PHARAOH

son and successor of .... RAMSES II

setoff .... OFFSET

setose .... BRISTLY

settee .... SEAT, SOFA, BENCH, LOUNGE

setter .... (GUN)DOG, RETRIEVER

setting .... ARENA, MOUNT, SCENE, LOCALE, MILIEU, SCENERY, BACKGROUND

jewels' .... PAVE

of As You Like It ...... ARDEN

scheme .... DECOR, MOTIF

used on stage .... SCENERY

settle .... END, FIX, PAY, SAG, SET, SIT, NEST, REST, SEAT, SINK, BENCH, CLEAR, COUCH, ALIGHT, DECIDE, ENCAMP, RESIDE, APPEASE, ARRANGE, CLARIFY, RESOLVE, COLONIZE, CONCLUDE, LIQUIDATE

argument .... CLINCH

down .... ABATE, DESCEND, SUBSIDE

for the night .... BED DOWN

in cozily .... NEST

on land illegally .... SQUAT

snugly .... ENSCONCE

settled .... LIT ON, SQUARE

in law .... VESTED

settlement ...... AWARD, COLONY, OUTPOST, PAYMENT, VILLAGE, JUDGMENT, AGREEMENT, PLANTATION

settler .... BOOMER, SOONER, PIONEER, COLONIST, HOMESTEADER

land .... HOMESTEAD

settlers led by Kok .... GRIQUA

settlings ...... LEES, DRAFF, DREGS, SEDIMENT

set-to .... BOUT, BRAWL, FIGHT, HASSLE, CONTEST, QUARREL

setup .... PLAN, LAYOUT, MAKEUP

Sevastopol is in .... CRIMEA

seven .... VII, SEPT, HEPTAD

against Thebes, one of .... TYDEUS

combining form .... HEPT(A)

companion of .... ELEVEN

days .... HEBDOMAD

deadly sins, one of the .... ENVY, LUST, ANGER, PRIDE, SLOTH, GLUTTONY,

COVETOUSNESS
-foot dunkers .... CAGERS
group of .... HEPTAD
of eleven, on offense ..... LINE
of number .... SEPTIMAL,
SEPTENARY
on the first cast ...... NATURAL
series of .... HEPTAD
-year period .... TEENS
Seven Dwarfs, one of .... DOC,
DOPEY, HAPPY, GRUMPY,
SLEEPY, SNEEZY, BASHFUL
Hills of Rome, one of the
.... CAELIAN, VIMINAL,
AVENTINE, PALATINE,
QUIRINAL, ESQUILINE,
CAPITOLINE
Wonders of the World, one
of .... PHAROS, COLOSSUS,
PYRAMIDS, MAUSOLEUM,
STATUE OF ZEUS
sevenfold .... SEPTUPLE
seventeen XVII
-year locust .... CICADA
17th century opener .... MDCI
seventh son .... SEER
sever .... CUT, PART, CLEAVE,
DIVIDE, SUNDER, DISJOIN,
BREAK(OFF), SEPARATE
several .... FEW, SUNDRY,
DIVERS(E), VARIOUS,
DISTINCT, SEPARATE
severe .... DOUR, HARD, ACUTE,
HARSH, RIGID, STERN, TOUGH,
STRICT, DRASTIC, SERIOUS,
RIGOROUS
not .... BENIGN, LENIENT
Severn river .... USK
severity .... RIGOR, FEROCITY,
AUSTERITY, HARSHNESS
sew .... FELL, MEND, SEAM, TACK,
BASTE, QUILT, STITCH,
SUTURE
lightly .... BASTE
together .... ENSEAM
up .... CLOSE, MONOPOLIZE
up the market .... ENJOY A
MONOPOLY
sewage .... OFFAL, WASTE, REFUSE,
RUBBISH, DRAINAGE
disposal .... SANITATION
hole .... CESSPOOL
sewan .... SHELL
Seward's "folly" .... JUNEAU
(ALASKA)
sewer .... PIPE, DRAIN, GUTTER,
KENNEL, CLOACA, PASSAGE,
STITCHER, SEAMSTRESS
entrance .... MANHOLE
sewing .... NEEDLEWORK
case .... ETUI, ETWEE

kit .... HUSSY, HOUSEWIFE
machine inventor .... HOWE
part .... LOOPER
technique .... CROSS-STITCH
sex .... GENDER
appeal .... CHARM, OOMPH
glands .... GONADS
glands, female .... OVARIES
glands, male .... TESTES
hormone .... STEROID
of a .... MALE, FEMALE,
FEMININE, MASCULINE
sexes, common to both
.... EPICENE
sexism .... BIAS, BIGOTRY,
INEQUITY, PREJUDICE
sexless .... FRIGID, NEUTER,
IMPOTENT
sext .... HOUR
sextant .... QUADRANT, ALTIMETER
sextet .... HEXAD
sexton .... BEADLE, VERGER,
SACRIST(AN), BELLRINGER,
GRAVEDIGGER
sextuple .... SIXFOLD
sexual .... GAMIC, CARNAL,
SENSUAL
attraction to either sex
.... BISEXUALITY
attraction toward the
opposite sex
.... HETEROSEXUALITY
attraction toward the same
sex .... HOMOSEXUALITY
continence .... CHASTITY
desire, of .... EROTIC
excitement .... RUT, HEAT,
(O)ESTRUS
inclination/urge .... LIBIDO
pervert .... DEVIATE
sexually cold .... FRIGID
ineffective .... STERILE
transmitted disease .... AIDS,
HERPES, SYPHILIS, GONORRHEA
unable .... IMPOTENT
sexy .... HOT, EROTIC, STEAMY,
WANTON, AMOROUS
picture .... PINUP
movie, describing a
.... X-RATED
Seychelles, capital of
.... VICTORIA
city/town .... CASCADE, ANSE
ROYALET
island .... MAHE, NORTH,
ASTOVE, FRIGATE, LA DIGUE,
PRASLIN
Sforza, Ital. statesman
.... CARLO
Sgts. and Cpls. .... NCOS
shabby ...... MEAN, WORN, DINGY,

DOWDY, MANGY, RATTY,
SEEDY, SORRY, TACKY,
CRUMMY, RAGGED,
RUNDOWN, UNKEMPT,
THREADBARE, DISGRACEFUL
color .... CHEESY
woman .... DOWD, SLOVEN,
SLATTERN
shack .... HUT, SHED, CABIN,
HOVEL, SHANTY
figure .... HAM
shackle .... BOND, CURB, GYVE,
BILBO, CHAIN, IRON(S),
FETTER, HAMPER, HOBBLE,
PINION, LEG-IRON, MANACLE,
TRAMMEL, HANDCUFF,
RESTRAIN
shad .... ALLIS, ALOSA, ALOSE,
ALEWIFE
fish like .... MENHADEN
running upriver
.... ANADROMOUS
shadbush ...... ROSE, JUNEBERRY,
SASKATOON, SERVICE(BERRY)
shaddock .... POMELO
family .... RUE
shade .... HUE, TINT, TONE,
COLOR, TOUCH, TRACE,
UMBER, UMBRA, BLIND(S),
SCREEN, SHADOW
bamboo ...... SCREEN, CURTAIN
blue .... SKY, ALICE, AZURE
canvas .... AWNING, CANOPY
cap's .... VISOR
fabric .... VEIL
for the eyes .... VISOR,
GOGGLES, SPECTACLES
for windshield .... VISOR
green .... AQUA, BICE, JADE,
EMERALD
lines .... HATCH
of color, pale .... PASTEL
of difference/meaning
.... NUANCE
orange ...... MADDER, PUMPKIN
pink .... ROSE, ORCHID,
SALMON
purple .... GRAPE, LILAC,
ORCHID, VIOLET, FUCHSIA,
AMETHYST
red .... WINE, OCHER,
CRIMSON, CARDINAL
tree .... ELM, LIN, ACACIA,
POPLAR, MAGNOLIA
used in church processions
.... BALDACHIN, BALDAQUIN
yellow .... AMBER, LEMON,
GOLDEN
shaded .... SHELTERED
walk .... MALL, ARBOR,
ALAMEDA, CLOISTER

Shades, the .... HADES
shadow .... DOG, SPY, OMEN,
TAIL, CLOUD, GHOST, GLOOM,
SHADE, TRACE, TRAIL,
UMBER, UMBRA, FOLLOW,
OUTLINE, VESTIGE,
REFLECTION, SILHOUETTE
astronomer's .... UMBRA
fighting .... SCIAMACHY
man without .... ASCIAN
Shadow, The
.... (LAMONT)CRANSTON
shadowbox .... SPAR
shadowy appearance
.... UMBRAGE
Shadrach's fellow-captive
.... MESHACH, ABEDNEGO
shady .... DARK, UMBRAL,
DUBIOUS, DOUBTFUL,
SINISTER, DISHONEST, ILLICIT
retreat .... NOOK, ARBOR,
KIOSK
SHAEF commander .... (IKE)
EISENHOWER
theater .... ETO, EUROPE
shaft .... BEAM, BOLT, FLUE, POLE,
ARBOR, ARROW, SHANK,
SPEAR, SPIRE, THILL, ARROYO,
COLUMN, HANDLE, CONDUIT,
JAVELIN, MISSILE, OBELISK,
SPINDLE, FLAGPOLE
bearing .... HOTBOX
building .... WELL
column's .... FUST, SCAPE,
TRUNK, VERGE
connecting .... AXLE
feather's .... SCAPE
give someone the ...... CHEAT,
TRICK
handle .... HELVE
mine .... PIT
part of .... BOSS, GUDGEON,
JOURNAL, TRUNNION
shag .... NAP, PILE, TOBACCO,
CORMORANT
shagbark ...... WALNUT, HICKORY
shaggy .... BUSHY, FUZZY, HAIRY,
NAPPY, WOOLY, HIRSUTE,
UNKEMPT, SCRUBBY,
THRUMMY
shagreen .... RAWHIDE,
(SHARK)SKIN
Shah Jahan's masterpiece .... TAJ
MAHAL
of Iran .... PAHLEVI
shaitan ...... DEVIL, FIEND, SATAN
shake .... JAR, RID, JOLT, LOSE,
ROCK, SWAY, WAVE, QUAKE,
MOMENT, QUIVER, SHIVER,
THRILL, TREMOR, WOBBLE,
SUCCUSS, TREMBLE, UNNERVE,

VIBRATE, CONVULSE
down .... EXTORT, SEARCH,
PRY LOOSE
due to cold .... SHIVER
due to fear, horror
.... SHUDDER
—— (hurry) .... A LEG
in a menacing way
.... BRANDISH, FLOURISH
up .... CHANGE, RATTLE,
REVAMP, AGITATE
shakedown: sl. .... BLACKMAIL,
EXTORTION
shaken .... RATTLED, STARTLED
Shakespeare .... THE BARD,
WILLIAM
enough of .... ENOW
form used by .... BLANK
VERSE
wife of ...... ANNE(HATHAWAY)
Shakespearean actor .... BURTON,
GIELGUD, OLIVIER,
BARRYMORE, WILLIAMSON
Athenian .... TIMON
character .... IAGO, KATE,
LEAR, CASCA, DIANA, PARIS,
REGAN, ROMEO, BRUTUS,
CICERO, CLITUS, HAMLET,
HELENA, JULIET, LUCIUS,
OBERON, OSWALD, PORTIA,
TYBALT, BERTRAM, CASSIUS,
HORATIO, OCTAVIA, OPHELIA,
ORLANDO, OTHELLO, SHYLOCK,
SOLINUS, TITANIA, BENVOLIO,
CORDELIA, FALSTAFF,
MERCUTIO
clown .... FESTE, GOBBY,
COSTARD
Danish Prince .... HAMLET
elf .... PUCK
forest .... ARDEN, SHERWOOD
king .... LEAR, HAMLET
play .... HAMLET, MACBETH,
OTHELLO, KING LEAR,
PERICLES, CYMBELINE, THE
TEMPEST, JULIUS CAESAR, AS
YOU LIKE IT, ROMEO AND
JULIET, MERCHANT OF VENICE,
TAMING OF THE SHREW,
ANTONY AND CLEOPATRA
river .... AVON
seven .... AGES
shrew .... KATE
songwriter .... ARNE
theatre .... GLOBE
villain .... IAGO
witch .... CYCORAX
shaking .... ASPEN, PALSIED
shako decoration .... POMPON
Shakti .... DEVI, POWER
shaky ...... WEAK, DOTTY, LOOSE,

QUAKY, ROCKY, CRANKY,
FLIMSY, UNSURE, WOBBLY,
JITTERY, RICKETY, UNSOUND,
UNSTEADY
shale .... ROCK, PELITE
product .... TARE
shall .... MUST
shallop .... BOAT, DINGHY
shallot .... BULB, ONION,
ESCHALOT, SCALLION
kin .... LEEK
shallow .... DULL, SHOAL, SIMPLE,
SUPERFICIAL
container .... TRAY
cut .... SCRATCH
lake .... LAGOON, LAGUNE
sham .... FAKE, HOAX, BOGUS,
FALSE, FEIGN, HUMBUG,
PHON(E)Y, BASTARD,
PRETENSE, IMITATION,
ARTIFICIAL, COUNTERFEIT
fight .... SCIAMACHY
knife .... SNEE
ridiculous .... FARCE
shaman .... PRIEST, MEDICINE
MAN
Shamash .... SUN GOD
shamble .... GAIT, WALK,
LUMBER, SHUFFLE
shambles .... MESS, CHAOS,
ABATTOIR, DISORDER,
SLAUGHTERHOUSE
shame ...... FIE, ABASH, MORTIFY,
BLACKEYE, DISGRACE,
DISHONOR, HUMILIATE
shamefaced .... SHY, BASHFUL,
BLUSHING
shameful .... BASE, MEAN,
ARRANT, IGNOBLE, INDECENT,
SHOCKING, OFFENSIVE,
SCANDALOUS
shameless .... BRAZEN
shammy .... CHAMOIS
Shamo .... GOBI
shampoo .... SOAP, WASH,
MASSAGE, LOMILOMI
shamrock .... CLOVER
country .... EIRE, ERIN,
IRELAND
describing .... GREENEST
Shan .... T(H)AI
shandrydan .... CART, CHAISE
Shandy's creator .... STERNE
Shanghai .... KIDNAP, CHICKEN,
SEAPORT
Shangri-la ...... UTOPIA, PARADISE
shank .... LEG, CRUS, SHIN,
GAMB(E), SHAFT
in botany .... FOOTSTALK
shanny .... BLENNY
Shantung .... TUSSA(H)

637

capital of .... TSINAN
city .... CHEFOO
shanty .... HUT, SHED, HOVEL,
HUTCH, SHACK
shantytown .... SLUM
shape .... CAST, FORM, GUISE,
MODEL, MO(U)LD, STATE,
FIGURE, CONTOUR, PATTERN,
CONDITION
abalone .... EAR
bust's .... TAILLE
for a dunce cap .... CONE
illusory .... PHANTOM
jinxed? .... HEXAGON
like a teapot .... OBLATE
tondo .... ROUND
shaped .... SET, CAST, MADE,
FORMED, MOLDED, DEVISED
roughly, as stone
.... SCABBLED
shapeless .... VAGUE, AMORPHOUS
shapely ...... NEAT, LITHE, SVELTE,
CURVACEOUS
shaping machine .... EDGER,
LATHE
shard .... PIECE, PLATE, SHELL,
FRAGMENT, POTSHERD
share .... BIT, CUT, LOT, METE,
PART, ALLOT, QUOTA, STAKE,
MOIETY, RATION, DOLE OUT,
PARTAKE, (AP)PORTION
in common .... JOINT, MUTUAL
slang .... DIVVY
shark .... GATA, MAKO, TOPE,
CHEAT, DOGFISH, MAN-EATER,
SWINDLER, THRESHER,
ANGELFISH, PORBEAGLE,
HAMMERHEAD, SHOVELHEAD
eating fish .... PEGA
genus .... LAMNA, SPHYRNA
loan .... USURER
nurse .... GATA
of northern seas
.... PORBEAGLE
rider/sucker .... REMORA
skin .... SHAGREEN
slang .... EXPERT
voracious .... MAN-EATER
young .... PUPPY
sharp .... GLEG, KEEN, ACERB,
ACUTE, CLEAR, EDGED, NIPPY,
SMART, SPINY, CLEVER,
CUSPED, PEAKED, SEVERE,
ACIFORM, CUTTING, NIPPING,
POINTED, PUNGENT, DISTINCT,
HANDSOME, INCISIVE,
PIERCING, TRENCHANT,
VITRIOLIC
as a tack .... HEP, HIP, IN-THE-
KNOW
at the end .... ACUATE

blade .... RAZOR
colloquial .... ADEPT, EXPERT
combining form .... ACET(O)
cornered .... ANGULAR
cry .... YELP
edged .... KEEN
end .... POINT
eyed one .... LYNX, EAGLE
horn .... ANTLER
in phonetics .... VOICELESS
metal device on a gamecock
.... SPUR
pain .... STING
point on a leaf .... MUCRO
rejoinder .... REPARTEE
reply .... RETORT
ridge .... ARETE
spot .... RAZOR'S EDGE
taste .... TANG, TART
tooth .... FANG, TUSH, TUSK,
CANINE, CUSPID
toothed wheel .... RATCHET
turn .... ZIG
witted .... KEEN
sharpen ...... EDGE, HONE, WHET,
GRIND, STROP, ACUATE
sharpening device .... HONE,
STEEL, STONE, STRAP, STROP,
GRINDER, ABRASIVE,
WHETSTONE, GRINDSTONE
sharper .... GYP, KITE, CROOK,
SHARK, CHEAT(ER), CON-MAN,
SWINDLER
sharpness .... BARB, EDGE,
ACUITY, ACERBITY,
PUNGENCY, ALERTNESS
of temper .... ASPERITY
Shasta .... DAISY, VOLCANO
sharpshooter .... SNIPER,
MARKSMAN, RIFLEMAN,
(CRACK)SHOT, TIRAILLEUR
shatter ...... DASH, BREAK, BURST,
CRASH, SMASH, WRECK,
SHIVER, DESTROY
shave ...... CUT, CROP, PARE, SKIM,
TRIM, GRAZE, PLANE, SHEAR,
SKIVE, SCRAPE, WHITTLE
the jowls .... BARBER CHOPS
shaveling .... MONK, PRIEST
shaven .... TONSURED
shaver .... BOY, LAD, RAZOR,
YOUTH, YOUNGSTER
shavetail .... MULE, LIEUTENANT
Shavian forte .... WIT
shaving ...... CHIP, FLAKE, PARING,
SAWDUST
shaw .... COPSE, THICKET
shawl .... CAPE, MAUD, WRAP,
MANTA, SCARF, STOLE,
MANTLE, PEPLOS, SERAPE,
MUFFLER, PAISLEY, TALLITH,

CASHMERE, MANTILLA
shepherd's .... MAUD
woolen .... CASHMERE
shawn .... OBOE
Shawnee .... INDIAN
bread .... PONE, JOHNNYCAKE
chief .... TECUMSEH,
TECUMTHA
shay .... BUGGY, CHAISE,
CARRIAGE, STANHOPE
puller of song .... HOSS
"Shazam!" .... PRESTO
she .... HER, FEMALE, FEMININE
carved it .... SCULPSIT
-demon .... LAMIA
died .... OBIT
escaped with "Declaration
of Independence"
.... DOLLEY MADISON
let down her hair
.... RAPUNZEL
opened a box of evils
.... PANDORA
painted it .... PNXT, PINXIT
pulled a switch on a witch
.... GRETEL
raised Cain with an apple
.... ERIS
reads and writes in her sleep
.... LADY MACBETH
speaks .... LOQUITUR
was born free .... ELSA
wrote it .... SCRIPSIT
sheaf .... BALE, BATCH, BUNCH,
BUNDLE, PACKET
of arrows .... QUIVER
of twigs .... FAGOT
shear .... CUT, LOP, MOW, CLIP,
CROP, POLL, SNIP, TRIM,
SHAVE, STRIP, FLEECE
Shearer, _____ .... MOIRA, NORMA
shearing machine .... MOWER,
CROPPER
tool .... CLIPPER(S), SCISSORS
sheatfish .... CATFISH
sheath .... COT, DRESS, OCREA,
STALL, THECA, CASING,
(EN)CASE, FASCIA, SLEEVE,
SPATHE, CAPSULE, SCABBARD
metalplate on .... CHAPE
sheathe .... COVER, ENCLOSE,
RETRACT
sheathed ...... OCREATE, THECATE
sheaves of grain .... SHOCK,
STOCK
Sheba .... SABA
people .... SAB(A)EAN
queen of .... BALKIS
shebang .... THING, AFFAIR,
MATTER, BUSINESS,
CONTRIVANCE

shed .... COTE, EMIT, MOLT, SHACK, LEAN-TO, SCONCE, SHANTY, CAST(OFF), DROP OFF, DIFFUSE, DISCARD, FALL OUT, RADIATE, SHELTER
aircraft ..... HANGAR, AIRDOCK, AIRDROME
animal .... HOVEL, HUTCH
chicken/sheep .... COTE
for storing grain .... CRIB
guard .... SENTRY BOX
livestock .... STALL
newsstand .... KIOSK
skin/feathers .... MEW, PEEL, MO(U)LT, SLOUGH OFF
temporary .... BOOTH
train .... DEPOT
shedding leaves annually
.... DECIDUOUS
Sheean, writer .... VINCENT
sheen .... GLOW, GLEAM, GLOSS, SHINE, LUSTER, LUSTRE, POLISH
Sheen, Bishop .... FULTON
Sheena's domain .... JUNGLE
sheep ...... SHA, TEG, ARUI, URIAL, MERINO, OORIAL, NAHOOR, BLEATER, CARACUL, CHEVIOT, KARAKUL, BROADTAIL, LEICESTER
brain ailment .... GID
breed .... MERINO, OXFORD, PANAMA, ROMNEY, CHEVIOT, KARAKUL, LINCOLN, TARGHEE, LEICESTER
caretaker .... SHEPHERD
castrated .... WETHER
cry of .... BAA, MAA, BLAT, BLEAT
descriptive of .... MEEK, TIMID
disease .... COE, GID, ROT, LOCO, SHAKES, STURDY, ANTHRAX, SCRAPIE, STAGGERS, RINDERPEST
dog .... COLLIE, SHELTY, SHELTIE, SHEPHERD
enclosure/pen .... FOLD, KRAAL
fat .... SUET, TALLOW
female/mama .... EWE
flesh/meat .... LAMB, VEAL, MUTTON
flock .... FOLD, DRYBAND
flock leader .... BELLWETHER
foot of .... TROTTER
fur .... MOUTON, CARACUL, KARAKUL
genus .... BOS, OVIS
grease .... SUINT
group of .... FOLD, FLOCK
head .... JEMMY

infectious disease of
.... RINDERPEST
intestinal disorder ...... BRAXY
killing bird .... KEA
like/pertaining to .... OVINE
like animal .... SAIGA
male .... RAM, TUP, WETHER
mountain .... IBEX
mutton .... SUFFOLK
neck growth of .... POKE
parasite ..... FLUKE, COENURUS
sexual excitement .... RUT, HEAT, ESTRUS
shelter .... COTE, FOLD
stomach trouble .... BRAXY
tender .... SHEPHERD
tick .... KED
unshorn .... HOG
walk .... SLAITH
white .... WILTSHIRE
white-faced .... CORRIEDALE
wild .... SHA, SNA, ARUI, UDAD, RASSE, URIAL, ARGALI, AOUDAD, NAHOOR, OORIAL, MOUF(F)LON
wool .... FLEECE
wool secretion .... YOLK
young .... HOG, TEG, LAMB, (Y)EANLING
sheepfold .... PEN, REE, COTE, KRAAL
sheepish .... COY
sheeplike .... MEEK, OVINE, TIMID, DOCILE
sheepshank .... KNOT
sheepshead .... SPAR(O)ID
sheepskin .... ROAN, SKIVER, DIPLOMA, PARCHMENT
cap .... KALPAK, CALPAC(K)
dealer .... FELLMONGER
disease .... SCAB, MANGE
sheepwalk .... SLAITH, PASTURE
sheer .... MERE, PURE, THIN, TURN, VEER, STARK, STEEP, UTTER, SIMPLE, SWERVE, DEVIATE, ABSOLUTE, DIAPHANOUS
delight ..... ECSTASY, RAPTURE
joy .... GLEE
legs .... SHEARS
sheet .... LEAF, PAGE, SAIL, LAYER, LINEN, BEDDING, EXPANSE, NEWSPAPER
bend .... KNOT
blurred .... MACKLE
metal(piece) .... LATH, LEAF, PLATE
metal cutter .... SNIP
of lava .... COULEE
of matted cotton .... BATT
sheeting material .... LINEN,

SATIN, PERCALE
shekel .... MONEY
3000 .... TALENT
sheldrake ...... DUCK, MERGANSER
shelf .... REEF, BERM(E), LEDGE, MANTEL, BEDROCK, GRADIN(E), RETABLE, SANDBAR
drapery .... VALANCE, LAMBREQUIN
shell ...... POD, CASE, HULL, HUSK, BIELD, CONCH, COVER, SHARD, SHUCK, STRIP, LORICA, STRAFE, TUNICA, BOMBARD, MISSILE, MOLLUSK, CARAPACE, CARTRIDGE, INTEGUMENT, RACING BOAT
abalone .... ORMER
artillery .... OBUS, SHRAPNEL
bean .... FAVA, LIMA
boat .... HULL
cone-shaped .... LIMPET, PERIWINKLE
corn .... HUSK
crab, clam, etc. .... TEST
defective .... DUD
dish, baking .... SCALLOP
ear .... ORMER, ABALONE
enclosed in a .... OBTECTED
explosive .... BOMB, GRENADE, SHRAPNEL
fragments .... SHRAPNEL
fruit .... PEEL, RIND
game .... THIMBLERIG
hole .... CRATER
hurling device .... MORTAR
invertebrate's .... TEST
kernel .... NUT
kind of .... EGG, NUT, SEA, COCKLE
many-chambered
.... NAUTILUS
mollusk's .... CONCH
money .... COWRY, PEAG(E), COWRIE, SE(A)WAN, WAMPUM
of .... TESTACEOUS
of the burrito .... TORTILLA
1/20 of .... GERAH
out .... PAY, GIVE, FORK OUT
oysters .... SHUCK
pastry .... TART
seed .... HUSK, TEST(A)
shock .... AMNESIA, COMBAT FATIGUE
slow-moving .... SNAIL, WHELK
spiral .... CONCH, SNAIL, WHELK, NAUTILUS
structures resembling a
.... CONCHA
tip of .... WARNOSE

trumpet .... CONCH
turtle/tortoise .... CARAPACE,
　　　　　　　　　　　　　PLASTRON
used for cameo .... CONCH
shellac(k) ...... BEAT, DRUB, FLOG,
　　　　WHIP, RESIN, LAC(QUER),
　　　　　　　　　　　　　VARNISH
shellacking .... BEATING,
　　　　CREAMING, WHIPPING,
　　　　　　　　　　　　CLOBBERING
shellback .... SAILOR
shellbark ...... WALNUT, HICKORY,
　　　　　　　　　　　　SHAGBARK
Shelley, poet .... ARIEL, PERCY
elegy by .... ADONAIS
shellfish .... CLAM, CRAB, NACRE,
　　　COCKLE, OYSTER, SHRIMP,
　　　ABALONE, LOBSTER,
　　　MOLLUSK, SCALLOP,
　　　BARNACLE, MOSSBACK
spawn .... SPAT
trap .... CREEL
shelter .... ROOF, SHED, BIELD,
　　　HAVEN, CABANA, COVER(T),
　　　NESTLE, REFUGE, SHIELD,
　　　RETREAT, (EN)SCONCE
aircraft .... HANGAR,
　　　　　　　　　　　　AIRDROME
airraid .... ABRI, DUGOUT
auto .... GARAGE, CARPORT
canvas/collapsible .... TENT
cattle .... KRAAL, CORRAL
decorative .... PAVILION
dove's .... COTE
hillside .... ABRI
movable .... MANT(E)LET
overhanging .... AWNING,
　　　　　　　　　　　　CANOPY
portable .... TENT
rain .... UMBRELLA
refugee's .... ASYLUM,
　　　　　　　　　　　SANCTUARY
ship's .... HARBOR
small .... COT(E), CABANA
soldier's .... FOXHOLE,
　　　　　　　　　　　(PUP)TENT
sheltered area/side .... LEE
shelty .... PONY, (SHEEP)DOG
shelve .... DEFER, RETIRE, LAY
　　　　　　ASIDE, POSTPONE
Shem's descendants
　　　　.................... S(H)EMITES
father .... NOAH
son .... LUD, ARAM, ELAM,
　　　　　　　　　　AS(S)HUR
shenanigan(s) .... PRANK, FROLIC,
　　　MISCHIEF, NONSENSE,
　　　　　　　　　TRICK(ERY)
Shensi, capital of .... SIAN
sheol .... HELL, HADES,
　　　　　　　　　　UNDERWORLD

shepherd .... LEAD, TEND,
　　　HERDER, PASTOR, CORYDON,
　　　DAPHNIS, ENDYMION,
　　　MINISTER, SHEEP DOG,
　　　　　　　LEADING MAN
concern of .... SHEEP
dog .... COLLIE
kings .... HYKSOS
pie of .... MASHED POTATOES
pipe .... OAT, REED
plaid .... MAUD
staff of .... KENT, PEDA,
　　　　　　　　　　　　CROOK
shepherdess .... AMARYLLIS
shepherds, god of .... PAN,
　　　　　　　　　　　　FAUNUS
pertaining to .... BUCOLIC,
　　　　　　　　　　　PASTORAL
sherbet .... DRINK, SORBET,
　　　DESSERT, BEVERAGE,
　　　　　　　ICE(CREAM)
Sheridan, Union general
　　　.................................. PHILIP
sherif .... EMIR
ancestor of .... FATIMA,
　　　　　　　　　MOHAMMED
sheriff .... REEVE, MARSHAL,
　　　　　　　　　　VISCOUNT
aid of .... YEOMAN, BAILIFF,
　　　BULLDOG, CATCHPOLL
armed group of .... POSSE
badge of .... STAR
deputy .... BAILIFF
Sheriff Pusser's story
　　　.................... WALKING TALL
Sherlock Holmes, creator of
　　　.................................. DOYLE
man of .... WATSON
sherry .... WINE, JEREZ, OLOROSO,
　　　　　　　　AMONTILLADO
Sherwood Forest hero .... ROBIN
　　　　　　　　　　　　HOOD
Shetland .... PONY, WOOL
fishing grounds .... HAAF
island .... MAINLAND
island tax .... SCAT(T)
pony .... SHELTY, SHELTIE
sheep dog .... COLLIE, SHELTY,
　　　　　　　　　　SHELTIE
shibboleth .... SLOGAN,
　　　PASSWORD, TEST WORD
shield .... ECU, (A)EGIS, ARMOR,
　　　COVER, MULGA, PAVIS,
　　　SCUTA, TARGE, DEFEND,
　　　SCREEN, SCUTUM, BUCKLER,
　　　PROTECT, MANT(E)LET,
　　　　　　　ESCUTCHEON
arm/hand .... BUCKLER
Athena's/Zeus' .... (A)EGIS
band across .... FESS
bar, heraldic .... GEMEL

bearer .... SQUIRE, ARMIGER
border .... ORLE
boss/knob of .... UMBO
bulletproof .... MANT(E)LET
center point .... FESS
of shields .... TESTUDO
rawhide .... PARFLECHE
Roman .... TESTUDO
shaped ..... PELTATE, SCUTATE,
　　　CLYPEATE, CLYPEIFORM
spike of .... UMBO
strap .... ENARME
shift .... MOVE, VARY, VEER,
　　　SHUNT, TRICK, CHANGE,
　　　SWITCH, CHEMISE, DEVIATE,
　　　TRANSFER, ASSIGNMENT
descriptive of a work
　　　........................... GRAVEYARD
direction .... HAUL, DIVERT
for oneself .... FREE-LANCE
from side to side .... JIBE
shiftless .... LAZY
shifty .... ALERT, TRICKY,
　　　CUNNING, EVASIVE, FURTIVE
Shiite .... SHIAH, MOSLEM
opposed to .... SUNNITE
shikar .... HUNT(ING)
shikari .... GUIDE, HUNTER
shill .... DECOY, PLANT,
　　　　　　　　　ACCOMPLICE
confederate of a ...... BARKER,
　　　　　　　　　　GAMBLER
shillelagh .... CLUB, CUDGEL
shilling: sl. .... BOB
shillings, 21 .... GUINEA
shilly-shally .... HEDGE, TARRY,
　　　WAVER, DAWDLE, HESITATE,
　　　FLUCTUATE, VACILLATE,
　　　　　　　(DILLY)DALLY
shimmer .... FLASH, GLINT,
　　　GLIMMER, TWINKLE
shimmy .... DANCE, WOBBLE,
　　　　　　　　　　CHEMISE
shin .... LEG, SHANK, CLIMB(UP)
Shinar .... SUMER, BABYLONIA
shinbone .... TIBIA
shindig .... GALA, DANCE, PARTY,
　　　　　SPREE, AFFAIR
shindy .... ROW, RIOT, BRAWL,
　　　HUBBUB, RACKET,
　　　　　　　COMMOTION
shine .... WAX, GLOW, EXCEL,
　　　GLEAM, GLOSS, LIGHT,
　　　LUSTER, POLISH, FLICKER,
　　　GLITTER, RADIATE, TWINKLE
shiner .... MINNOW
slang .... MOUSE, BLACKEYE
shingle .... BOB, CLIP, SHIM,
　　　FACIA, SLAT(E), GRAVEL,
　　　SIDING, SIGN(BOARD)
man with .... DOCTOR,

LAWYER
use of .... ROOF, SIGN
shingles .... ZONA,
      HERPES(ZOSTER)
drug treatment ..... ACYCLOVIR
shining ...... LUCID, NITID, SUNNY,
   BRIGHT, GLOSSY, LUCENT,
     EMINENT, RADIANT,
    LUMINOUS, LUSTROUS
example .... HERO
"star of the Carribean"
.... PUERTO RICO
shinleaf .... WINTERGREEN
shinny ...... CLUB, STICK, HOCKEY
shinplaster .... SCRIP, POULTICE
Shinto .... SINTU
deity .... KAMI
temple .... SHA
temple gate .... TORII
text .... KOJIKI, NAHONGI
ship .... BARK, BOAT, BRIG, DHOW,
   HULK, SAIL, SCOW, SEND,
   LINER, PINKY, YACHT,
   EMBARK, HOOKER, PINKIE,
   TARTAN, VESSEL, WHERRY,
    CARRACK, CLIPPER,
    DROMON(D), GALLEON,
    (AIR)CRAFT, BILANDER
abandoned .... DERELICT
accommodation .... CABIN,
       PASSAGE
accommodation, no frills
.... STEERAGE
afterpart of .... QUARTER
anchor rope .... HAWSER
anchorage .... MARINA,
      ROAD(STEAD)
ancient .... BIREME
balance of .... TRIM
ballast .... LASTAGE,
      KENTLEDGE
beak .... ROSTRUM
big, unwieldy .... HULK
biscuit .... (HARD)TACK
boat on .... GIG, YAWL, JOLLY,
   DINGHY, LAUNCH, PINNACE
body of .... HULK, HULL
boom .... BUMPKIN
bottom .... KEEL
bow flag .... JACK
breadth .... BEAM
cabin .... CUDDY
canal .... GOTA, KIEL, SUEZ,
    ALBERT, PANAMA
canvas .... SAIL
capacity .... TONNAGE
captain .... MASTER, SKIPPER
captive .... PRIZE
cargo .... FREIGHTER
cargo/passenger, from port to
  port .... COASTER

carpenter .... CHIPS
chains .... TYES
change course of .... TACK
channel .... GAT
clean bottom of .... BREAM
clean hull of .... GRAVE
cleaning tool .... HOG
clock .... NEF
clumsy .... ARK, TUB,
       DROGHER
coal .... COLLIER
coal bin .... BUNKER
crane .... DAVIT
crew-member .... HAND,
   MATE, OILER, STOKER,
       YEOMAN
crosspiece .... BEAM
device for raising sunken
.... CAMEL, CAISSON
dimension .... ABEAM
direct a .... NAVIGATE
drain hole .... SCUPPER
entrance of .... GANGWAY
equipped with sails .... SAILER
fender .... SKID
fictional .... CAINE
fishing .... TRAWLER
flag ..... JACK, BURGEE, ENSIGN
flat-bottomed .... KEEL
fleet .... ARGOSY
for transporting oil ..... OILER,
       TANKER
forward part .... BOW, PROW,
        STEM
framework ..... HULL, CARCASS
fraud .... BARRATRY
fuel tank of .... BUNKER
galley .... CUDDY, CABOOSE,
       KITCHEN
gun platform .... SPONSON
heave of .... SCEND
hold .... BULK
hospital .... SICK BAY
hunting .... RAIDER, SEALER,
   WHALER, WHALEBOAT
jail/prison .... BRIG, HULK
Jason's .... ARGO
ladder .... RATLINE
land from .... DEBARK
lateen-sailed .... TARTAN
left-side .... PORT, LARBOARD
line on side .... PLIMSOLL
list .... MANIFEST
load .... BULK, CARGO,
       FREIGHT
logbook .... JOURNAL
lookout point of .... CROW'S
        NEST
lowest deck .... ORLOP
made smaller .... RAZEE
master .... CAPTAIN, SKIPPER

master's declaration
.... PROTEST
merchant .... ARGOSY,
  TRADER, CARRACK, GALLEON,
       GAL(L)IOT
metal plating .... STRAKE
mooring place/slip ...... DOCK,
  BERTH, MARINA, ANCHORAGE
mythical/legendary .... ARGO
not sea-going .... HULK
of 1492 .... NINA, PINTA,
     SANTA MARIA
of the desert .... CAMEL
officer .... BOS'N, MATE,
   MASTER, PURSER, CAPTAIN,
   SKIPPER, BOATSWAIN
opening .... HATCH(WAY)
part of ...... BOW, BEAM, BRIG,
   HULL, KEEL, MAST, PROW,
   HAWSE, SALON, STERN,
   WHEEL, BUNKER, GALLEY,
    RUDDER, SCUPPER,
   (POOP)DECK, STEERAGE,
      PROMENADE
passage .... GAT, STEERAGE
passenger, clandestine
.... STOWAWAY
path of .... LANE
peg .... KEVEL
permit .... PRATIQUE
personnel .... CREW,
      COMPLEMENT
petty officer .... BOS'N,
   BOSUN, BOATSWAIN
pirate .... CORSAIR, FRIGATE,
      PRIVATEER
planking .... STRAKE
platform .... DECK, SPONSON
poetic .... BARK, KEEL
pole .... MAST
position finder .... LORAN
provisioner .... CHANDLER
prow's front .... CUTWATER
pull .... KEDGE
pursuit .... CHASER
rear of .... AFT
record .... LOG
rib .... FUTTOCK
rigging .... GEAR, TACKLE
rope .... TYE
sailing .... TARTAN, CLIPPER,
   GALLEON, SCHOONER
sails .... KITES
scout .... PINNACE
side opening .... PORTHOLE
side scaffold .... FLAKE
sidewise motion of .... ROLL
single-masted .... TARTAN
sink a .... SCUTTLE
skipper .... MASTER, CAPTAIN
slow .... TUB, BUCKET

small .... LUGGER, TARTAN, GALLIOT

small, armed .... CUTTER

smoke pipe .... STACK, FUNNEL

space for provisions .... LAZARETTO

speed measuring device .... LOG

square-masted .... BRIG

square-rigged .... CLIPPER

steer a .... CONN, NAVIGATE

stern section .... POOP, BUTTOCKS

supplier .... CHANDLER

supply .... TENDER, COLLIER, TRANSPORT

table railing .... FIDDLE

tender .... PINNACE, COCKBOAT

tax on .... TONNAGE

the .... SHE

timber .... SNY, BITT, CARLING, FUTTOCK, KEELSON, STEMSON

torpedoed May 1915 .... LUSITANIA

track .... WAKE

trading ..... ARGOSY, GALLEON, GAL(L)IOT

troop .... TRANSPORT

two-masted .... BRIG, GRAB

water in the hold .... BILGE

waterline .... PLIMSOLL

wheel .... HELM

whistle .... HORN, BLAST

windlass .... CAPSTAN

"window" .... PORTHOLE

with two or more masts .... SCHOONER

wrecked .... WRACK

shipbuilding peg .... TRUNNEL, TRE(E)NAIL

shipjack .... SHAD

shipment .... LOAD, CARGO, LADING, FREIGHT

shipping hazard .... FOG, REEF, STORM, ICEBERG, TYPHOON

list .... MANIFEST

news .... SAILINGS

ships, collectively .... CRAFT

group of ...... FLEET, FLOTILLA

shipshape ...... NEAT, SNUG, TIDY, TRIM, TIGHT, TIPTOP, ORDERLY

shipworm .... BORER, TEREDO

shipwreck goods .... JETSAM, FLOTSAM

shipwrecked .... SUNK, WRACK, GROUNDED, MAROONED

person .... CASTAWAY

shire .... COUNTY

shirk .... FUNK, SHUN, AVOID,

DODGE, EVADE, SKULK, NEGLECT, MALINGER

slang .... GOLDBRICK

shirker .... DODGER, EVADER, TRUANT, SLACKER, GOLDBRICK(ER)

shirr .... GATHER

shirt .... SARK, PARKA, CAMISE, JERSEY, SKIVVY, CHEMISE, GUERNSEY

broadcloth .... PIMA

closefitting, worn by seamen .... GUERNSEY

collar stiffener .... STAY

front ...... DICK(E)Y, PLASTRON

front ornament .... STUD, BUTTON

loose, long-sleeved .... CAMISE

sleeve .... PLAIN, SIMPLE, HOMESPUN

sleeve button .... CUFFLINK

shittah .... ACACIA

shiv .... KNIFE

shivaree .... SERENADE, CHARIVARI

shive .... CORK, FRAGMENT, SPLINTER

shiver ...... BREAK, BURST, QUAKE, SHAKE, QUIVER, CHITTER, SHATTER, SHUDDER, TREMBLE, FRAGMENT, SPLINTER

shivery .... COLD, CHILLY, BRITTLE, CHILLING

Shkoder .... SCUTARI

shoal .... BANK, HOST, MASS, REEF, SPIT, CROWD, HORDE, RIFFLE, SCHOOL, (SAND)BAR, SHALLOW

shoat .... SHOTE, PIG(LET)

shock .... JAR, BLOW, JOLT, STUN, BRUNT, SHAKE, APPAL(L), IMPACT, STROKE, TRAUMA, DISGUST, HORRIFY, STARTLE, PARALYZE, SURPRISE, CONCUSSION

absorber .... CUSHION, SNUBBER

dog .... POODLE

electric .... SPARK, CHARGE, ELECTRIFY

emotional .... TRAUMA

gather into a .... STOOK

main .... BRUNT

of grain sheaves .... SHOOK

sudden, brief .... START

tactics .... BLITZKRIEG

therapy drug .... INSULIN, METRAZOL

to action .... ENERGIZE, GALVANIZE

shocked .... AGHAST

shocking .... GHASTLY, OUTRAGEOUS, SCANDALOUS

shod .... SHOED, BOOTED, CALCED

shoddy .... JUNK, SHAM, CHEAP, SEEDY, SHABBY

shoe .... BOOT, CLOG, PUMP, BROGAN, BROGUE, GAITER, LOAFER, OXFORD, STEP-IN, STOG(E)Y, GALOSH(E), CLODHOPPER

armor .... SOLLERET

canvas .... SNEAKER, ESPADRILLE

cloglike .... PATTEN

designer ...... VIVIER, PERUGIA, FERRAGAMO

fastener .... LATCHET

flap .... TONGUE

form/model .... LAST

front .... VAMP

heavy .... SABOT, GALOSH(E)

high, thick-soled .... BUSKIN

house .... MULE, SLIPPER

implement .... HORN

insertion .... TREE

lace tag .... AGLET

leather .... SUEDE, FOXING

low .... PUMP, SANDAL, SLIPPER

material ..... KID, CORK, BARK, METAL, STRAW, SUEDE, RAFFIA, RUBBER, EELSKIN, LEATHER, SNAKESKIN, CROCODILE SKIN

mender .... COBBLER

moccasin-like .... PAC

ornament .... BUCKLE

oxford .... BROGAN

part .... FLAP, HEEL, LACE, LAST, RAND, SOLE, VAMP, WELT, THONG, UPPER, EYELET, (IN)SOLE, INSTEP, TASSEL, TOECAP, TONGUE

plate .... CALK, TRAMP, CLAMPER, CRAMPON, CREEPER

repair .... COBBLE

security .... LACING

sheepskin .... PAC

sole addition .... HOBNAIL

sole part .... SHANK

specialist .... SOLER

spike .... CLIMBER

sport .... LOAFER

style .... PUMP, LACED, WEDGE, SANDAL, BLUCHER, CHOPINE, PLATFORM, SLING(BACK), (CHUKKA)BOOT, ORIENTAL MULE

tennis/sports .... GUMSHOE, SNEAKER

uppers material .... CLOTH,

FOXING, LASTING, PRUNELLA
walking .... BALMORAL
wing-tipped .... BROGUE
woman's .... PUMP, STEP-IN,
CHOPINE
wooden .... CLOG, GETA,
SABOT, PATTEN
wooden-soled .... CLOG,
SABOT
shoebill .... HERON, STORK
shoelace tip .... TAG, AGLET
shoeless .... UNSHOD
shoemaker .... SNOB, SOLER,
SOUTER, COBBLER,
CORDWAINER
awl of .... ELSEN
block of .... LAST
need of .... WELT
patron saint of .... CRISPIN
shoes .... PUMPS, FOOTGEAR,
FOOTWEAR
brown .... TANS
for vehicle .... BRAKE LINING
golf .... CREEPERS
open-heeled .... STEP-INS
patent-leather .... SHINERS
rubber .... GUMS, SNEAKERS
work .... BOOTS, BROGANS
shoestring .... LACE(T)
shofar/shophar .... (RAM'S) HORN
shogun .... TYCOON, GOVERNOR
Sholem, author .... ASCH
shoo ...... GIT, SCAT, SCRAM, BEAT
IT, BEGONE, GET OUT, GET
LOST, DRIVE(AWAY)
shooi .... JAEGER
shoo-in ...... CINCH, (SURE)WINNER
shook .... UPSET, SHAKEN
shoot .... BUD, HIT, ROD, CAST,
CHIT, DART, EMIT, FILM, FIRE,
GROW, HURL, KILL, TEAR,
TWIG, SPRIG, THROW, WHISK,
PROPEL, SPROUT, TWINGE,
BURGEON, EXPLODE, PROJECT,
DETONATE, FLAGELLUM
a bullet into .... PLUG
a disk .... DISCUS
a marble .... TAW
down ...... KILL, SLAY, RIDDLE,
GUN DOWN
firearm .... FIRE
forth .... BURGEON
from cover ..... SNIPE, AMBUSH
game for food .... POT
grafting .... (S)CION
lichen .... FROND
long, flexible .... VIMEN
plant .... BUD, BINE, SLIP,
(S)CION, SPEAR, VIMEN,
RUNNER, STOLON, TENDRIL,
THALLUS

root/stem .... TILLER,
RAT(T)OON
scene again .... RETAKE
seaweed .... FROND
strawberry .... RUNNER
threadlike .... FLAGELLUM
up .... GROW, SPROUT
young, tender .... TENDRIL
shoot-out .... GUNFIGHT
shooter .... TAW, ALLEY, MARBLE
arrow .... AMOR
bow and arrow .... ARCHER,
BOWMAN
expert .... MARKSMAN
infantry .... RIFLEMAN
shooting .... FIRING, GUNFIRE,
KILLING
iron .... GAT, GUN, ROD, RIFLE,
PISTOL, CARBINE, FIREARM,
REPEATER, REVOLVER,
DERRINGER
match .... TIR, DUEL, SKEET
pain .... SPASM, TWINGE,
TWITCH
star .... BOLIDE, LEONID,
FIREBALL, METEOR(OID)
shoots .... BROWSE
shop .... MART, MILL, STORE,
BAZAAR, MARKET, PARLOR,
FACTORY, BOUTIQUE,
EMPORIUM
girl .... GRISETTE
nameplate of .... FACIA
shoplifter .... THIEF, BOOSTER,
STEALER
shopman/shopkeeper .... CLERK,
DEALER, MERCHANT,
RETAILER
shopping .... BUY(ING), EMPTION,
PURCHASE
aid .... CART, BASKET
center .... MALL, PLAZA,
MARKET(PLACE)
shoptalk .... SLANG, JARGON
shoran .... RADAR
part of .... SHORT, RANGE,
NAVIGATION
shore .... SAND, BANK, PROP,
BEACH, RIVAGE, SEASIDE,
COAST(LINE), WATERSIDE
along .... LITTORAL
bird .... RAIL, RUFF, SNIPE,
STILT, AVOCET, CURLEW,
PLOVER, DOTT(E)REL,
DOWITCHER, SANDPIPER
dinner attire .... BIBS
dinner item .... ROE
feature .... SAND
of the ..... COASTAL, LITTORAL
poetic .... STRAND
short ...... LOW, SHY, CURT, BRIEF,

BREVI, SCANT, ABRUPT,
CONCISE, FRIABLE, LACKING
air/aria .... ARIETTA
and fat .... PODGY, PUDGY,
SQUAT, TUBBY
and not so sweet .... CURT
and plumply round
.... ROLYPOLY
and stout .... SQUAB
and thick ..... PODGY, CHUNKY
branch .... SNAG
bristly haircut .... CREW
cake .... BISCUIT
combining form .... BRACHY
comedy .... SKIT, SKETCH
dowel .... PEG
drink .... DRAM, SNORT,
QUICKIE
fibers removed in combing
.... NOILS
for .... IN BRIEF
for a physical .... EXAM
for Augustus .... GUS
for Henry .... HANK
for throat infection ...... STREP
in .... BRIEFLY
in loan money ...... STRINGENT
jacket .... ETON, BOLERO,
REEFER
laughs .... HOS
-lived ...... FLEETING, FLITTING,
DECIDUOUS, EPHEMERAL,
TRANSIENT, TRANSITORY
-lived Arab confederation
.... UAR
musical passage ..... MORCEAU
-necked duck .... TEAL
of .... LACKING, WANTING
order .... TOAST, OMELET
overcoat .... REEFER
poem .... LAY, RONDEL
projecting part .... STUB
race .... DASH, SPRINT
reminder .... MEMO
rest .... NAP, SIESTA
ride .... SPIN
_____ (scant consideration)
.... SHRIFT
seller .... BEAR
shrift .... ABRUPT, REBUFF
skirt .... MINI
slang .... SHY
snort .... SHOT
sock .... ANKLET
song ..... ODE, DITTY, ARIETTA,
ARIETTE
sound .... SNAP
spoken .... CURT, BRIEF,
TERSE, LACONIC
stature .... DWARFISM
story .... CONTE

story: var. .... NOVELA
supply, in .... SCARCE
swim .... DIP
tail .... SCUT
-tempered .... TESTY
term .... TEMPORARY
time .... TRICE
visit .... CALL
wave .... PERM
-winded .... PUFFY, PURSY
window drapery ..... VALANCE
shortage .... LACK, NEED, DEFICIT,
DEFICIENCY
shortchange .... CON, GYP, CHEAT
shortcoming ...... FAULT, DEFECT,
FAILING, WEAKNESS, WEAK
POINT
shorten .... BOB, CUT, LOP, CHOP,
CLIP, CROP, DOCK, ELIDE,
PRUNE, REEVE, DIGEST,
REDUCE, ABRIDGE, CURTAIL,
CONDENSE, ABBREVIATE
mast/bowsprit .... REEF
shortened .... CUT, CONCISE,
CURTATE, ABSTRACT
shortening .... FAT, OIL, LARD,
OLEO, SUET
shortest route to anywhere
.... BEELINE
shortfall .... LACK, DEFICIT
shorthand .... GREGG, PITMAN,
STENOTYPE, STENOGRAPHY
character .... POT, HOOK
girl .... STENO
sign .... PHONOGRAM
shortly .... ANON, SOON, RUDELY,
ABRUPTLY
shorts .... BRIEFS, TROUSERS,
LEFT-OVERS
shortsighted .... MYOPY, MYOPIC,
NEARSIGHTED
person .... MYOPE
shorty .... RUNT
Shoshonean Indian .... UTE,
HOPI, OTOE, P(A)IUTE,
COMANCHE
Shostakovich, composer
.... DMITRI
shot ...... TRY, BALL, DOSE, DRINK,
GUESS, RANGE, SCOPE, SHELL,
BULLET, PELLET, FLECKED,
LANGREL, LANGRAGE,
MARKSMAN
and shell .... AMMO,
AMMUNITION
give it a .... GO, TRY, FLING
of booze .... SLUG, JIGGER
of liquid into the body
.... INJECTION
that hits target .... CLOUT
shote .... SHOAT, PIG(LET)

shotgun sport .... SKEET
shoulder .... BEAR, PUSH, CARRY,
EPAUL, ASSUME, JOSTLE,
SCAPULA, SUPPORT
armor .... PAULDRON
belt .... BALDRIC
blade .... SCAPULA
blade part .... ACROMION
bone .... HUMERUS
combining form .... OMO
muscle .... DELTOID
of the .... ALAR, SCAPULAR
ornament .... EPAULET(TE)
pack .... KNAPSACK
protection for .... PAULDRON
road's .... BERM(E)
wrap .... SCARF, SHAWL, STOLE
shoulders, covering for .... NUBIA
draw up .... SHRUG
fur piece .... PALATINE
of the .... HUMERAL
squared .... ERECT
shout .... CRY, CALL, ROAR, YELL,
YOHO, CHEER, WHOOP,
HOLLER, SCREAM
down .... SILENCE
of derision .... HOOT
of greeting .... HULLO
of joy/approval .... OLE, HEAR,
VIVA, BRAVO, HUZZA, HURRAH
shove ...... JAR, JOG, BUNT, CRAM,
PUSH, ELBOW, FORCE, NUDGE,
HUSTLE, JOSTLE, THRUST
off .... LEAVE, DEPART, BEAT
IT, HIT THE ROAD
shovel .... DIP, VAN, LADLE,
SCOOP, SPADE, DIG(GER),
TROWEL
baker's .... PEEL
shovelhead .... SHARK, STURGEON
show .... PLAY, FLASH, GUIDE,
PROVE, SIGHT, APPEAR,
ESCORT, EVINCE, EXPOSE,
PARADE, DISPLAY, EXHIBIT,
PAGEANT, MANIFEST,
PRETENSE
amusement .... GRIN, TEHEE
anger .... FUME
bill .... PLACARD
biz assn. .... ASCAP
biz award .... OBIE, EMMY,
OSCAR
biz report, famed .... STIX-
NIX-HIX-PIX
contrition .... RUE
empty .... FARCE
excessive fondness .... DOTE
fatigue .... NOD
gumption .... DARE
hit .... SMASH
hypocritical .... MUMMERY

in .... USHER
in a way .... COME IN THIRD
in law .... PLEAD, ALLEGE
indecision .... WAVER, FALTER,
VACILLATE
likeness .... MIRROR
mercy .... SPARE
of embarrassment ..... SQUIRM
off .... SWANK, FLAUNT,
PARADE
opener .... ACT ONE
partiality .... SIDE
peep .... RAREE
pleasure .... SMILE
restraint .... PLAY IT COOL
scorn .... SNEER
stage .... REVUE, FOLLIES
street .... RAREE
up ...... COME, APPEAR, ARRIVE
vain .... POMP
water .... AQUACADE
shower .... BATH, HAIL, POUR,
PARTY, SLEET, SPRAY, PEPPER,
FALLOUT, SCATTER,
RAIN(FALL), SPRINKLE
fall in a .... CASCADE
fine, mistlike .... DRIZZLE
kind of .... BABY, BRIDAL
of meteors .... LEONID,
ANDROMID
sudden .... BRASH
sudden heavy rain .... SPATE
showing .... DISPLAY
good taste .... DECOROUS
sorrow .... PENITENT
showman, famous .... ROSE,
BARNUM, CARROLL, RINGLING,
ZIEGFELD
showmanship .... STYLE,
FANFARE
show-off .... HOTSHOT
showpiece .... SAMPLE, EXAMPLE,
EXHIBIT
showroom model .... DEMO
showy .... ARTY, LOUD, GAUDY,
FLASHY, FLORID, GARISH,
ORNATE, SWANKY, TAWDRY,
DASHING, COLORFUL,
FLAUNTING, FLAMBOYANT,
OSTENTATIOUS
display .... BLAZON, SPLURGE
display in dress ...... FRIPPERY
display of daring .... DASH,
BRAVURA
gaities .... GAUDS
pretense .... TINSEL
show .... PAGEANT(RY),
SPECTACLE, EXTRAVAGANZA
style .... FLAIR
thing, worthless .... TRUMPERY
shrapnel .... SHELL, FRAGMENT

shred .... BIT, DAG, RAG, RIP, SNIP, TEAR, WISP, GRATE, SCRAP, SPECK, STRIP, TRACE, TATTER, FRAZZLE, MAMMOCK, VESTIGE, FRAGMENT
shredded cabbage .... SLAW
shrew .... ERD, HAG, NAG, HARPY, SCOLD, VIXEN, VIRAGO, BELDAM(E), FISHWIFE, TERMAGANT
domineering .... HENPECKER
like .... SORICINE
mouse .... HYRAX
name of Shakespeare's .... KATE
sister of Shakespeare's .... BIANCA
shrewd .... SLY, FOXY, KEEN, WILY, ACUTE, CAGEY, CANNY, SHARP, SMART, ARTFUL, ASTUTE, CLEVER, CUNNING, PRUDENT, SAGACIOUS
person .... FOX, CUTIE, SMOOTHIE
shrewdness .... ACUMEN
shrewish .... BITCHY, CRANKY, NAGGING, IRASCIBLE, TERMAGANT
shriek .... CRY, YELL, SCREAM, SQUEAL, SCREECH
shrieve .... SHERIFF
shrift .... ABSOLUTION
shrike .... BIRD, OSCINE, WOODCHAT
shrill .... PIPY, NASAL, SHARP, STRIDENT, HIGH-PITCHED
sound/voice ..... REEDY, SKIRL, PIPING, SCREAM, SHRIEK, SQUEAL, TREBLE
shrimp .... RUNT, MACRURAN, CRUSTACEAN
appendage .... UROPOD
covering .... MAIL
kin .... GRIBBLE
like crustacean .... PRAWN
shrine .... TOMB, ALTAR, DAGOBA, GROTTO, TEMPLE, MARTYRY, TABERNACLE
for relics .... FERETORY, RELIQUARY
visitor .... PILGRIM
Shrine bowl team .... EAST, WEST
shrink .... COWER, WINCE, WIZEN, CRINGE, FLINCH, RECOIL, REDUCE, SHRIVEL, CONTRACT
from .... FUNK, RECOIL
shrinkage .... LOSS
shrinkee .... ANALYSAND
shrinker, head ...... PSYCHIATRIST
shrinking .... SHY, TIMID

one .... CRINGER
violet .... MOUSE
shrive .... ABSOLVE
shrivel .... CURL, SEAR, WIZEN, SHRINK, WITHER, MUMMIFY, WRINKLE
shroff .... BANKER, MONEYCHANGER
Shropshire .... SALOP
river .... SEVERN
shroud .... PALL, VEIL, CLOAK, COVER, SHEET, SCREEN, CEREMENT
Shrove Tuesday ...... MARDI GRAS
Shroyer role .... ENOS
shrub .... BUSH, ALDER, ELDER, GORSE, LILAC, PLANT, SALAL, SENNA, SUMAC, ALTHEA, LAUREL, SMILAX, SPIREA, BRAMBLE, RHODORA, TREELET, MAGNOLIA, OLEASTER, MISTLETOE, CASCARILLA
aromatic .... MINT, BERGAMOT, LAVENDER, ROSEMARY
bean family .... BROOM, RETEM
berry .... HOLLY, COFFEE, CURRANT
birch family .... HAZEL
bushy .... TOD, CADE, SAVIN
climbing .... LIANA, CLEMATIS, AMPELOPSIS
dwarfed .... BONSAI
ericaceous .... SHEEP-LAUREL
evergreen ..... YEW, ILEX, TITI, ERICA, FURZE, HEATH, SALAL, SAVIN, TOYON, LAUREL, MYRTLE, JASMINE, JUNIPER, CAMELLIA, OLEANDER, OLEASTER, LAURUSTINE
fence .... HEDGE(ROW)
fiber source .... HEMP, JUTE, SISAL
flowering .... ITEA, LILAC, AZALEA, JASMINE, SYRINGA, GARDENIA, HIBISCUS, MAGNOLIA, OLEANDER, MOCK ORANGE
genus .... EVEA, ITEA, OLEA, RHUS, ERICA, SPIREA, LANTANA, SYRINGA
grape family .... AMPELOPSIS
grown flat .... ESPALIER
heath family .... KALMIA
holly family .... ILEX
honeysuckle .... WEIGELA, VIBURNUM
legume family .... INDIGO
madder family .... COFFEE
mallow family ..... ALTH(A)EA,

HIBISCUS, HOLLYHOCK
mint family .... ROSEMARY
olive ..... OLEA, LILAC, PRIVET, JASMIN(E)
Pacific Coast .... SALAL
pea family ...... LOTOS, LOTUS, CASSIA, MIMOSA, LABURNUM, MESQUIT(E), WISTERIA
pepper family .... KAVA, CUBEB
poisonous .... SUMAC(H), OLEANDER
prickly .... CAPER, CHICO, BRAMBLE
rose family .... SPIR(A)EA, HARDHACK
rubber source .... GUAYULE
spiny .... CHICO, FURZE, GORSE
spurge family ..... CASCARILLA
stunted .... SCRUB, BONSAI
tea family .... CAMELLIA
tropical .... INGA, HENNA, ABELIA, JASMIN(E), LANTANA, HIBISCUS, JESSAMINE
shrubbery .... TOD, BRIER, GARDEN, BOSCAGE, COPPICE
shrubby .... FRUTICOSE, FRUTESCENT
shrubs, clump of .... SCRUB
collectively .... SHRUBBERY
shrug .... GESTURE
one's shoulders .... DISLIKE, DISAPPROVE
shuck .... POD, HUSK, SHELL
shudder .... QUAKE, SHAKE, QUIVER, SHIVER, TREMOR, TREMBLE
shuffle .... MIX, DRAG, EVADE, SCUFF, SHIFT, TRICK, FIDGET, JUMBLE, RIFFLE, SWITCH, DECEIVE, SHAMBLE
shuffler .... COOT, DUCK
Shufu .... KASHGAR
Shumagin islander .... ALEUT
shun .... AVOID, DODGE, ELUDE, EVADE, IGNORE
shunt ...... SHIFT, DIVERT, SWITCH, TURN OFF, SIDETRACK
shush .... HIST, HUSH, QUIET, SILENCE
Shushan .... SUSA
shut .... BAR, FOLD, CLOSE, SECURED
in .... PENT(UP), CONFINE, INVALID
out .... BAN, BLANKED, EXCLUDE, OSTRACIZE
up ..... MEW, CLOSET, IMMURE, IMPRISON
with force .... SLAM
shutdown .... END, CLOSURE,

STOPPAGE
shuteye .... SLEEP
shutout .... (TOTAL)DEFEAT
shutter .... SHADE, SLIDE,
　　　BLIND(S), GRILLE, LOUVER,
　　　PERSIENNES
shutterbug .... PHOTOGRAPHER
shuttle .... SWING, SEESAW,
　　　TEETER
　　bobbin/spool .... PIRN
　　thread .... WEFT
shuttlecock .... BIRD
shy .... COY, JIB, MIM, BALK,
　　　WARY, CHARY, SHORT, START,
　　　TIMID, DEMURE, MODEST,
　　　RECOIL, BASHFUL, LACKING,
　　　RESERVED, RETIRING,
　　　TIMOROUS, VERECUND,
　　　DIFFIDENT
　　and cautious .... TIMID
　　and fearful .... TIMOROUS
　　and mistrustful .... SUSPICIOUS
　　and modest .... DEMURE
　　off .... DUCK, DODGE
Shylock .... USURER,
　　　MONEYLENDER
　　daughter of .... JESSICA
　　money of .... DUCATS
shylocking .... USURY
shyster .... PETTIFOGGER
sialid .... INSECT, DOBSONFLY
Siam .... THAILAND
siamang .... GIBBON
Siamese. See also **Thailand**
　　capital .... AYUDHYA,
　　　BANGKOK, THONBURI
　　coin .... ATT, BAHT, TICAL
　　dynasty .... CHAKRI
　　isthmus .... KRA
　　king ...... MAHIDOL, MONGKUT,
　　　ADULYADEJ, PRACHATIPOK,
　　　CHULALONGKORN
　　kingdom capital
　　　.............................. CHIENGMAI
　　measure ...... KUP, SOK, NGAN,
　　　NIOU, SISTI
　　monetary unit .... BAHT, TICAL
　　premier .... THANARAT
　　queen .... SIRIKIT
　　river .... MENAM, CHAUPAYA
　　tongue .... LAO, TAI
　　tribe .... MEO
　　twins, one of ..... ENG, CHANG
　　weight .... PAI, KLAM, KLOM,
　　　TICAL
Sian is capital of .... SHENSI
sib .... SISTER, BROTHER,
　　　KIN(SMAN), RELATIVE
Sibelius, composer .... JEAN
　　work ..... FINLANDIA, SWAN OF
　　　TUONELA

Siberian .... VOGUL, SAMOYED(E)
　　antelope .... SAIGA
　　city .... OMSK, TOMSK
　　dog .... SAMOYED(E)
　　forests .... TAIGA
　　fur .... CALABAR, CALABER
　　ibex .... TEK
　　leopard .... OUNCE
　　mountains .... ALTAI
　　native .... YUIT, TATAR,
　　　YAKUT, KIRGIZ
　　peninsula .... TAIMIR,
　　　KAMCHATKA
　　plain .... STEPPE
　　region .... OMSK, TA(R)TARY
　　river .... OB, AMUR, LENA,
　　　TOBOL, IRTISH, KOLIMA,
　　　YENISEI
　　sheep .... ARGALI
　　squirrel .... CALABAR,
　　　CALABER, MINIVER
　　tent .... YURT
　　warehouse .... ETAPE
　　wasteland .... STEPPE
　　wild cat .... MANUL
　　windstorm .... BURAN
sibilance/sibilate .... HISS
sibling .... KIN, SIS(TER), BROTHER
sibyl .... WITCH, ORACLE, SEERESS,
　　　SORCERESS, FORTUNETELLER
sibylline .... ORACULAR
　　sign .... OMEN
sic .... SO, SUCH, THUS, ATTACK,
　　　INCITE, JUST SO, RIGHTLY
sicca .... SEAL
siccative .... DRIER, DRYING
Sicilian .... SICANIAN, TRINACRIAN
　　cape .... PASSERO
　　capital .... PALERMO
　　city/town .... ENNA, GELA,
　　　NOTO, MODICA, RAGUSA,
　　　CATANIA, MARSALA,
　　　MAZZARO, TRAPANI,
　　　CORLEONE, SYRACUSE,
　　　VITTORIA, AGRIGENTO
　　code of silence .... OMERTA
　　evergreen .... MAQUIS
　　gulf .... CASTELLAMMARE
　　hero .... ENTELLUS
　　inhabitant, legendary
　　　................................. CYCLOPS
　　king .... RENE
　　landmark .... ETNA
　　resort .... ENNA
　　river .... SALSO, BELICE,
　　　SIMETO
　　seaport .... MARSALA,
　　　MESSINA, MILAZZO, PALERMO
　　secret society .... MAFIA
　　shotgun .... LUPARA
　　sizzler .... ETNA

　　strait .... SICILY, MESSINA
　　volcano .... (A)ETNA
　　whirlpool .... CHARYBDIS
　　wine .... MARSALA
sick .... ILL, AILING, ATTACK,
　　　UNWELL, UNSOUND,
　　　NAUSEOUS, NAUSEATED,
　　　SURFEITED, INDISPOSED
　　and tired .... FED UP
　　of .... BORED
　　person .... INVALID, PATIENT
sickbed, of a .... CLINICAL
sicken .... AIL, AFFLICT, NAUSEATE
sickening .... GROSS, NASTY,
　　　DISGUSTING
sickle .... HOOK, SIVE, SCYTHE,
　　　BUSHWHACKER
　　shaped .... FALCATE
sickly .... WAN, PALE, FAINT,
　　　AILING, LANGUID
sickness .... MALADY, NAUSEA,
　　　AILMENT, DISEASE, ILLNESS,
　　　COMPLAINT
Sid .... CAESAR
　　Caesar's dog .... CONUS
　　Caesar's partner ...... IMOGENE
　　　COCA
　　Caesar's wife .... FLORENCE
Siddhartha .... BUDDHA
side .... EDGE, PART, VIEW, FACET,
　　　FLANK, ASPECT, BORDER,
　　　FACTION, SURFACE, POSITION
　　arm(s) .... SWORD, DAGGER,
　　　PISTOL, BAYONET, REVOLVER
　　by one's .... NEAR, CLOSE
　　by side .... BESIDE, ABREAST,
　　　ALONGSIDE, COLLATERAL
　　dish .... SLAW, SOUP, SALAD,
　　　ENTREE, TRIMMING,
　　　ENTREMETS
　　effect .... REACTION
　　hill .... SLOPE
　　interest .... HOBBY, AVOCATION
　　meat .... BACON
　　of a .... LATERAL
　　pain .... STITCH
　　person's .... LEFT, RIGHT
　　portion .... RASHER
　　road .... BYWAY
　　trip .... SALLY, EXCURSION
　　view .... PROFILE
　　with .... AGREE, ALINE
sideboard .... CABINET, CREDENZA
sideburns .... WHISKERS, MUTTON
　　　CHOPS
sidecar .... COCKTAIL
sidekick ...... PAL, CHUM, BUDDY,
　　　FRIEND, PARTNER, ALTER EGO
　　of Red Ryder .... LITTLE
　　　BEAVER
sideline .... BENCH, BY-WORK

sidelong look .... GLANCE, SQUINT
sidereal .... STARRY, STELLAR
siderite .... IRON(ORE), METEORITE
sidero, as combining form
.... IRON, STAR
sides, _____ (everywhere) .... ON
ALL
unequal .... SCALENE
sideslip .... SKID
sidesplitter ...... JOKE, LAUGHTER
sidesplitting .... FUNNY, HEARTY,
CONVULSIVE
sidestep .... SHUN, AVOID, DODGE,
EVADE, CIRCUMVENT
sidetrack .... TURN, AVERT,
DETER, SHUNT, DIVERT,
SIDING, SWITCH
sidewalk .... FOOTPATH,
PAVEMENT, BANQUETTE
entrepreneur .... ARTIST,
BEGGAR, HAWKER, VENDOR,
NEWSBOY, PEDDLER
sideways, move .... EDGE, SKID,
SIDLE
walker .... CRAB
sidewinder .... CROTALUS,
RATTLESNAKE
sidewise .... ASKANCE, LATERAL
move .... SKEW, SIDLE
siding .... SPUR, SHINGLE,
PANELING, CLAPBOARD
sidle .... JIB, EDGE, SKEW, FLANK,
SLITHER
Sidon's name now .... SAIDA
siecle .... AGE, ERA, PERIOD,
CENTURY
siege ...... BLOCKADE, CORDONING,
INVESTMENT
lay .... BESET, INVEST, SUBJECT
TO
siegers' shelter .... CAT, MANTLET
Siegfried .... SIGURD
follower .... NIBELUNG
Line .... LIMES, WESTWALL
sword of .... BALMUNG
wife of .... KRIEMHILD
sienna .... PIGMENT
color .... REDDISH-BROWN
Sierra .... LEONE, MADRE, RANGE,
NEVADA, PINTADO, KINGFISH
fish resembling ..... MACKEREL
Leone capital .... FREETOWN
mountain .... DANA
Nevada fog .... POGONIP
Nevada lake .... TAHOE
Nevada peak .... WHITNEY,
MULHACEN
siesta .... NAP, REST, SNOOZE
sieur .... SIR
sieve ...... LAWN, LAUNE, BOLTER,
FILTER, RIDDLE, SCREEN,

SIFTER, CRIBBLE, TROMMEL,
COLANDER, STRAINER
coal, ore .... TROMMEL
like a .... ETHMOID
sift .... BOLT, SORT, WEIGH,
FILTER, SCREEN, WINNOW,
SEPARATE
dialect .... REE
sifter .... SIEVE, BOLTER,
COLANDER, STRAINER
siftings .... DREGS, RESIDUE
sigh ...... SOB, LONG, MOAN, SOUF,
SOUGH, YEARN, MURMUR,
SUSPIRE
sight .... AIM, EYE, ESPY, LOOK,
VIEW, SCENE, VISTA, VISION,
DISPLAY, GLIMPSE, PICTURE,
SPECTACLE
by .... VISUAL(LY)
colloquial ...... UGLY, EYESORE
come into .... LOOM, APPEAR
gun .... BEAD
of .... OCULAR, VISUAL
sightless .... BLIND
sightly .... COMELY
sightsee .... TOUR
sightseer .... TOURIST, VISITING
FIREMAN
sightseeing .... RUBBERNECKING
sigil .... SEAL, SIGNET
sigmoid .... ESS, SIGMATE
sign .... INK, MARK, NEON, OMEN,
BADGE, INDEX, TOKEN,
TRACE, EMBLEM, SYMBOL,
EARMARK, GESTURE, INDICIA,
PORTENT, VESTIGE, SYMPTOM,
EVIDENCE, INDICATION
affirmative .... NOD
arithmetical .... PLUS, MINUS
away .... CONVEY
Blue Eagle .... NRA
display ..... PLACARD, SHINGLE
handicapped person's
.... WHEELCHAIR
homage .... BOW, KNEEL,
CURTSY, SALAAM,
GENUFLECTION
in magic .... SIGIL
in music .... BAR, SLUR,
NEUM(E), PRESA, SEGNO,
STAFF, (TREBLE)CLEF
language .... AMESLAN
language science
.... SEMIOLOGY
of a hit .... SRO
a skunk .... ODOR
assent .... NOD
disapproval .... SHRUG
pleasure .... GRIN, SMILE
possession .... APOSTROPHE
sorrow .... RED EYES

omission .... CARET
road/street .... STOP, ARROW,
FLARE, YIELD
up .... HIRE, JOIN, EMPLOY,
ENGAGE, ENLIST, ENROL(L)
signal .... CUE, BUZZ, FLAG, SIGN,
WARN, ALARM, ARROW,
TOKEN, WIGWAG, NOTABLE,
STRIKING
actor's .... CUE
assembly .... REVEILLE
bell .... GONG
board .... SHINGLE
danger .... SIREN, SYMPTOM,
RED FLAG, RED LIGHT
entrance/exit .... SENNET
eye .... WINK
flag .... ABLE, JACK, WAIF,
ENSIGN
for parley .... CHAMADE,
WHITE FLAG
Indian .... SMOKE
light .... FLARE, BEACON
lights out .... TAPS
of quarantine .... YELLOW
FLAG, YELLOW JACK
railroad .... FUSEE
retirement .... TAPS, CURFEW
retreat .... CHAMADE
seance .... TAP
set .... CODE, LORAN
stage .... CUE, SENNET
to attract attention .... PST
tone, short high-pitched
.... PIP
warning .... WINK, ALARM,
ALERT, SIREN, CAUTION, RED
LIGHT
signaling apparatus ...... BEACON,
HOWLER, BLINKER, FOGHORN,
SEMAPHORE
system of .... SEMAPHORE
trumpet ..... SHOFAR, SHOPHAR
signatory .... CO-MAKER, (CO-
)SIGNER
signature .... HAND, SEAL,
AUTOGRAPH
faked .... FORGERY
flourish .... PARAPH, SCROLL
historic .... RELEE
in radio/musical .... THEME
of a sort .... THUMBMARK,
CRISS-CROSS
slang ..... FIST, JOHN HANCOCK
signboard .... SHINGLE
signet .... SEAL, SIGIL
significance ...... VALUE, WEIGHT,
MOMENT, MEANING,
IMPORT(ANCE)
significant .... TELLING,
EVENTFUL, IMPORTANT,

MOMENTOUS, MEANINGFUL
signify .... BODE, MEAN, SHOW, IMPLY, DENOTE, INDICATE
Signoret, actress .... SIMONE
signpost .... CLUE, GUIDE, HERMA
signs, of .... SEMIOTIC
Sigurd .... SIEGFRIED
father of .... REGIN
victim of .... FAFNIR
Sikh religion founder .... NANAK
Sikkim capital .... GANGTOK
inhabitants .... NEPALESE
king .... CHOGYAL
queen .... GYALMO
woman's dress .... KHO
Sikorsky, airplane builder
.... IGOR
silage .... FODDER
Silas Marner author .... ELIOT
ward of .... EPPIE
silence .... GAG, LULL, OYEZ, PEACE, APHONY, MUFFLE, (S)HUSH, (W)HIST, STIFLE, REPRESS, MUTE(NESS), THROTTLE, STILLNESS, QUIET(UDE)
slang .... SHUT UP
silencer ...... GAG, MUTE, HUSHER, MUZZLE, MUFFLER
judge's .... GAVEL
silent ...... MUM, MUTE(D), QUIET, STILL, TACIT, WHIST, INACTIVE, NOISELESS, SOUNDLESS
actor .... MIMER
habitually .... TACITURN
it is .... TACET
killer .... HYPERTENSION
one .... CLAM
Silenus .... DEITY, SATYR
foster son of .... BACCHUS, DIONYSUS
Silesia .... LINEN, SLASK
silex .... FLINT, QUARTZ, SILICA
silhouette ...... SHADOW, OUTLINE, PORTRAIT
silica .... MICA, SAND, SILEX, QUARTZ, MINERAL
deposit .... SINTER
silicate ...... MICA, ESTER, CERITE, EPIDOTE, TREMOLITE
silique .... POD
silk ...... TULLE, FABRIC, ALAMODE
and cotton cloth ..... EOLIENNE
and wool cloth .... BARATHEA, EOLIENNE
cloth, damask-like .... LAMPAS
cloth for ribbons, etc.
.... SARCENET
cloth, striped .... TABARET
coarse .... TUSSA(H), TUSSAR,

TUSSER
cocoon .... BAVE
color of raw .... ECRU
corded .... REPP, REP(S), FAILLE, OTTOMAN, PADUASOY
cotton (tree) .... CEIBA, KAPOK
crinkled cloth of .... CREPE
fabric .... GROS, CAFFA, MOIRE, PEKIN, QIANA, SATIN, SURAH, VOILE, BAREGE, MADRAS, PONGEE, SENDAL, SAMITE, VELVET, TAFFETA, VELOUR(S), SHANTUNG, CHARMEUSE, MESSALINE
fiber .... FLOSS
filament .... BRIN
fine, thin .... SARCENET, SARSENET
finely woven ...... LANSDOWNE
floss .... SLEAVE
for mourning .... ALMAS
glossy .... SATIN, TAFFETA, LUSTRING, LUTESTRING
hat .... TILE, TOPPER
heavy .... GROS
hit the .... PARACHUTE
knitted .... JERSEY
like .... SERICEOUS
lining material ...... SARCENET, SARSENET
lustrous .... PANNE
net .... MALINE(S)
netting .... TULLE
patterned .... MOIRE
prefix meaning .... SERIC
producing moth
.... AILANTHUS
raw .... GREGE, MARABOU
ribbed .... REPP, REP(S), FAILLE
ribbonlike .... GIMP
screen print .... SERIGRAPH
sheer .... VOILE, CHIFFON
shreds .... NOIL
source of .... ERIA, COCOON, AILANTHUS
-stocking .... WHIG, ELITE, ELEGANT, WEALTHY
synthetic .... NYLON, ORLON, RAYON, DACRON
taffeta with stripes ..... TABBY
thread .... TRAM, FLOSS, SLEAVE
thread, twisted .... TRAM, FLOSS
thread, very fine quality
.... ORGANZINE
threadmaker .... THROWSTER
tree .... SIRIS, MIMOSA
twilled .... ALMA, SERGE, SURAH
twisted .... ROVE

veil .... TULLE
waste .... KNUB, NOIL, FLOSS, FRISON
watered .... MOIRE, TABBY, MOREEN
weight .... PARI
with metal threads .... LAME
with raised design
.... BROCADE
Silkeborg Museum site
.... JUTLAND
silken .... SOFT, SERIC, GLOSSY, SMOOTH, ELEGANT
silkworm .... ERI(A), BOMBYX, TUSSA(H), TUSSER, TUSSORE
cocoon covering .... FLOSS
covering .... COCOON
disease .... UJI
food/leaves .... MULBERRY, AILANTHUS
moth .... BOMBYCID, CECROPIA
raising .... SERICULTURE
silky .... SOFT, SLEEK, SATINY, SMOOTH, LUSTROUS, SERICEOUS
furred animal .... TAMARIN, MARMOSET, CHINCHILLA
sill .... FRAME, LEDGE, SHELF
counterpart .... LINTEL
projection .... DRIP
sillabub ...... DESSERT, BEVERAGE
siller .... MONEY
sillier .... INANER
silliness .... INANITY
Sills, singer .... BEVERLY
silly .... DAFT, ANILE, DAFFY, INANE, KOOKY, SAPPY, ABSURD, KOOKIE, ASININE, FATUOUS, FOOLISH, PUERILE, IMBECILE, SLAP-HAPPY
language .... BOMBAST
one .... GOOSE
smile .... SIMPER
silo .... BIN, PIT, CRIB, TOWER
silt ...... WASH, LOESS, ALLUVIUM, SEDIMENT
silurid .... CATFISH
silva .... WOODS
silver .... COIN, MONEY, SYCEE, SILLER, ARGENT(UM)
abbreviation .... STER
alloy .... ALBATA, BILLON
containing .... LUNAR, ARGENTOL
dollar: sl. .... CARTWHEEL
fluoride .... TACHIOL
fox fur .... PLATINA
gilded .... VERMEIL
in alchemy .... LUNA
ingot .... SYCEE, BULLION
lacework .... FILIGREE

like/of .... ARGENTINE
oxidizer .... TARNISHER
screen .... CINEMA, MOVIES
sulfide .... ARGENTITE
symbol .... AG
telluride .... HESSITE
-tongued .... ELOQUENT
-tongued person .... ORATOR
unminted ...... SYCEE, BULLION
wire work .... FILIGREE
Silver Age writer .... JUVENAL,
            MARTIAL, TACITUS
State .... NEVADA
silverfish .... SARGO, TARPON
Silverheels' role .... TONTO
silverside(s) .... MINNOW, TINKER,
            GRUNION
silverware decoration
            .... GADROON
silverweed .... TANSY
silvery .... ARGENT(INE)
silviculture .... FORESTRY
simar .... ROBE, JACKET
Simenon, author .... GEORGES
detective .... MAIGRET
novel .... MAIGRET
simian .... APE, MONKEY
astronaut .... BONNY,
            ASTROMONK
similar ...... AKIN, NEAR, (A)LIKE,
            CLOSE, AGNATE, SUCH(AS),
            ANALOGOUS
combining form .... HOMEO
similarity .... ANALOGY,
            LIKENESS, SAMENESS
similarly .... LIKEWISE
simile .... METAPHOR
similitude .... IMAGE, DOUBLE,
            LIKENESS, FACSIMILE
simmer .... COOK, FUME, STEW,
            BROOD, SEETHE, (PAR)BOIL
down .... COOL, SUBSIDE
simnel .... BISCUIT, FRUITCAKE
simoleon .... DOLLAR
Simon .... PETER, APOSTLE
pure .... REAL, AMATEUR,
            GENUINE
the overseer .... LEGREE
Simon's acquaintance .... PIEMAN
sporty slob .... OSCAR
simoom/simoon .... WIND,
            SAMIEL, TEBBAD
simp .... DOLT, SIMPLETON
simper .... SMILE, SMIRK
simple .... BARE, EASY, MERE,
            SNAP, CLEAR, GREEN, LOWLY,
            NAIVE, PLAIN, COMMON,
            HOMELY, SINGLE, ARTLESS,
            NATURAL
in law .... ABSOLUTE
machine .... AXLE, LEVER,

SCREW, WHEEL, PULLEY
minded .... STUPID, FOOLISH
organism ..... MONAD, AMOEBA
simpleton .... DAW, OAF, SAP,
            COOT, DOLT, DOPE, FOOL,
            GABY, GAUP, GAWK, GOWK,
            ZANY, BOOBY, DUNCE, GOOSE,
            MORON, NINNY, NODDY,
            DIMWIT, DOODLE, GANDER,
            NITWIT, GOMERAL, IMBECILE,
            SOFTHEAD, NINCOMPOOP
Simplon _____ .... PASS
simply ...... JUST, ONLY, MERELY,
            PURELY, SOLELY
simulacrum .... SHAM, IMAGE,
            TRAVESTY
simular .... FEIGNED
simulate .... ACT, APE, FAKE,
            SHAM, FEIGN, MIMIC, AFFECT,
            ASSUME, IMITATE, PRETEND
simulation .... FEINT, FEIGNING,
            PRETENSE
simultaneous .... COINCIDENT
simurgh .... ROC
sin .... ERR, ENVY, EVIL, VICE,
            FAULT, GREED, GUILT, SLOTH,
            OFFENSE, INIQUITY, TRESPASS,
            TRANSGRESS
against a person, place or
            thing .... SACRILEGE
capable of .... PECCABLE
petty .... PECCADILLO
repentance for .... REMORSE,
            ATTRITION, PENITENCE,
            CONTRITION
Sinai .... HOREB, MOUNT
sinalbin .... GLUCOSIDE
Sinaloa capital .... CULIACAN
sinapism .... PLASTER
Sinatra, former Mrs. .... AVA,
            MIA
since .... AGO, SITH, HENCE,
            BEFORE NOW, INASMUCH AS
sincere .... OPEN, FRANK, CANDID,
            HEARTY, HONEST, EARNEST,
            GENUINE, FAITHFUL,
            HEARTFELT
sincerely .... WITH ALL MY HEART
sinciput .... FOREHEAD
Sinclair, novelist .... MAY, LEWIS,
            UPTON, CATHERINE
character .... CASS, BABBITT,
            DOREMUS
Sind, capital of .... KARACHI
Sin(d)bad the _____ ...... SAILOR
number of voyages taken by
            .... SEVEN
supposed birthplace of
            .... SOHAR
transport of .... ROC
sine .... WITHOUT

prole .... CHILDLESS
qua _____ .... NON
sinecure .... SNAP, CINCH
sinew(s) .... FORCE, THEWS,
            MUSCLE, TENDON, STRENGTH
sinewy .... WIRY, TOUGH,
            BRAWNY, ROBUST, STRONG,
            MUSCULAR
sinful .... EVIL, WICKED,
            IMMORAL, PECCANT
sing .... HUM, BUZZ, CAROL,
            CHANT, WARBLE, WHISTLE
cheerfully .... LILT
in certain way .... HUM,
            CROON, YODEL
in full rolling voice .... TROLL
praises to .... LAUD, EXTOL,
            GLORIFY
slang .... SQUEAL, CONFESS,
            BLOW THE WHISTLE
the opening phrase of a
            canticle .... INTONE
Singapore founder .... RAFFLES
garment .... SARI, KEBAYA,
            SAMFOO, CHEONGSAM
nickname of .... LION CITY
old name .... TEMASEK
president .... YUSOF
prime minister .... LEE
soup .... SOTO
singe .... BURN, SEAR, SCORCH
singer .... BIRD, POET, CANTOR,
            CAROLER, WARBLER,
            YODELER, MINSTREL,
            VOCALIST, CHORIST(ER)
Arnold .... EDDY
Bennett .... TONY
Brewer .... TERESA
Brooks .... GARTH
Campbell .... GLEN
Cash .... JOHNNY
choir .... ALTO, SOLOIST
Como .... PERRY
Donkey Serenade .... NANETTE
            FABRAY
female .... DIVA, COLE, LIND,
            JONES, PRICE, SILLS, SMITH,
            SOPRANO, STEVENS,
            CHANTEUSE, MADONNA,
            CHANTRESS, STREISAND,
            CANTATRICE, COLORATURA
Iglesias .... JULIO
Jones .... TOM, GEORGE
male .... COMO, JONES, LANZA,
            NEWTON, ROGERS, JACKSON,
            PRESLEY, SINATRA, BARITONE,
            CAMPBELL, IGLESIAS,
            MINSTREL
Manilow .... BARRY
Mathis .... JOHNNY
Moffo .... ANNA

Nabors .... JIM
Nelson .... WILLIE
Newton .... WAYNE
of a chantey .... SEAMAN
of Israel .... DAVID
opera ..... ALDA, PONS, GLUCK,
   HORNE, MELBA, PATTI, PINZA,
   SILLS, CALLAS, CARUSO,
   TAUBER, TIBBET, TUCKER,
   DOMINGO, NILSSON, STEVENS,
   TEBALDI, TRAUBEL
Orbison .... RAY
Parton .... DOLLY
pop .... ANKA
Presley .... ELVIS
Price .... LEONTYNE
Pride .... CHARLEY
Richie .... LIONEL
Rogers .... KENNY
Robbins .... MARTY
Sinatra .... FRANK, NANCY
stock of .... REPERTORY,
   REPERTOIRE
Streisand .... BARBRA
sweet .... LARK
Twitty .... CONWAY
wandering .... BUSKER,
   MINSTREL
Whittaker .... ROGER
Williams .... ANDY, HANK
singers' aid .... MIKE
group .... CHOIR, CHORUS,
   TROUPE, ENSEMBLE
singing voice .... ALTO, BASSO,
   TENOR, SOPRANO, BARITONE,
   FALSETTO, COLORATURA
single ...... ACE, ONE, SOLE, SOLO,
   UNAL, (A)LONE, UNWED,
   SOLITARY, UNMARRIED,
   INDIVIDUAL
combining form .... UNI,
   MONO, HAPLO
family dwelling, descriptive
   of .... DETACHED
file .... TANDEM
foot .... RACK
footed .... MONOPODE
handed .... UNAIDED
in baseball .... BASE HIT
in biology .... UNIVALENT
in telegraphy .... SIMPLEX
instance/time .... ONCE
man .... BACHELOR
-minded .... ONE-TRACK
out ...... PICK, CHOOSE, SELECT
period in office ..... ONE TERM
point .... ACE
rack railway .... MONORAIL
service charge .... ONE FEE
sticker .... SLOOP, SAILBOAT
thing .... UNIT

unit .... MONAD
singlet .... JERSEY, UNDERSHIRT
singly .... SOLO, ALONE, UNAIDED,
   ONE BY ONE
singsong recitation .... CHIME
singular .... ODD, RARE, SOLE,
   QUEER, UNIQUE, CURIOUS,
   STRANGE, UNUSUAL,
   PECULIAR, INDIVIDUAL
opposed to .... PLURAL
sinigrin .... GLUCOSIDE
sinister .... BAD, EVIL, GRIM,
   LEFT, WICKED, BALEFUL,
   HARMFUL, OMINOUS,
   INJURIOUS, PORTENTOUS
opposed to .... DEXTER
sink .... DIP, EBB, SAG, BOWL,
   FALL, WANE, BASIN, DROOP,
   DROWN, LAPSE, LOWER,
   SEWER, SLUMP, DEEPEN,
   RECEDE, SETTLE, DECLINE,
   DESCEND, IMMERSE, SUBSIDE,
   SUBMERGE
capital in a venture .... RISK,
   GAMBLE, PLUNGE
hole .... CESSPOOL
in .... PENETRATE
ship deliberately ...... SCUTTLE
-side convenience .... TOWEL
   RACK
sinker .... DONUT, DOUGHNUT
Sinkiang capital .... URUMCHI
sinking in the mud .... MIRING
sinless .... INNOCENT
Sinn _____, **Irish society** .... FEIN
sinople .... CINNABAR
sinuate .... WAVY, SINUOUS
sinuous .... WAVY, CURVED,
   DEVIOUS, WINDING, SLITHERY,
   SERPENTINE
sinus .... BEND, ANTRA, CURVE,
   TRACT, ANTRUM, CAVITY
_____ (dark moon plain)
   .... RORIS
kind of .... FRONTAL,
   ETHMOIDAL, MAXILLARY,
   SPHENOIDAL
sinuses .... AIR SPACES
drainage organ of .... NOSE
inflammation .... SINUSITIS
location of .... NOSE,
   FOREHEAD, CHEEKBONE
Sioux .... CROW, IOWA, OTO(E),
   OSAGE, PONCA, TETON,
   DAKOTA, MANDAN, CATAWBA,
   TUTELOS
chief .... SITTING BULL
sip .... NIP, SUCK, TIFF, DRINK,
   TASTE, IMBIBE, SAMPLING
siphon .... DRAW, STRAW,
   EXTRACT

sipid .... SAVORY
sipper .... STRAW
sippet .... TOAST, CROUTON,
   FRAGMENT
sipping tube .... STRAW
sir .... MR, SRI, TUAN, BWANA,
   SAHIB, SENOR, MISTER,
   EFFENDI, SEIGNOR,
   (MON)SIEUR
sire .... BEGET, PROCREATE,
   (FORE)FATHER
siren .... VAMP, CIRCE, NYMPH,
   WITCH, CHARMER,
   (FOG)HORN, LORELEI,
   WHISTLE, PARTHENOPE,
   ENCHANTRESS
like a .... SEDUCTIVE
Rhine .... LURLEI, LORELEI
sirenian .... DUGONG, SEA COW,
   MANATEE
Sirius .... DOG STAR, CANICULA
of .... SOTHIC
sirloin beef .... BARON
sirocco .... WIND
Madeira island .... LESTE
sirup. See **syrup**
sisal .... HEMP, AGAVE, FIBER,
   HENEQUIN
Sisera's enemy .... BARAK
murderer .... JAEL
soldiers .... CANAANITES
siskin .... FINCH, TARIN
sissy .... MILKSOP, WEAKLING,
   MAMA'S BOY, PANTYWAIST
like a .... EFFIMINATE
slang .... CHICKEN
sister .... NUN, SIB, NANCE,
   NURSE, SOROR, TITTY,
   WOMAN, TITTIE
fictional .... CARRIE
headdress of a .... CORNET
sisterhood .... SODALITY,
   SORORITY
Sistine Chapel feature
   .... FRESCOES
Madonna painter ..... RAPHAEL
sistrum .... RATTLE
sit .... POSE, BROOD, PERCH,
   ROOST
down to meet .... CONVENE
in .... ATTEND
in on .... LISTEN
on ..... PERCH, STIFLE, REPRESS
tight .... WAIT
Sita's husband .... RAMA
site .... SEAT, ARENA, SCENE,
   STEAD, LOCALE, LOCATION
for a drum .... EAR
for a lot of bucks .... RODEO
of abortive Cuban invasion
   .... BAY OF PIGS

Apollo oracle .... DELOS
Disneyland .... TOKYO, ANAHEIM
Disney World ...... ORLANDO
famous California aquarium
.... MONTEREY
famous Florida aquarium
.... MARINELAND
rods and cones ,...... RETINA
sitology .... DIETETICS
Sitsang .... TIBET
sitter .... NURSE, BROODER
sitting .... SEATED, MEETING, SESSION
of the court .... SESSION
room .... SALA, PARLOR, BOUDOIR
spiritual .... SEANCE
Sitting Bull's antagonist
.... CUSTER
sobriquet .... MEDICINE MAN
son .... CROWFOOT
situate .... PUT, SET, PLACE, POSIT, LOCATE
situation .... PLACE, STATE, LOCATION, POSITION
advantageous .... CAT-BIRD SEAT
difficult .... FIX, JAM, PINCH, PLIGHT, STRAIT, DISTRESS, HARDSHIP
entrapping .... NET, WEB
situs .... LOCATION, POSITION
Sitwell, poet .... EDITH, OSBERT
Siva's wife .... DEVI, MAYA, S(H)AKTI
six .... HEXAD, SESTET
combining form .... HEXA
footed .... HEXAPOD
group of ...... HEXAD, SENARY, SESTET, SEXTET(TE), SEXTUPLET
in dice game .... SICE, SISE
line stanza .... SESTET
of .... SENARY
pointed figure .... STAR
prefix .... HEXA
shooter .... REVOLVER
-sided figure .... HEXAGON
-sided solid .... CUBE
years, lasting .... SEXENNIAL
16-½ feet .... ROD, POLE, PERCH
sixth day, occurring every
.... SEXTAN
sense .... INTUITION
sense for short .... ESP
60's musical .... HAIR
sixty grains .... DRAM
sizable .... BIG, HUGE, VAST, AMPLE, GREAT, HEFTY,

LARGE, BULKY, PORTLY, IMMENSE, MASSIVE, SUBSTANTIAL
size .... AREA, BULK, EXTENT, DEGREE, VOLUME, CAPACITY, MAGNITUDE
exceeding the usual
.... ENORMOUS, GIGANTIC
of a bullet .... CALIBER
book page .... OCTAVO
great .... TITANIC
hole .... BORE
measurements
.... DIMENSION
paper .... DEMY, ROYAL, FOOLSCAP
of type .... AGATE
prefix .... DEMI
up .... EYE
sizy .... VISCOUS, GLUTINOUS
sizzle ...... FRY, BURN, HISS, SEAR, FRIZZ(LE), SPUTTER
sizzling .... ANGRY, (RED)HOT
skate .... RAY, CHAP, GLIDE, ROCKER
blade .... RUNNER
slang .... NAG, HORSE
skater's leap .... AXEL
skating arena .... RINK
sign .... REDBALL
skean .... SWORD, DAGGER
skedaddle ...... RUN, BLOW, BOLT, FLEE, DECAMP
skee .... SKI
skeg .... FIN
skein .... RAP, HANK, MESH
of yarn .... HASP
skeletal .... LEAN, THIN, SKINNY
disease ...... RICKETS, RACHITIS
skeleton .... ATOMY, BONES, DRAFT, CARCASS, OUTLINE, FRAME(WORK)
additional small bones in the
.... SESAMOIDS
bone, appendicular ...... ULNA, FEMUR, TIBIA, FIBULA, RADIUS, HUMERUS, PATELLA, SCAPULA, CLAVICLE, PHALANGE, (META)CARPAL, (META)TARSAL
bone, axial .... RIB, SPINE, SKULL, COCCYX, SACRUM, STERNUM, MANDIBLE, VERTEBRA(E)
connective tissue ..... TENDON, LIGAMENT
copy in printing .... DUMMY
force .... CADRE
hiding place of .... CLOSET
in the closet ..... PAST, SECRET
key .... MASTER(KEY)

limb girdle of the ...... PELVIS, SHOULDER
main part of the .... AXIAL, APPENDICULAR
sea animal .... CORAL
skellum .... SCAMP, RASCAL
skelp .... SMACK
skelter .... RUSH
Skelton, comedian .... RED
skep .... BASKET, HAMPER, BEEHIVE
skeptic .... CYNIC, LUCIAN, PYRRHO, DOUBTER, AGNOSTIC
Biblical .... THOMAS
skeptical .... WAVY, LEERY, DUBIOUS, PYRRHONIC
skepticism .... DOUBT, MISTRUST, UNBELIEF, AGNOSTICISM
skerry .... REEF
sketch .... MAP, SKIT, CHART, DRAFT, DESIGN, DRAW(ING), OUTLINE, PLAYLET, AFTERPIECE
aimlessly .... DOODLE
exaggerated .... CARICATURE
out .... DELINEATE
sketchy .... ROUGH, UNEVEN
skete member .... MONK, HERMIT
skew .... SIDLE, TWIST, SQUINT, SWERVE, DISTORT, OBLIQUE
on a .... SLANTWISE
skewer .... PIN, SPIT, TRUSS, BROACH, PIERCE, SKIVER, BROCHETTE
ski .... RUNNER, SNOWSHOE
lift .... T-BAR
mecca .... ASPEN
move .... RUADE
resort, famed .... ASPEN
run .... JUMP, SCHUSS, SLALOM, DOWNHILL
trail .... PISTE
skid ...... SLUE, SPIN, TRIG, BRAKE, SLIDE, (SIDE)SLIP
skiddoo .... LEAVE, DEPART
skid row character .... HOBO, BEGGAR, VAGRANT, DERELICT
skier's garment .... PARKA
hazard .... WINDBURN
transport .... T-BAR
skiff .... CAIQUE, ROWBOAT
skiing fan .... SNOWBIRD
race .... SLALOM
skill .... ART, GIFT, CRAFT, ADROIT, TALENT, FINESSE, KNOW-HOW, PROWESS, DEXTERITY, EXPERTISE, PROFICIENCY
combining form .... TECHNO
manual .... HANDICRAFT
skilled .... DEFT, WISE, ADEPT,

SHARP, ASTUTE, EXPERT, GIFTED, MASTER, VERSED, EDUCATED, SURE-FOOTED

skillet .... SPIDER, (FRYING)PAN

skillful .... APT, ABLE, DEFT, ADEPT, CLEVER, HANDY, ADROIT, EXPERT, DEXT(E)ROUS, ACCOMPLISHED

one .... PRO

workmanship .... D(A)EDAL

skim .... FLIT, SCAN, SCUD, SCUM, CREAM, GLIDE, BROWSE, GLANCE, COAT(ING)

skimmer .... SCISSORBILL

skimp .... SAVE, PINCH, SCAMP, SCANT, STINT, SCRIMP, ECONOMIZE

skimpy .... MEAGER, SCANTY, STINGY, NIGGARDLY

skin .... BARK, COAT, CUTIS, DERM(A), SHELL, STRIP, LAMINA, PLATING, COVERING, (EPI)DERMIS

abscess .... FURUNCLE

allergy .... ECZEMA, URTICARIA, DERMATITIS

analysis .... BIOPSY

animal .... FUR, KID, FELL, HIDE, PELT, SUEDE, PELLAGE

benign tumor .... CYST, KERATOSIS, PAPILLOMA

blemish .... MOLE, WART, NEVUS, FRECKLE

bulge .... INION

cast off .... SLOUGH

colloquial .... CHEAT, DEFRAUD, SWINDLE

coloration .... CYANOSIS

combining form .... DERMA, DERM(O), DERMAT(O)

condition/disorder .... RASH, HIVES, UREDO, ALLERGY, BLISTER, LENTIGO, URTICARIA

container .... KENCH

covering .... FUR, HAIR

cut away .... PARE, PEEL

dark .... MELANIC

decoration/design ...... TATTOO

-deep ..... CURSORY, SHALLOW, EPIDERMAL, SUPERFICIAL

deer antler's .... VELVET

discoloration .... BRUISE

disease ..... ACNE, ITCH, YAWS, FAVUS, HIVES, LUPUS, MANGE, PINTA, PSORA, SCALL, SCURF, TINEA, TUMOR, ULCER, ARAKIS, CANCER, ECZEMA, HERPES, LICHEN, TETTER, LEPROSY, PURPURA, PRURIGO, SCABIES, SERPIGO, IMPETIGO, MILIARIA, RINGWORM,

VITILIGO, PSORIASIS, ERYSIPELAS

disease drug .... RETIN-A, NEOMYCIN, ANTIBIOTIC

disease, oil for .... CAJUPUT

diver's aid .... SCUBA

diving device .... AQUALUNG

drying frame .... HERSE

dryness .... XEROSIS

duct dirt .... COMEDO

elevation .... WALE, WELT, WHEAL, PAPULE, PIMPLE, BLISTER, PUSTULE

eruption .... EXANTHEMA

flaw .... WRINKLE

flick .... PORNO

fold .... PLICA

fruit .... PEEL, RIND, ZEST

hemangioma .... BIRTHMARK

horny growth .... CORN, KERATOSIS

infection .... RINGWORM, ATHLETE'S FOOT

inflammation .... BOIL, PAPULE, PIMPLE, PUSTULE, SHINGLES, CARBUNCLE

injury ...... BRUISE, CONTUSION

irritating rash .... PRICKLY HEAT

layer .... CUTIS, CORIUM, DERM(A), (EPI)DERMIS

like ...... DERMOID, DERMATOID

lotion .... CALAMINE

nodule .... MILIUM

of the/pertaining to .... DERMAL, DERMIC, CUTANEOUS

oil .... SEBUM

opening .... PORE

outer layer .... CUTICLE, EPICARP, EPIDERMIS

peel off .... EXCORIATE

person with abnormal white .... ALBINO

pigment .... MELANIN

redness ..... RUBOR, ERYTHEMA

scales .... SCURF

scar ...... BRAND, VACCINATION

shed .... MOLT

shed by snake .... SLOUGH

shedding .... ECDYSIS

sheep's/goat's ..... PARCHMENT

ship's .... ARMOR, PLATE, SHELL

slang .... BLEED, SCREW, FLEECE

sore .... GALL

specialist ...... DERMATOLOGIST

spot .... N(A)EVUS

strip the .... FLAY, PEEL

swelling .... BLEB

tough .... BARK, RIND

treat .... TAN, TAW

tree .... BARK, RIND

true .... DERMIS

tumor .... WEN, CYST

untanned .... KIP, SHAGREEN

whip mark .... WALE, WELT, WHEAL, STRIPE

skinflint .... MISER, HOARDER, NIGGARD, TIGHTWAD

skink .... ADDA, SEPS, LIZARD

like/of the .... SCINCOID

skinless .... APELLOUS

skinner ...... MULETEER, STRIPPER, SWINDLER, (MULE)DRIVER

Skinner, actress/writer .... CORNELIA (OTIS)

skinny .... LANK, LEAN, SLIM, THIN, SCRAGGY, SLENDER, SKELETAL, EMACIATED

skip .... DAP, HOP, JUMP, LEAP, OMIT, CAPER, DECAMP, SPRING, ABSCOND, SKITTER, PASS OVER, RICOCHET

skipjack .... FISH, BEETLE, ELATER

skipper .... RAS, RAIS, PILOT, SAURY, MASTER, CAPTAIN, BUTTERFLY

Biblical .... NOAH

fictional sub .... NEMO

skirmish ...... SPAR, TILT, BRUSH, CLASH, MELEE, FIGHT, (AF)FRAY, BATTLE

skirr .... GLIDE, SCOUR

skirt ...... EDGE, BORDER, DIRNDL, FRINGE, KIRTLE, CHOGORI, PANNIER, PURLIEU, PETTICOAT

armor .... TASSE

ballet dancer's .... TUTU

expander .... HOOP

feature .... GORE

he wears one .... SCOT

men's .... KILT

slang .... GIRL, WOMAN

slit .... PLACKET

swish of silk .... FROUFROU

triangular part .... GORE

waist .... PEPLUM

skit .... GIBE, PARODY, SATIRE, SKETCH, LAMPOON, PLAY(LET), SLAPSTICK

skitter .... RUN, SKIP, SCAMPER

skittish ...... COY, JUMPY, FICKLE, LIVELY, JITTERY, NERVOUS, PLAYFUL

skittle(s) .... PIN, BOWL, NINEPINS

skive .... PARE, SHAVE, SLICE

skivvy .... UNDIES, UNDERWEAR, UNDERSHIRT

skoal .... TOAST

skua .... JAEGER, (SEA)GULL

skulduggery .... TRICKERY

skulk .... HIDE, LURK, MICHE, PROWL, SHIRK, SLINK, SNEAK, MALINGER

skull .... HEAD, MAZARD, SCONCE, CRANIUM

and _____ (death symbol) .... CROSSBONES

back part .... OCCIPUT

bone .... ZYGOMA, MAXILLA, SPHENOID, PARIETAL (BONE), OCCIPITAL (BONE)

bulge .... INION

cavity .... FOSSA, SINUS

domed part .... CALVARIA, CALVARIUM

first cervical vertebra of .... ATLAS

holes in the .... FORAMENS

injury .... FRACTURE

of the .... INIAL, CRANIAL, CEPHALIC

part of ..... BREGMA, CRANIUM, BRAINPAN, CALVARIA

protuberance .... INION

second cervical vertebra of .... AXIS

study of the ...... CRANIOLOGY

surgical saw for .... TREPAN, TREPHINE

skullcap .... COIF, BEANIE, IVETTA, PILEUS, CALOT(TE)

Jewish .... YARMULKE

Roman Catholic .... ZUCCHETTO

skunk .... CHINCHE, POLECAT, STINKER, CONEPATE, MEPHITIS

animal resembling .... TELEDU, ZORIL(A)

colloquial ...... SCAMP, RASCAL

kin of .... MINK, OTTER

slang .... BLANK, SHUT OUT

spray of .... MUSK

sky .... COPE, VAULT, CLIMATE, HEAVEN(S), OLYMPUS, EMPYREAN, FIRMAMENT

altar .... ARA

bear .... URSA

blue .... AZURE, CERULEAN

curved vault of .... WELKIN

highest point .... ZENITH

of the .... CELESTIAL

pilot .... PADRE, AVIATOR, CHAPLAIN, CLERGYMAN

prefix .... SCIO

rare phenomenon .... LUNAR ECLIPSE

sight .... SUN, MOON, STAR, CLOUD, PLANE

strange sight .... UFO

skylark .... FROLIC, HORSE AROUND

genus .... ALAUDA

skylight .... DORMER

skyline .... HORIZON

sight .... SPIRE

skyrocket .... JET, SOAR, ZOOM, POP UP

skyways .... AIR LANES

slab .... TILE, CHUNK, DALLE, PIECE, SLICE, STELE, TABLE(T), VISCID

atop column .... ABACUS

slack ...... LAX, DUFF, DULL, IDLE, LAZE, LULL, SLOW, WEAK, LOOSE, MORASS, REMISS, RELAXED, CARELESS, SLUGGISH

time for newspapers .... SILLY SEASON

slacken .... ABATE, LET UP, RELAX, EASE(UP), LESSEN, LOOSEN, RETARD, DWINDLE, SLOW DOWN

slacker ...... SPIV, IDLER, EVADER, LOAFER, TRUANT, QUITTER, SHIRKER

slacks .... PANTS, TROUSERS

slag .... LAVA, DROSS, CINDER, SCORIA

slake ...... SATE, ALLAY, QUENCH, HYDRATE, SATISFY

slalom .... SKI

slam .... HIT, PAN, BANG, BASH, SHUT, SWAT, VOLE, CLOSE, POUND, BATTER

-dunker .... CAGER

slammer .... JAIL, CLINK

slander .... MUD, LIBEL, SMEAR, DEFAME, MALIGN, REVILE, ASPERSE, CALUMNY, TRADUCE, CALUMNIATE, MALEDICTION

slanderous story ...... ROORBACK

slang .... CANT, ARGOT, LINGO, JARGON, PATOIS, DIALECT, SHOPTALK

suffix .... EROO

slant .... BIAS, CANT, COCK, HEEL, KEEL, RAKE, SKEW, TILT, ANGLE, SLOPE, GLANCE, INCLINE, OPINION

a nail .... TOE

combining form .... CLINO

line .... SOLIDUS

slanted .... ATILT

edge .... BEVEL

slanting .... ASKEW, ATILT, ASLOPE, OBLIQUE

type .... ITALIC

slap .... HIT, RAP, BIFF, BLOW, CUFF, SPAT, SWAT, SMACK, SPANK, WHACK, INSULT, REBUFF, THWACK

-happy .... GIDDY, SILLY, GROGGY, FOOLISH

slapdash .... OFFHAND, HIT OR MISS

slapjack .... PANCAKE

slapstick .... COMEDY, HORSEPLAY

slash ...... CUT, JAG, GASH, HACK, LASH, SLIT, SEVER, SCOURGE

prices .... LOWER, MARK DOWN

Slask .... SILESIA

slat ...... BEAT, FLAP, LATH, STRIP, SPLINE, STRIKE

barrel .... STAVE

movable .... LOUVER

slate .... BOOK, LIST, ROCK, ROOF, TILE, ABUSE, BRICK, SCOLD, BALLOT, ENROLL, TABLET, TICKET

ax/trimmer .... SAX, ZAX

excavation site .... QUARRY

roofing .... RAG

slater .... WOOD LOUSE

tool of .... STAKE

slatted box .... CRATE

slattern ...... DRAB, SLUT, SLOVEN, TROLLOP

slaughter ...... MURDER, POGROM, CARNAGE, KILLING, BUTCHER(Y), HECATOMB, MASSACRE

slaughterhouse .... ABATTOIR, BUTCHERY, SHAMBLES

waste .... TANKAGE

Slav .... POLE, SORB, WEND, CROAT, CZECH, SLOVAK, RUSSIAN, SERB(IAN), SLOVENE, BULGAR(IAN)

slave .... PEON, SERF, TOIL, HELOT, DRUDGE, THRALL, VASSAL, SERVANT, BOND(S)MAN

Biblical .... HAGAR

block .... CATASTA

driver .... TASKMASTER

educated .... HETAERA

female ..... HETAERA, HETAIRA, ODALISK, ODALISQUE

feudal .... ESNE

liberate .... MANUMIT

mark of .... BRAND, STIGMA

Moslem .... MAMELUKE

runaway .... MAROON

Scott .... DRED

ship .... SLAVER

soldier .... MAMELUKE

temple .... HIERODULE

to a habit .... ADDICT

slaver .... DROOL, DRIVEL, HUMBUG, TRADER, SLOBBER, NONSENSE

slavery .... CHAINS, BONDAGE, HELOTRY, SERFDOM, DRUDGERY, SERVITUDE, THRAL(L)DOM
free from .... MANUMIT, EMANCIPATE
to drugs, vice .... ADDICTION
slaves, dealer in .... MANGO
tied together .... COFFLE
slavish .... MENIAL, SERVILE
slaw .... SALAD
slay .... DO IN, KILL, MURDER, DESTROY, ASSASSINATE
slayer .... KILLER, ASSASSIN
of Castor .... IDAS
of Goliath .... DAVID
sleave .... FLOSS, TANGLE, THREAD
sleazy .... CHEAP, FLIMSY, SHABBY, TAWDRY
sled .... LUGE, PUNG, TODE, CUTTER, JUMPER, HURDLE, SLEDGE, SLEIGH, BOBSLED, GO-DEVIL, TOBOGGAN, TRAVOIS(E), DOUBLE-RIPPER
dog .... HUSKY
dog, command to .... MUSH
logging .... TODE
slider .... RUNNER
sledge ...... DRAG, SLED, HAMMER, SLEIGH, TRAVOIS(E)
sleek .... CHIC, OILY, SLICK, SUAVE, GLOSSY, POLISH, SMOOTH, UNCTUOUS
sleep .... NOD, BUNK, DOSS, REST, DROWSE, REPOSE, SHUTEYE, SLUMBER
cessation of breathing during .... (SLEEP)APNEA
combining form .... HYPNO
deep .... COMA, SOPOR, STUPOR
disturber .... PEE(PEE), WEE-WEE
drugged .... NARCOSIS
god of .... HYPNOS, HYPNUS, SOMNUS
inability to .... INSOMNIA
inducing drug .... OPIATE, NARCOTIC, SEDATIVE
last .... DEATH
lightly .... NAP, DOZE
midday .... SIESTA
restlessly .... TOSS
short .... DOZE, WINK, (CAT)NAP, SIESTA, SNATCH, SNOOZE
type of .... REM, NREM
unnatural .... COMA, SOPOR, STUPOR, TRANCE, LETHARGY
winter .... HIBERNATION
sleeper .... TIE, BEAM, TRAIN,

AMTRAK, PULLMAN, RACE HORSE
long .... RIP, SLUGABED
sleeper's production? .... ZEES
sleepiness .... SOMNOLENCE
sleeping bag .... SACK
car business .... PULLMAN
car part .... BERTH
compartment .... CUBICLE
dress .... PJ, NIGHTIE, PAJAMAS, NIGHTGOWN
pill .... SECONAL, VERONAL, BARBITAL, GOOF BALL
place .... BED, COT, PAD, BUNK, DOSS, FLOP, BERTH, COUCH, CUBICLE, LODGING
schedule, disruption of .... JET LAG
sickness carrier .... TSETSE
sickness cause .... TRYPANOSOME
sickness remedy ..... SURAMIN
sleepless one .... INSOMNIAC
sleeplike state .... COMA, TRANCE
sleepwalker .... SOMNAMBULIST
sleepy .... DOZY, DROWSY, LANGUID, OSCITANT, LETHARGIC, SOMNOLENT
Sleepy Hollow Crane .... ICHABOD
sleet .... ICE, HAIL, RAIN, GRAUPEL
sleety .... ICY, BRUMAL, WINTRY
sleeve .... GIGOT, ARM(LET), BUSHING
bar on .... CHEVRON
end of .... CUFF
hole .... SCYE, SKYE
kind of .... DOLMAN, LANTERN, LEG-OF-MUTTON
sleeveless garment .... ABA, CAPE, VEST, CLOAK, MANTLE
sleigh ...... SLED, CUTTER, SLEDGE
boxlike .... PUNG
puller .... REINDEER
rider .... SANTA
slider .... RUNNER
sleight .... FEINT, SKILL, TRICK(ERY), CHICANERY
of hand .... PASS, MAGIC, HOCUS-POCUS, ILLUSIONISM, LEGERDEMAIN
of hand artist .... JUGGLER, SHARPER, MAGICIAN
slender .... LANK, LEAN, SLIM, THIN, FRAIL, LITHE, SVELT, WISPY, FEEBLE, LISSOM, MEAGER, SKINNY, SLIGHT, GRACILE, TENUOUS, WILLOWY
and graceful .... LITHE, SVELT(E)
finial .... EPI

in phonetics .... CLOSE
waisted .... WASPISH
sleuth .... TEC, HAWKSHAW, DETECTIVE, OPERATIVE, PRIVATE EYE
fictional .... CHAN, MOTO, NERO, TRENT, HOLMES, HERCULE
slang .... DICK
slew .... LOT(S), SLUE, WAD(S), RAFTS, SPATE, SWAMP, SLOUGH
Slezsko .... SILESIA
slice ...... CUT, CHIP, GASH, HUNK, SLAB, CHUNK, LAYER, PIECE, SHAVE, SKIVE, SLASH, CANTLE, COLLOP, PORTION, SPATULA
a roast/a turkey .... CARVE
of bacon/ham .... RASHER
of meat, small .... COLLOP
of thrice .... ONCE
thick .... SLAB
slicer's cry .... FORE
slick .... OILY, SHINY, SLEEK, SMART, SUAVE, CLEVER, GLOSSY, SMOOTH, SLIPPERY, UNCTUOUS
colloquial .... SLY
slang .... MAGAZINE
slicker .... PONCHO, OILCOAT, (RAIN)COAT
colloquial .... SHARPER, SWINDLER
slide .... SKID, SLIP, SLUE, CHUTE, COAST, GLIDE, PLATE, LAWINE, AVALANCHE
by a mountain climber .... GLISSADE
by force of gravity ..... COAST
fastener .... ZIPPER
photograph .... TRANSPARENCY
rule .... SLAPSTICK
slight .... CUT, GO-BY, SLIM, SNUB, THIN, FAINT, FRAIL, SCANT, WISPY, IGNORE, MEAGER, AFFRONT, FRAGILE, NEGLECT, TENUOUS
cast .... TINGE
trace .... WHIFF
slightest .... LEAST
amount .... GRAIN
slightly .... SOMEWHAT
slim .... THIN, SCANT, SPARE, MEAGER, SLIGHT, SVELTE, GRACILE, SLENDER
slime .... MUD, MIRE, MUCK, OOZE, FILTH, SLUDGE, SEDIMENT
combining form .... MYX(O)
slimsy .... FLIMSY, SLIGHT,

slimy .... SLENDER, EELY, VISCID, VISCOUS

fish .... EEL, LAMPREY

matter ...... GOB, OOZE, GLEET, SLUDGE

sling .... CAST, HANG, HURL, DRINK, FLING, PITCH, SHOOT

barrel/log .... PARBUCKLE

slingshot .... CATAPULT

killer with .... DAVID

slink .... LURK, CREEP, SKULK, SNEAK, STEAL, SLITHER

slinky .... FELINE, SHIFTY, SNEAKY, FURTIVE, SINUOUS, STEALTHY

slip .... SKID, TRIP, BONER, ERR(OR), FAULT, GAFFE, LAPSE, LEASH, REEVE, SCION, SLIDE, LAPSUS, TUMBLE, CUTTING, MISTAKE, PETTICOAT

away .... ELOPE, ELAPSE

back .... RELAPSE

knot .... NOOSE

loose, short .... CHEMISE

-on garment .... SWEATER

out of place .... PROLAPSE

stream .... RACE, WASH

up .... ERROR, BOOBOO, OVERSIGHT

slipcase, book .... FOREL

slipover .... SWEATER

slipper .... MULE, SCUFF, STEP-IN, PANTOF(F)LE

flat-heeled .... MARY JANE

lounging .... MULE

strap .... SANDAL

slippery .... SLY, EELY, SLICK, SLIMY, GREASY, SHIFTY, ELUSIVE, EVASIVE

customer .... EEL, DEBTOR

slipshod .... SLOPPY, CARELESS, SLOVENLY, WISHY-WASHY

slipstream .... (PROP)WASH

slit ...... CUT, GASH, SLASH, SLICE, SPLIT

slither .... SLIP, CRAWL, CREEP, GLIDE, SLIDE

sliver .... CHIP, FIBER, SHARD, SLICE, FRAGMENT, SPLINTER

slob .... PIG, SLATTERN

slobber .... DROOL, DRIVEL, SLAVER

sloe .... GIN, HAW, PLUM, BLACKTHORN

slog .... PLOD, SLUG, TOIL

slogan .... MAXIM, MOTTO, BYWORD, PASSWORD, (BATTLE)CRY, CATCHWORD, SHIBBOLETH

sloop .... DANDY, CUTTER, SAILBOAT

of war .... FRIGATE

vessel like a .... HOY

slop .... MUD, MUCK, SNOW, SLIME, SLOSH, SLUSH, SWILL, WASTE, REFUSE, GARBAGE

over .... GUSH, SPILL

slang .... CHOW

slope .... BANK, BRAE, CANT, RAMP, RISE, TILT, GRADE, SLANT, SPLAY, TALUS, INCLINE, GRADIENT, DECLIVITY

combining form .... CLINO

gradual .... GLACIS

of a mountain .... VERSANT

steep .... SCARP

sloped .... BEVELED

sloping angle/surface ...... BEVEL, SPLAY

edge .... BEZEL, BISEL

runway .... RAMP

sloppy .... MESSY, MUDDY, UNTIDY, CARELESS, SLIPSHOD

slops .... SMOCK, BREECHES, TROUSERS, COVERALLS

slosh .... SLOP, WADE, SPILL, SPLASH

slot .... TRACK, TRAIL, GROOVE, KEYWAY

machine .... ONE-ARMED BANDIT

machine coin .... SLUG

machine windfall ..... JACKPOT

sloth .... BEAR, MAMMAL, INERTIA, EDENTATE, IDLENESS, LAZINESS, SLOWNESS, INDOLENCE

three-toed .... AI

two-toed .... UNAU

slothful .... LAZY

slouch .... SAG, HULK, SLUMP, DROOP(ING)

slough ...... SHED, MARSH, SWAMP, MORASS, CAST OFF, DISCARD

Slovakian city .... KOSICE

sloven .... SLOB

slovenly .... LAX, DOWDY, TACKY, FROWZY, SLOPPY, UNTIDY, UNKEMPT, SLIPSHOD

Slovensko .... SLOVAKIA

slow .... DULL, SLACK, TARDY, RETARD, GRADUAL, LANGUID, SLUGGISH

as _____ .... MOLASSES

boat's destination .... CHINA

down .... EASE

footed creature .... SLUG, UNAU, LORIS, SLOTH, SNAIL, TURTLE, TORTOISE

in music .... LARGO, LENTO, TARDO, ANDANTE

leak .... DRIP

learner .... DUNCE

mover .... SNAIL

moving-person .... IDLER, LAGGARD

progress/tempo .... SNAIL'S PACE

train .... LOCAL

up .... BRAKE, DELAY

walk .... STROLL, TRUDGE

witted .... DULL, DENSE

witted person ..... DOLT, DOPE, DUMMY, DUNCE, DIMWIT

slowly .... LEISURELY

slowpoke .... IDLER, SLOTH, SNAIL, LAGGARD, LOITERER, SLUGGARD

slubber .... DAUB, BOTCH, SMEAR, STAIN

sludge .... MUD, MIRE, FLOE, OOZE, SLAG, FILTH, SLEET, SLUSH, SEWAGE, (DRIFT)ICE, SEDIMENT

slue .... LOT(S), SLEW, PIVOT, SLOUGH

slug .... HIT, BELT, BASH, BLOW, SWAT, SMASH, SNAIL, TOKEN, BULLET, PELLET, MOLLUSK, TREPANG, GASTROPOD

genus .... LIMAX

sluggard .... LAZY, DRONE, IDLE(R), SNAIL, LOAFER

object lesson of .... ANT

slugger .... PUG(ILIST), PRIZEFIGHTER

sluggish .... DULL, LAZY, LOGY, SLOW, INERT, LEADEN, TORPID, LANGUID, STAGNANT, LETHARGIC, TARDIGRADE

condition .... TORPOR

creek .... BAYOU

slugs, of/like .... LIMACINE

sluice .... SOW, FLUME, TROUGH, CHANNEL, PENSTOCK, (FLOOD)GATE

slum .... GHETTO

kid .... GUTTERSNIPE

slumber .... NAP, DOZE, SLEEP, REPOSE

sound .... SNORE

slump .... SAG, DROP, FALL, SINK, WANE, DROOP, SPRAWL, DECLINE

business .... RECESSION

slur .... BLUR, ELIDE, SMEAR, STAIN, SULLY, SLIGHT, SMIRCH, ASPERSE, DISCREDIT, DISPARAGE

slush .... MUD, MIRE, SLOP, PATCH, DRIVEL

fund's use .... BRIBE(RY)

slut ...... DOG, DOXY, DRAB, JADE, SLOB, BITCH, QUEAN, TROLLOP, SLATTERN, PROSTITUTE

sly .... FOXY, WILY, CAGEY, ARTFUL, CRAFTY, TRICKY, CUNNING, FURTIVE, INSIDIOUS

look .... LEER

on the .... COVERTLY, SECRETLY

one .... FOX

very .... AS CUNNING AS A FOX

Slye, pathologist .... MAUD

smack .... HIT, BLOW, BUSS, KISS, SLAP, TANG, GUSTO, SAVOR, SLOOP, SMITE, TASTE, TRACE, WHACK, FLAVOR, STRIKE, THWACK, (SAIL)BOAT

slang .... HEROIN

smacking .... ALIVE, BRISK, LIVELY, SPANKING

small .... LIL, LOW, WEE, MEAN, PUNY, TINY, DINKY, PETTY, SHORT, TEENY, BANTAM, LITTLE, MINUTE, PALTRY, PETIT(E), TRIVIAL, MINIATURE, MINUSCULE

allowance .... PITTANCE

amount ...... DAB, DOIT, DRAM, GRAM, IOTA, MITE, GRAIN, MINIM, PINCH, MORSEL, MODICUM, FRACTION

and active .... DAPPER

and trim .... PETITE

animal .... RUNT

anything .... PINHEAD

armadillo .... PEBA

arms .... RIFLES, PISTOLS, CARBINES, REVOLVERS

bag .... SATCHEL

barracuda .... SPET

bite .... NIP

blisters .... CHICKENPOX

body of land .... ISLE

body of water .... POND

bottle .... VIAL, PHIAL

boy .... TAD

bright object .... SPANGLE

brook .... RILL

bunch .... WISP

burg .... DORP

cactus .... MESCAL

canyon .... CANADA

car .... COMPACT

case .... ETUI

cask .... KEG

cavity atop a volcano .... CRATERLET

cavity in the body .... FOLLICLE

change .... COIN(S), PETTY CASH

chest .... COFFRET

children .... TADS

cloud .... CLOUDLET

cobra .... ASP

combining form .... LEPTO, MICR(O), STENO

contribution .... MITE

cottage .... BUNGALOW

craft threat .... GALE

cube .... DICE

cucumber .... GHERKIN

cyst .... WEN

dam .... WEIR

demon .... IMP

distance .... HAIR

donkey .... BURRO

drink .... SNORT

drop .... GLOB

drum .... BONGO, SNARE

egg .... OVULE

error .... SLIP

fastener .... THUMBTACK

featured role .... CAMEO

finch .... SERIN

fish .... FRY, ID(E), DACE, SMELT, MINNOW, SARDINE, FINGERLING

flag .... FANION, PENNANT

flock .... COVEY

fly .... GNAT

fry .... TAD, KIDS, CHILDREN, YOUNGSTERS

generator .... MAGNETO

glass .... VIAL, JIGGER

handbill .... FLYER, DODGER

heater .... ETNA

hen .... BANTY

hill .... KNOLL

hollow .... AREOLA

horse .... PONY, BIDET, SHETLAND

house of yore .... COT

in law .... PETIT

in worth .... POOR

immature mushroom .... BUTTON

island .... AIT, CAY

lake .... POND

lemur .... ANGWANTIBO

letter(s) .... MINUSCULE

lie .... FIB

lump .... NODULE

mammal .... COON, HARE

margin .... HAIR

marsh bird .... RAIL

mass .... WAD

minded .... MEAN, PETTY

monkey .... TITI

mound .... TEE

nail .... BRAD, FOUR PENNY

napkin .... DOILY

opening .... PORE, STOMA

parakeet .... LORIKEET

part .... BIT, DETAIL, FRACTION

particle .... ATOM

passerine bird .... VIREO

pastry shell .... TIMBALE

perforated glass object .... BEAD

person .... RUNT, DWARF, MIDGE, PYGMY, BANTAM, SHRIMP

pest .... IMP, GNAT

piano .... SPINET

pie .... TART

piece .... CHIP, SNIP(PET)

plateau .... MESA

point .... DOT

porch .... STOOP

portion .... NIP, MODICUM

quantity .... BIT, IOTA, SPOT

ring .... ANNULET

sailboat .... YAWL

salmon .... GRILSE

sculpture .... CAMEO

shield .... ECU

shops .... ARCADE

shot .... COG

something extremely .... MINIM

space .... AREOLA

spot .... DOT

stream .... BAYOU, RUNLET, RIVULET

suitcase .... GRIP

table .... STAND

talk .... CHITCHAT

telescope .... SPYGLASS

thing to pick .... NIT

time .... MINOR, PETTY

tool .... AWL, BIT

tower .... TURRET

town .... BURGH, VILLAGE

town paper .... WEEKLY

truck .... PICKUP

unspecified number .... BAKER'S DOZEN

very .... WEE

violin .... KIT

yard, old style .... GARTH

smallage .... CELERY, PARSLEY

smallest .... LEAST, MINIM, TINIEST

amount .... LEAST

bird .... HUMMINGBIRD

carnivore .... WEASEL

finger .... PINKIE

liquid measure .... MINIMUM

of all mammals .... SHREW

of the Dionne quintuplets
.... MARIE
offspring .... RUNT
particle of an element
.... ATOM, MOLECULE
planet .... MERCURY
rabbit .... PYGMY
sovereign state .... VATICAN
CITY
smallpox .... VARIOLA, VARICELLA
disease of .... ZYMOTIC
mark .... POCK
resembling .... VARIOLOID
smalt .... BICE, BLUE, GLASS,
PIGMENT
smalto .... ENAMEL
smaragd .... EMERALD
smart .... APT, CHIC, KEEN, NEAT,
PERT, TRIM, BRISK, NIFTY,
QUICK, SHARP, SLICK, STING,
WITTY, CLEVER, DAPPER,
SHREWD, SPRUCE, SUFFER,
SWANKY, DASHING, STYLISH
aleck .... QUACK, WISE GUY
alecky ...... SAUCY, FLIP(PANT)
as a ____ .... WHIP
blow .... RAP
elegance .... CHIC
guy .... SLICK
set .... ELITE, LITERATI
slang .... SPIFFY
smartly dressed .... NATTY
phrased .... NEAT
smash .... HIT, DASH, ROUT,
BREAK, CRUSH, WRECK,
DEFEAT, STRIKE, SHATTER
sign .... SRO
smashup .... RUIN, CRASH,
WRECK, ACCIDENT, DISASTER,
COLLISION
smaze .... SOOT
relative of .... SMOG
smear .... DAB, DAUB, SOIL, SPOT,
DEFAME, GREASE, MALIGN,
SMUDGE, SLANDER, SLUBBER
smearcase .... CHEESE
smee .... POCHARD
smell ...... NOSE, ODO(U)R, SCENT,
SENSE, SNIFF, WHIFF, DETECT,
FLAVOR, INHALE
fats' .... RANCID
goatlike .... HIRCINE
loss of .... ANOSMIA
of the sense of .... OLFACTORY
offensive .... FOUL, OLID,
ODOR, RANK, REEK, FETOR,
STINK, STENCH
organ of .... NOSE, OLFACTORY
NERVE
perception, abnormal
.... DYSOSMIA

pleasant/savory .... AROMA
stale .... FUSTY, MUSTY
smeller .... NOSE, FEELER,
ANTENNA
smelling .... REDOLENT
salts ...... AMMONIA, INHALANT
smelly: var. .... REEKIE
smelt .... FISH, FUSE, MELT,
REFINE, CAP(E)LIN, SPARLING
fish like .... TROUT
smelter .... BLAST, FORGE,
FURNACE
smelting by-product .... SLAG,
DROSS, SPEISS
waste .... TUTTY
Smetana, composer .... BEDRICH
opera .... DANCE OF THE
COMEDIANS
smew .... DUCK, SCOTER,
MERGANSER
smidgen .... BIT, IOTA, MITE
smilax .... VINE, SARSAPARILLA
smile .... BEAM, GRIN, LAUGH,
SMIRK, SNEER, SIMPER,
GRIMACE
broadly .... GRIN
certain .... TOOTHY
Mona Lisa .... CRYPTIC,
ENIGMATIC
scornful .... SNEER
self-satisfied .... SMIRK
silly .... SIMPER
smiling .... RIANT, RIDENT
smirch ...... BLOT, DIRTY, SMEAR,
STAIN, SULLY, SMUDGE,
SMUT(CH), TARNISH,
DISCOLOR
smirk .... GRIN, LEER, SMILE,
SIMPER, GRIMACE
smite .... HIT, CUFF, AFFECT,
DEFEAT, ENAMOR, PUMMEL,
STRIKE, AFFLICT, DISTRESS
smith .... FORGE, TINKER,
VULCAN, METALWORKER
block of .... ANVIL
furnace of .... FORGE
invisible .... WAYLAND
Smith, confederate general
.... KIRBY
smithereens .... BITS, PIECES,
FRAGMENTS
smithsonite .... CALAMINE
smithy .... FORGE, STITHY,
BLACKSMITH
smitten .... TAKEN, ENAMORED,
STRICKEN, AFFLICTED
smock .... APRON, FROCK, CAMISE,
CHEMISE
smog .... MIST, SMAZE
ingredient .... SOOT, SMOKE
smoke .... CURE, FLOC, FUME,

LUNT, MIST, PUFF, REEF,
SMOG, VAPOR, INHALE,
CIGARET, POLLUTE,
CIGAR(ETTE)
a pipe .... WHIFF
and mist .... SMOG, SMAZE
country boy's .... CORNSILK
fragrant .... INCENSE
go up in .... EVAPORATE
meat .... REEST
out .... FLUSH, FORCE OUT
pipe .... STACK, FUNNEL
screen .... CAMOUFLAGE
tree .... YELLOWWOOD
smokeless power .... FILITE,
CORDITE
smoker .... STAG, PARTY
smokestack .... FLUE, FUNNEL,
CHIMNEY
worker .... STEEPLEJACK
smooking pipe .... BRIAR,
HOOKAH, CALUMET,
NARGHILE
room .... DIVAN
smoky .... HAZY
quartz .... CAIRNGORM
smolder .... BURN, FUME
Smollett, novelist .... TOBIAS
smolt .... SALMON
smooch .... KISS, SMUTCH
old style .... SPOON
smooth .... CALM, EVEN, IRON,
OILY, SAND, SOFT, BLAND,
GRIND, SLEEK, SUAVE,
REFINE, SERENE, SLICK,
SOOTHE, URBANE, VELVETY,
GLABROUS, POLISH(ED)
and lustrous .... SILKY
and white .... ALABASTER
combining form .... LIO
consonant .... LENE
feathers/with beak .... PREEN
in mechanics .... FRICTIONLESS
in music .... LEGATO
in performance .... DOLCE
in phonetics .... LENE
over .... GLOSS
pated .... BALD
talker .... CHARMER
tongued/talking .... GLIB,
OILY, SUAVE
with an abrasive .... SAND
smoother .... PLANE, BUFFER,
MANGLE
smoothing rock .... PUMICE
smorgasbord .... BUFFET
treat .... EELS, CANAPE,
DESSERT, KICKSHAW
smother .... CHOKE, DEADEN,
STIFLE, WELTER, REPRESS,
SUFFOCATE

smudge .... BLOT, BLUR, DIRT, SLUR, SOIL, SOOT, SPOT, GRIME, SMEAR, SMOKE, STAIN, SMUTCH

smug .... NEAT, TRIM, SLEEK, CONCEITED, COMPLACENT

one .... PRIG

smuggle .... RUN, SNEAK IN, BOOTLEG

smuggled goods .... CONTRABAND

whisk(e)y .... MOONSHINE

smuggler .... GUNRUNNER, (RUM)RUNNER, BOOTLEGGER

ship of .... RUNNER

smugness .... VANITY, CONCEIT

smut ...... ROT, BUNT, DIRT, SOOT, CROCK, FILTH, FUNGUS, MILDEW, OBSCENITY

smutch .... DIRT, SMUT, SOOT, GRIME, SMUDGE

Smuts, S. African statesman .... JAN

smutty .... OBSCENE, INDECENT

Smyrna .... IZMIR

fig .... ELEME

snack .... EAT, BITE, LUNCH, CANAPE, REPAST, TIFFIN

bar .... CAFETERIA

snaffle .... BIT, CURB

snafu .... CHAOS, MIX-UP, BOOBOO, FOUL-UP, MUDDLE, SCREW-UP

snag .... TEAR, HITCH, TOOTH, OBSTACLE, FLY-IN-THE-OINTMENT

snail ...... HELIX, WHELK, NERITA, MOLLUSK, ESCARGOT, SLUG(GARD), GASTROPOD

genus .... NERITA, OLEACINA

oyster-killer .... DRILL

shell .... CARACOLE, PERIWINKLE

snails, of/like .... LIMACINE

snake .... ASP, LORA, (A)BOMA, COBRA, VIPER, PYTHON, REPTILE, SERPENT, OPHIDIAN

big .... BOA, PYTHON, ANACONDA, PUFF ADDER, FER-DE-LANCE, CONSTRICTOR

bite remedy .... GUACO, CEDRON

black .... KRAIT, RACER

burrowing .... GOPHER

castoff of .... SLOUGH

charmer's flute .... PUNGI

charmer's tool .... MUSIC

combining form .... OPHI(O)

common .... ADDER

coral .... HARLEQUIN

crusher .... PYTHON, ANACONDA, BOA

(CONSTRICTOR)

deity .... ZOMBI(E)

doctor .... DRAGONFLY

eyes .... CRAPS, AMBSACE

fish like .... EEL, LAMPREY, OARFISH, LIZARD FISH

genus .... NAJA, ELAPS, ELAPHE, NATRIX, PYTHON, HETERODON, COLUBER, BUNGARUS, PITUOPHIS, DENDRASPIS

haired woman .... GORGON, MEDUSA

harmless .... MILK, RACER, GARTER, HOGNOSE

hooded .... COBRA

horned .... RATTLER, CERASTES, SAND VIPER

in the grass ..... RAT, DOUBLE-CROSSER

killer .... SECRETARY BIRD

kind of .... RAT, BULL, MILK, PINE, CORAL, WATER, RACER, HOODED, HORNED

king ...... COBRA, HAMADRYAD

like .... APODAL, ANGUINE, SINUOUS, COLUBRINE

movement .... SLITHER

non-poisonous .... BULL, GARTER, PYTHON

pit .... BEDLAM, JUNGLE, MADHOUSE

poison .... VENOM, VIRUS

poisonous .... ASP, SEPS, COBRA, KRAIT, MAMBA, VIPER, CERASTES, MOCCASIN, PUFF ADDER, COPPERHEAD, FER-DE-LANCE, COTTONMOUTH

root .... STEVIA, SANICLE

sand .... SIDEWINDER

sea .... KERRIL

skin(s) .... EXUVIA(E)

skin shedding .... ECDYSIS

slain by Apollo .... PYTHON

small .... ASP, ADDER, GARTER, HOGNOSE, SIDEWINDER

space on head of .... LORE

teeth .... FANGS

tempter of Eve .... SERPENT

tree .... MAMBA

type of .... BOA, ADDER, RACER, VIPER, PYTHON, RATTLER, CONSTRICTOR

(warning) sound of .... HISS, RATTLE

water .... MOCCASIN, COTTONMOUTH

snakebird .... DARTER, PLOTUS, WRYNECK

snakehead .... FIGWORT

snakemouth .... ORCHID

snakes, study of ...... OPHIOLOGY

snakestone .... AMMONITE

snaky .... ANGUINE, WINDING, SERPENTINE

snap .... NIP, PEP, POP, BARK, BITE, CLAP, CLIP, DASH, EASY, KNAP, BREAK, COOKY, CRACK, FLICK, SNARL, SPELL, WAFER, FILLIP, SIMPLE, SNATCH, FASTENER, SINECURE

a coin in the air .... FLIP

colloquial .... CINCH

of fingers .... FILLIP

snapdragon .... FIGWORT

snapper .... SESI, BEETLE, TAMURE, TURTLE

kin of .... SCUP

snappish ...... EDGY, RUDE, TART, CROSS, TESTY, SNARLY, UNCIVIL, IRRITABLE

snappy ...... BRISK, CROSS, QUICK, SHARP, SMART, STYLISH

answer .... RETORT

make it .... HURRY

snare .... GIN, WEB, MESH, BENET, CATCH, NOOSE, (EN)TRAP, (DRAG)NET, PIT(FALL), RATTRAP, SPRINGE

snared .... BAGGED

snark .... BOOJUM

snarl .... GIRN, KNOT, GNAR(L), GROWL, GRUMBLE, (EN)TANGLE

snatch ...... BIT, GET, NAB, GRAB, JERK, TAKE, GRASP, PLUCK, SEIZE, SPELL, SWIPE, WREST, KIDNAP(PING)

sneak ...... LURK, MOOCH, SKULK, SLINK, STEAL

sneakers .... GUMSHOES, (CANVAS)SHOES

sneaking .... FURTIVE, COWARDLY

snee .... DIRK

sneer .... MOCK, FLEER, SCOFF, SCORN, SMILE

sneering ...... DERISIVE, SCORNFUL

sneeze ...... SNUFF, STERNUTATION

at .... BRUSH OFF, DISREGARD

sound .... ACHOO

sneezewort .... YARROW

sneezing, cause of .... COLD, ALLERGY, HAY FEVER

snell .... GUT, KEEN, ACUTE, HARSH, QUICK, SMART, LEADER, SEVERE

Snerd, dummy .... MORTIMER

snick .... CUT, NICK, CLICK, NOTCH

and _____ .... SNEE

snicker .... LAUGH, NEIGH, TEHEE, GIGGLE, TITTER

snickersnee .... KNIFE

snide .... SLY, BASE, MEAN, NASTY, ORNERY, CYNICAL, MALICIOUS, SARCASTIC

sniff .... NOSE, SCENT, SMELL, SNORT, DETECT, INHALE, BREATHE

sniffles .... (HEAD)COLD

sniffy ...... SCORNFUL, DISDAINFUL

snifter ...... NIP, SIP, SHOT, DRINK, GOBLET

snigger .... LAUGH, GIGGLE, CHUCKLE, SNICKER

sniggle ...... HOOK, NOOSE, SNARE

snip .... BIT, CUT, CLIP, PIECE, SHEAR, SHRIMP

snipe .... BIRD, CIGAR, GODWIT, WOODCOCK

sniper .... AMBUSHER

snippet .... TAG, CHIP, SCRAP, DOLLOP, FRAGMENT

snippy .... CURT, GRUFF, BRUSQUE

snit .... PIQUE, TIZZY, DITHER

snitch .... TELL, PEACH, STEAL, SWIPE, PILFER, SQUEAL, INFORM(ER)

snivel .... CRY, FRET, WEEP, SNIFF, WHINE, SNUFFLE, WHIMPER, COMPLAIN

snob .... PRIG, PRUDE, TOADY, HIGH-HAT, PARVENU, UPSTART

snobbery .... HAUTEUR, PRIGGERY

snobbish .... PROUD, RITZY, SELECT, SNOOTY, SNOTTY, UPPISH, UPPITY, HIGH-HAT, STUCK-UP, PRIGGISH

snood ...... SNELL, FILLET, RIBBON, (HAIR)NET

snook .... ROBALO

snoop .... PRY, LURK, PROWL, SKULK, SPIER, NOSE AROUND

snooper .... PRY, MEDDLER, BUSYBODY

electronic .... BUG

snoopy one .... PRIER

snoot .... FACE, NOSE, SNUB, GRIMACE

snooty .... ALOOF, PROUD, HAUGHTY, SNOBBISH

one .... SNOB

snooze .... NAP, DOZE, SLEEP, CATNAP, DROWSE

snore .... RALE, SNIFF, WHEEZE, RHONCUS, STERTOR

snorer .... SAWER

loud .... GRAMPUS

snort .... NIP, DRINK, LAUGH, SNIFF, SNUFF

snorter .... HUMDINGER

snot .... MUCUS, PHLEGM

snotty .... MUCOID, HAUGHTY, IMPUDENT, OFFENSIVE

snout ...... NEB, BEAK, BILL, JAWS, NOSE, SERRA, MUZZLE, NOZZLE, ROSTRUM

dig with .... ROOT, ROUT

elephant's .... TRUNK

push/rub with .... NUZZLE

tapir's .... PROBOSCIS

snouted creature .... HOG, PIG, TAPIR, DESMAN, ECHIDNA, ANTEATER, AARDVARK, ELEPHANT

snow .... SNA, FIRN, HAIL, PASH, DRIFT, SLEET

become heaped with .... DRIFT

briefly .... SPIT

bunting .... FINCH

field .... NEVE

granular .... FIRN, NEVE

growing under .... NIVAL

gust of .... FLURRY

house .... HOLE, IGLOO, IG(D)LU

job .... SONG-AND-DANCE

leopard .... OUNCE

of .... NIVAL

on a glacier .... NEVE

partly melted .... SLUSH

pellets .... HAIL

runner/glider .... SKI, SKEE, (BOB)SLED, TOBOGGAN

slang .... HEROIN, COCAINE

slide, mass .... AVALANCHE

small feathery piece of .... FLAKE

travel through .... MUSH

vehicle .... SLED, SLEDGE, SLEIGH, SNOWMOBILE

watery .... SLOP, SLUSH

Snow White's friends .... DWARFS

snowbird .... FINCH, JUNCO, LERWA, ADDICT

snowbird's need .... DOPE, DRUG, HEROIN, COCAINE

snowdrift .... NEVE

snowdrop .... ANEMONE

snowfall .... HAIL, SLEET

snowflake .... FINCH, BUNTING

snowlike .... NIVEOUS

snowshoe .... PAC, SKI, RACKET

snowstorm .... BLIZZARD

snowy .... WHITE, BRUMAL, WINTRY, NIVEOUS, SPOTLESS

weather need .... MITTEN, EARMUFF, MUFFLER, OVERSHOES

snub .... CUT, CURB, STOP, CHECK, SCORN, IGNORE, REBUFF, SLIGHT, AFFRONT, HIGH-HAT, SET DOWN, UPSTAGE, TURNED-UP

nose(d) .... PUG

snubber .... PRIG, SNOB

snuff .... ODOR, PINCH, SCENT, SMELL, SNIFF, SNORT, INHALE, POWDER, PUT OUT, RAPPEE, TOBACCO, MACCOBOY

out .... DOUSE, EXTINGUISH

perfumed .... MACCABOY, MACCOBOY

snuffle ...... SMELL, SNIFF, SNORT, TWANG, SNIVEL

snug .... COSY, COZY, NEAT, SAFE, TAUT, TRIM, WARM, SECURE, FRIENDLY, COMFORTABLE

as a bug _____ .... IN A RUG

retreat .... DEN, NEST

spot .... CUBBYHOLE

snuggle .... CUDDLE, NESTLE, NUZZLE

so .... SIC, ERGO, THEN, THUS, TRUE, VERY, HENCE, LIKEWISE, THEREFORE

and so .... SOMEONE, SOMEBODY

be it .... AMEN

long! .... TATA, GOOD-BY

on, and .... ETCETERA

or .... NEARLY, ROUGHLY

-so .... AVERAGE, ORDINARY, PASSABLE

that .... PROVIDED

what! .... NO MATTER, ALL THE SAME

So Big author .... FERBER

Big heroine .... SELINA

Red the _____ .... ROSE

soak .... RET, SOG, SOP, WET, IMBUE, SOUSE, STEEP, DRENCH, SODDEN, IMMERSE, SATURATE

as fiber/flax .... RET

colloquial .... DRINK

customer .... BLEED, GOUGE, OVERCHARGE

in brine/vinegar .... MARINATE

in liquid .... STEEP, SOUSE

slang .... BOX, HIT, PAWN, TIPPLER, DRUNKARD

to soften .... RET, STEEP, MACERATE

up .... (AB)SORB, SPONGE

with blood .... IMBRUE

soaked .... SOGGY, SODDEN, SOPPING

soaker .... SOT, DELUGE, GUZZLER, TIPPLER, RAINSTORM

soaking medium .... BATH

pit .... FURNACE

soap ...... SAPO, LATHER, CASTILE, CLEAN(S)ER, DETERGENT

acid of .... OLEIC
bar frame .... SESS
convert into .... SAPONIFY
cresol mixture .... LYSOL
foam .... SUDS, BUBBLES
ingredient .... LYE
kind of .... BAR, BATH, LIQUID,
POWDER, LAUNDRY
material ...... POTASH, TALLOW
no .... NOTHING DOING
oil .... CITRONELLA
olive oil .... CASTILE
opera .... SOAPER, MELODRAMA
opera sphere .... DAYTIME
plant .... AMOLE
segment .... EPISODE
slang .... (BRIBE)MONEY
substitute ...... AMOLE, QUILIAI
vine .... GOGO
soapbark .... MIMOSA, QUILIAI
glucoside .... SAPONIN(E)
soapberry .... LICHEE, LITCHI,
RAMBUTAN
soapbox character .... QUACK,
ORATOR, RANTER, AGITATOR,
DEMAGOGUE
race .... DERBY
soapstone .... TALC, STEATITE
soapsuds .... FOAM, LATHER,
BUBBLES
soapy .... OILY, FOAMY, SUAVE,
UNCTUOUS, SAPONACEOUS
water .... SUDS
soar .... FLY, RISE, SAIL, GLIDE,
TOWER
in a way .... FLY OFF THE
HANDLE
soaring .... HIGH, LOFTY,
MOUNTING, TOWERING
sob ...... CRY, BAWL, MOAN, SIGH,
WEEP
story .... TEAR-JERKER
sober .... CALM, SANE, GRAVE,
PLAIN, QUIET, SOUND, STAID,
FRUGAL, SEDATE, SOLEMN,
SOMBER, SERIOUS, MODERATE,
TEMPERATE
sobriety .... GRAVITY, FRUGALITY,
MODERATION, TEMPERANCE
sobriquet .... ALIAS, AGNAME,
BYNAME, PET-NAME,
COGNOMEN, NICKNAME
of the Supreme Court
(former) .... THE NINE
OLD MEN
soccer .... FOOTBALL
player, famed .... PELE,
CHARLTON
Soche .... YARKAND
sociable .... NICE, CHATTY,
FOLKSY, JOVIAL, SOCIAL,

AFFABLE, FRIENDLY,
OUTGOING, HOSPITABLE,
NEIGHBORLY
colloquial .... CLUBBY
social .... BEE, CIVIC, PARTY,
PUBLIC, COMMUNAL,
CONVIVIAL, GATHERING
affair .... TEA, SOIREE,
SHINDIG, MUSICALE
appointment .... DATE
asset .... TACT, GRACE,
DIPLOMACY
call .... GAM
class .... CASTE
climber .... SNOB, UPSTART,
ADVENTURER, TUFTHUNTER,
NAME-DROPPER
contract theorist .... HOBBS,
LOCKE, ROUSSEAU
disease in short .... VD
error ...... FAUX PAS, SOLECISM
event .... BALL, DANCE, DEBUT,
MARDIGRAS
event of 1773 .... BOSTON TEA
PARTY
evil .... PROSTITUTION
finesse .... TACT
gathering .... BALL, LEVEE,
PARTY, SOIREE, REUNION,
RECEPTION
gathering, costumed
.... MASQUERADE
gathering for men .... STAG,
SMOKER
gathering for women ...... HEN
PARTY
grace .... ETIQUETTE
grace, lacking .... GAUCHE
group .... CLAN, CLUB, CLIQUE,
CIRCLE, COTERIE
hierarchy .... CASTE
insect .... ANT, BEE, WASP,
VESPID, TERMITE
order .... REGIME
outcast .... LEPER, PARIAH
outdoors gathering .... BBQ,
FRY, BARBECUE
person .... JOINER
reformer, American ..... MOTT
rules of conduct .... DECORUM
science .... SOCIOLOGY
security .... INSURANCE
service .... WELFARE
standing .... STATION
system .... CASTE, REGIME
unit .... FAMILY
virtue .... TACT
visit .... GAM, CALL
wasp .... VESPID
Social Contract author
.... ROUSSEAU

Register .... BLUEBOOK
socialist .... MARX, ENGELS,
FOURIER
socialite .... JET-SETTER,
TRENDSETTER, CLOTHESHORSE
potential .... DEB(UTANTE)
socialize .... VISIT, HOBNOB,
MINGLE, FRATERNIZE
in restaurant .... TABLE-HOP
society .... BODY, CLUB, GUILD,
ORDER, VEREIN, COMPANY,
COMMUNITY, ASSOCIATION
bigwig .... NOB
bow .... DEBUT
bud ..... (SUB)DEB, DEBUTANTE
combining form .... SOCIO
doings .... SOCIALS
entrance into .... DEBUT
fashionable .... BONTON
for animals .... SPCA
of the learned .... ACADEMY
page figure ..... DEB, SWINGER,
SOCIALITE
with government .... POLITY
Society Islands' capital
.... PAPEETE
Islands, one of the .... TAHAA,
MOOREA, TAHITI, BORA-BORA
of Friends .... QUAKERS
of Friends founder .... FOX
of Jesus founder ..... IGNATIUS
(OF LOYOLA)
socials .... GALAS, PARTIES
sociology .... DEMOTICS
sock .... BOP, BOX, HIT, BLOW,
HOSE, SHOE, ANKLET,
COMEDY, WALLOP, STOCKING
sockdolager .... ONER, FINISHER
socket .... CUP, PAN, HOLE,
MORTISE
bit .... POD
roof beam .... OPA
sockeye .... (RED)SALMON
socko .... HIT, SMASH
socks .... SOX, HOSE, ARGYLE,
BOOTEES
Socrate composer .... SATIE
Socrates' disciple .... PLATO
wife .... XANTHIPPE
sod .... DIRT, PEAT, SOIL, TURF,
EARTH, GLEBE, SWARD
clod .... DIVOT
soda .... SELTZER, BEVERAGE,
(CARBONATED)DRINK
_____ .... POP, JERK, FOUNTAIN
adjunct .... STRAW
ash .... ALKALI, BARILLA
ash source .... SEAWEED
baking .... SALERATUS, SODIUM
BICARBONATE
caustic .... LYE, SODIUM

HYDROXIDE
fountain .... COUNTER
fountain order .... MALT,
SHAKE, SUNDAE
jerk .... COUNTERMAN
water .... FIZZ
sodality .... FELLOWSHIP
sodden .... SOGGY, STEEP,
POACHY, SOAKED, DRUNKEN
sodium and aluminum
.... NATROLITE
benzoate use .... ANTISEPTIC,
PRESERVATIVE
bicarbonate ...... BAKING SODA
borate .... BORAX
bromide use .... SEDATIVE
carbonate .... TRONA, NATRON,
SAL SODA, SODA(ASH)
chloride .... SALT
chloride works .... SALTERN
combining form .... NATRO
hydroxide .... LYE, CAUSTIC
SODA
nitrate .... NITER, CALICHE,
SALTPETER, SALTPETRE
oxide .... SODA
thiosulfate .... HYPO
Sodom forsaker .... LOT
inhabitant .... SODOMITE
instrument of God's
punishment on ...... FIRE,
BRIMSTONE
neighbor of .... GOMORRAH
sodomite .... BUGGER
sodomy .... BUGGERY
form of .... PEDERASTY,
BESTIALITY
sofa .... COUCH, DIVAN, SQUAB,
DAYBED, SETTEE, SETTLE,
VIS-A-VIS, DAVENPORT,
CHESTERFIELD
backless .... LOUNGE
boxy, overstuffed ..... LAWSON
covering .... TIDY
small .... SETTEE, LOVE-SEAT
soft ...... LOW, EASY, HUSH, MILD,
WEAK, BLAND, PAPPY, SILKY,
GENTLE, MELLOW, PLIANT,
SMOOTH, TENDER, SUBDUED,
VELVETY, TEMPERATE
and limp .... FLABBY
and sweet .... DOLCE
breeze .... AURA
-cover .... PAPERBACK
drink .... ADE, POP, COKE,
MEAD, SODA, PEPSI, COCA-
COLA, GATORADE
fabric ..... SILK, PANNE, SATIN,
VELVET, CASHMERE
feathers .... DOWN, EIDER
food .... PAP, SOUP

goods ..... CLOTHING, TEXTILES
hair .... VILLUS
ice .... LOLLY
in music .... PIANO
in phonetics .... SIBILANT
in the head .... STUPID,
FOOLISH
job .... SNAP, SINECURE
mass .... PULP
metal .... TIN, LEAD
mineral .... TALC
palate .... UVULA, VELUM
pedal .... EASE, MUTE,
MODERATE, PLAY DOWN, TONE
DOWN
roll .... BUN
rustling sound .... WHISPER
saddle .... PANEL
shoe .... PAC, DANCE
shoulder .... BERM(E)
-soap .... SNOW, URGE,
CAJOLE, BLARNEY, FLATTER
sound .... HUM, BUZZ, SIGN,
MURMUR
sound of leaves .... RUSTLE
spoken .... QUIET, SUAVE,
GENTLE, SMOOTH
spot ..... FONTANEL, WEAKNESS
tissue .... BREI
toned organ stop .... DOLCE
touch .... TAP, EASY MARK,
PUSHOVER
soften .... EASE, MELT, RELAX,
YIELD, LOOSEN, RELENT,
TEMPER, MOLLIFY, MITIGATE
by soaking .... RET, STEEP,
MACERATE
softening .... LENITIVE
of the brain .... DEMENTIA
softhead .... SIMPLETON
softie .... SISSY, WEAKLING
softly .... LOW, MUTED, PIANO,
FAINTLY
softness .... LAXITY, LOWNESS,
PLIANCY, LENIENCY,
WEAKNESS, MELLOWNESS
Sogdian .... IRANIAN
soggy .... WET, DOUGHY, POACHY,
SOAKED, SODDEN
Soho feature .... RESTAURANTS
optimism .... OPE
radial .... TYRE
soigne .... CHIC, NEAT, TIDY,
MODISH, STYLISH
soil ...... SOD, CLAY, DAUB, LAND,
LOAM, MARL, DIRT(Y),
EARTH, GLEBE, GUMBO,
LOESS, PURGE, STAIN, SULLY,
BLOTCH, DEFILE, GROUND,
SMIRCH, SMUDGE, (BE)SMEAR,
COUNTRY

good .... LOAM
hard layer of .... PAN
hole-making tool .... DIBBLE
in combination .... AGRO
infertile .... PODZOL
organic part of .... HUMUS
poetic .... GLEBE
restorer .... VETCH
science .... PEDOLOGY
unfruitful .... BARREN
wind-deposited .... LOESS
soja .... SAUCE, SOY(BEAN)
sojourn .... REST, STAY, VISIT,
LODGE, TARRY
sojourner ...... LODGER, BOARDER,
PILGRIM
Sojourner .... TRUTH
sol .... COIN, GOLD, NOTE
Sol .... SUN(GOD)
impresario .... HUROK
sola .... ALONE
solace ...... CALM, ALLAY, CHEER,
RELIEF, SOOTHE, ASSUAGE,
COMFORT, CONSOLE
solan goose .... GANNET
solanaceous family
.... NIGHTSHADE
plant .... POTATO, TOMATO,
PETUNIA, TOBACCO
solano .... WIND
solanum .... NIGHTSHADE
family .... TREES, VINES,
SHRUBS
solar .... HELIACAL
companion .... PLEXUS
deity .... SOL, LLEU, HELIOS
disk .... ATEN
disk: var. .... ATON
furnace site .... ODEILLO
phenomenon .... CORONA,
ECLIPSE
spot/streak .... FACULA
system model .... ORRERY
system, part of .... SUN, MARS,
EARTH, PLUTO, VENUS,
SATURN, URANUS, JUPITER,
MERCURY, NEPTUNE
solarium .... PORCH, PARLOR,
SUNROOM
solder .... BOND, FUSE, JOIN,
MEND, WELD, BORAX, BRAZE,
PATCH, ROSIN, UNITE, CEMENT
soldering tool .... GUN, IRON
soldier .... POILU, FIGHTER,
TERMITE, WARRIOR,
COMMANDO, MAN-AT-ARMS
artillery .... GUNNER,
CANNONEER, BOMBARDIER
bag of .... DUFFEL, DUFFLE,
MUSETTE, KNAPSACK,
HAVERSACK

brutal .... PANDOUR

call to quarters .... TATTOO

cap of .... BERET, SHAKO

cavalry .... UHLAN, SPAHI,
HUSSAR, TROOPER

civies of .... MUFTI

employed to lay mines
.... SAPPER

fellow .... BUDDY

fighting on horseback or on
foot .... DRAGOON

food of .... CHOW, MESS,
K-RATION

foot .... INFANTRY

forced into military service
.... DRAFTEE, SELECTEE,
CONSCRIPT

freebooting .... RAPPAREE

from Down Under ..... ANZAC

headgear .... CAP, BERET,
SHAKO, HELMET

hired to serve in foreign
army .... MERCENARY

involved in a series of
military operations
.... CAMPAIGNER

infantry .... RIFLEMAN,
GRENADIER, MUSKETEER

killed .... CASUALTY

kind of .... FOOT, LANCE(R),
CAVALRY, INFANTRY,
LEGIONARY, MERCENARY

mercenary .... HESSIAN,
SWISSER, SWITZER

mounted ..... SPAHI, CAVALRY,
TROOPER

not on active duty
.... RESERVE, RESERVIST

of fortune .... ADVENTURER

old .... VET(ERAN)

pack of .... KIT

recently enlisted ...... RECRUIT,
ENLISTEE

shelter of .... BUNKER,
FOXHOLE

slang ...... DOGFACE, SADSACK,
DOUGHBOY

subject to call .... RESERVE,
RESERVIST

the President as
.... COMMANDER-IN-CHIEF

trainee .... CADET, DRAFTEE

volunteer .... ZOUAVE,
GUERRILLA

who served in the armed
forces .... VET(ERAN)

who shoots from hidden
position .... SNIPER

with musket .... DRAGO(O)N,
MUSKETEER

wounded in battle
.... CASUALTY

soldierly .... ERECT, MARTIAL

soldiers, body of .... ARRAY

collectively .... TROOPS,
MILITIA, MILITARY, RESERVES,
ARMED FORCES

rebellion of .... MUTINY

Soldiers Three author
.... KIPLING

sole .... ONE, ONLY, MERE,
(A)LONE, PLAICE, SINGLE,
UNIQUE, HALIBUT, (FLAT)FISH,
SOLITARY

foot's .... VOLA, PLANTAR

of the foot's .... VOLAR

plow's .... SLADE

solecism ...... SLIP, ERROR, LAPSE,
BLUNDER, MISTAKE,
BARBARISM, IMPROPRIETY

Soleil, _____ (Louis XIV)
.... LEROI

solely ...... ONLY, ALONE, MERELY,
EXCLUSIVELY

solemn .... GRAVE, SOBER,
FORMAL, SACRED, SOMBER,
SERIOUS, REVERENT,
DIGNIFIED

wonder .... AWE

looking .... OWLISH

word .... VOW, OATH, TROTH,
PAROL(E), PLEDGE

solemnity .... WEIGHT, DIGNITY,
GRAVITY, SOBRIETY,
FORMALITY

solemnize .... OBSERVE, PERFORM,
CELEBRATE

solfatara emission .... GAS,
VAPOR

solferino .... DYE, FUCHSIN

solicit .... ASK, BEG, BID, SEEK,
APPLY, ENTREAT, PETITION

business .... CALL ON
CUSTOMERS

customers .... TOUT, INVITE,
CANVASS

solicitation .... ENTREATY,
PETITION, PERSUASION

soliciting .... PANDERING,
PROSTITUTION

solicitor ...... LAWYER, PETITIONER

solicitous .... EAGER, ANXIOUS,
CAREFUL, CONCERNED

solicitude .... CARE, WORRY,
ANXIETY, CONCERN

solid .... FIRM, HARD, REAL,
DENSE, MASSY, RIGID, SOUND,
THICK, WHOLE, STABLE,
COMPACT, GENUINE, MASSIVE,
RELIABLE

blow .... WHAM

ground .... TERRA FIRMA

six-sided .... CUBE

solidago .... GOLDENROD

solidarity .... UNION, UNITY

solidified lava .... COULEE

solidify .... GEL, SET, CAKE, JELL,
HARDEN, COMBINE, CONGEAL

solidity .... DENSITY, FIRMNESS,
SOLVENCY, STABILITY

solidus .... BEZANT, VIRGULE,
DIAGONAL, SLANT(LINE)

soliloquist .... MONOLOGIST

soliloquy .... MONOLOGUE

solipsism, core of .... SELF

solitaire .... GEM, HERMIT,
RECLUSE, CANFIELD, CARD
GAME, PATIENCE, DIAMOND
RING

solitary .... ONE, ONLY, SOLE,
SOLO, ALONE, APART,
HERMIT, LONE(LY), REMOTE,
SINGLE, HERMITIC, ISOLATED,
CONFINEMENT

solitude ...... PRIVACY, ISOLATION,
SECLUSION, LONELINESS

sollar .... GALLERY, BRATTICE

solleret .... SHOE

solo .... ONE, ARIA, ALONE,
SINGLE, UNAIDED, SURAKARTA

Solomon .... KING, SAGE, WISE
MAN

island .... BUKA, MALAITA,
CHOISEUL, GUADALCANAL,
BOUGAINVILLE

Islands' capital .... HONIARA

Islands' city/town .... AUKI,
KIETA, SOHANO

of rhyme .... GRUNDY

seaport .... LAE

Solomon's brother .... AMNON,
ABSALOM, ADONIJAH

chariot cities, one of
.... GEZER, HAZOR, TAMAR,
BAALATH, MEGGIDO

famous structure .... TEMPLE

father .... DAVID

kingdom .... ISRAEL

land .... OPHIR

mines location .... TIMNAH
VALLEY

mother .... BATHSHEBA

sayings .... MAXIMS, PROVERBS

seal .... STAR OF DAVID

son .... MENELIK, REHOBOAM

supplier of architects,
masons and skilled
builders ..... (KING)HIRAM

solon .... SAGE, SENATOR,
WISEMAN, LAWGIVER,
LAWMAKER, LEGISLATOR

soluble salt .... SALAR

solus .... ALONE
solution .... KEY, OUT, CLUE,
BREAK, ANSWER, SEPARATION,
EXPLANATION
in pharmacy .... AQUA
part of ...... SOLUTE, SOLVENT
photographer's .... REAGENT
strength of .... TITER, TITRE
solve .... CLEAR UP, EXPLAIN,
UNRAVEL, WORK OUT
a message .... DECODE,
DECIPHER
a problem .... IRON OUT,
RESOLVE
solvent .... SOUND, WATER,
HEXONE, ACETONE, DILUENT,
DISSOLVER, MENSTRUUM
abuse .... GLUE SNIFFING,
INHALING FUMES
abuse effect ...... COMA, HIGH,
STUPOR
financially .... MONEYED
wood tar .... FURAN(E)
Solway Firth tributary .... EDEN
soma .... BODY, TRUNK
related to the .... SOMATIC
type of .... ECTOMORPH,
ENDOMORPH, MESOMORPH
Somalia bay .... NEGRO
cape .... ASER, SURA, HAFUN
capital .... MOGADISHU
city/town ...... BRAVA, BURAO,
MARKA, MERKA, AFMADU,
ZEILA, BORAMA, GIOHAR,
JAMAMA, BERBERA, CORIOLE,
ERIGABO, HARGEYSA,
CHISIMAYU
coin .... BESA
gulf .... ADEN
language ...... ARABIC, SOMALI
measure .... CABA
money ...... SOMALO, SHILLING
mountain .... SURUD AD
plateau .... HAUD
premier .... EGAL
president .... (SIAD) BARRE
province ..... BAY, BARI, GEDO,
MUDUG, SANAAG, TOGDHEER,
MOGADISCIO
region .... GUBAN, NOGAL
river .... GIUBA
Somaliland antelope .... BEIRA
——— Guiba .... OLTRE
somatic .... BODILY, PARIETAL,
PHYSICAL, CORPOREAL
somatization disorder
.... HYSTERIA
somatoform disorder
.... HYPOCHONDRIASIS
somber .... SAD, DARK, DULL,
GRAVE, DISMAL, GLOOMY,

SOLEMN
sombrero .... HAT
some .... ANY, A FEW, ABOUT,
CERTAIN, VARIOUS
are black, some are green
.... TEAS
are fine .... ARTS
are golden .... OLDIES
are green .... BERETS
are liberal .... ARTS
are purple .... PASSAGES
are spilled .... BEANS
are tight .... ENDS
are wild .... OATS
band leaders .... CAKE
WALKERS
bears .... GRISLY
books .... DOGEARED
carriers .... MAILMEN
controls ...... DUALS, REMOTES
eateries .... TEAROOMS
economic downers ...... STOCK
MARKET TIPS
future fliers .... EGGS
get this kind of deal
.... ROTTEN
haymakers .... LEFTS
kind of nut .... FADDIST
legislatures .... DIETS
MDs .... GPS
other time .... MANANA
putti .... CUPIDS
reviews .... RAVES
saws .... RIPPERS
time .... LATER, ONE DAY
somersault ...... TOPPLE, TUMBLE,
CAPSIZE, TWISTER, FLIP(FLOP),
SOMERSET
something .... PART, MATTER,
ANYTHING
done for effect ...... EYEWASH
easy .... PIE
else .... OTHER, ANOTHER
for thought .... FOOD
imagined .... FIGMENT
kept .... RETENT
monstrous .... FREAK, PRODIGY
notable/outstanding ..... DAISY
often copped .... PLEA
stated .... PAROL
that links .... COPULA
to bend .... EAR
carry .... ONUS
do with notes ...... COMPARE
pump .... IRON
purfle .... BORDER
set .... PACE
stand on .... LEG, FOOTING
sometime .... ONCE, FORMER,
ERST(WHILE)
in the future .... ONE DAY

sometimes .... NOW AND THEN,
OCCASIONALLY
bald .... PATE
Blue .... NUN(S)
found in the fire .... FAT
gold .... LEAF, LEAVES
it is bitter .... END
of woe .... TALE
raves, too .... RANTS
somewhat ...... KIND OF, NEARLY,
PARTLY, RATHER
ill .... POORLY
suffix .... ISH
somewhere .... SOMEPLACE
somite .... TELSON, SEGMENT,
MATAMERE
somnambulist ...... SLEEPWALKER
somniferous .... SOPORIFIC
somnolence .... LETHARGY,
DROWSINESS, SLEEPINESS
somnolent ...... DOZING, DROWSY,
SLEEPY, LETHARGIC
son .... HEIR, SCION, JUNIOR,
PROGENY, INHERITOR,
OFFSPRING
favorite .... BENJAMIN
in law .... GENER
kind of .... GOD, STEP, IN-LAW,
PRODIGAL
of: prefix .... MAC, FITZ
of a .... FILIAL
prodigal ...... WASTREL, GOOD-
FOR-NOTHING
rey's .... INFANTE
roi's .... DAUPHIN
younger .... CADET
sonance .... TUNE, SOUND
sonant .... VOICED, SOUNDING
opposed to .... SURD,
VOICELESS
sonata, part of .... CODA, RONDO,
SCHERZO, MOVEMENT
short .... SONATINA
sonderclass .... YACHT
song .... AIR, LAY, ARIA, GLEE,
LILT, POEM, RUNE, SOLO,
CAROL, CHANT, DITTY, LYRIC,
VERSE, BALLAD, LIED(ER),
MELODY, POETRY, CANZONE,
CHANSON, CANTICLE
accompaniment .... VAMP
after .... EPODE
-and-dance performer
.... DISEUSE
baby's .... LULLABY
Christmas .... NOEL, CAROL
contrapuntal .... FUGUE,
MOTET, MADRIGAL
dirgelike .... REQUIEM
evening ...... SERENA, VESPERS
flourish .... CADENZA

gay .... LILT
Goodnight girl of .... IRENE
handy .... ST. LOUIS BLUES
identification .... THEME,
    SIGNATURE
improvisation .... VAMP
joyful .... P(A)EAN
kind of .... POP, FOLK, SOUL,
    BLUES, P(A)EAN, TORCH,
    COUNTRY, SPIRITUAL
last words .... TAG
like .... ARIOSE, CANOROUS,
    CANTABILE
lively .... CANZONET
love .... AUBADE, SERENA,
    SERENADE
merry .... GLEE, LILT
minstrel's .... LAY, BALLAD
monotonous .... CHANT
morning .... MATIN
mystical .... RUNE
of .... MELIC
    gondoliers .... BARCAROLE
    joy .... CAROL
    lamentation .... DIRGE,
        THRENODE, THRENODY
    praise .... HYMN, LAUD,
        PAEAN, (H)ALLELUIA,
        MANIFICAT, HALLELUJAH
    sailors .... CHANTEY
    the 30's, popular
    .... COCKTAILS FOR TWO
    triumph .... PAEAN
    WW II .... MADELON
offered for a .... DIRT-CHEAP
operatic .... ARIA
part .... MADRIGAL
part of opera .... CAVATINA
poetic .... RUNE
prefix .... MELO
radio program .... THEME,
    SIGNATURE
refrain .... FALLA, BURDEN,
    CHORUS
religious .... ORATORIO
romantic, old .... RAMONA
sacred .... HYMN, MOTET,
    PSALM, ANTHEM
sad .... BLUES, DIRGE
section .... FIT
sentimental .... BALLAD
set of verses of .... STAVE
sheikdom of .... ARABY
short .... ODE, DITTY, ARIETTA,
    CANZONET, CAVATINA
syllable .... TRA
thrush .... MAVIE, MAVIS
with a refrain ..... ROUNDELAY
words of .... LYRIC
writer .... LYRICIST
Song of Solomon ...... CANTICLES

of Songs .... SONG OF
    SOLOMON, CANTICLE OF
    CANTICLES
songbird .... LARK, WREN, MAVIS,
    PIPIT, VIREO, BULBUL,
    CANARY, LINNET, ORIOLE,
    SINGER, THRUSH, VEERIE,
    BUNTING, REDWING,
    ROBIN(ET), SPARROW,
    TANAGER, WARBLER,
    BOBOLINK, CARDINAL,
    REDSTART, THRASHER,
    WHINCHAT, GOLDFINCH,
    NIGHTINGALE
    mewing .... CATBIRD
    of the .... TURDINE
    vocal organ .... SYRINX
songfest .... CONCERT
songlike .... LYRIC, MELIC,
    ARIOSE, CANOROUS,
    CANTABILE
songs, a collection of
    .... MINSTRELSY
    anthology of .... GARLAND
    composer of .... SONGSMITH
    made up of various
    .... MEDLEY
    medley of .... FANTASIA,
    POTPOURRI
songster .... CANTOR, SINGER,
    WARBLER
    of melodies .... MELODIST
songstress ...... SINGER, WARBLER,
    VOCALIST, CHANTRESS
    Bryant .... ANITA
    Clark .... PETULA
    Cline .... PATSY
    Clooney .... ROSEMARY
    Cole .... NATALIE
    Day .... DORIS
    Durbin .... DEANNA
    Farrell .... EILEEN
    Flack .... ROBERTA
    Froman .... JANE
    Gayle .... CRYSTAL
    Horne .... MARILYN
    Houston .... WHITNEY
    Jones .... SHIRLEY
    Judd .... NAOMI, WYNONNA
    Lynn .... LORETTA
    Mandrell .... BARBARA
    McEntire .... REBA
    Murray .... ANNE
    of popular ballads
    .... CHANTEUSE
    Page .... PATTI
    Reddy .... HELEN
    Ronstadt .... LINDA
    Ross .... DIANA
    Sills .... BEVERLY
    Smith .... KATE

    Steber .... ELEANOR
    Warwick .... DIONNE
    West .... DOTTIE
    Wynette .... TAMMY
    Yuru .... TIMI
Sonja of the ice .... HENIE
sonnet's last six lines .... SESTET
Sonora, capital of
    .... HERMOSILLO
    Indian .... YAQUI
sonority .... RESONANCE
sonorous ...... ROTUND, MAJESTIC,
    RESONANT, HIGH-FLOWN
sonsy .... BUXOM, LUCKY,
    HANDSOME
soon .... ANON, ENOW, EARLY,
    BETIME, PRONTO, ERELONG,
    QUICKLY, READILY, SHORTLY,
    PROMPTLY, BEFORE LONG
    afterward .... THEN
sooner .... RATHER, EARLIER,
    OKLAHOMAN, HOMESTEADER
    than .... ERE
soosoo .... DOLPHIN
soot .... COOM, GRIT, SMUT,
    COLLY, CROCK, GRIME,
    SMAZE, SMOKE, CARBON,
    LAMPBLACK
    full of .... FULIGINOUS
    holder .... FLUE
    pigment .... BISTER, BISTRE
sooth .... FACT, REAL, TRUTH,
    SMOOTH
soothe .... EASE, LULL, ALLAY,
    SALVE, (BE)CALM, PACIFY,
    APPEASE, ASSUAGE, COMFORT,
    MOLLIFY, PLACATE, RELIEVE
soother ...... ANODYNE, SOLACER,
    CONSOLER, TRANQUILIZER
soothing .... BALMY, EASING,
    CALMING, LENITIVE
soothsay .... PREDICT, FORETELL
soothsayer .... SEER, AUGUR,
    MANTIS, ORACLE, DIVINER,
    PROPHET, (H)ARUSPEX,
    TIRESIAS
    blind .... TIRESIAS
    brew of a .... HELLBROTH
soothsaying .... AUGURY
sooty .... DARK, BLACK, DUSKY
    matter .... DUST, SMUT
sop .... DIP, WET, OOZE, SOAK,
    BRIBE, STEEP, MORSEL,
    PACIFIER, INDUCEMENT
Sophia Scicolone .... LOREN
sophism .... FALLACY, IDOLISM
sophist .... CASUIST
sophisticate .... CORRUPT,
    FALSIFY, SLICKER,
    ADULTERATE, COSMOPOLITAN,
    MAN OF THE WORLD

sophisticated ...... HEP, HIP, CHIC, BLASE, SUBTLE, COMPLEX, REFINED, WORLDLY, ADVANCED, INTELLECTUAL

sophistication ...... WORLDLINESS

sophistry ...... FALLACY, IDOLISM, ABSURDITY, CHICANERY

sophomore .... HAZER

sophomoric ...... INANE, CALLOW

sopor .... STUPOR, LETHARGY

soporific .... DULL, SLOW, OPIATE, NARCOSE, SOMNIFIC, SULFONAL

sopping .... WET, SOAKED, DRENCHED

soppy ...... WET, RAINY, MAUDLIN, MAWKISH, SENTIMENTAL

soprano .... PONS, AMARA, HORNE, MOFFO, PATTI, VOICE, CALLAS, FARRAR, SINGER, TREBLE, FARRELL, NILSSON, ALBANESE

Sopwith plane .... TABLOID

sora .... BIRD, RAIL, CRAKE, ORTOLAN

Sorata .... ILLAMPU

Sorb .... SLAV, APPLE

descendants .... WENDS

Sorbonne, the .... PARISU

sorcerer .... HEX, MAGUS, WIZARD, WARLOCK, CHALDEAN, CONJURER, MAGICIAN

attendant .... FAMULUS

sorceress .... CIRCE, LAMIA, MEDEA, SYBIL, WITCH

sorcery .... OBE(AH), HOODOO, VOODOO, ALCHEMY, THEURGY, WIZARDRY, DIABLERIE, DIABOLISM, SORTILEGE, (BLACK)MAGIC, WITCHCRAFT, CONJURATION

sordid .... BASE, MEAN, DIRTY, GROSS, FILTHY, IGNOBLE, SQUALID, WRETCHED

sordino .... MUTE

sordor .... DREGS

sore .... DIRE, ANGRY, ACHING, FESTER, LESION, TENDER, TOUCHY, PAINFUL, PUSTULE, RESENTFUL, DISGRUNTLED

dressing .... GAUZE, PATCH

inflamed .... BLAIN

mustard application on .... POULTICE

open .... ULCER, WOUND

throat, kind of .... STREP

ulcer-like .... CANCER

sorehead .... CRANK, LOSER, GRIPER, GROUCH, MALCONTENT

sorghum .... MILO, GRASS, SYRUP, FODDER, KAF(F)IR, FETERITA

grain .... DURRA, SORGO, DOURA(H), MILLET, KAOLIANG

millet-like .... MILO

soricine animal .... SHREW

sorority .... SODALITY, FELLOWSHIP, SISTERHOOD

sorosis .... FRUIT, MULBERRY

sorrel .... HORSE, REDDISH-BROWN

wood .... OCA

sorrow .... WOE, DOLOR, GRIEF, ANGUISH, SADNESS, DISTRESS

sorrowful expression .... ALAS, WOE IS ME, ALACK(ADAY)

sinner .... PENITENT

sorry .... SAD, MEAN, POOR, DISMAL, PALTRY, RUEFUL, CONTRITE, INFERIOR, PENITENT, WRETCHED, MISERABLE, REGRETFUL, REMORSEFUL

sort .... ILK, KIND, SIFT, TYPE, CLASS, GRADE, GROUP, MATCH, NATURE, VARIETY, CLASSIFY

of .... SOMEWHAT

of appeal .... SNOB

sortie .... RAID, FORAY, SALLY, ATTACK, MISSION

sortilege .... SORCERY, PROPHECY, DIVINATION

sorts, out of .... ILL, CROSS, INDISPOSED

SOS .... HELP WANTED

sotol, plant like .... YUCCA

sot .... BLOAT, RUMMY, SOUSE, TOPER, TIPPLER, DRUNKARD

soubise .... SAUCE

soubrette .... MAID, FLIRT, ACTRESS, COQUETTE

soucar .... BANKER

souchong .... TEA

souffle .... PUFFY, MOUSSE, MERINGUE, SPOONBREAD

sough ...... MOAN, SIGH, MURMUR, RUSTLE

soul .... AME, EGO, ELAN, MIND, ANIMA, ATMAN, BEING, ESPRIT, PNEUMA, SPIRIT, ESSENCE, EMBODIMENT, INDIVIDUAL

dead person's .... MANES

dwelling place .... (THE)BODY, TABERNACLE

lost ...... THE DAMNED, FALLEN ANGEL

mate .... LOVER

personified .... PSYCHE

seller .... FAUST

singer ...... (ARETHA)FRANKLIN

timid .... LAMB

soulful .... EMOTIONAL

soulless .... HEARTLESS

sound .... FIT, GOOD, HALE, HONK, PURL, SAFE, SANE, SEEM, SONO, TONE, TRIG, WELL, AUDIO, INLET, NOISE, PLUMB, SOLID, VALID, APPEAR, FATHOM, SECURE, STABLE, STRAIT, HEALTHY, PERFECT, STRIDOR, RELIABLE

a bubbling .... HUBBLE-BUBBLE

a horn .... BEEP, TOOT

after-dinner .... BURP

amplifier .... RESONATOR

auto horn .... BEEP, HONK

bagpipe .... SKIRL

banging door .... SLAM

Banshee .... WAIL

barnyard .... BAA, BRAY

beating with a loud .... PLANGENT

bee's/insect .... HUM, DRONE

bell-like .... TING

bell's ...... PEAL, TOLL, CHIME, CLANG, JINGLE, TINKLE, DING-(DONG)

bird .... PEEP, CHIRP, TWEET, TWITTER

black sheep .... BAA-BAA

bomb .... WHINE

branch of physics dealing in .... ACOUSTICS

breathing .... RALE, STRIDOR

breathy .... PANT

bullet .... ZIP, PING, PHUT

butterfingers' .... OOPS

buzzing .... WHIR(R)

by reflection of sound waves .... ECHO

cats'/household .... PURR, MEOW, MEWL, MIAOW

Christmas .... TINKLE

chuckling/gleeful .... CHORTLE

clock .... CHIME

combining form ...... AUDI(O), PHON(O)

comic strip .... BAM

continued clanging .... CLANGOR

cooing .... CURR

deep .... BOOM, RUMBLE, CAVERNOUS

depth .... PLUMB

discordant .... DIN, JANGLE

disturbing motor .... PING

donkey's .... BRAY, HEEHAW

dove's .... COO, CURR

drum .... RATATAT, RATYTAT

dull .... THUD

effect .... ECHO
elephant's ..... ROAR, TRUMPET
escaping steam .... HISS
explosive .... POP
faster than .... SUPERSONIC
feline fight .... CATERWAUL
for quiet .... SSH
from a corner .... AMEN
from a steamwinder ...... TICK
from cold .... CHATTER
from spirits .... HIC
gentle flute .... TOOTLE
grating .... JAR, SCROOP
grimalkin .... MEOW
guttural .... GRATE, GRUNT
harsh .... JAR, RASP, GRIDE,
JANGLE
heard .... ACOUSTIC
hesitation .... ER
hissing ...... ZIP, FIZ(Z), SWISH,
FIZZLE, SIZZLE
hog's .... GRUNT
in harmony .... CHIME
in mind .... SANE
kennel .... YAP, YELP
large bell's .... DONG
light .... SWISH
loud, brassy .... BLARE
loud, prolonged .... PEAL
loud enough to be heard
.... AUDIBLE
loud in .... SONOROUS
low buzzing .... HUM
lung .... RALE
making crackling
.... CREPITATING
may be heard, distance
.... EARSHOT
menacing ..... GR-R-R, GROWL,
SNARL
metallic .... TING, CLANG,
monotonous buzzing
.... DRONE
mournful .... SOB, KNELL
murmuring .... COO, HUM,
CURR, SOUGH
mystery .... SCREAM
nocturnal .... SNORE
of .... SONIC, TONAL, PHONIC,
SONANT
a quiet motor .... PURR
activity .... HUM
bells, ringing
.... TINTINNABULATION
contentment .... PURR
delight .... SQUEAL
disapproval .... BOO, HISS,
HOOT, CATCALL
footsteps ..... CLUMP, TRAMP
goose .... HISS
gunfire/laughter .... PEAL

heart, abnormal .... MURMUR
heavy guns .... BOOM
indignation .... SNORT
merriment .... HA-HA
pain ..... MOAN, OUCH, YELL,
GROAN, SHRIEK
silence, meaning .... NO
surprise .... AH, OHO, GASP
thunder .... CLAP
time .... TICK
violence .... WHAM
warning .... HISS, ALARM,
SIREN, RATTLE, TOCSIN
whale .... MEW, CLICK,
SQUEAL, CHIRRUP
yearning .... SIGH
off .... ORATE, SPEAK
ominous .... KNELL
opposite of .... SILENCE
out .... PROBE, FEEL OUT
out the public .... POLL
paddock .... NEIGH
painful .... OW, OUCH
pastoral .... BAA
pertaining to .... SONIC
pertaining to speech
.... PHONETIC
plosive .... SPUTTER
-proofing material .... PUG
repetitive .... TICTAC, TOM-
TOM, DRUMBEAT, TICKTACK,
TICKTOCK, RAT-TAT-TAT
resonant .... TONE
reverberating .... ROLL
ringing .... TANG
rolling .... RUMBLE
rooster's .... CROW
rustling .... SWOOSH
sabot's .... CLOP
science of .... ACOUSTIC(S)
scolding .... TSK(TSK)
sharp .... SPANG
short, sharp .... CLACK
shrill ..... ZING, SKIRL, SQUEAK
signaling .... BEEP
slapping .... SPLAT
sleeper's .... ZEEZ, SNORE
slight .... CLICK
snake .... HISS, RATTLE
sob .... BLUB
soft, rubbing .... SWISH
stadium .... ROAR
storm .... ROAR, BLUSTER
sty .... OINK, GRUNT
surf .... ROTE
swelterer's .... PHEW
thin, sharp .... SQUEAK,
SQUEAL
thinking .... LOGIC
throat-clearing .... AHEM
thunder .... BOOM, CLAP, PEAL,

ROLL, (G)RUMBLE
trumpet .... BLARE
undignified .... WHINE
unit of measurement
.... MACH, DECIBEL
usually in triplicate .... RAH
veldt .... ROAR
voiceless .... CEDILLA
warbling .... CHIRM
warning: poet. .... ALARUM
wave, bend .... REFRACT
wave reflection phenomenon
.... ECHO
wavy .... ROTES
whiplash .... WHISH
whirring ...... BIRR, BURR, ZIZZ
whispering/rustling
.... SUSURRUS
wind .... PUFF, WAFT, WHIFFLE,
WHISTLE
Sound, _____ .... PUGET
soundless .... MUTE, STILL,
SILENT, ASONANT
soundly .... FULLY, TOTALLY,
COMPLETELY, THOROUGHLY
soundness .... SOLVENCY,
VALIDITY, STABILITY
soundproof .... QUIET,
NOISEPROOF
make .... PUG, DEADEN,
INSULATE
sounds in ear, ringing
.... TINNITUS
soup ...... BROTH, GUMBO, BISQUE,
BORSCHT, CHOWDER,
POT(T)AGE, BOUILLON,
CONSOMME, JULIENNE
accompaniments
.... CRACKERS, SALTINES,
BREAD STICKS
base for .... STOCK
bread .... CROUTON, MELBA
TOAST
clear .... CONSOMME
clear, Scotch style .... BROO
cold .... GAZPACHO,
VICHYSSOISE
dish .... TUREEN
flavor ..... DILL, CHIVE, CURRY,
ONION, CHEESE
flavored with curry
.... MULLIGATAWNY
garnish .... EGG, CHEESE,
ALMONDS, PARSLEY, BACON
BITS
in the .... IN TROUBLE
ingredient .... BEAN, BEEF,
CLAM, LENTIL, NOODLE,
MACARONI, VEGETABLE
kind of .... POTATO, CHOWDER,
NAVY BEAN, (SPLIT-)PEA,

BLACK BEAN, MINESTRONE, FRENCH ONION

meat .... BISQUE, BURGOO

plant .... LEEK

pods .... OKRA

potato .... VICHYSSOISE

slang .... OVERCAST, NITROGLYCERIN

spoon .... LADLE

thick .... GUMBO, PUREE, BISQUE, CHOWDER, POTTAGE

thickener .... EGG, FLOUR, CORNSTARCH

thickening mixture ...... ROUX, RIVELS

thin .... BROTH

to ____ .... NUTS

to nuts .... MEAL, MENU

vegetable ...... GUMBO, BISQUE, BURGOO, MINESTRONE

yegg's: sl. .... NITRO

soupçon .... TASTE, TRACE, SUSPICION

souped-up cars .... RACERS

sour .... RANK, TART, ACRID, CROSS, ACIDIC, BITTER, RANCID, ACERB(IC), ACETOSE, ACETOUS, ACID(ULOUS)

ale .... ALEGAR, VINEGAR

disposition, of .... CROSS, TESTY, CRANKY, MOROSE, SULLEN, PEEVISH, LIVERISH

gourd .... BAOBAB

grass .... SORREL

gum .... NYSSA, TUPELO

milk drink .... LEBAN

source ...... ROOT, CAUSE, ORIGIN, SPRING, FOUNT(AIN), HEADSPRING

of genius/inspiration .... MUSE

guidance .... ORACLE

iodine .... KELP

nuclear energy .... FISSION

spirits .... POTSTILLS

sourdine .... MUTE

sourdough ...... LEAVEN, SETTLER, PROSPECTOR

sourdough's town .... NOME

sourpuss .... CRAB, PRUNE, GROUCH, BROODER

Sousa, composer .... JOHN PHILIP

employment of .... (MARINE)BANDLEADER

sobriquet of .... (THE)MARCH KING

work of .... WASHINGTON POST MARCH, STARS AND STRIPES FOREVER

sousaphone .... HORN

souse .... SOAK, BRINE, STEEP, SWOOP, PICKLE, PLUNGE,

DRUNKARD, INTOXICATE

soused ...... DRUNK, TIPSY, STINKO

soutache .... BRAID, TRIMMING

soutane .... TUNIC, CASSOCK

South Africa, foreigner in
.... UITLANDER

South African .... BOER, AFRIKANER

animal ..... QUAGGA, SURICATE

antelope .... GNU, SASSABY, BUSHBACK

archbishop .... TUTU

assembly .... RAAD

aunt .... TANTA

bay .... FALSE, TABLE, WALVIS, SAINT HELENA

beverage .... MATE

camp .... LAAGER

cape .... AGULHAS, GOOD HOPE

capital .... CAPE TOWN, PRETORIA

city/town .... DURBAN, SOWETO, WELKOM, BRAKPAN, SPRINGS, BOKSBURG, GERMISTON, KIMBERLEY, JOHANNESBURG

coin .... CENT, POND, RAND, FLORIN, DAALDER

district .... RAND

Dutch .... BOER, TAAL

farmer .... BOER, WERF

field marshal .... SMUTS

fox .... ASSE

golfer ..... PLAYER, SEWGOLUM

grassland .... VELD(T)

hill .... KOP

island .... ROBBEN

issue .... APARTHEID

javelin .... ASSAGAI

lake .... SAINT LUCIA

language .... ZULU, SESOTHO, AFRIKAANS

legislature .... RAAD

monetary unit .... RAND

monkey .... VERVET

mountain .... TABLE, SNEEUWKOP

mulatto .... GRIQUA

native .... ZULU, BANTU, KAFFIR

plain .... VELD(T)

plateau ...... (GREAT)KAR(R)OO

polecat .... MUSANG

policeman .... ZARP

president .... DONGES, DE KLERK, MANDELA

prime minister .... SMUTS, HERTZOG, VORSTER, VERWOERD

province .... CAPE, NATAL, TRANSVAAL

racial policy .... APARTHEID

republic .... VENDA, CISKEI, TRANSKEI

river .... BOT, SAK, KLIP, SAND, VAAL, GROOTE, MOLOPO, ORANGE, LIMPOPO, PALMIET, HARTBEES, OLIFANTS, CROCODILE, ZONDEREND

road .... KLIP

settler .... BOER

spear .... ASSAGAI

swamp .... VLEI

tableland .... KAR(R)OO

thong .... RIEM

town .... STAD

tribal council .... INDABA

valley .... VAAL, KLOOP

village .... KRAAL

weapon .... KNOBKERPIE

workmen .... VOLK

South American animal
.... LLAMA, TAPIR, TAYRA, ALPACA, VICUNA

alligator ..... CAIMAN, CAYMAN

arid ground .... ESPINAL

armadillo .... POYOU, MATACO, TATOUAY

bean .... TONKA

bird .... GUAN, JACU, RHEA, AGAMI, TOPAZ, TURCO, JACANA, ARACARI, MANAKIN, SERIEMA, TINAM(O)U, CURASSOW, GUACHARO, HOA(C)TZIN, SCREAMER

butternut .... SOUARI

city/town .... LIMA, LA PAZ, BOGOTA, MEDELLIN, SAO PAULO, MONTEVIDEO, BUENOS AIRES, RIO DE JANEIRO

coin .... CONTO, CONDOR, ESCUDO, (MIL)REIS

crocodile .... YACARE

dance .... SAMBA, TANGO, CHA-CHA, BEGUINE, CARIOCA

deer .... GEMUL

desolate region .... PUNA

duck .... PATO

fish .... PIRANHA, ARAPAIMA, CHARACIN

guinea pig .... PACA

hare .... TAPETI

hat .... JIPIJAPA

hawk .... CARACARA

herdsman .... LLANERO

hog .... TAPIR

hummingbird .... WARRIOR

Indian .... ONA, INCA, CARIB, MAYAN, GUARANI, TEHUELCHE, PATAGONIAN

Indian, pertaining to
.... PEBAN

knife .... MACHETE
laborer .... PEON, BRACERO
lake .... MERIN, MIRIM,
      VIEDMA, TITICACA,
      MARACAIBO
lapwing .... TREUTERO
liberator .... SUCRE
lizard .... TEJU
mammal .... GRISON,
      KINKAJOU, PACARANA
marmoset .... TAMARIN
missile weapon .... BOLA
monkey .... TITI, ACARI,
      ARABA, TETEE, SAPAJOU,
      CAPUCHIN, MARMOSET
mountain .... HUILA, TOLIMA,
      RORAIMA, BANDEIRA,
      ACONCAGUA, CHIMBORAZO,
      HUASCARAN
nightbird .... GUACHARO
opossum ..... QUICA, YAPO(C)K
ostrich .... RHEA
palm .... ITA, GRUGRU
parrot .... MACAW, AMAZON(A)
plain .... CAMPO, LLANO,
      PAMPA(S), PARAMO
plant .... GUACO, COPAIBA,
      PAREIRA, RHATANY, JIPIJAPA,
      JABORANDI
raccoon .... COATI
reptile .... ABOMA
river .... PARA, META, PLATA,
      JURUA, NEGRO, PURUS,
      AMAZON, ARAUCA, CHUBUT,
      CUYUNI, GRANDE, IGUACU,
      JAPURA, MORONI, PARANA,
      DESEADO, GUAPORE, MADEIRA,
      ORINOCO, OYAPOCK,
      URUGUAY, PARAGUAI,
      PUTUMAYO
rock .... TALPATATE
rodent .... PIG, PACA, COYPU,
      RATEL, TAPIR, AGOUTI,
      AGOUTY, GUINEA, NUTRIA,
      TAPETI, CAPYBARA
ruminant .... LLAMA
seed .... TONKA, GUAIAC
snake .... BOA, ABOMA,
      BUSHMASTER
tanager .... YENI, LINDO
tea leaf .... MATE
tick .... CARAPATO
tortoise/turtle .... MATAMATA
toucan .... ARACARI
tree .... MORA, TOLU, BALSA,
      CAROB, CEBIL, BEBEERU
trumpeter .... AGAMI
tuber .... OCA
ungulate .... TAPIR
weapon .... BOLAS
wild cat .... EYRA, MARGAY

wind .... PAMPERO
wood sorrel .... OCA
South Carolina Air Force base
      .... SHAW, DONALDSON,
      CHARLESTON, MYRTLE BEACH
bay .... BULLS, WINYAH
cape .... ROMAIN
capital .... COLUMBIA
city/town .... CAYCE, CONWAY,
      EASLEY, LADSON, SUMTER,
      LAURENS, PICKENS, ANDERSON,
      FLORENCE, ROCK HILL,
      CHARLESTON, GREENVILLE,
      ORANGEBURG, SPARTANBURG
county ...... LEE, YORK, AIKEN,
      HORRY, UNION, DILLON,
      JASPER, ANDERSON, BEAUFORT,
      BERKELEY, FLORENCE,
      RICHLAND, LEXINGTON,
      CHARLESTON
dam .... SANTEE, HARTWELL,
      BUZZARD ROOST
island .... BULL, CAPE, CAPERS,
      FRIPP, JAMES, JOHNS, DEWEES,
      EDISTO, KIAWAH, MORRIS,
      MURPHY, WADMALAW, HILTON
      HEAD, PRITCHARDS
lake .... WYLIE, KEOWEE,
      MARION, MORRIS, MURRAY,
      WATEREE, HARTWELL,
      MOULTRIE, ROBINSON
Marine Air Station
      .... BEAUFORT
mountain .... SASSAFRAS
mountain range .... BLUE
      RIDGE
river .... NEW, BUSH, BLACK,
      BROAD, REEDY, SANDY,
      TYGER, WANDO, ASHLEY,
      COOPER, COOSAW, EDISTO,
      ENOREE, LUMBER, PEE DEE,
      SALUDA, SANTEE, SENECA,
      ASHEPOO, CATAWBA,
      LYNCHES, PACOLET, TUGALOO,
      WATEREE, WACCAMAW
state bird .... WREN
state flower .... JASMINE,
      JESSAMINE
state nickname ...... PALMETTO
South Dakota Air Force base
      .... ELLSWORTH
capital .... PIERRE
city/town .... HURON, SALEM,
      SELBY, CANTON, WINNER,
      BRITTON, IPSWICH, MADISON,
      YANKTON, ABERDEEN,
      DEADWOOD, MITCHELL,
      BROOKINGS, WATERTOWN,
      RAPID CITY, SIOUX FALLS,
      VERMILLION
county .... DAY, LAKE, BROWN,

      BUTTE, GRANT, MEADE,
      UNION, HUGHES, TURNER,
      DAVISON, LINCOLN, SHANNON,
      LAWRENCE, WALWORTH,
      CODINGTON, MINNEHAHA,
      PENNINGTON
creek .... ELK, CAIN, NASTY,
      WOUNDED KNEE
dam .... OAHE, BIG BEND
lake .... DRY, MUD, RED, LONG,
      OAHE, REID, SWAN, ANDES,
      BRANT, BYRON, PIYAS, WHITE,
      HERMAN, PLATTE, SHARPE,
      SPIRIT, WAUBAY, BUFFALO,
      KAMPESKA, POINSETT, LEWIS
      AND CLARK
mountains .... BLACK HILLS
river .... BAD, ELM, GRAND,
      JAMES, MAPLE, WHITE, BIG
      SIOUX, KEYA PAHA, MISSOURI,
      MINNESOTA
state bird .... PHEASANT
state flower
      .... PASQUEFLOWER
state nickname .... COYOTE
tourist site .... MOUNT
      RUSHMORE
South Pacific craft .... PROA
garment .... PAREU
island .... FIJI, SAMOA, TONGA,
      TAHITI
star .... PINZA
South Pole explorer
      .... AMUNDSEN
South Sea canoe .... PROA, PRAU
garment .... SARONG
island ...... ARU, BALI, SAMOA,
      TAHITI
island drink .... KAVA(KAVA)
loincloth .... LAVA-LAVA
native .... KANAKA, SAMOAN,
      BALINESE, TAHITIAN,
      POLYNESIAN
novel .... OMOO
shrub .... KAVA(KAVA)
staple .... TARO
South wind .... NOTUS, AUSTER
southerly .... AUSTRAL
southern .... AUSTRAL
beauty .... BELLE
Southern Cross .... CRUX
France .... MIDI
States .... DIXIE
southpaw .... LEFTY, SINISTRAL,
      LEFT-HANDED, LEFT-HANDER
souvenir .... FAVOR, RELIC,
      SCRAP, MEMENTO, KEEPSAKE
sou'westers .... STORMHATS
sovereign ...... KING, LORD, QUID,
      CHIEF, LIEGE, POUND, ROYAL,
      RULER, PRINCE, SOVRAN,

EMPEROR, MONARCH, SUPREME, POTENTATE

dignity .... MAJESTY

female .... LADY, QUEEN, EMPRESS, TSARINA

of a .... REGNAL

power .... SWAY

sovereignty .... RULE, EMPERY, THRONE, ROYALTY, SCEPTRE, DOMINION

Soviet. See also **Russian**

.... COUNCIL

administrative body

.... PRESIDIUM

caucasian .... KURD

government .... KREMLIN

gulf .... RIGA, ANADYR, SAKHALIN

island .... AYON, BELYY, WIESE, PIONER, WRANGEL, PARAMUSHIR

lake .... ONEGA, BAYKAL, BELOYE, LADOGA, TAYMYR, PEIPUS, TENGIZ, IMANDRA

money .... RUBLE, KOPECK

mountains .... URAL, ALTAY, SAYAN, ULUTAU

news agency .... TASS

newspaper .... PRAVDA

peninsula .... KOLA, YAMAL, CRIMEA

poet .... YEVTUSHENKO

president .... KALININ, MIKOYAN, PODGORNY, GORBACHEV

range .... OLOY, URAL, VILYUY

republic .... UZBEK, KAZAKH, KIRGIZ, LATVIA, RUSSIA, ARMENIA, ESTONIA, GEORGIA, TADZHIK, TURKMEN, UKRAINE, MOLDAVIA, LITHUANIA, AZERBAIDZHAN

river .... OB, CHU, DON, ILI, OKA, PUR, TAZ, TYM, UDA, AMGA, AMUR, EMBA, KUMA, KURA, LENA, MAYA, URAL, VAKH, YANA, ZEYA, ALDAN, ATREK, CHUNA, ISHIM, KHETA, MEZEN, NADYM, TOBOL, VITIM, VOLGA, DONETS, IRTYSH, MURGAB, TAYMYR

Russia .... USSR

sea .... ARAL, AZOV, KARA, WHITE, LAPTEV, CASPIAN, OKHOTSK

Union founder .... LENIN

workers' collective/group

.... ARTEL

sovran .... SOVEREIGN

sow .... HOG, PIG, SEED, PLANT, STREW, SWINE, SLUICE,

SCATTER, BROADCAST, PROPAGATE, DISSEMINATE

bug .... ISOPOD, SLATER, WOOD LOUSE

young .... GILT

sowens .... PORRIDGE

sox .... SOCKS

soy(a) .... BEAN, SOJA, SAUCE

soybean cake .... TAHURE

enzyme .... URASE

product .... OIL, MISO, SUFU, TAHO, NAT(T)O, TAUSI, TOKUA

sauce .... SOY, SOJA, TOYO

spa .... BATH, RESORT, SPRING, BALNEUM

space .... GAP, AREA, ROOM, RANGE, EXTENT, SPHERE, SPREAD, EXPANSE

agcy. .... NASA

beacon .... QUASAR, PULSAR

between .... DISTANCE

between bird's eye and bill

.... LORE

between vocal cords

.... GLOTTIS

blank .... GAP, LACUNA

critter .... ALIEN

dog .... STREIKA

empty .... HOLE, VOID, BLANK, CAVITY, HOLLOW, VACUUM

filled with matter ..... PLENUM

filler .... SHIM

for freedom of action

.... LEEWAY, ELBOW ROOM

for goods .... STORAGE

in biology .... LACUNA

in from margin .... INDENT

monkey .... ENOS, ASTROMONK

of time .... SPAN, INTERVAL

on a written sheet, blank

.... MARGIN

overhead .... HEADWAY, HEADROOM

pertaining to .... AMPLE, ROOMY, SPATIAL, SPACIOUS

science .... ASTRONAUTICS

ship blister .... MODULE

suit .... G-SUIT

travel .... FLIGHT

traveler .... SPACEMAN, ASTRONAUT, COSMONAUT

triangular .... SPANDREL

unlimited .... INFINITY

vehicle .... SOYUZ, APOLLO, COSMOS, GEMINI, SKYLAB, VOSTOK, FREEDOM, MARINER, SPUTNIK, COLUMBIA, EXPLORER, SATELLITE, CHALLENGER

void .... VACUUM

Space Age initials .... NASA

launcher .... SPUTNIK

spacecraft .... ROCKET, SATELLITE

capsule .... SPECS

first .... SPUTNIK

instrumented .... PROBE

into the earth, insertion of

.... REENTRY

landing on water of

.... SPLASHDOWN

launch site .... CAPE KENNEDY, CAPE CANAVERAL

launch site, Soviet Union

.... COSMODROME

launching of a ...... BLAST-OFF

on the moon, first ..... APOLLO

part .... MODULE, CAPSULE

path taken by .... ORBIT

point nearest to earth in orbit of .... PERIGEE

point nearest to moon in orbit of .... PERILUNE

schedule of operations just before launching

.... COUNTDOWN

small rocket on a large

.... RETRO

to Venus .... MARINER

unit .... LEM

spacer .... BAR

spacious .... VAST, AMPLE, LARGE, ROOMY, SPATIAL, INFINITE, SWEEPING

spade .... DIG, SAM, SCOOP

tool like .... SPUD, SHOVEL

spadefoot .... TOAD

spades .... SUIT

spaghetti .... PASTA, NOODLES

associate .... MEATBALLS

food like .... MACARONI

ingredient .... DURUM

spahi/spahee .... CAVALRYMAN

Spain .... ESPANA, IBERIA, HESPERIA

capital of .... MADRID

district of .... GALICIA, GRANADA, ASTURIAS, NAVARRE, ANDALUSIA

kingdom of .... LEON, ARAGON, CASTILE

Olympic site in

.... BARCELONA

Spalato .... SPLIT

spale .... LATH

spall .... CHIP, FLAKE, SPLIT, GALLET

spalpeen .... SCAMP, RASCAL

span .... ARCH, PAIR, TEAM, YOKE, CROSS, REACH, BRIDGE, EXTENT, PERIOD, MEASURE, STRETCH, WINGSPAN, WINGSPREAD

669

in inches .... NINE
of man's life .... LIFETIME
spang .... ABRUPTLY, DIRECTLY
spangle ...... BEAD, STUD, SEQUIN,
GLITTER, TRINKET, SPARKLER,
PAILLETTE
Spaniard .... SENOR, IBERIAN,
CASTILIAN
16th century
.... CONQUISTADOR
spaniel .... DOG, COCKER,
CLUMBER, PAPILLON,
SPRINGER
kind of .... TOY, WATER
Spanish .... ESPANOL, LANGUAGE,
CASTILIAN
abbot .... ABAD
above .... ARRIBA
absent .... AUSENTE
according to .... SEGUN
ache/pain .... DOLOR
add .... SUMAR
address .... DIRECCION
after .... DESPUES
afternoon .... TARDE
again .... OTRA VEZ
against .... CONTRA
aid .... AYUDA
airplane .... AVION
airport .... AEROPUERTO
alarm clock ..... DESPERTADOR
all .... TODA, TODO
all at once .... PRONTO
all right .... BIEN
almond .... JORDAN
almost .... CASI
alone .... SOLA, SOLO
also .... TAMBIEN
always .... SIEMPRE
American country .... MEXICO
mestizo .... LADINO
plain .... LLANO
town .... PUEBLO
war soldier ..... ROUGHRIDER
amiable .... SIMPATICO
and .... Y
another/other ...... OTRA, OTRO
answer .... RESPONDE
ant .... HORMIGA
any .... CUALQUIER
apple .... MANZANA
April .... ABRIL
apron .... DELANTAL
arm .... BRAZO
armada .... FLOTA
art .... ARTE
article .... EL, LA, LAS, EN, UN,
LOS, UNA
as .... COMO
asphalt .... BREA
August .... AGOSTO

aunt .... TIA
author of Don Quixote
.... CERVANTES
avenue .... AVENIDA
baby .... BEBE, NINA, NINO
back .... ESPALDA
bad .... MALO
bag .... BOLSA
baker .... PANADERO
bakery .... PANADERIA
ball .... PELOTA
balloon .... GLOBO
banana .... PLATANO
bank .... BANCO
barrel .... TONEL
basket .... CESTA, CESTO
bath .... BANO, BANARSE
bay .... BISCAY, ALCUDIA
bayonet .... YUCCA
beach .... PLAYA
beak .... PICO
bean .... HABA, FRIJOL
bear .... OSO
beautiful .... BELLA, BELLO,
HERMOSA, HERMOSO
because .... PORQUE
bed .... CAMA
bee .... ABEJA
beer .... CERVEZA
before .... ANTES
behave .... PORTARSE
believe .... CREER
bell .... CAMPANA
berry, dried .... PASA
best .... MUY BUENO
bet .... PONER, PARAR
better .... MEJOR
between .... ENTRE
bib .... BABERO
big .... GRANDE
bird .... AVE, PAJARO
birth .... NACIMIENTO
birthday .... CUMPLEANOS
bishop .... OBISPO
black .... NEGRA, NEGRO
blackboard .... PIZARRA
blanket .... MANTA, COBIJA,
PONCHO, SERAPE
blind .... CIEGA, CIEGO
blond .... RUBIA, RUBIO
blood .... SANGRE
blow .... GOLPE
blue .... AZUL
boat .... BARCO, VAPOR,
LANCHA
body .... CUERPO
bonnet .... GORRA
book .... LIBRO
boot .... BOTA
booth .... TIENDA, CASILLA
born .... MACIDA, MACIDO

boss .... AMO
botanist .... MONARDES
box .... CAJA
boy .... NINO, CHICO
branch .... RAMA
bread .... PAN
break .... ROMPER
breakfast .... DESAYUNO
-bred sheep .... MERINO
breech .... BRAGA
bridge .... PUENTE
broom .... ESCOBA
brother .... HERMANO
brown .... CAFE, PARDO
brush .... CEPILLO
buffoon/clown .... COMICO,
GRACIOSO
building .... EDIFICIO
bull .... TORO
bullfight/race .... CORRIDA
bullfighter .... MATADOR
bullfighter's cloak .... CAPA
burglar/thief .... LADRON
but .... PERO
butcher .... CARNICERO
butter .... MANTEQUILLA
button .... BOTON
cabbage .... COL, REPOLLO
cake .... TORTA
candy/sweet .... DULCE
cape .... NAO, GATA, CREUS,
MAYOR, PALOS, PENAS,
TORTOSA, FORMENTOR,
TRAFALGAR, FINISTERRE
capital .... MADRID
car .... COCHE
card .... TARJETA
card game .... MONTE, OMBER,
OMBRE
carnation .... CLAVEL
castle .... TORRE, ALCAZAR,
ALHAMBRA, CASTILLO
cat .... GATO
cathedral city .... AVILA,
SEVILLE
cellar .... BODEGA
cellist .... CASALS
center .... CENTRO
certain .... SEGURO
chair .... SILLA
chalk .... TIZA
change .... CAMBIO
cheap .... BARATO
cheer .... OLE, BRAVO
cheese .... QUESO
chest .... PECHO
chicken .... POLLO
chickpea .... GARBANZO
chop/cutlet .... CHULETA
church .... IGLESIA
cigar .... PURO

city/town .... TOL, ADRA, ARTA, ASPE, BAZA, ELDA, LEON, LUGO, REUS, TORO, VIGO, ALCOY, AVILA, CADIZ, ELCHE, GIJON, JEREZ, LORCA, OLIVA, PALMA, YECLA, AVILES, BILBAO, BURGOS, CIUDAD, CUENCA, GERONA, HUELVA, LERIDA, MALAGA, MURCIA, ORENSE, OVIEDO, TOLEDO, ZAMORA, ·ALMERIA, CORDOBA, GRANADA, LEGANES, SEGOVIA, SEVILLE, TARRASA, VITORIA, ALBACETE, ALICANTE, BADALONA, GUERNICA, LA CORUNA, PAMPLONA, SABADELL, VALENCIA, ZARAGOZA, BARCELONA, CARTAGENA, SALAMANCA, SARAGOSSA

clean .... LIMPIA, LIMPIO

clear .... CLARA, CLARO

clever .... LISTA, LISTO

cloak .... CAPA

clock/watch .... RELOJ

closed/shut .... CERRADO

cloth/dress .... VESTIDOS

clothing .... ROPA

cloud .... NUBE

club(house) .... CASINO

coal .... CARBON

coat .... ABRIGO

coffee .... CAFE

coffeepot .... CAFETERIA

coin ...... DURO, REAL, PESETA, CENTAVO, CENTIMO, PISTOLE, MARAVEDI

coin, obsolete .... DOUBLOON

coin, old .... DOBLA, PISTOLE

cold .... FRIA, FRIO

cold (illness) .... CATARRO

collar/neck .... CUELLO

colony in Africa .... IFNI

comb .... PEINE

composer .... FALLA

conqueror .... CORTEZ, PIZARRO, CONQUISTADOR

cookie .... GALLETA

cord/rope .... CUERDA

corn .... MAIZ

corner .... ESQUINA

cot .... CATRE

cotton .... ALGODON

cough .... TOS

council .... JUNTA

country/nation .... PAIS

countryman .... PAISANO

court .... CORTE, JUZGADO

courtyard .... PATIO

cousin .... PRIMA, PRIMO

cow .... VACA

cowboy .... GAUCHO, VAQUERO

cradle .... CUNA

cucumber .... PEPINO

cultivated/plowed land .... ARADO

cup .... TAZA

Cupid .... AMORINO, AMORETTO

dance .... JOTA, BAILE, DANZA, PAVIN, TANGO, VALSE, BOLERO, CANARY, PAVAN(E), CARIOCA, CACHUCHA, CHACONNE, FANDANGO, FLAMENCO, GUARACHA, SARABAND(E)

date .... FECHA

daughter .... HIJA

daughter-in-law .... NUERA

Davis Cupper .... ARILLA, GIMENO, GISBERT, SANCHEZ, SANTANA

day .... DIA

dear (beloved) .... QUERIDA, QUERIDO

dear (expensive) .... CARO

December .... DICIEMBRE

desert .... DESIERTO

desire .... GANA

dessert .... POSTRE

dialect .... CATALAN, ASTURIAN, ARAGONESE, CASTILIAN, ANDALUSIAN

dictator .... FRANCO

dictionary .... DICCIONARIO

difficult .... DIFICIL

dining-room .... COMEDOR

dinner/meal .... CENA, COMIDA

dish .... OLLA, PLATO, PAELLA, BACALAO

doctor .... MEDICO

dock .... MUELLE

dog .... PERRO

doll .... MUNECA

donkey .... ASNO, BURRO

door .... PUERTA

doorbell .... TIMBRE

doubloon .... ONZA

dramatist .... TELLEZ

dress suit .... TRAJE

dressing gown .... BATA

driver .... CHOFER

drink .... VINO

drop .... GOTA

dry .... SECO

drugstore .... FARMACIA

drum .... TAMBOR

duck .... PATO

each/every .... CADA

ear .... OREJA

early .... TEMPRANO

earn .... GANAR

earth/land .... TIERRA

east .... ESTE

easy .... FACIL

egg .... HUEVO

eight .... OCHO

eighth .... OCTAVO

end .... FIN

England .... INGLATERRA

enough .... BASTANTE

envelope .... SOBRE

equal .... PAR, IGUAL

error .... FALTA

estuary .... RIA

evening .... NOCHE

event .... CASO

everything .... TODO

evidence .... PRUEBA

evil .... MALIGNO

ex-queen .... ENA

execution .... GARROTE

exhibit .... MOSTRAR

expense .... GASTO

explorer .... ONATE, BALBOA, CORTES, DESOTO, CORONADO, MAGELLAN, MENENDEZ

eye .... OJO

eyebrow .... CEJA

eyeglasses .... GAFAS, ANTEOJOS

eyesight .... VISTA

face .... CARA

factory .... FABRICA

fair .... FERIA, JUSTA, JUSTO

fairy .... HADA

fan .... AFICIONADO, VENTILADOR

far .... LEJOS

farm .... FINCA, GRANJA, RANCHO, HACIENDA

fascist .... FALANGIST

fast/quick ..... PRONTO, RAPIDO

fat .... GORDA, GORDO

father .... PADRE

fear .... MIEDO

feast .... FIESTA

February .... FEBRERO

fellow .... ENTE, COMPADRE

fellow, young .... CHICO

fiance(e) .... NOVIA, NOVIO

field .... CAMPO

fight .... LUCHA

film .... PELICULA

fine arts .... BELLAS ARTES

finger .... DEDO

fire .... FUEGO

fireman .... BOMBERO

fireplace .... FOGON

first .... PRIMERA, PRIMERO

fish .... PEZ, PESCADO

fish tank .... ACUARIO

fisherman .... PESCADOR

five .... CINCO
flag .... BANDERA
flask/bottle .... FRASCO
fleet .... FLOTA, ARMADA
flesh/meat .... CARNE
flight .... VUELO
flower .... FLOR
floor .... PISO, SUELO
flour .... HARINA
fly .... MOSCA
foot .... PIE
for .... POR, PARA
forehead .... FRENTE
forest .... MONTE, BASQUE
fork .... TENEDOR
fortress official .... ALCAIDE
four .... CUATRO
fourth .... CUARTO
France .... FRANCIA
freedom .... LIBERTAD
Friday .... VIERNES
fried .... FRITO
friend .... AMIGO
frog .... RANA
from .... DE
fox .... ZORRO
game .... JUEGO, PELOTA, JAI
ALAI
garden .... JARDIN
gay/happy .... ALEGRE
general .... ALVA
gentleman .... DON, SENOR,
CABALLERO
German .... ALEMAN
giant .... GIGANTE
gift .... REGALO
girl .... NINA, CHICA
glad .... FELIZ
glass .... VASO, CRISTAL
glove .... GUANTE
goat .... CABRA, CHIVO
goblet .... COPA
God .... DIOS
god of love .... AMADIS
gold .... ORO
good .... BUENA, BUENO
good afternoon .... BUENAS
TARDES
goodbye/so long/farewell
.... ADIOS, HASTA LA VISTA
good gracious! ...... CARAMBA
good luck .... BUENA SUERTE
good morning .... BUENOS
DIAS
good night .... BUENAS
NOCHES
goose .... GANSO
gossip .... CHISME
governess .... AYA, DUENNA
granddaughter .... NIETA
grandfather .... ABUELO

grandmother .... ABUELA
grandson .... NIETO
grape .... UVA, MALAGA
grapefruit .... POMELO
grass .... YERBA, HIERBA,
ESPARTO
grasshopper .... CHAPULIN
gray .... GRIS
great .... GRAN(DE)
great! .... MAGNIFICO
green .... VERDE
greeting .... HOLA
grocer .... TENDERO
grocery .... TIENDA
guest .... INVITADO,
CONVIDADO
guide .... GUIA
guitarist .... SEGOVIA
gulf .... CADIZ, ROSAS, SAN
JORGE, VALENCIA
gun .... FUSIL
gypsy .... GITANO
dance .... FLAMENCO
lingo .... CALO
habit .... MANANA, SIESTA
hair .... PELO, CABELLO
half .... MEDIO, MITAD
half-breed .... LADINO
hall .... SALA
ham .... JAMON
hamlet .... ALDEA
hammer .... MARTILLO
hand .... MANO
hand of clock ...... MANECILLA
handkerchief .... PANUELO
handsome .... GUAPO
harbor/port ..... ASILO, PUERTO
hard .... DURO, FIRME
harm .... MAL
hat .... SOMBRERO
he .... EL
head .... CABEZA
headdress .... MANTILLA
health .... SALUD
heart .... CORAZON
heat .... CALOR
heavy .... PESADO
Hebrew dialect .... LADINO
hello .... HOLA, QUE TAL
help! .... SOCORRO
her .... LA, LE, SU, SUS
herdsman .... PASTORES
here .... AQUI
hero .... (EL)CID, AMADIS
high .... ALTA, ALTO
high society .... ALTA
SOCIEDAD
highest peak .... PICO DE
TEIDE
highway .... CARRETERA
hill .... ALCOR

him .... LE, LO
his .... SU, SUS
hole .... AGUJERO
holiday .... DIA DE FIESTA
home/house .... CASA
horse .... GENET, JENNET,
CABALLO
horseman .... JINETE,
CAVAL(I)ERO
hot/warm .... CALIENTE
hour/time .... LA HORA
how much .... CUANTO
hunger .... HAMBRE
hunter .... CAZADOR
hunter's cap .... MONTERO
hurray! .... OLE, BRAVO
husband .... ESPOSO
I .... YO
immediately .... ENSEGUIDA
in/into .... EN
inn .... FONDA, MESON, VENTA,
POSADO
ink .... TINTA
inkwell .... TINTERO
Inquisition prey .... HERETIC
introduce .... PRESENTA
invite .... CONVIDA
iron .... HIERRO
is ...... EL ES, UNO ES, ELLA ES
island .... ISLA, IBIZA,
GOMERA, HIERRO, ALBORAN,
CABRERA, LA PALMA,
MAJORCA, MENORCA
islands .... CANARY, BALEARIC,
COLUMBRETES
it .... LA, LO
its .... SU
jacket .... SACO, CHAQUETA
jail/prison .... CALABOZO
janitor .... PORTERO
January .... ENERO
jar .... OLLA, JARRO, TARRO,
TINAJA
jeopardy .... PELIGRO
jewel ...... JOYA, JUGO, ALHAJA
job .... PUESTO, TRABAJO
joke .... BROMA
joker .... BROMISTA
journey .... VIAJE
joy .... ALEGRIA
Juan Carlos .... EL REY
judge .... JUEZ
July .... JULIO
jump .... SALTA, SALTO
June .... JUNIO
jungle .... SELVA
jury .... JURADO
kettle .... OLLA, CALDERA
kettledrum .... TIMPANO
key .... LLAVE
killer .... MATADOR

kind .... CLASE, AMABLE

king ...... REY, JUAN, ALFONSO, MILESIAN

kingdom .... LEON, ARAGON, CASTILE, NAVARRE

kiss .... BESO

kitchen .... COCINA

kite .... PAPALOTE

kitten .... GATITO

knapsack .... MOCHILA

knee .... RODILLA

knife .... CUCHILLO

knight .... CABALLERO

know .... SABER

lady .... DONA, SENORA, SENORITA

lagoon .... MAR MENOR

lake .... LAGO

lamb .... CORDERO

lame .... COJO

lamp .... LAMPARA

landlady .... DUENA, CASERA

landmark .... ALHAMBRA, ESCORIAL

language/tongue ...... LENGUA, CATALAN, CASTILIAN

lantern .... FAROLA

lapel .... SOLAPA

large .... GRANDE

lasso .... LAZAR, REATO, RIATA

last/latest .... ULTIMO

late .... TARDE

later .... LUEGO, MAS TARDE

laugh .... REI(R)

laughter .... RISA

lawyer .... ABOGADO

lazy .... PEREZOSO

lead .... GUIAR

leader .... JEFE

leaf .... HOJA

leather .... CUERO

left .... IZQUIERDA

leftover .... SOBRAS

leg .... PIERNA

legislature .... CORTES

Lent .... CUARESMA

less/least .... MENOS

lesson .... LECCION

letter .... CARTA, LETRA

lettuce .... LECHUGA

library .... BIBLIOTECA

lie .... MENTIRA

life .... VIDA

light ...... LUZ, CLARO, LIGERO, CLARIDAD

lighthouse .... FARO

lightning .... RELAMPAGO

lily .... LIRIO

linen .... CREA, HILO

lip .... LABIO

little/small ..... POCO, PEQUENO

long .... LARGO

love .... AMOR, CARINO

lover .... AMADOR

low .... BAJA, BAJO

luck .... SUERTE

luggage .... EQUIPAJE

lung .... PULMON

machine .... MAQUINA

mackerel .... SIERRA

mad/crazy .... LOCA, LOCO, FURIOSO

Madrid boulevard .... PRADO

magazine/review ...... REVISTA

magician .... MAGO

maid .... DONCELLA, MUCHACHA, SIRVIENTA

mailbox .... BUZON

mailman .... CARTERO

Main .... CARRIBEAN

man .... HOMBRE

manager .... GERENTE

mantle .... CAPA

many .... MUCHAS, MUCHOS

marble .... CANICA, MARMOL

March .... MARZO

market .... MERCADO

marriage .... MATRIMONIO

marriage ceremony ...... BODA

married .... CASADO

marry .... CASAR

match .... FOSFORO

matchless .... SIN PAR

mate .... PAREJA

matter .... CASO

Matthew .... MATEO

May .... MAYO

maybe .... QUIZAS

mayor .... ALCALDE

me/my .... MI

meadow .... PRADO

meal .... COMIDA

measure ..... PIE, VARA, LINEA, MILLA, CANTARA, PULGADA, KILOMETRO, CENTIMETRO

measurement .... MEDIDA

melody .... AIRE, COPIA

member .... SOCIO, MIEMBRO

merchant .... MERCADER

merchantship .... GALLEON

mercy .... GRACIA, PIEDAD

mermaid .... SIRENA

merry-go-round .... TIOVIVO

midnight .... MEDIANOCHE

mile .... MILLA

milk .... LECHE

mine .... MIO, MINA

mirror .... ESPEJO

mischief .... MAL, DANO

misfortune .... DESGRACIA

Mister/Mr. .... SENOR

model .... TIPO, PARANGON

mole .... TOPO

Monday .... LUNES

monetary unit .... PESETA

money .... PLATA, DINERO, MONEDA

monkey .... MONO

month .... MES

moon .... LUNA

Moorish .... MORO

Moorish capital ...... CORDOBA

more .... MAS

morning .... MANANA

Morocco .... MARRUECOS

Morocco seaport .... TETUAN

Moss .... MOHO, TILLANDSIA

most .... MUY

moth .... POLILLA

mother .... MAMA, MADRE, MAMACITA

mother-in-law .... SUEGRA

mountain .... MONTE, MONTANA, PERDIDO, ALMANZOR, MULHACEN, PENALARA, BALAITOUS, PENA VIEJA, MONTSERRAT

mountain pass .... ABRA

mountain range .... GUDAR, CUENCA, GREDOS, MORENA, ALCARAZ, DEMANDA, MONCAYO, PYRENESS, CANTABRIAN

mountains ...... GATA, TOLEDO, SIERRA NEVADA

mouse .... RATON

mouth .... BOCA

movies .... CINE

mower .... SEGADORA

much .... MUCHO

mud .... LODO

muffler .... BUFANDA

muralist .... SERT

museum .... MUSEO, PRADO

music .... MUSICA, MELODIA

musician .... MUSICO

mustard .... MOSTAZA

mute .... MUDO

mutineer .... REBELDE

muzzle .... BOZAL

my .... MI, MIO, MIS

myself .... YO MISMO

nail (finger) .... UNA

nail (metal) .... CLAVO

name .... NOMBRE

namesake .... TOCAYO

napkin .... SERVILLETA

narrow ..... ESCASO, ESTRECHO

naught .... CERO, NADA

naughty .... PICARA, PICARO

near/close .... CERCA, JUNTO

neat .... LIMPIO

necktie .... CORBATA

needle .... AGUJA
needy .... POBRE
neighbor .... VECINA, VECINO
neither .... NI
nephew .... SOBRINO
nest .... NIDO
never .... NUNCA
new .... NUEVA, NUEVO
newcomer .... NOVATO
news .... NOVEDAD
newspaper .... DIARIO,
    PERIODICO
next/nearest .... DESPUES,
    PROXIMA, PROXIMO
nice .... AGRADABLE,
    SIMPATICO
nickname .... MOTE, APODO
niece .... SOBRINA
night .... NOCHE
nightmare .... PESADILLA
nine .... NUEVE
ninth .... NOVENO
no admittance ..... NO ENTRAR
    longer .... YA NO
    one .... NADIE
    smoking .... PROHIBIDO
    FUMAR
nobleman .... DON, CONDE,
    DUQUE, GRANDEE, HIDALGO,
    CABALLERO
nobody .... NADIE
none/nothing .... NADA
noise .... RUIDO
noon .... MEDIODIA
north .... NORTE
nose .... NARIZ
notebook .... CUADERNO
novelist .... BAROJA, IBANEZ,
    CERVANTES
November .... NOVIEMBRE
now .... AHORA
number .... NUMERO
nun .... MONJA
nurse .... ENFERMERA
nymph .... NINFA, ZAGALA
oar .... REMO
object .... COSA
obscene .... VERDE, GROSERO
October .... OCTUBRE
octopus .... PULPO
odor/smell .... OLOR
of .... DE
oil .... GRASA, ACEITE, CRISMA,
    PETROLEO
old .... VIEJA, VIEJO
omelet .... TORTILLA
on .... EN, ENCIMA DE
once again .... UNA VEZ MAS
one .... UNA, UNO
onion .... CEBOLLA
only .... SOLA, SOLO, UNICA,

UNICO, SOLAMENTE
open .... ABIERTA, ABIERTO
or .... O
orange .... NARANJA
order .... MANDA(R)
other .... OTRA, OTRO
our .... NUESTRA(S),
    NUESTRO(S)
outside .... AFUERA
over there .... ALLA
owl .... BUHO
own .... PROPIA, PROPIO
ox .... BUEY
oyster .... OSTRA
pack .... FARDO, PAQUETE
    back .... MOCHILA
    of cards .... BARAJA
    saddle .... ALBARDA
package .... BULTO, FARDO,
    PAQUETE
page .... PAGINA
pail ..... CUBO, BALDE, CUBETA
painter ..... DALI, GOYA, MIRO,
    SERT, PINTOR, MURILLO,
    PICASSO, VELASQUEZ
pair .... PAR(EJA)
palace ...... PALACIO, ESCORIAL
palm .... PALMA, PALMERA
pant .... PALPITAR, RESUELLO
pants .... PANTALON(ES)
paper .... PAPEL
paprika .... PIMIENTO
parade .... FASTO, PARADA,
    DESFILE, REVISTA
paradise .... PARAISO
pardon me .... PERDON(E)
park .... PARQUE
parrot .... LORO
party .... FIESTA
pass .... PASA(R)
past .... PASADO
paste .... PEGA
path .... SENDA, VEREDA
pawn in game .... PEON
pay .... PAGA(R)
payer .... PAGADOR
peace .... PAZ, SOSIEGO
peach .... DURAZNO
peacock .... PAVOREAL
peak .... ANETO, ESTATS,
    MULHACEN, PICO DE TEIDE
peanut .... MANI, CACAHUETE
pear .... PERA
pearl .... PERLA
peas .... CHICHAROS,
    GUISANTES
pebble .... GUIJA
pedestal .... BASA
pen .... PLUMA
pen, ballpoint ...... BOLIGRAFO
penal colony .... PRESIDIO

penalty .... MULTA
pencil .... LAPIZ
peninsula .... IBERIA
people .... GENTE
pianist .... ITURBE
picture .... RETRATO
pie .... PASTEL
piece .... PEDAZO
pig .... PUERCO, COCHINO
piggy-bank .... ALCANCIA
pillow .... ALMOHADA
pin .... BROCHE
pin, straight .... ALFILER
pineapple .... PINA
pitch .... BREA, BITUN
place .... LUGAR
plague .... PESTE
plain .... LLANO
plantation .... ARBOLEDA,
    HACIENDA
play .... JUEGO, JUGAR
please .... POR FAVOR
pocket/purse .... BOLSA
poem .... ODA
poet .... BARDO
point .... PUNTO
poison .... VENENO
police .... RURALE, POLICIA,
    GENDARME
pool .... ALBERCA
poor .... POBRE
Pope .... PAPA
porridge .... ATOLE, GACHAS
port .... CADIZ, PALOS,
    MALAGA, PUERTO
post office .... CORREO
pot .... OLIA, OLLA
potato .... PATATA
prefix .... HISPANO
pretty .... LINDO, BONITA,
    BONITO
price .... VALOR, PRECIO
priest .... CURA, PADRE,
    SACERDOTE
prince .... PRINCIPE
princess .... INFANTA,
    PRINCESA
prize .... PREMIO
profile .... CORTE, SILUETA
promenade .... PASEO
prompt .... PRONTO
property .... BIENES
province .... JAEN, LEON,
    ALAVA, CADIZ, BURGOS,
    CUENCA, GERONA, HUELVA,
    MADRID, MALAGA, MURCIA,
    ORENSE, OVIEDO, TERUEL,
    TOLEDO, ZAMORA, BADAJOZ,
    CACERES, CORDOBA,
    GRANADA, SEVILLA, VIZCAYA,
    ALICANTE, BALEARES, LA

CORUNA, VALENCIA, ZARAGOZA, BARCELONA, LAS PALMAS, SALAMANCA, SANTANDER, PONTEVEDRA, VALLADOLID
pump .... BOMBA
pumpkin .... CALABAZA
pupil .... NINA, ALUMNA, ALUMNO
puppy .... PERRITO
pure .... CASTO, VIRGEN
purple ...... MORADA, MORADO, VIOLETA
purse .... CARTERA
puzzle .... ENIGMA, EMBARAZO
quantity .... CANTIDAD
quarrel .... PLEITO, DISPUTA
quarter .... CUARTO
queen .... ELENA, REINA
queer .... RARO
question .... PREGUNTA
quickly .... PRONTO, RAPIDO
quiet ...... CALLADA, CALLADO, TRANQUILA
quilt .... SOBRECAMA
rabbi .... RABINO, MAIMONIDES
rabbit .... CONEJO
Railroad .... FERROCARRIL
rain .... LLUVIA
rainbow .... ARCO IRIS
raisin .... PASA
read .... LEER
reader .... LECTOR
ready .... LISTA, LISTO
record .... DISCO
red .... ROJA, ROJO
Red Cross .... CRUZ ROJA
region .... ARAGON, CASTILE, ASTURIAS, LA MANCHA, VALENCIA, ANDALUSIA, CATALONIA, COSTA BRAVA, ESTREMADURA
relative .... PARIENTE
relief .... SOCORRO
rest .... DESCANSO
return .... VUELTA
rib .... COSTILLA
ribbon .... CINTA
rice .... ARROZ
rich .... RICA, RICO
right .... JUSTO, DERECHA, DERECHO
ring .... ANILLO, SORTIJA
riot .... MOTIN, ALBOROTO
river .... RIO, SIL, TER, EBRO, ESLA, MINO, TAJO, ULLA, CINCA, DOURO, DUERO, GENIL, JALON, JUCAR, NAVIA, SEGRE, TAGUS, TINTO, TURIA, ERESMA, JARAMA, ORBIGO, SEGURA, BARBATE, HENARES,

GUADIANA, ALMANZORA, LLOBREGAT, GUADALIMAR, GUADARRAMA, MANZANARES
river, longest/to the Mediterranean .... EBRO
road .... VIA, CAMINO
roast beef .... CARNE ASADA
robber .... LADRON
robe .... TOGA, MANTO
roof .... TECHO
room .... SALA, CUARTO
rooster .... GALLO
round ..... REDONDA, REDONDO
row .... FILA
rubber .... GOMA, HULE, CAUCHO
rug .... ALFOMBRA
ruler .... REGLA, FRANCO
ruling house .... BOURBON
sack .... SACO, COSTAL
sad .... TRISTE
safe and sound .... SANO Y SALVO
Sahara .... RIO DE ORO
sailing vessel .... CARVEL, GALLEON, CARAVEL(LE)
sale .... VENTA
saltwort .... BARILLA
sand .... ARENA
Saturday .... SABADO
school .... ESCUELA
scissors .... TIJERAS
sea .... MAR
seaport .... ADRA, VIGO, CADIZ, PALOS, BILBAO, MALAGA, ALMERIA, ALGECIRAS
seaport in Africa .... CEUTA
season/station .... ESTACION
second .... SEGUNDA, SEGUNDO
September .... SEPTIEMBRE
seven .... SIETE
several .... VARIAS, VARIOS
shadow .... SOMBRA
shawl .... MANTA, SERAPE, MANTILLA
she .... ELLA
she-bear .... OSA
sheep .... OVEJA, MERINO
sheepfold .... REDIL
sheepskin .... ZALEA
sheet .... HOJA, PLIEGO, SABANA
shell .... CONCHA
shepherd .... PASTORES
sherry .... JEREZ
ship .... BARCO, BUQUE
shirt .... CAMISA
shirtwaist .... BLUSA
shoe .... BOTIN, ZAPATO
shoot .... TIRA
shop .... TALLER, TIENDA

short .... CORTO
shoulder .... HOMBRO
shovel .... PALA
shower .... REGADERA
shrimp .... CAMARON
shrine .... URNA, TEMPLO
shy .... HURANO, TIMIDO
sick .... MALO, ENFERMO
sickle .... HOZ
side .... LADO
sidewalk .... ACERA
sign(al) .... SENA, SENAL
signature .... FIRMA
silk .... SEDA
silly .... BOBO, TONTO
silver .... PLATA
sing .... CANTA
sister .... HERMANA
sitting room .... (ANTE)SALA
six .... SEIS
size .... TAMANO
skate .... PATIN
skin .... PIEL, CASCARA
skipper .... PATRON, CAPITAN
skirt .... FALDA
sky .... CIELO
skyscraper .... RASCACIELOS
sled .... TRINEO
sleep .... SUENO
slowly .... DESPACIO
smoke .... FUMAR
snack .... MERIENDA
snake .... CULEBRA
snow .... NIEVE
soap .... JABON
soil .... TIERRA
soldier .... SOLDADO
some .... ALGUN
somebody .... ALGUIEN
something .... ALGO
sometimes .... ALGUNAS VECES
son .... HIJO
song .... CANTO, CANCION
sorrow .... DOLOR
soup .... SOPA, CALDO, GAZPACHO
sour .... ACIDO, AGRIO
south .... SUD, SUR
souvenir .... RECUERDO
spider .... ARANA
spoon .... CUCHARA
sport .... DEPORTE
spot/stain .... MANCHA
spring .... PRIMAVERA
square .... CUADRADO
stairs/staircase .... ESCALERA
stamp .... SELLO
star .... ESTRELLA
state .... ESTADO
statesman .... AZANA
steel .... ACERO

step .... ESCALON
stick .... PALO
stock farm .... RANCHO
stockings .... MEDIAS
stomach .... ESTOMAGO
stone .... PIEDRA
stopover .... PARADA
stopper .... TAPON
store .... TIENDA, ALMACEN
storeroom/warehouse
.... BODEGA
storm .... TORMENTA
story .... CUENTO
stove .... ESTUFA
strange .... RARO, EXTRANO
strawberry .... FRESA
street .... CALLE
streetcar .... TRANVIA
strong .... FUERTE
student .... ESTUDIANTE
subway .... METRO
suddenly .... DE REPENTE
sugar .... AZUCAR
suit .... TRAJE
suitcase .... MALETA
summer .... VERANO
sun .... SOL
Sunday .... DOMINGO
sweet .... DULCE
swing .... COLUMPIO
switch .... ENCHUFE
sword .... ESPADA, TOLEDO
table .... MESA
tablecloth .... MANTEL
tail .... COLA, RABO
tailor .... SASTRE
tall .... ALTO, GRANDE
tape recorder .... GRABADOR
taste .... GUSTO
tea .... TE
teakettle .... TETERA
teacher .... MAESTRA,
                            MAESTRO
team .... EQUIPO
tear .... LAGRIMA
ten .... DIEZ
tennis star .... ARILLA,
    GIMENO, GISBERT, SANCHEZ,
                            SANTANA
test .... EXAMEN
thank you/thanks ..... GRACIAS
that .... ESO
the .... EL, LA, LAS, LOS
their .... SU, SUS
them .... LAS, LOS
then .... ENTONCES
there .... ALLI
these .... ESTAS, ESTOS
they .... ELLAS, ELLOS
thick .... GRUESO
thimble .... DEDAL

thin .... FLACO
thing .... COSA
third .... TERCERO
thirst .... SED, ANSIA
this .... ESTA, ESTE
those .... ESAS
three .... TRES
throat .... GARGANTA
thunder .... TRUENO
Thursday .... JUEVES
ticket .... BILLETE
tiger .... TIGRE
time .... VEZ, HORA, TIEMPO
tin can .... LATA
tip .... PROPINA
tired .... CANSADO
title .... DON, DONA, CONDE,
    DUQUE, SENOR, SENORA,
                            TITULO
to add .... SUMAR
aid .... AYUDAR
answer/reply ..... RESPONDER
arrange/fix .... ARREGLAR
arrest .... ARRESTAR
arrive .... LLEGAR
ask .... PEDIR, PREGUNTAR
attend .... ASISTIR
be .... SER, ESTAR
be born .... NACER
begin .... EMPEZAR
believe .... CREER
borrow .... PRESTAR
burn .... QUEMAR
buy .... COMPRAR
call .... LLAMAR
carry .... CARGAR
clean .... LIMPIAR
climb .... SUBIR, TREPAR
come .... VENIR
come into .... ENTRAR
cook .... COCINAR
count/to tell .... CONTAR
cry .... LLORAR
cut .... CORTAR
dance .... BAILAR
deceive .... ENGANAR
do/to make .... HACER
drink .... BEBER, TOMAR
drive .... MANEJAR
feel .... SENTIR
finish .... TERMINAR
fly .... VOLAR
follow .... SEGUIR
forget .... OLVIDAR
go down .... BAJAR
go out .... SALIR
grow .... CRECER
have .... TENER
keep .... GUARDAR
kill .... MATAR
know .... CONOCER

leap .... SALTAR
look .... MIRAR
lose .... PERDER
love .... AMAR, QUERER
open .... ABRIR
pay .... PAGAR
play .... JUGAR
play a musical instrument
.... TOCAR
put .... PONER
raise .... LEVANTAR
rest .... DESCANSAR
run .... CORRER
save .... SALVAR
say .... DECIR
shout/to scream ...... GRITAR
see .... VER
sell .... VENDER
send .... ENVIAR
sing .... CANTAR
sit down .... SENTARSE
sleep .... DORMIR
smile .... SONREIR
stay .... QUEDARSE
take .... LLEVAR
take a bath .... BANARSE
talk/to speak .... HABLAR
think .... PENSAR
travel .... VIAJAR
try .... TRATAR DE
turn off .... APAGAR, CERRAR
understand .... ENTENDER
wait .... ESPERAR
wash .... LAVAR
work .... TRABAJAR
write .... ESCRIBIR
today .... HOY
toe .... DEDO
tomorrow .... MANANA
tooth .... DIENTE
top .... TROMPO
towel .... TOALLA
tower .... TORRE
toy .... JUGUETE
tree .... ARBOL
truck .... CAMION
true .... VERDAD
Tuesday .... MARTES
turkey .... PAVO
turtle .... TORTUGA
twice .... DOS VECES
two .... DOS
ugly .... FEO
umbrella .... PARAGUAS
uncle .... TIO
until .... HASTA
valley .... HOYA
versifier .... POETA
very .... MUY
vessel .... GALLEON
waiter .... MOZO

waitress .... MOZA
walking cane .... BASTON
wall .... MURO, PARED
wallet .... CARTERA
want .... QUIERO
war .... GUERRA
warm .... CALLENTE
watchman .... SERENO
watchtower .... MIRADOR
watchword .... LEMA
water .... AGUA
waterfall .... CASCADA,
CATARATA
watermelon .... SANDIA
wave .... OLA, ONDA
wax .... CERA
we .... NOSOTROS
weak .... DEBIL, FLOJO
weapon .... ARMA, BOLA
weather .... TIEMPO
web .... TELA
wedding .... BODA
Wednesday .... MIERCOLES
wee .... CHIQUITO
week .... SEMANA
weight .... PESA, PESO, CARGA,
MARCO, ARROBA, TONELADA,
KILO(GRAMO)
weighty .... GRAVE
welcome .... BIENVENIDA,
BIENVENIDO
well .... BIEN
West .... OESTE
wet .... HUMEDA, HUMEDO,
MOJADA, MOJADO
whale .... BALLENA
what .... QUE, COMO
is the matter? ..... QUE PASA
will be, will be .... QUE
SERA SERA
wheat .... TRIGO
wheel .... RUEDA
when .... CUANDO
where .... DONDE
which .... CUAL(ES)
whim .... CAPRICHO
whip .... LATIGO
whistle .... SILBA(TO)
white .... PURO, BLANCA,
BLANCO
who .... QUIEN
who knows .... QUIEN SABE
whole .... ENTERO
why .... POR QUE
wide .... ANCHA, ANCHO
widow(er) .... VIUDA, VIUDO
wife .... MUJER, ESPOSA
wig .... PELUCA
wild .... FEROZ, SALVAJE
win .... GANAR, VENCER
wind .... VIENTO

windy .... VENTOSO
window .... VENTANA
wine .... VINO, TINTO,
MALAGA, SHERRY
wine-making center ..... JEREZ
wing .... ALA
winner .... GANADOR
winter .... INVIERNO
wire .... ALAMBRE
wisdom .... SABIDURIA
wise .... SABIA, SABIO
wish .... DESEO, RUEGO
witch .... BRUJA
with .... CON
without .... SIN
witness .... TESTIGO
wolf .... LOBO
woman .... MUJER, HEMBRA,
SENORA
wonderful ..... DIVINA, DIVINO,
PEREGRINO
wood .... MADERA
woodland .... MONTE, SELVA
wool .... LANA
word .... PALABRA
work .... OBRA, TRABAJO
workman .... OBRERO
world .... MUNDO
worm .... GUSANO
worship .... CULTO
wrinkle .... ARRUGA
writer .... AUTOR, IBANEZ,
ALARCON, ESCRITOR
year .... ANO
yellow .... AMARILLO
yes .... SI
yesterday .... AYER
you .... TU, USTED, USTEDES
you're welcome ..... DE NADA,
POR NADA
young .... JOVEN
your .... SU, TU, SUS, TUS
youth .... JUVENTUD
youthful .... JOVEN, JUVENIL
zealot .... FANATICO
zero .... CERO
zest .... GUSTO
zoo .... ZOOLOGICO
spank .... CUFF, SLAP, SMACK,
PADDLE, WALLOP
spanker .... SAIL, DRIVER
spanking .... BRISK, QUICK,
RAPID, THRASHING
spanner .... WRENCH
spar .... ROD, BEAM, BOOM, GAFF,
MAST, POLE, YARD, ARGUE,
SPRIT, BARITE, BICKER,
RAFTER, DISPUTE, WRANGLE,
LONGERON, (SHADOW)BOX
branch of service .... USCG,
COAST GUARD

for stowing .... STEEVE
lower a .... REEF
part of .... SEMPER, PARATUS
spare .... BONY, LEAN, SAVE,
THIN, EXTRA, LANKY,
EXEMPT, FOREGO, MEAGER,
SCANT(Y), RESERVE
time .... LEISURE
tire: sl. .... POTBELLY
sparge .... SPLASH, SPRINKLE
sparing .... FRUGAL, MEAGER,
SCANTY, THRIFTY
spark ...... ARC, JOT, WOO, BEAU,
IOTA, COURT, FLASH, LOVER,
SWAIN, TRACE, KINDLE,
ACTIVATE, PARTICLE,
SCINTILLA
gives off .... IGNESCENT
plug of a sort .... CATALYST
stream .... ARC
sparked .... ARCED
sparkle .... GLOW, FLASH, GLEAM,
GLINT, GLISTEN, GLITTER,
TWINKLE, VIVACITY,
CORUSCATE, BRILLIANCE,
EFFERVESCE
sparkler .... EYE, DIAMOND,
FIREWORK, BRILLIANT
sparkling .... FIZZY, BUBBLY,
LIVELY, GLITTERING
water .... FIZZ, SODA WATER
Sparks .... NED
Sparky, baseballer .... LYLE
sparling .... SMELT, HERRING
spar(o)id .... GAR, TAI, SCUP,
PORGY, GILTHEAD,
(SEA)BREAM, SHEEPSHEAD
sparrow .... FINCH, CHIPPY,
RICEBIRD, PASSERINE,
WEAVERBIRD
hawk .... KESTREL
hedge .... DUNNOCK
house .... PASSER
sparry .... SPATHIC, FOLIATED,
SPATHOSE
sparrowgrass .... ASPARAGUS
sparse .... FEW, THIN, MEAGER,
SCANTY, SCARCE
opposite of .... DENSE,
CROWDED
Sparta .... LACEDAEMON
Spartan .... BRAVE, HARDY,
FRUGAL, HEROIC, SEVERE,
SIMPLE, STOIC(AL), WARLIKE
admiral .... LYSANDER
bondman .... HELOT
king .... LEONIDAS, AGESILAUS,
CLEOMENES, TYNDAREUS
lawgiver .... LYCURGUS
magistrate .... EPHOR
queen .... LEDA

677

serf/slave .... HELOT
spasm ...... FIT, TIC, KINK, SPELL,
    THROE, CHOREA, CONVULSION
    caused by calcium deficiency
    .... TETANY
    diaphragm .... HICCUP
    facial .... TIC
    muscle .... CRAMP, CRICK
    nervous system .... CHOREA,
         MYOCLONUS
    of distress .... PANG
    of pain .... SHOOT
    twitch .... TIC
spasmodic .... JERKY, FITFUL,
    SPORADIC, INTERMITTENT
spasms, series of .... CLONUS
Spassky, chess champ .... BORIS
spastic paralysis, cause of
    .... STROKE
spat .... ROW, SLAP, TIFF, GAITER,
    OYSTER, DISPUTE, QUARREL
spate .... FLOOD, STORM, DELUGE,
    FRESHET, DOWNPOUR,
    INUNDATION, OUTPOURING
spathe .... GLUME
    enclosure .... SPADIX
spathic .... SPARRY
spatial .... DIMENSIONAL
spatiate .... RAMBLE
spatter ...... SOIL, SPRAY, DEFAME,
    SPLASH, SCATTER, SPRINKLE
spatterdash .... LEGGING
spatterdock .... LILY
spatula .... SLICE, BLUNGER
    shaped like a ...... SPATULATE,
         SPOONLIKE
spavined .... LAME
spawn .... OVA, ROE, EGGS, SPAT,
    BEGET, BREED, SPORE
    obs. dial. .... RAUN
spay .... CASTRATE, STERILIZE
spayed hen .... FOULARD
S.P.C.A. concern .... STRAY
speak .... SAY, TALK, TELL,
    ORATE, UTTER, ADDRESS,
    DELIVER, CONVERSE,
    DISCOURSE
    angrily .... SNARL
    at length .... LECTURE,
         EXPATIATE
    evasively .... HEDGE, STALL
    from the bench .... RULE
    from memory .... RECITE
    imperfectly .... LISP,
         STAMMER, STUTTER
    in dramatic way ...... DECLAIM
    in silly way .... DROOL,
         SLOBBER
    inability to .... ALALIA
    incoherently .... GIBBER
    irreverently .... BLASPHEME

    lengthily .... PERORATE
    loudly .... EXCLAIM
    noisily .... RANT, RAVE,
         BLUSTER
    of .... MENTION
    off the cuff/without
        preparation .... AD LIB,
        IMPROVISE
    one's thoughts .... EXPRESS
    sharply .... SNAP, SNARL
    slowly .... DRAWL
    softly .... MURMUR, WHISPER
    unable to .... DUMB, MUTE
    under the breath ...... MUTTER
speakeasy .... BLINDPIG, BLIND
         TIGER
speaker .... SAYER, ORATOR,
    TALKER, UTTERER
    baseball's .... TRIS
    bete noire of .... HECKLER
    loud .... STENTOR
    place of/spot of .... DAIS,
        PODIUM, ROSTRUM
speaking in a blase manner
    .... SOUNDING BORED
    in a certain way .... ALISP
    many tongues .... POLYGLOT
    style .... DELIVERY, PARLANCE,
        PERSIFLAGE
spear .... DART, GAFF, PIKE, STAB,
    BLADE, LANCE, SHAFT,
    SHOOT, PIERCE, ASSAGAI,
    HARPOON, JAVELIN
    barbed .... GAFF
    body of a .... SHAFT
    fish .... GIG, GAFF, LEISTER
    Neptune's .... TRIDENT
    of grass .... BLADE
    point .... PIKE
    shaped .... HASTATE
    three-pronged .... LEISTER,
        TRIDENT
    thrower .... WOMERA
spearfish .... MARLIN
spearhead .... VAN, LEAD,
    VANGUARD
spearwort .... CROWFOOT
special .... UNIQUE, UNLIKE,
    CERTAIN, UNUSUAL, DISTINCT,
    PECULIAR, SPECIFIC,
    EXCLUSIVE, PARTICULAR
    ability .... TALENT
    knowledge .... LORE
    talent .... FORTE
specialist, aquatint .... ETCHER
    foot diseases .... PODIATRIST
    glasses .... OPTICIAN
    in crime .... SAFECRACKER
specialize .... LIMIT, CONFINE,
    SPECIFY, RESTRICT
    in a subject .... MAJOR IN

specialized .... TECHNICAL
specialty .... AREA, LINE, FIELD,
    FORTE, METIER
    fountain ..... SUNDAE, BANANA
        SPLIT
    of parrots and doctors
    .... HOUSE CALL
    of some sharks .... USURY
    shop .... FLORIST, JEWELER,
    CLOTHIER, MILLINER,
    BOOKSTORE, STATIONER,
    HABERDASHERY
specie .... COIN
    factory .... MINT
species .... KIND, SORT, CLASS,
    VARIETY, CATEGORY
    grouping(s) .... GENUS,
        GENERA
specific .... EXACT, PRECISE,
    SPECIAL, CONCRETE, DEFINITE,
    EXPLICIT
    gravity scale .... BAUME
specify ...... NAME, ORDER, STATE,
    DEFINE, DETAIL, IDENTIFY,
    STIPULATE
specimen .... MODEL, SAMPLE,
    TASTE(R), EXAMPLE
    of body fluids .... BLOOD
    of waste products ...... STOOL,
        URINE
specious .... GILDED, SEEMING,
    APPARENT, PLAUSIBLE
    reasoning .... IDOLISM,
    SOPHISM, SYLLOGISM
speck .... BIT, JOT, IOTA, MARK,
    MITE, MOTE, SPOT, FLECK,
    STAIN, BLEMISH, PARTICLE
speckle .... DOT, SPOT, FLECK,
    DAPPLE, MOTTLE, MACULATE
specs .... EYEGLASSES
spectacle .... SHOW, VIEW, SCENE,
    SIGHT, PARADE, DISPLAY,
    PAGEANT, EXHIBITION
spectacles .... SPECS, LENSES,
    GOGGLES, EYEGLASSES,
    SUNGLASSES
    opera .... LORGNON,
        LORGNETTE
    part .... ARM, RIM, LENS
spectacular .... AMAZING,
    GLARING, STRIKING, BREATH-
    TAKING
    musical show
    .... EXTRAVAGANZA
    parade .... PAGEANT
spectator ...... VIEWER, WATCHER,
    BEHOLDER, LOOKER(-ON),
    OBSERVER, ONLOOKER
    devoted .... FAN, BUFF,
    AFICIONADO
    frequent .... HABITUE

mere .... BYSTANDER
seatless .... STANDEE
specter .... AURA, BOGEY, GHOST,
SPOOK, SHADOW, SPIRIT,
VISION, WRAITH, FANTASM,
PHANTOM, PHANTASM(A),
APPARITION
spectral .... EERY, SPOOKY,
GHOSTLY, PHANTOM,
WRAITHY
spectrum .... RAINBOW
colors, one of the .... RED,
BLUE, GREEN, INDIGO,
ORANGE, VIOLET, YELLOW
speculate .... GUESS, THINK,
GAMBLE, PONDER, REFLECT,
THEORIZE, CONSIDER,
MEDITATE, CONJECTURE
speculation, reckless .... FLIER,
FLYER
speculative .... IFFY, RISKY,
CHANCY, THEORETICAL
art .... THEORETICS
business scheme ..... WILDCAT
idea .... THEORY
speculator .... GAMBLER,
GUESSER, PLUNGER, THEORIST,
THINKER
inexperienced .... LAMB
kind of .... SCALPER,
ADVENTURER
welshing .... LAME DUCK
speculum .... DEVICE, MIRROR
shape of .... FUNNEL,
SHOEHORN
type of .... METAL, PLASTIC
speech .... LIP, LINE, TALK,
SERMON, TONGUE, BLARNEY,
DIALECT, OENOMEL, ORATION,
WHISPER, EPILOGUE,
PARLANCE, DISCOURSE,
SOLILOQUY, UTTERANCE,
EXPRESSION, DECLAMATION
abusive .... TIRADE, DIATRIBE
art .... ORATORY, RHETORIC
at beginning of special
occasion ..... INVOCATION
brevity of .... LACONISM
combining form .... LOG(O)
defect .... LISP, STAMMER,
STUTTER
delirious .... RAVING
disorder .... ALALIA, ALEXIA,
APHASIA, DYSPHASIA,
DYSPHONIA, DYSARTHRIA,
IMPEDIMENT
disorder: comb. form .... DYS,
LALIA
disorder treatment
.... THERAPY, PATHOLOGY
ecstatic .... RHAPSODY

emphatic .... BIRR
exalted to trivial .... BATHOS
farewell .... VALEDICTORY
figure of .... TROPE, SIMILE,
LITOTES, METAPHOR
formal ...... ADDRESS, ORATION
graduation .... VALEDICTORY
human .... LANGUAGE
incoherent .... JARGON,
GIBBERISH
ill-tempered .... VINEGAR
last words .... TAG
loss of .... MUTISM, APHASIA,
APHONIA
loud, wild .... RANT
manner of .... SLUR, DRAWL
Marc Antony's .... ELOGE
narrative part ...... CATASTASIS
noisy, blustering .... TIRADE,
HARANGUE
of praise .... PANEGYRIC
opening part .... EXORDIUM
organ .... LARYNX, TONGUE,
VOICE BOX, VOCAL CORDS
ornamental ending .... TAG
part of .... (AD)VERB,
(PRO)NOUN, ADJECTIVE
pattern of words
.... PHRASEOLOGY
plain in .... OUTSPOKEN,
POINT-BLANK
pompous .... BOMBAST
regional style .... BURR,
TWANG, ACCENT, BROGUE
slang .... JIVE, SPIEL
sound .... LENIS, FORTIS,
SONANT, CADENCE,
ALLOPHONE, PHONE(ME)
sounds, ability to produce
.... ARTICULATION
sounds, system of
.... PHONETICS, PHONOLOGY
style of .... EUPHUISM,
LOCUTION
surplusage .... PADDING
tiresome .... SCREED
voiceless sound .... SURD
wild .... RANT
speechify .... ORATE
speechless .... DUMB, MUTE,
SURD, SILENT, APHASIC,
APHONIC, VOICELESS,
TONGUE-TIED
speed .... FLY, HIE, REV, ZIP,
RACE, RATE, RUSH, TEAR,
HASTE(N), VELOCITY
drug .... METHEDRINE,
AMPHETAMINE
full .... AMAIN
measuring device
.... TACHOMETER,

SPEEDOMETER
of sound .... MACH, SONIC
setter .... PACER
unit, proposed .... VELO
up .... HURRY, HASTEN,
ACCELERATE
writing .... SHORTHAND
speed(st)er .... RACER
speedily .... AMAIN, APACE, BY
EXPRESS, POSTHASTE
speedway .... TRACK, RACECOURSE
speedwell .... PLANT, VERONICA
speedy ...... FAST, AMAIN, APACE,
QUICK, RAPID, SWIFT,
PROMPT, EXPRESS
spelean .... CAVE-LIKE
speleology, subject of .... CAVES
spell .... FIT, HEX, MEAN, TIME,
TERM, TURN, CHARM, MAGIC,
PERIOD, STREAK, TRANCE,
SIGNIFY, SORCERY
of activity .... SPURT, SPRINT
out .... READ, INTERPRET
spellbind .... HOLD, CHARM,
ENCHANT, ENTRANCE,
FASCINATE
spellbinder .... ORATOR
Spellbound Concert composer
.... ROZSA
director .... HITCHCOCK
star .... PECK, BERGMAN
spelldown .... BEE
spelling _____ .... BEE
incorrect .... CACOGRAPHY
spelt .... WHEAT
spelter .... ZINC, INGOTS
spelunker's interest .... CAVE
spence .... LARDER, PANTRY
spencer .... JACKET, TRYSAIL
spend .... USE, LOSE, PASS,
EXPEND, PAY OUT, CONSUME,
EXHAUST, WEAR OUT,
DISBURSE
lavishly .... DISPEND, SLATHER,
SQUANDER
more than one has
.... OVERDRAW
the night .... SHACK UP
the summer .... ESTIVATE
time for a special purpose
.... DEVOTE, DEDICATE
uselessly .... WASTE
spendthrift .... WASTER,
ROUNDER, SPENDER,
WASTREL, PRODIGAL,
WASTEFUL, SQUANDERER,
SCATTERGOOD
Spengler, philosopher
.... OSWALD
Spenser, poet .... EDMUND
spent .... WORN, ALL IN, TIRED,

WEARY, FAGGED, DRAINED,
USED UP, CONSUMED, BURNED
OUT, EXHAUSTED
and sterile .... EFFETE,
IMPOTENT
sperm .... GERM, SEED, SEMEN,
WHALE, SPERMATOZOON
fish .... MILT
flower .... POLLEN
whale .... CACHALOT
spermary .... GONAD, TESTIS
spermatozoid .... GAMETE
spermophile .... GOPHER, SUSLIK,
CHIPMUNK
spew ...... EMIT, GUSH, SPIT, SPUE,
EJECT, EXPEL, RETCH, VOMIT,
THROW UP
Speyer .... SPIRES
sphacelate .... MORTIFY
sphagnous .... PEATY
sphagnum .... (PEAT)MOSS
sphene .... TITANITE
sphere .... ORB, SKY, BALL, STAR,
FIELD, GLOBE, ORBIT, RANGE,
REALM, DOMAIN, PLANET,
RONDURE, PROVINCE
celestial .... ORB
of action .... ARENA
spherical .... CUBIC, OVOID,
ROUND, GLOBATE, GLOBOID,
GLOBOSE, GLOBOUS,
GLOBULAR
spheroid, example of a .... BALL,
EARTH
spherule .... GLOBULE
sphery .... STARLIKE, CELESTIAL
sphincter .... CONSTRICTOR
sphinx .... MONSTER,
(HAWK)MOTH
body of .... LION
head of ...... MAN, RAM, HAWK
query of .... RIDDLE
site of .... GIZA, GIZEH,
THEBES
sphinxlike .... PUZZLING,
ENIGMATIC
sphragistics' subject .... SEALS
sphygmus .... PULSE
spica .... STAR, SPIKE
spice .... MACE, MINT, AROMA,
CHILE, CLOVE, CURRY,
CHIL(L)I, FLAVOR, GINGER,
NUTMEG, PEPPER, SEASON,
STACTE, CANELLA,
CINNAMON, TURMERIC,
SASSAFRAS
anise-like flavor .... BASIL,
FENNEL, TARRAGON
"bean herb" .... SAVORY
berries .... ALLSPICE
bud .... CAPER, CLOVE,

SAFFRON
heat with/flavor with .... MULL
kingly .... BASIL
leaf .... BAY, MINT, SAGE,
BASIL, THYME, BORAGE,
BURNET, CHIVES, SAVORY,
CHERVIL, OREGANO, PARSLEY,
ANGELICA, MARJORAM,
ROSEMARY, TARRAGON
legendary .... ROSEMARY
lemony flavor ...... CORIANDER
licorice flavor .... ANISE
mint family .... SPEARMINT,
PEPPERMINT
of life .... VARIETY
onion family .... CHIVES
parsley family .... CHERVIL
powder .... CHILI, CURRY,
PAPRIKA
root .... GINGER, TURMERIC,
SASSAFRAS
seed .... DILL, MACE, ANISE,
CUMIN, POPPY, CELERY,
FENNEL, SESAME, CARAWAY,
MUSTARD, CARDAMOM,
CORIANDER
slightly bitter flavor ...... DILL,
CUMIN, CELERY, TURMERIC
sticks .... CINNAMON
sweet marjoram's cousin
.... OREGANO
up .... LIVEN
used as a tonic .... CANELLA
used in incense preparation
.... STACTE
whole pods .... CHILI,
CARDAMOM
whole nail-shaped buds
.... CLOVES
"wild marjoram"
.... OREGANO
wisdom .... SAGE
Spice Island(s) .... TERNATE,
MOLUCCAS
spiceberry .... WINTERGREEN
spiced .... SEASONED
ale .... WASSAIL
dish .... OLLA, SALMI, TAMALE,
CHILI(BEANS), CHILI CON
CARNE
meat .... SAUSAGE, BRATWURST
sausage .... SALAMI, KIELBASA,
PEPPERONI
spick and span ...... NEAT, TRIM,
CLEAN, FRESH
spiculate .... NEEDLELIKE
spicule .... SPIKE, ACTINE,
SCLERITE
spicy .... RACY, JUICY, SALTY,
RISQUE, GINGERY, PIQUANT,
PUNGENT, AROMATIC,

FRAGRANT
joke, describing a .... OFF-
COLOR
sensation .... HEAT
taste .... TANG
spider .... MITE, TRIVET, SKILLET,
ARACHNID, ARTHROPOD,
(FRYING)PAN
class .... ARACHNIDA
crab .... MAIA, MAJA,
THORNBACK
dangerous type of
.... RECLUSE, FUNNEL WEB,
BLACK WIDOW
fear of .... ARACHNOPHOBIA
girl turned into .... ARACHNE
habitat .... SHEDS, HOUSES,
CREVICES, WOODPILES
job of ..... WEAVING, SPINNING
largest .... TARANTULA
like .... ARACHNOID
monkey .... QUATA, ATELES
nest of .... NIDUS
poison .... VENOM
poison antidote ..... ANTIVENIN
poison injectors of ...... FANGS
poisonous .... TARANTULA,
FUNNEL WEB, BLACK WIDOW,
BROWN RECLUSE
trap of .... WEB
spiegel .... MIRROR, PIG IRON
spiel .... LINE, SPEECH,
(SALES)TALK, SALES PITCH
spiffy .... CHIC, NEAT, NIFTY,
SMART, CLASSY, SPRUCE
spigot ...... PEG, TAP, PLUG, SPILE,
VALVE, FAUCET
spike .... GAD, BROB, FOIL, GOAD,
NAIL, PROD, RIVET, SPINE,
ANTLER, IMPALE, PIERCE,
SKEWER, THWART, MACKEREL
broken grain .... CHOB
cereal .... EAR
fork's .... TINE, PRONG
heels .... STILETTO
lavender .... MINT
like .... SPINATE
mountain climber's ...... PITON
of flowers ...... AMENT, SPADIX
of plantain .... CHAT
shield's .... UMBO
slang .... LACE WITH
soles' .... CLEAT
spikelet .... SPINULE
spikenard .... GINSENG, OINTMENT
spile .... TAP, PLUG, SPOUT,
STAKE, SPIGOT
spill .... PEG, PIN, ROD, FALL,
PLUG, SLOP, SPILE, TUMBLE,
OVERFLOW, OVERTURN,
SPLINTER

the beans: sl. .... SING, TELL, SQUEAL, CONFESS, DIVULGE, DISCLOSE
Spillane's hero .... HAMMER
spin ...... BIRL, EDDY, REEL, RIDE, TURN, SWIRL, TWIRL, WEAVE, WHIRL, GYRATE, ROTATE, DRAW OUT, REVOLVE
a _____ .... WEB, DISK, TALE, YARN, BATON, TOY, WHEEL
spina bifida, type of .... OCCULTA, MYELOCELE, MENINGOCELE
spinaceous plant .... SPINACH
spinach .... GREENS, ORACH(E), TALINUM, GOOSEFOOT
like .... SANDY
spinal .... RACHIDIAN
anesthesia method .... EPIDURAL
column ...... SPINE, R(H)ACHIS, BACKBONE
column, having .... VERTEBRATE
cord .... MYELON
cord cut .... PITH
cord inflammation .... MYELITIS, RACHITIS
cord membrane .... EPENDYMA
cord sheath .... MATER, MYELIN(E)
cord tumor .... GLIOMA
curvature ..... KYPHOSCOLIOSIS
injury result .... PARALYSIS
marrow .... NUCHA
nerves, group of ..... LUMBAR, SACRAL, CERVICAL, THORACIC
nerves network .... PLEXUS
surgical procedure ..... FUSION
tap .... LUMBAR PUNCTURE
spindle .... PIN, ROD, AXIS, AXLE, BUFF, STEM, ARBOR, SHAFT, SPIKE, STALK, STICK, DISTAFF, MANDREL, TRIBLET, HYDROMETER
flywheel .... WHARVE
shaped like .... FUSIFORM
weaver's .... QUILL
spindling .... BONY, LEAN, GAUNT, LANKY, GANGLY, GANGLING
spindrift .... FOAM, SCUD, FROTH, SPUME, (SEA)SPRAY
spine .... RAY, CHINE, QUILL, SPIKE, THORN, CHAETA, NEEDLE, RACHIS, PRICKLE, BACKBONE
curvature, backward .... KYPHOSIS
inward .... LORDOSIS
to one side .... SCOLIOSIS

cylindrical bones of the .... VERTEBRAE
inflammation .... RACHITIS
section ...... COCCYX, LUMBAR, SACRUM, CERVICAL, THORACIC
spinel .... BALAS, STONE, SAPPHIRINE
gem .... RUBY
spineless .... LIMP, WEAK, BONELESS, INVERTEBRATE
slang .... CHICKEN, GUTLESS
spines, covered with .... HISPID
spinet .... ORGAN, PIANO, VIRGINAL, HARPSICHORD
spinnaker .... SAIL
spinner .... TOP, LURE, SPIDER, WEAVER, SILKWORM
of life's thread .... CLOTHO
spinney .... GROVE, THICKET
spinning apparatus .... BOBBIN, COILER
machine .... MULE, WHEEL, JENNY, THROTTLE
mule inventor .... CROMPTON
platform .... TURNTABLE
toy .... TOP, FRISBEE
wheel .... CHARK(H)A
wheel part .... DISTAFF, TREADLE
spinster .... FILLE, MAIDEN, SINGLE, VIRGIN, SPINNER, (OLD)MAID, FEMME SOLE
spiny .... HISPID, THORNY, PRICKLY, SPINOSE, ACICULAR, ACANTHOID
spiracle .... AIR HOLE, OPENING, BLOWHOLE
spiraea .... HARDHACK, MEADOWSWEET
spiral .... HELIX, HELICAL, WINDING
combining form .... HELICO
curl .... RINGLET
downward .... TAILSPIN
like a .... SPIROID
motion .... GYRE
of wire .... COIL
scroll .... VOLUTE
shaped .... HELICOID, TURBINATE
shaped device ..... CORKSCREW
shell whorl .... VOLUTE
spiraled .... VOLUTE, SCROLLED
spiraling .... SKYROCKETING
spirant .... FRICATIVE
spire .... APEX, PEAK, CROWN, SHAFT, STALK, FLECHE, SPROUT, STEEPLE
mountain .... ARETE, PINNACLE
ornament .... FINIAL

shaped like a needle .... AIGUILLE
topper .... EPI
tower .... PAGODA, MINARET
spirit .... PEP, VIM, DASH, ELAN, GALL, LIFE, MIND, MOOD, SOUL, WILL, ARDOR, BOGEY, BOGIE, DEMON, GHOST, HEART, SPUNK, VERVE, VIGOR, ENERGY, METTLE, MORALE, COURAGE, ESSENCE, PIZ(Z)AZZ, VITALITY, VIVACITY
cane .... RUM
chief evil .... SATAN
good .... DEVA, ANGEL
guiding .... ANGEL
heralding death ...... BANSHEE, BANSHIE
in a jar .... GENIE
living in fire ..... SALAMANDER
mischievous .... GOBLIN, ERLKING, GREMLIN
of chivalry .... ERRANTRY
of evil .... AHRIMAN
of good .... ORMAZD
of the sea .... DAVY JONES
presiding .... NUMEN
the .... GOD, HOLY GHOST
spirited .... BOLD, RACY, BRISK, FIERY, PERKY, ARDENT, BLITHE, LIVELY, SPUNKY, ANIMATED, VIGOROUS, ENERGETIC
self-assurance .... ELAN
spiritless ...... COLD, DEAD, DULL, LIFELESS, LISTLESS, DEPRESSED, LACKADAISICAL
spirits .... MOOD, HUMOR, LIQUOR, TEMPER, ALCOHOL, ETHANOL, LIQUEURS, DISPOSITION
alcoholic strength of .... PROOF
believer .... ANIMIST
night-walking .... LEMURES
of hartshorn .... AMMONIA
of the dead .... MANES
of wine .... ALCOHOL
out of .... SAD
spiritual .... PIOUS, SACRED, FOLK SONG, SUPERNATURAL
being .... ENS, ANGEL
charge .... CURE
guide .... FATHER, PRIEST, CONFESSOR
knowledge .... GNOSIS
mother .... AMMA
opposite of .... CORPOREAL
sitting .... SEANCE
spiritualism .... OCCULTISM
third party in .... MEDIUM

681

well-known champion of
.... DOYLE
spiritualist's equipment
.... OUIJA
spirituous drink .... WINE
spiritus frumenti .... WHISKY
spirochete .... TREPONEMA
disease .... YAWS
spirogyra .... ALGA
spirt .... GUSH, SPURT
spirula .... MOLLUSK
kin of .... SQUID, CUTTLEFISH
spiry .... COILED, CURLED
spit .... EMIT, HISS, RAIN, SNOW,
STAB, SHOAL, BROACH,
IMPALE, PIERCE, SALIVA,
SKEWER, DRIZZLE, SANDBANK,
EXPECTORATE
spital .... HOSTEL, SHELTER,
HOSPITAL
spitball .... WAD, CURVE, SINKER,
SLIDER
spitchcock .... EEL
spite .... VENOM, GRUDGE,
HATRED, MALICE, RANCOR,
SPLEEN, ILL WILL
spiteful ...... MEAN, CATTY, SNIDE,
HOSTILE, VENOMOUS,
VIPERINE, VIPEROUS,
MALICIOUS, SPLENETIC,
VINDICTIVE
woman .... CAT
spitefulness ...... ANGER, CHOLER,
SPLEEN, CATTINESS
spitfire .... HELLCAT, HOTHEAD
Mexican .... (LUPE)VELEZ
spitter .... DEER, BROCK, PITCHER,
SPITBALL
spitting image .... LIKENESS,
DEAD RINGER
spittle .... SALIVA
insect .... FROGHOPPER
spittoon .... CUSPIDOR
spitz dog .... POMERANIAN
spiv .... IDLER
splanchnic .... VISCERAL
splash .... LAP, DASH, DAUB,
PLOP, SLOP, SPILL, SWASH,
SPARGE, SPATTER, SPLOTCH,
SPLATTER, SPRINKLE
the fingers .... DABBLE
splashboard .... MUDGUARD
splashdown .... REENTRY
splashy .... SHOWY
splat .... LATH, SLAT
splatter .... DAB, SPLASH,
SPATTER, SPRINKLE
splay ...... AWRY, BEVEL, CLUMSY,
EXPAND, EXTEND, AWKWARD,
OBLIQUE, DISLOCATE,
SPREAD(ING)

spleen .... MILT, WHIM, ENNUI,
SPITE, MALICE, BOREDOM,
CAPRICE, MELANCHOLY
production .... ANTIBODIES,
PHAGOCYTES, LYMPHOCYTES
site .... ABDOMEN
surgery .... LIENECTOMY,
SPLENECTOMY
splendid .... FINE, GRAND,
SUPERB, RADIANT, GLORIOUS,
GORGEOUS, LUSTROUS,
EXCELLENT, GRANDIOSE,
MAGNIFICENT
slang .... RIPPING
splendor .... POMP, ECLAT,
GLORY, LUSTER, GLITTER,
RADIANCE, GRANDEUR,
BRILLIANCE
splenetic .... PEEVISH, SPITEFUL,
IRRITABLE
splice .... WED, JOIN(T), MARRY,
UNITE
splint .... CAST, LATH, SLAT,
BRACE, SUPPORT
use of .... FIRST AID
splinter ...... CHIP, SHARD, SHIVE,
SPILL, SPLIT, SHIVER, SLIVER,
FLINDER, FRAGMENT
splinters .... MATCHWOOD
split ...... CHAP, REND, RIFT, RIVE,
BREAK, BURST, CLEFT,
BREACH, CLEAVE, DIVIDE,
SCHISM, SLIVER, SPALATO,
DISUNITE, SEPARATE(D)
a marriage legally
.... DIVORCE
asunder .... REND
capable of being .... FISSILE
colloquial .... SHARE
hairs .... QUIBBLE, STRAIN AT
A GNAT
into thirds .... TRISECT
open .... BREAK, DEHISCE
personality, of .... MULTIPLE
pulse .... DAL
rattan .... CANE
slang .... LEAVE, PEACH,
DEPART, SQUEAL
the difference .... COMPROMISE
with violence .... REND
splitsville .... RENO
splitting .... ACHING, SEVERE
apart .... FISSION
splotch .... BLOB, BLOT, SPOT,
STAIN, SPLASH
splurge .... SPLASH, SHOW OFF,
OSTENTATION
spode .... CHINAWARE, PORCELAIN
Spohr, composer .... LOUIS
opera by .... JESSONDA
spoil .... MAR, ROB, ROT, LOOT,

MESS, RUIN, SACK, DECAY, GO
BAD, HUMOR, SEIZE, TAINT,
DAMAGE, IMPAIR, FERMENT,
LOUSE UP, PILLAGE, PLUNDER,
VITIATE, (OVER)INDULGE
liable to .... PERISHABLE
spoiled .... WASTED, PAMPERED
_____ .... ROTTEN
child .... BRAT
spoiler .... BANE
spoils .... LOOT, BOOTY, PRIZE,
TROPHY
spoilsport .... KILLJOY, MARPLOT,
SOURPUSS, WET BLANKET
spoke .... BAR, PIN, RUNG,
RUNDEL
spoken .... ORAL, VOCAL, VERBAL,
UTTERED
clearly .... ARTICULATED
merely .... LIP
spokes .... RADII
spokeshave .... PLANE
spokesman/spokesperson
.... AGENT, PROXY, VOICE,
MOUTHPIECE
spoliate .... ROB, DESPOIL,
PLUNDER
sponge .... BUM, MOP, SOP, BLOT,
SOAK, SWAB, ASCON, CADGE,
LEECH, MOOCH, ABSORB,
BLOTTER, PUDDING, PARASITE,
TRENCHER, PORIFERAN
cake .... JELLYROLL
gourd .... LOOF(A), LOOFAH
opening .... OSCULUM
pertaining to .... PORIFEROUS
slang .... MOOCHER, DEAD
BEAT, FREELOADER
spicule .... OXEA, TOXA,
ACTINE
substitute .... LUFFA, LOOFAH
throw in the .... YIELD, GIVE
UP, SUBMIT, CONCEDE,
SURRENDER
sponger .... DRUNK, LEECH,
CADGER, MOOCHER, HANGER-
ON, PARASITE
spongy .... POROUS, ELASTIC,
ABSORBENT
sponsor .... ANGEL, BACKER,
PATRON, SURETY, GODFATHER
beneficiary of .... PROTEGE
slang .... ANGEL
sponsorship .... (A)EGIS, AUSPICES
spontaneous .... AUTOMATIC,
IMPULSIVE
spontoon .... PIKE, HALBERD
spoof .... FOOL, JOKE, HOAX,
TRICK, BANTER, PARODY,
SATIRE, DECEIVE, LAMPOON,
HOODWINK, BAMBOOZLE

spook .... GHOST, SPECTER, FRIGHTEN

spooky .... EERIE, WEIRD, GHOSTLY, HAUNTED, SPECTRAL

spool .... COP, PIRN, REEL, BOBBIN, SPINDLE

out .... UNREEL

weaver's shuttle .... PIRN

spoon .... DIP, PET, LIFT, KISS, NECK, SCOOP, CARESS, CUTLERY

large .... LADLE

like implement .... OAR, SPADE, PADDLE, SPATULA

out .... DOLE, METE

shaped .... CONCAVE, SPATULATE

spoonbill .... AIAIA, AJAJA, PADDLEFISH

spoonfed .... CODDLED, PAMPERED

spooning .... SMOOCHING

spoony .... SILLY, AMOROUS, FOOLISH, MAWKISH, KISSABLE, LOVESICK, SENTIMENTAL

spoor .... TRACK, TRAIL

Sporades island .... SAMOS

sporadic .... RARE, FITFUL, SCARCE, ERRATIC, IRREGULAR, DESULTORY, OCCASIONAL

sporangium .... SPORE CASE

spore .... GERM, SEED, ZYGOTE

capsule .... URN

case .... ASCI, SORI, ASCUS, THECA, SPORANGIUM

cluster(s) .... SORUS, SORI

producer .... FERN, MOSS

sac .... ASCUS, THECA

small .... SPORULE

sporran .... PURSE, POUCH

sport .... FUN, GAME, JEST, FREAK, FROLIC, MUTANT, TRIFLE, DISPLAY, JESTING, PASTIME, ATHLETICS, DIVERSION, MERRIMENT, RECREATION

for short .... REC

group .... TEAM, COUPLE, TWOSOME

slang .... JOCK, SPENDER

sporting .... FAIR, GAMING, ATHLETIC, GAMBLING

chance .... BEST BET

events, certain .... ROUND-ROBIN

house .... HALL, ALLEY, CASINO

sportive .... FRISKY, FESTIVE, PLAYFUL, TRICKSY, WAGGISH

sports attendance .... GATE

devotee/fan .... ROOTER

"English" .... SPIN

event .... BOUT, HUNT, RACE, MEET, MATCH, CONTEST

meet .... GYMKHANA, OLYMPICS

nickname: Crazy Legs .... ELROY HIRSCH

Galloping Ghost .... RED GRANGE

Magic ...... EARVIN JOHNSON

Nasty .... ELIE NASTASE

Say Hey Kid .... WILLIE MAYS

Super Mex ..... LEE TREVINO

The Golden Bear .... JACK NICKLAUS

The Great White Shark .... GREG NORMAN

The King .... ARNOLD PALMER

The Stilt .... WILT CHAMBERLAIN

Yankee Clipper .... JOE DIMAGGIO

of kings .... HORSE RACING

of skill .... CHESS

official .... JUDGE, TIMER, UMP(IRE), REFEREE, COMMISSIONER

permit for a series of games .... SEASON TICKET

shirt .... TEE, JERSEY

shoe .... LOAFER, SNEAKER

site .... GYM, GRID, OVAL, POOL, RING, RINK, ARENA, COURT, FIELD, GREEN, LINKS, TRACK, COURSE, DIAMOND, STADIUM, COLISEUM, HIPPODROME

team .... CREW, FIVE, NINE, SQUAD, ELEVEN, STRING, FOURSOME

team, in charge of ..... COACH, MANAGER, TRAINER

type of/game .... POLO, CATCH, CHESS, RUGBY, TRACK, BOXING, DISCUS, SOCCER, TENNIS, BOWLING, HUNTING, BASEBALL, FOOTBALL, PING-PONG, SOFTBALL, (ICE)HOCKEY, BASKETBALL, VOLLEYBALL

sportscast .... ANNOUNCE, BROADCAST, GO ON THE AIR

sportscaster .... HILL, GOWDY, HEARN, GUMBEL, HODGES, MADDEN, SCULLY, COSSELL, GIFFORD, DIERDORF, BRADSHAW, MICHAELS, MUSBURGER

sportsmanship .... FAIRNESS

sporty .... SHOWY, CASUAL,

DRESSY, FLASHY, SNAZZY

spot .... BIT, SEE, DAUB, FLAW, MARK, SITE, FLECK, PLACE, SMEAR, STAIN, BLOTCH, DAPPLE, SMUT(CH), BLEMISH, SPECKLE, (FLY)SPECK, MACULA(TE)

colloquial .... JAM, PINCH, TROUBLE

domino .... PIP

hot .... OVEN

in diamond .... CARBON

in mineral .... MACLE

in the ocean .... ISLET

of color .... BLOB

on animal's face .... BLAZE

on lunar halo ..... PARASELENE

on solar halo .... PARHELION

playing card .... PIP

skin .... MOLE, SCAR, MACULA, STIGMA, BIRTHMARK

small .... DOT, FLECK, PRICK, (PIN)POINT

sun .... FRECKLE

spotless .... PURE, CLEAN, CHASTE, HONEST, INNOCENT, IMMACULATE, SPIC AND SPAN

reputation, of .... ABOVEBOARD

spotlight .... FOCUS, BEACON, EMPHASIZE, LIMELIGHT

spotted .... EYED, PIED, DAPPLE(D), MOTTLED, PIEBALD, MACULATE

animal .... CAVY, PACA, HYENA, CHITAL, DAPPLE, OCELOT, CHEETAH, (LEO)PARD

dog .... DALMATIAN

fever .... TICK, TYPHUS

with drops .... GUTTATE

spotter ...... LOOKOUT, DETECTIVE

spotty .... DOTTED, PATCHY, UNEVEN, IRREGULAR

spousal .... NUPTIAL

spouse .... MATE, WIFE, CONSORT, HUSBAND, PARTNER

spout .... JET, GUSH, SNOUT, SPILE, NOZZLE, STREAM, ELEVATOR

slang .... PAWN(SHOP)

steam .... JET, GEYSER

water .... GARGOYLE

whale's .... BLOWHOLE

spraddle .... SPAN

sprag .... TRIG, BLOCK, CHOCK, WEDGE

sprain .... TWIST, WRICK, WRENCH, TEARING

most common spot of .... ANKLE

sprat .... BRIT, HERRING, BRISLING

Sprat's diet no-no .... FAT
predilection .... LEAN
sprawl .... LIE, LOLL, CRAWL,
LOUNGE, SPREAD
spray .... MIST, TWIG, SPRIG,
SPUME, LIPPER, PEPPER,
SHOWER, BOUQUET,
ATOMIZE(R), NEBULIZE,
SPRINKLE
products .... AEROSOLS
with bullets .... RIDDLE
with medicated liquid
.... NEBULIZE
spread .... FAN, JAM, OLEO,
BRUIT, COVER, JELLY, SPLAY,
STREW, BUTTER, EXTEND,
UNFOLD, UNFURL, EXHIBIT,
OVERLAY, SCATTER, STRETCH,
DISPERSE, PROPAGATE
abroad .... RADIATE,
DISSEMINATE
apart .... SPLAY, EXPAND
by scattering .... STREW
colloquial .... MEAL, FEAST,
BANQUET, DISPLAY
eagle .... SPRAWL
false rumors .... ASPERSE
for drying .... TED
from person to person
.... CIRCULATE
grass/hay .... TED
here and there .... STREW,
SCATTER
linen .... COVERLET,
BEDSPREAD
newspaper .... LAYOUT
out .... FAN, FLARE, DEPLOY,
EFFUSE, DIFFUSE
out awkwardly .... SPRAWL
out freely .... POUR
perfume .... CENSE
rapidly .... MUSHROOM
rumors .... HAWK, BRUIT
thick .... SLATHER
thin .... BRAY
through .... PERMEATE
troops .... DEPLOY
spreading .... PATULOUS
from the center .... RADIAL
implement .... TEDDER,
MULCHER, SPATULA
spree .... BOUT, LARK, ORGY,
TEAR, FLING, SPELL, FROLIC,
REVELRY, WASSAIL,
CAROUSAL, (HELL)BENDER
drunken .... WASSAIL,
CAROUSAL, BACCHANAL(IA)
kind of .... SHOPPING
slang .... BAT, JAG, TOOT,
BINGE, BUST(ER)
sprig .... BRAD, TWIG, SHOOT,

SPRAY, BRANCH, FELLOW,
STRIPLING
sprightly .... GAY, TID, AIRY,
PERT, AGILE, BRISK, SAUCY,
SMART, BLITHE, JAUNTY,
LIVELY, CHIPPER, ANIMATED
spring .... BEND, BOLT, JUMP,
LEAP, STEM, WELL, (A)RISE,
VAULT, BOUNCE, DART(LE),
ORIGIN, SEASON, SOURCE,
EMANATE, REBOUND,
FOUNT(AIN)
Apollo's .... CASTALIA
artificial .... FOUNTAIN
back .... BOUNCE, RECOIL,
RESILE, REBOUND
biblical .... AIN
bloomer/flower .... PANSY,
TULIP, CROCUS
chicken .... FRYER, BROILER
deposit .... TUFA, TRONA,
TRAVERTIN
festival .... MAYDAY
fever .... BLAHS
guard .... MIMIR
herald .... ROBIN
holiday .... EASTER
like/of .... FONTAL, VERNAL
lizard .... SALAMANDER
mineral .... SPA
month .... MAY, APRIL, MARCH
phenomenon .... THAW
poet's .... CASTALIA
poetic .... FONT
sign of .... BUDS, SWALLOW
slang ..... BAIL, FREE, RELEASE
small .... GEYSER
tide .... FLOOD
water .... LYMPH, SELTZER
springboard .... BATULE
springbok .... GAZELLE, SPRINGER
springe .... TRAP, SNARE
springer .... IMPOST, GRAMPUS,
SPANIEL
springhead .... SOURCE
springing back .... ELASTIC,
RESILIENT
springs .... SPA, BATHS, THERMAE
springtime .... MAY
springy .... PLIANT, ELASTIC,
FLEXIBLE
sprinkle .... DEG, SOW, WET,
DUST, RAIN, SPRAY, STREW,
DREDGE, SHOWER, SPLASH,
DRIZZLE, SCATTER
as holy water .... SPARGE
water to purify .... BAPTIZE
with flour .... DREDGE
with sieve .... SIFT
sprinkling .... ASPERSION
in heraldry .... SEME

with holy water ..... ASPERGES
sprint .... RUN, DASH, RACE,
RUSH, SPEED
sprinter .... DASHER, RUNNER,
TRACKMAN, SPEEDSTER
sprit .... BOOM, SPAR
sprite .... ELF, FAY, HOB, NIX,
PIXY, ARIEL, FAIRY, GHOST,
GNOME, PIXIE, SPIRIT,
BROWNIE
helpful .... KOBOLD
mischievous .... IMP, PUCK,
GOBLIN, KOBOLD
prankish .... ELF
water .... NIS, NIX, UNDINE
spritelike .... ELFIN
sprout .... BUD, CHIT, GROW,
(S)CION, SHOOT, BURGEON,
SAPLING, GERMINATE,
PULLULATE
root/stem .... TILLER,
RAT(T)OON
spruce .... CHIC, NEAT, TIDY,
TRIM, NATTY, PICEA, SMART
fruit .... CONE
slang .... DAPPER, JAUNTY,
SPIFFY, SHIPSHAPE
tree .... FIR, PINE, CEDAR,
LARCH, CONIFER, EPINETTE
up .... FRESHEN, TITIVATE
sprue .... PSILOSIS
form of ...... CELIAC, TROPICAL
organ affected by
.... INTESTINE
spry .... AGILE, ALERT, BRISK,
QUICK, ACTIVE, LIVELY,
NIMBLE
spud .... TATER, POTATO
tool like .... SPADE, CHISEL
spue .... SPEW
spumante, _____ .... ASTI
spume .... FOAM, SCUM, FROTH
spun .... WOVE(N)
sugar .... COTTON CANDY
spunk .... GRIT, PUNK, PLUCK,
SPARK, AMADOU, KINDLE,
METTLE, SPIRIT, TINDER,
COURAGE
spunky .... GAME, BRAVE,
PLUCKY, SPIRITED
spur .... GOAD, URGE, BRACE,
ERGOT, HURRY, PRICK, RIDGE,
STRUT, CALCAR, GRIFFE,
INCITE, SIDING, STIMULUS
adjunct/wheel .... ROWEL
gamecock's .... GAFF
mountain .... ARETE
spurge .... MILKWEED, EUPHORBIA
spurious .... TIN, FAKE, SHAM,
BOGUS, FALSE, PSEUD,
FORGED, PHON(E)Y, BASTARD,

ARTIFICIAL, COUNTERFEIT

spurn .... KICK, FLOUT, REPEL,
SCORN, REFUSE, REJECT,
DECLINE

spurr(e)y .... (CHICK)WEED

spurt .... JET, DART, GUSH, BURST,
SPOUT, SPRAY, SQUIRT,
STREAM

of energy .... LICK

Sputnik .... SATELLITE

proprietor .... USSR, RUSSIA

sputter .... SPEW, SPIT, BLURT,
EJECT, DABBLE, FIZZLE,
JABBER, SPLUTTER

sputum .... SALIVA, SPIT(TLE)

spy .... PRY, SEE, FINK, KEEK,
NOSE, ANDRE, FUCHS, SCOUT,
WATCH, ARNOLD, CAVELL,
CICERO, GEISLER, STEIBER,
DISCERN, INFORMER,
(MATA)HARI, SPOTTER,
PERCEIVE, RINTELEN,
OPERATIVE, ROSENBERG,
PRIVATE EYE, (SECRET)AGENT,
UNDERCOVER MAN

Andre .... JOHN

Arnold .... BENEDICT

Arnold's wife .... PEGGY

glass .... BINOCULARS

in one's midst .... MOLE,
INSIDE MAN

lure of .... SECRETS

numerals .... OOVII

obsolete .... ESPIAL

slang .... FINK, MOLE, TAIL,
STOOLIE

who thwarts enemy
espionage
.... COUNTERSPY, DOUBLE
AGENT

woman .... MATA HARI,
(EDITH)CAVELL

work of a .... BUGGING,
STAKEOUT, SHADOWING,
OBSERVATION, WIRETAP(PING)

spying .... PRYING, SNOOPING,
WATCHING, ESPIONAGE,
INTELLIGENCE, SURVEILLANCE

work, of .... CLOAK AND
DAGGER

Spyri's heroine .... HEIDE

squab .... SOFA, COUCH, PIPER,
PIGEON, CUSHION

squabble .... ROW, MUSS, SPAT,
BICKER, HASSLE, DISPUTE,
QUARREL, WRANGLE,
COMMOTION

squad .... BAND, CREW, TEAM,
UNIT, PATROL

car adjunct .... SIREN

leader .... SERGEANT

squadron, navy .... FLEET,
ARMADA

of airplanes .... ESCADRILLE

squads, two or more
.... PLATOON

squalid ...... FOUL, DINGY, DIRTY,
MANGY, FILTHY, SORDID,
UNCLEAN, WRETCHED,
UNSIGHTLY

squall .... CRY, BAWL, BLOW,
FLAW, GALE, GUST, WAIL,
WAUL, WAWL, SCREAM,
TROUBLE, TURMOIL,
(WIND)STORM

squally .... GUSTY, STORMY

squalor ...... DIRT, FILTH, MISERY

squama(e) .... SCALE(S)

squamate/squamous .... SCALY

cell carcinoma .... TUMOR,
SKIN CANCER

squander .... LOSE, WASTE,
LAVISH, CONSUME, EXHAUST,
(DI)SPEND, MISSPEND,
DISSIPATE

slang .... BLOW, PISS AWAY

square .... FIT, FAIR, PARK,
AGREE, BLOCK, COURT,
FORUM, LEVEL, PLAZA,
TALLY, EVEN(UP), HONEST,
PIAZZA, SETTLE, CUBICAL,
BALANCE(D), QUADRATE,
TETRAGON, RECONCILE

all .... EVEN

college campus
.... QUADRANGLE

column .... PILASTER

dance .... REEL, HOEDOWN,
LANC(I)ERS, QUADRILLE

dance, four couples in a
.... (SQUARE) SET

dance need .... CALLER

feet .... AREA

nearly .... RECTANGLE

off .... CLASH, DISAGREE

one, back to .... IMPASSE,
DEADLOCK

person .... FOGY, MISFIT,
FUDDY-DUDDY

-rigged feature ..... YARD ARM

root of nine .... THREE

shooter .... FAIR DEALER

slang .... BRIBE, HUNKY,
WHITE, STRAIGHT, OLD-
FASHIONED

small .... QUADRILLE

the score .... TIE

up .... REPAY

squared circle .... ARENA,
(PRIZE)RING

quantities that are
.... QUADRATIC

squarehead ...... BOCHE, GERMAN,
SCANDINAVIAN

squaring circle ...... CYCLOTOMY,
CYCLOMETRY

squarrose .... SCALY

squash .... MASH, PEPO, CRUSH,
GOURD, PRESS, QUELL, SPORT,
SQUISH, FLATTEN, SILENCE,
SQUEEZE, SQUELCH

crookneck .... CASHAW,
CUSHAW

family .... GOURD

genus .... CURCUBITA

summer .... ZUCCHINI

winter .... HUBBARD,
BUTTERNUT

squashy .... MUSHY, PULPY

squat ...... DUMPY, FUBSY, PUDGY,
TUBBY, CROUCH

and pudgy .... ROLY-POLY

fat and .... FUBSY, PLUMP

on public land .... SETTLE

squatter .... CATCHER, SETTLER

squatter's domain
.... HOMEPLATE

squaw .... WOMAN, MAHALA

Indian .... WIFE

squawbush .... SUMAC

squawk .... CRY, CALL, KICK,
GRIPE, HERON, GROUSE,
OBJECT, SCREAM, GRUMBLE,
PROTEST, COMPLAIN

squeak .... CRY, PEEP, CHEEP,
CREAK, SQUEAL

squeal .... CRY, BLAB, SING, YELL,
YELP, PEACH, RAT ON,
INFORM, SHRIEK, TELL ON,
CONFESS, DIVULGE

squealer .... THIRD EAR, STOOL
PIGEON

of a sort .... CANARY

squeamish .... PICKY, DAINTY,
QUEASY, FINICAL, NERVOUS,
NAUSEOUS, QUALMISH,
SKITTISH, FASTIDIOUS

person .... PRUDE

squeezable container .... TUBE

squeeze .... EKE, HUG, JAM, NIP,
CRAM, CRUSH, WRING, EXACT,
EXTORT, SQUASH, EXTRACT,
(COM)PRESS

chin .... CHUCK

payment by threat
.... BLACKMAIL

squeezer, elongated .... BOA

juice .... REAMER

squelch .... CRUSH, SIT ON,
KIBOSH, MUFFLE, (S)QUASH,
STIFLE, SUBDUE, SILENCE,
SUPPRESS

squeteague .... CROAKER,

GRUNT(ER)

squib ...... LAMPOON, DETONATOR, PASQUINADE, FIRECRACKER

squid .... MOLLUSK, CALAMARY, CUTTLEFISH

arm of .... TENTACLE

relative .... SPIRULA

shell of .... PEN

squilgee .... SQUEEGEE

squill .... LILY, SEA ONION

squilla .... CRAB, PRAWN, MANTIS, SHRIMP, CRUSTACEAN, STOMATOPOD

squinch .... LINTEL, CORBELING

squint .... PEEK, PEER, SKEW, GLANCE, STRABISMUS

convergent .... CROSS-EYE

divergent .... WALLEYE

sideways .... SKEW

squire .... BEAU, DONZEL, ESCORT, ARMIGER, GALLANT, HENCHMAN, ATTEND(ANT), GENTLEMAN, ARMOR-BEARER

squirm .... TWIST, WIGGLE, WRITHE, WRIGGLE

squirrel .... XERUS, MARMOT, RODENT, STORER, HOARDER, TAMARIN, CHIPMUNK, CHICKAREE, PHALANGER, WOODCHUCK, SPERMOPHILE

away .... CACHE

burrowing .... GOPHER, MARMOT

flying .... ASSAPAN, PHALANGER

flying aid .... PATAGIUM

fodder .... ACORN

fur .... VAIR, SUSLIK

ground .... SISEL, GOPHER, SUSLIK

like rodent .... DORMOUSE

monkey .... TAMARIN

nest .... DRAY, DREY

parasite of .... WABBLE

red .... CHICKAREE

shrew .... TANA

skin fold .... PATAGIUM, PARACHUTE

stash of .... NUTS, ACORN

squirt .... JET, HOSE, SHOOT, SPIRT, SPRAY, STREAM

colloquial .... IMP, RUNT

gun .... WATER PISTOL

sri .... MISTER

Sri Lanka. See also **Ceylon**

former name of .... CEYLON

monetary unit .... RUPEE

SRO, part of .... STANDING, ROOM, ONLY

charge .... STANDAGE

patron? .... SEATLESS

sign .... SOLDOUT

SS Nazi .... BLACK SHIRTS

head .... HIMMLER

St. See also **Saint** .... SAINT, STREET

Anthony's cross .... TAU

Anthony's fire ..... ERYSIPELAS

Catherine's commune
.... SIENA

Elmo's fire .... CORPOSANT

Francis' birthplace ...... ASSISI

John's bread .... CAROB

Lawrence river discoverer
.... (JACQUES)CARTIER

Lawrence river feature
.... 1000 ISLANDS

Valentine's way ..... HEART TO HEART

stab ...... GORE, HURT, PINK, SPIT, PUNCH, STICK, WOUND, PIERCE, THRUST

colloquial .... TRY, ATTEMPT

stabile .... STATIONARY

opposite of .... LABILE

stabilize(r) .... BALLAST

stable .... BARN, FAST, FIRM, MEWS, FIXED, LODGE, SECURE, STEADY, CONSTANT, ENDURING, STEADFAST

compartment .... STALL

field .... PADDOCK

member .... BOXER, FIGHTER, RACEHORSE

part .... HAYMOW, HAYLOFT

sound .... NEIGH, SNORT, (W)HINNY

stableman ...... GROOM, CURRIER, (H)OSTLER

stables, royal .... MEWS

staccato, opposed to .... LEGATO

stack ...... FIX, MOW, HEAP, LOAD, PILE, RICK, RUCK, MOUND, BUNDLE, ARRANGE, CHIMNEY

as of fuel .... RUCK

as of papers .... SHEAF

base of .... STADDLE

blow one's ..... FLARE UP, FLY INTO A RAGE, HIT THE CEILING

of grain .... MOW

of hay/straw .... RICK

of iron/steel .... FA(G)GOT

steamship/factory .... FLUE, CHIMNEY, SMOKESTACK

the cards .... CHEAT

stacked .... CURVACEOUS, VOLUPTUOUS

deck .... SETUP

stacte .... SPICE

staddle .... BASE, FRAME, CRUTCH, SUPPORT

stadia .... ROD, TRANSIT,

RANGEFINDER

stadium .... BOWL, PARK, ARENA, FIELD, COLISEUM

passageway .... RAMP

plural of .... STADIA

receipts .... GATE

section .... TIER

shape .... OVAL

staff ...... MAN, ROD, CANE, CLUB, POLE, WAND, ANKUS, BATON, STAVE, STICK, VERGE, CUDGEL, OFFICE, RETINUE, TRUNCHEON

again .... REMAN

bearer .... VERGER

bishop's .... ROD, CROOK, CROSIER

flag .... FLAGPOLE

for leading an elephant
.... ANKUS

household .... DOMESTIC

in music .... STAVE

member .... AIDE

metal cap .... SHOE

mountain climber's
.... ALPENSTOCK

of an aircraft .... CREW

of attendants .... RETINUE

office ...... FORCE, MANPOWER, PERSONNEL

officer, in short .... ADC

officer's .... CADRE

plural of .... STAVES

shepherd's .... CROOK

symbol .... CLEF

symbol of authority .... MACE, WARDER

symbol of sovereignty
.... SCEPTER

teaching .... FACULTY

winged .... CADUCEUS

Stafford, singer .... JO

stag ...... HART, WAPITI, POLLARD, (RED)DEER

horn's tine .... BROCKET

mate of .... HIND

party .... SMOKER

stage .... DAIS, DOCK, SHOW, STEP, DRAMA, PHASE, DEGREE, PRESENT, PRODUCE, THEATER, PLATFORM, SCAFFOLD, FOOTLIGHTS, (THE)BOARDS

act on .... EMOTE, PERFORM

advanced .... WORSE

ancient Greek/Roman
.... PROSCENIUM

assignment .... PART, ROLE

assistant .... PROMPTER

curtain .... BACKDROP

direction .... EXIT, ASIDE, ENTER, MANET, EXEUNT,

SENNET
extra .... SUPE(R)
for public speaking
.... ROSTRUM, PLATFORM
fright .... BUCK FEVER
front .... PIT, APRON,
ORCHESTRA
group: abbr. .... ANTA
in lunar cycle .... PHASE
kind of .... REVOLVING
lighting .... FLOATS,
SPOTLIGHT, FOOTLIGHTS
name .... PSEUDONYM
of change .... PHASE
disease/illness .... PHASE,
DEGREE, PERIOD
life .... ESTATE
psychosexual development
.... ANAL
overact on .... HAM, MUG
part of ..... PIT, APRON, WINGS,
BOARDS, PODIUM, COULISSE,
PROSCENIUM
piece .... SKIT, SKETCH,
RECITAL, VARIETY
play .... DRAMA, COMEDY,
MUSICAL
elaborate .... OPERA,
OPERETTA, EXTRAVAGANZA
first showing of a
.... PREMIERE
held in the afternoon
.... MATINEE
part in .... LEAD, ROLE,
STAR, HEAVY, VILLAIN
part in, minor .... EXTRA,
WALK-ON
pause .... INTERMEZZO,
INTERMISSION
performance between acts
of .... INTERLUDE
players .... CAST
profession .... ACTING,
DRAMATICS, HISTRIONICS
prop .... (BACK)DROP,
FOOTLIGHTS, CURTAIN(RISER)
setting ...... DECOR, SCENE(RY)
show .... REVUE, MUSICAL,
BURLESQUE, VAUDEVILLE
side scene .... COULISSE
slang .... LEGIT
trumpet call .... SENNET
vehicle ..... DRAMA, PLAY(LET)
whisper .... SIGH, AD LIB,
ASIDE
stagecoach .... CONCORD
travel by .... STAGING
stagehand .... GRIP, CALLBOY,
PROMPTER, TECHNICIAN
stager .... OLD HAND, VETERAN
Stagg, Amos _____ .... ALONZO

stagger ...... REEL, SWAY, LURCH,
WAVER, FALTER, TOTTER,
WAMBLE, STARTLE,
FLOUNDER, ALTERNATE,
OVERWHELM, VACILLATE
staggered arrangement
.... ZIGZAG
staggering .... AMBLING,
SHOCKING, STUNNING,
SURPRISING, ASTONISHING
stagger(s) .... GID, MEGRIM(S)
cause of .... COENURUS
staghorn _____ .... CORAL
Stagirite .... ARISTOTLE
stagnant ...... DULL, FOUL, INERT,
STALE, TORPID, DORMANT,
SLUGGISH, STANDING
stagnate .... VEGETATE
stagnation .... STASIS
stagy ...... AFFECTED, THEATRICAL
staid .... FIXED, SOBER, SEDATE,
STEADY, SETTLED
stain .... DYE, BLOT, SOIL, SPOT,
TINT, BRAND, SMEAR, SPOIL,
SULLY, TAINT, TINGE,
BLOTCH, IMB(R)UE, SMUDGE,
STIGMA, BLEMISH, CORRUPT,
SPLOTCH, TARNISH,
DISHONOR, MACULA(TE)
escutcheon .... BLOT
remover .... LEMON, PUMICE
stainer for microscope
.... SAFRANIN(E)
staining .... DYEING
art of .... MARBLING
method .... PAP(ANICOLAOU)
stair .... STEP, STILE
edge .... NOSER
face .... RISER
lights .... FOOTS
post .... NEWEL
slope .... INCLINE
staircase .... PERRON, STAIRS
bend .... RAMP
guard .... HANDRAIL
landing .... HALFPACE
part ...... POST, RISER, RUNDLE,
RAILING, BALUSTRADE
post .... NEWEL, BALUSTER
railing .... BALUSTRADE
spiral .... CARACOLE
step .... WINDER
stairs pillar .... NEWEL
plane .... RAMP
set of .... FLIGHT
shaft .... WELL
stairway, horizontal surface of a
step .... TREAD
mechanical .... ESCALATOR
outside building .... FIRE
ESCAPE

step .... FLIER
vertical piece between steps
.... RISER
stake .... BET, PEG, POT, ANTE,
PALE, PILE, POST, RISK,
CLAIM, HITCH, SHARE, SPILE,
GAMBLE, IMPONE, PICKET,
TETHER, FINANCE, INTEREST
fence .... PALE, WEIR, PICKET
for foundation .... SPILE
for swordplay practice .... PEL
out ..... TAIL, WATCH, OBSERVE
played for .... MAIN
wooden .... PEG, TREE
stakeout ...... BUG, SURVEILLANCE
stakes .... BETS, KITTY, PRIZE,
WAGERS
driver .... MAUL
fence of .... PALISADE
stalactite site .... CAVE
stalag inmate .... POW, PRISONER
stale .... DRAB, DULL, FLAT, HACK,
HOAR, BANAL, FUSTY, MUSTY,
PASSE, TRITE, VAPID, RANCID,
INSIPID, NOT FRESH,
STAGNANT, HACKNEYED,
TASTELESS
slang .... CORNY
stalemate .... JAM, TIE, DRAW,
CHECK, STALL, IMPASSE,
DEADLOCK, STAND-OFF
Stalin's daughter .... (SVETLANA)
ALLILUYEVA
now a.k.a. .... LANA PETERS
Stalinabad .... DUSHANBE
Stalingrad .... VOLGOGRAD
Stalinism .... COMMUNISM
Stalino, former .... DONETSK
stalk .... CULM, LURK, STEM,
HAULM, PROWL, SCAPE, STIPE,
STRUT, CAULIS, PRANCE,
STOVER, PEDICEL, PETIOLE,
STRIPE(S), FILAMENT,
PEDUNCLE
eyed crustacean .... CRAB,
PRAWN, SHRIMP, LOBSTER,
CRAYFISH
flower .... PEDUNCLE
grass .... CULM, HA(U)LM,
STRAW
having a .... PETIOLATE
leaf .... PETIOLE
like structure .... PEDICEL,
PEDICLE
stalking horse .... BLIND, DECOY,
PRETEXT, SMOKE-SCREEN
stall .... COT, CRIB, LOGE, SEAT,
BOOTH, DELAY, HEDGE,
KIOSK, NICHE, STAND,
ALCOVE, MANGER, PUT OFF,
STABLE, CHAMBER,

TEMPORIZE, COMPARTMENT
covering .... TILT
shop's front .... BULK
stallion .... STEED, MORGAN,
STUD(HORSE), ENTIRE(HORSE)
Stallone's nickname .... SLY
stalwart .... FIRM, HUSKY,
ROBUST, STRONG, LOYALIST,
TIRELESS, DAUNTLESS,
SUPPORTER
Stamboul .... ISTANBUL
stamen .... STALK, ANTHER,
FILAMENT, POLLEN SAC
stamina ...... GRIT, PLUCK, VIGOR,
BACKBONE, HARDNESS,
STRENGTH, VITALITY,
ENDURANCE, TOUGHNESS
staminate .... MALE
stammer .... HALT, PAUSE,
FALTER, STUTTER, HESITATE,
HEM (AND HAW)
stamp .... DIE, MARK, SIGN, TAMP,
BRAND, SIGIL, CACHET,
IMPRESS, IMPRINT
Chinese .... CHOP
mail .... POSTAGE
official/ornamental .... SEAL
on coin .... MINTAGE
out .... CRUSH, CANCEL,
SCOTCH, ELIMINATE,
ANNIHILATE
stampede ...... RUN, ROUT, PANIC,
CHARGE, FLIGHT, ONRUSH,
RAMPAGE
stamper .... DATER
stamping device .... DATER,
PUNCHEON
ground .... TURF, HAUNT,
RESORT, FOOTING, HANGOUT
stamps, substitute for
.... INDICIA
Stan, the Man .... MUSIAL
stance .... POSE, POST, BEARING,
POSTURE, CARRIAGE, POSITION
stanch .... STEM, STOP, CHECK,
QUELL, QUENCH, SUPPRESS
stanchion .... POST, BRACE,
PILLAR
stand .... BEAR, BIER, FACE, HALT,
LAST, RACK, STAY, VIEW,
ABIDE, BOOTH, STALL,
CASTER, ENDURE, REMAIN,
RESIST, OPINION, STATION,
UNDERGO, ATTITUDE,
POSITION, TANTALUS,
TOLERATE
against .... OPPOSE
apart .... VARY, DIFFER
artist's/painter's .... EASEL
behind ...... BACK UP, SUPPORT
by ...... BACK, AWAIT, DEFEND,

MAINTAIN
conductor's .... PODIUM
fast .... RESIST
for .... MEAN, REPRESENT
for election .... RUN
in .... PROXY, SUBSTITUTE
in the way .... FOIL, BLOCK,
THWART, OBSTRUCT
high .... TOWER
kind of ...... LAST, NEWS, ONE-
NIGHT
on hind legs .... RAMP, REAR
orator's .... SOAPBOX
ornamental .... TABORET,
PEDESTAL
out .... GLARE, PROJECT,
DISSENTER
priest's .... PULPIT
sacrificial .... ALTAR
stockstill .... FREEZE
three-legged .... TEAPOY,
TRIPOD, TRIVET
two-legged .... BIPOD
standard .... FLAG, NORM,
CANON, GRADE, MODEL,
NORIA, BANNER, COLORS,
EMBLEM, ENSIGN, NORMAL,
CLASSIC, EXAMPLE, REGULAR,
TYPICAL, UNIFORM,
GONFALON, CRITERION,
YARDSTICK
battle .... ORIFLAME
bearer .... CHIEF, ENSIGN,
LEADER, CHAMPION,
CANDIDATE
of a .... VEXILLARY
of excellence/of perfection
.... IDEAL
pasha's .... HORSETAIL
standby .... STAPLE, MAINSTAY,
ALTERNATE
at airport .... PASSENGER
standee, bus/subway
.... STRAPHANGER
standing .... RANK, ERECT,
RATING, STATUS, UPRIGHT,
POSITION, PRESTIGE,
STAGNANT, REPUTATION
order .... SOP
out .... GLARING, SALIENT
room area .... AISLES
room charge .... STANDAGE
with feet on ground
.... STATENT
Standish, colonist .... MILES
standoff .... TIE, DRAW
standoffish ...... ALOOF, DISTANT,
RESERVED, WITHDRAWN
standout .... ONER
standpat(ter) .... TORY, DIEHARD,
CONSERVATIVE

standpoint .... ANGLE, ASPECT,
VIEWPOINT
standstill .... HALT, IMPASSE,
DEADLOCK, (DEAD)STOP,
CESSATION
stang .... PAIN
stanhope .... SHAY, CARRIAGE
Stanley _____ (early auto)
.... STEAMER
stannite .... ORE
stannum .... TIN
Stanovoi mountain ...... ANADYR,
KOLYMA, YABLONOI
Stan's pal .... OLLIE
stanza ...... ENVOI, STAVE, VERSE,
(L)ENVOY, DISTICH,
STROP(H)E
eight-line .... OCTAVE,
TRIOLET, OCTONARY
four-line .... QUATRAIN,
TETRASTICH
seven-line .... HEPTASTICH
six-line .... SESTET, SEXTAIN,
HEXASTICH
stapelia .... MILKWEED
stapes .... STIRRUP
location .... MIDDLE EAR
staple .... SALT, CHIEF, FIBER,
FLOUR, SUGAR, POPULAR,
REGULAR, COMMODITY,
PRINCIPAL
food .... CORN, RICE, POTATO
star ...... ACE, SUN, NOVA, EXCEL,
PLANET, LEADING, ASTERISK
apple .... CAIMITO
binary .... ALGOL, ALBIREO,
ANTARES
blue .... VEGA
brightest .... COR, LUCIDA,
SIRIUS
cluster .... GALAXY, ASTERISM,
MILKY WAY
combining form .... ASTRO,
SIDER(O)
Cygnus .... DENEB
evening .... VENUS, VESPER,
HESPER(US)
fallen .... ALGA, HAS-BEEN
five-pointed .... PENTACLE,
PENTAGRAM
grazer .... BOVINE
group .... DIPPER, MILKY WAY,
CONSTELLATION
in an opera ...... PRIMA DONNA
in Cetus .... MIRA
in Perseus, fixed .... ALGOL
in Serpens .... ALYA
like a/of a .... ASTRAL,
STELLAR
Lyra .... VEGA
Mars .... ANTARES

morning .... VENUS, PHOSPHOR

neutron .... PULSAR

new .... NOVA

Orion .... RIGEL

path of .... ORBIT

pertaining to a .... SIDEREAL, CELESTIAL

poetic .... LAMP

pulsating ..... CEPHEID, PULSAR

red .... RUSSIA, ANTARES

rising .... COMER

Scorpio .... ANTARES

shaped .... ASTROSE, ASTEROID, STELLATE, ASTERIATED

shell .... FLARE

shooting .... METEOR

show-biz ...... ACTOR, ACTRESS

six-pointed .... HEXAGRAM

small .... STARLET

spangled, in heraldry .... SEME

sports .... ACE, CHAMPION

temperamental .... PRIMA DONNA

thistle .... WEED, CALTRAP, CALTROP

with long luminous tail .... COMET

yellow .... CAPELIA

Star Chamber .... COURT, TRIBUNAL

of David .... HEXAGRAM

Spangled Banner, The, writer .... FRANCIS SCOTT KEY

_____: The New Generation .... TREK

Trek creator .... (GENE) RODDENBERRY

Trek's milieu .... SPACE

starch .... SAGO, MANIOC, AMYL(UM), AMIDINE, AMYLOSE, CASSAVA, TAPIOCA, GLYCOGEN, ARROWROOT, CARBOHYDRATE

food .... FARINA

grain nucleus .... HILUM

grain part .... GRANULOSE

like .... AMYLOID

pudding .... SAGO

source .... ARUM, SAGO, TARO, CANNA, MANIOC, CASSAVA, COONTIE, CURCUMA

to sugar, enzyme that changes .... AMYLASE

starchy .... RIGID, STIFF, FORMAL, AMYLACEOUS

food/substance .... AMYLOID

plant .... AROID

root/tuber .... YAM, TARO, (SWEET)POTATO

stare .... GAPE, GAWK, GAZE, OGLE, GLARE, GOGGLE

down .... OUTFACE

open-mouthed .... GAPE

stupidly .... GAWK

starfish .... SEA STAR, FIVE-FINGER, ASTEROID(EAN)

arm/limb .... RAY

relative .... COMATULID

starflower .... PRIMROSE

stargazer .... ASTROLOGER, ASTRONOMER

staring .... AGAPE

stark .... BLEAK, RIGID, SHEER, STIFF, BARREN, UTTER(LY), DESOLATE, DOWNRIGHT

naked ..... BARE, NUDE, IN THE RAW

raving-mad .... WILD, MANIAC, FURIOUS

starlet .... ACTRESS, INGENUE

starling .... MINO, REDWING, OXPECKER, (BLACK)BIRD

kin of .... MYNA(H), ORIOLE

starnose .... MOLE

Starr, bandit queen .... BELLE

husband of Belle .... SAM

of comic strips .... BRENDA

of football fame .... BART

starry .... SHINY, ASTRAL, STELLAR, SIDEREAL, GLITTERING

stars .... FATE, DESTINY, FORTUNE

dotted with .... SEME

group of .... CONSTELLATION

in Ursa Major, group of .... BIG DIPPER

large group of .... GALAXY, MILKY WAY

of the .... ASTRAL, STELLAR, SIDEREAL, CELESTIAL

visible winter nights, group of .... ORION, PLEIADES

worshiper of .... SABAIST

Stars and Stripes Forever composer .... (JOHN PHILIP)SOUSA

start .... JIB, SHY, EDGE, JERK, BIRTH, LEAD, OPEN, BEGIN, CRACK, ROUSE, ONSET, SET IN, SHOCK, LAUNCH, COMMENCE, INCEPTION

a set .... SERVE

anew .... REOPEN

card game .... DEAL

of a refrain .... TRA

of a tale .... ONCE

to take off .... UNZIP

START concerns, informally .... NUKES

starting point .... GATE, SCRATCH

startle .... ALARM, AMAZE, SCARE, SHOCK, EXCITE, AFFRIGHT, FRIGHTEN, SURPRISE, GALVANIZE

starvation .... FASTING

widespread .... FAMINE

starve .... DIET, DENY, FAST, PINE, FAMISH, HUNGER, SCRIMP

starved .... HUNGRY, FAMISHED

starwort .... ALGA, ASTER

stash .... HIDE, CACHE, HOARD, CONCEAL, SECRETE

cash .... IRA

state .... SAY, AVER, AVOW, ETAT, FORM, MODE, MOOD, POSIT, UTTER, NATION, PLIGHT, POLITY, STATUS, COUNTRY, DECLARE, EXPRESS, NARRATE, SPECIFY, CONDITION, SITUATION, TERRITORY

admitted to the Union in the 20th century .... ALASKA, HAWAII, ARIZONA, OKLAHOMA, NEW MEXICO

attorney .... DA

council .... SENATE

dependent .... SATELLITE

dial. .... GAUP

dominant .... SUPERPOWER

medium's .... TRANCE

of affairs .... CASE, DOINGS, CONCERNS

agitation .... SNIT

balance .... EQUIPOISE

being fat .... ADIPOSITY

body and mind .... FETTLE

continuing .... ABIDANCE

equilibrium .... STASIS

excitement .... FERMENT

mind .... MOOD, MORALE, SPIRITS, DISPOSITION

suspended animation .... ANABIOSIS

over and over .... REITERATE

police .... TROOPER

positively .... AVER, ASSERT

proposed by the Mormons: 1849 .... DESERET

treasury .... FISC

troops .... MILITIA

under oath .... SWEAR, DEPOSE

with confidence .... ASSURE

without proof .... CLAIM, ALLEGE

State, Aloha .... HAWAII

Badger .... WISCONSIN

Bay .... MASSACHUSETTS

Beaver .... OREGON

Beehive .... UTAH

Blue Hen .... DELAWARE

Bluegrass .... KENTUCKY

Buckeye .... OHIO
Centennial .... COLORADO
Constitution ..... CONNECTICUT
Cornhusker .... NEBRASKA
Cotton .... ALABAMA
Coyote .... SOUTH DAKOTA
Creole .... LOUISIANA
Department endorsement
.... VISA
El Dorado .... CALIFORNIA
Empire .... NEW YORK
Equality .... WYOMING
Evergreen .... WASHINGTON
Fair author .... STONG
First .... DELAWARE
Free .... MARYLAND
Garden .... NEW JERSEY
Gem .... IDAHO
Golden .... CALIFORNIA
Gopher .... MINNESOTA
Grand Canyon .... ARIZONA
Granite .... NEW HAMPSHIRE
Green Mountain .... VERMONT
Hawkeye .... IOWA
Hoosier .... INDIANA
Keystone .... PENNSYLVANIA
Land of Enchantment .... NEW
                              MEXICO
Little Rhody .... RHODE
                               ISLAND
Lone Star .... TEXAS
Magnolia .... MISSISSIPPI
Mountain .... WEST VIRGINIA
Nutmeg .... CONNECTICUT
Old Colony
.... MASSACHUSETTS
Old Dominion .... VIRGINIA
Old Line .... MARYLAND
Palmetto ..... SOUTH CAROLINA
Peach .... GEORGIA
Pelican .... LOUISIANA
Pine Tree .... MAINE
Prairie .... ILLINOIS
Show Me .... MISSOURI
Silver .... NEVADA
Sioux .... NORTH DAKOTA
Sooner .... OKLAHOMA
Sunflower .... KANSAS
Sunshine .... FLORIDA
Tar Heel ..... NORTH CAROLINA
The Last Frontier ..... ALASKA
Treasure .... MONTANA
Volunteer .... TENNESSEE
Wolverine .... MICHIGAN
statehood .... NATIONALITY
statehouse .... CAPITOL
stately .... GRAND, LOFTY, NOBLE,
    REGAL, ROYAL, AUGUST,
    FORMAL, COURTLY, IMPOSING,
    MAJESTIC, DIGNIFIED,
    GRANDIOSE, MAGNIFICENT

house .... DOME, VILLA,
    PALACE, CHATEAU, MANSION
music .... LARGO
statement .... BILL, WORD, PRECIS,
    REMARK, REPORT, THESIS,
    ACCOUNT, ADDRESS,
    BULLETIN, ASSERTION,
    TESTIMONY, DECLARATION
absurd, self-contradictory
.... PARADOX
authoritative .... DICTUM
brief, casual .... REMARK,
                              COMMENT
defamatory .... LIBEL
ex-employer's ...... REFERENCE
false, malicious .... CANARD
formal .... CITATION,
    AFFIDAVIT, COMMUNIQUE,
    DEPOSITION, DECLARATION
in belief .... CREDO, CREED
lying witness' .... PERJURY
of account, final .... AUDIT
of facts .... CASE
of principles, systematic
.... THEORY
positive .... ASSERTION
preliminary .... PREFACE
sanctimonious .... CANT
unsupported/without proof
.... SAY-SO, ALLEGATION
stater .... COIN
stateroom .... CABIN
statesman ...... SOLON, DIPLOMAT,
                              POLITICIAN
archaic .... STATIST
in Japan .... GENRO
retired ..... ELDER(STATESMAN)
static ...... FIXED, INERT, PASSIVE,
    FEEDBACK, INACTIVE,
    STATIONARY, ATMOSPHERICS
on radio reception
.... STRAY(S)
opposed to .... DYNAMIC,
                              KINETIC
result on TV set .... SNOW
station .... POST, RANK, DEPOT,
    PLACE, ASSIGN, STATUS,
    LOCATION, POSITION,
    TERMINAL, TERMINUS,
    STOP(PING) PLACE
wagon .... AUTO(MOBILE)
stationary .... FIXED, AT REST,
    ROOTED, STATIC, STABILE,
    CONSTANT, IMMOBILE
combining form .... STAT
stationer .... PUBLISHER,
    BOOKSELLER, SHOPKEEPER
stationery .... LINEN, PAPETERIE
item .... PEN, CARD, PAPER,
    PENCIL, ENVELOPE
statistician ...... FIGURER, STATIST

insurance .... ACTUARY
statistics .... DATA
statoscope .... BAROMETER
statuary ...... STATUES, SCULPTOR
piece of .... BUST, TORSO
statue .... IMAGE, EFFIGY,
    CARVING, ACROLITH,
    FIGULINE, FIGURINE,
    SCULPTURE
Aphrodite bestowed life on
    this .... GALATEA
base of ...... PLINTH, PEDESTAL
gigantic .... COLOSSUS
goddess of victory .... NIKE
ledgelike foundation
.... SOCLE
London .... GOG, MAGOG
mold .... (PLASTER)CAST
of _____ .... ZEUS, LIBERTY
Galatea sculptor
.... PYGMALION
Mary .... MADONNA
Sun god Helios
.... COLOSSUS OF RHODES
Sun god Helios sculptor
.... CHARES
Zeus sculptor .... PHEIDIAS
Zeus site .... OLYMPIA
religious .... PIETA
with arms raised in prayer
.... ORANTE
Statue of Liberty poetess
.... LAZARUS
sculptor .... BARTHOLDI
statuesque .... TALL, STATELY,
                              GRACEFUL
dimness .... MONUMENTAL
                              STUPIDITY
woman .... JUNO
statuette .... FIGURINE
award .... EMMY, OSCAR
stature .... RANK, HEIGHT,
                              IMPORTANCE
status .... AGE, RANK, STATE,
    POSITION, STANDING,
    CONDITION
asthmaticus
.... ASTHMA(ATTACK)
epilepticus .... SEIZURE,
                              EPILEPSY
seeker .... SOCIAL CLIMBER
symbol .... MINK, POOL,
    YACHT, DIAMONDS, ROLLS
                              ROYCE
symbol of retiree?
.... ROCKING CHAIR
statute .... ACT, LAW, RULE, EDICT
part of .... TITLE, ARTICLE
staunch .... FIRM, TRUE, LOYAL,
    SOLID, SOUND, STABLE,
    STEADY, FAITHFUL, RELIABLE,

WATERTIGHT

supporter .... LOYALIST

stave ...... BAR, LAG, RUNG, SLAT, STAP, STAFF, STICK, PIERCE, STANZA, VERSES, PUNCTURE

off .... FEND, WARD, AVERT, STALL, HOLD OFF, DELAY, PREVENT

staves, bundle of .... SHOOK

hold .... HOOP

stavesacre .... LARKSPUR

stay .... GUY, HALT, KEEP, LAST, LIVE, PROP, STOP, TACK, WAIT, (A)BIDE, BRACE, CEASE, CHECK, DEFER, DELAY, DWELL, STICK, TARRY, ENDURE, LINGER, REMAIN, RESIDE, SUPPORT, SUSPEND

continue to .... LINGER

longer .... TARRY

out of mischief .... BEHAVE, TOE THE LINE

to the end .... SIT OUT

staying .... ARRESTING

power .... STAMINA, STRENGTH, ENDURANCE

staylace .... A(I)GLET

stays .... CORSET

Ste. See also **Saint** ...... SAINT(E)

stead .... LIEU, SITE, PLACE, SERVICE

steadfast .... FIRM, FIXED, STABLE, CONSTANT, RESOLUTE

steady .... CALM, EVEN, FIRM, FIXED, STAID, SECURE, STABLE, EQUABLE, REGULAR, UNIFORM, CONSTANT, HABITUAL

colloquial .... BEAU, BOY FRIEND, SWEETHEART

opposite of .... JERKY, ADRIFT, FICKLE, ROVING, ASTATIC, ERRATIC, RESTLESS

steak .... CLUB, FLANK, T-BONE, NEW YORK, SIRLOIN, FILET MIGNON, PORTERHOUSE

steal .... DIP, NIM, ROB, CRIB, HOOK, LOOT, PALM, PRIG, SACK, FILCH, MOOCH, PINCH, POACH, BURGLE, FORAGE, PILFER, SNITCH, THIEVE, PURLOIN, ABSTRACT

cattle, etc. .... RUSTLE

colloquial .... CRIB, BARGAIN

ideas, writings .... CRIB, PIRATE, PLAGIARIZE

slang .... LIFT, HEIST, SWIPE, SNITCH

trust money .... EMBEZZLE, PECULATE

stealer .... CROOK, THIEF, ROBBER,

BURGLAR, FILCHER, SHOPLIFTER

compulsive .... KLEPTOMANIAC

literary .... PIRATE, PLAGIARIST, PLAGIARIZER

tricky ...... CONMAN, SWINDLER

who loves crowds .... DIP, PICKPOCKET

stealthy ...... SLY, FELINE, SECRET, SNEAKY, CUNNING, FURTIVE, CLANDESTINE, SURREPTITIOUS

steam .... GAS, BOIL, COOK, FUME, CLEAN, VAPOR

above earth's surface .... FOG, MIST

boiler safety device .... HYDROSTAT

burn with .... SCALD

colloquial ...... FORCE, POWER, ENERGY

engine .... LOCOMOTIVE

give off .... REEK

steamboat stateroom ...... TEXAS

steamer ...... SHIP, LINER, BOILER, LAUNCH, RIVERBOAT, STEAMBOAT, WHALEBACK

Steamer, Stanley

.... AUTOMOBILE

steaming .... BOILING, EXCITED, SEETHING

hot, descriptive of .... PIPING

under high pressure .... AUTOCLAVING

vapor from decomposing matter .... MIASMA, MEPHITIS

steamroll(er) .... RAZE, BULLY, CRUSH, LEVEL, OVERRIDE, OVERWHELM, BULLDOZE(R)

steamship .... LINER, GREYHOUND

abbreviation .... SS

family, noted .... DOLLARS

part of ..... BOW, KEEL, DAVIT, BRIDGE, ENGINE, GUNNEL, RUDDER, BOLLARD, FANTAIL, FUTTOCK, SCUPPER, TRANSOM, LARBOARD, POOPDECK, PORTHOLE, GANGPLANK, PROPELLER, STARBOARD, STOKEHOLD, STEAM PIPE

smokestack of .... FUNNEL

steamy ...... HOT, SEXY, LUSTFUL, PASSIONATE

stearin .... SUET, TALLOW

steatite .... TALC, SOAPSTONE

steed .... MOUNT, CHARGER, PRANCER, STALLION, (STUD)HORSE

steel ...... INURE, METAL, HARDEN, TEMPER, FORTIFY, TOUGHEN

alloy .... INVAR

beam/bar .... HBAR, IBAR, IBEAM, IRAIL, GIRDER

change to .... ACIERATE

covering .... ARMOR

kind of ...... DAMASK, TOLEDO, TEMPERED

making plant .... (RE)FINERY

making process .... DUPLEX, CEMENTATION

oneself for action .... GIRD

poetic .... SWORD, DAGGER

shape .... H-BAR, I-BAR, T-BAR, I-BEAM

with inlaid gold .... DAMASK

steelhead ...... TROUT, SALMONOID

steelyard .... SCALE, BALANCE

Steen, painter .... JAN

steenbok .... ANTELOPE

steep ...... RET, SOP, SOAK, HILLY, IMBUE, LOFTY, SHEER, ABRUPT, IMMERSE, MACERATE, SATURATE, EXCESSIVE, PRECIPITOUS

colloquial .... EXPENSIVE

slope .... CHUTE, SCARP

steeple .... TOWER, BELFRY, FLECHE, MINARET

kind of .... CAMPANILE

part of ..... EPI, SPIRE, BELFRY, FINIAL

steeplebush .... HARDHACK

steeplechase .... HORSERACE

steer .... GUIDE, PILOT, DIRECT, MANAGE, CONTROL

cattle .... YAK, BEEF, COWS, OX(EN), STOT, STIRK, BOVINE, BULL(OCK)

clear of .... SNUB, AVOID

ship .... CONN

slang .... TIP(OFF)

zigzag course .... PLY, YAW

steering gear ...... HELM, WHEEL, RUDDER, TILLER

steersman .... PILOT, WHEELER, HELMSMAN, COX(SWAIN), NAVIGATOR

steeve .... SPAR, STOW, DERRICK

stegomyia .... MOSQUITO

stegosaurus .... DINOSAUR

stein .... (BEER)MUG

Stein, writer .... GERTRUDE

song town ...... ORONO(MAINE)

Steinbeck, author .... JOHN

character .... OKIE

work .... THE GRAPES OF WRATH

steinbok .... ANTELOPE

stele .... LAT, PILLAR, MONUMENT, HEADSTONE

stella .... STAR

stellar .... CHIEF, ASTRAL,

LEADING, RADIANT, STARRING
stellate .... STARRY
stem ...... AXIS, BINE, REIN, STOP,
TUBE, ARISE, CHECK, STALK,
ARREST, SPRING, PEDICEL,
PETIOLE, PEDUNCLE
angle .... AXIL
climbing .... BINE
covering .... OCREA
cylinder .... STELE
fleshy .... TUBER
for grafting .... SLIP
fore part of a ship's
.... CUTWATER
hollow .... CANE
joint .... NODE
leaf's .... FOOTSTALK
main .... TRUNK
of arrow/of spear .... SHAFT
palm .... CAUDEX
plant .... AXIS, CAULIS
raceme's .... R(H)ACHIS
rootlike .... RHIZOME
rudimentary .... CAULICLE
ship's .... BOW, PROW
shoot .... TILLER
trailing .... RUNNER
twining .... BINE
underground ..... CORM, TUBER
stench .... REEK, STINK, F(O)ETOR,
MIASMA, (MAL)ODOR,
MEPHITIS, (ROTTEN)SMELL
Stendhal hero .... SOREL
Stengel, baseball's .... CASEY
steno, combining form .... THIN,
SMALL, NARROW
stenosis .... NARROWING,
STRICTURE
form of .... AORTIC, PYLORIC
stenography .... SHORTHAND
Stentor .... HERALD
stentorian .... LOUD
step .... GAIT, PACE, RANK, RUNG,
WALK, STAGE, STAIR, TREAD,
ACTION, GRADIN, STRIDE,
FOOTBALL, FOOTPRINT
as in course of action
.... MEASURES
by step .... GRADUALLY
dance .... PAS, CHASSE,
ELECTRIC SLIDE
down .... REDUCE, RESIGN,
ABDICATE
fence .... STILE
forward .... VOLUNTEER
giant .... STRIDE
in .... ENTER, MEDIATE,
INTERVENE
in a rustic dance ..... DOUBLE-
TROUBLE
ins ...... SLIPPERS, UNDERPANTS

ladder .... RUNG
lightly .... TRIP
mincingly .... SASHAY
on heavily ..... PLOD, TRAMPLE
on it ...... HIE, HURRY, HASTEN
on the gas .... REV
part of a .... RISER
projecting part .... NOSING
softly .... PAD, TIPTOE
substitute .... RAMP
to success .... RUNG
up ..... INCREASE, ACCELERATE
stepmother, of/like a
.... NOVERCAL
steppe .... PLAIN, WASTELAND
plain like a .... LLANO,
PAMPAS, SAVANNA(H)
stepper .... DANCER
steps, outdoor .... STILE, PERRON
sterculiaceous tree .... KOLA,
CACAO
stere .... CUBIC METER
stereo .... HI-FI, BINAURAL
stereotype .... LINOTYPE
printing plate .... CLICHE
stereotyped .... ALIKE, TRITE,
COMMON, FAMILIAR,
HACKNEYED
sterile .... BARREN, EFFETE,
MULISH, OTIOSE, ASEPTIC,
GERM-FREE, INFERTILE,
UNFRUITFUL
in botany .... ACARPOUS
sterility .... INFERTILITY
sterilization, female
.... LAPAROTOMY,
HYSTERECTOMY
male .... VASECTOMY
means of .... BOILING,
STEAMING, AUTOCLAVING
sterilize .... GELD, SPAY,
CASTRATE, SANITIZE,
EMASCULATE
sterlet .... STURGEON
sterling .... PURE, PENNY, SILVER,
GENUINE, EXCELLENT,
UNALLOYED
stern ...... AFT, DOUR, FIRM, GRIM,
HARD, REAR, HARSH, SEVERE,
STRICT, AUSTERE, RIGOROUS,
FORBIDDING
opposite of .... BOW, PROW,
STEM
section of a ship .... COUNTER,
POOP(DECK)
toward the .... AFT, REAR,
ABAFT
wheeler .... STEAMBOAT
sternum .... BREASTBONE
attachment ...... RIB, CLAVICLE
joint in the .... SYMPHYSIS

part of .... BODY, MANUBRIUM,
XIPHOID PROCESS
site .... CHEST
sternutation .... SNEEZE,
SNEEZING
sternutatory .... ERRHINE
substance .... SNUFF
steroid drug .... NANDROLONE,
STANOZOLOL, OXANDROLONE
drug abuser .... ATHLETE
possible effect of .... ACNE,
EDEMA, IMPOTENCE,
INFERTILITY
protein-building .... ANABOLIC
stertor .... SNORE
stet .... LET IT STAND
Stettin river .... ODER
stevedore .... LADER, NAVVY,
DOCKER, LUMPER, STOWER,
DOCKMAN, (UN)LOADER,
LONGSHOREMAN
Stevens-Johnson syndrome
...... RASH, HIVES, URTICARIA,
ERYTHEMA MULTIFORME
singer .... RISE
Steven's modifier .... EVEN
Stevenson, statesman ...... ADLAI
stew ...... BOIL, DISH, HASH, OLIO,
OLLA, CURRY, BURGOO,
POTPIE, RAGOUT, SIMMER,
GOULASH, HARICOT, POTTAGE,
POTPOURRI, HODGEPODGE
colloquial .... FRET, FUME,
SNIT, SWEAT, WORRY, DITHER,
AGITATION
dish ...... GOULASH, MULLIGAN,
BRUNSWICK, FRICASSEE,
HOTCHPOTCH, BOURGUIGNON
flavor .... CHIVE, CURRY,
ONION, CHERVIL, BAY LEAF
highly seasoned .... RAGOUT,
HARICOT
highly spiced .... OLIO, OLLA
hobo's .... MULLIGAN
Hungarian .... GOULASH
in one's own _____ ...... JUICE
meat .... BEEF, LAMB, PORK,
VEAL
pan ...... SKILLET, DUTCH OVEN
sailor's .... LOBSCOU(R)SE
slang .... TANK
steward .... REEVE, BUTLER,
FACTOR, BAILIFF, MANAGER,
TRUSTEE, MAJOR DOMO,
SENESCHAL, MAITRE D'HOTEL
college/monastery
.... MANCIPLE
stewardess .... HOSTESS,
ATTENDANT
stewardship .... MANAGEMENT
stewed fruit .... FOOL

slang .... DRUNK, PISSED, SOUSED, TANKED
stibium .... ANTIMONY
stich .... LINE, VERSE
stick ...... BAT, ROD, CANE, CLUB, GLUE, POKE, POLE, STAB, WAND, ABIDE, BATON, CLING, PASTE, PRICK, STAFF, ADHERE, CLEAVE, COHERE, CUDGEL, FERULE, IMPALE, PADDLE, PIERCE, THRUST, PUNCTURE
around .... STAY, LINGER
celery .... STALK
colloquial .... PUT, SET, STUMP, BAFFLE, PUZZLE
conductor's/cheerleader's .... BATON
fairy's .... WAND
for leveling grain .... STRICKLE
in-the-mud .... FOGY, IDLER
insect .... EMESA, PHASMID
jab with a .... POKE
jumping .... POGO
match .... LINSTOCK
measuring .... YARD, METER, RULER
metal cap .... FERRULE
out .... JUT, EXTRUDE, PROJECT, PROTRUDE
pointer .... FESCUE
policeman's .... BILLY, TRUNCHEON
primitive/caveman's ...... CLUB
propelling .... POLE
revertible .... BOOMERANG
sharp-pointed .... GOAD
slang .... CHEAT, DEFRAUD, CIGARETTE, OVERCHARGE
steering .... OAR
stirring ..... PADDLE, MUDDLER
throwing .... DINGBAT, BOOMERANG
to one's guns ...... NEVER SAY DIE
together ..... FUSE, JOIN, CLING
up .... ROB
up for .... DEFEND
stick-to-itiveness .... NOSE TO THE GRINDSTONE
sticker ...... BARB, BUR(R), DECAL, KNIFE, LABEL, THORN, PUZZLE
stickler .... MARTINET, QUIBBLER, PERFECTIONIST, DISCIPLINARIAN
of a sort .... PURIST
stickpin's place .... LAPEL, CRAVAT, NECKTIE
sticks, bundle of .... FAGOT
golf ..... CLUBS, IRONS, WOODS
the ...... COUNTRY, BOONDOCKS

sticktight (fruit) .... (COCKLE)BUR
stickum ...... GLUE, GUNK, PASTE, CEMENT, MUCILAGE
stickup .... HEIST, HOLDUP, ROBBERY
sticky .... GLUEY, GOOEY, GUMMY, HUMID, MUGGY, PASTY, TACKY, SWEATY, VISCID, TREACLY, VISCOUS, ADHESIVE, GLUTINOUS
sleuth .... GUMSHOE
substance .... GOO, GUM, GLUE, PASTE, MOLASSES
stiff ...... FIRM, HARD, HIGH, TAUT, WIRY, HARSH, RIGID, TENSE, TIGHT, FORMAL, SEVERE, WOODEN, STILTED
neck .... WRYNECK, TORTICOLLIS
neck cause .... SPASM, WHIPLASH
necked ..... PROUD, STUBBORN, DIFFICULT, OBSTINATE
slang .... HOBO, CORPSE
stiffen .... GIRD, PRIM, STEEL, HARDEN, TAUTEN, BRACE(UP), TOUGHEN
the punch .... LACE
stiffened .... STARCHY
stiffening material .... STAY
stiffly .... WOODENLY, AWKWARDLY
stiffness .... RIGOR, PRIMNESS
stifle ...... CHECK, CHOKE, SCOTCH, PUT DOWN, REPRESS, SILENCE, SMOTHER, SUPPRESS, SUFFOCATE
stigma .... BLOT, MARK, PORE, SCAR, BRAND, STAIN, BLEMISH, (EYE)SPOT
stigmatize .... MARK, SLUR, BRAND, DEFILE, VILIFY
stile .... STEP(S)
stiletto .... DIRK, DAGGER, STYLET
still ...... YET, CALM, EVEN, INERT, PHOTO, QUIET, WHIST, HUSHED, PLACID, SERENE, SILENT, WITHAL, ALEMBIC, DISTILLERY, MOTIONLESS, STATIONARY, NEVERTHELESS
existing .... EXTANT
stillbirth ...... LATE FETAL DEATH
stillborn .... DEAD, ABORTIVE, LIFELESS
Stillenacht composer .... GRUBER
stillness .... HUSH, PEACE, SILENCE, QUIETUDE
Still's disease .... JUVENILE ARTHRITIS
stilt .... BIRD, POST, PLOVER,

(BEAN)POLE, SANDPIPER
stilted .... PRIM, RIGID, STIFF, STUFFY, POMPOUS, PEDANTIC, BOMBASTIC
stiltlike toy .... POGO STICK
stilton .... CHEESE
Stilwell's nickname .... VINEGAR JOE
stimulant .... TONIC, BRACER, COFFEE, EXCITANT
drug .... CAFFEINE, DOXAPRAM, AMPHETAMINE
stimulate .... FAN, SPUR, STIR, URGE, WHET, ELATE, (A)ROUSE, AWAKEN, EXCITE, INCITE, ANIMATE
by electric shock .... GALVANIZE
colloquial .... PEP UP
slang .... REV UP
stimulating .... ROUSING, REFRESHING
stimulus .... BASE, GOAD, SPUR, BASIS, DRIVE, STING, FILLIP, MOTIVE, IMPULSE, CATALYST, ENERGIZER, INCENTIVE, INCITEMENT, INDUCEMENT
tantalizing, deceptive .... CARROT
sting .... BITE, GOAD, PAIN, SMART, WOUND, NETTLE, TINGLE, PRICK(LE), STIMULUS, URTICATE
in zoology .... ACULEUS
ray .... BATFISH, STINGAREE
relief .... CALAMINE
slang .... DUPE, CHEAT, GOUGE
stinger .... BEE, GNAT, WASP, CORAL, GADFLY, HORNET, ANEMONE, SCORPION, STINGRAY, JELLYFISH
plant .... RAMIE, NETTLE
stinging .... NIPPY, CAUSTIC, SCATHING, SMARTING, TINGLING
ant .... KELEP
creature .... ANT, BEE, RAY, WASP, GADFLY, HORNET, SCORPION, JELLYFISH
hairs, plant with .... RAMIE, NETTLE
sensation .... TINGLE, URTICATION
taste .... PUNGENT
stingo ...... ALE, VIM, BEER, ZEST, ENERGY
stingy .... NEAR, CLOSE, TIGHT, MEAGER, SCANTY, SKIMPY, MISERLY, NIGGARDLY, PENURIOUS
stink .... ODOR, REEK, FETOR,

SMELL, STENCH

stinker .... SKUNK, STOAT,
PETREL, POLECAT

stinking/stinky ...... FOUL, RANK,
FETID, FUSTY, GASSY, GOATY,
MUSTY, STALE, PUTRID,
RANCID, SMELLY, MIASMIC,
NOISOME, MEPHITIC,
MALODOROUS, BAD-SMELLING

smut .... BUNT

stinko .... BLOTTO

stint ...... JOB, BOUT, DUTY, TASK,
TURN, CHORE, SHIFT,
RESTRICT, SANDPIPER,
ASSIGNMENT, LIMIT(ATION)

stipe .... STEM, STALK, PETIOLE

stipel .... STIPULE

stipend ...... FEE, WAGE, SALARY,
PENSION, PREBEND,
ALLOWANCE

stipes ...... (EYE)STALK, PEDUNCLE

stipple .... DOT, DAPPLE, MOTTLE,
SPECKLE

stipulate ...... DEMAND, ARRANGE,
PROVIDE, REQUIRE, SPECIFY

stipulation ...... CLAUSE, PROVISO,
AGREEMENT, CONDITION,
PROVISION

stir .... ADO, FUSS, ROIL, TO-DO,
CHURN, ROUST, SHAKE,
(A)ROUSE, (A)WAKEN, EXCITE,
INCITE, TUMULT, AGITATE,
INFLAME, PROVOKE,
MOVE(MENT)

slang .... JAIL, PRISON

slightly .... BUDGE

up .... RILE, ROIL, AROUSE,
FOMENT

stirabout .... PORRIDGE

stirk .... HEIFER, BULLOCK

stirps .... RACE, STOCK, FAMILY

stirring .... BUSY, ACTIVE,
MOVING, ROUSING

stirrup ...... GAMBADO, FOOTREST

bone .... STAPES

cup .... DRINK, TOAST

stitch .... HEM, ACHE, DARN,
MEND, PAIN, SEAM, TACK,
BASTE, CRICK, QUILT,
SEW(UP), FASTEN, SUTURE

bird .... IHI

colloquial .... BIT

line .... SEAM

stitching material .... GUT, CORD,
WIRE, STAPLE, THREAD

stitchwort .... CHICKWEED

stithy ...... ANVIL, FORGE, SMITHY

stoa .... WALK, PORTICO

stoat .... ERMINE

like animal .... MINK, OTTER,
MARTEN, WEASEL

stoccado .... STAB, THRUST

stock .... BUTT, FUND, RACE,
BREED, GOODS, STORE, TRITE,
TRUNK, STIRPS, SUPPLY,
CAPITAL, LINEAGE, PLENISH,
PROVIDE, RHIZOME,
ANCESTRY, ORDINARY,
INVENTORY, REPERTORY,
REPERTOIRE

exchange .... BOURSE

dealer .... BEAR, BULL,
BROKER, JOBBER

member(ship) .... SEAT,
TRADER

speculator .... LAMEDUCK

telegraph device ...... TICKER

trick .... WASH SALE

farm .... STUD, RANCH(O)

high-priced .... BLUE CHIP

in .... ON HAND, AVAILABLE

in trade .... LINE, STAPLE

keep in .... CARRY

laughing .... BUTT, GOAT

kind of .... CAPITAL,
FLOATING, TREASURY,
PREFERRED

market .... CURB, BOURSE,
EXCHANGE

market event .... CRASH, PANIC

market figures .... BEARS

market gamble .... FLYER

market maneuver .... RAID

of inferior .... LOWBRED

of special skills
.... REPERTORY, REPERTOIRE

purebred .... PEDIGREE

replace .... REPLENISH

still .... MOTIONLESS

"strip" .... WALL STREET

take .... COUNT, APPRAISE,
INVENTORY

stockade .... PEN, BOMA, FORT,
ETAPE, CORRAL, BARRIER,
COMPOUND, BARRICADE,
ENCLOSURE

stockbroker .... AGENT

concern of .... BONDS, STOCKS

stockfish .... COD, HADDOCK

stocking ...... HOSE, SOCK, NYLON

stockish .... DULL, STUPID

stockman .... RANCHER

stockpile .... AMASS, CACHE,
HOARD, STORE, SUPPLY,
RESERVE, SURPLUS,
RESERVOIR

stockroom .... STORAGE,
STOREHOUSE

stocky .... DUMPY, PLUMP, SQUAT,
STOUT, CHUNKY, STUBBY,
STURDY, STUBBED, THICKSET

stodgy ...... DULL, BULKY, SHORT,

STOCKY, STOLID, TEDIOUS

stogie .... BOOT, SHOE, CIGAR,
CORONA

stoic .... ASCETIC, PATIENT,
SPARTAN, IMPASSIVE,
UNFEELING

Stoic, first .... ZENO

philosopher .... SENECA,
EPICTETUS

stoke ...... FEED, FIRE, FUEL, POKE,
STIR, TEND

stoker .... POKER, TEASER,
FIREMAN

Stoker, Count Dracula's
creator .... BRAM

Stokowski, conductor
.... LEOPOLD

stola .... PALLA

stole .... BOA, CAPE, SCARF,
ROBBED

stolen goods buyer .... FENCE

money, riches .... FILTHY
LUCRE

property .... LOOT, PELF, SWAG

stolid ...... CALM, DULL, WOODEN,
SLUGGISH, LETHARGIC,
IMPASSIVE, PHLEGMATIC

stolon .... RUNNER, RHIZOME

stoma ...... PORE, MOUTH, ORIFICE

stomach .... SAC, BEAR, CRAW,
CROP, BELLY, DESIRE,
ENDURE, ABDOMEN, CRAVING,
APPETITE, TOLERATE

abscess .... PEPTIC ULCER,
GASTRIC ULCER

animal's .... MAW, CRAW,
OMASUM, PAUNCH

colloquial ..... BELLY, TUMMY,
GIZZARD, CORPORATION

combining form ...... GASTRO

disease .... TUMOR, ULCER,
CANCER

disorder .... BRASH, NAUSEA,
PYROSIS, HEARTBURN

enzyme .... PEPSIN

gas .... FLATUS, FLATULENCE

inflammation .... GASTRITIS

opening .... PYLORUS

opening, surgically produced
.... GASTROSTOMY

part .... ANTRUM, FUNDUS,
LINING, MUSCLE, PYLORIC
SPHINCTER

passage tube to the
.... ESOPHAGUS

pertaining to .... GASTRIC

protruding .... BAYWINDOW

removal, partial/whole
.... GASTRECTOMY

ruminants' .... MAW, TRIPE,
OMASUM, PAUNCH,

PSALTERIUM

secretion .... GASTRIN,
GASTRIC JUICE

slang .... BREADBASKET

stony concretion
.... GASTROLITH

upset .... DYSPEPSIA,
INDIGESTION

wall movement
.... PERISTALSIS

washing out of .... LAVAGE

stomachache .... COLIC, GRIPE(S),
BELLYACHE, TUMMYACHE,
COLLYWOBBLES

reliever ..... ANTACID, ASPIRIN,
MAGNESIA

stomatic .... ORAL

stomatopod .... SQUILLA,
CRUSTACEAN

stomp .... CLUMP, STAMP,
TRAMPLE

stone .... GEM, PIT, PELT, ROCK,
JEWEL, LAPIS, MARBLE,
PEBBLE, PYRENE, DORNICK,
GRANITE

azure-blue .... LAPIS LAZULI

bright green, transparent
.... EMERALD

broke .... PENNILESS, DOWN
AND OUT

cameo .... ONYX

carver .... GRAVER

carved in relief .... CAMEO

cavity, crystal-lined .... GEODE

change into .... PETRIFY

chip .... SPALL, GALLET

chisel .... CELT

clay .... SHALE

clear, deep-red .... RUBY

combining form .... LITE,
LYTE, LITH(O), PETR(O)

crop .... ORPIN, SEDUM

cubic measure for .... PERCH

dark-green .... OLIVINE

dark-green with red spots
.... BLOODSTONE

deep-blue, transparent
.... SAPPHIRE

dress .... NIG, TRIM, SCABBLE

dressing tool .... ADZ(E),
HACKHAMMER

drupe .... NUTLET

engraved on .... LAPIDARY

engraving .... INTAGLIO

excavation site .... QUARRY

fire-starting .... FLINT

flake .... SPALL

flintlike .... HORNSTONE

for pavement
.... COBBLE(STONE)

for throwing .... DINGBAT,

DORNICK

fragments .... BRASH, DEBRIS

fruit .... PIP, PIT, PYRENE,
PUTAMEN

fruit with .... PLUM, APPLE,
DRUPE, OLIVE, PEACH,
CHERRY, APRICOT

green or white .... JADE

greenish-blue .... TURQUOISE

grinding .... MANO

hammer .... MASH

hard .... FLINT, ADAMANT

headed ax .... TOMAHAWK

heap .... CARN(E), SCREE,
CAIRN(E)

hearted .... CRUEL

huge .... MENHIR, BOULDER,
MEGALITH

hurling apparatus .... ONAGER,
CATAPULT, MANGONEL,
TREBUCHET

implement .... MANO, EOLITH

in chemistry .... LAPIS

jar .... CROCK

kidney/gallbladder
.... CALCULUS

kissable .... BLARNEY

lifting device .... LEWIS(SON)

like .... LITHOID(AL)

marker/pillar .... STELE

marker of a grave
.... HEADSTONE

masses .... SARSENS

monument .... CAIRN, STELE,
DOLMEN, MENHIR, CROMLECH

monument with inscription
.... TOMBSTONE

nodule .... GEODE

of a structure, uppermost
.... CAPSTONE

of an arch, central
.... KEYSTONE

of great brilliance
.... DIAMOND

oil .... PETROLEUM

ornamental .... JADE,
SODALITE, TIGER'S EYE

parsley .... HONEWORT

particles .... GRIT

paving .... FLAG, SETT, SLAB,
MACADAM

pertaining to .... LITHIC

pestle .... MULLER

philosopher's .... CARMOT

piece(s) .... SPALL, GALLET,
RUBBLE

pile .... TALUS

precious .... GEM, OPAL, RUBY,
PEARL, DIAMOND, EMERALD,
SAPPHIRE

prefix .... LITHO

red .... RUBY, GARNET, SPINEL,
CARNELIAN

roller .... CARP, DACE, TOTER

roller, eternal .... SISYPHUS

semi-precious .... JADE, ONYX,
AGATE, BERYL, CORAL, TOPAZ,
GARNET, JASPER, SPINEL,
ZIRCON, OLIVINE, PERIDOT,
AMETHYST, SARDONYX,
TURQUOISE, AQUAMARINE,
BLOODSTONE, CHALCEDONY,
CHRYSOLITE, TOURMALINE,
ALEXANDRITE, CHRYSOPRASE,
LAPIS LAZULI

sharpening .... HONE, WHET,
OILSTONE

slab ..... STELA, STELE, TABLET

small .... PEBBLE

spark-producing .... FLINT

square hewn .... ASHLAR,
ASHLER

tablet .... STELE

throwing device .... ONAGER,
CATAPULT, MANGONEL,
SLING(SHOT)

to death .... LAPIDATE

tool .... NEOLITH, PALEOLITH

trim .... NIG, DRESS

turn to .... PETRIFY, LAPIDIFY

unbreakable .... ADAMANT

upright prehistoric .... MENHIR

used in optical equipment
.... TOURMALINE

used to better one's position
.... STEPPING(STONE)

variety of jade .... JADEITE,
NEPHRITE

wall .... FENCE, BRICKWALL

wall-facing .... ASHLAR,
ASHLER

with brilliant play of colors
.... GIRASOL(E), FIRE OPAL

woman turned to .... NIOBE

worker .... MASON

Stone Age human ...... CAVEMAN

Age period .... EOLITHIC,
NEOLITHIC

Age tools .... (N)EOLITH

author .... IRVING

author-director of ''JFK''
.... OLIVER

Chief Justice .... HARLAN

site of Blarney .... CORK
(IRELAND)

stonechat .... BIRD, THRUSH

stonecrop .... PLANT, SEDUM,
ORPIN(E)

stonecutter ...... MASON, CARVER,
ENGRAVER, LAPIDARY,
LAPIDARIST

chisel of .... DROVE

disease of .... SILICOSIS, PNEUMOCONIOSIS
stoned ...... HIGH, DRUNK, ZONKED
Stonehenge, for one ...... CIRCLE
stones, cast .... ATTACK, CONDEMN, CRITICIZE
heap of .... CAIRN, SCREE, TALUS
roadbuilding .... MACADAM
stonewall .... FOIL, EVADE, THWART, FRUSTRATE
Stonewall, general ...... JACKSON
stoneware .... GRES, CERAMIC, POTTERY, CLAYWARE, EARTHENWARE
stonework ...... MASONRY, BRICK-LAYING
stonily .... COLDLY, HARSHLY
stony .... HARD, ROCKY, ROUGH, CALLOUS, PETROUS, PETROSAL, PITILESS
deposit in body ..... CALCULUS
stood .... AROSE, UPROSE
stooge .... DUPE, FOIL, PAWN, TOOL, DUMMY, LACKEY, HECKLER, UNDERLING
Stooges, one of the Three .... MOE, LARRY, CURLY
stook .... SHOCK
stool .... SEAT, PRIVY, STUMP, FOOTREST, PRIE-DIEU, TABO(U)RET
foot .... CRICKET, HASSOCK, OTTOMAN
pigeon .... SPY, LURE, MARK, DECOY, PEACHER, BETRAYER, INFORMER
stoolie, e.g. .... RAT
stoop .... BEND, LOUT, DEIGN, PORCH, STOUP, SWOOP, CROUCH, SUBMIT, VERANDA(H), CONDESCEND
greeting .... WELCOME
stop .... END, CLOG, HALT, WHOA, BELAY, BLOKE, BRAKE, CEASE, CHECK, CLOSE, LET UP, DEFEAT, DESIST, PULL UP, TERMINATE, BLOW THE WHISTLE
course of .... INTERCEPT
flow of blood or tears ...... QUELL, STANCH, STAUNCH
football carrier .... TACKLE
hole .... COVER, PLUG UP
legally .... ESTOP
nautical .... AVAST
overnight .... LAY OVER
progress of .... IMPEDE, STYMIE
resisting .... YIELD, SURRENDER, CAPITULATE

short .... BALK
spread of .... ARREST
talking .... DRY UP, SHUT UP
temporarily .... REST, PAUSE
to, put a .... NIP IN THE BUD
stopcock .... VALVE, FAUCET
stopgap .... EXPEDIENT, MAKESHIFT, SUBSTITUTE
stoppage .... GAP, BREAK, EMBARGO, DISRUPTION, DISCONTINUANCE
legal .... ESTOPPEL
of a death penalty, temporary .... REPRIEVE
activity, authorized .... MORATORIUM
body fluid .... STASIS
breath .... CHOKING, STRANGULATION
debate .... CLOSURE, CLOTURE
execution .... STAY
hostilities .... TRUCE, RESPITE, ARMISTICE
movement/traffic .... BOTTLENECK
progress .... BARRIER, OBSTACLE
right/privilege .... DEBARMENT
operation .... SHUTDOWN
phonetic .... OCCLUSION
stopped diapason .... MELODIA
stopper/stopple .... TAP, BUNG, CORK, PLUG, CAULK, COVER, SHIVE, TAMPON, TAMPION, TOMPION
stopwatch .... TIMER
storage .... STORING, SAFE-KEEPING, WAREHOUSING
computer .... MEMORY
device .... BATTERY
fee/charge .... CELLARAGE, DEMURRAGE
for small savings .... PIGGY BANK
kind of .... DRY, COLD
place .... LOFT, CACHE, HUTCH, VAULT, LOCKER, STOREROOM
below ground level .... CELLAR, BASEMENT
below the roof .... ATTIC, GARRET
place for:
bus/train .... DEPOT
clothes .... CHEST, CLOSET, DRAWER
dishes .... CUPBOARD
fodder .... CRIB
food .... BIN

food, ingredient, utensils .... LARDER, PANTRY
funds, public/private .... TREASURY
grain .... SILO, GRANARY
historical objects .... MUSEUM
long-range ballistic missile .... SILO
merchandise .... WAREHOUSE
personal valuables .... SAFE-DEPOSIT BOX
public records .... ARCHIVE(S)
streetcars/trucks/taxicabs .... BARN
wine/liquor .... CELLAR, BUTTERY
temporary .... DUMP
underground .... PIT, SILO
water .... TANK, CISTERN, RESERVOIR
storax .... BALSAM, STYRENE, GUMRESIN
store .... FUND, HOLD, SAVE, SHOP, AMASS, CACHE, HOARD, STOCK, GARNER, OUTLET, SUPPLY, DEPOSIT, PUT(AWAY), RESERVE, BOUTIQUE, LAY(ASIDE), STOW(AWAY), WAREHOUSE
ammo .... MAG
army .... PX, CANTEEN, COMMISSARY, POST EXCHANGE
away .... STASH
fodder/in a silo .... ENSILE
helper .... CLERK, CHECKER
kind of .... BOOK, DRUG, BAZAAR, GROCERY, SPECIALTY, FIVE-AND-TEN, HEALTH FOODS, SPORTING GOODS
manager .... FLOOR-WALKER
small articles .... NOTIONS
stiff .... MANNEQUIN
storehouse .... BARN, DEPOT, GRANARY, REPERTORY, DEPOSITARY, DEPOSITORY
public .... ETAPE
weapons .... ARMORY, ARSENAL, MAGAZINE
storekeeper .... GROCER, MERCHANT
storeroom .... VAULT, CELLAR, CLOSET, PANTRY, BUTTERY
storied ...... FAMOUS, LEGENDARY
stork .... AYAYA, JABIRU, MARABOU, ADJUTANT
delivery of .... BABY
kin of .... IBIS, HERON, HAMMERHEAD

stork's bill .... GERANIUM
storm .... BLOW, FUME, RACE,
RAGE, RANT, STOUR, ASSAIL,
ATTACK, ASSAULT, BLUSTER,
TEMPEST, RIPSNORTER
accompaniment .... HAIL,
RAIN, SNOW, WIND, FLOOD,
SLEET, THUNDER, LIGHTNING
center .... EYE
certain kind .... NOR'EASTER,
NOR'WESTER, SOU'EASTER,
SOU'WESTER
cloud formation
.... WATERSPOUT
cyclonic .... TYPHOON,
BLIZZARD, HURRICANE
with rotating winds
.... CYCLONE, TORNADO
Storm Country girl .... TESS
stormed about .... RAMPAGED
storming .... IRATE
stormy ...... FOUL, WILD, RAGING,
FURIOUS, VIOLENT,
INCLEMENT, TURBULENT,
TEMPESTUOUS
Storting .... PARLIAMENT
sits in .... OSLO
story .... REDE, TALE, TIER,
FABLE, FLOOR, LEVEL,
RUMOR, GOSSIP, REPORT,
ACCOUNT, MARCHEN,
NARRATION, NARRATIVE
animal .... FABLE
bedtime .... YARN
colloquial .... FIB
complication in a .... NODE,
NODUS
correspondent's ...... DISPATCH
exaggerated .... YARN
exclusive .... BEAT, SCOOP
false .... HOAX, FABLE,
CANARD
heroic .... SAGA
imagined .... FICTION
long .... NOVEL
newspaper ...... ITEM, ARTICLE,
PRESS RELEASE
of past events .... HISTORY
of person's life .... BIOGRAPHY
of person's life written by
oneself
.... AUTOBIOGRAPHY
of some personal happening
.... ANECDOTE
part of .... PASSUS
romantic .... GEST(E)
short .... CONTE, PARABLE
tell a .... SPIN
traditional ...... MYTH, LEGEND
with moral lesson ...... FABLE,
PARABLE, ALLEGORY

storyteller ...... AUTHOR, RECITER,
RACONTEUR, ALLEGORIST,
MUNCHAUSEN, SCHEHERAZADE
colloquial .... LIAR, FIBBER
stoss, opposite of .... ALEE
stound .... ACHE, PAIN, SMART
stoup .... FONT, PAIL, BUCKET,
TANKARD
stour .... STORM, COMBAT,
TURMOIL
stout .... ALE, FAT, BEER, BOCK,
BOLD, BURLY, BRAVE, HUSKY,
OBESE, BRAWNY, PORTER,
PORTLY, ROBUST, STOCKY,
STURDY, THICKSET,
CORPULENT
Stout hero .... NERO(WOLFE)
novelist .... REX
stouthearted .... BOLD, BRAVE,
DAUNTLESS
stove .... ETNA, OVEN, RANGE,
COOKER, HEATER, FURNACE,
CHAUFFER, HOT PLATE,
KITCHENER
stovepipe .... FLUE, SILK(HAT)
stover .... FODDER, CORNSTALKS
stow .... CAN, CRAM, LADE, PACK,
CHUCK, STASH, STORE,
CONCEAL
away .... STASH, STORE,
SECRETE
away again .... RESTASH
cargo .... STEEVE
it away .... EAT
stowage .... LADING, PACKING,
STORAGE, TANKAGE
stowaway .... DEADBEAT, FREE
RIDER
of a sort ..... SQUATTER, GATE-
CRASHER
Stowe, author .... HARRIET
(BEECHER)
book of .... UNCLE TOM'S
CABIN
brother of .... EDWARD, HENRY
(WARD)
character .... ELIZA, TOPSY,
LITTLE EVA, (UNCLE)TOM,
SIMON LEGREE
nickname of .... HATTIE
strabismic .... CROSS-EYED
strabismus .... SQUINT, WALLEYE,
CROSS-EYE
"Strad" .... VIOLIN
straddle .... BYPASS, BESTRIDE
colloquial .... HEDGE
Stradivarius .... VIOLIN
strafe .... RAKE, ATTACK, PEPPER,
RIDDLE, BOMBARD, CHASTISE
straggle ...... DRAG, ROVE, STRAY,
TRAIL, DAWDLE, RAMBLE,

SPRAWL, WANDER, MEANDER
straggler .... ROVER, STRAY,
ROAMER, DRIFTER, RAMBLER,
GADABOUT, WANDERER
straggling ...... ERRANT, SHIFTING
straight .... EVEN, FAIR, NEAT,
PURE, TRUE, ERECT, FRANK,
DIRECT, HONEST, UNBENT,
ALIGNED, UNMIXED,
(UP)RIGHT
as an _____ .... ARROW
away .... DIRECT, AT ONCE,
POINT-BLANK
combining form .... RECT(I)
edge .... LINER, RULER
face .... DEAD-PAN, LONG
FACE, POKER FACE
faced .... GRIM, GRAVE, SOBER,
SEDATE, EARNEST, SERIOUS,
IMPASSIVE
jacket .... CAMISOLE,
RESTRAINT, RESTRAINER
liner .... BEE, RULER
man .... FOIL, STOOGE
man's companion
.... COMEDIAN
out .... CLEAR, DIRECT,
EXPLICIT, OUTRIGHT
passage .... ENFILADE
route .... BEELINE
row .... RANK
up .... VERTICAL
straighten .... ALIGN, UNBEND,
RECTIFY, UNRAVEL
as hair .... UNCURL
as rope strands .... UNLAY
variant .... ALINE
straightforward .... OPEN, BLUNT,
FRANK, CANDID, DIRECT,
HONEST, SINCERE,
FORTHRIGHT
strain .... LINE, PULL, RACE, SIFT,
BREED, EXERT, HEAVE, PRESS,
STOCK, TRACE, EFFORT,
FILTER, REFINE, STREAK,
STRIVE, DESCENT, LINEAGE,
STRETCH, TENSION, FILTRATE
commonly affected by
.... ATHLETE(S)
of muscle fibers ...... TEARING
strained .... TAUT, TENSE,
UPTIGHT, UNFRIENDLY
strainer .... SIEVE, STRUM, TAMIS,
FILTER, SIFTER, COLANDER,
PERCOLATOR, CHEESECLOTH
strains .... AIR, TUNE
strait ...... NECK, TIGHT, CHANNEL,
EURIPUS, ISTHMUS,
NARROW(S), PASSAGE,
WATERWAY

697

between Alaska and USSR .... BERING
between Corsica and Sardinia .... BONIFACIO
between Spain and Morocco .... GIBRALTAR
between Sumatra and Malaysia .... MALACCA
in Argentina .... MAGELLAN
Australia .... BASS
British Columbia .... HECATE, JUAN DE FUCA
China .... TAIWAN
Indonesia .... BANGKA
Iran .... HORMUZ
Ireland .... DAVIS, HUDSON
Italy .... SICILY, OTRANTO, MESSINA
Michigan .... MACKINAC
Newfoundland .... MCLELAN, BELLE ISLE
Northwest Territories ..... HAZEN, NARES, BARROW, BALLANTYNE
Nova Scotia .... CANSO
Papua New Guinea .... TORRES, VITIAZ, DAMPIER, BOUGAINVILLE
Philippines .... LUZON, TANON, TABLAS, BASILAN, MINDORO, SURIGAO
Saudi Arabia .... TIRAN
Solomon Islands .... MANNING
Sri Lanka .... PALK
Tasmania .... BANKS
Turkey .... BOSPORUS
USSR .... TATAR, LA PEROUSE, SANNIKOVA
Virgin Islands .... THE NARROWS
Washington .... HARO, GEORGIA
jacket .... HOGTIE, RESTRAINER
laced .... DOUR, PRIM, STAID, STRICT, FORMAL, PROPER, STRICT, STUFFY, PRUDISH, PRIGGISH
seaport on a .... KERCH
straiten .... LIMIT, HAMPER, ENCLOSE, CONTRACT, DISTRESS
straits .... PLIGHT, POVERTY, DISTRESS, HARDSHIP, DIFFICULTY
financial .... BIND, PINCH, CLUTCH, CRISIS, CRUNCH, EMBARRASSMENT
Straits of Messina rock .... SCYLLA

Settlement, part of .... LUBUAN, PENANG, MALACCA, SINGAPORE
weight .... CHEE, CATTY
strand .... ROPE, BEACH, FIBER, SHORE, GROUND, MAROON, STRING, THREAD, NECKLACE
stranded .... PENNILESS, HIGH AND DRY
strange ...... FEY, ODD, OFF, RARE, UNCO, ALIEN, EERIE, FREMD, NOVEL, OUTRE, QUEER, EXOTIC, QUAINT, FOREIGN, UNCANNY, UNKNOWN, UNUSUAL, PECULIAR, SINGULAR, ECCENTRIC
mysteriously .... WEIRD, UNEARTHLY
very .... BIZARRE, OUTLANDISH
strangely beautiful .... EXOTIC
stranger .... ALIEN, GUEST, ODDER, EMIGRE, NOVICE, NEWCOMER, OUTSIDER, FOREIGNER, OUTLANDER, TRAMONTANE
combining form .... XENO
strangle .... KILL, CHOKE, SCRAG, STIFLE, GARROTE, REPRESS, SMOTHER, SQUEEZE, JUGULATE, SUPPRESS, THROTTLE, CONSTRICT, SUFFOCATE
hold .... DEATH GRIP
strangler .... THUG, BRAVO, GARROTER
strangulate .... CHOKE, GARROTE, SQUEEZE, THROTTLE
strangulation .... STRICTURE, CONSTRICTION
means of .... HANDS, LIGATURE
strangury .... URINATION
cause of .... CYSTITIS, PROSTATITIS
strap .... TAB, TIE, BAND, BELT, LASH, REIN, ROPE, TAPE, LEASH, THONG, THRASH, FASTEN(ER)
falcon's .... JESS
for leading animal .... HALTER
shaped ...... LORATE, LIGULATE
shoulder .... HALTER
waist, hips .... GIRDLE
straphanger .... STANDEE, COMMUTER
strapped .... NEEDY, FLAT-BROKE
strapping .... HARDY, ROBUST, STEELY, FLOGGING, WHIPPING, WELL-BUILT
Strasberg or Sontag ...... SUSAN
strass .... PASTE, (LEAD)GLASS

stratagem ...... PLOY, RUSE, WILE, FEINT, GUILE, TRICK, DEVICE, DESIGN, GAMBIT, SCHEME, TACTIC, TRAPAN, TREPAN, ARTIFICE, CHICANERY, MANEUVER, DECEPTION
strategic position .... VANTAGE
strategy .... PLAN, SCHEME, GIMMICK, TACTICS, ARTIFICE, MANEUVER, (WAR)CRAFT
Stratford's river .... AVON
stratified .... TIERED, LAYERED, LAMINATED
stratum ...... BED, LAYER, LEVEL, LAMELLA
horizontal, in geology .... TABLE
of mineral .... STREAK
soft, crumbly .... MARL
Straus, composer .... OSCAR, OSKAR
work .... THE CHOCOLATE SOLDIER
Strauss, composer .... JOHANN
sobriquet ..... THE WALTZ KING
wife of .... JETTY
work of .... INDIGO, SALOME, DIE FLEDERMAUS, THE BLUE DANUBE
Stravinsky, composer .... IGOR
work .... AGON, FIREBIRD, OEDIPUS REX, PERSEPHONE, PULCINELLA, THE RITE OF SPRING
straw .... CULM, REED, STEM, TUBE, STALK, FODDER, TRIFLE
bale of .... TRUSS
bed .... PALLET
boss .... ASSISTANT
bunch of .... WISP, TRUSS, WHISK
coat .... MINO
colored .... BLOND, FLAXEN
cover around plant ..... MULCH
fine-cut/for fodder .... CHAFF
for pointing .... FESCUE
hat .... PANAMA, SAILOR
in the wind .... OMEN, SIGN, PORTENT
like .... STRAMINEOUS
man ...... DUMMY, JACKSTRAW, NONENTITY, SCARECROW
plaited .... SENNIT
spread .... MULCH
stack .... MOW, RICK
thatching .... HA(U)LM
unsplit for hats .... YEDDA
vote .... POLL
vote man ...... ROPER, GALLUP, HARRIS, POLLSTER
vote objective ...... CONSENSUS

worm .... CADDIS
strawberry bush .... WAHOO
like fruit .... ETAERIO
nevus .... BIRTHMARK
stray .... ERR, LOST, ROAM, ROVE,
RAMBLE, WANDER, DEVIATE,
DIGRESS, MEANDER,
STRAGGLE
animal .... WAIF, MAVERICK
animal's place .... POUND,
PINFOLD
strays .... STATIC
streak .... RUN, BAND, TEAR,
VEIN, FREAK, HURRY, LAYER,
SMEAR, SPELL, STRIA, TRAIT,
MOTTLE, STRAIN, STRIPE
streaked ...... LINEATE, BRINDLED,
STRIATED, STRIGOSE
streaker .... HARE, GREYHOUND
heavenly .... COMET,
LIGHTNING
streaks, full of .... LIN(E)Y,
STRIPY
streaky .... TABBY, UNEVEN,
VARYING
stream .... RUN, BECK, FLOW,
GUSH, RILL, RUSH, BROOK,
CREEK, RIVER, ARROYO,
BOURN(E), OUTLET,
POUR(OUT), RUNNEL,
CURRENT, TORRENT
bed .... RUNWAY, CHANNEL
fence .... WEIR
limestone deposit .... TUFA
little/small .... BECK, RILL,
BAYOU, BROOK, CREEK
of lava .... COULEE
of light .... RAY, BEAM
overflow .... FRESHET
rocky obstruction .... RIFFLE
sound .... PURL, MURMUR
source .... FOUNTAIN-HEAD
swift, violent .... TORRENT
streamer .... FLAG, BANNER,
BURGEE, BUNTING, PENNANT,
HEADLINE, SCAREHEAD
streamlet ...... BECK, RILL, CREEK,
RUNNER, RIVULET,
BROOK(LET)
streamlined .... FAST, TRIM,
SPEEDY, UP-TO-DATE,
EFFICIENT, SIMPLIFIED
Streep, actress .... MERYL
street .... RUE, VIA, WAY, LANE,
ROAD, CALLE, DRIVE,
AVENUE, CAUSEWAY,
BOULEVARD
Arab .... WAIF, GAMIN,
URCHIN, MUDLARK
designating a ..... EASY, MAIN,
ONE-WAY, DEAD-END

ditch .... GUTTER
fight .... (AF)FRAY, RUMBLE
hydrant .... FIREPLUG
market .... CURB
musician ...... ORGAN-GRINDER
musician's employer
.... PADRONE
musician's organ ...... HURDY-
GURDY
narrow .... ALLEY
of flophouses in NYC
.... (THE)BOWERY
of shops .... BAZ(A)AR
of theatrical world in NYC
.... BROADWAY
open at both ends
.... THOROUGHFARE
principal: sl. .... MAIN DRAG,
MAIN STEM
private .... DRIVEWAY
public .... FREEWAY, HIGHWAY,
TURNPIKE, TOLL ROAD,
EXPRESSWAY
short .... COURT
show .... RAREE
sign ..... STOP, YIELD, DETOUR,
ONE-WAY, NO-U-TURN,
SCHOOL ZONE
sound of old .... CLOP
stray .... DOG, ARAB, WAIF,
GAMIN, URCHIN
urchin .... ARAB, WAIF, GAMIN,
MUDLARK, GUTTERSNIPE
W. C. Handy's .... BEALE
with houses both sides
.... ROW
streetcar .... TRAM(CAR),
TROLL(E)Y
cowcatcher .... FENDER
driver .... MOTORMAN
streetwalker .... ARAB, GAMIN,
WHORE, HARLOT, HOOKER,
PEDESTRIAN, PROSTITUTE
strength .... FORCE, MIGHT,
POWER, VIGOR, ENERGY,
FOISON, POTENCY, INFLUENCE,
MAIN(FORCE)
degree of .... INTENSITY
having manly .... VIRILE
mental/physical .... ABILITY,
VITALITY
muscular .... BRAWN, SINEW,
THEWS
of endurance .... STAMINA
of the body .... PHYSIQUE
regain .... RALLY
slang .... GRIT
to resist .... TOUGHNESS
strengthen .... GIRD, PROP,
BRACE, REMAN, STEEL,
HARDEN, FORTIFY, TOUGHEN,

ENERGIZE
as spirits .... LIFT, ENLIVEN
as thread .... MERCERIZE
by adding alcohol ..... NEEDLE
slang .... PEP UP
with more troops
.... REINFORCE
strengthener .... ROBORANT
strenuous ...... ACTIVE, ARDUOUS,
VIGOROUS, EXHAUSTING
strep throat .... SORE THROAT
streptomycin discoverer
.... WAKSMAN
stress .... ACCENT, STRAIN,
TENSION, URGENCY,
EMPHASIS, PRESSURE,
EMPHASIZE
in music .... ARSIS, ACCENT
metrical .... ICTUS
result of continued ..... ULCER
symptom of .... ANXIETY,
DEPRESSION
stretch ...... SPAN, FORCE, RANGE,
REACH, SWEEP, TRACT,
EXPAND, EXTEND, SPREAD,
STRAIN, TAUTEN, EXPANSE
a point .... MAGNIFY,
EXAGGERATE
mark(s) .... STRIA(E)
of water .... RIFFLE
out .... EXPAND, SPRAWL,
LENGTHEN
stretched one's neck .... CRANED
out .... PROLATE, ELONGATED
stretcher .... FRAME, LITTER,
TENTER, CARRIER, CROSSPIECE
sophisticated .... TROLLEY BED
stretching muscle .... TENSOR
strew .... SPREAD, SCATTER,
DISPERSE, SPRINKLE
stria ...... RIDGE, FILLET, GROOVE,
STREAK, STRIPE, STRETCH-
MARK
common site of .... THIGH,
ABDOMEN
striated .... LINY
stricken .... ILL, HURT, BESET,
STRUCK, AFFLICTED
strict .... RIGID, STERN, PRECISE,
ACCURATE, EXACT(ING),
RIGOROUS, STRINGENT,
METICULOUS, PUNCTILIOUS
adherence to law
.... LEGALISM, BY THE BOOK
disciplinarian .... SPARTAN,
MARTINET, STICKLER
stricture .... BLAME, CENSURE,
STENOSIS, CRITICISM
stride .... GAIT, LOPE, PACE, STEP,
MARCH, STRADDLE
cowhand's .... SIDLE

strident .... LOUD, HARSH, SHRILL, GRATING, RAUCOUS

sound .... STRIDOR

strides .... PROGRESS, ADVANCEMENT

stridulate .... CHIRR

strife .... FEUD, CONTEST, DISCORD, DISPUTE, QUARREL, RIVALRY, WAR(FARE), CONFLICT, STRUGGLE, CONTENTION

strigil .... FLUTING

strigose .... HISPID

strike .... DAB, HIT, BEAT, BITE, BLOW, BUMP, FIND, HOOK, LASH, OCCUR, SMITE, THUMP, TOUCH, ATTACK, IGNITE, IMPRESS, WALKOUT, HAUL DOWN

a bargain .... AGREE

back .... REACT, RETALIATE

caller .... UMP

demonstrator, etc. ...... PICKET

dumb .... AMAZE, ASTOUND, CONFOUND, FLABBERGAST

feature .... LOCKOUT

gently .... PAT, TAP

it rich .... SUCCEED, HIT THE JACKPOT

kind of .... SIT-IN, HUNGER, SIT-DOWN, WILDCAT, SYMPATHY, SLOW-DOWN

lightly .... DAB, BUMP

of a sort .... BOYCOTT

off .... ERASE, DELETE, EXPUNGE

out .... FAN, FAIL, DELE, CANCEL, DELETE, EXPUNGE

the Gold's prize .... ROSES

violently .... RIP, BASH

violently against each other .... CRASH, COLLIDE

weapon .... PICKET

with closed fist .... PUNCH

with open palm .... SLAP

with the foot .... KICK, SPURN, TRAMPLE

strikebreaker .... RAT, FINK, GOON, SCAB, BLACKLEG

strikebreakers' leader .... NOBLE

striker .... BAT, HAMMER, MALLET, CLAPPER, HARPOONER

of a sort .... HOLDOUT

striking .... VIVID, ATTRACTIVE, IMPRESSIVE, REMARKABLE

string .... ROW, SET, CORD, HANG, LACE, LINE, ROPE, CHAIN, THREAD, CATGUT, SERIES, THREAD

along .... DUPE, FOOL, HOAX,

JOSH, DECEIVE

in horse racing .... STABLE

of beads ..... ROSARY, STRAND, CHAPLET, NECKLACE

out ...... DRAW, PULL, STRETCH

quartet member .... VIOLA, VIOLONCELLO

section mezzo .... VIOLA

tipped end .... TAG, A(I)GLET

up .... HANG, SCRAG

stringed instrument .... HARP, KOTO, LUTE, LYRE, BANJO, CELLO, REBEC, VIOL(A), CITOLE, GUITAR, ZITHER, CITHARA, CITHER(N), CITTERN, PANDORA, SAMISEN, UKE(LELE), DULCIMER, MANDOLIN, PSALTERY, CLAVICHORD

instrument player ...... LUTIST, CELLIST, BANJOIST, LUTANIST, LUTENIST, STRUMMER, GUITARIST

instrument ridge .... NUT

toy .... TOP, KITE, YOYO

stringency .... RARITY, SCARCITY, SEVERITY

stringent .... STERN, TIGHT, SEVERE, STRICT, EXACTING, DEMANDING

strings attached: colloq.

.... TERM(S), PROVISO, CONDITION

stringy .... LONG, ROPY, WIRY, FIBROUS, THREADY, VISCOUS

strip ...... TAB, BARE, LATH, PEEL, TAPE, SPOIL, SWATH, BATTEN, DENUDE, DIVEST, FASCIA, FLENSE, DISROBE, UNDRESS, DISARRAY, DISMANTLE

from tree trunk .... FLITCH

in a way .... DEPRIVE, DISPOSSESS

landing .... RUNWAY

metal/wood .... LIST, SLAT

of land .... NECK

of leaves .... DEFOLIATE

of silk, velvet, etc. .... RIBBON

skin .... FLAY, EXCORIATE

slang .... SKIN

wool from sheep .... FLEECE

stripe .... BAR, BAND, BELT, KIND, LINE, MARK, SORT, TYPE, FILLET, STREAK, CHEVRON

colored .... STRIA

of color .... LIST

on skin .... WALE, WELT, WHEAL, STRETCH-MARK

on the sleeve, as of military or police uniform

.... CHEVRON

service: sl. .... HASH MARK

striped .... STRIPY, ZONATE(D), STREAKED, STRIATE(D)

animal .... BONGO, ZEBRA

cloth .... MADRAS

lengthwise .... VITTATE

squirrel .... CHIPMUNK

stripling .... BOY, KID, LAD, SPRIG, YOUTH, SHAVER

stripped .... NEEDY, DENUDED, FLEECED, SHORN(OF), DEPRIVED, DIVESTED

stripteaser .... STRIPPER, ECDYSIAST, (SALLY)RAND

covering for .... FAN, G-STRING

strive ...... TRY, VIE, COPE, EXERT, FIGHT, LABOR, STRAIN, CONTEND, ENDEAVOR, STRUGGLE

ambitiously .... SEEK, ASPIRE

strobil(e) .... CONE

stroke .... FIT, PET, PAT, BEAT, BLOW, BOLT, MARK, SHOT, ICTUS, THROB, CARESS, FONDLE, STRIPE, SEIZURE, APOPLEXY, CONVULSION

brilliant ...... ACE, COUP, FEAT, EXPLOIT

cutting .... CHOP, SLICE

finishing .... COUP DE GRACE

indirect/oblique .... BRICOLE

lucky .... COUP, FLUKE

of luck .... WINDFALL

on hand's palm .... PANDY

tender .... CARESS

with a whip ...... WELT, STRIPE

stroll .... WALK, RAMBLE, WANDER, SAUNTER, PROMENADE

stroller .... ROVER, ROAMER, WALKER, DRIFTER, VAGRANT, CARRIAGE

occupant .... TOT, BABY

Stromboli ...... ISLAND, VOLCANO

strong .... HALE, FIRM, BURLY, HARDY, HUSKY, LUSTY, STOUT, TOUGH, ROBUST, SINEWY, STURDY, VIRILE, HEALTHY, INTENSE, VIOLENT, ATHLETIC, FORCEFUL, POWERFUL, PUISSANT, VIGOROUS

arm .... BULLY, COERCE, INTIMIDATE

arm man ..... GOON, BOUNCER, GANGSTER

articulation .... FORTIS

as an ox .... HUSKY

attachment .... ADHESION

current .... RIPTIDE, UNDERTOW

desire .... HUNGER, THIRST

drink .... LIQUOR, SPIRITS

feeling .... FIRE, HATRED,
PASSION

giant .... ANTAEUS, GOLIATH

man .... ATLAS, TITAN,
SAMSON, DICTATOR, HERCULES

man: colloq. .... HE-MAN

masculine woman .... AMAZON

muscled ..... THEWY, BRAWNY,
HERCULEAN

odor .... REEK

passion .... FLAME

point .... FORTE, TALENT

scented .... OLID

smelling ...... ACRID, PIQUANT,
PUNGENT

yearning .... ACHE

strongbox .... SAFE, CHEST,
VAULT, COFFER

slang .... PETE

stronghold .... KEEP, AERIE,
CASTLE, REFUGE, BULWARK,
CITADEL, REDOUBT, FASTNESS,
FORT(RESS)

strongroom .... VAULT

strongyl(e) .... ROUNDWORM

strontium sulfite .... CELESTITE

strop .... STRAP, SHARPEN

strophe .... STANZA

strophulus .... MILIARIA

struck .... SMIT, SMOKE,
SHUTDOWN

paydirt .... MINED

structural .... TECTONIC

beam .... GIRDER

order .... TEXTURE

structure .... MAKEUP, ANATOMY,
EDIFICE, BUILDING

basic .... CADRE

containing Buddha relics
.... DAGOBA

defensive .... FORT

enclosed .... CAGE

strudel .... PASTRY

struggle .... TRY, TOIL, FIGHT,
LABOR, BATTLE, SQUIRM,
STRAIN, STRIFE, STRIVE,
TUSSLE, WRITHE, CONTEST,
WRESTLE, CONFLICT,
EXERTION

strum .... TIRL, PLUCK, THRUM,
FINGER

struma .... GOITER, SCROFULA

strummer ...... LUTIST, GUITARIST

strumpet .... HARLOT

strut .... GAIT, SPUR, BRACE,
STALK, SASHAY, SWAGGER

struthious bird .... EMU, RHEA,
OSTRICH, SPARROW

struts .... CABANE, SUPPORT

strutter .... PEACOCK

strychnine source .... NUX
VOMICA

tropical plant .... STRYCHNOS

stub .... END, BUTT, STUMP,
UPROOT, RECEIPT, STUBBLE

stubble .... BEARD, STALKS,
STUMPS, BRISTLES, REMNANTS

stubborn .... TOUGH, DOGGED,
MULISH, ORNERY, DIEHARD,
FROWARD, WILLFUL,
OBDURATE, OBSTINATE,
HARDHEADED

animal ..... ASS, MULE, BURRO,
DONKEY

hair tuft .... COWLICK

individual .... PIGHEAD,
STICKLER

ones .... MISSOURI MULES

stubbornly disagreeable
.... CONTRARY

disobedient .... UNYIELDING

refusing to go on .... BALKY

stubbornness .... HARDNESS,
TENACITY, WILLPOWER,
PERSISTENCE, PERTINACITY

stubby .... STOCKY, BRISTLY

stuckup .... VAIN, ALOOF, MIRED,
PROUD, SNOOTY, UPPISH,
UPPITY, HAUGHTY,
ARROGANT, SNOBBISH, HIGH-
NOSED

stud .... DOT, PIN, PEG, BOSS,
ADORN, BUTTON, SUPPORT,
NAILHEAD, PROJECTION

horse .... BREEDER, STALLION

shoe .... HOBNAIL

studded .... SPANGLY, TEEMING,
SPANGLED, BEJEWELED

student .... COED, PUPIL,
LEARNER, SCHOLAR, TRAINEE,
DISCIPLE, COLLEGIAN,
SCHOOLBOY, SCHOOLGIRL

Annapolis .... MIDSHIPMAN

bane of .... TEST

class exercise of
.... RECITATION

failing .... FLUNKEE

first year .... PLEBE, FRESHMAN

former .... DROPOUT

fourth year .... SENIOR

group .... CLASS, SEMINAR

high school: sl. .... TEENER

in charge .... MONITOR

initiate .... HAZE

international law .... PUBLICIST

military school .... CADET

of words .... LEXICOLOGIST

population .... ENROLLMENT

second year .... SOPHOMORE

third year .... JUNIOR

university .... COED,
VARSITARIAN

West Point .... CADET

wise .... SCHOLAR, THINKER

students' bugaboo .... EXAM

job schedule .... PART-TIME

scrimmage .... RUSH

second chance .... RETEST

studied .... ADVISED, CAREFUL,
MEDITATED, DELIBERATE(D)

studies .... LEARNING, EDUCATION,
SCHOOLING

studio .... SALON, ATELIER,
WORKSHOP

studious .... BOOKISH, DILIGENT

study .... CON, DEN, READ, ROOM,
ESSAY, ETUDE, WEIGH,
PERUSE, PONDER, EXAMINE,
CONSIDER, MEMORIZE,
PORE(OVER), RESEARCH,
SCRUTINIZE

assignment .... LESSON

by candlelight ..... LUCUBRATE

colloquial .... DIG, GRIND

frequently/repeatedly
.... DRILL, PRACTICE

group .... CLASS, SEMINAR

hard .... BONE, CRAM

intensely .... FOCUS,
CONCENTRATE

layout of .... CASE

musical .... ETUDE

of cells .... CYTOLOGY

creative processes
.... SYNECTICS

drugs and effects
.... PHARMACOLOGY

tissues .... HISTOLOGY

values .... EXIOLOGY

the Bible .... ISAGOGICS

over again .... REVIEW

private .... DEN, SANCTUM

product of .... ESSAY, THESIS

superficially .... SMATTER

up ..... BONE, CRAM, BRUSH UP

with .... TRAIN

stuff .... JAM, PAD, WAD, CRAM,
FILL, JUNK, PACK, PLUG,
SATE, THINGS, ESSENCE,
OVEREAT, SATIATE,
MATERIAL, SUBSTANCE

oneself: sl. .... PIG OUT

slang .... WHAT IT TAKES

the stomach .... GORGE,
OVEREAT

stuffed .... FULL, BLOCKED,
CRAMMED, REPLETE

stuffing .... WAD, KAPOK, COTTON,
FILLING, CONTENTS, DRESSING

stuffy .... DULL, PRIM, CLOSE,
MUSTY, STIFF, AIRLESS,

STRAIT-LACED

nose .... CONGESTION

Stuka .... (DIVE)BOMBER

stulm .... ADIT

stum .... MUST, GRAPE-JUICE

stumble .... ERR, SLIP, TRIP, HOBBLE, BLUNDER, FLOUNDER

upon .... FIND, DISCOVER

stumblebum .... MUFFER, BUTTERFINGERS

stumbling block .... SNAG, HURDLE, DRAWBACK, OBSTACLE, HINDRANCE

stump ...... END, LOP, BUTT, FOIL, STUB, TREAD, BAFFLE, PULPIT, PUZZLE, NONPLUS, PERPLEX, REMNANT, STUBBLE, TRAMPLE

colloquial .... ELECTIONEER

stumper ...... PUZZLE, CANDIDATE, CAMPAIGNER

stumps: sl. .... LEGS

stumpy .... STUBBY, SQUATTY

stun .... DAZE, FLOOR, SHOCK, BENUMB, DEADEN, ASTOUND, STARTLE, STUPEFY

stunning .... NIFTY, CUTESY, LOVELY, CUTESIE, DAZZLING, STRIKING, ATTRACTIVE, REMARKABLE, DEVASTATING

stunt .... FEAT, CHECK, DWARF, TRICK, RETARD

flying tour .... BARNSTORM

stunted tree .... SCRAG, SCRUB, BONSAI

stuntman .... ACROBAT, DAREDEVIL

or substitute .... STAND-IN

stupa .... MOUND, TOWER, SHRINE

stupe .... COMPRESS

stupefacient .... NARCOTIC

stupefy .... DAZE, DOPE, PALL, STUN, AMAZE, BESOT, DEADEN, ASTOUND, ASTONISH, BEWILDER, NARCOTIZE, OBFUSCATE

stupendous .... VAST, IMMENSE, COLOSSAL, ENORMOUS, OVERWHELMING

stupid .... DULL, DUMB, BANAL, CRASS, DENSE, DOPEY, INANE, INEPT, SILLY, ABSURD, ASININE, FOOLISH, TEDIOUS, TOMFOOL, TIRESOME, INSIPIENT

blunder .... BONER

from overdrinking .... SOTTISH

person .... ASS, CLOD, COOT, DOLT, LOON, DUMMY, DUNCE, GOOSE, IDIOT, LOOBY, MORON, NINNY, NITWIT, FATHEAD, DUMBBELL, BLOCKHEAD,

LAMEBRAIN, NINCOMPOOP

stupor .... COMA, DAZE, SOPOR, APATHY, TORPOR, TRANCE, LETHARGY, NARCOSIS, OSCITANCY

combining form .... NARCO

in a .... DOPEY

"Stupor Mundi" .... WORLD'S WONDER

to his followers .... FREDERICK II

sturdy .... GID, FIRM, HARDY, HUSKY, STOUT, ROBUST, STRONG, DURABLE, STAGGERS

sturgeon .... BELUGA, GANOID, HAUSEN, STERLET, SHOVELHEAD

eggs .... ROE

eggs relish .... CAVIAR(E)

Sturm und _____ .... DRANG

stutter .... FALTER, STAMMER, HESITATE

Stutz competitor .... REO

sty .... HAW, PEN, BOIL, SHED, STYE, HOVEL, PIGPEN, PIGSTY

Stygian .... DARK, GLOOMY, HELLISH, INFERNAL

style .... FAD, TON, WAY, CALL, CHIC, FORM, MAKE, MODE, NAME, RAGE, BRAND, GENRE, HABIT, VOGUE, DESIGN, MANNER, METHOD, NEEDLE, STYLUS, ENTITLE, FASHION, POINTER, VARIETY, TECHNIQUE

architectural .... ROMAN, GOTHIC, ROCOCO, BAROQUE, SPANISH, BYZANTINE, ROMANESQUE, RENAISSANCE

artistic .... GUSTO

bombastic .... TUMID

decorative .... ART DECO

dress .... COSTUME

furniture .... EMPIRE, RUSTIC, ARCADIAN, FRENCH-PROVINCIAL

genderless .... UNISEX

literary .... ATTIC, ROCOCO, CICERONIAN, SURREALISM

of abstract painting .... OP ART

out of .... DATED, PASSE

painting .... GENRE, CUBISM, DADAISM, FAUVISM, ABSTRACT

type .... DORIC, IONIC, ROMAN, FUTURA, GOTHIC, ITALIC, SCRIPT, CURSIVE, GROTESQUE

styled .... NAMED, CALLED, YCLEPT

stylet .... PROBE, DAGGER, LANCET, STILETTO

surgical .... PROBE, TROCAR

stylish .... CHIC, TONY, NOBBY, NIFTY, SMART, DRESSY, JAUNTY, MODISH, TRENDY, A LA MODE, ELEGANT, VOGUISH, FASHIONABLE

dresser .... FOP, DUDE, TOFF, DANDY, SPARK, SWELL, SOCIALITE, (BEAU)BRUMMEL, TRENDSETTER, CLOTHESHORSE

ostentatiously .... SWANK(Y)

stylist ...... DESIGNER, MANNERIST

stylite .... ASCETIC

stylized flower .... LIS

stylograph .... PEN

stylus .... PEN, NEEDLE, SCRIBER

stymie/stymy .... BALK, FOIL, BLOCK, BAFFLE, HINDER, IMPEDE, THWART, OBSTRUCT

colloquial .... FLOOR

styptic .... ALUM, AMADOU, ASTRINGENT

action of .... STYPSIS

substance .... ALUM

Styx .... LETHE, RIVER

ferryman of .... CHARON

suave .... OILY, AULIC, BLAND, SOAPY, POLITE, SMOOTH, URBANE, COURTLY, GRACIOUS, POLISHED, COURTEOUS

sub .... BELOW, UNDER, SUBMARINE, SUBSTITUTE

rosa ..... COVERTLY, SECRETLY, PRIVATELY

subaltern .... AIDE, JUNIOR, UNDERLING, SUBORDINATE

subalternate .... SUCCESSIVE

subaqueous .... UNDERWATER

subatomic ...... MINUTE, INVISIBLE

subclavian steal syndrome .... DIZZINESS, DOUBLE VISION

subconscious ...... ID, SUBLIMINAL

mind .... ANIMA, PSYCHE

psychic energy .... LIBIDO

subcontinent .... INDIA, NEW GUINEA

subcontract .... SUBLET, SUBLEASE

subdivide ...... DISSECT, SPLIT UP, TRANSECT, PARCEL OUT

subdue ...... CALM, TAME, QUELL, SOBER, MASTER, SOFTEN, CONQUER, CONTROL, REPRESS, HOLD BACK, OVERCOME, RESTRAIN, VANQUISH, OVERPOWER, SUBJUGATE

by reverence .... OVERAWE

subdued .... DOWNED

subereous ...... CORKY, CORKLIKE

subgum dish .... CHOW MEIN

subject .... NOUN, TEXT, BASIS,
SLAVE, THEMA, THEME,
TOPIC, MOTIVE, SERVANT,
OCCASION, SUBJUGATE,
SUBSTANCE
all courses, collectively, in a
particular
.... CURRICULUM
change to another
.... METASTASIS
main .... MOTIF
Markham's .... HOER
matter .... CASE, GIST, ISSUE,
TOPIC
of a famed 1897 editorial
.... SANTA
a musical composition
.... THEME
a nation/state .... CITIZEN
a sentence
.... NOUN(PHRASE)
an Aesop fable
.... SOURGRAPES
an essay, lecture, sermon,
etc. .... THEME
to an action/ radiation
.... EXPOSE
another's control
.... TRIBUTARY
defects .... FAULTY
depression .... SAD, GLUM,
MOODY, SULLEN
difficult circumstances
.... REDUCE
discussion .... MOOT,
DEBATABLE
dispute .... QUESTIONABLE
horseplay .... HAZE
obligation .... MORTGAGE
possibility of something
unpleasant .... LIABLE
reversal .... INVERTIBLE
severe questioning .... GRILL
something uncertain
.... CONTINGENT
taxation .... DUTIABLE,
ASSESSABLE
third degree .... SWEAT
under the feudal system
.... LIEGE, VASSAL
subjection .... YOKE, THRALL
subjective ...... IN-GOING, SELFISH,
INTERNAL, PERSONAL
subjoin ...... ADD, ANNEX, APPEND
subjugate .... TAME, SUBDUE,
CONQUER, ENSLAVE,
VANQUISH, OVERTHROW
subjugation .... BONDAGE,
CONQUEST
subleased .... RELET
sublimate .... PURIFY, REFINE

sublime .... HIGH, GRAND, LOFTY,
NOBLE, DIVINE, EXALTED,
STATELY, GLORIOUS,
MAJESTIC
submachine gun ...... THOMPSON
submarine .... TUB, U-BOAT,
U-BOOT, SUBMERSIBLE,
TORPEDO-BOAT
chaser .... CORVET(TE)
colloquial .... SUB
device against .... PARAVANE
"eye" of .... PERISCOPE
locator .... SONAR
nuclear .... GATO
slang .... PIGBOAT
submaxilla .... JAW(BONE)
submerge/submerse .... DIP,
DIVE, HIDE, SINK, SOAK,
DROWN, SWAMP, WHELM,
DELUGE, DRENCH, ENGULF,
PLUNGE, IMMERSE, INUNDATE
submerged continent
.... ATLANTIS
submersible .... U-BOAT, U-BOOT,
SUBMARINE
submission .... CESSION,
PATIENCE, OBEDIENCE,
SURRENDER, COMPLIANCE,
RESIGNATION
act of/sign of .... BOW, VAIL,
KNEEL, CURTSY, KOWTOW,
SALAAM
submissive .... MEEK, TAME,
LOWLY, DOCILE, DUTIFUL,
PASSIVE, OBEDIENT, YIELDING,
PROSTRATE
submit .... BOW, BEND, CEDE,
OBEY, REFER, STATE, STOOP,
YIELD, ACCEDE, COMPLY,
GIVE IN, RESIGN, PROPOSE,
RETREAT, SUCCUMB,
SURRENDER
subordinate .... AIDE, LOWER,
UNDER, INFERIOR, ASSISTANT,
DEPENDENT, SECONDARY
an unquestioning
.... MYRMIDON
suborn .... BRIBE, CORRUPT,
PERJURE
subpoena .... WRIT, ORDER,
SUMMONS, CITATION
subrogate .... SUBSTITUTE
subscribe .... AID, ABET, BACK,
SIGN, AGREE, PLEDGE,
CONSENT, ENDORSE, SUPPORT
subscription .... DONATION,
ENDORSEMENT
subsequent ...... LATER, ENSUING,
FOLLOWING
to .... AFTER, BEYOND
subsequently .... ANON, LATER,

AFTERWARDS, THEREAFTER
subservience .... SERVILITY
subservient ...... ABJECT, SERVILE,
OBEISANT
subside .... EBB, FALL, SINK,
WANE, ABATE, LOWER,
LESSEN, SETTLE
subsidiary .... BRANCH,
ANCILLARY, AUXILIARY,
SECONDARY, SUCCURSAL,
TRIBUTARY, PENSIONARY
subsidize .... AID, BACK, FINANCE,
SPONSOR, UNDERWRITE
subsidy .... AID, GRANT, BACKING,
FUNDING, PENSION, SUPPORT,
SUBVENTION
subsist ...... BE, FARE, FEED, LIVE,
ABIDE, EXIST, CONTINUE
subsistence ...... BEING, (UP)KEEP,
EXISTENCE, PROVISION,
LIVELIHOOD
substance ...... BODY, GIST, MEAT,
PITH, STUFF, ENTITY, MATTER,
WEALTH, ESSENCE, MEANING,
PURPORT, REALITY, MATERIAL
drying .... DESSICANT
recording-tape .... MYLAR
resinous .... LAC
sticky .... GOO
substances, one of the four
"natural" .... AIR, FIRE,
EARTH, WATER
substandard .... POOR, BELOW
PAR, INFERIOR
substantial .... REAL, AMPLE,
SOLID, SOUND, MASSIVE
substantially .... BASICALLY,
ESSENTIALLY
substantiate .... PROVE, EMBODY,
VERIFY, BEAR OUT, CONFIRM
substantiation .... PROOF,
EVIDENCE
substantive .... NOUN, BASIC,
SOLID, ACTUAL, CONCRETE
substitute .... VICE, PROXY,
DEPUTY, FILL-IN, REPLACE,
STAND-IN, EXCHANGE,
SUPPLANT, ALTERNATE,
SUBROGATE
closely resembling another
.... RINGER
empowered .... PROXY
food .... ERSATZ
for .... PINCHHIT
for a name .... DINGUS
for actor/actress
.... UNDERSTUDY
for the real thing ...... DUMMY
give up for a .... EXCHANGE
person for father or mother
.... SURROGATE

703

pitcher .... RELIEF
slang .... PATSY, DOUBLE
standing by as a ...... BACK-UP
temporary .... STOPGAP,
MAKESHIFT
substitution .... METONYMY,
REPLACEMENT
of obligation .... NOVATION
subterfuge .... RUSE, BLIND,
TRICK, DEVICE, EVASION,
PRETEXT, ARTIFICE, PRETENSE,
DECEPTION
subterranean .... HIDDEN,
NETHER, SECRET, INFERNAL,
UNDERGROUND
subtile .... KEEN, RARE, THIN,
DAINTY, SUBTLE, TENUOUS
subtitle .... SUBHEAD(ING)
subtle .... SLY, DEFT, KEEN, NICE,
RARE, THIN, WILY, ACUTE,
DAINTY, ARTFUL, CLEVER,
CRAFTY, CUNNING, DEVIOUS,
FRAGILE, REFINED, SUBTILE,
DELICATE, FINESPUN,
(SUPER)FINE
emanation .... AURA,
ATMOSPHERE
variation .... SHADE, NUANCE
subtlety .... ART, CRAFT, GUILE,
ACUMEN, NICETY, FINESSE,
QUILLET, DELICACY
subtract .... DEDUCT, LESSEN,
REMOVE, DETRACT, TAKE
AWAY
suburb(s) .... BURG, TOWN,
BARRIO, VILLAGE, ENVIRONS,
FAUBOURG, PURLIEU(S),
OUTSKIRTS
suburban residence .... VILLA
society .... VILLADOM
sward .... LAWN
subvention .... AID, GRANT,
RELIEF, SUBSIDY
subversion .... MUTINY,
REBELLION
subversive .... RED, REBEL,
RADICAL, MUTINEER,
REVOLTER, DISSIDENT
subvert .... RUIN, REVOLT, UP-
END, DEFEAT, CORRUPT,
OVERTHROW, UNDERMINE
subway .... TUBE, METRO,
TUNNEL, RAILWAY,
UNDERGROUND
entrance .... COVER, KIOSK,
TURNSTILE
fare .... TOKEN
rider, sometimes ..... STANDEE
stairway .... ESCALATOR
succeed ...... WIN, ENSUE, ARRIVE,
FOLLOW, THRIVE, ACHIEVE,

ADVANCE, INHERIT, PREVAIL,
PROSPER, REPLACE, FLOURISH,
SUPPLANT, SUPERSEDE,
ACCOMPLISH
colloquial .... CLICK
succeeding .... NEXT,
SEQUENT(IAL)
success .... TRIUMPH, VICTORY,
CONQUEST, PROSPERITY,
BREAKTHROUGH
colloquial .... (SMASH)HIT
easy .... PICNIC, RUNAWAY
great .... BEST SELLER
overwhelming ...... LANDSLIDE
sign of .... RANK, RICHES,
WEALTH
sure .... WINNER, NATURAL
successful .... ON TOP, DOMINANT,
UNBEATEN, EFFECTIVE,
FORTUNATE, OUT IN FRONT,
PROSPEROUS, VICTORIOUS
person .... HERO, COMER,
NABOB, VICTOR, WINNER,
CHAMP(ION), CONQUEROR
successfully reach one's ends
.... ARRIVE, ACHIEVE,
COMPASS, ACCOMPLISH
succession ...... SERIES, SEQUENCE
of rulers .... DYNASTY,
HERITAGE
successive .... LINEAL,
CONSECUTIVE
successively .... SERIALLY
successor .... HERES, HEIR(ESS),
FOLLOWER, (IN)HERITOR,
REPLACEMENT
Babist's .... BAHAI
to Caligula .... CLAUDIUS
Claudius .... NERO
David .... SOLOMON
Genghis Khan .... KUBLAI
KHAN, UGUDAI KHAN
Julius Caesar .... AUGUSTUS,
OCTAVIAN
Philip II .... ALEXANDER
(THE GREAT)
Queen Hatshepsut
.... THUTMOSE III
Saul .... DAVID
Solomon .... REHOBOAM
succinct .... BRIEF, CRISP, MEATY,
PITHY, SHORT, TERSE,
CONCISE, LACONIC
succor .... AID, HELP, SERVE,
RELIEF, COMFORT,
ASSIST(ANCE)
succory .... CHICORY
succubus .... INCUBUS,
DEMON(ESS), CACODEMON
succulent .... JUICY, MOIST, TASTY
plant .... ALOE

succumb .... DIE, FALL, YIELD,
EXPIRE, GIVE IN, SUBMIT,
SURRENDER
succursal .... AUXILIARY,
SUBSIDIARY
succus .... JUICE
succuss .... SHAKE(UP)
such .... SIC, LIKE
suck ...... SIP, DRAW, LURE, PULL,
BLEED, DRAIN, ABSORB,
GUZZLE, INHALE, EXTRACT
sucker .... BABY, DUPE, GULL,
PIPE, LEECH, PATSY, SHOOT,
SPROUT, LOLLIPOP, PUSHOVER
suck(er)fish .... REMORA
suckers, having/producing
.... SURCULOSE
suckle ...... REAR, NURSE, FOSTER,
LACTATE, NOURISH, NURTURE,
BREAST-FEED
suckler .... CHILD, NURSE,
MAMMAL, SUCKLING
suckling .... BABY, NEONATE,
TODDLER, NURSLING,
WEANLING
sucrose ...... SUGAR, SACCHAROSE
suction ...... SUCKING, SIPHONAGE
device .... REED, LEECH,
STRAW
Sudan cape .... KASAR, ABU DARA
capital .... KHARTOUM
chief of state .... AZHARI
city/town .... WAU, KODOK,
KOSTI, NYALA, ATBARA,
RUMBEK, DAMAZIN, EL OBEID,
GEDAREF, KASSALA, MALAKAL,
OMDURMAN
desert .... LIBYAN, NUBIAN,
SAHARA
lake .... NUBIA
language .... BEJA, NUER,
DINKA, ARABIC, NUBIAN
monetary unit .... POUND
mountain .... KINYETI, JEBEL
ODA, JEBEL MARRA
prime minister .... SADIG,
KHALIL, MAHGOUB
province .... DARFUR,
KHARTOUM, KORDOFAN
region .... DAR HAMID, EL
GEZIRA
river .... JUR, SUE, ADDA, NILE,
AKOBO, PIBOR, SETIT, ATBARA,
BARAKA, DINDER
swamp .... SUDD
Sudanese .... FULAH, MOSSI,
NILOT, HAUSSA
antelope .... OTEROP
inhabitant .... NILOTE
medicine man .... MUMBO
JUMBO

natives, of the .... NILOTIC
sultanate .... WADAI
Sudanic language .... TOSHI,
    YORUBA, MANDINGO
sudarium/sudary ...... VERONICA,
    HANDKERCHIEF
sudden ...... RASH, HASTY, QUICK,
    ABRUPT, PRECIPITATE
attack .... SORTIE
change/twist .... QUIRK
feeling of longing .... PANG
outpouring .... SPATE
spell of activity .... SPASM
thrust .... LUNGE
sudor .... SWEAT, PERSPIRATION
sudorific .... CLAMMY, SWEATY,
    HIDROTIC, PERSPIRY
sud(s) .... BEER, FOAM, FROTH,
    SPUME, LATHER, BUBBLES
sudsy .... FOAMY, SOAPY, BUBBLY,
    FROTHY
in a way .... ALEY
sue .... WOO, COURT, PLEAD,
    APPEAL, SOLICIT, LITIGATE,
    PETITION, BRING SUIT,
    PROSECUTE
suede .... LEATHER
source .... KID, CALF
suer .... SUITOR, LITIGANT,
    PLAINTIFF
suet .... FAT, TALLOW
Suez Canal builder ...... LESSEPS
suffer ...... AIL, LET, ACHE, BEAR,
    DREE, ALLOW, ENDURE,
    PERMIT, SUSTAIN, UNDERGO,
    TOLERATE, EXPERIENCE
punishment .... FACE THE
    MUSIC
sufferable .... BEARABLE
sufferance .... PATIENCE,
    ENDURANCE, TOLERATION
sufferer .... PREY, MARTYR,
    VICTIM, PATIENT, INVALID
suffering .... PAIN, DOLOR,
    THROES, DISTRESS
as of hopelessness
    .... DESPAIR
as of pressure .... STRESS
as through great loss
    .... SHOCK
intense .... GRIEF, SORROW
martyr's .... PASSION
suffice ...... DO, SATE, SERVE, GET
    BY, SATISFY
sufficiency .... FULLNESS,
    ABUNDANCE, PROFUSION,
    REPLETION
colloquial .... LOTS, OODLES
excessive .... GLUT, FLOOD,
    SURFEIT
kind of .... QUORUM,

AFFLUENCE
slang .... SCADS
sufficient .... ENOW, AMPLE,
    ENOUGH, PLENTY, ADEQUATE
barely .... MINIMAL
suffix .... ENDING, POSTFIX,
    SUBINDEX, DESINENCE
action .... URE, ANCE, XION
adjective .... ENT, IAL, ISH,
    IST, OUS, IBLE, PATHIC
alcohol .... OL
aphid .... IDAE
believer .... IST, ARIAN
boy .... ISH
capable of .... ILE
carbohydrate .... OSE
changing one .... TROPE
chemical .... ANE, ENE, IUM,
    OLE, ENOL, ITOL, OLIC
common .... ENT, INE, ING,
    ION
comparative .... IER, IOR
condition .... ATE, ILE, ISE,
    ANCE, EMIA, SION, STER
denoting agent .... STER
depend .... ENT
diminutive .... ULE, CULE,
    ETTE
disease .... PATHIC
enzyme .... ASE
fear .... PHOBIA
female/feminine .... ESS, ELLA,
    ETTE, GYNY
follower .... IST, ITE
good .... NESS
having to do with a
    .... SUFFIXAL
icy/cold .... CRYO
indicating quality .... ISE
inflammation .... ITIS
inhabitant/native .... ITE
intensifying: sl. .... AROO
killer .... CIDE
lacking .... LESS
like .... OID
lover .... PHILE
make .... ISE
meaning cavity .... COELE
enlargement .... MEGALY
government .... ARCHY
like .... ISH
recent .... CENE
mineral(ogical) .... ITE, LITE
noun .... EE, TUDE, ATION,
    ILITY, OSITY
number .... TEEN
occupational .... ARIAN
oil .... OLE
one connected with .... AST
one who .... IST, STER
ordinal .... ETH

pain .... ALGIA
plural .... IES
resembling .... PHANE
science .... OLOGY
skin .... DERM
snake .... OPHIS
state of being .... TUDE
stone .... LITH, LITHIC
sugar .... OSE
superlative .... EST
transfer .... ENCE
tumor .... OMA
used with para .... NOIA
used with song or prank
    .... STER
verb .... IRE, ISE, ESCE
voice .... PHONIA
way .... ODE
with ecto or proto ...... PLASM
worship .... LATRY
zoological .... ATA, ACEA
suffocate .... CHOKE, STIFLE,
    SMOTHER, OBSTRUCT,
    STRANGLE, SUPPRESS,
    ASPHYXIATE
suffocating .... AIRLESS, STIFLING
suffocation .... CHOKING,
    STRANGULATION
first aid .... CPR, ARTIFICIAL
    RESPIRATION
medical term for
    .... ASPHYXIA
result of untreated ...... DEATH
temporary .... APNEA
suffragan ...... BISHOP, AUXILIARY
suffrage ...... VOTING, FRANCHISE,
    (RIGHT TO)VOTE
woman supporter of
    .... LIBBER, FEMINIST,
    SUFFRAGIST, SUFFRAGETTE
suffragist Lucy _____ ...... STONE
U.S. .... CATT
suffuse .... WASH, BATHE, COLOR,
    IMBUE, TINGE, PERVADE,
    OVERSPREAD
suffusion .... GLOW, TINT, BLUSH,
    FLUSH, DIFFUSION
Sufi disciple .... MURID
wandering dervish
    .... CALENDER
sugar .... OSE, HEXOSE, GLUCOSE,
    LACTOSE, MALTOSE,
    MANNOSE, DEXTROSE,
    FLATTERY, FRUCTOSE,
    ARABINOSE, MUSCOVADO,
    SWEETEN(ER), SACCHAROSE
alcohol .... SORBITOL
apple .... SWEETSOP
beets .... SUCROSE
beets refuse .... BAGASSE
burnt .... CARAMEL

candy .... TAFFY, BONBON, NOUGAT, CARAMEL, DIVINITY, LOLLIPOP
cane .... SUCROSE
cane, crushed .... MEGASS(E)
cane cutting tool .... MACHETE
cane disease .... ILIAU
cane refuse .... TRASH, BAGASSE
cane sprout .... RATOON
can waste juice .... VINEGAR
coating .... ICING, FROSTING
combining form .... SACCHAR(O)
company personnel .... REFINERS
convert into .... SACCHARIZE
crude .... GUR
crystalline .... GLUCOSE, LACTOSE, MALTOSE, FRUCTOSE
crystalline, white .... TREHALOSE
cube .... LUMP
daddy .... BOYFRIEND, SANTA CLAUS
flavoring .... CARAMEL
form of/type of .... RAW, BROWN, WHITE, POWDERED, GRANULATED, CONFECTIONERS'
foundation for candy .... FONDANT
fruit .... KETOSE, FRUCTOSE, LEVULOSE
mass of hard refined .... LOAF
measure .... CUP, SPOON
mill/factory .... REFINERY, SUGARWORKS
mushroom .... TREHALOSE
of lead .... ACETATE
of milk .... LACTOSE
orchard .... PLANTATION
palm sap .... JAGGERY
pentose .... RIBOSE
raw .... CASSONADE, MUSCOVADO
simple .... OSE
slang .... MONEY, MOOLAH
solution .... SIRUP, SYRUP
source of .... BEET, CANE, MAPLE
sprinkler .... DUSTER
substitute .... ASPARTAME, SACCHARIN
syrup ..... TREACLE, MOLASSES
tree .... MAPLE
without .... DRY, SEC, SUGARLESS, UNSWEETENED
yeast .... TREHALOSE
sugared/sugary .... SWEET, SYRUPY, CANDIED, HONEYED

pastry .... DONUT, COOKIE, DOUGHNUT
sugarplum .... KISS, BONBON, COMFIT
suggest ...... HINT, IMPLY, ADVISE, SUBMIT, CONNOTE, PROPOSE, INTIMATE, INSINUATE
suggestion .... HINT, TRACE, ADVICE, INKLING, PROPOSAL, INDICATION
open to .... LIBERAL, AMENABLE, PERVIOUS, BROADMINDED
subtle .... INSINUATION
suggestive .... INDICATIVE
of something improper .... RISQUE, OFF-COLOR
suggests separate bedrooms .... SNORE
sui _____ .... JURIS, GENERIS
generis .... RARE, UNIQUE
juris .... SANE, COMPETENT
suicidal .... DEADLY, DESOLATE, MURDEROUS, DESPONDENT
charge .... BANZAI, WAR CRY
dive, bomber's .... KAMIKAZE
suicide .... SEPPUKU, HARAKARI, HARAKIRI, SELF-RUIN, SELF-MURDER
commit .... BLOW OUT ONE'S BRAINS
describing an attempted .... NON-FATAL
Hindu widow's .... SUTTEE
in law .... FELO-DE-SE
sacrificial .... IMMOLATION
suint .... GREASE
derivative .... POTASH
Suisse .... SWITZERLAND
suit .... SET, ADAPT, AGREE, (BE)FIT, GROUP, APPEAL, OUTFIT, PLEASE, WOOING, SATISFY, PETITION
beneficiary .... USEE
bring .... SUE
court .... CASE, ACTION
fabric for a .... SUITING
maker .... SARTOR
of armor .... PANOPLY
of mail .... ARMOR
part of a .... COAT, VEST, PANTS, TROUSERS
playing card .... CLUBS, HEARTS, SPADES, DIAMONDS
tarot card .... CUPS, WANDS, SWORDS, PENTACLES
to a _____ .... TEE
type of .... ZOOT
suitable .... APT, MEET, RIGHT, FIT(TED), PROPER, APROPOS, FITTING, BECOMING,

EXPEDIENT, COMPATIBLE, APPROPRIATE
for .... ELIGIBLE
for the block .... SALABLE
too exactly .... PAT
suitability .... FITNESS, PROPRIETY
suitably .... MEETLY, TIMELY
suitcase .... BAG, GRIP, VALISE, LUGGAGE
suite .... SET, FLAT, GROUP, STAFF, TRAIN, ESCORT, RETINUE
suited .... FITTED, APPROPRIATE
for tilling .... ARABLE
suiting .... SERGE
suitor .... BEAU, SUER, WOOER, FELLOW, ADMIRER, PETITIONER
song of .... SERENADE
Sulawesi .... CELEBES
sulcate .... FLUTED, GROOVED, FURROWED
sulcus .... FURROW, GROOVE
Suleiman soubriquet .... MAGNIFICENT
sulfate .... ALUM, COPPERAS
sulfide mixture .... MATTE
sulfonal .... SOPORIFIC
sulfur .... BRIMSTONE
alloy .... NIELLO
combining form .... THI(O)
sulfuric acid .... VITRIOL
sulk ...... PET, MOPE, POUT, GRIPE, GROUCH, GRUMBLE
sulky .... GIG, GLUM, MOROSE, SULLEN, CARRIAGE
puller .... HORSE
sullage .... SILT, SEWAGE
sullen .... DOUR, DULL, GLUM, GRIM, SOUR, DORTY, MOODY, SULKY, SURLY, CRUSTY, MOROSE, BALEFUL, CRABBED
Sullivan, _____ .... ED, BARRY
Sullivan's collaborator .... GILBERT
forte .... COMIC OPERA
sully .... BLOT, SOIL, SMEAR, STAIN, TAINT, DEFILE, BLEMISH, TARNISH, BESMIRCH
sulphate barium .... BARYTE
calcium .... GYPSUM
double .... ALUM
sulphide arsenic .... ORPIMENT
lead .... GALENA
zinc .... BLENDE
sulphur .... BUTTERFLY
alloy .... NIELLO
bottom .... WHALE
color .... LEMON
sulphuric acid .... VITRIOL
sulphurous .... ANGRY, FIERY, HEATED, HELLISH, PROFANE,

INFERNAL, PASSIONATE

sultan .... EMIR, IMAM, KHAN, MURAD, RULER, SELIM, CALIPH, CHICKEN, SALADIN, PADISHAH, SULEIMAN

chamberlain of .... EUNUCH

decree of .... IRADE

palace .... SERAI

wives' apartment .... HAREM

Sultan of Swat .... BABE(RUTH)

specialty of ...... GRAND-SLAM, FOUR-BAGGER

sultana .... GRAPE, RAISIN

sultanate .... OMAN, KUWAIT, MUSCAT, KINGDOM

sultry .... HOT, SEXY, CLOSE, FIERY, HUMID, MUGGY, STUFFY, TORRID, GLOWING, SENSUAL, STIFLING, TROPICAL, PASSIONATE, SWELTERING, VOLUPTUOUS

Sulu capital .... JOLO

Moslem .... MORO

sum .... ADD, GIST, TOTAL, AMOUNT, SUMMARY, QUANTITY, AGGREGATE, SUBSTANCE

and substance .... EPITOME

of money .... POT, BANK, LUMP-SUM

subtracted .... DEDUCTION

up .... RECAP, SUMMATE, SUMMARIZE

up a speech .... PERORATE

sumac .... RHUS, TEREBINTH, POISON IVY

family .... CASHEW

genus .... RHUS

Sumatra burrowing animal .... TELEDU

cape .... PUTING

city/town .... MEDAN, (D)JAMBI, LANGSA, PADANG, PALEMBANG

deerlike animal .... NAPU, CHEVROTAIN

gibbon .... SIAMANG

gutta .... SIAK

island near .... BATU, NIAS, BANYAK

lake .... TOBA

mountain ...... DEMPO, LEUSER, KERINCI

mountain range .... BARISAN

native .... BAT(T)AK, MALAYAN

primate .... ORANG

river ..... HARI, MUSI, ROKAN

shrew/squirrel .... TANA

volcano .... SARIKMERAPI

wild cat .... BALU

Sumbara volcano ...... TAMBORA

Sumerian god .... ABU

sumless .... VAST, COUNTLESS, INCALCULABLE

summarily ...... CURTLY, SWIFTLY

summarize .... SUM UP, RECOUNT, RESTATE

briefly/concisely .... RECAP(ITULATE)

summary .... GIST, BRIEF, SHORT, DIGEST, PRECIS, RESUME, CONCISE, EPITOME, RUN-DOWN, ABSTRACT, SYNOPSIS, ABRIDGMENT, COMPEND(IUM)

of main points .... SYLLABUS

summer ailment ...... HEAT-RASH, PRICKLY HEAT

beverage .... ADE

headliner .... HEATWAVE

house .... KIOSK, MAHAL, ALCOVE, CASINO, GAZEBO, COTTAGE, PAVILION, BELVEDERE

insect .... FLY, GNAT

pertaining to/of .... (A)ESTIVAL

place for furs .... STORAGE

porch hazard .... ROLLERSKATE

problem .... HEATWAVE

refresher .... LEMONADE, ORANGEADE

resort state .... MAINE

squash .... ZUCCHINI

suit fabric .... PALM BEACH

theater .... STOCK

time .... DST

triangle stars, one of the .... VEGA, DENEB, ALTAIR

summery .... SUNNY, TOASTY, AESTIVAL, SUNSHINY

summit .... TOP, ACME, APEX, KNAP, PEAK, CLIMAX, ZENITH, PINNACLE, ULTIMATE

summon .... BID, CALL, CITE, EVOKE, ROUSE, SERVE, ARRAIGN, CONVENE, SEND FOR, SUBPOENA

back .... RECALL

up .... ELICIT, PROMPT

summons ...... CALL, WRIT, CITAL, NOTICE, BIDDING, WARRANT, MONITION, SUBPOENA, EVOCATION, CONVOCATION

carrier .... PROCESS SERVER

summonses/serenades ...... LOVE CALLS

sump ...... PIT, WELL, (CESS)POOL, SEPTIC TANK

mine .... TUNNEL

oil .... RESERVOIR

sumpter .... PACKHORSE

animal ...... OX, MULE, CAMEL,

HORSE

horse .... BIDET

mule .... HINNY, JENNET

sumptuous .... RICH, GRAND, COSTLY, LAVISH, DE LUXE, IMPOSING, SPLENDID

sun .... DRY, SOL, TAN, (DAY)STAR, LUMINARY

baked .... DRIED, PARCHED

bittern .... HELIAS

bow .... IRIS, RAINBOW

burn .... TAN

clock .... SUNDIAL

combining form .... HELI(O)

cured .... DRIED

darkening of the .... ECLIPSE

deck .... PORCH, TERRACE

disk .... ATEN

dried brick .... DOBIE, (A)DOBE

for drying .... INSOLATE

god .... RA, SHU, SOL, TUM, AMON, ATEN, HORUS, TITAN, APOLLO, HELIOS, MURDUK, VARUNA, MITHRA(S), PHOEBUS, SHAMASH, HYPERION

greatest distance from .... APSIS

halo of .... CORONA

helmet .... TOPI, TOPEE

helmet scarf .... PUGGRY, PUGGREE

in the morning .... RISER

mirror .... HELIOSTAT

mock .... PARHELION

moon differential .... EPACT

orbit/path .... ECLIPTIC

overexposure to the .... SUNBURN

personification of .... TITAN

pertaining to the/of the .... SOLAR, HELIACAL

poetic .... LAMP, PHOEBUS

point farthest from .... APHELION

radiation .... INSOLATION

shadow .... UMBRA

shield .... VISOR, PARASOL

shield, window .... AWNING (VENETIAN)BLIND

spot .... FACULA, MACULA, FRECKLE

spurge .... TURNSOLE

streak .... FACULA

vitamin, so-called .... (COD) LIVER OIL

worship .... HELIOLATRY

worshipers .... NUDES, NUDISTS

Sun, Chinese president .... YAT-SEN

The Rising, author ..... (JOHN) TOLAND

Yat-Sen's party .... KUOMINTANG
sunbath, in a way .... FRY
sunbeam .... RAY
sunburn .... TAN
sunblock .... SUNSCREEN
ingredient .... PABA
sunburnt .... ADUST
sunburst-like jewelry
.... BROOCH
Sunda island .... BALI, JAVA,
FLORES, LOMBOK, SUMATRA
sundae .... PARFAIT, ICE CREAM
Sunday ...... HOLIDAY, HOLY DAY,
FIRST DAY, LORD'S DAY,
(CHRISTIAN)SABBATH
best .... FINERY, CLOTHES
evangelist .... BILLY (GRAHAM)
holy .... PALM, EASTER
school .... CHURCH
treat .... PICNIC, JOYRIDE
sunder .... PART, REND, RIVE,
TEAR, BREAK, SEVER, SPLIT,
CLEAVE, DIVIDE, SEPARATE
sundial .... CLOCK, HOROLOGE
gnomon .... STYLE
pointer .... GNOMON
sundog .... PARHELION
sundown .... SUNSET, TWILIGHT
sundowner .... DRINK, TRAMP,
DRIFTER
sundries .... NOTIONS, KNICK-
KNACKS, ODDS AND ENDS
sundry .... DIVERS, VARIOUS,
MISCELLANEOUS
sunfish ...... MOLA, OPAH, BREAM,
ROACH, CICHLID, CRAPPIE,
CROPPIE, BLUEGILL
genus .... MOLA
relative .... CARP, PERCH
sunflower .... GIRASOL(E),
MARIGOLD, TURNSOLE,
HELIANTHUS, HELIOTROPE
family .... COMPOSITE
Sunflower State .... KANSAS
sunk .... IN DAVY JONES'S LOCKER
sunken .... HOLLOW
fence .... HAHA
place .... SAG
sunket .... DAINTY, TIDBIT
Sunkian capital .... HARBIN
sunless .... DARK, SHADY
sunn .... HEMP, FIBER
sunny .... GAY, WARM, PALMY,
BRIGHT, CHEERY, CHEERFUL
sunrise .... DAWN, SUNUP,
AURORA, DAYBREAK
sunroom .... PORCH, SOLARIUM
sunset .... DUSK, SUNDOWN,
TWILIGHT, NIGHTFALL
occurring at .... ACRONICAL

sunshade .... VISOR, AWNING,
PARASOL, UMBRELLA,
SUNSCREEN
slang .... SUNGLASS(ES)
sunshine .... WARMTH,
(DAY)LIGHT, HAPPINESS, FAIR
WEATHER
bit of .... RAY
days .... ROSY ERA
Sunshine State .... FLORIDA, NEW
MEXICO, SOUTH DAKOTA
sunshiny .... ROSY, HAPPY,
BRIGHT, CHEERFUL
sunspot .... FACULA, MACULA
dark part .... UMBRA
sunstroke .... ICTUS, HELIOSIS,
HEATSTROKE, INSOLATION
suntan color ...... BROWN, KHAKI
sunwise .... CLOCKWISE
Suomi .... FINLAND
sup .... EAT, SIP, DINE, DRINK
super .... ACTOR, EXTRA,
SUPERIOR, EXCELLENT
ego .... CONSCIENCE, (ETHICAL)
SELF
patriot ..... JINGO, NATIONALIST
superabundance .... EXCESS,
PLEONASM, PLETHORA,
SUPERFLUX, OVERSUPPLY,
BUMPER CROP
superabundant .... RANK, RIFE,
LAVISH, REPLETE, TEEMING,
SWARMING, PLETHORIC
superannuate .... RETIRE,
(OUT)DATE, ANTIQUATE,
FOSSILIZE, OBSOLESCE
superannuated ...... AGED, ANILE,
ANTIQUE, RETIRED, OBSOLETE,
OUTDATED
superb .... FINE, RICH, FANCY,
ELEGANT, STATELY,
GORGEOUS, SPLENDID,
EXCELLENT, EXQUISITE,
GRAND(IOSE)
supercilious .... PROUD, SNIFFY,
SNOBBY, SNOOTY, SNOTTY,
HAUGHTY, ARROGANT,
CAVALIER, SCORNFUL,
SNOBBISH
person .... SNOB
superficial ...... LIP, GLIB, HASTY,
INANE, CASUAL, FLIMSY,
SLIGHT, SQUARE, CURSORY,
OUTWARD, PASSING,
SHALLOW, SKETCHY,
SURFACE, TRIVIAL, EXTERNAL,
SKIN-DEEP
blood vessel .... CAPILLARY
knowledge .... NOTION
polish .... VENEER
wound .... GASH, NICK,

SCRATCH
superficially .... SLAPDASH
superfine .... FANCY, DE LUXE,
SUBTLE, SUPERB, DELICATE,
GLORIOUS, OVERNICE,
EXQUISITE
superfluity .... REDUNDANCE
superfluous .... DE TROP, OTIOSE,
SURPLUS, NEEDLESS,
OVERMUCH, EXCESSIVE,
REDUNDANT
Superfort .... BOMBER,
B-TWENTY-NINE
superhighway .... FREEWAY,
AUTOBAHN, SPEEDWAY,
TURNPIKE, AUTOROUTE
superhuman ...... GODLY, DIVINE,
GODLIKE, SUBLIME
superimpose .... COVER, OVERLAY
superimposed .... OBSCURED
superintend .... DIRECT, MANAGE,
CONTROL, OVERSEE,
SUPERVISE, ADMINISTER
superintendent .... BOSS,
FOREMAN, MANAGER,
OVERSEER, SURVEYOR,
CONTROLLER
colloquial .... STRAW BOSS
police .... CHIEF, INSPECTOR,
COMMISSIONER
school .... PRINCIPAL
superior .... BOSS, ABOVE, MAJOR,
ULTRA, UPPER, BETTER,
HIGHER, UTMOST, GREAT(ER),
TOPNOTCH, EXCELLENT,
FIRST-RATE
slang .... TOPS
superiority .... EDGE, POWER,
SUPREMACY
superiors .... CHIEFS, BETTERS,
LEADERS, MASTERS
superlative .... ACME, ULTRA,
EXTREME, SUPREME,
EXCEEDING, EXCESSIVE
absolute .... ELATIVE
ending/suffix .... EST
Superman's city .... METROPOLIS
Lois .... LANE
other identity .... (CLARK)
KENT
portrayer .... (DEAN) CAIN,
(CHRISTOPHER) REEVE
supernal .... DIVINE, ETHEREAL,
HEAVENLY, CELESTIAL
supernatural ...... MAGIC, DIVINE,
OCCULT, ABNORMAL,
UNEARTHLY, MIRACULOUS
being ...... ELF, DEMON, FAIRY,
GHOST, PIXIE, GENIUS, GOBLIN,
SPIRIT, SPRITE, PHANTOM,
SPECTER

force .... MANA
happening .... MIRACLE
supernumerary .... ACTOR,
EXTRA, WALK-ON, STAND-IN,
FIGURANT(E)
superpower, a .... USA, USSR,
AMERICA, SOVIET UNION
economic .... JAPAN
superscribe ...... WRITE, ADDRESS
supersede .... REPLACE, SUCCEED,
DISPLACE, SUPPLANT
superseded .... OBSOLETE
supersensitive .... SORE,
OVERTENDER, THIN-SKINNED
reaction .... ALLERGY
supersonic noise .... BOOM
transport .... SST
superstar .... HERO, STANDOUT
superstition .... FEAR, BELIEF,
PHOBIA, (FOLK)LORE,
TRADITION
superstitious .... CREDULOUS
unlucky number ..... THIRTEEN
supervene .... ENSUE, HAPPEN,
EMANATE
supervise .... BOSS, DIRECT,
GOVERN, MANAGE, OVERSEE
supervision .... SURVEILLANCE
supervisor .... HEADMAN,
MANAGER, DIRECTOR,
OVERSEER
college .... PROCTOR,
PRINCIPAL
corporation .... SYNDIC
government .... MAGISTRATE
morals .... CENSOR
prison .... WARDEN
town/district .... REEVE
very exacting .... TASKMASTER
wildlife .... RANGER, GAME-
WARDEN
supination, opposed to
.... PRONATION
supine .... TORPID, PASSIVE,
INACTIVE, LISTLESS,
SLUGGISH, PROSTRATE,
RECUMBENT
opposite of .... PRONE
supper .... MEAL, FEAST, DINNER,
REPAST, REFECTION
club .... NITERY, NIGHTCLUB
supplant .... OUST, REPLACE,
SUCCEED, DISPLACE,
SUPERSEDE
supple .... SOFT, LITHE, LIMBER,
LISSOM(E), PLIABLE, SERVILE,
FLEXIBLE, YIELDING,
(COM)PLIANT
supplement .... EKE, ADJUNCT,
ADD(ITION), APPENDIX

supplemental material
...... INDEX, TABLE, ADDENDA,
GLOSSARY, ADDENDUM,
APPENDIX
supplementary .... ADDED,
EXTRA, SECOND, ADDITIONAL
rail .... EASER
story .... SEQUEL
suppliant/supplicant .... BEGGAR,
SUITOR, PLEADER, PETITIONER,
WORSHIP(P)ER
supplicate .... BEG, PRAY, PLEAD,
APPEAL, OBTEST, BESEECH,
ENTREAT, REQUEST, PETITION
supplication ...... BID, PLEA, SUIT,
APPEAL, ORISON, PRAYER,
REQUEST, ENTREATY,
PETITION, ROGATION,
DEVOTIONS
supplier .... PROVIDER, PURVEYOR
food .... GROCER, CATERER
ship .... CHANDLER
supplies .... STOCK, ISSUES,
STORES, PROVENDER,
PROVISIONS
office .... STATIONERY
supply .... FEED, GIVE, EQUIP,
STOCK, STORE, AFFORD,
FURNISH, PROVIDE
food .... CATER, PURVEY,
PROVISION
for consumption .... FEED
hidden .... HOARD
ship .... OILER, TENDER,
VICTUAL(L)ER
weapons .... ARM
workers .... MAN
support .... AID, ABET, BEAR,
STAY, BRACE, CARRY, SHORE,
TRUSS, BACK(UP), HOLD(UP),
SECOND, UPHOLD, (UP)KEEP,
BOLSTER, SUSTAIN, BUTTRESS,
MAINTAIN, SHOULDER,
UNDERPIN
chief .... KEYSTONE, MAINSTAY
idea/cause .... ESPOUSE,
SPONSOR
in a way ..... SIDE WITH, STICK
UP FOR
kind of .... LEG, PEG, BASE,
LIMB, POST, PROP, MORAL,
TABLE, PILLAR, TRIPOD,
UNIPOD, PEDESTAL, FINANCIAL
main .... PILLAR, BACKBONE
oar .... THOLEPIN
rim .... SPOKE
roof .... BEAM, RAFTER
supporter .... FAN, ALLY, DONOR,
GIVER, BACKER, BEARER,
PATRON, ROOTER, SECOND,
ABETTOR, CARRIER,

ADHERENT, ADVOCATE,
FOLLOWER, PARTISAN
athletic .... JOCKSTRAP
figure .... CORSET, GIRDLE
financial .... ANGEL, FUNDER,
PATRON, SPONSOR
of some big wheels ...... AXLE
zealous .... BOOSTER,
DEVOTEE, ENTHUSIAST
supporting framework .... EASEL,
TRELLIS, TRESTLE, SKELETON
member .... LEG, MAST,
STRUT, BRACER, GUY(LINE),
PILASTER
role .... HEAVY, VILLAIN,
SOUBRETTE
supportive .... CHEERING,
REASSURING, SUSTAINING
suppose ...... DEEM, TROW, WEEN,
FANCY, GUESS, OPINE, THINK,
ASSUME, DIVINE, GATHER,
RECKON, BELIEVE, IMAGINE,
PRESUME, SURMISE, THEORIZE,
CONJECTURE
supposed .... GIVEN, IMPLIED,
REPUTED, INFERRED,
PUTATIVE
supposition .... IF, HUNCH,
BELIEF, NOTION, THEORY,
INKLING, SURMISE, THEOREM,
GUESS(WORK), HYPOTHESIS
suppository .... PESSARY
shape .... CONE, BULLET,
CYLINDER
suppress .... BAN, HIDE, STOP,
CHECK, CRUSH, QUASH,
QUELL, CENSOR, SUBDUE,
CONCEAL, REPRESS, SILENCE,
THROTTLE
suppression .... LOCKING-IN,
BOTTLING-UP
of emotion .... INHIBITION
of memories .... REPRESSION
suppurate .... FESTER, RANKLE,
PUTREFY, MATURATE
suppuration .... PUS, PYOSIS
supra .... ABOVE
suprarenal .... ADRENAL
gland .... CORTEX, MEDULLA
glands location .... KIDNEYS
glands secretion
.... HORMONES
supremacy .... MASTERY
supreme ...... LAST, CHIEF, FINAL,
PRIME, UTMOST, HIGHEST,
FOREMOST, GREATEST,
DOMINANT, ULTIMATE,
PARAMOUNT
power .... IMPERIUM
Supreme Being .... GOD

709

Court nickname (former)
.... NINE OLD MEN
supremo .... COMMANDER,
GENERALISSIMO
Surakarta .... SOLO
Surat river .... TAPTI
surcease .... END, STOP, LET UP,
DESIST
surcingle .... GIRDLE
surcoat ...... CLOAK, GIPON, JUPON
surd .... RADICAL, VOICELESS,
IRRATIONAL
sure .... SAFE, TRUE, SECURE,
STABLE, CERTAIN, POSITIVE,
UNERRING, CONFIDENT,
CONVINCED, INFALLIBLE
grip .... CINCH
success .... WINNER
thing .... CINCH, (LEAD)PIPE,
CERT, IN THE BAG, TRUMP
CARD
surely ...... YES, INDEED, REALLY,
CLEARLY, OF COURSE,
CERTAINLY, ABSOLUTELY,
DEFINITELY
surety .... BAIL, BOND, PLEDGE,
SAFETY, HOSTAGE, SPONSOR,
GUARANTY, SECURITY,
ASSURANCE, GUARANTEE,
GUARANTOR
surf .... WAVES, SWELL(S),
ROLLERS, BREAKERS,
WHITECAPS
duck .... SCOTER
noise .... ROTE, THUNDER
part .... CAP, FOAM, CREST
surface .... AREA, OUTER,
OUTSIDE, EXTERIOR,
EXTERNAL, SUPERFICIAL
antique .... PATINA
curve .... CAMBER
flat .... PLANE
front/main .... OBVERSE
gem's .... FACET
in aeronautics .... AIRFOIL
lower .... FLOOR
rise to the ..... EMERGE, FLOAT
UP
slanting/sloping .... CANT,
RAMP
thing with smooth .... EGG,
FACE, GLASS
transit .... LAND, WATER
surfacing .... PAVING, ARISING,
EMERGING, FLOORING,
PAVEMENT
material .... ASPHALT,
MACADAM
surfactant .... WETTING-AGENT
kind of ..... SOAP, DETERGENT,
EMULSIFIER

surfbird .... PLOVER
surfcaster .... FISHERMAN
surfeit .... CLOY, GLUT, JADE,
PALL, SATE, GORGE, EXCESS,
SATIATE, SATIETY, PLETHORA
surfeited .... BLASE, FED-UP,
SATED, REPLETE, STUFFED
surge .... GUSH, GUST, RISE, RUSH,
TIDE, WAVE, HEAVE, SWELL,
SWIRL, BILLOW, SEETHE,
UNDULATION
surgeon .... PHYSICIAN, SPECIALIST
colloquial .... DOCTOR,
MEDIC(O)
extractor of .... FORCEPS
hammer of .... PLESSOR
head and neck
.... OTOLARYNGOLOGIST
knife of ..... LANCET, SCALPEL,
BISTOURY
of a kind .... AMPUTATOR,
UROLOGIST
probe of .... STYLET
saw of .... TREPAN, TREPHINE
slang .... SAWBONES
starter .... NEURO
surgery ...... EXCISION, OPERATION
abdominal .... LAPAROTOMY
abortion .... HYSTEROTOMY
blood clot removal
.... THROMBECTOMY
body contour .... LIPECTOMY
bone .... OSTEOTOMY,
AMPUTATION
breast removal
.... MASTECTOMY
breast reshaping
.... MAMMOPLASTY
childbirth .... CESAREAN
SECTION
chin .... MENTOPLASTY
cosmetic .... FACELIFT, HAIR-
TRANSPLANT
eyelid .... BLEPHAROPLASTY
gall bladder removal
.... CHOLECYSTECTOMY
goiter removal
.... THYROIDECTOMY
heart .... OPEN-HEART,
BALLOON-ANGIOPLASTY
heart valve
.... VALVULOPLASTY
kidney removal
.... NEPHRECTOMY
kind of .... MAJOR, MINOR
lip defect .... CHILOPLASTY
male sterilization
.... VASECTOMY
nose .... RHINOPLASTY
outer ear .... OTOPLASTY
perform .... OPERATE

skull .... CRANIOTOMY
specialty division .... ORAL,
NEURO, PLASTIC, COSMETIC,
GYNECOLOGY, OBSTETRICS,
ORTHOPEDICS,
OPHTHALMOLOGY
starter .... MICRO, NEURO
suffix meaning reshaping by
.... PLASTY
technique, plastic
.... IMPLANT, BONE GRAFT,
SKIN GRAFT
testis removal
.... ORCHIECTOMY
to correct infertility
.... TUBOPLASTY
to improve appearance
.... COSMETIC
to repair eardrum
.... TYMPANOPLASTY
to replace a diseased organ
.... TRANSPLANT
uterus removal
.... HYSTERECTOMY
voice box ..... LARYNGECTOMY
windpipe ...... TRACHEOSTOMY
surgical appliance .... BRACES,
CRUTCH, SPLINT, COLOSTOMY
BAG
compress ..... STUPE, ICE PACK
cut .... INCISION
electronic device
.... PACEMAKER
incision, closing of
.... STAPLING, SUTURING
instrument ...... FLEAM, PROBE,
LANCE(T), NEEDLE, STYLET,
TREPAN, TROCAR, LEVATOR,
SCALPEL, SYRINGE, BISTOURY,
OTOSCOPE, SPECULUM,
TREPHINE, OSTEOTOME
instrument to hold incision
open .... RETRACTOR
knife .... FLEAM, LANCET,
SCALPEL, BISTOURY,
PHLEBOTOME
operation .... RESECT,
EXCISION, PROCEDURE
operation, brain
.... LOBOTOMY
operation: comb. form
.... TOMY
operation, common
.... BIOPSY, COLECTOMY,
MASTECTOMY,
APPENDECTOMY, HERNIA
REPAIR
operation to relieve pressure
in muscles
.... FASCIOTOMY
pad .... SWAB, SPONGE

painkiller .... ANESTHESIA
pincers/extractor ...... FORCEPS
removal of diseased tissue or
    body part .... ABLATION
stitch .... SETON, SUTURE,
    STAPLING
thread .... WIRE, CATGUT,
    LIGATURE
wound plug .... TAMPON
Suribachi, site of .... IWO JIMA
suricate, kin of .... CIVET,
    MONGOOSE
Surinam capital .... PARAMARIBO
city/town .... ALBINA,
    MOENGO, DOMBURG, TOTNESS,
    CALCUTTA, LELYDORP
district .... PARA, CORONIE,
    NICKERIE, PARAMARIBO
governor of .... VRIES
lake .... BLOMMESTEIN
language .... DUTCH, HINDI
monetary unit .... GUILDER
mountain .... JULIANATOP
mountain range .... LELY,
    KAYSER, ORANGE,
    WILHELMINA
prime minister .... PENGEL
river .... LITANI, COTTICA,
    COEROENI, NICKERIE,
    SURINAME, SARAMACCA
toad .... PIPA
tree .... BALATA
surly .... RUDE, CROSS, GRUFF,
    SULKY, CRUSTY, GRUMPY,
    MOROSE, SULLEN, BOORISH,
    UNCIVIL, ARROGANT,
    CHURLISH
surmise ...... GUESS, INFER, OPINE,
    IMAGINE, PRESUME, SUPPOSE,
    SUSPECT, CONJECTURE
surmount ...... CAP, TOP, CROWN,
    SCALE, EXCEED, HURDLE,
    MASTER, CONQUER, SURPASS,
    OVERCOME
surmounting .... ATOP
surname .... AGNOMEN,
    COGNOMEN, FAMILY NAME,
    PATRONYMIC
surpass .... CAP, TOP, BEST,
    EXCEL, OUTDO, BETTER,
    EXCEED, ECLIPSE, OUTCLASS,
    OUTSHINE, OUTSTRIP,
    TRANSCEND
in marketing .... OUTSELL
surpassing .... PEERLESS,
    EXCELLENT, MATCHLESS,
    UNMATCHED, CONSUMMATE
surplice .... GOWN, COTTA
vestment like .... ROCHET
surplus ...... GLUT, EXTRA, SPARE,
    EXCESS, BALANCE, RESERVE,

OVER(AGE), RESIDUE,
    REMAINDER, OVERSUPPLY
value .... PROFIT
surprise .... AWE, DAZE, JOLT,
    STUN, TURN, AMAZE, SHOCK,
    DAZZLE, WONDER, ASTOUND,
    STARTLE, ASTONISH,
    DUMBFOUND, EYE-OPENER,
    FLABBERGAST,
    CATCH(NAPPING)
attack .... RAID
surprised .... UNWARNED,
    UNSUSPECTING
surpriser's cry .... AHA
surprising .... SUDDEN,
    UNEXPECTED, UNFORESEEN,
    THUNDERCLAP
**Surratt, first woman hanged in
U.S.** .... MARY
surrealist painter .... DALI
surrender ...... CEDE, YIELD, GIVE
    UP, REMISE, RESIGN, SUBMIT,
    CESSION, SUBMISSION
a citizenship .... RENOUNCE
a throne .... RELINQUISH
conditionally .... CAPITULATE
sign of .... HANDS UP, WHITE
    FLAG
surreptitious .... SLY, COVERT,
    SECRET, SNEAKY, BOOTLEG,
    FURITVE, STEALTHY,
    DECEITFUL, UNDERCOVER,
    CLANDESTINE
surrey .... CARRIAGE
Surrey village .... KEW
surrogate .... JUDGE, DEPUTY,
    STAND-IN, SUBSTITUTE
concern of .... WILLS
surround .... LAP, GIRT, RING,
    INVEST, WRAP, BESET,
    HEM(IN), CORRAL, ENFOLD,
    GIRD(LE), BESIEGE, EMBRACE,
    ENCLOSE, ENVELOP, ENVIRON,
    (EN)CIRCLE, BELEAGUER,
    ENCOMPASS
surrounded (by) .... AMID
surrounding .... MIDST, MILIEU,
    AMBIENT, SETTING,
    ENVIRONMENT,
    CIRCUMSTANCE
surtax .... DUTY, LEVY
surtout .... (OVER)COAT
surveillance ...... WATCH, PATROL,
    SCRUTINY, VIGILANCE,
    OBSERVATION
slang .... STAKEOUT
survey ...... POLL, VIEW, LOOK AT,
    EXAMINE, INSPECT, CANVASS,
    MEASURE, APPRAISE
surveying instrument ...... LEVEL,
    ALIDADE, CALIPER, TRANSIT,

STADIA(ROD), VERNIER,
    TACHYMETER, THEODOLITE
method .... STADIA, DIALING
personnel .... RODMEN
surveyor's assistant .... RODMAN,
    LINEMAN
map .... PLAT
transit .... STADIA
survive .... ABIDE, ENDURE,
    REMAIN, (OUT)LAST,
    (OUT)LIVE, WEATHER
surviving .... LEFT, REMANENT
survivor .... ORPHAN, RELICT,
    WIDOW(ER)
Susa, location of .... ELAM, IRAN
Susan, diminutive of .... SUE,
    SUZY, SUSIE
susceptibilities .... EMOTIONS,
    FEELINGS, PASSIONS,
    SENTIMENTS
susceptible .... SOFT, LIABLE,
    OPEN TO, ALLERGIC,
    RECEPTIVE, SENSITIVE,
    RESPONSIVE
to attack .... VULNERABLE
to mistake .... FALLIBLE
suslik .... SISEL, GOPHER,
    SQUIRREL, SPERMOPHILE
suspect .... INFER, ACCUSED,
    IMAGINE, PRESUME, SUPPOSE,
    SURMISE, DISTRUST,
    MISTRUST, PRISONER,
    QUESTIONABLE
suspect's defense .... ALIBI
suspecting .... SHY, WARY, LEERY,
    SKEPTICAL
suspend ...... HALT, HANG, HOLD,
    STOP, DEBAR, DEFER,
    DANGLE, RECESS, ADJOURN,
    EXCLUDE, POSTPONE,
    INTERRUPT
suspended .... HUNG, UNUSED,
    HANGING, PENDANT, PENDENT,
    PENDING, PENSILE
suspenders .... BRACERS,
    GARTERS, HANGERS,
    GALLUSES
suspense .... PAUSE, STRAIN,
    ANXIETY, TENSION,
    ABEYANCE, INACTION
suspenseful .... AGAPE, TENSE,
    ANXIOUS, ALL AGOG,
    APPREHENSIVE
suspension .... DELAY, PAUSE,
    ABEYANCE, PENDENCY,
    STOPPAGE, CESSATION,
    POSTPONEMENT
of court sentence
    .... PROBATION
of hostilities .... TRUCE,
    ARMISTICE

of proceedings .... RECESS, ADJOURNMENT

suspicion .... FEAR, HINT, DOUBT, HUNCH, SHADE, TRACE, ANXIETY, INKLING, MISTRUST, MISGIVING

emotional .... JEALOUSY

suspicious .... LEERY, DUBIOUS, ENVIOUS, FEARFUL, JEALOUS, DOUBTFUL, PARANOID, WATCHFUL, CONCERNED, SKEPTICAL

one .... ALARMIST, PARANOIAC, PESSIMIST

suspiration .... SIGH

Susskind, TV man .... DAVID

sustain .... BUOY, ASSIST, ENDURE, RATIFY, SUFFER, UPHOLD, CONFIRM, NOURISH, PROLONG, SUPPORT, MAINTAIN

sustenance .... FOOD, BREAD, UPKEEP, ALIMENT, SUPPORT, NUTRITION, PROVISION, SUBSISTENCE

susu .... DOLPHIN

domain .... INDUS, GANGES

susurrant .... RUSTLING, MURMURING, MUTTERING, WHISPERING

susurration/susurrus .... DRONE, JABBER, MUMBLE, MURMUR, MUTTER, RUSTLE, WHISPER

sutler .... MERCHANT, TRADESMAN, VICTUAL(L)ER

customer of .... SOLDIER

sutor .... BOOTER, SOUTER, COBBLER

sutra .... TEXT, VERSE, DISTICH

suttee .... SUICIDE, SACRIFICE, SELF-CREMATION, (SELF)IMMOLATION

suture .... SEW, SEAM, RAPHE, JOINT, STITCH, CLOSURE, JUNCTION

relating to a .... SUTURAL

suzerain .... LORD, LIEGE, RULER, SOVEREIGN

svelte .... SLIM, LITHE, SLINKY, GIRLISH, LISSOM(E), SLENDER, WILLOWY, WASP-WAISTED

Svengali .... HYPNOTIST, MESMERIST, HYPNOTIZER

Sverige .... SWEDEN

neighbor of .... NORGE

swab ...... DAB, MOP, DAUB, WIPE, Q-TIP, BRUSH, SCRUB, MALKIN, SPONGE, CLEANSE

swabbie .... GOB

swaddle .... BIND, TAPE, WRAP, CLOTHE, SWATHE, BANDAGE

swaddling clothes .... DUDS, BANDS

swag .... CANT, LIST, REEL, ROCK, SWAY, LURCH, DANGLE, FESTOON

slang ..... HAUL, LOOT, BOOTY, SPOILS, PLUNDER

swage .... DIE, STAMP

swagger .... BLUFF, BOAST, BULLY, STALK, STRUT, PRANCE, RUFFLE, BLUSTER, FLOUNCE, ROISTER

garment .... (SPORTS)COAT

swaggerer .... BRAVO, BUCKO, BULLY, PEACOCK, SWASHER, STRUTTER, SWASHBUCKLER

swaggering .... SWASH(ING), BOISTEROUS

Swahili .... BANTU

cheer word .... HARAMBEE

swain .... BEAU, LOVER, YOUTH, FELLOW, SUITOR, (E)SQUIRE, GALLANT, CAVALIER, BOYFRIEND

swallow .... BEAR, BIRD, BOLT, GULP, TERN, QUAFF, ABSORB, ACCEPT, DEVOUR, ENDURE, ENGULF, INGEST, TAKE IN, CONSUME, ENVELOP, RETRACT

bird like a ..... SWIFT, MARTIN, NIGHTJAR, STARLING

genus ...... HIRUNDO, PHEDINA, RIPARIA, PETROCHELIDON

greedily .... GORGE, DEVOUR

like .... HIRUNDINE

well known species of .... PURPLE MARTIN

swallowing difficulty .... DYSPHAGIA

swallowtail .... COAT, BUTTERFLY

swallowwort .... CELANDINE

family .... MILKWEED

swami ...... LORD, FAKIR, EXPERT, MASTER, PUNDIT, TEACHER

swamp .... BOG, FEN, MOOR, SINK, SOAK, FLOOD, MARSH, DELUGE, DRENCH, MORASS, IMMERSE, SLOUGH, WETLAND, INUNDATE, (QUAG)MIRE, OVERWHELM

air .... MIASMA, MALARIA

bird .... ROBIN, TOWHEE, REDWING, SPARROW

fever .... MALARIA

flower .... AZALEA, HONEYSUCKLE

forest site .... FLORIDA, GEORGIA

plant .... SOLA, COWSLIP, MAGNOLIA, MARIGOLD

trees .... MANGROVE

vapor ..... MIASM(A), MEPHETIS

Swamp Fox soubriquet .... MARION

swamped .... FLOODED, WHELMED, GROUNDED, SNOWED UNDER

swampland .... EVERGLADES

swamps .... SLEW, WETLAND, EVERGLADES, OVERSUPPLY

denizen of .... ALLIGATOR

swampy .... BOGGY, FENNY, MOIST, MARSHY, PALUDAL

area .... SLASH

region .... FLORIDA, GEORGIA

swan .... ANSA, BIRD, BARD, POET, SWEAR, WHOOPER, COSCOROBA, TRUMPETER, WATERFOWL

black-necked .... MELANOCORYPHUS

constellation .... CYGNUS

family .... ANATIDAE

female .... PEN

goose .... CYGNOIDES

largest .... CYGNUS OLOR

like a .... PURE, GRACEFUL

lover .... LEDA

male .... COB

mute .... CYGNUS OLOR

relative .... DUCK, GOOSE

song .... VALEDICTORY

sub-family .... ANSERINAE

trumpeter .... BUCCINATOR

whistling .... COLUMBIANUS

young .... CYGNET

Swan Lake role .... ODILE

swanky ...... POSH, FANCY, PLUSH, SHOWY, SMART, STYLISH

slang .... RITZY

swap .... TRADE, BARTER, EXCHANGE

swaraj .... HOME RULE

sward .... SOD, LAWN, TURF

swarm .... HIVE, HOST, NEST, TEEM, CROWD, GROUP, HORDE, COLONY, THRONG, CLUSTER, MIGRATE, OVERRUN, ASSEMBLE, MULTITUDE

cell .... ZOOSPORE

of birds .... FLOCK

of locusts .... CLOUD

off .... LEAVE, MIGRATE

up a tree .... SHIN

with .... INFEST, PLAGUE

swarmer .... ANT, BEE, INSECT, LOCUST

swarming .... TEEMING

swart(hy) .... DUN, DUSKY, DARK(-COMPLEXIONED)

swash ...... DASH, STRUT, PRANCE, SPLASH, SWAGGER

swashbuckling .... DARING

swastika .... FYLFOT, GAMMADION

swat .... HIT, RAP, BLOW, CLIP, SLAP, SLUG, CLOUT, WHACK

Swat, King of .... (BABE) RUTH

SWAT, part of .... SPECIAL, WEAPONS, ATTACK, TEAM

swatch .... SAMPLE, SPECIMEN

swath .... TIER, QUEUE, STRIP, TRACK, STRING, (WIND)ROW

swathe .... BIND, CLOTHE, BANDAGE, ENVELOP, SWADDLE, WRAP(PING)

sway .... BIAS, REEL, ROCK, RULE, VEER, WARP, LURCH, POWER, SWING, DANGLE, DIRECT, CONTROL, DOMINION, FLOUNDER, FLUCTUATE, OSCILLATE

swayback .... SAG, CURVATURE

sweal .... BURN, MELT(AWAY), WASTE(AWAY)

swear ...... (A)VOW, CUSS, CURSE, AFFIRM, DEPONE, DEPOSE, PLEDGE, PROMISE, BLASPHEME

by .... BET ON, TRUST

falsely .... PERJURE

in court ...... TESTIFY, WITNESS

off .... GIVE UP, ABANDON, RENOUNCE

to .... VOUCH, ATTEST, CERTIFY

word .... VOW, CUSS, OATH, CURSE, EXPLETIVE, BLASPHEMY, PROFANITY

words .... I DO

swearing .... JURANT, OATH-TAKING

sweat .... WET, BEAD, DRIP, HEAT, OOZE, SEEP, EXUDE, SUDOR, EGESTA, LATHER, EXCRETE, FERMENT, SWELTER, EXERCISE, OVERWORK, PERSPIRE, TRANSUDE, PERSPIRATION

causing .... HIDROTIC

colloquial .... STEW

drenched with .... CLAMMY, SWEATY, WILTED, SWELTER

it out .... STICK IT OUT, AWAIT(ANXIOUSLY)

no .... NO EFFORT, NO PROBLEM, NO TROUBLE

shirt .... JERSEY

sweater .... JERSEY, SLIP-ON, CARDIGAN, GUERNSEY, KNITWEAR, PULLOVER, SUDORIFIC

sweating .... SLAVING, TOILING

sweaty .... PERSPIRY, TOILSOME, LABORIOUS

Sweden .... SVERIGE

bay .... HANOBUKTEN

canal .... GOTA

capital .... STOCKHOLM

city/town .... LUND, ORSA, TABY, UMEA, BODEN, BORAS, ESLOV, FALUN, GAVLE, LULEA, MALMO, VAXJO, VISBY, YSTAD, AVESTA, OREBRO, LIDINGO, UPPSALA, BORLANGE, GOTEBORG, HALMSTAD, HUDDINGE, VASTERAS, JONKOPING, LINKOPING, OSTERSUND, SUNDSVAIL, NORRKOPING, HELSINGBORG

county .... KALMAR, OREBRO, HALLAND, UPPSALA, ALVSBORG, GOTEBORG, MALMOHUS, VARMLAND, JONKOPING, KRONOBERG, STOCKHOLM

gulf .... BOTHNIA

island .... FARO, ORNO, GRASO, OLAND, GOTLAND

lake .... ASNEN, BOLMEN, SILJAN, SOMMEN, VANERN, MALAREN, UDDJAUR, VATTERN, STORSJON, HJALMAREN

mountain .... SULITELMA, KEBNEKAISE

mountain range .... K(J)OLEN

peninsula .... HORNSLANDET

region .... LAPLAND

river .... GOTA, UME(ALV), KLAR(ALV), LJUSNAN, LULE(ALV), PITE(ALV), DALALVEN, KALIX(ALV), TORNE(ALV), MUONIO(ALV)

sea .... BALTIC

seaport .... MALMO, VISBY, KALMAR, GOTEBORG, HELSINGBORG

sound .... ORESUND, KALMARSUND

strait .... KATTEGAT, SKAGERRAK

Swedish .... LANGUAGE

balloonist, North Pole casualty .... ANDREE

clover .... ALSIKE

coin ..... ORE, CROWN, KRONA, KRONE(R), KRONOR

district .... LA(E)N

dwelling/hut .... CHALET

explorer .... HEDIN

farm .... TORP

hero .... WASA

import .... SAAB

island resident .... OLANDER, GOTLANDER

king .... ERIC, GUSTAV, BERNADOTTE

manual training .... SLOYD

measure, area .... MORGEN

measure, distance/length .... ALN, FOT, REF, FAMN

measure, liquid .... AM(AR), KAPP

monetary unit .... KRONA

native .... LAPP, SWEDE

"nightingale" .... (JENNY)LIND

Nobel Prize winner .... LAGERLOF

noble's title .... GRAF

novelist .... LAGERLOF

painter .... ZORN

parliament .... RIKSDAG

prime minister ...... ERLANDER

prime minister murdered 1985 .... PALME

rug .... RYA

ruler of Kiev .... OLEG

singer .... YODLER, YODEL(L)ER

soprano .... LIND, NILSSON

thimble .... FINGERBORG

turnip .... RUTABAGA

weight .... ASS, ORT, PUND, STEN, UNTZ, NYLAST

sweeny .... ATROPHY

sweep .... OAR, BLOW, DRAG, DUST, PUSH, RAKE, SKIM, SCAN, BROOM, BRUSH, CLEAN, CLEAR, GLIDE, IMPEL, RANGE, TRAIL, STRETCH

away .... REMOVE

out .... CLEAN, EJECT, UNCLOG, VACUUM

sweeper .... WHITEWING

sweeping .... BROAD, TOTAL, RADICAL, EXTENSIVE, WIDE(-RANGING)

blow .... SWIPE

movement .... SWOOP

sweepstakes .... DRAW, RAFFLE, LOTTERY, (HORSE)RACE

sweet ...... LUSH, CANDY, DULCET, SIRUPY, SUGARY, CANDIED, LUSCIOUS, HONEY(ED), PLEASANT, SUGAR-COATED

and soft .... DOLCE

anise .... FENNEL, FINOCCHIO

bay .... MAGNOLIA

chervil .... ANISE

cicely .... MYRRH, PARSLEY

clover .... MELILOT

drink .... PUNCH, NECTAR

flag .... SEDGE, CALAMUS

gum .... BALSAM, COPALM, BILSTED, LIQUIDAMBAR

liqueur .... CREME, CORDIAL, RATAFIA

natured .... DOUCE, GENTLE

nothings .... BLARNEY, FLATTERY, FLUMMERY

pepper ...... PAPRIKA, PIMIENTO

potato .... YAM, BATATA, CAMOTE, OCARINA

sap source .... GOMUTI

smelling .... OLENT, ODOROUS, FRAGRANT

sound .... MUSIC, MELODY

sounding .... DULCET, MELODIC, MUSICAL, MELODIOUS

stream .... AFTON

talk .... URGE, CAJOLE, SOFT-SOAP

tempered .... GENIAL, AFFABLE, AMIABLE, CORDIAL

Sweet, actress .... BLANCHE

sweetbread .... RUSK, THYMUS, PANCREAS

sweetbriar ...... ROSE, EGLANTINE

sweeten .... CANDY, GLAZE, FRESHEN, DULCIFY, SUGARCOAT

and spice .... MULL

the pot .... RAISE

sweetened drink ...... FLIP, JULEP

sweetener .... SUGAR, SYRUP, REWARD, GLUCOSE, SUCARYL, SUCROSE, ASPARTAME, CYCLAMATE, INCENTIVE, SACCHARIN

sweetening .... HONEY, SIRUP, SUGAR, SYRUP, MOLASSES, STIMULUS

sweetheart ...... JO(E), GIRL, JILL, LOVE, AMOUR, DEAR(Y), LEMAN, LOVER, POPSY, LASS(IE), SUITOR, BELOVED, LADYLOVE, TRUELOVE, VALENTINE

colloquial .... BEAU, SWAIN, DARLING, BOY FRIEND, GIRL FRIEND

idealized .... DULCINEA

in pastoral poetry ..... PHILLIS, PHYLLIS

slang .... GAL, FLAME, FELLOW, STEADY, HONEY(BUNCH), SWEETIE(PIE), LOLLAPALOOSA

sweetly .... BONHOMOUSLY

sweetmeat(s) .... CAKE, MINT, CANDY, TAFFY, BONBON, COMFIT, DRAGEE, JUJUBE, NOUGAT, TOFFEE, CARAMEL, LICORICE, PRESERVE, CONFECTION

sweetness .... HONEY, SUGAR, NECTAR

sweetsop .... ATES, ATTA

swell .... GROW, HUFF, RISE, SNOB, WAVE, BLOAT, BULGE, HEAVE, SURGE, BILLOW, DILATE, EXPAND, PUFF(UP), TUMEFY, DISTEND, INFLATE, INTUMESCE

box .... ORGAN

colloquial .... FOP, CHIC, NATTY, NOBBY, DAPPER, STYLISH, EXCELLENT

dresser .... FOP, DUDE, TOFF, DANDY, SPARK, BRUMMEL

in the ground .... LIFT

sea .... SURF

slang .... COOL, DANDY, GREAT, GROOVY

the pot .... RAISE

with water .... BLOAT

swelled .... TUMID, TURGID, SWOLLEN

swellfish .... PUFFER

swellhead .... EGOTIST, BRAGGART, NARCISSIST

swellheaded .... COCKY, STUCK UP, PUFFED UP, BOASTFUL, CONCEITED

swelling .... BLEB, BUMP, LUMP, NODE, PUFF, BULGE, EDEMA, TORUS, TUMOR, GOITER, GROWTH, TUMESCENT, TURGESCENCE

armpit/groin .... BUBO

combining form .... C(O)ELE

foot .... CHILBLAIN

harmony .... DIAPASON

pertaining to a .... NODAL

wave .... ROLLER

swelter ...... HEAT, ROAST, SWEAT, SCORCH, PERSPIRE

sweltering .... HOT, HEATED, SULTRY, TORRID, SIZZLING

swerve .... SKEW, VEER, DODGE, SHEER, SHIFT, STRAY, CAREEN, DEFLECT, DEVIATE, DIVERGE

away .... SHY

swift .... BIRD, FAST, ALERT, FLEET, QUICK, RAPID, PROMPT, SPEEDY

combining form .... TACHY

footed animal .... DEER, GAZELLE

footed maiden ...... ATALANTA

footed reptile .... IGUANA, LIZARD

ride .... TANTIVY

runner of myth ..... ATALANTA

rush .... WHOOSH

Swift, satirist .... JONATHAN

swiften .... HASTEN

swiftly .... APACE

swiftness .... HASTE, SPEED, VELOCITY

Swift's "flying island" .... LAPUTA

hero .... GULLIVER

imaginary island ...... LILLIPUT

name for himself .... CADENUS

pen name .... DRAPIER

swig .... GULP, DRINK, SWILL, GUZZLE

swiler .... SEALER

swill .... GULP, MESS, SOAK, DRINK, FILTH, OFFAL, QUAFF, SLOP(S), SLOSH, WASTE, GARBAGE, (HOG)WASH, SWALLOW, OUT-RINSE

swim .... DIP, KICK, REEL, BATHE, CRAWL, FLOAT, STEEP, SWOON, WHIRL, PADDLE, STROKE, (FEEL)DIZZY

in the nude .... SKINNY-DIP

of things, in the .... FLOW, STREAM, CURRENT

with the stream .... GO WITH THE TIDE

swimmer .... FISH, NAIAD, MERMAN, MERMAID, NATATOR

swimmer's ear .... OTITIS-EXTERNA

swimming .... CTENE, NATANT, AQUATICS

act of ..... BATHING, NATATION

bird .... DUCK, LOON, SWAN

of the head .... VERTIGO

pool .... TANK, WATERHOLE, NATATORIUM

stroke/style .... CRAWL, PADDLE, FLOATING, BUTTERFLY, BACKSTROKE, SIDESTROKE, BREASTSTROKE

suit .... BIKINI, MAILLOT

swimmingly ...... EASILY, SIMPLY, LIGHTLY, SUCCESSFULLY

swimmy .... DIZZY, GIDDY, BLURRED

Swinburne, poet ...... ALGERNON

swindle .... CON, GIP, GYP, ROB, BILK, CLIP, GULL, HOAX, ROOK, SKIN, BUNCO, BUNKO, CHEAT, COZEN, FUDGE, GOUGE, TRICK, WELSH, DIDDLE, FLEECE, (DE)FRAUD, VICTIMIZE, HORNSWOGGLE

sheet: sl. .... EXPENSE ACCOUNT

slang .... GYP, SCAM

swindler .... HAWK, CHEAT, (C)ROOK, FAKER, GOUGE, SHARK, THIEF, BILKER, CONMAN, FORGER, GYPPER, JACKAL, TREPAN, COZENER,

SHARPER, SKIN(NER), BLACKLEG, TRICKSTER
swindling scheme .... PLANT
swine .... HOG, PIG, PORCINE
breed .... DUROC, CHESTER, CHESHIRE, LANDRACE, TAMWORTH, BERKSHIRE, HAMPSHIRE, YORKSHIRE
characteristic of ...... PORCINE, SWINISH
colloquial .... SLOB, SLUT, SLOVEN, SLATTERN
disease .... GARGET, ROUGET
disease, infectious .... POX, PLAGUE
feeding of .... PANNAGE
female .... SOW
fever .... CHOLERA
flesh .... PORK
flu .... INFLUENZA
genus .... SUS
litter of .... FARROW
male .... BOAR
tender ..... HOGHERD, PIGHERD, SWINEHERD
wild .... PECCARY
young .... PIGLET, PORKER
swinelike .... PORCINE
swing .... FLAP, HANG, LILT, REEL, SWAY, TURN, WAVE, LURCH, CAREEN, RHYTHM, SWITCH, (WIG)WAG, STRETCH, BRANDISH, OSCILLATE
and miss .... STRIKE
around ...... SLUE, SPIN, PIVOT, SWIVEL
at .... FLAIL, SWIPE, THRUST
fan .... HEPCAT
in full .... ABSOLUTE, CAREFREE, UNCHAINED, UNRESTRAINED
music .... JAZZ, JIVE
the deal .... PUT OVER, PUT THROUGH
vote .... NEUTRAL
swinge .... BEAT, FLOG, LASH, WHIP
swinger .... JET-SETTER
swinging .... PENDULOUS
swingle .... SWIP(P)LE
swingman Goodman ...... BENNY
swingy .... JAZZY
swinish .... DIRTY, COARSE, FILTHY, GREEDY, HOGGISH, PIGGISH
swink .... TOIL, LABOR, SLAVE, DRUDGE, OVERWORK
swipe .... HIT, BLOW, GLOM, LIFT, CRACK, FILCH, LEVER, SMACK, STEAL, WHACK, PILFER, SNATCH, STRIKE,

THWACK
swipes .... BEER
swip(p)le .... FLAIL, SWINGLE
swirl .... CURL, EDDY, PURL, STIR, GURGE, SURGE, TWIRL, TWIST, WHIRL, WHORL
swirling ...... TURNING, GYRATION, ROTATION
aircraft .... HELICOPTER
hub .... PROPELLER
mass of water .... VORTEX, WHIRLPOOL
movement .... EDDY, TWIST, WHIRL
object .... WINDMILL
part of motor .... ROTOR
toy .... TOP, WHIRLIGIG
windstorm .... TORNADO
swirly .... KNOTTY, GNARLED, KNOTTED, TANGLED, TWISTED
swish .... CANE, FLOG, WHIP, SLOSH, RUSTLE, SPLASH, WHOOSH
swishy: sl. .... EFFEMINATE
Swiss architect .... (LE)CORBUSIER
army .... LANDWEHR
cake .... JELLYROLL
castle .... CHILLON
chard .... BEET
cheese .... GRUYERE, SAPSAGO, RACLETTE, EMMENTHALER
coin ...... BATZ, FRANC, RAPPE, CENTIME
cottage .... CHALET
district .... CANTON
Family Robinson author
.... WYSS
federal council .... BUNDESRAT
herdsman .... SENN
highest Alp .... BLANC
Italian enclave .... CAMPIONE
Italian-speaking canton
.... TICINO
language .... FRENCH, GERMAN, ITALIAN, ROMANS(C)H
largest city .... ZURICH
man of story .... TELL
mathematician .... EULER
measure ...... POT, AUNE, FUSS, IMMI, MUID, PIED, SAUM, ZOLL, POUCE, SCHUH, STAAB, TOISE, PERCHE, SETIER, KLAFTER
mercenary soldier
.... SWISSER, SWITZER
money .... FRANC
mountaineer's horn
.... ALP(EN)HORN
national flower ..... EDELWEISS
native .... BRISON, VAUDOIS

Nobel Prize winner,
medicine .... KOCHER
painter .... KLEE
patroit .... ZWINGLI
plant .... EDELWEISS
political division ...... CANTON
president .... BONVIN
Protestant .... HELVETIC
psychologist .... JUNG
resort .... YVERDON, INTERLAKEN
Rhine port .... BASEL, BASLE
scientist .... HALLER
shepherd .... SENN
sled .... LUGE
song .... YODEL
state .... CANTON
state council .... STANDERAT
union .... SONDERBUND
wind .... BISE
Swisser .... SWITZER
switch .... ROD, CANE, LASH, TURN, TWIG, WHIP, BIRCH, SHIFT, SHUNT, SPRAY, SPRIG, STICK, DIVERT, RAT(T)AN, TOGGLE, DEFLECT, HICKORY, (EX)CHANGE, TRANSFER, TRANSPOSE
blade knife .... SHIV
position .... ON, OFF, LOW, MED, HIGH
switchback ...... ROLLER COASTER
switchboard feature .... PLUG, PANEL
switchman .... SHUNTER
Switzerland .... SUISSE, HELVETIA
canton .... URI, ZUG, BERN, JURA, VAUD, AARGAU, GENEVA, GLARUS, LUZERN, SCHWYZ, TICINO, VALAIS, ZURICH, GRISONS, LUCERNE, SOLEURE, THURGAU, FRIBOURG, BASELLAND, NEUCHATEL, SOLOTHURN, BASELSTADT
capital of .... BERN(E)
city/town .... EGG, WIL, ZUG, ARTH, BIEL, CHUR, ELGG, NYON, THUN, VISP, WALD, WORB, ZOUZ, AARAU, ARBON, BADEN, BASEL, DAVOS, EMMEN, KONIZ, LANCY, PULLY, USTER, VEVEY, GENEVA, HORGEN, LUGANO, LUZERN, MORGES, RENENS, RIEHEN, WOHLEN, ZURICH, CAROUGE, HERISAU, LIESTAL, LOCARNO, LUCERNE, SOLEURE, YVERDON, BURGDORF, FRIBOURG, GRENCHEN, LAUSANNE, MONTREUX,

DUBENDORF, NEUCHATEL, RORSCHACH, WINTERTHUR

lake .... SIHL, AGERI, BODEN, LEMAN, MORAT, UNTER, ZUGER, BIELER, GENEVA, LUGANO, SARNEN, THUNER, ZELLER, ZURICH, GREIFEN, LUCERNE, SEMPACH, BRIENZER, MAGGIORE, CONSTANCE

mountain .... DOM, NAPF, RIGI, ROSA, TODI, JORAT, LEONE, VELAN, VORAB, DOLENT, HORNLI, LA DOLE, OCHSEN, RISOUX, SANTIS, TAMARO, TITLIS, MUTTLER, PILATUS, ROTHORN, BALMHORN, CLARIDEN, GENEROSO, HOCHWANG, JUNGFRAU, NAAFKOPF, NOIRMONT, OFENHORN, ROSSTOCK, BREITHORN, CHASSERON, GLARNISCH, KAISEREGG, MARMONTANA, MATTERHORN

mountain pass .... OFEN, FURKA, FLUELA, GREINA, PRAGEL, SUSTEN, BERNINA, GRIMSEL, OBERALP, SIMPLON, SPLUGEN, SEPTIMER

mountains .... JURA, LINDEN, BUCHEGG, RHATIKON, SILVRETTA, GLARUS ALPS

peak .... ERR, AULT, BUIN, KESCH, TERRI, LINARD, TENDRE, VADRET, BERNINA, UMBRAIL, SESVENNA

range .... PENNINE ALPS, RHAETIAN ALPS, LEPONTINE ALPS

region .... UNTERWALDEN, BERNESE-OBERLAND

river ...... AA, INN, AARE, BIRS, ORBE, SEEZ, THUR, TOSS, VISP, BROYE, DOUBS, LINTH, MOESA, MUOTA, REUSS, RHINE, RHONE, SAANE, SIMME, BORGNE, DRANCE, LAMMAT, MAGGIA, SARINE, TAMINO, TICINO, PLESSUR, EMMENTAL, LANDQUART, HINTERRHEIN

tunnel .... SIMPLON, LOTSCHBERG, SAINT GOTTHARD

valley .... DAVOS, ENGADINE

swivel .... TURN, VEER, PIVOT, SWING, ROTATE

swivet .... DITHER, FRENZY

in a .... AGOG

swizzle .... STIR

stick .... STIRRER

swollen .... BLOWN, PUFFY, TUMID,

BOLLEN, EDEMIC, TOROSE, TOROUS, TURGID, BLOATED, BULGING, TURGENT, ENLARGED, VARICOSE, DISTENDED

swoon .... SYNCOPE, FAINT(ING)

swoop .... FLY, DIVE, CLUTCH, PLUNGE, POUNCE, SNATCH, DESCEND, DESCENT, SWEEP UP, CARRY OFF

sword ...... BLADE, ESTOC, SABER, SKEAN, GLA(I)VE, RAPIER, ATAGHAN, CUTLAS(S), FALCHION, SCIMITAR

archaic .... TUCK, BILBO, GLAIVE

belt .... BALDRIC

blade, weaker part of .... FOIBLE

bullfighter's .... ESTOQUE

cavalry .... SABER, SABRE

curved .... SABER, CUTLASS, SCIMITAR

fencing .... EPEE, FOIL

fine-tempered .... TOLEDO

grass .... SEDGE

handle .... HAFT, HILT

Highlander's .... CLAYMORE

hilt's knob .... POMMEL

legendary .... BALMUNG, EXCALIBUR

lily .... GLADIOLUS

poetic .... STEEL

pointless/duelling .... EPEE

put to the .... KILL, SLAUGHTER

shaped .... ENSATE, XIPHOID, ENSIFORM, GLADIATE

short .... ESTOC, SKEAN

Siegfried's .... BALMUNG

St. George's .... ASCALON

strongest part of .... FORTE

thin .... TUCK, RAPIER

swordfish .... AUS, DORADO

saw of .... SERRA

swordplay .... FENCING

swords, cross .... DUEL, FIGHT

swordsman .... BLADE, FENCER

sworn .... BOUND, PLEDGED, ATTESTED, PROMISED, CERTIFIED

statement .... AFFIDAVIT, TESTIMONY, DEPOSITION

word .... VOW, OATH

swound .... FAINT, SWOON

sybarite .... EPICURE, HEDONIST, SENSUALIST, VOLUPTUARY

sybarite's delight .... EASE, LUXURY

sycamine .... MULBERRY

sycamore .... BUTTONWOOD

syce .... GROOM, ATTENDANT

sycee .... SILVER

syconium .... FIG

sycophant .... TOADY, FAWNER, YES-MAN, FLUNK(E)Y, SPANIEL, HANGER-ON, PARASITE, FLATTERER, TOADEATER, BOOTLICKER, COOKIE PUSHER

sycophantic .... PARASITIC(AL)

sycosis victim .... BEARD

vulgaris .... BARBERS' ITCH

Syene .... ASWAN

syllabic .... SONANT

syllable, accented/unaccented .... TONIC, THESIS

contraction of a .... SYNALEPHA

last .... ULTIMA

metrical stress on .... ICTUS

musical .... LA, TRA

omission of last ...... APOCOPE

short .... MORA

shortening of a .... SYSTOL

syllables, contraction of .... SYNERESIS

syllabus ...... OUTLINE, PROGRAM, SUMMARY, ABSTRACT, SYNOPSIS

syllogism ...... LOGIC, REASONING

major or minor in .... PREMISE

master of .... SOCRATES

middle term of .... MEAN

syllogisms, elliptical series of .... SORITES

sylph ...... FAIRY, GNOME, UNDINE

sylphlike .... SLIM, THIN, GRACILE, SLENDER, WILLOWY, GRACEFUL

sylvan .... RURAL, WOODY, WOODED, BUCOLIC

area .... WOODS, FOREST

diety .... PAN, SATYR, FAUN(US)

sight .... LEA

symbol. See also **emblem** .... MARK, SIGN, TOKEN, TOTEM, EMBLEM

American .... EAGLE, UNCLE SAM

bad luck .... OPAL

British .... LION, JOHN BULL

Indian .... TOTEM POLE

Libra's .... SCALES

of achievement .... MEDAL, RIBBON, TROPHY, DIPLOMA

attenuation .... SLAT

authority .... ROD, MACE, BADGE, CROWN, GLOBE, STAFF, SWORD, ENSIGN,

FASCES, SCEPTER

benevolence .... SANTA
CLAUS

birth .... STORK

bondage .... YOKE

comedy .... SOCK

death .... CROSS BONES

excellence .... ACADEMY
AWARD

family authority, once
.... PANTS

fortune/success .... RAINBOW

grief .... RUE

hardness .... NAIL

immortality .... PH(O)ENIX

Michael Arlen heroine
.... GREEN HAT

mourning .... CREPE,
CYPRESS

Ms. Nightingale .... LAMP

office .... VERGE

peace .... DOVE

"plain speaking" ..... SPADE

purity .... LILY

rank .... BADGE

remoteness .... TIMBUKTU

renewal ..... SNAKE, SERPENT

rigidity .... STEEL

royal power .... ORB,
SCEPTER

saintliness .... HALO

servitude .... YOKE

sovereignty .... MOUND,
URAEUS

strength .... ATLAS, SINEW

sun .... ATEN

swiftness .... BLUE STREAK

sword of Damocles
.... MENACE, THREAT

universe .... MANDALA

victory .... PALM, LAUREL

war .... ARES, MARS

wisdom .... OWL

phallic .... LINGA(M)

physician's .... CADUCEUS

picture used as a
.... PICTOGRAM, PICTOGRAPH

Pope's .... PALLIUM

registered .... TRADEMARK

remembrance .... ROSEMARY

shorthand .... LOGOGRAM

single speech sound
.... PHONOGRAM

status .... MINK, YACHT

suburban status .... POOL

symbolic .... ICONIC, TYPICAL,
EMBLEMATIC, FIGURATIVE

light .... HALO

representation ...... ICONOLOGY

symbolize .... MEAN, IMPLY,

FIGURE, TYPIFY, BETOKEN,
EXPRESS, SIGNIFY, STAND FOR

symmetric(al) ...... EVEN, EQUAL,
ORDERLY, REGULAR, SPHERAL,
BALANCED, PARALLEL

symmetry ...... ORDER, BALANCE,
HARMONY, EURYTHMY,
CONGRUITY, PROPORTION,
UNIFORMITY

many-sided .... MULTILATERAL

of similarity ..... PARALLELISM

three-sided .... TRILATERAL

sympathetic .... KIND, TENDER,
MERCIFUL, AGREEABLE,
CONDOLENT, CONGENIAL,
COMFORTING, COMPASSIONATE

response .... ECHO

sympathize .... CONDOLE, FEEL
FOR, UNDERSTAND,
COMMISERATE

sympathizer .... WELL-WISHER

sympathy .... PITY, RUTH,
ACCORD, CONCORD, EMPATHY,
HARMONY, KINSHIP, RAPPORT,
AFFINITY, GOODWILL,
RESPONSE, COMPASSION

expression of .... CLEMENCY,
CONDOLENCE

symphonic jazz leader
.... WHITEMAN

movement ..... LARGO, FINALE,
STRETTO

symphonize .... HARMONIZE

symphony .... CONCERT,
CONCORD, HARMONY,
SINFONIA

division of .... MOVEMENT

form .... SONATA

intended for Napoleon
.... EROICA

orchestra, particular
.... PHILHARMONIC

orchestra, philharmonic
.... VIENNA, NEW YORK

third section of .... SCHERZO

symposium .... FEAST, FORUM,
BANQUET, MEETING,
COLLOQUY, GATHERING,
CONFERENCE

kind of .... CONSENSUS

like a .... SYMPOSIAC

purpose .... DISCUSSION

symptom ...... HINT, MARK, SIGN,
TOKEN, WARNING, INDICATION

of illness .... PAIN, FEVER,
PRODROME, TEMPERATURE

of pregnancy, usually
.... MORNING SICKNESS

symptoms appearing together
.... SYNDROME

branch of medicine dealing
with .... SEM(E)IOLOGY

pertaining to ...... SEM(E)IOTIC,
SYMPTOMATIC

synagogue .... SHUL, TEMPLE,
TABERNACLE, CONGREGATION

figure .... RABBI

official .... HAZZAN, PARNAS

singer .... CANTOR, CHAZZAN

synchronize .... JIBE, MESH,
AGREE, MATCH, CONCUR,
COEXIST, COINCIDE,
HARMONIZE, COORDINATE,
CORRESPOND

synchronous .... COEVAL,
COINCIDENT, SIMULTANEOUS

syncopation .... JAZZ, BLUES,
RAGTIME

syncope .... SWOON, ELISION,
FAINTING

syncretize .... COMBINE,
RECONCILE

syncrisis .... CONTRAST

syndic .... JUDGE, MANAGER,
MAGISTRATE

syndicate .... POOL, TRUST,
CARTEL, COMBINE, COUNCIL,
MONOPOLY, CONSORTIUM,
ASSOCIATION

syndrome .... SIGNS, SYMPTOMS

syne .... AGO, SINCE

synergistic .... COACTING,
COACTIVE, CONCURRENT

synergy .... CONCERT,
COINCIDENCE

synod .... COUNCIL, MEETING,
ASSEMBLY, CONCLAVE

synonymous .... SIMILAR,
ANALOGOUS

synopsis ...... GIST, BRIEF, DIGEST,
PRECIS, REVIEW, SUMMARY,
ABSTRACT

synoptic gospel .... LUKE, MARK,
MATTHEW

syntax .... STRUCTURE

synthesis .... BLEND, UNION,
FUSION, MERGER

synthesized by means of light
.... PHOTOSYNTHESIS

synthetic .... SHAM, ERSATZ, MAN-
MADE, IMITATION, ARTIFICIAL

fabric .... NYLON, ORLON,
RAYON, DACRON, ACETATE

organic compound .... PLASTIC

rubber .... BUNA, NEOPRENE

silk .... NYLON, RAYON

syntony .... RESONANCE

syphilis .... POX, LUES

lesion .... CHANCRE

remedy .... SALVARSAN

slang .... CUPID'S ITCH
stage .... LATENT, PRIMARY,
    TERTIARY, SECONDARY
test for .... HAHN
syphilitic .... POCKY, LUETIC
Syria .... ARAM
Syriac script .... SERTA
Syrian .... ALAWITE, HITTITE,
    DAMASCENE, LEVANTINE
antelope .... ADDAX
bear .... DUBB
capital .... ANTIOCH,
    DAMASCUS
city/town .... AZAZ, DERA,
    DUMA, HAMA, HOMS, EL BAB,
    HALEB, HARIM, IDLIB, JEBLE,
    RAQQA, ALEPPO, MEMBIJ,
    SAFITA, TADMUR, TARTUS,
    BANIYAS, LATAKIA, MEYADIN,
    ZEBDANI, EL HASEKE, EL
    RASHID, SELEMIYA
goddess .... ASHTORETH
head of state .... AL-ATASSI
island .... RUAD, ARWAD
king .... ANTIOCHUS
measure ...... MAKUK, GARAVA
mountain .... HERMON
political party .... BAATH
premier .... ZAEYEN
president .... (HAFEZ)ASSAD
province .... DEIR, DERA,
    HAMA, HOMS, IDLIB, ALEPPO,
    HASEKE, RASHID, TARTUS,
    LATAKIA, DAMASCUS
religious follower .... DRUSE
river .... KHABUR, EL FURAT,

ORONTES, EUPHRATES
ruins .... A'MRIT, TADMOR,
    PALMYRA
ruler .... ATASSI
seaport .... TRIPOLI
sect member .... SUNNI, SHIITE
storm god .... HADAD
tribe .... AMALEK, SARACEN
tribesman .... DRUSE, SARACEN
weight .... COLA, MINA
syringa .... LILAC, MOCK ORANGE
syringe .... NEEDLE, SPRAYER,
    INJECTOR
kind of .... ENEMA, DOUCHE,
    HYPODERMIC
syrinx .... PANPIPE
syrphus fly .... GNAT
syrtis .... QUICKSAND
syrup .... SIRUP, ORGEAT,
    EXTRACT, GLUCOSE,
    SORGHUM, TREACLE,
    MOLASSES, SWEETENER
cane molasses:
    first extraction .... LIGHT
    third extraction
    .... BLACKSTRAP
kind of .... CORN, KARO,
    MAPLE
source .... SORGO
type of .... THIN, FUDGE
syrupy .... SWEET, SACCHARINE
system .... ISM, WAY, PLAN,
    ORDER, METHOD, SCHEME,
    ROUTINE, PROCEDURE,
    ARRANGEMENT

betting .... PARIMUTUEL
for classifying blood groups
    .... ABO, RH FACTORS
for sharing ideas
    .... INTERCOM
for the entire ..... SYSTEMWIDE
of government/rule
    .... REGIME
magnitude .... SOLAR
priorities .... TRIAGE
weights .... TROY
worship .... CULT
orderly .... COSMOS
part of the digestive
    .... LIVER, MOUTH, STOMACH,
    PANCREAS, ESOPHAGUS,
    INTESTINES, GALLBLADDER
political/social ...... REGIME(N)
signals .... CODE
voting .... BALLOT
systematic .... ORDERLY,
    REGULAR, ORGANIZED,
    METHODICAL, REGIMENTAL
arrangement .... SCHEMA
systematics .... TAXONOMY
systematize ...... PLAN, ARRANGE,
    ORGANIZE, STANDARDIZE
systole .... PULSE, CONTRACTION
syzygy .... DIPODY
Szczecin .... STETTIN
location .... POLAND
Szechwan .... SICHUAN
capital .... CHENGDU, CHENGTU
lyricist .... LIPO
szopelka .... OBOE

T

T-bone .... PORTERHOUSE
Greek .... TAU
Hebrew .... TAU, TAV, TAW,
    TETH
letter .... TEE
shaped cross .... TAU
Ta in chemistry .... TANTALUM
taa .... PAGODA
Taal .... AFRIKAANS
tab .... LUG, TAG, BILL, CHIT,
    FLAP, LOOP, CHECK, LABEL,
    STRIP, CHARGE, TICKET,
    ACCOUNT
colloquial .... CHOOSE,
    RECORD, SELECT, RECKONING
in aeronautics .... AIRFOIL
shoe .... STRAP, LATCHET
slang .... FINGER
Tab, actor .... HUNTER

tabanid ...... GADFLY, (HORSE)FLY
tabard ...... CAPE, CLOAK, JACKET,
    MANTLE
tabaret .... CLOTH, TABBY, FABRIC
Tabasco .... (HOT)SAUCE
capital of .... VILLAHERMOSA
tabby .... SILK, MOIRE, FELINE,
    MOREEN, TAFFETA, BRINDLED,
    BUSYBODY, GOSSIP(ER),
    (PUSSY)CAT, SPINSTER,
    GRIMALKIN
taberna .... HUT, SHED, TAVERN
tabernacle .... SHUL, TENT, HILET,
    NICHE, MOSQUE, PAGODA,
    SHRINE, TEMPLE, SANCTUARY,
    SYNAGOGUE
tabes .... ATROPHY, MARASMUS,
    PHTHISIS, EMACIATION,
    CONSUMPTION, TUBERCULOSIS

dorsalis .... SYPHILIS
tabescent .... WASTING,
    WITHERING
tabetic .... TABID, CONSUMPTIVE
Tabitha .... DORCAS
table .... DESK, DIET, FARE, FOOD,
    MENU, PEND, SLAB, BOARD,
    CHART, DEFER, FREEZE,
    SHELVE, COUNTER, LIST(ING),
    POSTPONE, TABULATION,
    COMPILATION
centerpiece .... EPERGNE
cloth .... TAPIS, RUNNER,
    SPREAD
communion .... ALTAR,
    CREDENCE
companion .... MESSMATE
cover .... BAIZE, SCARF,
    SPREAD

decoration .... DOILY, EPERGNE, PLACEMAT
decorative cloth .... RUNNER
d'hote .... MEAL
formal setting item .... CANDELABRUM
game .... POOL, CARDS, MAHJONG, PINGPONG, BILLIARDS
in architecture .... PANEL, CORNICE, MOLDING
insert .... LEAF
linen .... DAMASK, NAPERY, NAPKIN
napkin .... SERVIETTE
of contents .... INDEX
of the .... MENSAL
on wheels .... TEA WAGON
opposite of .... ACT ON
scrap .... ORT
server .... WAITER, WAITRESS
subject with Junior .... SPINACH
tennis .... PINGPONG
three-legged .... TRIVET
time- .... SCHEDULE
-top hand cleaner .... FINGER BOWL
top's section .... LEAF
tray .... LAZY SUSAN
with drawers .... DESK
writing .... SECRETARY, ESCRITOIRE
tableau .... SET, ARRAY, SCENE, DIORAMA, PICTURE
tableland .... MESA, PUNA, KAR(R)OO, PLATEAU
tablet .... PAD, PILL, SLAB, FACIA, SLATE, STELE, STONE, BOOKLET, TESSERA, MEMORIAL
blank/erased .... TABULA RASA
medicinal .... PILL, WAFER, TROCHE, LOZENGE, TABLOID, PASTILLE, COUGH DROP
ornamental .... PLAQUE
religious .... PAX
reused .... PALIMPSEST
scroll-like .... CARTOUCH(E)
writing .... PAD, SLATE, TRIPTYCH
tableware item .... DISH, FORK, KNIFE, PLATE, SPOON
tabloid .... PILL, TROCHE, NEWSPAPER
taboo/tabu ...... BAN, DON'T, NO-NO, DEBAR, BAR(OUT), EXCLUDE, PROHIBIT, VERBOTEN, FORBID(DEN), PROHIBITION
opposite of .... NOA

tabor .... DRUM, SNARE, AT(T)ABAL, TIMBREL, TABOURET
small .... TABRET
taboret .... STAND, STOOL
Tabriz native .... IRANI(AN)
tabula .... TABLE(T)
____ (clean slate) .... RASA
tabular .... FLAT
tabulate ...... LIST, CHART, TALLY, FIGURE
TAC, part of ...... TACTICAL, AIR, COMMAND
tacamahac .... GUM, RESIN, POPLAR
tache .... HOOK, BUCKLE
tachina .... FLY
tachometer meas. .... RPM
tacit .... MUTE, STILL, SILENT, UNSAID, IMPLIED, IMPLICIT, WORDLESS, UNSPOKEN, SOUNDLESS, UNUTTERED, UNEXPRESSED
for a certain time, in music .... TACET
taciturn ...... CURT, MUTE, SHORT, STILL, TERSE, SILENT, LACONIC, RESERVED, RETICENT, SATURNINE, TIGHT-LIPPED, CLOSE(-MOUTHED)
one .... CLAM, INDIAN
opposite of .... GLIB, GUSHY, CHATTY, GOSSIPY, GARRULOUS, TALKATIVE, LOQUACIOUS
tack .... ADD, PIN, SEW, YAW, BRAD, JIBE, NAIL, PATH, VEER, BASTE, ROUTE, ATTACH, COURSE, FASTEN, STITCH, ZIGZAG
kind of .... THUMB, CARPET
machine ..... DRIVER, HAMMER
on .... APPEND
room item ...... SPUR, SADDLE, STIRRUP
slang .... FARE, FOOD
tackle ...... RIG, TRY, GEAR, LUFF, GRASP, SEIZE, ADDRESS, ATTEMPT, APPARATUS, EQUIPMENT, UNDERTAKE
for lifting weights ..... PULLEY
hoisting .... CAT, GARNET
in football .... STOP, THROW, GRAPPLE WITH
kind of .... FISHING
ship's .... LUFF, JEERS
small .... JIGGER
tacky ...... CHEAP, DOWDY, SEEDY, SHABBY, SHODDY, SLEAZY, STICKY, TAWDRY, ADHESIVE
Tacoma mount .... RAINIER

tact ...... GRACE, POISE, CONCERN, FINESSE, DELICACY, DIPLOMACY, SAVOIR-FAIRE
tactical .... STRATEGIC
unit .... BRIGADE
tactics .... PLOY, METHOD, POLICY, SYSTEM, DEVICES, PROCESS, STRATEGY, MANEUVERS, STRATAGEM
warfare .... AERIAL, MANEUVER, GUERRILLA, BLITZKRIEG
tactics, ____ .... SHOCK, AERIAL, GUERRILLA
tactile .... TACTUAL, PALPABLE, TANGIBLE, TOUCHABLE
taction .... TOUCH, CONTACT
tactless .... RUDE, BLUNT, DIRECT, GAUCHE, CALLOUS, IMPOLITE, THOUGHTLESS
act .... FAUX PAS, GAUCHERIE
tad .... TOT, CHIT, CHILD, PEEWEE, URCHIN, YOUNGSTER
of salt .... PINCH
Tadmor .... PALMYRA
tadpole .... LARVA, POLLIWOG, POLLYWOG
Tadzhik's capital .... STALINABAD
taels, 16 .... CATTY
taenia .... FILLET, HEADBAND, TAPEWORM
taffarel .... (TAFF)RAIL
taffeta ...... SILK, GAUDY, TABBY, DAINTY, FLORID, SAMITE
characteristic .... GLOSSY
taffy .... CANDY, TOFFEE
colloquial .... BLARNEY, FLATTERY
Taffy .... WELSHMAN
tafia .... RUM
Taft, sculptor .... LORADO
U.S. president .... WILLIAM (HOWARD)
tag ...... TAB, LOCK, STUB, LABEL, TALLY, A(I)GLET, APPEND, FOLLOW, TAIL(END)
end .... STUB, SCRAP, STUMP, REMNANT
game chaser .... IT
line .... CATCHWORD, CATCH-PHRASE
rag .... SHRED, RABBLE, TATTER
Tagalog. See also Philippines .... MALAYAN, FILIPINO, LANGUAGE
Tagore's forte .... POETRY
Tagus .... TAJO, TEJO, RIVER
city on the .... TOLEDO
taha .... BAYA, WEAVER(BIRD)

black-headed ..... CUCULLATUS

genus .... PLOCEUS

habitat .... AFRICA, ETHIOPIA

Tahiti, capital of .... PAPEETE

former name .... OTAHEITE

lake .... VAIHIRIA

mountain .... OROHENA

neighbor island .... MOOREA

point .... TATAA, VENUS

port .... PHAETON

seaport .... PAPEETE

town .... FAAA, PAPARA,

MAHAENA, PAPENOO

Tahitian .... POLYNESIAN

canoe .... PAHI

god .... ORO, TAAROA

people .... POLYNESIAN

Tai .... THAI, SIAMESE

taiga .... FORESTS

Taihoku .... TAIPEH

tail .... CUE, END, TAG, TIP, BUNT,

BUSH, CODA, HIND, REAR,

SCUT, CAUDA, QUEUE,

FOLLOW, RETINUE,

APPENDAGE

bone .... COCCYX

breath on one's ...... TAILGATE

bushy .... BRUSH

coin's .... VERSO

colloquial .... STALK, TRAIL,

FOLLOW

combining form .... URO

deer's/hare's/rabbit's .... SCUT

docked .... BOB

end .... TAG, TIP, REAR

end of a ship, metal

.... RUDDER

ender .... LAST, FINAL

feathers .... TRAIN

hair .... BRAID, PIGTAIL

having a .... URA, CAUDATE

hood .... LIRIPIPE

like a/pertaining to a

.... CAUDAL

off .... FLEE

plane .... STABILIZER

short, erect .... SCUT

slang .... SHADOW(ER),

DETECTIVE, PRIVATE EYE

solid part .... DOCK

turn .... FLEE, RETREAT

word with .... BOB, CAT, HIGH,

COTTON

tailing .... SURVEILLANCE

tailings .... WASTE, REFUSE,

SCRAPS, REJECTS, RESIDUE

tailless .... ACAUDAL, ANUROUS,

ACAUDATE

amphibian .... FROG, TOAD,

BATRACHIA

monkey .... APE

tailor .... (OUT)FIT, DRAPER,

SARTOR, SNYDER, FASHION,

CLOTHIER, DESIGN(ER),

BUSHELMAN, COSTUMIER

concern of .... FIT, STYLE

of Coventry ...... PEEPING TOM

pattern of .... DELINEATOR

pressing iron of .... GOOSE

vent of .... SLIT

woman .... SEAMSTRESS

work of .... SARTORIAL,

TAILORING

tailors, of .... SARTORIAL

tails .... FORMAL, FULL DRESS

slang .... FISH AND SOUP

tailspin .... NOSE DIVE

tailwind welcomer .... SHIP,

AIRCRAFT

tain .... (TIN)FOIL, TIN PLATE

taint .... DYE, HUE, FLAW, COLOR,

SPOIL, STAIN, SULLY, TINGE,

DEFILE, POISON, STIGMA,

CORRUPT, POLLUTE, TARNISH,

INFECT(ION), CONTAMINATE

Taisho emperor .... YOSHIHITO

Taiwan .... FORMOSA

cape .... OLWAMPI

capital .... TAIPEH, TAIPEI

city/town .... ILAN, SUAO,

CHIAI, SINCHU, TAINAN,

TAOYUAN, CHANGHUA,

TAICHUNG, PINGTUNG,

CHUNGHSING

deer .... SIKA

government ...... KUOMINTANG

island .... HUNGTOW

islands .... PENGHU,

PESCADORES

legislature .... YUAN

mountain .... YU SHAN

port ..... KEELUNG, KAOHSIUNG

premier .... YEN

president .... CHIANG

strait port .... AMOY, XIAMEN

tea .... OOLONG

taj .... CAP, CROWN, DIADEM

Taj Mahal .... MAUSOLEUM

builder .... (SHAH) JAHAN

site of .... AGRA

take .... BUY, EAT, GET, USE, WIN,

RENT, ADOPT, CHARM, DRINK,

FETCH, GRASP, LEASE,

ABSORB, ACCEPT, ASSUME,

OBTAIN, OCCUPY, ACQUIRE,

PRESUME, RECEIVE

a breather .... REST, PAUSE

a crack at .... SNIPE

a dip .... BATHE

a liking to .... COTTON

a powder .... LEAVE, SCRAM

a risk .... DARE, GAMBLE

a stroll .... GO FOR A WALK

aback .... STARTLE, SURPRISE

——— (accept a challenge)

.... A DARE

action .... PROCEED

advantage of .... ABUSE,

IMPOSE, EXPLOIT

advice .... HEED, MIND

apart .... RUIN, UNDO

as one's own .... ADOPT

away .... DEDUCT, REMOVE,

SUBTRACT

back .... DENY, RECANT,

RETURN, RECOVER, RETRACT

by force .... GRAB, REAVE,

SEIZE, USURP, WREST, KIDNAP,

SNATCH, CAPTURE

by storm .... RAID, SEIZE,

ATTACK

care .... BEWARE

care of .... TEND, SEE TO,

NURSE, SERVE, WATCH

chances .... RISK, GAMBLE,

PLAY WITH FIRE

cover .... HIDE

——— (criticize) .... APART

dishonestly ..... STEAL, PILFER,

(SHOP)LIFT

down .... NOTE, LOWER,

WRITE, RECORD, HUMILIATE

edge off ..... DEADEN, OBTUND

effect .... INURE

exception ...... DEMUR, DIFFER,

DISAGREE

first .... PREEMPT

five .... REST, PAUSE, RELAX

for granted .... ASSUME,

EXPECT, IGNORE, NEGLECT,

PRESUME

heart .... REVIVE, CHEER UP

heed ..... MIND, RECK, BEWARE

in .... SEE, GAIN, ADMIT,

CHEAT, ACCEPT, DECEIVE,

INCLUDE, RECEIVE

in again .... RESORB

in livestock for feeding: obs.

.... AGIST

into custody .... ARREST,

IMPOUND

it easy .... LAZE, REST, LET UP,

GO SLOW

it on the lam .... FLEE, ESCAPE

——— (loll) .... IT EASY

notice .... SEE, HEED, LOOK,

NOTE, OBSERVE

off .... FLY, DOFF, FLEE, BEGIN,

LEAVE, START, DEDUCT,

DEPART, DETACH, REMOVE

offense/umbrage .... HUFF,

BRIDLE, RESENT

on .... HIRE, ADOPT, ASSUME,

EMPLOY, OPPOSE
on an obligation .... CO-SIGN
on cargo .... LADE
one's dust .... TAILGATE
one's way: poet. .... WEND
out .... ELIDE, DELE(TE),
   ESCORT, REMOVE, EXPUNGE,
   EXTRACT, ABSTRACT
out a policy .... INSURE
out again .... REDATE
over .... HAVE, ASSUME
over, unduly ...... SEIZE, USURP
part .... JOIN, PARTICIPATE
place .... OCCUR, HAPPEN,
   SUPERVENE
potshot at .... SNIPE
precedence over ..... OUTRANK
shape .... FORM, LOOM
side with .... GO TO BAT FOR
slang ..... GATE, CHEAT, TRICK,
   PROFIT, RECEIPTS
steps .... ACT
testimony from .... HEAR
the blame .... CONFESS
cake .... WIN
character of
   .... IMPERSONATE
helm .... STEER
law into one's hands
   .... COMMIT A CRIME
loss .... WRITE OFF
pits out .... DESTONE
roll .... COUNT NOSES
starch out of .... TAME
time ..... LOAF, DELAY, LINGER
to _____ .... TASK
court .... SUE
one's heels .... FLEE
task .... PUNISH
the bath .... TUB
the soapbox .... ORATE
turns .... ALTERNATE
unfair share .... HOG
up .... PURSUE, TACKLE,
   DISCUSS
up a dare .... VIE, DEFY,
   FIGHT, CONTEND
up again .... RENEW, RESUME
up as one's own .... ADOPT
voluntarily .... ADOPT
with a grain of salt
   .... DOUBT, DISTRUST,
   DISREGARD
without permission ..... STEAL
taken aback .... STARTLED,
   SURPRISED, DUMBFOUNDED
unawares .... UNPREPARED
with ..... CHARMED, IMPRESSED
taking .... WINNING, FETCHING,
   ACCEPTING, RECEIVING,
   RECEPTION, INFECTIOUS

money by intimidation
   .... BLACKMAIL, EXTORTION
turns .... ROTATIVE
takings .... PROFITS, RECEIPTS,
   WINNINGS
talapoin .... MONK, GUENON,
   MONKEY
talaria, location of .... ANKLES
of Hermes .... WINGS,
   SANDALS
talc .... POWDER, AGALITE,
   STEATITE, SOAPSTONE
talcum .... TALC, POWDER
tale .... REDE, YARN, FABLE,
   RUMOR, STORY, GOSSIP,
   LEGEND, REPORT, FICTION,
   MARCHEN, FALSEHOOD,
   NARRATIVE
adventure ...... CONTE, GEST(E)
bearer .... BUSYBODY,
   GOSSIP(ER), SCANDALMONGER
epic .... SAGA, ILIAD, AENEID
kind of .... TELL
medieval .... LAI
of lamentation/woe
   .... JEREMIAD
tall .... YARN, FISH STORY
Tale of Two Cities heroine
   .... LUCIE
talent .... ART, GIFT, FLAIR,
   KNACK, POWER, SKILL,
   GENIUS, METIER, ABILITY,
   FACULTY, APTITUDE,
   ENDOWMENT
founder .... SCOUT
natural .... DOWER, DOWRY
talented .... ABLE, SHARP,
   CLEVER, GIFTED, ENDOWED,
   ARTISTIC
tales ...... WRIT, JUROR(S), VENIRE
tales, _____ .... TWICE-TOLD
talesman .... JUROR
taleteller .... NARRATOR
Talien(wan) .... DALNY, DAIREN
taliera .... TARA
talion ...... REVENGE, PUNISHMENT
taliped .... CLUBFOOTED
talipes .... CLUBFOOT
talipot .... PALM
kind of .... BURI
talisman .... OBI, CHARM, OBEAH,
   AMULET, FETISH, GRIGRI
beetle .... SCARAB
talk ...... SAY, BLAB, BLAT, CHAT,
   CHIN, SPEAK, UTTER, SPEECH,
   YABBER, CONSULT, DECLAIM,
   DISCUSS, LECTURE, PALAVER,
   CONVERSE, CONFER(ENCE),
   CONVERSATION
abusive .... JAW
back .... LIP, SASS, RETORT,

PROVOKE, RIPOSTE,
   COMEBACK, REJOINDER
big .... BRAG, BOAST,
   MAGNIFY, EXAGGERATE
boastful .... GAS, BRAG,
   CRACK, BLUSTER, GASCONADE
chatty .... GAB, GOSSIP
childishly .... DROOL, SLOBBER
colloquial .... RAP
down .... OUTLAST, SILENCE
effusively .... GUSH
empty .... GAS, BULL, CANT,
   FUDGE, HUMBUG, PATTER,
   CHATTER, HOGWASH,
   BUNCOMBE, CLAPTRAP,
   MOONSHINE
evil .... CURSE, MALEDICTION
excited .... RANT, RAVE
flippant .... BANTER,
   PERSIFLAGE
foolish ..... GAB, BULL, DROOL,
   PRATE, BABBLE, DRIVEL,
   TATTLE, BLAB(BER), BLATHER,
   CHATTER, PRATTLE, TWADDLE,
   TWATTLE, FAPDOODLE,
   MOONSHINE, POPPYCOCK
fresh .... LIP
friendly ..... CHAT, COSE, COZE
from pulpit .... HOMILY,
   SERMON
glib .... PATTER, PALAVER
hearsay .... RUMOR, GOSSIP
idle .... GAS
impudent .... LIP, SASS
incoherent(ly) .... JABBER,
   MAUNDER, GIBBER(ISH)
informal .... CAUSERIE,
   (CHIT)CHAT
insincere .... BUNCOMBE
insincerely .... PALTER
light .... CHAFF, BANTER,
   RAILLERY, PERSIFLAGE
like an ass .... BRAY
made for effect .... BUNCOMBE
meaningless .... CANT,
   PATTER, PIFFLE, MALARK(E)Y
melodramatic .... HEROICS
moral/solemn .... HOMILY,
   SERMON
noisily .... YAP, RANT, YAUP,
   YAWP
noisy .... YAP, BLAT, RANT,
   JANGLE
nonsense .... DROOL
nonsensical .... JABBER, PIFFLE
offensive .... JAW
out of .... DISSUADE,
   PERSUADE, UNCONVINCE
over .... RERAP, DISCUSS
peevishly .... CARP

persistently on something
.... HARP
pert .... LIP
pointless .... TWADDLE,
SLIPSLOP
pompous .... BOMBAST,
FUSTIAN
quiet(ly) .... MURMUR,
WHISPER
rapid .... PATTER, CHATTER
sales .... SPIEL, PATTER
senseless .... BALDERDASH
sentimental .... SLUSH
show format .... PANEL
silly ...... BULL, DROOL, PRATE,
CACKLE, FLUMMERY
small .... GOSSIP, PATTER,
CHITCHAT
stupid .... DROOL
to .... ADDRESS, BESPEAK
to oneself .... MONOLOGIZE,
SOLILOQUIZE
vernacular .... CANT, LINGO,
JARGON
while crying .... BLUBBER
with .... CHIN
with another .... CONVERSE,
DIALOGUE, CONVERSATION
talkative .... GLIB, GABBY, GASSY,
WINDY, CHATTY, FLUENT,
MOUTHY, VOLUBLE,
GARRULOUS, LOQUACIOUS
bird .... MAGPIE, (BLUE)JAY
person .... JAY, GABBER,
GASBAG, MAGPIE, WINDBAG,
CHATTERBOX
talked about .... FAMOUS,
NOTORIOUS, WELL-KNOWN
slang .... SPIELED
talker .... SAYER, SPEAKER,
PARLEYER, CONVERSER
incessant .... GASBAG, MAGPIE,
WINDBAG, CHATTERBOX
talking dummy .... SNERD
fond of .... GABBY, WINDY,
GOSSIPY, GARRULOUS, LONG-
WINDED, LOQUACIOUS
picture .... TALKIE
to .... REBUKE, SCOLDING
tall ...... BIG, HIGH, HUGE, LARGE,
LOFTY, TAUNT, HIGHFLOWN,
LONG(LEGGED),
EXAGGERATED
and lean .... LANKY, LATHY,
GANGLY
chest .... HIGHBOY
drink with nutmeg
.... SANGAREE
order .... CHORE,
BACKBREAKER
story .... FIB

tale .... YARN
thin person .... STRINGBEAN
tallboy .... CHEST
Tallchief, ballerina .... MARIA
tallest animal .... GIRAFFE
tallier ...... SCORER, SCOREKEEPER
Tallinn .... REVAL, REVEL
tallith ...... COVER, SCARF, SHAWL,
MANTLE
tallow .... FAT, OIL, SEBO, SUET,
SEBUM, STEAT, GREASE,
STEARIN
product .... SOAP, CANDLE
tree .... CERA, ROKA
yielder .... SUET
tallowy .... LARDY, OLEIC,
UNCTUOUS
tally .... TAB, TAG, JIBE, SUIT,
TALE, AGREE, CHECK, COUNT,
LABEL, MATCH, NOTCH,
SCORE, RECORD, SQUARE,
ACCOUNT, CHALK UP,
REGISTER, CORRESPOND
tallyho .... CRY, COACH
crier .... HUNTER
pullers .... HORSES
Talmud, part of .... GEMARA,
HAGGADA, HALAKHA,
MISHNA(H)
version .... JERUSALEM,
BABYLONIAN
Talmudic .... GEMARIC, MISHNAIC,
RABBINIC
anecdote/parable
.... HAGGADA(H)
talon .... CLAW, FANG, HEEL,
NAIL, OGEE, SPUR, STOCK,
CLUTCH, HALLUX, POUNCE,
ZIPPER
taloned .... DENTATE
Talos .... MISSILE, WATCHMAN
killer of .... DAEDALUS
make of .... BRASS
talus .... SCREE, SLOPE,
ANKLE(BONE), ASTRAGALUS,
ANKLE-JOINT, HUCKLEBONE
part of .... ANKLE, TIBIA,
FIBULA
tam-o-shanter .... CAP, BERET
tam .... GONG
tamandu(a) .... ANTEATER
tamarack .... TREE, LARCH
tamarau ...... BUFFALO, CARABAO
tamarin .... MARMOSET
tamarind, Philippine
.... SAMPALOC
taste of .... ACERB
tamarisk salt tree .... ATLE(E)
tamasha .... SHOW, SPECTACLE
tambour .... DRUM, FRAME,
TABORET, EMBROIDERY

tambourine .... DRUM, RIKK,
TAAR, DAIRA, DAIRE, TABOR,
TIMBREL
Tamburlaine the Great author
...... (CHRISTOPHER) MARLOWE
tame ...... COW, DRY, BUST, DEAD,
DULL, MEEK, MILD, ACCOY,
BREAK, DAUNT, QUIET,
DOCILE, FEEBLE, GENTLE,
SOFTEN, SUBDUE, INSIPID,
SERVILE, DOMESTICATE
tamed .... BROKEN, GENTLE,
CRUSHED, CHASTENED
tameless .... WILD, FIERCE
tameness .... DOCILITY,
MEEKNESS, GENTLENESS,
MANSUETUDE
tamer .... BREAKER, TRAINER
wild horse .... COWBOY,
BRONC(H)OBUSTER
Tamerlane .... TIMUR-I-LENK
birthplace of ...... SAMARKAND
descendant of .... BABER
tomb of .... GUR AMIR
Tamil .... DRAVIDIAN
Taming of the Shrew author
.... SHAKESPEARE
Tamiroff, actor .... AKIM
Tammany Hall .... POLITICAL
MACHINE
Society official .... BOSS,
SACHEM, CACIQUE
tamp .... JAM, RAM, CRAM, DENT,
PACK, POUND, PUNCH, STAMP,
THUMP, (DE)PRESS
tamper .... PLOT, ALTER, BRIBE,
TAINT, CHANGE, DOCTOR,
MEDDLE, MONKEY, SEDUCE,
TINKER, CORRUPT, FALSIFY,
POUNDER
Tampico man .... SENOR
tampion .... PLUG, STOPPER
tampon .... PLUG, SPONGE,
PACKING, PADDING
tan .... DUN, TAW, BARK, BEAT,
BUFF, BURN, CURE, ECRU,
FLOG, HIDE, WHIP, BEIGE,
TAWNY, BRONZE, TANNIN,
THRASH, (EM)BROWN,
LEATHER
believe it or not! .... LUGGAGE
Tana .... LAKE
site .... ETHIOPIA
tanager .... REDBIRD, SONGBIRD
blue-gray .... THRAUPIS
family .... EMBERIZIDAE
paradise .... TANGARA
relative .... BUNTING, SPARROW
swallow .... TERSINA
Western .... PIRANGA
tanbark .... NAPA, ROSS

tandem .... BICYCLE, CARRIAGE
tandoor(i) .... (CLAY)OVEN
tandour .... HEATER
Tandy's husband .... CRONYN
Taney, U.S. chief justice
.... ROGER
tang .... NIP, BITE, GUST, ODOR,
ZEST, SAVOR, TASTE, TOUCH,
TRACE, FLAVOR, SHARPNESS
on chisel/knife .... POINT,
PRONG
ringing sound .... TWANG
Tanganyika merged with
Zanzibar .... TANZANIA
mountain .... KILIMANJARO
town .... UJIJI
tangent ...... ADJACENT, TOUCHING
tangerine .... ORANGE, MANDARIN
crossed with grapefruit/
pomelo .... TANGELO
tangible .... REAL, SOLID,
TACTILE, CONCRETE,
DEFINITE, MATERIAL,
PALPABLE, SENSIBLE,
TOUCHABLE, PERCEPTIBLE,
SUBSTANTIAL
tangle .... MAT, KNOT, TRAP,
CATCH, MIX(UP), SNARE,
SNARL, WEAVE, ENMESH,
JUMBLE, MUDDLE, SLEAVE,
EMBROIL, INVOLVE, PERPLEX,
SEAWEED, COMPLICATE,
INTERTWINE
foot .... WHISKEY
footed .... STUMBLING
legs: sl. .... BEER, LIQUOR
toad .... BUTTERCUP
tangled .... MESHED, COMPLEX,
BALLED UP, INTRICATE
mass .... MAT, SHAG, RAVEL
structure .... MAZE, LABYRINTH
tangy .... RACY, NIPPY, ZESTY,
SNAPPY, PIQUANT
Tanis .... ZOAN
tanist .... HEIR
tank ...... VAT, POND, POOL, STEW,
CISTERN, VEHICLE,
CONTAINER, RESERVOIR
destroyer .... BAZOOKA,
HALFTRACK
farming .... HYDROPONICS
fish .... AQUARIUM
gunner's place .... TURRET
hot water .... BOILER
military .... DD, MARK,
SHERMAN, DUPLEX DRIVE
oil .... BUNKER
rainwater .... CISTERN,
RESERVOIR
slang .... JAIL
top .... (UNDER)SHIRT

tankard .... CUP, MUG, STOUP,
POTTLE
tanker .... SHIP, OILER, BUNKER
tanned hide .... CROP, LEATHER
tannic acid .... TANNIN
source .... OAK, TEA, SUMAC,
MANGROVE
tanning bark .... KOA, ALDER
material .... KINO, FURAN,
CASHOO, SUMAC(H), CATECHU,
GAMBIER, CATECHIN,
QUEBRACHO
powdered leaves .... SUMAC(H)
tansy .... WEED
poisonous .... RAGWORT,
FELONWEED
tantalize .... VEX, BALK, TEASE,
TEMPT, EXCITE, HARASS,
PLAGUE, SEDUCE, BEWITCH,
TITILLATE
tantalizing .... ALLURING,
INVITING, TICKLING,
DESIRABLE, PROVOKING
Tantalus' daughter .... NIOBE
father .... ZEUS
kingdom .... PHRYGIA
punishment .... HUNGER,
THIRST
river of doom .... TARTARUS
son .... PELOPS
tantamount .... COEQUAL,
EQUIVALENT
tantara .... BLAST, FANFARE,
FLOURISH
tantivy .... CRY, FAST, RUSH,
SWIFT, GALLOP, HEADLONG
tantrum .... FIT, HUFF, RAGE,
RAVE, FRENZY, OUTBURST,
CONNIPTION
activity .... CRY, BITE, KICK,
SPIT, YELL, SCREAM
thrower .... CHILD, RAVER,
TODDLER
Tanzania cape .... KANZI
capital .... DAR ES SALAAM
city/town .... LINDI, MBEYA,
MOSHI, TANGA, ARUSHA,
BUKOBA, DODOMA, IRINGA,
MUSOMA, MWANZA, SONGEA,
TABORA, SINGIDA, ZANZIBAR
falls .... KALAMBO
island .... JUANI, MAFIA,
PEMBA, ZANZIBAR
lake .... EYASI, NYASA,
RUKWA, NATRON, MANYARA,
VICTORIA, TANGANYIKA
monetary unit .... SHILLING
mountain ...... MERU, RUNGWE,
KILIMANJARO
national park .... RUAHA,
MIKUMI, SERENGETI

part of .... ZANZIBAR,
TANGANYIKA
president .... NYERE
region .... MARA, LINDI,
MBEYA, PEMBA, PWANI,
RUKWA, TANGA, ARUSHA,
DODOMA, IRINGA, KAGERA,
KIGOMA, MWANZA, TABORA,
MOROGORO, ZANZIBAR,
SHINYANGA, DAR ES SALAAM,
KILIMANJARO
river .... WAMI, RUAHA,
NJOMBE, ROVUMA, RUFIJI,
RUNGWA, PANGANI, WEMBERE,
MBEMKURU, KILOMBERO
seaport .... ZANZIBAR
tap .... BAR, PAT, RAP, TIT, BUNG,
COCK, CORK, FLIP, OPEN,
PLUG, DRAFT, KNOCK, SPILE,
TOUCH, VALVE, BROACH,
DECANT, FAUCET, LIQUOR,
OUTLET, SPIGOT, STRIKE,
STOPPER
chin .... CHUCK
dance .... SOFT SHOE
dancer .... HOOFER, ASTAIRE
for an office/position
.... APPOINT, NOMINATE
tapa cloth source ...... MULBERRY
wearer .... POLYNESIAN
tape .... BAND, BIND, DEMO, STRIP,
RIBBON, BANDAGE
braided .... INKLE
kind of .... SCOTCH, TICKER,
MASKING, MEASURE,
ADHESIVE, FRICTION,
MAGNETIC, CELLOPHANE,
ELECTRICAL
record .... COPY
taper .... WANE, WICK, LIGHT,
CANDLE, LESSEN, NARROW,
SLACKEN, DECREASE,
DIMINISH
tapered .... CONOID, TERETE
tapering object ...... CONE, SHIM,
SPIRE, PYRAMID, VOLCANO
to a point .... SUBULATE
tapestry .... RUG, ARRAS, TAPIS,
DOSSAL, DOSSEL, DOSSER,
MOSAIC, GOBELIN, WEAVING
tapeworm .... T(A)ENIA, CESTODE,
CESTOID, PARASITE
disease .... HYDATID,
CYSTICERCOSIS
disease of cattle and hogs
.... MEASLES
disease of sheep .... STAGGERS
drug .... T(A)ENIACIDE,
T(A)ENIAFUGE, NICLOSAMIDE
habitat .... LIVER, LUNGS,
INTESTINES

head of .... SCOLEX
infestation .... T(A)ENIASIS
larva ..... MEASLES, COENURUS,
CYSTICERCUS
larva formation .... CYSTS
shape .... RIBBON
sucker .... HOOK, OSCULUM
type of .... BEEF, FISH, PORK,
DWARF
taphouse .... INN, TAVERN,
BAR(ROOM)
tapioca base/source .... MANIOC,
CAS(S)AVA, MANIHOT
tapir .... DANTA, MAMMAL,
UNGULATE
animal resembling ....HOG, PIG
pride of a .... SNOUT
relative .... HORSE,
RHINOCEROS
tapis .... TAPESTRY
tapper .... TELEGRAPHER
tappet .... ARM, CAM
tapping sound .... DRUM, TICK
tappings .... SAP
taproom .... BAR, SALOON
taps instrument .... DRUM, BUGLE
series of .... PATTER
tapster .... BARMAID, BARTENDER
Tapuyan .... GES, INDIAN,
LANGUAGE
tar .... GOB, GOO, BREA, SALT,
SOIL, PITCH, RESIN, SMEAR,
STAIN, DEFAME, MALTHA,
SAILOR, SEAMAN, SLUDGE,
ASPHALT, BITUMEN, BLACKEN,
MARINER, ALKITRAN,
ALCHITRAN
and _____ .... FEATHER
and feather ..... GRILL, PUNISH,
TORTURE
taramasalata .... APPETIZER
ingredient .... BREAD, POTATO,
FISH ROE
tarantas(s) .... CARRIAGE
tarantula .... SPIDER
tarboosh .... CAP, FEZ
tardy .... LATE, SLOW, SLACK,
BELATED, DELAYED,
OVERDUE, DILATORY,
SLUGGISH, BEHIND TIME
opposed to .... PROMPT
tare .... SEED, WEED, VETCH,
DISCOUNT, ALLOWANCE,
DEDUCTION
allowance additional to
.... TRET
noxious .... DARNEL
Tarentum .... TARANTO
targe .... SHIELD, BUCKLER
target ...... AIM, END, BUTT, GOAL,
MARK, QUARRY, OBJECT(IVE)

center of .... EYE, BLANK
circle .... INNER
circular central mark of a
.... BULL'S-EYE
date .... DEADLINE
easy .... SITTING DUCK
finder .... RADAR, SONAR
get on .... ZERO
in a game .... PIN
knight's .... QUINTAIN
mound behind .... BUTT
of a Patriot .... SCUD
of blame .... SCAPEGOAT
of ridicule .... BUTT,
LAUGHINGSTOCK
of white cloth .... CLOUT
practice place .... RANGE
range .... BUTTS
shooting gallery .... DUCK
shooting post ..... MANT(E)LET
towed .... DROGUE
Tarheel .... CAROLINIAN
State .... NORTH CAROLINA
tariff ...... TAX, COST, DUTY, LIST,
IMPOST, CUSTOMS
Tarkington, novelist ...... BOOTH
tarlatan .... MUSLIN
tarmac .... (AIRPORT)RUNWAY
tarn .... LAKE, LOCH, POND
location .... MOUNTAIN
'tarnal .... ETERNAL
tarnation .... DAMNED,
DAMNATION
tarnish .... DIM, DULL, SOIL, SPOT,
STAIN, SULLY, TAINT,
SMUDGE, BLEMISH,
(BE)SMIRCH
as reputation .... DEFAME,
DEFILE, MALIGN
as silverware .... DISCOLOR
taro .... TUBER, ELEPHANT EAR
dish .... POI
fermented in pit .... MOD
root .... ED(D)O, GABI, KALO
sprouts .... DASHEEN
tarot .... CARD
tarpaulin .... TARP, CANVAS,
OILCLOTH
raincoat ...... PONCHO, SLICKER
shelter .... TENT
tarpon .... SABALO, GAMEFISH,
MILKFISH, SILVERFISH
Tarquin's avenger ...... PORSENA
tar(r)adiddle .... FIB
tarring and feathering
.... PUNISHMENT
person subjected to .... CON-
MAN, WIFE-BEATER
person subjected to: 18th
century .... TAX
COLLECTOR

tarry .... IDLE, STAY, WAIT,
(A)BIDE, DELAY, DAWDLE,
LINGER, LOITER, REMAIN,
PERSIST, SOJOURN,
(DILLY)DALLY
tarsal bone .... CALCANEUS
tarsier's habitat .... INDONESIA,
PHILIPPINES
relative .... LEMUR
tarsus .... BONE, HOCK, ANKLE
combining form .... TARSO
tart .... FLAN, KEEN, SOUR, SHARP,
PASTRY, ACERBIC, CUTTING,
(FRUIT)PIE, ACID(ULOUS)
slang .... HUSSY, TRAMP,
HARLOT, WANTON, STRUMPET
tartan .... SHIP, CHECK, PLAID,
FREIGHTER, HIGHLANDER
pattern: var. .... SETT
trousers .... TREWS
wrap-around ..... KILT, FILIBEG
tartar, containing .... TARTAROUS
emetic .... MORDANT,
EXPECTORANT
teeth .... CALCULUS
Tartar .... TURK, TATAR, MONGOL
of/pertaining to a
.... TARTARIAN
wine cask .... ARGAL, ARGOL
Tartarus .... HELL, HADES
of/pertaining to ...... INFERNAL
Tartuf(f)e .... COMEDY,
HYPOCRITE
author .... MOLIERE
Tarzan .... JUNGLE HERO
cloth .... LOIN
friends of .... APES
mate of .... JANE
portrayer of .... CRABBE,
(RON)ELY
rope for .... LIANA
stories author ..... BURROUGHS
task .... JOB, TAX, DUTY, ONUS,
WORK, LABOR, STINT,
BURDEN, CHARGE, LESSON,
ASSIGNMENT
force .... COMMANDO
menial .... DRUDGERY
routine .... CHORE
take to .... SCOLD, REBUKE
tedious .... GRIND
taskmaster .... LEGREE,
MARTINET, OVERSEER, SLAVE-
DRIVER
Tasman, Dutch navigator
.... ABEL
discovery ...... TASMANIA, NEW
ZEALAND
Tasmanian bay .... FIRES, STORM,
MARION, OYSTER, ELLIOTT,
NORFOLK, PHOQUES,

cape ..... GRIM, RAOUL, SOUTH, ANDERSON
BARREN, PILLAR, SORELL,
WICKHAM, PORTLAND,
NATURALISTE
capital .... HOBART
city/town .... BURNIE,
WYNYARD, KINGSTON,
DEVONPORT, GLENORCHY,
LAUNCESTON
devil .... DASYURE
discoverer .... TASMAN
gulf ...... BATHURST, CIRCULAR
harbor .... MACQUARIE
island ...... DEAL, KING, SWAN,
BABEL, MARIA, HUNTER,
CLARKE, HUMMOCK, ROBBINS,
FLINDERS, SCHOUTEN, EAST
SISTER, WEST SISTER, NORTH
BRUNY, SOUTH BRUNY,
VANSITTART
island group .... KENT,
HOGAN, CURTIS, FURNEAUX
lake .... ECHO, GREAT,
ARTHUR, GORDON, SORELL,
CRESCENT, SAINT CLAIR, KING
WILLIAM
mountain .... ANNE, OSSA,
HARTZ, LYELL, MUNRO,
CRADLE, PICTON, RAMSEY,
STANLEY, BARN BLUFF,
LEGGES TOR, STRZELECKI,
FRENCHMAN'S CAP
ocean .... INDIAN
peninsula .... TASMAN,
FORESTIER, FREYCINET
phalanger .... TAPOA
pine .... HUON
range .... LOFTY, ARTHUR,
DENISON, D'AGUILAR,
FRANKLAND
river .... DEE, HUON, KING,
LAKE, NIVE, OUSE, CLYDE,
DAVEY, FORTH, LEVEN,
TAMAR, ARTHUR, GORDON,
MERSEY, PEDDER, PIEMAN,
SAVAGE, DERWENT, FLORENCE,
FRANKLIN, NORTH ESK,
MACQUARIE
sea .... TASMAN
strait .... BASS, BANKS
tiger/wolf .... THYLACINE
wolf: native name .... YABBI
tass .... CUP, DRAFT, GOBLET
tassel .... TUFT, TERCEL, ZIZITH,
CORNSILK
taste .... BIT, TRY, BENT, TANG,
ZEST, GUSTO, SAVOR, TINGE,
SNACK, TRACE, DEGUST,
FLAVOR, LIKING, PALATE,
SAPO(U)R, TIDBIT, SOUPCON,

PENCHANT, EXPERIENCE,
PREFERENCE
daintily .... SIP
delicacy of .... NICETY,
POLISH, REFINEMENT
distinctive .... TANG, SMACK,
FLAVOR
for artistic objects .... VIRTU
for some specific food
.... APPETITE
for something .... TOOTH
have a pleasing .... SAPID,
RELISH, SAVORY
having .... SAPOROUS
kind of .... SOUR, SALTY,
SHARP, SWEET, BITTER, SPICY,
PEPPERY, PUNGENT
offensive .... RANK
organ of .... TONGUE
quality of being delicate in
.... DELICACY, SOFTNESS
showing refined .... DAINTY,
FASTIDIOUS
stylish .... DASH, FLAIR,
ELEGANCE
try the .... SAMPLE
tasteful ...... KEEN, SAPID, TASTY,
DAINTY, SAVORY, ELEGANT,
REFINED, CULTURED,
DELICATE, PARTICULAR,
DISCRIMINATING
luxury .... ELEGANCE
tasteless ...... DULL, FLAT, BLAND,
STALE, VAPID, INSIPID
taster .... SIPPER, SAMPLER,
SAVORER
kind of .... JUDGE, CRITIC,
GOURMET
tasty .... SAPID, SAVORY, STRONG,
PUNGENT, FLAVORED,
GUSTABLE, LUSCIOUS,
DELICIOUS, FLAVORFUL,
PALATABLE, SAPORIFIC,
TOOTHSOME
and delicious .... AMBROSIAL
colloquial .... YUMMY
dish .... MORSEL
food, small portion of
.... ANTIPASTO, APPETIZER,
HORS D'OEUVRE(S)
Tatar .... TURK, TARTAR,
MONGOL(IAN)
capital .... KAZAN
drink .... KUMISS, KOUMIS(S)
ruler .... CHAM
Strait feeder .... AMUR
tater .... POTATO
tatouay .... ARMADILLO
tatter ...... DAG, RAG, TAG, PIECE,
SCRAP, SHRED, FRAGMENT
tattered .... DUDDY, DUDDIE,

RAGGED, SHABBY, MANGLED
tatterdemalion ...... RAGAMUFFIN
tattersall .... CHECKERED
tatters .... RAGS, RIBBONS,
FRAGMENTS, ODDS AND ENDS
tatting .... LACE
tattle .... BLAB, TALK, PEACH,
PRATE, GOSSIP, JABBER,
INFORM, SNITCH, CHAT(TER),
DIVULGE, PRATTLE, DISCLOSE
tattler .... GOSSIP, TELL-TALE,
INFORMER, SANDPIPER,
CHATTERBOX
tattoo .... DOT, MARK, PINK,
PRICK, SALVO, SIGNAL,
SUMMON, VOLLEY, DRUBBING,
PUNCTURE
tau .... TAV, TEE
cross .... ANKH, CRUX
taunt .... GIBE, JAPE, JEER, JEST,
MOCK, TWIT, CHAFF, FLOUT,
SCOFF, DERIDE, NEEDLE,
REVILE, PROVOKE, REPROACH,
RIDICULE
as a ship's mast .... HIGH,
TALL
slang .... POOH-POOH
taupe .... GRAY, BROWNISH-GRAY,
GRAYISH-BROWN
taurine .... BOVINE, BULLISH
animal .... BULL
tauromachy ...... BULLFIGHT(ING)
Taurus .... BULL, CONSTELLATION
cluster .... HYAD(E)S
taut .... EDGY, FIRM, NEAT, SNUG,
TIDY, TRIM, STIFF, TENSE,
TIGHT, NERVOUS, STRAINED,
SHIPSHAPE, STRETCHED
tautog .... CHUB, MOLL,
BLACKFISH
tautology .... PLEONASM,
VERBOSITY, REDUNDANCE,
REPETITION
tav .... TAU, TEE
tavern .... BAR, INN, PUB, CAFE,
KHAN, BISTRO, HOSTEL,
SALOON, TAPROOM,
ALEHOUSE, ORDINARY,
POTHOUSE, ROADHOUSE
character .... SOT, TOPER,
BARFLY
keeper .... PROPRIETOR
server .... POTBOY, BARMAID,
BARTENDER
taw .... MIB, LINE, AGATE, ALLEY,
MARBLE
tawdry .... CHEAP, GAUDY,
SHOWY, FLASHY, GARISH,
SLEAZY, VULGAR, RAFFISH,
GINGERBREAD
tawny .... TAN, DUSKY, SWART,

FULVOUS, RUBIATE,
BROWNISH-YELLOW
tax ...... CESS, DUTY, LEVY, RATE,
SCOT, SESS, TOLL, SCAT(T),
TITHE, ASSESS, BURDEN,
CHARGE, EXCISE, IMPOST,
STRAIN
agency .... IRS
allowance .... DEDUCTIBLE
church .... TITHE
collector .... TAXER, OCTROI,
CATCHPOLE, CATCHPOLL
evader's nemesis .... TMAN
export/import .... TARIFF
extra .... SURTAX
feudal .... TALLAGE, TRIBUTE
forms .... RETURNS
man .... AGENT, ASSESSOR,
PUBLICAN
municipal .... OCTROI
official .... CUSTOMS,
ASSESSOR, REVENUER,
COLLECTOR
on imports according to
value .... AD VALOREM
on ship .... TONNAGE
ploy .... IRA
privilege .... TOLL
protection .... TRIBUTE
schedule .... TARIFF
stratagem .... DODGING,
EVASION
substitute .... SCUTAGE
type of .... SALES, INCOME,
CUSTOMS, ROAD USE,
PROPERTY
voluntary .... TITHE
taxable .... DUTIABLE,
RAT(E)ABLE, CHARGEABLE
taxation .... ASSESSMENT,
IMPOSITION
taxeme .... ORDER, ARRANGEMENT
taxi .... CAB, HACK, FIACRE,
JITNEY, DROSHKY
adjunct .... METER
driver .... HACK, CABMAN,
CABETTE
driver: colloq. .... CABBY,
CABBIE, HACKIE
rider .... FARE
three-wheeled .... PEDICAB
two-wheeled .... HANSOM,
RICKSHAW, (JIN)RIKISHA
taxicab .... HACK
parking space .... STAND
taximeter for one .... ODOGRAPH,
ODOMETER
taxonomy subject
.... SYSTEMATICS,
CLASSIFICATION
Taygeta .... STAR, PLEIAD

Taylor, actor .... ROD, ROBERT
actress .... LIZ, ELIZABETH
Caldwell play .... MELISSA
comedian .... RIP
comedienne .... RENEE
composer, critic .... DEEMS
poet, writer .... BAYARD
U.S. president .... ZACHARY
Tay-Sachs disease .... IDIOCY
symptom .... DEAFNESS,
DEMENTIA, SEIZURES,
BLINDNESS, PARALYSIS
tazza .... CUP, BOWL, VASE
TB .... TUBERCULOSIS
Tchaikovsky ballet: 1890 .... THE
SLEEPING BEAUTY
opus .... PATHETIQUE
Te Deum .... HYMN
Kanawa's talent .... VOICE
tea .... CHA(A), MATE, TCHA, TSIA,
LEDUM, PARTY, PEKOE,
SNACK, YERBA, OSWEGO,
PTISAN, CAMBRIC, LAPSANG,
PARAGUAY, COLLATION,
GATHERING, RECEPTION
add liquor to .... LACE
alkaloid .... CAFFEIN(E)
beverage like .... BEEF(TEA),
CAMOMILE
biscuit .... COOKY,
SHORTBREAD
bitter principle .... THEINE
black .... BOHEA, OOPAK,
PEKOE, OOLONG, CONGO(U),
SOUCHONG
bowl .... CHAWAN
box/container .... CADDY,
CANISTER
brand .... LIPTON, NESTEA,
SALADA, TETLEY, BIGELOW
caffeine .... THEINE
cake .... SCONE
decoction .... TISANE
drink .... CAMBRIC
family .... THEACEAE
family shrub .... BAY,
CAMELLIA, LOBLOLLY
for two .... DUET
from meat .... BROTH,
BEEF(TEA), BOUILLON
garden .... PLANTATION
green .... HYSON
medicinal .... YERBA BUENA
party: sl. .... BRAWL
plant .... THEA
pot .... URN, KETTLE,
SAMOVAR
rolled .... CHA
serve .... POUR
slang .... MARIJUANA
substitute .... YAUPON

table .... TEAPOY
waterboiler for ...... POT, URN,
KETTLE, SAMOVAR
with mint flavor .... OSWEGO
with smoky flavor
.... LAPSANG
Tea and _____ .... SYMPATHY
teaberry .... WINTERGREEN
teach .... FORM, REAR, BREED,
COACH, DRILL, EDIFY, INURE,
TRAIN, TUTOR, INFUSE,
PREACH, SCHOOL, DEVELOP,
EDUCATE, EXPOUND,
NURTURE, PREPARE, INSTRUCT
Teach, Edward .... PIRATE,
PRIVATEER, BLACKBEARD
teacher .... DON, GURU, COACH,
GUIDE, RABBI, TUTOR,
MASTER, MENTOR, READER,
MULLA(H), PUNDIT, ADVISER,
TRAINER, DIRECTOR,
EDUCATOR, EXPONENT,
LECTURER, PREACHER,
PEDAGOG(UE), PRECEPTOR,
PROFESSOR, INSTRUCTOR
bird .... VIREO, WARBLER
favorite of .... PET
gift to .... APPLE
goal of .... TENURE
job security .... TENURE
movie .... (MR.) CHIPS
narrow-minded .... PEDANT
of music, great .... MAESTRO
of the deaf .... ORALIST
old style name for
.... SCHOOLMARM
pointer of .... FESCUE
project of .... EXAM
unattached .... DOCENT
teacher's group .... NEA
teaching ...... TUITION, GUIDANCE,
TRAINING, TUTELAGE,
DIRECTION, SCHOOLING,
TUTORSHIP, INSTRUCTION
science of .... PEDAGOGY,
DIDACTICS
teachings ...... PRECEPT, DOCTRINE
teak .... TECA, TEGA, TREE, WOOD
family .... VERBENA
teakettle spout .... NOZZLE
teal .... BLUE, DUCK
team. See also **baseball;**
football; basketball
.... CREW, PAIR, GROUP,
JOIN(UP), SIDE(WITH)
athletic .... SQUAD
baseball .... NINE
basketball .... FIVE, QUINTET
cricket .... ELEVEN
diamond .... NINE
football .... ELEVEN

manager .... COACH
of ducks/pigs .... BROOD
of two animals .... SPAN,
    YOKE
pet .... MASCOT
play .... COOPERATION
rowing .... CREW
second placer ...... RUNNER-UP
teacher .... TRAINER
valuable player .... MVP,
    SUPERSTAR
winning .... CHAMPION
working .... CREW, GANG
teamster .... CARTER, DRIVER,
    CARRIER, TRUCKER,
    TRUCKMAN
teapot .... KETTLE, SAMOVAR
cover .... COS(E)Y
tear .... GAP, JAG, RIP, DASH,
    PART, RACE, RAZE, REND,
    RENT, RIVE, BREAK, BURST,
    REAVE, SPEED, SHRED, SPLIT,
    REMOVE, TATTER, DISRUPT,
    RAMPAGE, LACERATE,
    SEPARATE, LANCINATE
apart .... RIP, OPEN
down .... RAZE, WRECK,
    BULLDOZE, DEMOLISH,
    DISMANTLE
from violently .... WREST,
    WRING, WRENCH
gas .... LAC(H)RIMATOR,
    LACHRYMATOR
gas grenade secretion
    .... SMOKE
into ...... RIP, ATTACK, TACKLE
jerker .... NOSTALGIA, SOB
    STORY, SOAP(OPERA)
jerking .... SAD, NOSTALGIC,
    SENTIMENTAL
limb from limb
    .... DISMEMBER
loose .... FREE, UPROOT,
    DISLODGE
out .... REMOVE, EXTRACT
skin .... CRACK, WOUND,
    FISSURE
slang .... BINGE, SPREE,
    BENDER, CAROUSAL
to pieces .... SHRED, SMASH,
    SHATTER
teardrop diamond cut
    .... BRIOLETTE
tearful ...... SAD, TEARY, CRYING,
    RUEFUL, TRISTE, ELEGIAC,
    UNHAPPY, WEEPING,
    MOURNFUL, LAMENTING,
    SORROWFUL, LAC(H)RYMOSE
mother .... NIOBE
person .... MOURNER,
    LAMENTER

tale .... JEREMIAH
tearing .... RUSHING, VIOLENT,
    RECKLESS
apart .... DIVULSION,
    SEPARATION
for .... LANIARY
tearless .... DRY-EYED,
    UNEMOTIONAL
tears .... LACHRYMA, SECRETION
characteristic of .... SALTY
combining form .... DACRY(O)
condition, deficiency of
    .... DRY EYE
condition, excessive shedding
    of .... WATERING EYE
excessive secretion of
    .... LACRIMATION
inclined to shed many
    .... LACHRYMOSE
of .... LACHRIMAL,
    LACHRYMAL
producer .... LACRIMAL
    GLANDS
teary lady .... NIOBE
Teasdale, poetess .... SARA
tease .... BEG, IRK, KID, RAG, RIB,
    VEX, CARD, COMB, MOCK,
    RAZZ, RIDE, TWIT, ANNOY,
    CHAFF, TAUNT, BOTHER,
    EXCITE, HARASS, HECTOR,
    PESTER, NEEDLE(R),
    IMPORTUNE, TANTALIZE,
    TITILLATE
teasel .... BURR, HERB, FLOWER,
    BONESET
teaser .... JOKER, POSER, COME-
    ON, KIDDER, NEEDLER,
    PUZZLE(R), TEMPTER, LEG-
    PULLER
teasing, critical but playful
    .... ROAST
good-natured .... CHAFF,
    BANTER
humiliating .... HAZE,
    RIDICULE
teat .... DUG, PAP, TIT, UDDER,
    NIPPLE, MAMMILLA
Tebaldi, Met star .... RENATA
technetium .... MASURIUM
technical .... SKILLED, SCIENTIFIC,
    SPECIALIZED
technicality ...... DETAIL, NUANCE,
    RUBRIC, LOOPHOLE,
    MINUTIAE, FORMALITY
technician .... EXPERT
technique .... ART, STYLE,
    METHOD, SYSTEM, PROCEDURE
technology .... CRAFT, SKILL,
    TECHNICS, AUTOMATION
colloquial .... KNOW-HOW
subject .... SCIENCE,

MECHANICS, ENGINEERING
techy. See **tetchy**
tectonics .... STRUCTURE,
    ARCHITECTURE
ted .... SPREAD, SCATTER
Teddy .... BEAR
Roosevelt word .... BULLY
tedious .... DRY, DULL, PROSY,
    BORING, DREARY, HUMDRUM,
    IRKSOME, TIRESOME,
    WEARISOME, MONOTONOUS
tedium .... ENNUI, BOREDOM,
    MONOTONY
tee .... TAU, MOUND
hee .... HA-HA, GIGGLE, HEE-
    HAW, TITTER, SNICKER
off .... BEGIN, DRIVE, START
shaped thing ...... ANKH, CRUX
to green .... HOLE
teel .... SESAME(OIL)
teem .... BEAR, POUR, EMPTY,
    SWARM, ABOUND, PRODUCE,
    MULTIPLY
teeming .... RAINING, REPLETE,
    ABUNDANT, CHOCKFUL, JAM-
    PACKED, PLENTIFUL
teen's term of approval ..... FAR
    OUT
teenage trouble .... ACNE
teenager .... YOUTH, ADOLESCENT,
    BOBBYSOXER
favorite record of ..... TOP TEN
teeny .... WEE, TINY
bopper .... TEENER, TEENAGER,
    YOUNGSTER, BOBBYSOXER
weeny .... PEEWEE
teepee ...... HUT, LODGE, WIGWAM,
    WICKIUP
teeter .... REEL, ROCK, SWAY,
    WAVER, SEESAW, TOTTER,
    WOBBLE, TREMBLE, HESITATE,
    VACILLATE
teeth. See also **tooth** .... MOLARS,
    CANINES, CUSPIDS, INCISORS
appearance of new
    .... ERUPTION
arrangement .... DENTITION
artificial .... PLATE, DENTURE
chisel-shaped .... INCISORS
cleaning substance
    .... DENTIFRICE
clenching/grinding of the
    .... BRUXISM
click of .... CHATTER
coating .... ENAMEL
colloquial .... GRINDERS
combining form .... DENT(I),
    ODONT(O)
decay .... CARIES
deciduous ...... MILK, PRIMARY
deposit .... TARTAR

doctor .... DENTIST
extraction .... EXODONTIA
eye .... UPPER CANINES
hard tissue surrounding pulp
of .... IVORY, DENTIN(E)
having ..... DENTATE, TOOTHED
having large .... MACRODONT
having small .... MICRODONT
last to erupt .... WISDOM,
　　　　　　　THIRD MOLARS
long pointed .... FANGS,
　　　　　　　TUSKS, TUSHES
of/for the .... DENTAL
premolar .... BICUSPIDS
roots covering ...... CEMENTUM
rough sticky coating on
.... PLAQUE
science dealing with
.... DENTISTRY, ODONTOLOGY
sets of .... PRIMARY,
　　　　　　　PERMANENT
shaped .... DENTOID,
　　　　　　　DENTIFORM
sharp .... FANGS
shock absorber of
.... PERIODONTAL LIGAMENT
slang .... IVORIES
small .... DENTICLES
sockets .... ALVEOLI
sound .... GNASH, CHATTER
tearing .... LANIARY
use of .... CHEWING,
　　　　　　　MASTICATION
without .... EDENTATE
teething .... ERUPTION
process .... DENTITION
toy .... RING
teethridge .... ALVEOLUS
teetotal .... ALL, ENTIRE,
　　　　　　　COMPLETE
teetotaler .... DRY, NAZARITE,
　　　　ABSTAINER, NON-DRINKER
beverage of .... ADAM'S ALE
teetotalism .... ABSTINENCE,
　　　　　　　TEMPERANCE
teetotum .... TOP
tegmen ...... COATING, COVERING,
　　　　　　　TEGUMENT
Tegucigalpa is capital of
.... HONDURAS
tegula .... TILE, ALULA
tegular .... TILE-LIKE
tegument ...... ARIL, SKIN, SHELL,
　　　COCOON, TEGMEN, CAPSULE
Tehuelche .... PATAGONIAN
teil .... LINDEN
Tejo .... TAGUS
Tel Aviv greeting .... SHALOM
tela ...... WEB, TISSUE, MEMBRANE
telar .... WEBLIKE
Telamon .... ATLAS, BEARER,

COLUMN, ATLANTES
son of .... AJAX
telecast .... TELEVISE
telegram .... WIRE, TELEX,
　　　　　　　MESSAGE
slower .... DAYLETTER,
　　　　　　　NIGHTLETTER
word .... STOP
telegraph .... CABLE, SIGNAL
code .... MORSE
jungle .... TOM-TOM
kind of .... GRAPEVINE
lever .... KEY, TAPPER
signal .... DOT, DASH
wire support .... PYLON
telegraphic dash .... DAH
device for quotations
.... TICKER
Telemachus' father ...... ULYSSES,
　　　　　　　ODYSSEUS
mother .... PENELOPE
telemeter .... RANGE-FINDER
teleost fish .... EEL
telepathic .... PSYCHIC
telepathy, mental .... MIND
　　　　　　　READING
telephone .... BUZZ, CALL, PHONE,
　　　　　　　RING(UP)
book .... DIRECTORY
book classified section
.... YELLOW PAGES
diaphragm .... TYMPANUM
emergency number .... NINE-
　　　　　　　ONE-ONE
exchange .... CENTRAL,
　　　　　　　SWITCHBOARD
inventor .... BELL
main line .... TRUNK
on freeways for emergency
.... CALL BOX
operator .... CENTRAL,
　　　　　　　TELEPHONIST
part .... CORD, DIAL, RINGER,
　　　　CRADLE, RECEIVER,
　　　　　　　MOUTHPIECE
shared by a number of
people .... PARTY LINE
structure for a public
.... BOOTH
type of .... DIAL, WALL,
　　RADIO, UNLISTED, WIRELESS,
　　EXTENSION, PUSH-BUTTON
wire .... LINE
telescope .... TUBE, ABRIDGE,
　　BINOCLE, SHORTEN,
　　CONDENSE, (SPY)GLASS,
　　REFRACTOR, FIELD GLASS,
　　　　　　　BINOCULARS
attached to another .... FINDER
measuring device
.... MICROMETER

opening .... APERTURE
part .... LENS, MIRROR,
　　　　　　　EYEPIECE
telescopic .... FARSEEING
telestic(h) .... POEM, ACROSTIC
telethon moderator .... STAR,
　　CELEBRITY, POLITICIAN
purpose of .... FUND-RAISING
televiewer .... VIDEO-GAZER
television/TV .... SET, TELLY,
　　VIDEO, TELESCREEN
ad .... COMMERCIAL
adjunct ...... AERIAL, ANTENNA
annoyance .... SNOW
award .... EMMY
Bart of .... SIMPSON
blurb .... AD
broadcast .... TELECAST
cabinet .... CONSOLE
camera move .... PAN
camera plate .... MOSAIC
camera platform .... DOLLY
caveman .... FLINTSTONE
classic, Mary Martin
.... PETER PAN
commercial cat .... MORRIS
cop .... STONE, KELLER,
　　COLUMBO, WILLIAMS,
　　(PETER)GUNN, MCGARRETT
deletion .... BLEEP
doctor, early .... WELBY,
　　　　　　　KILDARE
dragon .... OLLIE
educational channel .... PBS,
　　　　　　　DISCOVERY
emcee .... COMPERE
Endora of .... AGNES
excellent interviewer
.... (LARRY)KING,
　　(BARBARA)WALTERS
extra terrestrial of .... ALF
fare ...... GAME, MOVIE, SOAPS,
　　SPORTS, SERIALS
fare, monotonous .... RERUN
game show host .... CLARK,
　　PERRY, SAJAK, WHITE,
　　BARKER, COOMBS, DAWSON,
　　TREBEK, EUBANKS, WOOLERY,
　　DAVIDSON, TOMARKEN,
　　　　　　　MARTINDALE
hook-up .... CABLE
horse .... MISTER ED
host, avuncular early
.... MILTIE
host, former .... PAAR,
　　　　　　　CARSON
interference .... SNOW
inventor of
.... (VLADIMIR)ZWORYKIN
Jeannie of .... EDEN
lawyer .... BEN MATLOCK,

PERRY MASON

letter turner ..... VANNA WHITE

lines on tube .... RASTER

"Love Connection" star .... (CHUCK) WOOLERY

"magic" .... (TECHNI)COLOR

movie channel .... HBO, CINEMAX, SHOWTIME

name .... LUCY, RHODA, IMOGENE

network .... ABC, CBS, NBC, CNN, PBS, USA, ESPN

no-no .... CIGARETTE AD(VERTISEMENT)

pickup tube .... ORTHICON

plug .... COMMERCIAL

priest, old-time .... SHEEN

"Private Eye" .... CANON, JONES, HAMMER, ROCKFORD

radar air navigation .... TELERAN

receiver .... SET

role for Burt Reynolds .... DAN AUGUST

room .... DEN, FAMILY

series, popular .... MASH, DALLAS, DYNASTY, IRONSIDE, FALCON CREST, HAWAII FIVE-O, KNOTS LANDING, MURDER SHE WROTE

"shopping" channel ...... QVC

show .... GAME, LIVE, NEWS, QUIZ, MOVIE, PANEL, RERUN, SPORTS, PAGEANT, GIVEAWAY, DOCUDRAMA, DOCUMENTARY

sound .... AUDIO

specialty .... SOAP OPERA

Spock portrayer .... NIMOY

spoiler .... SNOW

spoof .... SOAP

stand .... ROLLAWAY

street for tots .... SESAME

talk show host .... HALL, KING, LENO, JONES, CARSON, POVICH, RIVERA, RIVERS, DONAHUE, RAPHAEL, WINFREY, WOOLERY, WILLIAMS

talk show pair ...... REGIS AND KATHIE LEE

technique .... VIDEOTAPE

time .... SLOT

time buyer .... SPONSOR

topper, old-time ..... ANTENNA

tube .... KINESCOPE, ICONOSCOPE

visual element .... VIDEO

waitress .... ALICE

weathercasters .... STORM TEAM

weatherman .... NANCE, SCOTT, PEREZ, MCKUEN,

COLEMAN

witch ..... ENDORA, SAMANTHA

witch portrayer .... MOOREHEAD, MONTGOMERY

tell .... SAY, DEEM, MEAN, ORDER, SPEAK, STATE, IMPART, INFORM, UTTER, NUMBER, RECITE, RECKON, RELATE, REPEAT, REPORT, REVEAL, DECLARE, DIVULGE, EXPRESS, MENTION, NARRATE, (RE)COUNT, ACQUAINT

a story .... SPIN A YARN

all .... BLAB

apart .... DISCERN, DISTINGUISH

as by appearance .... RECOGNIZE

in detail .... RELATE, NARRATE, RECOUNT

it like it is ...... CALL A SPADE A SPADE

it to ____ .... SWEENEY

it to the ____ .... JUDGE, MARINES

off .... RATE, CHIDE, SCOLD, REBUKE, LECTURE, CHASTISE

on ...... BLAB, PEACH, BETRAY, INFORM, SQUEAL, TATTLE

privately .... CONFIDE, WHISPER

publicly .... PUBLISH, ANNOUNCE, PROCLAIM

slang .... RAT, SING, SNITCH

the truth .... CONFESS, DISCLOSE

teller .... CLERK, CASHIER, INFORMER, NARRATOR, REPORTER, ANNOUNCER, MONEY-COUNTER

place of .... CAGE

slang ..... RAT, FINK, SNITCHER

window of .... WICKET

telling .... COGENT, FORCEFUL, STRIKING, EFFECTIVE

tales on someone .... RATTING

Tell's canton .... URI

telltale .... HINT, TATTLER, INDICATOR, REVEALING

tellurian .... EARTHLY, EARTHMAN, TERRESTRIAL

telluride .... HESSITE

Tellus' domain .... EARTH

telson .... SOMITE, SEGMENT

Telugu .... DRAVIDIAN

temblor .... TREMOR, (EARTH)QUAKE

temerarious ...... RASH, RECKLESS

temerity .... GALL, BRASS, CHEEK, NERVE, DARING, AUDACITY, BOLDNESS, RASHNESS, EFFRONTERY

temper .... PET, MOOD, TONE,

HUMOR, (AN)NEAL, NATURE, SOFTEN, SPIRIT, QUALITY, TANTRUM, MODERATE, CHARACTER, COMPOSURE, DISPOSITION

bad ...... BILE, CHOLER, SPLEEN

colloquial ..... ANGER, DANDER

kind of .... ILL, IRISH

of ugly .... ORNERY

tantrum .... FIT, CONNIPTION

violent .... FURY, RAGE

tempera painting .... SECCO

temperament ...... MOOD, ETHOS, GAMUT, NATURE, DISPOSITION

condition of .... BILIOUS, CHOLERIC, SANGUINE, IRRITABLE, PHLEGMATIC, MELANCHOLIC

temperamental .... MOODY, TESTY, INNATE, EXCITABLE, IRRITABLE, SENSITIVE, HIGH-STRUNG

temperance .... SOBRIETY, ABSTINENCE, CONTINENCE, MODERATION, (SELF)RESTRAINT

temperate .... COOL, MILD, SOBER, ASCETIC, CAUTIOUS, MODERATE, CONTINENT, ABSTEMIOUS

temperature .... HEAT, FEVER, HOTNESS, COLDNESS

measuring instrument .... CRYOMETER, THERMOMETER

regulator .... CRYOSTAT, THERMOSTAT

tempered ...... MELLOWED, HEAT-TREATED

tempest .... GALE, STORM, SQUALL, TUMULT, TURMOIL, BLIZZARD, OUTBURST, HURRICANE

tempestuous .... WILD, GUSTY, WINDY, RAGING, STORMY, FURIOUS, VIOLENT, TURBULENT

Templar ...... KNIGHT, CRUSADER, BARRISTER

Templar, ____ .... SIMON

portrayer .... MOORE

temple ...... FANE, NAOS, CHAPEL, CHURCH, MOSQUE, PAGODA, RATH(A), CATHEDRAL, SANCTUARY, TABERNACLE

ancient .... NAOS

Aztec .... TEOPAN

chamber .... NAOS, CELLA

Chinese .... PAGODA, JOSS HOUSE

for all gods .... PANTHEON

for private prayer
.... ORATORY
gateway .... TORII
girl ..... BAYADEER, BAYADERE
Jewish .... SYNAGOGUE
Jupiter's .... CAPITOL
secret/innermost parts
.... PENETRALIA
shrine ...... ADYTUM, SANCTUM

Temple's (Shirley) first spouse
.... AGAR

Templeton, —— .... ALEC

tempo .... BEAT, PACE, RATE,
TIME, SPEED, RHYTHM

temporal .... CIVIL, CARNAL,
EARTHLY, MUNDANE,
SECULAR, WORLDLY,
POLITICAL, TEMPORARY,
TRANSIENT, TRANSITORY

temporary .... BRIEF, ACTING,
INTERIM, STOPGAP, FLEETING,
SEASONAL, MAKESHIFT,
TENTATIVE, PROVISIONAL
amnesia .... FUGUE
bridge .... PONTOON,
GANGPLANK
property holder: law
.... BAILEE
quiet .... LULL
refuge .... ASYLUM
relief .... RESPITE
sale .... RENTAL
stopping of activity
.... MORATORIUM
warfare cessation, mutual
.... TRUCE, CEASE-FIRE

temporize .... DELAY, HEDGE,
STALL, PROCRASTINATE

tempt .... BAIT, COAX, LURE,
APPEAL, CAJOLE, ENTICE,
INCITE, INDUCE, SEDUCE,
ATTRACT, PROVOKE

temptation ...... BAIT, SEDUCTION,
ENTICEMENT

tempter .... DEVIL, SATAN,
TEASER, CHARMER, SERPENT

tempting .... ALLURING,
SEDUCTIVE, TOOTHSOME,
ATTRACTIVE, APPETIZING

temptress ...... EVE, VAMP, FLIRT,
CIRCE, SIREN, DELILAH,
LORELEI, ENCHANTRESS

ten .... IO, DECAD(E)
ares .... DECARE
cents .... DIME
combining form .... DEC(A),
DECI, DEKA
cubic meters .... DECASTERE
decibels .... BEL
dollar bill .... SAWBUCK
dollar gold piece .... EAGLE

gallon hat .... SOMBRERO
group of .... DECADE
legged .... DECAPOD
legged crustacean .... CRAB,
PRAWN, SHRIMP, LOBSTER,
MACRURAN
men, company of .... DECURIA
men, officer in charge of
.... DECURION
per center .... AGENT
pfennig coin .... GROSCHEN
plane surfaced figure
.... DECAHEDRON
rins .... SEN
Roman numeral for X
sided .... DECAGONAL
sided and ten angled figure
.... DECAGON
slang .... TENNER
square meters .... DECIARE
thousand .... MYRIAD
times as large .... DECUPLE,
TENFOLD
to one .... ODDS
year period .... DECADE,
DECEN(N)ARY, DECENNIAL,
DECENNIUM

Ten Commandments
.... DECALOG(UE)

10%er .... AGT

tenable .... VIABLE, CREDIBLE,
PLAUSIBLE

tenace .... KING-JACK, QUEENLACE

tenacious .... BOLD, TOUGH,
CLINGY, DOGGED, STICKY,
ADHESIVE, COHESIVE,
CONSTANT, RESOLUTE,
STUBBORN, OBSTINATE,
RETENTIVE, PERSISTENT
animal .... BULLDOG
follower .... TAIL, SHADOW

tenacity ...... HOLDING, PATIENCE,
STRENGTH, CONSTANCY,
OBSTINACY, RESISTANCE,
PERSISTENCE

tenancy .... OCCUPANCY

tenant .... INMATE, LESSEE,
RENTER, VASSAL, VILLEIN,
OCCUPANT, OCCUPIER,
RESIDENT, INHABITANT

tench .... CARP

tend .... BEND, KEEP, LEAN, MIND,
BE APT, GUARD, SERVE,
WATCH, MANAGE, WAIT ON,
CARE FOR, INCLINE, OPERATE,
MINISTER
toward .... PREFER

tendency ...... BENT, BIAS, MOOD,
TONE, TURN, DRIFT, TENOR,
TREND, APTNESS, LEANING,
PENCHANT, LIKELIHOOD,

PROPENSITY, DISPOSITION,
INCLINATION

tender .... BID, BOAT, KIND, SOFT,
SORE, FRAIL, LIGHT, OFFER,
YOUNG, FEEBLE, GENTLE,
LOVING, FRAGILE, PAINFUL,
PRESENT, PROFFER, PROPOSE,
DELICATE, SENSITIVE,
(SUPPLY)SHIP
feeling .... FONDNESS,
SENTIMENT
loving care .... CONCERN,
SUPPORT
ship's ..... PINNACE, COCKBOAT
sort of .... SORER
spot .... SORE POINT
yacht .... DINGHY

tenderfoot .... NOVICE, ROOKIE,
RECRUIT, BEGINNER, BOY
SCOUT, NEWCOMER

tenderhearted ...... SOFT, KINDLY,
HUMANE, LOVING, AMOROUS,
COMPASSIONATE

tenderizing sauce ...... MARINADE

tenderloin .... MEAT, STEAK, RED-
LIGHT DISTRICT

tenderness .... PAIN, LENITY,
SENSITIVITY
of mood .... LANGUOR

tending ...... APT, PRONE, LIABLE,
LEANING(TO),
CONDUCTIVE(TO)

tendon .... CORD, THEW, SINEW,
LEADER, MUSCLE, TISSUE,
LIGAMENT
combining form .... TENO
composition of a .... FIBERS,
PROTEIN, COLLAGEN
disorder ...... RUPTURE, TENNIS
ELBOW, TRIGGER FINGER
division of .... TENOTOMY
heel .... ACHILLES
inflammation .... TENDINITIS
knee .... HAMSTRING
nodule .... SESAMOID
of/like a .... TENDINOUS
operation .... TENDOLYSIS
shape .... CYLINDRICAL
sheets of fibers in a
.... APONEUROSES

tendrac .... TENREC

tendril .... BINE, CURL, CIRRUS,
BRANCH, STIPULE
having .... CAPREOLATE
resembling a ..... TENDRILLAR,
TENDRILOUS

tendron .... BUD, SHOOT

tenebrific .... OBSCURING

tenebrous .... DIM, SAD, DARK,
DUSKY, MURKY, GLOOMY

tenement .... FLAT, SLUM, ABODE,

BUILDING, DWELLING, (APARTMENT)HOUSE
district/house .... ROOKERY
Tenerife mountain .... TEYDE
tenet .... ISM, CREDO, CREED, DOGMA, MAXIM, BELIEF, OPINION, DOCTRINE, PRINCIPLE
tenfold .... DENARY, DECUPLE
Tennessee Air Force base
.... SEWART
capital .... NASHVILLE
city/town .... ALAMO, BRISTOL, JACKSON, JOHNSON, MEMPHIS, CLEVELAND, KINGSPORT, OAK RIDGE, KNOXVILLE, COOKEVILLE, CHATTANOOGA, CLARKSVILLE
college .... LEE, LANE, BELMONT, LAMBUTH, SCARRITT, MARYVILLE
county .... DYER, KNOX, MAURY, OBION, ROANE, BLOUNT, CARTER, COFFEE, GIBSON, GREENE, MCMINN, SHELBY, SUMNER, TIPTON, WARREN, WILSON, BRADLEY, HAWKINS, WEAKLEY, SULLIVAN
dam .... NORRIS, CHEROKEE, GREAT FALLS
federal agency .... TVA
Indian .... CHICKASAW
lake .... BOONE, NORRIS, DOUGLAS, WATAUGA, CHEROKEE, KENTUCKY, PICKWICK, REELFOOT, TIMS FORD, WATTS BAR, MELTON HILL, OLD HICKORY
mountain .... GUYOT, CHILHOWEE, CLINGMANS DOME
mountain inhabitant
.... MELUNGEON
mountain range .... BALD, IRON, STONE, UNAKA, UNICOI, GREAT SMOKY, APPALACHIAN
national park .... SHILOH
national military park
.... FORT DONELSON
native .... TENNESSEAN
Naval Air Station .... MEMPHIS
plateau .... CUMBERLAND
playwright .... WILLIAMS
river .... ELK, RED, DUCK, OBED, WOLF, EMORY, GREEN, OBION, OCOEE, CLINCH, POWELL, STONES, BUFFALO, COLLINS, HARPETH, HATCHIE, HOLSTON, TELLICO, BIG SANDY, FORKED DEER, FRENCH BROAD, MISSISSIPPI
state bird .... MOCKINGBIRD

state flower .... IRIS
state nickname .... VOLUNTEER
tourist attraction
...... DOLLYWOOD, GRACELAND, THE HERMITAGE, GRAND OLE OPRY
university .... FISK, UNION, VANDERBILT, LINCOLN MEMORIAL
tennis .... RACKETS
career most singles title holder .... CONNORS
champ ...... ASHE, BETZ, BORG, CASH, GRAF, HOAD, KING, NOAH, BUDGE, BUENO, CHANG, COURT, EVERT, KODES, LAVER, LENDL, PERRY, RIGGS, SELES, SMITH, WADE, STICH, WILLS, AGASSI, AUSTIN, BECKER, EDBERG, FORGET, GIBSON, GIMENO, KRAMER, MARBLE, STOLLE, TILDEN, CONNORS, COURIER, LACOSTE, MCENROE, SANCHEZ, SANTANA, TRABERT, WHEATON, SHRIVER, CAPRIATI, GONZALES, ROSEWALL, SABATINI, GERULAITAS, NAVRATILOVA, SAMPRAS, SANCHEZ-VICARIO
competition ...... TOURNAMENT
competition, four-player
.... DOUBLES
competition, two-player
.... SINGLES
court surface .... CLAY, GRASS
equipment .... BAT, NET, PADDLE, RACKET, RACQUET
first ball .... SERVICE
ground .... COURT
handicap .... BISQUE
"Little Mo" of
.... (MAUREEN)CONNOLY
love in .... ZERO
modified .... SQUASH, HANDBALL
player, Agassi .... ANDRE
Ashe .... ARTHUR
Austin .... TRACY
Becker .... BORIS
Borg .... BJORN
Bruguera .... SERGI
Capriati .... JENNIFER
Casals .... ROSIE
Cash .... PAT
Chang .... MICHAEL
Coetzer .... AMANDA
Connors .... JIMMY
Courier .... JIM
Court .... MARGARET
Date .... KIMIKO
Davenport .... LINDSAY

Drysdale .... CLIFF
Edberg .... STEFAN
Enqvist .... THOMAS
Evert .... CHRIS
Fendick .... PATTY
Fernandez .... GIGI, MARY-JOE
Ferreira .... WAYNE
Fleming .... PETER
Forget .... GUY
Frazier .... AMY
Garrison .... ZINA
Gerulaitis .... VITAS
Gibson .... ALTHEA
Gilbert .... BRADLEY
Graf .... STEFFI
Haarhuis .... PAUL
Huber .... ANKE
Ivanisevic .... GORAN
King .... BILLIE JEAN
Korda .... PETR
Krajicek .... RICHARD
Krickstein .... AARON
Kriek .... JOHAN
Larsson .... MAGNUS
Laver .... ROD
Lendl .... IVAN
Maleeva .... MAGDALENA
Martin .... TODD
Martinez .... CONCHITA
Mayotte .... TIM
McEnroe ..... JOHN, PATRICK
McNeil .... LORI
Muster .... THOMAS
Nagelsen .... BETSY
Navratilova .... MARTINA
Newcombe .... JOHN
Noah .... YANNICK
Novotna .... JANA
Palmer .... JARED
Perry .... FRED
Pierce .... MARY
Pugh .... JIM
Raymond .... LISA
Reneberg .... RICHEY
Riggs .... BOBBY
Rostagno .... DERRICK
Sabatini .... GABRIELA
Sampras .... PETE
Sanchez .... EMILIO
Sanchez-Vicario
.... ARANTXA
Schultz .... BRENDA
Seles .... MONICA
Shriver .... PAM
Stich .... MICHAEL
Stolle .... FRED, SANDON
Tanner .... ROSCOE
Vilas .... GUILLERMO
Washington .... MALIVAI
Wheaton .... DAVID

Wilander .... MATS
Woodforde .... MARK
Zvereva .... NATASHA
player, forward .... NETMAN
player's nemesis .... NET
racket string .... CATGUT
replay .... LET
score .... LOVE, DEUCE, FORTY,
      THIRTY, FIFTEEN
score of 40 each .... DEUCE
scoring system .... VASS
series of games .... SET
shoes .... SNEAKERS
stroke .... ACE, BAT, CUT, LOB,
  CHOP, DRIVE, SLICE, SMASH,
  VOLLEY, SERVICE, BACKHAND,
       FOREHAND
table .... PINGPONG
term .... ACE, BYE, LET, SET,
  LOVE, BREAK, DEUCE, FAULT,
  LINER, MATCH, DOUBLES,
  LOVE SET, SINGLES, BASELINE,
  (AD)VANTAGE, TIE BREAKER,
     SERVICE(LINE)
uncounted service .... LET
world championship cup
 .... DAVIS
Tennyson, poet .... ALFRED
heroine .... ENID, ISOLT,
    ELAINE(THE FAIR)
heroine's home .... ASTOLAT
tenon, companion of
 .... MORTISE
tenor .... GIST, MOOD, TONE,
  DRIFT, SENSE, COURSE,
  IMPORT, MANNER, NATURE,
  SINGER, MEANING, PURPORT,
   TENDENCY, VOCALIST
counter .... ALTO
great .... CARUSO, MELCHIOR
kind of .... FALSETTO
violin .... ALTO, VIOLA
tenpins .... BOWLS, BOWLING
tenpounder .... TARPON,
      LADYFISH
tenrec .... TENDRAC
food of .... INSECTS
habitat .... MADAGASCAR
tense .... FLEX, TAUT, DRAWN,
  RIGID, STIFF, UNEASY,
  ANXIOUS, EXCITED, NERVOUS,
  (UP)TIGHT, FRENETIC,
      STRAINED
change .... ABLAUT
opposite of .... LAX, LOOSE,
  SLACK, PLIANT, RELAXED,
      EASY-GOING
verb .... PAST, FUTURE,
       PRESENT
very .... ELECTRIC, EXCITING,
      ELECTRIFYING

tensile .... DUCTILE, FLEXILE,
  PLASTIC, PLIABLE, FLEXIBLE,
      STRETCHABLE
strength .... ELASTICITY,
      RESISTANCE
tensimeter .... MANOMETER
tension .... STRAIN, STRESS,
  ANXIETY, PRESSURE
tent ...... YURT, CANVAS, ENCAMP,
  SHELTER, TABERNACLE
arena enclosed in a
 .... CIRCUS
circus .... BIG TOP
cone-shaped .... TEPEE
dweller .... ARAB, KEDAR,
  NOMAD, INDIAN, BEDOUIN,
       SCENITE
felt .... YURT
flap .... FLY
Indian .... LODGE, TE(E)PEE,
       WIGWAM
kind of .... PUP, OXYGEN,
      UMBRELLA
large .... PAVILION
of animal skins .... TUPIK
of Meeting .... TABERNACLE
show .... CIRCUS, MARQUEE,
       MARQUISE
show man .... CARNIE, CARNEY
surgical .... PLUG, DOSSIL
tentacle .... PALP, GRASP, POWER,
  FEELER, ANTENNA
feature .... SUCKER
tentacles, creature with
 .... SQUID, OCTOPUS,
  CEPHALOPOD, CUTTLE(FISH)
tentative .... TRIAL, INTERIM,
  MAKESHIFT, TEMPORARY,
  CONDITIONAL, PROVISIONAL
tenterhook .... NAIL
tenterhooks, on .... TENSE,
       ANXIOUS
tenth .... DIME, TITHE, DENARY
muse .... SAPPHO
part, a .... TITHE
revolutionary year
 .... MESSIDOR
wave .... DECUMAN
wedding anniversary gift
 .... TIN
tenths, pertaining to
 .... DECIMAL
tentmaker .... OMAR
Aquila's wife .... PRISCILLA
tenuity .... RARITY, FINENESS,
  THINNESS, FAINTNESS
tenuous ...... RARE, THIN, FLIMSY,
  SLIGHT, SLENDER, RAREFIED
tenure .... TERM, HOLDING,
      DURATION
land .... SOCAGE

of office .... INCUMBENCY
teocalli .... TEMPLE
teosinte .... GRASS
tepee ...... TENT, LODGE, WIGWAM
tepid .... MILD, (LUKE)WARM
tequila .... AGAVE, DRINK,
  LIQUOR, MESCAL, PULQUE
drinker .... MEXICAN(O)
Terah's son ...... ABRAM, HARAN,
       NAHOR
teraphim .... IDOLS
teratism .... FETUS, FREAK,
      MONSTROSITY
teratoid .... MONSTER,
      MONSTROUS
tercel .... HAWK, PEREGRINE
tercet .... TRIPLET
terebinth ...... TEIL, TREE, SUMAC,
       LINDEN
yield .... TURPENTINE
teredo .... BORER, MOLLUSK,
      SHIPWORM
tergal .... BACK, DORSAL
tergiversate .... LIE, DUCK,
  EVADE, DODGE, HEDGE,
  PARRY, SIDESTEP,
  APOSTATIZE, EQUIVOCATE,
      PREVARICATE
tergiversation .... EVASION,
  APOSTASY, SUBTERFUGE
tergum .... BACK
term .... CALL, NAME, TIME,
  WORD, LIMIT, BOUND(ARY),
  DURATION, SEMESTER,
      EXPRESSION
bookbinding .... QUIRE
geometric .... SECANT
mod .... AGOGO
of address for a young boy
 .... SONNY
of endearment .... BABY,
  TOOTS, HON(EY), DEARIE
of imprisonment: sl.
 .... STRETCH
of office .... TENURE
paper .... THESIS
school .... SEMESTER
termagant .... SHREW, VIXEN,
      HELLCAT
termer .... PRISONER
terminal .... END, LAST, DEPOT,
  FINAL, CLOSING, STATION,
  TERMINUS, EXTREMITY
negative .... CATHODE
positive .... ANODE
terminate .... END, HALT, STOP,
  ABATE, CEASE, CLOSE,
  EXPIRE, COMPLETE, CONCLUDE
at point of contact .... ABUT
prematurely .... ABORT
termination .... END(ING),

EXPIRY, FINISH, RESULT,
CONCLUSION, EXPIRATION
in grammar .... DESINENCE
of pregnancy .... ABORTION
of right .... LAPSE
word .... SUFFIX
terminology .... WORDING,
NOMENCLATURE
terminus ...... END, GOAL, DEPOT,
LIMIT, MARKER, STATION,
BOUNDARY, EXTREMITY
termite .... ANAY, WHITE ANT
terms .... AGREEMENT,
CONDITIONS, PROVISIONS,
STIPULATIONS
come to .... AGREE
make .... TREAT, NEGOTIATE
tern .... NODDY, (SEA)BIRD, SEA
SWALLOW, (LOTTERY)PRIZE
Arctic .... PARADISAEA
common .... HIRUNDO
genus .... ANOUS, STERNA
Inca .... LAROSTERNA
largest .... CASPIA
Little .... ALBITRONS
relative .... GULL
roseate .... DOUGALLII
ternary .... TRIO, THIRD, TRIAD,
TRIPLE, THREE(FOLD)
terpene alcohol .... LINALOOL
derivative .... CAMPHOR
isomeric .... LIMONENE
Terpsichore .... MUSE
concern of .... DANCE,
DANCING
terra .... SOIL, EARTH
alba .... GYPSUM, KAOLIN,
MAGNESIA
cotta .... CLAY
firma .... SOLID GROUND
incognita .... UNEXPLORED
LAND, UNEXPLORED REGION
sigil lata .... SEALED EARTH
Terra Nova ...... NEWFOUNDLAND
terrace .... BERM(E), LEVEL,
PATIO, PLANE, PORCH,
BALCONY, GALLERY,
PLATEAU, PORTICO
staircase .... PERRON
terrain .... FIELD, GROUND,
SPHERE
terramycin .... ANTIBIOTIC
terrapin .... EMYD, TURTLE,
CHELONIAN
type of .... DIAMONDBACK
terrazo .... FLOORING
material ...... CEMENT, MARBLE
terrene .... LAND, EARTH(Y),
MUNDANE, WORLDLY,
TERRITORY
terrestrial ...... GAEAL, EARTHLY,

MUNDANE, WORLDLY,
SECULAR, TEMPORAL
planet .... MARS, EARTH,
VENUS, MERCURY
terret .... LOOP, RING
terrible ...... BAD, DIRE, AWFUL,
HORRID, SEVERE, AWESOME,
FEARFUL, HIDEOUS, INTENSE,
ALARMING, DREADFUL,
HORRIBLE, SHOCKING,
APPALLING, FRIGHTFUL
colloquial .... EXCESSIVE,
UNPLEASANT
one/tsar .... IVAN
terribly: colloq. .... VERY,
EXTREMELY, EXCEEDINGLY
terrier ...... AIREDALE, WIREHAIR,
SCHNAUZER, (HUNTING)DOG
kind of .... FOX, RAT, SKYE,
CAIRN, IRISH, SILKY, WELSH,
LAKELAND, SEALYHAM,
SCOTTISH, KERRY BLUE,
YORKSHIRE, BEDLINGTON,
AUSTRALIAN, (BOSTON)BULL
terrific .... GREAT, EXCELLENT,
FABULOUS, WONDERFUL
terrified .... AGHAST, STUNNED,
PETRIFIED
terrify ...... COW, ALARM, DAUNT,
SCARE, SHOCK, APPAL(L),
DISMAY, FREEZE, STUPEFY,
FRIGHTEN, TERRORIZE,
INTIMIDATE
terrifying .... SCARY, HORRID,
GRIS(T)LY, CHILLING,
DREADFUL
terrigenous .... EARTHBORN
terrine .... STEW
territorial .... AREAL, ZONAL,
REGIONAL
division .... AMT, SHIRE,
CANTON, COUNTY
territory .... REALM, STATE,
DOMAIN, REGION, TERRENE,
DISTRICT, PROVINCE,
POSSESSION
disputed ..... SABAH, CHENPAO,
KASHMIR, DAMANSKY
terror .... FEAR, DREAD, PANIC,
FRIGHT, HORROR
colloquial ..... PEST, NUISANCE
terrorism ...... THREAT, ANARCHY,
TYRANNY, SABOTAGE,
VIOLENCE
terrorist .... GOON, OGRE,
BOMBER, ALARMIST,
ASSASSIN, VIGILANTE,
NIGHTRIDER
1836 .... SEPTEMBRIST
terrorize .... COW, BULLY, SCARE,
BROWBEAT, FRIGHTEN,

THREATEN
terse .... CURT, BRIEF, CRISP,
PITHY, SHORT, COMPACT,
CONCISE, LACONIC, SUCCINCT
tertiary .... THIRD
tessellate ...... TILE, INFIX, INLAY,
CHECKER
tesselation .... MOSAIC
tessera .... TILE
test .... FEEL, ASSAY, CHECK,
PROVE, TRIAL, TRY(OUT),
EXAMINE, WORKOUT,
EXPERIMENT
by which something is
judged .... STANDARD,
CRITERION
colloquial ..... EXAM, MIDTERM
clam's/crab's .... SHELL
device ...... WIND TUNNEL
diagnostic .... BIOPSY
flight .... TRIAL RUN
general, medical ..... PHYSICAL
kind of .... ORAL, MEDICAL,
WRITTEN
knowledge, oral or written
.... QUIZ
match .... CONTEST
of patience .... TRIAL
operation .... SHAKEDOWN
ore .... ASSAY
paper .... LITMUS
print .... PROOF
quality of ...... ESSAY, SAMPLE
severe .... ORDEAL, STRAIN,
CRUCIBLE, TRIBULATION
vessel .... CUPEL, CRUCIBLE
testa .... SHELL, INTEGUMENT
testacean .... RHIZOPOD
testament .... WILL, COVENANT
testator .... LEGATOR
beneficiary of .... HEIR(ESS),
(IN)HERITOR
tester .... CIEL, CANOPY, SIPPER,
ASSAYER, EXAMINER
testifier .... WITNESS, DEPONENT
statement of .... AFFIDAVIT,
DEPOSITION
testify ...... AVOW, STATE, SWEAR,
AFFIRM, DEPONE, DEPOSE,
DECLARE, WITNESS, MANIFEST
testimonial .... GALA, TRIBUTE,
EVIDENCE, REFERENCE,
COMPLIMENT, CERTIFICATE
testimony ...... PROOF, EVIDENCE,
ATTESTATION, DECLARATION
testing place ...... LAB(ORATORY)
testis .... GONAD
teston .... COIN
testudinate .... TURTLE, TORTOISE
testudo .... SCREEN, SHIELD,
SHELTER

testy .... CROSS, ORNERY, TOUCHY, PEEVISH, PEPPERY, WASPISH, HOTHEADED, IRASCIBLE, IRRITABLE

tetanus .... LOCKJAW, TRISMUS, INFECTION

tetany .... SPASMS

tetched .... LOCO, WITLESS, DEMENTED

tetchy .... TOUCHY, PEEVISH, PRICKLY, IRRITABLE, SENSITIVE

tete-a-tete ...... CHAT, SEAT, FACE TO FACE, HEAD TO HEAD, CONVERSATION

tether .... TIE, ROPE, LEASH, LONGE, STAKE, FASTEN, LARIAT, PICKET

Tethys .... TITANESS

father of .... URANUS

husband of .... OCEANUS

tetracaine .... ANESTHETIC

tetrad .... FOUR

tetragon .... SQUARE, QUADRANGLE

Tetragrammaton .... ADONAI, ELOHIM, YAHWEH, JEHOVAH

tetrarch .... HEROD

tetter .... ECZEMA, HERPES, LICHEN

Teucrian .... TROJAN

Teutoburger ____ in Germany .... WALD

Teuton(ic) .... DUTCH, NORDIC, ENGLISH, GERMAN(IC)

Fate .... NORN

god .... TYR, ULL, ODIN, THOR, AESIR, WODEN, BALDER

goddess .... MERTHUS

hero .... OFFA

metal collar .... TORQUE

Teutonism .... GERMANISM

Tevere .... TIBER

tew .... TOIL

tewel .... BORE, PIPE, FUNNEL, TUYERE

Texas Air Force Base ...... DYESS, KELLY, REESE, CARSWELL, LACKLAND, LAUGHLIN, SHEPPARD, BERGSTROM, ELLINGTON, GOODFELLOW

battlesite town .... RESACA

bay .... WEST, BAFFIN, COPANO, TRINITY, GALVESTON, MATAGORDA, SAN ANTONIO

capital .... AUSTIN

city/town .... WACO, BRYAN, PLANO, TYLER, DALLAS, DENTON, EL PASO, IRVING, LAREDO, ODESSA, TEMPLE, ABILENE, DENISON, GARLAND,

HOUSTON, KILLEEN, LUBBOCK, MCALLEN, MIDLAND, AMARILLO, BEAUMONT, LONGVIEW, PASADENA, VICTORIA, ARLINGTON, FORT WORTH, GALVESTON, SAN ANGELO, SAN ANTONIO, WICHITA FALLS, CORPUS CHRISTI

college ...... BISHOP, MCMURRY

county .... BEE, BELL, CASS, CLAY, COKE, HILL, HUNT, WEBB, BEXAR, BOWIE, DELTA, ECTOR, ELLIS, GREGG, AUSTIN, BRAZOS, COLLIN, DALLAS, DENTON, EL PASO, HARRIS, ORANGE, POTTER, TAYLOR, CAMERON, CORYELL, GRAYSON, HIDALGO, LUBBOCK, MIDLAND, TRAVIS, TARRANT, ANGELINA, BRAZORIA, MCLENNAN, VICTORIA, DEAF SMITH, GALVESTON, JEFFERSON

dam .... DENISON

fever victim .... CATTLE

Indian tribe .... CADDO(AN)

island .... PADRE, MUSTANG, GALVESTON, MATAGORDA

lagoon .... MADRE

lake .... KEMP, CADDO, CEDAR, LAVON, TOYAH, WORTH, MEDINA, TEXOMA, TRAVIS, HOUSTON, STAMFORD, ARLINGTON, GRAPEVINE, LIVINGSTON, CORPUS CHRISTI

leaguer .... HIT, FLY BALL

mission .... ALAMO

mountain .... LOCKE, ELEPHANT, CATHEDRAL, LIVERMORE, CERRO ALTO, SAN ANTONIO

mountain range .... DAVIS, GLASS, HUECO, VIEJA, APACHE, CHISOS, DIABLO, FINLAY, CHINATI, QUITMAN, DELAWARE, SANTIAGO, GUADALUPE

mounted state police .... RANGER

national park .... BIG BEND

native .... TEXAN

Naval Air Station ...... CHASE, KINGSVILLE, CORPUS CHRISTI

peak .... EAGLE, EMORY, CHINATI, SANTIAGO, GUADALUPE

peninsula .... BOLIVAR, MATAGORDA

plant .... LOCO

plateau .... EDWARDS, STOCKTON

ranger John Reed's secret identity .... THE LONE RANGER

river .... RED, FRIO, LEON, LLANO, PEASE, PECOS, WHITE, BRAZOS, DEVILS, MEDINA, NECHES, NUECES, SABINE, ELM FORK, NAVIDAD, SAN SABA, SULPHUR, TRINITY, WASHITA, WICHITA, COLORADO, LAMPASAS, NAVASOTA, GUADALUPE, RIO GRANDE, PEDERNALES

seaport .... GALVESTON

shrine .... ALAMO

shrub .... GUAYULE

state bird .... MOCKINGBIRD

state flower .... BLUEBONNET

state motto .... FRIENDSHIP

state nickname ..... LONE STAR

state tree .... PECAN

strip of land .... PANHANDLE

university .... A AND M, LAMAR, BAYLOR, DALLAS, EASTERN, CHRISTIAN, ST. THOMAS

winter wind .... NORTHER

text .... BOOK, THEME, TOPIC, VERSE, MATTER, SUBJECT, VERSION, WORDING, LETTERPRESS

textile .... RAG, FLAG, WOOL, CLOTH, LINEN, WOVEN, COTTON, FABRIC, DRAPERY, MATERIAL

dealer .... MERCER, CLOTHIER

goods .... LINENS, NAPERY, MERCERY, KNITWEAR, SPORTSWEAR

machine regulating device .... EVENER

making apparatus .... LOOM, WEAVER, SHUTTLE

pattern, broken-check .... HOUND'S TOOTH

printing material .... CATECHIN

shop .... MERCERY

worker .... DYER, WEAVER, INTERLACER

textual .... LITERAL

texture .... WEB, FEEL, WALE, WEFT, WOOF, GRAIN, WEAVE, STUFF, FABRIC, FINISH, TISSUE, STRUCTURE, COMPOSITION

kind of .... FINE, ROUGH, COARSE, RIBBED, SMOOTH, TOOTHED, TWILLED

TFR, part of .... TERRAIN, RADAR, FOLLOWING

T.G.I.F., part of .... THANK,

GOD, IT'S, FRIDAY
Thackeray character ...... BECKY SHARP
Thailand .... SIAM, SHAN
air base .... KORAT
canal .... KLONG
cape .... LAEM PHO, LAEM TALUMPHUK
capital .... BANGKOK
city/town .... LAE, NAN, TAK, YALA, TRANG, HAT YAI, HUA HIN, KHORAT, BURIRAM, KALASIN, LAMPANG, PATTANI, SINGORA, RAT BURI, CHON BURI, SARA BURI, THON BURI, AYUTTHAYA, CHIANG MAI, UDON THANI
coin .... ANNA, BAHT, TICAL, SATANG
gulf .... SIAM
island .... KUT, TAO, CHANG, LANTA, SAMUI, PHUKET
islands .... THALU
king .... ANANDA, BHUMIBOL, NARESUAN
language .... LAO, SHAN, THAI, KHMER, MALAY
lake .... NONG LAHAN
measure .... KWIEN, TANAN
monetary unit .... BAHT
mountain .... KAO PRAWA, (KHAO)LUANG, DOI PIA FAI, DOI INTHANON
mountains .... DANGREK, DONGRAK
native ..... LAO, THAI, SIAMESE
palace .... OHITRA LADA
pass .... AMYA, THREE PAGODAS
premier .... THANARAT, KITTIKACHORN
queen .... SIRIKIT
range .... BILAUKTAUNG
religion .... BUDDHISM
resort .... HUA HIN, PATTAYA
river ..... CHI, MUN, NAN, PING, TAPI, WANG, PASAK, MEKONG, MAE NAM, PAKCHAN, THA CHIN, MAE KLONG, CHAO PHRAYA
state guesthouse .... BOROMABIMAN
strait .... SAMUI
temple .... WAT
throne room .... CHAKRI
twin city of Bangkok .... THON BURI
weight .... PAI, BAHT, HAPH, KATI, KLAM, CATTY, FUANG, PICUL, TICAL, SALUNG, SOMPAY

Thais .... OPERA, COURTESAN
composer .... MASSENET
thalamus .... TORUS
thalassic .... MARINE
Thalia .... GRACE, (COMIC)MUSE
sister of .... CLIO, ERATO, URANIA, EUTERPE, CALLIOPE, MELPOMENE, POLYHYMNIA, TERPSICHORE
sphere of .... BLOOM, COMEDY, POETRY
thallophyte .... ALGA(E), FUNGUS, LICHEN, BACTERIA
Thames landmark .... ETON, BRIDGE
than .... AS, OR, NOR, TILL, BESIDE, OR ELSE, ASIDE FROM
Thanatos personified ...... DEATH
thane .... THEGN, FREEMAN
latter-day equivalent of .... BARON, KNIGHT
thankful .... BEHOLDEN, GRATEFUL
thankless .... UNGRATEFUL
person .... INGRATE
thanks .... GRACE, GRAMERCY, GRATITUDE, APPRECIATION
deserving of .... THANKWORTHY
thanksgiving ...... GRACE, PAEAN, PRAISE, PRAYER, THANK(S)-OFFERING
Thanksgiving day .... THURSDAY
fruit .... CRANBERRY
main course at the first .... FOUR WILD TURKEYS
pie .... MINCED, PUMPKIN
tuber .... YAM
vehicle .... SNOWPLOW
VIP .... COOK
Thant, U .... SITHU
nationality .... BURMESE
Thapsus, victor at .... CAESAR
that .... WHO, WHEN, WHOM, WHICH, YON(DER)
identical one .... ITSELF
is (to say) .... ID, I.E., EST, VIZ, IN OTHER WORDS
man .... HE
place .... THERE
so .... BECAUSE
woman .... SHE
"that rocks the cradle, ____" .... THE HAND
thatch .... HAIR, PALM, ROOF(ING), COVER(ING)
thatched beach shelter .... RAMADA
Thatcher, English prime minister .... MARGARET
thatching material .... NIPA,

COGON, GRASS, HA(U)LM, STRAW, RUSHES
thaumatology subject .... MIRACLE(S)
thaumaturge's working .... MIRACLE
thaumaturgy .... MAGIC
thaw .... EASE, MELT, RELENT, SOFTEN, UNBEND, LIQUEFY, DISSOLVE
subject of a .... ICE, BERG, SNOW, RESERVE
the affluent vote .... SILK STOCKING DISTRICTS
Babe .... RUTH
"Bandit Queen" .... BELLE STARR
bears .... TRIO
"Beautiful Whistler" .... ALICE SHAW
bench .... COURT
best offense .... DEFENSE
Big Board .... NYSE
Big Dipper .... CHARLES'S WAIN
"Bird Man of Alcatraz" .... (ROBERT)STROUD
"Blessed One" .... BUDDHA
Book .... BIBLE
"bottom of the sea" .... DAVY JONES'S LOCKER
bounding main .... OCEAN
busy bee .... HONEYMAKER
"Catholic" .... ISABELLA
Crooner .... BING(CROSBY)
Crossroads of the Pacific .... HAWAII
day of surprise attack on Pearl Harbor ..... DAY OF INFAMY
____ Decade: 1890's .... MAUVE
Draft: abbr. .... SSS
____ Eagle .... LONE
Edge author .... FRANCIS
1890's .... MAUVE DECADE
Elder and the Younger: ancient Romans .... CATOS
Enchanted Isle .... ERIN
____ (end) .... PITS
____ (English channel) .... SOLENT
"Enlightened One" .... BUDDHA
external world .... NATURE
Father of the Waltz .... STRAUSS
"few, the proud, the ____" .... MARINES
First State .... DELAWARE

735

Flintstones' pet .... DINO
Gloomy Dean .... INGE
golden shiner .... WINDFISH
Grateful ____ .... DEAD
Great Commoner and son
.... PITTS
"greatest": boxing .... ALI
heavens .... ETHER
in crowd .... THE HAVES
"Killer Whale" .... NAMU,
ORCA
king .... LE ROI
latest .... CURRENT, NEW
MODEL
law's appendage .... LONG
ARM
least bit .... FICO
Little Corporal ..... NAPOLEON
Little Paris of the Balkans
.... BUCHAREST
Lone Eagle's monogram
.... CAL
Lord .... REDEEMER
Lord ____ me up .... TAKETH
Louvre is here .... PARIS
"____ made me do it!"
.... DEVIL
"march king" .... SOUSA
master chemistry lab
.... LIVER
Messiah, e.g. ...... ORATORIO
mother of all living .... EVE
mother of civil rights
movement .... ROSA
PARKS
musical Count .... BASIE
"Northern Bear" ...... RUSSIA
one that got away .... ESCAPEE
ones at hand .... THESE
"Original Private Eye"
.... (ALLAN)PINKERTON
Ould Sod .... EIRE, IRELAND
"peanut" president
.... CARTER
period after midnight ..... WEE
HOURS, SMALL HOURS
preponderance .... MOST
"red" explorer .... ERIC
Rhine of America .... HUDSON
rite thing to say .... I DO
rocks near Gibraltar
.... ROCAS
same .... ONE, IDEM, DITTO
"Scorpion's" eye
.... ANTARES
Scouts: abbr. .... BSA
seducer .... LOTHARIO
"Seeress of Washington"
.... JEAN DIXON
ship of the desert .... CAMEL
"Spruce Goose" designer

.... (HOWARD)HUGHES
"Steel King" .... CARNEGIE
Ten Commandments
.... TORAH, DECALOG(UE)
"tentmaker" .... OMAR
____ the limit .... SKY'S
____, the merrier .... MORE
Thin Man's pooch .... ASTA
365th day .... YEAR-END
Tight Little Isle ...... ENGLAND
top grossing film studio in
the 40's .... DISNEY
trachea .... WINDPIPE
two .... BOTH
____ (walking papers)
.... SACK
"Waltz King"
.... (JOHANN)STRAUSS
"Witch of Wall Street"
.... (HETTY)GREEN
whole enchilada .... ALL
Word .... LOGOS
works .... SOUP TO NUTS
world over .... UNDER THE SUN
yuppies .... INS
The Bells interpreter .... POE
____ Brothers Show
.... SMOTHERS
____ Carson Show
.... JOHNNY
____ Clooney Show
.... ROSEMARY
Dance of Life author
.... ELLIS
____ DeLuise Show ..... DOM
Fair Penitent author ..... ROWE
Golden Lotus setting
.... CHINA
Good ____ .... EARTH
Grass Harp author .... CAPOTE
Green Hat author .... ARLEN
Gulag Archipelago author
.... SOLZHENITSYN
Jungle Book author
.... KIPLING
Kiss sculptor .... RODIN
Lodger author .... LOUNDES
____: Nolte film .... DEEP
____: Philip Barry play
.... ANIMAL KINGDOM
Prince author .... (NICCOLO)
MACHIAVELLI
Raven author .... POE
"Saga of an American
Family" is subtitle
of ____ .... ROOTS
Snake Charmer painter
.... O'HUSSO
Sons of Katie ____
.... ELDER
Source author .... MICHENER

Source character .... ELIAV,
CULLINANE, DR. VERED BAR-EL
Star Spangled Banner writer
.... (FRANCIS SCOTT)KEY
Unmade Bed author
.... SAGAN
Untouchables' Eliot ...... NESS
____ Year Itch .... SEVEN
Thea's daughter ...... EOS, SELENE
husband .... HYPERION
son .... HELIOS
theaceous tree .... TEA
thearchic .... SUPREME,
SOVEREIGN
thearchy .... THEOCRACY
theater .... ARENA, DRAMA,
STAGE, BOARDS, STUDIO,
PLAYHOUSE, MOVIEHOUSE,
OPERA(HOUSE)
audience .... GOER, HOUSE,
ATTENDER, SPECTATOR
award .... TONY
awning .... MARQUEE
box/compartment .... LOGE
call .... CURTAIN
central stage .... ARENA, FIELD
OF ACTION
cheap .... GAFF
cheapest seat .... GALLERY
club .... LAMBS
crew .... CAST
curtain .... DROP, TEASER
district .... SOHO, RIALTO,
BROADWAY
drop .... SCRIM
entrance hall .... FOYER,
LOBBY
famous .... PALACE
figure in the .... THESPIAN,
DRAMATURGE
fixture .... PROP, MARQUEE,
CALLBOARD
goer .... FAN, BUFF, PATRON,
SPECTATOR, AFICIONADO
goer on free ticket
.... DEADHEAD
ground floor/area .... PIT,
PARQUET, ORCHESTRA
group .... ANTA
light .... SPOT
of combat/war .... FRONT
LINE, BATTLEFIELD, KILLING
FIELD
of sports .... ARENA,
DIAMOND, STADIUM
of war, 1945 .... ETO
part below balcony
.... PARTERRE
presentation .... FILM, PLAY,
DRAMA, MOVIE, OPERA,
REVUE, BALLET, CONCERT,

LECTURE, MUSICAL, VARIETY
program .... (PLAY)BILL
seat .... LOGE, STALL,
  BALCONY, GALLERY,
  ORCHESTRA
sign .... SRO, EXIT
slang .... GAFF, LEGIT,
  SHOWBIZ
stage scenery .... COULISSE
street .... BROADWAY
the .... STAGE, BOARDS,
  PLAYLAND, FOOTLIGHTS
theatrical .... SHOWY, STAGY,
  VIVID, SCENIC, POMPOUS,
  AFFECTED, DRAMATIC,
  HISTRIONIC
company .... STOCK
curtain .... DROP
employee .... CALLBOY,
  PROMPTER, STAGEHAND
exciting event .... SHOW-
  STOPPER
extra .... SUPER
financier ...... ANGEL, BACKER,
  PATRON
group ...... ANTA, CAST, CREW,
  TROUPE
itinerary .... ROAD, TOUR, TRIP
lights .... FOOTS, FLOATS,
  MARQUEE, LIMELIGHT,
  SPOTLIGHT, FLOODLIGHT
nickname .... FLO, BILLY
producer .... ROSE, COHAN,
  ZIEGFELD
production ...... PLAY, DRAMA,
  REVUE, BALLET, PAGEANT,
  EXTRAVAGANZA
profession .... STAGE
role .... LEAD, STAR, HEAVY,
  INGENUE, VILLAIN
show .... PLAY, DRAMA,
  OPERA, REVUE, BALLET,
  CONCERT, VARIETY, MUSICAL,
  BURLESQUE, PANTOMIME,
  VAUDEVILLE
sketch .... SKIT
Theban blind soothsayer
  .... TIRESIAS
deities .... CABIRI
general .... PELOPIDAS
god .... AMUN-RE
goddess .... MUT
king .... CREON, LAIUS
poet .... PINDAR
queen .... JOCASTA
town .... LUXOR
Thebes, founder of ...... CADMUS
is ancient capital of .... EGYPT
one of seven against
  .... TYDEUS
site of .... KARNAK

(talking) statue of ...... VOCAL
  MEMNON
theca .... SAC, CASE, COCOON,
  CAPSULE
content .... PUPA, SPORE
thecate .... SHEATHED
Theda, actress .... BARA
theelin .... ESTRONE, HORMONE
theelol .... ESTRIOL, HORMONE
theft .... LARCENY, ROBBERY,
  BURGLARY, STEALING,
  THIEVERY
describing one .... GRAND,
  PETTY, QUALIFIED,
  EMBEZZLEMENT
literary .... PLAGIARISM
theine .... CAFFEINE
source .... TEA
theism .... PIETY
Thelma of filmdom .... RITTER
variation of .... SELMA
them .... THEY
thematic .... TOPICAL, PERIODIC
theme .... TEXT, ESSAY, TOPIC,
  THESIS, SUBJECT, (LEIT)MOTIF
heading .... LEMMA
in a design/art, etc. ..... MOTIF
in music .... TEMA
in radio/song .... SIGNATURE
Themis .... GODDESS, TITANESS
concern of .... LAW, JUSTICE
father of .... URANUS
mother of .... GAEA
what she holds .... SCALE
then .... NEXT, SOON, AGAIN,
  ALORS, HENCE, THEREFORE,
  AFTERWARDS
thenar .... PALM, SOLE
thence .... THUSLY, HEREAFTER,
  THEREFROM
thenceforth .... THEREAFTER,
  CONSEQUENTLY
theodolite .... TRANSIT
user of a .... SURVEYOR
theologian .... BEDE, CALVIN,
  DIVINE, LUTHER, ORIGEN,
  AQUINAS
theological .... DIVINE,
  CANONICAL, RELIGIOUS
list .... SEVEN DEADLY SINS
virtues, one of the .... HOPE,
  FAITH, CHARITY
theology .... CREED, DOGMA,
  BELIEF, DOCTRINE
theopany .... REVELATION,
  APOCALYPSE
theorbo .... LUTE
theorem .... PREMISE, PREPOSITION
expression of a ..... FORMULA,
  EQUATION
theoretical .... ABSTRACT,

ACADEMIC, PLATONIC,
  SPECULATIVE, HYPOTHETICAL
force .... OD(YLE), ODYL(E)
opposed to .... APPLIED,
  PRACTICAL
theorize .... GUESS, SPECULATE
theory ...... ISM, LAW, IDEA, PLAN,
  GUESS, DOCTRINE, PRINCIPLE,
  CONJECTURE, (HYPO)THESIS,
  SUPPOSITION
Darwin's .... EVOLUTION
Einstein's .... RELATIVITY
Malthusian .... POPULATION
Newton's .... GRAVITY
suffix .... ISM
therapeutic .... HEALING,
  CURATIVE
agent .... REMEDY
draught .... DOSAGE
therapy .... CURE, REMEDY,
  TREATMENT
for cancer .... RADIATION
for mental, emotional
  disorder .... PSYCHOTHERAPY
there .... AT, THEN, TOWARD,
  YON(DER), THITHER
thereabouts .... CLOSE, NEAR(BY)
thereafter .... NEXT, LATER,
  SINCE, SUBSEQUENTLY
thereby .... UPON, THROUGH
therefor ...... FOR THAT, FOR THIS
therefore .... SO, ERGO, THEN,
  HENCE, ACCORDINGLY,
  CONSEQUENTLY
therefrom ...... THENCE, THEREOF
thereto .... ALSO, BESIDES,
  MOREOVER
theriac(a) .... TREACLE,
  ANTIDOTE, MOLASSES
therianthropic being .... HARPY,
  THOTH, SPHINX, TRITON,
  CENTAUR, MERMAID
therm .... CALORIE
Therma .... SALONIKA
thermae ...... BATHS, BATHHOUSES
thermal .... HOT, WARM
underwear: sl. .... LONG JOHNS
unit ..... BTU, THERM, CALORIE
thermion, negative .... ELECTRON
positive .... ION
thermometer .... GLASS,
  MERCURY, HEAT DETECTOR
type of .... CELSIUS, DIGITAL,
  REAUMUR, CLINICAL,
  CRYOMETER, CENTIGRADE,
  FAHRENHEIT
thermoplastic .... SARAN
Thermopylae protagonist(s)
  .... XERXES, LEONIDAS,
  PERSIANS, SPARTANS
thermos .... JUG, FLASK

theroid .... BEASTLIKE

Thersites' slayer .... ACHILLES
  target of abuse .... ULYSSES,
    ODYSSEUS

thersitical .... LOUD, ABUSIVE,
  REVILING, SCURRILOUS

thesaurus .... LEXICON,
  TREASURY, DICTIONARY,
  STOREHOUSE, ENCYCLOPEDIA
  compiler .... ROGET

these days .... TIMES

Theseus' father .... AEGEUS
  friend .... PIRITHOUS
  mother .... AETHRA
  victim .... MINOTAUR
  wife .... PHAEDRA

thesis ...... ESSAY, TOPIC, THEORY,
  ARGUMENT, TREATISE,
  MONOGRAPH, POSTULATE,
  STATEMENT, COMPOSITION,
  PREPOSITION, DISSERTATION

Thespian .... ACTOR, PLAYER,
  ACTRESS, PERFORMER,
  TRAGEDIAN
  quest of .... LEAD,
    (RECOGNITION)AWARD
  whisper .... ASIDE

Thespis' forte .... TRAGEDY

Thessalian city .... LARISSA
  mountain .... OSSA, PELION
  river .... SALAMBRIA
  tribe .... MYRMIDON
  valley .... TEMPE
  warrior .... MYRMIDON

thetic .... PRESCRIBED

Thetis .... NEREID
  husband of .... PELEUS
  son of .... ACHILLES

theurgist .... MAGICIAN

theurgy .... MAGIC

thews .... SINEWS, MUSCLES

thewy .... MUSCULAR

they .... THEM, PEOPLE, THINGS,
  ANIMALS, PERSONS
  once were checkered
    .... CABS, TAXIS
  revere ratings .... TV
    NETWORKS
  ring twice .... POSTMEN
  rode with Jesse James
    .... YOUNGER BROTHERS
  speak for themselves
    .... FACTS
  used to be carried by four
    .... SEDANS
  used to clang .... TROLLEYS

thiamine .... VITAMIN B(COMPLEX)
  deficiency disease
    .... BERIBERI
  source .... BRAN, FISH, NUTS,
  PORK, BEANS, PASTA, CEREAL,
    WHEAT GERM

thick .... FAT, DULL, WIDE,
  BROAD, CRASS, DENSE,
  GROSS, HEAVY, SOLID, STOUT,
  STUPID, TURBID, COMPACT,
  MASSIVE, LUXURIANT
  as thieves .... CLOSE
  colloquial .... FRIENDLY,
    INTIMATE
  consistency .... CREAMY
  end .... BUTT
  lay it on .... EXAGGERATE
  lipped .... LABROSE
  liqueur .... CREAM
  skin .... SHELL
  skinned .... HARD, NUMB,
    CALLOUS, SHAMELESS
  slang .... GOOKY
  slice .... SLAB
  sound of voice .... HOARSE,
    THROATY, GUTTURAL
  soup .... PUREE
  sticky consistency, having
    .... VISCOUS
  sticky fluid .... GRUME
  with .... TEEMING,
    (JAM)PACKED

thicken .... CURDLE, DEEPEN,
  CONGEAL, CONDENSE,
  SOLIDIFY, COAGULATE,
    INSPISSATE

thicket .... TOD, BOSK, BUSH,
  RONE, SHAW, BRAKE, COPSE,
  GROVE, BOSCAGE, COPPICE,
  SPINNEY, CHAPARRAL,
    (UNDER)BRUSH

thickhaired .... TRESSY

thickhead .... FOOL, DUNCE, IDIOT

thickheaded .... DENSE, STUPID,
  FOOLISH, WITLESS, HEBETATE

thickly populated ...... CROWDED,
    POPULOUS

thickness .... PLY, LAYER,
    STRATUM

thickset .... BEEFY, STOUT,
  CHUBBY, CHUNKY, PORTLY,
  STOCKY, SQUATTY, HEAVYSET

thief .... CROOK, GANEF, GANOF,
  GONOF, GONOV, GONOPH,
  FILCHER, LURCHER, POACHER,
  STEALER, LARCENER,
  PICAROON, PILFERER,
  LARCENIST, PURLOINER
  building/house .... BURGLAR,
    HOUSEBREAKER
  buyer of his loot .... FENCE
  cattle .... RUSTLER
  compulsive
    .... KLEPTO(MANIAC)
  discards of a .... WAIF
  fraudulent .... EMBEZZLER
    high seas .... PIRATE,
  PICAROON, BUCCANEER
  literary .... LIFTER, PIRATE,
    USURPER, PLAGIARIST
  petty .... FILCHER, PILFERER
  slang .... DIP, PRIG, YEGG
  store .... SHOPLIFTER
  trainer .... FAGIN
  tricky ...... CONMAN, SWINDLER
  violent .... ROBBER
  wallet .... PICKPOCKET

thieve .... ROB, FILCH, STEAL,
  PILFER, RUSTLE, DEFRAUD,
  SWINDLE, SHOPLIFT
  slang .... SWIPE, SNATCH

thievery .... FRAUD, THEFT,
  PLUNDER, ROBBERY, SWINDLE

thieves' language .... CANT,
  ARGOT, SLANG, JARGON

thievish .... SLY

thig .... BEG, CADGE, BORROW

thigh, and buttock .... HAM
  animal's .... HAM
  armor plate .... TUILLE
  back of .... HAM
  bone .... FEMUR
  combining form .... MER(O)
  muscle .... SARTORIUS
  of the .... FEMORAL
  pains .... SCIATICA
  part .... FLANK
  upper .... HIP

thill .... POLE, SHAFT

thimble .... THUMBSTALL

thimbleful .... SIP

thimblerig .... SHELL GAME, CON,
  GYP, GULL, CHEAT,
    (DE)FRAUD
  bettor .... SUCKER

thimblerigger .... CHEAT,
    SWINDLER

thimbleweed .... ANEMONE,
  RUDBECKIA, CONEFLOWER

thin ...... FINE, LEAN, RARE, SLIM,
  WEAK, LANKY, LIN(E)Y,
  REEDY, SCANT, SHEER, SPARE,
  DILUTE, FLIMSY, MEAGER,
  NARROW, SLIGHT, SPARSE,
  SUBTLE, SLENDER, TENUOUS,
  DELICATE, HAIRLINE
  and bony .... GAUNT,
    EMACIATED
  as air .... RARE
  as an excuse ..... LAME, POOR,
    FLIMSY, SHALLOW
  become .... SHRINK,
    ATTENUATE
  cake .... WAFER
  coating .... FILM, VENEER
  combining form .... STENO
  glue .... SIZE

layer .... FILM, LAMINA, VENEER

line/stripe .... HAIRLINE

man .... SLATS

man's nickname .... SLIM, LANKY, SLATS

nail .... BRAD

narrow strip .... SLAT

paper .... TISSUE

skinned .... DELICATE, SENSITIVE

stratum .... SEAM

soup .... BROTH, CONSOMME

tall person: colloq. .... BEANPOLE

tuft .... WISP

Thin Man's dog .... ASTA

thine .... YOUR(S)

thing .... ACT, DEED, ITEM, BEING, ISSUE, AFFAIR, DETAIL, DEVICE, ENTITY, MATTER, OBJECT, ARTICLE, CONCERN, BUSINESS

chosen .... CHOICE, OPTION, PREFERENCE

decisively forceful .... SOCKDOLOGER

dimpled .... GOLF BALL

easy to do .... SNAP, CINCH

emitted .... EMANATION

excreted .... SWEAT, URINE, WASTE

feared by elephants? .... MOUSE

hard to handle .... HOT POTATO

imaginary .... MYTH, IDEAL

in law .... RES

ineffectual .... DUD

insubstantial .... STRAW

of same class .... CONGENER

of small value .... STIVE, TRIFLE

of value .... ASSET

out of place .... ESTRAY

slang .... BAG, CUP OF TEA

sometimes spared .... ROD

thought of .... IDEA, PLAN, BRAINCHILD

to lend .... EAR

worthless .... CHIP, JUNK, LEES, SCUM, WEED, CHAFF, DREGS, FROTH, TRASH, WASTE, REFUSE

thingamabob/thingumabob .... DEVICE, GADGET, THINGAMAJIG

thingamajig/thingumajig ...... GIZMO, DEVICE, DOODAD, GADGET, DOOHICKEY, CONTRIVANCE

things .... PERSONAL EFFECTS

authentic .... REALIA

one thousand .... CHILIAD

that should meet .... ENDS

to be done .... CHORE, AGENDA

to be sold .... WARES

think .... DEEM, MUSE, TROW, WEEN, BROOD, DREAM, FANCY, JUDGE, OPINE, WEIGH, IDEATE, REASON, RECKON, IMAGINE, REFLECT, CEREBRATE, STIR GREY MATTER, USE THE OLD NOODLE

about intently .... CONTEMPLATE

ahead .... PLAN

back .... RECALL, REMEMBER, RECOLLECT

deeply ...... PONDER, MEDITATE

in a morbid way .... BROOD, WORRY

nothing of it .... DISREGARD

of .... REGARD, CONSIDER, REMEMBER

over .... MULL, PONDER, DELIBERATE

seriously .... COGITATE, MEDITATE

slang .... KICK AROUND

tank product .... IDEA, INVENTION

things out .... PLAN, STUDY, RATIONALIZE

twice .... HESITATE

up .... CREATE, IDEATE, INVENT, CONCEIVE

thinker .... PHILOSOPHER, INTELLECTUAL

Thinker sculptor .... RODIN

thinness .... RARITY, TENUITY

thinnest .... RAREST

discernible layer .... LAMINA

thiol .... MERCAPTAN

thiosulfate .... HYPO

Thira .... SANTORINI

third .... TERNARY, TIERCE(L), TERTIARY

day, every .... TERTIAN

degree .... GRILLING

degree user .... POLICE, PROBER, INTERROGATOR, INVESTIGATOR

estate .... COMMONS, BOURGEOISIE

in music .... TIERCE

largest island, world's .... BORNEO

man mentioned in the Bible .... ABEL

man, the .... REF(EREE)

power .... CUBE

rate .... POOR, COMMON, SHABBY, INFERIOR

son of Adam .... SETH

string .... SUB(STITUTE)

widow's .... DOWER

Third International .... COMINTERN

Reich .... GERMAN EMPIRE

Worlder .... ASIAN, AFRICAN

Thirkell, writer .... ANGELA

thirl .... PIERCE, THRILL

thirst .... DESIRE, CRAVING, DRYNESS, PARCHEDNESS

abnormal, excessive .... POLYDIPSIA

quencher .... POP, LIQUID

relieve .... SLAKE

stimulant .... SALT

thirsty .... DRY, ARID, FERVID, PARCHED, PRURIENT

boon to the .... OASIS

cat or dog .... LAPPER

Thirsty's wife .... IRMA

thirteen .... XIII, LONG DOZEN, BAKER'S DOZEN

witches .... COVEN

"30" on copy .... END

39.37 inches .... METER

thirty-two are a mouthful .... TEETH

this and no more .... ONLY

has class .... SCHOOLROOM

minute .... NOW, AT ONCE, PRONTO

world .... HERE

Thisbe's love .... PYRAMUS

thistle ...... BURR, ASTER, ARNICA, COSMOS, HYSSOP

like plant .... CARDOON, ARTICHOKE

plant .... SAFFLOWER

thistledown .... PAPPUS

thither ...... YON, THERE, FARTHER

thole .... PIN, OARLOCK

purpose of .... FULCRUM

Thomas, ____ .... DANNY, MARLO

archaelogist .... CYRUS

clockmaker .... SETH

Fr. composer .... AMBROISE

opera by .... MIGNON

thong .... RIEM, KNOUT, LEASH, STRAP, WHIP(LASH)

strangling .... GAROTTE, GARROTE

Thor .... SISECH

father of .... ODIN

noise of .... THUNDER

sphere of .... WAR

weapon of
.... (MAGIC)HAMMER
wife of .... SIF
thorax .... CHEST
insect's .... TRUNK
thorn .... ETH, STOB, TREE, BRIAR,
BRIER, SPINA, SPINE, TORUN,
NETTLE, BRAMBLE, PRICKLE
apple .... HAW, METEL,
DATURA
thornback ...... RAY, SPIDER-CRAB
Thorne Smith's novel .... TOPPER
Topper .... COSMO
thorny .... SPINY, BRAMBLY,
PRICKLY, SPINATE, SPINOSE
pig .... PORCUPINE
plant .... BRIAR, BRIER
thorough .... DEEP, EXACT,
CAREFUL, ABSOLUTE,
COMPLETE, SWEEPING, OUT-
AND-OUT
thoroughbred .... NOBLE,
HIGHBORN, PUREBRED,
PEDIGREED, BLUEBLOOD(ED),
ARISTOCRATIC
thoroughfare .... ROAD, AVENUE,
STREET, HIGHWAY,
BOULEVARD, TURNPIKE,
CONCOURSE, (PASSAGE)WAY
thoroughgoing .... ARRANT,
PRECISE, COMPLETE
thoroughly ...... FULLY, WHOLLY,
SOUNDLY
thoroughwort .... PLANT,
BONESET
thorp(e) .... DORP, HAMLET,
VILLAGE
Thorstein's (Ericsson) brother
.... LEIF
father .... ERIC THE RED
wife .... GUDRID
Thorvald's grandson .... LEIF,
THORSTEIN
hometown .... JAEDEREN
place of death .... ICELAND
son .... EIRIK, ERIC THE RED
those at the helm ...... STEERSMEN
in office .... INS
who are extremely loyal
.... DIEHARDS
boast loudly .... GASCONS,
BLOW-HARDS
comprehend .... GRASPERS
corroborate
.... (EYE)WITNESSES
exaggerate .... FIBBERS
flirt .... COQUETTES
Thoth's head .... IBIS, BABOON
sphere .... MAGIC, SPEECH,
WISDOM
thou .... YOU, THOUSAND

though ...... YET, STILL, EVEN(IF),
HOWEVER, NEVERTHELESS,
NOTWITHSTANDING
thought .... HEED, IDEA, LOGIC,
STUDY, WEIGH, BELIEF,
NOTION, CONCEPT, INTELLECT,
IMAGINATION
combining form .... IDEO
deep, continued
.... MEDITATION
disorder .... SCHIZOPHRENIA
distorted .... DELUSION
formulated .... IDEA,
JUDGMENT, SOLUTION
out .... CONSIDERED
representation of ...... SPEECH,
WRITING, BEHAVIOR
seat of .... BRAIN
transference of .... TELEPATHY
thoughtful .... KIND, HEEDFUL,
PENSIVE, TACTFUL,
CONSIDERATE
thoughtless .... RASH, SLACK,
REMISS, STUPID, RECKLESS
act .... FOLLY
thousand .... FIFTY SCORE
dollars: sl. .... THOU, YARD,
GRAND
prefix .... MILLI
years .... CHILIAD, MILLENNIUM
thousandth .... MILLESIMAL
anniversary .... MILLENARY
of an inch .... MIL
Thracian king .... TEREUS
slave .... SPARTACUS
soldier .... MYRMIDON
thrall ...... ESNE, SERF, BONDMAN,
(EN)SLAVE, SLAVERY,
SUBJECTION
thralldom .... BONDAGE,
SLAVERY, CAPTIVITY,
SERVITUDE, DOMINATION
thrash .... LAM, TAN, BEAT, CANE,
DRUB, FLOG, HIDE, LACE,
LASH, LICK, ROUT, WHIP,
FLAIL, POUND, WHALE,
DEFEAT, LARRUP, STRIKE,
WALLOP, BELABOR, CONQUER,
TROUNCE, LAMBAST(E)
out .... ARGUE, DISCUSS
over .... ANALYZE
thrasher .... (SONG)BIRD
genus .... TOXOSTOMA
relative .... MOCKINGBIRD
thrashing .... FLAGELLATION
thrasonical .... BOASTFUL
thread .... DUD, CORD, YARN,
FIBER, FILUM, INKLE, LINEN,
LISLE, STRAND, STRING,
FILAMENT
a needle .... REEVE

appendage like .... CIRRUS
ball of .... CLEW
bits of .... LINT
combining form .... NEMAT(O)
cotton .... LISLE
cutters, screws .... TAP
discharge .... SETON
end .... THRUM
fine .... FILM
holder .... SPOOL, BOBBIN,
SHUTTLE
knot .... BURL
like .... FILAR, FILOSE, FIBROID
like part ..... FILUM, FILAMENT
linen .... INKLE
loosely twisted .... FLOSS
lump .... BURL, KNOT
material .... FLAX, SILK, YARN,
LINEN, NYLON, COTTON
metal .... LAME, WIRE
producer .... SPIDER,
SILKWORM
pulled .... SNAG
quantity .... SKEIN
rubber .... LASTEX
separate .... SLEAVE
silk .... TRAM
skein of .... COIL, HASP
spun by a spider ...... COBWEB
surgical .... SETON, CATGUT,
LIGATURE
tangled .... RAVEL(L)ING
thick .... STRING
use of .... SEWING, SUTURE,
WEAVING
used in labyrinth .... CLEW
weight to measure fineness
of .... DENIER
threadbare .... SEEDY, TRITE,
WEARY, FRAYED, RAGGED,
SCANTY, SHABBY,
WORN(OUT), TATTERED
joke, describing a .... STALE
threadlike outgrowth .... HAIR
threadworm .... FILARIA,
PINWORM, NEMATODE
thready .... ROPY, WIRY, FIBROUS,
STRINGY
threap ...... ARGUE, CHIDE, SCOLD,
REBUKE
threat .... DANGER, MENACE,
NOTICE, PROMISE, WARNING
empty .... BLUFF, BLUSTER
getting money by
.... BLACKMAIL, EXTORTION
threaten .... COW, BULLY,
HARASS, HECTOR, MENACE,
BLUDGEON, BROWBEAT,
TERRORIZE, INTIMIDATE
threatening .... DARK, AWFUL,
BLACK, SULLEN, LOOMING,

OMINOUS, WARNING, IMMINENT, MENACING, MINATORY, SINISTER, MINACIOUS

three ...... TER, TREY, TRIO, TRIAD

an association of ...... TROIKA, TRIUMVIR(ATE)

angled .... TRIGONOUS

banded armadillo .... APAR

base hit .... TRIPLE, THREE-BAGGER

biblical symbolic meaning of .... TOTALITY

card's .... TREY

cut into .... TRISECT

cornered .... TRIGONAL, TRIGONOUS, TRIANGULAR

days, man in whale's belly for .... JONAH

decker .... TRIREME, SANDWICH

dimensional .... CUBIC, STEREO

feet .... YARD

group of .... TRIO, TRIAD, TRINE, TRINARY, TRINITY, TRIPLE(T), TRIPLEX, TRIPLICATE

hand card game .... SKAT

horned .... TRICORN

in dice/domino .... TREY, DEUCE-ACE

in one .... TRIUNE, TRINITY

in sequence, same suit .... TIERCE

languages, using .... TRILINGUAL

leafed .... TERNATE, TRIFOLIATE

leafed clover .... TREFOIL, SHAMROCK

legged seat .... STOOL

legged stand .... EASEL, TEAPOY, TRIPOD

legged table .... TRIVET

lines, group of .... TERCET

lobes/parts, divided into .... TRIFID

lobbed .... TRILOBATE

metrical feet, verse of .... TRIPODY

month period .... QUARTER, TRIMESTER

mountain peaks island .... TRINIDAD

pairs of leaflets, having .... TRIJUGATE

parts, having .... TRINAL, TRIFORM

parts of completeness, one of .... END, MIDDLE, BEGINNING

performers .... TRIO

pointed .... TRICUSPID

prefix .... TER, TRI

pronged .... TRIDENT, TRIDENTATE

pronged spear .... LEISTER, TRIDENT

related plays, set of .... TRILOGY

rhyming lines, group of .... TERCET

ribbed .... TRICOSTATE

set of .... TRIAD, TERNION

shakes .... SECS

sided figure .... TRIGON, TRIANGLE

significance of the number .... COMPLETENESS

song for .... TRIO

times .... THRICE, TREBLE, TRIPLE

toed sloth .... AI

trios .... NINE

wheeled vehicle .... TRICYCLE, MOTORCYCLE

years, happening every .... TRIENNIAL

years, period of .... TRIENNIUM

three blind mice .... MCEMCEMCE

300, in Rome CCC

Three Wise Men, gift of .... GOLD, MYRRH, FRANKINCENSE

one of the .... GASPAR, MELCHIOR, BALTHASAR

threefold .... TER(N), TRINE, THRICE, TREBEL, TRINAL, TRIPLE, TRIPLEX, TRIPARTITE

threepenny .... PALTRY

threes, arranged in .... TERNATE

threescore .... SIXTY

threesome .... TRIO

threnody .... SONG, DIRGE, REQUIEM, CORONACH

thresh .... FLOG, POUND, WINNOW, THRASH, BEAT(OUT)

out .... ARGUE, DISCUSS

over .... DWELL ON

thresher .... FLAIL, SHARK

shark .... SEAFOX

threshing implement ...... FLAIL, COMBINE

threshold .... EVE, LIMEN, OUTSET, GATEWAY, (DOOR)SILL, ENTRANCE

of consciousness .... LIMEN

threw ...... CAST, FLUNG, HURLED, TOSSED, PITCHED

thrice .... VERY, GREATLY, THREEFOLD

combining form .... TER

thrift .... WORK, LABOR, VIGOR, GROWTH, SAVING, ECONOMY, FRUGALITY

thrifty .... CANNY, CHARY, FRUGAL, SAVING, STINGY, CAREFUL, SPARING, THRIVING, PROVIDENT, ECONOMICAL

opposite of .... LAVISH, WASTEFUL

person .... MISER, HOARDER, NIGGARD, SKINFLINT, PENNY PINCHER

thrill .... STIR, FLUSH, THIRL, THROB, EXCITE, QUIVER, TINGLE, TREMOR, TREMBLE, VIBRATE, ELECTRIFY, SENSATION, EXHILARATE

thrilled .... PLEASED

thriller .... CHILLER, SHOCKER, SUSPENSE, WHODUNIT

thrilling ...... ELECTRIC, EXCITING

thrips .... WOODWORM

thrive .... WAX, GROW, ADDLE, BLOOM, BATTEN, FATTEN, FLOWER, PROSPER, SUCCEED, FLOURISH

thriving .... SITTING PRETTY

throat .... MAW, CRAG, NECK, GORGE, FAUCES, GULLET, PHARYNX, WEASAND, THROTTLE, WINDPIPE

armor .... GORGET

clearing .... HEM, HAWK

condition .... GOITER

cut competitor's .... UNDERSELL

cut the .... JUGULATE

disease .... CROUP, ANGINA, CANCER, GARGET, THRUSH

inflammation ..... PHARYNGITIS

lozenge .... PASTIL(E)

middle section of .... OROPHARYNX

of the .... (JU)GULAR, GUTTURAL

part .... LARYNX, PHARYNX, TRACHEA, ESOPHAGUS, VOICE BOX

skin, animal .... DEWLAP, WATTLE

sore .... PHARYNGITIS

sound .... CROAK

troublesome growths .... TONSILS

uppermost part of .... NASOPHARYNX

wrapper .... MUFFLER

throaty .... HOARSE, GUTTURAL

throb .... ACHE, BEAT, PAIN, PUMP, POUND, PULSE, THUMP, PULSATE, VIBRATE, PALPITATE, PULSATION

throbber .... HEART
throbbing .... ACHY, ACHING,
BEATING, PITAPAT, PULSING,
STACCATO, PALPITANT,
SALTATION
throe(s) ...... PANG, RACK, AGONY,
CRAMP, QUALM, SPASM,
SCRUPLE
childbirth .... LABOR PAINS
thrombocyte .... PLATELET
reduction in the number of
.... THROMBOCYTOPENIA
thrombosis .... COAGULATION,
BLOOD-CLOTTING
thrombus .... FIBRIN, BLOOD CLOT
combining form ..... THROMBO
formation in veins
.... THROMBOPHLEBITIS
fragment .... EMBOLUS
removal of a
.... THROMBECTOMY
throne .... CHAIR, RULER,
SCEPTER, ROYAL SEAT,
SOVEREIGN(TY)
bishop's .... CATHEDRA
covering .... CANOPY
seat of a .... DAIS, TRANSOM
sitter .... CZAR, KING, POPE,
TSAR, QUEEN, RULER,
EMPEROR, CARDINAL
throng .... MOB, ARMY, HOST,
CROWD, HORDE, PRESS,
SWARM, CONCOURSE,
MULTITUDE
throstle .... (SONG)THRUSH
throttle ...... GAG, CHOKE, CLOSE,
SCRAG, VALVE, STIFLE,
SILENCE, STRANGLE,
SUPPRESS, SUFFOCATE
engine .... GUN
hold .... STRANGLEHOLD
through ...... BY, PER, VIA, DONE,
OVER, WITH, AMONG, DURING,
FINISH, BY WAY OF
and through .... FULLY,
ENTIRELY, COMPLETELY
force .... BY DINT OF
throughout .... EVERYWHERE
throw .... CAST, DASH, HURL,
SHED, TOSS, FLING, HEAVE,
PITCH, SLING, UPSET
a monkey wrench into
.... SABOTAGE
a party .... HOST
about .... STREW, SCATTER
at .... PROJECT
at a mark .... COCKSHY
away .... WASTE, DISCARD,
SQUANDER
back .... RETURN, REVERT
back light .... REFLECT

dice .... CAST, MAIN, ROLL
football opponent .... STOP,
TACKLE
in .... INSERT, SUPPLEMENT
in with .... JOIN
into confusion ...... BEWILDER,
CONFOUND, EMBARRASS,
DEMORALIZE, DISCONCERT
lava .... ERUPT
obstacles at .... HAMPER,
HINDER, IMPEDE, OBSTRUCT
of ball .... PITCH, DELIVERY
off .... SHED, UNSEAT, SHAKE
OFF
out .... OUST, EJECT, EXPEL,
BOUNCE, REJECT, DISCARD
over .... JILT, ABANDON
overboard .... JETTISON
snake eyes .... LOSE
so as to make it roll .... BOWL
stones at .... LAPIDATE
the book at criminal
.... MAXIMUM PENALTY
the towel .... QUIT, YIELD
together .... MIX, ASSEMBLE,
IMPROVISE
up .... PUKE, SPEW, EJECT,
RETCH, VOMIT, REJECT,
REGORGE
with a short, quick motion
.... CHUCK
throwaway .... LEAFLET,
HANDBILL
throwback .... ATAVISM, RELAPSE,
SETBACK, REVERSION
thrower .... BOWLER, HEAVER,
HURLER, TOSSER, PITCHER,
SLINGER
discus .... DISCOBOLUS
kind of .... JAVELIN,
SHOTPUTTER
thrown .... CAST, FLUNG, OUSTED,
PITCHED, DEPORTED,
UNSEATED
thrum .... DRUM, TIRL, STRUM,
FRINGE
thrummy .... SHAGGY
thrush ...... MAVIS, OUZEL, PITTA,
ROBIN, VEERY, MISTLE,
REDWING, BLUEBIRD,
(SONG)BIRD, THROSTLE,
STONECHAT, NIGHTINGALE
blackbird .... MERULA
disease .... APHTHA,
CANDIDIASIS
family .... TURDIDAE
genus .... BABAX, TURDUS,
TURDOIDES
genus, bluebird .... SIALIA
genus, ground- ..... ZOOTHERA

genus, laughing-
.... GARRULAX
long distance migrant
.... WHINCHAT, NIGHTINGALE
mistle .... VISCIVORUS
of the .... TURDINE
relative .... BLACKCAP,
FERNBIRD, FLYCATCHER,
WHITETHROAT
rock .... SAXATILIS
slang .... WARBLER
song .... PHILOMELOS
water .... WAGTAIL
with one leg .... BLACKBIRD
wood .... MUSTELINA
thrust ...... DIG, JAB, RAM, BLOW,
POKE, PUSH, STAB, TILT,
DRIVE, FORCE, LUNGE, SHOVE,
ATTACK, COMPEL, DARTLE,
EXSERT, PIERCE
answer of .... PARRY
aside .... PUSH, SHOVE,
BRUSH(OFF)
away ..... DETRUDE, CHASE OFF
back .... REPEL, REBUFF
down .... DEPRESS, DETRUDE
in .... ENTER, INTRUDE
in fencing ...... FOIN, PASSADO
out .... EJECT, EXSERT,
EXTEND, STRETCH
out lips .... POUT
thruster .... RAM, CUDGEL,
FENCER, LUNGER, PLUNGER,
SWATTER
thruway .... AISLE
Thsombe, Congo premier
.... MOISE
thud .... BLOW, CLOP, CLUMP,
THUMP
thug ...... TOUGH, DACOIT, KILLER,
HOOD(LUM), RUFFIAN,
ASSASSIN, HOOLIGAN,
CUTTHROAT, STRANGLER
slang .... GOON, YEGG,
MUGGER, GORILLA
thuja .... PINE, CEDAR,
ARBORVITAE
Thule, part of .... NORWAY,
ICELAND
thumb .... DIGIT, FINGER, POLLEX
a ride .... HITCHHIKE
fleshy bulge of .... THENAR
in architecture .... OVOLO
index .... TAB
one's nose at .... FLOUT,
SCOFF, SNEER, DISDAIN
protector .... STALL, THIMBLE
through .... SCAN, BROWSE
thumbnail .... BRIEF, SMALL
thumbs, all .... CLUMSY
down ...... NO DICE, REJECTION

up .... NOD, OKS, YES,
AFFIRMATIVE
thumbstall .... THIMBLE
thump .... BEAT, THUD, POUND,
THROB, CUDGEL, POMMEL,
THRASH
thumper .... JUMBO, WHALE,
WHOPPER
thumping: colloq. .... HUGE,
LARGE, WHOPPING,
WALLOPING
thunder .... BOOM, PEAL, ROAR,
NOISE, FULMINATE
and lightning .... STORM
at the beach .... SURF
forth .... FULMINATE
god .... THOR, DONAR
sound .... CLAP, PEAL, ROAR,
ROLL, CRASH, MUTTER,
RUMBLE
thigh thinner ..... LIPOSUCTION
thunderbolt .... LIGHTNING
thunderer .... ZEUS, JUPITER
thunderfish .... RAAD, LOACH
thundering .... AROAR, BOOMING,
GROWLING, TONITRUANT
thunderous .... LOUD, DEAFENING
thunderstone .... BELEMITE,
CUTTLEFISH
thunderstruck .... AGHAST,
SPELLBOUND
Thurber, humorist .... JAMES
hero .... MITTY
thurible .... CENSER
thurifer .... ACOLYTE, ALTAR BOY
thurify .... CENSE
Thuringian capital .... ERFURT
castle .... WARTBURG
city ..... JENA, GOTHA, WEIMAR
forest .... THURINGER WALD
Thurman, actress .... UMA
thus .... SO, SIC, ERGO, HENCE,
THEREFORE, CONSEQUENTLY
far .... YET
thwack ...... SLAP, SMACK, WHACK
thwart .... BALK, FOIL, BLOCK,
SPITE, BAFFLE, DEFEAT,
HINDER, HOGTIE, OBLIQUE,
OBSTRUCT, FRUSTRATE
thy .... YOUR
Thyestes' brother .... ATREUS
father .... PELOPS
grandfather .... TANTALUS
son .... AEGISTHUS
thyme .... HERB, MINT
thymus .... GLAND
animal's .... SWEETBREAD
part .... FAT, LOBE,
EPITHELIUM, LYMPHOCYTE
site .... CHEST, THORAX
tumor .... THYMOMA

thyroid gland disease
...... CANCER, GOITER, GOITRE,
CRETINISM
hormone .... THYROXINE,
CALCITONIN
inflammation ...... THYROIDITIS
location .... NECK
scanning method
.... ULTRASOUND,
RADIONUCLIDE
surgical removal of
.... THYROIDECTOMY
thysanuran .... BRISTLETAIL
Ti, in chemistry .... TITANIUM
tiara .... CROWN, DIADEM,
CORONET, HEADDRESS
pope's .... TRIPLE CROWN
wearer .... POPE, QUEEN,
DUCHESS, EMPRESS, PEERESS,
PRINCESS
Tiber .... TEVERE
Tiberias Sea .... GALILEE
Tibet .... XIZANG, SITSANG
capital of .... LHASA
lake .... NAMCO, SILINGCO,
NGANGZECO, TANGRA YUMCO
mountain .... NANSHAN
mountain pass ..... LEKH, LIPU,
MANA, NITI
mountain range .... GANGDISE,
HIMALAYA
river .... INDUS, SUTLEJ,
SALWEEN
Tibetan antelope .... GOA, SUS,
CHIRU
chief lama .... DALAI,
PANCHEN
coin .... TANGA
deer .... SHOU
dog .... TERRIER
gazelle .... GOA
general .... CHANG
goat wool .... CASHMERE
high priest .... BLAMA
monastery .... LAMASERY
monk .... LAMA
ox .... YAK
oxlike animal .... ZEBU
priest .... LAMA
religion .... LAMAISM
wild sheep .... SHA, BHARAL,
NAHOOR
zoo animal .... PANDA
tibia .... FLUTE, CNEMIS,
SHIN(BONE)
common disorder of
.... FRACTURE
location of .... LEG
Tibur .... TIVOLI
tic .... SPASM, TWITCH,
CONTRACTION

douloureux ...... (TRIGEMINAL)
NEURALGIA
organ commonly affected by
.... ARM, FACE, SHOULDER
typical ..... JERKING, BLINKING,
SHRUGGING, TWITCHING
tic-tac-toe .... GAME
number of squares in .... NINE
win .... OOO, XXX
tical's replacement .... BAHT
Ticino .... TESSIN
tick .... BUG, DOT, BEAT, MITE,
CLICK, ACARID, INSECT,
JIGGER, MOMENT, ARACHNID,
PARASITE, (CHECK)MARK,
PILLOW CASE
British .... TRUST, CREDIT
broad category of .... HARD,
SOFT
colloquial .... TICKING
disease spread by .... LYME, Q
FEVER, TULAREMIA
food .... BLOOD
host of ...... DOG, MAN, SHEEP,
CATTLE
of the clock .... SECOND
off .... CHECK, COUNT,
ENUMERATE
ticked off .... MAD, IRATE, PISSED,
INCENSED
ticker .... TAPPER
slang .... CLOCK, HEART,
WATCH, TIMEPIECE
tape figures .... QUOTATIONS
tape man .... STOCKBROKER
ticket .... TAG, LIST, PASS, LABEL,
DOCKET, NOTICE, RECORD,
LICENSE
baggage .... TAG, CHECK
candidates' .... SLATE, BALLOT
free .... PASS, ANNIE OAKLEY
losing-lottery .... BLANK
of leave .... PAROLE
part .... STUB
slang .... DUCAT, DOCKET,
PASTEBOARD
speculator, theater
.... SCALPER
stub .... RAINCHECK
to go ashore, sailor's
.... LIBERTY
traffic .... SUMMONS
tickle .... STIR, AMUSE, EXCITE,
PLEASE, TINGLE, DELIGHT,
GRATIFY, OVERJOY, TITILLATE
tickler .... POSER, PUZZLE,
REMINDER
ticklish .... RISKY, FICKLE,
TOUCHY, CRITICAL, DELICATE,
SENSITIVE
tickseed .... DAISY, COREOPSIS

tid plus two .... BITS
tidal flow .... EBB, NEAP
   wave .... BORE, EAGRE,
            TSUNAMI
tidbit .... CATE, OLIVE, CANAPE,
   BONBON, GOSSIP, MORSEL,
            KICKSHAW
   for a pangolin .... ANT,
            TERMITE
tiddly .... DIZZY, TIPSY
tide .... FLOW, CURRENT
   designation of a ...... EBB, RIP,
      NEAP, FLOOD, SPRING
   over .... LAST, ENDURE
tidings ...... NEWS, WORD, ADVICE,
   GOSPEL, REPORT, EVANGEL,
         INFORMATION
tidy ...... NEAT, PRIM, TAUT, TRIG,
   TRIM, LARGE, NIFTY, SPRUCE,
   ORDERLY, SHIPSHAPE,
   STRAIGHTEN, CONSIDERABLE
tie ...... BEAM, BIND, BOND, EVEN,
   JOIN, KNOT, LASH, LINK,
   ASCOT, EQUAL, HITCH,
   TACH(E), TRUSS, UNION,
   ATTACH, CRAVAT, FASTEN,
   TETHER, LIGATURE, RELATION,
   STANDOFF, STALEMATE
   beam .... BALK
   between individuals of a
      group .... NEXUS
   boat/ship .... MOOR, ANCHOR
   connecting .... LIGAMENT
   contest .... DRAW, STANDOFF
   down .... HOLD, CONFINE,
          RESTRAIN
   down securely .... LASH
   fabric .... REP
   game to break .... RUBBER
   in .... JOIN, CONNECT
   in a race .... DEAD HEAT
   kind of .... BOW, ASCOT,
         FOUR-IN-HAND
   situation .... DEADLOCK,
         STALEMATE
   up .... HALT, STOP, SNARL,
   DELAY, HINDER, LIAISON,
   BLOCKADE, CONNECTION
   up, traffic .... JAM
tieback .... SASH
tied .... WED, EVEN, RELATED
   feet and hands .... HOGTIED
   one up .... BOUND, KNOTTED
   up .... BUSY
Tientsin river .... HAI
tier ...... ROW, BANK, DECK, RANK,
   FLOOR, LAYER, LEVEL, STAGE,
      STORY, PINAFORE
   of bare benches
   .... BLEACHERS
   theater seats .... BOX, LOGE,

    BALCONY, GALLERY
tierce .... CASK, HOUR, THIRD
Tierra del Fuego Indian .... ONA
ties .... OXFORDS
   support .... ROADBED
Tietze's syndrome .... CHEST
            PAIN
tiff .... FIT, ROW, HUFF, MIFF,
   SPAT, PUNCH, LIQUOR,
   TEMPER, BICKER, QUARREL,
   TANTRUM, WRANGLE,
   ARGUMENT, SQUABBLE
tiffany .... SILK, GAUZE, MUSLIN
tiffin .... TEA, LUNCH, SNACK
tig .... TAP, DALLY, TOUCH,
         MEDDLE
tiger .... PUMA, COUGAR, JAGUAR,
   LEOPARD, SABERTOOTH
   cat ..... LYNX, CHATI, MARGAY,
   OCELOT, SERVAL, PANTHER
   female .... TIGRESS
   of Malaya, so-called
   .... YAMASHITA
   of the sea .... BARRACUDA
   Persian .... SHER, SHIR
   young .... CUB, WHELP
tigerish .... CRUEL, FIERCE,
   VALIANT, FEROCIOUS,
   BELLIGERENT, BLOODTHIRSTY
tight .... SNUG, TAUT, CLOSE,
   TENSE, SCARCE, SEVERE,
   COMPACT, HERMETIC
   colloquial .... STINGY,
   MISERLY, SOUNDLY
   in .... FAMILIAR, INTIMATE
   manner, in a .... SECURE
   place .... FIX, JAM, SPOT
   slang .... DRUNK, TIPSY,
   LOADED, INEBRIATED
   spot .... PINCH, SCRAPE
tighten ...... FRAP, CLAMP, SCREW,
   TAUTEN, SQUEEZE, STRAITEN
tightfisted .... CHEAP, STINGY,
   FRUGAL, MISERLY, PENNY-
        PINCHING
tightlipped .... MUM, SILENT,
   TACITURN, SECRETIVE
tightness .... TENACITY,
       PARSIMONY
tightrope walker .... ACROBAT,
   AERIALIST, EQUILIBRIST,
   FUNAMBULIST
tightwad .... HUNKS, MISER,
   PIKER, NIGGARD, SCROOGE,
   SKINFLINT, CHEAPSKATE,
      PENNY-PINCHER
"Tijuana Brass" boss
   .... ALPERT
til .... SESAME
tilbury .... COACH, CARRIAGE
tile .... BRICK, DALLE, SLATE,

    QUARRY, TEGULA, CERAMIC,
    PANTILE, TESSERA
   arranged in a mosaic pattern
   .... TESSELLATED
   game .... DOMINO, MAHJONG
   like/of .... TEGULAR
   making art .... CERAMICS
   material .... CLAY, STONE,
   KAOLIN, RUBBER, ARGILLI,
   PLASTIC, CONCRETE, PETUNTSE
   mosaic .... TESSERA
   roofing .... SLATE, PANTILE
   square-shaped/diamond-
     shaped .... QUARRY
   structure .... TILING
   use .... ROOFING, COVERING,
         FLOORING
tiler .... DOORKEEPER
till .... FARM, PLOW, UNTO, UP TO,
   UNTIL, CULTIVATE,
   CASH(REGISTER)
   land .... SUBDUE
tilled land .... FARM, ARADA,
   TILTH, TILLAGE
tiller ...... HELM, SHOOT, FARMER,
   GRANGER, PEASANT,
   PLOWMAN, CULTIVATOR,
   HUSBANDMAN
Tillie the _____ .... TOILER
Tillis, _____ .... MEL
tilt .... TIP, HEEL, LIST, JOUST,
   SLANT, SLOPE, AWNING,
   CANOPY, DEBATE, SEESAW,
   DISPUTE, INCLINE, TOURNEY,
   TOURNAMENT
   and pour .... DECANT
tilted .... ACOCK
tilth .... FARM, ARADA, TILLAGE
tilting arena .... LISTS
   target .... QUINTAIN
   tournament .... CAR(R)OUSEL
timarau .... BUFFALO
timbal .... KETTLEDRUM
timber .... LOG, BEAM, BITT,
   STUD, WOOD, TREES, LUMBER
   above keel .... DEADWOOD
   arched .... CAMBER
   borer .... GRIBBLE
   crack .... ANEMOSIS
   deciduous .... HARDWOOD
   down bend .... SNY
   dressed .... PUNCHEON
   foundation .... SPILE
   grooved .... COULISSE
   heartwood .... DURAMEN
   hewn piece .... BALK
   hitch .... KNOT
   joining peg .... TRUNNEL,
      TRE(E)NAIL
   natural split in .... SHAKE
   nautical .... BITT

prop .... STULL
roof .... RAFTER
rot .... CONK, DODDER
sawn .... LUMBER
small .... SCANTLING
soak .... RET
standing .... STUMPAGE
state .... OREGON
support .... CORBEL
tree .... YEW
upward bend in .... SNY
wolf .... LOBO
timberland .... FOREST,
WOODLAND
Timberlane, Judge .... CASS
timbre .... RING, TONE, SOUND
timbrel ...... TABOR, TAMBOURINE
Timbuktu .... TOMBOUCTOU
location .... MALI
slang .... BOONDOCKS,
(THE)STICKS, (THE)TULLIES
time .... AGE, EON, ERA, DATE,
SPAN, CLOCK, EPOCH, SPELL,
MOMENT, PERIOD, INSTANT,
DURATION, INTERVAL,
OCCASION
A.D., part of .... ANNO,
DOMINI
all the .... ALWAYS
at no .... NEVER
at the same .... MEANTIME,
MEANWHILE
B.C., part of .... BEFORE,
CHRIST
bearish .... DROP
beating device
.... METRONOME
between .... INTERIM,
INTERVAL
comb. form .... CHRON(O)
Coronation .... MAY DAY
differential .... EPACT
extension .... GRACE
for an egg hunt .... EASTER
(SUN)DAY
for pistols .... SUNRISE
free .... BREAK, LEISURE
honored .... TRADITIONAL
in history .... ERA
in music .... BEAT, TEMPO,
VOLTA
incalculable .... EON
indefinite period of ...... SPELL
indicating device .... CLOCK,
WATCH, SUNDIAL, CLEPSYDRA,
HOURGLASS
limit .... DEADLINE
of day .... MORNING,
(AFTER)NOON
greatest vigor .... HEYDAY
imprisonment .... TERM

judgment .... DOOMSDAY
life .... TEENS, DOTAGE,
NONAGE, PUBERTY
rejoicing .... JUBILEE
the year .... SEASON
want .... FAMINE
yearly event .... BIRTHDAY,
NATAL DAY, ANNIVERSARY
youth and inexperience
.... SALAD DAYS
out .... REST, BREAK, RECESS,
RESPITE
pass the .... WHILE AWAY
period .... DAY, WEEK, YEAR,
HOUR, MONTH, SECOND
pertaining to .... FAST, LATE,
SLOW, EARLY, HORAL,
AORISTIC, PERIODIC
poetic .... EVENTIDE
prosperous .... BOOM, HEYDAY
science of .... HOROLOGY
span .... HOUR
spend .... WHILE
teller .... SUNDIAL
waster .... IDLER, LOAFER,
SLACKER, LINGERER, LOITERER
without end .... ETERNITY
timeless .... ENDLESS, ETERNAL,
IMMORTAL, LEGENDARY,
PERPETUAL, EVERLASTING
timely .... SOON, EARLY, RIGHT,
PROMPT, EXPEDIENT,
OPPORTUNE, AUSPICIOUS,
SEASONABLE
caravel .... NINA, PINTA, SANTA
MARIA
king .... FERDINAND
queen .... ISABELLA
observance .... HOLIDAY,
COLUMBUS DAY, VETERANS
DAY, THANKSGIVING DAY
painting of 1912
.... SEPTEMBER MORN
reminder .... TAX TIME,
SCHOOL DAYS AGAIN
treat .... LONG WEEKEND
visitors .... DWARFS AND
GNOMES, GHOSTS AND
SHADES, GOBLINS AND ELVES
timepiece .... CLOCK, WATCH,
HOROLOGE, TIMEKEEPER
art of making .... HOROLOGY
kind of .... SUNDIAL,
HOURGLASS
timer .... STOPWATCH
timeserver ...... TOADY, TRIMMER,
OPPORTUNIST
timetable .... SKED, SCHEDULE
timeworn .... OLD, AGED,
SHABBY, RAGGED(Y), OUT-OF-
DATE

timid .... SHY, WEAK, PAVID,
AFRAID, BASHFUL, CHICKEN,
COWARDLY, HESITANT,
RESERVED, RETIRING,
SHEEPISH, TIMOROUS
timidity, symbol of .... MOUSE
timing .... PACE, PACING,
CLOCKING
device .... METRONOME,
STOPWATCH
timon .... HELM, TILLER,
MISANTHROPE
Timon of Athens author
.... SHAKESPEARE
Timor Archipelago part
.... SUMBA, FLORES, SUMBAWA
capital .... DILI, KUPANG
city/town .... SOE, AUBA,
BAUKAU, ATAMBUA
coin .... AVO
timorous ...... SHY, PAVID, TIMID,
TREPID, BASHFUL, FEARFUL
Timoshenko, Soviet Marshal
.... SEMYON
timothy .... HAY, GRASS
Timothy, actor .... BOTTOMS
timpani .... KETTLEDRUMS
tin ...... CAN, STANNUM, PRESERVE
alloy .... BRONZE, PEWTER
and lead alloy .... TERNE
box .... TRUMMEL
coated sheet metal .... TAGGER
describing thing made of
.... CHEAP
fish .... TORPEDO
foil .... TAIN
hat .... HELMET
(metal) sheet .... LATTEN
mine .... STANNARY
of .... STANNOUS
plate .... FOIL, TAIN
pyrite .... STANNITE
slang .... MONEY
smeltery .... STANNARY
strips .... TINSEL
symbol for .... SN
threads, decorative ..... TINSEL
Tin Lizzie .... CRATE, MODEL T
FORD
Pan Alley character
.... COMPOSER, PROMOTER
Pan Alley females .... GALS
Pan Alley group .... ASCAP
tinamou family .... TINAMIDAE
genus .... NOTHOPROCTA
-like bird .... QUAIL,
PARTRIDGE
relative .... RHEA
tincal .... BORAX
tinct .... COLOR, TINGED, TINT(ED)
tincture .... DASH, TINT, VERT,

COLOR, SHADE, TINGE, TOUCH, TRACE, ELIXIR, SOUPCON, VESTIGE

tind .... KINDLE

tinder .... PUNK, AMADOU

tinderbox, like a .... POWDER KEG

tine ...... BIT, FORK, TYND, PRONG, SPIKE, ANTLER

tinea .... (FUNGAL)INFECTION

corporis .... RINGWORM

cruris .... JOCK ITCH

fungi causing .... DERMATOPHYTES

pedis .... ATHLETE'S FOOT

tinge .... DYE, DASH, TINT, COLOR, SHADE, STAIN, TAINT, TOUCH, TRACE, FLAVOR

tinged .... TINCT

tingle .... NIP, DIRL, STING, THIRL, DINDLE, THRILL, PRICKLE

tingling feeling ...... PARESTHESIA

sensation, describing a .... PINS AND NEEDLES

tinhorn .... CHEAP, PIKER, SHOWY, GAMBLER, TWO-BIT, SMALL-TIME

tiniest .... MINIM

tinker .... FUSS, BOTCH, CAIRD, PATCH, MEND(ER), PUTTER, REPAIR, TAMPER, BUNGLER, MACKEREL, SILVERSIDES

colloquial .... DOCTOR

jargon of .... SHELTA

Shakespearean .... SNOUT

slang .... MR. FIXIT

target of .... EVERS

to chance connector .... EVERS

Tinker Bell, for one .... FAIRY

tinkering ...... TOYING, DABBLING, PIDDLING

tinkle .... CLINK, JINGLE, URINATE

tinkling .... GRACKLE

tinned .... CANNED, PRESERVED

tinnitus (noise) .... BUZZING, HISSING, RINGING, WHISTLING

tin(s)man .... (TIN)SMITH

tinsel .... GAUDY, SHOWY, BAUBLES, GLITTER, SPANGLE

tinseled .... CLINQUANT

tinstone .... CASSITERITE

tint .... DYE, HUE, CAST, TONE, COLOR, SHADE, STAIN, TINGE

Tintagel Head's famous son .... ARTHUR

tinted .... TINCT

tinter .... DYER

tintinnabula .... BELLS

tintinnabulate .... RING

tinware .... PANS, POTS

tiny .... WEE, SMALL, TEENY,

ATOMIC, LITTLE, MINUTE, PETITE, MINUSCULE, DIMINUTIVE

being/creature .... RUNT, ATOMY, DWARF

bit .... IOTA, MORSEL

copy/model .... MINIATURE

extremely .... MICROSCOPIC

gold particles .... DUST

letter .... MINUSCULE

margin .... HAIR

opening .... PORE

person/thing .... DIMINUTIVE

portion .... MINIM

slang .... HALFPINT

speck .... MOTE

Tiny, singer .... TIM

tip .... END, FEE, NEB, TAP, TOP, APEX, CANT, CLUE, GIFT, HEEL, HINT, LIST, TILT, VAIL, SLANT, STEER, UPSET, ADVICE, GREASE, REWARD, TOPPLE, CUMSHAW, POINT(ER), GRATUITY

as of a hill or mountain .... PEAK, CREST, SUMMIT

off .... HINT, INFORM, WARN(ING)

one's hat .... DOFF

over .... UPEND, UPSET, TOPPLE, CAPSIZE, OVERTURN

pen's .... CAP, NEB, NIB

tipped .... CAPPED, CRESTED

rod .... CUE

"Tipper" .... MRS. AL GORE

tippet .... AMICE, SCARF, ALMUCE, CAMAIL, LIRIPIPE

tipping .... ALIST

hats .... DOFFING

tipple .... BIB, DRAM, DRINK, GUZZLE, IMBIBE, LIQUOR

tippler .... SOT, DRUNK, TOPER, BARFLY, BIBBER, SOAKER

tippler's haunt .... PUB, BAR(ROOM), TAPROOM, ALEHOUSE

tippy .... SHAKY

tips seller .... TOUT

tipstaff .... BAILIFF, CONSTABLE

tipster .... TOUT(ER), ADVISER, DOPESTER

tipsy .... AWRY, DRUNK, GROGGY, LOADED, CROOKED, INTOXICATED

slang .... HIGH, TIGHT

tiptoe .... LURK, CREEP, SNEAK

tiptop .... FIT, A-ONE, BEST, SHIPSHAPE

tirade ...... RANT, SPATE, SCREED, SPEECH, DIATRIBE, HARANGUE, JEREMIAD,

PHILIPPIC

tirailleur .... MARKSMAN, SHARPSHOOTER

tire ...... FAG, BORE, CLOY, DO IN, JADE, PNEU, SHOE, WEARY, EXHAUST, WHITEWALL

burst .... BLOWOUT

casing .... SHOE

filled with compressed air .... PNEUMATIC

iron .... STRAKE

kind of ...... RADIAL, TUBELESS

out .... FAG, EXHAUST

part of .... RIM, SHOE, TUBE, FELLY, TREAD, CASING

puncturer .... CALTRAP, CALTROP

tread mold .... MOULAGE

with low air pressure .... BALLOON

tired .... WEAK, JADED, WEARY, WORN-OUT, BREATHLESS

easily .... FATIGABLE

feeling .... ENNUI, FATIGUE, LANGUOR, WEARINESS

looking .... WAN, DRAWN, HAGGARD

of .... BORED

very ...... BEAT, ALL IN, SPENT, BUSHED, POOPED

tiredness, cause of .... OVERWORK

tireless .... INDEFATIGABLE

Tiresias .... SOOTHSAYER

tiresome .... DRY, DRAB, DULL, BORING, DREARY, HUMDRUM, IRKSOME, TEDIOUS, MONOTONOUS

person .... BORE, DRIP, NUISANCE

tiring .... TRYING, ANNOYING, DRAINING, GRUELING, STRAINING, STRESSFUL, WEARISOME

tirl .... STRUM, THRUM, QUIVER, THRILL, TREMOR

tisane .... TEA, PTISAN, DECOCTION

Tisiphone .... FURY

tissue .... WEB, BAST, MESH, TELA, CLOTH, FLESH, GAUZE, PAPER, PHLOEM, GRISTLE, NET(WORK)

animal .... GRISTLE, CARTILAGE

area of dead .... INFARCT

breaking down of organic .... HISTOLYSIS

cavity ...... LOCULUS, VACUOLE

cell in connecting .... HISTIOCYTE

change in .... CATAPLASIA

combining form .... HIST(O)

connecting ..... PONS, STROMA, TENDON, LIGAMENT

contracting .... MUSCLE

cutting instrument .... MICROTOME

decay .... CARIES, GANGRENE

development process .... HISTOGENESIS

divider .... SEPTUM, SEPTA (PL.)

elastic .... TENDON, CARTILAGE

fluid content ...... ION, WASTE, NUTRIENT

hardening .... SCLEROMA, SCLERIASIS

healed .... SCAR

horny: comb. form .... KERATO

inflammation .... CELLULITIS

like .... HISTOID

matching for transplant .... TYPING

nerve .... ALBA

orange/grapefruit .... PITH

plant .... BAST, LIGNIN, PHLOEM

sagging .... FLAB

skin .... EPITHELIUM

study of .... HISTOLOGY, HISTOPATHOLOGY

under epidermis .... HYPODERMA

wood .... LIGNIN, PHELLODERM, PHELLOGEN, CORK-CAMBIUM

tit .... NAG, TAP, BIRD, BLOW, GIRL, JADE, TEAT, HORSE, BREAST, NIPPLE

kapok .... ANTHOSCOPUS

long-tailed .... AEGITHALOS

penduline .... REMIZIDAE

Titan .... ZEUS, ATLAS, COEUS, CREUS, GIANT, CRONUS, HELIOS, IAPETUS, OCEANUS, COLOSSUS, HYPERION, PHAETHON, EPIMETHEUS, PROMETHEUS

father .... URANUS

female ...... LETO, MAIA, RHEA, DIONE, THEIA, AMAZON, PHOEBE, TETHYS, GIANTESS, EURYNOME, TITANESS

in lexicography .... ROGET, WEBSTER

in wrestling .... ANTAEUS

mother .... GE, GAEA, GAIA

noted for great strength .... SAMSON, HERCULES

place of consignment .... TARTARUS

Titania .... FAIRY-QUEEN

husband of .... OBERON

titanic .... HUGE, GIGANTIC

titanium dioxide .... RUTILE

titanite .... SPHENE, MINERAL

Titans' war with Olympians .... TITANOMACHY

tithe .... TAX, CESS, LEVY, TENTH, CHARGE, DONATION

tithing .... DECENARY

Tithonus' brother .... PRIAM

father .... LAOMEDON

love .... EOS

transformation .... GRASSHOPPER

titi .... TREE, MONKEY, IRONWOOD

titian .... AUBURN

titillate .... AMUSE, EXCITE, TICKLE, STIMULATE, TANTALIZE

titivate .... DRESS(UP), SPRUCE(UP)

titlark .... PIPIT

title .... NAME, CLAIM, RIGHT, LEGEND, PARENT, CAPTION, HEADING, PEERAGE, APPELLATION, DESIGNATION, CHAMPIONSHIP

colloquial .... HANDLE

degree .... MASTER, BACHELOR, EMERITUS, DOCTORATE

descriptive .... EPITHET, SURNAME, COGNOMEN

ecclesiastical ..... DOM, PADRE, RABBI, FATHER, SISTER, BROTHER, CARDINAL, HOLINESS, HIS GRACE, REVEREND, MONSIGNOR, MOTHER SUPERIOR

holder .... OWNER, TITLIST, CHAMPION, PROPRIETOR

inaccurate .... MISNOMER

of a noble .... RAS, DAME, DUKE, EARL, LADY, LORD, MILADY, DUCHESS, MARQUISE, BARON(ESS), COUNT(ESS), MARCHIONESS, VISCOUNT(ESS)

of a parliament's chief executive .... PRIME MINISTER

of a ruler .... EMIR, EMEER, CALIPH, PRINCE, SULTAN, (PADI)SHAH

of respect .... AGA, BEY, SIR, MILADY, MADAM(E), MONSIEUR

of Roman Catholic Church dignitary .... MONSIGNOR, (ARCH)BISHOP

of Roman Catholic Church head .... PAPA, POPE

of royalty .... KING, BEGUM, QUEEN, PRINCE, EMPEROR, EMPRESS, PRINCESS,

MAHARANI, MAHARAJA(H), MAHARANEE

of Shiite leader .... AYATOLLAH

of the highest executive officer .... PRESIDENT

of UK's highest state officer .... LORD CHANCELLOR

ownership .... DEED, CERTIFICATE

pages .... ODDMENTS

sports .... TITLIST, CHAMPION(SHIP)

subordinate .... SUBHEAD

to property .... DEED, MUNIMENT

transfer .... CEDE

titled person .... NOBLE, PEER(ESS)

titmouse .... MAG, NUN, TIT, VERDIN, BLUECAP, CHICKADEE

family .... PARIDAE

genus .... PARUS

relative .... NUTHATCH

Tito, Marshal .... (JOSIP)BROZ

country of .... YUGOSLAVIA

position held by .... PRESIDENT, PRIME MINISTER

resistance followers .... PARTISANS

titter .... GIGGLE, TEE-HEE, SNICKER, LAUGH(TER)

tittie .... SISTER

tittle .... DOT, JOT, IOTA, WHIT, SPECK, PARTICLE

tattle .... GOSSIP, JABBER, CHATTER, CHITCHAT

tittup .... CAPER, FRISK, FROLIC, PRANCE

titular .... NOMINAL, HONORIFIC

Titus' father .... VESPASIAN

Tiu .... TYR

Tivoli .... TIBUR

neighbor .... ROME

tizzy .... FUSS, SNIT, SWEAT, DITHER, SWIVET, FLUSTER, FOOFARAW, CONFUSION

Tlingit .... TONGA, INDIAN

Tman .... AGENT

tmesis .... DIACOPE

TNT .... TROTYL, DYNAMITE, EXPLOSIVE

part of .... NITRO

to .... AT, ON, UPON, WITH, UNTIL, TOWARD, AS FAR AS, THITHER

a degree .... SOMEWHAT

a point in time .... UNTIL

a T .... EXACTLY

adapt to new conditions .... ACCLIMATE

and fro .... UP AND DOWN,

BACK AND FORTH
any extent .... AT ALL
be .... ESSE
be continually thoughtful
.... REMEMBER
be evasive .... EQUIVOCATE
be frugal .... STINT
blame .... GUILTY,
RESPONSIBLE
boot .... AND
calm/quiet .... SEDATE
come .... LATER, FUTURE,
IMMINENT
-do .... ADO, FUSS, STIR,
BOTHER, BUSTLE, AGITATION,
COMMOTION
dwarf .... STUNT
hang .... NOOSE
help you bear it .... GRIN
_____ (just so) .... A TEE
now .... AS YET
open .... LANCE
opposite of .... FRO
rack .... WRING
send away .... RELEGATE
some extent .... SORT OF,
SOMEWHAT
stow cargo .... STEEVE
the letter .... VERBATIM
the other side (of) ..... ACROSS
the point .... APT, GERMANE,
RELATED, RELEVANT,
PERTINENT
the point at issue .... ADREM
the point that .... UNTIL
the port/the left .... APORT
the rear .... AFT
this .... HERETO
_____ (videlicet) .... WIT
wit .... NAMELY, SCILICET
your health ..... SKOAL, PROSIT
to, _____ (agree with)
.... COTTON
To Kill a Mockingbird author
.... LEE
toad .... AGUA, BUFO, FROG,
HYLA, PIPA, ANURAN, PEEPER,
CROAKER, PADDOCK,
AMPHIBIAN, BATRACHIA,
SPADEFOOT, NATTERJACK,
SALIENTIAN
back "wart" of ...... VERRUCA
larva ...... TADPOLE, POLLIWOG
poisonous secretion of
.... BUFOTENINE
sound .... CROAK
toadeater .... TOADY, HANGER-ON,
PARASITE, SYCOPHANT
toadfish .... SAPO
toadflax .... WEED
toadstone's use .... CHARM

toadstool .... AGARIC, FUNGUS,
BOLETUS, MUSHROOM,
PUFFBALL
toady .... SNOB, FAWNER, LACKEY,
FLUNK(E)Y, PARASITE,
TRUCKLE(R), FLATTERER,
SYCOPHANT, BOOTLICKER,
LICKSPIT(TLE)
toast .... DRY, HEAT, LEEP, WARM,
BREAD, BROWN, DRINK,
HONOR, PARCH, ROAST,
PLEDGE, SALUTE, SIPPET,
CAROUSE, COMPLIMENT
British .... CHEERS, CHEERIO
German .... PROSIT
Norwegian .... SKOAL
object of a .... HERO, LION,
BELLE, AWARDEE, HONOREE,
CELEBRANT, CELEBRITY
served in salad .... CROUTON
Spanish .... SALUD
type of .... RUSK, MELBA,
ZWIEBACK
used as a garnish .... SIPPET
toastmaster .... MC, EMCEE,
SYMPOSIARCH
toasty .... COZY, WARM
tobacco ...... CHEW, SHAG, WEED,
BURLEY, LATAKIA, PERIQUE,
MUNDUNGO, (BROAD)LEAF,
MUNDUNGUS
addiction .... TABACOSIS
and paper .... MAKING
bit of .... SCREW
box .... HUMIDOR
cake of .... PLUG
chewing .... PLUG, QUID
colloquial .... WEED
corporal's/soldier's
.... CAPORAL
Cuban .... CAPA, HAVANA,
VUELTA
dealer .... TOBACCONIST
juice .... PRAISS
kiln .... OAST
kind of .... DARKS
leaf bundle .... HAND
left in pipe .... DOTTEL,
DOTTLE
odor .... FUNK
peace pipe .... CALUMET
pipe .... DUDEEN, HOOKAH,
CHIBOUK, CORNCOB,
CHIBOUQUE, NARG(H)ILE,
MEERSCHAUM
plant pest .... THRIPS
poisonous alkaloid
.... NICOTINE
pouch .... SPLEUCHAN
powdered .... SNUFF
product .... PLUG, SNUFF,

STOGIE, CHEROOT,
CIGAR(ETTE)
rolled, twisted .... PIGTAIL
shredded .... SHAG
smoke .... WHIFF
snuff .... RAPPEE
Turkish .... LATAKIA
use of .... SMOKE, SNUFF,
CHEWING, SMOKING
toboggan .... SLED, GLIDE,
COASTER, DECLINE
like vehicle .... BOBSLED
runway of .... CHUTE
toby .... JUG, MUG, CIGAR
content of .... ALE, BEER
tock .... HORNBILL
tocology .... MIDWIFERY,
OBSTETRICS
tocsin .... BELL, ALARM, SIGNAL
tod .... FOX, BUSH, CLUMP
toddle .... PADDLE, TOTTER,
WADDLE
toddler .... TOT, BABY, CHILD,
MOPPET
toddy ...... SAP, DRINK, BEVERAGE
toe .... DIGIT, DACTYL(US)
bird's .... HALLUX
dance ...... BALLET, PIROUETTE
dancer .... BALLERINA
infection ..... FELON, WHITLOW
membrane .... WEB(BING)
sore .... AGNAIL
the line .... OBEY, BEHAVE,
CONFORM
woe .... CORN
toehold .... GRIP, FOOTING
toenails, work on .... PEDICURE
toes, on one's .... ALERT
step on someone's
.... INTERLOPE
whirling on the ..... PIROUETTE
toff .... DANDY
toffee/toffy .... CANDY, TAFFY
toft .... KNOLL, HILLOCK,
MESSUAGE, HOMESTEAD
tog(s) .... COAT, DUDS, DRESS,
OUTFIT, CLOTHES
toga .... GOWN, ROBE, CLOAK
together .... JOINTLY, MUTUALLY,
ASSOCIATED, HAND IN HAND
in music .... ADUE
toggery ...... CLOTHES, CLOTHING,
HABERDASHERY
toggle .... PIN, ROD, BOLT, COTTER
Togo, capital of .... LOME
city/town ...... KPEME, MANGO,
SOKODE, ATAKPAME
coin .... CENTIME
gulf .... GUINEA
language .... EWE, TWI,
HAUSA, FRENCH

monetary unit .... FRANC
mountain .... AGOU
president .... EYADEMA,
      OLYMPIO
river .... OTI, MONO
tribe .... EWE, MINA
Togoland plus Gold Coast
   .... GHANA
toil ...... MOIL, SLOG, TASK, WORK,
     LABOR, SLAVE, DRUDGE,
     EFFORT, STRIVE, TRAVAIL
toile .... CLOTH, LINEN, CRETONNE
toilet .... COMMODE, LATRINE,
     LAVATORY
case .... ETUI, ETWEE, MUSETTE
outdoor .... JAKES, PRIVY
slang .... CAN, HEAD, JOHN
water ...... BAYRUM, COLOGNE,
     LAVENDER
toiletry item .... SOAP, LOTION,
     CREAM, POWDER, COLOGNE,
     COSMETICS
toils .... GIN, NET, WEB, MESH,
     TRAP, SNARES
toilsome .... ARDUOUS,
     LABORIOUS, STRENUOUS
Tojo, Japan premier ...... HIDEKI
tokay .... WINE, GRAPE
token .... SIGN, SLUG, INDEX,
     EMBLEM, PLEDGE, SYMBOL,
     KEEPSAKE, INDICATION
currency .... SCRIP
of servitude .... YOKE
payment ..... ARLES, ADVANCE,
     EARNEST
tokens .... INDICIA
Tokyo .... EDO, YEDO
center .... SHIMBASI
coin .... SEN
Fifth Avenue of .... GINZA
fork .... CHOPSTICK
formerly .... EDO, YEDO
is capital of ____ .... JAPAN
Shogun's .... EDO
tole .... ALLURE, ENTICE
Toledo .... BLADE, SWORD
tolerable .... SO-SO, BEARABLE,
     PASSABLE, ENDURABLE
tolerably .... FAIRLY,
     MODERATELY
tolerance .... MARGIN,
     ALLOWANCE, LENIENCY,
     ENDURANCE
tolerate .... BEAR, ALLOW, BROOK,
     STAND, ENDURE, PERMIT,
     SUFFER
Tolkien badlands .... MORDOR
tree creature .... ENT
toll .... FEE, TAX, RING, KNELL,
     CHARGE, EXACTION
collector .... PUBLICAN

road .... (TURN)PIKE
tol(l)booth .... PEN, JAIL, LOCKUP,
     PRISON
toller .... DOG, BELL RINGER
Toller, German poet ...... ERNST
Tolstoy, Russian novelist
   .... LEO, LEV
Toltec .... NAHUATL(AN)
Tom .... TURKEY, MALE-CAT
Bosley role .... FATHER
     DOWLING
Dick and Harry ...... ANYONE,
     EVERYONE
the General .... THUMB
Thumb .... DWARF, MIDGET
Thumb's bride .... LAVINIA
     (WARREN)
tom tom .... DRUM
tomahawk .... HATCHET,
     (BATTLE)AX
tomalley .... LIVER
tomato .... GIRL, BERRY, FRUIT,
     WOMAN, LOVE-APPLE
blend of potato and
   .... POMATO
eaten whole .... CHERRY
juice jelly/salad .... ASPIC
sauce .... CATSUP, KETCHUP
variety .... TAXI, PEACH,
     ZEBRA, RED-ROMA, LEMON-
     BOY, BEEFSTEAK, EARLY GIRL,
     (RED)CHERRY, GREEN GRAPE,
     RED CURRANT, MARVEL-STRIPE
tomb .... CIST, CRYPT, GRAVE,
     VAULT, BURIAL, DOLMEN,
     OSSUARY, CROMLECH,
     MASTABA(H), SEPULCHER,
     SARCOPHAGUS
commemorative .... CENOTAPH
cover .... PALL
empty .... CENOTAPH,
     MONUMENT
famous Indian ..... TAJ MAHAL
flag .... BANDEROL(E)
for absent dead ..... CENOTAPH
heroes' .... PANTHEON
imposing .... MAUSOLEUM
inscription on .... EPITAPH, HIC
     JACET, HERE LIES, IN
     MEMORIAM
mummy's .... MASTABA(H)
prehistoric/rock .... CIST
room .... CRYPT
royal .... PYRAMID
saint's .... SHRINE
stone over .... LEDGER,
     MENHIR, MEGALITH, MONOLITH
towerlike .... STUPA
underground .... PIT,
     CATACOMB(S)
tomblike .... GRIM, BLEAK,

     DISMAL, DOLEFUL, FUNEREAL,
     SEPULCHRAL
tomboy .... ROMP, HOIDEN,
     HOYDEN
tomboyish .... MANNISH, ROMPISH
tombstone .... CAIRN, STELA,
     STELE, MARKER, TABLET
marshal .... (WYATT) EARP
tomcat .... GIB
tomcod or pollock ...... GAD(O)ID
tome .... BOOK, VOLUME
tomentose .... FLEECY, MATTED
tomfool .... ZANY, CLOWN, SILLY,
     STUPID, BUFFOON, FOOLISH
tomfoolery .... BANTER,
     NONSENSE, SILLINESS,
     BUFFOONERY
Tomlin, ____ .... LILY
Tommy, Brit. soldier .... ATKINS
tommyrot .... BOSH, RUBBISH,
     NONSENSE
tomography .... X-RAY
tomorrow .... MANANA
tomtit .... BIRD, WREN,
     CHICKADEE
ton .... STYLE, VOGUE, FASHION
unit of measure:
   1,000 kg. .... METRIC
   2,000 lbs. .... SHORT
   2,240 lbs. .... LONG
tonal .... TONIC, PHONIC
tonality .... TONE, MELODY,
     HARMONICS
tondo .... PAINTING
tone .... HUE, KEY, TINT, TUNE,
     PITCH, SHADE, SOUND, STYLE,
     ACCENT, QUALITY
arm .... PICKUP
certain kind of .... DIAL
color .... TIMBRE
combination .... CHORD
down .... MUTE, SOFTEN
lack of .... ATONY
quality of .... TONALITY
reiteration .... TREMOLO
shade of .... NUANCE
toneless .... ATONY
Tong member .... CHINESE
Tonga capital .... NUKUALOFA
city/town ...... NEIAFU, PANGAI
coin .... SENITI
king .... TUPOU
language .... TONGAN, ENGLISH
monetary unit .... PAANGA
tongs .... CLAMP, PLIERS, FORCEPS,
     NIPPERS, PINCERS
tongue .... TAB, FLAP, IDIOM,
     ORGAN, GLOSSA, LINGUA,
     SPEECH, DIALECT, LANGUAGE
bell's .... CLAPPER
bone of .... HYOID

buckle's .... PIN
coating .... FUR(RING)
combining form ..... GLOSS(O)
curbing device .... BRANKS
disorder .... TUMOR, ULCER,
CANCER, FISSURE
elevation on .... PAPILLA
examining instrument
.... DEPRESSOR
fold under the .... FRENUM,
FRENULUM
in cheek .... INSINCERE
inflammation .... GLOSSITIS
lashing ...... JAWING, REPROOF,
(BE)RATING, SCOLDING,
REPRIMAND
of the .... GLOSSAL, LINGUAL
"of vanity" .... EGO
part of .... BLADE, NODULE,
PAPILLA(E), EPIGLOTTIS
sensory organs of the
.... TASTE BUDS
-shaped .... LANGUET(TE),
LINGULATE
shoe's .... TAB
thickened patches on
.... LEUKOPLAKIA
-tied .... MUM, SHY, SILENT,
WORDLESS, DUMB(STRUCK),
SPEECHLESS
use of .... TASTE, SPEECH,
INGESTION, SWALLOWING,
MASTICATION, ARTICULATION
wagon's .... NEAP, POLE
tongueless .... MUM, DUMB, MUTE
tonguelike .... GLOSSAL, LINGUAL
organ .... LINGUA, PROBOSCIS
tongue-tie .... ANKYLOGLOSSIA
tonic ...... BRACER, ELIXIR, FILLIP,
PICKUP, REMEDY, BRACING,
BEVERAGE, MEDICINE,
ROBORANT, INVIGORATING
bark .... CANELLA
content .... VITAMIN, MINERAL,
HERBAL EXTRACT
effect, medically ..... PLACEBO
in medicine .... IRON
tonka bean .... GUAIAC
flavor .... COUMARIN
Tonkin .... BAMBOO
city .... HANOI
tonneau, later .... CHASSIS
tons and tons .... SCADS
tonsil .... AMYGDALA
abscess on the .... QUINSY
inflammation .... TONSILLITIS
instrument for .... FORCEPS,
GUILLOTINE
neighbor .... TONGUE,
ADENOID

surgical removal of
.... TONSILLECTOMY
tonsorial artist .... BARBER
tenet? .... BARBARISM
tonsured person .... MONK,
PRIEST
tontine .... ANNUITY
tonus .... TONICITY
tony .... CLASSY, STYLISH,
LUXURIOUS
Tony, actor .... CURTIS, RANDALL
too .... ALSO, VERY, AS WELL,
OVER(LY), BESIDES, LIKEWISE,
EXTREMELY, ADDITIONALLY
large ..... OUTSIZE, MONSTROUS
many/much .... DE TROP
much .... EXCESSIVE
much, in music .... TANTO
old .... OVERAGE
soon .... EARLY, UNTIMELY,
PREMATURE
tool ...... MEANS, DEVICE, GADGET,
STOOGE, MACHINE, UTENSIL,
APPARATUS, IMPLEMENT,
INSTRUMENT, INTERMEDIARY
adz-shaped .... MATTOCK
binding .... STAPLER, STAPLE
GUN
bookbinding .... GOUGE
boring .... AWL, AUGER, DRILL,
GIMLET, JUMPER, TREPAN
carpenter's .... SAW, BEVEL,
DRILL, LEVEL, PLANE,
HAMMER, NAILSET
case .... KIT
cleaving: var. .... FROE
cobbler's .... AWL
cutting .... SAW, ADZ(E), BOLO,
BLADE, KNIFE, CUTTER,
SCYTHE, SHEARS, SICKLE,
MACHETE, SCISSORS
digging ..... SHOVEL, MATTOCK
docking .... ANCHOR, BOAT-
HOOK
engraver's .... BURIN
fastening .... RIVETER,
STAPLER
finishing .... PLANER
garden ...... HOE, RAKE, SPADE,
SHOVEL, TROWEL,
BUSHWHACKER
grinding .... FILE
handle .... HAFT, HELVE
hoisting .... JACK, PULLEY
holding .... HAWK, VISE
hole-enlarging .... REAMER
hole-making .... BODKIN,
DIBBLE
knifelike .... SPATULA
lifting .... CRANE

lifting and tossing
.... PITCHFORK
lumberman's .... PEAVEY
mason's .... CHISEL, CUTTER
measuring .... CALIPER(S)
metal worker's .... SWAGE
mining .... CRADLE
molding .... DIE
person as a .... DUPE, PAWN,
DUMMY, PATSY, PUPPET,
STOOGE, CAT'S-PAW
pincers .... PLIERS, FORCEPS,
TWEEZER(S)
pipe-bending .... HICKEY
polishing ..... BUFFER, SANDER
pruning .... SHEARS, BILLHOOK
prying .... LEVER, CROWBAR
reaper's .... FLAIL
rotary .... REAMER
sculptor's .... CARVER, CHISEL,
MOLDER, WHITTLE
set .... KIT
shaping .... DIE, LATHE
sharpening .... HONE, STEEL,
STROP, GRINDER, WHETSTONE,
(GRIND)STONE
shaving .... (SAFETY)RAZOR
smoothing .... BUFFER
soil-breaking .... PICK
spike-toothed .... HARROW
surgical ...... LANCET, SCALPEL
surveyor's .... Y-LEVEL,
TRANSIT
toothed .... SAW,
RATCHET(WHEEL)
trimming .... SHEARS,
SCISSORS
turning .... WRENCH,
SCREWDRIVER
with serrated jaws ...... PLIERS
toolmaker .... MACHINIST
toon .... TREE, WOOD
family .... MAHOGANY
toot .... HORN, WHISTLE
sound .... HONK, BLAST,
WHISTLE
tooth .... PEG, TUSH, TUSK, IVORY,
MOLAR, TASTE, CUSPID,
CHOPPER, INCISOR, APPETITE
and _____ .... NAIL
and nail .... FIERCELY
back .... WISDOM(TOOTH)
boar's .... TUSK
broken .... SNAG
canine .... FANG, CUSPID,
LANIARY
combining form .... DENT(I),
ODONT(O)
covering .... ENAMEL
crooked .... SNAG
crust .... CEMENT

decay .... CARIES
deposit .... CRUST, TOPHUS
doctor .... DENTIST,
              ORTHODONTIST
dog's .... FANG
elephant .... TUSK
filler .... CEMENT
filling .... INLAY
for a tooth .... TALION
gear .... COG
growth on .... EXOSTOSIS
hollow in .... CAVITY
horse canine .... TUSH
like .... DENTOID, ODONTOID
long, projecting .... TUSK
long, sharp .... FANG
molar .... GRINDER
of the .... DENTAL
part .... PULP, CROWN,
    CEMENT, ENAMEL, DENTIN(E)
prefix .... DENTI
pre-molar .... BICUSPID
puller .... DENTIST
root tissue layer
    .... CEMENTUM
shaped .... DENTOID,
                DENTIFORM
small .... DENTIL, DENTICLE
snake's .... FANG
socket .... ALVEOLUS
substance .... PULP
upper canine .... EYETOOTH
use of ..... BITE, CHEW, GNAW,
             GRIND, PIERCE
walrus .... TUSK
wheel .... COG, GEAR
toothache .... ODONTALGIA
toothed .... DENTED, DENTATE,
                SERRATED
wheel .... GEAR, RATCHET,
                SPROCKET
toothlike part .... COG, TINE,
                PRONG
projection .... JAG, DENTIL,
    DENTICLE, DENT(ATION)
toothless .... EDENTATE
toothpaste .... ZIRCATE,
              DENTIFRICE
toothsome .... TASTY, DAINTY,
      SAVORY, LUSCIOUS,
    PALATABLE, APPETIZING
toothy look .... GRIN
tool .... HARROW
wheel .... RATCHET
tootle .... WHISTLE
toots: slang .... DEAR, DARLING
tootsy .... FOOT
top .... COP, LID, TOY, ACME,
    APEX, HEAD, LEAD, PICK,
    ROOF, COVER, ELITE, EXCEL,
    OUTDO, ZENITH, HIGHEST,

SURPASS, DOMINATE,
                PINNACLE
—— (A-One) .... DRAWER
altar .... MENSA
ballerina .... PRIMA
banana .... STAR
blow one's .... ERUPT
bottle .... CAP, CROWN
brass .... OFFICER, OFFICIAL(S),
           MANAGEMENT
carriage's .... CAPOTE
cover .... CAP, LID
dog .... ACE, BOSS, HEAD
drawer .... A-ONE, TOPS, FIRST-
                RATE
flight ...... BEST, A-ONE, FIRST-
                RATE
gallant .... ACME
grade .... BEST, CHOICE
hat .... GIBUS
hill .... COP, BROW
hole .... FIRST-RATE
kick: sl. .... SERGEANT
mast support .... FID
of head .... CROWN
of mountain ...... PEAK, CREST,
              SUMMIT
of the front page
    .... HEADLINE
of wave .... FOAM, CREST
off a room .... CEIL
priority ..... URGENT, URGENCY
quality .... SUPERIOR, FIRST-
                RATE
row on a form .... LINE-A
secret .... CLASSIFIED
shaped .... TURBINATE
spun with the fingers
    .... TEETOTUM
the next guy .... ONE-UP
topaz .... GEM, QUARTZ,
           HUMMINGBIRD
Topaz, author of .... URIS
topazolite .... GARNET
topcoat ...... RAGLAN, OVERCOAT,
           CHESTERFIELD
tope .... DRINK, SHARK, SHRINE
topee/topi ...... CAP, HAT, HELMET
toper .... SOT, SOAK, WINO,
    RUMMY, SOUSE, BIBBER,
    TOSSPOT, DRUNK(ARD)
topgallant .... MAST
tophat .... GIBUS
toph(e) .... TUFA, TUFF
Tophet(h) .... HELL
topic .... ITEM, TEXT, THEME,
    THESIS, HEAD(ING), SUBJECT
topical .... LOCAL
topkick .... SARGE, SERGEANT
topknot .... TUFT, HEADDRESS
topnotch ...... A-ONE, BEST, ONER,

TOPS, EXCELLENT, FIRST-RATE
toponym .... NAME
topper .... HAT, COAT, BERET,
                STETSON
beer glass .... FOAM, SUDS
topping ...... CRUST, ICING, LAYER
topple .... FAIL, FALL, TRIP,
    LEVEL, DEFEAT, TOTTER,
    TUMBLE, COLLAPSE,
              OVERTURN
tops .... A-ONE, BEST, SUPER
topsail .... RAFFE
topside .... DECK
topsoil .... LOAM, LAYER
Topsy's friend .... EVA
topsy-turvy .... CHAOTIC,
    CONFUSED, INVERTED,
    DISORDERLY, UPSIDE-DOWN
toque .... CAP, HAT, BONNET
tor .... CRAG, HILL, KNOLL
relative of .... ALP
Torah .... TETEL, PENTATEUCH
torch .... BURN, LINK, LUNT,
    IGNITE, CRESSET, FLAMBEAU,
         (FLASH)LIGHT
bearer ...... LINKBOY, LINKMAN
for lure .... JACK
material .... TOW, PITCH,
    TAPER, CANDLE, TALLOW
song .... BALLAD
tore .... RACED, TORUS
toreador .... BULLFIGHTER
assistant of .... PICADOR
torero .... MATADOR, BULLFIGHTER
queue of .... COLETA
torii .... GATEWAY
Torino .... TURIN
Torme, singer .... MEL
torment .... VEX, BAIT, PAIN,
    RACK, AGONY, ANNOY,
    HARRY, TEASE, BADGER,
    HARASS, PLAGUE, ANGUISH,
    HAGRIDE, TORTURE, AGITATE,
    DISTRESS, SUFFERING
archaic .... HASE
tormentor .... NAG, PEST, BULLY,
    TEASER, HARRIER, HECKLER
torn .... REFT, RENT, RIVEN,
    DAMAGED, SEVERED,
            TATTERED
tornado .... CYCLONE, TWISTER,
    TYPHOON, HURRICANE,
    WHIRLWIND, WIND(STORM)
toro .... BULL, COWFISH,
            TRUNKFISH
torose .... BULGING, KNOBBED,
    SWOLLEN, CYLINDRICAL
torpedo .... NUMBFISH,
    CRAMPFISH, PROJECTILE,
        (ELECTRIC)RAY
boat .... WARSHIP

colloquial .... EGG, ATTACK, DESTROY, SABOTAGE

part of .... FIN, RUDDER, TRIGGER, WARHEAD, EXPLOSIVE, PROPELLER

slang .... FISH, GUNMAN, ASSASSIN, GANGSTER, BODYGUARD

type of .... HOMING, ROCKET, BANGALORE

torpid .... DULL, NUMB, INERT, STILL, SLEEPY, STUPID, DORMANT, LISTLESS, SLUGGISH, STAGNANT, LETHARGIC

torpor .... APATHY, STUPOR, INERTIA, LANGUOR, LETHARGY

torquate .... COLLARED

torque .... CHAIN, TWIST, COLLAR, STRESS, TORSION, NECKLACE

torques .... RUFF

torrefy .... DRY, PARCH

torrent ...... RUSH, FLOOD, RIVER, SPATE, SPURT, SURGE, DELUGE, RAPID(S), CASCADE, DOWNPOUR

torrential ...... COPIOUS, ERUPTIVE

torrid .... HOT, ARID, ARDENT, STEAMY, SULTRY, BURNING, PARCHED, SIZZLING, TROPICAL, SCORCHING, PASSIONATE

torsion .... STRESS, PRESSURE, TWISTING, CONTORTION

torsk .... CUSK, BURBOT, CODFISH

torso .... TRUNK

tort .... WRONG, DAMAGE, INJURY, MISDEED, OFFENSE, MISDEMEANOR

torte .... CAKE, PASTRY

torticollis .... WRYNECK, STIFF NECK

tortile .... COILED, TWISTED

tortilla .... BREAD, CORNCAKE, CORNMEAL, FLAT(STONE)

tortoise .... EMYD, TURTLE, HICATEE, TESTUDO, GALAPAGO, TERRAPIN, CHELONIAN

burrowing/land .... GOPHER

of .... CHELONIAN, TESTUDINAL, TESTUDINATE

shell .... CARAPACE, BUTTERFLY

Tortue .... TORTUGA

tortuous .... SPIRAL, CROOKED, DEVIOUS, SINUOUS, WINDING

torture .... PAIN, RACK, AGONY, TWIST, PUNISH, ANGUISH, CRUELTY, DISTORT, TORMENT,

MARTYR(DOM), THIRD-DEGREE

for information .... SWEAT

instrument of .... RACK, WHEEL, STRAPPADO

method of .... WATERCURE, KEELHAUL(ING), TAR-AND-FEATHERING

torus .... TORE, MOLDING, SWELLING, THALAMUS, ELEVATION

Tory .... RIGHTIST, REACTIONARY, CONSERVATIVE

Toscana .... TUSCANY

Toscanini, conductor .... ARTURO

Tosca's love .... MARIO

toss .... LOB, PEG, CAST, FLIP, HURL, JERK, ROLL, SNAP, STIR, SWAY, FLING, PITCH, THROW, BUFFET, TUMBLE, AGITATE

about .... BANDY, FLOUNDER

and turn .... STAY AWAKE

out .... CHUCK, EJECT, DISCARD

side to side .... CAREEN

tossing expert .... JUGGLER

tosspot .... SOT, SOAK, SOUSE, TOPER, DRINKER, DRUNK(ARD)

tossup .... STANDOFF

tot .... TAD, ADD UP, CHILD, COUNT, DRINK, TOTAL, TODDLER

total .... ADD, SUM, GROSS, UTTER, WHOLE, AMOUNT, ENTIRE, ABSOLUTE, COMPLETE, OUTRIGHT, AGGREGATE

loss .... BOMB, FLOP

slang .... WRECK

tonal effect .... TUTTI

wipeout .... MASSACRE

totalitarian ruler ...... DICTATOR

totality .... ALL, ENTIRETY

totalizator .... TOTE-BOARD, PARI-MUTUEL

tote .... ADD, HAUL, LOAD, CARRY, COUNT, TOTALIZER

board word .... WIN, SHOW, PLACE

totem .... PHYLE, EMBLEM, MOIETY

pole .... XAT

toter .... LUGGER, CARRIER

totipalmate bird .... DUCK, GOOSE, PELICAN, CORMORANT

tot's "little piggy" .... TOE

-totsy, ____ .... HOTSY

totter .... REEL, ROCK, SHAKE, WAVER, DODDER, FALTER, TODDLE, STAGGER

toucan .... TOCO, ARACARI

family .... RAMPHASTIDAE

food .... FRUITS

genus .... ANDIGENA, RAMPHASTOS, PTEROGLOSSUS

mountain .... ANDIGENA

small green .... TOUCANET

toucanet genus .... SELENIDERA

touch .... HIT, LAP, PAT, RAP, RUB, TAP, ABUT, FEEL, LICK, LOAN, TINT, TINGE, TRACE, ADJOIN, AFFECT, FINGER, STROKE, CONTACT, MENTION

and go .... HASTY, RISKY, CASUAL, GAMBLE, TOSS-UP, UNSURE, UNCERTAIN

at .... STOP

bottom .... GO-TO-POT

caused by .... TACTUAL

closely .... OSCULATE

clumsily .... PAW

doctor's .... PALPATE

examine by .... FEEL

excite by .... TICKLE

for medical diagnosis .... PALPATE

ground with forehead .... KOWTOW

having sense of .... TACTILE

light, passing .... BRUSH

lightly .... KISS, GRAZE

lovingly .... CARESS, FONDLE

-me-not .... IMPATIENS, JEWELWEED

means of/organ of .... PAW, TOE, HAND, PALM, FEELER, FINGER, PALPUS, TONGUE, ANTENNA, VIBRISSA

microscopic structures of .... RECEPTORS

of .... TANG, HAPTIC, TACTIC, TACTILE

off .... FIRE, START, IGNITE

perceptible by .... TACTILE

prefix .... TAC

soft: sl. .... DUPE, GULL, SUCKER, PUSHOVER

stimulating .... MASSAGE

system for the blind .... BRAILLE

system worker .... STENO, TYPER, TYPIST

the emotions .... MOVE, AFFECT

up .... FIX, REFINE, FRESHEN, IMPROVE

upon .... CITE, MENTION

with the hand ...... RUB, PALM, CLASP, KNEAD, HANDLE, STROKE, MASSAGE

touchable ...... TACTILE, TANGIBLE

touchdown .... GOAL, SCORE, LANDING

touched .... MOVED, HUMBLED,

AFFECTED, DEMENTED, SOFTENED

touching .... MOVING, TENDER, PITIFUL, TACTION, TANGENT, PATHETIC, POIGNANT

touchstone ...... TEST, STANDARD, CRITERION

touchwood .... PUNK, AMADOU, TINDER

touchy .... SORE, HUFFY, RISKY, CRITICAL, DELICATE, TICKLISH, IRRITABLE, SENSITIVE, PRECARIOUS

king .... MIDAS

tough .... FIRM, WIRY, HARDY, ROUGH, STIFF, SEVERE, STICKY, STRONG, VISCOUS, COHESIVE, HARDENED, GLUTINOUS, HARDBOILED

colloquial .... DIFFICULT

guy .... GOON, THUG, BULLY, BUTCH, RUFFIAN

it out .... NEVER SAY DIE

job .... BACKBREAKER

luck .... BAD BREAK

minded .... WISE, DOGGED, WILLFUL

situation .... FIX, PINCH, PICKLE

street .... HOODLUM, HOOLIGAN

toughen .... STEEL, ANNEAL, TEMPER, STIFFEN

Toulouse, painter .... LAUTREC

toupee .... WIG, PERUKE, HAIRPIECE

slang .... RUG

tour ...... EYRE, TREK, TRIP, TURN, JAUNT, ROUND, SHIFT, JUNKET, TRAVEL, CIRCUIT, JOURNEY

de force .... FEAT

touraco kin .... CUCKOO

tourbillion .... FIREWORK, WHIRLWIND

tourist .... TREKKER, TRIPPER, VOYAGER, TRAVELER, SIGHTSEER

court .... MOTEL

guide of .... CICERONE, DRAGOMAN

mecca ..... LINCOLN MEMORIAL

stopping place .... INN, HOTEL, MOTEL, HOSTELRY

travel schedule ...... ITINERARY

tourmaline .... GEM(STONE)

black variety .... SCHORL

red variety .... RUBELLITE

tournament .... JOUST, MATCH, CONTEST, TOURNEY, COMPETITION

draw .... BYE

fighting area .... LIST

kind of .... PRO, OPEN, AMATEUR, CAR(R)OUSEL

knights' .... TILT, JOUST

tourney .... TILT, JOUST, TOURNAMENT

tourniquet .... PAD, BINDER, GARROT, BANDAGE, COMPRESS

tousle .... MUSS, RUFFLE, RUMPLE, TANGLE, DISHEVEL

tousled .... UNTIDY, SNARLED, UNKEMPT, MESSED-UP

tout .... SPY, PUFF, PRAISE, TIP(STER), DOPESTER, PITCHMAN, BALLYHOO(ER), SOLICITOR

subject of .... WAGER

tovarisch .... COMRADE

tow .... LUG, TUG, DRAG, DRAW, HALE, HAUL, PULL, FIBER, HARDS

and pitch torch .... LINK

-away zone .... NO PARKING

rope .... HAWSER, CORDELE, TOWLINE

towage .... FEE

toward .... NEAR, ABOUT, DOCILE, FACING, FORWARD, DIRECT(LY)

center .... ENTAD, INNER

exterior .... ECTAD

mouth .... ORAD

the rear .... AFT

the stern .... ABAFT

towardly .... WILLINGLY

towboat .... MULE, TUG(BOAT)

towel .... DRY, SWAB, WIPE(R), DIAPER, NAPKIN, ABSORBENT

church service .... LAVABO

fabric .... TERRY(CLOTH)

kind of ...... BATH, DISH, FACE, HAND, BEACH, PAPER

small .... SERVIETTE, TOWELETTE

tower .... LOOM, REAR, RISE, SILO, SOAR, SPIRE, CASTLE, PILLAR, PULLER, TURRET, DRAGGER, BASTIL(L)E, TOURELLE, ZIGGURAT, SKYSCRAPER

a kind of .... IVORY

above .... EXCEL, EXCEED, TRANSCEND

ancient .... BABEL, ZIGGURAT

bell .... BELFRY, CAMPANILE

Biblical .... BABEL, DAVID'S

canal boat's .... MULE

castle .... DONJON, BARBICAN

church .... STEEPLE

famed .... PISA, BABEL, EIFFEL, LONDON

feature .... SPIRAL STAIRCASE

fodder .... SILO

fortified .... PEEL, DONJON, CITADEL, DUNGEON, FORTRESS, STRONGHOLD

fortress, four- .... HERODIUM

gate .... BARBICAN

guide of ships .... LIGHTHOUSE

marker .... PYLON

mosque .... MINARET

observation ...... WATCHTOWER

of Babel .... MADHOUSE

of confusion .... BABEL

of strength .... ROCK

pointed .... SPIRE

portable .... TURRET, BASTIL(L)E

pyramidal .... PAGODA

signal .... BEACON

small .... TURRET, MIRADOR

tapering .... SPIRE, STEEPLE

towering .... LOFTY, HIGH(-UP), EMINENT

Towers, The Pool of .... HEZEKIAH'S POOL

towhead .... BLOND

towhee .... FINCH, CHEWINK

kin .... BUNTING, SPARROW

town .... CITY, WICK, BURG(H), HAMLET, PUEBLO, BOROUGH, VILLAGE

———— .... CRIER

fortified/walled .... BURG, BURH

imaginary .... PODUNK

in Tamil Nadu, historic .... ARCOT

league .... HANSEATIC

magistrate .... REEVE

map .... PLAT

near castle .... BOURG

of WWI fame .... ARMENTIERES

on the Po .... CREMONA

prefix .... TRE

section .... WARD

square .... CAMPO, PLAZA

street .... MAINDRAG

"Too Tough to Die" .... TOMBSTONE

township .... DEME, MUNICIPALITY

townsman .... CIT(IZEN), OPPIDAN, RESIDENT

toxic .... VENOMOUS, POISONOUS

toxicant .... POISON(OUS)

toxin .... VENOM, POISON

bacterial .... EXOTOXIN, ENDOTOXIN, ENTEROTOXIN

canned food .... BOTULIN

toxocariasis .... INFESTATION

toxophilite .... ARCHER

toxoplasmosis .... INFECTION

toy .... DOLL, PLAY, DALLY, FLIRT, BAUBLE, FIDDLE, PUPPET, TRIFLE, TRINKET, TEETOTUM, PLAYTHING
bear .... TEDDY
"brought to life" .... VELVETEEN RABBIT
dog .... PEKE, POODLE, TERRIER, CHIHUAHUA
musical instrument .... KAZOO
stilt-like .... POGO-STICK
stringed .... TOP, YOYO, DIABOLO
tra la la .... REFRAIN
trace .... COPY, DRAW, HINT, MARK, SIGN, SLOT, TANG, SCENT, SHADE, TINGE, TOUCH, TRACK, TRAIL, DETECT, ENGRAM, FOLLOW, VESTIGE, DELINEATE
trachea ...... WEASAND, WINDPIPE
trachoma .... CONJUNCTIVITIS
track .... RUT, WAY, PATH, ROUTE, TRACE, TRAIL, COURSE, FOLLOW, RUNWAY, CIRCUIT, VESTIGE
back .... RETRACE
circuit .... LAP
down .... HUNT, SEARCH
event .... FLAT RACE
game .... PUG, SPOOR
horse racing .... TURF, HIPPODROME
man .... TOUT, RUNNER, ATHLETE
mark .... RUT, SLOT, SPUR, SPOOR, FOOTPRINT
racing .... CINDERS, SPEEDWAY, CINDER PATH
run .... MILE
ship's .... WAKE
speedster .... KELSO
tipster .... TOUT
tracker .... TAIL, HOUND, HUNTER, DETECTIVE
tracks connection .... TIE
train .... RAILS
tract .... AREA, EXTENT, STEPPE, ENTERON, LEAFLET, STRETCH, PAMPHLET, TREATISE
tractable .... EASY, TAME, DOCILE, PLASTIC, WILLING, OBEDIENT, YIELDING, COMPLIANT, MALLEABLE, FLEXI(B)LE, (COM)PLIANT
tractate .... TREATISE
tractile .... DUCTILE, TENSILE
traction .... GRIP, DRAWING, PULLING, FOOTHOLD
tractor .... MULE, AIRPLANE, BULLDOZER

and trailer .... SEMI
for short .... CAT
type of .... FARM, LAWN, PLOW, TRUCK, GRADER, TRAILER
trademark for a .... CATERPILLAR
Tracy, _____ .... DICK, SPENCER
trade .... DEAL, SELL, SWAP, WORK, CRAFT, BARTER, METIER, BUSINESS, COMMERCE, EXCHANGE, CLIENTELE, CUSTOMERS, LIVELIHOOD, OCCUPATION
agreement .... CARTEL
association .... CARTEL, SYNDICATE
exclusive control .... MONOPOLY
of .... MERCANTILE
questionable .... TRAFFIC
route ...... AIR LANE, SEA LANE
union member .... UNIONIST, CARDHOLDER
union strategy .... RATTEN
unlawful .... CONTRABAND
variant .... SWOP
wind .... MONSOON
trademark .... LOGO, BRAND, LABEL, SYMBOL
publisher's .... COLOPHON
R with a circle around it .... REGISTERED
trader .... SHIP, MONGER, MERCHANT
of illegal commodity .... TRAFFICKER
ploy of .... HARD BARGAIN
unauthorized .... INTERLOPER
tradesman ...... DEALER, ARTISAN, HUCKSTER, SHOPKEEPER, STOREKEEPER
trading .... BUSINESS, COMMERCE, SWAPPING, COMMERCIAL, MERCHANDISING
center .... PIT, FAIR, MALL, MART, RIALTO, EMPORIUM, EXCHANGE, (FLEA)MARKET
directly to consumers .... RETAIL
grains .... PIT
in large quantities .... WHOLESALE
place, stocks .... EXCHANGE
post currency .... WAMPUM
settlement .... FACTORY
ship .... CRAY
stamp .... PREMIUM
tradition .... USAGE, BELIEF, CUSTOM, CULTURE, (FOLK)LORE, PRACTICE

traditional .... ROOTED, CUSTOMARY, LEGENDARY, ESTABLISHED, CONVENTIONAL
knowledge .... LORE
tales .... FOLKLORE
traduce .... SLUR, DEFAME, MALIGN, REVILE, VILIFY, ASPERSE, SLANDER, CALUMNIATE
traffic .... TRADE, BARTER, BUSINESS, COMMERCE, DEALINGS, TRANSPORTATION
circle .... ROTARY
crush .... JAM
direction ...... UTURN, DETOUR, ONE-WAY
jam .... GRIDLOCK
light ...... RED, AMBER, GREEN, BLINKER
stopper .... LIGHT, SIREN
summons .... TICKET
violator .... MOTORIST, JAYWALKER, SPEED(ST)ER
trafficker .... DEALER, TRADER, MERCHANT
kind of .... PUSHER
tragacanth .... GUM
tragedian .... ACTOR, THESPIAN, SHAKESPEARE
tragedy .... PLAY, DRAMA, CALAMITY, DISASTER, CATASTROPHE
tragic ...... SAD, FATAL, PATHETIC, CALAMITOUS, DISASTROUS, (MELO)DRAMATIC
tragopan .... PHEASANT
trail .... LAG, DRAG, DRAW, HEEL, HUNT, PATH, HOUND, TRACK, TRAIPSE, VESTIGE
along .... TAG, FOLLOW
animal .... PUG, FOIL, SLOT, SCENT, SPOOR
behind .... LAG, CRAWL, STRAGGLE
marker .... BLAZE
of scent .... DRAG
of wild animal .... SPOOR
secretly .... TAIL, SHADOW
slowly .... DAWDLE
through mud .... DAGGLE
trailblazer .... PIONEER, PATHFINDER
trailer .... VAN, CART, TAIL, WAGON, TRACER, TRACKER
arbutus .... MAYFLOWER
branch .... RUNNER, STOLON, RHIZOME
trailing .... AREAR, DECUMBENT
train .... AIM, CHAIN, DRILL, SUITE, TEACH, SERIES, RETINUE, INSTRUCT,

JERKWATER, PROCESSION
desert .... CARAVAN
designating a .... FLIER,
    LOCAL, EXPRESS, FREIGHT,
    LIMITED, SPECIAL, COMMUTER
for position .... GROOM
of attendants .... SUITE,
    CORTEGE, RETINUE,
    ENTOURAGE
overhead .... EL, MONORAIL
rider with free ticket
    .... DEADHEAD
track .... RAIL
trained canine dog ...... GERMAN
    POLICE DOG
trainee .... PUPIL, NOVICE,
    BEGINNER, NOVITIATE,
    APPRENTICE
trainer .... COACH, GYMNAST,
    HANDLER, TEACHER,
    INSTRUCTOR
trainmen's car .... CABOOSE
traipse .... GAD, TRAIL, TRAMP,
    WANDER
trait .... CUSTOM, FEATURE,
    QUALITY, CHARACTERISTIC
traitor .... RAT, JUDAS, APOSTATE,
    BETRAYER, DESERTER,
    INFORMER, ISCARIOT,
    RECREANT, RENEGADE,
    TURNCOAT, FIFTH COLUMNIST
American ..... HISS, CHAMBERS
Austrian .... REDL
Czechoslovakian
    .... GOTTWALD
Finnish .... KUSHNEN
French .... LAVAL, PETAIN,
    ESTERHAZY
Hungarian .... RAKOSI
Norwegian .... QUISLING
Romanian .... PAUKER
traject .... CAST, THROW
trajectory .... ARC, CURVE,
    PARABOLA
tram ...... CAR, WAGON, TROLLEY,
    STREETCAR
cargo .... ORE, COAL
coal mine .... TUB
trammel .... CHAIN, FETTER,
    HAMPER, CONFINE, MANACLE,
    POTHOOK, SHACKLE,
    RESTRAIN
tramontane .... ALIEN, STRANGER,
    FOREIGNER
tramp .... BUM, HIKE, HOBO,
    HOOF, PLOD, TART, YEGG,
    CLUMP, RAMBLE, TRUDGE,
    VAGRANT, VAGABOND
identification mark
    .... MONI(C)KER
offering to .... HANDOUT

trample .... CRUSH, STOMP, TREAD
trampolin(e) .... NET
user .... ACROBAT, TUMBLER
Tramp's girlfriend .... LADY
trance .... COMA, DAZE, SPELL,
    STUPOR, HYPNOSIS
tranquil ...... CALM, QUIET, STILL,
    PLACID, SERENE, COMPOSED,
    PEACEFUL
tranquility .... REST, PEACE,
    POISE, CALMNESS, SERENITY
of the mind .... ATARAXY,
    ATARAXIA
of the spirit .... QUIETISM
Tranquility Base site ...... MOON
tranquilize(r) .... CALM, QUIET,
    OPIATE, PACIFY, SEDATE,
    SOOTHE, APPEASE, ATARAXIC,
    SEDATIVE, DEPRESSANT
drug .... VALIUM
for hypertension
    .... RESERPINE
transact .... DEAL, TREAT,
    CONDUCT, PERFORM,
    NEGOTIATE
transaction .... ACT, DEAL, DEED,
    SALE, AFFAIR, BUSINESS
binding .... COMPACT,
    COVENANT
favorable to buyer
    .... BARGAIN
formal .... CONTRACT
garage/lawn .... RESALE
law enactment .... PASSAGE
transcend .... EXCEL, OUTDO,
    EXCEED, SURPASS, OVERPASS,
    OVERSTEP
transcendental .... ECLIPSING
transcribe .... COPY, WRITE,
    RECORD
transcriber .... CLERK, COPIER,
    COPYIST, STENO(GRAPHER)
transcript(ion) .... COPY,
    RECORDING, REPRODUCTION
transect .... (SUB)DIVIDE
transeunt, opposed to
    .... IMMANENT
transfer .... CEDE, DEED, GIVE,
    PASS, SEND, DECAL, GRANT,
    ASSIGN, CONFER, CONVEY,
    REMOVE
blood .... TRANSFUSE
by will ..... LEGACY, BEQUEST,
    BEQUEATH
from one position to another
    .... SHIFT
of court suit .... REMOVER
of disease .... CONTAGION
of property to an
    organization
    .... MORTMAIN

of sovereignty .... DEMISE,
    SUCCESSION
property .... DEED, GRANT,
    CONVEY
residence .... MOVE
sticker .... DECAL
transference .... SWITCH
of heat .... CONVECTION
transfigure ...... EXALT, GLORIFY,
    TRANSFORM
transfix .... PIN, NAIL, STAB,
    FASTEN, IMPALE, PIERCE,
    IMMOBILIZE
transform .... ALTER, CHANGE,
    CONVERT, TRANSMUTE,
    TRANSFIGURE,
    METAMORPHOSE
transformation .... CHANGE,
    SWITCH, ALTERATION,
    METASTASIS, TRANSITION,
    METAMORPHOSIS
transformer .... CONVERTER
type of .... STEP-UP, STEP-
    DOWN
transfuse .... POUR, IMBUE,
    INFUSE, INJECT, INSERT,
    INSTILL
transgress .... ERR, SIN, INFRACT,
    VIOLATE, INFRINGE,
    OVERSTEP, TRESPASS,
    CONTRAVENE
transgression .... SIN, SLIP,
    CRIME, FAULT, LAPSE,
    MISDEED, OFFENSE, TRESPASS,
    VIOLATION
transgressor .... SINNER, CULPRIT,
    OFFENDER, DELINQUENT
transient .... MORTAL, ELUSIVE,
    PASSING, FLEETING, FLITTING,
    EPHEMERAL, FUGACIOUS,
    MOMENTARY, TEMPORARY,
    EVANESCENT
ball of gas .... BUBBLE
be .... VANISH, EVAPORATE
burst of energy .... SPURT
laborer ...... DRIFTER, FLOATER
lodger .... PASSERBY,
    SOJOURNER
runaway .... FUGITIVE
transit .... RAPID, CHANGE,
    PASSAGE, CONVEYANCE,
    THEODOLITE
transition ...... FALL, RISE, SHIFT,
    CHANGE, PASSAGE, PASSING,
    TRANSFER, SWITCH-OVER
transitional .... CONVERTIBLE
transitive .... VERBAL, TRANSEUNT
transitory .... BRIEF, MUTABLE,
    FLEETING, TEMPORARY,
    TRANSIENT, CHANGEABLE
translate .... CHANGE, DECODE,

RENDER, CONSTRUE, TRANSFER, INTERPRET

a coded message ..... DECODE, DECIPHER

literally .... METAPHRASE

translation .... VERSION, RENDITION, PARAPHRASE, INTERPRETATION

of foreign writing .... CRIB, PONY

translations of the Scriptures in Aramaic .... TARGUMS

translator .... EXEGETE, INTERPRETER

translucent .... CLEAR, LUCID, FROSTY, PELLUCID, DIAPHANOUS, TRANSPARENT

transmit .... BEAM, MAIL, POST, SEND, WIRE, CARRY, CONVEY, IMPART, FORWARD, BROADCAST

in a way .... RADIO

transmogrify .... ALTER

transmute .... CONVERT

transom .... SLAT, TRAVE, LINTEL, LOUVER, TRESTLE, CROSSPIECE

transparent .... OPEN, THIN, CLEAR, GAUZY, SHEER, CANDID, FLIMSY, GLASSY, LIMPID, LIQUID, HYALINE, HYALOID, OBVIOUS, GOSSAMER, (PEL)LUCID, DIAPHANOUS, TRANSLUCENT

combining form ...... HYAL(O)

not .... OPAQUE

transpire .... PASS, OCCUR, SWEAT, EXHALE, HAPPEN, UNFOLD, LEAK OUT, TAKE PLACE

transplant .... GRAFT, REPLANT, RELOCATE, RESETTLE, TRANSFER

of a kind .... ALIEN

transport ..... CART, MOVE, TOTE, CARRY, BANISH, CONVEY, CARRIER, ECSTASY, EMOTION, AIRPLANE, ENTRANCE, TRANSFER, (EN)RAPTURE, (TROOP)SHIP

transportation .... WHEELS, PASSAGE, MOVEMENT, TRANSFER, CONVEYANCE, DEPORTATION

Arctic .... REINDEER

charge .... FARE

route .... LINE, AIRLANE

service/system ...... BUS, TAXI, TRAM, FERRY, TRAIN, SUBWAY, AIRLINE, RAILWAY, STREETCAR

transported .... RAPT, CARRIED, ENTRANCED, DELIVERED

transporter .... MOVER

transporting, act of .... CARTAGE, PORTAGE, DELIVERY

transpose .... INVERT, REVERSE, EXCHANGE, INTERCHANGE

transposition .... METATHESIS

transude .... DRIP, OOZE, SEEP, EXUDE, SWEAT, SECRETE

Transvaal capital .... PRETORIA

city .... BENONI

gold region .... RAND

transverse .... OBLIQUE, CROSS(ING), CROSSWISE

Transylvania city .... CLUJ

trap .... GIN, NET, FOOL, LURE, NAIL, TOIL, WHIN, CATCH, SNARE, ENMESH, TREPAN, LUGGAGE, PIT(FALL), CARRIAGE, CAPARISON

fish .... GIN, WEIR

game .... GIN

kind of .... WEB, DECOY, AMBUSH, DEADFALL

lobster .... POT

slang .... MOUTH

trapan .... TRAP, TRICK

trapdoor .... DROP, HATCH

trapeze .... BAR

locale .... GYM, CIRCUS

performer .... ACROBAT, GYMNAST, AERIALIST

trapper .... HUNTER, SNARER, TREPAN

trappings .... DUDS, FRILLS, OUTFIT, REGALIA, TRICKERY, CAPARISON, ADORNMENTS

Trappist .... MONK

trait .... AUSTERITY

writer .... MERTON

traps, orchestra .... BELLS, DRUMS, CYMBALS

trapshooting .... SKEET

target .... (CLAY)PIGEON

trash .... LAM, JUNK, OFFAL, SCRAP, TRIPE, WASTE, COLLAR, DEBRIS, LITTER, REFUSE, GARBAGE, RUBBISH, NONSENSE, (RIFF)RAFF, RESTRAIN(T)

gaudy .... KITSCH

receptacle .... ASHCAN, (DUST)BIN

slang .... TRIPE

trashy .... CHEAP, JUNKY, SHABBY, SHODDY, WORTHLESS

trattoria .... EATERY

trauma .... SHOCK, WOUND, INJURY

travail .... PAIN, TASK, TOIL, WORK, AGONY, LABOR, ANGUISH, TORMENT, DRUDGERY

trave .... CROSSBEAM

travel .... GO, PAD, HIKE, MOVE, RIDE, TOUR, TRIP, WEND, DRIVE, JOURNEY, TRAFFIC

back and forth .... COMMUTE

business .... RENT-A-CAR

by car .... DRIVE, MOTOR

by ox wagon .... TREK

class of .... COACH, ECONOMY, BUSINESS, STEERAGE, FIRST(CLASS)

extended .... ODYSSEY

for pleasure .... SIGHTSEE(ING)

from place to place .... DRIFT, CRUISE, MIGRATE

in circle .... ORBIT

of .... VIATIC

on foot .... JOG, PAD, HIKE, WALK, TRAMP

on foot over snow .... MUSH

swiftly .... JET

to holy place ...... PILGRIMAGE

what it does .... BROADENS, EDUCATES

widely .... SAIL THE SEVEN SEAS

traveler .... RIDER, ROVER, VIATOR, TOURIST, TREKKER, TRIPPER, MOTORIST, VOYAGE(U)R

aid of ...... COURIER, CICERONE

from place to place .... CRUISER, DRIFTER, EMIGRANT, ITINERANT

fun-seeking .... GADABOUT

guidebook for .... BAEDEKER

kind of .... HOBO, GYPSY, NOMAD, TRAMP, PILGRIM, SALESMAN, VAGABOND

on foot .... PEDESTRIAN

refuge of .... OASIS, HOSPICE

stopping place of .... INN, HOTEL, MOTEL, SERAI, HOSPICE, ROADHOUSE

who asks for ride .... HITCHHIKER

who reneges .... NO-SHOW

travelers, company of .... CARAVAN

travelers' diarrhea .... TOKYO TROTS, MONTEZUMA'S REVENGE

hunting expedition ..... SAFARI

traveling .... GADDING, FOOTLOOSE

bag .... VALISE, HOLDALL, GRIP(SACK), BRIEFCASE

companion .... ESCORT, COURIER, CHAPERON
group .... TROUPE
show .... CIRCUS
yen for .... WANDERLUST
traverse .... DENY, PIVOT, RANGE, COURSE, OPPOSE, PATROL, SURVEY, SWIVEL, EXAMINE, OBSTRUCT, CROSS(PIECE)
traversely .... ACROSS
travertine .... LIMESTONE
travesty .... FARCE, FIASCO, PARODY, SATIRE, LAMPOON, MOCKERY, BURLESQUE, CARICATURE
travois .... SLEDGE
trawl .... FISH, HAUL, SEINE, (DRAG)NET
trawler .... BOAT
trawling .... FISHING
tray .... TILL, SALVER, SERVER, COASTER, PLATTER
agriculture .... HYDROPONICS
dish .... SALVER, WAITER
for types .... GALLEY
liquids .... CAPSULE
wooden .... TRENCHER
treacherous ...... SHIFTY, SNEAKY, TRICKY, CUNNING, DEVIOUS, FURTIVE, DISLOYAL, TWO-FACED, DECEITFUL, FAITHLESS, PERFIDIOUS
greedy person .... BARRACUDA
person .... CROOK, BASTARD, TRAITOR, BETRAYER, RENEGADE, TURNCOAT
treachery .... DECEIT, FALSITY, PERFIDY, TREASON, BETRAYAL
treacle .... REMEDY, ANTIDOTE, MOLASSES
treacly .... STICKY
tread .... PAD, PACE, STEP, WALK, CRUSH, STAMP, CHALAZA, TRAMP(LE), FOOTPRINT, CICATRICLE
sound .... CRUNCH
treadle .... LEVER, PEDAL
treadmill .... WHEEL
treason ...... BETRAYAL, SEDITION, TREACHERY
kind of .... LESE MAJESTE
treasure .... HOARD, PRIZE, STORE, TROVE, VALUE, ESTEEM, RICHES, WEALTH, CHERISH, REMEMBER, APPRECIATE
container .... CHEST
isle of fiction .... MONTE CRISTO
Treasure Island author .... STEVENSON
Island character ...... BEN, JIM,

PEW
State .... MONTANA
treasurer .... BANKER, BURSAR, PURSER, PAYMASTER
treasury .... BOX, BANK, FISC, SAFE, CHEST, PURSE, VAULT, COFFER(S), BURSARY, EXCHEQUER, THESAURUS, DEPOSITORY, POCKETBOOK
agent .... TMAN
treat ...... USE, CURE, DEAL, DOSE, HEAL, ATTEND, HANDLE, PARLEY, PAY FOR, REGALE, BARGAIN, DELIGHT, DISCUSS, ENTERTAIN, NEGOTIATE, FOOT THE BILL
a broken bone .... RESET
a wound .... DRESS
as a celebrity .... LIONIZE
badly .... MOCK, ABUSE, SCORN, ILL-USE, INSULT
disdainfully .... UPSTAGE
flour .... AGENIZE
handsomely .... REGALE
hides again .... RETAN
insolently .... HUFF, ABUSE, BLUSTER, SWAGGER, PATRONIZE
lightly .... FIDDLE, PALTER, BELITTLE, DOWNPLAY
shabbily .... STEP ON
tenderly .... PET, SPOIL, CODDLE, DOTE ON, PAMPER, INDULGE
with .... BARGAIN, MEDIATE
with contempt .... CONTEMN
with warm application .... FOMENT
wrongfully .... HARM
treatise .... ESSAY, PAPER, TRACT, THESIS, (TEXT)BOOK, DISCOURSE, MONOGRAPH, COMPOSITION, DISSERTATION
opening part .... EXORDIUM
prelude/introduction .... ISAGOGE
treatment ...... USE, CARE, STUDY, USAGE, REMEDY, ANALYSIS, APPROACH, HANDLING, MANAGEMENT
before doctor's arrival .... FIRST AID
by physical means .... THERAPY
harsh .... ABUSE
hormone for short stature .... SOMATREM
kind of .... DRUG, BED REST, SURGERY, THERAPY
sprain .... ARNICA
water .... TORTURE

treaty .... MISE, (COM)PACT, PACTION, CONTRACT, DOCUMENT, COVENANT, PROTOCOL, AGREEMENT, CONCORDAT, NEGOTIATION
acronym .... NATO, SALT, SEATO
kind of .... PEACE, LEAGUE, CONCORD, ENTENTE, ALLIANCE
Trebizond ...... EMPIRE, SEAPORT, TRABZON
treble .... SHRILL, TRIPLE, SOPRANO, THREEFOLD
trebuchet's kin .... CATAPULT
missile .... STONE
tree .... BUSH, POLE, POST, WOOD, ARBOR, PLANT, SHRUB, STAKE, CORNER, TIMBER, GALLOWS, HATRACK
American larch .... TAMARACK
American olive .... DEVILWOOD
aromatic .... BALSAM, BAYBERRY, EUCALYPTUS, CANDLEBERRY
Asiatic, tall .... ACLE
Asiatic, with fan-shaped leaves .... GINGKO, GINKGO
Australian eucalyptus .... IRONBARK
balsam .... TOLU
bark .... CORTEX
bark remover .... SPUDDER
beech .... ROBLE, CHESTNUT, CHINQUAPIN
betelnut .... ARECA
biblical .... FIG, OLIVE
birch family .... ALDER, HAZEL, HORNBEAM
bombacaceous .... BALSA
bombax family .... SILKCOTTON
boxwood .... SERON
branch(es) .... TWIG, SPRAY, SPRIG, RAMAGE
Brazilian .... SERINGA
buckwheat .... TITI
bully .... BALATA
butter .... SHEA
California .... REDWOOD, SEQUOIA
cashew family .... PISTACHIO
caucho .... ULE
Central American ...... AMATE
Chinese evergreen ...... LITCHI
citrus .... LIME, LEMON, ORANGE
climber, Himalayan .... PANDA
climbing .... HOP
-climbing bird .... WOODPECKER

757

coffee .... CHICOT
combining form ..... DENDR(I),
                       DENDR(O)
cone-bearing/coniferous
.... FIR, YEW, PINE, CEDAR,
          SPRUCE, SEQUOIA
cottonwood .... ALAMO,
                       POPLAR
covering .... BARK
crook .... KNEE
custard apple .... SOURSOP,
                    SWEETSOP
cutting .... LOP(PING)
cypress family .... JUNIPER
decay .... NECROSIS
desert .... DATE PALM
disease .... KNOT, MOSAIC
dogwood ..... TUPELO, ASSAGAI
driller .... WOODPECKER
dwarf(ing)/stunting .... BONSAI
-dwelling creature
.... OPOSSUM
East Indian .... TEAK, BANIAN,
          BANYAN, NUTMEG
ebony family .... KAKI,
                PERSIMMON
European .... SERVICE TREE,
              SERVICEBERRY
evergreen .... BAY, FIR, YEW,
     PINE, TITI, CAROB, OLIVE,
   THUJA, SPRUCE, REDWOOD,
     SEQUOIA, EUCALYPTUS
excrescence .... OAKAPPLE
exudation .... GUM, SAP, MILK,
   COPAL, LATEX, RESIN, ROSIN,
                    BALATA
family .... LINEAGE,
    ANCESTRY, PEDIGREE
fiber ..... BASS, BAST, BAOBAB,
                      RAFFIA
flowering .... TITI, MAPLE,
      LOCUST, CATALPA,
   HAWTHORN, MAGNOLIA
fragrant .... HENNA, LINDEN
fragrant wood ...... BASSWOOD
fraxinus .... ASH
frog .... HYLA, TOAD, PEEPER
fruit .... FIG, DATE, PEAR,
   PLUM, APPLE, GUAVA, MANGO,
   PAPAW, PEACH, CHERRY,
   LITCHI, ORANGE, PAPAYA,
   APRICOT, AVOCADO, COCONUT,
   NECTARINE, PERSIMMON,
   TANGERINE, POMEGRANATE
fustic .... MORA
gamboge family .... CALABA
genus .... ACER, ALNUS,
    CARYA, HEVEA, KHAYA,
   LARIX, MORUS, PICEA, PINUS,
   SALIX, TAXUS, TILIA, ULMUS,
    CASSIA, CEDRUS, CORNUS,

LAURUS, CATALPA, JUGLANS,
   QUERCUS, AESCULUS,
   CASTANEA, FRAXINUS,
   SAMBUCUS, BOSWELLIA,
   CRATAEGUS, DIOSPYROS,
   SWIETENIA, EUCALYPTUS,
              FORTUNELLA
giant .... REDWOOD, SEQUOIA
gingko .... ICHO
graceful .... ELM
group .... GROVE, ORCHARD
grown flat .... ESPALIER
gum .... BUMBO, ICICA,
   XYLAN, ACACIA, BALATA,
   CHICLE, RUBBER, SAPOTA,
   TUPELO, WALNUT, SAPODILLA,
   SATINWOOD, EUCALYPTUS,
            PEPPERIDGE
gum resin .... ANTRA,
        FRANKINCENSE
hardwood ...... ASH, ELM, OAK,
   IPIL, TEAK, BEECH, BIRCH,
   PLANE, TULIP, MOLAVE,
   WALNUT, WILLOW, DOGWOOD,
   BASSWOOD, LIGNUMVITAE
head of/top .... CROWN
heart-shape leafed
.... CATALPA
heath family .... MADRONO
hive .... BEEGUM
holly family .... ILEX
horse-chestnut family
.... BUCKEYE
honeysuckle family ..... ELDER
icy coating of .... SLEET
iron .... ACLE
ironwood .... HOP, TITI,
          HORNBEAM
Javanese .... UPAS
juice ...... SAP, MANNA, CHICLE
kapok .... CEIBA
knot .... BURL
laurel family .... CASSIA,
   CINNAMON, SASSAFRAS
lawn .... ELM
legume family .... ACACIA,
   CASSIA, LOCUST, LOGWOOD,
   LABURNUM, ROSEWOOD
leguminous .... MIMOSA,
          TAMARIND
lemon/lime .... CITRUS
lightwood .... BALSA
like a .... PINY, ARBOREAL,
   DENDROID, DECIDUOUS,
   DENDRITIC, ARBORESQUE
linden family ...... LIME, LINN,
      TEIL, BASSWOOD
lily family .... DRACAENA
locust .... ACACIA
lotus .... SADR
madder family .... BANCAL

magnolia .... TULIP, CHAMPAC,
   CHAMPAK, CUCUMBER,
          WHITEWOOD
mark on .... BLAZE
marmalade .... CHICO, MAMEY,
    MAMMEE, SAPODILLA
Mediterranean .... CAROB
mimosa family .... ACACIA
moss .... USNEA
mulberry family .... UPAS,
   FUSTIC, SYCAMORE,
         BREADFRUIT
myrtle family .... CLOVE,
   LEHUA, CAJEPUT, CAJUPUT
nut .... PECAN, ALMOND,
   CASHEW, WALNUT, HICKORY,
   CHESTNUT, HAZELNUT,
   PISTACHIO, CHINQUAPIN
oak .... ROBLE, ENCINA
of a .... CEDARN, CITROUS,
   ARBOREAL, ARBOREOUS
of heaven .... AILANTHUS
of life .... ARBORVITAE
of life site .... EDEN
of the Lord .... ACACIA,
   ALMOND, LAUREL, CYPRESS,
   HOLM OAK, TAMARISK, CEDAR
          OF LEBANON
oil .... BEN
olive .... OLEA
olive family .... ASH
orange .... OSAGE
ornamental .... HOLLY
palm .... ARECA, RAFFIA,
   CALAMUS, COCONUT, TALIPOT
palm-like .... ZAMIA
pea family .... CASSIA,
   MIMOSA, DIVI-DIVI, LABURNUM
pear .... NOPAL
Philippine .... DAO, IPIL,
   DUHAT, MANGO, NARRA,
   YAKAL, ACACIA, PAPAYA,
   MOLAVE, SANTOL, SAMPALOC
pine .... CEDAR, LARCH, PINON,
   THUJA, SPRUCE, CYPRESS,
     HEMLOCK, JUNIPER
plum .... DAMSON
poisonous .... UPAS, SASSY,
   HEMLOCK, LABURNUM, NUX
               VOMICA
pomegranate .... BLAUSTINE
poplar .... ASPEN,
       COTTONWOOD
powder .... ARAROBA
product .... GUM, NUT, OIL,
   CONE, FRUIT, LUMBER,
     RUBBER, TIMBER
protuberance .... KNOT
pulse family .... LOCUST
rain .... SAMAN, ZAMIA
remnant .... STUB, STUMP

resin .... FIR, PINE, BALSAM

rose family .... PEAR, PEACH, LOQUAT, MEDLAR, QUINCE, HAWTHORN, JUNEBERRY

rue family .... LEMON, CITRON, KUMQUAT, SATINWOOD

rubber .... ULE, SERINGA

salicaceae family ...... POPLAR, WILLOW

salt .... ATLE

sandarac .... ARAR

sapodilla family .... BUSTIC

screw pine .... PANDANUS

shade .... ASH, ELM, LINN, LINDEN, WALNUT, SYCAMORE

shaped .... DENDROID, DENDRIFORM

shoots .... TWIGS, BROWSE

shrew .... TANA

silk .... SIRIS

silk-cotton .... CEIBA

smoke .... SUMAC

soapberry .... LITCHI

softwood .... FIR, PINE, CEDAR, SPRUCE, HEMLOCK, REDWOOD

sorrel .... TITI

specialist .... ARBORIST

spiny .... LOCUST

stock .... STEM, TRUNK

stump ..... RUNT, SNAG, STOOL

stunted .... SCRAG, SCRUB

sumac .... TEREBINTH

swamps .... TAMARACK

sweet-smelling/used for incense .... SANDALWOOD, FRANKINCENSE

toad .... PEEPER

toad genus .... HYLA

treatment of diseased .... SURGERY

"trembling" .... ASPEN

trimmings .... BRASH

tropical ...... ULE, ATTA, PALM, ARECA, CACAO, LEHUA, MANGO, PAPAYA, COCONUT, LOGWOOD, DATE PALM, MANGROVE, CINCHONA, TAMARISK, LANCEWOOD, BREADFRUIT

trunk .... BOLE

trunk, growth on .... LICHEN

trunk protuberance .... KNAR

trunk ring .... GIRDLE

trunk strip .... FLITCH

trunk wood .... DURAMEN

tulip .... POPLAR

verbena family .... TEAK

walnut family .... PECAN, HICKORY

wide-spreading .... CEDAR, WALNUT, JUNIPER

with apple-like fruit .... MEDLAR

buoyant wood .... BALSA

dark hard wood ...... EBONY, MAHOGANY

drooping branches .... WEEPING-WILLOW

elastic wood .... YEW

orange wood .... OSAGE

pliant branches .... WITCH-HAZEL

plum-like fruit .... LOQUAT

striped wood .... ARAROBA

winged fruit .... ASH, ELM, MAPLE, SAMARA

young ...... SAPLING, SEEDLING

treeless plain ...... WOLD, LLANO, PAMPAS, STEPPE, TUNDRA, SAVANNA

treelike .... ARBOREAL, BRANCHED, DENDRITIC

in form .... DENDROID

plant .... BANANA

vegetable .... BROCCOLI

treenail .... PEG, PIN, SPIKE, TRUNNEL

trees ...... WOODS, FOREST, TIMBER

book on .... SILVA, SYLVA

clump of .... BOSK, TUFT, GROVE, SCRUB

grove of pine .... PINETUM

of .... ARBOROUS

of a region .... SILVA

pertaining to .... ARBOREAL

place where sold .... NURSERY

study of .... DENDROLOGY

stunted .... SCRUB

treatise on .... SILVA

Trees poet .... KILMER

trefoil .... CLOVER, SHAMROCK, TRIFOLIUM

trehalose .... SUGAR

source ...... YEAST, MUSHROOM

trek .... HIKE, WALK, TRAMP, TRAVEL, TRUDGE, JOURNEY, MIGRATION

trellis .... ARBOR, BOWER, LATTICE, ESPALIER

part .... LATH

trelliswork .... PERGOLA, NETWORK, LATTICEWORK

trematode .... FLUKE, FLATWORM

larva .... CERCARIA

tremble .... QUAKE, SHAKE, QUIVER, SHIVER, TOTTER, WOBBLE, PULSATE, SHUDDER, VIBRATE, VACILLATE

trembling .... PALPITANT

tremendous .... HUGE, GREAT, COLOSSAL, ENORMOUS, GIGANTIC, EXTRAORDINARY

tremolite .... AMPHIBOLE

tremolo .... CRACK, TRILL, QUAVER, TWITTER, VIBRATO

tremor .... QUAKE, SHIVER, THRILL, SHAKING, TREMBLING, VIBRATION, TREPIDATION

tremulous .... ASPEN, SHAKY, TIMID, FEARFUL, QUAVERY, UNSTEADY, QUIVERING, TREMBLING, TREMULANT

trenail. See **treenail**

trench .... CUT, SAP, LEAT, DITCH, FOSSE, DUGOUT, FURROW

embankment .... PARADOS

knife .... BAYONET

moon .... RILL(E)

strengthener .... FASCINE

trenchant .... KEEN, CRISP, SHARP, BITING, CUTTING, CLEAR-CUT, FORCEFUL, INCISIVE, ENERGETIC, PENETRATING

trencher .... BOARD, DIGGER, SAPPER, PLATTER

trencherman .... EATER, GLUTTON, SPONGER, HANGER-ON, PARASITE

trend .... FLOW, DRIFT, TENOR, VOGUE, COURSE, STREAM, FASHION, TENDENCY, DIRECTION

bearish .... SAG

trendy one .... HIPSTER

trepan .... AUGER, TREPHINE, TRICK(STER)

trepang .... ECHINODERM, SEA CUCUMBER

trephine .... SAW, TREPAN

trepidation .... FEAR, ALARM, DREAD, DISMAY, TREMOR, QUAKING, AGITATION, TREMBLING

treponema .... SPIROCHETE

trespass ...... SIN, POACH, INROAD, INVADE, OFFEND, INTRUDE, OFFENSE, ENCROACH, INFRINGE, TRANSGRESS

trespasser .... INVADER, POACHER, INTRUDER, (GATE)CRASHER

tres _____ .... BIEN, CHIC

tress .... CURL, HAIR, LOCK, BRAID, PLAIT, QUEUE, STRAND, PIGTAIL, RINGLET

trestle .... (SAW)HORSE

Treves .... TRIER

trews .... TROUSERS

trey, thing with .... DIE, CARD, DICE, DOMINO

triad ...... TRINE, TRIUNE, TRINITY

trial .... TEST, CROSS, ESSAY, TRY(OUT), ATTEMPT, HEARING, INQUEST,

PROBATION, AFFLICTION, EXPERIMENT
ancient method of .... ORDEAL
and _____ .... ERROR
balloon .... KITE, FEELER
by _____ .... FIRE, JURY, COMBAT
decisive .... ACID TEST
panel .... JURY
performance .... PROLUSION, REHEARSAL
scene of .... COURT
severe .... ORDEAL, CRUCIBLE
site .... VENUE
trials and _____

.... TRIBULATIONS
triangle .... TRIO, TRIAD, TRIGON, SCALENE, TRIQUETRA
for example .... IDIOPHONE
kind of .... LOVE, ETERNAL, ISOSCELES
love .... ADULTERY, INFIDELITY
part .... BASE, SIDE, HYPOTENUSE
side of .... LEG
word for a love .... ETERNAL
triangular .... DELTOID, TRIGONAL, TRIGONOUS, TRIQUETROUS, THREE-CORNERED
aircraft structure .... DELTA WING
blower .... FAN
brace .... GUSSET
deposit of sand/soil .... DELTA
flag .... PENNON, BUNTING, PENNANT
insert in seam .... GUSSET
muscle of a shoulder
.... DELTOID
piece in a sail .... GORE
piece of land .... GORE
sail .... JIB, LATEEN, SPINNAKER
sides, structure with
.... PYRAMID
triarchy .... TRIUMVIRATE
tribal sign .... TOTEM
tribe .... CLAN, FOLK, GENE, RACE, SECT, GROUP, FAMILY, NATION, PEOPLE
Boadicea's .... ICENI
leader .... CHIEFTAIN, PATRIARCH
wandering .... HORDE
tribulation .... WOE, CARE, TRIAL, MISERY, SORROW, TROUBLE, DISTRESS, AFFLICTION
tribunal .... BAR, ROTA, SEAT, BENCH, BOARD, COURT, FORUM

mock .... KANGAROO COURT
tribune .... DAIS, PULPIT, ROSTRUM, PLATFORM, MAGISTRATE
tributary .... RIVER, SOURCE, STREAM, SUBJECT, SUBSIDIARY
creek .... BAYOU
of the Rhone .... ISERE
to the Elbe .... EGER, ISER
tribute .... TAX, GIFT, HOMAGE, PRAISE, OVATION, PAYMENT, OFFERING, COMPLIMENT
to a dead person ..... EULOGY, EPITAPH
to a victor .... ENCOMIUM
trice ...... TIE, MOMENT, SEC(OND), INSTANT, TWINKLE, TWINKLING
tricentennial ...... TERCENTENARY
triceps ..... THREE HEADS, TRIPLE-HEADED
muscle site .... (UPPER)ARM
triceratops .... DINOSAUR
trichoid .... HAIRLIKE
trichome .... BRISTLE, PRICKLE, ROOT HAIR
trichord .... LYRE
trick .... CON, FOB, FUB, GAG, DIDO, DUPE, FOOL, GAFF, GULL, HOAX, JAPE, JEST, JOKE, RUSE, SCAM, WILE, CHEAT, CRAFT, DODGE, FRAUD, KNACK, PRANK, SHIFT, STUNT, ENTRAP, TREPAN, DECEIVE, ARTIFICE, (FLIM)FLAM, HOODWINK, ILLUSION, CHICANE(RY), DECEPTION, STRATAGEM, SUBTERFUGE
device .... GIMMICK
easy to .... GULLIBLE
person easy to .... DUPE, GOOF, GULL, CULLY
trickery ...... ART, CRAFT, FRAUD, DECEIT, JAPERY, DODGERY, SLEIGHT, ARTIFICE, JUGGLING, CHICANE(RY), DECEPTION, HOCUS-POCUS
kind of .... SWINDLE
trickle .... FEW, DRIP, DROP, FLOW, LEAK, OOZE, SEEP, DRIBBLE
tricks, win all .... CAPOT
trickster ...... FOX, CHEAT, JOKER, TREPAN, JUGGLER, SHYSTER, CONJURER, MAGICIAN, SWINDLER, PRANKSTER, ILLUSIONIST
tricksy .... SMART, CLEVER, CUNNING, PLAYFUL,

MISCHIEVOUS
tricktrack .... BACKGAMMON
tricky .... SLY, WILY, SMART, ARTFUL, CATCHY, CLEVER, CRAFTY, SHIFTY, SNEAKY, CUNNING, FURTIVE, DECEITFUL, DECEPTIVE, INTRICATE
and sly .... DEEP
condition .... CATCH
tricolor .... FLAG
tricorn .... HAT
tricresyl phosphate: abbr.
.... TCP
tricycle .... IRON HORSE, VELOCIPEDE
trident .... SPEAR, LEISTER
bearer ..... NEPTUNE, POSEIDON
warrior with .... RETIARUS
tridentate .... TRIFID
Tridentum .... TRENT
tried .... PROVED, PROVEN, TESTED, SAMPLED
and true .... RELIABLE, DEPENDABLE, TRUSTWORTHY
trierarch's command
.... GALLEY, TRIREME
trifle .... BIT, DAB, PIN, SOU, TOY, DOIT, FICO, FOOL, MOTE, PLAY, DALLY, FLIRT, TRACE, DIDDLE, FRIVOL, GEWGAW, LITTLE, MONKEY, MORSEL, PALTER, PEWTER, DESSERT, TRINKET, FALDERAL, FALDEROL, GIMCRACK, KICKSHAW, BAGATELLE
trifler .... IDLER, DALLIER, PIDDLER, PUTTERER
trifles .... TRIVIA
trifling ...... MERE, PETTY, SMALL, FLIMSY, PALTRY, SLIGHT, TRIVIAL, PIDDLING, FRIVOLOUS
amount .... FIG, PEANUTS
objection .... CAVIL, QUIBBLE
sum .... GROAT
with danger .... PLAYING WITH FIRE
trifoliate .... TERNATE, THREE-LEAFED
plant .... CLOVER, TREFOIL, SHAMROCK, TRILLIUM, TRIFOLIUM
trifolium .... CLOVER, TREFOIL, SHAMROCK
trig .... FIT, CHIC, NEAT, PRIM, PROP, TIDY, TRIM, WELL, CHOKE, SMART, SOUND, WEDGE, SPRUCE
trigeminal .... TRIFACIAL
trigger .... FIRE, TRIP, SPARK,

KINDLE, LAUNCH, INITIATE

-happy .... JUMPY

triggerfish .... OLDWIFE

trigo .... WHEAT

trigon .... HARP, LYRE, TRINE,
TRIANGLE

trigonal .... TRIANGULAR

trigonometric function
.... (CO)SINE, SECANT

line .... SECANT, TANGENT

term .... COSEC

trigonous .... TRIANGULAR,
THREE-CORNERED

trilateral .... THREE-SIDED

trill .... ROLL, SING, QUAVER,
WARBLE, MORDENT, TIRALEE,
TREMOLO, VIBRATO,
VIBRATION

trilogy writer .... ASCH,
GALSWORTHY

trim .... CUT, LOP, CLIP, DECK,
DOCK, NEAT, PARE, TAUT,
TIDY, TRIG, ADORN, CHEAT,
CHIDE, DRESS, NATTY, NIFTY,
PRUNE, SCOLD, ADJUST,
DAPPER, DEFEAT, FETTLE,
ORDERLY, DECORATE

and simple .... TAILOR-MADE

beard/hair .... CLIP, BARBER

coin .... NIG

feathers .... PREEN

in curves .... ESCALOP,
SCALLOP

lumber .... DRESS

rosebush .... PRUNE

shrubbery/wool .... SHEAR

trimmer .... TOADY, ADJUSTER,
TIMESERVER, OPPORTUNIST

trimming .... GIMP, EXTRA,
RUCHE, EDGING, GUIPURE,
ORNAMENT, DECORATION

braid/ribbon .... GALLOON

coat of arms .... BORDURE

colloquial .... DEFEAT,
BEATING, CHEATING

food .... PARSLEY,
GARNISH(EE)

for dresses ..... RUCHE, PIPING,
RUFFLE, FLOUNCE, RICKRACK

of lace .... FRILL, GUIPURE

showy .... FURBELOW

tool .... ZAX, SHEARS,
CLIP(PER), SCISSORS

window drapes .... VALANCE

zigzag .... RICKRACK

Trimurti .... TRINITY

Trinacrian .... SICILIAN

trinal .... TRIPLE, THREEFOLD

trinary ...... TERNARY, THREEFOLD

trine ...... TRIAD, TRIGON, TRIPLE,
TRINITY, FAVORABLE,

THREEFOLD

Trinidad & Tobago bay
.... ERIN, COCOS, GUAPO,
MARACAS

capital .... PORT OF SPAIN

city/town .... TOCO, ARIMA,
COUVA, LA BREA, SIPARIA,
TUNAPUNA, CHAGUANAS,
MARABELLA, SAN FERNANDO

dance .... CALYPSO

fish .... GUPPY

island .... CHACACHACARE

lake .... PITCH

language .... HINDI, ENGLISH

monetary unit .... DOLLAR

mountain .... ARIPO, EL
TUCUCHE

music .... CALYPSO

native .... TRINIDADIAN

passage .... BOCA GRANDE

point .... GALERA, ICACOS,
GALEOTA

river .... ORTOIRE

strait .... DRAGON'S MOUTH

Trinidad's partner ...... TOBAGO

Trinity College scholar .... SIZAR,
SIZER

of Hindu gods .... TRIMURTI

trinitrotoluene ...... TNT, TROTYL,
DYNAMITE, EXPLOSIVE

trinket .... TOY, GAUD, BIJOU,
BAUBLE, GEWGAW, TRIFLE,
JEWELRY, GIMCRACK,
KICKSHAW, ORNAMENT,
KNICKNACK, PLAYTHING

seller .... FAKER

trio .... THREE(SOME)

alphabetic .... ABC, LMN

cards .... TIERCE

classical .... THE THREE B'S

mythical .... FATES, FURIES,
GRACES

of fiction .... MUSKETEERS

of sizes .... SML

one of a .... TOM, DICK,
HARRY, HOPE, FAITH,
CHARITY, CALM, COOL,
COLLECTED, ATHOS, ARAMIS,
PORTHOS, CLOTHO, ATROPOS,
LACHESIS

trioxide of arsenic .... RATSBANE

trip .... HALT, SKIP, SLIP, TILT,
CAPER, ERR(OR), JAUNT,
OUTING, TUMBLE, VOYAGE,
BLUNDER, JOURNEY,
STUMBLE, OBSTRUCT,
EXCURSION

slang .... HALLUCINATIONS

the light fantastic .... DANCE

tripartite .... THREEFOLD

tripe .... TRASH, RUBBISH

triple .... TRIAD, TRINE, TREBLE,
TRINAL, TERNARY,
THREEFOLD, TRIPLICATE

alliance .... AXIS, DREIBUND

crown .... TIARA

crown winner .... OMAHA,
ASSAULT, AFFIRMED,
CITATION, SEATTLE SLEW,
SECRETARIAT

for draft .... SSS

for motorists .... AAA

for school .... RRR

from Minnesota .... HHH

time .... TRIPLEX

triplet .... TRISTICH

in music .... TERCET

tripod .... CAT, STAND, SPIDER,
TRIPOS, TRIVET

part .... LEG

Tripoli .... ROCK, ABRASIVE,
ROTTENSTONE

badmen, former .... PIRATES

ruler .... DEY, PASHA

where it is .... LIBYA,
LEBANON

tripos .... TRIPOD

tripper ...... CAM, PAWL, DETENT,
TOURER, TREKKER, TOURIST,
TRAVELER, WAYFARER

slang .... DOPER, ADDICT

trippet .... CAM

triptych .... TABLET

triquetrous .... TRIHEDRAL,
TRIANGULAR

trireme .... GALLEY

commander .... TRIERARCH

propellant .... OAR

Tris, baseball player
.... SPEAKER

trisaccharide .... TRIOSE

trismus .... LOCKJAW, TETANUS

is symptom of _____
.... MUMPS, QUINSY

triste .... SAD, BLEAK, GLOOMY

tristesse .... SADNESS

tristful .... SAD, RUEFUL, WOEFUL,
MOURNFUL, SORROWFUL

tristich .... TRIPLET

Tristram's beloved .... ISEULT,
ISOLDE

trite .... OLD, DULL, BANAL,
CORNY, MUSTY, PASSE,
STALE, STOCK, JEJUNE,
ORDINARY, SHOPWORN,
HACK(NEYED), COMMONPLACE

expression ...... CORN, CLICHE,
BANALITY, PLATITUDE

opposite of .... FRESH,
ORIGINAL

triton .... EFT, NEWT, SNAIL,
SALAMANDER

Triton .... (SEA)GOD
   father of .... POSEIDON
   lower extremity of .... TAIL
   mother of .... AMPHITRITE
   trumpet of .... CONCH
triturate ...... RUB, BRAY, CRUSH,
   GRIND, PULVERIZE
triumph ...... JOY, WIN, CONQUER,
   PREVAIL, REJOICE, SUCCEED,
   SUCCESS, VICTORY,
   CONQUEST, CELEBRATE,
   EXULT(ATION)
triumphant .... FLUSHED,
   EXULTANT, JUBILANT,
   SUCCESSFUL, VICTORIOUS
triumvirate .... TRIARCHY
   member of a .... TRIUMVIR
   member of the first
   ..... CAESAR, POMPEY, CRASSUS
triune .... TRIAD, TRINITY
trivet .... SPIDER, TRIPOD
trivia .... TRIFLES, MINUTIAE
trivial ...... MEAN, BANAL, PETTY,
   SMALL, FLIMSY, LITTLE,
   PALTRY, SLIGHT, ONE-HORSE,
   PICAYUNE, PIDDLING,
   TRIFLING
   objection .... CAVIL
trivium, part of .... LOGIC,
   MUSIC, GRAMMAR,
   GEOMETRY, RHETORIC,
   ASTRONOMY, ARITHMETIC
troche .... ROTULA, LOZENGE,
   PASTIL(LE), COUGH-DROP
trochee .... TROCHAIC
   and iamb .... CHORIAMB
trochilus .... SCOTIA, WARBLER,
   HUMMINGBIRD
trochlear nerve
   .... CRANIAL(NERVE)
   damage result .... DOUBLE
   VISION
   location .... BRAIN
troglodyte .... APE, HERMIT,
   SAVAGE, CAVEMAN, GORILLA,
   RECLUSE, BARBARIAN,
   CHIMPANZEE
trogon .... BIRD, QUE(T)ZAL
   family .... TROGONIDAE
   genus .... NARINA, HARPACTES,
   APALODERMA, EUPTILOTIS,
   PHAROMACHRUS
   habitat .... FORESTS
troika ...... VEHICLE, TRIUMVIRATE
Troilus' brother .... PARIS,
   HECTOR
   father .... PRIAM
   killer .... ACHILLES
   love .... CRESSIDA
   mother .... HECUBA
   sister .... CASSANDRA

Trojan .... ILIAN, TEUCRIAN,
   DARDAN(IAN)
   commander .... ANTENOR
   country .... TROY, ILIUM
   epic .... ILIAD
   epic poet .... HOMER
   hero .... (A)ENEAS
   horse builder .... EPE(I)US
   king .... PRIAM
   peace offering
   .... (WOODEN)HORSE
   prince .... PARIS, HECTOR,
   TROILUS
War allies .... DARDANOI
   cause .... HELEN(OF TROY)
   hero .... AJAX, MEMNON
   protagonist .... PARIS,
   AGENOR, (A)ENEAS,
   DARDAN, HECTOR, ACHILLES
   warriors .... MYRMIDON(E)S
troll .... IMP, WAG, FISH, ROLL,
   SING, SPIN, CHANT, DWARF,
   GIANT, GNOME, WHIRL, REVOLVE
trolley ...... CART, TRAM, PULLEY,
   CARRIAGE
   car .... DINKEY, STREETCAR
   hand .... WHEELBARROW
   line .... ROUTE
trollop ...... SLUT, HUSSY, WHORE,
   HARLOT, SLATTERN
   slang .... HOOKER
trombone .... HORN, SAMBUKE
   forerunner of .... SACKBUT
   mouthpiece .... BOCAL
   part .... SLIDE
trommel .... SIEVE, SCREEN
trona .... NATRON
Trondheim .... NIDAROS
   type .... NORSE
trone .... SCALE
troop ...... GO, BAND, UNIT, WALK,
   FLOCK, GROUP, MARCH,
   PARTY, NUMBER, COMPANY
   barracks .... CASERN(E)
   disposition .... DEPLOYMENT
   formation .... HERSE, ECHELON
   member .... SOLDIER, BOY
   SCOUT, GIRL SCOUT
   quarters .... BILLET, CASERN,
   BARRACKS, CANTON(MENT)
   theatrical .... TROUPE
trooper .... MOUNTIE, POLICEMAN,
   CAVALRYMAN
troops .... ARMY, FORCES
troops' halting place .... ETAPE
   quarters .... BILLET, CANTON,
   BARRACKS
   screen .... BLINDAGE
   spread .... DEPLOY
   station .... POST, GARRISON

   temporary encampment
   .... BIVOUAC
   turning movement ...... WHEEL
troopship .... TRANSPORT
trop .... TOO, TOO MANY, TOO
   MUCH
trope .... METAPHOR
trophy ...... PALM, AWARD, PRIZE,
   LAUREL, PLAQUE, SPOILS,
   MEMENTO, MEMORIAL,
   (LOVING)CUP
   athletic contest .... MEDAL
   Indian .... SCALP
   matador's .... EARS
   trapping .... SKIN
   war .... ARMS, FLAG, BANNER
tropic .... SOLAR, CIRCLE
   circle ..... CANCER, CAPRICORN
tropical .... HOT, WARM, FIERY,
   SULTRY, TORRID,
   EQUATORIAL, FIGURATIVE
   affliction .... HEAT STROKE,
   MALNUTRITION
   animal .... TAPIR, ANTBEAR,
   CARABAO, ECHIDNA,
   ANTEATER, TAMANDUA,
   RHINOCEROS
   bird .... COLY, RHEA, CRANE,
   MACAW, BARBET, MOTMOT,
   TOUCAN, TROGON, HOATZIN,
   JACAMAR, OSTRICH, QUETZAL,
   TINAMOU, COCKATOO,
   FLAMINGO
   disease .... AGUE, BUBO,
   YAWS, SPRUE, DENGUE,
   CHOLERA, MALARIA, MEASLES,
   BERIBERI, PSILOSIS, AMEBIASIS,
   DIPTHERIA, FRAMB(O)ESIA,
   TUBERCULOSIS
   evergreen .... PALM, CASHEW
   fever .... YELLOW, TYPHOID,
   CALENTURE
   fish .... OPAH, COBIA, GUPPY,
   SNOOK, WAHOO, PUFFER,
   GROUPER, SNAPPER
   flower .... EVERLASTING
   fruit .... DATE, GUAVA,
   MANGO, BANANA, PAPAYA,
   PA(W)PAW, POMELO,
   COCONUT, TAMARIND,
   PINEAPPLE
   grass .... BAMBOO
   herb .... LOOFAH
   infectious disease .... DENGUE,
   DIPTHERIA, TUBERCULOSIS
   lizard .... SKINK, SCINCOID
   snake .... FER-DE-LANCE
   tree .... ULE, ATTA, PALM,
   BALSA, CACAO, LEHUA,
   MANGO, CASHEW, CASSIA,
   COLIMA, ACACIA, PAPAYA,

SAPOTA, COCONUT, LOGWOOD, MANGROVE, CINCHONA, TAMARIND, LANCEWOOD, BREADFRUIT

trot .... JOG, RUN, GAIT, LOPE, AMBLE, HURRY, CANTER, HASTEN

troth .... VOW, FAITH, PLEDGE, PLIGHT, PROMISE

Trotsky, Russian revolutionist .... LEON

trotter .... PACER, MORGAN

trotyl .... TNT

troubadour .... BARD, LAUREATE, MINSTREL, MUSICIAN, BALLADEER, (LYRIC)POET, MINNESINGER, (STREET)SINGER

forte of .... POEMS, SONGS, SINGING, RECITING

song .... BALLAD, SERENADE

theme of ...... LOVE, CHIVALRY

traveling/wandering .... JONGLEUR

trouble .... ADO, AIL, ILL, IRK, VEX, WOE, CARE, FASH, ANNOY, PAINS, WORRY, BOTHER, EFFORT, HARASS, OBSESS, PESTER, AFFLICT, AILMENT, DISTURB, DISORDER, INCOMMODE

cause .... RAISE CAIN

troublemaker .... IMP, ERIS, PEST, RIOTER, ROUSER, HELLION, INCITER, AGITATOR, PROVOKER, PROVOCATEUR

troubleshooter .... FIXER

troublesome .... HARD, TRYING, ANNOYING, DIFFICULT

situation .... SCRAPE

trough .... BIN, HOD, BOSH, CHUTE, DITCH, DRAIN, HUTCH, SHOOT, FURROW, GUTTER, MANGER, RUNWAY, SLUICE, VALLEY

brining .... SALTER

fodder .... CRIB

for cooling hot metal .... BOSH

for logs .... FLUME

for washing ore .... BUDDLE, LAUNDER

mining .... HUTCH, BUDDLE, LAUNDER

water wheel .... PENSTOCK

trounce .... BEAT, FLOG, HIDE, LASH, WHIP, DEFEAT, PUNISH, THRASH, DESTROY

troupe .... BAND, GROUP, TROOP

trouper .... ACTOR, PLAYER, SINGER, ACTRESS, PERFORMER

troupial .... ORIOLE, COWBIRD, CACIQUE, GRACKLE

trousers .... JEANS, PANTS, SLOPS, SLACKS, PAJAMAS, PEGTOPS

below the knees .... BREECHES

bottom fold .... CUFF

close-fitting, denim ...... LEVIS

cotton .... CHINO(S), DUCKS

leather .... CHAPS, CHAPARAJOS

tight-fitting .... PANTALOON

trousseau .... BUNDLE, BRIDE'S OUTFIT

item .... GOWN, VEIL, LINGERIE

trout .... CHAR(R), DOLLY, VARDEN, OQUASSA, BLUEBACK, NAMAYCUSH, SALMONOID, STEELHEAD

family .... SALMON

fish like .... SMELT

flap .... FLY

sea .... KIPPER

trowel ...... DARBY, FLOAT, PLANE

Troy .... ILION, ILIUM, WEIGHT

defender of: var. .... ENEAS

environs of ancient ..... TROAS

founder of .... ILUS, LAOMEDON

tale of .... ILIAD

truant .... ERRANT, SHIRKER, SLACKER, TRIVANT, VAGRANT, ABSENTEE, DESERTER

play .... MICHE

truce .... LULL, DELAY, PEACE, RESPITE, ARMISTICE, CEASEFIRE

signal .... WHITE FLAG

Trucial Coast region ...... OMAN

truck .... VAN, BOGY, CART, DRAY, BOGIE, LORRY, BARROW, BARTER, WAGON, CAMION, RUBBISH, TROLLEY, TRUNDLE, VEHICLE, WHEELER, DEALINGS, EXCHANGE

area .... CAB

army .... HALF-TRACK

artillery .... CAMION, WEAPONS-CARRIER

dump .... TILLER

factory .... DOLLY

farm product ..... VEGETABLES

low-temperature .... REEFER

part .... SEMI

rail .... LORRY

small .... PICKUP

-stop sight ...... CAFE, TRAILER

Truckee city .... RENO

truckle .... TOADY, YIELD, CASTER, CRINGE, KOWTOW, SUBMIT, TRUNDLE

truculent .... MEAN, RUDE, CRUEL, HARSH, DEADLY, FIERCE,

SAVAGE, BESTIAL, SCATHING, BELLIGERENT

trudge .... PLOD, SLOG, WALK, ANKLE, MARCH, TRAMP, TRAIPSE

true .... REAL, SURE, ALINE, EXACT, ACTUAL, LAWFUL, CERTAIN, CORRECT, GENUINE, SINCERE, ACCURATE, RIGHT(FUL), STRAIGHT

blue .... LOYAL, STANCH

copy .... ESTREAT

level .... GEOID

love ...... LOVER, SWEETHEART, SPECIAL ONE

skin .... DERMIS

thing/happening .... FACT

up .... ALIGN, ALINE

True Grit is one .... OATER

Truffaut's _____ Kisses .... STOLEN

truffle .... FUNGUS, EARTHNUT, MUSHROOM, TUCKAHOE

Truk island .... TOL, MOEN

truism .... FACT, AXIOM, PLATITUDE, COMMONPLACE

trull .... TART, TROLLOP, STRUMPET, PROSTITUTE

truly .... QUITE, SOOTH, TIGHT, INDEED, IN FACT, REALLY, VERILY, ACTUALLY, FAITHFULLY

relevant .... GERMANE

Truman, birthplace of Harry S .... LAMAR

cabinet member .... SNYDER, ACHESON, KIMBALL, STIMSON

daughter of Harry S .... MARGARET

playwright .... CAPOTE

president .... HARRY

wife of Harry S .... BESS

trump .... EXCEL, OUTDO, SURPASS

in card game .... RUFF

Trump, businessman .... DONALD

trumpery .... TRASH, PALTRY, RUBBISH, NONSENSE

trumpet .... HORN, BUGLE, CORNET, CLARION, PROCLAIM

belt .... BALDRIC

blast .... BLARE, FANFARE

call .... TAPS, SENNET, REVEILLE

caller .... GABRIEL

flourish ..... TUCKET, FANFARE, TANTARA

muffler .... MUTE

muting device .... WAWA

shell .... CONCH, TRITON

signal .... CHAMADE, FLOURISH
sound .... TOOT, BLARE
trumpeter .... SWAN, AGAMI,
BUGLER, HERALD, PIGEON,
GABRIEL, ELEPHANT
Baker .... CHET
from New Orleans .... HIRT
trumps, five of .... PEDRO
truncate .... LOP, TRIM, STUMP,
REDUCE, ABRIDGE, CURTAIL
truncheon .... CLUB, MACE,
BATON, STAFF, CUDGEL
trundle ...... CART, ROLL, WHEEL,
CASTER, ROTATE, REVOLVE
trunk .... BOX, STEM, CHEST,
SNOUT, STOCK, CIRCUIT, MAIN
LINE, PROBOSCIS,
COMPARTMENT
animal's .... SOMA
human .... BODY, TORSO
insect's .... THORAX
knot .... BURL
tree .... BOLE, BURL
trunkfish .... TORO, CHAPIN,
COWFISH
trunks .... SHORTS, BREECHES
trunnel .... TRE(E)NAIL
trunnion .... PIVOT, GUDGEON,
JOURNAL
truss .... TIE, BIND, PACK, PROP,
BRACE, STRAP, BUCKLE,
BUNDLE, SKEWER
trust .... DUTY, HOPE, RELY,
FAITH, BELIEF, CARTEL,
CHARGE, CREDIT, CUSTODY,
MONOPOLY, RELIANCE,
CONFIDENCE
betrayal of .... PERFIDY
of/like a .... FIDUCIAL,
FIDUCIARY
territory .... MANDATE
to the British .... TICK
trustee .... WARDEN, GUARDIAN,
OVERSEER, CUSTODIAN,
GARNISHEE
trustful .... CONFIDING
trustworthy .... SAFE, TRUE,
LOYAL, TRIED, TESTED,
STA(U)NCH, CONSTANT,
CREDIBLE, RELIABLE,
DEPENDABLE
trusty .... CONVICT, PRISONER
truth ...... FACT, VERITY, REALITY,
VERITAS, VERACITY,
ACTUALITY, CERTAINTY
accepted as .... GOSPEL
assumed in theology
.... MYSTERY
drug .... PENTOTHAL
obvious .... AXIOM, MAXIM
personified .... UNA

self-evident .... AXIOM,
TRUISM
stretcher .... LIAR
truthful .... PURE, HONEST,
SINCERE, UP FRONT,
VERACIOUS
boy .... (GEORGE) WASHINGTON
truthfulness .... HONESTY,
ACCURACY, FIDELITY,
VERACITY
try ...... MELT, STAB, TEST, ASSAY,
ESSAY, PURIFY, REFINE,
STRAIN, STRIVE, AFFLICT,
ATTEMPT, ENDEAVOR,
EXPERIMENT
again .... RETEST
cooked food .... SAMPLE
in court .... HEAR
to do .... TACKLE
to extract information
.... PUMP
trygon .... RAY
trying .... DULL, BORING,
IRKSOME, PAINFUL,
ANNOYING, IRRITATING
experience .... ORDEAL,
TRAUMA
time .... CRISIS
tryma .... NUT, HICKORY,
DRUPELET
tryout .... TEST, TRIAL, AUDITION,
EXPERIMENT
trypsin .... ENZYME
trysail .... SPENCER
tryst .... DATE, MEETING,
RENDEZVOUS
Tsaritsyn .... STALINGRAD
tsaritza .... CZARINA, TSARINA
Tschaikowsky, composer
.... PET(E)R
tsetse .... FLY, MAU, KIVU, MUSCID
caused disease .... NAGANA,
SLEEPING SICKNESS
Tse-tung, Chinese leader
.... MAO
tsine .... OX, BANTENG
Tuareg .... BERBER
tuatara .... REPTILE
tub ...... HOD, KEG, KID, KIT, POT,
SOE, TUN, VAT, BOAT, CASK,
KNOP, SHIP, TRAM, BARGE,
BASIN, BATH(E), KEEVE,
SKEEL, BUCKET, FIRKIN,
KEELER, CAULDRON,
HOGSHEAD
shaped like a .... TUBBY
slang ..... BLIMP, FATSO, ROLY-
POLY
-thump .... ORATE
2-handled .... COWL
tuba .... HELICON, SAXHORN,

BASSHORN, BOMBARDON
alcoholic drink source
.... COCONUT-PALM
ancient Romans' .... WAR
TRUMPET
instrument resembling
.... EUPHONIUM
mouthpiece .... BOCAL
tubal ligation ...... STERILIZATION
tubby .... BULKY, SQUAT, ROLY-
POLY
tube .... DUCT, HOSE, PIPE,
CONDUIT, HUMIDOR,
CYLINDER, TELESCOPE,
(ELECTRIC)RAILROAD
cannon/gun .... BARREL
draining .... CATHETER
electric wires' .... CONDUIT
electron .... DIODE
for gas, smoke, etc. ...... FLUE
glass .... PIPET(TE)
graduated .... HYDROMETER
joint of .... ELL
slang .... TELEVISION
tapering .... BURETTE
underground .... SUBWAY,
TUNNEL
vacuum .... DIODE
tuber .... OCA, YAM, BULB, CORM,
EDDO, TARO, JALAP, ONION,
MANIOC, POTATO, CASSAVA,
RHIZOME
dried orchid .... SALEP
tubercle .... GROWTH, NODULE,
PROCESS, PROJECTION
tubercular .... LUNGER,
CONSUMPTIVE
tuberculosis .... PHTHISIS,
CONSUMPTION, WHITE PLAGUE
bovine .... GRAPE
lymphatic gland .... SCROFULA
tuberculous .... PHTHISIC,
CONSUMPTIVE
tuberous .... KNOBBY, BULBOUS
tubular .... TUBATE, FISTULOUS
tuck .... HEM, LAP, TAP, CRAM,
FOLD, WRAP, COVER, PLEAT,
RUCHE, SWORD, PUCKER
companion of .... NIP
tuckahoe .... PORIA, FUNGUS,
TRUFFLE
tucker .... FAG, APRON, STUFF,
WEARY, COLLAR, EXHAUST,
TIRE(OUT), VITTLES,
CHEMISETTE
companion of .... BIB
tuckered out .... SPENT, WORN-
OUT
tucket .... TANTARA, FLOURISH
Tuesday, actress .... WELD
Shrove .... MARDIGRAS

tufa .... TUFF, TOPH(E), LIMESTONE
tuff .... ROCK, TUFA
tuft .... CLUMP, FLECK, FLOCK, CLUSTER
  having a .... COMOSE, CRESTED
  of feathers .... COP, CREST, PLUME, TOPKNOT
  feathers on helmet .... PANACHE
  grass ..... HASSOCK, TUSSOCK
  hair .... BEARD, GOATEE, MUTTON CHOPS
  seed hairs .... COMA
  threads, etc. .... TASSEL
  on woman's hat .... POMPON
tufted .... HAIRY, MOSSY, COMATE, COMOSE, SWARDY, CRESTED, C(A)ESPITOSE
tufthunter .... SNOB, TOADY, SYCOPHANT, SOCIAL CLIMBER
tug ...... DRAG, HAUL, PULL, TOIL, LABOR, DRUDGE, STRAIN, STRIVE, TOW(BOAT)
  boat pulled by .... SCOW, SHIP, BARGE
  -of-war ...... POWER-STRUGGLE, PULLING CONTEST
Tuileries .... PALACE
tuition .... BILL, COST, FEE(S), CHARGE, TUTELAGE, INSTRUCTION
tuitional .... EDUCATIONAL
tule .... BULRUSH
tulip .... BULB, FLOWER
  family .... LILY
  genus .... TULIPA
  shape .... CUP
  -shaped glass .... BRANDY SNIFTER
  tree .... POPLAR
tulle .... LACE, NET(TING), ILLUSION
tullibee .... WHITEFISH
Tully .... CICERO
tumble .... FALL, FLOP, LEAP, ROLL, TOSS, TRIP, PITCH, PLASH, SPILL, THROW, SPRING, OVERTURN, SOMERSAULT
  bug .... BEETLE
tumbler .... COG, DOVE, LEVER, PIGEON, TURNER, ACROBAT, GYMNAST, JUGGLER, TOPPLER, (DRINKING)GLASS
  dog .... GREYHOUND
  net of .... TRAMPOLIN(E)
tumbleweed .... THISTLE, AMARANTH
tumbling box .... DRUM, BARREL, RUMBLE(R)
tumbo fly-bite disease .... MYIASIS

tumbrel .... WAGON, CAISSON, (DUMP)CART
tumefy .... SWELL
tumescence .... SWELLING
tumid .... TURGID, BULGING, POMPOUS, SWOLLEN, TEEMING, ENLARGED, INFLATED, BOMBASTIC, DISTENDED
tummy .... STOMACH
  ache .... COLIC
tumor .... YAW, CYST, GUMMA, GROWTH, ANGIOMA, NEUROMA, HEMATOMA, MELANOMA, NEOPLASM, SCIRRHUS, SWELLING
  anal .... PILES, HEMORRHOID
  benign .... WEN, CORN, ADENOMA
  blood vessel .... ANGIOMA
  bony tissue .... OSTEOMA
  brain .... GLIOMA
  cartilaginous ...... CHONDROMA
  classification .... BENIGN, MALIGNANT
  combining form .... C(O)ELE
  epithelial .... CARCINOMA
  fat tissue .... LIPOMA
  fibrous .... KELOID, FIBROID, CHELOID, FIBROMA
  filled with blood .... HEMATOMA
  glandular .... ADENOMA
  liver .... HEPATOMA
  malignant .... CANCER, SARCOMA, TERATOMA, CARCINOMA
  not malignant .... BENIGN
  scar tissue .... KELOID, CHELOID
  secondary growth .... METASTASIS
  skin .... WEN, WART, MELANOMA, PAPILLOMA
  spinal cord .... GLIOMA
  tendon .... GANGLION
tumult .... DIN, RIOT, STIR, BABEL, NOISE, HUBBUB, UPROAR, TURMOIL, DISORDER, AGITATION, COMMOTION, CONFUSION
tumultuous .... AROAR, NOISY, RIOTOUS, VIOLENT, TURBULENT, BLUSTERING, BOISTEROUS
tumulus .... MOUND, BARROW
tun .... VAT, CASK
tuna .... PEAR, TUNNY, CACTUS, BLUEFIN, OPUNTIA, MACKEREL
  like fish .... BONITO, ALBACORE

tundra .... PLAIN, WASTELAND
  dweller .... LAPP
  like wasteland .... PAMPAS, STEPPE
tune .... AIR, ARIA, LILT, TONE, ADJUST, MELODY, CONCORD, HARMONY, MODULATE
tuneful .... MELODIC, MUSICAL, MELODIOUS
  in music .... ARIOSO
tuneless .... OFF-KEY, OUT-OF-TUNE
tunesmith .... COMPOSER, SONGWRITER
tungsten .... WOLFRAM, CARBOLOY
  mineral .... SCHEELITE, WOLFRAMITE
  part of bulb made of .... FILAMENT
tungstite .... OCHER
Tungus .... MANCHU, MONGOLIAN
tunic .... COAT, JAMA, ROBE, TOGA, VEST, FROCK, GIPON, JUPON, STOLE, WAIST, CHITON, KIRTLE
  of mail .... CHITON
  over armor ...... GIPON, JUPON, TABARD
  woman's tight-fitting .... BASQUE
tunicate .... SALPA, ASCIDIAN
  bulb .... ONION
tunicle .... VESTMENT
tuning fork .... DIAPASON
Tunisian Berber .... KABYLE
  cape .... BON, BLANC
  capital .... TUNIS
  city/town .... BEJA, GABES, GAFSA, MAHDIA, MSAKEN, NABEUL, SOUSSE, BIZERTE, KAIROUAN
  diplomat .... (MONGI) SLIM
  gulf .... GABES, TUNIS, HAMMAMET
  island .... DJERBA
  island group .... KERKENNAH
  measure .... SAA(H), UEBA, CAFIZ
  monetary unit .... DINAR
  mountain .... CHAMBI
  oasis .... GAFSA
  port ...... SFAX, GABES, SOUSSE
  president .... BOURGUIBA
  region .... JEFARA
  river .... MEDJERDA
  ruler .... BEY, DEY, PASHA
  weight .... UCKIA, KANTAR
tunnel ...... DIG, SAP, ADIT, CAVE, FLUE, LAIR, TUBE, BURROW, SUBWAY, CHANNEL,

PASSAGEWAY

disease .... BENDS,
CAISSON(DISEASE)

in the Alps .... SIMPLON

vision .... BLINDNESS

vision cause .... GLAUCOMA

tunneler .... ANT, DIGGER,
SAPPER, BURROWER

tunny .... AMIA, TUNA, ALBACORE,
MACKEREL

tup .... RAM, SHEEP

tupelo .... NYSSA, DOGWOOD,
LIME(TREE), WATER GUM,
PEPPERIDGE

Tupi .... INDIAN, GUARANI

tupik, e.g. .... TENT

tuque .... CAP

Turandot character .... PONG
composer .... (GIACOMO)
PUCCINI

turban .... HAT, MANDIL,
HEADDRESS

cloth .... LUNGI, LUNGEE

turbid .... ROILY, MUDDY,
CLOUDY, OPAQUE, ROILED,
CLOUDED, MUDDLED,
CONFUSED

turbine .... MOTOR, ROTOR,
ENGINE, PROPELLER

turbit .... PIGEON

turbot ...... BUTT, BRILL, FLATFISH

flatfish like .... SOLE, HALIBUT,
FLOUNDER

turbulence .... CHAOS, TUMULT,
UNREST, UPROAR, DISORDER,
VIOLENCE, COMMOTION

airplane .... BURBLE,
BUMP(INESS), AIR-POCKET

dizzying .... SWIRL

turbulent .... WILD, RAGING,
STORMY, UNRULY, CHAOTIC,
FURIOUS, RIOTOUS, AGITATED,
FRENZIED, TEMPESTUOUS

affair .... RIOT

turdine bird .... THRUSH

tureen .... (SOUP)DISH
adjunct .... LADLE

turf .... SOD, PEAT, SWARD,
DOMAIN, (RACE)TRACK,
TERRITORY

of/like .... CEPITOSE

piece of .... DIVOT

turfy .... GRASSY

Turgenev, novelist .... IVAN
heroine .... ELENA

turgid .... TUMID, TOROSE,
TOROUS, BLOATED, BULGING,
POMPOUS, SWOLLEN,
INFLATED, BOMBASTIC

Turin .... TORINO

Turk .... HORSE, TATAR, TURCO,
MOSLEM, TARTAR, OSMANLI,
OTTOMAN

Turkestan inhabitant .... SART
Moslem .... SALAR
mountain .... ALAI, PAMIRS
river ILI
tribe .... USBEG, KIRGHIZ

turkey, bird like .... CURASSOW
buzzard .... AURA, VULTURE
chin adornment of
.... WATTLE, CARUNCLE
cock .... TOM
male .... TOM, GOBBLER
slang ..... BUST, FLOP, FAILURE
sound .... GOBBLE
talk .... GOBBLE
trot .... DANCE
wild .... BUSTARD
young .... POULT

Turkey, Asiatic .... ANATOLIA
cape .... BABA, INCE, SINOP,
ANAMUR, HELLES, GELIDONYA
capital of .... ANKARA
capital, former name
.... ANGORA
city/town .... VAN, ICEL, PERA,
RIZE, URFA, USAK, ZARA, ZILE,
ADANA, AYDIN, BAFRA,
BURSA, HATAY, IZMIR, IZMIT,
TOKAT, ADALIA, BATMAN,
BEYKOZ, CEYHAN, EDESSA,
EDIRNE, EREGLI, MANISA,
MERSIN, SAMSUN, SMYRNA,
TARSUS, ANTALYA, ANTIOCH,
BEYOGLU, CANKAYA,
ERZURUM, ISPARTA, KADIKOY,
KARABUK, MALATYA,
SAKARYA, TRABZON,
USKUDAR, ALTINDAG,
BAKIRKOY, ISTANBUL,
BALIKESIR, ESKISEHIR,
GALLIPOLI, GAZIANTEP,
KARSIYAKA
gulf .... KERME, SAROS,
ANTALYA, CANDARLI,
MANDALYA, ALEXANDRETTA
island .... ADALAR, BURGAZ,
HEYBELI, MARMARA,
BOZCAADA, PRINKIPO
lake .... ACI, TUZ, VAN,
BEYSEHIR
mountain .... CILO, AKDAG,
ALADAG, ARARAT, KACKAR,
SUPHAN, ERCIYAS
mountains .... KURE, CANIK,
AMANOS, PONTIC, TAURUS,
KOROGLU
province ...... MUS, VAN, AGRI,
BOLU, ICEL, KARS, ORDU,
RIZE, URFA, ADANA, AYDIN,
BURSA, CORUM, HATAY, IZMIR,

KONYA, NIGDE, SIVAS, TOKAT,
ANKARA, BURDUR, MANISA,
SAMSUN, YOZGAT, DENIZLI,
ISPARTA, KAYSERI, TRABZON,
ISTANBUL, GAZIANTEP,
ZONGULDAK
red dye .... MADDER, ALIZARIN
region .... ANATOLIA,
KURDISTAN
river ...... ARPA, KOCA, ARAKS,
CORUH, DICLE, FIRAT, GEDIZ,
GOKSU, MERIC, MURAT,
SIMAV, CEYHAN, ERGENE,
KELKIT, PORSUK, SEYHAN,
TIGRIS, SAKARYA, MENDERES,
EUPHRATES
ruins .... TROY, ILIUM,
ABYDOS, EPHESUS
sea .... BLACK, AEGEAN,
MARMARA
seaport .... TRABZON,
TREBIZOND
strait .... BOSPORUS,
DARDANELLES

Turki .... OSMANLI, TURKOMAN

Turkic language .... TATAR
people .... UZBEG, UZBEK

Turkish bathhouse .... BAGNIO
cab/carriage .... ARABA
cap ...... FEZ, CALPAC, KALPAK
caravansary .... IMARET
cavalryman ..... SPAHI, SPAHEE
chamber .... ODA(H)
chieftain .... ZAIM
coin .... LIRA, PARA, ALTUN,
ASPER, YUZLUK, PIASTER,
PIASTRE
college/school .... ULEMA
commander .... SIRDAR
confection .... HALVAH
court .... PORTE
decree .... IRADE
delight .... CANDY
dialect .... JAGATAI
dispute with Greece
.... CYPRUS
district .... VILAYET
dulcimer .... CANUN
dynasty/tribe .... SELJUK
emblem .... CRESCENT
emissary .... CHIAUS
ensign .... CRESCENT,
HORSETAIL
father .... BABA
fig .... ELEME
flag .... ALEM, CRESCENT
float .... KALAK
foreign quarter .... PERA,
BEYOGLU
garment ...... CAFTAN, KAFTAN
general .... AGA, INONU,

government .... PORTE KEMAL

governor .... BEY, MALI, WALI, PASHA

harem resident .... KADEIN

hat .... FEZ

hell .... DAGH

hospice .... IMARET

house for men ...... SELAM LIK

inn .... KHAN, SERAI, IMARET

island .... TENEDOS

javelin ..... JER(R)ID, JER(R)EED

judge .... CADI, KADI

legendary leader .... SELCUK

liqueur .... RAKI

liquor .... MASTIC

magistrate .... CADI

major .... AGA

master .... EFFENDI

measure .... PIK, DRA(H), HATT, KHAT, KILE, ZIRA, ALMUD, BERRI, ARSHIN

messenger .... CHIAUS

military district .... ORDO

milk food .... YOG(H)URT

minister .... VIZI(E)R

mock battle .... JER(R)ID, JER(R)EED

monetary unit .... LIRA

money .... PARA

money of account .... ASPER

monk .... DERVISH

non-Moslem .... RAIA, RAYAH, GIAOUR

oak .... CERRIS

official .... EMIR, EMEER, PACHA, PASHA, BASHAW

opium .... AFYON

oxcart .... ARABA

palace .... SERAI, SERAGLIO

parade .... ALAI

pasha's standard .... HORSETAIL

pavilion .... KIOSK

peasant .... RAYA

peninsula .... GALLIPOLI

people .... KURD, TURKI, OSMANLI

policeman .... ZAPTIAH

pound .... LIRA

prayer rug .... MELAS

premier .... DEMIREL

president .... BAYAR, SUNAY, INONU, ATATURK

province .... VILAYET

regiment .... ALAI

rice dish .... PILAF, PILAU, PILAW

robe .... DOLMAN, CAFTAN, KAFTAN

royal court .... DIVAN

ruler .... KHAN, CALIPH, SULTAN

saber .... YATAG(H)AN

scholar .... ULEMA

sergeant .... CHIAUS

sir .... EFFENDI

slave .... MAMELUKE

soldier .... NIZAM, JANIZARY, JANISSARY

standard ..... ALEM, HORSETAIL

statesman .... INONU

sultan .... CALIF, SELIM, CALIPH, PADISHAH

sultan's guard .... JANIZARY

sultan's palace .... SERAGLIO

sultan's visit to mosque .... SELAM LIK

summerhouse .... KIOSK

sword .... SCIMITAR, YATAGHAN

teacher .... MULLA(H)

title .... BEY, AG(H)A, EMIR, EMEER, GHAZI, PACHA, PASHA, EFFENDI

tobacco .... LATAKIA

tower ..... MANARAT, MENARET

tribesman .... TATAR

veil .... YASHMAC, YASHMAK

viceroy .... KHEDIVE

"victorious warrior" .... GHAZI

vilayet. See **Turkey**, province

vilayet subdivision .... SANJAK

weight .... OKA, OKE, ROTL, CEQUI, CHEKE, KERAT, MAUND, DIRHAM, KANTAR, MISKAL

whip .... KURBASH

zither .... CANUM

Turko .... ABO

-Tartar tribe .... BASHKIR

turmeric .... REA, GINGER, CURCUMA

turmoil .... ADO, STOUR, HUBBUB, TUMULT, UPROAR, WELTER, AGITATION, COMMOTION, CONFUSION

turn ...... BEND, CANT, COIL, REEL, SPIN, AVERT, BLUNT, CURVE, PIVOT, REPEL, SCREW, SHIFT, TREND, TWIRL, TWIST, DIVERT, ROTATE, SWITCH, VOLUTE, DEVIATE, REVOLVE

a deaf ear to .... IGNORE

a new leaf .... CHANGE, REFORM

about .... BY TURNS, ALTERNATE

against .... CROSS, BETRAY

against one's benefactor .... BITE THE HAND THAT FEEDS ONE

around .... SLUE, PIVOT, ROTATE, REVOLVE

aside ...... DAFF, VEER, BRUSH, AVERT, DETER, SHUNT, DEFLECT, DEVIATE, FEND(OFF)

away .... SHOO, AVERT, REFUSE, REJECT, ESTRANGE

back .... PUSH, REPEL, REFLEX, RETURN, REPULSE, RETREAT

combining form .... TROPO

complete .... LAP, CIRCLE

course/off course .... YAW

down ..... DENY, VETO, SPURN, REFUSE, REJECT

equestrian/horsemanship .... CARACOLE

in .... ENTER, BETRAY, REPORT, DELIVER, HIT THE SACK

in music .... VOLTA

inside out ...... EVERT, INVERT, RANSACK

into .... BECOME, CONVERT

into money .... (EN)CASH

left .... HAW

loose .... FREE, RELEASE, LIBERATE

loose an inmate .... PAROLE

of mind .... CAPRICE

off .... REPEL, DAMPEN, DISCOURAGE

on .... (A)ROUSE, AWAKEN, EXCITE

on an axis .... ROLL

one side .... DEFLECT

one's back upon .... SNUB, REBUFF

out .... ARRAY, EJECT, EVICT, BECOME, OUTPUT, DISMISS, EQUIPAGE, GATHERING

outward .... EVERT

over .... KEEL, CAPSIZE, DELIVER, TRANSFER

over a new leaf .... MEND ONE'S WAYS

over by tossing .... FLAP

over in the mind ...... PONDER, REFLECT

page over .... LEAF

red .... BLUSH

right .... GEE, JEE

ship's .... YAW, TACK

single .... WINDING

-the-page dir. .... PTO

to .... BEGIN, DIVE IN, EMBARK, CONSULT

topsy-turvy .... UPEND

toward .... FACE

unfriendly .... MADDEN, ENVENOM, PROVOKE, ALIENATE, EMBITTER,

ESTRANGE, ANTAGONIZE

up .... COME, SHOW, APPEAR, ARRIVE, EXPOSE

up one's nose at .... SPURN, FROWN AT, DISAPPROVE

upside down .... SUBVERT, OVERTHROW

white .... PALE, BLANCH

turnabout .... SHIFT, REVERSAL, VOLTE-FACE

turnaround .... FLIP-FLOP

contrivance .... CARROUSEL, MERRY-GO-ROUND

turncoat .... RAT, BOLTER, TRAITOR, APOSTATE, DESERTER, RECREANT, RENEGADE, RUNAGATE

turndown .... VETO, REBUFF, BRUSH-OFF, REJECTION

turned back piece .... REVERSE

down page corners
.... DOGEARED

in mathematics .... VERSED

on .... ENTHUSIASTIC

traitor .... SOLD OUT

unfriendly .... ICY, COLD, CHILLY, HOSTILE

up .... SNUB, ACOCK, TILTED

turner .... ACROBAT, GYMNAST, TUMBLER

Turner, _____ .... IKE, NAT, LANA, TINA

turning joint .... HINGE

machine .... LATHE, SPANNER

point .... CRUX, PIVOT, CLIMAX, CRISIS, SOLSTICE

turnip .... NEEP, ROOT, SWEDE, RUTABAGA

shaped .... NAPIFORM

turnip's lack .... BLOOD

turnix .... (GAME)BIRD

turnkey .... GAOLER, JAILER, WARDER

turnout .... RIG, EQUIPAGE, ATTENDANCE

turnover .... PIE, TART, SPILL, UPSET, PASTRY

turnpike .... HIGHWAY, THRUWAY, TOLLGATE, TOLLROAD

exit .... RAMP

turnsole .... DYE, SUNFLOWER, HELIOTROPE

turnstile .... GATE

turnstone .... WADER, PLOVER, (SHORE)BIRD

genus .... ARENARIA

relative .... CURLEW, SANDPIPER

turntable operator .... DISC JOCKEY

Turnverein member .... TURNER, GYMNAST, TUMBLER

turpentine .... OIL, GAL(L)IPOT, OLEORESIN

distillate .... ROSIN

substance like .... ELEMI

tree .... PINE, TARATA, TEREBINTH

turpeth .... EMETIC, CATHARTIC

turpitude .... BASENESS, VILENESS, DEPRAVITY

moral .... CORRUPTION

turquoise .... GEM, STONE, GREENISH-BLUE

turret .... TOWER, BARBICAN

gun .... CUPOLA

open-roofed .... BELVEDERE

opening .... LOUVER

tower ..... BARTISAN, BARTIZAN

viewing .... GAZEBO

turtle ...... EMYD, ARRAU, JURARA, REPTILE, SNAPPER, MOSSBACK, CHELONIAN, TERRAPIN, HAWK(S)BILL, LOGGERHEAD, LEATHERBACK

descriptive of a
.... SLOW(FOOT)

enclosure for .... CRAWL

fresh-water .... TERRAPIN

genus .... EMYS, CARETTA

land .... TESTUDO, TORTOISE

largest living
.... LEATHERBACK

medium-sized ...... HAWKSBILL

of a/like a .... CHELONIAN

old .... MOSSBACK

protective covering .... MAIL

refuge of .... SHELL

shell .... PEE, CARAPACE, PLASTRON

shell substance .... CALIPEE, CALIPASH

turn .... CAPSIZE

Tuscany .... TOSCANA

city .... PISA, LUCCA, PRATO, SIENA, AREZZO, FIRENZE, LEGHORN, LIVORNO, FLORENCE

island .... ELBA

river .... ARNO, ORCIA, OMBRONE

wine .... CHIANTI

tush .... CANINE-TOOTH

tusk .... FANG, HORN, IVORY, TOOTH

small elephant's
.... SCRIVELLO

wound with a .... GORE

tusker .... BOAR, WALRUS, NARWHAL, PECCARY, WARTHOG, ELEPHANT

tussah .... SHANTUNG, SILK(WORM)

tussis .... COUGH

tussle ...... FIGHT, SCRAP, BICKER, CONTEND, GRAPPLE, SCUFFLE, WRESTLE, STRUGGLE

tussock .... TUFT, CLUMP, THICKET

tut .... TSK

Tutankhamon's former name
.... TUTANKHATON

god .... ATON

kingdom .... AMARNA

predecessor .... AKHENATON, AMENHOTEP

tutelage .... CARE, AEGIS, AUSPICES, GUIDANCE, TEACHING, WARDSHIP, PROTECTION, INSTRUCTION

tutelary deity .... LAR(ES), GENIUS, PENATES

tutor ...... COACH, GUIDE, MASTER, MENTOR, TEACH(ER), GUARDIAN, PEDAGOG(UE), DISCIPLINE, INSTRUCT(OR)

tutto .... ALL, ENTIRE

Tutuila city .... PAGO PAGO

Tuvalu capital .... FUNAFUTI, FONGAFALE

island/atoll .... NUI, NIUTAO, NANUMEA

tuxedo .... TUX, BLACK TIE, (DINNER)JACKET

tuyere .... TEW, PIPE, TUBE, TEWEL, NOZZLE

TV. See **television**

TVA, part of .... TENNESSEE, VALLEY, AUTHORITY

Tver .... KALININ

twaddle .... ROT, BUNK, PRATE, DRIVEL, GABBLE, FUSTIAN, PRATTLE, NONSENSE

twain .... TWO

Twain, humorist .... MARK

character .... SAWYER

invention .... SCRAPBOOK

twang .... TANG, PLUNK

twangy .... NASAL

tweak .... JERK, PINCH, PLUCK, TWIST, TWITCH

Tweeddale .... PEEBLES

tweeg .... HELLBENDER

tweet .... PEEP, CHIRP

tweeter .... LOUDSPEAKER

tweeze .... PLUCK

tweezers .... PINCERS

Twelfth Night .... EPIPHANY

character .... FESTE, VIOLA, ORSINO, MALVOLIO

composer .... AMRAM

twelve .... XII, DOZEN

Biblical .... APOSTLES, DISCIPLES

by twelve .... GROSS

dozen .... GROSS

relating to .... DUODECIMAL

Twelve Apostles, one of the

.... JOHN, JUDE, JAMES, JUDAS, PETER, SIMON, ANDREW, PHILIP, THOMAS, MATTHEW, BARTHOLOMEW

twelvemo .... DUODECIMO

Twelvetrees or Hayes ...... HELEN

twentieth .... VIGESIMAL

twenty .... XX, SCORE

combining form .... ICOS(A), ICOSI, VIGINTI

dinars .... BISTI

-fifth anniversary ...... JUBILEE

-fifth wedding anniversary .... SILVER(WEDDING)

five pounds .... PONY

four carat .... PURE

-minute walk .... MILE

of/based on .... VICENARY, VIGESIMAL

one .... BLACK JACK

one merit badge wearer .... EAGLE SCOUT

plane surfaces, figure with .... ICOSAHEDRON

quires .... REAM

years, period of .... VICENNIAL

twerp .... CLOD, DOLT, LOUT, CREEP, DULLARD

twibill .... MATTOCK, (BATTLE)AX

twice ..... BIS, DOUBLY, TWOFOLD, TWO TIMES

halved .... ONCE

prefix .... BI, DI

-told .... REPEATED, REITERATED

twiddle .... TOY, TWIRL, TRIFLE

one's ——— .... THUMBS

with .... PLAY

twig .... ROD, SLIP, LAYER, (S)CION, SHOOT, SPRIG, BRANCH, TENDRIL

abnormal enlargement of a .... GALL

and branch angle .... AXIL

British: sl. .... NOTICE, OBSERVE

broom .... BARSOM

dead .... STICK

flexible .... OSIER, WITHE, SWITCH, WICKER, WILLOW

for grafting .... CION, SLIP

like a .... TWIGGY

willow .... SALLOW

young .... SHOOT

twiggy .... SLENDER, VIRGATE, DELICATE

Twiggy, Britain's .... MODEL

twigs, bunch of .... FAGOT, WHISK

clump of .... TUSSOCK

having .... VIRGATE

of .... VIMINAL

twilight .... EVE, DUSK, SHADE, EVENFALL, EVENTIDE, GLOAM(ING), CREPUSCLE, NIGHTFALL

like .... DIM

of the Gods .... RAGNAROK

poet .... EEN

sleep inducer ..... SCOPOLAMIN

twill .... PRUNELLA

twilled .... CORDED

fabric ...... REP, DENIM, SERGE, CORDUROY

twin .... TWO, COPY, LIKE, GEMEL, COUPLE, DOUBLE, PAIR(ED), DIDYMOUS, IDENTICAL

artists Raphael and Moses .... SOYERS

biblical .... ESAU, JACOB

bill .... DOUBLEHEADER

brother of Romulus .... REMUS

crystal .... MACLE

genetically identical .... MONOVULAR, MONOZYGOTIC

non-identical ...... BINOVULAR, DIZYGOTIC

of Pollux, mortal ...... CASTOR

of sorts .... CLONE

sister of Apollo .... ARTEMIS

sons of Zeus, one of .... CASTOR, POLLUX

Twin Cities, one of .... ST. PAUL, MINNEAPOLIS

twinberry .... HONEYSUCKLE

twine .... CORD, LINE, SNARL, TWIST, WEAVE, ENFOLD, ENLACE, STRING, TANGLE, THREAD, WREATHE, ENCIRCLE, FILAMENT, INTERLACE

material .... HEMP, JUTE, ABACA, OAKUM, MAGUEY

twinge .... ACHE, PAIN, PANG, DOUBT, PINCH, SHOOT, THROB

of conscience .... QUALM, SHAME, REMORSE, SCRUPLE, COMPUNCTION

twining stem .... BINE

twinkle ...... WINK, BLINK, GLINT, SHINE, FLICKER, GLIMMER, SHIMMER, SPARKLE

twinkling .... INSTANT, (SPLIT)SECOND

twins .... GEMINI

conjoined ..... SIAMESE(TWINS)

one of the Siamese .... ENG, CHANG

twirl ...... COIL, SPIN, TURN, WIND, TWIST, WHIRL, ROTATE,

FLOURISH

twist .... TIC, SKEW, TURN, WARP, WIND, CURVE, SCREW, TWINE, WRICK, WRING, SPRAIN, SQUIRM, WRENCH, WRITHE, CONTORT

a joint .... SPRAIN

and turn .... W(R)IGGLE

around .... COIL, CURL

around one's finger .... DOMINATE, SPELLBIND

given to a ball .... SPIN

in a tree .... GNARL

into thread .... THROW

of fiction .... OLIVER

one's arm ...... URGE, COMPEL, PERSUADE

out of shape .... DISTORT

the meaning of .... PERVERT, MISINTERPRET

twisted .... WRY, AWRY, SKEW, COMPLEX, TORTILE, CONTORTED

cord .... TORSADE

doughnut .... CRULLER

inclination .... BIAS

mind, person with a .... ODDBALL, SCREWBALL

roll of cotton .... SLUB

roll of tobacco .... PIGTAIL

rope/wire strands .... CABLE

thread .... LISLE

twister .... CYCLONE, TORNADO

twisting .... SPIRAL, TORSION

pinch/pluck .... TWEAK

twit .... RAG, RIB, GIBE, JEER, JOSH, MOCK, CHAFF, SCOFF, TAUNT, TEASE, BANTER, DERIDE, UPBRAID, REPROACH, RIDICULE

twitch .... TIC, TUG, JERK, PAIN, PULL, PLUCK, SHAKE, SPASM, TWEAK, FIDGET, SNATCH, TWINGE, SQUEEZE, VELLICATE

of a muscle .... TIC, FASCICULATION

twitter .... GIGGLE, TITTER, CHATTER, CHIRRUP, FLUTTER, CHIRP(ING)

twittering .... QUIVERING, TREMBLING

"of the sparrows" .... MAHJONG

twixt .... BETWEEN

ifs and buts .... ANDS

two ...... DUO, DUET, PAIR, BRACE, TWAIN, COUPLE, LOWEST CARD IN THE DECK

aces in dice .... CRABS, CRAPS, SNAKE EYES

Americans who shared Nobel Prize for medicine,
one of: 1992 .... (EDWIN) KREBS, (EDMOND) FISCHER
archaic .... TWAIN
at a time .... DOUBLY
-base hit .... DOUBLE, TWO-BAGGER
bells .... ONE O'CLOCK
bends or curves, having .... BIFLEX
-bit: sl. .... CHEAP, TAWDRY, SMALL-TIME, WORTHLESS
bits .... QUARTER
branches, having ...... FORKED, BIFURCATE
-by-four .... SMALL, LUMBER, NARROW, CRAMPED, LIMITED
by two .... BINAL
-celled .... BILOCULAR
-colored .... TWO-TONE, DICHROMATIC
-colored bird .... OWL, TERN, EAGLE, PARROT, PETREL, PENGUIN, SWALLOW
combining form .... BI, DI, BIS, DUO, DYO, TWI
consisting of .... DYAD(IC)
-continent nation .... RUSSIA
contrary states of the human soul, one of the (per Blake) .... INNOCENCE, EXPERIENCE
cups .... PINT
different focus, having .... BIFOCAL
divide by .... FIFTY-FIFTY
-edged .... ANCIPITAL, ANCIPITOUS
-element semiconductor .... DIODE
equal parts, divide into .... HALVE
-faced .... FALSE, BIFACIAL, DECEIVING, INSINCERE, DUPLICITOUS, HYPOCRITICAL
-faced being .... JANUS, HYPOCRITE
-fisted .... POTENT, VIRILE, VIGOROUS
-footed animal .... BIPED(AL)
for the price of one .... TWOFER
-forked .... BIFURCATE
groups/classes, division into .... DICHOTOMY
-handed .... BIMANOUS, AMBIDEXTROUS
-handed animal .... BIMANE
-headed .... BICEPHALOUS

-headed muscle .... BICEPS
heads, having .... DICEPHALOUS
-horned .... BICORN
-horse chariot .... BIGA
hundred milligrams .... CARAT
-leaf paper sheet .... FOLIO
-legged .... BIPED
legislative chambers, having .... BICAMERAL
magistrates, either of .... DUUMVIR
-masted squarerigger ..... BRIG
-month period .... BIMESTER
of .... DUAL
of a kind .... BRACE
of similar things ..... DOUBLET
-part mollusk .... CLAM, MUSSEL, BIVALVE
partners with joint authority .... DUUMVIRATE
people, conversation between .... DUOLOGUE, TETE-A-TETE
plus tid .... BITS
punches in quick succession .... ONE-TWO
-seater .... TANDEM, ROADSTER
shillings .... FLORIN
-sided .... BILATERAL
similar parts, having .... DUPLICATE
song for .... DUET
-spot .... DEUCE
-step .... DANCE
-striper .... CORPORAL
successive lines of verse .... COUPLET, DISTICH
-supplier controlled market .... DUOPOLY
-syllable foot .... TROCHEE
teeth, having .... BIDENTATE
the .... BOTH
thousand pounds .... NET TON, SHORT TON
-time .... DOUBLE-CROSS
-timer ...... SPY, CHEAT, JUDAS, INFIDEL, ADULTERER, ADULTERESS, DOUBLE-AGENT
-toed sloth .... UNAU
together .... DUAD, PAIR
-tusked animal .... WALRUS, ELEPHANT, (WILD)BOAR
units regarded as one .... DYAD, PAIR
vertical rows, arranged in .... DISTICHOUS
-way .... DUAL
-week period .... FORTNIGHT
-wheeled cab .... HANSOM
-wheeled carriage .... GIG, CART, CALASH, HANSOM,

CALECHE, TILBURY
-wheeled vehicle .... TONGA, BICYCLE
-year old sheep .... TEG(G)
Two-Faced Woman star .... (GRETA) GARBO
Women star .... (SOPHIA) LOREN
Years Before the Mast author .... DANA
twofold .... DUAL, BINAL, BINARY, DOUBLE, DUPLE(X)
twosome .... COUPLE
Ty, baseball great .... COBB
Tyburn event .... HANGING, EXECUTION
Tyche .... FORTUNA, GODDESS
tycoon ...... TSAR, BARON, MOGUL, SHOGUN, MAGNATE, FINANCIER
Tydeus' son .... DIOMEDES
tyke .... CUR, DOG, LAD, BOOR, CHILD, MONGREL
Tyler, English rebel .... WAT
U.S. president .... JOHN
tympan .... DRUM
tympani .... KETTLEDRUMS
tympanic membrane .... EARDRUM
tympanist .... DRUMMER
tympanum .... MIDDLE EAR
tympany .... PRIDE, BOMBAST, CONCEIT, ARROGANCE
Tyndareus .... SPARTAN
wife of .... LEDA
Tyne river city .... JARROW
type .... KIND, SIGN, SORT, BREED, CLASS, GROUP, IDEAL, MODEL, TOKEN, EMBLEM, FIGURE, NATURE, VARIETY, CLASSIFY, (TYPE)WRITE
assortment of .... FO(U)NT
blank .... QUAD(RAT)
body measure .... POINT
break in .... BATTER
case .... LOWER, UPPER
disarrange .... SQUABBLE
face like writing ...... CURSIVE
face projection .... KERN
jumbled/mixed .... PI(E)
lead-in .... PROTO
line of .... SLUG
measure .... EM, EN
metal .... QUAD
mold .... MATRIX
of acid .... AMINO
button .... PANIC
clock .... ALARM, BANJO, GRANDFATHER
coat .... SPORT, DUFFEL,

TUXEDO, SWAGGER, SPIKETAIL, SWALLOWTAIL
diving board .... FLAT, SPRING
hands? .... DISHPAN
intelligence test .... IQ, BINET-SIMON, STANFORD-BINET
law .... DRY, GAG, BLUE, COMMON, UNWRITTEN
law enforcement agency .... SWAT
police operation .... STING
sleeve .... DOLMAN, LANTERN, LEG-OF-MUTTON
space .... AERO
surgeon .... HEART, NEURO, PLASTIC
trip .... EGO
ornamental line .... SERIF
part .... KERN
set .... COMPOSE
size .... FONT, PICA, AGATE, RUBY, ELITE, ROMAN, MINION, BREVIER, DIAMOND, PARAGON, EXCELSIOR, NONPAREIL, LONG PRIMER
style .... ROMAN, BODONI, CASLON, GOTHIC, ITALIC, GARAMOND, GROTESQUE
tray .... GALLEY
type .... IONIC, ROMAN, ITALIC, SCRIPT, CURSIVE, BOLDFACE, OLD ENGLISH
typescript .... COPY
typesetter .... PRINTER,

COMPOSITOR, LINOTYPIST
typesetting .... COMPOSING
machine: colloq. .... LINO
typewriter, kind of .... TELEX, MANUAL, ELECTRIC, TELETYPE
part ..... KEY, PLATEN, ROLLER, SPACER, CARRIAGE, TABULATOR
type .... PICA, ELITE
typhlosis .... BLINDNESS
Typhoeus' killer .... ZEUS
typhoid fever bacterium .... SALMONELLA
drug treatment .... AMPICILLIN, ANTIBIOTICS
symptom ..... FEVER, MALAISE, HEADACHE
"Typhoid Mary" .... (MARY) MALLON
occupation of .... COOK
typhoon .... WIND, STORM, CYCLONE, TORNADO, HURRICANE
typhus carrier .... FLEA, LOUSE
cause of .... RICKETTSIA(E)
type of .... SCRUB, MURINE, ENDEMIC
typical .... IDEAL, MODEL, USUAL, NORMAL, GENERAL, REGULAR, SYMBOLIC, CHARACTERISTIC
typify .... EMBODY, EXEMPLIFY, SYMBOLIZE
typographer .... PRINTER
typographical error .... ERRATUM
Tyr .... TIU

father of .... ODIN
tyramine source .... ERGOT, MISTLETOE
tyrannical .... CRUEL, HARSH, UNJUST, DESPOTIC, OPPRESSIVE
tyrannize .... OPPRESS, DOMINEER
tyrannosaurus .... DINOSAUR
tyranny .... RIGOR, CRUELTY, SEVERITY, AUTOCRACY, DESPOTISM, OPPRESSION, TOTALITARIANISM
tyrant .... CZAR, TSAR, DESPOT, PHARAOH, USURPER, AUTOCRAT, DICTATOR, OPPRESSOR
Tyre, king of .... HIRAM
princess of .... DIDO
renowned export of .... PURPLE-DYE
tyro .... PUPIL, NOVICE, AMATEUR, LEARNER, BEGINNER, NEOPHYTE
Tyrol topography .... ALPS
Tyrolean city ...... ZAMS, PFUNDS, LANDECK, INNSBRUCK
hat wearer .... PINOCCHIO
mountains .... OTZTAL ALPS
pass .... BRENNER
patriot .... HOFER
refrain/song .... YODEL
river .... INN, ISAR(CO)
singer .... YOD(E)LER
tzar .... CZAR, TSAR, RULER, TYRANT
tzigane .... GYPSY

U

U-boat .... SUBMARINE
boat locator .... SONAR
Greek .... UPSILON
in chemistry .... URANIUM
in mathematics ...... UNIVERSE
letter .... EU
_____ of the U.N. .... THANT
-shaped bone .... HYOID
-shaped frame .... OXBOW
-turn, describing a .... HAIRPIN
Ubangi tributary .... UELE
Ubermensch .... OVERMAN, SUPERMAN
ubication .... LOCATION
ubiety .... LOCATION, POSITION, WHERENESS
ubique .... EVERYWHERE
ubiquitous .... PERVASIVE, INESCAPABLE, OMNIPRESENT

ubiquity .... OMNIPRESENCE
Ucayali tributary ...... APURIMAC
udder .... BAG, MAMMA
inflammation .... GARGET
product .... MILK
protuberance .... TEAT, NIPPLE
udometer .... RAIN GAUGE
Uffizi Museum site ... FLORENCE
UFO, part of ...... UNIDENTIFIED, FLYING, OBJECT
Uganda capital .... KAMPALA
capital, former .... ENTEBBE
city/town .... ARUA, GULU, MOYO, JINJA, MBALE, MASAKA, MOROTI, SOROTI, TORORO
city on Lake Victoria .... ENTEBBE
dam .... OWEN FALLS

falls .... KABALEGA
islands .... SESE
kingdom .... BUGANDA
lake .... KIOGA, ALBERT, EDWARD, GEORGE, VICTORIA
language .... SOGA, TESO, NYORO, ACHOLI, SWAHILI
monetary unit .... SHILLING
mountain .... ELGON, MARGHERITA
president .... OBOTE, MUSEVENI
range .... VIRUNGA, RUWENZORI
religion .... ISLAM
ugly .... FOUL, VILE, CROSS, NASTY, PLAIN, GRISLY, HOMELY, HORRID, HIDEOUS, OMINOUS, DEFORMED,

GRUESOME, UNGAINLY, DANGEROUS, GROTESQUE, REPULSIVE, UNSIGHTLY

as _____ .... SIN

customer ..... CRANK, DRAGON, GROUCH, HOTHEAD, SOREHEAD

disposition, having .... ORNERY

duckling once .... SWAN

face expression .... MOUE, POUT, FROWN, SCOWL, GLOWER, GRIMACE

figure in a field .... SCARECROW

hopper .... TOAD

humpback/hunchback .... QUASIMODO

make .... MAR, DEFACE, UGLIFY, DISFIGURE

object of fear .... SPECTER

ones .... HAGS, TOADS, WITCHES

savage creature .... CALIBAN

sight .... EYESORE

-tempered .... CROSS, HUFFY, TESTY, BITCHY, CRANKY, PEEVISH, IRRITABLE

Ugudai Khan's father .... GENGHIS KHAN

nephew .... KUBLAI KHAN

uh-huh .... YES

uh-uh .... NOPE

uhlan .... GERMAN, SOLDIER, CAVALRYMAN

weapon of .... LANCE

uintaite ...... ASPHALT, GILSONITE

uitlander .... FOREIGNER

ukase .... DECREE

kin .... IRADE

Ukrainian capital .... KIEV

city/town .... KHARKOB, KHERSON

farmer .... KULAK

holy city .... KIEV

legislature .... RADA

money of account ..... GRIVNA

native .... COSSACK

port .... KHERSON

president .... (LEONID)KRAVCHUK

sea .... BLACK

seaport .... ODESSA

ukulele, for short .... UKE

instrument like .... GUITAR

player .... HAWAIIAN

Ulalume poet .... POE

Ulan Bator .... URGA, KHOTO, KULUN

ulcer ...... SORE, ABSCESS, FISTULA

decubitus .... BEDSORE

discharge .... PUS, ICHOR,

SANIES

in the mouth .... APHTHOUS, CANKER-SORE

site, peptic .... STOMACH, DUODENUM

type of .... MOUTH, PEPTIC, CORNEAL, GASTRIC

venereal .... CHANCRE

ulcerate .... FESTER

ule .... CAUCHO

fluid .... LATEX

ulema .... MUFTI, SCHOLARS

Ullmann, actress LIV

ulmaceous tree .... ELM

ulmus .... ELM

ulna projection ...... OLECRANON

Ulster .... OVERCOAT

lake .... ERNE

ult. .... ULTIMO, ULTIMATE

ulterior .... BEYOND, HIDDEN, LATENT, REMOTE, FARTHER, CONCEALED

motive .... NISUS, DESIGNS

Ultima Thule .... ICELAND

ultimate .... LAST, FINAL, ENDALL, EXTREME, MAXIMUM, PRIMARY, EVENTUAL, FARTHEST

degree .... NTH

slang .... THE MOST

ultimatum .... DEMAND, WARNING, LAST OFFER

words .... OR ELSE

ultra .... EXTREME, RADICAL, EXCESSIVE, SUPERLATIVE

modern ...... FAR-OUT, AVANT-GARDE

nationalistic .... JINGO(ISTIC), CHAUVINIST(IC)

ultramarine .... (BLUE)PIGMENT

ultrasonic .... FASTER-THAN-SOUND

ulu .... KNIFE

ululant .... HOWLING

ululate .... BAY, CRY, HOWL, PULE, MEWL, WAIL, WEEP, LAMENT

Ulyanov, Vladimir .... LENIN

Ulysses .... ODYSSEUS

author of .... JOYCE

country/kingdom of .... ITHACA

father of .... LAERTES

name given to Cyclops .... NOMAN

son of .... TELEMACHUS

wife of .... PENELOPE

umbelliferous plant .... CARROT, PARSLEY

umber .... SHADE, SHADOW, PIGMENT, GRAYLING

bird .... UMBRETTE

umbilical cord .... FUNICULUS

umbilicus .... NAVEL

umbles .... ENTRAILS

umbo .... BEAK, BOSS, KNOB

umbra .... SHADE, SHADOW

umbrage .... HUFF, PIQUE, SHADOW, FOLIAGE, OFFENSE, RESENTMENT

umbrella .... GAMP, COVER, CHATTA, PARASOL, (SUN)SHADE

cloth for .... GLORIA

like flower .... UMBEL

like fungus .... MUSHROOM

of leaves .... TALIPOT

part .... RIB

style .... BUBBLE

thing like .... CANOPY, (PARA)CHUTE

tree .... MAGNOLIA

umbrette .... UMBER, HAMMERHEAD

Umbria town .... ASSISI

umiak .... CANOE, KAYAK

umlaut .... DIERESIS

in linguistics .... MUTATION

umpire .... UMP, JUDGE, ARBITER, DAYSMAN, REFEREE

UN adopted official language .... ARABIC, FRENCH, CHINESE, ENGLISH, RUSSIAN, SPANISH

agency .... FAO, IDA, WHO, GATT, ICAO, UNRRA, UNESCO

goal .... PEACE

president .... ARCE, MAZA, SLIM, EVATT, MALIK, MUNRO, NERVO, SPAAK, ARANHA, PANDIT, ROMULO, MANESCU

secretary-general .... (U)THANT, DE CUELLAR, (TRYGVE)LIE, BOUTROS-GHALI, (DAG)HAMMARSKJOLD

workers' org. .... ILO

una .... CATBOAT

unabashed .... COOL, BRAZEN

unable .... UNFIT, INCAPABLE

to act: sl. ...... OVER A BARREL

unaccented .... ATONIC, STRESSLESS

vowel sound .... SCHWA

unacceptable .... UNSUITABLE, INADMISSIBLE

unaccompanied .... SOLO, ALONE, SOLITARY, UNESCORTED

unaccustomed .... NEW, RARE

unadorned .... BALD, BARE, NAKED, PLAIN, STARK, SIMPLE

unadulterated .... NEAT, PURE, TRUE, GENUINE

unaffected .... NAIVE, PLAIN,

SIMPLE, ARTLESS, NATURAL, SINCERE, UNMOVED
unaided .... ALONE
Unalaskan .... ALEUT
unalloyed .... PURE
unanimity .... ACCORD, ONE-VOICE
unanimous .... SOLID
opinion .... CONSENSUS
unanimously .... AS ONE MAN
unapproachable .... COLD, ALOOF, DISTANT, INACCESSIBLE
unarmed .... WEAPONLESS, DEFENSELESS
unaspirated consonant .... LENE
unassuming .... SHY, MEEK, MODEST, NATURAL, RESERVED, RETIRING
unattached .... FREE, (A)LONE, LOOSE, SINGLE, VAGILE, INDEPENDENT
unau .... SLOTH
unauthorized .... ILLEGAL
departure .... FRENCH LEAVE
unavailing .... IDLE, VAIN, FUTILE, USELESS
unavoidable .... CERTAIN, INEVITABLE
unaware .... IGNORANT
unawares, take .... SURPRISE
unbalanced .... MAD, UNEVEN, DERANGED, LOPSIDED
unbearable .... ODIOUS
unbecoming .... UGLY, IMPROPER, ILL-SUITED, INDECOROUS
unbelievable .... FAR-FETCHED, INCREDIBLE
unbeliever .... PAGAN, ATHEIST, DOUBTER, HERETIC, INFIDEL, SKEPTIC, AGNOSTIC, MISCREANT
unbelieving .... INCREDULOUS
unbend .... THAW, RELAX, YIELD, RELENT, STRAIGHTEN
unbending ...... SET, FIRM, RIGID, ADAMANT, RESOLUTE
unbiased .... FAIR, JUST, IMPARTIAL, OBJECTIVE
unbleached .... ECRU
muslin .... MANTA
wool fabric .... BEIGE
unblemished .... CLEAN, FLAWLESS, SPOTLESS, STAINLESS
unblessed .... UNHAPPY, ACCURSED
unborn young in womb .... FETUS
unbosom .... TELL, REVEAL
unbounded .... INFINITE,

LIMITLESS
unbranded cow .... MAVERICK
unbreakable .... TOUGH, DURABLE
unbridled .... UNRULY, UNCONTROLLED
unbroken .... WILD, WHOLE, INTACT, UNTAMED, CONTINUOUS
unburden .... RID, REVEAL, UNLOAD, LIGHTEN, RELIEVE
unburnt brick .... ADOBE
uncalled-for .... UNDUE, ILL-TIMED, GRATUITOUS, IMPERTINENT, UNNECESSARY
uncanny ...... EERY, UNCO, EERIE, WEIRD, STRANGE, MYSTERIOUS
uncared-for .... NEGLECTED
Uncas' beloved .... CORA
unceasing .... ENDLESS, ETERNAL, PERPETUAL, CONTINUOUS
unceremonious .... CURT, ABRUPT, INFORMAL
uncertain ...... VAGUE, DOUBTFUL, UP IN THE AIR
uncertainty .... DOUBT, DUBIETY, QUESTION MARK
unchanged .... ORIGINAL, PRISTINE
uncharacteristic .... UNREALISTIC
of the upper class .... NONU
unchaste .... LEWD, WANTON
unchecked .... RIFE, LOOSE, RAMPANT
uncheerful .... DREAR
unchristian .... WICKED
unciform .... HOOK-SHAPED
uncinate .... HAMATE, HOOKED, HOOKLIKE
uncivil .... RUDE
uncivilized .... SAVAGE, BARBARIC, PRIMITIVE
unclad .... NUDE, NAKED
uncle ...... EAM, OOM, UNK, UNCS, NUNKS, NUNCLE
American .... SAM
cry .... YIELD, SURRENDER
of fiction .... REMUS
pertaining to ...... AVUNCULAR
Sandy's .... EME
slang .... PAWNBROKER
Uncle Fester's family ...... ADAMS
Remus' author .... HARRIS
Remus' rabbit .... BRE'R
Tom's ____ .... CABIN
Tom's Cabin author ...... (HARRIET BEECHER)STOWE
Tom's Cabin character .... ELIZA, TOPSY, LITTLE EVA, SIMON LEGREE
unclean .... BAD, FOUL, VILE,

DINGY, DIRTY, DUSTY, FETID, FUSTY, GRIMY, MOLDY, MUSTY, NASTY, SOOTY, FILTHY, FROWZY, IMPURE, SMUTTY, SOILED, UNTIDY, LEPROUS, OBSCENE, SQUALID, UNKEMPT
immoral dealings .... CORRUPTION
one: biblical .... LEPER
person .... SLOB
place .... DUMP, SEWER, PIGPEN, (PIG)STY, CESSPOOL
unclear .... DIM, VAGUE
uncloak .... EXPOSE, REVEAL
unclose .... OPE(N), REVEAL
unclothe .... STRIP, DIVEST, UNCOVER, UNDRESS
unclothed partially .... TOPLESS, DISHABILLE
uncluttered .... TIDY
unclouded .... CLEAR
unco .... VERY, NOVEL, WEIRD, NOTABLE, STRANGE, UNCANNY, UNKNOWN
uncoil .... UNWIND
uncoined metal .... BULLION
uncombed .... UNKEMPT
uncomely .... UGLY, PLAIN
uncomfortable .... UNEASY
feeling .... ACHE
uncommitted .... FREE, NEUTRAL, UNPLEDGED
uncommon .... ODD, RARE, EXOTIC, SCARCE, STRANGE, UNUSUAL, ORIGINAL, SINGULAR
thing .... RARITY
uncommunicative .... SILENT, RESERVE, RETICENT, TACITURN, SECRETIVE
uncompromising ...... SET, RIGID, STRICT, ADAMANT, AUSTERE, DETERMINED, INFLEXIBLE
unconcerned .... ALOOF, UNMOVED, DETACHED, INSOUCIANT, INDIFFERENT
unconditional .... FULL, TOTAL, ABSOLUTE, TERMLESS
unconfined .... FREE, LOOSE
unconfirmed news ...... RUMOR, GOSSIP, REPORT, HEARSAY
unconformity .... ODDITY, ECCENTRICITY
unconnected .... DETACHED, DISCRETE, SEPARATE, UNRELATED
unconquerable .... INVINCIBLE
unconscionable .... WRONG, UNETHICAL
unconscious .... OUT, ASLEEP,

BLOTTO, UNAWARE, MINDLESS, UNWITTING

state .... COMA, SWOON, TRANCE, SYNCOPE, HYPNOSIS, NARCOSIS

unconstitutional .... UNFAIR, UNJUST, ILLEGAL

unconstrained ...... FREE, DEGAGE

uncontrolled .... WILD, UNRULY

unconventional .... OUTRE, UNUSUAL, BOHEMIAN, INFORMAL, OUT-OF-STEP

one .... REBEL

uncooked .... RAW

uncooperative .... CONTRARY, DIFFICULT, RELUCTANT

uncos .... NEWS

uncouth .... RUDE, CRUDE, GAWKY, CLUMSY, GAUCHE, SAVAGE, VULGAR, AWKWARD, BOORISH, AGRESTIC, UNREFINED

person .... CAD, OAF, BOOR, GAWK, LOUT, CHURL, YOKEL, CODGER, RUSTIC, BUM(P)KIN

variant .... UNCOS

uncover .... BARE, OPEN, DENUDE, EXPOSE, REVEAL

hat .... DOFF

uncovered .... BARE, NUDE, NAKED, EXPOSED, DISCOVERED

unction .... OIL, UNGUENT, OINTMENT

give extreme .... ANELE

unctuous .... OILY, BLAND, SLEEK, SOAPY, SUAVE, GREASY, SMOOTH, PINGUID, PLASTIC

as of soil .... RICH

substance .... CERATE, GREASE, LANOLIN, UNGUENT, OINTMENT

uncultivated .... WILD, COARSE, FALLOW, VIRGIN, UNTILLED, UNREFINED, ILLITERATE

uncultured .... RUDE, COARSE, BOORISH, ILL-BRED, UNCOUTH, UNREFINED, UNPOLISHED

uncurl .... STRAIGHTEN

und so weiter .... ETC, ET CETERA

undaunted ...... BOLD, FEARLESS, INTREPID, COURAGEOUS, UNDISMAYED

unde, in heraldry .... WAVY

undecided .... PENDENT, PENDING, DOUBTFUL, HESITANT, WAVERING, UNCERTAIN, IRRESOLUTE, UP IN THE AIR

undefeated .... CHAMPION, UNBEATEN

undefiled .... PURE, CHASTE

undemonstrative .... CALM, RESERVED

undeniable .... REAL, TRUE, FACTUAL, IRREFUTABLE

undeniably .... INDEED

under .... BELOW, LOWER, NETHER, (BE)NEATH

average .... INFERIOR

no circumstances ..... NOWAY, NOWISE

obligation ...... BOUND, OWING, INDEBTED

par .... ILL, SICK

poetic .... NEATH

prefix .... HYP, SUB

the influence .... STONED

the power of another .... SUBORDINATE

the Washington bridges .... POTOMAC RIVER

underage ...... MINOR, IMMATURE

underbrush .... BOSCAGE, THICKET

undercooked .... RARE

undercover ...... MASKED, SECRET, INCOGNITO

person .... SPY, SLEUTH, DETECTIVE

undercroft .... CRYPT

undercurrent .... INNUENDO

underdog .... LOSER, ALSO-RAN

victory of .... UPSET

underdone .... RARE

underestimate .... BELITTLE, MINIMIZE, DEPRECATE

undergarment .... SLIP, SHIRT, TEDDY, CHEMISE

man's .... SINGLET

undergo .... BEAR, STAND, ENDURE, SUFFER, EXPERIENCE

undergraduate .... FROSH, PLEBE, JUNIOR, FRESHMAN, SOPHOMORE

underground .... HIDDEN, SECRET

being .... DWARF, GNOME, TROLL

burial place .... CRYPT, CATACOMB

drain .... SEWER

fighter ..... EDES, ELAS, MAQUI, PARTISAN

foundation .... ROOTAGE

fungus .... TRUFFLE, EARTHNUT, TUCKAHOE

organization .... MAFIA

passage .... SAP, TUBE, BURROW, TUNNEL

railway .... TUBE, METRO, SUBWAY

resident .... DWARF, GNOME, TROLL

stem .... ONION, SALEP, STOCK, TUBER, MANIOC, POTATO, CASSAVA, RHIZOME

volunteer soldier .... GUER(R)ILLA

worker .... MINER, SANDHOG

underhand .... SLY, COVERT, SECRET, CLANDESTINE

underhanded .... SLY, TRICKY, DEVIOUS, FURTIVE, DECEITFUL, FRAUDULENT

underline .... MARK, STRESS, EMPHASIZE, UNDERSCORE

underling .... AIDE, SLAVE, FLUNKY, ASSISTANT, SUBALTERN, SUBORDINATE

underlying .... BASIC, ESSENTIAL, FUNDAMENTAL

principle .... ELIXIR

undermine .... SAP, ERODE, THWART, WEAKEN, SUBVERT, WEAR AWAY, FRUSTRATE

undernourish .... FAMISH, STARVE

undernourished .... UNFED, EMACIATED

underpin .... PROP

underpinning .... SUPPORT

colloquial .... LEGS

underrate .... BELITTLE

underscore ...... ACCENT, STRESS, EMPHASIZE, UNDERLINE

undersea craft .... UBOAT, SUBMARINE

explorer .... PICARD

undershirt .... VEST, JERSEY, SKIVVY, SINGLET

undersigned, the .... WRITER

undersized .... RUNTY, SMALL, SCRUBBY

being .... RUNT, DWARF, PIGMY

underskirt .... PETTICOAT

undersong .... REFRAIN

understand ...... KEN, SEE, KNOW, CATCH, GRASP, INFER, ASSUME, GATHER, DISCERN, REALIZE, CONSTRUE, PERCEIVE, APPREHEND, INTERPRET, APPRECIATE, COMPREHEND

colloquial .... DIG, GET, SAVVY

thoroughly .... FATHOM

understanding ...... CODE, NOUS, SENSE, ACCORD, INSIGHT, AGREEMENT, KNOWLEDGE, OPEN-MINDED

between nations, etc. .... ENTENTE

understate .... PLAY DOWN

understood .... TACIT, AGREED, SENSED, ASSUMED, IMPLIED,

IMPLICIT, PRESUMED

readily .... CLEAR, LUCID, LUCULENT

understrapper .... UNDERLING, SUBORDINATE

understudy .... STAND-IN, ALTERNATE, APPRENTICE, SUBSTITUTE

undertake .... TRY, OFFER, ASSUME, PLEDGE, TACKLE, ATTEMPT, PROMISE, CONTRACT, VOLUNTEER

undertaker .... EMBALMER, MORTICIAN

job of .... PALL-BEARING

undertaking .... JOB, TASK, CAPER, PROJECT, PROMISE, VENTURE, BUSINESS, ENDEAVOR, GUARANTEE, ENTERPRISE

undertow .... RIPTIDE

underwater .... SUNKEN, SUBMARINE, SUBMERGED

apparatus .... SCUBA, CAISSON, SNORKEL, BATHYSCAPH, BATHYSPHERE

craft .... UBOAT, PIGBOAT, SUBMARINE

eye of sort .... HYDROSCOPE

ledge .... REEF

plants .... BENTHOS

prefix .... HYP(O)

projectile .... TORPEDO

sound detection device .... SOFAR, SONAR

swimmer .... FROGMAN, (SKIN)DIVER, SNORK(E)LER

worker .... SANDHOG

underwear .... BRA, SLIP, PANTY, BRIEFS, CORSET, GIRDLE, SCANTY, SHORTS, UNDIES, DRAWERS, FLANNELS, LINGERIE, BRASSIERE

underworld .... HEL, EARTH, HADES, SHEOL, EREBUS, GANGLAND, ANTIPODES

character .... CRIMINAL, GANGSTER

king .... YAMA

queen .... HEL

underwrite ...... ASSUME, INSURE, AGREE(TO), FINANCE, SUBSCRIBE

slang .... BANKROLL

underwriter .... INSURER, SPONSOR, INSURANCE MAN

undeserving .... INDIGN, UNWORTHY

undesirable .... DISLIKED, UNWANTED, OBJECTIONABLE

person ..... BORE, BOOR, LOUT,

FELON, LEPER, PARIAH, OUTCAST, DERELICT

person: biblical .... HAGAR, ISHMAEL

undeveloped .... LATENT

quality .... POTENTIAL

undies .... PANTIES, LINGERIE, UNDERWEAR

undignified ...... MEAN, ILL-BRED, DEGRADING

undiluted .... NEAT, PURE, SHEER, STRAIGHT

undiminished .... WHOLE, UNABATED, UNSHAKEN, UNREDUCED

undine ...... NIX, GNOME, NYMPH, SYLPH, KELPIE, SEAMAID

undisciplined ...... WILD, SAVAGE, CHAOTIC, LAWLESS

undiscovered .... UNDETECTED

undisguised .... OPEN, TRUE, FRANK, OVERT, CANDID

undisputed .... ACCEPTED, UNCONTESTED, UNQUESTIONED

undisturbed .... CALM, COOL, QUIET

undivided .... ONE, WHOLE, ENTIRE, INTACT, SINGLE, UNITED

undo .... OPEN, UNTIE, CANCEL, UNFASTEN

a breach .... REUNIFY

undoer .... NEMESIS

undoing .... RUIN, DEFEAT, DOWNFALL

undomesticated .... WILD, FERAL, UNTAMED

undone ...... RUINED, ABANDONED, NEGLECTED, UNFINISHED

undoubtedly .... SURELY, CERTAINLY, ADMITTEDLY

undraped .... BARE, NUDE

undress .... STRIP, DISROBE, DISARRAY

slang .... PEEL

stage of .... DISHABILLE

undressed skin .... KIP, PELT

Undset, Norwegian novelist .... SIGRID

undue .... UNJUST, EXTREME, IMPROPER, EXCESSIVE, INORDINATE

undulant fever ...... BRUCELLOSIS

undulate .... RISE, ROLL, WAVE, SURGE, SWELL, BILLOW, RIPPLE

undulating .... WAVY

object .... WAVE, WORM, SNAKE, RIPPLE

undulation .... WAVE, HEAVE,

SURGE, RIPPLE, PULSATION

unduly .... UNJUSTLY, IMPROPERLY, EXCESSIVELY, UNREASONABLY

undyed .... PLAIN, TINTLESS

undying .... ABIDING, ETERNAL, IMMORTAL, UNENDING, EVERLASTING

unearth .... DIG UP, EXHUME, EXPOSE, UPROOT, DISCLOSE, DISCOVER

unearthly .... EERIE, WEIRD, GHOSTLY, UNCANNY, UNUSUAL

sight .... UFO

uneasiness .... FEAR, WORRY, UNREST, ANXIETY, MALAISE, DISCOMFORT

slang .... HEEBIE-JEEBIES

uneasy .... JUMPY, ANXIOUS, FEARFUL, FIDGETY, JITTERY, FRETFUL, NERVOUS, RESTIVE, RESTLESS, CONCERNED, DISTURBED, DISQUIETED

feeling .... MALAISE

uneducated .... IGNORANT, UNLEARNED, ILLITERATE, UNLETTERED

unemotional .... CALM, COOL, NUMB, APATHETIC, UNFEELING

unemployed .... FREE, IDLE, JOBLESS, AVAILABLE

unending .... ETERNAL, CEASELESS, PERPETUAL, CONTINUOUS

unenlightened .... BENIGHTED

unenthusiastic .... COLD, COOL, UNEAGER, LISTLESS, RELUCTANT, INDIFFERENT

unequal .... ROUGH, UNEVEN, UNFAIR, UNLIKE, IRREGULAR, INADEQUATE, UNBALANCED

angled .... SCALENE

combining form .... ANISO

unequalled .... SUPREME, PEERLESS, MATCHLESS, NONPAREIL

unequitable .... UNJUST

unequivocal .... CLEAR, PLAIN, CANDID, DEFINITE

unerring .... SURE, EXACT, CERTAIN, ACCURATE, CONSTANT

unescorted .... SOLO, ALONE

unessential .... NEEDLESS, DISPENSABLE

uneven .... ODD, EROSE, LUMPY, ROUGH, HUBBLY, RAGGED, RUGGED, SPOTTY, CROOKED, UNEQUAL, IRREGULAR

contest .... LOPSIDED

uneventful .... DULL, HUMDRUM
unexcited .... UNRUFFLED
unexciting .... DULL, TAME,
    VAPID, BORING, LIFELESS
unexpected .... ABRUPT, SUDDEN,
    UNFORESEEN
astonishment .... SURPRISE
attack .... AMBUSH
candidate .... DARK HORSE
defeat .... UPSET
event .... ACCIDENT
gain .... WINDFALL
meeting .... ENCOUNTER
source of delight .... TREAT
unexploded .... LIVE
unexpressive .... DULL, BLAND
unfading .... FAST
flower .... AMARANTH,
    EVERLASTING
unfailing .... SURE, CERTAIN,
    REGULAR, CONSTANT,
    STEADFAST
unfair ...... FOUL, BIASED, UNJUST,
    PARTIAL, DISHONEST,
    PREJUDICED
unfaithful .... FICKLE, UNTRUE,
    CHEATING, DISLOYAL
unfamiliar .... NEW, STRANGE
unfasten .... OPEN, UNDO,
    DISCONNECT
poetic .... OPE
unfavorable .... BAD, ILL,
    ADVERSE, CONTRARY,
    INIMICAL, NEGATIVE
weather, describing
    .... INCLEMENT
unfeasible .... IMPRACTICAL
unfeeling .... NUMB, CRUEL,
    STONY, CALLOUS, HEARTLESS,
    INSENSATE, INSENSIBLE,
    HARD(-HEARTED)
unfeigned .... DIRECT, HONEST,
    UNDISGUISED
unfermented grape juice
    .... STUM
unfettered .... LOOSE, UNCHAINED
unfinished .... CRUDE, ROUGH,
    SKETCHY, INCOMPLETE
unfit .... INAPT, INEPT, UNABLE,
    UNSUITED
to eat .... INEDIBLE
unfix .... DETACH, LOOSEN
unflappable .... CALM, FIRM
unflattering .... BLUNT, FRANK,
    CANDID, DEROGATORY
unflawed .... IDEAL
unfledged .... CALLOW
bird .... EYAS, NESTLING
unflinching ...... FIRM, RESOLUTE,
    STEADFAST
unfold .... OPEN, EVOLVE, EXPOSE,

REVEAL, SPREAD, UNFURL,
UNROLL, DEVELOP, DISCLOSE
in a verse .... OPE
unforeseen .... SUDDEN,
    UNEXPECTED, OUT-OF-THE-
    BLUE
unforgettable .... MEMORABLE
unforgiving .... VENGEFUL
unfortunate .... HAPLESS,
    UNLUCKY, ILL-STARRED
unfounded .... IDLE, BASELESS,
    GROUNDLESS
unfrequented .... LONELY,
    SOLITARY
unfriendly .... ILL, COLD,
    HOSTILE, INIMICAL,
    UNGENIAL, UNSOCIAL,
    ANTAGONISTIC
unfrock .... OUST, DEPOSE
unfruitful .... BARREN, STERILE,
    INFERTILE
unfulfilled .... UNATTAINED,
    UNSATISFIED
unfurl .... WAVE, SPREAD,
    UNFOLD, UNROLL, DISPLAY
ungainly .... UGLY, GAWKY,
    CLUMSY, AWKWARD
ungenerous .... STINGY
unglorified .... UNSUNG
unglued .... UPSET
ungodly .... BAD, PAGAN,
    UNHOLY, WICKED, IMPIOUS,
    PROFANE, SATANIC, DREADFUL
ungovernable ...... WILD, UNRULY,
    HEADSTRONG, REBELLIOUS
ungracious .... RUDE, UNCIVIL,
    IMPOLITE, UNFRIENDLY
ungrateful .... INGRATE
ungual growth ...... CLAW, HOOF,
    NAIL, TALON
unguarded .... CARELESS,
    UNDEFENDED, THOUGHTLESS
unguent .... BALM, SALVE,
    CHRISM, POMADE, OINTMENT
unguis .... CLAW, HOOF, NAIL,
    TALON, UNGULA
ungula .... CLAW, HOOF, NAIL,
    TALON, UNGUIS
ungulate ...... COW, HORSE, TAPIR,
    CATTLE, HOOFED
unhappy ...... SAD, BLUE, DISMAL,
    GLOOMY, MOROSE, JOYLESS,
    WRETCHED, MISERABLE
unharmed .... SAFE
unhealthy .... FRAIL, AILING,
    MORBID, SICKLY, OMINOUS
unheard-of .... UNBELIEVABLE
unhidden .... OPEN, FOUND,
    EXPOSED
unhinge .... DERANGE
unhinged .... DAFT, CRAZY

unhitch .... DETACH, RELEASE,
    UNFASTEN
unholy .... WICKED, IMPIOUS,
    PROFANE, UNGODLY
unhorse .... SPILL, UPSET,
    OVERTHROW
unhurried .... EASY
unicellular animal .... AM(O)EBA,
    PROTOZOAN
unicorn .... LIN, REEM,
    MONOCERO
fish .... UNIE
whale .... NARWHAL
unidentified flying object
    .... UFO
uniform .... EVEN, HABIT, OUTFIT,
    STABLE, STEADY, EQUABLE,
    STANDARD, UNVARYING,
    CONSISTENT
servant's .... LIVERY
shoulder ornament
    .... EPAULET(TE)
unify .... JOIN, WELD, UNITE,
    COMBINE, INTEGRATE,
    CONSOLIDATE
unilateral .... ONE-SIDED
unimpeachable .... CLEAN,
    INNOCENT, RELIABLE,
    BLAMELESS
unimportant .... PETTY, PUERILE,
    TRIVIAL, WORTHLESS,
    IMMATERIAL
item .... NOTION
slang .... PUNK
things .... TRIVIA
uninformed .... IN-THE-DARK
uninhabited .... DESOLATE,
    TENANTLESS
uninhibited ...... FREE, NATURAL,
    UNRESERVED, UNSUPPRESSED
unintelligible .... MUMBLED,
    INCOHERENT, MEANINGLESS
chatter .... GIBBER(ISH)
handwriting ...... CACOGRAPHY
language .... JARGON, PIDGIN
unintentional .... FORCED,
    UNPLANNED, UNWITTING,
    ACCIDENTAL, INADVERTENT
uninterested .... BORED
uninteresting .... DRY, DULL
uninterrupted .... CONSTANT,
    UNBROKEN, CONTINUOUS
unintimidated .... UNCOWED
uninvited .... UNASKED,
    UNWANTED, UNWELCOME
person in a party .... GATE-
    CRASHER
uninvolved .... FREE, NEUTRAL
union .... UNITY, FUSION, LEAGUE,
    MERGER, CONCORD, LIAISON,
    ONE(NESS), ALLIANCE,

JUNCTION, MARRIAGE, COALITION, CONNECTION, COMBINATION

business .... CARTEL, SYNDICATE

collection .... DUES

dues deduction ...... CHECKOFF

from birth .... CONNATION

jack .... FLAG

labor .... ARTEL

member .... FELLOW, CARDHOLDER

merchants' .... HANSE

of nations, states ..... LEAGUE, FEDERATION

of political intriguers .... CABAL, JUNTA

of South Africa town .... MAFEKING

political ...... BLOC, COALITION

soldier .... YANKEE

trade .... GUILD

unionist .... TORY, JOINER, FEDERALIST, CONSERVATIVE

unique .... LONE, ONLY, RARE, SOLE, SINGLE, SPECIAL, UNUSUAL, PECULIAR, SINGULAR, MATCHLESS, UNEQUALED

altogether .... SUIGENERIS

person .... ONER

unisexual .... DICLINOUS, DIOECIOUS

unison ...... CONCORD, HARMONY, AGREEMENT, UNANIMITY

utter in .... CHORUS

Unisphere, part of .... ASIA

unit .... ACE, ONE, ATOM, ITEM, DIGIT, MONAD, PIECE, MODULE, SINGLE, INTEGER, STANDARD

Army Advance .... VAN

caloric .... THERM

capacitance .... FARAD

charge .... RATE

electrical .... REL, VOLT, WATT, AMPERE

electro-magnetic .... FARAD

factor .... GENE

for measure of motor power .... HORSEPOWER

for measure of thermonuclear weapon power .... KILOTON

in medicine .... DOSE, DOSAGE

of acceleration .... GAL

astronomical distance .... PARSEC, SECPAR, LIGHT YEAR

brightness, c g s .... LAMBERT

capacity .... PINT, LITRE, QUART, GALLON, KILOBYTE, (KILO)LITER

conductance .... MHO

distance .... ROD, MILE, SPAN, LEAGUE, FURLONG, KILOMETER

dry measure ..... PECK, PINT, QUART, BUSHEL

electric power .... KILOWATT

electrical resistance .... OHM

energy .... ERG, ERGON, JOULE, KILERG

fluidity .... RHE

force .... OD, DENE, DYNE

heat .... THERM, CALORIE

illumination .... PHOT

instruction .... LESSON

length ..... FOOT, INCH, MILE, YARD, CUBIT, DIGIT, METER, METRE, MICRON, ANGSTROM, KILOMETER

length of a stride .... PACE

light .... LUX, LUMEN

loudness .... SONE

luminous intensity .... NIT

magnetic intensity .... OERSTED

magnetism .... GAUSS

measure for angles .... DEGREE

metric measure .... ARE, METER, HECTARE, CENTIARE

metrical time .... MORA

parliament follower .... ARIAN

pressure .... TORR, BARAD, BARYE, KILOBAR

quantity of electricity .... FARADAY

radioactivity .... CURIE

reluctance .... REL

speed .... KNOT

value .... POINT

verse .... QUATRAIN

volume .... CUBIC-FEET, CUBIC-INCH, CUBIC-YARD, CUBIC-METER, CUBIC-CENTIMETER

weight ..... KEG, TON, DRAM, GRAM, KEEL, CARAT, MAUND, OUNCE, POUND, BUSHEL, KILO(GRAM), MILLIGRAM

weight, smallest .... GRAIN

work .... ERG(ON), JOULE, KILERG, KILOGRAMMETER

ultimate .... MONAD

wire .... MIL

unite .... MIX, ONE, WED, FUSE, JOIN, WELD, BLEND, MARRY,

MERGE, PIECE, COMBINE, COALESCE, FEDERATE

united .... ATONE

United Arab Republic country .... EGYPT, SYRIA

Kingdom national flag .... UNION JACK

Kingdom, part of .... IRELAND, GREAT BRITAIN

Nations (see **UN**)

States (see **US/American**)

unity ...... PEACE, UNION, ACCORD, FUSION, UNISON, CONCORD, HARMONY, ONENESS, COHERENCE, SOLIDARITY

univalent .... SINGLE, UNPAIRED

univalve .... SNAIL, MOLLUSK

shell's edge .... LABRUM

universal .... ASTRAL, COSMIC, ENTIRE, GLOBAL, EARTHLY, GENERAL, GENERIC, CATHOLIC, PANDEMIC, ECUMENIC(AL)

language .... IDO, VOLAPUK, ESPERANTO

remedy .... AZOTH

ruler, 12th century .... GENGHIS KHAN

universe .... EARTH, WORLD, COSMOS, CREATION, MACROCOSM

of the .... VAST, COSMIC

university .... ACADEMY, INSTITUTE

business agent .... SYNDIC

composition of .... SCHOOLS, COLLEGES

for clergy .... SEMINARY

grounds .... CAMPUS

group .... SORORITY, FRAT(ERNITY)

lecturer .... PRELECTOR

official .... DEAN, BEADLE, BURSAR, RECTOR, REGENT, PROCTOR, PROVOST, TRUSTEE, REGISTRAR

professorship .... CHAIR

program of studies .... CURRICULUM

rank .... DEGREE

teacher .... PROFESSOR, INSTRUCTOR

team .... VARSITY

unjust .... UNDUE, BIASED, UNFAIR, PARTIAL

unjustly .... UNDULY

unkempt .... CRUDE, MESSY, RATTY, ROUGH, SEEDY, SHABBY, SHAGGY, UNTIDY, SLOVENLY, UNCOMBED

unkind .... CRUEL, HARSH,

BRUTAL, SEVERE, INHUMAN

unknown .... UNCO, OBSCURE, STRANGE, NAMELESS, INCOGNITO

person .... ANONYM, JANE DOE, JOHN DOE

writer, describing an
.... ANONYMOUS

Unknown Soldier's Tomb inscription ending: Known But to ____ .... GOD

unlace .... UNTIE, LOOSEN, UNFASTEN

unlatch .... OPEN

unlawful ...... CROOKED, ILLEGAL, ILLICIT, CRIMINAL

act .... CRIME

goods/trade .... CONTRABAND

hunting .... POACHING

importation .... SMUGGLING

intrusion .... TRESPASS, ENCROACHMENT

liquor .... BOOTLEG

seizure of power
.... USURPATION

unlearned .... IGNORANT, ILLITERATE

unleash .... RELEASE, SET FREE, (UN)LOOSE, UNSHACKLE

unleavened .... AZYMOUS

unless .... BUT, SAVE, EXCEPT, BARRING

unlettered .... IGNORANT, ILLITERATE, UNEDUCATED

unlike .... DISTINCT, DIFFERENT, DISSIMILAR

unlikely .... FAR-FETCHED

unlimited .... FULL, VAST, ABSOLUTE, INFINITE, BOUNDLESS

limit .... SKY

unload .... RID, DUMP, EMPTY, REMOVE, OFFLOAD, UNBURDEN

unlock ...... OPEN, UNDO, REVEAL, UNBOLT

unloose .... UNDO, UNTIE, RELEASE, UNFASTEN

unlucky .... DOOMED, HAPLESS, HOPELESS, ILL-FATED, ILL-STARRED, UNFORTUNATE

fighters ...... POWS, PRISONERS-OF-WAR

gem, believed to be ...... OPAL

unmake .... RUIN, DESTROY

unman .... WEAKEN, UNNERVE, CASTRATE, ENERVATE

unmanageable .... UNRULY

unmanly .... EFFEMINATE

unmannerly ...... RUDE, CADDISH, IMPOLITE, DISCOURTEOUS

unmarried .... UNWED, SINGLE, DIVORCED

in law .... SOLE

man ...... BACHELOR, CELIBATE

state .... CELIBACY, MAIDENHOOD

woman ...... MAIDEN, SPINSTER

unmask .... REVEAL, DISCLOSE

unmentionables ...... UNDERWEAR

unmerciful .... COLD-BLOODED, HARD-HEARTED

unmistakable ...... CLEAR, OVERT, PLAIN, EVIDENT, OBVIOUS, APPARENT

unmitigated .... SHEER, UTTER, ARRANT

unmixed drink .... NEAT

unmoved .... FIRM, INSENSATE, UNAFFECTED, UNCONVINCED

unnatural .... STAGY, ABNORMAL, AFFECTED, ARTIFICIAL

unnecessary .... NEEDLESS, SUPERFLOUS

unnerve .... SHAKE, SHOCK, UNMAN, RATTLE, UNHINGE

unobtrusive .... SHY, TIMID, MODEST

unoccupied .... IDLE, EMPTY, VACANT

unofficial .... TENTATIVE

unorganized .... DISORDERLY

unorthodox .... HERETICAL, NONCONFORMIST

unowing .... SOLVENT

unpaid .... DUE, OWING

unpaired .... ODD, SINGLE, UNIVALENT

unpalatable .... INSIPID, INEDIBLE, UNSAVORY, TASTELESS

unperturbed .... SERENE

unpleasant .... BAD, MESSY, NASTY, SURLY, NOISOME, UNSAVORY, OFFENSIVE, SICKENING, UNFRIENDLY, DISAGREEABLE

unpleasantness .... SPAT, QUARREL

unplowed ...... FALLOW, UNTILLED

unpolished .... RAW, CRUDE, COARSE, AGRESTIC

unpopular .... DISLIKED

unprecedented ...... NEW, NOVEL

unpredictable .... CASUAL, FICKLE, CAPRICIOUS

unprejudiced .... FAIR, UNBIASED, IMPARTIAL

unpremeditated ...... IMPROMPTU, IMPULSIVE, SPONTANEOUS

unprepared .... COLD, UNFIT, UNREADY, HAPHAZARD, SURPRISED

unpressed .... BAGGY, SEEDY, RUMPLED

unpretentious .... MODEST

unprincipled .... EVIL, WICKED, IMMORAL, UNSCRUPULOUS

unprintable usually .... OBSCENE, OBSCENITY, VULGAR(ITY)

unproductive .... BARREN, STERILE, IMPOTENT, INFERTILE

unprofessional ...... AMATEURISH

unprofitable ...... FUTILE, OTIOSE, USELESS, BOOTLESS, WORTHLESS

unpromising .... HOPELESS

unpropitious .... INOPPORTUNE

unqualified .... SHEER, UNFIT, ABSOLUTE, COMPLETE, OUTRIGHT

unquenchable .... ARID, PARCHED, THIRSTY

unquestionable .... SURE, CERTAIN

unravel .... FEAZE, SOLVE, TEASE, UNFOLD, DEVELOP, UNTANGLE

unreadable .... ILLEGIBLE

unreal .... FALSE, FANCIED, FANCIFUL, IMAGINARY, FICTITIOUS

unreasonable ...... INANE, UNDUE, ABSURD, STUBBORN, ILLOGICAL, SENSELESS, IRRATIONAL

unreasoning devotion .... FETISH

unredeemed territory
.... IRREDENTA

unreel .... UNWIND

unrefined .... RAW, RUDE, BRUTE, CRASS, CRUDE, GROSS, COARSE, COMMON, VULGAR, NATURAL

unrelenting .... STERN, ADAMANT, UNYIELDING

unreliable .... UNSURE, FALLIBLE, UNCERTAIN

unremitting .... CHRONIC, ENDLESS, NON-STOP, INCESSANT, PERSISTENT

unrequited .... IGNORED, SCORNED

unreserved .... OUTSPOKEN

unresolved .... UP-IN-THE-AIR

unrest .... FERMENT, DISQUIET, AGITATION, INSURGENCE

unrestrained .... LAX, FREE, LOOSE

unrestraint .... CANDOR

unrestricted .... WIDE-OPEN

unripe .... CRUDE, GREEN, IMMATURE, PREMATURE

unrivaled .... PEERLESS, MATCHLESS, NONPAREIL,

UNEQUALED
unroll .... OPEN, UNFURL, DISPLAY
unroot .... STUB, ERADICATE
unruffled .... CALM, COOL,
POISED, SEDATE, SERENE,
SMOOTH, UNFAZED
unruly .... WILD, BALKY, RESTIVE,
FRACTIOUS, BOISTEROUS,
DISORDERLY, INTRACTABLE
child .... BRAT
hair .... COWLICK
unsafe .... RISKY
unsatisfactory .... FAILING,
WANTING, INADEQUATE
unsavory .... VILE, ACERB, ACRID,
HARSH, NASTY, INSIPID,
OFFENSIVE, REPULSIVE,
TASTELESS, UNPLEASANT
unsay .... DENY, RETRACT,
DISCLAIM
unscathed .... SAFE, UNHARMED
unschooled .... ILLITERATE,
UNEDUCATED
unscientific .... UNTRUE,
UNSOUND, UNPROVED
unscramble .... CRACK, SOLVE,
DECODE, CLEAR UP, UNRAVEL,
DECIPHER, UNTANGLE
unscrupulous .... DISHONEST,
UNETHICAL, UNPRINCIPLED
person .... CHEAT(ER),
SWINDLER
unseal .... OPEN
unseasonable .... UNTIMELY
unseasoned .... RAW, GREEN,
UNVERSED, FLEDGLING
unseat .... OUST, DEPOSE,
UNHORSE, DISLODGE,
DISPLACE
unseemly ...... UNDUE, IMPROPER,
UNFITTING, INDECOROUS,
UNBECOMING
unseen .... INVISIBLE
unselfish .... LIBERAL, GENEROUS,
SELFLESS, ALTRUISTIC
unselfishness .... ALTRUISM,
FAIRNESS, GENEROSITY
unsettle .... UPSET, DISTURB,
DISPLACE
unsettled .... MOOT, SHAKY,
UNPAID, TROUBLED,
UNSTABLE, UNCERTAIN
unsettling ...... JARRING, JOLTING,
UPSETTING
unshaken .... TRUE, FIXED,
STEELY
unshaven .... BEARDED,
WHISKERED
unsheathe .... DRAW, DIVEST
unsightly .... UGLY, MESSY,
UNGAINLY, UNATTRACTIVE

unskilled .... INAPT, INEPT,
CLUMSY, AMATEUR,
AWKWARD, HALF-BAKED
one .... KLUTZ
one at sports .... HACKER
unsmiling .... GRAVE, SOLEMN,
SERIOUS
and grim .... DOUR
unsociable .... SHY, ALOOF,
DISTANT
unsolicited .... VOLUNTARY
unsophisticated .... NAIVE,
SIMPLE, SQUARE, ARTLESS,
INNOCENT, INGENIOUS
unsound .... FAULTY, SICKLY,
ILLOGICAL
unsounded .... MUM, MUTE,
HUSHED
unsparing .... LAVISH, SEVERE,
LIBERAL, PROFUSE
unspeakable .... VILE, WICKED,
SHOCKING
unspoiled .... FRESH,
WHOLE(SOME)
unspoken .... TACIT, SILENT,
UNSAID, IMPLIED
unstable .... FICKLE, LABILE,
ASTATIC, ERRATIC, VARIABLE,
CHANGEABLE, INCONSTANT
unsteady .... SHAKY, INFIRM,
ERRATIC, WOBBLY, UNSTABLE,
WAVERING
unsubstantial .... FLIMSY,
PAPERY, SLIGHT, UNREAL,
IMMATERIAL, INTANGIBLE
unsuccessful .... LICKED,
ABORTIVE, BOOTLESS
unsuitable .... INAPT, UNFIT(TING)
name .... MISNOMER
unsullied .... PURE, CHASTE,
INNOCENT, VIRGIN(AL)
unsung .... IGNORED
unsure ...... DOUBTFUL, IGNORANT
unsurpassed ...... BEST, PEERLESS
unsusceptible .... CONSTANT,
INFLEXIBLE
to disease .... IMMUNE
unsuspecting .... UNAWARE,
TRUSTING
unswayable .... FIRM
unswayed .... UNBIASED,
IMPARTIAL
unsweet .... SOUR, TART, ACERB
unsweetened .... DRY, SEC
unswerving .... FIRM, DIRECT,
STEADY, STRAIGHT
unsymmetrical .... ALOP
unsympathetic ...... COLD, HARD,
UNKIND, OBDURATE,
HEARTLESS, UNCOMPASSIONED
untamed .... WILD, FERAL,

FERINE, SAVAGE, UNRULY
state .... FERITY
untangle .... COMB, (UN)RAVEL,
STRAIGHTEN
untanned hide .... KIP, PELT,
SHAGREEN
untenable .... INDEFENSIBLE
untenanted ...... EMPTY, VACANT,
AVAILABLE
untended .... UNCARED,
NEGLECTED
unterseeboot .... UBOAT,
SUBMARINE
untested .... UNTRIED
unthinkable .... ABSURD, BEYOND
BELIEF
untidy .... DOWDY, MESSY,
MUSSY, SLOPPY, LITTERY,
UNKEMPT, LITTERED,
SLIPSHOD, SLOVENLY
animal .... PIG
person .... SLOB, SLOVEN,
SLATTERN
place .... PIGPEN, (PIG)STY
untie ...... FREE, UNDO, LOOSE(N),
UNBIND
until .... TILL, UNTO, (UP)TO,
BEFORE, PENDING
now .... AS YET
untimely .... LATE, EARLY,
PREMATURE, INOPPORTUNE
unto .... TO, TILL, UNTIL
untold .... LEGION, UNKNOWN,
COUNTLESS, INNUMERABLE,
UNDISCLOSED, INCALCULABLE
untouchable ...... LEPER, EXEMPT,
BRAHMAN, SACRED COW
Untouchables' Eliot .... NESS
untouched .... PURE, VIRGIN,
PRISTINE
untoward .... ADVERSE, PERVERSE,
UNFAVORABLE, UNFORTUNATE
untrained ...... GREEN, UNTAMED,
UNSKILLED
untreated .... RAW, UNPROCESSED
untrue .... FALSE, NOT SO,
WRONG, DISLOYAL,
FAITHLESS, FALSIFIED,
UNFOUNDED, UNFAITHFUL
untruth .... FIB, LIE, FABLE,
LYING, CANARD, FICTION,
FALSEHOOD, MENDACITY
on the witness stand
.... PERJURY
untwine .... (UN)RAVEL
untwist .... FEAZE, (UN)RAVEL,
STRAIGHTEN
unusual .... ODD, RARE, NOVEL,
OUTRE, QUEER, UNIQUE,
ABNORMAL, PECULIAR,
SINGULAR, UNCOMMON

be .... TAKE THE CAKE

unvarnished .... PLAIN, SIMPLE, LITERAL

unvarying .... EVEN

sound .... DRONE, MONOTONE

unveil .... REVEAL, UNMASK, UNCOVER, DISCLOSE

unvoiced .... SURD, MUTED, ELIDED

unwanted fat .... FLAB

unwary .... RASH, UNWISE, CARELESS

unwed .... SINGLE

unwell .... ILL, SICK, AILING

unwholesome .... HARMFUL, NOXIOUS, NOISOME, PECCANT, DISEASED, STINKING, UNHEALTHY, DISTASTEFUL

unwieldy .... BULKY, CLUMSY, AWKWARD, UNGAINLY, PONDEROUS, CUMBERSOME

colloquial .... HULKING

ship .... ARK, HULK

unwilling .... BALKY, LOATH, AVERSE, FORCED, OPPOSED, GRUDGING, RELUCTANT

in days of yore .... NILL

to be photographed
.... CAMERA-SHY

unwind .... RAVEL, RELAX, UNCOIL, UNREEL

unwise .... FOOLISH, UNSOUND, TACTLESS, IMPOLITIC, ILL-ADVISED

unwitting .... BLIND, UNAWARE, INNOCENT, UNCONSCIOUS

unwonted .... RARE, UNUSED, UNUSUAL, UNACCUSTOMED

unworldly .... ASTRAL, SPIRITUAL

unworthy .... INDIGN, WORTHLESS, UNDESERVED, UNDESERVING

of .... BENEATH

unwrinkled .... SMOOTH

unwritten .... BLANK, UNRECORDED

but understood .... TACIT

law .... CUSTOM, TRADITION

unyielding .... PAT, SET, FAST, FIRM, GRIM, HARD, IRON, RIGID, STEELY, ADAMANT, AUSTERE, OBDURATE, STUBBORN

up .... OVER, ABOVE, ALOFT, ARISEN, HIGHER

and about .... ASTIR

-and-coming .... PROMISING

front .... AHEAD

in ____ (aged) .... YEARS

in arms .... ANGRY, IRATE

prefix .... ANA

to ____ (in debt) .... OUR

EARS

-to-the-minute .... RED-HOT

up, ____ (impede) .... GUM

(wroth) .... HET

Upanishad .... ISHA

upas tree poison .... ANTIAR

upbeat ...... ARSIS, BRISK, LIVELY

upbraid .... TWIT, CHIDE, SCOLD, SCORE, ACCUSE, BERATE, REBUKE, REVILE, CENSURE, REPROVE, ADMONISH, REPROACH

upbringing .... BREEDING, TRAINING

upcountry .... INLAND

update .... REVISE, MODERNIZE

Updike novel .... COUPLES, RABBIT REDUX

upend .... UPSET, TOPPLE, OVERTHROW

upgrade .... RAISE, BETTER, IMPROVE

upheaval .... STORM, REVOLT, UNREST, DEBACLE, AGITATION, CONVULSION

uphill .... RISING, DIFFICULT

uphold .... BACK, CONFIRM, SUPPORT, SUSTAIN, ADVOCATE, CHAMPION

upholstery ...... DOSSAL, DOSSEL, GOBELIN

material .... FRISE, SCRIM, LAMPAS, MOHAIR, MOREEN, VELURE, TABARET, VALANCE, VELOUR(S), MOQUETTE

stuffing .... FLOCK

upkeep .... CARE, REPAIR, PENSION, MAINTENANCE

upland .... MESA, PLATEAU

country .... TIBET

plover .... SANDPIPER

uplift .... RAISE, ELEVATE, BRASSIERE

Upolu town/seaport .... APIA

upon .... BY, ON, ATOP, OVER, ABOUT, ABOVE, UP AND ON, AGAINST, THROUGH, REGARDING

oxygen .... EPOXY

upper ...... VAMP, BERTH, HIGHER, SUPERIOR

air .... ETHER, OZONE

Amazon .... MARANON

case .... CAPITAL

class .... ELITE, MONEYED

classman .... JUNIOR, SENIOR

crust .... HIGH SOCIETY

hand .... LEAD, MASTERY, ADVANTAGE

house .... SENATE

limit .... CEILING

Upper Volta capital
.... QUAGADOUGOU

city/town .... PO, LEO, KAYA, PAMA, YAKO, BANFORA, QUAHIGOUYA

language .... LOBI, SAMO, MOSSI, GOUROUNSI

monetary unit .... FRANC

president .... YAMEOGO, LAMIZAME

region .... SUDAN

river .... OTI, COMOE, RED VOLTA, BLACK VOLTA, WHITE VOLTA

uppermost .... FIRST

uppish/uppity .... PROUD, HAUGHTY, ARROGANT, SNOBBISH

one .... SNOOT

upright .... JUST, ERECT, ON END, HONEST, VERTICAL, HONORABLE

colloquial .... STRAIGHT

timber .... GATEPOST

uprise .... REBEL, SWELL, ASCEND

uprising .... COUP, RIOT, (E)MEUTE, MUTINY, PUTSCH, REVOLT, REBELLION

1794 tax .... WHISKY REBELLION

uproar .... ADO, DIN, RIOT, BABEL, NOISE, BEDLAM, BUSTLE, CLAMOR, HUBBUB, RACKET, RUCKUS, TUMULT, DISCORD, TURMOIL, BROUHAHA, COMMOTION, PANDEMONIUM

uproot ...... GRUB, STUB, ABOLISH, DESTROY, SUPPLANT, ERADICATE, DERACINATE

upset .... ADO, SPOIL, SWAGE, BOTHER, DEFEAT, TOPPLE, CAPSIZE, DISTURB, PERTURB, TOP OVER, DISORDER, DISTRESS, OVERTURN, REVERSAL

in one way .... DERAIL(ED)

upshot .... EFFECT, RESULT, OUTCOME

upside down .... UPENDED, INVERTED, TOPSY-TURVY

upsilon-shaped bone ...... HYOID

upstage ...... SNUB, ALOOF, SHOW UP, SNOOTY, CONCEITED

upstart .... SNOB, PARVENU, WHIPPERSNAPPER

upswing .... PICKUP

uptight .... TENSE

up-to-date .... NEW, FRESH, MODERN, MODISH, TIMELY, CURRENT

energy .... SOLAR
slang .... HIP, MOD
upturned nose .... PUG, SNUB
upward .... MORE, ALOFT
movement .... LIFT, SCEND
Ur location .... MESOPOTAMIA
Royal Cemetery discoverer
.... (LEONARD) WOOLLEY
Uraeus .... ASP, COBRA
place of an .... HEADDRESS
symbol .... ASP
Ural Altaic branch .... TATAR
Urania .... MUSE, APHRODITE
sphere of .... ASTRONOMY
uranic .... CELESTIAL
Uranus' discoverer .... HERSCHEL
mother .... GAEA, GAIA
offspring .... RHEA, CRONUS,
FURIES, SATURN, TITANS,
CYCLOPES
satellite .... ARIEL
wife .... GAEA
urban ...... CITY, TOWN, OPPIDAN,
METROPOLITAN
blight .... SMOG
plague .... CRIME
urbane .... SUAVE, SMOOTH,
AFFABLE, DEBONAIR,
POLISHED
urbanize .... CITIFY, POLISH,
REFINE
urchin .... IMP, BRAT, CHILD,
GAMIN, MUDLARK,
HEDGEHOG, (STREET)ARAB
urd .... PYROL
urde .... CLECHE
Urdu .... HINDUSTANI
uredo .... HIVES, URTICARIA
urethane .... HYPNOTIC, SEDATIVE
uretic .... URINARY, DIURETIC
Urfa .... EDESSA
Urga .... ULAN BATOR
urge ...... EGG, YEN, COAX, GOAD,
PROD, PUSH, SPUR, PLEAD,
PRESS, ALLEGE, EXHORT,
INCITE, INDUCE, ENTREAT,
IMPULSE, SOLICIT, ADVOCATE,
IMPORTUNE
urgency .... EXIGENCY
urgent .... RUSH, GRAVE, EXIGENT,
PRESSING, INSISTENT
Uriah .... HEEP
wife of .... BATHSHEBA
urial .... SHA, CORIAL
Uriel .... ARCHANGEL
urinary .... URIC, URETIC,
URINOUS, DIURETIC
calculus .... STONE, UROLITH
diversion device .... CATHETER
duct .... URETER, URETHRA
funnel-shaped ducts .... RENAL

PELVES
inflammation .... CYSTITIS
tract, branch of medicine
concerning ..... UROLOGY
filtering units .... GLOMERULI
imaging of the
.... UROGRAPHY
infection .... URETHRITIS
part of .... BLADDER,
KIDNEYS, URETERS, URETHRA
specialist .... UROLOGIST
stone .... CALCULUS
tube .... URETHRA
urinate .... PEE, WET, PIDDLE,
MICTURATE
urination, difficult
.... STRANGURY
excessive .... POLYURIA
involuntary .... ENURESIS
painful .... DYSURIA
urine .... PEE, PISS, WATER
blood in the .... HEMATURIA
composition, part of .... SALT,
UREA, WATER
container for .... BEDPAN,
URINAL
high level of glucose in
.... DIABETES(MELLITUS)
inherited disorder
.... PORPHYRIA
lack of production by
kidneys .... ANURIA
low production of
.... OLIGURIA
passage of .... MICTURITION
substance giving yellow
color to ...... UROCHROME
substance giving orange
color to .... RIFAMPIN
suffix .... URIA
test .... URINALYSIS
thrombolytic drug prepared
from human
.... UROKINASE
unrestrained natural
discharge of
.... INCONTINENCE
waste product in .... UREA,
URIC ACID, CREATININE
Uris, author .... LEON
Urkel, for one .... NERD
urn .... JAR, KIST, VASE, STEEN,
VESSEL
figurative .... GRAVE
for bones .... OSSUARY
handle .... EAR
shaped .... URCEOLATE
uroxanthin .... INDICAN
Ursa .... BEAR
Major .... GREAT BEAR
Minor .... LITTLE BEAR

ursine animal .... BEAR
birthplace .... DEN
howler .... MONKEY,
ARAGUATO
Urth .... NORN
urticaria .... HIVES, UREDO
urticate .... STING
Uruguay cape .... POLONIO,
SANTA MARIA
capital .... MONTEVIDEO
city/town .... LA PAZ, MINAS,
ROCHA, SALTO, RIVERA,
ARTIGAS, CARMELO, DOLORES,
DURAZNO, MERCEDES,
PAYSANDU, TRINIDAD,
MALDONADO, LAS PIEDRAS
cowboy .... GAUCHO
dam .... BONETE
department .... ROCHA, SALTO,
RIVERA, COLONIA, FLORIDA,
SAN JOSE, SORIANO,
PAYSANDU, CANELONES,
MONTEVIDEO
discoverer .... DIAZ
falls .... SALTO GRANDE
first colony .... COLONIA
island .... LOBOS, TIGRE,
FLORES
lagoon .... MERIN, NEGRA,
ROCHA, SAUCE, GARZON,
CASTILLOS
language .... SPANISH
measure ...... CUADRA, SUERTE
monetary unit .... PESO
president .... GESTIDO
river .... YI, AIGUA, NEGRO,
PANDO, PARAO, DAYMAN,
ARAPEY, OLIMAR, ALFEREZ,
CUAREIM, LA PLATA,
QUEQUAY, SAN JOSE, TACUARI,
URUGUAY, CORDOBES,
YAGUARON, CARAGUATA,
CEBOLLATI
weight .... QUINTAL
urus .... OX, TUR, AUROCHS
US. See also **American**
.... AMERICA, NEW WORLD,
UNCLE SAM, UNITED STATES
Air Force mascot ...... FALCON
Army mascot .... MULE
capitalist, famous .... ASTOR
capitol lobbyist
.... RAINMAKER
chemist .... UREY
-China relations .... PINGPONG
DIPLOMACY
consumer advocate ..... RALPH
NADER
educator .... NEILSON
expatriate in Paris .... STEIN
first aviatrix .... HARRIET

QUIMBY

black Supreme Court
Justice .... THURGOOD
MARSHALL

black woman elected to
Congress .... SHIRLEY
CHISHOLM

casualty of the Cold War
.... JOHN BIRCH

Catholic president .... JFK,
(JOHN FITZGERALD)
KENNEDY

city with cable cars ..... SAN
FRANCISCO

Navy veteran elected
president .... JOHN
KENNEDY

Secretary of Energy
.... SCHLESINGER

Supreme Court Chief
Justice .... JOHN JAY

flag .... OLD GLORY

foreign broadcasts: abbr.
.... VOA

General Eisenhower ...... IKE,
DWIGHT

M. Smith .... HOLLAND,
"HOWLIN' MAD"

MacArthur .... DOUGLAS

Schwarzkopf .... NORMAN,
"STORMIN' NORMAN"

Stilwell .... JOSEPH,
"VINEGAR JOE"

von _____ .... STEUBEN

of Vietnam War
.... WESTMORELAND

Gov't security .... E BOND

Great Lakes, largest of the
.... SUPERIOR

one of the ..... ERIE, HURON,
ONTARIO, MICHIGAN,
SUPERIOR

smallest of the ..... ONTARIO

lawyers' assn. .... ABA

Marine Corps emblem, part
of ..... EAGLE, GLOBE, ANCHOR

fighting knife .... KA-BAR

mascot .... BULLDOG

motto .... SEMPER FIDELIS,
ALWAYS FAITHFUL

remarkable airplane
.... (THE) HARRIER

Military branch .... ARMY,
NAVY, AIR FORCE, MARINE
CORPS, NATIONAL GUARD

missile ..... ABLE, ARGO, JUNO,
NIKE, THOR, AGENA

naturalist .... THOREAU

Navy mascot .... GOAT

or USSR .... SUPERPOWER

personified as a woman
.... COLUMBIA

president, first .... GEORGE
WASHINGTON

Washington's chef
.... HERCULES

who fathered 15 children
.... JOHN TYLER

who received the Pulitzer
Prize .... KENNEDY

who resigned .... NIXON

presidential retreat .... CAMP
DAVID

former name of
.... SHANGRI-LA

principal mountains,
highest of the .... MCKINLEY

one of the .... ELBERT,
SHASTA, RAINIER, WHITNEY,
MAUNA KEA, MAUNA LOA,
MCKINLEY, MITCHELL

railroad .... AMTRAK

reformer .... RIIS

region ..... MIDWEST, SUNBELT,
DIXIELAND, EAST(COAST),
WEST(COAST), NEW ENGLAND

river .... RED, OHIO, GREEN,
SNAKE, HUDSON, MOBILE,
PEEDEE, ALABAMA, POTOMAC,
ARKANSAS, COLORADO,
COLUMBIA, MISSOURI,
SAVANNAH, CUMBERLAND,
SACRAMENTO, MISSISSIPPI

**state admitted to the
Union:**

1787 .... DELAWARE, NEW
JERSEY, PENNSYLVANIA

1788 .... GEORGIA, NEW
YORK, MARYLAND, VIRGINIA,
CONNECTICUT, NEW
HAMPSHIRE,
MASSACHUSETTS, SOUTH
CAROLINA

1789 .... NORTH CAROLINA

1790 .... RHODE ISLAND

1791 .... VERMONT

1792 .... KENTUCKY

1796 .... TENNESSEE

1803 .... OHIO

1812 .... LOUISIANA

1816 .... INDIANA

1817 .... MISSISSIPPI

1818 .... ILLINOIS

1819 .... ALABAMA

1820 .... MAINE

1821 .... MISSOURI

1836 .... ARKANSAS

1837 .... MICHIGAN

1845 .... TEXAS, FLORIDA

1846 .... IOWA

1848 .... WISCONSIN

1850 .... CALIFORNIA

1858 .... MINNESOTA

1859 .... OREGON

1861 .... KANSAS

1863 .... WEST VIRGINIA

1864 .... NEVADA

1867 .... NEBRASKA

1876 .... COLORADO

1889 .... MONTANA,
WASHINGTON, NORTH
DAKOTA, SOUTH DAKOTA

1890 .... IDAHO, WYOMING

1896 .... UTAH

1907 .... OKLAHOMA

1912 .... ARIZONA, NEW
MEXICO

1959 .... ALASKA, HAWAII

state with one-syllable name
.... MAINE

Surgeon General .... KOOP,
NOVELLO, ELDERS

traditional data
.... AMERICANA

watchdog agency .... FDA

watchdog for animals
.... ASPCA

waterway .... RED, OHIO,
PECOS, YUKON, BRAZOS,
COLORADO, COLUMBIA,
MISSOURI, MISSISSIPPI

USA in France .... EUA

USAF Academy cadet
.... DOOLIE

USSR, official language of
.... RUSSIAN

usage .... USE, HABIT, CUSTOM,
MANNER, PRACTICE,
TREATMENT

usance .... USE, USAGE

use .... WEAR, AVAIL, ENJOY,
HABIT, TREAT, USAGE,
WORTH, EMPLOY, CONSUME,
PURPOSE, SERVICE, UTILITY,
UTILIZE, EXERCISE, FUNCTION

a dabber .... INK

davit .... HOIST

gripping device .... TONG

hammer .... NAIL

hose .... WATER

pawnshop .... HOCK

stiletto .... STAB

stopwatch .... TIME

strop .... HONE

stump .... ORATE

all one's energy for a
purpose .... DEVOTE

anti-freeze .... DE-ICE

art gum .... ERASE

as a remedy .... ADHIBIT

as example .... CITE

cosmetics .... PAINT
divining rod .... DOWSE
efforts .... EXERT, STRIVE
experimentally .... TRY OUT
galoshes .... SLOSH
litotes .... UNDERSTATE
of another's property
.... USUFRUCT
of extreme pressure,
    influence .... ARM-
    TWISTING
profanity .... SWEAR
salve on skin .... APPLY
the needle .... SEW
to make profit, unethical
.... EXPLOIT
up .... EAT, DRAIN, SPEND,
    EXPEND, CONSUME, EXHAUST
wastefully .... SQUANDER
with the hand(s) .... HANDLE
used .... SECONDHAND
at a Western necktie party
.... NOOSE
the PA system .... PAGED
to .... ACCUSTOMED
up .... EATEN, SPENT,
    DEPLETED, EXHAUSTED
useful .... UTILE, HELPFUL,
    PRACTICAL, BENEFICIAL,
    FUNCTIONAL, SERVICEABLE
for drivers .... MAP
for snapshots .... ALBUM
quality .... ASSET
useless .... IDLE, VAIN, FUTILE,
    OTIOSE, INUTILE, NEEDLESS,
    POINTLESS, WORTHLESS
user .... BUYER, CONSUMER,
    EMPLOYER, UTILIZER,
    EXPLOITER, PURCHASER
of exit .... GOER
usher .... ESCORT, INDUCT,
    DOORMAN, FORERUN,
    INTRODUCE, DOORKEEPER
in .... HERALD, ANNOUNCE
Uskudar .... SCUTARI
Usnach, son of .... NOISE
Uspallata Pass .... LA CUMBRE
location .... ANDES
usquebaugh .... WHISK(E)Y
ustulate .... BLACKENED,
    DISCOLORED
usual .... NORMAL, WONTED,
    REGULAR, TYPICAL,
    EVERYDAY, HABITUAL,
    ORDINARY, CUSTOMARY
openers .... PAIRS
usually .... AS A RULE,
    COMMONLY, NORMALLY,
    GENERALLY, ORDINARILY
usurer .... SHYLOCK, VAMPIRE,

LOAN-SHARK, MONEYLENDER
usurp .... SEIZE, ASSUME,
    ARROGATE
usurper .... TYRANT, ARROGATOR,
    OPPRESSOR
usury .... SHYLOCKING, LOAN-
    SHARKING
slang .... HIGHWAY ROBBERY
Utah asphalt .... GILSONITE,
    UINTA(H)ITE
canyon ..... GRAY, DESOLATION
capital .... SALT LAKE CITY
city/town .... LOA, ROY, OREM,
    DELTA, LOGAN, MAGNA,
    OGDEN, PRICE, PROVO,
    KEARNS, LAYTON, MURRAY,
    TOOELE, VERNAL, BRIGHAM,
    HOLLADAY, BOUNTIFUL,
    TAYLORSVILLE
county ...... IRON, JUAB, KANE,
    RICH, UTAH, CACHE, DAVIS,
    EMERY, GRAND, PIUTE, WEBER,
    CARBON, MORGAN, SEVIER,
    SUMMIT, TOOELE, UINTAH,
    SANPETE, SALT LAKE
desert ...... SEVIER, ESCALANTE
Indian .... NAVAHO, NAVAJO,
    P(A)IUTE
lake .... BEAR, FISH, SWAN,
    UTAH, CLEAR, NORTH,
    POWELL, SEVIER, GREAT SALT,
    LITTLE SALT
lily .... SEGO
mountain .... NEBO, WAAS,
    ELLEN, KINGS, PEALE,
    DUTTON, EMMONS, NAVAJO,
    AGASSIZ, HILGARD, HILLERS,
    MARVINE, PENNELL
mountain range .... ABAJO,
    CEDAR, HENRY, UINTA,
    BEAVER, PAVANT, WAHWAH,
    MINERAL
national park .... ZION,
    ARCHES, CANYONLANDS
natives .... MORMONS
peak .... BALDY, KINGS,
    PROVO, DELANO, MONROE
plateau .... AQUARIUS,
    TAVAPUTS
river .... BEAR, GREEN, MALAD,
    PARIA, PRICE, UINTA, WEBER,
    WHITE, BEAVER, JORDAN,
    SEVIER, VIRGIN, DOLORES,
    FREMONT, SAN JUAN,
    COLORADO, DUCHESNE, SAN
    PITCH, ESCALANTE
salt flats .... BONNEVILLE
speedway .... SALT FLATS
state bird .... SEA GULL
state flower .... SEGO LILY

state nickname .... BEEHIVE
state tree .... SPRUCE
university .... BRIGHAM YOUNG
utensil .... TOOL, IMPLEMENT
kitchen .... TONG, KNIFE,
    LADLE, SCOOP, SIEVE, BEATER,
    FUNNEL, GRATER, SIFTER,
    SKIMMER, STRAINER, CAN
    OPENER
maker .... COPPERSMITH
uterus .... WOMB, MATRIX
condition .... TIPPED
disorder .... PROLAPSE,
    MENORRHAGIA,
    DYSMENORRHEA
growth .... MOLE, TUMOR
infection/inflammation
.... ENDOMETRITIS
lining .... ENDOMETRIUM
pain .... METRALGIA
part .... CERVIX, MUSCLE,
    ENDOMETRIUM
swelling .... MOLE
tumor .... POLYP, FIBROID
Uther's son .... ARTHUR
utile .... PRACTICAL
doubly .... REVERSIBLE
utility .... AID, VALUE, WORTH,
    BENEFIT, SERVICE, FUNCTION
craft .... JOLLY BOAT
utilize .... USE, AVAIL, SERVE,
    EMPLOY, HARNESS
utmost .... BEST, FULL, FINAL,
    TOTAL, EXTREME, VERIEST,
    FARTHEST, GREATEST,
    MAXIMUM, REMOTEST
extent .... LIMIT
Uto Aztecan Indian .... YAQUI
utopia .... HEAVEN, ARCADIA,
    PARADISE
almost literally .... NOWHERE
imaginary .... SHANGRI-LA
Utopia author .... (THOMAS)MORE
Utopian .... ROSY, IDEAL, EDENIC,
    DREAMER, ARCADIAN,
    VISIONARY, IDEALIST(IC)
land of the Israelites
.... CANAAN, GOSHEN
place .... PROMISED LAND
scheme .... BUBBLE
visions .... IDEALS
utricle .... SAC, VESICLE
Uttar Pradesh capital
.... LUCKNOW
city .... AGRA, MEERUT
part of .... OUDH
utter .... SAY, EMIT, RANK, ISSUE,
    MOUTH, SHEER, SPEAK,
    STARK, TOTAL, VOICE,
    BROACH, ENTIRE, DIVULGE,

EXPRESS, ABSOLUTE, COMPLETE, DOWNRIGHT, PRONOUNCE
defeat .... ROUT
in unison .... CHORUS
lovingly .... COO
utterance .... DICTUM, REMARK, EXPRESSION

uttered ...... ORAL, SAID, SPOKEN, VERBAL, VOICED
utterly .... FULLY, STARK, ENTIRELY, COMPLETELY
uttermost .... LAST, FINAL, UTMOST
U-turn .... ABOUT-FACE
uvarovite .... GARNET

color .... GREEN
uvea, inflammation of the
.... IRITIS, UVEITIS, CYCLITIS
part of the ...... IRIS, CHOROID, CILIARY BODY
uxorial .... WIFELY
Uzbek capital .... TASHKENT
city .... KHIVA

V

V .... VERSUS, VOLUME, VOLT(AGE)
author of .... PYNCHON
formation flyers .... GEESE
Greek .... UPSILON
Hebrew .... VAV
in chemistry .... VANADIUM
in math .... VECTOR, VELOCITY
letter/shaped .... VEE
Roman numeral for _____
.... FIVE
shaped cut .... NOTCH
shaped piece .... PIE, WEDGE
symbol .... VICTORY
V.A., part of .... VETERANS, ADMINISTRATION
vaca .... COW
vacancy .... GAP, VOID, BLANK, BREAK, SPACE, VACUUM, OPENING, VACUITY, EMPTINESS
vacant .... FREE, IDLE, OPEN, VOID, BLANK, EMPTY, HOLLOW, VACUOUS, UNOCCUPIED, UNTENANTED
vacate .... QUIT, VOID, ANNUL, EMPTY, LEAVE, DEPART
a throne formally
.... ABDICATE
dangerous area ..... EVACUATE
out of necessity .... ABANDON, RELINQUISH
quickly .... FLEE
suddenly .... DECAMP
vacation .... REST, LEAVE, RECESS, HOLIDAY, RESPITE, TIME OFF
military personnel's
.... FURLOUGH
vacationer, short-stay
.... WEEKENDER
vaccinate ...... INJECT, IMMUNIZE, INOCULATE
vaccination .... SHOT(S), IMMUNIZATION
pioneer .... JENNER
vaccine .... SERO, VIRUS, ANTIDOTE

developer, injected polio
.... (JONAS)SALK
developer, oral polio
.... (ALBERT)SABIN
discoverer .... (EDWARD) JENNER
vaccinia .... COWPOX
vacillate .... WAVER, FALTER, TEETER, WHIFFLE, HESITATE, FLUCTUATE, BLOW HOT AND COLD
vacuity .... VOID, VACUUM, INANITY, EMPTINESS
vacuous .... DULL, IDLE, INANE, STUPID, EMPTY(-HEADED)
vacuum ...... VOID, SPACE, SWEEP, VACANCY, EMPTINESS
-packed .... AIRTIGHT
opposed to .... PLENUM
tube .... DIODE, OCTODE, TRIODE, ELECTRODE
tube element .... GRID, ANODE, PLATE, CATHODE
vade mecum .... MANUAL, HANDBOOK
vagabond .... BUM, VAG, (HO)BO, WAFFIE, LOREL, TRAMP, BEGGAR, RASCAL, TRUANT, DRIFTER, VAGRANT, RUNAGATE, WANDERER, WANDERING, LANDLO(U)PER
vagabondage .... VAGRANCY, VAGRANTS, WANDERING
vagary .... WHIM, FANCY, FOIBLE, NOTION, ODDITY, CAPRICE
vagrancy .... NOMADISM
vagrant .... BUM, HOBO, SPIV, CAIRD, ROVER, STRAY, TRAMP, BEGGAR, AIMLESS, NOMAD(IC), WAYWARD, VAGABOND, WANDERER
bedding carried by .... BINDLE
fortune-telling .... GYPSY
greeting of ..... HOBO, HOBEAU
jargon of .... SHELTA
place in city .... SKID ROW
slang .... BINDLE-STIFF

vague .... DIM, HAZY, LOOSE, MISTY, BLURRY, BLURRED, OBSCURE, SKETCHY, UNCLEAR, NEBULOUS, AMORPHOUS, UNCERTAIN, INDEFINITE
become .... BLUR
vagus .... NERVE
nerve disorder .... MENINGITIS, PEPTIC ULCER
nerve surgery ...... VAGOTOMY
vail .... TIP, DOFF, GRATUITY
vain .... IDLE, PERT, SMUG, COCKY, EMPTY, PROUD, FUTILE, OTIOSE, HAUGHTY, USELESS, CONCEITED, FRUITLESS
and affected .... FOPPISH
bird .... PEACOCK
colloquial .... STUCK-UP
manners .... AIRS
person ...... FOP, PRIG, DANDY, EGOIST, COXCOMB, EGOTIST, COCKSCOMB, CHAUVINIST
quest .... WILD-GOOSE-CHASE
vainglorious .... BOASTFUL, CONCEITED, OVERPROUD
vainglory ...... AIRS, POMP, PRIDE, VANITY, CONCEIT, ARROGANCE
vair .... FUR
valance .... CURTAIN, DRAPERY
vale .... DALE, GLEN, ADIEU, DINGLE, VALLEY, FAREWELL
valediction .... ADIEU, SPEECH, GOODBY(E), FAREWELL
valedictory .... ADDRESS, ORATION
Valence's river .... RHONE
valentine .... BELOVED, SWEETHEART, (GREETING) CARD
figure on a .... EROS, CUPID
Valera (Eamon de) nickname
.... DEV
valerian .... PLANT, BENNET, ALLHEAL, HEMLOCK

valet .... DRESSER, MANSERVANT
valetudinarian .... INFIRM,
SICKLY, INVALID,
HYPOCHONDRIAC
Valetta native .... MALTESE
valgus .... KNOCK-KNEE(D)
Valhalla group .... AESIR
healer at .... EIR
maiden .... VALKYR(IE)
presider at .... ODIN
valiant .... BOLD, BRAVE, DARING,
GALLANT, LIONHEARTED
valid .... JUST, LEGAL, SOUND,
COGENT, LAWFUL, BINDING,
IN FORCE, DEFENSIBLE
not .... NULL, VOID
validate .... SEAL, ATTEST,
RATIFY, CONFIRM, LEGALIZE,
SANCTION, AUTHORIZE
validity .... FORCE, WEIGHT,
COGENCY, LEGALITY,
SOUNDNESS
valise .... BAG, SATCHEL,
SUITCASE, GRIP(SACK),
PORTMANTEAU
Valjean, ____ (Hugo's) .... JEAN
pursuer of .... (DETECTIVE)
JAVERT
what he stole .... LOAF
Valkyrie .... BRYNHILD,
BRUN(N)HILD(E)
love of .... SIGURD
vallation .... WALL, TRENCH,
RAMPART, EARTHWORK
valley .... DALE, DELL, GLEN,
VALE, WADI, COMB(E),
COOMB, GLADE, GULCH,
KLOOF, SWALE, BOLSON,
CANYON, DINGLE, GUTTER,
HOLLOW, STRATH
a deep narrow .... GORGE,
KLOOF, COULEE
a wide river .... STRATH
Apollo's .... TEMPE
Argolis .... NEMEA
between cliffs .... CAN(Y)ON
entrance of .... JAWS
moon .... RILL(E)
rich in coal .... SAAR
where David fought Goliath
.... ELAH
valor .... VIRTUE, BRAVERY,
COURAGE, HEROISM,
BOLDNESS, CHIVALRY
valorous .... BOLD, BRAVE,
HEROIC, GALLANT, VALIANT,
STOUT(HEARTED)
valse .... WALTZ, TRISTE
valuable .... DEAR, COSTLY,
PRIZED, USEFUL, WORTHY,
PRECIOUS

discovery .... FIND
valuation .... ESTIMATE,
APPRAISAL
value .... COST, RATE, MERIT,
PRICE, PRIZE, WORTH,
ADMIRE, ASSESS, ESTEEM,
RATING, APPRAISE, TREASURE,
APPRECIATE
beyond amount owed
.... EQUITY
highly .... CHERISH
more .... PREFER
of little .... TRIFLE, TRIVIAL,
FARTHING, TRIFLING
valued seashell .... CONCH
valueless .... CHEAP, PALTRY,
WORTHLESS
valve .... COCK, CUSP, PLUG,
CUTOFF, DAMPEN, POPPET,
SPIGOT, PETCOCK, STOPCOCK,
FLOODGATE
defect, heart .... STENOSIS
engine .... CHOKE, THROTTLE
heart .... MITRAL
reconstructive operation,
heart .... VALVULOPLASTY
sliding .... PISTON
surgery, heart .... VALVOTOMY
vamo(o)se .... GO, LAM, BLOW,
SCAT, LEAVE, SCRAM, BEAT
IT, DECAMP, DEPART, BUZZ
OFF, SKIDDOO, SKEDADDLE
vamp .... FLIRT, TEMPT, UPPER,
REPAIR, SEDUCE, BEGUILE,
BEWITCH, COQUETTE,
PATCH(WORK)
in music .... DESCANT
name, silent .... POLA
vampire ...... BAT, FLIRT, GHOUL,
HARPY, LAMIA, SIREN, LILITH,
MONSTER, TEMPTER,
PARASITE, TEMPTRESS,
SEDUCTRESS, BLOODSUCKER
insect .... FLEA
kind of .... USURER,
BLACKMAILER, EXTORTIONIST
Pericles' .... ASPASIA
Samson's .... DELILAH
singing .... LORELEI,
PARTHENOPE
Transylvania's .... DRACULA
who leads men to ruin
.... FEMME FATALE
who turned men into swine
.... CIRCE
wicked, shameless .... JEZEBEL
worm .... LEECH
vampirism .... BLOODSUCKING
van .... FORE, LEAD, WING, FRONT,
LORRY, TRUCK, WAGON,
CARAVAN, TRAILER,

VANGUARD
kind of .... MAIL, MOVING
man .... MOVER
Van Buren, U.S. president
.... MARTIN
Diemen's land ...... TASMANIA
Doren, critic ...... CARL, MARK
Druten character .... MAMA
Gogh, painter .... VINCENT
Vance, sleuth .... PHILO
vandal .... HUN, MARRER, RUINER
vandalism .... SAVAGERY,
SPOLIATION,
DESTRUCTIVENESS
vandalize .... MAR, WRECK,
DAMAGE, DEFACE, SABOTAGE
Vanderbilt, industrialist
.... CORNELIUS
of perfume fame .... GLORIA
Vandyke .... BEARD, COLLAR,
GOATEE
forte of .... PORTRAITS
painter .... ANTHONY
vane .... WIND GAUGE,
ANEMOMETER,
(WEATHER)COCK
of arrow .... FEATHER
of feather .... VEXILLUM
of windmill .... TAIL,
WINDSAIL
vanguard .... VAN, LEAD(ER),
FRONT(LINE)
military forces .... MARINES
of the arts .... AVANT-GARDE
vanilla .... ORCHID, FLAVORING
vanish .... FADE, MELT, DISSOLVE,
EVANESCE, DISAPPEAR
vanity ...... AIRS, PRIDE, CONCEIT,
EGO(T)ISM, FUTILITY, SELF-
LOVE, VAINGLORY, DRESSING
TABLE
case .... ETUI, COMPACT
Vanity Fair author
.... THACKERAY
ex-editor of .... TINA BROWN
vanquish .... BEAT, BEST, LICK,
ROUT, QUELL, DEFEAT,
MASTER, SUBDUE, THRASH,
SILENCE, CONQUER,
OVERCOME, SURMOUNT,
OVERPOWER, SUBJUGATE
vantage point .... COIGN
Vanzetti's partner .... SACCO
vapid .... DULL, FLAT, PALL,
TAME, INANE, STALE, BORING,
INSIPID, LIFELESS, TASTELESS
vapor ...... AIR, GAS, BRAG, DAMP,
FUME, MIST, REEK, BRUME,
CLOUD, ETHER, SMOKE,
STEAM, BLUSTER, HALITUS
aircraft's .... CONTRAIL

colorless .... NEON, ARGON
combining form .... ATMO
in air .... FOG, HAZE, MIST,
SMOG
in stomach .... FLATUS
mass of .... WRACK
pressure instrument
.... TONOMETER, TENSIMETER
pure, fresh .... OZONE
vaporize .... SPRAY, STEAM,
GASIFY, ATOMIZE, DISTILL
vaporizer .... ETNA, STILL,
SPRAYER, ATOMIZER
example of .... INHALER
vaporous .... FUMY, FOGGY,
GASSY, MISTY, CLOUDY,
STEAMY, GASEOUS, REEKING,
HALITOUS
vaquero .... COWBOY, HERDER
Varangian .... RO, SCANDINAVIAN
Vargas, Brazilian president
.... GETULIO
variable .... FICKLE, UNEVEN,
MUTABLE, PROTEAN,
ABERRANT, SHIFTING,
VOLATILE, CHANGEABLE
star .... CEPHEID
variance .... ODDS, DISCORD,
DISSENT, DIVISION,
DIFFERENCE
variation .... CHANGE, VARIETY,
DEVIATION, DIVERSITY
slight .... SHADE, NUANCE
varicella .... CHICKENPOX
varicolored .... MOTTLED,
POLYCHROME, MULTICOLORED
cloth .... MOTLEY
phenomenon .... RAINBOW
varicose .... VARIX, CIRSOID,
DILATED, SWOLLEN
veins in the anus
.... HEMORRHOIDS
in the esophagus
.... VARICES
in the scrotum
.... VARICOCELE
surgery .... VARICOTOMY
treatment
.... SCLEROTHERAPY
varied .... MIXED, D(A)EDAL,
DIVERSE, VARIOUS, ASSORTED,
MISCELLANEOUS
tunes, musical piece from
.... MEDLEY
variegate .... VARY, DIVERSIFY
variegated .... PIED, VARIED,
CHECKED, DAPPLED, DIVERSE,
MOTTLED, SPOTTED, STRIPED,
VARICOLORED,
MULTICOLORED
animal .... ZEBRA, LEOPARD

bed cover .... QUILT
bits of paper .... CONFETTI
cloth .... PLAID, CALICO,
MOTLEY
design .... MOSAIC
horse .... PINTO, PIEBALD
insect .... BUTTERFLY
instrument ...... KALEIDOSCOPE
variety .... KIND, SORT, BRAND,
CLASS, DIVERSITY
act .... TURN
show .... SKIT, VAUDEVILLE
word .... SOCKO
variola .... SMALLPOX
scar .... POCKMARK
vaccination .... VARIOLATION
various .... MANY, SUNDRY,
DIVERSE, SEVERAL, DIFFERENT
items .... SUNDRIES
varlet .... CUR, PAGE, KNAVE,
RASCAL, COISTREL,
SCOUNDREL
varmint .... BEAST, BRUTE,
VERMIN
varnish .... COLOR, GLOSS, JAPAN,
ENAMEL, LACQUER,
BRIGHTEN, SHELLAC(K),
EMBELLISH, WHITEWASH
and linseed oil mix
.... MEGILP
material .... COPAL, ELEMI,
RESIN, MASTIC, SHELLAC,
TUNG(OIL), OLEORESIN,
TURPENTINE
resin .... LAC
varsity .... TEAM, COLLEGIATE
varus .... BOWLEG(GED)
opposite of .... VALGUS
vary ..... ALTER, CHANGE, DIFFER,
MODIFY, DEVIATE, DIVERGE,
DIVERSIFY, FLUCTUATE
vas .... DUCT, VESSEL
vascular organ .... PLACENTA
vase .... CUP, JAR, JUG, URN,
TAZZA, AMPHORA, CHALICE,
POTICHE, LACRIMAL,
JARDINIERE
base .... STOOL
making material .... MURRHINE
support .... PEDESTAL
vasectomy .... STERILIZATION
Vaseline .... JELLY, OINTMENT,
LUBRICANT, PETROLATUM
Vashti's successor .... ESTHER
vassal .... SERF, SLAVE, BONDMAN,
SERVANT, SUBJECT,
LIEGE(MAN), (FEUDAL)TENANT
heritable land by a .... FIEF
loyalty/service required of a
.... FEALTY, VASSALAGE
of/like a .... SERVILE

tax paid by .... TRIBUTE
vassalage .... FIEF, FEALTY,
SERVITUDE
Vassar's pride .... MILLAY
vast .... HUGE, LARGE, COSMIC,
IMMENSE, MASSIVE, OCEANIC,
SIZ(E)ABLE, ENORMOUS,
INFINITE
chasm .... ABYSS
vat .... BAC, KEG, TUB, TUN, CASK,
DRUM, KIER, TANK, KEEVE,
BARREL, CALDRON, CISTERN
for beer/wine .... CASK,
PUNCHEON
used in making dairy
product .... CHESSEL
vatic .... PROPHETIC
Vatican .... PAPACY, POPEDOM
art gallery .... BELVEDERE
basilica .... ST. PETER'S
chapel .... SISTINE
guard's nationality .... SWISS
sculpture .... PIETA
vaticinate .... PREDICT, FORETELL,
PROPHESY
vaticinator .... SEER, ORACLE,
PROPHET
Vaud .... CANTON
capital of .... LAUSANNE
vaudeville .... BURLESQUE,
VARIETY(SHOW)
performer .... HOOFER
Vaughn role .... SOLO
vault .... ARCH, CELL, COPE,
DOME, JUMP, LEAP, SAFE,
BOUND, SPRING, CATACOMB
burial .... TOMB, CRYPT,
GRAVE, SEPULCHER
concave .... COVE
for bones .... OSSUARY
horse's .... CURVET
inside curve/surface
.... INTRADOS
of heaven .... SKY
underground .... DONJON,
DUNGEON
vaulted .... ARCHED
roof .... DOME
vaunt .... BRAG, CROW, BOAST,
VAPOR, BLUSTER
vaunty .... VAIN, PROUD
vavasor .... VASSAL
veal .... GIGOT
of/like .... VITULINE
neck .... SCRAG
sausage .... BOLOGNA
slice .... SCHNITZEL
stew .... GOULASH
Veda, Atharva- .... HYMNS
Rig- .... PSALMS
Sama- .... CHANTS

Yajur- .... SACRED FORMULAS

Vedas, language of the
.... VED(A)IC, SANSKRIT
one of the .... RIG, SAMA,
YAJUR, ATHARVA

vedette .... SENTINEL,
SCOUT(BOAT)

Vedic .... PALI, SANSKRIT
god .... AGNI, DYAUS
goddess .... USHAS
sky serpent .... AHI

vee .... FIN, FIVER

veer .... YAW, SLUE, TURN, SHEER,
SHIFT, SWERVE, DEVIATE

veery .... THRUSH

Vega constellation .... LYRA
for one .... STAR

Veganova .... FIXED STARS

vegetable .... PEA, POD, BEAN,
BEET, LEEK, OKRA, SASS,
PLANT, SAUCE, TUBER,
CARROT, ENDIVE, LEGUME,
POTATO, TOMATO, CABBAGE,
LETTUCE
basket .... SCUTTLE
boiled, buttered .... VICHY
decaying matter .... DUFF
farmer .... TRUCKER
garden ...... TRUCK, KAILYARD,
KALEYARD
gas .... METHANE
growing art .... HORTICULTURE
leafstalk .... CHARD
life .... FLORA, GREENERY,
VEGETATION
marrow .... SQUASH
oyster .... SALSIFY
poison .... PTOMAIN(E)
pulse .... PEAS, BEANS,
LEGUME, LENTILS
root ..... BULB, ONION, TURNIP,
PARSNIP
sponge .... LOOFA, LUFFA,
LOOFAH

vegetables, garden .... SASS
grown for sale .... TRUCK

vegetarian ...... VEGAN, MEATLESS
colloquial .... HEALTH NUT
sea mammal .... DUGONG,
SEACOW, MANATEE

vegetate .... EXIST, STAGNATE

vegetation, combining form
.... PHYTO
covered with green
.... VERDANT
green .... VERDURE
luxuriant .... LUSH

vegetative state .... COMA

vehemence .... FIRE, FURY, RAGE,
ZEAL, ARDOR, FORCE, VIGOR,
FERVOR, WARMTH, PASSION,
VIOLENCE

vehement .... HOT, LOUD, ANGRY,
FIERY, ARDENT, BITTER,
FERVID, FERVENT, IMPETUOUS,
PASSIONATE, IMPASSIONED

vehemently .... EAGERLY,
STRONGLY, EARNESTLY

vehicle .... BUS, CAB, CAR, VAN,
AUTO, CART, JEEP, BUGGY,
TRAIN, WAGON, CAMPER,
SLED(GE), TRAILER,
CARRIAGE, CONVEYANCE
air .... GLIDER, BALLOON,
AIRCRAFT, AIRPLANE,
DIRIGIBLE, HELICOPTER,
CONVERTIPLANE
air cushion .... HOVERCRAFT
armored .... TANK, HALF-
TRACK
baby's/infant's .... PRAM,
STROLLER, PERAMBULATOR
covered .... AUTO, COUPE,
SEDAN, CARAVAN, HARDTOP,
SCHOONER
decrepit .... SHANDRYDAN
farm .... TRACTOR
for Clydesdales .... DRAY
for handicapped
.... WHEELCHAIR
for sick, wounded ..... LITTER,
STRETCHER
funeral .... HEARSE
horse-drawn .... SULKY,
CALASH, CALESA, CHARIOT,
PHAETON
hospital .... AMBULANCE
"last ride" .... HURDLE,
TUMBREL, TUMBRIL
luxurious .... LIMO(USINE)
man-drawn .... (JIN)RICKSHA
of a kind ...... TRAM, SUBWAY,
TROLLEY, CABLE-CAR,
STREETCAR, TOURING CAR
old, ramshackle .... JALOPY
on runners .... SLED(GE),
SLEIGH, TOBOGGAN
open .... ROADSTER,
CONVERTIBLE
parade .... FLOAT
pedalled .... BIKE, MOPED,
BICYCLE, TRICYCLE
running on rails .... LORRY
sightseeing .... CHARABANC
slow-moving .... SLUG
space .... ROCKET, SHUTTLE,
SATELLITE
two-wheeled .... SULKY,
CHARIOT, BAROUCHE
with runners, water
.... SCOOTER, SAILBOAT

without wheels/runnered
.... PUNG, SLED, SLEIGH,
TRAVOIS, TOBOGGAN

veil ...... CAUL, HAZE, HIDE, MASK,
MESH, CLOAK, COVER,
SCREEN, SHROUD, WIMPLE,
CONCEAL, CURTAIN,
YAS(H)MAK, MANTILLA
having a .... VELATE
in botany .... VELUM
material .... TULLE, BAREGE,
ILLUSION
papal .... ORALE

veiled .... HIDDEN, VELATE,
COVERED, DISGUISED

veiling .... TULLE, CURTAIN

vein .... LODE, MOOD, VENA,
HUMOR, TENOR, INTIMA,
PHLEBO, STREAK, TEMPER,
BLOOD VESSEL
blood clotting in a
.... THROMBOPHLEBITIS
branch .... VENULE
diagnostic procedure on a
.... VENOGRAPHY,
PHLEBOGRAPHY
disorder .... SWELLING,
VARICOSE, DISTORTION
formation in a .... CLOT
heart .... VENA CAVA
inflammation .... PHLEBITIS
kind of .... RENAL, AZYGOS,
HEPATIC, JUGULAR,
SUBCLAVIAN
layer .... INNER, OUTER,
MIDDLE, MUSCULAR
leaf .... RIB
mine .... LODE, REEF, LEDGE
mineral .... LODE
of ore .... SEAM
process of withdrawing
blood from a
.... PHLEBOTOMY,
VENESECTION
rich ore .... BONANZA
swollen/varicose .... VARIX

veining, art of .... MARBLING

veinless .... AVENOUS

veins collectively .... VENATION
having .... VENOSE, VENOUS,
NERVATE

veinstone .... GANGUE

velamen .... MEMBRANE

velar .... GUTTURAL

veld(t) .... GRASSLAND

Velez, actress .... LUPE

velleity .... WISH, DESIRE,
VOLITION

vellicate .... PLUCK, TWITCH

vellication .... TIC, JERK,
TWITCH(ING)

vellum .... PARCHMENT, (SHEEP)SKIN
velocipede .... BICYCLE, HANDCAR, TRICYCLE
velocity .... RATE, SPEED, CELERITY, RAPIDITY, SWIFTNESS
measuring device .... TACHOMETER
velum .... VELAMEN, SOFT PALATE
velure .... PAD, VELVET
velutinous .... VELVETY
velvet .... SILK, PLUSH, PANNE, VELOUR
slang .... GAIN, PROFIT, WINNINGS
velveteen .... FUSTIAN
velvety .... MILD, SOFT, MOSSY, MELLOW, SMOOTH
vena .... VEIN
venal .... SORDID, CORRUPT, VENDIBLE, MERCENARY
vend .... SELL, ISSUE, PURVEY, PUBLISH
vendace .... WHITEFISH
vendee .... BUYER
vender .... SELLER, ALIENOR
vendetta .... FEUD, GRUDGE, VENGEANCE
vendible ...... VENAL, SAL(E)ABLE
vendition .... SALE
vendor .... HAWKER, SELLER, PEDDLER, HUCKSTER, SALESMAN
route of a .... WALK
vendue .... AUCTION
veneer .... BURL, LAYER, SHELL, ENAMEL, FACADE, FACING, COATING, OVERLAY, VARNISH
venerable .... OLD, AGED, HOARY, REVERED
man .... SAGE, PATRIARCH
monk .... BEDE
venerate .... ADORE, HALLOW, REVERE, RESPECT, WORSHIP
venerated .... HOLY, SACRED
veneration .... AWE, ESTEEM, HOMAGE, RESPECT, WORSHIP, ADORATION, REVERENCE
venereal disease .... SYPHILIS, CHANCROID, GONORRHEA
infection .... HERPES
infection: sl. .... CLAP, DOSE
sore/ulcer .... CHANCRE
venery .... CHASE, HUNTING
venesection .... PHLEBOTOMY
Venetia .... VENETO
Venetian barge .... BUCENTAUR
boat .... GONDOLA
boatman .... GONDOLIER

bridge/business center .... RIALTO
canals .... RII
(chief) magistrate .... DOGE
gondolier's song .... BARCAROL(L)E
island .... RIALTO
nobleman .... MAGNIFICO
painter .... TITIAN, TIEPOLO, VERONESE, TINTORETTO
red .... SIEN(N)A
resort .... LIDO
ruler/official .... DOGE
song .... BARCAROL(L)E
street .... CANAL
traveler .... (MARCO) POLO
Venezia .... VENICE
Venezuela cape .... CODERA
capital .... CARACAS
city/town .... CORO, RUBIO, TOVAR, UPATA, CUMANA, MERIDA, TARIBA, VALERA, ZARAZA, BARINAS, CABIMAS, BOLIVAR, EL TIGRE, GUACARA, TURMERO, ACARIGUA, CALABOZO, CARUPANO, POZUELOS, TUCUPITA, TRUJILLO, VALENCIA, BARCELONA, MARACAIBO
city on the lake .... MARACAIBO
copper center .... AROA
dam .... GURI
discoverer of .... COLUMBUS
falls .... (SALTO)ANGEL
fish .... GUPPY
gulf .... PARIA, TRISTE
Indian .... CARIB, TIMOTE
island .... COCHE, CUBAGUA, LA ORCHILA, LA TORTUGA, MARGARITA
lake .... VALENCIA, MARACAIBO
language .... SPANISH
mining center .... AROA
minister .... IZAGUIRRE
monetary unit .... BOLIVAR
mountain ..... DUIDA, VENAMO, BOLIVAR, RORAIMA
mountain range .... IMERI, GUAMPI, PARIMA, IMATACA, TURAGUA, PACARAIMA
passage .... SERPENTS MOUTH
patriot .... BOLIVAR
peninsula .... PARIA, MACANAO, PARAGUANA
plain .... LLANO, GRAN SABANA
president ...... LEONI, CALDERA
river .... ARO, PAO, TUY, CUAO, META, APURE, BARIA,

CAURA, GUERE, NEGRO, OCAMO, SIAPA, TIGRE, UNARE, ZUATA, ZULIA, ARAUCA, CAPARO, CARONI, CARRAO, CURUTU, CUYUNI, SARARE, TOCUCO, TOCUYO, VENAMO, VOTAMO, AMACURO, CANAGUA, EREBATO, GUANARE, GUANIPA, GUARICO, ICABARU, ORINOCO, APONGUAO, CUQUENAN, VENTUARI
seaport .... MARACAIBO
snake .... LORA
state ..... LARA, APURE, SUCRE, ZULIA, ARAGUA, FALCON, MERIDA, BARINAS, BOLIVAR, GUERICO, MIRANDA, TACHIRA, CARABOBO, TRUJILLO
strait .... DRAGONS MOUTH
tree .... BALATA
Venezuelan god .... TSUMA
vengeance .... TALION, WANION, REVENGE, REPRISAL, REQUITAL, RETALIATION
vengeful .... SPITEFUL, VINDICTIVE
veni, vidi, _____ VICI
venial .... MINOR, TRIVIAL, EXCUSABLE, PARDONABLE
opposed to .... MORTAL
Venice famous district .... RIALTO
"Little" .... VENEZUELA
race in .... REGATTA
state barge .... BUCENTAUR
venireman .... JUROR
Venite .... PSALM, CANTICLE
venom .... BANE, GALL, SPITE, TOXIN, VIRUS, MALICE, POISON
antidote .... ANTIVENIN
venomous .... TOXIC, DEADLY, BANEFUL, NOXIOUS, SPITEFUL, VIPERINE, VIPERISH, VIRULENT, MALICIOUS, MALIGNANT, POISONOUS
arthropod .... SPIDER, CENTIPEDE, MILLIPEDE
fish ...... LION(FISH), SCORPION, STINGRAY, WEEVER(FISH)
reptile .... SNAKE, LIZARD
venous .... VEINY
vent .... EMIT, FLUE, HOLE, EXPEL, ISSUE, ESCAPE, FUNNEL, OUTLET, OPENING, ORIFICE, PASSAGE, APERTURE, UTTERANCE, EXPRESSION
in earth's crust .... GEYSER, VOLCANO
tailor's .... SLIT
whale's .... BLOWHOLE, SPIRACLE

ventage .... (FINGER)HOLE
venter ...... WAME, WOMB, BELLY,
    ABDOMEN
ventilate .... FAN, AERATE,
    AIR(OUT), EXPOSE, FRESHEN
ventilating shaft ...... DOWNCAST
ventilation .... AIRING
    opening .... LOUVER
ventilator .... FAN, BLOWER
ventral ...... H(A)EMAD, STERNAL,
    ABDOMINAL
ventriloquist .... BERGEN
    Bergen's daughter
    .... CANDICE
    Bergen's dummy .... SNERD,
    CHARLIE
    medium of .... DUMMY,
    PUPPET
venture ...... RISK, BRAVE, STAKE,
    CHANCE, HAZARD, DARE(SAY),
    SPECULATE, ENTERPRISE
venturesome one .... DARER
Venus .... PLANET, CYTHEREA,
    PHOSPHOR, APHRODITE
    as morning star .... LUCIFER
    beloved of .... ADONIS
    flytrap of .... DIONAEA
    girdle .... CESTUS
    in alchemy .... COPPER
    island .... MELOS
    Milo's .... STATUE
    or Vesta .... DEA
    planet .... VESPER
    poetical .... LUCIFER,
    HESPERUS
    son of .... CUPID, AENEAS
    tree sacred to .... MYRTLE
    whence .... MILO
veracious .... TRUE, HONEST,
    ACCURATE, TRUTHFUL
veracity .... TRUTH, HONESTY
veranda(h) .... STOA, LANAI,
    PORCH, LOGGIA, PIAZZA,
    BALCONY, PORTICO
    in Dixie .... GALLERY
verb, biblical .... WAST
    ending .... ATE, ESCE
    expression of a .... ACTION,
    EXISTENCE, OCCURRENCE
    kind of .... AUXILIARY,
    TRANSITIVE
verbal .... ORAL, VOCAL, SPOKEN,
    UNWRITTEN
    attack .... SERMON, TIRADE,
    OBLOQUY, DIATRIBE,
    HARANGUE, INVECTIVE
    noun ...... GERUND, INFINITIVE,
    PARTICIPLE
    suffix .... ATE, ESCE
    thrust .... DIG
verbalize .... EXPRESS

verbatim ...... EXACTLY, LITERAL,
    WORD FOR WORD
verbenaceous plant .... LANTANA,
    VERBENA, VERVAIN
    tree .... TEAK
verbiage ...... DICTION, PROLIXITY,
    WORDINESS
verbose .... WINDY, WORDY,
    PROLIX, TALKATIVE, LONG-
    WINDED
verboten .... TABU, TABOO,
    FORBIDDEN, PROHIBITED
verbs, derived from
    .... RHEMATIC
verd .... GREEN
    antique .... MARBLE, PATINA,
    VERDIGRIS
verdancy ...... NAIVETE, NAIVETY,
    VIRIDITY, GREENNESS,
    INEXPERIENCE
verdant .... FRESH, GREEN, NAIVE,
    IMMATURE
Verdi, composer .... GIUSEPPE
    opus .... OPERA
    work .... AIDA, ERNANI,
    OTELLO, NABUCCO, DON
    CARLO, FALSTAFF,
    (IL)TROVATORE
verdict .... DECREE, RULING,
    FINDING, OPINION, DECISION,
    JUDGMENT, SENTENCE
verdigris .... RUST, VERD, PATINA,
    ANTIQUE
verdin .... BIRD, TITMOUSE
verditer .... BICE
Verdugo, actress .... ELENA
verdure .... GREENERY,
    GREENNESS
verecund .... SHY, MODEST,
    BASHFUL
Vereen .... BEN
verein .... SOCIETY
verge .... EVE, RIM, ROD, EDGE,
    BRINK, MARGE, POINT, STAFF,
    BORDER, MARGIN
Vergil's/Virgil's birthplace
    .... MANTUA
    family name .... MARO
    hero .... (A)ENEAS
    queen .... DIDO
    word .... TIMEO
    work .... (A)ENEID
veriest .... UTMOST, GREATEST
verify .... CHECK, PROVE, AFFIRM,
    ATTEST, CONFIRM, IDENTIFY
verily ...... AMEN, TRULY, CERTES,
    INDEED, IN FACT, REALLY
veritable .... REAL, VALID,
    ACTUAL, GENUINE
veritas .... TRUTH
Verite author .... ZOLA

verity ...... FACT, TRUTH, REALITY
vermeil .... VERMILION
vermiform .... WORM-SHAPED
    process .... APPENDIX
vermilion .... RED, MINIUM,
    VERMEIL, PIGMENT, CINNABAR
vermin .... BUGS, LICE, MICE,
    RATS, SCUM, FLIES, PESTS,
    WEASEL, VARMENT, VARMINT,
    RIFFRAFF
Vermont capital ...... MONTPELIER
    city/town .... BARRE, DERBY,
    ESSEX, JERICHO, NEWPORT,
    RUTLAND, HARTFORD,
    WOODSTOCK, BENNINGTON,
    BURLINGTON, COLCHESTER,
    MIDDLEBURY, SPRINGFIELD
    college .... GODDARD
    county .... ESSEX, ORANGE,
    ADDISON, ORLEANS, RUTLAND,
    WINDHAM, WINDSOR,
    FRANKLIN, BENNINGTON,
    CHITTENDEN, WASHINGTON
    dam .... MOORE, WILDER,
    COMERFORD
    lake ..... ECHO, CARMI, SALEM,
    GROTON, CASPIAN, CRYSTAL,
    DUNMORE, HARVEYS,
    SEYMOUR, BOMOSEEN,
    HARDWICK, HORTONIA,
    IROQUOIS, CHAMPLAIN,
    MAIDSTONE
    mountain .... BALD, GORE,
    SNOW, BURKE, ELLEN, TABOR,
    BOLTON, HUNGER, SPRUCE,
    ABRAHAM, BROMLEY,
    EQUINOX, ASCUTNEY,
    HAYSTACK, STRATTON,
    BELVIDERE, BLOODROOT,
    MANSFIELD, CAMELS HUMP,
    WHITE FACE
    mountain range .... GREEN
    river .... MAD, MILL, WEST,
    BLACK, CLYDE, MOOSE,
    TROUT, WAITS, WELLS, WHITE,
    BARTON, HOOSIC, LITTLE,
    LAMOILLE, NULHEGAN,
    POULTNEY, WINOOSKI,
    MISSISQUOI, PASSUMPSIC,
    CONNECTICUT
    state bird .... THRUSH
    state flower .... RED CLOVER
    state nickname .... GREEN
    MOUNTAIN
    state tree .... SUGAR MAPLE
    university .... NORWICH
vermouth .... WINE
vernacular .... ARGOT, IDIOM,
    JARGON, DIALECT
vernal .... GREEN, AESTIVAL,
    YOUTHFUL, SPRINGLIKE

Verne, author .... JULES
    character .... NEMO
    submarine .... NAUTILUS
veronal .... BARBITAL
veronica .... SUDARY, FIGWORT,
    SUDARIUM, SPEEDWELL
verruca .... WART
verrucose .... WARTY
versant .... SLOPE
versatile ...... SKILLED, TALENTED,
    ADAPTABLE, MANY-SIDED
verse .... ALBA, EPIC, LINE, POEM,
    RIME, RUNE, SONG, CANTO,
    IONIC, RHYME, POETRY,
    STANZA, DIMETER, TRIPODY,
    TROCHEE
    accented .... ARSIS
    accented and unaccented
    .... TROCHEE
    analysis .... SCANSION
    book of .... GARLAND
    comic .... DOGGEREL
    form ...... ODE, IAMB, PANTUN,
    SONNET, ANAPEST, COUPLET,
    DIMETER, (DI)STICH, PANTOUM,
    SPONDEE, VIRELAY, MADRIGAL
    free .... VERS LIBRE
    group .... TERCET
    half line of .... HEMISTICH
    imaginative .... POESY
    inside ring .... POSY
    kind of .... EPIC, ELEGY,
    EPODE, JINGLE, DOGGEREL,
    LIMERICK, MADRIGAL
    measure .... MORA
    mournful .... ELEGY
    musical .... STAFF
    of a lyric sort .... STRAIN
    eight metrical feet
    .... OCTAMETER
    farewell .... ENVOI
    five lines .... PENTASTICH
    four lines .... QUATRAIN,
    TETRASTICH
    fourteen lines .... SONNET
    love .... MADRIGAL
    seven lines .... HEPTASTICH
    six lines .... HEXASTICH
    three metrical feet
    .... TRIPODY
    one-line .... MONOSTICH
    rhythm in .... METER,
    MEASURE
    satirical .... IAMBIC
    set to music .... LYRICS
    terse, witty .... EPIGRAM
    two-feet ...... DIPODY, SYZYGY,
    DIMETER
    two-line ..... COUPLET, DISTICH
    unit .... FOOT
    with nosegay .... POSY

versed .... ADEPT, TURNED,
    LEARNED, SKILLED, TRAINED,
    FAMILIAR, CONVERSANT,
    PROFICIENT, ACCOMPLISHED,
    KNOWLEDGEABLE
verses, set of .... STAVE, PANTUN,
    STANZA, STROPHE
versifier .... RIMER, RHYMER,
    POETESS, POET(ASTER),
    RHYMESTER
versify .... RHYME, METRIFY,
    POETIZE
version .... ACCOUNT, RECENSION,
    RENDITION, TRANSLATION
    of Bible .... DOUAY, VULGATE,
    APOCRYPHA, KING JAMES,
    SEPTUAGINT, NEW TESTAMENT,
    OLD TESTAMENT
verso, opposed to .... RECTO,
    OBVERSE
versus .... AGAINST
vertebra, body of .... CENTRUM
    combining form
    .... SPONDYL(O)
    top .... ATLAS
vertebral bone .... COCCYX,
    SACRUM
vertebrate .... AVIS, FISH,
    MAMMAL, REPTILE
vertex .... CAP, TOP, ACME, APEX,
    HEAD, CROWN, HEIGHT,
    SUMMIT, ZENITH, PINNACLE
vertical .... PLUMB, APLOMB,
    ERECT, UPRIGHT,
    PERPENDICULAR
vertically .... UP, APEAK
verticil .... WHORL
vertiginous .... DIZZY, GIDDY,
    SPINNING
vertigo .... GID, DINUS, MEGRIM,
    DIZZINESS, GIDDINESS
Vertigo actress ...... (KIM)NOVAK
Vertumnus' wife .... POMONA
verve .... PEP, DASH, ELAN,
    GUSTO, VIGOR, FERVOR,
    SPIRIT, VIVACITY,
    ENTHUSIASM
vervet .... MONKEY
    relative .... GRIVET
very .... EVEN, REAL, SAME, TRES,
    QUITE, TRULY, ACTUAL, EVER
    SO, HIGHLY, REALLY,
    GENUINE, EXTREMELY,
    EXCEEDINGLY
    accurate .... EXACT, PRECISE
    brave .... LION-HEARTED
    bright light .... FLARE,
    SPOTLIGHT
    bright star .... NOVA
    close .... NOSE-TO-NOSE
    colloquial .... AWFULLY,

    TERRIBLY
    dark .... INKY
    dry .... ARID
    dry champagne .... BRUT
    flamboyant pianist
    .... LIBERACE
    friendly .... PALSY-WALSY
    good reviews .... RAVES
    hard .... STONY, DIFFICULT
    important person .... STAR,
    BIGWIG, BIG WHEEL, TOP
    BRASS, CELEBRITY, DIGNITARY
    in English slang .... BALLY
    justifiable .... LEGAL,
    LEGITIMATE
    large .... DECUMAN
    little .... PETTY, MINUTE,
    PICAYUNE, MINIATURE
    lowest level ..... ROCK-BOTTOM
    neat .... TRIG
    new .... RED-HOT
    pleasing .... GROOVY
    powerful .... MIGHTY
    red .... BLOODY, CRIMSON
    red-complexioned ...... BURNT,
    SUNBURNED
    sharp .... QUICK-WITTED, AS
    HOT AS A PISTOL
    signal .... FLARE
    small .... WEE, TINY, DWARF,
    PIGMY, PYGMY, INSIGNIFICANT
    small cucumber .... GHERKIN
    small dog .... CHIHUAHUA
    small donkey .... BURRO
    tense .... TAUT, TIGHT
    true .... HONEST, VERACIOUS,
    UNMISTAKABLY SO
    well .... FINE, FIRST-RATE
vesica .... BLADDER
vesicant .... EPISPASTIC, MUSTARD
    GAS
vesicate .... BLISTER
vesicle .... SAC, BLEB, CYST,
    BULLA, CAVITY, BLISTER,
    UTRICLE
vespa .... WASP, YELLOWJACKET
vesper .... EVE, STAR, VENUS,
    EVENING, EVENTIDE,
    HESPERUS
vespers .... EVENSONG,
    CANONICAL HOUR
vespertilione .... BAT
vespiary inhabitant .... WASP,
    HORNET, VESPID
vespid .... WASP, HORNET,
    YELLOWJACKET
vespine insect .... WASP
Vespucci, explorer ...... AMERIGO
    friend of .... COLUMBUS
    nation named after
    .... AMERICA

vessel .... CAN, JUG, PAN, TUB, VAS, VAT, BOWL, CASK, DUCT, BOAT, SHIP, TUBE, BARGE, BASIN, CANAL, CRAFT, CRUSE, BARREL, GALLEY, LATEEN, LUGGER, AIRSHIP, CAR(R)ACK, CARRIER, (CAT)BOAT, FRIGATE, GALLEON, UTENSIL, CONTAINER

ancient .... TRIREME

anti-smuggling .... CUTTER

assayer's .... CUPEL

baptismal/holy water ..... FONT, PISCINA, SACRARIUM

body of a .... HULK, HULL

butter-making .... CHURN

cargo/commercial ...... BARGE, OILER, TANKER, STEAMER, FREIGHTER

carried on a warship .... DINGHY

Chinese .... JUNK, SAMPAN

clumsy .... ARK, HOOKER, DROGHER

combining form .... VASO

cooking .... PAN, POT, FRYPAN, KETTLE, TEAPOT, CALDRON, SKILLET, STEAMER, CROCKPOT, STOCKPOT, RICE COOKER

cylindrical .... KEG, TUBE, BARREL

deck of a .... ORLOP

decorative .... VASE

deep-sea diving .... BATHYSCAPH(E)

drinking .... CUP, MUG, GLASS, GOBLET, TANKARD, TUMBLER

druggist's .... JAR, GALLIPOT

Ecclesiastical .... AMA, PYX

Eucharist .... CRUET

fishing .... SMACK, HOOKER, SEALER, WHALER, TRAWLER

for burning oil .... CRESSET

for coal .... HOD, SCUTTLE

for medicine .... VIAL, PHIAL

freight .... TRAMP, PACKET, FREIGHTER, WHALEBACK

funnel-shaped .... HOPPER

Holy Communion .... CHALICE

John Barleycorn's ..... BOTTLE

Levantine .... SAIC, KETCH

lightweight .... RAFT, BALSA, BATEAU

made of wicker .... BASKET, HAMPER, PANNIER

mail .... PACKET(BOAT)

Malay .... PRAU, PROA

merchant .... ARGOSY, GALLIOT

of the Vikings .... KNORR

part .... DECK, STERN

passenger .... FERRY, LINER, PACKET, AIRPLANE, STEAMSHIP

pleasure .... YACHT

racing .... SLOOP

sailing .... HOY, BARK, BRIG, SHIP, YAWL, KETCH, CARAVEL

single-decked .... GALLEY

single-masted .... GALLIOT

small .... JAR, TUBE, VIAL, CRUSE, PHIAL, CANISTER

small sailing ..... HOY, BARGE, PINNACE

supply .... COALER, TENDER

the Jumblies' .... SIEVE

thermos bottle .... DEWAR

three-masted .... BARK, ZEBEC, GALLEASS

trader .... GALLEON

transporting cars, people .... FERRY(BOAT)

two-masted ..... BRIG, HOOKER

type of .... BOX, PAN, POT, CASE, CADDY, TRAMP, BOTTLE, BASKET, BUSHEL, HOLDER, CONTAINER, RECEPTACLE

used in photometry .... CUVETTE

warship .... CRUISER, GALLEON, MONITOR, HYDROFOIL, SUBMARINE, ENTERPRISE, SUPERTANKER

water/liquid .... JUG, CASK, PAIL, FLASK, BOTTLE, BUCKET, CANTEEN, PITCHER, RUNDLET, PUNCHEON, KILDERKIN

vessels, having .... VASCULAR

vest .... ENDOW, BODICE, BOLERO, WESKIT, EMPOWER, FURNISH, WAISTCOAT, TATTERSALL

pocket .... SMALL

Vesta .... MATCH, HESTIA

vestal .... NUN, PURE, CHASTE, VIRGIN(AL)

virgin .... TUCCIA, AEMILIA, CLAUDIA, URBINIA, PRIESTESS

virgin Urbinia's burial place .... COLLINE GATE

Vestal Virgins .... ROMAN CULT

disciplinarian of the .... PONTIFEX-MAXIMUS

dwelling place .... ATRIUM-VESTAE

one of highly revered .... URBINIA

Roman goddess of the .... VESTA

who escaped, one of .... TUCCIA, AEMILIA, CLAUDIA

vested .... FIXED, ROBED, ENDUED, GOWNED, SETTLED,

ABSOLUTE, RAIMENTED, ENTRENCHED

vestibule .... HALL, ENTRY, FOYER, LOBBY, ALCOVE, HALLWAY

vestige(s) .... BIT, MARK, SIGN, RELIC, SHRED, TRACE, TRACK, SHADOW, NARTHEX, REMAINS, EVIDENCE, REMAINDER

of burn .... ESCHAR

vestment .... GOWN, ROBE, FROCK, GARMENT, RAIMENT, TUNICLE

clerical .... ALB, COPE, AMICE, TUNIC, TIPPET, CASSOCK, CHASUBLE, SURPLICE

English king's coronation .... DALMATIC

eucharistic .... MANIPLE

Jewish priest's .... EPHOD

papal .... FANON

place for .... AMBRY

vestments .... CANONICALS

vestry .... CHAPEL, SACRISTY

Vesuvian .... FUSEE, MATCH, VOLCANIC

vesuvianite .... EGERAN, IDOCRASE

vesuviate .... ERUPT

Vesuvius .... VOLCANO

city destroyed by ..... POMPEII, HERCULANEUM

site .... NAPLES

vetch .... ERS, AKRA, TARE, SATIVA

vet(eran) .... ELDER, STAGER, OLD HAND, OLDSTER, TROUPER, OLDTIMER, SEASONED, EX-SOLDIER, EXPERIENCED

of battles .... WAR HORSE

veterinarian .... LEECH, FARRIER, (ANIMAL)DOCTOR

colloquial .... VET

vetiver .... BENA, GRASS

veto .... NO, KILL, QUASH, TABOO, FORBID, KIBOSH, NEGATE, DISALLOW, PROHIBIT, DISAPPROVE

vetoer .... NOER

vex .... IRE, IRK, CARK, FASH, GALL, RILE, ROIL, ANNOY, CHAFE, PEEVE, PIQUE, TEASE, HARASS, NEEDLE, NETTLE, OFFEND, DISTURB, TORMENT, TROUBLE, ACERBATE, IRRITATE

vexation .... WOE, BANE, BOTHER, PLAGUE, ANXIETY, NUISANCE, AGITATION, ANNOYANCE

vexatious .... PESKY, IRKSOME, ANNOYING, IRRITABLE, PROVOKING, BOTHERSOME,

via ...... PER, ALONG, BY(WAY OF), TROUBLESOME THROUGH

viable .... VITAL, ALIVE, CAPABLE, WORKABLE, PRACTICAL

viaduct .... BRIDGE, TRESTLE

vial .... PHIAL, BOTTLE, AMP(O)ULE

viand(s) .... DISH, FARE, FOOD, VICTUALS

viaticum .... EUCHARIST

viator ...... TRAVELER, WAYFARER

Viaud's pseudonym .... LOTI

vibes .... ECHO, VIBRATION

vibrant .... VITAL, ROBUST, DYNAMIC, HEALTHY, PULSING, RESONANT, ENERGETIC, QUIVERING

vibrate .... JAR, TIRL, THROB, DINDLE, QUIVER, SHIMMY, THRILL, FLUTTER, RESOUND, TREMBLE, RESONATE, OSCILLATE

vibration .... THROB, QUIVER, THRILL, SHAKING, TREMOLO, PULSATION

check .... DAMP

chest .... FREMITUS

vibrator .... OSCILLATOR

vibrissa .... WHISKERS

viburnum .... LIANA, LIANE, SHRUB, LANTANA, HONEYSUCKLE

vicar ...... AGENT, DEPUTY, PRIEST, MINISTER, VICEGERENT

assistant of .... CURATE

Christ's .... POPE

residence of .... VICARAGE

vicarious .... PROXY, DEPUTY, INDIRECT, DELEGATED, SUBSTITUTE

vice .... SIN, CRIME, ERROR, FAULT, STEAD, FRAILTY, INIQUITY, WEAKNESS, INSTEAD OF, ADDICTION

chairman, public dinner .... CROUPIER

companion of .... VERSA

president .... VEEP

versa .... CONVERSELY, OPPOSITELY

vicegerent .... VICAR, DEPUTY

vicenary number .... TWENTY

viceroy ...... REGENT, BUTTERFLY, VICEGERENT

of a .... VICEREGAL

wife of a .... VICEREINE

Vichy and others .... EAUX, SPAS, WATERS

vichyssoise .... SOUP

vicinage .... AREA, VICINITY, NEIGHBORHOOD

vicinal .... LOCAL

vicinity ...... ENVIRONS, LOCALITY, NEIGHBORHOOD

vicious ...... MEAN, VILE, WRONG, SINFUL, UNRULY, WICKED, CORRUPT, HEINOUS, IMMORAL, DEPRAVED, MALICIOUS

act .... CRIME, OUTRAGE

vicissitude .... CHANGE, UP AND DOWN

victim .... DUPE, GULL, LAMB, MARK, PREY, LOSER, QUARRY, WRETCH, SUFFERER

accident .... CASUALTY

blamed for others' mistakes .... SCAPEGOAT

Cain's .... ABEL

Corday's .... MARAT

easily cheated .... DUPE, GULL, SUCKER

left to face consequences .... FALL GUY

long-suffering .... MARTYR

of Bellerophon .... CHIMERA

of pranks .... STOOGE

used for dangerous work .... TOOL, CAT'S PAW

victimize ...... DUPE, FOOL, GULL, CHEAT, DECEIVE, SWINDLE, HOODWINK

victor .... MASTER, WINNER, CHAMPION, CONQUEROR

actor .... JORY, MATURE

character .... AXEL, LENA, HEYST

Victoria .... QUEEN, EMPRESS, CARRIAGE, WATERLILY, AUTO(MOBILE)

and Reichenbach .... FALLS

consort of Queen .... (PRINCE)ALBERT

goddess .... NIKE

manservant of Queen .... JOHN BROWN

Victoria (Australia) bay .... HOBSONS, WARATAH, PORTLAND, DISCOVERY, PORT PHILLIP

cape .... OTWAY, NELSON, BRIDGEWATER

capital .... MELBOURNE

city/town .... ALTONA, COBURG, ELTHAM, KEILOR, BENDIGO, CROYDON, GEELONG, PRAHRAN, PRESTON, BALLARAT, ESSENDON, SUNSHINE, WAVERLEY, BRUNSWICK, DANDENONG, LILLYDALE, MOORABBIN, CAMBERWELL

island .... FRENCH, PHILLIP

lake .... HUME, EILDON, TYRRELL, HINDMARSH, WELLINGTON, CORANGAMITE

mountain .... BOGONG, BULLER, DANDENONG, DIFFICULT

peninsula .... MORNINGTON

river .... AVOCA, OVENS, SNOWY, YARRA, LODDON, MURRAY, GLENEIG, HOPKINS, WIMMERA, CAMPASPE, MITCHELL

Victorian vice .... BIGOTRY, PRUDERY

victorious .... PALMARY, TRIUMPHAL, SUCCESSFUL, TRIUMPHANT

number .... ONE

victory .... MASTERY, SUCCESS, TRIUMPH, WINNING, CONQUEST

celebration .... SNAKE DANCE

costly .... PYRRHIC

crown of .... ANADEM, LAUREL

easy .... RUNAWAY, WALKAWAY

goddess of ...... NIKE, ATHENA

kind of .... ROUT, CADMEAN, PYRRHIC, LANDSLIDE

sign .... VEE

symbol .... VEE, PALM, LAUREL, TROPHY, CHAPLET

Victory, author of .... CONRAD

Victrola .... PHONOGRAPH

kin of .... GRAMOPHONE

victual(s) .... EAT, FEED, FOOD, VIAND, VITTLE, PROVISIONS

victualer .... SUTLER, CATERER, INNKEEPER

vicuna .... ALPACA

vide .... SEE

videliet .... NAMELY

video .... TV, TELEVISION

meaning .... I SEE

vie .... BET, WAGER, STRIVE, COMPETE, CONTEND, EMULATE

vier .... RIVAL, ENTRANT

Vienna .... WIEN

park .... PRATER

Woods composer ..... STRAUSS

Viennese dress .... DIRNDL, LEDERHOSEN

Vientiane citizen .... LAO

money .... KIP

Vietnam bay .... VINH CAM RANH, VUNG CHON MAY

Buddhist sect .... HAO, HOA, CAO-DAI

cape .... MUI LAY, MUI DINH, MUI VARELLA, MUI NAM TRAM

capital .... HANOI
capital, former (South)
.... SAIGON
city/town .... HUE, VINH,
    DALAT, MYTHO, TAMKY,
    TANAN, DANANG, CANTHO,
    HONGAI, KONTUM, PLEIKU,
    SAIGON, BACLIEU, BIENHOA,
    CAMRANH, LACGIAO, PHUVINH,
    QUINHON, RACHGIA, TRAVINH,
    VUNGTAU, HAIPHONG,
    NHATRANG, PHANRANG,
    KHANH HUNG, LONG XUYEN,
    PHAN THIET, HO CHI MINH
economic reform program
.... DOI MOI
general (North) .... GIAP
guerrillas (South)
.... VIETCONG
gulf .... TONKIN
holiday/New Year .... TET
island .... PHU QUOC, DAO CAT
    BA, HON KHOAI, NIGHTINGALE
language .... MEO, YAO,
    KHMER, MUONG, FRENCH,
    CHINESE, VIETNAMESE
monetary unit .... DONG
monetary unit, former
    (South) .... PIASTRE
mountain .... RAOCO, NUI BA
    DEN, FAN SI PAN, CHU YANG
    SIN
native .... MEO
newspaper .... NHANDAN
offensive .... TET
plain .... JONCS
plateau .... KONTUM
premier (North) .... (PHAM
    VAN) DONG
premier (South) .... CAO KY,
    KHANH
president (North) .... (HO CHI)
    MINH
president, former (South)
.... DIEM, THIEU
river ...... RED, BLACK, SE SAN,
    SONG BA, SONG CA, IA DRANG,
    SONG CAI
Saigon's new name .... HO
    CHI MINH
section of .... ANNAM
view .... AIM, SEE, GOAL, SCAN,
    ANGLE, SCAPE, SCENE, SIGHT,
    VISTA, WATCH, ASPECT,
    BELIEF, NOTION, SURVEY,
    VISION, GLIMPSE, OPINION,
    PURPOSE, WITNESS,
    PANORAMA, PROSPECT
viewpoint .... ANGLE, OPINION,
    OUTLOOK, ATTITUDE
vigesimal .... TWENTIETH

vigil .... EVE, WAKE, WATCH,
    SURVEILLANCE
vigilance, in medicine
.... INSOMNIA
vigilant .... WARY, ALERT,
    CAREFUL, CAUTIOUS,
    WATCHFUL
vigilante .... NIGHTRIDER
vignette .... SQUIB, SKETCH,
    PICTURE, DEPICTION
vignettist .... ARTIST, AUTHOR,
    WRITER
vigor .... SAP, VIM, VIS, ZIP, DASH,
    SNAP, FORCE, MIGHT, POWER,
    VERVE, ENERGY, STAMINA,
    STRENGTH, VITALITY,
    INTENSITY
    slang .... PEP
vigorous .... HALE, ALERT,
    HARDY, SOUND, STOUT,
    MIGHTY, POTENT, ROBUST,
    STRONG, STURDY, VIRILE,
    FORCEFUL, ENERGETIC
    scuffle .... TUSSLE
Viking .... ROVER, PIRATE,
    SAILOR, NORSEMAN
    famed .... ERIC, OLAF, ROLLO
    hero .... RURIK
    literature .... SAGAS
    poet .... SKALD
Vikings, name given by
  Finnish to .... RUS
vilayet .... EYALET, PROVINCE
    subdivision of .... SANJAK
vile .... BAD, LOW, BASE, EVIL,
    FOUL, MEAN, NASTY, PALTRY,
    SCURVY, VULGAR, WICKED,
    OBSCENE, DEPRAVED,
    CONTEMPTIBLE
vilify .... SLUR, ABUSE, LIBEL,
    SMEAR, DEFAME, MALIGN,
    REVILE, ASPERSE, SLANDER,
    TRADUCE, CALUMNIATE
vilipend .... REVILE, VILIFY,
    BELITTLE, DISPARAGE
villa .... CHATEAU, MANSION
Villa, Mexican leader .... PANCHO
_____, near Rome .... DESTE
    of Herod .... MASADA
village .... BURG, BURH, DORP,
    KAIK, STAD, TOWN, WICK,
    KRAAL, BARRIO, CASALE,
    HAMLET, THROP(E), CLACHAN,
    MUNICIPALITY
    Biblical .... CANA
    near castle .... BOURG
villain .... FELON, KNAVE, ROGUE,
    MEANIE, RASCAL, CRIMINAL,
    MISCREANT, SCOUNDREL
    Dickens .... SIKES
    expression of .... LEER

    movie: sl. .... HEAVY, BAD
    GUY
    of story .... LEGREE,
    RASSENDALE
    "Star Wars" .... VADER
villainy .... CRIME
villatic .... RURAL, RUSTIC
villein .... ESNE, SERF, CARL(E),
    TENANT, PEASANT
Villon, Fr. poet .... FRANCOIS
Vilnius .... VILNA, WILNO
vim .... PEP, ZIP, ELAN, ZEST,
    VERVE, VIGOR, ENERGY,
    SPIRIT, STINGO
vimen .... SHOOT
vin .... WINE
vina .... ZITHER
vinaceous .... RED, VINOUS
    fruit .... GRAPE
vinaigrette .... BOX, BOTTLE
Vincent's disease .... GINGIVITIS,
    TRENCH MOUTH
Vinci's patron .... SFORZA
vincible .... BEATABLE
vincit omnia _____ ...... VERITAS
vindicate .... CLEAR, ACQUIT,
    ABSOLVE, JUSTIFY
vindication .... APOLOGY,
    EXONERATION
vindicator .... AVENGER
vindictive .... BITTER, SPITEFUL,
    MALICIOUS, (RE)VENGEFUL
vine .... HOP, IVY, PEA, BINE,
    GRAPE, LIANA, LIANE,
    RUNNER, CLIMBER,
    COW(H)AGE, CREEPER,
    ANGLEPOD, WISTERIA
    coil of .... TENDRIL
    dresser .... PRUNER
    gourd .... COLOCYNTH
    support ..... LATTICE, TENDRIL,
    TRELLIS
    tuberous .... TAMUS
    type of .... GRAPE, JASMINE,
    CLEMATIS, WISTERIA, POISON
    IVY, MORNING GLORY
    used in making leis .... MAILE
    with twining stems .... BINE
    woody .... SMILAX
    young .... VINELET
vinegar .... EISEL, ACETUM,
    ALEGAR
    bottle .... CRUET, CASTER,
    CASTOR
    change to .... ACETIFY
    dregs .... MOTHER
    eel .... NEMATODE
    formation in .... ROPE,
    MOTHER
    from ale .... ALEGAR
    kind of .... MALT, PALM, CIDER

like/of .... SOUR, ACETIC, ACETOSE, ACETOUS
pickling .... MARINADE
preserve in .... MARINATE
producing .... ACETOUS
spiced .... MARINADE
stringy substance ..... MOTHER
worm .... EEL
vinegarroon .... SCORPION
vinegary .... SOUR, ACETIC, ILL-HUMORED, ILL-TEMPERED
vinery ...... HOTHOUSE, VINEYARD, GREENHOUSE
vineyard ...... CRU, CLOS, VINERY, GRAPERY
vingt et un .... BLACKJACK, TWENTY ONE
vino .... WINE
vinous .... WINY, VINACEOUS
vinta .... CANOE
vintage .... AGE, CROP, TIME, WINE, YIELD, MODEL, CHOICE, PERIOD, HARVEST
autos, e.g. .... ANTIQUES
vintner's assistant ...... GOURMET
study .... (O)ENOLOGY
viol .... SARINDA
viola .... PANSY, PLANT, VIOLET
clef .... ALTO
violate ...... RAPE, ABUSE, BREAK, USURP, RAVISH, INFRACT, PROFANE, ENCROACH, INFRINGE, TRESPASS, DESECRATE
trust .... BETRAY
violation .... BREACH, OFFENSE, INFRACTION, DESECRATION
kind of law ...... RAPE, ARSON, MURDER, BURGLARY, KIDNAPING
of the law ...... CRIME, DELICT, FELONY, DELINQUENCY
violator .... LAWBREAKER
violence .... ROW, RIOT, FORCE, TURMOIL, SEVERITY
violent .... WILD, FIERY, ROUGH, FIERCE, RAGING, STORMY, STRONG, FURIOUS, TEARING, FORCEFUL
anger .... FURY
blow .... BASH
contact ..... IMPACT, COLLISION
disturbance ...... RIOT, RUMPUS
jar .... SHOCK
outburst/storm .... TEMPEST
stream .... TORRENT
struggle .... AGONY
temporary activity ...... SPASM
violently agitated .... TURBULENT
violet .... MAUVE, FLOWER, PURPLE

blue .... INDIGO
cousin of .... PANSY
violin ...... CELLO, VIOLA, FIDDLE, VIOL(ONCELLO)
bow .... ARCO, FIDDLESTICK
bow's knob .... NUT
companion of .... BOW
E-string .... QUINT
famous ...... AMATI, CREMONA, STRAD(IVARIUS)
forerunner of the .... REBEC(K)
inlaid border .... PURFLING
instrument resembling .... REBEC(K)
maker ..... AMATI, STRADIVARI, GUARNERI(US)
maker Amati .... NICOLO
part of ..... NUT, NECK, WAIST, BRIDGE, BUTTON, PEG(BOX), SCROLL, CHINBOARD, TAILPIECE, FINGERBOARD
piano piece .... SONATA
player .... FIDDLER
rare .... KIT, AMATI, STRAD
small .... KIT
stroke .... UPBOW
violinist .... AUER, ELMAN, STERN, YSAYE, HEIFETZ, MENUHIN, KREISLER
comedian .... BENNY
direction to .... SPICCATO
Elman .... MISCHA
Menuhin .... YEHUDI
Roman .... NERO
so-called .... (JACK) BENNY
violone .... CONTRABASS
VIP .... BIGWIG, BIGSHOT, MAGNATE, NOTABLE, TOPBRASS, CELEBRITY, DIGNITARY
bullring .... TORERO, MATADOR, TOREADOR
Easter .... BUNNY
June .... DAD
May .... MOM
part of .... VERY, PERSON, IMPORTANT
wheels for .... LIMO(USINE)
VIPs, assembly of .... GALAXY
viper .... ASP, BOA, ADDER, SNAKE, REPTILE, SERPENT, BUSHMASTER, COPPERHEAD, FER-DE-LANCE, RATTLESNAKE
horned .... CERASTES
viper's bugloss .... BLUEWEED
viperine .... VENOMOUS
viperous .... ASPISH, SPITEFUL, VENOMOUS, MALICIOUS
virago ...... FURY, SCOLD, SHREW, VIXEN, AMAZON, MAENAD, HELLCAT, TERMAGANT

virelay .... POEM, VERSE
vireo .... RUDD, REDEYE, GREENLET, (SONG)BIRD
virescent .... GREENISH
virgate ...... TWIGGY, ROD-SHAPED
Virgil. See **Vergil**
virgin .... NUN, PURE, UNCUT, VIRGO, CHASTE, MAID(EN), VESTAL, INITIAL, MADONNA, PARTHENOS, UNTOUCHED
queen .... ELIZABETH
unblemished .... CAMILLA
woman .... OLD MAID, SPINSTER
Virgin Islands' discoverer .... COLUMBUS
the .... MARY
Vestal .... RHEA, TUCCIA, CLAUDIA, URBINIA
virginal .... NEW, PURE, FRESH, SPINET, MAIDENLY, UNSULLIED, UNEXPLORED, HARPSICHORD
membrane .... HYMEN
Virginia bay .... BACK, MOBJACK, CHESAPEAKE
cape .... HENRY, CHARLES
capital .... RICHMOND
city/town .... SALEM, BEDFORD, BRISTOL, EMPORIA, FAIRFAX, HAMPTON, NORFOLK, ROANOKE, SUFFOLK, DANVILLE, GROVETON, HOPEWELL, MANASSAS, STAUNTON, ANNANDALE, ARLINGTON, LEXINGTON, LYNCHBURG, ALEXANDRIA, CHESAPEAKE, PORTSMOUTH, MOUNT VERNON, NEWPORT NEWS, SPRINGFIELD
college ..... AVERETT, HOLLINS, RADFORD, LONGWOOD, MARYMOUNT
county .... LEE, BATH, PAGE, WISE, YORK, BLAND, FLOYD, GILES, SCOTT, SMYTH, SURRY, WYTHE, AMELIA, ORANGE, AMHERST, AUGUSTA, FAIRFAX, HALIFAX, PULASKI, ROANOKE, RUSSELL, ACCOMACK, CAMPBELL, CULPEPER, POWHATAN, TAZEWELL, ARLINGTON, CHESTERFIELD
cowslip .... BLUEBELL
creeper .... IVY, VINE, WOODBINE
dance .... REEL
island ...... HOG, COBB, CEDAR, SMITH, TANGIER, WALLOPS, METOMPKIN, PARRAMORE, FISHERMANS

lake .... ANNA, GASTON, CLAYTOR, DRAMMOND, PHILPOTT, BLUESTONE, SOUTH HOLSTON, SMITH-MOUNTAIN

mount .... VERNON

mountain .... ROGERS, CUMBERLAND, SHENANDOAH, MASSANUTTEN

mountain range .... ALLEGHENY, BLUE RIDGE, APPALACHIAN

national cemetery .... ARLINGTON

pine .... LOBLOLLY

river .... NI, PO, DAN, NEW, HYCO, PIGG, YORK, JAMES, MAURY, SLATE, SMITH, CLINCH, LITTLE, POWELL, WILLIS, JACKSON, POTOMAC, RAPIDAN, RIVANNA, ROANOKE, TUG FORK, MEHERRIN, NOTTOWAY, PAMUNKEY, MATTAPONI

seaport .... NORFOLK

settlement .... JAMESTON

state bird .... CARDINAL

state flower .... DOGWOOD

state nickname .... OLD DOMINION

truffle .... TUCKAHOE

university .... OLD DOMINION

virginity .... PURITY, MAIDENHOOD, SPINSTERHOOD

virgin's-bower .... CLEMATIS

Virgo .... VIRGIN, CONSTELLATION

star .... SPICA

virgulate .... VIRGATE, ROD-SHAPED

viridian .... PIGMENT

viridity .... VERDANCY, GREENNESS

virile .... MACHO, MANLY, POTENT, VIGOROUS, MASCULINE

fellow .... HE-MAN

Virna, actress .... LISI

virtu ...... CURIO, RARITY, BIBELOT

virtual .... LITERAL, IMPLICIT, POTENTIAL

virtually .... ALMOST, NEARLY, LITERALLY

virtue .... MERIT, WORTH, QUALITY, CHASTITY, GOODNESS, MORALITY, EXCELLENCE

virtues, one of the .... HOPE, FAITH, CHARITY, JUSTICE, PRUDENCE

virtuous .... PURE, MORAL, NOBLE, RIGHT, WORTHY, LAUDABLE, DESERVING, EXCELLENT

virtuosity .... FLAIR, SKILL, KNOW-HOW, EXPERTISE

virtuoso .... ARTIST(E), MAESTRO, AESTHETE, CONNOISSEUR

virulence .... VENOM, DEADLINESS, MALIGNANCY

virulent .... RABID, TOXIC, DEADLY, CAUSTIC, NOXIOUS, VENOMOUS, MALIGNANT, POISONOUS, INFECTIOUS

virus ...... GERM, VENOM, POISON, VACCINE, PATHOGEN

disease .... FLU, AIDS, COLD, POLIO, GRIP(PE), HERPES, RABIES, MEASLES, VARIOLA, VIROSIS, SHINGLES, SMALLPOX, INFLUENZA, VARICELLA, CHICKEN POX

particle, single .... VIRION

type of .... POX, TOGA, ADENO, ARENA, RETRO, HERPES, CORONA, PAPOVA, PICOMA, RHABDO

vis ...... FORCE, POWER, STRENGTH

-a-vis .... FACE TO FACE

visa .... ENDORSEMENT

visage .... MAP, FACE, LOOK, GUISE, ASPECT, COUNTENANCE

viscera .... GUTS, VITALS, INNARDS, ENTRAILS, INTESTINES

viscid .... GUMMY, SYRUPY, STICKY, VISCOSE, VISCOUS

viscosity .... STICKINESS

viscount .... PEER, SHERIFF, NOBLE(MAN)

heir of .... MASTER

viscous .... ROPY, SIZY, GLUEY, MUCID, PASTY, SLIMY, STICKY, GREASY, VISCID, SYRUPY

product ..... GUM, GLUE, PASTE

substance .... TAR, PITCH, RESIN, SLIME, SYRUP, MOLASSES

vise .... CLAM, DIAL, CLAMP, CLINCH, GRIPPER

part of .... JAW

Vishinsky, Soviet diplomat .... ANDREI

Vishnu .... (THE) PRESERVER

avatar of .... KRISHNA

incarnation of .... RAMA, KRISHNA

wife of .... SRI

visible .... IN VIEW, VISUAL, EVIDENT, IN SIGHT, OBVIOUS, SEEABLE, DISCERNIBLE, PERCEPTIBLE

to naked eye .... MACROSCOPIC

Visigoth .... TEUTON

king/chief .... ALARIC

vision .... DREAM, FANCY, IMAGE, ESPIAL, OPTICS, IMAGINE, PICTURE, (EYE)SIGHT

blurred/distorted .... ASTIGMATISM

component of ...... EYE, BRAIN

deceptive, unreal ...... MIRAGE, ILLUSION

defect .... ANOPIA, MYOPIA, DIPLOPIA, HYPEROPIA, ASTIGMATISM

double .... DIPLOPIA, AMBLYOPIA

far-sighted .... PRESBYOPIA

focusing factor .... CORNEA

loss .... BLINDNESS

nearsightedness .... MYOPIA

night blindness .... NYCTALOPIA

pertaining to .... OCULAR, VISUAL, OPTIC(AL)

range .... KEN, EYESHOT, EYESIGHT

reduced in bright light .... HEMERALOPIA

scope .... SCAN

sharpness of .... VISUAL ACUITY

starting point .... RETINA

test, kind of ...... REFRACTION, VISUAL FIELD, VISUAL ACUITY, ACCOMMODATION

tri-dimensional .... STEREOPSIS

visionary .... FEY, DREAMER, FANTAST, UTOPIAN, IDEALIST, QUIXOTIC, THEORIST, IMAGINARY, STARRY-EYED, ILLUSIONIST, IMPRACTICAL

visit .... GO TO, STAY, TARRY, ASSAIL, CALL(ON), DROP IN, INFLICT, SOJOURN, STOPOVER

between whalers .... GAM(MING)

frequently .... HAUNT

kind of ...... SOCIAL, BUSINESS, OFFICIAL, PROFESSIONAL

short .... CALL, LOOK-IN

social .... GAM

visitant .... GUEST, VISITOR

visitation .... BLOW, CALAMITY, DISASTER, HARDSHIP, AFFLICTION

visitor .... GUEST, CALLER, COMPANY, VISITANT

seasonal .... SANTA(CLAUS)

supernatural .... GHOST

visor .... BRIM, MASK, VISARD, VIZARD, EYESHADE, SUNSHADE, EYESHIELD

site .... CAP, HELMET,

WINDSHIELD

vista ...... VIEW, SCENE, OUTLOOK, PANORAMA, LANDSCAPE

Vistula River .... WISLA

city on .... TORUN

tributary .... SAN

visual .... OCULAR, OPTICAL, VISIBLE

Acuity Test aid ..... SNELLEN'S CHART

aids device .... CHART, GRAPH, MOVIE, SLIDE

disorder .... SQUINT, SCOTOMA, STRABISMUS

indication of a submerged problem .... TIP OF THE ICEBERG

perception area .... FIELD

purple .... RHODOPSIN

yellow .... RETINENE

visualize .... SEE, IMAGINE, PICTURE, ENVISION

vita .... LIFE

Vita Nuova author .... DANTE

vital .... ALIVE, FATAL, DEADLY, MORTAL, ESSENTIAL, IMPORTANT

element .... GERM

fluid .... SAP, BLOOD

organ ..... LUNG, HEART, LIVER

principle .... SOUL

statistics of beauty contestant .... MEASUREMENTS

vitality .... LIFE, ZEST, ZING, POWER, VIGOR, ENERGY, VIRILITY

vitalize .... LIVEN, ANIMATE, ENERGIZE

vitamin A .... CAROTENE

deficiency disease .... KWASHIORKOR

-like compounds .... RETINOIDS

source .... EGGS, FISH, MILK, LIVER, CARROT, APRICOT

vitamin B .... CHOLINE

B complex constituent ...... BIOTIN, NIACIN, THIAMINE, FOLIC ACID, PYRIDOXINE

B component .... PABA

B deficiency disease .... ECZEMA, BERIBERI, PELLAGRA, CHLOROSIS, (PERNICIOUS)ANEMIA

B_1 .... THIAMINE

B_2 .... RIBOFLAVIN

B_6 .... PYRIDOXINE

B_{12} .... CYANOCOBALAMIN

B_{12} deficiency patient .... VEGAN

B_{12} source .... BEEF, BRAN,

EGGS, FISH, MILK, PEAS, PORK, LIVER, YOGURT, PEANUTS, POULTRY, SPINACH

B_{12} storage .... LIVER

vitamin C .... ASCORBIC ACID

deficiency disease ..... SCURVY

excessive intake result .... NAUSEA, DIARRHEA, KIDNEY STONE

source .... LIME, LEMON, ORANGE, POTATO, TOMATO, CANTALOUPE, STRAWBERRY

vitamin D .... CALCIFEROL

deficiency disease .... RICKETS, OSTEOMALACIA

source ..... EGGS, TUNA, LIVER, SALMON, HERRING, SARDINE, ULTRAVIOLET RAYS

vitamin E .... TOCOPHEROL

deficiency disease ..... EDEMA, ANEMIA

source ...... EGGS, MEAT, NUTS, CEREALS, WHEAT GERM

vitamin H .... BIOTIN

vitelline .... EGG YOLK

vitellus .... YOLK

vitiate .... UNDO, VOID, SPOIL, TAINT, DEBASE, IMPAIR, WEAKEN, CORRUPT, PERVERT, INVALIDATE

vitreous .... GLASSY, BRITTLE, HYALINE, HYALOID, TRANSPARENT

vitrics .... GLASSWARE

vitrify .... BAKE

vitrine .... SHOWCASE

vitriol .... SORY, SULFATE, BLUEJACK, BLUESTONE

vitriolic .... SHARP, BITING, CAUSTIC, SARCASTIC

vitta .... RIBBON, HEADBAND

vittle .... FOOD, VICTUAL

vituline animal .... CALF

vituperate .... RAIL, ABUSE, SCOLD, BERATE, REBUKE, REVILE, VILIFY, UPBRAID

vituperation ...... ABUSE, TIRADE, INVECTIVE, TONGUE-LASHING

vituperative .... ABUSIVE, SCOLDING

viva .... CHEER, ACCLAIM, EXCLAMATION

voce .... ORAL(LY)

vivacious .... GAY, BREEZY, LIVELY, ANIMATED, CHEERFUL, SPIRITED, SPORTIVE

vivacity .... PEP, BRIO, DASH, ELAN, ARDOR, VERVE, VIGOR, GAIETY, ANIMATION

vivandiere .... SUTLER

vivarium .... HOTHOUSE, GREENHOUSE

vive le _____ .... ROI

vivid .... FRESH, BRIGHT, LIVE(LY), GRAPHIC, ANIMATED, STRIKING

vivify .... ANIMATE, ENLIVEN, REFRESH

vixen .... FOX, HARPY, SCOLD, SHREW, WITCH, VIRAGO, HELLCAT, TERMAGANT

viz. .... NAMELY, VIDELICET

vizard .... MASK, VISOR

Vladimir Ilyich Ulyanov .... LENIN

pianist .... HOROWITZ

vocabulary .... ARGOT, SLANG, WORDS, JARGON, LEXICON, GLOSSARY, WORDBOOK, DICTIONARY

of a .... LEXICAL

vocal .... ORAL, SUNG, SONANT, SPOKEN, VERBAL, VOICED, UTTERED, ARTICULATE

composition .... SONG

cords inflammation .... LARYNGITIS

cords site .... LARYNX

expression .... UTTERANCE

group .... CHOIR, OCTET

ornament .... ROULADE

solo .... ARIA, ARIOSO

vocalist .... SINGER, CROONER, WARBLER

slang .... NIGHTINGALE

vocalize .... SAY, UTTER, PHONATE, ENUNCIATE

vocally .... ALOUD

vocation .... WORK, CRAFT, TRADE, CAREER, METIER, CALLING, OCCUPATION, PROFESSION

voce, _____ .... VIVA

voces .... VOX, VOICE

vociferation .... RANT, CLAMOR

vociferous .... LOUD, NOISY, BLATANT, CLAMOROUS, BOISTEROUS

vodka cocktail .... SCREWDRIVER

mixture .... ORANGE JUICE

vogue .... FAD, TON, MODE, RAGE, STYLE, FASHION

voguish .... POPULAR, FASHIONABLE

voice .... SAY, VOX, UTTER, TONGUE, VOCALITY, UTTER(ANCE), EXPRESS(ION), ARTICULATION

between bass and tenor .... BARITONE

box .... LARYNX

change in tone of
...... INFLECTION, MODULATION
colloquial .... SPOKESMAN,
MOUTHPIECE
female .... ALTO, SOPRANO,
CONTRALTO
highest female singing
.... SOPRANO
highest male singing .... ALTO
impairment .... DYSPHONIA
intonation .... TONE, PITCH
kind of .... ALTO, BASS(O),
TENOR, SOPRANO, BARITONE,
FALSETTO
loud, strident .... FOGHORN
lowest female singing
.... ALTO
male .... BASSO, TENOR
organ .... LARYNX
overused ...... HUSKY, HOARSE,
CROAKING
person with loud ..... STENTOR
pertaining to .... VOCAL,
PHONETIC
practice .... SOLFEGGIO
quality .... TIMBRE
range .... DIAPASON
range, artificial ...... FALSETTO
roaming .... VAGANS
temporary loss of
.... DYSPHONIA
total loss of .... APHONIA
voiced sound ...... SONG, SONANT,
SPEECH, VIBRANT, UTTERANCE
stop .... MEDIA
voiceful .... VOCAL
voiceless ...... MUM, DUMB, MUTE,
SILENT, APHONIC, SPIRATE,
SPEECHLESS, TONGUELESS
sound .... SURD, TENUIS
sound sign .... CEDILLA
voices, for all .... TUTTI
void .... NULL, ANNUL, BLANK,
EMPTY, CANCEL, HOLLOW,
NEGATE, VACANT, VACATE,
VACUUM, INVALID, LACKING,
NULLIFY, NULLITY
of infinite space .... INANE
voidance .... VETO, REPEAL,
VACANCY, ANNULMENT
voided escutcheon .... ORLE
voilà .... LO, SEE, BEHOLD
voile .... FABRIC
voiture .... WAGON, VEHICLE,
CARRIAGE
volant ...... AGILE, QUICK, FLYING,
NIMBLE
jumbo .... AIRLINER
Volapuk, inventor of
.... SCHLEYER
volar .... PALMAR

volatile .... AIRY, GIDDY, LIGHT,
FICKLE, BUOYANT, GASEOUS,
MUTABLE, MERCURIAL
liquid .... ETHER, ALCOHOL
volcanic .... FIERY, VESUVIAN,
EXPLOSIVE, EXTRUSIVE
activity .... BELCHING,
ERUPTION
ash .... TUFF
cinder .... SCORIA
crater .... MAAR
dust .... TUFF
earth .... TRASS
ejection .... LAVA, BELCH,
COULEE, PUMICE, SCORIA,
LAPILLUS
glass .... PUMICE, OBSIDIAN
island .... FAROE, LIPARI,
IWO(JIMA)
landform .... MAAR
mud .... SALSE
opening .... FUMAROLE
rock .... TUFF, WACK, TRASS,
BASALT, LATITE, PUMICE,
TAXITE, PERLITE, LAPILLUS,
OBSIDIAN, RHYOLITE,
TRACHYTE, TEPHRITE,
PROPYLITE, TALPATATE
rock cavity .... VESICLE
slag .... CINDER, SCORIA
soil .... TALPATATE
vent .... CRATER, SOLFATARA
volcano, cone of ...... MONTICULE
crater-like basin ...... CALDERA
island .... IWO JIMA
kind of ..... ACTIVE, DORMANT,
EXTINCT
molten rock .... LAVA, MAGMA
mouth of .... CRATER,
FUMAROLE
well known .... APO, ETNA,
FUJI, TAAL, ASAMA, MAYON,
PELEE, SHASTA, MAUNA LOA,
PINATUBO, VESUVIUS
vole .... RAT, SLAM, RODENT,
(FIELD)MOUSE
volery .... AVIARY
Volga figure .... BOATMAN
tributary .... OKA, KAMA
volitant .... FLYING, FLITTING
volitient .... WILLING
volition .... WILL, CHOICE, OPTION,
VELLEITY
volk .... NATION, PEOPLE
volley ...... BURST, ROUND, SALVO,
BROADSIDE, FUSILLADE
volplane .... COAST, GLIDE
Volstead Act dissenters .... WETS
supporters .... DRYS
Volsunga _____ .... SAGA
Saga dwarf .... NIBELUNG

Saga hero .... SIGURD,
SIEGFRIED
Saga king .... ATLI
volta, in music .... TIME, TURN
Voltaire .... AROUET
character .... PANGLOSS
novel by .... CANDIDE
volt-ampere .... WATT
volte-face ...... REVERSAL, ABOUT-
FACE
voluble .... GLIB, FLUENT,
VERBOSE, GARRULOUS,
TALKATIVE
volume .... BOOK, BULK, MASS,
SIZE, TOME, CUBAGE,
CAPACITY, CONTENTS,
CUBATURE, QUANTITY
of sound unit .... DECIBEL
voluminous .... BIG, AMPLE,
BULKY, LARGE, COPIOUS
dress .... MUMU, MUUMUU
voluntarily .... FREELY,
WILLINGLY
voluntary .... UNASKED, WILLFUL,
WILLING
volunteer .... OFFER, DONATE,
ENLIST, PROFFER
opposed to .... DRAFTEE,
CONSCRIPT
voluptuary .... HEDONIST,
SYBARITE, SENSUALIST
voluptuous ...... FLESHY, LYDIAN,
SENSUAL, WORLDLY,
SENSUOUS
slang .... SEXY
volute .... CURL, ROLL, TURN,
WHORL, SPIRAL(ED)
volution .... COIL, GYRE, HELIX,
SCROLL, ROLLING
vomica .... PUS
vomit .... PUKE, SPEW, BELCH,
EJECT, EMETIC, REJECT,
REGORGE, THROW UP,
DISGORGE
effort to .... RETCH
vomiting .... EMESIS
blood .... HEMATEMESIS
in pregnancy .... MORNING
SICKNESS
Vonnegut novel .... CAT'S
CRADLE
voodoo .... HEX, OBI, BEAH,
CHARM, HOODOO, FETISHISM,
BLACK MAGIC, WITCHCRAFT
deity .... ZOMBI(E)
spell .... MOJO
voracious ...... GREEDY, HUNGRY,
EDACIOUS, ESURIENT,
RAVENOUS, RAPACIOUS,
GLUTTONOUS, INSATIABLE
voracity .... GREED, EDACITY,

GLUTTONY, RAPACITY

Voroshilov, USSR president .... KLEMENTI

vortex .... EDDY, GYRE, WHIRLPOOL, WHIRLWIND

votary .... FAN, NUN, MONK, DEVOTEE, BELIEVER, CELIBATE, WORSHIPER, ENTHUSIAST

vote .... BALLOT, SUFFRAGE

by gesture .... THUMBS UP, THUMBS DOWN

counting .... POLL

in .... ELECT

in opposition .... CON

kind of .... CON, HAND, PROXY, STRAW, SECRET

non-candidate's ...... WRITE-IN

of assent .... AYE, PLACET

presiding officer's .... CASTING

right to .... SUFFRAGE, FRANCHISE

solicitation for a bill .... LOBBY

survey .... POLL

voiced .... AYE, NAY, YEA

voter .... ELECTOR

voting amendment beneficiaries as of 1971 ...... EIGHTEEN OR OLDER

method .... VOICE, BALLOT

vouch .... BACK, AFFIRM, ASSURE, ATTEST, CERTIFY, SPONSOR, GUARANTEE

voucher .... CHIT, RECEIPT, EVIDENCE, DEBENTURE

vouchsafe .... GIVE, DEIGN, GRANT, BESTOW, CONCEDE, GUARANTEE

vouge .... TON

vow .... OATH, SWEAR, PLEDGE, PROMISE, DEDICATE

taker .... NUN, MONK, VOTARY, WITNESS, CELIBATE, OFFICIAL, DEFENDANT

to inflict harm .... THREATEN

vowel .... LETTER

change in sound ..... UMLAUT

contraction of .... SYNERESIS

gradation .... ABLAUT

mark .... BREVE, TILDE, MACRON, UMLAUT, DI(A)ERESIS, CIRCUMFLEX

slurring .... ELISION

vox .... VOICE

voyage .... SAIL, TRAVEL, JOURNEY, PASSAGE, (SEA)TRIP

pleasure .... JAUNT, CRUISE

short .... EXCURSION

voyager .... SAILOR

voyageur .... BOATMAN, TRAVELER

voyeur .... PEEPING TOM

vrouw .... LADY, WOMAN, HOUSEWIFE

vs. .... VERSUS

Vulcan .... HEPHAESTUS, HEPHAISTOS

Star Trek .... (MR) SPOCK

vulcanite .... RUBBER, EBONITE

vulgar ...... LOUD, CRASS, CRUDE, GROSS, RANDY, COARSE, COMMON, RIBALD, BOORISH, LOW-BRED, OBSCENE, UNCOUTH, PLEBEIAN

vulgarian .... CAD, LOUT, SLUT, CHURL, BARBARIAN, ROUGHNECK

vulgarity .... ILL-BREEDING

Vulgate, author of the .... JEROME

vulnerable .... WEAK, ASSAILABLE

Vulpecula .... LITTLE FOX, CONSTELLATION

vulpine ...... FOXY, WILY, CRAFTY, TRICKY, CUNNING, VULPECULAR

vulture .... URUBU, ATRATA, CONDOR, BUZZARD, GRIFFON, PREDATOR, SCAVENGER, LAMMERGEI(E)R

food .... CARRION

hawk resembling .... CARACARA

W

W, Arabic .... WAW

in chemistry .... TUNGSTEN

old English .... WEN

Waadt .... VAUD

Wabash Cannonball composer .... (ROY)ACUFF

Wabash River City .... TERRE HAUTE

tributary .... TIPPECANOE

wabble .... LARVA, WOBBLE

wacker .... QUAKER

wacky ...... ODD, QUEER, ERRATIC, ECCENTRIC

person .... WACKO

wad .... BAT, PAD, CRAM, LUMP, MASS, PLUG, BUNDLE, DOSSIL, FILLING, STUFF(ING)

of paper money .... (BANK)ROLL

used as wound dressing .... PLEDGET

wadding material .... HEMP, KAPOK, COTTON

waddle .... WAG, SWAY, LURCH, TODDLE, WOBBLE

waddler ...... BABY, DUCK, GOOSE, TODDLER

waddy ...... CANE, CLUB, COWBOY, WALKING STICK

wade .... FORD, SLOG, SLOSH, PADDLE, WALLOW

wader .... COOT, IBIS, RAIL, CRANE, EGRET, HERON, SNIPE

waders .... BOOTS

wadi ...... OASIS, RAVINE, VALLEY, CHANNEL, WATERCOURSE

wading bird. See also **bird** .... IBIS

wadset .... MORTGAGE

wafer .... CAKE, DISK, SNAP, CANDY, COOKIE, TABLET, BISCUIT, CRACKER, LOZENGE

container .... PIX, PYX

of the Eucharist .... HOST

waff .... GUST, PUFF, WAVE, GHOST, WHIFF, SOLITARY, WORTHLESS

waffie .... VAGABOND

waffle .... PRATTLE, (BATTER)CAKE

like .... PANCAKE

waft .... BUOY, GUST, ROLL, WAIF, WAVE, FLOAT, BREATH, CONVEY, CARRY(OVER), TRANSPORT

wag .... NOD, WIT, CARD, JERK, SWAY, WAVE, JOKER, SHAKE, JESTER, WAGGLE, WIGGLE, FARCEUR, PUNSTER

wage .... PAY, HIRE, MAKE, SALARY, CARRY ON, CONDUCT, STIPEND, ENGAGE(IN), EMOLUMENT

boost .... RAISE

deduct from .... DOCK

earner .... CARPENTER, STEVEDORE, BRICKLAYER, STONEMASON, LONGSHOREMAN

earners collectively .... LABOR

war .... LEVY

wager ...... BET, VIE, ANTE, GAGE, RISK, STAKE, GAMBLE, HAZARD, IMPONE, PARLAY

wages .... INCOME, REWARD, STIPEND, EARNINGS, EMOLUMENT, RECOMPENSE, COMPENSATION

after deductions .... TAKE-HOME

describing some .... LIVING, STARVATION

payment in kind .... TRUCK

wagged, thing that's .... FLAG, HEAD, TAIL, FINGER, TONGUE

wagger .... DOG, PIPIT

waggery .... WIT, JEST, JOKE, MERRIMENT

waggish .... DROLL, MERRY, JOCULAR, PLAYFUL, ROGUISH, SPORTIVE

waggle .... TOTTER

dancer .... BEE

Wagner, composer ...... RICHARD

father-in-law of .... LISZT

forte of .... OPERA

heroine of .... EVA, ELSA, ISOLDE

tetralogy of .... RING CYCLE

wife of .... COSIMA

work of .... LIEBESTOD, LOHENGRIN

Wagnerian earth goddess .... ERDA

heroine .... EVA, ELSA

music festival city .... BAYREUTH

opus .... RIENZI, PARSIFAL, LIEBESTOD, LOHENGRIN

role ...... ELSA, HAGEN, SENTA, WOTAN, ISOLDE, TRISTAN

soprano .... NILSSON

wagon .... CAR, VAN, DRAY, TRAM, WAIN, LORRY, (T)CART, TRUCK, CAMION, TRAILER, TUMBREL, TUMBRIL, VOITURE

ammunitions .... CAISSON

baggage .... FOURGON

battle .... DREADNAUGHT

box-like .... TRAM

builder .... WAINWRIGHT

Charlemagne's .... WAIN

driver .... CARTER, CHARIOTEER

for hauling .... DRAY

freight charge .... CARTAGE

horse .... POLER

horse-drawn .... CHARIOT

open four-wheeled .... T-CART, WAGONETTE

oriental .... ARABA

pin .... CLEVIS

police .... BLACK MARIA

prairie .... SCHOONER

repairer .... WAINWRIGHT

shaft .... THILL

tongue .... NEAP

track .... RUT

yoke .... INSPAN

Wagoner .... AURIGA, BIG DIPPER, CHARLES'S WAIN

wagons, convoy of .... WAGON TRAIN

wagtail .... BIRD, LARK, PIPIT, THRUSH

wahoo .... ELM, SHRUB, BASSWOOD, BURNING BUSH

fish .... ONO, PETO

waif .... WAFT, GAMIN, STRAY, SIGNAL, VAGRANT, MAVERICK, FOUNDLING, (STREET)ARAB

Waikiki .... BEACH

site .... HONOLULU

wail ...... CRY, SOB, HOWL, MOAN, WAWL, YOWL, MOURN, LAMENT, ULULATE, COMPLAIN, (CATER)WAUL

Wailing Wall chore ...... PRAYER, LAMENTATION

devotee .... JEW

site .... JERUSALEM

wain .... CART, WAGON

wainscot .... CEIL, LINING, PANEL(ING), WALLBOARD

waist ...... LOIN, BASQUE, BLOUSE, BODICE, MIDDLE, MIDRIFF

circumference .... GIRTH

garment .... SARONG, LOINCLOTH

molding garment .... GIRDLE

of dress .... TAILLE

wasters .... DIET

waistband .... OBI, BELT, SASH, GIRDLE, CINCTURE

waistcloth .... PAREUS, SARONG, LAVA-LAVA

waistcoat .... VEST, GILET, JACKET, WESKIT

waistline .... GIRTH

wait .... BIDE, STAY, DALLY, DELAY, SERVE, TARRY, ATTEND, LINGER, REMAIN

in ambush .... COUCH

lie in .... TRAP, AMBUSH

near at hand .... HOVER

on .... SERVE, VISIT, ATTEND

until a future time .... POSTPONE, PROCRASTINATE

waiter .... TRAY, GARCON, POTMAN, SALVER, SERVER, STEWARD, ATTENDANT

drive-in .... CARHOP

female .... WAITRESS

portable .... DUMB

waiter's delight .... TIPPER

waiting line .... CUE, QUEUE

waitresses, chief of ...... HOSTESS

waive .... DEFER, GIVE UP, FOR(E)GO, ABANDON, DISCLAIM, RENOUNCE, RELINQUISH

right or title .... QUITCLAIM

Wakashan people .... AHT, NOOTKA

wake .... PATH, STIR, TRACK, VIGIL, WATCH, AROUSE, EXCITE

periscope's .... FEATHER

robin .... ARUM, PLANT, SARAH, TRILLIUM, CUCKOOPINT, JACK-IN-THE-PULPIT

submarine's .... FEATHER

up from this .... COMA, DREAM, SLEEP, STUPOR, TRANCE, NIGHTMARE

wakeful .... ALERT, RESTLESS, INSOMNIAC, SLEEPLESS

Wake Island .... OTORI

waken .... STIR, AWAKE, (A)ROUSE, EXCITE, SHAKE UP

Waldheim, UN secretary-general .... KURT

nationality of .... AUSTRIAN

Waldorf .... SALAD

-Astoria .... HOTEL

-Astoria site .... NEW YORK

wale .... RIB, BLOW, WELT, W(H)EAL, WHELK, CHOICE, BLEMISH, TEXTURE, SELECT(ION)

on a fabric .... RIDGE

waled fabric .... CORDUROY

Waler .... HORSE

Wales bay .... CARDIGAN, TREMADOC, CARMARTHEN, SAINT BRIDES

capital .... CARDIFF

city/town .... BALA, RHYL, BARRY, CHIRK, FLINT, NEATH, NEFYN, BANGOR, HARLECH, MAESTEG, NEWPORT, PENARTH, SWANSEA, WREXHAM, ABERDARE, HAWARDEN, LLANELLI, RHONDDA, PEMBROKE, TREDEGAR

county .... CLWYD, DYFED, GWENT, POWYS, GWYNEDD, GLAMORGAN

dog .... (WELSH)CORGI, (WELSH)TERRIER

floral emblem .... LEEK

head .... CEMMAES

island .... HOLY, CALDY, BARDSEY, ANGLESEY
language .... CYMRIC, BRYTHONIC
mountain .... SNOWDON, PLYNLIMON
mountain range .... BLACK, BERWYN, PRESELI, CAMBRIAN
national park ...... SNOWDONIA
patron saint .... DAVID
peninsula .... GOWER, LLEYN
people of .... WELSH
poetic name .... CAMBRIA
port .... TALBOT
river ...... DEE, ELY, USK, WYE, TAFF, TOWY, DOVEY, TEIFI, SEVERN, RHYMNEY
seaport .... SWANSEA
strait .... MENAI
Walesa, Polish leader ...... LECH
walk .... GAIT, HIKE, HOOF, PLOD, STEP, STOA, TREK, ALLEY, AMBLE, MARCH, TRAMP, TREAD, RAMBLE, SPHERE, STROLL, TRAVEL
a beat .... PATROL
about .... AMBULATE
about idly .... STROLL, SAUNTER
about ostentatiously .... PARADE
across a street carelessly .... JAYWALK
aimlessly .... ROAM, ROVE, RAMBLE, WANDER
along .... MOSEY
around .... SKIRT
awkward, halting .... LIMP, HOBBLE
awkwardly .... SHAMBLE
baby's .... TODDLE, WADDLE
beach .... ESPLANADE
clumsily .... LUMBER, SHUFFLE
coating .... PARGET, PLASTER
covered .... STOA, ARCADE, PORTICO, CLOISTER
daintily .... MINCE
furtively .... STALK
kind of .... HIKE, LIMP, MINCE, STRUT, TRAMP, LUMBER, PRANCE, SASHAY, STRIDE, TODDLE, WADDLE, WOBBLE, LAMBETH, SWAGGER
leisurely ...... AMBLE, STROLL, TRUDGE, SAUNTER, TRAIPSE, PROMENADE
like a crab .... SIDLE
long .... HIKE, MARCH
of life .... SPHERE
off .... LEAVE, DEPART
off with .... WIN, STEAL

on .... TREAD, TRAMPLE
on stilts .... TRAMPOLIO
out on .... LEAVE, DESERT, ABANDON
over .... BULLY, HENPECK, BULLDOZE
pompously .... STRUT
precariously .... TEETER
public .... PARADE, ESPLANADE, PROMENADE
self-importantly .... SASHAY
shaded .... MALL, ALAMEDA
slang .... HIT THE ROAD
softly .... PAD, TIPTOE
taken for one's health .... CONSTITUTIONAL
this in Boston .... FREEDOM TRAIL
through mud .... SLOSH, WALLOW, SQUELCH
through water .... WADE
to and fro .... PACE
unsteadily .... TOTTER, STAGGER
vain .... STRUT, PEACOCK, SWAGGER
with a lame leg .... LIMP, HOBBLE
with heavy steps .... STAMP, STUMP, TRAMP, TRAMPLE
walkaway ...... TRIUMPH, VICTORY
walker .... HIKER, PACER, TREKKER, VAGRANT, AMBULANT, STROLLER, PEDESTRIAN
idle .... FLANEUR
walking .... HIKING, HOOFING, AMBULANT, FOOTWORK, GRADIENT, AMBULATORY, PEDESTRIAN
adapted for .... GRESSORIAL
aid .... CANE, WALKER, CRUTCHES
idle .... FLANERIE
miss one's step in .... STUMBLE
on air .... ELATED
on all fours ...... PRONOGRADE
papers .... PINK SLIP, DISMISSAL
shoes .... RUBBERS, BALMORAL, SNEAKERS
stick .... CANE, POGO, STAFF, STILT, WADDY, MALAGA, RATTAN, MALACCA, SUPPLEJACK
vendor .... PEDDLER
walkout .... STRIKE
wall .... DIKE, SIDE, FENCE, LEVEE, PARIES, SEPTUM, BARRIER, PARAPET, PARTITION

aboard ship .... BULKHEAD
band .... CORDON
bench .... PODIUM
binder .... PERPEND
border .... DADO
bracket .... CORBEL, SCONCE
coating .... PAINT, PLASTER
column .... PILASTER
cover .... PAPER, MANTLE, LAG(GING), PANELING
dividing .... SEPTUM, PARTITION
end of .... ANTA
facing .... VENEER, REVETMENT
for defense .... RAMPART, PALISADE, VALLATION
fort .... RAMPART
garden .... HAHA
hanging cloth .... ARRAS, TAPESTRY
in .... CONFINE, ENCLOSE
indentation .... CRENEL(LE)
inscription .... GRAFFITO
kind of .... JETTY, STONE, RIPRAP
lining .... STEEN, WAINSCOT
lizard .... GECKO
loophole .... CRENEL(LE)
mine .... BRATTICE
molding .... CORNICE
opening .... BAY, SCUTTLE, CRENEL(LE), EMBRASURE
painter .... MURALIST
park .... HAHA
pertaining to .... MURAL
pier .... ANTA
protective .... PARAPET, RAMPART, PALISADE
recess .... BAY, NICHE
river ..... LEVEE, EMBANKMENT
rue .... FERN
sea .... DAM, DIKE, MOLE, PIER, BREAKWATER
section .... PANEL
step .... STILE
stone .... ASHLAR
tapestry .... ARRAS
top layer .... COPING
top slab .... CAPSTONE
water .... DAM, DIKE, PIER, WEIR, EMBANKMENT
wood lining .... WAINSCOT
wooden pin .... NOG
writing .... GRAFFITO
Wall Street ...... MONEY MARKET, STOCK EXCHANGE
operator .... BEAR, BULL, BROKER, SPECULATOR
transaction .... TRADE
watchdog .... SEC
Wall Streeter .... (STOCK)BROKER

wallaba ...... APA, TREE, ARAWAK
wallaby .... KANGAROO
Wallace, novelist .... LEW, IRVING
   work ..... BEN HUR, THE WORD
Wallach, actor .... ELI
Wal(l)achian 15th century
   ruler ...... VLAD TEPES, VLAD
                 DRACUL
wallaroo .... EURO, KANGAROO
wallboard .... WAINSCOT, GYPSUM
                    BOARD
walled .... ENCLOSED,
                PARTITIONED
   town .... BURG
wallet .... POUCH, PURSE, SCRIP,
   BILLFOLD, (KNAP)SACK,
   (MONEY)BAG, POCKETBOOK
walleye .... ALEWIFE, STRABISMUS
walleyed .... CROSSEYED
   fish ..... PIKE, PERCH, ALEWIFE,
                 POLLACK
   pike .... DORE, DORY
   slang .... DRUNK
wallflower .... CUBA, HEARTSEASE
wallies .... FINERY
wallop .... HIT, BEAT, BELT,
   PASTE, SMITE, THRASH
walloper .... WHOPPER
walloping .... STRONG, POWERFUL,
               WHOPPING
wallow .... TOSS, REVEL, GROVEL,
   PUDDLE, WELTER, MUDHOLE,
   FLOUNDER, LUXURIATE,
             ROLL(ABOUT)
walls, behind the .... IN PRISON
   dividing .... SEPTA
wally .... TOY, FINE, GEWGAW,
   PLEASING, FIRST-RATE
"Wally" .... DUCHESS OF
                 WINDSOR
walnut ...... TREE, WOOD, BROWN,
   TRYMA, HICKORY, SHAGBARK
Walpurgis Night revelers
   .... WITCHES
walrus .... BRUT, SEAL, MORSE,
   SEACOW, TUSKER, PINNIPED,
   SEAHORSE, ROSMARINE
   herd .... POD
   male .... BULL
   tooth .... TUSK
   tusk .... IVORY
   weapon .... RUSK
Walton, basketball player
   .... BILL
   business tycoon .... SAM
   fisherman .... IZAAK
waltz .... DANCE, MUSIC, VALSE,
                  WHIRL
   a kind of .... BOSTON
   dance like .... REDOWA
   king .... STRAUSS

wamble .... REEL, STAGGER
wame ...... WOMB, BELLY, VENTER
wampum .... BEADS, MONEY,
   PEAG(E), SE(A)WAN
wamus .... JACKET, CARDIGAN
wan .... ASHY, PALE, WAXY,
   ASHEN, WAXEN, PALLID,
               COLORLESS
wand .... ROD, MACE, BATON,
   SHOOT STAFF, VERGE, WITHE,
   SWITCH, WATTLE, SCEPTER
   conductor's .... BATON
   shaped like a .... VIRGATE
   symbol of medical
      profession ..... CADUCEUS
   symbol of sovereignty
   .... SCEPTER
wander .... GAD, ROAM, ROVE,
   DRIFT, STRAY, RAMBLE,
   STROLL, MEANDER, TRAIPSE,
              DIVAGATE
   about idly .... GAD
   from main subject in talking
   .... RAMBLE, DIGRESS,
                DIVAGATE
   over a wide area
   .... STRAGGLE
   predatorily .... PROWL
wanderer .... ARAB, HOBO,
   GYPSY, NOMAD, ROVER,
   TRAMP, BEDOUIN, VAGRANT,
   VAGABOND, ITINERANT,
            LANDLO(U)PER
wandering ...... ERRANT, ERRATIC,
   NOMADIC, ODYSSEY,
   VAGRANT, DEVIATING,
             FOOTLOOSE
   beggar .... FAKIR, ROGUE,
              VAGABOND
   caliph .... AL RASCHID
   dervish .... CALENDER
   extended .... ODYSSEY
   from what is normal
   .... ABERRANT
   mental state .... DELIRIUM
   minstrel/student .... GOLIARD
   tribe .... GYPSY
wanderings .... ODYSSEY,
               TRAVELS
wanderoo ...... LANGUR, MONKEY,
              MACAQUE
wandle ...... AGILE, LITHE, SUPPLE
wane .... EBB, FADE, SINK, ABATE,
   LESSEN, DECLINE, DWINDLE,
   SLACKEN, SUBSIDE, DIMINISH
wangle .... GET, COAX, WRING,
   OBTAIN, FALSIFY, FINAGLE,
   JUGGLE, WHEEDLE,
   W(R)IGGLE, CONTRIVE
wanigan .... ARK
want .... LACK, MISS, NEED, WISH,

   CRAVE, DEARTH, DESIRE,
   NEGLECT, POVERTY,
   SCARCITY, SHORTAGE,
   NECESSITY, DESTITUTION,
   REQUIRE(MENT)
wanted man .... OUTLAW,
   ESCAPEE, DESPERADO, PUBLIC
                ENEMY
wanting .... MINUS, ABSENT,
               WITHOUT
wanton .... LEWD, RASH, TART,
   WILD, LOOSE, IMMORAL,
   PLAYFUL, WAYWARD,
   WILLFUL, HEEDLESS,
   RECKLESS, UNCHASTE,
            FROLICSOME
   destroyer .... VANDAL
   kittens make _____ ..... SOBER
                  CATS
   man .... LIBERTINE
   woman .... FLIRT, HUSSY,
             TRAMP, TROLLOP
wapiti .... ELK, DEER
Wapner's bailiwick .... PEOPLE'S
                 COURT
   wrap .... ROBE
war .... COMBAT, STRIFE,
   CONFLICT, HOSTILITY,
   BELLICOSITY, HOSTILITIES,
           BELLIGERENCE
   acquisition .... SPOILS
   advocate for an all-out
   .... HAWK, JINGO
   against abuse .... CRUSADE
   agency .... OSS
   agreement .... TRUCE, CARTEL,
              CEASEFIRE
   ammo wagon .... CAISSON
   arrange forces for battle in
   .... MARSHAL
   at .... BELLICOSE, BELLIGERENT
   attack by military force
   .... INVASION
   between armed forces
   .... BATTLE, COMBAT,
              STRUGGLE
   boat: abbr. .... LST
   bonnet wearer .... INDIAN
   casualty symbol .... GOLD
                 STAR
   chariot .... ESSED
   chief, name meaning
   .... CEDRIC
   cry ...... YELL, ALALA, AMORT,
   WHOOP, BANZAI, SLOGAN
   dance .... PYRRHIC
   describing a mutually
     destructive
   .... INTERNECINE
   drums .... TAM-TAM, TOM-TOM

engine, stone-throwing .... CATAPULT, TREBUCHET
event provoking .... CASUS BELLI
fleet .... ARMADA
foot soldiers .... INFANTRY
galley beak .... ROSTRUM
games .... MANEUVERS
gas .... MUSTARD, YPERITE, ADAMSITE
god .... TYR, ARES, IRRA, MARS, ODIN, WOTAN
goddess .... ENYO, ATHENA, BELLONA, MINERVA
holy .... JIHAD, CRUSADE
horse ...... CHARGER, COURSER, VET(ERAN), DESTRIER
horse head armor .... CHAMFRON, CHAMFRAIN
long-continued, between families .... FEUD
maneuvering of military forces .... TACTICS
mounted troops ...... CAVALRY
of words .... DEBATE
operation .... CAMPAIGN
paint: sl. .... REGALIA, COSMETICS
paint wearer .... INDIAN
participant .... GUNNER, MARINE, SAILOR, FIGHTER, SOLDIER, VETERAN, WARRIOR, COMBATANT, ANTAGONIST, BELLIGERENT
pertaining to .... MARTIAL
planning of large-scale operations ...... STRATEGY
preparation ...... MOBILIZATION
pretext for .... CASUS BELLI
religious .... CRUSADE
scheme to deceive enemy .... STRATAGEM
slogan of Marine Raiders .... GUNG-HO
symbol of .... MARS
-torn land .... IRAQ, IRAN, KUWAIT, CROATIA, LEBANON
troops' resurgence ...... RALLY
troops' withdrawal .... RETREAT
vehicle .... JEEP, TANK, HALFTRACK
vessel .... U-BOAT, PT-BOAT, CRUISER, FLATTOP, TRIREME, CORVETTE, DESTROYER, SUB(MARINE), DREADNAUGHT, AIRCRAFT CARRIER
volunteer forces .... GUERRILLAS
weapon ..... GAS, BOMB, GUNS, CANNON, ROCKET, MISSILE, TORPEDO, ARTILLERY
within nation .... CIVIL WAR, REVOLUTION

War and Peace author .... TOLSTOI
heroine .... NATASHA
warble ...... SING, CAROL, LARVA, TRILL, TREMOR, YODEL, BABBLE, QUAVER
warbler. See also **songbird** .... SINGER, REDSTART, SONGSTER, BECCAFICO, TROCHILUS
warbling .... CHIRM, TWITTER
Warbucks .... DADDY
ward .... CARE, FEND, AVERT, GUARD, PARRY, WATCH, CHARGE, CUSTODY, DISTRICT, PROTEGE(E), DEPENDENT
heelers .... POLITICOS
kind of .... MINOR, INCOMPETENT
off .... AVERT, STAVE OFF
part of a .... PRECINCT
person (entrusted) with a .... PATRON, TRUSTEE, GUARDIAN
politician .... HEELER
warden ...... PEAR, JAILER, JAILOR, ALCAIDE, TRUSTEE, KEEPER, GUARDIAN, CONSTABLE, CUSTODIAN, GATEKEEPER
famous .... LAWES
forest .... RANGER
kind of .... FIRE, GAME, FOREST, PRISON, AIR-RAID
of a minor .... CURATOR
warder .... ROD, GUARD, STAFF, TURNKEY, WATCHMAN, CUSTODIAN
wardrobe .... DUDS, ATTIRE, CLOSET, APPAREL, ARMOIRE, CLOTHES
bride's .... TROUSSEAU
room, clergy's .... VESTRY
servant's .... LIVERY, UNIFORMS
slang .... FINERY
wardship .... CUSTODY
ware .... WARY, WISE, AWARE, READY, DISHES, POTTERY, PRUDENT, CAUTIOUS, CONSCIOUS OF
warehouse .... HONG, DEPOT, ETAPE, STORE, BODEGA, GODOWN, CAMARIN, ELEVATOR, ENTREPOT, MAGAZINE
for candles .... CHANDLERY
items .... STORABLES
platform .... PALLET

public .... ETAPE
receipt ..... QUEDAN, WARRANT
vehicle .... FORKLIFT
weapons .... ARSENAL
wares .... GOODS, MERCHANDISE
warfare .... CLASH, COMBAT, POLEMY, STRIFE, CONFLICT, FIGHTING, STRUGGLE, HOSTILITIES
kind of .... AIR, LAND, NAVAL, AERIAL, ATOMIC, MISSILE, CHEMICAL, AMPHIBIOUS, UNDERGROUND
temporary stoppage of ..... TRUCE, ARMISTICE, CEASE-FIRE
Warfield, duchess .... WALLIS
warhead of missile .... PAYLOAD
Warhol .... ANDY
warlike .... ODINIC, HOSTILE, MARTIAL, MILITANT, TACTICAL, BELLICOSE, COMBATIVE, BELLIGERENT
warlock .... WIZARD, CONJURER, MAGICIAN, SORCERER
warm .... MILD, FRESH, MUGGY, SUNNY, ARDENT, FERVID, HEAT(ED), LIVELY, CORDIAL, THERMAL, ZEALOUS
and stuffy .... CLOSE
baths .... THERMAE
-blooded .... ARDENT, FERVENT, PASSIONATE
compress .... STUPE
-hearted .... KIND, LOVING, TENDER, CORDIAL
make moderately .... TEPEFY
moderately .... TEPID, WARMISH, LUKEWARM
springs .... THERMAE
state of being made .... CALEFACTION
very .... HOT, CANDENT
warmed-over .... (RE)HEATED
warmer .... STOVE, BURNER, HEATER, FURNACE
warmly lit .... AGLOW
warmonger .... HAWK, WARLORD, JINGO(IST), DEMAGOGUE, FIREBRAND, MILITARIST, RABBLEROUSER
warmth ...... HEAT, ZEAL, ARDOR, ENTHUSIASM
increasing in .... CALESCENT
of emotion ..... ARDOR, SPARK, VIVACITY, EAGERNESS
sensation of .... GLOW
warn .... FLAG, ALERT, ADVISE, DEMAND, EXHORT, NOTIFY, SIGNAL, CAUTION, PORTEND, ADMONISH, FOREBODE,

warning .... OMEN, ALARM, THREATEN, CHECK, AUGURY, LESSON, NOTICE, THREAT, TIP-OFF, PORTENT, PRESAGE, (AD)MONITION
from dermatologist .... SKIN-DONT(S)
in law .... CAVEAT
old style .... LARUM
signal ...... HISS, ALERT, SIREN, ALAR(U)M, BEACON, TOCSIN
signal device .... BELL, FLARE, SIREN, FOGHORN, RED FLAG
snake's .... HISS, RATTLE
system, for short .... DEWS
weather .... ADVISORY
word(s) of .... FORE, HALT, STOP, BEWARE, FREEZE, LOOK OUT, WATCH OUT, OFF LIMIT(S)
warp ...... MUD, BIAS, SILT, TWIST, DEFORM, CONTORT, DEVIATE, INCLINE, PERVERT, ABERRATION, DISTORT(ION), (BEND) OUT OF SHAPE
and woof .... WEAVE
thread ends .... THRUM
warped .... UNJUST, PREJUDICED
warplane .... SPAD, ZERO, STUKA, BOMBER, FIGHTER, SPITFIRE, FLYING FORTRESS
warplanes, fleet of .... (AIR)ARMADA
warrant .... PASS, WRIT, MERIT, ORDER, STATE, ASSURE, CAVEAT, PERMIT, PLEDGE, PLEVIN, SURETY, TICKET, CERTIFY, JUSTIFY, PRECEPT, VOUCHER, GUARANTEE, AUTHORIZATION
convict's .... MITTIMUS
of arrest .... CAPIAS
officer .... BOSUN
one's ability, character .... AVOUCH, VOUCH FOR
royal .... BERAT, EDICT
to appear in court .... SUMMONS, SUBPOENA
warranty .... PROMISE, ASSURANCE, GUARANTEE
warren .... HUTCH, SLUM(S), RABBITRY
inhabitant .... GAME, RABBIT
Warren, Chief Justice ...... EARL
warrigal .... DINGO
warring nations' agreement ...... TRUCE, CARTEL, TREATY, ARMISTICE
warrior .... JINGO, SINGH, FIGHTER, KURIPAN, SOLDIER, COMBATANT, SERVICEMAN
arena .... GLADIATOR
Algerian .... SPAHI
female .... AMAZON
frenzied for battle .... BERSERK(ER)
Indian .... BRAVE
Japanese .... SAMURAI
noted: poet. .... THANE
Philippine .... MAHARLIKA
warsaw .... FISH, GROUPER
warship .... RAZEE, GALLEY, CRUISER, FLATTOP, FRIGATE, GALLEON, MAN O'WAR, TRIREME, IRONCLAD, DESTROYER, BATTLEWAGON, DREADNAUGHT, DREADNOUGHT
armored .... MONITOR, IRONCLAD, MERRIMAC
boat on .... DINGHY, LAUNCH
convoy .... CORVET(TE)
deck, lowest .... ORLOP
eating quarters .... WARDROOM
gun emplacement ...... TURRET
gun shield .... CUPOLA
kitchen .... GALLEY
lookout .... CROW'S NEST
prison .... BRIG
ram .... BEAK
station for wounded .... COCKPIT
tower .... TURRET
warships, fleet of .... ARMADA
involving .... NAVAL
wart .... BULGE, TUMOR, GROWTH, PAPULE, BLEMISH, VERRUCA, KERATOSIS, PAPILLOMA
on eyelids/armpit, describing .... FILIFORM
on foot sole, describing .... PLANTAR
type of .... FLAT, GENITAL, PLANTAR, DIGITATE, FILIFORM
Wartburg's important resident .... LUTHER
wartime detainee .... INTERNEE
detention .... INTERNMENT
sea hazard .... MINE
warts, covered with .... VERRUCOSE
wary .... SHY, ALERT, CAG(E)Y, CANNY, CHARY, LEERY, CAREFUL, GUARDED, PRUDENT, CAUTIOUS, DISCREET, SUSPICIOUS, CIRCUMSPECT
wash .... LAP, WET, LAVE, SLOP, BATHE, DRIFT, ELUTE, FLOOD, RINSE, SWILL, DRENCH, PURIFY, DETERGE, MOISTEN, HOSE(DOWN)
away .... ERODE
and iron .... LAUNDER
basin/bowl .... LAVER, LAVABO, LABATORY
by rubbing hard .... SCOUR, SCRUB
hair/scalp .... SHAMPOO
in lye .... BUCK
kind of .... MOUTH, LOTION
lightly .... RINSE
one's hands of ...... ABANDON, GIVE UP, CAST OFF, DISCARD
out .... FADE, ELUTE
out with swift current of water .... FLUSH
to remove dirt, impurities .... CLEAN(SE)
washbowl in church .... LAVABO
washed out .... FADED, BLEACHED
up ..... BEAT, BUSHED, POOPED, THROUGH, EXHAUSTED
washer .... GASKET, SCRUBBER
washerwoman .... LAUNDRESS
washing ...... ELUTION, FLUSHING, LAVATION, SCRUBBING, LAUNDERING
act/process of .... LAVATION
board .... DOLLY
body, in religious ceremony .... ABLUTION
out of an organ .... ENEMA, LAVAGE
soapsuds .... LATHER
sound of .... SLOSH
water for .... LAVATION
Washington Air Force Base .... MCCHORD, FAIRCHILD
airport .... DULLES
author .... IRVING
bay .... DABOB, PADILLA, WILLAPA, BOUNDARY
bills .... ONES
bloomer .... CHAT
cape .... ALAVA, FLATTERY, SHOALWATER, DISAPPOINTMENT
capital .... OLYMPIA
city/town ..... KELSO, AUBURN, BURIEN, RENTON, TACOMA, WAPATO, YAKIMA, EDMONDS, EVERETT, PULLMAN, REDMOND, SEATTLE, SPOKANE, ABERDEEN, BELLEVUE, LYNNWOOD, BREMERTON, KENNEWICK, VANCOUVER, BELLINGHAM, WALLA WALLA, MOUNT VERNON
college .... WHITMAN
county .... KING, ADAMS, CLARK, GRANT, LEWIS,

MASON, BENTON, CHELAN,
ISLAND, KITSAP, PIERCE,
SKAGIT, YAKIMA, COWLITZ,
SPOKANE, WHATCOM,
THURSTON, SNOHOMISH,
WALLA WALLA
dam ..... ROSS, WELLS, ASOTIN,
MCNARY, BOUNDARY, DRY
FALLS, ICE HARBOR,
O'SULLIVAN, THE DALLES,
BONNEVILLE, GRAND COULEE
DC Air Force Base
.... BOLLING
art gallery .... FREER
hostess .... HOWAR, MESTA
pressure group
.... LOBBY(IST)
river .... ANACOSTIA
seeress .... DIXON
university ...... GEORGETOWN
educator .... BOOKER (T)
first U.S. president
.... GEORGE
aide of .... (TOBIAS)LEAR
brother of .... LAWRENCE
chef of .... HERCULES
home of .... MOUNT VERNON
mother of ...... MARY (BALL)
physician of
.... (JAMES)CRAIK
portrait painter
.... (CHARLES)PEALE,
(GILBERT)STUART
wife of .... MARTHA
football team .... REDSKINS
initials .... AID
Irving character .... RIP VAN
WINKLE
island ..... LONG, SAND, LOPEZ,
LUMMI, ORCAS, PUGET, SUCIA,
CAMANO, BLALOCK, FIDALGO,
TATOOSH, BAINBRIDGE,
DESTRUCTION
lake .... BLUE, DEER, LONG,
OMAK, ROCK, ROSS, SOAP,
ALDER, BAKER, BANKS,
MOSES, RIFLE, UNION, CELILO,
CHELAN, CURLEW, DIABLO,
ENTIAT, MERWIN, PALMER,
SAMISH, SILVER, SPIRIT,
SYLVAN, WALUPT, BUMPING,
CUSHMAN, DIAMOND,
OSOYOOS, PATEROS, SACHEEN,
SPRAGUE, WALLULA,
WANAPUM, CRESCENT,
UMATILLA, QUINAULT,
CAVANAUGH, VANCOUVER,
WYNOOCHEE, BONNEVILLE
-Moscow telephone
.... HOTLINE
mountain .... AIX, JACK,

ADAMS, LOGAN, DANIEL,
REMMEL, STUART, GARDNER,
OLYMPUS, RAINIER, SHUKSAN,
SPOKANE, TIFFANY,
BONAPARTE, SKOKOMISH,
ABERCROMBIE, SAINT HELENS,
TWIN SISTERS
mountain range .... BLUE,
ROCKY, ENTIAT, CASCADE,
OLYMPIC, WENATCHEE
national park .... OLYMPIC,
SAN JUAN, MOUNT RAINIER
peak .... SNOW, BONANZA,
SNOWFIELD
peninsula .... EDIZ HOOK
river .... HOH, SAUK, BAKER,
CEDAR, GREEN, LEWIS, NORTH,
SNAKE, TWISP, WHITE, CISPUS,
ENTIAT, KALAMA, NACHES,
SKAGIT, SULTAN, TIETON,
TOUTLE, YAKIMA, CASCADE,
CHIWAWA, COWLITZ, NASELLE,
SANPOIL, SPOKANE, TOUCHET,
CHEHALIS, COLUMBIA,
COLVILLE, NOOKSACK,
OKANOGAN, PASAYTEN,
TUCANNON, DESCHUTES,
NISQUALLY, SNOQUALMIE,
WALLA WALLA
sound .... PUGET
state bird .... GOLDFINCH
state flower
.... RHODODENDRON
state motto .... AL-KI
state nickname .... EVERGREEN
strait .... GEORGIA, ROSARIO,
JUAN DE FUCA
university .... GONZAGA
washout .... FIASCO, FAILURE
washroom .... BATHROOM,
LAVATORY, RESTROOM
washstand .... COMMODE
wasp .... WHAMP, DIGGER,
HORNET, VESPID, STINGER,
COW KILLER, MUDDAUBER,
YELLOW JACKET
like a .... VESPINE, WASPISH
nest .... VESPIARY
prick of .... STING
waspish .... TESTY, SNAPPISH,
IRASCIBLE, IRRITABLE, BAD-
TEMPERED, SLIM-WAISTED,
SLENDER-WAISTED
wassail .... SPREE, TOAST, GUZZLE,
CAROUSE, REVEL(RY),
CAROUSAL, CELEBRATION,
DRINKING BOUT
Wasserman test subject
.... SYPHILIS
waste .... EBB, LOSS, RUIN, CHAFF,
DECAY, OCEAN, SPILL, SPOIL,

BARREN, DESERT, MISUSE,
REFUSE, FRITTER, GARBAGE,
RUBBISH, LEAK(AGE),
LEFTOVER, (MIS)SPEND,
SQUANDER, WEAR AWAY,
EXCRETION, WILDERNESS
allowance .... TRET
arctic .... TUNDRA
away .... ROT, GNAW, PEAK,
DECAY, MO(U)LDER,
EMACIATE, MACERATE
cause of .... HASTE
colloquial .... BLOW
deposit .... SLUDGE
drain/duct .... SEWER
fiber .... NOIL, FLOSS
glass .... CULLET
lay .... RAZE, RAVAGE,
DESTROY
maker .... HASTE
matter .... ASH, CULL, LEES,
DREGS, FECES, SWEAT,
REFUSE, GARBAGE, REJECTS
metal .... SLAG, DROSS
of time .... WILD-GOOSE-CHASE
piece of cloth .... RAG
pipe .... DRAIN, SEWER
product .... RUN-OFF
sugar cane/beets ..... BAGASSE,
MEGASS(E)
time ...... IDLE, LOAF, DABBLE,
DAWDLE, DIDDLE, FIDDLE,
FRIVOL, LINGER, LOITER,
PUTTER, FRIBBLE
wasted .... THIN, GAUNT,
CONSUMED, EMACIATED
wasteful .... LAVISH, PRODIGAL,
PROFLIGATE, CONSUMPTIVE,
EXTRAVAGANT
wasteland .... MOOR, HEATH,
DESERT, FOREST, STEPPE,
TUNDRA, DUST BOWL,
HINTERLAND, WILDERNESS
reclamation .... INNING
Waste Land author .... ELIOT
waster .... SPENDER, PRODIGAL,
PROFLIGATE, SPENDTHRIFT
wasting .... DECAY, DEVASTATING
away .... TABID, ATROPHY,
TABETIC, MARASMUS,
TABESCENT, EMACIATION
disease .... TB, TABES,
LEUKEMIA, CONSUMPTION,
TUBERCULOSIS
disease, pertaining to
.... HECTIC
wastrel .... BUM, WASTER,
SPENDER, PRODIGAL,
SPENDTHRIFT, GOOD-FOR-
NOTHING
wat .... STEW, TEMPLE

watch .... EYE, LOOK, OGLE, TEND, VIEW, STARE, VIGIL, FOLLOW, SENTRY, SURVEY, LOOKOUT, OBSERVE, OVERSEE, GUARD(ING), HOROLOGE, TIMEPIECE
a person or thing .... MONITOR
act of keeping .... ESPIAL
bearing .... JEWEL
chain .... FOB
children .... BABYSIT
covering .... CRYSTAL
death .... WAKE, VIGIL
during exams .... INVIGILATE
duty .... VIGIL, PATROL
graveyard .... NIGHT SHIFT
kind of .... WRIST, POCKET, REPEATER
mounted .... VEDETTE
movement units .... LIGNES
night .... NEW YEAR'S EVE
over .... TEND, SUPERVISE
part .... BAND, CASE, DIAL, PAWL, STEM, STUD, CLICK, DETENT, PALLET, CRYSTAL, (HOUR)HAND, MINUTE HAND, SECOND HAND
pawl .... JUMPER
pocket .... FOB
secretly .... SPY, SHADOW
slang .... TICKER
soldier on .... SENTRY, SENTINEL
sound .... TICK
time .... HOROLOGE
undercover .... SPYING, ESPIONAGE
watchdog ...... BANDOG, MASTIFF, CERBERUS, GUARD(IAN), BLOODHOUND
kind of .... CHAPERON(E)
movie industry .... CENSOR
peace and order .... POLICE(MAN)
three-headed .... CERBERUS
warning .... GRR
watcher .... GUARD, LOOKOUT, SPOTTER, OBSERVER, OVERSEER
ballroom .... WALLFLOWER
secret ..... SPY, TAIL, SHADOW, DETECTIVE, PRIVATE EYE
watchful ...... ALERT, OPEN-EYED, VIGILANT, ATTENTIVE, OBSERVANT
man .... IRA
watchmaker .... HOROLOGIST
watchman .... GUARD, SCOUT, SENTRY, WARDEN, WARDER, LOOKOUT, VEDETTE, SENTINEL
mythological .... ARGUS,

TALOS, HEIMDALL
watchtower .... BEACON, LOOKOUT, MIRADOR, BARBICAN, LIGHTHOUSE
watchword .... CRY, MOTTO, SLOGAN, PASSWORD, BATTLECRY, CATCHWORD, SHIBBOLETH
person concerned with ...... GUARD, SENTRY, SENTINEL
water .... EAU, WET, AQUA, BATH, RAIN, DILUTE, DILUENT, IRRIGATE, SPRINKLE
animal .... HYDRA, POLYP, ROTIFER, BRYOZOAN, POLYZOAN, SEA ANEMONE
as source of power ..... WHITE COAL
baptismal .... LAVER
barely above .... AWASH
barrier ...... DAM, BOOM, DIKE, MOLE, WEIR, LEVEE, EMBANKMENT
bearer, in astronomy .... AQUARIUS
borne .... AFLOAT, FLOATING
bottle .... CARAFE, DECANTER
brash .... PYROSIS, HEARTBURN
buffalo .... ARNA, ARNEE, CARABAO
bug .... BEETLE, COCKROACH
capable of uniting with ..... HYDROPHILE, HYDROPHILIC
carrier .... CLOUD
carrier bird .... ALBATROSS
channel .... CANAL, DRAIN, FLUME, GULLY, GULLET, GUTTER, SLUICE, RACEWAY, AQUEDUCT
chestnut .... LING, CALTRAP, CALTROP
chinquapin .... LOTUS
clock .... CLEPSYDRA
closet .... STOOL, CLOACA, TOILET
cloud .... RAIN
color .... PAINTING, AQUARELLE
color painting .... FRESCO
coloring technique .... GOUACHE
combining form ...... HYDR(O)
conduit .... AQUEDUCT
container .... JUG, GOGLET, BREAKER, CANTEEN, CISTERN, GURGLET, PITCHER
containing .... HYDROUS
corral .... CRAWL
crake .... OUZEL
cress .... MUSTARD, POTHERB
cure .... TORTURE,

HYDROPATHY, HYDROTHERAPY
current .... RACE
deposit .... SILT, SEDIMENT
dog ..... SPANIEL, SALAMANDER
element .... OXYGEN, HYDROGEN
excursion .... CRUISE
exhibition .... AQUACADE
fairy .... NIX
fear of .... HYDROPHOBIA
floating on .... AWASH
foam on .... SUDS
gate .... SLUICE, WICKET
gauge .... UDOMETER
glass .... GOBLET, TUMBLER
gum .... TUPELO
heater .... SAMOVAR
hemlock .... COWBANE
hen .... COOT
hole .... POND, POOL
hunger for .... THIRST
ice .... SHERBET
in sheep's brain .... GID
jar .... EWER, OLLA, BANGA, HYDRIA
jet, revolving .... GIRANDOLE
journey .... CRUISE, VOYAGE, PASSAGE
jug/pitcher .... EWER, OLLA
keg .... BREAKER
kind of .... SEA, TAP, HOLY, RAIN, SALT, FRESH, SPRING, JAVELLE, MINERAL, DRINKING
like .... WET, AQUEOUS
lily ..... LOTOS, LOTUS, WOCAS, FANWORT, NELUMBO, VICTORIA
living in .... AQUATIC
logged .... SOGGY, SWAMPY
marker .... DANDY ROLL
mill .... CLOW
moccasin .... SNAKE, VIPER, COTTONMOUTH
move across a body of .... SWIM(MING)
movement .... EBB, TIDE, SEICHE
natural mineral .... SELTZER
not capable of absorbing .... HYDROPHOBIC
nymph .... NAIAD, NEREID, OCEANID
of .... AQUEOUS
on the brain .... HYDROCEPHALUS
opossum .... YAPOK
ouzel .... PIET, DIPPER, THRUSH
overflowing of .... FLOOD, DELUGE
parting .... DIVIDE
passage .... SLUICE, STRAIT,

CHANNEL

pepper .... SMARTWEED

pimpernel .... BROOKWEED

pipe .... HOSE, MAIN, DRAIN,
HOOKA(H), AQUEDUCT,
NARGHILE

plant .... LOTUS, BULRUSH,
CABOMBA, CALTROP, CATTAIL,
PAPYRUS, SEAWEED,
DUCKWEED, EELGRASS,
HYACINTH, PLANTAIN,
PONDWEED, WATERLILY,
CHINQUAPIN, WATERCRESS

plant leaf .... PAD

plant leaf walker .... JACANA

power .... HYDRAULIC

pump .... RAM

purify .... CHLORINATE

raising device .... RAM, NORIA,
TABUT

rat ...... VOLE, THIEF, MUSKRAT

rejection of .... OIL

rodent ...... NUTRIA, CAPYBARA

sapphire .... IOLITE

scented .... BAYRUM, COLOGNE

science of .... HYDROLOGY

scorpion .... NEPA

search for source of
.... DOWSE

shallow part of river/sea
.... SHOAL

snake .... MOCCASIN

soak in .... STEEP, IMMERSE,
SATURATE

soaked .... DRENCHED

soluble stuff .... HYDROGEN

sound .... (S)PLASH

sparkling mineral .... VICHY

spirit .... ARIEL, KELPY,
NIX(IE), KELPIE, UNDINE

sports .... AQUATICS

spout .... GUSH, SPATE,
GEYSER, GARGOYLE

spring .... LYMPH

sprite .... KELPY, NAIAD,
NIX(IE), NYMPH, KELPIE,
NEREID

standing .... PUDDLE

storage .... TANK, CISTERN,
RESERVOIR

stone .... HYDROLITE

surface .... RYME

surge of .... BILLOW

the garden .... HOSE

thin down with .... DILUTE

thrush .... OUZEL

transportation .... FERRY

trough, mining .... LAUNDER

tube .... HOSE

user .... BOAT, SHIP

vessel/pot .... LOTA(H)

washing .... LAVATION

wave .... BILLOW

wheel .... NORIA, TURBINE

witch .... GREBE, DOWSER

without .... DRY, ARID,
PARCHED, ANHYDROUS

worm .... NAID

Water Lilies painter ...... MONET

waterbuck .... KOB, ANTELOPE

watercourse .... DIKE, RACE,
BROOK, CANAL, FIORD,
GORGE, GULLY, NULLA,
CAN(Y)ON, RAVINE, RUNNEL,
CHANNEL

dry .... WADI

watercraft ...... BOAT, RAFT, SHIP

watercress .... POTHERB

watered ...... DILUTED, SPRINKLED,
ADULTERATED

down .... MILD, THIN, WEAK

fabric/silk .... MOIRE, TABBY

Wateree .... CAWTABA

waterfall .... FOSS, LIN(N), CHUTE,
FALLS, CASCADE, CHIGNON,
CATARACT

waterfinder .... DOWSER,
DOWSING ROD, DIVINING ROD

waterfront laborer
...... STEVEDORE, ROUSTABOUT

structure .... PIER

watergate .... FLOODGATE

Watergate scandal perpetrator
.... (RICHARD)NIXON

watering .... ADULTERATION

can .... SPRINKLER

eye .... EPIPHORA

place .... SPA, WELL, BATHS,
OASIS, SPRING(S)

waterless .... ARID, BARREN,
(BONE-)DRY, ANHYDROUS

Waterloo, victor of
.... WELLINGTON

waterproof .... SEALED,
HERMETIC, LEAKPROOF,
WATER-REPELLENT

covering .... PONCHO,
GOSSAMER, RAINCOAT,
TARP(AULIN)

garment .... WADER, RAINCOAT

material ...... RUBBER, PLASTIC

to .... PAY, CALK

Waters, _____ .... ETHEL

Waters of _____: Douay Bible
.... SILOE

watershed .... DIVIDE, RUNOFF,
RESERVOIR, CROSSROAD

waterside .... BEACH, COAST,
SHORE

watertight .... IRONCLAD

box .... CAISSON, COFFERDAM

make .... CA(U)LK

waterway .... RILL, CANAL,
CREEK, RIVER, CHANNEL,
CULVERT, STREAM, RIVULET,
AQUEDUCT, SHIP-ROUTE,
IRRIGATION DITCH

Antarctic .... ROSS SEA

waterworks: sl. .... TEARS

waterwort .... ELATINE

watery .... WET, THIN, RAINY,
SOGGY, WASHY, LIQUID,
SEROUS, AQUEOUS, HYDROUS

discharge .... RHEUM

grave .... SEA

wattle .... ROD, GILL, TWIG,
WAND, DEWLAP, LAPPET

birds' .... JOWL, GILL(S),
CARUNCLE

fish .... BARBEL

tree .... BOREE

Waugh, novelist .... EVELYN

waul .... HOWL, WAIL, SQUALL

waur .... WORSE

wave .... FLAP, SURF, SWAY, TIDE,
WAFF, CURVE, SURGE, SWELL,
BILLOW, COMBER, MOTION,
RIPPLE, ROLLER, SEESAW,
BREAKER, FLUTTER, GESTURE,
BRANDISH, FLOURISH,
UNDULATION

action .... LAP

back and forth .... WAG

channel .... BORE, EAGRE

controller .... HAIRNET

finger .... CURL

foam .... WHITECAP

hair .... PERMANENT

heave of a .... SCEND

hollow of .... VALLEY

large ..... SEA, SWELL, ROLLER,
DECUMAN

little .... RIPPLE

movement .... CHOP,
UNDULATION, CONVOLUTION

off .... SHOO

signaling .... WAFF

tidal .... BORE, EAGRE

to and fro .... WAG, FLAP

top of .... CREST

tossed .... AWASH

with foamy crest
.... WHITECAP

wavelet .... RIPPLE

Wavell, Earl .... ARCHIBALD

waver ...... SWAY, HOVER, FALTER,
QUAVER, TEETER, TOTTER,
FLUTTER, TREMBLE, HESITATE,
UNDULATE, FLUCTUATE,
VACILLATE

wavering .... FICKLE, UNSURE,
DOUBTFUL, UNSTEADY

sound .... TREMOLO

waves, breaking on shore .... SURF
move in .... RIPPLE, UNDULATE
sound of .... ROAR
space between .... TROUGH
tidal .... EAGRE
tossing and tumbling
.... WELTER
wavy .... CURLY, SPIRAL, SINUATE,
SINUOUS, UNDULOUS
edged ...... REPAND, UNDULATE
form .... UNDULATION
in heraldry .... UNDE(E)
state .... UNDULANCY
wax .... CERA, CERE, GROW, PELA,
CERATE, GREASE, POLISH,
SEALER, CERESIN, CERUMEN,
PARAFFIN
and pitch mixture .... MALTHA
candle .... TAPER, CIERGE,
PARAFFIN
cloth treated with
.... CEREMENT, CERECLOTH
cobbler's .... CODE
combining form .... CER(O)
covered with .... CERATED
eloquent .... ORATE
figure .... CEROPLAST
like secretion .... CERUMEN
match .... VESTA
mineral .... OZOCERITE
modeled in .... CEROPLASTIC
myrtle .... BAYBERRY
ointment .... CERATE
palm .... CARNAUBA
producing .... CERIFEROUS
prolix .... SPOUT
source .... BEE, CARNAUBA
waxbill .... WEAVERBIRD
waxed runner .... SKI
waxen .... ASHY, PALE, ASHEN,
SALLOW
waxwing .... CEDARBIRD,
CHATTERER
waxwork artist .... TUSSAUD
waxy .... CERACEOUS
substance ...... CUTIN, SUBERIN
way .... LANE, MODE, PATH, PLAN,
ROAD, WONT, ROUTE, STYLE,
TREND, USAGE, AVENUE,
COURSE, CUSTOM, MANNER,
METHOD, STREET, PRACTICE
easy/direct .... STREET,
HIGHWAY, HIGHROAD
for people on foot .... PATH,
TRAIL
give .... YIELD
in the family .... PREGNANT,
PARTURIENT
of approaching .... ACCESS
of passage .... ALLEY,

CHANNEL
of walking/running .... GAIT
on the .... MOVING,
PROCEEDING
out .... AFAR, EXIT, EGRESS
station town .... WHISTLE STOP
train .... LOCAL
under .... MOVING, IN TRANSIT,
PROCEEDING, PROGRESSING
up .... STEP, ASCENT, STAIRS
usual .... HABIT, CUSTOM
waybill .... MANIFEST
wayfarer .... HIKER, VIATOR,
WALKER, PILGRIM, TRAVELER
shelter for .... INN, SPITAL
wayfaring tree .... VIBURNUM,
HOBBLEBUSH
waylay .... ACCOST, AMBUSH,
ATTACK, DETAIN, AMBUSCADE
Wayne, actor .... JOHN
nickname of .... DUKE
Wayne's The _____ .... GREEN
BERETS
wayward .... UNRULY, WANTON,
ERRATIC, VAGRANT, WILLFUL,
ACCIDENTAL, CAPRICIOUS,
HEADSTRONG, REBELLIOUS
WCTU bane .... ALCOHOL
We Are the World target
.... HUNGER
weak .... WAN, LAME, PUNY,
ANILE, FAINT, FRAIL, ANEMIC,
EFFETE, FEEBLE, FLABBY,
FLIMSY, INFIRM, POORLY,
SICKLY, FLACCID, FRAGILE,
DECREPIT, DELICATE,
HELPLESS, VULNERABLE,
INEFFECTIVE
drink .... TIFF
grow .... FLAG, DROOP,
COLLAPSE
-hearted .... AFRAID
-kneed .... SOFT, TIMID
-kneed: sl. .... CHICKEN
link .... ACHILLES' HEEL
-minded .... DAFT, FICKLE,
STUPID, FOOLISH, IDIOTIC,
MORONIC, WITLESS, IMBECILE,
INDECISIVE, WISHY-WASHY
morally .... FRAIL, CORRUPT
physically .... TIRED, WEARY,
PALSIED, FATIGUED, IMPOTENT
point .... FAULT, DEFECT,
FAILING
slang .... WOOZY
weaken .... EBB, SAP, BATE, FADE,
FLAG, WILT, ABATE, DAMAGE,
DILUTE, IMPAIR, CRIPPLE,
DEPLETE, EXHAUST, SLACKEN,
ENERVATE, ENFEEBLE,
ATTENUATE, UNDERMINE,

DEBILITATE
morally .... VITIATE
the spirit .... DEMORALIZE
weakened .... UNSOUND,
FATIGUED, UNHEALTHY
and disabled person
.... INVALID
body condition ...... CACHEXIA
weakener .... SAPPER, ENERVATOR
weakening .... SAPPING, DRAINING
weaker ones .... PREY
sex .... FEMALE,
WOMAN(HOOD)
weakfish .... ACOUPA, TOTUAVA
weakling .... SOP, WIMP, SISSY,
SOFTY, SOFTIE, WHINER,
CRYBABY, WALLYDRAG,
PANTYWAIST, MOLLYCODDLE
weakness .... FAULT, DEFECT,
FETISH, LIKING, FAILING,
FRAILTY, DEBILITY, DELICACY,
FONDNESS, IMPOTENCE,
INFIRMITY
bodily .... ATONY, ASTHENIA,
CACHEXIA
in behavior .... VICE
in character .... FOIBLE
moral .... FRAILTY
of an organ .... ATONY
small .... FOIBLE, FRAILTY
weal .... WALE, WELT, WHEAL,
STRIPE, WELFARE, WELL-
BEING
weald .... FOREST
wealth .... GOLD, MEANS, MONEY,
ASSET(S), RICHES, FORTUNE,
OPULENCE, PROPERTY,
ABUNDANCE, AFFLUENCE,
PLENITUDE
accumulated .... TREASURE
benefits/income from
.... USANCE
blind god of .... PLUTUS
ill-gotten .... PELF
personified .... MAMMON,
CROESUS
symbol of .... MONEYBAG
wealthy .... RICH, MONEYED,
OPULENT, WELL-OFF,
AFFLUENT, WELL-TO-DO,
PROSPEROUS
government by the
.... PLUTOCRACY
king .... MIDAS, CROESUS
person .... DIVES, NABOB,
MONEYBAGS, PLUTOCRAT,
CAPITALIST, BILLIONAIRE,
MILLIONAIRE
slang .... FILTHY RICH
wean ...... BABY, CHILD, DEPRIVE,
ESTRANGE, WITHDRAW

weapon .... ARM, GUN, CLUB, MACE, LANCE, SABER, SWORD, ARQUEBUS, CROSSBOW, SLINGSHOT
animal's .... HORN, TUSK
Australian aborigines' .... WOMERA, BOOMERANG
bigot's .... STEREOTYPE
bird's ..... BEAK, CLAW, TALON
David's, that killed Goliath .... STONE
duelist's .... PISTOL
for negotiation .... BARGAINING CHIP
gaucho's .... BOLA(S)
"handy" .... FISTS
hood's .... SHIV
hoplite .... SPEAR
Indian .... TOMAHAWK
King Arthur's .... SWORD, EXCALIBUR
medieval ...... MACE, GISARME, HALBERD, ARBALEST, CATAPULT
old-time .... SNEE
pampas .... BOLAS
plant's .... SPINE
primitive .... SPEAR
Samson's .... JAWBONE
shafted .... SPONTOON
throwing stick .... BOOMERANG
Vikings' .... AX, SWORD
war .... GUN, RIFLE, CANNON, BAYONET, REPEATER
weaponry .... ORDNANCE
weapons: colloq. ...... HARDWARE
wear ...... DON, USE, GARB, SHOW, CHAFE, ERODE, PUT ON, SPORT, CLOTHES, DISPLAY
away .... FRET, ERODE, ABRADE, CORRODE
down .... TIRE, ABRADE, DEPLETE, EXHAUST
on .... LINGER
out .... HACK, POOP
ragged .... FRAY, FRAZZLE
thin .... WEAKEN
to tatters .... FRAZZLE
well .... LAST, ENDURE
wearer, Arab headdress .... VALENTINO
beret .... CHE GUEVARA
crash-helmet .... EVEL KNIEVEL
flier's helmet .... SNOOPY
hobo-hat .... EMMETT KELLY
peaked-cap .... JIM COURIER
plumed-hat .... CYRANO
Stetson .... JOHN WAYNE
top-hat .... FRED ASTAIRE

wearied .... ALL IN, BORED, JADED, TIRED, FAGGED
person .... JADED ONE
weariness .... ENNUI, TEDIUM, FATIGUE, LANGUOR, BOREDOM, MONOTONY, WEAKNESS, LASSITUDE
wearing apparel .... GARB, DRESS, ATTIRE, CLOTHES, RAIMENT, CLOTHING, GARMENTS
apparel at a masquerade .... COSTUME
apparel, distinctive ...... HABIT
apparel: sl. .... RAGS
shoe gaiters .... SPATTED
shoes .... SHOD
wearisome ...... BORING, DREARY, TIRING, HUMDRUM, IRKSOME, TEDIOUS, TOILSOME, TIRESOME
grow .... BORE, PALL
person .... BORE, PEST
talker .... PROSER
weary .... BORE(D), FED-UP, JADE(D), SPENT, TIRE(D), FAG(GED), POOPED, IRKSOME, TEDIOUS, WORNOUT, FATIGUED, TUCKER(ED), CHAPFALLEN
weasand .... THROAT, TRACHEA, WINDPIPE, ESOPHAGUS
weasel ...... VARE, PEKAN, SNEAK, ERMINE, FERRET, HEDGER, VERMIN, ZORIL(A), SKULKER, MUSTELINE
family .... MUSTELA
like animal .... SABLE, MARTEN
relative .... MINK, OTTER, STOAT, FERRET, MARTEN
slang .... WELSH, PUSSYFOOT
words .... AMBIGUITIES, EQUIVOCATIONS
weather ...... SKY, CLIME, SEASON, CLIMATE, SURVIVE
-beaten .... WORN, FADED, INURED, SEASONED
become accustom to a different .... ACCLIMATE
condition .... CLIMATE
indicator .... BAROMETER
indoors .... RAINY DAY
item ..... HUMIDITY, MOISTURE, TEMPERATURE
map line .... ISOBAR, ISALLOBAR
personified .... JACK FROST
phenomenon .... SMOG, SNOW, FLOOD, SLEET, SMAZE, STORM, CYCLONE, TORNADO, HAIL(STONE)

phrase .... HEAVY RAINS, SUNNY SKIES, CEILING ZERO, STRONG WINDS
prevailing .... CLIMATE
prolonged dry .... DROUT, DROUGHT
radar system .... SODAR
report .... ADVISORY
satellite .... TIROS
scientist .... METEOROLOGIST
season with heavy rains .... MONSOON
study of .... METEOROLOGY
under the ..... ILL, SICK, TIPSY, AILING, UNWELL, INDISPOSED
warning .... ADVISORY
word .... FAIR, GALE, RAIN, SNOW, WARM, GUSTY, SLEET, FOGGY, SUNNY, WINDY, STORMY, SHOWER(S), THUNDER, TWISTER, HUMIDITY, TYPHOON, BLIZZARD, HURRICANE, LIGHTNING
weathercock .... FANE, VANE
weathered .... ENDURED, SURVIVED, OUTLASTED
weatherglass .... BAROMETER
weatherman .... FORECASTER, METEOROLOGIST
weathervane figure .... COCK
weave .... MAT, KNIT, SPIN, BRAID, PLAIT, PLEAT, TWIST, PLEACH, ENTWINE, CONTRIVE, INTERLACE, (INTER)TWINE
ornamental .... LACE
type of .... LENO, NETTING, NETWORK
weaver .... LOOM, WEBSTER, FABRICATOR
bobbin of .... PIRN
girl .... IRENE
material of/need of ...... REED, SLEY, YARN, FIBER, WICKER
twisted silk thread of .... TRAM
weaverbird .... MAYA, TAHA, FINCH, WHIDAH, SPARROW, WAXBILL
weaving art .... LOOM
contestant .... ARACHNE
device ..... REED, REEL, SPOOL, SHUTTLE
machine/frame .... LOOM
occupation .... HANDICRAFT
reed .... SLEY
thread running horizontally .... WOOF
thread running lengthwise .... WARP
yarn .... WARP, WEFT, WOOF
web .... MESH, TRAP, SNARE,

TISSUE, NET(WORK), GOSSAMER
feather's .... VEXILLUM
footed/toed .... PALMATE
footed bird .... DUCK, SWAN, GOOSE, AVOCET
footed creature .... FROG, TOAD, OTTER, BEAVER, MUSKRAT
in anatomy .... TISSUE, MEMBRANE
kind of .... COB, SPIDER
like membrane .... TELA
pertaining to .... RETIARY
spinner .... SPIDER, ARACHNE
Webb, actor .... CLIFTON
webbed .... PALMATE
weber .... MAXWELL
weblike .... TELAR
wed ...... ONE, JOIN, WIVE, BLEND, MARRY, UNITE, ESPOUSE, TIE THE KNOT
wedding ...... BRIDAL, MARRIAGE, NUPTIALS
anniversary designation:
1st year .... PAPER
5th year .... WOOD
10th year .... TIN, ALUMINUM
15th year .... CRYSTAL
20th year .... CHINA
25th year .... SILVER
30th year .... PEARL
35th year .... JADE, CORAL
40th year .... RUBY
45th year .... SAPPHIRE
50th year .... GOLDEN
55th year .... EMERALD
75th year .... DIAMOND
announcement .... BAN(N)S
couple .... NEWLYWEDS
couple's holiday
.... HONEYMOON
March bride .... ELSA
party member .... MATRON, BESTMAN, RINGBOY, SPONSOR, BRIDESMAID, FLOWER GIRL, RING BEARER
place, biblical .... CANA
rite/sacrament ..... MATRIMONY
sight at a .... TRAIN
song .... AVE MARIA, HYMENEAL, OH PROMISE ME
word, one-time .... OBEY
wedge ...... JAM, KEY, SHIM, TRIG, BLOCK, CLEAT, QUOIN, COIGN(E), COTTER
driver .... MAUL, BEETLE
shaped ..... CUNEAL, CUNEATE, SPHENIC, SPHENOID, CUNEIFORM

shaped piece .... PIE, VEE, SHIM, CHOCK, QUOIN
shaped writing .... CUNEIFORM
to prevent rolling ...... CHOCK, QUOIN, SCOTCH
used in masonry .... SHIM
wedlock .... MARRIAGE, MATRIMONY
Wednesday .... MIDWEEK
Wednesday's child, lot of
.... WOE
god ..... ODIN, WODEN, WOTAN
wee .... TINY, SMALL, TEENY, LITTLE, MINUTE, TEENSY
hours .... DAWN
wee .... URINE, URINATE
weed .... BUR, RID, CULL, DOCK, BROME, COCKLE, NETTLE, QUITCH, REMOVE, SPURR(E)Y, CHARLOCK, PURSLANE, SANDBUR(R), TOADFLAX, DANDELION
biblical .... TARE
buckwheat .... DOCK
colloquial .... CIGAR, TOBACCO
digging tool .... SPUD
genus .... PORTULACA, TARAXACUM
killer .... HERBICIDE
Klamath .... EOLA
mourning ...... CRAPE, WEEPER
narcotic .... MARIHUANA, MARIJUANA
noxious/of grainfields
.... TARE
of mustard family
.... CHARLOCK
out .... UPROOT, EXTIRPATE
pickling .... DILL
poisonous ...... LOCO, DARNEL, JIMSON, HEMLOCK
roadside .... DOGFENNEL
weeding tool .... HOE, SPUD
weeds .... CRAPE, WRACK, WEEPER
wearer .... WIDOW
weedy .... SCRAWNY, GANGLING
plant ..... CELANDINE, BUTTER-AND-EGGS
week .... HEBDOMAD, SENNIGHT
weekday .... FERIA
weekly .... HEBDOMADAL, PERIODICAL
bonanza .... PAY
magazine .... TIME, PEOPLE, NEWSWEEK
portion .... DAY
weeks, 52 .... YEAR
two .... FORTNIGHT
Weems, bandleader .... TED
preacher .... PARSON
ween .... THINK, EXPECT, IMAGINE,

SUPPOSE
weenie .... SAUSAGE, FRANKFURTER, WIENER(WURST)
weeny .... TINY, TEENY
weep ...... CRY, SOB, BAWL, WAIL, MOURN, BEWAIL, GRIEVE, LAMENT, BLUBBER, LAPWING
weeper output .... TEARDROP
weeping goddess .... NIOBE
philosopher .... HERACLITUS
weevil .... KIS, BOLL, BORER, BEETLE, CURCULIO
larva .... GRUGRU
wing cover .... SHARD
weft .... WOOF, YARN, FILLING
Weiscsel .... VISTULA
weigh .... BEAR, HEFT, MULL, TELL, COUNT, HOIST, POISE, RAISE, BURDEN, PONDER, BALANCE, REFLECT, CONSIDER
anchor .... SAIL
down ...... DRAG, LOAD, PRESS, BURDEN, HAMPER
weighing device .... SCALE, TRONE, BALANCE, FAIRBANKS, STEELYARD, (WEIGH)BEAM
weight .... HEFT, LOAD, ROTL, OBOLE, POWER, VALUE, BURDEN, OBOLUS, STRESS, TON(NAGE), EMPHASIS, POUNDAGE, HEAVINESS, INFLUENCE, IMPORTANCE
allowance .... TARE, TRET
apothecaries .... DRAM, OUNCE, POUND, SCRUPLE
atomic .... MOLECULAR
avoirdupois .... TON, OUNCE, POUND
balance .... RIDER
balloon's .... BALLAST
boxer's .... HEAVY, LIGHT, BANTAM, MIDDLE, FEATHER
clock .... PEISE
coal .... KEEL
colloquial .... HEFT
deduction .... TARE
diamond .... CARAT
4,000-pound .... LAST
hundred pounds .... CENTAL, CENTNER
leaden .... PLUMB
lifting machine .... CRANE
measure .... TON, KILO, METAGE
metric .... TON, GRAM, KILO, CENTNER, QUINTAL, MYRIAGRAM
on animal's leg .... CLOG
pertaining to .... BARIC
problem .... OBESITY

stabilizer .... BALLAST

system .... TROY, METRIC, AVOIRDUPOIS, APOTHECARIES

3.086 grains .... (ONE)CARAT

troy .... CARAT, GRAIN, PENNYWEIGHT

200 milligrams .... CARAT

unit .... TON, GRAM, KILO, ROTL, CARAT, GRAIN, OUNCE, POUND, SHEKEL, QUINTAL

watcher .... BOXER, MODEL, DIETER, MILADY, ATHLETE

wool .... TOD

weightless .... LIGHT, FEATHERY

weights and measures, science of .... METROLOGY

weighty .... HEAVY, ONEROUS, SERIOUS, MOMENTOUS, PONDEROUS, BURDENSOME, OPPRESSIVE, INFLUENTIAL

weir .... TRAP, FENCE, GARTH, BARRIER, (MILL)DAM

weird .... ODD, EERY, UNCO, EERIE, QUEER, SPOOKY, BIZARRE, GHOSTLY, STRANGE, UNCANNY, ELDRITCH, SPECTRAL, UNEARTHLY, MYSTERIOUS

sister .... FATE, CLOTHO, ATROPOS, LACHESIS

weirdo .... NUT, KOOK, SCREWBALL

wejack .... PEKAN, WEASEL

weka .... RAIL

Welch, actress .... RAQUEL

welcome .... HAIL, SALUTE, EMBRACE, RECEIVE, GREET(ING), AGREEABLE, DESIRABLE, ACCEPT(ABLE)

benefit .... BOON

welcoming .... CORDIAL, RECEPTIVE, HOSPITABLE

weld .... FUSE, JOIN, UNITE, SOLDER, MIGNONETTE

Weld, actress .... TUESDAY

welding material .... SOLDER, THERMIT

welfare .... EASE, SAKE, COMFORT, WELL-BEING, (COMMON)WEAL, PROSPERITY

organization ...... CARE, YMCA, YWCA, RED CROSS, SALVATION ARMY

work .... SOCIAL SERVICE

Welfare Island's name change .... ROOSEVELT ISLAND

welkin .... SKY, HEAVEN, FIRMAMENT, ATMOSPHERE

well .... FIT, PIT, FLOW, GUSH, HALE, HOLE, SUMP, TRIG, SHAFT, HEARTY, PROPER, ROBUST, SPRING, STRONG, HEALTHY, EXPERTLY, FOUNT(AIN)

advised .... WISE

along .... FAR

balanced .... SANE, POISED, SENSIBLE

being .... WEAL, WELFARE, HAPPINESS

bred .... GENTEEL, EDUCATED

built .... STRONG

doer .... (BOY) SCOUT

done .... OVERCOOKED

done! .... BRAVO, HURRAH, RIGHT ON

dressed .... CHIC

earned .... WORTHY

favored .... PRETTY, HANDSOME

fed .... FAT, FULL, PLUMP

feeling .... EUPHORIA

groomed .... TRIG, SLEEK, SLICK, SOIGNE, SPRUCE

grounded .... SOUND, VALID, LOGICAL, INFORMED

heeled .... RICH, MONEYED, WEALTHY

kind of .... OIL, STAIR, ARTESIAN

known .... FAMOUS, FAMILIAR, RENOWNED, NOTORIOUS

beach .... LIDO

person .... CELEBRITY

ranger .... LONE

lining .... STEAN, STEEN

mannered .... POLITE, COURTEOUS

nigh .... ALMOST, NEARLY

off .... RICH, PROSPEROUS

ordered .... NEAT

pit .... SUMP

preserved .... GOOD AS NEW

proportioned .... TRIM

read person .... BOOKWORM

reported variable .... DOW JONES AVERAGE

set .... FIXED

settled .... ENSCONCED

suited .... CONVENIENT

supplied with money .... LOADED

thought of .... ESTEEMED, REPUTABLE

timed ...... TIMELY, EXPEDIENT, OPPORTUNE, AUSPICIOUS, SEASONABLE

to-do .... RICH, MONEYED, WEALTHY, AFFLUENT

versed .... INFORMED, SCHOOLED

watered .... IRRIGUOUS

worn .... TRITE, OVERUSED

Welland .... CANAL

wellaway .... ALAS, ALACK

Welle river .... UELE

Welles, actor .... ORSON

diplomat .... SUMNER

Wellington's soubriquet .... OLD NOSY, IRON DUKE

wellspring .... FOUNTAINHEAD

Welsh .... CYMRY, TAFFY, CELT(IC), CYMRIC, CAMBRIAN

astronomer .... MEE

boat .... CORACLE

buccaneer .... MORGAN

cheese dish .... RABBIT

dog .... CORGI, TERRIER

god of sea .... BRAN, DYLAN

onion .... CIBOL

poppy .... CAMBRICA

rabbit .... RAREBIT

slang .... CHEAT, SWINDLE

welsher .... CHEAT, SHIRKER, DEADBEAT, SWINDLER

Welshman .... CELT, CAMBRIAN

nickname for a .... TAFFY

welt .... BELT, LASH, WALE, RIDGE, W(H)EAL, STRIPE, THRASH

welter .... ROLL, RUCK, JUMBLE, SOAKED, WALLOW, FERMENT, TURMOIL, CONFUSION

wen .... CYST, MOLE, TALPA, TUMOR

wench .... LASS, MAID, HUSSY, WOMAN, WANTON, SERVANT

disreputable ..... BAWD, DOXY, SLUT, HARLOT, TROLLOP

wend .... GO (ON), TRAVEL, JOURNEY, PROCEED

Wendell, presidential candidate .... WILLKIE

Wendy's dog .... NANA

pal .... PETER PAN

went .... LEFT

out .... DIED

wer(e)gild .... CRO, BLOOD MONEY

werewolf .... LOUP-GAROU, LYCANTHROPE

wernard .... LIAR

wernerite .... SCAPOLITE

weskit .... VEST

Wesley (John) follower .... METHODIST

West .... OCCIDENT

English novelist ...... REBECCA

from the East .... MAE

newcomer to the .... TENDERFOOT

of Broadway .... MAE

wind .... ZEPHYR

wind, of the .... FAVONIAN

West African .... ASHANTI

baboon .... (MAN)DRILL
fetish .... JUJU
Gold Coast city .... ACCRA,
                AKKRA
magic/taboo .... JUJU
secessionist state .... BIAFRA
tribe .... IBO
weaverbird .... WHIDAH
West Bengal capital
.... CALCUTTA
language .... HINDI, TAMIL,
                BENGALI
West Flanders capital
.... BRUGES
West German capital .... BONN
chancellor .... BRANDT,
                ADENAUER
president .... LUBKE
West Indian food plant
.... RIMA(S), BREADFRUIT
rodent .... HUTIA
West Indies African ...... EBO(E),
                MAROON
bird .... TODY, COURLAN,
                LIMPKIN
capital:
   Barbados .... BRIDGETOWN
   Dominica .... ROSEAU
   Grenada .... ST. GEORGE'S
   Saint Kitts & Nevis
   .... BASSETERRE
   Saint Lucia .... CASTRIES
   Saint Vincent
   .... KINGSTOWN
coin .... PISTAREEN
egret .... GAULIN
fish .... BANG, BOGA, CERO,
   PEGA, SESI, TESTAR, BACALAO,
                CABRILLA
flea .... CHIGOE, CHIGGER
grouper .... BONACI
heron .... GAULIN
hog plum .... AMRA, JOBO
Indian .... CARIB, TAINO,
                ESTERON
island ..... CUBA, HAITI, NEVIS,
   CAICOS, TOBAGO, BAHAMA(S),
   CURACAO, GRENADA, JAMAICA,
     LEEWARD, ANTILLES,
     BARBADOS, DOMINICA,
   TRINIDAD, HISPANIOLA, SAINT
     KITTS, SAINT LUCIA, SAINT
                VINCENT
liquor .... RUM, MOBBY
lizard ..... ARBALO, GALLIWASP
magic .... OBI, OBEAH
mahogany .... CAOBA
music .... CALYPSO
native .... CARIB, CREOLE
native chief .... CACIQUE
patois .... GUMBO

plant .... ANIL
rodent .... AGOUTI
rum .... TAF(F)IA
sailboat .... DROGHER
shark .... GATA
shrub .... ANIL, CASCARILLA
state .... ANTIGUA, GRENADA,
   DOMINICA, SAINT LUCIA, SAINT
                VINCENT
talisman .... OBEAH
taro .... TANIA
tree .... ARALIE, BALATA,
   BONACE, CALABA, GENIP(AP),
            GREENHEART
vessel .... DROGHER
volcano .... PELEE
"white man" .... BUCKRA
witchcraft .... OBI, OBEAH
West Irian capital
.... KOTABARU, HOLLANDIA
West Point motto, word in
officer candidates' .... DUTY,
   HONOR, COUNTRY
West Pointer .... CADET, PLEB(E),
                YEARLING
West Virginia capital
.... CHARLESTON
city/town .... LOGAN, NITRO,
   WAYNE, WELCH, ELKINS,
   HINTON, KEYSER, RIPLEY,
   ROMNEY, SUTTON, VIENNA,
   WESTON, BECKLEY, GRAFTON,
   WEIRTON, FAIRMONT,
   WHEELING, BLUEFIELD,
   PRINCETON, CLARKSBURG,
   HUNTINGTON, MORGANTOWN,
   MARTINSBURG, PARKERSBURG
college .... SALEM, BETHANY,
   CONCORD, WESLEYAN
county ...... CLAY, OHIO, WIRT,
   WOOD, BOONE, GRANT,
   HARDY, LOGAN, MASON,
   WAYNE, CABELL, MARION,
   MERCER, PUTNAM, WETZEL,
   FAYETTE, HANCOCK,
   KANAWHA, PRESTON, RALEIGH,
   WYOMING, HARRISON,
                JEFFERSON
lake .... SUTTON, TYGART,
   EAST LYNN, BLUESTONE,
   MOUNT STORM, SUMMERSVILLE
mountain .... SPRUCE KNOB
river .... ELK, MUD, NEW,
   COAL, OHIO, CHEAT, STONY,
   CHERRY, GAULEY, HUGHES,
   MEADOW, CACAPON,
   KANAWHA, BUCKHANNON,
   GREENBRIER, GUYANDOTTE,
            POCATALICO
state bird .... CARDINAL
state flower .... ROSEBAY

         RHODODENDRON
state nickname .... MOUNTAIN,
            PANHANDLE
state tree .... SUGAR MAPLE
university .... MORGANTOWN
western .... MOVIE, OATER,
   HESPERIAN, OCCIDENTAL
land .... HESPERIA
lawman .... MARSHAL, SHERIFF
movie character .... SCOUT,
   COWBOY, INDIAN, DESPERADO,
            FRONTIERSMAN
ocean .... ATLANTIC
soil .... GUMBO
Western Alliance .... NATO
Australia capital .... PERTH
Dvina .... RIVER
Islands .... HEBRIDES
Westerner .... PLAINSMAN
Westmacott, Mary ...... AGATHA
                CHRISTIE
Westminster Abbey
.... PANTHEON
clock .... BIG BEN
landmark .... ABBEY
rite .... CORONATION
street .... WHITEHALL
wet .... DIP, RET, ASOP, DAMP,
   DANK, DEWY, (A)SOAK,
   BATHE, FOGGY, MISTY, MOIST,
   EMBRUE, SOAKED, DRENCHED
a line .... FISH
all .... WRONG, MISTAKEN
blanket .... KILLJOY,
   SPOILSPORT, PARTY POOPER
combining form .... HYGRO
lowland .... FEN
plaster painting .... FRESCO
with falling drops .... RAINY
wetback .... PEON, BRACERO
nationality of .... MEXICAN
wether .... SHEEP
wetland(s) .... SWAMPS, MARSHES
wetter .... BABY, CHILD
Weygand, French general
.... MAXIME
whack .... BEAT, BLOW, SLAP,
   SMACK, WHANG, THWACK
in .... IN LINE
out of .... DISORDERED
slang .... TRY, TRIAL, ATTEMPT
up .... SHARE, DIVIDE
whacked .... EXHAUSTED
whacky .... WILD, MADCAP,
   FOOLISH, ECCENTRIC
whale .... CETE, BEAT, FLOG,
   WHIP, SPERM, THRASH,
   BOWHEAD, FINBACK,
   CACHALOT, CETACEAN,
   BLACKFISH, LEVIATHAN
Arctic .... NARWHAL

baby .... CALF
biggest .... BLUE
blowhole .... SPIRACLE
carcass .... KRENG
colloquial .... WHOPPER
combining form .... CETO
cut blubber of .... FLENSE
dolphin .... ORCA
fat .... BLUBBER
female .... COW
finback .... RORQUAL,
PORPOISE
fishing .... WHALING
food .... BRIT, SHRIMP
food strainer .... BALEEN
grampus .... ORC(A)
growth on jaw .... BALEEN
herd .... GAM
hunter of fiction .... AHAB
killer .... ORC(A), DOLPHIN,
GRAMPUS
kind of ...... SEI, BLUE, SCRAG,
FIN(BACK), HUMPBACK
male .... BULL
mammal resembling
.... DUGONG, MANATEE
Melville's .... MOBY DICK
oil cask .... RIER
river .... DOLPHIN
shark .... MHOR
small .... DOLPHIN, HOGFISH,
PORPOISE, BLACKFISH
sound ...... MEW, BARK, CLICK,
WHINE, SQUEAL, CHIRRUP,
WHISTLE
sperm .... CACHALOT
tail part .... FLUKE
tusked .... NARWHAL
white .... HUSE, HUSO, BELUGA
young .... CALF
whaleback .... FREIGHTER
whalebone .... BALEEN
decorative article
.... SCRIMSHAW
whaleman .... HARPOONER
whaler's spear .... HARPOON
visit .... GAM
whales, pertaining to .... CETIC,
CETACEAN
school/herd of .... GAM, POD
skin .... SCULP
whaling ship .... PEQUOD
first to be sunk .... ESSEX
post .... LOGGERHEAD
whammy .... JINX, EVIL EYE
whang .... WHACK, STRIKE,
THRASH
whangee .... BAMBOO-(CANE),
WALKING-STICK
wharf .... DOCK, PIER, QUAI,
QUAY, JETTY, LANDING,

WATERFRONT
loafer .... RAT
Wharton, novelist .... EDITH
Wharton's Frome .... ETHAN
what .... HOW, WHICH, SORT OF
a CPA does .... AUDITS
a dentist can prettify
.... SMILE
a panhandle is
.... ELONGATION
a priest says .... MASS
a waiter waits for .... TIP,
ORDER
an accountant is .... BEAN
COUNTER
barflies do .... TIPPLE
Caesar's "Veni" means I
CAME
daily life is .... STRUGGLE
Don Juan wasn't
.... MISOGYNIC
for .... WHY
Godiva lacked .... HABIT
little shavers don't have
.... BEARDS
many heads make .... LIGHT
WORK
muses do .... INSPIRE
oneirocritics give
.... INTERPRETATIONS
questions do .... ARISE
setters do .... POINT
some do to a quarry
.... STALK
some say we all are
.... SINNERS
tempts a discount offer
.... CASH
the K.P. peel .... SPUDS
to pay a hero .... HOMAGE
tyros must learn .... ROPES
whatchamacallit
.... THINGAMAJIG
whatnot .... CABINET, ETAGERE,
WHATEVER
what's his name .... SO-AND-SO
left of fading hopes
.,.............. GLIMMERING HOPES
what .... FACT, TRUTH
whaup .... CURLEW
wheal .... WALE, WELT, PIMPLE,
STRIPE, PUSTULE
wheat ...... CORN, DURRA, DURUM,
GRAIN, GRASS, SPELT, TRIGO,
CEREAL
beard .... AWN, ARISTA
beer .... WEISS
coat .... BRAN
cracked .... GROATS
disease .... BUNT, RUST, SMUT,
AECIA, ERGOT

flour foodstuff .... PASTA,
MACARONI, SPAGHETTI
flour substance .... GLUTEN
grass resembling .... CHEAT,
CHESS
ground .... MEAL, FLOUR
hard-grained .... DURUM,
SPELT
head .... EAR
hulled .... GROATS
liquor .... WHISK(E)Y
meal .... SEMOLINA
milling by-product .... SHORTS
stalk part .... AWN
wheatear .... CHAT, CHACK,
WHITETAIL
Wheatley, slave poetess
laureate .... PHILLIS
husband of .... (JOHN)PETERS
master of .... JOHN(WHEATLEY)
mistress of .... SUSANNAH
wheedle .... COAX, COURT,
HUMOR, CAJOLE, WANGLE,
BLARNEY, FLATTER
wheel .... DISK, HELM, SPIN, TURN,
CYCLE, PIVOT, TWIRL, WHIRL,
CIRCLE, PULLEY, ROLL(ER),
ROTATE, RUNDLE, REVOLVE
animalcule .... ROTIFER
band .... STRAKE
big: sl. .... VIP, BIGWIG,
(TOP)BRASS
block ..... TRIG, SPRAG, WEDGE
break .... DRAG, SKID, TRIG
center of .... HUB, NAVE
collar .... FLANGE
furniture .... CASTER
grooved .... SHEAVE
hoop .... TIRE
horse .... POLER
hub .... NAVE
like .... TROCHAL
little .... CASTER
motion .... ROLL, ROTATION
part ...... CAM, HOB, HUB, RIM,
AXLE, TIRE, FELLY, SPOKE
projection .... CAM
pulley .... SHEAVE
resembling a .... TROCHAL
rim .... FELLY, FELLOE,
FLANGE
shaft .... AXLE
shaped ..... ROTATE, ROTIFORM
small .... CASTER, TRUCKER,
TRUNDLE
spindle .... AXLE, ARBOR
spoke .... RUNG, RADIUS
spur .... ROWEL
swivel .... CASTER
tire .... STRAKE
tooth .... SPROCKET

toothed .... COG
turner in Hades .... IXION
turning around an axis
.... ROTARY
water .... NORIA
Wheel of Fortune host
.... (PAT)SAJAK
hostess .... (VANNA)WHITE
White's stint .... LETTER-
TURNER
wheeler .... PILOT, STEERSMAN
wheelman .... PILOT, CYCLIST
wheels, move on .... ROLL, DRIVE
of .... ROTAL
set of swiveled .... CASTER
shoe with .... SKATE
slang .... CAR, AUTO(MOBILE)
wheen .... FEW
wheeze .... GAG, GASP, JOKE,
PUFF, CHOKE
wheezy weather ...... ASTHMATIC
whelk .... MUREX, SNAIL, PAPULE,
PIMPLE, PUSTULE, GASTROPOD
whelm .... BURY, SINK, DROWN,
ENGULF, SUBMERGE
whelp .... CUR, LAD, PUP, BEAR,
HOUND, POOCH, PUPPY,
YOUTH, MONGREL
when ...... TIME, WHILE, MOMENT,
WHEREAS
both hands are up .... NOON,
MIDNIGHT
whenever .... ANYTIME
where .... WHITHER, WHAT PLACE,
WHEREABOUTS
a banner flies .... HEADLINE
a pest pains .... NECK
Aida premiered .... CAIRO
alligators are found
.... SWAMP
Bowie fell .... ALAMO
cappuccino is served
.... TRATTORIA
Charon labored .... STYX
Crockett fell .... ALAMO
Daniel was cast .... DEN OF
LIONS
David slew Goliath ...... ELAH
edelweiss bloom .... ALPS
Gideon defeated Midian
.... ENDOR
Ike commanded .... ETO
it rains mainly in the plain
.... SPAIN
Kipling's road leads
.... MANDALAY
loving couples get taken
.... ALTAR
lunettes sit .... NOSES
pants bag .... KNEE
Peter put his wife .... (IN

A)PUMPKIN SHELL
ships ply .... SEA LANES
some bettors to .... TO THE
DOGS
the action is .... ARENA,
CASINO
the buffalo roam .... RANGE
the Ganges flows .... INDIA
the heart is .... HOME
the Liffey flows .... ERIN
the tall corn grows
.... KANSAS, NEBRASKA,
OKLAHOMA
there is no opportunity to
advance .... BLIND ALLEY
there's ____, there's a way
.... A WILL
to read hidden meanings
.... BETWEEN THE LINES
to soul-search .... INWARD
Twain often summered
.... ELMIRA
wishes are fulfilled .... IN
DREAMS
whereabouts .... LOCATION
whereas .... WHILE
wherefore .... WHY, HENCE,
BECAUSE
wherefrom .... WHENCE
whereness .... UBIETY
whereupon .... WHEN, AFTER
WHICH
wherewithal .... CASH, FUNDS,
MEANS, MONEY, RESOURCES
wherry .... BARGE, SCULL,
LIGHTER, ROWBOAT
whet .... HONE, GRIND, EXCITE,
INSPIRE, SHARPEN, STIMULATE
the appetite .... TEASE, TEMPT,
TICKLE
whether .... IF, EITHER, IN CASE
whetstone .... BURR, HONE,
BUHR(STONE)
whey-faced .... PALE
of milk .... SERUM
which .... WHAT, WHATEVER
animal talked: biblical
.... DONKEY, SERPENT
whichever .... ANYONE, NO
MATTER WHAT
whidah .... WIDOW-BIRD,
WEAVERBIRD
whiff .... GUST, PUFF, WAFF,
WAFT, SMELL, SMOKE,
BREATH
whiffet .... DOG, PUFF
whiffle .... BLOW, VEER, SHIFT,
VACILLATE
Whig conspiracy, 1863
.... RYEHOUSE PLOT
opposed to .... TORY

whigmaleerie .... GEWGAW
while .... AS, YET, UNTIL, ALBEIT,
DURING, OCCUPY, WHEREAS
away .... KILL TIME
lead-in .... ERST, MEAN
whilom .... ONCE, QUONDAM,
FORMER(LY), ERST(WHILE)
whim .... KINK, CRANK, FANCY,
FREAK, QUIRK, DESIRE,
MAGGOT, NOTION, VAGARY,
CAPRICE, IMPULSE, CAPRICCIO
peculiar .... CROTCHET
wham ..... TRINKET, GIMCRACK
whimper .... CRY, MEWL, PULE,
WHINE, YAMMER
whimsical .... ODD, DROLL,
QUEER, QUAINT, CURIOUS,
FLIGHTY, WAGGISH, FANCIFUL,
FREAKISH, PECULIAR,
FANTASTIC, CAPRICIOUS
whimsicality .... ODDITY, CAPRICE
whimsy .... FANCY, HUMOR,
NOTION, CAPRICE
whin .... ROCK, TRAP, FURZE,
GORSE, GREENSTONE
whinchat .... SONGBIRD
whine .... CRY, MEWL, MOAN,
PULE, SNIVEL, YAMMER,
GRUMBLE, WHIMPER,
COMPLAIN
slang .... BELLYACHE
whiner .... PULER, GRIPER
whinny ...... FURZY, HINNY, NEIGH
whip ...... TAN, BEAT, BELT, FLAP,
FLAY, FLOG, LACE, LASH,
LICK, SNAP, WALE, FLAIL,
SWISH, WHALE, WHISK,
DEFEAT, LARRUP, SUBDUE,
THRASH, BELABOR, CONQUER,
PULLOUT, SCOURGE,
FLAGELLATE
Biblical .... SCORPION
blow .... FLICK
braided .... QUIRT, COWHIDE,
BLACKSNAKE
cream/egg whites .... WHISK
leather .... KNOUT, QUIRT,
COWHIDE, KURBASH
made of rhino hide
.... SJAMBOK
made of untanned hide
.... RAWHIDE
mark .... WALE, WELT,
W(H)EAL, STRIPE
riding .... CROP, QUIRT
severely .... TAN, FLOG,
THRASH, FLAGELLATE
stroke .... FLICK
to a froth .... MILL
up .... ROUSE, EXCITE

used by cattle drivers .... BULLWHIP

whipcord .... CATGUT

whiplash .... FLOG, THONG, INJURY, THRASH

snapper .... COSAQUE

sound .... WHISH

whippersnapper .... SQUIRT, UPSTART, JACKANAPES

whippet .... DOG, GREYHOUND

whipping boy .... SCAPEGOAT

stick .... ROD, CANE, SWITCH

whippoorwill .... GOATSUCKER

feathers .... VIBRISSA

whir(r) ...... BIRR, BUZZ, VIBRATE

whirl .... EDDY, GYRE, REEL, SPIN, STIR, TURN, DANCE, SWIRL, TWIRL, CIRCLE, GYRATE, ROTATE, UPROAR, REVOLVE, PIROUETTE

whirler and howler ...... DERVISH

whirligig .... TOP, ROTOR, BEETLE, CAROUSEL, MERRY-GO-ROUND

whirling _____ .... DERVISH

man .... DERVISH

motion .... SPIN, SWIRL

on toes .... PIROUETTE

wind .... CYCLONE, TORNADO

whirlpool .... EDDY, GULF, WEEL, VORTEX, CHARYBDIS, MAELSTROM

bath: trademark .... JACUZZI

whirlwind ...... ANE, EDDY, FAST, SPEEDY, CYCLONE, TORNADO, TWISTER, TYPHOON, DIZZYING, HURRICANE, TOURBILLION

Faroes .... OES

whirlybird .... CHOPPER, AUTOGYRO, HELICOPTER

whish .... WHIZ, SWISH

whisht .... QUIET, STILL, HUSH(ED), WHISPER

whisk .... BEAT, WHIP, BROOM, BRUSH, CARRY, FROTH, (EGG-)BEATER

broom .... WISP

whiskers .... HAIR, BEARD, BRISTLES, MUSTACHE, BURNSIDES, SIDEBURNS

cat's .... VIBRISSA

chin .... GOATEE

closely trimmed, pointed .... VANDYKE BEARD

insect's .... ANTENNA, FEELERS

short growth .... STUBBLE

side .... MUTTONCHOPS

whisk(e)y .... RYE, LIQUOR, SCOTCH, ALCOHOL, BOURBON, POT(H)EEN, SPIRITS

and soda .... HIGHBALL

colloquial .... BOOZE, BOOTLEG, MOONSHINE

illegally distilled ...... POTEEN, MOONSHINE, MOUNTAIN DEW

kind of .... BLENDED, PURE MALT, SINGLE MALT

slang .... HOOCH, REDEYE, ROTGUT

storeroom .... BUTTERY

to an Indian .... FIREWATER

whisper .... SIGH, MURMUR, BREATH(E)

actor's .... ASIDE

whispered, something .... TIP, HINT, RUMOR, GOSSIP, SECRET, CONFIDENCE

whist ...... STILL, SILENT, SILENCE, CARD GAME

game series .... RUBBER

game similar to .... RUFF, BRIDGE

term .... MORT, SLAM, VOLE, MISERI

whistle .... PIPE, TOOT, FLUTE, SQUEAL, TOTTLE, FOGHORN, TWEEDLE

blower .... SNITCH, INFORMER

holder .... LANYARD

stop .... STUMP, CAMPAIGN

time .... FIVE O'CLOCK

whistler .... OUSEL, MARMOT, GOLDENEYE

whistling sound .... WHIZZ, STRIDOR

in the ears .... TINNITUS

whit .... BIT, JOT, ATOM, DOIT, IOTA, TITTLE, PARTICLE

white .... WAN, FAIR, PALE, ASHEN, HOAR(Y), LIGHT, MILKY, SNOWY, SILVER

admiral .... BUTTERFLY

alkali .... SODA ASH

and-pink-skinned .... BLOND

Anglo-Saxon Protestant .... WASP

animal .... ALBINO

ant .... ANAY, TERMITE

bear .... POLAR

cabbage .... BACHOY

cedar .... ARBORVITAE

cliffs site .... DOVER

clouds .... CERRI

coal .... WATER

collar employee .... CLERK, OFFICE WORKER

combining form .... ALBO, LEUK(O)

creamy .... IVORY

earth .... GYPSUM, KAOLIN, MAGNESIA, TERRA ALBA

egg's .... GLAIR, ALBUMEN

elephant: sl. .... LEMON

eye .... SONGBIRD

faced .... PALE, PALLID

flag signal .... TRUCE, SURRENDER

gum .... EUCALYPTUS

gypsum .... ALABASTER

haired .... HOARY

hot .... INCANDESCENT

lead .... CERUSE, CERUSSITE

lie .... FIB

limestone .... CHALK

livered person .... COWARD

make .... BLANCH, BLEACH

mammary gland secretion .... MILK

man .... BUCKRA

man's burden .... IMPERIALISM

meat .... VEAL, CHICKEN

men in .... DOCTORS

oak .... ROBLE

person .... PALEFACE, CAUCASIAN

plague .... TUBERCULOSIS

poplar .... ABELE

race .... CAUCASIAN

-sale items .... LINENS

shade of off- .... BONE

slang .... FAIR, HONEST

smooth, hard gem .... PEARL

soap .... IVORY

spruce .... EPINETTE

thorn .... MAYFLOWER

tie .... DRESS

turning .... ALBESCENT

wax ...... CARNAUBA, PARAFFIN

whale .... BELUGA

women in .... NUNS, NURSES

yellowish .... CREAM, EGGSHELL

White Friar .... ALSATIAN, CARMELITE

Hart .... INN

House nickname .... ABE, CAL, IKE, WOODY

office .... OVAL

resident .... PRESIDENT

room .... OVAL OFFICE

of ''The Golden Girls'' .... BETTY

Rose house .... YORK

Sea gulf .... ARCHANGEL

whitebait .... BRIT, SMELT, SPRAT, HERRING

whitecap .... WAVE

whitefish .... CISCO, ATINGA, BELUGA, POLLAN, VENDACE, MENHADEN, TULLIBEE

whitehead .... MILIA, BLEMISH

Whitelaw, American journalist and diplomat .... REID

whiten .... BLANCH, BLEACH,

ETIOLATE

whitening .... CANESCENT

whitetail .... DEER, WHEATER

whitewall .... TIRE

whitewash .... FUDGE, PARGET, CONCEAL, PLASTER, VARNISH

whitewood .... TULIP, LINDEN

whither .... WHERE, WHEREVER

whiting .... COD, HAKE, CHALK, POLLACK, WALLEYE, DRUMFISH, MENHADEN, WEAKFISH

whitlow .... FELON, AGNAIL, ABSCESS

kind of .... HERPETIC

location .... TOE, FINGER

Whitman, poet .... WALT(ER)

Whitney, cotton gin inventor .... ELI

Whitsunday .... PENTECOST

Whitsuntide .... PINKSTER

whittle .... CUT, DOCK, PARE, CARVE, ERODE, SHAVE, SLICE, DEDUCT, REDUCE

whittling refuse .... SHAVINGS

whiz(z) .... ZIP, HISS, WHIR(R), EXPERT, BARGAIN, SPEED BY

kid .... PRODIGY

kin .... LULU

whizzing sound .... PIRR

who a loaner likes .... PAYER

authorized Jesus of Nazareth's execution? .... PILATE

claimed he shot John Wilkes Booth? .... ''BOSTON'' CORBETT

escaped with the Declaration of Independence? .... DOLLEY MADISON

goes there? .... CHALLENGE

ordered John the Baptist's execution? .... ANTIPAS

refused to grow up, boy .... PETER PAN

replaced Judas? ..... MATTHIAS

whoa .... STOP, HOLLA

whodunit .... MYSTERY

character .... DICK, BUTLER, SLEUTH, VICTIM, DETECTIVE

coiner of .... GORDON

movie ...... CHILLER, SUSPENSE

serial .... COLUMBO, PERRY MASON, HAWAII FIVE-O, MURDER SHE WROTE

staple .... CLUES, CRIME, MURDER

whoever .... ANYONE

whole .... BULK, LUMP, MASS, TOTO, UNCUT, INTACT, COMPLETE, ENTIRE(TY),

TOTAL(ITY), AGGREGATE, 100 PERCENT

as a .... ALTOGETHER

combining form .... HOLO

costume .... ENSEMBLE

note .... SEMIBREVE

number .... INTEGER

slang .... THE WORKS

wholehearted .... SINCERE

wholesale .... BULK, MASS, GROSS, CHEAPER, SWEEPING

house .... DISCOUNT STORE

opposed to .... RETAIL

wholesaler .... JOBBER, MIDDLEMAN, DISTRIBUTOR

wholesome ...... SOUND, HEALTHY, SALUTARY, HEALTHFUL, BENEFICIAL

wholly .... ALL, FULLY, PLUMB, IN TOTO, TOTALLY, ENTIRELY

whoooo cares? .... DON'T GIVE A HOOT

whoop .... CRY, CALL, HOOT, YELL, SHOUT, HOLLER

Hoople .... EGAD

it up .... CELEBRATE

whoopee ...... HOOPLA, FESTIVITY, MERRIMENT

whooper .... SWAN

whooping cough .... CHINCOUGH, PERTUSSIS

whop .... HIT, BEAT, FLOG, STRIKE, WALLOP, CLOBBER

whopper .... JUMBO, BIG (LIE)

whore ...... BAWD, HARLOT, CALL-GIRL, STRUMPET, PROSTITUTE

whorehouse .... BROTHEL

whorl .... VOLUTE, FLYWHEEL, VERTICIL, VOLUTION

fingerprint .... RIDGE

Who's station .... FIRST

why .... HOW COME

wick ...... TAPER, THORP, HAMLET, VILLAGE

kind of .... LAMP, CANDLE

lead-in .... BAILI

wicked .... BAD, EVIL, CRUEL, SINFUL, GODLESS, IMPIOUS, NAUGHTY, SATANIC, VICIOUS

act .... SIN, CRIME, MISDEED

city .... SODOM, BABYLON, GOMORRAH

colloquial .... NAUGHTY, MISCHIEVOUS

wickedness .... VICE

wicker .... BURI, TWIG, STRAW, WITHE, RAFFIA, RATTAN

basket .... CORE, KISH, SKEP, CRATE, CREEL, HAMPER, KIPSEY, PANNIER

cradle .... BASSINET

tree .... OSIER, WILLOW

wickerwork material .... BURI, OSIER, STRAW, WITHE, RAFFIA, RAT(T)AN, WILLOW

wicket .... ARCH, DOOR, GATE, HOOP, WINDOW

in cricket .... INNING

in croquet .... ARCH, HOOP

part .... BAIL

wickiup .... TEPEE, WIGWAM

wicopy .... BASSWOOD

wide .... VAST, AMPLE, BROAD, LARGE, ROOMY, SPACIOUS

awake .... KEEN, ALERT, SLEEPLESS

eyed .... ASTARE

inlet .... BAY

open .... AGAPE, CLEAR

open break ..... ABYSS, CHASM

open space ..... PLAIN, DESERT

widely .... FAR-AND-NEAR, EXTENSIVELY

known .... FAMED

widen .... DILATE, SPREAD, BROADEN, ENLARGE, INCREASE

widespread .... RIFE, COMMON, GLOBAL, GENERAL, RAMPANT, REGNANT, PREVALENT, UNIVERSAL

disease .... EPIDEMIC

fear .... PANIC

widgeon ...... DUCK, SMEE, SMEW, GOOSE, ZUISIN, BALDPATE

genus .... MARECA

kin .... POCHARD, REDHEAD

widow .... MATRON, RELICT, SUTTEE, BEREAVE, FEME SOLE, SURVIVOR

bird .... WHIDAH

black .... SPIDER

grass .... DIVORCEE

Hindu .... SUTTEE

inheritance of .... DOWER

man .... WIDOWER

of a king .... QUEEN DOWAGER

titled, wealthy .... DOWAGER

widowhood .... VIDUAGE, VIDUITY

widow's dream cocktail .... BENEDICTINE

mites .... LEPTA

mourning clothes .... WEEDS

third .... DOWER, DOWRY

width .... BEAM, SPAN, EXTENT, BREADTH, EXPANSE, LATITUDE, WIDENESS, BROADNESS

wield .... PLY, WAVE, EXERT, EMPLOY, HANDLE, MANAGE, CONTROL, BRANDISH, EXERCISE

815

wielder, authority .... BOSS, RULER, DICTATOR, GOVERNOR

blue pencil .... EDITOR, REDACTOR

wieldy .... PLIANT, DUCTILE, PLIABLE, FLEXIBLE, YIELDING

Wien .... VIENNA

wiener .... HOTDOG, FRANKFURTER

schnitzel .... VEAL

wurst .... SAUSAGE

wienie .... RED-HOT

Wiesbaden's location ...... HESSE

wife .... MRS., RIB, FEME, FERE, FRAU, FROW, BRIDE, MATRON, MISSIS, MISSUS, SPOUSE, HELPMATE, HELPMEET, YOKEFELLOW

beating .... ABUSE

bequest to .... DOS

common-law .... MISTRESS

domineering: sl. .... BATTLEAX

dowry of .... DOT

duke's, e.g. .... PEERESS

in law .... FEME

Indian .... SQUAW

killer .... UXORICIDE

king's .... QUEEN-CONSORT

knight's .... DAME

lord's .... LADY

man's prospective .... INTENDED

of a .... UXORIAL

of Peter the Great .... EUDOXIA

one .... MONOGAMY

rajah's .... RANI, RANEE

secondary .... CONCUBINE

slang .... OLD LADY, BETTER HALF, LITTLE WOMAN, BALL AND CHAIN

submissive to one's .... UXORIOUS

take to .... WED, MARRY

wifely .... LOVING, UXORIAL

wig ...... TETE, PERUKE, TO(U)PEE, PERIWIG, POSTICHE, HAIRPIECE, HEADDRESS

gray .... GRIZZLE

small .... TOUPEE, WIGLET

used as part of coiffure .... FALL, SWITCH, WIGLET

wigeon .... SMEE, WIDGEON

wigging .... REBUKE, SCOLDING

wiggle ...... WAG, SHAKE, SQUIRM, WANGLE, WOBBLE, WRIGGLE

wiggler .... LARVA, WRIGGLER

wigwag .... CODE, WAVE, SIGNAL, ALTERNATE

wigwam .... HUT, TENT, LODGE, TE(E)PEE, WICKIUP

wild .... GAGA, RANK, RASH, FERAL, WASTE, DARING, FERINE, FIERCE, SAVAGE, STORMY, UNRULY, RIOTOUS, UNTAMED, VIOLENT, DESOLATE, RECKLESS, PHRENETIC, PRIMITIVE, UNBRIDLED, DISORDERLY, LICENTIOUS, HARUM-SCARUM

animal .... BEAST

apple .... CRAB, CREEPER

ass .... ONAGER

boar .... HOG

brier .... DOG ROSE

buffalo .... ARNA, ARNEE

cat .... EYRA, LYNX, BOBCAT, MARGAY, MARGOT, OCELOT, SERVAL

cattle .... GAUR, BANTENG

celery .... EELGRASS, SMALLAGE

country .... WEALD

cry .... EVOE, WHOOP, SCREAM, SHRIEK, SCREECH

dog .... CUON, DHOLE, DINGO

duck .... SCAUP, GADWALL, MALLARD, REDHEAD, GOLDENEYE, CANVASBACK

eyed .... HAGGARD

fowl .... DUCK, QUAIL, PHEASANT, PARTRIDGE

fowl flock .... SKEIN

goat .... IBEX, TAHR, TAIR

goose .... BRANT

goose's call .... HONK

guess .... STAB

hog ..... BENE, BOAR, PECCARY

honey source .... BEETREE

horse .... CAYUSE, TARPAN, BRONC(H)O, BRUMBIE, MUSTANG

hyacinth .... BLUEBELL

life .... GAME

life preserve .... WETLAND

madder .... BEDSTRAW

mint, e.g. .... POTHERB

mustard .... CHARLOCK

olive .... OLEASTER

ox ...... ANOA, REEM, BANTENG

ox hunter .... BUCCANEER

parsley .... LOVAGE

pig .... BOAR

plum .... SLOE

revelry .... ORGY

rose .... EGLANTINE, (SWEET)BRIER

sheep .... SHA, ARUI, UDAD, URIAL, AOUDAD, ARGALI, NAHOOR, BIGHORN, MOUFLON

sown .... OATS

state of being .... FERITY

swan .... ELKE

talker .... RAVER

the .... NATURE

time .... SPREE

try .... STAB

Wild Bill _____ .... HICKOK

Bill Hickok's burial place .... MOUNT MORIAH

Bill Hickok's killer .... (JACK) MCCALL

Duck author .... IBSEN

Huntsman .... ODIN

West show .... RODEO

wildcat: colloq. .... RISKY, SPECULATIVE

grayish .... JAGUARUNDI

wildcatter's quest .... OIL

Wilde, actor .... CORNEL

dramatist .... OSCAR

ballad's subject .... GAOL

play .... SALOME

wildebeest .... GNU, ANTELOPE

country? .... GNUENGLAND

wilderness ...... WILD(S), DESERT, JUNGLE, STEPPE, TUNDRA, BOONDOCKS, WASTE(LAND)

biblical .... SIN

road traveler .... BOONE

wildfire .... LIGHTNING, ERYSIPELAS

wildlife preserve .... WETLAND, SANCTUARY

wildness .... FERITY

wile .... ART, LURE, DECEIT, BEGUILE, ARTIFICE, TRICK(ERY)

wiles .... CHARM

wilier .... ASTUTER, CRAFTIER

Wilkes, Antarctic explorer .... CHARLES

ship of .... VINCENNES

will .... MIND, WISH, LEAVE, POWER, CHOICE, CHOOSE, DECREE, DESIRE, OPTION, BEQUEATH, PLEASURE, VOLITION

addition to a .... CODICIL

bequeathed by .... TESTAMENTARY

convey by .... DEMISE

exercise of the .... VOLITION

handwritten .... HOLOGRAPH

having made a .... TESTATE

having no .... INTESTATE

in law .... TESTAMENT

maker ..... DEVISOR, TESTATOR

of one's free .... ACCORD

o'-the-wisp .... CHIMERA, WILDFIRE, IGNIS FATUUS

power .... SELF-CONTROL

power, loss of .... ABULIA

Willard, boxing champion
.... JESS
organization of Mrs. .... WCTU
temperance leader
.... FRANCES
willful .... WAYWARD, STUBBORN,
OBSTINATE, HEADSTRONG
William, actor .... HOLDEN
Howard _____, U.S.
president .... TAFT
in German .... WILHELM
Jefferson Blythe, born
.... BILL CLINTON
Williams, ballplayer .... TED
Williamson, Shakespearean
actor .... NICOL
Williamson, Texas judge
.... ROBERT
nickname of .... THREE-
LEGGED WILLIE
willies .... CREEPS, JITTERS,
NERVOUSNESS
willing .... BAIN, GAME, LIEF,
EAGER, READY, DOCILE,
MINDED, PLIANT, CONTENT,
DISPOSED, INCLINED,
UNFORCED, ASSENTING,
CONSENTING
reluctantly .... FAIN
variant: poet. .... FAINE
willingly .... LIEF, GLADLY,
READILY, VOLUNTARILY
archaic .... FAIN
willingness .... ASSENT, DESIRE,
ALACRITY, PENCHANT
Willkie, presidential candidate
.... WENDELL
utopian dream of .... ONE
WORLD
willow .... ITEA, OSIER, SALIX,
SALLOW
ament .... CHAT
bark, glucoside from
.... SALICIN
basket .... PRICKLE
catkin .... CHAT
herb .... ROSEBAY
of the .... SALICACEOUS
run product .... AUTO
shoot .... WAND
spike .... CHAT, AMENT,
CATKIN
twig .... OSIER, WITHE,
SALLOW
twigs, woven .... WICKER
willowy .... SLIM, LITHE, SVELT,
PLIANT, SUPPLE, SLENDER
Willy, bold peacemaker
.... BRANDT
Brandt's award: 1971
.... NOBEL PEACE PRIZE

birthplace .... LIBECK
bold policy .... OSTPOLITIK
real name .... HERBERT
FRAHM
willy-nilly .... PERFORCE,
INDECISIVE, IRRESOLUTE,
WHETHER OR NOT
Wilms' tumor
.... NEPHROBLASTOMA
locale .... KIDNEY
Wilson, U.S. president
.... WOODROW
nickname of .... WOODY
wife of .... EDITH
Wilson's thrush .... VEERY
wilt .... SAG, DROOP, WITHER,
SHRIVEL, COLLAPSE,
LANGUISH
Wilt of basketball fame
.... CHAMBERLAIN
the _____ .... STILT
wily .... SLY, FOXY, ARTFUL,
ASTUTE, CLEVER, CRAFTY,
SHIFTY, SUBTLE, TRICKY,
CROOKED, CUNNING,
INSIDUOUS
wimble .... AUGER, GIMLET
Wimbledon event .... TENNIS
wimp .... WEAKLING
wimple .... RIPPLE
wearer of .... NUN
win .... GET, HIT, BEAT, EARN,
GAIN, SWAY, REACH, MASTER,
OBTAIN, ACHIEVE, CONQUER,
PREVAIL, SUCCEED, TRIUMPH
a point .... ACE
acceptance .... SELL
all games .... SWEEP
all tricks .... SLAM, VOLE
overwhelming ..... KNOCKOUT,
LANDSLIDE
wince .... SHY, REEL, QUAIL,
FLINCH, RECOIL, ROLLER,
SHRINK, GRIMACE
winch .... WHIM, CRANK, HOIST,
WINDLASS
Winchester .... RIFLE
wind ...... AIR, AURA, BLOW, COIL,
GALE, GUST, HINT, PUFF,
REEL, BLAST, NOSER, SCENT,
STORM, WHIFF, BUSTER,
DUSTER, SAMIEL, SIMOOM,
ZEPHYR, PAMPERO, LEVANTER,
NONSENSE, CORKSCREW
away from .... ALEE
blowing down from the Alps
.... BISE
borne by the .... EOLIC
breath of .... WAFT, FLATUS
combining form .... ANEMO

coming across the mountains
.... TRAMONTANE
cone .... SLEEVE
crack in timber made by
.... ANEMOSIS
deposit .... LOESS, SEDIMENT
desert .... SAMIEL, SIMOOM,
SIROCCO
direction recorder
.... ANEMOGRAPH,
ANEMOSCOPE
driven clouds .... SCUD
dry .... FOEHN
east .... EURUS
equatorial .... TRADE
gauge .... ANEMOMETER
gentle .... AURA, BREEZE,
ZEPHYR
gust of .... PUFF, WAFT
high, strong .... GALE
Indian Ocean .... MONSOON
indicator .... CONE, SLEEVE,
(WIND)SOCK, (WEATHER)COCK,
(WEATHER)VANE
instrument .... HORN, OBOE,
PIPE, REED, TUBA, BUGLE,
FLUTE, SHAWM, CORNET,
BASSOON, OCARINA, SACKBUT,
CLARINET, TROMBONE,
HARMONICA
instrument finger hole
.... VENTAGE
instrument mouthpiece .... LIP
mythical .... SANSAR
north .... BISE, AQUILO,
BOREAS
northeast .... EURAQUILO,
EUROCLYDON
of the north .... BOREAL
puff .... FLATUS
Rocky Mountain ..... CHINOOK
run before the .... SCUD
scale .... BEAUFORT
science of the .... ANEMOLOGY
shifting .... VARIABLE
side away from .... LEE
side toward .... WEATHER,
WINDWARD
sign of .... MARE'S TAIL
sound .... SOB, ROAR, SOUGH
south .... AUSTER
southeast .... EURUS
southwest .... AFER
strong .... GALE, STORM,
PAMPERO, TEMPEST, LEVANTER
sudden, brief .... FLAW,
FLURRY
sudden, violent .... SQUALL
up ..... END, FINISH, CONCLUDE
warm, dry .... FOEHN
wave .... RIPPLE

west .... FAVONIAN,
ZEPHYR(US)
whirling .... CYCLONE,
TORNADO, TWISTER
with snow/rain .... FLAW
Wind in the Willows animal
.... OTTER
windbag .... GASBAG, BRAGGART,
CHATTERER
windblown dust .... STOUR
windbreaker .... JACKET
winded .... BREATHLESS
windfall .... BOON, FIND, VAIL,
BONUS, MANNA, PRIZE,
BONANZA, FORTUNE,
GODSEND
windflower .... ANEMONE
windhover ...... FALCON, KESTREL
windigo .... OGRE
winding .... MAZY, SNAKY,
SPIRAL, TURNING, TORTUOUS,
TWISTING, MEANDROUS,
LABYRINTHINE
gait of horse .... CARACOLE
line .... ZIGZAG
passages, structure with
.... LABYRINTH
pathway .... AMBAGE
sheet .... SHROUD, CEREMENT
structure .... SPIRAL STAIRCASE
windjammer .... SAILBOAT,
SAILING SHIP
slang .... WINDBAG
windlass .... REEL, CRANK, HOIST,
WINCH, LIFTER, PINION,
CAPSTAN
cylinder .... BARREL
windless .... CALM, STUFFY,
WINDED, AIRLESS, STIFLING
windmill fighter
.... (DON)QUIXOTE
part .... SAIL, VANE, SHAFT
pump .... GIN
Windmills of the Gods author
.... (SIDNEY)SHELDON
window bar .... MULLION
bay .... ORIEL
cleaned .... SQUEEGEED
door .... TRANSOM
dormer .... LUTHERN
drapery .... VALANCE,
LAMBREQUIN
dresser .... DECORATOR
dressing .... TRIM, FACADE,
DISPLAY, FALSE FRONT
fastener .... HASP, LATCH
frame .... CASEMENT
frame piece .... STILE
of a .... FENESTRAL
on a fort's wall .... LOOPHOLE,
EMBRASURE

part .... PANE, SASH, SILL,
FRAME, JAMB(E), GRILL(E),
LINTEL, GRATING
roof .... DORMER, SKYLIGHT
round .... ROUNDEL
sash sidepiece .... STILE
shade .... BLIND, SHUTTER
ship's .... PORTHOLE,
DEADLIGHT
shopping .... BROWSE,
LOOKING, BROWSING
small ..... WICKET, FENESTELLA
trellised .... LATTICE
with sloping slats ..... LOUVER
windpipe .... TRACHEA, WEASAND,
THROTTLE
part of .... LARYNX, THROAT
windrow .... SWATH, FURROW
winds, Alpine .... FOEHNS
annual .... ETESIAN
deviation caused by ..... DRIFT
god of .... AEOLUS
study of .... ANEMOLOGY
windshake .... ANEMOSIS
windshield .... WINDSCREEN
gadget .... WIPER, DEICER
Windsor's novel, 1944
.... FOREVER AMBER
windstorm .... BLOW, GALE,
BURAN, SQUALL, CYCLONE,
TORNADO, TWISTER, TYPHOON
of Central Asia .... BURA(N)
windup .... CLIMAX, END(ING),
FINALE, CLOSURE
Windward island ...... GRENADA,
DOMINICA, ST. LUCIA, ST.
VINCENT, MARTINIQUE
opposed to .... LEEWARD
windy ...... AIRY, BLOWY, GABBY,
GASSY, GUSTY, STORMY,
VERBOSE, BOASTFUL,
TALKATIVE, LONG-WINDED
city .... CHICAGO
spate .... GUST
wine .... PORT, DRINK, YQUEM,
CANARY, LIQUOR, NECTAR,
SHERRY, CATAWBA, MADEIRA,
VINTAGE, MUSCADEL,
MUSCATEL
addicted to .... VINOUS
addiction .... VINOSITY
age of .... VINTAGE
and dine .... TREAT,
ENTERTAIN
beverage ..... NEGUS, SILLABUB
bottle ..... MAGNUM, DECANTER
bottle indentation .... KICK
Burgundy .... CHABLIS
burning of .... USTULATION
cask .... TUN, BOSS, BUTT, PIPI,
PUNCHEON

cask deposit .... ARGAL,
ARGOL, TARTAR
choice .... VINTAGE
colored .... VINACEOUS
combining form .... OENO,
VINI
cup .... BEAKER
deposit .... LEES, GRIFFE
disorder .... CASSE
distillate .... BRANDY, COGNAC
drink, cold .... COBBLER,
SANGAREE, SILLABUB
dry .... SEC, BRUT, SACK,
CLARET, CHABLIS, CHIANTI,
TUSCANY, VERMOUTH
effervescent .... CHAMPAGNE
film on .... BEESWING
flavor .... MULL
flavoring .... DOSE, DOSAGE
formation in .... ROPE
fragrance of .... BOUQUET
glass .... RUMMER
god .... BACCHUS
grapes harvester .... VINTAGER
grower's patron .... VINCENT
indicating .... OENO
jug .... OLPE
kind of .... DRY, RED, PORT,
CIDER, PERRY, WHITE,
BRANDY, COOKING, CORDIAL,
MUSCATEL, SAUTERNE,
VERMOUTH, SPARKLING
like .... VINACEOUS
loss of color .... CASSE
measure .... ORNE
merchant .... VINTNER
mixture .... KIR, NEGUS
new .... MUST
of .... VINIC, VINOUS,
VINACEOUS
pitcher .... OLPE
prized .... VINTAGE
punch .... SANGRIA
receptacle .... AMA
red .... PORT, MEDOC, TINTA,
CLARET, CHIANTI, TUSCANY,
BURGUNDY, DUBONNET
refuse .... LEES, DREGS
revived .... STUM
Rhine .... HOCK, MOSELLE
sauterne .... YQUEM
seller .... VINTNER
sherry .... JEREZ, OLOROSO
shop .... BISTRO, TABERNA,
ESTAMINET
spiced .... NEGUS, BISHOP,
MARINADE, SANGAREE,
HIPPOCRAS
stock .... CELLAR
storage place .... CELLAR,
BUTTERY

strength .... SEVE
strengthen .... DOSE
sweet .... PORT, TOKAY,
CANARY, MADEIRA, MALMSEY,
ALICANTE, MUSCATEL,
SAUTERNE, VERMOUTH
sweeten .... MULL
taster .... GOURMET
term .... DRY, SEC, BODY,
BRUT, FLINTY, BOUQUET,
VINTAGE
unfermented .... MUST
vessel .... AMA, TUN, VAT,
BARREL, AMPULLA, CHALICE
white .... HOCK, SACK,
BARSAC, MALAGA, CHABLIS,
MADEIRA, MALMSEY,
MARSALA, MOSELLE,
BURGUNDY, SAUTERNE,
VERMOUTH
with honey .... MULSE
wines, study of .... OENOLOGY,
VINOLOGY
winesap .... (WINTER)APPLE
wing .... ALA, ARM, FLY, PINNA,
PENNON, PINION
bastard .... ALULA
bind the .... PINION
combining form .... PTERO
control .... AILERON
cover .... SHARD, ELYTRON,
ELYTRUM
feather .... REMEX, PINION
footed .... SWIFT, ALIPED
footed creature .... BAT,
LEMUR
furnish with .... IMP
having the form of a
.... PTERYGOID
in anatomy .... ALA
it, verbally .... AD LIB
length .... SPAN
movement .... BEAT, FLAP,
FLUTTER
of building .... BAY, ELL,
ANNEX, ALETTE, EXTENSION
protuberance .... CALCAR
shaped ...... ALAR(Y), ALIFORM
small .... ALULA
span of airplane .... SPREAD
support of airplane
.... CABANE
three-quilled .... ALULA
type of .... DELTA
winged .... ALAR, FLEW,
ALATE(D), PENNATE,
FEATHERED
being .... AMOR, ANGEL,
SERAPH(IM)
figure .... ICARUS, IDOLON,
IDOLUM

fruit .... SAMARA
goddess .... NIKE
hat .... PETASOS, PETASUS
hat wearer
.... HERMES(MERCURY)
horse .... PEGASUS
monster: myth. .... HARPY
sandals .... TALARIA
sandals wearer
.... MERCURY(HERMES)
staff .... CADUCEUS
two .... DIPTERAL, DIPTEROUS
wingless ...... APTERAL, APTEROUS
bird .... EMU, KIWI, APTERYX
winglet .... ALULA
winglike .... ALA(R), ALATE,
PTERYGOID
part .... FIN
wings, flap the .... WINNOW
furnish .... IMP
having .... ALATE(D)
having two .... BIPENNATE
wingspread .... SPAN
wink .... BAT, HINT, BLINK,
SIGNAL, SQUINT, INSTANT,
NICTATE, TWINKLE
at .... CONDONE, CONSENT
winker .... BLINDER, EYE(LASH)
winkle .... SNAIL
winks, forty .... NAP, DOZE
winner .... VICTOR, CHAMPION,
CONQUEROR
long shot/surprise
.... SLEEPER, DARK HORSE
Winnie ____ Pu .... ILLE
Winnie the Pooh author
.... MILNE
was his nickname
.... (WINSTON)CHURCHILL
winning .... AHEAD, TAKING,
CHARMING, DOMINANT,
ENGAGING, SPORTIVE,
ATTRACTIVE, CAPTIVATING
disposition .... SWEET,
PLEASANT
lottery combination ...... TERN
margin .... HAIR, NOSE
point .... ACE
winnings .... GAINS, RETURNS
slang .... VELVET
winnow .... FAN, SIFT, SCATTER,
SEPARATE
Winona, actress .... RYDER
winsome .... GAY, BONNY,
MERRY, LIVELY, LOVABLE,
WINNING, CHARMING,
ENGAGING
winter .... COLD, SEASON,
YULE(TIDE), HIBERNATE
apple .... ROME, RUSSET,
WINESAP, DELICIOUS

cap .... TUQUE
cover/blanket .... SNOW
cutter .... ICEBOAT
eave hanger .... ICICLE
festival .... POTLATCH
fodder .... SILAGE
glider .... SKI, SLED
hazard .... SKID, SLEET
melon .... CASABA
of/like .... BRUMAL, HIEMAL,
HIBERNAL
pear .... BOSC, WARDEN
precipitation ...... SNOW, SLEET
product .... SNOW, FROST
sleep .... HIBERNATION
solstice festival
.... SATURNALIA
spend the .... HIBERNATE
sport .... SKIING, SLALOM,
SKIJORING
squash .... CUSHAW
torpid in .... DORMANT
vehicle ...... SLED(GE), SLEIGH,
TOBOGGAN
wear .... GLOVES, MITTENS,
EARMUFFS, SNOWSHOES
weather .... SLEETY
winterberry .... HOLLY
wintergreen .... OIL, SHINLEAF,
TEABERRY
false .... PYROLA
Winters, actress .... SHELLEY
Winter's Tale shepherdess
.... MOPSA, DORCAS
wintertime creation
.... SNOWMAN
wintry .... COLD, SNOWY,
BRUMAL, HIEMAL, HIBERNAL
winze .... SHAFT
wipe ...... DRY, MOP, DUST, SWAB,
BRUSH, CLEAN, TOWEL,
EFFACE
out ...... KILL, ERASE, REMOVE,
ELIMINATE, ERADICATE,
LIQUIDATE, EXTERMINATE
wiper ...... CAM, TOWEL, DUSTER,
DISHRAG
finger/lip .... NAPKIN,
SERVIETTE
wire ...... CORD, LINE, TELEGRAM,
CABLE(GRAM), TELEGRAPH
brush .... CARD
coil .... SPRING
cutting tool .... PLIERS
drum's .... SNARE
insulated, electric .... FLEX
light bulb .... FILAMENT
measure .... MIL, STONE
nail .... BRAD
pen/enclosure .... CAGE
rope .... CABLE

service .... API, INS, UPI, REUTERS
spiral of .... COIL
tapper .... TOUT, BUGGER
wiredancer .... AERIALIST
wirehair .... (FOX)TERRIER
wireless .... RADIO
adjunct ...... AERIAL, ANTENNA
devotee .... HAM
wirepuller .... PUPPETEER
wirework .... GRILLAGE
wireworm .... MILLIPEDE
wiry .... STIFF, TOUGH, SINEWY, STRONG, MUSCULAR
Wisconsin bay .... GREEN, CHEQUAMEGON
capital .... MADISON
city/town .... ALMA, ANTIGO, BELOIT, JUNEAU, RACINE, WAUSAU, ASHLAND, BARABOO, ELKHORN, OSHKOSH, APPLETON, KENOSHA, GREEN BAY, LA CROSSE, SUPERIOR, WAUKESHA, WEST BEND, EAU CLAIRE, FOND DU LAC, GREENDALE, MARINETTE, MILWAUKEE, NEW BERLIN, SHEBOYGAN, GREENFIELD, JANESVILLE, INDEPENDENCE
college .... MILTON, LAKELAND, NORTHLAND
county .... DANE, DOOR, DUNN, IOWA, IRON, SAUK, BROWN, CLARK, DODGE, GRANT, BARRON, CALUMET, KENOSHA, OZAUKEE, WAUPACA, CHIPPEWA, COLUMBIA, LA CROSSE, MARATHON, MANITOWOC, MILWAUKEE, OUTAGAMIE, SHEBOYGAN, WINNEBAGO, WASHINGTON
football team .... GREEN BAY PACKERS
Indian .... SAC, WINNEBAGO
island .... CAT, OAK, BEAR, SAND, OUTER, CHAMBERS, MADELINE, MICHIGAN, STOCKTON, WASHINGTON
islands .... APOSTLE
lake .... CLAM, LONG, OWEN, PINE, WIND, DU BAY, EAGLE, MOOSE, NORTH, PEPIN, ROUND, SHELL, TROUT, BARDON, BEULAH, CHETAC, DENOON, GENEVA, GOLDEN, POYGAN, SPIDER, YELLOW, KEGONSA, MENDOTA, METONGA, PELICAN, PHANTOM, SHAWAMO, THUNDER, CHIPPEWA, MICHIGAN, SUPERIOR, WINNEBAGO

mountain .... RIB, TIMMS HILL, SUGARBUSH HILL
native .... BADGER
river .... FOX, CLAM, JUMP, ROCK, WOLF, APPLE, BLACK, SUGAR, OCONTO, YELLOW, FLAMBEAU, KICKAPOO, MONTREAL, PESHTIGO, MENOMINEE, NAMEKAGON, WISCONSIN, PECATONICA, SAINT CROIX
state animal .... BADGER
state bird .... ROBIN
state fish .... MUSKY
state flower ..... WOOD VIOLET, BUTTERFLY VIOLET
state nickname .... BADGER
strait .... PORTE DES MORTS
university .... LAWRENCE, MARQUETTE
wisdom .... WIT, LORE, LEARNING, SAGACITY, SAGENESS, SAPIENCE, ERUDITION, KNOWLEDGE
a love of .... PHILOSOPHY
Books of the Old Testament .... JOB, PROVERBS, ECCLESIASTES
goddess of .... ATHENA, MINERVA
infinite .... OMNISCIENCE
source of .... LAMP
symbol of .... OWL
tooth .... MOLAR
universal .... PANSOPHY
words of ..... MAXIM, PROVERB
wise .... DEEP, SAGE, WITTY, SHREWD, CUNNING, ERUDITE, LEARNED, SAPIENT, INFORMED, JUDICIOUS, SAGACIOUS
adviser .... MENTOR
and pithy .... GNOMIC
guy .... SMART ALECK
lawmaker .... SOLON
leader .... STATESMAN
man .... SAGE, SOLON, MASTER, MENTOR, NESTOR, PUNDIT, SAVANT, MAHATMA, SCHOLAR, SOLOMON
men, biblical .... MAGI
saying ..... SAW, REDE, ADAGE, MAXIM, PROVERB
slang .... FRESH, SAVVY, KNOWING, CONCEITED
wiseacre ...... QUACK, SMART ASS, KNOW-IT-ALL, SMART ALECK
wisecrack .... GAG, GIBE, JEST, JOKE, QUIP, RETORT
wisent .... BISON
wish ...... BID, HOPE, WANT, WILL,

CRAVE, DREAM, YEARN, BEHEST, DESIRE
mere .... VELLEITY
undone .... RUE
wishbone .... FURCULA, FURCULUM, FOURCHETTE
wishful .... HOPEFUL, LONGING
wishy-washy .... THIN, WEAK, BLAND, FEEBLE, WATERY, INSIPID, SLIPSHOD, SLOVENLY, SPINELESS, NAMBY-PAMBY
Wisla .... VISTULA
wisp .... LOCK, TATE, TUFT, BUNCH, SHRED, BUNDLE
wispy .... FRAIL, SLIGHT, SLENDER
wisteria .... PEA, SHRUB, FLOWER, VIOLET
wistful .... EAGER, MUSING, PENSIVE, YEARNING
wit .... WAG, MIND, IRONY, SENSE, CUNNING, SARCASM, HUMOR(IST)
bit of .... EPIGRAM
descriptive of .... QUICK, NIMBLE
graceful, piercing .... ATTIC SALT
lively .... ESPRIT
lowest form of .... PUN
sharp .... SALT
soul of .... BREVITY
sting of .... BARB
witch .... HAG, HEX, CRONE, HARPY, LAMIA, SHREW, SIREN, SYBIL, BELDAM(E), CARLINE, CHARMER, HELLCAT, WARLOCK, SORCERESS, ENCHANTRESS
brew of .... HELLBROTH
city .... SALEM
doctor .... MEDICINE MAN
folklore .... LILITH
Homer's .... CIRCE
hunt .... PERSECUTION
in "Damn Yankees" .... LOLA
male equivalent of a .... WARLOCK
means of transportation .... BROOM
Shakespeare's .... DUESSA
who helped Jason ...... MEDEA
with snakes for hair ..... GORGON, MEDUSA, STHENO
witchcraft ...... MAGIC, SORCERY, WIZARDRY, NECROMANCY
charm .... JUJU
talisman .... OBI, OBEAH
witchery .... CHARM, HOODOO, VOODOO, SORCERY, FASCINATION
witches' broom ...... HEXENBESEN

Sabbath .... ORGY, MEETING
witching .... MAGICAL, ENCHANTING
witchy words .... INCANTATION
wite .... BLAME, FAULT
with ...... BY, CUM, PLUS, AMONG, USING, THROUGH, ALONG(SIDE)
bated breath .... TENSE, ANXIOUS
child .... PREGNANT, EXPECTING
competence .... ABLY
cruel tendencies ...... SADISTIC
finesse .... ADEPTLY
force .... AMAIN
great ineptness .... SADLY
haste: poet. .... AMAIN
humility .... MEEKLY
it: sl. .... HEP, HIP
more decibels .... LOUDER
open arms .... WILLINGLY
prefix .... SYN
regard to .... AS FOR
spirit, in music ...... CON BRIO
the result .... SO AS
withal .... ALSO, STILL, BESIDES
withdraw .... QUIT, WEAN, LEAVE, DECAMP, DEPART, RECALL, RECANT, REMOVE, RESIGN, RETIRE, SECEDE, BACKOUT, PULLOUT, RETRACT, RETREAT, TAKE OUT, EVACUATE
withdrawn .... SHY, RESERVED, ISOLATED, RETIRING
withe .... OSIER, WICKER
wither .... BURN, FADE, SEAR, WILT, BLAST, DECAY, DROOP, DRY UP, WASTE, WIZEN, SCATHE, SCORCH, SHRIVEL
withered .... SERE
withering .... SARCASTIC
away .... TABESCENT
remark .... SARCASM
withershins .... COUNTER-CLOCKWISE
withhold .... DENY, CHECK, DETAIN, HINDER, REFUSE, HOLD BACK, KEEP(BACK), RESERVE, RESTRAIN
approval .... DISSENT
information .... CLAM UP
within .... BEN, INNER, INSIDE, INTERNAL
audible frequencies ..... SONIC
comb. form .... ESO, ENDO
easy reach .... HANDY
without .... EX, SANS, SINE, MINUS, BEREFT, LACKING, OUTSIDE, DEVOID OF, NOT HAVING, EXTERNALLY

a bit of light .... PITCH-DARK
a mixer .... NEAT
adequate help .... SHORT-HANDED
charge .... FREE, GRATIS
combining form .... ECTO
delay ..... AT ONCE, PROMPTLY, FORTHWITH, IMMEDIATELY
doubt .... POSITIVE(LY)
embellishment .... PLAIN
exception .... EXPRESS, UNQUALIFIED
fail .... RELIGIOUSLY
feet .... APOD
fluid .... DRY, ANEROID, DEHYDRATED
foundation .... FLIMSY
gender .... NEUTER
guile .... OPENLY
legal force .... NULL
life .... AZOIC
modulation .... TONELESS
ornamentation .... STARK
passengers: colloq. .... DEADHEAD
preparation .... EXTEMPORE, IMPROMPTU
rhyme or reason .... SENSELESS, IRRATIONAL
saddles, in geological parlance .... ASELLATE
skill .... INEPT(LY)
sound .... MUTE, SILENT
teeth .... EDENTATE, EDENTULOUS
warning .... ABRUPTLY, SUDDENLY, ALL OF A SUDDEN
written records .... PRELITERATE
without a paddle, _____ ...... UP THE CREEK
withstand ...... BEAR, DEFY, FACE, ENDURE, OPPOSE, RESIST, CONFRONT
witless .... DULL, DUMB, SILLY, STUPID, FOOLISH, IDIOTIC
witness .... SEE, SIGN, PROOF, TASTE, ATTEST, TESTIFY, BEHOLD(ER), OBSERVE(R), ONLOOKER, TESTIFIER
bear .... ATTEST, TESTIFY
kind of .... EYE, HOSTILE
perjured .... STRAWMAN
place in court .... STAND
witticism .... GAG, PUN, JEST, JOKE, QUIP, SALLY, (BON)MOT, WISECRACK
Witt's planetoid .... EROS
witty .... DROLL, PITHY, SALTY, CLEVER, JOCOSE, AMUSING, JOCULAR, HUMOROUS,

FACETIOUS
exchange .... REPARTEE
poem .... EPIGRAM
remarks .... MOTS
reply .... SALLY, RETORT, RIPOSTE
sayings .... BONS MOTS
wive .... MARRY
wivern .... DRAGON
wizard ...... MAGE, SAGE, MAGIAN, PELLAR, SHAMAN, CONJURER, MAGICIAN, SORCERER, ARCHIMAGE
Arthurian .... MERLIN
colloquial .... EXPERT, MASTER
Wizard of Menlo Park .... EDISON
wizardry .... MAGIC, SORCERY
wizen .... BURN, SEAR, DRY UP, WITHER, SHRIVEL
wizened .... SERE
woad ...... DYE, PASTEL, MUSTARD
woald .... WELD
wobble .... REEL, ROCK, ROLL, SWAY, SHAKE, WAVER, SHIMMY, TEETER, TOTTER, WADDLE, STAGGER, TREMBLE, VACILLATE
"Wobblies" of 1905 .... IWW
wobbly .... ROCKY, SHAKY, GROGGY
Woden .... ODIN, OTHIN
woe .... BANE, BLUES, DOLOR, DUMPS, GRIEF, MISERY, SORROW, CHAGRIN, DESPAIR, TROUBLE, AFFLICTION
is me! .... ALAS
tale of .... JEREMIAD, LAMENTATION
woebegone .... SAD, DOLEFUL, PENSIVE, PITIFUL, TEARFUL, DESOLATE, LACHRYMOSE
woeful .... SAD, BLUE, GRAY, TRISTE, MELANCHOLY
wolaba .... KANGAROO
wold .... PLAIN, FLOWER, MIGNONETTE
wolf .... CANID, LARVA, LUPUS
bound with magic rope .... FENRIR
cry of .... HOWL
female .... BITCH
foot(print) .... PAD
hunter .... WOLFER, WOLVER
in sheep's clothing .... HYPOCRITE
large .... LOBO, GRAYWOLF
male .... DOG
of a .... LUPINE
pack leader .... AKELA

person changed into a
.... WER(E)WOLF,
LYCANTHROPE
prairie .... COYOTE
slang .... RAKE, ROUE,
PHILANDERER
timber .... LOBO
up .... GULP, RAVEN, GOBBLE
young .... CUB, WHELP,
WOLFKIN
Wolfe, fiction detective ...... NERO
victim of .... MONTCALM
Wolfert, writer .... IRA
wolfish .... GREEDY, RAVENOUS,
RAPACIOUS
wolframite .... CAL TUNGSTEN
wolfhound .... ALAN, BORZOI
wolflike .... FIERCE, LUPINE,
SAVAGE, RAVENOUS
animal .... HYENA
wolfsbane .... ACONITE,
MONKSHOOD
Wollaston, physicist .... WILLIAM
mineral named after
.... WOLLASTONITE
wolverine .... GLUTTON,
CARCAJOU
relative .... BADGER, WEASEL
Wolverine State .... MICHIGAN
woman ...... MS, EVE, SHE, DAME,
FRAU, GIRL, JILL, LADY, WIFE,
MUJER, SQUAW, FEMALE,
MULIER, DISTAFF
adviser .... EGERIA
annoyer .... OGLER, MASHER
attendant .... MATRON
bad-tempered .... SHREW,
VIXEN, VIRAGO, HELLCAT,
SPITFIRE, TERMAGANT
bearing second child
.... MULTIPARA
beautiful .... BELLE, FREYA,
HELEN, HOURI, SIREN, VENUS,
VISION, STUNNER
birth control advocate
.... SANGER
bold, brazen .... HUSSY,
QUEAN
British: sl. .... BIRD
chaser ..... RAKE, ROUE, WOLF,
CASANOVA, LOTHARIO, LADY-
KILLER
chaste .... VESTAL, VIRGIN
colloquial .... HEN, BROAD,
FILLY, FRAIL, PETTICOAT
combining form .... GYN(O)
companion .... CUMMER
conductor .... QUACH
country ...... GAFFER, GAMMER
deadly, alluring .... FEMME
FATALE

dirty ..... DRAB, SLOB, MALKIN,
SLOVEN, SLATTERN
domineering .... BATTLE-AX
dowdy .... FRUMP
elderly ...... GRANNY, MATRON,
DOWAGER
escort of .... CHAPERON,
(E)SQUIRE
evil .... HAG, HELLCAT,
JEZEBEL
fairest .... HELEN
fascinating .... WITCH
flyer .... AVIATRIX
frenzied .... M(A)ENAD
graceful .... SYLPH
guard .... MATRON
half fish .... MERMAID
hater .... MISOGYNIST,
MISANTHROPE
hideous .... WITCH, GORGON,
MEDUSA, STHENO, BELDAME
homosexual .... LESBIAN
houseworker .... MARTHA
in the doll house .... NORA
in 30's song ..... LADY IN RED
in uniform .... WAC, WAF,
SPAR, WAVE, WREN, NURSE
jungle .... SHEENA
kept .... DOXY, MISTRESS,
PARAMOUR, CONCUBINE
killing .... FEMICIDE
little ...... JO, AMY, MEG, BETH,
WIFE, SPOUSE
loose ..... BAWD, TART, HUSSY,
QUEAN, TRULL, WENCH,
WHORE, TROLLOP, STRUMPET
married .... MS, MRS.,
MADAM(E), MATRON, MISSUS
meek .... GRISELDA
member of U.S. Coast Guard
.... SPAR
model .... MANNIKIN,
MANNEQUIN
nagging .... SHREW
noble .... DUCHESS, BARONESS,
COUNTESS, MARQUISE,
PRINCESS
of Athens, influential
.... ASPASIA
of poor repute .... DEMIREP,
COURTESAN
of song .... AMY, MAMA,
IRENE, LOUISE, ADELINE
old .... HAG, CRONE, WITCH,
GAMMER, CARLINE,
GRANDAM(E)
old, unmarried ..... OLD MAID,
SPINSTER
opera comic .... BUFFA
patient .... GRISELDA
performer .... ACTRESS,

ARTISTE, DISEUSE, FARCEUSE,
COMEDIENNE
pert .... MINX
pioneer aviatrix
.... (AMELIA)EARHART
popular .... BELLE
pretty .... MODEL, PEACH,
LOOKER, DAZZLER, STUNNER,
KNOCKOUT
quarrelsome .... BITCH,
SHREW, VIRAGO, HARRIDAN,
TERMAGANT, XANTHIPPE
religious .... NUN, SISTER
repulsive .... GORGON
ruler .... QUEEN, REINE,
EMPRESS, MATRIARCH
scolding .... NAG, SHREW,
VIRAGO, FISHWIFE, HARRIDAN,
TERMAGANT, XANTHIPPE
seducer .... SIREN, VAMPIRE,
TEMPTRESS
sexually abnormal
.... NYMPHO(MANIAC)
shameless .... JEZEBEL
shrewish .... HARRIDAN
singer .... SOPRANO,
CHANTEUSE, CHANTRESS,
CANTATRICE
slang .... HEN, BABE, DAME,
BROAD, FRAIL, SKIRT, SQUAW,
FLOSSY, HEIFER, TOOTS(Y),
FLOSSIE, TOOTSIE
slave in a harem ..... ODALISK,
ODALISQUE
soothsayer .... SEERESS,
PYTHONESS
spiteful .... CAT
spy .... MATA HARI
stately .... JUNO
street .... WHORE, HOOKER,
PROSTITUTE
suckling another's baby
.... WET NURSE
treacherous .... DELILAH,
SEDUCER, VAMPIRE,
TEMPTRESS
ugly .... HAG, CRONE, WITCH,
GORGON, BELDAM(E)
unattractive .... BAG, FRUMP
unfruitful, descriptively
.... BARREN, JEJUNE, STERILE,
CHILDLESS
untidy .... DRAB, SLOB,
MALKIN, SLOVEN, SLATTERN
vagrant, homeless .... BAG
LADY
violent .... FURY
warrior ..... AMAZON, CAMILLA
warrior of Israel: biblical
.... DEBORAH

who advocates voting rights .... SUFFRAGETTE
who rode horse naked .... GODIVA
who rules a family .... MATRIARCH
wicked .... JEZEBEL
yellow-haired .... BLONDE
young .... BABE, GIRL, LASS, MISS, NYMPH, DAMSEL, MAIDEN, DEMOISELLE
zodiac .... VIRGO
womanhood .... FEMININITY, MULIEBRITY
womanish .... WEAK, FEMININE, EFFEMINATE
womanizer .... RAKE, ROUE, LOTHARIO, LIBERTINE
woman's baggy trousers .... BLOOMERS
blouse .... BASQUE
bonnet .... CAPOTE
cape .... MANTLE, MANTEAU, PELERINE
cloak ...... MANTUA, MANTEAU, PALETOT, CAPUCHIN, CARDINAL
coat .... MINK, MANDARIN, REDINGOTE, CHESTERFIELD
collar .... BERTHA
coronet .... TIARA
dowry .... DOT
drawers .... PANTALET(TES)
dressing gown .... FROCK, CAMISE, KIMONO
evening dress .... GOWN, FORMAL
hairstyle .... BOB, BANGS, CHIGNON, PAGEBOY, SHINGLE, UPSWEEP, POMPADOUR
hat .... TOQUE, BRETON, CLOCHE, TURBAN, PILLBOX
head and shoulder covering .... NUBIA
headdress .... FRET, POUF, PINNER
jacket .... SACK, SIMAR, BLAZER, BOLERO, SACQUE, PALETOT, CAMISOLE
light housecoat .... DUSTER
mantle .... MANTEAU
masculine traits .... VIRILISM
neckwear .... STOLE, CHOKER
one-piece undergarment .... TEDDY
origin .... RIB
pants .... CULOTTES, PEDAL-PUSHERS
riding costume .... HABIT, JOSEPH
robe .... SIMAR

scarf/veil .... MANTILLA
shoe .... PUMP, CHOPINE
shoe style ..... WEDGIE, CUBAN HEEL, SLING-BACK
short negligee .... CAMISOLE
short overskirt .... PEPLUM
skirt .... KIRTLE
skirt stretcher .... PANNIER
title ...... DONA, LADY, DONNA, MADAM, MADONNA
tongue, iron curb for .... BRANKS
unacquainted annoyer .... MASHER
undergarment .... BRA, SLIP, PANTY, TEDDY, CORSET, GIRDLE, UNDIES, STEP-IN, CHEMISE, BLOOMERS, KNICKERS, LINGERIE
vest .... JERKIN
weapon of yore .... HATPIN
work/concerns .... DISTAFF
wrap .... MANTA, NUBIA, DOLMAN
womb .... WAME, BELLY, MATRIX, UTERUS, VENTER
wombat ...... BADGER, MARSUPIAL
feature .... POUCH
like animal .... BEAR
women, club of .... SOROSIS, SORORITY
fondness for women .... PHILOGYNY
government by .... MATRIARCHY
in U.S. Army .... WACS
in U.S. Air Force .... WAFS
in U.S. Navy .... WAVES
lover of .... PHILOGYNIST
organization of .... NOW, NAFE, WCTU
preoccupation of .... DIET, STYLE, FIGURE, MAKE-UP, WEIGHT, FASHION
reformatory .... MAGDALENE
rights movement .... FEMINISM, LIB(ERATION)
seclusion of .... PURDAH
with questionable ethics .... DEMIMONDE
wonder .... AWE, MUSE, STUN, MARVEL, MIRACLE, SURPRISE, AMAZEMENT, ELECTRIFY
boy .... PRODIGY
world's .... PHAROS, PYRAMIDS, COLOSSUS, GRAND CANYON, CATACOMBS, STONEHENGE, HANGING GARDENS, GREAT WALL OF CHINA, LEANING TOWER OF PISA

wonderful .... COLOSSAL, TERRIFIC, OUT-OF-SIGHT
wonderwork .... MIRACLE
won't .... SHANT
wont .... USE, HABIT, CUSTOM, ROUTINE, ACCUSTOMED
wonted .... USUAL
woo .... COAX, LURE, SEEK, URGE, COURT, SPARK, PURSUE, ENTREAT, ROMANCE
musically .... SERENADE
wood .... LOG, BOARD, COPSE, GROVE, XYLEM, BOSQUE, FOREST, LUMBER, TIMBER
alcohol .... METHANOL
anemone .... THIMBLEWEED
aromatic .... LINALOA
ash oxide .... POTASH
ashes extract .... LYE
axe breaker .... QUEBRACHO
bar .... FID
batted for distance ..... TIPCAT
bend in .... SNY, WARP
betony .... LOUSEWORT
bits .... KINDLING
black .... TEAK, EBONY
block .... NOG, DOOK, TRIG, SPRAG, WEDGE
borer .... TEREDO
building .... TIMBER
burning piece .... FIREBRAND
charred .... BRAY
coal .... LIGNITE, CHARCOAL
combining form .... HYL(O), XYL(O), LIGNI, LIGN(O)
cutter .... RIPSAW
cutting .... HAG
destroying insect .... ANAY, TERMITE
destroying mollusk .... TEREDO
dressed .... TIMBER
dresser/trimmer .... ADZ(E)
drug .... QUASSIA
dust .... COOM(B)
easily burned .... SPUNK
eater/wrecker .... ANAY, TERMITE
elastic .... YEW
engraving .... XYLOGRAPH
flat piece .... SPLAT
fluting .... CHAMFER
for bows .... YEW
for bridges/piles .... ALDER
for dagger hilt .... DUDGEON
for flooring .... MAPLE
for furniture .... OAK, TEAK, EBONY, NARRA, WALNUT, MAHOGANY, CALAMANDER
fragrant .... ALOES, CEDAR
groove .... CHAMFER

gum .... XYLAN
hard .... ASH, ELM, OAK,
  ASPEN, BIRCH, EBONY, MAPLE,
  NARRA, LOCUST, MOLAVE,
  WALNUT, WILLOW, HICKORY,
  MAHOGANY
hyacinth .... BLUEBELL,
  HAREBELL
ibis .... STORK, JABIRU
inlaid .... BUHL
kind of .... DEAL
knot .... KNAR
layer .... VENEER
light .... BALSA
louse .... SLATER, SOW BUG
made of .... OAKEN, XYLOID
make into .... LIGNIFY
mark .... ROE
measure .... CORD, FOOT
nymph ..... MOTH, BUTTERFLY,
  (HAMA)DRYAD, HUMMINGBIRD
of .... XYLOID, LIGNEOUS
oil .... TUNG
partially burned .... CINDER
piece of .... SLAT, BOARD,
  PLANK, STAVE, BILLET
pigeon .... CULVER, CUSHAT,
  RINGDOVE
pin .... FID, NOG, PEG
pin in boat .... THOLE
plug .... SPILE
preservative .... CREOSOTE
quantity .... CORDAGE
reddish .... CHERRY
reddish-brown ..... MAHOGANY
resinous .... SANDARAC,
  LIGNALOES
small .... GROVE
soft .... FIR, PINE, CEDAR,
  SPRUCE, HEMLOCK, REDWOOD
sorrel .... OCA, OXALIS
stand, top of .... CRISS
strip .... LATH, LIST, SLAT,
  SLIP, SPLIT, STAVE, BATTEN,
  SPLINT
striped .... TULIP, ARAROBA
tar distillate .... PITCH,
  CREOSOTE
twist in .... WARP
type of .... HARD, SOFT
veneer .... BURL
warbler .... WAGTAIL
wheel brake .... NOG, TRIG,
  SPRAG, WEDGE
worker .... SAWYER,
  CARPENTER
worm .... THRIPS
wood, _____ (superstitious
  statement) .... KNOCK ON
Wood, actress .... NATALIE
woodbine .... IVY, CREEPER,

PERIDOT, HONEYSUCKLE
woodchat .... SHRIKE
woodchuck .... MARMOT, WEJACK,
  GROUNDHOG
woodcock relative .... PEWEE,
  SNIPE, SANDPIPER
woodcraft .... HUNTING, TRAPPING
woodcutter .... LOGGER, SAWYER,
  LUMBERJACK
wooded .... SYLVAN
  area .... WEALD, BOONDOCKS
  hill .... HOLT
wooden .... DULL, RIGID, STIFF,
  TREEN, STOLID, XYLOID,
  DEADPAN, LIFELESS,
  LIGNEOUS, INFLEXIBLE,
  INSENSITIVE
bar .... TREE
bench .... SETTEE
board for meat-carving
  .... TRENCHER
bowl .... KITTY, MAZER,
  MAZARD
brick .... DOOK
bucket .... CANNIKIN
club .... BILLET
collar .... CANGUE
hammer .... MALLET
horse giver .... TROJAN
Indian's place .... CIGAR
  STORE
limb .... PEG LEG
nutmeg trick .... FRAUD
pail .... PIGGIN
peg/pin ...... FID, NOG, DOWEL,
  SPILE, THOLE, TRE(E)NAIL
pole/post .... TREE
seat .... BENCH
shoe .... CLOG, SABOT, PATTEN
spool toy .... DIABOLO
stake .... TREE
strip .... LATH
time-beater .... CASTANETS
woodenware .... BOWLS, ROLLING
  PIN
woodland .... GROVE, WOODS,
  FOREST, SYLVAN
clearing .... GLADE
deity .... PAN, FAUN, SATYR,
  SILENUS, SILVANUS
woodlark genus .... LULLULA
woodpecker .... CHAB, COLY,
  FLICKER, REDHEAD, HIGH-
  HOLE, POPINJAY, SAPSUCKER,
  YELLOWHAMMER
cartoon creator
  .... (WALTER)LANTZ
family .... PICIDAE
feature
  .... (PROTRUSILE)TONGUE
genus .... SASIA, DINOPIUM,

PICOIDES, DENDROCOPOS
green .... COLY, ECCLE
green: genus .... PICUS VIRIDIS
lifestyle .... WOOD-BORING,
  TREE-CLIMBING
specie .... ACORN, BLACK,
  GREEN, WHITE, WRYNECK,
  ARROWHEAD, RED-HEADED,
  THREE-TOED, GOLDEN-NAPED,
  IVORY-BILLED, RED-
  COCKADED, GREAT SPOTTED
true .... PICINAE
wryneck .... JUNGINAE
woods ...... GROVE, SILVA, FOREST
attraction toward the
  .... NEMOPHILA
out of the .... SAFE, CLEAR
woodsia .... FERN
wood(s)man .... HUNTER, LOGGER,
  RANGER, TRAPPER, FORESTER,
  VOYAGEUR, LUMBERJACK
woodsy .... SYLVAN
woodwaxen .... DYEWEED
woodwind .... OBOE, SAXE, FLUTE,
  BASSOON, SAXHORN,
  CLARINET, SAXOPHONE
woodwork .... DOORS, DIDOES,
  FRAMES, MOLDING, PANELING
woody .... XYLOID, LIGNEOUS
fiber .... BAST
fiber substance .... LIGNIN
plant .... TREE, SHRUB
tissue .... XYLEM
vine .... LIANA, CLEMATIS,
  WISTERIA, HONEYSUCKLE
vine bearing fruit .... GRAPE
Woody of the movies ...... ALLEN
Woody's boy .... ARLO
wooer .... SUITOR, PURSUER
woof .... ABB, BARK, WEFT,
  CLOTH, FABRIC, FILLING,
  TEXTURE
companion of .... WARP
woofer .... DOG, LOUDSPEAKER
wooing .... SUIT, COURTSHIP
wool .... HAIR, LANA, PILE,
  ALPACA, ANGORA, FLEECE,
  MERINO
and cashmere .... CASHA
and silk cloth .... CAMLET,
  EOLIENNE
animal with .... RAM, GOAT,
  LLAMA, SHEEP, ALPACA,
  MERINO, VICUNA, GUANACO
bearing .... LANIFEROUS
blemish .... MOTE
cleaning machine
  .... WILLOW(ER)
cluster .... NEP
coarse/matted .... SHAG
comb .... CARD

combed knot of .... NOIL
combining form .... LANI
covered with .... LANATE,
FLOCCOSE
cuttings .... KERFS
fabric ..... REPP, REP(S), BEIGE,
CASHA, BEAVER, TWEED,
FRIEZE, HODDEN, TARTAN,
CHALLIE, CHALLIS, DELAINE,
ETAMINE, STAMMEL,
VELOUR(S), LANDSDOWNE
fat .... LANOLIN(E)
felted .... CASHA, BEAVER
fiber .... NOIL, PILE, FLOCK,
SLIVER
fiber, batted .... BATTING
gathering .... MOONING,
STARGAZING, DAYDREAMING
goat's .... CASHMERE
grease .... SUINT
implement .... SHEARS,
PICKLOCK
knitted .... JERSEY
knot .... BURL, NOIL
like .... DOWNY, HAIRY,
FLEECY, FLUFFY
like fabric .... LANITAL
lock of .... TAG
matted .... SHAG, DAGLOCK
measure .... HEER
nemesis of .... LINT
oily substance .... GREASE
pack .... BALE
particles .... DOWN
piece of .... NOIL
produced one year .... CLIP
refuse .... COTT
roll of .... SLUB
rug fibers .... NAP, PILE
salvage .... MUNGO
seller .... STAPLER
sheared at one time ...... CLIP,
FLEECE
sheep/fine .... MERINO
sheer .... VOILE
shreds of .... NOIL
spinning machine
.... THROSTLE
still on animal ...... WOOLFELL
substitute .... ORLON
synthetic .... LANITAL
thread .... YARN, WORSTED
tuft .... LOCK, FLOCCUS,
FLOCCULE
twisted .... ROVE
unbleached .... BEIGE
unravel .... CARD, TEASE
waste ..... FUD, FLOCK, MUNGO
watered .... MOREEN
weight .... TOD
yarn .... WORSTED

woolen blanket .... SERAPE,
MACKINAW
cloth/fabric .... BAIZE, CASHA,
LODEN, MUNGO, TWEED,
CAMLET, DUFFEL, DUFFLE,
FRIEZE, HODDEN, JERSEY,
KERSEY, MELTON, MERINO,
MOREEN, RATINE, SHODDY,
TARTAN, DOESKIN, ETAMINE,
RATTEEN, WORSTED,
CAS(S)IMIRE, CALAMANCO,
PETERSHAM, TRICOT(INE)
cheap .... MUNGO, SHODDY
coarse .... DUFFEL, DUFFLE
glossy .... CALAMANCO
loosely woven ...... FLANNEL
of silk and wool .... CAMLET
resembling gabardine
.... TRICOTINE
ribbed .... KERSEY
silky .... MERINO
twilled .... SERGE, TWEED,
RATINE, RATTEEN,
CASHMERE, SHALLOON,
CAS(S)IMIRE, TRICOTINE
undyed .... HODDEN
used for billiard tables
.... BAIZE
jacket .... CARDIGAN
material .... CADDIS,
CADDICE
shawl .... PAISLEY
sweater .... CARDIGAN,
CASHMERE
woolly .... DOWNY, HAIRY,
FLEECY, FLUFFY, LANATE,
LANOSE, FLOCCULENT
bear .... CATERPILLAR
cud-chewing animal
.... VICUNA
haired .... ULOTRICHOUS
haired people ...... ULOTRICHI
Peruvian animal .... ALPACA
tuft .... FLOCCULUS
wild, reddish-brown animal
.... GUANACO
woorali .... URARI, CURARE
woozy .... DOPEY, TIPSY, GROGGY,
MUDDLED, CONFUSED,
BEFUDDLED
word .... NEWS, TALK, TERM,
ORDER, PAROL(E), PLEDGE,
REMARK, SIGNAL, PROMISE,
TIDINGS, LOCUTION,
UTTERANCE, INFORMATION
action .... VERB
addition to beginning of
.... PREFIX
addition to end of ..... SUFFIX,
PARAGOGE
appropriate .... MOT JUSTE

auctioneer's .... GONE, SOLD,
GOING
blindness .... ALEXIA
book .... LEXICON, LIBRETTO,
THESAURUS, DICTIONARY
Captain Marvel's magic
.... SHAZAM
change in a .... METAPLASM
coined and used for a single
occasion .... NONCE
WORD
derivation .... PARONYM
disapproving .... TUT
division .... INTO
dropping of middle sound of
.... SYNCOPE
dropping of last sound/letter
of .... APOCOPE
figurative .... TROPE, SIMILE,
METAPHOR
final .... AMEN, ULTIMATUM
first of doxology .... GLORIA
for second base .... KEYSTONE
for word .... VERBAL, LITERAL,
TEXTUAL, VERBATIM,
METAPHRASE
formative ending
.... DESINENCE
formed from another
.... DERIVATIVE
four-letter .... TETRAGRAM
game .... RIDDLE, ANAGRAM,
CHARADE, ACROSTIC,
SCRABBLE, CONUNDRUM
hard to pronounce
.... JAWBREAKER
in a .... BRIEFLY, IN SHORT
in an ultimatum .... ELSE
invented .... COINAGE
inventor .... NEOLOGIST
inversion .... ANASTROPHE
last .... AMEN
last syllable of .... ULTIMA
long: colloq. .... MOUTHFUL
Major Hoople's .... EGAD
meaning, study of
...... SEMANTICS, SEMASIOLOGY
misused .... BARBARITY
mystical, biblical .... SELAH
new or new meaning of
.... NEOLOGY, NEOLOGISM
of admonition .... DON'T
agreement .... SURE
assent .... YEA, YES, AMEN
excitement .... WOW
honor .... PAROLE, PLEDGE,
PROMISE
impatience .... PISH
inquiry .... HOW, WHO, WHY,
WHAT, WHEN, WHICH,
WHERE

lament .... ALAS
mouth .... ORAL, PAROL
only one .... MONOMIAL
opposite meaning
.... ANTONYM
rebuke .... TUT
similar meaning
.... SYNONYM
two or more base
   morphemes
.... COMPOUND
warning .... BEWARE,
              CAUTION
on the wall .... MENE
ordinary meaning ..... LITERAL
origin of a .... ETYMOLOGY
original form .... ETYMON
prisoner's .... PAROLE
puzzle .... REBUS, CHARADE,
   ACROSTIC, CROSSWORD,
            LOGOGRAPH
reading same backward
.... PALINDROME
roll-call .... HERE, PRESENT
ruer's .... ALAS
same pronunciation, different
   meaning .... HOMONYM,
            HOMOPHONE
same spelling, different
   meaning .... HETERONYM,
            HOMOGRAPH
shorten a .... SYNCOPE
sorority .... TAU
square .... PALINDROME
substitute .... METONYM
symbol .... LOGOGRAM
the .... BIBLE, LOGOS
ultimatum .... ELSE
unprintable, usually ..... FOUR-
            LETTER
vowel omission .... APHESIS
wedding announcement
.... NEE
with back or hands ...... BARE
beat or stick .... DRUM
Big or Gentle .... BEN
bird or print .... BLUE
Black or White .... SEA
cake or change .... SHORT
car or maid .... PARLOR
common or horse ..... SENSE
cross .... ROADS
deep or bitter .... END
egg or pie .... PLANT
fire or transit .... RAPID
flower or fish .... STAR
friend or fellow .... SHIP
gas or ivy .... POISON
golf or cuff .... LINK
high or hole .... KNEE
in or out .... TURN

Inchcape or Plymouth
.... ROCK
jacket or lace .... STRAIT
Lear or Kong .... KING
lord or lady .... LAND
maker or breaker .... LAW
on or out .... TRY
out or off .... RIP
over or upon .... ONCE
side or edge .... WISE
sun or moon .... LIT
tail .... BOB, CAT, HIGH
term or time .... LONG
to or through .... SEE
up or down .... SHUT
vegetable or victory
.... GARDEN
view or fix .... PRE
water or tea .... WAGON
well or ill .... BRED
wordiest language .... ENGLISH
wordiness .... PLEONISM,
   VERBIAGE, PROLIXITY,
           VERBOSITY
wording .... TEXT, DICTION,
   PHRASING, PHRASEOLOGY
wordless .... MUM, MUTE, TACIT
comment .... SIGH
words .... TALK, TEXT, LYRICS,
   DISPUTE, ARGUMENT
argument about
.... LOGOMACHY
Almanac author .... ESPY
attack with ..... ABUSE, BASTE,
   SCOLD, CRITICIZE
author's .... TEXT
battle of .... DEBATE,
          LOGOMACHY
brush-off .... SOME OTHER
          TIME
choice of .... DICTION
clever exchange of
.... REPARTEE
doctrine of .... NEOLOGY
eat one's .... EAT CROW,
   RETRACT, SWALLOW, EAT
         HUMBLE PIE
for indefinite adjournment
.... SINE DIE
incorrect use of
.... CATACHRESIS
manner of expression
.... DICTION, ENUNCIATION
misuse of .... MALAPROPISM
of .... VERBAL
approximation .... OR SO,
   MORE OR LESS
determination .... I CAN
few .... CURT, TERSE,
         LACONIC
flattery .... PALAVER

understanding .... I SEE
wisdom .... SAW, GNOME,
   MAXIM, SAYING
on airmail envelope .... PAR
         AVION
on the Tomb of the
   Unknown Soldier
.... KNOWN BUT TO GOD
play on .... PUN
prefix .... LOGO
preprandial .... GRACE
put into .... EXPRESS
ridiculous user of
.... (MRS.)MALAPROP
slang .... BULL SESSION
to a convalescent .... GET
         WELL
vengeful .... TIT FOR TAT
wordy .... WINDY, PROLIX,
   VERBOSE, REDUNDANT,
   TALKATIVE, LONG-WINDED
work .... DO, JOB, MOIL, OPUS,
   TASK, TOIL, CRAFT, ERGON,
   GRIND, LABOR, EFFORT,
   BUSINESS, EMPLOYMENT,
         OCCUPATION
against .... MILITATE
aimlessly ...... POTTER, PUTTER
amount of .... LOAD
arduously .... TOIL
artist's .... MASTER
assignment .... JOB, BEAT,
   TASK, SHIFT, STINT, TRICK
at .... PLY, PURSUE
avoid .... SHIRK, SKULK,
         MALINGER
clothes .... UNIFORM,
   COVERALL, OVERALLS
clothes cloth .... DENIM,
   DRILL, OSNABURG
crew .... GANG
delicate interlacing
.... TRACERY
energetically .... HUSTLE
evade .... MALINGER
for .... EARN
fussily .... NIGGLE
great .... MASTER(PIECE)
group .... BEE, CREW, GANG,
        TEAM, DETAIL
hard .... GRUB, PLUG, TOIL,
   LABOR, SWEAT, HUSTLE
house/farm .... CHORE
in .... INSERT
in a smokehouse .... CURE
incentive .... TIP, PERK,
   BONUS, RAISE, GRATUITY,
        PERQUISITE
life .... CAREER
measures .... MAN-HOURS,
        MAN-YEARS

of art .... OIL, OPUS, MUSIC, CARVING, ETCHING, PAINTING, SCULPTURE, COMPOSITION

of wonder .... MIRACLE

on antiques .... RESTORE

out .... SOLVE, TRAIN, EVOLVE, DEVELOP, EXERCISE, PRACTICE

pants .... LEVIS

parties .... BEES

patiently ..... PLY, PLOD, PLUG, TOIL

schedule .... STINT

second job .... MOONLIGHT

shift .... TRICK

shirker .... BUCK PASSER

shoes .... BROGAN

suitable .... METIER

tedious .... CHORE, GRIND, TRAVAIL, DRUDGERY

time-out from .... BREAK, RECESS, VACATION

trainee .... APPRENTICE

trousers .... DUNGAREES

together: slogan ...... GUNG HO

under compulsion .... SLAVE

unit of .... ERG(ON)

unskillfully .... DABBLE

with lead .... PLUMB

your fingers to the _____ (to the point of exhaustion) .... BONE

workable .... FEASIBLE, OPERABLE, PRACTICAL

workaday .... DRAB, USUAL, HUMDRUM, PROSAIC, ROUTINE, ORDINARY, QUOTIDIAN, COMMONPLACE

workaholic .... ERGOPHILE

workbag .... KIT

workbench adjunct .... VISE

workbook .... MANUAL

workbox .... ETUI, (TOOL)KIT

worked up .... AGOG, FIRED, RILED, EXCITED, INFLAMED

worker ...... DOER, HAND, MOILER, TOILER, ARTISAN, LABORER, EMPLOYE(E), WAGE-EARNER

agricultural ...... OKIE, FARMER

agricultural, illegal .... WETBACK

Atlantic City .... DEALER, CROUPIER

beginner .... NOVICE, APPRENTICE

coal mine .... COLLIER

dell ..... FARMER, AGRONOMIST

farm .... HIND, PEON

garage .... MECHANIC

gem .... JEWELER

hard .... SCRUB

hotel .... VALET, PORTER, BELLBOY

in a caisson .... SANDHOG

in a royal household .... GROOM, YEOMAN, FOOTMAN

in a skilled trade .... ARTIST, WRITER, ARTISAN, MUSICIAN, ARTIFICER, CRAFTSMAN, MACHINIST, PROGRAMMER, TECHNICIAN

in accounting office .... ADDER, BOOKKEEPER

in oil fields .... RIGGER

iron .... SMELTER

itinerant .... BOOMER

kind of .... BREADWINNER

maintenance .... JANITOR

menial ..... DRUDGE, SERVANT, DOMESTIC

migratory .... HOBO, OKIE, PEON, BRACERO

non-union .... SCAB

of the working class .... PROLETARIAN

odd job ...... JACK, HANDYMAN

on strike, union .... PICKET

pavement .... BRICKLAYER

respite of .... VACATION

restless .... FLOATER

stone .... MASON, JEWELER

telephone .... OPERATOR

transient .... HOBO, OKIE, FLOATER, WETBACK

unskilled .... PEON, COOLIE, TINKER, COBBLER, LABORER

water system .... PLUMBER

waterfront .... STEVEDORE, LONGSHOREMAN

white collar .... CLERK

who had served apprenticeship .... JOURNEYMAN

who replaces striker ...... RAT, SCAB

workers .... STAFF, PERSONNEL, WORK FORCE

certain illicit .... MOONSHINERS

collectively .... LABOR

group: abbr. .... ILO

group, retired .... AARP

railroad track .... SPIKERS

working .... ACTIVE, RUNNING, OPERATING, FUNCTIONAL, FUNCTIONING

class .... PROLETARIAT

no longer .... RETIRED

not .... IDLE, UNEMPLOYED

workhorse .... HACK, SLAVE, DRUDGE, TOILER, PLODDER

workhouse .... ASYLUM, ALMSHOUSE

Workman, explorer .... FANNY

workmanlike .... EXPERT, SKILLED, SKILLFUL, PROFESSIONAL

workmanship .... FINISH, ARTIFICE, ARTISTRY, TECHNIQUE

workout ...... TEST, ESSAY, TRIAL, EXERCISE, PRACTICE, REHEARSAL

workroom .... DEN, STUDY

works, the .... OEUVRES, EVERYTHING

slang .... WHOLE SHEBANG

workshop ...... LAB, MILL, STORE, OFFICE, STUDIO, ATELIER

government department .... BUREAU

lumber .... SAWMILL

manufacturing .... PLANT, FACTORY

metal .... FOUNDRY

money .... MINT

remedial .... CLINIC

smelting .... IRONWORKS

with poor working conditions .... SWEATSHOP

world ...... EARTH, GLOBE, REALM, COSMOS, DOMAIN, NATURE, MANKIND, CREATION, UNIVERSE

bearer of the .... ATLAS

beater .... ONER

domain ..... ANIMAL, MINERAL, VEGETABLE

first national park in the .... YELLOWSTONE

largest clothing manufacturer of the .... LEVI STRAUSS

most populous nation of the .... CHINA

most populous democracy of the .... INDIA

nicknamed "oldest teenager" of the .... DICK CLARK

of the .... MUNDANE, SECULAR, TEMPORAL, TERRESTRIAL

out of this .... OUTRE

power .... RUSSIA, ENGLAND, UNITED STATES

-shaking .... GREAT, SIGNAL, BIG-TIME, MOMENTOUS

spinner .... LOVE

supporter .... ATLAS

trade agreement: abbr. .... RTA

workers group: abbr. .... ILO

World War I machine gun .... POMPOM

plane .... SPAD, TAUBE,

NIEUPORT

U.S. president .... WILSON

World War II. See **WW II**

worldly .... PROUD, CARNAL,
SORDID, EARTHLY, MUNDANE,
SECULAR, SELFISH, TERRENE,
TEMPORAL, MERCENARY,
TERRESTRIAL,
MATERIAL(ISTIC)

wise .... KNOWING,
EXPERIENCED, SOPHISTICATED

worldwide .... COMMON, GLOBAL,
GENERAL, CATHOLIC,
PANDEMIC, SWEEPING,
UNIVERSAL, ECUMENIC(AL),
ALL-EMBRACING

worm ...... ESS, LOA, NAID, TINEA,
INSECT, WRETCH, ANNELID,
ASCARID, CRAWLER,
HELMINTH, NEMATODE

bait .... LURG

bloodsucking .... LEECH

combining form .... VERMI

drug .... VERMICIDE

eaten ...... RAGGED, WORN-OUT

feeler of a .... PALP(US)

flat .... FLUKE, PLANARIAN,
TREMATODE

freshwater .... TUBIFEX

genus .... NEREIS, ASCARIS,
PLANARIA, LUMBRICUS

in .... EDGE IN, INTRUDE

in zoology .... LYTTA

infestation .... ASCARIASIS

larva .... GRUB, MAGGOT,
CERCARIA, CATERPILLAR

marine .... NEREIS, NEMERTEAN

measuring .... LOOPER

move like a .... CRAWL, CREEP

out (of) .... ELICIT, EXTRACT

out of trouble .... WRIGGLE

parasite of plants
.... PINWORM, HOOKWORM,
NEMATODE

parasitic ...... FLUKE, ASCARID,
CESTODE, CESTOID,
TAPEWORM, ROUNDWORM

round .... ASCARID

round, segmented .... LEECH,
ANNELID, EARTHWORM

sea .... ANNELID

segment .... SOMITE,
METAMERE

shaped .... VERMIFORM

ship .... CLAM, BORER,
TEREDO, COPPERWORM

silk .... ERIA, TUSSAH,
CATERPILLAR

slang .... PEST, INSECT

snail resembling .... SLUG

sucker .... LEECH

sucking organ of
.... PROBOSCIS

threadlike .... FILARIA

track .... NEREITE

used as fishing bait
.... ANGLEWORM, EARTHWORM,
HELLGRAMMITE

water .... LEECH, TEREDO,
TUBIFEX

worms, can of .... PROBLEM,
TROUBLE, HEADACHE

disease caused by parasitic
.... HELMINTHIASIS

medicine for intestinal
.... SANTONIN(E)

of the Nile .... ASPS

parasitic .... FILARIA,
HOOKWORM, TAPEWORM,
ROUNDWORM

wormseed .... SANTONICA

wormwood ...... MOXA, CHAGRIN,
ABSINTH(E), TARRAGON,
EMBARRASSMENT,
MORTIFICATION

wormy .... ROTTEN

worn .... OLD, USED, EROSE,
RAGGED, SHABBY, TATTERED

by friction .... ATTRITE

clothes .... RAGS

down .... TRODDEN

end .... FRAZZLE

look .... HAGGARD

out .... BEAT, SHOT, WEAK,
JADED, SEEDY, SPENT, TIRED,
WEARY, BUSHED, EFFETE,
FRAYED, POOPED, DECREPIT,
DOG-TIRED, EXHAUSTED

worried .... BESET, ANXIOUS,
CAREWORN, TROUBLED

worrier's crop .... ULCERS,
WRINKLES

worrisome .... IRKSOME,
ANNOYING

worry .... VEX, CARE, FEAR, FRET,
STEW, ANNOY, TEASE, UPSET,
HARASS, PESTER, ANXIETY,
DISTURB, GRIZZLE, DISTRESS

colloquial .... CONCERN,
LOOKOUT

worship .... PRAY, ADORE, DEIFY,
HOMAGE, REVERE, ADULATE,
IDOLIZE, RESPECT, DEVOTION,
ENSHRINE, VENERATE,
ADORATION

animal .... ZOOLATRY

bend the knee, as in
.... GENUFLECT

combining form .... LATRY

due to God alone ...... LATRIA

object of .... HERO, IDOL,
SWEETHEART

of all gods .... PANTHEISM

of idols .... IDOLISM,
IDOLATRY

of saints .... HAGIOLATRY

place of .... ALTAR, CHAPEL,
CHURCH, PAGODA, SHRINE,
TEMPLE, SYNAGOGUE

ritual .... LITURGY

system .... CULT, FETISH

worshiper .... DEIST, ADORER,
ADMIRER, DEIFIER, DEVOTEE,
VENERATOR

affected .... RELIGIONIST

devout .... VOTARY

exaggeratedly pious
.... PIETIST

of idols .... IDOLIST, IDOLATER

of the sun god .... INCA

of stars .... SABAIST

worshipful .... PIOUS, DEVOUT,
RELIGIOUS, REVERENTIAL

worst .... BEAT, BEST, DEFEAT,
CONQUER, POOREST

Worst Dressed Woman Awards

creator .... BLACKWELL

worsted .... BESTED

cloth .... WOOL, SERGE,
ETAMINE

ribbon/yarn .... CADDIS

wort .... HERB, PLANT

worth .... COST, MERIT, PRICE,
VALUE, ESTIMATION,
IMPORTANCE

having .... ASSET, DESIRABLE

of little .... TRIFLE, TRIFLING

person's character ...... CREDIT

worthless .... RIP, BASE, POOR,
VAIN, LOSEL, USELESS,
NUGATORY, GOOD-FOR-
NOTHING

almost .... PETTY, PALTRY,
PIDDLE

chap/fellow .... BUM, DOG,
IDLER, LOSER

horse .... NAG, RIP, JADE,
PLATER

ideas .... BILGE

remains .... DREGS, SCRAPS,
CARCASE, CARCASS

scrap .... ORT

slang .... LOUSY

thing .... RIP, CHIP, FICO, TRIPE

worthwhile .... GOOD, WORTHY,
GAINFUL, OF VALUE,
LUCRATIVE, BENEFICIAL

worthy .... HONEST, UPRIGHT,
VALUABLE, ADMIRABLE,
DESERVING, MERITORIOUS

Wouk, author .... HERMAN

ship .... CAINE

would be ...... HOPEFUL, ASPIRING

dialectical .... WOD
wound .... CUT, GASH, HURT,
PAIN, SORE, STAB, INJURY,
INSULT, LESION, OFFEND,
PIERCE, TRAUMA, LACERATE
adhesion .... SCAR
blood shed from .... GORE,
SANIES
discharge from a .... PUS,
ICHOR, SANIES
dressing .... PATCH
edge of .... LIP
in a way .... SPOOLED
jagged .... LACERATION
mark .... SCAR
on a bobbin .... SPOOLED
plug .... TENT, DOSSIL
woven ...... KNIT, LACED, TWINED,
WEBBED
double .... TWO-PLY
goods dealer .... HOSIER
material, netlike .... MESH
with raised design .... BROCHE
work made of sticks
.... WATTLE
wow .... HIT, AMUSE,
INTERJECTION
wowser .... PRUDE
wrack .... RUIN, CLOUDS,
SEAWEED, WRECKAGE
wraith .... FETCH, GHOST,
SPECTER, SPECTRE,
APPARITION
wrangle .... ROW, SPAR, ARGUE,
BRAWL, BICKER, DEBATE,
HIGGLE, DISPUTE, QUARREL,
SQUABBLE
wrangler ...... ARGUER, COWBOY,
BRAWLER
wrap .... LAP, FOLD, HIDE, CLOAK,
COVER, NUBIA, CLOTHE,
SWATHE, ENCLOSE, CONCEAL,
ENVELOP, SWADDLE
around .... SARONG,
LOINCLOTH
in burial cloth .... CERE
shoulder .... CAPE, SHAWL
snugly .... TUCK
tightly: naut. .... FRAP
to deaden sound .... MUFFLE
up .... ENFOLD, FINISH,
ENVELOP
woman's .... ROBE, SHAWL,
DOLMAN, PELISSE
wrapped up .... COMPLETED
wrapper .... BINDER, VESTURE
book's .... JACKET
candy's .... TINFOIL
wrapping material .... LEAF,
PAPER, KRAFT, MATTING,
CELLOPHANE

wrasse .... CUNNER, FISHES,
TAUTOG, HOGFISH
wrath .... IRE, FURY, RAGE,
ANGER, CHOLER, VENGEANCE
wrathy .... ANGRY, INDIGNANT
wreak .... EXACT, PUNISH,
INFLICT, OPPRESS
wreath .... LEI, ORLE, TORSE,
ANADEM, CHAPLET, FESTOON,
FLOWERS, GARLAND
bridal .... SPIREA
for achievement .... CORONA
for head .... ANADEM, LAUREL,
CHAPLET
hanging .... FESTOON
heraldic .... ORLE
victor's .... CORONA, LAUREL
wreathe .... COIL, TWIST,
ENTWINE, ENVELOP, ENCIRCLE
wreck .... RAZE, RUIN, CRASH,
DAMAGE, DESTROY, CRACK-
UP, SMASH(UP), UNDOING,
ACCIDENT, DISASTER,
COLLISION
building .... DEMOLISH, TEAR
DOWN
wreckage .... (W)RACK, DEBRIS,
JETSAM, FLOTSAM
wren .... JENNY, TOMTIT,
SONGBIRD
wrench .... JERK, PULL, YANK,
TWIST, WREST, WRICK,
WRING, SPRAIN, SPANNER
kind of .... MONKEY, STILLSON
wrest .... GRAB, TURN, TWIST,
WRING, EXTORT, SNATCH,
STRAIN, USURP, WRENCH,
EXTRACT
wrestle .... STRIVE, TUSSLE,
CONTEND, GRAPPLE,
STRUGGLE
wrestler .... MATMAN, MAULER,
GRAPPLER, SCUFFLER
Hulk .... HOGAN
pad of .... MAT
wrestling champion Rowan
.... CHAD
champion Rowan's name in
Japan .... AKEBONO
down for the three-count in
.... PINNED
highest rank in .... YOKUZUNA
hold .... SCISSORS, WRISTLOCK,
(HEAD)LOCK, (HALF)NELSON
match division .... FALL
oriental .... SUMO
place/school ...... PAL(A)ESTRA
score .... FALL
sound .... THUD, GROAN,
GRUNT
trick throw .... CHIP

wretch .... WORM, KNAVE, MISER,
ROGUE, BEGGAR, PARIAH,
RASCAL, CAITIFF, HILDING,
OUTCAST, VILLAIN, SCULLION
wretched .... SAD, MEAN, ABJECT,
DISMAL, PALTRY, SHABBY,
WOEFUL, FORLORN, PITIFUL,
UNHAPPY, MISERABLE
wriggle .... DODGE, SHAKE,
SHIMMY, SQUIRM, WANGLE,
WIGGLE
wriggler .... LARVA, TADPOLE,
HULA DANCER
Wright, airplane inventor
.... WILBUR, ORVILLE
wring .... PAIN, PRESS, TWIST,
WREST, EXTORT, WRENCH,
SQUEEZE, COMPRESS
neck of .... SCRAG
wrinkle .... FOLD, RUCK, RUGA,
SEAM, ANGLE, CRIMP, RIDGE,
TWIST, COCKLE, CREASE,
FURROW, PUCKER, RIMPLE,
RUMPLE, CRINKLE, CRUMPLE,
NOVELTY, SHRIVEL
remover .... IRON
wrinkled .... LINED, RUGAL,
RUGATE, RUGOSE
wrinkles around the eyes
.... CROW'S FEET
wrist .... JOINT, CARPUS,
CARPAL(E)
bone .... HAMATE, LUNATE,
CAPITATE, PISIFORM,
SCAPHOID, TRAPEZIUM,
TRAPEZOID, TRIQUETRAL
bones, collectively .... CARPUS
guard .... BRACER
injury ..... SPRAIN, WRISTDROP,
(COLLES')FRACTURE
number of bones in ..... EIGHT
wristband .... CUFF, BRACER
wristlet .... BRACELET, HANDCUFF
writ .... VENIRE, PRECEPT,
PROCESS, SUMMONS,
WARRANT, DOCUMENT,
ALLOCATUR, OYER BREVE,
INJUNCTION
Holy .... BIBLE
judicial .... TALES
of ____ .... RIGHT, VENIRE,
MANDAMUS, EXECUTION,
CERTIORARI, PROHIBITION
of execution .... ELEGIT
of right's issue .... MISE
order of arrest .... CAPIAS
to call up .... CERTIORARI
to serve in court .... VENIRE,
SUMMONS, SUBPOENA
write .... PEN, COPY, INDITE,
SCRAWL, SCRIVE, COMPOSE,

INSCRIBE, SCRIBBLE
a check .... DRAW
at length .... EXPATIATE
compose and .... INDITE
down .... JOT, LIST, RECORD
effusively .... GUSH
hurriedly .... SCRAWL,
DASH(OFF), SCRATCH
illegibly .... SCRIBBLE
in scholarly manner
.... LUCUBRATE
into law .... ENACT
on a surface .... INSCRIBE
on his own .... FREELANCE
one's name .... SIGN
out in large letters
.... ENGROSS
out in full (notes, speeches)
.... TRANSCRIBE
the screenplay for a book
.... ADAPT
up .... REPORT, SKETCH
writer ...... POET, CLERK, EDITOR,
PENMAN, SCRIBE, COPYIST,
AUTHOR(ESS), SCRIVENER,
AMANUENSIS, JOURNALIST
Dahl .... ROALD
Davis .... GWEN
for motion pictures
.... SCRIPTWRITER
"Fourth Estate"
.... JOURNALIST
inferior ..... HACK, POETASTER,
SCRIBBLER
kind of .... COPY, GHOST,
COPYIST, COMPILER,
REPORTER, COLUMNIST
of articles, speeches for
another ..... GHOSTWRITER
long fictional prose
.... NOVELIST
morals .... AESOP
news .... REPORTER
news from a distant place
.... CORRESPONDENT
plays .... DRAMATIST,
PLAYWRIGHT
research paper ..... ESSAYIST
text of an opera
.... LIBRETTIST
trilogies .... ASCH
unscrupulous .... PLAGIARIST
verse .... POET, RHYMER,
VERSIFIER
who indulges in faultfinding
and censure .... CRITIC
writer's bugaboo .... DEADLINE
cramp ..... SCRIVENER'S PALSY
own signature ..... AUTOGRAPH
writers' group .... PEN
writhe ...... WARP, TWIST, SQUIRM,

CONTORT, DISTORT
writing ...... BOOK, POEM, DIARY,
VERSE, LETTER, ARTICLE,
DOCUMENT, TREATISE,
MONOGRAPH, NARRATIVE
as a profession .... PEN
bad hand(writing)
.... CACOGRAPHY
beautiful hand(writing)
.... CALLIGRAPHY
characters .... ALPHABET
cipher .... CRYPTOGRAPHY
combining form .... LOG(UE)
desk ..... BUREAU, SECRETARY,
ESCRITOIRE
exalted to trivial .... BATHOS
expert .... GRAPHOLOGIST
flippant style of
.... PERSIFLAGE
flourish .... TAG, CURLICUE,
CURLYCUE
foolish .... HOGWASH,
TWADDLE
hand- .... PENMANSHIP,
CHIROGRAPHY
implement .... NIB, PEN,
BRUSH, CHALK, QUILL,
CRAYON, PENCIL, STYLUS,
BALLPOINT, (FOUNTAIN)PEN
instrument, ancient ...... STYLE
long tiresome piece of
.... SCREED
machine .... COMPUTER,
TELETYPE, STENOTYPE,
TYPEWRITER
mark .... CHARACTER
material .... STATIONERY
material, box for
.... PAPETERIE
mystic(al) .... RUNE
paper .... PAD, BOND, TABLET,
PAPYRUS, TALIPOT,
STATIONERY
roll of .... SCROLL
size .... DEMY, LEGAL,
LETTER, FOOLSCAP, IMPERIAL
specially treated
.... PARCHMENT
thin .... FLIMSY, ONIONSKIN
parchment .... VELLUM
pompous .... FUSTIAN
preliminary .... DRAFT
pretentious .... KITSCH
secret .... CODE, CIPHER
senseless .... BALDERDASH
sentimental .... SLUSH
stroke .... SERIF
style .... PROSE, POETRY
system of speed
.... SHORTHAND, STENOGRAPHY
table .... DESK, BUREAU,

ESCRITOIRE
tablet .... DIPTYCH
wall .... GRAFFITO
wedge-shaped
.... CUNEI(FORM)
writings .... LITERATURE,
COMPILATION, COMPOSITION
collection of .... PAPERS
sacred .... SCRIPTURE
unpublished .... REMAINS
written author's copy of work
.... MANUSCRIPT
copy .... TRANSCRIPT
copy by reporter .... FLIMSY
document, formal .... WRIT
in person's own handwriting
.... HOLOGRAPH(IC)
not .... ORAL, TACIT, VERBAL
off .... CANCELLED, CHARGED
OFF
order: law ...... WRIT, PRECEPT,
WARRANT, RESCRIPT
order issued by bank
.... CHECK, DRAFT
opposite of .... ORAL, TACIT,
SPOKEN, VERBAL, LINGUAL
plans, for short .... SKEDS
release .... QUITCLAIM
wrong .... BAD, EVIL, HARM,
ABUSE, AMISS, DAMAGE,
INJURE, OFFEND, SINFUL,
WICKED, IMMORAL, VICIOUS,
ERRONEOUS, INCORRECT
act .... CRIME, MISDEED,
VIOLATION, MISCONDUCT
civil/legal .... TORT
do .... SIN
do woman ..... ABUSE, SEDUCE
habit .... VICE
impression .... MISBELIEF
name .... MISNOMER
way, the .... AGAINST THE
GRAIN
"Wrong Way" Corrigan
.... DOUGLAS
wrongdoer .... CROOK, FELON,
THIEF, KILLER, OUTLAW,
RAPIST, SINNER, VANDAL,
CONVICT, HOODLUM,
MOBSTER, ARSONIST,
CRIMINAL, GANGSTER,
KIDNAPER, OFFENDER,
SCOFFLAW, SWINDLER,
TERRORIST, MALEFACTOR
wrongful .... UNFAIR, UNJUST,
HARMFUL, ILLEGAL, LAWLESS,
IMPROPER, UNLAWFUL
wrongheaded .... STUBBORN,
MISGUIDED
wrongly .... FALSELY,
MISTAKENLY

wroth .... MAD, SORE, ANGRY, CROSS, IRATE, INCENSED
wrought .... D(A)EDAL, SHAPED, DECORATED, FASHIONED
up .... AGOG, ANGRY, RILED, TENSE, EXCITED, DISTURBED
wry ...... ASKEW, IRONIC, WARPED, CROOKED, TWISTED, CONTRARY, PERVERSE, DISTORTED
wryneck .... WEET, LOXIA, (SNAKE)BIRD, TORTICOLLIS
genus .... JYNX
relative .... WOODPECKER
Wuthering Heights author .... BRONTE
WW II Allies .... FRANCE, SOVIET UNION, GREAT BRITAIN, UNITED STATES
Axis power ...... ITALY, JAPAN, GERMANY
battle site .... GUAM, ST. LO, LEYTE, BATAAN, MIDWAY, SAIPAN, TARAWA, IWOJIMA, OKINAWA, NORMANDY, KWAJALEIN, CORREGIDOR, GUADALCANAL
beachhead .... ANZIO, NORMANDY
bomb site .... NORDEN, NAGASAKI, HIROSHIMA
British Prime Minister .... (WINSTON) CHURCHILL
date .... D-DAY
Greek group .... EDES, ELAS
Japanese admiral .... ITO, OKA, OTA, TOGO, KIMURA, TAKAGI, TANAKA, TOYODA, YAMADA, YAMAMOTO, YAMAGUCHI
admiral, head of kamikaze units .... UGAKI
admiral, originator of kamikaze corps .... ONISHI
Army Commander .... HOMMA
battle cry .... BANZAI
battleship ...... FUSO, KONGO, HARUNA, MOGAMI, YAMATO, MUSASHI, YAMASHIRO
carrier .... AOBA, AKAGI, HOSHO, TAIHO, CHIYODA, ZUIKAKU
Commander of Pearl Harbor striking force .... NAGUMO
cruiser .... YURA, NACHI, CHOKAI, HAGURO, FURUTAKA
death by suicide .... HARA-KIRI
destroyer .... FUBUKI, AKIZUKI, SHIGURE
emperor .... HIROHITO
general .... CHO, NASU, SATO, TOJO, HOMMA, NAGAI, OSUGA, UMEZU, SUZUKI, TANAKA, NISHINO, MIYAZAKI, TOMINAGA, WATANABE, YAMASHITA
suicide pilot .... KAMIKAZE
warplane .... ZERO
"Little Tokyo" .... SAIPAN
Nazi dictator .... (ADOLF)HITLER
org. .... OPA, OSS
powers .... AXIS
refugees, post .... DPS
Russian generalissimo .... STALIN
sector/area: abbr. .... ETO
shouts .... HEILS
site of Japan's formal surrender .... MISSOURI
"The Big Three," one of the .... STALIN, CHURCHILL, ROOSEVELT
title .... SCAP
"Tokyo Rose" ..... IVA IKUKO TOGURI
WW II, U.S. admiral ...... HART, BLOCH, HALSEY, KIMMEL, NIMITZ, ROCKWELL, SPRUANCE
atomic bomb assembly place .... TINIAN
bomber .... ENOLA GAY, BOCK'S CAR
expert .... (WILLIAM)PARSONS
battleship ...... UTAH, NEVADA, ARIZONA, MARYLAND, MISSOURI, OKLAHOMA, SARATOGA, TENNESSEE, CALIFORNIA, WHITE PLAINS, PENNSYLVANIA, WEST VIRGINIA
"Bock's Car" bombardier .... (KERMIT)BEAHAN
bomb site .... NAGASAKI
Commander .... (CHARLES)SWEENEY
co-pilot .... ALBURY
cargo plane ..... C-FIFTY FOUR, C-FORTY SEVEN
carrier .... HORNET, YORKTOWN, LEXINGTON, ENTERPRISE
Commander-in-Chief who ordered use of atomic bomb on Japan .... (HARRY)TRUMAN
cruiser .... BOISE, DENVER, DUNCAN, HELENA, AUGUSTA, HOUSTON, NASHVILLE, PENSACOLA, MINNEAPOLIS
D-Day top secret code word .... UTAH, OMAHA, NEPTUNE, MULBERRY, OVERLORD
destroyer ...... BLUE, FLETCHER
draft classification .... ONE-A
engineer .... SEABEE
"Enola Gay" bombardier .... (THOMAS)FEREBEE
bomb site .... HIROSHIMA
Commander .... (PAUL)TIBBETS
co-pilot .... (ROBERT)LEWIS
navigator ..... "DUTCH" VAN KIRK
general .... KING, SMITH, GROVES, PARKER, PATTON, PULLER, SPAATZ, FARRELL, MARSHALL, PERSHING, STILWELL, MACARTHUR, EISENHOWER, WAINWRIGHT
"Howlin' Mad" Smith's command ship .... ELDORADO
in command of atomic bomb project .... (THOMAS)FARRELL
of the Army ...... (DOUGLAS) MACARTHUR
landing craft .... LCI, LCV, LSD, LST, HIGGIN'S BOAT
last battleship sunk by enemy ...... INDIANAPOLIS
MacArthur-Halsey two-pronged drive .... OPERATION CARTWHEEL
marine: nickname .... GYRENE, JARHEAD, LEATHERNECK
motor torpedo boat .... PT-BOAT
nickname of General Eisenhower .... IKE
Puller .... CHESTY
Smith .... HOWLIN' MAD
Spaatz .... TOOEY
Stilwell .... VINEGAR JOE
Wainwright .... SKINNY
Old ____ .... SARGE
president .... TRUMAN, ROOSEVELT
sailor: nickname .... SWAB(BIE)
service woman ..... WAC, WAF, SPAR, WAVE
soldier: nickname .... DOGFACE, DOUGHBOY
submarine .... CAVALLA,

ALBACORE, STINGRAY
war plan .... ORANGE-THREE
warplane .... B-SEVENTEEN,
P-FIFTY ONE, B-TWENTY FIVE,
B-TWENTY FOUR, B-TWENTY
NINE, P-THIRTY EIGHT,
GRUMMAN HELLCAT,
GRUMMAN WILDCAT
warplane's monicker
.... BOCK'S CAR, ENOLA GAY,
DINAH MIGHT, LONESOME
LADY, MEMPHIS BELLE,
DAUNTLESS DOTTY
Wolf pack unit .... U-BOAT
Wyandot .... HURON
Wycliffe, reformer .... JOHN
disciple .... LOLLARD
Wylie, novelist .... ELINOR
Wyoming basin .... BIGHORN,
SHIRLEY
capital .... CHEYENNE
cavern .... SHOSHONE
city/town .... CODY, CASPER,

LANDER, BUFFALO, DOUGLAS,
JACKSON, LARAMIE, RAWLINS,
WORLAND, EVANSTON,
GILLETTE, SHERIDAN,
SUNDANCE, WHEATLAND,
TORRINGTON
county .... PARK, CROOK,
TETON, UINTA, ALBANY,
GOSHEN, FREMONT, LARAMIE,
NATRONA, CAMPBELL,
SHERIDAN, SWEETWATER
dam .... BUFFALO BILL
lake .... LEWIS, BIGHORN,
FREMONT, JACKSON,
SHOSHONE, YELLOWSTONE
mountain .... HUNT, GREEN,
LEIDY, CROSBY, HOLMES,
ISABEL, NEEDLE, BURWELL,
DEADMAN, FORTRESS,
WASHBURN, INYAN KARA,
BONNEVILLE, TEAPOT DOME
mountain range .... ASPEN,
ROCKY, BIGHORN, GRANITE,

LARAMIE, SEMINOE
national monument .... DEVILS
TOWER
national park .... GRAND
TETON, YELLOWSTONE
peak .... CLOUD, EAGLE,
HOBACK, FREMONT, GANNETT,
LARAMIE, ATLANTIC
plateau .... MADISON
river .... BEAR, SALT, WIND,
WOOD, GREEN, GREYS, LAMAR,
SNAKE, HOBACK, POWDER,
BIGHORN, LARAMIE,
GREYBULL, MEDICINE BOW,
YELLOWSTONE, LITTLE
MISSOURI
state bird .... MEADOWLARK
state flower .... INDIAN
PAINTBRUSH
state nickname .... EQUALITY
state tree .... COTTONWOOD
Wystan Hugh .... AUDEN
wyvern .... DRAGON

X

X .... TEN, MARK, CROSS,
SIGNATURE
Greek XI
letter .... EX
marker, usually .... ILLITERATE
marks the _____ .... SPOT
shaped .... EX
word "dill" .... ANET
xanthic ...... TAWNY, YELLOW(ISH)
Xanthippe's husband
.... SOCRATES
prototype .... SHREW, NAGGER,
VIRAGO, TERMAGANT
xanthous .... FAIR, BLOND(E),
YELLOW(ISH)
Xavier, bandleader .... CUGAT
Saint .... FRANCIS

Xe, in chemistry .... XENON
xebec .... SHIP
common users .... CORSAIRS
xema .... GULL
xeno .... GUEST
as prefix .... FOREIGN,
STRANGE
xenophobe .... WARMONGER
Xeres .... JEREZ
xerophilous animal .... CAMEL
plant ...... CACTUS, XEROPHYTE
xerotic .... DRY
Xerxes I, father of .... DARIUS
wife .... ESTHER
xiphoid .... ENSIFORM, SWORD-
SHAPED
xiphosuran ...... ARACHNID, KING

CRAB
Xmas .... CHRISTMAS, YULE(TIDE)
X-rated feature .... NUDITY
X-ray ...... EXAMINE, PHOTOGRAPH
discoverer of ...... RO(E)NTGEN
Xtian .... CHRISTIAN
XV .... FIFTEEN
xylan .... PENTOSAN
xyloid .... WOOD(Y), LIGNEOUS
xylonite .... CELLULOID
xylophone-like instrument
.... SARON, MARIMBA
xylotomous insect .... ANAY,
TERMITE
xyst .... WALK, PORTICO
xyster .... (BONE)SCRAPER

Y

Y, Greek .... UPSILON
Hebrew .... YOD(H)
in mathematics ...... ORDINATE
letter .... WYE
men .... ELIS
yabber .... TALK, GIBBER, JABBER,
CHATTER
yacht .... SAIL, CUTTER,
CRUISE(R), KNOCKABOUT

club president
.... COMMODORE
flag .... BURGEE
haven of .... COVE
racing .... SONDERCLASS
racing champion ..... INTREPID
sail .... SPINNAKER
tender .... DINGHY
yachting center .... COWES

yachtsman .... LIPTON, YACHTER,
CORINTHIAN
Yadkin .... PEEDEE RIVER
yaffle .... WOODPECKER
yager .... RIFLEMAN
yahoo .... LOUT, BRUTE, KNAVE,
BUMPKIN
creator .... SWIFT
Yahwe(h) .... GOD, JEHOVAH

yak .... OX, SARLAK
   where found .... TIBET
yaki .... CAYMAN
Yakutsk river .... LENA
Yale .... ELI, LOCK, UNIVERSITY
   Bowl sound .... BOOLA
   elite secret society ..... SKULL
       AND BONES
   clubhouse .... (THE)TOMB
   clubhouse member
     .... BONESMAN
   Mr. .... (ELIHU)ROOT
Yalie .... ELI
Yalta conference member
    .... STALIN, CHURCHILL,
       ROOSEVELT
   native .... CRIMEAN
yam .... HOI, UBE, UBI, ROOT,
       POTATO
   bean .... KAMA, BONIATA
Yamashita, Japanese general
    .... TOMOYUKI
   sobriquet .... TIGER
yamen resident .... MANDARIN
yammer .... CRY, HOWL, PULE,
    WAIL, YELL, GRIPE, WHINE,
    CLAMOR, WHIMPER, COMPLAIN
Yangtze River city .... WUHU,
       NANKING
Yank .... JERK, PULL, TWIST,
       AMERICAN
Yankee .... AMERICAN,
       NORTHERNER
yap .... NAG, YIP, BARK, TALK,
    YAWP, YELP, JABBER,
       SQUAWK
   slang .... MOUTH, ROWDY,
       HOODLUM
Yaqui .... RIVER, INDIAN
yard .... AREA, SPAR, GROUNDS
   enclosed .... GARTH
   in law .... CURTILAGE
   kind of .... QUAD, COURT,
       PATIO
   section .... FOOT
yards, 220 .... FURLONG
yardstick ...... RULE(R), MEASURE,
    STANDARD, CRITERION
yarn ...... FIB, SLUB, TALE, FABLE,
    FIBER, GEARN, INKLE, STORY,
    ANGORA, BOUCLE, SPINEL,
       THREAD
   ball of .... CLEW, SKEIN
   count .... TYPP
   560 yards .... HANK
   flax .... LINEN
   knot .... BURL
   knitting .... SAXONY
   machine .... MULE
   measure .... COP, LEA, CLEW,
    CLUE, HANK, SKEIN, SPINDLE

   mule .... SPINNING JENNY
   quantity .... SKEIN
   roll of .... COP
   skein of .... HASP
   teller .... ANGLER,
       MUNCHAUSEN
   twilled/twisted .... CREWEL
   warp .... ABB
   waste .... THRUM
   winder .... PIRNER
   with protruding pile
    .... CHENILLE
   woolen, inferior .... SHODDY
   worsted .... CADDIS
yarrow .... HERB, MILFOIL
yashmak .... VEIL
yatag(h)an .... SABER
yaud .... JADE, MARE
yaupon .... ASSI, HOLLY,
    CASSENA, CASSINE
   use of .... TEA
yaw .... JIBE, TACK, VEER, TUMOR,
       DEVIATE
yawl .... DANDY, KETCH,
    SAILBOAT, JOLLYBOAT
yawn .... GAPE, PART, CHASM,
    SPLIT, OSCITATE
   aloud .... YAUP, YAWP
   meaning of, usually
   .... ENNUI, BOREDOM, FATIGUE,
       DROWSINESS
yawner .... SLEEPYHEAD
yawning .... GAPING
   depth of .... ABYSS
   fit of .... GAPES
yawp ...... CRY, YAP, BAWL, GAPE,
    HOWL, WAIL, YAWN
yaws .... FRAMB(O)ESIA
   cause of .... SPIROCHETE
Yb, in chemistry .... YTTERBIUM
yclept .... NAMED, CALLED,
       KNOWN(AS)
ye .... THEE, THOU
yea(h) .... YES, TRULY, INDEED
yean .... REAR, BRING FORTH
yeanling .... KID, LAMB, NEWBORN
year .... AGE, ANNO, TIME,
       TWELVEMONTH
   continuing for a
   .... YEARLONG, YEAR-ROUND
   designating a .... LEAP,
    LUNAR, SOLAR, FISCAL,
    NATURAL, CALENDAR,
    SIDEREAL, TROPICAL,
       EQUINOCTIAL
   every .... ANNUALLY, PER
       ANNUM
   good or bad .... VINTAGE
   half .... SEMESTER
   in the past .... IAD

   of plenary indulgence
    .... JUBILEE
   with a bonus day .... LEAP
yearbook .... ANNAL, ANNUAL,
       ALMANAC
yearling .... CUB, TEG, COLT,
    FILLY, WHELP, LEVERET
yearly .... ETESIAN, ANNUALLY
   calendar .... ALMANAC
yearn .... ACHE, HOPE, LONG,
    PINE, SIGH, CRAVE, MOURN,
       HANKER
yearning ...... YEN, WISH, DESIRE,
    THIRST, LONGING
   for family .... HOMESICK
years, happening every eight
    .... OCTENNIAL
   ten .... DECENNIAL
   two .... BIENNIAL
   old, 65 (usually) ...... RETIREE
   70 .... SEPTUAGENARIAN
   80 .... OCTOGENARIAN
   90 .... NONAGENARIAN
   100 .... CENTENNIAL
   period of 5 .... PENTAD
   10 .... DECADE, DECENARY,
       DECENNIUM
   100 .... CENTURY,
       CENTENARY
   1000 .... CHILIAD,
       MILLENIUM
   thousands and thousands of
    .... (A)EON
yeast .... BARM, BEES, FOAM,
    FROTH, SPUME, FUNGUS,
    LEAVEN, ANAMITE, FERMENT
   disease-causing ...... CANDIDA-
       ALBICANS
   disease caused by
    .... CANDIDIASIS
   enzyme .... ZYMASE
yeasty .... BARMY, LIGHT, BUBBLY,
    BUBBLING, EBULLIENT
Yeats' _____ and the Swan
    .... LEDA
yecchy .... ICKY, FILTHY
Yed(d)o .... EDO, TOKYO
yegg .... THIEF, ROBBER, BURGLAR,
       SAFECRACKER
yeld .... BARREN
yell ...... CRY, BAWL, ROAR, YELP,
    CHEER, SHOUT, BELLOW,
    HALLOO, HOLLER, OUTCRY,
    SCREAM, SHRIEK, YAMMER
   college .... RAH, CHEER
   ending cheers .... TIGER
yellow ...... DYE, AMBER, CHROME,
    GAMBOGE, LUTEOUS,
    PIGMENT, XANTHIC,
       XANTHOUS
   bird .... CANARY, MELINE,

ORIOLE, FLICKER, WARBLER, GOLDFINCH
bright .... GOLDEN, GAMBOGE
brown ..... DUN, ECRU, SORREL
bugle .... IVA
calla .... AROID
clay .... OCHER, OCHRE
colloquial .... AFRAID, CRAVEN, COWARDLY
color .... GOLD, ALOMA, AMBER, LEMON, OCHER, BUTTERY, SAFFRON, XANTHIC
colored fruit .... LEMON, MANGO, BANANA, CITRON, AZAROLE
combining form .... CHRYS(O), LUTEO, XANTH(O)
compound .... LUTEOLIN
daisy .... BLACK-EYED SUSAN
dark .... OCHRE
deep .... GOLD
dull brownish .... TAN, BUFF, ECRU, BEIGE
dye stuff .... MORIN, FLAVONE, FLAVONOL, PHOSPHINE, QUERCETIN
egg's .... YOLK
eyed .... ENVIOUS, JEALOUS, JAUNDICED
fever .... VOMITO, INFECTION
fever carrier .... AEDES, MOSQUITO
fever mosquito .... STEGOMYIA, AEDES-AEGYPTI
flag signal .... QUARANTINE
flower .... IRIS, CROCUS, JASMINE, JONQUIL, DANDELION, GOLDENROD, SUNFLOWER, CHRYSANTHEMUM
gem .... TOPAZ
green .... NILE
greenish .... CHAMPAGNE
gum resin .... GAMBOGE, CAMBOGIA
haired .... BLOND
jacket .... WASP, VESPA, HORNET, VESPID
journalism .... MELODRAMA(TICS)
journalism staple .... SCANDAL
lead ore .... WULFENITE
light ...... CANARY, PRIMROSE
man .... MONGOLIAN
metal .... GOLD, BRASS
orange .... PEACH, CROCUS, SAFFRON
pale ...... BUFF, MAIZE, STRAW, FALLOW, FLAXEN
pigment .... SIL, OCHER, OCHRE, FLAVIN, ETIOLIN,

GAMBOGE, ORPIMENT, QUERCETIN
quartz .... CITRINE
race .... CHINESE, MONGOL(IAN)
red .... CORAL
reddish .... SANDY
river .... HWANG HO
sickly, pale .... SALLOW
skin, cause of .... JAUNDICE
somewhat .... YELLOWISH
streak .... FEAR, FUNK, COWARDICE
turning .... ICTERUS, FLAVESCENT
Yellow Kid Weil .... JOSEPH
Pages .... DIRECTORY, PHONEBOOK
Peril harbinger .... CHINESE, MONGOLIANS
Sea .... HWANG HAI
Sea gulf .... POHAI
Sea port .... TSINGTAO
Sea, river into .... YALU
yellowhammer .... BIRD, YITE, VERDIN, BUNTING, FLICKER, WOODPECKER
Yellowhammer State .... ALABAMA
yellowish brown .... DRAB, FAWN, HAZEL, KHAKI, STRAW, TAWNY, CHAMOIS, CINNAMON
green .... CHARTREUSE
orange .... PEACH, CADMIUM
pale complexion .... SALLOW
part of milk .... CREAM
red .... RUFOUS
semi-precious stone .... CHRYSOBERYL
white .... CREAM
yellowlegs .... SANDPIPER
Yellowstone Park denizen .... BEAR
Park employee .... RANGER
sight .... LAKE, PARK, FALLS
yellowtail .... MENHADEN, ROCKFISH, CARANGOID
relative .... CAVALLA, POMPANO
yellowthroat ...... BIRD, WARBLER
yellowweed .... RAGWORT, CROWFOOT, GOLDENROD
yelp .... CRY, YAP, YIP, BARK, YAWP, SQUAWK, SQUEAL
Yemen Arab Republic capital .... SANA
city/town .... IBB, TAIZZ, DHAMAR, HODEIDA
dynasty .... RASSITE
island .... ZUQAR, HANISH
king .... IMAM, (AL)BADR

language .... ARABIC
monetary unit .... RIYAL
mountain .... MANAR, SABIR
neighbor of .... OMAN
president/premier .... (AL)SALAL
region .... TIHAMA
religion .... ISLAM
sea .... RED
seaport .... MOCHA
seat of government ...... TAIZZ
sect .... ZAIDI
strait .... MANDEB
Yemen, People's Democratic Republic cape .... FARTAK
capital .... ADEN
city/town .... SELYUN, MUKALLA
island .... PERIM, KAMARAN, SOCATRA
language .... ARABIC
monetary unit .... DINAR
religion .... ISLAM
Yemenite .... ARAB(IAN), BEDOUIN
garment .... ABA
yen .... URGE, TASTE, DESIRE, HUNGER, LIKING, CRAVING, LONG(ING), PASSION, YEARNING
is monetary unit of ____ .... JAPAN
yenite .... LIVAITE
yenta ...... BUSYBODY, GOSSIP(ER)
yeoman .... SQUIRE, DECKHAND, MYRMIDON, ASSISTANT, ATTENDANT, BODYGUARD, FREEHOLDER, MANSERVANT, SUBORDINATE
yeomanly .... BRAVE, LOYAL, STURDY
yep .... YES
opposite of .... NOPE
yes .... AYE, YEP, YUP, SURE, YEA(H), AGREEMENT, AFFIRMATIVE
man .... TOADY, SYCOPHANT
yeshiva .... SEMINARY
yeso .... GYPSUM
yet .... NOW, ALSO, STILL, BESIDES, HOWEVER, NOTWITHSTANDING
to be published ...... UNEDITED
yeti ...... (ABOMINABLE) SNOWMAN
yew ...... TREE, CONIFER, HEMLOCK
fruit .... CONE, BERRY
genus .... TAXUS
Yezd is in ____ .... IRAN
Yezo .... HOKKAIDO
Yggdrasil .... ASH TREE
Yiddish .... JEWISH, LANGUAGE
noodles .... FARFEL, FERFEL

synagogue .... SHUL
thief .... GANEF, GANOF
yield .... OBEY, DEFER, GRANT,
    COMPLY, GIVE(IN), GIVE UP,
    RELENT, RETURN, SOFTEN,
    SUBMIT, (CON)CEDE,
    PRODUCT, SUCCUMB,
    SURRENDER, CAPITULATE
a profit .... PAY
farm .... CROP, PRODUCE
gold .... PAN OUT
point .... CONCEDE
to Morpheus .... SLEEP
yielding .... SOFT, DOCILE, PLIANT,
    FERTILE, PRODUCTIVE
yill .... ALE
yip .... CRY, YAP, BARK, YELP
Ymir .... GIANT
yo-heave-ho, for example
    .... CHANT
yodel .... SING, WARBLE
yodeler .... SWISS, TYROLEAN
milieu of .... ALPS
yoga, form of .... HATHAYOGA
need .... CONCENTRATION
originator ...... HINDU, HINDOO
person who practices .... YOGI
posture/squat .... ASANA
yogi ...... SWAMI, MYSTIC, ASCETIC
Yogi, ballplayer .... BERRA
yoke .... TIE, BIND, BOND, LINK,
    PAIR, CHAIN, CANGUE,
    COUPLE, HALTER, INSPAN,
    BONDAGE, ENSLAVE,
    HARNESS, SLAVERY,
    SERVITUDE, THRALLDOM
large, wooden .... CANGUE
part of .... OXBOW
yokefellow .... MATE, WIFE,
    HUSBAND, PARTNER,
    ASSOCIATE
yokel .... HICK, RUBE, YAHOO,
    RUSTIC, BUMPKIN, PEASANT
Yoko .... ONO
Yokum's creator .... CAPP
yolk, egg ...... YELLOW, VITELLUS
of the egg .... VITELLINE
protein .... VITELLIN
yolked .... LECITHAL
yom .... DAY
Yom ____, Jewish holiday
    .... KIPPUR
yon(der) .... THERE
yore .... ELD, LONG AGO, WAY
    BACK, OLDEN TIMES
York, ____ .... SERGEANT
yorker, game associated with
    .... CRICKET
Yorkshire native .... DALESMAN
port .... HULL, WHITBY

river .... AIRE
Yoruba native .... EGBA
Yosemite sight ...... PARK, FALLS,
    CLIFFS, REDWOOD
Yoshihito's empire .... JAPAN
reign .... TAISHO
son .... HIROHITO
title .... EMPEROR
young .... NEW, RAW, FRESH,
    GREEN, PUERILE, TEEN-AGE,
    IMMATURE, JUVENILE,
    YOUTHFUL, ADOLESCENT
animal .... CUB, KID, CALF,
    TOTO, PUPPY, SLINK, WHELP,
    SUCKLING
beef .... VEAL
bird .... CHICK, OWLET,
    NESTLING, FLEDGLING
blood .... YOUTH
branch .... TWIG, SHOOT
bull .... CALF
cat .... KITTY, PUSSY, KITTEN
chicken .... FRYER
cod .... SCROD
cow .... CALF, HEIFER
deer .... DOE, FAWN
dog .... PUP(PY), WHELP
Duroc .... SHOAT
eagle .... AERIE, EYRIE
eel .... SNIG, ELVER
falcon .... EYAS
fish .... FRY, PARR, SMELT,
    GRILSE, FINGERLING
fowl .... POULT
fox .... CUB
frog .... TADPOLE
girl .... LASS, MISS, MAIDEN,
    MOPPET
goat .... KID
goose .... GOSLING
hare .... LEVERET
hawk .... EYAS, AERIE, EYRIE
hen .... CHICK, PULLET,
    POULARD
herring .... BRIT, SPRAT,
    SARDINE
hog .... GILT, SHOAT, SHOTE,
    PORKER
hooter .... OWLET
horse .... COLT, FOAL, FILLY
kangaroo .... JOEY
lion .... CUB, WHELP, LIONET
male .... BUCK
man .... YOUTH, CHIEL(D),
    MASTER
man of high birth ...... SQUIRE
man's fancy .... BEARD
moose .... CALF
oyster .... SPAT
ox .... STEER

pig .... FARROW
pigeon .... SQUAB
salmon .... PARR, SMOLT,
    GRILSE
seal .... PUP
sheep .... LAMB
squab .... PIPER
swan .... CYGNET
tiger .... CUB, WHELP
turkey/pheasant .... POULT
whale .... CUB
with .... PREGNANT, ON THE
    WAY
wolf .... WHELP
Young, actor .... GIG
actress .... LORETTA
Mormon church head
    .... BRIGHAM
Turks, so-called .... REBELS
young of animals born at one
time .... LITTER
younger son .... CADET
youngster .... KID, LAD, TAD, TOT,
    TIKE, TYKE, CHILD, MINOR,
    YOUTH, SHAVER, URCHIN,
    SAPLING, BUNTLING, SMALL
    FRY, TEENAGER
colloquial .... BOBBY SOXER
with a sweet innocent face
    .... CHERUB
yours truly .... ME, MYSELF
youth .... LAD, BABY, TEENS,
    CHIEL(D), NONAGE, SHAVER,
    BOY(HOOD), INFANCY,
    PUBERTY, GIRL(HOOD),
    MINORITY, TEENAGE(R),
    CHILD(HOOD), PUERILITY,
    STRIPLING, YOUNGSTER,
    ADOLESCENCE
beautiful .... NARCISSUS
group: abbr. .... BSA, GSA
of a .... MINOR
who fell in love with his
    image .... NARCISSUS
youthful ...... NEW, FRESH, GREEN,
    YOUNG, ACTIVE, TENDER,
    VERNAL, BUDDING, PUERILE,
    IMMATURE, JUVENILE,
    UNDERAGE
works .... JUVENALIA
yow .... OUCH
yowl .... CRY, WAIL, YELL
yperite .... MUSTARD GAS
where used in battle
    .... YPRES
Yquem .... WINE, SAUTERNE(S)
Yseult .... ISOLDE
yuan .... TAEL, DYNASTY
is monetary unit of ____
    .... CHINA

yuca .... MANIOC, CASSAVA
Yucatan capital .... MERIDA
   Indian/people .... MAYA
   leaf fiber .... SISAL
   Mayan city .... USMAL
   native .... MAYAN
yucca .... FLAT, LILY, PITA
   fiber .... ISTLE
   plant like .... SOTOL
Yuga .... AGE, ERA
   period .... KALI, KRITA, TRETA,
      DVAPARA
Yugoslavia cape .... KAMENJAK
   capital .... BEOGRAD,
      BELGRADE
   city/town .... BOR, NIS, PEC,
      POLA, STIP, ZARA, PIROT,
      SENTA, SPLIT, TUZLA, ZADAR,
      APATIN, OSIJEK, PRILEP,
      RIJEKA, SKOPJE, SOMBOR,
      ZAGREB, ZENICA, MARIBOR,
      NOVI SAD, SARAJEVO,
      SUBOTICA, TITOGRAD, BANJA
      LUKA, KRAGUJEVAC
   coin .... PARA, DINAR
   commune .... STIP
   division ...... BOSNIA, KOSOVO,
      SERBIA, CROATIA, SLOVENIA,
      MACEDONIA, MONTENEGRO,
      HERCEGOVINA
   guerrillas .... CHETNIKS,
      PARTISANS
   gulf .... KVARNER
   island ..... KRK, PAG, RAB, VIS,
      BRAC, CRES, HVAR, MLJET,
      SOLTA, ZIRJE, KORNAT,

      LASTOVO
   lake .... OHRID, PRESPA,
      SCUTARI
   language .... ALBANIAN,
      CROATIAN, SLOVENIAN,
      MACEDONIAN
   measure .... OKA, RIF, AKOV,
      DONUM, KHVAT, LANAZ,
      PALAZ, STOPA
   monetary unit .... DINAR
   mountain .... KORAB, RUJEN,
      MIDZHUR, TRIGLAV, CVRSNICA
   mountain range .... DINARIC
      ALPS
   native .... SERB, CROAT,
      SLOVENE
   news agency .... TANJUG
   peninsula .... ISTRIA
   port .... RIJEKA
   premier .... PANIC, SPILJAK
   president .... TITO (BROZ)
   region .... DALMATIA,
      SLAVONIA
   republic ...... SERBIA, CROATIA,
      SLOVENIA, MACEDONIA,
      MONTENEGRO
   river .... LIM, MUR, UNA, IBAR,
      KUPA, SAVA, TARA, TISA,
      CAZMA, DRAVA, DRINA,
      TIMOK, VRBAS, BOSNIA,
      DANUBE, MORAVA, VARDAR,
      NERETVA
   sea .... ADRIATIC
   seaport ..... POLA, PULA, ZARA,
      RIJEKA, DUBROVNIK
   weight .... TOVAR, WAGON,

      DRAMMA, SATLIJK
Yukon Territory capital
      .... WHITEHORSE
   city/town .... ELSA, FARO,
      MAYO, DAWSON, TESLIN, OLD
      CROW, CARCROSS
   flower .... FIREWEED
   island .... HERSCHEL
   lake .... MAYO, KLUANE,
      TESLIN, FRANCES
   mining town .... SKAGWAY
   mountain ...... LOGAN, SELOUS,
      CAMPBELL, SAINT ELIAS
   mountain range .... PELLY,
      ROCKY, SELWYN, BRITISH,
      CASSIAR, OGILVIE, MACKENZIE
   peak .... KEELE, LOGAN
   region .... KLONDIKE
   river .... HESS, PEEL, ALSEK,
      LIARD, PELLY, WHITE, YUKON,
      HYLAND, TESLIN, OGILVIE,
      STEWART, KLONDIKE,
      MACMILLAN, PORCUPINE
   tributary .... TANANA
yule .... CHRISTMAS
   short for .... XMAS
   symbol .... LOG, MISTLETOE
   tipple .... NOG
Yum Yum's friend .... KOKO
Yuma .... INDIAN, MOHAVE,
      MOJAVE
yummy .... TASTY, DELICIOUS,
      DELECTABLE
Yunnan capital .... KUNMING
yurt, e.g. .... TENT
Yutang, writer .... LIN

Z

Z, Arabic .... ZE
   English .... ZED
   Greek .... ZETA
   Hebrew .... ZAYIN
   in the UK .... ZED
   letter .... ZED, ZEE, IZZARD
   mark of ____ .... ZORRO
Zabrze is in ____ .... POLAND
zac .... IBEX
Zac Starr, father of .... RINGO
zacaton .... GRASS
Zaccur's father .... IMRI
Zaire capital .... KINSHASA
   city/town .... ABA, BENI,
      BOMA, BUTA, GOMA, KAMA,
      AKETI, BUMBA, BUNIA,
      DEMBA, ILEBO, ISIRO, WAMBA,
      WATSA, BUKAVU, KABALO,
      KALIMA, KAMINA, KIKWIT,

      MANONO, MATADI, BUTEMBO,
      KABINDA, KALEMIE, KANANGA,
      KASONGO, KOLWEZI, VIRUNGA,
      BANDUNDU, MBANDAKA,
      TSHIKAPA, YANGAMBI,
      KISANGANI, MWENE-DITU,
      LUBUMBASHI, PANDA-LIKASI
   falls .... BOYOMA, STANLEY,
      LIVINGSTONE
   lake .... KIVU, MWERU, TUMBA,
      ALBERT, EDWARD, MALEBO,
      UPEMBA, TANGANYIKA
   language .... MONGO, ZANDE,
      FRENCH, KIKONGO, LINGALI,
      SWAHILI
   monetary unit .... ZAIRE
   mountain .... KARISIMBI,
      MARGHERITA
   mountain range .... MURUNGU,

      VIRUNGA, RUWENZORI
   national park .... UPEMBA,
      GARAMBA, VIRUNGA
   president .... MOBUTO SESE
      SEKO
   province .... KIVU, KASAI,
      SHABA, BANDUNDU, BAS-
      ZAIRE, EQUATEUR, KINSHASA,
      HAUT-ZAIRE
   river .... KWA, LUA, BOMU,
      FIMI, GIRI, LOWA, UELE,
      CONGO, ELILA, KASAI, KWILU,
      LINDI, LULUA, LUVUA,
      KWANGO, LOANGE, LOKORO,
      LOMANI, LOMELA, LUFIRA,
      LUKUYA, RUZIZI, UBANGI,
      ULINDI, ARUWIMI, CHICAPA,
      LUALABA, LUAPULA, TSHUAPA,
      ITIMBIRI

Zambal .... MALAY
Zambezi tributary .... SHIRE
Zambia capital .... LUSAKA
city/town .... KABWE, KITWE,
MANSA, MONGU, NDOLA,
KASAMA, ZAMBEZI, BANCROFT,
CHINGOLA, LUANSHYA,
MUFULIRA
dam .... KARIBA
falls .... KALAMBO, VICTORIA
lake .... MWERU, KARIBA
language .... LOZI, BEMBA,
TONGA, LUVALE
monetary unit .... KWACHA
mountain .... SUNZU
national park .... KAFUE
president .... KAUNDA
region .... BAROTSELAND
river .... KAFUE, CUANDO,
DONGWE, LUAPULA, ZAMBEZI
Zamenhof's invention
.... ESPERANTO
Zane Grey locale .... MESA
zany .... DOLT, FOOL, CLOWN,
COMIC, DUNCE, JESTER,
MADCAP, NITWIT, BUFFOON,
SIMPLETON
Lucille .... BALL
Zanzibar island .... PEMBA
zap .... END, KAYO, KILL, BLAST
Zarathustra .... ZOROASTER
Zardari, Pakistan legislator
.... ASIF ALI
wife of ...... (BENAZIR)BHUTTO
zarf .... CUP
Zasu, comedienne .... PITTS
Zauberflote, ___ .... DIE
Zea .... KEOS, ISLAND
zeal .... ELAN, SOUL, ARDOR,
VERVE, ENERGY, FERVOR,
SPIRIT, PASSION, DEVOTION,
ENTHUSIASM
Zealand city .... COPENHAGEN
fiord .... ISSE
zealot .... FAN, BIGOT, ADDICT,
DEVOTEE, DREAMER, FANATIC,
PARTISAN, ENTHUSIAST,
EAGER BEAVER
zealotry .... BIGOTRY, FANATICISM
Zealots' conqueror .... TITUS,
VESPASIAN
zealous .... RABID, ARDENT,
FERVID, FANATIC, FERVENT,
INTENSE, HARD-CORE,
SPIRITED
zebec(k) .... SHIP
Zebedee's son .... JOHN, JAMES
zebra and ass offspring
.... ZEBRASS
and horse offspring
.... ZEBRULA

animal resembling .... ASS,
HORSE, QUAGGA
extinct .... QUAGGA
of the .... ZEBRINE
wood .... ARAROBA
young .... COLT
zebu .... BRAHMA
and yak offspring .... BO(H),
ZOBO
cousin of .... ANGONI
zebuder .... ZAC, IBEX
zecchin(o) .... COIN, SEQUIN
Zechariah's hymn .... (THE)
BENEDICTUS
son .... JOHN THE BAPTIST
wife .... ELIZABETH
zed, equivalent of .... ZEE,
IZZARD
zee .... IZZARD
Zeeland, capital of
.... MIDDELBURG
island .... WALCHEREN
**Zeiger, talk show hosts' top
banana** .... LARRY KING
Zen .... CHAN
Buddhism, central figure of
.... SHAKA MUNI
zenana .... HAREM, SERAGLIO
factotum .... EUNUCH
resident .... ODALISK,
CONCUBINE, ODALISQUE
room .... ODA
zenith .... TOP, ACME, APEX,
PEAK, APOGEE, CLIMAX,
HEIGHT, SUMMIT, VERTEX,
PINNACLE
opposed to .... NADIR
sun's .... NOON
Zeno follower .... CYNIC, STOIC
of ___ .... ELEA, CITIUM
philosophy .... STOICISM
Zenobia .... QUEEN
domain of .... PALMYRA
zephyr ...... SOFT, WIND, BREATH,
BREEZE, GENTLE
Zephyrus .... DEITY, FAVONIUS
zeppelin .... BLIMP, AIRSHIP,
DIRIGIBLE
zero .... NIL, NONE, ZILCH, CIPHER,
(N)AUGHT, (N)OUGHT,
NOTHING, NULLITY
colloquial .... ZIP
in tennis .... LOVE
on a compass .... NORTH
Zero Hour .... D-DAY
Zerulah's son .... ABISHAI
zest .... VIM, BRIO, TANG, ZEAL,
ZING, GUSTO, TASTE, VIGOR,
PEEL, FLAVOR, RELISH,
STINGO, THRILL, APPETITE,

PIQUANCY, VITALITY,
VIVACITY, ANIMATION
for life, with a .... LUSTY
zestful .... RACY, BRISK, SAPID,
SPICY, ZIPPY, BREEZY,
LIVELY, BRACING, PIQUANT
zeta .... ZED, ZEE, IZZARD
Zeus .... JUPITER
attendant of .... NIKE
beloved of .... IO, LEDA,
EUROPA
breastplate of .... (A)EGIS
brother of .... HADES,
POSEIDON
changed her to stone
.... NIOBE
daughter of .... HEBE, IRENE,
ATHENA
disguise of .... SWAN
Egyptian's .... AMMON
epithet .... AMMON, SOTER
father of .... CRONUS
father of: var. .... KRONOS
festival .... NEMEAN
gift to Minos .... TALOS
grandfather of .... URANUS
messenger of .... IRIS
monster killed by
.... TYPHOEUS
mother of .... RHEA
mountain birthplace of
.... IDA
nurse of .... GOAT
nymph loved by ..... CALLISTO
oracle seat .... DODONA
Phoenician princess loved by
.... EUROPA
punishment to mankind of
.... PANDORA
sacred tree of .... OAK
shield of .... (A)EGIS
sister of .... HERA, HESTIA,
DEMETER
son of .... ARES, ARCAS,
ARGUS, MINOS, AEACUS,
APOLLO, HERMES, AMPHION,
PERSEUS, SARPEDON,
TANTALUS, HEPHAESTUS
surname of .... ALASTOR
wife/lover of ...... HERA, JUNO,
LEDA, LETO, MAIA, AEGLE,
CERES, DANAE, DIONE, METIS,
AEGINA, EUROPA, LATONA,
SEMELE, THEMIS, ALCMENE,
ANTIOPE, DEMETER, CALLISTO,
EURYNOME
Zhivago's love .... LARA
Zhou ___ .... EN LAI
Zhukov, marshal .... GRIGORI
Zibeline .... (SABLE)FUR

Zibeon's son .... AIAH, ANAH

Ziegfeld show .... RIO RITA, SHOWGIRL

theatrical producer .... FLO(RENZ)

ziggurat .... PYRAMID

zigzag .... YAW, FORKED, JAGGED, CRANK(LE), CROOKED, STAGGER, SERRATED

course .... PLY, TACK

road .... SWITCHBACK

skiing race .... SLALOM

what it has plenty of .... ANGLES

zilch .... NIL, ZIP, NONE, ZERO, NAUGHT, NOTHING

courtwise .... LOVE

Zilpah's son .... GAD, ASHER

Zimbabwe .... STONE HOUSES

capital .... HARARE

capital, former ..... SALISBURY

city/town .... GWERU, HWANGA, KADOMA, KWEKWE, MUTARE, BINDURA, BULAWAYO, CHINHOYI

falls .... VICTORIA

former name of ..... RHODESIA

lake .... KARIBA

language .... BANTU, SHONA

monetary unit .... DOLLAR

mountain .... INYANGA(NI)

native .... BANTU, MBIRE

president .... MUGABE

river ...... SABI, LUNDI, MAZOE, SHASHE, SHANGAN, ZAMBEZI, MTILIKWE

tribe .... ILAS

Zimbalist, violinist .... EFREM

zinc .... SPELTER

alloy .... BIDRI, OROIDE, TOMBAK, TOMBAC(K)

aluminate .... GAHNITE

blende .... SPHALERITE

carbonate .... CALAMINE, SMITHSONITE

ingots .... SPELTER

oxide .... TUTTY

ore .... BLENDE

silicate .... CALAMINE

symbol .... ZN

zing .... PEP, VIM, DASH, ELAN, ZEST, FORCE, VIGOR, ENERGY, VITALITY

zingara/zingaro .... GYPSY

zingel .... PERCH

zinnia .... ASTER

Zion .... JEW, HILL, HEAVEN

site of .... JERUSALEM

Zionism, founder of .... HERZL

Zionist leader .... WEIZMANN

revolutionary group .... IRGUN

zip .... PEP, VIM, ZEST, VIGOR, ENERGY, FASTEN

and _____ .... ZING

colloquial .... ZERO, ZILCH

slang .... HISS, SWISH, WHIZZ

up .... CLOSE

Zipangu .... JAPAN, CIPANGO

namer of .... (MARCO)POLO

zipper .... CLASP, TALON, (SLIDE)FASTENER

site .... FLY, BOOT, PLACKET, OVERSHOE

zippy ...... ZESTY, FRISKY, LIVELY, SNAPPY, ZESTFUL

zircon .... AZORITE, JACINTH

zither, instrument like ...... KOTO, LYRE, ROTA, VINA, CITHARA

of yore .... ASOR

zizany .... TARES, COCKLE

zizith .... TASSELS

zloty is money of _____ .... POLAND

zoa, singular of .... ZOON

Zoan .... TANIS

zodiac .... CIRCLE, GIRDLE, CIRCUIT

sign, 1st .... ARIES

2nd .... TAURUS

3rd .... GEMINI

4th .... CANCER

5th .... LEO

6th .... VIRGO

7th .... LIBRA

8th .... SCORPIO

9th .... SAGITTARIUS

10th .... CAPRICORN

11th .... AQUARIUS

12th .... PISCES

starter .... ARIES

zodiacal archer ...... SAGITTARIUS

bull .... TAURUS

chart .... HOROSCOPE

crab .... CANCER

fish .... PISCES

goat .... CAPRICORN

lion .... LEO

ram .... ARIES

scale .... LIBRA

scorpion .... SCORPIO

twins .... GEMINI

virgin .... VIRGO

water carrier .... AQUARIUS

Zohar's son .... EPHRON

Zola, _____ .... EMILE

defender of .... DREYFUS

heroine .... NANA

novel .... NANA, VERITE, GERMINAL, THERESE RAQUIN

zombi(e) .... SNAKE, PYTHON,

WEIRDO, COCKTAIL, WALKING DEAD

subject of .... CORPSE

zone .... AREA, BELT, WARD, CLIME, GIRDLE, REGION, SECTOR, CINCTURE, DISTRICT

designation .... FRIGID, TORRID, TEMPERATE

zoo .... VIVARIUM, MENAGERIE

animal ..... BEAR, LION, COATI, TIGER, MONKEY, ELEPHANT

attraction .... APE, GNU, MACAW, GORILLA, MACAQUE, SERPENT, WILDCAT

clean-up person .... POOPER-SCOOPER

equipment .... CAGE

floating .... ARK

sounds .... YIPS, ROARS, YELPS

zooid .... CORAL, HYDRANTH, POLYPITE

zoological region ...... NOTOGAEA

zoologist's concern .... ANIMAL(IA)

zoology branch on shells .... CONCHOLOGY

zoom .... FLY, SOAR

zoophyte .... ECTOPRACT

coral .... FUNGIA, ASTRANGIA

glass .... FARREA

horny .... CLIONA, GEODIA, SPONGILLA

sponge .... SCYPHA, GRANTIA

zoot _____ .... SUIT

Zorba the Greek composer .... THEODORAKIS

zoril(a) .... WEASEL, MARIPUT, POLECAT

animal like .... SKUNK

Zoroastrian .... YEMA, PARSI, PARSEE

bible .... AVESTA

demon .... DEVA

evil spirit .... AHRIMAN, ANGRA MAINYU

fire worshiper .... PARSI, CHEBER

god .... AHURA MAZDA

sacred writings .... (ZEND)AVESTA

supreme deity .... ORMAZD, ORMUZD

teaching .... HUMATA, HUKHATA, HUVARSHTA

Zoroastrianism, commentary on .... ZEND

zoster .... BELT, GIRDLE

zucetto .... SKULLCAP

zucchini .... SQUASH

Zug .... CANTON

Zuider _____ .... ZEE
zuisin .... WIDGEON
Zulu ...... BANTU, ISLAND, KAFFIR,
                       MATABELE
   band of warriors .... IMPI
   headman .... INDUNA

language .... BANTU
spear .... ASSAGAI, ASSEGAI
Zululand capital .... ESHOWE
Zuni .... PUEBLO
Zweig, novelist .... ARNOLD,
                       STEFAN

zwieback .... TOAST
zygodactyl bird .... PARROT
zygote .... OOSPERM, OOSPORE
zymase .... ENZYME
zymone .... GLUTEN
zythepsary .... BREWER

ABOUT THE AUTHOR

Born in the Philippines, Edy Garcia Schaffer has studied at the Edison Technical School in Seattle and the American Institute of Banking in San Francisco, and has been a senior stenographer, secretary, liaison officer, and an executive administrator at trade firms and banking institutions in the Philippines, Guam, and California.

She migrated to the United States in 1969, following her marriage to Art Schaffer, her husband of twenty-six years. They have five children: Karl, Bobby, Lynn, Ruby, and Venus; and eleven grandchildren: Tanya, Liza, Jacquelyn, Eddie, Joel, Ricky, Eric, Robert, Jennifer Camille, Jade Benae, and Jon Benjamin.

Mrs. Schaffer is a member of the National Association of Female Executives (NAFE) and devotes her time to the pleasures of grannyhood and traveling with her husband all over America.